Features

Visit us on the Web at
http://www.census.gov/statab/www/

ACKNOWLEDGMENTS

Lars B. Johanson was responsible for the technical supervision and coordination of this volume under the general direction of **Glenn W. King**, Chief, Statistical Compendia Branch. Assisting in the research and analytical phases of assigned sections and in the development aspects of new tables were **Rosemary E. Clark, Richard P. Kersey**, and **Jean F. Maloney. Catherine Lavender** provided primary editorial assistance. Other editorial assistance was rendered by **Susan Antroinen, Samuel E. Santos**, and **Barbara Shugart**.

Maps were designed and produced by **Connie Beard** and **Jessica Dobrowolski** of the Cartographic Products Management Branch within the Geography Division.

Catherine M. Raymond, Patricia Edwards, Linda Chen, and **Diane Oliff-Michael** of the Administrative and Customer Services Division, **Walter C. Odom**, Chief, provided publications and printing management, graphics design and composition, and editorial review for print and electronic media. General direction and production management were provided by **James R. Clark**, Assistant Division Chief, and **Wanda K. Cevis**, Chief, Publications Services Branch.

The cooperation of many contributors to this volume is gratefully acknowledged. The source note below each table credits the various government and private sector agencies that have collaborated in furnishing the information for the *Statistical Abstract.*

Statistical Abstract
of the United States: 2007

Issued October 2006

U.S. Department of Commerce
Carlos M. Gutierrez,
Secretary

David A. Sampson,
Deputy Secretary

Economics and Statistics
Administration
Cynthia A. Glassman,
Under Secretary for Economic Affairs

U.S. CENSUS BUREAU
Charles Louis Kincannon,
Director

SUGGESTED CITATION

U.S. Census Bureau,
*Statistical Abstract of the
United States: 2007*
(126th Edition)
Washington, DC,
2006

ECONOMICS
AND STATISTICS
ADMINISTRATION

**Economics
and Statistics
Administration**

Cynthia A. Glassman,
Under Secretary
for Economic Affairs

U.S. CENSUS BUREAU

Charles Louis Kincannon,
Director

Hermann Habermann,
Deputy Director and
Chief Operating Officer

Ted A. Johnson, Associate Director
for Administration
and Chief Financial Officer

Walter C. Odom, Chief, Administrative
and Customer Services Division

For sale by National Technical Information Service (NTIS), Springfield, VA
Internet: www.ntis.gov   Phone (toll-free): 1-800-553-NTIS (6847)
Phone (local area): 703-605-6000   Fax: 703-605-6900

Reprinted without alteration on acid-free paper
December 2006

ISBN (case) 978-1-59888-147-9   (paper) 978-1-59888-146-2
PB Number (case) PB2007-965301   (paper) PB2007-965801

Preface

The *Statistical Abstract of the United States*, published since 1878, is the standard summary of statistics on the social, political, and economic organization of the United States. It is designed to serve as a convenient volume for statistical reference and as a guide to other statistical publications and sources. The latter function is served by the introductory text to each section, the source note appearing below each table, and Appendix I, which comprises the Guide to Sources of Statistics, the Guide to State Statistical Abstracts, and the Guide to Foreign Statistical Abstracts.

This volume includes a selection of data from many statistical sources, both government and private. Publications cited as sources usually contain additional statistical detail and more comprehensive discussions of definitions and concepts. Data not available in publications issued by the contributing agency but obtained from the Internet or unpublished records are identified in the source notes. More information on the subjects covered in the tables so noted may generally be obtained from the source.

Except as indicated, figures are for the United States as presently constituted. Although emphasis in the *Statistical Abstract* is primarily given to national data, many tables present data for regions and individual states and a smaller number for metropolitan areas and cities. Appendix II, Metropolitan and Micropolitan Statistical Areas: Concepts, Components, and Population, presents explanatory text, a complete current listing and population data for metropolitan and micropolitan areas defined as of December 2005. Statistics for the Commonwealth of Puerto Rico and for island areas of the United States are included in many state tables and are supplemented by information in Section 29. Additional information for states, cities, counties, metropolitan areas, and other small units,

as well as more historical data are available in various supplements to the *Abstract* (see inside back cover).

Statistics in this edition are generally for the most recent year or period available by summer 2006. Each year over 1,400 tables and charts are reviewed and evaluated; new tables and charts of current interest are added, continuing series are updated, and less timely data are condensed or eliminated. Text notes and appendices are revised as appropriate. In addition, two special features—*Mini Historical Statistics*, and *State Rankings*—can be found on our Web site: <http://www.census.gov/compendia/statab/>.

Changes in this edition—This year we have introduced 72 new tables covering a wide range of subject areas. These cover a variety of topics including: learning disability for children, people impacted by the hurricanes in the Gulf Coast area, employees with alternative work arrangements, adult computer and Internet users by selected characteristics, North America cruise industry, women- and minority-owned businesses, and the percentage of the adult population considered to be obese by country. For a complete list of new tables, see section titled "New Tables," p. xi.

In addition to the above new tables, there are other changes to note for this edition. The title for Section 22, "Domestic Trade" has been changed to "Wholesale and Retail Trade." Tables displaying Service sector and County Business Patterns data have been adjusted using the results of the 2002 Economic Census.

Statistical Abstract on other media— The *Abstract* is available on the Internet and on CD-ROM. Both versions contain the same material as the book, except for a few copyrighted tables for which we did not receive permission to release in these

v

formats. Our Internet site <http://www .census.gov/compendia/statab/> contains this 2007 edition plus selected earlier editions in Adobe Acrobat .pdf format. The CD-ROM version and Internet site also include spreadsheet files for each table in the book.

Statistics for states and metropolitan areas—Extensive data for the states and metropolitan areas of the United States can be found in the *State and Metropolitan Area Data Book: 2006*. This publication minus some data items, as well as selected rankings of the states and metropolitan areas, is available on our Internet site at <http://www.census.gov /compendia/smadb>.

Statistics for counties and cities— Extensive data for counties can be found in the *County and City Data Book: 2000*. It features 191 data items covering everything from age and agriculture to water use and wholesale trade for all states and counties with U.S. totals for comparison. Also included are 103 data items for cities with population of 25,000 or more. The primary sources are Census 2000 and the 1997 Economic Census. Two tables present 11 data items from Census 2000 for all places and minor civil divisions with a population of 2,500 or more.

This publication, as well as selected rankings, is available on our Internet site at <http://www.census.gov/statab/www /ccdb.html>. Some data items that appear in the book from private sources are not available on the Internet or CD-ROM versions because we did not receive copyright permission to release the data items in these formats. For a database with over 5,000 county items, check out USA Counties at <http://censtats.census.gov/usa /usa.shtml>.

Limitations of the data—The contents of this volume were taken from many sources. All data from censuses and surveys or from administrative records are subject to error arising from a number of factors: Sampling variability (for statistics based on samples), reporting errors in the data for individual units, incomplete coverage, nonresponse, imputations, and processing error. (See also Appendix III, p. 914.) The Census Bureau cannot accept the responsibility for the accuracy or limitations of the data presented here, other than those for which it collects. The responsibility for selection of the material and for proper presentation, however, rests with the Census Bureau.

For additional information on data presented—Please consult the source publications available in local libraries or write to the agency indicated in the source notes. Write to the Census Bureau only if it is cited as the source.

Suggestions and comments—Users of the Statistical Abstract and its supplements (see inside back cover) are urged to make their data needs known for consideration in planning future editions. Suggestions and comments for improving coverage and presentation of data should be sent to the Director, U.S. Census Bureau, Washington, DC 20233.

vi

Contents

[Numbers following subjects are page numbers]

New Tables

xi

xii New Tables

Guide to Tabular Presentation

Example of Table Structure

Table 519. **Border Patrol Enforcement Activities: 2000 to 2004**

[As of September 30. Excludes Immigration and Customs Enforcement (ICE) investigations' data. The source of the data is administrative records that come from the Performance Analysis System (PAS)]

Activities	2000	2001	2002	2003	2004
Persons processed by the Border Patrol [1]	1,689,195	1,277,577	967,044	946,684	1,179,296
Deportable aliens located by the Border Patrol	1,676,438	1,266,214	955,310	931,557	1,160,395
Mexican aliens	1,636,883	1,224,046	917,994	882,012	1,085,006
Working in agriculture	1,330	1,248	1,821	1,908	1,647
Working in trades, crafts, industry, and service	2,167	2,678	2,897	3,856	3,634
Seeking employment	1,525,422	1,107,550	822,161	810,671	997,986
Canadian aliens	2,211	2,539	1,836	1,611	1,497
All others.	37,344	39,629	35,480	47,934	73,892
Smugglers of aliens located	14,406	8,720	8,701	11,128	16,074
Aliens located who were smuggled into the United States	236,782	112,927	68,192	110,575	193,122
Seizures (conveyances)	17,269	5,892	7,250	9,355	18,024
Value of seizures (mil. dol.)	**1,945**	**1,581**	**1,564**	**1,680**	**1,696**
Narcotics.	1,848	1,519	1,499	1,608	1,620
Other	97	62	65	72	75

[1] Includes deportable aliens located and nondeportable (e.g., U.S. citizens).

Source: U.S. Department of Homeland Security, Office of Immigration Statistics, *Yearbook of Immigration Statistics, 2004*. See also <http://uscis.gov/graphics/shared/aboutus/statistics/ybpage.htm>. Data as of 8 May 2006.

Headnotes immediately below table titles provide information important for correct interpretation or evaluation of the table as a whole or for a major segment of it.

Footnotes below the bottom rule of tables give information relating to specific items or figures within the table.

Unit indicators show the *specified quantities* in which data items are presented. They are used for two primary reasons. Sometimes data are not available in absolute form and are estimates (as in the case of many surveys). In other cases we round the numbers in order to save space to show more data, as in the case above.

EXAMPLES OF UNIT INDICATOR INTERPRETATION FROM TABLE

Year	Item	Unit Indicator	Number shown	Multiplier
2000	Value of seizures	$ Millions	1,945	1,000,000

To Determine the Figure it is Necessary to Multiply the Number Shown by the Unit Indicator:

Value of seizures by Border Patrol – 1,945 x $1,000,000 – $1,945,000,000
(over $1.9 billion)

When a table presents data with more than one unit indicator, they are found in the headnotes and column headings (Tables 2 and 31), spanner (Table 44), stub (Table 29), or unit column (Table 128). When the data in a table are shown in the same unit indicator, it is shown in boldface as the first part of the headnote (Table 2). If no unit indicator is shown, data presented are in absolute form (Table 1).

Vertical rules are used to separate independent sections of a table (Table 1), or in tables where the stub is continued into one or more additional columns (Table 2).

Averages—An average is a single number or value that is often used to represent the "typical value" of a group of numbers. It is regarded as a measure of "location" or "central tendency" of a group of numbers.

The *arithmetic mean* is the type of average used most frequently. It is derived by summing the individual item values of a particular group and dividing the total by the number of items. The arithmetic mean is often referred to as simply the "mean" or "average."

The *median* of a group of numbers is the middle number or value when each item in the group is arranged according to size (lowest to highest or visa versa); it generally has the same number of items above it as well as below it. If there is an even number of items in the group, the median is taken to be the average of the two middle numbers.

Per capita (or per person) quantities—a per capita figure represents an average computed for every person in a specified group (or population). It is derived by taking the total for an item (such as income, taxes, or retail sales) and dividing it by

U.S. Census Bureau, Statistical Abstract of the United States: 2007

the number of persons in the specified population.

Index numbers—An index number is the measure of difference or change, usually expressed as a percent, relating one quantity (the variable) of a specified kind to another quantity of the same kind. Index numbers are widely used to express changes in prices over periods of time, but may also be used to express differences between related subjects for a single point in time.

To compute a price index, a base year or period is selected. The base year price (of the commodity or service) is then designated as the base or reference price to which the prices for other years or periods are related. Many price indexes use the year 1982 as the base year; in tables this is shown as "1982 = 100." A method of expressing the price relationship is: The price of a set of one or more items for a related year (e.g. 1990) **divided by** the price of the same set of items for the base year (e.g. 1982). The result multiplied by 100 provides the index number. When 100 is subtracted from the index number, the result equals the percent change in price from the base year.

Average annual percent change— Unless otherwise stated in the *Abstract* (as in Section 1, Population), average annual percent change is computed by use of a *compound interest formula*. This formula assumes that the rate of change is constant throughout a specified compounding period (1 year for average annual rates of change). The formula is similar to that used to compute the balance of a savings account that receives compound interest. According to this formula, at the end of a compounding period the amount of accrued change (e.g., school enrollment or bank interest) is added to the amount that existed at the beginning of the period. As a result, over time (e.g., with each year or quarter), the same rate of change is applied to a larger and larger figure.

The *exponential formula,* which is based on continuous compounding, is often used to measure population change. It is preferred by population experts, because they view population and population-related subjects as changing without interruption, ever ongoing. Both exponential and compound interest formulas assume a constant rate of change. The former, however, applies the amount of change continuously to the base rather than at the end of each compounding period. When the average annual rates are small (e.g., less than 5 percent) both formulas give virtually the same results. For an explanation of these two formulas as they relate to population, see U.S. Census Bureau, *The Methods and Materials of Demography,* Vol. 2, 3d printing (rev.), 1975, pp. 372–381.

Current and constant dollars— Statistics in some tables in a number of sections are expressed in both current and constant dollars (see, e.g., Table 660 in Section 13, Income, Expenditures, and Wealth). Current dollar figures reflect actual prices or costs prevailing during the specified year(s). Constant dollar figures are estimates representing an effort to remove the effects of price changes from statistical series reported in dollar terms. In general, constant dollar series are derived by dividing current dollar estimates by the appropriate price index for the appropriate period (e.g., the Consumer Price Index). The result is a series as it would presumably exist if prices were the same throughout, as in the base year—in other words, as if the dollar had constant purchasing power. Any changes in this constant dollar series would reflect only changes in real volume of output, income, expenditures, or other measure.

Explanation of Symbols

The following symbols, used in the tables throughout this book, are explained in condensed form in footnotes to the tables where they appear:

– Represents zero or rounds to less than half the unit of measurement shown.

B Base figure too small to meet statistical standards for reliability of a derived figure.

D Figure withheld to avoid disclosure pertaining to a specific organization or individual.

NA Data not enumerated, tabulated, or otherwise available separately.

S Figure does not meet publication standards for reasons other than that covered by symbol B, above.

X Figure not applicable because column heading and stub line make entry impossible, absurd, or meaningless.

Z Entry would amount to less than half the unit of measurement shown.

In many tables, details will not add to the totals shown because of rounding.

U.S. Census Bureau, Statistical Abstract of the United States: 2007

Telephone & Internet Contacts

To help *Abstract* users find more data and information about statistical publications, we are issuing this list of contacts for federal agencies with major statistical programs. The intent is to give a single, first-contact point-of-entry for users of statistics. These agencies will provide general information on their statistical programs and publications, as well as specific information on how to order their publications. We are also including the Internet (World Wide Web) addresses for many of these agencies. These URLs were current in July 2006.

Executive Office of the President
Office of Management and Budget
Administrator
Office of Information and Regulatory
Affairs
Office of Management and Budget
725 17th Street, NW
Washington, DC 20503
Information: 202-395-3080
Internet address:
http://www.whitehouse.gov/omb

Department of Agriculture
Economic Research Service
Information Center
U.S. Department of Agriculture
1800 M Street, NW
Washington, DC 20036-5831
Information and Publications:
202-694-5050
Internet address:
http://www.ers.usda.gov/

National Agricultural Statistics Service
National Agricultural Statistics Service
USDA–NASS
Room 5038-South Building
12th St. and Independence Ave., SW
Washington, DC 20250
Information hotline: 1-800-727-9540
Internet address:
http://www.nass.usda.gov/

Department of Commerce
U.S. Census Bureau
Customer Services Branch
U.S. Census Bureau
4700 Silver Hill Road
Washington, DC 20233-0001
Information and Publications:
301-763-4636
Internet address:
http://www.census.gov/

Bureau of Economic Analysis
Bureau of Economic Analysis
1441 L Street, NW
Washington, DC 20230
Information and Publications:
202-606-9900
Internet address: http://www.bea.gov/

Department of Commerce —Con.
International Trade Administration
International Trade Administration
1401 Constitution Ave., NW
U.S. Department of Commerce
Washington, DC 20230
Information: 1-800-872-8723
Internet address: http://trade.gov

National Oceanic and Atmospheric Administration
National Oceanic and Atmospheric
Administration Central Library
U.S. Department of Commerce
1315 East-West Highway
SSMC3, 2nd Floor
Silver Spring, MD 20910
Library: 301-713-2600 x.124
Internet address:
http://www.lib.noaa.gov/

Department of Defense
Department of Defense
Directorate for Public Inquiry and
Analysis
Office of the Assistant Secretary of
Defense, Public Affairs
Room 2E565 the Pentagon
1400 Defense Pentagon
Washington, DC 20301-1400
Information: 703-428-0711
Internet address:
http://www.defenselink.mil

Department of Education
National Library of Education
U.S. Department of Education
400 Maryland Avenue, SW
Washington, DC 20202
Education Information and Statistics:
1-800-872-5327
Education Publications:
1-877-433-7827
Internet address: http://www.ed.gov/

Department of Energy

Energy Information Administration
National Energy Information Center
U.S. Department of Energy
1000 Independence Ave., SW
Washington, DC 20585
Information and Publications:
202-586-8800
Internet address:
http://www.eia.doe.gov/

Department of Health and Human Services

Health Resources and Services Administration
HRSA Information Center
P. O. Box 2910
Merrifield, VA 22116
Information Center: 1-888-275-4772
Internet address: http://www.hrsa.gov/

Substance Abuse and Mental Health Services Administration
U.S. Department of Health and Human Services
1 Choke Cherry Road
Rockville, MD 20857
Information: 240-276-2000
Publications: 1-800-729-6686
Internet address:
http://www.samhsa.gov/

Centers for Disease Control and Prevention
Public Inquiries/MASO
1600 Clifton Road
Atlanta, GA 30333
Public Inquiries: 1-800-311-3435
Internet address: http://www.cdc.gov/

Centers for Medicare and Medicaid Services (CMS)
U.S. Department of Health and Human Services
7500 Security Boulevard
Baltimore, MD 21244
1-877-267-2323
Internet address:
http://www.cms.hhs.gov/

National Center for Health Statistics
National Center For Health Statistics
3311 Toledo Road
Hyattsville, MD 20782
301-458-4000
Internet address:
http://www.cdc.gov/nchs

Department of Homeland Security

U.S. Citizenship and Immigration Services
20 Massachusetts Avenue, NW
Washington, DC 20529
Information and Publications:
1-800-375-5283
Internet address:
http://uscis.gov/graphics/

Department of Homeland Security —Con.
Department of Housing and Urban Development

Office of the Assistant Secretary for Community Planning and Development
451 7th Street, SW
Washington, DC 20410
Information:
1-800-998-9999
Publications:
1-800-767-7468
Internet address:
http://www.hud.gov/

Department of the Interior

U.S. Geological Survey
USGS National Center
12201 Sunrise Valley Drive
Reston, VA 20192
Information and Publications:
1-888-275-8747
Internet address for minerals:
http://minerals.usgs.gov/
Internet address for other materials:
http://ask.usgs.gov/

Department of Justice

Bureau of Justice Statistics
Statistics Division
810 7th Street, NW
Washington, DC 20531
Information and Publications:
1-800-851-3420
Datasets and Codebooks: 1-800-999-0960
Internet address:
http://www.ojp.usdoj.gov/bjs/

National Criminal Justice Reference Service
P.O. Box 6000
Rockville, MD 20849-6000
Publications: 1-800-851-3420
Internet address: http://www.ncjrs.org/

Federal Bureau of Investigation
U.S. Department of Justice
J. Edgar Hoover Building
935 Pennsylvania Avenue, NW
Washington, DC 20535-0001
Information: 202-324-3000
Internet address: http://www.fbi.gov/

U.S. Census Bureau, Statistical Abstract of the United States: 2007

Department of Labor

Bureau of Labor Statistics
Office of Publications and Special Studies
Services
Bureau of Labor Statistics
Postal Square Building
2 Massachusetts Avenue, NE
Washington, DC 20212-0001
Information and Publications:
202-691-5200
Internet address: http://www.bls.gov/

Employment and Training Administration
U.S. Department of Labor
Francis Perkins Building
200 Constitution Avenue, NW
Washington, DC 20210
Information and Publications:
1-877-872-5627
Internet address: http://www.doleta.gov/

Department of Transportation

Federal Aviation Administration
U.S. Department of Transportation
800 Independence Avenue, SW
Washington, DC 20591
Information and Publications:
1-866-835-5322
Internet address: http://www.faa.gov/

Bureau of Transportation Statistics
400 7th Street, SW, Room 3430
Washington, DC 20590
Products and Statistical Information:
1-800-853-1351
Internet address: http://www.bts.gov/

Federal Highway Administration
Office of Public Affairs
U.S. Department of Transportation
400 7th Street, SW
Washington, DC 20590
Information: 1-866-835-5322
Internet address:
http://www.fhwa.dot.gov/

*National Highway Traffic Safety
Administration*
Office of Public & Consumer Affairs
U.S. Department of Transportation
400 7th Street, SW
Washington, DC 20590
Information and Publications:
1-888-327-4236
Internet address:
http://www.nhtsa.dot.gov/

Department of the Treasury

Internal Revenue Service
Statistics of Income Division
Internal Revenue Service
P. O. Box 2608
Washington, DC 20013-2608
Information and Publications:
202-874-0410
Internet address:
http://www.irs.gov/taxstats/

Department of Veterans Affairs

Office of Public Affairs
Department of Veterans Affairs
810 Vermont Avenue, NW
Washington, DC 20420
Internet address: http://www.va.gov/

Independent Agencies

Administrative Office of the U.S. Courts
Statistics Division
Washington, DC 20544
Information: 202-502-2600
Internet address:
http://www.uscourts.gov/

Environmental Protection Agency
Environmental Protection Agency
Ariel Rios Building
1200 Pennsylvania Avenue, NW
Washington, DC 20460
Information: 1-800-490-9198
Internet address: http://www.epa.gov/

Federal Reserve Board
Division of Research and Statistics
Federal Reserve Board
20th & C Streets, NW
Washington, DC 20551
Information: 202-452-3301
Publications: 202-452-3245
Internet address:
http://www.federalreserve.gov/

National Science Foundation
Office of Legislation and Public Affairs
National Science Foundation
4201 Wilson Boulevard
Arlington, VA 22230
Information: 703-292-5111
Publications: 703-292-7827
Internet address: http://www.nsf.gov/

Securities and Exchange Commission
Office of Public Affairs
Securities and Exchange Commission
100 F Street, NE
Washington, DC 20549
Information: 202-942-8088
Publications: 202-551-4040
Internet address: http://www.sec.gov/

Social Security Administration
Social Security Administration
Office of Research, Evaluation and
Statistics
6401 Security Boulevard
Baltimore, MD 21235
Information and Publications:
1-800-772-1213
Internet address:
http://www.socialsecurity.gov/

Section 1
Population

This section presents statistics on the growth, distribution, and characteristics of the U.S. population. The principal source of these data is the U.S. Census Bureau, which conducts a decennial census of population, a monthly population survey, a program of population estimates and projections, and a number of other periodic surveys relating to population characteristics. For a list of relevant publications, see the Guide to Sources of Statistics in Appendix I.

Decennial censuses—The U.S. Constitution provides for a census of the population every 10 years, primarily to establish a basis for apportionment of members of the House of Representatives among the states. For over a century after the first census in 1790, the census organization was a temporary one, created only for each decennial census. In 1902, the Census Bureau was established as a permanent federal agency, responsible for enumerating the population and also for compiling statistics on other population and housing characteristics.

Historically, the enumeration of the population has been a complete count. That is, an attempt is made to account for every person, for each person's residence, and for other characteristics (sex, age, family relationships, etc.). Since the 1940 census, in addition to the complete count information, some data have been obtained from representative samples of the population. In the 1990 and 2000 censuses, variable sampling rates were employed. For most of the country, 1 in every 6 households (about 17 percent) received the long form or sample questionnaire; in governmental units estimated to have fewer than 2,500 inhabitants, every other household (50 percent) received the sample questionnaire to enhance the reliability of sample data for small areas. Exact agreement is not to be expected between sample data and the 100-percent count. Sample data may be used with confidence where large numbers are involved and assumed to indicate trends and relationships where small numbers are involved.

Current Population Survey (CPS)—This is a monthly nationwide survey of a scientifically selected sample representing the noninstitutionalized civilian population. The sample is located in 754 areas with coverage in every state and the District of Columbia and is subject to sampling error. At the present time, about 60,000 occupied households are eligible for interview every month; of these, between 6 and 7 percent are, for various reasons, unavailable for interview.

While the primary purpose of the CPS is to obtain monthly statistics on the labor force, it also serves as a vehicle for inquiries on other subjects. Using CPS data, the Census Bureau issues a series of publications under the general title of *Current Population Reports,* which cover population characteristics (P20), consumer income (P60), special studies (P23), and other topics.

Estimates of population characteristics based on the CPS will not agree with the counts from the census because the CPS and the census use different procedures for collecting and processing the data for racial groups, the Hispanic population, and other topics. Caution should also be used when comparing estimates for various years because of the periodic introduction of changes into the CPS. Beginning in January 1994, a number of changes were introduced into the CPS that effect all data comparisons with prior years. These changes included the results of a major redesign of the survey questionnaire and collection methodology and the introduction of 1990 census population controls, adjusted for the estimated undercount. Beginning with the 2001 CPS Annual Demographic Supplement, the independent estimates used as control totals for the CPS are based on civilian population benchmarks consistent with Census 2000. In March 2002, the sample size of the Annual Demographic Supplement was increased to approximately 78,000. In 2003 the name of the March supplement was changed to Annual Social and Economic Supplement. These changes in population controls had relatively little impact on derived measures such as means, medians, and percent distribution, but did have a significant impact on levels.

American Community Survey (ACS)—This is a nationwide survey to obtain data about demographic, social, economic, and housing information of people, households, and housing units. The survey collects the same type of information that has been collected every 10 years from the long-form questionnaire of the census, which the American Community Survey will replace. The estimates are limited to the household population and exclude the population living in institutions, college dormitories, and other group quarters.

Population estimates and projections—Estimates of the United States population are derived by updating the resident population enumerated in Census 2000 with information on the components of population change: births, deaths, and net international migration. The April 1, 2000, population used in these estimates reflects modifications to the Census 2000 population as documented in the Count Question Resolution program.

Registered births and deaths are estimated from data supplied by the National Center for Health Statistics. The net international migration component consists of three parts: (1) net migration of the foreign born, (2) emigration of natives, and (3) net movement from Puerto Rico to the United States (50 states and DC). Data from the American Community Survey are used to estimate the annual net migration of the foreign-born population. Estimates of native emigration and net movement between Puerto Rico and the United States are derived from the Demographic Analysis and Population Estimates (DAPE) project (see Population Division Working Paper Series, No. 63 and No. 64).

Estimates for state and county areas are based on the same components of change data and sources as the national estimates with the addition of net internal migration. School enrollment statistics from state departments of education and parochial school systems, federal income tax returns from the Internal Revenue Service, group quarters data from the Federal-State Cooperative Program, and Medicare data from the Centers for Medicare and Medicaid Services are also included.

The population by age for April 1, 1990, (shown in Table 11) reflects modifications to the 1990 census data counts. The review of detailed 1990 information indicated that respondents tended to report age as of the date of completion of the questionnaire, not as of April 1, 1990. In addition, there may have been a tendency for respondents to round up their age if they were close to having a birthday. A detailed explanation of the age modification procedure appears in 1990 Census of Population and Housing, Data Paper Listing CPH-L74.

Population estimates and projections are available on the Census Bureau Internet site <http://www.census.gov>. These estimates and projections are consistent with official decennial census figures with no adjustment for estimated net census coverage. However, the categories for these estimates and projections by race have been modified and are not comparable to the census race categories (see section below under "Race"). For details on methodology, see the sources cited below the individual tables.

Immigration—Immigration (migration *to* a country) is one component of international migration; the other component is emigration (migration *from* a country). In its simplest form, international migration is defined as any movement across a national border. In the United States, federal statistics on international migration are produced primarily by the U.S. Census Bureau and the Office of Immigration Statistics (located in the Department of Homeland Security).

The Census Bureau collects data used to estimate international migration through its decennial censuses and numerous surveys of the U.S. population.

The Office of Immigration Statistics publishes immigration data in the *Yearbook of Immigration Statistics* and collects these data from several administrative records such as the Immigrant Visa and Alien Registration (OF-155, U.S. State Department) for new arrivals, and the Memorandum of Creation of Record of Lawful Permanent Residence (I-181, INS) for persons adjusting migrant status. Immigrants are aliens admitted for legal permanent residence in the United States. The category, immigrant, includes persons who may have entered the United States as nonimmigrants or refugees, but who subsequently changed their status to that of a permanent resident. Nonresident aliens admitted to the United States for a temporary period are nonimmigrants. Refugees are considered nonimmigrants when initially admitted into the United States but are not included in nonimmigrant admission data. A refugee is an alien outside the United States who is unable or unwilling to return to his or her country of nationality because of persecution or a well-founded fear of persecution. After 1 year of residence in the United States, refugees are eligible for immigrant status.

U.S. immigration law gives preferential immigration status to persons with a close family relationship with a U.S. citizen or legal permanent resident, persons with needed job skills, or persons who qualify as refugees. Immigration to the United States can be divided into two general categories: (1) those subject to the annual worldwide limitation and (2) those exempt from it. Numerical limits are imposed on visas issued and not on admissions. The maximum number of visas allowed to be issued under the preference categories in 2005 was 374,449—226,000 for family-sponsored immigrants and 148,449 for employment-based immigrants. Those exempt from the worldwide limitation include immediate relatives of U.S. citizens, refugees and asylees adjusting to permanent residence, and other various classes of special immigrants (see Table 6).

Metropolitan and micropolitan areas—The United States Office of Management and Budget (OMB) defines metropolitan and micropolitan statistical areas according to published standards that are applied to Census Bureau data. The general concept of a metropolitan or micropolitan statistical area is that of a core area containing a substantial population nucleus, together with adjacent communities having a high degree of economic and social integration with that core. Currently defined metropolitan and micropolitan statistical areas are based on application of 2000 standards to 2000 decennial census data as updated by application of those standards to more recent Census Bureau population estimates. The term "metropolitan area" (MA) was used to refer collectively to metropolitan statistical areas (MSAs), consolidated metropolitan statistical areas (CMSAs), and primary metropolitan statistical areas (PMSAs) as defined according to 1980 and 1990 standards. The term "core-based statistical area" (CBSA) became effective in 2003 and refers collectively to metropolitan and micropolitan statistical areas.

Over time, new statistical areas are created and the components of others change. Because of historical changes in geographic definitions, users must be cautious in comparing data for these statistical areas from different dates. For some purposes, comparisons of data for areas as defined at given dates may be appropriate; for other purposes, it may be preferable to maintain consistent area definitions. For descriptive details and a list of titles and components of metropolitan and micropolitan statistical areas, see Appendix II.

Urban and rural—For Census 2000, the Census Bureau classified as urban all territory, population, and housing units located within urbanized areas (UAs) and urban clusters (UCs). A UA consists of densely settled territory that contains 50,000 or more people, while a UC consists of densely settled territory with at least 2,500 people but fewer than 50,000 people. (UCs are a new type of geographic entity for Census 2000.) From the 1950 census through the 1990 census, the urban population consisted of all people living in UAs and most places outside of UAs with a census population of 2,500 or more.

UAs and UCs encompass territory that generally consists of:

- A cluster of one or more block groups or census blocks each of which has a population density of at least 1,000 people per square mile at the time.

- Surrounding block groups and census blocks each of which has a population density of at least 500 people per square mile at the time.
- Less densely settled blocks that form enclaves or indentations, or are used to connect discontiguous areas with qualifying densities.

They also may include an airport located adjacent to qualifying densely settled area if it has an annual enplanement (aircraft boarding) of at least 10,000 people.

"Rural" for Census 2000 consists of all territory, population, and housing units located outside of UAs and UCs. Prior to Census 2000, rural consisted of all territory, population, and housing outside of UAs and outside of other places designated as "urban." For Census 2000, many more geographic entities, including metropolitan areas, counties, county subdivisions, and places, contain both urban and rural territory, population, and housing units.

Residence—In determining residence, the Census Bureau counts each person as an inhabitant of a usual place of residence (i.e., the place where one lives and sleeps most of the time). While this place is not necessarily a person's legal residence or voting residence, the use of these different bases of classification would produce the same results in the vast majority of cases.

Race—For the 1990 census, the Census Bureau collected and published racial statistics as outlined in Statistical Policy Directive No. 15 issued by the U.S. Office of Management and Budget (OMB). This directive provided standards on ethnic and racial categories for statistical reporting to be used by all federal agencies. According to the directive, the basic racial categories were American Indian or Alaska Native, Asian or Pacific Islander, Black, and White. (The directive identified Hispanic origin as an ethnicity.) The question on race for Census 2000 was different from the one for the 1990 census in several ways. Most significantly, respondents were given the option of selecting one or more race categories to indicate their racial identities. Because of these changes, the Census 2000 data on race are not directly comparable with data from the 1990 census or earlier censuses.

Caution must be used when interpreting changes in the racial composition of the United States population over time. Census 2000 adheres to the federal standards for collecting and presenting data on race and ethnicity as established by OMB in October 1997. Starting with Census 2000, the OMB requires federal agencies to use a minimum of five race categories: White, Black or African American, American Indian or Alaska Native, Asian, and Native Hawaiian or Other Pacific Islander. Additionally, to collect data on individuals of mixed race parentage, respondents were allowed to select one or more races. For respondents unable to identify with any of these five race categories, OMB approved and included a sixth category—"Some other race" on the Census 2000 questionnaire. The Census 2000 question on race included 15 separate response categories and three areas where respondents could write in a more specific race group. The response categories and write-in answers can be combined to create the five minimum OMB race categories plus "Some other race." People who responded to the question on race by indicating only one race are referred to as the *race alone* population, or the group that reported only one race category. Six categories make up this population: White alone, Black or African American alone, American Indian and Alaska Native alone, Asian alone, Native Hawaiian and Other Pacific Islander alone, and Some other race alone. Individuals who chose more than one of the six race categories are referred to as the *Two or More Races* population, or as the group that reported more than one race. Additionally, respondents who reported one race together with those who reported the same race plus one or more other races are combined to create the *race alone or in combination* categories. For example, the *White alone or in combination group* consists of those respondents who reported only White or who reported White combined with one or more other race groups, such as "White and Black or African American," or "White and Asian and American Indian and Alaska Native." Another way to think of the group who reported White alone or in combination is as the total number of people who identified entirely or partially as White. This group is also described as people who reported White, whether or not they reported any other race.

The *alone or in combination* categories are tallies of *responses* rather than *respondents*. That is, the alone or in combination categories are not mutually exclusive. Individuals who reported two races were counted in two separate and distinct alone or in combination race categories, while those who reported three races were counted in three categories, and so on. Consequently, the sum of all alone or in combination categories equals the number of races reported (i.e., responses) which exceeds the total population.

The concept of race, as used by the Census Bureau, reflects self-identification by people according to the race or races with which they most closely identify. These categories are sociopolitical constructs and should not be interpreted as being scientific or anthropological in nature. Furthermore, the race categories include both racial and national-origin groups. Additionally, data are available for the American Indian and Alaska Native tribes. A detailed explanation of race can be found at <http://www.census.gov/prod/cen2000/doc/sf1.pdf>.

Data for the population by race for April 1, 2000, (shown in Tables 13, 14, and 15) are modified counts and are not comparable to Census 2000 race categories. These numbers were computed using Census 2000 data by race that had been modified to be consistent with the 1997 Office of Management and Budget's, "Revisions to the Standards for the Classification of Federal Data on Race and Ethnicity," (Federal Register Notice, Vol. 62, No 210, October 1997). A detailed explanation of the race modification procedure appears on the Census Web page <http://www.census.gov/popest/topics/methodology/2003_nat_char_meth.html>.

In the CPS and other household sample surveys in which data are obtained through personal interview, respondents are asked to classify their race as: (1) White; (2) Black, African American, or Negro; (3) American Indian or Alaska Native; (4) Asian; (5) Native Hawaiian or Other Pacific Islander. Beginning January 2003, respondents were allowed to report more than one race to indicate their mixed racial heritage.

Hispanic population—The Census Bureau collected data on the Hispanic origin population in the 2000 census by using a self-identification question. Persons of Spanish/Hispanic/Latino origin are those who classified themselves in one of the specific Hispanic origin categories listed on the questionnaire—Mexican, Puerto Rican, Cuban, as well as those who indicated that they were of Other Spanish/Hispanic/Latino origin. Persons of Other Spanish/Hispanic/Latino origin are those whose origins are from Spain, the Spanish-speaking countries of Central or South America, or the Dominican Republic.

In the CPS, information on Hispanic persons is gathered by using a self-identification question. Based on a two-part question, the respondents are first asked whether or not they are of Hispanic, Spanish, or Latino origin and based on their response are further classified into the following categories: Mexican or Mexican-American or Chicano; Puerto Rican; Cuban; Central or South American; or Other Hispanic, Spanish, or Latino origin group.

Traditional and current data collection and classification treat race and Hispanic origin as two separate and distinct concepts in accordance with guidelines from the OMB. Race and Hispanic origin are two separate concepts in the federal statistical system. People who are Hispanic may be any race and people in each race group may be either Hispanic or Not Hispanic. Also, each person has two attributes, their race (or races) and whether or not they are Hispanic. The overlap of race and Hispanic origin is the main comparability issue. For example, Black Hispanics (Hispanic Blacks) are included in both the number of Blacks and in the number of Hispanics. For further information, see Census Web page <http://www.census.gov/population/www/socdemo/compraceho.html>.

Foreign-born and native populations—The Census Bureau separates the U.S. resident population into two groups based on whether or not a person was a U.S. citizen or U.S. national at the time of birth. Anyone born in the United States, Puerto Rico, or a U.S. Island Area (such as Guam) or born abroad to a U.S. citizen parent is a U.S. citizen at the time of birth and consequently included in the *native population*. The term *foreign-born population* refers to anyone who is not a U.S. citizen or U.S. national at birth. This includes naturalized U.S. citizens, legal permanent resident aliens (immigrants), temporary migrants (such as foreign students), humanitarian migrants (such as refugees), and people illegally present in the United States. The Census Bureau provides a variety of demographic, social, economic, geographic, and housing information on the foreign-born population in the United States. More information on the foreign-born population collected from censuses and surveys is available at <http://www.census.gov /population /www/socdemo/foreign .html>.

Mobility status—The U.S. population is classified according to mobility status on the basis of a comparison between the place of residence of each individual at the time of the survey or census and the place of residence at a specified earlier date. Nonmovers are all persons who were living in the same house or apartment at the end of the period as at the beginning of the period. Movers are all persons who were living in a different house or apartment at the end of the period than at the beginning of the period. Movers are further classified as to whether they were living in the same or different county, state, or region or were movers from abroad. Movers from abroad include all persons, either U.S. citizens or noncitizens, whose place of residence was outside the United States at the beginning of the period; that is, in Puerto Rico, another U.S. Island Area, or a foreign country.

Living arrangements—Living arrangements refer to residency in households or in group quarters. A "household" comprises all persons who occupy a "housing unit," that is, a house, an apartment or other group of rooms, or a single room that constitutes "separate living quarters." A household includes the related family members and all the unrelated persons, if any, such as lodgers, foster children,

wards, or employees who share the housing unit. A person living alone or a group of unrelated persons sharing the same housing unit is also counted as a household. See text, Section 20, Construction and Housing, for definition of housing unit.

All persons not living in housing units are classified as living in group quarters. These individuals may be institutionalized, e.g., under care or custody in juvenile facilities, jails, correctional centers, hospitals, or nursing homes; or they may be residents in noninstitutional group quarters such as college dormitories, group homes, or military barracks.

Householder—The householder is the person in whose name the home is owned or rented. If a home is owned or rented jointly by a married couple, either the husband or the wife may be listed first.

Family—The term family refers to a group of two or more persons related by birth, marriage, or adoption and residing together in a household. A family includes among its members the householder.

Subfamily—A subfamily consists of a married couple and their children, if any, or one parent with one or more never-married children under 18 years old living in a household. Subfamilies are divided into "related" and "unrelated" subfamilies. A related subfamily is related to, but does not include, the householder. Members of a related subfamily are also members of the family with whom they live. The number of related subfamilies, therefore, is not included in the count of families. An unrelated subfamily may include persons such as guests, lodgers, or resident employees and their spouses and/or children; none of whom is related to the householder.

Married couple—A married couple is defined as a husband and wife living together in the same household, with or without children and other relatives.

Statistical reliability—For a discussion of statistical collection and estimation, sampling procedures, and measures of statistical reliability applicable to Census Bureau data, see Appendix III.

Table 1. Population and Area: 1790 to 2000

[Area figures represent area on indicated date including in some cases considerable areas not then organized or settled, and not covered by the census. Beginning 1870, area data include Alaska and Hawaii. Total area figures for 1790 to 1970 have been recalculated on the basis of the remeasurement of states and counties for the 1980 census, but not on the basis of the 1990 census. The land and water area figures for past censuses have not been adjusted and are not strictly comparable with the total area data for comparable dates because the land areas were derived from different base data, and these values are known to have changed with the construction of reservoirs, draining of lakes, etc. Density figures are based on land area measurements as reported in earlier censuses]

Census date	Resident population		Increase over preceding census		Area (square miles)		
	Number	Per square mile of land area	Number	Percent	Total	Land	Water [1]
1790 (Aug. 2)	3,929,214	4.5	(X)	(X)	891,364	864,746	24,065
1800 (Aug. 4)	5,308,483	6.1	1,379,269	35.1	891,364	864,746	24,065
1810 (Aug. 6)	7,239,881	4.3	1,931,398	36.4	1,722,685	1,681,828	34,175
1820 (Aug. 7)	9,638,453	5.5	2,398,572	33.1	1,792,552	1,749,462	38,544
1830 (June 1)	12,866,020	7.4	3,227,567	33.5	1,792,552	1,749,462	38,544
1840 (June 1)	17,069,453	9.8	4,203,433	32.7	1,792,552	1,749,462	38,544
1850 (June 1)	23,191,876	7.9	6,122,423	35.9	2,991,655	2,940,042	52,705
1860 (June 1)	31,443,321	10.6	8,251,445	35.6	3,021,295	2,969,640	52,747
1870 (June 1)	[2]39,818,449	[2]11.2	8,375,128	26.6	3,612,299	3,540,705	68,082
1880 (June 1)	50,189,209	14.2	10,370,760	26.0	3,612,299	3,540,705	68,082
1890 (June 1)	62,979,766	17.8	12,790,557	25.5	3,612,299	3,540,705	68,082
1900 (June 1)	76,212,168	21.5	13,232,402	21.0	3,618,770	3,547,314	67,901
1910 (Apr. 15)	92,228,496	26.0	16,016,328	21.0	3,618,770	3,547,045	68,170
1920 (Jan. 1)	106,021,537	29.9	13,793,041	15.0	3,618,770	3,546,931	68,284
1930 (Apr. 1)	123,202,624	34.7	17,181,087	16.2	3,618,770	3,554,608	60,607
1940 (Apr. 1)	132,164,569	37.2	8,961,945	7.3	3,618,770	3,554,608	60,607
1950 (Apr. 1)	151,325,798	42.6	19,161,229	14.5	3,618,770	3,552,206	63,005
1960 (Apr. 1)	179,323,175	50.6	27,997,377	18.5	3,618,770	3,540,911	74,212
1970 (Apr. 1)	[3]203,302,031	57.5	23,978,856	13.4	3,618,770	3,536,855	78,444
1980 (Apr. 1)	[3]226,542,199	64.0	23,240,168	11.4	3,618,770	3,539,289	79,481
1990 (Apr. 1)	[4]248,718,302	70.3	22,176,103	9.8	[5]3,717,796	3,536,278	[5]181,518
2000 (Apr. 1)	[6]281,424,603	79.6	32,706,301	13.1	3,794,083	3,537,438	256,645

X Not applicable. [1] Data for 1790 to 1980 cover inland water only. Data for 1990 comprise Great Lakes, inland, and coastal water. Data for 2000 comprise Great Lakes, inland, territorial, and coastal water. [2] Revised to include adjustments for underenumeration in southern states; unrevised number is 38,558,371 (10.9 per square mile). [3] Total population count has been revised since the 1980 census publications. Numbers by age, race, Hispanic origin, and sex have not been corrected. [4] The April 1, 1990, census count includes count question resolution corrections processed through December 1997, and does not include adjustments for census coverage errors. [5] Data reflect corrections made after publication of the results. [6] Reflects modifications to the Census 2000 population as documented in the Count Question Resolution program.

Source: U.S. Census Bureau, 2000 Census of Population and Housing, *Population and Housing Counts,* Series PHC-3-1, United States Summary; *Notes and Errata, 2000* SF/01-ER ; <http://www.census.gov/prod/cen2000/notes/errata.pdf>; *Areas of the United States: 1940;* Area data for 1990: unpublished data from TIGER®; and Davis, Warren; personal e-mail; U.S. Census Bureau; 23 June 2006.

Table 2. Population: 1960 to 2005

[In thousands, except percent (180,671 represents 180,671,000). Estimates as of July 1. Total population includes Armed Forces abroad; civilian population excludes Armed Forces. For basis of estimates, see text of this section]

Year	Total		Resident population	Civilian population	Year	Total		Resident population	Civilian population
	Population	Percent change [1]				Population	Percent change [1]		
1960	180,671	1.60	179,979	178,140	1983	234,307	0.91	233,792	232,097
1961	183,691	1.67	182,992	181,143	1984	236,348	0.87	235,825	234,110
1962	186,538	1.55	185,771	183,677	1985	238,466	0.90	237,924	236,219
1963	189,242	1.45	188,483	186,493	1986	240,651	0.92	240,133	238,412
1964	191,889	1.40	191,141	189,141	1987	242,804	0.89	242,289	240,550
1965	194,303	1.26	193,526	191,605	1988	245,021	0.91	244,499	242,817
1966	196,560	1.16	195,576	193,420	1989	247,342	0.95	246,819	245,131
1967	198,712	1.09	197,457	195,264	1990	250,132	1.13	249,623	247,983
1968	200,706	1.00	199,399	197,113	1991	253,493	1.34	252,981	251,370
1969	202,677	0.98	201,385	199,145	1992	256,894	1.34	256,514	254,929
1970	205,052	1.17	203,984	201,895	1993	260,255	1.31	259,919	258,446
1971	207,661	1.27	206,827	204,866	1994	263,436	1.22	263,126	261,714
1972	209,896	1.08	209,284	207,511	1995	266,557	1.18	266,278	264,927
1973	211,909	0.96	211,357	209,600	1996	269,667	1.17	269,394	268,108
1974	213,854	0.92	213,342	211,636	1997	272,912	1.20	272,647	271,394
1975	215,973	0.99	215,465	213,789	1998	276,115	1.17	275,854	274,633
1976	218,035	0.95	217,563	215,894	1999	279,295	1.15	279,040	277,841
1977	220,239	1.01	219,760	218,106	2000	282,403	1.11	282,193	280,970
1978	222,585	1.06	222,095	220,467	2001	285,335	1.04	285,108	283,893
1979	225,055	1.11	224,567	222,969	2002	288,216	1.01	287,985	286,739
1980	227,726	1.19	227,225	225,621	2003	291,089	1.00	290,850	289,599
1981	229,966	0.98	229,466	227,818	2004	293,908	0.97	293,657	292,416
1982	232,188	0.97	231,664	229,995	2005	296,639	0.93	296,410	295,194

[1] Percent change from immediate preceding year.

Source: U.S. Census Bureau, 1960 to 1979: *Current Population Reports* P25-802 and P25-917; 1980 to 1989: "Monthly Estimates of the United States Population: April 1, 1980, to July 1, 1999, with Short-Term Projections to November 1, 2000"; published 2 January 2001; <http://www.census.gov/popest/archives/1990s/nat-total.txt>; 1990 to 1999: "national intercensal estimates (1990-2000)"; published 13 August 2004; <http://www.census.gov/popest/archives/EST90INTERCENSAL/US-EST90INT-datasets.html>; 2000 to 2005: "Monthly Population Estimates for the United States: April 1, 2000, to May 1, 2006"; published 22 December 2005 (revised May 2006); <http://www.census.gov/popest/national/tables/NA-EST2005-01.xls>.

Population 7

Table 3. Resident Population Projections: 2006 to 2050

[298,217 represents 298,217,000. As of July 1. The projections are based on assumptions about future childbearing, mortality, and migration. The level of childbearing among women is assumed to remain close to present levels, with differences by race and Hispanic origin diminishing over time. Mortality is assumed to decline gradually with less variation by race and Hispanic origin than at present. International migration is assumed to vary over time and decrease generally relative to the size of the population]

Year	Number (1,000)	Percent change [1]	Year	Number (1,000)	Percent change [1]	Year	Number (1,000)	Percent change [1]
2006	298,217	0.9	2021	338,490	0.8	2036	380,716	0.7
2007	300,913	0.9	2022	341,195	0.8	2037	383,537	0.7
2008	303,598	0.9	2023	343,921	0.8	2038	386,348	0.7
2009	306,272	0.9	2024	346,669	0.8	2039	389,151	0.7
2010	308,936	0.9	2025	349,439	0.8	2040	391,946	0.7
2011.	311,601	0.9	2026	352,229	0.8	2041	394,734	0.7
2012	314,281	0.9	2027	355,035	0.8	2042	397,519	0.7
2013	316,971	0.9	2028	357,862	0.8	2043	400,301	0.7
2014	319,668	0.9	2029	360,711	0.8	2044	403,081	0.7
2015	322,366	0.8	2030	363,584	0.8	2045	405,862	0.7
2016	325,063	0.8	2031	366,466	0.8	2046	408,646	0.7
2017	327,756	0.8	2032	369,336	0.8	2047	411,435	0.7
2018	330,444	0.8	2033	372,196	0.8	2048	414,230	0.7
2019	333,127	0.8	2034	375,046	0.8	2049	417,035	0.7
2020	335,805	0.8	2035	377,886	0.8	2050	419,854	0.7

[1] Percent change from immediate preceding year. 2006, change from 2005.

Source: U.S. Census Bureau, "U.S. Interim Projections by Age, Sex, Race, and Hispanic Origin"; published 18 March 2004; <http://www.census.gov/ipc/www/usinterimproj/>.

Table 4. Components of Population Change: 2000 to 2005

[In thousands (281,425 represents 281,425,000), except as indicated. Resident population]

Period	Population as of beginning of period	Net increase		Births	Deaths	Net international migration [2]	Population as of end of period
		Total	Percent [1]				
April 1, 2000 to July 1, 2000 [3] . . .	281,425	769	0.3	989	561	341	282,193
July 1, 2000 to July 1, 2001	282,193	2,914	1.0	4,047	2,419	1,286	285,108
July 1, 2001 to July 1, 2002	285,108	2,877	1.0	4,007	2,430	1,300	287,985
July 1, 2002 to July 1, 2003	287,985	2,865	1.0	4,053	2,423	1,235	290,850
July 1, 2003 to July 1, 2004	290,850	2,807	1.0	4,105	2,420	1,122	293,657
July 1, 2004 to July 1, 2005	293,657	2,754	0.9	4,129	2,425	1,050	296,410

[1] Percent of population at beginning of period.   [2] Includes net migration of the foreign-born, emigration of natives, net movement from Puerto Rico to the United States, and Armed Forces movement.   [3] The April 1, 2000, Population Estimates base reflects changes to the Census 2000 population from the Count Question Resolution program and geographic program revisions.

Source: U.S. Census Bureau, "Population, population change and estimated components of population change: April 1, 2000 to July 1, 2005"; published December 2005; <http://www.census.gov/popest/national/files/NST_EST2005_ALLDATA.csv>.

Table 5. Immigration: 1901 to 2005

[In thousands, except rate (8,795 represents 8,795,000). For fiscal years ending in year shown; see text, Section 8. For definition of immigrants, see text of this section. Data represent immigrants admitted. Rates based on Census Bureau estimates as of July 1 for resident population through 1929 and for total population thereafter (excluding Alaska and Hawaii prior to 1959)]

Period	Number	Rate [1]	Year	Number	Rate [1]
1901 to 1910	8,795	10.4	1990	1,536	6.1
1911 to 1920	5,736	5.7	1991	1,827	7.2
1921 to 1930	4,107	3.5	1992	973	3.8
			1993	904	3.5
1931 to 1940	528	0.4	1994	804	3.1
1941 to 1950	1,035	0.7	1995	720	2.7
			1996	916	3.4
1951 to 1960	2,515	1.5	1997	798	2.9
1961 to 1970	3,322	1.7	1998	653	2.4
			1999	645	2.3
1971 to 1980	4,399	2.0	2000	841	3.0
1981 to 1990	7,256	3.0	2001	1,059	3.7
			2002	1,059	3.7
1991 to 2000	9,081	3.4	2003	704	2.4
2001 to 2005	4,902	3.4	2004	958	3.3
			2005	1,122	3.8

[1] Annual rate per 1,000 U.S. population. Rate computed by dividing sum of annual immigration totals by sum of annual U.S. population totals for same number of years.

Source: U.S. Department of Homeland Security, Office of Immigration Statistics, *2005 Yearbook of Immigration Statistics*. See also <http://uscis.gov/graphics/shared/statistics/yearbook/index.htm>.

Table 6. Immigrants Admitted by Class of Admission: 2000 to 2005

[For fiscal year ending September 30. For definition of immigrants, see text of this section]

Class of admission	2000	2001	2002	2003	2004	2005
Total	841,002	1,058,902	1,059,356	703,542	957,883	1,122,373
New arrivals.	407,279	410,816	384,289	358,333	373,962	384,071
Adjustments.	433,723	648,086	675,067	345,209	583,921	738,302
Family-sponsored preferences.	235,092	231,699	186,880	158,796	214,355	212,970
Unmarried sons/daughters of U.S. citizens and their children	27,635	27,003	23,517	21,471	26,380	24,729
Spouses, unmarried sons/daughters of alien residents and their children . . . . , ...	124,540	112,015	84,785	53,195	93,609	100,139
Married sons/daughters of U.S. citizens [1]	22,804	24,830	21,041	27,287	28,695	22,953
Brothers or sisters of U.S. citizens [1]	60,113	67,851	57,537	56,843	65,671	65,149
Employment-based preferences	106,642	178,702	173,814	81,727	155,330	246,878
Priority workers [1].	27,566	41,672	34,168	14,453	31,291	64,731
Professionals with advanced degrees or aliens of exceptional ability [1]	20,255	42,550	44,316	15,406	32,534	42,597
Skilled workers, professionals, unskilled workers [1]	49,589	85,847	88,002	46,415	85,969	129,070
Special immigrants [1]	9,014	8,442	7,186	5,389	5,407	10,134
Employment creation (investors) [1]	218	191	142	64	129	346
Immediate relatives of U.S. citizens	346,350	439,972	483,676	331,286	417,815	436,231
Spouses [2]	196,405	268,294	293,219	183,796	252,193	259,144
Children [2]	82,638	91,275	96,941	77,948	88,088	94,974
Parents	67,307	80,403	93,516	69,542	77,534	82,113
Refugees [1]	56,091	96,870	115,601	34,362	61,013	112,676
Asylees.	6,837	11,111	10,197	10,402	10,217	30,286
Diversity [3]	50,920	41,989	42,820	46,335	50,084	46,234
Cancellation of removal	12,154	22,188	23,642	28,990	32,702	20,785
Parolees	3,162	5,349	6,018	4,196	7,121	7,715
Nicaraguan Adjustment and Central American Relief Act (NACARA)	20,364	18,663	9,307	2,498	2,292	1,155
Haitian Refugee Immigration Fairness Act (HRIFA) . . .	435	10,064	5,345	1,406	2,451	2,820
Other	2,955	2,295	2,056	3,544	4,503	4,623

[1] Includes spouses and children. [2] Includes orphans. [3] Includes categories of immigrants admitted under three laws intended to diversify immigration: P.L. 99-603, P.L. 100-658, and P.L. 101-649.

Source: U.S. Dept. of Homeland Security, Office of Immigration Statistics, *2005 Yearbook of Immigration Statistics*. See also <http://uscis.gov/graphics/shared/statistics/yearbook/index.htm>.

Table 7. Immigrants by Selected Country of Birth and Selected Characteristics: 2004

[For year ending September 30. Unrevised data. For definition of immigrants, see text of this section]

Age, marital status, class of admission	Total [1]	Mexico	India	Philippines	China	Vietnam	Dominican Republic	El Salvador	Cuba
Total	946,142	175,364	70,116	57,827	51,156	31,514	30,492	29,795	20,488
Under 18 years	182,355	33,867	8,826	12,001	9,432	5,707	11,068	2,489	4,709
18 to 24 years	119,733	27,357	6,010	5,641	4,010	4,491	4,869	2,769	1,673
25 to 34 years	268,327	51,930	30,253	14,356	11,135	8,555	4,865	8,292	4,625
35 to 44 years	183,655	28,009	11,567	10,006	11,974	6,544	4,321	10,364	4,741
45 to 54 years	94,884	13,988	5,973	6,599	6,580	3,924	2,520	3,969	2,128
55 to 64 years	53,866	10,366	4,439	5,302	3,733	1,461	1,597	1,261	1,369
65 years and over.	43,282	9,830	3,047	3,922	4,289	831	1,252	649	1,241
Unknown.	40	17	1	–	3	1	–	2	2
Single.	346,185	61,635	15,479	23,006	14,442	13,215	20,380	12,994	9,150
Married	561,886	108,068	52,532	32,399	34,863	16,854	9,171	15,454	8,769
Other	35,770	5,507	1,981	2,386	1,803	1,343	885	1,302	2,498
Unknown.	2,301	154	124	36	48	102	56	45	71
Family-sponsored preferences.	214,355	62,463	13,307	17,406	13,658	14,890	18,099	3,744	2,340
Employment-based preferences.	155,330	7,225	38,443	15,497	15,583	(D)	212	996	34
Immediate relatives of U.S. citizens . .	406,074	99,718	16,942	24,708	20,947	10,338	12,087	4,874	976
Diversity programs	50,084	12	90	11	76	(D)	8	–	298
Refugee and asylee adjustments	71,230	122	1,181	35	876	2,831	32	263	16,678
Other	49,069	5,824	153	170	16	3,247	54	19,918	162

- Represents zero. D Data withheld to avoid disclosure. [1] Includes other countries not shown separately.

Source: U.S. Department of Homeland Security, Office of Immigration Statistics, "Profiles on Legal Permanent Residents: 2004"; published 5 August 2005; <http://uscis.gov/graphics/shared/statistics/data/DSLPR04c.htm>.

Population 9

Table 8. **Immigrants by Country of Birth: 1981 to 2005**

[In thousands (7,256.0 represents 7,256,000). For fiscal years ending Sept. 30. Number of immigrants by country prior to 1996 are unrevised. For definition of immigrants, see text of this section]

Country of birth	1981–1990, total	1991–2000, total	2001–2004, total	2005	Country of birth	1981–1990, total	1991–2000, total	2001–2004, total	2005
All countries. . . .	7,256.0	9,080.5	3,779.7	1,122.4	Syria	20.6	26.1	10.1	2.8
Europe [1]	705.6	1,309.1	581.6	176.6	Taiwan	([5])	106.3	37.8	9.2
Albania	(NA)	26.2	15.3	5.9	Thailand	64.4	48.4	15.8	5.5
Armenia	(X)	[2]26.6	6.7	2.6	Turkey	20.9	26.3	13.5	4.6
Belarus	(X)	[2]28.9	9.9	3.5	Vietnam	401.4	420.8	122.6	32.8
Bosnia and					**Africa** [1]	192.3	382.5	228.9	85.1
Herzegovina	(X)	[2]38.8	65.6	14.1	Egypt	31.4	46.7	18.9	7.9
Bulgaria	(NA)	23.1	16.1	5.6	Ethiopia	27.2	49.3	27.6	10.6
France	23.1	27.4	14.3	4.4	Ghana	14.9	35.6	18.0	6.5
Germany	70.1	67.6	30.8	9.3	Nigeria	35.3	67.2	33.6	10.6
Ireland	32.8	58.9	5.4	2.1	Somalia	(NA)	20.1	13.9	5.8
Italy	32.9	22.5	9.7	3.1	South Africa	15.7	22.6	13.5	4.5
Poland	97.4	169.5	49.3	15.4	**Oceania**	(NA)	47.9	21.9	6.5
Portugal	40.0	22.7	4.8	1.1	**North America** [1]	3,125.0	3,910.1	1,401.0	345.6
Romania	38.9	57.5	19.7	7.1	Canada	119.2	137.2	68.0	21.9
Russia	(X)	[2]127.8	72.4	18.1	Mexico	1,653.3	2,250.5	715.4	161.4
Serbia and					Cuba	159.2	178.7	85.4	36.3
Montenegro [3, 4] . . .	19.2	25.8	22.9	5.2	Dominican				
Soviet Union [3]	84.0	[2]103.8	7.1	2.9	Republic	251.8	340.8	100.4	27.5
Ukraine	(X)	[2]141.0	67.9	22.8	Haiti	140.2	181.7	73.7	14.5
United Kingdom	142.1	135.6	59.0	19.8	Jamaica	213.8	173.4	57.9	18.3
Asia [1]	2,817.4	2,890.2	1,267.2	400.1	Trinidad and				
Bangladesh	15.2	66.0	25.3	11.5	Tobago	39.5	63.2	21.9	6.6
Cambodia	116.6	18.5	11.1	4.0	El Salvador	214.6	217.3	120.2	21.4
China	[5]388.8	424.4	213.4	70.0	Guatemala	87.9	103.0	63.0	16.8
Hong Kong	63.0	74.0	21.9	3.7	Honduras	49.5	66.7	23.2	7.0
India	261.9	383.0	261.2	84.7	Nicaragua	44.1	94.6	38.4	3.3
Iran	154.8	112.5	41.0	13.9	Panama	29.0	24.0	6.1	1.8
Iraq	19.6	40.7	16.1	4.1	**South America** [1]	455.9	539.3	269.7	103.1
Israel	36.3	31.9	14.5	5.8	Argentina	25.7	24.3	14.9	7.1
Japan	43.2	61.4	31.5	8.8	Brazil	23.7	52.2	35.8	16.7
Jordan [6]	32.6	39.7	14.9	3.7	Colombia	124.4	130.8	69.0	25.6
Korea	338.8	171.1	73.4	26.6	Ecuador	56.0	76.3	35.9	11.6
Laos	145.6	43.5	4.7	1.2	Guyana	95.4	73.8	31.4	9.3
Lebanon	41.6	43.4	15.3	4.3	Peru	64.4	105.6	44.2	15.7
Pakistan	61.3	124.5	51.6	14.9	Venezuela	17.9	29.9	20.6	10.6
Philippines	495.3	505.3	207.1	60.7					

NA Not available. X Not applicable. [1] Includes countries not shown separately. [2] Covers years 1992–2000. [3] Prior to 1992, data include independent republics; beginning in 1992, data are for unknown republic only. [4] Yugoslavia (unknown republic) prior to February 7, 2003. [5] Data for Taiwan included with China. [6] Prior to 2003, includes Palestine; beginning in 2003, Palestine included in Unknown.

Source: U.S. Department of Homeland Security, Office of Immigration Statistics, *2005 Yearbook of Immigration Statistics*. See also <http://uscis.gov/graphics/shared/statistics/yearbook/index.htm>.

Table 9. **Immigrants Admitted as Permanent Residents Under Refugee Acts by Country of Birth: 1991 to 2005**

[For fiscal years ending September 30. Data prior to 2005 are unrevised]

Country of birth	1991–2000, total	2001–2004, total	2005	Country of birth	1991–2000, total	2001–2004, total	2005
Total [1]	1,021,266	350,747	142,962	India	2,544	5,198	2,331
Europe [1]	426,565	160,880	46,588	Iran	24,313	12,166	6,480
Albania	3,255	915	1,137	Iraq	22,557	9,465	2,169
Armenia	2,161	921	811	Laos	37,265	1,319	317
Azerbaijan	[2]12,072	1,644	938	Pakistan	1,650	1,571	967
Belarus	[2]24,581	4,134	1,677	Thailand	22,759	1,621	414
Bosnia and				Vietnam	206,857	21,689	5,818
Herzegovina	[2]37,591	64,243	13,298	**Africa** [1]	51,649	40,526	25,143
Croatia	1,807	7,555	1,258	Ethiopia [6]	17,865	5,525	3,802
Germany	1,309	4,286	464	Liberia	3,839	4,907	3,548
Kazakhstan	[2]4,269	1,750	634	Sierra Leone	272	2,203	1,793
Moldova	[2]11,717	3,742	2,351	Somalia	16,837	12,365	5,478
Poland	7,500	187	60	Sudan	5,191	6,191	4,619
Romania	15,708	377	163	**Oceania**	291	98	55
Russia	[2]60,404	14,156	5,335	**North America** [1]	185,333	78,280	35,709
Serbia and				Cuba	144,612	71,305	32,555
Montenegro [3, 4] . . .	6,274	15,842	3,078	Haiti	9,364	2,512	1,118
Soviet Union [3]	90,533	4,094	18	El Salvador	4,073	839	(D)
Ukraine	[2]109,739	30,061	12,421	Guatemala	2,033	1,490	(D)
Uzbekistan	[2]19,539	2,906	866	Nicaragua	22,486	937	208
Asia [1]	351,347	65,626	32,009	**South America** [1]	5,857	4,826	3,312
Afghanistan	9,725	3,435	4,049	Colombia	1,132	1,434	1,270
Cambodia	6,388	251	302	Peru	2,507	1,581	900
China [5]	7,608	3,191	5,335				

D Data withheld to avoid disclosure. [1] Includes other countries and unknown, not shown separately. [2] Covers years 1992–2000. [3] Prior to 1992, data include independent republics; beginning in 1992, data are for unknown republic only. [4] Yugoslavia (unknown republic) prior to February 7, 2003. [5] Includes Taiwan. [6] Prior to 1993, data include Eritrea.

Source: U.S. Department of Homeland Security, Office of Immigration Statistics, *2005 Yearbook of Immigration Statistics*. See also <http://uscis.gov/graphics/shared/statistics/yearbook/index.htm>.

Table 10. **Immigrants Admitted by State and Leading Country of Birth: 2005**

[**For year ending September 30.** For definition of immigrants, see text of this section]

State and other area	Total [1]	Mexico	India	China	Philip-pines	Cuba	Vietnam	Domini-can Republic	Korea
Total	1,122,373	161,445	84,681	69,967	60,748	36,261	32,784	27,504	26,562
Alabama.	4,200	569	431	328	178	22	86	5	203
Alaska	1,525	96	15	92	435	(D)	8	42	75
Arizona.	18,988	8,373	739	543	636	311	495	22	235
Arkansas	2,698	870	215	202	132	6	116	(D)	80
California	232,023	63,092	14,724	17,668	23,993	428	12,047	82	6,660
Colorado.	11,977	2,891	516	765	247	18	452	6	343
Connecticut.	15,335	316	1,571	894	367	32	188	319	208
Delaware	2,992	357	439	279	114	3	32	34	178
District of Columbia	2,457	37	60	113	98	8	33	29	15
Florida	122,918	4,236	3,714	1,891	2,766	30,624	1,078	2,064	638
Georgia	31,535	3,377	3,671	1,376	694	193	1,308	114	1,622
Hawaii	6,480	45	28	625	3,447	3	207	(D)	280
Idaho	2,768	992	75	126	76	8	29	8	59
Illinois	52,419	9,838	5,978	2,571	2,989	184	673	95	1,311
Indiana.	6,915	941	621	541	424	25	134	21	125
Iowa	4,536	647	315	249	146	6	275	8	83
Kansas.	4,514	955	460	278	137	12	352	9	105
Kentucky	5,267	288	511	393	228	318	127	12	110
Louisiana	3,777	214	318	285	147	70	342	41	91
Maine.	1,908	23	108	124	107	5	38	4	13
Maryland	22,870	624	1,785	1,600	1,180	34	470	159	1,070
Massachusetts.	34,236	268	3,100	3,000	418	41	998	1,946	577
Michigan.	23,597	1,189	3,595	1,293	575	240	362	91	648
Minnesota.	15,456	696	830	675	399	19	583	12	234
Mississippi	1,831	256	224	147	154	20	107	10	31
Missouri	8,744	535	786	530	307	41	343	11	166
Montana.	589	28	14	41	65	(D)	(D)	–	8
Nebraska	2,997	538	168	141	52	18	189	6	65
Nevada	9,823	2,424	253	518	1,725	416	174	29	127
New Hampshire	3,298	53	459	221	76	–	57	40	82
New Jersey.	56,180	1,072	9,624	2,539	3,354	637	532	3,688	2,056
New Mexico	3,513	1,828	150	176	81	128	110	(D)	49
New York	136,828	1,972	6,693	14,505	3,476	629	770	14,226	2,445
North Carolina	16,715	1,901	1,774	1,112	569	103	1,245	77	447
North Dakota.	864	10	49	43	43	–	14	–	24
Ohio	16,897	700	1,984	1,271	611	30	338	74	264
Oklahoma.	4,702	1,238	373	257	204	4	351	7	86
Oregon.	9,623	1,632	405	823	288	118	464	6	203
Pennsylvania	28,908	1,222	3,362	2,359	844	201	970	894	1,163
Rhode Island.	3,852	73	165	209	64	3	21	639	35
South Carolina.	5,029	448	529	315	257	10	102	14	88
South Dakota	881	30	23	51	57	(D)	8	(D)	18
Tennessee	8,962	1,093	900	637	521	114	183	22	286
Texas.	95,958	38,040	7,139	4,139	3,353	794	3,919	119	1,551
Utah	5,082	922	147	217	128	21	127	11	84
Vermont	1,042	(D)	74	50	16	–	23	(D)	36
Virginia.	27,100	870	2,776	1,327	1,420	143	926	90	1,265
Washington.	26,482	2,330	1,747	1,508	1,670	33	1,253	18	728
West Virginia.	847	30	133	101	39	(D)	15	6	14
Wisconsin.	7,909	1,054	876	593	234	11	93	39	151
Wyoming	321	75	(D)	28	23	–	–	–	8
Armed Services posts . . .	128	(D)	(D)	13	17	–	(D)	(D)	12
U.S. possessions	5,868	129	24	184	1,167	171	8	2,346	107
Unknown	9	–	1	1	–	–	–	–	–

– Represents zero.   D Data withheld to avoid disclosure.   [1] Includes other countries, not shown separately.

Source: U.S. Department of Homeland Security, Office of Immigration Statistics, *2005 Yearbook of Immigration Statistics*, See also <http://uscis.gov/graphics/shared/statistics/yearbook/index.htm>.

Table 11. Resident Population by Age and Sex: 1980 to 2005

[In thousands, except as indicated (226,546,000). 1980, 1990, and 2000 data are enumerated population as of April 1; data for other years are estimated population as of July 1. Excludes Armed Forces overseas. For definition of median, see Guide to Tabular Presentation]

Age group	1980 [1] Total	Male	Female	1990 [2] Total	Male	Female	1995, total	1999, total	2000 [3] Total	Male	Female	2001, total	2002, total	2003, total	2004, total	2005 Total	Male	Female
Total	**226,546**	**110,053**	**116,493**	**248,791**	**121,284**	**127,507**	**266,278**	**279,040**	**281,425**	**138,056**	**143,368**	**285,108**	**287,985**	**290,850**	**293,657**	**296,410**	**146,000**	**150,411**
Under 5 years	16,348	8,362	7,986	18,765	9,603	9,162	19,627	19,136	19,176	9,811	9,365	19,349	19,976	19,761	19,614	20,304	10,381	9,922
5 to 9 years	16,700	8,539	8,161	18,042	9,236	8,806	19,438	20,606	20,550	10,523	10,026	20,233	20,891	21,199	20,724	19,539	9,993	9,545
10 to 14 years	18,242	9,316	8,926	17,067	8,742	8,325	19,207	20,213	20,528	10,520	10,008	20,891	20,366	20,768	20,487	20,858	10,682	10,176
15 to 19 years	21,168	10,755	10,413	17,893	9,178	8,714	18,300	20,085	20,219	10,391	9,828	19,801	20,338	20,726	20,973	21,039	10,790	10,249
20 to 24 years	21,319	10,663	10,655	19,143	9,749	9,394	18,680	18,591	18,963	9,688	9,275	18,937	20,815	21,413	21,050	21,038	10,857	10,181
25 to 29 years	19,521	9,705	9,816	21,336	10,708	10,629	19,680	19,575	19,382	9,799	9,583	18,914	19,133	20,726	20,467	20,066	10,268	9,798
30 to 34 years	17,561	8,677	8,884	21,838	10,866	10,973	22,372	20,603	20,511	10,322	10,189	20,730	20,815	20,726	20,077	20,077	10,153	9,924
35 to 39 years	13,965	6,862	7,104	19,851	9,837	10,014	22,492	22,883	22,707	11,319	11,388	22,279	22,014	21,840	21,413	21,002	10,563	10,439
40 to 44 years	11,669	5,708	5,961	17,593	8,679	8,914	20,219	22,194	22,442	11,129	11,313	21,840	22,947	22,991	23,055	22,861	11,377	11,484
45 to 49 years	11,090	5,388	5,702	13,747	6,741	7,006	17,624	19,654	20,093	9,890	10,203	20,709	21,275	21,991	22,121	22,485	11,107	11,378
50 to 54 years	11,710	5,621	6,089	11,315	5,494	5,821	13,856	16,924	17,586	8,608	8,978	18,662	18,696	19,041	19,496	19,998	9,789	10,209
55 to 59 years	11,615	5,482	6,133	10,489	5,009	5,480	11,182	13,085	13,469	6,509	6,961	13,933	15,083	15,723	16,488	17,354	8,425	8,929
60 to 64 years	10,088	4,670	5,418	10,627	4,947	5,679	10,138	10,693	10,806	5,137	5,669	11,104	11,501	12,111	12,589	13,002	6,202	6,800
65 to 74 years	15,581	6,757	8,824	18,048	7,908	10,140	18,866	18,419	18,391	8,303	10,088	18,322	18,282	18,351	18,478	18,640	8,529	10,110
75 to 84 years	7,729	2,867	4,862	10,014	3,745	6,268	11,222	12,225	12,361	4,879	7,482	12,590	12,760	12,885	12,987	13,054	5,279	7,775
85 years and over	2,240	682	1,559	3,022	841	2,181	3,681	4,154	4,240	1,227	3,013	4,418	4,547	4,716	4,867	5,096	1,604	3,492
5 to 13 years	31,159	15,923	15,237	31,839	16,301	15,538	34,825	36,804	37,026	18,964	18,062	37,077	36,971	36,765	36,371	36,087	18,468	17,619
14 to 17 years	16,247	8,298	7,950	13,345	6,860	6,485	15,013	16,007	16,093	8,285	7,808	16,354	16,354	16,504	16,826	17,079	8,752	8,327
18 to 24 years	30,022	15,054	14,969	26,961	13,744	13,217	25,482	26,685	27,141	13,873	13,268	27,971	28,463	28,947	29,246	29,307	15,102	14,205
18 years and over	162,791	77,473	85,321	184,841	88,519	96,322	196,814	207,094	209,130	100,996	108,133	212,498	215,123	217,803	220,399	222,940	108,398	114,542
55 years and over	47,253	20,458	26,796	52,200	22,450	29,748	55,089	58,576	59,267	26,055	33,212	60,368	62,173	63,786	65,409	67,146	30,039	37,106
65 years and over	25,550	10,306	15,245	31,084	12,494	18,589	34,798	34,798	34,992	14,410	20,582	35,330	35,589	35,952	36,333	36,790	15,413	21,377
75 years and over	9,969	3,549	6,421	13,036	4,586	8,449	14,903	16,379	16,601	6,106	10,495	17,008	17,307	17,601	17,855	18,150	6,883	11,267
Median age (years)	30.0	28.8	31.3	32.8	31.6	34.0	34.2	35.2	35.3	34.0	36.5	35.6	35.7	35.9	36.0	36.2	34.9	37.6

[1] Total population count has been revised since the 1980 census publications. Numbers by age and sex have not been corrected. [2] The data shown here have been modified from the official 1990 census counts. See text of this section for explanation. The April 1, 1990, estimates base (248,790,925) includes count resolution corrections processed through August 1997. It generally does not include adjustments for census coverage errors. However, it includes adjustments estimated for the 1995 Test Census in various localities in California, New Jersey, and Louisiana; and the 1998 census dress rehearsals in localities in California and Wisconsin. These adjustments amounted to a total of 81,052 persons. [3] The April 1, 2000, population estimates base reflects changes to the Census 2000 population from the Count Question Resolution program and geographic program revisions.

Source: U.S. Census Bureau, Current Population Reports, P25-1095; "Table US-EST90INT-04—Intercensal Estimates of the United States Resident Population by Age Groups and Sex, 1990-2000: Selected Months"; published 13 September 2002; <http://www.census.gov/popest/archives/EST90INTERCENSAL/US-EST90INT-04.html>; and "Table 1: Annual Estimates of the Population by Sex and Five-Year Age Groups for the United States: April 1, 2000 to July 1, 2005"; published 10 May 2006; <http://www.census.gov/popest/national/asrh/NC-EST2005/NC-EST2005-01.xls>.

Table 12. Resident Population Projections by Sex and Age: 2010 to 2050

[In thousands, except as indicated (308,936 represents 308,936,000). As of July 1. For assumptions, see Table 3. For definition of median, see Guide to Tabular Presention]

Age	2010 Total	2010 Male	2010 Female	2015 Total	2015 Male	2015 Female	2020	2025	2030	2035	2040	2045	2050	Percent distribution 2010	2015	2020	2025	2030	2035	2040	2045	2050
Total	308,936	151,815	157,121	322,366	158,489	163,877	335,805	349,439	363,584	377,886	391,946	405,862	419,854	100.0	100.0	100.0	100.0	100.0	100.0	100.0	100.0	100.0
Under 5 years	21,426	10,947	10,479	22,358	11,423	10,935	22,932	23,518	24,272	25,262	26,299	27,233	28,080	6.9	6.9	6.8	6.7	6.7	6.7	6.7	6.7	6.7
5 to 9 years	20,706	10,575	10,131	21,623	11,044	10,579	22,564	23,163	23,790	24,562	25,550	26,586	27,521	6.7	6.7	6.7	6.6	6.5	6.5	6.5	6.6	6.6
10 to 14 years	19,767	10,109	9,658	20,984	10,718	10,265	21,914	22,888	23,539	24,182	24,953	25,938	26,974	6.4	6.5	6.5	6.5	6.5	6.4	6.4	6.4	6.4
15 to 19 years	21,336	10,938	10,398	20,243	10,366	9,877	21,478	22,457	23,503	24,182	24,824	25,587	26,572	6.9	6.3	6.4	6.4	6.5	6.4	6.3	6.3	6.3
20 to 24 years	21,676	11,075	10,602	21,810	11,137	10,673	20,751	22,052	23,136	24,227	24,897	25,534	26,297	7.0	6.8	6.2	6.3	6.4	6.4	6.4	6.3	6.3
25 to 29 years	21,375	10,868	10,507	22,195	11,269	10,926	22,361	21,390	22,810	23,943	25,024	25,690	26,327	6.9	6.9	6.7	6.1	6.3	6.3	6.4	6.3	6.3
30 to 34 years	20,271	10,238	10,034	21,858	11,075	10,783	22,704	22,955	22,125	23,605	24,731	25,808	26,477	6.6	6.8	6.8	6.6	6.1	6.2	6.3	6.4	6.3
35 to 39 years	20,137	10,091	10,046	20,543	10,337	10,206	22,143	23,046	23,399	22,627	24,101	25,223	26,300	6.5	6.4	6.6	6.6	6.4	6.0	6.2	6.2	6.3
40 to 44 years	20,984	10,462	10,523	20,250	10,108	10,142	20,673	23,305	23,277	23,669	22,907	24,376	25,496	6.8	6.3	6.2	6.7	6.4	6.3	5.8	6.0	6.1
45 to 49 years	22,654	11,190	11,464	20,926	10,387	10,539	20,219	20,678	23,352	23,350	23,734	23,001	24,466	7.3	6.5	6.0	5.9	6.4	6.2	6.1	5.7	5.8
50 to 54 years	22,173	10,874	11,299	22,376	10,992	11,383	20,702	20,043	20,550	23,234	23,234	23,641	22,917	7.2	6.9	6.2	5.7	5.7	6.1	5.9	5.8	5.5
55 to 59 years	19,507	9,456	10,051	21,649	10,532	11,117	21,876	20,291	19,702	20,241	21,370	22,916	23,337	6.3	6.7	6.5	5.8	5.4	5.4	5.5	5.6	5.6
60 to 64 years	16,679	7,982	8,696	18,761	8,985	9,776	20,856	21,128	19,676	19,156	19,719	21,370	22,384	5.4	5.8	6.2	6.0	5.4	5.1	5.0	5.3	5.3
65 to 69 years	12,172	5,686	6,486	15,621	7,336	8,285	17,618	19,647	19,980	18,683	18,237	18,829	20,444	3.9	4.8	5.2	5.6	5.5	4.9	4.7	4.6	4.9
70 to 74 years	9,097	4,111	4,987	10,987	4,988	5,998	14,161	16,041	17,968	18,350	17,233	16,879	17,499	2.9	3.4	4.2	4.6	4.9	4.9	4.4	4.2	4.2
75 to 79 years	7,186	3,066	4,120	7,761	3,351	4,409	9,450	12,268	13,989	15,764	16,192	15,304	15,067	2.3	2.4	2.8	3.5	3.8	4.2	4.1	3.8	3.6
80 to 84 years	5,665	2,206	3,459	5,600	2,226	3,374	6,134	7,557	9,914	11,414	12,978	13,449	12,835	1.8	1.7	1.8	2.2	2.7	3.0	3.3	3.3	3.1
85 to 89 years	3,713	1,274	2,439	3,857	1,363	2,494	3,897	4,353	5,451	7,259	8,476	9,768	10,254	1.2	1.2	1.2	1.2	1.5	1.9	2.2	2.4	2.4
90 to 94 years	1,727	510	1,218	2,059	629	1,440	2,221	2,312	2,651	3,395	4,621	5,510	6,473	0.6	0.6	0.7	0.7	0.7	0.9	1.2	1.4	1.5
95 to 99 years	569	137	432	723	185	537	909	1,018	1,102	1,310	1,731	2,430	2,984	0.2	0.2	0.3	0.3	0.3	0.3	0.4	0.6	0.7
100 years and over	114	21	93	173	35	138	241	327	399	467	581	790	1,150	(Z)	0.1	0.1	0.1	0.1	0.1	0.1	0.2	0.3
5 to 13 years	36,439	18,618	17,821	38,418	19,621	18,796	40,148	41,501	42,627	43,922	45,536	47,379	49,138	11.8	11.9	12.0	11.9	11.7	11.6	11.6	11.7	11.7
14 to 17 years	16,566	8,492	8,074	16,243	8,313	7,930	17,220	18,079	18,809	19,311	19,847	20,505	21,330	5.4	5.0	5.1	5.2	5.2	5.1	5.1	5.1	5.1
18 to 24 years	30,461	15,587	14,884	30,000	15,331	14,669	29,339	30,980	32,533	33,924	34,841	35,763	36,895	9.9	9.3	8.7	8.9	8.9	9.0	8.9	8.8	8.8
16 years and over	242,936	118,082	124,854	253,361	123,235	130,126	264,085	275,339	287,281	299,051	310,182	320,974	331,940	78.6	78.6	78.6	78.8	79.0	79.1	79.1	79.1	79.1
18 years and over	234,504	113,758	120,746	245,347	119,132	126,216	255,505	266,341	277,877	289,391	300,264	310,746	321,305	75.9	76.1	76.1	76.2	76.4	76.6	76.6	76.6	76.5
16 to 64 years	202,693	101,071	101,622	206,570	103,120	103,450	209,453	211,815	215,828	222,410	230,132	238,015	245,234	65.6	64.1	62.4	60.6	59.4	58.9	58.7	58.6	58.4
55 years and over	76,429	34,450	41,980	87,201	39,632	47,569	97,363	104,944	110,831	116,039	121,679	127,245	132,427	24.7	27.1	29.0	30.0	30.5	30.7	31.0	31.4	31.5
65 years and over	40,244	17,011	23,233	46,791	20,115	26,676	54,632	63,524	71,453	76,641	80,050	82,959	86,706	13.0	14.5	16.3	18.2	19.7	20.3	20.4	20.4	20.7
75 years and over	18,974	7,214	11,760	20,182	7,790	12,393	22,853	27,836	33,506	39,609	44,580	47,251	48,763	6.1	6.3	6.8	8.0	9.2	10.5	11.4	11.6	11.6
85 years and over	6,123	1,942	4,182	6,822	2,213	4,609	7,269	8,011	9,603	12,430	15,409	18,498	20,861	2.0	2.1	2.2	2.3	2.6	3.3	3.9	4.6	5.0
Median age (years)	37.0	35.6	38.4	37.4	36.0	38.8	38.0	38.5	39.0	39.2	39.1	39.1	39.1	(X)	(X)	(X)	(X)	(X)	(X)	(X)	(X)	(X)

X Not applicable.   Z Less than 0.05 percent.

Source: U.S. Census Bureau, "U.S. Interim Projections by Age, Sex, Race, and Hispanic Origin"; published March 2004; <http://www.census.gov/ipc/www/usinterimproj/>.

Table 13. Resident Population by Sex, Race, and Hispanic Origin Status: 2000 to 2005

[281,425 represents 281,425,000. As of July, except as noted. Data shown are modified race counts; see text, this section]

Characteristic	2000 [1] (April 1)	Number (1,000) 2002	2003	2004	2005	Percent change, 2000 to 2005
BOTH SEXES						
Total	281,425	287,985	290,850	293,657	296,410	5.3
One race	277,527	283,804	286,539	289,213	291,831	5.2
White	228,107	232,375	234,241	236,064	237,855	4.3
Black or African American	35,705	36,671	37,082	37,496	37,909	6.2
American Indian and Alaska Native	2,664	2,750	2,788	2,825	2,863	7.5
Asian	10,589	11,523	11,933	12,321	12,687	19.8
Native Hawaiian and Other Pacific Islanders	463	485	496	506	517	11.7
Two or more races	3,898	4,181	4,311	4,444	4,579	17.5
Race alone or in combination: [2]						
White	231,436	235,962	237,947	239,892	241,807	4.5
Black or African American	37,105	38,244	38,733	39,229	39,724	7.1
American Indian and Alaska Native	4,225	4,324	4,368	4,411	4,454	5.4
Asian	12,007	13,052	13,514	13,956	14,377	19.7
Native Hawaiian and Other Pacific Islanders	907	944	960	975	990	9.1
Not Hispanic or Latino	246,118	249,485	250,915	252,319	253,723	3.1
One race	242,712	245,843	247,166	248,459	249,749	2.9
White	195,577	196,827	197,340	197,843	198,366	1.4
Black or African American	34,314	35,201	35,574	35,950	36,325	5.9
American Indian and Alaska Native	2,097	2,155	2,181	2,207	2,233	6.5
Asian	10,357	11,277	11,680	12,061	12,421	19.9
Native Hawaiian and Other Pacific Islanders	367	384	391	398	405	10.3
Two or more races	3,406	3,642	3,750	3,861	3,974	16.7
Race alone or in combination: [2]						
White	198,477	199,940	200,551	201,156	201,782	1.7
Black or African American	35,499	36,530	36,970	37,414	37,859	6.6
American Indian and Alaska Native	3,456	3,519	3,546	3,574	3,603	4.3
Asian	11,632	12,650	13,099	13,527	13,934	19.8
Native Hawaiian and Other Pacific Islanders	752	779	791	802	812	8.0
Hispanic or Latino	35,306	38,500	39,935	41,338	42,687	20.9
One race	34,815	37,960	39,373	40,754	42,082	20.9
White	32,530	35,548	36,901	38,221	39,489	21.4
Black or African American	1,391	1,471	1,508	1,547	1,585	13.9
American Indian and Alaska Native	566	594	607	619	630	11.2
Asian	232	246	253	260	267	14.8
Native Hawaiian and Other Pacific Islanders	95	102	105	108	112	16.9
Two or more races	491	540	561	583	605	23.2
Race alone or in combination: [2]						
White	32,959	36,022	37,396	38,736	40,025	21.4
Black or African American	1,606	1,713	1,763	1,815	1,866	16.2
American Indian and Alaska Native	770	805	821	836	851	10.6
Asian	375	402	415	429	443	18.2
Native Hawaiian and Other Pacific Islanders	155	165	169	173	177	14.5
MALE						
Total	138,056	141,542	143,058	144,535	146,000	5.8
One race	136,146	139,488	140,937	142,347	143,742	5.6
White	112,478	114,825	115,843	116,832	117,814	4.7
Black or African American	16,972	17,457	17,663	17,869	18,079	6.5
American Indian and Alaska Native	1,333	1,377	1,396	1,415	1,435	7.6
Asian	5,128	5,583	5,783	5,973	6,152	20.0
Native Hawaiian and Other Pacific Islanders	235	247	252	258	263	11.9
Two or more races	1,910	2,054	2,121	2,188	2,257	18.2
Race alone or in combination: [2]						
White	114,116	116,593	117,672	118,723	119,768	5.0
Black or African American	17,644	18,217	18,463	18,711	18,963	7.5
American Indian and Alaska Native	2,088	2,139	2,161	2,183	2,205	5.6
Asian	5,834	6,346	6,573	6,790	6,996	19.9
Native Hawaiian and Other Pacific Islanders	456	475	483	491	498	9.2
Not Hispanic or Latino	119,894	121,685	122,442	123,181	123,934	3.4
Hispanic or Latino	18,162	19,857	20,616	21,354	22,065	21.5
FEMALE						
Total	143,368	146,442	147,792	149,121	150,411	4.9
One race	141,381	144,315	145,602	146,866	148,089	4.7
White	115,628	117,550	118,398	119,232	120,041	3.8
Black or African American	18,733	19,214	19,419	19,627	19,830	5.9
American Indian and Alaska Native	1,331	1,373	1,392	1,410	1,429	7.3
Asian	5,461	5,940	6,150	6,348	6,535	19.7
Native Hawaiian and Other Pacific Islanders	227	239	244	249	253	11.5
Two or more races	1,987	2,127	2,190	2,256	2,322	16.8
Race alone or in combination: [2]						
White	117,321	119,369	120,275	121,168	122,039	4.0
Black or African American	19,461	20,027	20,270	20,518	20,761	6.7
American Indian and Alaska Native	2,137	2,185	2,207	2,228	2,249	5.2
Asian	6,173	6,706	6,942	7,166	7,380	19.6
Native Hawaiian and Other Pacific Islanders	451	469	477	484	492	9.1
Not Hispanic or Latino	126,224	127,799	128,473	129,138	129,789	2.8
Hispanic or Latino	17,144	18,643	19,319	19,984	20,622	20.3

[1] See footnote 3, Table 11. [2] In combination with one or more other races. The sum of the five race groups adds to more than the total population because individuals may report more than one race.

Source: U.S. Census Bureau, "Annual Estimates of the Population by Sex, Race and Hispanic or Latino Origin for the United States: April 1, 2000 to July 1, 2005 (NC-EST2005-03)"; published 10 May 2006; <http://www.census.gov/popest/national/asrh/NC EST2005/NC-EST2005-03.xls>.

Table 14. Resident Population by Race, Hispanic Origin, and Age: 2000 and 2005

[In thousands (281,425 represents 281,425,000); except as indicated. 2000, as of April and 2005, as of July. For definition of median, see Guide to Tabular Presentation]

Age group	Total		White alone		Black or African American alone		American Indian, Alaska Native alone		Asian alone		Native Hawaiian, Other Pacific Islander alone		Two or more races		Hispanic or Latino origin [1]		Not Hispanic or Latino White alone	
	2000 [2]	2005	2000 [2]	2005	2000 [2]	2005	2000 [2]	2005	2000 [2]	2005	2000 [2]	2005	2000 [2]	2005	2000 [2]	2005	2000 [2]	2005
Total	281,425	296,410	228,107	237,855	35,705	37,909	2,664	2,863	10,589	12,687	463	517	3,898	4,579	35,306	42,687	195,577	198,366
Under 5 years	19,176	20,304	14,657	15,515	2,925	3,047	233	199	708	861	41	36	613	647	3,718	4,532	11,288	11,258
5 to 9 years	20,550	19,539	15,688	14,920	3,320	2,942	258	234	716	782	44	42	524	618	3,624	3,952	12,392	11,322
10 to 14 years	20,528	20,858	15,843	15,898	3,221	3,331	264	259	715	792	42	45	443	532	3,163	3,859	12,961	12,379
15 to 19 years	20,219	21,039	15,745	16,193	3,024	3,280	251	269	776	800	44	44	380	453	3,172	3,461	12,836	13,032
20 to 24 years	18,963	21,038	14,826	16,357	2,729	3,077	218	260	848	906	46	47	297	392	3,385	3,732	11,681	12,917
25 to 29 years	19,382	20,066	15,217	15,608	2,645	2,799	204	228	1,019	1,069	42	50	254	312	3,410	4,029	12,077	11,875
30 to 34 years	20,511	20,077	16,349	15,629	2,710	2,676	202	208	980	1,256	39	44	231	264	3,125	3,798	13,451	12,096
35 to 39 years	22,707	21,002	18,372	16,645	2,910	2,727	217	208	937	1,147	38	41	233	239	2,825	3,389	15,753	13,498
40 to 44 years	22,442	22,861	18,346	18,427	2,772	2,894	202	217	870	1,046	33	39	219	237	2,304	3,002	16,213	15,642
45 to 49 years	20,093	22,485	16,615	18,344	2,330	2,735	169	202	770	949	27	34	183	221	1,775	2,423	14,973	16,098
50 to 54 years	17,586	19,998	14,794	16,530	1,846	2,268	135	167	641	822	21	27	149	183	1,361	1,846	13,530	14,820
55 to 59 years	13,469	17,354	11,479	14,591	1,332	1,781	95	133	443	678	15	21	106	149	960	1,403	10,582	13,287
60 to 64 years	10,806	13,002	9,214	11,085	1,082	1,240	70	91	350	467	11	15	78	104	750	975	8,511	10,174
65 to 69 years	9,534	10,131	8,238	8,639	895	976	52	66	279	365	8	11	61	74	599	745	7,675	7,941
70 to 74 years	8,858	8,508	7,799	7,346	742	769	38	48	224	282	6	8	49	56	477	576	7,348	6,804
75 to 79 years	7,416	7,412	6,634	6,523	557	592	27	35	159	214	4	6	36	43	327	443	6,325	6,105
80 to 84 years	4,945	5,643	4,466	5,040	350	407	15	23	90	140	2	3	22	29	180	286	4,296	4,769
85 to 89 years	2,790	3,211	2,525	2,887	200	223	8	12	43	72	1	2	12	16	98	143	2,432	2,751
90 to 94 years	1,113	1,415	1,007	1,268	82	104	3	6	15	29	1	1	4	7	39	65	970	1,207
95 to 99 years	287	400	254	354	27	34	1	2	4	8	–	–	1	2	11	20	243	335
100 years and over	50	70	41	58	7	9	–	1	1	1	–	–	–	1	3	5	39	54
5 to 13 years	37,026	36,087	28,381	27,527	5,923	5,578	471	438	1,288	1,416	78	78	885	1,049	6,186	7,057	22,754	21,099
14 to 17 years	16,093	17,079	12,523	13,081	2,426	2,720	205	219	590	639	33	36	315	384	2,438	2,871	10,290	10,462
18 to 24 years	27,141	29,307	21,197	22,759	3,944	4,332	315	365	1,178	1,225	64	65	444	562	4,744	5,076	16,827	18,089
16 years and over	217,151	231,324	178,790	188,171	25,633	27,881	1,857	2,115	8,304	10,091	328	385	2,237	2,681	24,204	29,600	156,352	160,733
18 years and over	209,130	222,940	172,546	181,732	24,431	26,565	1,755	2,007	8,003	9,771	311	367	2,084	2,499	22,964	28,227	151,245	155,548
16 to 64 years	182,159	194,534	147,826	156,055	22,773	24,768	1,713	1,923	7,489	8,981	305	354	2,051	2,453	22,471	27,316	127,023	130,767
55 years and over	59,267	67,146	51,656	57,791	5,274	6,134	310	417	1,608	2,256	48	67	371	481	3,444	4,663	48,422	53,426
65 years and over	34,992	36,790	30,964	32,115	2,860	3,113	144	192	815	1,111	23	31	186	228	1,734	2,284	29,329	29,966
75 years and over	16,601	18,150	14,927	16,131	1,223	1,368	55	78	312	464	8	12	77	98	657	963	14,306	15,221
85 years and over	4,240	5,096	3,827	4,567	316	369	13	20	63	109	2	3	18	26	151	234	3,685	4,347
Median age (years)	35.3	36.2	36.6	37.6	30.0	30.9	27.7	29.6	32.5	34.5	26.8	29.4	19.8	20.5	25.8	27.2	38.6	40.3

– Represents or rounds to zero. [1] Persons of Hispanic origin may be of any race. [2] April 1, 2000, population estimates base reflects changes to the Census 2000 population from the Count Question Resolution program and geographic program revisions.

Source: U.S. Census Bureau, "Annual Estimates of the Population by Sex, Age and Race for the United States: April 1, 2000 to July 1, 2005/NC-EST2005-04)"; published 10 May 2006; <http://www.census.gov/popest/national/asrh/NC-EST2005-asrh.html>.

Table 15. **Resident Population by Race, Hispanic Origin, and Single Years of Age: 2005**

[In thousands, except as indicated (296,410 represents 296,410,000). As of July 1. For derivation of estimates, see text of this section]

Age	Total	Race						Hispanic or Latino origin [1]	Not-Hispanic or Latino White alone
		White alone	Black or African American alone	American Indian, Alaska Native alone	Asian alone	Native Hawaiian and Other Pacific Islander alone	Two or more races		
Total........	296,410	237,855	37,909	2,863	12,687	517	4,579	42,687	198,366
Under 5 yrs. old....	20,304	15,515	3,047	199	861	36	647	4,532	11,258
Under 1 yr. old ...	4,107	3,134	612	41	176	8	136	932	2,262
1 yr. old	4,086	3,118	611	40	175	7	133	936	2,243
2 yrs. old.......	4,042	3,093	599	40	175	7	129	911	2,237
3 yrs. old.......	4,007	3,066	604	39	166	7	125	885	2,231
4 yrs. old.......	4,062	3,104	620	39	169	7	124	869	2,285
5 to 9 yrs. old	19,539	14,920	2,942	234	782	42	618	3,952	11,322
5 yrs. old.......	3,908	2,985	587	45	154	8	130	821	2,234
6 yrs. old.......	3,865	2,950	578	47	152	9	129	785	2,239
7 yrs. old.......	3,876	2,955	586	47	156	8	124	781	2,246
8 yrs. old.......	3,903	2,980	590	47	159	8	119	779	2,271
9 yrs. old.......	3,986	3,049	602	48	162	9	116	786	2,333
10 to 14 yrs. old....	20,858	15,898	3,331	259	792	45	532	3,859	12,379
10 yrs. old......	4,051	3,093	629	48	159	9	113	786	2,376
11 yrs. old	4,086	3,110	650	50	158	9	109	777	2,401
12 yrs. old......	4,170	3,171	674	52	158	9	105	774	2,466
13 yrs. old......	4,241	3,233	683	54	159	9	104	768	2,533
14 yrs. old......	4,309	3,290	695	55	158	9	102	755	2,603
15 to 19 yrs. old....	21,039	16,193	3,280	269	800	44	453	3,461	13,032
15 yrs. old......	4,386	3,352	708	56	161	9	100	744	2,674
16 yrs. old......	4,223	3,236	670	54	161	9	93	692	2,604
17 yrs. old......	4,160	3,203	647	54	159	9	89	681	2,581
18 yrs. old......	4,119	3,185	629	52	157	9	86	670	2,573
19 yrs. old......	4,150	3,217	625	53	162	9	84	674	2,599
20 to 24 yrs. old....	21,038	16,357	3,077	260	906	47	392	3,732	12,917
20 yrs. old......	4,181	3,249	622	53	166	9	82	688	2,617
21 yrs. old......	4,117	3,197	608	52	171	9	79	704	2,550
22 yrs. old......	4,199	3,267	613	53	178	9	78	748	2,577
23 yrs. old......	4,245	3,301	616	51	189	10	77	786	2,575
24 yrs. old......	4,296	3,342	617	51	200	10	75	806	2,598
25 to 29 yrs. old....	20,066	15,608	2,799	228	1,069	50	312	4,029	11,875
25 yrs. old......	4,288	3,331	619	50	206	11	71	831	2,563
26 yrs. old......	4,084	3,173	581	47	208	10	66	803	2,431
27 yrs. old......	3,965	3,093	548	45	209	10	61	803	2,349
28 yrs. old......	3,913	3,047	536	44	218	10	58	800	2,305
29 yrs. old......	3,815	2,965	514	42	229	9	55	793	2,227
30 to 34 yrs. old....	20,077	15,629	2,676	208	1,256	44	264	3,798	12,096
30 yrs. old......	3,928	3,052	524	42	246	9	54	792	2,315
31 yrs. old......	3,817	2,960	507	41	248	9	52	761	2,252
32 yrs. old......	3,909	3,025	528	41	255	9	52	757	2,320
33 yrs. old......	4,097	3,191	546	42	257	9	52	748	2,496
34 yrs. old......	4,327	3,400	570	43	251	9	53	740	2,713
35 to 39 yrs. old....	21,002	16,645	2,727	204	1,147	41	239	3,389	13,498
35 yrs. old......	4,412	3,479	574	43	254	9	53	741	2,792
36 yrs. old......	4,170	3,304	530	41	238	8	49	686	2,667
37 yrs. old......	4,094	3,239	533	40	228	8	46	672	2,615
38 yrs. old......	4,104	3,268	531	40	212	8	45	645	2,670
39 yrs. old......	4,222	3,354	558	41	214	8	46	646	2,754
40 to 44 yrs. old....	22,861	18,427	2,894	217	1,046	39	237	3,002	15,642
40 yrs. old......	4,511	3,598	593	44	220	8	48	653	2,992
41 yrs. old......	4,581	3,677	586	44	217	8	48	627	3,095
42 yrs. old......	4,565	3,677	576	43	214	8	47	596	3,125
43 yrs. old......	4,578	3,712	570	43	199	8	47	576	3,173
44 yrs. old......	4,625	3,763	570	43	195	8	47	551	3,252
45 to 49 yrs. old....	22,485	18,344	2,735	202	949	34	221	2,423	16,098
45 yrs. old......	4,707	3,810	593	44	205	8	47	555	3,295
46 yrs. old......	4,514	3,677	555	41	190	7	45	500	3,214
47 yrs. old......	4,516	3,690	544	40	190	7	44	476	3,249
48 yrs. old......	4,461	3,653	535	39	183	6	43	458	3,229
49 yrs. old......	4,287	3,512	509	37	181	6	41	434	3,111

See footnote at end of table.

U.S. Census Bureau, Statistical Abstract of the United States: 2007

[In thousands, except as indicated (296,410 represents 296,410,000). As of July 1. For derivation of estimates, see text of this section]

Age	Total	Race						Hispanic or Latino origin [1]	Not-Hispanic or Latino White alone
		White alone	Black or African American alone	American Indian, Alaska Native alone	Asian alone	Native Hawaiian and Other Pacific Islander alone	Two or more races		
50 to 54 yrs. old. . . .	19,998	16,530	2,268	167	822	27	183	1,846	14,820
50 yrs. old	4,306	3,533	507	37	182	6	41	425	3,139
51 yrs. old	4,119	3,398	473	35	170	6	38	388	3,039
52 yrs. old	3,981	3,298	444	33	164	5	37	364	2,961
53 yrs. old	3,847	3,195	424	32	156	5	34	340	2,880
54 yrs. old	3,746	3,106	420	30	151	5	33	329	2,802
55 to 59 yrs. old. . . .	17,354	14,591	1,781	133	678	21	149	1,403	13,287
55 yrs. old	3,731	3,082	421	30	160	5	33	327	2,779
56 yrs. old	3,583	2,991	383	28	145	5	31	294	2,718
57 yrs. old	3,549	2,991	360	27	137	4	30	281	2,730
58 yrs. old	3,721	3,191	341	27	127	4	31	267	2,943
59 yrs. old	2,770	2,336	276	21	109	4	24	235	2,118
60 to 64 yrs. old. . . .	13,002	11,085	1,240	91	467	15	104	975	10,174
60 yrs. old	2,757	2,329	275	21	105	4	23	224	2,121
61 yrs. old	2,709	2,308	259	19	98	3	22	207	2,115
62 yrs. old	2,797	2,406	256	19	92	3	22	196	2,222
63 yrs. old	2,461	2,103	231	17	88	3	19	179	1,935
64 yrs. old	2,278	1,939	219	16	83	3	18	169	1,781
65 to 69 yrs. old. . . .	10,131	8,639	976	66	365	11	74	745	7,941
65 yrs. old	2,209	1,871	220	15	83	3	17	168	1,714
66 yrs. old	2,092	1,787	198	14	75	2	16	155	1,642
67 yrs. old	2,044	1,746	195	13	73	2	15	149	1,607
68 yrs. old	1,916	1,636	183	12	69	2	14	139	1,506
69 yrs. old	1,871	1,599	180	12	66	2	13	134	1,473
70 to 74 yrs. old. . . .	8,508	7,346	769	48	282	8	56	576	6,804
70 yrs. old	1,863	1,595	179	11	64	2	13	133	1,470
71 yrs. old	1,693	1,452	159	10	58	2	12	118	1,341
72 yrs. old	1,683	1,449	155	10	57	2	11	112	1,344
73 yrs. old	1,650	1,433	143	9	52	1	10	108	1,331
74 yrs. old	1,619	1,417	133	8	50	1	10	105	1,318
75 to 79 yrs. old. . . .	7,412	6,523	592	35	214	6	43	443	6,105
75 yrs. old	1,627	1,420	137	8	50	1	10	105	1,321
76 yrs. old	1,516	1,332	122	7	45	1	9	94	1,243
77 yrs. old	1,491	1,315	117	7	43	1	9	88	1,231
78 yrs. old	1,429	1,263	111	6	39	1	8	80	1,187
79 yrs. old	1,349	1,194	105	6	36	1	8	75	1,122
80 to 84 yrs. old. . . .	5,643	5,040	407	23	140	3	29	286	4,769
80 yrs. old	1,311	1,163	100	6	35	1	7	71	1,096
81 yrs. old	1,218	1,086	89	5	31	1	6	63	1,026
82 yrs. old	1,114	994	81	4	28	1	6	57	941
83 yrs. old	1,045	937	73	4	25	1	5	51	888
84 yrs. old	954	860	64	4	22	–	5	45	818
85 to 89 yrs. old. . . .	3,211	2,887	223	12	72	2	16	143	2,751
90 to 94 yrs. old. . . .	1,415	1,268	104	6	29	1	7	65	1,207
95 to 99 yrs. old. . . .	400	354	34	2	8	–	2	20	335
100 yrs. old and over	70	58	9	1	1	–	1	5	54
Median age (yr.). . . .	36.2	37.6	30.9	29.6	34.5	29.4	20.5	27.2	40.3

– Represents or rounds to zero.   [1] Persons of Hispanic origin may be of any race.

Source: U.S. Census Bureau, "Annual Estimates of the Population by Sex, Age and Race for the United States: April 1, 2000 to July 1, 2005(NC-EST2005-04)"; published 10 May 2006; <http://www.census.gov/popest/national/asrh/NC-EST2005-asrh.html>.

Table 16.

Table 16. Resident Population by Race, Hispanic Origin Status, and Age—Projections: 2010 and 2015

[In thousands (308,936 represents 308,936,000), except as indicated. As of July 1. For definition of median, see Guide to Tabular Presentation. Projections are based on middle series of assumptions; see headnote, Table 3]

Age group	Total 2010	Total 2015	White alone 2010	White alone 2015	Black alone 2010	Black alone 2015	Asian alone 2010	Asian alone 2015	All other races [1] 2010	All other races [1] 2015	Hispanic origin [2] 2010	Hispanic origin [2] 2015	White alone, not of Hispanic origin 2010	White alone, not of Hispanic origin 2015
Total	**308,936**	**322,366**	**244,995**	**252,850**	**40,454**	**42,927**	**14,241**	**16,099**	**9,246**	**10,489**	**47,756**	**53,647**	**201,112**	**203,649**
Under 5 years	21,426	22,358	15,995	16,556	3,332	3,498	919	987	1,181	1,318	4,824	5,201	11,647	11,884
5 to 9 years	20,706	21,623	15,639	16,114	3,127	3,347	888	976	1,052	1,186	4,515	4,927	11,553	11,668
10 to 14 years	19,767	20,984	15,049	15,799	2,976	3,163	834	963	909	1,059	4,057	4,660	11,361	11,577
15 to 19 years	21,336	20,243	16,203	15,341	3,396	3,043	886	937	851	922	4,162	4,338	12,401	11,390
20 to 24 years	21,676	21,810	16,591	16,473	3,357	3,451	943	1,020	785	866	3,927	4,472	12,992	12,380
25 to 29 years	21,375	22,195	16,495	16,890	3,130	3,413	1,041	1,093	709	799	3,878	4,162	12,919	13,069
30 to 34 years	20,271	21,858	15,654	16,727	2,856	3,180	1,166	1,231	595	720	3,769	4,035	11,977	13,004
35 to 39 years	20,137	20,543	15,597	15,758	2,701	2,880	1,319	1,303	520	601	3,343	4,052	12,096	13,009
40 to 44 years	20,543	20,250	15,566	15,616	2,724	2,697	1,208	1,414	486	523	2,939	3,799	13,466	12,088
45 to 49 years	20,984	20,926	16,566	16,473	2,844	2,685	1,105	1,282	492	486	2,371	3,342	15,489	13,374
50 to 54 years	22,654	22,376	18,213	17,966	2,657	2,768	997	1,154	453	487	1,806	2,916	15,870	15,264
55 to 59 years	22,173	21,649	18,066	17,637	2,176	2,546	857	1,023	372	444	1,365	2,331	14,431	15,479
60 to 64 years	19,507	18,761	16,102	15,484	1,674	2,044	706	873	295	359	941	1,755	12,736	13,860
65 to 69 years	16,679	15,621	14,004	13,125	1,127	1,518	489	701	199	278	694	1,301	9,477	11,918
70 to 74 years	12,172	10,987	10,357	9,363	838	979	355	463	138	181	510	870	7,117	8,552
75 to 79 years	9,097	7,761	7,767	6,641	622	688	244	313	94	119	359	617	5,747	6,065
80 to 84 years	7,186	5,600	6,226	4,861	440	471	158	194	61	74	204	423	4,666	4,464
85 to 89 years	5,665	3,857	5,005	3,404	274	303	83	108	34	42	84	268	3,128	3,152
90 to 94 years	3,713	2,069	3,321	1,839	136	165	31	46	14	19	28	128	1,467	1,718
95 to 99 years	1,727	723	1,546	636	53	68	8	13	4	6	6	41	476	598
100 years and over	569	173	503	147	14	22	1	2	1	1		10	92	138
	114		98											
5 to 13 years	36,439	38,418	27,613	28,744	5,491	5,885	1,550	1,747	1,786	2,041	7,760	8,670	20,580	20,909
14 to 17 years	16,566	16,243	12,589	12,301	2,597	2,430	695	742	685	770	3,291	3,513	9,586	9,108
18 to 24 years	30,481	30,000	23,280	22,682	4,768	4,689	1,307	1,408	1,125	1,221	5,611	6,214	18,142	16,998
16 years and over	242,936	253,361	195,194	201,321	30,383	32,319	11,427	12,988	5,933	6,733	33,541	37,977	164,179	166,259
18 years and over	234,504	245,347	188,799	195,250	29,034	31,114	11,077	12,623	5,594	6,361	31,881	36,263	159,300	161,747
16 to 64 years	202,693	206,570	160,372	161,303	26,877	28,106	10,056	11,147	5,387	6,013	30,715	34,321	132,007	129,655
55 years and over	76,429	87,201	64,928	73,139	7,355	8,802	2,934	3,737	1,213	1,523	5,997	7,742	59,339	65,942
65 years and over	40,244	46,791	34,821	40,018	3,505	4,212	1,371	1,841	546	720	2,826	3,656	32,171	36,604
75 years and over	18,974	20,182	16,698	17,529	1,540	1,716	527	676	209	261	1,191	1,485	15,577	16,134
85 years and over	6,123	6,822	5,467	6,027	478	558	125	169	54	69	322	446	5,163	5,606
Median age (yrs.)	37.0	37.4	38.6	38.9	31.5	32.4	36.7	38.3	24.0	24.4	28.1	28.8	41.3	42.1

[1] Includes 2 or more races.   [2] Persons of Hispanic origin may be of any race.

Source: U.S. Census Bureau, "U.S. Interim Projections by Age, Sex, Race, and Hispanic Origin"; published March 2004; <http://www.census.gov/ipc/www/usinterimproj/>.

Figure 1.1
Center of Population: 1790 to 2000

[Prior to 1960, excludes Alaska and Hawaii. The median center is located at the intersection of two median lines, a north-south line constructed so that half of the nation's population lives east and half lives west of it, and an east-west line selected so that half of the nation's population lives north and half lives south of it. The mean center of population is that point at which an imaginary, flat, weightless, and rigid map of the United States would balance if weights of identical value were placed on it so that each weight represented the location of one person on the date of the census]

Year	Median center		Mean center		
	Latitude-N	Longitude	Latitude-N	Longitude-W	Approximate location
1790 (August 2)	(NA)	(NA)	39 16 30	76 11 12	In Kent County, MD, 23 miles E of Baltimore MD
1850 (June 1)..	(NA)	(NA)	38 59 00	81 19 00	In Wirt County, WV, 23 miles SE of Parkersburg, WV[1]
1900 (June 1)..	40 03 32	84 49 01	39 09 36	85 48 54	In Bartholomew County, IN, 6 miles SE of Columbus, IN
1950 (April 1)..	40 00 12	84 56 51	38 50 21	88 09 33	In Richland County, IL, 8 miles NNW of Olney, IL
1960 (April 1)..	39 56 25	85 16 60	38 35 58	89 12 35	In Clinton County, IL, 6.5 miles NW of Centralia, IL
1970 (April 1)..	39 47 43	85 31 43	38 27 47	89 42 22	In St. Clair County, IL, 5.3 miles ESE of Mascoutah, IL
1980 (April 1)..	39 18 60	86 08 15	38 08 13	90 34 26	In Jefferson County, MO, .25 mile W of DeSoto, MO
1990 (April 1)..	38 57 55	86 31 53	37 52 20	91 12 55	In Crawford County, MO, 10 miles SE of Steelville, MO
2000 (April 1)..	38 45 23	86 55 51	37 41 49	91 48 34	In Phelps County, MO, 3 miles E of Edgar Springs, MO

NA Not available.   [1]West Virginia was set off from Virginia, Dec. 31, 1862, and admitted as a state, June 19, 1863.

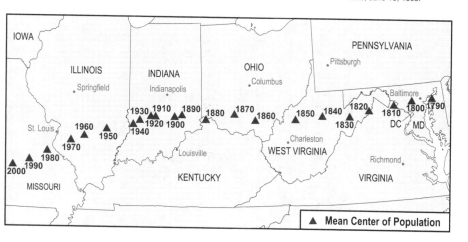

▲ Mean Center of Population

▲ Median Center of Population

Population   19

Table 17. **Resident Population—States: 1980 to 2005**

[In thousands (226,546 represents 226,546,000). 1980, 1990, and 2000 data as of April 1, data for other years as of July 1. Insofar as possible, population shown for all years is that of present area of state. See Appendix III]

State	1980 [1]	1990 [2]	1995	2000 [3]	2001	2002	2003	2004	2005
United States	226,546	248,791	266,278	281,425	285,108	287,985	290,850	293,657	296,410
Alabama.	3,894	4,040	4,297	4,447	4,467	4,480	4,502	4,525	4,558
Alaska	402	550	604	627	632	641	649	658	664
Arizona.	2,718	3,665	4,432	5,131	5,296	5,438	5,578	5,740	5,939
Arkansas	2,286	2,351	2,535	2,673	2,692	2,707	2,726	2,750	2,779
California	23,668	29,811	31,697	33,872	34,527	34,988	35,457	35,842	36,132
Colorado.	2,890	3,294	3,827	4,302	4,427	4,498	4,548	4,602	4,665
Connecticut.	3,108	3,287	3,324	3,406	3,432	3,458	3,486	3,499	3,510
Delaware	594	666	730	784	795	806	818	830	844
District of Columbia	638	607	581	572	569	565	558	554	551
Florida	9,746	12,938	14,538	15,983	16,351	16,678	16,993	17,385	17,790
Georgia	5,463	6,478	7,328	8,187	8,416	8,582	8,747	8,918	9,073
Hawaii	965	1,108	1,197	1,212	1,222	1,234	1,248	1,262	1,275
Idaho	944	1,007	1,177	1,294	1,321	1,344	1,368	1,395	1,429
Illinois	11,427	11,431	12,008	12,420	12,519	12,587	12,650	12,712	12,763
Indiana.	5,490	5,544	5,851	6,081	6,126	6,155	6,196	6,227	6,272
Iowa	2,914	2,777	2,867	2,926	2,931	2,934	2,941	2,953	2,966
Kansas.	2,364	2,478	2,601	2,689	2,701	2,712	2,724	2,734	2,745
Kentucky	3,661	3,687	3,887	4,042	4,067	4,089	4,117	4,142	4,173
Louisiana	4,206	4,222	4,379	4,469	4,465	4,475	4,490	4,507	4,524
Maine.	1,125	1,228	1,243	1,275	1,286	1,297	1,308	1,315	1,322
Maryland	4,217	4,781	5,070	5,297	5,380	5,442	5,512	5,561	5,600
Massachusetts.	5,737	6,016	6,141	6,349	6,395	6,412	6,418	6,407	6,399
Michigan	9,262	9,295	9,676	9,938	10,003	10,039	10,078	10,104	10,121
Minnesota.	4,076	4,376	4,660	4,919	4,985	5,024	5,062	5,097	5,133
Mississippi	2,521	2,575	2,723	2,845	2,858	2,866	2,881	2,901	2,921
Missouri	4,917	5,117	5,378	5,597	5,643	5,681	5,719	5,760	5,800
Montana.	787	799	877	902	906	910	918	927	936
Nebraska	1,570	1,578	1,657	1,711	1,719	1,727	1,738	1,748	1,759
Nevada	800	1,202	1,582	1,998	2,095	2,168	2,242	2,333	2,415
New Hampshire	921	1,109	1,158	1,236	1,259	1,275	1,288	1,299	1,310
New Jersey.	7,365	7,748	8,083	8,414	8,505	8,576	8,640	8,685	8,718
New Mexico	1,303	1,515	1,720	1,819	1,833	1,855	1,879	1,903	1,928
New York	17,558	17,991	18,524	18,977	19,091	19,165	19,228	19,281	19,255
North Carolina	5,882	6,632	7,345	8,046	8,198	8,313	8,422	8,540	8,683
North Dakota.	653	639	648	642	640	636	634	633	637
Ohio	10,798	10,847	11,203	11,353	11,385	11,405	11,432	11,450	11,464
Oklahoma.	3,025	3,146	3,308	3,451	3,466	3,487	3,505	3,524	3,548
Oregon.	2,633	2,842	3,184	3,421	3,473	3,522	3,563	3,591	3,641
Pennsylvania	11,864	11,883	12,198	12,281	12,296	12,324	12,365	12,394	12,430
Rhode Island.	947	1,003	1,017	1,048	1,058	1,069	1,076	1,080	1,076
South Carolina.	3,122	3,486	3,749	4,012	4,060	4,103	4,147	4,198	4,255
South Dakota	691	696	738	755	758	760	765	771	776
Tennessee	4,591	4,877	5,327	5,689	5,747	5,790	5,842	5,893	5,963
Texas	14,229	16,986	18,959	20,852	21,334	21,722	22,099	22,472	22,860
Utah	1,461	1,723	2,014	2,233	2,288	2,337	2,379	2,421	2,470
Vermont	511	563	589	609	613	616	619	621	623
Virginia.	5,347	6,189	6,671	7,079	7,192	7,286	7,383	7,481	7,567
Washington	4,132	4,867	5,481	5,894	5,992	6,066	6,131	6,207	6,288
West Virginia.	1,950	1,793	1,824	1,808	1,801	1,805	1,810	1,813	1,817
Wisconsin.	4,706	4,892	5,185	5,364	5,404	5,439	5,472	5,504	5,536
Wyoming	470	454	485	494	494	499	502	506	509

[1] See footnote 3, Table 1.   [2] The April 1, 1990, census counts include corrections processed through August 1997, results of special censuses and test censuses, and do not include adjustments for census coverage errors.   [3] Reflects modifications to the Census 2000 population as documented in the Count Question Resolution program and geographic program revisions.

Source: U.S. Census Bureau, Current Population Reports, P25-1106; "Table CO-EST2001-12-00—Time Series of Intercensal State Populaton Estimates: April 1, 1990 to April 1, 2000"; published 11 April 2002; <http://www.census.gov/popest/archives/2000s /vintage2001/CO-EST2001-12/CO-EST2001-12-00.html>; and "Table 1: Annual Estimates of the Population for the United States and States, and for Puerto Rico: April 1, 2000 to July 1, 2005 (NST-EST2005-01)"; published 22 December 2005; <http://www.census.gov/popes /states/NST-ann-est.html>.

Table 18. State Population—Rank, Percent Change, and Population Density: 1980 to 2005

[As of April 1, except 2005, as of July 1. Insofar as possible, population shown for all years is that of present area of state. For area figures of states, see Table 345. Minus sign (–) indicates decrease. See Appendix III]

State	Rank				Percent change			Population per sq. mile of land area [1]		
	1980	1990	2000	2005	1980–1990	1990–2000	2000–2005	1990	2000	2005
United States.	(X)	(X)	(X)	(X)	9.8	13.1	5.3	70.3	79.6	83.8
Alabama	22	22	23	23	3.8	10.1	2.5	79.6	87.6	89.8
Alaska	50	49	48	47	36.9	14.0	5.9	1.0	1.1	1.2
Arizona.	29	24	20	17	34.8	40.0	15.8	32.3	45.2	52.3
Arkansas.	33	33	33	32	2.8	13.7	4.0	45.1	51.3	53.4
California.	1	1	1	1	26.0	13.6	6.7	191.1	217.2	231.7
Colorado.	28	26	24	22	14.0	30.6	8.4	31.8	41.5	45.0
Connecticut	25	27	29	29	5.8	3.6	3.1	678.5	702.9	724.5
Delaware.	47	46	45	45	12.1	17.6	7.6	341.0	401.1	431.8
District of Columbia. . .	(X)	(X)	(X)	(X)	–4.9	–5.7	–3.8	9,884.4	9,316.4	8,966.1
Florida	7	4	4	4	32.7	23.5	11.3	239.9	296.4	329.9
Georgia	13	11	10	9	18.6	26.4	10.8	111.9	141.4	156.7
Hawaii	39	41	42	42	14.9	9.3	5.3	172.6	188.6	198.5
Idaho	41	42	39	39	6.7	28.5	10.4	12.2	15.6	17.3
Illinois.	5	6	5	5	(Z)	8.7	2.8	205.6	223.4	229.6
Indiana	12	14	14	15	1.0	9.7	3.1	154.6	169.5	174.9
Iowa.	27	30	30	30	–4.7	5.4	1.4	49.7	52.4	53.1
Kansas.	32	32	32	33	4.8	8.5	2.1	30.3	32.9	33.5
Kentucky.	23	23	25	26	0.7	9.6	3.2	92.8	101.7	105.0
Louisiana	19	21	22	24	0.4	5.9	1.2	96.9	102.6	103.8
Maine.	38	38	40	40	9.2	3.8	3.7	39.8	41.3	42.8
Maryland.	18	19	19	19	13.4	10.8	5.7	489.1	541.9	573.0
Massachusetts	11	13	13	13	4.9	5.5	0.8	767.4	809.8	816.2
Michigan	8	8	8	8	0.4	6.9	1.8	163.6	175.0	178.2
Minnesota	21	20	21	21	7.4	12.4	4.3	55.0	61.8	64.5
Mississippi.	31	31	31	31	2.2	10.5	2.7	54.9	60.6	62.3
Missouri	15	15	17	18	4.1	9.4	3.6	74.3	81.2	84.2
Montana	44	44	44	44	1.6	12.9	3.7	5.5	6.2	6.4
Nebraska	35	36	38	38	0.5	8.4	2.8	20.5	22.3	22.9
Nevada.	43	39	35	35	50.1	66.3	20.8	10.9	18.2	22.0
New Hampshire	42	40	41	41	20.5	11.4	6.0	123.7	137.8	146.1
New Jersey	9	9	9	10	5.2	8.6	3.6	1,044.5	1,134.4	1,175.3
New Mexico.	37	37	36	36	16.3	20.1	6.0	12.5	15.0	15.9
New York	2	2	3	3	2.5	5.5	1.5	381.0	401.9	407.8
North Carolina	10	10	11	11	12.8	21.3	7.9	136.2	165.2	178.3
North Dakota	46	47	47	48	–2.1	0.5	–0.9	9.3	9.3	9.2
Ohio.	6	7	7	7	0.5	4.7	1.0	264.9	277.3	280.0
Oklahoma	26	28	27	28	4.0	9.7	2.8	45.8	50.3	51.7
Oregon	30	29	28	27	7.9	20.4	6.4	29.6	35.6	37.9
Pennsylvania	4	5	6	6	0.2	3.4	1.2	265.1	274.0	277.3
Rhode Island	40	43	43	43	5.9	4.5	2.7	960.3	1,003.2	1,029.9
South Carolina	24	25	26	25	11.7	15.1	6.1	115.8	133.2	141.3
South Dakota	45	45	46	46	0.8	8.5	2.8	9.2	9.9	10.2
Tennessee.	17	17	16	16	6.2	16.7	4.8	118.3	138.0	144.7
Texas	3	3	2	2	19.4	22.8	9.6	64.9	79.6	87.3
Utah	36	35	34	34	17.9	29.6	10.6	21.0	27.2	30.1
Vermont	48	48	49	49	10.0	8.2	2.3	60.8	65.8	67.4
Virginia	14	12	12	12	15.8	14.4	6.9	156.3	178.8	191.1
Washington	20	18	15	14	17.8	21.1	6.7	73.1	88.6	94.5
West Virginia	34	34	37	37	–8.0	0.8	0.5	74.5	75.1	75.5
Wisconsin	16	16	18	20	4.0	9.6	3.2	90.1	98.8	101.9
Wyoming	49	50	50	50	–3.4	8.9	3.1	4.7	5.1	5.2

X Not applicable.   Z Less than 0.05 percent.   [1] Persons per square mile were calculated on the basis of land area data from the 2000 census.

Source: U.S. Census Bureau, Current Population Reports, P25-1106; "ST-99-3 State Population Estimates: Annual Time Series, July 1, 1990, to July 1, 1999"; published 29 December 1999; <http://www.census.gov/population/estimates/state /st-99-3.txt>; *Population Change and Distribution: 1990 to 2000, Census 2000 Brief*, (C2KBR/01-2), April 2001; and "Table 2: Cumulative Estimates of Population Change for the United States and States, and for Puerto Rico and State Rankings: April 1, 2000 to July 1, 2005 (NST-EST2005-02);" published 22 December 2005; <http://www.census.gov/popest/states/NST-pop -chg.html>.

Population   21

Table 19. **State Resident Population—Projections: 2010 to 2030**

[As of July 1. These projections were produced in correspondence with the U.S. interim projections released in March 2004 (see Table 3). They were developed for each of the 50 states and the District of Columbia by age and sex for the years 2000 to 2030, based on Census 2000 results. These projections differ from forecasts in that they represent the results of the mathematical projection model given that current state-specific trends in fertility, mortality, internal migration and international migration continue. The projections to 2005 have been superseded by population estimates which are shown in Table 17. Minus sign (–) indicates decrease]

| State | Number (1,000) | | | | | Change, 2000–2030 | | Rank | |
	2010	2015	2020	2025	2030	Number (1,000)	Percent	Total population, 2030	Percent change, 2000–2030
United States . . .	308,936	322,366	335,805	349,439	363,584	82,163	29.2	(X)	(X)
Alabama.	4,596	4,663	4,729	4,800	4,874	427	9.6	24	35
Alaska	694	733	774	821	868	241	38.4	46	12
Arizona.	6,637	7,495	8,456	9,532	10,712	5,582	108.8	10	2
Arkansas	2,875	2,969	3,060	3,151	3,240	567	21.2	32	21
California	38,067	40,123	42,207	44,305	46,445	12,573	37.1	1	13
Colorado.	4,832	5,049	5,279	5,523	5,792	1,491	34.7	22	14
Connecticut.	3,577	3,635	3,676	3,691	3,689	283	8.3	30	38
Delaware	884	927	963	991	1,013	229	29.2	45	18
District of Columbia .	530	506	481	455	433	–139	–24.2	(X)	(X)
Florida	19,252	21,204	23,407	25,912	28,686	12,703	79.5	3	3
Georgia	9,589	10,231	10,844	11,439	12,018	3,831	46.8	8	8
Hawaii	1,341	1,386	1,412	1,439	1,466	255	21.0	41	22
Idaho	1,517	1,630	1,741	1,853	1,970	676	52.2	37	6
Illinois	12,917	13,097	13,237	13,341	13,433	1,014	8.2	5	39
Indiana.	6,392	6,518	6,627	6,721	6,810	730	12.0	18	31
Iowa	3,010	3,026	3,020	2,993	2,955	29	1.0	34	48
Kansas.	2,805	2,853	2,891	2,919	2,940	252	9.4	35	36
Kentucky	4,265	4,351	4,424	4,490	4,555	513	12.7	27	30
Louisiana	4,613	4,674	4,719	4,762	4,803	334	7.5	26	41
Maine.	1,357	1,389	1,409	1,414	1,411	136	10.7	42	32
Maryland	5,905	6,208	6,498	6,763	7,022	1,726	32.6	16	16
Massachusetts.	6,649	6,759	6,856	6,939	7,012	663	10.4	17	33
Michigan.	10,429	10,599	10,696	10,714	10,694	756	7.6	11	40
Minnesota.	5,421	5,668	5,901	6,109	6,306	1,387	28.2	20	20
Mississippi	2,971	3,014	3,045	3,069	3,092	248	8.7	33	37
Missouri	5,922	6,070	6,200	6,315	6,430	835	14.9	19	27
Montana.	969	999	1,023	1,037	1,045	143	15.8	44	25
Nebraska	1,769	1,789	1,803	1,813	1,820	109	6.4	38	42
Nevada	2,691	3,058	3,452	3,863	4,282	2,284	114.3	28	1
New Hampshire	1,386	1,457	1,525	1,586	1,646	411	33.2	40	15
New Jersey	9,018	9,256	9,462	9,637	9,802	1,388	16.5	13	24
New Mexico	1,980	2,042	2,084	2,107	2,100	281	15.4	36	26
New York	19,444	19,547	19,577	19,540	19,477	501	2.6	4	46
North Carolina	9,346	10,011	10,709	11,449	12,228	4,178	51.9	7	7
North Dakota.	637	635	630	621	607	–36	–5.5	49	50
Ohio	11,576	11,635	11,644	11,606	11,551	197	1.7	9	47
Oklahoma.	3,592	3,662	3,736	3,821	3,913	463	13.4	29	29
Oregon.	3,791	4,013	4,260	4,536	4,834	1,413	41.3	25	10
Pennsylvania.	12,584	12,711	12,787	12,802	12,768	487	4.0	6	45
Rhode Island.	1,117	1,140	1,154	1,158	1,153	105	10.0	43	34
South Carolina.	4,447	4,642	4,823	4,990	5,149	1,137	28.3	23	19
South Dakota	786	797	802	802	800	46	6.0	47	43
Tennessee	6,231	6,502	6,781	7,073	7,381	1,691	29.7	15	17
Texas	24,649	26,586	28,635	30,865	33,318	12,466	59.8	2	4
Utah	2,595	2,783	2,990	3,226	3,485	1,252	56.1	31	5
Vermont	653	673	691	703	712	103	16.9	48	23
Virginia	8,010	8,467	8,917	9,364	9,825	2,747	38.8	12	11
Washington.	6,542	6,951	7,432	7,996	8,625	2,731	46.3	14	9
West Virginia.	1,829	1,823	1,801	1,766	1,720	–88	–4.9	39	49
Wisconsin.	5,727	5,883	6,005	6,088	6,151	787	14.7	21	28
Wyoming	520	528	531	529	523	29	5.9	50	44

X Not applicable.

Source: U.S. Census Bureau, "Table A1: Interim Projections of the Total Population for the United States and States: April 1, 2000 to July 1, 2030"; published 21 April 2005; <http://www.census.gov/population/www/projections/projectionsagesex.html>.

Table 20. **State Resident Population—Components of Change: 2000 to 2005**

[Covers period April 1, 2000, to July 1, 2005. Minus sign (–) indicates net decrease or net outflow]

State	Numeric population change [1]	Births	Deaths	Natural increase (births minus deaths)	Net internal migration	Net international migration
United States	**14,985,802**	**21,329,804**	**12,677,943**	**8,651,861**	**(X)**	**6,333,941**
Alabama.	110,457	319,544	242,126	77,418	10,521	25,936
Alaska	36,730	53,132	16,542	36,590	–4,619	5,800
Arizona.	808,660	462,739	221,007	241,732	408,160	168,078
Arkansas	105,756	198,800	146,586	52,214	35,664	21,947
California	2,260,494	2,781,539	1,224,427	1,557,112	–664,460	1,415,879
Colorado.	363,162	353,091	147,770	205,321	47,740	112,217
Connecticut.	104,695	222,222	154,795	67,427	–34,273	75,991
Delaware	59,924	58,699	36,721	21,978	27,912	11,226
District of Columbia	–21,538	42,502	30,109	12,393	–53,550	20,618
Florida	1,807,040	1,115,565	869,507	246,058	1,057,619	528,085
Georgia	885,760	718,764	342,659	376,105	232,666	192,844
Hawaii	63,657	96,028	47,917	48,111	–13,112	30,068
Idaho	135,140	111,131	52,247	58,884	61,273	14,522
Illinois	343,724	959,470	553,045	406,425	–391,031	328,020
Indiana.	191,456	451,681	292,193	159,488	–17,000	55,656
Iowa	39,952	197,163	143,457	53,706	–41,140	29,386
Kansas.	55,863	204,663	128,525	76,138	–57,763	38,222
Kentucky	131,120	287,222	210,066	77,156	32,169	27,435
Louisiana	54,670	350,818	220,929	129,889	–89,547	20,174
Maine.	46,582	71,276	64,863	6,413	36,804	5,004
Maryland	303,882	395,775	230,068	165,707	9,752	108,972
Massachusetts.	49,638	426,232	294,903	131,329	–236,415	162,674
Michigan.	182,380	691,897	456,137	235,760	–165,084	122,901
Minnesota.	213,307	358,012	196,760	161,252	–16,768	70,800
Mississippi	76,432	228,849	148,116	80,733	–10,578	10,653
Missouri	203,627	401,148	285,745	115,403	26,979	42,690
Montana.	33,475	58,001	44,327	13,674	18,933	2,141
Nebraska	47,522	132,394	80,290	52,104	–26,206	22,199
Nevada	416,550	170,451	88,790	81,661	270,945	66,098
New Hampshire	74,154	75,060	51,188	23,872	40,861	11,107
New Jersey.	303,578	604,110	383,890	220,220	–194,901	290,194
New Mexico	109,338	143,617	69,220	74,397	9,527	27,974
New York	277,809	1,345,482	817,606	527,876	–1,001,100	667,000
North Carolina.	636,751	627,309	379,212	248,097	232,448	158,224
North Dakota.	–5,527	40,890	30,607	10,283	–18,568	3,687
Ohio	110,897	789,312	571,435	217,877	–177,150	75,142
Oklahoma.	97,232	264,324	183,571	80,753	–15,418	36,546
Oregon.	219,620	236,557	161,361	75,196	77,821	72,263
Pennsylvania.	148,562	761,887	674,287	87,600	–28,012	102,470
Rhode Island.	27,870	66,973	51,753	15,220	–4,964	18,965
South Carolina.	243,267	295,425	197,710	97,715	115,084	36,401
South Dakota	21,093	56,247	37,048	19,199	–735	3,957
Tennessee	273,697	414,305	297,102	117,203	109,707	49,973
Texas.	2,008,176	1,948,398	793,216	1,155,182	218,722	663,161
Utah	236,387	254,433	68,022	186,411	–33,822	49,995
Vermont	14,223	33,606	26,458	7,148	3,530	4,359
Virginia.	488,435	531,476	300,421	231,055	103,521	139,977
Washington.	393,619	418,055	237,895	180,160	80,974	134,242
West Virginia.	8,506	108,292	111,588	–3,296	10,518	3,691
Wisconsin.	172,486	361,534	242,187	119,347	14,595	46,106
Wyoming	15,512	33,704	21,539	12,165	1,771	2,264

X Not applicable.   [1] The estimated components of population change will not sum to the numerical population change due to the process of controlling to national totals.

Source: U.S. Census Bureau, "Table 4: Cumulative Estimates of the Components of Population Change for the United States and States: April 1, 2000 to July 1, 2005 (NST-EST2005-04);" published 22 December 2005; <http://www.census.gov/popest /states/NST-comp-chg.html>.

Population   23

Table 21. **Resident Population by Age and State: 2005**

[In thousands, except percent (296,410 represents 296,410,000). **As of July.** Includes Armed Forces stationed in area]

State	Total	Under 5 years	5 to 17 years	18 to 24 years	25 to 34 years	35 to 44 years	45 to 54 years	55 to 64 years	65 to 74 years	75 to 84 years	85 years and over	Percent 65 years and over
U.S.	296,410	20,304	53,166	29,307	40,143	43,862	42,482	30,356	18,640	13,054	5,096	12.4
AL	4,558	297	793	452	607	647	659	499	329	207	68	13.3
AK	664	51	138	77	80	100	109	66	27	13	4	6.6
AZ	5,939	460	1,121	586	858	822	752	582	410	257	91	12.8
AR	2,779	187	488	279	365	385	384	305	208	127	49	13.8
CA	36,132	2,686	7,016	3,586	5,175	5,500	4,938	3,363	1,967	1,359	543	10.7
CO	4,665	340	840	463	725	709	678	443	248	158	60	10.0
CT	3,510	211	624	316	402	554	543	386	214	174	86	13.5
DE	844	55	141	83	112	127	122	91	59	38	14	13.3
DC	551	38	75	52	109	82	71	57	34	24	10	12.2
FL.	17,790	1,119	2,949	1,590	2,167	2,540	2,473	1,959	1,508	1,086	399	16.8
GA	9,073	693	1,670	920	1,400	1,428	1,238	853	491	279	100	9.6
HI	1,275	90	209	128	158	179	189	147	78	69	28	13.7
ID	1,429	106	268	159	191	195	201	145	87	54	23	11.5
IL	12,763	898	2,343	1,252	1,790	1,885	1,811	1,255	762	541	228	12.0
IN	6,272	430	1,172	622	835	898	900	637	389	280	109	12.4
IA	2,966	181	490	310	377	412	445	315	202	158	75	14.7
KS	2,745	188	486	297	364	382	399	271	170	129	58	13.0
KY	4,173	270	710	408	571	617	615	457	286	179	61	12.6
LA	4,524	322	825	498	605	632	650	460	281	189	62	11.8
ME	1,322	68	210	126	144	201	219	162	96	70	26	14.6
MD	5,600	381	1,021	532	703	880	843	595	330	226	89	11.5
MA	6,399	397	1,061	591	868	1,011	945	672	390	320	142	13.3
MI	10,121	650	1,874	990	1,293	1,490	1,509	1,056	611	463	184	12.4
MN	5,133	336	894	533	684	781	772	510	303	217	103	12.1
MS	2,921	212	537	315	397	402	405	295	195	122	41	12.3
MO	5,800	376	1,002	590	760	836	848	616	396	273	104	13.3
MT	936	54	151	100	109	125	155	113	67	42	19	13.8
NE	1,759	123	308	191	233	240	254	175	111	86	37	13.3
NV	2,415	174	447	219	362	365	322	252	160	87	26	11.3
NH	1,310	73	230	123	148	211	214	148	82	57	24	12.5
NJ	8,718	582	1,580	757	1,066	1,395	1,297	913	537	421	171	13.0
NM	1,928	134	355	209	239	263	282	211	128	79	28	12.2
NY	19,255	1,249	3,297	1,819	2,600	2,958	2,780	2,037	1,224	921	370	13.1
NC	8,683	606	1,535	830	1,254	1,303	1,206	896	565	362	127	12.1
ND	637	37	100	75	83	83	99	67	42	34	17	14.7
OH	11,464	732	2,027	1,120	1,457	1,657	1,721	1,220	742	570	217	13.3
OK	3,548	244	609	382	479	484	505	376	252	162	55	13.2
OR	3,641	226	624	353	514	514	541	400	234	162	75	12.9
PA	12,430	725	2,092	1,180	1,472	1,793	1,899	1,376	850	738	305	15.2
RI	1,076	64	181	108	140	162	159	113	63	59	28	13.9
SC	4,255	281	746	426	577	612	607	472	295	176	64	12.6
SD	776	52	136	86	95	104	114	78	52	40	19	14.2
TN	5,963	387	1,003	576	834	889	869	654	415	249	86	12.6
TX	22,860	1,871	4,455	2,417	3,372	3,351	3,070	2,052	1,236	778	257	9.9
UT	2,470	235	507	319	424	302	282	184	116	73	27	8.8
VT	623	32	101	64	72	93	104	77	41	29	12	13.2
VA	7,567	513	1,312	756	1,015	1,170	1,121	817	462	294	109	11.4
WA	6,288	394	1,090	645	865	957	950	666	367	243	111	11.5
WV	1,817	102	281	168	229	248	285	226	144	101	33	15.3
WI	5,536	340	956	572	702	825	844	575	349	257	115	13.0
WY	509	31	83	57	62	68	85	61	33	21	8	12.2

Source: U.S. Census Bureau, "Age and Sex for States and for Puerto Rico: April 1, 2000 to July 1, 2005"; published 4 August 2006; <http://www.census.gov/popest/states/asrh/SC-EST2005-02.html>.

Table 22. **Resident Population by Age and State—Projections: 2010 and 2015**

[As of July 1. **74,432 represents 74,432,000.** These projections were produced in correspondence with the U.S. interim projections released in March 2004 (see Tables 3 and 12). They were developed for each of the 50 states and the District of Columbia by age and sex for the years 2000 to 2030, based on Census 2000 results. These projections differ from forecasts in that they represent the results of the mathematical projection model given that current state-specific trends in fertility, mortality, internal migration and international migration continue. The projections to 2005 have been superseded by population estimates which are shown in Table 21]

State	Population (1,000)										Percent of population, 2015	
	Under 18 years old		18 to 44 years old		45 to 64 years old		65 to 74 years old		75 years old and over		Under 18 years old	65 years old and over
	2010	2015	2010	2015	2010	2015	2010	2015	2010	2015		
U.S.	74,432	77,018	113,248	114,845	81,012	83,711	21,270	26,608	18,974	20,182	23.9	14.5
AL	1,092	1,089	1,605	1,575	1,251	1,259	354	427	295	312	23.4	15.9
AK	184	199	270	280	184	178	35	49	21	26	27.2	10.2
AZ	1,688	1,892	2,349	2,529	1,678	1,892	516	711	406	470	25.2	15.8
AR	703	721	996	998	765	782	227	274	185	194	24.3	15.8
CA	9,497	9,820	14,787	15,240	9,391	9,835	2,333	2,972	2,060	2,256	24.5	13.0
CO	1,189	1,256	1,863	1,886	1,263	1,280	282	369	235	258	24.9	12.4
CT	814	807	1,257	1,251	990	1,001	253	308	262	270	22.2	15.9
DE	202	210	309	305	249	264	68	87	57	61	22.6	16.0
DC	114	112	237	225	118	108	32	34	29	27	22.1	12.2
FL	4,086	4,455	6,315	6,614	5,431	6,002	1,773	2,345	1,646	1,789	21.0	19.5
GA	2,502	2,679	3,724	3,822	2,382	2,543	564	723	417	464	26.2	11.6
HI	316	330	477	479	357	350	101	131	90	96	23.8	16.3
ID	400	427	554	583	381	400	99	129	82	91	26.2	13.5
IL	3,197	3,215	4,842	4,798	3,277	3,307	826	979	774	799	24.5	13.6
IN	1,596	1,614	2,328	2,333	1,656	1,664	425	508	386	398	24.8	13.9
IA	711	707	1,049	1,031	800	794	217	259	233	236	23.4	16.3
KS	699	708	1,004	1,001	727	724	185	225	190	194	24.8	14.7
KY	1,002	1,007	1,540	1,526	1,165	1,181	309	376	249	262	23.1	14.6
LA	1,172	1,176	1,665	1,642	1,194	1,192	313	379	270	285	25.2	14.2
ME	269	269	462	455	413	415	110	142	102	108	19.3	18.0
MD	1,406	1,487	2,212	2,283	1,568	1,601	386	478	332	359	23.9	13.5
MA	1,484	1,474	2,440	2,402	1,817	1,857	454	567	454	458	21.8	15.2
MI	2,487	2,479	3,822	3,799	2,785	2,814	699	852	635	654	23.4	14.2
MN	1,290	1,349	2,027	2,069	1,433	1,475	343	429	327	346	23.8	13.7
MS	759	753	1,052	1,028	781	801	209	254	170	179	25.0	14.4
MO	1,411	1,436	2,111	2,123	1,578	1,589	432	518	390	404	23.7	15.2
MT	212	216	324	326	287	284	77	100	68	74	21.6	17.4
NE	446	454	619	608	460	455	119	145	125	126	25.4	15.2
NV	665	752	961	1,033	735	851	199	264	131	158	24.6	13.8
NH	304	313	494	508	408	418	97	129	82	88	21.5	14.9
NJ	2,088	2,104	3,252	3,239	2,446	2,528	632	760	600	625	22.7	15.0
NM	479	485	669	654	553	560	153	201	126	142	23.7	16.8
NY	4,421	4,353	7,227	7,077	5,144	5,173	1,346	1,589	1,306	1,354	22.3	15.1
NC	2,269	2,438	3,471	3,586	2,445	2,611	641	810	520	565	24.4	13.7
ND	142	139	223	219	174	169	46	56	51	51	21.8	17.0
OH	2,744	2,723	4,123	4,054	3,121	3,093	816	980	771	786	23.4	15.2
OK	895	915	1,264	1,260	938	933	266	316	229	238	25.0	15.1
OR	863	916	1,412	1,470	1,022	1,036	263	348	231	242	22.8	14.7
PA	2,748	2,741	4,385	4,334	3,496	3,487	960	1,159	997	990	21.6	16.9
RI	249	248	410	412	300	304	76	94	82	81	21.8	15.4
SC	1,036	1,061	1,579	1,581	1,226	1,271	343	439	263	290	22.9	15.7
SD	194	196	269	264	209	209	55	67	60	61	24.6	16.1
TN	1,479	1,539	2,249	2,275	1,673	1,720	461	570	368	399	23.7	14.9
TX	6,785	7,376	9,417	9,848	5,859	6,248	1,426	1,826	1,162	1,287	27.7	11.7
UT	819	872	1,021	1,073	520	556	127	162	108	119	31.3	10.1
VT	132	132	232	235	195	193	50	67	43	46	19.6	16.9
VA	1,880	1,982	2,997	3,085	2,139	2,207	554	703	441	490	23.4	14.1
WA	1,488	1,561	2,481	2,591	1,777	1,833	429	567	367	399	22.5	13.9
WV	382	373	618	595	536	525	156	190	136	140	20.4	18.1
WI	1,319	1,343	2,076	2,067	1,561	1,591	392	487	380	395	22.8	15.0
WY	116	115	177	174	154	150	40	52	33	37	21.9	16.8

Source: U.S. Census Bureau, "File 2. Annual projections by 5-year and selected age groups by sex;" published 21 April 2005; http://www.census.gov/population/www/projections/projectionsagesex.html>.

Population 25

Table 23. Resident Population by Race, Hispanic or Latino Origin, and State: 2005

[In thousands (296,410 represents 296,410,000). As of July. Persons of Hispanic or Latino origin may be of any race. Due to the complexities associated with the production of detailed characteristics' estimates at the state level, the values of the estimates at lower levels of geography may not necessarily sum to estimates at higher levels of geography]

State	Total population	White alone	Black or African American alone	American Indian/ Alaska Native alone	Asian alone	Native Hawaiian and Other Pacific Islander alone	Two or more races	Hispanic or Latino origin	Non-Hispanic White alone
				One race					
U.S.	296,410	237,855	37,909	2,863	12,687	517	4,579	42,687	198,366
AL	4,558	3,253	1,203	23	38	2	40	105	3,159
AK	664	468	24	106	30	4	31	34	441
AZ	5,939	5,188	216	300	132	11	91	1,693	3,589
AR	2,779	2,261	437	19	27	2	33	131	2,139
CA	36,132	27,823	2,434	422	4,424	152	878	12,723	15,829
CO	4,665	4,211	191	52	120	7	85	908	3,363
CT	3,510	2,982	354	12	112	3	48	382	2,646
DE	844	631	174	3	23	(Z)	11	51	587
DC	551	209	314	2	17	(Z)	9	47	171
FL.	17,790	14,307	2,799	76	372	15	220	3,467	11,052
GA	9,073	6,001	2,700	27	244	7	94	647	5,411
HI	1,275	342	30	4	529	114	256	102	299
ID	1,429	1,365	8	20	15	2	19	130	1,243
IL	12,763	10,131	1,928	39	519	8	139	1,826	8,393
IN	6,272	5,554	555	17	75	3	68	285	5,289
IA	2,966	2,816	69	10	43	1	27	109	2,715
KS	2,745	2,453	162	26	58	2	45	228	2,239
KY	4,173	3,771	313	9	38	2	41	82	3,698
LA	4,524	2,898	1,497	27	62	2	37	128	2,786
ME	1,322	1,281	10	7	11	(Z)	12	13	1,269
MD	5,600	3,587	1,640	18	267	3	85	319	3,313
MA	6,399	5,549	439	18	302	5	85	506	5,139
MI	10,121	8,230	1,451	60	226	4	149	385	7,884
MN	5,133	4,601	218	60	177	3	74	187	4,431
MS	2,921	1,788	1,079	13	22	1	18	51	1,745
MO	5,800	4,952	667	26	77	4	75	156	4,811
MT	936	852	4	60	5	(Z)	14	23	833
NE	1,759	1,619	76	17	27	1	19	125	1,502
NV	2,415	1,981	187	34	138	13	62	568	1,450
NH	1,310	1,258	13	3	23	1	12	29	1,232
NJ.	8,718	6,680	1,262	27	630	7	112	1,327	5,510
NM	1,928	1,630	47	197	24	2	28	837	832
NY	19,255	14,217	3,347	104	1,281	18	287	3,102	11,717
NC	8,683	6,434	1,889	112	155	6	87	553	5,929
ND	637	588	5	34	4	(Z)	6	10	578
OH	11,464	9,759	1,368	25	164	4	144	261	9,530
OK	3,548	2,785	275	289	55	3	142	234	2,573
OR	3,641	3,305	66	50	126	10	86	360	2,970
PA	12,430	10,688	1,318	22	276	6	120	506	10,262
RI	1,076	957	66	6	29	1	16	115	861
SC	4,255	2,911	1,245	16	46	2	36	140	2,787
SD	776	687	6	68	5	(Z)	9	16	673
TN	5,963	4,810	1,003	16	74	3	57	181	4,645
TX	22,860	19,017	2,673	155	746	25	244	8,030	11,243
UT	2,470	2,316	24	33	47	18	32	268	2,063
VT	623	604	4	2	6	(Z)	7	7	598
VA	7,567	5,567	1,505	24	345	6	121	453	5,164
WA	6,288	5,343	222	104	402	29	188	551	4,845
WV	1,817	1,730	58	3	10	(Z)	15	15	1,716
WI	5,536	4,986	331	52	108	2	57	247	4,759
WY	509	483	4	12	3	(Z)	6	34	451

Z Less than 500.

Source: U.S. Census Bureau, "Table 4: Estimates of the Population by Race and Hispanic or Latino Origin for the United States and States: July 1, 2005 (SC-EST2005-04)"; published 15 July 2006; <http://www.census.gov/popest/states/asrh/SC-EST2005-04.html>.

Table 24. Resident Population by Region, Race, and Hispanic Origin: 2000

[As of April (281,422 represents 281,422,000). For composition of regions, see map, inside front cover]

Race and Hispanic origin	Population (1,000) United States	North-east	Mid-west	South	West	Percent distribution United States	North-east	Mid-west	South	West
Total population	**281,422**	**53,594**	**64,393**	**100,237**	**63,198**	**100.0**	**19.0**	**22.9**	**35.6**	**22.5**
One race.	274,596	52,366	63,370	98,390	60,470	100.0	19.1	23.1	35.8	22.0
White	211,461	41,534	53,834	72,819	43,274	100.0	19.6	25.5	34.4	20.5
Black or African American . . .	34,658	6,100	6,500	18,982	3,077	100.0	17.6	18.8	54.8	8.9
American Indian and Alaska Native	2,476	163	399	726	1,188	100.0	6.6	16.1	29.3	48.0
Asian	10,243	2,119	1,198	1,922	5,004	100.0	20.7	11.7	18.8	48.8
Asian Indian	1,679	554	293	441	391	100.0	33.0	17.5	26.3	23.3
Chinese	2,433	692	212	343	1,186	100.0	28.4	8.7	14.1	48.8
Filipino	1,850	202	151	245	1,253	100.0	10.9	8.2	13.2	67.7
Japanese	797	76	63	77	580	100.0	9.6	7.9	9.7	72.8
Korean.	1,077	246	132	224	474	100.0	22.9	12.3	20.8	44.0
Vietnamese.	1,123	115	107	336	564	100.0	10.3	9.5	29.9	50.3
Other Asian [1]	1,285	233	239	257	556	100.0	18.2	18.6	20.0	43.2
Native Hawaiian and Other Pacific Islander	399	21	22	51	304	100.0	5.2	5.6	12.8	76.3
Native Hawaiian.	141	4	6	12	118	100.0	3.2	4.1	8.9	83.8
Guamanian or Chamorro. .	58	5	5	15	34	100.0	7.9	7.9	25.1	59.1
Samoan.	91	4	5	9	73	100.0	4.2	5.6	9.7	80.5
Other Pacific Islander [2] . . .	109	8	7	15	79	100.0	7.3	6.4	14.0	72.2
Some other race	15,359	2,430	1,417	3,889	7,623	100.0	15.8	9.2	25.3	49.6
Two or more races	6,826	1,228	1,022	1,847	2,728	100.0	18.0	15.0	27.1	40.0
Hispanic or Latino [3]	35,306	5,254	3,125	11,587	15,341	100.0	14.9	8.8	32.8	43.5
Mexican.	20,641	479	2,200	6,548	11,413	100.0	2.3	10.7	31.7	55.3
Puerto Rican	3,406	2,075	325	759	247	100.0	60.9	9.6	22.3	7.2
Cuban.	1,242	169	45	921	106	100.0	13.6	3.6	74.2	8.5
Other Hispanic or Latino . . .	10,017	2,531	554	3,358	3,574	100.0	25.3	5.5	33.5	35.7
Not Hispanic or Latino	246,116	48,340	61,268	88,650	47,857	100.0	19.6	24.9	36.0	19.4
White alone	194,553	39,327	52,386	65,928	36,912	100.0	20.2	26.9	33.9	19.0

[1] Other Asian alone, or two or more Asian categories. [2] Other Pacific Islander alone, or two or more Native Hawaiian and Other Pacific Islander categories. [3] Persons of Hispanic origin may be any race.

Source: U.S. Census Bureau, "Demographic Profiles: Census 2000"; <http://www.census.gov/Press-Release/www/2001/demoprofile.html>.

Table 25. Large Metropolitan Statistical Areas—Population: 1990 to 2005

[1990 and 2000, as of April 1; beginning 2003 as of July 1 (658 represents 658,000). Covers metropolitan statistical areas with 250,000 and over population in 2005, as defined by the U.S. Office of Management and Budget as of December 2005. For definitions and components of all metropolitan and micropolitan areas, see Appendix II. Minus sign (–) indicates decrease]

Metropolitan statistical area	Number (1,000) 1990	2000, esti-mates base [1]	2003	2004	2005	Percent change 1990–2000	2000–2005 [1]	Rank, 2005
Akron, OH.	658	695	701	702	702	5.7	1.0	69
Albany-Schenectady-Troy, NY	810	826	841	845	849	2.0	2.8	57
Albuquerque, NM	599	730	767	781	798	21.7	9.4	61
Allentown-Bethlehem-Easton, PA-NJ	687	740	769	780	791	7.8	6.8	63
Anchorage, AK	266	320	340	346	351	20.1	9.8	138
Ann Arbor, MI	283	323	336	339	342	14.1	5.9	141
Asheville, NC.	308	369	382	387	393	19.9	6.4	125
Atlanta-Sandy Springs-Marietta, GA.	3,069	4,248	4,675	4,796	4,918	38.4	15.8	9
Atlantic City, NJ	224	253	264	268	271	12.6	7.3	164
Augusta-Richmond County, GA-SC	436	500	510	516	520	14.7	4.1	95
Austin-Round Rock, TX	846	1,250	1,376	1,411	1,453	47.7	16.2	38
Bakersfield, CA	545	662	713	734	757	21.4	14.4	66
Baltimore-Towson, MD	2,382	2,553	2,628	2,645	2,656	7.2	4.0	19
Baton Rouge, LA	624	706	721	727	734	13.2	3.9	67
Beaumont-Port Arthur, TX	361	385	383	383	384	6.6	–0.4	126
Birmingham-Hoover, AL.	957	1,051	1,074	1,082	1,090	9.9	3.7	48
Boise City-Nampa, ID	320	465	511	525	544	45.4	17.1	88
Boston-Cambridge-Quincy, MA-NH	4,134	4,392	4,429	4,419	4,412	6.3	0.4	11
Boulder, CO [2]	225	270	278	280	280	19.7	3.9	161
Bridgeport-Stamford-Norwalk, CT	828	883	900	902	903	6.6	2.3	54
Brownsville-Harlingen, TX	260	335	362	371	378	28.9	12.9	129
Buffalo-Niagara Falls, NY.	1,189	1,170	1,158	1,154	1,148	–1.6	–1.9	47
Canton-Massillon, OH	394	407	410	410	410	3.3	0.8	115
Cape Coral-Fort Myers, FL.	335	441	492	515	545	31.6	23.6	87
Charleston, WV	308	310	307	307	306	0.6	–1.0	150
Charleston-North Charleston, SC	507	549	572	583	595	8.3	8.4	81
Charlotte-Gastonia-Concord, NC-SC	1,025	1,330	1,439	1,475	1,521	29.8	14.3	36
Chattanooga, TN-GA	433	477	486	489	492	10.0	3.3	98
Chicago-Naperville-Joliet, IL-IN-WI	8,182	9,099	9,331	9,393	9,443	11.2	3.8	3
Cincinnati-Middletown, OH-KY-IN	1,845	2,010	2,046	2,057	2,070	8.9	3.0	25

See footnotes at end of table.

U.S. Census Bureau, Statistical Abstract of the United States: 2007

[1990 and 2000, as of April 1; beginning 2003 as of July 1 (**658 represents 658,000**). Covers metropolitan statistical areas with 250,000 and over population in 2005, as defined by the U.S. Office of Management and Budget as of December 2005. For definitions and components of all metropolitan and micropolitan areas, see Appendix II. Minus sign (–) indicates decrease]

Metropolitan statistical area	Number (1,000)					Percent change		Rank, 2005
	1990	2000, esti-mates base [1]	2003	2004	2005	1990–2000	2000–2005 [1]	
Cleveland-Elyria-Mentor, OH.	2,102	2,148	2,140	2,134	2,126	2.2	–1.0	23
Colorado Springs, CO	409	537	572	579	588	31.3	9.3	84
Columbia, SC.	549	647	672	680	690	17.9	6.6	70
Columbus, GA-AL.	266	282	280	284	284	5.7	0.9	158
Columbus, OH.	1,405	1,613	1,675	1,691	1,709	14.8	5.9	32
Corpus Christi, TX	368	403	406	410	414	9.7	2.5	111
Dallas-Fort Worth-Arlington, TX	3,989	5,162	5,585	5,696	5,819	29.4	12.7	5
Davenport-Moline-Rock Island, IA-IL.	368	376	375	375	376	2.1	0.1	130
Dayton, OH.	844	848	845	845	844	0.5	–0.5	59
Deltona-Daytona Beach-Ormond Beach, FL	371	443	468	479	490	19.6	10.5	100
Denver-Aurora, CO [2].	1,650	2,179	2,300	2,326	2,360	32.0	8.3	22
Des Moines-West Des Moines, IA	416	481	504	512	522	15.6	8.5	93
Detroit-Warren-Livonia, MI	4,249	4,453	4,486	4,490	4,488	4.8	0.8	10
Duluth, MN-WI.	269	275	276	276	275	2.3	(Z)	162
Durham, NC	345	424	445	450	456	23.0	7.6	103
El Paso, TX.	592	680	703	713	722	14.9	6.2	68
Erie, PA	276	281	283	281	280	1.9	–0.1	160
Eugene-Springfield, OR.	283	323	330	332	335	14.2	3.8	143
Evansville, IN-KY.	325	343	346	348	350	5.5	2.0	139
Fayetteville, NC.	298	337	345	346	346	13.1	2.7	140
Fayetteville-Springdale-Rogers, AR-MO	239	347	378	391	405	44.9	16.7	117
Flint, MI	430	436	442	443	444	1.3	1.8	107
Fort Collins-Loveland, CO	186	251	266	269	272	35.1	8.1	163
Fort Smith, AR-OK	234	273	280	282	285	16.7	4.3	157
Fort Wayne, IN.	354	390	400	402	404	10.1	3.7	118
Fresno, CA.	667	799	850	866	878	19.8	9.8	56
Grand Rapids-Wyoming, MI	646	740	762	766	771	14.6	4.1	65
Green Bay, WI.	244	282	292	295	297	15.9	5.3	154
Greensboro-High Point, NC	540	643	662	666	675	19.2	4.8	73
Greenville, SC.	472	560	578	584	591	18.6	5.6	83
Gulfport-Biloxi, MS	208	246	249	253	255	18.4	3.7	170
Hagerstown-Martinsburg, MD-WV	193	223	238	244	251	15.6	12.8	171
Harrisburg-Carlisle, PA.	474	509	517	519	522	7.3	2.5	94
Hartford-West Hartford-East Hartford, CT	1,124	1,149	1,179	1,183	1,188	2.2	3.4	44
Hickory-Lenoir-Morganton, NC	292	342	350	353	356	16.9	4.0	136
Holland-Grand Haven, MI.	188	238	250	253	255	26.9	7.2	169
Honolulu, HI.	836	876	893	900	905	4.8	3.3	53
Houston-Sugar Land-Baytown, TX	3,767	4,715	5,074	5,177	5,280	25.2	12.0	7
Huntington-Ashland, WV-KY-OH	288	289	287	286	286	0.2	–0.9	156
Huntsville, AL.	293	343	358	363	369	16.9	7.6	133
Indianapolis-Carmel, IN	1,294	1,525	1,600	1,617	1,641	17.8	7.6	34
Jackson, MS	447	497	510	517	523	11.2	5.1	92
Jacksonville, FL	925	1,123	1,196	1,224	1,248	21.4	11.2	42
Kalamazoo-Portage, MI	293	315	320	318	319	7.3	1.4	145
Kansas City, MO-KS	1,637	1,836	1,908	1,927	1,948	12.2	6.1	27
Killeen-Temple-Fort Hood, TX	269	331	344	346	352	23.0	6.3	137
Kingsport-Bristol-Bristol, TN-VA	276	298	300	300	301	8.3	0.9	152
Knoxville, TN	535	616	640	647	655	15.2	6.4	78
Lakeland, FL	405	484	511	524	543	19.4	12.2	89
Lancaster, PA.	423	471	483	486	491	11.3	4.2	99
Lansing-East Lansing, MI.	433	448	454	454	455	3.5	1.7	104
Las Vegas-Paradise, NV	741	1,376	1,575	1,649	1,711	85.6	24.3	31
Lexington-Fayette, KY	348	408	421	425	430	17.2	5.3	110
Lincoln, NE	229	267	277	279	282	16.5	5.5	159
Little Rock-North Little Rock, AR	535	611	629	636	643	14.1	5.4	80
Los Angeles-Long Beach-Santa Ana, CA	11,274	12,366	12,817	12,899	12,924	9.7	4.5	2
Louisville-Jefferson County, KY-IN	1,056	1,162	1,190	1,199	1,208	10.1	4.0	43
Lubbock, TX	230	250	257	258	259	8.6	3.7	167
Madison, WI	432	502	525	531	537	16.1	7.0	90
Manchester-Nashua, NH	336	381	395	398	401	13.4	5.4	120
McAllen-Edinburg-Mission, TX.	384	569	635	657	678	48.5	19.1	72
Memphis, TN-MS-AR.	1,067	1,205	1,238	1,248	1,261	12.9	4.6	41
Miami-Fort Lauderdale-Miami Beach, FL.	4,056	5,008	5,276	5,356	5,422	23.5	8.3	6
Milwaukee-Waukesha-West Allis, WI	1,432	1,501	1,513	1,513	1,513	4.8	0.8	37
Minneapolis-St. Paul-Bloomington, MN-WI.	2,539	2,969	3,083	3,113	3,143	16.9	5.9	16
Mobile, AL.	379	400	400	400	401	5.6	0.4	119
Modesto, CA.	371	447	491	498	506	20.6	13.1	97
Montgomery, AL.	305	347	353	354	357	13.6	3.1	135
Naples-Marco Island, FL	152	251	286	297	307	65.3	22.2	149
Nashville-Davidson—Murfreesboro, TN.	1,048	1,312	1,371	1,395	1,423	25.1	8.4	39
New Haven-Milford, CT	804	824	841	844	847	2.5	2.8	58
New Orleans-Metairie-Kenner, LA	1,264	1,317	1,315	1,318	1,319	4.1	0.2	40

See footnotes at end of table.

[1990 and 2000, as of April 1; beginning 2003 as of July 1 (**658 represents 658,000**). Covers metropolitan statistical areas with 250,000 and over population in 2005, as defined by the U.S. Office of Management and Budget as of December 2005. For definitions and components of all metropolitan and micropolitan areas, see Appendix II. Minus sign (–) indicates decrease]

Metropolitan statistical area	Number (1,000)					Percent change		Rank, 2005
	1990	2000, esti- mates base [1]	2003	2004	2005	1990– 2000	2000– 2005 [1]	
New York-Northern New Jersey-Long Island, NY-NJ-PA	16,846	18,323	18,687	18,755	18,747	8.8	2.3	1
Norwich-New London, CT	255	259	265	266	267	1.6	2.9	166
Ocala, FL	195	259	281	292	303	32.9	17.2	151
Ogden-Clearfield, UT	352	443	469	477	487	25.8	10.0	101
Oklahoma City, OK	971	1,095	1,132	1,142	1,157	12.8	5.6	46
Omaha-Council Bluffs, NE-IA	686	767	792	802	813	11.9	6.0	60
Orlando-Kissimmee, FL	1,225	1,645	1,802	1,863	1,933	34.3	17.6	28
Oxnard-Thousand Oaks-Ventura, CA	669	753	790	796	796	12.6	5.7	62
Palm Bay-Melbourne-Titusville, FL	399	476	505	519	531	19.4	11.6	91
Pensacola-Ferry Pass-Brent, FL	344	412	430	435	440	19.7	6.7	109
Peoria, IL	359	367	366	367	369	2.3	0.6	132
Philadelphia-Camden-Wilmington, PA-NJ-DE-MD	5,436	5,687	5,771	5,799	5,823	4.6	2.4	4
Phoenix-Mesa-Scottsdale, AZ	2,238	3,252	3,593	3,713	3,865	45.3	18.9	14
Pittsburgh, PA	2,468	2,431	2,408	2,398	2,386	–1.5	–1.9	21
Portland-South Portland-Biddeford, ME	441	488	507	511	514	10.5	5.5	96
Portland-Vancouver-Beaverton, OR-WA	1,524	1,928	2,040	2,062	2,096	26.5	8.7	24
Port St. Lucie-Fort Pierce, FL	251	319	349	365	381	27.2	19.3	128
Poughkeepsie-Newburgh-Middletown, NY	567	622	656	663	668	9.6	7.4	75
Providence-New Bedford-Fall River, RI-MA	1,510	1,583	1,622	1,627	1,623	4.8	2.5	35
Provo-Orem, UT	269	377	431	443	453	39.9	20.2	105
Raleigh-Cary, NC	544	797	888	915	950	46.5	19.2	51
Reading, PA	337	374	386	391	396	11.0	6.1	123
Reno-Sparks, NV	257	343	375	384	394	33.3	14.9	124
Richmond, VA	949	1,097	1,141	1,157	1,176	15.6	7.2	45
Riverside-San Bernardino-Ontario, CA	2,589	3,255	3,645	3,786	3,910	25.7	20.1	13
Roanoke, VA	269	288	290	291	293	7.4	1.6	155
Rochester, NY	1,002	1,038	1,041	1,041	1,039	3.5	0.1	49
Rockford, IL	284	320	331	335	339	12.9	5.9	142
Sacramento—Arden-Arcade—Roseville, CA	1,481	1,797	1,975	2,015	2,042	21.3	13.7	26
St. Louis, MO-IL [3]	2,581	2,699	2,753	2,769	2,779	4.6	3.0	18
Salem, OR	278	347	365	370	376	24.9	8.2	131
Salinas, CA	356	402	414	415	412	13.0	2.6	112
Salt Lake City, UT	768	969	1,006	1,019	1,034	26.1	6.8	50
San Antonio, TX	1,408	1,712	1,815	1,853	1,890	21.6	10.4	29
San Diego-Carlsbad-San Marcos, CA	2,498	2,814	2,921	2,935	2,933	12.6	4.3	17
San Francisco-Oakland-Fremont, CA	3,684	4,124	4,155	4,147	4,153	11.9	0.7	12
San Jose-Sunnyvale-Santa Clara, CA	1,534	1,736	1,732	1,738	1,755	13.1	1.1	30
San Luis Obispo-Paso Robles, CA	217	247	253	254	255	13.6	3.6	168
Santa Barbara-Santa Maria, CA	370	399	403	402	401	8.0	0.4	121
Santa Rosa-Petaluma, CA	388	459	467	468	466	18.1	1.7	102
Sarasota-Bradenton-Venice, FL	489	590	634	652	673	20.5	14.1	74
Savannah, GA	258	293	305	310	314	13.7	7.0	148
Scranton—Wilkes-Barre, PA	575	561	552	551	551	–2.6	–1.8	86
Seattle-Tacoma-Bellevue, WA	2,559	3,044	3,143	3,168	3,203	18.9	5.2	15
Shreveport-Bossier City, LA	360	376	378	381	383	4.5	1.9	127
South Bend-Mishawaka, IN-MI	297	317	317	317	318	6.8	0.5	146
Spartanburg, SC	227	254	262	264	267	11.9	5.1	165
Spokane, WA	361	418	431	435	441	15.7	5.4	108
Springfield, MA	673	680	687	687	687	1.0	1.1	71
Springfield, MO	299	368	384	391	398	23.3	8.1	122
Stockton, CA	481	564	631	649	664	17.3	17.8	76
Syracuse, NY	660	650	653	653	652	–1.5	0.2	79
Tallahassee, FL	259	320	328	331	335	23.6	4.6	144
Tampa-St. Petersburg-Clearwater, FL	2,068	2,396	2,530	2,586	2,648	15.9	10.5	20
Toledo, OH	654	659	659	658	657	0.8	–0.4	77
Trenton-Ewing, NJ	326	351	361	364	366	7.7	4.4	134
Tucson, AZ	667	844	890	907	925	26.5	9.6	52
Tulsa, OK	761	860	879	881	888	12.9	3.3	55
Utica-Rome, NY	317	300	298	299	298	–5.3	–0.7	153
Vallejo-Fairfield, CA	339	395	411	412	412	16.2	4.3	113
Virginia Beach-Norfolk-Newport News, VA-NC	1,451	1,577	1,625	1,642	1,647	8.7	4.5	33
Visalia-Porterville, CA	312	368	391	401	411	18.0	11.6	114
Washington-Arlington-Alexandria, DC-VA-MD-WV	4,122	4,796	5,085	5,158	5,215	16.3	8.7	8
Wichita, KS	511	571	582	584	587	11.8	2.8	85
Wilmington, NC	200	275	294	303	315	37.2	14.8	147
Winston-Salem, NC	361	422	437	441	449	16.7	6.3	106
Worcester, MA	710	750	775	779	783	5.7	4.4	64
York-Hanover, PA	340	382	395	401	409	12.4	7.1	116
Youngstown-Warren-Boardman, OH-PA	614	603	593	596	593	–1.7	–1.6	82

Z Less than 0.05 percent. [1] Reflects modifications to the Census 2000 population as documented in the Count Question Resolution program, updates to the Boundary and Annexation Survey, and geographic program revisions. [2] Broomfield County, CO was formed from parts of Adams, Boulder, Jefferson, and Weld Counties, CO on November 15, 2001, and is coextensive with Broomfield city. For purposes of defining and presenting data for metropolitan statistical areas, Broomfield city is treated as if it were a county at the time of the 1990 and 2000 censuses. [3] The portion of Sullivan city in Crawford County, Missouri, is legally part of the St. Louis, MO-IL MSA. Data shown here do not include this area.

Source: U.S. Census Bureau, "July 1, 2005 Population Estimates for Metropolitan, Micropolitan, and Combined Statistical Areas (Areas defined by the Office of Management and Budget as of December 2005)"; published 21 August 2006; <http://www.census.gov/population/www/estimates/Estimates%20pages_final.html>.

Population 29

Table 26. 50 Largest Metropolitan Statistical Areas—Population Change: 2000 to 2005

[Covers period April 1, 2000, to July 1, 2005 (670 represents 670,000). Covers metropolitan statistical areas as defined by the U.S. Office of Management and Budget as of December 2005. For definitions and components of all metropolitan and micropolitan areas, see Appendix II. Minus sign (–) indicates decrease]

Metropolitan statistical area	Number (1,000)							Percent change
	Total change [1]	Natural increase			Net migration			
		Total	Births	Deaths	Total	Inter-national	Internal migration	
Atlanta-Sandy Springs-Marietta, GA	670	252	397	146	330	145	186	15.8
Austin-Round Rock, TX	203	83	117	35	122	47	75	16.2
Baltimore-Towson, MD	103	57	181	124	22	28	-5	4.0
Birmingham-Hoover, AL	39	20	79	58	18	7	11	3.7
Boston-Cambridge-Quincy, MA-NH	19	116	304	188	-90	133	-223	0.4
Buffalo-Niagara Falls, NY	-22	4	69	65	-25	8	-33	-1.9
Charlotte-Gastonia-Concord, NC-SC	191	63	118	54	130	34	96	14.3
Chicago-Naperville-Joliet, IL-IN-WI	345	379	747	368	-36	307	-343	3.8
Cincinnati-Middletown, OH-KY-IN	61	60	153	92	3	14	-11	3.0
Cleveland-Elyria-Mentor, OH	-22	31	143	112	-52	20	-71	-1.0
Columbus, OH	96	65	132	67	30	24	6	5.9
Dallas-Fort Worth-Arlington, TX	658	334	504	170	332	232	100	12.7
Denver-Aurora, CO [2]	181	120	191	71	64	74	-10	8.3
Detroit-Warren-Livonia, MI	36	114	320	206	-74	72	-146	0.8
Hartford-West Hartford-East Hartford, CT	40	19	72	53	22	20	2	3.4
Houston-Sugar Land-Baytown, TX	565	298	454	156	273	210	63	12.0
Indianapolis-Carmel, IN	115	64	130	66	53	17	36	7.6
Jacksonville, FL	126	34	89	54	94	12	82	11.2
Kansas City, MO-KS	111	70	149	79	41	23	17	6.1
Las Vegas-Paradise, NV	335	65	125	60	272	53	219	24.3
Los Angeles-Long Beach-Santa Ana, CA	558	633	1,032	400	-57	647	-704	4.5
Louisville-Jefferson County, KY-IN	46	26	84	58	22	10	12	4.0
Memphis, TN-MS-AR	56	48	104	56	10	11	-1	4.6
Miami-Fort Lauderdale-Miami Beach, FL	414	131	374	243	291	332	-41	8.3
Milwaukee-Waukesha-West Allis, WI	12	45	113	68	-30	19	-49	0.8
Minneapolis-St. Paul-Bloomington, MN-WI	174	135	234	99	42	58	-16	5.9
Nashville-Davidson--Murfreesboro, TN	111	46	104	58	67	20	47	8.4
New Orleans-Metairie-Kenner, LA	3	37	102	65	-32	9	-41	0.2
New York-Northern New Jersey-Long Island, NY-NJ-PA	424	634	1,388	753	-286	866	-1,151	2.3
Oklahoma City, OK	61	38	89	51	25	17	8	5.6
Orlando-Kissimmee, FL	289	61	131	71	229	51	178	17.6
Philadelphia-Camden-Wilmington, PA-NJ-DE-MD	136	120	402	282	24	76	-52	2.4
Phoenix-Mesa-Scottsdale, AZ	613	184	314	131	436	134	301	18.9
Pittsburgh, PA	-45	-16	133	149	-26	13	-39	-1.9
Portland-Vancouver-Beaverton, OR-WA	168	68	146	78	103	55	48	8.7
Providence-New Bedford-Fall River, RI-MA	40	23	102	79	19	23	-5	2.5
Richmond, VA	79	28	80	52	52	11	41	7.2
Riverside-San Bernardino-Ontario, CA	655	169	298	129	492	79	413	20.1
Rochester, NY	1	18	65	47	-15	11	-26	0.1
Sacramento—Arden-Arcade—Roseville, CA	245	68	142	74	180	51	129	13.7
St. Louis, MO-IL [3]	80	58	191	134	1	22	-21	3.0
Salt Lake City, UT	66	74	103	29	-9	32	-41	6.8
San Antonio, TX	178	87	152	65	93	27	66	10.4
San Diego-Carlsbad-San Marcos, CA	120	130	232	103	-6	92	-98	4.3
San Francisco-Oakland-Fremont, CA	29	138	292	154	-104	199	-302	0.7
San Jose-Sunnyvale-Santa Clara, CA	19	96	143	47	-75	129	-204	1.1
Seattle-Tacoma-Bellevue, WA	159	102	213	111	55	86	-32	5.2
Tampa-St. Petersburg-Clearwater, FL	252	7	156	149	249	47	202	10.5
Virginia Beach-Norfolk-Newport News, VA-NC	70	61	126	64	12	11	1	4.5
Washington-Arlington-Alexandria, DC-VA-MD-WV	418	245	405	160	160	200	-40	8.7

[1] Based on the April 1, 2000, Population Estimates base which reflects changes to the Census 2000 population from the Count Question Resolution program and geographic program revisions. Includes residual not shown separately. [2] Broomfield County, CO, was formed from parts of Adams, Boulder, Jefferson, and Weld Counties, CO, on November 15, 2001, and is coextensive with Broomfield city. For purposes of defining and presenting data for metropolitan statistical areas, Broomfield city is treated as if it were a county at the time of the 2000 census. [3] The portion of Sullivan city in Crawford County, Missouri, is legally part of the St. Louis, MO-IL MSA. Data shown here do not include this area.

Source: U.S. Census Bureau, "Table 2: Cumulative Estimates of the Components of Population Change for Metropolitan and Micropolitan Statistical Areas: April 1, 2000 to July 1, 2005 (CBSA-EST2005-02)"; published 21 August 2006; <http://www.census.go /population/www/estimates/Estimates%20pagesfinal.html>.

Table 27.
50 Largest Metropolitan Statistical Areas—Population by Race and Hispanic Origin: 2005

[In thousands (4,918 represents 4,918,000). As of July 1. Covers metropolitan statistical areas as defined by the U.S. Office of Management and Budget as of December 2005. For definitions and components of all metropolitan and micropolitan areas, see Appendix II]

Metropolitan statistical area	Total persons	White alone	Black or African American alone	American Indian and Alaska Native alone	Asian alone	Native Hawaiian and Other Pacific Islander alone	Two or more races	Hispanic or Latino origin [1]
Atlanta-Sandy Springs-Marietta, GA	4,918	3,129	1,516	15	196	3	59	424
Austin-Round Rock, TX	1,453	1,244	114	10	63	2	20	421
Baltimore-Towson, MD	2,656	1,761	756	8	94	2	36	71
Birmingham-Hoover, AL	1,090	762	307	3	10	(Z)	8	28
Boston-Cambridge-Quincy, MA-NH	4,412	3,749	336	11	253	3	60	331
Buffalo-Niagara Falls, NY	1,148	969	141	8	19	(Z)	11	36
Charlotte-Gastonia-Concord, NC-SC	1,521	1,104	356	7	39	1	15	113
Chicago-Naperville-Joliet, IL-IN-WI	9,443	7,087	1,735	33	474	8	107	1,773
Cincinnati-Middletown, OH-KY-IN	2,070	1,767	244	4	32	1	23	31
Cleveland-Elyria-Mentor, OH	2,126	1,635	423	4	36	1	28	80
Columbus, OH	1,709	1,386	241	4	48	1	29	42
Dallas-Fort Worth-Arlington, TX	5,819	4,604	829	37	268	6	77	1,491
Denver-Aurora, CO	2,360	2,075	133	24	80	3	45	510
Detroit-Warren-Livonia, MI	4,488	3,234	1,036	16	136	2	65	153
Hartford-West Hartford-East Hartford, CT	1,188	1,002	129	3	36	1	16	123
Houston-Sugar Land-Baytown, TX	5,280	4,005	889	29	297	4	57	1,703
Indianapolis-Carmel, IN	1,641	1,349	240	4	26	1	21	66
Jacksonville, FL	1,248	910	281	5	34	1	18	62
Kansas City, MO-KS	1,948	1,626	240	10	38	2	32	125
Las Vegas-Paradise, NV	1,711	1,349	172	16	114	10	48	446
Los Angeles-Long Beach-Santa Ana, CA	12,924	9,718	1,017	131	1,778	44	236	5,625
Louisville-Jefferson County, KY-IN	1,208	1,014	162	3	14	1	15	28
Memphis, TN-MS-AR	1,261	657	569	3	20	1	11	39
Miami-Fort Lauderdale-Miami Beach, FL	5,422	4,090	1,132	20	112	4	65	2,034
Milwaukee-Waukesha-West Allis, WI	1,513	1,195	249	9	38	1	21	114
Minneapolis-St. Paul-Bloomington, MN-WI	3,143	2,707	198	24	153	2	59	134
Nashville-Davidson—Murfreesboro, TN	1,423	1,156	217	5	27	1	16	66
New Orleans-Metairie-Kenner, LA	1,319	765	503	5	31	(Z)	14	66
New York-Northern New Jersey-Long Island, NY-NJ-PA	18,747	12,968	3,692	91	1,684	21	291	3,925
Oklahoma City, OK	1,157	914	124	46	32	1	40	98
Orlando-Kissimmee, FL	1,933	1,519	303	9	68	2	32	406
Philadelphia-Camden-Wilmington, PA-NJ-DE-MD	5,823	4,276	1,220	13	237	3	73	350
Phoenix-Mesa-Scottsdale, AZ	3,865	3,435	166	95	100	8	62	1,124
Pittsburgh, PA	2,386	2,134	196	3	32	1	21	21
Portland-Vancouver-Beaverton, OR-WA	2,096	1,844	59	20	110	7	56	195
Providence-New Bedford-Fall River, RI-MA	1,623	1,465	86	8	38	2	23	141
Richmond, VA	1,176	771	359	5	28	1	13	38
Riverside-San Bernardino-Ontario, CA	3,910	3,227	314	55	204	17	93	1,678
Rochester, NY	1,039	882	119	3	23	(Z)	13	50
Sacramento—Arden-Arcade—Roseville, CA	2,042	1,553	153	23	222	12	79	358
St. Louis, MO-IL [2]	2,779	2,185	506	6	48	1	32	51
Salt Lake City, UT	1,034	955	14	10	28	13	15	148
San Antonio, TX	1,890	1,692	123	19	31	3	22	989
San Diego-Carlsbad-San Marcos, CA	2,933	2,340	163	28	299	17	87	864
San Francisco-Oakland-Fremont, CA	4,153	2,681	383	26	904	28	130	806
San Jose-Sunnyvale-Santa Clara, CA	1,755	1,126	48	14	515	7	46	452
Seattle-Tacoma-Bellevue, WA	3,203	2,531	175	38	323	20	117	212
Tampa-St. Petersburg-Clearwater, FL	2,648	2,234	300	11	65	2	35	346
Virginia Beach-Norfolk-Newport News, VA-NC	1,647	1,033	523	6	49	2	34	59
Washington-Arlington-Alexandria, DC-VA-MD-WV	5,215	3,269	1,389	18	426	5	109	581

Z Less than 500.   [1] Persons of Hispanic origin may be any race.   [2] The portion of Sullivan city in Crawford County, Missouri, is legally part of the St. Louis, MO-IL MSA. Data shown here do not include this area.

Source: U.S. Census Bureau, USA Counties; <http://censtats.census.gov/usa/usa.shtml>; (31 August 2006).

Table 28. **Population by Core-Based Statistical Area Status and State: 1990 to 2005**

[1990 and 2000, as of April 1; 2005 as of July 1 (230,779 represents 230,779,000). Covers metropolitan and micropolitan statistical areas as defined by the U.S. Office of Management and Budget as of December 2005. For definitions and components of all metropolitan and micropolitan areas, see Appendix II. Minus sign (–) indicates decrease]

State	Core-Based Statistical Area (metropolitan and micropolitan) population						Population outside Core-Based Statistical Area					
	Number (1,000)			Percent of total		Percent change, 2000–2005	Number (1,000)			Percent of total		Percent change, 2000–2005
	1990	2000 [1]	2005	2000	2005	2005	1990	2000 [1]	2005	2000	2005	2005
U.S. ...	230,779	262,114	276,889	93.1	93.4	5.6	17,939	19,310	19,521	6.9	6.6	1.1
AL	3,559	3,945	4,066	88.7	89.2	3.1	482	503	492	11.3	10.8	–2.1
AK	398	461	496	73.6	74.7	7.5	152	166	168	26.4	25.3	1.2
AZ	3,512	4,944	5,741	96.4	96.7	16.1	153	187	198	3.6	3.3	6.1
AR	1,802	2,082	2,191	77.9	78.8	5.2	549	591	588	22.1	21.2	–0.5
CA	29,540	33,628	35,873	99.3	99.3	6.7	218	243	259	0.7	0.7	6.6
CO	2,989	[2]3,922	4,272	91.2	91.6	8.9	306	380	394	8.8	8.4	3.5
CT	3,287	3,406	3,510	100.0	100.0	3.1	–	–	–	–	–	–
DE	666	784	844	100.0	100.0	7.6	–	–	–	–	–	–
DC	607	572	551	100.0	100.0	–3.8	–	–	–	–	–	–
FL	12,645	15,620	17,398	97.7	97.8	11.4	293	363	392	2.3	2.2	8.1
GA	5,822	7,411	8,254	90.5	91.0	11.4	656	776	818	9.5	9.0	5.5
HI	1,108	1,211	1,275	100.0	100.0	5.3	–	–	–	–	–	–24.5
ID	846	1,103	1,231	85.2	86.1	11.6	161	191	198	14.8	13.9	3.8
IL	10,809	11,796	12,147	95.0	95.2	3.0	622	624	616	5.0	4.8	–1.2
IN	5,198	5,715	5,904	94.0	94.1	3.3	346	366	368	6.0	5.9	0.6
IA	1,939	2,090	2,147	71.4	72.4	2.7	838	836	819	28.6	27.6	–2.1
KS	2,029	2,248	2,325	83.6	84.7	3.4	448	440	419	16.4	15.3	–4.8
KY	2,734	3,036	3,155	75.1	75.6	3.9	953	1,006	1,018	24.9	24.4	1.2
LA	3,917	4,156	4,216	93.0	93.2	1.4	303	312	307	7.0	6.8	–1.6
ME	845	893	932	70.0	70.5	4.3	383	382	390	30.0	29.5	2.1
MD	4,708	5,218	5,519	98.5	98.5	5.8	73	79	82	1.5	1.5	3.6
MA	5,999	6,325	6,373	99.6	99.6	0.8	18	25	26	0.4	0.4	5.1
MI	8,601	9,153	9,323	92.1	92.1	1.9	694	785	798	7.9	7.9	1.6
MN	3,750	4,266	4,474	86.7	87.2	4.9	626	654	659	13.3	12.8	0.8
MS	1,969	2,196	2,273	77.2	77.8	3.5	606	648	648	22.8	22.2	–
MO	4,392	4,810	5,001	85.9	86.2	4.0	725	787	799	14.1	13.8	1.6
MT	495	574	607	63.7	64.8	5.6	304	328	329	36.3	35.2	0.4
NE	1,198	1,339	1,402	78.2	79.7	4.7	381	373	357	21.8	20.3	–4.2
NV	1,157	1,950	2,367	97.6	98.0	21.4	44	48	48	2.4	2.0	–0.6
NH	1,074	1,192	1,263	96.5	96.4	5.9	35	44	47	3.5	3.6	8.6
NJ	7,730	8,414	8,718	100.0	100.0	3.6	–	–	–	–	–	–
NM	1,442	1,737	1,850	95.5	95.9	6.5	73	82	79	4.5	4.1	–4.4
NY	17,574	18,547	18,821	97.7	97.7	1.5	417	430	433	2.3	2.3	0.8
NC	6,030	7,352	7,965	91.4	91.7	8.3	602	695	718	8.6	8.3	3.3
ND	410	435	440	67.7	69.2	1.3	228	208	196	32.3	30.8	–5.5
OH	10,377	10,849	10,951	95.6	95.5	0.9	470	504	513	4.4	4.5	1.7
OK	2,610	2,891	2,987	83.8	84.2	3.3	536	560	561	16.2	15.8	0.2
OR	2,719	3,281	3,500	95.9	96.1	6.7	123	140	141	4.1	3.9	0.8
PA	11,518	11,899	12,046	96.9	96.9	1.2	365	382	384	3.1	3.1	0.4
RI	1,003	1,048	1,076	100.0	100.0	2.7	–	–	–	–	–	–
SC	3,230	3,735	3,980	93.1	93.5	6.6	256	277	275	6.9	6.5	–0.5
SD	469	527	553	69.8	71.3	5.0	227	228	222	30.2	28.7	–2.3
TN	4,350	5,080	5,339	89.3	89.5	5.1	527	610	624	10.7	10.5	2.4
TX	15,723	19,465	21,445	93.4	93.8	10.2	1,264	1,386	1,415	6.6	6.2	2.0
UT	1,618	2,107	2,341	94.4	94.8	11.1	105	126	128	5.6	5.2	2.0
VT	417	449	459	73.8	73.7	2.2	146	159	164	26.2	26.3	2.7
VA	5,434	6,269	6,742	88.6	89.1	7.6	755	810	825	11.4	10.9	1.8
WA	4,689	5,678	6,063	96.3	96.4	6.8	178	216	225	3.7	3.6	4.1
WV	1,315	1,348	1,362	74.5	75.0	1.1	478	461	455	25.5	25.0	–1.3
WI	4,205	4,604	4,757	85.8	85.9	3.3	687	759	779	14.2	14.1	2.6
WY	320	352	364	71.3	71.5	3.5	133	142	145	28.7	28.5	2.3

– Represents or rounds to zero.   [1] Reflects modifications to the Census 2000 population as documented in the Count Question Resolution program and geographic program revisions.   [2] Includes Broomfield city.

Source: U.S. Census Bureau, "Annual Estimates of the Population for Counties: April 1, 2000 to July 1, 2005" (CO-EST2005-01); published 16 March 2006; <http://www.census.gov/popest/counties/CO-EST2005-01.html>; and 2000 Census of Population and Housing, *Population and Housing Unit Counts*, PHC-1.

Table 29. **Population in Coastal Counties: 1980 to 2005**

[Population as of April 1, except as indicated (3,537 represents 3,537,000). Areas as defined by U.S. National Oceanic and Atmospheric Administration, 1992. Covers 673 counties and equivalent areas with at least 15 percent of their land area either in a coastal watershed (drainage area) or in a coastal cataloging unit (a coastal area between watersheds). See Appendix III]

Year	Total	Counties in coastal regions					Balance of United States
		Total	Atlantic	Gulf of Mexico	Great Lakes	Pacific	
Land area, 2000 (1,000 sq. mi.)	3,537	889	148	115	115	511	2,649
POPULATION							
1980 (mil.).	226.5	119.8	53.7	13.1	26.0	27.0	106.7
1990 (mil.).	248.7	133.4	59.0	15.2	25.9	33.2	115.3
2000 (mil.).	281.4	148.3	65.2	18.0	27.3	37.8	133.1
2005 (July 1) (mil.)	296.4	155.2	68.1	19.5	27.5	40.0	141.2
1980 (percent).	100	53	24	6	11	12	47
1990 (percent).	100	54	24	6	10	13	46
2000 (percent).	100	53	23	6	10	13	47
2005 (July 1) (percent)	100	53	23	6	10	14	47

Source: U.S. Census Bureau, 1980 Census of Population, Vol. 1, Chapter A (PC80-1-A-1), *U.S. Summary*; 1990 Census of Population and Housing (CPH1); and unpublished data.

Table 30. **States With Coastal Counties—Population, Housing Units, Establishments, and Employees by Coastal Region and State: 2000 to 2005**

[281,425 represents 281,425,000. Population and housing as of July 1, except 2000 as of April 1. See headnote, Table 29]

Coastal region and state	Population					Housing units			Private nonfarm [3]—	
		2005		Percent change, 2000– 2005	Per square mile, 2005 [2]	Number (1,000)		Percent change, 2000– 2004	Estab- lish- ments, 2004 (1,000)	Employ- ees, 2004 (1,000)
	2000 [1] (1,000)	Number (1,000)	Percent of state total			2000	2004			
United States, total . .	281,425	296,410	(X)	5.3	84	116,299	122,672	5.5	7,388	115,075
Interior U.S.	133,103	141,218	(X)	6.1	53	56,150	59,795	6.5	3,442	54,256
Coastal counties, total . .	148,322	155,193	(X)	4.6	175	60,148	62,877	4.5	3,946	60,819
Atlantic.	65,198	68,132	(X)	4.5	461	26,890	28,016	4.2	1,839	27,591
Maine	1,184	1,231	93.1	4.0	61	601	624	3.8	39	465
New Hampshire	1,007	1,071	81.8	6.4	254	433	456	5.4	32	440
Massachusetts	6,125	6,173	96.5	0.8	934	2,534	2,580	1.8	170	2,903
Rhode Island	1,048	1,076	100.0	2.7	1,030	440	446	1.4	30	434
Connecticut	3,406	3,510	100.0	3.1	725	1,388	1,414	1.9	93	1,535
New York	13,573	13,851	71.9	2.0	1,787	5,291	5,384	1.8	389	5,424
New Jersey	8,312	8,608	98.7	3.6	1,219	3,277	3,371	2.9	238	3,556
Pennsylvania	5,750	5,889	47.4	2.4	855	2,338	2,400	2.7	143	2,555
Delaware.	784	844	100.0	7.6	432	344	367	6.7	25	391
Maryland.	4,865	5,134	91.7	5.5	677	1,975	2,061	4.4	124	1,962
District of Columbia.	572	551	100.0	-3.8	8,966	275	277	0.6	20	437
Virginia.	4,794	5,143	68.0	7.3	370	1,920	2,054	7.0	129	2,169
North Carolina	1,985	2,062	23.7	3.9	105	909	971	6.9	47	630
South Carolina	1,653	1,764	41.5	6.7	116	755	816	8.1	44	595
Georgia.	822	862	9.5	4.9	71	347	369	6.2	19	269
Florida	9,320	10,364	58.3	11.2	554	4,063	4,427	8.9	298	3,827
Gulf of Mexico	18,003	19,524	(X)	8.4	170	7,752	8,364	7.9	445	6,620
Florida	6,249	6,985	39.3	11.8	222	3,090	3,386	9.6	177	2,272
Georgia.	95	98	1.1	3.3	61	40	42	3.7	2	30
Alabama	712	734	16.1	3.0	84	320	339	6.0	17	247
Mississippi.	588	614	21.0	4.4	91	248	263	6.0	12	178
Louisiana	3,510	3,566	78.8	1.6	139	1,442	1,498	3.9	82	1,299
Texas	6,850	7,527	32.9	9.9	187	2,612	2,836	8.6	154	2,595
Great Lakes	27,325	27,514	(X)	0.7	238	11,428	11,792	3.2	665	11,311
New York	3,650	3,627	18.8	-0.6	169	1,587	1,611	1.5	83	1,384
Pennsylvania	281	280	2.3	-0.1	350	114	116	1.6	7	118
Ohio	4,418	4,397	38.4	-0.5	417	1,872	1,919	2.5	111	1,872
Michigan	8,859	9,025	89.2	1.9	176	3,794	3,957	4.3	214	3,476
Indiana	1,378	1,417	22.6	2.8	348	558	585	4.9	32	574
Illinois	6,021	6,006	47.1	-0.3	4,311	2,325	2,377	2.2	149	2,662
Wisconsin	2,469	2,514	45.4	1.8	163	1,057	1,103	4.3	62	1,130
Minnesota	248	248	4.8	-0.3	23	121	125	3.0	7	95
Pacific	37,796	40,022	(X)	5.9	78	14,078	14,705	4.5	997	15,297
Washington	4,587	4,897	77.9	6.8	198	1,927	2,048	6.3	137	1,851
Oregon	1,808	1,883	51.7	4.2	90	796	828	4.1	58	768
California.	29,660	31,405	86.9	5.9	404	10,674	11,116	4.1	754	12,015
Hawaii	1,212	1,275	100.0	5.3	199	462	483	4.6	32	469
Alaska	530	561	84.6	6.0	1	220	229	4.3	17	193

X Not applicable.   [1] Reflects modifications to the Census 2000 population as documented in the Count Question Resolution program and geographic program revisions.   [2] Calculated on the basis of land area data from the 2000 census.   [3] Covers establishments with payroll. Excludes most government employees railroad employees, self-employed persons. Employees are for the week including March 12.

Source: U.S. Census Bureau, USA Counties; <http://censtats.census.gov/usa/usa.shtml>; (10 August 2006); and County Business Patterns, annual. See <http://www.census.gov/epcd/cbp/view/cbpview.html>.

Population   33

Table 31. Incorporated Places With 150,000 or More Inhabitants in 2005—Population: 1980 to 2005

[In thousands, except as indicated (237 represents 237,000). As of April 1, except 2005 as of July 1. 2005 data refer to boundaries in effect on January 1, 2005; 1990 and 2000 data, boundaries in effect on January 1, 2000; 1980 data, boundaries in effect for 1980 census. Minus sign (–) indicates decrease. See Appendix III]

Incorporated place	1980	1990	2000 Total	2000 Percent change, 1990–2000	2005 Total	2005 Rank	2005 Percent change, 2000–2005 [1]
Akron, OH	237	223	217	–2.7	211	89	–2.9
Albuquerque, NM	332	387	449	15.9	494	33	10.2
Amarillo, TX	149	158	174	10.0	183	118	5.4
Anaheim, CA	219	267	328	23.0	332	55	1.2
Anchorage, AK	174	226	260	15.0	275	68	5.7
Arlington, TX	160	262	333	27.1	363	50	8.9
Arlington, VA [2]	153	171	189	10.9	196	103	3.4
Atlanta, GA	425	394	416	5.8	471	35	13.0
Augusta-Richmond County, GA	[4]48	186	195	4.8	191	113	–2.3
Aurora, CO	159	222	276	24.6	297	60	7.7
Aurora, IL	81	100	143	42.6	168	131	17.5
Austin, TX	346	497	657	32.1	690	16	4.6
Bakersfield, CA	106	188	247	31.4	296	61	21.5
Baltimore, MD	787	736	651	–11.5	636	18	–2.4
Baton Rouge, LA	220	223	228	2.2	222	82	–2.6
Birmingham, AL	284	266	243	–8.7	231	79	–4.6
Boise City, ID	102	142	186	30.8	193	111	2.3
Boston, MA	563	575	589	2.5	559	24	–5.1
Brownsville, TX	85	114	140	22.6	167	132	17.9
Buffalo, NY	358	328	293	–10.8	280	66	–4.4
Chandler, AZ	30	91	177	94.7	235	75	32.7
Charlotte, NC	315	428	541	26.4	611	20	8.7
Chattanooga, TN	170	153	156	1.8	155	143	–0.8
Chesapeake, VA	114	152	199	31.1	219	85	9.9
Chicago, IL	3,005	2,783	2,896	4.1	2,843	3	–1.8
Chula Vista, CA	84	135	174	28.3	210	90	21.3
Cincinnati, OH	385	365	331	–9.1	309	58	–6.8
Cleveland, OH	574	506	478	–5.5	452	39	–5.3
Colorado Springs, CO	215	282	361	28.0	370	49	2.4
Columbus, GA	169	[3]179	[3]186	4.0	185	115	–0.5
Columbus, OH	565	639	711	11.3	731	15	2.6
Corpus Christi, TX	232	258	277	7.4	283	64	2.2
Dallas, TX	905	1,007	1,189	18.1	1,214	9	2.1
Dayton, OH	194	182	166	–8.9	159	140	–4.4
Denver, CO	493	468	555	18.6	558	25	0.8
Des Moines, IA	191	193	199	2.8	194	106	–2.3
Detroit, MI	1,203	1,028	951	–7.5	887	11	–6.8
Durham, NC	101	149	187	25.5	205	94	9.1
El Paso, TX	425	516	564	9.3	599	21	6.2
Fontana, CA	37	88	129	46.7	164	138	26.9
Fort Lauderdale, FL	153	150	152	1.6	167	133	8.5
Fort Wayne, IN	172	206	206	–0.1	223	81	–0.7
Fort Worth, TX	385	449	535	19.1	624	19	15.3
Fremont, CA	132	173	203	17.3	200	96	–1.4
Fresno, CA	217	355	428	20.3	461	36	7.5
Garden Grove, CA	123	144	165	15.0	166	136	0.5
Garland, TX	139	181	216	19.3	216	86	0.3
Gilbert, AZ	6	30	110	265.6	174	127	58.1
Glendale, AZ	97	151	219	45.0	239	73	9.4
Glendale, CA	139	180	195	8.3	200	98	2.6
Grand Rapids, MI	182	189	198	4.7	194	107	–2.0
Greensboro, NC	156	192	224	16.9	232	77	3.3
Henderson, NV	24	65	175	169.4	232	76	32.3
Hialeah, FL	145	188	226	20.5	220	84	–2.6
Honolulu, HI [2]	365	376	372	–1.2	377	47	1.5
Houston, TX	1,595	1,697	1,954	15.1	2,017	4	3.0
Huntington Beach, CA	171	181	190	4.7	194	105	2.5
Huntsville, AL	143	161	158	–1.7	166	134	4.2
Indianapolis, IN [3]	701	732	782	6.9	784	12	0.3
Irvine, CA	62	111	143	28.4	187	114	30.5
Irving, TX	110	155	192	23.5	194	110	1.0
Jackson, MS	203	197	184	–6.3	178	123	–3.4
Jacksonville, FL	541	635	736	15.8	783	13	6.4
Jersey City, NJ	224	229	240	4.8	240	72	–0.2
Kansas City, MO	448	435	442	1.5	445	40	0.8
Knoxville, TN	175	174	174	–0.1	180	119	2.7
Laredo, TX	91	126	177	40.1	209	92	17.5
Las Vegas, NV	165	259	478	84.7	545	29	13.6
Lexington-Fayette, KY	204	225	261	15.6	268	69	2.9
Lincoln, NE	172	193	226	17.0	239	74	5.7
Little Rock, AR	159	177	183	3.4	185	116	0.8
Long Beach, CA	361	430	462	7.4	474	34	2.7
Los Angeles, CA	2,969	3,486	3,695	6.0	3,845	2	4.1
Louisville-Jefferson County, KY [3]	[5]299	[5]269	[5]256	–4.7	556	26	1.0
Lubbock, TX	174	187	200	6.9	210	91	5.1
Madison, WI	171	191	208	9.0	222	83	5.9
Memphis, TN	646	664	650	–2.1	672	17	–1.6
Mesa, AZ	152	291	396	36.2	443	41	11.3
Miami, FL	347	359	362	1.0	386	45	6.6
Milwaukee, WI	636	629	597	–5.1	579	22	–3.0

See footnotes at end of table.

Table 31. **Incorporated Places With 150,000 or More Inhabitants in 2005—**
Population: 1980 to 2005—Con.

[In thousands, except as indicated (237 represents 237,000). **As of April 1, except 2005 as of July 1.** 2005 data refer to boundaries in effect on January 1, 2005; 1990 and 2000 data, boundaries in effect on January 1, 2000; 1980 data, boundaries in effect for 1980 census. Minus sign (–) indicates decrease. See Appendix III]

Incorporated place	1980	1990	2000 Total	2000 Percent change, 1990–2000	2005 Total	2005 Rank	2005 Percent change [1], 2000–2005
Minneapolis, MN	371	368	383	3.9	373	48	–2.6
Mobile, AL	200	198	199	0.3	192	112	–3.8
Modesto, CA	107	166	189	13.5	207	93	9.6
Montgomery, AL	178	191	202	5.6	200	97	–0.8
Moreno Valley, CA	(6)	119	142	19.9	178	121	25.3
Nashville-Davidson, TN [3]	456	488	546	11.7	549	28	0.7
New Orleans, LA	558	497	485	–2.5	455	38	–6.2
New York, NY	7,072	7,323	8,008	9.4	8,143	1	1.7
Newark, NJ	329	275	274	–0.6	281	65	3.0
Newport News, VA	145	171	180	5.1	180	120	–0.4
Norfolk, VA	267	261	234	–10.3	232	78	–1.0
North Las Vegas, NV	43	48	115	140.8	177	125	52.9
Oakland, CA	339	372	399	7.4	395	44	–1.1
Oceanside, CA	77	128	161	25.8	166	135	3.1
Oklahoma City, OK	404	445	506	13.8	531	31	5.0
Omaha, NE	314	373	390	4.6	415	43	5.9
Ontario, CA	89	135	158	17.0	173	128	9.3
Orlando, FL	128	166	186	12.0	213	87	10.8
Overland Park, KS	82	111	149	34.3	165	137	10.3
Oxnard, CA	108	142	170	19.6	184	117	7.6
Pembroke Pines, FL	36	65	137	110.0	150	148	9.4
Philadelphia, PA	1,688	1,586	1,518	–4.3	1,463	5	–3.6
Phoenix, AZ	790	989	1,321	33.6	1,462	6	10.6
Pittsburgh, PA	424	370	335	–9.6	317	57	–5.3
Plano, TX	72	128	222	73.5	250	70	12.7
Pomona, CA	93	132	149	13.0	154	144	4.0
Portland, OR	368	486	529	8.9	533	30	0.8
Providence, RI	157	161	174	7.8	177	124	1.9
Raleigh, NC	150	221	276	24.9	342	53	19.9
Rancho Cucamonga, CA	55	101	128	26.0	169	129	32.6
Reno, NV	101	139	180	29.8	204	95	12.5
Richmond, VA	219	203	198	–2.4	194	108	–2.1
Riverside, CA	171	227	255	12.6	290	62	13.7
Rochester, NY	242	230	220	–4.4	211	88	–4.0
Rockford, IL	140	144	150	4.3	153	146	1.4
Sacramento, CA	276	370	407	10.0	456	37	12.1
Salt Lake City, UT	163	160	182	13.6	178	122	–2.0
San Antonio, TX	786	998	1,145	14.7	1,257	7	9.1
San Bernardino, CA	119	171	185	8.3	199	100	6.8
San Diego, CA	876	1,111	1,223	10.1	1,256	8	2.6
San Francisco, CA	679	724	777	7.3	739	14	–4.8
San Jose, CA	629	783	895	14.2	912	10	1.9
Santa Ana, CA	204	294	338	14.8	340	54	0.7
Santa Clarita, CA	(6)	123	151	22.8	168	130	11.3
Santa Rosa, CA	83	121	148	22.0	153	145	3.4
Scottsdale, AZ	89	130	203	55.8	226	80	11.5
Seattle, WA	494	516	563	9.1	574	23	1.9
Shreveport, LA	206	199	200	0.6	199	99	–0.9
Spokane, WA	171	178	196	9.8	197	101	0.6
Springfield, MA	152	157	152	–3.1	152	147	–0.2
Springfield, MO	133	141	152	7.4	150	149	–1.1
St. Louis, MO	453	397	348	–12.2	344	52	–1.1
St. Paul, MN	270	272	287	5.5	275	67	–4.1
St. Petersburg, FL	239	240	248	3.3	249	71	0.1
Stockton, CA	150	212	244	15.0	287	63	17.6
Tacoma, WA	159	177	194	9.1	196	104	1.2
Tallahassee, FL	82	126	151	19.5	159	141	4.1
Tampa, FL	272	280	303	8.4	326	56	7.4
Tempe, AZ	107	142	159	11.7	161	139	1.6
Toledo, OH	355	333	314	–5.8	301	59	–4.0
Tucson, AZ	331	418	487	16.4	516	32	5.8
Tulsa, OK	361	367	393	7.0	382	46	–2.7
Vancouver, WA	43	104	144	38.0	157	142	9.6
Virginia Beach, VA	262	393	425	8.2	438	42	3.1
Washington, DC	638	607	572	–5.7	551	27	–3.8
Wichita, KS	280	311	344	10.7	355	51	1.0
Winston–Salem, NC	132	168	186	10.6	194	109	4.3
Worcester, MA	162	170	173	1.8	176	126	1.9
Yonkers, NY	195	188	196	4.2	196	102	0.2

[1] The April 1, 2000, Population Estimates base reflects changes to the Census 2000 population from the Count Question Resolution program and geographic program revisions.   [2] The population shown is for the census designated place (CDP).   [3] Represents the portion of a consolidated city before consolidation of the city and county governments.   [4] Number is for the incorporated place of Augusta city before consolidation of the city and county governments.   [5] Data are for the incorporated place of Louisville city before consolidation of the city and county governments.   [6] Not incorporated.

Source: U.S. Census Bureau, 2000 Census of Population and Housing, *Population and Housing Unit Counts* PHC-3; and "Population Estimates for Places Over 100,000: 2000 to 2005"; published June 2006; <http://www.census.gov/popest/cities /SUB-EST2005.html>.

Population **35**

Table 32. Incorporated Places by Population Size: 1980 to 2005

[140.3 represents 140,300,000. See Appendix III]

Population size	Number of incorporated places				Population (mil.)				Percent of total			
	1980	1990	2000	2005	1980	1990	2000 [1]	2005	1980	1990	2000 [1]	2005
Total	19,097	19,262	19,471	19,471	140.3	152.9	176.1	183.8	100.0	100.0	100.0	100.0
1,000,000 or more. . . .	6	8	9	9	17.5	20.0	23.0	23.5	12.5	13.0	13.0	12.8
500,000 to 999,999 . . .	16	15	21	23	10.9	10.1	13.5	14.7	7.8	6.6	7.7	8.0
250,000 to 499,999 . . .	33	41	37	38	11.8	14.2	13.5	13.7	8.4	9.3	7.6	7.5
100,000 to 249,999 . . .	114	131	177	184	16.6	19.1	26.2	27.8	11.8	12.5	14.9	15.1
50,000 to 99,999.	250	309	370	411	17.6	21.2	25.4	28.5	12.3	13.9	14.4	15.5
25,000 to 49,999.	526	567	653	674	18.4	20.0	22.9	23.5	13.1	13.0	13.0	12.8
10,000 to 24,999.	1,260	1,290	1,447	1,488	19.8	20.3	22.8	23.4	14.1	13.3	13.0	12.8
Under 10,000	16,892	16,901	16,757	16,644	28.0	28.2	28.9	28.8	20.0	18.4	16.4	15.6

[1] The April 1, 2000, Population Estimates base reflects modifications to the Census 2000 population as documented in the Count Question Resolution program and geographic program revisions.

Source: U.S. Census Bureau, *Census of Population: 1980*, Vol. I; *1990 Census of Population and Housing, Population and Housing Unit Counts* (CPH-2-1); and "Population Estimates for All Places: 2000 to 2005"; published June 2006; <http://www.census.gov/popest/cities>.

Table 33. Urban and Rural Population by State: 1990 and 2000

[222,361 represents 222,361,000. As of April 1. Resident population. For urban definitions; see text, this section]

State	Urban population				Rural population, 2000 (1,000)	State	Urban population				Rural population, 2000 (1,000)
	1990 Former definition (percent)	1990 Current definition (percent)	2000, current definition Number (1,000)	2000, current definition Percent			1990 Former definition (percent)	1990 Current definition (percent)	2000, current definition Number (1,000)	2000, current definition Percent	
US, total . .	75.2	78.0	222,361	79.0	59,061	MS.	47.1	49.1	1,387	48.8	1,457
AL	60.4	56.8	2,466	55.4	1,981	MO	68.7	69.6	3,883	69.4	1,712
AK	67.5	61.0	411	65.6	216	MT.	52.5	56.4	488	54.1	414
AZ	87.5	86.5	4,524	88.2	607	NE	66.1	67.2	1,194	69.8	518
AR	53.5	52.0	1,404	52.5	1,269	NV	88.3	87.4	1,829	91.5	170
CA	92.6	93.7	31,990	94.4	1,882	NH	51.0	57.2	732	59.3	503
CO	82.4	83.8	3,633	84.5	668	NJ	89.4	93.5	7,939	94.4	475
CT	79.1	87.0	2,988	87.7	418	NM	73.0	75.0	1,364	75.0	456
DE	73.0	79.2	628	80.1	156	NY	84.3	87.4	16,603	87.5	2,374
DC	100.0	100.0	572	100.0	–	NC	50.4	57.8	4,849	60.2	3,200
FL	84.8	88.0	14,270	89.3	1,712	ND	53.3	53.4	359	55.9	283
GA	63.2	68.7	5,864	71.6	2,322	OH	74.1	77.5	8,782	77.4	2,571
HI	89.0	90.5	1,108	91.5	103	OK	67.7	65.2	2,255	65.3	1,196
ID	57.4	62.2	859	66.4	434	OR	70.5	74.9	2,694	78.7	727
IL	84.6	86.4	10,910	87.8	1,510	PA	68.9	76.8	9,464	77.1	2,817
IN	64.9	69.1	4,304	70.8	1,776	RI	86.0	89.9	953	90.9	95
IA	60.6	59.4	1,787	61.1	1,139	SC	54.6	61.5	2,427	60.5	1,585
KS	69.1	69.5	1,921	71.4	768	SD	50.0	50.3	391	51.9	363
KY	51.8	55.9	2,254	55.8	1,788	TN	60.9	62.7	3,620	63.6	2,069
LA	68.1	72.9	3,246	72.6	1,223	TX	80.3	81.2	17,204	82.5	3,648
ME	44.6	42.6	513	40.2	762	UT	87.0	86.8	1,970	88.2	263
MD	81.3	85.0	4,559	86.1	738	VT	32.2	40.2	232	38.2	376
MA	84.3	90.5	5,801	91.4	548	VA	69.4	71.5	5,170	73.0	1,909
MI	70.5	75.2	7,419	74.7	2,519	WA	76.4	79.9	4,831	82.0	1,063
MN	69.9	69.0	3,490	70.9	1,429	WV	36.1	46.9	833	46.1	976
						WI	65.7	67.3	3,664	68.3	1,700
						WY	65.0	67.1	321	65.1	172

– Represents zero.

Source: U.S. Census Bureau, 2000 Census of Population and Housing, *Population and Housing Unit Counts* PHC-3.

U.S. Census Bureau, Statistical Abstract of the United States: 2007

Table 34. **Mobility Status of the Population by Selected Characteristics: 1981 to 2005**

[As of March (221,641 represents 221,641,000). For persons 1 year old and over. Based on comparison of place of residence in immediate prior year and year shown. Excludes members of the Armed Forces except those living off post or with their families on post. Based on Current Population Survey, Annual Social and Economic Supplement; see text of this section and Appendix III. For composition of regions, see map, inside front cover]

Mobility period and characteristic	Total (1,000)	Non-movers	Movers (different house in United States)		Different county			Movers from abroad
			Total	Same county	Total	Same state	Different state	
1981.	221,641	83	17	10	6	3	3	1
1991.	244,884	83	16	10	6	3	3	1
2001.	275,611	86	14	8	6	3	3	1
2005, total	**287,136**	**86**	**13**	**8**	**5**	**3**	**3**	**1**
1 to 4 years old.	16,243	79	21	13	7	4	4	1
5 to 9 years old.	19,546	84	15	10	6	3	3	1
10 to 14 years old.	20,922	88	12	7	4	2	2	1
15 to 19 years old.	20,661	87	12	7	5	3	2	1
20 to 24 years old.	20,402	70	29	17	11	6	5	1
25 to 29 years old.	19,499	72	26	16	10	6	5	1
30 to 44 years old.	63,158	85	14	8	6	3	3	1
45 to 64 years old.	71,491	93	7	4	3	2	2	(Z)
65 to 74 years old.	18,388	95	5	2	2	1	1	(Z)
75 to 84 years old.	12,981	96	4	2	2	1	1	(Z)
85 years old and over	3,845	96	4	2	2	1	1	(Z)
Northeast.	53,388	90	9	5	4	2	2	1
Midwest.	63,983	88	12	7	5	2	2	(Z)
South.	103,556	85	14	8	6	3	3	1
West.	66,209	84	15	9	6	3	3	1
Persons 16 years and over	226,105	87	13	7	5	3	3	1
Civilian labor force.	147,451	85	14	8	6	3	3	1
Employed.	139,277	86	14	8	5	3	2	1
Unemployed.	8,174	77	21	13	9	4	5	1
Armed Forces.	869	71	24	9	16	6	10	5
Not in labor force	77,786	90	10	5	4	2	2	1
Employed civilians, 16 years and over	139,277	86	14	8	5	3	2	1
Management, business, and financial	19,878	89	11	7	4	2	2	(Z)
Professional.	28,464	87	12	7	6	3	3	(Z)
Service	22,609	83	16	10	6	3	3	1
Sales	16,138	85	15	9	6	3	3	(Z)
Office and administrative support	19,301	87	13	8	5	3	2	(Z)
Farming, fishing, and forestry	944	79	15	11	4	2	2	6
Construction and extraction.	8,634	80	18	11	7	4	3	2
Installation, maintenance, and repair.	5,149	87	13	7	5	3	2	(Z)
Production	9,598	86	13	8	5	3	2	1
Transportation and material moving	8,561	86	13	8	5	3	2	1
Tenure:								
Owner-occupied units	207,326	93	7	4	3	2	1	(Z)
Renter-occupied units	79,810	70	28	18	11	5	5	2

Z Less than 0.5 percent.

Source: U.S. Census Bureau, "Geographical Mobility: 2004 to 2005, Detailed Tables"; <http://www.census.gov/population/www/socdemo/migrate.html>.

Table 35. **Movers by Type of Move and Reason for Moving: 2005**

[As of March (39,421 represents 39,421,000). For persons 1 year old and over. Based on comparison of place of residence in 2004 and 2005. Excludes members of the Armed Forces except those living off post or with their families on post. Based on Current Population Survey, Annual Social and Economic Supplement; see text of this section and Appendix III]

Reason for move	All movers	Intra-county	Inter-county	From abroad	Reason for move	All movers	Intra-county	Inter-county	From abroad
Total (1,000)	**39,421**	**22,443**	**15,142**	**1,836**	Other job-related reason	1.4	0.4	2.0	7.8
					Housing-related reasons	47.1	61.8	29.8	10.1
PERCENT DISTRIBUTION					Wanted to own home/ not rent.	9.3	12.2	5.9	1.6
Total.	100.0	100.0	100.0	100.0	New/better house/ apartment	17.8	24.5	9.7	3.3
Family-related reasons	27.2	26.4	29.4	19.6	Better neighborhood/ less crime	4.0	4.8	3.3	0.4
Change in marital status	7.1	7.0	7.8	3.4	Cheaper housing	6.6	8.7	4.2	1.2
To establish own household.	7.8	9.5	5.7	3.5	Other housing	9.4	11.6	6.7	3.6
Other family reasons.	12.3	9.8	15.9	12.6	Other reasons.	8.0	5.2	11.3	15.3
Work-related reasons	17.6	6.6	29.5	55.0	Attend/leave college	3.2	1.8	4.9	6.5
New job/job transfer	10.4	2.3	20.1	30.6	Change of climate	0.6	0.2	1.3	0.1
To look for work/lost job.	1.9	0.5	2.4	14.9	Health reasons	1.6	1.4	2.0	1.0
Closer to work/ easier commute	3.4	3.2	3.9	1.3	Other reason.	2.6	1.9	3.1	7.7
Retired.	0.6	0.2	1.1	0.4					

Source: U.S. Census Bureau, "Geographic Mobility: 2004 to 2005, Detailed Tables"; <http://www.census.gov/population/www/socdemo/migrate.html>.

Table 36. **Mobility Status of Households by Household Income: 2005**

[As of March (113,155 represents 113,155,000). Covers householders 15 years old and over. Based on comparison of place of residence in 2004 and 2005. Excludes members of the Armed Forces except those living off post or with their families on post. Based on Current Population Survey, Annual Social and Economic Supplement; see text of this section and Appendix III]

Household income in 2004	Total (1,000)	Non-movers	Percent distribution					Movers from abroad
			Movers (different house in United States)					
			Total	Same county	Different county			
					Total	Same state	Different state	
Householders, 15 years and over...	113,155	87	13	8	5	3	2	(Z)
Less than $5,000	3,956	79	19	11	8	4	4	2
$5,000 to $9,999	5,850	84	15	10	5	2	3	1
$10,000 to $14,999	7,557	86	14	9	5	3	2	1
$15,000 to $24,999	14,634	85	15	9	6	3	3	1
$25,000 to $34,999	13,475	85	15	9	6	3	3	(Z)
$35,000 to $49,999	16,739	85	14	8	6	3	3	(Z)
$50,000 to $74,999	20,699	88	12	7	5	3	2	(Z)
$75,000 and over	30,245	91	9	5	4	2	2	(Z)

Z Less than 0.5 percent.

Source: U.S. Census Bureau, "Geographical Mobility: 2004 to 2005, Detailed Tables"; <http://www.census.gov/population/www/socdemo/migrate.html>.

Table 37. **Mobility Status of Resident Population by State: 2004**

[In percent, except as indicated (281,762 represents 281,762,000). Based on comparison of place of residence in 2003 and 2004. The American Community Survey universe is limited to the household population and excludes the population living in institutions, college dormitories, and other group quarters. Based on a sample and subject to sampling variability; see text, this section and Appendix III]

State	Population 1 year old and over [1] (1,000)	Same house in 2003	Different house in United States in 2003		State	Population 1 year old and over [1] (1,000)	Same house in 2003	Different house in United States in 2003	
			Same county	Different county				Same county	Different county
U.S...	281,762	84.3	9.7	5.4	MO	5,514	82.9	10.0	6.7
AL......	4,358	83.9	10.8	4.9	MT......	893	84.2	9.1	6.4
AK......	627	82.3	10.9	6.3	NE......	1,671	83.6	9.3	6.6
AZ......	5,543	78.8	14.1	6.1	NV......	2,267	77.9	14.2	7.1
AR......	2,642	80.9	12.2	6.5	NH......	1,248	86.1	8.3	5.4
CA......	34,534	84.2	10.6	4.4					
					NJ......	8,405	88.7	6.8	4.0
CO......	4,438	79.8	11.1	8.4	NM......	1,841	82.3	11.2	6.0
CT......	3,342	87.6	8.6	3.4	NY......	18,389	89.4	6.8	3.2
DE......	796	85.7	8.9	4.8	NC......	8,157	84.2	9.3	5.9
DC......	512	82.7	9.4	6.7	ND......	603	85.5	8.9	5.2
FL......	16,771	80.5	11.4	7.1					
					OH......	11,024	85.1	10.0	4.6
GA......	8,445	82.5	9.1	7.5	OK......	3,362	81.7	10.9	6.7
HI......	1,207	85.9	9.5	3.5	OR......	3,469	80.2	11.5	7.8
ID......	1,337	79.7	12.0	7.6	PA......	11,811	88.4	7.2	4.1
IL......	12,228	85.8	9.4	4.1	RI......	1,025	86.8	8.2	4.5
IN......	5,972	83.2	11.1	5.1					
					SC......	4,006	84.0	8.6	6.9
IA......	2,817	84.7	9.1	5.9	SD......	730	84.7	8.9	6.2
KS......	2,615	82.3	11.1	6.1	TN......	5,666	83.2	10.8	5.6
KY......	3,982	83.9	10.0	5.7	TX......	21,569	82.4	11.4	5.5
LA......	4,320	85.3	9.4	5.1	UT......	2,301	81.4	11.5	6.3
ME......	1,266	87.2	7.6	5.0					
					VT......	595	86.7	7.8	5.2
MD......	5,342	86.1	7.4	6.1	VA......	7,116	83.5	7.0	8.8
MA......	6,112	87.3	8.0	4.0	WA......	5,985	80.7	12.3	6.3
MI......	9,736	86.0	9.1	4.4	WV......	1,752	88.2	7.3	4.4
MN......	4,884	86.0	7.6	6.1	WI......	5,287	85.6	9.2	5.0
MS......	2,765	83.5	10.4	5.8	WY......	487	81.0	11.6	7.2

[1] Includes persons moving from abroad, not shown separately.

Source: U.S. Census Bureau, 2004 American Community Survey; B07003. Residence 1 Year Ago by Sex; using American FactFinder®; <http://factfinder.census.gov/>; (25 January 2006).

Table 38. Persons 65 Years Old and Over—Characteristics by Sex: 1990 to 2005

[As of March, except as noted (29.6 represents 29,600,000). Covers civilian noninstitutional population. Excludes members of Armed Forces except those living off post or with their families on post. Data for 1990 are based on 1980 census population controls; 1995 and 2000 data based on 1990 census population controls; 2004 and 2005 data based on 2000 census population controls and an expanded sample of households. Based on Current Population Survey; see text of this section and Appendix III]

Characteristic	Total				Male				Female			
	1990	1995	2000	2005	1990	1995	2000	2005	1990	1995	2000	2005
Total (million)	29.6	31.7	32.6	35.0	12.3	13.2	13.9	14.4	17.2	18.5	18.7	20.6
PERCENT DISTRIBUTION												
Marital status:												
Never married	4.6	4.2	3.9	4.1	4.2	4.2	4.2	4.4	4.9	4.2	3.6	3.9
Married	56.1	56.9	57.2	57.7	76.5	77.0	75.2	74.9	41.4	42.5	43.8	44.7
Spouse present	54.1	54.7	54.6	54.8	74.2	74.5	72.6	71.7	39.7	40.6	41.3	42.0
Spouse absent	2.0	2.2	2.6	2.9	2.3	2.5	2.6	3.2	1.7	1.9	2.5	2.7
Widowed	34.2	33.2	32.1	30.3	14.2	13.5	14.4	13.7	48.6	47.3	45.3	42.9
Divorced	5.0	5.7	6.7	7.9	5.0	5.2	6.1	7.0	5.1	6.0	7.2	8.5
Educational attainment:												
Less than ninth grade	28.5	21.0	16.7	[1]13.9	30.0	22.0	17.8	[1]13.8	27.5	20.3	15.9	[1]14.0
Completed 9th to 12th grade, but no high school diploma	[2]16.1	15.2	13.8	[1]13.0	[2]15.7	14.5	12.7	[1]12.1	[2]16.4	15.6	14.7	[1]13.7
High school graduate	[3]32.9	33.8	35.9	[1]36.0	[3]29.0	29.2	30.4	[1]30.9	[3]35.6	37.1	39.9	[1]39.8
Some college or associate's degree	[4]10.9	17.1	18.0	[1]18.4	[4]10.8	17.1	17.8	[1]17.8	[4]11.0	17.0	18.2	[1]18.8
Bachelor's or advanced degree	[5]11.6	13.0	15.6	[1]18.7	[5]14.5	17.2	21.4	[1]25.4	[5]9.5	9.9	11.4	[1]13.7
Labor force participation: [6]												
Employed	11.5	11.7	12.4	14.5	15.9	16.1	16.9	19.1	8.4	8.5	9.1	11.1
Unemployed	0.4	0.4	0.5	0.5	0.6	0.7	0.6	0.7	0.3	0.3	0.3	0.4
Not in labor force	88.1	87.9	87.2	84.9	83.6	83.2	82.5	80.2	91.3	91.2	90.6	88.5
Percent below poverty level [7]	11.4	11.7	9.7	9.8	7.8	7.2	6.9	7.0	13.9	14.9	11.8	12.0

[1] Data for 2004. [2] Represents those who completed 1 to 3 years of high school. [3] Represents those who completed 4 years of high school. [4] Represents those who completed 1 to 3 years of college. [5] Represents those who completed 4 years of college or more. [6] Annual averages of monthly figures. Source: U.S. Bureau of Labor Statistics, *Employment and Earnings*, January issues. See footnote 2, Table 573. [7] Poverty status based on income in preceding year.

Source: Except as noted, U.S. Census Bureau, *Current Population Reports*, P20-546, and earlier reports; P60-226; "Educational Attainment in the United States: 2004, Detailed Tables"; published March 2005; <http://www.census.gov/population/www/socdemo/education/cps2004.html>; "America's Families and Living Arrangements: 2005, Table A1. Marital Status of People 15 Years and Over, by Age, Sex, Personal Earnings, Race, and Hispanic Origin, 2005"; published 25 May 2006; <http://www.census.gov/population/www/socdemo/hh-fam/cps2005.html>; and "POV01. Age and Sex of All People, Family Members and Unrelated Individuals Iterated by Income-to-Poverty Ratio and Race"; published 19 May 2005; <http://pubdb3.census.gov/macro/032005/pov/new01000.htm>.

Table 39. Persons 65 Years Old and Over—Living Arrangements and Disability Status: 2005

[In thousands (34,761 represents 34,761,000), except as indicated. The American Community Survey universe is limited to the household population and excludes the population living in institutions, college dormitories, and other group quarters. Based on a sample and subject to sampling variability; see text of this section and Appendix III]

Relationship by household type	Number	Percent distri- bution	Type of disability	Total	65 to 74 years old	75 years old and over
Total	**34,761**	**100.0**	**People 65 years and over with a disability**	**14,064**	**5,556**	**8,508**
In family households	23,553	67.8				
Householder	12,205	35.1				
Spouse	8,620	24.8	With a sensory disability	5,707	1,871	3,836
Parent	1,571	4.5	With a physical disability	10,712	4,286	6,426
Other relatives	1,026	3.0	With a mental disability	3,988	1,329	2,659
Nonrelatives	130	0.4	With a self-care disability	3,358	1,061	2,297
In nonfamily households	11,208	32.2	With a go-outside-home disability	5,778	1,636	4,142
Householder	10,799	31.1				
Living alone	10,299	29.6				
Not living alone	500	1.4				
Nonrelatives	409	1.2				

Source: U.S. Census Bureau, 2005 American Community Survey; B09017. Relationship by Household Type (Including Living Alone) for the Population 65 Years and Over; B18002. Sex by Age by Disability Status for the Civilian Noninstitutionalized Population 5 Years and Over; B18003. Sex by Age by Sensory Disability for the Civilian Noninstitutionalized Population 5 Years and Over; B18004. Sex by Age by Physical Disability for the Civilian Noninstitutionalized Population 5 Years and Over; B18005. Sex by Age by Mental Disability for the Civilian Noninstitutionalized Population 5 Years and Over; B18006. Sex by Age by Self-Care Disability for the Civilian Noninstitutionalized Population 5 Years and Over; B18007. Sex by Age by Go-Outside-Home Disability for the Civilian Noninstitutionalized Population 16 Years and Over; using American FactFinder®; <http://factfinder.census.gov/>; (23 August 2006).

Table 40. Selected Characteristics of Racial Groups and Hispanic/Latino Population: 2004

[In thousands (186,534 represents 186,534,000), except as indicated. The American Community Survey universe is limited to the household population and excludes the population living in institutions, college dormitories, and other group quarters. Based on a sample and subject to sampling variability; see text of this section and Appendix III]

Characteristic	Total population	White alone	Black or African American alone	American Indian and Alaska Native alone	Asian alone
EDUCATIONAL ATTAINMENT					
Persons 25 years old and over, total	**186,534**	**146,327**	**20,271**	**1,277**	**8,242**
Less than 9th grade	11,699	7,481	1,197	97	691
9th to 12th grade, no diploma	18,277	12,847	3,003	201	559
High school graduate (includes equivalency)	55,055	43,812	6,685	400	1,425
Some college, no degree	37,875	30,198	4,523	296	1,044
Associate's degree	13,217	10,594	1,362	101	549
Bachelor's degree	32,030	26,279	2,324	118	2,377
Graduate degree	18,381	15,116	1,177	63	1,597
Percent high school graduate or higher.	83.9	86.1	79.3	76.6	84.8
Percent bachelor's degree or higher.	27.0	28.3	17.3	14.2	48.2
OCCUPATION					
Employed civilian population, 16 years old and over, total	**134,259**	**105,048**	**14,127**	**855**	**5,812**
Management, professional, and related occupations	45,845	37,581	3,769	217	2,661
Management, business and financial operations occupations	18,529	15,609	1,354	77	847
Professional and related occupations	27,316	21,972	2,415	140	1,815
Service occupations	21,750	15,381	3,325	184	901
Sales and office occupations.	35,117	27,774	3,790	199	1,391
Farming, fishing, and forestry occupations.	902	676	44	6	16
Construction, extraction, and maintenance occupations	13,109	10,758	866	125	215
Construction and extraction occupations	8,279	6,773	496	86	96
Installation, maintenance, and repair occupations	4,830	3,985	370	38	119
Production, transportation, and material moving occupations	17,536	12,878	2,333	124	627
Production occupations	9,360	6,920	1,072	62	440
Transportation and material moving occupations	8,176	5,958	1,261	63	186
FAMILY INCOME IN THE PAST 12 MONTHS					
Total families.	**73,886**	**57,841**	**8,411**	**526**	**2,915**
Less than $10,000	4,054	2,294	1,187	54	145
$10,000 to $19,999	6,473	4,311	1,272	88	213
$20,000 to $29,999	7,944	5,741	1,220	83	245
$30,000 to $39,999	8,046	6,173	1,005	56	244
$40,000 to $49,999	7,580	6,001	814	54	253
$50,000 to $59,999	6,955	5,624	687	51	230
$60,000 to $74,999	8,772	7,223	745	47	337
$75,000 to $99,999	9,967	8,349	744	43	438
$100,000 to $124,999	5,794	4,909	369	24	305
$125,000 to $149,999	3,035	2,589	180	8	175
$150,000 to $199,999	2,709	2,341	119	10	178
$200,000 or more	2,557	2,285	70	7	152
Median family income in the past 12 months (dol.).	53,692	57,427	34,851	35,981	65,132
POVERTY STATUS IN THE PAST 12 MONTHS [2]					
Persons below poverty level	37,162	22,125	8,865	526	1,420
Percent below poverty level.	13.1	10.3	25.6	24.6	11.8
Families below poverty level	7,444	4,323	1,937	108	273
Percent below poverty level.	10.1	7.5	23.0	20.5	9.4
HOUSING TENURE					
Total householders	109,902	86,665	12,964	771	3,967
Owner-occupied	73,754	62,442	5,978	428	2,286
Renter-occupied	36,148	24,223	6,986	343	1,681

See footnotes at end of table.

U.S. Census Bureau, Statistical Abstract of the United States: 2007

Table 40. **Selected Characteristics of Racial Groups and Hispanic/Latino Population: 2004**—Con.

[See headnote, page 40]

Characteristic	Native Hawaiian and Other Pacific Islander alone	Some other race alone	Two or more races	Hispanic/ Latino [1]	White alone, not Hispanic or Latino
EDUCATIONAL ATTAINMENT					
Persons 25 years old and over, total	236	8,021	2,161	21,683	133,459
Less than 9th grade	13	2,086	133	5,157	4,505
9th to 12th grade, no diploma	25	1,410	232	3,612	10,768
High school graduate (includes equivalency)	83	2,103	547	5,676	40,451
Some college, no degree	58	1,195	561	3,342	28,249
Associate's degree	20	409	181	1,150	9,909
Bachelor's degree	28	579	326	1,869	25,057
Graduate degree	8	240	181	877	14,520
Percent high school graduate or higher	83.9	56.4	83.1	59.6	88.6
Percent bachelor's degree or higher	15.4	10.2	23.5	12.7	29.7
OCCUPATION					
Employed civilian population, 16 years old and over, total	181	6,503	1,735	17,242	94,925
Management, professional, and related occupations	41	1,045	531	3,103	35,660
Management, business and financial operations occupations	19	421	202	1,262	14,817
Professional and related occupations	21	624	329	1,840	20,843
Service occupations	37	1,582	339	4,083	13,020
Sales and office occupations	59	1,423	482	3,822	25,546
Farming, fishing, and forestry occupations	1	151	8	365	469
Construction, extraction, and maintenance occupations	18	969	159	2,672	9,123
Construction and extraction occupations	9	713	105	2,042	5,496
Installation, maintenance, and repair occupations	9	256	53	630	3,626
Production, transportation, and material moving occupations	25	1,333	216	3,198	11,107
Production occupations	11	738	116	1,770	5,936
Transportation and material moving occupations	14	594	100	1,428	5,171
FAMILY INCOME IN THE PAST 12 MONTHS					
Total families	91	3,217	887	8,689	52,705
Less than $10,000	6	290	77	771	1,854
$10,000 to $19,999	9	476	104	1,299	3,540
$20,000 to $29,999	9	535	111	1,414	4,903
$30,000 to $39,999	10	455	103	1,209	5,469
$40,000 to $49,999	7	362	89	960	5,433
$50,000 to $59,999	12	267	84	730	5,194
$60,000 to $74,999	11	310	100	798	6,764
$75,000 to $99,999	10	277	105	757	7,901
$100,000 to $124,999	7	132	47	360	4,694
$125,000 to $149,999	5	53	25	182	2,468
$150,000 to $199,999	3	36	23	123	2,258
$200,000 or more	1	23	19	86	2,226
Median family income in the past 12 months (dol.)	53,806	36,488	45,412	36,820	59,907
POVERTY STATUS IN THE PAST 12 MONTHS [2]					
Persons below poverty level	73	3,234	919	8,847	16,949
Percent below poverty level	18.1	22.0	17.2	22.0	8.8
Families below poverty level	14	651	138	1,738	3,309
Percent below poverty level	15.1	20.2	15.6	20.0	6.3
HOUSING TENURE					
Total householders	116	4,054	1,365	11,256	79,949
Owner-occupied	54	1,842	725	5,375	59,110
Renter-occupied	62	2,212	641	5,881	20,839

[1] Persons of Hispanic/Latino origin may be of any race.   [2] For explanation of poverty level, see text, Section 13.

Source: U.S. Census Bureau, 2004 American Community Survey; B15002. Sex by Educational Attainment for the Population 25 Years and Over, B24010. Sex by Occupation for the Employed Civilian Population 16 Years and Over, B19101. Family Income in the Past 12 Months (In 2004 Inflation-Adjusted Dollars), B19113. Median Family Income in the Past 12 Months (In 2004 Inflation-Adjusted Dollars), B17001. Poverty Status in the Past 12 Months by Sex by Age, B17010. Poverty Status in the Past 12 Months of Families by Family Type by Presence of Related Children Under 18 Years by Age of Related Children, B25003. Tenure; using American FactFinder®; <http://factfinder.census.gov/>; (8 May 2006).

Table 41. Social and Economic Characteristics of the White and Black Populations: 1990 to 2004

[As of March, except labor force status, annual average (134,687 represents 134,687,000). Excludes members of Armed Forces except those living off post or with their families on post. Data for 1990 are based on 1980 census population controls; 2000 data (except for income and poverty) based on 1990 census population controls; 2004 data and 2000 data for income and poverty based on 2000 census population controls and an expanded sample of households. Based on Current Population Survey; see text of this section and Appendix III]

Characteristic	Number (1,000)						Percent distribution			
	White		White alone[1]	Black		Black alone[1]	White,	White alone[1]	Black,	Black alone[1]
	1990	2000	2004	1990	2000	2004	2000	2004	2000	2004
EDUCATIONAL ATTAINMENT										
Persons 25 years old and over	134,687	147,067	154,150	16,751	20,036	20,812	100.0	100.0	100.0	100.0
Less than ninth grade	14,131	10,035	9,566	2,701	1,417	1,197	6.8	6.2	7.1	5.8
Completed 9th to 12th grade, but no high school diploma	[2]14,080	12,153	12,292	[2]2,969	2,899	2,833	8.3	8.0	14.5	13.6
High school graduate	[3]52,449	49,105	49,579	[3]6,239	7,050	7,493	33.4	32.2	35.2	36.0
Some college or associate's degree	[4]24,350	37,353	39,311	[4]2,952	5,366	5,623	25.4	25.5	26.8	27.0
Bachelor's or advanced degree	[5]29,677	38,421	43,402	[5]1,890	3,303	3,667	26.1	28.2	16.5	17.6
LABOR FORCE STATUS [6]										
Civilians 16 years old and over	160,625	176,220	182,643	21,477	24,902	26,065	100.0	100.0	100.0	100.0
Civilian labor force	107,447	118,545	121,086	13,740	16,397	16,638	67.3	66.3	65.8	63.8
Employed	102,261	114,424	115,239	12,175	15,156	14,909	64.9	63.1	60.9	57.2
Unemployed	5,186	4,121	5,847	1,565	1,241	1,729	2.3	3.2	5.0	6.6
Unemployment rate [7]	4.8	3.5	4.8	11.4	7.6	10.4	(X)	(X)	(X)	(X)
Not in labor force	53,178	57,675	61,558	7,737	8,505	9,428	32.7	33.7	34.2	36.2
FAMILY TYPE										
Total families	56,590	60,251	62,609	7,470	8,664	8,912	100.0	100.0	100.0	100.0
With own children [8]	26,718	28,107	28,410	4,378	4,782	4,973	46.6	45.4	55.2	55.8
Married couple	46,981	48,790	50,021	3,750	4,144	4,146	81.0	79.9	47.1	46.5
With own children [8]	21,579	21,809	21,769	1,972	2,093	2,035	36.2	34.8	24.2	22.8
Female householder, no spouse present	7,306	8,380	9,050	3,275	3,814	3,984	13.9	14.5	45.1	44.7
With own children [8]	4,199	4,869	5,203	2,232	2,409	2,582	8.1	8.3	27.8	29.0
Male householder, no spouse present	2,303	3,081	3,537	446	706	782	5.1	5.6	7.8	8.8
With own children [8]	939	1,429	1,438	173	280	356	2.4	2.3	3.2	4.0
FAMILY INCOME IN PREVIOUS YEAR IN CONSTANT (2003) DOLLARS										
Total families [9]	56,590	61,074	62,620	7,470	8,653	8,914	100.0	100.0	100.0	100.0
Less than $5,000	(NA)	(NA)	1,382	(NA)	(NA)	593	(NA)	2.2	(NA)	6.7
$5,000 to $9,999	(NA)	(NA)	1,302	(NA)	(NA)	627	(NA)	2.1	(NA)	7.0
$10,000 to $14,999	(NA)	(NA)	2,235	(NA)	(NA)	692	(NA)	3.6	(NA)	7.8
$15,000 to $24,999	(NA)	(NA)	6,610	(NA)	(NA)	1,407	(NA)	10.6	(NA)	15.8
$25,000 to $34,999	(NA)	(NA)	7,049	(NA)	(NA)	1,187	(NA)	11.3	(NA)	13.3
$35,000 to $49,999	(NA)	(NA)	9,367	(NA)	(NA)	1,402	(NA)	15.0	(NA)	15.7
$50,000 or more	(NA)	(NA)	34,675	(NA)	(NA)	3,005	(NA)	55.4	(NA)	33.7
Median income (dol.) [10]	51,539	56,383	55,768	28,952	35,157	34,369	(X)	(X)	(X)	(X)
POVERTY STATUS IN PREVIOUS YEAR [11]										
Families below poverty level	4,409	4,377	5,058	2,077	1,898	1,985	7.3	8.1	21.9	22.3
Persons below poverty level	20,785	21,922	24,280	9,302	8,360	8,801	9.8	10.5	23.6	24.5
HOUSING TENURE										
Total occupied units	80,163	87,671	91,962	10,486	12,849	13,629	100.0	100.0	100.0	100.0
Owner-occupied	54,094	62,077	66,681	4,445	6,055	6,749	70.8	72.5	47.1	49.5
Renter-occupied	24,685	24,253	24,045	5,862	6,563	6,687	27.7	26.1	51.1	49.1
No cash rent	1,384	1,340	1,234	178	231	193	1.5	1.3	1.8	1.4

NA Not available.   X Not applicable.   [1] Beginning 2003, the Current Population Survey asked respondents to choose one or more races. Refers to people who reported specified race and did not report any other race category.   [2] Represents those who completed 1 to 3 years of high school.   [3] Represents those who completed 4 years of high school.   [4] Represents those who completed 1 to 3 years of college.   [5] Represents those who completed 4 years of college or more.   [6] Source: U.S. Bureau of Labor Statistics, *Employment and Earnings*, January issues. See footnote 2, Table 573.   [7] Total unemployment as percent of civilian labor force.   [8] Children under 18 years old.   [9] Includes families in group quarters.   [10] For definition of median, see Guide to Tabular Presentation.   [11] For explanation of poverty level, see text, Section 13.

Source: Except as noted, U.S. Census Bureau, Current Population Reports, P60-226 and earlier reports; "Educational Attainment"; <http://www.census.gov/population/www/socdemo/educ-attn.html>; "Families and Living Arrangements"; <http://www.census.gov/population/www/socdemo/hh-fam.html>; "Table F-5. Race and Hispanic Origin of Householder— Families by Median and Mean Income: 1947 to 2003"; published 13 May 2005; <http://www.census.gov/hhes/www/income/histinc/f05.html>; "Table FINC-01. Selected Characteristics of Families, by Total Money Income in 2003"; published 26 August 2004; <http://pubdb3.census.gov/macro/032004/faminc/new01000.htm>; "Table 4. Poverty Status Status of Families, by Type of Family, Presence of Related Children, Race, and Hispanic Origin: 1959 to 2003"; published 26 August 2004; <http://www.census.gov/hhes/www/poverty/histpov/hstpov4.html>; and unpublished data.

Table 42. American Indian and Alaska Native Population by Tribe: 2000

[**As of April.** This table shows data for American Indian and Alaska Native tribes alone or in combination of tribes or races. Respondents who identified themselves as American Indian or Alaska Native were asked to report their enrolled or principal tribe. Therefore, data shown here reflect the written tribal entries reported on the questionnaire. Some of the entries (for example, Iroquois, Sioux, Colorado River, and Flathead) represent nations or reservations. The information on tribe is based on self-identification and includes federally- or state-recognized tribes, as well as bands and clans]

American Indian and Alaska Native tribe	Number	American Indian and Alaska Native tribe	Number
Total persons [1]	**4,119,301**	Osage.	15,897
Apache	96,833	Ottawa	10,677
Blackfeet	85,750	Paiute	13,532
Cherokee.	729,533	Pima.	11,493
Cheyenne	18,204	Potawatomi	25,595
Chickasaw	38,351	Pueblo	74,085
Chippewa	149,669	Puget Sound Salish.	14,631
Choctaw	158,774	Seminole	27,431
Colville	9,393	Shoshone	12,026
Comanche	19,376	Sioux	153,360
Cree	7,734	Tohono O'odham.	20,087
Creek	71,310	United Houma Nation.	8,713
Crow.	13,394	Ute	10,385
Delaware	16,341	Yakama	10,851
Iroquois	80,822	Yaqui	22,412
Kiowa	12,242	Yuman	8,976
Latin American Indian	180,940	Alaskan Athabascan	18,838
Lumbee.	57,868	Aleut.	10,548
Menominee	9,840	Eskimo	54,761
Navajo	298,197	Tlingit-Haida.	22,365

[1] Includes other tribes not shown separately.

Source: U.S. Census Bureau, *The American Indian and Alaska Native Population: 2000*, Census 2000 Brief (C2KBR/01-15), February 2002.

Table 43. Population Living on Selected Reservations and Trust Lands: 2000

[**As of April**. OTSA = Oklahoma Tribal Statistical Area; SDAISA = State Designated American Indian Statistical Area; ANRC = Alaska Native Regional Corporation]

Reservation, Trust Land, or Other Area	Total population	American Indian and Alaska Native population alone	American Indian and Alaska Native population alone or in combination with one or more races
Navajo Nation Reservation and Off-Reservation Trust Land, AZ—NM—UT.	180,462	173,987	175,228
Cherokee OTSA, OK	462,327	76,041	104,482
Creek OTSA, OK	704,565	51,296	77,253
Lumbee SDAISA, NC	474,100	58,238	62,327
Choctaw OTSA, OK	224,472	29,521	39,984
Cook Inlet ANRC, AK	364,205	24,923	35,972
Chickasaw OTSA, OK	277,416	22,946	32,372
Calista ANRC, AK.	23,032	19,617	20,353
United Houma Nation SDAISA, LA	839,880	11,019	15,305
Sealaska ANRC, AK	71,507	11,320	15,059
Pine Ridge Reservation and Off-Reservation Trust Land, SD—NE . . .	15,521	14,304	14,484
Doyon ANRC, AK.	97,190	11,182	14,128
Kiowa-Comanche-Apache-Fort Sill Apache OTSA, OK	193,260	9,675	13,045
Fort Apache Reservation, AZ	12,429	11,702	11,854
Citizen Potawatomi Nation-Absentee Shawnee OTSA, OK.	106,624	6,733	10,617
Gila River Reservation, AZ.	11,257	10,353	10,578
Cheyenne-Arapaho OTSA, OK	157,869	7,402	10,310
Tohono O'odham Reservation and Off-Reservation Trust Land, AZ . . .	10,787	9,718	9,794
Osage Reservation, OK.	44,437	6,410	9,209
Rosebud Reservation and Off-Reservation Trust Land, SD	10,469	9,040	9,165
San Carlos Reservation, AZ.	9,385	8,921	9,065
Blackfeet Reservation and Off-Reservation Trust Land, MT	10,100	8,507	8,684
Yakama Reservation and Off-Reservation Trust Land, WA.	31,799	7,411	8,193
Turtle Mountain Reservation and Off-Reservation Trust Land, MT—ND—SD	8,331	8,009	8,043
Flathead Reservation, MT	26,172	6,999	7,883
Zuni Reservation and Off-Reservation Trust Land, NM—AZ	7,758	7,426	7,466
Bering Straits ANRC, AK	9,196	6,915	7,274
Sac and Fox OTSA, OK	55,690	5,334	7,232
Eastern Cherokee Reservation, NC.	8,092	6,665	6,898
Wind River Reservation and Off-Reservation Trust Land, WY.	23,250	6,544	6,864
Hopi Reservation and Off-Reservation Trust Land, AZ.	6,946	6,573	6,633
Fort Peck Reservation and Off-Reservation Trust Land, MT	10,321	6,391	6,577
Cheyenne River Reservation and Off-Reservation Trust Land, SD. . . .	8,470	6,249	6,346
NANA ANRC, AK	7,208	5,944	6,181
Standing Rock Reservation, SD—ND.	8,250	5,964	6,054
Bristol Bay ANRC, AK.	7,892	5,336	5,749
Arctic Slope ANRC, AK.	7,385	5,050	5,453
Crow Reservation and Off-Reservation Trust Land, MT	6,894	5,165	5,275
Red Lake Reservation, MN	5,162	5,071	5,087

Source: U.S. Census Bureau, 2000 Census of Population and Housing, *Profiles of General Demographic Characteristics.* See also <http://factfinder.census.gov/home/aian/index.html>.

Population 43

Table 44. **Social and Economic Characteristics of the Hispanic Population: 2005**

[As of March, except labor force status, annual average (41,839 represents 41,839,000). Excludes members of the Armed Forces except those living off post or with their families on post. Based on Current Population Survey; see text of this section and Appendix III]

Characteristic	Number (1,000)					Percent distribution				
	His-panic, total [1]	Mexi-can	Puerto Rican	Cuban	Cen-tral, South Ameri-can	His-panic, total [1]	Mexi-can	Puerto Rican	Cuban	Central South Ameri-can
Total persons	**41,839**	**27,617**	**3,607**	**1,540**	**6,909**	**100.0**	**100.0**	**100.0**	**100.0**	**100.0**
Under 5 years	4,464	3,262	267	120	602	10.7	11.8	7.4	7.8	8.7
5 to 14 years old............	7,771	5,464	719	187	1,004	18.6	19.8	20.0	12.1	14.5
15 to 44 years old............	20,933	13,881	1,712	625	3,773	50.0	50.3	47.5	40.7	54.6
45 to 64 years old............	6,478	3,848	680	308	1,207	15.4	13.9	18.9	20.1	17.5
65 years old and over	2,194	1,161	230	298	322	5.2	4.2	6.4	19.4	4.7
EDUCATIONAL ATTAINMENT										
Persons 25 years old and over...............	**22,551**	**14,136**	**1,998**	**1,084**	**4,118**	**100.0**	**100.0**	**100.0**	**100.0**	**100.0**
High school graduate or more	13,183	7,383	1,444	797	2,571	58.9	52.2	72.3	73.5	62.4
Bachelor's degree or more	2,696	1,167	276	268	762	12.1	8.3	13.8	24.7	18.5
LABOR FORCE STATUS [2]										
Civilians 16 years old and over...............	**28,109**	**17,900**	**2,547**	**1,264**	**6,207**	**100.0**	**100.0**	**100.0**	**100.0**	**100.0**
Civilian labor force............	19,272	12,340	1,610	769	4,422	68.6	68.9	63.2	60.8	71.2
Employed.................	17,930	11,449	1,481	735	4,146	63.8	64.0	58.1	58.1	66.8
Unemployed .... [3]	1,342	892	130	34	277	4.8	5.0	5.1	2.7	4.5
Unemployment rate [3]	7.0	7.2	8.1	4.5	6.3	(X)	(X)	(X)	(X)	(X)
Male.................	6.5	6.5	8.2	4.9	6.2	(X)	(X)	(X)	(X)	(X)
Female...............	7.6	8.5	7.9	3.8	6.3	(X)	(X)	(X)	(X)	(X)
Not in labor force	8,837	5,559	936	495	1,785	31.4	31.1	36.7	39.2	28.8
HOUSEHOLDS										
Total	**12,181**	**7,586**	**1,214**	**579**	**2,119**	**100.0**	**100.0**	**100.0**	**100.0**	**100.0**
Family households	9,537	6,146	852	397	1,639	78.3	81.0	70.2	68.6	77.3
Married-couple families [4]......	6,367	4,228	470	300	1,051	52.3	55.7	38.7	51.8	49.6
Male householder, no spouse present	930	603	76	29	161	7.6	7.9	6.3	5.0	7.6
Female householder, no spouse present	2,240	1,315	306	68	427	18.4	17.3	25.2	11.7	20.2
Nonfamily households	2,644	1,440	362	182	479	21.7	19.0	29.8	31.4	22.6
Male householder	1,467	856	193	85	248	12.0	11.3	15.9	14.7	11.7
Female householder.........	1,177	584	169	97	232	9.7	7.7	13.9	16.8	10.9
Size:										
One person	1,921	1,016	280	157	321	15.8	13.4	23.1	27.1	15.1
Two people..............	2,651	1,524	312	155	448	21.8	20.1	25.7	26.8	21.1
Three people	2,365	1,397	246	115	464	19.4	18.4	20.2	19.9	21.9
Four people	2,527	1,652	219	97	465	20.7	21.8	18.0	16.7	22.0
Five people	1,558	1,119	91	38	259	12.8	14.8	7.5	6.6	12.2
Six people	712	527	47	11	107	5.8	6.9	3.9	2.0	5.0
Seven people or more	447	352	20	5	55	3.7	4.6	1.7	0.9	2.6
FAMILY INCOME IN 2004										
Total families [5]............	**9,537**	**6,146**	**852**	**396**	**1,606**	**100.0**	**100.0**	**100.0**	**100.0**	**100.0**
Less than $5,000	398	253	48	12	64	4.1	4.2	5.8	2.9	3.9
$5,000 to $14,999...........	1,111	753	117	37	149	11.7	12.2	13.7	9.3	9.3
$15,000 to $24,999..........	1,714	1,193	137	66	250	18.0	19.4	16.1	16.5	15.6
$25,000 to $34,999..........	1,492	990	120	58	264	15.6	16.1	14.1	14.6	16.4
$35,000 to $49,999..........	1,579	1,015	126	54	310	16.6	16.5	14.8	13.7	19.3
$50,000 to $74,999..........	1,660	1,072	137	52	270	17.4	17.4	16.0	13.0	16.8
$75,000 and over	1,583	870	167	119	298	16.6	14.2	19.6	29.9	18.5
POVERTY STATUS IN 2004										
Families below poverty level [6]....	1,958	1,389	182	49	263	20.5	22.6	21.4	12.3	16.
Persons below poverty level [6]....	9,132	6,543	823	224	1,225	21.9	23.8	22.9	14.5	17.8
HOUSEHOLD TENURE										
Total occupied units	**12,181**	**7,586**	**1,214**	**579**	**2,077**	**100.0**	**100.0**	**100.0**	**100.0**	**100.0**
Owner-occupied [7]...........	6,022	3,900	481	355	814	49.4	51.4	39.7	61.3	39.2
Renter-occupied [7]...........	6,159	3,686	732	224	1,264	50.6	48.6	60.3	38.7	60.8

X Not applicable.   [1] Includes other Hispanic groups not shown separately.   [2] Source: U.S. Bureau of Labor Statistics Employment and Earnings, January 2006.   [3] Total unemployment as percent of civilian labor force.   [4] In married-couple families, Hispanic origin refers to the householder.   [5] Includes families in group quarters.   [6] For explanation of poverty level, see text, Section 13.   [7] Includes no cash rent.

Source: Except as noted, U.S. Census Bureau, "America's Families and Living Arrangements: 2005"; published 25 May 2006 <http://www.census.gov/population/www/socdemo/hh-fam/cps2005.html>; "Table FINC-01. Selected Characteristics of Families by Total Money Income in 2004"; published 5 May 2005; <http://pubdb3.census.gov/macro/032005/faminc/new01000.htm> "POV01. Age and Sex of All People, Family Members and Unrelated Individuals Iterated by Income-to-Poverty Ratio and Race" and "POV04. Families by Age of Householder, Number of Children, and Family Structure"; published 10 June 2005 <http://pubdb3.census.gov/macro/032005/pov/toc.htm>; and unpublished data.

Table 45. Native and Foreign-Born Population by State: 2004

[In thousands, except percent (251,412 represents 251,412,000). The American Community Survey universe is limited to the household population and excludes the population living in institutions, college dormitories, and other group quarters. Based on a sample and subject to sampling variability; see text of this section and Appendix III]

State	Native population	Foreign-born population			State	Native population	Foreign-born population		
		Number	Percent of total population	Percent entered 2000 or later			Number	Percent of total population	Percent entered 2000 or later
U.S., total . . .	251,412	34,280	12.0	18.3	MO	5,409	177	3.2	29.8
AL	4,305	110	2.5	39.0	MT	887	15	1.6	18.9
AK	597	39	6.1	24.6	NE	1,613	83	4.9	30.7
AZ	4,824	810	14.4	24.9	NV	1,887	414	18.0	16.6
AR	2,578	98	3.6	35.1	NH	1,200	62	4.9	17.8
CA	25,669	9,386	26.8	13.9					
CO	4,064	435	9.7	27.9	NJ	6,903	1,601	18.8	17.3
CT	2,995	395	11.6	18.3	NM	1,692	171	9.2	16.0
DE	744	61	7.6	23.0	NY	14,723	3,912	21.0	13.9
DC	450	68	13.1	22.8	NC	7,733	537	6.5	28.7
FL	13,945	3,045	17.9	19.6	ND	594	15	2.5	23.0
GA	7,857	725	8.4	30.8	OH	10,767	387	3.5	23.1
HI	1,000	227	18.5	14.5	OK	3,261	151	4.4	23.8
ID	1,280	80	5.9	30.8	OR	3,189	325	9.2	20.5
IL	10,738	1,653	13.3	17.7	PA	11,393	565	4.7	18.9
IN	5,821	237	3.9	33.6	RI	909	128	12.3	17.3
IA	2,762	89	3.1	20.6	SC	3,901	159	3.9	34.4
KS	2,527	127	4.8	27.3	SD	729	13	1.7	18.4
KY	3,934	97	2.4	32.9	TN	5,531	217	3.8	26.6
LA	4,255	126	2.9	19.1	TX	18,603	3,309	15.1	19.1
ME	1,240	39	3.0	12.2	UT	2,186	164	7.0	21.1
MD	4,827	595	11.0	19.9	VT	577	24	3.9	21.7
MA	5,353	848	13.7	18.5	VA	6,535	689	9.5	22.5
MI	9,260	598	6.1	23.3	WA	5,378	685	11.3	19.1
MN	4,655	304	6.1	20.1	WV	1,756	15	0.8	19.7
MS	2,769	36	1.3	27.5	WI	5,130	221	4.1	23.7
					WY	478	15	3.0	23.2

Source: U.S. Census Bureau, 2004 American Community Survey; B05002. Place of Birth by Citizenship Status; B05005. Year of Entry by Citizenship Status; using American FactFinder; <http://factfinder.census.gov/>; (accessed: 25 January 2006).

Table 46. Nativity and Place of Birth of Resident Population—25 Largest Cities: 2004

[In thousands except percent (653 represents 653,000). The American Community Survey universe is limited to the household population and excludes the population living in institutions, college dormitories, and other group quarters. Based on a sample and subject to sampling variability; see text of this section and Appendix III]

City	Native population			Foreign-born population		Entered 2000 or later	
	Total population	Total	Born in United States	Born outside United States	Total Number	Percent of total population	Number	Percent of foreign-born population
Austin, TX	653	538	529	9	115	17.5	37	32.2
Baltimore, MD	610	581	576	5	29	4.7	11	38.5
Charlotte, NC	583	518	512	6	65	11.1	24	36.4
Chicago, IL	2,719	2,139	2,100	39	580	21.3	104	17.9
Columbus, OH	701	637	630	7	64	9.1	20	31.3
Dallas, TX	1,193	876	863	13	318	26.6	91	28.6
Denver, CO	544	444	439	5	100	18.4	27	27.1
Detroit, MI	840	798	792	6	42	5.0	16	36.8
El Paso, TX	579	424	412	11	155	26.7	25	16.4
Fort Worth, TX	625	520	514	6	105	16.7	19	18.4
Houston, TX	1,946	1,421	1,407	14	526	27.0	107	20.4
Indianapolis, IN [1]	766	718	712	6	48	6.2	18	38.2
Jacksonville, FL	766	714	697	17	52	6.7	11	22.0
Los Angeles, CA	3,746	2,231	2,203	28	1,514	40.4	215	14.2
Louisville-Jefferson County, KY	539	519	518	1	20	3.8	6	31.6
Memphis, TN	628	601	598	3	26	4.2	8	29.4
Milwaukee, WI	555	501	485	15	54	9.8	16	30.1
New York, NY	7,919	5,079	4,749	330	2,840	35.9	378	13.3
Philadelphia, PA	1,414	1,253	1,211	42	161	11.4	35	21.6
Phoenix, AZ	1,331	1,027	1,016	12	304	22.8	87	28.7
San Antonio, TX	1,198	1,053	1,033	20	146	12.1	22	15.2
San Diego, CA	1,241	904	885	20	337	27.1	51	15.1
San Francisco, CA	725	454	443	12	270	37.3	33	12.3
San Jose, CA	874	543	535	8	331	37.9	31	9.4
Seattle, WA	557	441	427	15	116	20.8	32	28.0

[1] Represents the portion of a consolidated city that is not within one or more separately incorporated places.

Source: U.S. Census Bureau, 2004 American Community Survey; B05002. Place of Birth by Citizenship Status; B05005. Year of Entry by Citizenship Status; using American FactFinder; <http://factfinder.census.gov/>; (accessed: 27 January 2006).

Population   45

Table 47. Foreign-Born Population—Selected Characteristics by Region of Origin: 2005

[In thousands (35,157 represents 35,157,000). As of March. The term foreign-born refers to anyone who is not a U.S. citizen at birth. This includes naturalized U.S. citizens, legal permanent residents (immigrants), temporary migrants (such as foreign students), humanitarian migrants (such as refugees), and persons illegally present in the United States. Based on Current Population Survey, Annual Social and Economic Supplement; see text this section and Appendix III]

Characteristic	Total foreign-born	Europe	Asia	Latin America Total	Caribbean	Central America [1]	South America	Other areas
Total	**35,157**	**4,519**	**8,970**	**18,898**	**3,211**	**13,447**	**2,241**	**2,769**
Under 5 years old	379	37	91	227	15	192	21	24
5 to 14 years old	1,906	170	409	1,129	123	874	132	199
15 to 24 years old	4,426	364	835	2,893	339	2,272	282	333
25 to 34 years old	8,060	663	1,900	4,921	496	3,923	500	576
35 to 44 years old	7,787	704	2,096	4,367	777	3,086	505	619
45 to 54 years old	5,437	712	1,586	2,688	587	1,681	421	453
55 to 64 years old	3,411	695	1,098	1,376	370	792	214	241
65 to 74 years old	2,077	558	601	791	292	386	113	127
75 to 84 years old	1,297	467	294	388	164	182	41	148
85 years old and over	378	150	59	118	48	58	12	50
EDUCATIONAL ATTAINMENT								
Persons 25 years old and over . . .	**28,446**	**3,949**	**7,635**	**14,650**	**2,734**	**10,109**	**1,806**	**2,213**
Less than ninth grade	6,002	324	648	4,817	456	4,188	172	213
Ninth to twelfth grade (no diploma)	3,247	204	368	2,502	336	2,015	151	173
High school graduate	7,182	1,208	1,588	3,813	885	2,330	597	573
Some college or associate's degree . . .	4,389	782	1,200	1,915	549	995	371	491
Bachelor's degree	4,818	766	2,407	1,156	367	447	341	489
Advanced degree	2,809	664	1,424	448	141	134	174	274
High school graduate or more	19,198	3,420	6,618	7,332	1,942	3,906	1,484	1,828
Bachelor's degree or more	7,627	1,430	3,830	1,604	507	581	516	763
INCOME IN 2004								
Total family households	**11,167**	**1,456**	**2,925**	**5,934**	**1,080**	**4,216**	**638**	**851**
Under $15,000	1,276	101	218	888	185	638	65	68
$15,000 to $24,999	1,596	147	228	1,109	164	866	81	111
$25,000 to $34,999	1,521	157	227	1,026	184	764	77	111
$35,000 to $49,999	1,801	214	418	1,044	143	776	124	125
$50,000 to $74,999	2,024	273	589	1,003	177	685	141	159
$75,000 and over	2,950	563	1,246	864	227	488	150	277
POVERTY STATUS IN 2004 [2]								
Persons below poverty level	**6,006**	**450**	**962**	**4,203**	**613**	**3,294**	**296**	**391**
Persons above poverty level	29,109	4,068	8,007	14,659	2,594	10,121	1,945	2,375

[1] Includes Mexico.   [2] Persons for whom poverty status is determined. Excludes unrelated individuals under 15 years old.

Source: U.S. Census Bureau, unpublished data.

Table 48. Foreign-Born Population by Place of Birth and Citizenship Status: 2004

[In thousands, except percent (34,280 represents 34,280,000). The term foreign-born refers to anyone who is not a U.S. citizen at birth. This includes naturalized U.S. citizens, legal permanent residents (immigrants), temporary migrants (such as foreign students), humanitarian migrants (such as refugees), and persons illegally present in the United States. The survey universe is limited to the household population and excludes the population living in institutions, college dormitories, and other group quarters. Based on a sample and subject to sampling variability; see text of this section and Appendix III]

Region	Foreign-born population, total	Naturalized citizen	Not U.S. citizen Number	Percent of foreign-born
Total	**34,280**	**14,399**	**19,880**	**58**
Latin America	17,973	5,511	12,462	69
Caribbean	3,147	1,694	1,453	46
Central America	12,546	2,900	9,646	77
Mexico	10,268	2,221	8,046	78
Other Central America	2,278	679	1,599	70
South America	2,280	917	1,363	60
Asia	9,255	5,165	4,090	44
Europe	4,890	2,849	2,042	42
Africa	1,147	(NA)	(NA)	(NA)
Northern America	824	(NA)	(NA)	(NA)
Oceania	190	(NA)	(NA)	(NA)

NA Not available.

Source: U.S. Census Bureau, 2004 American Community Survey; B05006. Place of Birth for the Foreign-Born Population; B05007. Place of Birth by Year of Entry by Citizenship Status for The Foreign-Born Population, using American FactFinder®; <http://factfinder.census.gov>; (accessed: 9 August 2006).

Table 49. Native and Foreign-Born Populations by Selected Characteristics: 2005

[In thousands (291,155 represents 291,155,000). As of March. The foreign-born population includes anyone who is not a U.S. citizen at birth. This includes legal permanent residents (immigrants), temporary migrants (such as students), humanitarian migrants (such as refugees), and persons illegally present in the United States. Based on Current Population Survey, Annual Social and Economic Supplement which includes the civilian noninstitutional population plus Armed Forces living off post or with their families on post; see text, this section, and Appendix III]

Characteristic	Total population	Native population	Foreign-born population			
			Total	Natural-ized citizen	Not U.S. citizen	Year of entry: 2000 to March 2005
Total..........................	291,155	255,999	35,157	13,498	21,659	7,926
Under 5 years old...................	20,262	19,884	379	73	305	379
5 to 14 years old...................	40,468	38,563	1,906	264	1,641	1,041
15 to 24 years old..................	41,063	36,637	4,426	785	3,641	1,887
25 to 34 years old..................	39,307	31,246	8,060	1,829	6,231	2,362
35 to 44 years old..................	43,350	35,563	7,787	2,955	4,832	1,291
45 to 54 years old..................	41,960	36,522	5,437	2,765	2,673	563
55 to 64 years old..................	29,532	26,121	3,411	2,136	1,274	208
65 to 74 years old..................	18,388	16,312	2,077	1,448	628	141
75 to 84 years old..................	12,981	11,684	1,297	966	331	51
85 years old and over...............	3,845	3,467	378	276	102	4
Male.............................	142,750	124,967	17,783	6,458	11,324	4,140
Female...........................	148,405	131,031	17,374	7,040	10,334	3,785
MARITAL STATUS						
Persons 15 years old and over.........	230,425	197,552	32,872	13,160	19,712	6,507
Married...........................	122,615	102,611	20,004	8,571	11,433	3,501
Widowed..........................	13,859	12,312	1,548	974	573	141
Divorced..........................	22,227	20,124	2,103	1,184	919	196
Separated.........................	4,825	3,865	960	336	624	149
Never married.....................	66,899	58,641	8,258	2,094	6,164	2,520
EDUCATIONAL ATTAINMENT						
Persons 25 years old and over.........	189,362	160,915	28,446	12,375	16,072	4,620
Not high school graduate............	28,041	18,793	9,249	2,617	6,631	1,480
High school graduate/some college.........	109,019	97,448	11,571	5,744	5,827	1,635
Bachelor's degree..................	34,219	29,401	4,818	2,534	2,283	956
Advanced degree...................	18,083	15,274	2,809	1,479	1,331	548
EARNINGS IN 2004 [1]						
Persons 15 yrs old and over with earnings.....................	102,400	86,599	15,801	6,652	9,149	2,548
Under $15,000.....................	8,871	6,586	2,284	570	1,715	531
$15,000 to $24,999..................	19,283	15,055	4,228	1,269	2,958	855
$25,000 to $34,999..................	20,152	17,153	2,999	1,367	1,633	402
$35,000 to $49,999..................	21,891	19,328	2,563	1,304	1,259	325
$50,000 to $74,999..................	18,313	16,309	2,004	1,154	850	212
$75,000 and over...................	13,890	12,167	1,723	989	734	223
HOUSEHOLD SIZE [2]						
Total households...................	113,146	98,681	14,466	6,731	7,735	2,209
One person........................	29,859	27,280	2,580	1,488	1,091	358
Two persons.......................	37,247	33,835	3,412	1,769	1,642	541
Three persons......................	18,347	15,599	2,748	1,150	1,598	510
Four persons.......................	16,506	13,607	2,900	1,197	1,703	480
Five persons.......................	7,230	5,621	1,609	675	934	181
Six persons........................	2,522	1,803	719	277	442	90
Seven persons or more...............	1,435	936	499	174	325	49
INCOME IN 2004 [2]						
Total family households...............	77,010	65,844	11,167	5,037	6,130	1,630
Under $15,000.....................	6,693	5,418	1,276	397	879	289
$15,000 to $24,999..................	8,003	6,406	1,596	543	1,053	275
$25,000 to $34,999..................	8,310	6,789	1,521	576	944	231
$35,000 to $49,999..................	11,471	9,670	1,801	771	1,030	258
$50,000 to $74,999..................	16,167	14,144	2,024	981	1,043	258
$75,000 and over...................	26,366	23,417	2,950	1,769	1,181	319
POVERTY STATUS IN 2004 [3]						
Persons at or below poverty level..........	36,997	30,991	6,006	1,328	4,678	2,006
Persons above poverty level..............	253,608	224,499	29,109	12,168	16,941	5,882
HOUSEHOLD TENURE [2, 4]						
Owner-occupied unit.................	78,573	71,023	7,551	4,590	2,961	484
Renter-occupied unit.................	33,090	26,334	6,756	2,062	4,694	1,702

[1] Covers only year-round full-time workers. [2] Based on citizenship of householder. [3] Persons for whom poverty status is determined. Excludes unrelated individuals under 15 years old. [4] Excludes occupiers who paid no cash rent.

Source: U.S. Census Bureau, unpublished data.

Population 47

Table 50. Population by Selected Ancestry Group and Region: 2004

[In thousands (285,692 represents 285,692,000). Covers single and multiple ancestries. The American Community Survey universe is limited to the household population and excludes the population living in institutions, college dormitories, and other group quarters. Based on a sample and subject to sampling variability; see text, this section and Appendix III. For composition of regions, see map, inside front cover]

Ancestry group	Total (1,000)	North-east	Mid-west	South	West
Total population . . .	**285,692**	**19**	**22**	**36**	**23**
Acadian/Cajun	105	3	2	88	7
Afghan	60	13	5	29	53
Albanian	173	53	34	7	7
Arab [1]	1,320	26	27	26	21
Egyptian	148	40	13	25	23
Iraqi	53	6	64	6	24
Jordanian.	51	17	23	26	35
Lebanese.	435	24	28	28	19
Moroccan	44	32	11	36	21
Palestinian	67	12	34	24	30
Syrian	144	41	22	20	17
Arab/Arabic	252	23	34	24	19
Armenian	448	24	7	10	59
Assyrian/Chaldean/Syriac . .	60	4	60	4	32
Australian	81	19	16	32	33
Austrian	781	32	24	22	22
Basque.	53	9	2	10	79
Belgian.	393	12	56	16	15
Brazilian	293	48	5	33	14
British.	1,222	16	17	40	27
Bulgarian	76	25	31	23	21
Canadian	704	28	18	24	30
Celtic	47	16	17	37	29
Croatian	412	25	43	12	20
Czech.	1,462	12	44	27	17
Czechoslovakian . .	346	26	31	24	18
Danish	1,477	9	32	15	44
Dutch	5,087	16	37	26	21
Eastern European. .	311	41	11	24	23
English	28,411	18	21	37	24
European	2,305	15	20	31	35
Finnish	826	10	56	10	23
French (except Basque)	9,497	25	23	31	20
French Canadian.	2,234	42	20	23	15
German	48,208	16	39	26	19
Greek.	1,310	35	23	23	19
Guyanese	215	81	2	14	3
Hungarian	1,527	33	32	20	15
Icelander.	50	7	23	16	53
Iranian	365	11	8	23	58
Irish	34,488	26	25	31	18
Israeli	99	44	10	15	31

Ancestry group	Total (1,000)	North-east	Mid-west	South	West
Italian	16,823	47	17	21	16
Latvian	90	36	19	22	23
Lithuanian	719	38	29	19	13
Macedonian.	49	27	47	14	12
Norwegian.	4,585	6	50	11	33
Pennsylvania German.	357	53	26	12	8
Polish	9,385	34	37	17	12
Portuguese	1,336	47	3	11	38
Romanian	433	29	28	19	24
Russian	3,017	38	18	21	24
Scandinavian	583	7	34	18	41
Scotch-Irish	5,324	15	19	45	21
Scottish	5,753	17	20	37	26
Serbian	150	15	50	15	20
Slavic.	124	35	23	22	20
Slovak	809	44	35	14	7
Slovene	179	16	60	11	13
Subsaharan African [1]	2,077	23	16	45	16
Cape Verdean . .	69	86	1	7	6
Ethiopian	109	5	16	39	40
Ghanian	74	53	4	35	8
Nigerian.	199	21	20	50	9
South African . . .	48	27	13	37	24
Sudanese	42	8	39	38	15
African	1,320	19	15	49	16
Swedish	4,326	14	39	16	31
Swiss	1,033	16	35	19	31
Turkish	150	40	13	26	21
Ukrainian.	894	43	21	16	20
United States or American	20,061	10	21	54	15
Welsh.	1,913	21	23	28	28
West Indian [1,2] . . .	2,182	50	4	42	4
Barbadian	59	68	4	28	1
Belizean	55	23	26	23	28
British West Indian	95	67	2	30	1
Dutch West Indian	50	4	13	68	15
Haitian.	680	45	2	52	1
Jamaican.	786	52	5	38	5
Trinidadian and Tobagonian	170	61	2	33	5
West Indian	230	57	2	35	6
Yugoslavian.	388	24	32	18	27

[1] Includes other groups not shown separately. [2] Excludes Hispanic origin groups.

Source: U.S. Census Bureau, 2004 American Community Survey; B04003. Total Ancestry Reported; using American FactFinder®; <http://factfinder.census.gov/>; (accessed: 8 May 2006).

Table 51. Languages Spoken at Home by Language: 2004

[265,683 represents 265,683,000. Covers population 5 years old and over. The American Community Survey universe is limited to the household population and excludes the population living in institutions, college dormitories, and other group quarters. Based on a sample and subject to sampling variability; see text of this section and Appendix III]

Language	Number (1,000)	Language	Number (1,000)
Total population 5 years old and over	**265,683**	Other Indic languages	531
Speak only English	216,050	Other Indo-European languages	384
Spanish or Spanish Creole	30,522	Chinese.	2,309
French (incl. Patois, Cajun).	1,323	Japanese.	479
French Creole	495	Korean	987
Italian	783	Mon-Khmer, Cambodian.	167
Portuguese or Portuguese Creole	586	Miao, Hmong	154
German.	1,087	Thai	115
Yiddish	135	Laotian	189
Other West Germanic languages	329	Vietnamese	1,060
Scandinavian languages.	132	Other Asian languages	567
Greek	369	Tagalog	1,293
Russian	746	Other Pacific Island languages	294
Polish	631	Navajo	127
Serbo-Croatian	271	Other Native North American languages	171
Other Slavic languages	273	Hungarian	96
Armenian	231	Arabic	636
Persian	300	Hebrew	161
Gujarathi	280	African languages	557
Hindi	437	Other and unspecified languages	115
Urdu	310		

Source: U.S. Census Bureau, 2004 American Community Survey; B16001. Language Spoken at Home for the Population 5 Years and Over; using American FactFinder®; <http://factfinder.census.gov/>; (accessed: 8 May 2006).

Table 52. Language Spoken at Home by State: 2004

[In thousands, except percent (265,683 represents 265,683,000). The American Community Survey universe is limited to the household population and excludes the population living in institutions, college dormitories, and other group quarters. Based on a sample and subject to sampling variability; see text, this section and Appendix III]

State	Population 5 years and over	English only	Language other than English — Number	Language other than English — Percent of population 5 years and over	State	Population 5 years and over	English only	Language other than English — Number	Language other than English — Percent of population 5 years and over
U.S...	265,683	216,050	49,633	18.7	MO	5,215	4,942	273	5.2
AL.....	4,119	3,977	142	3.4	MT.....	847	817	30	3.6
AK.....	587	512	75	12.7	NE.....	1,576	1,446	130	8.2
AZ.....	5,182	3,864	1,318	25.4	NV.....	2,131	1,588	543	25.5
AR.....	2,494	2,355	139	5.6	NH.....	1,188	1,096	92	7.7
CA.....	32,416	19,030	13,385	41.3	NJ.....	7,939	5,830	2,109	26.6
CO.....	4,161	3,492	670	16.1	NM.....	1,730	1,100	631	36.4
CT.....	3,181	2,580	600	18.9	NY.....	17,394	12,637	4,757	27.3
DE.....	752	668	83	11.1	NC.....	7,674	7,007	668	8.7
DC.....	483	405	78	16.2	ND.....	574	543	32	5.5
FL.....	15,903	12,046	3,857	24.3	OH.....	10,427	9,816	611	5.9
GA.....	7,914	7,048	867	11.0	OK.....	3,168	2,930	238	7.5
HI.....	1,140	861	278	24.4	OR.....	3,289	2,866	423	12.9
ID.....	1,252	1,120	132	10.6	PA.....	11,239	10,279	960	8.5
IL.....	11,498	9,153	2,345	20.4	RI.....	976	783	194	19.8
IN.....	5,630	5,131	499	8.9	SC.....	3,788	3,588	201	5.3
IA.....	2,672	2,528	145	5.4	SD.....	689	660	29	4.2
KS.....	2,468	2,272	197	8.0	TN.....	5,362	5,070	292	5.5
KY.....	3,767	3,610	157	4.2	TX.....	20,071	13,642	6,429	32.0
LA.....	4,064	3,750	313	7.7	UT.....	2,116	1,859	256	12.1
ME.....	1,209	1,120	89	7.4	VT.....	569	540	30	5.2
MD.....	5,051	4,356	694	13.8	VA.....	6,727	5,867	859	12.8
MA.....	5,809	4,676	1,134	19.5	WA.....	5,670	4,809	861	15.2
MI.....	9,203	8,389	815	8.9	WV.....	1,672	1,637	35	2.1
MN.....	4,624	4,153	471	10.2	WI.....	5,016	4,639	376	7.5
MS.....	2,595	2,531	64	2.5	WY.....	462	435	27	5.9

Source: U.S. Census Bureau, 2004 American Community Survey; B16005. Nativity by Language Spoken at Home by Ability to Speak English for the Population 5 Years and Over; using American FactFinder; <http://factfinder.census.gov/>; (accessed 25 January 2006).

Table 53. Language Spoken at Home—25 Largest Cities: 2004

[In thousands, except percent (602 represents 602,000). The American Community Survey universe is limited to the household population and excludes the population living in institutions, college dormitories, and other group quarters. Based on a sample and subject to sampling variability; see text, this section and Appendix III]

City	Population 5 years and over	English only	Language other than English, total [1] — Number	Language other than English, total [1] — Percent of population 5 years and over	Speak English less than "very well"	Spanish	Other Indo-European languages	Asian and Pacific Island languages
Austin, TX	602	407	195	32.4	94	157	15	20
Baltimore, MD	564	525	39	7.0	16	17	14	6
Charlotte, NC	537	466	71	13.2	46	45	13	11
Chicago, IL	2,504	1,645	859	34.3	427	609	144	80
Columbus, OH	644	569	75	11.7	37	20	19	20
Dallas, TX	1,080	608	472	43.7	266	417	23	19
Denver, CO	494	356	138	28.0	65	117	9	7
Detroit, MI	777	712	65	8.4	31	37	14	2
El Paso, TX	529	123	406	76.8	148	393	9	3
Fort Worth, TX	567	396	171	30.2	92	143	12	14
Houston, TX.......	1,771	954	817	46.1	445	674	51	72
Indianapolis, IN [2].....	700	636	63	9.1	37	44	9	7
Jacksonville, FL	705	644	61	8.6	21	29	9	19
Los Angeles, CA	3,462	1,335	2,127	61.4	1,111	1,574	237	268
Louisville-Jefferson County, KY	503	476	27	5.5	15	13	7	5
Memphis, TN	577	542	35	6.1	17	19	8	4
Milwaukee, WI	509	426	83	16.3	49	57	9	14
New York, NY.......	7,336	3,951	3,385	46.1	1,695	1,758	928	557
Philadelphia, PA	1,310	1,049	261	19.9	116	117	77	52
Phoenix, AZ	1,211	800	410	33.9	209	359	29	12
San Antonio, TX	1,097	632	465	42.4	149	441	13	10
San Diego, CA	1,152	723	430	37.3	217	251	46	125
San Francisco, CA ...	686	368	318	46.3	175	82	45	187
San Jose, CA.......	795	366	429	54.0	206	193	46	185
Seattle, WA	530	409	122	23.0	64	26	18	68

[1] Includes other language groups not shown separately. [2] Represents the portion of a consolidated city that is not within one or more separately incorporated places.

Source: U.S. Census Bureau, 2004 American Community Survey; B16005. Nativity by Language Spoken at Home by Ability to Speak English for the Population 5 Years and Over; using American FactFinder; <http://factfinder.census.gov/>; (accessed 27 January 2006).

Population 49

Table 54. Marital Status of the Population by Sex, Race, and Hispanic Origin: 1990 to 2005

[In millions, except percent (181.8 represents 181,800,000). As of March. Persons 18 years old and over. Excludes members of Armed Forces except those living off post or with their families on post. Population controls for 2005 based on Census 2000 and an expanded sample of households. Based on Current Population Survey, see text of this section, and Appendix III]

Marital status, race, and Hispanic origin	Total				Male				Female			
	1990	1995	2000	2005	1990	1995	2000	2005	1990	1995	2000	2005
Total [1]	181.8	191.6	201.8	217.2	86.9	92.0	96.9	104.8	95.0	99.6	104.9	112.3
Never married	40.4	43.9	48.2	53.9	22.4	24.6	26.1	29.6	17.9	19.3	22.1	24.3
Married.	112.6	116.7	120.1	127.4	55.8	57.7	59.6	63.3	56.7	58.9	60.4	64.0
Widowed.	13.8	13.4	13.7	13.8	2.3	2.3	2.6	2.7	11.5	11.1	11.1	11.1
Divorced	15.1	17.6	19.8	22.1	6.3	7.4	8.5	9.2	8.8	10.3	11.3	12.9
Percent of total	100.0	100.0	100.0	100.0	100.0	100.0	100.0	100.0	100.0	100.0	100.0	100.0
Never married	22.2	22.9	23.9	24.8	25.8	26.8	27.0	28.2	18.9	19.4	21.1	21.6
Married.	61.9	60.9	59.5	58.6	64.3	62.7	61.5	60.4	59.7	59.2	57.6	56.9
Widowed.	7.6	7.0	6.8	6.4	2.7	2.5	2.7	2.6	12.1	11.1	10.5	9.9
Divorced	8.3	9.2	9.8	10.2	7.2	8.0	8.8	8.8	9.3	10.3	10.8	11.5
White [2], total	155.5	161.3	168.1	177.5	74.8	78.1	81.6	86.6	80.6	83.2	86.6	90.9
Never married	31.6	33.2	36.0	39.7	18.0	19.2	20.3	22.6	13.6	14.0	15.7	17.0
Married.	99.5	102.0	104.1	108.3	49.5	50.6	51.8	54.0	49.9	51.3	52.2	54.2
Widowed.	11.7	11.3	11.5	11.5	1.9	1.9	2.2	2.3	9.8	9.4	9.3	9.2
Divorced	12.6	14.8	16.5	18.1	5.4	6.3	7.2	7.6	7.3	8.4	9.3	10.4
Percent of total	100.0	100.0	100.0	100.0	100.0	100.0	100.0	100.0	100.0	100.0	100.0	100.0
Never married	20.3	20.6	21.4	22.3	24.1	24.6	24.9	26.1	16.9	16.9	18.1	18.7
Married.	64.0	63.2	62.0	61.0	66.2	64.9	63.5	62.4	61.9	61.7	60.3	59.7
Widowed.	7.5	7.0	6.8	6.5	2.6	2.5	2.7	2.6	12.2	11.3	10.8	10.2
Divorced	8.1	9.1	9.8	10.2	7.2	8.1	8.8	8.8	9.0	10.1	10.7	11.5
Black [2], total	20.3	22.1	24.0	25.2	9.1	9.9	10.7	11.2	11.2	12.2	13.3	13.9
Never married	7.1	8.5	9.5	10.2	3.5	4.1	4.3	4.7	3.6	4.4	5.1	5.5
Married.	9.3	9.6	10.1	10.3	4.5	4.6	5.0	5.0	4.8	4.9	5.1	5.2
Widowed.	1.7	1.7	1.7	1.7	0.3	0.3	0.3	0.3	1.4	1.4	1.4	1.4
Divorced	2.1	2.4	2.8	2.9	0.8	0.8	1.1	1.1	1.3	1.5	1.7	1.8
Percent of total	100.0	100.0	100.0	100.0	100.0	100.0	100.0	100.0	100.0	100.0	100.0	100.0
Never married	35.1	38.4	39.4	40.6	38.4	41.7	40.2	42.0	32.5	35.8	38.3	39.5
Married.	45.8	43.2	42.1	41.0	49.2	46.7	46.7	45.5	43.0	40.4	38.3	37.4
Widowed.	8.5	7.6	7.0	6.6	3.7	3.1	2.8	2.7	12.4	11.3	10.5	10.0
Divorced	10.6	10.7	11.5	11.7	8.8	8.5	10.3	9.8	12.0	12.5	12.8	13.3
Asian [2], total	(NA)	(NA)	(NA)	9.4	(NA)	(NA)	(NA)	4.5	(NA)	(NA)	(NA)	4.9
Never married	(NA)	(NA)	(NA)	2.3	(NA)	(NA)	(NA)	1.3	(NA)	(NA)	(NA)	1.0
Married.	(NA)	(NA)	(NA)	6.2	(NA)	(NA)	(NA)	2.9	(NA)	(NA)	(NA)	3.3
Widowed.	(NA)	(NA)	(NA)	0.4	(NA)	(NA)	(NA)	0.1	(NA)	(NA)	(NA)	0.3
Divorced	(NA)	(NA)	(NA)	0.5	(NA)	(NA)	(NA)	0.2	(NA)	(NA)	(NA)	0.3
Percent of total	100.0	100.0	100.0	100.0	100.0	100.0	100.0	100.0	100.0	100.0	100.0	100.0
Never married	(NA)	(NA)	(NA)	24.8	(NA)	(NA)	(NA)	29.7	(NA)	(NA)	(NA)	20.3
Married.	(NA)	(NA)	(NA)	65.6	(NA)	(NA)	(NA)	64.7	(NA)	(NA)	(NA)	66.5
Widowed.	(NA)	(NA)	(NA)	4.3	(NA)	(NA)	(NA)	1.3	(NA)	(NA)	(NA)	6.7
Divorced	(NA)	(NA)	(NA)	5.3	(NA)	(NA)	(NA)	4.1	(NA)	(NA)	(NA)	6.4
Hispanic, [3] total	13.6	17.6	21.1	27.5	6.7	8.8	10.4	14.1	6.8	8.8	10.7	13.4
Never married	3.7	5.0	5.9	8.6	2.2	3.0	3.4	5.2	1.5	2.1	2.5	3.4
Married.	8.4	10.4	12.7	15.6	4.1	5.1	6.2	7.8	4.3	5.3	6.5	7.8
Widowed.	0.5	0.7	0.9	1.0	0.1	0.2	0.2	0.2	0.4	0.6	0.7	0.8
Divorced	1.0	1.4	1.6	2.2	0.4	0.6	0.7	0.9	0.6	0.8	1.0	1.3
Percent of total	100.0	100.0	100.0	100.0	100.0	100.0	100.0	100.0	100.0	100.0	100.0	100.0
Never married	27.2	28.6	28.0	31.3	32.1	33.8	32.3	36.7	22.5	23.5	23.4	25.6
Married.	61.7	59.3	60.2	57.0	60.9	57.9	59.7	55.6	62.4	60.7	60.7	58.7
Widowed.	4.0	4.2	4.2	3.7	1.5	1.8	1.6	1.5	6.5	6.6	6.5	6.1
Divorced	7.0	7.9	7.6	7.9	5.5	6.6	6.4	6.3	8.5	9.2	9.3	9.7
Non-Hispanic White [2, 3] total	(NA)	(NA)	(NA)	151.9	(NA)	(NA)	(NA)	73.4	(NA)	(NA)	(NA)	78.5
Never married	(NA)	(NA)	(NA)	31.8	(NA)	(NA)	(NA)	17.8	(NA)	(NA)	(NA)	13.9
Married.	(NA)	(NA)	(NA)	93.5	(NA)	(NA)	(NA)	46.6	(NA)	(NA)	(NA)	47.0
Widowed.	(NA)	(NA)	(NA)	10.6	(NA)	(NA)	(NA)	2.1	(NA)	(NA)	(NA)	8.5
Divorced	(NA)	(NA)	(NA)	16.0	(NA)	(NA)	(NA)	6.8	(NA)	(NA)	(NA)	9.2
Percent of total	100.0	100.0	100.0	100.0	100.0	100.0	100.0	100.0	100.0	100.0	100.0	100.0
Never married	(NA)	(NA)	(NA)	20.9	(NA)	(NA)	(NA)	24.3	(NA)	(NA)	(NA)	17.7
Married.	(NA)	(NA)	(NA)	61.5	(NA)	(NA)	(NA)	63.5	(NA)	(NA)	(NA)	59.7
Widowed.	(NA)	(NA)	(NA)	6.9	(NA)	(NA)	(NA)	2.8	(NA)	(NA)	(NA)	10.8
Divorced	(NA)	(NA)	(NA)	10.6	(NA)	(NA)	(NA)	9.3	(NA)	(NA)	(NA)	11.7

NA Not available. [1] Includes persons of other races, not shown separately. [2] 2005 data represent persons who selected this race group only and exclude persons reporting more than one race. The CPS in prior years only allowed respondents to report one race group. See also comments on race in the text for this section. [3] Hispanic persons may be of any race.

Source: U.S. Census Bureau, Current Population Reports, P20-537, and earlier reports; and "America's Families and Living Arrangements: 2005, Table A1. Marital Status of People 15 Years and Over, by Age, Sex, Personal Earnings, Race, and Hispanic Origin, 2005"; published 25 May 2006; <http://www.census.gov/population/www/socdemo/hh-fam/cps2005.html>.

Table 55. **Marital Status of the Population by Sex and Age: 2005**

[As of March (104,848 represents 104,848,000). See headnote, Table 54]

Sex and age	Number of persons (1,000)					Percent distribution				
	Total	Never married	Married	Wid-owed	Divorced	Total	Never married	Married	Wid-owed	Divorced
Male	**104,848**	**29,608**	**63,318**	**2,723**	**9,200**	**100.0**	**28.2**	**60.4**	**2.6**	**8.8**
18 to 19 years old	3,760	3,701	55	–	3	100.0	98.4	1.4	–	0.1
20 to 24 years old	10,282	8,868	1,304	8	103	100.0	86.2	12.6	0.1	1.0
25 to 29 years old	9,812	5,399	4,060	4	348	100.0	55.0	41.3	–	3.6
30 to 34 years old	9,842	3,138	6,031	21	652	100.0	31.9	61.3	0.2	6.6
35 to 39 years old	10,260	2,304	6,904	45	1,006	100.0	22.5	67.4	0.4	9.8
40 to 44 years old	11,189	1,964	7,827	56	1,343	100.0	17.5	70.0	0.5	12.0
45 to 54 years old	20,526	2,665	14,865	176	2,820	100.0	13.0	72.4	0.9	13.7
55 to 64 years old	14,032	899	10,932	344	1,857	100.0	6.4	77.9	2.4	13.2
65 to 74 years old	8,463	408	6,646	692	717	100.0	4.8	78.6	8.2	8.5
75 years old and over . . .	6,682	262	4,694	1,377	351	100.0	4.0	70.3	20.6	5.3
Female	**112,329**	**24,318**	**63,971**	**11,105**	**12,932**	**100.0**	**21.6**	**56.9**	**9.9**	**11.5**
18 to 19 years old	3,805	3,622	168	3	13	100.0	95.2	4.4	–	0.3
20 to 24 years old	10,110	7,546	2,376	17	171	100.0	74.6	23.5	0.2	1.7
25 to 29 years old	9,674	3,995	5,084	31	563	100.0	41.3	52.5	0.3	5.8
30 to 34 years old	9,956	2,347	6,709	53	847	100.0	23.6	67.3	0.5	8.5
35 to 39 years old	10,376	1,616	7,326	87	1,347	100.0	15.6	70.5	0.8	13.0
40 to 44 years old	11,489	1,387	8,183	185	1,734	100.0	12.1	71.3	1.6	15.1
45 to 54 years old	21,399	2,073	14,841	661	3,822	100.0	9.7	69.4	3.1	17.9
55 to 64 years old	15,481	946	10,331	1,474	2,730	100.0	6.1	66.7	9.5	17.6
65 to 74 years old	9,913	406	5,655	2,772	1,079	100.0	4.1	57.0	28.0	10.9
75 years old and over . . .	10,126	380	3,298	5,822	626	100.0	3.8	32.6	57.5	6.2

– Represents or rounds to zero.

Source: U.S. Census Bureau, "America's Families and Living Arrangements: 2005, Table A1. Marital Status of People 15 Years and Over, by Age, Sex, Personal Earnings, Race, and Hispanic Origin, 2005"; published 25 May 2006; <http://www.census.gov/population/www /socdemo/hh-fam/cps2005.html>.

Table 56. **Living Arrangements of Persons 15 Years Old and Over by Selected Characteristics: 2005**

[In thousands (230,261 represents 230,261,000). As of March. See headnote, Table 54]

Living arrangement	Total	15 to 19 years old	20 to 24 years old	25 to 34 years old	35 to 44 years old	45 to 54 years old	55 to 64 years old	65 to 74 years old	75 years old and over
Total [1]	**230,261**	**20,652**	**20,392**	**39,283**	**43,313**	**41,924**	**29,513**	**18,375**	**16,808**
Alone	29,859	135	1,367	3,772	3,912	5,162	4,922	4,212	6,378
With spouse	119,026	201	3,248	20,268	28,084	27,752	20,194	11,752	7,526
With other persons	81,376	20,316	15,777	15,243	11,317	9,010	4,397	2,411	2,904
White [2]	**187,550**	**15,949**	**15,959**	**30,764**	**34,727**	**34,496**	**24,975**	**15,741**	**14,940**
Alone	24,148	90	1,008	2,779	3,004	4,004	4,045	3,525	5,693
With spouse	102,435	173	2,843	16,988	23,569	23,753	17,702	10,467	6,941
With other persons	60,967	15,686	12,108	10,997	8,154	6,739	3,228	1,749	2,306
Black [2]	**27,184**	**3,152**	**2,847**	**5,093**	**5,373**	**4,853**	**2,906**	**1,715**	**1,243**
Alone	4,332	38	249	669	701	958	643	555	519
With spouse	8,555	13	214	1,524	2,199	2,194	1,401	696	314
With other persons	14,297	3,101	2,384	2,900	2,473	1,701	862	464	410
Asian [2]	**9,930**	**789**	**823**	**2,249**	**2,175**	**1,707**	**1,094**	**645**	**447**
Alone	774	5	52	209	124	79	137	66	104
With spouse	5,732	5	88	1,240	1,681	1,324	748	439	209
With other persons	3,424	779	683	800	370	304	209	140	134
Hispanic origin [3]	**29,601**	**3,378**	**3,675**	**7,636**	**6,242**	**4,159**	**2,316**	**1,316**	**878**
Alone	1,921	14	135	367	300	325	288	255	237
With spouse	13,719	78	821	3,969	3,836	2,535	1,407	733	340
With other persons	13,961	3,286	2,719	3,300	2,106	1,299	621	328	301
Non-Hispanic White [2,3] .	**160,084**	**12,881**	**12,612**	**23,651**	**28,903**	**30,618**	**22,814**	**14,509**	**14,097**
Alone	22,402	80	885	2,447	2,734	3,715	3,780	3,300	5,461
With spouse	89,570	103	2,086	13,281	19,955	21,375	16,381	9,773	6,618
With other persons	48,112	12,698	9,641	7,923	6,214	5,528	2,653	1,436	2,018

[1] Includes other races and persons not of Hispanic origin, not shown separately.   [2] See footnote 2, Table 54.   [3] Persons of Hispanic origin may be of any race.

Source: U.S. Census Bureau, "America's Families and Living Arrangements: 2005, Table A2. Family Status and Household Relationship of People 15 Years and Over, by Marital Status, Age, Sex, Race, and Hispanic Origin: 2005"; published 25 May 2006; <http://www.census.gov/population/www/socdemo/hh-fam/cps2005.html>.

Population   51

Table 57. Households, Families, Subfamilies, and Married Couples: 1980 to 2005

[In thousands, except as indicated (80,776 represents 80,776,000). **As of March.** Excludes members of Armed Forces except those living off post or with their families on post. Beginning 2003, population controls based on Census 2000 and an expanded sample of households. Based on Current Population Survey, see text of this section, and Appendix III. Minus sign (–) indicates decrease]

Type of unit	1980	1990	1995	2000	2003	2004	2005	Percent change 1980– 1990	Percent change 1990– 2000	Percent change 2000– 2005
Households	80,776	93,347	98,990	104,705	111,278	112,000	113,146	16	12	8
Persons per household . . .	2.76	2.63	2.65	2.62	2.57	2.57	2.57	(X)	(X)	(X)
White [1]	70,766	80,163	83,737	87,671	91,645	91,962	92,702	13	9	6
Black [1]	8,586	10,486	11,655	12,849	13,465	13,629	13,792	22	23	7
Hispanic [2]	3,684	5,933	7,735	9,319	11,339	11,339	12,181	61	57	31
Family households.	59,550	66,090	69,305	72,025	75,596	76,217	77,010	11	9	7
Married couple	49,112	52,317	53,858	55,311	57,320	57,719	58,109	7	6	5
Male householder [3]	1,733	2,884	3,226	4,028	4,656	4,716	4,893	66	40	21
Female householder [3]	8,705	10,890	12,220	12,687	13,620	13,781	14,009	25	17	10
Nonfamily households	21,226	27,257	29,686	32,680	35,682	35,783	36,136	28	20	11
Male householder	8,807	11,606	13,190	14,641	16,020	16,136	16,344	32	26	12
Female householder.	12,419	15,651	16,496	18,039	19,662	19,647	19,792	26	15	10
One person.	18,296	22,999	24,732	26,724	29,431	29,586	29,859	26	16	12
Families	59,550	66,090	69,305	72,025	75,596	76,217	77,010	11	9	7
Persons per family	3.29	3.17	3.19	3.17	3.13	3.13	3.13	(X)	(X)	(X)
With own children [4]	31,022	32,289	34,296	34,605	35,968	35,944	36,520	4	7	5
Without own children [4]	28,528	33,801	35,009	37,420	39,628	40,273	40,491	18	11	8
Married couple	49,112	52,317	53,858	55,311	57,320	57,719	58,109	7	6	5
With own children [4] . . .	24,961	24,537	25,241	25,248	25,914	25,793	26,180	–2	3	4
Without own children [4] . . .	24,151	27,780	28,617	30,062	31,406	31,926	31,929	15	8	6
Male householder [3]	1,733	2,884	3,226	4,028	4,656	4,716	4,893	66	40	21
With own children [4] . . .	616	1,153	1,440	1,786	1,915	1,931	2,034	87	55	14
Without own children [4] . . .	1,117	1,731	1,786	2,242	2,741	2,786	2,859	55	30	28
Female householder [3]	8,705	10,890	12,220	12,687	13,620	13,781	14,009	25	17	10
With own children [4] . . .	5,445	6,599	7,615	7,571	8,139	8,221	8,305	21	15	10
Without own children [4] . . .	3,261	4,290	4,606	5,116	5,481	5,560	5,703	32	19	11
Unrelated subfamilies	360	534	674	571	525	509	518	48	7	–9
Married couple	20	68	64	37	34	42	62	(B)	(B)	(B)
Male reference persons [3] . .	36	45	59	57	84	61	61	(B)	(B)	(B)
Female reference persons [3] .	304	421	550	477	407	406	395	39	13	–17
Related subfamilies.	1,150	2,403	2,878	2,984	3,089	3,309	3,444	109	24	15
Married couple	582	871	1,015	1,149	1,232	1,303	1,342	50	32	17
Father-child [3]	54	153	195	201	260	296	391	(B)	31	95
Mother-child [3]	512	1,378	1,668	1,634	1,596	1,710	1,711	169	19	5
Married couples	49,714	53,256	54,937	56,497	58,586	59,064	59,513	7	6	5
With own household	49,112	52,317	53,858	55,311	57,320	57,719	58,109	7	6	5
Without own household	602	939	1,079	1,186	1,266	1,345	1,406	56	26	13
Percent without	1.2	1.8	2.0	2.1	2.2	2.3	2.4	(X)	(X)	(X)

B Not shown; base less than 75,000. X Not applicable. [1] Beginning with the 2003 Current Population Survey (CPS), respondents could choose more than one race. Beginning 2003, data represent persons who selected this race group only and exclude persons reporting more than one race. The CPS in prior years only allowed respondents to report one race group. See also comments on race in the text for this section. [2] Persons of Hispanic origin may be of any race. [3] No spouse present. [4] Under 18 years old.

Source: U.S. Census Bureau, "Families and Living Arrangements"; <http://www.census.gov/population/www/socdemo/hh-fam.html>.

Table 58. Married Couples by Race and Hispanic Origin of Spouses: 1980 to 2005

[In thousands (49,714 represents 49,714,000). **As of March. Persons 15 years old and over.** Persons of Hispanic origin may be of any race. Based on Current Population Survey; see headnote, Table 57 and Appendix III]

Race and origin of spouses	1980	1990	2000	2005
Married couples, total [1]	49,714	53,256	56,497	59,513
Interracial married couples, total	651	964	1,464	2,276
White [2]/Black [2]	167	211	363	422
Black husband/White wife	122	150	268	288
White husband/Black wife	45	61	95	134
White [2]/other race [3]	450	720	1,051	1,709
Black [2]/other race [3]	34	33	50	145
HISPANIC ORIGIN				
Hispanic/Hispanic	1,906	3,085	4,739	5,762
Hispanic/other origin (not Hispanic).	891	1,193	1,743	2,195
All other couples (not of Hispanic origin)	46,917	48,979	50,015	51,556

[1] Includes other married couples not shown separately. [2] See footnote 2, Table 54. [3] "Other race," is any race other than White or Black, such as American Indian, Japanese, Chinese, etc. This total excludes combinations of other races by other races.

Source: U.S. Census Bureau, Table MS-3. Interracial Married Couples: 1980 to 2002; published 15 September 2004; <http://www.census.gov/population/www/socdemo/hh-fam.html>; and unpublished data.

Table 59. Households and Persons Per Household by Type of Household: 1990 to 2005

[As of March (93,347 represents 93,347,000). See headnote, Table 57]

Type of household	Households						Persons per household		
	Number (1,000)			Percent distribution					
	1990	2000	2005	1990	2000	2005	1990	2000	2005
Total households	**93,347**	**104,705**	**113,146**	**100**	**100**	**100**	**2.63**	**2.62**	**2.57**
Family households.	66,090	72,025	77,010	71	69	68	3.22	3.24	3.19
Married couple family	52,317	55,311	58,109	56	53	51	3.25	3.26	3.21
Male householder, no spouse present	2,884	4,028	4,893	3	4	4	3.04	3.16	3.17
Female householder, no spouse present. . .	10,890	12,687	14,009	12	12	12	3.10	3.17	3.15
Nonfamily households.	27,257	32,680	36,136	29	31	32	1.22	1.25	1.25
Living alone.	22,999	26,724	29,859	25	26	26	1.00	1.00	1.00
Male householder.	11,606	14,641	16,344	12	14	14	1.33	1.34	1.34
Living alone.	9,049	11,181	12,652	10	11	11	1.00	1.00	1.00
Female householder.	15,651	18,039	19,792	17	17	17	1.14	1.17	1.17
Living alone.	13,950	15,543	17,207	15	15	15	1.00	1.00	1.00

Source: U.S. Census Bureau, Current Population Reports, P20-537, and earlier reports; and "America's Families and Living Arrangements: 2005"; published 25 May 2006; <http://www.census.gov/population/www/socdemo/hh-fam/cps2005.html>.

Table 60. Households by Age of Householder and Size of Household: 1990 to 2005

[In millions (93.3 represents 93,300,000). As of March. Based on Current Population Survey; see headnote, Table 57]

Age of householder and size of household	1990	1995	2000	2005					
				Total [1]	White [2]	Black [2]	Asian [2]	His-panic [3]	Non-Hispanic White [3]
Total.	**93.3**	**99.0**	**104.7**	**113.1**	**92.7**	**13.8**	**4.1**	**12.2**	**81.4**
Age of householder:									
15 to 24 years old	5.1	5.4	5.9	6.7	5.1	1.1	0.2	1.2	4.0
25 to 29 years old	9.4	8.4	8.5	9.1	7.2	1.3	0.4	1.6	5.7
30 to 34 years old	11.0	11.1	10.1	10.1	7.8	1.4	0.5	1.7	6.2
35 to 44 years old	20.6	22.9	24.0	23.2	18.6	3.0	1.1	3.1	15.7
45 to 54 years old	14.5	17.6	20.9	23.4	19.1	3.0	0.8	2.1	17.1
55 to 64 years old	12.5	12.2	13.6	17.5	14.7	1.9	0.6	1.3	13.5
65 to 74 years old	11.7	11.8	11.3	11.5	9.8	1.2	0.3	0.7	9.1
75 years old and over . . .	8.4	9.6	10.4	11.6	10.4	0.9	0.2	0.5	9.9
One person	23.0	24.7	26.7	29.9	24.1	4.3	0.7	1.9	22.4
Male	9.0	10.1	11.2	12.7	10.2	1.8	0.3	0.9	9.3
Female.	14.0	14.6	15.5	17.2	13.9	2.5	0.4	1.0	13.0
Two persons.	30.1	31.8	34.7	37.2	31.7	3.7	1.1	2.7	29.3
Three persons.	16.1	16.8	17.2	18.3	14.6	2.4	0.9	2.4	12.4
Four persons	14.5	15.3	15.3	16.5	13.4	1.9	0.8	2.5	11.1
Five persons	6.2	6.6	7.0	7.2	5.8	0.9	0.3	1.6	4.4
Six persons	2.1	2.3	2.4	2.5	1.9	0.4	0.1	0.7	1.2
Seven persons or more. . . .	1.3	1.4	1.4	1.4	1.0	0.2	0.1	0.4	0.6

[1] Includes other races, not shown separately. [2] Beginning with the 2003 Current Population Survey (CPS), respondents could choose more than one race. 2005 data represent persons who selected this race group only and exclude persons reporting more than one race. The CPS in prior years only allowed respondents to report one race group. See also comments on race in the text for this section. [3] Hispanic persons may be of any race.

Source: U.S. Census Bureau, Current Population Reports, P20-537, and earlier reports; and "America's Families and Living Arrangements: 2005"; published 25 May 2006; <http://www.census.gov/population/www/socdemo/hh-fam/cps2005.html>.

Table 61. Unmarried-Partner Households by Sex of Partners: 2004

[The American Community Survey universe is limited to the household population and excludes the population living in institutions, college dormitories, and other group quarters. Based on a sample and subject to sampling variability; see text, this section and Appendix III]

Item	Number
Total households	**109,902,090**
Unmarried-partner households.	5,840,833
Male householder and male partner	374,397
Male householder and female partner	2,544,546
Female householder and female partner	332,799
Female householder and male partner.	2,589,091
All other households	104,061,257

Source: U.S. Census Bureau, 2004 American Community Survey; B11009. Unmarried-Partner Households and Household Type by Sex of Partner; using American FactFinder®; <http://factfinder.census.gov/>; (accessed: 31 January 2006).

Population   53

Table 62. Family Groups With Children Under 18 Years Old by Race and Hispanic Origin: 1990 to 2005

[In thousands. As of March (34,670 represents 34,670,000). Family groups comprise family households, related subfamilies, and unrelated subfamilies. Excludes members of Armed Forces except those living off post or with their families on post. Population controls for 2005 based on Census 2000 and an expanded sample of households. Based on Current Population Survey, see text of this section, and Appendix III]

Race and Hispanic origin of householder or reference person	1990	1995	2000	2005 Total	2005 Family house- holds	2005 Subfamilies Total	2005 Subfamilies Related	2005 Subfamilies Unrelated
All races, total [1]............	34,670	37,168	37,496	39,646	36,520	3,126	2,635	491
Two-parent family groups...........	24,921	25,640	25,771	26,749	26,180	568	533	35
One-parent family groups...........	9,749	11,528	11,725	12,897	10,339	2,558	2,102	456
Maintained by mother...........	8,398	9,834	9,681	10,411	8,305	2,106	1,711	395
Maintained by father............	1,351	1,694	2,044	2,487	2,034	452	391	61
White, total [2]...............	28,294	29,846	30,079	31,272	29,117	2,155	1,748	407
Two-parent family groups...........	21,905	22,320	22,241	22,562	22,139	423	388	35
One-parent family groups...........	6,389	7,525	7,838	8,710	6,978	1,732	1,360	372
Maintained by mother...........	5,310	6,239	6,216	6,796	5,368	1,428	1,109	319
Maintained by father............	1,079	1,286	1,622	1,913	1,610	303	251	52
Black, total [2]...............	5,087	5,491	5,530	5,502	4,833	669	614	55
Two-parent family groups...........	2,006	1,962	2,135	2,077	2,035	42	42	–
One-parent family groups...........	3,081	3,529	3,396	3,425	2,798	627	572	55
Maintained by mother...........	2,860	3,197	3,060	3,033	2,509	524	475	49
Maintained by father............	221	332	335	392	289	103	97	6
Asian, total [2]...............	(NA)	(NA)	1,469	1,771	1,618	153	149	5
Two-parent family groups...........	(NA)	(NA)	1,184	1,485	1,409	76	76	–
One-parent family groups...........	(NA)	(NA)	285	286	209	77	73	5
Maintained by mother...........	(NA)	(NA)	236	224	159	65	62	3
Maintained by father............	(NA)	(NA)	49	62	50	12	10	2
Hispanic, total [3]............	3,429	4,527	5,503	6,763	6,001	762	660	102
Two-parent family groups...........	2,289	2,879	3,625	4,355	4,172	183	168	15
One-parent family groups...........	1,140	1,647	1,877	2,408	1,829	579	492	87
Maintained by mother...........	1,003	1,404	1,565	1,964	1,503	462	385	77
Maintained by father............	138	243	313	444	326	118	108	10
Non-Hispanic White, total [2, 3]....	(NA)	(NA)	24,847	25,028	23,575	1,452	1,145	307
Two-parent family groups...........	(NA)	(NA)	18,750	18,486	18,235	251	232	19
One-parent family groups...........	(NA)	(NA)	6,096	6,542	5,340	1,201	913	288
Maintained by mother...........	(NA)	(NA)	4,766	5,031	4,030	1,001	755	246
Maintained by father............	(NA)	(NA)	1,331	1,511	1,310	200	158	42

– Represents or rounds to zero.   NA Not available.   [1] Includes other races, not shown separately.   [2] Beginning with the 2003 Current Population Survey (CPS), respondents could choose more than one race. 2005 data represent persons who selected this race group only and exclude persons reporting more than one race. CPS prior to 2003 allowed respondents to report only one race group. See also comments on race in the text for this section.   [3] Hispanic persons may be of any race.

Source: U.S. Census Bureau, Current Population Reports, P20-537, and earlier reports; and "America's Families and Living Arrangements: 2005"; published 25 May 2006; <http://www.census.gov/population/www/socdemo/hh-fam/cps2005.html>.

Table 63. Parents and Children in Stay-At-Home Parent Family Groups: 1995 to 2005

[In thousands (22,973 represents 22,973,000). Family groups with children include those families that maintain their own household (family households with own children); those that live in the home of a relative (related subfamilies); and those that live in the home of a nonrelative (unrelated subfamilies). Stay-at-home family groups are married-couple family groups with children under 15 where one parent is in the labor force all of the previous year and their spouse is out of the labor force for the entire year with the reason 'taking care of home and family.' Only married couples with children under 15 are included. Based on Current Population Survey; see Appendix III]

Year	Married-couple family groups with children under 15 years old Total	With stay-at-home mothers	With stay-at-home fathers	Children under 15 years old in married-couple family groups Total in married-couple family groups	With stay-at-home mothers	With stay-at-home fathers
1995	22,973	4,440	64	41,008	9,106	125
1996	22,808	4,633	49	40,739	9,693	115
1997	22,779	4,617	71	40,798	9,788	140
1998	22,881	4,555	90	41,038	9,432	196
1999	22,754	4,731	71	41,003	9,796	143
2000	22,953	4,785	93	41,860	10,087	180
2001	22,922	4,934	81	41,862	10,194	148
2002	23,339	5,206	106	41,802	10,573	189
2003	23,209	5,388	98	41,654	11,028	175
2004	23,160	5,571	147	41,409	11,205	268
2005	23,530	5,638	143	41,170	11,246	245

Source: U.S. Census Bureau, Table SHP-1. Parents and Children in Stay-At-Home Parent Family Groups: 1994 to Present; published 25 May 2006; <http://www.census.gov/population/www/socdemo/hh-fam.html>.

Table 64. Children Under 18 Years Old by Presence of Parents: 1990 to 2005

[As of **March (64,137 represents 64,137,000).** Excludes persons under 18 years old who maintained households or family groups. Based on Current Population Survey; see headnote, Table 57]

Race Hispanic origin, and year	Number (1,000)	Both parents	Total	Divorced	Married, spouse absent	Never married	Widowed	Father only	Neither parent
ALL RACES [1]									
1990	64,137	72.5	21.6	8.0	5.3	6.8	1.5	3.1	2.8
1995	70,254	68.7	23.5	8.6	5.6	8.3	1.0	3.5	4.3
2000	72,012	69.1	22.4	7.9	4.5	9.2	1.0	4.2	4.2
2005	73,523	67.4	23.4	7.9	4.6	10.1	0.8	4.7	4.5
WHITE [2]									
1990	51,390	79.0	16.2	(NA)	(NA)	(NA)	(NA)	3.0	1.8
1995	55,327	75.8	17.8	(NA)	(NA)	(NA)	(NA)	3.4	3.0
2000	56,455	75.3	17.3	(NA)	(NA)	(NA)	(NA)	4.3	3.1
2005	56,259	73.6	18.4	7.9	4.0	5.8	0.7	4.7	3.4
BLACK [2]									
1990	10,018	37.7	51.2	(NA)	(NA)	(NA)	(NA)	3.5	7.5
1995	11,301	33.1	52.0	(NA)	(NA)	(NA)	(NA)	4.1	10.8
2000	11,412	37.6	49.0	(NA)	(NA)	(NA)	(NA)	4.2	9.2
2005	11,295	35.1	50.1	8.6	8.1	32.0	1.3	4.9	9.8
ASIAN [2]									
2005	2,860	83.7	10.2	4.0	2.3	2.7	1.3	3.6	2.5
HISPANIC [3]									
1990	7,174	66.8	27.1	(NA)	(NA)	(NA)	(NA)	2.9	3.2
1995	9,843	62.9	28.4	(NA)	(NA)	(NA)	(NA)	4.2	4.4
2000	11,613	65.1	25.1	(NA)	(NA)	(NA)	(NA)	4.4	5.4
2005	14,248	64.7	25.4	6.1	7.1	11.4	0.8	4.8	5.1
NON-HISPANIC WHITE [2, 3]									
2005	43,122	76.0	16.4	8.4	3.1	4.2	0.7	4.8	2.9

NA Not available. [1] Includes other races not shown separately. [2] Beginning with the 2003 Current Population Survey, (CPS) respondents could choose more than one race. 2005 data represent persons who selected this race group only and exclude persons reporting more than one race. The CPS prior to 2003 allowed respondents to report only one race group. See also comments on race in the text for this section. [3] Hispanic persons may be of any race.

Source: U.S. Census Bureau, "America's Families and Living Arrangements: 2005"; published 25 May 2006; <http://www.census.gov/population/www/socdemo/hh-fam/cps2005.html>.

Table 65. Adopted Children of Householder—Summary: 2000

[In thousands (2,059 represents 2,059,000), except as indicated. As of April 1. Based on a sample from the 2000 Census of Population and Housing; see text of this section and Appendix III]

Characteristic of adopted child	Total	Under 18 years old	18 years old and over	Characteristic	Adopted children	Step-children	Biological children
Total	2,059	1,586	473	Total	1,586	3,292	59,774
Place of birth:				CHARACTERISTIC OF CHILDREN			
Native	1,801	1,387	414				
Foreign born [1]	258	199	59	Under 5 years old	307	214	16,034
Korea	57	48	9	5 to 13 years old	892	1,940	30,999
Mexico	28	18	10	14 to 17 years old	387	1,138	12,741
China	22	21	1				
Russia	20	20	1	Male	751	1,655	30,741
Philippines	10	6	4	Female	835	1,638	29,033
Colombia	10	7	3				
India	10	8	2	CHARACTERISTIC OF HOUSEHOLDER			
Different race than householder [2]	321	271	50	Median household income	$56,138	$50,900	$48,200
				Percent bachelor's degree or more	33.4	15.7	25.9
Different Hispanic origin than householder [3]	125	105	20	Percent owning home	77.8	66.8	66.8

[1] Includes other countries not shown separately. [2] Child and householder do not report the same group, where race groups are: White alone, Black alone, American Indian and Alaska Native alone, Asian alone, Native Hawaiian or Pacific Islander alone, Some Other Race alone, or either the child or householder reports multiple race groups. [3] Child is Hispanic and householder is not Hispanic, or vice versa.

Source: U.S. Census Bureau, Adopted Children and Stepchildren: 2000, Census 2000 Special Reports (CENSR-6RV), October 2003.

U.S. Census Bureau, Statistical Abstract of the United States: 2007

Table 66. Families by Number of Own Children Under 18 Years Old: 1990 to 2005

[As of March (66,090 represents 66,090,000). Based on Current Population Survey; see headnote, Table 62]

Race, Hispanic origin, and year	Number of families (1,000)					Percent distribution				
	Total	No children	One child	Two children	Three or more children	Total	No children	One child	Two children	Three or more children
ALL FAMILIES [1]										
1990	66,090	33,801	13,530	12,263	6,496	100	51	20	19	10
1995	69,305	35,009	14,088	13,213	6,995	100	51	20	19	10
2000	72,025	37,420	14,311	13,215	7,080	100	52	20	18	10
2005, total	77,010	40,491	15,194	13,865	7,461	100	53	20	18	10
Married couple	58,109	31,929	9,885	10,676	5,619	100	55	17	18	10
Male householder [2]	4,893	2,859	1,227	563	244	100	58	25	12	5
Female householder [2]	14,009	5,703	4,081	2,626	1,597	100	41	29	19	11
WHITE FAMILIES [3]										
1990	56,590	29,872	11,186	10,342	5,191	100	53	20	18	9
1995	58,437	30,486	11,491	10,983	5,478	100	52	20	19	9
2000	60,251	32,144	11,496	10,918	5,693	100	53	19	18	9
2005, total	63,222	34,105	11,992	11,243	5,881	100	54	19	18	9
Married couple	50,260	28,121	8,256	9,073	4,810	100	56	16	18	10
Male householder [2]	3,726	2,116	979	450	181	100	57	26	12	5
Female householder [2]	9,236	3,868	2,757	1,720	890	100	42	30	19	10
BLACK FAMILIES [3]										
1990	7,470	3,093	1,894	1,433	1,049	100	41	25	19	14
1995	8,093	3,411	1,971	1,593	1,117	100	42	24	20	14
2000	8,664	3,882	2,101	1,624	1,058	100	45	24	19	12
2005, total	8,904	4,071	2,061	1,647	1,126	100	46	23	18	13
Married couple	4,180	2,145	803	784	448	100	51	19	19	11
Male householder [2]	734	445	169	79	41	100	61	23	11	6
Female householder [2]	3,991	1,482	1,089	784	636	100	37	27	20	16
ASIAN FAMILIES [3]										
2005, total	3,155	1,537	734	650	234	100	49	23	21	7
Married couple	2,560	1,151	605	591	213	100	45	24	23	8
Male householder [2]	248	198	27	17	6	100	80	11	7	2
Female householder [2]	347	188	101	42	15	100	54	29	12	4
HISPANIC FAMILIES [4]										
1990	4,840	1,790	1,095	1,036	919	100	37	23	21	19
1995	6,200	2,216	1,408	1,406	1,171	100	36	23	23	19
2000	7,561	2,747	1,791	1,693	1,330	100	36	24	22	18
2005, total	9,537	3,536	2,135	2,163	1,702	100	37	22	23	18
Married couple	6,367	2,195	1,327	1,604	1,240	100	34	21	25	19
Male householder [2]	930	604	175	104	47	100	65	19	11	5
Female householder [2]	2,240	737	633	455	414	100	33	28	20	18
NON-HISPANIC WHITE FAMILIES [3, 4]										
2005, total	54,383	30,808	10,040	9,267	4,269	100	57	18	17	8
Married couple	44,296	26,060	7,015	7,602	3,618	100	59	16	17	8
Male householder [2]	2,888	1,578	819	354	137	100	55	28	12	5
Female householder [2]	7,200	3,170	2,205	1,311	514	100	44	31	18	7

[1] Includes other races, not shown separately. [2] No spouse present. [3] Beginning with the 2003 Current Population Survey (CPS), respondents could choose more than one race. 2005 data represent persons who selected this race group only and exclude persons reporting more than one race. The CPS prior to 2003 only allowed respondents to report one race group. See also comments on race in the text for this section. [4] Hispanic persons may be of any race.

Source: U.S. Census Bureau, Current Population Reports, P20-537 and earlier reports; and "America's Families and Living Arrangements: 2005"; published 25 May 2006; <http://www.census.gov/population/www/socdemo/hh-fam/cps2005.html>.

Table 67. Families by Size and Presence of Children: 1990 to 2005

[As of March (66,090 represents 66,090,000). See headnote, Table 62]

Characteristic	Number (1,000)				Percent distribution			
	1990	1995	2000	2005	1990	1995	2000	2005
Total	66,090	69,305	72,025	77,010	100	100	100	100
Size of family:								
Two persons	27,606	29,176	31,455	33,888	42	42	44	44
Three persons	15,353	15,903	16,073	17,235	23	23	22	22
Four persons	14,026	14,624	14,496	15,635	21	21	20	20
Five persons	5,938	6,283	6,526	6,699	9	9	9	9
Six persons	1,997	2,106	2,226	2,301	3	3	3	3
Seven or more persons	1,170	1,213	1,249	1,252	2	2	2	2
Own children under age 6:								
None	50,905	53,695	57,039	61,039	77	77	79	79
One	10,304	10,733	10,454	10,919	16	15	15	14
Two or more	4,882	4,876	4,533	5,052	7	7	6	7

Source: U.S. Census Bureau, Current Population Reports, P20-537 and earlier reports; and "America's Families and Living Arrangements: 2005"; published 25 May 2006; <http://www.census.gov/population/www/socdemo/hh-fam/cps2005.html>.

Table 58. Families by Type, Race, and Hispanic Origin: 2005

[In thousands (77,010 represents 77,010,000). As of March. Excludes members of Armed Forces except those living off post or with their families on post. Population controls based on Census 2000 and an expanded sample of households. Based on Current Population Survey, see text of this section and Appendix III]

Characteristic	All families	Married couple families — All races[1]	White[2]	Black[2]	Asian[2]	Hispanic[3]	Non-Hispanic White[2,3]	Female family householder[4] — All races[1]	White[2]	Black[2]	Asian[2]	Hispanic[3]	Non-Hispanic White[2,3]	Male family householder[4], all races
All families	**77,010**	**58,109**	**50,260**	**4,180**	**2,560**	**6,367**	**44,296**	**14,009**	**9,236**	**3,991**	**347**	**2,240**	**7,200**	**4,893**
Age of householder:														
Under 25 years old	3,633	1,411	1,224	104	32	351	898	1,437	869	463	38	286	611	786
25 to 34 years old	13,695	9,577	8,084	738	507	1,824	6,388	2,974	1,778	1,016	62	607	1,234	1,145
35 to 44 years old	18,266	13,652	11,498	1,032	818	1,802	9,800	3,518	2,300	1,035	84	608	1,764	1,095
45 to 54 years old	17,298	13,546	11,684	1,055	572	1,190	10,561	2,812	1,943	713	77	383	1,587	939
55 to 64 years old	11,977	10,051	8,794	747	345	675	8,165	1,467	1,015	361	61	211	814	459
65 to 74 years old	7,108	5,998	5,381	338	199	355	5,050	858	585	235	13	78	508	252
75 years old and over	5,033	3,875	3,595	165	87	171	3,433	943	746	167	11	66	680	215
Without own children under 18	40,491	31,929	28,121	2,145	1,151	2,195	26,060	5,703	3,868	1,482	188	737	3,170	2,859
With own children under 18	36,520	26,180	22,139	2,035	1,409	4,172	18,235	8,305	5,368	2,509	159	1,503	4,030	2,034
One own child under 18	15,194	9,885	8,256	803	605	1,327	7,015	4,081	2,757	1,089	101	633	2,205	1,227
Two own children under 18	13,865	10,676	9,073	784	591	1,604	7,602	2,626	1,720	784	42	455	1,311	563
Three or more own children under 18	7,461	5,619	4,810	448	213	1,240	3,618	1,597	890	636	15	414	514	244
Average per family with own children under 18	1.81	1.86	1.87	1.93	1.72	1.98	1.84	1.72	1.65	1.91	1.47	1.82	1.57	1.50
Age of own children:														
Of any age	47,084	32,227	27,195	2,560	1,763	4,814	22,682	11,945	7,932	3,402	244	1,918	6,195	2,912
Under 25 years	42,101	30,005	25,402	2,342	1,603	4,558	21,137	9,679	6,270	2,905	202	1,702	4,746	2,417
Under 12 years	26,731	19,460	16,441	1,486	1,087	3,373	13,289	5,869	3,714	1,862	97	1,131	2,704	1,401
Under 6 years	15,971	11,905	10,065	881	689	2,244	7,957	3,232	1,991	1,076	54	659	1,392	835
Under 3 years	9,366	7,166	6,112	482	410	1,306	4,868	1,695	1,044	550	27	356	730	504
Under 1 year	3,415	2,595	2,251	173	126	402	1,866	614	393	185	7	136	269	206
Members 65 and older:														
Without members 65 and older	61,700	46,144	39,622	3,482	2,081	5,611	34,366	11,536	7,450	3,421	293	1,976	5,670	4,020
With members 65 and older	15,311	11,966	10,639	698	478	756	9,930	2,473	1,786	570	54	264	1,530	872
Marital status of householder:														
Married, spouse present	58,109	58,109	50,260	4,180	2,560	6,367	44,296	(X)	(X)	(X)	(X)	(X)	(X)	(X)
Married, spouse absent	2,647	(X)	(X)	(X)	(X)	(X)	(X)	2,011	1,341	541	69	527	870	636
Separated	1,854	(X)	(X)	(X)	(X)	(X)	(X)	1,492	1,019	400	41	403	663	362
Other	793	(X)	(X)	(X)	(X)	(X)	(X)	519	322	141	28	124	207	274
Widowed	2,644	(X)	(X)	(X)	(X)	(X)	(X)	2,229	1,664	464	47	251	1,426	415
Divorced	6,454	(X)	(X)	(X)	(X)	(X)	(X)	4,938	3,811	880	111	584	3,266	1,516
Never married	7,156	(X)	(X)	(X)	(X)	(X)	(X)	4,831	2,420	2,106	119	877	1,639	2,325

X Not applicable. [1] Includes other races not shown separately. [2] Beginning with the 2003 Current Population Survey (CPS), respondents could choose more than one race. Data represent persons who selected this race group only and exclude persons reporting more than one race. See also comments on race in the text for this section. [3] Persons of Hispanic origin may be of any race. [4] No spouse present.

Source: U.S. Census Bureau, "America's Families and Living Arrangements: 2005"; published 25 May 2006; <http://www.census.gov/population/www/socdemo/hh-fam/cps2005.html>.

Table 69.

Table 69. Family Households With Own Children Under Age 18 by Type of Family, 1990 to 2005, and by Age of Householder, 2005

[As of March (32,289 represents 32,289,000). Excludes members of Armed Forces except those living off post or with their families on post. Population controls for 2005 based on Census 2000 and an expanded sample of households. Based on Current Population Survey, see text of this section and Appendix III]

Family type	1990	2000	2005 Total	15 to 24 years old	25 to 34 years old	35 to 44 years old	45 to 54 years old	55 to 64 years old	65 years old and over
NUMBER (1,000)									
Family households with children	32,289	34,605	36,520	2,051	10,525	14,665	7,919	1,121	239
Married couple.	24,537	25,248	26,180	850	7,193	10,980	6,101	893	163
Male householder [1]	1,153	1,786	2,034	177	596	706	449	78	29
Female householder [1]	6,599	7,571	8,305	1,024	2,735	2,979	1,369	151	46
HOUSEHOLDS WITH CHILDREN, AS A PERCENT OF ALL FAMILY HOUSEHOLDS BY TYPE									
Family households with children, total ...	49	48	47	56	77	80	46	9	2
Married couple.	47	46	45	60	75	80	45	9	2
Male householder [1]	40	44	42	23	52	64	48	17	6
Female householder [1]	61	60	59	71	92	85	49	10	3

[1] No spouse present.

Source: U.S. Census Bureau, Current Population Reports, P20-537 and earlier reports; and "America's Families and Living Arrangements: 2005"; published 25 May 2006; <http://www.census.gov/population/www/socdemo/hh-fam/cps2005.html>.

Table 70. Nonfamily Households by Sex and Age of Householder: 2005

[In thousands (16,344 represents 16,344,000). As of March. See headnote, Table 69]

Item	Male householder Total	15 to 24 yrs. old	25 to 44 yrs. old	45 to 64 yrs. old	65 yrs. old and over	Female householder Total	15 to 24 yrs. old	25 to 44 yrs. old	45 to 64 yrs. old	65 yrs. old and over
Total	16,344	1,556	6,289	5,398	3,102	19,792	1,497	4,230	6,174	7,890
One person (living alone) . .	12,652	746	4,439	4,565	2,903	17,207	756	3,246	5,518	7,686
Nonrelatives present	3,691	810	1,850	833	199	2,585	741	984	656	204
Never married.	8,160	1,496	4,366	1,814	485	6,354	1,422	2,967	1,458	507
Married [1]	1,534	30	540	635	327	1,209	41	271	555	342
Widowed	1,815	6	37	275	1,495	7,024	5	85	1,085	5,852
Divorced	4,835	23	1,345	2,672	795	5,205	30	907	3,078	1,191

[1] No spouse present.

Source: U.S. Census Bureau, "America's Families and Living Arrangements: 2005"; published 25 May 2006; <http://www.census.gov/population/www/socdemo/hh-fam/cps2005.html>.

Table 71. Persons Living Alone by Sex and Age: 1990 to 2005

[As of March (22,999 represents 22,999,000). Excludes members of Armed Forces except those living off post or with their families on post. Beginning 2004, population controls based on Census 2000 and an expanded sample of households. Based on Current Population Survey, see text of this section and Appendix III]

Sex and age	Number of persons (1,000) 1990	1995	2000	2004	2005	Percent distribution 1990	1995	2000	2004	2005
Both sexes	22,999	24,732	26,724	29,586	29,859	100	100	100	100	100
15 to 24 years old	1,210	1,196	1,144	1,530	1,502	5	5	4	5	5
25 to 34 years old	3,972	3,653	3,848	3,888	3,772	17	15	14	13	13
35 to 44 years old	3,138	3,663	4,109	3,883	3,912	14	15	15	13	13
45 to 64 years old	5,502	6,377	7,842	9,626	10,084	24	26	29	33	34
65 to 74 years old	4,350	4,374	4,091	4,198	4,212	19	18	15	14	14
75 years old and over	4,825	5,470	5,692	6,461	6,378	21	22	21	22	21
Male	9,049	10,140	11,181	12,562	12,652	39	41	42	42	42
15 to 24 years old	674	623	556	769	746	3	3	2	3	2
25 to 34 years old	2,395	2,213	2,279	2,229	2,146	10	9	9	8	7
35 to 44 years old	1,836	2,263	2,569	2,400	2,293	8	9	10	8	8
45 to 64 years old	2,203	2,787	3,422	4,380	4,565	10	11	13	15	15
65 to 74 years old	1,042	1,134	1,108	1,293	1,356	5	5	4	4	5
75 years old and over	901	1,120	1,247	1,491	1,547	4	5	5	5	5
Female	13,950	14,592	15,543	17,024	17,207	61	59	58	58	58
15 to 24 years old	536	572	588	762	756	2	2	2	3	3
25 to 34 years old	1,578	1,440	1,568	1,660	1,626	7	6	6	6	5
35 to 44 years old	1,303	1,399	1,540	1,482	1,626	6	6	6	5	5
45 to 64 years old	3,300	3,589	4,420	5,246	5,518	14	15	17	18	18
65 to 74 years old	3,309	3,240	2,983	2,904	2,856	14	13	11	10	10
75 years old and over	3,924	4,351	4,444	4,970	4,830	17	18	17	17	16

Source: U.S. Census Bureau, Current Population Reports, P20-553 and earlier reports; and "Families and Living Arrangements"; <http://www.census.gov/population/www/socdemo/hh-fam.html>.

Table 72. Population in Group Quarters by State: 2000 and 2005

[In thousands (7,780 represents 7,780,000). 2000, as of April; 2005, as of July. For definition of group quarters, see text, this section]

State	2000	2005	State	2000	2005	State	2000	2005
U.S.	7,780	8,032	KS	82	82	ND	24	27
AL	115	115	KY	115	115			
AK	19	22	LA	136	134	OH	299	308
AZ	110	109	ME	35	38	OK	112	114
AR	74	78				OR	77	81
CA	820	853	MD	134	139	PA	433	450
CO	103	103	MA	221	216	RI	39	44
CT	108	116	MI	250	255			
DE	25	25	MN	136	143	SC	135	141
DC	36	35	MS	95	97	SD	28	30
FL	389	407	MO	164	168	TN	148	152
			MT	25	25	TX	561	590
GA	234	251	NE	51	52	UT	40	42
HI	36	37	NV	34	34			
ID	31	33	NH	36	37	VT	21	21
IL	322	323	NJ	195	196	VA	231	235
IN	178	179	NM	36	41	WA	136	141
			NY	581	599	WV	43	45
IA	104	104	NC	254	272	WI	156	160
						WY	14	14

Source: U.S. Census Bureau, "County Population Estimates and Estimated Components of Change: April 1, 2000 to July 1, 2005;" published March 16, 2006; <http://www.census.gov/popest/datasets.html>.

Table 73. Self-Described Religious Identification of Adult Population: 1990 and 2001

[In thousands (175,440 represents 175,440,000). The American Religious Identification Survey (ARIS) 2001 was based on a random digit-dialed telephone survey of 50,281 American residential households in the continental U.S.A. (48 states). Respondents were asked to describe themselves in terms of religion with an open-ended question. Interviewers did not prompt or offer a suggested list of potential answers. Moreover, the self-description of respondents was not based on whether established religious bodies, institutions, churches, mosques, or synagogues considered them to be members. Quite the contrary, the survey sought to determine whether the respondents themselves regarded themselves as adherents of a religious community. Subjective rather than objective standards of religious identification were tapped by the surveys]

Religious group	1990	2001	Religious group	1990	2001
Adult population, total [1]	**175,440**	**207,980**	Fundamentalist	27	61
			Salvation Army	27	25
Total Christian	151,496	159,506	Independent Christian Church	25	71
Catholic	46,004	50,873			
Baptist	33,964	33,830	Total other religions	5,853	7,740
Protestant-no denomination supplied	17,214	4,647	Jewish	3,137	2,831
Methodist/Wesleyan	14,174	14,150	Muslim/Islamic	527	1,104
Lutheran	9,110	9,580	Buddhist	401	1,082
Christian-no denomination supplied	8,073	14,150	Unitarian/Universalist	502	629
Presbyterian	4,985	5,596	Hindu	227	766
Pentecostal/Charismatic	3,191	4,407	Native American	47	103
Episcopalian/Anglican	3,042	3,451	Scientologist	45	55
Mormon/Latter-Day Saints	2,487	2,787	Baha'i	28	84
Churches of Christ	1,769	2,593	Taoist	23	40
Jehovah's Witness	1,381	1,331	New Age	20	68
Seventh-Day Adventist	668	724	Eckankar	18	26
Assemblies of God	660	1,106	Rastafarian	14	11
Holiness/Holy	610	569	Sikh	13	57
Congregational/United Church of Christ	599	1,378	Deity	8	134
Church of the Nazarene	549	544	Druid	6	49
Church of God	531	944	Santeria	(NA)	33
Orthodox (Eastern)	502	645	Pagan	(NA)	22
Evangelical [2]	242	1,032	Spiritualist	(NA)	140
Mennonite	235	346	Ethical Culture	(NA)	116
Christian Science	214	194	Other unclassified	837	386
Church of the Brethren	206	358			
Born Again [2]	204	56	No religion specified, total	14,331	29,481
Nondenominational [2]	195	2,489	Atheist	(NA)	902
Disciples of Christ	144	492	Agnostic	1,186	991
Reformed/Dutch Reform	161	289	Humanist	29	49
Apostolic/New Apostolic	117	254	Secular	(NA)	53
Quaker	67	217	No religion	13,116	27,486
Full Gospel	51	168			
Christian Reform	40	79	Refused to reply to question	4,031	11,246
Foursquare Gospel	28	70			

NA Not available. [1] Refers to the total number of adults in all fifty states. All other figures are based on projections from surveys conducted in the continental United States (48 states). [2] Because of the subjective nature of replies to open-ended questions, these categories are the most unstable as they do not refer to clearly identifiable denominations as much as underlying feelings about religion. Thus they may be the most subject to fluctuation over time.

Source: 1990 data, Barry A. Kosmin and Seymour P. Lachman, "One Nation Under God: Religion in Contemporary American Society", 1993; 2001 data, Barry A. Kosmin and Ariela Keysar, Institute for the Study of Secularism in Society and Culture, Trinity College, Hartford, CT, <http://www.trincoll.edu/secularisminstitute> (Copyright).

Population   59

Table 74. **Religious Bodies—Selected Data**

[**Membership data: 2,500 represents 2,500,000.** Includes the self-reported membership of religious bodies with 750,000 or more as reported to the *Yearbook of American and Canadian Churches*. Groups may be excluded if they do not supply information. The data are not standardized so comparisons between groups are difficult. The definition of "church member" is determined by the religious body]

Religious body	Year reported	Churches reported	Membership (1,000)
African Methodist Episcopal Church.	1999	4,174	2,500
African Methodist Episcopal Zion Church, The.	2004	3,251	1,436
American Baptist Churches in the U.S.A.	2004	5,793	1,425
Assemblies of God.	2004	12,277	2,779
Baptist Bible Fellowship International	2003	4,500	1,200
Catholic Church, The	2004	19,297	67,821
Christian Churches and Churches of Christ.	1988	5,579	1,072
Christian Methodist Episcopal Church	2002	3,300	850
Church of God (Cleveland, Tennessee)	2004	6,511	990
Church of God in Christ, The	1991	15,300	5,500
Church of Jesus Christ of Latter-day Saints, The	2004	12,463	5,599
Churches of Christ	1999	15,000	1,500
Episcopal Church.	2003	7,220	2,284
Evangelical Lutheran Church in America.	2004	10,585	4,930
Greek Orthodox Archdiocese of America	2004	563	1,500
Jehovah's Witnesses	2004	12,317	1,030
Lutheran Church—Missouri Synod (LCMS), The	2004	6,151	2,464
National Baptist Convention of America, Inc.	2000	(NA)	3,500
National Baptist Convention, U.S.A., Inc.	(NA)	9,000	5,000
National Missionary Baptist Convention of America.	1992	(NA)	2,500
Orthodox Church in America, The	2004	737	1,064
Pentecostal Assemblies of the World, Inc..	1998	1,750	1,500
Presbyterian Church (U.S.A.)	2004	11,019	3,190
Progressive National Baptist Convention, Inc.	1995	2,000	2,500
Seventh-day Adventist Church	2003	4,683	935
Southern Baptist Convention	2004	43,465	16,267
United Church of Christ.	2004	5,682	1,266
United Methodist Church, The	2003	34,892	8,186

NA Not available.

Source: National Council of Churches, New York, NY, *2006 Yearbook of American & Canadian Churches*, annual (copyright). (For more church-related information visit <http://www.ncccusa.org> or call 888-870-3325).

Table 75. **Christian Church Adherents, 2000, and Jewish Population, 2003—States**

[**133,377 represents 133,377,000.** Christian church adherents were defined as "all members, including full members, their children and the estimated number of other regular participants who are not considered as communicant, confirmed or full members." The Jewish population includes Jews who define themselves as Jewish by religion as well as those who define themselves as Jewish in cultural terms. Data on Jewish population are based primarily on a compilation of individual estimates made by local Jewish federations. Additionally, most large communities have completed Jewish demographic surveys from which the Jewish population can be determined]

State	Christian adherents 2000		Jewish population 2003		State	Christian adherents 2000		Jewish population 2003	
	Number (1,000)	Percent of population [1]	Number (1,000)	Percent of population [1]		Number (1,000)	Percent of population [1]	Number (1,000)	Percent of population [1]
U.S.	133,377	47.4	6,155	2.2	MO	2,813	50.3	63	1.1
AL	2,418	54.4	9	0.2	MT.	401	44.4	1	0.1
AK	210	33.6	3	0.5	NE.	995	58.2	7	0.4
AZ	1,946	37.9	82	1.6	NV	604	30.2	77	3.8
AR	1,516	56.7	2	0.1	NH.	571	46.2	10	0.8
CA	14,328	42.3	999	2.9	NJ	4,262	50.7	485	5.8
CO	1,604	37.3	73	1.7	NM.	1,041	57.2	12	0.6
CT	1,828	53.7	111	3.3	NY	9,569	50.4	1,657	8.7
DE	299	38.2	14	1.7	NC	3,598	44.7	26	0.3
DC.	331	57.8	26	4.5	ND.	468	72.9	(Z)	0.1
FL	5,904	36.9	620	3.9	OH.	4,912	43.3	149	1.3
GA	3,528	43.1	94	1.1	OK.	2,079	60.3	5	0.1
HI	431	35.6	7	0.6	OR.	1,029	30.1	32	0.9
ID	624	48.3	1	0.1	PA	6,751	55.0	282	2.3
IL	6,457	52.0	270	2.2	RI	646	61.7	16	1.5
IN	2,578	42.4	18	0.3	SC.	1,874	46.7	11	0.3
IA	1,698	58.0	6	0.2	SD.	510	67.6	(Z)	(Z)
KS	1,307	48.6	14	0.5	TN	2,867	50.4	18	0.3
KY	2,141	53.0	12	0.3	TX	11,316	54.3	131	0.6
LA	2,599	58.2	16	0.4	UT.	1,659	74.3	5	0.2
ME.	450	35.3	9	0.7	VT.	230	37.8	6	0.9
MD.	2,012	38.0	213	4.0	VA	2,807	39.7	66	0.9
MA	3,725	58.7	275	4.3	WA	1,872	31.8	43	0.7
MI	3,970	39.9	110	1.1	WV	646	35.7	2	0.1
MN.	2,974	60.5	42	0.9	WI	3,198	59.6	28	0.5
MS.	1,549	54.5	1	0.1	WY	229	46.4	(Z)	0.1

Z Fewer than 500 or .05 percent. [1] Based on U.S. Census Bureau data for resident population enumerated as of April 1, 2000, and estimated as of July 1, 2003.

Source: Christian church adherents—Dale E. Jones, Sherri Doty, Clifford Grammich, James E. Horsch, Richard Houseal, John P. Marcum, Kenneth M. Sanchagrin, and Richard H. Taylor, *Religious Congregations and Membership in the United States: 2000,* Glenmary Research Center, Nashville, TN <www.glenmary.org/grc>, 2002 (copyright); Jewish population—American Jewish Committee, New York, NY, *American Jewish Year Book* (copyright).

Section 2
Vital Statistics

This section presents vital statistics data on births, deaths, abortions, fetal deaths, fertility, life expectancy, marriages, and divorces. Vital statistics are compiled for the country as a whole by the National Center for Health Statistics (NCHS) and published in its annual report, *Vital Statistics of the United States*, in certain reports of the *Vital and Health Statistics* series, and in the *National Vital Statistics Reports* (formerly *Monthly Vital Statistics Report*). Reports in this field are also issued by the various state bureaus of vital statistics. Data on fertility, on age of persons at first marriage, and on marital status and marital history are compiled by the U.S. Census Bureau from its Current Population Survey (CPS; see text, Section 1) and published in *Current Population Reports,* P20 Series. Data on abortions are published by the Alan Guttmacher Institute, New York, NY, in selected issues of *Perspectives on Sexual and Reproductive Health* online at <www.agi-usa.org/sections/abortion.php>.

Registration of vital events—The registration of births, deaths, fetal deaths, and other vital events in the United States is primarily a state and local function. The civil laws of every state provide for a continuous and permanent birth- and death-registration system. Many states also provide for marriage- and divorce-registration systems. Vital events occurring to U.S. residents outside the United States are not included in the data.

Births and deaths—The live-birth, death, and fetal-death statistics prepared by NCHS are based on vital records filed in the registration offices of all states, New York City, and the District of Columbia. The annual collection of death statistics on a national basis began in 1900 with a national death-registration area of ten states and the District of Columbia; a similar annual collection of birth statistics for a national birth-registration area began in 1915, also with ten reporting states and the District of Columbia. Since 1933, the birth- and death-registration areas have comprised the entire United States, including Alaska (beginning 1959) and Hawaii (beginning 1960). National statistics on fetal deaths were first compiled for 1918 and annually since 1922.

Prior to 1951, birth statistics came from a complete count of records received in the Public Health Service (now received in NCHS). From 1951 through 1971, they were based on a 50-percent sample of all registered births (except for a complete count in 1955 and a 20- to 50-percent sample in 1967). Beginning in 1972, they have been based on a complete count for states participating in the Vital Statistics Cooperative Program (VSCP) (for details, see the technical appendix in *Vital Statistics of the United States*) and on a 50-percent sample of all other areas. Beginning in 1986, all reporting areas participated in the VSCP. Mortality data have been based on a complete count of records for each area (except for a 50-percent sample in 1972). Beginning in 1970, births to and deaths of nonresident aliens of the United States and U.S. citizens outside the United States have been excluded from the data. Fetal deaths and deaths among Armed Forces abroad are excluded. Data based on samples are subject to sampling error; for details, see annual issues of *Vital Statistics of the United States*.

Mortality statistics by cause of death are compiled in accordance with World Health Organization regulations according to the *International Classification of Diseases* (ICD). The ICD is revised approximately every 10 years. The tenth revision of the ICD was employed beginning in 1999. Deaths for prior years were classified according to the revision of the ICD in use at the time. Each revision of the ICD introduces a number of discontinuities in mortality statistics; for a discussion of those between the ninth and tenth revisions of the ICD, see *National Vital Statistics Reports*, Vol. 49, Nos. 2 and 8. Preliminary mortality data are based on a percentage of death records weighted up to the total number of deaths reported for the given year; for a discussion of preliminary data, see *National Vital Statistics Reports*, Vol. 49, No. 3. Information on tests of statistical significance, differences between death rates, and standard errors can also be found in the reports mentioned above.

Some of the tables present age-adjusted death rates in addition to crude death rates. Age-adjusted death rates shown in this section were prepared using the direct method, in which age-specific death rates for a population of interest are applied to a standard population distributed by age. Age adjustment eliminates the differences in observed rates between points in time or among compared population groups that result from age differences in population composition.

Fertility and life expectancy—The total fertility rate, defined as the number of births that 1,000 women would have in their lifetime if, at each year of age, they experienced the birth rates occurring in the specified year, is compiled and published by NCHS. Other data relating to social and medical factors that affect fertility rates, such as contraceptive use and birth expectations, are collected and made available by both NCHS and the Census Bureau. NCHS figures are based on information in birth and fetal death certificates and on the periodic National Surveys of Family Growth; Census Bureau data are based on decennial censuses and the CPS.

Data on life expectancy, the average remaining lifetime in years for persons who attain a given age, are computed and published by NCHS. For details, see *National Vital Statistics Reports*, Vol. 52, No. 3.

Marriage and divorce—The compilation of nationwide statistics on marriages and divorces in the United States began in 1887–88, when the National Office of Vital Statistics prepared estimates for the years 1867–86. Although periodic updates took place after 1888, marriage and divorce statistics were not collected and published annually until 1944 by that office. In 1957 and 1958 respectively, the same office established marriage- and divorce-registration areas. Beginning in 1957, the marriage-registration area comprised 30 states, plus Alaska, Hawaii,

Puerto Rico, and the Virgin Islands; it currently includes 42 states and the District of Columbia. The divorce-registration area, starting in 1958 with 14 states, Alaska, Hawaii, and the Virgin Islands, currently includes a total of 31 states and the Virgin Islands. Procedures for estimating the number of marriages and divorces in the registration states are discussed in *Vital Statistics of the United States*, Vol. III—Marriage and Divorce. Total counts of events for registration and nonregistration states are gathered by collecting already summarized data on marriages and divorces reported by state offices of vital statistics and by county offices of registration. The collection and publication of detailed marriage and divorce statistics (for example: by age and race) was suspended beginning in January 1996. For additional information, contact the National Center for Health Statistics online at <http://www.cdc.gov/nchs /datawh/datasite/frnotice.htm>.

Vital statistics rates—Except as noted, vital statistics rates computed by NCHS are based on decennial census population figures as of April 1 for 1940, 1950, 1960, 1970, 1980, 1990, and 2000; and on midyear population figures for other years, as estimated by the Census Bureau (see text, Section 1).

Race—Data by race for births, deaths, marriages, and divorces from NCHS are based on information contained in the certificates of registration. The Census Bureau's Current Population Survey obtains information on race by asking respondents to classify their race as (1) White, (2) Black, (3) American Indian or Alaska Native, (4) Native Hawaiian or other Pacific Islander, and (5) Asian.

Beginning with the 1989 data year, NCHS is tabulating its birth data primarily by race of the mother. In 1988 and prior years, births were tabulated by race of the child, which was determined from the race of the parents as entered on the birth certificate.

Trend data by race shown in this section are by race of mother beginning with the 1980 data. Hispanic origin of the mother is reported and tabulated independently of race. Thus, persons of Hispanic origin may be any race. In 1994, 91 percent of women of Hispanic origin were reported as White.

Table 76. **Live Births, Deaths, Marriages, and Divorces: 1950 to 2004**

[**3,632 represents 3,632,000.** Prior to 1960, excludes Alaska and Hawaii. Beginning 1970, excludes births to, and deaths of, non-residents of the United States. See Appendix III]

Year	Number (1,000)					Rate per 1,000 population				
	Births [1]	Deaths		Marriages [3]	Divorces [4]	Births [1]	Deaths		Marriages [3]	Divorces [4]
		Total	Infant [2]				Total	Infant [2]		
1950	3,632	1,452	104	1,667	385	24.1	9.6	29.2	11.1	2.6
1955	4,097	1,529	107	1,531	377	25.0	9.3	26.4	9.3	2.3
1960	4,258	1,712	111	1,523	393	23.7	9.5	26.0	8.5	2.2
1965	3,760	1,828	93	1,800	479	19.4	9.4	24.7	9.3	2.5
1970	3,731	1,921	75	2,159	708	18.4	9.5	20.0	10.6	3.5
1975	3,144	1,893	51	2,153	1,036	14.6	8.8	16.1	10.0	4.8
1976	3,168	1,909	48	2,155	1,083	14.6	8.8	15.2	9.9	5.0
1977	3,327	1,900	47	2,178	1,091	15.1	8.6	14.1	9.9	5.0
1978	3,333	1,928	46	2,282	1,130	15.0	8.7	13.8	10.3	5.1
1979	3,494	1,914	46	2,331	1,181	15.6	8.5	13.1	10.4	5.3
1980	3,612	1,990	46	2,390	1,189	15.9	8.8	12.6	10.6	5.2
1981	3,629	1,978	43	2,422	1,213	15.8	8.6	11.9	10.6	5.3
1982	3,681	1,975	42	2,456	1,170	15.9	8.5	11.5	10.6	5.1
1983	3,639	2,019	41	2,446	1,158	15.6	8.6	11.2	10.5	5.0
1984	3,669	2,039	40	2,477	1,169	15.6	8.6	10.8	10.5	5.0
1985	3,761	2,086	40	2,413	1,190	15.8	8.8	10.6	10.1	5.0
1986	3,757	2,105	39	2,407	1,178	15.6	8.8	10.4	10.0	4.9
1987	3,809	2,123	38	2,403	1,166	15.7	8.8	10.1	9.9	4.8
1988	3,910	2,168	39	2,396	1,167	16.0	8.9	10.0	9.8	4.8
1989	4,041	2,150	40	2,403	1,157	16.4	8.7	9.8	9.7	4.7
1990	4,158	2,148	38	2,443	1,182	16.7	8.6	9.2	9.8	4.7
1991	4,111	2,170	37	2,371	1,187	16.2	8.6	8.9	9.4	4.7
1992	4,065	2,176	35	2,362	1,215	15.8	8.5	8.5	9.3	4.8
1993	4,000	2,269	33	2,334	1,187	15.4	8.8	8.4	9.0	4.6
1994	3,953	2,279	31	2,362	1,191	15.0	8.8	8.0	9.1	4.6
1995	3,900	2,312	30	2,336	1,169	14.6	8.7	7.6	8.9	4.4
1996	3,891	2,315	28	2,344	1,150	14.4	8.6	7.3	8.8	4.3
1997	3,881	2,314	28	2,384	1,163	14.2	8.5	7.2	8.9	4.3
1998 [5] . .	3,942	2,337	28	2,244	1,135	14.3	8.5	7.2	8.4	4.2
1999 [5] . .	3,959	2,391	28	2,358	(NA)	14.2	8.6	7.1	8.6	4.1
2000 [5] . .	4,059	2,403	28	2,329	(NA)	14.4	8.5	6.9	8.3	4.1
2001 [5] . .	4,026	2,416	28	2,345	(NA)	14.1	8.5	6.8	8.2	4.0
2002 [6] . .	4,022	2,443	28	2,254	(NA)	13.9	8.5	7.0	7.8	3.9
2003 [6] . .	4,090	2,448	28	2,245	(NA)	14.1	8.4	6.9	7.7	3.8
2004 [6, 7]. .	4,116	2,398	28	2,279	(NA)	14.0	8.2	6.8	7.8	3.7

NA Not available. [1] Prior to 1960, data adjusted for underregistration. [2] Infants under 1 year, excluding fetal deaths; rates per 1,000 registered live births. [3] Includes estimates for some states through 1965 and also for 1976 and 1977 and marriage licenses for some states for all years except 1973 and 1975. Beginning 1978, includes nonlicensed marriages in California. [4] Includes reported annulments and some estimated state figures for all years. [5] Divorce rate excludes data for California, Colorado, Indiana, and Louisiana; population for this rate also excludes these states. [6] Divorce rates exclude data for California, Georgia, Hawaii, Indiana, and Louisiana, in 2004; California, Hawaii, Indiana, and Oklahoma in 2003; and California, Indiana, and Oklahoma in 2002. Populations for these rates also exclude these states. [7] Births and deaths are based on preliminary data.

Source: U.S. National Center for Health Statistics, *Vital Statistics of the United States*, annual; *National Vital Statistics Reports (NVSR)* and unpublished data.

Table 77. **Live Births, Birth Rates, and Fertility Rates by Hispanic Origin Status: 1990 to 2003**

[**4,093 represents 4,093,000.** Represents registered births. Excludes births to nonresidents of the United States. Data are based on Hispanic origin and race of mother. Persons of Hispanic origin may be any race. See Appendix III]

Hispanic origin status and race of mother	Number of births (1,000)				Birthrate per 1,000 population				Fertility rate [2]			
	1990 [1]	2000	2002	2003	1990 [1]	2000	2002	2003	1990 [1]	2000	2002	2003
Total [3]	4,093	4,059	4,022	4,090	16.7	14.4	13.9	14.1	71.0	65.9	64.8	66.1
Hispanic origin	595	816	877	912	26.7	23.1	22.6	22.9	107.7	95.9	94.4	96.9
Mexican	386	582	628	655	28.7	25.0	24.2	24.7	118.9	105.1	102.8	105.5
Puerto Rican	59	58	57	58	21.6	18.1	16.5	15.1	82.9	73.5	65.4	61.6
Cuban	11	13	14	15	10.9	9.7	10.0	9.9	52.6	49.3	59.0	61.7
Central and South American [4]	83	113	126	136	27.5	21.8	22.4	23.0	102.7	85.1	86.1	91.2
Other and unknown Hispanic	56	49	51	49	([4])	([4])	([4])	([4])	([4])	([4])	([4])	([4])
Non-Hispanic [5]	3,457	3,200	3,120	3,149	15.7	13.2	12.6	12.7	67.1	61.1	59.6	60.5
White	2,627	2,363	2,298	2,322	14.4	12.2	11.7	11.8	62.8	58.5	57.4	58.5
Black	662	604	578	576	23.0	17.3	16.1	15.9	89.0	71.4	67.4	67.1

[1] Excludes data for New Hampshire and Oklahoma, which did not report Hispanic origin. [2] Live births per 1,000 women age 15 to 44 years in specified group. [3] Includes status of Hispanic origin not stated. [4] Rates for the Central and South American population include other and unknown Hispanic. [5] Includes other races not shown separately.

Source: U.S. National Center for Health Statistics; *National Vital Statistics Reports (NVSR)*, vol. 54, No. 2, September 8, 2005.

Vital Statistics 63

Table 78. Births and Birth Rates by Race, Sex, and Age: 1980 to 2004

[**Births in thousands (3,612 represents 3,612,000).** Births by race of mother. Excludes births to nonresidents of the United States. For population bases used to derive these data, see text this section, and Appendix III]

Item	1980	1985	1990	1995	1998	1999	2000	2001	2002	2003	2004, prel.
Live births [1]	3,612	3,761	4,158	3,900	3,942	3,959	4,059	4,026	4,022	4,090	4,116
White	2,936	3,038	3,290	3,099	3,119	3,133	3,194	3,178	3,175	3,226	3,230
Black	568	582	684	603	610	606	623	606	594	600	612
American Indian, Eskimo, Aleut	29	34	39	37	40	41	42	42	42	43	44
Asian or Pacific Islander	74	105	142	160	173	182	201	200	211	221	229
Male	1,853	1,928	2,129	1,996	2,016	2,027	2,077	2,058	2,058	2,094	(NA)
Female	1,760	1,833	2,029	1,903	1,925	1,933	1,982	1,968	1,964	1,996	(NA)
Males per 100 females	105	105	105	105	105	105	105	105	105	105	(NA)
Age of mother:											
Under 20 years old	562	478	533	512	494	485	478	454	433	421	422
20 to 24 years old	1,226	1,141	1,094	966	965	982	1,018	1,022	1,022	1,032	1,035
25 to 29 years old	1,108	1,201	1,277	1,064	1,083	1,078	1,088	1,058	1,060	1,086	1,105
30 to 34 years old	550	696	886	905	889	892	929	943	951	976	967
35 to 39 years old	141	214	318	384	425	434	452	452	454	468	476
40 to 44 years old	(NA)	(NA)	(NA)	(NA)	81	83	90	93	96	101	104
45 to 49 years old	(NA)	(NA)	(NA)	(NA)	4	4	4	5	5	6	6
Birth rate per 1,000 population	**15.9**	**15.8**	**16.7**	**14.6**	**14.3**	**14.2**	**14.4**	**14.1**	**13.9**	**14.1**	**14.0**
White	15.1	15.0	15.8	14.1	13.8	13.7	13.9	13.7	13.5	13.6	(NA)
Black	21.3	20.4	22.4	17.8	17.1	16.8	17.0	16.3	15.7	15.7	(NA)
American Indian, Eskimo, Aleut	20.7	19.8	18.9	15.3	14.8	14.2	14.0	13.7	13.8	13.8	14.0
Asian or Pacific Islander	19.9	18.7	19.0	16.7	15.9	15.9	17.1	16.4	16.5	16.8	16.8
Age of mother:											
10 to 14 years old	1.1	1.2	1.4	1.3	1.0	0.9	0.9	0.8	0.7	0.6	0.7
15 to 19 years old	53.0	51.0	59.9	56.0	50.3	48.8	47.7	45.3	43.0	41.6	41.2
20 to 24 years old	115.1	108.3	116.5	107.5	108.4	107.9	109.7	106.2	103.6	102.6	101.8
25 to 29 years old	112.9	111.0	120.2	108.8	110.2	111.2	113.5	113.4	113.6	115.6	115.5
30 to 34 years old	61.9	69.1	80.8	81.1	85.2	87.1	91.2	91.9	91.5	95.1	95.5
35 to 39 years old	19.8	24.0	31.7	34.0	36.9	37.8	39.7	40.6	41.4	43.8	45.4
40 to 44 years old	3.9	4.0	5.5	6.6	7.4	7.4	8.0	8.1	8.3	8.7	9.0
45 to 49 years old [2]	0.2	0.2	0.2	0.3	0.4	0.4	0.5	0.5	0.5	0.5	0.6
Fertility rate per 1,000 women [3]	**68.4**	**66.2**	**70.9**	**64.6**	**64.3**	**64.4**	**65.9**	**65.3**	**64.8**	**66.1**	**66.3**
White [3]	65.6	64.1	68.3	63.6	63.6	64.0	65.3	65.0	64.8	66.1	66.2
Black [3]	84.9	78.8	84.8	71.0	69.4	68.5	70.0	67.6	65.8	66.3	67.2
American Indian, Eskimo, Aleut [3]	82.7	78.6	76.2	63.0	61.3	59.0	58.7	58.1	58.0	58.4	58.9
Asian or Pacific Islander [3]	73.2	68.4	69.6	62.6	60.1	60.9	65.8	64.2	64.1	66.3	67.2

NA Not available. [1] Includes other races not shown separately. [2] Beginning 1998, rates computed by relating births to women age 45 to 54 years to women 45 to 49 years old. [3] Number of live births per 1,000 women, 15 to 44 years old in specified group.

Source: U.S. National Center for Health Statistics, *Vital Statistics of the United States,* annual; *National Vital Statistics Reports (NVSR)*; and unpublished data.

Table 79. Live Births and Ratios by Plurality of Birth and Race of Mother: 1995 to 2003

[See Appendix III]

Plurality and race of mother	1995	1999	2000	2001	2002	2003
NUMBER						
Live births, total [1]	3,899,589	3,959,417	4,058,814	4,025,933	4,021,726	4,089,950
White	3,098,885	3,132,501	3,194,005	3,177,626	3,174,760	3,225,848
Black	603,139	605,970	622,598	606,156	593,691	599,847
Live births in single deliveries [1]	3,797,880	3,837,789	3,932,573	3,897,216	3,889,191	3,953,622
White	3,018,184	3,035,757	3,094,249	3,075,683	3,069,915	3,117,818
Black	585,787	586,027	601,451	585,189	572,659	578,564
Live births in twin deliveries [1]	96,736	114,307	118,916	121,246	125,134	128,665
White	76,196	90,191	93,235	95,315	98,304	101,297
Black	17,000	19,374	20,626	20,414	20,423	20,633
Live births in higher-order multiple deliveries [1,2]	4,973	7,321	7,325	7,471	7,401	7,663
White	4,505	6,553	6,551	6,628	6,541	6,733
Black	352	569	521	553	609	650
RATIO PER 1,000 LIVE BIRTHS						
All multiple births [1]	26.1	30.7	31.1	32.0	33.0	33.3
White	26.0	30.9	31.2	32.1	33.0	33.5
Black	28.8	32.9	34.0	34.6	35.4	35.5
Twin births [1]	24.8	28.9	29.3	30.1	31.1	31.5
White	24.6	28.8	29.2	30.0	31.0	31.4
Black	28.2	32.0	33.1	33.7	34.4	34.4
RATIO PER 100,000 LIVE BIRTHS						
Higher-order multiple births [1,2]	127.5	184.9	180.5	185.6	184.0	187.4
White	145.4	209.2	205.1	208.6	206.0	208.7
Black	58.4	93.9	83.7	91.2	102.6	108.4

[1] Includes races other than White and Black. [2] Births in greater than twin deliveries.

Source: U.S. National Center for Health Statistics, *National Vital Statistics Reports (NVSR)*.

Table 80. **Live Births by State and Island Areas: 2004**

[Number of births, except rate. Registered births. Excludes births to nonresidents of the United States. By race and Hispanic origin of mother. Data are preliminary. See Appendix III]

State and Island Area	All races [1]	White	Black	Asian or Pacific Islander	American Indian, Eskimo, Aleut	Hispanic [2]	Birth rate [3]	Fertility rate [4]
United States.	**4,115,590**	**3,229,814**	**612,493**	**229,352**	**43,931**	**944,993**	**14.0**	**66.3**
Alabama.	59,549	40,550	18,057	762	179	3,346	13.1	62.5
Alaska	10,338	6,588	397	765	2,588	877	15.8	74.4
Arizona.	93,672	81,171	3,426	2,801	6,274	41,427	16.3	79.5
Arkansas	38,602	30,363	7,396	598	245	3,510	14.0	68.4
California	545,071	441,315	32,106	68,749	2,902	275,365	15.2	70.4
Colorado.	68,520	62,514	2,929	2,480	597	21,746	14.9	68.8
Connecticut.	42,099	34,454	5,279	2,116	250	7,598	12.0	58.8
Delaware	11,299	7,919	2,895	452	33	1,519	13.6	63.4
District of Columbia	7,932	2,302	5,392	229	9	998	14.3	58.2
Florida	218,034	157,701	52,758	6,834	740	55,407	12.5	64.1
Georgia	138,851	89,771	44,001	4,804	275	20,113	15.7	70.1
Hawaii	18,280	5,177	573	12,463	67	2,679	14.5	74.0
Idaho	22,527	21,710	109	309	399	3,241	16.2	77.2
Illinois	180,934	140,867	30,874	8,903	289	42,608	14.2	66.7
Indiana	86,733	75,418	9,655	1,543	116	7,257	13.9	66.7
Iowa	38,439	35,727	1,478	983	251	2,835	13.0	63.8
Kansas	39,581	35,089	2,837	1,156	498	5,472	14.5	69.6
Kentucky	54,451	48,665	4,878	813	95	2,177	13.1	62.2
Louisiana	65,399	37,144	26,732	1,096	426	1,954	14.5	66.7
Maine.	13,945	13,382	225	222	116	180	10.6	52.4
Maryland	74,605	43,909	25,721	4,806	169	7,637	13.4	62.3
Massachusetts.	78,566	64,031	8,720	5,650	165	9,847	12.2	56.5
Michigan.	129,768	102,802	21,705	4,580	681	7,826	12.8	61.4
Minnesota.	70,615	59,565	4,646	4,710	1,693	5,330	13.8	64.5
Mississippi	42,810	23,558	18,516	431	304	1,052	14.7	68.3
Missouri	77,780	64,152	11,455	1,790	383	3,844	13.5	64.3
Montana.	11,525	9,827	53	125	1,520	374	12.4	62.8
Nebraska	26,331	23,703	1,573	606	449	3,446	15.1	72.6
Nevada	35,188	29,032	2,958	2,666	532	13,060	15.1	72.6
New Hampshire	14,566	13,767	256	519	24	461	11.2	53.4
New Jersey.	114,916	84,139	19,730	10,875	172	27,312	13.2	64.0
New Mexico	28,386	23,856	502	410	3,618	15,163	14.9	71.9
New York	250,894	178,771	49,765	21,662	696	57,081	13.0	60.9
North Carolina	119,851	87,414	27,623	3,237	1,577	17,295	14.0	66.0
North Dakota.	8,189	7,017	96	101	975	167	12.9	63.2
Ohio	149,154	121,516	23,910	3,418	312	5,737	13.0	62.8
Oklahoma.	51,283	40,042	4,705	1,134	5,401	6,007	14.6	70.2
Oregon.	45,693	41,251	1,057	2,510	875	8,836	12.7	61.8
Pennsylvania.	145,768	117,754	22,081	5,597	337	11,686	11.7	58.5
Rhode Island.	12,778	10,874	1,196	544	164	2,429	11.8	55.0
South Carolina.	56,592	35,789	19,613	970	220	4,334	13.5	63.6
South Dakota	11,340	9,199	147	120	1,874	395	14.7	72.4
Tennessee	79,641	60,406	17,401	1,671	163	5,838	13.5	63.4
Texas.	384,389	327,511	42,422	13,587	869	189,586	17.1	78.0
Utah	50,669	48,256	299	1,454	660	7,180	21.2	92.3
Vermont	6,565	6,383	58	112	12	75	10.6	51.8
Virginia.	103,915	73,953	22,899	6,911	151	11,691	13.9	65.0
Washington.	81,740	67,157	4,059	8,385	2,139	14,254	13.2	61.7
West Virginia.	20,855	19,992	673	170	19	151	11.5	58.3
Wisconsin.	70,154	59,998	6,601	2,446	1,109	5,888	12.7	60.7
Wyoming	6,807	6,359	55	75	318	699	13.4	66.5
Puerto Rico	51,099	46,325	4,753	(NA)	(NA)	(NA)	13.1	59.8
Virgin Islands	1,413	281	1,060	1	71	258	13.0	62.6
Guam	3,419	273	32	3,108	6	51	20.6	92.1
American Samoa	1,714	4	–	1,710	–	(NA)	29.6	132.4
Northern Marianas . . .	1,358	20	–	1,338	–	(NA)	17.4	43.6

– Represents zero.   NA Not available.   [1] Includes other races not shown separately.   [2] Persons of Hispanic origin may be of any race. Births by Hispanic origin of mother.   [3] Per 1,000 estimated population.   [4] Number of births per 1,000 women aged 15 to 44 years estimated.

Source: U.S. National Center for Health Statistics, *National Vital Statistics Reports (NVSR)*, Vol. 54, No. 8, December 29, 2005.

Vital Statistics 65

Table 81. Total Fertility Rate by Race and Hispanic Origin: 1980 to 2004

[Based on race of mother. Excludes births to nonresidents of United States. The *total fertility rate* is the number of births that 1,000 women would have in their lifetime if, at each year of age, they experienced the birth rates occurring in the specified year. A total fertility rate of 2,110 represents "replacement level" fertility for the total population under current mortality conditions (assuming no net immigration). See Appendix III]

Race and Hispanic origin	1980	1990	1995	2000	2001	2002	2003	2004 [1]
Total [2]	1,840	2,081	1,978	2,056	2,034	2,013	2,043	2,049
White.....................	1,773	2,003	1,955	2,051	2,040	2,028	2,061	(NA)
Black.....................	2,177	2,480	2,128	2,129	2,051	1,991	1,999	(NA)
American Indian, Eskimo, Aleut. . .	2,165	2,185	1,879	1,773	1,747	1,735	1,732	1,735
Asian or Pacific Islander	1,954	2,003	1,796	1,892	1,840	1,820	1,873	1,901
Hispanic [3]...............	(NA)	2,960	2,799	2,730	2,749	2,718	2,786	2,821

NA Not available.   [1] Preliminary data.   [2] For 1980 and 1990, includes births to races not shown separately. Beginning 1995 unknown race of mother is imputed.   [3] Persons of Hispanic origin may be any race.

Source: U.S. National Center for Health Statistics, *National Vital Statistics Reports (NVSR)*, Volume 54, Number 2, September 8, 2005 and Volume 54, Number 8, December 29, 2005.

Table 82. Teenagers—Births and Birth Rates by Age, Race, and Hispanic Origin: 1990 to 2004

[Birth rates per 1,000 women in specified group, see text, this section]

Age, race, and Hispanic origin	Number of births					Birth rate				
	1990	1995	2000	2003	2004 [1]	1990	1995	2000	2003	2004 [1]
All races, total [2]	521,826	499,873	468,990	414,580	415,408	59.9	56.0	47.7	41.6	41.2
15 to 17 years old	183,327	192,508	157,209	134,384	133,987	37.5	35.5	26.9	22.4	22.1
18 and 19 years old	338,499	307,365	311,781	280,196	281,421	88.6	87.7	78.1	70.7	70.0
White.....................	354,482	349,635	333,013	298,347	297,931	50.8	49.5	43.2	38.3	37.8
Black.....................	151,613	133,694	118,954	100,951	102,087	112.8	94.4	77.4	63.8	62.9
American Indian, Eskimo, Aleut	(NA)	7,764	8,055	7,690	7,699	81.1	72.9	58.3	53.1	52.5
Asian or Pacific Islander	(NA)	8,780	8,968	7,592	7,691	26.4	25.5	20.5	17.4	17.4
Hispanic [2]	(NA)	118,449	129,469	128,524	132,983	100.3	99.3	87.3	82.3	82.6
Non-Hispanic White	(NA)	230,024	204,056	172,620	169,528	42.5	39.3	32.6	27.4	26.8
Non-Hispanic Black	(NA)	130,907	116,019	97,509	96,718	116.2	97.2	79.2	64.7	62.7

NA Not available.   [1] Preliminary data.   [2] Persons of Hispanic origin may be any race.

Source: U.S. National Center for Health Statistics, *National Vital Statistics Reports (NVSR)*.

Table 83. Births to Unmarried Women by Race, Hispanic Origin and Age of Mother: 1990 to 2004

[(1,165 represents 1,165,000). Excludes births to nonresidents of United States. Persons of Hispanic origin may be any race. Marital status is inferred from a comparison of the child's and parents' surnames on the birth certificate for those states that do not report on marital status. No estimates included for misstatements on birth records or failures to register births. See also Appendix III]

Race and age of mother	Number (1,000)				2004, prel.	Percent distribution			Birth rate [1]				2004, prel.
	1990	1995	2000	2003		1990	2000	2003	1990	1995	2000	2003	
Total live births [2]. . .	1,165	1,254	1,347	1,416	1,470	100.0	100.0	100.0	43.8	44.3	44.1	44.9	46.1
White...............	670	785	866	947	(NA)	57.5	64.3	66.9	32.9	37.0	38.2	40.4	(NA)
Black...............	455	421	427	409	(NA)	39.1	31.7	28.9	90.5	74.5	70.5	66.3	(NA)
American Indian, Eskimo, Aleut.......	(NA)	(NA)	(NA)	26	(NA)	(NA)	(NA)	1.9	(NA)	(NA)	(NA)	(NA)	(NA)
Asian or Pacific Islander......	(NA)	(NA)	(NA)	33	(NA)	(NA)	(NA)	2.3	(NA)	(NA)	20.9	22.2	(NA)
Hispanic............	[3]219	278	348	411	(NA)	[3]18.8	25.8	29.0	[3]89.6	88.8	87.3	92.2	(NA)
Non-Hispanic White	[3]443	504	522	547	(NA)	[3]38.0	38.7	38.6	[3]24.4	28.1	28.0	28.6	(NA)
Non-Hispanic Black ...	(NA)	(NA)	415	395	(NA)	(NA)	30.8	27.9	(NA)	(NA)	(NA)	(NA)	(NA)
Under 15 years	11	11	8	6	7	0.9	0.6	0.5	(NA)	(NA)	(NA)	(NA)	(NA)
15 to 19 years	350	376	369	337	342	30.0	27.4	23.8	42.5	43.8	39.0	34.8	(NA)
20 to 24 years.......	404	432	504	549	(NA)	34.7	37.4	38.8	65.1	68.7	72.2	71.2	(NA)
25 to 29 years.......	230	229	255	287	(NA)	19.7	18.9	20.3	56.0	54.3	58.5	65.7	(NA)
30 to 34 years.......	118	133	130	148	(NA)	10.1	9.7	10.4	37.6	38.9	39.3	44.0	(NA)
35 to 39 years.......	44	60	65	69	(NA)	3.8	6.0	4.9	17.3	19.3	19.7	22.3	(NA)
40 years and over	9	13	16	19	(NA)	0.7	1.2	1.4	3.6	4.7	5.0	5.8	(NA)

NA Not available.   [1] Rate per 1,000 unmarried women (never-married, widowed, and divorced) estimated as of July 1. Total rate and rates by race/Hispanic origin cover women 15 to 44 years old.   [2] Includes other races not shown separately.   [3] Excludes data for New Hampshire and Oklahoma, which did not report Hispanic origin.

Source: U.S. National Center for Health Statistics, *National Vital Statistics Reports (NVSR)*.

Table 84. **Births to Teens, Unmarried Mothers, and Prenatal Care: 1990 to 2004**

[Represents registered births. Excludes births to nonresidents of the United States. Data are based on race and Hispanic origin of mother. See Appendix III]

Race and Hispanic origin	1990	1995	2000	2001	2002	2003	2004, prel.
Percent of births to teenage mothers ...	**12.8**	**13.1**	**11.8**	**11.3**	**10.8**	**10.3**	**10.3**
White.	10.9	11.5	10.6	10.2	9.8	9.4	9.3
Black.	23.1	23.1	19.7	18.9	18.0	17.3	17.1
American Indian, Eskimo, Aleut	19.5	21.4	19.7	19.3	18.5	18.2	17.8
Asian or Pacific Islander [1]	5.7	5.6	4.5	4.3	3.8	3.5	3.4
Filipino	6.1	6.2	5.3	5.1	4.5	(NA)	(NA)
Chinese	1.2	0.9	0.9	1.0	0.9	(NA)	(NA)
Japanese	2.9	2.5	1.9	1.7	1.7	(NA)	(NA)
Hawaiian.	18.4	19.1	17.4	16.2	14.6	(NA)	(NA)
Hispanic origin [2]	16.8	17.9	16.2	15.6	14.9	14.3	14.3
Mexican	17.7	18.8	17.0	16.5	15.9	15.3	(NA)
Puerto Rican	21.7	23.5	20.0	19.2	17.8	17.9	(NA)
Cuban	7.7	7.7	7.5	7.5	8.1	7.9	(NA)
Central and South American.	9.0	10.6	9.9	9.4	8.5	8.3	(NA)
Percent of births to unmarried mothers . .	**26.6**	**32.2**	**33.2**	**33.5**	**34.0**	**34.6**	**35.7**
White.	16.9	25.3	27.1	27.7	28.5	29.4	(NA)
Black.	66.7	69.9	68.5	68.4	68.2	68.2	(NA)
American Indian, Eskimo, Aleut	53.6	57.2	58.4	59.7	59.7	61.3	62.3
Asian or Pacific Islander [1]	13.2	16.3	14.8	14.9	14.9	15.0	15.5
Filipino	15.9	19.5	20.3	20.4	20.0	(NA)	(NA)
Chinese	5.0	7.9	7.6	8.4	9.0	(NA)	(NA)
Japanese	9.6	10.8	9.5	9.2	10.3	(NA)	(NA)
Hawaiian.	45.0	49.0	50.0	50.6	50.4	(NA)	(NA)
Hispanic origin [2]	36.7	40.8	42.7	42.5	43.5	45.0	46.4
Mexican	33.3	38.1	40.7	40.8	42.1	43.7	(NA)
Puerto Rican	55.9	60.0	59.6	58.9	59.1	59.8	(NA)
Cuban	18.2	23.8	27.3	27.2	29.8	31.4	(NA)
Central and South American.	41.2	44.1	44.7	44.3	44.8	46.0	(NA)
Percent of mothers beginning prenatal care 1st trimester	**74.2**	**81.3**	**83.2**	**83.4**	**83.7**	**84.1**	**(NA)**
White.	77.7	83.6	85.0	85.2	85.4	85.7	(NA)
Black.	60.7	70.4	74.3	74.5	75.2	75.9	(NA)
American Indian, Eskimo, Aleut	57.9	66.7	69.3	69.3	69.8	70.8	(NA)
Asian or Pacific Islander [1]	(NA)	79.9	84.0	84.0	84.8	85.4	(NA)
Filipino	77.1	80.9	84.9	85.0	85.4	(NA)	(NA)
Chinese	81.3	85.7	87.6	87.0	87.2	(NA)	(NA)
Japanese	87.0	89.7	91.0	90.1	90.5	(NA)	(NA)
Hawaiian.	65.8	75.9	79.9	79.1	78.1	(NA)	(NA)
Hispanic origin [2]	60.2	70.8	74.4	75.7	76.8	77.5	(NA)
Mexican	57.8	69.1	72.9	74.6	75.7	76.5	(NA)
Puerto Rican	63.5	74.0	78.5	79.1	79.9	81.2	(NA)
Cuban	84.8	89.2	91.7	91.8	92.0	92.1	(NA)
Central and South American.	61.5	73.2	77.6	77.4	78.7	79.2	(NA)
Percent of mothers beginning prenatal care 3d trimester or no care. . .	**6.0**	**4.2**	**3.9**	**3.7**	**3.6**	**3.5**	**(NA)**
White.	4.9	3.5	3.3	3.2	3.1	3.0	(NA)
Black.	10.9	7.6	6.7	6.5	6.2	6.0	(NA)
American Indian, Eskimo, Aleut	12.9	9.5	8.6	8.2	8.1	7.6	(NA)
Asian or Pacific Islander [1]	(NA)	4.3	3.3	3.4	3.1	3.1	(NA)
Filipino	4.5	4.1	3.0	3.0	2.8	(NA)	(NA)
Chinese	3.4	3.0	2.2	2.4	2.1	(NA)	(NA)
Japanese	2.9	2.3	1.8	2.0	2.1	(NA)	(NA)
Hawaiian.	8.7	5.1	4.2	4.8	4.7	(NA)	(NA)
Hispanic origin [2]	12.0	7.4	6.3	5.9	5.5	5.3	(NA)
Mexican	13.2	8.1	6.9	6.2	5.8	5.6	(NA)
Puerto Rican	10.6	5.5	4.5	4.6	4.1	3.7	(NA)
Cuban	2.8	2.1	1.4	1.3	1.3	1.3	(NA)
Central and South American.	10.9	6.1	5.4	5.7	4.9	4.7	(NA)
Percent of births with low birth weight [3]	**7.0**	**7.3**	**7.6**	**7.7**	**7.8**	**7.9**	**8.1**
White.	5.7	6.2	6.5	6.7	6.8	6.9	(NA)
Black.	13.3	13.1	13.0	13.0	13.3	13.4	(NA)
American Indian, Eskimo, Aleut	6.1	6.6	6.8	7.3	7.2	7.4	7.5
Asian or Pacific Islander [1]	(NA)	6.9	7.3	7.5	7.8	7.8	7.9
Filipino	7.3	7.8	8.5	8.7	8.6	(NA)	(NA)
Chinese	4.7	5.3	5.1	5.3	5.5	(NA)	(NA)
Japanese	6.2	7.3	7.1	7.3	7.6	(NA)	(NA)
Hawaiian.	7.2	6.8	6.8	7.9	8.1	(NA)	(NA)
Hispanic origin [2]	6.1	6.3	6.4	6.5	6.5	6.7	6.8
Mexican	5.5	5.8	6.0	6.1	6.2	6.3	(NA)
Puerto Rican	9.0	9.4	9.3	9.3	9.7	10.0	(NA)
Cuban	5.7	6.5	6.5	6.5	6.5	7.0	(NA)
Central and South American.	5.8	6.2	6.3	6.5	6.5	6.7	(NA)

NA Not available. [1] Includes other races not shown separately. [2] Hispanic persons may be any race. Includes other types, not shown separately. [3] Births less than 2,500 grams (5 lb.–8 oz.).

Source: U.S. National Center for Health Statistics, *National Vital Statistics Reports (NVSR)*.

Table 85. Births to Teenage Mothers and Unmarried Women and Births With Low Birth Weight—States and Island Areas: 1990 to 2003

[Represents registered births. Excludes births to nonresidents of the United States. Based on 100 percent of births in all states and the District of Columbia. See Appendix III]

State and Island Area	Births to teenage mothers, percent of total [1]			Births to unmarried women, percent of total			Percent of births with low birth weight [2]		
	1990	2000	2003	1990	2000	2003	1990	2000	2003
United States	**12.8**	**11.8**	**10.3**	**26.6**	**33.2**	**34.6**	**7.0**	**7.6**	**7.9**
Alabama.	18.2	15.7	13.9	30.1	34.3	35.0	8.4	9.7	10.0
Alaska	9.7	11.8	10.6	26.2	33.0	34.6	4.8	5.6	6.0
Arizona.	14.2	14.3	12.9	32.7	39.3	41.5	6.4	7.0	7.1
Arkansas	19.7	17.3	15.1	29.4	35.7	38.0	8.2	8.6	8.9
California	11.6	10.6	9.3	31.6	32.7	33.5	5.8	6.2	6.6
Colorado.	11.3	11.7	9.8	21.2	25.0	26.7	8.0	8.4	9.0
Connecticut.	8.2	7.8	6.7	26.6	29.3	30.0	6.6	7.4	7.5
Delaware	11.9	12.3	10.8	29.0	37.9	41.9	7.6	8.6	9.4
District of Columbia	17.8	14.2	11.4	64.9	60.3	53.6	15.1	11.9	10.9
Florida	13.9	12.6	10.9	31.7	38.2	39.9	7.4	8.0	8.5
Georgia	16.7	13.9	11.9	32.8	37.0	38.1	8.7	8.6	9.0
Hawaii	10.5	10.3	8.4	24.8	32.2	33.5	7.1	7.5	8.6
Idaho.	12.3	11.6	9.6	16.7	21.6	22.3	5.7	6.7	6.5
Illinois	13.1	11.4	9.7	31.7	34.5	35.3	7.6	7.9	8.3
Indiana.	14.5	12.5	11.0	26.2	34.7	37.1	6.6	7.4	7.9
Iowa	10.2	10.0	8.7	21.0	28.0	29.9	5.4	6.1	6.6
Kansas	12.3	12.0	10.5	21.5	29.0	31.6	6.2	6.9	7.4
Kentucky	17.5	14.1	12.4	23.6	31.0	33.8	7.1	8.2	8.7
Louisiana	17.6	17.0	14.9	36.8	45.6	47.5	9.2	10.3	10.7
Maine	10.8	9.4	8.2	22.6	31.0	33.5	5.1	6.0	6.5
Maryland	10.5	9.9	8.6	29.6	34.6	34.8	7.8	8.6	9.1
Massachusetts.	8.0	6.6	5.9	24.7	26.5	27.8	5.9	7.1	7.6
Michigan.	13.5	10.5	9.5	26.2	33.3	34.6	7.6	7.9	8.2
Minnesota.	8.0	8.3	7.1	20.9	25.8	27.7	5.1	6.1	6.2
Mississippi	21.3	18.8	16.0	40.5	46.0	47.0	9.6	10.7	11.4
Missouri	14.4	13.1	11.4	28.6	34.6	35.6	7.1	7.6	8.0
Montana	11.5	11.6	10.6	23.7	30.8	32.2	6.2	6.2	6.8
Nebraska	9.8	10.2	9.0	20.7	27.2	29.7	5.3	6.8	6.9
Nevada	12.6	12.7	11.3	25.4	36.4	39.1	7.2	7.2	8.1
New Hampshire	7.2	6.8	5.7	16.9	24.7	24.8	4.9	6.3	6.2
New Jersey.	8.4	7.1	6.2	24.3	28.9	29.3	7.0	7.7	8.1
New Mexico	16.3	17.4	16.5	35.4	45.6	48.4	7.4	8.0	8.5
New York	9.1	8.2	7.0	33.0	36.6	36.5	7.6	7.7	7.9
North Carolina	16.2	13.0	11.4	29.4	33.3	35.3	8.0	8.8	9.0
North Dakota.	8.6	9.2	8.0	18.4	28.3	28.5	5.5	6.4	6.5
Ohio	13.8	12.1	10.5	28.9	34.6	36.2	7.1	7.9	8.3
Oklahoma.	16.2	15.9	13.9	25.2	34.3	37.1	6.6	7.5	7.8
Oregon.	12.0	11.3	9.1	25.7	30.1	31.7	5.0	5.6	6.1
Pennsylvania.	10.9	9.9	9.0	28.6	32.7	33.9	7.1	7.7	8.1
Rhode Island.	10.5	10.2	8.3	26.3	35.5	35.8	6.2	7.2	8.5
South Carolina.	17.1	15.3	13.3	32.7	39.8	41.1	8.7	9.7	10.1
South Dakota	10.8	11.6	9.4	22.9	33.5	34.2	5.1	6.2	6.6
Tennessee	17.6	14.7	13.2	30.2	34.5	37.2	8.2	9.2	9.4
Texas.	15.6	15.3	13.8	17.5	30.5	34.3	6.9	7.4	7.9
Utah	10.3	8.9	6.7	13.5	17.3	17.2	5.7	6.6	6.5
Vermont	8.5	8.0	6.4	20.1	28.1	30.0	5.3	6.1	7.0
Virginia.	11.7	9.9	8.9	26.0	29.9	30.4	7.2	7.9	8.2
Washington.	10.8	10.2	8.5	23.7	28.2	28.8	5.3	5.6	6.0
West Virginia.	17.8	15.9	12.3	25.4	31.7	34.6	7.1	8.3	8.6
Wisconsin.	10.2	10.2	9.0	24.2	29.3	30.4	5.9	6.5	6.8
Wyoming	13.6	13.5	12.0	19.8	28.8	32.6	7.4	8.3	8.9
Puerto Rico	(NA)	(NA)	17.8	(NA)	49.7	53.2	(NA)	10.8	11.5
Virgin Islands	(NA)	(NA)	14.7	(NA)	66.7	68.8	(NA)	9.1	10.8
Guam.	(NA)	(NA)	13.2	(NA)	54.8	55.5	(NA)	7.6	9.2
American Samoa	(NA)	(NA)	6.9	(NA)	35.5	37.9	(NA)	2.7	4.2
Northern Marianas . . .	(NA)	(NA)	8.8	(NA)	(NA)	57.8	(NA)	8.9	7.6

NA Not available. [1] Defined as mothers who are 19 years of age or younger. [2] Less than 2,500 grams (5 pounds–8 ounces).

Source: U.S. National Center for Health Statistics, *National Vital Statistics Reports (NVSR).*

Table 86. Births by Race, Hispanic Origin Status and Method of Delivery: 1990 to 2003

[In thousands (4,111 represents 4,111,000), except rate. 1990 excludes data for Oklahoma, which did not report method of delivery on the birth certificate. Persons of Hispanic origin may be any race. See Appendix III]

Method of delivery	1990	2000	2002	2003					
				Total [1]	White	Black	Hispanic	Non-Hispanic White	Non-Hispanic Black
Births, total	**4,111**	**4,059**	**4,022**	**4,090**	**3,226**	**600**	**912**	**2,322**	**576**
Vaginal.................	3,111	3,108	2,958	2,950	2,333	423	668	1,671	406
After previous caesarean ..	84	90	59	52	40	8	11	29	8
Caesarean deliveries	914	924	1,044	1,119	877	174	241	637	168
Primary..............	575	578	634	684	531	108	134	398	104
Repeat..............	339	346	409	435	345	66	107	239	64
Not stated.............	85	27	19	21	17	3	4	13	3
Caesarean delivery rate [2] ...	22.7	22.9	26.1	27.5	27.3	29.1	26.5	27.6	29.2
Primary [3]	16.0	16.1	18.0	19.1	18.8	20.6	17.0	19.5	20.7
Rate of vaginal birth after previous caesarean [4] ..	19.9	20.6	12.6	10.6	10.3	11.4	9.4	10.7	11.3

[1] Includes other races not shown separately. [2] Caesarean rates are the number of caesarean deliveries per 100 total deliveries for specified category. [3] Number of primary caesareans per 100 live births to women who have not had a previous caesarean. [4] Number of vaginal births after previous caesarean delivery per 100 live births to women with a previous caesarean delivery.

Source: U.S. National Center for Health Statistics, *National Vital Statistics Reports (NVSR)*, Volume 54, Number 2, September 8, 2005.

Table 87. Births—Percent With Low Birth Weight by Age, Race, Hispanic Origin and Smoking Status of Mother: 2003

[Low birth weight is defined as weight of less than 2,500 grams (5 lb.–8 oz.). Excludes data for California, Pennsylvania, and Washington]

Smoking status, Hispanic origin status, and race of mother	All ages [1]	Under 15 years	15–19 years			20–24 years	25–29 years	30–34 years	35–39 years
			Total	15–17 years	18 and 19 years				
All races [2, 3]	8.2	13.0	10.0	10.8	9.7	8.3	7.3	7.6	8.9
Smoker	12.4	12.2	11.8	12.8	11.5	11.1	11.9	13.8	17.4
Nonsmoker.............	7.7	13.0	9.7	10.5	9.3	7.7	6.8	7.1	8.3
White [3]	7.1	10.2	8.6	9.2	8.3	7.0	6.4	6.8	8.0
Smoker	11.3	12.9	11.2	12.2	10.9	10.2	10.8	12.5	15.3
Nonsmoker.............	6.5	9.8	7.9	8.7	7.5	6.2	5.9	6.3	7.4
Black [3]	13.4	16.3	14.2	14.4	14.0	13.1	12.3	13.4	15.5
Smoker	20.2	(B)	17.5	17.4	17.5	17.4	19.2	23.9	30.1
Nonsmoker.............	12.8	16.4	13.9	14.2	13.7	12.6	11.7	12.6	14.2
Hispanic [3, 4]	7.0	10.0	8.1	8.7	7.8	6.6	6.2	6.9	8.1
Smoker	13.0	(B)	12.1	12.5	11.9	12.2	12.7	14.0	16.7
Nonsmoker.............	6.8	9.7	8.0	8.6	7.6	6.4	6.1	6.8	7.9
Non-Hispanic, White [3]	7.2	10.3	8.8	9.6	8.5	7.2	6.4	6.7	8.0
Smoker	11.2	11.9	11.2	12.2	10.8	10.1	10.7	12.3	15.2
Nonsmoker.............	6.5	9.9	7.8	8.8	7.5	6.2	5.8	6.2	7.3
Non-Hispanic, Black [3]	13.6	16.4	14.3	14.5	14.1	13.3	12.5	13.6	15.8
Smoker	20.3	(B)	17.6	17.5	17.6	17.5	19.3	24.0	30.2
Nonsmoker.............	13.0	16.4	14.0	14.3	13.8	13.2	11.8	12.8	14.4

B Base figure too small to meet statistical standards for reliability of a derived figure. [1] Includes other age groups not shown separately. [2] Includes races other than White and Black and non-Hispanics. [3] Includes those with smoking status not stated. [4] Persons of Hispanic origin may be any race.

Source: U.S. National Center for Health Statistics, *National Vital Statistics Reports (NVSR)*, Volume 54, Number 2, September 8, 2005.

Table 88. Women Who Have Had a Child in the Last Year by Age: 1990 to 2004

[3,913 represents 3,913,000. As of June. See headnote, Table 89]

Age of mother	Women who had a child in last year (1,000)			Total births per 1,000 women			First births per 1,000 women		
	1990	2000	2004	1990	2000	2004	1990	2000	2004
Total	**3,913**	**3,934**	**3,746**	**67.0**	**64.6**	**60.8**	**26.4**	**26.7**	**23.9**
15 to 29 years old ...	2,568	2,432	2,205	90.8	85.9	74.7	43.2	43.1	35.1
15 to 19 years old ..	338	586	385	39.8	59.7	38.7	30.1	38.7	22.1
20 to 24 years old ..	1,038	850	882	113.4	91.8	87.6	51.8	47.1	43.0
25 to 29 years old ..	1,192	996	938	112.1	107.9	98.7	46.2	43.7	40.2
30 to 44 years old ...	1,346	1,502	1,542	44.7	46.1	48.1	10.6	12.5	13.7
30 to 34 years old ..	892	871	946	80.4	87.9	93.8	21.9	27.5	28.4
35 to 39 years old ..	377	506	443	37.3	45.1	42.4	6.5	9.6	11.5
40 to 44 years old ..	77	125	153	8.6	10.9	13.2	1.2	2.3	2.8

Source: U.S. Census Bureau, *Current Population Reports*, P20-555.

Vital Statistics 69

Table 89. **Women Who Had a Child in the Last Year by Selected Characteristics: 1990 to 2004**

[58,381 represents 58,381,000. As of June. Covers civilian noninstitutional population. Since the number of women who had a birth during the 12-month period was tabulated and not the actual numbers of births, some small underestimation of fertility for this period may exist due to the omission of: (1) Multiple births, (2) Two or more live births spaced within the 12-month period (the woman is counted only once), (3) Women who had births in the period and who did not survive to the survey date, (4) Women who were in institutions and therefore not in the survey universe. These losses may be somewhat offset by the inclusion in the CPS of births to immigrants who did not have their children born in the United States and births to nonresident women. These births would not have been recorded in the vital registration system. Based on Current Population Survey (CPS); see Appendix III]

Characteristic	Total women (1,000)	Percent childless	Women who had a child in the last year			
			Total births		First births	
			Number (1,000)	Per 1,000 women	Number (1,000)	Per 1,000 women
1990	58,381	41.6	3,913	67.0	1,540	26.4
2000	60,873	42.8	3,934	64.6	1,626	26.7
2004, total [1]	61,588	44.6	3,746	60.8	1,474	23.9
15 to 19 years old.	9,964	93.3	385	38.7	221	22.1
20 to 24 years old.	10,068	68.9	882	87.6	433	43.0
25 to 29 years old.	9,498	44.2	938	98.7	382	40.2
30 to 34 years old.	10,082	27.6	946	93.8	286	28.4
35 to 39 years old.	10,442	19.6	443	42.4	120	11.5
40 to 44 years old.	11,535	19.3	153	13.2	33	2.8
White alone	47,984	45.1	2,881	60.0	1,115	23.2
White alone, non-Hispanic.	39,120	47.0	2,114	54.0	875	22.4
Black alone	8,798	40.5	515	58.5	192	21.8
Asian alone	3,035	47.2	230	75.8	116	38.1
Hispanic [2]	9,618	37.1	817	84.9	269	28.0
Married, husband present.	27,586	18.7	2,416	87.6	894	32.4
Married, husband absent [3]	2,323	22.1	142	61.1	33	14.2
Widowed or divorced.	5,294	20.8	145	27.3	37	7.0
Never married	26,385	78.5	1,044	39.6	510	19.3
Educational attainment:						
Not a high school graduate	12,965	61.4	748	57.7	235	18.1
High school, 4 years	16,137	31.8	1,086	67.3	397	24.6
Some college, no degree	12,667	47.6	671	53.0	242	19.1
Associate's degree	5,335	31.0	295	55.3	143	26.8
Bachelor's degree	10,807	47.4	681	63.0	331	30.7
Graduate or professional degree	3,678	42.5	267	72.5	125	33.9
Labor force status:						
Employed	39,441	44.0	1,824	46.2	797	20.2
Unemployed	3,180	50.5	223	70.0	84	26.3
Not in labor force.	18,967	44.9	1,700	89.6	593	31.3
Family income:						
Under $10,000	3,979	42.4	381	95.8	110	27.7
$10,000 to $19,999	5,098	39.6	401	78.7	138	27.0
$20,000 to $24,999	2,931	37.6	222	75.6	66	22.6
$25,000 to $29,999	3,242	41.0	193	59.6	81	24.9
$30,000 to $34,999	3,468	44.9	227	65.3	84	24.3
$35,000 to $49,999	8,149	44.5	465	57.1	198	24.3
$50,000 to $74,999	10,659	46.0	588	55.2	249	23.3
$75,000 and over	13,812	47.2	750	54.3	316	22.9

[1] Includes women of other races and women with family income not reported, not shown separately. [2] Persons of Hispanic origin may be any race. [3] Includes separated women.

Source: U.S. Census Bureau, *Current Population Reports*, P20-555 and "Fertility of American Women Current Population Survey—June 2004 Detailed Tables;" last revised December 20, 2005; <http://www.census.gov/population/www/socdemo/fertility/cps2004.html>.

Table 90. **Women Who Have Had a Child in the Last Year by Age and Labor Force Status: 1980 to 2004**

[3,247 represents 3,247,000. See headnote, Table 89. See Appendix III]

Year	Total, 15 to 44 years old			15 to 29 years old			30 to 44 years old		
	Number (1,000)	In the labor force		Number (1,000)	In the labor force		Number (1,000)	In the labor force	
		Number (1,000)	Percent		Number (1,000)	Percent		Number (1,000)	Percent
1980 [1]	3,247	1,233	38	2,476	947	38	770	287	37
1990	3,913	2,068	53	2,568	1,275	50	1,346	793	59
1995	3,696	2,034	55	2,252	1,150	51	1,444	884	61
1998	3,671	2,155	59	2,274	1,275	56	1,397	880	63
2000	3,934	2,170	55	2,432	1,304	54	1,502	866	58
2002	3,766	2,056	55	2,318	1,175	51	1,448	881	61
2004	3,746	2,045	55	2,205	(NA)	(NA)	1,542	(NA)	59

NA Not available. [1] Lower age limit is 18 years old.

Source: U.S. Census Bureau, *Current Population Reports,* P20-555; and earlier reports.

70 Vital Statistics

Table 91. Persons Who Have Ever Had Sexual Contact by Selected Characteristics: 2002

[In percent except as indicated (61,147 represents 61,147,000). Based on the National Survey of Family Growth, see Appendix III]

Characteristic	Number (1,000)	Number of opposite-sex partners in lifetime							Any same-sex sexual contact[2]
		Any	One	Two	3 to 6	7 to 14	15 or more	Median number[1]	
Males, 15 to 44 years old[3]	61,147	90.3	12.8	8.1	27.5	19.3	22.6	5.4	6.0
15 to 19 years old	10,208	61.6	23.0	9.2	20.7	6.2	2.5	1.9	4.5
20 to 24 years old	9,883	91.1	15.9	11.7	33.5	14.1	15.9	3.8	5.5
25 to 44 years old	41,056	97.3	9.6	7.0	27.8	23.7	29.2	6.7	6.5
25 to 29 years old	9,226	95.2	10.0	8.8	29.4	23.2	23.8	5.9	5.7
30 to 34 years old	10,138	97.2	10.7	6.9	28.5	21.9	29.2	6.4	(NA)
35 to 39 years old	10,557	98.2	8.9	7.0	28.0	25.5	28.8	6.9	(NA)
40 to 44 years old	11,135	98.2	8.8	5.4	25.6	24.2	34.2	8.2	(NA)
White only, non-Hispanic	38,738	90.3	13.4	8.3	27.1	19.2	22.3	5.3	(NA)
Black only, non-Hispanic	6,940	91.8	5.8	5.9	24.1	22.2	33.8	8.3	(NA)
Hispanic or Latino origin	10,188	91.8	13.7	8.6	32.8	18.6	18.1	4.5	(NA)
Currently married	25,808	100.0	15.4	8.5	30.5	22.3	23.3	5.2	3.4
Currently cohabiting	5,653	100.0	4.7	6.4	34.1	26.6	28.3	6.6	5.3
Never married, not cohabiting	25,412	76.8	13.9	8.7	24.0	13.8	16.4	4.3	8.6
Formerly married, not cohabiting	4,274	100.0	0.7	3.6	22.5	24.6	46.8	11.9	7.1
Females, 15 to 44 years old[3]	61,561	91.4	22.5	10.8	32.6	16.3	9.2	3.3	11.2
15 to 19 years old	9,834	62.2	27.2	9.0	19.1	5.0	1.9	1.4	10.6
20 to 24 years old	9,840	91.1	24.6	13.0	32.2	14.4	6.9	2.8	14.2
25 to 44 years old	41,887	98.4	20.9	10.7	36.0	19.4	11.4	3.8	10.7
25 to 29 years old	9,249	97.5	22.5	11.7	31.3	20.1	11.9	3.5	14.1
30 to 34 years old	10,272	98.0	20.5	9.4	38.8	18.0	11.3	3.8	(NA)
35 to 39 years old	10,853	98.9	20.2	11.2	35.8	20.5	11.2	3.9	(NA)
40 to 44 years old	11,512	98.6	20.4	10.5	37.4	19.1	11.2	3.8	(NA)
White only, non-Hispanic	39,498	92.1	21.0	10.6	32.1	18.2	10.2	3.6	(NA)
Black only, non-Hispanic	8,250	92.4	12.4	8.4	44.8	18.0	8.8	4.1	(NA)
Hispanic or Latino origin	9,107	89.5	34.6	14.9	27.2	8.2	4.6	1.7	(NA)
Currently married	28,327	100.0	30.8	12.2	34.0	15.6	7.4	2.7	7.2
Currently cohabiting	5,570	100.0	13.7	12.2	39.2	20.4	14.5	4.3	17.6
Never married, not cohabiting	21,568	75.4	18.3	9.4	27.7	12.8	7.2	3.1	13.5
Formerly married, not cohabiting	6,096	100.0	6.5	8.1	37.8	28.5	19.1	5.6	16.3

NA Not available. [1] Excludes those who have never had sexual intercourse with a person of the opposite sex. For definition of median, see Guide to Tabular Presentation. [2] Same-sex sexual contact was measured using significantly different questions for males and females. [3] Includes persons of other or multiple race and origin groups, not shown separately.

Source: U.S. National Center for Health Statistics, *Advance Data*, No. 362; September 15, 2005, and unpublished data.

Table 92. Males and Females by Number and Sex of Partners in Last 12 Months: 2002

[In percent except as indicated (61,147 represents 61,147,000). Based on the National Survey of Family Growth, see Appendix III]

Sex and age	Number (1,000)	Percent distribution							Number of partners not ascertained
		Total	No partners in last 12 months	One partner		Two or more partners			
				Same sex[1]	Opposite sex	Same sex only	Opposite sex only	Both same and opposite sex[1]	
Males 15 to 44 years old	61,147	100.0	14.8	0.7	62.2	0.9	17.6	1.0	2.6
15 to 19 years old	10,208	100.0	45.1	0.8	29.7	(S)	21.8	0.9	1.4
20 to 24 years old	9,883	100.0	14.2	0.4	48.8	0.9	30.9	1.5	3.2
25 to 44 years old	41,056	100.0	7.4	0.7	73.6	1.1	13.4	1.0	2.8
25 to 29 years old	9,226	100.0	10.0	0.5	66.6	0.9	18.4	1.1	2.5
30 to 34 years old	10,138	100.0	5.6	0.9	74.3	1.0	14.5	1.3	2.4
35 to 39 years old	10,557	100.0	7.1	0.7	76.5	1.2	11.4	0.5	2.5
40 to 44 years old	11,135	100.0	7.0	0.7	75.9	1.3	10.1	1.0	3.8
Females 15 to 44 years old	61,561	100.0	13.9	1.1	66.8	0.2	12.7	3.1	2.2
15 to 19 years old	9,834	100.0	42.9	1.7	30.5	(S)	16.8	5.8	2.1
20 to 24 years old	9,840	100.0	12.5	0.4	58.9	(S)	21.1	4.8	1.9
25 to 44 years old	41,887	100.0	7.4	1.1	77.2	0.2	9.8	2.0	2.2
25 to 29 years old	9,249	100.0	6.1	0.5	74.1	0.4	14.1	2.8	2.0
30 to 34 years old	10,272	100.0	7.1	0.5	78.5	(S)	9.7	2.1	1.9
35 to 39 years old	10,853	100.0	7.3	1.8	76.8	(S)	9.4	2.5	2.0
40 to 44 years old	11,512	100.0	9.0	1.4	78.8	(S)	6.7	0.9	3.0

S Does not meet standards for reliability or precision. [1] Same-sex sexual contact was measured using significantly different questions for males and females.

Source: U.S. National Center for Health Statistics, *Advance Data*, No. 362; September 15, 2005.

Table 93. Contraceptive Use by Women 15 to 44 Years of Age Who Have Ever Had Sexual Intercourse: 1982 to 2002

[46,684 represents 46,684,000. Based on the National Survey of Family Growth, see Appendix III]

Contraceptive status and method	1982	1995	2002 Total [1]	2002 Non-Hispanic White	2002 Non-Hispanic Black	Hispanic [2]
Women who have had sexual intercourse (1,000) ..	46,684	53,800	54,190	35,789	7,693	7,887
PERCENT DISTRIBUTION						
Ever used any method...................	94.8	98.2	98.2	98.8	97.3	96.5
Female sterilization...........................	22.3	23.4	20.7	19.4	26.6	24.1
Male sterilization	10.1	14.6	13.0	16.7	4.9	4.4
Pill..	76.3	82.2	82.3	87.1	79.2	68.5
Norplant implant..............................	(X)	2.1	2.1	1.4	3.2	4.0
1-month injectable (Lunelle ™).................	(X)	(X)	0.9	0.5	0.9	3.1
3-month injectable (Depo-Provera ™)	(X)	4.5	16.8	13.7	23.9	24.3
Emergency contraception	(X)	0.8	4.2	4.3	4.0	3.8
Contraceptive patch	(X)	(X)	0.9	0.7	1.3	1.1
Today ™...................................	18.4	12.0	7.3	8.8	6.2	2.7
Intrauterine device	17.1	10.0	5.8	4.7	5.5	10.0
Diaphragm	51.8	15.2	8.5	10.3	6.9	3.4
Condom...................................	(X)	82.0	89.7	92.2	92.0	78.2
Female condom.............................	17.0	1.2	1.9	1.2	5.3	1.4
Periodic abstinence—calendar rhythm	2.3	24.3	16.2	16.6	13.9	16.2
Periodic abstinence—natural family planning.........	24.5	4.2	3.5	3.6	1.9	4.7
Withdrawal	24.9	40.6	56.1	59.7	50.6	47.2
Foam alone................................	5.8	18.3	12.1	12.7	15.4	8.2
Jelly/cream alone...........................	9.7	9.1	7.3	7.8	9.7	3.4
Suppository/insert...........................	9.3	10.6	7.5	8.1	8.6	4.5
Other methods.............................		0.3	1.0	0.8	1.3	1.3

X Not applicable.   [1] Includes other races, not shown separately.   [2] Persons of Hispanic origin may be any race.

Source: U.S. National Center for Health Statistics, *Advance Data*, Number 350, "*Use of Contraception and Use of Family Planning Services in the United States: 1982–2002*," December 10, 2004.

Table 94. Select Family Planning and Medical Service Use by Women 15 to 44 Years of Age: 2002

[61,561 represents 61,561,000. Based on the National Survey of Family Growth, see Appendix III]

Characteristic	Number (1,000)	Family planning services: At least one family planning service	Family planning services: Birth control method	Family planning services: Birth control checkup or test	Medical services: At least one medical service	Medical services: Pregnancy test	Medical services: Pap smear	Medical services: Pelvic exam	Medical services: Counseling/ test/ treatment for STD [1]
All women [2]............	61,561	41.7	33.9	23.6	69.1	19.7	64.4	59.7	12.6
15 to 19 years..............	9,834	39.9	31.1	22.0	40.6	18.3	34.6	27.0	15.2
15 to 17 years............	5,819	31.8	22.2	15.8	28.0	11.4	23.2	17.9	11.1
18 to 19 years	4,016	51.6	43.9	31.0	58.9	28.2	51.2	40.2	21.1
20 to 24 years..............	9,840	63.3	54.0	35.7	75.7	31.5	69.7	60.6	22.3
25 to 29 years..............	9,249	55.4	46.3	30.2	75.9	30.2	70.7	66.0	16.6
30 to 34 years..............	10,272	47.0	39.1	27.2	78.1	22.2	72.7	69.7	12.2
35 to 39 years..............	10,853	30.5	23.9	18.6	71.5	13.6	68.3	65.9	6.9
40 to 44 years..............	11,512	19.5	14.0	10.8	71.8	5.9	69.4	67.0	4.4
Currently married	28,327	39.5	31.5	21.3	77.2	21.1	73.1	69.8	8.1
Currently cohabiting	5,570	50.4	43.2	30.2	77.2	31.0	72.2	64.7	20.3
Never married, not cohabiting....	21,568	44.4	36.4	25.4	55.8	16.5	50.7	43.9	15.9
Formerly married, not cohabiting..	6,096	34.5	28.0	22.0	71.0	14.1	66.0	64.0	14.4
Non-Hispanic White	40,420	43.2	36.4	25.4	70.0	17.5	64.9	63.1	12.0
Non-Hispanic Black	8,587	39.6	30.6	21.5	74.5	23.7	69.2	58.9	16.1
Hispanic[3]	9,107	39.7	28.9	20.6	63.4	24.3	57.1	48.5	12.5

[1] STD stands for sexually transmitted disease.   [2] Includes other races, not shown separately.   [3] Persons of Hispanic origin may be any race.

Source: U.S. National Center for Health Statistics, *Advance Data* , Number 350, "*Use of Contraception and Use of Family Planning Services in the United States: 1982-2002*," December 10, 2004.

Table 95. Current Contraceptive Use by Women, 15 to 44 Years of Age: 1995 and 2002

[In percent, except total (60,201 represents 60,201,000.) Based on the National Survey of Family Growth; see Appendix III]

Contraceptive status and method	All women, 1995	All women [1,2] (2002)	15–19 years	20–24 years	25–29 years	30–34 years	35–39 years	40–44 years	Non-Hispanic White	Black	Hispanic [3]	Never married, not cohabiting	Currently married	Formerly married, not cohabiting
					Age					Race/ethnicity			Marital status	
All women (1,000)	60,201	61,561	9,834	9,840	9,249	10,272	10,853	11,512	40,420	8,587	9,107	21,568	28,327	6,096
PERCENT DISTRIBUTION														
Using contraception (contraceptors) [4]	64.2	61.9	31.5	60.7	68.0	69.2	70.8	69.1	64.5	57.4	59.0	44.0	72.9	64.4
Female sterilization	17.8	16.7	–	2.2	10.3	19.0	29.2	34.7	15.5	22.3	19.9	4.4	21.7	35.3
Male sterilization	7.0	5.7	–	0.5	2.8	6.4	10.0	12.7	7.5	1.4	2.6	0.4	11.2	2.2
Pill	17.3	18.9	16.7	31.9	25.6	18.9	13.2	7.6	22.2	12.9	13.0	21.8	17.2	12.3
Implant, Lunelle (™), 3-month injectable	0.9	0.8	0.4	0.9	1.7	0.9	0.5	0.2	0.5	0.5	1.8	0.4	1.0	0.5
(Depo-Provera (™))	1.9	3.3	4.4	6.1	4.4	2.9	1.5	1.1	2.7	5.6	4.3	4.2	2.2	1.7
Intrauterine device (IUD)	0.5	1.3	0.1	1.1	2.5	2.2	1.0	0.8	0.9	0.8	3.2	0.2	1.9	1.9
Diaphragm	1.2	0.2	–	0.1	0.3	0.1	–	0.4	0.2	0.1	–	0.2	0.2	–
Condom	13.1	11.1	8.5	14.0	14.0	11.8	11.1	8.0	10.7	11.4	10.9	10.3	12.0	8.0
Periodic abstinence-calendar rhythm	1.3	0.7	–	0.8	0.3	0.9	1.1	1.2	0.8	0.3	0.6	0.2	1.3	0.3
Periodic abstinence-natural family planning	0.2	0.2	–	–	0.4	0.2	0.3	0.4	0.2	0.1	0.3	0.0	0.4	–
Withdrawal	2.0	2.5	0.8	3.1	5.3	2.6	2.4	1.0	2.5	1.5	2.2	1.6	3.0	1.3
Other methods [5]	1.1	0.6	0.6	0.2	0.4	0.4	0.5	1.1	0.7	0.5	0.3	0.2	0.7	0.9
Not using contraception	35.8	38.1	68.5	39.3	32.0	30.8	29.2	30.9	35.5	42.6	41.0	56.0	27.1	35.6
Surgically sterile-female (noncontraceptive)	3.0	1.5	–	–	0.4	0.9	2.1	4.9	1.7	1.5	0.9	0.4	2.1	3.0
Nonsurgically sterile-female or male [6]	1.7	1.6	0.7	0.7	0.9	1.4	1.2	4.4	1.7	1.5	1.7	1.0	2.0	2.5
Pregnant or postpartum	4.6	5.3	3.5	9.5	8.4	6.9	3.8	0.8	4.6	5.9	6.9	2.3	7.5	2.2
Seeking pregnancy	4.0	4.2	1.2	2.8	5.5	7.0	5.1	3.3	3.9	4.2	5.2	0.8	6.9	2.0
Other nonuse	22.5	25.5	63.1	26.3	16.9	14.6	16.9	17.6	23.7	29.7	26.4	51.4	8.6	26.0
Never had intercourse or no intercourse in 3 months before interview	17.1	18.1	56.2	17.9	8.9	7.6	9.1	10.8	17.0	19.4	18.7	42.9	2.3	17.7
Had intercourse in 3 months before interview	5.2	7.4	6.9	8.4	8.0	7.0	7.7	6.7	6.7	10.2	7.7	8.5	6.3	8.2
All other nonusers	0.2	–	–	–	–	–	0.1	0.1	–	0.1	–	–	–	0.1

– Represents or rounds to zero.   [1] Includes other races, not shown separately.   [2] Includes women who are currently cohabiting, not shown separately.   [3] Persons of Hispanic origin may be any race.   [4] Percents may not add to the total who were using contraception because more than one method could have been used in the month of interview.   [5] Includes implants, injectables, morning-after pill, suppository, Today (™) sponge, and less frequently used methods.   [6] Persons sterile from illness, accident, or congenital conditions.

Source: U.S. National Center for Health Statistics, Advance Data, Number 350, "Use of Contraception and Use of Family Planning Services in the United States: 1982–2002," December 10, 2004.

Vital Statistics   73

Table 96. Abortions—Number, Rate, and Ratio by Race: 1975 to 2002

(47,606 represents 47,606,000)

Year	Women 15–44 years old (1,000)	All races Abortions Number (1,000)	All races Abortions Rate per 1,000 women	All races Ratio per 1,000 live births [1]	Women 15 to 44 years old (1,000)	White Abortions Number (1,000)	White Abortions Rate per 1,000 women	White Ratio per 1,000 live births [1]	Women 15 to 44 years old (1,000)	Black and other Abortions Number (1,000)	Black and other Abortions Rate per 1,000 women	Black and other Ratio per 1,000 live births [1]
1975...	47,606	1,034	21.7	331	40,857	701	17.2	276	6,749	333	49.3	565
1980...	53,048	1,554	29.3	428	44,942	1,094	24.3	376	8,106	460	56.5	642
1985...	56,754	1,589	28.0	422	47,512	1,076	22.6	360	9,242	513	55.5	659
1986 [2]..	57,483	1,574	27.4	416	48,010	1,045	21.8	350	9,473	529	55.9	661
1987...	57,964	1,559	27.1	405	48,288	1,017	21.1	338	9,676	542	56.0	648
1988...	58,192	1,591	27.3	401	48,325	1,026	21.2	333	9,867	565	57.3	638
1989 [2]..	58,365	1,567	26.8	380	48,104	1,006	20.9	309	10,261	561	54.7	650
1990 [2]..	58,700	1,609	27.4	389	48,224	1,039	21.5	318	10,476	570	54.4	655
1991...	59,305	1,557	26.2	379	48,560	982	20.2	303	10,745	574	53.5	661
1992...	59,417	1,529	25.7	380	48,435	943	19.5	298	10,982	585	53.3	681
1993 [2]..	59,712	1,495	25.0	376	48,497	908	18.7	290	11,215	587	52.4	698
1994 [2]..	60,020	1,423	23.7	362	48,592	856	17.6	275	11,429	567	49.6	696
1995...	60,368	1,359	22.5	350	48,719	817	16.8	265	11,648	542	46.6	684
1996...	60,704	1,360	22.4	349	48,837	797	16.3	258	11,867	563	47.5	699
1997 [2]..	61,041	1,335	21.9	341	48,942	777	15.9	251	12,099	558	46.1	684
1998 [2]..	61,326	1,319	21.5	334	49,012	762	15.5	244	12,313	557	45.2	678
1999...	61,475	1,315	21.4	327	48,974	743	15.2	234	12,501	572	45.8	674
2000...	61,631	1,313	21.3	324	48,936	733	15.0	230	12,695	580	45.7	676
2001 [2]..	61,673	1,303	21.1	325	48,868	723	14.8	229	12,805	579	45.3	686
2002 [2]..	62,044	1,293	20.8	319	48,998	719	14.7	225	13,046	574	44.0	672

[1] Live births are those which occurred from July 1 of year shown through June 30 of the following year (to match time of conception with abortions). Births are classified by race of child 1975–1988, and by race of mother after 1988. [2] Total numbers of abortions in 1986, 1989, 1990, 1993, 1994, 1997, and 1998 have been estimated by interpolation; 2001 and 2002 have been estimated using trends in Centers for Disease Control data.

Source: 1975–1988, S.K. Henshaw and J. Van Vort, eds., *Abortion Factbook, 1992 Edition: Readings, Trends, and State and Local Data to 1988*, The Alan Guttmacher Institute, New York, NY, 1992 (copyright); 1989–2000, L.B. Finer and S.K. Henshaw, "Abortion Incidence and Services in the United States in 2000," *Perspectives on Sexual and Reproductive Health*, 35:6; 2001–2002, L.B. Finer and S.K. Henshaw, "Estimates of U.S. abortion incidence in 2001 and 2002," New York: The Alan Guttmacher Institute, 2005, <http://www.guttmacher.org/pubs/2005/05/18/abincidence.pdf>; and unpublished data from Guttmacher Institute.

Table 97. Abortions by Selected Characteristics: 1990 to 2002

[(1,609 represents 1,609,000). Number of abortions from surveys conducted by source; characteristics from the U.S. Centers for Disease Control's (CDC) annual abortion surveillance summaries, with adjustments for changes in states reporting data to the CDC each year]

Characteristic	Number (1,000) 1990	Number (1,000) 2000	Number (1,000) 2002	Percent distribution 1990	Percent distribution 2000	Percent distribution 2002	Abortion ratio [1] 1990	Abortion ratio [1] 2000	Abortion ratio [1] 2002
Total abortions	1,609	1,313	1,293	100	100	100	280	245	242
Age of woman:									
Less than 15 years old	13	9	8	1	1	1	515	512	527
15 to 19 years old	351	235	215	22	18	17	403	339	338
20 to 24 years old	532	430	431	33	33	33	328	296	296
25 to 29 years old	360	303	295	22	23	23	224	220	215
30 to 34 years old	216	190	196	13	15	15	196	169	169
35 to 39 years old	108	110	108	7	8	8	249	195	191
40 years old and over.......	29	37	40	2	3	3	354	276	278
Race of woman:									
White...................	1,039	733	719	65	56	56	241	187	184
Black and other	570	580	574	35	44	44	396	403	403
Marital status of woman:									
Married	341	246	233	21	19	18	104	84	80
Unmarried	1,268	1,067	1,060	79	81	82	516	443	433
Number of prior live births:									
None...................	780	533	516	49	41	40	316	248	243
One....................	396	361	359	25	28	28	230	216	214
Two....................	280	260	255	17	20	20	292	278	272
Three	102	104	107	6	8	8	279	285	287
Four or more............	50	56	56	3	4	4	223	250	246
Number of prior induced abortions:									
None...................	891	699	694	55	53	54	(NA)	(NA)	(NA)
One....................	443	355	343	28	27	26	(NA)	(NA)	(NA)
Two or more	275	259	256	17	20	20	(NA)	(NA)	(NA)
Weeks of gestation:									
Less than 9 weeks..........	825	757	788	51	58	61	(NA)	(NA)	(NA)
9 to 10 weeks	416	266	238	26	20	18	(NA)	(NA)	(NA)
11 to 12 weeks	195	138	124	12	11	10	(NA)	(NA)	(NA)
13 weeks or more	173	153	143	11	12	11	(NA)	(NA)	(NA)

NA Not available. [1] Number of abortions per 1,000 abortions and live births. Live births are those which occurred from July 1 of year shown through June 30 of the following year (to match time of conception with abortions).

Source: L.B. Finer and S.K. Henshaw, "Estimates of U.S. abortion incidence in 2001 and 2002," New York: The Alan Guttmacher Institute, 2005, <http://www.guttmacher.org/pubs/2005/05/18/abincidence.pdf>; and unpublished data, Guttmacher Institute.

Table 98. **Expectation of Life at Birth, 1970 to 2004, and Projections, 2010 and 2015**

[**In years.** Excludes deaths of nonresidents of the United States. See Appendix III]

Year	Total			White			Black		
	Total	Male	Female	Total	Male	Female	Total	Male	Female
1970	70.8	67.1	74.7	71.7	68.0	75.6	64.1	60.0	68.3
1971	71.1	67.4	75.0	72.0	68.3	75.8	64.6	60.5	68.9
1972	71.2	67.4	75.1	72.0	68.3	75.9	64.7	60.4	69.1
1973	71.4	67.6	75.3	72.2	68.5	76.1	65.0	60.9	69.3
1974	72.0	68.2	75.9	72.8	69.0	76.7	66.0	61.7	70.3
1975	72.6	68.8	76.6	73.4	69.5	77.3	66.8	62.4	71.3
1976	72.9	69.1	76.8	73.6	69.9	77.5	67.2	62.9	71.6
1977	73.3	69.5	77.2	74.0	70.2	77.9	67.7	63.4	72.0
1978	73.5	69.6	77.3	74.1	70.4	78.0	68.1	63.7	72.4
1979	73.9	70.0	77.8	74.6	70.8	78.4	68.5	64.0	72.9
1980	73.7	70.0	77.4	74.4	70.7	78.1	68.1	63.8	72.5
1981	74.1	70.4	77.8	74.8	71.1	78.4	68.9	64.5	73.2
1982	74.5	70.8	78.1	75.1	71.5	78.7	69.4	65.1	73.6
1983	74.6	71.0	78.1	75.2	71.6	78.7	69.4	65.2	73.5
1984	74.7	71.1	78.2	75.3	71.8	78.7	69.5	65.3	73.6
1985	74.7	71.1	78.2	75.3	71.8	78.7	69.3	65.0	73.4
1986	74.7	71.2	78.2	75.4	71.9	78.8	69.1	64.8	73.4
1987	74.9	71.4	78.3	75.6	72.1	78.9	69.1	64.7	73.4
1988	74.9	71.4	78.3	75.6	72.2	78.9	68.9	64.4	73.2
1989	75.1	71.7	78.5	75.9	72.5	79.2	68.8	64.3	73.3
1990	75.4	71.8	78.8	76.1	72.7	79.4	69.1	64.5	73.6
1991	75.5	72.0	78.9	76.3	72.9	79.6	69.3	64.6	73.8
1992	75.8	72.3	79.1	76.5	73.2	79.8	69.6	65.0	73.9
1993	75.5	72.2	78.8	76.3	73.1	79.5	69.2	64.6	73.7
1994	75.7	72.4	79.0	76.5	73.3	79.6	69.5	64.9	73.9
1995	75.8	72.5	78.9	76.5	73.4	79.6	69.6	65.2	73.9
1996	76.1	73.1	79.1	76.8	73.9	79.7	70.2	66.1	74.2
1997	76.5	73.6	79.4	77.2	74.3	79.9	71.1	67.2	74.7
1998	76.7	73.8	79.5	77.3	74.5	80.0	71.3	67.6	74.8
1999	76.7	73.9	79.4	77.3	74.6	79.9	71.4	67.8	74.7
2000	77.0	74.3	79.7	77.6	74.9	80.1	71.9	68.3	75.2
2001	77.2	74.4	79.8	77.7	75.0	80.2	72.2	68.6	75.5
2002	77.3	74.5	79.9	77.7	75.1	80.3	72.3	68.8	75.6
2003	77.5	74.8	80.1	78.0	75.3	80.5	72.7	69.0	76.1
2004 [1]	77.9	75.2	80.4	78.3	75.7	80.8	73.3	69.8	76.5
Projections [2]:									
2010	78.5	75.6	81.4	79.0	76.1	81.8	74.5	70.9	77.8
2015	79.2	76.2	82.2	80.9	78.0	83.8	75.5	71.9	78.9

[1] Preliminary data.   [2] Based on middle mortality assumptions; for details, see source. Source: U.S. Census Bureau, Population Division Working Paper No. 38.

Source: Except as noted, U.S. National Center for Health Statistics, *Vital Statistics of the United States*, annual, and *National Vital Statistics Reports (NVSR)* .

Vital Statistics   75

Table 99. Selected Life Table Values: 1979 to 2003

[See Appendix III]

Age and sex	Total 1979-1981	Total 1985	Total 1990	Total 1995	Total 2000	Total 2001	Total 2002	Total 2003	White 1979-1981	White 1985	White 1990	White 1995	White 2000	White 2001	White 2002	White 2003	Black 1979-1981	Black 1985	Black 1990	Black 1995	Black 2000	Black 2001	Black 2002	Black 2003
AVERAGE EXPECTATION OF LIFE IN YEARS																								
At birth: Male	70.1	71.1	71.8	72.5	74.3	74.4	74.5	74.8	70.8	71.8	72.7	73.4	74.9	75.0	75.1	75.3	64.1	65.0	64.5	65.2	68.3	68.6	68.8	69.0
Female	77.6	78.2	78.8	78.9	79.7	79.8	79.9	80.1	78.2	78.7	79.4	79.6	80.1	80.2	80.3	80.5	72.9	73.4	73.6	73.9	75.2	75.5	75.6	76.1
Age 20: Male	51.9	52.6	53.3	53.8	55.3	55.5	55.6	55.8	52.5	53.2	54.0	54.5	55.8	56.0	56.1	56.3	46.4	47.1	46.7	47.3	50.0	50.3	50.5	50.7
Female	59.0	59.3	59.8	60.5	60.7	60.7	60.7	60.9	59.4	59.8	60.3	60.3	60.9	60.9	61.0	61.2	54.9	55.2	55.3	55.5	56.6	56.8	57.0	57.4
Age 40: Male	33.6	34.2	35.1	35.6	36.7	37.0	37.0	37.3	34.0	34.7	35.6	36.1	37.1	37.3	37.4	37.6	29.5	29.8	30.1	30.6	32.3	32.6	32.6	32.9
Female	39.8	40.0	40.6	41.6	41.3	41.4	41.4	41.6	40.2	40.4	41.0	41.0	41.5	41.6	41.6	41.9	36.3	36.4	36.8	37.0	37.8	38.0	38.1	38.6
Age 50: Male	25.0	25.5	26.4	27.0	27.9	28.1	28.1	28.5	25.3	25.8	26.7	27.3	28.2	28.3	28.4	28.8	22.0	22.1	22.5	22.5	24.2	24.5	24.6	24.8
Female	30.7	30.8	31.3	32.4	32.0	32.1	32.2	32.4	31.0	31.1	31.6	31.7	32.0	32.2	32.4	32.6	27.8	27.8	28.2	28.5	29.1	29.4	29.5	29.9
Age 65: Male	14.2	14.5	15.1	15.6	16.2	16.4	16.4	16.6	14.3	14.5	15.2	15.7	16.3	16.5	16.6	16.9	13.3	13.0	13.2	13.7	14.2	14.4	14.6	14.9
Female	18.4	18.5	18.9	18.9	19.3	19.4	19.5	19.8	18.6	18.7	19.1	19.0	19.4	19.5	19.5	19.8	17.1	16.9	17.2	17.2	17.7	17.9	18.0	18.5
EXPECTED DEATHS PER 1,000 ALIVE AT SPECIFIED AGE [2]																								
At birth: Male	13.9	12.0	10.3	8.3	7.5	7.5	7.5	7.6	12.3	10.6	8.6	7.0	6.2	6.2	6.4	6.4	23.0	19.9	19.7	16.2	15.6	15.4	15.4	15.6
Female	11.2	9.4	8.2	6.8	6.2	6.1	6.1	6.1	9.7	8.0	6.6	5.6	5.1	5.1	5.1	5.1	19.3	16.5	16.3	13.8	12.7	12.5	13.2	12.4
Age 20: Male	1.8	1.5	1.6	(NA)	1.3	1.4	1.4	1.4	1.6	1.4	1.4	(NA)	1.2	1.2	1.3	1.3	2.2	1.9	2.7	(NA)	2.0	2.1	2.1	2.1
Female	0.6	0.5	0.5	(NA)	0.5	0.4	0.4	0.5	0.6	0.5	0.5	(NA)	0.4	0.4	0.4	0.4	0.7	0.6	0.7	(NA)	0.6	0.6	0.6	0.7
Age 40: Male	3.0	2.8	3.1	(NA)	2.6	2.6	2.7	2.7	2.5	2.5	2.7	(NA)	2.4	2.4	2.5	2.4	6.9	6.5	7.1	(NA)	4.6	4.3	4.3	4.0
Female	1.6	1.4	1.4	(NA)	1.5	1.5	1.5	1.5	1.4	1.3	1.2	(NA)	1.3	1.3	1.3	1.4	3.2	2.9	3.1	(NA)	2.8	2.9	2.6	2.9
Age 50: Male	7.8	6.8	6.2	(NA)	5.7	5.7	5.7	5.8	7.1	6.2	5.6	(NA)	5.2	5.2	5.2	5.3	14.9	13.3	12.8	(NA)	11.2	10.6	10.4	10.7
Female	4.2	3.8	3.5	(NA)	3.3	3.2	3.2	3.3	3.8	3.5	3.2	(NA)	2.9	2.9	2.8	3.0	7.7	6.8	6.8	(NA)	6.2	6.2	6.2	6.0
Age 65: Male	28.2	26.1	22.9	(NA)	20.0	19.3	18.9	18.5	27.4	25.2	23.0	(NA)	19.2	18.5	18.2	17.7	38.5	28.5	36.8	(NA)	29.6	30.0	29.3	29.1
Female	14.3	14.1	13.5	(NA)	12.7	12.3	12.1	11.9	13.6	13.5	12.8	(NA)	12.2	11.8	11.7	11.4	21.6	21.4	21.4	(NA)	18.2	18.0	17.8	18.0
NUMBER SURVIVING TO SPECIFIED AGE PER 1,000 BORN ALIVE																								
Age 20: Male	973	977	979	981	984	984	984	985	975	979	981	981	986	986	986	986	961	966	963	967	973	973	974	974
Female	982	985	986	987	989	989	989	990	984	986	986	987	990	991	991	991	972	976	976	978	981	982	981	982
Age 40: Male	933	941	938	940	953	953	953	954	940	946	946	940	958	958	958	958	885	897	880	885	918	920	920	923
Female	965	970	971	971	975	975	975	975	969	973	975	971	978	978	978	978	941	948	944	944	955	957	957	958
Age 50: Male	890	902	899	899	917	918	918	918	901	911	912	899	925	925	925	925	801	820	801	803	855	859	862	864
Female	941	948	950	950	954	954	954	954	947	953	957	950	960	959	959	959	896	908	904	902	915	918	918	919
Age 65: Male	706	727	741	750	779	785	786	787	724	744	760	750	794	799	799	780	551	571	571	581	640	656	657	659
Female	835	844	851	855	863	866	867	867	848	855	864	855	874	875	876	876	733	746	751	758	780	796	785	786

NA Not available. [1] Includes other races not shown separately. [2] See footnote 1, Table 100.

Source: U.S. National Center for Health Statistics, *U.S. Life Tables and Actuarial Tables, 1979–81*; *Vital Statistics of the United States*, annual; and unpublished data.

[See Appendix III]

Age (years)	Expectation of life in years					Expected deaths per 1,000 alive at specified age [2]				
	Total [1]	White Male	White Female	Black Male	Black Female	Total [1]	White Male	White Female	Black Male	Black Female
At birth	77.5	75.3	80.5	69.0	76.1	6.87	6.37	5.05	15.57	12.45
1	77.0	74.8	79.9	69.1	76.0	0.47	0.46	0.37	0.85	0.60
2	76.1	73.8	78.9	68.2	75.1	0.33	0.33	0.27	0.53	0.45
3	75.1	72.9	78.0	67.2	74.1	0.26	0.27	0.20	0.45	0.34
4	74.1	71.9	77.0	66.2	73.1	0.20	0.20	0.17	0.30	0.19
5	73.1	70.9	76.0	65.3	72.2	0.17	0.18	0.13	0.25	0.21
6	72.1	69.9	75.0	64.3	71.2	0.15	0.17	0.11	0.21	0.20
7	71.1	68.9	74.0	63.3	70.2	0.14	0.14	0.13	0.22	0.17
8	70.2	67.9	73.0	62.3	69.2	0.14	0.15	0.11	0.22	0.16
9	69.2	66.9	72.0	61.3	68.2	0.13	0.13	0.13	0.19	0.15
10	68.2	66.0	71.0	60.3	67.2	0.17	0.16	0.13	0.29	0.20
11	67.2	65.0	70.0	59.3	66.2	0.15	0.15	0.11	0.25	0.21
12	66.2	64.0	69.1	58.4	65.2	0.18	0.21	0.12	0.30	0.19
13	65.2	63.0	68.1	57.4	64.3	0.21	0.24	0.16	0.32	0.20
14	64.2	62.0	67.1	56.4	63.3	0.26	0.31	0.17	0.42	0.19
15	63.2	61.0	66.1	55.4	62.3	0.34	0.41	0.25	0.54	0.24
16	62.3	60.0	65.1	54.4	61.3	0.53	0.68	0.37	0.90	0.28
17	61.3	59.1	64.1	53.5	60.3	0.66	0.90	0.41	1.06	0.37
18	60.3	58.1	63.2	52.5	59.3	0.86	1.14	0.50	1.67	0.51
19	59.4	57.2	62.2	51.6	58.4	0.92	1.28	0.46	1.91	0.50
20	58.4	56.3	61.2	50.7	57.4	0.96	1.29	0.45	2.13	0.73
21	57.5	55.4	60.2	49.8	56.4	0.96	1.34	0.47	1.98	0.63
22	56.5	54.4	59.3	48.9	55.5	0.99	1.34	0.48	2.24	0.71
23	55.6	53.5	58.3	48.0	54.5	0.95	1.24	0.46	2.47	0.72
24	54.7	52.6	57.3	47.2	53.6	0.96	1.24	0.48	2.42	0.74
25	53.7	51.6	56.3	46.3	52.6	0.92	1.18	0.46	2.39	0.72
26	52.8	50.7	55.4	45.4	51.6	0.96	1.21	0.49	2.63	0.94
27	51.8	49.7	54.4	44.5	50.7	0.95	1.16	0.50	2.60	1.02
28	50.9	48.8	53.4	43.6	49.7	0.93	1.20	0.51	2.32	0.85
29	49.9	47.9	52.5	42.7	48.8	1.00	1.24	0.54	2.53	1.16
30	48.9	46.9	51.5	41.8	47.8	1.01	1.28	0.55	2.47	1.14
31	48.0	46.0	50.5	40.9	46.9	1.05	1.31	0.61	2.46	1.13
32	47.0	45.0	49.5	40.0	45.9	1.11	1.39	0.62	2.75	1.28
33	46.1	44.1	48.6	39.1	45.0	1.16	1.38	0.72	2.70	1.42
34	45.2	43.2	47.6	38.2	44.1	1.23	1.48	0.74	2.72	1.65
35	44.2	42.2	46.6	37.3	43.1	1.36	1.58	0.86	3.07	1.84
36	43.3	41.3	45.7	36.5	42.2	1.46	1.73	0.91	3.24	1.99
37	42.3	40.4	44.7	35.6	41.3	1.58	1.87	1.01	3.31	2.11
38	41.4	39.4	43.8	34.7	40.4	1.67	1.96	1.08	3.64	2.20
39	40.5	38.5	42.8	33.8	39.5	1.85	2.18	1.21	3.89	2.46
40	39.5	37.6	41.9	32.9	38.6	2.03	2.40	1.34	3.96	2.87
41	38.6	36.7	40.9	32.1	37.7	2.21	2.61	1.46	4.70	2.97
42	37.7	35.8	40.0	31.2	36.8	2.41	2.81	1.61	5.24	3.22
43	36.8	34.9	39.0	30.4	35.9	2.55	2.99	1.72	5.52	3.24
44	35.9	34.0	38.1	29.6	35.0	2.85	3.37	1.90	5.89	3.94
45	35.0	33.1	37.2	28.7	34.1	3.01	3.53	2.03	6.32	4.13
46	34.1	32.2	36.3	27.9	33.3	3.37	3.95	2.19	7.49	4.75
47	33.2	31.3	35.3	27.1	32.4	3.59	4.27	2.35	7.87	4.81
48	32.3	30.5	34.4	26.3	31.6	3.84	4.53	2.49	8.89	5.20
49	31.4	29.6	33.5	25.6	30.8	4.18	4.92	2.75	9.61	5.50
50	30.6	28.8	32.6	24.8	29.9	4.49	5.30	2.96	10.72	5.98
51	29.7	27.9	31.7	24.1	29.1	4.80	5.63	3.15	11.66	6.62
52	28.8	27.1	30.8	23.3	28.3	5.20	6.03	3.45	12.62	7.06
53	28.0	26.2	29.9	22.6	27.5	5.37	6.29	3.61	12.32	7.12
54	27.1	25.4	29.0	21.9	26.7	6.06	7.12	4.10	13.95	8.12
55	26.3	24.6	28.1	21.2	25.9	6.33	7.41	4.41	15.02	8.44
56	25.5	23.7	27.2	20.5	25.1	7.23	8.60	5.16	15.83	9.20
57	24.7	22.9	26.4	19.8	24.3	7.10	8.27	5.10	15.81	9.35
58	23.8	22.1	25.5	19.2	23.6	8.34	9.63	6.13	18.38	10.63
59	23.0	21.3	24.7	18.5	22.8	9.13	10.66	6.72	19.66	11.24
60	22.2	20.6	23.8	17.9	22.1	10.21	11.92	7.55	21.85	12.91
61	21.5	19.8	23.0	17.3	21.4	10.49	12.42	7.73	22.10	12.96
62	20.7	19.0	22.2	16.6	20.6	11.97	14.05	8.90	25.36	14.71
63	19.9	18.3	21.4	16.1	19.9	12.70	15.03	9.57	24.94	15.22
64	19.2	17.6	20.6	15.5	19.2	14.03	16.43	10.79	27.94	16.62
65	18.4	16.9	19.8	14.9	18.5	15.00	17.71	11.40	29.10	17.99
70	14.9	13.5	16.0	12.1	15.3	23.23	27.82	18.42	39.73	25.68
75	11.8	10.5	12.6	9.8	12.4	35.77	43.92	28.73	58.83	37.18
80	9.0	8.0	9.6	7.9	9.8	56.85	69.33	48.36	84.92	55.48

[1] Includes other races not shown separately.　[2] Based on the proportion of the cohort who are alive at the beginning of the indicated age who will die before reaching the age shown plus 1. For example, out of every 1,000 people alive and exactly 50 years old at the beginning of the period, between 4 and 5 (4.49) will die before reaching their 51st birthdays.

Source: U.S. National Center for Health Statistics, *Vital Statistics of the United States*, annual; and *National Vital Statistics Report (NVSR)*, Vol. 54, No. 14.

Table 101. Deaths and Death Rates by Sex, Race, and Hispanic Origin: 1980 to 2004

[1,990 represents 1,990,000. Rates are per 1,000 population for specified groups. Excludes deaths of nonresidents of the United States and fetal deaths. For explanation of age-adjustment, see text, this section. The standard population for age-adjustment is the projected year 2000 population of the United States. See Appendix III. Data for Hispanic origin and specified races other than White and Black should be interpreted with caution because of inconsistencies between reporting Hispanic origin and race on death certificates and censuses and surveys]

Sex, race, and Hispanic origin	1980	1990	1995	1997	1998	1999	2000	2001	2002	2003	2004, prel.
Deaths [1] (1,000)	1,990	2,148	2,312	2,314	2,337	2,391	2,403	2,416	2,443	2,448	2,398
Male [1] (1,000)	1,075	1,113	1,173	1,154	1,157	1,175	1,178	1,183	1,199	1,202	1,180
Female [1] (1,000)	915	1,035	1,139	1,160	1,180	1,216	1,226	1,233	1,244	1,246	1,218
White (1,000)	1,739	1,853	1,987	1,996	2,016	2,061	2,071	2,080	2,103	2,104	2,060
Male (1,000)	934	951	997	987	990	1,005	1,007	1,011	1,025	1,026	1,007
Female (1,000)	805	902	990	1,010	1,026	1,056	1,064	1,068	1,077	1,078	1,053
Black (1,000)	233	265	286	277	278	285	286	288	290	291	285
Male (1,000)	130	145	154	144	143	146	145	145	146	147	145
Female (1,000)	103	120	132	132	135	139	141	142	143	143	140
Asian or Pacific Islander (1,000)	11	21	28	31	32	34	35	37	38	40	40
Male (1,000)	7	12	16	17	18	18	19	20	20	21	21
Female (1,000)	4	9	12	14	14	15	16	17	18	19	19
American Indian, Eskimo, Aleut (1,000)	7	8	10	11	11	11	11	12	12	13	13
Male (1,000)	4	5	6	6	6	6	6	6	7	7	7
Female (1,000)	3	3	4	5	5	5	5	6	6	6	6
Hispanic origin [2] (1,000)	(NA)	(NA)	(NA)	95	98	104	107	113	117	122	121
Male (1,000)	(NA)	(NA)	(NA)	54	56	58	60	63	66	68	68
Female (1,000)	(NA)	(NA)	(NA)	41	43	46	47	50	51	54	53
Non-Hispanic, White (1,000)	(NA)	(NA)	(NA)	1,895	1,913	1,953	1,960	1,963	1,982	1,979	1,937
Male (1,000)	(NA)	(NA)	(NA)	930	932	945	945	946	958	956	939
Female (1,000)	(NA)	(NA)	(NA)	966	981	1,008	1,015	1,017	1,024	1,023	999
Death rates [1]	8.8	8.6	8.7	8.5	8.5	8.6	8.5	8.5	8.5	8.4	8.2
Male [1]	9.8	9.2	9.0	8.6	8.6	8.6	8.5	8.5	8.5	8.4	8.2
Female [1]	7.9	8.1	8.4	8.3	8.4	8.5	8.6	8.5	8.5	8.4	8.2
White	8.9	8.9	9.0	8.9	8.9	9.0	9.0	9.0	9.0	8.9	8.6
Male	9.8	9.3	9.3	8.9	8.9	9.1	8.9	8.8	8.8	8.8	8.5
Female	8.1	8.5	8.5	8.9	8.9	9.2	9.1	9.1	9.1	9.0	8.7
Black	8.8	8.7	8.5	7.9	7.8	7.9	7.8	7.7	7.7	7.6	7.4
Male	10.3	10.1	9.8	8.7	8.5	8.8	8.3	8.2	8.2	8.1	7.8
Female	7.3	7.5	7.6	7.2	7.2	7.6	7.3	7.3	7.2	7.2	7.0
Asian or Pacific Islander	3.0	2.8	2.9	2.9	2.9	3.0	3.0	3.0	3.0	3.0	3.0
Male	3.8	3.3	3.4	3.4	3.4	3.3	3.3	3.4	3.3	3.3	3.2
Female	2.2	2.3	2.5	2.5	2.5	2.6	2.6	2.7	2.7	2.8	2.8
American Indian, Eskimo, Aleut	4.9	4.0	4.1	4.0	4.0	4.0	3.8	3.9	4.0	4.2	4.1
Male	6.0	4.8	4.6	4.6	4.4	4.3	4.2	4.2	4.4	4.6	4.5
Female	3.8	3.3	3.6	3.5	3.5	3.7	3.5	3.6	3.7	3.9	3.8
Hispanic origin [2]	(NA)	(NA)	(NA)	3.1	3.0	3.1	3.0	3.1	3.0	3.1	2.9
Male	(NA)	4.1	(NA)	3.4	3.3	3.7	3.3	3.3	3.3	3.3	3.2
Female	(NA)	2.9	(NA)	2.7	2.7	2.9	2.7	2.8	2.7	2.8	2.7
Non-Hispanic, White	(NA)	(NA)	(NA)	9.7	9.7	9.9	9.9	9.9	10.0	9.9	9.7
Male	(NA)	(NA)	(NA)	9.7	9.7	9.8	9.8	9.8	9.8	9.8	9.6
Female	(NA)	(NA)	(NA)	9.6	9.8	10.0	10.1	10.1	10.1	10.1	9.8
Age-adjusted death rates [1]	10.4	9.4	9.2	8.8	8.7	8.8	8.7	8.5	8.5	8.3	8.0
Male [1]	13.5	12.0	11.5	10.9	10.7	10.7	10.5	10.3	10.1	9.9	9.6
Female [1]	8.2	7.5	7.5	7.3	7.2	7.3	7.3	7.2	7.2	7.1	6.8
White	10.1	9.1	8.9	8.6	8.5	8.5	8.5	8.4	8.3	8.2	7.9
Male	13.2	11.7	11.1	10.6	10.4	10.4	10.3	10.1	9.9	9.7	9.4
Female	8.0	7.3	7.3	7.1	7.1	7.2	7.2	7.1	7.0	6.9	6.7
Black	13.1	12.5	12.2	11.4	11.3	11.4	11.2	11.0	10.8	10.7	10.2
Male	17.0	16.4	15.8	14.6	14.3	14.3	14.0	13.8	13.4	13.2	12.6
Female	10.3	9.8	9.7	9.2	9.2	9.3	9.3	9.1	9.0	8.9	8.5
Asian or Pacific Islander	5.9	5.8	6.2	5.3	5.2	5.2	5.1	4.9	4.7	4.7	4.5
Male	7.9	7.2	7.9	6.6	6.5	6.4	6.2	6.0	5.8	5.6	5.3
Female	4.3	4.7	4.9	4.3	4.3	4.3	4.2	4.1	4.0	3.9	3.8
American Indian, Eskimo, Aleut	8.7	7.2	7.2	7.7	7.7	7.8	7.1	6.9	6.8	6.9	6.5
Male	11.1	9.2	8.6	9.7	9.4	9.3	8.4	8.0	7.9	8.0	7.5
Female	6.6	5.6	5.9	6.3	6.4	6.7	6.0	5.9	5.8	5.9	5.6
Hispanic origin [2]	(NA)	(NA)	(NA)	6.7	6.7	6.8	6.7	6.6	6.3	6.2	5.8
Male	(NA)	8.9	(NA)	8.4	8.3	7.4	8.2	8.0	7.7	7.5	7.0
Female	(NA)	5.4	(NA)	5.4	5.4	4.9	5.5	5.4	5.2	5.2	4.8
Non-Hispanic, White	(NA)	(NA)	(NA)	8.6	8.5	8.6	8.6	8.4	8.4	8.3	8.0
Male	(NA)	(NA)	(NA)	10.6	10.5	10.5	10.4	10.1	10.0	10.0	9.5
Female	(NA)	(NA)	(NA)	7.1	7.1	7.2	7.2	7.1	7.1	7.0	6.8

NA Not available.   [1] Includes other races, not shown separately.   [2] Persons of Hispanic origin may be any race.

Source: U.S. National Center for Health Statistics, *Vital Statistics of the United States*, annual; and *National Vital Statistics Reports (NVSR)*.

Table 102. **Death Rates by Age, Sex, and Race: 1950 to 2004**

[**Rates per 100,000 population.** See headnote, Table 101 and Appendix III]

Characteristic	All ages [1]	Under 1 year	1–4 years	5–14 years	15–24 years	25–34 years	35–44 years	45–54 years	55–64 years	65–74 years	75–84 years	85 years and over
MALE												
1950	1,106	3,728	152	71	168	217	429	1,067	2,395	4,931	10,426	21,636
1960	1,105	3,059	120	56	152	188	373	992	2,310	4,914	10,178	21,186
1970	1,090	2,410	93	51	189	215	403	959	2,283	4,874	10,010	17,822
1980	977	1,429	73	37	172	196	299	767	1,815	4,105	8,817	18,801
1990	918	1,083	52	29	147	204	310	610	1,553	3,492	7,889	18,057
2000	853	807	36	21	115	139	255	543	1,231	2,980	6,973	17,501
2003	840	777	35	20	117	141	255	552	1,166	2,772	6,642	15,794
2004 [2]	816	752	32	19	113	137	240	539	1,121	2,647	6,409	15,100
White:												
1990	931	896	46	26	131	176	268	549	1,467	3,398	7,845	18,268
2000	888	668	33	20	106	124	234	497	1,163	2,906	6,933	17,716
2003	878	659	32	18	109	129	238	509	1,102	2,707	6,621	16,038
2004 [2]	854	635	29	18	107	125	226	501	1,061	2,589	6,406	15,322
Black:												
1990	1,008	2,112	86	41	252	431	700	1,261	2,618	4,946	9,130	16,955
2000	834	1,568	55	28	181	261	453	1,018	2,080	4,254	8,486	16,791
2003	814	1,410	54	27	171	256	427	991	2,011	3,981	8,067	14,903
2004 [2]	785	1,385	49	26	161	249	392	946	1,932	3,792	7,648	14,422
Asian or Pacific Islander [3]:												
1990	334	605	45	21	76	80	131	287	789	2,041	5,009	12,446
2000	333	529	23	13	55	55	105	250	642	1,661	4,328	12,125
2003	330	497	25	15	56	54	96	243	566	1,473	4,041	10,392
2004 [2]	319	463	20	14	53	50	88	229	528	1,363	3,766	10,341
American Indian, Eskimo, Aleut [3]:												
1990	476	1,057	77	33	220	256	365	620	1,211	2,462	5,389	11,244
2000	416	700	45	20	136	179	295	520	1,090	2,478	5,351	10,726
2003	458	912	57	29	153	185	338	584	1,058	2,237	4,644	9,584
2004 [2]	450	1,076	55	24	133	186	322	543	1,065	2,174	4,448	7,984
FEMALE												
1950	824	2,855	127	49	89	143	290	642	1,405	3,333	8,400	19,195
1960	809	2,321	98	37	61	107	229	527	1,196	2,872	7,633	19,008
1970	808	1,864	75	32	68	102	231	517	1,099	2,580	6,678	15,518
1980	785	1,142	55	24	58	76	159	413	934	2,145	5,440	14,747
1990	812	856	41	19	49	74	138	343	879	1,991	4,883	14,274
2000	855	663	29	15	43	64	143	313	772	1,921	4,815	14,719
2003	843	619	28	14	44	65	149	318	733	1,823	4,676	14,063
2004 [2]	817	610	28	14	43	63	142	311	706	1,761	4,539	13,355
White:												
1990	847	690	36	18	46	62	117	309	823	1,924	4,839	14,401
2000	912	551	26	14	41	55	126	281	731	1,868	4,785	14,891
2003	902	521	26	13	43	58	133	287	694	1,781	4,672	14,241
2004 [2]	875	511	25	13	42	56	129	283	671	1,725	4,536	13,531
Black:												
1990	748	1,736	68	28	69	160	299	639	1,453	2,866	5,688	13,310
2000	733	1,280	45	20	58	122	272	588	1,227	2,690	5,697	13,941
2003	718	1,132	40	19	54	114	270	582	1,179	2,487	5,386	13,617
2004 [2]	696	1,138	41	21	53	110	254	554	1,126	2,365	5,272	12,861
Asian or Pacific Islander [3]:												
1990	234	518	32	13	29	38	70	183	483	1,089	3,128	10,254
2000	262	434	20	12	22	28	66	156	391	996	2,882	9,052
2003	279	428	20	12	29	30	58	151	359	990	2,682	8,329
2004 [2]	276	399	20	9	23	27	53	138	335	942	2,571	8,400
American Indian, Eskimo, Aleut [3]:												
1990	330	689	38	26	69	102	156	381	806	1,679	3,073	8,201
2000	346	492	40	18	59	85	172	285	772	1,900	3,850	9,118
2003	388	676	43	18	62	89	196	364	785	1,711	3,920	7,920
2004 [2]	379	725	56	20	63	103	188	338	702	1,712	3,525	7,108

[1] Figures for age not stated are included in "All ages" but not distributed among age groups. [2] Preliminary data. [3] The death rates for specified races other than White and Black should be interpreted with caution because of inconsistencies between reporting race on death certificates and censuses and surveys.

Source: U.S. National Center for Health Statistics, *Vital Statistics of the United States,* annual and National Vital Statistics Reports (NVSR).

Table 103. Age-Adjusted Death Rates by Sex, Race, and Hispanic Origin: 1950 to 2003

[Age-adjusted rates per 100,000 population; see headnote, Table 101. Populations enumerated as of April 1 for census years and estimated as of July 1 for all other years. Beginning 1970, excludes deaths of nonresidents of the United States. Data for Hispanic origin and specified races other than White and Black should be interpreted with caution because of inconsistencies reporting race on death certificates and on censuses and surveys. See Appendix III]

Sex, race, and Hispanic origin	1950	1960	1970	1980	1990	1995	2000	2001	2002	2003
ALL RACES [1]										
Total	1,446	1,339	1,223	1,039	939	919	869	855	845	833
Male	1,674	1,609	1,542	1,348	1,203	1,150	1,054	1,029	1,014	994
Female.	1,236	1,105	971	818	751	748	731	722	715	706
WHITE										
Total	1,411	1,311	1,193	1,013	910	890	850	837	829	817
Male	1,643	1,586	1,514	1,318	1,166	1,113	1,029	1,006	993	974
Female.	1,198	1,074	944	796	729	727	715	707	701	693
BLACK										
Total	(NA)	1,578	1,518	1,315	1,250	1,225	1,121	1,101	1,083	1,066
Male	(NA)	1,811	1,874	1,698	1,645	1,582	1,404	1,375	1,341	1,319
Female.	(NA)	1,370	1,229	1,033	975	970	928	913	902	886
ASIAN OR PACIFIC ISLANDER										
Total	(NA)	(NA)	(NA)	590	582	616	506	492	474	466
Male	(NA)	(NA)	(NA)	787	716	788	624	597	578	563
Female.	(NA)	(NA)	(NA)	426	469	488	417	412	396	393
AMERICAN INDIAN, ESKIMO, ALEUT										
Total	(NA)	(NA)	(NA)	867	716	717	709	687	677	685
Male	(NA)	(NA)	(NA)	1,112	916	864	842	799	794	797
Female.	(NA)	(NA)	(NA)	662	562	593	605	594	581	592
HISPANIC ORIGIN [2]										
Total	(NA)	(NA)	(NA)	(NA)	(NA)	(NA)	666	659	629	621
Male	(NA)	(NA)	(NA)	(NA)	886	(NA)	818	803	767	748
Female.	(NA)	(NA)	(NA)	(NA)	537	(NA)	546	544	518	516
NON-HISPANIC, WHITE										
Total	(NA)	(NA)	(NA)	(NA)	(NA)	(NA)	856	843	838	826
Male	(NA)	(NA)	(NA)	(NA)	(NA)	(NA)	1,035	1,013	1,002	984
Female.	(NA)	(NA)	(NA)	(NA)	(NA)	(NA)	722	714	710	702

NA Not available.   [1] For 1950 to 1990 includes deaths among races not shown separately.   [2] Persons of Hispanic origin may be any race.

Source: U.S. National Center for Health Statistics, *Vital Statistics of the United States,* annual and National Vital Statistics Reports (NVSR).

Table 104. Death Rates by Hispanic Origin Status, Sex, and Age: 1990 to 2004

[Rates per 100,000 population. Rates are based on populations enumerated as of April 1 for census years and estimated as of July 1 for all other years. Excludes deaths of nonresidents of the United States. Data for Hispanic origin should be interpreted with caution because of inconsistencies between reporting Hispanic origin and race on death certificates and censuses and surveys]

Age	Hispanic male				Hispanic female				Non-Hispanic White male		Non-Hispanic White female	
	1990	2000	2003	2004 [1]	1990	2000	2003	2004 [1]	2003	2004 [1]	2003	2004 [1]
Age-adjusted [2].	886	818	748	703	537	546	516	484	984	950	702	679
Crude.	412	331	331	317	285	275	279	268	979	958	1,008	981
Under 1 year.	922	637	666	634	747	554	552	525	647	629	503	499
1 to 4 years.	54	32	34	30	42	28	26	25	30	29	25	25
5 to 14 years.	26	18	18	16	17	13	13	12	18	18	13	13
15 to 24 years	159	108	113	112	41	32	36	30	106	104	44	45
25 to 34 years	234	120	118	106	63	43	43	41	130	129	61	60
35 to 44 years	342	211	190	177	109	101	96	86	244	233	138	135
45 to 54 years	534	439	436	411	253	224	219	205	513	507	293	291
55 to 64 years	1,124	966	921	862	608	548	528	502	1,111	1,072	705	683
65 to 74 years	2,368	2,288	2,116	1,983	1,454	1,423	1,343	1,293	2,739	2,624	1,808	1,754
75 to 84 years	5,369	5,395	4,949	4,782	3,351	3,625	3,506	3,325	6,692	6,484	4,721	4,593
85 years and over.	12,272	13,086	11,029	10,022	10,099	11,203	10,128	9,251	16,234	15,558	14,377	13,691

[1] Preliminary data.   [2] See headnote, Table 101.

Source: U.S. National Center for Health Statistics, *Vital Statistics of the United States,* annual and National Vital Statistics Reports (NVSR).

Table 105. Deaths and Death Rates by State and Island Areas: 1990 to 2004

[2,148 represents 2,148,000. By state of residence. Excludes deaths of nonresidents of the United States. Caution should be used in comparing death rates by state; rates are affected by the population composition of the area. For explanation of age adjustment, see table 101. See also Appendix III]

State and Island Areas	Number of deaths (1,000)						Crude rate per 1,000 population [1]						Age-adjusted rate, 2004 [2]
	1990	1995	2000	2002	2003	2004 [2]	1990	1995	2000	2002	2003	2004 [2]	
United States . .	2,148	2,312	2,403	2,443	2,448	2,398	8.6	8.7	8.5	8.5	8.4	8.2	8.0
Alabama	39	42	45	46	47	46	9.7	10.0	10.1	10.3	10.4	10.2	9.9
Alaska	2	3	3	3	3	3	4.0	4.2	4.6	4.7	4.9	4.6	7.5
Arizona	29	35	41	43	43	43	7.9	8.4	7.9	7.8	7.8	7.5	7.6
Arkansas	25	27	28	29	28	28	10.5	10.8	10.6	10.6	10.2	10.0	9.2
California	214	224	230	235	239	(NA)	7.2	7.1	6.8	6.7	6.7	(NA)	(NA)
Colorado	22	25	27	29	30	28	6.6	6.7	6.3	6.5	6.5	6.1	7.4
Connecticut	28	29	30	30	30	29	8.4	9.0	8.8	8.7	8.5	8.4	7.0
Delaware	6	6	7	7	7	7	8.7	8.8	8.8	8.5	8.6	8.6	8.2
Dist. of Columbia . .	7	7	6	6	6	5	12.0	12.4	10.5	10.2	9.9	9.8	9.7
Florida	134	153	164	168	169	169	10.4	10.8	10.3	10.0	9.9	9.7	7.6
Georgia	52	58	64	65	66	66	8.0	8.1	7.8	7.6	7.7	7.4	9.2
Hawaii	7	8	8	9	9	9	6.1	6.4	6.8	7.1	7.1	7.1	6.2
Idaho . .	7	9	10	10	10	10	7.4	7.3	7.4	7.4	7.6	7.2	7.5
Illinois	103	108	107	107	105	(NA)	9.0	9.2	8.6	8.5	8.3	(NA)	(NA)
Indiana	50	53	55	55	56	54	8.9	9.2	9.1	9.0	9.0	8.7	8.5
Iowa	27	28	28	28	28	27	9.7	9.9	9.6	9.5	9.5	9.1	7.3
Kansas	22	24	25	25	25	24	9.0	9.3	9.2	9.2	9.0	8.7	8.0
Kentucky	35	37	40	41	40	39	9.5	9.6	9.8	9.9	9.8	9.3	9.3
Louisiana	38	40	41	42	43	42	8.9	9.1	9.2	9.4	9.5	9.4	9.9
Maine	11	12	12	13	13	12	9.0	9.5	9.7	9.8	9.6	9.4	8.0
Maryland	38	42	44	44	44	43	8.0	8.3	8.3	8.1	8.1	7.8	8.0
Massachusetts . . .	53	55	57	57	56	55	8.8	9.1	8.9	8.9	8.8	8.5	7.4
Michigan	79	84	87	88	87	85	8.5	8.8	8.7	8.7	8.6	8.4	8.1
Minnesota	35	38	38	39	38	37	7.9	8.1	7.7	7.7	7.4	7.3	6.9
Mississippi	25	27	29	29	28	28	9.8	10.0	10.1	10.0	9.9	9.6	10.0
Missouri	50	54	55	56	56	54	9.8	10.2	9.9	9.9	9.7	9.4	8.7
Montana	7	8	8	9	8	8	8.6	8.8	9.0	9.4	9.2	8.7	7.8
Nebraska	15	15	15	16	15	15	9.4	9.3	8.8	9.1	8.9	8.4	7.5
Nevada	9	13	15	17	18	18	7.8	8.2	7.6	7.8	8.0	7.6	8.8
New Hampshire . . .	8	9	10	10	10	10	7.7	8.0	7.8	7.7	7.5	7.8	7.6
New Jersey	70	74	75	74	74	(NA)	9.1	9.3	8.9	8.6	8.5	(NA)	(NA)
New Mexico	11	13	13	14	15	14	7.0	7.4	7.4	7.7	7.9	7.5	7.8
New York	169	168	158	158	156	153	9.4	9.3	8.3	8.3	8.1	7.9	7.3
North Carolina	57	65	72	72	73	72	8.6	9.0	8.9	8.7	8.7	8.5	8.7
North Dakota	6	6	6	6	6	6	8.9	9.3	9.1	9.3	9.6	8.8	7.0
Ohio	99	106	108	110	109	106	9.1	9.5	9.5	9.6	9.5	9.3	8.5
Oklahoma	30	33	35	36	36	34	9.7	10.0	10.2	10.2	10.2	9.8	9.5
Oregon	25	28	30	31	31	30	8.8	9.0	8.6	8.8	8.7	8.4	7.8
Pennsylvania	122	128	131	130	130	128	10.3	10.6	10.7	10.6	10.5	10.3	8.1
Rhode Island	10	10	10	10	10	10	9.5	9.8	9.6	9.6	9.3	9.0	7.4
South Carolina . . .	30	34	37	38	38	37	8.5	9.1	9.2	9.2	9.2	8.9	9.0
South Dakota	6	7	7	7	7	7	9.1	9.5	9.3	9.1	9.3	8.9	7.5
Tennessee	46	51	55	57	57	56	9.5	9.8	9.7	9.8	9.8	9.5	9.5
Texas	125	138	150	156	155	153	7.4	7.4	7.2	7.1	7.0	6.8	8.4
Utah	9	11	12	13	13	13	5.3	5.6	5.5	5.7	5.7	5.6	7.6
Vermont	5	5	5	5	5	5	8.2	8.5	8.4	8.2	8.3	8.0	7.3
Virginia	48	53	56	57	58	57	7.8	8.0	8.0	7.8	7.9	7.6	8.1
Washington	37	41	44	45	46	45	7.6	7.5	7.5	7.5	7.5	7.2	7.4
West Virginia	19	20	21	21	21	21	10.8	11.1	11.7	11.7	11.8	11.4	9.7
Wisconsin	43	45	46	47	46	46	8.7	8.8	8.7	8.6	8.4	8.3	7.5
Wyoming	3	4	4	4	4	4	7.1	7.7	7.9	8.4	8.3	7.8	7.8
Puerto Rico	26	30	28	28	28	29	7.3	8.1	7.2	7.2	7.3	7.4	7.4
Virgin Islands . . .	(Z)	1	1	1	1	1	4.6	5.8	5.3	5.7	5.8	5.7	5.7
Guam	1	1	1	1	1	1	3.9	4.1	4.2	4.0	4.2	4.1	4.1
American Samoa	(NA)	(NA)	(Z)	(Z)	(Z)	(Z)	(NA)	(NA)	3.3	5.0	4.4	4.9	5.0
Northern Marianas	(NA)	(NA)	(Z)	(Z)	(Z)	(Z)	(NA)	(NA)	1.9	2.2	1.9	2.1	2.1

NA Not available. Z Less than 500. [1] Rates based on enumerated resident population as of April 1 for 1990 and 2000; estimated resident population as of July 1 for all other years. [2] Preliminary data.

Source: U.S. National Center for Health Statistics, *Vital Statistics of the United States*, annual; and *National Vital Statistics Reports (NVSR)*.

Vital Statistics   81

Table 106. Infant, Maternal, and Neonatal Mortality Rates by Race: 1980 to 2003

[**Deaths per 1,000 live births, except as noted.** Excludes deaths of nonresidents of U.S. Infant and maternal deaths are based on race of the decedent. For infant and neonatal mortality rates live births are based on race of mother. See also Appendix III]

Item	1980	1990	1995	1999	2000	2001	2002	2003
Infant deaths [1]	12.6	9.2	7.6	7.1	6.9	6.8	7.0	6.9
White	10.9	7.6	6.3	5.8	5.7	5.7	5.8	5.7
Black and other	20.2	15.5	12.6	11.9	11.4	11.3	11.4	11.1
Black	22.2	18.0	15.1	14.6	14.1	14.0	14.4	14.0
Maternal deaths [2]	9.2	8.2	7.1	9.9	9.8	9.9	8.9	[3]12.1
White	6.7	5.4	4.2	6.8	7.5	7.2	6.0	[3]8.7
Black and other	19.8	19.1	18.5	21.4	18.0	20.2	19.7	[3]24.9
Black	21.5	22.4	22.1	25.4	22.0	24.7	24.9	[3]30.5
Neonatal deaths [4]	8.5	5.8	4.9	4.7	4.6	4.5	4.7	4.6
White	7.4	4.8	4.1	3.9	3.8	3.8	3.9	3.9
Black and other	13.2	9.9	8.1	7.9	7.6	7.4	7.5	7.4
Black	14.6	11.6	9.8	9.8	9.4	9.2	9.5	9.4

[1] Represents deaths of infants under 1 year old, exclusive of fetal deaths. [2] Per 100,000 live births from deliveries and complications of pregnancy, childbirth, and the puerperium. Deaths are classified according to the tenth revision of the *International Classification of Diseases*; earlier years classified according to the revision in use at the time; see text, this section. [3] Increase partially reflects the use of a separate item on the death certificate on pregnancy status by an increasing number of states. [4] Represents deaths of infants under 28 days old, exclusive of fetal deaths.

Source: U.S. National Center for Health Statistics, *Vital Statistics of the United States*, annual; *National Vital Statistics Reports (NVSR)*, Volume 54, Number 13; <http://www.cdc.gov/nchs/data/nvsr/nvsr54/nvsr54_13.pdf>.

Table 107. Infant Mortality Rates by Race—States: 1980 to 2003

[**Deaths per 1,000 live births, by place of residence.** Represents deaths of infants under 1 year old, exclusive of fetal deaths. Excludes deaths of nonresidents of the United States. See headnote, Table 106 and Appendix III]

State	Total [1]				White				Black			
	1980	1990	2000	2003	1980	1990	2000	2003	1980	1990	2000	2003
U.S.	12.6	9.2	6.9	6.9	10.9	7.6	5.7	5.7	22.2	18.0	14.1	14.0
Alabama	15.1	10.8	9.4	8.7	11.6	8.1	6.6	6.5	21.6	16.0	15.4	14.1
Alaska	12.3	10.5	6.8	7.0	9.4	7.6	5.8	5.7	19.5	(B)	(B)	(B)
Arizona	12.4	8.8	6.7	6.5	11.8	7.8	6.2	6.2	18.4	20.6	17.6	14.7
Arkansas	12.7	9.2	8.4	8.7	10.3	8.4	7.0	7.6	20.0	13.9	13.7	13.5
California	11.1	7.9	5.4	5.2	10.6	7.0	5.1	4.9	18.0	16.8	12.9	12.6
Colorado	10.1	8.8	6.2	6.1	9.8	7.8	5.6	5.5	19.1	19.4	19.5	20.4
Connecticut	11.2	7.9	6.6	5.4	10.2	6.3	5.6	4.7	27.9	20.1	14.8	18.2
Delaware	13.9	10.1	9.2	9.4	9.8	9.7	7.9	6.7	26.7	24.6	16.1	12.4
District of Columbia	25.0	20.7	12.0	10.5	17.8	(B)	(B)	(B)	22.8	16.8	12.6	13.7
Florida	14.6	9.6	7.0	7.5	11.8	6.7	5.4	5.8	21.0	18.3	13.9	13.8
Georgia	14.5	12.4	8.5	8.5	10.8	7.4	5.9	6.1	19.8	17.3	14.8	13.8
Hawaii	10.3	6.7	8.1	7.5	11.6	6.1	6.5	6.5	(B)	(B)	(B)	(B)
Idaho	10.7	8.7	7.5	6.3	10.7	8.6	7.5	6.5	(NA)	(B)	(B)	(B)
Illinois	14.8	10.7	8.5	7.7	11.7	7.9	6.6	6.2	26.3	22.4	17.1	16.2
Indiana	11.9	9.6	7.8	7.7	10.5	7.9	6.9	6.7	23.4	17.4	15.8	15.8
Iowa	11.8	8.1	6.5	5.6	11.5	7.9	6.0	5.2	27.2	21.9	21.1	19.4
Kansas	10.4	8.4	6.8	6.6	9.5	8.0	6.4	6.2	20.6	17.7	12.2	14.5
Kentucky	12.9	8.5	7.2	6.9	12.0	8.2	6.7	6.5	22.0	14.3	12.7	11.8
Louisiana	14.3	11.1	9.0	9.3	10.5	8.1	5.9	6.4	20.6	16.7	13.3	13.7
Maine	9.2	6.2	4.9	4.9	9.4	6.7	4.8	4.9	(B)	(B)	(B)	(B)
Maryland	14.0	9.5	7.6	8.2	11.6	6.8	4.8	5.4	20.4	17.1	13.2	14.2
Massachusetts	10.5	7.0	4.6	4.8	10.1	6.1	4.0	4.4	24.2	21.6	18.2	17.4
Michigan	12.8	10.7	8.2	8.5	10.6	7.4	6.0	6.7	20.0	23.7	14.6	17.7
Minnesota	10.0	7.3	5.6	4.6	9.6	6.7	4.8	4.3	23.7	16.2	15.3	15.3
Mississippi	17.0	12.1	10.7	10.7	11.1	7.4	6.8	6.9	20.7	18.2	14.7	15.1
Missouri	12.4	9.4	7.2	7.9	11.1	7.9	5.9	6.8	20.7	18.2	14.7	15.1
Montana	12.4	9.0	6.1	6.8	11.8	6.0	5.5	6.5	(NA)	(B)	(B)	(B)
Nebraska	11.5	8.3	7.3	5.4	10.7	6.9	6.4	4.8	25.2	18.9	20.3	15.7
Nevada	10.7	8.4	6.5	5.7	10.0	8.2	6.0	5.3	20.6	14.2	12.7	12.1
New Hampshire	9.9	7.1	5.7	4.0	9.9	6.0	5.5	4.0	22.5	(B)	(B)	(B)
New Jersey	12.5	9.0	6.3	5.7	10.3	6.4	5.0	4.5	21.9	18.4	13.6	11.8
New Mexico	11.5	9.0	6.6	5.8	11.3	7.6	6.3	5.5	23.1	(B)	(B)	(B)
New York	12.5	9.6	6.4	6.0	10.8	7.4	5.4	5.0	20.0	18.1	10.9	11.4
North Carolina	14.5	10.6	8.6	8.2	12.1	8.0	6.3	6.1	20.0	16.5	15.7	15.7
North Dakota	12.1	8.0	8.1	7.3	11.7	7.2	7.5	7.0	27.5	(B)	(B)	(B)
Ohio	12.8	9.8	7.6	7.7	11.2	7.8	6.3	6.5	23.0	19.5	15.4	15.4
Oklahoma	12.7	9.2	8.5	7.8	12.1	9.1	7.9	7.3	21.8	14.3	16.9	14.9
Oregon	12.2	8.3	5.6	5.6	12.2	7.0	5.5	5.5	15.9	(B)	(B)	(B)
Pennsylvania	13.2	9.6	7.1	7.3	11.9	7.4	5.8	6.2	23.1	20.5	15.7	14.9
Rhode Island	11.0	8.1	6.3	6.7	10.9	7.0	5.9	6.4	(B)	(B)	(B)	(B)
South Carolina	15.6	11.7	8.7	8.3	10.8	8.1	5.4	5.9	22.9	17.3	14.8	13.5
South Dakota	10.9	10.1	5.5	6.7	9.0	8.0	4.3	4.9	(NA)	(B)	(B)	(B)
Tennessee	13.5	10.3	9.1	9.3	11.9	7.3	6.8	7.0	19.3	17.9	18.0	18.0
Texas	12.2	8.1	5.7	6.6	11.2	6.7	5.1	5.7	18.8	14.7	11.4	13.8
Utah	10.4	7.5	5.2	5.0	10.5	6.0	5.1	4.9	27.3	(B)	(B)	(B)
Vermont	10.7	6.4	6.0	5.0	10.7	5.9	6.1	5.0	(B)	(B)	(B)	(B)
Virginia	13.6	10.2	6.9	7.7	11.9	7.4	5.4	6.2	19.8	19.5	12.4	13.6
Washington	11.8	7.8	5.2	5.6	11.5	7.3	4.9	5.5	16.4	20.6	9.4	9.7
West Virginia	11.8	9.9	7.6	7.3	11.4	8.1	7.4	6.9	21.5	(B)	(B)	(B)
Wisconsin	10.3	8.2	6.6	6.5	9.7	7.7	5.5	5.4	18.5	19.0	17.2	15.7
Wyoming	9.8	8.6	6.7	5.8	9.3	7.5	6.5	4.9	25.9	(B)	(B)	(B)

B Base figure too small to meet statistical standards for reliability. NA Not available. [1] Includes other races, not shown separately.

Source: U.S. National Center for Health Statistics, *Vital Statistics of the United States*, annual; and *National Vital Statistics Reports (NVSR)*.

Table 108. Age-Adjusted Death Rates by Major Causes: 1960 to 2004

[**Rates per 100,000 population**; see headnote, Table 101. Beginning 1999, deaths classified according to tenth revision of International Classification of Diseases; for earlier years, causes of death were classified according to the revisions then in use. Changes in classification of causes of death due to these revisions may result in discontinuities in cause-of-death trends. See Appendix III]

Year	Diseases of heart	Malignant neoplasms (cancer)	Cerebro-vascular diseases	Chronic lower respira-tory diseases	Acci-dents [1]	Diabetes mellitus	Influenza and pneu-monia	Nephritis, nephrotic syndrome and nephrosis	Septi-cemia	Intentional self harm (suicide)
1960	559.0	193.9	177.9	12.5	63.1	22.5	53.7	10.6	1.2	12.5
1961	545.3	193.4	173.1	12.6	60.6	22.1	43.4	10.0	1.2	12.2
1962	556.9	193.3	174.0	14.2	62.9	22.6	47.1	9.6	1.3	12.8
1963	563.4	194.7	173.9	16.5	64.0	23.1	55.6	9.2	1.5	13.0
1964	543.3	193.6	167.0	16.3	64.1	22.5	45.4	8.9	1.5	12.7
1965	542.5	195.6	166.4	18.3	65.8	22.9	46.8	8.3	1.5	13.0
1966	541.2	196.5	165.8	19.2	67.6	23.6	47.9	7.9	1.6	12.7
1967	524.7	197.3	159.3	19.2	66.2	23.4	42.2	7.3	1.6	12.5
1968	531.0	198.8	162.5	20.7	65.5	25.3	52.8	6.1	1.7	12.4
1969	516.8	198.5	155.4	20.9	64.9	25.1	47.9	6.0	1.7	12.7
1970	492.7	198.6	147.7	21.3	62.2	24.3	41.7	5.5	2.0	13.1
1971	492.9	199.3	147.6	21.8	60.3	23.9	38.4	5.2	2.2	13.1
1972	490.2	200.3	147.3	22.8	60.2	23.7	41.3	5.2	2.4	13.3
1973	482.0	200.0	145.2	23.6	59.3	23.0	41.2	5.0	2.6	13.1
1974	458.8	201.5	136.8	23.2	52.7	22.1	35.5	4.7	3.0	13.2
1975	431.2	200.1	123.5	23.7	50.8	20.3	34.9	4.7	3.1	13.6
1976	426.9	202.5	117.4	24.9	48.7	19.5	38.8	4.9	3.5	13.2
1977	413.7	203.5	110.4	24.7	48.8	18.2	31.0	4.8	3.8	13.7
1978	409.9	204.9	103.7	26.3	48.9	18.3	34.5	4.8	4.2	12.9
1979	401.6	204.0	97.1	25.5	46.5	17.5	26.1	8.6	4.3	12.6
1980	412.1	207.9	96.4	28.3	46.4	18.1	31.4	9.1	5.0	12.2
1981	397.0	206.4	89.5	29.0	43.4	17.6	30.0	9.1	5.4	12.3
1982	389.0	208.3	84.2	29.1	40.1	17.2	26.5	9.4	5.9	12.5
1983	388.9	209.1	81.2	31.6	39.1	17.6	29.8	9.6	6.7	12.4
1984	378.8	210.8	78.7	32.4	38.8	17.2	30.6	10.0	7.4	12.5
1985	375.0	211.3	76.6	34.5	38.5	17.4	34.5	10.4	8.3	12.5
1986	365.1	211.5	73.1	34.8	38.6	17.2	34.8	10.4	9.0	13.0
1987	355.9	211.7	71.6	35.0	38.2	17.4	33.8	10.4	9.3	12.8
1988	352.5	212.5	70.6	36.5	38.9	18.0	37.3	10.4	9.7	12.5
1989	332.0	214.2	66.9	36.6	37.7	20.5	35.9	9.6	8.8	12.3
1990	321.8	216.0	65.3	37.2	36.3	20.7	36.8	9.3	8.6	12.5
1991	312.5	215.2	62.9	37.9	34.7	20.7	34.7	9.3	8.6	12.3
1992	304.0	213.5	61.5	37.7	33.2	20.7	32.8	9.4	8.4	12.0
1993	308.1	213.5	62.7	40.7	34.2	21.9	35.0	9.7	8.6	12.1
1994	297.5	211.7	62.6	40.3	34.2	22.6	33.6	9.4	8.3	11.9
1995	293.4	209.9	63.1	40.1	34.4	23.2	33.4	9.5	8.4	11.8
1996	285.7	206.7	62.5	40.6	34.5	23.8	32.9	9.6	8.4	11.5
1997	277.7	203.4	61.1	41.1	34.2	23.7	33.3	9.8	8.6	11.2
1998	267.4	202.1	62.8	43.8	35.6	24.2	24.2	9.8	8.9	11.1
1999	266.5	200.8	61.6	45.4	35.3	25.0	23.5	13.0	11.3	10.5
2000	257.6	199.6	60.9	44.2	34.9	25.0	23.7	13.5	11.3	10.4
2001	247.8	196.0	57.9	43.7	35.7	25.3	22.0	14.0	11.4	10.7
2002	240.8	193.5	56.2	43.5	36.9	25.4	22.6	14.2	11.7	10.9
2003	232.3	190.1	53.5	43.3	37.3	25.3	22.0	14.4	11.6	10.8
2004 [2]	217.5	184.6	50.0	41.8	36.6	24.4	20.4	14.3	11.2	10.7

[1] Unintentional injuries.   [2] Preliminary data.

Source: U.S. National Center for Health Statistics, *Vital Statistics of the United States*, annual; *Health, United States, 2005*; and *National Vital Statistics Reports (NVSR)*, Volume 54, Number 13; <http://www.cdc.gov/nchs/data/nvsr/nvsr54/nvsr54_13.pdf>.

Vital Statistics   83

Table 109. **Deaths and Death Rates by Selected Causes: 2003 and 2004**

[**Rates per 100,000 population.** Figures are weighted data rounded to the nearest individual, so categories may not add to total or subtotal. Excludes deaths of nonresidents of the United States. Deaths classified according to tenth revision of International Classification of Diseases. See also Appendix III]

Cause of death	2003			2004 [2]		
	Number	Rate	Age-adjusted rate [1]	Number	Rate	Age-adjusted rate [1]
All causes [3]	**2,448,288**	**841.9**	**832.7**	**2,398,365**	**816.7**	**801.1**
Major cardiovascular diseases [3]	902,443	310.3	306.1	862,800	293.8	287.0
Diseases of heart	685,089	235.6	232.3	654,062	222.7	217.5
Acute rheumatic fever and chronic rheumatic heart disease	3,624	1.2	1.2	3,248	1.1	1.1
Hypertensive heart disease	28,345	9.7	9.6	28,262	9.6	9.3
Hypertensive heart and renal disease	3,108	1.1	1.1	2,971	1.0	1.0
Ischemic heart disease.	480,028	165.1	162.9	452,327	154.0	150.5
Other heart diseases	169,984	58.5	57.6	167,285	57.0	55.6
Essential (primary) hypertension and hypertensive renal disease	21,940	7.5	7.4	22,953	7.8	7.6
Cerebrovascular diseases	157,689	54.2	53.5	150,147	51.1	50.0
Atherosclerosis.	13,053	4.5	4.4	11,898	4.1	3.9
Malignant neoplasms [3]	556,902	191.5	190.1	550,270	187.4	184.6
Malignant neoplasms of lip, oral cavity, and pharynx . .	7,778	2.7	2.6	7,712	2.6	2.6
Malignant neoplasms of colon, rectum, and anus	55,958	19.2	19.1	53,614	18.3	17.9
Malignant neoplasms of trachea, bronchus, and lung. .	158,086	54.4	54.1	157,218	53.5	52.9
Malignant neoplasm of breast	42,000	14.4	14.2	40,880	13.9	13.6
Malignant neoplasms of kidney and renal pelvis	12,286	4.2	4.2	12,127	4.1	4.0
Malignant neoplasms of lymphoid, hematopoietic, and related tissue	55,679	19.1	19.1	54,485	18.6	18.3
Leukemia	21,535	7.4	7.4	21,367	7.3	7.2
Accidents (unintentional injuries) [3]	109,227	37.6	37.3	108,694	37.0	36.6
Motor vehicle accidents	44,757	15.4	15.3	43,974	15.0	14.8
Accidental discharge of firearms	730	0.3	0.2	661	0.2	0.2
Accidental drowning and submersion	3,306	1.1	1.1	3,180	1.1	1.1
Accidental exposure to smoke, fire, and flames	3,369	1.2	1.2	3,223	1.1	1.1
Accidental poisoning and exposure to noxious substances	19,457	6.7	6.7	19,250	6.6	6.5
Other acute lower respiratory infections	421	0.1	0.1	310	0.1	0.1
Chronic lower respiratory diseases	126,382	43.5	43.3	123,884	42.2	41.8
Bronchitis, chronic and unspecified	850	0.3	0.3	798	0.3	0.3
Emphysema.	14,861	5.1	5.1	13,913	4.7	4.7
Asthma.	4,099	1.4	1.4	3,780	1.3	1.3
Other chronic lower respiratory diseases	106,572	36.6	36.5	105,393	35.9	35.5
Influenza and pneumonia.	65,163	22.4	22.0	61,472	20.9	20.4
Influenza.	1,792	0.6	0.6	1,265	0.4	0.4
Pneumonia	63,371	21.8	21.4	60,207	20.5	20.0
Tuberculosis	711	0.2	0.2	662	0.2	0.2
Septicemia	34,069	11.7	11.6	33,464	11.4	11.2
Human immunodeficiency virus (HIV) disease	13,658	4.7	4.7	12,995	4.4	4.4
Anemias.	4,594	1.6	1.6	4,569	1.6	1.5
Diabetes mellitus	74,219	25.5	25.3	72,815	24.8	24.4
Nutritional deficiencies	3,338	1.1	1.1	3,042	1.0	1.0
Meningitis	730	0.3	0.3	720	0.2	0.2
Parkinson's disease	17,997	6.2	6.2	18,018	6.1	6.1
Alzheimer's disease	63,457	21.8	21.4	65,829	22.4	21.7
Chronic liver disease and cirrhosis	27,503	9.5	9.3	26,549	9.0	8.8
Alcoholic liver disease	12,360	4.3	4.2	12,283	4.2	4.1
Other chronic liver disease and cirrhosis	15,143	5.2	5.2	14,265	4.9	4.7
Nephritis, nephrotic syndrome and nephrosis [3]	42,453	14.6	14.4	42,762	14.6	14.3
Renal failure	41,737	14.4	14.2	42,000	14.3	14.0
Other disorders of kidney	31	(Z)	(Z)	39	(Z)	(Z)
Infections of kidney.	823	0.3	0.3	769	0.3	0.3
Pregnancy, childbirth, and the puerperium.	545	0.2	0.2	654	0.2	0.2
Congenital malformations, deformations, and chromosomal abnormalities	10,518	3.6	3.6	10,459	3.6	3.5
Intentional self-harm (suicide).	31,484	10.8	10.8	31,647	10.8	10.7
Assault (homicide)	17,732	6.1	6.0	16,611	5.7	5.6
Legal intervention.	423	0.1	0.1	356	0.1	0.1
Events of undetermined intent	5,072	1.7	1.7	4,750	1.6	1.6
Operations of war and their sequelae.	14	(B)	(B)	28	(Z)	(Z)
Complications of medical and surgical care	2,855	1.0	1.0	2,889	1.0	1.0
Injury by firearms [4]	30,136	10.4	10.3	29,036	9.9	9.8
Drug-induced deaths [4]	28,723	9.9	9.9	28,457	9.7	9.7
Alcohol-induced deaths [4]	20,687	7.1	7.0	20,398	6.9	6.8
Injury at work.	5,025	2.2	2.2	4,971	2.1	2.1

B Base figure too small to meet statistical standards for reliability; see text, this section.   Z Less than 0.05.   [1] See headnote, Table 101.   [2] Preliminary data.   [3] Includes other causes not shown separately.   [4] Included in selected categories.

Source: U.S. National Center for Health Statistics, *Vital Statistics of the United States*, annual; *National Vital Statistics Reports (NSVR)*, Volume 54, Number 13,<http://www.cdc.gov/nchs/data/nvsr/nvsr54_13.pdf> and Volume 54, Number 19, <http://www.cdc.gov/nchs/data/nvsr/nvsr54_19.pdf>..

Table 110. Deaths by Age and Selected Causes: 2003

[Deaths are classified according to the Tenth Revision of the International Classification of Diseases. See Appendix III]

Cause of death	All ages	Under 1 year	1 to 4 years	5 to 14 years	15 to 24 years	25 to 34 years	35 to 44 years	45 to 54 years	55 to 64 years	65 to 74 years	75 to 84 years	85 years and over
All causes	2,448,288	28,025	4,965	6,954	33,568	41,300	89,461	176,781	262,519	413,497	703,024	687,852
Septicemia	34,069	278	85	77	154	309	910	2,157	3,651	5,970	10,932	9,543
Human immunodeficiency virus (HIV) disease	13,658	5	–	–	178	1,588	5,340	4,442	1,517	438	95	14
Malignant neoplasms	556,902	75	392	1,076	1,651	3,741	15,509	49,843	95,692	141,248	167,617	80,046
Malignant neoplasm of esophagus	12,860	–	–	–	5	29	288	1,210	2,765	2,940	3,619	1,180
Malignant neoplasm of stomach	12,110	–	–	1	19	89	480	1,407	1,874	2,793	3,549	2,057
Malignant neoplasms of colon, rectum, and anus	55,958	–	–	1	40	127	1,315	4,442	8,304	12,934	17,331	11,296
Malignant neoplasms of liver and intrahepatic bile ducts	14,706	6	–	1	36	291	395	2,223	2,765	3,630	3,949	1,576
Malignant neoplasm of pancreas	30,777	–	–	–	10	60	548	2,540	5,320	8,104	8,104	4,486
Malignant neoplasms of trachea, bronchus, and lung	158,086	–	–	–	25	154	2,478	12,374	30,956	49,386	48,619	14,088
Malignant neoplasm of breast	42,000	–	–	–	16	407	2,716	5,320	8,267	8,338	9,644	6,245
Malignant neoplasm of ovary	14,657	–	–	–	28	84	452	1,629	2,891	3,569	4,194	1,810
Malignant neoplasm of prostate	29,554	–	–	–	–	–	25	418	2,074	6,033	9,708	8,717
Malignant neoplasms of kidney and renal pelvis	12,286	–	23	–	1	84	321	1,201	2,498	3,090	3,475	1,567
Malignant neoplasm of bladder	12,483	1	–	–	1	1	98	522	1,391	2,736	4,679	3,052
Malignant neoplasms of meninges, brain, and other parts of central nervous system	12,901	18	104	336	236	405	1,079	1,962	2,698	2,836	2,510	717
Malignant neoplasms of lymphoid, hematopoietic and related tissue	55,679	31	138	394	606	865	1,728	3,785	7,471	12,885	18,442	9,334
Non-Hodgkins lymphoma	21,475	–	5	45	140	252	630	1,548	3,007	4,919	7,217	3,712
Leukemia	21,535	30	133	342	402	433	796	1,365	2,605	4,706	6,937	3,786
Diabetes mellitus	74,219	3	8	31	160	657	2,049	5,658	10,731	16,656	23,299	14,964
Parkinson's disease	17,997	–	–	–	–	2	11	64	352	2,330	8,723	6,513
Alzheimer's disease	63,457	–	–	–	–	–	11	78	554	3,836	21,157	37,821
Major cardiovascular diseases	902,443	555	234	347	1,447	4,089	16,930	46,279	79,497	137,220	279,358	336,449
Diseases of heart	685,089	439	186	264	1,133	3,250	13,600	37,732	65,060	107,263	207,331	248,796
Hypertensive heart disease	28,345	–	–	–	53	305	1,306	3,230	3,651	4,045	6,565	9,189
Ischemic heart diseases	480,028	–	–	–	160	1,082	7,547	25,361	47,377	78,880	149,370	170,164
Acute myocardial infarction	170,564	–	–	–	73	413	3,094	10,420	19,767	30,923	53,108	52,734
Essential (primary) hypertension and hypertensive renal disease	21,940	–	–	–	–	98	372	1,031	1,755	3,104	6,649	8,904
Cerebrovascular diseases	157,689	101	46	69	221	583	2,460	6,127	9,946	20,708	52,847	64,579
Atherosclerosis	13,053	–	–	–	3	7	47	190	466	1,211	3,841	7,288
Influenza and pneumonia	65,163	322	163	147	224	373	992	2,140	3,130	6,831	19,442	31,397
Chronic lower respiratory diseases	126,382	31	55	118	191	282	950	3,537	12,077	29,919	49,286	29,934
Emphysema	14,861	–	–	–	4	5	87	450	1,755	4,063	3,837	2,574
Pneumonitis due to solids and liquids	17,335	13	10	16	46	69	166	392	773	1,754	5,789	8,307
Chronic liver disease and cirrhosis	27,503	2	–	–	16	358	3,020	7,466	6,428	5,406	3,858	946
Nephritis, nephrotic syndrome and nephrosis	42,453	181	14	22	95	282	796	2,001	3,806	7,345	14,093	13,816
Renal failure	41,737	170	11	21	82	266	771	1,944	3,741	7,206	13,870	13,653
Certain conditions originating in the perinatal period	14,378	14,254	79	19	16	3	3	2	–	–	2	–
Congenital malformations, deformations, and chromosomal abnormalities	10,518	5,621	541	386	451	426	564	667	666	413	464	319
Accidents (unintentional injuries)	109,277	945	1,717	2,618	15,272	12,541	16,766	15,837	9,170	8,081	13,108	13,146
Motor vehicle accidents	44,757	145	621	1,642	10,972	6,833	6,961	6,074	3,958	2,967	3,210	1,358
Falls	17,229	14	54	45	230	285	636	1,043	1,220	2,048	5,249	6,404
Accidental poisoning and exposure to noxious substances	19,457	20	49	61	1,999	3,435	6,230	5,434	1,370	403	284	166
Intentional self-harm (suicide)	31,484	(X)	(X)	250	3,988	5,065	6,602	6,481	3,843	2,335	2,115	798
Assault (homicide)	17,732	341	376	324	5,368	4,516	3,110	2,017	786	432	317	104

– Represents zero. X Not applicable.
Source: U.S. National Center for Health Statistics, *National Vital Statistics Reports (NSVR)*, Volume 54, Number 13, <http://www.cdc.gov/nchs/data/nvsr/nvsr54/nvsr54_13.pdf>.

Vital Statistics 85

Table 111. Deaths and Death Rates by Leading Causes of Death and Age: 2003

[Data are based on the tenth revision of the International Classification of Diseases (ICD). **Rates per 100,000 population** in specified group. Numbers are based on weighted data rounded to the nearest individual, so categories may not add to totals. See Appendix III]

Age	Number	Rate	Age	Number	Rate
ALL AGES [1]			**35 TO 44 YEARS**		
All causes.	**2,448,288**	**841.9**	All causes.	89,461	201.6
Diseases of heart	685,089	235.6	Accidents	16,766	37.8
Malignant neoplasms.	556,902	191.5	Malignant neoplasms.	15,509	35.0
Cerebrovascular diseases	157,689	54.2	Diseases of heart	13,600	30.7
Chronic lower respiratory diseases. . .	126,382	43.5	Intentional self-harm (suicide)	6,602	14.9
Accidents (unintentional injuries)	109,277	37.6	Human immunodeficiency virus (HIV)		
Diabetes mellitus	74,219	25.5	disease	5,340	12.0
Influenza and pneumonia	65,163	22.4	Assault (homicide)	3,110	7.0
Alzheimer's disease	63,457	21.8	Chronic liver disease and cirrhosis. . .	3,020	6.8
Nephritis, nephrotic syndrome, and			Cerebrovascular diseases	2,460	5.5
nephrosis	42,453	14.6	Diabetes mellitus	2,049	4.6
Septicemia	34,069	11.7	Chronic lower respiratory diseases. . .	950	2.1
			45 TO 54 YEARS		
1 TO 4 YEARS			All causes.	176,781	433.2
			Malignant neoplasms.	49,843	122.2
All causes.	**4,965**	**31.5**	Diseases of heart	37,732	92.5
Accidents (unintentional injuries)	1,717	10.9	Accidents	15,837	38.8
Congenital malformations,			Chronic liver disease and cirrhosis. . .	7,466	18.3
deformations, and chromosomal			Intentional self-harm (suicide)	6,481	15.9
abnormalities	541	3.4	Cerebrovascular diseases	6,127	15.0
Malignant neoplasms.	392	2.5	Diabetes mellitus	5,658	13.9
Assault (homicide)	376	2.4	Human immunodeficiency virus (HIV)		
Diseases of heart	186	1.2	disease	4,442	10.9
Influenza and pneumonia	163	1.0	Chronic lower respiratory diseases. . .	3,537	8.7
Septicemia	85	0.5	Viral hepatitis	2,259	5.5
Certain conditions originating in the			**55 TO 64 YEARS**		
perinatal period.	79	0.5	All causes.	262,519	940.9
Chronic lower respiratory diseases. . .	55	0.3	Malignant neoplasms.	95,692	343.0
In situ neoplasms [2]	51	0.3	Diseases of heart	65,000	233.2
			Chronic lower respiratory diseases. . .	12,077	43.3
5 TO 14 YEARS			Diabetes mellitus	10,731	38.5
			Cerebrovascular diseases	9,946	35.6
All causes.	**6,954**	**17.0**	Accidents (unintentional injuries)	9,170	32.9
Accidents (unintentional injuries)	2,618	6.4	Chronic liver disease and cirrhosis. . .	6,428	23.0
Malignant neoplasms.	1,076	2.6	Intentional self-harm (suicide)	3,843	13.8
Congenital malformations,			Nephritis, nephrotic syndrome, and		
deformations, and chromosomal			nephrosis	3,806	13.6
abnormalities	386	0.9	Septicemia	3,651	13.1
Assault (homicide)	324	0.8	**65 TO 74 YEARS**		
Diseases of heart	264	0.6	All causes.	413,497	2,255.0
Intentional self-harm (suicide)	250	0.6	Malignant neoplasms.	141,248	770.3
Influenza and pneumonia	147	0.4	Diseases of heart	107,263	585.0
Chronic lower respiratory diseases. . .	118	0.3	Chronic lower respiratory diseases. . .	29,919	163.2
In situ neoplasms [2]	79	0.2	Cerebrovascular diseases	20,708	112.9
Septicemia	77	0.2	Diabetes mellitus	16,656	90.8
			Accidents (unintentional injuries)	8,081	44.1
15 TO 24 YEARS			Nephritis, nephrotic syndrome, and		
			nephrosis	7,345	40.1
All causes.	**33,568**	**81.5**	Influenza and pneumonia	6,831	37.3
Accidents (unintentional injuries)	15,272	37.1	Septicemia	5,970	32.6
Assault (homicide)	5,368	13.0	Chronic liver disease and cirrhosis. . .	5,406	29.5
Intentional self-harm (suicide)	3,988	9.7	**75 TO 84 YEARS**		
Malignant neoplasms.	1,651	4.0	All causes.	703,024	5,463.1
Diseases of heart	1,133	2.7	Diseases of heart	207,331	1,611.1
Congenital malformations,			Malignant neoplasms.	167,617	1,302.5
deformations, and chromosomal			Cerebrovascular diseases	52,847	410.7
abnormalities	451	1.1	Chronic lower respiratory diseases. . .	49,286	383.0
Influenza and pneumonia	224	0.5	Diabetes mellitus	23,299	181.1
Cerebrovascular diseases	221	0.5	Alzheimer's disease	21,157	164.4
Chronic lower respiratory diseases. . .	191	0.5	Influenza and pneumonia	19,442	151.1
Human immunodeficiency virus (HIV)			Nephritis, nephrotic syndrome, and		
disease	178	0.4	nephrosis	14,093	109.5
			Accidents (unintentional injuries)	13,108	101.9
25 TO 34 YEARS			Septicemia	10,932	85.0
			85 YEARS AND OVER		
All causes.	**41,300**	**103.6**	All causes.	687,852	14,593.3
Accidents	12,541	31.5	Diseases of heart	248,796	5,278.4
Intentional self-harm (suicide)	5,065	12.7	Malignant neoplasms.	80,046	1,698.2
Assault (homicide)	4,516	11.3	Cerebrovascular diseases	64,579	1,370.1
Malignant neoplasms.	3,741	9.4	Alzheimer's disease	37,821	802.4
Diseases of heart	3,250	8.2	Influenza and pneumonia	31,397	666.1
Human immunodeficiency virus (HIV)			Chronic lower respiratory diseases. . .	29,934	635.1
disease	1,588	4.0	Diabetes mellitus	14,964	317.5
Diabetes mellitus	657	1.6	Nephritis, nephrotic syndrome, and		
Cerebrovascular diseases	583	1.5	nephrosis	13,816	293.1
Congenital malformations,			Accidents (unintentional injuries)	13,146	278.9
deformations, and chromosomal			Septicemia	9,543	202.5
abnormalities	426	1.1			
Chronic liver disease and cirrhosis. . .	358	0.9			

[1] Includes deaths under 1 year of age. [2] Includes benign neoplasms and neoplasms of uncertain or unknown behavior.

Source: U.S. National Center for Health Statistics, *Vital Staistics of the United States*, annual; *National Vital Statistics Report (NSVR)*, Volume 54, Number 13, <http://www.cdc.gov/nchs/data/nvsr/nvsr54/nvsr54_13.pdf> and unpublished data.

Table 112. Death Rates for Major Causes of Death—States and Island Areas: 2003

[Deaths per 100,000 resident population estimated as of July 1. By place of residence. Excludes nonresidents of the United States. Causes of death classified according to tenth revisions of International Classification of Diseases. See Appendix III]

State and Island Areas	Total	Disease of heart	Malig-nant neo-plasms (cancer)	Cerebro-vascular diseases	Accidents Total	Motor vehicle acci-dents	Chronic lower respira-tory diseases	Diabetes mellitus	Influ-enza and pneu-monia	Alz-heimer's disease	Nephritis, nephrotic syndrome and nep-hrosis
U.S. . .	841.9	235.6	191.5	54.2	37.6	15.4	43.5	25.5	22.4	21.8	14.6
AL.......	1,038.0	292.2	218.0	67.3	48.4	23.8	54.1	31.4	25.7	28.2	23.6
AK.......	490.1	96.5	113.3	28.5	49.5	18.3	22.7	15.7	9.2	8.6	4.3
AZ.......	777.5	195.1	172.5	43.5	48.3	19.7	45.9	20.7	23.0	30.5	10.1
AR.......	1,024.2	285.6	224.5	77.3	47.8	26.4	55.0	32.4	33.8	20.3	19.3
CA.......	674.6	194.1	153.1	49.9	29.5	12.6	37.9	20.0	23.1	18.6	6.6
CO	648.4	142.8	141.0	39.8	39.7	15.5	42.4	15.6	17.8	19.8	9.0
CT.......	850.5	240.8	204.7	52.5	31.9	8.1	41.5	19.1	24.7	17.6	16.3
DE.......	864.8	248.0	210.3	49.8	35.1	16.0	41.5	29.2	15.5	18.0	15.9
DC	987.5	288.8	198.8	45.5	41.3	11.3	24.3	31.7	15.4	16.8	14.4
FL.......	991.0	282.9	231.5	58.2	46.5	19.1	53.4	28.0	17.6	25.4	13.3
GA	765.5	197.9	161.6	49.5	40.6	16.5	37.5	19.8	19.4	18.8	16.9
HI	713.9	195.7	169.6	59.8	33.0	11.3	22.8	16.1	18.8	12.8	9.8
ID	759.7	187.8	169.9	55.8	44.3	20.7	44.0	26.2	24.4	26.0	7.1
IL	832.4	235.6	193.3	54.6	31.2	11.9	38.4	24.1	22.7	20.8	18.2
IN	903.3	249.6	208.7	58.5	35.4	15.3	52.7	27.9	22.0	24.5	19.9
IA	953.2	266.3	219.7	70.7	39.5	15.6	56.9	24.7	35.1	30.1	8.2
KS.......	903.0	238.3	195.8	64.5	40.0	18.1	53.0	24.8	25.5	28.7	19.5
KY.......	977.2	274.9	227.7	59.3	55.1	22.8	58.1	31.5	25.1	26.0	20.4
LA.......	950.1	256.7	212.0	56.2	49.1	21.4	38.5	38.7	20.3	26.3	23.7
ME	960.4	237.9	238.9	61.4	39.5	15.4	59.9	30.5	25.0	35.8	20.3
MD	807.8	220.8	186.8	49.6	26.0	12.9	36.1	26.4	21.3	15.7	10.6
MA	875.0	227.5	210.6	53.0	22.1	8.2	43.0	22.1	31.4	25.0	20.0
MI	860.4	258.0	195.6	54.3	33.0	13.8	44.4	26.2	19.3	21.2	16.5
MN	743.6	161.0	181.5	50.4	37.8	13.9	36.2	25.2	17.0	24.6	12.9
MS	988.8	301.4	206.9	60.3	57.5	31.2	48.4	23.6	26.3	20.2	23.5
MO	974.4	287.7	216.6	62.8	48.8	21.5	51.5	29.2	28.1	22.7	19.3
MT	922.7	216.2	201.3	62.8	56.5	28.1	64.1	28.4	27.9	25.6	11.0
NE.......	889.2	227.3	192.0	62.9	40.0	17.7	51.4	23.4	25.0	26.5	17.4
NV.......	796.8	205.2	184.6	45.9	40.6	16.6	52.3	13.4	18.3	13.8	19.6
NH	753.9	211.6	193.0	41.6	31.5	10.1	41.2	23.3	15.8	22.2	11.6
NJ.......	853.0	255.2	207.9	45.9	27.4	9.1	33.7	28.8	21.1	18.9	19.6
NM	789.8	181.5	165.5	41.1	65.5	23.2	49.9	32.0	19.7	19.2	11.6
NY.......	812.3	288.0	188.8	37.9	24.5	8.2	35.0	22.0	27.8	9.7	12.6
NC	873.8	222.1	192.0	61.9	45.6	19.8	46.2	28.4	23.7	25.5	16.5
ND	960.8	257.5	210.5	75.1	44.5	19.1	47.6	33.3	29.8	53.0	8.8
OH	954.1	268.2	219.3	60.4	32.9	11.8	51.8	32.6	20.4	25.4	18.3
OK	1,017.2	315.0	209.0	70.8	49.8	20.5	61.5	31.4	27.0	22.6	16.1
OR	868.4	198.0	203.2	71.7	39.4	15.3	51.1	29.0	17.8	32.5	8.6
PA	1,049.4	307.9	241.3	66.8	40.5	13.4	48.9	30.2	24.3	23.9	24.4
RI	932.8	279.8	216.3	52.5	36.5	9.6	46.0	23.4	24.8	28.2	13.8
SC.......	919.0	229.3	205.2	66.3	46.8	22.8	46.1	28.0	21.9	26.5	19.2
SD.......	933.1	254.2	214.0	62.3	53.1	27.5	49.6	26.6	29.7	22.8	16.2
TN.......	981.1	272.5	215.9	66.5	51.4	22.4	52.5	31.8	31.1	25.1	11.6
UT.......	570.4	128.3	103.9	37.3	38.1	18.2	34.2	25.6	16.3	18.2	12.1
VT.......	827.0	217.9	195.4	49.4	29.9	13.1	24.2	22.1	19.3	14.1	8.8
VA.......	789.1	199.8	186.6	53.3	38.0	12.0	48.6	29.6	18.7	27.6	8.6
WA	748.9	182.4	180.4	58.6	35.8	13.7	40.4	21.5	21.1	19.8	16.8
WV	1,176.9	341.7	254.6	72.3	36.5	11.7	43.3	24.6	17.7	38.8	5.0
WI	843.8	228.0	194.6	58.8	55.5	22.2	71.6	44.6	29.6	26.0	25.3
WY.......	832.3	194.5	188.1	50.5	42.9	16.2	42.0	24.3	21.3	25.8	16.0
					54.5	27.1	55.5	27.5	28.9	28.3	11.4
PR.......	727.1	156.6	122.6	40.0	26.9	12.9	29.9	64.9	27.1	26.1	24.6
VI	579.9	166.3	102.0	40.4	19.3	(S)	(S)	31.2	(S)	(S)	(S)
GU.....	415.7	119.2	70.3	31.2	28.1	12.8	(S)	(S)	(S)	(S)	(S)
AS	442.6	69.2	60.5	38.0	(S)	(S)	(S)	51.9	(S)	(S)	(S)
MP.....	186.5	(S)	(S)	(S)	(S)	(S)	(S)	(S)	(S)	(S)	(S)

S Figure does not meet standards of reliability or precision.

Source: U.S. National Center for Health Statistics, *National Vital Statistics Reports (NSVR)*, Volume 54, Number 13, <http://www.cdc.gov/nchs/data/nvsr/nvsr54/nvsr54_13.pdf> and unpublished data.

Vital Statistics 87

Table 113. **Death Rates from Heart Disease by Selected Characteristics: 1970 to 2003**

[Rates per 100,000 population. See headnote, Tables 101 and 108. See Appendix III]

Characteristic	1970	1980	1985	1990	1995	2000	2001	2002	2003
Total, age adjusted	492.7	412.1	375.0	321.8	293.4	257.6	247.8	240.8	232.3
Total, crude	362.0	336.0	324.1	289.5	277.0	252.6	245.8	241.7	235.6
Under 1 year	13.1	22.8	25.0	20.1	17.4	13.0	11.9	12.4	11.0
1 to 4 years	1.7	2.6	2.2	1.9	1.6	1.2	1.5	1.1	1.2
5 to 14 years	0.8	0.9	1.0	0.9	0.8	0.7	0.7	0.6	0.6
15 to 24 years	3.0	2.9	2.8	2.5	2.8	2.6	2.5	2.5	2.7
25 to 34 years	11.4	8.3	8.3	7.6	8.2	7.4	8.0	7.9	8.2
35 to 44 years	66.7	44.6	38.1	31.4	31.8	29.2	29.6	30.5	30.7
45 to 54 years	238.4	180.2	153.8	120.5	109.6	94.2	92.9	93.7	92.5
55 to 64 years	652.3	494.1	443.0	367.3	320.1	261.2	246.9	241.5	233.2
65 to 74 years	1,558.2	1,218.6	1,089.8	894.3	795.4	665.6	635.1	615.9	585.0
75 to 84 years	3,683.8	2,993.1	2,693.1	2,295.7	2,050.5	1,780.3	1,725.7	1,677.2	1,611.1
85 years and over	7,891.3	7,777.1	7,384.1	6,739.9	6,391.5	5,926.1	5,664.2	5,446.8	5,278.4
Male, age adjusted	634.0	538.9	488.0	412.4	371.0	320.0	305.4	297.4	286.6
Male, crude	422.5	368.6	344.1	297.6	278.5	249.8	242.5	240.7	235.0
Under 1 year	15.1	25.5	27.8	21.9	17.7	13.3	11.8	12.9	12.1
1 to 4 years	1.9	2.8	2.2	1.9	1.7	1.4	1.5	1.1	1.1
5 to 14 years	0.9	1.0	0.9	0.9	0.8	0.8	0.7	0.7	0.7
15 to 24 years	3.7	3.7	3.5	3.1	3.5	3.2	3.2	3.3	3.4
25 to 34 years	15.2	11.4	11.6	10.3	11.0	9.6	10.3	10.5	10.5
35 to 44 years	103.2	68.7	58.6	48.1	46.9	41.4	41.7	43.1	42.8
45 to 54 years	376.4	282.6	237.8	183.0	166.1	140.2	136.6	138.4	136.2
55 to 64 years	987.2	746.8	659.1	537.3	460.1	371.7	349.8	343.4	331.7
65 to 74 years	2,170.3	1,728.0	1,535.8	1,250.0	1,095.3	898.3	851.3	827.1	785.3
75 to 84 years	4,534.8	3,834.3	3,496.9	2,968.2	2,622.9	2,248.1	2,177.3	2,110.1	2,030.3
85 years and over	8,426.2	8,752.7	8,251.8	7,418.4	6,993.5	6,430.0	6,040.5	5,823.5	5,621.5
White	640.2	539.6	487.3	409.2	367.0	316.7	301.8	294.1	282.9
Black	607.3	561.4	533.9	485.4	451.3	392.5	384.5	371.0	364.3
American Indian, Alaska Native	(NA)	320.5	280.5	264.1	256.4	222.2	200.7	201.2	203.2
Asian, Pacific Islander	(NA)	286.9	258.9	220.7	214.5	185.5	169.8	169.8	158.3
Hispanic origin [1]	(NA)	(NA)	296.6	270.0	260.8	238.2	232.6	219.8	206.8
Non-Hispanic, White [1]	(NA)	(NA)	480.4	413.6	369.1	319.9	304.8	297.7	286.9
Female, age adjusted	381.6	320.8	294.5	257.0	236.6	210.9	203.9	197.2	190.3
Female, crude	304.5	305.1	305.2	281.8	275.5	255.3	249.0	242.7	236.2
Under 1 year	10.9	20.0	22.0	18.3	17.0	12.5	12.0	11.8	9.8
1 to 4 years	1.6	2.5	2.2	1.9	1.5	1.0	1.4	1.0	1.3
5 to 14 years	0.8	0.9	1.0	0.8	0.7	0.5	0.7	0.6	0.5
15 to 24 years	2.3	2.1	2.1	1.8	2.1	2.1	1.8	1.7	2.1
25 to 34 years	7.7	5.3	5.0	5.0	5.4	5.2	5.6	5.2	5.7
35 to 44 years	32.2	21.4	18.3	15.1	17.0	17.2	17.6	18.0	18.6
45 to 54 years	109.9	84.5	74.4	61.0	55.4	49.8	50.7	50.6	50.2
55 to 64 years	351.6	272.1	252.1	215.7	192.6	159.3	151.8	147.2	141.9
65 to 74 years	1,082.7	828.6	746.1	616.8	554.9	474.0	455.9	440.1	417.5
75 to 84 years	3,120.8	2,497.0	2,220.4	1,893.8	1,692.7	1,475.1	1,428.9	1,389.7	1,331.1
85 years and over	7,591.8	7,350.5	7,037.6	6,478.1	6,159.6	5,720.9	5,506.8	5,283.3	5,126.7
White	376.7	315.9	289.1	250.9	230.8	205.6	198.7	192.1	185.4
Black	435.6	378.6	357.7	327.5	304.0	277.6	269.8	263.2	253.8
American Indian, Alaska Native	(NA)	175.4	170.0	153.1	164.8	143.6	127.0	123.6	127.5
Asian, Pacific Islander	(NA)	132.3	149.4	149.2	137.6	115.7	112.9	108.1	104.2
Hispanic origin [1]	(NA)	(NA)	195.9	177.2	173.8	163.7	161.0	149.7	145.8
Non-Hispanic, White [1]	(NA)	(NA)	287.2	252.6	231.5	206.8	200.0	193.7	187.1

NA Not available. [1] Persons of Hispanic origin may be any race. Data for 1970 to 1995 exclude data from states lacking an Hispanic-origin item on their death certificates.

Source: U.S. National Center for Health Statistics, *Health, United States, 2005.*

Table 114. **Death Rates from Cerebrovascular Diseases by Sex and Age: 1990 to 2003**

[Rates per 100,000 population. See headnote, Tables 101 and 108. See Appendix III]

Age	Total				Male				Female			
	1990	1995	2000	2003	1990	1995	2000	2003	1990	1995	2000	2003
All ages, age adjusted	65.3	63.1	60.9	53.5	68.5	65.9	62.4	54.1	62.6	60.5	59.1	52.3
All ages, crude	57.8	59.2	59.6	54.2	46.7	47.2	46.9	42.9	68.4	70.7	71.8	65.1
Under 1 year	3.8	5.9	3.3	2.5	4.4	6.4	3.8	2.8	3.1	5.3	2.7	2.2
1 to 4 years	0.3	0.4	0.3	0.3	0.3	0.4	(B)	0.3	0.3	0.3	0.4	0.3
5 to 14 years	0.2	0.2	0.2	0.2	0.2	0.2	0.2	0.2	0.2	0.1	0.2	0.1
15 to 24 years	0.6	0.5	0.5	0.5	0.7	0.5	0.5	0.5	0.6	0.4	0.5	0.5
25 to 34 years	2.2	1.7	1.5	1.5	2.1	1.8	1.5	1.6	2.2	1.6	1.5	1.4
35 to 44 years	6.4	6.5	5.8	5.5	6.8	7.0	5.8	5.8	6.1	6.0	5.7	5.3
45 to 54 years	18.7	17.4	16.0	15.0	20.5	19.5	17.5	16.7	17.0	15.3	14.5	13.4
55 to 64 years	47.9	45.6	41.0	35.6	54.3	52.7	47.2	40.8	42.2	39.1	35.3	30.9
65 to 74 years	144.2	136.2	128.6	112.9	166.6	154.7	145.0	127.8	126.7	121.4	115.1	100.5
75 to 84 years	498.0	477.1	461.3	410.7	551.1	517.7	490.8	431.4	466.2	451.8	442.1	396.8
85 years and over	1,628.9	1,607.2	1,589.2	1,370.1	1,528.5	1,522.1	1,484.3	1,236.0	1,667.6	1,640.0	1,632.0	1,429.4

B Base figure too small to meet statistical standards for reliability.

Source: U.S. National Center for Health Statistics, *Health, United States, 2005.*

Table 115. **Death Rates from Malignant Neoplasms, by Selected Characteristics: 1990 to 2003**

[Rates per 100,000 population. Beginning 2000, cause of death is coded according to ICD-10; for explanation, see text, this section. For explanation of age adjustment, see headnote, Table 101. See Appendix III]

Characteristic	1990	1995	2000	2001	2002	2003
Total, age adjusted	216.0	209.9	199.6	196.0	193.5	190.1
Total, crude	203.2	202.2	196.5	194.4	193.2	191.5
Under 1 year.	2.3	1.8	2.4	1.6	1.8	1.9
1 to 4 years.	3.5	3.1	2.7	2.7	2.6	2.5
5 to 14 years.	3.1	2.7	2.5	2.5	2.6	2.6
15 to 24 years.	4.9	4.5	4.4	4.3	4.3	4.0
25 to 34 years.	12.6	11.6	9.8	10.1	9.7	9.4
35 to 44 years.	43.3	40.1	36.6	36.8	35.8	35.0
45 to 54 years.	158.9	140.4	127.5	126.5	123.8	122.2
55 to 64 years.	449.6	412.3	366.7	356.5	351.1	343.0
65 to 74 years.	872.3	863.3	816.3	802.8	792.1	770.3
75 to 84 years.	1,348.5	1,355.4	1,335.6	1,315.8	1,311.9	1,302.5
85 years and over	1,752.9	1,797.7	1,819.4	1,765.6	1,723.9	1,698.2
AGE-ADJUSTED RATES						
Male	280.4	267.5	248.9	243.7	238.9	233.3
Female	175.7	173.6	167.6	164.7	163.1	160.9
White male	272.2	260.6	243.9	239.2	235.2	230.1
Black male	397.9	374.3	340.3	330.9	319.6	308.8
American Indian, Alaska Native male	145.8	169.0	155.8	155.3	141.9	139.9
Asian, Pacific Islander male	172.5	164.3	150.8	147.0	137.9	137.2
Hispanic male, [1]	174.7	180.9	171.7	168.2	161.4	156.5
Non-Hispanic, White male, [1]	276.7	263.5	247.7	243.1	239.6	234.6
White female	174.0	172.1	166.9	163.9	162.4	160.2
Black female	205.9	203.8	193.8	191.3	190.3	187.7
American Indian, Alaska Native female. . . .	106.9	117.7	108.3	114.1	112.9	105.6
Asian, Pacific Islander female.	103.0	107.4	100.7	99.3	95.9	96.7
Hispanic female, [1]	111.9	110.8	110.8	108.6	106.1	105.9
Non-Hispanic, White female, [1]	177.5	174.7	170.0	167.2	165.9	163.8
DEATH RATES FOR MALIGNANT NEOPLASM OF BREASTS FOR FEMALES						
All ages, age adjusted	33.3	30.5	26.8	26.0	25.6	25.3
All ages, crude.	34.0	32.2	29.2	28.6	28.3	28.2
Under 25 years	(B)	(B)	(B)	(B)	(B)	(B)
25 to 34 years	2.9	2.6	2.3	2.4	2.1	2.1
35 to 44 years	17.8	14.9	12.4	12.4	12.0	12.2
45 to 54 years	45.4	41.0	33.0	32.8	31.4	30.4
55 to 64 years	78.6	69.4	59.3	57.5	56.2	56.6
65 to 74 years	111.7	102.8	88.3	85.8	84.4	82.6
75 to 84 years	146.3	140.1	128.9	125.8	125.9	123.7
85 years and over	196.8	200.2	205.7	188.9	191.5	189.4
DEATH RATES FOR MALIGNANT NEOPLASM OF TRACHEA, BRONCHUS, AND LUNG						
All ages, age adjusted	59.3	58.4	56.1	55.3	54.9	54.1
All ages, crude.	56.8	56.8	55.3	54.8	57.7	54.4
Under 25 years	(Z)	(Z)	(Z)	(Z)	(Z)	(Z)
25 to 34 years	0.7	0.6	0.5	0.4	0.4	0.4
35 to 44 years	6.8	6.0	6.1	6.2	6.0	5.6
45 to 54 years	46.8	37.5	31.6	30.7	30.3	30.3
55 to 64 years	160.6	141.6	122.4	117.7	115.3	111.0
65 to 74 years	288.4	295.4	284.2	279.7	275.0	269.3
75 to 84 years	333.3	358.9	370.8	371.4	377.6	377.8
85 years and over	242.5	279.9	302.1	302.7	297.2	298.9

B Base figure too small to meet statistical standards for reliability of a derived figure.   Z Less than 0.05.   [1] Excludes data from states lacking an Hispanic-origin item on their death certificates. See text, this section. Persons of Hispanic origin may be any race.

Source: U.S. National Center for Health Statistics, *Health, United States, 2005.*

Vital Statistics   89

Table 116. Death Rates From Suicide, by Selected Characteristics: 1990 to 2003

[Rates per 100,000 population. Beginning 2000, cause of death is coded according to ICD-10; for explanation, see text this section. For explanation of age adjustment, see headnote, Table 101. See Appendix III]

Characteristic	1990	1995	2000	2001	2002	2003
All ages, age adjusted	**12.5**	**11.8**	**10.4**	**10.7**	**10.9**	**10.8**
All ages, crude	**12.4**	**11.7**	**10.4**	**10.8**	**11.0**	**10.8**
Under 1 year.	(X)	(X)	(X)	(X)	(X)	(X)
1 to 4 years.	(X)	(X)	(X)	(X)	(X)	(X)
5 to 14 years.	0.8	0.9	0.7	0.7	0.6	0.6
15 to 24 years.	13.2	13.0	10.2	9.9	9.9	9.7
25 to 34 years.	15.2	15.0	12.0	12.8	12.6	12.7
35 to 44 years.	15.3	15.1	14.5	14.7	15.3	14.9
45 to 54 years.	14.8	14.4	14.4	15.2	15.7	15.9
55 to 64 years.	16.0	13.2	12.1	13.1	13.6	13.8
65 to 74 years.	17.9	15.7	12.5	13.3	13.5	12.7
75 to 84 years.	24.9	20.6	17.6	17.4	17.7	16.4
85 years and over	22.2	21.3	19.6	17.5	18.0	16.9
AGE ADJUSTED						
Male	21.5	20.3	17.7	18.2	18.4	18.0
Female.	4.8	4.3	4.0	4.0	4.2	4.2
White male	22.8	21.6	19.1	19.6	20.0	19.6
Black male	12.8	12.4	10.0	9.8	9.8	9.2
American Indian, Alaska Native male	20.1	17.4	16.0	17.4	16.4	16.6
Asian, Pacific Islander male	9.6	9.6	8.6	8.4	8.0	8.5
Hispanic male [1]	13.7	12.7	10.3	10.1	9.9	9.1
Non-Hispanic, White male [1]	23.5	22.3	20.2	21.0	21.4	21.0
White female.	5.2	4.7	4.3	4.5	4.7	4.6
Black female.	2.4	2.0	1.8	1.8	1.6	1.9
American Indian, Alaska Native female. . . .	3.6	3.9	3.8	4.0	4.1	3.5
Asian, Pacific Islander female.	4.1	4.1	2.8	2.9	3.0	3.
Hispanic female [1]	2.3	2.0	1.7	1.6	1.8	1.
Non-Hispanic, White female [1]	5.4	4.9	4.7	4.9	5.1	5.

X Not applicable.   [1] Excludes data from states lacking an Hispanic-origin item on their death certificates. Persons of Hispani origin may be any race.

Source: U.S. National Center for Health Statistics, *Health, United States, 2005.*

Table 117. Death Rates from Human Immunodeficiency Virus (HIV) Disease by Selected Characterstics: 1990 to 2003

[Rates per 100,000 population. Beginning 2000, cause of death is coded according to ICD-10; for explanation, see text this section. For explanation of age adjustment, see headnote, Table 101. See Appendix III]

Characteristic	1990	1995	2000	2001	2002	2003
All ages, age adjusted	**10.2**	**16.2**	**5.2**	**5.0**	**4.9**	**4.**
All ages, crude	**10.1**	**16.2**	**5.1**	**5.0**	**4.9**	**4.**
Under 1 year.	2.7	1.5	(B)	(B)	(B)	(B)
1 to 4 years.	0.8	1.3	(B)	(B)	(B)	(B)
5 to 14 years.	0.2	0.5	0.1	0.1	0.1	0.
15 to 24 years.	1.5	1.7	0.5	0.6	0.4	0.
25 to 34 years.	19.7	28.3	6.1	5.3	4.6	4.
35 to 44 years.	27.4	44.2	13.1	13.0	12.7	12.
45 to 54 years.	15.2	26.0	11.0	10.5	11.2	10.
55 to 64 years.	6.2	10.9	5.1	5.2	5.1	5.
65 to 74 years.	2.0	3.6	2.2	2.1	2.2	2.
75 to 84 years.	0.7	0.7	0.7	0.7	0.8	0.
85 years and over	(B)	(B)	(B)	(B)	(B)	(B)
AGE ADJUSTED						
Male	18.5	27.3	7.9	7.5	7.4	7.
Female.	2.2	5.3	2.5	2.5	2.5	2.
White male	15.7	20.4	4.6	4.4	4.3	4.
Black male	46.3	89.0	35.1	33.8	33.3	31.
American Indian, Alaska Native male	3.3	10.5	3.5	4.2	3.4	3.
Asian or Pacific Islander male.	4.3	6.0	1.2	1.2	1.5	1.
Hispanic male [1]	28.8	40.8	10.6	9.7	9.1	9.
Non-Hispanic, White male [1]	14.1	17.9	3.8	3.6	3.5	3.
White female.	1.1	2.5	1.0	0.9	0.9	0
Black female.	10.1	24.4	13.2	13.4	13.4	12
American Indian, Alaska Native female. . . .	(B)	2.5	1.0	(B)	(B)	1
Asian or Pacific Islander female	(B)	0.6	0.2	(B)	(B)	(B)
Hispanic female [1]	3.8	8.8	2.9	2.7	2.6	2.
Non-Hispanic, White female [1]	0.7	1.7	0.7	0.6	0.6	0

B Base figure too small to meet statistical standards for reliability of a derived figure.   [1] Excludes data from states lacking an Hispanic-origin item on their death certificates. Persons of Hispanic origin may be any race.

Source: U.S. National Center for Health Statistics, *Health, United States, 2005.*

Table 118. Deaths—Life Years Lost and Mortality Costs by Age, Sex, and Cause: 2000 and 2002

[(2,403 represents 2,403,000). **Life years lost:** Number of years person would have lived in absence of death. **Mortality cost:** value of lifetime earnings lost by persons who die prematurely]

Characteristic	Number of deaths (1,000)	Life years lost [1] Total (1,000)	Life years lost [1] Per death	Mortality cost [2] Total (mil. dol.)	Mortality cost [2] Per death (dol.)
2000, total	2,403	38,843	16.2	431,992	179,772
Under 5 years old	33	2,522	76.4	30,421	921,471
5 to 14 years old	7	513	69.2	8,331	1,123,778
15 to 24 years old	31	1,835	58.6	43,039	1,374,751
25 to 44 years old	130	5,604	43.1	144,409	1,108,713
45 to 64 years old	346	10,555	30.5	168,201	486,146
65 years old and over	1,855	17,815	9.6	37,591	20,265
Heart disease	711	8,917	12.5	72,224	101,623
Cancer	553	10,028	18.1	107,501	194,367
Cerebrovascular diseases	168	1,934	11.5	12,103	72,187
Accidents and adverse effects	98	3,303	33.8	69,429	709,801
Other	874	14,661	16.8	170,736	195,408
Male	1,177	20,415	17.3	316,850	269,135
Under 5 years old	19	1,373	74.0	19,287	1,040,197
5 to 14 years old	4	295	67.0	5,540	1,258,796
15 to 24 years old	23	1,319	57.2	34,230	1,483,692
25 to 44 years old	85	3,549	41.7	107,638	1,263,555
45 to 64 years old	244	6,098	25.0	123,301	505,917
65 years old and over	802	7,781	9.7	26,853	33,467
Heart disease	345	4,709	13.7	56,883	164,989
Cancer	286	5,333	18.6	75,819	265,036
Cerebrovascular diseases	65	777	12.0	7,861	121,377
Accidents and adverse effects	64	2,259	35.4	55,756	874,831
Other	418	7,336	17.6	120,531	288,386
Female	1,226	18,428	15.0	115,142	93,939
Under 5 years old	14	1,149	79.4	11,134	769,356
5 to 14 years old	3	218	72.4	2,791	926,495
15 to 24 years old	8	516	62.6	8,809	1,069,584
25 to 44 years old	45	2,054	45.6	36,770	815,994
45 to 64 years old	102	4,457	43.6	44,899	439,031
65 years old and over	1,053	10,034	9.5	10,738	10,201
Heart disease	366	4,208	11.5	15,341	41,923
Cancer	267	4,695	17.6	31,681	118,653
Cerebrovascular diseases	103	1,157	11.2	4,241	41,223
Accidents and adverse effects	34	1,044	30.6	13,673	401,183
Other	456	7,325	16.1	50,205	110,150
2002, total	2,443	40,216	16.5	475,101	194,472
Under 5 years old	33	2,526	76.8	31,176	947,825
5 to 14 years old	7	497	69.5	8,247	1,153,363
15 to 24 years old	33	1,947	58.9	46,412	1,404,461
25 to 44 years old	132	5,743	43.3	153,188	1,156,179
45 to 64 years old	369	11,381	30.8	195,403	529,031
65 years old and over	1,868	18,123	9.7	40,677	21,774
Heart disease	697	8,965	12.9	79,541	114,136
Cancer	557	10,288	18.5	118,618	212,858
Cerebrovascular diseases	163	1,909	11.7	12,771	78,511
Accidents and adverse effects	107	3,594	33.7	77,859	729,992
Other	920	15,460	16.8	186,312	202,614
Male	1,199	21,137	17.6	340,827	284,264
Under 5 years old	19	1,379	74.4	19,341	1,044,188
5 to 14 years old	4	282	67.3	5,312	1,265,460
15 to 24 years old	24	1,404	57.5	36,464	1,493,433
25 to 44 years old	86	3,626	42.0	111,931	1,296,567
45 to 64 years old	259	6,584	25.4	140,248	541,322
65 years old and over	806	7,862	9.7	27,530	34,138
Heart disease	341	4,762	14.0	61,487	180,367
Cancer	289	5,481	19.0	81,952	283,805
Cerebrovascular diseases	63	763	12.2	8,041	128,410
Accidents and adverse effects	69	2,444	35.3	61,311	886,215
Other	438	7,687	17.6	128,036	292,642
Female	1,244	19,080	15.3	134,274	107,933
Under 5 years old	14	1,147	79.8	11,834	823,603
5 to 14 years old	3	215	72.7	2,934	993,950
15 to 24 years old	9	543	62.9	9,948	1,152,744
25 to 44 years old	46	2,116	45.8	41,257	893,658
45 to 64 years old	110	4,798	43.5	55,154	500,156
65 years old and over	1,062	10,261	9.7	13,147	12,383
Heart disease	356	4,203	11.8	18,055	50,715
Cancer	269	4,807	17.9	36,666	136,557
Cerebrovascular diseases	100	1,146	11.5	4,730	47,279
Accidents and adverse effects	37	1,150	30.7	16,548	441,578
Other	482	7,774	16.1	58,276	120,899

[1] Based on life expectancy at year of death. [2] Cost estimates based on the person's age, sex, life expectancy at the time of death, labor force participation rates, annual earnings, value of homemaking services, and a 3 percent discount rate by which to convert to present worth the potential aggregate earnings lost over the years.

Source: Institute for Health and Aging, University of California, San Francisco, CA, unpublished data.

Table 119. **Marriages and Divorces—Number and Rate by State: 1990 to 2004**

[2,443.5 represents 2,443,500. By place of occurence. See Appendix III]

State	Marriages [1] Number (1,000) 1990	2000	2004	Rate per 1,000 population [2] 1990	2000	2004	Divorces [3] Number (1,000) 1990	2000	2004	Rate per 1,000 population [2] 1990	2000	2004
U.S. [4]	2,443.5	2,329.0	2,279.0	9.8	8.3	7.8	1,182.0	(NA)	(NA)	4.7	4.1	3.7
Alabama.	43.1	45.0	42.5	10.6	10.3	9.4	25.3	23.5	22.4	6.1	5.4	5.0
Alaska	5.7	5.6	5.6	10.2	8.9	8.5	2.9	2.7	2.8	5.5	4.4	4.3
Arizona [5]	36.8	38.7	37.9	10.0	7.9	6.6	25.1	21.6	24.4	6.9	4.4	4.3
Arkansas	36.0	41.1	36.8	15.3	16.0	13.4	16.8	17.9	16.9	6.9	6.9	6.1
California	237.1	196.9	227.5	7.9	5.9	6.3	128.0	(NA)	(NA)	4.3	(NA)	(NA)
Colorado.	32.4	35.6	33.8	9.8	8.6	7.4	18.4	(NA)	20.2	5.5	(NA)	4.4
Connecticut.	26.0	19.4	20.2	7.9	5.9	5.8	10.3	6.5	10.9	3.2	2.0	3.1
Delaware	5.6	5.1	5.1	8.4	6.7	6.1	3.0	3.2	3.1	4.4	4.2	3.7
Dist. of Columbia . . .	5.0	2.8	2.5	8.2	5.4	4.5	2.7	1.5	1.0	4.5	3.0	1.9
Florida	141.8	141.9	156.4	10.9	9.3	9.0	81.7	81.9	82.7	6.3	5.3	4.8
Georgia	66.8	56.0	68.9	10.3	7.1	7.7	35.7	30.7	(NA)	5.5	3.9	(NA)
Hawaii	18.3	25.0	28.8	16.4	21.2	22.9	5.2	4.6	(NA)	4.6	3.9	(NA)
Idaho	14.1	14.0	15.0	13.9	11.0	10.7	6.6	6.9	6.9	6.5	5.4	5.0
Illinois	100.6	85.5	77.8	8.8	7.0	6.1	44.3	39.1	33.1	3.8	3.2	2.6
Indiana.	53.2	34.5	48.4	9.6	5.8	7.8	(NA)	(NA)	(NA)	(NA)	(NA)	(NA)
Iowa	24.9	20.3	20.5	9.0	7.0	6.9	11.1	9.4	8.3	3.9	3.3	2.8
Kansas	22.7	22.2	19.1	9.2	8.3	7.0	12.6	10.6	9.1	5.0	4.0	3.3
Kentucky	49.8	39.7	36.4	13.5	10.0	8.8	21.8	21.6	20.3	5.8	5.4	4.9
Louisiana	40.4	40.5	36.3	9.6	9.3	8.1	(NA)	(NA)	(NA)	(NA)	(NA)	(NA)
Maine.	11.9	10.5	11.2	9.7	8.3	8.5	5.3	5.8	5.7	4.3	4.6	4.3
Maryland	46.3	40.0	38.3	9.7	7.7	6.9	16.1	17.0	17.8	3.4	3.3	3.2
Massachusetts.	47.7	37.0	41.5	7.9	6.0	6.5	16.8	18.6	14.1	2.8	3.0	2.2
Michigan.	76.1	66.4	61.9	8.2	6.7	6.1	40.2	39.4	34.7	4.3	4.0	3.4
Minnesota.	33.7	33.4	30.4	7.7	6.9	6.0	15.4	14.8	14.2	3.5	3.1	2.8
Mississippi	24.3	19.7	17.7	9.4	7.1	6.1	14.4	14.4	13.1	5.5	5.2	4.5
Missouri	49.1	43.7	40.8	9.6	7.9	7.1	26.4	26.5	21.7	5.1	4.8	3.8
Montana	6.9	6.6	6.9	8.6	7.4	7.5	4.1	2.1	3.5	5.1	2.4	3.8
Nebraska	12.6	13.0	12.5	8.0	7.8	7.1	6.5	6.4	6.0	4.0	3.8	3.4
Nevada	120.6	144.3	145.8	99.0	76.7	62.5	13.3	18.1	14.8	11.4	9.6	6.4
New Hampshire	10.5	11.6	10.4	9.5	9.5	8.0	5.3	7.1	5.1	4.7	5.8	3.9
New Jersey.	58.7	50.4	50.7	7.6	6.1	5.8	23.6	25.6	26.0	3.0	3.1	3.0
New Mexico [5]	13.3	14.5	14.1	8.8	8.3	7.4	7.7	9.2	8.8	4.9	5.3	4.6
New York [5]	154.8	162.0	130.8	8.6	8.9	6.8	57.9	62.8	57.8	3.2	3.4	3.0
North Carolina	51.9	65.6	62.2	7.8	8.5	7.3	34.0	36.9	35.9	5.1	4.8	4.2
North Dakota.	4.8	4.6	4.4	7.5	7.3	7.0	2.3	2.0	2.0	3.6	3.2	3.1
Ohio	98.1	88.5	75.3	9.0	7.9	6.6	51.0	49.3	40.8	4.7	4.4	3.6
Oklahoma.	33.2	15.6	22.8	10.6	4.6	6.5	24.9	12.4	17.1	7.7	3.7	4.9
Oregon.	25.3	26.0	29.0	8.9	7.8	8.1	15.9	16.7	14.8	5.5	5.0	4.1
Pennsylvania.	84.9	73.2	73.6	7.1	6.1	5.9	40.1	37.9	36.7	3.3	3.2	3.0
Rhode Island.	8.1	8.0	8.2	8.1	8.0	7.6	3.8	3.1	3.3	3.7	3.1	3.0
South Carolina.	55.8	42.7	34.5	15.9	10.9	8.2	16.1	14.4	13.4	4.5	3.7	3.2
South Dakota	7.7	7.1	6.5	11.1	9.6	8.4	2.6	2.7	2.4	3.7	3.6	3.1
Tennessee	68.0	88.2	67.1	13.9	15.9	11.4	32.3	33.8	28.9	6.5	6.1	4.9
Texas	178.6	196.4	178.5	10.5	9.6	7.9	94.0	85.2	81.3	5.5	4.2	3.6
Utah	19.4	24.1	23.8	11.2	11.1	9.8	8.8	9.7	9.8	5.1	4.5	4.1
Vermont	6.1	6.1	5.8	10.9	10.2	9.4	2.6	5.1	2.4	4.5	8.6	3.9
Virginia.	71.0	62.4	62.0	11.4	9.0	8.3	27.3	30.2	29.4	4.4	4.3	3.9
Washington	46.6	40.9	40.2	9.5	7.0	6.5	28.8	27.2	26.7	5.9	4.7	4.3
West Virginia	13.0	15.7	13.6	7.2	8.7	7.5	9.7	9.3	9.1	5.3	5.2	5.0
Wisconsin	38.9	36.1	34.1	7.9	6.8	6.2	17.8	17.6	16.8	3.6	3.3	3.1
Wyoming	4.9	4.9	4.7	10.7	10.3	9.4	3.1	2.8	2.7	6.6	5.9	5.3

NA Not available. [1] Data are counts of marriages performed, except as noted. [2] Based on total population residing in area; population enumerated as of April 1 for 1990 and 2000; estimated as of July 1 for all other years. [3] Includes annulments. [4] U.S. total for the number of divorces is an estimate which includes states not reporting. Beginning 2000, divorce rates based solely on the combined counts and populations for reporting states and the District of Columbia. [5] Some figures for marriages are marriage licenses issued.

Source: U.S. National Center for Health Statistics, *Vital Statistics of the United States*, annual; and *National Vital Statistics Reports (NVSR)*.

Section 3
Health and Nutrition

This section presents statistics on health expenditures and insurance coverage, including Medicare and Medicaid, medical personnel, hospitals, nursing homes and other care facilities, injuries, diseases, disability status, nutritional intake of the population, and food consumption. Summary statistics showing recent trends on health care and discussions of selected health issues are published annually by the U.S. National Center for Health Statistics (NCHS) in *Health, United States*. Data on national health expenditures, medical costs, and insurance coverage are compiled by the U.S. Centers for Medicare & Medicaid Services (CMS) (formerly Health Care Financing Administration), and appear on the CMS Web site at <http://www.cms.hhs.gov /NationalHealthExpendData/> and in the annual *Medicare and Medicaid Statistical Supplement* to the *Health Care Financing Review*. Statistics on health insurance are also collected by NCHS and are published in Series 10 of *Vital and Health Statistics*. U.S. Census Bureau also publishes data on utilization of insurance coverage. Statistics on hospitals are published annually by the Health Forum, L.L.C., an American Hospital Association Company, in *Hospital Statistics*. Primary source for data on nutrition is the annual *Food Consumption, Prices, and Expenditures*, issued by the U.S. Department of Agriculture. NCHS also conducts periodic surveys of nutrient levels in the population, including estimates of food and nutrient intake, overweight and obesity, hypercholesterolemia, hypertension, and clinical signs of malnutrition.

National health expenditures—Please be advised that the most recent release of the National Health Expenditure Accounts (NHEA) was a benchmark (comprehensive) revision. All estimates were open to revision for the entire time series, which now runs from 1960 to 2004. For NHEA Tables 120 through 127, all data have been revised.

CMS compiles estimates of national health expenditures (NHE) to measure spending for health care in the United States. The NHE accounts are structured to show spending by type of expenditure (i.e., hospital care, physician and clinical care, dental care, and other professional care; home health care; retail sales of prescription drugs; other medical nondurables; vision products and other medical durables; nursing home care and other personal health expenditures; plus other health expenditures such as public health activities, administration, and the net cost of private health insurance; plus medical sector investment, the sum of noncommercial medical research and capital formation in medical sector structures and equipment; and by source of funding (e.g., private health insurance, out-of-pocket payments, and a range of public programs including Medicare, Medicaid, and those operated by the Department of Veterans Affairs (VA)).

Data used to estimate health expenditures come from existing sources, which are tabulated for other purposes. The type of expenditure estimates rely upon statistics produced by such groups as the American Hospital Association, the Census Bureau, and the Department of Health and Human Services (HHS). Source of funding estimates are constructed using administrative and statistical records from the Medicare and Medicaid programs, the Department of Defense and VA medical programs, the Social Security Administration, Census Bureau's *Governmental Finances*, state and local governments, other HHS agencies, and other nongovernment sources.

Medicare, Medicaid and SCHIP—Since July 1966, the federal Medicare program has provided two coordinated plans for nearly all people age 65 and over: (1) a hospital insurance plan, which covers hospital and related services and (2) a voluntary supplementary medical insurance plan, financed partially by monthly premiums paid by participants, which partly covers physicians' and related medical services. Such insurance also applies, since July 1973, to disabled beneficiaries of any age after 24 months of entitlement to cash benefits under the social security or railroad retirement programs and to persons with end stage renal disease. On January 1, 2006, Medicare began to provide coverage for prescription drugs as mandated by the Medicare Prescription Drug, Improvement, and Modernization Act of 2003 (MMA). This benefit is available on a voluntary basis to everyone with Medicare, and beneficiaries pay a monthly premium to enroll in one of Medicare's prescription drug plans.

Medicaid is a health insurance program for certain low-income people. These include: certain low-income families with children; aged, blind, or disabled people on supplemental security income; certain low-income pregnant women and children; and people who have very high medical bills. Medicaid is funded and administered through a state/federal partnership. Although there are broad federal requirements for Medicaid, states have a wide degree of flexibility to design their program. Congress created the State Children's Health Insurance Program (SCHIP) to address the growing problem of children without health insurance. SCHIP was designed as a federal/state partnership, similar to Medicaid, with the goal of expanding health insurance to children whose families earn too much money to be eligible for Medicaid, but not enough money to purchase private insurance.

Health resources—Hospital statistics based on data from the American Hospital Association's yearly survey are published annually in *Hospital Statistics* and cover all hospitals accepted for registration by the Association. To be accepted for registration, a hospital must meet certain requirements relating to number of beds, construction, equipment, medical and nursing staff, patient care, clinical records, surgical and obstetrical facilities, diagnostic and treatment facilities, laboratory services, etc. Data obtained from NCHS cover all U.S. hospitals that meet

certain criteria for inclusion. The criteria are published in *Vital and Health Statistics* reports, Series 13.

Statistics on the demographic characteristics of persons employed in the health occupations are compiled by the U.S. Bureau of Labor Statistics and reported in *Employment and Earnings* (monthly) (see Table 602, Section 12, Labor Force, Employment, and Earnings). Data based on surveys of health personnel and utilization of health facilities providing long-term care, ambulatory care, and hospital care are presented in NCHS Series 13, *Data on Health Resources Utilization and Advance Data from Vital and Health Statistics.* Statistics on patient visits to health care providers, as reported in health interviews, appear in NCHS Series 10, *National Health Interview Survey Data.*

The CMS's *Health Care Financing Review* and its annual *Medicare and Medicaid Statistical Supplement* present data for hospitals and nursing homes as well as extended care facilities and home health agencies. These data are based on records of the Medicare program and differ from those of other sources because they are limited to facilities meeting federal eligibility standards for participation in Medicare.

Disability and illness—General health statistics, including morbidity, disability, injuries, preventive care, and findings from physiological testing are collected by NCHS in its National Health Interview Survey and its National Health and Nutrition Examination Surveys and appear in *Vital and Health Statistics,* Series 10 and 11, respectively. The Department of Labor compiles statistics on occupational injuries (see Section 12, Labor Force, Employment, and Earnings). Annual incidence data on notifiable diseases are compiled by the Public Health Service (PHS) at its Centers for Disease Control and Prevention in Atlanta, Georgia, and are published as a supplement to its *Morbidity and Mortality Weekly Report.* The list of diseases is revised annually and includes those which, by mutual agreement of the states and PHS, are communicable diseases of national importance.

Nutrition—Statistics on annual per capita consumption of food and its nutrient value are estimated by the U.S. Department of Agriculture. Data are available online at <http://www.ers.usda.gov /data/foodconsumption>. NCHS collects physical examination data to assess the population's nutritional status, including growth, overweight/ obesity, nutritional deficiencies, and prevalence of nutrition-related conditions, such as hypertension, hypercholesterolemia, and diabetes.

Statistical reliability—For discussion of statistical collection, estimation, and sampling procedures and measures of reliability applicable to data from NCHS and CMS, see Appendix III.

Table 120. National Health Expenditures—Summary, 1960 to 2004, and Projections: 2005 to 2015
[In billions of dollars (28 represents $28,000,000,000). Excludes Puerto Rico and island areas]

Year	Total expenditures [1]	Private expenditures			Public expenditures			Health services and supplies				
		Total [2]	Out-of-pocket	Insurance	Total	Federal	State and local	Total [3]	Hospital care	Physician and clinical services	Prescription drugs	Nursing home care
1960	28	21	13	6	7	3	4	25	9	5	3	1
1961	29	22	13	7	8	3	4	27	10	6	3	1
1962	32	24	14	7	8	4	4	29	11	6	3	1
1963	35	26	15	8	9	4	5	31	12	7	3	1
1964	39	29	17	9	10	5	5	34	13	8	3	1
1965	42	32	18	10	11	5	6	37	14	8	4	1
1966	47	33	19	10	14	8	7	41	16	9	4	2
1967	52	33	19	11	20	12	7	47	18	10	4	2
1968	59	37	21	12	22	14	8	53	21	11	5	3
1969	67	41	23	13	25	16	9	59	24	12	5	3
1970	75	47	25	16	28	18	11	67	28	14	6	4
1971	84	51	26	18	32	21	12	74	31	16	6	5
1972	93	57	29	21	36	23	13	83	34	17	6	5
1973	103	63	32	23	41	25	15	93	38	19	7	6
1974	117	69	34	26	48	31	17	106	45	22	7	7
1975	134	77	37	30	56	36	20	121	52	25	8	9
1976	153	89	41	37	64	43	21	139	60	28	9	10
1977	173	102	45	45	71	47	24	159	67	33	9	12
1978	195	114	48	52	81	54	27	179	76	35	10	14
1979	221	129	53	61	92	61	31	203	87	41	11	16
1980	255	148	59	69	107	72	36	234	101	47	12	19
1981	295	172	66	81	124	83	41	271	118	55	13	21
1982	332	195	72	94	137	92	45	305	134	61	15	23
1983	367	216	79	105	151	103	49	336	145	68	17	27
1984	404	239	87	119	165	113	52	372	155	77	20	29
1985	442	263	96	131	179	123	56	409	165	90	22	32
1986	474	278	104	136	196	133	63	440	177	100	24	35
1987	515	301	109	149	215	144	71	478	191	112	27	36
1988	577	344	119	176	233	155	77	535	207	127	31	41
1989	642	383	126	205	259	174	85	596	227	142	35	46
1990	717	427	136	234	290	194	96	667	252	158	40	53
1991	785	456	140	255	329	223	106	732	277	175	44	58
1992	853	486	143	275	367	253	114	794	300	190	48	62
1993	917	514	145	297	402	278	125	854	317	201	51	65
1994	966	528	143	309	438	303	135	901	330	211	54	68
1995	1,020	554	146	327	467	325	141	953	341	221	61	74
1996	1,073	580	152	342	493	349	144	1,003	352	229	69	80
1997	1,130	614	162	359	516	365	151	1,054	365	241	78	85
1998	1,196	662	175	385	533	373	161	1,112	376	256	89	90
1999	1,270	710	184	418	560	390	170	1,180	395	270	105	91
2000	1,359	756	193	455	602	418	184	1,265	417	289	121	95
2001	1,474	807	200	498	667	465	202	1,376	451	313	139	102
2002	1,608	881	211	552	727	510	217	1,499	489	338	158	106
2003	1,741	957	224	606	783	554	229	1,625	526	367	174	110
2004	1,878	1,030	236	659	847	600	247	1,753	571	400	189	115
2005, proj.	2,016	1,101	249	706	915	646	269	1,882	616	430	204	122
2006, proj.	2,164	1,148	246	745	1,016	742	279	2,020	663	463	219	128
2007, proj.	2,320	1,237	262	806	1,083	790	299	2,165	709	497	237	135
2008, proj.	2,498	1,336	279	876	1,162	847	322	2,332	763	534	256	143
2009, proj.	2,689	1,444	298	951	1,245	907	346	2,511	821	572	277	151
2010, proj.	2,879	1,545	316	1,018	1,335	971	371	2,688	882	611	299	161
2011, proj.	3,078	1,649	336	1,087	1,429	1,040	398	2,873	947	651	324	170
2012, proj.	3,298	1,762	356	1,163	1,536	1,120	426	3,078	1,013	696	351	181
2013, proj.	3,533	1,879	377	1,242	1,654	1,209	455	3,298	1,082	745	380	192
2014, proj.	3,776	1,997	398	1,320	1,779	1,304	486	3,525	1,154	796	412	204
2015, proj.	4,032	2,116	421	1,397	1,915	1,408	519	3,763	1,231	850	446	217

[1] Includes medical research and medical structures and equipment, not shown separately. [2] Includes other private expenditures, not shown separately. [3] Includes other objects of expenditure, not shown separately.

Source: U. S. Centers for Medicare & Medicaid Services, Office of the Actuary, "Health Accounts"; <http://www.cms.hhs.gov /NationalHealthExpendData/>.

U.S. Census Bureau, Statistical Abstract of the United States: 2007

Table 121. **National Health Expenditures by Type: 1990 to 2004**

[In billions of dollars (717.3 represents $717,300,000,000), except percent. Excludes Puerto Rico and island areas]

Type of expenditure	1990	1995	1999	2000	2001	2002	2003	2004
Total	717.3	1,020.4	1,270.3	1,358.5	1,474.2	1,607.9	1,740.6	1,877.6
Annual percent change [1]	11.8	5.6	6.3	6.9	8.5	9.1	8.2	7.9
Percent of gross domestic product	12.4	13.8	13.7	13.8	14.6	15.4	15.9	16.0
Private expenditures	427.3	553.8	710.2	756.3	807.2	881.4	957.2	1,030.3
Health services and supplies	400.9	518.4	660.1	705.3	755.0	822.5	894.8	964.2
Out-of-pocket payments	136.1	146.4	183.9	192.6	199.8	210.8	223.5	235.7
Insurance premiums [2]	233.7	327.0	417.8	454.8	497.7	552.2	606.3	658.5
Other	31.1	45.0	58.4	57.9	57.5	59.5	65.0	70.0
Medical research	1.0	1.6	2.2	2.5	2.8	3.1	3.2	3.4
Medical structures and equipment [3]	25.4	33.8	47.9	48.5	49.4	55.9	59.3	62.7
Public expenditures	290.0	466.6	560.1	602.2	667.0	726.5	783.4	847.3
Percent federal of public	66.8	69.7	69.6	69.5	69.7	70.1	70.8	70.8
Health services and supplies	265.8	434.6	519.9	559.2	620.5	676.7	729.8	788.8
Medicare [4]	109.5	182.4	213.2	225.2	248.3	266.3	283.8	309.0
Public assistance medical payments [5]	78.7	150.3	189.1	207.5	233.2	258.2	281.2	303.7
Temporary disability insurance [6]	0.1	0.1	–	–	0.1	0.1	0.1	0.1
Workers' compensation (medical) [6]	17.4	21.7	22.2	24.9	28.1	30.1	31.5	33.5
Defense Dept. hospital, medical	10.4	12.0	12.6	13.7	15.4	18.7	21.8	24.4
Maternal, child health programs	1.7	2.2	2.6	2.7	2.7	2.7	2.7	2.7
Public health activities	20.0	31.0	40.7	43.4	46.8	51.7	54.0	56.1
Veterans' hospital, medical care	10.8	14.6	17.3	18.9	20.9	22.6	26.3	28.9
Medical vocational rehabilitation	0.3	0.4	0.4	0.4	0.4	0.5	0.5	0.5
State and local hospitals [7]	13.2	14.0	14.0	13.6	14.7	15.4	16.8	18.4
Other [8]	3.8	6.0	7.7	8.8	9.9	10.4	11.0	11.6
Medical research	11.7	16.8	21.2	23.1	26.0	29.5	32.5	35.6
Medical structures and equipment [3]	12.5	15.2	19.0	19.9	20.6	20.4	21.2	22.9

– Represents zero. [1] Change from immediate prior year. For explanation of average annual percent change, see Guide to Tabular Presentation. [2] Covers insurance benefits and amount retained by insurance companies for expenses, additions to reserves, and profits (net cost of insurance). [3] Represents expenditures for total medical sector acquisitions of structures and equipment including structures that house medical professionals' offices. [4] Represents expenditures for benefits and administrative cost from federal hospital and medical insurance trust funds under old-age, survivors, disability, and health insurance programs; see text, of this section. [5] Payments made directly to suppliers of medical care (primarily Medicaid). [6] Includes medical benefits paid under public law by private insurance carriers, state governments, and self-insurers. [7] Expenditures not offset by other revenues. [8] Covers expenditures for Substance Abuse and Mental Health Services Administration, Indian Health Service; school health and other programs.

Source: U. S. Centers for Medicare & Medicaid Services, Office of the Actuary, "National Health Expenditure Accounts"; See also <http://www.cms.hhs.gov/NationalHealthExpendData/>

Table 122. **National Health Expenditures by Object, 1990 to 2004, and Projections, 2005**

[In billions of dollars (717.3 represents $717,300,000,000). Excludes Puerto Rico and outlying areas]

Object of expenditure	1990	1995	1999	2000	2001	2002	2003	2004	2005, proj.
Total	717.3	1,020.4	1,270.3	1,358.5	1,474.2	1,607.9	1,740.6	1,877.6	2,016.0
Spent by—									
Consumers	369.8	473.4	601.7	647.4	697.5	763.0	829.7	894.2	955.2
Out-of-pocket	136.1	146.4	183.9	192.6	199.8	210.8	223.5	235.7	248.8
Private insurance	233.7	327.0	417.8	454.8	497.7	552.2	606.3	658.5	706.4
Public	290.0	466.6	560.1	602.2	667.0	726.5	783.4	847.3	914.6
Other [1]	57.5	80.4	108.6	108.9	109.7	118.4	127.5	136.1	146.2
Spent for—									
Health services and supplies	666.7	953.0	1,180.0	1,264.5	1,375.5	1,499.2	1,624.5	1,753.0	1,882.2
Personal health care expenses	607.5	863.7	1,068.3	1,139.9	1,239.1	1,341.4	1,445.7	1,560.2	1,677.8
Hospital care	251.6	340.7	395.0	417.0	451.4	488.6	525.5	570.8	616.1
Physician and clinical services	157.5	220.5	269.6	288.6	313.1	337.9	367.0	399.9	429.9
Dental services	31.5	44.5	57.1	62.0	67.5	73.3	76.9	81.5	87.4
Other professional services [2]	18.2	28.5	37.1	39.1	42.8	45.7	49.1	52.7	55.8
Home health care	12.6	30.5	31.6	30.6	32.2	34.3	38.1	43.2	48.9
Prescription drugs	40.3	60.9	104.7	120.8	138.6	157.9	174.1	188.5	203.5
Other nondurable medical products	22.5	25.7	29.8	30.2	30.3	30.9	32.1	32.3	32.6
Durable medical equipment [3]	11.2	15.3	19.0	19.3	19.6	20.8	22.1	23.0	23.7
Nursing home care	52.6	74.1	90.5	95.3	101.5	105.7	110.4	115.2	121.7
Other personal health care	9.6	23.0	34.0	37.1	41.9	46.3	50.4	53.3	58.1
Public administration and net cost of private health insurance [4]	39.2	58.4	70.9	81.2	89.6	106.1	124.9	136.7	142.4
Public health activities	20.0	31.0	40.7	43.4	46.8	51.7	54.0	56.1	62.0
Medical research [5]	12.7	18.3	23.4	25.6	28.8	32.5	35.6	39.0	42.0
Medical structures and equipment [6]	38.0	49.1	66.8	68.4	69.9	76.2	80.5	85.7	91.8

[1] Includes nonpatient revenues, privately funded construction, and industrial inplant. [2] Includes services of registered and practical nurses in private duty, podiatrists, optometrists, physical therapists, clinical psychologists, chiropractors, naturopaths, and Christian Science practitioners. [3] Includes expenditures for eyeglasses, hearing aids, orthopedic appliances, artificial limbs, crutches, wheelchairs, etc. [4] Includes administrative expenses of federally financed health programs. [5] Research and development expenditures of drug companies and other manufacturers and providers of medical equipment and supplies are excluded from research expenditures, but are included in the expenditure class in which the product falls. [6] Represents expenditures for total medical sector acquisitions of structures and equipment including structures that house medical professionals' offices.

Source: U. S. Centers for Medicare & Medicaid Services, Office of the Actuary, "National Health Expenditure Accounts"; See also <http://www.cms.hhs.gov/NationalHealthExpendData/>.

Table 123. Health Services and Supplies—Per Capita Consumer Expenditures by Object: 1990 to 2004

[In dollars, except percent. Based on U. S. Census Bureau estimates of total U.S. population as of July 1, excluding Armed Forces and federal employees abroad and civilian population of outlying areas. Excludes medical research, medical structures and equipment]

Object of expenditure	1990	1995	1999	2000	2001	2002	2003	2004
Total, national	**2,621**	**3,513**	**4,154**	**4,402**	**4,739**	**5,114**	**5,487**	**5,864**
Annual percent change [1]	10.6	4.6	4.9	6.0	7.7	7.9	7.3	6.9
Hospital care	989	1,256	1,390	1,452	1,555	1,667	1,775	1,909
Physician and clinical services	619	813	949	1,005	1,079	1,152	1,240	1,338
Dental services	124	164	201	216	233	250	260	273
Other professional services [2]	71	105	131	136	147	156	166	176
Home health care	49	113	111	106	111	117	129	144
Prescription drugs	158	224	368	421	477	539	588	630
Other nondurable medical products	88	95	105	105	104	105	109	108
Durable medical equipment [2]	44	56	67	67	68	71	75	77
Nursing home care	207	273	319	332	350	361	373	385
Other personal health care	38	85	120	129	144	158	170	178
Public administration and net cost of private health insurance	154	215	250	283	309	362	422	457
Public health activities	78	114	143	151	161	176	182	188
Total, private consumer [3]	**1,454**	**1,745**	**2,118**	**2,254**	**2,403**	**2,603**	**2,803**	**2,991**
Hospital care	429	446	508	547	589	637	686	742
Physician and clinical services	383	487	558	588	629	675	726	783
Dental services	120	156	192	205	219	235	244	256
Other professional services [2]	49	67	83	87	92	95	103	109
Home health care	20	38	49	43	38	34	34	34
Prescription drugs	130	176	287	324	364	405	432	457
Other nondurable medical products	86	91	101	100	99	100	103	102
Durable medical equipment [2]	36	43	51	51	50	50	51	53
Nursing home care	86	98	125	127	127	130	132	137
Public administration and net cost of private health insurance	114	143	162	181	195	240	292	318

[1] Change from immediate prior year.   [2] See footnotes for corresponding objects in Table 122.   [3] Represents out-of-pocket payments and private health insurance.

Source: U. S. Centers for Medicare and Medicaid Services, Office of the Actuary, "National Health Expenditure Accounts"; See also <http://www.cms.hhs.gov/NationalHealthExpendData/>.

Table 124. Public Expenditures for Health Services and Supplies: 2004

[In millions of dollars (788,827 represents $788,827,000,000). Excludes Puerto Rico and island areas. Excludes medical research, medical structures, and equipment]

Type of service	Total [1]	Federal	State and local	Medicare [2] (OASDHI)	Public assistance [3]	Other health services		
						Veterans	Defense Dept. [4]	Workers' compensation [5]
Total [1]	**788,827**	**561,664**	**227,163**	**308,957**	**303,725**	**28,883**	**24,350**	**33,479**
Hospital care	321,098	258,725	62,373	163,397	103,006	18,567	13,134	6,582
Physician and clinical services	138,274	113,825	24,449	81,848	29,520	2,637	4,883	13,068
Prescription drugs	51,869	31,880	19,989	3,373	40,111	2,584	3,340	2,250
Nursing home care	70,022	48,393	21,629	16,005	51,301	2,717	–	–
Public administration and net cost of private health insurance	40,313	23,340	16,974	9,388	20,815	133	1,745	7,949
Public health activities	56,117	9,119	46,998	–	–	–	–	–

– Represents zero.   [1] Includes other items not shown separately.   [2] Covers hospital and medical insurance payments and administrative costs under old-age, survivors, disability, and health insurance program.   [3] Covers Medicaid and other medical public assistance. Excludes funds paid into Medicare trust fund by states to cover premiums for public assistance recipients and medically indigent persons.   [4] Includes care for retirees and military dependents.   [5] Medical benefits.

Source: U. S. Centers for Medicare and Medicaid Services, Office of the Actuary, "National Health Expenditure Accounts"; See also <http://www.cms.hhs.gov/NationalHealthExpendData/>.

Table 125. Personal Health Care—Third Party Payments and Private Consumer Expenditures, 1990 to 2004, and Projections, 2005

[In billions of dollars (607.5 represents $607,500,000,000), except percent. See headnote, Table 126]

Item	1990	1995	1999	2000	2001	2002	2003	2004	2005, proj.
Personal health care expenditures	607.5	863.7	1,068.3	1,139.9	1,239.1	1,341.4	1,445.7	1,560.2	1,677.8
Third party payments, total	**471.4**	**717.4**	**884.5**	**947.3**	**1,039.3**	**1,130.6**	**1,222.2**	**1,324.5**	**1,429.0**
Percent of personal health care	77.6	83.1	82.8	83.1	83.9	84.3	84.5	84.9	85.2
Private insurance payments	204.6	288.2	371.8	402.7	441.0	481.8	519.9	563.5	608.1
Public expenditures	236.2	384.8	455.3	487.7	542.0	590.6	638.6	692.4	747
Other [1]	30.5	44.3	57.5	56.8	56.3	58.2	63.8	68.6	73.4
Private consumer expenditures [2]	**340.7**	**434.5**	**555.6**	**595.4**	**640.8**	**692.6**	**743.3**	**799.2**	**856.9**
Percent met by private insurance	60.1	66.3	66.9	67.6	68.8	69.6	69.9	70.5	71.0
Hospital care	109.1	121.0	144.4	157.2	170.9	186.8	203.0	222.0	240.3
Percent met by private insurance	89.6	91.4	91.1	91.4	91.7	91.7	91.6	91.6	91.6
Physician and clinical services	97.5	132.1	158.6	169.0	182.6	197.9	215.0	234.0	251.5
Percent met by private insurance	69.0	80.3	80.6	80.9	81.6	82.2	82.6	82.9	83.3
Prescription drugs	33.0	47.8	81.6	93.2	105.5	118.7	128.0	136.6	148.0
Percent met by private insurance	32.2	51.1	62.7	64.1	65.7	66.3	65.8	65.7	65.8

[1] Includes nonpatient revenues and industrial inplant health services.   [2] Includes expenditures not shown separately. Represents out-of-pocket payments and private health insurance benefits. Excludes net cost of insurance.

Source: U. S. Centers for Medicare and Medicaid Services, Office of the Actuary, "National Health Expenditure Accounts"; See also <http://www.cms.hhs.gov/NationalHealthExpendData/>.

Health and Nutrition   97

Table 126. Personal Health Care Expenditures by Object and Source of Payment: 2004

[In millions of dollars (1,560,242 represents $1,560,242,000,000). Excludes Puerto Rico and island areas. Covers all expenditures for health services and supplies, except net cost of insurance and administration, government public health activities, and expenditures of philanthropic agencies for fund-raising activities]

Object of expenditure	Total	Private payments						Public	Third party payments [2]
		Total	Consumer				Other [1]		
			Total	Out-of-pocket payments	Private health insurance	Other [1]			
Total...................	1,560,242	867,845	799,198	235,709	563,489	68,647		692,397	1,324,533
Hospital care...............	570,756	249,658	221,953	18,601	203,352	27,706		321,098	552,156
Physician and clinical services	399,883	261,609	234,017	39,972	194,045	27,592		138,274	359,911
Dental services..............	81,532	76,651	76,602	36,082	40,520	49		4,881	45,450
Other professional services [3]	52,720	35,527	32,631	13,786	18,846	2,895		17,193	38,934
Home health care............	43,181	11,093	10,145	4,949	5,196	948		32,088	38,232
Prescription drugs............	188,452	136,583	136,583	46,855	89,728	–		51,869	141,597
Other nondurable medical products .	32,284	30,347	30,347	30,347	–	–		1,937	1,937
Durable medical equipment [3]	22,951	15,934	15,934	13,170	2,765	–		7,017	9,781
Nursing home care...........	115,210	45,188	40,985	31,948	9,038	4,202		70,022	83,262
Other personal health care.......	53,272	5,254	–	–	–	5,254		48,018	53,272

– Represents zero.   [1] Includes nonpatient revenues and industrial inplant.   [2] Covers private health insurance, other private payments, and government.   [3] See footnotes for corresponding items on Table 122.

Source: U. S. Centers for Medicare and Medicaid Services, Office of the Actuary "National Health Expenditure Accounts"; See also <http://www.cms.hhs.gov/NationalHealthExpendData/>.

Table 127. Hospital Care, Physician and Clinical Services, Nursing Home Care, and Prescription Drug Expenditures by Source of Payment: 1990 to 2004

[In billions of dollars (251.6 represents $251,600,000,000)]

Source of payment	1990	1995	1998	1999	2000	2001	2002	2003	2004
Hospital care, total...............	251.6	340.7	376.3	395.0	417.0	451.4	488.6	525.5	570.8
Out-of-pocket payments	11.3	10.4	12.0	12.8	13.6	14.2	15.5	17.0	18.6
Third-party payments	240.2	330.3	364.3	382.2	403.5	437.2	473.1	508.5	552.2
Private health insurance...........	97.8	110.6	121.9	131.6	143.6	156.7	171.3	186.0	203.4
Other private funds...............	10.4	14.5	19.9	21.1	21.8	20.8	21.4	24.9	27.7
Public.........................	132.0	205.2	222.5	229.4	238.1	259.7	280.3	297.6	321.1
Federal	101.7	166.0	180.9	186.6	192.9	210.9	227.2	242.3	258.7
State and local	30.3	39.2	41.6	42.8	45.2	48.9	53.2	55.4	62.4
Medicare [1].....................	67.8	106.9	120.3	122.5	125.5	137.6	146.7	154.0	163.4
Medicaid [2].....................	26.7	56.8	61.7	66.6	71.1	76.5	84.4	89.7	98.6
Physician and clinical services, total ...	157.5	220.5	256.4	269.6	288.6	313.1	337.9	367.0	399.9
Out-of-pocket payments	30.2	26.0	29.9	30.7	32.2	33.5	35.2	37.5	40.0
Third-party payments	127.3	194.5	226.5	238.9	256.4	279.6	302.7	329.5	359.9
Private health insurance...........	67.3	106.1	122.1	127.9	136.8	149.1	162.7	177.5	194.0
Other private funds...............	11.3	17.6	22.2	22.9	22.2	23.2	24.4	26.1	27.6
Public.........................	48.7	70.9	82.2	88.1	97.4	107.3	115.6	125.9	138.3
Federal	38.0	56.2	65.7	71.3	79.0	86.9	93.9	102.9	113.8
State and local	10.7	14.7	16.5	16.8	18.4	20.4	21.6	23.0	24.4
Medicare [1].....................	29.4	41.4	49.1	53.2	58.3	63.6	67.7	73.7	81.8
Medicaid [2].....................	7.0	14.8	16.8	17.4	19.1	21.6	23.8	25.4	27.4
Nursing home care, total	52.6	74.1	89.5	90.5	95.3	101.5	105.7	110.4	115.2
Out-of-pocket payments	19.0	20.8	26.8	27.4	28.6	28.8	29.5	30.5	31.9
Third-party payments	33.6	53.3	62.7	63.1	66.7	72.7	76.2	80.0	83.3
Private health insurance...........	2.9	5.8	7.9	8.2	7.9	8.1	8.6	8.7	9.0
Other private funds...............	3.8	5.0	5.0	5.0	4.5	4.0	4.0	4.0	4.2
Public.........................	26.9	42.5	49.8	50.0	54.3	60.6	63.6	67.2	70.0
Federal	16.3	27.4	33.4	33.0	36.5	42.2	44.6	46.5	48.4
State and local	10.6	15.0	16.4	17.0	17.8	18.4	18.9	20.7	21.6
Medicare [1].....................	1.7	6.7	10.5	9.1	10.3	12.6	14.1	14.9	16.0
Medicaid [2].....................	24.1	34.1	37.5	38.9	42.0	45.8	47.1	49.6	51.1
Prescription drugs, total............	40.3	60.9	88.6	104.7	120.8	138.6	157.9	174.1	188.5
Out-of-pocket payments	22.4	23.3	27.5	30.4	33.4	36.2	40.0	43.7	46.9
Third-party payments	17.9	37.5	61.1	74.3	87.4	102.4	117.9	130.4	141.6
Private health insurance...........	10.6	24.4	42.1	51.2	59.7	69.3	78.7	84.2	89.7
Other private funds...............	–	–	–	–	–	–	–	–	–
Public.........................	7.3	13.1	19.0	23.1	27.6	33.0	39.2	46.1	51.9
Federal	3.2	6.6	10.7	13.2	15.8	19.2	23.1	28.1	31.9
State and local	4.0	6.5	8.3	9.9	11.8	13.8	16.2	18.1	20.0
Medicare [1].....................	0.2	0.7	1.5	1.9	2.1	2.4	2.4	2.4	3.4
Medicaid [2].....................	5.1	9.7	14.1	17.0	20.2	23.8	27.8	32.7	36.3

– Represents zero.   [1] Medicare expenditures come from federal funds.   [2] Medicaid expenditures come from federal, state, and local funds.

Source: U. S. Centers for Medicare and Medicaid Services, Office of the Actuary, "National Health Expenditure Accounts"; See also <http://www.cms.hhs.gov/NationalHealthExpendData/>.

98   Health and Nutrition

Table 128. **Retail Prescription Drug Sales: 1995 to 2005**

[2,125 represents 2,125,000,000]

Sales outlet	Unit	1995	1998	1999	2000	2001	2002	2003	2004	2005
Number of prescriptions. . .	Mil.	**2,125**	**2,481**	**2,707**	**2,865**	**3,009**	**3,139**	**3,215**	**3,274**	**3,383**
Traditional chain	Mil.	914	1,129	1,246	1,344	1,415	1,474	1,494	1,510	1,562
Independent	Mil.	666	651	680	689	700	708	726	728	743
Mass merchant.	Mil.	238	272	289	293	314	339	345	353	365
Supermarkets	Mil.	221	306	357	394	418	444	462	470	469
Mail order	Mil.	86	123	134	146	161	174	189	214	244
Retail sales	**Bil. dol.. . . .**	**72.2**	**108.7**	**125.8**	**145.6**	**164.1**	**182.7**	**203.1**	**221.0**	**230.3**
Traditional chain	Bil. dol. . . .	28.8	45.5	53.8	61.2	67.7	75.9	85.4	90.6	94.5
Independent	Bil. dol. . . .	21.1	26.1	28.9	31.4	33.9	35.4	38.3	40.5	41.8
Mass merchant.	Bil. dol. . . .	7.7	10.9	11.8	13.5	15.2	18.0	19.5	21.5	22.5
Supermarkets	Bil. dol. . . .	7.4	12.0	13.8	17.4	19.8	23.1	25.1	27.0	27.6
Mail order	Bil. dol. . . .	7.4	14.3	17.4	22.1	27.6	30.2	34.9	41.3	43.9
Average Prices [1]										
All prescriptions	Dollars . . .	**30.01**	**38.43**	**42.42**	**45.79**	**50.06**	**55.37**	**59.52**	**63.59**	**64.86**
Brand drugs.	Dollars . . .	40.22	53.51	60.66	65.29	69.75	77.49	85.57	95.86	101.71
Generic drugs	Dollars . . .	14.84	17.33	18.16	19.33	21.72	24.89	27.69	28.71	29.82
Percentage of Number of Drug Prescriptions by Brand/Generic Mix										
Brand drugs.	Percent . . .	59.8	58.3	57.1	57.6	59.0	57.9	55.0	51.9	48.7
Generic drugs	Percent . . .	40.2	41.7	42.9	42.4	41.0	42.1	45.0	48.1	51.3

[1] Excludes mail order.

Source: National Association of Chain Drug Stores, Alexandria, VA, *NACDS Foundation Chain Pharmacy Industry Profile, 2006* (copyright); <http://www.nacds.org>.

Table 129. **Prescription Drug Use in the Past Month by Sex, Age, Race, and Hispanic Origin: 1988–1994 and 1999–2002**

[Data are based on National Health and Nutrition Examination Survey (NHANES), a sample of the civilian noninstitutionalized population]

Sex and age	Percent of population using at least one prescription drug in past month							
	All persons [1]		White		Black or African American		Mexican [3]	
			Not Hispanic or Latino [2]					
	1988–1994	1999–2002	1988–1994	1999–2002	1988–1994	1999–2002	1988–1994	1999–2002
Both sexes, age adjusted [4]	**39.1**	**45.3**	**41.1**	**48.9**	**36.9**	**40.1**	**31.7**	**31.7**
Male.	32.7	39.9	34.2	43.1	31.1	35.4	27.5	25.8
Female	45.0	50.4	47.6	54.5	41.4	43.8	36.0	37.8
Both sexes, crude	37.8	45.1	41.4	50.9	31.2	36.0	24.0	23.7
Male.	30.6	38.7	33.5	43.9	25.5	30.8	20.1	18.8
Female	44.6	51.2	48.9	57.6	36.2	40.6	28.1	28.9
Under 18 years old	20.5	24.2	22.9	27.6	14.8	18.6	16.1	15.9
18 to 44 years old	31.3	33.9	34.3	41.3	27.8	28.5	21.1	19.2
45 to 64 years old	54.8	64.1	55.5	66.1	57.5	62.3	48.1	49.3
65 years old and over	73.6	84.7	74.0	85.4	74.5	81.1	67.7	72.0
Male:								
Under 18 years old.	20.4	26.2	22.3	30.6	15.5	19.8	16.3	16.2
18 to 44 years old	21.5	27.1	23.5	31.2	21.1	21.5	14.9	13.0
45 to 64 years old	47.2	55.6	48.1	57.4	48.2	54.0	43.8	36.4
65 years old and over.	67.2	80.1	67.4	81.0	64.4	78.1	61.3	66.8
Female:								
Under 18 years old.	20.6	22.0	23.6	24.4	14.2	17.3	16.0	15.6
18 to 44 years old	40.7	44.6	44.7	51.7	33.4	34.2	28.1	26.2
45 to 64 years old	62.0	72.0	62.6	74.7	64.4	69.0	52.2	62.4
65 years old and over.	78.3	88.1	78.8	88.8	81.3	83.1	73.0	76.3

[1] Includes persons of other races and Hispanic origins, not shown separately. [2] Starting with data year 1999 race-specific estimates are not comparable with estimates for earlier years, see footnote 3, Table 156. [3] Persons of Mexican origin may be of any race. [4] Age adjusted to the 2000 standard population using four age groups: Under 18, 18–44, 45–64, and 65 years and over. See text Section 2.

Source: National Center for Health Statistics *Health, United States, 2005.* <http://www.cdc.gov/nchs/hus.htm>.

Health and Nutrition 99

Table 130. Consumer Price Indexes of Medical Care Prices: 1980 to 2005

[1982–1984 = 100. Indexes are annual averages of monthly data based on components of consumer price index for all urban consumers; for explanation, see text, Section 14, Prices. See Appendix III]

Year	Medical care services [1] Medical care total [1]	Total	Professional services Total	Physicians	Dental	Hospital and related services	Medical care commodities [2] Total	Prescription drugs and medical supplies	Annual percent change [3] Medical care, total	Medical care services	Medical care commodities
1980....	74.9	74.8	77.9	76.5	78.9	69.2	75.4	72.5	11.0	11.3	9.3
1985....	113.5	113.2	113.5	113.3	114.2	116.1	115.2	120.1	6.3	6.1	7.2
1990....	162.8	162.7	156.1	160.8	155.8	178.0	163.4	181.7	9.0	9.3	8.4
1995....	220.5	224.2	201.0	208.8	206.8	257.8	204.5	235.0	4.5	5.1	1.9
1998....	242.1	246.8	222.2	229.5	236.2	287.5	221.8	258.6	3.2	3.2	3.0
1999....	250.6	255.1	229.2	236.0	247.2	299.5	230.7	273.4	3.5	3.4	4.0
2000....	260.8	266.0	237.7	244.7	258.5	317.3	238.1	285.4	4.1	4.3	3.2
2001....	272.8	278.8	246.5	253.6	269.0	338.3	247.6	300.9	4.6	4.8	4.0
2002....	285.6	292.9	253.9	260.6	281.0	367.8	256.4	316.5	4.7	5.1	3.6
2003....	297.1	306.0	261.2	267.7	292.5	394.8	262.8	326.3	4.0	4.5	2.5
2004....	310.1	321.3	271.5	278.3	306.9	417.9	269.3	337.1	4.4	5.0	2.5
2005....	323.2	336.7	281.7	287.5	324.0	439.9	276.0	349.0	4.2	4.8	2.5

[1] Includes other services not shown separately.   [2] Includes other commodities not shown separately.   [3] Percent change from the immediate prior year.
Source: U.S. Bureau of Labor Statistics, *CPI Detailed Report*, monthly, <http://www.bls.gov/cpi/cpi_dr.htm>. See also *Monthly Labor Review* at <http://www.bls.gov/opub/mlr/MLRhome.htm>.

Table 131. Average Annual Expenditures Per Consumer Unit for Health Care: 1990 to 2004

[In dollars, except percent. See text, Section 13, Income, Expenditures, and Wealth, and headnote, Table 667. Consumer Expenditures Survey (CE) has implemented multiple imputation of income data, starting with the publication of the 2004 tables. Because of income imputation, data for 2004 are not strictly, comparable to data from previous years, especially for income tables. For more information go to <http://www.bls.gov/cex/csxann04.pdf>, page 4. For composition of regions, see map, inside front cover]

Item	Health care, total Amount	Percent of total expenditures	Health insurance	Medical services	Drugs and medical supplies [1]	Percent distribution Health insurance	Medical services	Drugs and medical supplies [1]
1990	1,480	5.2	581	562	337	39.3	38.0	22.8
1995	1,732	5.4	860	512	360	49.7	29.6	20.8
2000	2,066	5.4	983	568	515	47.6	27.5	24.9
2001	2,182	5.5	1,061	573	549	48.6	26.3	25.2
2002	2,350	5.8	1,168	590	592	49.7	25.1	25.2
2003	2,416	5.9	1,252	591	574	51.8	24.5	23.8
2004	**2,574**	**5.9**	**1,332**	**648**	**594**	**51.7**	**25.2**	**23.1**
Age of reference person:								
Under 25 years old	654	2.7	321	184	149	49.1	28.1	22.8
25 to 34 years old.......	1,519	3.6	842	403	274	55.4	26.5	18.0
35 to 44 years old.......	2,263	4.5	1,199	654	410	53.0	28.9	18.1
45 to 54 years old.......	2,695	5.1	1,291	809	594	47.9	30.0	22.0
55 to 64 years old.......	3,262	6.9	1,567	892	803	48.0	27.3	24.6
65 to 74 years old.......	3,799	10.4	2,171	631	998	57.1	16.6	26.3
75 years old and over	3,995	15.5	2,115	723	1,157	52.9	18.1	29.0
Race of reference person:								
White and other	2,736	6.1	1,397	706	634	51.1	25.8	23.2
Black	1,368	4.5	846	220	302	61.8	16.1	22.1
Origin of reference person:								
Hispanic	1,588	4.2	850	402	337	53.5	25.3	21.2
Non-Hispanic	2,691	6.1	1,389	678	624	51.6	25.2	23.2
Region of residence:								
Northeast	2,371	5.1	1,307	597	467	55.1	25.2	19.7
Midwest	2,861	6.6	1,492	714	654	52.1	25.0	22.9
South	2,508	6.4	1,287	583	639	51.3	23.2	25.5
West...............	2,560	5.3	1,261	731	569	49.3	28.6	22.2
Size of consumer unit:								
One person	1,697	6.7	850	391	456	50.1	23.0	26.9
Two or more persons.....	2,932	5.8	1,528	753	650	52.1	25.7	22.2
Two persons.........	3,212	7.0	1,648	768	797	51.3	23.9	24.8
Three persons	2,865	5.6	1,476	804	586	51.5	28.1	20.5
Four persons	2,635	4.6	1,443	686	507	54.8	26.0	19.2
Five persons or more ...	2,520	4.5	1,328	723	468	52.7	28.7	18.6
Income before taxes:								
Quintiles of income:								
Lowest 20 percent ...	1,421	8.0	745	265	410	52.4	18.6	28.9
Second 20 percent....	2,139	7.8	1,146	439	554	53.6	20.5	25.9
Third 20 percent	2,529	6.8	1,346	578	606	53.2	22.9	24.0
Fourth 20 percent....	2,969	5.8	1,556	778	635	52.4	26.2	21.4
Highest 20 percent...	3,810	4.8	1,864	1,181	765	48.9	31.0	20.1

[1] Includes prescription and nonprescription drugs.
Source: U.S. Bureau of Labor Statistics, *Consumer Expenditure Survey*, annual; <http://www.bls.gov/cex/>.

Table 132. **Medicare Benefits by Type of Provider: 1990 to 2005**

[In millions of dollars (65,721 represents $65,721,000,000). For years ending Sept. 30. Distribution of benefits by type is estimated and subject to change]

Type of provider	1990	1995	2000	2001	2002	2003	2004	2005
Hospital insurance benefits, total . .	65,721	113,395	125,992	135,979	144,140	153,144	163,764	180,973
Inpatient hospital	57,012	81,095	86,561	93,918	101,908	108,203	113,759	121,625
Skilled nursing facility	2,761	8,684	10,269	12,059	15,049	14,869	16,571	18,084
Home health agency	3,295	15,715	4,880	3,701	4,802	4,926	5,184	5,946
Hospice	318	1,854	2,818	3,464	4,516	5,879	7,319	8,318
Managed care	2,335	6,047	21,463	22,837	17,865	19,267	20,932	27,001
Supplementary medical insurance benefits, total.	41,498	63,490	88,876	100,514	108,068	119,455	131,364	148,472
Physician fee schedule	(NA)	31,110	35,958	40,447	44,217	47,486	52,206	57,281
Durable medical equipment	(NA)	3,576	4,577	5,222	6,132	7,432	7,727	7,841
Carrier lab [1]	(NA)	2,819	2,194	2,361	2,692	2,945	3,195	3,515
Other carrier [2]	(NA)	4,513	7,154	8,396	10,304	12,430	13,785	15,183
Hospital [3]	(NA)	8,448	8,516	11,696	13,464	14,687	16,925	19,605
Home health	(NA)	223	4,281	4,338	4,811	5,167	5,588	6,558
Intermediary lab [4]	(NA)	1,437	1,748	1,914	2,150	2,408	2,669	2,924
Other intermediary [5]	(NA)	5,110	6,099	6,891	8,245	9,697	10,455	11,768
Managed care	(NA)	6,253	18,348	19,249	16,052	17,203	18,816	23,797

NA Not available.   [1] Lab services paid under the lab fee schedule performed in a physician's office lab or an independent lab.   [2] Includes free-standing ambulatory surgical centers facility costs, ambulance, and supplies.   [3] Includes the hospital facility costs for Medicare Part B services which are predominantly in the outpatient department. The physician reimbursement associated with these services is included on the "Physician Fee Schedule" line.   [4] Lab fee services paid under the lab fee schedule performed in a hospital outpatient department.   [5] Includes end stage renal disease (ESRD) free-standing dialysis facility payments and payments to rural health clinics, outpatient rehabilitation facilities, psychiatric hospitals, and federally qualified health centers.

Source: U.S. Centers for Medicare and Medicaid Services, unpublished data. See also <http://www.cms.hhs.gov/ReportsTrustFunds/>.

Table 133. **Medicare—Enrollment by State and Other Areas: 2000 to 2004**

[(39,620 represents 39,620,000) Hospital and/or supplementary medical insurance enrollment as July 1]

State and area	2000	2002	2003	2004	State and area	2000	2002	2003	2004
All areas . . .	39,620	40,489	41,087	41,729	MT	137	140	142	145
					NE	254	256	257	259
U.S.	38,762	39,594	40,173	40,792	NV	240	261	274	286
AL	685	706	719	733	NH	170	176	180	183
AK	42	46	48	50	NJ	1,203	1,213	1,220	1,225
AZ	675	708	729	755	NM	234	244	250	257
AR	439	446	453	460	NY	2,715	2,747	2,763	2,775
CA	3,901	4,009	4,078	4,150	NC	1,133	1,178	1,205	1,235
CO	467	484	493	506	ND	103	103	103	103
CT	515	518	522	524	OH	1,701	1,713	1,727	1,739
DE	112	116	119	123	OK	508	515	521	529
DC	75	74	74	73	OR	489	504	513	527
FL	2,804	2,876	2,921	2,982	PA	2,095	2,101	2,110	2,118
GA	916	951	974	998	RI	172	172	172	173
HI	165	171	175	178	SC	568	592	606	624
ID	165	173	178	184	SD	119	121	122	123
IL	1,635	1,646	1,661	1,676	TN	829	855	872	891
IN	852	865	878	889	TX	2,265	2,338	2,390	2,451
IA	477	479	482	486	UT	206	215	220	227
KS	390	392	394	397	VT	89	91	93	94
KY	623	637	648	660	VA	893	927	946	967
LA	602	612	620	627	WA	736	759	775	799
ME	216	223	227	231	WV	338	343	347	351
MD	645	664	674	685	WI	783	794	804	814
MA	961	963	966	968	WY	65	67	69	70
MI	1,403	1,426	1,445	1,464					
MN	654	667	676	686	PR and island areas	537	562	575	613
MS	419	429	437	446	Other areas . .	321	333	340	324
MO	861	874	884	896					

Source: U.S. Centers for Medicare and Medicaid Services, Medicare Enrollment Reports. See also <http://www.cms.hhs.gov/MedicareEnrpts/>.

Health and Nutrition   101

Table 134. Medicare Enrollees: 1980 to 2005

[In millions (28.4 represents 28,400,000). As of July 1. Includes Puerto Rico and island areas and enrollees in foreign countries and unknown place of residence]

Item	1980	1990	1995	2000	2002	2003	2004	2005
Total	28.4	34.3	37.6	39.7	40.5	41.2	41.9	42.5
Aged	25.5	31.0	33.2	34.3	34.7	35.0	35.4	35.8
Disabled	3.0	3.3	4.4	5.4	5.8	6.2	6.4	6.7
Hospital insurance	28.0	33.7	37.2	39.3	40.1	40.7	41.4	42.0
Aged	25.0	30.5	32.7	33.8	34.2	34.6	35.0	35.4
Disabled	3.0	3.3	4.4	5.4	5.8	6.2	6.4	6.7
Supplementary medical insurance	27.3	32.6	35.6	37.3	38.0	38.6	39.1	39.6
Aged	24.6	29.6	31.7	32.6	32.9	33.2	33.4	33.7
Disabled	2.7	2.9	3.9	4.8	5.1	5.4	5.7	5.9

Source: U.S. Centers for Medicare and Medicaid Services, Medicare Enrollment Reports. See also <http://www.cms.hhs.gov /MedicareEnrpts/>.

Table 135. Medicare Disbursements by Type of Beneficiary: 1990 to 2005

[In millions of dollars (109,709 represents $109,709,000,000). For years ending Sept. 30. Distribution of benefits by type is estimated and subject to change. Minus sign (–) indicates decrease]

Type of beneficiary	1990	1995	2000	2001	2002	2003	2004	2005
Total disbursements	109,709	180,096	219,276	241,175	256,856	277,846	301,488	336,876
Hospital insurance disbursements	66,687	114,883	130,284	141,723	148,031	153,792	166,998	184,142
Benefits	65,722	113,394	125,992	135,979	144,140	153,144	163,764	180,973
Aged	58,503	100,107	110,261	118,816	125,248	132,415	141,277	155,135
Disabled	7,218	13,288	15,731	17,163	18,892	20,729	22,487	25,838
Disabled	6,467	12,300	14,705	16,029	17,627	19,341	20,954	24,148
ESRD [1]	751	988	1,026	1,134	1,265	1,388	1,533	1,690
Home health transfer [2]	–	–	1,706	3,103	1,168	-2,174	–	–
Quality improvement activity [3]	191	189	236	274	259	280	314	319
Administrative expenses [4]	774	1,300	2,350	2,368	2,464	2,542	2,920	2,850
Supplementary medical insurance disbursements (Parts B and D)	43,022	65,213	88,992	99,452	108,825	124,055	134,490	152,735
Benefits	41,498	63,489	88,875	100,514	108,068	119,455	131,581	149,670
Aged	36,837	54,830	76,340	86,108	91,667	100,505	109,893	123,681
Disabled	4,661	8,660	12,535	14,406	16,400	18,950	21,471	24,791
Disabled	3,758	7,363	11,683	13,657	15,523	17,981	20,479	23,755
ESRD [1]	903	1,297	852	749	877	969	992	1,037
Part D Transitional Assistance	–	–	–	–	–	–	216	1,198
Home health transfer [2]	–	–	-1,706	-3,103	-1,168	2,174	–	–
Quality improvement activity [3]	–	–	2	43	55	95	70	79
Administrative expenses	1,524	1,722	1,780	1,986	1,830	2,356	2,817	2,914
Cost/Demos	–	–	–	–	–	–	14	71

– Represents or rounds to zero. [1] Represents persons entitled because of End Stage Renal Disease only. Benefits for those who have ESRD, but would be entitled due to their age or disabled status are included in aged and disabled benefits. [2] Beginning 1998 home health agency transfers are excluded from total supplementary medical insurance disbursements and included in total hospital insurance disbursements. [3] Beginning in 2002, Peer Review Organizations were renamed Quality Improvement Organizations. [4] Includes costs of experiments and demonstration projects. Includes costs of the health care fraud and abuse control program.

Source: U.S. Centers for Medicare and Medicaid Services, Trustees Report and Trust Funds, and unpublished data. See also <http://www.cms.hhs.gov/ReportsTrustFunds/>.

Table 136. Medicare Trust Funds: 1990 to 2005

[In billions of dollars (126.3 represents $126,300,000,000). Minus sign (–) indicates a decrease]

Type of trust fund	1990	1995	1999	2000	2001	2002	2003	2004	2005
TOTAL MEDICARE									
Total income	126.3	175.3	232.5	257.1	273.3	284.8	291.6	317.7	357.5
Total expenditures	111.0	184.2	213.0	221.8	244.8	265.7	280.8	308.9	336.4
Assets, end of year	114.4	143.4	186.2	221.5	250.0	269.1	280.8	288.8	309.8
Net change in assets	15.3	–8.9	19.5	35.3	28.5	19.1	10.8	8.8	21.0
HOSPITAL INSURANCE (HI)									
Net contribution income [1]	72.1	103.3	140.3	154.5	160.9	162.7	159.2	167.2	182.6
Interest received [2]	8.5	10.8	10.1	11.7	14.0	15.1	15.8	16.0	16.1
Benefit payments [3]	66.2	116.4	128.8	126.8	138.1	148.8	154.3	167.6	180.0
Assets, end of year	98.9	130.3	141.4	177.5	208.7	234.8	256.0	269.3	285.8
SUPPLEMENTARY MEDICAL INSURANCE (SMI) Parts B and D									
Net premium income	11.3	19.7	[4]19.0	20.6	22.8	25.1	27.4	31.4	37.5
Transfers from general revenue [6]	33.0	39.0	[4]59.1	65.9	72.8	78.3	86.4	100.4	119.2
Interest received [2]	1.6	1.6	2.8	3.5	3.1	2.8	2.0	1.5	1.4
Benefit payments [3, 5]	42.5	65.0	80.7	88.9	99.7	111.0	123.8	135.0	150.3
Assets, end of year	15.5	13.1	44.8	44.0	41.3	34.3	24.0	19.4	24.0

[1] Includes income from taxation of benefits beginning in 1994. Includes premiums from aged ineligibles enrolled in HI. [2] Includes recoveries of amounts reimbursed from the trust fund. [3] Beginning 1998 monies transferred to the SMI trust fund for home health agency costs, as provided for by P.L. 105-33, are included in HI benefit payments but excluded from SMI benefit payments. [4] Premiums withheld from check and associated general revenue contributions that were to occur on Jan. 3, 1999, actually occurred on December 31, 1998. These amounts are therefore excluded from 1999 data. [5] These amounts for 2004 and 2005 include transitional assistance for Part D of Medicare. [6] These amounts for 2004 and 2005 include amounts transferred for transitional assistance for Part D of Medicare.

Source: U.S. Centers for Medicare and Medicaid Services, Annual Report of the Board of Trustees of the Federal Hospital Insurance Trust Fund and Annual Report of the Board of Trustees of the Federal Supplementary Medical Insurance Trust Funds. See also <http://www.cms.hhs.gov/ReportsTrustFunds/>.

Table 137. Medicaid—Selected Characteristics of Persons Covered: 2004

[In thousands, except percent (37,270 represents 37,270,000). Represents number of persons as of March of following year who were enrolled at any time in year shown. Excludes unrelated individuals under age 15. Person did not have to receive medical care paid for by Medicaid in order to be counted. See headnote, Table 553]

Poverty status	Total [1]	White alone [2]	Black alone [3]	Asian alone [4]	His- panic [5]	Under 18 years old	18 to 44 years old	45 to 64 years old	65 years old and over
Persons covered, total . . .	**37,270**	**25,425**	**8,880**	**1,266**	**9,073**	**19,603**	**9,739**	**4,631**	**3,297**
Below poverty level	15,398	9,688	4,621	368	4,040	8,554	4,164	1,755	924
Above poverty level	21,872	15,737	4,259	898	5,033	11,049	5,575	2,876	2,373
Percent of population covered	12.8	10.9	24.4	10.3	21.8	26.8	8.8	6.5	9.4
Below poverty level	41.6	38.3	51.3	30.4	44.2	65.7	29.2	28.1	26.7
Above poverty level	8.6	7.6	15.5	8.1	15.5	18.3	5.8	4.4	7.5

[1] Includes other races not shown separately.   [2] White alone refers to people who reported White and did not report any other race category.   [3] Black alone refers to people who reported Black and did not report any other race category.   [4] Asian alone refers to people who reported Asian and did not report any other race category.   [5] Persons of Hispanic origin may be of any race.

Source: U.S. Census Bureau, "Table HI02. Health Insurance Coverage Status and Type of Coverage by Selected Characteristics for People in the Poverty Universe: 2004"; published August 2005; <http://pubdb3.census.gov/macro/032005/health/h02000.htm>; and "Table HI03. Health Insurance Coverage Status and Type of Coverage by Selected Characteristics for Poor People in the Poverty Universe: 2004"; published August 2005; <http://pubdb3.census.gov/macro/032005/health/toc.htm>.

Table 138. Medicaid—Beneficiaries and Payments: 2000 to 2003

[For year ending September 30 (42,887 represents 42,887,000). Starting in 1999, states were required to submit all their eligibility and claims data to the Centers for Medicare & Medicaid Services (CMS) on a quarterly basis through the Medicaid Statistical Information System (MSIS). The federal requirement for the HCFA-Form 2082 (used for 1998 and preceding years) was eliminated.]

Basis of eligibility and type of service	Beneficiaries (1,000) [1]				Payments (mil. dol.)			
	2000	2001	2002	2003	2000	2001	2002	2003
Total	**42,887**	**46,164**	**49,329**	**51,971**	**168,443**	**186,914**	**213,497**	**233,206**
Age 65 and over	3,730	3,812	3,890	4,041	44,560	48,431	52,012	55,271
Blind/disabled	6,890	7,118	7,411	7,669	72,772	80,494	92,414	102,014
Children	19,018	20,340	22,421	23,992	23,490	26,771	31,595	35,080
Adults	8,671	9,769	11,253	11,679	17,671	20,097	23,525	26,689
Foster care children	761	775	815	839	3,309	3,773	4,311	4,791
Unknown	3,817	4,349	3,534	3,739	6,639	7,347	9,607	9,251
BCCA women [2]	(NA)	(Z)	5	12	(NA)	1	33	110
Capitated care [3]	21,292	23,356	25,527	27,574	25,026	29,368	33,635	37,405
Clinic services	7,678	8,464	9,491	10,162	6,138	5,603	6,704	7,312
Dental services	5,922	7,019	7,881	8,510	1,413	1,897	2,309	2,595
Home health services	1,007	1,014	1,064	1,184	3,133	3,521	3,926	4,404
ICF/MR services [4]	119	117	117	114	9,376	9,701	10,676	10,861
Inpatient hospital services	4,913	4,879	5,046	5,217	24,131	25,943	29,123	31,549
Lab and X-ray services	11,439	12,339	14,062	14,687	1,292	1,623	2,160	2,365
Mental health facility services [5] . . .	100	91	100	105	1,769	1,959	2,128	2,143
Nursing facility services	1,706	1,702	1,760	1,691	37,323	37,323	39,286	40,381
Other care [6]	9,022	9,709	10,934	11,742	14,755	16,617	19,877	21,809
Outpatient hospital services	13,170	13,731	14,831	15,511	7,082	7,496	8,469	9,252
Other practitioner services	4,758	5,103	5,566	5,746	664	762	842	882
PCCM services [7]	5,649	6,378	7,178	7,542	177	187	200	208
Prescribed drugs	20,325	21,911	24,380	26,075	19,898	23,764	28,404	33,714
Physician services	18,965	20,021	22,065	22,857	6,809	7,439	8,349	9,210
Personal support services [8]	4,559	4,978	5,681	6,022	11,629	13,115	15,362	17,245
Sterilizations	137	144	164	160	128	140	165	166
Unknown	74	45	73	88	496	438	1,882	1,702

NA Not available.   Z Less than 500.   [1] Beneficiaries' data do not add due to number of beneficiaries that are reported in more than one category.   [2] Women-Breast and Cervical Cancer Assistance.   [3] HMO payments and prepaid health plans.   [4] Intermediate care facilities for mentally retarded.   [5] Inpatient mental health-aged and inpatient mental health—under 21.   [6] Includes beneficiaries of, and payments for, other care not shown separately.   [7] Primary Care Case Management Services.   [8] Includes personal care services, rehabilitative services, physical occupational targeted case management services, speech therapies, hospice services, nurse midwife services, nurse practitioner services, private duty nursing services, and religious nonmedical health care institutions.

Source: U.S. Centers for Medicare and Medicaid Services, "Medicaid Program Statistics, Medicaid Statistical Information System (MSIS)"; <http://www.cms.hhs.gov/MedicaidDataSourcesGenInfo/>.

Table 139. **Medicaid—Summary by State: 2000 and 2003**

[In thousands (42,887 represents 42,887,000). For year ending September 30. See headnote, Table 138]

State	Beneficiaries [1] (1,000) 2000	2003	Payments [2] (mil. dol.) 2000	2003	State	Beneficiaries [1] (1,000) 2000	2003	Payments [2] (mil. dol.) 2000	2003
U.S.	42,887	51,971	168,443	233,206	MO	890	1,081	3,274	4,407
AL	619	781	2,393	3,471	MT	104	110	422	536
AK	96	116	473	836	NE	229	254	960	1,283
AZ	681	1,015	2,112	3,285	NV	138	220	516	881
AR	489	702	1,543	2,212	NH	97	112	651	786
CA	7,918	9,319	17,105	25,812	NJ	822	950	4,714	6,030
CO	381	459	1,809	2,269	NM	376	452	1,249	2,033
CT	420	497	2,839	3,359	NY	3,420	4,450	26,148	35,207
DE	115	150	529	750	NC	1,214	1,417	4,834	6,521
DC	139	158	793	1,200	ND	63	77	358	445
FL	2,373	2,743	7,433	11,104	OH	1,305	1,778	7,115	10,235
GA	1,369	1,732	3,624	5,358	OK	507	626	1,604	2,129
HI	194	209	600	753	OR	558	598	1,714	2,116
ID	131	193	594	867	PA	1,492	1,722	6,366	9,450
IL	1,519	1,830	7,807	9,391	RI	179	202	1,070	1,338
IN	706	896	2,977	3,951	SC	689	861	2,765	3,642
IA	314	362	1,477	1,996	SD	102	124	402	542
KS	263	316	1,227	1,615	TN	1,568	1,730	3,491	5,459
KY	764	848	2,921	3,558	TX	2,633	3,340	9,277	12,525
LA	761	995	2,632	3,615	UT	225	285	960	1,201
ME	194	307	1,310	2,074	VT	139	155	480	642
MD	626	726	3,003	4,398	VA	627	709	2,479	3,181
MA	1,060	1,042	5,413	6,392	WA	896	1,077	2,435	4,524
MI	1,352	1,590	4,881	6,479	WV	342	373	1,394	1,830
MN	558	668	3,280	4,702	WI	577	829	2,968	3,921
MS	605	717	1,808	2,570	WY	46	67	215	325

[1] Persons who had payments made on their behalf at any time during the fiscal year. [2] Payments are for fiscal year and reflect federal and state contribution payments. Data exclude disproportionate share hospital payments. Disproportionate share hospitals receive higher medicaid reimbursement than other hospitals because they treat a disproportionate share of Medicaid patients.

Source: U.S. Centers for Medicare and Medicaid Services, "Medicaid, Program Statistics, Medicaid Statistical Information System." <http://www.cms.hhs.gov/MedicaidDataSourcesGenInfo/02MSISData.asp#TopOfPage>.

Table 140. **State Children's Health Insurance Program (SCHIP)—Enrollment and Expenditures by State: 2000 and 2005**

[In thousands (3,357.4 represents 3,357,400) In millions (1,928.8 represents 1,928,800,000). For year ending September 30. This program provides health benefits coverage to children living in families whose incomes exceed the eligibility limits for Medicaid. Although it is generally targeted to families with incomes at or below 200 percent of the federal poverty level, each state may set its own income eligibility limits, within certain guidelines. States have three options: they may expand their Medicaid programs, develop a separate child health program that functions independently of Medicaid, or do a combination of both]

State	Enrollment [1] (1,000) 2000	2005	Expenditures [2] (mil. dol.) 2000	2005	State	Enrollment [1] (1,000) 2000	2005	Expenditures [2] (mil. dol.) 2000	2005
US	3,357.4	6,000.1	1,928.8	5,044.8	MO	72.8	115.4	41.2	88.7
AL	37.6	81.9	31.9	80.2	MT	8.3	15.8	4.3	12.8
AK	13.4	22.3	18.1	24.4	NE	11.4	44.7	6.1	34.0
AZ	59.6	88.0	29.4	198.0	NV	15.9	39.3	9.0	26.6
AR	1.9	1.2	1.5	63.0	NH	4.3	11.9	1.6	7.6
CA	484.4	1,109.6	187.3	760.0	NJ	89.0	129.6	46.9	204.9
CO	34.9	59.5	13.9	38.7	NM	8.0	24.3	3.4	23.2
CT	19.9	22.3	12.8	20.5	NY	769.5	619.0	401.0	362.5
DE	4.5	10.4	1.5	6.4	NC	103.6	196.2	65.5	211.0
DC	2.3	6.6	5.8	7.4	ND	2.6	5.7	1.8	8.3
FL	227.5	384.8	125.7	244.0	OH	118.3	216.5	53.1	172.3
GA	120.6	306.7	48.7	201.6	OK	57.7	108.1	51.3	63.6
HI	(Z)	20.6	0.4	13.0	OR	37.1	52.7	12.5	38.6
ID	12.4	21.8	7.5	16.6	PA	119.7	179.8	70.7	140.9
IL	62.5	281.4	32.7	320.2	RI	11.5	27.1	10.4	56.4
IN	44.4	129.5	53.7	76.1	SC	60.4	80.6	46.6	57.3
IA	20.0	46.6	15.5	40.8	SD	5.9	14.0	3.1	11.9
KS	26.3	47.3	12.8	43.1	TN	14.9	(NA)	41.7	3.4
KY	55.6	63.7	60.0	70.8	TX	131.1	526.4	41.4	287.7
LA	50.0	109.2	25.3	109.9	UT	25.3	43.9	12.8	28.7
ME	22.7	30.7	11.4	20.6	VT	4.1	6.6	1.4	3.7
MD	93.1	120.3	92.2	122.4	VA	37.7	124.1	18.6	79.8
MA	113.0	162.7	44.2	121.5	WA	2.6	15.5	0.6	40.3
MI	55.4	89.3	36.2	172.2	WV	21.7	38.6	9.7	33.3
MN	(Z)	5.1	(Z)	71.5	WI	47.1	57.2	21.4	86.3
MS	12.2	79.4	21.1	112.5	WY	2.5	6.1	1.0	5.7

NA Not available.　Z Less than 50 or $50,000. [1] Number of children ever enrolled during the year in SCHIP. [2] Expenditures for which states are entitled to federal reimbursement under Title XXI and which reconciles any advance of Title XXI federal funds made on the basis of estimates.

Source: U.S. Centers for Medicare & Medicaid Services, *The State Children's Health Insurance Program, Annual Enrollment Report* and the Statement of Expenditures for the SCHIP Program (CMS-21). See also <http://www.cms.hhs.gov/NationalSCHIPPolicy /SCHIPER/list.asp> and <http://www.cms.hhs.gov/MedicaidSCHIPBudExpInfSys/>.

Table 141. Medicaid Managed Care Enrollment by State and Other Areas: 1995 to 2005

[For year ending June 30. (33,373 represents 33,373,000)]

State and area	Total enroll-ment [1] (1,000)	Managed care enrollment [2] Number (1,000)	Managed care enrollment [2] Percent of total	State and area	Total enroll-ment [1] (1,000)	Managed care enrollment [2] Number (1,000)	Managed care enrollment [2] Percent of total	State and area	Total enroll-ment [1] (1,000)	Managed care enrollment [2] Number (1,000)	Managed care enrollment [2] Percent of total
1995	33,373	9,800	29.4	HI	201	160	79.9	NY	4,189	2,575	61.5
2000	33,690	18,786	55.8	ID	172	143	82.8	NC	1,138	807	70.9
2001	36,563	20,774	56.8	IL	1,827	175	9.6	ND	54	33	60.6
2002	40,148	23,118	57.6	IN	811	556	68.5	OH	1,711	534	31.2
2003	42,741	24,406	58.4	IA	298	274	92.0	OK	544	473	87.0
2004	44,356	26,914	60.7	KS	276	154	55.9	OR	411	373	90.6
2005, total	45,392	28,576	63.0	KY	692	636	92.0	PA	1,698	1,534	90.4
U.S.	44,515	27,710	62.2	LA	964	761	79.0	RI	180	125	69.4
AL	821	496	60.5	ME	266	165	61.9	SC	833	82	9.8
AK	98	–	–	MD	716	483	67.4	SD	101	98	97.5
AZ	997	885	88.8	MA	992	610	61.5	TN	1,350	1,350	100.0
AR	624	506	81.1	MI	1,435	1,290	89.9	TX	2,767	1,339	48.4
CA	6,553	3,291	50.2	MN	573	378	65.9	UT	203	185	91.0
CO	410	390	95.0	MS	633	85	13.5	VT	130	87	66.9
CT	403	302	75.0	MO	949	428	45.0	VA	674	421	62.5
DE	140	107	76.2	MT	84	57	68.2	WA	963	817	84.8
DC	141	91	64.8	NE	207	147	71.1	WV	296	141	47.5
FL	2,248	1,488	66.2	NV	175	175	100.0	WI	813	378	46.4
GA	1,378	1,320	95.8	NH	100	2	2.0	WY	61	–	–
				NJ	802	553	69.0	PR	867	865	99.9
				NM	411	249	60.6	VI	11	–	–

– Represents zero. [1] The unduplicated Medicaid enrollment figures include individuals in state health care reform programs that expand eligibility beyond traditional Medicaid eligibility standards. [2] The unduplicated managed care enrollment figures include enrollees receiving comprehensive and limited benefits.

Source: U.S. Centers for Medicare and Medicaid Services, 2005 Medicaid Managed Care Enrollment Report. See also <http://www.cms.hhs.gov/MedicaidDataSourcesGenInfo/04MdManCrEnrllRep.asp>.

Table 142. Health Maintenance Organizations (HMOs): 1990 to 2004

[As of January 1 (33.0 represents 33,000,000). An HMO is a prepaid health plan delivering comprehensive care to members through designated providers, having a fixed periodic payment for health care services, and requiring members to be in a plan for a specified period of time (usually 1 year). A group HMO delivers health services through a physician group that is controlled by the HMO unit or contracts with one or more independent group practices to provide health services. An individual practice association (IPA) HMO contracts directly with physicians in independent practice, and/or contracts with one or more associations of physicians in independent practice, and/or contracts with one or more multispecialty group practices. Data are based on a census of HMOs]

Model type	Number of plans 1990	1995	2000	2002	2003	2004	Enrollment [1] (mil.) 1990	1995	2000	2002	2003	2004
Total	572	550	568	500	454	412	33.0	46.2	80.9	76.1	71.8	68.8
IPA	360	323	278	229	203	176	13.7	17.4	33.4	31.6	28.0	24.6
Group	212	107	102	100	105	96	19.3	12.9	15.2	14.9	16.1	15.3
Mixed	(NA)	120	188	171	146	140	(NA)	15.9	32.3	29.5	27.7	28.9

NA Not available. [1] 1990–1995 exclude enrollees participating in open-ended plans; beginning 1999 includes open-ended enrollment.

Source: HealthLeaders-InterStudy, Nashville, TN, The Competitive Edge, copyright). See also <http://www.interstudypublications.com/>.

Table 143. Persons Enrolled in Health Maintenance Organizations (HMOs) by State: 2000 and 2004

[As of January 1 (67,665 represents 67,665,000). Data are based on a census of health maintenance organizations]

State	Number 2004 (1,000)	Percent of population 2000	Percent of population 2004 [1]	State	Number 2004 (1,000)	Percent of population 2000	Percent of population 2004 [1]	State	Number 2004 (1,000)	Percent of population 2000	Percent of population 2004 [1]
U.S.	67,665	29.7	23.0	KS	453	17.9	16.6	ND	3	2.5	0.4
AL	127	7.2	2.8	KY	422	31.5	10.2	OH	1,881	25.1	16.4
AK	–	–	–	LA	485	17.0	10.7	OK	253	14.7	5.1
AZ	944	30.9	16.4	ME	341	22.3	25.9	OR	581	41.1	16.2
AR	176	10.4	6.4	MD	1,557	43.9	28.0	PA	3,697	33.9	29.8
CA	17,623	53.5	49.1	MA	2,441	53.0	37.4	RI	280	38.1	25.9
CO	1,178	39.5	25.6	MI	2,660	27.1	26.3	SC	298	9.9	7.1
CT	1,266	44.6	36.1	MN	1,295	29.9	25.4	SD	61	6.7	7.9
DE	84	22.0	10.1	MS	3	1.1	0.1	TN	853	33.0	14.4
DC	233	35.2	42.2	MO	1,416	35.2	24.6	TX	2,652	18.5	11.8
FL	4,538	31.4	26.6	MT	75	7.0	8.1	UT	510	35.3	21.3
GA	1,452	17.4	16.4	NE	92	11.2	5.3	VT	100	4.6	16.1
HI	472	30.0	37.4	NV	589	23.5	25.2	VA	1,660	18.5	22.2
ID	41	7.9	2.9	NH	463	33.7	21.9	WA	1,124	15.2	18.1
IL	1,994	21.0	15.7	NJ	2,175	30.9	25.0	WV	147	10.3	8.1
IN	1,407	12.4	22.5	NM	463	37.7	24.3	WI	1,476	30.2	26.8
IA	321	7.4	10.9	NY	4,615	35.8	24.0	WY	11	1.4	2.1
				NC	897	17.8	10.5				

– Represents zero. [1] Starting with 2004, data for Guam and Puerto Rico not included in U.S. total.

Source: HealthLeaders-InterStudy, Nashville, TN, The Competitive Edge, copyright). See also <http://www.interstudypublications.com/>

Table 144. **Health Insurance Coverage Status by Selected Characteristics: 1990 to 2004**

[(**248.9 represents 248,900,000**). Persons as of following year for coverage in the year shown. Government health insurance includes medicare, medicaid, and military plans. Based on Current Population Survey; Annual Demographic Survey; see text, Section 1, Population, and Appendix III]

Characteristic	Number (mil.)							Percent			
	Total persons	Covered by private or government health insurance					Not covered by health insurance	Covered by private or government health insurance			Not covered by health insurance
		Total[1]	Private		Government			Total[1]	Private	Medicaid[3]	
			Total	Group health[2]	Medicare	Medicaid[3]					
1990	248.9	214.2	182.1	150.2	32.3	24.3	34.7	86.1	73.2	9.7	13.9
1995[4]	264.3	223.7	185.9	161.5	34.7	31.9	40.6	84.6	70.3	12.1	15.4
2000[4,5]	279.5	239.7	201.1	177.8	37.7	29.5	39.8	85.8	71.9	10.6	14.2
2003[4,5]	288.3	243.3	197.9	174.0	39.5	35.6	45.0	84.4	68.6	12.4	15.6
2004, total[4,5]	**291.2**	**245.3**	**198.3**	**174.2**	**39.7**	**37.5**	**45.8**	**84.3**	**68.1**	**12.9**	**15.7**
Age:											
Under 18 years	73.8	65.6	48.5	44.9	0.5	19.8	8.3	88.8	65.6	26.9	11.2
Under 6 years	24.1	21.7	14.8	13.9	0.2	7.8	2.4	89.9	61.4	32.5	10.1
6 to 11 years	23.8	21.2	15.9	14.9	0.2	6.3	2.6	89.0	66.6	26.6	11.0
12 to 17 years	25.9	22.6	17.8	16.2	0.1	5.7	3.2	87.5	68.8	22.0	12.5
18 to 24 years	28.0	19.2	16.2	13.0	0.2	3.2	8.8	68.6	58.0	11.4	31.4
25 to 34 years	39.3	29.1	25.8	24.0	0.5	3.4	10.2	74.1	65.5	8.7	25.9
35 to 44 years	43.4	35.2	31.9	29.8	0.9	3.1	8.1	81.3	73.5	7.2	18.7
45 to 54 years	42.0	35.7	32.4	30.1	1.5	2.6	6.3	85.1	77.2	6.2	14.9
55 to 64 years	29.5	25.6	22.2	19.9	2.7	2.0	3.9	86.7	75.1	6.9	13.3
65 years and over	35.2	34.9	21.3	12.5	33.5	3.3	0.3	99.2	60.6	9.4	0.8
Sex: Male	142.8	118.2	96.8	86.1	17.5	17.1	24.5	82.8	67.8	12.0	17.2
Female	148.4	127.1	101.5	88.1	22.3	20.4	21.3	85.7	68.4	13.7	14.3
Race: White alone	234.1	199.3	165.3	144.2	34.1	25.6	34.8	85.2	70.6	10.9	14.9
Black alone	36.5	29.4	19.6	18.1	3.9	8.9	7.2	80.3	53.6	24.5	19.7
Asian alone	12.3	10.2	8.7	7.6	1.1	1.3	2.1	83.2	70.7	10.3	16.8
Hispanic origin[6]	41.8	28.2	18.7	17.2	2.6	9.1	13.7	67.3	44.7	21.8	32.7
Household income:											
Less than $25,000	62.2	47.1	22.0	14.2	17.5	19.7	15.1	75.7	35.3	31.6	24.3
$25,000-$49,999	74.0	59.2	46.4	39.6	11.9	10.8	14.8	80.0	62.7	14.7	20.0
$50,000-$74,999	59.1	51.2	46.3	42.4	5.2	3.9	7.8	86.7	78.3	6.6	13.3
$75,000 or more	95.9	87.8	83.6	78.0	5.1	3.1	8.1	91.6	87.2	3.2	8.4
Persons below poverty	37.0	25.6	9.1	6.0	4.9	15.4	11.4	69.2	24.7	41.6	30.8

[1] Includes other government insurance, not shown separately. Persons with coverage counted only once in total, even though they may have been covered by more than one type of policy. [2] Related to employment of self or other family members.
[3] Beginning 1997, persons with no coverage other than access to Indian Health Service are no longer considered covered by health insurance; instead they are considered to be uninsured. The effect of this change on the overall estimates of health insurance coverage is negligible; however, the decrease in the number of people covered by Medicaid may be partially due to this change.
[4] Estimates reflect results of follow-up verification questions. [5] Implementation of Census 2000-based population controls. Sample expanded by 28,000 households. [6] Persons of Hispanic origin may be any race.
Source: U.S. Census Bureau, Health Insurance, Health Insurance Data, Health Insurance Coverage Status and Type of Coverage by Selected Characteristics: 2004; <http://www.census.gov/hhes/www/hlthins/hlthins04.html>.

Table 145. **Persons With and Without Health Insurance Coverage by State: 2004**

[**245,335 represents 245,335,000**. Based on the Current Population Survey Annual Demographic Supplement and subject to sampling error; see text, Section 1, Population, and Appendix III]

State	Total persons covered (1,000)	Total persons not covered		Children not covered		State	Total persons covered (1,000)	Total persons not covered		Children not covered	
		Number (1,000)	Percent of total	Number (1,000)	Percent of total			Number (1,000)	Percent of total	Number (1,000)	Percent of total
U.S.	245,335	45,820	15.7	8,269	11.2	MO	4,908	707	12.6	120	8.5
AL	3,902	609	13.5	81	7.4	MT	737	174	19.1	33	15.4
AK	538	110	17.0	20	10.9	NE	1,531	197	11.4	26	6.0
AZ	4,778	989	17.1	231	14.7	NV	1,947	443	18.5	100	16.1
AR	2,282	448	16.4	47	6.8	NH	1,142	152	11.7	24	7.8
CA	29,140	6,710	18.7	1,194	12.4	NJ	7,343	1,322	15.3	259	11.7
CO	3,756	767	17.0	175	15.0	NM	1,504	399	21.0	76	15.3
CT	3,086	407	11.6	71	8.5	NY	16,345	2,705	14.2	396	8.6
DE	707	120	14.5	24	12.6	NC	7,110	1,322	15.7	239	11.2
DC	474	73	13.3	9	7.6	ND	557	70	11.2	14	9.6
FL	13,987	3,479	19.9	611	15.1	OH	9,987	1,282	11.4	212	7.5
GA	7,193	1,513	17.1	273	11.7	OK	2,760	685	19.9	144	16.9
HI	1,130	120	9.6	15	5.4	OR	2,991	591	16.5	86	10.0
ID	1,164	212	15.4	33	8.6	PA	10,724	1,454	11.9	304	10.7
IL	10,832	1,764	14.0	368	11.4	RI	937	120	11.4	19	7.4
IN	5,264	872	14.2	144	8.9	SC	3,518	605	14.7	80	7.7
IA	2,629	277	9.5	41	6.0	SD	663	90	12.0	16	8.3
KS	2,377	297	11.1	45	6.5	TN	5,030	828	14.1	142	10.1
KY	3,492	582	14.3	82	8.4	TX	16,741	5,583	25.0	1,353	21.4
LA	3,661	761	17.2	92	8.0	UT	2,056	337	14.1	81	10.4
ME	1,164	130	10.0	17	5.8	VT	548	69	11.2	6	4.8
MD	4,739	810	14.6	134	9.6	VA	6,326	1,061	14.4	149	8.1
MA	5,625	748	11.7	97	6.5	WA	5,323	793	13.0	106	7.0
MI	8,816	1,156	11.6	174	6.8	WV	1,499	294	16.4	34	8.8
MN	4,667	458	8.9	85	6.8	WI	4,898	566	10.4	67	5.1
MS	2,379	489	17.1	109	14.2	WY	428	70	14.0	11	9.7

Source: U.S. Census Bureau, Current Population Survey 2005 Annual Social and Economic Supplement. Health Insurance Coverage in the United States: 2004, P60-229. Table HI05. Health Insurance Coverage Status and Type of Coverage by State for All People: 2004 <http://www.census.gov/hhes/www/hlthins/hlthin04.html>.

Table 146. People Without Health Insurance for the Entire Year by Selected Characteristics: 2000 and 2004

[In thousands, except as noted (279,517 represents 279,517,000). Based on the Current Population Survey, Annual Demographic Survey, and subject to sampling error; see text, Section 1 and Appendix III]

Characteristic	2000			2004		
		Uninsured persons			Uninsured persons	
	Total persons	Number	Percent distribution	Total persons	Number	Percent distribution
Total [1]	279,517	39,804	100.0	291,155	45,820	100.0
Under 18 years	72,314	8,617	21.6	73,821	8,269	18.0
18 to 24 years	26,815	7,406	18.6	27,972	8,772	19.1
25 to 34 years	38,865	8,507	21.4	39,307	10,177	22.2
35 to 44 years	44,566	6,898	17.3	43,350	8,110	17.7
45 to 64 years	63,391	8,124	20.4	71,492	10,196	22.3
65 years and over	33,566	251	0.6	35,213	297	0.6
Male	136,559	20,791	52.2	142,750	24,528	53.5
Female	142,958	19,013	47.8	148,405	21,293	46.5
White	228,208	30,075	75.6	(NA)	(NA)	(NA)
Non-Hispanic	193,931	18,683	46.9	(NA)	(NA)	(NA)
Black	35,597	6,683	16.8	(NA)	(NA)	(NA)
Asian and Pacific Islander	12,693	2,287	5.7	(NA)	(NA)	(NA)
White alone [2]	(NA)	(NA)	(NA)	234,077	34,788	75.9
Black alone [2]	(NA)	(NA)	(NA)	36,546	7,186	15.7
Asian alone [2]	(NA)	(NA)	(NA)	12,311	2,070	4.5
Hispanic [3]	36,093	11,883	29.9	41,839	13,678	29.9

NA Not available. [1] Includes other races not shown separately. [2] Refers to people who reported specified race and did not report any other race category. [3] Persons of Hispanic origin may be of any race.

Source: U.S. Census Bureau, Health Insurance, Health Insurance Data, Health Insurance Coverage: 2004, <http://www.census.gov/hhes/www/hlthins/hlthin04.html>.

Table 147. Percent of Workers Participating in Health Care Benefit Programs and Percent of Participants Required to Contribute: 2005

[Based on National Compensation Survey, a sample survey of 4,560 private industry establishments of all sizes, representing about 103 million workers; see Appendix III. See also Table 637]

Characteristic	Percent of workers participating—			Single coverage medical care			Family coverage medical care		
	Medical care	Dental care	Vision care	Employee contributions not required (percent)	Employee contributions required (percent)	Average monthly contribution [1] (dol.)	Employee contributions not required (percent)	Employee contributions required (percent)	Average monthly contribution [1] (dol.)
Total	53	36	22	24	76	68.96	12	88	273.03
White-collar occupations . .	58	42	24	22	78	68.60	9	91	281.73
Blue-collar occupations . .	61	39	25	29	71	67.25	18	82	252.22
Service occupations	27	17	12	21	79	76.21	11	89	287.17
Full-time [2]	66	45	27	24	76	68.37	12	88	271.12
Part-time [2]	12	9	6	20	80	79.19	17	83	310.50
Union [3]	83	67	51	43	57	55.71	35	65	198.19
Nonunion	49	33	19	21	79	70.80	8	92	282.98

[1] The average is presented for all covered workers and excludes workers without the plan provision. Averages are for plans stating a flat monthly cost. [2] Employees are classified as working either a full-time or part-time schedule based on the definition used by each establishment. [3] Union workers are those whose wages are determined through collective bargaining.

Source: U.S. Bureau of Labor Statistics, *National Compensation Survey: Employee Benefits in Private Industry in the United States*, March, 2005. See also <http://www.bls.gov/ncs/ebs/sp/ebsm0003.pdf> (accessed 18 July 2006).

Table 148. **Medical Care Benefits of Workers by Type and Amount of Employee Contribution: 2005**

[In percent. See headnote, Table 147]

Type and amount of contribution	Individual coverage				Type and amount of contribution	Family coverage			
	All employees	White-collar occupations	Blue-collar occupations	Service occupations		All employees	White-collar occupations,	Blue-collar occupations,	Service occupations
Total with contributory coverage	100	100	100	100	Total with contributory coverage	100	100	100	100
Flat monthly amount . .	75	75	75	70	Flat monthly amount. .	76	76	78	71
Less than $5.00 . . .	(Z)	(Z)	(Z)	(Z)	Less than $25.00 . .	1	1	1	1
$5.00–$9.99	1	1	2	1	$25.00–$49.99	2	2	4	3
$10.00–$14.99	2	1	3	1	$50.00–$74.99. . . .	3	3	3	4
$15.00–$19.99	2	2	2	1	$75.00–$99.99. . . .	3	3	3	3
$20.00–$29.99	6	7	5	8	$100.00–$124.99 . .	5	4	6	4
$30.00–$39.99	8	8	9	6	$125.00–$149.99 . .	5	6	5	1
$40.00–$49.99	9	9	8	8	$150.00–$174.99 . .	6	6	8	3
$50.00–$59.99	10	10	11	6	$175.00–$199.99 . .	6	6	6	5
$60.00–$69.99	8	8	8	8	$200.00–$224.99 . .	5	6	6	6
$70.00–$79.99	7	7	6	9	$225.00–$249.99 . .	4	5	5	3
$80.00–$89.99	5	6	5	6	$250.00–$274.99 . .	4	5	4	3
$90.00–$99.99	4	4	4	3	$275.00–$299.99 . .	4	4	3	4
$100.00–$124.99 . .	6	7	6	5	$300.00–$324.99 . .	2	4	4	4
$125.00 or more . . .	7	7	6	9	$325.00–$349.99 . .	2	2	1	5
					$350.00 or more . .	2	2	2	2
Composite rate [1]	1	1	(Z)	1	Composite rate [1]	1	1	(Z)	(Z)
Varies [2]	5	5	3	5	Varies [2]	4	5	3	5
Flexible benefits [3]	2	2	1	1	Flexible benefits [3] . . .	1	2	1	1
Percent of earnings . .	(Z)	(Z)	(Z)	1	Percent of earnings . .	(Z)	(Z)	(Z)	1
Exists, but unknown . .	16	15	17	19	Exists, but unknown . .	15	15	15	19
Other	2	2	4	2	Other	2	2	2	3

Z Less than 0.5 percent.   [1] A composite rate is a set contribution covering more than one benefit area; for example, health care and life insurance. Cost data for individual plans cannot be determined.   [2] Based on worker attributes. For example, employee contributions may vary based on earnings, length of service, or age.   [3] Amount varies by options selected under a "cafeteria plan" or employer-sponsored reimbursement account.

Source: U.S. Bureau of Labor Statistics, "National Compensation Survey, Employee Benefits in Private Industry, March 2005"; <http://www.bls.gov/ncs/ebs/sp/ebsm0003.pdf> (accessed 18 July 2006).

Table 149. **Annual Receipts/Revenue for Health Care Industries: 2000 to 2004**

[In millions of dollars (1,036,010 represents $1,036,010,000,000). Based on the North American Industry Classification System, 1997 (NAICS); see text, Section 15. All firms in NAICS 6211, 6212, 6213, and 6215 are defined as taxable. Estimates for the nonemployer portion are derived from administrative records data provided by other federal agencies. These data are available only at the total revenue level. See Appendix III]

Kind of business	1997 NAICS code	Total, all firms [1]			Employer firms		
		2000 [2]	2003 [2]	2004	2000 [2]	2003 [2]	2004
Health care and social assistance . . .	**62**	1,036,010	1,289,368	1,383,439	500,929	634,650	681,400
Ambulatory health care services	621	419,398	526,329	568,298	376,093	473,879	512,476
Offices of physicians	6211	213,806	270,326	290,782	213,806	270,326	290,782
Offices of dentists	6212	60,931	73,372	78,871	60,931	73,372	78,871
Offices of other health practitioners [3]	6213	32,037	39,675	42,930	32,037	39,675	42,930
Offices of chiropractors	62131	7,570	9,363	9,624	7,570	9,363	9,624
Offices of optometrists	62132	7,639	8,607	9,318	7,639	8,607	9,318
Offices of PT/OT/speech therapy & audiology [4]	62134	8,486	11,805	13,396	8,486	11,805	13,396
Outpatient care centers	6214	(S)	(S)	(S)	(S)	(S)	(S)
Medical & diagnostic laboratories.	6215	23,450	30,529	32,413	23,450	30,529	32,413
Home health care services	6216	26,841	34,001	38,311	16,879	22,051	25,477
Other ambulatory health care services	6219	15,565	19,352	21,410	9,421	11,610	12,804
Hospitals	622	423,888	529,202	569,444	42,907	62,613	65,714
General medical & surgical hospitals	6221	397,526	496,216	533,829	36,926	53,127	54,516
Psychiatric & substance abuse hospitals	6222	13,422	13,578	13,363	2,189	2,290	2,002
Other specialty hospitals	6223	12,940	19,408	22,252	3,793	7,196	9,196
Nursing and residential care facilities	623	112,706	132,994	138,068	66,245	77,484	80,827
Nursing care facilities.	6231	67,239	77,438	79,960	49,816	56,549	58,738
Residential mental retardation/health facilities [3]	6232	16,717	20,614	21,602	4,726	5,958	6,143
Residential mental retardation facilities . . .	62321	11,570	14,090	14,703	3,297	4,234	4,298
Community care facilities for the elderly	6233	22,104	26,984	28,333	10,812	13,878	14,822

S Figure does not meet publication standards.   [1] Includes taxable nonemployer firms, not shown separately.   [2] Estimates for 2003 and prior years have been revised.   [3] Includes other kinds of business not shown separately.   [4] Offices of physical, occupational, and speech therapists, and audiologists.

Source: U.S. Census Bureau, Current Business Reports, "Service Annual Survey," 2004. <http://www.census.gov/econ/www/servmenu.html>.

Table 150. Receipts for Selected Health Service Industries by Source of Revenue: 2000 and 2004

[In millions of dollars (202,059 represents $202,059,000,000). Based on the 1997 North American Industry Classification System (NAICS), see text, Section 15. Based on a sample of employer firms only and does not include nonemployer revenue. See Appendix III]

Source of revenue	Offices of physicians (NAICS 6211)		Offices of dentists (NAICS 6212)		Hospitals (NAICS 622)		Nursing and residential care facilities (NAICS 623)	
	2000 [1]	2004	2000 [1]	2004	2000 [1]	2004	2000 [1]	2004
Total	202,059	273,446	59,463	77,539	390,915	530,352	99,154	123,216
Medicare	51,030	71,726	(S)	(S)	137,322	177,440	13,130	19,025
Medicaid	14,624	20,072	1,467	2,680	51,049	67,813	45,956	56,069
Other government [2]	2,123	3,578	(S)	(S)	21,918	29,500	8,041	10,766
Worker's compensation	7,833	9,554	(S)	(S)	4,673	6,559	(S)	(S)
Private insurance	102,472	139,483	31,321	40,531	153,428	216,865	6,400	5,945
Patient (out-of-pocket)	23,977	29,033	26,675	34,328	22,525	32,175	[3]25,627	[3]31,411
Other patient care sources, n.e.c [4]	7,695	10,900	(S)	(S)	10,404	11,232	3,563	3,846
Nonpatient care revenue	4,054	6,436	(S)	(S)	22,570	27,861	7,410	7,939

S Figure does not meet publication standards.   [1] Estimates for 2003 and prior years have been revised.   [2] Veterans, National Institute of Health, Indian Affairs, etc.   [3] Represents payment from patients and their families plus patients' assigned social security benefits.   [4] N.e.c. represents not elsewhere classified.

Source: U.S. Census Bureau, Current Business Reports, "Service Annual Survey, 2004." <http://www.census.gov/econ/www/servmenu.html>.

Table 151. Employment in the Health Service Industries: 1990 to 2005

[In thousands (9,296 represents 9,296,000). See headnote, Table 618]

Industry	2002 NAICS code [1]	1990	1995	2000	2001	2002	2003	2004	2005
Health care and social assistance [2]	62	9,296	11,278	12,718	13,134	13,556	13,893	14,190	14,523
Ambulatory health care services	621	2,842	3,768	4,320	4,462	4,633	4,786	4,952	5,110
Offices of physicians	6211	1,278	1,540	1,840	1,911	1,968	2,003	2,048	2,101
Offices of dentists	6212	513	592	688	705	725	744	760	771
Offices of other health practitioners	6213	276	395	438	457	486	503	527	545
Medical and diagnostic laboratories	6215	129	146	162	170	175	182	190	199
Home health care services	6216	288	622	633	639	680	733	777	814
Hospitals	622	3,513	3,734	3,954	4,051	4,160	4,245	4,285	4,347
General medical and surgical hospitals	6221	3,305	3,520	3,745	3,833	3,930	4,005	4,042	4,099
Psychiatric and substance abuse hospitals	6222	113	101	86	87	90	92	92	92
Other hospitals	6223	95	112	123	132	140	148	151	156
Nursing and residential care facilities [2]	623	1,856	2,308	2,583	2,676	2,743	2,786	2,818	2,856
Nursing care facilities	6231	1,170	1,413	1,514	1,547	1,573	1,580	1,577	1,579

[1] Based on the North American Industry Classification System 2002 code; see text, Section 15.   [2] Includes other industries not shown separately.

Source: U.S. Bureau of Labor Statistics, Employment and Earnings, March issues. See also <http://stats.bls.gov/ces/home.htm>.

Table 152. Health Professions—Practitioners and Schools: 1990 to 2004

[573 represents 573,000]. Data on the number of schools and total enrollment are reported as of the beginning of the academic year; all other school data are reported as of the end of the academic year. Data are based on reporting by health professions schools]

Year	Medicine	Osteopathy	Registered nursing				Licensed practical nursing	Dentistry [1]	Optometry	Pharmacy
			Total	Baccalaureate	Associate's degree	Diploma				
ACTIVE PERSONNEL (1,000)										
1990	573	28	[2]1,790	682	1,107	(³)	441	148	26	168
1995	646	36	[2]2,116	881	1,235	(³)	399	159	29	181
2000	738	45	[2]2,249	983	1,267	(³)	374	168	32	196
2001	752	42	[2]2,262	1,000	1,262	(³)	(NA)	(NA)	(NA)	(NA)
NUMBER OF SCHOOLS [4]										
1990	126	15	1,470	489	829	152	1,154	56	17	74
1995	125	16	1,516	521	876	119	1,210	54	17	75
2000	125	19	(NA)	(NA)	(NA)	(NA)	(NA)	55	17	81
2001	125	19	(NA)	(NA)	(NA)	(NA)	(NA)	54	17	83
2002	125	19	1,459	526	857	76	(NA)	54	17	83
TOTAL ENROLLMENT										
1990	65,016	6,615	201,458	74,865	106,175	20,418	46,720	16,412	4,723	23,013
1995	66,788	8,146	268,350	112,659	135,895	19,796	59,428	16,353	5,201	27,667
2000	66,377	10,388	192,202	89,508	95,598	7,096	(NA)	17,242	5,464	29,586
2003	(NA)	11,432	221,698	94,739	117,192	9,767	(NA)	(NA)	(NA)	33,437
2004	67,013	11,857	244,769	105,907	127,709	11,153	(NA)	(NA)	(NA)	36,454

NA Not available.   [1] Personnel data exclude dentists in military service, U.S. Public Health Service, and U.S. Dept. of Veterans Affairs.   [2] Includes nurses with advanced degrees.   [3] Diploma nurses included with associate's degree nurses.   [4] Some nursing schools offer more than one type of program. Numbers shown for nursing are number of nursing programs.

Source: U.S. Dept. of Health and Human Services, Bureau of Health Professions, unpublished data; American Medical Association, Chicago, IL, Physician Characteristics and Distribution in the U.S., annual; and American Association of Colleges of Osteopathic Medicine, Rockville, MD, Annual Statistical Report.

Table 153. **Physicians by Sex and Specialty: 1980 to 2004**

[In thousands (467.7 represents 467,700). As of Dec. 31, except 1990 as of Jan. 1, and as noted. Includes Puerto Rico and island areas]

Activity	1980 Total [1]	1980 Office-based	1990 Total [1]	1990 Office-based	2000 Total [1]	2000 Office-based	2004 Total [1]	2004 Office-based
Doctors of medicine, total	**467.7**	**272.0**	**615.4**	**361.0**	**813.8**	**490.4**	**885.0**	**538.5**
Place of medical education:								
U.S. medical graduates	370.0	226.2	483.7	286.2	616.8	376.5	660.9	414.9
International medical graduates [2]	97.7	45.8	131.8	74.8	197.0	113.9	224.0	123.6
Sex: Male	413.4	251.4	511.2	311.7	618.2	382.3	649.3	401.1
Female	54.3	20.6	104.2	49.2	195.5	108.1	235.6	137.5
Allergy/immunology	1.5	1.4	3.4	2.5	4.0	3.1	4.1	3.2
Anesthesiology	16.0	11.3	26.0	17.8	35.7	27.6	38.8	30.0
Cardiovascular diseases	9.8	6.7	15.9	10.7	21.0	16.3	22.1	17.3
Child psychiatry	3.3	2.0	4.3	2.6	6.2	4.3	6.8	5.0
Dermatology	5.7	4.4	7.6	6.0	9.7	8.0	10.4	8.7
Diagnostic radiology	7.0	4.2	15.4	9.8	21.1	14.6	23.7	16.8
Emergency medicine	5.7	3.4	14.2	8.4	23.1	14.5	27.9	19.0
Family practice	27.5	18.4	47.6	37.5	71.6	54.2	80.3	63.3
Gastroenterology	4.0	2.7	7.5	5.2	10.6	8.5	11.7	9.4
General practice	32.5	29.6	22.8	20.5	15.2	13.0	11.7	9.9
General surgery	34.0	22.4	38.4	24.5	36.7	24.5	37.6	25.3
Internal medicine	71.5	40.6	98.3	58.0	134.5	89.7	150.9	101.8
Neurology	5.7	3.3	9.2	5.6	12.3	8.6	13.7	9.6
Neurological surgery	3.3	2.5	4.4	3.1	5.0	3.7	5.3	4.0
Obstetrics and gynecology	26.3	19.5	33.7	25.5	40.2	31.7	42.1	33.8
Ophthalmology	13.0	10.6	16.1	13.1	18.1	15.6	18.7	16.3
Orthopedic surgery	14.0	10.7	19.1	14.2	22.3	17.4	23.8	18.6
Otolaryngology	6.6	5.3	8.1	6.4	9.4	7.6	9.9	8.2
Pathology	13.6	6.1	16.6	7.5	18.8	10.6	19.2	11.0
Pediatrics	29.5	18.2	41.9	27.1	63.9	43.2	71.9	50.5
Physical medicine/rehabilitation.	2.1	1.0	4.1	2.2	6.5	4.3	7.3	5.2
Plastic surgery	3.0	2.4	4.6	3.8	6.2	5.3	6.9	5.8
Psychiatry	27.5	16.0	35.2	20.1	39.5	25.0	40.3	26.0
Pulmonary diseases	3.7	2.0	6.1	3.7	8.7	5.9	9.8	7.1
Radiology	11.7	7.8	8.5	6.1	8.7	6.7	4.3	3.3
Radiation oncology	1.6	1.0	2.8	2.0	3.9	3.0	8.7	6.9
Urological surgery	7.7	6.2	9.4	7.4	10.3	8.5	10.6	8.8
Other specialty	5.8	2.4	7.3	2.7	5.8	2.3	5.4	2.2
Other surgical specialty [3]	2.9	2.3	2.9	2.4	6.1	5.1	6.2	5.2
Other remaining specialty [4]	6.1	2.5	7.8	3.3	8.8	4.2	8.7	4.2
Not classified	20.6	(X)	12.7	(X)	45.1	(X)	48.0	(X)
Other categories [5]	32.1	(X)	55.4	(X)	75.2	(X)	92.8	(X)
Doctors of Osteopathy [6]	18.8	(X)	30.9	(X)	44.9	(X)	54.1	(X)

X Not applicable.   [1] Includes unspecified physicians.   [2] International medical graduates received their medical education in schools outside the United States and Canada.   [3] Includes Colon and Rectal Surgery and Thoracic Surgery.   [4] Includes Aerospace Medicine, General Preventive Medicine, Nuclear Medicine, Occupational Medicine, Medical Genetics, and Public Health.   [5] Includes inactive and address unknown.   [6] Total number of DOs as of June 1. This number includes all living DOs, including retired DOs, DOs in in postdoctoral training and federally employed DOs. Data from American Osteopathic Association Fact Sheet, American Osteopathic Association, Chicago, IL. <http://www.osteopathic.org/index.cfm?PageID=aoa_annualrprt>.
Source: Except as noted, American Medical Association, Chicago, IL, *Physician Characteristics and Distribution in the U.S.* annual (copyright).

Table 154. **Active Physicians and Nurses by State: 2004**

[As of December. Excludes doctors of osteopathy, physicians with addresses unknown, and inactive status. Includes all physicians not classified according to activity status]

State	Physicians [1] Total	Physicians [1] Rate [2]	Nurses Total	Nurses Rate [2]	State	Physicians [1] Total	Physicians [1] Rate [2]	Nurses Total	Nurses Rate [2]
United States. .	**780,662**	**266**	**2,421,000**	**824**	Missouri	13,790	239	57,400	997
Alabama.	9,627	213	36,500	807	Montana.	2,047	221	7,900	852
Alaska	1,463	222	6,800	1,034	Nebraska	4,181	239	18,500	1,059
Arizona.	11,955	208	39,100	681	Nevada	4,333	186	14,100	604
Arkansas	5,577	203	20,100	731	New Hampshire	3,372	260	13,600	1,047
California	92,907	259	211,600	590	New Jersey.	26,580	306	73,000	841
Colorado.	11,871	258	34,700	754	New Mexico	4,563	240	13,600	715
Connecticut.	12,716	363	32,700	935	New York	74,924	389	174,200	903
Delaware	2,061	248	8,600	1,036	North Carolina	21,609	253	76,800	899
District of Columbia .	4,423	798	11,600	2,093	North Dakota.	1,539	242	7,500	1,179
Florida	42,665	245	132,800	764	Ohio	29,833	261	112,800	985
Georgia	19,589	220	66,500	746	Oklahoma.	6,031	171	24,400	692
Hawaii	3,912	310	9,300	737	Oregon.	9,429	263	30,900	860
Idaho	2,351	169	8,800	631	Pennsylvania.	36,381	294	127,000	1,025
Illinois	34,514	272	113,800	895	Rhode Island.	3,786	351	11,400	1,056
Indiana.	13,283	213	54,600	877	South Carolina	9,646	230	30,700	731
Iowa	5,518	187	32,700	1,107	South Dakota	1,687	219	9,300	1,207
Kansas.	6,021	220	24,900	911	Tennessee	15,357	261	54,300	921
Kentucky	9,523	230	37,600	908	Texas.	47,617	212	145,300	647
Louisiana	11,898	264	35,400	785	Utah	5,061	209	15,800	653
Maine.	3,512	267	15,100	1,148	Vermont	2,249	362	6,400	1,030
Maryland	22,863	411	47,100	847	Virginia.	20,183	270	56,700	758
Massachusetts. . . .	28,827	450	75,400	1,177	Washington	16,443	265	48,400	780
Michigan.	24,287	240	85,000	841	West Virginia	4,150	229	16,000	883
Minnesota	14,303	281	51,900	1,018	Wisconsin	14,005	254	51,700	939
Mississippi	5,251	181	24,000	827	Wyoming	949	188	4,100	810

[1] 2002 and earlier data excluded federally employed persons.   [2] Per 100,000 resident population. Based on U.S. Census Bureau estimates as of July 1.
Source: Physicians: American Medical Association, Chicago, IL, *Physician Characteristics and Distribution in the U.S.*, annual (copyright); Nurses: U.S. Dept. of Health and Human Services, Health Resources and Services Administration, unpublished data.

110   Health and Nutrition

Table 155. Adults 18 Years and Over Who Used Complementary and Alternative Medicine (CAM), by Type of Therapy: 2002

[In thousands (149,271 represents 149,271,000). The denominators for statistics shown exclude persons with unknown CAM information. Estimates were age adjusted to the year 2000 U.S. standard population using four age groups: 18 to 24 years, 25 to 44 years, 45 to 64 years, and 65 years and over]

Therapy	Ever used	Used during past 12 months	Therapy	Ever used	Used during past 12 months
Any CAM use [1]	**149,271**	**123,606**	Manipulative and body-based therapies:		
Alternative medical systems: . . .			Chiropractic care	40,242	15,226
Acupuncture	8,188	2,136	Massage	18,899	10,052
Ayurveda.	751	154	Mind-body therapies:		
Homeopathic treatment	7,379	3,433	Biofeedback.	1,986	278
Naturopathy.	1,795	498	Meditation	20,698	15,336
Biologically based therapies: . . .			Guided imagery	6,067	4,194
Chelation therapy	270	(B)	Progressive relaxation	8,518	6,185
Folk medicine.	1,393	233	Deep breathing exercises.	29,658	23,457
Nonvitamin, nonmineral, natural			Hypnosis.	3,733	505
products	50,613	38,183	Yoga	15,232	10,386
Diet-based therapies [2]	13,799	7,099	Tai chi.	5,056	2,565
Vegetarian diet	5,324	3,184	Qi gong	950	527
Macrobiotic diet.	1,368	317	Prayer for health reasons [3]	110,012	89,624
Atkins diet	7,312	3,417	Prayed for own health	103,662	85,432
Pritikin diet.	580	137	Others ever prayed for your health .	62,348	48,467
Ornish diet.	290	(B)	Participate in prayer group	25,167	18,984
Zone diet.	1,062	430	Healing ritual for own health	9,230	4,045
Megavitamin therapy	7,935	5,739	Energy healing therapy/Reiki.	2,264	1,080

B Base figure too small to meet statistical standards for reliability of derived figures.   [1] Respondents may have reported using more than one type of therapy.   [2] The sum of the categories listed under "Diet-based therapies" are greater than the total number of "Diet-based therapies" because respondents could choose more than one diet-based therapy.   [3] The sum of the categories listed under "Prayer for health reasons" are greater than the total number of "Prayer for health reasons" because respondents could choose more than one method of prayer.

Source: U.S. National Center for Health Statistics, Advance Data, No. 343. May 27, 2004. <http://www.cdc.gov/nchs/data/ad/ad343.pdf>.

Table 156. Percent Distribution of Number of Visits to Health Care Professionals by Selected Characteristics: 2000 and 2004

[Covers ambulatory visits to doctor's offices and emergency departments, and home health care visits during a 12-month period. Based on the redesigned National Health Interview Survey, a sample survey of the civilian noninstitutionalized population. See Appendix III]

Characteristic	None		1–3 visits		4–9 visits		10 or more visits	
	2000	2004	2000	2004	2000	2004	2000	2004
All persons [1, 2].	**16.6**	**16.1**	**45.4**	**45.8**	**24.7**	**24.6**	**13.3**	**13.5**
AGE:								
Under 6 years	6.3	5.3	44.3	47.5	38.3	36.9	11.2	10.3
6 to 17 years old	15.1	13.1	58.2	59.0	20.7	21.1	6.0	6.8
18 to 44 years old.	23.2	23.8	45.3	45.6	19.2	19.2	12.2	11.5
45 to 64 years old.	15.0	15.0	43.4	43.3	25.7	25.3	15.8	16.3
65 to 74 years old.	9.0	6.8	34.5	36.0	34.4	34.5	22.1	22.6
75 years old and over	5.8	4.1	29.3	26.4	39.3	39.5	25.6	30.0
SEX: [2]								
Male.	21.5	20.9	46.0	46.6	22.4	21.6	10.1	10.9
Female	11.9	11.5	44.8	45.0	27.0	27.5	16.4	16.0
RACE: [2, 3]								
Race alone:								
White	16.0	16.0	45.1	45.4	25.3	24.8	13.7	13.8
Black or African American.	17.3	16.8	46.7	47.0	23.4	24.6	12.6	12.6
American Indian or Alaska Native.	21.2	17.7	42.9	41.7	20.0	25.0	15.8	15.5
Asian	20.2	20.8	49.2	51.5	20.9	19.7	9.7	8.1
Two or more races	12.1	13.6	41.6	42.9	28.3	26.2	17.9	17.3
HISPANIC ORIGIN AND RACE: [2, 3, 4]								
Hispanic or Latino	26.5	26.7	41.8	41.8	20.0	20.6	11.7	10.9
Mexican	30.7	29.7	40.9	41.0	18.0	18.9	10.4	10.4
Not Hispanic or Latino.	15.2	14.2	45.9	46.5	25.3	25.2	13.6	14.1
White, non-Hispanic	14.5	13.5	45.4	46.1	26.0	25.7	14.1	14.7
Black, non-Hispanic.	17.2	15.6	46.9	47.3	23.4	24.6	12.6	12.5

[1] Includes other categories not shown separately.   [2] Estimates are age adjusted to the year 2000 standard using six age groups: Under 18 years, 18–44 years, 45–54 years, 55–64 years, 65–74 years, and 75 years and over.   [3] Estimates by race and Hispanic origin are tabulated using the 1997 standards for federal data on race and ethnicity. Estimates for specific race groups are shown when they meet requirements for statistical reliability and confidentiality. The categories "White only," "Black or African American only," "American Indian and Alaska Native (AI/AN) only," and "Asian only" include persons who reported only one racial group; and the category "2 or more races" includes persons who reported more than one of the five racial groups in the 1997 standards or one of the five racial groups and "Some other race."   [4] Persons of Hispanic or Latino origin may be of any race or combination of races.

Source: U.S. National Center for Health Statistics, *Health, United States, 2006.* See also <www.cdc.gov/nchs/hus.htm>.

Health and Nutrition   111

Table 157. **Ambulatory Care Visits to Physicians' Offices and Hospital Outpatient and Emergency Departments: 2004**

[1,106.1 represents 1,106,100,000. Based on the annual National Ambulatory Medical Care Survey and National Hospital Ambulatory Medical Care Survey and subject to sampling error; see source for details]

Characteristic	Number of visits (mil.)				Visits per 100 persons			
	Total	Physi-cian offices	Outpa-tient dept.	Emer-gency dept.	Total	Physi-cian offices	Outpa-tient dept.	Emer-gency dept.
Total	1,106.1	910.9	85.0	110.2	383.6	315.9	29.5	38.2
Age:								
Under 15 years old	189.6	147.9	18.8	22.9	312.1	243.4	30.9	37.8
15 to 24 years old	98.5	70.6	10.0	17.9	242.4	173.8	24.5	44.1
25 to 44 years old	247.5	194.3	21.1	32.1	301.3	236.5	25.7	39.1
45 to 64 years old	307.7	264.1	22.1	21.5	438.4	376.2	31.5	30.6
65 to 74 years old	126.8	113.4	7.2	6.2	696.0	622.6	39.3	34.1
75 years old and over	135.9	120.6	5.9	9.5	827.1	733.6	35.6	57.9
Sex:								
Male	458.9	375.3	33.2	50.3	325.5	266.3	23.6	35.7
Female	647.2	535.5	51.8	59.9	439.0	363.3	35.1	40.6
Race:								
White	919.6	775.0	62.9	81.8	395.8	333.6	27.1	35.2
Black/African American.	141.1	98.0	18.2	24.9	390.5	271.3	50.3	68.9
Asian	34.1	29.1	2.9	2.2	278.6	237.7	23.3	17.6
Native Hawaiian/Other Pacific Islander	3.5	2.9	0.3	0.4	711.7	577.7	54.3	79.7
American Indian/Alaska Native.	3.8	2.6	[1]0.5	[1]0.7	138.4	94.4	[1]19.2	[1]24.8
More than one race reported	3.9	3.2	0.3	[1]0.3	87.9	73.5	7.2	[1]7.2
Primary source of payment:								
Private insurance	580.1	509.8	31.0	39.3	(X)	(X)	(X)	(X)
Medicare	236.8	206.7	13.2	16.9	(X)	(X)	(X)	(X)
Medicaid	140.3	89.6	26.2	24.5	(X)	(X)	(X)	(X)
Worker's compensation	16.2	13.5	0.8	2.0	(X)	(X)	(X)	(X)
Self-pay.	64.3	40.7	5.9	17.7	(X)	(X)	(X)	(X)
No charge	5.6	[1]2.7	[1]2.1	0.9	(X)	(X)	(X)	(X)
Other	26.2	20.2	2.9	3.1	(X)	(X)	(X)	(X)
Unknown	36.6	27.6	3.1	5.9	(X)	(X)	(X)	(X)

X Not applicable   [1] Figures do not meet standard of reliability or precision.

Source: U.S. National Center for Health Statistics, *Advance Data,* Nos. 372, 373, and 374; June 23, 2006. <http://www.cdc.gov/nchs/namcs.htm>.

Table 158. **Visits to Office-Based Physicians and Hospital Outpatient Departments by Diagnosis: 2000 and 2004**

[369.0 represents 369,000,000. See headnote, Table 157]

Leading diagnoses [1]	Number (mil.)		Rate per 1,000 persons [2]		Leading diagnoses [1]	Number (mil.)		Rate per 1,000 persons [2]	
	2000	2004	2000	2004		2000	2004	2000	2004
MALE					FEMALE				
All ages	**369.0**	**408.5**	**2,760**	**2,898**	**All ages . . . .**	**537.8**	**587.3**	**3,829**	**3,984**
Under 15 years old [3]	85.3	87.6	2,765	2,817	Under 15 years old [3].	75.4	79.1	2,556	2,666
Routine infant or child health check.	17.9	15.8	580	509	Routine infant or child health check.	17.5	17.1	593	575
Acute respiratory infections [4]. .	8.5	8.3	276	267	Acute respiratory infections [4]. .	8.1	7.2	276	241
Otitis media and Eustachian tube disorders	7.1	5.4	231	172	Otitis media and Eustachian tube disorders	6.6	4.1	222	137
Attention deficit disorder.	3.4	3.5	110	112	Allergic rhinitis	1.1	2.9	36	97
Asthma.	3.1	3.5	101	111	Asthma.	1.2	2.5	40	83
15 to 44 years old [3]	98.9	95.8	1,660	1,569	15 to 44 years old [3]	194.8	200.1	3,199	3,245
General medical examination . .	3.9	3.7	66	61	Normal pregnancy.	24.5	26.0	402	422
Spinal disorders	3.0	3.1	50	50	Gynecological examination . . .	6.1	9.4	100	152
Rheumatism, excluding back. . .	3.3	2.7	55	44	Acute respiratory infections [4]. .	6.0	5.6	98	91
Acute respiratory infections [4]. .	3.6	2.6	60	43	Complications of pregnancy, childbirth and the puerperium	6.2	5.1	102	83
Psychoses, excluding major depressive disorder	1.7	2.4	28	39	Spinal disorders	3.2	4.9	52	80
45 to 64 years old [3]	96.5	120.7	3,294	3,542	45 to 64 years old [3]	141.0	165.6	4,511	4,581
Essential hypertension.	6.8	8.8	233	259	Essential hypertension.	8.3	9.5	264	262
Diabetes mellitus	5.8	7.2	199	211	Diabetes mellitus	5.6	6.5	181	179
Spinal disorders	3.1	5.9	106	174	Arthropathies and related disorders	6.6	6.4	212	178
Arthropathies and related disorders	2.9	4.3	99	126	Spinal disorders	4.1	6.3	130	175
Malignant neoplasms.	2.7	4.0	93	119	Malignant neoplasms.	5.7	6.3	173	173
65 years old and over [3]	88.2	104.4	6,340	7,100	65 years old and over [3]	126.6	142.6	6,736	7,148
Malignant neoplasms.	7.1	9.5	507	646	Essential hypertension.	11.8	12.0	628	599
Essential hypertension.	6.6	6.3	478	425	Malignant neoplasms.	5.9	8.0	312	400
Diabetes mellitus	4.8	5.6	344	382	Diabetes mellitus	6.0	7.2	318	363
Heart disease, excluding ischemic	4.1	4.4	296	297	Arthropathies and related disorders	6.3	6.6	333	329
Ischemic heart disease	4.9	4.1	349	278	Heart disease, excluding ischemic	3.6	4.3	194	217

[1] Based on the International Classification of Diseases, 9th Revision, clinical modification, (ICD-9-CM).   [2] Based on U.S. Census Bureau estimated civilian population as of July 1.   [3] Includes other first-listed diagnoses, not shown separately.   [4] Excluding pharyngitis.

Source: U.S. National Center for Health Statistics, unpublished data. Nos. 372, and 373; June 23, 2006. <http://www.cdc.gov/nchs/namcs.htm>.

Table 159. Visits to Hospital Emergency Departments by Diagnosis: 2004

[**50,320 represents 50,320,000.** See headnote, Table 157]

Leading diagnoses [1] (MALE)	Number (1,000)	Rate per 1,000 persons [2]	Leading diagnoses [1] (FEMALE)	Number (1,000)	Rate per 1,000 persons [2]
All ages	**50,320**	**357**	**All ages**	**59,896**	**406**
Under 15 years old [3]	12,262	394	Under 15 years old [3]	10,681	360
Otitis media and Eustachian tube disorders	928	30	Acute respiratory infections [4]	813	27
Acute upper respiratory infections [4]	907	29	Otitis media and Eustachian tube disorders	809	27
Contusions with intact skin surfaces	674	22	Pyrexia of unknown origin	533	18
Open wound, excluding head	666	21	Contusions with intact skin surfaces	441	15
Open wound of head	642	21	Open wound of head	360	12
15 to 44 years old [3]	21,553	353	15 to 44 years old [3]	28,483	462
Open wound, excluding head	1,412	23	Abdominal pain	1,654	27
Contusions with intact skin surfaces	1,128	18	Complications of pregnancy, childbirth and the puerperium	1,216	20
Spinal disorders	754	12	Contusions with intact skin surfaces	1,188	19
Sprains and strains of neck and back	751	12	Chest pain	934	15
Chest pain	745	12	Spinal disorders	850	14
45 to 64 years old [3]	10,134	297	45 to 64 years old [3]	11,372	315
Chest pain	736	22	Chest pain	773	21
Open wound, excluding head	463	14	Abdominal pain	620	17
Spinal disorders	450	13	Spinal disorders	448	12
Abdominal pain	420	12	Contusions with intact skin surfaces	442	12
Contusions with intact skin surfaces	302	9	Rheumatism, excluding back	299	8
65 years old and over [3]	6,372	433	65 years old and over [3]	9,360	469
Chest pain	375	26	Chest pain	529	27
Heart disease, excluding ischemic	292	20	Heart disease, excluding ischemic	520	26
Abdominal pain	216	15	Contusions with intact skin surfaces	394	20
Pneumonia	200	14	Abdominal pain	350	18
Syncope and collapse	192	13	Fractures, excluding lower limb	340	17

[1] Based on the International Classification of Diseases, 9th Revision, Clinical Modification (ICD-9-CM). [2] Based on U.S. Census Bureau estimated civilian noninstitutional population as of July 1. [3] Includes other first-listed diagnoses, not shown separately. [4] Excluding pharyngitis.

Source: U.S. National Center for Health Statistics, Advance Data, No. 372, June 23, 2006. <http://www.cdc.gov/nchs/namcs.htm>.

Table 160. Skilled Nursing Facilities: 1980 to 2003

[**436 represents 436,000.** Covers facilities and beds certified for participation under Medicare and are deemed to meet Medicaid standards. Includes facilities which have transfer agreements with one or more participating hospitals, and are engaged primarily in providing skilled nursing care and related services for the rehabilitation of injured, disabled, or sick persons]

Item	Unit	1980 [1]	1990 [1]	1995	1999	2000	2001	2002 [2]	2003 [2]
Skilled nursing facilities	Number	5,052	8,937	13,122	14,913	14,913	14,841	14,755	14,838
Beds	1,000	436	509	652	837	837	939	1,050	1,261
Per 1,000 Medicare enrollees [3]	Rate	20.0	15.2	17.7	21.6	21.3	23.7	26.2	31.1

[1] Facility data are as of July 1. [2] Facility data are as of December 31. [3] Based on total number of beneficiaries enrolled in the medicare hospital insurance program as of July 1 of year stated.

Source: U.S. Centers for Medicare and Medicaid Services, Data Compendium 2003, Other Medicare Providers and Suppliers. <http://www.cms.hhs.gov/DataCompendium/022003DataCompendium.asp#TopOfPage>.

Table 161. Nursing Homes—Selected Characteristics: 2004

[**Beds: 1,730 represents 1,730,000.** Covers licensed and/or certified nursing homes in the conterminous United States that had three or more beds. Based on the 2004 National Nursing Home Survey, a two-stage survey sample of nursing homes and their residents. Subject to sampling variability. For composition of regions, see map, inside front cover]

Characteristic	Nursing homes	Beds Number (1,000)	Beds Per nursing home	Current residents Number (1,000)	Current residents Occupancy rate [1]	Full-time equivalent employees [2] Number (1,000)	Full-time equivalent employees Rate per 100 beds
2004, total	**16,081**	**1,730**	**108**	**1,492**	**86.3**	**1,053**	**60.9**
Certification:							
Medicare and medicaid certified	14,090	1,600	114	1,380	86.2	972	60.8
Medicare only	[2]653	33	51	28	85.0	20	59.7
Medicaid only	1,104	76	69	68	89.1	41	53.7
Not certified	[2]234	21	90	17	78.3	20	95.7
Bed size:							
Less than 50 beds	2,242	76	34	62	82.1	43	56.6
50–99 beds	6,005	455	76	423	92.9	254	55.8
100–199 beds	6,840	903	132	789	87.3	563	62.4
200 beds or more	994	296	298	219	73.9	193	65.3

[1] Number of residents divided by number of available beds multiplied by 100. [2] Includes only those employees providing direct health-related services to residents. Includes nurses, nurses aides, orderlies, dentists, dental hygenists, physical therapists, speech pathologists and /or audiologists, dieticians or nutritionists, podiatrists, and social workers. [3] Figure does not meet standards of reliability or precision.

Source: U.S. National Center for Health Statistics, National Health Care Survey, National Nursing Home Survey. See also <http://www.cdc.gov/nchs/fastats/nursingh.htm>.

Table 162. Hospitals—Summary Characteristics: 1980 to 2004

[For beds, (1,365 represents 1,365,000). Covers hospitals accepted for registration by the American Hospital Association; see text, this section. Short-term hospitals have an average patient stay of less than 30 days; long-term, an average stay of longer duration. Special hospitals include obstetrics and gynecology; eye, ear, nose, and throat; rehabilitation; orthopedic; and chronic and other special hospitals except psychiatric, tuberculosis, alcoholism, and chemical dependency hospitals]

Item	1980	1990	1995	1999	2000	2001	2002	2003	2004
Number:									
All hospitals	6,965	6,649	6,291	5,890	5,810	5,801	5,794	5,764	5,759
With 100 beds or more	3,755	3,620	3,376	3,140	3,102	3,084	3,032	3,007	2,972
Nonfederal [1]	6,606	6,312	5,992	5,626	5,565	5,558	5,554	5,525	5,520
Community hospitals [2]	5,830	5,384	5,194	4,956	4,915	4,908	4,927	4,895	4,919
Nongovernmental nonprofit	3,322	3,191	3,092	3,012	3,003	2,998	3,025	2,984	2,967
For profit	730	749	752	747	749	754	766	790	835
State and local government	1,778	1,444	1,350	1,197	1,163	1,156	1,136	1,121	1,117
Long-term general and special	157	131	112	129	131	136	124	126	108
Psychiatric	534	757	657	516	496	491	477	477	466
Tuberculosis	11	4	3	4	4	4	4	4	4
Federal	359	337	299	264	245	243	240	239	239
Beds (1,000) [3]:									
All hospitals	1,365	1,213	1,081	994	984	987	976	965	956
Rate per 1,000 population [4]	6.0	4.9	4.1	3.6	3.5	3.5	3.4	3.3	3.3
Beds per hospital	196	182	172	169	169	170	168	167	166
Nonfederal [1]	1,248	1,113	1,004	939	931	936	926	917	908
Community hospitals [2]	988	927	873	830	824	826	821	813	808
Rate per 1,000 population [4]	4.3	3.7	3.3	3.0	2.9	2.9	2.8	2.8	2.8
Nongovernmental nonprofit	692	657	610	587	583	585	582	575	567
For profit	87	102	106	107	110	109	108	110	112
State and local government	209	169	157	136	131	132	130	120	127
Long-term general and special	39	25	19	20	18	19	18	18	15
Psychiatric	215	158	110	87	87	89	85	85	86
Tuberculosis	2	(Z)	(Z)	(Z)	(Z)	(Z)	(Z)	(Z)	(Z)
Federal	117	98	78	55	53	53	50	47	58
Average daily census (1,000): [5]									
All hospitals	1,060	844	710	657	650	658	662	657	658
Community hospitals [2]	747	619	548	526	526	533	540	539	541
Nongovernmental nonprofit	542	455	393	381	382	385	391	389	388
For profit	57	54	55	58	61	63	64	65	99
State and local government	149	111	100	86	83	85	84	84	84
Expenses (bil. dol.): [6]									
All hospitals	91.9	234.9	320.3	372.9	395.4	426.8	462.2	498.1	533.8
Nonfederal [1]	84.0	219.6	300.0	349.2	371.5	399.3	432.5	467.2	499.0
Community hospitals [2]	76.9	203.7	285.6	335.2	356.6	383.7	416.6	450.1	481.2
Nongovernmental nonprofit	55.8	150.7	209.6	251.5	267.1	287.3	312.7	337.7	359.4
For profit	5.8	18.8	26.7	31.2	35.0	37.3	40.1	44.0	48.9
State and local government	15.2	34.2	49.3	52.5	54.5	59.1	63.8	68.4	72.8
Long-term general and special	1.2	2.7	2.2	2.8	2.8	3.3	3.6	3.6	2.3
Psychiatric	5.8	12.9	11.7	11.0	11.9	13.2	12.1	13.1	13.8
Tuberculosis	0.1	0.1	0.4	(Z)	(Z)	(Z)	(Z)	(Z)	(Z)
Federal	7.9	15.2	20.2	23.7	23.9	27.5	29.7	30.9	34.8
Personnel (1,000): [7]									
All hospitals	3,492	4,063	4,273	4,369	4,454	4,535	4,610	4,650	4,695
Nonfederal [1]	3,213	3,760	3,971	4,074	4,157	4,236	4,312	4,350	4,379
Community hospitals [2]	2,873	3,420	3,714	3,838	3,911	3,987	4,069	4,108	4,147
Nongovernmental nonprofit	2,086	2,533	2,702	2,862	2,919	2,971	3,039	3,058	3,076
For profit	189	273	343	362	378	379	380	391	404
State and local government	598	614	670	614	614	637	651	658	665
Long-term general and special	56	55	38	42	41	44	46	45	42
Psychiatric	275	280	215	191	200	201	193	194	185
Tuberculosis	3	1	1	1	1	1	1	1	1
Federal	279	303	301	295	297	299	299	300	315
Outpatient visits (mil.)	263.0	368.2	483.2	573.5	592.7	612.0	640.5	648.6	662.1
Emergency	82.0	92.8	99.9	103.8	106.9	109.8	114.2	115.1	116.9

Z Less than 500 beds or $50 million. [1] Includes hospital units of institutions. [2] Short-term (average length of stay less than 30 days) general and special (e.g., obstetrics and gynecology; eye, ear, nose and throat; rehabilitation etc. except psychiatric, tuberculosis, alcoholism and chemical dependency). Excludes hospital units of institutions. [3] Beginning 1990, number of beds at end of reporting period; prior years, average number in 12-month period. [4] Based on Census Bureau estimated resident population as of July 1. 1980, 1990, and 2000 based on enumerated resident population as of April 1. Estimates reflect revisions based on the 2000 census of population. [5] The average number of people served on an inpatient basis on a single day during the reporting period. [6] Excludes new construction. [7] Includes full-time equivalents of part-time personnel.

Source: Health Forum, An American Hospital Association Company, Chicago, IL, Hospital Statistics 2006 Edition, and prior years (copyright).

Table 163. **Average Cost to Community Hospitals Per Patient: 1980 to 2004**

[In dollars, except percent. Covers nonfederal short-term general or special hospitals (excluding psychiatric or tuberculosis hospitals and hospital units of institutions). Total cost per patient based on total hospital expenses (payroll, employee benefits, professional fees, supplies, etc.). Data have been adjusted for outpatient visits]

Type of expense and hospital	1980	1990	1995	1998	1999	2000	2001	2002	2003	2004
Average cost per day, total......	245	687	968	1,067	1,103	1,149	1,217	1,290	1,379	1,450
Annual percent change [1]......	12.9	7.8	4.0	3.3	3.3	4.2	5.9	6.0	6.9	5.1
Nongovernmental nonprofit	246	692	994	1,111	1,140	1,182	1,255	1,329	1,429	1,501
For profit...................	257	752	947	968	999	1,057	1,121	1,181	1,264	1,362
State and local government	239	635	878	949	1,007	1,064	1,114	1,188	1,238	1,291
Average cost per stay, total	1,851	4,947	6,216	6,386	6,512	6,649	6,980	7,346	7,796	8,166
Nongovernmental nonprofit	1,902	5,001	6,279	6,526	6,608	6,717	7,052	7,458	7,905	8,266
For profit..................	1,676	4,727	5,425	5,262	5,350	5,642	5,972	6,161	6,590	7,139
State and local government	1,750	4,838	6,445	6,612	6,923	7,106	7,400	7,773	8,205	8,473

[1] Change from immediate prior year.

Source: Health Forum, An American Hospital Association Company, Chicago, IL, *Hospital Statistics 2006 Edition*, and prior years (copyright). <http://www.healthforum.com/>.

Table 164. **Community Hospitals—States: 2000 and 2004**

[823.6 represents 823,600. For definition of community hospitals see footnote 2, Table 162]

State	Number of hospitals		Beds (1,000)		Patients admitted (1,000)		Average daily census [1] (1,000)		Outpatient visits (mil.)		Average cost per day (dol.)	
	2000	2004	2000	2004	2000	2004	2000	2004	2000	2004	2000	2004
United States ...	4,915	4,919	823.6	808.1	33,089	35,086	525.7	541.1	521.4	571.6	1,149	1,450
Alabama.........	108	108	16.4	15.3	680	716	9.8	10.0	8.0	8.3	980	1,142
Alaska..........	18	19	1.4	1.4	47	45	0.8	0.8	1.3	1.3	1,495	1,965
Arizona.........	61	62	10.9	11.2	539	625	6.8	7.6	5.3	5.4	1,311	1,678
Arkansas........	83	87	9.8	9.6	368	383	5.7	6.4	4.4	4.8	908	1,170
California........	389	361	72.7	71.9	3,315	3,469	47.8	50.3	44.9	47.5	1,438	1,878
Colorado........	69	70	9.4	9.3	397	435	5.4	5.9	6.7	7.0	1,280	1,699
Connecticut.......	35	35	7.7	7.8	349	390	5.8	6.2	6.7	7.0	1,373	1,668
Delaware.......	5	6	1.8	2.0	83	103	1.4	1.8	1.5	1.9	1,311	1,563
District of Columbia .	11	11	3.3	3.5	129	141	2.5	2.7	1.3	1.6	1,512	1,861
Florida..........	202	203	51.2	50.0	2,119	2,322	31.0	33.1	21.8	22.4	1,161	1,504
Georgia.........	151	146	23.9	24.7	863	944	15.0	16.7	11.2	13.4	978	1,144
Hawaii..........	21	24	3.1	3.1	100	114	2.3	2.4	2.5	1.9	1,088	1,219
Idaho...........	42	39	3.5	3.4	123	127	1.8	1.8	2.2	2.4	1,003	1,367
Illinois..........	196	191	37.3	34.8	1,531	1,586	22.4	23.0	25.1	28.3	1,278	1,544
Indiana..........	109	113	19.2	18.8	700	731	10.8	11.1	14.1	15.5	1,132	1,447
Iowa...........	115	115	11.8	10.9	360	360	6.8	6.4	9.2	9.7	740	985
Kansas.........	129	134	10.8	10.4	310	331	5.7	5.8	5.3	5.9	837	1,006
Kentucky........	105	105	14.8	15.3	582	606	9.1	9.3	8.7	8.9	929	1,140
Louisiana	123	131	17.5	17.2	654	696	9.8	10.5	10.0	10.4	1,075	1,191
Maine...........	37	37	3.7	3.5	147	151	2.4	2.2	3.2	4.1	1,148	1,562
Maryland	49	50	11.2	11.5	587	661	8.2	8.7	6.0	6.9	1,315	1,720
Massachusetts.....	80	78	16.6	16.2	740	801	11.7	12.1	16.7	19.0	1,467	1,723
Michigan........	146	144	26.1	26.0	1,106	1,190	16.9	17.2	24.9	27.7	1,211	1,468
Minnesota........	135	132	16.7	16.1	571	627	11.2	10.9	7.3	9.5	932	1,203
Mississippi	95	93	13.6	13.1	425	427	8.0	7.6	3.7	4.2	719	957
Missouri	119	119	20.1	19.1	773	832	11.7	12.0	14.8	16.2	1,185	1,459
Montana........	52	54	4.3	4.3	99	107	2.9	2.8	2.6	2.9	579	757
Nebraska	85	85	8.2	7.3	209	211	4.8	4.4	3.4	3.9	743	1,075
Nevada	22	30	3.8	4.8	199	233	2.7	3.4	2.2	2.4	1,285	1,524
New Hampshire....	28	28	2.9	2.8	111	117	1.7	1.8	2.8	3.0	1,201	1,460
New Jersey.......	80	80	25.3	22.0	1,074	1,104	17.3	16.2	16.3	17.7	1,299	1,691
New Mexico	35	37	3.5	3.7	174	163	2.0	2.1	3.1	5.0	1,388	1,581
New York	215	206	66.4	64.2	2,416	2,526	52.1	50.5	46.4	49.7	1,118	1,457
North Carolina.....	113	115	23.1	23.5	971	1,006	16.0	16.7	12.4	15.3	1,061	1,226
North Dakota......	42	40	3.9	3.6	89	88	2.3	2.1	1.7	1.8	747	880
Ohio...........	163	166	33.8	33.4	1,404	1,475	20.6	21.1	26.9	30.5	1,198	1,585
Oklahoma........	108	109	11.1	10.8	429	455	6.2	6.5	4.7	5.3	1,031	1,238
Oregon..........	59	58	6.6	6.5	330	341	3.9	4.0	7.3	7.9	1,461	1,977
Pennsylvania......	207	197	42.3	40.1	1,796	1,847	28.8	28.0	31.8	33.4	1,080	1,394
Rhode Island......	11	11	2.4	2.4	119	125	1.7	1.8	2.1	2.1	1,313	1,667
South Carolina.....	63	62	11.5	11.2	495	513	8.0	8.0	7.8	7.0	1,101	1,435
South Dakota	48	51	4.3	4.6	99	103	2.8	2.8	1.7	1.6	476	704
Tennessee	121	127	20.6	20.4	737	825	11.5	12.8	10.3	10.3	1,078	1,228
Texas..........	403	418	55.9	58.1	2,367	2,517	33.1	36.2	29.4	32.4	1,274	1,567
Utah	42	43	4.3	4.5	194	219	2.4	2.6	4.5	4.7	1,375	1,811
Vermont	14	14	1.7	1.5	52	53	1.1	0.9	1.2	2.3	888	1,084
Virginia..........	88	88	16.9	17.3	727	770	11.4	12.2	9.5	11.9	1,057	1,352
Washington.......	84	85	11.1	11.0	505	528	6.6	6.7	9.6	10.1	1,511	2,006
West Virginia......	57	57	8.0	7.4	288	298	4.8	8.9	5.2	6.0	844	1,075
Wisconsin........	118	121	15.3	14.6	558	599	9.1	9.1	10.9	11.8	1,055	1,380
Wyoming	24	24	1.9	2.0	48	51	1.1	1.1	0.9	0.9	677	833

[1] Inpatients receiving treatment each day; excludes newborn.

Source: Health Forum, An American Hospital Association Company, Chicago, IL, *Hospital Statistics 2006 Edition*, and prior years (copyright). <http://www.healthforum.com/>.

Table 165. **Hospital Use Rates by Type of Hospital: 1980 to 2004**

Type of hospital	1980	1990	1995	2000	2001	2002	2003	2004
Community hospitals: [1]								
Admissions per 1,000 population [2]	159	125	116	117	118	120	120	119
Admissions per bed	37	34	35	40	40	42	43	43
Average length of stay [3] (days)	7.6	7.2	6.5	5.8	5.7	5.7	5.7	5.6
Outpatient visits per admission	5.6	9.7	13.4	15.8	15.9	16.1	16.2	16.3
Outpatient visits per 1,000 population [2]	890	1,207	1,556	1,852	1,890	1,932	1,937	1,946
Surgical operations (million [4])	18.8	21.9	23.2	26.1	26.5	27.6	27.1	27.4
Number per admission	0.5	0.7	0.7	0.8	0.8	0.8	0.8	0.8
Nonfederal psychiatric:								
Admissions per 1,000 population [2]	2.5	2.9	2.7	2.4	2.6	2.5	2.6	2.7
Days in hospital per 1,000 population [2]	295	190	122	93	94	92	91	88

[1] For definition of community hospitals, see footnote 2, Table 162.   [2] Based on U.S. Census Bureau estimated resident population as of July 1. Estimates reflect revisions based on the 2000 census of population.   [3] Number of inpatient days divided by number of admissions.   [4] 18.8 represents 18,800,000.

Source: Health Forum, An American Hospital Association Company, Chicago, IL, *Hospital Statistics 2006 Edition*, and prior years (copyright). <http://www.healthforum.com/>.

Table 166. **Hospital Utilization Rates by Sex: 1990 to 2004**

[30,788 represents 30,788,000. Represents estimates of inpatients discharged from noninstitutional, short-stay hospitals, exclusive of federal hospitals. Excludes newborn infants. Based on sample data collected from the National Hospital Discharge Survey, a sample survey of hospital records of patients discharged in year shown; subject to sampling variability]

Item and sex	1990	1995	1998	1999	2000	2001	2002	2003	2004
Patients discharged (1,000).	30,788	30,722	31,827	32,132	31,706	32,653	33,727	34,738	34,864
Patients discharged per 1,000 persons,									
total [1]	122	116	117	117	114	115	118	120	119
Male	100	94	93	95	92	93	95	98	97
Female	143	136	139	138	135	137	139	141	141
Days of care per 1,000 persons, total [1] . .	784	620	589	581	560	562	572	578	574
Male	694	551	517	510	491	490	506	507	505
Female	869	686	658	649	627	631	635	646	641
Average stay (days).	6.4	5.4	5.1	5.0	4.9	4.9	4.9	4.8	4.8
Male	6.9	5.8	5.5	5.4	5.3	5.3	5.3	5.2	5.2
Female	6.1	5.0	4.7	4.7	4.6	4.6	4.6	4.6	4.5

[1] Rates are computed using Census Bureau estimates of the civilian population as of July 1. Rates for 1990 and 1995 were based on population estimates adjusted for the net undernumeration in the 1990 census. Rates for 2000 and 2003 were calculated using 2000-based postcensal estimates. Rates for 2000 differ from the ones shown in earlier reports because they were calculated using revised population estimates.

Source: U.S. National Center for Health Statistics, *Vital and Health Statistics*, Series 13; and unpublished data <http://www.cdc.gov/nchs/products/pubs/pubd/series/ser.htm>.

Table 167. **Hospital Utilization Measures for HIV Patients: 1990 to 2004**

[HIV represents human immunodeficiency virus. See headnote, Table 166]

Measure of utilization	Unit	1990	1995	2000	2002	2003	200
Number of patients discharged	1,000. . . .	146	249	173	189	207	20
Rate of patient discharges [1]	Rate	5.8	9.4	6.2	6.6	7.2	7.
Number of days of care	1,000. . . .	2,188	2,326	1,257	1,322	1,696	1,47
Rate of days of care [1]	Rate	86.9	87.6	45.2	46.0	58.6	50.
Average length of stay	Days	14.9	9.3	7.3	7.0	8.2	7.

[1] Per 10,000 population. Based on Census Bureau estimated civilian population as of July 1. Populations for 1990-99 were adjusted for the net undernumeration in the 1990 census. Populations for 2000-2003 were 2000-based postcensal estimates. Rates for 2000-2001 differ from rates shown in a previous report because they were calculated using revised population estimates.

Source: National Center for Health Statistics, *Vital and Health Statistics*, Series 13; and unpublished data <http://www.cdc.gov/nchs/products/pubd/series/ser.htm>

Table 168. Hospital Discharges and Days of Care: 2002 and 2004

[**33,727 represents 33,727,000.** See headnote, Table 166. For composition of regions, see map, inside front cover]

Age, race, and region	Discharges Number (1,000) 2002	2004	Per 1,000 persons [1] 2002	2004	Days of care per 1,000 persons [1] 2002	2004	Average stay (days) 2002	2004
Total [2]	33,727	34,864	118	119	572	575	4.9	4.8
Age:								
Under 1 year old.	810	842	201	207	1,134	1,244	5.6	6.0
1 to 4 years old	713	734	46	46	159	142	3.5	3.1
5 to 14 years old	1,016	995	25	24	109	106	4.4	4.3
15 to 24 years old.	3,083	3,062	77	74	266	257	3.5	3.5
25 to 34 years old.	3,897	4,046	99	102	328	343	3.3	3.4
35 to 44 years old.	3,757	3,692	84	84	368	363	4.4	4.3
45 to 64 years old.	7,723	8,323	116	118	575	592	5.0	5.0
65 to 74 years old.	4,642	4,786	254	259	1,412	1,405	5.6	5.4
75 years old and over	8,085	8,384	467	470	2,795	2,715	6.0	5.8
Race:								
White	20,806	20,979	90	89	436	431	4.9	4.8
Black	3,995	4,118	109	110	584	597	5.3	5.4
Asian/Pacific Islander.	538	592	45	46	243	230	5.4	5.0
American Indian/Eskimo/ Aleut.	173	135	63	48	330	202	5.2	4.2
Region:								
Northeast	6,990	7,388	129	136	727	732	5.6	5.4
Midwest	7,503	7,680	115	117	512	513	4.4	4.4
South	12,994	13,239	127	126	618	617	4.9	4.9
West.	6,239	6,557	96	98	430	439	4.5	4.5

[1] Based on U.S. Census Bureau estimated civilian population as of July 1. Population estimates based on the 2000 Census were used to calculate rates.   [2] Includes other races not shown separately.

Source: U.S. National Center for Health Statistics, *Vital and Health Statistics*, Series 13; and unpublished data. <http://www.cdc.gov/nchs/products/pubs/pubd/series/ser.htm>.

Table 169. Hospital Discharges and Days of Care by Sex: 2004

[**13,844 represents 13,844,000.** Represents estimates of inpatients discharged from noninstitutional, short-stay hospitals, exclusive of federal hospitals. Excludes newborn infants. Diagnostic categories are based on the International Classification of Diseases, Ninth Revision, Clinical Modification. See headnote, Table 166]

Sex, age, and first-listed diagnosis	Discharges Number (1,000)	Per 1,000 persons [1]	Days of care per 1,000 persons [1]	Average stay (days)	Sex, age, and first-listed diagnosis	Discharges Number (1,000)	Per 1,000 persons [1]	Days of care per 1,000 persons [1]	Average stay (days)
Male					**Female**				
All ages [2]	13,844	102.6	541.1	5.2	**All ages [2]**	21,020	134.9	599.6	4.5
Under 18 years [3]	1,637	43.6	201.5	4.6	Under 18 years [3]	1,516	42.4	184.4	4.4
Injuries and poisoning . . .	195	5.2	18.5	3.6	Injuries and poisoning . . .	122	3.4	12.6	3.7
Asthma	127	3.4	7.3	2.1	Pneumonia	86	2.4	7.9	3.3
Pneumonia	103	2.7	8.9	3.2	Asthma	71	2.0	4.6	2.3
18–44 years [3]	2,622	46.5	225.6	4.9	18–44 years [3]	7,597	136.2	445.5	3.3
Injuries and poisoning . . .	453	8.0	40.8	5.1	Delivery	3,980	71.4	186.2	2.6
Serious mental illness [5] . .	319	5.7	43.4	7.7	Serious mental illness [5] . .	331	5.9	43.1	7.3
Alcohol and drug [4]	182	3.2	14.3	4.4	Injuries and poisoning . . .	298	5.3	22.4	4.2
Diseases of heart	162	2.9	10.1	3.5	Alcohol and drug [4]	109	2.0	[6] 9.2	[6] 4.7
45–64 years [3]	4,073	118.4	612.4	5.2	45–64 years [3]	4,249	117.3	571.8	4.9
Diseases of heart	821	23.9	95.7	4.0	Diseases of heart	483	13.3	57.1	4.3
Injuries and poisoning . . .	374	10.9	68.9	6.3	Injuries and poisoning . . .	335	9.2	50.8	5.5
Malignant neoplasms . . .	206	6.0	38.6	6.4	Malignant neoplasms . . .	211	5.8	36.9	6.3
Serious mental illness [5] . .	162	4.7	42.2	9.0	Serious mental illness [5] . .	201	5.5	51.8	9.4
Alcohol and drug [4]	150	4.4	19.6	4.5	Pneumonia	118	3.3	18.8	5.8
65–74 years [3]	2,263	268.5	1,442.3	5.4	65–74 years [3]	2,523	251.4	1,374.0	5.5
Diseases of heart	547	65.0	280.9	4.3	Diseases of heart	428	42.6	199.7	4.7
Malignant neoplasms . . .	161	19.1	128.7	6.7	Injuries and poisoning . . .	197	19.6	114.6	5.8
Injuries and poisoning . . .	146	17.4	109.7	6.3	Osteoarthritis	152	15.1	60.9	4.0
Cerebrovascular diseases.	106	12.5	56.9	4.5	Malignant neoplasms . . .	138	13.8	101.3	7.3
Pneumonia	103	12.2	75.0	6.2	Pneumonia	125	12.5	72.3	5.8
					Cerebrovascular diseases.	92	9.1	44.4	4.9
75 years and over [3]	3,250	483.1	2,815.5	5.8	75 years and over [3] . . .	5,135	462.4	2,653.9	5.7
Diseases of heart	761	113.1	579.0	5.1	Diseases of heart	1,051	94.6	485.2	5.1
Pneumonia	261	38.8	232.5	6.0	Injuries and poisoning . . .	501	45.1	284.0	6.3
Injuries and poisoning . . .	225	33.4	207.8	6.2	Pneumonia	311	28.0	179.1	6.4
Cerebrovascular diseases.	168	24.9	129.9	5.2	Cerebrovascular diseases.	272	24.5	129.2	5.3
Malignant neoplasms . . .	144	21.3	149.0	7.0	Malignant neoplasms . . .	174	15.6	103.6	6.6

[1] Based on Census Bureau estimated civilian population as of July 1.   [2] Estimates are age adjusted to the year 2000 standard population using six age groups: under 18 years, 18–44 years, 45–54 years, 55–64 years, 65–74 years, and 75 years and over. See Appendix II, Age adjustment.   [3] Includes discharges with first-listed diagnoses not shown in table.   [4] Includes abuse, dependence, and withdrawal. These estimates are for nonfederal short-stay hospitals only and do not include alcohol and drug discharges from other types of facilities or or programs such as the Department of Veterans Affairs or day treatment programs.   [5] These estimates are for nonfederal short-stay hospitals only and do not include serious mental illness discharges from other types of facilities or programs such as the Department of Veterans Affairs or long-term hospitals.   [6] Estimates are considered unreliable.

Source: Centers for Disease Control and Prevention, National Center for Health Statistics, National Hospital Discharge Survey. <http://www.cdc.gov/nchs/about/major/hdasd/nhds.htm>.

Table 170. **Procedures for Inpatients Discharged From Short-Stay Hospitals: 1990 to 2004**

[23,051 represents 23,051,000. Procedure categories are based on the International Classification of Diseases, Ninth Revision, Clinical Modification. See headnote, Table 166]

Sex and type of procedure	Number of procedures (1,000)				Rate per 1,000 population [1]			
	1990	1995	2000	2004	1990	1995	2000	2004
Surgical procedures, total [2]	**23,051**	**22,530**	**23,244**	**26,632**	**92.4**	**86.2**	**83.6**	**91.1**
Cardiac catheterization	995	1,068	1,221	1,297	4.0	4.1	4.4	4.4
Removal of coronary artery obstruction [3]	285	434	1,025	1,285	1.2	1.7	3.7	4.4
Repair of current obstetric laceration	795	964	1,136	1,241	3.2	3.7	4.1	4.2
Cesarean section	945	785	855	1,236	3.8	3.0	3.1	4.2
Reduction of fracture [4]	609	577	628	667	2.4	2.2	2.3	2.3
Male, total [2]	**8,538**	**8,388**	**8,689**	**10,098**	**70.6**	**65.9**	**63.9**	**70.4**
Removal of coronary artery obstruction [3]	200	285	655	853	1.7	2.2	4.8	5.9
Cardiac catheterization	620	660	732	771	5.1	5.2	5.4	5.4
Ccronary artery bypass graft	286	423	371	303	2.4	3.3	2.7	2.1
Female, total [2]	**14,513**	**14,142**	**14,556**	**16,534**	**113.0**	**105.3**	**102.4**	**111.0**
Repair of current obstetric laceration	795	964	1,136	1,241	6.2	7.2	8.0	8.3
Cesarean section	945	785	855	1,236	7.4	5.8	6.0	8.3
Hysterectomy	591	583	633	617	4.6	4.3	4.5	4.1
Diagnostic and other nonsurgical procedures [5]	**17,455**	**17,278**	**16,737**	**18,391**	**70.0**	**66.1**	**60.2**	**62.9**
Angiocardiography and arteriography [6]	1,735	1,834	2,005	2,110	7.0	7.0	7.2	7.2
Respiratory therapy	1,164	1,127	991	1,157	4.7	4.3	3.6	3.8
Manual assisted delivery	750	866	898	1,000	3.0	3.3	3.2	3.5
CAT scan [7]	1,506	967	754	828	6.0	3.7	2.7	2.8
Diagnostic ultrasound	1,608	1,181	886	813	6.4	4.5	3.2	2.8
Male, total [5]	**7,378**	**7,261**	**6,965**	**7,573**	**61.0**	**57.1**	**51.2**	**52.8**
Angiocardiography and arteriography [6]	1,051	1,076	1,157	1,171	8.7	8.5	8.5	8.2
Respiratory therapy	586	572	507	588	4.9	4.5	3.7	4.1
CAT scan [7]	736	473	345	389	6.1	3.7	2.5	2.7
Female, total [5]	**10,077**	**10,016**	**9,772**	**10,818**	**78.5**	**74.6**	**68.8**	**72.6**
Manual assisted delivery	750	866	898	1,000	5.9	6.5	6.3	6.7
Fetal EKG and fetal monitoring	1,377	935	750	854	10.8	7.0	5.5	5.7
Diagnostic ultrasound	941	682	501	444	7.3	5.1	3.5	3.0

[1] Based on Census Bureau estimated civilian population as of July 1. Population estimates based on the 1990 Census were used to calculate rates for 1990 through 2000. Population estimates based on the 2000 census were used to calculate rates for 2001 through 2004.   [2] Includes other types of surgical procedures not shown separately.   [3] Beginning 1996 includes separately coded "insertion of stent."   [4] Excluding skull, nose, and jaw.   [5] Includes other nonsurgical procedures not shown separately.   [6] Using contrast material.   [7] Computerized axial tomography.

Source: U.S. National Center for Health Statistics, *Vital and Health Statistics,* series 13; and unpublished data. <http://www.cdc.gov/nchs/products/pubs/pubd/series/ser.htm>.

Table 171. **Organ Transplants and Grafts: 1990 to 2005**

[As of end of year. Based on reports of procurement programs and transplant centers in the United States, except as noted]

Procedure	Number of procedures						Number of centers		Number of people waiting, 2005	1-year patient survival rates, 2004 (percent)
	1990	1995	2000	2003	2004	2005	1990	2005		
Transplant: [1]										
Heart	2,095	2,342	2,172	2,057	2,016	2,127	148	135	2,993	87.7
Heart-lung	52	69	47	29	39	33	79	60	143	56.4
Lung	203	869	955	1,085	1,173	1,408	70	67	3,038	82.8
Liver	2,631	3,818	4,816	5,671	6,168	6,444	85	126	17,250	86.3
Kidney	9,358	10,957	13,258	15,129	16,000	16,477	232	247	66,701	98.0
Kidney-pancreas	459	915	910	871	880	903	(NA)	(NA)	2,506	95.5
Pancreas	60	103	420	502	604	540	84	145	1,747	94.2
Intestine	1	21	29	116	152	178	(NA)	48	220	82.4
Multi-organ [2]	71	124	213	350	441	518	(NA)	(NA)	(NA)	(NA)
Cornea grafts [2]	40,631	44,652	46,949	46,436	46,841	44,329	[3]107	[3]88	(NA)	(NA)
Bone grafts(1,000)	350	450	800	1,200	1,500	1,620	30	65	(X)	(NA)
Skin grafts [4]	5,500	5,500	13,000	16,000	19,000	20,000	25	45	(X)	(NA)

NA Not available.   X Not applicable.   [1] Kidney-pancreas and heart-lung transplants are each counted as one organ. All other multi-organ transplants, excluding kidney-pancreas and heart-lung, are included in the multi-organ row. Based on the Organ Procurement and Transplant Network (OPTN) as of July 28, 2006. The data have been supplied by UNOS under contract with HHS. This work was supported in part by Health Resources and Services Administration contract 231-00-0015. The authors alone are responsible for the reporting and interpretation of these data. Data subject to change based on future data submission or correction.   [2] 1990–1992, number of procedures and eye banks include Canada. From 1993 on, the data is for the U.S. only.   [3] Eye banks.   [4] Procedure data are shown in terms of square feet.

Source: U.S. Department of Health and Human Services, Health Resources and Services Administration, Office of Special Programs, Division of Transplantation, Rockville, MD; United Network for Organ Sharing (UNOS), Richmond, VA; University Renal Research and Education Association, Ann Arbor, MI; American Association of Tissue Banks, McLean, VA; and Eye Bank Association of America, Washington, DC; and unpublished data. See also <http://www.optn.org/>.

Table 172. Injury and Poisoning Episodes and Conditions by Age and Sex: 2004

[**33,173 represents 33,173,000.** Covers all medically attended injuries and poisonings occurring during the 5-week period prior to the survey interview. Age adjustment is used to adjust for differences in the age distribution of populations being compared. There may be more than one condition per episode. Based on the redesigned National Health Interview Survey, a sample survey of the civilian noninstitutionalized population; see Appendix III.]

External cause and nature of injury	Total	Total, age-adjusted [1]	Both sexes Under 12 years old	12 to 21 years old	22 to 44 years old	45 to 64 years old	65 years old and over	Male, total	Female, total
EPISODES									
Number (1,000)	33,173	(X)	4,816	6,977	10,569	7,314	3,496	17,273	15,900
Annual rate per 1,000 population, total [2]	115.1	111.9	100.7	168.8	112.1	104.2	101.1	122.6	107.9
Fall	41.7	41.0	43.2	41.3	29.9	46.0	64.0	36.9	46.4
Struck by or against a person or an object	13.4	11.9	11.8	35.5	10.6	8.9	[4]5.8	17.1	9.8
Transportation [3]	12.8	12.5	10.2	18.8	14.2	12.4	[4]6.2	12.9	12.7
Overexertion	16.5	16.1	[4]2.0	31.4	23.8	11.8	[4]8.7	17.8	15.3
Cutting, piercing instruments.	9.9	10.1	[4]6.9	[4]9.9	13.6	9.3	[4]4.7	13.0	6.9
Poisoning [5]	1.3	1.1	[4]1.1	[4]3.4	[4]0.9	[4]1.4	–	[4]1.3	[4]1.3
CONDITIONS									
Annual rate per 1,000 population, total [2]	149.8	145.9	120.5	207.9	144.6	147.6	139.2	154.3	145.4
Sprains/strains	48.7	47.7	14.9	79.2	64.3	45.6	22.7	45.8	51.5
Open wounds	19.1	19.3	22.3	18.8	21.6	16.5	13.0	24.7	13.7
Fractures	18.7	17.9	18.6	27.9	13.0	16.2	28.5	18.3	19.1
Contusions	29.0	27.6	18.4	36.4	15.7	37.6	53.8	26.5	31.4

– Represents zero.   X Not applicable.   [1] Data were age-adjusted using the 2000 standard population.   [2] Includes other items not shown separately.   [3] Includes the categories "Motor vehicle, bicycle, motorcycle; pedestrian, train, boat, and airplane."   [4] Figure does not meet standard of reliability or precision.   [5] Poisoning episodes are assumed to have a single condition resulting from the episode.
Source: U.S. National Center for Health Statistics, unpublished data. See also <http://www.cdc.gov/nchs/injury.htm>.

Table 173. Injuries Associated With Selected Consumer Products: 2004

[Estimates calculated from a representative sample of hospitals with emergency treatment departments in the United States. Data are estimates of the number of emergency room treated cases nationwide associated with various products . Product involvement does not necessarily mean the product caused the accident. Products were selected from the U.S. Consumer Product Safety Commission's National Electronic Injury Surveillance System (NEISS)]

Product	Number	Product	Number
Home workshop equipment:		Floors or flooring materials	1,112,226
Saws (hand or power)	101,420	Other doors (excl. garage)	327,041
Hammers.	36,066	Ceilings and walls	314,346
Household packaging and containers:		Home entertainment equipment:	
Household containers and packaging	223,260	Televisions	42,811
Bottles and jars.	72,107	Personal use items:	
Housewares:		Footwear	121,094
Knives	460,309	Wheelchairs	105,935
Tableware and flatware.	107,052	Jewelry	79,753
Drinking glasses	82,517	Yard and garden equipment:	
Home furnishing		Lawn mowers	81,948
Beds.	518,441	Sports and recreation equipment:	
Tables [1]	305,214	Bicycles	534,883
Chairs	306,523	Skateboards	113,329
Household cabinets, racks, and shelves . .	268,183	Trampolines	111,851
Home structures, construction:		Swimming pools	79,601
Stairs or steps.	1,138,196	Playground climbing equipment	80,206

[1] Excludes baby changing and television tables or stands.
Source: National Safety Council, Itasca, IL, *Accident Facts*, annual through 1998, beginning 1999, *Injury Facts, Annual* (copyright); <http://www.nsc.org/lrs/statstop.htm>.

Table 174. Costs of Unintentional Injuries: 2004

[**574.8 represents $574,800,000,000.** Covers costs of deaths or disabling injuries together with vehicle accidents and fires]

Cost	Amount (bil. dol.) Total [1]	Motor vehicle	Work	Home	Other	Percent distribution Total [1]	Motor vehicle	Work	Home	Other
Total	574.8	240.6	142.2	129.0	83.4	100.0	100.0	100.0	100.0	100.0
Wage and productivity losses [2]	298.4	86.4	73.3	85.1	57.6	51.9	35.9	51.5	66.0	69.1
Medical expense	98.9	30.0	26.0	27.7	17.0	17.2	12.5	18.3	21.5	20.4
Administrative expenses [3]	111.9	81.0	31.0	6.8	5.7	19.5	33.7	21.8	5.3	6.8
Motor vehicle damage	41.0	41.0	1.6	(NA)	(NA)	7.1	17.0	1.1	(NA)	(NA)
Employer uninsured cost [4]	14.8	2.2	7.9	3.3	1.8	2.6	0.9	5.6	2.6	2.2
Fire loss	9.8	(NA)	2.4	6.1	1.3	1.7	(NA)	1.7	4.7	1.6

NA Not available.   [1] Excludes duplication between work and motor vehicle ($20.4 billion in 2004).   [2] Actual loss of wages and household production, and the present value of future earnings lost.   [3] Home and other costs may include costs of administering medical treatment claims for some motor-vehicle injuries filed through health insurance plans.   [4] Estimate of the uninsured costs incurred by employers, representing the money value of time lost by noninjured workers.
Source: National Safety Council, Itasca, IL, *Accident Facts*, annual through 1998, beginning 1999, *Injury Facts, Annual* (copyright); <http://www.nsc.org/lrs/statstop.htm>.

Health and Nutrition   119

Table 175. **Specified Reportable Diseases—Cases Reported: 1980 to 2004**

[190.9 represents 190,900. Figures should be interpreted with caution. Although reporting of some of these diseases is incomplete, the figures are of value in indicating trends of disease incidence. Includes cases imported from outside the United States]

Disease	1980	1990	1995	1999	2000	2001	2002	2003	2004
AIDS [1]	(2)	41,595	71,547	45,104	40,758	41,868	42,745	44,232	44,108
Botulism [3]	89	92	97	154	138	155	118	129	133
Brucellosis (undulant fever)	183	85	98	82	87	136	125	104	114
Chickenpox (Varicella) [4] (1,000)	190.9	173.1	120.6	46.0	27.4	22.5	22.8	20.9	32.9
Coccidoidomycosis	(2)	(2)	(2)	2,826	2,867	3,922	4,968	4,870	6,449
Cholera	9	6	23	6	5	3	2	2	5
Cryptosporidiosis	(2)	(2)	(NA)	2,361	3,128	3,785	3,016	3,506	3,577
Diphtheria	3	4	–	1	1	2	1	1	–
Encephalitis/menigitis, arboviral West Nile	(2)	(2)	(2)	(2)	(2)	(2)	2,840	2,866	1,273
Enterohemorrhagic Escherichia coli 0157:H7	(2)	(2)	2,139	4,513	4,528	3,287	3,840	2,671	2,544
Giardiasis	(2)	(2)	(2)	(2)	(2)	(2)	21,206	19,709	20,636
Haemophilus influenza	(2)	(2)	1,180	1,309	1,398	1,597	1,743	2,013	2,085
Hansen disease (Leprosy)	223	198	144	108	91	79	96	95	105
Hepatitis: A (infectious) (1,000)	29.1	31.4	31.6	17.0	13.4	10.6	8.8	7.7	5.9
B (serum) (1,000)	19.0	21.1	10.8	7.7	8.0	7.8	8.0	7.5	6.2
C/Non-A, non-B (1,000) [5]	(2)	2.6	4.6	3.1	3.2	4.0	1.8	1.1	0.7
Legionellosis	(2)	1,370	1,241	1,108	1,127	1,168	1,321	2,232	2,093
Lyme disease	(2)	(2)	11,700	16,273	17,730	17,029	23,763	21,273	19,804
Malaria	2,062	1,292	1,419	1,666	1,560	1,544	1,430	1,402	1,458
Measles (1,000)	13.5	27.8	0.3	0.1	0.1	0.1	–	0.1	–
Meningococcal infections	2,840	2,451	3,243	2,501	2,256	2,333	1,814	1,756	1,361
Mumps (1,000)	8.6	5.3	0.9	0.4	0.3	0.3	0.3	0.2	0.3
Pertussis [6] (1,000)	1.7	4.6	5.1	7.3	7.9	7.6	9.8	11.6	25.8
Plague	18	2	9	9	6	2	2	1	3
Poliomyelitis, acute	9	6	7	2	–	–	–	–	–
Psittacosis	124	113	64	16	17	25	18	12	12
Rabies, animal	6,421	4,826	7,811	6,730	6,934	7,150	7,609	6,846	6,345
Rabies, human	–	1	5	–	4	1	3	2	7
Rocky Mountain spotted fever	1,163	651	590	579	495	695	1,104	1,091	1,713
Rubella [7]	3,904	1,125	128	267	176	23	18	7	10
Salmonellosis [8] (1,000)	33.7	48.6	46.0	40.6	39.6	40.5	44.3	43.7	42.2
Shigellosis [9] (1,000)	19.0	27.1	32.1	17.5	22.9	20.2	23.5	23.6	14.6
Streptococcal disease, invasive, Group A	(2)	(2)	(2)	2,667	3,144	3,750	4,720	5,872	4,395
Streptococcus pneumoniae, invasive: Drug-resistant	(2)	(2)	(2)	4,625	4,533	2,896	2,546	2,356	2,590
Age less than 5 years	(2)	(2)	(2)	(2)	(2)	498	513	845	1,162
Tetanus	95	64	41	40	35	37	25	20	34
Toxic-shock syndrome	(2)	322	191	113	135	127	109	133	95
Trichinosis	131	129	29	12	16	22	14	6	5
Tuberculosis [10] (1,000)	27.7	25.7	22.9	17.5	16.4	16.0	15.1	14.9	14.5
Typhoid fever	510	552	369	346	377	368	321	356	322
Sexually transmitted diseases: Chancroid	788	4,212	606	143	78	38	67	54	30
Chlamydia (1,000)	(2)	(2)	478	657	702	783	835	877	929
Gonorrhea (1,000)	1,004	690	393	360	359	362	352	335	330
Syphilis (1,000)	69	134	69	36	32	32	34	34	33

– Represents zero. [1] Acquired immunodeficiency syndrome was not a notifiable disease until 1984. Figures are shown for years in which cases were reported to the CDC. Beginning 1995, based on revised classification system and expanded surveillance case definition. [2] Disease was not notifiable. [3] Includes foodborne, infant, wound, and unspecified cases. [4] Chickenpox was taken off the nationally notifiable list in 1991 but many states continue to report. [5] Includes some persons positive for antibody to hepatitis C virus who do not have hepatitis. [6] Whooping cough. [7] German measles. Excludes rubella, congenital syndrome. [8] Excludes typhoid fever. [9] Bacillary dysentery. [10] Newly reported active cases.

Source: U.S. Centers for Disease Control and Prevention, Atlanta, GA, *Summary of Notifiable Diseases, United States, 2004, Morbidity and Mortality Weekly Report*, Vol. 53, No. 53, June 16, 2006. <http://www.cdc.gov/mmwr/PDF/wk/mm5353.pdf>.

Table 176. **AIDS, Syphilis, and Tuberculosis Cases Reported by State: 2004**

State	AIDS	Syphilis	Tuber-culosis	State	AIDS	Syphilis	Tuber-culosis	State	AIDS	Syphilis	Tuber-culosis
U.S.	[1]44,108	33,401	14,517	KS	118	87	62	ND	18	–	4
				KY	255	151	127	OH	685	571	219
AL	476	639	43	LA	1,027	1,645	249	OK	202	168	178
AK	55	15	211	ME	60	7	20	OR	282	108	106
AZ	607	974	272	MD	1,453	1,002	314	PA	1,663	574	327
AR	185	249	132	MA	576	517	283	RI	133	104	51
CA	4,764	4,586	2,989	MI	654	806	273	SC	768	523	234
CO	350	179	127	MN	220	145	199	SD	12	–	11
CT	653	169	101	MS	478	404	119	TN	777	799	279
DE	163	61	32	MO	408	268	127	TX	3,307	4,205	1,683
DC	990	357	81	MT	8	4	15	UT	81	78	36
FL	5,869	2,964	1,076	NE	68	15	39	VT	17	3	6
GA	1,682	1,588	536	NV	304	253	95	VA	798	610	329
HI	149	36	116	NH	45	26	24	WA	447	336	244
ID	20	78	11	NJ	1,849	826	482	WV	97	18	24
IL	1,702	1,345	569	NM	188	251	42	WI	178	127	95
IN	406	273	128	NY	7,624	4,468	1,363	WY	21	6	5
IA	64	36	47	NC	1,152	747	382				

– Represents zero. [1] Includes cases among persons with unknown state of residence.

Source: U.S. Centers for Disease Control and Prevention, Atlanta, GA, *Summary of Notifiable Diseases, United States, 2004, Morbidity and Mortality Weekly Report*, Vol. 53, No. 53, June 16, 2006. <http://www.cdc.gov/mmwr/PDF/wk/mm5353.pdf>.

120 Health and Nutrition

Table 177. Reported AIDS Cases for Adults and Adolescents by Transmission Category and Sex: Cumulative Through 2004

[Provisional. For cases reported in the year shown. Includes Puerto Rico, Virgin Islands, Guam, and U.S. Pacific Islands. Acquired immunodeficiency syndrome (AIDS) is a specific group of diseases or conditions which are indicative of severe immunosuppression related to infection with the human immunodeficiency virus (HIV). Data are subject to retrospective changes and may differ from those data in Table 175]

Exposure category	2004			Cumulative through 2004[1]		
	Total	Male	Female	Total	Male	Female
Persons 13 years old and over, total	**44,615**	**32,756**	**11,859**	**908,905**	**737,300**	**171,603**
Male-to-male sexual contact.	15,607	15,607	(X)	402,722	402,722	(X)
Injection drug use.	6,919	4,564	2,355	219,053	155,872	63,181
Male-to-male sexual contact and injection drug use	1,696	1,696	(X)	60,038	60,038	(X)
Hemophilia/coagulation disorder	92	71	21	5,427	5,096	331
Heterosexual contact	8,651	3,373	5,278	117,887	43,347	74,540
Sex with injection drug user	1,306	435	871	35,616	11,048	24,568
Sex with bisexual male	251	(X)	251	4,617	(X)	4,617
Sex with person with hemophilia	19	4	15	556	78	478
Sex with HIV-infected transfusion recipient.	66	29	37	1,250	517	733
Sex with HIV-infected person, risk factor not specified.	7,009	2,905	4,104	75,848	31,704	44,144
Receipt of blood transfusion, blood components, or tissue.	196	90	106	9,274	5,163	4,111
Other/risk not reported or identified	11,454	7,355	65,062	94,504	65,062	29,440

X Not applicable.   [1] Includes persons with a diagnosis of AIDS, reported from the beginning of the epidemic through 2004. Cumulative total includes persons with characteristics unknown.

Source: U.S. Centers for Disease Control and Prevention, Atlanta, GA, *HIV/AIDS Surveillance Report, 2004*, Volume 16. <http://www.cdc.gov/hiv/topics/surveillance/resources/reports/2004report/default.htm> (accessed 6 March 2006).

Table 178. Estimated Number of Persons Living With Acquired Immunodeficiency Syndrome (AIDS) by Year and Selected Characteristics: 2000 to 2004

[These numbers do not represent reported case counts. Rather, these numbers are point estimates, which result from adjustments of reported case counts. The reported case counts are adjusted for reporting delays and for redistribution of cases in persons initially reported without an identified risk factor. The estimates do not include adjustment for incomplete reporting. Data for years 2000 to 2003 have been revised. See the Commentary section in the 2004 report]

Age and characteristic	2000	2001	2002	2003	2004
Total [1]	**320,177**	**341,773**	**364,496**	**388,477**	**415,193**
AGE AS OF END OF YEAR					
Less than 13 years old	2,843	2,611	2,353	2,034	1,695
13 and 14 years old	513	640	718	759	776
15 to 24 years	4,944	5,201	5,614	6,268	6,985
25 to 34 years	54,473	51,685	49,672	48,228	47,390
35 to 44 years	143,920	150,625	156,011	160,559	164,263
45 to 54 years	85,445	97,796	110,412	123,385	137,972
55 to 64 years	22,089	26,179	31,415	37,364	44,261
65 years old and over	5,950	7,036	8,300	9,880	11,850
RACE/ETHNICITY					
White, not Hispanic	119,420	125,279	131,672	138,238	145,935
Black, not Hispanic	132,090	142,552	153,512	165,246	178,233
Hispanic	63,894	68,673	73,463	78,557	84,001
Asian/Pacific Islander	2,612	2,893	3,242	3,638	4,045
American Indian/Alaska Native	1,099	1,187	1,288	1,404	1,506
MALE ADULT/ADOLESCENT TRANSMISSION CATEGORY					
Males 13 years old and over, total	248,726	264,267	280,917	298,272	317,698
Male-to-male sexual contact.	142,069	151,511	161,937	173,086	185,326
Injection drug use.	57,778	60,150	62,335	64,432	67,091
Male-to-male sexual contact and injection drug use . . .	22,603	23,293	23,953	24,627	25,367
Heterosexual contact	22,568	25,480	28,738	32,071	35,671
Other [2]	3,708	3,833	3,954	4,057	4,242
FEMALE ADULT/ADOLESCENT TRANSMISSION CATEGORY					
Females 13 years old and over, total	67,601	73,610	79,639	86,262	93,566
Injection drug use.	26,656	27,924	28,955	30,033	31,472
Heterosexual contact	39,121	43,708	48,559	53,947	59,599
Other [2]	1,824	1,977	2,125	2,282	2,494
CHILD (LESS THAN 13 YEARS AT DIAGNOSIS)					
Child (under 13 years old) total.	3,848	3,895	3,939	3,941	3,927
Perinatal	3,706	3,753	3,799	3,807	3,797
Other [3]	142	142	140	134	131

[1] Includes persons of unknown or multiple race and of unknown sex. Because column totals were calculated independently of the values for the subpopulations, the values in each column may not sum to the column total.   [2] Includes hemophilia, blood transfusion, perinatal and risk not reported or not identified.   [3] Includes hemophilia, blood transfusion, and risk not reported or not identified.

Source: U.S. Centers for Disease Control and Prevention, Atlanta, GA, *HIV/AIDS Surveillance Report, 2004*, Volume 16. <http://www.cdc.gov/hiv/topics/surveillance/resources/reports/2004report/default.htm> (accessed 6 March 2006).

Health and Nutrition   121

Table 179. **Children Immunized Against Specified Diseases: 1995 to 2004**

[In percent. Covers civilian noninstitutionalized population ages 19 months to 35 months. Based on estimates from the National Immunization Survey. The health care providers of the children are contacted to verify and/or complete vaccination information. Results are based on race/ethnic status of the child]

Vaccination	1995, total	2000, total	2004 [1] Total	White, non-Hispanic	Black, non-Hispanic	His-panic [2]	American Indian/ Alaska Native [3]	Asian [3]
Diphtheria-tetanus-pertussis (DTP) diphtheria-tetanus:								
3+ doses	95	94	95.9	96.5	94.7	95.3	95.1	97.2
4+ doses	79	82	85.5	87.7	79.5	84.1	76.7	89.6
Polio: 3+ doses	88	90	91.6	92.1	90.4	91.2	86.5	92.8
Measles, mumps, rubella vaccine	90	91	93.0	93.5	90.7	93.2	88.8	94.1
Hib: 3+ doses [4]	92	93	93.5	94.7	90.9	92.6	90.2	91.5
Hepatitis B: 3+ doses	68	90	92.4	93.0	90.8	91.9	91.2	93.0
Varicella [5]	(NA)	68	87.5	86.5	86.3	89.1	84.0	91.1
PCV: 3+ doses [6]	(X)	(X)	73.2	75.3	68.2	70.4	75.0	76.0
4+ DTP/3+ polio/1+ MCV [7]	76	78	83.5	85.7	77.8	82.2	75.6	87.4
4+ DTP/3+ polio/1+ MCV/3+ Hib	74	76	82.5	85.1	76.0	81.2	74.6	83.5

NA Not available.   X Not Applicable.   [1] Children in the Q1 2004 - Q4 2004 National Immunization Survey were born between February 2001 and June 2003.   [2] Children of Hispanic ethnicity may be of any race.   [3] Non-Hispanic.   [4] Haemophilus influenzae type B.   [5] Data collection for varicella (chicken pox) began in July 1996.   [6] PCV = Pneumococcal conjugate vaccine.   [7] MCV = Measles containing vaccine.

Source: U.S. Centers for Disease Control and Prevention, Atlanta, GA, National Immunization Program, Data and Statistics, *"Immunization Coverage in the U.S."*; <http://www.cdc.gov/nip/coverage/default.htm>.

Table 180. **Learning Disability or Attention Deficit Hyperactivity Disorder for Children 3–17 Years of Age by Selected Characteristics: 2004**

[In thousands, except percent (61,285 represents 61,285,000). Learning Disability is based on the question, "Has a representative from a school or a health professional ever told you that (child's name) has a learning disability?" Attention Deficit Hyperactivity Disorder is based on the question, "Has a doctor or health professional ever told you that (child's name) had Attention Hyperactivity Disorder or Attention Deficit Disorder?"]

Selected characteristics	Total	Ever told had Learning disability Number	Percent	Attention deficit hyperactivity disorder Number	Percent
Total [1] (age-adjusted)	61,285	4,881	8.0	4,527	7.4
Total [1] (crude)	61,285	4,881	8.0	4,527	7.4
SEX:					
Male	31,476	2,989	9.5	3,194	10.2
Female	29,809	1,892	6.3	1,333	4.4
AGE: [2]					
3 to 4 years old	8,201	[4]202	[4]2.5	[4]151	[4]1.8
5 to 11 years old	28,110	2,063	7.4	1,822	6.5
12 to 17 years old	24,974	2,615	10.5	2,553	10.2
RACE:					
Race alone [3]	59,655	4,724	7.9	4,374	7.3
White	47,346	3,717	7.9	3,545	7.5
Black or African American	9,278	875	9.4	762	8.2
American Indian or Alaska Native	559	[4]79	[4]14.2	[4]22	[4]3.8
Asian	2,364	[4]46	[4]1.9	[4]38	[4]1.6
Native Hawaiian or Other Pacific Islander	108	(B)	(B)	(B)	(B)
2 or more races [5]	1,630	157	10.4	152	10.0
HISPANIC ORIGIN AND RACE: [6]					
Hispanic or Latino	11,491	647	5.8	462	4.1
Mexican or Mexican American	7,915	441	5.7	265	3.5
Not Hispanic or Latino	49,794	4,234	8.4	4,065	8.1
White, single race	36,685	3,115	8.4	3,147	8.5
Black or African American, single race	8,963	855	9.5	709	7.8

B Base figure too small to meet statistical standards for reliability of a derived figure.   [1] Includes other races not shown separately.   [2] Estimates for age groups are not age adjusted.   [3] Refers to persons who indicated only a single race group.   [4] Figures do not meet standard of reliability or precision.   [5] Refers to all persons who indicated more than one race group.   [6] Persons of Hispanic or Latino origin may be of any race or combination of races.

Source: National Center for Health Statistics, *Vital and Health Statistics, Series 10, Number 227, Summary Health Statistics for U.S. Children: National Health Interview Survey, 2004*; <http://www.cdc.gov/nchs/products/pubs/pubd/series/ser.htm>.

Table 181. **Number of Persons With a Disability by Age Group and by State: 2004**

[In thousands (37,859 represents 37,859,000). A disability is a long-lasting sensory, physical, mental, or emotional condition (see footnotes below). Data are limited to the household population and exclude the population living in institutions, college dormitories, and other group quarters. Based on data from the 2004 American Community Survey (ACS). See text, Section 1 and Appendix III]

State	Total	5 to 15 years [1]	16 to 64 years [2]	65 years and over [3]	State	Total	5 to 15 years [1]	16 to 64 years [2]	65 years and over [3]
U.S.	37,859	2,824	21,495	13,539	MO	818	54	472	292
AL	768	49	460	258	MT	128	7	75	46
AK	86	10	57	19	NE	224	17	125	83
AZ	723	58	401	265	NV	254	18	151	85
AR	534	37	323	174	NH	165	19	93	52
CA	3,978	261	2,276	1,441	NJ	955	82	495	378
CO	481	36	292	153	NM	283	17	170	97
CT	364	23	194	147	NY	2,297	171	1,276	850
DE	114	11	65	39	NC	1,191	97	668	425
DC	68	6	39	24	ND	80	6	43	31
FL	2,375	151	1,202	1,023	OH	1,596	132	905	559
GA	1,069	81	633	356	OK	582	37	352	192
HI	143	10	73	61	OR	528	41	306	181
ID	195	15	111	69	PA	1,781	132	967	681
IL	1,362	98	722	542	RI	150	14	83	53
IN	831	71	469	292	SC	632	47	375	209
IA	375	27	190	158	SD	90	6	47	37
KS	347	26	196	125	TN	925	59	557	308
KY	786	47	506	233	TX	2,636	230	1,513	894
LA	676	48	398	229	UT	240	24	141	74
ME	212	17	128	67	VT	88	9	51	28
MD	657	60	362	235	VA	909	71	527	311
MA	729	56	395	278	WA	826	57	507	262
MI	1,396	120	810	466	WV	394	19	238	137
MN	542	39	310	193	WI	675	55	387	233
MS	533	42	319	172	WY	70	5	43	22

[1] Persons aged 5 to 15 were classified as having a disability if they reported any one of the four conditions; sensory, physical, mental, or self-care disability. [2] Persons aged 16 to 64 were classified as having a disability if they reported any one of the six conditions; sensory, physical, mental, self-care disability, go-outside-home, or employment disability. [3] Persons 65 years and over were classified as having a disability if they reported any one of the five conditions; sensory, physical, mental, self-care disability, or go-outside-home disability.
Source: U.S. Census Bureau, "American Factfinder, 2004 American Community Survey, Summary Table, Sex by Age by Disability Status for the Civilian Noninstitutionalized Population 5 Years and Over.". <http://www.factfinder.census.gov/>.

Table 182. **Persons With Limitation of Activity Caused by Chronic Conditions: 2000 to 2004**

[In percent. Limitation of activity is assessed by asking respondents a series of questions about limitations in their ability to perform activities usual for their age group because of a physical, mental, or emotional problem. Based on the National Health Interview Survey, a sample survey of the civilian noninstitutionalized population; see Appendix III]

Characteristic	2000	2002	2003	2004	Characteristic	2000	2002	2003	2004
Total [1,2]	11.7	12.4	12.1	11.9	Male [2]	11.7	12.3	11.9	11.8
Under 18 years	6.0	7.1	6.9	7.0	Female [2]	11.5	12.3	12.2	11.9
18 to 44 years	5.8	6.3	6.0	6.0					
45 to 64 years	12.4	13.7	13.0	12.5	White, non-Hispanic [2]	11.5	12.1	11.8	12.1
55 to 64 years	19.7	21.1	21.1	19.9	Black, non-Hispanic [2]	14.3	14.9	15.3	15.3
65 to 74 years	26.1	25.2	26.3	25.5	Hispanic [2,3]	10.3	10.7	10.2	10.2
75 years and over	45.1	45.1	44.0	43.9	Mexican	10.4	10.8	9.7	10.1

[1] Includes all other races not shown separately. [2] Estimates for all persons are age adjusted to the year 2000 standard using six age groups: Under 18 years, 18–44 years, 45–54 years, 55–64 years, 65–74 years, and 75 years and over. [3] Persons of Hispanic origin may be of any race.
Source: U.S. National Center for Health Statistics, Health, United States, 2006. <http://www.cdc.gov/nchs/hus.htm>

Table 183. **Persons 65 Years Old and Over With Limitation of Activity Caused by Chronic Conditions: 2000 to 2004**

[In percent. Covers noninstitutionalized persons 65 years old and over. To determine activities of daily living (ADL) limitations respondents were asked "Because of a physical, mental, or emotional problem, does (this person) need the help of other persons with personal care needs, such as eating, bathing, dressing, or getting around inside this home?" Instrumental activities of daily living (IADL) were determined by asking respondents "Because of a physical, mental, or emotional problem, does (this person) need the help of other persons in handling routine needs, such as everyday household chores, doing necessary business, shopping, or getting around for other purposes?" See also headnote, Table 182]

Characteristic	Percent with ADL limitation				Percent with IADL limitation			
	2000	2002	2003	2004	2000	2002	2003	2004
Total [1,2]	6.3	6.1	6.4	6.1	12.7	12.2	12.2	11.5
55 to 74 years	3.3	2.7	3.1	2.9	6.6	6.0	6.5	5.5
75 years and over	9.5	9.8	9.9	9.5	19.3	18.9	18.4	18.1
Male [2]	5.1	4.7	5.2	4.8	9.2	7.8	8.6	8.4
Female [2]	7.0	7.0	7.2	6.9	15.1	15.2	14.6	13.6
Not Hispanic or Latino [2]	6.1	5.9	6.1	5.8	12.6	12.1	12.1	11.3
White	5.7	5.5	5.7	5.5	12.1	11.5	11.4	10.7
Black or African American	10.1	9.9	10.4	8.7	19.1	18.4	19.0	17.1
Hispanic or Latino [2,3]	8.6	9.2	10.3	10.4	13.4	13.1	13.8	14.8
Mexican	9.4	10.1	9.8	10.7	16.3	13.9	15.1	15.3

[1] Includes other races not shown separately. [2] Estimates are age adjusted to the year 2000 standard using two age groups: 55–74 years and 75 years and over. [3] Persons of Hispanic origin may be of any race.
Source: U.S. National Center for Health Statistics, Health, United States, 2006.

Health and Nutrition 123

Table 184. **Persons 18 Years and Over With Selected Diseases and Conditions, by Selected Characteristics: 2004**

[In thousands (215,191 represents 215,191,000). Based on the National Health Interview Survey, a sample survey of the civilian noninstitutionalized population; see Appendix III]

Selected characteristic	Total persons	Diabetes[1,2]	Ulcers[1]	Kidney disease[3,4]	Liver disease[3]	Arthritis diagnosis[5]	Chronic joint symptoms[5,6]
Total[7]	215,191	15,126	14,828	3,652	2,860	46,515	58,005
SEX:							
Male	103,552	7,541	7,129	1,447	1,293	18,497	25,797
Female	111,640	7,585	7,699	2,205	1,568	28,018	32,209
AGE:							
18 to 44 years old	110,417	2,173	4,956	972	878	8,841	17,349
45 to 64 years old	70,182	6,963	5,772	1,250	1,449	20,169	24,439
65 to 74 years old	18,360	3,393	2,002	629	263	8,496	8,181
75 years old and over	16,232	2,598	2,148	801	270	9,008	8,036
RACE:							
Race alone:[8]	212,861	14,952	14,649	3,595	2,828	45,926	57,275
White	178,552	11,811	12,956	2,920	2,412	40,163	50,285
Black or African American	24,602	2,387	1,333	531	338	4,567	5,434
American Indian or Alaska Native	1,501	194	129	[9]32	(B)	323	467
Asian	7,853	516	231	112	[9]59	866	1,060
Native Hawaiian or other Pacific Islander	352	(B)	–	–	–	(B)	(B)
2 or more races[10]	2,330	175	179	57	[9]32	589	730
HISPANIC ORIGIN AND RACE:[11]							
Hispanic or Latino origin	26,798	1,879	1,292	626	416	3,095	4,319
Mexican or Mexican American	17,139	1,148	759	365	228	1,641	2,496

– Represents zero.   B Figure too small to meet statistical standards for reliability of a derived figure.   [1] Respondents were asked if they had ever been told by a health professional that they had an ulcer or diabetes. A person may be represented in more than one column.   [2] Excludes borderline diabetes.   [3] Respondents were asked if they had been told in the last 12 months by a health professional that they had weak or failing kidneys or any kind of liver condition.   [4] Excludes kidney stones, bladder infections, or incontinence.   [5] Respondents were asked if they had ever been told by a health professional that they had some form of arthritis, rheumatoid arthritis, gout, lupus, or fibromyalgia.   [6] Respondents with joint symptoms that began more than 3 months ago prior to interview. Excludes back and neck.   [7] Total includes other races not shown separately.   [8] Refers to persons who indicated only a single race group.   [9] Figures do not meet standard of reliability or precision.   [10] Refers to all persons who indicated more than one race group.   [11] Persons of Hispanic or Latino origin may be of any race or combination of races.

Source: National Center for Health Statistics, *Vital and Health Statistics, Series 10, Number 228, Summary Health Statistics for U.S. Adults: National Health Interview Survey, 2004;* <http://www.cdc.gov/nchs/products/pubs/pubd/series/ser.htm>.

Table 185. **Persons 18 Years of Age and Over with Selected Circulatory Diseases, by Selected Characteristics: 2004**

[In thousands (215,191 represents 215,191,000). In separate questions, respondents were asked if they had ever been told by a doctor or other health professional that they had: hypertension (or high blood pressure); coronary heart disease, angina (or angina pectoris); heart attack (or myocardial infarction); any other heart condition or disease not already mentioned; or a stroke. A person may be represented in more than one column. Based on the National Health Interview Survey, a sample survey of the civilian noninstitutionalized population; see Appendix III]

Characteristic	Total persons	Heart disease[1] All types	Coronary[2]	Hypertension[3]	Stroke
Total[4]	215,191	24,666	13,621	47,493	5,519
SEX:					
Male	103,552	12,107	7,934	22,040	2,657
Female	111,640	12,559	5,688	25,453	2,862
AGE:					
18–44 years old	110,417	4,953	1,184	8,133	510
45–64 years old	70,182	8,636	4,858	21,303	1,750
65–74 years old	18,360	4,994	3,358	9,089	1,257
75 years old and over	16,232	6,082	4,221	8,968	2,002
RACE:					
Race Alone[5]	212,861	24,415	13,493	47,004	5,467
White	178,552	21,732	12,056	39,111	4,600
Black or African American	24,602	2,088	1,082	6,484	667
American Indian or Alaska Native	1,501	144	[6]88	318	(B)
Asian	7,853	436	253	1,038	131
Native Hawaiian or Other Pacific Islander	352	(B)	(B)	[6]42	(B)
2 or more races[7]	2,330	251	128	489	[6]52
HISPANIC ORIGIN AND RACE:[8]					
Hispanic or Latino	26,798	1,685	1,042	3,734	460
Mexican or Mexican American	17,139	1,007	642	2,216	309

B Figure too small to meet statistical standards for reliability of a derived figure.   [1] Heart disease includes coronary heart disease, angina pectoris, heart attack, or any other heart condition or disease.   [2] Coronary heart disease includes coronary heart disease, angina pectoris, or heart attack.   [3] Persons had to have been told on two or more different visits that they had hypertension, or high blood pressure, to be classified as hypertensive.   [4] Includes other races not shown separately.   [5] Refers to persons who indicated only a single race group.   [6] Figures do not meet standard of reliability or precision.   [7] Refers to all persons who indicated more than one race group.   [8] Persons of Hispanic or Latino origin may be of any race or combination of races.

Source: National Center for Health Statistics, *Vital and Health Statistics, Series 10, Number 228, Summary Health Statistics for U.S. Adults: National Health Interview Survey, 2004;* <http://www.cdc.gov/nchs/products/pubd/series/ser.htm>.

Table 186. Selected Respiratory Diseases Among Persons 18 Years of Age and Over by Selected Characteristics: 2004

[In thousands (215,191 represents 215,191,000). Respondents were asked in two separate questions if they had ever been told by a doctor or other health professional that they had emphysema or asthma. Respondents who had been told they had asthma were asked if they still had asthma. Respondents were asked in three separate questions if they had been told by a doctor or other health professional in the past 12 months that they had hay fever, sinusitis, or bronchitis. Based on the National Health Interview Survey, a sample survey of the civilian noninstitutionalized population; see Appendix III]

Selected characteristic	Total persons	Selected respiratory conditions [1]					
		Emphy- sema	Asthma		Hay fever	Sinusitis	Chronic bronchitis
			Ever	Still			
Total [2].	215,191	3,576	21,300	14,358	18,629	30,789	9,047
SEX:							
Male.	103,552	1,871	8,796	5,148	8,161	10,597	2,757
Female.	111,640	1,704	12,503	9,210	10,468	20,192	6,291
AGE:							
18 to 44 years old.	110,417	309	10,959	7,058	8,777	13,976	3,483
45 to 64 years old.	70,182	1,393	6,973	4,871	7,252	11,769	3,413
65 to 74 years old.	18,360	904	1,893	1,368	1,475	2,780	1,126
75 years old and over	16,232	970	1,474	1,061	1,126	2,265	1,026
RACE:							
Race alone: [3]							
White	212,861	3,541	20,945	14,106	18,331	30,368	8,904
Black or African American.	178,552	3,207	17,376	11,750	15,948	26,352	7,842
American Indian or Alaska Native.	24,602	237	2,755	1,890	1,667	3,278	878
Asian	1,501	[4]30	251	147	84	203	[4]45
Native Hawaiian or other Pacific Islander	7,853	[4]59	541	302	606	521	131
	352	(B)	(B)	(B)	(B)	(B)	(B)
2 or more races [5]	2,330	[4]35	355	252	298	421	143
HISPANIC ORIGIN AND RACE: [6]							
Hispanic or Latino.	26,798	155	2,013	1,163	1,561	1,979	669
Mexican or Mexican American.	17,139	82	997	604	873	1,064	354
Not Hispanic or Latino.	188,393	3,420	19,287	13,195	17,068	28,810	8,378
White, single race	153,365	3,061	15,635	10,740	14,499	24,525	7,233
Black or African American, single race . . .	23,806	235	2,648	1,831	1,615	3,184	865

B Figure too small to meet statistical standards for reliability of a derived figure.   [1] A person may be represented in more than one column.   [2] Total includes other races not shown separately.   [3] Refers to persons who indicated only a single race group.   [4] Figure does not meet standard of reliability or precision.   [5] Refers to all persons who indicated more than one race group.   [6] Persons of Hispanic or Latino origin may be of any race or combination of races.

Source: National Center for Health Statistics, *Vital and Health Statistics, Series 10, Number 228, Summary Health Statistics for U.S. Adult: National Health Interview Survey,* <http://www.cdc.gov/nchs/products/pubs/pubd/series/ser.htm>.

Table 187. Asthma Incidence Among Children Under 18 Years of Age by Selected Characteristics: 2004

[In thousands, except percent (73,067 represents 73,067,000). Based on the National Health Interview Survey, a sample survey of the civilian noninstitutionalized population; see Appendix III]

Selected characteristic	Total	Ever told had asthma		Had asthma attack in past 12 months	
		Number	Percent	Number	Percent
Total [1] (age-adjusted)	73,067	8,890	12.2	3,975	5.5
Total [1] (crude)	73,067	8,890	12.2	3,975	5.4
SEX:					
Male.	37,351	5,524	14.8	2,497	6.7
Female.	35,715	3,366	9.4	1,478	4.1
AGE: [2]					
0 to 4 years old	19,983	1,454	7.3	781	3.9
5 to 11 years old.	28,110	3,653	13.0	1,710	6.1
12 to 17 years old.	24,974	3,782	15.2	1,484	5.9
RACE:					
Race alone: [3]					
White	71,024	8,477	12.0	3,816	5.4
Black or African American.	56,340	6,328	11.3	2,844	5.1
American Indian or Alaska Native.	11,166	1,910	17.2	882	8.0
Asian	653	68	9.9	[4]29	(B)
Native Hawaiian or Other Pacific Islander	2,726	171	6.2	[4]61	[4]2.2
	139	–	–	–	–
2 or more races [5].	2,043	413	21.1	159	8.0
HISPANIC ORIGIN AND RACE: [6]					
Hispanic or Latino	13,956	1,423	10.4	568	4.2
Mexican or Mexican American.	9,673	851	9.1	277	3.0
Not Hispanic or Latino.	59,111	7,467	12.6	3,407	5.8
White, single race	43,405	5,059	11.6	2,329	5.3
Black or African American, single race . .	10,751	1,834	17.1	838	7.9

– Represents zero.   B Figure too small to meet statistical standards for reliability of a derived figure.   [1] Includes other races not shown separately.   [2] Estimates for age groups are not age adjusted.   [3] Refers to persons who indicated only a single race group.   [4] Figures do not meet standard of reliability or precision.   [5] Refers to all persons who indicated more than one race group.   [6] Persons of Hispanic or Latino origin may be of any race or combination of races.

Source: National Center for Health Statistics, *Vital and Health Statistics, Series 10, Number 227, Summary Health Statistics for U.S. Children: National Health Interview Survey, 2004;* <http://www.cdc.gov/nchs/products/pubs/pubd/series/ser.htm>.

Health   125

Table 188. **Cancer—Estimated New Cases, 2006, and Survival Rates, 1987–1989 to 1996–2002**

[1,400 represents 1,400,000. The 5-year relative survival rate, which is derived by adjusting the observed survival rate for expected mortality, represents the likelihood that a person will not die from causes directly related to their cancer within 5 years. Survival data shown are based on those patients diagnosed while residents of an area listed below during the time periods shown. Data are based on information collected as part of the National Cancer Institute's Surveillance, Epidemiology and End Results (SEER) program, a collection of population-based registries in five states (Connecticut, Hawaii, Iowa, New Mexico, Utah) and four metropolitan areas (Atlanta, Detroit, San Francisco-Oakland and Seattle-Puget Sound)]

| Site | Estimated new cases, [1] 2006 (1,000) | | | 5-year relative survival rates (percent) | | | | | | | |
| | | | | White | | | | Black | | | |
	Total	Male	Female	1987–1989	1990–1992	1993–1995	1996–2002	1987–1989	1990–1992	1993–1995	1996–2002
All sites [2]	1,400	720	680	57.7	62.4	64.0	67.5	43.7	48.3	53.4	57.2
Lung	174	93	82	13.8	14.6	15.3	15.8	11.2	10.8	13.2	12.8
Breast [3]	215	2	213	85.3	86.7	88.0	90.1	71.2	71.6	72.9	77.3
Colon and rectum	149	73	76	61.0	63.2	62.2	66.2	53.3	53.8	53.2	55.4
Colon	107	49	57	61.7	64.0	62.1	66.1	53.2	54.4	52.5	54.3
Rectum	42	24	18	59.5	61.3	62.4	66.4	53.6	52.0	55.4	58.6
Prostate	234	234	(X)	85.4	95.8	98.3	99.9	72.2	85.9	93.7	98.0
Bladder	61	45	17	81.4	82.0	83.4	82.9	63.4	64.8	62.7	64.5
Corpus uteri	41	(X)	41	85.7	87.2	86.6	87.0	59.3	57.1	62.3	62.2
Non-Hodgkin's lymphoma [4]	59	31	28	52.7	52.9	54.8	64.0	47.5	42.2	42.1	56.3
Oral cavity and pharynx	31	20	11	56.6	58.8	61.4	62.2	34.6	33.5	38.7	39.9
Leukemia [4]	35	20	15	45.3	47.8	49.6	50.3	37.0	37.2	42.2	38.7
Melanoma of skin	62	34	28	88.2	89.6	90.1	92.5	79.9	61.6	67.6	75.2
Pancreas	34	17	17	3.4	4.6	4.3	4.9	5.7	3.6	3.7	4.7
Kidney	39	25	14	58.5	62.2	63.6	65.8	55.8	57.9	59.2	66.0
Stomach	22	13	9	19.1	19.4	20.9	21.9	19.9	24.5	20.0	23.3
Ovary	20	(X)	20	39.9	42.5	42.6	44.6	35.5	36.8	42.6	38.9
Cervix uteri [5]	10	(X)	10	73.6	71.9	74.7	74.6	58.4	58.6	64.3	66.3

X Not applicable. [1] Estimates provided by American Cancer Society (www.cancer.org) are based on rates from the National Cancer Institute's SEER program. [2] Includes other sites not shown separately. [3] Survival rates for female only. [4] All types combined. [5] Invasive cancer only.

Source: U.S. National Institutes of Health, National Cancer Institute, <http://seer.cancer.gov/csr/19752003/>.

Table 189. **Cancer—Estimated New Cases and Deaths by State: 2006**

[In thousands (1,399.8 represents 1,399,800). Excludes basal and squamous cell skin cancers and in situ carcinomas except urinary bladder]

| State | New cases [1] | | | Deaths | | | State | New cases [1] | | | Deaths | | |
	Total [2]	Female breast	Lung	Total [2]	Female breast	Lung		Total [2]	Female breast	Lung	Total [2]	Female breast	Lung
U.S.	1,399.8	212.9	174.5	564.8	41.0	162.5	MO	31.1	4.6	4.1	12.5	0.9	3.9
AL	24.4	3.7	3.5	9.8	0.7	3.3	MT	4.8	0.6	0.6	1.9	0.1	0.6
AK	2.0	0.3	0.2	0.8	0.1	0.2	NE	8.5	1.2	1.0	3.4	0.2	0.9
AZ	25.5	3.7	3.1	10.3	0.7	2.9	NV	11.6	1.7	1.5	4.7	0.3	1.4
AR	15.2	2.0	2.4	6.1	0.4	2.2	NH	6.5	0.9	0.8	2.6	0.2	0.7
CA	138.7	21.2	14.9	56.0	4.1	13.9							
							NJ	43.9	8.1	5.0	17.7	1.6	4.6
CO	16.9	2.7	1.8	6.8	0.5	1.7	NM	8.2	1.1	0.8	3.3	0.2	0.8
CT	17.3	2.6	2.0	7.0	0.5	1.9	NY	88.2	14.4	9.9	35.6	2.8	9.2
DE	4.2	0.6	0.6	1.7	0.1	0.5	NC	40.9	6.3	5.5	16.5	1.2	5.1
DC	2.7	0.5	0.3	1.1	0.1	0.3	ND	3.2	0.5	0.3	1.3	0.1	0.3
FL	99.0	13.4	13.3	39.9	2.6	12.4							
							OH	61.3	9.6	7.9	24.7	1.9	7.4
GA	36.7	5.9	4.9	14.8	1.1	4.5	OK	18.6	2.9	2.6	7.5	0.6	2.4
HI	5.6	0.7	0.5	2.3	0.1	0.5	OR	18.3	2.8	2.3	7.4	0.5	2.1
ID	5.9	0.9	0.7	2.4	0.2	0.6	PA	73.6	12.3	8.5	29.7	2.4	7.9
IL	60.2	9.3	7.3	24.3	1.8	6.8	RI	5.9	0.8	0.7	2.4	0.2	0.6
IN	32.7	4.7	4.6	13.2	0.9	4.3							
							SC	22.5	3.2	3.0	9.1	0.6	2.8
IA	16.3	2.2	1.9	6.6	0.4	1.7	SD	4.1	0.5	0.4	1.6	0.1	0.4
KS	13.2	2.1	1.7	5.3	0.4	1.5	TN	32.1	4.6	4.7	13.0	0.9	4.4
KY	23.7	3.2	3.8	9.6	0.6	3.5	TX	85.6	13.2	10.8	34.5	2.5	10.0
LA	23.9	4.0	3.2	9.6	0.8	3.0	UT	6.6	1.2	0.5	2.7	0.2	0.5
ME	7.9	1.0	1.0	3.2	0.2	1.0							
							VT	3.0	0.5	0.4	1.2	0.1	0.4
MD	25.9	4.3	3.3	10.4	0.8	3.1	VA	35.0	6.1	4.8	14.1	1.2	4.5
MA	33.3	4.7	4.1	13.4	0.9	3.8	WA	28.4	4.0	3.5	11.4	0.8	3.3
MI	48.3	7.1	6.2	19.5	1.4	5.8	WV	11.3	1.4	1.6	4.6	0.3	1.5
MN	23.5	3.1	2.6	9.5	0.6	2.4	WI	26.4	4.0	3.0	10.7	0.8	3.0
MS	15.1	2.3	2.2	6.1	0.4	2.1	WY	2.5	0.3	0.3	1.0	0.1	0.3

[1] Estimates are offered as a rough guide and should be interpreted with caution. They are calculated according to the distribution of estimated cancer deaths by state. [2] Includes other types of cancer, not shown separately.

Source: American Cancer Society, Inc., Atlanta, Georgia, *Cancer Facts and Figures—2006* (copyright). <http://www.cancer.org/docroot /STT/stt0.asp>.

Table 190. **Use of Mammography for Women 40 Years Old and Over by Patient Characteristics: 1990 to 2003**

[Percent of women having a mammogram within the past 2 years. Covers civilian noninstitutional population. Based on National Health Interview Survey; see Appendix III. Data years 2001 and 2002 are not available]

Characteristic	1990	2000 [1]	2003 [2]	Characteristic	1990	2000 [1]	2003 [2]
Total [3]	51.4	70.4	69.7	Years of school completed:			
40 to 49 years old	55.1	64.3	64.4	Less than 12 years	36.4	57.7	58.1
50 years old and over . . .	49.7	73.6	72.4	12 years	52.7	69.7	67.8
50 to 64 years old	56.0	78.7	76.2	13 years or more.	62.8	76.2	75.1
65 years old and over . . .	43.4	67.9	67.7				
White, non-Hispanic	52.7	72.2	70.5	Poverty status: [5]			
Black, non-Hispanic.	46.0	67.9	70.5	Below poverty	28.7	54.8	55.3
Hispanic origin [4]	45.2	61.2	65.0	At or above poverty	54.8	72.1	71.5

[1] Adjusted data—data for 2000 have been reweighted using the 2000 census population controls. [2] Data for 2003 are weighted using the 2000 census population controls. [3] Includes all other races not shown separately and unknown education level and poverty status. [4] Persons of Hispanic origin may be of any race. [5] For explanation of poverty level, see text, Section 13, Income, Expenditures and Wealth.
Source: U.S. National Center for Health Statistics, *Health, United States*, annual. See also <http://www.cdc.gov/nchs/hus.htm>.

Table 191. **Current Cigarette Smoking: 1990 to 2004**

[In percent. Prior to 1992, a current smoker is a person who has smoked at least 100 cigarettes and who now smokes. Beginning 1995, definition includes persons who smoke only "some days." Excludes unknown smoking status. Based on the National Health Interview Survey; for details, see Appendix III]

Sex, age, and race	1990 [1]	1995 [1]	2000	2004	Sex, age, and race	1990 [1]	1995 [1]	2000	2004
Total smokers, age-adjusted [2]	**25.3**	**24.6**	**23.1**	**20.8**	Black, total	32.5	28.5	26.1	23.9
					18 to 24 years	21.3	[3]14.6	20.8	18.0
Male	28.0	26.5	25.2	23.0	25 to 34 years	33.8	25.1	23.3	21.2
Female	22.9	22.7	21.1	18.7	35 to 44 years	42.0	36.3	30.8	28.4
					45 to 64 years	36.7	33.9	32.2	29.2
White male.	27.6	26.2	25.5	23.0	65 years and over . .	21.5	28.5	14.2	14.1
Black male.	32.8	29.4	25.7	23.5	Female, total	22.8	22.6	21.0	18.5
White female.	23.5	23.4	22.0	19.5	18 to 24 years	22.5	21.8	25.1	21.5
Black female	20.8	23.5	20.7	16.9	25 to 34 years	28.2	26.4	22.5	21.0
					35 to 44 years	24.8	27.1	26.2	21.6
Total smokers.	**25.5**	**24.7**	**23.3**	**20.9**	45 to 64 years.	24.8	24.0	21.6	19.8
					65 years and over . .	11.5	11.5	9.3	8.1
Male, total	28.4	27.0	25.7	23.4	White, total	23.4	23.1	21.6	19.1
18 to 24 years.	26.6	27.8	28.5	25.6	18 to 24 years	25.4	24.9	28.7	22.9
25 to 34 years	31.6	29.5	29.0	26.1	25 to 34 years	28.5	27.3	25.1	22.6
35 to 44 years	34.5	31.5	30.2	26.5	35 to 44 years	25.0	27.0	26.6	22.7
45 to 64 years	29.3	27.1	26.4	25.0	45 to 64 years	25.4	24.3	21.4	20.1
65 years and over . . .	14.6	14.9	10.2	9.8	65 years and over . .	11.5	11.7	9.1	8.2
White, total	28.0	26.6	25.8	23.2	Black, total	21.2	23.5	20.8	17.3
18 to 24 years	27.4	28.4	30.9	26.7	18 to 24 years	[3]10.0	[3]8.8	14.2	15.6
25 to 34 years	31.6	29.9	29.9	26.3	25 to 34 years	29.1	26.7	15.5	18.3
35 to 44 years	33.5	31.2	30.6	26.6	35 to 44 years	25.5	31.9	30.2	18.9
45 to 64 years	28.7	26.3	25.8	24.4	45 to 64 years	22.6	27.5	25.6	20.9
65 years and over . .	13.7	14.1	9.8	9.4	65 years and over . .	11.1	13.3	10.2	6.7

[1] Data prior to 1997 are not strictly comparable with data for later years due to the 1997 questionnaire redesign. [2] Estimates are age adjusted to the year 2000 standard using five age groups: 18 to 24 years, 25 to 34 years, 35 to 44 years, 45 to 64 years, 65 years and over. [3] Data have a relative standard error of 20–30 percent.
Source: U.S. National Center for Health Statistics, *Health, United States*, annual. See also <www.cdc.gov/nchs/hus.htm>.

Table 192. **Current Cigarette Smoking by Sex and State: 2004**

[In percent. Current cigarette smoking is defined as persons 18 years and older who reported having smoked 100 or more cigarettes during their lifetime and who currently smoke every day or some days. Based on the Behavioral Risk Factor Surveillance System, a telephone survey of health behaviors of the civilian, noninstitutionalized U.S. population, 18 years old and over; for details, see source]

State	Total	Male	Female	State	Total	Male	Female	State	Total	Male	Female
U.S. [1] . .	**20.9**	**23.2**	**19.2**	KS	19.8	22.1	17.6	ND	19.9	24.1	15.8
				KY	27.6	29.3	25.9	OH	25.9	27.3	24.7
AL	24.9	29.0	21.2	LA	23.6	26.9	20.5	OK	26.1	28.1	24.2
AK	24.9	26.4	23.3	ME	21.0	22.6	19.5	OR	20.0	21.9	18.2
AZ	18.6	19.7	17.6	MD	19.7	22.7	16.9	PA	22.7	23.0	22.5
AR	25.7	28.1	23.4	MA	18.5	19.7	17.4	RI	21.3	23.7	19.2
CA	14.8	18.5	11.1	MI	23.4	25.0	21.8	SC	24.5	28.1	21.2
CO	20.1	22.3	17.8	MN	20.7	22.0	19.5	SD	20.3	22.0	18.7
CT	18.1	20.1	16.2	MS	24.6	29.1	20.5	TN	26.1	27.1	25.3
DE	24.5	28.4	20.9	MO	24.1	26.1	22.3	TX	20.6	23.7	17.5
DC	21.0	25.1	17.3	MT	20.4	20.6	20.2	UT	10.5	11.7	9.4
FL	20.4	23.3	17.7	NE	20.3	23.1	17.7	VT	20.0	21.8	18.3
GA	20.1	22.4	17.9	NV	23.2	24.7	21.7	VA	20.9	22.4	19.5
HI [2]	(NA)	(NA)	(NA)	NH	21.8	24.0	19.7	WA	19.2	20.1	18.3
ID	17.5	19.2	15.7	NJ	18.9	20.1	17.8	WV	26.9	27.4	26.4
IL	22.2	26.1	18.6	NM	20.3	22.8	17.9	WI	22.0	25.0	19.1
IN	25.0	26.8	23.2	NY	20.0	21.2	19.0	WY	21.7	21.6	21.9
IA	20.8	22.8	19.0	NC	23.2	26.6	20.0				

NA Not available. [1] Represents median value among the states and DC. For definition of median, see Guide to Tabular Presentations. [2] Hawaii completed 3 of 12 months of interviews in 2004; these data are not available in the aggregate 2004 dataset.
Source: U.S. Centers for Disease Control and Prevention, Atlanta, GA, *Morbidity and Mortality Weekly Report*, Vol. 54, No. 44, November 11, 2005; <http://www.cdc.gov/mmwr>.

Health and Nutrition 127

Table 193. **Substance Abuse Treatment Facilities and Clients: 1995 to 2005**

[As of October 2 (1995); As of October 1 (1996–2000), As of March 29 (2002), and as of March 31 (2003–2004). Based on the Uniform Facility Data Set (UFDS)/National Survey of Substance Abuse Treatment Services (N-SSATS) survey, a census of all known facilities that provide substance abuse treatment in the United States and associated jurisdictions. Selected missing data for responding facilities were imputed]

Primary focus	Number	Primary focus	Number	Type of care and type of problem	Number of clients
FACILITIES		CLIENTS		**2005, total** [1]	**1,080,437**
1995	10,746	1995	1,009,127	Outpatient rehab.	947,729
1996	10,641	1996	940,141	Outpatient detoxification. . .	13,464
1997	10,860	1997	929,086	24-hour rehab	105,557
1998	13,455	1998	1,038,378	24-hour detoxification	13,687
1999	15,239	2000	1,000,896		
2000	13,428	2002	1,136,287		
2002	13,720	2003	1,092,546	**2005, total** [1]	**1,066,248**
2003	13,623	2004	1,072,251	Drug only	366,334
2004	13,454			Alcohol only.	199,986
2005, total	**13,367**	**2005, total**	**1,080,437**	Both alcohol & drug.	499,928
Substance abuse treatment services	8,303	Substance abuse treatment services	747,068		
Mental health services. . .	1,063	Mental health services. . .	47,002	Total with a drug problem [2]	866,262
General health care	249	General health care	20,763	Total with an	
Both substance abuse and mental health.	3,568	Both substance abuse and mental health.	257,524	alcohol problem [3]	699,914
Other	184	Other	8,080		

[1] Excludes clients at facilities that did not provide data on type of substance abuse problem treated. [2] The sum of clients with a drug problem and clients with both diagnoses. [3] The sum of clients with an alcohol problem and clients with both diagnoses.

Source: U.S. Substance Abuse and Mental Health Services Administration, *Uniform Facility Data Set (UFDS): Annual surveys for 1995 – 1999* and National Survey of Substance Abuse Treatment Services (N-SSATS) 2000, and 2002–2005. <http://oas.samhsa.gov/oasftp.cfm#Data>.

Table 194. **Drug Use by Type of Drug and Age Group: 2002 and 2004**

[In percent. The 2002 survey changed names from the National Household Survey on Drug Abuse to the National Household Survey on Drug Use and Health (NSDUH). Due to the impact of Survey improvements, 2002 data should not be compared with data collected in 2001 or earlier years. Current users are those who used drugs at least once within month prior to this study. Based on a representative sample of the U.S. population age 12 and older, including persons living in households and in some group quarters such as dormitories and homeless shelters. Estimates are based on computer-assisted interviews of about 68,000 respondents. Subject to sampling variability; see source]

Age and type of drug	Ever used		Current user		Age and type of drug	Ever used		Current user	
	2002	2004	2002	2004		2002	2004	2002	2004
12 YEARS OLD AND OVER					**18 TO 25 YEARS OLD**				
Any illicit drug [1].	46.0	45.8	8.3	7.9	Any illicit drug [1].	59.8	59.2	20.2	19.4
Marijuana and hashish	40.4	40.2	6.2	6.1	Marijuana and hashish	53.8	52.8	17.3	16.1
Cocaine	14.4	14.2	0.9	0.8	Cocaine	15.4	15.2	2.0	2.1
Crack	3.6	3.3	0.2	0.2	Hallucinogens	24.2	21.3	1.9	1.5
Heroin	1.6	1.3	0.1	0.1	Inhalants	15.7	14.0	0.5	0.4
Hallucinogens	14.6	14.3	0.5	0.4	Any psychotherapeutic [2] . . .	27.7	29.2	5.4	6.1
LSD	10.4	9.7	–	0.1	Alcohol	86.7	86.2	60.5	60.5
PCP	3.2	2.8	–	–	"Binge" alcohol use [3]	(NA)	(NA)	40.9	41.2
Inhalants	9.7	9.5	0.3	0.3	Cigarettes	71.2	68.7	40.8	39.5
Any psychotherapeutic [2] . . .	19.8	20.0	2.6	2.5	Smokeless tobacco	23.7	21.4	4.8	4.9
Pain relievers.	12.6	13.2	1.9	1.8	Cigars	45.6	44.1	11.0	12.7
Tranquilizers	8.2	8.3	0.8	0.7					
Stimulants	9.0	8.3	0.5	0.5	**26 TO 34 YEARS OLD**				
Methamphetamine. . . .	5.3	4.9	0.3	0.2	Any illicit drug [1].	58.3	56.9	10.5	11.1
Sedatives	4.2	4.1	0.1	0.1	Marijuana and hashish	52.2	50.5	7.7	8.3
Alcohol	83.1	82.4	51.0	50.3	Cocaine	17.6	16.3	1.2	1.4
"Binge" alcohol use [3]	(NA)	(NA)	22.9	22.8	Hallucinogens	20.6	20.9	0.5	0.5
Cigarettes	69.1	67.3	26.0	24.9	Inhalants	14.1	13.1	0.1	0.2
Smokeless tobacco	19.9	18.6	3.3	3.0	Any psychotherapeutic [2] . . .	24.4	23.9	3.6	3.6
Cigars	37.4	36.3	5.4	5.7					
Pipes	17.0	16.4	0.8	0.8	**35 YEARS OLD AND OVER**				
					Any illicit drug.	42.7	42.9	4.6	4.2
12 to 17 YEARS OLD					Marijuana and hashish	38.0	38.7	3.1	3.1
Any illicit drug [1].	30.9	30.0	11.6	10.6	Cocaine	15.4	15.5	0.6	0.5
Marijuana and hashish	20.6	19.0	8.2	7.6	Hallucinogens	12.6	12.8	0.1	–
Cocaine	2.7	2.4	0.6	0.5	Inhalants	7.2	7.4	0.1	0.1
Hallucinogens	5.7	4.6	1.0	0.8	Any psychotherapeutic [2] . . .	18.0	18.1	1.6	1.3
Inhalants	10.5	11.0	1.2	1.2					
Any psychotherapeutic [2] . . .	13.7	13.5	4.0	3.6	**26 YEARS OLD AND OVER**				
Alcohol	43.4	42.0	17.6	17.6	Alcohol	88.0	87.3	53.9	53.0
"Binge" alcohol use [3]	(NA)	(NA)	10.7	11.1	"Binge" alcohol use [3]	(NA)	(NA)	21.4	21.1
Cigarettes	33.3	29.2	13.0	11.9	Cigarettes	73.7	72.3	25.2	24.1
Smokeless tobacco	8.0	7.1	2.0	2.3	Smokeless tobacco	20.9	19.6	3.2	2.7
Cigars	16.3	14.8	4.5	4.8	Cigars	39.0	37.9	4.6	4.6

– Represents or rounds to zero. NA Not available. [1] Illicit drugs include marijuana/hashish, cocaine (including crack), heroin, hallucinogens, inhalants, or prescription-type psychotherapeutics used nonmedically. [2] Nonmedical use of any prescription-type pain relievers, tranquilizers, stimulants, or sedatives; does not include over-the-counter drugs. [3] Binge alcohol use is defined as drinking five or more drinks on the same occasion (i.e., at the same time or within a couple of hours of each other) on at least 1 day in the past 30 days. Heavy alcohol use is defined as drinking five or more drinks on the same occasion on each of 5 or more days in the past 30 days; all heavy alcohol users are also binge alcohol users.

Source: U.S. Substance Abuse and Mental Health Services Administration, National Survey on Drug Use and Health, 2002, 2003, and 2004. <http://oas.samhsa.gov/nhsda.htm#Reports>

Table 195. **Estimated Use of Selected Drugs by State: 2003–2004**

[**19,272 represents 19,272,000**. Data in this table cover a 2-year period. The 2002 survey changed names from the National Household Survey on Drug Abuse to National Household Survey on Drug Use and Health (NSDUH). Due to the impact of survey improvements, 2002 data should not be compared with data collected in 2001 or earlier years. Current users are those persons 12 years old and over who used drugs at least once within month prior to this study. Based on national sample of respondents (see also headnote, Table 194). The state estimates were produced by combining the prevalence rate based on the state sample data and the prevalence rate based on a national regression model applied to local-area county and census block group/tract-level estimates from the state. The parameters of the regression model are estimated from the entire national sample. For comparison purposes, the data shown here display estimates for all 50 states and the District of Columbia utilizing the modeled estimates for all 51 areas.]

State	Estimated current users (1,000)					Current users as percent of population				
	Any illicit drug [1]	Mari- juana	Any illicit drug other than mari- juana [1]	Ciga- rettes	Binge alcohol [2]	Any illicit drug [1]	Mari- juana	Any illicit drug other than mari- juana [1]	Ciga- rettes	Binge alcohol [2]
U.S.	19,272	14,608	8,548	60,158	54,250	8.1	6.1	3.6	25.2	22.7
AL.	258	175	135	1,030	711	6.9	4.7	3.6	27.7	19.1
AK.	60	50	20	130	110	11.8	9.9	4.0	25.5	21.5
AZ.	377	268	182	1,128	1,095	8.3	5.9	4.0	24.8	24.1
AR.	170	130	85	674	464	7.5	5.8	3.8	30.0	20.7
CA.	2,571	1,933	1,079	5,141	5,941	8.9	6.7	3.7	17.8	20.6
CO.	379	273	173	985	919	10.2	7.3	4.7	26.5	24.7
CT.	247	204	93	683	701	8.5	7.1	3.2	23.6	24.3
DE.	58	43	27	169	155	8.6	6.3	3.9	24.9	22.8
DC.	45	35	16	122	118	9.6	7.4	3.3	25.9	24.9
FL.	1,110	840	502	3,436	3,030	7.8	5.9	3.5	24.0	21.2
GA	560	383	274	1,816	1,505	8.0	5.5	3.9	25.9	21.5
HI	81	66	29	206	232	8.0	6.5	2.8	20.3	22.8
ID	77	54	38	251	237	6.9	4.8	3.4	22.6	21.3
IL	788	594	337	2,808	2,693	7.6	5.7	3.3	27.1	26.0
IN	377	285	180	1,391	1,102	7.4	5.6	3.5	27.4	21.7
IA.	161	116	77	668	699	6.5	4.7	3.1	27.1	28.4
KS.	148	111	69	618	539	6.7	5.0	3.1	27.9	24.3
KY.	294	219	138	1,133	686	8.6	6.4	4.1	33.3	20.1
LA.	278	191	142	1,039	892	7.7	5.2	3.9	28.6	24.5
ME	104	93	40	298	240	9.3	8.3	3.6	26.6	21.5
MD	317	250	142	1,044	891	7.0	5.5	3.1	23.1	19.7
MA	547	468	192	1,177	1,528	10.2	8.7	3.6	21.9	28.4
MI	750	603	286	2,321	2,040	9.0	7.2	3.4	27.8	24.5
MN	313	258	136	1,053	1,098	7.4	6.1	3.2	25.0	26.0
MS	135	99	73	653	464	5.8	4.2	3.1	28.0	19.9
MO	384	301	177	1,444	1,185	8.1	6.4	3.7	30.6	25.1
MT	75	62	28	202	215	9.7	7.9	3.7	26.1	27.7
NE.	98	76	43	345	377	6.9	5.3	3.0	24.2	26.5
NV.	161	114	75	494	396	8.7	6.2	4.0	26.6	21.3
NH	108	95	40	268	277	9.9	8.7	3.7	24.6	25.4
NJ.	490	357	225	1,622	1,467	6.9	5.0	3.1	22.7	20.5
NM	173	133	70	363	353	11.2	8.7	4.6	23.6	23.0
NY.	1,451	1,186	495	3,967	3,735	9.1	7.4	3.1	24.9	23.4
NC	497	386	237	1,863	1,319	7.2	5.6	3.4	27.1	19.2
ND	39	30	17	145	168	7.5	5.6	3.2	27.5	31.8
OH	745	577	321	2,767	2,233	7.9	6.1	3.4	29.2	23.6
OK	241	160	118	879	591	8.4	5.6	4.1	30.8	20.7
OR	283	240	112	730	599	9.5	8.0	3.8	24.4	20.1
PA.	808	624	355	2,814	2,558	7.8	6.0	3.4	27.1	24.7
RI	98	83	38	236	251	10.8	9.1	4.2	26.1	27.7
SC.	261	196	123	919	724	7.6	5.7	3.6	26.9	21.2
SD.	44	31	19	189	179	7.0	4.9	3.0	30.2	28.6
TN.	331	245	170	1,360	739	6.8	5.0	3.5	28.0	15.2
TX.	1,226	825	676	4,605	4,147	7.0	4.7	3.8	26.1	23.6
UT.	126	77	75	324	276	6.9	4.2	4.1	17.6	15.0
VT.	56	48	20	135	126	10.4	9.0	3.7	25.3	23.7
VA.	434	323	201	1,520	1,327	7.2	5.4	3.4	25.4	22.2
WA	434	324	201	1,211	1,096	8.5	6.4	3.9	23.8	21.5
WV	113	86	60	493	297	7.4	5.6	3.9	32.1	19.3
WI	356	264	172	1,179	1,416	7.8	5.7	3.7	25.8	31.0
WY	33	24	16	107	107	7.9	5.7	3.8	25.5	25.5

[1] Illicit drugs include marijuana/hashish, cocaine (including crack), heroin, hallucinogens, inhalants, or prescription-type psychotherapeutics used nonmedically. Illicit drugs other than marijuana include cocaine (including crack), heroin, hallucinogens, inhalants, or prescription-type psychotherapeutics used nonmedically. [2] Binge alcohol use is defined as drinking five or more drinks on the same occasion (i.e., at the same time or within a couple of hours of each other) on at least 1 day in the past 30 days.

Source: U.S. Substance Abuse and Mental Health Services Administration, *National Household Survey on Drug Use and Health, 2003 and 2004.* <http://www.oas.samhsa.gov/nhsda.htm#Reports>.

Table 196. Cumulative Percent Distribution of Population by Height and Sex: 2003–2004

[Data are based on National Health and Nutrition Examination Survey (NHANES), a sample of the civilian noninstitutional population. For this survey, the respondent participates in an interview and a physical examination. For persons 20 years old and over. Height was measured without shoes. Based on sample and subject to sampling variability; see source]

Height	Males 20–29 years	30–39 years	40–49 years	50–59 years	60–69 years	70–79 years	Females 20–29 years	30–39 years	40–49 years	50–59 years	60–69 years	70–79 years
Percent under—												
4'10"	–	–	–	–	–	–	(B)	(B)	(B)	(B)	(B)	(B)
4'11"	–	–	–	(B)	–	(B)	(B)	(B)	(B)	(B)	3.2	5.1
5'	–	(B)	–	(B)	–	(B)	3.7	3.9	5.9	9.0	4.8	11.4
5'1"	–	(B)	(B)	(B)	(B)	(B)	8.2	10.0	12.3	14.5	11.8	24.6
5'2"	–	(B)	(B)	(B)	(B)	(B)	14.7	16.3	21.8	20.9	20.6	38.5
5'3"	(B)	2.5	(B)	(B)	(B)	(B)	29.8	26.7	32.1	33.3	35.4	55.9
5'4"	(B)	5.3	2.2	(B)	2.8	6.6	45.2	42.1	46.2	52.0	51.1	68.9
5'5"	5.4	9.2	3.4	(B)	6.5	13.8	57.8	60.9	60.2	63.9	66.7	86.5
5'6"	10.3	13.7	8.3	12.1	11.1	24.3	74.2	75.6	72.0	76.7	80.8	93.3
5'7"	15.2	20.0	15.2	18.2	20.1	33.3	84.5	86.5	84.2	87.4	89.0	96.8
5'8"	23.0	31.1	25.1	26.7	32.2	45.4	94.3	92.4	89.7	93.3	94.5	100.0
5'9"	33.9	43.4	38.0	41.7	44.7	56.7	97.5	96.6	95.9	97.8	96.0	100.0
5'10"	45.0	59.8	51.1	53.9	55.9	68.1	98.4	98.9	98.5	99.0	97.0	100.0
5'11"	60.9	72.3	63.9	67.6	68.6	84.7	99.4	99.4	100.0	99.5	98.9	100.0
6'	72.3	80.2	75.7	78.0	81.3	89.0	99.6	99.8	100.0	99.8	99.4	100.0
6'1"	85.1	87.8	86.1	85.0	89.1	94.5	99.6	99.8	100.0	100.0	100.0	100.0
6'2"	92.1	93.1	96.4	93.6	95.1	97.5	100.0	100.0	100.0	100.0	100.0	100.0
6'3"	95.7	97.3	98.4	96.8	98.0	98.7	100.0	100.0	100.0	100.0	100.0	100.0
6'4"	97.5	98.4	99.3	99.5	99.2	100.0	100.0	100.0	100.0	100.0	100.0	100.0
6'5"	98.8	99.5	99.3	99.5	99.8	100.0	100.0	100.0	100.0	100.0	100.0	100.0
6'6"	99.5	100.0	100.0	99.5	100.0	100.0	100.0	100.0	100.0	100.0	100.0	100.0

– Represents zero.   B Base figure too small to meet statistical standards of realiability of a derived figure.

Source: U.S. National Center for Health Statistics, unpublished data. <http://www.cdc.gov/nchs/nhanes.htm>.

Table 197. Cumulative Percent Distribution of Population by Weight and Sex: 2003–2004

[See headnote, Table 196. Data are based on National Health and Nutrition Examination Survey (NHANES). Weight was measured without shoes. Pregnant females were excluded from the analyses. Based on sample and subject to sampling variability; see source]

Weight	Males 20–29 years	30–39 years	40–49 years	50–59 years	60–69 years	70–79 years	Females 20–29 years	30–39 years	40–49 years	50–59 years	60–69 years	70–79 years
Percent under—												
100 lb.	(B)	(B)	–	–	(B)	(B)	2.2	(B)	(B)	(B)	(B)	(B)
110 lbs.	(B)	(B)	(B)	–	(B)	(B)	6.2	(B)	(B)	(B)	(B)	(B)
120 lbs.	(B)	(B)	(B)	–	(B)	(B)	17.6	10.8	10.5	10.2	5.8	9.2
130 lbs.	5.7	(B)	2.2	(B)	(B)	(B)	30.6	22.8	15.5	18.1	12.9	18.7
140 lbs.	10.6	6.9	3.8	(B)	5.1	9.6	47.5	34.1	26.7	24.8	22.4	31.2
150 lbs.	15.0	12.4	6.7	7.6	9.2	18.1	57.9	44.0	36.5	35.0	32.7	47.1
160 lbs.	26.9	23.7	13.3	14.5	14.2	27.1	66.8	55.4	48.5	47.7	46.2	59.0
170 lbs.	36.7	35.5	20.0	25.3	22.9	37.9	72.8	62.8	56.3	58.8	59.7	70.9
180 lbs.	49.8	46.5	31.2	38.9	31.0	49.0	78.1	72.8	64.2	66.5	69.2	82.0
190 lbs.	61.4	52.4	43.2	46.4	44.1	57.2	82.0	79.1	71.5	72.7	76.1	86.7
200 lbs.	69.2	61.7	54.4	57.7	52.7	67.3	86.7	81.6	78.0	79.8	81.9	89.1
210 lbs.	76.1	69.6	66.7	66.6	62.6	76.6	89.4	86.8	83.9	83.5	86.1	91.8
220 lbs.	79.5	76.8	77.3	74.7	73.3	86.6	90.3	89.0	86.1	86.9	90.6	95.4
230 lbs.	83.9	85.8	82.6	81.7	79.4	89.4	92.1	91.2	89.9	88.8	93.4	96.7
240 lbs.	86.8	91.5	87.7	86.9	85.4	92.0	93.5	92.7	92.2	91.9	94.6	98.5
250 lbs.	90.7	92.7	92.0	92.1	88.6	94.8	94.4	93.9	94.6	93.2	97.1	98.5
260 lbs.	93.4	94.3	95.3	92.9	92.2	95.8	95.3	95.0	95.6	95.9	97.6	99.3
270 lbs.	94.9	94.8	95.8	93.5	94.6	98.0	96.6	96.7	95.9	96.9	99.1	99.8
280 lbs.	96.0	95.9	97.0	96.5	95.5	98.2	98.3	97.7	96.5	97.7	99.2	99.8
290 lbs.	96.6	96.1	97.4	97.1	97.5	99.5	98.9	98.2	97.5	97.7	99.3	99.8
300 lbs.	96.9	97.6	98.0	98.2	97.5	100.0	99.1	98.7	97.7	98.7	99.6	100.0
320 lbs.	98.0	99.5	98.8	99.7	98.2	100.0	100.0	98.9	98.9	98.7	99.8	100.0
340 lbs.	98.7	99.6	99.4	99.7	99.1	100.0	100.0	99.8	99.3	99.5	99.8	100.0
360 lbs.	99.2	99.6	99.9	100.0	99.4	100.0	100.0	99.8	100.0	99.5	100.0	100.0
380 lbs.	99.2	99.7	100.0	100.0	100.0	100.0	100.0	100.0	100.0	99.5	100.0	100.0
400 lbs.	99.2	99.9	100.0	100.0	100.0	100.0	100.0	100.0	100.0	100.0	100.0	100.0
420 lbs.	99.2	99.9	100.0	100.0	100.0	100.0	100.0	100.0	100.0	100.0	100.0	100.0
440 lbs.	99.7	100.0	100.0	100.0	100.0	100.0	100.0	100.0	100.0	100.0	100.0	100.0

– Represents zero.   B Base figure too small to meet statistical standards of realiability of a derived figure.

Source: U.S. National Center for Health Statistics, unpublished data. <http://www.cdc.gov/nchs/nhanes.htm>.

Table 198. Age-Adjusted Percent Distributions of Body Mass Index (BMI) Among Persons 18 Years Old and Over by Selected Characteristics: 2003–2004

[See headnote, table 196. Body Mass Index (BMI) is a measure that adjusts body weight for height. It is calculated as weight in kilograms divided by height in meters squared. For both men and women, underweight is indicated by a BMI under 18.5; healthy weight is indicated by a BMI greater than or equal to 18.5 and less than 25.0; overweight is indicated by a BMI greater than or equal to 25.0 and less than 30.0; obesity is indicated by a BMI greater than or equal to 30.0. Based on the National Health and Nutrition Examination Survey (NHANES)]

Selected characteristic	Underweight	Healthy weight	Above healthy weight		
			Total	Overweight	Obese
Total [1] (age-adjusted)	1.8	32.9	65.3	33.7	31.6
Total [1] (crude)	1.8	32.6	65.6	33.8	31.8
Age: [2]					
18 to 44 years	2.7	38.0	59.3	29.5	29.8
45 to 64 years	(B)	26.0	73.1	37.2	35.9
65 to 74 years	(B)	25.5	74.0	39.4	34.6
75 years and over	0.8	33.3	65.9	42.4	23.5
Sex:					
Male	1.5	28.5	69.9	39.2	30.7
Female	2.0	36.6	61.5	28.7	32.8
Race/ethnicity and sex:					
Not Hispanic or Latino:					
White, male	1.5	27.8	70.7	39.6	31.1
White, female	2.2	39.2	58.6	28.4	30.2
Black alone or African American, male.	(B)	31.3	67.0	33.7	33.3
Black alone or African American, female	(B)	18.3	80.3	27.3	53.0
Mexican or Mexican American, male	(B)	26.3	73.4	42.0	31.4
Mexican or Mexican American, female	(B)	27.2	72.1	32.6	39.5
Education: [3]					
Less than a high school diploma	1.4	31.0	67.6	34.5	33.1
High school diploma or GED	(B)	27.2	71.8	36.6	35.2
Some college, bachelor's degree, or higher . . .	1.3	31.7	66.9	35.0	32.0

B Base figure too small to meet statistical standards for reliability of a derived figure.   [1] Total includes other race/ethnicities not shown separately and persons with unknown race/ethnicity.   [2] Estimates for age groups are not age adjusted.   [3] Education is shown only for persons 25 years old and over.

Source: U.S. National Center for Health Statistics, unpublished data.

Table 199. Percentage of Adults Engaging in Leisure-Time, Transportation-Related and Household-Related Physical Activity: 2005

[In percent. Covers persons 18 years old and over. Based on responses to questions about physical activity in prior month from the Behavioral Risk Factor Surveillance System. Estimates are age-adjusted to the year 2000 standard population. Based on a survey sample of approximately 350,000 persons in 50 states and the District of Columbia in 2005]

Characteristic	Persons who meet recommended activity [1]	Persons not meeting recommended activity [2]	Persons who are physically inactive [3]	Characteristic	Persons who meet recommended activity [1]	Persons not meeting recommended activity [2]	Persons who are physically inactive [3]
Total	**48.3**	**51.7**	**25.1**	30 to 44 years old . . .	50.3	49.7	24.3
				45 to 64 years old . . .	45.8	54.2	27.3
Male	49.9	50.1	22.9	65 to 74 years old . . .	41.2	58.8	31.7
Female	47.0	53.0	27.1	75 years old and			
				over	31.8	68.2	41.8
White, non-Hispanic . . .	50.9	49.1	21.4				
Black, non-Hispanic. . . .	40.2	59.8	32.8	School years completed:			
Hispanic	42.1	57.9	37.4	Less than 12 years . .	37.2	62.8	45.4
Other	46.2	53.8	25.5	12 years	45.6	54.4	31.4
				Some college (13 to			
Males:				15 years)	49.2	50.8	22.5
18 to 29 years old . . .	58.5	41.5	18.8	College (16 or more			
30 to 44 years old . . .	50.1	49.9	21.0	years)	54.2	45.8	13.8
45 to 64 years old . . .	46.6	53.4	24.6				
65 to 74 years old . . .	47.7	52.3	26.0	Household income:			
75 years old and				Less than $10,000. . .	36.9	63.1	44.6
over	40.3	59.7	32.0	$10,000 to $19,999 . .	38.7	61.3	39.8
				$20,000 to $34,999 . .	45.3	54.7	30.6
Females:				$35,000 to $49,999 . .	49.1	50.9	22.9
18 to 29 years old . . .	52.1	47.9	23.2	$50,000 and over . . .	55.0	45.0	15.0

[1] Recommended activity is physical activity at least 5 times/week x 30 minutes/time or vigorous physical activity for 20 minutes at a time at least 3 times/week.   [2] Persons whose reported physical activity does not meet recommended level or report no leisure-time, transportation-related, or household-related physical activity.   [3] Persons with no reported physical activity.

Source: U.S. National Center for Chronic Disease Prevention and Health Promotion, Nutrition and Physical Activity; and unpublished data; <http://www.cdc.gov/nccdphp/dnpa>.

Health and Nutrition   131

Table 200. Households and Persons Having Problems With Access to Food: 2000 to 2004

[106,043 represents 106,043,000. Food secure means that a household had access at all times to enough food for an active healthy life for all household members, with no need for recourse to socially unacceptable food sources or extraordinary coping behaviors to meet their basic food needs. Food insecure households had limited or uncertain ability to acquire acceptable foods in socially acceptable ways. Food insecure households with hunger were those with one or more household members who were hungry at least sometime during the period due to inadequate resources for food. The omission of homeless persons may be a cause of underreporting. The severity of food insecurity and hunger in households is measured through a series of questions about experiences and behaviors known to characterize households that are having difficulty meeting basic food needs. These experiences and behaviors generally occur in an ordered sequence as the severity of food insecurity increases. As resources become more constrained, adults in typical households first worry about having enough food, then they stretch household resources and juggle other necessities, then decrease the quality and variety of household members' diets, then decrease the frequency and quantity of adults' food intake, and finally decrease the frequency and quantity of children's food intake. All questions refer to the previous 12 months and include a qualifying phrase reminding respondents to report only those occurrences that resulted from inadequate financial resources. Restrictions to food intake due to dieting or busy schedules are excluded. Data are from the Food Security Supplement to the Current Population Survey (CPS); for details about the CPS, see text, Section 1 and Appendix III]

Household food security level	Number (1,000)					Percent distribution				
	2000	2001	2002	2003	2004	2000	2001	2002	2003	2004
Households, total	**106,043**	**107,824**	**108,601**	**112,214**	**112,967**	**100.0**	**100.0**	**100.0**	**100.0**	**100.0**
Food secure	94,942	96,303	96,543	99,631	99,473	89.5	89.3	88.9	88.8	88.1
Food insecure	11,101	11,521	12,058	12,583	13,494	10.5	10.7	11.1	11.2	11.9
Without hunger	7,786	8,010	8,259	8,663	9,045	7.3	7.4	7.6	7.7	8.0
With hunger	3,315	3,511	3,799	3,920	4,449	3.1	3.3	3.5	3.5	3.9
With hunger among children [1] . .	255	211	265	207	274	0.7	0.6	0.7	0.5	0.7
Adult members	**201,922**	**204,340**	**206,493**	**213,441**	**215,564**	**100.0**	**100.0**	**100.0**	**100.0**	**100.0**
In food secure households	181,586	183,398	184,718	190,451	191,236	89.9	89.8	89.5	89.2	88.7
In food insecure households	20,336	20,942	21,775	22,990	24,328	10.1	10.2	10.5	10.8	11.3
Without hunger	14,763	14,879	15,486	16,358	16,946	7.3	7.3	7.5	7.7	7.9
With hunger [2]	5,573	6,063	6,289	6,632	7,382	2.8	3.0	3.0	3.1	3.4
Child members	**71,763**	**72,321**	**72,542**	**72,969**	**73,039**	**100.0**	**100.0**	**100.0**	**100.0**	**100.0**
In food secure households	58,867	59,620	59,415	59,704	59,171	82.0	82.4	81.9	81.8	81.0
In food insecure households	12,896	12,701	13,127	13,265	13,868	18.0	17.6	18.1	18.2	19.0
Without hunger	12,334	12,234	12,560	12,845	13,323	17.2	16.9	17.3	17.6	18.2
With hunger among children [1] . . .	562	467	567	420	545	0.8	0.6	0.8	0.6	0.7

[1] One or more children in these households was hungry at some time during the year because of the household's food insecurity. Percent distribution of households with hunger among children excludes households with no child from the denominator. [2] One or more adults in these households was hungry at some time during the year because of the household's food insecurity.

Source: U.S. Dept. of Agriculture, Economic Research Service, *Household Food Security in the United States, 2004, Economic Research Report Number 11*; October 2005; <http://www.ers.usda.gov/briefing/foodsecurity/>.

Table 201. Per Capita Consumption of Selected Beverages by Type: 1980 to 2004

[In gallons. See headnote, Table 202. Per capita consumption uses U.S. resident population, July 1, for all beverages except coffee, tea, and fruit juices which use U.S. total population, July 1]

Commodity	1980	1985	1990	1995	2000	2001	2002	2003	2004
Nonalcoholic	104.9	114.6	128.2	130.6	135.4	134.5	134.2	135.8	137.5
Milk (plain and flavored)	27.1	26.1	25.3	23.6	22.2	21.8	21.7	21.3	21.0
Whole	17.0	14.3	10.5	8.6	8.1	7.8	7.7	7.6	7.3
Reduced-fat, light, and skim	10.1	11.8	14.8	15.0	14.2	14.0	13.9	13.7	13.7
Tea	7.3	7.1	6.9	7.9	7.8	8.2	7.8	7.5	7.3
Coffee	26.7	27.4	26.8	20.2	26.3	24.2	23.6	24.2	24.6
Bottled water	2.7	5.1	8.8	11.6	16.7	18.2	20.1	21.6	23.2
Carbonated soft drinks	33.6	41.2	47.1	50.6	53.2	52.9	52.8	52.5	52.3
Diet	(NA)	10.4	14.0	13.8	13.8	13.9	14.4	15.0	15.8
Regular	(NA)	30.8	33.1	36.8	39.4	39.0	38.4	37.5	36.5
Fruit juices	7.6	7.6	6.6	8.1	8.9	9.0	7.9	8.5	8.9
Fruit drinks, cocktails, and ades	(NA)	(NA)	6.3	7.7	(NA)	(NA)	(NA)	(NA)	(NA)
Canned iced tea	(NA)	(NA)	0.1	0.7	(NA)	(NA)	(NA)	(NA)	(NA)
Vegetable juices	(NA)	(NA)	0.3	0.3	0.2	0.2	0.2	0.2	0.2
Alcoholic	28.3	28.0	27.5	24.7	24.9	25.0	25.2	25.1	25.2
Beer	24.3	23.8	23.9	21.8	21.7	21.8	21.8	21.6	21.6
Wine [1]	2.1	2.4	2.0	1.7	2.0	2.0	2.1	2.2	2.3
Distilled spirits	2.0	1.8	1.5	1.2	1.3	1.3	1.3	1.3	1.4

NA Not available. [1] Beginning 1983, includes wine coolers.

Source: U.S. Department of Agriculture, Economic Research Service, *Food Consumption, Prices, and Expenditures, 1970–1997*; Food Consumption (Per Capita) Data System; <http://www.ers.usda.gov/data/foodconsumption/>.

Table 202. **Per Capita Consumption of Major Food Commodities: 1980 to 2004**

[In pounds, retail weight, except as indicated. Consumption represents the residual after exports, nonfood use and ending stocks are subtracted from the sum of beginning stocks, domestic production, and imports. Based on Census Bureau estimated population]

Commodity	Unit	1980	1990	1995	2000	2002	2003	2004
Red meat, total (boneless, trimmed weight) [1, 2]	Pounds	126.4	112.2	113.6	113.7	114.0	111.6	112.0
Beef	Pounds	72.1	63.9	63.5	64.5	64.5	61.9	62.9
Veal	Pounds	1.3	0.9	0.8	0.5	0.5	0.5	0.4
Lamb and mutton	Pounds	1.0	1.0	0.9	0.8	0.9	0.8	0.8
Pork	Pounds	52.1	46.4	48.4	47.8	48.2	48.4	47.8
Poultry (boneless, trimmed weight) [2]	Pounds	40.8	56.2	62.1	67.9	70.7	71.2	72.7
Chicken	Pounds	32.7	42.4	48.2	54.2	56.8	57.5	59.2
Turkey	Pounds	8.1	13.8	13.9	13.7	14.0	13.7	13.4
Fish and shellfish (boneless, trimmed weight)	Pounds	12.4	14.9	14.8	15.2	15.6	16.3	16.5
Eggs	Number	271	234	232	251	255	254	256
Shell	Number	236	186	172	178	180	182	180
Processed	Number	35	48	60	73	75	72	76
Dairy products, total [3]	Pounds	543.1	568.0	576.2	592.2	585.4	588.8	591.8
Fluid milk products [4]	Gallons	27.9	26.2	24.6	23.2	22.7	22.5	22.3
Beverage milks	Gallons	27.6	25.7	23.9	22.5	21.9	21.6	21.2
Plain whole milk	Gallons	16.5	10.2	8.3	7.7	7.3	7.2	6.9
Plain reduced-fat milk (2%)	Gallons	6.3	9.1	8.0	7.1	7.0	6.9	6.9
Reduced-fat milk (1%)and skim milk	Gallons	3.1	4.9	6.1	6.1	5.8	5.6	5.5
Flavored whole milk	Gallons	0.6	0.3	0.3	0.4	0.4	0.4	0.3
Flavored milks other than whole	Gallons	0.6	0.8	0.8	1.0	1.2	1.2	1.4
Buttermilk	Gallons	0.5	0.4	0.3	0.3	0.2	0.2	0.2
Yogurt (excl. frozen)	1/2 pints	4.6	7.8	11.4	12.0	13.7	15.2	17.0
Fluid cream products [5]	1/2 pints	10.5	14.3	15.6	18.3	19.7	22.2	23.5
Cream [6]	1/2 pints	6.3	8.7	9.4	11.6	12.1	13.9	14.8
Sour cream and dips	1/2 pints	3.4	4.7	5.4	6.1	6.7	7.5	7.9
Condensed and evaporated milks	Pounds	7.0	7.9	6.8	5.8	6.0	5.9	5.5
Whole milk	Pounds	3.8	3.1	2.3	2.0	2.3	2.6	2.2
Skim milk	Pounds	3.3	4.8	4.5	3.8	3.7	3.3	3.2
Cheese [7]	Pounds	17.5	24.6	26.9	29.8	30.5	30.4	31.3
American [8]	Pounds	9.6	11.1	11.7	12.7	12.8	12.5	12.9
Cheddar	Pounds	6.8	9.0	9.0	9.7	9.6	9.2	10.3
Italian [8]	Pounds	4.4	9.0	10.3	12.1	12.5	12.6	12.9
Mozzarella	Pounds	3.0	6.9	8.0	9.3	9.7	9.6	9.9
Other [8]	Pounds	3.3	4.3	5.0	4.8	4.8	5.1	5.3
Swiss	Pounds	1.3	1.4	1.1	1.0	1.1	1.2	1.2
Cream and Neufchatel	Pounds	0.9	1.6	2.2	2.3	2.3	2.4	2.3
Cottage cheese, total	Pounds	4.5	3.4	2.7	2.6	2.6	2.7	2.6
Lowfat	Pounds	0.8	1.2	1.2	1.3	1.3	1.3	1.3
Frozen dairy products	Pounds	26.4	28.5	29.0	28.0	26.6	27.1	26.4
Ice cream	Pounds	17.5	15.8	15.5	16.7	16.7	16.4	15.4
Lowfat ice cream	Pounds	7.1	7.7	7.4	7.3	6.5	7.5	7.8
Sherbet	Pounds	1.2	1.2	1.3	1.2	1.3	1.2	1.2
Frozen yogurt	Pounds	(NA)	2.8	3.4	2.0	1.5	1.4	1.8
Fats and oils:								
Total, fat content only	Pounds	56.9	62.3	64.2	82.3	88.6	88.0	87.5
Butter (product weight)	Pounds	4.5	4.4	4.4	4.5	4.4	4.5	4.6
Margarine (product weight)	Pounds	11.3	10.9	9.1	7.5	6.5	5.3	5.3
Lard (direct use)	Pounds	2.3	0.9	0.4	0.8	1.3	1.3	0.7
Edible beef tallow (direct use)	Pounds	1.1	0.6	2.7	4.0	3.4	3.8	4.0
Shortening	Pounds	18.2	22.2	22.2	31.6	33.3	32.8	32.6
Salad and cooking oils	Pounds	21.2	25.2	26.5	34.8	40.3	40.8	40.8
Other edible fats and oils [9]	Pounds	1.5	1.2	1.6	1.5	1.5	1.5	1.5
Flour and cereal products [9]	Pounds	144.9	181.0	188.7	199.2	191.7	193.1	191.5
Wheat flour	Pounds	116.9	135.9	140.0	146.3	136.8	136.7	134.3
Rice, milled	Pounds	9.5	15.8	17.1	18.9	19.5	20.3	20.4
Corn products	Pounds	12.9	21.4	24.9	28.4	29.7	30.3	30.9
Oat products	Pounds	3.9	6.5	5.5	4.4	4.5	4.7	4.7
Caloric sweeteners, total [10]	Pounds	120.2	132.4	144.1	148.8	146.1	141.4	141.0
Sugar, refined cane and beet	Pounds	83.6	64.4	64.9	65.5	63.2	60.9	61.5
Corn sweeteners [11]	Pounds	35.3	66.8	77.9	81.8	81.5	79.1	78.1
High-fructose corn syrup	Pounds	19.0	49.6	57.6	62.6	62.8	60.8	59.2
Other:								
Cocoa beans	Pounds	3.4	5.4	4.5	5.9	4.8	5.3	6.0
Coffee (green beans)	Pounds	10.3	10.3	7.9	10.3	9.2	9.5	9.6
Peanuts (shelled)	Pounds	5.1	6.1	5.7	5.9	5.9	6.4	6.7
Tree nuts (shelled)	Pounds	1.8	2.5	1.9	2.6	3.2	3.5	3.6

NA Not available. [1] Excludes edible offals. [2] Excludes shipments to Puerto Rico and the other U.S. possessions. [3] Milk-equivalent, milkfat basis. Includes butter. [4] Fluid milk figures are aggregates of commercial sales and milk produced and consumed on farms. [5] Includes eggnog, not shown separately. [6] Heavy cream, light cream, and half-and-half. [7] Excludes full-skim American, cottage, pot, and baker's cheese. [8] Includes other cheeses not shown separately. [9] Includes rye flour and barley products not shown separately. Excludes quantities used in alcoholic beverages. [10] Dry weight. Includes edible syrups (maple, molasses, etc.) and honey not shown separately. [11] Includes glucose and dextrose not shown separately.

Source: U.S. Department of Agriculture, Economic Research Service, *Food Consumption, Prices, and Expenditures, 1970–1997*; Food Consumption (Per Capita) Data System; <http://www.ers.usda.gov/data/foodconsumption/>.

Health and Nutrition 133

Table 203. Per Capita Utilization of Selected Commercially Produced Fruits and Vegetables: 1980 to 2004

[**In pounds, farm weight.** Domestic food use of fresh fruits and vegetables reflects the fresh-market share of commodity production plus imports and minus exports]

Commodity	1980	1985	1990	1995	2000	2001	2002	2003	2004
Fruits and vegetables, total [1]	608.8	632.2	660.2	692.5	711.7	685.3	685.4	704.0	694.3
Fruits, total	269.8	271.8	274.2	284.8	288.7	273.0	273.7	282.2	271.4
Fresh fruits	106.5	110.7	117.0	123.5	128.7	126.1	127.0	128.3	127.1
Noncitrus	80.5	89.2	95.6	99.6	105.2	102.1	103.7	104.4	104.4
Apples	19.4	17.4	19.8	18.9	17.6	15.8	16.2	17.1	18.8
Bananas	20.8	23.5	24.3	27.1	28.4	26.6	26.8	26.2	25.8
Cantaloupes	5.8	8.5	9.2	9.0	11.1	11.2	11.1	10.8	9.5
Grapes	4.0	6.9	7.9	7.5	7.5	7.5	8.5	7.7	7.9
Peaches and nectarines	7.1	5.5	5.5	5.3	5.3	5.2	5.2	5.2	5.1
Pears	2.6	2.8	3.3	3.4	3.4	3.3	3.1	3.1	3.1
Pineapples	1.5	1.5	2.0	1.9	3.2	3.2	3.8	4.4	4.4
Plums and prunes	1.5	1.4	1.5	0.9	1.2	1.3	1.3	1.2	1.1
Strawberries	2.0	3.0	3.2	4.1	4.9	4.2	4.6	5.3	5.5
Watermelons	10.7	13.5	13.3	15.2	13.8	15.0	14.0	13.6	13.0
Other [2]	5.1	5.3	5.4	6.3	8.7	9.0	9.1	9.8	10.3
Fresh citrus	26.1	21.5	21.4	23.8	23.5	23.9	23.4	23.9	22.7
Oranges	14.3	11.6	12.4	11.8	11.7	11.9	11.7	11.9	10.8
Grapefruit	7.3	5.5	4.4	6.0	5.1	4.8	4.6	4.1	4.1
Other [3]	4.5	4.4	4.6	6.0	6.7	7.2	7.0	8.0	7.8
Processed fruits	163.2	161.1	157.2	161.4	160.0	146.9	146.6	153.9	144.3
Frozen fruits [4]	3.3	3.5	4.3	5.2	4.2	7.0	4.1	5.4	5.0
Dried fruits [5]	11.3	12.9	12.2	12.8	10.5	10.3	10.5	10.2	9.8
Canned fruits [6]	24.8	21.1	21.2	17.5	17.7	17.8	16.9	17.4	15.8
Fruit juices [7]	123.1	123.3	119.3	125.7	127.2	111.5	114.9	120.4	113.4
Vegetables, total	339.0	360.4	386.0	407.6	423.0	412.3	411.8	421.8	422.8
Fresh vegetables	151.4	158.6	170.2	180.9	198.7	195.7	194.7	199.8	204.6
Asparagus (all uses)	0.3	0.5	0.6	0.6	1.0	0.9	1.0	1.0	1.0
Broccoli	1.4	2.6	3.4	4.3	5.9	5.4	5.4	5.5	5.9
Cabbage	8.0	8.7	8.3	8.1	8.9	8.8	8.3	7.5	8.3
Carrots	6.2	6.5	8.3	11.2	9.2	9.4	8.4	8.8	8.9
Cauliflower	1.1	1.8	2.2	1.6	1.7	1.5	1.4	1.6	1.8
Celery (all uses)	7.4	6.9	7.2	6.9	6.3	6.4	6.3	6.3	6.0
Corn	6.5	6.4	6.7	7.8	9.0	9.2	9.0	9.5	9.6
Cucumbers	3.9	4.4	4.7	5.6	6.4	6.3	6.5	6.1	6.3
Head lettuce	25.6	23.7	27.7	22.2	23.5	23.0	22.5	22.2	22.5
Mushrooms	1.2	1.8	2.0	2.0	2.6	2.6	2.6	2.6	2.6
Onions	11.4	13.6	15.1	17.8	18.9	18.5	19.3	19.5	21.7
Snap beans	1.3	1.3	1.1	1.6	2.0	2.2	2.1	2.0	1.9
Bell peppers (all uses)	2.9	3.8	4.5	6.2	7.0	6.9	6.8	6.9	7.1
Potatoes (all uses)	51.1	46.3	46.7	49.2	47.1	46.6	44.3	47.2	46.5
Sweet potatoes (all uses)	4.4	5.3	4.4	4.2	4.2	4.4	3.8	4.7	4.7
Tomatoes	12.8	14.9	15.5	16.8	19.0	19.2	20.3	19.5	19.3
Other fresh vegetables [8]	6.0	10.2	11.8	14.7	26.1	24.6	26.8	29.0	30.6
Processed vegetables	187.6	201.9	215.8	226.7	224.3	216.6	217.0	222.0	218.2
Selected vegetables for freezing [9]	51.5	64.5	66.8	78.8	79.3	78.6	76.7	78.3	77.6
Selected vegetables for canning [10]	103.2	99.4	110.8	108.5	103.4	96.9	100.5	101.7	102.4
Vegetables for dehydrating [11]	10.5	12.8	14.6	14.5	17.3	15.8	15.8	17.3	14.9
Potatoes for chips	16.5	17.6	16.4	16.4	15.9	17.6	16.5	17.3	16.5
Pulses [12]	5.9	7.6	7.2	8.4	8.5	7.8	7.5	7.3	6.7

[1] Excludes wine grapes. [2] Apricots, avocados, cherries, cranberries, kiwifruit, mangoes, papayas, and honeydew melons.
[3] Lemons, limes, tangerines, and tangelos. [4] Apples, apricots, blackberries, blueberries, boysenberries, cherries, loganberries, peaches, plums, prunes, raspberries, and strawberries. [5] Apples, apricots, dates, figs, peaches, pears, prunes, and raisins.
[6] Apples, apricots, cherries, olives, peaches, pears, pineapples, plums, and prunes. [7] Apple, cranberry, grape, grapefruit, lemon, lime, orange, pineapple, and prunes. [8] Artichokes, brussels sprouts, eggplant, escarole, endive, garlic, romaine, leaf lettuce, radishes, spinach, and squash. Beginning 2000, includes collard greens, kale, mustard greens, okra, pumpkin, and turnip greens. [9] Asparagus, snap beans, lima beans, broccoli, cauliflower, sweet corn, green peas, potatoes, spinach, and miscellaneous vegetables. [10] Asparagus, snap beans, beets, cabbage, carrots, chile peppers, sweet corn, cucumbers for pickling, green peas, lima beans, mushrooms, spinach, and tomatoes. [11] Onions and potatoes. [12] Dry peas, lentils, and dry edible beans.

Source: U.S. Department of Agriculture, Economic Research Service, *Food Consumption, Prices, and Expenditures, 1970–1997*; Food Consumption (Per Capita) Data System; online at <http://www.ers.usda.gov/data/foodconsumption/>.

Section 4

Education

This section presents data primarily concerning formal education as a whole, at various levels, and for public and private schools. Data shown relate to the school-age population and school enrollment, educational attainment, education personnel, and financial aspects of education. In addition, data are shown for charter schools, computer usage in schools, distance education, and adult education. The chief sources are the decennial census of population and the Current Population Survey (CPS), both conducted by the U.S. Census Bureau (see text, Section 1, Population); annual, biennial, and other periodic surveys conducted by the National Center for Education Statistics (NCES), a part of the U.S. Department of Education; and surveys conducted by the National Education Association.

The censuses of population have included data on school enrollment since 1840 and on educational attainment since 1940. The CPS has reported on school enrollment annually since 1945 and on educational attainment periodically since 1947.

The NCES is continuing the pattern of statistical studies and surveys conducted by the U.S. Office of Education since 1870. The annual *Digest of Education Statistics* provides summary data on pupils, staff, finances, including government expenditures, and organization at the elementary, secondary, and higher education levels. It is also a primary source for detailed information on federal funds for education, projections of enrollment, graduates, and teachers. *The Condition of Education,* issued annually, presents a summary of information on education of particular interest to policymakers. NCES also conducts special studies periodically.

The census of governments, conducted by the Census Bureau every 5 years (for the years ending in "2" and "7"), provides data on school district finances and state and local government expenditures for education. Reports published by the

Bureau of Labor Statistics contain data relating civilian labor force experience to educational attainment (see also Tables 578, 605, and 613 in Section 12, Labor Force, Employment, and Earnings).

Types and sources of data—The statistics in this section are of two general types. One type, exemplified by data from the Census Bureau, is based on direct interviews with individuals to obtain information about their own and their family members' education. Data of this type relate to school enrollment and level of education attained, classified by age, sex, and other characteristics of the population. The school enrollment statistics reflect attendance or enrollment in any regular school within a given period; educational attainment statistics reflect the highest grade completed by an individual, or beginning 1992, the highest diploma or degree received.

Beginning in 2001, the CPS used Census 2000 population controls. From 1994 to 2000, the CPS used 1990 census population controls plus adjustment for undercount. Also the survey changed from paper to computer-assisted technology. For years 1981 through 1993, 1980 census population controls were used; 1971 through 1980, 1970 census population controls had been used. These changes had little impact on summary measures (e.g., medians) and proportional measures (e.g., enrollment rates); however, use of the controls may have significant impact on absolute numbers.

The second type, generally exemplified by data from the NCES and the National Education Association, is based on reports from administrators of educational institutions and of state and local agencies having jurisdiction over education. Data of this type relate to enrollment, attendance, staff, and finances for the nation, individual states, and local areas.

Unlike the NCES, the Census Bureau does not regularly include specialized vocational, trade, business, or correspondence schools in its surveys. The NCES includes nursery schools and kindergartens that are part of regular grade schools in their enrollment figures. The Census Bureau includes all nursery schools and kindergartens. At the higher education level, the statistics of both agencies are concerned with institutions granting degrees or offering work acceptable for degree-credit, such as junior colleges.

School attendance—All states require that children attend school. While state laws vary as to the ages and circumstances of compulsory attendance, generally they require that formal schooling begin by age 6 and continue to age 16.

Schools—The NCES defines a school as "a division of the school system consisting of students composing one or more grade groups or other identifiable groups, organized as one unit with one or more teachers to give instruction of a defined type, and housed in a school plant of one or more buildings. More than one school may be housed in one school plant, as is the case when the elementary and secondary programs are housed in the same school plant."

Regular schools are those which advance a person toward a diploma or degree. They include public and private nursery schools, kindergartens, graded schools, colleges, universities, and professional schools.

Public schools are schools controlled and supported by local, state, or federal governmental agencies; private schools are those controlled and supported mainly by religious organizations or by private persons or organizations.

The Census Bureau defines *elementary* schools as including grades 1 through 8; *high* schools as including grades 9 through 12; and *colleges* as including junior or community colleges, regular 4-year colleges, and universities and graduate or professional schools. Statistics reported by the NCES and the National Education Association by type of organization, such as elementary level and secondary level, may not be strictly comparable with those from the Census Bureau because the grades included at the two levels vary, depending on the level assigned to the middle or junior high school by the local school systems.

School year—Except as otherwise indicated in the tables, data refer to the school year which, for elementary and secondary schools, generally begins in September of the preceding year and ends in June of the year stated. For the most part, statistics concerning school finances are for a 12-month period, usually July 1 to June 30. Enrollment data generally refer to a specific point in time, such as fall, as indicated in the tables.

Statistical reliability—For a discussion of statistical collection, estimation, and sampling procedures and measures of statistical reliability applicable to the Census Bureau and the NCES data, see Appendix III.

U.S. Census Bureau, Statistical Abstract of the United States: 2007

Table 204. School Enrollment: 1970 to 2015

[In thousands (59,838 represents 59,838,000). As of fall. Based on surveys of state education agencies and private schools; see source for details]

Year	All levels Total	Public	Private	Pre-K through grade 8 Public	Private	Grades 9 through 12 Public	Private	College [1] Public	Private
1970	59,838	52,322	7,516	32,558	4,052	13,336	1,311	6,428	2,153
1975	61,004	53,654	7,350	30,515	3,700	14,304	1,300	8,835	2,350
1980	58,305	50,335	7,971	27,647	3,992	13,231	1,339	9,457	2,640
1985	57,226	48,901	8,325	27,034	4,195	12,388	1,362	9,479	2,768
1986	57,709	49,467	8,242	27,420	4,116	12,333	1,336	9,714	2,790
1987	58,253	49,982	8,272	27,933	4,232	12,076	1,247	9,973	2,793
1988	58,485	50,349	8,136	28,501	4,036	11,687	1,206	10,161	2,894
1989	59,279	51,120	8,159	29,152	4,035	11,390	1,163	10,578	2,961
1990	60,269	52,061	8,208	29,878	4,084	11,338	1,150	10,845	2,974
1991	61,681	53,357	8,324	30,506	4,113	11,541	1,162	11,310	3,049
1992	62,633	54,208	8,425	31,088	4,175	11,735	1,147	11,385	3,103
1993	63,118	54,654	8,464	31,504	4,215	11,961	1,132	11,189	3,116
1994	63,888	55,245	8,643	31,898	4,335	12,213	1,163	11,134	3,145
1995	64,764	55,933	8,831	32,341	4,465	12,500	1,197	11,092	3,169
1996	65,744	56,733	9,011	32,764	4,551	12,847	1,213	11,121	3,247
1997	66,470	57,323	9,147	33,073	4,623	13,054	1,218	11,196	3,306
1998	66,983	57,677	9,306	33,346	4,702	13,193	1,235	11,138	3,369
1999	67,667	58,166	9,501	33,488	4,765	13,369	1,254	11,309	3,482
2000	68,670	58,956	9,713	33,688	4,867	13,515	1,287	11,753	3,560
2001	69,920	59,905	10,014	33,938	4,993	13,734	1,326	12,233	3,695
2002	71,188	60,935	10,253	34,116	5,034	14,067	1,359	12,752	3,860
2003	71,890	61,398	10,492	34,202	5,065	14,338	1,383	12,857	4,043
2004, proj. [2]	72,236	61,540	10,696	33,925	4,990	14,634	1,414	12,980	4,292
2005, proj.	72,576	61,912	10,664	33,823	4,997	14,887	1,441	13,202	4,226
2006, proj.	73,107	62,308	10,800	33,906	5,055	15,042	1,456	13,360	4,288
2007, proj.	73,544	62,647	10,897	33,990	5,074	15,101	1,463	13,555	4,361
2008, proj.	73,928	62,931	10,997	34,154	5,105	15,013	1,454	13,765	4,437
2009, proj.	74,332	63,235	11,097	34,350	5,139	14,917	1,446	13,968	4,511
2010, proj.	74,779	63,574	11,205	34,618	5,181	14,797	1,437	14,159	4,587
2011, proj.	75,252	63,948	11,304	34,907	5,224	14,730	1,435	14,311	4,645
2012, proj.	75,830	64,411	11,418	35,297	5,280	14,641	1,429	14,473	4,709
2013, proj.	76,497	64,953	11,545	35,724	5,341	14,569	1,424	14,659	4,780
2014, proj.	77,243	65,570	11,673	36,142	5,401	14,593	1,425	14,835	4,847
2015, proj.	77,981	66,193	11,787	36,439	5,448	14,780	1,440	14,974	4,900

[1] Data beginning 1996 based on new classification system. See footnote 1, Table 267.   [2] Pre-K through grade 12 are projections, college data are actual.

Source: U.S. National Center for Education Statistics, *Digest of Education Statistics*, annual, and *Projections of Education Statistics*, annual.

Table 205. School Expenditures by Type of Control and Level of Instruction in Constant (2003–2004) Dollars: 1970 to 2004

[In millions of dollars (316,401 represents $316,401,000,000). For school years ending in year shown. Data shown reflect historical revisions. Total expenditures for public elementary and secondary schools include current expenditures, interest on school debt and capital outlay. Data deflated by the Consumer Price Index, wage earners, and clerical workers through 1975; thereafter, all urban consumers, on a school year basis (supplied by the National Center for Education Statistics). See also Appendix III. Based on survey of state education agencies; see source for details]

Year	Total	Elementary and secondary schools Total	Public	Private [1]	Colleges and universities [2] Total	Public	Private
1970	316,401	212,736	200,420	12,316	103,665	65,272	38,394
1975	373,332	247,368	232,995	14,372	125,964	84,401	41,563
1980	383,712	247,286	230,027	17,259	136,426	90,533	45,893
1985	421,127	262,862	241,045	21,817	158,265	102,602	55,663
1986	443,500	276,700	254,126	22,574	166,800	108,070	58,729
1987	470,050	293,108	269,185	23,924	176,942	113,184	63,757
1988	484,799	302,007	277,429	24,578	182,792	116,693	66,097
1989	511,703	321,502	296,320	25,182	190,201	121,222	68,978
1990	535,853	338,504	311,831	26,674	197,348	125,704	71,645
1991	548,919	345,914	318,817	27,097	203,005	129,179	73,825
1992	562,073	351,770	324,571	27,199	210,303	133,094	77,209
1993	573,945	358,193	330,252	27,942	215,752	136,535	79,217
1994	586,538	365,913	337,659	28,254	220,625	139,119	81,506
1995	600,522	374,144	345,193	28,952	226,378	142,859	83,519
1996	612,746	383,321	353,691	29,630	229,425	143,965	85,460
1997	631,268	397,169	366,721	30,448	234,100	147,529	86,571
1998	656,124	415,825	384,646	31,180	240,299	152,846	87,453
1999	682,254	434,335	402,442	31,893	247,919	158,945	88,974
2000	712,660	452,378	419,731	32,647	260,282	167,441	92,841
2001	746,333	469,780	436,620	33,160	276,553	181,047	95,506
2002	781,663	488,502	454,666	33,836	293,161	191,568	101,592
2003	801,403	499,397	464,858	34,539	302,006	193,819	108,187
2004	826,600	511,200	475,500	35,700	315,400	200,100	115,300

[1] Estimated.   [2] Data beginning 1996 based on new classification system. See footnote 1, Table 267.

Source: U.S. National Center for Education Statistics, *Digest of Education Statistics*, annual.

Table 206. **School Enrollment, Faculty, Graduates, and Finances—Projections: 2005 to 2011**

[As of fall, except as indicated (55,148 represents 55,148,000)]

Item	Unit	2005	2006	2007	2008	2009	2010	2011
ELEMENTARY AND SECONDARY SCHOOLS								
School enrollment, total.	1,000. . .	55,148	55,460	55,628	55,726	55,852	56,034	56,296
Pre-kindergarten through grade 8 . . .	1,000. . .	38,820	38,961	39,064	39,259	39,489	39,799	40,131
Grades 9 through 12.	1,000. . .	16,328	16,498	16,564	16,467	16,363	16,234	16,165
Public.	1,000. . .	48,710	48,948	49,091	49,167	49,267	49,415	49,637
Pre-kindergarten through grade 8. .	1,000. . .	33,823	33,906	33,990	34,154	34,350	34,618	34,907
Grades 9 through 12	1,000. . .	14,887	15,042	15,101	15,013	14,917	14,797	14,730
Private	1,000. . .	6,438	6,512	6,536	6,559	6,585	6,619	6,659
Pre-kindergarten through grade 8. .	1,000. . .	4,997	5,055	5,074	5,105	5,139	5,181	5,224
Grades 9 through 12	1,000. . .	1,441	1,456	1,463	1,454	1,446	1,437	1,435
Classroom teachers, total FTE [1].	1,000. . .	3,534	3,575	3,608	3,639	3,670	3,706	3,746
Public.	1,000. . .	3,139	3,176	3,207	3,237	3,266	3,299	3,337
Private	1,000. . .	395	400	401	403	404	406	409
High school graduates, total [2]	1,000. . .	3,176	3,232	3,326	3,339	3,326	3,301	3,256
Public.	1,000. . .	2,861	2,912	2,995	3,008	2,996	2,973	2,933
Public schools: [2]								
Average daily attendance (ADA)	1,000. . .	45,269	45,491	45,624	45,694	45,787	45,925	46,131
Current dollars: [3]								
Teachers' average salary	Dol.	48,533	49,907	51,124	52,446	(NA)	(NA)	(NA)
Current school expenditure	Bil. dol. .	447.4	468.0	489.4	511.6	(NA)	(NA)	(NA)
Per pupil in fall enrollment.	Dol.	9,185	9,562	9,969	10,406	(NA)	(NA)	(NA)
Constant (2003–2004) dollars: [3, 4]								
Teachers' average salary	Dol.	46,561	47,017	47,185	47,373	(NA)	(NA)	(NA)
Current school expenditure	Bil. dol. .	429.2	440.9	451.7	462.1	(NA)	(NA)	(NA)
Per pupil in fall enrollment.	Dol.	8,812	9,008	9,201	9,399	(NA)	(NA)	(NA)
HIGHER EDUCATION								
Enrollment, total	1,000. . .	17,429	17,648	17,916	18,202	18,480	18,746	18,956
Male	1,000. . .	7,423	7,458	7,552	7,657	7,760	7,848	7,928
Full-time	1,000. . .	4,768	4,802	4,876	4,959	5,038	5,105	5,161
Part-time	1,000. . .	2,655	2,655	2,676	2,698	2,722	2,743	2,767
Female.	1,000. . .	10,005	10,190	10,365	10,545	10,720	10,897	11,028
Full-time	1,000. . .	5,974	6,133	6,283	6,440	6,588	6,740	6,826
Part-time	1,000. . .	4,031	4,057	4,081	4,104	4,132	4,157	4,202
Public.	1,000. . .	13,202	13,360	13,555	13,765	13,968	14,159	14,311
Four-year institutions	1,000. . .	6,892	6,990	7,106	7,230	7,351	7,472	7,561
Two-year institutions	1,000. . .	6,310	6,370	6,450	6,535	6,617	6,686	6,750
Private	1,000. . .	4,226	4,288	4,361	4,437	4,511	4,587	4,645
Four-year institutions	1,000. . .	3,930	3,987	4,054	4,124	4,193	4,263	4,318
Two-year institutions	1,000. . .	296	301	307	313	319	323	326
Undergraduate.	1,000. . .	14,914	15,105	15,340	15,595	15,845	16,073	16,233
Graduate	1,000. . .	2,165	2,188	2,215	2,239	2,262	2,293	2,333
First-time professional	1,000. . .	349	355	361	367	373	380	389
Full-time equivalent.	1,000. . .	13,141	13,343	13,583	13,840	14,085	14,320	14,487
Public	1,000. . .	9,538	9,681	9,852	10,035	10,211	10,375	10,490
Private	1,000. . .	3,603	3,662	3,731	3,804	3,874	3,945	3,996
Degrees conferred, total [2]	1,000. . .	2,857	2,915	2,977	3,043	3,102	3,146	3,190
Associate's	1,000. . .	682	686	694	704	714	721	726
Bachelor's.	1,000. . .	1,456	1,488	1,523	1,561	1,596	1,622	1,645
Master's	1,000. . .	584	603	619	635	647	657	670
Doctoral	1,000. . .	50	51	51	51	51	52	53
First-professional	1,000. . .	85	87	90	92	93	95	96

NA Not available.   [1] Full-time equivalent.   [2] For school year ending in June the following year.   [3] Limited financial projections are shown due to the uncertain behavior of inflation over the long term.   [4] Based on the Consumer Price Index (CPI) for all urban consumers, U.S. Bureau of Labor Statistics. CPI adjusted to a school year basis by NCES.

Source: U.S. National Center for Education Statistics, *Projections of Education Statistics to 2015*, NCES 2006-084 See Internet site <http://www.nces.ed.gov/surveys/AnnualReports/>.

Table 207. Federal Funds for Education and Related Programs: 2003 to 2005

[In millions of dollars (124,374,500,000), except percent. For fiscal years ending in September. Figures represent on-budget funds]

Level, agency, and program	2003	2004	2005 [1]
Total, all programs	**124,374.5**	**131,720.1**	**141,788.2**
Percent of federal budget outlays	5.8	5.7	5.7
Elementary/secondary education programs	**59,274.2**	**62,653.2**	**67,959.2**
Department of Education [2]	30,749.3	33,689.4	37,716.1
Grants for the disadvantaged	11,253.0	12,486.3	14,638.2
School improvement programs	6,752.9	7,459.8	8,419.0
Indian education	115.9	114.4	129.9
Special education	8,490.7	9,749.4	10,226.5
Vocational and adult education	1,942.7	1,945.2	2,030.4
Education reform—Goals 2000	531.9	50.8	102.8
Department of Agriculture [2]	11,215.3	11,725.3	12,643.0
Child nutrition programs	[3]10,828.3	[3]11,206.4	[3]12,163.9
Agricultural Marketing Service—commodities [4]	200.0	171.0	188.0
Special milk program [2]	([3])	([3])	([3])
Department of Defense [2]	1,684.3	1,642.1	1,698.6
Overseas dependents' schools	1,056.1	959.3	996.0
Section VI schools [5]	376.1	390.1	395.6
Department of Health and Human Services	7,571.0	7,727.5	7,785.4
Head Start	6,666.8	6,774.4	6,843.2
Social security student benefits	904.2	953.0	942.2
Department of the Interior [2]	0.5	0.5	0.6
Mineral Leasing Act and other funds	963.0	983.3	1,024.5
Indian Education	138.7	150.1	225.98
Department of Justice	823.3	832.2	797.53
Inmate programs	445.4	482.5	506.1
Department of Labor	437.4	478.5	506.1
Job Corps	5,972.0	5,675.0	5,778.0
Department of Veterans Affairs	1,423.0	1,438.0	1,688.0
Vocational rehab for disabled veterans	514.6	551.0	604.0
Other agencies and programs [6]	514.6	551.0	604.0
Department of the Interior [2]	159.0	176.7	202.9
Higher education programs [2]	**29,499.7**	**32,433.0**	**36,405.1**
Student financial assistance	22,706.4	25,341.0	28,769.6
Federal Family Education Loans [7]	14,092.4	14,968.6	14,667.8
Department of Agriculture	1,216.0	4,661.6	10,210.1
Department of Commerce	93.6	93.8	98.7
Department of Defense	4.2	4.0	4.0
Tuition assistance for military personnel	1,673.4	1,780.3	1,907.6
Service academies [8]	548.6	594.4	645.0
Senior ROTC	268.7	286.2	292.8
National Science Foundation	521.2	525.2	577.5
Professional development education [2]	334.9	374.5	392.3
Department of Health and Human Services [2]	1,692.8	1,535.3	1,559.2
Health professions training programs	882.4	698.3	700.0
National Health Service Corps scholarships [9]	46.3	45.0	45.0
National Institutes of Health training grants [9]	711.4	740.5	762.2
Department of Homeland Security [6]	33.9	41.1	42.5
Department of the Interior	234.2	246.2	269.6
Shared revenues, Mineral Leasing Act and other receipts—estimated education share	135.1	142.3	164.3
Indian education	99.1	103.9	105.3
Department of State	387.0	399.6	528.2
Department of Transportation	65.0	66.0	66.0
Department of Veterans Affairs [2]	2,005.3	2,294.0	2,533.3
Post-Vietnam veterans	1.2	1.0	1.0
All-volunteer-force educational assistance	1,712.6	1,942.8	2,109.6
Other agencies and programs [2]	603.8	631.7	626.4
National Endowment for the Humanities	34.1	29.8	29.0
National Science Foundation	535.0	566.0	561.0
Other education programs [2]	**6,532.5**	**6,576.8**	**7,207.5**
Department of Education [2]	3,435.2	3,437.8	3,896.8
Administration	548.3	525.2	525.5
Rehabilitative services and handicapped research	2,871.8	2,894.0	3,350.7
Department of Agriculture	473.8	462.1	467.6
Department of Health and Human Services [6]	300.0	310.0	325.0
Department of Homeland Security [6]	192.4	205.4	183.0
Department of Justice	19.6	25.2	25.8
Department of State	107.7	90.4	92.5
Agency for International Development	2,004.0	2,045.9	2,216.8
Library of Congress	489.2	536.0	513.2
National Endowment for the Arts	389.0	402.0	405.0
National Endowment for the Humanities	2.5	1.6	1.7
National Science Foundation	66.7	94.9	90.0
Research programs at universities and related institutions [2]	**29,068.1**	**30,057.1**	**30,216.3**
Department of Agriculture	641.1	728.4	599.0
Department of Defense	2,282.2	2,261.8	1,893.8
Department of Energy	4,053.6	4,116.4	4,145.9
Department of Health and Human Services	15,140.5	15,854.1	16,253.1
National Aeronautics and Space Administration	2,479.0	2,629.9	2,528.6
National Science Foundation	3,419.5	3,538.6	3,663.2

[1] Estimated except U.S. Department of Education, which are actual budget reports. [2] Includes other programs and agencies, not shown separately. [3] The Special Milk Program is included in the Child Nutrition Program. [4] Purchased under Section 32 of the Act of August 1935 for use in child nutrition programs. [5] Program provides for the education of dependents of federal employees residing on federal property where free public education is unavailable in the nearby community. [6] The U.S. Department of Homeland Security was created on January 24, 2003, under public law (107-296). [7] Includes Federal Direct Loans. [8] Instructional costs only including academics, audiovisual, academic computer center, faculty training, military training, physical education, and libraries. [9] Includes alcohol, drug abuse, and mental health training programs.

Source: U.S. National Center for Education Statistics, *Digest of Education Statistics*, annual.

Table 208. School Enrollment by Age: 1970 to 2004

[As of October (60,357 represents 60,357,000). Covers civilian noninstitutional population enrolled in nursery school and above. Based on Current Population Survey, see text, Section 1, and Appendix III]

Age	1970	1980	1985	1990	1995	2000	2001	2002	2003	2004
ENROLLMENT (1,000)										
Total 3 to 34 years old ..	60,357	57,348	58,013	60,588	66,939	69,560	70,271	71,003	72,116	72,418
3 and 4 years old	1,461	2,280	2,801	3,292	4,042	4,097	4,030	4,187	4,590	4,552
5 and 6 years old	7,000	5,853	6,697	7,207	7,901	7,648	7,526	7,353	7,309	7,561
7 to 13 years old	28,943	23,751	22,849	25,016	27,003	28,296	28,570	28,525	28,184	28,006
14 and 15 years old	7,869	7,282	7,362	6,555	7,651	7,885	7,914	8,022	8,329	8,327
16 and 17 years old	6,927	7,129	6,654	6,098	6,997	7,341	7,483	7,669	8,177	8,086
18 and 19 years old	3,322	3,788	3,716	4,044	4,274	4,926	4,871	5,007	4,856	4,961
20 and 21 years old	1,949	2,515	2,708	2,852	3,025	3,314	3,570	3,696	3,684	3,904
22 to 24 years old.	1,410	1,931	2,068	2,231	2,545	2,731	2,798	3,003	3,397	3,221
25 to 29 years old.	1,011	1,714	1,942	2,013	2,216	2,030	2,140	2,196	2,212	2,479
30 to 34 years old.	466	1,105	1,218	1,281	1,284	1,292	1,370	1,345	1,378	1,321
35 years old and over	(NA)	1,290	1,766	2,439	2,830	2,653	2,852	3,043	2,797	3,042
ENROLLMENT RATE										
Total 3 to 34 years old ..	56.4	49.7	48.3	50.2	53.7	55.8	55.7	56.1	56.2	56.2
3 and 4 years old	20.5	36.7	38.9	44.4	48.7	52.1	52.2	54.5	55.1	54.0
5 and 6 years old	89.5	95.7	96.1	96.5	96.0	95.6	95.3	95.2	94.5	95.4
7 to 13 years old	99.2	99.3	99.2	99.6	98.9	98.2	98.3	98.3	98.3	98.4
14 and 15 years old	98.1	98.2	98.1	99.0	98.9	98.7	98.1	98.4	97.5	98.5
16 and 17 years old	90.0	89.0	91.7	92.5	93.6	92.8	93.4	94.3	94.9	94.5
18 and 19 years old	47.7	46.4	51.6	57.3	59.4	61.2	61.0	63.3	64.5	64.4
20 and 21 years old	31.9	31.0	35.3	39.7	44.9	44.1	45.5	47.8	48.3	48.9
22 to 24 years old.	14.9	16.3	16.9	21.0	23.2	24.6	25.1	25.6	27.8	26.3
25 to 29 years old.	7.5	9.3	9.2	9.7	11.6	11.4	11.7	12.1	11.8	13.0
30 to 34 years old.	4.2	6.4	6.1	5.8	6.0	6.7	6.8	6.6	6.8	6.6
35 years old and over	(NA)	1.4	1.6	2.1	2.2	1.9	2.0	2.1	1.9	2.0

NA Not available.

Source: U.S. Census Bureau, Current Population Reports, PPL-148; and earlier PPL and P-20 reports; and data published on the Internet. See Internet site <http://www.census.gov/population/www/socdemo/school.html>.

Table 209. School Enrollment by Race, Hispanic Origin, and Age: 1980 to 2004

[(47,673 represents 47,673,000). See headnote, Table 208]

Age	White [1]			Black [1]			Hispanic origin [2]		
	1980	1990	2004	1980	1990	2004	1980	1990	2004
ENROLLMENT (1,000)									
Total 3 to 34 years old ..	47,673	48,899	55,327	8,251	8,854	11,014	4,263	6,073	12,193
3 and 4 years old	1,844	2,700	3,376	371	452	817	172	249	797
5 and 6 years old	4,781	5,750	5,784	904	1,129	1,131	491	835	1,455
7 to 13 years old	19,585	20,076	21,313	3,598	3,832	4,407	2,009	2,794	5,238
14 and 15 years old	6,038	5,265	6,403	1,088	1,023	1,316	568	739	1,437
16 and 17 years old	5,937	4,858	6,188	1,047	962	1,267	454	592	1,226
18 and 19 years old	3,199	3,271	3,919	494	596	659	226	329	636
20 and 21 years old	2,206	2,402	3,094	242	305	440	111	213	466
22 to 24 years old.	1,669	1,781	2,422	196	274	433	93	121	431
25 to 29 years old.	1,473	1,706	1,835	187	162	362	84	130	313
30 to 34 years old.	942	1,090	993	124	119	182	54	72	194
35 years old and over	1,104	2,096	2,259	186	238	528	(NA)	145	317
ENROLLMENT RATE									
Total 3 to 34 years old ..	48.9	49.5	55.5	53.9	51.9	59.0	49.8	47.4	50.7
3 and 4 years old	36.3	44.9	52.8	38.2	41.6	59.6	28.5	29.8	43.9
5 and 6 years old	95.8	96.5	95.5	95.4	96.3	94.1	94.5	94.8	93.0
7 to 13 years old	99.2	99.6	98.2	99.4	99.8	98.6	99.2	99.0	98.2
14 and 15 years old	98.3	99.1	98.5	97.9	99.2	99.0	94.3	99.0	98.2
16 and 17 years old	88.6	92.5	94.2	90.6	91.7	95.7	81.8	85.4	90.2
18 and 19 years old	46.3	57.1	64.9	45.7	55.2	59.2	37.8	44.1	50.1
20 and 21 years old	31.9	41.0	49.3	23.4	28.4	40.0	19.5	27.2	32.2
22 to 24 years old.	16.4	20.2	25.3	13.6	20.0	25.1	11.7	9.9	19.4
25 to 29 years old.	9.2	9.9	12.2	8.8	6.1	14.3	6.9	6.3	8.1
30 to 34 years old.	6.3	5.9	6.4	6.8	4.4	7.2	5.1	3.6	5.3
35 years old and over	1.3	2.1	1.9	1.8	2.1	3.3	(NA)	2.1	2.2

NA Not available. [1] 2004 for persons who selected this race group only. See footnote 2, Table 214. [2] Persons of Hispanic origin may be of any race.

Source: U.S. Census Bureau, Current Population Reports, PPL-148; and earlier PPL and P-20 reports; and data published on the Internet. See Internet site <http://www.census.gov/population/www/socdemo/school.html>.

Table 210. **Enrollment in Public and Private Schools: 1970 to 2004**

[In millions (52.2 represents 52,200,000), except percent. As of October. For civilian noninstitutional population. For **1970 to 1985**, persons 3 to 34 years old; **beginning 1986**, for 3 years old and over. For college enrollment 35 years old and over, see Table 270. See also headnote, Table 208]

Year	Public						Private					
	Total	Nur-sery	Kinder-garten	Ele-mentary	High school	College	Total	Nur-sery	Kinder-garten	Ele-mentary	High school	College
1970	52.2	0.3	2.6	30.0	13.5	5.7	8.1	0.8	0.5	3.9	1.2	1.7
1980	(NA)	0.6	2.7	24.4	(NA)	(NA)	(NA)	1.4	0.5	3.1	(NA)	(NA)
1985	49.0	0.9	3.2	23.8	12.8	8.4	9.0	1.6	0.6	3.1	1.2	2.5
1987 [1]	51.7	0.8	3.4	24.8	12.7	10.0	8.9	1.7	0.6	2.8	1.1	2.8
1988	52.2	0.9	3.4	25.5	12.2	10.3	8.9	1.8	0.5	2.8	1.0	2.8
1989	52.5	0.9	3.3	25.9	12.1	10.3	8.9	1.9	0.6	2.7	0.8	2.9
1990	53.8	1.2	3.3	26.6	11.9	10.7	9.2	2.2	0.6	2.7	0.9	2.9
1991	54.5	1.1	3.5	26.6	12.2	11.1	9.4	1.8	0.6	3.0	1.0	3.0
1992	55.0	1.1	3.5	27.1	12.3	11.1	9.4	1.8	0.6	3.1	1.0	3.0
1993	56.0	1.2	3.5	27.7	12.6	10.9	9.4	1.8	0.7	2.9	1.0	3.0
1994	58.6	1.9	3.3	28.1	13.5	11.7	10.7	2.3	0.6	3.4	1.1	3.3
1995	58.7	2.0	3.2	28.4	13.7	11.4	11.1	2.4	0.7	3.4	1.2	3.3
1996	59.5	1.9	3.4	28.1	14.1	12.0	10.8	2.3	0.7	3.4	1.2	3.2
1997	61.6	2.3	3.3	29.3	14.6	12.1	10.5	2.2	0.7	3.1	1.2	3.3
1998	60.8	2.3	3.1	29.1	14.3	12.0	11.3	2.3	0.7	3.4	1.2	3.6
1999	60.8	2.3	3.2	29.2	14.4	11.7	11.4	2.3	0.7	3.6	1.3	3.5
2000	61.2	2.2	3.2	29.4	14.4	12.0	11.0	2.2	0.7	3.5	1.3	3.3
2001	62.4	2.2	3.1	29.8	14.8	12.4	10.8	2.1	0.6	3.4	1.2	3.5
2002	62.8	2.2	3.0	29.7	15.1	12.8	11.3	2.2	0.6	3.5	1.3	3.7
2003	63.8	2.6	3.1	29.2	15.8	13.1	11.1	2.4	0.6	3.4	1.3	3.5
2004	64.3	2.5	3.4	29.2	15.5	13.7	11.3	2.3	0.6	3.4	1.3	3.7
Percent White:												
1970.	84.5	59.5	84.4	83.1	85.6	90.7	93.4	91.1	88.2	94.1	96.1	92.8
1980.	(NA)	68.2	80.7	80.9	(NA)	(NA)	(NA)	89.0	87.0	90.7	(NA)	(NA)
1990.	79.8	71.7	78.3	78.9	79.2	84.1	87.4	89.6	83.2	88.2	89.4	85.0
2000.	77.0	69.4	77.3	76.7	78.0	78.0	83.5	84.9	82.8	85.9	84.6	79.8
2001.	76.5	68.7	76.1	76.7	77.4	76.5	83.1	84.3	84.4	85.6	86.7	78.4
2002.	76.6	71.8	75.3	76.5	77.9	76.2	83.8	83.6	87.5	84.1	86.4	82.1
2003 [2]	75.6	74.7	76.4	75.0	75.6	77.1	82.3	84.3	80.3	83.8	86.0	79.0
2004 [2]	75.2	68.5	75.2	75.0	75.4	76.7	82.4	82.7	82.1	85.1	88.0	77.8

NA Not available.   [1] Beginning 1987, based on a revised edit and tabulation package.   [2] Beginning 2003, for persons who selected this race group only. See footnote 2, Table 214.

Source: U.S. Census Bureau, Current Population Reports, PPL-148; and earlier PPL and P-20 reports; and data published on the Internet. See Internet site <http://www.census.gov/population/www/socdemo/school.html>.

Table 211. **School Enrollment by Sex and Level: 1970 to 2004**

[In millions (60.4 represents 60,400,000). As of Oct. For the civilian noninstitutional population. 1970–1979, for persons 3 to 34 years old; **beginning 1980**, 3 years old and over. Elementary includes kindergarten and grades 1–8; high school, grades 9–12; and college, 2-year and 4-year colleges, universities, and graduate and professional schools. Data for college represent degree-credit enrollment. See headnote, Table 208]

Year	All levels [1]			Elementary			High school			College		
	Total	Male	Female	Total	Male	Female	Total	Male	Female	Total	Male	Female
1970	60.4	31.4	28.9	37.1	19.0	18.1	14.7	7.4	7.3	7.4	4.4	3.0
1980	58.6	29.6	29.1	30.6	15.8	14.9	14.6	7.3	7.3	11.4	5.4	6.0
1985	59.8	30.0	29.7	30.7	15.7	15.0	14.1	7.2	6.9	12.5	5.9	6.6
1986 [2]	60.5	30.6	30.0	31.1	16.1	15.0	14.2	7.2	7.0	12.7	6.0	6.7
1987	60.6	30.7	29.9	31.6	16.3	15.3	13.8	7.0	6.8	12.7	6.0	6.7
1988	61.1	30.7	30.5	32.2	16.6	15.6	13.2	6.7	6.4	13.1	5.9	7.2
1989	61.5	30.8	30.7	32.5	16.7	15.8	12.9	6.6	6.3	13.2	6.0	7.2
1990	63.0	31.5	31.5	33.2	17.1	16.0	12.8	6.5	6.4	13.6	6.2	7.4
1991	63.9	32.1	31.8	33.8	17.3	16.4	13.1	6.8	6.4	14.1	6.4	7.6
1992	64.6	32.2	32.3	34.3	17.7	16.6	13.3	6.8	6.5	14.0	6.2	7.8
1993	65.4	32.9	32.5	34.8	17.9	16.9	13.6	7.0	6.6	13.9	6.3	7.6
1994	69.3	34.6	34.6	35.4	18.2	17.2	14.6	7.4	7.2	15.0	6.8	8.2
1995	69.8	35.0	34.8	35.7	18.3	17.4	15.0	7.7	7.3	14.7	6.7	8.0
1996	70.3	35.1	35.2	35.5	18.3	17.3	15.3	7.9	7.4	15.2	6.8	8.4
1997	72.0	35.9	36.2	36.3	18.7	17.6	15.8	8.0	7.7	15.4	6.8	8.6
1998	72.1	36.0	36.1	36.4	18.7	17.7	15.6	7.9	7.6	15.5	6.9	8.6
1999	72.4	36.3	36.1	36.7	18.8	17.9	15.9	8.2	7.7	15.2	7.0	8.2
2000	72.2	35.8	36.4	36.7	18.9	17.9	15.8	8.1	7.7	15.3	6.7	8.6
2001	73.1	36.3	36.9	36.9	19.0	17.9	16.1	8.2	7.8	15.9	6.9	9.0
2002	74.0	36.8	37.3	36.7	18.9	17.8	16.4	8.3	8.0	16.5	7.2	9.3
2003	74.9	37.3	37.6	36.3	18.7	17.6	17.1	8.6	8.4	16.6	7.3	9.3
2004	75.5	37.4	38.0	36.5	19.0	17.6	16.8	8.4	8.4	17.4	7.6	9.8

[1] Includes nursery schools, not shown separately.   [2] Revised. Data beginning 1986, based on a revised edit and tabulation package.

Source: U.S. Census Bureau, Current Population Reports, PPL-148; and earlier PPL and P-20 reports; and data published on the Internet. See Internet site <http://www.census.gov/population/www/socdemo/school.html>.

Education   141

Table 212. School Enrollment by Control and Level: 1980 to 2004

[In thousands (58,305 represents 58,305,000). As of fall. Data below college level are for regular day schools and exclude subcollegiate departments of colleges, federal schools and home-schooled children. College data include degree-credit and nondegree-credit enrollment. Based on survey of state education agencies; see source for details. For more projections, see Table 206]

Control of school and level	1980	1990	1995	1998	1999	2000	2001	2002	2003	2004 [1], proj.
Total	58,305	60,269	64,764	66,982	67,667	68,671	69,920	71,188	71,890	72,236
Public.	50,335	52,061	55,933	57,677	58,167	58,956	59,905	60,935	61,398	61,540
Private	7,971	8,208	8,831	9,306	9,501	9,714	10,014	10,253	10,492	10,696
Pre-kindergarten through 8.	31,639	33,962	36,806	38,048	38,253	38,556	38,931	39,150	39,267	38,915
Public	27,647	29,878	32,341	33,346	33,488	33,688	33,938	34,116	34,202	33,925
Private	3,992	4,084	4,465	4,702	4,765	4,868	4,993	5,034	5,065	4,990
Grades 9 through 12	14,570	12,488	13,697	14,428	14,623	14,802	15,061	15,426	15,722	16,049
Public	13,231	11,338	12,500	13,193	13,369	13,515	13,734	14,067	14,338	14,634
Private	1,339	1,150	1,197	1,235	1,254	1,287	1,326	1,359	1,383	1,414
College [2]	12,097	13,819	14,262	14,507	14,791	15,312	15,928	16,612	16,900	17,272
Public	9,457	10,845	11,092	11,138	11,309	11,753	12,233	12,752	12,857	12,980
Private	2,640	2,974	3,169	3,369	3,482	3,560	3,695	3,860	4,043	4,292

[1] Pre-K through grade 12 are projections; college data are actual.   [2] Data beginning 1998, reflects new classification system. See footnote 1, Table 267.

Source: U.S. National Center for Education Statistics, *Digest of Education Statistics*, annual, and *Projections of Education Statistics*, annual.

Table 213. Students Who are Foreign Born or Who Have Foreign-Born Parents: 2004

[In thousands (49,347 represents 49,347,000), except percent. As of October. Covers civilian noninstitutional population enrolled in elementary school and above. Based on Current Population Survey, see text, Section 1 and Appendix III]

Characteristic	All students	Students with at least one foreign-born parent					
		Total		Foreign-born student		Native student	
		Number	Percent	Number	Percent	Number	Percent
ELEMENTARY AND HIGH SCHOOL							
Total [1]	49,347	10,887	22.1	2,558	5.2	8,328	16.9
White [2]	37,595	7,617	20.3	1,768	4.7	5,850	15.6
White, non-Hispanic.	29,359	2,123	7.2	388	1.3	1,735	5.9
Black [2]	7,818	1,038	13.3	289	3.7	750	9.6
Asian [2, 3]	1,888	1,727	91.5	466	24.7	1,261	66.8
Hispanic [4]	8,977	5,870	65.4	1,430	15.9	4,440	49.5
COLLEGE, 1 TO 4 YEARS							
Total [1]	14,004	3,127	22.3	1,488	10.6	1,639	11.7
White [2]	10,827	1,879	17.4	781	7.2	1,098	10.1
White, non-Hispanic.	9,201	821	8.9	328	3.6	493	5.4
Black [2]	1,958	409	20.9	244	12.5	165	8.4
Asian [2, 3]	782	717	91.7	410	52.4	307	39.3
Hispanic [4]	1,750	1,144	65.4	486	27.8	658	37.6
GRADUATE SCHOOL							
Total [1]	3,378	926	27.4	607	18.0	319	9.4
White [2]	2,554	418	16.4	214	8.4	203	7.9
White, non-Hispanic.	2,370	303	12.8	150	6.3	153	6.5
Black [2]	343	94	27.4	64	18.7	31	9.0
Asian [2, 3]	408	392	95.9	324	79.4	68	16.7
Hispanic [4]	225	139	61.8	75	33.3	64	28.4

[1] Includes other races, not shown separately.   [2] For persons who selected this race group only. See footnote 2, Table 214.   [3] Data are for Asians only; excludes Pacific Islanders.   [4] Persons of Hispanic origin may be of any race.

Source: U.S. Census Bureau, Current Population Survey, unpublished data. See Internet site See Internet site <http://www.census.gov/population/www/socdemo/school.html>

Table 214. Educational Attainment by Race and Hispanic Origin: 1960 to 2005

[In percent. **For persons 25 years old and over.** 1960, 1970, and 1980 as of **April 1** and based on sample data from the censuses of population. **Other years as of March** and based on the Current Population Survey; see text, Section 1, Population, and Appendix III.]

Year	Total [1]	White [2]	Black [2]	Asian and Pacific Islander [2]	Hispanic [3] Total [4]	Mexican	Puerto Rican	Cuban
HIGH SCHOOL GRADUATE OR MORE [5]								
1960	41.1	43.2	20.1	(NA)	(NA)	(NA)	(NA)	(NA)
1970	52.3	54.5	31.4	(NA)	32.1	24.2	23.4	43.9
1980	66.5	68.8	51.2	(NA)	44.0	37.6	40.1	55.3
1990	77.6	79.1	66.2	80.4	50.8	44.1	55.5	63.5
1995	81.7	83.0	73.8	(NA)	53.4	46.5	61.3	64.7
2000	84.1	84.9	78.5	85.7	57.0	51.0	64.3	73.0
2002	84.1	84.8	78.7	87.4	57.0	50.6	66.8	70.8
2003	84.6	85.1	80.0	[6]87.6	57.0	50.9	69.7	70.8
2004	85.2	85.8	80.6	86.8	58.4	51.9	71.8	72.1
2005	85.2	85.7	81.1	87.6	58.5	52.2	72.3	73.5
COLLEGE GRADUATE OR MORE [5]								
1960	7.7	8.1	3.1	(NA)	(NA)	(NA)	(NA)	(NA)
1970	10.7	11.3	4.4	(NA)	4.5	2.5	2.2	11.1
1980	16.2	17.1	8.4	(NA)	7.6	4.9	5.6	16.2
1990	21.3	22.0	11.3	39.9	9.2	5.4	9.7	20.2
1995	23.0	24.0	13.2	(NA)	9.3	6.5	10.7	19.4
2000	25.6	26.1	16.5	43.9	10.6	6.9	13.0	23.0
2002	26.7	27.2	17.0	47.2	11.1	7.6	14.0	18.6
2003	27.2	27.6	17.3	[6]49.8	11.4	7.8	12.3	21.6
2004	27.7	28.2	17.6	49.4	12.1	7.9	14.0	24.0
2005	27.6	28.0	17.6	50.1	12.0	8.3	13.8	24.7

NA Not available. [1] Includes other races, not shown separately. [2] The 2003 Current Population Survey (CPS) allowed respondents to choose more than one race. Beginning 2003 data represent persons who selected this race group only and exclude persons reporting more than one race. The CPS in prior years only allowed respondents to report one race group. See also comments on race in the text for Section 1. [3] Persons of Hispanic origin may be of any race. [4] Includes persons of other Hispanic origin, not shown separately. [5] Through 1990, completed 4 years of high school or more and 4 years of college or more. [6] Starting in 2003, data are for Asians only, excludes Pacific Islanders.

Source: U.S. Census Bureau, U.S. Census of Population, 1960, 1970, and 1980, Vol. 1; and Current Population Reports P20-550 and earlier reports; and data published on the Internet. See Internet site <http://www.census.gov/population/www/socdemo/educ-attn.html>.

Table 215. Educational Attainment by Race, Hispanic Origin, and Sex: 1960 to 2005

[**In percent.** See Table 214 for headnote and totals for both sexes]

Year	All races [1] Male	Female	White [2] Male	Female	Black [2] Male	Female	Asian and Pacific Islander [2] Male	Female	Hispanic [3] Male	Female
HIGH SCHOOL GRADUATE OR MORE [4]										
1960	39.5	42.5	41.6	44.7	18.2	21.8	(NA)	(NA)	(NA)	(NA)
1970	51.9	52.8	54.0	55.0	30.1	32.5	(NA)	(NA)	37.9	34.2
1980	67.3	65.8	69.6	68.1	50.8	51.5	(NA)	(NA)	67.3	65.8
1990	77.7	77.5	79.1	79.0	65.8	66.5	84.0	77.2	50.3	51.3
1995	81.7	81.6	83.0	83.0	73.4	74.1	(NA)	(NA)	52.9	53.8
2000	84.2	84.0	84.8	85.0	78.7	78.3	88.2	83.4	56.6	57.5
2002	83.8	84.4	84.3	85.2	78.5	78.9	89.5	85.5	56.1	57.9
2003	84.1	85.0	84.5	85.7	79.6	80.3	[5]89.5	[5]86.0	56.3	57.8
2004	84.8	85.4	85.3	86.3	80.4	80.8	88.7	85.0	57.3	59.5
2005	84.9	85.4	85.2	86.2	81.1	81.2	90.4	85.1	58.0	58.9
COLLEGE GRADUATE OR MORE [4]										
1960	9.7	5.8	10.3	6.0	2.8	3.3	(NA)	(NA)	(NA)	(NA)
1970	13.5	8.1	14.4	8.4	4.2	4.6	(NA)	(NA)	7.8	4.3
1980	20.1	12.8	21.3	13.3	8.4	8.3	(NA)	(NA)	9.4	6.0
1990	24.4	18.4	25.3	19.0	11.9	10.8	44.9	35.4	9.8	8.7
1995	26.0	20.2	27.2	21.0	13.6	12.9	(NA)	(NA)	10.1	8.4
2000	27.8	23.6	28.5	23.9	16.3	16.7	47.6	40.7	10.7	10.6
2002	28.5	25.1	29.1	25.4	16.4	17.5	50.9	43.8	11.0	11.2
2003	28.9	25.7	29.4	25.9	16.7	17.8	[5]53.9	[5]46.1	11.2	11.6
2004	29.4	26.1	30.0	26.4	16.6	18.5	53.7	45.6	11.8	12.3
2005	28.9	26.5	29.4	26.7	16.1	18.8	54.0	46.7	11.8	12.1

NA Not available. [1] Includes other races, not shown separately. See footnote 2, Table 214. [2] Beginning 2003, for persons who selected this race group only. See footnote 2, Table 214. [3] Persons of Hispanic origin may be of any race. [4] Through 1990, completed 4 years of high school or more and 4 years of college or more. [5] Starting in 2003, data are for Asians only, excludes Pacific Islanders.

Source: U.S. Census Bureau, U.S. Census of Population, 1960, 1970, and 1980, Vol. 1; and Current Population Reports P20-550 and earlier reports; and data published on the Internet. See Internet site <http://www.census.gov/population/www/socdemo/educ-attn.html>.

Education 143

Table 216. **Educational Attainment by Selected Characteristic: 2005**

[For persons 25 years old and over (189,362 represents 189,362,000). As of March. Based on the Current Population Survey; see text, Section 1, and Appendix III. For composition of regions, see map inside front cover]

Characteristic	Population (1,000)	Not a high school graduate	High school graduate	Some college, but no degree	Associate's degree [1]	Bachelor's degree	Advanced degree
Total persons	189,362	14.8	32.2	16.8	8.6	18.1	9.5
Age:							
25 to 34 years old	39,307	13.3	28.8	18.7	9.0	22.4	7.9
35 to 44 years old	43,350	11.6	31.7	16.8	10.0	20.2	9.7
45 to 54 years old	41,960	10.9	32.1	17.6	9.9	18.7	10.9
55 to 64 years old	29,532	13.7	32.5	16.9	8.5	16.3	12.1
65 to 74 years old	18,388	22.3	37.2	14.2	5.7	12.4	8.1
75 years old or over.	16,825	30.2	35.4	13.0	4.5	10.5	6.5
Sex:							
Male	90,896	15.1	32.1	16.4	7.6	18.3	10.6
Female	98,465	14.6	32.2	17.2	9.5	17.9	8.6
Race:							
White [2]	155,768	14.3	32.2	16.8	8.8	18.2	9.8
Black [2]	21,202	18.9	37.1	18.5	7.9	12.5	5.1
Other	12,391	14.6	23.5	14.2	7.8	26.1	13.8
Hispanic origin:							
Hispanic	22,551	41.5	27.6	13.3	5.6	8.4	3.5
Non-Hispanic	166,811	11.2	32.8	17.3	9.0	19.4	10.4
Region:							
Northeast.	36,117	13.3	34.8	12.6	7.9	19.4	12.0
Midwest.	42,245	11.5	35.5	17.3	9.5	17.3	8.8
South	68,147	17.0	32.7	16.9	8.2	16.7	8.4
West.	42,852	15.8	25.7	19.6	8.9	19.9	10.1
Marital status:							
Never married.	30,239	15.5	30.9	17.3	7.4	20.3	8.6
Married spouse present	115,590	12.1	31.4	16.5	9.1	19.8	11.1
Married spouse absent [3]	3,305	28.9	31.0	12.1	5.8	12.7	9.6
Separated	4,521	24.0	35.8	17.1	8.5	9.5	5.1
Widowed	13,823	31.7	36.7	12.8	5.3	8.9	4.7
Divorced	21,885	13.6	34.6	20.6	10.2	14.3	6.8
Civilian labor force status:							
Employed	120,148	9.6	29.9	17.7	10.0	21.2	11.6
Unemployed.	5,543	20.0	37.0	17.9	8.1	12.6	4.5
Not in the labor force	62,956	24.5	36.1	14.9	6.0	12.4	6.0

[1] Includes vocational degrees.   [2] For persons who selected this race group only. See footnote 2, Table 214.   [3] Excludes those separated.

Source: U.S. Census Bureau, Current Population Report P20-550; and data published on the Internet. See Internet site <http://www.census.gov/population/www/socdemo/educ-attn.html>.

Table 217. **Mean Earnings by Highest Degree Earned: 2004**

[In dollars. For persons 18 years old and over with earnings. Persons as of March the following year. Based on Current Population Survey; see text, Section 1, and Appendix III. For definition of mean, see Guide to Tabular Presentation]

Characteristic	Total persons	Not a high school graduate	High school graduate only	Some college, no degree	Associate's	Bachelor's	Master's	Professional	Doctorate
All persons [1]	37,897	19,182	28,631	30,173	36,021	51,568	67,073	114,878	93,033
Age:									
25 to 34 years old. . . .	33,057	19,436	26,984	29,316	31,740	42,836	47,832	76,664	61,425
35 to 44 years old. . . .	44,214	22,699	32,060	38,076	39,126	59,835	74,824	116,054	90,453
45 to 54 years old. . . .	46,968	22,742	33,700	39,841	41,253	59,919	79,232	133,654	107,130
55 to 64 years old . . .	44,706	22,087	31,042	38,712	39,508	57,196	64,981	130,748	102,885
65 years old and over .	30,352	18,924	21,976	31,408	24,856	32,766	45,293	105,991	67,951
Sex:									
Male.	46,008	22,537	34,050	37,561	44,130	63,753	84,017	137,050	104,848
Female	28,691	13,655	21,923	22,896	29,208	38,766	50,547	70,812	68,191
White [2]	38,930	19,365	29,590	30,895	36,694	52,893	67,435	116,823	95,279
Male.	47,404	22,598	35,360	38,604	45,361	65,652	85,732	138,763	108,621
Female	28,966	13,459	22,260	22,997	29,221	38,898	49,821	71,029	67,302
Black [2]	29,105	17,948	23,492	26,518	31,046	42,298	58,715	101,359	82,647
Male.	33,029	23,018	26,619	31,244	35,119	47,648	68,164	(B)	(B)
Female	25,747	12,807	20,265	23,012	28,310	38,612	49,581	(B)	(B)
Hispanic [3]	27,293	19,041	25,913	28,505	31,033	45,267	57,578	94,158	(B)
Male.	30,897	21,636	29,835	33,449	36,875	53,814	62,815	(B)	(B)
Female	21,936	13,832	20,046	23,132	25,339	34,849	52,406	(B)	(B)

B Base figure too small to meet statistical standards for reliability of a derived figure.   [1] Includes other races, not shown separately.   [2] For persons who selected this race group only. See footnote 2, Table 214.   [3] Persons of Hispanic origin may be of any race.

Source: U.S. Census Bureau, Current Population Report P20-550 and data published on the Internet. See Internet site <http://www.census.gov/population/www/socdemo/educ-attn.html>.

Table 218. **Educational Attainment by State: 1990 to 2005**

[In percent. **As of March, except 1990 as of April**. For persons 25 years old and over. Based on the 1990 Census of Population and the Current Population Survey; see text, Section 1, and Appendix III]

State	1990 High school graduate or more	1990 Bachelor's degree or more	1998 High school graduate or more	1998 Bachelor's degree or more	2000 High school graduate or more	2000 Bachelor's degree or more	2005 High school graduate or more	2005 Bachelor's degree or more
United States.	**75.2**	**20.3**	**82.8**	**24.4**	**84.1**	**25.6**	**85.2**	**27.6**
Alabama.	66.9	15.7	78.8	20.6	77.5	20.4	80.9	19.8
Alaska	86.6	23.0	90.6	24.2	90.4	28.1	91.7	28.7
Arizona.	78.7	20.3	81.9	21.9	85.1	24.6	85.7	27.9
Arkansas	66.3	13.3	76.8	16.2	81.7	18.4	81.4	17.5
California	76.2	23.4	80.1	26.4	81.2	27.5	80.3	30.4
Colorado.	84.4	27.0	89.6	34.0	89.7	34.6	89.2	35.4
Connecticut.	79.2	27.2	83.7	31.4	88.2	31.6	90.0	36.9
Delaware	77.5	21.4	85.2	25.1	86.1	24.0	86.8	25.6
District of Columbia	73.1	33.3	83.8	36.5	83.2	38.3	84.0	46.7
Florida	74.4	18.3	81.9	22.5	84.0	22.8	86.8	25.5
Georgia	70.9	19.3	80.0	20.7	82.6	23.1	85.7	26.9
Hawaii	80.1	22.9	84.6	24.0	87.4	26.3	87.3	30.6
Idaho.	79.7	17.7	82.7	20.3	86.2	20.0	89.1	25.9
Illinois.	76.2	21.0	84.2	25.8	85.5	27.1	87.3	29.5
Indiana.	75.6	15.6	83.5	17.7	84.6	17.1	87.2	22.5
Iowa	80.1	16.9	87.7	20.3	89.7	25.5	89.9	24.5
Kansas.	81.3	21.1	89.2	28.5	88.1	27.3	91.4	30.4
Kentucky	64.6	13.6	77.9	20.1	78.7	20.5	78.9	19.0
Louisiana	68.3	16.1	78.6	19.5	80.8	22.5	80.2	19.7
Maine.	78.8	18.8	86.7	19.2	89.3	24.1	87.2	24.2
Maryland	78.4	26.5	84.7	31.8	85.7	32.3	87.0	36.3
Massachusetts.	80.0	27.2	85.6	31.0	85.1	32.7	87.5	36.8
Michigan.	76.8	17.4	85.4	22.1	86.2	23.0	88.5	24.6
Minnesota.	82.4	21.8	89.4	31.0	90.8	31.2	92.7	34.3
Mississippi	64.3	14.7	77.3	19.5	80.3	18.7	79.9	21.9
Missouri	73.9	17.8	82.9	22.4	86.6	26.2	85.4	24.9
Montana.	81.0	19.8	89.1	23.9	89.6	23.8	92.1	25.4
Nebraska	81.8	18.9	87.7	20.9	90.4	24.6	89.7	25.1
Nevada	78.8	15.3	89.1	20.6	82.8	19.3	86.6	23.5
New Hampshire	82.2	24.4	84.0	26.6	88.1	30.1	91.9	32.8
New Jersey	76.7	24.9	86.5	30.1	87.3	30.1	87.0	36.3
New Mexico	75.1	20.4	79.6	23.1	82.2	23.6	81.0	27.2
New York	74.8	23.1	81.5	26.8	82.5	28.7	85.6	30.3
North Carolina	70.0	17.4	81.4	23.3	79.2	23.2	84.0	25.4
North Dakota.	76.7	18.1	84.3	22.5	85.5	22.6	90.0	27.2
Ohio	75.7	17.0	86.2	21.5	87.0	24.6	87.9	22.9
Oklahoma.	74.6	17.8	84.6	20.5	86.1	22.5	85.2	24.0
Oregon.	81.5	20.6	85.5	27.7	88.1	27.2	88.7	29.1
Pennsylvania.	74.7	17.9	84.1	22.1	85.7	24.3	86.3	25.8
Rhode Island.	72.0	21.3	80.7	27.8	81.3	26.4	84.0	29.2
South Carolina.	68.3	16.6	78.6	21.3	83.0	19.0	83.0	24.2
South Dakota	77.1	17.2	86.3	21.8	91.8	25.7	88.5	25.1
Tennessee	67.1	16.0	76.9	16.9	79.9	22.0	81.8	21.6
Texas.	72.1	20.3	78.3	23.3	79.2	23.9	78.2	25.4
Utah	85.1	22.3	89.3	27.6	90.7	26.4	92.7	29.8
Vermont	80.8	24.3	86.7	27.1	90.0	28.8	90.0	34.4
Virginia.	75.2	24.5	82.6	30.3	86.6	31.9	86.1	30.7
Washington.	83.8	22.9	92.0	28.1	91.8	28.6	91.5	30.9
West Virginia.	66.0	12.3	76.4	16.3	77.1	15.3	82.4	15.1
Wisconsin	78.6	17.7	88.0	22.3	86.7	23.8	90.5	25.1
Wyoming	83.0	18.8	90.0	19.8	90.0	20.6	90.9	22.0

Source: U.S. Census Bureau, 1990 Census of Population, CPH-L-96, and Current Population Reports, P20-550, and earlier reports; and data published on the Internet. See Internet site <http://www.census.gov/population/www/socdemo/educ-attn.html>.

Table 219. Tenth Grade Schools With Specified Safety or Security Measures: 2002

[In percent of schools. Data based on observers' physical inspection of the school property. Based on the Fast Response Survey System and subject to sampling error; see source for details]

School characteristic	Bars on class-room win-dows	Materials covering class room win-dows	Security guards	Metal detec-tors	Security cam-eras	Fencing around entire school	Student lockers	Exterior lights	Parking lots moni-tored by person	Parking lots locked during day
Total	**3.5**	**25.3**	**29.8**	**4.1**	**18.3**	**18.0**	**83.3**	**80.9**	**17.0**	**11.7**
Sector:										
Public	3.2	22.5	35.0	5.0	19.1	15.4	89.1	85.5	19.9	12.5
Private	4.1	32.8	15.1	1.8	16.0	25.5	67.0	67.7	8.5	9.6
Urbanicity: [1]										
Urban	12.7	22.4	39.0	8.5	16.4	36.2	84.6	73.9	21.3	11.4
Suburban.	1.4	23.4	33.1	3.1	22.7	13.1	79.9	79.9	16.9	17.1
Rural.	0.8	28.9	20.6	2.8	14.3	13.2	86.6	86.0	14.8	5.8
Enrollment:										
1 to 399.	2.4	27.0	16.4	1.2	8.3	10.9	82.7	74.1	9.6	5.5
400 to 799	2.7	23.2	24.1	6.5	20.0	18.5	83.7	88.2	13.9	11.0
800 to 1,999.	8.1	18.0	39.4	3.9	22.4	22.6	83.7	91.0	18.5	18.0
1,200 to 1,599	2.9	19.5	62.5	8.5	31.6	15.8	90.9	91.1	31.0	20.0
1,600 and over	7.6	22.8	70.3	5.1	35.3	42.9	82.2	84.4	42.4	24.0
Grade span:										
PK, K, 1, 2, 3,										
4, or 5 through 12	3.6	31.8	15.1	1.1	11.7	17.1	79.3	80.0	11.7	5.1
6, 7, 8 through 12	0.8	25.3	18.9	5.4	15.4	7.8	80.6	74.1	9.0	10.3
9 through 10, 11, or 12. . .	4.3	19.2	41.3	5.7	22.9	21.9	87.9	83.9	21.8	15.8
10 through 11 or 12	(Z)	36.1	30.8	(Z)	27.4	8.9	75.9	95.5	25.3	9.0
Percent of grade 10 students eligible for a free or reduced price lunch:										
5 percent or less	1.1	29.2	21.5	1.8	20.3	21.4	77.0	72.9	13.8	10.1
6 to 20 percent	1.9	30.1	28.0	4.5	19.1	14.8	89.3	87.8	15.0	18.5
21 to 50 percent	1.6	16.6	30.5	2.7	13.6	10.5	91.3	87.2	18.0	8.1
51 and 100 percent	16.0	14.3	44.9	12.8	15.6	36.6	82.7	78.6	21.7	11.4

Z Rounds to zero.   [1] Urban: school located in a large or midsize central city; Suburban: the school is located in a large or small town or is in the fringe of a large or midsize central city; Rural: the school is in a rural area, either inside or outside a metropolitan statistical area.

Source: U.S. National Center for Education Statistics, *An Examination of the Conditions of School Facilities Attended by 10th-Grade Students in 2002,* NCES 2006-302, October 2005.

Table 220. Students Who Reported Carrying a Weapon: 1993 to 2003

[In percent. For students in grades 9 to 12. Percentages are based on students who reported carrying a weapon at least one day during the previous thirty days. Weapons are such things as guns, knives, and clubs. Based on the Youth Risk Behavior Surveillance System. See source for details. See also <http://www.cdc.gov/HealthyYouth/yrbs/index.htm>]

Student Characteristics	Anywhere					On school property				
	1993	1995	1999	2001	2003	1993	1995	1999	2001	2003
Total	**22.1**	**20.0**	**17.3**	**17.4**	**17.1**	**11.8**	**9.8**	**6.9**	**6.4**	**6.1**
Sex:										
Male.	34.3	31.1	28.6	29.3	26.9	17.9	14.3	11.0	10.2	8.9
Female	9.2	8.3	6.0	6.2	6.7	5.1	4.9	2.8	2.9	3.1
Race/ethnicity:										
White, non-Hispanic	(1)	(1)	16.4	17.9	16.7	(1)	(1)	6.4	6.1	5.5
Black, non-Hispanic.	(1)	(1)	17.2	15.2	17.3	(1)	(1)	5.0	6.3	6.9
Hispanic [2]	(1)	(1)	18.7	16.5	16.5	(1)	(1)	7.9	6.4	6.0
Asian	(1)	(1)	13.0	10.6	11.6	(1)	(1)	6.5	7.2	6.6
American Indian	(1)	(1)	21.8	31.2	29.3	(1)	(1)	11.6	16.4	12.9
Pacific Islander.	(1)	(1)	25.3	17.4	16.3	(1)	(1)	9.3	10.0	4.9
More than one race.	(1)	(1)	22.2	25.2	29.8	(1)	(1)	11.4	13.2	13.3
Grade:										
9th	25.5	22.6	17.6	19.8	18.0	12.6	10.7	7.2	6.7	5.3
10th	21.4	21.1	18.7	16.7	15.9	11.5	10.4	6.6	6.7	6.0
11th	21.5	20.3	16.1	16.8	18.2	11.9	10.2	7.0	6.1	6.6
12th	19.9	16.1	15.9	15.1	15.5	10.8	7.6	6.2	6.1	6.4

[1] The response categories for race/ethnicity changed in 1999 making comparisons of some categories with earlier years problematic.   [2] Persons of Hispanic origin may be any race.

Source: U.S. National Center for Education Statistics and U.S. Bureau of Justice Statistics, *Indicators of School Crime and Safety: 2005,* November 2005, NCES 2006-001.

Table 221. Children's Involvement in Home Literacy Activities: 1993 and 2005

[In percent, except number of children (8,579 represents 8,579,000). For children 3 to 5 years old not yet enrolled in kindergarten who participated in activities with a family member. Based on the School Readiness Early Childhood Program Participation Surveys of the National Household Education Surveys Program; see source and Appendix III. See also Tables 224]

Characteristic	Children (1,000)		Read to [1]		Told a story [1]		Taught letters, words, or numbers [1]		Visited a library [2]	
	1993	2005	1993	2005	1993	2005	1993	2005	1993	2005
Total	8,579	9,066	78	86	43	54	58	77	38	42
Age:										
3 years old...............	3,889	4,070	79	86	46	54	57	75	34	40
4 years old...............	3,713	3,873	78	85	41	53	58	77	41	44
5 years old...............	976	1,123	76	86	36	55	58	80	38	46
Race/ethnicity:										
White, non-Hispanic..........	5,902	5,177	85	92	44	53	58	76	42	45
Black, non-Hispanic..........	1,271	1,233	66	78	39	54	63	81	29	44
Hispanic..................	1,026	1,822	58	72	38	50	54	74	26	32
Other....................	381	834	73	88	50	64	59	82	43	48
Mother's home language: [3]										
English	7,805	7,618	81	89	44	55	58	78	39	45
Not English..............	603	1,245	42	66	36	45	52	69	26	29
Mother's highest education: [3]										
Less than high school........	1,036	886	60	64	37	39	56	70	22	23
High school..............	3,268	2,687	76	82	41	51	56	78	31	33
Vocational ed or some college ...	2,624	2,461	83	88	45	57	60	79	44	45
College degree	912	1,832	90	92	48	56	56	75	55	52
Graduate/professional training or degree	569	997	90	94	50	64	60	76	59	60

[1] Three or more times in the past week.   [2] At least once in the past month.   [3] Excludes children with no mother in the household and no female guardian.

Source: U.S. National Center for Education Statistsics, Statistical Brief, NCES 2000-026, November 1999; and the Early Childhood Program Participation Survey, National Household Education Surveys Program, 2005, unpublished data. See Internet site <http://nces.ed.gov/nhes>.

Table 222. Children Who Speak a Language Other Than English at Home: 2000 to 2004

[In percent, except as indicated. For children 5 to 17 years old (9.5 represents 9,500,000). Based on the American Community Survey; see text Section 1, and Appendix III]

Characteristic	2000	2001	2002	2003	2004
Children who speak another language at home (mil.)	**9.5**	**9.8**	**9.8**	**9.9**	**10.0**
Percent of children 5 to 17 years old	18.1	18.5	18.5	18.6	18.9
Race and Hispanic origin:					
White alone, non-Hispanic..............	5.7	5.7	5.6	5.1	5.3
Black alone, non-Hispanic..............	4.4	4.5	4.5	5.0	4.7
American Indian and Alaska Native alone	19.9	23.8	22.5	20.8	17.0
Asian alone	68.4	67.9	65.8	64.5	63.4
Native Hawaiian and Other Pacific Islander alone	36.2	42.9	39.2	34.2	32.6
Two or more races..................	18.2	17.9	17.2	15.2	13.4
Hispanic [1]	68.6	68.7	67.8	67.6	67.4
Region: [2]					
Northeast..................	19.1	18.7	18.4	19.0	19.0
Midwest..................	9.5	9.9	10.0	9.9	10.5
South..................	14.6	15.1	15.4	15.7	15.6
West..................	31.0	31.1	31.3	31.0	31.4
Living in linguistically isolated household [3] (mil.)...........	2.4	2.6	2.6	2.8	2.8
Percent of children 5 to 17 years old	4.6	4.9	4.9	5.3	5.5
Children who speak another language at home and have difficulty speaking English [4] (mil.)...........	**2.9**	**2.8**	**2.8**	**2.9**	**2.8**
Percent of children 5 to 17 years old	5.5	5.4	5.3	5.4	5.2
Race and Hispanic origin:					
White alone, non-Hispanic..............	1.3	1.4	1.3	1.4	1.3
Black alone, non-Hispanic..............	1.2	1.0	1.2	1.3	1.2
American Indian and Alaska Native alone	4.6	4.5	4.2	3.9	3.1
Asian alone	20.4	21.1	19.3	17.9	16.9
Native Hawaiian and Other Pacific Islander alone	10.2	8.8	9.2	5.9	7.1
Two or more races..................	4.3	3.9	3.9	3.4	2.5
Hispanic [1]	22.8	21.3	20.5	20.9	19.7
Region: [2]					
Northeast..................	5.0	5.1	5.0	5.5	4.8
Midwest..................	2.8	2.9	3.0	3.2	3.2
South..................	4.4	4.1	4.3	4.7	4.4
West..................	10.0	9.7	9.0	8.7	8.8

[1] Persons of Hispanic origin may be of any race.   [2] For composition of regions, see map, inside front cover.   [3] No person in the household aged 14 or over speaks English at least "very well."   [4] Children who speak English less than "very well."

Source: Federal Interagency Forum on Child and Family Statistics, *America's Children: Key National Indicators of Well-Being, 2006.* See Internet site <http://www.childstats.gov/>.

Table 223. **Preprimary School Enrollment—Summary: 1970 to 2004**

[As of October. **Civilian noninstitutional population (10,949 represents 10,949,000).** Includes public and nonpublic nursery school and kindergarten programs. Excludes 5-year olds enrolled in elementary school. Based on Current Population Survey; see text, Section 1, and Appendix III]

Item	1970	1975	1980	1985	1990	1995	2000	2003	2004
NUMBER OF CHILDREN (1,000)									
Population, 3 to 5 years old.......	**10,949**	**10,183**	**9,284**	**10,733**	**11,207**	**12,518**	**11,858**	**12,204**	**12,362**
Total enrolled [1]	**4,104**	**4,954**	**4,878**	**5,865**	**6,659**	**7,739**	**7,592**	**7,921**	**7,968**
Nursery	1,094	1,745	1,981	2,477	3,378	4,331	4,326	4,859	4,672
Public...................	332	570	628	846	1,202	1,950	2,146	2,512	2,429
Private..................	762	1,174	1,353	1,631	2,177	2,381	2,180	2,347	2,244
Kindergarten	3,010	3,211	2,897	3,388	3,281	3,408	3,266	3,062	3,296
Public...................	2,498	2,682	2,438	2,847	2,767	2,799	2,701	2,539	2,813
Private..................	511	528	459	541	513	608	565	523	485
White [2]...................	3,443	4,105	3,994	4,757	5,389	6,144	5,861	6,204	5,976
Black [2]...................	586	731	725	919	964	1,236	1,265	1,156	1,332
Hispanic [3].................	(NA)	(NA)	370	496	642	1,040	1,155	1,320	1,438
3 years old	454	683	857	1,035	1,205	1,489	1,540	1,806	1,583
4 years old	1,007	1,418	1,423	1,765	2,086	2,553	2,556	2,785	2,969
5 years old	2,643	2,852	2,598	3,065	3,367	3,697	3,496	3,331	3,417
ENROLLMENT RATE									
Total enrolled [1]	**37.5**	**48.6**	**52.5**	**54.6**	**59.4**	**61.8**	**64.0**	**64.9**	**64.4**
White [2]...................	37.8	48.6	52.7	54.7	59.7	63.0	63.2	65.8	63.8
Black [2]...................	34.9	48.1	51.8	55.8	57.8	58.9	68.5	62.7	67.0
Hispanic [3].................	(NA)	(NA)	43.3	43.3	49.0	51.1	52.6	54.2	55.6
3 years old	12.9	21.5	27.3	28.8	32.6	35.9	39.2	42.4	38.7
4 years old	27.8	40.5	46.3	49.1	56.0	61.6	64.9	68.3	68.4
5 years old	69.3	81.3	84.7	86.5	88.8	87.5	87.6	86.1	86.9

NA Not available.   [1] Includes races not shown separately.   [2] Beginning 2003, for persons who selected this race group only. See footnote 2, Table 214.   [3] Persons of Hispanic origin may be of any race. The method of identifying Hispanic children was changed in 1980 from allocation based on status of mother to status reported for each child. The number of Hispanic children using the new method is larger.

Source: U.S. Census Bureau, Current Population Reports, PPL-148; and earlier PPL and P-20 reports; and data published on the Internet. See Internet site <http://www.census.gov/population/www/socdemo/school.html>.

Table 224. **Children's School Readiness Skills: 1993 and 2005**

[In percent. For children 3 to 5 years old not yet enrolled in kindergarden. Based on the School Readiness Survey of the National Household Education Survey Program; see source for details. See also Table 221]

Characteristic	Recognizes all letters		Counts to 20 or higher		Writes name		Reads or pretends to read storybooks		Has 3 to 4 skills	
	1993	2005	1993	2005	1993	2005	1993	2005	1993	2005
Total	**21**	**26**	**52**	**61**	**50**	**59**	**72**	**70**	**35**	**42**
Age:										
3 years old	11	16	37	46	22	32	66	67	15	24
4 years old	28	31	62	71	70	78	75	73	49	55
5 years old	36	44	78	81	84	91	81	72	65	66
Sex:										
Male	19	26	49	59	47	57	68	70	32	40
Female	23	26	56	64	53	60	76	71	39	45
Race/ethnicity:										
White, non-Hispanic	23	29	56	65	52	60	76	75	39	47
Black, non-Hispanic	18	24	53	69	45	61	63	67	31	44
Hispanic..................	10	16	32	42	42	51	59	55	22	26
Other....................	22	31	49	65	52	63	70	79	36	48
Mother's employment status: [1]										
Employed.................	23	28	57	65	52	62	75	72	39	46
Unemployed	17	18	41	49	46	53	67	61	29	32
Not in the labor force	18	24	49	57	47	55	68	69	32	39
Family type:										
Two parents	22	27	54	63	51	59	74	72	37	44
None or one parent	18	22	49	56	47	57	65	65	31	36
Poverty status: [2]										
Above threshold	24	29	57	64	53	61	74	75	40	47
Below threshold............	12	14	41	49	41	52	64	54	23	26

[1] Excludes children with no mother in the household and no female guardian.   [2] Children are considered poor if they lived in households with incomes below the poverty threshold which is a dollar amount determined by the federal government to meet the household's need, given its size and composition.

Source: U.S. Department of Education, U.S. National Center for Education Statistics, *Home Literacy Activities and Signs of Children's Emerging Literacy*, 1993, NCES 2000-026, November 1999; and the Early Childhood Program Participation Survey, National Household Education Surveys Program, 2005, unpublished data. See Internet site <http://nces.ed.gov/nhes>.

Table 225. Type of School Attended By Student and Household Characteristics: 1993 and 2003

[In percent, except total in thousands (33,900 represent 33,900,000. For students in grades 1 to 12. Includes homeschooled students enrolled in public or private school 9 or more hours per week. Based on the Parent and Family Involvement Survey of the National Household Education Survey Program; see source and Appendix III for details]

Characteristic	Public Assigned		Public Chosen		Private Church-related		Private Not church-related	
	1993	2003	1993	2003	1993	2003	1993	2003
Total students (1,000)	33,900	35,300	4,700	7,400	3,200	4,000	700	1,100
Percent distribution	79.9	73.9	11.0	15.4	7.5	8.4	1.6	2.4
Grade level:								
1 to 5	78.6	71.6	11.6	16.6	8.3	9.7	1.5	2.1
6 to 8	81.3	75.0	9.9	14.5	7.4	7.9	1.5	2.5
9 to 12	80.6	76.0	11.2	14.4	6.5	6.9	1.8	2.6
Race/ethnicity:								
White, non-Hispanic	81.0	74.7	8.6	12.9	8.6	9.7	1.8	2.7
Black, non-Hispanic	77.2	68.1	18.6	24.0	3.4	5.7	0.8	2.2
Other, non-hispanic	73.0	70.1	14.9	19.3	9.0	7.2	3.1	3.4
Hispanic [1]	79.2	77.9	13.7	15.1	6.4	6.2	0.7	0.8
Family type:								
Two-parent household	80.1	73.6	9.3	14.1	8.8	9.7	1.8	2.6
One-parent household	78.9	74.5	15.2	18.3	4.8	5.3	1.1	1.9
Nonparent guardians	83.7	74.7	13.5	20.0	2.1	3.7	0.7	1.5
Parents' education:								
Less than high school	83.6	77.6	13.7	19.7	2.4	2.1	0.2	0.6
High school diploma or equivalent	83.5	79.3	11.4	15.8	4.6	3.7	0.5	1.2
Some college, including vocational/technical	79.8	75.8	11.1	15.8	7.7	6.7	1.4	1.7
Bachelor's degree	75.8	69.0	9.2	13.7	12.5	14.5	2.6	2.8
Graduate/professional degree	72.7	66.2	9.8	14.1	13.1	14.1	4.4	5.6
Region: [2]								
Northeast	77.8	73.5	9.3	11.6	10.5	11.0	2.4	3.9
South	82.0	75.9	10.9	15.8	5.4	6.1	1.7	2.1
Midwest	79.6	71.6	10.4	14.4	9.2	12.1	0.8	1.9
West	78.7	73.6	13.4	18.6	6.5	5.8	1.5	2.0

[1] Persons of Hispanic origin may be of any race.   [2] For composition of regions see map, inside front cover.

Source: U.S. National Center for Education Statistics, *Condition of Education, 2004*, NCES 2004-077, June 2004.

Table 226. Public Charter and Traditional Schools—Selected Characteristics: 2003–2004

[46,689 represents 46,689,000. A public charter school is a public school that, in accordance with an enabling state statute, has been granted a charter exempting it from selected state and local rules and regulations. Schools open as public charter schools during 2002–03 and still open in the 2003–04 school year were surveyed. Based on the 2003–2004 School and Staffing Survey and subject to sampling error; see source for details]

Characteristic	All schools Traditional	Public charter	Elementary Traditional	Public charter	Secondary Traditional	Public charter	Combined Traditional	Public charter
Number of schools	85,934	2,179	60,419	1,152	19,365	521	6,150	505
Enrollment (1,000)	46,689	627	29,588	51	15,186	116	1,915	145
PERCENT DISTRIBUTION OF STUDENTS								
Race/ethnicity	100.0	100.0	100.0	100.0	100.0	100.0	100.0	100.0
White, non-Hispanic	60.6	43.4	58.0	42.9	63.6	34	75.9	51.8
Black, non-Hispanic	16.6	29.7	17.5	31.3	15.6	28	10.5	26.8
Hispanic [1]	17.6	21.7	19.6	20.6	14.9	33	8.5	15.8
Asian/Pacific Islander	3.9	3.8	3.7	4.5	4.7	1	1.4	4.0
American Indian/Alaska Native	1.3	1.4	1.2	0.7	1.2	3	3.7	1.7
PERCENT DISTRIBUTION OF SCHOOLS								
Size of enrollment	100.0	100.0	100.0	100.0	100.0	100.0	100.0	100.0
Less than 300	28.2	67.9	25.0	60.3	27.6	81.4	61.8	71.4
300 to 599	39.4	19.2	46.5	23.7	22.5	12.0	23.4	16.4
600 to 999	21.9	9.9	23.8	13.4	19.8	4.4	9.9	7.3
1,000 or more	10.5	3.0	4.8	2.6	30.0	2.1	4.9	4.9
Percent minority enrollment	100.0	100.0	100.0	100.0	100.0	100.0	100.0	100.0
Less than 10.0	32.5	14.8	30.3	13.8	36.3	12	42.4	20.1
10.0 to 24.9	18.5	19.7	19.3	19.5	17.9	16	12.5	24.2
25.0 to 49.9	17.0	16.1	17.2	17.3	17.3	13	14.1	16.4
50.0 to 74.9	13.1	12.3	12.3	13.0	13.8	11	18.1	11.6
75.0 or more	18.9	37.1	20.9	36.4	14.7	48	12.9	27.7
Percent of students eligible for free or reduced-price lunch [2]	100.0	100.0	100.0	100.0	100.0	100.0	100.0	100.0
Less than 15.0	17.1	28.3	16.3	20.8	22.1	(B)	8.3	37.3
15.0 to 29.9	18.2	14.3	16.2	22.2	26.0	(B)	14.2	8.1
30.0 to 49.9	23.7	16.4	23.5	19.5	23.1	(B)	28.4	16.2
50.0 to 74.9	22.3	18.6	23.6	16.7	16.4	(B)	27.6	12.3
75.0 or more	18.7	22.3	20.4	20.8	12.3	(B)	21.5	26.1

B Does not meet standard of reliability or precision.   [1] Persons of Hispanic origin may be of any race.   [2] Excludes data for schools not providing information on eligibility for free or reduced-price lunch.

Source: U.S. National Center for Education Statistics, Schools and Staffing Survey "Public School Questionnaire," 2003–04; and Common Core of Data, "Public Elementary/Secondary School Universe Survey," 2003–04.

Table 227. **Students Who are Homeschooled by Selected Characteristics: 2003**

[As of spring. (50,707 represents 50,707,000). For students 5 to 17 with a grade equivalent of K–12. Homeschoolers are students whose parents reported them to be schooled at home instead of a public or private school. Excludes students who were enrolled in school for more than 25 hours a week or were homeschooled due to a temporary illness. Based on the Parent and Family Involvement Survey of the National Household Education Surveys Program; see source and Appendix III for details]

Characteristic	Number of students			Percent distribution		
	Total (1,000)	Home-schooled (1,000)	Percent home-schooled	All students	Home-schooled	Non-home-schooled
Total	50,707	1,096	2.2	100.0	100.0	100.0
Grade equivalent: [1]						
K–5	24,269	472	1.9	47.9	43.3	48.0
Kindergarten	3,643	98	2.7	7.2	9.0	7.2
Grades 1 to 3	12,098	214	1.8	23.9	19.7	24.0
Grades 4 to 5	8,528	160	1.9	16.8	14.7	16.9
Grades 6 to 8	12,472	302	2.4	24.6	27.8	24.5
Grades 9 to 12	13,958	315	2.3	27.5	28.9	27.5
Sex:						
Male	25,819	569	2.2	50.9	51.9	50.9
Female	24,888	527	2.1	49.1	48.1	49.1
Race/ethnicity:						
White, non-Hispanic	31,584	843	2.7	62.3	77.0	62.0
Black, non-Hispanic	7,985	103	1.3	15.7	9.4	15.9
Hispanic [2]	8,075	59	0.7	15.9	5.3	16.2
Other	3,063	91	3.0	6.0	8.3	6.0
Number of children in the household:						
One child	8,005	110	1.4	15.8	10.1	16.0
Two children	20,510	306	1.5	40.4	28.0	40.8
Three or more children	22,192	679	3.1	43.8	62.0	43.3
Number of parents in the household:						
Two parents	35,936	886	2.5	70.9	80.8	70.7
One parent	13,260	196	1.5	26.2	17.9	26.3
Nonparental guardians	1,511	14	0.9	3.0	1.3	3.0
Parents' participation in the labor force:						
Two parents-one in labor force	10,545	594	5.6	20.8	54.2	20.1
Two parents-both in labor force	25,108	274	1.1	49.5	25.0	50.1
One parent in labor force	12,045	174	1.4	23.8	15.9	23.9
No parent in labor force	3,008	54	1.8	5.9	4.9	6.0
Household income:						
$25,000 or less	12,375	283	2.3	24.4	25.8	24.4
$25,001 to 50,000	13,220	311	2.4	26.1	28.4	26.0
$50,001 to 75,000	10,944	264	2.4	21.6	24.1	21.6
$75,001 or more	14,167	238	1.7	27.9	21.7	28.0
Parents' highest educational attainment:						
High school diploma or less	16,106	269	1.7	31.8	24.5	31.9
Voc/tech degree or some college	16,068	338	2.1	31.7	30.8	31.7
Bachelor's degree	9,798	274	2.8	19.3	25.0	19.2
Graduate/professional school	8,734	215	2.5	17.2	19.6	17.2

[1] Excludes those ungraded.   [2] Persons of Hispanic origin may be of any race.

Source: U.S. National Center for Education Statistics, Parent and Family Involvement in Education Survey of the 2003 National Household Education Surveys Porgram, unpublished data. See also <http://nces.ed.gov/nhes>.

Table 228. **Public Elementary and Secondary Schools by Type and Size of School: 2003–2004**

[Enrollment in thousands (48,354 represents 48,354,000). Data reported by schools, rather than school districts. Based on the Common Core of Data Survey; see source for details]

Enrollment size of school	Number of schools					Enrollment [1]				
	Total	Elemen-tary [2]	Second-ary [3]	Com-bined [4]	Other [5]	Total	Elemen-tary [2]	Second-ary [3]	Com-bined [4]	Other [5]
Total	95,726	65,758	22,782	5,437	1,749	48,354	31,205	15,752	1,310	87
PERCENT										
Total	100.00	100.00	100.00	100.00	100.00	100.00	100.00	100.00	100.00	100.00
Under 100 students	11.02	6.14	16.75	45.32	55.72	0.96	0.63	1.07	6.35	16.30
100 to 199 students	9.67	8.60	11.04	16.21	22.88	2.77	2.74	2.23	8.73	22.31
200 to 299 students	11.59	12.95	8.10	9.34	9.31	5.62	6.90	2.79	8.48	16.32
300 to 399 students	13.45	15.83	7.95	7.24	4.74	9.04	11.64	3.83	9.33	11.61
400 to 499 students	13.18	16.16	6.31	5.17	3.27	11.35	15.21	3.92	8.62	10.11
500 to 599 students	10.79	13.12	5.62	3.69	1.47	11.33	15.07	4.27	7.50	5.64
600 to 699 students	8.04	9.36	5.34	3.34	0.82	9.98	12.71	4.78	8.04	3.56
700 to 799 students	5.55	6.14	4.68	2.22	0.65	7.95	9.61	4.84	6.17	3.37
800 to 999 students	6.76	6.86	7.46	3.10	0.49	11.52	12.74	9.26	10.25	3.04
1,000 to 1,499 students . . .	6.09	4.18	12.73	2.73	0.33	13.96	10.23	21.55	12.31	2.88
1,500 to 1,999 students . . .	2.16	0.52	7.39	1.01	0.16	7.11	1.82	17.67	6.44	2.20
2,000 to 2,999 students . . .	1.38	0.13	5.42	0.33	0.16	6.25	0.61	17.73	2.87	2.65
3,000 or more students . . .	0.31	0.01	1.22	0.31	–	2.16	0.08	6.05	4.90	–
Average enrollment [1]	521	476	722	269	142	521	476	722	269	142

– Represents zero.   [1] Exclude data for schools not reporting enrollment.   [2] Includes schools beginning with grade 6 or below and with no grade higher than 8.   [3] Includes schools with no grade lower than 7.   [4] Includes schools beginning with grade 6 or below and ending with grade 9 or above.   [5] Includes special education, alternative, and other schools not classified by grade span.

Source: U.S. National Center for Education Statistics, *Digest of Education Statistics*, annual.

Table 229. **Public Elementary and Secondary Schools—Summary: 1980 to 2004**

[For school year ending in year shown, except as indicated (48,041 represents 48,041,000). Data are estimates]

Item	Unit	1980	1985	1990	1995	2000	2003	2004
School districts, total.	Number .	16,044	15,812	15,552	14,947	15,403	15,732	15,695
ENROLLMENT								
Population 5–17 years old [1]	1,000. . .	48,041	44,787	44,949	48,855	52,811	53,316	53,259
Percent of resident population	Percent .	21.4	19.0	18.2	18.6	18.9	18.5	18.3
Fall enrollment [2].	1,000. . .	41,778	39,354	40,527	43,898	46,581	47,804	48,133
Percent of population								
5–17 years old	Percent .	87.0	87.9	90.2	89.9	88.2	89.7	90.4
Elementary [3]	1,000. . .	24,397	23,830	26,253	28,148	29,245	29,590	29,628
Secondary [4].	1,000. . .	17,381	15,524	14,274	15,750	17,336	18,215	18,505
Average daily attendance (ADA)	1,000. . .	38,411	36,530	37,573	40,792	43,269	44,674	45,082
High school graduates	1,000. . .	2,762	2,424	2,327	2,282	2,540	2,706	2,772
INSTRUCTIONAL STAFF								
Total [5]	1,000. . .	2,521	2,473	2,685	2,919	3,273	3,448	3,469
Classroom teachers.	1,000. . .	2,211	2,175	2,362	2,565	2,891	3,030	3,044
Average salaries:								
Instructional staff.	Dollar . .	16,715	24,666	32,638	38,349	43,837	47,462	48,402
Classroom teachers.	Dollar . .	15,970	23,600	31,367	36,675	41,807	45,776	46,752
REVENUES								
Revenue receipts	Mil. dol. .	97,635	141,013	208,656	273,255	369,754	433,904	452,795
Federal	Mil. dol. .	9,020	9,533	13,184	18,764	26,346	35,598	38,856
State	Mil. dol. .	47,929	69,107	100,787	129,958	183,986	212,965	217,140
Local	Mil. dol. .	40,686	62,373	94,685	124,533	159,421	185,340	196,798
Percent of total:								
Federal	Percent .	9.2	6.8	6.3	6.9	7.1	8.2	8.6
State	Percent .	49.1	49.0	48.3	47.6	49.8	49.1	48.0
Local	Percent .	41.7	44.2	45.4	45.6	43.1	42.7	43.5
EXPENDITURES								
Total	Mil. dol. .	96,105	139,382	209,698	276,584	374,782	451,706	471,965
Current expenditures								
(day schools)	Mil. dol. .	85,661	127,230	186,583	242,995	320,954	385,557	397,015
Other current expenditures [6]	Mil. dol. .	1,859	2,109	3,341	5,564	6,618	8,273	8,309
Capital outlay	Mil. dol. .	6,504	7,529	16,012	21,646	37,552	44,577	47,707
Interest on school debt	Mil. dol. .	2,081	2,514	3,762	6,379	9,659	13,299	18,934
Percent of total:								
Current expenditures								
(day schools)	Percent .	89.1	91.3	89.0	87.9	85.6	85.4	84.1
Other current expenditures [6]	Percent .	1.9	1.5	1.6	2.0	1.8	1.8	1.8
Capital outlay	Percent .	6.8	5.4	7.6	7.8	10.0	9.9	10.1
Interest on school debt	Percent .	2.2	1.8	1.8	2.3	2.6	2.9	4.0
In current dollars:								
Revenue receipts per pupil								
enrolled	Dollar . .	2,337	3,583	5,149	6,225	7,938	9,077	9,407
Current expenditures per pupil								
enrolled	Dollar . .	2,050	3,233	4,604	5,535	6,890	8,065	8,248
In constant **(2004)** dollars: [7]								
Revenue receipts per pupil								
enrolled	Dollar . .	5,605	6,303	7,544	7,702	8,726	9,276	9,407
Current expenditures per pupil								
enrolled	Dollar . .	4,917	5,687	6,746	6,849	7,574	8,242	8,248

[1] Estimated resident population as of July 1 of the previous year, except 1980, 1990, and 2000 population enumerated as of April 1. Estimates reflect revisions based on the 2000 Census of Population. [2] Fall enrollment of the previous year. [3] Kindergarten through grade 6. [4] Grades 7 through 12. [5] Full-time equivalent. [6] Current expenses for summer schools, adult education, post-high school vocational education, personnel retraining, etc., when operated by local school districts and not part of regular public elementary and secondary day-school program. [7] Compiled by U.S. Census Bureau. Deflated by the Consumer Price Index, all urban consumers (for school year July through June) supplied by U.S. National Center for Education Statistics.

Source: Except as noted, National Education Association, Washington, DC, Estimates of School Statistics Database (copyright).

Education 151

Table 230. Tenth Grade Schools With Specified Physical or Structural Conditions: 2002

[In percent of schools. Conditions based on observers' physical inspection of the school property. Conditions may be at any location in the school. Based on the Fast Response Survey System and subject to sampling error; see source for details]

School characteristic	Trash on floor	Trash over-flowing	Graffiti	Ceiling in disrepair	Floors/walls not clean	Broken lights	Chipped paint on walls	Broken windows	Doors not on all bathroom stalls
Total	**16.0**	**5.5**	**10.4**	**10.6**	**32.7**	**3.2**	**8.3**	**0.4**	**29.6**
Sector:									
Public	17.9	5.2	13.3	12.7	31.8	3.8	9.7	0.6	29.3
Private	10.7	6.5	2.5	5.0	35.4	1.4	4.3	(Z)	30.2
Urbanicity: [1]									
Urban	26.4	9.6	15.3	7.2	32.8	5.1	11.1	0.8	38.1
Suburban.	14.3	5.9	11.0	9.4	34.3	2.7	6.8	0.6	23.8
Rural.	11.8	2.8	6.8	14.2	30.8	2.7	8.2	(Z)	31.3
Enrollment:									
1 to 399.	12.9	2.6	4.0	19.0	37.8	3.8	12.1	(Z)	35.5
400 to 799	13.3	4.0	15.6	4.7	27.2	2.7	2.9	0.3	29.6
800 to 1,999.	9.8	5.8	9.8	4.1	24.1	2.6	4.4	1.6	20.6
1,200 to 1,599	16.0	7.9	20.5	7.1	35.0	1.7	11.9	(Z)	19.5
1,600 and over	31.8	9.0	26.8	6.3	29.2	4.5	12.2	(Z)	18.9
Grade span:									
PK, K, 1, 2, 3,									
4 or 5 through 12.	4.2	3.7	0.5	11.4	39.7	(Z)	4.3	(Z)	24.7
6, 7, 8, through 12.	20.1	8.6	9.3	11.4	26.0	6.8	16.6	0.6	34.4
9 through 10, 11, or 12. . .	21.3	5.7	16.2	10.4	32.2	4.1	8.5	0.6	29.9
10 through 11 or 12	28.3	6.5	19.0	40.0	7.0	4.0	2.8	(Z)	25.1
Percent of grade 10 students eligible for a free or reduced price lunch:									
5 percent or less.	14.5	8.5	4.5	4.6	35.2	2.6	4.1	(Z)	26.4
6 to 20 percent	19.4	6.2	13.4	11.0	30.1	4.8	6.5	0.6	36.5
21 to 50 percent	9.0	1.2	13.6	16.6	32.9	1.2	7.9	0.7	19.6
51 and 100 percent	27.4	8.0	10.3	17.4	39.8	6.5	20.6	0.8	40.0

Z Rounds to zero. [1] Urban: school located in a large or midsize central city; Suburban: the school is located in a large or small town or is in the fringe of a large or midsize central city; Rural: the school is in a rural area, either inside or outside a metropolitan statistical area.

Source: U.S. National Center for Education Statistics, *An Examination of the Conditions of School Facilities Attended by 10th-Grade Students in 2002*, NCES 2006-302, October 2005.

Table 231. Tenth Grade Students in Schools With Specified Physical or Structural Conditions: 2002

[In percent of students. See headnote, Table 230]

School characteristic	Trash on floor	Trash over-flowing	Graffiti	Ceiling in disrepair	Floors/walls not clean	Broken lights	Chipped paint on walls	Broken windows	Doors not on all bathroom stalls
Total	**21.6**	**6.4**	**5.6**	**7.8**	**30.5**	**3.7**	**9.6**	**1.0**	**24.7**
Sex: Male	22.3	6.3	5.6	7.5	30.2	4.0	9.7	1.1	24.1
Female.	20.9	6.5	5.6	8.1	30.9	3.5	9.6	0.9	25.2
Race/ethnicity:									
White [1]	18.1	5.3	2.8	6.6	28.4	3.2	6.2	0.4	23.3
Black [1]	29.2	10.2	10.1	12.0	37.2	5.0	16.3	2.1	32.7
Amercian Indian [1]	18.2	2.5	(Z)	2.5	32.2	6.9	8.0	(Z)	24.0
Asian [1]	24.2	7.7	4.5	6.9	26.3	6.1	9.7	0.6	21.8
Pacific Islander [1].	12.3	(Z)	9.3	9.3	35.0	4.8	6.4	(Z)	50.4
Multiracial [1]	22.0	6.0	6.2	8.8	27.5	5.2	11.2	1.6	22.6
Hispanic	27.9	7.4	12.3	8.8	34.3	3.6	16.4	2.1	23.6
Sector:									
Public	22.5	6.8	6.0	8.1	30.8	4.0	10.2	1.1	24.7
Private	11.3	2.1	1.1	4.1	27.6	0.7	3.3	(Z)	23.7
Urbanicity: [2]									
Urban	27.5	7.9	7.6	9.3	35.0	4.5	16.7	0.9	26.9
Suburban.	20.5	5.7	5.8	6.3	29.4	3.2	6.6	1.4	22.7
Rural.	15.5	6.0	1.9	9.3	26.5	4.0	6.5	(Z)	26.2
Native language:									
English	20.2	6.1	4.6	7.7	29.7	3.6	8.5	0.8	24.7
Non-English	30.1	7.7	11.5	9.3	34.9	4.1	16.4	1.7	23.0

Z Rounds to zero. [1] Non-Hispanic. [2] Urban: school located in a large or midsize central city; Suburban: the school is located in a large or small town or is in the fringe of a large or midsize central city; Rural: the school is in a rural area, either inside or outside a metropolitan statistical area.

Source: U.S. National Center for Education Statistics, *An Examination of the Conditions of School Facilities Attended by 10th-Grade Students in 2002*, NCES 2006-302, October 2005.

Table 232. Public Elementary and Secondary Schools and Enrollment—States: 2003–2004

[**For schools with membership (48,541 represents 48,541,000).** Based on the Common Core of Data Program; see source for details]

State	Total number of schools with member-ship	Total number of students (1,000)	Regular Number of schools	Regular Percent of students	Special education [1] Number of schools	Special education [1] Percent of students	Vocational education [2] Number of schools	Vocational education [2] Percent of students	Alternative education [3] Number of schools	Alternative education [3] Percent of students
Total	92,816	48,541	85,910	98.1	1,771	0.4	347	0.4	4,788	1.1
Alabama	1,389	731	1,338	99.5	21	0.2	3	0.1	27	0.3
Alaska	500	134	476	97.8	3	0.4	–	–	21	1.8
Arizona	1,931	1,012	1,786	94.5	13	0.1	72	4.2	60	1.3
Arkansas	1,128	455	1,119	99.9	4	0.1	1	(Z)	4	(Z)
California	9,222	6,414	7,908	96.8	127	0.5	–	–	1,187	2.7
Colorado	1,658	758	1,578	98.5	8	0.1	2	(Z)	70	1.3
Connecticut	1,099	577	1,000	96.9	24	0.6	17	2.0	58	0.6
Delaware.	200	118	173	92.5	13	1.3	5	4.9	9	1.3
District of Columbia.	206	78	184	92.8	13	4.3	2	1.3	7	1.7
Florida	3,427	2,588	3,099	98.4	117	0.6	26	0.1	185	0.9
Georgia	2,032	1,523	2,002	99.6	4	0.1	–	–	26	0.4
Hawaii	284	184	280	99.9	3	0.1	–	–	1	0.1
Idaho	664	252	597	98.0	5	0.1	–	–	62	1.9
Illinois.	4,267	2,101	3,910	98.1	234	1.2	–	–	123	0.7
Indiana	1,911	1,011	1,855	99.5	21	0.2	1	(Z)	34	0.3
Iowa.	1,491	481	1,438	99.0	10	0.2	–	–	43	0.8
Kansas.	1,410	470	1,401	99.9	4	(Z)	–	–	5	0.1
Kentucky	1,370	664	1,227	98.9	9	0.1	1	(Z)	133	1.0
Louisiana	1,519	728	1,383	98.1	35	0.2	–	–	101	1.7
Maine.	662	202	660	100.0	2	(Z)	–	–	–	–
Maryland.	1,366	869	1,258	97.0	48	0.9	11	1.0	49	1.1
Massachusetts . . .	1,860	980	1,792	96.4	1	(Z)	40	3.3	27	0.3
Michigan.	3,869	1,758	3,473	96.9	163	1.6	16	0.1	217	1.4
Minnesota	2,187	843	1,616	96.6	240	1.4	1	(Z)	330	2.0
Mississippi.	897	494	896	99.9	–	–	1	0.1	–	–
Missouri	2,260	906	2,186	99.6	13	0.2	–	–	61	0.3
Montana	858	148	853	99.9	2	(Z)	–	–	3	0.1
Nebraska	1,228	286	1,187	99.3	41	0.7	–	–	–	0.0
Nevada.	545	385	499	98.4	12	0.3	2	0.5	32	0.8
New Hampshire . .	473	207	473	100.0	–	–	–	–	–	–
New Jersey	2,428	1,381	2,292	97.6	79	0.7	40	1.2	17	0.4
New Mexico	814	323	741	97.3	16	0.7	1	0.1	56	1.9
New York	4,514	2,865	4,230	97.1	73	0.7	25	1.2	186	1.0
North Carolina . . .	2,260	1,360	2,171	99.5	19	0.2	–	–	70	0.4
North Dakota	517	102	517	100.0	–	–	–	–	–	–
Ohio.	3,836	1,845	3,783	99.7	40	0.3	10	0.1	3	(Z)
Oklahoma	1,786	626	1,786	100.0	–	–	–	–	–	–
Oregon.	1,225	551	1,166	98.4	2	(Z)	–	–	57	1.5
Pennsylvania	3,189	1,821	3,149	98.3	12	1.0	15	0.7	13	0.1
Rhode Island	328	159	314	98.1	4	0.1	5	1.0	5	0.8
South Carolina . . .	1,091	699	1,069	99.6	10	0.1	–	–	12	0.3
South Dakota. . . .	734	126	707	99.0	4	0.1	–	–	23	0.8
Tennessee.	1,644	937	1,608	99.7	12	0.1	4	0.1	20	0.1
Texas	7,843	4,332	6,852	98.2	118	0.1	30	0.1	843	1.6
Utah.	886	496	753	98.1	41	0.4	2	(Z)	90	1.4
Vermont	358	99	316	98.4	40	1.6	–	–	2	(Z)
Virginia	1,856	1,192	1,819	99.5	12	0.1	–	–	25	0.4
Washington	2,241	1,021	1,890	96.2	82	0.3	10	0.1	259	3.3
West Virginia	755	281	727	99.6	7	0.1	3	(Z)	18	0.3
Wisconsin	2,218	880	2,020	97.0	10	0.1	1	(Z)	187	2.8
Wyoming.	380	87	353	97.8	–	–	–	–	27	2.2

– Represents zero. Z Less than 0.05 percent. [1] Focuses on special education with materials and instructional approaches adapted to meet the students' needs. [2] Focuses on vocational, technical, or career education and provides education and training in at least one semi–skilled or technical occupation. [3] Addresses the needs of students that typically cannot be met in the regular school setting, and provides nontraditional education.

Source: U.S. National Center for Education Statistics, *Public Elementary and Secondary Staff, Schools and School Districts: School Year 2003–04*, NCES 2006-307, February 2006.

Education   153

Table 233. **Selected Statistics for the Largest Public School Districts: 2003–2004**

[**For the 50 largest districts by enrollment size.** Based on reports from state education agencies in the spring 2004. Data from the Common Core Data Program; see source for details. School district boundaries are not necessarily the same as city or county boundaries]

School district	City	County	Number of students [1]	Number of full-time equivalent (FTE) teachers	Number of 2002–03 completers [2]	Number of schools
New York City, NY	Brooklyn	Kings	1,023,674	70,171	38,802	1,225
Los Angeles Unified, CA	Los Angeles	Los Angeles	747,009	35,493	27,655	693
Puerto Rico Department of Education, PR.	San Juan	San Juan	584,916	42,444	35,013	1,523
City of Chicago, IL	Chicago	Cook	434,419	22,951	16,186	633
Dade County, FL	Miami	Miami-Dade	371,785	18,887	18,236	375
Broward County, FL	Fort Lauderdale	Broward	272,835	14,264	12,866	264
Clark County, NV	Las Vegas	Clark	270,529	13,483	10,395	298
Houston ISD, TX	Houston	Harris	211,499	12,277	8,350	308
Philadelphia City, PA	Philadelphia	Philadelphia	189,779	10,194	9,507	263
Hawaii Department of Education, HI.	Honolulu	Honolulu	183,609	11,129	10,190	284
Hillsborough County, FL.	Tampa	Hillsborough	181,900	11,020	8,832	237
Palm Beach County, FL.	West Palm Beach	Palm Beach	170,260	9,359	9,219	213
Orange County, FL	Orlando	Orange	165,992	9,495	8,162	190
Fairfax County, VA	Fairfax	Fairfax	164,235	12,293	11,364	204
Dallas Independent School District, TX .	Dallas	Dallas	160,584	10,323	6,696	227
Detroit City, MI	Detroit	Wayne	153,034	6,719	5,975	261
Montgomery County, MD	Rockville	Montgomery	139,201	9,007	8,923	194
San Diego City Unified, CA.	San Diego	San Diego	137,960	7,421	6,622	185
Prince George's County, MD.	Upper Marlboro	Prince George's	137,285	8,119	7,762	203
Duval County, FL	Jacksonville	Duval	129,557	6,976	6,105	179
Gwinnett County, GA.	Lawrenceville	Gwinnett	129,014	8,221	6,571	98
Memphis City, TN	Memphis	Shelby	116,224	7,275	4,788	185
Pinellas County, FL.	Largo	Pinellas	114,510	6,632	6,013	169
Charlotte-Mecklenburg, NC.	Charlotte	Mecklenburg	114,071	7,350	5,368	137
Wake County, NC	Raleigh	Wake	109,424	7,302	6,185	126
Baltimore County, MD	Towson	Baltimore	108,523	7,292	7,123	167
Cobb County, GA	Marietta	Cobb	102,034	6,867	6,015	106
DeKalb County, GA.	Decatur	De Kalb	99,550	6,409	4,933	141
Long Beach Unified, CA.	Long Beach	Los Angeles	97,560	4,439	4,565	91
Milwaukee, WI	Milwaukee	Milwaukee	97,359	5,930	3,536	233
Jefferson County, KY.	Louisville	Jefferson	95,582	5,656	4,886	173
Baltimore City, MD	Baltimore	Baltimore City	94,049	6,268	3,878	189
Albuquerque, NM	Albuquerque	Bernalillo	90,537	6,191	4,158	148
Jefferson County, CO	Golden	Jefferson	87,172	4,765	5,840	167
Polk County, FL	Bartow	Polk	84,135	5,284	4,262	147
Fresno Unified, CA	Fresno	Fresno	81,408	3,927	3,950	103
Fort Worth ISD, TX	Fort Worth	Tarrant	80,335	4,793	3,495	145
Austin Independent School District, TX .	Austin	Travis	79,007	5,354	3,861	111
Virginia Beach City, VA	Virginia Beach	Virginia Beach	76,304	5,555	4,695	86
Mesa Unified, AZ	Mesa	Maricopa	75,401	3,704	4,090	91
Cypress-Fairbanks ISD, TX	Houston	Harris	74,877	4,884	4,238	60
Jordan, UT	Sandy	Salt Lake	74,761	3,054	4,485	85
Anne Arundel County, MD	Annapolis	Anne Arundel	74,508	4,501	4,760	119
Brevard County, FL.	Viera	Brevard	73,901	4,303	4,225	108
Fulton County, GA	Atlanta	Fulton	73,319	4,891	3,865	87
Denver County, CO.	Denver	Denver	72,100	4,218	2,724	145
Northside Independent School District, TX.	San Antonio	Bexar	71,798	4,594	4,293	93
Granite, UT	Salt Lake City	Salt Lake	70,771	3,206	4,161	109
Cleveland City, OH	Cleveland	Cuyahoga	69,655	5,109	2,542	122
Nashville-Davidson, TN	Nashville	Davidson	68,651	4,858	3,179	126

[1] Number of students receiving educational services from the school district. [2] Includes high school diploma recipients and other completers (for example certificates of attendance) but does not include high school equivalents (GEDs).

Source: U.S. National Center for Education Statistics, Common Core of Data (CCD) Data Files: "Public Elementary/Secondary School Universe Survey," 2003-04, Version 1a; "Local Education Agency Universe Survey," 2003–04, Version 1b; and "State Nonfiscal Survey of Public Elementary/Secondary Education," 2003–04.

Table 234. Public Elementary and Secondary School Enrollment by State: 1980 to 2003

[In thousands (27,647 represents 27,647,000), except rate. As of fall. Includes unclassified students. Based on survey of state education agencies; see source for details]

State	Enrollment								Enrollment rate [1]			
	Prekindergarten through grade 8				Grades 9 through 12							
	1980	1990	2000	2003	1980	1990	2000	2003	1980	1990	2000	2003
United States. . .	27,647	29,878	33,688	34,202	13,231	11,338	13,515	14,338	86.2	91.2	88.8	91.1
Alabama	528	527	539	525	231	195	201	206	87.6	93.2	89.6	90.7
Alaska	60	85	94	94	26	29	39	40	94.0	97.4	93.4	95.6
Arizona	357	479	641	704	157	161	237	308	88.9	93.3	88.4	94.0
Arkansas	310	314	318	322	138	123	132	133	90.3	95.8	90.2	91.9
California	2,730	3,615	4,408	4,540	1,347	1,336	1,733	1,874	87.1	92.6	90.5	92.9
Colorado	374	420	517	536	172	154	208	221	92.2	94.6	89.7	91.0
Connecticut	364	347	406	408	168	122	156	169	83.3	90.2	90.7	92.4
Delaware.	62	73	81	83	37	27	34	35	79.5	87.2	80.3	83.3
District of Columbia.	71	61	54	59	29	19	15	19	91.8	100.6	84.0	103.7
Florida	1,042	1,370	1,760	1,832	468	492	675	755	84.4	92.6	89.7	90.1
Georgia	742	849	1,060	1,103	327	303	385	419	86.8	93.7	91.4	93.0
Hawaii	110	123	132	130	55	49	52	54	83.4	87.4	84.8	86.9
Idaho	144	160	170	175	59	61	75	77	95.4	96.9	90.3	93.4
Illinois	1,335	1,310	1,474	1,493	649	512	575	608	82.6	86.9	86.4	89.4
Indiana	708	676	703	717	347	279	286	294	88.0	90.4	85.8	86.5
Iowa	351	345	334	327	183	139	161	154	88.4	92.1	91.3	94.4
Kansas	283	320	323	323	133	117	147	148	88.7	92.5	90.0	93.6
Kentucky	464	459	471	478	206	177	194	186	83.7	90.5	91.4	92.4
Louisiana	544	586	547	536	234	199	197	191	80.2	88.1	82.6	85.1
Maine	153	155	146	139	70	60	61	63	91.6	96.5	90.3	92.4
Maryland	493	527	609	606	258	188	244	263	83.9	89.1	84.9	85.5
Massachusetts	676	604	703	692	346	230	273	288	88.6	88.8	88.5	90.8
Michigan	1,227	1,145	1,222	1,229	570	440	498	528	86.9	90.3	89.5	92.9
Minnesota	482	546	578	564	272	211	277	279	87.2	91.3	89.5	91.4
Mississippi.	330	372	364	361	147	131	134	133	79.6	91.3	87.5	90.1
Missouri	567	588	645	632	277	228	268	274	83.8	86.5	86.5	88.2
Montana	106	111	105	100	50	42	50	48	92.9	94.1	89.1	92.5
Nebraska	189	198	195	195	91	76	91	90	86.6	88.7	86.2	89.9
Nevada	101	150	251	281	49	51	90	105	93.4	98.6	91.8	91.8
New Hampshire . . .	112	126	147	142	55	46	61	65	85.3	89.1	89.1	88.8
New Jersey	820	784	968	979	426	306	346	402	81.5	85.9	85.9	88.2
New Mexico.	186	208	225	226	85	94	95	97	89.5	94.4	85.0	88.6
New York	1,838	1,828	2,029	1,979	1,033	770	853	886	80.8	86.6	83.6	85.7
North Carolina	786	783	945	974	343	304	348	386	90.1	94.8	90.4	90.7
North Dakota	77	85	72	68	40	33	37	34	85.9	92.6	90.9	94.8
Ohio	1,312	1,258	1,294	1,278	645	514	541	567	84.8	88.0	86.1	89.0
Oklahoma	399	425	445	450	179	154	178	176	92.9	95.1	95.4	99.6
Oregon	319	340	379	378	145	132	167	173	88.5	90.6	87.5	87.9
Pennsylvania	1,231	1,172	1,258	1,236	678	496	556	586	80.4	83.5	82.8	85.3
Rhode Island	98	102	114	111	51	37	44	48	80.1	87.5	85.6	87.3
South Carolina	426	452	493	501	193	170	184	198	88.1	93.9	90.9	93.9
South Dakota.	86	95	88	86	42	34	41	40	87.4	89.9	85.3	88.1
Tennessee.	602	598	668	675	252	226	241	261	87.8	93.5	88.3	92.6
Texas	2,049	2,511	2,943	3,133	851	872	1,117	1,199	92.4	98.4	94.9	98.2
Utah	250	325	333	349	93	122	148	147	98.2	97.8	94.5	97.3
Vermont	66	71	70	67	29	25	32	32	87.9	94.3	90.5	93.6
Virginia	703	728	816	837	307	270	329	355	90.7	94.2	89.5	91.5
Washington	515	613	694	699	242	227	310	322	91.7	94.1	89.8	92.3
West Virginia	270	224	201	199	113	98	85	82	92.6	95.7	95.6	97.6
Wisconsin	528	566	595	590	303	232	285	290	82.1	86.1	86.0	89.2
Wyoming	70	71	60	60	28	27	30	28	97.3	97.7	92.7	98.1

[1] Percent of persons 5–17 years old. Based on enumerated resident population as of April 1, 1980, and 1990, and estimated resident population as of July 1 for 2000 and 2003.

Source: U.S. National Center for Education Statistics, *Digest of Education Statistics*, annual.

Education 155

Table 235. Public School Districts With Alternative Schools or Programs for at-Risk Students: 2000–2001

[For the school year. Alternative schools and programs are designed to address the needs of students that typically cannot be met in regular schools. The schools and programs in data shown here serve students who are typically at risk for educational failure (as indicated by poor grades or truancy, for example). Alternative schools are usually housed in a separate facility where students are removed from regular schools. Alternative programs are usually housed within regular schools. Based on the Fast Response Survey System; see source for details]

District characteristic	Percent of districts with schools or programs	Percent distribution of districts with schools or programs by—						
		Number of schools or programs			Percent of district students enrolled			
		One	Two	Three or more	Less than 1 percent	1 to 1.99 percent	2 to 2.99 percent	3 percent or more
Total	39	65	18	17	43	27	14	16
Metropolitan status: [1]								
Urban	66	33	15	52	36	30	17	16
Suburban.	41	63	19	18	49	26	12	13
Rural.	35	74	17	8	38	28	16	18
Enrollment size:								
Less that 2,500.	26	82	11	7	39	26	15	20
2,500 to 9,999	69	58	26	16	46	29	13	12
10,000 or more	95	27	17	56	46	25	17	12
Percent minority enrollment:								
5 percent or less	26	75	15	10	49	26	11	14
6 to 20 percent	43	63	20	17	48	22	14	16
21 to 50 percent	51	63	16	22	38	32	18	12
More than 50 percent. . .	62	58	20	22	34	28	16	22
Poverty concentration:								
10 percent or less	31	68	15	16	56	24	10	10
11 to 20 percent	43	59	22	20	40	27	17	16
More than 20 percent. . .	45	71	15	14	38	29	15	18

[1] Urban: Primarily serves the central city of a Metropolitan Statistical Area (MSA); suburban: serves an MSA, but not primarily the central city; rural: does not serve an MSA.

Source: U.S. National Center for Education Statistics, *Public School Alternative Schools and Programs for Students At Risk of Education Failure 2000–01*, September 2002, NCES 2002–004.

Table 236. Public Elementary and Secondary School Enrollment by Grade: 1980 to 2003

[In thousands (40,877 represents 40,877,000). As of fall of year. Based on survey of state education agencies; see source for details]

Grade	1980	1985	1990	1995	1996	1997	1998	1999	2000	2001	2002	2003
Pupils enrolled.	**40,877**	**39,422**	**41,217**	**44,840**	**45,611**	**46,127**	**46,539**	**46,857**	**47,204**	**47,672**	**48,183**	**48,541**
Pre-kindergarten to 8.	27,647	27,034	29,878	32,341	32,764	33,073	33,346	33,488	33,688	33,938	34,116	34,202
Pre-K and Kindergarten .	2,689	3,192	3,610	4,173	4,202	4,198	4,172	4,148	4,158	4,244	4,349	4,453
First	2,894	3,239	3,499	3,671	3,770	3,755	3,727	3,684	3,636	3,614	3,594	3,613
Second	2,800	2,941	3,327	3,507	3,600	3,689	3,681	3,656	3,634	3,593	3,565	3,544
Third	2,893	2,895	3,297	3,445	3,524	3,597	3,696	3,691	3,676	3,653	3,623	3,611
Fourth	3,107	2,771	3,248	3,431	3,454	3,507	3,592	3,686	3,711	3,695	3,669	3,619
Fifth	3,130	2,776	3,197	3,438	3,453	3,458	3,520	3,604	3,707	3,727	3,711	3,685
Sixth	3,038	2,789	3,110	3,395	3,494	3,492	3,497	3,564	3,663	3,769	3,788	3,772
Seventh	3,085	2,938	3,067	3,422	3,464	3,520	3,530	3,541	3,629	3,720	3,821	3,841
Eighth	3,086	2,982	2,979	3,356	3,403	3,415	3,480	3,497	3,538	3,616	3,709	3,809
Unclassified [1]	924	511	543	502	401	442	451	417	336	306	287	256
Grades 9 to 12.	13,231	12,388	11,338	12,500	12,847	13,054	13,193	13,369	13,515	13,734	14,067	14,338
Ninth	3,377	3,439	3,169	3,704	3,801	3,819	3,856	3,935	3,963	4,012	4,105	4,191
Tenth	3,368	3,230	2,896	3,237	3,323	3,376	3,382	3,415	3,491	3,528	3,584	3,675
Eleventh	3,195	2,866	2,612	2,826	2,930	2,972	3,021	3,034	3,083	3,174	3,229	3,277
Twelfth	2,925	2,550	2,381	2,487	2,586	2,673	2,722	2,782	2,803	2,863	2,990	3,047
Unclassified [1]	366	303	282	245	206	214	212	203	175	157	160	149

[1] Includes ungraded.

Source: U.S. National Center for Education Statistics, *Digest of Education Statistics,* annual.

U.S. Census Bureau, Statistical Abstract of the United States: 2007

Table 237. **School Enrollment Below Postsecondary—Summary by Sex, Race, and Hispanic Origin: 2004**

[In thousands (58,078 represents 58,078,000), except percent and rate. As of October. Covers civilian noninstitutional population enrolled in nursery school through high school. Based on Current Population Survey, see text, Section 1, and Appendix III]

Characteristic	Total			Race and Hispanic origin				
	Number [1]	Male	Female	White [2]		Black [2]	Asian [2]	Hispanic [3]
				Total	Non-Hispanic			
All students	**58,078**	**29,874**	**28,204**	**44,205**	**34,524**	**9,238**	**2,218**	**10,533**
Nursery.	4,739	2,501	2,239	3,566	2,840	825	165	787
Full day	2,368	1,239	1,130	1,586	1,250	589	102	358
Part day	2371	1,262	1,109	1,980	1,590	236	63	429
Kindergarten	3,992	2,141	1,851	3,043	2,325	596	164	769
Elementary.	32,556	16,834	15,722	24,774	19,093	5,158	1,239	6,184
High school	16,791	8,398	8,392	12,822	10,266	2,659	650	2,793
Students in public schools	50,568	26,036	24,533	37,848	28,738	8,624	1,995	9,870
Nursery.	2,487	1,311	1,176	1,703	1,153	600	71	591
Full day	1,252	633	619	748	504	405	47	256
Part day	1,235	678	557	955	649	195	24	335
Kindergarten.	3,417	1,829	1,588	2,571	1,917	535	152	699
Elementary.	29,166	15,140	14,027	21,889	16,447	4,905	1,153	5,895
High school	15,498	7,756	7,742	11,685	9,221	2,584	619	2,685
Population 15 to 17 years old	12,767	6,395	6,371	9,783	7,892	1,992	490	2,072
Percent below modal grade [4] . .	30.6	35.3	25.8	29.3	28.6	38.8	23.1	32.2
Students, 10th to 12th grade	11,166	5,624	5,542	8,585	7,015	1,716	452	1,723
Annual dropout rate.	4.4	4.7	4.0	4.2	3.5	5.2	0.9	8.0
Population 18 to 24 years old	27,948	14,018	13,930	21,897	17,327	3,940	1,152	4,941
Dropouts.	3,386	1,942	1,444	2,599	1,313	597	49	1,386
High school graduates	23,086	11,258	11,828	18,213	15,224	3,050	1,066	3,244
Enrolled in college	10,611	4,865	5,746	8,351	7,228	1,238	695	1,221

[1] Includes other races, not shown separately. [2] For persons who selected this race group only. See footnote 2, Table 214. [3] Persons of Hispanic origin may be of any race. [4] The modal grade is the grade most common for a given age.

Source: U.S. Census Bureau, Current Population Survey, unpublished data. See Internet site <http://www.census.gov/population/www/socdemo/school.html>.

Table 238. **Elementary and Secondary Schools—Teachers, Enrollment, and Pupil-Teacher Ratio: 1970 to 2004**

[In thousands (2,292 represents 2,292,000), except ratios. As of fall. Data are for full-time equivalent teachers. Based on surveys of state education agencies and private schools; see source for details]

Year	Teachers			Enrollment			Pupil-teacher ratio		
	Total	Public	Private	Total	Public	Private	Total	Public	Private
1970	2,292	2,059	233	51,257	45,894	5,363	22.4	22.3	23.0
1975	2,453	2,198	255	49,819	44,819	5,000	20.3	20.4	19.6
1976	2,457	2,189	268	49,478	44,311	5,167	20.1	20.2	19.3
1977	2,488	2,209	279	48,717	43,577	5,140	19.6	19.7	18.4
1978	2,479	2,207	272	47,637	42,551	5,086	19.2	19.3	18.7
1979	2,461	2,185	276	46,651	41,651	5,000	19.0	19.1	18.1
1980	2,485	2,184	301	46,208	40,877	5,331	18.6	18.7	17.7
1981	2,440	2,127	313	45,544	40,044	5,500	18.7	18.8	17.6
1982	2,458	2,133	325	45,166	39,566	5,600	18.4	18.6	17.2
1983	2,476	2,139	337	44,967	39,252	5,715	18.2	18.4	17.0
1984	2,508	2,168	340	44,908	39,208	5,700	17.9	18.1	16.8
1985	2,549	2,206	343	44,979	39,422	5,557	17.6	17.9	16.2
1986	2,592	2,244	348	45,205	39,753	5,452	17.4	17.7	15.7
1987	2,631	2,279	352	45,487	40,008	5,479	17.3	17.6	15.6
1988	2,668	2,323	345	45,430	40,189	5,242	17.0	17.3	15.2
1989	2,734	2,357	377	45,741	40,543	5,198	16.7	17.2	13.8
1990	2,753	2,398	355	46,451	41,217	5,234	16.9	17.2	14.7
1991	2,787	2,432	355	47,322	42,047	5,275	17.0	17.3	14.9
1992	2,822	2,459	363	48,145	42,823	5,322	17.1	17.4	14.7
1993	2,870	2,504	366	48,813	43,465	5,348	17.0	17.4	14.6
1994	2,926	2,552	374	49,609	44,111	5,498	17.0	17.3	14.7
1995	2,978	2,598	380	50,502	44,840	5,662	17.0	17.3	14.9
1996	3,054	2,667	387	51,375	45,611	5,764	16.8	17.1	14.9
1997	3,134	2,746	388	51,968	46,127	5,841	16.6	16.8	15.1
1998	3,221	2,830	391	52,475	46,539	5,937	16.3	16.4	15.2
1999	3,306	2,911	395	52,876	46,857	6,018	16.0	16.1	15.2
2000	3,331	2,941	390	53,358	47,204	6,155	16.0	16.0	15.8
2001	3,390	3,000	390	53,992	47,672	6,320	15.9	15.9	16.2
2002	3,428	3,034	394	54,576	48,183	6,393	15.9	15.9	16.2
2003	3,444	3,049	396	54,989	48,541	6,448	16.0	15.9	16.3
2004, proj.	3,504	3,111	393	54,964	48,560	6,404	15.7	15.6	16.3

Source: U.S. National Center for Education Statistics, *Digest of Education Statistics*, annual and *Projections of Educational Statistics*.

U.S. Census Bureau, Statistical Abstract of the United States: 2007

Table 239. Public Elementary and Secondary School Teachers—Selected Characteristics: 2003–2004

[For school year. (530 represents 530,000) Based on the 2003–2004 School and Staffing Survey and subject to sampling error; for details, see source Web site at <http://nces.ed.gov/surveys/sass/>. Excludes prekindergarten teachers. See Table 253 for similar data on private school teachers]

Characteristic	Unit	Age				Sex		Race/ethnicity		
		Under 30 years old	30 to 39 years old	40 to 49 years old	Over 50 years old	Male	Female	White [1]	Black [1]	Hispanic
Total teachers [2]	1,000	530	781	822	1056	804	2,385	2,669	257	198
Highest degree held:										
Bachelor's	Percent	76.9	54.2	47.5	40.4	50.4	52.1	50.7	52.4	65.3
Master's	Percent	21.4	41.5	45.2	50.3	41.9	42.0	43.3	40.2	26.6
Education specialist	Percent	1.2	2.9	4.2	6.2	3.4	4.3	3.9	3.6	5.3
Doctorate	Percent	0.1	0.6	1.5	1.9	1.7	1.0	1.1	1.9	1.4
Full-time teaching experience:										
Less than 3 years	Percent	41.7	10.5	6.8	2.8	11.9	12.3	11.5	14.6	17.1
3 to 9 years	Percent	58.3	55.4	23.4	10.8	33.9	32.6	32.0	35.3	39.0
10 to 20 years	Percent	(X)	34.1	39.2	23.2	23.4	27.1	26.7	20.9	26.7
20 years or more	Percent	(X)	(X)	30.5	63.2	30.8	28.1	29.8	29.2	17.1
Full-time teachers	1,000	484	712	743	962	743	2,158	2,420	240	183
Earned income	Dollars	37,733	43,804	48,656	54,772	50,936	46,543	47,820	46,516	47,428
Salary	Dollars	36,360	42,345	47,202	53,290	48,089	45,573	46,343	45,167	46,021

X Not applicable. [1] Non-Hispanic. [2] Includes teachers with no degrees and associate's degrees, not shown separately.

Source: U.S. National Center for Education Statistics, Schools and Staffing Survey, "Public School Teacher Questionnaire," 2003–04, unpublished data.

Table 240. Public Elementary and Secondary Schools—Number and Average Salary of Classroom Teachers, 1990 to 2004, and by State, 2004

[Estimates for school year ending in June of year shown (2,362 represents 2,362,000). Schools classified by type of organization rather than by grade-group; elementary includes kindergarten]

Year and state	Teachers [1] (1,000)			Avg. salary ($1,000)			Year and state	Teachers [1] (1,000)			Avg. salary ($1,000)		
	Total	Elementary	Secondary	All teachers	Elementary	Secondary		Total	Elementary	Secondary	All teachers	Elementary	Secondary
1990	2,362	1,390	972	31.4	30.8	32.0	MD	55.2	32.7	22.5	50.3	50.2	48.5
1995	2,565	1,517	1,048	36.7	36.1	37.5	MA	65.2	28.0	37.2	53.2	53.2	53.2
1996	2,605	1,543	1,062	37.6	37.1	38.4	MI	95.2	49.2	45.9	54.4	54.4	54.4
1997	2,671	1,586	1,086	38.4	38.0	39.2	MN	52.2	26.6	25.7	45.4	45.8	44.3
1998	2,746	1,630	1,116	39.4	39.0	39.9	MS	30.7	18.3	12.4	35.7	35.7	35.7
1999	2,814	1,650	1,164	40.5	40.1	41.3	MO	65.0	33.2	31.8	38.0	38.1	37.9
2000	2,891	1,696	1,195	41.8	41.3	42.5	MT	10.3	6.9	3.4	37.2	37.2	37.2
2001 [2]	2,947	1,739	1,211	43.4	42.9	44.0	NE	20.7	13.5	7.1	38.4	38.4	38.4
2002 [2]	2,992	1,759	1,236	44.7	44.2	45.3	NV	20.0	11.8	8.2	42.3	41.9	42.7
2003 [2]	3,030	1,779	1,254	45.8	45.5	46.1	NH	15.1	10.5	4.6	42.7	42.7	42.7
2004, U.S. [2]	3,044	1,782	1,265	46.8	46.4	47.1	NJ	107.5	39.7	67.8	55.6	54.4	56.3
AL [2]	45.9	28.0	20.5	38.3	37.9	38.7	NM	21.5	15.3	6.2	38.1	37.7	38.9
AK	7.8	5.1	2.7	51.7	51.5	52.2	NY	224.0	111.0	113.0	55.2	54.7	55.8
AZ	45.5	30.8	14.7	41.8	41.8	41.8	NC	87.9	61.7	26.3	43.2	43.2	43.2
AR	32.0	15.6	16.4	39.3	37.4	41.1	ND	7.7	5.2	2.5	35.4	35.8	34.8
CA	305.9	220.7	85.2	56.4	56.4	56.4	OH	117.8	80.6	37.2	47.5	47.5	47.4
CO	44.9	22.4	22.5	43.3	43.3	43.2	OK	39.2	20.4	18.8	35.1	34.8	35.3
CT	43.0	30.3	12.7	57.3	56.9	58.1	OR	27.7	17.8	9.9	49.2	49.2	49.2
DE	7.8	3.8	3.9	49.4	49.0	49.7	PA	118.3	61.9	56.5	51.8	51.9	51.8
DC	5.7	4.1	1.6	57.0	57.0	57.0	RI	13.7	8.3	5.3	52.3	52.3	52.3
FL	148.2	74.6	73.6	40.6	40.6	40.6	SC	45.2	31.8	13.3	41.2	39.3	40.0
GA	103.6	62.5	41.1	46.0	45.4	46.9	SD	9.0	6.3	2.7	33.2	33.3	33.1
HI	11.3	6.0	5.3	45.5	45.5	45.5	TN	58.6	42.4	16.2	40.3	40.0	41.1
ID	14.1	7.2	6.9	41.1	41.1	41.1	TX	289.5	148.9	140.6	40.5	40.0	40.9
IL	130.0	89.9	40.1	54.2	50.9	61.8	UT	21.7	11.7	9.9	39.0	39.0	39.0
IN	59.8	32.1	27.7	45.8	45.8	45.8	VT	9.0	4.7	4.3	42.0	41.7	42.3
IA	34.8	16.5	18.3	39.4	38.6	40.2	VA	98.7	56.9	41.7	43.7	42.8	44.9
KS	32.6	16.0	16.6	38.6	38.6	38.6	WA	52.9	29.3	23.6	45.4	45.5	45.4
KY	39.3	27.7	11.6	40.2	40.0	40.8	WV	19.9	13.7	6.1	38.5	38.2	39.0
LA	50.4	35.3	15.1	37.9	37.9	37.9	WI	60.0	41.3	18.8	42.9	42.7	43.3
ME	15.7	10.7	5.0	39.9	39.8	40.0	WY	6.5	3.2	3.4	39.5	39.6	39.5

[1] Full-time equivalent. [2] Total number of teachers excludes some duplication in elementary and secondary levels.

Source: National Education Association, Washington, DC, Estimates of School Statistics Database (copyright).

Table 241. Average Salary and Wages Paid in Public School Systems: 1985 to 2005

[In dollars. For school year ending in year shown. Data reported by a stratified sample of school systems enrolling 300 or more pupils. Data represent unweighted means of average salaries paid school personnel reported by each school system]

Position	1985	1990	1995	2000	2001	2002	2003	2004	2005
ANNUAL SALARY									
Central-office administrators:									
Superintendent (contract salary)...	56,954	75,425	90,198	112,158	118,496	121,794	126,268	125,609	128,770
Deputy/assoc. superintendent	52,877	69,623	81,266	97,251	104,048	107,458	112,104	113,790	116,186
Assistant superintendent........	48,003	62,698	75,236	88,913	94,137	96,627	98,623	100,808	103,212
Administrators for—									
Finance and business........	40,344	52,354	61,323	73,499	77,768	80,132	81,451	82,269	83,678
Instructional services	43,452	56,359	66,767	79,023	82,725	82,418	84,640	84,866	88,950
Public relations/information	35,287	44,926	53,263	60,655	65,505	67,170	67,298	70,291	70,502
Staff personnel services	44,182	56,344	65,819	76,608	80,969	83,035	85,041	86,333	86,966
Technology	(X)	(X)	(X)	(X)	(X)	72,962	73,931	76,139	76,308
Subject area supervisors........	34,422	45,929	54,534	63,103	64,659	66,351	66,582	67,098	68,714
School building administrators:									
Principals:									
Elementary..............	36,452	48,431	58,589	69,407	72,587	73,114	75,291	75,144	76,182
Junior high/middle	39,650	52,163	62,311	73,877	77,382	78,176	80,708	80,060	81,514
Senior high..............	42,094	55,722	66,596	79,839	83,367	83,944	86,452	86,160	86,938
Assistant principals:									
Elementary..............	30,496	40,916	48,491	56,419	59,080	60,672	62,230	62,213	63,140
Junior high/middle	33,793	44,570	52,942	60,842	63,709	64,375	67,288	66,360	67,600
Senior high	35,491	46,486	55,556	64,811	67,593	67,822	70,847	70,495	71,401
Classroom teachers...........	23,587	31,278	37,264	42,213	43,658	43,802	45,026	45,646	45,884
Auxiliary professional personnel:									
Counselors..............	27,593	35,979	42,486	48,195	50,003	50,022	51,706	52,303	52,500
Librarians...............	24,981	33,469	40,418	46,732	49,007	48,741	49,611	50,403	50,720
School nurses.............	19,944	26,090	31,066	35,540	37,188	38,221	39,165	40,201	40,520
Secretarial/clerical personnel:									
Central office:									
Secretaries..............	15,343	20,238	23,935	28,405	29,514	30,039	31,295	31,830	32,716
Accounting/payroll clerks......	15,421	20,088	24,042	28,498	29,898	30,551	32,154	32,632	33,217
Typists/data entry clerks	12,481	16,125	18,674	22,853	24,232	24,840	25,793	25,318	26,214
School building level:									
Secretaries..............	12,504	16,184	19,170	22,630	23,630	24,041	24,853	24,964	25,381
Library clerks.............	9,911	12,152	14,381	16,509	17,052	18,104	18,170	18,427	18,443
HOURLY WAGE RATE									
Other support personnel:									
Teachers' aides:									
Instructional	5.89	7.43	8.77	10.00	10.41	10.68	10.93	11.22	11.35
Noninstructional............	5.60	7.08	8.29	9.77	10.15	10.42	10.98	11.08	11.23
Custodians................	6.90	8.54	10.05	11.35	11.85	11.96	12.40	12.47	12.61
Cafeteria workers	5.42	6.77	7.89	9.02	9.41	9.71	9.98	10.18	10.33
Bus drivers...............	7.27	9.21	10.69	12.48	12.99	13.49	13.85	13.79	14.18

X Not applicable.

Source: Educational Research Service, Arlington, VA, *National Survey of Salaries and Wages in Public Schools*, annual. (All rights reserved. Copyright.)

Table 242. Public School Employment: 1982 and 2004

[In thousands (3,082 represents 3,082,000). Covers a sample of all public elementary-secondary school districts with 15 or more full-time employees in 1982, and covers all public elementary-secondary school districts with 100 or more full-time employees in 2004]

Occupation	1982					2004				
	Total	Male	Female	White [1]	Black [1]	Total	Male	Female	White [1]	Black [1]
All occupations	**3,082**	**1,063**	**2,019**	**2,498**	**432**	**4,499**	**1,170**	**3,329**	**3,424**	**582**
Officials, administrators	41	31	10	36	3	61	30	31	50	7
Principals and assistant principals................	90	72	19	76	11	122	57	65	91	20
Classroom teachers [2]	1,680	534	1,146	1,435	186	2,467	608	1,859	2,033	230
Elementary schools	798	129	669	667	98	1,246	173	1,073	1,019	109
Secondary schools	706	363	343	619	67	921	374	547	769	85
Other professional staff	235	91	144	193	35	373	76	297	300	42
Teachers' aides [3]	215	14	200	146	45	472	58	414	308	90
Clerical, secretarial staff.......	210	4	206	177	19	298	10	288	217	35
Service workers [4]...........	611	316	295	434	132	707	331	376	425	158

[1] Excludes individuals of Hispanic origin. [2] Includes other classroom teachers, not shown separately. [3] Includes technicians. [4] Includes craftworkers and laborers.

Source: U.S. Equal Employment Opportunity Commission, *Elementary-Secondary Staff Information (EEO-5)*, biennial.

Education 159

Table 243. Finances of Public Elementary and Secondary School Systems by Enrollment-Size Group: 2003–2004

[In millions of dollars (442,686 represents $442,686,000,000). Data are based on annual survey. For details, see source. See also Appendix III]

Item	All school systems	School systems with enrollment of—						
		50,000 or more	25,000 to 49,999	15,000 to 24,999	7,500 to 14,999	5,000 to 7,499	3,000 to 4,999	Under 3,000
General revenue	462,686	98,121	53,185	42,437	66,513	41,645	54,563	106,223
From federal sources	41,301	10,576	4,896	3,380	5,410	2,954	3,882	10,203
Through state	37,593	9,890	4,534	3,135	4,820	2,690	3,569	8,957
Child nutrition programs	7,917	2,171	1,055	746	1,078	618	791	1,458
Direct	3,708	686	363	246	590	264	314	1,246
From state sources [1]	218,099	43,891	26,132	21,754	32,116	18,661	24,266	51,278
General formula assistance	148,274	27,058	17,564	15,439	22,251	13,104	16,724	36,133
Compensatory programs	4,804	936	1,150	532	828	370	370	617
Special education	14,270	3,680	1,458	1,025	1,848	1,078	1,646	3,534
From local sources	203,286	43,654	22,156	17,303	28,987	20,031	26,414	44,742
Taxes	138,126	23,059	15,301	12,208	20,998	14,777	19,278	32,504
Contributions from parent government	35,116	14,974	3,304	2,297	3,867	2,747	3,806	4,121
From other local governments	4,649	521	678	321	411	373	617	1,729
Current charges	11,901	1,876	1,214	1,190	1,794	1,106	1,445	3,276
School lunch	6,322	932	666	662	1,026	667	853	1,517
Other	13,494	3,224	1,658	1,288	1,917	1,028	1,267	3,112
General expenditure	472,276	100,373	54,007	43,846	67,907	42,595	55,338	108,210
Current spending	405,232	85,810	45,851	36,817	58,017	36,841	47,670	94,226
By function: Instruction	245,193	52,878	27,701	22,408	35,280	22,494	29,026	55,405
Support services	138,497	28,162	15,625	12,363	19,674	12,527	16,286	33,860
Other current spending	21,543	4,770	2,525	2,046	3,063	1,820	2,358	4,961
By object: Total salaries and wages	251,822	53,258	29,252	23,615	36,641	23,124	29,691	56,240
Total employee benefits	74,889	15,682	8,132	6,902	10,958	6,969	8,998	17,248
Other	78,522	16,870	8,467	6,300	10,418	6,747	8,981	20,738
Capital outlay	52,269	11,408	6,544	5,762	7,668	4,216	5,814	10,856
Interest on debt	12,149	2,843	1,388	1,162	1,726	1,124	1,512	2,393
Payments to other governments	2,626	312	223	106	496	414	342	734
Debt outstanding	274,364	60,138	32,495	25,908	39,413	25,567	34,206	56,639
Long-term	265,242	59,056	31,723	25,387	38,052	24,517	32,844	53,662
Short-term	9,123	1,082	772	520	1,360	1,050	1,362	2,977
Long-term debt issued	44,827	9,696	6,608	4,608	6,314	3,899	5,091	8,611
Long-term debt retired	25,570	5,291	3,201	2,708	3,512	2,220	3,130	5,508

[1] Includes other sources, not shown separately.

Source: U.S. Census Bureau, *Public Education Finances, 2004*, March 2006. See Internet site <http://www.census.gov/govs /www/school.html>.

Table 244. Per Pupil Amounts of Finances of Public Elementary and Secondary School Systems by Enrollment-Size Group: 2003–2004

[In dollars, except as indicated (47,898 represents 47,898,000). Data are based on annual survey. For details, see source. See also Appendix III]

Item	All school systems	School systems with enrollment of—						
		50,000 or more	25,000 to 49,999	15,000 to 24,999	7,500 to 14,999	5,000 to 7,499	3,000 to 4,999	Under 3,000
Fall enrollment (1,000)	47,898	10,139	5,841	4,902	7,091	4,367	5,556	10,002
General revenue	9,660	9,678	9,106	8,656	9,380	9,537	9,820	10,620
From federal sources	862	1,043	838	690	763	676	699	1,020
From state sources [1]	4,553	4,329	4,474	4,437	4,529	4,273	4,368	5,127
General formula assistance	3,096	2,669	3,007	3,149	3,138	3,001	3,010	3,612
Special education	298	363	250	209	261	247	296	353
From local sources [1]	4,244	4,306	3,793	3,529	4,088	4,587	4,754	4,473
Taxes	2,884	2,274	2,620	2,490	2,961	3,384	3,470	3,250
Contributions from parent government	733	1,477	566	469	545	629	685	412
Current charges	248	185	208	243	253	253	260	328
School lunch	132	92	114	135	145	153	154	152
General expenditure [1]	9,687	9,685	9,077	8,810	9,424	9,597	9,800	10,637
Current spending	8,287	8,248	7,680	7,376	8,029	8,280	8,420	9,239
By function: Instruction	5,056	5,132	4,676	4,537	4,922	5,083	5,158	5,484
Support services	2,892	2,778	2,675	2,522	2,775	2,869	2,931	3,385
By object: Total salaries and wages	5,257	5,253	5,008	4,817	5,167	5,295	5,344	5,623
Total employee benefits	1,564	1,547	1,392	1,408	1,545	1,596	1,619	1,724
Capital outlay	1,091	1,125	1,120	1,175	1,081	966	1,046	1,085
Interest on debt	254	280	238	237	243	258	272	239
Debt outstanding	5,728	5,932	5,563	5,285	5,558	5,855	6,157	5,662
Long-term	5,538	5,825	5,431	5,179	5,366	5,614	5,911	5,365

[1] Includes other sources of revenue and expenditure categories, not shown separately.

Source: U.S. Census Bureau, *Public Education Finances, 2004*, March 2006. See Internet site <http//www.census.gov/govs /www/school.html>.

Table 245. Public Elementary and Secondary Estimated Finances, 1980 to 2004, and by State, 2004

[In millions of dollars (101,724 represents $101,724,000,000), except as noted. For school years ending in June of year shown]

Year and state	Receipts						Expenditures				
		Revenue receipts							Current expenditures		
			Source			Non-revenue re-ceipts [1]		Per capita [3] (dol.)	Ele-mentary and second-ary day schools	Average per pupil in ADA [4]	
	Total	Total	Federal	State	Local		Total [2]			Amount (dol.)	Rank
1980	101,724	97,635	9,020	47,929	40,686	4,089	96,105	427	85,661	2,230	(X)
1985	146,976	141,013	9,533	69,107	62,373	5,963	139,382	591	127,230	3,483	(X)
1990	218,126	208,656	13,184	100,787	94,685	9,469	209,698	850	186,583	4,966	(X)
1995	288,501	273,255	18,764	129,958	124,533	15,246	276,584	1,051	242,995	5,957	(X)
1997	325,007	303,400	19,965	148,184	135,251	21,607	310,719	1,153	269,824	6,401	(X)
1998	349,787	324,429	21,668	159,596	143,164	25,359	330,952	1,214	285,213	6,666	(X)
1999	370,735	345,901	23,583	170,606	151,711	24,835	350,539	1,271	301,380	7,011	(X)
2000	390,861	369,754	26,346	183,986	159,421	21,106	374,782	1,343	320,954	7,418	(X)
2001	425,283	396,395	28,009	198,310	170,076	28,888	402,809	1,431	342,911	7,841	(X)
2002	448,945	416,754	32,101	206,139	178,514	32,191	426,340	1,495	361,814	8,183	(X)
2003	469,785	433,904	35,598	212,965	185,340	35,882	451,706	1,569	385,557	8,630	(X)
2004, total	**488,447**	**452,795**	**38,856**	**217,140**	**196,798**	**35,653**	**471,965**	**1,623**	**397,015**	**8,807**	**(X)**
Alabama	5,613	5,328	639	2,977	1,711	285	5,499	1,221	4,887	6,953	43
Alaska	1,443	1,285	161	817	308	157	1,418	2,187	1,314	11,432	6
Arizona	7,145	7,049	552	3,589	2,907	96	6,346	1,137	5,154	5,595	49
Arkansas	3,596	3,535	391	1,851	1,293	61	3,160	1,158	2,715	6,663	45
California	70,408	60,595	6,501	35,401	18,692	9,813	58,752	1,657	47,771	7,860	32
Colorado	7,557	6,489	426	2,797	3,267	1,067	7,272	1,599	6,079	8,651	25
Connecticut	7,469	7,457	436	2,967	4,055	12	7,469	2,142	6,784	12,394	2
Delaware	1,429	1,254	82	804	369	175	1,380	1,687	1,161	10,347	11
District of Columbia	827	827	115	–	712	–	1,042	1,869	867	14,621	(X)
Florida	22,752	21,161	2,220	9,195	9,746	1,591	21,869	1,286	17,380	7,181	40
Georgia	14,299	13,883	1,227	6,335	6,320	416	14,299	1,648	12,347	8,671	24
Hawaii	2,138	2,106	173	1,901	32	32	1,683	1,347	1,510	9,019	22
Idaho	1,700	1,650	150	1,000	500	50	1,700	1,244	1,585	6,779	44
Illinois	20,325	18,240	1,408	5,546	11,286	2,085	29,528	2,334	20,299	10,866	9
Indiana	10,471	9,763	642	4,908	4,212	709	10,191	1,644	8,502	9,138	21
Iowa	4,535	4,251	312	1,965	1,974	285	4,139	1,407	3,503	7,696	35
Kansas	4,760	4,274	345	2,138	1,791	486	3,863	1,418	3,435	8,189	29
Kentucky	5,205	5,196	620	3,031	1,545	10	5,203	1,263	4,736	8,298	28
Louisiana	6,442	5,779	782	2,811	2,185	664	6,144	1,367	5,282	7,840	33
Maine	2,247	2,132	201	891	1,039	115	2,247	1,716	2,051	10,961	8
Maryland	9,278	9,074	663	3,458	4,953	205	8,971	1,627	7,983	9,824	16
Massachusetts . . .	12,228	12,227	838	4,722	6,667	1	11,602	1,807	10,562	11,445	5
Michigan	17,055	16,713	944	11,204	4,566	342	18,954	1,880	14,857	9,416	19
Minnesota	9,716	8,612	543	6,138	1,931	1,105	9,417	1,860	7,469	9,513	17
Mississippi	3,586	3,436	513	1,869	1,053	150	3,394	1,178	2,994	6,556	46
Missouri	8,609	7,972	697	2,577	4,698	637	7,366	1,288	6,203	7,548	37
Montana	1,279	1,251	148	590	512	28	1,205	1,312	1,141	8,631	26
Nebraska	2,230	2,209	157	892	1,159	21	2,385	1,373	2,089	7,947	30
Nevada	3,617	3,025	216	965	1,844	592	3,399	1,516	2,552	6,177	48
New Hampshire . .	2,309	2,075	121	961	993	234	2,103	1,632	1,878	9,902	15
New Jersey	18,297	18,143	520	6,892	10,731	154	16,449	1,903	15,728	11,847	4
New Mexico	2,998	2,901	512	2,002	387	97	3,022	1,608	2,547	8,772	23
New York	39,242	38,500	2,400	17,500	18,600	742	39,309	2,046	34,832	12,408	1
North Carolina . . .	10,268	9,422	1,015	6,035	2,371	846	10,382	1,233	9,344	7,511	38
North Dakota	938	847	111	307	429	91	833	1,316	676	7,112	41
Ohio	21,487	18,546	1,167	8,472	8,908	2,941	19,065	1,667	16,673	10,102	13
Oklahoma	4,600	4,343	553	2,358	1,432	257	4,078	1,163	3,740	6,405	47
Oregon	4,776	4,402	468	2,354	1,580	374	4,934	1,384	4,217	8,575	27
Pennsylvania	19,552	19,374	1,529	7,007	10,839	178	20,008	1,617	16,866	9,949	14
Rhode Island	1,496	1,496	55	553	888	–	1,715	1,594	1,640	10,976	7
South Carolina . . .	6,809	6,004	640	2,769	2,595	804	5,899	1,422	4,767	7,395	39
South Dakota	1,092	1,006	159	339	507	86	1,017	1,329	887	7,611	36
Tennessee	6,523	6,191	709	2,804	2,679	332	6,309	1,079	5,980	6,983	42
Texas	39,680	35,387	3,882	13,644	17,862	4,292	37,498	1,696	30,905	7,698	34
Utah	3,023	3,022	279	1,756	987	1	3,103	1,319	2,479	5,556	50
Vermont	1,232	1,182	95	801	286	50	1,206	1,948	1,055	12,157	3
Virginia	12,110	11,310	770	4,588	5,951	800	12,012	1,631	10,381	9,401	20
Washington	9,553	8,758	829	5,457	2,473	795	9,574	1,561	7,511	7,904	31
West Virginia	2,837	2,728	321	1,641	765	110	2,785	1,538	2,530	9,509	18
Wisconsin	10,675	9,413	522	5,052	3,838	1,262	9,813	1,792	8,345	10,293	12
Wyoming	991	970	94	506	370	20	952	1,896	820	10,413	10

– Represents zero. X Not applicable. [1] Amount received by local education agencies from the sales of bonds and real property and equipment, loans, and proceeds from insurance adjustments. [2] Includes interest on school debt and other current expenditures not shown separately. [3] Based on U.S. Census Bureau estimated resident population, as of July 1, the previous year, except 1980, 1990, and 2000 population enumerated as of April 1. [4] Average daily attendance.

Source: National Education Association, Washington, DC, Estimates of School Statistics Database (copyright).

Education 161

Table 246. Public Schools With Internet Access: 1995 to 2003

[In percent. As of fall. Excludes special education, vocational education, and alternative schools. Based on the Fast Response Survey System and subject to sampling error; see source for details]

School characteristic	Percent of schools with Internet access				Percent of instructional classrooms with Internet access				Students per instruc-tional computer with Internet access, 2003	Schools with Internet available to students outside of regular school hours, 2003
	1995	2000	2002	2003	1995	2000	2002	2003		
Total [1]	50	98	99	100	8	77	92	93	4.4	48
Instructional level:										
Elementary	46	97	99	100	8	76	92	93	4.9	41
Secondary	65	100	100	100	8	79	91	94	3.8	69
Size of enrollment:										
Less than 300	39	96	96	100	9	83	91	93	3.2	39
300 to 999	52	98	100	100	8	78	93	93	4.7	47
1,000 or more	69	99	100	100	4	70	89	94	4.3	74
Percent minority enrollment:										
Less than 6 percent	52	98	97	100	9	85	93	93	4.1	45
6 to 20 percent	58	100	100	100	10	83	94	95	4.1	50
21 to 49 percent	55	98	99	99	9	79	91	95	4.1	46
50 percent or more	39	96	99	100	3	64	89	92	5.1	51
Percent of students eligible for free or reduced-price lunch:										
Less than 35 percent	60	99	98	100	10	82	93	95	4.2	47
35 to 49 percent	48	99	100	100	6	81	90	93	4.4	48
50 to 74 percent	41	97	100	100	6	77	91	94	4.4	46
75 percent or more	31	94	99	99	3	60	89	90	5.1	53

[1] Includes combined schools.

Source: U.S. National Center for Education Statistics, *Internet Access in U.S. Public Schools and Classrooms: 1994–2003*, NCES 2005-015, February 2005.

Table 247. Public Schools With Broadband and Wireless Connections: 2000 to 2003

[In percent. As of fall. Excludes special education, vocational education, and alternative schools. Based on the Fast Response Survey System and subject to sampling error; see source for details]

School characteristic	Percent of schools with Internet access using broadband connections				Percent using any type of wireless Internet connection		Percent of instructional rooms with wireless Internet connections	
	2000	2001	2002	2003	2002	2003	2002	2003
Total [1]	80	85	94	95	23	32	15	11
Instructional level:								
Elementary	77	83	93	94	20	29	13	11
Secondary	89	94	98	97	33	42	19	11
Size of enrollment:								
Less than 300	67	72	90	90	17	28	12	15
300 to 999	83	89	94	96	23	30	14	10
1,000 or more	90	96	100	100	37	51	19	11
Percent minority enrollment:								
Less than 6 percent	76	81	92	90	21	31	14	14
6 to 20 percent	82	85	91	96	23	36	13	12
21 to 49 percent	84	85	96	98	25	35	15	10
50 percent or more	81	93	95	97	23	28	16	9
Percent of students eligible for free or reduced-price lunch:								
Less than 35 percent	81	84	93	95	24	36	15	13
35 to 49 percent	82	86	96	96	25	33	15	12
50 to 74 percent	79	84	93	96	23	28	17	9
75 percent or more	75	90	95	93	20	25	11	9

[1] Includes combined schools.

Source: U.S. National Center for Education Statistics, *Internet Access in U.S. Public Schools and Classrooms: 1994–2003*, NCES 2005-015, February 2005.

Table 248. **Computers for Student Instruction in Elementary and Secondary Schools: 2005–2006**

[54,848 represents 54,848,000. Market Data Retrieval collects student use computer information in elementary and secondary schools nationwide through a comprehensive annual technology survey that utilizes both mail, telephone, and Internet data methods]

Level	Total schools	Total enrollment (1,000)	Number of computers [1] (1,000)	Students per computer	Schools with a wireless network (percent)	Schools with distance learning programs for students (percent) [2]	Schools with laptop computers (percent) [3]	Schools with high speed Internet access (percent) [4]	Schools with video-streaming (percent)
U.S. total	114,749	54,848	14,165	3.9	54.2	19.1	59.7	84.3	43.4
Public schools, total.	91,977	49,567	12,914	3.8	54.4	20.3	60.0	85.7	45.0
Elementary	53,245	23,805	5,612	4.2	49.1	11.2	55.4	85.0	41.3
Middle/junior high.	14,310	9,376	2,503	3.7	61.6	15.6	66.2	85.8	53.2
Senior high	17,282	14,028	4,067	3.4	64.0	43.8	67.9	87.5	50.4
K to 12/other.	7,140	2,358	733	3.2	54.7	43.2	61.7	85.9	41.0
Catholic schools, total	7,673	2,481	554	4.5	51.0	7.1	60.3	74.0	29.7
Elementary	6,326	1,797	358	5.0	46.5	3.8	57.9	71.6	27.3
Secondary	1,179	621	179	3.5	67.7	20.8	70.0	83.8	38.8
K to 12/other.	168	63	17	3.8	73.1	7.7	65.4	73.1	38.5
Other private schools, total .	15,099	2,800	697	4.0	52.1	6.5	50.1	66.4	24.1
Elementary	7,426	1,171	283	4.1	52.9	2.0	51.4	67.6	26.5
Secondary	1,274	265	77	3.4	67.5	18.1	54.2	68.7	24.1
K to 12/other.	6,399	1,363	338	4.0	47.1	9.5	47.4	64.2	20.8

[1] Includes estimates for schools not reporting number of computers. [2] Distance learning programs as determined by respondents. [3] For student instruction. [4] Statistics based on responses to those indicating type of Internet connection. High speed includes Internet connection types: T1, T3, and cable modem.

Source: Market Data Retrieval, Shelton, CT, unpublished data (copyright).

Table 249. **Computer and Internet Use by Children and Adolescents: 2003**

[For persons 5 to 17 years old (53,561 represents 53,561,000). As of September. Based on the Current Population Survey; see source and Appendix III for details]

User characteristics	Number of children (1,000)	Percent using computers at school	Percent using computers at home [1]	Home use activity (percent)				
				Word processing	Connect to the Internet	E-mail	Complete school assignments	Play games
Total	53,561	84.5	68.6	33.4	46.6	32.9	49.2	56.9
Age: 5 to 7 years old	11,785	72.2	59.3	9.6	23.3	7.7	16.6	51.7
8 to 10 years old	11,849	86.3	66.1	23.5	38.2	19.5	42.7	58.0
11 to 14 years old.	17,173	89.0	72.0	42.7	54.8	40.9	61.8	61.0
15 to 17 years old.	12,753	87.9	75.0	51.9	64.7	57.7	68.1	55.4
Sex: Male	27,422	84.2	68.0	31.2	45.5	30.2	47.5	57.8
Female	26,139	84.7	69.3	35.6	47.7	35.7	50.9	56.0
Race/ethnicity:								
White alone, non-Hispanic	32,279	86.6	79.6	40.1	56.9	41.1	56.6	67.3
Black alone, non-Hispanic	8,048	82.6	47.2	20.5	28.0	18.6	35.9	39.1
Hispanic	9,503	79.7	48.3	20.2	27.2	17.1	34.4	37.8
Other	3,731	82.1	71.4	35.9	46.4	32.6	50.8	54.7
Parent educational attainment:								
Less than high school credential . . .	10,001	77.9	43.7	17.7	24.2	16.3	29.5	34.6
High school credential	15,270	84.1	61.4	26.9	39.9	28.2	43.7	50.6
Some college.	14,384	86.8	75.4	35.5	51.9	35.7	54.1	63.4
Bachelor's degree	9,410	86.9	86.5	47.4	62.9	45.2	63.2	73.0
Graduate education.	4,495	87.6	89.5	53.8	67.9	50.5	66.0	73.6
Household language:								
Spanish-only	2,680	75.3	33.6	12.7	14.3	9.0	24.1	26.7
Not Spanish-only	50,881	84.9	70.5	34.4	48.3	34.1	50.5	58.5
Family income:								
Under $20,000	16,459	81.3	51.7	23.1	30.7	21.7	36.2	41.2
20,000 to 34,999	8,615	81.9	55.7	22.9	33.3	23.2	38.2	45.4
35,000 to 49,999	6,993	85.9	72.2	33.2	46.7	32.3	50.5	60.5
50,000 to 74,999	9,053	86.0	80.5	38.6	56.7	39.2	57.6	67.1
75,000 or more.	12,441	88.5	89.3	50.5	69.3	50.1	67.0	76.4

[1] Includes other home activities, not shown separately.

Source: U.S. National Center for Education Statistics, CPS October (Education) Supplement, October 2003, special tabulation.

U.S. Census Bureau, Statistical Abstract of the United States: 2007

Table 250. Distance Education in Public Elementary and Secondary Schools: 2002–2003

[For the school year. Distance education courses are for-credit classes offered to students enrolled in the district where the teacher and student were in different locations. They could be delivered via audio, video, Internet, or other computer technologies. Reasons for districts providing these courses include offering courses not otherwise available, offering Advanced Placement courses, addressing growing populations and space limitations, reducing scheduling conflicts for students, and permitting students who failed a course to take the course again. Excludes such things as virtual field trips, online homework, or a course delivered mainly by written correspondence. Based on the Fast Response Survey System and subject to sampling error; see source for details]

District characteristic	Number of districts		Enrollments in distance education courses							
		With students enrolled in distance education courses		Curriculum						
	Total		Total [1]	English/ language arts	Social studies/ social sciences	Computer sciences	Natural/ physical sciences	Math	Foreign language	High school level
All public school districts [2] . .	15,040	5,480	327,670	61,590	74,570	11,660	38,920	49,210	39,090	222,090
District enrollment size:										
Less than 2,500	11,080	4,060	117,730	21,480	25,550	3,060	12,900	15,060	22,300	74,160
2,500 to 9,999	3,100	1,010	85,640	15,810	18,950	1,970	11,090	13,480	9,290	44,780
10,000 or more	820	410	124,300	24,300	30,070	6,630	14,930	20,670	7,500	103,150
Region: [3]										
Northeast	3,040	640	42,070	6,060	8,280	3,020	4,830	4,730	5,300	17,420
South	1,750	790	59,010	10,240	12,490	1,420	5,400	8,920	11,120	50,410
Midwest	5,390	2,500	108,140	21,250	21,500	2,750	14,270	17,040	14,250	60,560
West	4,850	1,540	118,450	24,040	32,290	4,470	14,420	18,520	8,410	93,700
Poverty concentration: [4]										
Less than 10 percent	4,850	1,620	77,380	15,300	17,350	2,140	6,900	10,590	9,600	57,320
10 to 19 percent	5,330	2,220	97,300	18,370	23,820	3,000	10,720	15,030	10,600	77,810
20 percent or more	3,690	1,560	93,280	17,800	22,770	6,290	11,800	14,150	15,330	83,100

[1] Includes other curriculum not shown separately. [2] Includes districts and enrollments where enrollment size and poverty concentration were not known. [3] For composition or regions, see map inside front cover. [4] Percentage of children in the district ages 5 to 17 in families living below the poverty level.

Source: U.S. National Center for Education Statistics, *Distance Education Courses for Public Elementary and Secondary School Students: 2002–03* NCES 2005-010, March 2005.

Table 251. Children and Youth With Disabilities Served by Selected Programs: 1995 to 2004

[In thousands (5,078.8 represents 5,078,800). As of December 1. Excludes children and youth ages 6 to 21 served under the Individuals with Disabilities Education Act (IDEA) Part B. Excludes outlying areas]

Disability	1995	1998	1999	2000	2001	2002	2003	2004
Total	**5,078.8**	**5,539.7**	**5,677.9**	**5,773.9**	**5,861.4**	**5,959.1**	**6,045.1**	**6,118.4**
Specific learning disabilities.	2,601.8	2,815.5	2,867.7	2,881.6	2,878.3	2,878.6	2,866.9	2,839.7
Speech impairments	1,026.9	1,074.1	1,087.8	1,093.4	1,093.2	1,110.9	1,127.9	1,151.3
Mental retardation	585.6	610.7	614.3	613.4	605.0	591.7	582.6	567.8
Emotional disturbance	439.2	462.8	469.8	474.3	477.8	482.0	484.5	484.5
Multiple disabilities.	94.5	107.8	113.0	122.9	128.7	130.8	132.7	133.4
Hearing impairments	68.0	70.9	71.4	70.8	71.2	72.0	72.0	72.6
Orthopedic impairments	63.2	69.4	71.4	73.0	73.7	74.0	68.2	65.5
Other health impairments	134.2	221.8	255.3	294.0	341.3	393.0	452.7	511.9
Visually impaired.	25.5	26.1	26.4	26.0	25.8	26.1	25.9	26.2
Autism.	29.1	54.1	66.0	79.6	98.6	118.8	141.1	166.4
Deaf-blind	1.4	1.6	1.7	1.3	1.6	1.6	1.7	1.7
Traumatic brain injury.	9.6	13.0	13.9	14.9	20.8	21.5	22.5	23.2
Developmental delay [1]	(X)	11.9	19.3	28.6	45.3	58.3	66.3	74.377

X Not applicable. [1] States had the option of reporting children ages 3 to 9 under developmental delay beginning 1997–98.

Source: U.S. Department of Education, Office of Special Education Programs, Data Analysis System (DANS). See Internet site <http://www.ideadata.org/index.html>.

Table 252. **Private Schools: 2003–2004**

[5,123 represents 5,123,000. Based on the Private School Survey, conducted every 2 years; see source for details. For composition of regions, see map, inside front cover]

Characteristic	Schools				Students (1,000)				Teachers (1,000) [1]			
	Number	Ele-mentary	Sec-ondary	Com-bined	Total	Ele-mentary	Sec-ondary	Com-bined	Total	Ele-mentary	Sec-ondary	Com-bined
Total.	**28,384**	**17,197**	**2,694**	**8,494**	**5,123**	**2,694**	**845**	**1,583**	**425**	**199**	**68**	**158**
School type:												
Catholic	7,919	6,539	1,096	284	2,365	1,659	610	97	153	101	43	9
Parochial	4,074	3,852	171	51	1,097	1,006	75	17	67	60	6	1
Diocesan	2,947	2,367	504	76	909	593	291	25	57	36	19	2
Private	897	319	420	157	359	60	244	55	28	5	18	5
Other religious	13,659	7,278	758	5,623	1,836	734	117	984	163	63	11	88
Conservative												
Christian	5,060	1,838	195	3,026	774	216	25	533	65	18	2	45
Affiliated	3,398	2,110	329	959	553	264	61	229	51	24	6	22
Unaffiliated.	5,201	3,330	234	1,637	508	255	31	222	47	22	3	22
Nonsectarian	6,806	3,380	840	2,587	922	301	118	502	110	35	14	61
Regular.	2,963	1,606	320	1,036	603	179	87	337	67	19	10	38
Special												
emphasis.	2,392	1,550	303	539	214	109	21	84	25	13	3	9
Special												
education.	1,451	223	217	1,011	105	14	10	81	18	3	2	14
Program emphasis:												
Regular el/sec	22,896	14,709	1,981	6,206	4,639	2,511	784	1,345	365	177	61	127
Montessori	1,318	1,195	(B)	118	83	72	(B)	10	10	9	(B)	1
Special program												
emphasis	961	465	126	369	170	59	28	84	18	6	3	9
Special education . . .	1,634	272	233	1,129	115	16	11	88	20	3	2	15
Vocational/tech . . .	(B)	(B)	(B)	(B)	(B)	(B)	(B)	(B)	(B)	(B)	(B)	(B)
Alternative.	1,454	443	343	668	110	32	21	57	12	4	2	6
Early childhood . . .	116	112	(X)	(B)	5	4	(X)	(B)	(Z)	(Z)	(X)	(B)
Size:												
Less than 50	8,741	5,053	654	3,033	224	129	16	79	33	17	3	13
50 to 149	8,206	5,190	605	2,411	760	490	55	215	81	48	7	27
150 to 299	6,324	4,465	424	1,435	1,352	953	92	307	106	66	9	31
300 to 499	3,000	1,823	399	778	1,154	699	155	300	85	44	13	27
500 to 749	1,298	562	278	458	777	328	169	281	55	18	12	25
750 or more	816	103	334	378	856	95	358	403	64	5	24	35
Region:												
Northeast	6,558	4,035	844	1,679	1,273	683	296	294	111	50	25	36
Midwest	7,226	5,169	644	1,413	1,271	818	233	220	94	56	17	21
South	8,820	4,467	573	3,780	1,612	657	160	795	143	54	13	76
West	5,780	3,526	633	1,621	967	537	155	275	77	38	12	26

B Does not meet standard of reliability or precision.   X Not applicable.   Z Less than 500.   [1] Full-time equivalents.

Source: U.S. National Center for Education Statistics, *Characteristics of Private Schools in the United States: Results from the 2003–2004 Private School Universe Survey*, NCES 2006-319, March 2005. See Internet site <http://nces.ed.gov/surveys/pss/>.

Table 253. **Private Elementary and Secondary School Teachers—Selected Characteristics: 2003–2004**

[For school year (84 represents 84,000). Based on the 2003–2004 School and Staffing Survey and subject to sampling error; for details, see source Web site at <http://nces.ed.gov/surveys/sass/>. Excludes prekindergarten teachers. See Table 239 for similar data on public school teachers]

Characteristic	Unit	Age				Sex		Race/ethnicity		
		Under 30 years old	30 to 39 years old	40 to 49 years old	50 years old and over	Male	Fe-male	White [1]	Black [1]	His-panic
Total teachers [2] . . .	**1,000 . . .**	**84**	**96**	**110**	**149**	**106**	**333**	**390**	**18**	**20**
Highest degree held:										
Bachelor's	Percent .	71.4	57.3	53.7	48.6	48.5	58.6	56.0	59.3	57.5
Master's	Percent .	14.3	30.2	32.1	39.2	38.1	28.4	31.6	20.0	26.1
Education specialist .	Percent .	0.3	2.1	2.1	3.7	2.8	2.1	2.2	2.1	1.4
Doctorate	Percent .	0.6	1.7	3.3	2.8	4.1	1.6	2.2	2.2	2.9
Full-time teaching										
experience:										
Less than 3 years . .	Percent .	54.9	25.3	19.2	10.1	25.0	24.0	23.2	29.9	34.3
3 to 9 years	Percent .	44.8	52.8	30.7	15.3	32.7	33.1	32.9	32.6	34.0
10 to 20 years.	Percent .	(X)	21.9	35.4	25.7	20.1	23.2	22.8	20.0	20.4
20 years or more . . .	Percent .	(X)	(X)	14.7	48.9	22.3	19.7	21.1	17.6	11.3
Full-time teachers . .	1,000 . . .	71	76	83	118	82	265	308	15	15
Earned income	Dollars . .	29,032	33,299	34,766	38,955	40,740	32,827	34,659	32,038	36,212
Salary	Dollars . .	27,202	31,581	33,383	37,250	37,345	31,707	33,039	29,778	34,554

X Not applicable.   [1] Non-Hispanic.   [2] Includes teachers with no degrees and associate's degrees, not shown separately.

Source: U.S. National Center for Education Statistics, Schools and Staffing Survey, "Private School Teacher Questionnaire," 2003–04, unpublished data.

Table 254. **SAT Scores and Characteristics of College-Bound Seniors: 1967 to 2005**

[For school year ending in year shown. Data are for the SAT I: Reasoning Tests. SAT I: Reasoning Test replaced the SAT in March 1994. Scores between the two tests have been equated to the same 200–800 scale and are thus comparable. Scores for 1995 and prior years have been recentered and revised]

Type of test and characteristic	Unit	1967	1970	1975	1980	1985	1990	1995	2000	2004	2005
AVERAGE TEST SCORES [1]											
Verbal, total [2]	Point . . .	543	537	512	502	509	500	504	505	508	508
Male	Point . . .	540	536	515	506	514	505	505	507	512	513
Female	Point . . .	545	538	509	498	503	496	502	504	504	505
Math, total [2]	Point . . .	516	512	498	492	500	501	506	514	518	520
Male	Point . . .	535	531	518	515	522	521	525	533	537	538
Female	Point . . .	495	493	479	473	480	483	490	498	501	504
PARTICIPANTS											
Total [3]	1,000 . . .	(NA)	(NA)	996	922	977	1,026	1,068	1,260	1,419	1,476
Male	Percent . .	(NA)	(NA)	49.9	48.2	48.3	47.8	46.4	46.2	46.5	46.5
White	Percent . .	(NA)	(NA)	86.0	82.1	81.0	73.0	69.2	66.4	62.7	62.3
Black	Percent . .	(NA)	(NA)	7.9	9.1	7.5	10.0	10.7	11.2	12.0	11.6
Obtaining scores [1] of—											
600 or above:											
Verbal	Percent . .	(NA)	(NA)	(NA)	(NA)	(NA)	20.3	21.9	21.1	22.2	22.5
Math	Percent . .	(NA)	(NA)	(NA)	(NA)	(NA)	20.4	23.4	24.2	25.5	26.5
Below 400:											
Verbal	Percent . .	(NA)	(NA)	(NA)	(NA)	(NA)	17.3	16.4	15.9	15.2	15.5
Math	Percent . .	(NA)	(NA)	(NA)	(NA)	(NA)	15.8	16.0	14.7	13.9	13.8
Selected intended area of study:											
Business and commerce	Percent . .	(NA)	(NA)	11.5	18.6	21.0	20.9	13.3	13.6	13.5	13.6
Engineering	Percent . .	(NA)	(NA)	6.7	11.1	11.7	10.2	8.8	8.5	9.1	8.3
Social science	Percent . .	(NA)	(NA)	7.7	7.8	7.5	12.6	11.6	10.6	9.6	9.2
Education	Percent . .	(NA)	(NA)	9.1	6.1	4.7	7.5	8.1	8.8	8.2	8.0

NA Not available. [1] Minimum score 200; maximum score, 800. [2] 1967 and 1970 are estimates based on total number of persons taking SAT. [3] 996 represents 996,000.
Source: The College Board, New York, NY, *College Bound Seniors*. Copyright 1967 to 2006. Reproduced with permission. All rights reserved. See Internet site <http://www.collegeboard.com/>.

Table 255. **ACT Program Scores and Characteristics of College-Bound Students: 1970 to 2005**

[For academic year ending in year shown. Except as indicated, test scores and characteristics of college-bound students. Through 1980, data based on 10 percent sample; thereafter, based on all ACT tested graduating seniors]

Type of test and characteristic	Unit	1970	1975	1980	1985	1990 [1]	1995 [1]	2000 [1]	2003 [1]	2004 [1]	2005 [1]
TEST SCORES [2]											
Composite	Point . . .	19.9	18.6	18.5	18.6	20.6	20.8	21.0	20.8	20.9	20.9
Male	Point . . .	20.3	19.5	19.3	19.4	21.0	21.0	21.2	21.0	21.0	21.1
Female	Point . . .	19.4	17.8	17.9	17.9	20.3	20.7	20.9	20.8	20.9	20.9
English	Point . . .	18.5	17.7	17.9	18.1	20.5	20.2	20.5	20.3	20.4	20.4
Male	Point . . .	17.6	17.1	17.3	17.6	20.1	19.8	20.0	19.8	19.9	20.0
Female	Point . . .	19.4	18.3	18.3	18.6	20.9	20.6	20.9	20.7	20.8	20.8
Math	Point . . .	20.0	17.6	17.4	17.2	19.9	20.2	20.7	20.6	20.7	20.7
Male	Point . . .	21.1	19.3	18.9	18.6	20.7	20.9	21.4	21.2	21.3	21.3
Female	Point . . .	18.8	16.2	16.2	16.0	19.3	19.7	20.2	20.1	20.2	20.2
Reading [3]	Point . . .	19.7	17.4	17.2	17.4	(NA)	21.3	21.4	21.2	21.3	21.3
Male	Point . . .	20.3	18.7	18.2	18.3	(NA)	21.1	21.2	21.0	21.1	21.0
Female	Point . . .	19.0	16.4	16.4	16.6	(NA)	21.4	21.5	21.4	21.5	21.5
Science reasoning [4]	Point . . .	20.8	21.1	21.1	21.2	(NA)	21.0	21.0	20.8	20.9	20.9
Male	Point . . .	21.6	22.4	22.4	22.6	(NA)	21.6	21.6	21.3	21.3	21.4
Female	Point . . .	20.0	20.0	20.0	20.0	(NA)	20.5	20.6	20.4	20.5	20.5
PARTICIPANTS [5]											
Total [6]	1,000 . . .	788	714	822	739	817	945	1,065	1,175	1,171	1,186
Male	Percent . .	52	46	45	46	46	44	43	44	44	44
White	Percent . .	(NA)	77	83	82	79	75	76	73	72	71
Black	Percent . .	4	7	8	8	9	10	11	12	12	13
Obtaining composite scores of—[7]											
27 or above	Percent . .	14	14	13	14	12	13	14	14	14	14
18 or below	Percent . .	21	33	33	32	35	34	32	35	34	34
Planned educational major:											
Business [8]	Percent . .	18	21	20	21	20	14	11	11	11	11
Engineering [9]	Percent . .	8	6	8	9	9	9	6	5	5	5
Social science [9]	Percent . .	10	9	6	7	10	9	8	9	8	8
Education	Percent . .	16	12	9	6	8	9	9	9	8	8

NA Not available. [1] Beginning 1990, not comparable with previous years because a new version of the ACT was introduced. Estimated average composite scores for prior years: 1989, 20.6; 1988, 1987, and 1986, 20.8. [2] Minimum score, 1; maximum score, 36. [3] Prior to 1990, social studies; data not comparable with previous years. [4] Prior to 1990, natural sciences; data not comparable with previous years. [5] Beginning 1985, data are for seniors who graduated in year shown and had taken the ACT in their junior or senior year. Data by race are for those responding to the race question. [6] 788 represents 788,000. [7] Prior to 1990, 26 or above and 15 or below. [8] Includes political and persuasive (e.g. sales) fields through 1975; 1980 and 1985 business and commerce; thereafter, business and management and business and office. [9] Includes religion through 1975.
Source: ACT, Inc., Iowa City, IA, *High School Profile Report*, annual.

Table 256. Proficiency Levels on Selected NAEP Tests for Students in Public Schools, by State: 2005

[Represents percent of public school students scoring at or above Basic and Proficient levels. Basic denotes mastery of the knowledge and skills that are fundamental for proficient work at a given grade level. Proficient represents solid academic performance. Students reaching this level demonstrated competency over challenging subject matter. For more detail see <http://www.nagb.org/pubs/pubs.html>. Based on The National Assessment of Educational Progress (NAEP) tests which are administered to a representative sample of students in public schools, private schools, and Department of Defense schools. Data shown here are for public school students only]

State	Grade 4 Math		Grade 8 Math		Grade 4 Reading		Grade 8 Reading	
	At or above basic	At or above proficient	At or above basic	At or above proficient	At or above basic	At or above proficient	At or above basic	At or above proficient
U.S. average	79	35	68	28	62	30	71	29
Alabama	66	21	53	15	53	22	63	22
Alaska	77	34	69	29	58	27	70	26
Arizona	70	28	64	26	52	24	65	23
Arkansas	78	34	64	22	63	30	69	26
California	71	28	57	22	50	21	60	21
Colorado	81	39	70	32	69	37	75	32
Connecticut	84	42	70	35	71	38	74	34
Delaware	84	36	72	30	73	34	80	30
District of Columbia	45	10	31	7	33	11	45	12
Florida	82	37	65	26	65	30	66	25
Georgia	76	30	62	23	58	26	67	25
Hawaii	73	27	56	18	53	23	58	18
Idaho	86	40	73	30	69	33	76	32
Illinois	74	32	68	29	62	29	75	31
Indiana	84	38	74	30	64	30	73	28
Iowa	85	37	75	34	67	33	79	34
Kansas	88	47	77	34	66	32	78	35
Kentucky	75	26	64	23	65	31	75	31
Louisiana	74	24	59	16	53	20	64	20
Maine	84	39	74	30	71	35	81	38
Maryland	79	38	66	30	65	32	69	30
Massachusetts	91	49	80	43	78	44	83	44
Michigan	79	38	68	29	63	32	73	28
Minnesota	88	47	79	43	71	38	80	37
Mississippi	69	19	52	14	48	18	60	18
Missouri	79	31	68	26	67	33	76	31
Montana	85	38	80	36	71	36	82	37
Nebraska	80	36	75	35	68	34	80	35
Nevada	72	26	60	21	52	21	63	22
New Hampshire	89	47	77	35	74	39	80	38
New Jersey	86	45	74	36	68	37	80	38
New Mexico	65	19	53	14	51	20	62	19
New York	81	36	70	31	69	33	75	33
North Carolina	83	40	72	32	62	29	69	27
North Dakota	89	40	81	35	72	35	83	37
Ohio	84	43	74	33	69	34	78	36
Oklahoma	79	29	63	21	60	25	72	25
Oregon	80	37	72	34	62	29	74	33
Pennsylvania	82	41	72	31	69	36	77	36
Rhode Island	76	31	63	24	62	30	71	29
South Carolina	81	36	71	30	57	26	67	25
South Dakota	86	41	80	36	70	33	82	35
Tennessee	74	28	61	21	59	27	71	26
Texas	87	40	72	31	64	29	69	26
Utah	83	37	71	30	68	34	73	29
Vermont	87	44	78	38	72	39	79	37
Virginia	83	39	75	33	72	37	78	36
Washington	84	42	75	36	70	36	75	34
West Virginia	75	25	60	18	61	26	67	22
Wisconsin	84	40	76	36	67	33	77	35
Wyoming	87	43	76	29	71	34	81	36

Source: U.S. Department of Education, National Center for Education Statistics, National Assessment of Educational Progress (NAEP), 2005 Mathematics and Reading Assessments. See Internet site <http://nces.ed.gov/nationsreportcard/> (accessed 15 March 2006).

Education 167

Table 257. Public High Schools Offering Dual Credit and Exam-Based Courses and Course Enrollments: 2002–2003

[For the school year. Includes public schools with a grade of 11 or 12. Excludes schools with the highest grade lower than 11, special education, vocational and alternative/other schools. Based on the Fast Response Survey System and subject to sampling error; for details, see source]

School characteristic	Number of high schools	Schools offering—			Enrollments in—		
		Dual credit courses [1]	AP courses [2]	IB courses [3]	Dual credit courses [1]	AP courses [2]	IB courses [3]
All public high schools [4] . . .	**16,500**	**11,700**	**11,000**	**390**	**1,162.0**	**1,795.4**	**165.1**
Enrollment size:							
Fewer than 500	7,400	4,700	3,000	(B)	185.3	81.1	(B)
500 to 1,199	5,000	3,700	4,100	70	335.1	481.0	24.8
1,200 or more	4,100	3,300	3,900	290	641.6	1,233.3	140.2
School locale: [5]							
City	2,700	1,800	2,100	150	246.3	548.4	58.7
Urban fringe	4,100	3,100	3,600	180	458.8	853.2	97.6
Town	2,400	1,900	1,700	(NA)	201.7	143.2	(NA)
Rural	7,200	5,000	3,600	(B)	255.2	250.6	(B)
Region: [6]							
Northeast	2,800	1,600	2,300	30	144.8	390.9	(NA)
Southeast	3,500	2,400	2,400	170	194.0	386.1	65.8
Central	5,200	4,100	2,800	50	333.9	319.3	(NA)
West	5,100	3,600	3,500	150	489.4	699.1	66.4
Percent minority enrollment:							
Less than 6 percent	5,600	4,300	3,300	(Z)	317.4	267.1	(Z)
6 to 20 percent	3,800	3,000	2,600	90	380.9	463.8	16.7
21 to 49 percent	3,200	2,300	2,400	150	228.9	528.5	64.3
50 percent or more	3,600	2,100	2,500	150	231.4	497.7	84.1

B Base too small to meet statistical standards for reliability of a derived figure. NA Not available. Z Rounds to zero. [1] Courses where students can earn both secondary and postsecondary credit. [2] Advanced Placement courses follow the content and curricular goals developed by the College Board. [3] International Baccalaureate courses compose a 2-year liberal arts curriculum that leads to a diploma and meets requirements established by the International Baccalaureate program. [4] Includes schools whose minority enrollment was not available. [5] City: a large or midsize central city of a Consolidated Metropolitan Statistical Area (CMSA) or Metropolitan Statistical Area (MSA); Urban fringe: any incorporated place, census-designated place, or nonplace territory within a CSMA or MSA of a large midsize city, and defined as urban by the Census Bureau; Town: any incorporated place or census-designated place with a population greater than or equal to 2,500 and located outside a CMSA or MSA; Rural: any incorporated place, census-designated place, or nonplace territory defined as rural by the Census Bureau. [6] For compositions of regions, see map inside front cover.

Source: U.S. National Center for Education Statistics, *Dual Credit and Exam-Based Courses in U.S. Public High Schools: 2002–03* NCES 2005-009, April 2005.

Table 258. Foreign Language Enrollment in Public High Schools: 1970 to 2000

[In thousands (13,301.9 represents 13,301,900), except percent. As of fall, for grades 9 through 12]

Language	1970	1974	1978	1982	1985	1990	1994	2000
Total enrollment	**13,301.9**	**13,648.9**	**13,941.4**	**12,879.3**	**12,466.5**	**11,099.6**	**11,847.5**	**13,457.8**
Enrolled in all foreign languages . . .	**3,779.3**	**3,294.5**	**3,200.1**	**2,909.8**	**4,028.9**	**4,256.9**	**5,001.9**	**5,899.4**
Percent of all students	28.4	24.1	23.0	22.6	32.3	38.4	42.2	43.8
Enrolled in modern foreign languages [1] . . .	3,514.1	3,127.3	3,048.3	2,740.2	3,852.0	4,093.0	4,813.0	5,721.9
Spanish	1,810.8	1,678.1	1,631.4	1,562.8	2,334.4	2,611.4	3,219.8	4,057.6
French	1,230.7	977.9	856.0	858.0	1,133.7	1,089.4	1,105.9	1,075.4
German	410.5	393.0	330.6	266.9	312.2	295.4	326.0	283.3
Italian	27.3	40.2	45.5	44.1	47.3	40.4	43.8	64.1
Japanese	(NA)	(NA)	(NA)	6.2	8.6	24.1	42.3	50.9
Russian	20.2	15.1	8.8	5.7	6.4	16.5	16.4	10.6
Percent of all students [1]	26.4	22.9	21.9	21.3	30.9	36.9	40.6	42.5
Spanish	13.6	12.3	11.7	12.1	18.7	23.5	27.2	30.2
French	9.3	7.2	6.1	6.7	9.1	9.8	9.3	8.0
German	3.1	2.9	2.4	2.1	2.5	2.7	2.8	2.1
Italian	0.2	0.3	0.3	0.3	0.4	0.4	0.4	0.5
Japanese	(NA)	(NA)	(NA)	0.1	0.1	0.2	0.4	0.1
Russian	0.2	0.1	0.1	(Z)	0.1	0.2	0.1	0.1

NA Not available. Z Less than 0.05 percent. [1] Includes other foreign languages, not shown separately.

Source: The American Council on the Teaching of Foreign Languages, Alexandria, VA, *Foreign Language Enrollments in Public Secondary Schools, fall 1994 and fall 2000.*

Table 259. Public High School Graduates by State: 1980 to 2004

[In thousands (2,747.7 represents 2,747,700). For school year ending in year shown]

State	1980	1990	2000	2004, proj.
United States ...	2,747.7	2,320.3	2,553.8	2,757.5
Alabama	45.2	40.5	37.8	37.6
Alaska	5.2	5.4	6.6	7.1
Arizona	28.6	32.1	38.3	57.0
Arkansas	29.1	26.5	27.3	26.9
California	249.2	236.3	309.9	342.6
Colorado	36.8	33.0	38.9	42.9
Connecticut	37.7	27.9	31.6	34.4
Delaware	7.6	5.6	6.1	6.8
District of Columbia	5.0	3.6	2.7	3.2
Florida	87.3	88.9	106.7	129.0
Georgia	61.6	56.6	62.6	69.7
Hawaii	11.5	10.3	10.4	10.3
Idaho	13.2	12.0	16.2	15.5
Illinois	135.6	108.1	111.8	121.3
Indiana	73.1	60.0	57.0	57.6
Iowa	43.4	31.8	33.9	33.8
Kansas	30.9	25.4	29.1	30.0
Kentucky	41.2	38.0	36.8	36.2
Louisiana	46.3	36.1	38.4	36.2
Maine	15.4	13.8	12.2	13.4
Maryland	54.3	41.6	47.8	53.0
Massachusetts	73.8	55.9	53.0	57.9
Michigan	124.3	93.8	97.7	106.3
Minnesota	64.9	49.1	57.4	59.8
Mississippi	27.6	25.2	24.2	23.6
Missouri	62.3	49.0	52.8	57.0
Montana	12.1	9.4	10.9	10.5
Nebraska	22.4	17.7	20.1	20.0
Nevada	8.5	9.5	14.6	16.2
New Hampshire	11.7	10.8	11.8	13.3
New Jersey	94.6	69.8	74.4	88.3
New Mexico	18.4	14.9	18.0	18.1
New York	204.1	143.3	141.7	150.9
North Carolina	70.9	64.8	62.1	71.4
North Dakota	9.9	7.7	8.6	7.8
Ohio	144.2	114.5	111.7	116.3
Oklahoma	39.3	35.6	37.6	36.7
Oregon	29.9	25.5	30.2	32.5
Pennsylvania	146.5	110.5	114.0	121.6
Rhode Island	10.9	7.8	8.5	9.3
South Carolina	38.7	32.5	31.6	32.1
South Dakota	10.7	7.7	9.3	9.1
Tennessee	49.8	46.1	41.6	43.6
Texas	171.4	172.5	212.9	236.7
Utah	20.0	21.2	32.5	29.9
Vermont	6.7	6.1	6.7	7.0
Virginia	66.6	60.6	65.6	71.7
Washington	50.4	45.9	57.6	60.4
West Virginia	23.4	21.9	19.4	17.1
Wisconsin	69.3	52.0	58.5	62.3
Wyoming	6.1	5.8	6.5	5.7

Source: U.S. National Center for Education Statistics, *Digest of Education Statistics*, annual.

Table 260. High School Dropouts by Race and Hispanic Origin: 1975 to 2004

[In percent. As of October]

Item	1975	1980	1985	1990 [1]	1995	1998	1999	2000	2001	2002	2003	2004
EVENT DROPOUTS [2]												
Total [3]	5.8	6.0	5.2	4.5	5.4	4.4	4.7	4.5	4.7	3.3	3.8	4.4
White [4]	5.4	5.6	4.8	3.9	5.1	4.4	4.4	4.3	4.6	3.0	3.7	4.2
Male	5.0	6.4	4.9	4.1	5.4	4.4	4.1	4.7	5.3	3.0	3.9	4.9
Female	5.8	4.9	4.7	3.8	4.8	4.4	4.7	4.0	3.8	3.0	3.4	3.5
Black [4]	8.7	8.3	7.7	7.7	6.1	5.0	6.0	5.6	5.7	4.4	4.5	5.2
Male	8.3	8.0	8.3	6.9	7.9	4.6	5.2	7.6	6.1	5.1	4.1	4.8
Female	9.0	8.5	7.2	8.6	4.4	5.5	6.8	3.8	5.4	3.8	4.9	5.7
Hispanic [5]	10.9	11.5	9.7	7.7	11.6	8.4	7.1	6.8	8.1	5.3	6.5	8.0
Male	10.1	16.9	9.3	7.6	10.9	8.6	6.9	7.1	7.6	6.2	7.7	11.5
Female	11.6	6.9	9.8	7.7	12.5	8.2	7.3	6.5	8.7	4.4	5.4	4.6
STATUS DROPOUTS [6]												
Total [3]	15.6	15.6	13.9	14.4	13.9	13.9	13.1	12.4	13.0	12.3	11.8	12.1
White [4]	13.9	14.4	13.5	14.1	13.6	13.7	12.8	12.2	13.4	12.2	11.6	11.9
Male	13.5	15.7	14.7	15.4	14.3	15.7	13.9	13.5	15.3	13.7	13.3	13.7
Female	14.2	13.2	12.3	12.8	13.0	11.7	11.8	10.9	11.4	10.6	9.8	10.0
Black [4]	27.3	23.5	17.6	16.4	14.4	17.1	16.0	15.3	13.8	14.6	14.2	15.1
Male	27.8	26.0	18.8	18.6	14.2	20.5	16.3	17.4	16.9	16.9	16.7	17.9
Female	26.9	21.5	16.6	14.5	14.6	14.3	15.7	13.5	11.0	12.5	12.0	12.7
Hispanic [5]	34.9	40.3	31.5	37.7	34.7	34.4	33.9	32.3	31.7	30.1	28.4	28.0
Male	32.6	42.6	35.8	40.3	34.2	39.7	36.4	36.8	37.1	33.8	31.7	33.5
Female	36.8	38.1	27.0	35.0	35.4	28.6	31.1	27.3	25.5	25.6	24.7	21.7

[1] Beginning 1990, reflects new editing procedures for cases with missing data on school enrollment. [2] Percent of students who drop out in a single year without completing high school. For grades 10 to 12. [3] Includes other races, not shown separately. [4] Beginning 2003, for persons who selected this race group only. See footnote 2, Table 214. [5] Persons of Hispanic origin may be of any race. [6] Percent of the population who have not completed high school and are not enrolled, regardless of when they dropped out. For persons 18 to 24 years old.

Source: U.S. Census Bureau, Current Population Reports, PPL-148; and earlier PPL and P-20 reports; and data published on the Internet. See Internet site <http://www.census.gov/population/www/socdemo/school.html>.

Table 261. High School Dropouts by Age, Race, and Hispanic Origin: 1980 to 2004

[As of October (5,212 represents 5,212,000). For persons 14 to 24 years old. See Table 263 for definition of dropouts]

Age and race	Number of dropouts (1,000)					Percent of population				
	1980	1990	1995	2000	2004	1980	1990	1995	2000	2004
Total dropouts [1,2] . . .	5,212	3,854	3,963	3,883	3,597	12.0	10.1	9.9	9.1	7.9
16 to 17 years.	709	418	406	460	303	8.8	6.3	5.4	5.8	3.4
18 to 21 years.	2,578	1,921	1,980	2,005	1,669	15.8	13.4	14.2	12.9	10.5
22 to 24 years.	1,798	1,458	1,491	1,310	1,485	15.2	13.8	13.6	11.8	12.4
White [2,3]	4,169	3,127	3,098	3,065	2,785	11.3	10.1	9.7	9.1	7.9
16 to 17 years.	619	334	314	366	223	9.2	6.4	5.4	5.8	3.3
18 to 21 years.	2,032	1,516	1,530	1,558	1,299	14.7	13.1	13.8	12.6	10.4
22 to 24 years.	1,416	1,235	1,181	1,040	1,167	14.0	14.0	13.4	11.7	12.6
Black [2,3]	934	611	605	705	616	16.0	10.9	10.0	10.9	9.2
16 to 17 years.	80	73	70	84	64	6.9	6.9	5.8	7.0	4.7
18 to 21 years.	486	345	328	383	351	23.0	16.0	15.8	16.0	15.9
22 to 24 years.	346	185	194	232	245	24.0	13.5	12.5	14.3	14.2
Hispanic [2,4]	919	1,122	1,355	1,499	1,467	29.5	26.8	24.7	23.5	18.6
16 to 17 years.	92	89	94	121	93	16.6	12.9	10.7	11.0	6.3
18 to 21 years.	470	502	652	733	672	40.3	32.9	29.9	30.0	24.5
22 to 24 years.	323	523	598	602	663	40.6	42.8	37.4	35.5	30.8

[1] Includes other groups not shown separately. [2] Includes persons 14 to 15 years, not shown separately. [3] For 2004, for persons who selected this race group only. See footnote 2, Table 214. [4] Persons of Hispanic origin may be of any race.
Source: U.S. Census Bureau, *Current Population Reports*, PPL-148; and earlier PPL and P-20 reports; and data published on the Internet. See Internet site <http://www.census.gov/population/www/socdemo/school.html>.

Table 262. Enrollment Status by Race, Hispanic Origin, and Sex: 1975 and 2004

[As of October (15,693 represents 15,693,000). For persons 18 to 21 years old. For the civilian noninstitutional population. Based on the Current Population Survey; see text, Section 1, and Appendix III]

Characteristic	Total persons 18 to 21 years old (1,000)		Percent distribution							
			Enrolled in high school		High school graduates				Not high school graduates	
					Total		In college			
	1975	2004	1975	2004	1975	2004	1975	2004	1975	2004
Total [1]	15,693	15,677	5.7	8.9	78.0	79.4	33.5	47.6	16.3	11.7
White [2]	13,448	12,325	4.7	8.4	80.6	80.4	34.6	48.4	14.7	11.2
Black [2]	1,997	2,213	12.5	11.7	60.4	72.3	24.9	37.9	27.0	16.0
Hispanic [3]	899	2,718	12.0	10.3	57.2	64.2	24.4	30.0	30.8	25.5
Male [1]	7,584	7,865	7.4	9.8	76.6	76.6	35.4	43.5	15.9	13.6
White [2]	6,545	6,255	6.2	8.9	79.7	77.9	36.9	43.9	14.1	13.2
Black [2]	911	1,023	15.9	15.5	55.0	65.5	23.9	32.6	29.0	19.0
Hispanic [3]	416	1,437	17.3	9.7	54.6	58.1	25.2	26.7	27.9	32.2
Female [1]	8,109	7,812	4.2	8.0	79.2	82.2	31.8	51.7	16.6	9.8
White [2]	6,903	6,069	3.2	8.0	81.4	82.9	32.4	53.0	15.3	9.1
Black [2]	1,085	1,190	9.7	8.5	65.0	78.2	25.8	42.4	25.4	13.3
Hispanic [3]	484	1,281	7.6	10.9	59.3	71.1	25.2	33.7	33.1	18.1

[1] Includes other races not shown separately. [2] For 2004, for persons who selected this race group only. See footnote 2, Table 214. [3] Persons of Hispanic origin may be of any race.
Source: U.S. Census Bureau, Current Population Reports, PPL-148; and earlier PPL and P-20 reports; and data published on the Internet. See Internet site <http://www.census.gov/population/www/socdemo/school.html>.

Table 263. Employment Status of High School Graduates and School Dropouts: 1980 to 2005

[In thousands (11,622 represents 11,622,000), except percent. As of October. For civilian noninstitutional population 16 to 24 years old. Based on Current Population Survey; see text, Section 1, and Appendix III]

Employment status, sex, and race	Graduates [1]				Dropouts [3]			
	1980	1990	2000 [2]	2005 [2]	1980	1990	2000 [2]	2005 [2]
Civilian population	11,622	8,370	7,351	7,068	5,254	3,800	3,776	3,458
In labor force	9,795	7,107	6,195	5,736	3,549	2,506	2,612	2,378
Percent of population.	84.3	84.9	84.3	81.1	67.5	66.0	69.2	68.8
Employed.	8,567	6,279	5,632	5,101	2,651	1,993	2,150	1,968
Percent of labor force	87.5	88.3	90.9	88.9	74.7	79.5	82.3	82.8
Unemployed.	1,228	828	563	634	898	513	463	410
Unemployment rate, total [4]	12.5	11.7	9.1	11.1	25.3	20.5	17.7	17.3
Male.	13.5	11.1	9.3	10.7	23.5	18.8	16.3	15.3
Female	11.5	12.3	8.8	11.5	28.7	23.5	20.3	21.2
White [5]	10.8	9.0	7.2	9.4	21.6	17.0	15.0	14.4
Black [5]	26.1	26.0	18.1	18.3	43.9	43.3	33.2	34.3
Not in labor force	1,827	1,262	1,156	1,332	1,705	1,294	1,163	1,080
Percent of population	15.7	15.1	15.7	18.8	32.5	34.1	30.8	31.2

[1] For persons not enrolled in college who have completed 4 years of high school only. [2] Data not strictly comparable with data for earlier years. See text, this section, and February 2000 and 2005 issues of *Employment and Earnings*. [3] For persons not in regular school and who have not completed the 12th grade nor received a general equivalency degree. [4] Includes other races not shown separately. [5] For 2004, for persons who selected this race group only. See footnote 2, Table 214.
Source: U.S. Bureau of Labor Statistics, Bulletin 2307; *News*, USDL06-514, March 24, 2006; and unpublished data. See Internet site <http://www.bls.gov/news.release/hsgec.toc.htm>.

Table 264. General Educational Development (GED) Credentials Issued: 1975 to 2003

[GEDs issued in thousands (340 represents 340,000). For the 50 states and DC]

Year	GEDs issued	Percent distribution by age of test taker				
		19 years old or under	20 to 24 years old	25 to 29 years old	30 to 34 years old	35 years old and over
1975	340	33	26	14	9	18
1980	479	37	27	13	8	15
1985	413	32	26	15	10	16
1990	410	36	25	13	10	15
1999	498	44	25	11	7	13
2000	487	45	25	11	7	13
2001	648	41	26	11	8	14
2002	330	49	25	10	6	11
2003	387	47	26	10	7	11

Source: U.S. National Center for Education Statistics, *Digest of Education Statistics*, annual.

Table 265. College Enrollment of Recent High School Completers: 1970 to 2004

[2,758 represents 2,758,000. For persons 16 to 24 who graduated from high school in the preceding 12 months. Includes persons receiving GEDs. Based on surveys and subject to sampling error; data will not agree with data in other tables]

Year	Number of high school completers (1,000)						Percent enrolled in college [5]					
	Total [1]	Male	Female	White [2]	Black [2, 3]	His-panic [3, 4]	Total [1]	Male	Female	White [2]	Black [2, 3]	His-panic [3, 4]
1970 . .	2,758	1,343	1,415	2,461	(NA)	(NA)	51.7	55.2	48.5	52.0	(NA)	(NA)
1975 . .	3,185	1,513	1,672	2,701	302	132	50.7	52.6	49.0	51.1	41.7	58.0
1980 . .	3,088	1,498	1,589	2,554	350	130	49.3	46.7	51.8	49.8	42.7	52.3
1985 . .	2,668	1,287	1,381	2,104	332	141	57.7	58.6	56.8	60.1	42.2	51.0
1990 . .	2,362	1,173	1,189	1,819	331	121	60.1	58.0	62.2	63.0	46.8	42.7
1991 . .	2,276	1,140	1,136	1,727	310	154	62.5	57.9	67.1	65.4	46.4	57.2
1992 . .	2,397	1,216	1,180	1,724	354	198	61.9	60.0	63.8	64.3	48.2	55.0
1993 . .	2,342	1,120	1,223	1,719	304	201	62.6	59.9	65.2	62.9	55.6	62.2
1994 . .	2,517	1,244	1,273	1,915	316	178	61.9	60.6	63.2	64.5	50.8	49.1
1995 . .	2,599	1,238	1,361	1,861	349	288	61.9	62.6	61.3	64.3	51.2	53.7
1996 . .	2,660	1,297	1,363	1,875	406	227	65.0	60.1	69.7	67.4	56.0	50.8
1997 . .	2,769	1,354	1,415	1,909	384	336	67.0	63.6	70.3	68.2	58.5	65.6
1998 . .	2,810	1,452	1,358	1,980	386	314	65.6	62.4	69.1	68.5	61.9	47.4
1999 . .	2,897	1,474	1,423	1,978	436	329	62.9	61.4	64.4	66.3	58.9	42.3
2000 . .	2,756	1,251	1,505	1,938	393	300	63.3	59.9	66.2	65.7	54.9	52.9
2001 . .	2,549	1,277	1,273	1,834	381	241	61.8	60.1	63.5	64.3	55.0	51.7
2002 . .	2,796	1,412	1,384	1,903	382	344	65.2	62.1	68.4	69.1	59.4	53.6
2003 . .	2,677	1,306	1,372	1,832	327	314	63.9	61.2	66.5	66.2	57.5	58.6
2004 . .	2,752	1,327	1,425	1,854	398	286	66.7	61.4	71.5	68.8	62.5	61.8

NA Not available. [1] Includes other races, not shown separately. [2] Beginning 2003, for persons of this race group only. See footnote 2, Table 214. [3] Due to small sample size, data are subject to relatively large sampling errors. [4] Persons of Hispanic origin may be any race. [5] As of October.

Source: U.S. National Center for Education Statistics, *Digest of Education Statistics*, annual.

Table 266. College Enrollment by Sex and Attendance Status: 1983 to 2004

[As of fall. In thousands (12,465 represents 12,465,000)]

Sex and age	1983		1988		1993		1998 [1]		2004 [1]	
	Total	Part-time	Total	Part-time	Total	Part-time	Total	Part-time	Total	Part-time
Total	12,465	5,204	13,055	5,619	14,305	6,177	14,507	5,944	17,272	6,662
Male	6,024	2,264	6,002	2,340	6,427	2,537	6,369	2,436	7,387	2,648
14 to 17 years old	102	16	55	5	83	10	45	5	82	17
18 to 19 years old	1,256	158	1,290	132	1,224	138	1,535	296	1,628	288
20 to 21 years old	1,241	205	1,243	216	1,294	209	1,374	245	1,637	281
22 to 24 years old	1,158	382	1,106	378	1,260	392	1,127	350	1,435	410
25 to 29 years old	1,115	624	875	485	950	564	908	485	918	416
30 to 34 years old	570	384	617	456	661	484	463	322	543	351
35 years old and over . .	583	494	816	668	955	739	917	733	1,145	886
Female	6,441	2,940	7,053	3,278	7,877	3,640	8,138	3,508	9,885	4,014
14 to 17 years old	142	16	115	17	93	6	74	21	116	20
18 to 19 years old	1,496	179	1,536	195	1,416	172	1,847	292	2,043	343
20 to 21 years old	1,125	204	1,278	218	1,414	279	1,437	295	1,871	319
22 to 24 years old	884	378	932	403	1,263	493	1,250	463	1,704	630
25 to 29 years old	947	658	932	633	1,058	689	1,083	617	1,362	677
30 to 34 years old	721	553	698	499	811	575	732	506	776	476
35 years old and over . .	1,126	953	1,563	1,313	1,824	1,427	1,715	1,315	2,012	1,550

[1] In this table, data beginning in 1998 reflect the new classification of institutions. See footnote 1, Table 267.

Source: U.S. National Center for Education Statistics, *Digest of Education Statistics*, annual.

Table 267. **Higher Education—Summary: 1980 to 2004**

[**Institutions, staff, and enrollment as of fall (686 represents 686,000). Finances for fiscal year ending in the following year.**]
Covers universities, colleges, professional schools, junior and teachers colleges, both publicly and privately controlled, regular session. Includes estimates for institutions not reporting. See also Appendix III]

Item	Unit	1980	1985	1990	1995	2000	2001	2002	2003	2004
ALL INSTITUTIONS										
Number of institutions [1]	Number ..	3,231	3,340	3,559	3,706	4,182	4,197	4,168	4,236	4,216
4-year.	Number...	1,957	2,029	2,141	2,244	2,450	2,487	2,466	2,530	2,533
2-year.	Number...	1,274	1,311	1,418	1,462	1,732	1,710	1,702	1,706	1,683
Instructional staff—										
(lecturer or above) [2]	1,000	686	715	817	932	(NA)	1113	(NA)	1175	(NA)
Percent full-time	Percent ...	66	64	61	59	(NA)	56	(NA)	54	(NA)
Total enrollment [3,4]	1,000	12,097	12,247	13,819	14,262	15,312	15,928	16,612	16,900	17,272
Male	1,000	5,874	5,818	6,284	6,343	6,722	6,961	7,202	7,256	7,387
Female	1,000	6,223	6,429	7,535	7,919	8,591	8,967	9,410	9,645	9,885
4-year institutions	1,000	7,571	7,716	8,579	8,769	9,364	9,677	10,082	10,408	10,726
2-year institutions	1,000	4,526	4,531	5,240	5,493	5,948	6,251	6,529	6,493	6,546
Full-time	1,000	7,098	7,075	7,821	8,129	9,010	9,448	9,946	10,312	10,610
Part-time	1,000	4,999	5,172	5,998	6,133	6,303	6,480	6,665	6,589	6,662
Public	1,000	9,457	9,479	10,845	11,092	11,753	12,233	12,752	12,857	12,980
Private	1,000	2,640	2,768	2,974	3,169	3,560	3,695	3,860	4,043	4,292
Not-for-profit	1,000	2,528	2,572	2,760	2,929	3,109	3,167	3,265	3,341	3,412
For profit	1,000	112	196	213	240	450	528	594	703	880
Undergraduate [4]	1,000	10,475	10,597	11,959	12,232	13,155	13,716	14,257	14,474	14,781
Men	1,000	5,000	4,962	5,380	5,401	5,778	6,004	6,192	6,224	6,340
Women	1,000	5,475	5,635	6,579	6,831	7,377	7,711	8,065	8,250	8,441
First-time freshmen	1,000	2,588	2,292	2,257	2,169	2,428	2,497	2,571	2,605	(NA)
First professional	1,000	278	274	273	298	307	309	319	329	335
Men	1,000	199	180	167	174	164	161	163	166	168
Women	1,000	78	94	107	124	143	148	156	163	166
Graduate [4]	1,000	1,343	1,376	1,586	1,732	1,850	1,904	2,036	2,098	2,157
Men	1,000	675	677	737	768	780	796	847	865	879
Women	1,000	670	700	849	965	1,071	1,108	1,189	1,233	1,278
Public institutions:										
Current funds revenues [5] ...	Mil. dol. ...	43,196	65,005	94,905	123,501	176,645	174,503	(NA)	(NA)	(NA)
Tuition and fees	Mil. dol....	5,570	9,439	15,258	23,257	31,919	31,464	(NA)	(NA)	(NA)
Federal government.	Mil. dol....	5,540	6,852	9,763	13,672	19,744	18,668	(NA)	(NA)	(NA)
State government	Mil. dol....	19,676	29,221	38,240	44,243	62,895	62,543	(NA)	(NA)	(NA)
Auxiliary enterprises.	Mil. dol....	4,615	6,685	9,059	11,595	16,501	16,379	(NA)	(NA)	(NA)
Public institutions:										
Current funds										
expenditures [5]	Mil. dol. ...	42,280	63,194	92,961	119,525	170,345	168,296	(NA)	(NA)	(NA)
Educational and general ...	Mil. dol....	34,173	50,873	74,395	96,086	136,613	135,549	(NA)	(NA)	(NA)
Auxiliary enterprises.	Mil. dol....	4,658	6,830	9,050	11,309	16,377	16,245	(NA)	(NA)	(NA)
2-YEAR INSTITUTIONS										
Number of institutions [1,6] ...	Number ..	1,274	1,311	1,418	1,462	1,732	1,710	1,702	1,706	1,683
Public	Number...	945	932	972	1,047	1,076	1,085	1,081	1,086	1,061
Private	Number...	329	379	446	415	656	625	621	620	622
Instructional staff—										
(lecturer or above) [2]	1,000	192	211	(NA)	285	(NA)	349	(NA)	359	(NA)
Enrollment [3,4]	1,000	4,526	4,531	5,240	5,493	5,948	6,251	6,529	6,493	6,546
Public	1,000	4,329	4,270	4,996	5,278	5,697	5,997	6,270	6,208	6,244
Private	1,000	198	261	244	215	251	254	259	285	302
Male	1,000	2,047	2,002	2,233	2,329	2,559	2,675	2,753	2,689	2,698
Female	1,000	2,479	2,529	3,007	3,164	3,390	3,575	3,776	3,804	3,848

NA Not available. [1] Number of institutions includes count of branch campuses. Due to revised survey procedures, data beginning 1990 are not comparable with previous years. Beginning 1996 (2000 for data in this table), data reflect a new classification of institutions; this classification includes some additional, primarily 2-year, colleges and excludes a few institutions that did not award degrees. Includes institutions that were eligible to participate in Title IV federal financial aid programs. [2] Due to revised survey methods, data beginning 1990 not comparable with previous years. [3] Branch campuses counted according to actual status, e.g., 2-year branch in 2-year category. [4] Includes unclassified students. (Students taking courses for credit, but are not candidates for degrees.) [5] Includes items not shown separately. [6] Includes schools accredited by the National Association of Trade and Technical Schools. See footnote 1 for information pertaining to data beginning 2000.

Source: U.S. National Center for Education Statistics, *Digest of Education Statistics*, annual; and unpublished data.

Table 268. College Enrollment by Selected Characteristics: 1990 to 2004

[In thousands (13,818.6 represents 13,818,600). As of fall. Nonresident alien students are not distributed among racial/ethnic groups]

Characteristic	1990	1995	1999 [1]	2000 [1]	2001 [1]	2002 [1]	2003 [1]	2004 [1]
Total	13,818.6	14,261.8	14,791.2	15,312.3	15,928.0	16,611.7	16,900.5	17,272.0
Male	6,283.9	6,342.5	6,490.6	6,721.8	6,960.8	7,202.1	7,255.6	7,387.3
Female	7,534.7	7,919.2	8,300.6	8,590.5	8,967.2	9,409.6	9,644.9	9,884.8
Public	10,844.7	11,092.4	11,309.4	11,752.8	12,233.2	12,752.0	12,857.1	12,980.1
Private	2,973.9	3,169.4	3,481.8	3,559.5	3,694.8	3,859.7	4,043.4	4,291.9
2-year	5,240.1	5,492.5	5,592.7	5,948.4	6,250.6	6,529.4	6,492.9	6,545.9
4-year	8,578.6	8,769.3	9,198.5	9,363.9	9,677.4	10,082.3	10,407.6	10,726.2
Undergraduate.	11,959.2	12,232.0	12,681.2	13,155.4	13,715.6	14,257.1	14,473.9	14,780.6
Graduate	1,586.2	1,732.0	1,806.8	1,850.3	1,903.7	2,035.7	2,097.5	2,156.9
First professional	273.4	297.6	303.2	306.6	308.6	319.0	329.1	334.5
White [2]	10,722.5	10,311.2	10,282.1	10,462.1	10,774.5	11,140.2	11,275.4	11,422.8
Male	4,861.0	4,594.1	4,551.1	4,634.6	4,762.3	4,897.9	4,927.9	4,988.0
Female	5,861.5	5,717.2	5,731.0	5,827.5	6,012.2	6,242.3	6,347.5	6,434.8
Public	8,385.4	7,945.4	7,803.2	7,963.4	8,214.0	8,490.5	8,531.4	8,546.3
Private	2,337.0	2,365.9	2,478.8	2,498.7	2,560.5	2,649.8	2,744.1	2,876.5
2-year	3,954.3	3,794.0	3,672.0	3,804.1	3,955.7	4,086.5	4,076.7	4,063.8
4-year	6,768.1	6,517.2	6,610.1	6,658.0	6,818.8	7,053.8	7,198.7	7,359.0
Undergraduate.	9,272.6	8,805.6	8,805.7	8,983.5	9,278.7	9,564.9	9,662.5	9,771.3
Graduate	1,228.4	1,282.3	1,256.5	1,258.5	1,275.1	1,348.0	1,378.6	1,413.3
First professional	221.5	223.3	219.9	220.1	220.8	227.4	234.3	238.2
Black [2]	1,247.0	1,473.7	1,643.2	1,730.3	1,850.4	1,978.7	2,068.9	2,164.7
Male	484.7	555.9	604.2	635.3	672.4	708.6	730.6	758.4
Female	762.3	917.8	1,038.9	1,095.0	1,178.0	1,270.2	1,338.2	1,406.3
Public	976.4	1,160.6	1,253.4	1,319.2	1,397.1	1,487.2	1,533.5	1,574.6
Private	270.6	313.0	389.8	411.1	453.2	491.6	535.3	590.1
2-year	524.3	621.5	679.1	734.9	795.7	859.1	879.9	905.8
4-year	722.8	852.2	964.1	995.4	1,054.7	1,119.7	1,189.0	1,258.9
Undergraduate.	1,147.2	1,333.6	1,471.9	1,548.9	1,657.1	1763.8	1,838.2	1918.5
Graduate	83.9	118.6	148.7	157.9	169.4	189.6	204.9	220.4
First professional	15.9	21.4	22.5	23.5	23.9	25.3	25.8	25.9
Hispanic	782.4	1,093.8	1,319.1	1,461.8	1,560.6	1,661.7	1,716.0	1,809.6
Male	353.9	480.2	563.6	627.1	664.2	699.0	709.1	745.1
Female	428.5	613.7	755.5	834.7	896.4	962.7	1,006.9	1,064.5
Public	671.4	937.1	1,099.1	1,229.3	1,308.8	1,388.7	1,414.6	1,477.4
Private	111.0	156.8	220.0	232.5	251.8	273.1	301.4	332.2
2-year	424.2	608.4	735.7	843.9	904.3	958.9	932.6	972.4
4-year	358.2	485.5	583.4	617.9	656.3	702.9	783.4	837.2
Undergraduate.	724.6	1,012.0	1,214.0	1,351.0	1,444.4	1,533.3	1,579.6	1,666.9
Graduate	47.2	68.0	90.4	95.4	100.5	112.3	119.5	125.8
First professional	10.7	13.8	14.7	15.4	15.6	16.1	16.9	17.0
American Indian/ Alaska Native	102.8	131.3	145.5	151.2	158.2	165.9	172.7	176.1
Male	43.1	54.8	58.6	61.4	63.6	65.7	67.1	68.6
Female	59.7	76.5	86.8	89.7	94.5	100.2	105.6	107.5
Public	90.4	113.8	124.2	127.3	133.6	140.0	144.3	144.4
Private	12.4	17.5	21.3	23.9	24.6	25.9	28.3	31.8
2-year	54.9	65.6	72.1	74.7	78.2	81.3	82.2	82.2
4-year	47.9	65.7	73.4	76.5	80.0	84.6	90.4	93.9
Undergraduate.	95.5	120.7	133.4	138.5	144.8	151.7	157.8	160.3
Graduate	6.2	8.5	10.0	10.3	11.2	11.9	12.5	13.4
First professional	1.1	2.1	2.1	2.3	2.1	2.2	2.3	2.4
Asian/ Pacific Islander	572.4	797.4	913.0	978.2	1,019.0	1,074.2	1,075.7	1,108.7
Male	294.9	393.3	437.1	465.9	480.8	503.9	498.1	511.6
Female	277.5	404.1	475.8	512.3	538.3	570.2	577.6	597.1
Public	461.0	638.0	716.1	770.5	806.1	851.6	845.2	866.1
Private	111.5	159.4	196.9	207.7	213.0	222.6	230.5	242.6
2-year	215.2	314.9	356.2	401.9	417.5	441.0	425.3	430.7
4-year	357.2	482.4	556.8	576.3	601.6	633.1	650.4	678.0
Undergraduate.	500.5	692.2	786.0	845.5	883.9	927.4	922.7	949.9
Graduate	53.2	75.6	90.7	95.8	97.4	107.1	111.7	115.9
First professional	18.7	29.6	36.3	36.8	37.7	39.6	41.3	42.9
Nonresident alien . . .	391.5	454.4	488.5	528.7	565.3	590.9	591.8	590.2
Male	246.3	264.3	276.0	297.3	317.4	327.0	322.7	315.6
Female	145.2	190.1	212.4	231.4	247.8	263.9	269.2	274.6
Public	260.0	297.5	313.3	343.1	373.6	394.1	388.0	371.4
Private	131.4	156.9	175.1	185.6	191.6	196.8	203.9	218.8
2-year	67.1	88.1	77.6	89.0	99.2	102.6	96.2	90.9
4-year	324.3	366.2	410.8	439.7	466.1	488.3	495.6	499.2
Undergraduate.	218.7	267.6	270.3	288.0	306.7	316.0	313.0	313.8
Graduate	167.3	179.5	210.6	232.3	250.1	266.6	270.4	268.1
First professional	5.4	7.3	7.6	8.4	8.4	8.3	8.4	8.2

[1] In this table, data beginning 1999 reflect a new classification of institutions; see footnote 1, Table 267.   [2] Non-Hispanic.

Source: U.S. National Center for Education Statistics, Digest of Education Statistics, annual.

Education   173

Table 269. Degree-Granting Institutions, Number and Enrollment by State: 2004

[**17,272 represents 17,272,000.** Number of institutions beginning in academic year. Opening fall enrollment of resident and extension students attending full-time or part-time. Excludes students taking courses for credit by mail, radio, or TV, and students in branches of U.S. institutions operated in foreign countries. See Appendix III]

State	Number of institutions [1]	Enrollment (1,000)							Minority enrollment			Nonresident alien
		Total	Male	Female	Public	Private	Full-time	White [2]	Total [3]	Black [2]	Hispanic	
United States . . .	4,216	17,272	7,387	9,885	12,980	4,292	10,610	11,423	5,259	2,165	1,810	590
Alabama.	69	256	107	149	227	29	173	167	83	74	4	6
Alaska	8	31	12	19	30	1	13	22	8	1	1	1
Arizona.	77	491	211	280	318	173	304	316	148	35	78	27
Arkansas	47	138	55	83	124	14	92	105	31	25	2	2
California	399	2,374	1,043	1,331	1,987	387	1,204	1,040	1,259	183	610	75
Colorado.	77	301	133	168	239	62	176	231	63	14	33	7
Connecticut.	45	173	72	101	110	62	109	127	40	18	14	7
Delaware	10	50	20	30	38	12	32	36	12	9	2	1
District of Columbia .	15	100	41	59	5	95	61	49	45	33	4	7
Florida	163	867	360	507	650	217	484	493	344	157	154	30
Georgia	128	434	176	259	336	98	292	262	159	131	11	13
Hawaii	20	67	27	40	51	17	40	18	44	2	2	5
Idaho.	14	76	34	42	61	16	53	67	6	1	3	3
Illinois	172	801	343	458	564	238	450	525	252	111	92	24
Indiana.	99	357	160	197	267	90	246	296	47	29	10	13
Iowa	64	218	95	123	150	68	145	190	21	10	5	7
Kansas.	63	192	85	107	170	21	113	157	29	11	8	6
Kentucky	76	240	102	138	198	42	153	209	27	21	3	4
Louisiana	90	246	98	149	208	38	179	150	88	76	6	8
Maine.	30	65	26	39	47	18	40	60	4	1	1	1
Maryland	57	312	127	185	257	56	166	182	117	85	12	13
Massachusetts.	122	439	186	253	188	251	299	319	94	34	26	27
Michigan.	105	621	264	357	501	120	360	475	122	80	17	23
Minnesota.	105	349	149	200	241	108	225	292	47	22	7	9
Mississippi	40	152	59	93	138	15	116	89	61	58	1	2
Missouri	125	365	155	210	215	151	220	290	65	44	10	10
Montana.	23	47	21	26	42	5	36	40	6	(Z)	1	1
Nebraska	39	121	54	67	93	28	80	105	13	5	4	3
Nevada	20	106	46	60	97	9	50	69	34	8	14	3
New Hampshire	26	70	29	41	41	30	47	63	5	2	2	2
New Jersey.	59	380	162	218	305	75	226	229	136	54	49	15
New Mexico	43	132	54	78	121	10	69	57	71	4	54	3
New York	307	1,142	478	664	623	518	799	698	381	161	128	63
North Carolina.	127	473	189	283	389	84	300	320	141	113	11	12
North Dakota.	21	50	24	26	43	6	38	43	5	1	1	2
Ohio.	194	614	264	350	454	160	412	498	98	71	12	18
Oklahoma.	54	208	91	117	179	28	136	146	51	19	7	10
Oregon.	59	200	89	111	165	35	122	164	31	5	10	5
Pennsylvania.	260	689	300	389	385	304	495	546	120	70	19	23
Rhode Island.	14	80	35	46	40	40	57	65	13	5	5	3
South Carolina.	63	209	82	127	172	37	141	140	65	58	3	3
South Dakota	26	49	21	28	38	11	33	42	6	1	1	1
Tennessee	97	278	116	162	200	78	201	208	65	54	5	5
Texas.	208	1,229	534	695	1,072	157	687	646	533	151	316	50
Utah.	27	194	99	95	145	49	119	170	18	2	9	6
Vermont	25	39	17	22	23	16	28	35	3	1	1	1
Virginia.	99	425	181	245	343	82	257	293	121	81	15	11
Washington.	81	344	150	193	293	50	214	263	71	15	18	10
West Virginia.	43	98	43	55	83	15	73	88	7	5	1	2
Wisconsin	67	332	142	189	267	65	212	286	39	17	9	9
Wyoming	9	34	15	19	32	2	20	31	3	(Z)	2	(Z)
U.S. military [4]. . . .	5	15	12	3	15	(X)	15	12	3	1	1	(Z)

X Not applicable. Z Fewer than 500. [1] Branch campuses counted as separate institutions. [2] Non-Hispanic. [3] Includes other races not shown separately. [4] Service schools.

Source: U.S. National Center for Education Statistics, *Digest of Education Statistics,* annual.

U.S. Census Bureau, Statistical Abstract of the United States: 2007

Table 270. College Enrollment by Sex, Age, Race, and Hispanic Origin: 1980 to 2004

[In thousands (11,387 represents 11,387,000). **As of October** for the civilian noninstitutional population, 14 years old and over. Based on the Current Population Survey; see text, Section 1, and Appendix III]

Characteristic	1980	1985	1990 [1]	1995	1998	1999	2000	2001	2002	2003	2004
Total [2]	11,387	12,524	13,621	14,715	15,546	15,203	15,314	15,873	16,497	16,638	17,383
Male [3]	5,430	5,906	6,192	6,703	6,905	6,956	6,682	6,875	7,240	7,318	7,575
18 to 24 years	3,604	3,749	3,922	4,089	4,403	4,397	4,342	4,437	4,629	4,697	4,866
25 to 34 years	1,325	1,464	1,412	1,561	1,500	1,458	1,361	1,476	1,460	1,590	1,604
35 years old and over . .	405	561	772	985	953	1,024	918	908	1,071	970	1,033
Female [3]	5,957	6,618	7,429	8,013	8,641	8,247	8,631	8,998	9,258	9,319	9,808
18 to 24 years	3,625	3,788	4,042	4,452	4,919	4,863	5,109	5,192	5,404	5,667	5,742
25 to 34 years	1,378	1,599	1,749	1,788	1,915	1,637	1,846	1,946	1,941	1,904	2,091
35 years old and over . .	802	1,100	1,546	1,684	1,732	1,675	1,589	1,776	1,797	1,660	1,850
White [3, 4]	9,925	10,781	11,488	12,021	12,401	12,053	11,999	12,208	12,781	12,870	13,381
18 to 24 years	6,334	6,500	6,635	7,011	7,541	7,446	7,566	7,548	7,921	8,150	8,354
25 to 34 years	2,328	2,604	2,698	2,686	2,568	2,345	2,339	2,469	2,515	2,545	2,748
35 years old and over . .	1,051	1,448	2,023	2,208	2,199	2,174	1,978	2,103	2,236	2,075	2,143
Male	4,804	5,103	5,235	5,535	5,602	5,562	5,311	5,383	5,719	5,714	5,944
Female	5,121	5,679	6,253	6,486	6,799	6,491	6,689	6,826	7,062	7,155	7,438
Black [3, 4]	1,163	1,263	1,393	1,772	2,016	1,998	2,164	2,230	2,278	2,144	2,301
18 to 24 years	688	734	894	988	1,115	1,146	1,216	1,206	1,227	1,225	1,238
25 to 34 years	289	295	258	426	539	453	567	562	542	503	522
35 years old and over . .	156	213	207	334	340	354	361	429	454	388	502
Male	476	552	587	710	770	833	815	781	802	798	776
Female	686	712	807	1,062	1,247	1,164	1,349	1,449	1,476	1,346	1,525
Hispanic origin [3, 5]	443	580	748	1,207	1,363	1,307	1,426	1,700	1,656	1,714	1,975
18 to 24 years	315	375	435	745	820	740	899	1,035	979	1,115	1,223
25 to 34 years	118	189	168	250	336	334	309	392	414	380	460
35 years old and over . .	(NA)	(NA)	130	193	198	226	195	260	249	207	271
Male	222	279	364	568	550	568	619	731	705	703	852
Female	221	299	384	639	814	739	807	969	951	1,011	1,123

NA Not available. [1] Beginning 1990, based on a revised edit and tabulation package. [2] Includes other races not shown separately. [3] Includes persons 14 to 17 years old, not shown separately. [4] Beginning 2003, for persons who selected this race group only. See footnote 2, Table 214. [5] Persons of Hispanic origin may be of any race.

Source: U.S. Census Bureau, *Current Population Reports*, PPL-148; and earlier PPL and P-20 reports. See Internet site <http://www.census.gov/population/www/socdemo/school.html>.

Table 271. Foreign (Nonimmigrant) Student Enrollment in College: 1976 to 2005

[In thousands (179 represents 179,000). For fall of the previous year]

Region of origin	1976	1980	1985	1990	1995	1996	1997	1998	1999	2000	2001	2002	2003	2004	2005
All regions . . .	179	286	342	387	453	454	458	481	491	515	548	583	586	573	565
Africa.	25	36	40	25	21	21	22	23	26	30	34	38	40	38	36
Nigeria	11	16	18	4	2	2	2	2	3	4	4	4	6	6	6
Asia [1]	97	165	200	245	292	290	291	308	308	315	339	363	367	356	356
China: Taiwan . . .	11	18	23	31	36	33	30	31	31	29	29	29	28	26	26
Hong Kong	12	10	10	11	13	12	11	10	9	8	8	8	8	7	7
India	10	9	15	26	34	32	31	34	37	42	55	67	75	80	80
Indonesia	1	2	7	9	12	13	12	13	12	11	12	12	10	9	8
Iran	20	51	17	7	3	3	2	2	2	2	2	2	2	2	2
Japan	7	12	13	30	45	46	46	47	46	47	46	47	46	41	42
Malaysia	2	4	22	14	14	14	15	15	12	9	8	7	7	6	6
Saudi Arabia	3	10	8	4	4	4	4	5	5	5	5	6	4	4	3
South Korea	3	5	16	22	34	36	37	43	39	41	46	49	52	52	53
Thailand	7	7	7	7	11	12	13	15	12	11	11	12	10	9	9
Europe.	14	23	33	46	65	67	68	72	74	78	81	82	78	74	72
Latin America [2]	30	42	49	48	47	47	50	51	55	62	64	68	69	70	68
Mexico	5	6	6	7	9	9	9	9	10	10	11	11	13	13	13
Venezuela	5	10	10	3	4	4	5	5	5	5	5	6	5	6	5
North America	10	16	16	19	23	24	24	23	23	24	26	27	27	28	29
Canada.	10	15	15	18	23	23	23	22	23	24	24	25	27	27	28
Oceania	3	4	4	4	4	4	4	4	4	5	5	5	5	5	4

[1] Includes countries not shown separately. [2] Includes Central America, Caribbean, and South America.

Source: Institute of International Education, New York, NY, *Open Doors Report on International Educational Exchange*, annual (copyright).

Table 272. College Enrollment—Summary by Sex, Race and Hispanic Origin: 2004

[In thousands (17,383 represents 17,383,000), except percent. As of October. Covers civilian noninstitutional population 15 years old and over enrolled in colleges and graduate schools. Based on Current Population Survey, see text, Section 1, Population and Appendix III]

Characteristic	Total			Race and Hispanic origin				
				White [2]				
	Number [1]	Male	Female	Total	Non-Hispanic	Black [2]	Asian [2]	Hispanic [3]
Total enrollment	**17,383**	**7,575**	**9,808**	**13,381**	**11,571**	**2,301**	**1,192**	**1,975**
15 to 17 years old.	198	75	122	134	111	40	20	23
18 to 19 years old.	3,685	1,610	2,074	2,946	2,596	440	182	384
20 to 21 years old.	3,777	1,811	1,966	3,016	2,618	398	245	431
22 to 24 years old.	3,149	1,444	1,705	2,389	2,014	400	269	407
25 to 29 years old.	2,403	1,068	1,335	1,776	1,513	352	217	280
30 to 34 years old.	1,287	533	753	974	814	170	113	179
35 years old and over	2,884	1,034	1,850	2,146	1,905	501	146	271
Type of school:								
2-year.	4,340	1,756	2,584	3,303	2,681	656	218	659
15 to 19 years old	1,243	537	705	962	801	162	70	177
20 to 24 years old	1,371	651	720	1,068	830	181	76	247
25 years old and over . .	1,727	567	1,159	1,273	1,050	312	73	235
4-year.	9,664	4,401	5,264	7,524	6,519	1,303	563	1,090
15 to 19 years old	2,620	1,137	1,484	2,101	1,888	316	133	230
20 to 24 years old	4,761	2,261	2,499	3,734	3,251	552	331	532
25 years old and over . .	2,283	1,002	1,281	1,690	1,379	434	101	328
Graduate school	3,378	1,419	1,959	2,554	2,370	343	409	225
15 to 24 years old	815	354	461	621	569	66	107	58
25 to 34 years old	1,433	630	803	1,054	965	133	223	108
35 years old and over . .	1,131	434	696	879	836	145	79	60
Public.	13,652	5,871	7,781	10,477	8,929	1,831	928	1,676
2-year	3,940	1,569	2,371	3,007	2,427	590	202	613
4-year	7,445	3,379	4,066	5,747	4,920	1,016	460	907
Graduate	2,267	923	1,344	1,723	1,582	225	266	156
Percent of students:								
Employed full-time.	17.8	17.3	18.2	17.9	18.1	19.9	14.7	16.9
Employed part-time	25.4	23.4	27.3	27.7	29.1	14.9	19.9	20.0

[1] Includes other races, not shown separately. [2] For persons who selected this race group only. See footnote 2, Table 214.
[3] Persons of Hispanic origin may be of any race.

Source: U.S. Census Bureau, unpublished data. See Internet site <http://www.census.gov/population/www/socdemo/school.html>.

Table 273. Higher Education Enrollments in Foreign Languages: 1970 to 2002

[As of fall (1,111.5 represents 1,111,500). For credit enrollment]

Enrollment	1970	1977	1980	1983	1986	1990	1995	1998	2002
Registrations [1] **(1,000)**	**1,111.5**	**933.5**	**924.8**	**966.0**	**1,003.2**	**1,184.1**	**1,138.8**	**1,193.8**	**1,397.3**
By selected language (1,000):									
Spanish	389.2	376.7	379.4	386.2	411.3	533.9	606.3	656.6	746.3
French	359.3	246.1	248.4	270.1	275.3	272.5	205.4	199.1	202.0
German	202.6	135.4	126.9	128.2	121.0	133.3	96.3	89.0	91.1
Italian	34.2	33.3	34.8	38.7	40.9	49.7	43.8	49.3	63.9
American Sign Language	(X)	(X)	(X)	(X)	(X)	1.6	4.3	11.4	60.8
Japanese	6.6	10.7	11.5	16.1	23.5	45.7	44.7	43.1	52.2
Chinese	6.2	9.8	11.4	13.2	16.9	19.5	26.5	28.5	34.2
Latin.	27.6	24.4	25.0	24.2	25.0	28.2	25.9	26.1	29.8
Russian	36.2	27.8	24.0	30.4	34.0	44.6	24.7	23.8	23.9
Hebrew.	16.6	19.4	19.4	18.2	15.6	13.0	13.1	15.8	22.8
Ancient Greek	16.7	25.8	22.1	19.4	17.6	16.4	16.3	16.4	20.4
Arabic.	1.3	3.1	3.5	3.4	3.4	3.5	4.4	5.5	10.6
Portuguese	5.1	5.0	4.9	4.4	5.1	6.2	6.5	6.9	8.4
Korean	0.1	0.2	0.4	0.7	0.9	2.3	3.3	4.5	5.2
Index (1965 = 100).	107.3	90.1	89.3	93.2	96.8	114.3	109.9	115.2	134.9

X Not applicable. [1] Includes other foreign languages, not shown separately.

Source: Association of Departments of Foreign Languages, New York, NY, ADFL Bulletin, Vol. 35, No. 2-3, Winter-Spring 2004 (copyright). For 1970 to 1998, consult prior ADFL Bulletins.

Table 274. **College Freshmen—Summary Characteristics: 1970 to 2005**

[In percent, except as indicated (12.8 represents $12,800). **As of fall** for first-time full-time freshmen in 4-year colleges and universities. Based on sample survey and subject to sampling error; see source]

Characteristic	1970	1980	1985	1990	1995	2000	2003	2004	2005
Sex: Male	52.1	48.8	48.9	46.9	45.6	45.2	45.1	44.9	45.0
Female	47.9	51.2	51.1	53.1	54.4	54.8	55.0	55.1	55.0
Applied to three or more colleges	(NA)	31.5	35.4	42.9	44.4	50.5	54.2	52.8	55.4
Average grade in high school:									
A- to A+	19.6	26.6	28.7	29.4	36.1	42.9	46.6	47.5	46.6
B- to B+	62.5	58.2	57.1	57.0	54.2	50.5	48.3	47.6	48.0
C to C+	17.7	14.9	14.0	13.4	9.6	6.5	5.0	5.0	5.4
D	0.3	0.2	0.2	0.2	0.1	0.1	0.1	0.1	0.1
Political orientation:									
Liberal	35.7	21.0	22.4	24.6	22.9	24.8	24.2	26.1	27.1
Middle of the road	43.4	57.0	53.1	51.7	51.3	51.9	50.3	46.4	45.0
Conservative	17.3	19.0	21.3	20.6	21.8	18.9	21.1	21.9	22.6
Probable field of study:									
Arts and humanities	(NA)	10.5	10.1	10.5	11.2	12.1	12.3	12.0	12.8
Biological sciences	(NA)	4.5	4.5	4.9	8.3	6.6	7.3	7.7	7.6
Business	(NA)	21.2	24.6	21.1	15.4	16.7	15.9	16.0	17.4
Education	(NA)	8.4	6.9	10.3	10.1	11.0	10.1	9.6	9.9
Engineering	(NA)	11.2	11.0	9.7	8.1	8.7	9.3	9.6	8.3
Physical science	(NA)	3.2	3.2	2.8	3.1	2.6	2.7	3.0	3.1
Social science	(NA)	8.2	9.4	11.0	9.9	10.0	10.5	10.3	10.7
Professional	(NA)	15.5	13.1	13.0	16.5	11.6	14.3	15.1	14.6
Technical	(NA)	3.1	2.4	1.1	1.2	2.1	1.5	1.5	1.2
Data processing/computer programming	(NA)	1.7	1.7	0.7	0.8	1.5	0.7	0.6	0.5
Other [1]	(NA)	14.0	15.1	15.8	16.0	17.9	16.0	15.0	14.1
Communications	(NA)	2.4	2.8	2.9	1.8	2.7	2.4	1.9	2.0
Computer science	(NA)	2.6	2.4	1.7	2.2	3.7	1.7	1.4	1.1
Personal objectives—very important or essential:									
Being very well off financially	36.2	62.5	69.2	72.3	72.8	73.4	73.8	73.6	74.5
Developing a meaningful philosophy of life	79.1	62.5	46.9	45.9	45.4	42.4	39.3	42.1	45.0
Keeping up to date with political affairs	57.2	45.2	(NA)	46.6	32.3	28.1	33.9	34.3	36.4
Attitudes—agree or strongly agree:									
Capital punishment should be abolished	59.4	34.8	27.6	23.1	22.0	31.2	32.6	33.2	33.3
Legalize marijuana	40.6	37.1	21.4	18.8	33.4	34.2	38.8	37.2	37.7
There is too much concern for the rights of criminals	50.7	65.0	(NA)	65.1	73.2	66.5	61.1	58.1	57.9
Abortion should be legalized	85.7	53.7	56.4	65.5	59.9	53.9	54.5	53.9	55.2
Median family income ($1,000)	12.8	24.5	37.3	46.6	54.8	64.4	71.3	71.9	73.2

NA Not available.   [1] Includes other fields, not shown separately.

Source: The Higher Education Research Institute, University of California, Los Angeles, CA, *The American Freshman: National Norms,* annual.

Table 275. **Students Reported Disability Status by Selected Characteristic: 2003–2004**

[(19,054 represents 19,054,000). Disabled students reported that they had one or more of the following conditions: a specific learning disability, a visual handicap, hard of hearing, deafness, a speech disability, an orthopedic handicap, or a health impairment. Based on the 2003–2004 National Postsecondary Student-Aid Study; see source for details. Includes Puerto Rico. See also Appendix III]

Student characteristic	Undergraduate			Graduate and first-professional		
	All students	Disabled students	Nondisabled students	All students	Disabled students	Nondisabled students
Total students (1,000)	19,054	2,156	16,897	2,826	189	2,637
PERCENT DISTRIBUTION						
Total	100.0	100.0	100.0	100.0	100.0	100.0
Age:						
15 to 23	56.8	45.8	58.2	11.2	8.5	11.4
24 to 29	17.3	15.5	17.5	39.6	33.9	40.0
30 or older	25.9	38.7	24.3	49.2	57.6	48.6
Sex:						
Male	42.4	42.1	42.4	41.9	38.0	42.2
Female	57.6	57.9	57.6	58.1	62.0	57.8
Race/ethnicity of student:						
White, non-Hispanic	63.1	65.1	62.9	68.3	67.0	68.4
Black, non-Hispanic	14.0	13.2	14.1	9.6	12.5	9.3
Hispanic	12.7	12.3	12.8	7.7	7.9	7.6
Asian/Pacific Islander	5.9	3.8	6.2	11.0	5.9	11.3
American Indian/Alaska Native	0.9	1.2	0.9	0.6	0.4	0.6
Other	3.3	4.4	3.2	2.9	6.3	2.7
Attendance status:						
Full-time, full-year	38.6	33.5	39.2	32.7	28.9	32.9
Part-time or part-year	61.4	66.5	60.8	67.3	71.1	67.1
Student housing status:						
On-campus	13.8	10.7	14.2	(NA)	(NA)	(NA)
Off-campus	55.2	61.5	54.4	(NA)	(NA)	(NA)
With parents or relatives	31.0	27.7	31.4	(NA)	(NA)	(NA)
Dependency status:						
Dependent	49.7	39.4	51.0	(NA)	(NA)	(NA)
Independent, unmarried	15.2	19.5	14.7	47.5	48.1	47.5
Independent, married	7.9	9.1	7.8	18.8	15.7	19.0
Independent with dependents	27.1	32.0	26.5	33.7	36.2	33.6

NA Not available.

Source: U.S. National Center for Education Statistics, *Digest of Education Statistics, 2005.*

Education   177

Table 276. Average Total Price of Attendance of Undergraduate Education: 2003-2004

[In dollars. Excludes students attending more than one institution. Price of attendance includes tuition and fees, books and supplies, room and board, transportation, and personal and other expenses allowed for federal cost of attendance budgets. Based on the 2003-2004 National Postsecondary Student-Aid Study; see source for details. Includes Puerto Rico. See also Appendix III]

Student characteristic	Total [1]	Public 2-year	Public 4-year		Private not-for-profit 4-year		Private for-profit
			Non-doctorate	Doctorate	Non-doctorate	Doctorate	
Total.	**11,256**	**6,149**	**10,812**	**13,809**	**18,700**	**30,340**	**15,657**
Age: [2]							
18 years or younger	13,534	6,899	12,055	15,611	23,937	33,287	18,370
19 to 23 years	13,193	6,565	11,618	14,499	22,693	31,870	16,464
24 to 29 years	9,545	6,073	9,628	11,688	14,746	18,664	15,373
30 to 39 years	8,589	5,880	9,096	10,046	12,846	13,833	15,132
40 years or older	7,480	5,195	8,330	8,800	11,371	15,525	14,814
Sex:							
Male	11,567	6,138	10,762	13,877	18,910	30,559	16,839
Female	11,025	6,157	10,848	13,746	18,553	30,161	14,697
Race:							
One race:							
White	11,625	6,161	10,698	13,922	19,778	30,659	15,736
Black or African American	10,511	6,321	11,445	13,516	16,163	25,451	14,551
Asian	12,486	6,577	11,455	14,936	21,310	33,496	18,956
American Indian/Alaska Native	9,124	5,791	10,420	11,451	19,113	28,756	14,100
Native Hawaiian or other Pacific Islander. . .	9,517	4,922	10,353	14,110	19,198	33,392	18,365
Other race	11,734	7,084	10,779	13,424	19,854	31,805	16,234
More than one race	11,375	6,086	11,339	13,990	19,775	30,899	16,946
Hispanic or Latino: [3]							
Not Hispanic or Latino	11,454	6,213	10,846	13,946	19,200	30,444	15,591
Hispanic or Latino	9,910	5,772	10,505	12,224	15,102	29,088	16,001
Attendance pattern:							
Full-time, full-year	17,151	10,482	13,632	16,446	24,516	34,721	21,134
Full-time, part-year	9,801	5,723	7,519	9,628	14,265	23,622	13,158
Part-time, full-year	8,711	6,509	9,501	11,514	14,884	20,540	14,040
Part-time, part-year	4,157	3,234	4,479	5,586	6,918	9,247	8,812
Local residence:							
On campus	19,867	7,085	12,786	15,816	25,346	33,986	19,329
Off campus	10,034	6,062	10,532	13,350	15,434	24,517	15,412
With parents/other relatives	9,063	6,268	9,734	11,614	16,728	24,976	16,340

[1] Includes public less-than-2-year and private not-for-profit less-than-4-year. [2] As of December 31, 2003. [3] Persons of Hispanic origin may be of any race.

Source: U.S. National Center for Education Statistics, 2003-04 National Postsecondary Student Aid Study (NPSAS:04) data file, special tabulation.

Table 277. Average Amount of Aid Received by Undergraduates Receiving Aid: 2003-2004

[Average amount in dollars. Based on the 2003-2004 Student Postsecondary Aid Study and subject to sampling error; see source for details. Includes Puerto Rico. See also Appendix III]

Characteristic	Total aid [1]		Total grants		Total loans [2]	
	Percent receiving aid	Average amount	Percent receiving grants	Average amount	Percent receiving loans	Average amount
Total	**63.0**	**7,400**	**50.4**	**4,000**	**35.1**	**5,800**
Attendance pattern:						
Full-time, full-year	76.2	9,900	62.2	5,600	49.5	6,200
Part-time or part-year	54.3	4,900	42.7	2,400	24.9	5,300
Institution type: [3]						
Public 2-year	46.8	3,200	39.8	2,200	12.1	3,600
Public 4-year	68.5	7,600	51.5	4,000	44.8	5,600
Private not-for-profit 4-year	83.2	13,500	73.1	7,900	57.4	7,000
Private for-profit	89.2	8,900	65.3	3,300	74.5	6,800
Dependency status: [4]						
Dependent	63.8	8,600	50.4	5,200	38.1	5,300
Independent	62.7	6,100	51.0	2,900	32.0	6,400
Dependent student parents income: [5]						
Less than 32,000	78.5	8,500	74.6	5,500	39.2	5,000
32,000 to 92,000	62.5	8,400	46.6	4,800	40.7	5,300
More than 92,000	51.9	9,000	34.0	5,400	31.6	5,600
Independent student income: [5, 6]						
Less than 25,000	71.6	6,800	63.3	3,300	38.9	6,200
25,000 or more	54.0	5,200	39.1	2,200	25.2	6,700

[1] Includes other aid not shown separately. [2] Includes only loans to students. [3] Excludes students attending more than one institution. [4] Dependent or independent for federal aid purposes. [5] Income in 2002. [6] Including spouse.

Source: U.S. National Center for Education Statistics, *Undergraduate Financial Aid Estimates for 2003-04 by Type of Institution,* June 2005, NCES 2005-163.

178   Education

Table 278. **Higher Education Price Indexes: 1970 to 2006**

[1983 = 100. **For years ending June 30.** Reflects prices paid by colleges and universities. Minus sign (–) indicates decrease]

Year	Total	Personnel compensation					Contracted services, supplies, and equipment		
		Faculty salaries	Adminis- trative salaries	Clerical salaries	Service employee salaries	Fringe benefits	Miscel- laneous services	Supplies and materials	Utilities
INDEXES									
1970	39.5	(NA)	(NA)	(NA)	(NA)	24.7	(NA)	37.6	16.3
1980	77.5	(NA)	(NA)	(NA)	(NA)	72.6	(NA)	84.6	64.1
1990	140.8	(NA)	(NA)	(NA)	(NA)	171.4	(NA)	119.6	90.1
2000	196.9	(NA)	(NA)	(NA)	(NA)	254.8	(NA)	145.0	104.9
2001	206.5	214.5	229.2	197.7	182.6	261.7	199.8	130.4	140.7
2002	215.0	222.7	236.4	205.4	189.6	277.1	205.8	130.6	149.4
2003	221.2	229.4	255.7	211.1	193.9	292.3	209.5	129.0	127.0
2004	231.5	234.2	263.3	217.1	197.6	312.8	216.4	133.8	174.6
2005	239.5	240.7	274.0	223.4	201.4	327.2	222.7	140.2	190.1
2006	251.9	248.2	287.7	229.7	206.1	343.7	229.5	151.7	241.6
ANNUAL PERCENT CHANGE [1]									
1970	6.7	(NA)	(NA)	(NA)	(NA)	(NA)	(NA)	(NA)	(NA)
1980	9.9	(NA)	(NA)	(NA)	(NA)	12.6	(NA)	18.0	27.4
1990	6.0	(NA)	(NA)	(NA)	(NA)	7.9	(NA)	5.5	5.6
2000	4.1	(NA)	(NA)	(NA)	(NA)	6.5	(NA)	–0.1	4.4
2001	4.9	(NA)	(NA)	(NA)	(NA)	2.7	(NA)	6.0	34.1
2002	4.1	3.8	3.1	3.9	3.8	5.9	3.0	0.2	6.2
2003	2.9	3.0	8.2	2.8	2.3	5.5	1.8	–1.2	–15.0
2004	4.7	2.1	3.0	2.8	1.9	7.0	3.3	3.7	37.5
2005	3.5	2.8	4.1	2.9	1.9	4.6	2.9	4.8	8.9
2006	5.0	3.1	5.0	2.8	2.3	5.0	3.0	8.2	27.1

NA Not available. [1] Percent change from the immediate prior year.

Source: The Commonfund Institute, Wilton, CT, (copyright). See Internet site <http://www.commonfund.org>.

Table 279. **Federal Student Financial Assistance: 1995 to 2006**

[**For award years July 1 of year shown to the following June 30 (35,477 represents ($35,477,000,000).** Funds utilized exclude operating costs, etc., and represent funds given to students]

Type of assistance	1995	2000	2002	2003	2004	2005	2006, est.
FUNDS UTILIZED (mil. dol.)							
Total	**35,477**	**44,007**	**55,525**	**62,275**	**69,053**	**72,112**	**76,604**
Federal Pell Grants	5,472	7,956	11,640	12,707	13,149	12,594	12,745
Federal Supplemental Educational Opportunity Grant	764	907	1,033	1,064	1,065	985	975
Federal Work-Study	764	939	1,097	1,106	1,082	1,184	1,172
Federal Perkins Loan	1,029	1,144	1,460	1,638	1,651	1,135	1,135
Federal Direct Student Loan (FDSL) . .	8,296	10,348	11,689	11,969	12,840	12,930	13,874
Federal Family Education Loans (FFEL)	19,152	22,712	28,606	33,791	39,266	43,284	46,703
NUMBER OF AWARDS (1,000)							
Total	**13,667**	**15,043**	**17,976**	**19,414**	**20,825**	**21,052**	**21,845**
Federal Pell Grants	3,612	3,899	4,953	5,139	5,308	5,129	5,213
Federal Supplemental Educational Opportunity Grant	1,083	1,175	1,354	1,389	1,408	1,287	1,274
Federal Work-Study	702	713	759	764	810	818	810
Federal Perkins Loan	688	639	728	756	748	524	524
Federal Direct Student Loan (FDSL)	2,339	2,739	2,908	2,937	3,001	2,971	3,092
Federal Family Education Loans (FFEL)	5,243	5,878	7,274	8,429	9,550	10,323	10,932
AVERAGE AWARD (dol.)							
Total	**2,596**	**2,925**	**3,089**	**3,208**	**3,316**	**3,425**	**3,507**
Federal Pell Grants	1,515	2,041	2,350	2,473	2,477	2,456	2,445
Federal Supplemental Educational Opportunity Grant	705	772	763	766	759	766	766
Federal Work-Study	1,088	1,318	1,446	1,447	1,335	1,447	1,447
Federal Perkins Loan	1,496	1,790	2,003	2,166	2,206	2,166	2,166
Federal Direct Student Loan (FDSL)	3,547	3,778	4,020	4,075	4,279	4,352	4,487
Federal Family Education Loans (FFEL)	3,653	3,864	3,933	4,009	4,112	4,193	4,272
COHORT DEFAULT RATE [1]							
Federal Perkins Loan	12.6	9.9	8.9	8.3	8.1	(NA)	(NA)

NA Not available. [1] As of June 30. Represents the percent of borrowers entering repayment status in year shown who defaulted in the following year.

Source: U.S. Dept. of Education, Office of Postsecondary Education, unpublished data.

Education 179

Table 280. State and Local Financial Support for Higher Education by State: 2004–2005

[For 2004–2005 fiscal year, except as indicated (10,102.2 represents 10,102,200). Data for the 50 states]

State	FTE enrollment [1] (1,000)	Educational appropriations per FTE [2] (dol.)	Appropriations for higher ed. as a percent of state and local tax revenue 2002–2003 [3]	State	FTE enrollment [1] (1,000)	Educational appropriations per FTE [2] (dol.)	Appropriations for higher ed. as a percent of state and local tax revenue 2002–2003 [3]
Total . . .	10,102.2	5,825	7.4	MO	167.9	5,906	6.8
				MT	35.3	3,873	6.7
AL	181.2	4,902	11.8	NE	71.9	5,911	10.1
AK	37.4	5,671	9.8	NV	59.6	7,890	5.3
AZ	217.5	5,925	8.1	NH	30.9	3,296	2.8
AR	100.6	4,691	9.7	NJ	202.8	8,602	5.1
CA	1,651.7	5,844	9.4	NM	79.2	7,641	14.4
CO	162.7	3,360	4.6	NY	499.8	7,240	5.0
CT	72.3	9,150	4.7	NC	304.0	6,995	11.0
DE	30.5	6,350	6.8	ND	36.7	4,319	11.1
FL	531.1	4,854	5.5	OH	380.9	4,702	5.8
GA	291.6	7,445	8.5	OK	136.4	4,874	9.8
HI	35.7	9,666	8.3	OR	123.1	4,221	1.5
ID	46.5	6,768	9.7	PA	326.7	5,514	5.3
IL	380.0	6,851	7.9	RI	28.1	6,169	4.4
IN	220.9	5,282	7.2	SC	136.9	5,710	8.2
IA	117.7	5,280	9.6	SD	28.5	4,561	7.8
KS	111.9	6,136	9.6	TN	169.4	6,263	8.1
KY	144.3	5,969	9.5	TX	812.7	5,384	9.2
LA	183.4	5,200	9.5	UT	107.7	5,287	9.9
ME	35.2	5,982	4.9	VT	18.0	3,019	3.2
MD	196.6	4,544	6.9	VA	260.8	4,934	6.3
MA	137.4	7,712	4.5	WA	213.8	5,873	6.8
MI	372.0	5,687	8.1	WV	70.8	4,196	9.1
MN	190.1	5,495	6.8	WI	210.9	6,202	7.9
MS	118.5	4,849	11.3	WY	22.4	12,354	13.4

[1] Full-time equivalent. Includes degree enrollment and enrollment in public postsecondary programs resulting in a certificate or other formal recognition. Includes summer sessions. Excludes medical enrollments. [2] State and local appropriations for general operating expenses of public postsecondary education. Includes state-funded financial aid to students attending in-state public institutions. Excludes sums for research, agricultural extension, and teaching hospitals and medical schools. [3] Includes state and local appropriations for public and independent postsecondary education (including sums for research, agricultural extension, and teaching hospitals and medical schools).

Source: State Higher Education Executive Officers, Boulder, CO (copyright). See Internet site <http://www.sheeo.org>.

Table 281. Distance Education in Degree-Granting Postsecondary Institutions: 2000–2001

[For the school year (3,077 represents 3,077,000). Distance education is education or training courses delivered to off-campus sites via audio, video (live or prerecorded), or computer technologies (simultaneous or not simultaneous). Based on the Postsecondary Education Quick Information System; see source for details]

Institution type and size		Institutions offering distance education courses		Enrollments in distance education courses (1,000)			
						Enrollments in college-level courses	
	Number of institutions	Number	Percent	Total [1]	Total [2]	Under-graduate enrollments	Graduate enrollments [3]
All institutions.	4,130	2,320	56	3,077	2,876	2,350	510
Type:							
Public 2-year	1,070	960	90	1,472	1,436	1,435	(B)
Private 2-year	640	100	16	(B)	(B)	(B)	(B)
Public 4-year	620	550	89	945	888	566	308
Private 4-year	1,800	710	40	589	480	278	202
Enrollment size:							
Less than 3,000	2,840	1,160	41	486	460	368	91
3,000 to 9,999	870	770	88	1,171	1,132	932	197
10,000 or more	420	400	95	1,420	1,284	1,049	222

B Base figure too small to meet statistical standards of reliability for a derived figure. [1] Includes all levels and audiences (for example, adult education and continuing education). [2] Includes duplication for students enrolled in more than one course. [3] Includes first-professional.

Source: U.S. National Center for Education Statistics, *Distance Education at Degree-Granting Postsecondary Institutions: 2000–2001*, NCES 2003-017, July 2003.

Table 282. Institutions of Higher Education—Charges: 1985 to 2005

[In dollars. Estimated. **For the entire academic year ending in year shown.** Figures are average charges per full-time equivalent student. Room and board are based on full-time students]

Academic control and year	Tuition and required fees [1]				Board rates [2]				Dormitory charges			
	All institutions	2-yr. colleges	4-yr. colleges	Other 4-yr. schools	All institutions	2-yr. colleges	4-yr. colleges	Other 4-yr. schools	All institutions	2-yr. colleges	4-yr. colleges	Other 4-yr. schools
Public:												
1985	971	584	1,386	1,117	1,241	1,302	1,276	1,201	1,196	921	1,237	1,200
1990	1,356	756	2,035	1,608	1,635	1,581	1,728	1,561	1,513	962	1,561	1,554
1995	2,057	1,192	2,977	2,499	1,949	1,712	2,108	1,866	1,959	1,232	1,992	2,044
2000	2,506	1,338	3,768	3,091	2,364	1,834	2,628	2,239	2,440	1,549	2,516	2,521
2001	2,562	1,333	3,979	3,208	2,455	1,906	2,686	2,358	2,569	1,600	2,657	2,652
2002	2,700	1,380	4,273	3,409	2,598	2,036	2,835	2,504	2,723	1,722	2,838	2,801
2003	2,903	1,483	4,686	3,668	2,669	2,164	2,895	2,580	2,930	1,954	3,023	3,032
2004	3,319	1,702	5,363	4,141	2,823	2,233	3,084	2,724	3,107	2,086	3,232	3,198
2005, prel. . . .	3,638	1,847	5,948	4,520	2,935	2,333	3,226	2,813	3,304	2,154	3,431	3,409
Private:												
1985	5,315	3,485	6,843	5,135	1,462	1,294	1,647	1,405	1,426	1,424	1,753	1,309
1990	8,147	5,196	10,348	7,778	1,948	1,811	2,339	1,823	1,923	1,663	2,411	1,774
1995	11,111	6,914	14,537	10,653	2,509	2,023	3,035	2,362	2,587	2,233	3,469	2,347
2000	14,081	8,235	19,307	13,361	2,882	2,922	3,157	2,790	3,224	2,808	4,070	2,976
2001	15,000	9,067	20,106	14,233	2,993	3,000	3,300	2,893	3,374	2,722	4,270	3,121
2002	15,742	10,076	21,176	14,923	3,104	2,633	3,462	2,996	3,567	3,116	4,478	3,301
2003	16,383	10,651	22,716	15,416	3,206	3,870	3,602	3,071	3,752	3,232	4,724	3,478
2004	17,327	11,546	24,128	16,298	3,364	4,432	3,778	3,222	3,945	3,581	4,979	3,647
2005, prel. . . .	18,374	12,182	25,600	17,261	3,486	3,556	3,854	3,371	4,165	4,162	5,244	3,849

[1] For in-state students. [2] Beginning 1990, rates reflect 20 meals per week, rather than meals served 7 days a week.

Source: U.S. National Center for Education Statistics, *Digest of Education Statistics,* annual.

Table 283. Voluntary Financial Support of Higher Education: 1990 to 2005

[For school years ending in years shown (9,800 represents $9,800,000,000); enrollment as of fall of preceding year. Voluntary support, as defined in Gift Reporting Standards, excludes income from endowment and other invested funds as well as all support received from federal, state, and local governments and their agencies and contract research]

Item	Unit	1990	1995	2000	2001	2002	2003	2004	2005
Estimated support, total	Mil. dol. . .	**9,800**	**12,750**	**23,200**	**24,200**	**23,900**	**23,900**	**24,400**	**25,600**
Individuals	Mil. dol. . . .	4,770	6,540	12,220	12,030	11,300	11,150	11,900	12,100
Alumni	Mil. dol. . . .	2,540	3,600	6,800	6,830	5,900	6,600	6,700	7,100
Business corporations	Mil. dol. . . .	2,170	2,560	4,150	4,350	4,370	4,250	4,400	4,400
Foundations	Mil. dol. . . .	1,920	2,460	5,080	6,000	6,300	6,600	6,200	7,000
Fundraising consortia and other organizations	Mil. dol. . . .	700	940	1,380	1,450	1,570	1,540	1,550	1,730
Religious organizations	Mil. dol. . . .	240	250	370	370	360	360	350	370
Current operations	Mil. dol. . . .	5,440	7,230	11,270	12,200	12,400	12,900	13,600	14,200
Capital purposes.	Mil. dol. . . .	4,360	5,520	11,930	12,000	11,500	11,000	10,800	11,400
Enrollment, higher education [1] .	1,000	13,819	14,262	15,312	15,928	16,611	17,435	18,050	18,397
Support per student.	Dollars . . .	709	894	1,515	1,519	1,439	1,371	1,352	1,392
In **2004–2005** dollars	Dollars . . .	1,059	1,145	1,717	1,674	1,561	1,454	1,397	1,392
Expenditures, higher education.	Bil. dol. . . .	105.59	144.16	203.32	222.24	228.91	248.23	258.85	266.47
Expenditures per student	Dollars . . .	7,641	10,108	13,278	13,953	13,780	14,237	14,341	14,485
In **2004–2005** dollars	Dollars . . .	11,409	12,944	15,048	15,375	14,949	15,100	14,815	14,485
Institutions reporting support . . .	Number. . .	1,056	1,086	945	960	955	994	971	1,005
Total support reported	Mil. dol. . .	**8,214**	**10,992**	**19,419**	**20,569**	**19,824**	**19,823**	**19,630**	**20,940**
Private 4-year institutions	Mil. dol. . . .	5,072	6,500	11,047	11,391	10,953	10,318	10,695	11,007
Public 4-year institutions.	Mil. dol. . . .	3,056	4,382	8,254	9,026	8,754	9,400	8,802	9,757
2-year colleges.	Mil. dol. . . .	85	110	117	152	117	105	133	176

[1] Excludes proprietary schools.

Source: Council for Aid to Education, New York, NY, *Voluntary Support of Education,* annual.

Table 284. Average Salaries for College Faculty Members: 2004 to 2006

[In thousands of dollars (65.0 represents $65,000). For academic year ending in year shown. Figures are for 9 months teaching for full-time faculty members in 2-year and 4-year institutions with ranks. Fringe benefits averaged in 2004, $17,090 in public institutions and $20,565 in private institutions; in 2005, $17,966 in public institutions and $21,332 in private institutions; and in 2006, $18,677 in public institutions and $22,170 in private institutions]

Type of control and academic rank	2004	2005	2006	Type of control and academic rank	2004	2005	2006
Public: All ranks.	65.0	66.9	68.4	Private: [1] All ranks	76.6	79.3	81.5
Professor	85.8	88.5	91.4	Professor	104.0	108.2	111.8
Associate professor	62.4	64.4	66.3	Associate professor	68.5	71.0	73.3
Assistant professor	52.5	54.3	55.9	Assistant professor	57.5	59.4	61.0
Instructor	37.9	39.4	40.1	Instructor	41.8	42.2	44.5

[1] Excludes church-related colleges and universities.

Source: American Association of University Professors, Washington, DC, *AAUP Annual Report on the Economic Status of the Profession.*

Table 285. Employees in Higher Education Institutions by Sex and Occupation: 1976 to 2003

[In thousands (1,863.8 represents 1,863,800). As of fall. Based on survey and subject to sampling error; see source]

Year and status	Total	Professional staff									Nonpro-fessional staff, total
		Total	Executive, administrative, and managerial		Faculty [1]		Research/instruction assistants		Other		
			Male	Female	Male	Female	Male	Female	Male	Female	
1976, total	1,863.8	1,073.1	74.6	26.6	460.6	172.7	106.5	53.6	87.5	91.0	790.7
Full-time	1,339.9	709.4	72.0	25.0	326.8	107.2	18.6	9.4	76.2	74.1	630.5
Part-time	523.9	363.7	2.6	1.7	133.7	65.4	87.9	44.2	11.3	16.9	160.2
1991, total	2,545.2	1,595.5	85.4	59.3	525.6	300.7	119.1	78.6	165.4	261.3	949.8
Full-time	1,812.9	1,031.8	82.9	56.2	366.2	169.4	–	–	142.2	214.8	781.1
Part-time	732.3	563.7	2.5	3.1	159.4	131.2	119.1	78.6	23.2	46.4	168.7
2003, total [2]	3,194.2	2,272.6	91.8	94.7	664.8	510.1	157.4	135.7	248.4	369.8	921.6
Full-time	2,085.9	1,340.4	89.3	90.9	382.8	248.8	–	–	216.1	312.5	745.5
Part-time	1,108.2	932.2	2.5	3.8	282.0	261.3	157.4	135.7	32.3	57.3	176.1

– Represents zero.   [1] Instruction and research.   [2] In this table, 2003 data reflect the new classification of institutions. See footnote 1, Table 267.

Source: U.S. National Center for Education Statistics, *Digest of Education Statistics,* annual.

Table 286. Faculty in Institutions of Higher Education: 1975 to 2003

[In thousands (628 represents 628,000), except percent. As of fall. Based on survey and subject to sampling error; see source]

Year	Total	Employment status		Control		Level		Percent		
		Full-time	Part-time	Public	Private	4-Year	2-Year or less	Part-time	Public	2-Year or less
1975 [1]	628	440	188	443	185	467	161	30	71	26
1980 [1]	686	450	236	495	191	494	192	34	72	28
1985 [1]	715	459	256	503	212	504	211	36	70	30
1991 [2]	826	536	291	581	245	591	235	35	70	28
1993	915	546	370	650	265	626	290	40	71	32
1995	932	551	381	657	275	647	285	41	70	31
1997 [3]	990	569	421	695	295	683	307	43	70	31
1999 [3]	1,028	591	437	713	315	714	314	43	69	31
2001 [3]	1,113	618	495	771	342	764	349	44	69	31
2003 [3]	1,175	632	543	793	382	816	359	46	67	31

[1] Estimated on the basis of enrollment.   [2] Data beginning 1991 not comparable to prior years.   [3] In this table, data beginning in 1997 reflect the new classification of institutions. See footnote 1, Table 267.

Source: U.S. National Center for Education Statistics, *Digest of Education Statistics,* annual.

Table 287. Salary Offers to Candidates for Degrees: 2003 to 2005

[In dollars. Data are average beginning salaries based on offers made by business, industrial, government, nonprofit, and educational employers to graduating students. Data from representative colleges throughout the United States]

Field of study	Bachelor's			Master's [1]			Doctoral		
	2003	2004	2005	2003	2004	2005	2003	2005	2005
Accounting.	40,647	41,058	42,940	42,241	43,042	45,992	(NA)	(NA)	(NA)
Business administration/ management [2]	36,012	38,254	39,480	[3]50,835	[3]44,807	[3]50,513	[3]87,000	[3]75,125	[3]66,500
Marketing.	34,038	34,712	36,409	[3]35,000	[3]65,000	[3]47,000	(NA)	(NA)	(NA)
Engineering:									
Civil.	41,669	42,056	43,774	47,245	48,852	48,619	[3]69,079	[3]53,067	[3]59,216
Chemical	52,384	52,539	53,639	[3]57,857	[3]53,920	62,845	[3]70,729	[3]72,613	[3]73,317
Computer	51,343	51,297	52,242	[3]64,200	[3]63,563	58,631	(NA)	(NA)	[3]69,625
Electrical	49,794	51,124	51,773	64,556	63,413	64,781	74,283	73,674	[3]75,066
Mechanical	48,585	48,578	50,175	59,098	58,298	60,223	[3]69,904	[3]68,003	69,757
Nuclear [4]	[3]50,104	[3]47,914	[3]51,225	(NA)	[3]66,350	[3]59,059	(NA)	(NA)	(NA)
Petroleum.	55,987	[3]58,518	62,236	[3]67,500	[3]71,332	[3]65,000	(NA)	(NA)	(NA)
Engineering technology. .	44,930	43,425	45,790	(NA)	(NA)	(NA)	(NA)	(NA)	(NA)
Chemistry	37,733	37,618	38,635	[3]52,583	[3]59,043	(NA)	58,481	60,986	55,874
Mathematics.	40,512	43,567	43,304	[3]42,348	[3]37,805	[3]34,500	[3]58,778	[3]49,254	[3]55,047
Physics	[3]42,365	[3]38,945	[3]44,700	(NA)	[3]37,440	[3]62,500	[3]55,485	[3]54,729	[3]54,897
Humanities.	[3]29,694	30,626	31,565	[3]32,465	[3]33,049	[3]35,212	[3]41,100	[3]47,500	[3]43,728
Social sciences [5].	29,098	31,698	31,621	[3]36,992	[3]35,174	[3]40,575	[3]43,603	[3]42,727	[3]46,838
Computer science	47,109	49,036	50,664	62,806	60,457	64,840	[3]64,640	[3]74,598	[3]84,025

NA Not available.   [1] Candidates with 1 year or less of full-time nonmilitary employment.   [2] For master's degree, offers are after nontechnical undergraduate degree.   [3] Fewer than 50 offers reported.   [4] Includes engineering physics.   [5] Excludes economics.

Source: National Association of Colleges and Employers, Bethlehem, PA (copyright). Reprinted with permission from Fall 2003, 2004, amd 2005 *Salary Survey.* All rights reserved.

Table 288. **Earned Degrees Conferred by Level and Sex: 1960 to 2004**

[In thousands (477 represents 477,000), except percent. Based on survey; see Appendix III]

Year ending	All degrees Total	All degrees Percent male	Associate's Male	Associate's Female	Bachelor's Male	Bachelor's Female	Master's Male	Master's Female	First professional Male	First professional Female	Doctoral Male	Doctoral Female
1960 [1]	477	65.8	(NA)	(NA)	254	138	51	24	(NA)	(NA)	9	1
1970	1,271	59.2	117	89	451	341	126	83	33	2	26	4
1975	1,666	56.0	191	169	505	418	162	131	49	7	27	7
1980	1,731	51.1	184	217	474	456	151	147	53	17	23	10
1985	1,828	49.3	203	252	483	497	143	143	50	25	22	11
1987	1,823	48.4	191	245	481	510	141	148	47	25	22	12
1988	1,835	48.0	190	245	477	518	145	154	45	25	23	12
1989	1,873	47.3	186	250	483	535	149	161	45	26	23	13
1990	1,940	46.6	191	264	492	560	154	171	44	27	24	14
1991	2,025	45.8	199	283	504	590	156	181	44	28	25	15
1992	2,108	45.6	207	297	521	616	162	191	45	29	26	15
1993	2,167	45.5	212	303	533	632	169	200	45	30	26	16
1994	2,206	45.1	215	315	532	637	176	211	45	31	27	17
1995 [2]	2,218	44.9	218	321	526	634	179	219	45	31	27	18
1996 [2]	2,248	44.2	220	336	522	642	179	227	45	32	27	18
1997 [2]	2,288	43.6	224	347	521	652	181	238	46	33	27	19
1998 [2]	2,298	43.2	218	341	520	664	184	246	45	34	27	19
1999 [2]	2,323	42.7	218	342	519	682	186	254	44	34	25	19
2000 [2]	2,385	42.6	225	340	530	708	192	265	44	36	25	20
2001 [2]	2,416	42.4	232	347	532	712	194	274	43	37	25	20
2002 [2]	2,494	42.2	238	357	550	742	199	283	43	38	24	20
2003 [2]	2,621	42.1	253	380	573	775	211	301	42	39	24	22
2004 [2]	2,755	41.8	260	405	595	804	230	329	42	41	25	23

NA Not available. [1] First-professional degrees are included with bachelor's degrees. [2] Data beginning in 1996 reflect the new classification of institutions. See footnote 1, Table 267.

Source: U.S. National Center for Education Statistics, *Digest of Education Statistics*, annual.

Table 289. **Degrees Earned by Level and Race/Ethnicity: 1981 to 2004**

[For school year ending in year shown. Based on survey; see Appendix III]

Level of degree and race/ethnicity	Total 1981 [1]	Total 1985 [1]	Total 1990	Total 1995	Total 2000 [2]	Total 2004 [2]	Percent distribution 1981	Percent distribution 2004 [2]
Associate's degrees, total	410,174	429,815	455,102	539,691	564,933	665,301	100.0	100.0
White, non-Hispanic	339,167	355,343	376,816	420,656	408,772	456,047	82.7	68.5
Black, non-Hispanic	35,330	35,791	34,326	47,067	60,221	81,183	8.6	12.2
Hispanic.	17,800	19,407	21,504	35,962	51,573	72,270	4.3	10.9
Asian or Pacific Islander	8,650	9,914	13,066	20,677	27,782	33,149	2.1	5.0
American Indian/Alaska Native . . .	2,584	2,953	3,430	5,482	6,497	8,119	0.6	1.2
Nonresident alien.	6,643	6,407	5,960	9,847	10,088	14,533	1.6	2.2
Bachelor's degrees, total	934,800	968,311	1,051,344	1,160,134	1,237,875	1,399,542	100.0	100.0
White, non-Hispanic	807,319	826,106	887,151	914,610	929,106	1,026,114	86.4	73.3
Black, non-Hispanic	60,673	57,473	61,046	87,236	108,013	131,241	6.5	9.4
Hispanic.	21,832	25,874	32,829	54,230	75,059	94,644	2.3	6.8
Asian or Pacific Islander	18,794	25,395	39,230	60,502	77,912	92,073	2.0	6.6
American Indian/Alaska Native . . .	3,593	4,246	4,390	6,610	8,719	10,638	0.4	0.8
Nonresident alien.	22,589	29,217	26,698	36,946	39,066	44,832	2.4	3.2
Master's degrees, total.	294,183	280,421	324,301	397,629	457,056	558,940	100.0	100.0
White, non-Hispanic	241,216	223,628	254,299	293,345	320,485	369,582	82.0	66.1
Black, non-Hispanic	17,133	13,939	15,336	24,166	35,874	50,657	5.8	9.1
Hispanic.	6,461	6,864	7,892	12,905	19,253	29,666	2.2	5.3
Asian or Pacific Islander	6,282	7,782	10,439	16,847	23,218	30,952	2.1	5.5
American Indian/Alaska Native . . .	1,034	1,256	1,090	1,621	2,246	3,192	0.4	0.6
Nonresident alien.	22,057	26,952	35,245	48,745	55,980	74,891	7.5	13.4
Doctoral degrees, total.	32,839	32,307	38,371	44,446	44,808	48,378	100.0	100.0
White, non-Hispanic	25,908	23,934	26,221	27,846	27,843	28,214	78.9	58.3
Black, non-Hispanic	1,265	1,154	1,149	1,667	2,246	2,900	3.9	6.0
Hispanic.	456	677	780	984	1,305	1,662	1.4	3.4
Asian or Pacific Islander	877	1,106	1,225	2,689	2,420	2,632	2.7	5.4
American Indian/Alaska Native . . .	130	119	98	130	160	217	0.4	0.4
Nonresident alien.	4,203	5,317	8,898	11,130	10,834	12,753	12.8	26.4
First-professional degrees, total . .	71,340	71,057	70,988	75,800	80,057	83,041	100.0	100.0
White, non-Hispanic	64,551	63,219	60,487	59,402	59,637	60,379	90.5	72.7
Black, non-Hispanic	2,931	3,029	3,409	4,747	5,555	5,930	4.1	7.1
Hispanic.	1,541	1,884	2,425	3,231	3,865	4,273	2.2	5.1
Asian or Pacific Islander	1,456	1,816	3,362	6,396	8,584	9,964	2.0	12.0
American Indian/Alaska Native . . .	192	248	257	413	564	565	0.3	0.7
Nonresident alien.	669	861	1,048	1,611	1,852	1,930	0.9	2.3

[1] Excludes some persons whose race/ethnicity was unknown and are slight undercounts of degrees awarded. [2] In this table, data beginning in 2000 reflect the new classification of institutions. See footnote 1, Table 267.

Source: U.S. National Center for Education Statistics, *Digest of Education Statistics*, annual.

Education 183

Table 290. Degrees and Awards Earned Below Bachelor's by Field: 2004

[Covers associate's degrees and other awards based on postsecondary curriculums of less than 4 years in institutions of higher education. Based on survey; see Appendix III. See headnote, Table 291]

Field of study	Less than 1-year awards Total	Women	1- to less than 4-year awards Total	Women	Associate's degrees Total	Women
Total	**210,368**	**115,900**	**169,497**	**100,842**	**665,301**	**405,268**
Agriculture and natural resources, total	3,258	934	1,851	730	6,283	2,355
Architecture and related services	124	69	172	118	492	312
Area, ethnic, cultural, and gender studies	316	249	94	71	105	65
Biological and biomedical sciences	36	27	31	22	1,456	985
Business, management, and marketing	26,882	18,514	18,555	14,487	92,065	64,155
Communications and communications technologies	1,064	491	1,199	533	5,845	2,731
Computer and information sciences	12,853	4,992	9,559	3,698	41,845	13,128
Construction trades	5,661	300	7,092	312	3,560	200
Education	2,700	2,357	2,039	1,863	12,465	10,267
Engineering and engineering technologies	7,071	1,177	8,002	1,112	39,652	6,040
English language and literature/letters	430	295	153	114	828	562
Family and consumer sciences	9,025	7,802	3,708	3,154	9,478	9,084
Foreign languages and literatures	544	405	325	303	1,047	867
Health professions and related sciences	77,640	61,357	65,429	57,122	106,208	92,371
Legal professions and studies	1,701	1,436	2,620	2,299	9,466	8,527
Liberal arts and sciences, general studies, and humanities	211	165	3,166	1,955	227,650	144,434
Library science	214	200	82	70	114	101
Mathematics	45	10	8	2	801	299
Mechanics and repairers	13,118	976	20,361	865	12,553	728
Military technologies	76	32	-	-	293	53
Multi/interdisciplinary studies	393	225	348	252	14,794	8,390
Parks, recreation, leisure, and fitness studies	287	137	138	69	923	383
Personal and culinary services	6,792	4,817	9,009	7,052	14,239	6,429
Philosophy and religion	14	12	46	20	404	300
Physical sciences and science technologies	325	137	245	105	2,676	1,136
Precision production trades	4,583	260	4,987	243	1,968	140
Psychology	143	117	30	28	1,887	1,453
Public administration and social services	786	657	475	384	3,728	3,284
Security and protective services	19,966	4,747	4,844	1,450	20,573	8,571
Social sciences and history	222	113	108	51	6,245	4,157
Theology and religious vocations	79	48	456	227	492	272
Transportation and material moving	11,588	1,647	881	81	1,217	182
Visual and performing arts	2,221	1,195	3,484	2,050	23,949	13,307

- Represents zero.

Source: U.S. National Center for Education Statistics, *Digest of Education Statistics,* annual.

Table 291. Bachelor's Degrees Earned by Field: 1980 to 2004

[The new Classification of Instructional Programs was introduced in 2002–03. Data for previous years has been reclassified where necessary to conform to the new classifications. Based on survey; see Appendix III]

Field of study	1980	1990	2000	2002	2003	2004
Total	**929,417**	**1,051,344**	**1,237,875**	**1,291,900**	**1,348,503**	**1,399,542**
Agriculture and natural resources	22,802	12,900	24,238	23,331	23,294	22,835
Architecture and related services	9,132	9,364	8,462	8,808	9,054	8,838
Area, ethnic, cultural, and gender studies	2,840	4,447	6,212	6,390	6,629	7,181
Biological and biomedical sciences	46,190	37,204	63,005	59,415	60,072	61,509
Business	186,264	248,568	256,070	278,217	293,545	307,149
Communication, journalism, and related programs [1]	28,616	51,572	57,058	64,036	69,792	73,002
Computer and information sciences	11,154	27,347	37,788	50,365	57,439	59,488
Education	118,038	105,112	108,034	106,295	105,790	106,278
Engineering and engineering technologies	69,387	82,480	73,419	74,679	77,267	78,227
English language and literature/letters	32,187	46,803	50,106	52,375	53,670	53,984
Family and consumer sciences/human sciences	18,411	13,514	16,321	16,938	18,166	19,172
Foreign languages, literatures, and linguistics	12,480	13,133	15,886	16,258	16,901	17,754
Health professions and related clinical sciences	63,848	58,983	80,863	72,887	71,223	73,934
Legal professions and studies	683	1,632	1,969	2,003	2,466	2,841
Liberal arts and sciences, general studies, and humanities	23,196	27,985	36,104	39,333	40,221	42,106
Mathematics and statistics	11,378	14,276	11,418	11,950	12,493	13,327
Multi/interdisciplinary studies	11,457	16,557	28,561	28,943	28,757	29,162
Parks, recreation, leisure and fitness studies	5,753	4,582	17,571	18,885	21,428	22,164
Philosophy and religious studies	7,069	7,034	8,535	9,473	10,344	11,152
Physical sciences and science technologies	23,407	16,056	18,331	17,799	17,940	17,983
Psychology	42,093	53,952	74,194	76,775	78,613	82,098
Public administration and social services	16,644	13,908	20,185	19,392	19,878	20,552
Security and protective services	15,015	15,354	24,877	25,536	26,189	28,175
Social sciences and history	103,662	118,083	127,101	132,874	143,218	150,357
Theology and religious vocations	6,170	5,185	6,789	7,762	7,926	8,126
Transportation and materials moving	213	2,387	3,395	4,020	4,567	4,824
Visual and performing arts	40,892	39,934	58,791	66,773	71,474	77,181
Other and unclassified	436	2,992	2,592	388	147	143

[1] Includes technologies.

Source: U.S. National Center for Education Statistics, *Digest of Education Statistics,* annual; and unpublished data.

184 Education

Table 292. **Master's and Doctoral Degrees Earned by Field: 1980 to 2004**

[The new Classification of Instructional Programs was introduced in 2002–03. Data for previous years has been reclassified where necessary to conform to the new classifications. Based on survey; see Appendix III]

Field of study	1980	1990	2000	2002	2003	2004
MASTER'S DEGREES						
Total.	**298,081**	**324,301**	**457,056**	**482,118**	**512,645**	**558,940**
Agriculture and natural resources	3,976	3,382	4,360	4,503	4,492	4,783
Architecture and related services.	3,139	3,499	4,268	4,566	4,925	5,424
Area, ethnic, cultural, and gender studies	852	1,191	1,544	1,541	1,509	1,683
Biological and biomedical sciences	6,322	4,906	6,781	6,937	6,990	7,657
Business	55,008	76,676	111,532	119,725	127,545	139,347
Communication, journalism, and related programs [1] .	3,082	4,353	5,525	5,980	6,495	6,900
Computer and information sciences.	3,647	9,677	14,990	17,173	19,503	20,143
Education.	101,819	84,890	123,045	135,189	147,448	162,345
Engineering and engineering technologies	16,765	25,294	26,726	27,057	30,669	35,197
English language and literature/letters	6,026	6,317	7,022	7,097	7,413	7,956
Family and consumer sciences/human sciences . . .	2,690	1,679	1,882	1,683	1,610	1,794
Foreign languages, literatures, and linguistics	3,067	3,018	3,037	3,075	3,049	3,124
Health professions and related clinical sciences. . . .	15,374	20,406	42,593	43,560	42,715	44,939
Legal professions and studies	1,817	1,888	3,750	4,053	4,126	4,243
Liberal arts and sciences, general studies, and humanities	2,646	1,999	3,256	2,754	3,312	3,697
Library science	5,374	4,341	4,577	5,113	5,314	6,015
Mathematics and statistics.	2,860	3,624	3,208	3,350	3,626	4,191
Multi/interdisciplinary studies	2,494	3,182	3,487	3,708	3,780	4,047
Parks, recreation, leisure and fitness studies	647	529	2,322	2,580	2,978	3,199
Philosophy and religious studies	1,204	1,327	1,376	1,371	1,578	1,578
Physical sciences and science technologies	5,167	5,410	4,810	5,012	5,109	5,570
Psychology.	9,938	10,730	15,740	16,357	17,123	17,898
Public administration and social services	17,560	17,399	25,594	25,448	25,894	28,250
Security and protective services	1,805	1,151	2,609	2,935	2,955	3,717
Social sciences and history	12,176	11,634	14,066	14,112	14,634	16,110
Theology and religious vocations.	3,872	4,941	5,534	4,909	5,099	5,486
Visual and performing arts	8,708	8,481	10,918	11,595	11,986	12,906
Other and unclassified	46	2,377	2,504	735	768	741
DOCTORAL DEGREES						
Total.	**32,615**	**38,371**	**44,808**	**44,160**	**46,024**	**48,378**
Agriculture and natural resources	991	1,295	1,168	1,148	1,229	1,185
Architecture and related services.	79	103	129	183	152	173
Area, ethnic, cultural, and gender studies	151	125	205	212	186	209
Biological and biomedical sciences	3,527	3,837	5,180	4,823	5,003	5,242
Business	767	1,093	1,194	1,156	1,251	1,481
Communication, journalism, and related programs [1] .	193	272	357	383	398	426
Computer and information sciences.	240	627	779	752	816	909
Education.	7,314	6,503	6,409	6,549	6,835	7,088
Engineering and engineering technologies	2,546	5,030	5,421	5,245	5,333	5,981
English language and literature/letters	1,196	986	1,470	1,291	1,246	1,207
Family and consumer sciences/human sciences . . .	192	273	327	311	372	329
Foreign languages, literatures, and linguistics	857	816	1,086	1,003	1,042	1,031
Health professions and related clinical sciences. . . .	821	1,449	2,053	2,913	3,328	4,361
Legal professions and studies	40	111	74	79	105	119
Liberal arts and sciences, general studies, and humanities	192	63	83	113	78	95
Mathematics and statistics.	724	917	1,075	923	1,007	1,060
Multi/interdisciplinary studies	318	442	792	765	899	876
Parks, recreation, leisure and fitness studies	21	35	134	151	199	222
Philosophy and religious studies	374	445	598	610	662	595
Physical sciences and science technologies	3,044	4,116	3,963	3,760	3,858	3,815
Psychology.	3,395	3,811	4,731	4,759	4,831	4,827
Public administration and social services	342	508	537	571	596	649
Security and protective services	18	38	52	49	72	54
Social sciences and history	3,230	3,010	4,095	3,902	3,850	3,811
Theology and religious vocations.	1,315	1,317	1,630	1,350	1,321	1,304
Visual and performing arts	655	849	1,127	1,114	1,293	1,282
Other and unclassified	73	300	139	45	62	47

[1] Includes technologies.

Source: U.S. National Center for Education Statistics, *Digest of Education Statistics,* annual; and unpublished data.

U.S. Census Bureau, Statistical Abstract of the United States: 2007

Table 293. **First Professional Degrees Earned in Selected Professions: 1970 to 2004**

[First professional degrees include degrees which require at least 6 years of college work for completion (including at least 2 years of preprofessional training). Based on survey; see Appendix III]

Type of degree and sex of recipient	1970	1975	1980	1985	1990	1995	2000	2002	2003	2004
Medicine (M.D.):										
Institutions conferring degrees.....	86	104	112	120	124	119	118	118	118	118
Degrees conferred, total..........	8,314	12,447	14,902	16,041	15,075	15,537	15,286	15,237	15,034	15,442
Percent to women	8.4	13.1	23.4	30.4	34.2	38.8	42.7	44.4	45.3	46.4
Dentistry (D.D.S. or D.M.D.):										
Institutions conferring degrees.....	48	52	58	59	57	53	54	53	53	53
Degrees conferred, total..........	3,718	4,773	5,258	5,339	4,100	3,897	4,250	4,239	4,344	4,335
Percent to women	0.9	3.1	13.3	20.7	30.9	36.4	40.1	38.5	38.9	41.6
Law (LL.B. or J.D.):										
Institutions conferring degrees.....	145	154	179	181	182	183	190	192	194	195
Degrees conferred, total..........	14,916	29,296	35,647	37,491	36,485	39,349	38,152	38,981	39,067	40,209
Percent to women	5.4	15.1	30.2	38.5	42.2	42.6	45.9	48.0	49.0	49.4
Theological (B.D., M.Div., M.H.L.):										
Institutions conferring degrees....	(NA)	(NA)	(NA)	(NA)	(NA)	192	198	191	196	200
Degrees conferred, total..........	5,298	5,095	7,115	7,221	5,851	5,978	6,129	5,195	5,351	5,332
Percent to women	2.3	6.8	13.8	18.5	24.8	25.7	29.2	32.9	34.6	34.2

NA Not available.

Source: U.S. National Center for Education Statistics, *Digest of Education Statistics*, annual.

Table 294. **Participation in Adult Education: 2004–2005**

[In thousands (211,607 represents 211,607,000), except percent. For the civilian noninstitutional population 16 years old. Adult education includes enrollment in formal education activities in the previous 12 months. Excludes participants in only postsecondary degree, certificate or diploma programs as full-time students. Based on the Adult Education Survey of the National Household Education Survey Program and subject to sampling error; see source and Appendix III for details]

Characteristic	Adult population (1,000)	Number taking adult education courses [1] (1,000)	Percent of total [1]	College or university degree program	Work-related course	Personal interest course
				Participants in adult education — Type of course (percent)		
Total, 2005................	**211,607**	**93,939**	**44**	**4**	**27**	**21**
Age:						
16 to 30 years old............	48,544	25,040	52	8	25	23
31 to 40 years old............	40,009	20,839	52	6	34	23
41 to 50 years old............	45,662	21,983	48	3	36	20
51 to 65 years old............	46,211	18,767	41	2	28	20
66 years old and over	31,181	7,310	23	–	5	19
Sex:						
Male.....................	101,596	41,724	41	4	24	18
Female...................	110,011	52,216	47	4	29	24
Race/ethnicity:						
White, non-Hispanic	146,614	66,909	46	4	29	22
Black, non-Hispanic...........	23,467	10,878	46	4	27	24
Hispanic	26,101	9,824	38	4	17	15
Other	15,426	6,328	41	5	24	22
Educational attainment:						
Less than high school	31,017	6,851	22	–	4	11
High school diploma or GED......	64,334	20,955	33	2	17	16
Some college................	58,545	30,070	51	6	31	25
Bachelor's degree or higher	57,711	36,063	62	7	46	29
Marital status:						
Married...................	132,008	58,748	45	3	29	21
Living with partner, unmarried	12,498	4,879	39	4	26	16
Separated/divorced/widowed......	30,170	10,874	36	2	20	19
Never married	36,930	19,439	53	8	23	26
Employment/occupation						
Employed	152,450	78,879	52	5	36	22
Professional or managerial	48,647	34,138	70	8	56	29
Services, sales, or support	65,289	31,609	48	5	31	22
Trades..................	38,514	13,132	34	2	19	13
Unemployed or not in labor force in past 12 months	59,157	15,060	25	1	4	20
Household income:						
$20,000 or less	34,670	9,552	28	2	11	16
$20,001 to $35,000	35,839	12,866	36	4	18	17
$35,001 to $50,000	33,376	14,122	42	2	23	22
$50,001 to $75,000	47,114	22,494	48	5	33	21
$75,001 or more.............	60,607	34,904	58	5	39	27
Children under 10 in household:						
Yes	57,560	26,746	46	5	29	20
No	154,047	67,193	44	4	26	22

– Represents or rounds to zero. [1] Includes English as a Second Language, basic education skills, vocational or technical diploma programs, and apprenticeship programs each with a total participation rate of about 1 percent.

Source: U.S. Department of Education, National Center for Education Statistics, Adult Education Survey of the National Household Education Surveys Program 2005, unpublished data.

Section 5
Law Enforcement, Courts, and Prisons

This section presents data on crimes committed, victims of crimes, arrests, and data related to criminal violations and the criminal justice system. The major sources of these data are the Bureau of Justice Statistics (BJS), the Federal Bureau of Investigation (FBI), and the Administrative Office of the U.S. Courts. BJS issues several reports, including *Sourcebook of Criminal Justice Statistics, Criminal Victimization, Prisoners* (annual), *Census of State and Federal Correctional Facilities, Survey of Prison Inmates, Census of Jails, Survey of Prison Inmates, Probation and Parole in the United States, Capital Punishment,* and the annual *Justice Expenditure and Employment Data for the Criminal Justice System.* The Federal Bureau of Investigation's major annual reports are *Crime in the United States, Law Enforcement Officers Killed and Assaulted,* annual, and *Hate Crimes,* annual, which presents data on reported crimes as gathered from state and local law enforcement agencies.

Legal jurisdiction and law enforcement—Law enforcement is, for the most part, a function of state and local officers and agencies. The U.S. Constitution reserves general police powers to the states. By act of Congress, federal offenses include only offenses against the U.S. government and against or by its employees while engaged in their official duties and offenses which involve the crossing of state lines or an interference with interstate commerce. Excluding the military, there are 52 separate criminal law jurisdictions in the United States: one in each of the 50 states, one in the District of Columbia, and the federal jurisdiction. Each of these has its own criminal law and procedure and its own law enforcement agencies. While the systems of law enforcement are quite similar among the states, there are often substantial differences in the penalties for like offenses.

Law enforcement can be divided into three parts: Investigation of crimes and arrests of persons suspected of committing them; prosecution of those charged with crime; and the punishment or treatment of persons convicted of crime.

Crime—The U.S. Department of Justice administers two statistical programs to measure the magnitude, nature, and impact of crime in the nation: the Uniform Crime Reporting (UCR) Program and the National Crime Victimization Survey (NCVS). Each of these programs produces valuable information about aspects of the nation's crime problem. Because the UCR and NCVS programs are conducted for different purposes, use different methods, and focus on somewhat different aspects of crime, the information they produce together provides a more comprehensive panorama of the nation's crime problem than either could produce alone.

Uniform Crime Reports (UCR)—The FBI's UCR Program, which began in 1929, collects information on the following crimes reported to law enforcement authorities: murder and nonnegligent manslaughter, forcible rape, robbery, aggravated assault, burglary, larceny-theft, motor vehicle theft, and arson. Law enforcement agencies report arrest data for 21 additional crime categories. For UCR definitions of criminal offenses (including those listed), please go to: <www.fbi.gov/ucr/cius_04/appendices/appendix_02.html>.

The UCR Program compiles data from monthly law enforcement reports or individual crime incident records transmitted directly to the FBI or to centralized state agencies that then report to the FBI. The Program thoroughly examines each report it receives for reasonableness, accuracy, and deviations that may indicate errors. Large variations in crime levels may indicate modified records procedures, incomplete reporting, or changes in a jurisdiction's boundaries. To identify any unusual fluctuations in an agency's crime counts, the Program compares monthly reports to previous submissions of the agency and with those for similar agencies.

The UCR Program presents crime counts for the nation as a whole, as well as for regions, states, counties, cities, towns, tribal law enforcement, and colleges and universities. This permits studies among neighboring jurisdictions and among those with similar populations and other common characteristics.

The UCR Program annually publishes its findings in a preliminary release in the spring of the following calendar year, followed by a detailed annual report, *Crime in the United States*, issued in the fall. In addition to crime counts and trends, this report includes data on crimes cleared, persons arrested (age, sex, and race), law enforcement personnel (including the number of sworn officers killed or assaulted), and the characteristics of homicides (including age, sex, and race of victims and offenders; victim-offender relationships; weapons used; and circumstances surrounding the homicides). Other periodic reports are also available from the UCR Program.

National Crime Victimization Survey (NCVS)—A second perspective on crime is provided by this survey of the Bureau of Justice Statistics. Details about the crimes come directly from the victims. No attempt is made to validate the information against police records or any other source.

The NCVS measures rape/sexual assault, robbery, assault, pocket-picking, purse snatching, burglary, and motor vehicle theft. The NCVS includes offenses reported to the police, as well as those not reported.

Police reporting rates (percent of victimizations) varied by type of crime. In 2005, for instance, 38 percent of rapes/sexual assaults were reported; 52 percent of robberies; 47 percent of assaults; 32 percent of personal thefts; 35 percent of pocket-pickings/purse snatchings; 56 percent of household burglaries; and 83 percent of motor vehicle thefts.

Murder and kidnaping are not covered. Commercial burglary and robbery were dropped from the program during 1977. The so-called victimless crimes, such as drunkenness, drug abuse, and prostitution, also are excluded, as are crimes for which it is difficult to identify knowledgeable respondents or to locate data records.

Crimes of which the victim may not be aware also cannot be measured effectively. Buying stolen property may fall into this category, as may some instances of embezzlement. Attempted crimes of many types probably are under recorded for this reason. Events in which the victim has shown a willingness to participate in illegal activity also are excluded.

In any encounter involving a personal crime, more than one criminal act can be committed against an individual. For example, a rape may be associated with a robbery, or a household offense, such as a burglary, can escalate into something more serious in the event of a personal confrontation. In classifying the survey-measured crimes, each criminal incident has been counted only once—by the most serious act that took place during the incident and ranked in accordance with the seriousness classification system used by the Federal Bureau of Investigation. The order of seriousness for crimes against persons is as follows: rape, robbery, assault, and larceny. Personal crimes take precedence over household offenses.

A *victimization*, basic measure of the occurrence of crime, is a specific criminal act as it affects a single victim. The number of victimizations is determined by the number of victims of such acts. Victimization counts serve as key elements in computing rates of victimization. For crimes against persons, the rates are based on the total number of individuals age 12 and over or on a portion of that population sharing a particular characteristic or set of traits. As general indicators of the danger of having been victimized during the reference period, the rates are not sufficiently refined to represent true measures of risk for specific individuals or households.

An *incident* is a specific criminal act involving one or more victims; therefore the number of incidents of personal crimes is lower than that of victimizations.

Courts—Statistics on criminal offenses and the outcome of prosecutions are incomplete for the country as a whole, although data are available for many states individually.

Since 1982, through its National Judicial Reporting Program, the Bureau of Justice Statistics has surveyed a nationally representative sample of 300 counties every 2 years and collected detailed information on demographic characteristics of felons, conviction offenses, type of sentences, sentence lengths, and time from arrest to conviction and sentencing.

The bulk of civil and criminal litigation in the country is commenced and determined in the various state courts. Only when the U.S. Constitution and acts of Congress specifically confer jurisdiction upon the federal courts may civil or criminal litigation be heard and decided by them. Generally, the federal courts have jurisdiction over the following types of cases: suits or proceedings by or against the United States; civil actions between private parties arising under the Constitution, laws, or treaties of the United States; civil actions between private litigants who are citizens of different states; civil cases involving admiralty, maritime, or private jurisdiction; and all matters in bankruptcy.

There are several types of courts with varying degrees of legal jurisdiction. These jurisdictions include original, appellate, general, and limited or special. A court of original jurisdiction is one having the authority initially to try a case and pass judgment on the law and the facts; a court of appellate jurisdiction is one with the legal authority to review cases and hear appeals; a court of general jurisdiction is a trial court of unlimited original jurisdiction in civil and/or criminal cases, also called a "major trial court"; a court of limited or special jurisdiction is a trial court with legal authority over only a particular class of cases, such as probate, juvenile, or traffic cases.

The 94 federal courts of original jurisdiction are known as the U.S. district courts. One or more of these courts is established in every state and one each in the District of Columbia, Puerto Rico, the Virgin Islands, the Northern Mariana Islands, and Guam. Appeals from the district courts are taken to intermediate appellate courts of which there are 13, known as U.S. courts of appeals and the United States Court of Appeals for the Federal Circuit. The Supreme Court of the United States is the final and highest appellate court in the federal system of courts.

Juvenile offenders—For statistical purposes, the FBI and most states classify as juvenile offenders persons under the age of 18 years who have committed a crime or crimes.

Delinquency cases are all cases of youths referred to a juvenile court for violation of a law or ordinance or for seriously "antisocial" conduct. Several types of facilities are available for those adjudicated delinquents, ranging from the short-term physically unrestricted environment to the long-term very restrictive atmosphere.

Prisoners and jail inmates—Bureau of Justice Statistics started to collect annual data in 1979 on prisoners in federal and state prisons and reformatories. Adults convicted of criminal activity may be given a prison or jail sentence. A *prison* is a confinement facility having custodial authority over adults sentenced to confinement of more than 1 year. A *jail* is a facility, usually operated by a local law enforcement agency, holding persons detained pending adjudication and/or persons committed after adjudication to 1 year or less.

Data on inmates in local jails were collected by the Bureau of Justice Statistics for the first time in 1970. Since then, BJS has conducted censuses of facilities and inmates every 5 to 6 years. In 1984, BJS initiated an annual survey of jails conducted in noncensus years.

Statistical reliability—For discussion of statistical collection, estimation and sampling procedures, and measures of statistical reliability pertaining to the National Crime Victimization Survey and Uniform Crime Reporting Program, see Appendix III.

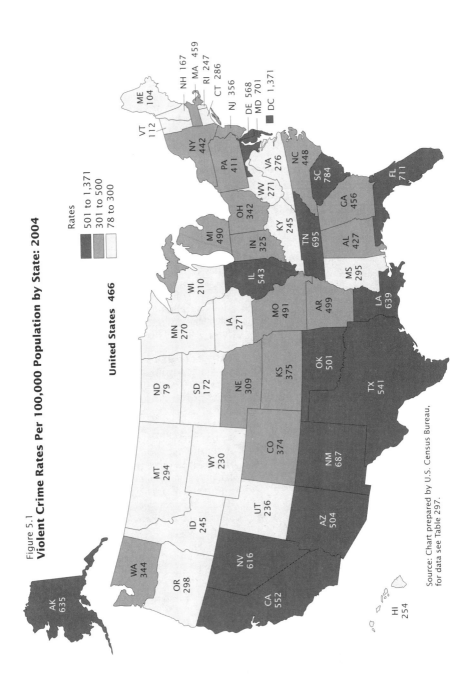

Figure 5.1
Violent Crime Rates Per 100,000 Population by State: 2004

Rates

501 to 1,371
301 to 500
78 to 300

United States 466

Source: Chart prepared by U.S. Census Bureau,
for data see Table 297.

AK 635
WA 344
OR 298
ID 245
MT 294
WY 230
NV 616
UT 236
CA 552
AZ 504
NM 687
CO 374
ND 79
SD 172
NE 309
KS 375
OK 501
TX 541
MN 270
IA 271
MO 491
AR 499
LA 639
WI 210
IL 543
MI 490
IN 325
KY 245
TN 695
MS 295
AL 427
GA 456
OH 342
WV 271
VA 276
NC 448
SC 784
FL 711
PA 411
NY 442
VT 112
ME 104
NH 167
MA 459
RI 247
CT 286
NJ 356
DE 568
MD 701
DC 1,371
HI 254

Table 295. Crimes and Crime Rates by Type of Offense: 1980 to 2004

[**1,345 represents 1,345,000.** Data refer to offenses known to the police. Rates are based on Census Bureau estimated resident population as of **July 1; 1980, 1990, and 2000, enumerated as of April 1.** See source for details. For definitions of crimes, go to <http://www.fbi.gov/ucr/cius_04/appendices/appendix_02.html>]

Item and year	Violent crime					Property crime			
	Total	Murder [1,2]	Forcible rape	Robbery	Aggravated assault	Total	Burglary	Larceny/ theft	Motor vehicle theft
Number of offenses (1,000):									
1980	1,345	23	83	566	673	12,064	3,795	7,137	1,132
1985	1,328	19	88	498	723	11,103	3,073	6,926	1,103
1989	1,646	22	95	578	952	12,605	3,168	7,872	1,565
1990	1,820	23	103	639	1,055	12,655	3,074	7,946	1,636
1991	1,912	25	107	688	1,093	12,961	3,157	8,142	1,662
1992	1,932	24	109	672	1,127	12,506	2,980	7,915	1,611
1993	1,926	25	106	660	1,136	12,219	2,835	7,821	1,563
1994	1,858	23	102	619	1,113	12,132	2,713	7,880	1,539
1995	1,799	22	97	581	1,099	12,064	2,594	7,998	1,472
1996	1,689	20	96	536	1,037	11,805	2,506	7,905	1,394
1997	1,636	18	96	499	1,023	11,558	2,461	7,744	1,354
1998	1,534	17	93	447	977	10,952	2,333	7,376	1,243
1999	1,426	16	89	409	912	10,208	2,101	6,956	1,152
2000	1,425	16	90	408	912	10,183	2,051	6,972	1,160
2001	1,439	16	91	424	909	10,437	2,117	7,092	1,228
2002	1,424	16	95	421	891	10,455	2,151	7,057	1,247
2003	1,384	17	94	414	859	10,443	2,155	7,027	1,261
2004	1,367	16	95	401	855	10,328	2,143	6,948	1,237
Rate per 100,000 population:									
1980	597	10.2	36.8	251	299	5,353	1,684	3,167	502
1985	558	8.0	36.8	209	304	4,666	1,292	2,911	464
1989	667	8.7	38.3	234	386	5,107	1,284	3,190	634
1990	730	9.4	41.1	256	423	5,073	1,232	3,185	656
1991	758	9.8	42.3	273	433	5,140	1,252	3,229	659
1992	758	9.3	42.8	264	442	4,904	1,168	3,104	632
1993	747	9.5	41.1	256	441	4,740	1,100	3,034	606
1994	714	9.0	39.3	238	428	4,660	1,042	3,027	591
1995	685	8.2	37.1	221	418	4,591	987	3,043	560
1996	637	7.4	36.3	202	391	4,451	945	2,980	526
1997	611	6.8	35.9	186	382	4,316	919	2,892	506
1998	568	6.3	34.5	166	361	4,053	863	2,730	460
1999	523	5.7	32.8	150	334	3,744	770	2,551	423
2000	507	5.5	32.0	145	324	3,618	729	2,477	412
2001	505	5.6	31.8	149	319	3,658	742	2,486	431
2002	494	5.6	33.1	146	310	3,631	747	2,451	433
2003	476	5.7	32.3	143	295	3,591	741	2,417	434
2004	466	5.5	32.2	137	291	3,517	730	2,366	421

[1] Includes nonnegligent manslaughter. [2] The murder and nonnegligent homicides that occurred as a result of the events of September 11, 2001, were not included in this table.

Source: U.S. Department of Justice, Federal Bureau of Investigation, *Crime in the United States,* annual. See also <http://www.fbi.gov/ucr/cius_04/offenses_reported/index.html>.

Table 296. Crimes and Crime Rates by Type and Area: 2004

[**In thousands (1,367 represents 1,367,000), except rate. Rate per 100,000 population;** see headnote, Table 295. Estimated totals based on reports from city and rural law enforcement agencies representing 96 percent of the national population. For definitions of crimes, go to <http://www.fbi.gov/ucr/cius_04/appendices/appendix_02.html>)]

Type of crime	United States		Metropolitan areas [1]		Other cities		Rural areas	
	Total	Rate	Total	Rate	Total	Rate	Total	Rate
Violent crime	1,367	466	1,231	506	75	377	61	202
Murder and nonnegligent manslaughter	16	6	14	6	1	4	1	4
Forcible rape	95	32	80	33	8	39	7	24
Robbery	401	137	385	158	11	58	5	16
Aggravated assault	855	291	752	309	55	277	48	158
Property crime	10,328	3,517	8,995	3,697	819	4,110	514	1,691
Burglary	2,143	730	1,812	745	164	823	167	550
Larceny-theft	6,948	2,366	6,026	2,477	615	3,089	307	1,008
Motor vehicle theft	1,237	421	1,157	476	39	198	40	133

[1] For definition, see Appendix II.

Source: U.S. Department of Justice, Federal Bureau of Investigation, *Crime in the United States,* annual. See also <http://www.fbi.gov/ucr/cius_04/offenses_reported/index.html>.

Law Enforcement, Courts, and Prisons 191

Table 297. **Crime Rates by State, 2003 and 2004, and by Type, 2004**

[**Offenses known to the police per 100,000 population.** Based on Census Bureau estimated resident population as of **July 1.**
For definitions of crimes, go to <http:www.fbi.gov/ucr/cius_04/appendices;appendix_02.html>]

State		Violent crime						Property crime				
	2003, total	2004					2003, total	2004				
		Total	Mur- der [1]	Forc- ible rape	Rob- bery	Aggra- vated assault		Total	Burglary	Lar- ceny/ theft	Motor vehicle theft
United States..	476	466	6	32	137	291	3,591	3,517	730	2,366	421
Alabama	429	427	6	39	133	249	4,046	4,025	986	2,730	310
Alaska.	598	635	6	85	68	476	3,762	3,383	576	2,465	342
Arizona	513	504	7	33	134	329	5,634	5,341	990	3,387	963
Arkansas	456	499	6	42	86	364	3,632	4,013	1,094	2,684	236
California	580	552	7	27	172	346	3,426	3,419	685	2,030	704
Colorado	347	374	4	43	82	245	3,952	3,919	717	2,679	523
Connecticut	317	286	3	21	121	143	2,667	2,627	444	1,868	315
Delaware	675	568	2	42	147	378	3,415	3,164	648	2,257	259
District of Columbia [2]	1,625	1,371	36	40	579	717	5,864	4,859	713	2,627	1,519
Florida.	731	711	5	38	172	496	4,457	4,180	956	2,773	450
Georgia	455	456	7	27	155	267	4,260	4,266	940	2,825	501
Hawaii.	272	254	3	26	75	151	5,275	4,793	857	3,253	683
Idaho	246	245	2	41	17	185	2,929	2,794	547	2,052	196
Illinois [3]	556	543	6	33	177	326	3,288	3,186	597	2,271	317
Indiana	352	325	5	29	102	189	3,356	3,398	676	2,384	338
Iowa	278	271	2	27	38	205	2,976	2,905	615	2,107	183
Kansas	398	375	5	40	66	263	4,010	3,974	731	2,934	308
Kentucky	249	245	6	30	79	131	2,510	2,538	625	1,701	212
Louisiana.	637	639	13	36	145	445	4,311	4,410	1,005	2,969	437
Maine	109	104	1	24	22	56	2,450	2,410	481	1,829	99
Maryland	704	701	9	24	230	438	3,799	3,640	660	2,335	645
Massachusetts . . .	473	459	3	28	116	312	2,563	2,460	537	1,579	344
Michigan	511	490	6	54	112	318	3,279	3,058	637	1,921	500
Minnesota	263	270	2	42	80	146	3,113	3,039	550	2,224	265
Mississippi.	324	295	8	40	86	161	3,707	3,479	953	2,254	271
Missouri.	491	491	6	26	115	343	4,084	3,904	703	2,750	450
Montana	365	294	3	30	25	236	3,096	2,936	379	2,382	175
Nebraska.	294	309	2	36	65	206	3,752	3,521	562	2,656	303
Nevada	616	616	7	41	210	358	4,287	4,207	991	2,246	970
New Hampshire . .	150	167	1	35	39	92	2,053	2,040	382	1,509	149
New Jersey	364	356	5	15	150	186	2,550	2,429	472	1,609	348
New Mexico	667	687	9	55	108	516	4,089	4,198	1,047	2,736	415
New York	466	442	5	19	174	244	2,249	2,199	368	1,618	213
North Carolina	454	448	6	27	138	276	4,271	4,160	1,185	2,659	316
North Dakota	80	79	1	25	6	47	2,110	1,917	301	1,473	143
Ohio	334	342	5	41	153	144	3,650	3,673	846	2,471	357
Oklahoma	506	501	5	44	88	363	4,312	4,242	1,000	2,874	368
Oregon	295	298	3	36	77	184	4,766	4,631	837	3,279	516
Pennsylvania	398	411	5	29	149	228	2,430	2,415	439	1,727	250
Rhode Island	286	247	2	30	68	148	2,995	2,884	506	2,001	377
South Carolina . . .	806	784	7	41	130	607	4,522	4,505	1,034	3,098	373
South Dakota	174	172	2	44	15	111	2,003	1,934	409	1,415	110
Tennessee	691	695	6	38	150	502	4,389	4,307	1,020	2,867	419
Texas	553	541	6	37	159	338	4,600	4,494	979	3,097	418
Utah	250	236	2	39	52	143	4,255	4,086	637	3,128	320
Vermont	114	112	1	25	12	73	2,229	2,308	545	1,671	93
Virginia	278	276	5	24	93	154	2,722	2,677	386	2,057	233
Washington	347	344	3	46	95	200	4,755	4,849	977	3,175	697
West Virginia	255	271	4	18	42	208	2,339	2,506	602	1,698	206
Wisconsin	221	210	3	21	74	112	2,880	2,663	433	2,024	207
Wyoming	262	230	2	22	13	192	3,316	3,334	541	2,636	158

[1] Includes nonnegligent manslaughter.   [2] Includes offenses reported by the Zoological Police and the Metro Transit Police.
[3] Limited data for 2004 were available for Illinois.

Source: U.S. Department of Justice, Federal Bureau of Investigation, *Crime in the United States,* annual. See also <http://www.fbi.gov/ucr/cius_04/offenses_reported/index.html>

Table 298. Crime Rates by Type—Selected Large Cities: 2004

[Offenses known to the police per 100,000 population. Based on U.S. Census Bureau estimated resident population as of July 1. For definitions of crimes, go to <http://www.fbi.gov/ucr/cius_04/appendices/appendix_02.html>]

City ranked by population size, 2004	Violent crime					Property crime			
	Total	Murder	Forcible rape	Robbery	Aggra-vated assault	Total	Burglary	Larceny-theft	Motor vehicle theft
New York, NY	687	7.0	17.6	301	362	2,113	322	1,531	260
Los Angeles, CA	1,107	13.4	29.3	367	698	3,240	600	1,865	776
Chicago, IL [1]	(NA)	15.5	(NA)	552	650	4,877	847	3,239	791
Houston, TX	1,146	13.3	44.4	498	590	6,040	1,327	3,658	1,055
Philadelphia, PA	1,408	22.2	67.4	657	661	4,105	710	2,547	848
Phoenix, AZ	662	14.1	34.3	261	353	6,607	1,154	3,712	1,740
San Diego, CA	529	4.8	29.1	129	366	3,546	570	1,964	1,012
Las Vegas MPD Jurisidiction, NV	789	10.6	48.8	301	429	4,812	1,147	2,360	1,304
San Antonio, TX	635	7.6	54.8	172	401	6,579	1,192	4,928	459
Dallas, TX	1,316	20.2	47.9	608	640	7,656	1,882	4,481	1,293
Detroit, MI [2]	1,740	42.1	78.6	596	1,023	6,279	1,334	2,257	2,687
San Jose, CA	372	2.6	28.2	86	255	2,454	398	1,559	497
Honolulu, HI	277	2.9	24.5	90	159	4,867	799	3,255	813
Indianapolis, IN	883	13.6	59.8	345	464	5,870	1,364	3,543	964
Jacksonville, FL	826	13.1	26.4	281	505	5,466	1,146	3,723	597
San Francisco, CA	757	11.6	20.0	400	326	4,717	802	2,855	1,060
Columbus, OH [2]	814	10.7	81.9	460	261	7,845	2,003	4,673	1,169
Austin, TX	525	3.8	44.3	206	271	6,057	997	4,674	386
Charlotte-Mecklenburg, NC	1,099	8.9	47.1	421	622	7,090	1,816	4,250	1,024
Memphis, TN	1,547	16.4	68.7	578	883	8,314	2,244	4,942	1,127
Baltimore, MD	1,839	43.5	28.7	639	1,129	5,685	1,258	3,369	1,058
Louisville Metro, KY [3]	525	10.6	34.6	236	244	4,191	1,100	2,608	484
Fort Worth, TX	636	8.7	48.4	238	341	6,503	1,440	4,453	610
El Paso, TX	546	1.9	33.8	96	414	3,510	388	2,812	310
Milwaukee, WI	785	14.7	29.8	432	309	5,427	767	3,700	960
Boston, MA	1,192	10.5	46.4	419	717	4,761	784	3,021	956
Seattle, WA	660	4.2	25.2	276	354	7,432	1,343	4,482	1,607
Denver, CO	797	15.4	43.1	256	482	5,402	1,299	2,766	1,337
Nashville, TN	1,552	10.6	71.2	383	1,087	6,507	1,231	4,533	743
Washington, DC	1,325	35.8	39.4	552	698	4,667	712	2,485	1,470
Portland, OR	742	5.3	57.6	237	442	7,630	1,331	5,208	1,092
Oklahoma City, OK	823	7.4	71.2	223	521	8,683	1,584	6,369	730
Tucson, AZ	933	10.5	74.1	297	551	9,004	1,206	6,585	1,213
Long Beach, CA	781	10.0	28.5	319	424	3,017	675	1,546	796
Albuquerque, NM	985	8.6	49.1	258	669	6,170	1,094	4,273	803
New Orleans, LA	948	56.0	40.1	390	462	5,162	1,112	2,663	1,387
Cleveland, OH [2]	1,299	17.1	116.0	713	454	5,869	1,760	2,850	1,259
Fresno, CA	766	11.6	39.6	270	445	5,772	875	3,749	1,149
Sacramento, CA	1,050	11.1	43.3	425	571	6,239	1,190	3,431	1,618
Kansas City, MO	1,444	19.9	70.7	431	923	7,851	1,556	5,105	1,190
Mesa, AZ	562	4.9	27.9	95	434	5,250	827	3,581	842
Virginia Beach, VA	227	3.4	31.8	108	84	3,054	400	2,482	172
Atlanta, GA	1,842	25.8	62.1	725	1,029	7,716	1,564	4,814	1,338
Omaha, NE	642	4.9	46.0	203	388	5,549	897	3,814	838
Oakland, CA	(NA)	(NA)	(NA)	(NA)	(NA)	(NA)	(NA)	(NA)	(NA)
Tulsa, OK	1,205	12.3	76.8	266	850	6,928	1,708	4,263	957
Miami, FL	1,677	17.9	26.5	615	1,018	6,362	1,442	3,804	1,116
Minneapolis, MN	1,256	14.1	103.4	597	541	5,379	1,266	3,142	970
Colorado Springs, CO	431	3.7	72.6	93	261	5,430	1,019	3,858	554
Arlington, TX	524	3.9	55.4	183	282	5,425	935	4,067	423
Wichita, KS	811	8.1	67.7	176	559	6,083	1,106	4,478	500

NA Not available. [1] Forcible rape figures furnished by the state-level Uniform Crime Reporting (UCR) Program administered by the Illinois Department of State Police were not in accordance with national UCR guidelines. Therefore, the figures were excluded from the forcible rape and Violent Crime and Crime Index total categories. [2] Due to reporting changes or annexations, figures are not comparable to previous years. [3] Louisville, KY, and Jefferson County, KY, Police Departments merged forming the Louisville Metro Police Department.

Source: U.S. Department of Justice, Federal Bureau of Investigation, Crime in the United States, annual. See also <http://www.fbi.gov/ucr/cius_04/offenses_reported/index.html>

Law Enforcement, Courts, and Prisons 193

Table 299. **Murder Victims—Circumstances and Weapons Used or Cause of Death: 1990 to 2004**

[Based solely on police investigation. For definition of murder, go to <http://www.fbi.gov/ucr/cius_04/appendices/appendix_02.html>]

Characteristic	1990	2000	2003	2004	Characteristic	1990	2000	2003	2004
Murders, total. . . .	**20,273**	**13,230**	**14,493**	**14,249**	Other motives	19.4	20.2	20.5	21.3
Percent distribution	100.0	100.0	100.0	100.0	Unknown.	24.8	30.8	33.6	35.0
CIRCUMSTANCES					TYPE OF WEAPON OR CAUSE OF DEATH				
Felonies, total	20.8	16.8	16.5	14.8	Guns	64.3	65.5	66.8	66.0
Robbery	9.2	8.1	7.3	7.0	Handguns	49.8	51.2	53.5	51.3
Narcotics	6.7	4.5	4.7	3.9	Cutting or stabbing	17.4	13.5	12.6	13.1
Sex offenses	1.1	0.6	0.5	0.4	Blunt objects [1]	5.4	4.7	4.5	4.7
Other felonies.	3.7	3.7	4.0	3.4	Personal weapons [2] . . .	5.5	7.0	6.6	6.6
Suspected felonies	0.7	0.5	0.6	0.8	Strangulations, asphyxiations	2.0	2.0	2.2	1.9
Argument, total.	34.4	31.8	28.8	28.8	Fire	1.4	1.0	1.2	0.8
Property or money. . .	2.5	1.6	1.5	1.6	All other [3]	4.0	6.4	6.1	6.8
Romantic triangle . . .	2.0	0.9	0.7	0.7					
Other arguments	29.8	29.3	26.6	26.5					

[1] Refers to club, hammer, etc.   [2] Hands, fists, feet, etc.   [3] Includes poison, drowning, explosives, narcotics, and unknown.

Source: U.S. Department of Justice, Federal Bureau of Investigation, *Crime in the United States,* annual. See also <http://www.fbi.gov/ucr/cius_04/offenses_reported/index.html>.

Table 300. **Murder Victims by Age, Sex, and Race: 2004**

Age	Total	Sex			Race			
		Male	Female	Unknown	White	Black	Other	Unknown
Murders, total	**14,249**	**11,077**	**3,137**	**35**	**7,005**	**6,680**	**367**	**197**
Percent of total	100.0	77.7	22.0	0.2	49.2	46.9	2.6	1.4
Under 18 yrs. old	1,381	939	436	6	696	626	33	26
18 yrs. old and over	12,608	9,963	2,641	4	6,182	5,980	330	116
Infant (under 1 year old)	177	86	88	3	111	53	4	9
1 to 4 years old	337	183	151	3	187	134	8	8
5 to 8 years old	71	33	38	–	41	29	–	1
9 to 12 years old	81	48	33	–	40	36	3	2
13 to 16 years old	416	329	87	–	178	222	10	6
17 to 19 years old	1,251	1,070	181	–	560	652	37	2
20 to 24 years old	2,654	2,305	348	1	1,080	1,484	65	25
25 to 29 years old	2,148	1,842	306	–	891	1,200	38	19
30 to 34 years old	1,560	1,242	317	1	697	805	47	11
35 to 39 years old	1,240	935	304	1	625	568	33	14
40 to 44 years old	1,148	812	336	–	630	480	31	7
45 to 49 years old	922	648	273	1	539	348	23	12
50 to 54 years old	653	507	146	–	385	239	21	8
55 to 59 years old	394	288	106	–	244	132	11	7
60 to 64 years old	278	189	89	–	184	79	10	5
65 to 69 years old	208	135	73	–	158	38	10	2
70 to 74 years old	148	102	46	–	98	41	8	1
75 years old and over	303	148	155	–	230	66	4	3
Age unknown	260	175	60	25	127	74	4	55

– Represents zero.

Source: U.S. Department of Justice, Federal Bureau of Investigation, *Crime in the United States,* annual. See also <http://www.fbi.gov/ucr/cius_04/offenses_reported/index.html>.

Table 301. **Murder Victims of September 11, 2001, Terrorist Attacks, by Race, Sex, and Location**

Race	Total	Sex			Race	Total	Sex		
		Male	Female	Unknown			Male	Female	Unknown
All locations					Pentagon				
Total	**2,973**	**2,256**	**712**	**5**	**Total . . . .**	**184**	**108**	**71**	**5**
White.	2,401	1,879	522	–	White.	120	79	41	–
Black.	265	162	103	–	Black	49	21	28	–
Other.	173	117	56	–	Other.	2	2	–	–
Unknown	134	98	31	5	Unknown	13	6	2	5
World Trade Center					Somerset County, Pennsylvania				
Total	**2,749**	**2,128**	**621**	**–**	**Total . . . .**	**40**	**20**	**20**	**–**
White.	2,245	1,782	463	–	White.	36	18	18	–
Black.	213	140	73	–	Black	3	1	2	–
Other.	170	114	56	–	Other	1	1	–	–
Unknown	121	92	29	–	Unknown	–	–	–	–

– Represents zero.

Source: U.S. Federal Bureau of Investigation, *Crime in the United States,* annual. See also<http://www.fbi.gov/ucr/cius_01/01crime.pdf> (accessed 28 October 2002).

194   Law Enforcement, Courts, and Prisons

Table 302. **Homicide Trends: 1980 to 2002**

[**Rate per 100,000 population.** Not all agencies which report offense information to the FBI also submit supplemental data on homicides. To account for the total number of homicide victims, the data was weighted to match national and state estimates prepared by the FBI; hence, columns may not equal total]

Year	Number of victims						Rate					
	Total	Male	Female	White	Black	Other	Total	Male	Female	White	Black	Other
1980	23,040	17,788	5,232	12,275	9,767	327	10.2	16.2	4.5	6.3	37.7	5.7
1985	18,976	14,079	4,880	10,590	7,891	399	8.0	12.2	4.0	5.2	27.6	5.5
1988	20,675	15,414	5,238	10,184	9,959	344	8.5	12.9	4.2	4.9	33.5	4.0
1989	21,500	16,407	5,085	10,325	10,566	390	8.7	13.6	4.0	5.0	35.1	4.3
1990	23,438	18,304	5,115	11,279	11,488	400	9.4	15.0	4.0	5.4	37.6	4.2
1991	24,703	19,270	5,394	11,661	12,226	608	9.8	15.7	4.2	5.5	39.3	6.0
1992	23,760	18,513	5,217	11,229	11,777	573	9.3	14.9	4.0	5.3	37.2	5.4
1993	24,526	18,937	5,550	11,278	12,435	601	9.5	15.0	4.2	5.3	38.7	5.5
1994	23,326	18,294	5,007	10,773	11,856	526	9.0	14.4	3.8	5.0	36.4	4.6
1995	21,606	16,552	5,022	10,376	10,444	581	8.2	12.9	3.7	4.8	31.6	4.9
1996	19,645	15,153	4,469	9,483	9,476	512	7.4	11.7	3.3	4.3	28.3	4.1
1997	18,208	14,057	4,125	8,620	8,842	524	6.8	10.7	3.0	3.9	26.0	4.1
1998	16,974	12,753	4,139	8,389	7,931	393	6.3	9.7	3.0	3.8	23.0	2.9
1999	15,522	11,704	3,800	7,777	7,139	458	5.7	8.8	2.7	3.5	20.5	3.3
2000	15,586	11,818	3,733	7,560	7,425	399	5.5	8.6	2.6	3.3	20.5	2.7
2001	16,037	12,232	3,775	7,884	7,522	424	5.6	8.8	2.6	3.4	20.4	2.8
2002	16,204	12,410	3,764	7,784	7,758	437	5.6	8.8	2.6	3.3	20.8	2.7

Source: U.S. Department of Justice, Office of Justice Programs, Bureau of Justice Statistics, *Homicide Trends in the United States, 1976–2002*. See also: <http://www.ojp.usdoj.gov/bjs/pub/pdf/htius.pdf>

Table 303. **Homicide Victims by Race and Sex: 1980 to 2003**

[**Rates per 100,000 resident population in specified group.** Excludes deaths to nonresidents of United States. Beginning 1999, deaths classified according to the tenth revision of the *International Classification of Diseases;* see text, Section 2, and footnote 3]

Year	Homicide victims					Homicide rate [2]				
		White		Black			White		Black	
	Total [1]	Male	Female	Male	Female	Total [1]	Male	Female	Male	Female
1980	24,278	10,381	3,177	8,385	1,898	10.7	10.9	3.2	66.6	13.5
1985	19,893	8,122	3,041	6,616	1,666	8.3	8.2	2.9	48.4	11.0
1989	22,909	8,337	2,971	8,888	2,074	9.2	8.2	2.8	61.1	12.9
1990	24,932	9,147	3,006	9,981	2,163	10.0	9.0	2.8	69.2	13.5
1991	26,513	9,581	3,201	10,628	2,330	10.5	9.3	3.0	72.0	14.2
1992	25,488	9,456	3,012	10,131	2,187	10.0	9.1	2.8	67.5	13.1
1993	26,009	9,054	3,232	10,640	2,297	10.1	8.6	3.0	69.7	13.6
1994	24,926	9,055	2,921	10,083	2,124	9.6	8.5	2.6	65.1	12.4
1995	22,895	8,336	3,028	8,847	1,936	8.7	7.8	2.7	56.3	11.1
1996	20,971	7,570	2,747	8,183	1,800	7.9	7.0	2.5	51.5	10.2
1997	19,846	7,343	2,570	7,601	1,652	7.4	6.7	2.3	47.1	9.3
1998	18,272	6,707	2,534	6,873	1,547	6.8	6.1	2.2	42.1	8.6
1999 [3]	16,889	6,162	2,466	6,214	1,434	6.2	5.6	2.2	37.5	7.8
2000	16,765	5,925	2,414	6,482	1,385	6.1	5.3	2.1	38.6	7.5
2001	20,308	8,254	3,074	6,780	1,446	7.1	7.2	2.6	38.3	7.4
2002	17,638	6,282	2,403	6,896	1,391	6.1	5.4	2.0	38.4	7.0
2003	17,732	6,337	2,372	7,083	1,309	6.1	5.4	2.0	38.9	6.6

[1] Includes races not shown separately.   [2] Rate based on enumerated population figures as of April 1 for 1980, 1990 and 2000; estimated resident population as of July 1 for other years.   [3] Effective with data for 1999, causes of death are classified by The Tenth Revision International Classification of Diseases (ICD-10), replacing the Ninth Revision (ICD-9) used for 1979–98 data. Breaks in the comparability of some cause of death statistics result from changes in category titles, changes in the structure and content of the classification, and changes in coding rules used to select the underlying cause of death. In ICD-9, the category Homicide also inludes death as a result of legal intervention. ICD-10 has two separate categories for these two causes of death. Some caution should be used in comparing data between 1998 and 1999.

Source: U.S. National Center for Health Statistics, *Vital Statistics of the United States,* annual; and *National Vital Statistics Reports (NVSR)* (formerly *Monthly Vital Statistics Report*); and unpublished data.

Table 304. **Forcible Rape—Number and Rate: 1980 to 2004**

[Minus sign (–) indicates decrease. For definition of rape, go to <http://www.fbi.gov/ucr/cius_04/appendices/appendix_02.html>]

Item	1980	1990	1995	1998	1999	2000	2001	2002	2003	2004
NUMBER										
Total.	82,990	102,560	97,460	93,144	89,411	90,186	90,863	95,235	93,883	94,635
By force	63,599	86,541	85,249	82,823	79,697	81,111	82,004	86,655	85,837	86,847
Attempt.	19,391	16,019	12,211	10,321	9,714	9,075	8,859	8,580	8,046	7,788
RATE										
Per 100,000 population	36.8	41.1	37.1	34.5	32.8	32.0	31.8	33.1	32.3	32.2
Per 100,000 females	71.6	80.5	72.5	67.4	64.1	62.7	62.6	65.0	63.5	63.5
AVERAGE ANNUAL PERCENT CHANGE IN RATE [1]										
Per 100,000 population	6.1	8.1	–5.6	–3.9	–4.9	–2.4	–0.6	4.1	–3.0	–0.3

[1] Represents annual average from immediate prior year.

Source: U.S. Department of Justice, Federal Bureau of Investigation, *Population-at-Risk Rates and Selected Crime Indicators,* annual. <http://www.fbi.gov/ucr/cius_04/offenses_reported/violent_crime/forcible_rape.html>

Law Enforcement, Courts, and Prisons   195

Table 305. Violence by Intimate Partners by Sex, 1993 to 2003, and by Type of Crime, 2003

[Violent acts covered include murder, rape, sexual assault, robbery, and aggravated and simple assault. Intimate partners involve current spouses, former spouses, current boy/girlfriends, and former boy/girlfriends. Based on the National Criminal Victimization Survey; see text, this section, and Appendix III]

Year and type of crime	All persons		Female victims		Male victims	
	Number	Rate per 100,000 [1]	Number	Rate per 100,000 [1]	Number	Rate per 100,000 [1]
1993	1,228,760	580.9	1,072,090	982.0	156,670	153.1
1994	1,148,210	537.2	1,003,190	908.9	145,020	140.3
1995	1,063,520	493.0	953,700	855.8	109,820	105.3
1996	1,008,860	462.8	879,290	781.7	129,570	122.8
1997	953,780	432.7	848,480	747.3	105,300	98.5
1998	1,054,260	475.7	896,030	780.9	158,230	146.7
1999	783,120	347.7	672,330	578.4	110,790	101.6
2000	630,530	277.2	547,310	466.5	83,220	75.5
2001	693,321	301.4	589,692	497.1	103,629	92.8
2002	568,690	245.4	495,772	214.0	72,918	31.5
2003, total	**521,760**	**218.0**	**437,990**	**183.0**	**83,750**	**35.0**
Rape or sexual assault	27,380	11.4	(B)	(B)	(B)	(B)
Robbery	37,120	15.5	(B)	(B)	(B)	(B)
Aggravated assault	123,310	51.5	101,400	42.4	(B)	(B)
Simple assault	333,950	139.5	284,170	118.7	49,780	20.8

B Base figure too small to meet statistical standards for reliability of derived figure. In this case, 10 or fewer sample cases.
[1] Rates are the number of victimizations per 100,000 persons.

Source: U.S. Department of Justice, Office of Justice Programs, Bureau of Justice Statistics, *Intimate Partner Violence,* Series NCJ-206348, October 2004 and unpublished data. See also<http://www.ojp.usdoj.gov/bjs/abstract/cv04.htm>.

Table 306. Robbery and Property Crimes by Type and Selected Characteristic: 1990 to 2004

[For definition of crime, go to <http://www.fbi.gov/ucr/cius_04/appendices/appendix_02.html>]

Characteristic of offenses	Number of offenses (1,000)				Rate per 100,000 population				Average value lost (dol.)	
	1990	2000	2003	2004	1990	2000	2003	2004	2003	2004
Robbery, total [1]	**639**	**408**	**414**	**401**	**256.3**	**144.9**	**142.5**	**136.7**	**1,244**	**1,283**
Type of crime:										
Street or highway	359	188	180	172	144.2	66.7	61.8	58.5	898	913
Commercial house	73	57	61	59	29.5	20.1	20.8	20.1	1,778	1,521
Gas station	18	12	11	11	7.1	4.1	3.9	3.7	690	1,698
Convenience store	39	26	26	25	15.6	9.3	8.9	8.4	813	642
Residence	62	50	57	56	25.1	17.7	19.5	18.9	1,472	1,444
Bank	9	9	10	10	3.8	3.1	3.3	3.3	4,767	4,153
Weapon used:										
Firearm	234	161	174	163	94.1	57.0	59.8	55.4	(NA)	(NA)
Knife or cutting instrument	76	36	37	36	30.7	12.8	12.6	12.1	(NA)	(NA)
Other dangerous weapon	61	53	39	38	24.5	18.9	13.4	13.4	(NA)	(NA)
Strongarm	268	159	165	165	107.7	56.4	56.6	56.6	(NA)	(NA)
Burglary, total	**3,074**	**2,050**	**2,155**	**2,143**	**1,232.2**	**728.4**	**741.0**	**729.9**	**1,626**	**1,726**
Forcible entry	2,150	1,297	1,340	1,310	864.5	460.7	460.9	446.0	(NA)	(NA)
Unlawful entry	678	615	677	701	272.8	218.7	232.9	238.6	(NA)	(NA)
Attempted forcible entry	245	138	137	133	98.7	49.0	47.2	45.4	(NA)	(NA)
Residence	2,033	1,335	1,418	1,409	817.4	474.3	487.8	479.7	1,600	1,737
Nonresidence	1,041	715	736	734	418.5	254.1	253.2	250.2	1,676	1,702
Occurred during the night	1,135	699	719	713	456.4	248.3	247.4	242.8	(NA)	(NA)
Occurred during the day	1,151	836	890	889	462.8	297.2	306.1	302.7	(NA)	(NA)
Larceny-theft, total	**7,946**	**6,972**	**7,027**	**6,948**	**3,185.1**	**2,477.3**	**2,416.5**	**2,365.9**	**698**	**733**
Pocket picking	81	36	32	30	32.4	12.7	11.0	10.2	293	350
Purse snatching	82	37	42	42	32.8	13.2	14.5	14.4	367	417
Shoplifting	1,291	959	1,013	1,011	519.1	340.7	348.5	344.2	163	155
From motor vehicles	1,744	1,754	1,858	1,761	701.3	623.3	638.8	599.7	680	702
Motor vehicle accessories	1,185	677	781	750	476.3	240.6	268.7	255.5	442	428
Bicycles	443	312	272	250	178.2	110.9	93.5	85.2	247	241
From buildings	1,118	914	869	863	449.4	324.6	298.7	294.7	1,030	1,114
From coin-operated machines . . .	63	46	52	46	25.4	16.2	18.0	15.7	262	238
Other	1,940	2,232	2,108	2,195	780.0	793.0	724.8	747.4	1,012	1,052
Motor vehicles, total [2]	**1,636**	**1,160**	**1,261**	**1,237**	**655.8**	**412.2**	**433.7**	**421.3**	**6,797**	**6,019**
Automobiles	1,304	877	927	903	524.3	311.5	318.9	307.4	(NA)	(NA)
Trucks and buses	238	209	230	226	95.5	74.1	78.9	76.9	(NA)	(NA)

NA Not available. [1] Includes other crimes not shown separately. [2] Includes other types of motor vehicles not shown separately.

Source: U.S. Department of Justice, Federal Bureau of Investigation, *Population-at-Risk Rates and Selected Crime Indicators,* annual. <http://www.fbi.gov/ucr/ucr.htm>.

Table 307. **State Trends in Fraud and Identity Theft: 2005**

[Rate per 100,000 population. **As of December 31.** Based on Census Bureau population estimates.]

Consumer State	Fraud complaints		Identity theft complaints	
	Number	Rate	Number	Rate
United States [1]	**371,448**	**125.3**	**248,524**	**83.8**
Alabama	4,840	106.2	2,675	58.7
Alaska	1,654	249.2	421	63.4
Arizona	9,789	164.8	9,320	156.9
Arkansas	2,155	77.5	1,617	58.2
California	48,707	134.8	45,175	125.0
Colorado	7,551	161.9	4,535	97.2
Connecticut	4,688	133.5	2,313	65.9
Delaware	1,091	129.3	583	69.1
District of Columbia	1,243	225.8	842	152.9
Florida	24,796	139.4	17,048	95.8
Georgia	10,285	113.4	7,918	87.3
Hawaii	1,852	145.2	810	63.5
Idaho	1,899	132.9	745	52.1
Illinois	14,885	116.6	11,137	87.3
Indiana	9,572	152.6	4,201	67.0
Iowa	2,981	100.5	1,090	36.7
Kansas	3,323	121.1	1,606	58.5
Kentucky	4,149	99.4	1,815	43.5
Louisiana	3,724	82.3	2,831	62.6
Maine	1,714	129.7	491	37.2
Maryland	8,413	150.2	4,848	86.6
Massachusetts	7,363	115.1	3,999	62.5
Michigan	11,618	114.8	7,139	70.5
Minnesota	6,224	121.3	3,015	58.7
Mississippi	2,114	72.4	1,458	49.9
Missouri	7,912	136.4	3,920	67.6
Montana	1,253	133.9	398	42.5
Nebraska	2,278	129.5	919	52.3
Nevada	3,770	156.1	3,144	130.2
New Hampshire	2,008	153.3	645	49.2
New Jersey	10,180	116.8	6,582	75.5
New Mexico	2,168	112.4	1,634	84.7
New York	20,868	108.4	17,387	90.3
North Carolina	9,765	112.5	5,830	67.1
North Dakota	632	99.3	158	24.8
Ohio	14,075	122.8	7,155	62.4
Oklahoma	3,917	110.4	2,403	67.7
Oregon	5,938	163.1	2,973	81.7
Pennsylvania	15,996	128.7	7,908	63.6
Rhode Island	1,127	104.7	626	58.2
South Carolina	6,312	148.3	2,416	56.8
South Dakota	709	91.4	233	30.0
Tennessee	6,261	105.0	3,412	57.2
Texas	23,184	101.4	26,624	116.5
Utah	3,829	155.0	1,668	67.5
Vermont	651	104.5	201	32.3
Virginia	11,234	148.5	5,163	68.2
Washington	11,008	175.1	5,810	92.4
West Virginia	1,849	101.8	677	37.3
Wisconsin	7,215	130.3	2,782	50.3
Wyoming	679	133.3	224	44.0

[1] U.S. total represents only complaints from state consumers.

Source: U.S. Federal Trade Commission, *Consumer Fraud and Identity Theft complaint data, January–December 2005.*
Issued January 2006. See also <http://www.consumer.gov/sentinel/pubs/Top10Fraud2005.pdf>.

Law Enforcement, Courts, and Prisons 197

Table 308. Hate Crimes—Number of Incidents, Offenses, Victims, and Known Offenders by Bias Motivation: 2000 to 2004

[The FBI collected statistics on hate crimes from 12,723 law enforcement agencies representing over 254 million inhabitants in 2004. Hate crime offenses cover incidents motivated by race, religion, sexual orientation, ethnicity/national origin, and disability]

Bias motivation	Incidents reported	Offenses	Victims[1]	Known offenders[2]
2000, Total.	8,213	9,619	10,117	7,690
2001, Total.	9,728	11,480	12,067	9,258
2002, Total.	7,484	8,849	9,238	7,289
2003, Total.	7,529	8,773	9,164	6,979
2004, Total.	7,679	9,065	9,561	7,175
Race, total	4,067	4,889	5,148	4,203
Anti-White	828	998	1,027	1,090
Anti-Black	2,751	3,299	3,494	2,713
Anti-American Indian/Alaska native.	84	99	102	98
Anti-Asian/Pacific Islander	220	256	272	191
Anti-multiracial group.	184	237	253	111
Ethnicity/national origin, total	974	1,204	1,257	1,046
Anti-Hispanic	475	611	646	584
Anti-other ethnicity/national origin.	499	593	611	462
Religion, total.	1,382	1,486	1,592	605
Anti-Jewish	963	1,013	1,086	337
Anti-Catholic	57	57	68	37
Anti-Protestant	38	43	48	28
Anti-Islamic	157	194	202	124
Anti-other religious group	126	135	142	62
Anti-multireligious group.	35	37	39	14
Anti-atheism/agnosticism/etc.	6	7	7	3
Sexual orientation, total	1,192	1,401	1,477	1,256
Anti-male homosexual	738	855	902	831
Anti-female homosexual.	165	202	213	163
Anti-homosexual.	245	297	314	224
Anti-heterosexual	29	31	32	21
Anti-bisexual	15	16	18	17
Disability, total	57	71	73	54
Anti-physical	23	23	24	16
Anti-mental	34	48	49	38
Multiple bias	7	14	14	9

[1] The term "victim" may refer to a person, business, institution, or a society as a whole. [2] The term "known offender" does not imply that the identity of the suspect is known, but only that an attribute of the suspect is identified which distinguishes him/her from an unknown offender.

Source: U.S. Department of Justice, Federal Bureau of Investigation, *Offenses reported, Hate Crime Statistics*, annual. See also <http://www.fbi.gov/ucr/cius_04/offenses_reported/hate_crime/index.html>.

Table 309. Hate Crimes Reported by State: 2004

[In thousands for population (254,193 represents 254,193,000). See headnote, Table 308]

State	Number of participating agencies	Population covered (1,000)	Agencies submitting incidents	Incidents reported	State	Number of participating agencies	Population covered (1,000)	Agencies submitting incidents	Incidents reported
United States . . .	12,723	254,193	2,057	7,679	Missouri	260	3,535	29	71
					Montana	105	927	25	56
Alabama	51	527	3	3	Nebraska	207	1,494	15	62
Alaska	1	274	1	9	Nevada	35	2,335	4	81
Arizona	83	5,558	20	225	New Hampshire	141	936	30	49
Arkansas	192	1,633	48	83	New Jersey	513	8,699	249	769
California	725	35,894	245	1,394	New Mexico	49	1,172	4	22
Colorado	205	4,444	27	60					
Connecticut	100	3,504	49	119	New York	520	19,199	42	386
Delaware	53	830	12	37	North Carolina	418	8,027	35	66
District of Columbia . . .	2	554	2	49	North Dakota	69	560	6	10
Florida	490	17,351	95	274	Ohio	410	8,992	74	354
Georgia	77	1,576	7	29	Oklahoma	297	3,524	29	51
Hawaii	([1])	([1])	([1])	([1])	Oregon	170	3,592	23	155
Idaho	119	1,392	12	37	Pennsylvania	864	11,447	34	105
Illinois	63	5,088	48	187	Rhode Island	48	1,081	8	29
Indiana	137	3,017	13	63	South Carolina	468	4,196	50	102
Iowa	219	2,906	18	23					
Kansas	357	2,110	21	49	South Dakota	156	767	6	7
Kentucky	326	3,709	32	71	Tennessee	453	5,901	70	136
Louisiana	148	3,499	12	24	Texas	987	22,466	84	297
Maine	147	1,317	29	68	Utah	55	1,841	17	60
Maryland	150	5,558	32	245	Vermont	74	603	12	28
					Virginia	395	7,400	69	310
Massachusetts	301	5,837	93	359	Washington	253	6,204	51	175
Michigan	602	8,996	173	559	West Virginia	431	1,815	11	45
Minnesota	318	5,083	63	239	Wisconsin	369	5,509	19	37
Mississippi	68	1,013	2	2	Wyoming	42	349	4	4

[1] Did not report.

Source: U.S. Department of Justice, Federal Bureau of Investigation, *Offenses reported, Hate Crime Statistics*, annual. See also <http://www.fbi.gov/ucr/cius_04/offenses_reported/hate_crime/index.html>

Table 310. Criminal Victimizations and Victimization Rates: 1995 to 2004

[Based on National Crime Victimization Survey; see text, this section and Appendix III. For definitions of crimes, go to <http://www.ojp.usdoj.gov/bjs/abstract/cvus/definitions.htm>]

Type of crime	Number of victimizations (1,000)				Victimization rates [1]			
	1995	2000	2003	2004	1995	2000	2003	2004
All crimes, total	39,926	25,893	24,213	24,061	(X)	(X)	(X)	(X)
Personal crimes [2]	10,436	6,597	5,586	5,407	46.2	29.1	23.3	22.4
Crimes of violence	10,022	6,323	5,402	5,183	44.5	27.9	22.6	21.4
Completed violence	2,960	2,044	1,655	1,737	12.9	9.0	6.9	7.2
Attempted/threatened violence . . .	7,061	4,279	3,747	2,446	31.6	18.9	15.7	14.3
Rape/sexual assault	363	261	199	210	1.6	1.2	0.8	0.9
Rape/attempted rape	252	147	117	101	1.1	0.6	0.5	0.4
Rape	153	92	72	59	0.7	0.4	0.3	0.2
Attempted rape	99	55	45	42	0.4	0.2	0.2	0.2
Sexual assault	112	114	82	109	0.5	0.5	0.3	0.5
Robbery	1,171	732	596	502	5.3	3.2	2.5	2.1
Completed/property taken	753	520	378	299	3.5	2.3	1.6	1.2
With injury.	224	160	160	110	1.0	0.7	0.7	0.5
Without injury	529	360	218	189	2.4	1.6	0.9	0.8
Attempted to take property	418	212	218	203	1.8	0.9	0.9	0.8
With injury.	84	66	54	71	0.4	0.3	0.2	0.3
Without injury	335	146	165	132	1.4	0.6	0.7	0.5
Assault	8,487	5,330	4,607	4,471	37.6	23.5	19.3	18.5
Aggravated.	2,050	1,293	1,101	1,030	8.8	5.7	4.6	4.3
With injury.	533	346	362	378	2.4	1.5	1.5	1.6
Threatened with weapon	1,517	946	740	652	6.4	4.2	3.1	2.7
Simple.	6,437	4,038	3,506	3,441	28.9	17.8	14.6	14.2
With minor injury	1,426	989	769	898	6.0	4.4	3.2	3.7
Without injury	5,012	3,048	2,737	2,543	22.9	13.4	11.4	10.5
Personal theft [3]	414	274	185	224	1.7	1.2	0.8	0.9
Property crimes	29,490	19,297	18,626	18,654	279.5	178.1	163.2	161.1
Household burglary.	5,004	3,444	3,396	3,428	47.4	31.8	29.8	29.6
Completed.	4,232	2,909	2,811	2,909	40.0	26.9	24.6	25.1
Attempted forcible entry	773	534	585	518	7.4	4.9	5.1	4.5
Motor vehicle theft	1,717	937	1,032	1,015	16.2	8.6	9.0	8.8
Completed.	1,163	642	764	779	10.8	5.9	6.7	6.7
Attempted	554	295	269	236	5.5	2.7	2.4	2.0
Theft	22,769	14,916	14,198	14,212	215.9	137.7	124.4	122.8
Completed [4].	21,857	14,300	13,719	13,584	207.6	132.0	120.2	117.3
Attempted	911	616	479	628	8.4	5.7	4.2	5.4

X Not applicable.   [1] Per 1,000 persons age 12 or older or per 1,000 households.   [2] The victimization survey cannot measure murder because of the inability to question the victim.   [3] Includes pocket picking, purse snatching, and attempted purse snatching.   [4] Includes thefts in which the amount taken was not ascertained.
Source: U.S. Department of Justice, Office of Justice Programs, Bureau of Justice Statistics, *Criminal Victimization*, annual; and *Criminal Victimization 2004, Trends 1994–2004*, Series NCJ-211511. See also http://www.ojp.usdoj.gov/bjs/abstract/cnh04.htm.

Table 311. Victimization Rates by Type of Violent Crime and Characteristic of the Victim: 2003

[**Rate per 1,000 persons age 12 years or older**. Based on National Crime Victimization Survey; see text, this section, and Appendix III. For definition of crimes, go to <http://www.ojp.usdoj.gov/bjs/abstract/cvus/definitions.htm>]

Characteristic of the victim	All crimes	Crimes of violence						Personal theft
		Total	Rape/ sexual assault	Robbery	Assault			
					Total	Aggra- vated	Simple	
Total	23.3	22.6	0.8	2.5	19.3	4.6	14.6	0.8
Male	26.7	26.3	0.2	[1]3.2	23.0	5.9	17.1	0.4
Female	20.2	19.0	1.5	1.9	15.7	3.3	12.4	1.1
12 to 15 years old	53.1	51.6	1.2	[1]5.2	45.3	8.9	36.4	[1]1.5
16 to 19 years old	54.4	53.0	1.3	[1]5.1	46.6	11.9	34.7	[1]1.4
20 to 24 years old	45.0	43.3	1.7	6.4	35.3	9.8	25.5	1.6
25 to 34 years old	27.4	26.4	1.6	2.5	22.3	6.0	16.3	1.0
35 to 49 years old	19.0	18.5	0.6	1.7	16.1	3.8	12.3	0.5
50 to 64 years old	10.5	10.3	0.4	[1]1.4	8.5	1.6	[1]7.0	[1]0.3
65 years old and over	2.5	2.0	0.1	[1]0.7	[1]1.2	0.1	[1]1.1	[1]0.5
White	22.1	21.5	0.8	1.9	18.8	4.2	14.7	0.6
Black	30.7	29.1	0.8	[1]5.9	22.3	6.0	16.3	1.7
Other	16.9	16.0	0.2	[1]3.4	12.4	5.4	7.0	[1]0.9
Hispanic	25.3	24.2	0.4	[1]3.1	20.8	4.6	16.1	[1]1.1
Non-Hispanic	23.0	22.3	0.9	2.4	19.0	4.6	14.4	0.7
Household income:								
Less than $7,500	51.1	49.9	1.6	[1]9.0	39.3	10.8	28.5	[1]1.2
$7,500 to $14,999	31.9	30.8	1.8	[1]4.0	25.0	7.9	17.0	[1]1.1
$15,000 to $24,999	27.0	26.3	0.8	[1]4.0	21.5	4.5	17.0	[1]0.7
$25,000 to $34,999	25.8	24.9	0.9	[1]2.2	21.8	5.0	16.9	[1]0.8
$35,000 to $49,999	22.0	21.4	0.9	[1]2.1	18.3	4.8	13.5	[1]0.7
$50,000 to $74,999	23.3	22.9	0.5	[1]2.0	20.4	5.2	15.2	[1]0.5
$75,000 or more	18.5	17.5	0.5	[1]1.7	15.4	2.7	12.6	1.0

[1] Based on 10 or fewer sample cases.
Source: U.S. Department of Justice, Office of Justice Programs, Bureau of Justice Statistics, *Criminal Victimization*, annual; and Series NCJ-199994. See also <http://www.ojp.usdoj.gov/bjs/pub/pdf/cv03.pdf>.

Law Enforcement, Courts, and Prisons   199

Table 312. **Criminal Victimizations by Age of Victim: 1993 to 2002**

[In percent. Covers period 1993 to 2002. Offender characteristics are based on victim's perception. See source for details. Fo definitions of crimes, see text, this section and also <http://www.ojp.usdoj.gov/bjs/abstract/cvus/definitions.htm>]

Characteristic	12–64 years old	65 years old or older	Characteristic	12–64 years old	65 years old or older
NONFATAL VIOLENT VICTIMIZATIONS			Casual acquaintance	18.2	15.7
Victims facing weapons	25.7	30.2	Stranger	46.3	52.5
Firearm	9.4	12.7	Don't know relationship.	3.7	8.2
Victims resisting	71.0	55.5	Age 30 or older	30.2	48.3
Threatened/attacked			Male.	78.8	75.6
without weapon.	27.9	15.3	CHARACTERISTICS OF CRIMES		
Victims not resisting	29.0	44.5	Occurring at night:		
Victims injured	25.9	21.8	Violence	45.8	27.2
CHARACTERISTIC OF OFFENDER			Occurring at/near home:		
Relationship to victim:			Violence	27.0	45.5
Known to victim.	31.7	23.6	Crime reported to police:		
Well-known person.	15.8	13.9	Violence	43.9	53.0

Source: Department of Justice, Office of Justice Programs, Bureau of Justice Statistics, *Crimes Against Persons Age 65 (Older: 1993–2002*, Series NCJ 206154, January 2005; <http://www.ojp.usdoj.gov/bjs/cvict_v.htm#publications>.

Table 313. **State and Local Government Expenditures Per Capita by Criminal Justice Function and State: 2002**

[In dollars]

State	Total justice system	Police protec- tion	Judicial and legal	Correc- tions	State	Total justice system	Police protec- tion	Judicial and legal	Correc- tions
Total.	**524**	**225**	**109**	**191**	Missouri	389	180	66	144
Alabama	332	159	71	103	Montana	405	187	84	134
Alaska	889	412	204	273	Nebraska	369	155	65	149
Arizona.	558	231	120	206	Nevada	680	300	148	232
Arkansas.	358	149	72	137	New Hampshire . . .	333	166	76	90
California.	749	290	201	257	New Jersey	596	282	126	187
Colorado.	514	238	86	190	New Mexico.	525	221	103	201
Connecticut	550	226	140	184	New York	738	351	143	244
Delaware.	673	237	132	304	North Carolina	389	181	67	141
District of Columbia. .	2,162	1,348	205	609	North Dakota	295	122	79	94
Florida	563	263	99	202	Ohio.	490	212	119	159
Georgia	468	182	80	207	Oklahoma	389	163	65	161
Hawaii	504	205	172	127	Oregon.	568	219	114	235
Idaho	442	179	92	171	Pennsylvania	490	199	93	199
Illinois.	494	256	88	149	Rhode Island	468	224	97	147
Indiana	344	145	62	137	South Carolina	367	176	52	139
Iowa.	367	156	98	112	South Dakota	318	139	57	123
Kansas	396	176	87	133	Tennessee.	361	169	73	119
Kentucky	357	133	77	147	Texas	449	171	75	203
Louisiana	471	199	99	173	Utah.	456	190	104	162
Maine	314	140	62	112	Vermont	347	149	69	129
Maryland.	571	245	95	231	Virginia	460	180	90	191
Massachusetts	515	224	116	175	Washington	463	180	94	189
Michigan	516	197	109	210	West Virginia	284	104	69	112
Minnesota	436	203	104	129	Wisconsin	537	234	87	216
Mississippi	329	161	55	113	Wyoming.	578	243	114	220

Source: U.S. Department of Justice, Office of Justice Programs, Bureau of Justice Statistics, *Expenditures and Employme Statistics. Series NCJ 209179*, July 2005. See also <http://www.ojp.usdoj.gov/bjs/eande.htm>

Table 314. **Violent Victimizations of College Students 18 to 24 Years Old: 1995 to 2002**

[Average annual rates per 1,000 persons ages 18–24 except as indicated. Covers period 1995 to 2002. Based on Natior Crime Victimization Survey; see text, this section, and Appendix III. For definitions of crimes, go to <http://www.ojp.gov/bjs/abstract/cvi /definitions.htm>]

Sex, Race, and Ethnicity	Population [1]	Violent crime	Rape/ sexual assault	Robbery	Aggravated assault	Simple assault	Seriou viole crim
College students, total . .	**7,894,930**	**60.7**	**3.8**	**5.0**	**13.5**	**38.4**	**22**
Gender:							
Male.	3,796,380	80.2	1.4	7.4	21.4	49.9	30
Female	4,098,550	42.7	6.0	2.7	6.2	27.7	15
Race/ethnicity: [2]							
White	5,592,920	64.9	4.0	4.4	13.2	43.3	21
Black	934,160	52.4	(B)	8.7	15.6	24.9	27
Other	580,700	37.2	(B)	7.0	9.8	18.4	18
Hispanic	811,370	56.1	(B)	8.0	15.4	33.4	22

B Base figure too small to meet statistical standards for reliability. In this case, 10 or fewer sample cases.   [1] Represents t total number of full and part-time college or university students who experience violence.   [2] All racial categories do not inclu Hispanics. "Other" includes Asian, Pacific Islanders, and Native Americans.

Source: U.S. Department of Justice, Office of Justice Programs, Bureau of Justice Statistics, *Violent Victimizations of Colle Students, 1995–2002*, Series NCJ 206836, January 2005. <http://www.ojp.usdoj.gov/bjs/cvict_v.htm#publications>

Table 315. Victim-Offender Relationship in Crimes of Violence by Characteristics of the Criminal Incident: 2004

[In percent. Covers only crimes of violence. Based on National Crime Victimization Survey; see text, this section, and Appendix III]

Characteristics of incident	Total	Rape/ sexual assault	Robbery	Assault Total	Assault Aggra-vated[1]	Assault Simple
Total	**100.0**	**100.0**	**100.0**	**100.0**	**100.0**	**100.0**
Victim/offender relationship: [2]						
Relatives	11.1	3.6	7.6	11.8	13.2	11.4
Well-known	23.5	27.1	23.2	23.4	22.6	23.6
Casual acquaintance	15.6	26.1	6.2	16.2	10.6	17.9
Stranger	43.3	33.5	56.4	42.3	47.5	40.8
Time of day: [3]						
6 a.m. to 6 p.m.	50.9	34.8	45.1	52.4	42.9	55.0
6 p.m. to midnight	35.8	34.3	41.4	35.3	39.8	34.0
Midnight to 6 a.m.	10.5	24.3	13.0	9.6	13.2	8.5
Location of crime:						
At or near victim's home or lodging	30.5	33.8	29.2	30.5	32.1	30.1
Friend's/relative's/neighbor's home	6.9	20.2	5.2	6.4	9.2	5.6
Commercial places	13.9	9.6	5.2	15.1	13.9	15.4
Parking lots/garages	7.7	9.9	8.4	7.5	7.9	7.4
School	14.2	6.5	5.9	15.5	6.5	18.0
Streets other than near victim's home . . .	15.2	1.7	32.5	14.0	16.0	13.4
Other [4]	11.5	18.2	13.6	11.1	14.6	10.1
Victim's activity: [5]						
At work or traveling to or from work	19.9	10.4	11.3	(NA)	21.8	21.2
School	12.4	7.6	10.1	(NA)	7.3	14.5
Activities at home	24.8	38.2	20.3	(NA)	25.7	24.4
Shopping/errands	3.8	1.2	9.6	(NA)	2.3	3.5
Leisure activities away from home	22.4	40.3	13.4	(NA)	25.4	21.7
Traveling	8.1	0.0	21.0	(NA)	9.6	6.4
Other [6]	8.1	2.3	12.9	(NA)	7.7	7.9
Distance from victim's home: [7]						
Inside home or lodging	17.2	31.0	20.9	16.1	17.9	15.6
Near victim's home	15.2	3.7	13.3	16.0	18.3	15.4
1 mile or less	20.7	9.2	32.7	19.9	17.8	20.5
5 miles or less	21.6	24.5	16.7	22.0	17.7	23.2
50 miles or less	21.8	28.0	12.4	22.6	24.6	22.0
More than 50 miles	2.5	3.6	3.5	2.4	2.8	2.2
Weapons:						
No weapons present	69.3	86.9	47.9	70.8	6.4	88.7
Weapons present	22.1	7.9	46.3	20.1	92.2	–
Firearm	5.9	–	18.5	4.8	21.9	–
Other type of weapon [8]	16.2	8.0	27.8	15.2	70.4	–

NA Not available. – Represents zero. [1] An aggravated assault is any assault in which an offender possesses or uses a weapon or inflicts serious injury. [2] Excludes "don't know" relationships. [3] Excludes "not known and not available" time of day. [4] Includes areas on public transportation or inside station, in apartment yard, park, field, playground, or other areas. [5] Excludes "don't know" and "not available" victim activity. [6] Includes sleeping. [7] Excludes "don't know" and "not available" distance from victim's home. [8] Includes knives, other sharp objects, blunt objects, and other types of weapons.

Source: U.S. Department of Justice, Office of Justice Programs, Bureau of Justice Statistics, *Criminal Victimization*, annual; and series NCJ-210265, September 2005. See also <http://www.ojp.usdoj.gov/bjs/abstract/cv04.htm>.

Table 316. Property Victimization Rates by Selected Household Characteristic: 2004

[Victimizations per 1,000 households. Based on National Crime Victimization Survey; see text, this section, and Appendix III]

Characteristic	Total	Burglary	Motor vehicle theft	Theft
Total	**161.1**	**29.6**	**8.8**	**122.8**
Race:				
White	156.8	27.6	7.6	121.6
Black	190.6	44.3	15.6	130.6
Other	137.9	22.8	11.4	103.7
Ethnicity:				
Hispanic	203.8	36.5	19.5	147.9
Non-Hispanic	156.4	28.9	7.5	120.0
Household income:				
Less than $7,500	197.1	59.3	[1]4.9	132.8
$7,500 to $14,999	181.5	38.5	9.7	133.3
$15,000 to $24,999	167.8	4.1	8.7	119.0
$25,000 to $34,999	169.3	27.6	11.1	130.6
$35,000 to $49,999	176.2	33.4	9.3	133.6
$50,000 to $74,999	167.0	21.8	9.0	136.2
$75,000 or more	176.5	23.9	7.4	145.1
Residence:				
Urban	214.7	41.9	13.4	159.4
Suburban	143.2	23.2	8.8	111.2
Rural	134.4	27.8	3.4	103.2
Form of tenure:				
Home owned	142.8	24.9	7.1	110.8
Home rented	201.4	39.9	12.5	148.9

[1] Based on 10 or fewer sample cases.

Source: U.S. Department of Justice, Office of Justice Programs, Bureau of Justice Statistics, *Criminal Victimization*, annual; and series NCJ-210674, September 2005. See also <http://www.ojp.usdoj.gov/bjs/abstract/cv04.htm>.

Law Enforcement, Courts, and Prisons 201

Table 317. **Persons Arrested by Charge and Selected Characteristics: 2004**

[In thousands (10,047.3 represents 10,047,300). Represents arrests (not charges) reported by approximately 10,830 agencies with a total 2004 population of approximately 210 million as estimated by FBI. Age and sex data are mandatory, while race data are optional and not always reported with arrest data; hence, two different total number of arrests]

Offense	Total arrests	Male	Female	Total arrests	White	Black	American Indian or Alaska Native	Asian or Pacific Islander
Total	10,047.3	7,659.4	2,387.9	10,021.1	7,067.4	2,714.0	131.5	108.1
Serious crimes:								
Murder and nonnegligent manslaughter	10.0	8.8	1.2	10.0	4.9	4.8	0.1	0.2
Forcible rape	18.7	18.4	0.3	18.6	12.2	6.0	0.2	0.2
Robbery	79.3	70.6	8.7	79.2	35.6	42.5	0.5	0.7
Aggravated assault	316.6	251.0	65.6	316.0	203.9	104.6	4.0	3.6
Burglary.	211.5	181.4	30.1	211.2	149.7	57.4	2.1	2.0
Larceny/theft	866.2	534.8	331.4	863.9	596.8	243.7	11.0	12.4
Motor vehicle theft.	105.7	87.7	18.1	105.6	67.0	36.1	1.1	1.5
Arson	11.1	9.3	1.8	11.1	8.5	2.3	0.1	0.1
All other nonserious crimes:								
Other assaults	923.1	695.7	227.4	920.8	607.0	291.0	12.2	10.6
Forgery and counterfeiting	86.1	51.9	34.2	86.0	60.3	24.2	0.5	1.0
Fraud	200.0	110.2	89.7	199.3	143.8	52.8	1.3	1.4
Embezzlement	12.6	6.3	6.4	12.6	8.7	3.6	0.1	0.2
Stolen property—buying, receiving, possessing.	93.3	75.9	17.4	93.2	58.5	33.0	0.7	0.9
Vandalism	199.1	165.4	33.6	198.5	150.4	43.3	2.8	2.0
Weapons; carrying, possessing etc.	127.5	117.1	10.5	127.3	79.4	45.7	1.0	1.2
Prostitution and commercialized vice.	64.8	20.0	44.8	64.7	37.0	26.0	0.4	1.2
Sex offenses (except forcible rape and prostitution)	65.3	59.8	5.5	65.2	48.0	15.8	0.6	0.8
Drug abuse violations.	1,251.1	1,015.0	236.1	1,249.1	822.3	410.6	7.9	8.4
Gambling.	7.7	7.0	0.7	7.7	2.1	5.4	–	0.2
Offenses against family and children.	88.7	67.4	21.4	88.5	60.4	26.2	1.4	0.5
Driving under the influence	1,014.1	824.7	189.4	1,011.1	894.2	91.9	14.6	10.5
Liquor laws.	439.6	325.5	114.1	437.3	376.6	44.5	11.6	4.6
Drunkenness	399.1	339.7	59.4	398.2	335.5	51.9	8.7	2.1
Disorderly conduct.	494.2	367.4	126.8	492.6	317.5	163.5	7.5	4.1
Vagrancy	25.7	20.7	4.9	25.7	16.0	9.0	0.5	0.2
Suspicion.	2.5	1.9	0.6	2.5	1.7	0.8	–	–
Curfew and loitering law violations	99.7	68.8	30.9	99.6	65.6	32.2	0.6	1.3
Runaways	86.1	35.3	50.8	85.9	63.1	18.3	1.4	3.2
All other offenses (except traffic)	2,747.5	2,121.5	626.0	2,739.7	1,840.7	827.3	38.7	33.0

– Represents zero.

Source: U.S. Department of Justice, Federal Bureau of Investigation, *Crime in the United States,* annual. See also <http://www.fbi.gov/ucr/cius_04/persons_arrested/index.html> (accessed 17 February 2006).

Table 318. **Juvenile Arrests for Selected Offenses: 1980 to 2004**

[169,439 represents 169,439,000. Juveniles are persons under 18 years of age]

Offense	1980	1990	1995	1998	1999	2000	2001	2002	2003	2004
Number of contributing agencies	8,178	10,765	10,037	9,589	9,502	9,904	10,281	10,946	11,368	11,437
Population covered (1,000) . . .	169,439	204,543	206,762	194,612	195,324	204,965	215,380	220,157	219,562	222,147
NUMBER										
Violent crime, total	77,220	97,103	123,131	90,201	81,715	78,450	78,443	71,059	69,060	68,247
Murder.	1,475	2,661	2,812	1,587	1,131	1,027	1,069	1,014	960	829
Forcible rape	3,668	4,971	4,556	3,988	3,544	3,402	3,504	3,553	3,195	3,186
Robbery	38,529	34,944	47,240	29,989	26,125	24,206	23,408	19,491	18,950	19,000
Aggravated assault.	33,548	54,527	68,523	54,637	50,915	49,815	50,462	47,001	45,955	45,232
Weapon law violations	21,203	33,123	46,506	34,122	31,307	28,514	29,290	26,786	29,512	30,530
Drug abuse, total	86,685	66,300	149,236	148,066	138,774	146,594	146,758	133,557	134,746	135,056
Sale and manufacturing. . . .	13,004	24,575	34,077	29,312	26,134	26,432	24,649	22,086	21,987	21,136
Heroin/cocaine	1,318	17,511	19,187	15,094	12,686	11,000	10,535	8,832	7,848	7,852
Marijuana	8,876	4,372	10,682	10,808	10,770	11,792	10,552	9,962	10,463	9,743
Synthetic narcotics	465	346	701	813	722	945	911	974	1,043	1,119
Dangerous nonnarcotic drugs	2,345	2,346	3,507	2,597	1,956	2,695	2,651	2,318	2,633	2,422
Possession	73,681	41,725	115,159	118,754	112,640	120,432	122,109	111,471	112,759	113,920
Heroin/cocaine	2,614	15,194	21,253	16,278	13,445	12,586	11,734	10,969	9,932	10,805
Marijuana	64,465	20,940	82,015	91,467	89,523	95,962	97,088	85,769	87,909	87,717
Synthetic narcotics	1,524	1,155	2,047	1,916	1,581	2,052	2,237	2,805	2,872	3,279
Dangerous nonnarcotic drugs	5,078	4,436	9,844	9,093	8,091	9,832	11,050	11,928	12,046	12,119

Source: U.S. Department of Justice, Federal Bureau of Investigation, *Crime in the United States,* annual. See also <http://www.fbi.gov/ucr/cius_04/persons_arrested/index.html> (accessed 17 February 2006).

Table 319. Drug Use by Arrestees in Major U.S. Cities by Type of Drug and Sex: 2003

[Percent testing positive. Based on data from the Arrestee Drug Abuse Monitoring Program]

City	Male Any drug [1]	Marijuana	Cocaine	Opiates	Female Any drug [1]	Marijuana	Cocaine	Opiates
Albuquerque, NM	70.3	41.6	35.0	11.2	70.0	29.4	38.1	13.8
Atlanta, GA	73.5	41.8	49.8	3.0	(NA)	(NA)	(NA)	(NA)
Chicago, IL	86.0	53.2	50.6	24.9	66.7	38.9	33.3	22.2
Cleveland, OH	74.9	48.9	39.0	5.4	72.4	27.2	52.7	6.7
Dallas, TX	63.8	39.1	32.7	6.9	(NA)	(NA)	(NA)	(NA)
Denver, CO	72.6	42.3	38.3	6.8	75.1	34.3	52.5	6.1
Indianapolis, IN	66.4	44.8	35.3	5.1	79.9	42.0	55.7	5.7
Las Vegas, NV	70.0	34.4	21.9	6.4	(NA)	(NA)	(NA)	(NA)
Los Angeles, CA	68.9	40.7	23.5	2.0	63.0	29.6	25.9	0.0
New Orleans, LA	79.6	50.8	47.6	14.0	62.2	30.3	37.3	13.3
New York, NY	72.7	43.1	35.7	15.0	73.3	36.7	50.0	23.3
Oklahoma City, OK	73.5	54.9	24.6	3.0	78.4	43.3	35.3	5.6
Philadelphia, PA	68.8	45.8	30.3	11.5	(NA)	(NA)	(NA)	(NA)
Phoenix, AZ	76.8	40.9	23.4	4.4	78.5	31.6	28.1	6.1
Portland, OR	72.7	38.4	29.7	15.0	84.4	35.2	39.6	22.0
Sacramento, CA	81.1	49.2	21.6	6.9	(NA)	(NA)	(NA)	(NA)
San Antonio, TX	65.2	41.9	30.5	9.1	(NA)	(NA)	(NA)	(NA)
San Diego, CA	71.2	41.0	10.3	5.1	72.6	29.1	15.2	8.7
San Jose, CA	63.7	35.4	12.9	3.1	72.8	29.1	10.1	3.4
Seattle, WA	69.4	37.2	36.6	6.8	(NA)	(NA)	(NA)	(NA)
Tucson, AZ	76.4	44.1	42.5	4.2	73.2	29.0	40.0	9.7
Washington, DC	65.8	37.4	26.5	9.8	66.7	29.1	30.9	10.9

NA Not available. [1] Includes other drugs not shown separately.

Source: U.S. National Institute of Justice, *ADAM 2003 Annual Report on Drug Use Among Adult and Juvenile Arrestees*, June 2004. See also <http://www.ncjrs.org/drgswww.html#top>.

Table 320. Drug Arrest Rates for Drug Abuse Violations, 1990 to 2004, and by Region, 2004

[Rate per 100,000 inhabitants. Based on Census Bureau estimated resident population as of July 1, except 1990 and 2000, enumerated as of April 1. For composition of regions, see map, inside front cover]

Offense	1990	1995	2000	2004 Total	North-east	Mid-west	South	West
Drug arrest rate, total	435.3	564.7	587.1	555.0	481.8	399.7	606.6	661.0
Sale and/or manufacture	139.0	140.7	122.7	101.7	116.3	73.7	111.4	101.4
Heroin or cocaine [1]	93.7	83.7	60.8	46.3	76.3	20.8	53.0	37.2
Marijuana	26.4	32.7	34.2	27.8	29.6	29.0	27.3	26.5
Synthetic or manufactured drugs	2.7	3.9	6.4	8.7	4.8	6.1	16.0	4.7
Other dangerous nonnarcotic drugs	16.2	20.3	21.3	18.9	5.6	17.8	15.1	33.1
Possession	296.3	423.9	464.4	453.3	365.5	326.0	495.2	559.6
Heroin or cocaine [1]	144.4	157.4	138.7	121.1	121.2	56.6	136.7	150.7
Marijuana	104.9	192.7	244.4	219.9	204.9	201.0	284.9	169.0
Synthetic or manufactured drugs	6.6	8.5	12.0	19.3	8.7	13.9	27.4	21.5
Other dangerous nonnarcotic drugs	40.4	65.4	69.4	93.0	30.6	54.5	46.1	218.3

[1] Includes other derivatives such as morphine, heroin, and codeine.

Source: U.S. Department of Justice, Federal Bureau of Investigation, *Crime in the United States*, annual. See also http://www.fbi.gov/ucr/cius_04/persons_arrested/index.html> (accessed 17 February 2006).

Table 321. Federal Drug Seizures by Type of Drug: 1990 to 2005

[In pounds. For fiscal years ending in year shown. Reflects the combined drug seizure effort of the Drug Enforcement Administration, the Federal Bureau of Investigation, the U.S. Customs Services, and beginning October 1995, the U.S. Border Patrol within the jurisdiction of the United States as well as maritime seizures by the U.S. Coast Guard. Based on reports to the Federal-wide Drug Seizure System, which eliminates duplicate reporting of a seizure involving more than one federal agency. Data have been revised for years through 2004]

Drug	1990	1995	1999	2000	2001	2002	2003	2004	2005
Total	464,583	1,574,890	2,568,899	2,888,169	2,922,543	2,649,756	2,956,580	3,047,047	2,821,890
Heroin	1,704	2,971	2,727	3,341	4,358	6,859	5,920	4,078	4,294
Cocaine	235,891	234,342	282,207	248,894	237,857	225,368	245,623	336,365	398,842
Cannabis	226,988	1,337,577	2,283,965	2,635,934	2,680,328	2,417,529	2,705,037	2,706,604	2,418,754
Marijuana	219,249	1,305,701	2,282,287	2,611,947	2,679,898	2,417,343	2,703,664	2,706,031	2,418,754
Hashish	7,739	31,876	1,678	23,987	430	186	1,373	573	818

Source: U.S. Drug Enforcement Administration, unpublished data from Federal-wide Drug Seizure System.

Law Enforcement, Courts, and Prisons 203

Table 322. **Authorized Intercepts of Communication—Summary: 1980 to 2005**

[Data for jurisdictions with statutes authorizing or approving interception of wire or oral communication]

Item	1980	1985	1990	1995	1999	2000	2001	2002	2003	2004	2005
Jurisdictions: [1]											
With wiretap statutes	28	32	40	41	45	45	46	47	47	47	47
Reporting interceptions	22	22	25	19	28	26	25	20	24	20	23
Intercept applications authorized	564	784	872	1,156	1,489	1,266	1,561	1,358	1,442	1,710	1,773
Intercept installations	524	722	812	1,024	1,277	1,139	1,405	1,273	1,367	1,633	1,694
Federal	79	235	321	527	595	472	481	490	576	723	624
State	445	487	491	497	682	667	924	783	791	910	1,070
Intercepted communications, average [2]	1,058	1,320	1,487	2,028	1,921	1,769	1,565	1,708	3,004	3,017	2,835
Incriminating, average [2]	315	275	321	459	390	402	333	403	993	619	629
Persons arrested [3]	1,871	2,469	2,057	2,577	4,372	3,411	3,683	3,060	3,674	4,056	4,674
Convictions [3]	259	660	420	494	654	736	732	493	843	634	776
Major offense specified:											
Gambling	199	206	116	95	60	49	82	82	49	90	42
Drugs	282	434	520	732	978	894	1,167	1,052	1,104	1,308	1,433
Homicide and assault	13	25	21	30	62	72	52	58	80	48	82
Racketeering	(NA)	(NA)	(NA)	98	139	76	70	72	96	138	94
Other	70	119	215	201	250	175	190	94	113	126	122

NA Not available   [1] Jurisdictions include federal government, states, and District of Columbia.   [2] Average per authorized installation.   [3] Based on information received from intercepts installed in year shown; additional arrests/convictions will occur in subsequent years but are not shown here.

Source: Administrative Office of the U.S. Courts, *Report on Applications for Orders Authorizing or Approving the Interception of Wire, Oral or Electronic Communications* (Wiretap Report), annual. See also <http://www.uscourts.gov/wiretap05/contents.html> (accessed April 2006).

Table 323. **Background Checks for Firearm Transfers: 1994 to 2004**

[In thousands (61,632 represents 61,632,000), except rates. For "Interim period" of 1994 to November 29, 1998, covered handgun purchases from licensed firearm dealers; beginning November 29, 1998, (effective date for the Brady Handgun Violence Prevention Act, P.L. 103-159,1993) covers the transfer of both handguns and long guns from a federal firearms licensee, as well as purchases from pawnshops and retail gun shops]

Inquiries and rejections	1994–2004 period [1]	Interim period		Permanent Brady					
		1995	1998 [2]	1999	2000	2001	2002	2003	2004
Applications and rejections:									
Applications received	61,632	2,706	3,277	8,621	7,699	7,958	7,806	7,831	8,084
Applications rejected	1,228	41	90	204	153	151	136	126	126
Rejection rate	2.0	1.5	2.9	2.4	2.0	1.9	1.7	1.6	1.6

[1] Represents from the inception of the Brady Act on February 29, 1994, to 2004.   [2] For period January 1 to November 29, 1998. Counts are from the National Instant Criminal Background Check System and may include multiple transactions for the same application.

Source: U.S. Department of Justice, Office of Justice Programs, Bureau of Justice Statistics, Presale Handgun Checks, The Brady Interim Period 1994–1998, Series NCJ 175034, June 1999. Background Checks for Firearm Transfers, 2003: Trends for Permanent Brady Period, 1999–2003, Series NCJ 204428, September 2004. Background Checks for Firearm Transfers, 2004, Series NCJ 210117, October 2005. <http://www.ojp.usdoj.gov/bjs/guns.htm>.

Table 324. **Requests for Forensic Services: 2002**

Type of function	Back-logged request [1]	New requests	Requests completed [2]	Type of function	Back-logged request [1]	New requests	Requests completed [2]
Total	289,938	2,706,785	2,495,313	Trace	9,997	41,531	36,878
Controlled substances	95,404	1,291,488	1,154,221	DNA analysis	29,516	60,887	41,592
Biology screening	18,456	88,857	76,332	Toxicology	17,523	467,752	455,624
Firearms/toolmarks	22,636	104,068	88,997	Questioned documents	3,391	16,683	15,562
Crime scene	1,579	166,588	165,461	Computer crimes	952	2,839	2,757
Latent prints	50,245	274,225	238,135	Other functions	40,239	191,867	219,754

[1] As of January 2, 2002.   [2] As of December 31, 2002

Source: U.S. Department of Justice, Office of Justice Programs, Bureau of Justice Statistics, *Census of Publicly Funded Forensic Crime Laboratories, 2003* Series NCJ 207205, February 2005.

Table 325. Law Enforcement Officers Killed and Assaulted: 1990 to 2004

[Covers officers killed feloniously and accidentally in line of duty; includes federal officers. For composition of regions, see map, inside front cover]

Item	1990	1995	1998	1999	2000	2001 [1]	2002	2003	2004
OFFICERS KILLED									
Total killed	132	133	142	107	134	218	132	133	139
Northeast	13	16	6	11	13	79	10	13	18
Midwest	20	19	19	17	32	26	22	20	25
South.................	68	63	70	56	67	68	65	66	66
West	23	32	36	22	19	38	28	31	24
Puerto Rico...........	8	2	9	1	3	7	7	3	6
Island areas, foreign countries..............	–	1	2	–	–	–	–	–	–
Feloniously killed	65	74	61	42	51	142	56	52	57
Firearms	56	62	58	41	47	61	51	45	54
Handgun	47	43	40	25	33	46	38	34	36
Rifle	8	14	17	11	10	11	10	10	13
Shotgun............	1	5	1	5	4	4	3	1	5
Knife	3	2	1	–	1	–	1	–	1
Bomb	–	8	1	–	–	–	–	–	–
Personal weapons	2	–	–	–	–	1	–	–	–
Other	4	2	–	1	3	80	4	7	2
Accidentally killed.........	67	59	81	65	83	76	76	81	82
OFFICERS ASSAULTED									
Population (1,000) [2]	197,426	191,759	193,098	207,124	204,599	213,645	219,425	225,770	225,598
Number of—									
Agencies represented	9,343	8,503	8,153	9,832	8,940	9,773	10,164	10,539	10,459
Police officers.........	410,131	428,379	452,361	462,782	452,531	471,096	491,009	501,738	499,396
Total assaulted	72,091	57,762	60,673	55,971	58,398	57,463	59,526	58,600	59,373
Firearm	3,651	2,354	2,126	1,772	1,749	1,841	1,927	1,879	2,109
Knife or cutting instrument ...	1,647	1,356	1,098	999	1,015	1,168	1,061	1,084	1,121
Other dangerous weapon ...	7,423	6,414	7,415	7,560	8,132	8,233	8,526	8,180	8,598
Hands, fists, feet, etc	59,370	47,638	50,034	45,640	47,502	46,221	48,012	47,457	47,545

– Represents zero. [1] The 72 officers feloniously slain during the events of September 11, 2001, are included in data for 2001.
[2] Represents the number of persons covered by agencies shown.

Source: U.S. Department of Justice, Federal Bureau of Investigation, *Law Enforcement Officers Killed and Assaulted*, annual. <http://www.fbi.gov/ucr/killed/2004/openpage.htm>.

Table 326. U.S. Supreme Court—Cases Filed and Disposition: 1980 to 2004

[Statutory term of court begins first Monday in **October**]

Action	1980	1990	1995	1999	2000	2001	2002	2003	2004
Total cases on docket	5,144	6,316	7,565	8,445	8,965	9,176	9,406	8,882	8,588
Appellate cases on docket...........	2,749	2,351	2,456	2,413	2,305	2,210	2,190	2,058	2,041
From prior term	527	365	361	321	351	324	321	336	300
Docketed during present term	2,222	1,986	2,095	2,092	1,954	1,886	1,869	1,722	1,741
Cases acted upon	2,324	2,042	2,130	2,096	2,024	1,932	1,899	1,798	1,727
Granted review	167	114	92	78	85	82	83	74	69
Denied, dismissed, or withdrawn	1,999	1,802	1,945	1,958	1,842	1,751	1,727	1,641	1,529
Summarily decided	90	81	62	34	63	57	46	37	89
Cases not acted upon	425	309	326	317	281	278	291	260	314
Pauper cases on docket	2,371	3,951	5,098	6,024	6,651	6,958	7,209	6,818	6,543
Cases acted upon [1].............	2,027	3,436	4,514	5,273	5,736	6,139	6,488	6,036	5,815
Granted review	17	27	13	14	6	6	8	13	11
Denied, dismissed, or withdrawn	1,968	3,369	4,439	5,239	5,658	6,114	6,459	6,005	5,061
Summarily decided	32	28	55	16	61	13	17	13	737
Cases not acted upon	344	515	584	751	915	819	721	782	728
Original cases on docket	24	14	11	8	9	8	7	6	4
Cases disposed of during term	7	3	5	–	2	1	1	2	–
Total cases available for argument .	264	201	145	124	138	137	139	140	128
Cases disposed of	162	131	93	87	89	90	87	93	87
Cases argued	154	125	90	83	86	88	84	91	87
Cases dismissed or remanded without argument	8	6	3	4	3	2	3	2	–
Cases remaining	102	70	52	37	49	47	52	47	41
Cases decided by signed opinion	144	121	87	79	83	85	79	89	85
Cases decided by per curiam opinion.....	8	4	3	4	4	3	5	2	2
Number of signed opinions.	123	112	75	74	77	76	71	73	74

– Represents zero. [1] Includes cases granted review and carried over to next term, not shown separately.

Source: Office of the Clerk, Supreme Court of the United States, unpublished data.

Table 327. **U.S. District Courts—Civil Cases Commenced and Pending: 2000 to 2005**

[For years ending June 30]

Type of case	Cases commenced				Cases pending			
	2000	2003	2004	2005	2000	2003	2004	2005
Cases total [1]	263,049	254,499	258,117	282,758	249,692	261,608	267,881	267,270
Contract actions [1]	54,494	32,356	29,687	28,590	38,262	30,789	28,413	26,712
Recovery of overpayments [2]	25,636	3,466	2,914	3,380	12,107	2,713	2,146	1,953
Real property actions	6,481	7,503	6,341	4,541	4,249	6,302	5,651	4,512
Tort actions	40,877	46,295	51,881	75,273	63,116	65,562	74,589	76,821
Personal injury [1]	36,867	42,233	45,948	52,215	59,232	61,496	68,928	72,716
Personal injury product liability [1]	15,349	24,255	29,089	35,615	31,772	34,655	42,886	46,575
Asbestos	7,893	3,718	1,208	1,628	4,949	5,606	2,528	1,073
Other personal injury	21,518	17,978	16,859	16,600	27,460	26,841	26,042	26,141
Personal property damage	4,010	4,062	5,933	23,058	3,884	4,066	5,661	4,105
Actions under statutes [1]	161,187	168,332	170,168	171,922	144,053	158,943	159,200	157,357
Civil rights [1]	41,226	40,567	40,118	36,724	44,259	43,981	43,431	40,596
Employment	21,404	20,777	19,670	17,998	24,456	23,618	22,964	21,344
Bankruptcy suits	3,378	3,342	3,982	3,428	2,555	2,522	2,684	2,650
Commerce (ICC rates, etc.)	1,007	574	483	492	444	455	427	395
Environmental matters	894	935	999	726	1,355	2,296	2,282	1,193
Prisoner petitions	57,706	55,112	53,132	62,698	43,560	44,306	44,317	47,870
Forfeiture and penalty	2,246	2,120	2,112	2,214	1,772	1,932	2,017	2,156
Labor laws	14,229	17,290	18,189	18,643	11,267	14,621	15,131	15,725
Protected property rights [3]	8,745	8,613	9,289	11,809	7,858	8,654	8,992	10,507
Securities commodities and exchanges	2,500	3,449	3,081	2,371	3,578	5,227	5,325	5,192
Social Security laws	14,365	17,483	15,935	16,066	13,667	17,526	14,853	15,420
Tax suits	938	1,232	1,291	1,348	1,068	1,106	1,158	1,222
Freedom of information	335	266	300	426	380	347	360	378

[1] Includes other types not shown separately.   [2] Includes enforcement of judgments in student loan cases, and overpayments of veterans benefits.   [3] Includes copyright, patent, and trademark rights.

Source: Administrative Office of the U.S. Courts, *Statistical Tables for the Federal Judiciary,* annual.

Table 328. **U.S. District Courts—Offenders Convicted and Sentenced to Prison and Length of Sentence: 2003**

Most serious offense of conviction	Offenders convicted	Convicted offenders sentenced to prison	Mean length of sentence (mo.) [1]	Most serious offense of conviction	Offenders convicted	Convicted offenders sentenced to prison	Mean length of sentence (mo.) [1]
Total [2]	75,805	57,629	58.7	Possession	2,061	1,840	82.7
Violent offenses	2,643	2,462	97.2	Trafficking and manufacturing	23,521	21,704	81.2
Property offenses	13,311	7,948	27.3	Public-order offenses	4,331	3,036	42.9
Fraudulent offenses [3]	11,323	6,737	24.8	Regulatory offenses	1,136	542	33.2
Embezzlement	786	391	16.9	Other offenses	3,195	2,494	45.0
Fraud [4]	9,373	5,599	25.4	Tax law violations [5]	404	250	21.9
Forgery	77	33	20.3	Weapons	6,970	6,431	83.7
Other offenses [3]	1,988	1,211	41.1	Immigration	14,199	12,390	26.7
Larceny	1,442	781	31.7	Misdemeanors	8,767	1,818	9.1
Drug offenses [3]	25,582	23,544	81.4				

[1] Excludes sentences of life, death, and indeterminate sentences.   [2] Total may include offenders for whom offense category could not be determined.   [3] Includes offenses not shown separately.   [4] Excludes tax fraud.   [5] Includes tax fraud.

Source: U.S. Department of Justice, Office of Justice Programs, Bureau of Justice Statistics, *Compendium of Federal Justice Statistics, 2003,* Series NCJ 210299, October 2005; <http://www.ojp.usdoj.gov/bjs/abstract/cfjs03.htm>.

Table 329. **Federal Prosecutions of Public Corruption: 1980 to 2004**

[As of Dec. 31. Prosecution of persons who have corrupted public office in violation of Federal Criminal Statutes]

Prosecution Status	1980	1985	1990	1995	1997	1998	1999	2000	2001	2002	2003	2004
Total: [1] Charged	727	1,157	1,176	1,051	1,057	1,174	1,134	1,000	1,087	1,136	1,150	1,213
Convicted	602	997	1,084	878	853	1,014	1,065	938	920	1,011	868	1,020
Awaiting trial	213	256	300	323	327	340	329	327	437	413	412	419
Federal officials: Charged	123	563	615	527	459	442	480	441	502	478	479	424
Convicted	131	470	583	438	392	414	460	422	414	429	421	381
Awaiting trial	16	90	103	120	83	85	101	92	131	119	129	98
State officials: Charged	72	79	96	61	51	91	115	92	95	110	94	111
Convicted	51	66	79	61	49	58	80	91	61	132	87	81
Awaiting trial	28	20	28	23	20	37	44	37	75	50	38	48
Local officials: Charged	247	248	257	236	255	277	237	211	224	299	259	268
Convicted	168	221	225	191	169	264	219	183	184	262	119	252
Awaiting trial	82	49	98	89	118	90	95	89	110	118	106	105
Others involved: Charged	285	267	208	227	292	364	302	256	266	249	318	410
Convicted	252	240	197	188	243	278	306	242	261	188	241	306
Awaiting trial	87	97	71	91	106	128	89	109	121	126	139	168

[1] Includes individuals who are neither public officials nor employees but were involved with public officials or employees in violating the law, not shown separately.

Source: U.S. Department of Justice, *Federal Prosecutions of Corrupt Public Officials, 1970-1980* and *Report to Congress on the Activities and Operations of the Public Integrity Section,* annual; <http://www.usdoj.gov/criminal/pin.html>.

Table 330. Delinquency Cases Disposed by Juvenile Courts by Reason for Referral: 1990 to 2002

[In thousands (1,318 represents 1,318,000), except rate. A delinquency offense is an act committed by a juvenile for which an adult could be prosecuted in a criminal court. Disposition of a case involves taking a definite action such as waiving the case to criminal court, dismissing the case, placing the youth on probation, placing the youth in a facility for delinquents, or such actions as fines, restitution, and community service. Data has been revised through 2001]

Reason for referral	1990	1993	1994	1995	1996	1997	1998	1999	2000	2001	2002
All delinquency cases	1,318	1,521	1,667	1,763	1,807	1,822	1,755	1,670	1,624	1,621	1,615
Case rate [1]	51.4	55.2	59.3	61.5	62.2	61.8	58.9	55.3	52.9	52.2	51.6
Violent offenses	93	116	128	133	125	106	98	86	80	78	75
Criminal homicide	2	3	3	3	3	2	2	2	2	2	2
Forcible rape	5	7	6	6	6	5	5	4	5	5	5
Robbery	27	35	38	40	38	34	30	25	22	22	22
Aggravated assault	58	72	81	84	78	64	60	54	51	49	47
Property offenses	772	833	871	891	884	853	782	703	663	628	625
Burglary	562	592	610	632	629	607	543	484	459	433	431
Larceny-theft	143	149	144	141	145	141	131	112	105	101	100
Motor vehicle theft	340	373	395	426	419	402	356	322	308	286	284
Arson	72	63	62	55	55	55	48	40	37	38	39
Delinquency offenses	664	813	928	998	1,054	1,109	1,114	1,101	1,085	1,110	1,109
Simple assault	132	178	199	220	226	255	261	258	254	270	271
Vandalism	99	118	128	124	122	116	114	107	102	95	95
Drug law violations	73	92	130	164	183	192	192	190	192	202	193
Obstruction of justice	80	95	111	123	151	166	170	171	180	187	183
Other [2]	280	331	360	367	372	380	378	375	357	356	368

[1] Number of cases disposed per 1,000 youth (ages 10 to 17) at risk of referral to juvenile court. [2] Includes such offenses as stolen property offenses, trespassing, weapons offenses, other sex offenses, liquor law violations, disorderly conduct, and miscellaneous offenses.

Source: National Center for Juvenile Justice, Pittsburgh, PA, *Juvenile Court Statistics*, annual. See also <http://www.ojjdp.ncjrs.org /ojstatbb/index.html>.

Table 331. Delinquency Cases and Case Rates by Sex and Race: 1992 to 2002

[Data has been revised through 2000. See headnote, Table 330]

Sex, race, and offense	Number of cases disposed			Case rate [1]		
	1992	2000	2002	1992	2000	2002
Male, total	1,196,100	1,218,900	1,192,300	86.6	77.4	74.3
Person	243,600	270,800	277,900	17.7	17.2	17.3
Property	693,600	497,400	460,400	50.3	31.6	28.7
Drugs	64,600	159,800	158,100	4.6	10.1	9.8
Public order	194,400	291,000	296,000	14.0	18.5	18.4
Female, total	285,500	404,700	423,100	21.9	27.1	27.7
Person	64,100	103,000	109,700	5.0	6.9	7.2
Property	166,600	165,900	164,500	12.8	11.1	10.8
Drugs	8,700	32,300	35,100	0.7	2.2	2.3
Public order	46,100	103,500	113,800	3.5	6.9	7.5
White, total	979,400	1,108,100	1,086,700	45.3	46.0	44.4
Person	177,600	230,400	233,700	8.2	9.6	9.5
Property	608,700	460,900	427,700	28.2	19.1	17.5
Drugs	37,500	144,100	146,300	1.7	6.0	6.0
Public order	155,700	272,700	279,100	7.1	11.3	11.4
Black, total	449,600	461,300	473,100	112.1	95.5	94.0
Person	120,800	132,300	141,900	30.1	27.4	28.2
Property	217,500	176,000	172,000	54.7	36.4	34.2
Drugs	34,100	43,300	41,400	8.3	9.0	8.2
Public order	77,200	109,700	117,800	19.1	22.7	23.4
Other races, total	52,700	54,200	55,600	40.5	31.0	30.9
Person	9,400	11,100	12,000	7.4	6.3	6.7
Property	34,000	26,300	25,100	26.0	15.1	14.0
Drugs	1,600	4,700	5,500	1.2	2.7	3.1
Public order	7,600	12,100	13,000	5.8	6.9	7.2

[1] Cases per 1,000 youth (ages 10 to 17) at risk.

Source: National Center for Juvenile Justice, Pittsburgh, PA, *Juvenile Court Statistics*, annual. See also <http://www.ojjdp.ncjrs.org /ojstatbb/index.html>.

Law Enforcement, Courts, and Prisons   207

Table 332. Child Abuse and Neglect Cases Substantiated and Indicated—Victim Characteristics: 1990 to 2004

[Based on reports alleging child abuse and neglect that were referred for investigation/assessment by the respective child protective services agency in each state. The reporting period may be either calendar or fiscal year. Children are counted each time they were subjects of an investigation report. Victims are children whose alleged maltreatments have been substantiated, indicated, or assessed as maltreatments. A substantiated case represents a type of investigation disposition that determines that there is sufficient evidence under state law to conclude that maltreatment occurred or that the child is at risk of maltreatment. An indicated case represents a type of disposition that concludes that there was a reason to suspect maltreatment had occurred. An alternative response-victim case represents a type of disposition that identifies a child as a victim within the alternative response system]

ITEM	1990		2000		2003		2004	
	Number	Percent	Number	Percent	Number	Percent	Number	Percent
TYPES OF SUBSTANTIATED MALTREATMENT [1]								
Victims, total [2]	690,658	(X)	864,837	(X)	893,296	113.3	872,088	113.4
Neglect	338,770	49.1	517,118	59.8	550,178	61.6	544,050	62.4
Physical abuse	186,801	27.0	167,713	19.4	164,689	18.4	152,250	17.5
Sexual abuse	119,506	17.3	87,770	10.2	87,078	9.8	84,398	9.7
Emotional maltreatment	45,621	6.6	66,965	7.7	57,391	6.4	61,272	7.0
Medical neglect	(NA)	(NA)	25,498	3.0	17,945	2.0	17,968	2.1
SEX OF VICTIM								
Victims, total	742,519	100.0	864,837	100.0	893,296	100.0	872,088	100.0
Male	323,339	43.5	413,744	47.8	428,948	48.0	419,743	48.1
Female	369,919	49.8	446,230	51.6	461,068	51.6	449,416	51.5
AGE OF VICTIM								
Victims, total	731,282	100.0	864,837	100.0	893,296	100.0	872,088	100.0
1 year and younger	97,101	13.3	133,094	15.4	144,508	16.2	145,773	16.7
2 to 5 years old	172,791	23.6	205,790	23.8	219,725	24.6	217,297	24.9
6 to 9 years old	157,681	21.6	212,186	24.5	202,070	22.6	192,941	22.1
10 to 13 years old	135,130	18.5	176,071	20.4	185,995	20.8	176,485	20.2
14 to 17 years old	103,383	14.1	126,207	14.6	135,998	15.2	135,858	15.6
18 and over	4,880	0.7	992	0.1	589	0.1	475	0.1

NA Not available.   X Not applicable.   [1] Not all types of maltreatment are shown.   [2] A child may be a victim of more than one maltreatment. Therefore, the total for this item adds up to more than 100%.

Source: U.S. Department of Health and Human Services, Administration for Children and Families, Statistics and Research, *Child Maltreatment 2004*, annual; <http://www.acf.hhs.gov/programs/cb/pubs/cm04/index.htm>.

Table 333. Child Abuse and Neglect Cases Reported and Investigated by State: 2004

[See headnote, Table 332]

State	Population under 18 years old	Number of children subject of an investigation [1]	Number of reports [2]	Number of child victims [3]	State	Population under 18 years old	Number of children subject of an investigation [1]	Number of reports [2]	Number of child victims [3]
U.S. [4]	73,277,998	3,423,347	1,859,386	872,088	MO	1,384,542	82,442	54,216	9,616
					MT	208,093	12,406	7,450	1,753
AL	1,094,533	31,300	19,118	9,414	NE	434,566	24,235	10,962	4,785
AK	188,229	(NA)	(NA)	(NA)	NV	603,596	24,004	13,061	4,377
AZ	1,547,260	81,121	35,623	7,344	NH	304,994	9,037	6,400	948
AR	676,550	44,472	20,748	7,276	NJ	2,156,059	79,057	44,127	8,159
CA	9,596,463	442,741	234,035	98,201					
CO	1,178,889	45,121	29,540	9,578	NM	492,287	26,095	16,005	6,150
CT	838,788	48,657	32,097	13,285	NY	4,572,363	250,459	148,244	74,483
DE	193,506	12,307	5,276	1,581	NC	2,118,492	108,636	53,668	29,085
DC	109,547	12,074	4,977	2,378	ND	138,955	6,818	3,912	1,668
FL	4,003,290	329,158	145,393	129,914	OH	2,779,212	110,972	70,280	43,093
GA	2,332,567	203,671	85,817	52,851	OK	859,870	63,684	36,070	12,483
					OR	852,357	37,865	23,529	11,759
HI	298,693	7,186	3,608	3,629	PA	2,837,009	23,862	23,862	4,647
ID	372,411	9,669	6,502	1,856	RI	243,813	9,920	6,707	3,068
IL	3,238,150	142,727	64,784	29,150	SC	1,024,700	38,462	17,186	9,950
IN	1,600,295	54,679	35,817	18,869					
IA	680,437	37,163	24,366	13,804	SD	190,874	8,355	4,620	1,917
KS	683,491	24,140	15,729	4,895	TN	1,391,289	74,835	48,622	14,840
KY	980,187	73,375	46,951	19,186	TX	6,266,779	226,614	140,038	50,891
LA	1,164,961	39,337	23,843	10,862	UT	740,114	33,746	21,132	13,559
ME	282,129	9,543	5,358	4,235	VT	134,894	3,361	2,690	1,138
MD	1,394,808	(NA)	(NA)	15,180	VA	1,804,900	56,088	28,105	6,959
MA	1,464,189	81,219	38,940	36,201	WA	1,486,020	50,865	32,314	6,730
MI	2,533,439	196,873	74,333	28,035	WV	384,641	40,916	18,508	8,446
MN	1,240,280	25,595	17,471	8,183	WI	1,307,986	40,205	40,205	9,325
MS	749,569	24,546	15,801	5,674	WY	116,932	3,734	2,018	678

NA Not available.   [1] Investigations represent the screening of referrals. The number is based on the total number of children for whom an alleged maltreatment was substantiated, indicated, or assessed to have occurred or the child was at risk of occurrence.   [2] Accepted or screened-in referrals are termed reports.   [3] Victims are defined as children subject of a substantiated, indicated, or alternative response-victim maltreatment.   [4] Includes estimates for states that did not report.

Source: U.S. Department of Health and Human Services, Administration for Children and Families, Statistics and Research, *Child Maltreatment 2004*, annual; <http://www.acf.hhs.gov/programs/cb/pubs/cm04/index.htm>.

Table 334. Prisoners Under Jurisdiction of Federal or State Correctional Authorities—Summary by State: 1990 to 2004

[For years ending December 31. Minus sign (–) indicates decrease]

State	1990	2000	2003	2004, advance Total	2004, advance Percent change, 2003–2004	State	1990	2000	2003	2004, advance Total	2004, advance Percent change, 2003–2004
U.S. [1]	773,919	1,391,261	1,468,601	1,496,629	1.9	MO	14,943	27,543	30,303	31,081	2.6
AL	15,665	26,332	27,913	25,887	-7.3	MT.....	1,425	3,105	3,620	3,877	7.1
AK [2]....	2,622	4,173	4,527	4,554	0.6	NE.....	2,403	3,895	4,040	4,130	2.2
AZ [3]	14,261	26,510	31,170	32,515	4.3	NV.....	5,322	10,063	10,543	11,365	7.8
AR.....	7,322	11,915	13,315	13,807	3.7	NH.....	1,342	2,257	2,434	2,448	0.6
CA.....	97,309	163,001	164,487	166,556	1.3	NJ.....	21,128	29,784	27,246	26,757	-1.8
CO.....	7,671	16,833	19,671	20,293	3.2	NM.....	3,187	5,342	6,223	6,379	2.5
CT [2]....	10,500	18,355	19,846	19,497	-1.8	NY.....	54,895	70,199	65,198	63,751	-2.2
DE [2]....	3,471	6,921	6,794	6,927	2.0	NC.....	18,411	31,266	33,560	35,434	5.6
DC [4, 5]..	9,947	7,456	(NA)	(NA)	(NA)	ND.....	483	1,076	1,239	1,327	7.1
FL [3]....	44,387	71,319	82,012	85,533	4.3	OH.....	31,822	45,833	44,778	44,806	0.1
GA [3]....	22,411	44,232	47,208	51,104	8.3	OK.....	12,285	23,181	22,821	23,319	2.2
HI [2]....	2,533	5,053	5,828	5,960	2.3	OR.....	6,492	10,580	12,715	13,183	3.7
ID	1,961	5,535	5,737	6,375	11.1	PA.....	22,290	36,847	40,890	40,963	0.2
IL.....	27,516	45,281	43,418	44,054	1.5	RI [2]....	2,392	3,286	3,527	3,430	-2.8
IN.....	12,736	20,125	23,069	24,008	4.1	SC.....	17,319	21,778	23,719	23,428	-1.2
IA [3]....	3,967	7,955	8,546	8,525	-0.2	SD.....	1,341	2,616	3,026	3,095	2.3
KS.....	5,775	8,344	9,132	8,966	-1.8	TN.....	10,388	22,166	25,403	25,884	1.9
KY.....	9,023	14,919	16,622	17,814	7.2	TX.....	50,042	166,719	166,911	168,105	0.7
LA.....	18,599	35,207	36,047	36,939	2.5	UT [2]....	2,496	5,637	5,763	5,989	3.9
ME.....	1,523	1,679	2,013	2,024	0.5	VT [2]....	1,049	1,697	1,944	1,968	1.2
MD.....	17,848	23,538	23,791	23,285	-2.1	VA.....	17,593	30,168	35,067	35,564	1.4
MA [5]....	8,345	10,722	10,232	10,144	-0.9	WA.....	7,995	14,915	16,148	16,614	2.9
MI [5]....	34,267	47,718	49,358	48,883	-1.0	WV.....	1,565	3,856	4,758	5,067	6.5
MN.....	3,176	6,238	7,865	8,758	11.4	WI.....	7,465	20,754	22,604	22,966	1.6
MS.....	8,375	20,241	20,589	20,983	1.9	WY	1,110	1,680	1,872	1,980	5.8

NA Not available. [1] For table 334 U.S.total includes Federal prisoners not distributed by State. This total includes all inmates held in public and private adult correctional facilities. [2] Includes both jail and prison inmates (state has combined jail and prison system). [3] Numbers are for custody rather than jurisdiction counts. [4] The transfer of responsibility for sentenced felons from the District of Columbia to the federal system was completed by the year end 2001. Since June 30, 2000, the inmate population in the District of Columbia has dropped by 5,825 inmates. Approximately 58% of the growth in the federal system in the last 6 months of 2001 was the result of this transfer of responsibility. [5] The District of Columbia inmates sentenced to more than 1 year are now under the responsibility of the Bureau of Prisons.

Source: U.S. Department of Justice, Office of Justice Programs, Bureau of Justice Statistics, *Prisoners in 2004*, Series NCJ 210677; and earlier reports. <http://www.ojp.usdoj.gov/bjs/prisons.htm>

Table 335. Adults on Probation, in Jail or Prison, or on Parole: 1980 to 2004

[As of December 31, except jail counts as of June 30]

Year	Total [1]	Percent of adult population	Probation	Jail	Prison	Parole	Male	Female
1980.........	1,840,400	(NA)	1,118,097	[2]182,288	319,598	220,438	(NA)	(NA)
1981.........	2,006,600	(NA)	1,225,934	[2]195,085	360,029	225,539	(NA)	(NA)
1982.........	2,192,600	(NA)	1,357,264	207,853	402,914	224,604	(NA)	(NA)
1983.........	2,475,100	(NA)	1,582,947	221,815	423,898	246,440	(NA)	(NA)
1984.........	2,689,200	(NA)	1,740,948	233,018	448,264	266,992	(NA)	(NA)
1985.........	3,011,500	1.7	1,968,712	254,986	487,593	300,203	2,606,000	405,500
1986.........	3,239,400	1.8	2,114,621	272,735	526,436	325,638	2,829,100	410,300
1987.........	3,459,600	1.9	2,247,158	294,092	562,814	355,505	3,021,000	438,600
1988.........	3,714,100	2.0	2,356,483	341,893	607,766	407,977	3,223,000	491,100
1989.........	4,055,600	2.2	2,522,125	393,303	683,367	456,803	3,501,600	554,000
1990.........	4,348,000	2.3	2,670,234	403,019	743,382	531,407	3,746,300	601,700
1991.........	4,535,600	2.4	2,728,472	424,129	792,535	590,442	3,913,000	622,600
1992.........	4,762,600	2.5	2,811,611	441,781	850,566	658,601	4,050,300	712,300
1993.........	4,944,000	2.6	2,903,061	455,500	909,381	676,100	4,215,800	728,200
1994.........	5,141,300	2.7	2,981,022	479,800	990,147	690,371	4,377,400	763,900
1995.........	5,342,900	2.8	3,077,861	507,044	1,078,542	679,421	4,513,000	822,100
1996.........	5,482,700	2.8	3,164,996	510,400	1,127,528	679,733	4,629,900	852,800
1997.........	5,725,800	2.9	3,296,513	557,974	1,176,564	694,787	4,825,300	900,500
1998.........	6,126,100	3.1	3,670,441	584,372	1,224,469	696,385	(NA)	(NA)
1999.........	6,331,400	3.1	3,779,922	596,485	1,287,172	714,457	(NA)	(NA)
2000.........	6,445,100	3.1	3,826,209	621,149	1,316,333	723,898	(NA)	(NA)
2001.........	6,581,700	3.1	3,931,731	631,240	1,330,007	732,333	(NA)	(NA)
2002.........	6,758,800	3.1	4,024,067	665,475	1,367,547	750,934	(NA)	(NA)
2003.........	6,936,600	3.2	4,144,782	691,301	1,392,796	745,125	(NA)	(NA)
2004, advance ...	6,996,500	3.2	4,151,125	713,990	1,421,911	765,355	(NA)	(NA)

NA Not available. [1] Totals may not add due to individuals having multiple correctional statuses. [2] Estimated.

Source: U.S. Department of Justice, Office of Justice Programs, Bureau of Justice Statistics, *Correctional Populations in the United States*, annual; <http://www.ojp.usdoj.gov/bjs/correct.htm>.

Law Enforcement, Courts, and Prisons **209**

Table 336. Jail Inmates by Sex, Race, and Hispanic Origin: 1990 to 2004

[As of June 30. Excludes federal and state prisons or other correctional institutions; institutions exclusively for juveniles; state-operated jails in Alaska, Connecticut, Delaware, Hawaii, Rhode Island, and Vermont; and other facilities which retain persons for less than 72 hours. Data based on the Annual Survey of Jails, which is a sample survey and subject to sampling variability. Due to rounding, inmates may not add to total]

Characteristic	1990	1995	1999	2000	2001	2002	2003	2004
Total inmates	405,320	507,044	605,943	621,149	631,240	665,475	691,301	713,990
Male	365,821	448,000	528,998	543,120	551,007	581,411	602,781	626,407
Female	37,198	51,300	67,487	70,414	72,621	76,817	81,650	87,583
Juveniles	2,301	7,800	9,458	7,613	7,613	7,248	6,869	7,083
White, non-Hispanic	169,600	203,300	249,900	260,500	271,700	291,800	301,200	317,400
Black, non-Hispanic	172,300	220,600	251,800	256,300	256,200	264,900	271,000	275,400
Hispanic	58,100	74,400	93,800	94,100	93,000	98,000	106,600	108,300
Other [1]	5,400	8,800	10,400	10,200	10,300	10,800	12,500	12,900

[1] Includes American Indians, Alaska Natives, Asians, and Pacific Islanders.

Source: U.S. Department of Justice, Office of Justice Programs, Bureau of Justice Statistics, Jail Inmates, annual; beginning 1995, Prison and Jail Inmates at Midyear, annual; <http://www.ojp.usdoj.gov/bjs/jails.htm>.

Table 337. Federal and State Prisoners by Sex: 1980 to 2004

[Prisoners, as of December 31. Includes all persons under jurisdiction of federal and state authorities rather than those in the custody of such authorities. Represents inmates sentenced to maximum term of more than a year]

Year	Total [1]	Rate [2]	State	Male	Female	Year	Total [1]	Rate [2]	State	Male	Female
1980 . . .	315,974	139	295,363	303,643	12,331	1993 . . .	932,074	359	857,675	878,037	54,037
1982 . . .	395,516	171	371,864	379,075	16,441	1994 . . .	1,016,691	389	936,896	956,566	60,125
1983 . . .	419,346	179	393,015	401,870	17,476	1995 . . .	1,085,022	411	1,001,359	1,021,059	63,963
1984 . . .	443,398	188	415,796	424,193	19,205	1996 . . .	1,137,722	427	1,048,907	1,068,123	69,599
1985 . . .	480,568	202	447,873	459,223	21,345	1997 . . .	1,195,498	445	1,100,511	1,121,663	73,835
1986 . . .	522,084	217	485,553	497,540	24,544	1998 . . .	1,245,402	461	1,141,720	1,167,802	77,600
1987 . . .	560,812	231	521,289	533,990	26,822	1999 . . .	1,304,074	476	1,189,799	1,221,611	82,463
1988 . . .	603,732	247	560,994	573,587	30,145	2000 . . .	1,331,278	[3]470	1,204,323	1,246,234	85,044
1989 . . .	680,907	276	633,739	643,643	37,264	2001 . . .	1,345,217	470	1,208,708	1,260,033	85,184
1990 . . .	739,980	297	689,577	699,416	40,564	2002 . . .	1,380,516	476	1,237,476	1,291,450	89,066
1991 . . .	789,610	313	732,914	745,808	43,802	2003 . . .	1,408,361	482	1,256,442	1,315,790	92,571
1992 . . .	846,277	332	780,571	799,776	46,501	2004 . . .	1,433,793	486	1,274,656	1,337,668	96,125

[1] Includes federal. [2] Rate per 100,000 estimated population. Based on U.S. Census Bureau estimated resident population. [3] Decrease in incarceration rate from 1999 to 2000 due to use of new Census numbers.

Source: U.S. Department of Justice, Office of Justice Programs, Bureau of Justice Statistics, Prisoners in State and Federal Institutions on December 31, Series NCJ 210677 annual; <http://www.ojp.usdoj.gov/bjs/abstract/p04.htm>.

Table 338. Prisoners Under Sentence of Death by Characteristic: 1980 to 2004

[As of December 31. Excludes prisoners under sentence of death who remained within local correctional systems pending exhaustion of appellate process or who had not been committed to prison]

Characteristic	1980	1990	1995	1996	1997	1998	1999	2000	2001	2002	2003	2004
Total [1, 2]	688	2,346	3,064	3,242	3,328	3,465	3,540	3,601	3,577	3,562	3,377	3,314
White	418	1,368	1,732	1,833	1,864	1,917	1,960	1,989	1,968	1,939	1,882	1,850
Black and other	270	978	1,332	1,409	1,464	1,548	1,580	1,612	1,609	1,623	1,495	1,464
Under 20 years	11	8	20	17	16	16	16	11	4	4	1	1
20 to 24 years	173	168	264	288	275	273	251	237	192	153	133	95
25 to 34 years	334	1,110	1,068	1,088	1,077	1,108	1,108	1,103	1,099	1,058	965	896
35 to 54 years	186	1,006	1,583	1,711	1,809	1,897	1,958	2,019	2,043	2,069	1,969	1,977
55 years and over	10	64	119	138	151	171	194	223	243	273	306	345
Years of school completed:												
7 years or less	68	178	191	196	205	208	201	214	212	215	213	207
8 years	74	186	195	201	206	218	221	233	236	234	227	221
9 to 11 years	204	775	979	1,040	1,069	1,122	1,142	1,157	1,145	1,130	1,073	1,053
12 years	162	729	995	1,037	1,084	1,128	1,157	1,184	1,183	1,173	1,108	1,091
More than 12 years	43	209	272	282	288	301	307	315	304	294	270	262
Unknown	163	279	422	486	476	488	499	490	501	511	483	480
Marital status:												
Never married	268	998	1,412	1,507	1,555	1,645	1,689	1,749	1,763	1,746	1,641	1,622
Married	229	632	718	739	740	752	731	739	716	709	684	658
Divorced [3]	217	726	924	996	1,033	1,068	1,107	1,105	1,102	1,102	1,049	1,034
Time elapsed since sentencing:												
Less than 12 months	185	231	287	306	262	293	259	208	151	147	137	117
12 to 47 months	389	753	784	816	844	816	800	786	734	609	495	421
48 to 71 months	102	438	423	447	456	482	499	507	476	468	451	388
72 months and over	38	934	1,560	1,673	1,766	1,874	1,969	2,092	2,220	2,333	2,291	2,388
Legal status at arrest:												
Not under sentence	384	1,345	1,764	1,881	1,957	2,036	2,088	2,202	2,189	2,165	2,048	2,026
Parole or probation [4]	115	578	866	894	880	879	886	921	918	909	845	809
Prison or escaped	45	128	110	112	116	127	125	126	135	141	137	145
Unknown	170	305	314	355	375	423	428	334	339	342	344	334

[1] Revisions to the total number of prisoners were not carried to the characteristics except for race. [2] Includes races not shown separately. [3] Includes persons married but separated, widows, widowers, and unknown. [4] Includes prisoners on mandatory conditional release, work release, leave, AWOL or bail. Covers 28 prisoners in 1990, and 29 in 1991 and 1992, 33 in 1993 and 1995, 31 in 1994 and 1996, 30 in 1997, 26 in 1998, 21 in 1999 and 2000, and 17 in 2001, 2002, and 2003.

Source: U.S. Department of Justice, Office of Justice Programs, Bureau of Justice Statistics, Capital Punishment, 2004, Series NCJ 211349, November 2005. See also <http://www.ojp.usdoj.gov/bjs/cp.htm>.

210   Law Enforcement, Courts, and Prisons

U.S. Census Bureau. Statistical Abstract of the United States: 2007

Table 339. Movement of Prisoners Under Sentence of Death: 1980 to 2004

[Prisoners reported under sentence of death by civil authorities. The term "under sentence of death" begins when the court pronounces the first sentence of death for a capital offense]

Status	1980	1990	1995	1996	1997	1998	1999	2000	2001	2002	2003	2004
Under sentence of death, Jan. 1 . .	595	2,346	3,064	3,242	3,328	3,465	3,540	3,601	3,577	3,562	3,377	3,314
Received death sentence [1]	203	244	327	322	282	306	282	235	166	169	152	125
White	125	147	168	174	146	145	157	122	89	83	92	75
Black	77	94	138	119	106	132	104	86	61	73	44	50
Dispositions other than executions	101	108	105	99	89	93	112	76	109	108	267	129
Executions	–	23	56	45	74	68	98	85	66	71	65	59
Under sentence of death, Dec. 31 [1,2]	688	2,346	3,054	3,242	3,335	3,452	3,527	3,593	3,581	3,562	3,377	3,314
White	425	1,368	1,730	1,833	1,876	1,906	1,948	1,990	1,969	1,939	1,882	1,850
Black	268	940	1,275	1,358	1,406	1,486	1,514	1,535	1,538	1,551	1,417	1,390

– Represents zero. [1] Includes races other than White or Black. [2] Revisions to total number of prisoners under death sentence not carried to this category.

Source: U.S. Department of Justice, Office of Justice Programs, Bureau of Justice Statistics, *Capital Punishment, Series NCJ 211349*, annual. See also <http://www.ojp.usdoj.gov/bjs/abstract/cp04.htm>.

Table 340. Prisoners Executed Under Civil Authority by Sex and Race: 1930 to 2005

[Excludes executions by military authorities. The Army (including the Air Force) carried out 160 (148 between 1942 and 1950; 3 each in 1954, 1955, and 1957; and 1 each in 1958, 1959, and 1961). Of the total, 106 were executed for murder (including 21 involving rape), 53 for rape, and 1 for desertion. The Navy carried out no executions during the period]

Year or period	Total [1]	Male	Female	White	Black	Executed for murder		
						Total [1]	White	Black
All years, 1930–2005 . .	**4,863**	**4,820**	**43**	**2,399**	**2,407**	**4,338**	**2,312**	**1,971**
1930 to 1939	1,667	1,656	11	827	816	1,514	803	687
1940 to 1949 [2]	1,284	1,272	12	490	781	1,064	458	595
1950 to 1959 [2]	717	709	8	336	376	601	316	280
1960 to 1967	191	190	1	98	93	155	87	68
1968 to 1976	–	–	–	–	–	–	–	–
1977 to 2005	1,004	993	11	648	341	1,004	648	341
1985	18	18	–	11	7	18	11	7
1989	16	16	–	8	8	16	8	8
1990	23	23	–	16	7	23	16	7
1991	14	14	–	7	7	14	7	7
1992	31	31	–	19	11	31	19	11
1993	38	38	–	23	14	38	23	14
1994	31	31	–	20	11	31	20	11
1995	56	56	–	33	22	56	33	22
1996	45	45	–	31	14	45	31	14
1997	74	74	–	45	27	74	45	27
1998	68	66	2	48	18	68	48	18
1999	98	98	–	61	33	98	61	33
2000	85	83	2	49	35	85	49	35
2001	66	63	3	48	17	66	48	17
2002	71	69	2	53	18	71	53	18
2003	65	65	–	44	20	65	44	20
2004	59	59	–	39	19	59	39	19
2005	60	59	1	41	19	60	41	19

– Represents zero. [1] Includes races other than White or Black. [2] Includes 25 armed robbery, 20 kidnapping, 11 burglary, 8 espionage (6 in 1942 and 2 in 1953), and 6 aggravated assault.

Source: Through 1978, U.S. Law Enforcement Assistance Administration; thereafter, U.S. Department of Justice, Office of Justice Programs, Bureau of Justice Statistics, *Correctional Populations in the United States*, annual; <http://www.ojp.usdoj.gov/bjs/correct.htm> and *Capital Punishment*, annual; <http://www.ojp.usdoj.gov/bjs/abstract/cp04.htm>.

Table 341. Prisoners Executed Under Civil Authority by State: 1977 to 2005

[Alaska, District of Columbia, Hawaii, Iowa, Maine, Massachusetts, Michigan, Minnesota, New York, North Dakota, Rhode Island, Vermont, West Virginia, and Wisconsin are jurisdictions without a death penalty]

State	1977 to 2005	2002	2003	2004	2005	State	1977 to 2005	2002	2003	2004	2005	State	1977 to 2005	2002	2003	2004	2005
U.S. .	**1,004**	**71**	**65**	**59**	**60**	IL	12	–	–	–	–	OK . . .	79	7	14	6	4
						IN	16	–	2	–	5	OR . . .	2	–	–	–	–
AL . . .	34	2	3	2	4	KY . . .	2	–	–	–	–	PA . . .	3	–	–	–	–
AZ . . .	22	–	–	–	–	LA . . .	27	1	–	–	–	SC . . .	35	3	–	4	3
AR . . .	27	–	1	1	1	MD . . .	5	–	–	1	1	TN . . .	1	–	–	–	–
CA . . .	12	1	–	–	2	MS . . .	7	2	–	–	1	TX . . .	355	33	24	23	19
DE . . .	14	–	–	–	–	MO . . .	66	6	2	–	5	UT . . .	6	–	–	–	–
FL . . .	60	3	3	2	1	NE . . .	3	–	–	–	–	VA . . .	94	4	2	5	–
GA . . .	39	4	3	2	3	NV . . .	11	–	2	–	–	WA . . .	4	–	–	–	–
ID	1	–	–	–	–	NC . . .	39	2	7	4	5	WY . . .	1	–	–	–	–

– Represents zero.

Source: Through 1978, U.S. Law Enforcement Assistance Administration; thereafter, U.S. Department of Justice, Office of Justice Programs, Bureau of Justice Statistics, *Capital Punishment, Series NCJ 211349*, annual; <http://www.ojp.usdoj.gov/bjs/cp.htm>.

Law Enforcement, Courts, and Prisons 211

Table 342. Fire Losses—Total and Per Capita: 1980 to 2004

[5,579 represents $5,579,000,000. Includes allowance for uninsured and unreported losses]

Year	Total (mil. dol.)	Per capita [1] (dol.)	Year	Total (mil. dol.)	Per capita [1] (dol.)	Year	Total (mil. dol.)	Per capita [1] (dol.)
1980	5,579	24.56	1989	9,514	38.33	1997	12,940	48.32
1982	5,894	25.61	1990	9,495	38.07	1998	11,510	45.59
1983	6,320	27.20	1991	11,302	44.82	1999	12,428	45.58
1984	7,602	32.35	1992	13,588	53.28	2000	13,457	47.68
1985	7,753	32.70	1993	11,331	43.96	2001 [2]	17,118	60.04
1986	8,488	35.21	1994	12,778	49.08	2002	17,586	61.07
1987	8,504	34.96	1995	11,887	45.23	2003	21,129	72.66
1988	9,626	39.11	1996	12,544	47.29	2004	18,874	64.27

[1] Based on U.S. Census Bureau estimated resident population as of July 1. Enumerated population as of April 1 for 1980, 1990 and 2000. [2] Does not include insured fire losses related to terrorism.

Source: Insurance Information Institute, New York, NY, *The Fact Book, Property/Casualty Insurance Facts*, annual (copyright) <http://www.iii.org/>.

Table 343. Fires—Number and Loss by Type and Property Use: 2001 to 2004

[1,734 represents 1,734,000 and property loss of 44,023 represents $44,023,000,000. Based on annual sample survey of fire departments. No adjustments were made for unreported fires and losses]

Type and property use	Number (1,000)				Direct property loss (mil. dol.) [1]			
	2001	2002	2003	2004	2001	2002	2003	2004
Fires, total	1,734	1,688	1,584	1,550	[2]44,023	10,337	12,367	9,794
Structure	521	519	520	526	42,314	8,742	8,678	8,314
Outside of structure [3]	75	71	66	69	86	121	162	108
Brush and rubbish	623	603	550	514	–	–	–	–
Vehicle	351	330	312	297	1,512	1,392	1,356	1,304
Other	164	165	136	144	111	82	[4]2,171	68
Structure by property use:								
Public assembly	15	14	14	13	336	342	302	316
Educational	7	7	7	7	170	92	69	68
Institutional	7	7	7	6	27	26	28	25
Stores and offices	26	24	25	24	34,155	604	721	586
Residential	396	401	402	411	5,643	6,055	6,074	5,948
1–2 family units [5]	295	301	297	302	4,652	5,005	5,052	4,948
Apartments	88	88	92	94	864	926	897	885
Other residential [6]	13	12	13	15	127	124	125	115
Storage [6]	34	32	32	32	930	627	675	748
Industry, utility, defense [7] . .	13	12	11	12	858	658	625	423
Special structures	23	22	22	21	195	338	184	200

– Represents zero. [1] Direct property damage figures do not include indirect losses, like business interruption, and adjustments for inflation. [2] Includes $33.4 billion in property loss that occured due to the events of September 11, 2001. [3] Includes outside storage, crops, timber, etc. [4] Includes Southern California wildfires where there was an estimated $2.044 billion in property loss. [5] Includes mobile homes. [6] Includes hotels and motels, college dormitories, boarding houses, etc. [7] Data underreported as some incidents were handled by private fire brigades or fixed suppression systems which do not report.

Source: National Fire Protection Association, Quincy, MA, 2004 U.S. Fire Loss, *NFPA Journal*, November 2005, and prior issues (copyright 2005); <http://www.nfpa.org/index.asp>.

Table 344. Fires and Property Loss for Incendiary and Suspicious Fires and Civilian Fire Deaths and Injuries by Selected Property Type: 2001 to 2004

[521 represents 521,000. Based on sample survey of fire departments]

Characteristic	2001	2002	2003	2004	Characteristic	2001	2002	2003	2004
NUMBER (1,000)					CIVILIAN FIRE DEATHS				
Structure fires, total .	521	519	520	526	Deaths, total [3]	[4]6,196	3,380	3,925	3,900
Structure fires of incendiary or suspicious origin	–	–	–	–	Residential property	3,140	2,695	3,165	3,225
					One- and two-family dwellings	2,650	2,280	2,735	2,680
Fires of incendiary origin .	46	45	38	37	Apartments	460	390	410	510
Fires of suspicious origin .	–	–	–	–	Vehicles	485	565	475	550
PROPERTY LOSS [1] (mil. dol.)					CIVILIAN FIRE INJURIES				
Structure fires, total .	[2]42,314	8,742	8,678	8,314	Injuries, total [3]	[5]21,100	18,425	18,125	17,785
Structure fires of incendiary or suspicious origin	–	–	–	–	Residential property	15,575	14,050	14,075	14,175
					One- and two-family dwellings	11,400	9,950	10,000	10,500
Fires of incendiary origin .	[2]34,453	919	692	714	Apartments	3,800	3,700	3,650	3,200
Fires of suspicious origin .	–	–	–	–	Vehicles	1,875	1,125	1,600	1,500

– Represents zero. [1] Direct property loss only. [2] Includes $33.44 billion in property loss due to the events of September 11, 2001. [3] Includes other not shown separately. [4] Includes 2,451 civilian deaths due to the events of September 11, 2001. [5] Includes 800 civilian injuries due to the events of September 11, 2001.

Source: National Fire Protection Association, Quincy, MA, 2004 U.S. Fire Loss, *NFPA Journal*, November 2005, and prior issues (copyright 2005); <http://www.nfpa.org/index.asp>.

Section 6
Geography and Environment

This section presents a variety of information on the physical environment of the United States, starting with basic area measurement data and ending with climatic data for selected weather stations around the country. The subjects covered between those points are mostly concerned with environmental trends but include related subjects such as land use, water consumption, air pollutant emissions, toxic releases, oil spills, hazardous waste sites, municipal waste and recycling, threatened and endangered wildlife, and the environmental industry.

The information in this section is selected from a wide range of federal agencies that compile the data for various administrative or regulatory purposes, such as the Environmental Protection Agency (EPA), U.S. Geological Survey (USGS), National Oceanic and Atmospheric Administration (NOAA), Natural Resources Conservation Service (NRCS), and General Services Administration (GSA). New information on waste generation recycling, wetlands, and Hurricane Katrina may be found in Tables 349, 364, 375, and 376.

Area—For the 2000 census, area measurements were calculated by computer based on the information contained in a single, consistent geographic database, the Topologically Integrated Geographic Encoding & Referencing system (TIGER®) database, rather than relying on historical, local, and manually calculated information. Information from the 2000 census may be found in Table 346.

Geography—The USGS conducts investigations, surveys, and research in the fields of geography, geology, topography, geographic information systems, mineralogy, hydrology, and geothermal energy resources as well as natural hazards. The USGS provides United States cartographic data through the Earth Sciences Information Center, water resources data through

the National Water Data Exchange (NAW-DEX), and a variety of research and Open-File reports which are announced monthly in *New Publications of the USGS.*

In a joint project with the U.S. Census Bureau, during the 1980s, the USGS provided the basic information on geographic features for input into a national geographic and cartographic database prepared by the Census Bureau, called TIGER® database. Since then, using a variety of sources, the Census Bureau has updated these features and their related attributes (names, descriptions, etc.) and inserted current information on the boundaries, names, and codes of legal and statistical geographic entities; very few of these updates added aerial water features. Maps prepared by the Census Bureau using the TIGER® database show the names and boundaries of entities and are available on a current basis.

An inventory of the nation's land resources by type of use/cover was conducted by the National Resources Inventory Conservation Service every 5 years beginning in 1977. The most recent survey results, which were published in the 1997 National Resources Inventory, cover all nonfederal land in Puerto Rico, the Virgin Islands, and the United States except Alaska. Tables 347 to 350 provide results from the survey. Beginning with the release of the 2001 estimates, this program will shift to become an annual release of land use data.

Environment—The principal federal agency responsible for pollution abatement and control activities is the Environmental Protection Agency (EPA). It is responsible for establishing and monitoring national air quality standards, water quality activities, solid and hazardous waste disposal, and control of toxic substances. Many of these series now appear in the Envirofacts portion of the EPA Web site at <http://www.epa.gov/enviro/>. In 2003, EPA released a major compilation of

Geography and Environment   213

environmental indicators, entitled *Draft Report on the Environment: 2003,* found at <http://www.epa.govindicators/roe/htm/roeTOC.htm>.

National Ambient Air Quality Standards (NAAQS) for suspended particulate matter, sulfur dioxide, photochemical oxidants, carbon monoxide, and nitrogen dioxide were originally set by the EPA in April 1971. Every 5 years, each of the NAAQS is reviewed and revised to include any additional or new health or welfare data. The standard for photochemical oxidants, now called ozone, was revised in February 1979. Also, a new NAAQS for confining lead was promulgated in October 1978 and for suspended particulate matter in 1987. Table 358 gives some of the health-related standards for the six air pollutants having NAAQS. Data gathered from state networks are periodically submitted to EPA's National Aerometric Information Retrieval System (AIRS) for summarization in annual reports on the nationwide status and trends in air quality. For details, see *National Air Quality and Emissions Trends Report.* More current information on emissions may be found on the EPA Web site at <http://www.epa.gov/airtrends>.

The Toxics Release Inventory (TRI), published by the EPA, is a valuable source of information on nearly 650 chemicals that are being used, manufactured, treated, transported, or released into the environment. Sections 313 of the Emergency Planning and Community Right-to-Know Act (EPCRA) and 6607 of the Pollution Prevention Act (PPA), mandate that a publicly-accessible toxic chemical database be developed and maintained by EPA. This database, known as the TRI, contains information concerning waste management activities and the release of toxic chemicals by facilities that manufacture, process, or otherwise use said materials. Data on the release of these chemicals are collected from over 23,000 facilities and facilities added in 1998 that have the equivalent of 10 or more full-time employees and meet the established thresholds for manufacturing, processing or "other use" of listed chemicals. Facilities must report their releases and other waste management quantities. Since 199 federal facilities have been required to report their data regardless of industry classification. In May 1997, EPA added seven new industry sectors that reported to the TRI for the first time in July 1999 for the 1998 reporting year.

Climate—NOAA, through the National Weather Service and the National Environmental Satellite, Data, and Information Service, is responsible for climate data. NOAA maintains about 11,600 weather stations, of which over 3,000 produce autographic precipitation records, about 600 take hourly readings of a series of weather elements, and the remainder record data once a day. These data are reported monthly in the Climatological Data and Storm Data, published monthly and annually in the Local Climatological Data (published by location for major cities).

The normal climatological temperatures, precipitation, and degree days listed in this publication are derived for comparative purposes and are averages for the 30-year period, 1971–2000. For stations that did not have continuous records for the entire 30 years from the same instrument site, the normals have been adjusted to provide representative values for the current location. The information in all other tables is based on data from the beginning of the record at that location through 2004.

Table 345. Land and Water Area of States and Other Entities: 2000

[One square mile = 2.59 square kilometers. Area is calculated from the specific boundary recorded for each entity in the U.S. Census Bureau's geographic TIGER ™ database]

State and other area	Total area		Land area		Water area Total		Inland (sq. mi.)	Coastal (sq. mi.)	Great Lakes (sq. mi.)	Territorial (sq. mi.)
	Sq. mi.	Sq. km.	Sq. mi.	Sq. km.	Sq. mi.	Sq. km.				
Total.............	3,800,286	9,842,696	3,540,999	9,171,146	259,287	671,550	79,018	42,241	60,251	77,777
United States ...	3,794,083	9,826,630	3,537,438	9,161,923	256,645	664,707	78,797	42,225	60,251	75,372
Alabama..........	52,419	135,765	50,744	131,426	1,675	4,338	956	519	–	200
Alaska...........	663,267	1,717,854	571,951	1,481,347	91,316	236,507	17,243	27,049	–	47,024
Arizona..........	113,998	295,254	113,635	294,312	364	942	364	–	–	–
Arkansas.........	53,179	137,732	52,068	134,856	1,110	2,876	1,110	–	–	–
California........	163,696	423,970	155,959	403,933	7,736	20,037	2,674	222	–	4,841
Colorado	104,094	269,601	103,718	268,627	376	974	376	–	–	–
Connecticut	5,543	14,357	4,845	12,548	699	1,809	161	538	–	–
Delaware..........	2,489	6,447	1,954	5,060	536	1,388	72	371	–	93
District of Columbia ...	68	177	61	159	7	18	7	–	–	–
Florida...........	65,755	170,304	53,927	139,670	11,828	30,634	4,672	1,311	–	5,845
Georgia...........	59,425	153,909	57,906	149,976	1,519	3,933	1,016	48	–	455
Hawaii............	10,931	28,311	6,423	16,635	4,508	11,677	38	–	–	4,470
Idaho	83,570	216,446	82,747	214,314	823	2,131	823	–	–	–
Illinois	57,914	149,998	55,584	143,961	2,331	6,037	756	–	1,575	–
Indiana	36,418	94,321	35,867	92,895	551	1,427	316	–	235	–
Iowa	56,272	145,743	55,869	144,701	402	1,042	402	–	–	–
Kansas	82,277	213,096	81,815	211,900	462	1,197	462	–	–	–
Kentucky	40,409	104,659	39,728	102,896	681	1,763	681	–	–	–
Louisiana.........	51,840	134,264	43,562	112,825	8,278	21,440	4,154	1,935	–	2,189
Maine	35,385	91,646	30,862	79,931	4,523	11,715	2,264	613	–	1,647
Maryland	12,407	32,133	9,774	25,314	2,633	6,819	680	1,843	–	110
Massachusetts	10,555	27,336	7,840	20,306	2,715	7,031	423	977	–	1,314
Michigan	96,716	250,494	56,804	147,121	39,912	103,372	1,611	–	38,301	–
Minnesota	86,939	225,171	79,610	206,189	7,329	18,982	4,783	–	2,546	–
Mississippi........	48,430	125,434	46,907	121,489	1,523	3,945	785	590	–	148
Missouri..........	69,704	180,533	68,886	178,414	818	2,120	818	–	–	–
Montana	147,042	380,838	145,552	376,979	1,490	3,859	1,490	–	–	–
Nebraska..........	77,354	200,345	76,872	199,099	481	1,247	481	–	–	–
Nevada	110,561	286,351	109,826	284,448	735	1,903	735	–	–	–
New Hampshire	9,350	24,216	8,968	23,227	382	989	314	–	–	68
New Jersey	8,721	22,588	7,417	19,211	1,304	3,377	396	401	–	507
New Mexico........	121,590	314,915	121,356	314,309	234	606	234	–	–	–
New York..........	54,556	141,299	47,214	122,283	7,342	19,016	1,895	981	3,988	479
North Carolina	53,819	139,389	48,711	126,161	5,108	13,229	3,960	–	–	1,148
North Dakota	70,700	183,112	68,976	178,647	1,724	4,465	1,724	–	–	–
Ohio	44,825	116,096	40,948	106,056	3,877	10,040	378	–	3,499	–
Oklahoma	69,898	181,036	68,667	177,847	1,231	3,189	1,231	–	–	–
Oregon	98,381	254,805	95,997	248,631	2,384	6,174	1,050	80	–	1,254
Pennsylvania	46,055	119,283	44,817	116,075	1,239	3,208	490	–	749	–
Rhode Island	1,545	4,002	1,045	2,706	500	1,295	178	9	–	314
South Carolina	32,020	82,932	30,110	77,983	1,911	4,949	1,008	72	–	831
South Dakota	77,117	199,731	75,885	196,540	1,232	3,191	1,232	–	–	–
Tennessee	42,143	109,151	41,217	106,752	926	2,399	926	–	–	–
Texas	268,581	695,621	261,797	678,051	6,784	17,570	5,056	404	–	1,324
Utah	84,899	219,887	82,144	212,751	2,755	7,136	2,755	–	–	–
Vermont	9,614	24,901	9,250	23,956	365	945	365	–	–	–
Virginia	42,774	110,785	39,594	102,548	3,180	8,237	1,006	1,728	–	446
Washington	71,300	184,665	66,544	172,348	4,756	12,317	1,553	2,537	–	666
West Virginia	24,230	62,755	24,078	62,361	152	394	152	–	–	–
Wisconsin	65,498	169,639	54,310	140,663	11,188	28,976	1,830	–	9,358	–
Wyoming..........	97,814	253,336	97,100	251,489	713	1,847	713	–	–	–
Other areas:										
Puerto Rico.......	5,325	13,790	3,425	8,870	1,900	4,921	67	16	–	1,817
U.S. minor outlying islands ...	141	365	3	7	138	359	138	–	–	–
Virgin Islands of the U.S	737	1,910	134	346	604	1,564	16	–	–	588

– Represents or rounds to zero.

Source: U.S. Census Bureau, 2000 Census of Population and Housing, *Summary Population and Housing Characteristics,* Series PHC-1; and unpublished data from the Census TIGER ™ data base.

Geography and Environment 215

Table 346. Total and Federally Owned Land by State: 2004

[(2,271,343 represents 2,271,343,000). As of September 30. See text, Section 8. Total land area figures are not comparable with those in Table 345]

State	Total (1,000 acres)	Not owned by federal government (1,000 acres)	Owned by federal government [1] Acres (1,000)	Owned by federal government [1] Percent	State	Total (1,000 acres)	Not owned by federal government (1,000 acres)	Owned by federal government [1] Acres (1,000)	Owned by federal government [1] Percent
United States..	2,271,343	1,618,044	653,299	28.8	Mississippi.	30,223	28,026	2,197	7.3
					Missouri	44,248	42,024	2,225	5.0
Alabama	32,678	32,164	514	1.6	Montana	93,271	65,361	27,910	29.9
Alaska	365,482	112,986	252,496	69.1	Nebraska	49,032	48,366	665	1.4
Arizona	72,688	37,755	34,933	48.1	Nevada.	70,264	10,902	59,363	84.5
Arkansas.	33,599	31,191	2,408	7.2	New Hampshire . . .	5,769	4,993	776	13.4
California.	100,207	54,813	45,393	45.3	New Jersey	4,813	4,665	148	3.1
Colorado.	66,486	42,131	24,355	36.6	New Mexico.	77,766	45,283	32,484	41.8
Connecticut	3,135	3,121	14	0.4	New York	30,681	30,447	234	0.8
Delaware.	1,266	1,240	26	2.0	North Carolina	31,403	27,693	3,710	11.8
District of Columbia	39	29	10	24.7	North Dakota	44,452	43,267	1,186	2.7
					Ohio.	26,222	25,774	448	1.7
Florida	34,721	31,862	2,859	8.2	Oklahoma	44,088	42,502	1,586	3.6
Georgia	37,295	35,886	1,409	3.8	Oregon	61,599	28,883	32,716	53.1
Hawaii	4,106	3,309	797	19.4	Pennsylvania	28,804	28,085	720	2.5
Idaho	52,933	26,368	26,565	50.2	Rhode Island	677	674	3	0.4
Illinois.	35,795	35,153	642	1.8	South Carolina	19,374	18,813	561	2.9
Indiana	23,158	22,695	463	2.0	South Dakota	48,882	45,854	3,028	6.2
Iowa.	35,860	35,587	274	0.8	Tennessee	26,728	25,862	866	3.2
Kansas	52,511	51,879	631	1.2	Texas	168,218	165,087	3,130	1.9
Kentucky.	25,512	24,134	1,379	5.4	Utah.	52,697	22,425	30,272	57.4
Louisiana	28,868	27,393	1,475	5.1	Vermont	5,937	5,493	443	7.5
Maine	19,848	19,639	208	1.1	Virginia	25,496	22,962	2,534	9.9
Maryland.	6,319	6,141	179	2.8	Washington	42,694	29,744	12,950	30.3
Massachusetts	5,035	4,941	94	1.9	West Virginia	15,411	14,264	1,146	7.4
Michigan	36,492	32,854	3,638	10.0	Wisconsin	35,011	33,039	1,972	5.6
Minnesota	51,206	48,332	2,874	5.6	Wyoming.	62,343	35,952	26,391	42.3

[1] Excludes trust properties.

Source: U.S. General Services Administration, *Federal Real Property Profile*, annual. For most recent report, see <http://www.gsa.gov/gsa/cm_attachments/GSA_DOCUMENT/Annual%20Report%20%20FY2004%20FINAL_R2M-n11_0Z5RDZ-i34K-pR.pdf>.

Table 347. Land Cover/Use by Type: 1982 to 2002

[In millions of acres (1,937.7 represents 1,937,700,000), except percent. Excludes Alaska, Hawaii, and District of Columbia]

Year	Total surface area	Rural land, total [1]	Nonfederal rural land Crop- land	Nonfederal rural land Pasture land	Nonfederal rural land Range- land	Nonfederal rural land Forest land	Nonfederal rural land Other rural land	Devel- oped land	Water areas	Fed- eral land
Land										
1982	1,937.7	1,417.2	420.4	131.4	414.5	402.6	48.3	72.8	48.6	399.1
1992	1,937.6	1,400.2	381.2	125.1	406.6	404.0	49.3	86.5	49.4	401.5
2002	1,937.7	1,378.1	368.4	117.3	405.3	404.9	50.6	107.3	50.4	401.9
Percent of total land										
1982	100.0	73.1	21.7	6.8	21.4	20.8	2.5	3.8	2.5	20.6
1992	100.0	72.3	19.7	6.5	21.0	20.9	2.5	4.5	2.5	20.7
2002	100.0	71.1	19.0	6.1	20.9	20.9	2.6	5.5	2.6	20.7

[1] Includes Conservation Reserve Program land not shown separately.

Source: U.S. Department of Agriculture, Natural Resources and Conservation Service, *National Resources Inventory 2002 Annual NRI, Land Use*, April 2004. See also <http://www.nrcs.usda.gov/technical/land/nri02/landuse.pdf>.

Table 348. Developed Land by Type: 1982 to 2001

[In millions of acres (1,937.7 represents 1,937,700,000), except percent. Excludes Alaska, Hawaii, and District of Columbia]

Year	Total surface area	Developed land Developed land, total	Developed land Large urban and built-up areas	Developed land Small built-up areas	Developed land Rural transportation land
Land 1982	1,937.7	72.8	46.9	4.7	21.2
1992	1,937.7	86.5	59.6	5.4	21.5
2001	1,937.7	106.3	77.6	6.7	22.0
Percent of total land					
1982	100.0	3.8	2.4	0.2	1.1
1992	100.0	4.5	3.1	0.3	1.1
2001	100.0	5.5	4.0	0.3	1.1

Source: U.S. Department of Agriculture, Natural Resources and Conservation Service, *National Resources Inventory 2001 Annual NRI, Urbanization and Development of Rural Land*, July 2003. See also <http://www.nrcs.usda.gov/technical/land/nri01/urban.pdf> (released July 2003).

216   Geography and Environment

Table 349. Wetlands on Nonfederal Land and Water Areas by Land Cover/Use and Farm Production Region: 2003

[In thousands of acres (110,760 represents 110,760,000). Represents palustrine and estuarine wetlands; see source. For information on farm production regions, see source]

Farm production region	Total	Cropland [1]	Forest land	Rangeland	Other rural land	Developed land	Water area
Wetlands, total	**110,760**	**16,730**	**65,440**	**7,740**	**15,800**	**1,590**	**3,460**
Lake states	22,460	2,710	15,480	–	3,880	160	230
Southeast	22,360	940	16,010	970	3,460	420	560
Delta states.	17,950	3,240	11,020	270	2,730	190	500
Northeast	14,150	1,250	10,890	–	1,550	240	220
Northern plains	7,640	3,020	210	2,870	1,090	80	370
Appalachian	7,460	400	6,080	–	570	110	300
Southern plains	5,590	970	2,350	970	520	230	550
Mountain	4,780	1,570	220	2,010	820	30	130
Corn belt	4,690	1,330	2,440	–	380	100	440
Pacific	3,680	1,300	740	650	800	30	160

– Represents or rounds to zero. [1] Includes pastureland and Conservation Reserve Program (CRP) lands.

Source: U.S. Department of Agriculture, Natural Resources Conservation Service, *2003 Annual National Resources Inventory*. See also <http://www.nrcs.usda.gov/technical/NRI/>.

Table 350. Land Cover/Use by State: 1997

[In thousands of acres (1,944,130 represents 1,944,130,000), except percent. Excludes Alaska and District of Columbia]

State	Total surface area	Nonfederal rural land, percent of total			State	Total surface area	Nonfederal rural land, percent of total		
		Cropland	Rangeland	Forest land			Cropland	Rangeland	Forest land
Total	**1,944,130**	**19.4**	**20.9**	**20.9**					
					Montana	94,110	16.1	39.1	5.8
United States .	**1,941,823**	**19.4**	**20.9**	**20.9**	Nebraska.	49,510	39.3	46.6	1.7
					Nevada.	70,763	1.0	11.8	0.4
Alabama	33,424	8.8	0.2	63.6	New Hampshire . .	5,941	2.3	0.0	66.2
Arizona	72,964	1.7	44.3	5.8	New Jersey	5,216	11.3	0.0	32.6
Arkansas	34,037	22.4	0.1	44.1					
California.	101,510	9.5	18.0	13.7	New Mexico	77,823	2.4	51.4	7.0
					New York	31,361	17.3	0.0	56.4
Colorado	66,625	13.2	36.9	5.2	North Carolina . .	33,709	16.7	0.0	47.3
Connecticut	3,195	6.4	0.0	55.0	North Dakota . . .	45,251	55.3	23.6	1.0
Delaware	1,534	31.6	0.0	22.9	Ohio	26,445	44.0	0.0	26.8
Florida.	37,534	7.3	8.6	33.4					
Georgia.	37,741	12.6	0.0	57.1	Oklahoma	44,738	21.8	31.4	16.3
					Oregon	62,161	6.1	14.9	20.3
Hawaii.	4,158	5.9	24.3	39.3	Pennsylvania . . .	28,995	18.9	0.0	53.4
Idaho	53,488	10.3	12.2	7.4	Rhode Island . . .	813	2.6	0.0	47.6
Illinois	36,059	66.6	0.0	10.5	South Carolina . .	19,939	12.9	0.0	56.1
Indiana	23,158	57.9	0.0	16.3					
Iowa	36,017	70.3	0.0	6.1	South Dakota . . .	49,358	33.9	44.3	1.1
					Tennessee	26,974	17.2	0.0	44.6
Kansas	52,661	50.4	29.9	2.9	Texas	171,052	15.7	56.0	6.3
Kentucky	25,863	20.0	0.0	41.2	Utah	54,339	3.1	19.8	3.5
Louisiana.	31,377	18.0	0.9	42.2	Vermont	6,154	9.9	0.0	67.4
Maine	20,966	2.0	0.0	84.4					
Maryland	7,870	20.5	0.0	30.2	Virginia	27,087	10.8	0.0	49.2
					Washington	44,035	15.1	13.3	29.1
Massachusetts . .	5,339	5.2	0.0	51.4	West Virginia . . .	15,508	5.6	0.0	68.2
Michigan	37,349	22.9	0.0	43.8	Wisconsin	35,920	29.5	0.0	40.2
Minnesota	54,010	39.6	0.0	30.1	Wyoming	62,603	3.5	43.6	1.6
Mississippi	30,527	17.5	0.0	53.1					
Missouri.	44,614	30.8	0.2	27.9	Caribbean . . .	2,307	16.0	6.3	27.7

Source: U.S. Department of Agriculture, Natural Resources and Conservation Service, and Iowa State University, Statistical Laboratory, *Summary Report, 1997 National Resources Inventory*, revised December 2000. See also <http://www.nrcs.usda.gov/technical/NRI/1997/summaryreport/> (revised December 2000).

Geography and Environment 217

Table 351. **Extreme and Mean Elevations by State and Other Area**

[One foot = .305 meter]

State and other areas	Highest point Name	Highest Elevation Feet	Highest Elevation Meters	Lowest point Name	Lowest Elevation Feet	Lowest Elevation Meters	Approximate mean elevation Feet	Approximate mean elevation Meters
United States	Mt. McKinley (AK)	20,320	6,198	Death Valley (CA). . . .	-282	-86	2,500	763
AL	Cheaha Mountain	2,407	734	Gulf of Mexico	(1)	(1)	500	153
AK	Mount McKinley	20,320	6,198	Pacific Ocean	(1)	(1)	1,900	580
AZ	Humphreys Peak	12,633	3,853	Colorado River	70	21	4,100	1,251
AR	Magazine Mountain.	2,753	840	Ouachita River	55	17	650	198
CA	Mount Whitney	14,494	4,419	Death Valley.	-282	-86	2,900	885
CO	Mt. Elbert	14,433	4,402	Arikaree River.	3,315	1,011	6,800	2,074
CT	Mt. Frissell on south slope . . . Ebright Road, [2]	2,380	726	Long Island Sound . . .	(1)	(1)	500	153
DE	at. . . . . DE-PA state line . . . . Tenleytown at Reno	448	137	Atlantic Ocean	(1)	(1)	60	18
DC	Reservoir	410	125	Potomac River	1	(Z)	150	46
FL	Britton Hill	345	105	Atlantic Ocean	(1)	(1)	100	31
GA	Brasstown Bald	4,784	1,459	Atlantic Ocean	(1)	(1)	600	183
HI	Pu'u Wekiu, Mauna Kea.	13,796	4,208	Pacific Ocean.	(1)	(1)	3,030	924
ID	Borah Peak	12,662	3,862	Snake River.	710	217	5,000	1,525
IL	Charles Mound.	1,235	377	Mississippi River	279	85	600	183
IN	Hoosier Hill	1,257	383	Ohio River	320	98	700	214
IA	Hawkeye Point.	1,670	509	Mississippi River	480	146	1,100	336
KS	Mount Sunflower.	4,039	1,232	Verdigris River	679	207	2,000	610
KY	Black Mountain.	4,145	1,264	Mississippi River	257	78	750	229
LA	Driskill Mountain.	535	163	New Orleans	-8	-2	100	31
ME	Mount Katahdin	5,268	1,607	Atlantic Ocean	(1)	(1)	600	183
MD	Hoye Crest	3,360	1,025	Atlantic Ocean	(1)	(1)	350	107
MA	Mount Greylock	3,491	1,065	Atlantic Ocean	(1)	(1)	500	153
MI	Mount Arvon	1,979	604	Lake Erie.	571	174	900	275
MN	Eagle Mountain	2,301	702	Lake Superior.	601	183	1,200	366
MS	Woodall Mountain	806	246	Gulf of Mexico	(1)	(1)	300	92
MO	Taum Sauk Mountain.	1,772	540	St. Francis River	230	70	800	244
MT	Granite Peak	12,799	3,904	Kootenai River	1,800	549	3,400	1,037
NE	Panorama Point	5,424	1,654	Missouri River.	840	256	2,600	793
NV	Boundary Peak	13,140	4,007	Colorado River	479	146	5,500	1,678
NH	Mount Washington	6,288	1,918	Atlantic Ocean	(1)	(1)	1,000	305
NJ	High Point	1,803	550	Atlantic Ocean	(1)	(1)	250	76
NM	Wheeler Peak	13,161	4,014	Red Bluff Reservoir . . .	2,842	867	5,700	1,739
NY	Mount Marcy	5,344	1,630	Atlantic Ocean	(1)	(1)	1,000	305
NC	Mount Mitchell	6,684	2,039	Atlantic Ocean	(1)	(1)	700	214
ND	White Butte	3,506	1,069	Red River of the North .	750	229	1,900	580
OH	Campbell Hill	1,550	473	Ohio River	455	139	850	259
OK	Black Mesa	4,973	1,517	Little River	289	88	1,300	397
OR	Mount Hood.	11,239	3,428	Pacific Ocean.	(1)	(1)	3,300	1,007
PA	Mount Davis	3,213	980	Delaware River.	(1)	(1)	1,100	336
RI	Jerimoth Hill.	812	248	Atlantic Ocean	(1)	(1)	200	61
SC	Sassafras Mountain	3,560	1,086	Atlantic Ocean	(1)	(1)	350	107
SD	Harney Peak	7,242	2,209	Big Stone Lake	966	295	2,200	671
TN	Clingmans Dome	6,643	2,026	Mississippi River	178	54	900	275
TX	Guadalupe Peak.	8,749	2,668	Gulf of Mexico	(1)	(1)	1,700	519
UT	Kings Peak	13,528	4,126	Beaverdam Wash	2,000	610	6,100	1,861
VT	Mount Mansfield	4,393	1,340	Lake Champlain	95	29	1,000	305
VA	Mount Rogers	5,729	1,747	Atlantic Ocean	(1)	(1)	950	290
WA	Mount Rainier	14,411	4,395	Pacific Ocean.	(1)	(1)	1,700	519
WV	Spruce Knob	4,863	1,483	Potomac River	240	73	1,500	458
WI	Timms Hill	1,951	595	Lake Michigan	579	177	1,050	320
WY	Gannett Peak.	13,804	4,210	Belle Fourche River. . .	3,099	945	6,700	2,044
Other areas:								
Puerto Rico	Cerro de Punta.	4,390	1,339	Atlantic Ocean	(1)	(1)	1,800	549
American Samoa. . .	Lata Mountain	3,160	964	Pacific Ocean.	(1)	(1)	1,300	397
Guam	Mount Lamlam.	1,332	406	Pacific Ocean.	(1)	(1)	330	101
Virgin Is. . . .	Crown Mountain.	1,556	475	Atlantic Ocean	(1)	(1)	750	229

Z Less than 0.5 meter.   [1] Sea level.   [2] At DE-PA state line.   [3] "Sec." denotes section; "T," township; "R," range; "N," north; and "W," west.

Source: U.S. Geological Survey, for highest and lowest points, "Elevations and Distances in the United States" at <http://erg.usgs.gov/isb/pubs/booklets/elvadist/elvadist.html> (released 29 April 2005). for mean elevations, *Elevations and Distances in the United States,* 1983 edition.

Table 352. U.S. Wetland Resources and Deepwater Habitats by Type: 1986 and 1997

[In thousands of acres (144,673.3 represents 144,673,300). Wetlands and deepwater habitats are defined separately because the term wetland does not include permanent water bodies. Deepwater habitats are permanently flooded land lying below the deepwater boundary of wetlands. Deepwater habitats include environments where surface water is permanent and often deep, so that water, rather than air, is the principal medium within which the dominant organisms live, whether or not they are attached to the substrate. As in wetlands, the dominant plants are hydrophytes; however, the substrates are considered nonsoil because the water is too deep to support emergent vegetation. In general terms, wetlands are lands where saturation with water is the dominant factor determining the nature of soil development and the types of plant and animal communities living in the soil and on its surface. The single feature that most wetlands share is soil or substrate that is at least periodically saturated with or covered by water. Wetlands are lands transitional between terrestrial and aquatic systems where the water table is usually at or near the surface or the land is covered by shallow water]

Wetland or deepwater category	1986	1997	Change, 1986 to 1997
All wetlands and deepwater habitats, total	**144,673.3**	**144,136.8**	**-536.5**
All deepwater habitats, total	38,537.6	38,645.1	107.5
Lacustrine [1]	14,608.9	14,725.3	116.4
Riverine [2]	6,291.1	6,255.9	-35.2
Estuarine subtidal [3]	17,637.6	17,663.9	26.3
All wetlands, total	106,135.7	105,491.7	-644.0
Intertidal wetlands [4]	5,336.6	5,326.2	-10.4
Marine intertidal	133.1	130.9	-2.2
Estuarine intertidal nonvegetated	580.4	580.1	-0.3
Estuarine intertidal vegetated	4,623.1	4,615.2	-7.9
Freshwater wetlands	100,799.1	100,165.5	-633.6
Freshwater nonvegetated	5,251.0	5,914.3	663.3
Freshwater vegetated	95,548.1	94,251.2	-1,296.9
Freshwater emergent [5]	26,383.3	25,157.1	-1,226.2
Freshwater forested [6]	51,929.6	50,728.5	-1,201.1
Freshwater shrub [7]	17,235.2	18,365.6	1,130.4

[1] The lacustrine system includes deepwater habitats with all of the following characteristics: (1) situated in a topographic depression or a dammed river channel; (2) lacking trees, shrubs, persistent emergents, emergent mosses or lichens with greater than 30 percent coverage; (3) total area exceeds 20 acres.   [2] The riverine system includes deepwater habitats contained within a channel, with the exception of habitats with water containing ocean derived salts in excess of 0.5 parts per thousand.   [3] The estuarine system consists of deepwater tidal habitats and adjacent tidal wetlands that are usually semi-enclosed by land but have open, partly obstructed, or sporadic access to the open ocean, and in which ocean water is at least occasionally diluted by freshwater runoff from the land. Subtidal is where the substrate is continuously submerged by marine or estuarine waters.   [4] Intertidal is where the substrate is exposed and flooded by tides. Intertidal includes the splash zone of coastal waters.   [5] Emergent wetlands are characterized by erect, rooted, herbaceous hydrophytes, excluding mosses and lichens. This vegetation is present for most of the growing season in most years. These wetlands are usually dominated by perennial plants.   [6] Forested wetlands are characterized by woody vegetation that is 20 feet tall or taller.   [7] Shrub wetlands include areas dominated by woody vegetation less than 20 feet tall. The species include true shrubs, young trees, and trees or shrubs that are small or stunted because of environmental conditions.

Source: U.S. Fish and Wildlife Service, *Status and Trends of Wetlands in the Conterminous United States, 1986 to 1997,* January 2001. See also <www.fws.gov.nwi>.

Table 353. Flows of Largest U.S. Rivers—Length, Discharge, and Drainage Area

River	Location of mouth	Source stream (name and location)	Length (miles) [1]	Average discharge at mouth (1,000 cubic ft. per second)	Drainage area (1,000 sq. mi.)
Missouri	Missouri	Red Rock Creek, MT	2,540	76.2	[2]529
Mississippi	Louisiana	Mississippi River, MN	[3]2,340	[4]593	[2, 5]1,150
Yukon	Alaska	McNeil River, Canada	1,980	225	[2]328
St. Lawrence	Canada	North River, MN.	1,900	348	[2]396
Rio Grande	Mexico-Texas	Rio Grande, CO	1,900	([7])	336
Arkansas	Arkansas	East Fork Arkansas River, CO . . .	1,460	41	161
Colorado	Mexico	Colorado River, CO	1,450	([7])	246
Atchafalaya [6]	Louisiana	Tierra Blanca Creek, NM	1,420	58	95.1
Ohio	Illinois-Kentucky.	Allegheny River, PA	1,310	281	203
Red	Louisiana	Tierra Blanca Creek, NM	1,290	56	93.2
Brazos	Texas	Blackwater Draw, NM	1,280	([7])	45.6
Columbia	Oregon-Washington . . .	Columbia River, Canada	1,240	265	[2]258
Snake	Washington	Snake River, WY	1,040	56.9	108
Platte	Nebraska	Grizzly Creek, CO	990	([7])	84.9
Pecos	Texas	Pecos River, NM	926	([7])	44.3
Canadian	Oklahoma	Canadian River, CO	906	([7])	46.9
Tennessee	Kentucky	Courthouse Creek, NC	886	68	40.9
Colorado (of Texas) . . .	Texas	Colorado River, TX.	862	([7])	42.3
North Canadian	Oklahoma	Corrumpa Creek, NM	800	([7])	17.6
Mobile	Alabama	Tickanetley Creek, GA	774	67.2	44.6
Kansas	Kansas	Arikaree River, CO.	743	([7])	59.5
Kuskokwim	Alaska	South Fork Kuskokwim River, AK . . .	724	67	48
Yellowstone	North Dakota	North Folk Yellowstone River, WY. . .	692	([7](	70
Tanana	Alaska	Nabesna River, AK	659	41	44.5
Gila	Arizona	Middle Fork Gila River, NM	649	([7])	58.2
Porcupine	Alaska	Porcupine River, Canada.	569	23	45.1
Susquehanna	Maryland	Hayden Creek, NY	447	38.2	27.2

- Represents zero.   [1] From source to mouth.   [2] Drainage area includes both the United States and Canada.   [3] The length from the source of the Missouri River to the Mississippi River and thence to the Gulf of Mexico is about 3,710 miles.   [4] Includes about 167,000 cubic ft. per second diverted from the Mississippi into the Atchafalaya River but excludes the flow of the Red River, but exclude all water diverted into the Atchafalaya from the Mississippi River.   [5] Excludes the drainage areas of the Red and Atchafalaya Rivers.   [6] In east-central Louisiana, the Red River flows into the Atchafalaya River, a distributary of the Mississippi River. Data on average discharge, length, and drainage area include the Red River, but exclude all water diverted into the Atchafalaya from the Mississippi River.   [7] Less than 15,000 cubic feet per second.

Source: U.S. Geological Survey, *Largest Rivers in the United States,* <http://pubs.usgs.gov/of/1987/ofr87-242/>.

Geography and Environment   219

Table 354. U.S. Water Withdrawals and Consumptive Use Per Day by End Use: 1940 to 2000

[In billions of gallons, except as indicated. (140 represents 140,000,000,000). Includes Puerto Rico. Withdrawal signifies water physically withdrawn from a source. Includes fresh and saline water; excludes water used for hydroelectric power]

Year	Total (bil. gal.)	Per capita [1] (gal.)	Irrigation (bil. gal.)	Public supply (bil. gal.) [2]	Rural (bil. gal.) [3]	Industrial and misc. [4] (bil. gal.)	Steam electric utilities (bil. gal.)
WITHDRAWALS							
1940	140	1,027	71	10	3.1	29	23
1950	180	1,185	89	14	3.6	37	40
1955	240	1,454	110	17	3.6	39	72
1960	270	1,500	110	21	3.6	38	100
1965	310	1,602	120	24	4.0	46	130
1970	370	1,815	130	27	4.5	47	170
1975	420	1,972	140	29	4.9	45	200
1980	440	1,953	150	34	5.6	45	210
1985	399	1,650	137	38	7.8	31	187
1990	408	1,620	137	41	7.9	30	195
1995	402	1,500	134	40	8.9	29	190
2000	408	1,430	137	43	9.2	23	196
CONSUMPTIVE USE							
1960	61	339	52	3.5	2.8	3.0	0.2
1965	77	403	66	5.2	3.2	3.4	0.4
1970	87	427	73	5.9	3.4	4.1	0.8
1975	96	451	80	6.7	3.4	4.2	1.9
1980	100	440	83	7.1	3.9	5.0	3.2
1985	92	380	74	(5)	9.2	6.1	6.2
1990	94	370	76	(5)	8.9	6.7	4.0
1995	100	374	81	(5)	9.9	4.8	3.7
2000	(NA)	(NA)	(NA)	(NA)	(NA)	(NA)	(NA)

NA Not available   [1] Based on U.S. Census Bureau resident population as of July 1.   [2] Includes commercial water withdrawals.   [3] Rural farm and nonfarm household and garden use, and water for farm stock and dairies.   [4] For 1940 to 1960, includes manufacturing and mineral industries, rural commercial industries, air-conditioning, resorts, hotels, motels, military, and other state and federal agencies, and miscellaneous; thereafter, includes manufacturing, mining and mineral processing, ordnance, construction, and miscellaneous.   [5] Public supply consumptive use included in end-use categories.

Source: 1940–1960, U.S. Bureau of Domestic Business Development, based principally on committee prints, *Water Resources Activities in the United States,* for the Senate Committee on National Water Resources, U.S. Senate, thereafter, U.S. Geological Survey, *Estimated Use of Water in the United States in 2000,* circular 1268. See also <http://pubs.usgs.gov/circ/2004/circ1268/> (released 12 March 2004).

Table 355. Water Withdrawals by Source, Type, and Use—State and Other Areas: 2000

[Withdrawals in millions of gallons per day(408,000 represents 408,000,000,000). Figures may not add due to rounding. Withdrawal signifies water physically withdrawn from a source. Includes fresh and saline water. For information on methodology and differences with prior surveys, see <http://water.usgs.gov/pubs/circ/2004/circ1268/htdocs/text-intro.html>]

State and other area	Withdrawals, total [1]	Source, percent— Ground water	Source, percent— Surface water	Selected major uses, percent— Public supply	Selected major uses, percent— Irrigation	State and other area	Withdrawals, total [1]	Source, percent— Ground water	Source, percent— Surface water	Selected major uses, percent— Public supply	Selected major uses, percent— Irrigation
Total [2]	**408,000**	**20.7**	**79.2**	**10.6**	**33.6**	MT	8,290	2.3	97.7	1.8	95.9
						NE	12,300	63.9	35.7	2.7	71.5
AL	9,990	4.4	95.6	8.3	0.4	NV	2,810	26.9	73.0	22.4	75.1
AK	305	46.2	53.8	26.2	0.3	NH	1,210	7.0	92.6	8.0	0.4
AZ	6,730	51.0	49.0	16.0	80.2	NJ	5,560	10.5	89.6	18.9	2.5
AR	10,900	63.5	36.2	3.9	72.6	NM	3,260	47.2	52.5	9.1	87.7
CA	51,200	30.1	69.9	12.0	59.6	NY	12,100	7.4	92.6	21.2	0.3
						NC	11,400	5.1	94.7	8.3	2.5
CO	12,600	18.4	81.7	7.1	90.5	ND	1,140	10.8	89.5	5.6	12.7
CT	4,150	3.4	96.6	10.2	0.7						
DE	1,320	8.7	91.7	7.2	3.3	OH	11,100	7.9	92.8	13.2	0.3
DC	10	0.0	100.0	0.0	1.8	OK	2,020	51.0	49.0	33.4	35.5
FL	20,100	25.0	75.1	12.1	21.3	OR	6,930	14.3	85.7	8.2	87.7
						PA	9,950	6.7	93.4	14.7	0.1
GA	6,500	22.3	77.8	19.2	17.5	RI	429	6.7	93.2	27.7	0.8
HI	641	67.7	32.4	39.0	56.8						
ID	19,500	21.2	78.5	1.3	87.7	SC	7,170	4.6	95.4	7.9	3.7
IL	13,700	5.9	94.2	12.8	1.1	SD	528	42.0	58.0	17.7	70.6
IN	10,100	6.5	93.7	6.6	1.0	TN	10,800	3.9	96.3	8.2	0.2
						TX	29,600	30.3	69.9	14.3	29.2
IA	3,360	20.2	79.8	11.4	0.6	UT	4,970	21.1	78.9	12.8	77.7
KS	6,610	57.3	42.7	6.3	56.1						
KY	4,160	4.5	95.4	12.6	0.7	VT	447	9.7	90.4	13.4	0.8
LA	10,400	15.7	83.9	7.2	9.8	VA	8,830	3.6	96.5	8.2	0.3
ME	799	10.1	89.9	12.8	0.7	WA	5,310	27.7	72.3	19.2	57.3
						WV	5,150	1.8	98.3	3.7	0.0
MD	7,910	2.8	97.2	10.4	0.5	WI	7,590	10.7	89.3	8.2	2.6
MA	4,660	5.8	94.2	15.9	2.7	WY	5,170	14.8	85.1	2.1	87.0
MI	10,000	7.3	92.6	11.4	2.0						
MN	3,870	18.6	81.4	12.9	5.9						
MS	2,960	73.6	26.4	12.1	47.6	PR	2,810	4.9	95.0	18.3	3.4
MO	8,230	21.6	78.4	10.6	17.4	VI	148	0.7	99.3	4.1	0.3

[1] Represents both fresh and saline water.   [2] Includes Puerto Rico and Virgin Islands.

Source: U.S. Geological Survey, *Estimated Use of Water in the United States in 2000,* circular 1268. See also <http://pubs.usgs.gov/circ/2004/circ1268/> (released March 2004).

220   Geography and Environment

Table 356. U.S. Water Quality Conditions by Type of Waterbody: 2000

[Section 305(b) of the Clean Water Act requires states and other jurisdictions to assess the health of their waters and the extent to which their waters support water quality standards. Section 305(b) requires that states submit reports describing water quality conditions to the Environmental Protection Agency every two years. Water quality standards have three elements (designated uses, criteria developed to protect each use, and an antidegradation policy). For information on survey methodology and assessment criteria, see report]

Item	Rivers and streams (miles)	Lakes, reservoirs, and ponds (acres)	Coastal resources[1] (sq. miles)	Great Lakes shoreline (miles)	Ocean shoreline (miles)
Total size	3,692,830	40,603,893	87,369	5,521	58,618
Amount accessed [2]	699,946	17,339,080	31,072	5,066	3,221
Percent of total size	19	43	36	92	6
Amount accessed as—					
Good [3]	463,441	8,026,988	13,850	–	2,176
Good but threatened [4]	85,544	1,343,903	1,023	1,095	193
Polluted [5]	291,264	7,702,370	15,676	3,955	434
Percent of accessed as—					
Good [3]	53	47	45	–	79
Good but threatened [4]	8	8	4	22	7
Polluted [5]	39	45	51	78	14
Amount impaired by leading sources of pollution: [6]					
Agriculture	128,859	3,158,393	2,811	75	(NA)
Atmospheric deposition	(NA)	983,936	3,692	71	(NA)
Construction	(NA)	(NA)	(NA)	(NA)	29
Contaminated sediments	(NA)	(NA)	(NA)	(NA)	(NA)
Forestry	28,156	(NA)	(NA)	519	(NA)
Habitat modification	37,654	(NA)	(NA)	62	(NA)
Hydrologic modification	53,850	1,413,624	2,171	(NA)	(NA)
Industrial discharges/point sources . . .	(NA)	(NA)	4,116	(NA)	76
Land disposal of wastes	(NA)	856,586	(NA)	(NA)	(NA)
Municipal point sources	27,988	943,715	5,779	61	123
Nonpoint sources	(NA)	1,045,036	(NA)	(NA)	89
Resource extraction	27,695	(NA)	1,913	(NA)	142
Septic tanks	(NA)	(NA)	(NA)	(NA)	(NA)
Urban runoff and storm sewers	34,871	13,699,327	5,045	61	103
				152	241

– Represents zero. NA Not available. [1] Includes tidal estuaries, shoreline waters, and coral reefs. [2] Includes waterbodies assessed as not attainable for one or more uses. Most states do not assess all their waterbodies during the 2-year reporting cycle, but use a "rotating basin approach" whereby all waters are monitored over a set period of time. [3] Based on assessment of available data, water quality supports all designated uses. Water quality meets narrative and/or numeric criteria adopted to protect and support a designated use. [4] Although all assessed uses are currently met, data show a declining trend in water quality. Projections based on this trend indicate water quality will be impaired in the future, unless action is taken to prevent further degradation. [5] Impaired or not attainable. The reporting state or jurisdiction has performed a "use-attainability analysis" and demonstrated that support of one or more designated beneficial uses is not attainable due to specific biological, chemical, physical, or economic/social conditions. [6] Excludes unknown and natural sources.

Source: U.S. Environmental Protection Agency, *National Water Quality Inventory: 2000 Report*, EPA-841-R-02-001, August 2002. See also <http://www.epa.gov/305b/2000report>.

Table 357. Oil Spills in U.S. Water—Number and Volume: 1998 to 2001

[Based on reported discharges into U.S. navigable waters, including territorial waters (extending 3 to 12 miles from the coastline), tributaries, the contiguous zone, onto shoreline, or into other waters that threaten the marine environment. Data found in Marine Safety Management System]

Spill characteristic	Number of spills				Spill volume (gallons)			
	1998	1999	2000	2001	1998	1999	2000	2001
Total	8,315	8,539	8,354	7,559	885,303	1,172,449	1,431,370	854,520
Size of spill (gallons):								
1–100	7,962	8,212	8,058	7,256	38,093	39,119	39,355	33,276
101–1,000	259	240	219	216	86,606	86,530	78,779	86,955
1,001–3,000	54	42	37	45	96,743	74,582	67,529	77,447
3,001–5,000	15	18	12	16	64,609	73,798	45,512	67,241
5,001–10,000	15	10	16	11	108,148	66,274	112,415	89,224
10,001–50,000	8	12	6	14	216,335	301,510	108,400	376,057
50,001–100,000	–	4	4	–	–	245,406	266,380	–
100,001–1,000,000	2	1	2	1	274,769	285,230	713,000	124,320
1,000,000 and over	–	–	–	–	–	–	–	–
Waterbody:								
Atlantic ocean	109	148	150	83	6,674	29,440	135,010	7,168
Pacific ocean	644	758	623	493	192,775	150,694	36,301	53,295
Gulf of Mexico	2,190	1,756	1,838	1,728	181,372	45,786	112,069	133,872
Great Lakes	119	129	96	109	3,006	906	4,535	1,600
Lakes	25	31	32	35	63	624	349	244
Rivers and canals	1,944	1,924	1,816	1,682	280,651	504,264	663,404	237,980
Bays and sounds	891	1,299	1,248	1,140	24,234	136,650	49,783	139,300
Harbors	790	907	801	893	97,223	105,213	273,095	158,667
Other	1,603	1,587	1,750	1,396	99,305	198,872	156,824	122,394
Source:								
Tankship	104	92	111	95	56,673	8,414	608,176	125,217
Tankbarge	220	227	229	246	248,089	158,977	133,540	212,298
All other vessels	4,848	5,361	5,220	4,680	316,473	409,084	291,927	232,341
Facilities	937	1,019	1,054	995	166,269	367,537	311,604	201,025
Pipelines	45	25	25	34	47,863	36,140	17,021	13,577
All other non-vessels	571	571	566	436	32,584	147,704	45,136	55,921
Unknown	1,590	1,244	1,149	1,073	17,352	44,593	23,966	14,141

– Represents or rounds to zero.

Source: U.S. Coast Guard, <http://www.uscg.mil/hq/g-m/nmc/response/stats/Summary.htm> and <http://www.uscg.mil/hq/g-m/nmc/response/stats/c2data.htm> (released August 2003).

Geography and Environment   221

Table 358. National Ambient Air Pollutant Concentrations by Type of Pollutant: 1990 to 2004

[Data represent annual composite averages of pollutant based on daily 24-hour averages of monitoring stations, except carbon monoxide is based on the second-highest, nonoverlapping, 8-hour average; ozone, the second-highest daily maximum 1-hour value or the fourth-highest maximum 8-hour value; and lead, the maximum quarterly average of ambient lead levels. Based on data from the Air Quality System. $\mu g/m^3$ = micrograms of pollutant per cubic meter of air; ppm = parts per million. Also see document at <http://www.epa.gov/airtrends/>]

Pollutant	Unit	Monitoring stations, number	Air quality standard[1]	1990	1995	2000	2001	2002	2003	2004
Carbon monoxide	ppm	293	9[2]	5.9	4.7	3.4	3.2	2.9	2.7	2.6
Ozone	ppm	634	.12[3]	0.125	0.114	0.111	0.108	0.107	0.107	0.105
Ozone	ppm	633	0.08[4]	0.090	0.085	0.084	0.083	0.082	0.083	0.080
Sulfur dioxide	ppm	351	.03	0.0083	0.0055	0.0050	0.0047	0.0044	0.0043	0.0042
Particulates (PM-10)	$\mu g/m^3$	545	50[5]	31.4	26.4	25.2	24.3	23.7	23.8	22.6
Fine Particulates (PM-2.5)	$\mu g/m^3$	785	15[6]	(NA)	(NA)	13.5	13.1	12.6	12.2	11.8
Nitrogen dioxide	ppm	190	.053	0.020	0.019	0.017	0.017	0.016	0.016	0.015
Lead	$\mu g/m^3$	66	1.5[7]	0.12	0.06	0.06	0.08	0.03	0.05	0.05

[1] Refers to the primary National Ambient Air Quality Standard that protects the public health. [2] Based on 8-hour standard of 9 ppm. [3] Based on 1-hour standard of .12 ppm. [4] Based on 8-hour standard of .08 ppm. [5] The particulates (PM-10) standard replaced the previous standard for total suspended particulates in 1987. [6] The PM-2.5 national monitoring network was deployed in 1999. National trend data prior to that time is not available. [7] Based on 3-month standard of 1.5 $\mu g/m^3$.

Source: U.S. Environmental Protection Agency, National Emissions Inventory (NEI) Air Pollution Emissions Trends Data, 1970-2002; Released August 2005: <http://www.epa.gov/ttn/chief/trends/index.html#tables>.

Table 359. Selected National Air Pollutant Emissions: 1970 to 2002

[In thousands of tons (13,042 represents 13,042,000), except as indicated. PM-10 = Particulate matter of less than ten microns; PM-2.5 = particulate matter of less than 2.5 microns effective diameter. Methodologies to estimate data for 1970 to 1980 period and 1985 to present emissions differ. Beginning with 1985, the methodology for more recent years is described in the document available at <http://www.epa.gov/ttn/chief/net/2002inventory.html>.

Year	PM-10	PM-10, fugitive dust[1]	PM-2.5	Sulfur dioxide	Nitrogen dioxides	Volatile organic compounds	Carbon monoxide	Lead (tons)[2]
1970	13,042	(NA)	(NA)	31,218	26,883	34,659	204,043	220,869
1975	7,671	(NA)	(NA)	28,043	26,337	30,765	188,398	159,659
1980	7,013	(NA)	(NA)	25,925	27,079	31,106	185,407	74,153
1985	11,590	29,734	(NA)	23,307	25,757	27,404	176,844	22,890
1990	9,689	18,063	7,559	23,076	25,529	24,108	154,186	4,975
1995	8,807	17,012	6,929	18,619	24,956	22,041	126,777	3,929
1996	9,014	13,844	6,725	18,385	24,787	20,871	128,858	2,627
1997	8,393	14,516	6,256	18,840	24,705	19,530	117,910	(NA)
1998	8,343	14,550	6,261	18,944	24,348	18,782	115,380	(NA)
1999	9,391	14,112	7,333	17,545	22,845	18,776	114,541	(NA)
2000	9,440	14,307	7,288	16,347	22,598	17,512	114,467	(NA)
2001	9,118	13,769	6,632	15,932	21,547	17,118	106,295	(NA)
2002	8,882	13,272	6,803	15,353	21,102	16,544	112,049	(NA)

NA Not available. [1] Sources such as agricultural tilling, construction, mining and quarrying, paved roads, unpaved roads, and wind erosion. [2] Beginning 1996, lead and lead compounds are inventoried through the hazardous air pollutants (HAPs) portion of the National Emission Inventory (NEI) every three years; data for 1997 forward are currently not available.

Source: U.S. Environmental Protection Agency, National Emissions Inventory (NEI) Air Pollution Emissions Trends Data, 1970-2002; Released August 2005: <http://www.epa.gov/ttn/chief/trends/index.html#tables>.

Table 360. Selected Air Pollutant Emissions by Pollutant and Source: 2002

[In thousands of tons, except as indicated. See headnote, Table 359]

Source	PM-10[1]	PM-2.5	Sulfur dioxide	Nitrogen dioxides	Volatile organic compounds	Carbon monoxide
Total emissions	22,153	6,802	15,351	21,103	16,544	112,049
Fuel combustion, stationary sources	1,369	1,157	13,167	8,294	1,012	4,433
Electric utilities	695	582	10,293	4,699	52	499
Industrial	269	191	2,299	2,870	170	1,436
Other fuel combustion	405	384	575	725	790	2,498
Residential	177	319	150	360	765	2,331
Industrial processes	586	368	1,363	825	1,064	2,394
Chemical and allied product manufacturing	36	27	328	105	214	337
Metals processing	118	81	271	84	69	1,294
Petroleum and related industries	34	20	348	149	375	128
Other	398	240	416	487	406	635
Solvent utilization	16	14	2	8	4,692	51
Storage and transport	82	33	5	16	1,205	215
Waste disposal and recycling	443	419	28	152	457	1,847
Highway vehicles	204	149	275	7,366	4,543	62,161
Light-duty gas vehicles and motorcycles	52	27	93	2,166	2,496	34,400
Light-duty trucks	30	16	65	1,401	1,638	24,191
Heavy-duty gas vehicles	9	7	12	404	201	2,554
Diesels	113	99	105	3,395	208	1,016
Off highway[2]	311	285	420	4,086	2,688	24,450
Miscellaneous[3]	19,142	4,377	91	356	883	16,498

[1] Represents both PM-10 and PM-10 fugitive dust; see Table 359. [2] Includes emissions from farm tractors and other farm machinery, construction equipment, industrial machinery, recreational marine vessels, and small general utility engines such as lawn mowers. [3] Includes emissions such as from forest fires and other kinds of burning, various agricultural activities, fugitive dust from paved and unpaved roads, and other construction and mining activities, and natural sources.

Source: U.S. Environmental Protection Agency, National Emissions Inventory (NEI) Air Pollution Emissions Trends Data, 1970-2002; Released August 2005: <http://www.epa.gov/ttn/chief/trends/index.html#tables>.

Table 361. Emissions of Greenhouse Gases by Type and Source: 1990 to 2004

[6,148.8 represents 6,148,800,000 tons. Emission estimates were mandated by Congress through Section 1605(a) of the Energy Policy Act of 1992 (Title XVI). Gases that contain carbon can be measured either in terms of the full molecular weight of the gas or just in terms of their carbon dioxide equivalent. Both measures are utilized below]

Type and source	Unit	1990	2000	2001	2002	2003	2004, est.
CARBON DIOXIDE EQUIVALENT							
Total emissions	Mil. metric tons . . .	6,148.8	6,970.8	6,884.1	6,912.9	6,983.2	7,122.1
Carbon dioxide, total	Mil. metric tons	5,002.3	5,845.5	5,785.5	5,808.5	5,871.8	5,973.0
Energy sources	Mil. metric tons	4,996.6	5,802.3	5,728.4	5,746.0	5,795.5	5,899.9
CO_2 in natural gas	Mil. metric tons	14.0	18.2	18.6	17.9	18.0	17.8
Cement production.	Mil. metric tons	33.3	41.3	41.5	43.0	43.2	44.8
Gas flaring	Mil. metric tons	9.1	5.5	5.9	6.0	5.9	5.9
Other industrial	Mil. metric tons	26.8	29.4	27.4	26.4	27.6	28.7
Waste combustion	Mil. metric tons	5.1	7.9	8.0	6.2	7.5	7.8
Other, adjustments.	Mil. metric tons	-82.6	-59.1	-44.2	-37.1	-25.9	-31.9
Methane	Mil. metric tons	721.4	639.8	625.8	626.2	633.9	639.5
Nitrous oxide	Mil. metric tons	337.0	343.5	338.8	335.1	335.2	353.7
HFCs, PFCs, and SF_6[1].	Mil. metric tons	88.1	142.1	133.9	143.1	142.4	155.9
GAS							
Carbon dioxide	Mil. metric tons	5,002.3	5,845.5	5,785.5	5,808.5	5,871.8	5,973.0
Methane, total	Mil. metric tons	31.36	27.82	27.21	27.23	27.56	27.80
Nitrous oxide, total.	Mil. metric tons	1.139	1.160	1.145	1.132	1.133	1.195
HFCs, PFCs, and SF_6[1].	Mil. metric tons	(2)	(2)	(2)	(2)	(2)	(2)

[1] Hyrdofluorocarbons, perfluorocarbons, and sulfur hexafluoride.   [2] Mixture of gases.

Source: U.S. Energy Information Administration, *Emissions of Greenhouse Gases in the United States*, Series DOE/EIA-0573(2004), annual. See also <ftp://ftp.eia.doe.gov/pub/oiaf/1605/cdrom/pdf/ggrpt/057304.pdf> (released 19 December 2005).

Table 362. Municipal Solid Waste Generation, Recovery, and Disposal: 1980 to 2003

[In millions of tons (151.6 represents 151,600,000), except as indicated. Covers post-consumer residential and commercial solid wastes which comprise the major portion of typical municipal collections. Excludes mining, agricultural and industrial processing, demolition and construction wastes, sewage sludge, and junked autos and obsolete equipment wastes. Based on material-flows estimating procedure and wet weight as generated]

Item and material	1980	1990	1995	2000	2001	2002	2003
Waste generated	151.6	205.2	211.4	234.0	231.2	235.5	236.2
Per person per day (lb.)	3.7	4.5	4.4	4.5	4.4	4.5	4.4
Materials recovered	14.5	33.2	54.9	68.9	69.3	70.5	72.3
Per person per day (lb.)	0.35	0.7	1.1	1.3	1.3	1.3	1.4
Combustion for energy recovery	2.7	31.9	35.5	33.7	33.6	33.4	33.1
Per person per day (lb.)	0.06	0.7	0.7	0.7	0.7	0.6	0.6
Combustion without energy recovery	11.0	(1)	(1)	(1)	(1)	(1)	(1)
Per person per day (lb.)	0.27	(1)	(1)	(1)	(1)	(1)	(1)
Landfill, other disposal.	123.4	140.1	120.9	131.4	128.3	131.7	130.8
Per person per day (lb.)	3.0	3.1	2.5	2.6	2.5	2.5	2.5
Percent distribution of generation:							
Paper and paperboard	36.4	35.4	38.6	37.5	35.7	35.8	35.2
Glass	10.0	6.4	6.1	5.4	5.4	5.4	5.3
Metals.	10.2	8.1	7.5	7.8	7.9	7.8	8.0
Plastics	4.5	8.3	8.9	10.5	10.9	11.2	11.3
Rubber and leather	2.8	2.8	2.9	2.8	2.9	2.8	2.9
Textiles	1.7	2.8	3.5	4.0	4.2	4.4	4.5
Wood	4.6	6.0	4.9	5.5	5.7	5.7	5.8
Food wastes	8.6	10.1	10.3	11.3	11.7	11.6	11.7
Yard wastes	18.1	17.1	14.0	11.8	12.1	12.0	12.1
Other wastes	3.2	3.0	3.3	3.2	3.4	3.3	3.2

[1] Combustion without energy recovery is no longer available separately.

Source: Franklin Associates, a Division of ERG, Prairie Village, KS, *Municipal Solid Waste Generation, Recycling, and Disposal in the United States: Facts and Figures for 2003*. Prepared for the U.S. Environmental Protection Agency. See also <http://www.epa.gov/epaoswer/non-hw/muncpl/msw99.htm>.

Geography and Environment   223

Table 363. Generation and Recovery of Selected Materials of Municipal Solid Waste: 1980 to 2003

[In millions of tons (151.6 represents 151,600,000), except as indicated. Covers post-consumer residential and commercial solid wastes which comprise the major portion of typical municipal collections. Excludes mining, agricultural and industrial processing, demolition and construction wastes, sewage sludge, and junked autos and obsolete equipment wastes. Based on material-flows estimating procedure and wet weight as generated]

Item and material	1980	1990	1995	2000	2001	2002	2003
Waste generated, total	151.6	205.2	211.4	234.0	231.2	235.5	236.2
Paper and paperboard.	55.2	72.7	81.7	87.7	82.7	84.2	83.1
Ferrous metals.	12.6	12.6	11.6	13.5	13.5	13.6	14.0
Aluminum	1.7	2.8	3.0	3.1	3.2	3.2	3.2
Other nonferrous metals	1.2	1.1	1.3	1.6	1.6	1.6	1.6
Glass.	15.1	13.1	12.8	12.6	12.6	12.8	12.5
Plastics.	6.8	17.1	18.9	24.7	25.3	26.3	26.7
Yard waste	27.5	35.0	29.7	27.7	28.0	28.3	28.6
Other wastes.	31.5	50.7	52.4	63.1	64.4	65.5	66.5
Materials recovered, total	14.5	33.2	54.9	68.9	69.3	70.5	72.3
Paper and paperboard.	11.9	20.2	32.7	37.6	37.7	38.3	40.0
Ferrous metals.	0.4	2.2	4.1	4.6	4.6	4.9	5.1
Aluminum	0.3	1.0	0.9	0.9	0.8	0.8	0.7
Other nonferrous metals	0.5	0.7	0.8	1.1	1.1	1.1	1.1
Glass.	0.8	2.6	3.1	2.7	2.4	2.5	2.4
Plastics.	–	0.4	1.0	1.4	1.4	1.4	1.4
Yard waste	–	4.2	9.0	15.8	15.8	16.0	16.1
Other wastes.	0.6	1.8	3.2	4.9	5.6	5.6	5.6
Percent of generation recovered, total . . .	9.6	16.2	26.0	29.4	30.0	29.9	30.6
Paper and paperboard.	21.6	27.8	40.0	42.8	45.6	45.5	48.1
Ferrous metals.	3.2	17.5	35.3	34.1	34.1	36.0	36.4
Aluminum	17.6	35.7	30.0	28.7	25.0	23.8	21.4
Other nonferrous metals	41.7	63.6	61.5	67.9	67.5	67.5	66.7
Glass.	5.3	19.8	24.2	21.4	19.0	19.1	18.8
Plastics.	–	2.3	5.3	5.5	5.5	5.2	5.2
Yard waste	–	12.0	30.3	57.0	56.4	56.5	56.3
Other wastes.	1.9	3.6	6.1	7.8	8.6	8.6	8.5

– Represents zero.

Source: Franklin Associates, a Division of ERG, Prairie Village, KS, *Municipal Solid Waste Generation, Recycling, and Disposal in the United States: Facts and Figures for 2003.* Prepared for the U.S. Environmental Protection Agency. Prepared for the U.S. Environmental Protection Agency. See also <http://www.epa.gov/epaoswer/non-hw/muncpl/msw99.htm>.

Table 364. Municipal Solid Waste—Generation and Recovery by Type of Product: 2003

[See headnote, Table 363]

Type of product	Generation (1,000 tons)	Recovery		Discards (1,000 tons)
		Products recovered (1,000 tons)	Percent of generation	
Paper and paperboard products [1]	83,090	39,960	48.1	43,130
Newspapers.	12,640	10,410	82.4	2,230
Magazines.	2,270	750	33.0	1,520
Office papers	7,150	3,990	55.8	3,160
3rd class mail.	5,400	1,750	32.4	3,650
Other commercial printing.	6,950	880	12.7	6,070
Containers and packaging [1]	38,830	21,890	56.4	16,940
Corrugated boxes	29,710	21,180	71.3	8,530
Folding cartons	5,560	450	8.1	5,110
Glass products [1]	12,470	2,350	18.8	10,120
Containers and packaging	10,690	2,350	22.0	8,340
Beer and soft drink bottles	6,440	1,250	19.4	5,190
Wine and liquor bottles.	1,520	350	23.0	1,170
Food and other bottles and jars	2,730	750	27.5	1,980
Metal products [1]	18,820	6,840	36.3	11,980
Ferrous metals.	11,160	3,370	30.2	7,790
Aluminum	1,060	(Z)	(Z)	1,060
Lead.	1,140	1,060	93.0	80
Containers and packaging	4,780	2,410	50.4	2,370
Steel	2,840	1,720	60.6	1,120
Aluminum.	1,940	690	35.6	1,250
Plastics	26,650	1,390	5.2	25,260
Plastics in durable goods	8,390	330	3.9	8,060
Plastics in nondurable goods	6,350	–	0.0	6,350
Containers and packaging [1]	11,910	1,060	8.9	10,850
Soft drink bottles	1,070	270	25.2	800
Rubber and leather [1]	6,820	1,100	16.1	5,720
Rubber in tires	3,080	1,100	35.7	1,980

– Represents zero or rounds to zero.   Z Less than 5,000 tons or .05 percent.   [1] Includes products not shown separately.

Source: Franklin Associates, a Division of ERG, Prairie Village, KS, *Municipal Solid Waste Generation, Recycling, and Disposal in the United States: Facts and Figures for 2003.* Prepared for the U.S. Environmental Protection Agency. See also <http://www.epa.gov/epaoswer/non-hw/muncpl/msw99.htm>.

Table 365. **Toxic Chemical Releases and Transfers by Media: 1998 to 2004**

[In millions of pounds (6,734.6 represents 6,734,600,000), except as indicated. Based on reports filed as required by section 313 of the Emergency Planning and Community Right-to-Know Act (EPCRA, or Title III of the Superfund Amendments and Reauthorization Act of 1986), Public Law 99-499. Owners and operators of facilities that are classified within Standard Classification Code groups 20 through 39, have 10 or more full-time employees, and that manufacture, process, or otherwise use any listed toxic chemical in quantities greater than the established threshold in the course of a calendar year are covered and required to report. Excludes all Persistent, Bioaccumulative, Toxic (PBT) chemicals and vanadium and vanadium compounds]

Media	1998	2000	2002	2003	2004
Total facilities reporting	23,367	23,021	21,532	20,816	20,444
Total on-and off-site disposal or other releases	**6,734.6**	**6,184.4**	**4,262.8**	**3,902.6**	**3,735.5**
On-site releases	6,336.9	5,709.5	3,794.4	3,429.1	3,236.9
Air emissions.	2,040.4	1,880.8	1,606.6	1,569.7	1,545.3
Surface water discharges	255.8	269.1	232.1	218.6	240.3
Underground injection class I	232.0	239.9	205.3	205.8	208.6
Underground injection class II–V.	26.1	29.7	13.6	14.7	19.2
RCRA subtitle C landfills [1]	190.7	201.9	106.9	120.3	110.4
Other landfills	261.2	275.6	229.9	220.0	217.9
Land treatment/application farming	9.7	13.8	20.4	15.1	18.5
Surface impoundments	1,289.5	963.0	631.4	666.1	588.0
Other land disposal	2,031.6	1,835.7	748.2	398.7	288.7
Off-site releases	397.7	474.9	468.4	473.5	498.6
Total transfers offsite for further waste management	3,747.3	3,803.5	3,528.0	3,367.2	3,853.7
Tranfers to recycling	1,755.1	1,876.8	1,679.7	1,625.0	1,977.2
Transfers to energy recovery	835.3	745.8	737.7	649.4	652.7
Transfers to treatment	316.6	268.6	262.9	276.7	324.2
Transfers to POTWs [2]	332.9	341.2	303.2	269.4	257.7
Transfers to POTWs metal and metal compounds [2].	3.5	2.9	1.9	1.8	1.6
Other off-site transfers	0.6	1.1	0.8	0.9	72.3
Transfers off-site for disposal or other releases	503.3	567.1	541.7	544.0	568.0
Total production-related waste managed	27,642.3	31,798.8	24,635.9	23,680.1	24,789.9
Recycled on-site	7,319.8	7,536.7	7,196.0	6,666.4	6,766.9
Recycled off-site	1,813.5	1,939.4	1,669.5	1,627.8	1,976.4
Energy recovery on-site	2,636.3	2,689.3	2,776.7	2,621.7	2,601.0
Energy recovery off-site	828.2	759.8	738.4	649.2	647.7
Treated on-site	7,549.2	12,219.0	7,332.3	7,594.0	8,415.2
Treated off-site	672.5	599.9	550.8	516.3	562.0
Quantity disposed or otherwise release of on- and off-site. . .	6,822.8	6,054.7	4,372.2	4,004.8	3,820.6
Non-production-related waste managed	25.7	240.0	15.4	23.4	18.9

[1] RCRA = Resource Conservation and Recovery Act.   [2] POTW (Publicly Owned Treatment Work) is a wastewater treatment facility that is owned by a state or municipality.

Source: U.S. Environmental Protection Agency, 2004 TRI Public Data Release eReport, See also <http://www.epa.gov/tri/tridata/tri04/index.htm> (released 12 April 2006).

Table 366. **Toxic Chemical Releases by Industry: 2004**

[In millions of pounds (4,244.4 represents 4,244,400,000), except as indicated. "Original Industries" include owners and operators. Covers facilities that are classified within Standard Classification Code groups 20 through 39, 10, 12, 49, 5169, 5171, and 4953/7169 that have 10 or more full-time employees, and that manufacture, process, or otherwise use any listed toxic chemical in quantities greater than the established threshold in the course of a calendar year are covered and required to report]

Industry	1987 SIC[1] code	Total on- and off-site releases	On-site release Total [2]	On-site release Point source air emissions	On-site release Other surface impoundments	Off-site releases/ transfers to disposal
Total [3]	**(X)**	**4,244.4**	**3,708.1**	**1,349.7**	**720.8**	**536.3**
Metal mining	10	1,072.9	1,071.3	1.9	534.4	1.6
Coal mining.	12	14.6	14.6	0.1	2.7	–
Food and kindred products	20	164.9	154.3	33.0	0.1	10.6
Tobacco products	21	2.2	1.9	1.6	–	0.4
Textile mill products	22	6.2	5.2	3.7	0.4	1.0
Apparel and other textile products	23	0.4	0.2	0.2	–	0.2
Lumber and wood products	24	28.7	27.6	24.5	–	1.0
Furniture and fixtures	25	5.1	5.1	4.1	–	0.1
Paper and allied products	26	228.5	222.7	149.6	4.1	5.8
Printing and publishing	27	14.2	13.9	6.0	–	0.3
Chemical and allied products	28	556.1	504.6	173.7	14.8	51.5
Petroleum and coal products	29	81.2	76.3	39.8	0.1	4.9
Rubber and miscellaneous plastic products. . .	30	72.7	61.5	49.9	–	11.1
Leather and leather products	31	2.2	0.9	0.7	–	1.4
Stone, clay, glass products.	32	52.4	47.1	37.7	0.2	5.3
Primary metal industries	33	492.8	195.9	38.5	36.9	296.9
Fabricated metals products	34	55.7	35.0	21.0	–	20.7
Industrial machinery and equipment.	35	10.6	6.5	3.6	–	4.1
Electronic, electric equipment	36	18.8	11.8	5.2	–	7.0
Transportation equipment	37	74.6	61.8	47.6	–	12.9
Instruments and related products	38	7.7	6.8	4.5	–	0.8
Miscellaneous	39	5.7	4.2	3.3	–	1.5
Electric utilities.	49	1.4	1.3	0.6	–	0.1
Chemical wholesalers	5169	2.8	2.5	1.5	–	0.2
Petroleum bulk terminals	5171	194.9	165.9	0.5	1.5	29.0

– Represents or rounds to zero.   X Not applicable.   [1] Standard Industrial Classification, see text, Section 12, Labor Force.   [2] Includes several types of on-site releases, not shown separately.   [3] Includes industries with no specific industry identified and several small industries in terms of releases, not shown separately.

Source: U.S. Environmental Protection Agency, 2004 TRI Public Data Release eReport, See also <http://www.epa.gov/tri/tridata/tri04/index.htm> (released 12 April 2006).

Geography and Environment   225

Table 367. **Toxic Chemical Releases by State: 2004**

[In millions of pounds (4,244.4 represents 4,244,400,000). Excludes delisted chemicals, chemicals added in 1990, 1994, and 1995, and aluminum oxide, ammonia, hydrochloric acid, PBT chemicals, sulfuric acid, vanadium, and vanadium compounds. See headnote, Table 366]

State and outlying areas	Total on- and off-site re- leases	On-site release Total [1]	Point source air emis- sions	Sur- face water dis- charges	Off-site releases/ transfers to disposal	State and outlying areas	Total on- and off-site re- leases	On-site release Total [1]	Point source air emis- sions	Sur- face water dis- charges	Off-site releases/ transfers to disposal
Total	**4,244.4**	**3,708.1**	**1,349.7**	**720.8**	**536.3**	NV	269.3	268.1	1.2	152.3	1.2
U.S. total	**4,233.7**	**3,697.8**	**1,341.1**	**720.7**	**535.9**	NH	5.2	4.7	4.5	(Z)	0.6
AL	122.9	95.8	42.0	16.0	27.1	NJ	21.3	17.5	10.2	(Z)	3.8
AK	512.3	512.0	1.3	216.2	0.3	NM	10.7	10.5	0.7	1.2	0.2
AZ	56.6	55.8	3.2	8.0	0.8	NY	42.4	35.8	20.6	(Z)	6.7
AR	49.5	41.4	14.2	2.1	8.0	NC	133.5	118.6	92.7	6.3	14.9
CA	46.6	38.8	14.9	0.3	7.8	ND	22.9	14.4	4.4	6.3	8.5
CO	24.3	18.9	2.0	3.2	5.4	OH	244.8	186.9	117.9	12.7	58.0
CT	5.0	3.4	2.1	0.0	1.7	OK	29.6	25.0	13.2	0.7	4.5
DE	14.2	10.3	7.6	0.0	3.9	OR	39.7	38.6	10.3	(Z)	1.1
DC	(Z)	(Z)	(Z)	(Z)	(Z)	PA	160.6	109.5	82.7	1.7	51.1
FL	123.4	118.6	66.7	7.6	4.8	RI	0.6	0.5	0.3	0.0	0.1
GA	118.7	116.0	78.3	17.2	2.7	SC	80.8	69.1	48.8	2.2	11.7
HI	3.2	2.9	2.2	–	0.3	SD	8.5	8.4	1.0	(Z)	0.2
ID	64.1	62.7	3.2	7.3	1.4	TN	157.8	150.5	83.1	27.8	7.2
IL	135.0	102.2	45.3	10.1	32.8	TX	277.5	254.2	59.5	4.3	23.3
IN	239.4	128.8	63.6	7.9	110.6	UT	167.8	163.9	8.2	86.8	3.9
IA	43.1	35.4	24.2	2.2	7.7	VT	0.4	0.2	(Z)	(Z)	0.2
KS	25.8	22.7	10.7	2.5	3.1	VA	71.8	62.2	42.5	1.4	9.7
KY	95.9	87.7	54.2	7.5	8.2	WA	32.8	29.8	10.5	14.1	3.0
LA	132.9	125.8	43.2	3.8	7.1	WV	91.6	84.0	64.9	3.1	7.6
ME	10.5	9.6	4.0	(Z)	0.9	WI	46.0	26.1	17.2	(Z)	19.9
MD	43.6	40.5	34.6	(Z)	3.1	WY	16.1	15.3	1.8	1.2	0.9
MA	8.8	6.4	5.3	0.1	2.4	American Samoa	(Z)	(Z)	(Z)	–	–
MI	98.3	62.5	44.5	5.9	35.7	Guam	0.7471	0.7419	0.6556	–	(Z)
MN	26.2	23.8	9.8	2.3	2.3	Northern Marianas	(Z)	(Z)	(Z)	–	–
MS	73.7	71.7	30.0	10.0	2.1	Puerto Rico	8.6748	8.2516	7.0771	–	0.4232
MO	128.0	114.1	24.1	52.9	13.9	Virgin Islands	1.2558	1.2463	0.8224	0.0165	0.0095
MT	61.1	60.1	3.9	15.3	1.0						
NE	38.8	36.2	10.1	0.0	2.6						

– Represents zero. Z Less than 50,000. [1] Includes other types of release not shown separately.

Source: U.S. Environmental Protection Agency, *2003 TRI Public Data Release eReport*,(released May 2005). See also <http://www.epa.gov/tri/tridata/tri04/index.htm> (released 12 April 2006).

Table 368. **Hazardous Waste Sites on the National Priority List by State and Outlying Area: 2004**

[As of December 31. Includes both proposed and final sites listed on the National Priorities List for the Superfund program as authorized by the Comprehensive Environmental Response, Compensation, and Liability Act of 1980 and the Superfund Amendments and Reauthorization Act of 1986]

State and outlying area	Total sites	Rank	Per- cent distri- bution	Fed- eral	Non- fed- eral	State and outlying area	Total sites	Rank	Per- cent distri- bution	Fed- eral	Non- fed- eral
Total	**1,302**	(X)	(X)	164	1,138	Montana	15	27	1.2	–	15
United States	**1,286**	(X)	100.0	162	1,124	Nebraska	12	35	0.9	1	11
Alabama	15	25	1.2	3	12	Nevada	1	49	0.1	–	1
Alaska	6	44	0.5	5	1	New Hampshire	20	20	1.6	1	19
Arizona	9	41	0.7	2	7	New Jersey	114	1	8.9	8	106
Arkansas	10	40	0.8	–	10	New Mexico	13	32	1.0	1	12
California	95	3	7.4	23	72	New York	91	4	7.1	4	87
Colorado	18	21	1.4	3	15	North Carolina	30	14	2.3	2	28
Connecticut	16	23	1.2	1	15	North Dakota	–	50	0.0	–	–
Delaware	14	28	1.1	1	13	Ohio	37	11	2.9	5	32
District of Columbia	1	(X)	0.1	1	–	Oklahoma	11	37	0.9	1	10
Florida	52	6	4.0	6	46	Oregon	11	38	0.9	2	9
Georgia	15	26	1.2	2	13	Pennsylvania	96	2	7.5	6	90
Hawaii	3	46	0.2	2	1	Rhode Island	12	36	0.9	2	10
Idaho	9	42	0.7	2	7	South Carolina	26	17	2.0	2	24
Illinois	47	7	3.7	5	42	South Dakota	2	47	0.2	1	1
Indiana	30	13	2.3	–	30	Tennessee	14	30	1.1	4	10
Iowa	13	31	1.0	1	12	Texas	43	9	3.3	4	39
Kansas	12	33	0.9	2	10	Utah	17	22	1.3	4	13
Kentucky	14	29	1.1	1	13	Vermont	11	39	0.9	–	11
Louisiana	16	24	1.2	1	15	Virginia	30	15	2.3	11	19
Maine	12	34	0.9	3	9	Washington	47	8	3.7	14	33
Maryland	20	19	1.6	9	11	West Virginia	9	43	0.7	2	7
Massachusetts	32	12	2.5	7	25	Wisconsin	39	10	3.0	–	39
Michigan	69	5	5.4	1	68	Wyoming	2	48	0.2	1	1
Minnesota	24	18	1.9	2	22	Guam	2	(X)	(X)	1	1
Mississippi	5	45	0.4	–	5	Puerto Rico	12	(X)	(X)	1	11
Missouri	26	16	2.0	3	23	Virgin Islands	2	(X)	(X)	–	2

– Represents zero. X Not applicable.

Source: U.S. Environmental Protection Agency, *Supplementary Materials: CERCLIS3/WasteLan Database* (25 April 2005).

Table 369. Federal Funding for the Superfund, Brownfields, and Related Programs: 1995 to 2005

[In millions of dollars (1,354 represents $1,354,000,000). For fiscal years ending in year shown; see text, Section 8, State and Local Government Finances and Employment. Represents either outlays or obligations; see footnotes below for further explanation. ATSDR = Agency for Toxic Substance and Disease Registry. NIEHS = National Institute for Environmental Health Sciences]

Program	1995	1996	1997	1998	1999	2000	2001	2002	2003	2004	2005
Current dollars											
Total	1,354	1,314	1,394	1,503	1,503	1,403	1,408	1,418	1,590	1,579	1,567
Superfund [1]	1,224	1,195	1,239	1,279	1,273	1,178	1,179	1,175	1,265	1,258	1,247
Brownfields [2]	2	8	37	89	91	92	91	95	167	170	164
ATSDR [3]	69	59	64	74	76	70	75	78	82	73	76
NIEHS [4]	59	52	54	61	63	63	63	70	76	78	80
Constant (2004) dollars [5]											
Total	1,589	1,514	1,578	1,682	1,660	1,519	1,489	1,473	1,622	1,579	1,537
Superfund [1]	1,437	1,377	1,403	1,431	1,406	1,275	1,247	1,220	1,290	1,258	1,223
Brownfields [2]	2	9	42	100	100	100	96	99	170	170	161
ATSDR [3]	81	68	72	83	84	76	79	81	84	73	75
NIEHS [4]	69	60	61	68	70	68	67	73	78	78	78

[1] Superfund program funding is the enacted appropriations excluding amounts designated for the Brownfields, Agency for Toxic Substances and Disease Registry (ATSDR), and National Institute for Environmental Health Sciences (NIEHS) programs. [2] Brownfields funding includes amounts received through the Superfund appropriations for fiscal years 1995 through 2002 and direct appropriations for fiscal years 2003 through 2005. [3] ATSDR and NIEHS funding includes amounts received through the Superfund appropriations for fiscal years 1995 through 2000 and direct appropriations for fiscal years 2001 through 2005. [4] The amount designated for the Brownfields program in fiscal year 1993 was 0.15 million in current year dollars and 0.18 in constant year 2004 dollars. [5] The current years' dollars adjusted for inflation using the Gross Domestic Product (Chained) Price Index, with 2004 as the reference year.

Source: U.S. Government Accountability Office, *Hazardous Waste Programs: Information on Appropriations and Expenditures for Superfund, Brownfields, and Related Programs*, series GAO-05-746R, June 30, 2005. See also <http://www.gao.gov/new.items /d05746r.pdf> (released 30 June 2005).

Table 370. Hazardous Waste Generated, Shipped, and Received by State and Outlying Area: 2003

[In thousands of tons (30,176.1 represents 30,176,100). Covers hazardous wastes regulated under the Resource Conservation and Recovery Act (RCRA) of 1976 as amended. The 2003 Report includes management and receipts data from both permitted treatment, storage and disposal facilities and generators that are not required to be permitted (e.g., those that recycle solvent hazardous waste generated on-site). For generation, based on reports from any large quantity generators (LQGs) as defined by the Federal government. For further information on coverage, see report]

State and outlying area	Generated	Shipped	Received	State and outlying area	Generated	Shipped	Received
Total	30,176.1	7,333.3	7,232.2	Montana	18.9	5.9	–
				Nebraska	43.5	37.7	34.1
United States. . . .	**29,944.1**	**7,264.3**	**7,170.5**	Nevada.	9.7	11.9	45.2
				New Hampshire . . .	8.1	8.1	–
Alabama	1,252.0	165.4	136.3	New Jersey	1,236.2	494.0	310.1
Alaska	4.8	3.2	(Z)	New Mexico.	727.3	5.6	1.6
Arizona	28.7	27.1	35.1	New York	1,130.6	229.0	417.8
Arkansas.	419.4	222.2	268.8	North Carolina . . .	112.6	99.0	20.1
California.	445.3	353.8	385.2	North Dakota	633.7	1.6	0.4
Colorado.	86.7	72.7	21.3	Ohio.	1,800.2	649.5	847.2
Connecticut	38.4	54.1	31.3	Oklahoma	242.7	31.3	47.9
Delaware.	19.1	16.7	2.7	Oregon	55.7	42.5	67.0
District of Columbia.	1.1	1.1	–	Pennsylvania	388.7	327.6	443.8
Florida	356.9	48.6	16.6	Rhode Island	6.8	6.7	6.5
Georgia	203.3	85.8	13.6	South Carolina	156.4	182.9	209.4
Hawaii	1.1	1.1	0.5	South Dakota	1.3	1.5	0.2
Idaho	5.4	5.7	127.9	Tennessee	572.3	566.1	54.5
Illinois.	1,125.5	311.6	467.4	Texas	6,585.1	767.5	803.5
Indiana	988.3	446.7	493.0	Utah.	50.2	56.3	222.4
Iowa.	48.3	47.1	0.7	Vermont	2.9	2.9	1.0
Kansas	104.2	103.9	115.2	Virginia	152.5	78.6	74.9
Kentucky.	2,441.4	143.2	58.0	Washington	91.9	67.6	37.9
Louisiana	4,559.7	181.4	193.8	West Virginia	87.3	35.3	5.6
Maine	7.3	3.9	0.6	Wisconsin	369.8	169.2	99.8
Maryland.	55.4	56.9	54.9	Wyoming.	2.4	1.7	–
Massachusetts	69.1	97.5	46.4				
Michigan	448.2	776.0	462.0	Guam	0.2	0.2	0.1
Minnesota	550.3	52.8	196.0	Puerto Rico	217.8	66.9	61.6
Mississippi.	2,004.6	26.6	63.2	Trust Territories . .	12.2	0.1	–
Missouri	192.9	79.2	229.4	Virgin Islands . . .	1.9	1.9	–

– Represents zero.

Source: U.S. Environmental Protection Agency, *The National Biennial RCRA Harardous Waste Report (Based on 2003 Data)*. See also <http://www.epa.gov/epaoswer/hazwaste/data/br03/index.htm> (released 23 February 2006).

Geography and Environment 227

Table 371. Environmental Industry—Revenues and Employment, by Industry Segment: 1990 to 2005

[148.8 represents $148,800,000,000. Covers approximately 59,000 private and public companies engaged in environmental activities]

Industry segment	Revenue (bil. dol.)				Employment			
	1990	1995	2000	2005	1990	1995	2000	2005
Industry total..............	148.8	186.3	214.2	255.2	1,171,700	1,358,600	1,451,400	1,501,400
Analytical services [1]...............	2.1	1.8	1.8	1.8	24,100	21,200	20,200	19,800
Wastewater treatment works [2]......	18.4	25.1	28.7	34.5	82,600	108,500	118,800	128,000
Solid waste management [3].........	26.1	32.5	39.4	46.4	205,500	243,400	266,300	282,100
Hazardous waste management [4].....	7.1	8.4	8.5	8.5	60,300	70,800	70,000	66,800
Remediation/industrial services......	9.9	9.9	10.1	10.4	118,900	112,000	100,200	93,300
Consulting and engineering........	12.5	15.5	17.4	22.4	147,100	180,300	184,000	195,800
Water equipment and chemicals.....	13.4	16.6	19.8	24.8	91,800	110,300	130,500	142,000
Instrument manufacturing	2.0	3.0	3.8	4.6	18,000	26,200	30,300	32,500
Air pollution control equipment [5].....	11.1	15.3	19.1	19.3	81,500	109,100	129,600	123,100
Waste management equipment [6].....	8.7	9.8	10.0	9.7	69,600	75,500	75,500	68,200
Process and prevention technology ...	0.4	0.8	1.2	1.5	9,300	19,500	29,000	27,600
Water utilities [7]	19.8	25.3	29.9	34.9	98,500	118,200	130,000	138,100
Resource recovery [8].............	13.1	16.9	16.0	16.0	142,900	136,000	127,000	128,500
Clean energy systems and power....	4.3	5.6	8.6	16.3	21,600	27,600	40,000	55,600

[1] Covers environmental laboratory testing and services. [2] Mostly revenues collected by municipal entities. [3] Covers such activities as collection, transportation, transfer stations, disposal, landfill ownership and management for solid waste. [4] Transportation and disposal of hazardous, medical, and nuclear waste. [5] Includes stationary and mobile sources. [6] Includes vehicles, containers, liners, processing and remediation equipment. [7] Revenues generated from the sale of water. [8] Revenues generated from the sale of recovered metals, paper, plastic, etc.

Source: Environmental Business International, Inc., San Diego, CA, *Environmental Business Journal*, monthly (copyright).

Table 372. Threatened and Endangered Wildlife and Plant Species—Number: 2006

[As of April. Endangered species: One in danger of becoming extinct throughout all or a significant part of its natural range. Threatened species: One likely to become endangered in the foreseeable future]

Item	Mammals	Birds	Reptiles	Amphibians	Fishes	Snails	Clams	Crustaceans	Insects	Arachnids	Plants
Total listings	357	273	118	32	149	37	72	22	49	12	748
Endangered species, total ..	324	252	79	21	87	25	64	19	40	12	600
United States..........	68	77	14	13	76	24	62	19	36	12	599
Foreign..............	256	175	65	8	11	1	2	–	4	–	1
Threatened species, total ..	33	21	39	11	62	12	8	3	9	–	148
United States..........	13	15	23	10	61	12	8	3	9	–	146
Foreign..............	20	6	16	1	1	–	–	–	–	–	2

– Represents or rounds to zero.

Source: U.S. Fish and Wildlife Service, *Endangered Species Bulletin*, <http://www.fws.gov/endangered/bulletin.html>; see also <http://www.fws.gov/endangered/wildlife.html>; (released 28 April 2006).

Table 373. Tornadoes, Floods, Tropical Storms, and Lightning: 1994 to 2004

Weather type	1994	1995	1996	1997	1998	1999	2000	2001	2002	2003	2004, prel.
Tornadoes: [1]											
Lives lost................	69	30	26	67	130	94	41	40	55	54	35
Injuries	(NA)	650	705	1,033	1,868	1,842	882	743	968	1,087	396
Property loss (mil. dol.)	(NA)	410.8	719.6	730.7	1,714.2	1,989.9	423.6	630.1	801.3	1,263.2	537.1
Floods and flash floods:											
Lives lost................	91	80	131	118	136	68	38	48	49	85	82
Injuries	(NA)	57	95	525	6,440	301	47	277	88	65	128
Property loss (mil. dol.)	(NA)	1,250.5	2,120.7	6,910.6	2,324.8	1,420.7	1,255.1	1,220.3	655.0	2,540.9	1,696.2
North Atlantic tropical storms and hurricanes [2]	7	19	13	7	14	12	15	15	12	21	16
Direct deaths on U.S. mainland .	9	17	37	1	9	19	–	24	51	14	34
Property loss in U.S. (mil.dol.)..............	973.0	5,932.3	1,436.1	667.6	3,546.6	4,190.1	8.1	5,187.8	1,104.4	1,879.5	18,901.8
Lightning:											
Deaths	69	85	52	42	44	46	51	44	51	44	32
Injuries	577	433	309	306	283	243	364	371	256	237	280

– Represents zero.   NA Not available.   [1] Source: U.S. National Weather Service, Internet site <http://www.noaa.gov/climo/torn/monthlytornstats.html>. A violent, rotating column of air descending from a cumulonimbus cloud in the form of a tubular- or funnel-shaped cloud, usually characterized by movements along a narrow path and wind speeds from 100 to over 300 miles per hour. Also known as a "twister" or "waterspout."   [2] Source: National Hurricane Center (NHC), Coral Gables, FL, unpublished data. For data on individual hurricanes, see the NHC Web site at <http://www.nhc.noaa.gov/>.

Source: Except as noted, U.S. National Oceanic and Atmospheric Administration (NOAA), *Storm Data*, monthly. See also NOAA Web site at <http://www.nws.noaa.gov/os/hazstats.shtml> and <http://www.spc.noaa.gov/climo/torn/monthlytornstats.pdf> (released 27 April 2006).

Table 374. **Major U.S. Weather Disasters: 2000 to 2005**

[**10 represents $10,000,000,000.** Covers only weather-related disasters costing $1 billion or more]

Event	Description	Time period	Estimated cost (bil.dol.)	Deaths
Hurricane Wilma	Category 3 hurricane makes landfall in southwest Florida, causing considerable damage from major flooding and strong winds in southeast Florida.	Oct. 2005	over 10	35
Hurricane Rita	Category 3 hurricane makes landfall on the Texas-Lousiana border coastal region, causing surge/wind damage along the coast and flood damage in FL, MS, LA, AR, and TX.	Sept. 2005	over 8	119
Hurricane Katrina	Category 3 hurricane makes landfall as a category 1 near Miami, FL, and on the LA, MS coast, causing massive damage in addition to flood and wind damage in Al, FL, TN, KY, OH, and GA.	Aug. 2005	over 100	1300+
Hurricane Dennis	Category 3 hurricane makes landfall in western Florida causing wind and surge damage, also causing wind and flood damage to GA, MS and TN.	July 2005	over 2	12+
Midwest drought	Midwest drought causing crop losses in AR, IL, IN, MO, OH, and WI.	Spring-summer 2005	over 1.0	–
Hurricane Jeanne	Category 3 hurricane makes landfall in east-central Florida, causing considerable damage in Florida and some flood damage in GA, SC, NC, VA, MD, DE, NJ, PA, and NY.	Sept. 2004	over 6.9	28
Hurricane Ivan	Category 3 hurricane makes landfall on Gulf coast of Alabama causing significant damage in AL and FL and wind/flood damage in GA, SC, NC, LA, MS, WV, MD, TN, KY, OH, DE, NJ, PA, & NY.	Sept. 2004	over 14	57
Hurricane Frances	Category 2 hurricane makes landfall in east-central Florida causing significant damage in FL and considerable flood damage in GA, SC, NC, and NY.	Sept. 2004	over 9	48
Hurricane Charly	Category 4 hurricane makes landfall in southwest FL resulting in major damage in FL and some damage in SC and NC.	Aug. 2004	15	34
Southern California wildfires	Dry weather, high winds, and resulting wildfires in southern CA burned 743,000 acres and destroyed 3700 homes.	Oct.– Nov. 2003	2.5	22
Hurricane Isabel	Category 2 hurricane makes landfall in eastern NC, causing damage along coasts of NC, VA, and MD with wind damage and flooding in NC, VA, MD, DE, WV, NJ, NY, and PA.	Sept. 2003	5	55
Midwest severe storms and tornadoes	Numerous tornadoes over the midwest, MS River valley, and OH/TN River valleys with record 400 tornadoes in one week.	May 2003	over 3.4	51
Storms and hail	Severe storms and large hail over southern plains, lower MS River valley, and TX.	April 2003	over 1.6	3
Widespread drought	Moderate to extreme drought over large portions of 30 states.	Spring to fall 2002	over 10	–
Western fire season	Major fires over 11 western states from Rockies to west coast.	Spring to fall 2002	over 2.0	21
Tropical Storm Allison	Tropical storm produced rainfall and severe flooding in coastal portions of TX & LA & damage in MS, FL, VA, and PA.	June 2001	5.0	43
Midwest and Ohio Valley hail and tornadoes	Storms, tornadoes, and hail in TX, OK, KS, NE, IA, MO, IL, IN, WI, MI, OH, KY, and PA.	April 2001	over 1.9	3
Southern drought/heat wave	Severe drought and heat over south-central and south-eastern states cause significant losses in agriculture and related industries.	Spring-summer 2000	over 4.0	140
Western fire season	Severe fire season in western states.	Spring-summer 2000	over 2.0	–

– Represents zero.

Source: U.S. National Oceanic and Atmospheric Administration, National Climatic Data Center, *"Billion Dollar U.S. Weather Disasters, 1980–2005"* (release date: 01 January 2006). See also <http://www.ncdc.noaa.gov/img/reports/billion/billionz-2005-1.pdf> (released 01 January 2006).

Geography and Environment   229

Table 375. **Household Population Estimates for Impacted States and Counties in the Gulf Coast Area from Hurricanes Katrina and Rita: 2005 and 2006**

[Covers 117 counties as identified by the Federal Emergency Management Agency as eligible for Individual and Public Assistance (IPA). For information on methodology, see <http://www.census.gov/Press-Release/www/emergencies/impacted_gulf_methodology.html>]

County	July 1, 2005	Jan. 1, 2006	County	July 1, 2005	Jan. 1, 2006	County	July 1, 2005	Jan. 1, 2006
Gulf coast area .	**11,928.2**	**11,677.8**	St. John the Baptist.......	46.0	48.6	Madison	82.1	83.8
Alabama			St. Landry ...	88.4	89.6	Marion........	24.3	24.3
counties......	**855.9**	**855.7**	St. Martin.....	49.6	50.0	Neshoba	29.3	29.3
Baldwin.......	160.4	160.6	St. Mary......	50.8	50.7	Newton	21.7	21.5
Choctaw.......	14.7	14.4	St. Tammany ..	218.0	220.7	Noxubee	12.0	11.9
Clarke........	26.9	27.0	Tangipahoa	103.3	109.5	Oktibbeha	37.5	38.2
Greene	9.6	9.6	Terrebonne....	106.1	107.3	Pearl River.....	51.9	55.7
Hale	16.9	17.0	Vermilion	54.4	54.5	Perry.........	12.1	12.0
Marengo	21.7	21.8	Vernon	45.3	45.8	Pike	38.5	39.3
Mobile........	393.6	391.3	Washington	43.0	43.5	Rankin	126.6	128.0
Pickens.......	20.0	20.0	West Baton Rouge.......	21.1	20.8	Scott.........	28.4	28.3
Sumter	13.6	13.6	West Feliciana ..	10.1	10.3	Simpson	27.0	27.0
Tuscaloosa....	160.9	162.8	**Mississippi**			Smith	15.9	16.1
Washington ...	17.7	17.6	**counties......**	**1,882.2**	**1,839.8**	Stone	13.9	14.2
Lousiana			Adams	31.6	31.5	Walthall.......	15.3	15.7
parishes.......	**3,330.6**	**2,985.8**	Amite	13.3	13.7	Warren	48.5	48.0
Acadia.......	58.6	58.7	Attala	19.2	19.0	Wayne........	21.1	21.0
Allen.........	21.3	21.4	Choctaw	9.3	9.2	Wilkinson......	9.1	9.4
Ascension	89.9	94.1	Claiborne.....	10.0	10.0	Winston	19.3	19.2
Assumption	23.0	23.4	Clarke.......	17.5	17.4	Yazoo	25.6	25.4
Beauregard ...	33.4	33.0	Copiah	27.9	28.1	**Texas counties ...**	**5,859.6**	**5,996.5**
Calcasieu.....	180.7	174.6	Covington	20.0	20.0	Angelina	78.8	79.2
Cameron	9.5	7.5	Forrest	69.6	69.3	Brazoria.......	267.4	273.0
East Baton Rouge......	396.7	413.7	Franklin......	8.3	8.3	Chambers	28.1	28.4
East Feliciana...	18.2	18.5	George	20.6	21.1	Fort Bend	457.2	472.6
Evangeline.....	33.8	33.8	Greene	10.7	10.8	Galveston	273.2	277.9
Iberia	72.8	72.8	Hancock	46.2	35.1	Hardin.......	50.5	51.2
Iberville	29.1	29.7	Harrison......	186.5	155.8	Harris........	3,647.7	3,740.5
Jefferson	448.6	411.3	Hinds	239.9	238.2	Jasper........	34.7	34.9
Jefferson Davis..	30.9	30.6	Jackson......	134.2	126.3	Jefferson	231.3	233.6
Lafayette	192.4	194.9	Jasper.......	18.0	18.3	Liberty.......	70.1	70.5
Lafourche	90.5	91.2	Jefferson	8.8	8.8	Montgomery....	376.1	387.3
Livingston	108.6	111.9	Jefferson Davis..	13.1	13.1	Nacogdoches ...	56.1	56.8
Orleans	437.2	158.4	Jones	64.4	64.3	Newton	13.7	13.9
Plaquemines ...	28.3	20.2	Kemper.......	9.6	9.6	Orange	84.0	85.0
Pointe Coupee ..	22.0	22.6	Lamar........	44.1	45.0	Polk	43.3	43.7
Sabine	23.4	23.8	Lauderdale.....	73.6	72.6	Sabine	10.3	10.4
St. Bernard ...	64.6	3.4	Lawrence......	13.4	13.5	San Augustine ...	8.6	8.6
St. Charles ...	50.2	52.3	Leake	21.0	20.9	San Jacinto	24.7	24.8
St. Helena	10.2	10.9	Lincoln	33.3	33.4	Shelby........	26.0	26.2
St. James	20.9	21.8	Lowndes	58.1	58.1	Trinity	14.2	14.3
						Tyler.........	19.0	19.0
						Walker.......	44.6	44.8

Source: U.S. Census Bureau, "Special Population Estimates for Impacted Counties in the Gulf Coast Area" (released 25 May 2006). See <http://www.census.gov/Press-Release/www/emergencies/impacted_gulf_estimates.html>.

Table 376. **Characteristics of People and Households Impacted by Hurricanes Katrina and Rita in the Gulf Coast Area: 2005**

[In percent, except as indicated. Annualized estimates for period shown. Covers mostly the 117 counties (see Table 375) as identified by the Federal Emergency Management Agency as eligible for Individual and Public Assistance (IPA). For information on methodology, coverage, and the American Community Survey, see <http://www.census.gov/acs/www/Products/Profiles/gulf_coast/methodology.htm>]

Characteristic	Jan.– Aug. 2005	Sept.– Dec. 2005	Characteristic	Jan.– Aug. 2005	Sept.– Dec. 2005
Total population (1,000)......	**11,092**	**10,708**	Social security	25.6	26.2
			Retirement income.........	15.0	15.4
Under 20 years old..........	30.5	30.5	Supplemental security income .	4.6	4.3
65 years old and over........	10.7	10.8	Cash public assistance......	1.7	2.5
White only................	66.7	66.9	Food stamp benefits	10.1	17.9
Black or African American only ..	24.5	23.3	Median family income (dol.)	49,227	48,224
Hispanic or Latino...........	15.8	17.2	Per capita income (dol.).......	22,060	21,378
Total households (1,000).....	**4,310**	**4,078**	Poverty rate: [2]		
Family households.........	69.0	70.0	All families.............	14.3	13.8
With own children under 18 years.	33.6	33.2	With related children under 18 years..............	21.1	20.8
Nonfamily households........	31.0	30.0	All people..............	17.7	18.0
Householder living alone.....	26.5	25.3	Under 18 years	25.5	26.2
65 years and over	8.4	8.2	65 years and over	13.3	12.2
Civilian labor force (1,000)....	5,339	5,155	**Housing units, total (1,000) ...**	**4,914**	**4,730**
Unemployment rate [1]......	8.1	8.3	Owner-occupied	67.1	66.7
Median household income (dol.) .	40,688	40,432	Median value (dol.).......	107,511	113,136
Households with—			Median gross rent (dol.)	633	668
Earnings	80.7	81.2			

[1] Percent unemployed of the civilian labor force.   [2] Represents the percentage of families or people whose income in the past 12 months was below the poverty level.
Source: U.S. Census Bureau, "2005 American Community Survey Gulf Coast Area Data Profiles, Total FEMA Designated IPA Area Data Profiles"; <http://www.census.gov/acs/www/Products/Profiles/gulf_coast/tables/tab1_katrinaK0500US01v.htm> (released 19 July 2006).

Table 377. **Highest and Lowest Temperatures by State Through 2000**

State	Highest temperatures Station	Tempera-ture (F)	Date	Lowest temperatures Station	Tempera-ture (F)	Date
U.S.	Greenland Ranch, CA. . . .	134	Jul. 10, 1913	Prospect Creek, AK	-80	Jan. 23, 1971
AL.	Centerville	112	Sep. 5, 1925	New Market	-27	Jan. 30, 1966
AK.	Fort Yukon.	100	[1]Jun. 27, 1915	Prospect Creek Camp . . .	-80	Jan. 23, 1971
AZ.	Lake Havasu City	128	Jun. 29, 1994	Hawley Lake.	-40	Jan. 7, 1971
AR.	Ozark	120	Aug. 10, 1936	Pond.	-29	Feb. 13, 1905
CA.	Greenland Ranch	134	Jul. 10, 1913	Boca.	-45	Jan. 20, 1937
CO	Bennett	118	Jul. 11, 1888	Maybell	-61	Feb. 1, 1985
CT.	Danbury	106	Jul. 15, 1995	Falls Village	-32	Feb. 16, 1943
DE.	Millsboro	110	Jul. 21, 1930	Millsboro	-17	Jan. 17, 1893
FL.	Monticello	109	Jun. 29, 1931	Tallahassee	-2	Feb. 13, 1899
GA	Greenville	112	Aug. 20, 1983	CCC Camp F-16	-17	[1]Jan. 27, 1940
HI	Pahala	100	Apr. 27, 1931	Mauna Kea Obs. 111.2 . . .	12	May 17, 1979
ID	Orofino	118	Jul. 28, 1934	Island Park Dam	-60	Jan. 18, 1943
IL	East St. Louis.	117	Jul. 14, 1954	Congerville	-36	Jan. 5, 1999
IN	Collegeville	116	Jul. 14, 1936	New Whiteland	-36	Jan. 19, 1994
IA	Keokuk	118	Jul. 20, 1934	Elkader	-47	[2]Feb. 3, 1996
KS.	Alton (near)	121	[2]Jul. 24, 1936	Lebanon	-40	Feb. 13, 1905
KY.	Greensburg	114	Jul. 28, 1930	Shelbyville	-37	Jan. 19, 1994
LA.	Plain Dealing	114	Aug. 10, 1936	Minden	-16	Feb. 13, 1899
ME	North Bridgton	105	[2]Jul. 10, 1911	Van Buren	-48	Jan. 19, 1925
MD	Cumberland & Frederick. . .	109	[2]Jul. 10, 1936	Oakland.	-40	Jan. 13, 1912
MA	New Bedford & Chester . . .	107	Aug. 2, 1975	Chester	-35	Jan. 12, 1981
MI	Mio.	112	Jul. 13, 1936	Vanderbilt.	-51	Feb. 9, 1934
MN	Moorhead	114	[2]Jul. 6, 1936	Tower	-60	Feb. 2, 1996
MS	Holly Springs	115	Jul. 29, 1930	Corinth.	-19	Jan. 30, 1966
MO	Warsaw & Union.	118	[2]Jul. 14, 1954	Warsaw	-40	Feb. 13, 1905
MT	Medicine Lake	117	Jul. 5, 1937	Rogers Pass.	-70	Jan. 20, 1954
NE.	Minden	118	[2]Jul. 24, 1936	Camp Clarke.	-47	Feb. 12, 1899
NV.	Laughlin	125	Jun. 29, 1994	San Jacinto	-50	Jan. 8, 1937
NH	Nashua	106	Jul. 4, 1911	Mt. Washington	-47	Jan. 29, 1934
NJ	Runyon	110	Jul. 10, 1936	River Vale	-34	Jan. 5, 1904
NM	Waste Isolat Pilot Plt	122	Jun. 27, 1994	Gavilan	-50	Feb. 1, 1951
NY.	Troy	108	Jul. 22, 1926	Old Forge.	-52	[2]Feb. 18, 1979
NC	Fayetteville.	110	Aug. 21, 1983	Mt. Mitchell.	-34	Jan. 21, 1985
ND	Steele.	121	Jul. 6, 1936	Parshall	-60	Feb. 15, 1936
OH	Gallipolis (near).	113	[2]Jul. 21, 1934	Milligan	-39	Feb. 10, 1899
OK	Tipton	120	[2]Jun. 27, 1994	Watts.	-27	Jan. 18, 1930
OR	Pendleton	119	Aug. 10, 1898	Seneca	-54	[2]Feb. 10, 1933
PA.	Phoenixville	111	[2]Jul. 10, 1936	Smethport	-42	[1]Jan. 5, 1904
RI	Providence.	104	Aug. 2, 1975	Kingston	-23	Jan. 11, 1942
SC.	Camden	111	[2]Jun. 28, 1954	Caesars Head.	-19	Jan. 21, 1985
SD.	Gannvalley.	120	Jul. 5, 1936	McIntosh	-58	Feb. 17, 1936
TN.	Perryville	113	[2]Aug. 9, 1930	Mountain City	-32	Dec. 30, 1917
TX.	Seymour	120	Aug. 12, 1936	Seminole	-23	[2]Feb. 8, 1933
UT.	Saint George	117	Jul. 5, 1985	Peter's Sink	-69	Feb. 1, 1985
VT.	Vernon	105	Jul. 4, 1911	Bloomfield	-50	Dec. 30, 1933
VA.	Balcony Falls	110	Jul. 15, 1954	Mtn. Lake Bio. Stn.	-30	Jan. 22, 1985
WA	Ice Harbor Dam	118	[2]Aug. 5, 1961	Mazama & Winthrop.	-48	Dec. 30, 1968
WV	Martinsburg	112	[2]Jul. 10, 1936	Lewisburg.	-37	Dec. 30, 1917
WI	Wisconsin Dells	114	Jul. 13, 1936	Couderay	-55	Feb. 4, 1996
WY	Basin	114	Jul. 12, 1900	Riverside R.S.	-66	Feb. 9, 1933

[1] Estimated.   [2] Also on earlier dates at the same or other places.

Source: U.S. National Oceanic and Atmospheric Administration, website at <http://www.ncdc.noaa.gov/oa/climate/severeweather/temperatures.html>.

Geography and Environment   231

Table 378. Normal Daily Mean, Maximum, and Minimum Temperatures—Selected Cities

[In Fahrenheit degrees. Airport data except as noted. Based on standard 30-year period, 1971 through 2000]

State	Station	Daily mean temperature			Daily maximum temperature			Daily minimum temperature		
		Jan.	July	Annual average	Jan.	July	Annual average	Jan.	July	Annual average
AL	Mobile	50.1	81.5	66.8	60.7	91.2	77.4	39.5	71.8	56.2
AK	Juneau	25.7	56.8	41.5	30.6	64.3	47.6	20.7	49.2	35.3
AZ	Phoenix	54.2	92.8	72.9	65.0	104.2	84.5	43.4	81.4	61.1
AR	Little Rock	40.1	82.4	62.1	49.5	92.8	72.7	30.8	72.0	51.5
CA	Los Angeles	57.1	69.3	63.3	65.6	75.3	70.6	48.6	63.3	56.1
	Sacramento	46.3	75.4	61.1	53.8	92.4	73.7	38.8	58.3	48.4
	San Diego	57.8	70.9	64.4	65.8	75.8	70.8	49.7	65.9	58.1
	San Francisco	49.4	62.8	57.3	55.9	71.1	65.1	42.9	54.5	49.6
CO	Denver	29.2	73.4	50.1	43.2	88.0	64.2	15.2	58.7	35.8
CT	Hartford	25.7	73.7	50.2	34.1	84.9	60.5	17.2	62.4	40.0
DE	Wilmington	31.5	76.6	54.4	39.3	86.0	63.6	23.7	67.3	45.1
DC	Washington	34.9	79.2	57.5	42.5	88.3	66.4	27.3	70.1	48.6
FL	Jacksonville	53.1	81.6	68.0	64.2	90.8	78.4	41.9	72.4	57.6
	Miami	68.1	83.7	76.7	76.5	90.9	84.2	59.6	76.5	69.1
GA	Atlanta	42.7	80.0	62.2	51.9	89.4	72.0	33.5	70.6	52.3
HI	Honolulu	73.0	80.8	77.5	80.4	87.8	84.7	65.7	73.8	70.2
ID	Boise	30.2	74.7	52.0	36.7	89.2	62.6	23.6	60.3	41.3
IL	Chicago	22.0	73.3	49.1	29.6	83.5	58.3	14.3	63.2	39.8
	Peoria	22.5	75.1	50.8	30.7	85.7	60.7	14.3	64.6	40.9
IN	Indianapolis	26.5	75.4	52.5	34.5	85.6	62.3	18.5	65.2	42.7
IA	Des Moines	20.4	76.1	50.0	29.1	86.0	59.8	11.7	66.1	40.2
KS	Wichita	30.2	81.0	56.4	40.1	92.9	67.4	20.3	69.1	45.2
KY	Louisville	33.0	78.4	57.0	41.0	87.0	66.0	24.9	69.8	47.9
LA	New Orleans	52.6	82.7	68.8	61.8	91.1	78.0	43.4	74.2	59.6
ME	Portland	21.7	68.7	45.8	30.9	78.8	55.2	12.5	58.6	36.3
MD	Baltimore	32.3	76.5	54.6	41.2	87.2	65.1	23.5	65.8	44.2
MA	Boston	29.3	73.9	51.6	36.5	82.2	59.3	22.1	65.5	43.9
MI	Detroit	24.5	73.5	49.8	31.1	83.4	58.4	17.8	63.6	41.0
	Sault Ste. Marie	13.2	63.9	40.1	21.5	75.7	49.6	4.9	52.0	30.5
MN	Duluth	8.4	65.5	39.1	17.9	76.3	48.7	-1.2	54.6	29.3
	Minneapolis-St. Paul . . .	13.1	73.2	45.4	21.9	83.3	54.7	4.3	63.0	35.9
MS	Jackson	45.0	81.4	64.1	55.1	91.4	75.0	35.0	71.4	53.2
MO	Kansas City	26.9	78.5	54.2	36.0	88.8	64.3	17.8	68.2	44.0
	St. Louis	29.6	80.2	56.3	37.9	89.8	65.7	21.2	70.6	46.9
MT	Great Falls	21.7	66.2	43.8	32.1	82.0	56.4	11.3	50.4	31.1
NE	Omaha	21.7	76.7	50.7	31.7	87.4	61.5	11.6	65.9	39.8
NV	Reno	33.6	71.3	51.3	45.5	91.2	67.4	21.8	51.4	35.2
NH	Concord	20.1	70.0	45.9	30.6	82.9	57.7	9.7	57.1	34.1
NJ	Atlantic City	32.1	75.3	53.5	41.4	85.1	63.6	22.8	65.4	43.3
NM	Albuquerque	35.7	78.5	56.8	47.6	92.3	70.4	23.8	64.7	43.2
NY	Albany	22.2	71.1	47.6	31.1	82.2	57.6	13.3	60.0	37.5
	Buffalo	24.5	70.8	48.0	31.1	79.6	55.9	17.8	62.1	39.9
	New York [1]	32.1	76.5	54.6	38.0	84.2	61.7	26.2	68.8	47.5
NC	Charlotte	41.7	80.3	61.4	51.3	90.1	71.7	32.1	70.6	51.0
	Raleigh	39.7	78.8	59.6	49.8	89.1	70.6	29.6	68.5	48.6
ND	Bismarck	10.2	70.4	42.3	21.1	84.5	54.5	-0.6	56.4	30.1
OH	Cincinnati	29.7	76.3	54.2	38.0	86.4	64.0	21.3	66.1	44.3
	Cleveland	25.7	71.9	49.7	32.6	81.4	58.1	18.8	62.3	41.2
	Columbus	28.3	75.1	52.9	36.2	85.3	62.6	20.3	64.9	43.2
OK	Oklahoma City	36.7	82.0	60.1	47.1	93.1	71.1	26.2	70.8	49.2
OR	Portland	39.9	68.1	53.5	45.6	79.3	62.1	34.2	56.9	44.8
PA	Philadelphia	32.3	77.6	55.3	39.0	85.5	63.2	25.5	69.7	47.4
	Pittsburgh	27.5	72.6	51.0	35.1	82.7	60.4	19.9	62.4	41.5
RI	Providence	28.7	73.3	51.1	37.1	82.6	60.2	20.3	64.1	42.0
SC	Columbia	44.6	82.0	63.6	55.1	92.1	74.8	34.0	71.8	52.5
SD	Sioux Falls	14.0	73.0	45.1	25.2	85.6	57.2	2.9	60.3	33.0
TN	Memphis	39.9	82.5	62.4	48.6	92.1	72.1	31.3	72.9	52.5
	Nashville	36.8	79.1	58.9	46.3	88.7	69.0	27.9	69.5	48.8
TX	Dallas-Fort Worth	44.1	85.0	65.5	54.1	95.4	75.8	34.0	74.6	55.1
	El Paso	45.1	83.3	64.7	57.2	94.5	77.1	32.9	72.0	52.1
	Houston	51.8	83.6	68.8	62.3	93.6	79.4	41.2	73.5	58.2
UT	Salt Lake City	29.2	77.0	52.0	37.0	90.6	62.9	21.3	63.4	41.2
VT	Burlington	18.0	70.6	45.2	26.7	81.4	54.5	9.3	59.8	35.8
VA	Norfolk	40.1	79.1	59.6	47.8	86.8	67.8	32.3	71.4	51.4
	Richmond	36.4	77.9	57.6	45.3	87.5	67.8	27.6	68.3	47.4
WA	Seattle-Tacoma	40.9	65.3	52.3	45.8	75.3	59.8	35.9	55.3	44.8
	Spokane	27.3	68.6	47.3	32.8	82.5	57.4	21.7	54.6	37.2
WV	Charleston	33.4	73.9	54.5	42.6	84.9	65.4	24.2	62.9	43.5
WI	Milwaukee	20.7	72.0	47.5	28.0	81.1	55.9	13.4	62.9	39.2
WY	Cheyenne	25.9	67.7	45.0	37.1	81.9	57.6	14.8	53.4	32.3
PR	San Juan	76.6	82.2	79.9	82.4	87.4	85.5	70.8	76.9	74.2

[1] City office data.

Source: U.S. National Oceanic and Atmospheric Administration, *Climatography of the United States*, No. 84. See also <http://www.ncdc.noaa.gov/oa/climate/online/ccd/nrmmax.txt>; and <http://www.ncdc.noaa.gov/oa/climate/online/ccd/nrmmin.txt>; and <http://www.ncdc.noaa.gov/oa/climate/online/ccd/nrmavg.txt>.

232   Geography and Environment

Table 379. Highest Temperature of Record—Selected Cities

[In Fahrenheit degrees. Airport data, except as noted. For period of record through 2004]

State	Station	Length of record (years)	Jan.	Feb.	Mar.	Apr.	May	June	July	Aug.	Sept.	Oct.	Nov.	Dec.	Annual
AL	Mobile	63	84	82	90	94	100	102	104	105	99	93	87	81	105
AK	Juneau	60	57	57	61	74	82	86	90	84	73	61	56	54	90
AZ	Phoenix	67	88	92	100	105	113	122	121	116	118	107	95	88	122
AR	Little Rock	63	83	85	91	95	98	105	112	109	106	97	86	80	112
CA	Los Angeles	69	91	92	95	102	97	104	97	98	110	106	101	94	110
	Sacramento	54	70	76	88	95	105	115	114	110	108	104	87	72	115
	San Diego	64	88	90	93	98	96	101	95	98	111	107	97	88	111
	San Francisco	77	72	78	85	92	97	106	105	100	103	99	85	75	106
CO	Denver	62	73	76	84	90	96	104	105	100	103	99	85	75	105
CT	Hartford	50	66	73	89	96	99	104	104	101	97	89	79	75	104
DE	Wilmington	57	75	78	86	94	96	99	100	102	99	91	81	76	102
DC	Washington	63	79	82	89	95	99	101	104	105	101	94	86	79	105
FL	Jacksonville	63	85	88	91	95	100	103	105	102	100	96	88	84	105
	Miami	62	88	89	93	96	96	98	98	98	97	95	91	87	98
GA	Atlanta	56	79	80	89	93	95	101	105	102	98	95	84	79	105
HI	Honolulu	35	88	88	88	91	93	92	94	93	95	94	93	89	95
ID	Boise	65	63	71	81	92	99	109	111	110	102	94	78	65	111
IL	Chicago	46	65	72	88	91	93	104	104	101	99	94	78	71	104
	Peoria	65	70	72	86	92	93	105	103	103	100	90	81	71	105
IN	Indianapolis	65	71	76	85	89	93	102	104	102	100	90	81	74	104
IA	Des Moines	65	67	73	91	93	98	103	105	108	101	95	81	69	108
KS	Wichita	52	75	87	89	96	100	110	113	110	108	95	85	83	113
KY	Louisville	57	77	77	86	91	95	102	106	101	104	92	84	76	106
LA	New Orleans	58	83	85	89	92	96	100	101	102	101	94	87	84	102
ME	Portland	64	64	64	88	85	94	98	99	103	95	88	74	71	103!
MD	Baltimore	54	75	79	89	94	98	101	104	105	100	92	83	77	105
MA	Boston	53	66	70	89	94	95	100	102	102	100	90	79	76	102
MI	Detroit	46	62	70	81	89	93	104	102	100	98	91	77	69	104
	Sault Ste. Marie	64	45	49	75	85	89	93	97	98	95	80	67	62	98
MN	Duluth	63	52	55	78	88	90	94	97	95	86	71	62	55	97
	Minneapolis-St. Paul	66	58	61	83	95	96	102	105	102	98	90	77	68	105
MS	Jackson	41	83	85	89	94	99	105	106	107	104	95	88	84	107
MO	Kansas City	32	71	77	86	93	95	105	107	109	106	92	82	74	109
	St. Louis	47	76	85	89	93	94	102	107	107	104	94	85	76	107
MT	Great Falls	67	67	70	78	89	93	101	105	106	98	91	76	69	106
NE	Omaha	68	69	78	89	97	99	105	114	110	104	96	83	72	114
NV	Reno	63	71	75	83	89	97	103	108	105	101	91	77	70	108
NH	Concord	61	68	75	87	94	99	98	102	101	98	90	80	73	102
NJ	Atlantic City	63	69	67	89	95	97	98	106	104	103	99	90	80	106
NM	Albuquerque	65	69	76	85	92	99	105	107	105	101	90	84	77	107
NY	Albany	58	65	68	89	92	99	98	100	101	100	91	77	72	100
	New York [1]	136	72	75	86	96	90	96	97	99	98	87	80	74	99
	Buffalo	61	72	71	81	94	90	96	97	99	100	89	82	71	100
NC	Charlotte	65	79	81	90	93	100	103	104	103	100	94	84	75	104
	Raleigh	60	80	84	92	95	97	100	105	105	103	98	85	78	105
ND	Bismarck	65	63	69	81	93	98	111	109	109	105	95	79	65	111
OH	Cincinnati	43	69	75	84	89	93	102	103	102	98	88	81	75	103
	Cleveland	63	73	74	83	88	92	104	103	102	101	90	82	77	104
	Columbus	65	74	75	85	89	94	102	100	101	100	90	80	76	102
OK	Oklahoma City	51	80	92	93	100	104	105	110	110	108	96	87	86	110
OR	Portland	64	63	71	80	90	100	102	105	107	105	92	73	65	107
PA	Philadelphia	63	74	74	87	95	97	100	104	101	100	96	81	73	104
	Pittsburgh	52	72	76	82	89	91	98	103	100	97	87	82	74	103
RI	Providence	51	69	72	85	88	95	97	102	104	100	90	78	77	104
SC	Columbia	57	84	84	91	94	101	107	107	104	100	86	78	77	107
SD	Sioux Falls	59	66	70	87	94	99	104	108	108	104	94	81	63	108
TN	Memphis	63	79	81	85	91	98	104	108	107	104	95	86	81	108
	Nashville	65	78	84	86	91	97	106	107	104	105	94	84	79	107
TX	Dallas-Fort Worth	51	88	95	96	95	103	113	110	109	111	102	89	88	113
	El Paso	65	80	83	89	94	104	114	112	108	104	96	87	80	114
	Houston	35	84	91	91	95	99	103	104	107	109	96	87	80	109
UT	Salt Lake City	76	63	69	78	86	99	103	107	106	100	89	75	69	107
VT	Burlington	61	66	62	84	91	93	100	101	100	98	89	75	69	101
VA	Norfolk	56	80	82	88	97	100	101	103	104	99	98	85	75	104
	Richmond	75	81	83	93	96	100	101	103	104	99	95	86	80	104
WA	Seattle-Tacoma	60	64	70	78	85	93	96	100	100	98	89	66	63	100
	Spokane	57	59	63	71	90	96	101	108	108	98	86	67	56	108
WV	Charleston	57	79	79	89	94	93	98	108	104	102	92	85	80	108
WI	Milwaukee	64	62	68	82	91	93	104	105	103	98	92	80	66	104
WY	Cheyenne	69	66	71	74	83	91	100	100	96	95	83	75	69	100
PR	San Juan	50	92	96	96	97	96	97	95	97	97	98	96	94	98

[1] City office data.

Source: U.S. National Oceanic and Atmospheric Administration, *Comparative Climatic Data*, annual. See also <http://www.ncdc.noaa.gov/oa/climate/online/ccd/hghtmp.txt>.

Table 380. Lowest Temperature of Record—Selected Cities

[**In Fahrenheit degrees.** Airport data, except as noted. For period of record through 2004]

State	Station	Length of record (years)	Jan.	Feb.	Mar.	Apr.	May	June	July	Aug.	Sept.	Oct.	Nov.	Dec.	Annual
AL	Mobile	63	3	11	21	32	43	49	60	59	42	30	22	8	3
AK	Juneau	60	−22	−22	−15	6	25	31	36	27	23	11	−5	−21	−22
AZ	Phoenix	67	17	22	25	32	40	50	61	60	47	34	25	22	17
AR	Little Rock	63	−4	−5	11	28	40	46	54	52	37	29	17	−1	−5
CA	Los Angeles	69	23	32	34	39	43	48	49	51	47	16	34	32	16
	Sacramento	54	23	23	26	31	36	41	48	49	43	36	26	18	18
	San Diego	64	29	36	39	41	48	51	55	57	51	43	38	34	29
	San Francisco	77	24	25	30	31	36	41	43	42	38	34	25	20	20
CO	Denver	62	−25	−30	−11	−2	22	30	43	41	17	3	−8	−25	−30
CT	Hartford	50	−26	−21	−6	9	28	35	44	36	30	17	1	−14	−26
DE	Wilmington	57	−14	−6	2	18	30	41	48	43	36	24	14	−7	−14
DC	Washington	63	−5	4	11	24	34	47	54	49	39	29	16	1	−5
FL	Jacksonville	63	7	19	23	34	45	47	61	59	48	36	21	11	7
	Miami	62	30	32	32	46	53	60	69	68	51	39	30	30	30
GA	Atlanta	56	−8	5	10	26	37	46	53	55	36	28	3	–	−8
HI	Honolulu	35	53	53	55	57	60	65	66	67	66	61	57	54	53
ID	Boise	65	−17	−15	6	19	22	31	35	34	23	11	−3	−25	−25
IL	Chicago	46	−27	−19	−8	7	24	36	40	41	28	17	1	−25	−27
	Peoria	65	−25	−19	−10	14	25	39	47	41	26	19	−2	−23	−25
IN	Indianapolis	65	−27	−21	−7	16	28	37	44	41	28	17	−2	−23	−27
IA	Des Moines	65	−24	−26	−22	9	30	38	47	40	26	14	−4	−22	−26
KS	Wichita	52	−12	−21	−2	15	31	43	51	48	31	18	1	−16	−21
KY	Louisville	57	−22	−19	−1	22	31	42	50	46	33	23	−1	−15	−22
LA	New Orleans	58	14	16	25	32	41	50	60	60	42	35	24	11	11
ME	Portland	64	−26	−39	−21	8	23	33	40	33	23	15	3	−21	−39
MD	Baltimore	54	−7	−3	6	20	32	40	50	45	35	25	13	–	−7
MA	Boston	53	−12	−4	6	16	34	45	50	47	38	28	15	−7	−12
MI	Detroit	46	−21	−15	−4	10	25	36	41	38	29	17	9	−10	−21
	Sault Ste. Marie	64	−36	−35	−24	−2	18	26	36	29	25	16	−10	−31	−36
MN	Duluth	63	−39	−39	−29	−5	17	27	35	32	22	8	−23	−34	−39
	Minneapolis-St. Paul . . .	66	−34	−32	−32	2	18	34	43	39	26	13	−17	−29	−34
MS	Jackson	41	2	10	15	27	38	47	51	54	35	26	17	4	2
MO	Kansas City	32	−17	−19	−10	12	30	42	51	43	31	17	1	−23	−23
	St. Louis	47	−18	−12	−5	22	31	43	51	47	36	23	1	−16	−18
MT	Great Falls	67	−37	−35	−29	−6	15	31	36	30	16	−11	−25	−43	−43
NE	Omaha	68	−23	−21	−16	5	27	38	44	43	25	13	−9	−23	−23
NV	Reno	63	−16	−16	−2	13	18	25	33	24	20	8	1	−16	−16
NH	Concord	63	−33	−37	−16	8	21	30	35	29	21	10	−5	−22	−37
NJ	Atlantic City	61	−10	−11	5	12	25	37	42	40	32	20	10	−7	−11
NM	Albuquerque	65	−17	−5	8	19	16	40	52	50	37	21	−7	−7	−17
NY	Albany	58	−28	−21	−21	10	26	36	40	34	24	16	5	−22	−28
	Buffalo	61	−16	−20	−7	12	26	35	43	38	32	20	9	−10	−20
	New York [1]	136	−6	−15	3	12	32	44	52	50	39	28	5	−13	−15
NC	Charlotte	65	−5	5	4	24	32	45	53	50	39	24	11	2	−5
	Raleigh	60	−9	–	11	23	31	38	48	46	37	19	11	4	−9
ND	Bismarck	65	−44	−43	−31	−12	15	30	35	33	11	−10	−30	−43	−44
OH	Cincinnati	43	−25	−11	−11	15	27	39	47	43	31	16	1	−20	−25
	Cleveland	63	−20	−15	−5	10	25	31	41	38	32	19	3	−15	−20
	Columbus	65	−22	−13	−6	14	25	35	43	39	31	20	5	−17	−22
OK	Oklahoma City	51	−4	−3	3	20	37	47	53	51	36	16	11	−8	−8
OR	Portland	64	−2	−3	19	29	29	39	43	44	34	26	13	6	−3
PA	Philadelphia	63	−7	−4	7	19	28	44	51	44	35	25	15	1	−7
	Pittsburgh	52	−22	−12	−1	14	26	34	42	39	31	16	−1	−12	−22
RI	Providence	51	−13	−7	1	14	29	41	48	40	33	20	6	−10	−13
SC	Columbia	57	−1	5	4	26	34	44	54	53	40	23	12	4	−1
SD	Sioux Falls	59	−36	−31	−23	5	17	33	38	34	22	9	−17	−28	−36
TN	Memphis	63	−4	−11	12	29	38	48	52	48	36	25	9	−13	−13
	Nashville	65	−17	−13	2	23	34	42	51	47	36	26	−1	−10	−17
TX	Dallas-Fort Worth	51	4	7	15	29	41	51	59	56	43	29	20	−1	−1
	El Paso	65	−8	8	14	23	31	46	57	56	41	25	1	5	−8
	Houston	35	12	20	22	31	44	52	62	60	48	29	19	7	7
UT	Salt Lake City	76	−22	−30	2	14	25	35	40	37	27	16	−14	−21	−30
VT	Burlington	61	−30	−30	−20	2	24	33	39	35	25	15	−2	−26	−30
VA	Norfolk	56	−3	8	18	28	36	45	54	49	45	27	20	7	−3
	Richmond	75	−12	−10	11	23	31	40	51	46	35	21	10	−1	−12
WA	Seattle–Tacoma	60	–	1	11	29	28	38	43	44	35	28	6	6	–
	Spokane	57	−22	−24	−7	17	24	33	37	35	22	7	−21	−25	−25
WV	Charleston	57	−16	−12	–	19	26	33	46	41	34	17	6	−12	−16
WI	Milwaukee	64	−26	−26	−10	12	21	33	40	44	28	18	−5	−20	−26
WY	Cheyenne	69	−29	−34	−21	−8	16	25	38	36	8	−1	−16	−28	−34
PR	San Juan	50	61	62	60	64	66	69	69	70	69	46	66	59	46

– Represents zero. [1] City office data.

Source: U.S. National Oceanic and Atmospheric Administration, *Comparative Climatic Data*, annual. See also <http://www.ncdc.noaa.gov/oa/climate/online/ccd/lowtmp.txt>.

Table 381. **Normal Monthly and Annual Precipitation—Selected Cities**

[**In inches.** Airport data, except as noted. Based on standard 30-year period, 1971 through 2000]

State	Station	Jan.	Feb.	Mar.	Apr.	May	June	July	Aug.	Sept.	Oct.	Nov.	Dec.	Annual
AL	Mobile............	5.75	5.10	7.20	5.06	6.10	5.01	6.54	6.20	6.01	3.25	5.41	4.66	66.29
AK	Juneau...........	4.81	4.02	3.51	2.96	3.48	3.36	4.14	5.37	7.54	8.30	5.43	5.41	58.33
AZ	Phoenix..........	0.83	0.77	1.07	0.25	0.16	0.09	0.99	0.94	0.75	0.79	0.73	0.92	8.29
AR	Little Rock	3.61	3.33	4.88	5.47	5.05	3.95	3.31	2.93	3.71	4.25	5.73	4.71	50.93
CA	Los Angeles	2.98	3.11	2.40	0.63	0.24	0.08	0.03	0.14	0.26	0.36	1.13	1.79	13.15
	Sacramento	3.84	3.54	2.80	1.02	0.53	0.20	0.05	0.06	0.36	0.89	2.19	2.45	17.93
	San Diego	2.28	2.04	2.26	0.75	0.20	0.09	0.03	0.09	0.21	0.44	1.07	1.31	10.77
	San Francisco.......	4.45	4.01	3.26	1.17	0.38	0.11	0.03	0.07	0.20	1.04	2.49	2.89	20.11
CO	Denver...........	0.51	0.49	1.28	1.93	2.32	1.56	2.16	1.82	1.14	0.99	0.98	0.63	15.81
CT	Hartford..........	3.84	2.96	3.88	3.86	4.39	3.85	3.67	3.98	4.13	3.94	4.06	3.60	46.16
DE	Wilmington........	3.43	2.81	3.97	3.39	4.15	3.59	4.28	3.51	4.01	3.08	3.19	3.40	42.81
DC	Washington	3.21	2.63	3.60	2.77	3.82	3.13	3.66	3.44	3.79	3.22	3.03	3.05	39.35
FL	Jacksonville	3.69	3.15	3.93	3.14	3.48	5.37	5.97	6.87	7.90	3.86	2.34	2.64	52.34
	Miami	1.88	2.07	2.56	3.36	5.52	8.54	5.79	8.63	8.38	6.19	3.43	2.18	58.53
GA	Atlanta...........	5.02	4.68	5.38	3.62	3.95	3.63	5.12	3.67	4.09	3.11	4.10	3.82	50.20
HI	Honolulu	2.73	2.35	1.89	1.11	0.78	0.43	0.50	0.46	0.74	2.18	2.26	2.85	18.29
ID	Boise............	1.39	1.14	1.41	1.27	1.27	0.74	0.39	0.30	0.76	0.76	1.38	1.38	12.19
IL	Chicago...........	1.75	1.63	2.65	3.68	3.38	3.63	3.51	4.62	3.27	2.71	3.01	2.43	36.27
	Peoria	1.50	1.67	2.83	3.56	4.17	3.84	4.02	3.16	3.12	2.76	2.99	2.40	36.03
IN	Indianapolis	2.48	2.41	3.44	3.61	4.35	4.13	4.42	3.82	2.88	2.76	3.61	3.03	40.95
IA	Des Moines	1.03	1.19	2.21	3.58	4.25	4.57	4.18	4.51	3.15	2.62	2.10	1.33	34.72
KS	Wichita	0.84	1.02	2.71	2.57	4.16	4.25	3.31	2.94	2.96	2.45	1.82	1.35	30.38
KY	Louisville	3.28	3.25	4.41	3.91	4.88	3.76	4.30	3.41	3.05	2.79	3.80	3.69	44.54
LA	New Orleans........	5.87	5.47	5.24	5.02	4.62	6.83	6.20	6.15	5.55	3.05	5.09	5.07	64.16
ME	Portland..........	4.09	3.14	4.14	4.26	3.82	3.28	3.32	3.05	3.37	4.40	4.72	4.24	45.83
MD	Baltimore..........	3.47	3.02	3.93	3.00	3.89	3.43	3.85	3.74	3.98	3.16	3.12	3.35	41.94
MA	Boston...........	3.92	3.30	3.85	3.60	3.24	3.22	3.06	3.37	3.47	3.79	3.98	3.73	42.53
MI	Detroit...........	1.91	1.88	2.52	3.05	3.05	3.55	3.16	3.10	3.27	2.23	2.66	2.51	32.89
	Sault Ste. Marie......	2.64	1.60	2.41	2.57	2.50	3.00	3.14	3.47	3.71	3.32	3.40	2.91	34.67
MN	Duluth	1.12	0.83	1.69	2.09	2.95	4.25	4.20	4.22	4.13	2.46	2.12	0.94	31.00
	Minneapolis-St. Paul...	1.04	0.79	1.86	2.31	3.24	4.34	4.04	4.05	2.69	2.11	1.94	1.00	29.41
MS	Jackson...........	5.67	4.50	5.74	5.98	4.86	3.82	4.69	3.66	3.23	3.42	5.04	5.34	55.95
MO	Kansas City	1.15	1.31	2.44	3.38	5.39	4.44	4.42	3.54	4.64	3.33	2.30	1.64	37.98
	St. Louis	2.14	2.28	3.60	3.69	4.11	3.76	3.90	2.98	2.96	2.76	3.71	2.86	38.75
MT	Great Falls.........	0.68	0.51	1.01	1.40	2.53	2.24	1.45	1.65	1.23	0.93	0.59	0.67	14.89
NE	Omaha...........	0.77	0.80	2.13	2.94	4.44	3.95	3.86	3.21	3.17	2.21	1.82	0.92	30.22
NV	Reno............	1.06	1.06	0.86	0.35	0.62	0.47	0.24	0.27	0.45	0.42	0.80	0.88	7.48
NH	Concord..........	2.97	2.36	3.04	3.07	3.33	3.10	3.37	3.21	3.16	3.46	3.57	2.96	37.60
NJ	Atlantic City	3.60	2.85	4.06	3.45	3.38	2.66	3.86	4.32	3.14	2.86	3.26	3.15	40.59
NM	Albuquerque	0.49	0.44	0.61	0.50	0.60	0.65	1.27	1.73	1.07	1.00	0.62	0.49	9.47
NY	Albany	2.71	2.27	3.17	3.25	3.67	3.74	3.50	3.68	3.31	3.23	3.31	2.76	38.60
	Buffalo...........	3.16	2.42	2.99	3.04	3.35	3.82	3.14	3.87	3.84	3.19	3.92	3.80	40.54
	New York [1]	4.13	3.15	4.37	4.28	4.69	3.84	4.62	4.22	4.23	3.85	4.36	3.95	49.69
NC	Charlotte	4.00	3.55	4.39	2.95	3.66	3.42	3.79	3.72	3.83	3.66	3.36	3.18	43.51
	Raleigh	4.02	3.47	4.03	2.80	3.79	3.42	4.29	3.78	4.26	3.18	2.97	3.04	43.05
ND	Bismarck..........	0.45	0.51	0.85	1.46	2.22	2.59	2.58	2.15	1.61	1.28	0.70	0.44	16.84
OH	Cincinnati.........	2.92	2.75	3.90	3.96	4.59	4.42	3.75	3.79	2.82	2.96	3.46	3.28	42.60
	Cleveland..........	2.48	2.29	2.94	3.37	3.50	3.89	3.52	3.69	3.77	2.73	3.38	3.14	38.71
	Columbus..........	2.53	2.20	2.89	3.25	3.88	4.07	4.61	3.72	2.92	2.31	3.19	2.93	38.52
OK	Oklahoma City	1.28	1.56	2.90	3.00	5.44	4.63	2.94	2.48	3.98	3.64	2.11	1.89	35.85
OR	Portland..........	5.07	4.18	3.71	2.64	2.38	1.59	0.72	0.93	1.65	2.88	5.61	5.71	37.07
PA	Philadelphia	3.52	2.74	3.81	3.49	3.88	3.29	4.39	3.82	3.88	2.75	3.16	3.31	42.05
	Pittsburgh..........	2.70	2.37	3.17	3.01	3.80	4.12	3.96	3.38	3.21	2.25	3.02	2.86	37.85
RI	Providence.........	4.37	3.45	4.43	4.16	3.66	3.38	3.17	3.90	3.70	3.69	4.40	4.14	46.45
SC	Columbia..........	4.66	3.84	4.59	2.98	3.17	4.99	5.54	5.41	3.94	2.89	2.88	3.38	48.27
SD	Sioux Falls	0.51	0.51	1.81	2.65	3.39	3.49	2.93	3.01	2.58	1.93	1.36	0.52	24.69
TN	Memphis	4.24	4.31	5.58	5.79	5.15	4.30	4.22	3.00	3.31	3.31	5.76	5.68	54.65
	Nashville	3.97	3.69	4.87	3.93	5.07	4.08	3.77	3.28	3.59	2.87	4.45	4.54	48.11
TX	Dallas-Ft. Worth	1.90	2.37	3.06	3.20	5.15	3.23	2.12	2.03	2.42	4.11	2.57	2.57	34.73
	El Paso	0.45	0.39	0.26	0.23	0.38	0.87	1.49	1.75	1.61	0.81	0.42	0.77	9.43
	Houston...........	3.68	2.98	3.36	3.60	5.15	5.35	3.18	3.83	4.33	4.50	4.19	3.69	47.84
UT	Salt Lake City	1.37	1.33	1.91	2.02	2.09	0.77	0.72	0.76	1.33	1.57	1.40	1.23	16.50
VT	Burlington..........	2.22	1.67	2.32	2.88	3.32	3.43	3.97	4.01	3.83	3.12	3.06	2.22	36.05
VA	Norfolk...........	3.93	3.34	4.08	3.38	3.74	3.77	5.17	4.79	4.06	3.47	2.98	3.03	45.74
	Richmond..........	3.55	2.98	4.09	3.18	3.95	3.54	4.67	4.18	3.98	3.60	3.06	3.12	43.91
WA	Seattle-Tacoma	5.13	4.18	3.75	2.59	1.77	1.49	0.79	1.02	1.63	3.19	5.90	5.62	37.07
	Spokane	1.82	1.51	1.53	1.28	1.60	1.18	0.76	0.68	0.76	1.06	2.24	2.25	16.67
WV	Charleston.........	3.25	3.19	3.90	3.25	4.30	4.09	4.86	4.11	3.45	2.67	3.66	3.32	44.05
WI	Milwaukee	1.85	1.65	2.59	3.78	3.06	3.56	3.58	4.03	3.30	2.49	2.70	2.22	34.81
WY	Cheyenne	0.45	0.44	1.05	1.55	2.48	2.12	2.26	1.82	1.43	0.75	0.64	0.46	15.45
PR	San Juan..........	3.02	2.30	2.14	3.71	5.29	3.52	4.16	5.22	5.60	5.06	6.17	4.57	50.76

[1] City office data.

Source: U.S. National Oceanic and Atmospheric Administration, *Comparative Climatic Data*, annual. See also
<http://www.ncdc.noaa.gov/oa/climate/online/ccd/nrmpcp.txt>.

Geography and Environment 235

Table 382. **Average Number of Days With Precipitation of 0.01 Inch or More— Selected Cities**

[Airport data, except as noted. For period of record through 2004]

State	Station	Length of record (years)	Jan.	Feb.	Mar.	Apr.	May	June	July	Aug.	Sept.	Oct.	Nov.	Dec.	Annual
AL	Mobile	62	11	9	10	7	8	12	16	14	10	6	8	10	121
AK	Juneau	59	19	17	18	17	17	16	17	18	21	24	20	21	223
AZ	Phoenix	64	4	4	4	2	1	1	4	5	3	3	2	4	36
AR	Little Rock	61	9	9	10	10	10	9	8	7	7	7	8	9	104
CA	Los Angeles	68	6	6	6	3	1	1	1	(Z)	1	2	3	5	35
	Sacramento	64	10	9	9	5	3	1	(Z)	(Z)	1	3	7	9	58
	San Diego	63	7	6	7	5	2	1	(Z)		1	2	4	6	41
	San Francisco	76	11	10	10	6	3	1	(Z)	(Z)	1	3	7	10	63
CO	Denver	61	6	6	9	9	11	9	9	9	6	5	6	5	89
CT	Hartford	49	11	10	12	11	12	11	10	10	10	9	11	12	128
DE	Wilmington	56	11	10	11	11	11	10	9	9	8	8	9	10	117
DC	Washington	62	10	9	11	10	11	10	10	9	8	7	8	9	113
FL	Jacksonville	62	8	8	8	6	8	13	14	15	13	9	6	8	116
	Miami	61	7	6	6	6	10	15	16	18	18	14	8	7	131
GA	Atlanta	69	12	10	11	9	9	10	12	9	8	7	8	10	115
HI	Honolulu	54	9	9	9	9	7	6	7	6	7	8	9	10	96
ID	Boise	64	12	10	10	8	8	6	2	3	4	6	10	11	89
IL	Chicago	45	11	9	12	13	11	10	10	9	9	9	11	11	125
	Peoria	64	9	8	11	12	12	10	9	8	8	8	9	10	114
IN	Indianapolis	64	12	10	13	12	12	10	10	9	8	8	10	12	126
IA	Des Moines	64	7	7	10	11	12	11	9	9	9	8	7	8	108
KS	Wichita	50	5	5	7	8	11	9	8	7	8	6	5	6	85
KY	Louisville	56	11	11	13	12	12	10	10	8	8	7	10	12	124
LA	New Orleans	55	10	9	9	7	8	11	14	13	10	6	8	10	114
ME	Portland	63	11	10	11	12	12	11	10	9	9	9	12	11	129
MD	Baltimore	53	10	9	11	11	11	10	9	9	8	7	9	9	115
MA	Boston	52	12	10	12	11	12	11	9	10	9	9	11	11	127
MI	Detroit	45	13	11	13	13	12	10	10	10	10	10	12	13	135
	Sault Ste. Marie	62	19	14	13	11	11	11	10	11	13	14	17	19	165
MN	Duluth	62	12	9	11	11	12	13	12	11	12	10	11	11	134
	Minneapolis-St. Paul	65	9	7	10	10	11	12	10	10	9	8	8	9	115
MS	Jackson	40	11	9	10	8	9	9	11	10	8	7	9	10	110
MO	Kansas City	31	7	7	10	11	12	10	9	8	8	8	8	7	104
	St. Louis	46	9	8	11	11	11	9	9	8	8	8	9	9	111
MT	Great Falls	66	9	8	9	9	11	12	8	8	7	6	7	7	100
NE	Omaha	67	6	7	9	10	12	11	9	9	8	6	6	6	99
NV	Reno	61	6	6	6	4	4	3	2	2	2	3	5	6	51
NH	Concord	62	11	9	11	12	12	11	10	10	9	9	11	11	127
NJ	Atlantic City	60	11	10	11	11	11	10	9	9	8	7	9	10	113
NM	Albuquerque	64	4	4	5	3	4	4	9	9	6	5	4	4	60
NY	Albany	57	13	11	12	12	13	11	10	10	10	9	12	12	136
	Buffalo	60	20	17	16	14	13	11	10	10	11	12	16	19	169
	New York [1]	134	11	10	11	11	11	10	11	10	8	8	9	10	121
NC	Charlotte	64	10	10	11	9	10	10	11	10	7	7	8	10	112
	Raleigh	59	10	10	10	9	10	10	11	10	8	7	8	9	113
ND	Bismarck	64	8	7	8	8	10	12	9	8	7	6	6	7	96
OH	Cincinnati	56	12	11	13	13	12	11	10	9	8	8	11	12	131
	Cleveland	62	16	14	15	14	13	11	10	10	10	11	14	16	155
	Columbus	64	13	12	13	13	13	11	11	9	8	9	11	13	137
OK	Oklahoma City	64	5	6	7	8	10	9	6	6	7	7	5	6	83
OR	Portland	63	18	16	17	15	12	9	4	5	7	12	18	19	153
PA	Philadelphia	63	11	9	11	11	11	10	9	9	8	8	9	10	117
	Pittsburgh	51	16	14	15	14	13	12	11	10	10	10	13	16	152
RI	Providence	50	11	10	12	11	11	11	9	10	9	9	11	12	124
SC	Columbia	56	10	9	10	8	8	10	12	11	8	6	7	9	109
SD	Sioux Falls	58	6	7	8	10	11	11	10	9	8	6	6	6	98
TN	Memphis	53	10	9	11	10	10	9	9	7	7	6	9	10	107
	Nashville	62	11	11	12	11	11	10	10	9	8	7	9	11	119
TX	Dallas-Ft. Worth	50	7	7	7	8	9	7	5	5	6	6	6	6	79
	El Paso	64	4	3	2	2	2	3	8	8	5	4	3	4	49
	Houston	34	10	8	9	7	8	10	9	9	9	8	8	9	105
UT	Salt Lake City	75	10	9	10	10	8	5	4	6	5	6	8	9	91
VT	Burlington	60	14	11	13	12	14	13	12	12	12	12	14	15	154
VA	Norfolk	55	11	10	11	10	10	9	11	10	8	8	8	9	116
	Richmond	66	10	9	11	10	11	10	11	10	8	7	8	9	114
WA	Seattle-Tacoma	59	19	16	17	14	11	9	5	6	9	13	18	19	155
	Spokane	56	14	11	11	9	9	8	5	5	5	8	13	14	112
WV	Charleston	56	15	14	15	14	13	12	13	11	9	9	12	14	151
WI	Milwaukee	63	11	9	12	12	12	11	10	9	9	9	10	11	125
WY	Cheyenne	68	6	6	9	10	12	11	11	10	8	6	6	6	100
PR	San Juan	48	17	13	12	13	16	15	19	19	18	17	19	19	198

– Represents zero.   Z Less than 1/2 day.   [1] City office data.

Source: U.S. National Oceanic and Atmospheric Administration, *Comparative Climatic Data*, annual. See also <http://www.ncdc.noaa.gov/oa/climate/online/ccd/prge01.txt>.

Table 383. Snow and Ice Pellets—Selected Cities

[In inches. Airport data, except as noted. For period of record through 2004. T denotes trace]

State	Station	Length of record (years)	Jan.	Feb.	Mar.	Apr.	May	June	July	Aug.	Sept.	Oct.	Nov.	Dec.	Annual
AL	Mobile	61	0.1	0.1	0.1	T	T	–	T	–	–	–	T	0.1	0.4
AK	Juneau	59	25.4	18.9	14.7	3.3	T	T	–	–	T	1.0	12.0	21.7	97.0
AZ	Phoenix[2]	62	T	–	T	T	T	–	–	–	T	T	0.0	T	T
AR	Little Rock[2]	56	2.4	1.5	0.5	T	T	T	–	–	–	T	0.2	0.6	5.2
CA	Los Angeles[2]	62	T	T	T	–	–	–	–	–	–	–	0.0	T	T
	Sacramento[2]	50	T	T	T	–	T	–	–	–	–	–	0.0	T	T
	San Diego[2]	60	T	–	T	T	–	–	–	–	–	–	T	T	T
	San Francisco[2]	69	–	T	T	–	–	–	–	–	–	–	–	–	T
CO	Denver[2]	61	8.1	7.5	12.5	8.9	1.6	–	T	T	1.6	3.7	9.1	7.3	60.3
CT	Hartford	46	13.0	12.4	10.1	1.5	–	T	–	–	–	0.1	2.1	10.4	49.6
DE	Wilmington	53	6.7	6.6	3.2	0.2	T	T	T	–	–	0.1	0.9	3.4	21.1
DC	Washington	60	5.5	5.5	2.3	T	T	T	T	T	–	–	0.8	3.0	17.1
FL	Jacksonville[2]	60	T	–	–	T	–	T	T	–	–	–	0.0	0.0	T
	Miami[2]	59	–	–	–	–	–	T	–	–	–	–	0.0	0.0	T
GA	Atlanta	65	1.0	0.5	0.4	T	–	–	T	–	–	T	T	0.2	2.1
HI	Honolulu[2]	52	–	–	–	–	–	–	–	–	–	–	–	–	–
ID	Boise	64	6.5	3.6	1.7	0.6	0.1	T	T	T	T	0.1	2.3	5.7	20.6
IL	Chicago	44	11.0	7.8	6.9	1.6	0.1	T	T	T	T	0.4	2.0	8.2	38.0
	Peoria	60	6.7	5.0	4.2	0.8	T	T	T	–	T	0.1	2.0	6.1	24.9
IN	Indianapolis	72	6.9	5.6	3.5	0.5	T	T	T	–	T	0.2	1.9	5.3	23.9
IA	Des Moines	60	8.2	7.2	6.0	1.9	–	T	T	T	–	0.3	3.1	6.6	33.3
KS	Wichita	50	4.1	4.1	2.8	0.2	T	T	T	T	–	T	1.3	3.4	15.9
KY	Louisville	56	5.4	4.3	3.1	0.1	T	T	T	T	–	0.1	1.0	2.4	16.4
LA	New Orleans[2]	51	T	0.1	T	T	T	–	–	–	–	–	T	0.1	0.2
ME	Portland	63	19.3	16.5	13.3	2.9	0.2	–	T	–	T	0.2	3.3	14.7	70.4
MD	Baltimore	53	6.3	7.1	3.8	0.1	T	T	–	T	–	T	1.0	3.2	21.5
MA	Boston	66	12.7	12.0	8.1	0.9	–	T	–	T	–	T	1.3	7.8	42.8
MI	Detroit	45	10.7	9.2	6.9	1.8	T	–	T	–	T	0.2	2.6	9.9	41.3
	Sault Ste. Marie[2]	57	29.2	18.2	14.6	5.8	0.5	T	T	T	0.1	2.4	15.6	31.0	117.4
MN	Duluth	60	17.5	11.8	13.9	6.9	0.7	T	T	T	0.1	1.6	13.0	15.1	80.6
	Minneapolis-St. Paul[2]	62	10.7	8.1	10.5	2.8	0.1	T	T	T	T	0.5	7.8	9.4	49.9
MS	Jackson[2]	38	0.5	0.2	0.2	T	–	–	–	T	–	–	T	0.1	1.0
MO	Kansas City	69	5.6	4.4	3.4	0.8	T	T	T	T	T	0.1	1.2	4.4	19.9
	St. Louis	67	5.4	4.5	3.8	0.5	0.0	T	T	–	–	T	1.4	4.0	19.6
MT	Great Falls	66	9.4	8.6	10.6	7.0	1.9	0.3	T	0.1	1.5	3.4	7.3	8.1	58.2
NE	Omaha	68	7.2	6.8	6.3	1.1	0.1	T	T	T	–	0.3	2.6	5.7	30.1
NV	Reno[2]	54	5.8	5.2	4.3	1.2	0.8	–	–	–	–	0.3	2.4	4.3	24.3
NH	Concord	62	18.0	14.2	11.5	2.7	0.1	T	–	–	T	0.1	3.9	14.0	64.5
NJ	Atlantic City	54	4.9	5.8	2.5	0.3	T	T	T	–	–	T	0.4	2.3	16.2
NM	Albuquerque	64	2.5	2.1	1.8	0.6	T	T	T	T	T	T	1.2	2.7	11.0
NY	Albany	57	17.0	13.8	11.5	2.8	0.1	T	–	T	T	0.2	4.2	14.8	64.4
	Buffalo	60	24.2	17.7	12.4	3.2	0.2	T	–	T	T	0.3	11.3	24.3	93.6
	New York[1]	135	7.5	8.6	5.1	0.9	T	–	–	–	–	T	0.9	5.6	28.6
NC	Charlotte	64	2.2	1.6	1.2	T	T	T	T	–	–	T	0.1	0.5	5.6
	Raleigh	59	2.8	2.5	1.3	T	T	T	T	–	–	T	0.1	0.8	7.5
ND	Bismarck	64	7.8	7.0	8.5	4.0	0.9	T	T	T	0.2	1.9	7.1	6.9	44.3
OH	Cincinnati	56	7.2	5.6	4.2	0.5	–	T	T	T	0.0	0.3	2.0	3.7	23.5
	Cleveland	62	13.8	12.3	10.8	2.4	0.1	T	T	–	T	0.6	5.3	12.3	57.6
	Columbus	56	8.9	6.3	4.4	0.9	T	T	T	–	T	0.1	2.2	5.4	28.2
OK	Oklahoma City	64	3.2	2.4	1.5	T	T	T	T	T	T	T	0.5	1.9	9.5
OR	Portland[2]	55	3.2	1.1	0.4	T	–	T	–	T	–	T	0.4	1.4	6.5
PA	Philadelphia	61	6.1	7.0	3.4	0.3	T	T	T	–	T	–	0.7	3.3	20.8
	Pittsburgh	51	11.9	9.2	8.4	1.7	0.1	T	T	T	T	0.4	3.5	8.4	43.6
RI	Providence	50	9.5	9.9	7.3	0.7	0.2	–	T	T	–	0.1	1.2	7.1	36.0
SC	Columbia[2]	55	0.6	0.8	0.2	T	T	–	–	–	T	–	T	0.3	1.9
SD	Sioux Falls[2]	58	6.9	8.0	9.2	3.0	T	T	T	T	T	0.9	6.1	7.1	41.2
TN	Memphis[2]	49	2.2	1.4	0.8	T	T	T	T	–	–	T	0.1	0.6	5.1
	Nashville[2]	58	3.8	3.0	1.5	–	T	–	–	–	–	T	0.4	1.4	10.1
TX	Dallas-Ft. Worth	45	1.1	1.0	0.2	T	T	–	–	–	–	T	0.1	0.2	2.6
	El Paso[2]	57	1.3	0.8	0.4	0.3	T	T	T	T	–	T	0.9	1.6	5.3
	Houston	69	0.2	0.2	T	T	T	–	–	–	–	–	T	T	0.4
UT	Salt Lake City	75	13.6	9.8	9.2	5.0	0.6	T	T	T	0.1	1.3	7.0	12.1	58.7
VT	Burlington	60	19.5	16.4	13.8	4.2	0.2	–	T	T	T	0.2	6.7	18.3	79.3
VA	Norfolk	53	3.0	2.9	1.0	T	–	T	T	–	–	–	0.0	T	7.8
	Richmond	64	5.0	3.9	2.4	0.1	T	–	T	–	–	T	0.4	2.0	13.8
WA	Seattle-Tacoma[2]	52	4.9	1.6	1.3	0.1	T	–	T	–	–	T	1.1	2.4	11.4
	Spokane	56	15.2	7.5	3.9	0.6	0.1	–	T	–	T	0.4	6.5	14.4	48.6
WV	Charleston[2]	49	11.1	8.7	5.4	0.9	–	T	T	T	T	0.4	2.4	5.3	34.0
WI	Milwaukee	63	13.7	9.2	8.4	1.9	0.1	T	T	T	T	0.2	3.0	10.5	47.0
WY	Cheyenne	68	6.3	6.4	12.0	9.3	3.4	0.2	T	T	1.1	3.8	7.1	6.2	55.8
PR	San Juan	48	–	–	–	–	–	–	–	–	–	–	–	–	–

– Represents zero or rounds to zero.   [1] City office data.   [2] Period of record through 2000.

Source: U.S. National Oceanic and Atmospheric Administration, *Comparative Climatic Data*, annual. See also <http://www.ncdc.noaa.gov/oa/climate/online/ccd/avgsnf.txt>.

Geography and Environment   237

Table 384. Sunshine, Average Wind Speed, Heating and Cooling Degree Days, and Average Relative Humidity—Selected Cities

[Airport data, except as noted. For period of record through 2004, except heating and cooling normals for period 1971–2000. M = morning. A = afternoon]

State	Station	Average percentage of possible sunshine [1]		Average wind speed (m.p.h.)				Heating degree days	Cooling degree days	Length of record (yr.)	Average relative humidity (percent)					
		Length of record (yr.)	Annual	Length of record (yr.)	Annual	Jan.	July				Annual		Jan.		July	
											M	A	M	A	M	A
AL	Mobile	47	59.7	56	8.8	10.1	6.9	1,667	2,548	42	87	63	82	66	90	67
AK	Juneau	47	23.3	59	8.2	8.1	7.5	8,574	–	38	80	70	78	75	79	67
AZ	Phoenix	57	81.1	59	6.2	5.3	7.1	1,040	4,355	44	49	23	64	32	43	20
AR	Little Rock	35	60.0	62	7.8	8.4	6.7	3,084	2,086	40	83	61	80	65	86	60
CA	Los Angeles	60	72.1	56	7.5	6.7	7.9	1,286	682	45	79	66	72	61	86	69
	Sacramento	49	72.6	54	7.8	6.9	8.9	2,666	1,248	18	83	46	91	70	77	30
	San Diego	55	72.1	64	7.0	6.0	7.5	1,063	866	44	77	63	72	58	82	67
	San Francisco	68	71.2	77	10.6	7.2	13.6	2,862	142	45	84	62	87	68	87	60
CO	Denver	61	67.1	48	8.6	8.6	8.3	6,128	695	36	67	40	63	49	68	34
CT	Hartford	41	52.1	50	8.4	8.9	7.3	6,104	759	45	77	53	72	57	79	51
DE	Wilmington	47	55.1	56	9.0	9.8	7.8	4,887	1,125	57	79	55	75	60	80	54
DC	Washington	48	55.3	56	9.4	10.0	8.3	3,999	1,560	44	75	54	71	56	77	54
FL	Jacksonville	47	60.5	55	7.8	8.1	7.0	1,353	2,636	68	89	56	87	59	89	59
	Miami	46	68.2	55	9.2	9.5	7.9	155	4,383	40	83	61	85	59	83	63
GA	Atlanta	61	59.5	66	9.1	10.4	7.7	2,827	1,810	44	82	56	78	59	88	59
HI	Honolulu	47	74.2	55	11.3	9.4	13.1	–	4,561	35	72	56	81	61	68	52
ID	Boise	56	57.5	65	8.7	7.9	8.4	5,809	769	65	69	43	81	71	54	21
IL	Chicago	37	51.8	46	10.3	11.6	8.4	6,493	835	46	80	63	77	70	82	61
	Peoria	52	52.6	61	9.8	10.9	7.8	6,095	998	45	83	66	80	72	86	64
IN	Indianapolis	64	51.2	56	9.6	10.9	7.5	5,521	1,042	45	84	62	81	71	87	60
IA	Des Moines	46	55.3	55	10.7	11.4	8.9	6,432	1,052	43	80	64	77	70	83	63
KS	Wichita	46	57.8	51	12.2	12.0	11.3	4,765	1,658	51	80	59	79	66	79	54
KY	Louisville	47	53.4	57	8.3	9.5	6.8	4,352	1,443	44	81	59	78	65	85	58
LA	New Orleans	47	60.0	56	8.2	9.3	6.1	1,417	2,776	56	87	66	84	69	91	69
ME	Portland	54	54.8	64	8.7	9.0	7.6	7,325	347	64	79	59	76	60	80	60
MD	Baltimore	45	58.4	54	8.8	9.4	7.6	4,634	1,220	51	78	54	73	57	80	53
MA	Boston	60	55.1	47	12.4	13.7	11.0	5,630	777	40	73	56	73	57	69	53
MI	Detroit	37	49.3	46	10.2	11.9	8.5	6,449	727	46	81	60	80	69	82	54
	Sault Ste. Marie	54	42.7	63	9.2	9.6	7.8	9,230	145	63	85	66	81	74	88	62
MN	Duluth	47	49.0	55	11.0	11.6	9.4	9,742	189	43	81	67	78	72	85	64
	Minneapolis- St. Paul	57	53.7	66	10.5	10.5	9.4	7,882	699	45	78	63	75	69	81	60
MS	Jackson	30	58.9	41	7.0	8.2	5.2	2,368	2,290	41	90	63	86	68	93	65
MO	Kansas City	23	59.2	32	10.6	11.1	9.2	5,249	1,325	32	81	65	77	68	84	65
	St. Louis	47	55.3	55	9.6	10.6	8.0	4,757	1,561	44	81	63	80	69	83	61
MT	Great Falls	57	50.7	63	12.5	14.9	10.0	7,675	326	43	68	45	67	61	68	31
NE	Omaha	49	59.2	68	10.5	10.9	9.8	6,312	1,095	40	81	64	78	68	84	64
NV	Reno	53	68.8	62	6.6	5.6	7.2	5,601	493	41	68	31	79	50	59	19
NH	Concord	54	54.5	62	6.7	7.2	5.7	7,485	442	39	81	53	76	59	84	51
NJ	Atlantic City	37	56.2	46	9.8	10.7	8.3	5,113	935	40	82	57	78	59	83	57
NM	Albuquerque	56	76.2	65	8.9	8.0	8.9	4,281	1,290	44	59	29	68	39	59	27
NY	Albany	57	49.3	66	8.9	9.8	7.5	6,861	544	39	80	58	78	64	81	55
	Buffalo	52	43.0	65	11.8	14.0	10.2	6,693	548	44	80	63	79	73	79	56
	New York [2]	42	64.1	67	9.3	10.6	7.6	4,744	1,160	70	72	56	68	60	75	55
NC	Charlotte	49	58.6	55	7.4	7.8	6.6	3,208	1,644	44	82	54	78	55	86	56
	Raleigh	47	59.5	55	7.6	8.2	6.7	3,465	1,521	40	85	54	79	55	89	58
ND	Bismarck	56	54.8	65	10.2	10.0	9.2	8,809	471	45	80	61	76	71	84	54
OH	Cincinnati	44	49.0	57	9.0	10.4	7.2	5,200	1,053	42	82	60	80	68	86	58
	Cleveland	54	44.7	63	10.5	12.2	8.6	6,097	712	44	80	62	79	70	82	57
	Columbus	46	47.9	55	8.3	9.8	6.5	5,546	925	45	81	59	78	68	84	56
OK	Oklahoma City	44	64.4	56	12.2	12.5	10.9	3,663	1,907	39	80	60	78	63	80	56
OR	Portland	47	38.9	56	7.9	9.9	7.6	4,366	398	64	85	59	85	76	82	45
PA	Philadelphia	55	56.2	64	9.5	10.3	8.2	4,759	1,235	45	77	55	73	59	79	54
	Pittsburgh	43	44.4	52	9.0	10.4	7.3	5,829	726	44	80	58	77	66	83	54
RI	Providence	42	55.1	51	10.4	10.9	9.4	5,754	714	41	76	55	71	57	77	56
SC	Columbia	48	59.7	56	6.8	7.2	6.3	2,595	2,063	38	86	51	82	54	89	56
SD	Sioux Falls	50	57.0	56	11.0	10.9	9.8	7,746	757	41	82	65	78	71	84	61
TN	Memphis	43	58.6	56	8.8	10.0	7.5	3,033	2,190	65	80	60	78	65	84	61
	Nashville	54	57.0	63	8.0	9.1	6.5	3,658	1,656	39	83	62	79	67	88	63
TX	Dallas-Ft. Worth	42	63.6	51	10.7	11.0	9.8	2,370	2,571	41	81	60	79	64	79	55
	El Paso	53	80.3	62	8.8	8.3	8.3	2,604	2,165	44	56	27	64	34	61	29
	Houston	26	53.9	35	7.6	8.1	6.6	1,525	2,893	35	89	66	85	69	92	65
UT	Salt Lake City	69	61.9	75	8.8	7.5	9.5	5,607	1,089	44	67	43	79	70	52	22
VT	Burlington	52	43.6	61	9.0	9.7	8.0	7,665	489	39	77	59	73	64	79	53
VA	Norfolk	47	58.4	56	10.5	11.4	9.1	3,342	1,630	56	78	58	75	59	82	59
	Richmond	50	56.4	56	7.7	8.1	6.9	3,878	1,466	70	83	53	80	57	85	56
WA	Seattle-Tacoma [3]	51	38.4	56	8.8	9.5	8.1	4,797	173	45	84	62	82	75	82	49
	Spokane	48	47.7	57	8.9	8.7	8.6	6,820	394	45	78	52	86	80	65	27
WV	Charleston	47	48.2	57	6.9	6.9	4.8	4,589	1,064	57	84	57	78	63	91	60
WI	Milwaukee	55	52.1	64	11.5	12.6	9.7	7,096	616	44	79	67	76	70	81	65
WY	Cheyenne	60	63.8	47	12.9	15.2	10.4	7,289	280	45	66	45	58	50	70	38
PR	San Juan	40	75.6	49	8.4	8.3	9.7	–	5,426	49	79	65	82	65	79	67

– Represents zero. [1] Percent of days that are either clear or partly cloudy. [2] Airport data for sunshine. [3] Does not represent airport data.

Source: U.S. National Oceanic and Atmospheric Administration, *Comparative Climatic Data*, annual. See also <http://www.ncdc.noaa.gov/oa/climate/online/ccd/pctpos.txt>; <http://www.ncdc.noaa.gov/oa/climate/online/ccd/wndspd.txt>; <http://www.ncdc.noaa.gov/oa/climate/online/ccd/nrmhdd.txt>; <http://www.ncdc.noaa.gov/oa/climate/online/ccd/nrmcdd.txt>; <http://www.ncdc.noaa.gov/oa/climate/online/ccd/relhum.txt>.

Elections

This section relates primarily to presidential, congressional, and gubernatorial elections. Also presented are summary tables on congressional legislation; state legislatures; Black, Hispanic, and female officeholders; population of voting age; voter participation; and campaign finances.

Official statistics on federal elections, collected by the Clerk of the House, are published biennially in *Statistics of the Presidential and Congressional Election* and *Statistics of the Congressional Election.* Federal and state elections data appear also in *America Votes,* a biennial volume published by CQ Press (a division of Congressional Quarterly, Inc.), Washington, DC. Federal elections data also appear in the U.S. Congress, *Congressional Directory,* and in official state documents. Data on reported registration and voting for social and economic groups are obtained by the U.S. Census Bureau as part of the Current Population Survey (CPS) and are published in Current Population Reports, Series P20 (see text, Section 1).

Almost all federal, state, and local governmental units in the United States conduct elections for political offices and other purposes. The conduct of elections is regulated by state laws or, in some cities and counties, by local charter. An exception is that the U.S. Constitution prescribes the basis of representation in Congress and the manner of electing the President and grants to Congress the right to regulate the times, places, and manner of electing federal officers. Amendments to the Constitution have prescribed national criteria for voting eligibility. The 15th Amendment, adopted in 1870, gave all citizens the right to vote regardless of race, color, or previous condition of servitude. The 19th Amendment, adopted in 1919, further extended the right to vote to all citizens regardless of sex. The payment of poll taxes as a prerequisite to voting in federal elections was banned by the 24th Amendment in 1964. In 1971, as a result of the 26th Amendment, eligibility to vote in national elections was extended to all citizens, 18 years old and over.

Presidential election—The Constitution specifies how the President and Vice President are selected. Each state elects, by popular vote, a group of electors equal in number to its total of members of Congress. The 23d Amendment, adopted in 1961, grants the District of Columbia three presidential electors, a number equal to that of the least populous state. Subsequent to the election, the electors meet in their respective states to vote for President and Vice President. Usually, each elector votes for the candidate receiving the most popular votes in his or her state. A majority vote of all electors is necessary to elect the President and Vice President. If no candidate receives a majority, the House of Representatives, with each state having one vote, is empowered to elect the President and Vice President, again, with a majority of votes required.

The 22nd Amendment to the Constitution, adopted in 1951, limits presidential tenure to two elective terms of 4 years each or to one elective term for any person who, upon succession to the Presidency, has held the office or acted as President for more than 2 years.

Congressional election—The Constitution provides that Representatives be apportioned among the states according to their population, that a census of population be taken every 10 years as a basis for apportionment, and that each state have at least one Representative. At the time of each apportionment, Congress decides what the total number of Representatives will be. Since 1912, the total has been 435, except during 1960 to 1962 when it increased to 437, adding one Representative each for Alaska and Hawaii. The total reverted to 435 after reapportionment following the 1960 census. Members are elected for 2-year terms, all terms covering the same period. The District of Columbia, American Samoa, Guam, and the Virgin Islands each elect one nonvoting Delegate, and Puerto Rico elects a nonvoting Resident Commissioner.

The Senate is composed of 100 members, 2 from each state, who are elected to serve for a term of 6 years. One-third of the Senate is elected every 2 years. Senators were originally chosen by the state legislatures. The 17th Amendment to the Constitution, adopted in 1913, prescribed that Senators be elected by popular vote.

Voter eligibility and participation— The Census Bureau publishes estimates of the population of voting age and the percent casting votes in each state for Presidential and congressional election years. These voting-age estimates include a number of persons who meet the age requirement but are not eligible to vote, (e.g. aliens and some institutionalized persons). In addition, since 1964, voter participation and voter characteristics data have been collected during November of election years as part of the CPS. These survey data include noncitizens in the voting age population estimates, but exclude members of the Armed Forces and the institutional population.

Statistical reliability— For a discussion of statistical collection and estimation, sampling procedures, and measures of statistical reliability applicable to Census Bureau data, see Appendix III.

Figure 7.1
Vote Cast for President by Major Political Party: 1996 to 2004

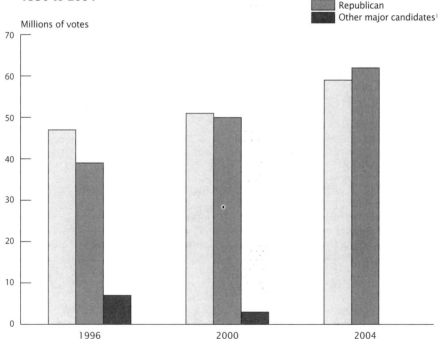

[1]Candidates with 1 million or more votes: 1996—Reform, Ross Perot; 2000—Green, Ralph Nader.

Source: Chart prepared by U.S. Census Bureau. For data, see Tables 385 and 386.

Table 385. **Vote Cast for President by Major Political Party: 1948 to 2004**

[In thousands (48,834 represents 48,834,000). Prior to 1960, excludes Alaska and Hawaii; prior to 1964, excludes DC. Vote cast for major party candidates includes the votes of minor parties cast for those candidates]

Year	Candidates for President		Vote cast for President						
				Democratic			Republican		
	Democratic	Republican	Total popular vote [1] (1,000)	Popular vote		Electoral vote	Popular vote		Electoral vote
				Number (1,000)	Per-cent		Number (1,000)	Per-cent	
1948....	Truman......	Dewey.......	48,834	24,106	49.4	303	21,969	45.0	189
1952....	Stevenson....	Eisenhower ...	61,552	27,315	44.4	89	33,779	54.9	442
1956....	Stevenson....	Eisenhower ...	62,027	26,739	43.1	73	35,581	57.4	457
1960....	Kennedy.....	Nixon........	68,836	34,227	49.7	303	34,108	49.5	219
1964....	Johnson......	Goldwater	70,098	42,825	61.1	486	27,147	38.7	52
1968....	Humphrey....	Nixon........	73,027	30,989	42.4	191	31,710	43.4	301
1972....	McGovern....	Nixon........	77,625	28,902	37.2	17	46,740	60.2	520
1976....	Carter.......	Ford........	81,603	40,826	50.0	297	39,148	48.0	240
1980....	Carter.......	Reagan.......	86,497	35,481	41.0	49	43,643	50.5	489
1984....	Mondale.....	Reagan......	92,655	37,450	40.4	13	54,167	58.5	525
1988....	Dukakis.....	Bush........	91,587	41,717	45.5	111	48,643	53.1	426
1992....	Clinton	Bush........	104,600	44,858	42.9	370	38,799	37.1	168
1996....	Clinton	Dole........	96,390	47,402	49.2	379	39,198	40.7	159
2000....	Gore........	Bush........	105,594	50,996	48.3	266	50,465	47.8	271
2004....	Kerry........	Bush........	122,349	58,895	48.1	251	61,873	50.6	286

[1] Include votes for minor party candidates, independents, unpledged electors, and scattered write-in votes.

Source: U.S. House of Representatives, Office of the Clerk, *Statistics of the Presidential and Congressional Election*, biennial. See also <http://clerk.house.gov/members/electionInfo/elections.html>.

Table 386. **Vote Cast for Leading Minority Party Candidates for President: 1948 to 2004**

[In thousands (1,169 represents 1,169,000). See headnote, Table 385. Data do not include write-ins, scatterings, or votes for candidates who ran on party tickets not shown]

Year	Candidate	Party	Popular vote (1,000)	Candidate	Party	Popular vote (1,000)
1948 . .	Strom Thurmond ...	States' Rights.......	1,169	Henry Wallace.....	Progressive........	1,156
1952 . .	Vincent Hallinan....	Progressive........	135	Stuart Hamblen	Prohibition.........	73
1956 [1]	T. Coleman Andrews.	States' Rights.......	91	Eric Hass	Socialist Labor	41
1960 . .	Eric Hass	Socialist Labor......	46	Rutherford Decker ..	Prohibition.........	46
1964 . .	Eric Hass	Socialist Labor......	43	Clifton DeBerry	Socialist Workers	22
1968 . .	George Wallace	American Independent.	9,446	Henning Blomen	Socialist Labor	52
1972 [1]	John Schmitz......	American........	993	Benjamin Spock....	People's	9
1976 . .	Eugene McCarthy ...	Independent	680	Roger McBride......	Libertarian........	172
1980 . .	John Anderson	Independent	5,251	Ed Clark..........	Libertarian........	920
1984 . .	David Bergland	Libertarian........	227	Lyndon H. LaRouche.	Independent	79
1988 . .	Ron Paul	Libertarian........	410	Lenora B. Fulani ...	New Alliance	129
1992 . .	H. Ross Perot	Independent	19,722	Andre Marrou	Libertarian........	281
1996 . .	H. Ross Perot	Reform	7,137	Ralph Nader	Green...........	527
2000 . .	Ralph Nader	Green...........	2,530	Pat Buchanan	Reform	324
2004 . .	Ralph Nader	Green...........	116	Michael Badnarik ...	Libertarian........	369

[1] Data include write-ins, scatterings, and/or votes for candidates who ran on party tickets not shown.

Source: U.S. House of Representatives, Office of the Clerk, *Statistics of the Presidential and Congressional Election*, biennial. See also <http://clerk.house.gov/members/electionInfo/elections.html>.

Table 387. **Democratic and Republican Percentages of Two-Party Presidential Vote by Selected Characteristics of Voters: 2000 and 2004**

[In percent. Covers citizens of voting age living in private housing units in the contiguous United States. Percentages for Democratic Presidential vote are computed by subtracting the percentage Republican vote from 100 percent; third-party or independent votes are not included as valid data. Data are from the National Election Studies and are based on a sample and subject to sampling variability; for details, see source]

Characteristic	2000		2004		Characteristic	2000		2004	
	Demo-cratic	Repub-lican	Demo-cratic	Repub-lican		Demo-cratic	Repub-lican	Demo-cratic	Repub-lican
Total [1]	52	48	50	50	Race:				
					White.............	46	54	42	58
Year of birth:					Black.............	92	8	90	10
1975 or later........	63	37	66	34	Education:				
1959 to 1974	46	54	45	55	Less than high school..	65	35	69	31
1943 to 1958	53	47	44	56	High school diploma/				
1927 to 1942	48	52	51	49	equivalent.........	53	47	46	54
1911 to 1926........	64	36	52	48	Some college, no				
1895 to 1910	–	100	–	–	degree...........	50	50	47	53
					College...........	50	50	50	50
Sex:					Union household......	61	39	64	36
Male	47	53	46	54	Nonunion household	50	50	46	54
Female	56	44	53	47					

– Represents zero. [1] Includes other characteristics, not shown separately.

Source: American National Election Studies; <www.electionstudies.org>.

U.S. Census Bureau, Statistical Abstract of the United States: 2007

Table 388. Electoral Vote Cast for President by Major Political Party—States: 1964 to 2004

[D = Democratic, R = Republican. For composition of regions, see map, inside front cover]

State	1964	1968 [1]	1972 [2]	1976 [3]	1980	1984	1988 [4]	1992	1996	2000 [5]	2004
Democratic . . .	486	191	17	297	49	13	111	370	379	266	25
Republican . . .	52	301	520	240	489	525	426	168	159	271	28
Northeast:											
Democratic	126	102	14	86	4	–	53	106	106	102	10
Republican	–	24	108	36	118	113	60	–	–	4	
Midwest:											
Democratic	149	31	–	58	10	10	29	100	100	68	5
Republican	–	118	145	87	135	127	108	29	29	61	6
South:											
Democratic	121	45	3	149	31	3	8	68	80	15	1
Republican	47	77	165	20	138	174	168	116	104	168	17
West:											
Democratic	90	13	–	4	4	–	21	96	93	81	7
Republican	5	82	102	97	98	111	90	23	26	38	4
AL.	R-10	(1)	R-9	D-9	R-9	R-9	R-9	R-9	R-9	R-9	R
AK.	D-3	R-3	R-3	R-3	R-3	R-3	R-3	R-3	R-3	R-3	R
AZ.	R-5	R-5	R-6	R-6	R-6	R-7	R-7	R-8	D-8	R-8	R-1
AR.	D-6	(1)	R-6	D-6	R-6	R-6	R-6	D-6	D-6	R-6	R
CA.	D-40	R-40	R-45	R-45	R-45	R-47	R-47	D-54	D-54	D-54	D-5
CO	D-6	R-6	R-7	R-7	R-7	R-8	R-8	D-8	R-8	R-8	R
CT.	D-8	D-8	R-8	R-8	R-8	R-8	R-8	D-8	D-8	D-8	D
DE.	D-3	R-3	R-3	D-3	R-3	R-3	R-3	D-3	D-3	D-3	D
DC	D-3	D-3	D-3	D-3	D-3	D-3	D-3	D-3	D-3	[5]D-2	D
FL.	D-14	R-14	R-17	D-17	R-17	R-21	R-21	R-25	R-25	R-25	R-2
GA	R-12	(1)	R-12	D-12	D-12	R-12	R-12	D-13	R-13	R-13	R-1
HI	D-4	D-4	R-4	D-4	D-4	R-4	D-4	D-4	D-4	D-4	D
ID	D-4	R-4	R-4	R-4	R-4	R-4	R-4	R-4	R-4	R-4	R
IL	D-26	R-26	R-26	R-26	R-26	R-24	R-24	D-22	D-22	D-22	D-2
IN	D-13	R-13	R-13	R-13	R-13	R-12	R-12	R-12	R-12	R-12	R-1
IA	D-9	R-9	R-8	R-8	R-8	R-8	D-8	D-7	D-7	D-7	R
KS.	D-7	R-7	R-7	R-7	R-7	R-7	R-7	R-6	R-6	R-6	R
KY.	D-9	R-9	R-9	D-9	R-9	R-9	R-9	D-8	D-8	R-8	R
LA.	R-10	(1)	R-10	D-10	R-10	R-10	R-10	D-9	D-9	R-9	R
ME	D-4	D-4	R-4	R-4	R-4	R-4	R-4	D-4	D-4	D-4	D
MD	D-10	D-10	R-10	D-10	D-10	R-10	R-10	D-10	D-10	D-10	D-1
MA	D-14	D-14	D-14	R-14	D-14	R-13	D-13	D-12	D-12	D-12	D-1
MI	D-21	D-21	R-21	R-21	R-21	R-20	R-20	D-18	D-18	D-18	D-1
MN	D-10	D-10	R-10	D-10	D-10	D-10	D-10	D-10	D-10	D-10	[6]D
MS	R-7	(1)	R-7	D-7	R-7	R-7	R-7	R-7	R-7	R-7	R
MO	D-12	R-12	R-12	D-12	R-12	R-11	R-11	D-11	D-11	R-11	R-
MT	D-4	R-4	R-4	R-4	R-4	R-4	R-4	D-3	R-3	R-3	R
NE.	D-5	R-5	R-5	R-5	R-5	R-5	R-5	R-5	R-5	R-5	R
NV.	D-3	R-3	R-3	R-3	R-3	R-4	R-4	D-4	D-4	R-4	R
NH	D-4	R-4	R-4	R-4	R-4	R-4	R-4	D-4	D-4	R-4	D
NJ.	D-17	R-17	R-17	R-17	R-17	R-16	R-16	D-15	D-15	D-15	D-
NM	D-4	R-4	R-4	R-4	R-4	R-5	R-5	D-5	D-5	D-5	R
NY.	D-43	D-43	R-41	D-41	R-41	R-36	D-36	D-33	D-33	D-33	D-3
NC.	D-13	[1]R-12	R-13	D-13	R-13	R-13	R-13	R-14	R-14	R-14	R-
ND	D-4	R-4	R-4	R-3	R-3	R-3	R-3	R-3	R-3	R-3	R
OH	D-26	R-26	R-25	D-25	R-25	R-23	R-23	D-21	D-21	R-21	R-2
OK	D-8	R-8	R-8	R-8	R-8	R-8	R-8	R-8	R-8	R-8	R
OR	D-6	R-6	R-6	R-6	R-6	R-7	D-7	D-7	D-7	D-7	D
PA	D-29	D-29	R-27	R-27	R-27	R-25	R-25	D-23	D-23	D-23	D-2
RI	D-4	D-4	R-4	D-4	D-4	R-4	D-4	D-4	D-4	D-4	D
SC.	R-8	R-8	R-8	D-8	R-8	R-8	R-8	R-8	R-8	R-8	R
SD.	D-4	R-4	R-4	R-4	R-4	R-3	R-3	R-3	R-3	R-3	R
TN.	D-11	R-11	R-11	D-10	R-10	R-11	R-11	D-11	D-11	R-11	R-
TX.	D-25	D-25	R-26	D-26	R-26	R-29	R-29	R-32	R-32	R-32	R-3
UT.	D-4	R-4	R-4	R-4	R-4	R-5	R-5	R-5	R-5	R-5	R
VT.	D-3	R-3	R-3	R-3	R-3	R-3	R-3	D-3	D-3	D-3	D
VA.	D-12	R-12	[2]R-11	R-12	R-12	R-12	R-12	R-13	R-13	R-13	R-
WA	D-9	D-9	R-9	[3]R-8	R-9	R-10	D-10	D-11	D-11	D-11	D-
WV	D-7	D-7	R-6	D-6	D-6	R-6	[4]D-5	D-5	D-5	R-5	R
WI	D-12	R-12	R-11	D-11	R-11	R-11	D-11	D-11	D-11	D-11	D-
WY	D-3	R-3	R-3	R-3	R-3	R-3	R-3	R-3	R-3	R-3	R

– Represents zero. [1] Excludes 46 electoral votes cast for American Independent George C. Wallace as follows: AL 10, A 6, GA 12, LA 10, MS 7, and NC 1. [2] Excludes one electoral vote cast for Libertarian John Hospers in Virginia. [3] Excludes o electoral vote cast for Ronald Reagan in Washington. [4] Excludes one electoral vote cast for Lloyd Bentsen for President in We Virginia. [5] Excludes one electoral vote left blank by a Democratic elector in the District of Columbia. [6] Excludes one electo vote cast for Democratic vice presidential nominee John Edwards in Minnesota.

Source: U.S. House of Representatives, Office of the Clerk, *Statistics of the Presidential and Congressional Election*, bienni See also <http://clerk.house.gov/members/electionInfo/elections.html>.

Table 389. **Popular Vote Cast for President by Political Party—States: 2000 and 2004**

[In thousands (105,594 represents 105,594,000), except percent]

State	2000					2004				
				Percent of total vote					Percent of total vote	
	Total [1]	Demo-cratic Party	Repub-lican Party	Demo-cratic Party	Repub-lican Party	Total [1]	Demo-cratic Party	Repub-lican Party	Demo-cratic Party	Repub-lican Party
United States. .	**105,594**	**50,996**	**50,465**	**48.3**	**47.8**	**122,349**	**58,895**	**61,873**	**48.1**	**50.6**
Alabama.	1,666	693	941	41.6	56.5	1,883	694	1,176	36.8	62.5
Alaska	286	79	167	27.7	58.6	313	111	191	35.5	61.1
Arizona.	1,532	685	782	44.7	51.0	2,013	894	1,104	44.4	54.9
Arkansas	922	423	473	45.9	51.3	1,055	470	573	44.5	54.3
California	10,966	5,861	4,567	53.4	41.7	12,421	6,745	5,510	54.3	44.4
Colorado.	1,741	738	884	42.4	50.8	2,130	1,002	1,101	47.0	51.7
Connecticut.	1,460	816	561	55.9	38.4	1,579	857	694	54.3	43.9
Delaware	328	180	137	55.0	41.9	375	200	172	53.3	45.8
District of Columbia .	202	172	18	85.2	9.0	228	203	21	89.2	9.3
Florida	5,963	2,912	2,913	48.8	48.8	7,610	3,584	3,965	47.1	52.1
Georgia	2,583	1,116	1,420	43.2	55.0	3,302	1,366	1,914	41.4	58.0
Hawaii	368	205	138	55.8	37.5	429	232	194	54.0	45.3
Idaho.	502	139	337	27.6	67.2	598	181	409	30.3	68.4
Illinois	4,742	2,589	2,019	54.6	42.6	5,274	2,892	2,346	54.8	44.5
Indiana.	2,199	902	1,246	41.0	56.6	2,468	969	1,479	39.3	59.9
Iowa	1,353	639	634	47.2	46.9	1,507	742	752	49.2	49.9
Kansas.	1,072	399	622	37.2	58.0	1,188	435	736	36.6	62.0
Kentucky	1,544	639	873	41.4	56.5	1,796	713	1,069	39.7	59.5
Louisiana	1,766	792	928	44.9	52.6	1,943	820	1,102	42.2	56.7
Maine.	652	320	287	49.1	44.0	741	397	330	53.6	44.6
Maryland	2,025	1,144	814	56.5	40.2	2,384	1,334	1,025	56.0	43.0
Massachusetts.	2,734	1,616	879	59.1	32.1	2,927	1,804	1,071	61.6	36.6
Michigan.	4,233	2,170	1,953	51.3	46.1	4,839	2,479	2,314	51.2	47.8
Minnesota	2,439	1,168	1,110	47.9	45.5	2,828	1,445	1,347	51.1	47.6
Mississippi	994	405	573	40.7	57.6	1,140	458	673	40.2	59.0
Missouri	2,360	1,111	1,190	47.1	50.4	2,731	1,259	1,456	46.1	53.3
Montana	411	137	240	33.4	58.4	450	174	266	38.6	59.1
Nebraska	697	232	434	33.3	62.2	778	254	513	32.7	65.9
Nevada	609	280	302	45.9	49.5	830	397	419	47.9	50.5
New Hampshire	569	266	274	46.8	48.1	678	341	331	50.2	48.8
New Jersey.	3,187	1,789	1,284	56.1	40.3	3,612	1,911	1,670	52.9	46.2
New Mexico	599	287	286	47.9	47.8	756	371	377	49.0	49.8
New York	6,960	4,108	2,403	59.0	34.5	7,448	4,181	2,807	56.1	37.7
North Carolina	2,915	1,258	1,631	43.1	56.0	3,501	1,526	1,961	43.6	56.0
North Dakota	288	95	175	33.1	60.7	313	111	197	35.5	62.9
Ohio	4,702	2,184	2,350	46.4	50.0	5,628	2,741	2,860	48.7	50.8
Oklahoma.	1,234	474	744	38.4	60.3	1,464	504	960	34.4	65.6
Oregon.	1,534	720	714	47.0	46.5	1,837	943	867	51.3	47.2
Pennsylvania.	4,912	2,486	2,281	50.6	46.4	5,770	2,938	2,794	50.9	48.4
Rhode Island.	409	250	131	61.0	31.9	437	260	169	59.4	38.7
South Carolina.	1,384	566	787	40.9	56.9	1,618	662	938	40.9	58.0
South Dakota	316	119	191	37.6	60.3	388	149	233	38.4	59.9
Tennessee	2,076	982	1,062	47.3	51.1	2,437	1,036	1,384	42.5	56.8
Texas.	6,408	2,434	3,800	38.0	59.3	7,411	2,833	4,527	38.2	61.1
Utah	771	203	515	26.3	66.8	928	241	664	26.0	71.5
Vermont	294	149	120	50.6	40.7	312	184	121	58.9	38.8
Virginia.	2,739	1,217	1,437	44.4	52.5	3,195	1,455	1,717	45.5	53.7
Washington.	2,487	1,248	1,109	50.2	44.6	2,859	1,510	1,305	52.8	45.6
West Virginia	648	295	336	45.6	51.9	756	327	424	43.2	56.1
Wisconsin.	2,599	1,243	1,237	47.8	47.6	2,997	1,490	1,478	49.7	49.3
Wyoming	214	60	148	28.3	69.2	244	71	168	29.0	68.7

[1] Includes other parties.

Source: U.S. House of Representatives, Office of the Clerk, *Statistics of the Presidential and Congressional Election*, biennial. See also <http://clerk.house.gov/members/electionInfo/elections.html>.

Elections 243

Table 390. Vote Cast for United States Senators, 2002 and 2004, and Incumbent Senators, 2006—States

[**1,353 represents 1,353,000.** D = Democrat; R = Republican]

State	2002 Total (1,000)[1]	2002 Percent for leading party	2004 Total (1,000)[1]	2004 Percent for leading party	Incumbent senators and year term expires — Name, party, and year	Incumbent senators and year term expires — Name, party, and year
Alabama	1,353	R-58.6	1,839	R-67.5	Jeffrey Sessions (R) 2009	Richard Shelby (R) 2011
Alaska	230	R-78.2	308	R-48.6	Lisa Murkowski (R) 2011	Ted Stevens (R) 2009
Arizona	(X)	(X)	1,962	R-76.7	Jon Kyl (R) 2007	John McCain (R) 2011
Arkansas	804	D-53.9	1,039	D-55.9	Blanche Lincoln (D) 2011	Mark Pryor (D) 2009
California	(X)	(X)	12,053	D-57.7	Barbara Boxer (D) 2011	Dianne Feinstein (D) 2007
Colorado	1,416	R-50.7	2,107	D-51.3	Wayne Allard (R) 2009	Ken Salazar (D) 2011
Connecticut	(X)	(X)	1,425	D-66.4	Christopher Dodd (D) 2011	Joseph Lieberman (D) 2007
Delaware	232	D-58.2	(X)	(X)	Joseph Biden (D) 2009	Thomas Carper (D) 2007
Florida	(X)	(X)	7,430	R-49.4	Mel Martinez (R) 2011	Bill Nelson (D) 2007
Georgia	2,032	R-52.7	3,221	R-57.8	Saxby Chambliss (R) 2009	Johnny Isakson (R) 2011
Hawaii	(X)	(X)	415	D-75.5	Daniel Akaka (D) 2007	Daniel Inouye (D) 2011
Idaho	409	R-65.2	504	R-99.2	Larry Craig (R) 2009	Michael Crapo (R) 2011
Illinois	3,487	D-60.3	5,142	D-70.0	Richard Durbin (D) 2009	Barack Obama (D) 2011
Indiana	(X)	(X)	2,428	D-61.6	Evan Bayh (D) 2011	Richard Lugar (R) 2007
Iowa	1,023	D-54.2	1,479	R-70.2	Chuck Grassley (R) 2011	Tom Harkin (D) 2009
Kansas	767	R-83.6	1,129	R-69.2	Sam Brownback (R) 2011	Pat Roberts (R) 2009
Kentucky	1,131	R-64.7	1,724	R-50.7	Jim Bunning (R) 2011	Mitch McConnell (R) 2009
Louisiana [2]	1,235	D-51.7	1,848	R-51.0	Mary Landrieu (D) 2009	David Vitter (R) 2011
Maine	505	R-58.4	(X)	(X)	Susan Collins (R) 2009	Olympia Snowe (R) 2007
Maryland	(X)	(X)	2,322	D-64.8	Barbara Mikulski (D) 2011	Paul Sarbanes (D) 2007
Massachusetts	2,220	D-72.3	(X)	(X)	Edward Kennedy (D) 2007	John Kerry (D) 2009
Michigan	3,129	D-60.6	(X)	(X)	Carl Levin (D) 2009	Debbie Stabenow (D) 2007
Minnesota	2,255	R-49.5	(X)	(X)	Norm Coleman (R) 2009	Mark Dayton (D) 2007
Mississippi	630	R-84.6	(X)	(X)	Thad Cochran (R) 2009	Trent Lott (R) 2007
Missouri	(X)	(X)	2,706	R-56.1	Christopher Bond (R) 2011	James Talent (R) 2007
Montana	327	D-62.7	(X)	(X)	Max Baucus (D) 2009	Conrad Burns (R) 2007
Nebraska	480	R-82.8	(X)	(X)	Chuck Hagel (R) 2009	Ben Nelson (D) 2007
Nevada	(X)	(X)	810	D-61.1	John Ensign (R) 2007	Harry Reid (D) 2011
New Hampshire	447	R-50.8	657	R-66.2	Judd Gregg (R) 2011	John Sununu (R) 2009
New Jersey	2,113	D-53.9	(X)	(X)	Robert Menendez (D) 2007	Frank Lautenberg (D) 2009
New Mexico	483	R-65.0	(X)	(X)	Jeff Bingaman (D) 2007	Pete Domenici (R) 2009
New York	(X)	(X)	7,448	D-58.9	Hillary Clinton (D) 2007	Charles Schumer (D) 2011
North Carolina	2,331	R-53.6	3,472	R-51.6	Richard Burr (R) 2011	Elizabeth Dole (R) 2009
North Dakota	(X)	(X)	311	D-68.3	Kent Conrad (D) 2007	Byron Dorgan (D) 2011
Ohio	(X)	(X)	5,426	R-63.8	Mike DeWine (R) 2007	George Voinovich (R) 2011
Oklahoma	1,018	R-57.3	1,447	R-52.8	Tom Coburn (R) 2011	James Inhofe (R) 2009
Oregon	1,267	R-56.2	1,781	D-63.4	Gordon Smith (R) 2009	Ron Wyden (D) 2011
Pennsylvania	(X)	(X)	5,559	R-52.6	Rick Santorum (R) 2007	Arlen Specter (R) 2011
Rhode Island	324	D-78.4	(X)	(X)	Lincoln Chafee (R) 2007	Jack Reed (D) 2009
South Carolina	1,103	R-54.4	1,597	R-53.7	Jim DeMint (R) 2011	Lindsey Graham (R) 2009
South Dakota	338	D-49.6	391	R-50.6	Tim Johnson (D) 2009	John Thune (R) 2011
Tennessee	1,642	R-54.3	(X)	(X)	Lamar Alexander (R) 2009	Bill Frist (R) 2007
Texas	4,514	R-55.3	(X)	(X)	John Cornyn (R) 2009	Kay Hutchison (R) 2007
Utah	(X)	(X)	912	R-68.7	Robert Bennett (R) 2011	Orrin Hatch (R) 2007
Vermont	(X)	(X)	307	D-70.6	James Jeffords (I) 2007	Patrick Leahy (D) 2011
Virginia	1,489	R-82.6	(X)	(X)	George Allen (R) 2007	John Warner (R) 2009
Washington	(X)	(X)	2,819	D-55.0	Maria Cantwell (D) 2007	Patty Murray (D) 2011
West Virginia	436	D-63.1	(X)	(X)	Robert Byrd (D) 2007	John Rockefeller (D) 2009
Wisconsin	(X)	(X)	2,950	D-55.4	Russell Feingold (D) 2011	Herb Kohl (D) 2007
Wyoming	183	R-73.0	(X)	(X)	Michael Enzi (R) 2009	Craig Thomas (R) 2007

X Not applicable.   [1] Includes vote cast for minor parties.   [2] Louisiana holds an open-primary election with candidates from all parties running on the same ballot. Any candidate who receives a majority is elected.

Source: U.S. House of Representatives, Office of the Clerk, *Statistics of the Presidential and Congressional Election*, biennial. See also <http://clerk.house.gov/members/electionInfo/elections.html>.

Table 391. **Vote Cast for United States Representatives by Major Political Party—States: 2000 to 2004**

[In thousands (98,800 represents 98,800,000), except percent. R = Republican,D = Democrat, and I = Independent. In each state, totals represent the sum of votes cast in each Congressional District or votes cast for Representative-at-Large in states where only one member is elected. In all years there are numerous districts within the state where either the Republican or Democratic party had no candidate. In some states the Republican and Democratic vote includes votes cast for the party candidate by endorsing parties]

State	2000				2002				2004			
	Total[1]	Demo-cratic	Repub-lican	Percent for leading party	Total[1]	Demo-cratic	Repub-lican	Percent for leading party	Total[1]	Demo-cratic	Repub-lican	Percent for leading party
U.S.	**98,800**	**46,412**	**46,750**	**R-47.3**	**74,707**	**33,642**	**37,091**	**R-49.6**	**113,192**	**52,745**	**55,713**	**R-49.2**
AL	1,439	486	849	R-59.0	1,269	507	695	R-54.7	1,793	708	1,080	R-60.2
AK	274	45	191	R-69.6	228	39	170	R-74.5	300	67	213	R-71.1
AZ [2]	1,466	558	855	R-58.3	1,194	472	682	R-57.1	1,871	598	1,128	R-60.3
AR [2]	633	355	277	D-56.2	688	392	284	D-57.0	791	426	358	D-53.9
CA	10,437	5,407	4,446	D-51.8	7,258	3,731	3,226	D-51.4	11,624	6,224	5,031	D-53.5
CO [2]	1,624	496	969	R-59.7	1,397	589	753	R-53.9	2,039	995	992	D-48.8
CT [2]	1,313	699	591	D-53.2	989	509	466	D-51.5	1,429	786	630	D-55.0
DE	313	96	212	R-67.6	228	61	165	R-72.1	356	106	246	R-69.1
FL [2]	5,011	1,976	2,852	R-56.9	3,767	1,537	2,161	R-57.4	5,627	2,212	3,319	R-59.0
GA	2,417	918	1,498	R-62.0	1,919	814	1,105	R-57.6	2,961	1,141	1,820	R-61.5
HI	340	221	111	D-65.0	360	232	117	D-64.5	417	262	148	D-62.9
ID	493	142	333	R-67.5	405	138	256	R-63.3	572	171	401	R-70.1
IL	4,393	2,454	1,907	D-55.9	3,429	1,741	1,657	D-50.8	4,989	2,675	2,272	D-53.6
IN	2,157	953	1,141	R-52.9	1,521	641	841	R-55.3	2,416	999	1,382	R-57.2
IA	1,276	532	717	R-56.2	1,013	454	546	R-54.0	1,458	625	823	R-56.4
KS	1,036	328	656	R-63.3	830	260	536	R-64.6	1,156	387	724	R-62.6
KY [2]	1,435	562	825	R-57.5	1,094	351	694	R-63.4	1,635	602	1,017	R-62.2
LA [2]	1,202	360	747	R-62.1	1,140	391	668	R-58.6	1,259	478	780	R-62.0
ME	638	423	203	D-66.2	495	290	206	D-58.5	710	418	283	D-58.9
MD	1,927	1,061	856	D-55.1	1,659	904	753	D-54.5	2,254	1,311	896	D-58.2
MA	2,734	1,968	343	D-72.0	2,220	1,529	290	D-68.8	2,927	2,060	435	D-70.4
MI	4,070	2,178	1,787	D-53.5	3,056	1,507	1,474	D-49.3	4,631	2,242	2,289	R-49.4
MN	2,364	1,234	993	D-52.2	2,202	1,098	1,030	D-49.9	2,722	1,400	1,236	D-51.4
MS	986	496	468	D-50.3	678	320	339	R-50.0	1,116	335	659	R-59.0
MO	2,326	1,136	1,136	D-48.8	1,854	829	986	R-53.2	2,667	1,193	1,430	R-53.6
MT	411	190	211	R-51.5	331	108	214	R-64.6	444	146	286	R-64.4
NE	683	178	487	R-71.2	474	47	387	R-81.6	765	231	515	R-67.3
NV	587	225	331	R-56.4	502	171	301	R-60.0	791	334	421	R-53.2
NH	556	239	303	R-54.5	443	176	255	R-57.5	652	244	396	R-60.8
NJ	2,988	1,532	1,384	D-51.3	2,006	1,030	934	D-51.4	3,285	1,721	1,515	D-52.4
NM	588	300	274	D-51.0	437	262	175	D-59.9	743	385	358	D-51.8
NY	6,949	3,052	2,235	D-43.9	4,701	1,778	1,526	D-37.8	7,448	3,457	2,209	D-46.4
NC	2,780	1,194	1,515	R-54.5	2,244	971	1,209	R-53.9	3,413	1,670	1,743	R-51.1
ND	286	151	127	D-52.9	231	121	110	D-52.4	311	185	126	D-59.6
OH	4,585	2,099	2,235	R-48.8	3,158	1,332	1,776	R-56.2	5,184	2,515	2,650	R-51.1
OK	1,088	337	702	R-64.5	1,002	392	547	R-54.6	1,375	389	875	R-63.7
OR	1,440	790	607	D-54.9	1,240	677	529	D-54.6	1,772	952	762	D-53.7
PA	4,552	2,279	2,229	D-50.1	3,310	1,349	1,859	R-56.2	5,151	2,478	2,565	R-49.8
RI	384	247	89	D-64.3	329	225	97	D-68.3	402	279	113	D-69.5
SC	1,321	523	730	R-55.2	984	345	569	R-57.8	1,439	486	913	R-63.5
SD	315	78	231	R-73.4	337	154	180	R-53.5	389	208	179	D-53.4
TN	1,854	819	992	R-53.5	1,529	708	771	R-50.4	2,219	1,032	1,161	R-52.3
TX	5,986	2,799	2,932	R-49.0	4,295	1,885	2,291	R-53.3	6,959	2,714	4,013	R-57.7
UT	759	305	427	R-56.2	557	221	322	R-57.8	909	362	520	R-57.3
VT	283	15	52	I-73.4	225	(X)	73	I-64.3	305	22	74	I-67.5
VA	2,422	1,060	1,132	R-46.7	1,516	440	956	R-63.0	3,004	1,023	1,817	R-60.5
WA	2,382	1,246	998	D-52.3	1,739	907	779	D-52.2	2,730	1,609	1,095	D-58.9
WV	580	421	109	D-72.6	400	264	136	D-66.0	722	415	303	D-57.6
WI	2,506	1,188	1,311	R-53.3	1,638	677	889	R-54.3	2,822	1,369	1,381	R-48.9
WY	212	61	142	R-66.8	182	66	110	R-60.5	239	100	132	R-55.2

X Not applicable. [1] Includes vote cast for minor parties. [2] State law does not require tabulation of votes for unopposed candidates.

Source: U.S. House of Representatives, Office of the Clerk, *Statistics of the Presidential and Congressional Election*, biennial. See also <http://clerk.house.gov/members/electionInfo/elections.html>.

U.S. Census Bureau, Statistical Abstract of the United States: 2007

Table 392. Vote Cast for United States Representatives by Major Political Party—Congressional Districts: 2004

[In some states the Democratic and Republican vote includes votes cast for the party candidate by endorsing parties]

State and district	Democratic candidate Name	Percent of total	Republican candidate Name	Percent of total
AL	(X)........	(X)	(X)........	(X)
1st...	Belk...	36.81	Bonner.....	63.12
2d...	James.....	28.46	Everett.....	71.42
3d...	Fuller.....	38.75	Rogers.....	61.20
4th...	Cole.......	25.14	Aderholt....	74.73
5th...	Cramer, Jr...	72.97	Wallace....	26.92
6th...	(¹)......	(¹)	Bachus....	98.80
7th...	Davis.....	74.97	Cameron...	24.94
AK	Higgins.....	22.36	Young.....	71.08
AZ	(X)........	(X)	(X)........	(X)
1st...	Babbitt.....	36.22	Renzi.....	58.54
2d...	Camacho...	38.46	Franks.....	59.17
3d...	(¹)........	(¹)	Shadegg....	80.10
4th...	Pastor.....	70.12	Karg......	25.66
5th...	Rogers.....	38.19	Hayworth...	59.50
6th...	(¹)........	(¹)	Flake......	79.38
7th...	Grijalva....	62.06	Sweeney...	33.67
8th...	Bacal.....	36.20	Kolbe......	60.36
AR	(X)........	(X)	(X)........	(X)
1st...	Berry.....	66.57	Humphrey...	33.43
2d...	Snyder.....	58.17	Parks.....	41.83
3d...	Judy.....	38.09	Boozman...	59.32
4th...	Ross.....	(²)	(¹)......	(¹)
CA	(X)........	(X)	(X)........	(X)
1st...	Thompson..	66.92	Wiesner....	28.26
2d...	Johnson...	33.15	Herger.....	66.85
3d...	Castillo.....	34.84	Lungren....	61.91
4th...	Winters....	34.61	Doolittle....	65.39
5th...	Matsui.....	71.36	Dugas.....	23.33
6th...	Woolsey....	72.65	Erickson....	27.35
7th...	Miller......	76.08	Hargrave...	23.92
8th...	Pelosi......	82.95	DePalma....	11.51
9th...	Lee.......	84.55	Bermudez...	12.26
10th...	Tauscher...	65.71	Ketelson....	34.29
11th...	McNerney...	38.77	Pombo.....	61.23
12th...	Lantos.....	68.03	Garza.....	20.82
13th...	Stark......	71.61	Bruno.....	23.99
14th...	Eshoo.....	69.77	Haugen....	26.56
15th...	Honda.....	72.03	Chukwu....	27.97
16th...	Lofgren.....	70.89	McNea.....	26.33
17th...	Farr.......	66.73	Risley.....	29.17
18th...	Cardoza....	67.49	Pringle.....	32.51
19th...	Bufford.....	27.22	Radanovich..	66.03
20th...	Costa.....	53.40	Ashburn....	46.60
21st...	Davis.....	26.83	Nunes.....	73.17
22d...	(¹)......	(¹)	Thomas.....	100.00
23d...	Capps.....	63.03	Regan.....	34.35
24th...	Wagner....	33.90	Gallegly....	62.82
25th...	Willoughby...	35.58	McKeon....	64.42
26th...	Matthews...	42.80	Dreier......	53.58
27th...	Sherman...	62.27	Levy......	33.27
28th...	Berman.....	70.95	Hernandez..	23.30
29th...	Schiff......	64.63	Scolinos....	30.40
30th...	Waxman....	71.24	Elizalde....	28.76
31st...	Becerra....	80.21	Vega......	19.79
32d...	Solis......	85.01	(¹)......	(¹)
33d...	Watson.....	88.58	(¹)......	(¹)
34th...	Roybal-Allard.	74.49	Miller......	25.51
35th...	Waters.....	80.53	Moen......	15.08
36th...	Harman....	61.96	Whitehead...	33.46
37th...	Millender-McDonald	75.05	Van.......	20.19
38th...	Napolitano...	100.00	(¹)......	(¹)
39th...	Sanchez....	60.70	Escobar....	39.30
40th...	Williams....	32.07	Royce.....	67.93
41st...	(¹)......	(¹)	Lewis.....	82.95
42d...	Myers.....	31.86	Miller......	68.14
43d...	Baca......	66.37	Laning.....	33.63
44th...	Vandenberg..	35.00	Calvert.....	61.64
45th...	Meyer.....	33.39	Bono......	66.61
46th...	Brandt.....	32.57	Rohrabacher.	61.92
47th...	Sanchez....	60.38	Coronado...	44.22
48th...	Graham....	32.15	Cox.......	64.98
49th...	Byron......	34.91	Issa.......	62.55
50th...	Busby.....	36.49	Cunningham.	58.42
51st...	Filner.....	61.61	Giorgino....	35.12
52d...	Keliher.....	27.58	Hunter.....	69.19
53d...	Davis......	66.14	Hunzeker...	28.86
CO ...	(X)........	(X)	(X)........	(X)
1st...	DeGette....	73.50	Chicas.....	24.35
2d...	Udall......	67.20	Hackman...	30.44
3d...	Salazar.....	50.55	Walcher....	46.56
4th...	Matsunaka...	44.78	Musgrave...	51.05
5th...	Hardee.....	27.04	Hefley.....	70.54
6th...	Conti......	39.10	Tancredo...	59.48
7th...	Thomas....	42.79	Beauprez...	54.72
CT	(X)........	(X)	(X)........	(X)
1st...	Larson.....	72.98	Halstead....	27.02
2d...	Sullivan....	45.77	Simmons...	54.19
3d...	DeLauro....	72.44	Elser......	24.97
4th...	Farrell.....	47.56	Shays.....	52.43
5th...	Gerratana...	38.17	Johnson....	59.79
DE	Donnelly....	29.69	Castle.....	69.09
FL	(X)........	(X)	(X)........	(X)
1st...	Coutu.....	23.46	Miller......	76.54
2d...	Boyd......	61.65	Kilmer.....	38.35
3d...	Brown.....	99.24	(¹)......	(¹)
4th...	(¹)........	(¹)	Crenshaw...	99.55
5th...	Whittel.....	34.06	Brown-Waite.	65.93
6th...	Bruderly....	35.59	Stearns....	64.40
7th...	(¹)........	(¹)	Mica......	(²)
8th...	Murray.....	39.48	Keller.....	60.52
9th...	(¹)........	(¹)	Bilirakis....	99.91
10th...	Derry......	30.67	Young.....	69.33
11th...	Davis.....	85.81	(¹)......	(¹)
12th...	Hagenmaier..	35.11	Putnam....	64.89
13th...	Schneider...	44.70	Harris.....	55.30
14th...	Neeld......	32.41	Mack......	67.59
15th...	Pristoop....	34.65	Weldon....	65.35
16th...	Fisher.....	31.96	Foley......	68.04
17th...	Meek......	99.59	(¹)......	(¹)
18th...	Sheldon....	35.27	Ros-Lehtinen.	64.73
19th...	Wexler.....	(²)	(¹)......	(¹)
20th...	Schultz.....	70.19	Hostetter...	29.81
21st...	(¹)........	(¹)	Balart.....	72.80
22d...	Rorapaugh...	35.29	Shaw......	62.79
23d...	Hastings....	(²)	(¹)......	(¹)
24th...	(¹)........	(¹)	Feeney.....	(²)
25th...	(¹)........	(¹)	Diaz-Balart...	(²)
GA	(X)........	(X)	(X)........	(X)
1st...	(¹)........	(¹)	Kingston....	100.00
2d...	Bishop, Jr...	66.79	Eversman...	33.21
3d...	Marshall....	62.88	Clay......	37.12
4th...	McKinney...	63.76	Davis.....	36.24
5th...	Lewis.....	100.00	(¹)......	(¹)
6th...	(¹)........	(¹)	Price......	99.97
7th...	(¹)........	(¹)	Linder.....	100.00
8th...	Delamar....	24.45	Westmore-land...	75.55
9th...	Ellis......	25.71	Norwood....	74.29
10th...	(¹)........	(¹)	Deal......	100.00
11th...	Crawford....	42.60	Gingrey....	57.40
12th...	Barrow.....	51.81	Burns.....	48.19
13th...	Scott......	100.00	(¹)......	(¹)
HI	(X)........	(X)	(X)........	(X)
1st...	Abercrombie.	62.97	Tanonaka...	33.98
2d...	Case......	62.77	Gabbard....	37.23
ID	(X)........	(X)	(X)........	(X)
1st...	Preston....	30.45	Otter......	69.55
2d...	Whitworth...	29.26	Simpson....	70.74

See footnotes at end of table.

U.S. Census Bureau, Statistical Abstract of the United States: 2007

Table 392. Vote Cast for United States Representatives by Major Political Party—Congressional Districts: 2004—Con.

[See headnote, p. 246]

State and district	Democratic candidate Name	Percent of total	Republican candidate Name	Percent of total
IL......	(X)	(X)	(X)	(X)
1st	Rush	84.86	Wardingley	15.14
2d	Jackson	88.49	[1]	[1]
3d	Lipinski	72.64	Chlada	25.15
4th	Gutierrez	83.71	Cisneros	12.41
5th	Emanuel	76.18	Best	23.82
6th	Cegelis	44.17	Hyde	55.83
7th	Davis	86.13	Davis-Fairman	13.87
8th	Bean	51.70	Crane	48.30
9th	Schakowsky	75.74	Eckhardt	24.26
10th	Goodman	35.86	Kirk	64.14
11th	Renner	41.33	Weller	58.67
12th	Costello	69.46	Zweigart	28.86
13th	Andersen	34.98	Biggert	65.02
14th	Zamora	31.37	Hastert	68.63
15th	Gill	38.95	Johnson	61.05
16th	Kutsch	58.25	Manzullo	69.08
17th	Evans	32.20	Zinga	39.32
18th	Waterworth	29.76	LaHood	70.24
19th	Bagwell	30.64	Shimkus	69.36
IN.....	(X)	(X)	(X)	(X)
1st	Visclosky	68.29	Leyva	31.71
2d	Donnelly	44.54	Chocola	54.17
3d	Parra	30.79	Souder	69.21
4th	Sanders	28.30	Buyer	69.47
5th	Carr	25.96	Burton	71.84
6th	Fox	31.29	Pence	67.09
7th	Carson	54.35	Horning	43.68
8th	Jennings	44.55	Hostettler	53.37
9th	Hill	48.96	Sodrel	49.46
IA.....	(X)	(X)	(X)	(X)
1st	Gluba	43.26	Nussle	55.16
2d	Franker	39.15	Leach	58.92
3d	Boswell	55.21	Thompson	44.72
4th	Johnson	39.02	Latham	60.93
5th	Schulte	36.64	King	63.30
KS.....	(X)	(X)	(X)	(X)
1st	[1]	[1]	Moran	90.72
2d	Boyda	41.28	Ryun	56.15
3d	Moore	54.82	Kobach	43.35
4th	Kinard	31.07	Tiahrt	66.11
KY.....	(X)	(X)	(X)	(X)
1st	Cartwright	32.61	Whitfield	67.32
2d	Smith	32.08	Lewis	67.92
3d	Miller	37.80	Northup	60.26
4th	Clooney	43.89	Davis	54.40
5th	[1]	[1]	Rogers	100.00
6th	Chandler	58.60	Buford	40.01
LA [3]	(X)	(X)	(X)	(X)
1st	Armstrong	6.69	Jindal	78.40
2d	Jefferson	79.01	Schwertz	20.99
3d	Melancon	50.25	Tauzin III	49.75
4th	[1]	[1]	McCrery	[2]
5th	Blakes	24.61	Alexander	59.44
6th	Craig, Jr.	19.37	Baker	72.21
7th	Mount	45.04	Boustany, Jr.	54.96
ME.....	(X)	(X)	(X)	(X)
1st	Allen	59.74	Summers, Jr.	40.26
2d	Michaud	58.03	Hamel	39.47
MD.....	(X)	(X)	(X)	(X)
1st	Alexakis	24.11	Gilchrest	75.89
2d	Ruppersberger	66.68	Brooks	30.68
3d	Cardin	63.44	Duckworth	33.80
4th	Wynn	75.23	McKinnis	20.22
5th	Hoyer	68.72	Jewitt	29.25
6th	Bosley	29.49	Bartlett	67.45
7th	Cummings	73.43	Salazar	24.63
8th	Van Hollen	74.91	Floyd	25.07
MA.....	(X)	(X)	(X)	(X)
1st	Olver	77.73	[1]	[1]
2d	Neal	75.62	[1]	[1]
3d	McGovern	67.15	Crews	28.04
4th	Frank	73.14	[1]	[1]
5th	Meehan	64.09	Tierney	31.48
6th	Tierney	66.35	O'Malley, Jr.	28.47
7th	Markey	69.27	Chase	20.65
8th	Capuano	76.85	[1]	[1]
9th	Lynch	73.25	[1]	[1]
10th	Delahunt	63.30	Jones	32.75
MI.....	(X)	(X)	(X)	(X)
1st	Stupak	65.57	Hooper	32.76
2d	Kotos	28.93	Hoekstra	69.34
3d	Hickey	31.48	Ehlers	66.58
4th	Huckleberry	34.77	Camp	64.36
5th	Kildee	67.17	Kirkwood	31.28
6th	Elliott	32.43	Upton	65.34
7th	Renier	36.31	Schwarz	58.36
8th	Alexander	36.87	Rogers	61.03
9th	Reifman	39.54	Knollenberg	58.45
10th	Casey	29.54	Miller	68.62
11th	Truran	41.04	McCotter	56.97
12th	Levin	69.32	Shafer	29.02
13th	Kilpatrick	78.16	Cassell	18.47
14th	Conyers	83.93	Pedraza	33.42
15th	Dingell	70.92	Reamer	26.57
MN.....	(X)	(X)	(X)	(X)
1st	Pomeroy	35.51	Gutknecht	59.60
2d	Daley	40.31	Kline	56.38
3d	Watts	35.29	Ramstad	64.61
4th	McCollum	57.48	Bataglia	33.24
5th	Sabo	69.67	Mathias	24.43
6th	Wetterling	45.94	Kennedy	53.99
7th	Peterson	66.07	Sturrock	33.84
8th	Oberstar	65.22	Groettum	32.15
MS.....	(X)	(X)	(X)	(X)
1st	[1]	[1]	Wicker	79.01
2d	Thompson	58.38	LeSueur	40.64
3d	[1]	[1]	Pickering	80.06
4th	Taylor	64.19	Lott	34.50
MO.....	(X)	(X)	(X)	(X)
1st	Clay	75.29	Farr, II	22.83
2d	Weber	32.97	Akin	65.37
3d	Carnahan	52.86	Federer	45.13
4th	Skelton	66.20	Noland	32.38
5th	Cleaver, II	55.19	Patterson	42.12
6th	Broomfield	34.75	Graves	63.83
7th	Newberry	28.29	Blunt	70.45
8th	Henderson	26.62	Emerson	72.21
9th	Jacobsen	33.84	Hulshof	64.60
MT.....	Velazquez	32.78	Rehberg	64.40
NE.....	(X)	(X)	(X)	(X)
1st	Connealy	43.00	Fortenberry	54.23
2d	Thompson	36.15	Terry	61.10
3d	Anderson	10.57	Osborne	87.45
NV.....	(X)	(X)	(X)	(X)
1st	Berkley	65.98	Mickelson	31.12
2d	Cochran	27.48	Gibbons	67.15
3d	Gallagher	40.40	Porter	54.46
NH.....	(X)	(X)	(X)	(X)
1st	Nadeau	36.56	Bradley	63.34
2d	Hodes	38.17	Bass	58.25
NJ.....	(X)	(X)	(X)	(X)
1st	Andrews	75.00	Hutchison	24.65
2d	Robb	32.70	LoBiondo	65.09
3d	Conaway	34.65	Saxton	63.44
4th	Vasquez	32.28	Smith	67.00
5th	Wolfe	41.11	Garrett	57.57
6th	Pallone, Jr.	66.90	Fernandez	30.82
7th	Brozak	41.66	Ferguson	56.88
8th	Pascrell, Jr.	69.46	Ajjan	28.68
9th	Rothman	67.53	Trawinski	31.71
10th	Payne	96.88		
11th	Buell	31.02	Frelinghuysen	67.88
12th	Holt	59.25	Spadea	39.69
13th	Menendez	75.85	Piatkowski	22.12

See footnotes at end of table.

U.S. Census Bureau, Statistical Abstract of the United States: 2007

Table 392. Vote Cast for United States Representatives by Major Political Party—Congressional Districts: 2004—Con.

[See headnote, p. 246]

State and district	Democratic candidate — Name	Percent of total	Republican candidate — Name	Percent of total
NM	(X)	(X)	(X)	(X)
1st...	Romero	45.53	Wilson	54.40
2d ...	King	39.80	Pearce	60.20
3d ...	Udall	68.68	Tucker	31.32
NY	(X)	(X)	(X)	(X)
1st...	Bishop	44.87	Manger	35.29
2d ...	Israel	51.93	Hoffmann	25.73
3d ...	Mathies	31.87	King	47.87
4th...	McCarthy	52.23	Garner	30.05
5th...	Ackerman	55.26	Graves	20.82
6th...	Meeks	67.65	(1)	(1)
7th...	Crowley	56.57	Cinquemain	12.31
8th...	Nadler	61.24	Hort	13.98
9th...	Weiner	53.60	Cronin	19.57
10th..	Towns	66.72	Clarke	5.68
11th..	Owens	66.41	(1)	(1)
12th..	Velazquez	61.47	Rodriguez	9.61
13th..	Barbaro	33.13	Fossella	47.14
14th..	Maloney	64.18	Srdanovic	15.30
15th..	Rangel	70.03	Jefferson, Jr.	5.65
16th..	Serrano	72.06	Mohamed	3.32
17th..	Engel	58.78	Brennan	17.60
18th..	Lowey	54.81	Hoffman	25.49
19th..	Jaliman	28.50	Kelly	49.57
20th..	Kelly	29.81	Sweeney	50.39
21st..	McNulty	53.63	Redlich	25.69
22d ..	Hinchey	51.70	Brenner	28.49
23d ..	Johnson	25.07	McHugh	51.40
24th..	Miller	29.70	Boehlert	44.82
25th..	(1)	(1)	Walsh	49.12
26th..	Davis	36.28	Reynolds	42.80
27th..	Higgins	42.46	Naples	41.80
28th..	Slaughter	57.37	Laba	18.68
29th..	Barend	34.16	Kuhl, Jr.	44.72
NC	(X)	(X)	(X)	(X)
1st...	Butterfield	63.98	Dority	36.02
2d ...	Etheridge	62.30	Creech	37.70
3d ...	Eaton	29.30	Jones	70.70
4th...	Price	64.10	Batchelor	35.88
5th...	Harrell, Jr.	41.17	Foxx	58.83
6th...	Jordan	26.85	Coble	73.15
7th...	McIntyre	73.19	Plonk	26.81
8th...	Troutman	44.46	Hayes	55.54
9th...	Flynn	29.76	Myrick	70.24
10th..	Fischer	35.85	McHenry	64.15
11th..	Keever	45.10	Taylor	54.90
12th..	Watt	66.83	Fisher	33.17
13th..	Miller	58.79	Johnson	41.21
ND	Pomeroy	59.56	Sand	40.44
OH	(X)	(X)	(X)	(X)
1st...	Harris	40.10	Chabot	59.83
2d ...	Sanders	28.29	Portman	71.70
3d ...	Mitakides	37.71	Turner	62.29
4th...	Konop	41.40	Oxley	58.60
5th...	Weirauch	32.95	Gillmor	67.05
6th...	Strickland	99.94	(1)	(1)
7th...	Anastasio	35.04	Hobson	64.96
8th...	Hardenbrook	30.99	Boehner	69.01
9th...	Kaptur	68.13	Kaczala	31.87
10th..	Kucinich	60.03	Herman	33.59
11th..	Jones	100.00	(1)	(1)
12th..	Brown	38.03	Tiberi	61.96
13th..	Brown	67.43	Lucas	67.65
14th..	Cafaro	40.16	LaTourette	51.82
15th..	Brown	34.51	Pryce	73.01
16th..	Seemann	33.45	Regula	66.55
17th..	Ryan	77.19	Cusimano	22.81
18th..	Thomas	33.84	Ney	66.16
OK	(X)	(X)	(X)	(X)
1st...	Dodd	37.54	Sullivan	60.19
2d ...	Boren	65.89	Smalley	34.11
3d ...	(1)	(1)	Lucas	82.21
4th...	(1)	(1)	Cole	77.77
5th...	Smith	33.94	Istook, Jr.	66.06
OR	(X)	(X)	(X)	(X)
1st...	Wu	57.51	Ameri	38.15
2d ...	McColgan	25.63	Walden	71.63
3d ...	Blumenauer	70.86	Mars	23.67
4th...	DeFazio	60.98	Feldkamp	37.58
5th...	Hooley	52.86	Zupancic	44.33
PA	(X)	(X)	(X)	(X)
1st...	Brady	86.27	Williams	13.38
2d ...	Fattah	88.04	Bolno	11.96
3d ...	Porter	39.92	English	60.08
4th...	Drobac, Jr.	35.91	Hart	63.08
5th...	(1)	(1)	Peterson	88.02
6th...	Murphy	48.99	Gerlach	51.01
7th...	Scoles	40.34	Weldon	58.76
8th...	Schrader	43.30	Fitzpatrick	55.31
9th...	Politis	30.47	Shuster	69.53
10th..	(1)	(1)	Sherwood	92.84
11th..	Kanjorski	94.42	(1)	(1)
12th..	Murtha	100.00	(1)	(1)
13th..	Schwartz	55.74	Brown	41.28
14th..	Doyle	100.00	(1)	(1)
15th..	Driscoll	39.38	Dent	58.61
16th..	Herr	34.49	Pitts	64.36
17th..	Holden	59.09	Paterno	38.93
18th..	Boles	37.24	Murphy	62.76
19th..	(1)	(1)	Platts	91.51
RI	(X)	(X)	(X)	(X)
1st...	Kennedy	64.06	Rogers	35.80
2d ...	Langevin	74.53	Barton, III	20.82
SC	(1)	(1)	Brown, Jr.	87.82
2d ...	Ellisor	33.32	Wilson	64.98
3d ...	(1)	(1)	Barrett	99.51
4th...	Brown	28.96	Inglis	69.77
5th...	Spratt, Jr.	63.03	Spencer	36.93
6th...	Clyburn	66.98	McLeod	31.20
SD	Daschle	53.36	Diedrich	45.91
TN	(X)	(X)	(X)	(X)
1st...	Leonard	24.13	Jenkins	73.88
2d ...	Greene	19.11	Duncan, Jr.	79.07
3d ...	Wolfe	32.85	Wamp	64.74
4th...	Davis	54.80	Bowling	43.54
5th...	Cooper	69.26	Knapp	30.73
6th...	Gordon	64.24	Demas	33.58
7th...	(1)	(1)	Blackburn	100.00
8th...	Tanner	74.34	Hart	25.63
9th...	Ford, Jr.	82.04	Fort	17.89

See footnotes at end of table.

U.S. Census Bureau, Statistical Abstract of the United States: 2007

Table 392. Vote Cast for United States Representatives by Major Political Party—Congressional Districts: 2004—Con.

[See headnote, p. 246]

State and district	Democratic candidate Name	Percent of total	Republican candidate Name	Percent of total	State and district	Democratic candidate Name	Percent of total	Republican candidate Name	Percent of total
TX	(X).	(X)	(X).	(X)	VA	(X).	(X)	(X).	(X)
1st..	Sandlin..	37.68	Gohmert..	61.47	1st...	(¹).	(¹)	Davis..	78.55
2d...	Lampson...	42.91	Poe..	55.53	2d...	Ashe..	44.82	Drake..	55.08
3d...	(¹)..	(¹)	Johnson..	85.62	3d...	Scott..	69.33	Sears..	30.53
4th..	Nickerson...	30.45	Hall..	68.25	4th...	Menefee..	35.48	Forbes..	64.46
5th..	Bernstein...	32.88	Hensarling..	64.47	5th...	Weed, III.	36.28	Goode, Jr.	63.68
6th..	Meyer..	32.71	Barton..	66.02	6th...	(¹).	(¹)	Goodlatte...	96.68
7th..	Martinez..	33.30	Culberson...	64.11	7th...	(¹).	(¹)	Cantor...	75.50
8th..	Wright..	29.67	Brady..	68.91	8th...	Moran..	59.73	Cheney..	36.90
9th..	Green..	72.19	Molina..	26.57	9th...	Boucher..	59.32	Triplett...	38.94
10th..	(¹)..	(¹)	McCaul..	78.62	10th..	Socas..	36.11	Wolf..	63.77
11th..	Raasch..	21.79	Conaway..	76.76	11th..	Longmyer...	38.26	Davis..	60.25
12th..	Alvarado...	27.68	Granger..	72.32	WA	(X).	(X)	(X).	(X)
13th..	(¹).	(¹)	Thornberry..	92.31	1st...	Inslee..	62.28	Eastwood..	35.96
14th..	(¹).	(¹)	Paul..	100.00	2d...	Larsen..	63.91	Sinclair..	33.58
15th..	Hinojosa..	57.76	Thamm..	40.83	3d...	Baird..	61.93	Crowson..	38.07
16th..	Reyes..	67.53	Brigham...	31.08	4th...	Matheson..	37.43	Hastings...	62.57
17th..	Edwards..	51.20	Wohlgemuth..	47.42	5th...	Barbieri..	40.32	McMorris..	59.68
18th..	Jackson-Lee..	88.91	(¹).	(¹)	6th...	Dicks..	68.99	Cloud..	31.01
19th..	Stenholm..	40.05	Neugebauer...	58.44	7th...	McDermott..	80.68	Cassady..	19.32
20th..	Gonzalez...	65.47	Scott..	32.00	8th...	Ross..	46.70	Reichert..	51.50
21st..	Smith..	35.51	Smith..	61.50	9th...	Smith..	63.28	Lord..	34.40
22d..	Morrison..	41.10	DeLay..	55.16	WV	(X).	(X)	(X).	(X)
23d..	Sullivan..	29.40	Bonilla..	69.26	1st...	Mollohan..	67.78	Parks..	32.22
24th..	Page..	34.22	Marchant...	63.98	2d...	Wells..	41.29	Capito..	57.46
25th..	Doggett..	67.60	Klein..	30.74	3d...	Rahall, II.	65.20	Snuffer..	34.80
26th..	Reyes..	32.71	Burgess..	65.75	WI	(X).	(X)	(X).	(X)
27th..	Ortiz..	63.13	Vaden..	34.90	1st...	Thomas..	32.57	Ryan..	65.37
28th..	Cuellar..	59.01	Hopson..	38.60	2d...	Baldwin..	63.27	Magnum...	36.66
29th..	Green..	94.14	(¹).	(¹)	3d...	Kind..	56.43	Schultz..	43.49
30th..	Johnson..	93.03	(¹).	(¹)	4th...	Moore..	69.60	Boyle..	28.16
31st..	Porter..	32.45	Carter..	64.77	5th...	Kennedy..	31.77	Sensenbrenner, Jr.	66.57
32d..	Frost..	44.02	Sessions...	54.32	6th...	Hall..	30.12	Petri..	67.03
UT	(X).	(X)	(X).	(X)	7th...	Obey..	85.64	(¹).	(¹)
1st..	Thompson..	29.13	Bishop..	67.91	8th...	Le Clair..	29.83	Green..	70.13
2d..	Matheson...	54.76	Swallow..	43.21	WY	Ladd..	41.81	Cubin..	55.24
3d..	Babka..	32.52	Cannon..	63.39					
VT⁴...	Drown..	7.11	Parke..	24.35					

X Not applicable. ¹ No candidate. ² According to state law, it is not required to tabulate votes for unopposed candidates. ³ Louisiana holds an open-primary election with candidates from all parties running on the same ballot. Any candidate who receives a majority is elected; if no candidate receives 50 percent, there is a run-off election in November between the top two finishers. ⁴ Sanders, an Independent, was elected with 67.5 percent of the vote in 2004.

Source: U.S. House of Representatives, Office of the Clerk, *Statistics of the Presidential and Congressional Election*, biennial. See also <http://clerk.house.gov/members/electionInfo/elections.html>.

Table 393. Composition of Congress by Political Party: 1975 to 2006

[D = Democratic, R = Republican. As of beginning of first session of each Congress, except as noted. Data reflect immediate result of elections. Vacancies are noted]

Year	Party and President	Congress	House Majority party	Minority party	Other	Senate Majority party	Minority party	Other
1975 [1]	R (Ford)	94th	D-291	R-144	–	D-61	R-37	2
1977 [2]	D (Carter)	95th	D-292	R-143	–	D-61	R-38	1
1979 [2]	D (Carter)	96th	D-277	R-158	–	D-58	R-41	1
1981 [2]	R (Reagan)	97th	D-242	R-192	1	R-53	D-46	1
1983	R (Reagan)	98th	D-269	R-166	–	R-54	D-46	–
1985	R (Reagan)	99th	D-253	R-182	–	R-53	D-47	–
1987	R (Reagan)	100th	D-258	R-177	–	D-55	R-45	–
1989	R (Bush)	101st	D-260	R-175	–	D-55	R-45	–
1991 [3]	R (Bush)	102d	D-267	R-167	1	D-56	R-44	–
1993 [3]	D (Clinton)	103d	D-258	R-176	1	D-57	R-43	–
1995 [4]	D (Clinton)	104th	R-230	D-204	1	R-52	D-48	–
1997 [3]	D (Clinton)	105th	R-226	D-207	2	R-55	D-45	–
1999 [4]	D (Clinton)	106th	R-223	D-211	1	R-55	D-45	–
2001 [5,6]	R (Bush)	107th	R-221	D-212	2	R-50	D-50	–
2003 [5,7]	R (Bush)	108th	R-229	D-204	1	R-51	D-48	1
2006 [5,7,8]	R (Bush)	109th	R-231	D-201	1	R-55	D-44	1

– Represents zero. ¹ Senate had one Independent, and one Conservative-Republican. ² Senate had one Independent. ³ House had one Independent-Socialist. ⁴ House had one Independent-Socialist and one Independent. ⁵ House and Senate each had one Independent. ⁶ House had one vacancy. ⁷ As of beginning of second session. ⁸ House had two vacancies.

Source: U.S. House of Representatives, Office of the Clerk, *Official List of Members*, annual. See also <http://clerk.house.gov/members/olm_109.pdf>.

Table 394. Composition of Congress by Political Party Affiliation—States: 1999 to 2006

[Figures are for the beginning of the first session (as of January 3), except as noted. Dem. = Democratic; Rep. = Republican]

State	Representatives								Senators							
	106th Cong.,[1] 1999		107th Cong.,[1,2,3] 2001		108th Cong.,[1] 2003		109th Cong.,[1,2,4,5] 2006		106th Cong., 1999		107th Cong.,[6] 2001		108th Cong.,[6] 2003		109th Cong.,[4,6] 2006	
	Dem.	Rep.	Dem.	Rep.	Dem.	Rep.	Dem.	Rep.	Dem.	Rep.	Dem.	Rep.	Dem.	Rep.	Dem.	Rep.
U.S. . . .	**212**	**222**	**211**	**221**	**205**	**229**	**201**	**231**	**45**	**55**	**50**	**50**	**48**	**51**	**44**	**55**
AL.	2	5	2	5	2	5	2	5	–	2	–	2	–	2	–	2
AK.	–	1	–	1	–	1	–	1	–	2	–	2	–	2	–	2
AZ.	1	5	1	5	2	6	2	6	–	2	–	2	–	2	–	2
AR.	2	2	3	1	3	1	3	1	1	1	1	1	2	–	2	–
CA.	28	24	31	20	33	20	33	19	2	–	2	–	2	–	2	–
CO	2	4	2	4	2	5	3	4	–	2	–	2	–	2	1	1
CT.	4	2	3	3	2	3	2	3	2	–	2	–	2	–	2	–
DE.	–	1	–	1	–	1	–	1	1	1	2	–	2	–	2	–
FL.	8	15	8	15	7	18	7	18	1	1	2	–	2	–	1	1
GA	3	8	3	8	5	8	6	7	1	1	2	–	1	1	–	2
HI	2	–	2	–	2	–	2	–	2	–	2	–	2	–	2	–
ID	–	2	–	2	–	2	–	2	–	2	–	2	–	2	–	2
IL	10	10	10	10	9	10	10	9	1	1	1	1	1	1	2	–
IN	4	6	4	6	3	6	2	7	1	1	1	1	1	1	1	1
IA	1	4	1	4	1	4	1	4	1	1	1	1	1	1	1	1
KS.	1	3	1	3	1	3	1	3	–	2	–	2	–	2	–	2
KY.	1	5	1	5	1	5	1	5	–	2	–	2	–	2	–	2
LA.	2	5	2	5	3	4	2	5	2	–	2	–	2	–	1	1
ME	2	–	2	–	2	–	2	–	–	2	–	2	–	2	–	2
MD	4	4	4	4	6	2	6	2	2	–	2	–	2	–	2	–
MA	10	–	10	–	10	–	10	–	2	–	2	–	2	–	2	–
MI.	10	6	9	7	6	9	6	9	1	1	2	–	2	–	2	–
MN	6	2	5	3	4	4	4	4	1	1	2	–	1	1	1	1
MS	3	2	3	2	2	2	2	2	–	2	–	2	–	2	–	2
MO	5	4	4	5	4	5	4	5	–	2	1	1	–	2	–	2
MT	–	1	–	1	–	1	–	1	1	1	1	1	1	1	1	1
NE.	–	3	–	3	–	3	–	3	1	1	1	1	1	1	1	1
NV.	1	1	1	1	1	2	1	2	2	–	1	1	1	1	1	1
NH	–	2	–	2	–	2	–	2	–	2	–	2	–	2	–	2
NJ.	7	6	7	6	7	6	6	6	2	–	2	–	2	–	2	–
NM	1	2	1	2	1	2	1	2	1	1	1	1	1	1	1	1
NY.	19	12	19	12	19	10	20	9	2	–	2	–	2	–	2	–
NC	5	7	5	7	6	7	6	7	1	1	1	1	1	1	–	2
ND	1	–	1	–	1	–	1	–	2	–	2	–	2	–	2	–
OH	8	11	8	11	6	12	6	12	–	2	–	2	–	2	–	2
OK	–	6	1	5	1	4	1	4	–	2	–	2	–	2	–	2
OR	4	1	4	1	4	1	4	1	1	1	1	1	1	1	1	1
PA.	11	10	10	11	7	12	7	12	–	2	–	2	–	2	–	2
RI.	2	–	2	–	2	–	2	–	1	1	1	1	1	1	1	1
SC.	2	4	2	4	2	4	2	4	1	1	1	1	1	1	–	2
SD.	–	1	–	1	–	1	1	–	2	–	2	–	2	–	1	1
TN.	4	5	4	5	5	4	5	4	–	2	–	2	–	2	–	2
TX.	17	13	17	13	17	15	11	21	–	2	–	2	–	2	–	2
UT.	–	3	1	2	1	2	1	2	–	2	–	2	–	2	–	2
VT.	–	–	–	–	–	–	–	–	1	1	1	1	1	–	1	–
VA.	6	5	4	6	3	8	3	8	1	1	–	2	–	2	–	2
WA	5	4	6	3	6	3	6	3	1	1	2	–	2	–	2	–
WV	3	–	2	1	2	1	2	1	2	–	2	–	2	–	2	–
WI	5	4	5	4	4	4	4	4	2	–	2	–	2	–	2	–
WY	–	1	–	1	–	1	–	1	–	2	–	2	–	2	–	2

– Represents zero.   [1] Vermont had one Independent Socialist Representative.   [2] California had one vacancy.   [3] Virginia had one Independent Representative.   [4] As of beginning of second session February 15, 2006.   [5] Vacancy due to the resignation of Robert Mendez (NJ) January 17, 2006.   [6] Vermont had one Independent Senator. (Jeffords was reelected in Vermont in 2000 as a Republican, but subsequently switched to Independent status in June 2001.)

Source: U.S. Congress, Joint Committee on Printing, *Congressional Directory*, biennial through 2001; Starting in 2003, Office of the Clerk, *Official List of Members by State*, annual. See also <http://clerk.house.gov/members/olm_109.pdf>.

Table 395. Members of Congress—Selected Characteristics: 1991 to 2005

[As of beginning of first session of each Congress, (January 3). Figures for Representatives exclude vacancies]

Members of Congress and year	Male	Female	Black[1]	API[2]	Hispanic[3]	Age[4] (in years) Under 40	40 to 49	50 to 59	60 to 69	70 and over	Seniority[5,6] Less than 2 yrs.	2 to 9 yrs.	10 to 19 yrs.	20 to 29 yrs.	30 yrs. or more
REPRESENTATIVES															
102d Cong., 1991[8] ...	407	28	[7]26	5	11	39	152	134	86	24	55	178	147	44	11
103d Cong., 1993[8] ...	388	47	[7]38	7	17	47	151	128	89	15	118	141	132	32	12
104th Cong., 1995. ...	388	47	[9]40	7	17	53	155	135	79	13	92	188	110	36	9
106th Cong., 1999. ...	379	56	[9]39	6	19	23	116	173	87	35	41	236	104	46	7
107th Cong., 2001. ...	376	59	[9]39	7	19	14	97	167	117	35	44	155	158	63	14
108th Cong., 2003. ...	376	59	[9]39	5	22	19	86	174	121	32	54	178	140	48	13
109th Cong., 2005. ...	369	65	[9]42	4	23	22	96	175	113	28	37	173	158	48	18
SENATORS															
102d Cong., 1991[8] ...	98	2	–	2	–	–	23	46	24	7	5	34	47	10	4
103d Cong., 1993[8] ...	93	7	1	2	–	1	16	48	22	12	15	30	39	11	5
104th Cong., 1995. ...	92	8	1	2	–	1	14	41	27	17	12	38	30	15	5
106th Cong., 1999. ...	91	9	–	2	–	1	14	38	35	13	8	39	33	14	6
107th Cong., 2001. ...	87	13	–	2	–	–	8	39	33	18	11	34	30	14	9
108th Cong., 2003. ...	86	14	–	2	–	1	12	29	34	24	9	42	29	13	7
109th Cong., 2005. ...	86	14	1	2	2	–	17	29	33	21	9	41	29	14	7

– Represents zero. [1] Source: Joint Center for Political and Economic Studies, Washington, DC, Black Elected Officials: Statistical Summary, annual (copyright). [2] Asian and Pacific Islanders. Source: Prior to 2005, Library of Congress, Congressional Research Service, "Asian Pacific Americans in the United States Congress," Report 94-767 GOV; starting 2005, U.S. House of Representatives, "House Press Gallery," <http://www.house.gov/daily/hpg.htm> (as of January 17, 2006) and U.S. Senate, "Minorities in the Senate," <http://www.senate.gov/artandhistory/history/common/briefing/minority_senators.htm>. [3] Source: National Association of Latino Elected and Appointed Officials, Washington, DC, National Roster of Hispanic Elected Officials, annual. [4] Some members do not provide date of birth. [5] Represents consecutive years of service. [6] Some members do not provide years of service. [7] Includes District of Columbia delegate but not Virgin Islands Delegate. [8] Includes members elected to fill vacant seats through June 14, 1993. [9] Includes District of Columbia and Virgin Islands delegate.

Source: Except as noted, compiled by U.S. Census Bureau from data published in Congressional Directory, biennial.

Table 396. U.S. Congress—Measures Introduced and Enacted and Time in Session: 1989 to 2005

[Excludes simple and concurrent resolutions]

Item	101st Cong., 1989–90	102d Cong., 1991–92	103d Cong., 1993–94	104th Cong., 1995–96	105th Cong., 1997–98	106th Cong., 1999–00	107th Cong., 2001–02	108th Cong., 2003–04	109th Cong., 2005
Measures introduced	6,664	6,775	8,544	6,808	7,732	9,158	9,130	8,625	6,924
Bills	5,977	6,212	7,883	6,545	7,532	8,968	8,953	8,468	6,822
Joint resolutions	687	563	661	263	200	190	177	157	102
Measures enacted	666	609	473	337	404	604	337	504	147
Public.............	650	589	465	333	394	580	331	498	147
Private	16	20	8	4	10	24	6	6	–
HOUSE OF REPRESENTATIVES									
Number of days	281	280	265	290	251	272	265	243	140
Number of hours	1,688	1,796	1,887	2,445	2,001	2,179	1,694	1,894	1,067
Number of hours per day...	6.0	6.4	7.1	8.4	8.0	8.0	6.4	7.8	7.6
SENATE									
Number of days	274	287	291	343	296	303	322	300	159
Number of hours	2,254	2,292	2,514	2,876	2,188	2,200	2,279	2,486	1,222
Number of hours per day...	8.2	8.0	8.6	8.4	7.4	7.3	7.1	8.3	7.7

Source: U.S. Congress, Congressional Record and Daily Calendar, selected issues. See also <http://www.senate.gov/pagelayout/reference/two_column_table/Resumes.htm>.

Table 397. Congressional Bills Vetoed: 1961 to 2006

Period	President	Total vetoes	Regular vetoes	Pocket vetoes	Vetoes sustained	Bills passed over veto
1961–63	John F. Kennedy	21	12	9	21	–
1963–69	Lyndon B. Johnson	30	16	14	30	–
1969–74	Richard M. Nixon	43	26	17	36	7
1974–77	Gerald R. Ford	66	48	18	54	12
1977–81	Jimmy Carter	31	13	18	29	2
1981–89	Ronald W. Reagan ...	78	39	39	69	9
1989–93	George Bush	44	29	15	43	1
1993–2001	William J. Clinton	38	37	1	36	2
2001–2006[1]	George W. Bush	–	–	–	–	2

– Represents zero. [1] Through April 10, 2006.

Source: U.S. Congress, Senate Library, Presidential Vetoes ... 1789–1968; U.S. Congress, Calendars of the U.S. House of Representatives and History of Legislation, annual. See also <http://clerk.house.gov/>.

Elections 251

Table 398. Number of Governors by Political Party Affiliation: 1975 to 2006

[Reflects figures after inaugurations for each year]

Year	Demo-cratic	Repub-lican	Indepen-dent/other	Year	Demo-cratic	Repub-lican	Indepen-dent/other	Year	Demo-cratic	Repub-lican	Indepen-dent/other
1975	36	13	1	1995	19	30	1	2001	19	29	2
1980	31	19	–	1996 [2] . . .	18	31	1	2002	22	27	1
1985	34	16	–	1997	17	32	1	2003	23	27	–
1990	29	21	–	1998	17	32	1	2004	22	28	–
1993 [1] . . .	30	18	2	1999	17	31	1	2005	22	28	–
1994	29	19	2	2000	18	30	2	2006	22	28	–

– Represents zero. [1] Alaska's Republican governor was succeeded midyear by a Democrat. [2] Arkansas's Democratic governor was succeeded midyear by a Republican.

Source: National Governors Association, Washington, DC, 1970–87 and 1991–2006, *Directory of Governors of the American States, Commonwealths & Territories,* annual; and 1988–90, *Directory of Governors,* annual (copyright).

Table 399. Vote Cast for and Governor Elected by State: 2002 to 2004

[In thousands (1,367 represents 1,367,000), except percent. D = Democratic, R = Republican, I = Independent]

State	2002				2004				Current governor [2]
	Total vote [1]	Repub-lican	Demo-crat	Percent leading party	Total vote [1]	Repub-lican	Demo-crat	Percent leading party	
AL. . . .	1,367	672	669	R-49.2	(X)	(X)	(X)	(X)	Bob Riley
AK. . . .	231	129	94	R-55.8	(X)	(X)	(X)	(X)	Frank H. Murkowski
AZ. . . .	1,226	554	566	D-46.2	(X)	(X)	(X)	(X)	Janet Napolitano
AR. . . .	806	427	378	R-53.0	(X)	(X)	(X)	(X)	Mike Huckabee
CA. . . .	7,476	3,170	3,533	D-47.3	(X)	(X)	(X)	(X)	[3]Arnold Schwarzenegger
CO . . .	1,413	885	475	R-62.6	(X)	(X)	(X)	(X)	Bill Owens
CT. . . .	1,023	574	449	R-56.0	(X)	(X)	(X)	(X)	M. Jodi Rell
DE. . . .	(X)	(X)	(X)	(X)	365	167	186	D-50.9	Ruth Ann Minner
FL. . . .	5,101	2,857	2,201	R-56.0	(X)	(X)	(X)	(X)	Jeb Bush
GA . . .	2,026	1,042	937	R-51.4	(X)	(X)	(X)	(X)	Sonny Perdue
HI	385	197	180	R-51.1	(X)	(X)	(X)	(X)	Linda Lingle
ID	411	232	172	R-56.3	(X)	(X)	(X)	(X)	Dirk Kempthorne
IL	3,539	1,595	1,847	D-52.2	(X)	(X)	(X)	(X)	Rod R. Blagojevich
IN	(X)	(X)	(X)	(X)	2,448	1,303	1,114	R-53.2	Mitch Daniels
IA	1,026	457	540	D-52.7	(X)	(X)	(X)	(X)	Thomas Vilsack
KS. . . .	836	377	442	D-52.9	(X)	(X)	(X)	(X)	Kathleen Sebelius
KY [4] . .	(X)	(X)	(X)	(X)	1,083	596	487	R-55.0	Ernie Fletcher
LA [4] . .	(X)	(X)	(X)	(X)	1,416	369	872	D-52.0	Kathleen Blanco
ME . . .	505	209	238	D-47.1	(X)	(X)	(X)	(X)	John Baldacci
MD . . .	1,706	880	813	R-51.6	(X)	(X)	(X)	(X)	Robert L. Erlich Jr.
MA . . .	2,194	1,092	986	R-49.8	(X)	(X)	(X)	(X)	Mitt Romney
MI	3,178	1,506	1,634	D-51.4	(X)	(X)	(X)	(X)	Jennifer M. Granholm
MN . . .	2,252	999	821	R-44.4	(X)	(X)	(X)	(X)	Tim Pawlenty
MS [4] .	(X)	(X)	(X)	(X)	894	470	410	R-52.6	Haley Barbour
MO . . .	(X)	(X)	(X)	(X)	2,720	1,382	1,301	R-50.8	Matt Blunt
MT . . .	(X)	(X)	(X)	(X)	456	205	225	D-50.4	Brian Schweitzer
NE. . . .	481	330	132	R-68.7	(X)	(X)	(X)	(X)	Dave Heineman
NV. . . .	504	344	111	R-68.2	(X)	(X)	(X)	(X)	Kenny Guinn
NH . . .	442	260	169	R-58.8	684	326	340	D-51.0	John Lynch
NJ [5] . .	2,227	928	1,257	D-56.4	2,290	985	1,225	D-53.5	Jon Corzine
NM . . .	484	189	269	D-55.5	(X)	(X)	(X)	(X)	Bill Richardson
NY. . . .	4,579	2,262	1,534	R-49.4	(X)	(X)	(X)	(X)	George E. Pataki
NC . . .	(X)	(X)	(X)	(X)	3,487	1,495	1,939	D-55.6	Michael F. Easley
ND . . .	(X)	(X)	(X)	(X)	310	221	85	R-71.3	John Hoeven
OH . . .	3,229	1,865	1,237	R-57.7	(X)	(X)	(X)	(X)	Bob Taft
OK . . .	1,036	441	448	D-43.3	(X)	(X)	(X)	(X)	Brad Henry
OR . . .	1,294	517	531	D-41.0	(X)	(X)	(X)	(X)	Theodore R. Kulongoski
PA. . . .	3,582	1,589	1,913	D-53.4	(X)	(X)	(X)	(X)	Edward G. Rendell
RI	332	182	150	R-54.8	(X)	(X)	(X)	(X)	Donald L. Carcieri
SC. . . .	1,108	585	521	R-52.8	(X)	(X)	(X)	(X)	Mark Sanford
SD. . . .	335	190	140	R-56.8	(X)	(X)	(X)	(X)	Mike Rounds
TN. . . .	1,653	787	837	D-50.6	(X)	(X)	(X)	(X)	Phil Bredesen
TX. . . .	4,554	2,633	1,820	R-57.8	(X)	(X)	(X)	(X)	Rick Perry
UT. . . .	(X)	(X)	(X)	(X)	907	525	374	R-57.8	Jon Huntsman Jr.
VT. . . .	227	103	98	R-45.5	309	182	117	R-58.7	James H. Douglas
VA [5] . .	1,887	887	984	D-52.2	1,984	912	1,026	D-52.0	Tim Kaine
WA . . .	(X)	(X)	(X)	(X)	2,883	1,373	1,373	D-48.8	Christine Gregoire
WV . . .	(X)	(X)	(X)	(X)	744	253	473	D-63.5	Joe Manchin III
WI	1,775	735	801	D-45.2	(X)	(X)	(X)	(X)	James E. Doyle
WY . . .	185	89	93	D-50.0	(X)	(X)	(X)	(X)	Dave Freudenthal

X Not applicable. [1] Includes minor party and scattered votes. [2] As of April 11, 2006. Source: National Governors Association, Washington, DC. See <http://www.nga.org/portal/site/nga/menuitem.5dbb9333fc52447ae8ebb856a11010a0/>. [3] Recall election in 2003; Arnold Schwarzenegger (Republican) was elected governor. [4] Voting year 2003. [5] Voting years 2001 and 2005.

Source: The Council of State Governments, Lexington, KY, *The Book of States 2005,* annual (copyright).

Table 400. Composition of State Legislatures by Political Party Affiliation: 2005 and 2006

[Data reflect election results as of February in year shown. Figures reflect immediate results of elections, including holdover members in state houses which do not have all of their members running for re-election. Dem. = Democrat, Rep. = Republican, Vac. = Vacancies. In general, Lower House refers to body consisting of state representatives; Upper House, of state senators]

State	Lower House 2005 Dem.	Rep.	Other	Vac.	Lower House 2006 Dem.	Rep.	Other	Vac.	Upper House 2005 Dem.	Rep.	Other	Vac.	Upper House 2006 Dem.	Rep.	Other	Vac.
U.S.	2,704	2,683	15	9	2,702	2,675	15	19	951	963	3	5	952	964	3	3
AL [1]	62	40	–	3	63	42	–	–	25	10	–	–	25	10	–	–
AK [3]	14	26	–	–	14	26	–	–	8	12	–	–	8	12	–	–
AZ [3]	22	38	–	–	21	39	–	–	12	18	–	–	12	18	–	–
AR [2]	72	28	–	–	72	28	–	–	27	8	–	–	27	8	–	–
CA [2]	48	32	–	–	48	32	–	–	25	15	–	–	25	15	–	–
CO [3]	35	30	–	–	35	30	–	–	18	17	–	–	18	17	–	–
CT [2]	99	52	–	–	99	52	–	–	24	12	–	–	24	12	–	–
DE [2]	15	25	1	–	15	25	1	–	13	8	–	–	13	8	–	–
FL [3]	36	84	–	–	36	84	–	–	14	26	–	–	14	26	–	–
GA [3]	80	99	1	–	80	99	1	–	22	34	–	–	22	34	–	–
HI [2]	41	10	–	–	41	10	–	–	20	5	–	–	20	5	–	–
ID [3]	13	57	–	–	13	57	–	–	7	28	–	–	7	28	–	–
IL [4]	65	53	–	–	65	53	–	–	31	27	1	–	31	27	1	–
IN [2]	48	52	–	–	48	52	–	–	17	33	–	–	17	33	–	–
IA [2]	49	51	–	–	49	51	–	–	25	25	–	–	25	25	–	–
KS [2]	42	83	–	–	42	83	–	–	10	30	–	–	10	30	–	–
KY [2]	57	43	–	–	57	43	–	–	15	22	1	–	15	22	1	–
LA [1]	67	37	1	–	67	37	1	–	24	15	–	–	24	15	–	–
ME [3]	76	73	2	–	76	73	2	–	19	16	–	–	19	16	–	–
MD [1]	98	43	–	–	98	43	–	–	33	14	–	–	33	14	–	–
MA [3]	136	21	–	3	137	20	–	3	34	6	–	–	34	6	–	–
MI [2]	52	58	–	–	50	58	–	2	16	22	–	–	16	22	–	–
MN [2]	66	68	–	–	66	68	–	–	35	31	1	–	35	31	1	–
MS [1]	75	47	–	–	74	47	–	1	28	24	–	–	28	24	–	–
MO [2]	66	97	1	–	64	96	–	3	10	22	–	2	11	22	–	1
MT [2]	49	50	1	–	50	50	–	–	27	23	–	–	27	23	–	–
NE [5]	(6)	(6)	(6)	(6)	(6)	(6)	(6)	(6)	(6)	(6)	(6)	(6)	(6)	(6)	(6)	(6)
NV [2]	26	16	–	–	26	15	–	1	9	12	–	–	9	12	–	–
NH [3]	147	250	–	3	149	247	–	4	8	16	–	–	8	16	–	–
NJ [2]	47	33	–	–	49	31	–	–	22	18	–	–	22	18	–	–
NM [2]	42	28	–	–	42	28	–	–	24	18	–	–	24	18	–	–
NY [3]	104	46	–	–	104	46	–	–	28	34	–	–	27	35	–	–
NC [3]	63	57	–	–	63	57	–	–	29	21	–	–	29	21	–	–
ND [1]	27	67	–	–	27	67	–	–	15	32	–	–	15	32	–	–
OH [2]	40	59	–	–	38	61	–	–	11	22	–	–	11	22	–	–
OK [2]	44	57	–	–	44	57	–	–	26	22	–	–	26	22	–	–
OR [2]	27	33	–	–	27	33	–	–	18	12	–	–	18	12	–	–
PA [2]	93	110	–	–	93	110	–	–	18	29	–	3	20	30	–	–
RI [3]	60	15	–	–	60	15	–	–	33	5	–	–	33	5	–	–
SC [2]	50	74	–	–	49	74	–	1	20	26	–	–	20	26	–	–
SD [3]	19	51	–	–	19	51	–	–	10	25	–	–	10	25	–	–
TN [2]	53	46	–	–	53	46	–	–	16	17	–	–	15	17	–	1
TX [2]	63	87	–	–	62	87	–	1	12	19	–	–	12	19	–	–
UT [2]	19	56	–	–	19	56	–	–	8	21	–	–	8	21	–	–
VT [3]	83	60	7	–	83	60	7	–	21	9	–	–	21	9	–	–
VA [2]	38	60	2	–	39	56	3	2	16	24	–	–	16	23	–	1
WA [2]	55	43	–	–	55	43	–	–	26	23	–	–	26	23	–	–
WV [2]	68	32	–	–	68	32	–	–	21	13	–	–	21	13	–	–
WI [2]	39	60	–	–	39	59	–	1	14	19	–	–	14	19	–	–
WY [2]	14	46	–	–	14	46	–	–	7	23	–	–	7	23	–	–

– Represents zero. [1] Members of both houses serve 4-year terms. [2] Upper House members serve 4-year terms and Lower House members serve 2-year terms. [3] Members of both houses serve 2-year terms. [4] Illinois—4- and 2-year term depending on district. [5] Nebraska—4-year term and only state to have a nonpartisan legislature.

Source: The Council of State Governments, Lexington, KY, The Book of States 2006, annual (copyright).

Table 401. Political Party Control of State Legislatures by Party: 1985 to 2006

[As of beginning of year. Nebraska has a nonpartisan legislature]

Year	Legislatures under— Democratic control	Split control or tie	Republican control	Year	Legislatures under— Democratic control	Split control or tie	Republican control	Year	Legislatures under— Democratic control	Split control or tie	Republican control
1985	27	11	11	1994	24	17	8	2001	16	15	18
1987	28	12	9	1995	18	12	19	2002	17	15	17
1989[1] ...	28	13	8	1996	16	15	18	2003	16	12	21
1990	29	11	9	1997	20	11	18	2004	17	11	21
1992	29	14	6	1999	20	12	17	2005	19	10	20
1993	25	16	8	2000	16	15	18	2006	19	10	20

[1] A party change during the year by a Democratic representative broke the tie in the Indiana House of Representatives, giving the Republicans control of both chambers.

Source: National Conference of State Legislatures, Denver, CO, *State Legislatures*, periodic.

Table 402. Women Holding State Public Offices by Office and State: 2005

[As of January. For data on women in U.S. Congress, see Table 395]

State	Total	State-wide elective executive office[1]	State legislature Number	Percent[2]	State	Total	State-wide elective executive office[1]	State legislature Number	Percent[2]
U.S. ...	1,755	81	1,674	23	MT......	38	1	37	25
AL......	20	5	15	11	NE......	14	2	12	(3)
AK......	11	–	11	18	NV......	23	2	21	33
AZ......	32	3	29	32	NH......	129	–	129	30
AR......	23	–	23	17	NJ......	20	–	20	17
CA......	37	–	37	31	NM......	38	3	35	31
CO......	35	2	33	33	NY......	48	1	47	22
CT......	59	4	55	29	NC......	43	4	39	23
DE......	23	2	21	34	ND......	25	–	25	16
FL......	40	1	39	24	OH......	28	2	26	20
GA......	46	3	43	18	OK......	27	5	22	15
HI......	24	1	23	30	OR......	26	1	25	28
ID......	30	1	29	28	PA......	35	1	34	13
IL......	51	2	49	28	RI......	19	–	19	17
IN......	29	3	26	17	SC......	15	1	14	8
IA......	32	2	30	20	SD......	17	–	17	16
KS......	57	3	54	33	TN......	24	–	24	18
KY......	18	1	17	12	TX......	39	3	36	20
LA......	26	1	25	17	UT......	21	–	21	20
ME......	43	–	43	23	VT......	61	1	60	33
MD......	67	–	67	36	VA......	22	1	21	15
MA......	51	1	50	25	WA......	51	2	49	33
MI......	32	2	30	20	WV.....	22	1	21	16
MN......	65	3	62	31	WI.....	37	3	34	26
MS......	23	1	22	13	WY.....	14	1	13	14
MO	45	3	42	21					

– Represents zero. [1] Excludes women elected to the judiciary, women appointed to state cabinet–level positions, women elected to executive posts by the legislature, and elected members of university Board of Trustees or Board of Education. [2] Calculated by U.S. Census Bureau based on total state legislature (both upper and lower houses) data from Table 400. [3] Nebraska—4-year term and only state to have a nonpartisan legislature.

Source: Center for the American Woman and Politics, Eagleton Institute of Politics, Rutgers University, New Brunswick, NJ, information releases, (copyright).

Table 403. Black Elected Officials by Office, 1970 to 2001, and State, 2001

[As of January 2001, no Black elected officials had been identified in Hawaii, Montana, North Dakota, or South Dakota]

State	Total	U.S. and state legisla-tures[1]	City and county offices[2]	Law enforce-ment[3]	Educa-tion[4]	State	Total	U.S. and state legisla-tures[1]	City and county offices[2]	Law enforce-ment[3]	Educa-tion[4]
1970 (Feb.)	1,469	179	715	213	362	MD	175	40	93	33	9
1980 (July)	4,890	326	2,832	526	1,206	MA	60	6	44	2	8
1990 (Jan.)	7,335	436	4,485	769	1,645	MI	346	25	147	55	119
1995 (Jan.)	8,385	604	4,954	987	1,840	MN	20	2	4	9	5
1998 (Jan.)	8,830	614	5,210	998	2,008	MS	892	46	607	109	130
1999 (Jan.)	8,896	618	5,354	997	1,927	MO	201	19	142	16	24
2000 (Jan.)	9,001	621	5,420	1,037	1,923	NE	8	1	4	–	3
2001 (Jan.)	**9,061**	**633**	**5,456**	**1,044**	**1,928**	NV	14	5	5	2	2
						NH	5	5	–	–	–
AL	756	36	569	57	94	NJ	249	16	139	1	93
AK	3	1	2	–	–	NM	4	1	–	2	1
AZ	12	1	1	5	5	NY	325	34	83	83	125
AR	502	15	298	67	122	NC	491	28	349	29	85
CA	224	10	70	67	77	OH	313	20	217	28	48
CO	18	4	4	9	1	OK	105	6	75	3	21
CT	72	14	47	3	8	OR	6	3	1	2	–
DE	24	4	16	1	3	PA	185	19	74	65	27
DC	176	5[5]	171	–	3	RI	8	7	1	–	–
FL	243	25	163	39	16	SC	534	32	335	9	158
GA	611	53	395	43	120	TN	180	18	108	27	27
ID	2	–	2	–	–	TX	460	19	302	44	95
IL	624	28	318	55	223	UT	5	1	3	1	–
IN	86	13	52	13	8	VT	1	1	–	–	–
IA	13	1	8	1	3	VA	246	16	130	15	85
KS	17	7	4	3	3	WA	26	2	12	11	1
KY	60	5	44	5	6	WV	19	2	13	3	1
LA	705	32	388	122	163	WI	33	8	15	5	5
ME	1	1	–	–	–	WY	1	1	–	1	–

– Represents zero. [1] Includes elected state administrators. [2] County commissioners and councilmen, mayors, vice mayors, aldermen, regional officials, and other. [3] Judges, magistrates, constables, marshals, sheriffs, justices of the peace, and other. [4] Members of state education agencies, college boards, school boards, and other. [5] Includes one shadow senator.

Source: Joint Center for Political and Economic Studies, Washington, DC, *Black Elected Officials: A Statistical Summary*, annual (copyright) and <http://www.jointcenter.org/publications1/PublicationsDetail.php?recordID=118> (accessed 17 April 2003).

Table 404. Hispanic Public Elected Officials by Office, 1985 to 2005, and State, 2005

[As of January of year shown. For states not shown, no Hispanic public officials had been identified]

State	Total	State execu-tives and legisla-tors[1]	County and munici-pal officials	Judicial and law enforce-ment	Educa-tion and school boards	State	Total	State execu-tives and legisla-tors[1]	County and munici-pal officials	Judicial and law enforce-ment	Educa-tion and school boards
1985	3,147	129	1,316	517	1,185	MA	20	4	12	–	4
1990	4,004	144	1,819	583	1,458	MI	18	2	7	3	6
1993	5,170	182	2,023	633	2,332	MN	4	1	1	1	1
1994	5,459	199	2,197	651	2,412	MO	1	–	1	–	–
2000	5,019	217	1,852	447	2,503	MT	1	–	–	1	–
2001	5,205	223	1,846	454	2,682	NE	3	1	1	1	–
2002	4,303	227	1,960	532	1,603	NV	12	3	5	3	1
2003	4,432	231	1,958	549	1,694	NH	3	2	1	–	–
2004	4,651	253	2,059	638	1,723	NJ	107	6	61	–	40
						NM	633	49	323	108	153
2005	**4,853**	**266**	**2,149**	**678**	**1,760**	NY	68	18	29	16	5
AK	1	–	1	–	–	NC	4	3	1	–	–
AZ	362	18	141	44	159	ND	1	–	1	–	–
CA	1,021	37	394	43	547	OH	7	–	6	1	–
CO	144	9	97	7	31	OK	1	–	–	–	1
CT	32	6	20	–	6	OR	17	3	9	5	–
DE	2	1	1	–	–	PA	16	1	10	2	3
DC	2	–	–	–	2	RI	7	4	3	–	–
FL	119	21	66	26	6	SC	1	1	–	–	–
GA	7	3	2	2	–	TN	2	1	1	–	–
HI	1	1	–	–	–	TX	2,082	43	867	401	771
ID	2	1	1	–	–	UT	5	2	3	–	–
IL	81	12	54	6	9	VA	1	–	1	–	–
IN	13	1	8	3	1	WA	15	3	6	–	6
KS	11	4	6	–	1	WI	13	1	4	4	4
LA	2	–	–	2	–	WY	3	1	2	–	–
MD	9	4	3	–	2						

– Represents zero. [1] Includes U.S. Senators and Representatives, not shown separately.

Source: National Association of Latino Elected and Appointed Officials, Washington, DC, *National Roster of Hispanic Elected Officials*, annual.

Elections 255

Table 405. **Voting-Age Population, Percent Reporting Registered, and Voted: 1992 to 2004**

[185.7 represents 185,700,000. As of November. Covers civilian noninstitutional population 18 years old and over. Includes aliens. Figures are based on Current Population Survey (see text, Section 1, Population, and Appendix III) and differ from those in Table 407 based on population estimates and official vote counts]

Characteristic	Voting-age population (mil.)							Percent reporting they registered							Percent reporting they voted						
								Presidential election years				Congressional election years			Presidential election years				Congressional election years		
	1992	1994	1996	1998	2000	2002	2004	1992	1996	2000	2004	1994	1998	2002	1992	1996	2000	2004	1994	1998	2002
Total [1]	185.7	190.3	193.7	198.2	202.6	210.4	215.7	68.2	65.9	63.9	65.9	62.0	62.1	60.9	61.3	54.2	54.7	58.3	44.6	41.9	42.3
18 to 20 years old	9.7	10.3	10.8	11.4	11.9	11.7	11.5	48.3	45.6	40.5	50.7	37.2	32.1	32.6	38.5	31.2	28.4	41.0	16.5	13.5	15.1
21 to 24 years old	14.6	14.9	13.9	14.1	14.9	15.6	16.4	55.3	51.2	49.3	52.1	45.5	35.0	42.5	45.7	33.4	35.4	46.9	22.3	19.2	18.7
25 to 34 years old	41.6	41.0	40.1	38.6	37.3	38.5	39.0	60.6	56.9	54.7	55.6	51.5	52.4	50.2	53.2	43.1	43.7	46.9	32.2	28.0	27.1
35 to 44 years old	39.7	41.9	43.3	44.4	44.5	43.7	43.1	69.2	66.5	63.8	64.0	63.3	62.4	60.0	63.6	54.9	55.0	56.9	46.0	40.7	40.2
45 to 64 years old	49.1	50.9	53.7	57.4	61.4	66.9	71.0	75.3	73.5	71.2	72.7	71.0	71.1	69.4	70.0	64.4	64.1	66.6	56.0	53.6	53.1
65 years old and over	30.8	31.1	31.9	32.3	32.8	33.9	34.7	78.0	77.0	76.1	76.9	75.6	75.4	75.8	70.1	67.0	67.6	68.9	60.7	59.5	61.0
Male	88.6	91.0	92.6	95.2	97.1	100.9	103.8	66.9	64.4	62.2	64.0	60.8	60.6	58.9	60.2	52.8	53.1	56.3	44.4	41.4	41.4
Female	97.1	99.3	101.0	103.0	105.5	109.5	111.9	69.3	67.3	65.6	67.6	63.2	63.5	62.8	62.3	55.5	56.2	60.1	44.9	42.4	43.0
White [2]	157.8	160.3	162.8	165.8	168.7	174.1	176.6	70.1	67.7	65.6	67.9	64.2	63.9	63.1	63.6	56.0	56.4	60.3	46.9	43.3	44.1
Black [2]	21.0	21.8	22.5	23.3	24.1	24.4	24.9	63.9	63.5	65.6	64.4	58.3	60.2	58.8	54.0	50.6	53.5	60.3	37.0	39.6	39.7
Asian [2,3]	(NA)	(NA)	(NA)	(NA)	8.0	9.6	9.3	(NA)	(NA)	30.7	34.9	(NA)	(NA)	30.7	(NA)	(NA)	25.4	29.8	(NA)	(NA)	19.4
Hispanic [4]	14.7	17.5	18.4	20.3	21.6	25.2	27.1	35.0	35.7	34.9	34.3	30.0	33.7	32.6	28.9	26.7	27.5	28.0	19.1	20.0	18.9
Region: [5]																					
Northeast	38.3	38.4	38.3	38.5	38.9	41.1	41.0	67.0	64.7	63.7	65.3	60.9	60.8	60.8	61.2	54.5	55.2	58.6	45.2	41.2	41.4
Midwest	44.4	44.5	45.2	45.9	46.4	48.8	48.4	74.6	71.6	70.2	72.8	68.7	68.2	66.5	67.2	59.3	60.9	65.0	48.8	47.3	47.1
South	63.7	66.4	68.1	70.1	71.8	74.2	77.2	67.2	65.9	64.5	65.5	60.7	62.7	61.6	59.0	52.2	53.5	56.4	40.5	38.6	41.6
West	39.3	41.0	42.1	43.7	45.5	46.3	49.1	63.6	60.8	56.9	60.1	58.1	56.0	54.0	58.5	51.8	49.9	54.4	46.4	42.3	39.0
School years completed:																					
8 years or less	15.4	14.7	14.1	13.3	12.9	12.3	12.6	43.9	40.7	36.1	32.5	40.1	40.2	32.4	35.1	28.1	26.8	23.6	23.2	24.6	19.4
High school:																					
Less than high school graduate	21.0	20.7	21.0	21.0	20.1	20.9	20.7	50.4	47.9	45.9	45.8	44.7	43.4	41.6	41.2	33.8	33.6	34.6	27.0	25.0	23.3
High school graduate or GED [6]	65.3	64.9	65.2	65.6	66.3	68.9	68.5	64.9	62.2	60.1	61.5	58.9	58.6	57.1	57.5	49.1	49.4	52.4	40.5	37.1	37.1
College:																					
Some college or associate's degree	46.7	50.4	50.9	52.9	55.3	57.3	58.9	75.4	72.9	70.0	73.7	68.4	68.3	66.7	68.7	60.5	60.3	66.1	49.1	46.2	45.8
Bachelor's or advanced degree	37.4	39.4	42.5	45.4	48.0	51.0	54.9	84.8	80.4	77.3	78.1	76.3	75.1	74.4	81.0	73.0	72.0	74.2	63.1	57.2	58.5
Employed	116.3	122.6	125.6	130.5	133.4	134.9	138.8	69.9	67.0	64.7	67.1	62.9	62.6	61.7	63.8	55.2	55.5	60.0	45.2	41.2	42.1
Unemployed	8.3	6.5	6.4	5.2	4.9	7.7	7.3	53.7	52.5	46.1	56.3	46.4	48.5	48.1	46.2	37.2	35.1	46.4	28.3	28.4	27.2
Not in labor force	61.1	61.2	61.6	62.5	64.2	67.8	69.6	66.8	65.1	63.8	64.3	64.6	62.1	60.9	58.7	54.1	54.5	56.2	45.3	44.5	44.2

NA Not available. [1] Includes other races not shown separately. [2] Beginning with the 2003 Current Population Survey (CPS), respondents could choose more than one race. 2004 data represent persons who selected this race group only and exclude persons reporting more than one race. The CPS in prior years only allowed respondents to report one race group. See also comments in the text for section 1. [3] Prior to 2004, this category was "Asian and Pacific Islanders," therefore rates are not comparable with prior years. [4] Hispanic persons may be any race. [5] For composition of regions, see map, inside cover. [6] The General Educational Development (GED) Test measures how well a non-high school graduate has mastered the skills and general knowledge that are acquired in a four-year high school education. Successfully passing the exam is a credential generally considered to be the equivalent of a high school diploma.

Source: U.S. Census Bureau, *Current Population Reports*, P20-552, and earlier reports; and "Voting and Registration in the Election of November 2004"; published 25 May 2005; <http://www.census.gov/population/www/socdemo/voting.html>.

Table 406. Persons Reported Registered and Voted by State: 2004

[215,694 represents 215,694,000. See headnote, Table 405]

State	Voting-age population (1,000)	Percent of voting-age population — Registered	Voted	State	Voting-age population (1,000)	Percent of voting-age population — Registered	Voted
U.S..	215,694	65.9	58.3	MO	4,243	78.6	66.3
AL	3,332	72.6	61.8	MT	690	75.2	69.9
AK	451	74.1	65.0	NE	1,294	70.9	61.3
AZ	4,122	60.3	54.3	NV	1,699	56.8	51.3
AR	2,010	66.1	56.7	NH	982	72.9	68.9
CA	26,085	54.4	49.1	NJ	6,413	63.7	57.6
CO	3,398	67.9	61.7	NM	1,375	68.1	60.9
CT	2,606	65.0	58.5	NY	14,492	59.5	53.1
DE	612	67.8	62.9	NC	6,250	68.7	58.2
DC	435	67.4	62.1	ND	466	88.4	70.8
FL	13,133	62.6	56.1	OH	8,469	70.9	64.8
GA	6,338	62.3	52.6	OK	2,602	68.4	59.2
HI	938	53.0	46.2	OR	2,727	75.1	70.6
ID	996	66.6	58.7	PA	9,356	69.3	62.5
IL	9,303	69.2	61.0	RI	813	64.2	57.4
IN	4,536	66.8	57.3	SC	3,061	73.1	62.0
IA	2,212	75.7	68.8	SD	564	75.4	67.0
KS	1,990	67.2	59.7	TN	4,402	62.2	52.7
KY	3,042	73.3	63.4	TX	15,813	61.2	50.3
LA	3,277	73.6	63.1	UT	1,629	70.0	62.7
ME	1,022	80.6	72.0	VT	482	73.4	65.6
MD	4,043	66.2	59.7	VA	5,364	64.1	58.4
MA	4,840	72.0	63.7	WA	4,596	68.2	62.0
MI	7,452	72.0	64.7	WV	1,395	67.0	57.2
MN	3,766	81.8	76.7	WI	4,126	78.2	73.0
MS	2,081	72.6	60.7	WY	373	71.0	66.2

Source: U.S. Census Bureau, *Current Population Reports*, P20-552 and earlier reports; and "Voting and Registration in the Election of November 2004"; published 25 May 2005; <http://www.census.gov/population/www/socdemo/voting.html>.

Table 407. Participation in Elections for President and U.S. Representatives: 1932 to 2004

[75,768 represents 75,768,000. As of November, except as noted. Estimated resident population 21 years old and over, 1932–70, except as noted, and 18 years old and over thereafter; includes Armed Forces. Prior to 1958, excludes Alaska and prior to 1960, excludes Hawaii. District of Columbia is included in votes cast for President beginning 1964]

Year	Resident population (incl. aliens) of voting age [1] (1,000)	Votes cast — For President [2] (1,000)	Per-cent of voting-age population	For U.S. Representatives (1,000) [2]	Per-cent of voting-age population	Year	Resident population (incl. aliens) of voting age [1] (1,000)	Votes cast — For President [2] (1,000)	Per-cent of voting-age population	For U.S. Representatives (1,000) [2]	Per-cent of voting-age population
1932 . . .	75,768	39,817	52.6	(NA)	(NA)	1970 . . .	124,498	(X)	(X)	54,259	43.6
1934 . . .	77,997	(X)	(X)	32,804	42.1	1972 . . .	140,777	77,625	55.1	71,188	50.6
1936 . . .	80,174	45,647	56.9	(NA)	(NA)	1974 . . .	146,338	(X)	(X)	52,313	35.7
1938 . . .	82,354	(X)	(X)	(NA)	(NA)	1976 . . .	152,308	81,603	53.6	74,259	48.8
1940 . . .	84,728	49,815	58.8	(NA)	(NA)	1978 . . .	158,369	(X)	(X)	54,584	34.5
1942 . . .	86,465	(X)	(X)	28,074	32.5	1980 . . .	163,945	86,497	52.8	77,874	47.5
1944 . . .	85,654	48,026	56.1	45,110	52.7	1982 . . .	169,643	(X)	(X)	63,881	37.7
1946 . . .	92,659	(X)	(X)	34,410	37.1	1984 . . .	173,995	92,655	53.3	82,422	47.4
1948 . . .	95,573	48,834	51.1	46,220	48.4	1986 . . .	177,922	(X)	(X)	59,758	33.6
1950 . . .	98,134	(X)	(X)	40,430	41.2	1988 . . .	181,956	91,587	50.3	81,682	44.9
1952 . . .	99,929	61,552	61.6	57,571	57.6	1990 . . .	185,812	(X)	(X)	62,355	33.6
1954 . . .	102,075	(X)	(X)	42,583	41.7	1992 . . .	189,493	104,600	55.2	97,198	51.3
1956 . . .	104,515	62,027	59.3	58,886	56.3	1994 . . .	193,010	(X)	(X)	70,494	36.5
1958 . . .	106,447	(X)	(X)	45,719	43.0	1996 . . .	196,789	96,390	49.0	90,233	45.9
1960 . . .	109,672	68,836	62.8	64,124	58.5	1998 . . .	201,270	(X)	(X)	66,605	33.1
1962 . . .	112,952	(X)	(X)	51,242	45.4	2000 . . .	[2]209,831	105,594	50.3	98,800	47.1
1964 . . .	114,090	70,098	61.4	65,879	57.7	2002 . . .	[2]215,077	(X)	(X)	74,707	34.7
1966 . . .	116,638	(X)	(X)	52,902	45.4	2004 . . .	[2]220,377	122,349	55.5	113,192	51.4
1968 . . .	120,285	73,027	60.7	66,109	55.0						

NA Not available.   X Not applicable.   [1] Population 18 and over in Georgia, 1944–70, and in Kentucky, 1956–70; 20 and over in Alaska and 20 and over in Hawaii, 1960–70. Source: Through 1992, U.S. Census Bureau, *Current Population Reports*, P25-1059 and earlier reports; also see <http://www.census.gov/population/www/socdemo/voting/past-voting.html#p25> (released July 31, 2000). For 1992–1998, "Projections of the Voting-Age Population for States: November 2000"; published 31 July 2000; also see <http://www.census.gov/population/socdemo/voting/proj00/tab03.txt>. Starting 2000, "Annual Estimates of the Population by Selected Age Groups and Sex for the United States: April 1, 2000, to July 1, 2004," (NC-EST2004-02); also see <http://www.census.gov/popest/states/asrh/>.   [2] As of July 1.

Source: U.S. House of Representatives, Office of the Clerk, *Statistics of the Presidential and Congressional Election*, biennial. See also <http://clerk.house.gov/members/electionInfo/elections.html>.

Table 408. Resident Population of Voting Age and Percent Casting Votes— States: 2000 to 2004

[209,831 represents 209,831,000. Estimated population, 18 years old and over. Includes Armed Forces stationed in each state, aliens, and institutional population]

State	Voting-age population (1,000) [1]			Percent casting votes for—				
				Presidential electors		U.S. Representatives		
	2000	2002	2004	2000	2004	2000	2002	2004
U.S.	**209,831**	**215,077**	**220,377**	**50.3**	**55.5**	**47.1**	**34.7**	**51.4**
AL.	3,330	3,370	3,436	50.0	54.8	43.2	37.7	52.2
AK.	437	451	467	65.3	66.9	62.8	50.5	64.2
AZ.	3,788	3,959	4,197	40.4	48.0	38.7	30.2	44.6
AR.	1,998	2,025	2,076	46.1	50.8	31.7	34.0	38.1
CA.	24,728	25,611	26,297	44.3	47.2	42.2	28.3	44.2
CO	3,219	3,351	3,423	54.1	62.2	50.4	41.7	59.6
CT.	2,570	2,620	2,665	56.8	59.2	51.1	37.8	53.6
DE.	592	611	637	55.3	58.9	52.9	37.4	55.9
DC	456	455	444	44.2	51.3	(NA)	(NA)	(NA)
FL.	12,383	12,824	13,394	48.2	56.8	40.5	29.4	42.0
GA	6,050	6,273	6,497	42.7	50.8	39.9	30.6	45.6
HI	917	939	964	40.1	44.5	37.1	38.3	43.2
ID	930	970	1,021	53.9	58.6	53.0	41.7	56.1
IL	9,192	9,353	9,475	51.6	55.7	47.8	36.7	52.6
IN	4,515	4,560	4,637	48.7	53.2	47.8	33.4	52.1
IA	2,198	2,232	2,274	61.5	66.3	58.0	45.4	64.1
KS.	1,981	2,013	2,052	54.1	57.9	52.3	41.2	56.4
KY.	3,055	3,100	3,166	50.5	56.7	47.0	35.3	51.7
LA.	3,253	3,291	3,351	54.3	58.0	37.0	34.6	37.6
ME	978	1,007	1,035	66.7	71.6	65.3	49.2	68.6
MD	3,953	4,069	4,163	51.2	57.3	48.7	40.8	54.1
MA	4,864	4,929	4,952	56.2	59.1	56.2	45.0	59.1
MI	7,362	7,482	7,579	57.5	63.8	55.3	40.8	61.1
MN	3,650	3,763	3,861	66.8	73.3	64.8	58.5	70.5
MS	2,076	2,107	2,153	47.9	52.9	47.5	32.2	51.8
MO	4,182	4,271	4,370	56.4	62.5	55.6	43.4	61.0
MT	675	692	719	60.9	62.7	60.8	47.9	61.8
NE.	1,264	1,284	1,313	55.1	59.3	54.0	36.9	58.3
NV.	1,500	1,602	1,731	40.6	47.9	39.1	31.3	45.7
NH	931	968	995	61.1	68.2	59.7	45.8	65.5
NJ.	6,342	6,458	6,543	50.3	55.2	47.1	31.1	50.2
NM	1,315	1,352	1,411	45.5	53.6	44.7	32.4	52.7
NY.	14,314	14,572	14,655	48.6	50.8	48.5	32.3	50.8
NC	6,104	6,254	6,423	47.8	54.5	45.5	35.9	53.1
ND	482	484	495	59.8	63.1	59.3	47.7	62.7
OH	8,480	8,580	8,680	55.4	64.8	54.1	36.8	59.7
OK	2,565	2,608	2,664	48.1	55.0	42.4	38.4	51.6
OR	2,583	2,670	2,742	59.4	67.0	55.7	46.4	64.6
PA.	9,371	9,472	9,569	52.4	60.3	48.6	34.9	53.8
RI	803	824	837	50.9	52.2	47.8	39.9	48.1
SC.	3,014	3,087	3,173	45.9	51.0	43.8	31.9	45.3
SD.	554	563	580	57.1	66.9	56.8	59.8	67.1
TN.	4,305	4,398	4,510	48.2	54.0	43.1	34.8	49.2
TX.	15,040	15,576	16,223	42.6	45.7	39.8	27.6	42.9
UT.	1,522	1,581	1,649	50.6	56.3	49.9	35.2	55.1
VT.	464	476	487	63.5	64.2	61.1	47.3	62.7
VA.	5,361	5,491	5,655	51.1	56.5	45.2	27.6	53.1
WA	4,398	4,561	4,718	56.6	60.6	54.2	38.1	57.9
WV	1,407	1,411	1,431	46.1	52.8	41.2	28.3	50.4
WI	4,010	4,099	4,201	64.8	71.3	62.5	39.9	67.2
WY	366	376	390	58.3	62.6	58.0	48.4	61.4

NA Not available.   [1] As of July 1. Source: U.S. Census Bureau, "Annual Estimates of the Population by Selected Age Groups and Sex for the United States: April 1, 2000, to July 1, 2004," (NC-EST2004-02); see also <http://www.census.gov/popest/states/asrh/>.

Source: U.S. House of Representatives, Office of the Clerk, *Statistics of the Presidential and Congressional Election,* biennial. See also <http://clerk.house.gov/members/electionInfo/elections.html>.

Table 409. Political Action Committees—Number by Committee Type: 1980 to 2005

[As of December 31]

Committee type	1980	1990	1995	2000	2001	2002	2003	2004	2005
Total...................	2,551	4,172	4,016	3,706	3,907	4,027	4,023	4,867	4,343
Corporate................	1,206	1,795	1,674	1,523	1,545	1,528	1,552	1,756	1,638
Labor...................	297	346	334	316	317	320	308	328	296
Trade/membership/health.........	576	774	815	812	860	975	877	986	912
Nonconnected...............	374	1,062	1,020	902	1,026	1,055	1,147	1,650	1,357
Cooperative................	42	59	44	39	41	39	36	38	37
Corporation without stock........	56	136	129	114	118	110	103	109	103

Source: U.S. Federal Election Commission, press release, January 2006.

Table 410. Political Action Committees—Financial Activity Summary by Committee Type: 2001 to 2006

[In millions of dollars (685.3 represents $685,300,000). Covers financial activity during 2-year calendar period indicated]

Committee type	Receipts			Disbursements [1]			Contributions to candidates		
	2001–02	2003–04	2005–06	2001–02	2003–04	2005–06	2001–02	2003–04	2005–06
Total	685.3	915.7	477.4	656.5	842.9	394.1	282.0	310.5	141.1
Corporate............	191.7	239.0	131.2	178.3	221.6	116.3	99.6	115.6	56.5
Labor...............	167.8	191.7	100.3	158.0	182.9	73.1	53.9	52.1	21.1
Trade/membership/health...	166.7	181.8	95.4	165.7	170.1	74.6	46.3	83.2	38.0
Nonconnected..........	145.8	289.4	141.6	141.3	255.2	122.6	75.1	52.5	22.0
Cooperative	3.7	4.2	2.7	3.6	3.9	1.9	2.7	2.9	1.4
Corporation without stock...	9.7	9.6	6.1	9.6	9.2	5.7	4.4	4.2	2.1

[1] Comprises contributions to candidates, independent expenditures, and other disbursements.

Source: U.S. Federal Election Commission, *FEC Reports on Financial Activity, Final Report, Party and Non-party Political Committees*, biennial.

Table 411. Presidential Campaign Finances—Federal Funds for General Election: 1992 to 2004

[In millions of dollars (110.4 represents $110,400,000). Based on FEC certifications, audit reports, and Dept. of Treasury reports]

1992		1996		2000		2004	
Candidate	Amount	Candidate	Amount	Candidate	Amount	Candidate	Amount
Total	110.4	Total......	152.6	Total......	147.7	Total......	150.1
Bush........	55.2	Clinton	61.8	Bush........	67.6	Bush........	74.6
Clinton.......	55.2	Dole........	61.8	Gore........	67.6	Kerry........	74.6
Perot........	–	Perot	29.0	Buchanan	12.6	Nader.......	0.9

– Represents zero.

Source: U.S. Federal Election Commission, periodic press releases.

Table 412. Presidential Campaign Finances—Primary Campaign Receipts and Disbursements: 1995 to 2004

[In millions of dollars (243.9 represents $243,900,000). Covers campaign finance activity during 2-year calendar period indicated. Covers candidates who received federal matching funds or who had significant financial activity]

Item	Total [1]			Democratic			Republican		
	1995–96	1999–00	2003–04	1995–96	1999–00	2003–04	1995–96	1999–00	2003–04
Receipts, total [2]......	243.9	351.6	673.9	46.2	96.6	401.8	187.0	236.7	269.6
Individual contributions....	126.4	238.2	611.4	31.3	66.7	351.0	93.1	159.1	258.9
Federal matching funds ...	56.0	61.6	28.0	14.0	29.3	27.2	41.6	26.5	
Disbursements	234.1	343.5	661.1	41.8	92.2	389.7	182.1	233.2	268.9

– Represents zero. [1] Includes other parties, not shown separately. [2] Includes other types of receipts, not shown separately.

Source: U.S. Federal Election Commission, *FEC Reports on Financial Activity, Final Report, Presidential Pre-Nomination Campaigns*, quadrennial.

Elections 259

Table 413. Congressional Campaign Finances—Receipts and Disbursements: 1999 to 2004

[610.4 represents $610,400,000. Covers all campaign finance activity during 2-year calendar period indicated for primary, general, run-off, and special elections. Data have been adjusted to eliminate transfers between all committees within a campaign. For further information on legal limits of contributions, see Federal Election campaign act of 1971, as amended]

Item	House of Representatives						Senate					
	Amount (mil. dol.)			Percent distribution			Amount (mil. dol.)			Percent distribution		
	1999–00	2001–02	2003–04	1999–00	2001–02	2003–04	1999–00	2001–02	2003–04	1999–00	2001–02	2003–04
Total receipts [1]	610.4	643.3	708.5	100	100	100	437.0	326.1	497.6	100	100	100
Individual contributions......	315.6	322.5	396.7	52	50	56	252.1	214.3	324.1	58	66	65
Other committees	193.4	214.1	225.4	32	33	32	52.0	60.2	63.7	12	18	13
Candidate loans	61.9	72.0	47.4	10	11	7	89.0	28.1	39.8	20	9	8
Candidate contributions	6.3	9.2	7.8	1	1	1	18.7	0.8	38.2	4	(Z)	8
Democrats..............	286.7	314.2	307.4	47	49	43	230.4	162.9	250.6	53	50	50
Republicans.............	317.7	326.3	399.2	52	51	56	203.8	162.7	246.1	47	50	49
Others	6.0	2.8	1.9	1	(Z)	(Z)	2.8	0.6	0.9	1	(Z)	(Z)
Incumbents	361.8	369.8	452.6	59	57	64	130.6	145.0	171.7	30	44	35
Challengers [2]	127.4	107.0	118.2	21	17	17	99.6	109.7	79.5	23	34	16
Open seats [2]	121.1	166.5	137.8	20	26	19	206.7	71.4	246.4	47	22	50
Total disbursements ...	572.3	613.9	660.3	100	100	100	434.7	322.4	496.4	100	100	100
Democrats..............	266.8	301.1	288.5	47	49	44	226.3	162.9	254.6	52	51	51
Republicans.............	299.7	310.0	370.0	52	50	56	205.7	158.9	241.0	47	49	49
Others	5.7	2.9	1.8	1	(Z)	(Z)	2.7	0.6	0.8	1	(Z)	(Z)
Incumbents	327.0	343.9	410.1	57	56	62	130.2	145.6	171.7	30	45	35
Challengers [2]	125.6	103.9	116.6	22	17	18	99.3	108.4	76.6	23	34	15
Open seats [2]	119.7	166.1	133.6	21	27	20	205.1	68.5	248.1	47	21	50

Z Less than $50,000 or 0.5 percent.   [1] Includes other types of receipts, not shown separately.   [2] Elections in which an incumbent did not seek re-election.

Source: U.S. Federal Election Commission, *FEC Reports on Financial Activity, Final Report, U.S. Senate and House Campaigns*, biennial.

Table 414. Contributions to Congressional Campaigns by Political Action Committees (PAC) by Type of Committee: 1995 to 2004

[In millions of dollars (155.8 represents $155,800,000). Covers amounts given to candidates in primary, general, run-off, and special elections during the 2-year calendar period indicated. For number of political action committees, see Table 409]

Type of committee	Total [1]	Democrats	Republicans	Incumbents	Challengers	Open seats [2]
HOUSE OF REPRESENTATIVES						
1995–96	155.8	77.3	77.7	113.9	21.4	20.5
1997–98	158.7	77.6	80.9	124.0	14.9	19.8
1999–00	193.4	98.2	94.7	150.5	19.9	23.0
2001–02	206.9	102.6	104.2	161.0	13.8	32.1
2003–04, total [3]	225.4	98.6	126.6	187.3	15.6	22.5
Corporate	79.1	24.8	54.3	72.6	1.9	4.6
Trade association [4]	63.2	23.0	40.1	55.5	2.3	5.4
Labor.................	42.8	37.3	5.4	33.0	5.2	4.6
Nonconnected [5]	35.2	11.4	23.8	21.6	6.0	7.6
SENATE						
1995–96	45.6	16.6	29.0	19.4	6.9	19.3
1997–98	48.1	20.7	27.3	34.3	6.6	7.2
1999–00	51.9	18.7	33.2	33.5	7.1	11.3
2001–02	59.2	25.4	33.8	37.0	14.2	8.1
2003–04, total [3]	63.7	28.4	35.3	39.3	5.6	18.8
Corporate	25.2	8.9	16.3	17.2	1.2	6.7
Trade association [4]	15.0	5.7	9.3	9.9	1.1	4.0
Labor.................	7.6	6.8	0.8	4.3	0.9	2.3
Nonconnected [5]	14.6	6.3	8.3	6.9	2.2	5.4

[1] Includes other parties, not shown separately.   [2] Elections in which an incumbent did not seek re-election.   [3] Includes other types of political action committees not shown separately.   [4] Includes membership organizations and health organizations.   [5] Represents "ideological" groups as well as other issue groups not necessarily ideological in nature.

Source: U.S. Federal Election Commission, *FEC Reports on Financial Activity, Party and Non-Party Political Committees, Final Report*, biennial.

Section 8
State and Local Government Finances and Employment

This section presents data on revenues, expenditures, debt, and employment of state and local governments. Nationwide statistics relating to state and local governments, their numbers, finances, and employment are compiled primarily by the U.S. Census Bureau through a program of censuses and surveys. Every fifth year (for years ending in "2" and "7"), the Census Bureau conducts a census of governments involving collection of data for all governmental units in the United States. In addition, the Census Bureau conducts annual surveys which cover all the state governments and a sample of local governments.

Annually, the Census Bureau releases information on the Internet which presents financial data for the federal government, nationwide totals for state and local governments, and state-local data by states. Also released annually is a series on state, city, county, and school finances and on state and local public employment. There is also a series of quarterly data releases covering tax revenue and finances of major public employee retirement systems.

Basic information for Census Bureau statistics on governments is obtained by mail canvass from state and local officials; however, financial data for each of the state governments and for many of the large local governments are compiled from their official records and reports by Census Bureau personnel. In over two-thirds of the states, all or part of local government financial data are obtained through central collection arrangements with state governments. Financial data on the federal government are primarily based on the *Budget* published by the Office of Management and Budget (see text, Section 9, Federal Government Finances and Employment).

Governmental units—The governmental structure of the United States includes, in addition to the federal government and the states, thousands of local governments—counties, municipalities, townships, school districts, and many "special districts." In 2002, 87,576 local governments were identified by the census of governments (see Tables 415–417). As defined by the census, governmental units include all agencies or bodies having an organized existence, governmental character, and substantial autonomy. While most of these governments can impose taxes, many of the special districts—such as independent public housing authorities and numerous local irrigation, power, and other types of districts—are financed from rentals, charges for services, benefit assessments, grants from other governments, and other nontax sources. The count of governments excludes semi-autonomous agencies through which states, cities, and counties sometimes provide for certain functions—for example, "dependent" school systems, state institutions of higher education, and certain other "authorities" and special agencies which are under the administrative or fiscal control of an established governmental unit.

Finances—The financial statistics relate to government fiscal years ending June 30 or at some date within the 12 previous months. The following governments are exceptions and are included as though they were part of the June 30 group; ending September 30, the state governments of Alabama and Michigan, the District of Columbia, and Alabama school districts; and ending August 31, the state governments of Nebraska, Texas, and Chicago school districts. New York State ends its fiscal year on March 31. The federal government ended the fiscal year June 30 until 1976 when its fiscal year, by an act of Congress, was revised to extend from Oct. 1 to Sept. 30. A 3-month quarter (July 1 to Sept. 30, 1976) bridged the transition.

Nationwide government finance statistics have been classified and presented in

U.S. Census Bureau, Statistical Abstract of the United States: 2007

terms of uniform concepts and categories, rather than according to the highly diverse terminology, organization, and fund structure utilized by individual governments.

Statistics on governmental finances distinguish among general government, utilities, liquor stores, and insurance trusts. *General government* comprises all activities except utilities, liquor stores, and insurance trusts. Utilities include government water supply, electric light and power, gas supply, and transit systems. Liquor stores are operated by 17 states and by local governments in 6 states. Insurance trusts relate to employee retirement, unemployment compensation, and other social insurance systems administered by the federal, state, and local governments.

Data for cities or counties relate only to municipal or county and their dependent agencies and do not include amounts for other local governments in the same geographic location. Therefore, expenditure figures for "education" do not include spending by the separate school districts which administer public schools within most municipal or county areas. Variations in the assignment of governmental responsibility for public assistance, health, hospitals, public housing, and other functions to a lesser degree also

have an important effect upon reported amounts of city or county expenditure, revenue, and debt.

Employment and payrolls—These data are based mainly on mail canvassing of state and local governments. Payroll includes all salaries, wages, and individual fee payments for the month specified, and employment relates to all persons on governmental payrolls during a pay period of the month covered—including paid officials, temporary help, and (unless otherwise specified) part-time as well as full-time personnel. Effective with the 1997 Census of Governments, the reference period for measuring government employment was changed from October of the calendar year to March of the calendar year. As a result, there was no annual survey of government employment covering the October 1996 period. The prior reference month of October was used from 1958 to 1995. Figures shown for individual governments cover major dependent agencies such as institutions of higher education, as well as the basic central departments and agencies of the government.

Statistical reliability—For a discussion of statistical collection and estimation, sampling procedures, and measures of statistical reliability applicable to Census Bureau data, see Appendix III.

Figure 8.1
Federal Aid to State and Local Governments: 1990 to 2006

Billions of dollars

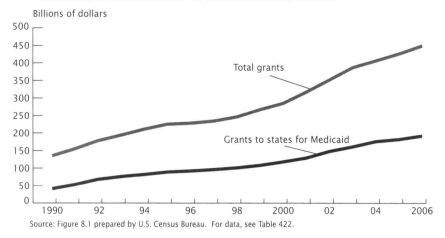

Total grants

Grants to states for Medicaid

Source: Figure 8.1 prepared by U.S. Census Bureau. For data, see Table 422.

Figure 8.2
Government Employees: 1990 to 2004

Millions

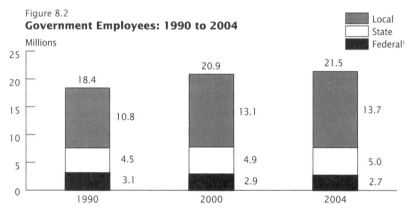

Legend: Local, State, Federal[1]

Figure 8.3
Government Payrolls: 1990 to 2004

Billions of dollars

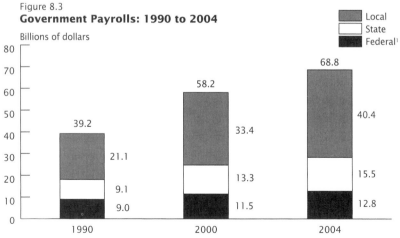

Legend: Local, State, Federal[1]

[1]Civilian employees only. Includes employees outside the United States.

Source: Figures 8.2 and 8.3 prepared by U.S. Census Bureau. For data, see Table 450.

State and Local Government Finances and Employment   263

Table 415. **Number of Governmental Units by Type: 1952 to 2002**

Type of government	1952 [1]	1962	1967	1972	1977	1982	1987	1992	1997	2002
Total units	116,807	91,237	81,299	78,269	79,913	81,831	83,237	85,006	87,504	87,576
U.S. government	1	1	1	1	1	1	1	1	1	1
State government	50	50	50	50	50	50	50	50	50	50
Local governments	116,756	91,186	81,248	78,218	79,862	81,780	83,186	84,955	87,453	87,525
County	3,052	3,043	3,049	3,044	3,042	3,041	3,042	3,043	3,043	3,034
Municipal	16,807	18,000	18,048	18,517	18,862	19,076	19,200	19,279	19,372	19,429
Township and town . . .	17,202	17,142	17,105	16,991	16,822	16,734	16,691	16,656	16,629	16,504
School district	67,355	34,678	21,782	15,781	15,174	14,851	14,721	14,422	13,726	13,506
Special district	12,340	18,323	21,264	23,885	25,962	28,078	29,532	31,555	34,683	35,052

[1] Adjusted to include units in Alaska and Hawaii which adopted statehood in 1959.

Source: U.S. Census Bureau, *Census of Governments, Volume 1, Number 1, Government Organization,* Series GC02(1)-1), quinquennial, <http://www.census.gov/govs/www/cog2002.html>.

Table 416. **Number of Local Governments by Type—States: 2002**

[Governments in existence in January. Limited to governments actually in existence. Excludes, therefore, a few counties and numerous townships and "incorporated places" existing as areas for which statistics can be presented as to population and other subjects, but lacking any separate organized county, township, or municipal government. See Appendix III]

State	All governmental units [1]	County	Municipal	Township [1]	School district	Special district [2] Total [3]	Natural resources	Fire protection	Housing & community development
United States . . .	87,525	3,034	19,429	16,504	13,506	35,052	6,979	5,725	3,399
Alabama	1,171	67	451	–	128	525	68	12	152
Alaska	175	12	149	–	–	14	–	–	13
Arizona	638	15	87	–	231	305	83	151	–
Arkansas	1,588	75	499	–	310	704	258	80	122
California	4,409	57	475	–	1,047	2,830	484	368	71
Colorado	1,928	62	270	–	182	1,414	178	250	91
Connecticut	580	–	30	149	17	384	1	64	93
Delaware	339	3	57	–	19	260	239	–	3
District of Columbia	2	–	1	–	–	1	–	–	–
Florida	1,191	66	404	–	95	626	124	57	105
Georgia	1,448	156	531	–	180	581	38	2	201
Hawaii	19	3	1	–	–	15	14	–	–
Idaho	1,158	44	200	–	116	798	176	142	10
Illinois	6,903	102	1,291	1,431	934	3,145	979	823	112
Indiana	3,085	91	567	1,008	294	1,125	141	1	63
Iowa	1,975	99	948	–	386	542	251	67	23
Kansas	3,887	104	627	1,299	324	1,533	261	–	199
Kentucky	1,439	119	424	–	176	720	166	163	17
Louisiana	473	60	302	–	66	45	4	–	–
Maine	826	16	22	467	99	222	15	–	23
Maryland	265	23	157	–	–	85	44	–	21
Massachusetts	841	5	45	306	82	403	16	16	250
Michigan	2,804	83	533	1,242	580	366	80	4	–
Minnesota	3,482	87	854	1,793	345	403	114	–	167
Mississippi	1,000	82	296	–	164	458	242	34	57
Missouri	3,422	114	946	312	536	1,514	183	317	136
Montana	1,127	54	129	–	352	592	125	155	12
Nebraska	2,791	93	531	446	575	1,146	80	421	125
Nevada	210	16	19	–	17	158	33	19	5
New Hampshire . . .	559	10	13	221	167	148	10	14	21
New Jersey	1,412	21	324	242	549	276	16	196	2
New Mexico	858	33	101	–	96	628	583	–	6
New York	3,420	57	616	929	683	1,135	3	911	–
North Carolina	960	100	541	–	–	319	155	–	91
North Dakota	2,735	53	360	1,332	226	764	79	281	39
Ohio	3,636	88	942	1,308	667	631	98	73	77
Oklahoma	1,798	77	590	–	571	560	97	26	105
Oregon	1,439	36	240	–	236	927	179	256	20
Pennsylvania	5,031	66	1,018	1,546	516	1,885	7	–	90
Rhode Island	118	–	8	31	4	75	3	34	25
South Carolina	701	46	269	–	85	301	48	86	46
South Dakota	1,866	66	308	940	176	376	102	72	40
Tennessee	930	92	349	–	14	475	108	–	98
Texas	4,784	254	1,196	–	1,089	2,245	442	141	398
Utah	605	29	236	–	40	300	81	19	16
Vermont	733	14	47	237	283	152	14	19	10
Virginia	521	95	229	–	1	196	47	–	–
Washington	1,787	39	279	–	296	1,173	170	387	41
West Virginia	686	55	234	–	55	342	15	–	39
Wisconsin	3,048	72	585	1,265	442	684	191	–	164
Wyoming	722	23	98	–	55	546	134	64	–

– Represents zero. [1] Includes "town" governments in the six New England States and in Minnesota, New York, and Wisconsin. [2] Single function districts. [3] Includes other special districts not shown separately.

Source: U.S. Census Bureau, *Census of Governments, Volume 1, Number 1, Government Organization,* Series GC02(1)–1), quinquennial, <http://www.census.gov/govs/www/cog2002.html>.

Table 417. County, Municipal, and Township Governments by Population Size: 2002

[Number of governments as of **January 2002**. Population enumerated as of **April 1, 2000. (252,051 represents 252,051,000).** Consolidated city-county governments are classified as municipal rather than county governments. Township governments include "towns" in the six New England states, Minnesota, New York, and Wisconsin. See Appendix III]

Population-size group	County governments			Municipal governments			Township governments		
		Population, **2000**			Population, **2000**			Population, **2000**	
	Number, 2002	Number (1,000)	Percent	Number, 2002	Number (1,000)	Percent	Number, 2002	Number (1,000)	Percent
Total	3,034	252,051	100	19,429	174,882	100	16,504	57,365	100
300,000 or more. . . .	161	131,575	52	58	47,768	27	3	1,527	3
200,000 to 299,999. . .	84	20,606	8	30	7,163	4	3	728	1
100,000 to 199,999. . .	228	31,576	13	153	21,076	12	30	3,974	7
50,000 to 99,999	383	27,160	11	364	24,960	14	97	6,588	11
25,000 to 49,999	638	22,913	9	643	22,576	13	273	9,275	16
10,000 to 24,999	869	14,488	6	1,436	22,589	13	773	12,067	21
5,000 to 9,999	385	2,911	1	1,637	11,644	7	1,085	7,560	13
2,500 to 4,999	173	643	(Z)	2,070	7,352	4	1,909	6,732	12
1,000 to 2,499	84	158	(Z)	3,677	5,951	3	3,679	5,905	10
Less than 1,000	29	21	(Z)	9,361	3,803	2	8,652	3,008	5

Z less than 0.5 percent.

Source: U.S. Census Bureau, *Census of Governments, Volume 1, Number 1, Government Organization,* Series GC02(1)-1), quinquennial. <http://www.census.gov/govs/www/cog2002.html>.

Table 418. Government Current Receipts and Expenditures by Type: 1990 to 2005

[**In billions of dollars (1,707.8 represents $1,707,800,000,000).** For explanation of national income, see text, Section 13. Minus sign (–) indicates decrease]

Item	1990	1995	2000	2001	2002	2003	2004	2005
Current receipts	1,707.8	2,212.6	3,125.9	3,113.1	2,958.7	3,018.1	3,208.2	3,557.2
Current tax receipts	1,161.9	1,517.2	2,206.8	2,168.0	2,004.5	2,031.8	2,169.9	2,486.3
Personal current taxes	592.8	744.1	1,235.7	1,237.3	1,051.8	999.9	1,049.1	1,209.7
Taxes on production and imports	425.5	558.2	708.9	728.6	762.8	801.4	852.8	903.1
Taxes on corporate income	140.6	211.0	255.0	194.9	182.6	221.9	258.9	363.9
Taxes from the rest of the world	3.0	3.9	7.3	7.1	7.3	8.5	9.2	9.6
Contributions for government social insurance	410.1	532.8	702.7	731.1	750.0	776.6	822.2	871.2
Income receipts on assets	98.7	92.1	117.4	113.7	98.4	97.6	99.0	102.3
Interest and miscellaneous receipts. . .	98.4	91.1	115.6	111.7	96.4	95.4	96.6	99.8
Dividends	0.2	1.0	1.9	2.0	2.0	2.1	2.4	2.5
Current transfer receipts	35.6	59.1	93.7	101.8	104.9	110.9	120.1	108.6
From business (net)	17.2	26.5	43.7	47.5	46.6	48.9	51.5	33.8
From persons	18.4	32.6	50.0	54.2	58.2	62.1	68.6	74.8
Current surplus of government enterprises	1.6	11.4	5.3	–1.4	0.9	1.3	–3.0	–11.3
Current expenditures	1,872.6	2,397.6	2,886.5	3,061.6	3,240.8	3,424.7	3,620.6	3,877.2
Consumption expenditures	964.4	1,136.5	1,417.1	1,501.6	1,616.9	1,736.7	1,843.4	1,962.6
Current transfer payments.	586.1	872.5	1,062.4	1,160.6	1,270.4	1,340.0	1,423.4	1,518.1
Government social benefits	574.8	860.3	1,044.1	1,146.6	1,251.6	1,316.4	1,397.5	1,487.0
To persons	573.1	858.4	1,041.6	1,143.9	1,248.9	1,313.5	1,394.5	1,483.7
To the rest of the world	1.8	1.9	2.5	2.7	2.7	2.8	3.0	3.3
Other current transfer payments to the rest of the world	11.3	12.1	18.3	13.9	18.8	23.6	25.9	31.1
Interest payments	295.3	354.6	362.8	344.1	315.1	301.4	310.3	341.3
To persons and business.	254.6	300.8	279.8	261.7	238.5	227.9	220.6	225.4
To the rest of the world	40.8	53.8	83.0	82.4	76.6	73.5	89.7	115.9
Subsidies.	26.8	34.0	44.3	55.3	38.4	46.7	43.5	55.2
Less: Wage accruals less disbursements	0.1	–	–	–	–	–	–	–
Net government saving	–164.8	–184.9	239.4	51.5	–282.1	–406.5	–412.3	–320.0
Social insurance funds	45.0	23.0	114.4	89.6	50.6	42.0	54.0	56.2
Other	–209.8	–208.0	125.1	–38.1	–332.7	–448.6	–466.3	–376.2
Addenda:								
Total receipts.	1,723.6	2,232.7	3,161.6	3,148.8	2,991.5	3,046.1	3,238.4	3,587.7
Current receipts	1,707.8	2,212.6	3,125.9	3,113.1	2,958.7	3,018.1	3,208.2	3,557.2
Capital transfer receipts	15.8	20.0	35.7	35.7	32.7	28.0	30.2	30.5
Total expenditures	1,969.6	2,464.9	3,002.6	3,188.2	3,388.2	3,589.4	3,792.0	4,062.5
Current expenditures	1,872.6	2,397.6	2,886.5	3,061.6	3,240.8	3,424.7	3,620.6	3,877.2
Gross government investment.	215.7	232.7	304.5	324.0	344.3	355.3	372.5	400.3
Capital transfer payments	7.2	0.4	0.0	0.0	3.8	16.9	16.3	20.0
Net purchases of nonproduced assets.	5.0	–0.8	8.5	8.5	10.9	11.1	11.8	12.0
Less: Consumption of fixed capital. .	130.9	165.0	197.0	206.0	211.6	218.5	229.1	247.0
Net lending or net borrowing (–). . .	–246.0	–232.3	159.0	–39.3	–396.7	–543.3	–553.6	–474.8

– Represents zero.

Source: U.S. Bureau of Economic Analysis, *Survey of Current Business,* April 2006. See also <http://www.bea.gov/bea/dn/nipaweb /index.asp> (released 30 March 2006).

State and Local Government Finances and Employment   265

Table 419. **Government Consumption Expenditures and Gross Investment in Current and Real (2000) Dollars by Level of Government and Type: 2000 to 2005**

[In billions of dollars (1,721.6 represents $1,721,600,000,000). Government consumption expenditures are services (such as education and national defense) produced by government that are valued at their cost of production. Excludes government sales to other sectors and government own-account investment (construction and software). Gross government investment consists of general government and government enterprise expenditures for fixed assets; inventory investment is included in government consumption expenditures. For explanation of national income, see text, Section 13.]

Item	Current dollars				Chained (2000) dollars			
	2000	2003	2004	2005	2000	2003	2004	2005
Government consumption expenditures and gross investment, total	1,721.6	2,091.9	2,215.9	2,362.9	1,721.6	1,911.1	1,952.3	1,987.1
Consumption expenditures	1,417.1	1,736.7	1,843.4	1,962.6	1,417.1	1,568.8	1,602.1	1,626.7
Gross investment	304.5	355.3	372.5	400.3	304.5	342.2	350.1	360.7
Structures	189.3	226.9	232.0	251.2	189.3	208.4	205.4	208.6
Equipment and software	115.2	128.3	140.5	149.1	115.2	134.3	146.4	154.6
Federal	578.8	754.8	827.6	877.7	578.8	687.8	723.7	740.5
Consumption expenditures	499.3	661.9	725.7	769.6	499.3	593.4	622.1	635.0
Gross investment	79.5	92.9	101.9	108.1	79.5	94.4	101.9	106.2
Structures	13.3	15.4	14.5	15.6	13.3	14.1	12.7	12.7
Equipment and software	66.2	77.6	87.4	92.5	66.2	80.3	89.7	94.0
National defense	370.3	496.7	552.7	587.1	370.3	449.7	481.3	493.6
Consumption expenditures	321.5	436.6	484.2	515.9	321.5	388.5	413.3	424.1
Gross investment	48.8	60.1	68.5	71.2	48.8	61.3	68.5	70.0
Structures	5.0	5.1	5.1	5.2	5.0	4.7	4.4	4.3
Equipment and software	43.8	55.0	63.4	66.0	43.8	56.7	64.4	66.0
Nondefense	208.5	258.2	274.9	290.6	208.5	238.0	242.2	246.6
Consumption expenditures	177.8	225.3	241.4	253.7	177.8	204.8	208.6	210.6
Gross investment	30.7	32.8	33.4	36.9	30.7	33.1	33.4	36.3
Structures	8.3	10.3	9.4	10.4	8.3	9.4	8.3	8.5
Equipment and software	22.3	22.6	24.0	26.5	22.3	23.6	25.3	28.0
State and local	1,142.8	1,337.1	1,388.3	1,485.2	1,142.8	1,223.3	1,228.4	1,246.6
Consumption expenditures	917.8	1,074.8	1,117.7	1,193.0	917.8	975.2	979.5	991.1
Gross investment	225.0	262.3	270.6	292.2	225.0	248.2	248.9	255.4
Structures	176.0	211.6	217.6	235.7	176.0	194.3	192.8	195.8
Equipment and software	49.0	50.8	53.0	56.6	49.0	53.9	56.6	60.5

Source: U.S. Bureau of Economic Analysis, *Survey of Current Business*, April 2006. See also <http://www.bea.gov/bea/dn/nipaweb /index.asp> (released 30 March, 2006).

Table 420. **State and Local Government Current Receipts and Expenditures in the National Income and Product Accounts: 1990 to 2005**

[In billions of dollars (737.8 represents $737,800,000,000). For explanation of national income, see text, Section 13. Minus sign (–) indicates decrease]

Item	1990	1995	1999	2000	2001	2002	2003	2004	2005
Current receipts	737.8	990.2	1,236.7	1,319.5	1,373.0	1,410.1	1,488.6	1,581.7	1,689.4
Current tax receipts.	519.1	672.1	840.4	893.2	915.8	929.0	972.6	1,047.6	1,139.2
Personal current taxes	122.6	158.1	214.5	236.6	242.7	221.3	225.6	247.2	274.7
Income taxes	109.6	141.7	195.5	217.3	223.1	200.8	203.7	224.0	249.7
Other	13.0	16.4	19.0	19.4	19.6	20.5	21.9	23.2	25.0
Taxes on production and imports	374.1	482.4	590.2	621.1	642.8	675.5	711.7	758.8	805.9
Sales taxes	184.3	242.7	301.6	316.6	321.1	330.2	347.9	370.4	392.1
Property taxes	161.5	202.6	242.8	254.6	269.3	290.1	303.4	322.8	341.4
Other	28.3	37.0	45.8	49.9	52.4	55.2	60.4	65.5	72.5
Taxes on corporate income	22.5	31.7	35.8	35.5	30.2	32.2	35.3	41.5	58.6
Contributions for government social insurance	10.0	13.6	9.8	11.0	13.6	15.8	17.5	19.7	19.9
Income receipts on assets	68.4	68.4	85.3	92.2	88.8	78.2	74.9	77.1	79.1
Interest receipts	64.1	62.9	78.4	84.0	80.3	69.6	65.4	67.0	68.3
Dividends.	0.2	1.0	1.8	1.9	2.0	2.0	2.1	2.4	2.5
Rents and royalties	4.2	4.5	5.1	6.3	6.5	6.6	7.3	7.7	8.3
Current transfer receipts.	133.5	224.1	290.8	315.4	350.8	384.7	424.3	439.8	458.6
Federal grants-in-aid	111.4	184.1	232.9	247.3	276.1	304.6	339.1	348.3	357.6
From business (net).	7.1	13.5	23.0	28.8	31.4	32.6	34.1	35.5	39.4
From persons.	14.9	26.5	34.9	39.2	43.3	47.5	51.1	56.0	61.6
Current surplus of government enterprises.	6.7	12.0	10.4	7.7	4.0	2.5	-0.6	-2.5	-7.5
Current expenditures	730.5	978.2	1,186.3	1,269.5	1,368.2	1,444.3	1,512.4	1,587.5	1,686.4
Consumption expenditures	544.6	696.1	858.9	917.8	969.8	1,025.3	1,074.8	1,117.7	1,193.0
Government social benefit payments to persons	127.7	217.6	252.4	271.7	305.2	332.0	351.3	380.5	400.7
Public assistance	111.1	195.8	228.3	245.4	275.9	300.3	317.8	345.2	(NA)
Medicaid	73.1	149.6	184.6	199.5	227.3	258.6	274.3	299.7	(NA)
Interest payments	57.9	64.2	74.6	79.5	85.5	86.0	86.2	88.9	92.2
Subsidies	0.4	0.3	0.4	0.5	7.7	0.9	0.1	0.5	0.5
Net state and local government . .	7.2	12.0	50.4	50.0	4.8	-34.2	-23.8	-5.9	3.0
Social insurance funds.	2.0	4.0	1.7	2.0	2.6	1.7	1.3	1.8	0.4
Other	5.3	8.0	48.7	47.9	2.2	-35.9	-25.1	-7.7	2.6

NA Not available.

Source: U.S. Bureau of Economic Analysis, *Survey of Current Business*, April 2006. See also <http://www.bea.gov/bea/dn/nipaweb /index.asp> (released 30 March 2006).

266 State and Local Government Finances and Employment

U.S. Census Bureau. Statistical Abstract of the United States: 2007

Table 421. **Federal Grants-in-Aid to State and Local Governments: 1990 to 2006**

[135,325 represents $135,325,000,000, except as indicated. For year ending September 30. Minus sign (–) indicates decrease]

Year	Current dollars							Constant (2000) dollars	
			Grants to individuals		Grants as percent of—				
	Total grants (mil. dol.)	Annual percent change [1]	Total (mil. dol.)	Percent of total grants	State/ local govt. expendi- tures [2]	Federal outlays	Gross domestic product	Total grants (bil. dol.)	Annual percent change [1]
1990	135,325	11.0	77,264	57.1	25.2	10.8	2.4	172.1	6.3
1993	193,612	8.7	124,155	64.1	29.6	13.7	3.0	223.9	5.9
1994	210,596	8.8	134,153	63.7	30.9	14.4	3.0	238.1	6.3
1995	224,991	6.8	144,427	64.2	31.5	14.8	3.1	247.9	4.1
1996	227,811	1.3	146,493	64.3	30.8	14.6	3.0	245.5	–1.0
1997	234,160	2.8	148,236	63.3	30.2	14.6	2.9	247.7	0.9
1998	246,128	5.1	160,305	65.1	30.3	14.9	2.9	257.3	3.9
1999	267,081	8.5	172,384	64.5	31.2	15.7	2.9	274.7	6.8
2000	284,659	6.6	182,592	64.1	27.2	15.9	2.9	284.7	3.6
2001	317,211	11.4	203,920	64.3	28.2	17.0	3.2	309.4	8.7
2002	351,550	10.8	227,373	64.7	29.3	17.5	3.4	337.2	9.0
2003	387,366	10.2	246,570	63.7	31.0	17.9	3.6	362.9	7.6
2004	406,330	4.9	262,177	64.5	31.3	17.7	3.5	371.7	2.4
2005	426,243	4.9	273,464	64.2	30.7	17.2	3.5	374.0	0.9
2006, est.. . .	449,277	5.4	287,634	64.0	(NA)	16.6	3.4	379.3	1.4

NA Not available. [1] Average annual percent change from prior year shown. For explanation, see Guide to Tabular Presentation. For 1990, change from 1989. [2] Expenditures from own sources as defined in the national income and product accounts.

Source: U. S. Office of Management and Budget, based on *Historical Tables, Budget of the United States Government*, annual <http://www.whitehouse.gov/omb/budget/>.

Table 422. **Total Outlays for Grants to State and Local Governments—Selected Agencies and Programs: 1990 to 2006**

[In millions of dollars (135,325 represents $135,325,000,000). For year ending September 30. Includes trust funds]

Program	1990	1995	2000	2002	2003	2004	2005	2006 est.
Total outlays for grants [1]	135,325	224,991	284,659	351,550	387,281	406,330	426,243	449,277
Energy [1].	461	492	433	528	589	608	636	650
Natural resources and environment [1].	3,745	4,148	4,595	5,085	5,593	6,009	5,858	5,846
Environmental Protection Agency [2].	2,874	2,912	3,490	3,588	3,917	4,018	3,734	3,691
Agriculture [1]	1,285	780	724	750	800	995	933	799
Transportation [1].	19,174	25,787	32,222	40,998	41,029	41,471	43,370	46,701
Grants for airports [2].	1,220	1,826	1,624	2,860	2,681	2,958	3,530	3,800
Federal-aid highways [3]	14,171	19,475	24,711	29,833	29,960	29,791	30,915	32,639
Urban mass transportation [2]	3,730	4,353	5,262	7,462	7,448	7,777	8,114	8,438
Community and regional development [2].	4,965	7,230	8,665	10,501	15,082	12,604	20,167	22,299
Rural community advance program	139	333	479	740	800	797	814	704
Community development fund.	2,818	4,333	4,955	5,429	5,569	5,388	4,985	6,906
Department of Homeland Security	1,184	1,772	2,439	3,456	7,861	5,490	13,541	13,804
State and local programs	(X)	(X)	(X)	(X)	550	1,535	2,116	1,407
Firefighter assistance grants	(X)	(X)	(X)	(X)	31	508	1,185	278
Operating expenses.	11	79	192	218	(X)	387	132	222
Mitigation grants	(X)	(X)	13	18	21	23	39	66
Disaster relief	1,173	1,693	2,234	3,220	7,529	3,037	10,069	11,881
Education, training, employment, social services [1]	23,359	34,125	42,125	44,827	51,543	54,201	57,247	60,337
Education for the disadvantaged [4].	4,437	6,785	8,511	9,211	11,204	12,417	14,539	14,812
School improvement programs [4]	1,080	1,288	2,394	3,401	5,964	6,542	6,569	5,808
Vocational and adult education	1,287	1,449	1,448	1,742	1,908	1,909	1,930	2,003
Special education	1,485	2,938	4,696	6,730	8,216	9,465	10,661	10,416
Social services-block grant	2,749	2,797	1,827	1,780	1,740	1,752	1,822	2,224
Children and family services programs	2,618	4,463	5,843	7,749	8,161	8,326	8,490	8,514
Training and employment services	3,042	3,620	2,957	4,206	4,291	3,883	3,372	3,077
Health [1].	43,890	93,587	124,843	158,677	173,814	189,883	197,848	210,580
Substance abuse, and mental health services [4]	1,241	2,444	1,931	2,193	2,171	2,241	3,203	2,326
Grants to states for Medicaid [4]	41,103	89,070	117,921	147,650	160,805	176,231	181,720	192,334
State children's health insurance fund [4]	(X)	(X)	1,220	3,682	4,355	4,607	5,129	5,775
Income security [1].	35,189	55,122	63,200	81,506	86,476	85,983	90,885	93,726
Food stamp program [4].	2,130	2,740	3,508	3,949	4,162	4,204	4,385	4,561
Child nutrition programs [4].	4,871	7,387	9,060	10,100	10,664	11,035	11,726	12,717
Temporary assistance for needy families [1,4] . . .	(X)	(X)	15,464	18,749	19,352	17,725	17,357	17,406
Veterans' benefits and services [1,4]	134	253	434	360	403	454	118	115
Administration of justice [1]	574	1,222	5,120	5,826	4,498	5,084	4,784	3,736

X Not applicable. [1] Includes items not shown separately. [2] Grants include trust funds. [3] Trust funds. [4] Includes grants for payments to individuals.

Source: U. S. Office of Management and Budget, *Budget of the United States Government, Historical Tables*, annual <http://www.whitehouse.gov/omb>.

State and Local Government Finances and Employment   267

Table 423. Federal Aid to State and Local Governments—Selected Programs by State: 2004

[In millions of dollars (408,143 represents $408,143,000,000). For fiscal year ending September 30]

State and island areas	Federal aid, total [1]	Department of Agriculture — Food and nutrition service — Total	Child nutrition programs	Food stamp programs [2]	Special supplemental food program (WIC)	Other	Department of Education — Total	Special education programs	Office of Elementary and Secondary Education — No child left behind act	Title 1 programs	Other
United States total....	408,143	23,184	11,132	4,060	4,858	3,133	31,251	7,936	4,318	9,052	9,945
Alabama	6,057	382	217	32	78	56	522	141	82	167	132
Alaska	2,433	116	31	8	22	54	148	–	8	–	139
Arizona...........	7,815	457	245	41	114	57	740	143	86	183	327
Arkansas..........	4,124	263	130	26	54	52	351	107	64	103	78
California..........	47,283	2,887	1,407	410	848	222	4,411	1,026	513	1,330	1,543
Colorado..........	4,606	229	107	29	51	42	472	118	63	101	189
Connecticut	5,015	160	83	20	34	22	354	104	57	106	87
Delaware..........	1,113	62	29	9	10	14	119	27	26	30	36
District of Columbia....	3,591	60	27	13	13	7	117	14	24	36	44
Florida	18,174	1,016	622	83	229	82	1,815	516	223	522	553
Georgia	9,540	729	445	59	150	75	97	2	12	–	83
Hawaii	1,805	128	49	10	29	40	233	44	24	34	131
Idaho	1,900	111	47	9	21	36	162	46	29	38	48
Illinois	14,949	771	431	91	167	81	1,529	450	203	472	404
Indiana	6,965	364	197	45	72	50	548	207	74	159	109
Iowa	3,612	209	95	21	39	54	355	102	50	71	132
Kansas	2,931	198	111	15	41	31	131	16	16	–	99
Kentucky..........	6,307	351	188	31	71	60	559	131	105	153	170
Louisiana	7,035	497	280	47	89	81	42	2	8	–	32
Maine............	2,641	108	38	12	12	47	186	50	27	50	59
Maryland	6,646	275	148	35	61	32	583	197	74	124	187
Massachusetts	10,649	294	165	36	61	33	724	199	96	247	182
Michigan..........	12,210	612	295	94	127	97	1,186	328	200	427	231
Minnesota	6,331	357	172	49	67	70	108	7	11	–	89
Mississippi.........	5,297	359	194	33	58	75	418	93	80	146	99
Missouri	7,717	383	206	32	76	70	98	1	14	–	83
Montana	1,883	100	34	10	13	43	208	34	32	38	104
Nebraska	2,322	140	70	16	23	31	214	66	29	36	83
Nevada...........	2,093	114	53	12	27	21	203	60	29	50	65
New Hampshire	1,508	63	22	5	10	26	144	43	27	29	46
New Jersey	10,856	435	219	88	91	37	932	301	115	274	242
New Mexico........	4,249	228	123	24	41	40	430	108	47	93	182
New York	42,576	1,425	748	236	338	104	2,722	612	376	1,050	684
North Carolina	11,354	659	366	65	133	96	939	269	123	248	298
North Dakota	1,316	81	27	8	10	36	143	22	27	29	65
Ohio............	14,500	700	317	158	153	72	84	5	13	–	65
Oklahoma	4,937	356	183	43	65	65	538	117	77	129	216
Oregon	4,969	415	117	54	64	179	437	124	58	116	139
Pennsylvania	18,033	694	323	139	137	95	1,164	342	158	409	255
Rhode Island	1,981	65	33	8	15	10	17	–	1	--	16
South Carolina	5,544	324	197	22	62	43	104	7	21	–	76
South Dakota.......	1,407	92	34	10	14	33	71	1	2	–	68
Tennessee	9,129	448	240	37	100	70	662	199	86	190	188
Texas	25,674	1,963	1,212	159	448	144	2,876	714	442	970	749
Utah............	2,639	171	85	21	33	33	259	77	40	37	105
Vermont	1,274	63	16	14	12	22	108	20	22	22	45
Virginia	6,598	65	6	3	5	51	765	208	78	172	307
Washington	7,855	427	169	46	103	109	624	181	101	152	190
West Virginia	3,384	163	79	15	31	37	229	49	55	75	51
Wisconsin	6,888	319	148	47	65	59	673	192	90	155	236
Wyoming..........	1,583	43	17	5	7	14	119	24	25	29	40
Island areas:											
American Samoa....	137	22	10	5	6	1	25	5	1	–	19
Micronesia	65	1	–	–	–	–	6	3	1	–	2
Guam	275	18	6	3	5	4	44	16	1	–	28
Marshall Islands	49	–	–	–	–	–	4	1	1	–	2
Northern Marianas...	86	14	5	7	–	2	14	5	–	–	8
Palau	43	–	–	–	–	–	4	1	–	–	2
Puerto Rico	4,854	1,788	154	1,431	175	28	475	58	70	249	98
Virgin Islands	575	369	162	79	78	50	5	1	–	–	4
Undistributed amounts ..	760	39	–	–	–	39	–	–	–	–	–

See footnote at end of table.

Table 423. Federal Aid to State and Local Governments—Selected Programs by State: 2004—Con.

[In millions of dollars (2,508 represents $2,508,000,000). For fiscal year ending September 30]

State and Island areas	FEMA total [3]	Department of Housing and Urban Development						Department of Labor			
		Total	Community development block grants	Public housing programs			Other	Total	State unemployment insurance and employment service	Workforce investment	Other
				Low rent housing assistance	Housing certificate program	Capital program					
United States total....	2,508	40,431	5,412	3,488	22,356	3,413	5,762	8,749	3,404	3,166	2,290
Alabama...........	44	534	70	109	213	75	66	138	43	71	28
Alaska............	10	161	14	8	36	3	100	57	21	16	20
Arizona...........	7	480	82	17	165	10	206	138	42	57	39
Arkansas..........	43	295	37	25	180	27	26	72	27	28	17
California..........	585	4,677	581	115	3,184	121	677	1,193	490	532	192
Colorado..........	12	444	49	17	303	12	63	103	50	27	27
Connecticut........	14	673	61	52	448	32	81	105	63	20	23
Delaware..........	8	113	9	9	65	8	22	22	11	5	6
District of Columbia....	6	700	77	53	215	276	79	306	150	17	140
Florida............	134	1,405	186	93	823	74	230	283	105	132	47
Georgia	26	919	118	109	495	88	108	174	69	67	39
Hawaii	3	167	28	10	93	16	20	48	19	11	18
Idaho	3	89	17	1	55	2	14	60	25	18	17
Illinois............	13	2,188	225	254	1,246	202	262	384	162	138	88
Indiana...........	21	591	83	40	359	29	79	130	51	39	39
Iowa.............	10	247	48	5	157	7	30	69	33	16	20
Kansas...........	14	223	44	15	118	13	33	56	24	20	11
Kentucky..........	44	524	56	46	304	51	67	127	38	45	44
Louisiana..........	20	571	84	58	253	62	114	125	36	77	14
Maine............	10	206	23	8	139	7	28	60	19	18	25
Maryland..........	42	840	81	69	475	60	155	190	66	41	82
Massachusetts......	43	1,866	148	106	1,335	79	198	170	80	43	47
Michigan..........	19	960	154	50	542	44	170	341	147	124	83
Minnesota.........	18	634	70	36	386	44	98	125	47	35	45
Mississippi........	18	315	54	27	164	26	44	87	35	36	16
Missouri..........	25	716	110	37	335	114	121	124	45	55	25
Montana	15	123	21	4	52	4	43	41	16	14	11
Nebraska..........	11	163	29	10	86	11	27	34	22	4	8
Nevada...........	6	178	22	15	107	5	29	61	32	20	9
New Hampshire.....	7	163	19	6	108	10	21	30	16	8	7
New Jersey........	33	1,518	128	160	965	98	168	204	126	42	38
New Mexico........	8	190	35	9	89	10	47	58	22	20	17
New York	156	5,420	958	874	2,515	563	511	531	205	229	130
North Carolina......	115	829	93	96	456	66	117	273	78	76	120
North Dakota.......	16	111	14	2	64	5	27	25	13	6	5
Ohio.............	33	1,601	227	154	868	130	222	260	92	108	61
Oklahoma.........	28	469	58	25	190	22	174	79	30	30	22
Oregon...........	34	376	46	16	232	13	71	140	61	48	31
Pennsylvania.......	33	1,913	290	243	941	194	245	373	156	130	91
Rhode Island.......	2	266	21	20	173	18	35	30	17	6	7
South Carolina......	15	380	51	30	219	28	52	109	41	43	27
South Dakota.......	5	125	20	3	55	2	46	34	13	8	14
Tennessee.........	50	609	62	89	291	70	97	163	54	55	54
Texas............	126	1,939	297	113	1,143	148	239	546	174	229	146
Utah.............	15	166	30	4	99	3	31	56	32	13	10
Vermont..........	4	91	13	3	60	3	13	25	12	5	9
Virginia...........	194	743	76	62	449	50	105	247	53	44	151
Washington	48	702	89	35	373	43	161	263	92	108	64
West Virginia.......	39	216	48	16	114	11	28	54	22	20	12
Wisconsin.........	9	525	103	18	287	17	100	205	85	53	71
Wyoming..........	2	38	7	1	22	1	7	20	10	6	3
Island areas:											
American Samoa....	3	2	1	–	–	–	–	1	–	–	1
Micronesia........	4	–	–	–	–	–	1	–	1	–	–
Guam	31	42	3	3	32	3	1	8	1	6	2
Marshall Islands	–	–	–	–	–	–	–	1	–	1	–
Northern Marianas...	7	3	–	–	2	–	–	1	7	1	–
Palau	–	–	–	–	–	–	–	1	–	–	–
Puerto Rico	52	663	138	96	261	115	53	182	27	140	13
Virgin Islands	2	49	3	19	17	8	2	6	3	1	2
Undistributed amounts..	216	278	–	–5	1	281	–	24	–	–	–

See footnote at end of table.

U.S. Census Bureau, Statistical Abstract of the United States: 2007

Table 423. **Federal Aid to State and Local Governments—Selected Programs by State: 2004**—Con.

[In millions of dollars (234,755 represents $234,755,000,000). For fiscal year ending September 30]

State and island areas	Total	Department of Health and Human Services					Department of Transportation				Other federal aid [4]
		Administration for children			Centers for Medicare and Medicaid Services	Other	Total	High-way trust fund	Federal transit admin-istration	Other	
		Chil-dren & family ser-vices (Head Start)	Foster care and adop-tion assis-tance	Tempo-rary assis-tance to needy families							
United States total. . . .	234,755	8,263	6,331	17,468	180,115	22,576	40,080	28,881	6,818	4,393	27,187
Alaska	944	56	23	61	667	136	572	373	18	181	426
Arizona	4,745	158	82	244	3,851	410	680	450	165	66	567
Arkansas.	2,416	90	48	41	2,045	192	459	375	17	67	224
California.	27,395	1,041	1,550	3,765	18,448	2,591	3,801	2,365	1,080	357	2,333
Colorado.	2,203	139	69	148	1,509	337	675	434	125	116	469
Connecticut	2,878	72	100	290	2,122	293	540	460	60	20	292
Delaware.	569	15	9	29	441	75	102	91	4	7	118
District of Columbia. . . .	1,295	62	33	106	859	235	378	131	237	10	730
Florida	10,560	315	200	642	8,163	1,240	1,982	1,563	262	156	980
Georgia	5,957	220	89	380	4,705	562	1,021	788	127	105	617
Hawaii	890	35	27	76	655	97	162	97	38	27	174
Idaho	977	43	11	37	764	121	295	231	8	57	204
Illinois.	8,245	343	358	688	5,928	928	1,067	611	341	115	750
Indiana	4,164	115	71	201	3,381	396	724	607	54	63	424
Iowa	2,056	71	52	135	1,587	211	397	339	23	35	269
Kansas	1,674	85	45	99	1,279	166	413	369	13	30	222
Kentucky	3,761	146	70	174	3,107	265	549	435	38	76	391
Louisiana	4,701	167	83	265	3,861	325	631	501	60	71	448
Maine	1,696	43	28	73	1,442	109	216	177	11	28	160
Maryland	3,611	108	128	265	2,677	432	624	426	74	124	481
Massachusetts	6,166	150	88	436	4,974	517	848	604	192	53	539
Michigan	7,372	297	226	803	5,256	791	1,019	799	88	133	700
Minnesota	3,981	119	93	247	3,120	401	671	453	139	78	437
Mississippi.	3,313	189	8	99	2,774	243	465	362	12	90	322
Missouri	4,974	155	86	212	4,097	424	928	723	93	112	470
Montana	734	46	16	34	539	99	380	314	1	64	283
Nebraska	1,273	49	23	56	984	161	299	257	10	33	187
Nevada	895	35	21	42	659	137	319	199	53	67	318
New Hampshire	802	24	19	26	643	91	142	128	4	10	157
New Jersey	5,753	165	87	429	4,447	624	1,357	752	537	68	624
New Mexico.	2,256	78	32	130	1,830	186	332	281	25	27	746
New York	28,156	528	726	2,480	22,518	1,903	2,610	1,470	1,011	129	1,555
North Carolina	6,819	202	93	332	5,551	641	1,110	977	73	59	610
North Dakota	524	37	15	25	368	80	245	181	3	61	171
Ohio.	9,753	310	389	722	7,486	846	1,257	958	152	148	812
Oklahoma	2,581	129	35	171	1,959	287	559	487	19	52	325
Oregon	2,431	114	66	151	1,842	258	672	355	131	186	464
Pennsylvania	11,149	299	440	935	8,535	940	1,819	1,224	448	147	887
Rhode Island	1,282	32	21	96	1,038	95	185	157	12	16	133
South Carolina	3,507	106	30	101	2,969	300	737	670	24	43	367
South Dakota	577	41	8	25	414	89	228	182	2	43	275
Tennessee	5,855	149	50	214	5,017	425	749	622	57	69	592
Texas	13,597	593	221	523	10,814	1,446	3,302	2,827	255	219	1,325
Utah	1,377	57	29	98	1,027	166	327	245	50	32	268
Vermont	714	23	21	48	564	59	145	122	11	12	123
Virginia	3,190	187	102	176	2,262	463	831	588	162	81	564
Washington	4,253	167	102	412	3,106	466	903	486	264	154	634
West Virginia	1,988	64	33	128	1,585	177	430	331	8	91	266
Wisconsin	3,962	131	130	398	2,889	414	686	518	75	92	508
Wyoming	370	24	3	31	261	50	273	225	3	46	718
Island areas:											
American Samoa. . . .	17	6	–	–	5	7	13	7	–	6	54
Micronesia	1	–	–	–	–	–	–	–	–	–	53
Guam	30	6	–	–	9	14	12	9	–	3	90
Marshall Islands	–	–	–	–	–	–	–	–	–	–	44
Northern Marianas. . .	10	3	–	–	3	4	9	1	–	8	29
Palau	–	–	–	–	–	–	–	–	–	–	39
Puerto Rico	898	265	14	54	273	291	188	47	127	14	609
Virgin Islands	44	12	–	3	8	20	4	–	1	3	97
Undistributed amounts. .	17	17	–	–	–	6	123	4	–	132	63

– Represents or rounds to zero   [1] Total includes programs not shown separately.   [2] For Puerto Rico, amount shown is for nutritional assistance grant program, all other amounts are grant payments for food stamp administration.   [3] FEMA = Federal Emergency Management Agency. FEMA is part of Department of Homeland Security.[4] Represents aid for other programs not shown.

Source: U.S. Census Bureau, *Federal Aid to States For Fiscal Year 2004* (issued January 2006.) See also <http://www.census.gov/prod/2006pubs/fas-04.pdf>

270   State and Local Government Finances and Employment

Table 424. State and Local Governments—Summary of Finances: 1990 to 2003

[In millions of dollars (1,032,115 represents $1,032,115,000,000), except as indicated. For fiscal year ending in year shown; see text, this section. Local government amounts are estimates subject to sampling variation; see Appendix III and source. Minus sign (–) indicates net loss]

Item	Total (mil. dol.)				Per capita [1] (dol.)			
	1990	2000	2002	2003	1990	2000	2002	2003
Revenue [2]	1,032,115	1,942,328	1,807,573	2,047,337	4,150	6,902	6,277	7,041
From federal government	136,802	291,950	360,534	389,264	550	1,037	1,252	1,339
Public welfare...................	59,961	148,549	183,868	199,789	241	528	638	687
Highways	14,368	24,414	30,382	30,052	58	87	106	103
Education	23,233	45,873	55,997	61,901	93	163	194	213
Health and hospitals	5,904	15,611	19,678	21,491	24	55	68	74
Housing and community development. . .	9,655	17,690	22,628	24,713	39	63	79	85
Other and unallocable	23,683	39,812	47,981	51,317	95	141	167	176
From state and local sources.	895,313	1,650,379	1,447,039	1,658,073	3,600	5,864	5,025	5,702
General, net intergovernmental	712,700	1,249,093	1,324,241	1,373,948	2,865	4,439	4,598	4,725
Taxes	501,619	872,351	904,971	938,972	2,017	3,100	3,143	3,229
Property	155,613	249,178	279,122	296,683	626	885	969	1,020
Sales and gross receipts	177,885	309,290	324,040	337,787	715	1,099	1,125	1,162
Individual income	105,640	211,661	202,858	199,407	425	752	704	686
Corporation income	23,566	36,059	28,152	31,369	95	128	98	108
Other.....................	38,915	66,164	70,800	73,726	156	235	246	254
Charges and miscellaneous........	211,081	377,022	419,270	434,976	849	1,340	1,456	1,496
Utility and liquor stores...........	58,642	89,546	107,387	108,388	236	318	373	373
Water supply system	17,674	30,515	33,207	34,736	71	108	115	119
Electric power system...........	29,268	42,436	54,404	53,938	118	151	189	185
Gas supply system	5,216	8,049	8,950	8,985	21	29	31	31
Transit system	3,043	3,954	5,762	5,391	12	14	20	19
Liquor stores	3,441	4,592	5,065	5,338	14	16	18	18
Insurance trust revenue [3]	123,970	311,460	15,410	175,737	498	1,107	54	604
Employee retirement	94,268	273,881	–29,261	120,157	379	973	–102	413
Unemployment compensation	18,441	23,366	27,086	35,335	74	83	94	122
Direct expenditure	972,695	1,742,914	2,044,331	2,159,772	3,911	6,193	7,099	7,427
By function:								
Direct general expenditure [3]	831,573	1,502,768	1,730,809	1,817,513	3,356	5,340	6,010	6,250
Education [3]	288,148	521,612	594,591	621,335	1,159	1,853	2,065	2,137
Elementary and secondary.......	202,009	365,181	411,073	428,503	812	1,298	1,427	1,474
Higher education............	73,418	134,352	156,810	164,187	295	477	545	565
Highways....................	61,057	101,336	115,467	117,696	245	360	401	405
Public welfare...............	107,287	233,350	279,598	306,463	444	829	971	1,054
Health	24,223	51,366	59,132	61,703	97	183	205	212
Hospitals	50,412	75,976	87,247	93,175	203	270	303	320
Police protection.............	30,577	56,798	64,492	67,361	123	202	224	232
Fire protection...............	13,186	23,102	25,978	27,854	53	82	90	96
Corrections.................	24,636	48,805	54,687	55,471	100	173	190	191
Natural resources	12,330	20,235	22,000	22,808	50	72	76	78
Sanitation and sewerage........	28,453	45,261	50,286	51,723	114	161	175	178
Housing and community development................	15,479	26,590	31,610	35,225	62	94	110	121
Parks and recreation	14,326	25,038	30,096	31,765	58	89	105	109
Financial administration	16,217	29,300	32,653	34,911	65	104	113	120
Interest on general debt [4]	49,739	69,814	75,303	77,277	200	248	261	266
Utility and liquor stores [4]	77,801	114,916	143,851	148,996	313	408	500	512
Water supply system	22,101	35,789	40,527	43,260	89	127	141	149
Electric power system..........	30,997	39,719	55,952	54,355	125	141	194	187
Gas supply system	2,989	3,724	5,720	5,300	12	13	20	18
Transit system	18,788	31,883	37,468	41,678	76	113	130	143
Liquor stores	2,926	3,801	4,183	4,402	12	14	15	15
Insurance trust expenditure [3]	63,321	125,230	169,672	193,263	255	445	589	665
Employee retirement	38,355	95,679	114,208	127,197	154	340	397	437
Unemployment compensation	16,499	18,648	42,166	51,547	66	66	146	177
By character and object:								
Current operation	700,131	1,288,746	1,497,216	1,579,290	2,815	4,579	5,199	5,431
Capital outlay..................	123,102	217,063	257,214	263,198	495	771	893	905
Construction.................	89,144	161,694	197,629	203,035	358	575	686	698
Equipment, land, and existing structures...................	33,958	55,369	59,585	60,162	137	197	207	207
Assistance and subsidies........	27,227	31,375	35,082	35,080	109	111	116	121
Interest on debt (general and utility)	58,914	80,499	86,948	88,940	237	286	302	306
Insurance benefits and repayments	63,321	125,230	169,672	193,263	255	445	589	665
Expenditure for salaries and wages [5] . . .	340,654	548,796	610,879	647,211	1,372	1,950	2,121	2,226
Debt outstanding, year end.	858,006	1,451,815	1,686,106	1,812,667	3,460	5,159	5,855	6,234
Long-term.......................	838,700	1,427,524	1,642,864	1,772,197	3,382	5,073	5,705	6,094
Short-term.....................	19,306	24,291	43,242	40,470	78	86	150	139
Long-term debt:								
Issued	108,468	184,831	262,339	345,784	436	657	911	1,189
Retired	64,831	121,849	162,463	215,218	261	433	564	740

[1] 1990 and 2000 based on enumerated resident population as of April 1. Other years based on estimated resident population as of July 1; see Table 17. [2] Aggregates exclude duplicative transactions between state and local governments; see source. [3] Includes amounts not shown separately. [4] Interest on utility debt included in "utility and liquor stores expenditure." For total interest on debt, see "Interest on debt (general and utility)." [5] Included in items above.

Source: U.S. Census Bureau, "Federal, State, and Local Governments, Finance, State and Local Government Finances," 2002–03; see also <http://www.census.gov/govs/www/estimate03.html> (accessed 21 June 2005).

Table 425. **State and Local Governments—Revenue and Expenditures by Function: 2003**

[In millions of dollars (2,047,337 represents $2,047,337,000,000) except as indicated. **For fiscal year ending in year shown;** see text, this section. Local government amounts are estimates subject to sampling variation; see Appendix III and source. Minus sign (-) indicates net loss]

Item	Amount (mil. dol.) State and local	State	Local	Per capita [1] (dol.) State and local	State	Local
Revenue [2]	**2,047,337**	**1,295,659**	**1,140,633**	**7,041**	**4,464**	**3,923**
Intergovernmental revenue [2]	389,264	361,617	416,601	1,339	1,246	1,433
Total revenue from own sources [2]	1,658,073	934,042	724,032	5,702	3,218	2,490
General revenue from own sources	1,373,948	750,732	623,216	4,725	2,587	2,143
Taxes [3]	938,972	548,991	389,981	3,229	1,892	1,341
Property	296,683	10,471	286,213	1,020	36	984
Individual income	199,407	181,933	17,475	686	627	60
Corporation income	31,369	28,384	2,985	108	98	10
Sales and gross receipts	337,787	273,811	63,975	1,162	943	220
General sales	229,222	184,597	44,626	788	636	153
Selective sales [3]	108,564	89,215	19,350	373	307	67
Motor fuel	33,379	32,269	1,110	115	111	4
Alcoholic beverages	4,757	4,399	358	16	15	1
Tobacco products	11,807	11,482	325	41	40	1
Public utilities	21,015	10,557	10,458	72	36	36
Motor vehicle and operators' licenses	19,098	17,727	1,372	66	61	5
Death and gift	6,715	6,685	30	23	23	–
Charges and miscellaneous [3]	434,976	201,741	233,235	1,496	695	802
Current charges [3]	269,560	106,357	163,204	927	366	561
Education [3]	78,522	60,215	18,307	270	207	63
School lunch sales	6,074	19	6,055	21	–	21
Higher education	66,831	59,392	7,440	230	205	26
Natural resources	3,018	2,160	857	10	7	3
Hospitals	68,927	24,131	44,796	237	83	154
Sewerage	28,237	27	28,210	97	–	97
Solid waste management	11,559	416	11,143	40	1	38
Parks and recreation	7,342	1,202	6,140	25	4	21
Housing and community development	4,589	565	4,024	16	2	14
Airports	12,759	871	11,888	44	3	41
Sea and inland port facilities	2,930	809	2,121	10	3	7
Highways	8,503	5,351	3,152	29	18	11
Interest earnings	58,317	29,730	28,587	201	102	98
Special assessments	5,808	306	5,502	20	1	19
Sale of property	1,773	608	1,165	6	2	4
Utility and liquor store revenue	108,388	17,036	91,352	373	59	314
Insurance trust revenue	175,737	166,274	9,463	604	573	33
Expenditure [2]	**2,164,176**	**1,359,048**	**1,194,932**	**7,442**	**4,683**	**4,109**
Intergovernmental expenditure [2]	4,404	382,197	12,011	15	1,317	41
Direct expenditure [2]	2,159,772	976,852	1,182,920	7,427	3,366	4,068
General expenditure [3]	1,817,513	781,772	1,035,741	6,250	2,694	3,562
Education [3]	621,335	170,685	450,650	2,137	588	1,550
Elementary and secondary education	428,503	4,691	423,812	1,474	16	1,457
Higher education	164,187	137,349	26,838	565	473	92
Public welfare	306,463	265,105	41,358	1,054	913	142
Hospitals	93,175	38,023	55,152	320	131	190
Health	61,703	30,351	31,353	212	105	108
Highways	117,696	72,455	45,241	405	250	156
Police protection	67,361	9,860	57,501	232	34	198
Fire protection	27,854	–	27,854	96	–	96
Corrections	55,471	36,938	18,533	191	127	64
Natural resources	22,808	17,110	5,699	78	59	20
Sewerage	32,540	1,003	31,537	112	3	108
Solid waste management	19,183	2,693	16,491	66	9	57
Housing and community development	35,275	4,608	30,668	121	16	105
Governmental administration	98,658	42,846	55,813	339	148	192
Parks and recreation	31,765	4,636	27,129	109	16	93
Interest on general debt	77,277	31,295	45,982	266	108	158
Utility	144,594	22,405	122,189	497	77	420
Liquor store expenditure	4,402	3,697	706	15	13	2
Insurance trust expenditure	193,263	168,979	24,285	665	582	84
By character and object:						
Current operation	1,579,290	656,989	922,301	5,431	2,264	3,172
Capital outlay	263,198	91,943	171,255	905	317	589
Construction	203,035	72,374	130,661	698	249	449
Equipment, land, and existing structures	60,162	19,568	40,594	207	67	140
Assistance and subsidies	35,080	25,901	9,179	121	89	32
Interest on debt (general and utility)	88,940	33,040	55,900	306	114	192
Insurance benefits and repayments	193,263	168,979	24,285	665	582	84
Expenditure for salaries and wages [4]	*647,211*	*183,386*	*463,826*	*2,226*	*632*	*1,595*

– Represents or rounds to zero. [1] Based on estimated resident population as of July 1. [2] Aggregates exclude duplicative transactions between levels of government; see source. [3] Includes amounts not shown separately. [4] Included in items shown above.

Source: U.S. Census Bureau, "Federal, State, and Local Governments, Finance, State and Local Government Finances," 2002–03; see also <http://www.census.gov/govs/www/estimate03.html> (accessed 21 June 2005).

Table 426. State and Local Governments—Capital Outlays: 1990 to 2003

[In millions of dollars (123,102 represents $123,102,000,000), except percent. For fiscal year ending in year shown; see text, this section. Local government amounts are subject to sampling variation; see Appendix III and source]

Level and function	1990	1995	1998	1999	2000	2001	2002	2003
State & local governments: Total . . .	123,102	151,440	181,871	198,483	217,063	233,258	257,214	263,198
Annual percent change [1]	4.9	10.1	6.1	9.1	9.4	7.5	10.3	2.3
By function:								
Education [2]	25,997	35,708	49,332	54,418	60,968	65,116	71,533	70,813
Elementary and secondary. . . .	18,057	24,808	36,198	40,768	45,150	48,404	53,151	51,118
Higher education	7,441	10,461	12,590	13,114	15,257	15,911	17,648	19,044
Highways.	33,867	42,561	48,067	51,906	56,439	60,108	66,170	65,523
Health and hospitals	3,848	4,883	5,692	5,699	5,502	5,630	6,136	7,158
Natural resources	2,545	2,891	3,206	3,359	4,347	4,908	4,247	4,244
Housing [3]	3,997	4,527	5,544	5,615	6,184	5,888	6,939	7,660
Air transportation	3,434	3,802	5,004	6,666	6,717	8,420	8,551	9,066
Water transportation [4]	924	1,101	1,252	1,487	1,618	4,306	1,691	3,721
Sewerage	8,356	8,894	9,061	9,718	10,093	9,224	11,574	12,467
Parks and recreation	3,877	4,085	6,154	6,486	6,916	8,540	9,093	9,224
Utilities	16,601	19,028	20,357	21,861	24,847	24,553	30,228	34,538
Water.	6,873	7,466	8,644	10,325	10,542	10,742	11,818	13,536
Electric.	3,976	3,715	3,026	3,613	4,177	4,812	6,538	6,438
Gas.	310	340	986	389	400	453	358	422
Transit	5,443	7,507	7,701	7,533	9,728	8,545	11,514	14,142
Other	19,657	23,961	28,202	31,268	33,431	36,566	41,053	38,784
State governments: Total.	45,524	57,829	64,441	68,509	76,233	81,881	89,919	91,943
Annual percent change [1]	5.6	9.3	8.1	6.3	11.3	7.4	9.8	2.3
By function:								
Education [2]	7,253	10,042	11,970	12,294	14,077	14,936	16,589	17,727
Highways	24,850	31,687	35,008	37,986	41,651	44,761	49,272	48,719
Health and hospitals	1,531	2,402	2,274	2,276	2,228	2,390	2,240	2,930
Natural resources	1,593	1,956	2,199	2,349	2,758	3,105	2,766	2,788
Housing [3]	119	187	202	202	860	600	582	774
Air transportation	339	356	339	536	561	667	525	846
Water transportation [4]	202	223	305	270	310	362	346	410
Sewerage	333	853	639	627	403	393	405	405
Parks and recreation	601	650	1,293	1,023	1,044	1,185	1,483	1,098
Utilities	2,605	2,226	2,758	3,034	4,232	3,641	5,145	7,084
Other	6,098	7,246	7,454	7,912	8,108	9,840	10,567	9,163
Local governments: Total	77,578	93,611	117,430	129,974	140,830	151,377	167,295	171,255
Annual percent change [1]	4.5	10.6	5.0	10.7	8.4	7.5	10.5	2.4
By function:								
Education [2]	18,744	29,858	37,362	42,124	46,890	50,180	54,944	53,087
Elementary and secondary. . . .	17,669	28,402	35,763	40,160	44,629	47,808	52,661	50,475
Higher education	1,076	1,456	1,600	1,964	2,261	2,372	2,283	2,612
Highways.	9,017	10,874	13,059	13,920	14,789	15,347	16,898	16,804
Health and hospitals	2,316	2,481	3,418	3,423	3,274	3,239	3,895	4,228
Natural resources	952	935	1,007	1,010	1,589	1,803	1,481	1,456
Housing [3]	3,878	4,340	5,342	5,413	5,324	5,288	6,357	6,886
Air transportation	3,095	3,446	4,665	6,129	6,156	7,753	8,026	8,221
Water transportation [4]	722	877	947	1,217	1,308	3,944	1,345	3,310
Sewerage	8,023	8,040	8,422	9,091	9,690	8,831	11,169	12,062
Parks and recreation	3,276	3,435	4,861	5,463	5,872	7,355	7,611	8,126
Utilities	13,996	16,801	17,599	18,827	20,615	20,912	25,083	27,455
Other	13,559	16,715	20,748	23,356	25,323	26,726	30,486	29,621

[1] Change from immediate/prior year except 1990, change from 1989. [2] Includes other education. [3] Includes community development. [4] Includes terminals.

Source: U.S. Census Bureau , "Federal, State, and Local Governments, Finance, State and Local Government Finances," 2002–03, and unpublished data; see also <http://www.census.gov/govs/www/estimate03.html> (accessed 21 June 2005).

Table 427. State and Local Governments—Expenditure for Public Works: 1995 to 2003

[In millions of dollars (180,148 represents $180,148,000,000), except as noted. Public works include expenditures for current operations and capital outlays on highways, airports, water transport terminals, and sewerage, solid waste management, water supply, and mass transit systems. Represents direct expenditures excluding intergovernmental grants]

Item	Total	Highways	Airport transportation	Water transport and terminals	Sewerage	Solid waste management	Water supply	Mass transit
1995, Total	180,148	77,109	8,397	2,309	23,583	14,990	28,041	25,719
State	56,392	46,893	783	604	1,462	1,658	178	4,814
Local	123,756	30,216	7,614	1,706	22,121	13,331	27,863	20,904
Capital expenditures (percent) . .	40.7	55.2	45.3	47.7	37.7	13.2	26.6	29.2
2000, Total	230,569	101,336	13,160	3,141	28,052	17,208	35,789	31,883
State	74,974	61,942	1,106	863	955	2,347	354	7,407
Local	155,595	39,394	12,054	2,277	27,098	14,861	35,435	24,476
Capital expenditures (percent) . .	41.9	55.7	51.0	51.5	36.0	8.9	29.5	30.5
2003, Total	277,278	117,696	17,046	5,875	32,540	19,183	43,260	41,678
State	89,911	72,455	1,565	1,150	1,003	2,693	353	10,694
Local	187,367	45,241	15,481	4,725	31,537	16,491	42,908	30,985
Capital expenditures (percent) . .	43.2	55.7	53.2	63.3	38.3	7.6	31.3	33.9

Source: U.S. Census Bureau, "Federal, State, and Local Governments, Finance, State and Local Government Finances," 2002–03, and unpublished data; see also <http://www.census.gov/govs/www/estimate03.html> (accessed 21 June 2005).

State and Local Government Finances and Employment 273

Table 428. **State and Local Governments—Indebtedness: 1980 to 2003**

[In billions of dollars (335.6 represents $335,600,000,000), except per capita. For fiscal year ending in year shown; see text, this section. Local government amounts are estimates subject to sampling variation; see Appendix III and source]

Item	Debt outstanding						Long-term		
				Long-term					
	Total	Per capita [1] (dol.)	Local schools [2]	Utilities	All other	Short-term	Net long-term [3]	Debt issued	Debt retired
1980: Total........	335.6	1,481	32.3	55.2	235.0	13.1	262.9	42.4	17.4
State......	122.0	540	3.8	4.6	111.5	2.1	79.8	16.4	5.7
Local......	213.6	943	28.5	50.6	123.5	11.0	183.1	25.9	11.7
1990: Total........	858.0	3,449	60.4	134.8	643.5	19.3	474.4	108.5	64.8
State......	318.3	1,282	4.4	12.3	298.7	2.8	125.5	43.5	22.9
Local......	539.8	2,169	56.0	122.4	344.8	16.5	348.9	65.0	42.0
1991: Total........	915.8	3,632	71.0	141.2	681.8	21.7	509.9	118.1	65.7
State......	345.6	1,374	5.9	12.5	323.7	3.4	139.9	50.5	25.4
Local......	570.2	2,261	65.1	128.7	358.1	18.3	369.9	67.6	40.3
1992: Total........	970.5	3,806	78.4	150.4	720.4	21.3	561.6	155.1	99.2
State......	372.3	1,463	7.6	13.7	348.1	2.9	125.4	70.2	45.0
Local......	598.1	2,345	70.9	136.7	373.1	18.4	409.1	85.0	54.3
1993: Total........	1,017.7	3,943	89.8	157.6	747.5	22.7	617.1	195.6	147.0
State......	389.7	1,515	9.4	14.8	361.7	3.9	176.9	77.1	60.7
Local......	628.0	2,436	80.5	142.8	385.8	18.8	440.1	118.4	86.3
1994: Total........	1,074.7	4,128	94.3	164.9	788.8	26.7	672.8	207.8	166.6
State......	411.0	1,582	10.4	16.7	379.0	4.9	200.8	78.5	61.3
Local......	663.7	2,549	83.9	148.2	409.7	21.8	472.0	129.3	105.3
1995: Total........	1,115.4	4,244	118.2	163.9	806.2	27.0	697.3	129.3	95.1
State......	427.2	1,629	11.3	17.0	392.8	6.1	205.3	52.6	37.5
Local......	688.1	2,618	107.0	146.9	413.4	20.9	491.9	76.8	57.6
1996: Total........	1,169.7	4,410	130.7	170.3	844.7	24.0	751.6	141.1	106.5
State......	452.4	1,709	11.2	16.3	419.1	5.8	220.3	60.2	42.4
Local......	717.3	2,705	119.5	154.0	425.6	18.2	531.3	80.9	64.1
1997: Total........	1,224.5	4,573	139.0	179.1	889.8	16.6	797.7	151.3	109.3
State......	456.7	1,709	11.7	16.0	426.8	2.1	222.7	54.4	41.1
Local......	767.9	2,867	127.3	163.1	463.0	14.5	575.1	96.8	68.2
1998: Total........	1,283.6	4,750	159.2	182.8	924.3	17.3	842.6	204.4	144.6
State......	483.1	1,791	13.6	16.7	450.6	2.2	237.2	83.4	58.1
Local......	800.4	2,962	145.5	166.1	473.8	15.1	605.4	120.9	86.5
1999: Total........	1,369.3	5,021	180.7	194.9	975.7	17.8	907.3	229.4	153.1
State......	510.5	1,876	15.4	16.7	475.8	2.7	249.4	83.2	55.6
Local......	858.8	3,149	165.3	178.3	500.0	15.2	657.9	146.2	97.5
2000: Total........	1,451.8	5,159	197.7	200.1	1,029.8	24.3	959.6	184.8	121.9
State......	547.9	1,951	18.7	17.9	505.0	6.4	266.9	75.0	44.4
Local......	903.9	3,212	179.0	182.2	524.8	17.9	692.7	109.8	77.5
2001: Total........	1,554.0	5,447	225.3	210.4	1,096.2	22.1	1,038.6	199.6	130.6
State......	576.5	2,025	21.5	18.7	532.6	3.7	287.4	81.3	50.7
Local......	977.5	3,426	203.8	191.7	563.5	18.5	751.2	118.3	79.9
2002: Total........	1,686.1	5,855	250.2	218.5	1,174.2	43.2	1,126.6	262.3	162.5
State......	642.2	2,234	23.8	26.1	573.6	18.6	317.8	103.7	65.3
Local......	1,043.9	3,625	226.4	192.4	600.5	24.6	808.8	158.6	97.2
2003: Total........	1,812.7	6,234	272.7	238.4	1,261.1	40.5	1,242.7	345.8	215.2
State......	697.9	2,405	24.0	36.1	621.7	16.1	366.2	148.8	85.9
Local......	1,114.7	3,833	248.7	202.3	639.4	24.3	876.5	196.9	129.3

[1] 1980, 1990, and 2000 based on enumerated resident population as of April 1; other years based on estimated resident population as of July 1. [2] Includes debt for education activities other than higher education. [3] Net long-term debt outstanding is the amount of long-term debt held by a government for which no funds have been set aside for its repayment.

Source: U.S. Census Bureau, 1990, *Government Finances*, Series GF, No. 5, annual; thereafter, "Federal, State, and Local Governments, Finance, State and Local Government Finances," 2002–03, and unpublished data. See also <http://www.census.gov /govs/www/estimate03.html> (accessed 21 June 2005).

Table 429. **New Security Issues, State and Local Governments: 1990 to 2005**

[In billions of dollars, (122.9 represents 122,900,000,000)]

Type of issue, issuer, or use	1990	1995	1998	1999	2000	2001	2002	2003	2004	2005
All issues, new and refunding [1].......	122.9	145.7	262.3	215.4	180.4	291.9	363.9	384.3	357.9	409.5
By type of issue:										
General obligation.................	39.5	57.0	87.0	73.3	64.5	118.6	145.3	144.1	130.5	146.2
Revenue........................	83.3	88.7	175.3	142.1	115.9	170.0	214.8	238.0	227.4	263.3
By type of issuer:										
State...........................	15.0	14.7	23.5	16.4	19.9	30.1	33.9	49.8	47.4	31.6
Special district of statutory authority [2]....	75.9	93.5	178.4	152.4	121.2	197.5	259.1	253.5	234.2	297.0
Municipality, county, or township.........	32.0	37.5	60.2	46.6	39.3	61.0	67.1	79.0	76.3	80.9
Issues for new capital..............	97.9	102.4	160.6	161.1	154.3	200.3	242.9	264.7	228.4	224.7
By use of proceeds:										
Education.......................	17.1	24.0	36.9	36.6	38.7	50.1	57.9	70.4	65.4	71.4
Transportation....................	11.8	11.9	19.9	17.4	19.7	21.4	22.1	23.8	20.5	25.3
Utilities and conservation.............	10.0	9.6	21.0	15.1	11.9	21.9	33.4	10.3	9.2	9.9
Industrial aid....................	6.6	6.6	8.6	9.1	7.1	6.6	7.2	22.3	19.1	18.7
Other purposes...................	31.7	30.8	42.5	47.9	47.3	55.7	73.0	97.7	80.4	60.9

[1] Par amounts of long-term issues based on date of sale. [2] Includes school districts.

Source: Board of Governors of the Federal Reserve System, *Statistical Supplement to the Federal Reserve Bulletin*, monthly. Based on data from Securities Data Company, <http://www.federalreserve.gov/pubs/supplement/2006/04/default.htm>.

274   State and Local Government Finances and Employment

U.S. Census Bureau. Statistical Abstract of the United States: 2007

Table 430. **State and Local Governments—Summary of Finances by State: 2002**

[In millions of dollars (1,807,573 represents $1,807,573,000,000), except as indicated. For fiscal year ending in year shown; see text, this section]

State	Revenue [1]						Expenditures		Debt outstanding	
	All revenue		General revenue		Taxes		Direct general expenditures	Per capita [2] (dol.)	Total	Per capita [2] (dol.)
	Total	Per capita [2] (dol.)	Total	Per capita [2] (dol.)	Total	Per capita [2] (dol.)				
United States ..	1,807,573	6,277	1,684,776	5,850	904,971	3,143	1,730,809	6,010	1,686,106	5,855
Alabama........	24,740	5,524	23,741	5,301	9,719	2,170	24,605	5,493	19,057	4,255
Alaska	6,993	10,909	7,209	11,246	2,070	3,229	8,443	13,172	8,646	13,488
Arizona........	30,083	5,529	25,524	4,691	14,420	2,650	25,252	4,641	26,606	4,890
Arkansas	13,616	5,032	13,260	4,900	6,461	2,388	13,068	4,829	8,754	3,235
California	250,725	7,163	226,644	6,475	120,424	3,440	235,627	6,732	209,299	5,980
Colorado.......	25,657	5,700	26,041	5,786	13,900	3,088	27,099	6,021	26,718	5,936
Connecticut.....	24,831	7,179	22,805	6,593	15,125	4,373	24,199	6,996	27,767	8,028
Delaware	5,972	7,410	5,600	6,948	2,687	3,334	5,357	6,646	5,533	6,864
District of Columbia	7,352	12,921	6,922	12,166	3,228	5,673	6,180	10,860	5,436	9,554
Florida	92,631	5,549	86,663	5,192	44,840	2,686	87,082	5,217	90,276	5,408
Georgia	46,166	5,403	44,360	5,192	24,058	2,816	44,951	5,261	34,301	4,015
Hawaii	7,452	6,005	7,429	5,986	4,240	3,416	8,289	6,680	8,448	6,808
Idaho..........	6,873	5,117	6,620	4,929	3,291	2,451	6,804	5,066	3,985	2,967
Illinois	73,588	5,847	69,098	5,490	41,570	3,303	73,819	5,865	80,936	6,431
Indiana........	34,221	5,558	32,363	5,256	16,987	2,759	32,796	5,327	24,071	3,910
Iowa	17,601	5,995	16,871	5,746	8,330	2,837	17,186	5,854	9,494	3,234
Kansas	15,985	5,894	14,635	5,396	7,975	2,941	14,876	5,485	12,313	4,540
Kentucky.......	22,475	5,495	21,231	5,191	10,781	2,636	21,592	5,279	28,994	7,089
Louisiana	27,373	6,115	26,048	5,819	12,182	2,722	24,321	5,434	20,986	4,688
Maine..........	8,019	6,193	8,077	6,237	4,541	3,507	7,948	6,137	6,346	4,901
Maryland	33,468	6,140	32,319	5,929	19,874	3,646	31,796	5,833	25,663	4,708
Massachusetts....	41,925	6,528	39,002	6,073	23,895	3,721	42,347	6,594	65,322	10,172
Michigan.......	63,099	6,283	57,942	5,769	30,644	3,051	60,723	6,046	54,195	5,396
Minnesota......	35,131	6,991	33,193	6,606	18,456	3,673	34,933	6,952	32,010	6,370
Mississippi	15,905	5,548	15,293	5,334	6,524	2,275	15,384	5,366	9,934	3,465
Missouri	30,621	5,400	29,062	5,126	15,123	2,667	29,045	5,123	24,244	4,276
Montana........	5,511	6,056	5,122	5,629	2,135	2,346	5,051	5,550	3,963	4,355
Nebraska	12,031	6,962	9,821	5,684	5,316	3,077	9,745	5,640	7,906	4,575
Nevada	12,809	5,911	11,417	5,269	6,433	2,968	11,766	5,430	15,773	7,279
New Hampshire...	6,729	5,281	6,406	5,028	3,599	2,825	6,343	4,979	7,221	5,668
New Jersey......	54,835	6,395	55,256	6,444	34,629	4,038	54,387	6,343	57,590	6,716
New Mexico	11,503	6,211	10,868	5,868	4,878	2,634	11,436	6,175	8,603	4,645
New York	170,982	8,936	155,541	8,129	88,878	4,645	161,130	8,421	197,195	10,306
North Carolina....	48,597	5,851	44,165	5,317	22,576	2,718	44,540	5,362	33,461	4,028
North Dakota.....	4,227	6,666	3,994	6,300	1,729	2,727	3,886	6,130	2,905	4,582
Ohio	72,627	6,366	65,568	5,747	36,165	3,170	67,047	5,877	51,344	4,500
Oklahoma.......	19,161	5,490	18,061	5,175	8,782	2,516	18,154	5,202	12,508	3,584
Oregon.........	23,201	6,591	21,625	6,144	9,003	2,558	22,990	6,531	18,827	5,349
Pennsylvania.....	73,694	5,977	71,961	5,837	37,627	3,052	73,312	5,946	83,809	6,798
Rhode Island.....	6,862	6,425	6,636	6,214	3,622	3,392	6,756	6,326	7,345	6,877
South Carolina....	24,985	6,088	21,239	5,175	9,752	2,376	23,820	5,804	22,873	5,573
South Dakota	3,964	5,216	3,902	5,134	1,841	2,423	3,885	5,111	3,451	4,540
Tennessee	33,483	5,783	27,484	4,747	12,974	2,241	28,952	5,000	21,128	3,649
Texas..........	114,018	5,245	109,128	5,020	58,981	2,713	111,604	5,134	122,810	5,650
Utah	13,789	5,946	12,499	5,390	6,026	2,599	12,861	5,546	13,250	5,714
Vermont	4,046	6,568	3,857	6,262	1,965	3,190	3,805	6,177	3,028	4,915
Virginia........	38,780	5,321	39,026	5,355	22,131	3,037	39,267	5,388	35,422	4,860
Washington......	42,124	6,943	36,345	5,991	19,514	3,216	38,646	6,370	45,561	7,510
West Virginia....	11,345	6,285	10,111	5,602	4,641	2,571	9,848	5,456	8,085	4,479
Wisconsin.......	31,424	5,776	32,555	5,984	18,610	3,421	34,003	6,251	30,327	5,575
Wyoming	4,346	8,710	4,237	8,491	1,818	3,644	3,853	7,722	2,388	4,786

[1] Includes items not shown separately.   [2] Based on estimated resident population as of July 1, see Table 17.

Source: U.S. Census Bureau; *Federal, State, and Local Governments, State and Local Government Finances* Census of Governments. <http://www.census.gov/govs/estimate/02.html>; (accessed 8 April 2005).

State and Local Government Finances and Employment   275

Table 431. **State and Local Governments—Revenue by State: 2002**

[In millions of dollars (1,807,573 represents $1,807,573,000,000). **For fiscal year ending in year shown;** see text, this section minus sign (-) indicates net loss]

State	Total revenue [1]	General revenue			Taxes					
		Total	Intergovernmental from federal government	General revenue own sources	Total [1]	Property	Sales and gross receipts	Individual income [2]	Motor vehicle	Other taxes
United States ..	1,807,573	1,684,776	360,534	1,324,241	904,971	279,122	324,040	231,010	16,944	53,856
Alabama	24,740	23,741	6,263	17,478	9,719	1,474	4,800	2,449	207	789
Alaska	6,993	7,209	1,789	5,420	2,070	830	311	269	47	613
Arizona	30,083	25,524	5,719	19,805	14,420	4,254	7,081	2,437	153	495
Arkansas	13,616	13,260	3,645	9,614	6,461	1,004	3,340	1,743	107	267
California	250,725	226,644	48,250	178,394	120,424	30,243	41,560	38,380	1,740	8,502
Colorado	25,657	26,041	4,269	21,772	13,900	4,162	5,302	3,681	184	571
Connecticut	24,831	22,805	4,039	18,766	15,125	5,995	4,516	3,835	241	538
Delaware	5,972	5,600	959	4,641	2,687	400	326	1,015	32	914
District of Columbia	7,352	6,922	2,840	4,082	3,228	803	936	1,160	19	309
Florida	92,631	86,663	14,956	71,707	44,840	15,754	22,936	1,219	957	3,974
Georgia	46,166	44,360	9,357	35,002	24,058	6,640	9,395	7,056	269	699
Hawaii	7,452	7,429	1,547	5,881	4,240	615	2,244	1,164	133	83
Idaho	6,873	6,620	1,415	5,204	3,291	959	1,135	919	116	162
Illinois	73,588	69,098	12,717	56,382	41,570	15,873	13,876	8,855	1,458	1,508
Indiana	34,221	32,363	6,283	26,080	16,987	5,976	5,522	4,831	301	357
Iowa	17,601	16,871	3,626	13,245	8,330	2,878	2,886	1,903	378	285
Kansas	15,985	14,635	3,098	11,537	7,975	2,525	3,066	1,977	145	262
Kentucky	22,475	21,231	5,414	15,817	10,781	1,977	3,942	3,798	214	849
Louisiana	27,373	26,048	6,485	19,563	12,182	1,940	6,949	2,053	118	1,121
Maine	8,019	8,077	1,901	6,176	4,541	1,912	1,242	1,150	105	132
Maryland	33,468	32,319	5,927	26,391	19,874	5,412	4,974	8,004	200	1,285
Massachusetts . . .	41,925	39,002	6,176	32,826	23,895	8,722	5,363	8,725	270	815
Michigan	63,099	57,942	12,543	45,398	30,644	9,793	10,238	8,663	891	1,059
Minnesota	35,131	33,193	6,088	27,105	18,456	5,215	5,918	5,977	497	850
Mississippi	15,905	15,293	4,625	10,667	6,524	1,647	3,255	1,181	112	329
Missouri	30,621	29,062	7,329	21,733	15,123	3,880	6,044	4,229	249	721
Montana	5,511	5,122	1,590	3,532	2,135	852	374	586	127	196
Nebraska	12,031	9,821	1,973	7,848	5,316	1,749	1,819	1,261	104	383
Nevada	12,809	11,417	1,632	9,785	6,433	1,702	3,840	–	130	761
New Hampshire. . .	6,729	6,406	1,296	5,110	3,599	2,169	605	449	77	299
New Jersey	54,835	55,256	8,949	46,307	34,629	16,050	8,804	7,969	372	1,435
New Mexico	11,503	10,868	3,124	7,744	4,878	756	2,319	1,107	119	576
New York	170,982	155,541	36,186	119,356	88,878	26,826	22,491	35,283	808	3,471
North Carolina. . . .	48,597	44,165	10,241	33,924	22,576	5,422	7,852	7,933	437	932
North Dakota	4,227	3,994	1,156	2,838	1,729	532	689	250	52	206
Ohio	72,627	65,568	13,863	51,704	36,165	10,643	10,766	12,555	718	1,483
Oklahoma	19,161	18,061	4,413	13,648	8,782	1,482	3,446	2,460	570	824
Oregon	23,201	21,625	6,438	15,187	9,003	3,139	889	3,871	275	829
Pennsylvania	73,694	71,961	16,026	55,935	37,627	10,911	11,291	10,708	771	3,945
Rhode Island . . .	6,862	6,636	1,766	4,870	3,622	1,462	1,164	852	53	91
South Carolina . . .	24,985	21,239	5,333	15,907	9,752	3,096	3,425	2,509	110	611
South Dakota	3,964	3,902	1,150	2,752	1,841	668	930	41	66	137
Tennessee	33,483	27,484	7,604	19,880	12,974	3,453	7,461	649	342	1,069
Texas	114,018	109,128	22,915	86,214	58,981	24,521	28,639	–	1,292	4,528
Utah	13,789	12,499	2,613	9,886	6,026	1,420	2,619	1,716	86	186
Vermont	4,046	3,857	1,087	2,770	1,965	824	573	445	41	83
Virginia	38,780	39,026	6,235	32,791	22,131	6,711	6,542	7,020	447	1,411
Washington	42,124	36,345	7,042	29,303	19,514	5,791	11,976	–	338	1,410
West Virginia	11,345	10,111	2,999	7,112	4,641	901	1,980	1,255	88	418
Wisconsin.	31,424	32,555	6,456	26,100	18,610	6,466	5,698	5,419	314	713
Wyoming	4,346	4,237	1,187	3,050	1,818	692	691	–	63	372

See footnote at end of table.

Table 431. **State and Local Governments—Revenue by State: 2002—Con.**

[See headnote page 276]

State	General revenue								Utility and liquor stores	Insurance trust revenue
	Current charges and miscellaneous revenue									
		Current charges				Miscellaneous revenue				
	Total	Total [1]	Education	Hospitals	Sewerage	Total [1]	Interest earnings	Special assessments		
United States ..	419,270	253,193	72,401	65,645	27,089	166,077	67,078	4,779	107,387	15,410
Alabama	7,759	5,992	1,457	3,519	257	1,767	678	3	2,138	−1,140
Alaska	3,350	696	146	65	53	2,654	1,226	8	225	−441
Arizona	5,385	2,893	1,099	265	386	2,492	1,064	73	3,193	1,367
Arkansas	3,153	1,960	707	640	171	1,194	493	8	595	−238
California	57,970	36,003	7,950	7,952	3,585	21,967	9,107	1,205	21,061	3,020
Colorado	7,872	4,603	1,618	834	488	3,269	1,323	142	1,755	−2,140
Connecticut	3,641	1,763	558	342	189	1,878	737	25	508	1,518
Delaware	1,954	908	313	33	113	1,046	364	1	170	202
District of Columbia	854	302	18	–	92	553	132	1	499	−69
Florida	26,867	15,022	2,741	3,635	1,614	11,844	4,333	1,207	5,689	278
Georgia	10,944	6,963	1,468	2,978	650	3,981	1,466	21	3,109	−1,303
Hawaii	1,642	1,037	224	180	145	605	291	17	197	−174
Idaho.	1,913	1,299	280	516	104	614	318	28	206	47
Illinois	14,812	7,886	2,868	912	831	6,926	3,089	145	2,781	1,708
Indiana	9,093	5,763	2,263	1,774	750	3,331	1,000	26	1,720	138
Iowa	4,915	3,288	1,271	1,295	255	1,626	479	17	731	−1
Kansas	3,562	2,084	757	546	190	1,478	683	82	864	486
Kentucky	5,037	2,824	998	586	282	2,213	1,304	34	951	292
Louisiana	7,381	4,441	995	2,308	235	2,940	1,114	5	900	425
Maine	1,635	802	311	64	116	833	308	2	174	−231
Maryland	6,517	3,920	1,800	86	590	2,597	868	108	701	448
Massachusetts . . .	8,930	3,823	1,198	323	682	5,107	2,006	32	2,288	636
Michigan	14,754	9,324	3,644	1,912	1,118	5,430	2,194	182	2,241	2,916
Minnesota	8,649	4,874	1,429	1,034	613	3,775	1,393	276	1,581	356
Mississippi	4,144	3,066	777	1,605	139	1,077	399	8	780	−168
Missouri.	6,610	3,882	1,423	1,133	395	2,728	1,309	18	1,240	319
Montana	1,397	748	325	41	50	649	315	45	122	266
Nebraska	2,532	1,435	563	353	102	1,097	419	37	2,348	−139
Nevada	3,352	2,196	392	496	235	1,156	586	47	835	557
New Hampshire. . .	1,511	805	388	6	76	706	388	1	404	−81
New Jersey	11,678	6,802	1,948	783	1,135	4,876	1,574	21	1,314	−1,734
New Mexico	2,867	1,230	393	385	114	1,636	722	20	367	268
New York	30,477	18,180	2,846	5,137	1,456	12,297	4,516	97	9,446	5,994
North Carolina. . . .	11,348	8,543	2,075	3,787	962	2,804	1,341	14	2,891	1,541
North Dakota	1,109	706	285	5	30	403	150	46	76	156
Ohio	15,539	9,107	3,653	1,793	1,362	6,432	2,604	157	2,478	4,581
Oklahoma	4,866	3,265	1,344	791	231	1,601	610	5	1,048	52
Oregon	6,184	3,894	1,073	745	525	2,290	652	58	1,319	257
Pennsylvania	18,308	11,080	3,355	2,938	1,489	7,229	3,190	83	3,184	−1,451
Rhode Island	1,248	555	252	4	59	693	289	4	135	90
South Carolina . . .	6,155	4,579	1,202	2,215	262	1,576	681	27	2,212	1,533
South Dakota	910	424	190	29	45	486	253	4	176	−113
Tennessee	6,906	5,141	1,451	1,959	417	1,765	662	17	5,670	330
Texas	27,233	16,160	5,025	4,448	1,959	11,073	4,818	93	7,220	−2,330
Utah	3,860	2,504	955	629	163	1,356	480	22	1,577	−288
Vermont.	805	437	294	–	36	368	169	3	200	−12
Virginia	10,660	6,520	2,063	1,602	741	4,140	1,604	73	1,596	−1,842
Washington	9,790	6,599	1,799	1,534	907	3,191	1,340	104	5,163	616
West Virginia	2,471	1,310	450	260	123	1,160	467	10	195	1,039
Wisconsin.	7,490	4,857	1,635	752	532	2,632	1,180	110	957	−2,088
Wyoming	1,231	696	132	413	33	535	391	11	156	−46

– Represents or rounds to zero.   [1] Includes items not shown separately.   [2] Includes individual and corporate income taxes.

Source: U.S. Census Bureau; *Federal, State, and Local Governments, State and Local Government Finances* Census of Governments. <http://www.census.gov/govs/estimate/02.html>;(accessed 8 April 2005).

State and Local Government Finances and Employment   277

Table 432. **State and Local Governments—Expenditures and Debt by State: 2002**

[In millions of dollars (2,048,719 represents $2,048,719,000,000), except as indicated. For fiscal year ending in year shown; see text, this section]

State	Total expenditure [1]	Total		Direct general expenditures, total	Education and social services				Public safety		
		Amount	Per capita [2] (dol.)		Education	Public welfare	Health and hospitals	Highways	Police protection	Fire protection	Corrections
United States .	**2,048,719**	**1,735,196**	**6,026**	**1,730,809**	**594,591**	**279,598**	**146,380**	**115,467**	**64,492**	**25,978**	**54,687**
Alabama	28,531	24,605	5,493	24,605	8,320	4,162	4,082	1,668	710	279	460
Alaska	9,397	8,443	13,172	8,443	2,107	1,035	263	916	264	85	175
Arizona	31,308	25,252	4,641	25,252	8,796	3,286	1,209	1,913	1,259	485	1,122
Arkansas	14,570	13,068	4,829	13,068	4,783	2,593	915	1,307	403	148	369
California	293,424	238,503	6,814	235,627	76,827	35,559	20,961	11,467	10,147	4,170	9,012
Colorado	31,891	27,102	6,021	27,099	9,011	2,823	2,040	2,836	1,072	424	856
Connecticut	27,592	24,199	6,996	24,199	7,852	3,472	1,903	1,224	781	391	638
Delaware	5,947	5,358	6,647	5,357	1,937	659	327	464	191	24	245
District of Columbia	7,832	6,180	10,860	6,180	1,175	1,462	555	69	385	136	174
Florida	99,307	87,082	5,217	87,082	25,795	12,500	7,491	6,720	4,393	1,856	3,365
Georgia	52,310	44,951	5,261	44,951	17,366	6,159	4,832	2,939	1,555	636	1,765
Hawaii	9,402	8,304	6,691	8,289	2,257	1,141	652	419	255	104	157
Idaho	7,565	6,804	5,066	6,804	2,423	1,035	605	618	241	82	229
Illinois	87,401	73,822	5,865	73,819	25,953	9,861	5,199	5,676	3,226	1,358	1,879
Indiana	36,302	32,796	5,327	32,796	12,193	5,313	2,876	2,031	895	503	841
Iowa	19,294	17,229	5,868	17,186	6,467	2,682	1,886	1,762	458	161	330
Kansas	16,718	14,876	5,485	14,876	5,501	2,003	1,231	1,528	478	189	361
Kentucky	24,839	21,592	5,279	21,592	6,878	4,816	1,445	1,952	543	266	599
Louisiana	27,668	24,321	5,434	24,321	7,994	3,362	3,621	1,531	889	359	774
Maine	8,677	7,984	6,166	7,948	2,491	1,792	500	618	181	84	146
Maryland	35,577	31,796	5,833	31,796	12,142	4,737	1,490	1,855	1,335	523	1,257
Massachusetts . .	51,146	42,527	6,622	42,347	13,443	5,731	3,174	3,257	1,441	848	1,125
Michigan	69,533	60,783	6,052	60,723	23,745	9,837	5,347	3,219	1,976	681	2,109
Minnesota	40,516	34,933	6,952	34,933	11,266	7,473	1,965	2,681	1,019	265	649
Mississippi	17,285	15,384	5,366	15,384	5,101	3,236	2,140	1,236	461	173	323
Missouri	33,036	29,048	5,123	29,045	10,556	5,520	2,433	2,473	1,018	476	816
Montana	5,616	5,052	5,552	5,051	1,792	671	378	542	170	42	122
Nebraska	12,492	9,759	5,648	9,745	3,797	1,703	607	924	268	126	258
Nevada	13,971	11,774	5,433	11,766	3,679	1,120	923	1,271	650	285	503
New Hampshire . .	7,066	6,343	4,979	6,343	2,439	1,030	184	504	212	119	115
New Jersey	64,289	54,467	6,352	54,387	20,544	6,608	2,736	2,963	2,419	700	1,607
New Mexico	12,689	11,436	6,175	11,436	4,176	2,077	829	1,143	410	146	371
New York	198,536	161,740	8,453	161,130	47,723	32,503	13,008	7,078	6,719	2,452	4,663
North Carolina. . .	51,839	44,540	5,362	44,540	15,262	7,657	6,087	3,017	1,504	573	1,172
North Dakota . . .	4,190	3,886	6,130	3,886	1,311	664	104	461	77	26	60
Ohio	79,972	67,050	5,877	67,047	23,623	12,278	5,454	4,092	2,414	1,202	1,814
Oklahoma	20,776	18,196	5,214	18,154	6,904	3,192	1,305	1,544	569	295	560
Oregon	27,731	22,990	6,531	22,990	7,543	4,045	2,194	1,197	772	376	828
Pennsylvania . . .	86,262	73,670	5,975	73,312	24,296	14,486	5,153	5,290	2,448	482	2,451
Rhode Island . . .	7,939	6,784	6,352	6,756	2,180	1,667	299	331	239	189	158
South Carolina . .	28,106	23,820	5,804	23,820	8,380	4,374	3,143	1,491	722	232	570
South Dakota . . .	4,276	3,885	5,111	3,885	1,360	605	171	580	105	36	93
Tennessee	36,638	28,952	5,000	28,952	9,468	6,458	3,300	1,773	977	423	690
Texas	129,874	111,604	5,134	111,604	45,703	14,903	10,104	7,527	3,728	1,496	4,401
Utah	15,523	12,861	5,546	12,861	5,196	1,595	858	1,017	441	147	375
Vermont	4,218	3,815	6,193	3,805	1,460	757	88	362	92	35	80
Virginia	43,688	39,269	5,388	39,267	15,149	4,674	3,184	3,102	1,309	623	1,388
Washington	50,431	38,657	6,372	38,646	12,866	6,198	4,013	2,376	1,092	663	1,146
West Virginia . . .	11,930	9,848	5,456	9,848	3,519	2,139	516	1,041	187	66	202
Wisconsin	39,262	34,003	6,251	34,003	12,565	5,560	2,082	2,986	1,272	490	1,176
Wyoming	4,337	3,853	7,722	3,853	1,277	381	516	477	121	42	110

See footnotes at end of table.

Table 432. State and Local Governments—Expenditures and Debt by State: 2002—Con.

[See headnote page 278]

State	Environment and housing				Govern-mental adminis-tration	Interest on general debt	Other	Utility and liquor store expendi-tures	Em-ployee retire-ment expendi-tures	Debt out-stand-ing
	Sewer-age	Solid waste man-age-ment	Parks and recre-ation	Housing[3]						
United States ..	31,238	19,047	30,096	31,610	92,789	75,303	169,532	143,851	114,208	1,686,106
Alabama.........	612	234	340	404	955	819	1,558	2,160	1,429	19,057
Alaska	53	49	100	175	523	427	2,271	290	537	8,646
Arizona..........	547	341	643	300	1,644	1,091	2,615	4,122	1,353	26,606
Arkansas	190	148	163	158	672	416	803	594	592	8,754
California	3,964	2,697	4,173	5,381	15,640	8,683	26,947	28,814	17,123	209,299
Colorado........	512	81	975	445	1,461	1,258	3,305	2,380	1,834	26,718
Connecticut.....	268	372	301	440	1,358	1,429	3,769	829	1,774	27,767
Delaware	104	44	76	104	408	326	447	222	257	5,533
District of Columbia	211	43	303	88	383	236	959	1,490	13	5,436
Florida	1,714	1,852	1,837	1,179	4,886	4,176	9,317	7,190	3,632	90,276
Georgia	1,081	493	746	740	2,400	1,132	3,107	4,244	2,204	34,301
Hawaii	168	147	260	221	529	573	1,406	336	569	8,448
Idaho...........	154	87	109	31	419	210	561	202	295	3,985
Illinois	1,480	466	2,524	1,788	4,148	3,926	6,333	4,842	6,156	80,936
Indiana.........	866	230	471	589	1,906	1,176	2,907	1,782	1,093	24,071
Iowa	299	146	296	151	838	376	1,334	845	839	9,494
Kansas.........	190	100	196	138	943	633	1,385	834	709	12,313
Kentucky.......	441	203	259	178	1,011	1,490	1,512	1,188	1,447	28,994
Louisiana	349	269	410	369	1,401	1,054	1,936	1,046	2,017	20,986
Maine..........	117	104	56	130	424	329	978	154	412	6,346
Maryland	485	440	696	754	1,645	1,368	3,069	1,104	1,953	25,663
Massachusetts....	836	393	280	1,344	2,053	3,236	5,184	3,495	2,976	65,322
Michigan........	1,426	539	1,057	372	2,860	2,382	5,172	2,778	3,972	54,195
Minnesota.......	613	273	733	763	1,744	1,455	4,034	2,009	2,587	32,010
Mississippi	116	118	160	145	634	497	1,045	761	929	9,934
Missouri	456	143	430	467	1,303	1,038	1,916	1,518	1,848	24,244
Montana........	51	55	43	82	335	210	557	122	294	3,963
Nebraska.......	114	67	147	113	435	256	932	2,306	312	7,906
Nevada	178	19	381	195	910	676	976	1,260	549	15,773
New Hampshire...	74	79	64	155	361	406	603	354	265	7,221
New Jersey.....	1,112	1,048	961	941	2,801	2,377	7,569	3,024	4,080	57,590
New Mexico	119	105	205	92	626	378	759	382	745	8,603
New York.......	2,244	2,367	2,006	3,766	7,470	8,329	20,801	17,282	14,140	197,195
North Carolina....	651	623	645	760	1,744	1,343	3,503	3,693	2,330	33,461
North Dakota.....	31	34	95	53	180	150	641	89	123	2,905
Ohio	1,598	456	1,038	1,449	4,651	2,695	4,283	2,909	6,628	51,344
Oklahoma.......	269	162	302	178	865	523	1,487	1,088	1,109	12,508
Oregon.........	602	132	318	483	1,590	737	2,174	1,667	1,800	18,827
Pennsylvania.....	1,563	620	678	1,645	3,423	4,046	6,731	4,539	5,123	83,809
Rhode Island.....	82	105	64	156	372	324	591	233	546	7,345
South Carolina....	229	235	261	270	1,291	1,159	1,462	2,277	1,372	22,873
South Dakota	44	25	104	51	199	173	339	164	198	3,451
Tennessee	366	317	442	496	1,247	922	2,074	5,808	1,185	21,128
Texas..........	1,777	907	2,050	1,564	4,509	4,999	7,935	9,107	6,910	122,810
Utah	237	111	323	180	915	425	1,040	1,796	452	13,250
Vermont........	42	35	31	90	255	164	315	224	97	3,028
Virginia	751	550	632	702	2,251	1,706	3,245	1,838	1,914	35,422
Washington.....	911	493	866	897	1,742	1,539	3,844	6,775	1,841	45,561
West Virginia.....	124	60	113	114	636	446	686	261	493	8,085
Wisconsin.......	776	396	655	314	1,551	1,457	2,725	1,239	2,980	30,327
Wyoming	44	36	78	9	243	128	391	185	172	2,388

[1] Includes items not shown separately. [2] Based on estimated resident population as of July 1; see Table 17. [3] Includes community development.

Source: U.S. Census Bureau; *Federal, State, and Local Governments, State and Local Government Finances* Census of Governments. <http://www.census.gov/govs/estimate/02.html>;(accessed 8 April 2005).

Table 433. **Bond Ratings for State Governments by State: 2005**

[As of fourth quarter. Key to investment grade ratings are in declining order of quality. The ratings from AA to CCC may be modified by the addition of a (+) or (−) sign to show relative standing within the major rating categories. *S&P:* AAA, AA, A, BBB, BB, B, CCC, CC, C; *Moody's:* Aaa, Aa, A, Baa, Ba, B, Caa, Ca, C; Numerical modifiers 1, 2, and 3 are added to letter-rating. *Fitch:* AAA, AA, A, BBB, BB, B, CCC, CC, CC, C]

State	Standard & Poor's	Moody's	Fitch	State	Standard & Poor's	Moody's	Fitch
Alabama	AA	Aa2	AA	Montana	AA−	Aa3	(NA)
Alaska	AA	Aa2	AA	Nebraska	(¹)	(NA)	(NA)
Arizona	AA	²Aa3	(NA)	Nevada	AA	Aa1	(NA)
Arkansas	AA	Aa2	(NA)	New Hampshire	AA	Aa2	AA
California	A	A2	A	New Jersey	AA	Aa3	AA−
Colorado	AA−	(NA)	(NA)	New Mexico	AA+	Aa1	(NA)
Connecticut	AA	Aa3	AA	New York	AA	Aa3	AA−
Delaware	AAA	Aaa	AAA	North Carolina	AAA	Aa1	AAA
Florida	AAA	Aa1	AA+	North Dakota	AA	²Aa2	(NA)
Georgia	AAA	Aaa	AAA	Ohio	AA+	Aa1	AA+
Hawaii	AA−	Aa2	AA	Oklahoma	AA	Aa3	AA
Idaho	AA−	²Aa2	(NA)	Oregon	AA−	Aa3	AA−
Illinois	AA	Aa3	AA	Pennsylvania	AA	Aa2	(NA)
Indiana	AA+	²Aa1	AAA	Rhode Island	AA	Aa3	AA
Iowa	AA+	²Aa1	(NA)	South Carolina	AA+	Aaa	AAA
Kansas	AA+	²Aa1	(NA)	South Dakota	(¹)	(NA)	(NA)
Kentucky	AA−	²Aa2	(NA)	Tennessee	AA	Aa2	AA+
Louisiana	A	A2	A	Texas	AA	Aa1	AA+
Maine	AA−	Aa3	AA	Utah	AAA	Aaa	AAA
Maryland	AAA	Aaa	AAA	Vermont	AA+	Aa1	AA+
Massachusetts	AA	Aa2	(NA)	Virginia	AAA	Aaa	(NA)
Michigan	AA	Aa2	AA	Washington	AA	Aa1	AA
Minnesota	AAA	Aa1	AAA	West Virginia	AA−	Aa3	AA−
Mississippi	AA	Aa3	AA	Wisconsin	AA−	Aa3	AA−
Missouri	AAA	Aaa	AAA	Wyoming	AA	(NA)	(NA)

NA Not available.   ¹ Not reviewed.   ² Issuer rating.

Sources: Standard & Poor's, New York, NY (copyright), <http://www2.standardandpoors.com/servlet/Satellite?pagename=sp /Page/HomePg>; Moody's Investors Service, New York, NY (copyright), <http://www.moodys.com/cust/defaultalt.asp>; Fitch Ratings, New York, NY (copyright), <http://www.fitchratings.com/>.

Table 434. **Bond Ratings for City Governments by Largest Cities: 2005**

[As of fourth quarter. See headnote in table 433]

Cities ranked by 2000 population	Standard & Poor's	Moody's	Fitch	Cities ranked by 2000 population	Standard & Poor's	Moody's	Fitch
New York, NY	A+	A1	A+	Oakland, CA	A+	A1	A+
Los Angeles, CA.	AA	Aa2	AA	Mesa, AZ	AA−	A1	(NA)
Chicago, IL	AA−	Aa3	AA	Tulsa, OK	AA	Aa2	(NA)
Houston, TX	AA−	Aa3	AA−	Omaha, NE	AAA	Aaa	(NA)
Philadelphia, PA	BBB	Baa1	(NA)	Minneapolis, MN	AAA	Aa1	(NA)
Phoenix, AZ	AA+	Aa1	(NA)	Honolulu, HI	AA−	Aa2	AA
San Diego, CA	(¹)	A3	BBB+	Miami, FL	A+	A3	(NA)
Dallas, TX	AA+	Aa1	(NA)	Colorado Springs, CO	AA	Aa3	(NA)
San Antonio, TX	AA+	Aa2	(NA)	St. Louis, MO	A−	A3	A−
Detroit, MI	BBB	Baa2	(NA)	Wichita, KS	AA	Aa2	(NA)
San Jose, CA	AA+	Aa1	(NA)	Santa Ana, CA	(¹)	(NA)	(NA)
Indianapolis, IN	AAA	(NA)	(NA)	Pittsburgh, PA	BBB−	Baa3	BBB
San Francisco, CA	AA	Aa3	AA−	Arlington, TX	AA	Aa2	(NA)
Jacksonville, FL	(¹)	Aa2	(NA)	Cincinnati, OH	AA+	Aa1	(NA)
Columbus, OH	AAA	Aaa	(NA)	Anaheim, CA	AA	Aa2	(NA)
Austin, TX	AA+	Aa2	(NA)	Toledo, OH	A	A3	(NA)
Baltimore, MD	A+	A1	A+	Tampa, FL	A	Aa3	(NA)
Memphis, TN	A+	A1	AA−	Buffalo, NY	BBB−	Baa3	(NA)
Milwaukee, WI	AA	Aa2	AA+	St. Paul, MN	AAA	Aa2	AA+
Boston, MA	AA	Aa1	AA	Corpus Christi, TX	A+	A1	AA−
Washington, DC	A+	A2	(NA)	Aurora, CO	AA	Aa2	(NA)
El Paso, TX	AA	Aa3	(NA)	Raleigh, NC	AAA	Aaa	AAA
Seattle, WA	AAA	Aaa	(NA)	Newark, NJ	AA	Baa2	(NA)
Denver, CO	AA+	Aa1	(NA)	Lexington-Fayette, KY	AA+	(NA)	(NA)
Nashville-Davidson, TN	AA	Aa2	(NA)	Anchorage, AK	(¹)	Aa3	(NA)
Charlotte, NC	AAA	Aaa	AAA	Louisville, KY	AA+	Aa2	(NA)
Fort Worth, TX	AA+	Aa1	(NA)	Riverside, CA	A+	(NA)	(NA)
Portland, OR	(¹)	Aaa	(NA)	St Petersburg, FL	(¹)	(NA)	(NA)
Oklahoma City, OK	AA	Aa2	(NA)	Bakersfield, CA	(¹)	Aa3	(NA)
Tucson, AZ	AA	Aa3	(NA)	Stockton, CA	A+	A1	(NA)
New Orleans, LA	B	Ba1	(NA)	Birmingham, AL	AA	Aa3	AA−
Las Vegas, NV	AA−	Aa3	(NA)	Jersey City, NJ	BBB	Baa3	(NA)
Cleveland, OH	A	A2	A+	Norfolk, VA	AA	A1	AA
Long Beach, CA	AA−	Aa3	(NA)	Baton Rouge, LA	(¹)	(NA)	(NA)
Albuquerque, NM	AA	Aa3	AA	Hialeah, FL	(¹)	(NA)	(NA)
Kansas City, MO.	AA	Aa3	(NA)	Lincoln, NE	AAA	Aaa	(NA)
Fresno, CA	AA−	A1	(NA)	Greensboro, NC	AAA	Aaa	AAA
Virginia Beach, VA	AA+	Aa1	AA+	Plano, TX	AAA	Aaa	(NA)
Atlanta, GA	AA−	Aa3	AA−	Rochester, NY	AA	A2	(NA)
Sacramento, CA	AA	Aa2	(NA)				

NA Not available.   ¹ Not reviewed.

Sources: Standard & Poor's, New York, NY (copyright), <http://www2.standardandpoors.com/servlet/Satellite?pagename=sp /Page/HomePg>; Moody's Investors Service, New York, NY (copyright), <http://www.moodys.com/cust/defaultalt.asp>; Fitch Ratings, New York, NY (copyright), <http://www.fitchratings.com/>.

Table 435. State Resources, Expenditures, and Balances: 2004 and 2005

[In millions of dollars (1,177,285 represents $1,177,285,000,000). For fiscal year ending in year shown; see text; this section. General funds exclude special funds earmarked for particular purposes, such as highway trust funds and federal funds; they support most on-going broad-based state services and are available for appropriation to support any governmental activity. Minus sign (–) indicates deficit]

| State | Expenditures by fund source | | | | State general fund | | | | | |
| | Total, 2004 | 2005 [1] | | | Resources [3,4] | | Expenditures [4] | | Balance [5] | |
		Total [2]	General fund	Federal fund	2004	2005 [1]	2004	2005 [1]	2004	2005 [1]
United States ..	1,177,285	1,260,174	535,654	371,076	547,672	594,796	522,869	557,051	20,653	32,170
Alabama	16,082	18,658	6,075	7,276	5,866	6,697	5,483	6,030	347	675
Alaska	7,650	9,787	2,383	3,409	2,346	3,055	2,319	3,046	27	9
Arizona	21,728	22,785	7,486	7,737	6,876	8,304	6,516	7,661	[6]360	[6]643
Arkansas	13,674	16,200	3,689	5,277	3,526	3,630	3,526	3,630	–	–
California	156,643	174,176	80,283	56,686	79,822	89,227	76,333	81,728	[6]3,489	[6]7,499
Colorado	13,633	13,797	5,799	3,227	6,035	6,363	5,689	6,211	[6]346	[6]152
Connecticut	20,314	20,732	13,361	3,603	12,973	14,212	12,671	13,909	302	303
Delaware	4,686	5,373	2,883	1,093	3,200	3,524	2,554	2,822	[6]646	[6]701
Florida	51,838	58,579	24,392	18,035	23,884	27,711	21,427	24,808	2,457	2,903
Georgia	28,670	30,368	14,633	13,992	16,774	17,657	15,906	16,429	[6]869	[6]1,228
Hawaii	7,949	9,007	4,166	1,678	4,025	4,671	3,840	4,185	185	486
Idaho	4,584	5,158	2,114	1,965	2,087	2,325	1,987	2,110	100	215
Illinois	50,336	46,889	17,743	8,220	27,140	26,342	23,448	22,187	182	497
Indiana	21,495	21,286	11,723	6,758	11,244	11,647	11,244	11,800	–	119
Iowa	13,456	14,177	4,519	4,107	4,683	4,826	4,517	4,590	166	76
Kansas	10,197	10,813	4,680	2,987	4,644	5,171	4,317	4,690	327	481
Kentucky	19,007	20,237	7,640	6,795	7,620	8,087	7,294	7,735	250	255
Louisiana	20,217	24,755	6,865	6,468	6,826	7,240	6,760	7,241	44	19
Maine	6,549	6,953	2,710	2,545	2,658	2,818	2,643	2,784	15	34
Maryland	16,902	18,468	8,294	5,060	10,703	12,438	10,250	11,264	453	1,174
Massachusetts . . .	25,683	26,685	19,311	4,849	24,100	25,129	22,848	23,779	[6]1,893	[6]1,955
Michigan	39,756	40,617	8,498	12,710	8,751	8,655	8,751	8,655	–	–
Minnesota	23,537	25,147	15,145	5,805	14,868	15,598	13,600	14,595	[6]1,269	1,003
Mississippi	10,799	11,535	3,490	4,358	3,541	3,945	3,591	3,632	3	52
Missouri	17,945	19,046	7,172	5,972	7,150	7,421	6,662	7,121	488	300
Montana	3,941	4,532	1,351	1,804	1,417	1,664	1,282	1,367	135	297
Nebraska	7,104	8,442	2,854	2,705	2,752	3,124	2,576	2,720	177	403
Nevada	6,769	7,524	2,721	1,794	2,610	3,213	2,389	3,076	221	137
New Hampshire. . .	4,316	4,352	1,293	1,439	1,311	1,407	1,295	1,325	15	82
New Jersey	37,031	40,977	27,117	8,581	25,198	28,250	24,364	27,612	[6]834	[6]638
New Mexico	9,591	11,034	4,417	3,894	4,612	4,969	4,422	4,748	[6]447	[6]682
New York	97,328	100,668	43,619	36,697	43,142	44,837	42,065	43,619	[6]1,077	[6]1,218
North Carolina. . . .	32,096	30,811	15,918	8,967	15,187	16,616	14,704	15,798	289	493
North Dakota	2,925	3,366	920	1,335	971	1,074	894	906	77	69
Ohio	48,154	55,039	25,020	9,147	24,083	25,708	23,839	24,831	157	138
Oklahoma	13,069	14,210	5,027	5,153	4,936	5,142	4,869	4,945	67	10
Oregon	17,134	18,532	4,995	4,564	5,036	5,479	5,479	4,777	–443	296
Pennsylvania	48,022	52,499	23,031	17,950	22,152	23,483	21,885	23,105	77	365
Rhode Island	5,760	6,246	2,963	1,932	2,761	3,007	2,727	2,966	24	41
South Carolina . . .	15,868	15,951	4,996	5,726	5,162	5,646	4,865	5,073	[6]55	[6]468
South Dakota	2,662	2,933	971	1,233	892	991	889	989	–	–
Tennessee	21,695	24,711	9,758	9,685	8,910	9,904	8,175	9,373	545	443
Texas	63,421	65,164	29,015	21,851	31,445	34,398	29,390	29,695	1,448	3,700
Utah	7,905	8,415	3,978	2,179	3,628	3,978	3,574	3,978	54	–
Vermont.	3,213	3,670	673	972	972	1,083	915	1,038	–	–
Virginia	28,231	31,714	12,328	5,682	12,660	14,442	12,387	13,879	274	563
Washington	25,966	27,384	11,788	6,188	11,952	13,196	11,452	12,220	500	977
West Virginia	16,669	16,702	3,165	3,471	3,319	3,803	3,019	3,410	291	361
Wisconsin.	32,911	31,869	11,860	6,976	10,759	11,889	10,784	11,758	[6]105	[6]6
Wyoming	2,175	2,201	762	538	463	1,207	453	1,202	10	5

– Represents zero [1] Estimated. [2] Includes bonds and other state funds not shown separately. [3] Includes funds budgeted, adjustments, and balances from previous year. [4] May or may not include budget stabilization fund transfers, depending on state accounting practices. [5] Resources less expenditures. [6] Ending balance includes the balance in a budget stabilization fund.

Source: National Association of State Budget Officers, Washington, DC, *2004 State Expenditure Report*, and *State General Fund from NASBO*, Fiscal Survey of the States, semi-annual (copyright).

Table 436. Estimated State and Local Taxes Paid by a Family of Four for Selected Largest City in Each State: 2004

[Data based on average family of four (two wage earners and two school-age children) owning their own home and living in a city where taxes apply. Comprises state and local sales, income, auto, and real estate taxes. For definition of median, see Guide to Tabular Presentation]

City	Total taxes paid by gross family income level (dollars)					Total taxes paid as percent of income				
	$25,000	$50,000	$75,000	$100,000	$150,000	$25,000	$50,000	$75,000	$100,000	$150,000
Albuquerque, NM	1,589	3,840	6,524	9,031	13,887	6.4	7.7	8.7	9.0	9.3
Atlanta, GA	1,969	4,949	8,326	11,262	16,839	7.9	9.9	11.1	11.3	11.2
Baltimore, MD	1,916	5,681	9,072	12,041	17,769	7.7	11.4	12.1	12.0	11.8
Boston, MA	1,843	4,713	7,689	10,068	14,833	7.4	9.4	10.3	10.1	9.9
Charlotte, NC	1,657	4,215	7,153	10,013	14,914	6.6	8.4	9.5	10.0	9.9
Chicago, IL	2,269	4,865	7,693	9,934	14,380	9.1	9.7	10.3	9.9	9.6
Columbus, OH	2,180	4,715	7,647	10,504	14,839	8.7	9.4	10.2	10.5	9.9
Denver, CO	1,299	3,395	5,804	7,609	11,098	5.2	6.8	7.7	7.6	7.4
Detroit, MI	2,440	5,253	8,280	11,010	16,377	9.8	10.5	11.0	11.0	10.9
Honolulu, HI	1,728	3,941	6,566	8,911	13,700	6.9	7.9	8.8	8.9	9.1
Houston, TX	1,681	3,295	5,134	6,518	9,145	6.7	6.6	6.8	6.5	6.1
Indianapolis, IN	2,403	5,221	8,076	10,535	15,423	9.6	10.4	10.3	10.5	10.3
Jacksonville, FL	676	1,956	3,464	4,588	6,791	2.7	3.9	4.6	4.6	4.5
Kansas City, MO	1,782	4,387	7,101	9,435	14,059	7.1	8.8	9.5	9.4	9.4
Las Vegas, NV	1,497	2,596	3,951	4,957	6,806	6.0	5.2	5.3	5.0	4.5
Los Angeles, CA	2,416	4,719	8,265	11,745	19,048	9.7	9.4	11.0	11.7	12.7
Memphis, TN	1,798	3,219	4,876	6,130	8,664	7.2	6.4	6.5	6.1	5.8
Milwaukee, WI	1,915	5,107	8,309	11,167	16,687	7.7	10.2	11.1	11.2	11.1
Minneapolis, MN	1,446	4,160	6,934	9,449	14,528	5.8	8.3	9.2	9.4	9.7
New Orleans, LA	1,070	3,607	6,908	9,671	14,802	4.3	7.2	9.2	9.7	9.9
New York City, NY	1,840	6,143	10,711	14,491	22,635	7.4	12.3	14.3	14.5	15.1
Oklahoma City, OK	1,801	4,096	6,722	8,670	13,421	7.2	8.2	9.0	8.7	8.9
Omaha, NE	1,924	4,325	7,378	10,166	15,626	7.7	8.7	9.8	10.2	10.4
Philadelphia, PA	2,858	6,237	10,149	13,133	19,077	11.4	12.5	13.5	13.1	12.7
Phoenix, AZ	1,348	3,321	5,655	7,582	11,371	5.4	6.6	7.5	7.6	7.6
Portland, OR	2,280	5,398	8,503	11,555	17,562	9.1	10.8	11.3	11.6	11.7
Seattle, WA	1,968	3,561	5,477	6,932	9,581	7.9	7.1	7.3	6.9	6.4
Virginia Beach, VA	1,905	4,056	6,540	8,723	12,863	7.6	8.1	8.7	8.7	8.6
Washington, DC	1,633	4,584	7,679	10,553	16,327	6.5	9.2	10.2	10.6	10.9
Wichita, KS	1,075	3,335	5,653	8,118	12,429	4.3	6.7	7.5	8.1	8.3
Average [1]	1,787	4,161	6,884	9,254	13,903	7.1	8.3	9.2	9.3	9.3
Median [1]	1,798	4,073	6,908	9,449	14,219	7.2	8.1	9.2	9.4	9.5

[1] Based on selected cities and District of Columbia. For complete list of cities, see Table 437.

Source: Government of the District of Columbia, Office of the Chief Financial Officer, *Tax Rates and Revenues, Tax Burden Comparisons, Nationwide Comparison*, annual. See <http://www.cfo.dc.gov/cfo/site/>.

Table 437. Residential Property Tax Rates for Largest City in Each State: 2004

[The real property tax is a function of housing values, real estate tax rates, assessment levels, homeowner exemptions and credits. Effective rate is the amount each jurisdiction considers based upon assessment level used. Assessment level is ratio of assessed value to assumed market value. Nominal rates represent the "announced" rates levied by the jurisdiction]

City	Effective tax rate per $100 Rank	Effective tax rate per $100 Rate	Assessment level (percent)	Nominal rate per $100	City	Effective tax rate per $100 Rank	Effective tax rate per $100 Rate	Assessment level (percent)	Nominal rate per $100
Houston, TX	1	2.99	100.0	2.99	Columbus, OH	28	1.49	30.3	4.91
Providence, RI	2	2.97	100.0	2.97	Portland, OR	29	1.43	64.2	2.23
Indianapolis, IN	3	2.78	100.0	2.78	Wilmington, DE	30	1.39	51.2	2.71
Bridgeport, CT	4	2.73	70.0	3.90	Little Rock, AR	31	1.38	20.0	6.90
Philadelphia, PA	5	2.64	32.0	8.26	Phoenix, AZ	32	1.32	10.0	13.21
Manchester, NH	6	2.64	100.0	2.64	Wichita, KS	33	1.31	11.5	11.43
Milwaukee, WI	7	2.54	96.8	2.63	Minneapolis, MN	34	1.31	88.6	1.48
Baltimore MD	8	2.46	100.0	2.46	Albuquerque, NM	35	1.27	33.3	3.80
Newark, NJ	9	2.30	94.7	2.43	Los Angeles, CA	36	1.25	100.0	1.25
Des Moines, IA	10	2.21	48.5	4.56	Boston, MA	37	1.23	100.0	1.23
Portland, ME	11	2.20	82.0	2.68	Oklahoma City, OK	38	1.20	11.0	10.91
Omaha, NE	12	2.08	94.0	2.21	Kansas City, MO	39	1.20	19.0	6.30
Jacksonville, FL	13	1.98	98.0	2.02	New York City, NY	40	1.16	8.0	14.46
Fargo, ND	14	1.89	3.9	48.41	Charlotte, NC	41	1.13	95.8	1.18
Detroit, MI	15	1.86	27.8	6.71	Louisville, KY	42	1.10	90.0	1.23
Columbia, SC	16	1.84	4.0	46.10	Las Vegas, NV	43	1.09	35.0	3.12
Chicago, IL	17	1.74	22.1	7.88	Virginia Beach, VA	44	1.08	88.7	1.22
New Orleans, LA	18	1.74	10.0	17.40	Seattle, WA	45	1.03	94.1	1.09
Memphis, TN	19	1.73	23.8	7.27	Washington, DC	46	0.96	100.0	0.96
Boise, ID	20	1.73	97.3	1.78	Charleston, SC	47	0.88	60.0	1.47
Atlanta, GA	21	1.72	40.0	4.29	Birmingham, AL	48	0.70	10.0	6.95
Jackson, MS	22	1.71	10.0	17.09	Cheyenne, WY	49	0.68	9.5	7.11
Anchorage, AK	23	1.63	100.0	1.63	Denver, CO	50	0.53	8.0	6.69
Sioux Falls, SD	24	1.56	85.0	1.84	Honolulu, HI	51	0.38	100.0	0.38
Billings, MT	25	1.55	80.0	1.94	Unweighted Average	(X)	1.62	59.3	6.29
Burlington, VT	26	1.54	67.6	2.28	Median	(X)	1.54	(X)	(X)
Salt Lake City, UT	27	1.51	99.0	1.53					

X Not applicable.

Source: Government of the District of Columbia, Office of the Chief Financial Officer, *Tax Rates and Revenues, Tax Burden Comparisons, Nationwide Comparison*, annual. See <http://www.cfo.dc.gov/cfo/site/>.

Table 438. Gross Revenue From Parimutuel and Amusement Taxes and Lotteries by State: 2002 to 2004

[In millions of dollars (43,653.3 represents $43,653,300,000). For fiscal years; see text, this section]

State	Gross revenue			2004					
						Lottery revenue			
							Apportionment of funds		
	2002	2003	2004	Amusement taxes [1]	Parimutuel taxes	Total [2]	Prizes	Administration	Proceeds available from ticket sales
United States..	43,653.3	46,673.7	50,758.5	4,990.7	301.9	45,465.9	27,654.7	2,790.2	15,021.1
Alabama.........	3.7	3.5	3.3	0.1	3.2	(X)	(X)	(X)	(X)
Alaska..........	2.5	2.6	2.4	2.4	(X)	(X)	(X)	(X)	(X)
Arizona..........	276.2	302.0	343.3	0.6	0.6	342.1	200.3	33.8	108.0
Arkansas........	4.4	4.4	4.6	(X)	4.6	(X)	(X)	(X)	(X)
California.......	2,743.4	2,634.0	2,810.6	(X)	42.1	2,768.5	1,566.0	156.7	1,045.8
Colorado........	478.2	464.6	510.8	99.1	4.5	407.2	242.5	51.0	113.7
Connecticut......	1,282.8	1,302.4	1,355.3	435.1	10.7	909.6	538.3	87.3	283.9
Delaware	397.1	367.3	379.6	(X)	0.2	379.4	53.2	42.3	283.9
Florida..........	2,232.9	2,743.5	2,928.5	(X)	26.7	2,901.7	1,724.5	134.9	1,042.3
Georgia	2,162.8	2,284.1	2,376.3	(X)	(X)	2,376.3	1,480.3	112.4	783.6
Hawaii	(X)	(X)	(X)	(X)	(X)	(X)	(X)	(X)	(X)
Idaho	92.7	90.8	101.4	(X)	(X)	101.4	64.7	10.7	25.9
Illinois	2,064.4	2,152.2	2,370.4	785.9	12.0	1,572.5	973.8	56.5	542.1
Indiana.........	1,094.8	1,281.2	1,439.4	765.7	4.8	668.9	436.5	31.6	200.8
Iowa	375.4	356.8	412.0	213.5	3.2	195.2	114.5	27.3	53.5
Kansas.........	184.3	196.7	215.7	0.7	3.5	211.5	120.8	20.7	70.0
Kentucky	656.8	650.7	695.8	0.2	15.5	680.1	439.2	44.6	196.3
Louisiana	787.8	809.9	855.6	524.1	20.4	311.1	169.8	19.5	121.8
Maine..........	157.7	164.3	193.5	(X)	4.5	189.0	116.8	29.6	42.6
Maryland	1,314.5	1,336.9	1,408.9	10.1	3.0	1,395.4	789.8	139.4	466.2
Massachusetts.....	4,214.9	4,214.1	4,386.5	5.3	5.7	4,375.6	3,148.5	73.2	1,153.9
Michigan........	1,662.9	1,666.0	1,952.7	99.5	11.8	1,841.4	1,099.7	56.8	684.9
Minnesota.......	410.0	370.5	403.2	55.8	1.5	345.9	240.7	22.6	82.6
Mississippi	184.2	184.6	167.3	167.3	(X)	(X)	(X)	(X)	(X)
Missouri	769.2	952.6	1,049.5	307.1	(X)	742.5	484.8	38.4	219.3
Montana........	75.5	78.6	85.2	50.5	0.1	34.6	18.7	6.8	9.2
Nebraska	81.2	88.1	99.0	6.1	0.3	92.6	52.6	20.6	19.4
Nevada	720.7	739.3	861.5	861.5	(X)	(X)	(X)	(X)	(X)
New Hampshire....	209.5	217.1	232.2	1.8	4.1	226.3	137.1	15.4	73.7
New Jersey......	2,306.0	2,307.6	2,533.7	468.1	(X)	2,065.7	1,196.8	73.1	795.9
New Mexico	158.2	168.8	178.2	38.5	1.2	138.4	85.2	17.3	36.0
New York	4,506.6	5,109.8	5,528.5	0.6	36.1	5,491.8	3,306.3	226.3	1,959.2
North Carolina....	11.1	11.1	11.5	11.5	(X)	(X)	(X)	(X)	(X)
North Dakota.....	16.6	16.9	12.7	10.1	2.6	(X)	(X)	(X)	(X)
Ohio	2,000.5	2,093.8	2,170.6	(X)	15.9	2,154.7	1,276.0	277.8	600.9
Oklahoma........	10.1	9.4	8.2	5.4	2.8	(X)	(X)	(X)	(X)
Oregon.........	1,421.8	1,526.5	1,612.5	0.1	2.9	1,609.5	1,148.9	264.7	195.9
Pennsylvania.....	1,805.7	1,987.6	2,189.5	0.6	26.6	2,162.4	1,305.9	19.2	837.3
Rhode Island.....	1,019.4	1,124.8	1,314.0	(X)	4.7	1,309.4	1,023.7	7.2	278.4
South Carolina....	364.5	709.0	922.7	39.6	(X)	883.1	552.3	39.9	290.9
South Dakota	132.6	137.0	141.6	–	0.9	140.7	19.1	5.0	116.6
Tennessee	(X)	(X)	(X)	(X)	(X)	(X)	(X)	(X)	(X)
Texas..........	2,847.7	3,164.3	3,522.8	23.1	11.8	3,487.9	2,068.6	356.2	1,063.1
Utah	(X)	(X)	(X)	(X)	(X)	(X)	(X)	(X)	(X)
Vermont	82.0	74.8	87.0	(X)	(X)	87.0	57.6	9.3	20.1
Virginia..........	1,104.9	1,137.4	1,262.4	0.1	(X)	1,262.4	707.2	132.9	422.2
Washington......	440.7	462.3	483.3	0.1	1.8	481.4	295.5	65.7	120.3
West Virginia.....	461.5	566.8	683.3	(X)	9.5	673.8	123.3	30.1	520.5
Wisconsin.......	399.9	406.7	451.2	0.4	1.8	449.0	275.2	33.3	140.6
Wyoming	0.2	0.2	0.2	(X)	0.2	(X)	(X)	(X)	(X)

– Rounds to zero.   X Not applicable.   [1] Represents nonlicense taxes.   [2] Excludes commissions.

Source: U.S. Census Bureau, Federal, State and Local Governments, State Government Finances, Lottery, and unpublished data; <http://www.census.gov/govs/www/state.html>.

Table 439. Lottery Sales—Type of Game: 1980 to 2005

[In millions of dollars (2,393 represents $2,393,000,000). For fiscal years]

Game	1980	1990	1995	2000	2002	2003	2004	2005
Total ticket sales.............	2,393	20,017	31,931	37,201	41,979	43,521	47,697	47,364
Instant [1]	527	5,204	11,511	15,459	18,509	20,387	23,011	25,946
Three-digit [2]	1,554	4,572	5,737	5,341	5,356	5,394	5,389	5,428
Four-digit [2]	55	1,302	1,941	2,711	2,916	3,059	3,195	3,300
Lotto [3]	52	8,563	10,594	9,160	9,564	9,655	10,472	9,707
Other [4].......................	206	376	2,148	4,530	5,633	5,026	5,630	2,983
State proceeds (net income) [5].....	978	7,703	11,100	11,404	12,478	13,991	15,094	15,779

[1] Player scratches a latex section on ticket which reveals instantly whether ticket is a winner.   [2] Players choose and bet on three or four digits, depending on game, with various payoffs for different straight order or mixed combination bets.   [3] Players typically select six digits out of a large field of numbers. Varying prizes are offered for matching three through six numbers drawn by lottery.   [4] Includes break-open tickets, spiel, keno, video lottery, etc.   [5] Sales minus prizes and expenses equal net government income.

Source: TLF Publications, Inc., Boyds, MD, 2006 World Lottery Almanac annual; LaFleur's Fiscal 2005 Lottery Interim & VLT Book (copyright) <http://www.lafleurs.com/>.

Table 440. **State Governments—Summary of Finances: 1990 to 2003**

[(673,119 represents $673,119,000,000), For fiscal year ending in year shown; see text; this section. Minus sign (–) indicates net loss]

Item	Total (million dollars)				Per capita (dollars) [1]			
	1990	2000	2002	2003	1990	2000	2002	2003
Borrowing and revenue	673,119	1,336,798	1,205,999	1,430,303	2,712	4,760	4,196	4,928
Borrowing...................	40,948	75,968	108,170	134,644	165	270	376	464
Total revenue	632,172	1,260,829	1,097,829	1,295,659	2,547	4,489	3,820	4,464
General revenue.............	517,429	984,783	1,062,305	1,112,349	2,085	3,506	3,696	3,833
Taxes..................	300,489	539,655	535,241	548,991	1,211	1,922	1,862	1,892
Sales and gross receipts.....	147,069	252,147	262,361	273,811	593	898	913	943
General...............	99,702	174,461	179,665	184,597	402	621	625	636
Motor fuels	19,379	29,968	31,968	32,269	78	107	111	111
Alcoholic beverages	3,191	4,104	4,249	4,399	13	15	15	15
Tobacco products	5,541	8,391	8,902	11,482	22	30	31	40
Other	19,256	35,222	37,576	41,065	78	125	131	141
Licenses................	18,842	32,598	35,391	35,863	76	116	123	124
Motor vehicles	9,848	15,099	15,641	16,009	40	54	54	55
Corporations in general	3,099	6,460	5,842	6,129	12	23	20	21
Other	5,895	11,039	13,908	13,725	24	39	48	47
Individual income	96,076	194,573	185,697	181,933	387	693	646	627
Corporation net income......	21,751	32,522	25,123	28,384	88	116	87	98
Property.................	5,848	10,996	9,702	10,471	24	39	34	36
Other..................	10,902	16,819	16,967	18,529	44	60	59	64
Charges and miscellaneous.....	90,612	170,747	191,641	201,741	365	608	667	695
Intergovernmental revenue	126,329	274,382	335,423	361,617	509	977	1,167	1,246
From federal government.....	118,353	259,114	317,581	343,308	477	923	1,105	1,183
Public welfare	59,397	147,150	181,517	196,954	239	524	632	679
Education	21,271	42,086	51,103	56,362	86	150	178	194
Highways	13,931	23,790	29,641	29,481	56	85	103	102
Health and hospitals	5,475	14,223	17,875	19,559	22	51	62	67
Other	18,279	31,865	37,445	40,951	74	113	130	141
From local governments	7,976	15,268	17,842	18,309	32	54	62	63
Utility revenue	3,305	4,513	11,935	12,518	13	16	42	43
Liquor store revenue	2,907	3,895	4,288	4,518	12	14	15	16
Insurance trust revenue [2].......	108,530	267,639	19,301	166,274	437	953	67	573
Employee retirement	78,898	230,166	-25,244	110,839	318	820	-88	382
Unemployment compensation ...	18,370	23,260	26,960	35,191	74	83	94	121
Expenditure and								
**debt redemption........... **	**592,213**	**1,125,828**	**1,334,969**	**1,426,715**	**2,386**	**4,009**	**4,645**	**4,916**
Total expenditure	572,318	1,084,097	1,280,290	1,359,048	2,306	3,860	4,455	4,683
General expenditure	508,284	964,723	1,109,227	1,163,968	2,048	3,435	3,859	4,010
Education................	184,935	346,465	389,390	411,094	745	1,234	1,355	1,416
Public welfare.............	104,971	238,890	287,016	314,407	423	851	999	1,083
Health	20,029	42,066	50,293	50,221	81	150	175	173
Hospitals	22,637	32,578	37,393	38,395	91	116	130	132
Highways................	44,249	74,415	84,198	85,726	178	265	293	295
Police protection	5,166	9,788	10,706	11,144	21	35	37	38
Corrections...............	17,266	35,129	38,918	39,188	70	125	135	135
Natural resources	9,909	15,967	17,821	18,577	40	57	62	64
Housing and community								
development...............	2,856	4,726	5,989	8,112	12	17	21	28
Other and unallocable	96,267	164,698	187,504	187,106	388	586	652	645
Utility expenditure	7,131	10,723	20,279	22,405	29	38	71	77
Liquor store expenditure. . .;.....	2,452	3,195	3,498	3,697	10	11	12	13
Insurance trust expenditure [2]	54,452	105,456	147,286	168,979	219	375	512	582
Employee retirement	29,562	75,971	91,971	103,049	119	271	320	355
Unemployment compensation ...	16,423	18,583	42,017	51,411	66	66	146	177
By character and object								
Intergovernmental expenditure	175,028	327,070	364,789	382,197	705	1,165	1,269	1,317
Direct expenditure.............	397,291	757,027	915,501	976,852	1,601	2,695	3,185	3,366
Current operation	258,046	523,114	620,763	656,989	1,040	1,863	2,160	2,264
Capital outlay	45,524	76,233	89,919	91,943	183	271	313	317
Construction	34,803	59,681	71,035	72,374	140	213	247	249
Land and existing structure ...	3,471	4,681	5,305	6,945	14	17	18	24
Equipment	7,250	11,871	13,579	12,623	29	42	47	43
Assistance and subsidies	16,902	22,136	24,313	25,901	68	79	85	89
Interest on debt. .;.........	22,367	30,089	33,220	33,040	90	107	116	114
Insurance benefits [3].........	54,452	105,456	147,286	168,979	219	375	512	582
Debt redemption	19,895	41,730	54,678	67,666	80	149	190	233
**Debt outstanding, year end.... **	**318,254**	**547,876**	**642,202**	**697,929**	**1,282**	**1,951**	**2,234**	**2,405**
Long-term....................	315,490	541,497	623,558	681,796	1,271	1,928	2,170	2,349
Full-faith and credit	74,972	138,525	159,502	179,372	302	493	555	618
Nonguaranteed................	240,518	402,972	464,056	502,424	969	1,435	1,615	1,731
Short-term...................	2,764	6,379	18,644	16,133	11	23	65	56
Net long-term [4]	125,524	266,870	317,829	366,207	506	950	1,106	1,262
Full-faith and credit only........	63,481	128,384	149,580	170,137	256	457	520	586

[1] 1990 and 2000 based on enumerated resident population as of April 1. Other years based on estimated resident population as of July 1.   [2] Includes other items not shown separately.   [3] Includes repayments.   [4] Less cash and investment assets specifically held for redemption of long-term debt.

Source: U.S. Census Bureau, *Federal State and Local Governments, State Government Finances*, series GF, No. 3 thereafter. <http://www.census.gov/govs/www/estimate03.html> (accessed 21 June 2005).

Table 441. **State Governments—Revenue by State: 2004**

[In millions of dollars (1,589,856 represents $1,589,856,000,000), except as noted. For fiscal year ending in year shown; see text, this section. Includes local shares of state imposed taxes. Minus sign (–) indicates net loss]

State	Total revenue [1,2]	General revenue			Intergovernmental				Utility and liquor store revenue	Insurance trust revenue
		Total	Per capita [3] Total (dol.)	Rank	Total	From federal government	Taxes	Current charges and miscellaneous revenue		
United States. .	1,589,856	1,197,347	4,085	(X)	394,497	374,694	593,822	209,028	17,821	374,689
Alabama	21,568	17,616	4,767	39	6,871	6,278	7,018	3,727	172	3,780
Alaska	8,848	6,626	13,446	1	2,194	2,189	1,339	3,093	14	2,208
Arizona	23,753	18,949	4,138	46	6,987	6,582	9,606	2,355	25	4,779
Arkansas.	14,225	11,680	5,173	29	4,042	4,019	5,581	2,057	–	2,545
California.	229,289	154,485	6,397	13	49,556	45,553	85,721	19,207	4,367	70,437
Colorado.	23,082	14,957	5,016	33	4,595	4,531	7,051	3,311	–	8,125
Connecticut	19,519	17,423	5,578	23	4,132	4,123	10,291	3,000	23	2,072
Delaware.	5,698	5,144	6,865	6	1,054	1,022	2,375	1,715	10	544
Florida	75,176	56,672	4,324	44	16,737	16,609	30,534	9,401	19	18,486
Georgia	34,814	28,205	3,904	50	9,096	9,040	14,571	4,538	2	6,607
Hawaii	8,229	6,675	6,521	10	1,640	1,633	3,849	1,186	–	1,554
Idaho	7,112	5,310	5,098	31	1,741	1,736	2,648	921	77	1,726
Illinois.	61,255	46,519	4,819	37	14,173	12,650	25,491	6,856	–	14,736
Indiana	26,917	23,465	4,323	45	7,057	6,912	11,957	4,450	–	3,452
Iowa.	15,292	11,845	5,178	28	4,038	3,912	5,143	2,664	136	3,310
Kansas	11,044	9,869	4,040	48	3,000	2,966	5,284	1,585	–	1,175
Kentucky.	20,180	17,382	4,872	36	5,796	5,894	8,463	3,123	–	2,798
Louisiana	23,730	19,156	5,265	26	6,996	6,900	8,030	4,130	5	4,569
Maine.	8,310	6,795	6,319	14	2,574	2,560	2,897	1,325	91	1,424
Maryland.	28,396	22,841	5,106	30	6,457	6,227	12,315	4,070	107	5,447
Massachusetts . . .	41,616	32,980	6,495	11	8,997	8,626	16,839	7,143	130	8,505
Michigan.	57,461	46,780	5,687	20	13,750	13,483	24,061	8,969	676	10,006
Minnesota	29,708	24,217	5,829	18	6,380	6,207	14,735	3,102	–	5,491
Mississippi.	15,351	12,196	5,292	25	5,425	5,229	5,125	1,647	194	2,961
Missouri	26,320	20,287	4,570	42	7,412	7,237	9,120	3,756	–	6,033
Montana	5,452	4,245	5,881	17	1,705	1,694	1,626	915	50	1,157
Nebraska	8,316	7,338	4,758	40	2,383	2,362	3,640	1,315	–	979
Nevada.	10,136	7,318	4,345	43	1,625	1,569	4,739	954	143	2,675
New Hampshire . .	6,175	5,024	4,753	41	1,677	1,456	2,005	1,342	372	779
New Jersey	50,589	37,904	5,825	19	9,580	9,006	20,981	7,343	591	12,093
New Mexico.	11,810	9,798	6,206	16	3,546	3,434	4,002	2,250	–	2,011
New York	136,521	106,300	7,081	4	47,838	41,219	45,826	12,636	6,091	24,129
North Carolina . . .	44,371	32,951	5,196	27	11,609	11,045	16,836	4,506	–	11,420
North Dakota	5,228	3,172	8,220	3	1,221	1,191	1,229	723	–	2,056
Ohio.	76,443	45,732	6,676	9	14,870	14,480	22,476	8,386	581	30,130
Oklahoma	17,520	13,700	4,972	35	4,566	4,483	6,427	2,708	353	3,467
Oregon	24,489	13,766	6,819	7	4,161	4,148	6,103	3,502	291	10,431
Pennsylvania	69,213	50,029	5,584	22	15,298	15,175	25,347	9,384	1,109	18,075
Rhode Island	7,266	5,619	6,728	8	2,096	1,987	2,409	1,114	22	1,625
South Carolina . . .	21,242	16,836	5,060	32	6,229	5,822	6,804	3,804	1,048	3,358
South Dakota. . . .	3,864	2,907	5,011	34	1,239	1,220	1,063	605	–	957
Tennessee.	23,921	20,901	4,059	47	9,017	8,772	9,529	2,355	–	3,020
Texas	90,570	71,568	4,030	49	25,640	24,864	30,752	15,176	–	19,003
Utah.	13,168	9,560	5,439	24	2,878	2,810	4,196	2,486	142	3,466
Vermont	4,303	3,795	6,928	5	1,315	1,314	1,767	713	35	472
Virginia	35,740	27,972	4,777	38	6,238	6,091	14,233	7,501	408	7,361
Washington	35,086	25,202	5,653	21	6,954	6,669	13,895	4,353	418	9,466
West Virginia	11,633	9,638	6,417	12	3,306	3,258	3,749	2,583	60	1,935
Wisconsin	34,753	23,934	6,314	15	6,832	6,596	12,638	4,464	–	10,819
Wyoming.	5,152	4,061	10,182	2	1,977	1,912	1,505	580	56	1,034

– Represents or rounds to zero. X Not applicable. [1] Includes categories not shown separately. [2] Duplicate intergovernmental transactions are excluded. [3] Based on estimated resident population July 1.

Source: U.S. Census Bureau, *Federal, State, and Local Governments, Finance, Survey of State Government Finances*, 2004, and unpublished data. See also <http://www.census.gov/govs/www/state04.html>. Accessed as of 10 April 2006.

State and Local Government Finances and Employment 285

Table 442. State Government Tax Collections by State: 2004

[In millions of dollars (593,822 represents 593,822,000,000)]

State	All taxes Total	Per capita Total (dol.)	Per capita Rank	Total property tax	Sales and gross receipts taxes Total	Total general sales and gross receipts	Selective sales tax Total	Alcoholic beverages sales	Insurance premiums	Motor fuels sales	Public utilities
United States. . .	593,822	2,026	(X)	11,425	293,776	198,209	95,567	4,615	13,914	33,709	10,609
Alabama	7,018	1,551	46	221	3,676	1,893	1,783	137	246	535	601
Alaska	1,339	2,035	22	47	168	(X)	168	28	50	41	4
Arizona.	9,606	1,674	41	346	6,071	4,720	1,351	56	313	672	35
Arkansas.	5,581	2,029	24	520	2,934	2,150	785	41	91	453	(X)
California.	85,721	2,392	9	2,079	33,984	26,507	7,477	313	2,115	3,325	521
Colorado.	7,051	1,532	48	(X)	2,894	1,909	985	31	178	598	9
Connecticut	10,291	2,941	3	(X)	4,900	3,127	1,773	44	218	457	196
Delaware.	2,375	2,862	5	(X)	383	(X)	383	13	68	112	36
Florida	30,534	1,756	36	277	23,409	17,129	6,281	592	711	2,022	1,712
Georgia	14,571	1,634	42	65	6,469	4,921	1,547	150	317	756	(X)
Hawaii	3,849	3,050	1	(X)	2,470	1,900	570	41	82	84	100
Idaho	2,648	1,898	32	(X)	1,403	1,037	366	7	82	218	2
Illinois.	25,491	2,005	25	57	12,527	6,923	5,604	148	379	1,422	1,705
Indiana	11,957	1,920	30	9	6,907	4,759	2,148	39	178	802	11
Iowa.	5,143	1,742	38	(X)	2,437	1,618	820	13	138	358	(X)
Kansas	5,284	1,933	28	58	2,723	1,933	790	88	122	429	0.7
Kentucky.	8,463	2,043	21	455	4,006	2,466	1,540	79	332	477	(X)
Louisiana	8,030	1,782	34	40	4,611	2,681	1,930	53	342	561	7
Maine	2,897	2,203	16	45	1,360	917	443	39	78	220	8
Maryland.	12,315	2,214	15	479	5,212	2,945	2,267	27	279	746	137
Massachusetts	16,839	2,628	7	0.1	5,603	3,743	1,859	69	400	684	(X)
Michigan	24,061	2,241	12	2,803	10,844	7,894	2,950	149	230	1,081	29
Minnesota	14,735	2,891	4	608	6,384	4,067	2,318	69	266	648	0.1
Mississippi.	5,125	1,767	35	40	3,391	2,483	908	40	161	465	12
Missouri	9,120	1,583	45	23	4,469	2,950	1,518	28	305	727	(X)
Montana	1,626	1,754	37	184	437	(X)	437	21	61	198	28
Nebraska	3,640	2,082	18	2	1,988	1,525	463	23	38	303	3
Nevada.	4,739	2,031	23	132	3,825	2,265	1,560	34	194	294	10
New Hampshire . . .	2,005	1,544	47	494	674	(X)	674	12	79	130	66
New Jersey	20,981	2,416	8	4	9,740	6,262	3,479	87	418	547	943
New Mexico.	4,002	2,103	17	53	2,038	1,443	595	38	87	211	18
New York	45,826	2,377	10	(X)	16,479	10,050	6,429	191	833	519	822
North Carolina	16,836	1,971	26	(X)	7,269	4,352	2,917	212	433	1,273	320
North Dakota	1,229	1,932	29	1	667	367	299	6	31	119	34
Ohio.	22,476	1,963	27	41	10,783	7,882	2,902	88	423	1,541	276
Oklahoma	6,427	1,824	33	(X)	2,339	1,594	745	68	144	415	21
Oregon	6,103	1,700	40	16	749	(X)	749	13	52	405	11
Pennsylvania	25,347	2,045	20	68	12,530	7,773	4,757	221	640	1,785	1,017
Rhode Island	2,409	2,230	14	12	1,305	805	501	11	43	133	89
South Carolina	6,804	1,621	43	12	3,690	2,727	963	147	107	489	45
South Dakota	1,063	1,378	49	(X)	865	586	279	12	55	126	2
Tennessee.	9,529	1,617	44	(X)	7,345	5,845	1,499	92	351	832	5
Texas	30,752	1,368	50	(X)	24,621	15,460	9,161	602	1,130	2,919	793
Utah.	4,196	1,733	39	(X)	2,142	1,561	581	29	107	342	14
Vermont	1,767	2,845	6	448	688	257	431	17	49	86	11
Virginia	14,233	1,903	31	21	5,212	2,977	2,235	146	351	909	129
Washington	13,895	2,239	13	1,527	10,865	8,423	2,441	193	346	926	353
West Virginia	3,749	2,068	19	3	2,093	1,021	1,072	9	102	309	188
Wisconsin	12,638	2,296	11	104	5,621	3,899	1,722	48	138	936	286
Wyoming.	1,505	2,974	2	140	574	463	111	1	18	70	3

See footnote at end of table.

U.S. Census Bureau, Statistical Abstract of the United States: 2007

Table 442. **State Government Tax Collections by State: 2004**

[See headnote, page 286]

State	License taxes Total	Corporation	Hunting and fishing	Motor vehicle operators	Occupancy and business n.e.c. [2]	Other taxes Total	Individual income	Corporation net income	Death and gift	Severance
United States...	**39,627**	**6,339**	**1,234**	**19,282**	**10,881**	**248,994**	**197,879**	**30,897**	**5,739**	**6,362**
Alabama........	397	73	15	190	107	2,724	2,244	292	29	114
Alaska.........	84	1	24	44	9	1,039	(X)	340	2	697
Arizona........	290	14	18	177	63	2,899	2,316	526	42	16
Arkansas.......	188	9	21	126	21	1,938	1,686	182	21	16
California.......	5,744	71	83	2,342	3,063	43,914	36,399	6,926	575	14
Colorado.......	338	7	66	207	50	3,820	3,414	240	50	116
Connecticut.....	385	16	4	236	118	5,006	4,320	380	130	(X)
Delaware........	882	568	1	34	221	1,110	781	218	12	(X)
Florida........	1,775	161	15	1,277	256	5,073	(X)	1,441	387	49
Georgia	618	53	24	317	117	7,419	6,830	495	66	(X)
Hawaii	123	2	0.3	89	19	1,256	1,169	58	10	(X)
Idaho..........	221	2	29	114	42	1,024	908	104	7	3
Illinois.........	2,386	169	30	1,448	719	10,521	8,140	2,069	222	0.3
Indiana........	448	5	17	371	40	4,593	3,808	645	140	0.6
Iowa...........	576	39	25	397	76	2,130	1,959	90	68	(X)
Kansas.........	275	47	18	176	23	2,228	1,916	167	48	98
Kentucky........	542	198	21	217	85	3,459	2,819	382	68	187
Louisiana	429	187	28	125	77	2,951	2,192	237	46	477
Maine..........	158	4	12	89	49	1,333	1,160	112	32	(X)
Maryland........	512	53	12	311	132	6,112	5,278	447	152	(X)
Massachusetts....	665	26	7	383	140	10,572	8,830	1,301	195	(X)
Michigan.......	1,545	19	48	1,131	172	8,868	6,576	1,841	76	58
Minnesota.......	942	7	57	555	284	6,801	5,710	637	87	15
Mississippi.......	318	90	13	141	60	1,375	1,062	244	15	54
Missouri........	606	91	30	271	135	4,023	3,721	224	70	0.1
Montana........	233	1	37	150	38	771	606	68	11	84
Nebraska	202	7	14	97	64	1,447	1,243	167	26	2
Nevada.........	623	53	7	154	309	158	(X)	(X)	25	37
New Hampshire ...	199	4	9	97	62	638	55	408	31	(X)
New Jersey	1,177	250	12	433	408	10,060	7,401	1,897	516	(X)
New Mexico......	170	3	17	127	22	1,740	1,007	138	7	588
New York	1,193	58	4	907	146	28,154	24,647	2,045	736	(X)
North Carolina	1,017	338	15	516	132	8,550	7,511	837	145	2
North Dakota	118	(X)	13	59	46	442	214	50	3	176
Ohio...........	1,813	297	31	781	667	9,838	8,705	1,061	64	8
Oklahoma	840	42	22	567	200	3,247	2,319	133	111	655
Oregon.........	651	4	40	451	132	4,687	4,271	320	74	17
Pennsylvania	2,548	788	65	853	763	10,201	7,323	1,678	709	(X)
Rhode Island	94	4	2	58	30	1,007	900	69	25	(X)
South Carolina	384	73	19	158	113	2,718	2,439	197	33	(X)
South Dakota.....	139	3	22	44	58	59	(X)	47	9	2
Tennessee.......	1,046	507	25	297	203	1,139	140	695	97	1
Texas..........	4,083	1,896	80	1,329	682	2,048	(X)	(X)	151	1,897
Utah...........	157	3	21	102	27	1,897	1,692	145	10	50
Vermont	99	5	6	67	19	532	430	62	15	(X)
Virginia	614	46	20	386	148	8,386	7,422	422	150	2
Washington	687	19	30	382	190	818	(X)	(X)	140	38
West Virginia	179	8	16	87	40	1,473	1,068	182	9	204
Wisconsin	812	14	61	361	290	6,102	5,251	682	86	5
Wyoming........	102	6	28	53	15	689	(X)	(X)	6	683

X Not applicable. [1] Details will not add to the totals shown because of rounding. [2] Not elsewhere classified.

Source: U.S. Census Bureau, *Federal, State, and Local Governments, Tax collections, State Governments Tax Collections,* Annual. See also <http://www.census.gov/govs/www/statetax.html> (accessed 10 April 2006).

State and Local Government Finances and Employment 287

Table 443. **State Governments—Expenditures and Debt by State: 2003**

[In millions of dollars (1,359,048 represents $1,359,048,000,000) except as indicated. For fiscal year ending in year shown; see text, this section]

State	Total expendi- ture [1]	Total Amount	Total Per capita [2] (dol.)	Inter- govern- mental	Total [1]	Educa- tion	Public welfare	Health and hospitals	High- ways	Police protec- tion
United States ..	1,359,048	1,163,968	4,010	382,197	781,772	170,685	265,105	68,374	72,455	9,860
Alabama	18,471	17,010	3,777	4,074	12,936	3,522	4,532	1,953	971	105
Alaska	8,122	7,111	10,975	1,091	6,020	981	1,193	154	802	68
Arizona	19,606	17,503	3,137	6,937	10,566	2,407	3,758	870	1,292	163
Arkansas	12,085	11,081	4,062	3,211	7,871	1,919	2,705	834	940	69
California	204,438	173,158	4,883	84,469	88,689	18,214	26,016	7,130	5,095	1,267
Colorado	17,691	14,793	3,253	4,666	10,126	3,088	2,547	957	1,106	102
Connecticut	20,721	17,885	5,129	3,030	14,855	2,533	3,715	1,915	678	169
Delaware	4,858	4,376	5,350	903	3,473	788	747	319	338	73
Florida	56,317	50,218	2,954	14,461	35,757	5,606	13,396	3,113	4,812	416
Georgia	32,527	29,291	3,376	9,016	20,275	5,360	7,530	1,226	1,837	244
Hawaii	7,611	6,852	5,486	125	6,726	2,332	1,215	642	259	8
Idaho	5,415	4,759	3,482	1,449	3,310	730	1,093	145	411	39
Illinois	51,291	43,954	3,475	13,370	30,584	6,129	9,739	3,384	3,155	370
Indiana	23,090	21,295	3,435	6,761	14,534	4,505	5,042	722	1,366	190
Iowa	13,088	11,715	3,982	3,443	8,272	2,105	2,747	905	936	85
Kansas	10,954	9,843	3,612	2,925	6,918	1,754	1,891	589	931	70
Kentucky	19,117	16,858	4,094	3,694	13,164	3,025	4,917	903	1,694	159
Louisiana	18,681	16,323	3,632	4,329	11,994	2,919	2,723	1,925	1,045	208
Maine	6,706	6,072	4,639	1,051	5,021	759	1,942	451	470	67
Maryland	24,592	21,789	3,953	5,358	16,431	3,582	5,052	1,342	1,273	307
Massachusetts . . .	32,710	27,871	4,341	6,436	21,435	3,338	4,992	2,373	2,304	296
Michigan	51,016	44,522	4,416	19,852	24,670	6,446	8,689	2,498	1,301	310
Minnesota	28,899	25,384	5,013	9,618	15,765	3,669	7,195	631	1,199	200
Mississippi	13,503	12,095	4,195	3,666	8,429	1,644	3,500	910	800	67
Missouri	21,566	19,137	3,346	5,159	13,978	2,530	5,486	1,459	1,569	154
Montana	4,437	3,917	4,267	938	2,979	688	646	288	479	28
Nebraska	6,824	6,494	3,739	1,785	4,709	1,149	1,793	313	558	52
Nevada	7,816	6,706	2,991	2,649	4,057	940	1,159	319	640	59
New Hampshire . . .	5,276	4,592	3,562	1,283	3,309	682	1,086	190	347	41
New Jersey	44,948	34,860	4,034	8,997	25,862	5,755	6,067	2,149	2,270	390
New Mexico	10,673	9,714	5,170	2,951	6,762	1,491	2,411	735	805	93
New York	127,475	101,825	5,300	40,875	60,951	7,849	28,116	4,963	3,847	531
North Carolina	34,361	30,428	3,613	10,356	20,072	4,952	6,562	1,731	2,580	334
North Dakota	3,121	2,898	4,577	606	2,291	611	649	75	302	12
Ohio	56,390	44,614	3,900	15,249	29,364	7,043	10,772	2,465	2,284	258
Oklahoma	15,125	13,306	3,795	3,395	9,910	2,859	3,131	551	1,020	92
Oregon	18,006	14,130	3,965	4,072	10,059	2,080	3,431	932	681	147
Pennsylvania	57,428	48,252	3,900	11,943	36,309	7,843	14,072	2,321	4,605	1,023
Rhode Island	5,977	5,026	4,671	828	4,198	669	1,774	299	229	50
South Carolina . . .	21,040	17,685	4,262	4,156	13,529	3,189	4,763	1,733	1,267	229
South Dakota	2,898	2,663	3,481	515	2,148	414	622	135	386	26
Tennessee	21,022	19,387	3,317	4,953	14,434	2,983	6,990	1,229	1,232	137
Texas	76,386	66,804	3,022	17,333	49,471	11,945	17,804	3,743	5,154	413
Utah	10,252	9,176	3,902	2,165	7,011	2,219	1,740	748	638	83
Vermont	3,859	3,594	5,806	938	2,656	601	914	92	238	57
Virginia	29,129	26,289	3,569	8,353	17,937	4,646	4,617	2,329	2,313	238
Washington	32,600	26,021	4,244	6,785	19,235	5,176	6,218	2,268	1,340	177
West Virginia	10,004	7,998	4,416	1,545	6,453	1,375	2,231	322	962	54
Wisconsin	27,658	23,813	4,350	9,478	14,335	3,319	4,731	977	1,261	103
Wyoming	3,264	2,881	5,740	953	1,929	321	445	116	436	28

See footnote at end of table.

U.S. Census Bureau, Statistical Abstract of the United States: 2007

Table 443. **State Governments—Expenditures and Debt by State: 2003**—Con.

[See headnote, page 288]

State	General expenditure—Con. / Direct expenditures—Con. Corrections	Natural resources	Parks and recreation	Govern-mental admin-istration	Interest on general debt	Expenditures Utility	Liquor stores	Insurance trust	Cash and security holdings	Debt outstanding, total	Per capita [2] (dollars)
United States. .	36,938	17,110	4,636	42,846	31,295	22,405	3,697	168,979	2,594,216	697,929	2,400
Alabama	351	223	25	439	252	–	173	1,288	28,661	6,285	1,396
Alaska	182	254	9	374	256	62	–	948	42,721	5,830	8,990
Arizona	641	230	60	434	192	29	–	2,074	34,307	5,554	996
Arkansas	305	160	72	443	115	–	–	1,003	17,000	3,295	1,209
California	5,480	3,033	367	8,060	3,558	5,126	–	26,155	382,874	95,210	2,685
Colorado	627	178	62	456	418	12	–	2,887	39,820	8,921	1,962
Connecticut	614	138	106	1,011	1,241	309	–	2,527	31,425	22,490	6,452
Delaware	206	63	48	291	253	87	–	395	10,615	4,358	5,329
Florida	2,141	1,696	196	1,846	1,016	58	–	6,041	138,711	21,993	1,294
Georgia	1,230	484	152	667	430	–	–	3,236	61,859	8,890	1,016
Hawaii	135	109	55	468	353	–	–	759	13,312	5,653	4,529
Idaho	163	161	24	200	142	–	54	602	10,509	2,603	1,902
Illinois	1,310	386	397	1,365	2,072	–	–	7,337	87,544	46,689	3,691
Indiana	627	273	44	521	447	31	–	1,764	33,491	11,854	1,913
Iowa	239	228	18	494	122	–	84	1,289	25,148	4,279	1,455
Kansas	282	182	6	527	129	–	–	1,111	12,194	2,472	907
Kentucky	452	290	123	623	436	–	–	2,259	32,922	7,109	1,727
Louisiana	469	382	214	610	571	9	–	2,350	36,969	9,773	2,176
Maine	107	152	10	241	234	–	60	574	11,980	4,417	3,377
Maryland	1,049	410	185	818	860	487	–	2,316	40,694	12,951	2,349
Massachusetts . . .	919	237	98	1,284	2,477	289	–	4,551	59,207	48,479	7,554
Michigan	1,614	471	125	798	1,045	–	521	5,973	65,432	22,479	2,230
Minnesota	327	461	114	651	386	112	–	3,403	50,296	7,150	1,413
Mississippi	272	209	42	258	200	–	149	1,259	22,100	4,167	1,446
Missouri	652	256	48	742	605	–	–	2,429	49,559	13,855	2,423
Montana	103	185	6	232	125	–	40	480	9,802	2,879	3,137
Nebraska	181	148	31	184	107	–	–	330	8,610	2,136	1,229
Nevada	215	91	17	200	132	150	–	961	19,162	3,604	1,608
New Hampshire . .	94	65	9	193	310	–	299	386	8,837	5,594	4,345
New Jersey	1,249	326	350	1,304	1,151	2,369	–	7,718	84,401	33,609	3,890
New Mexico	265	180	53	363	175	–	–	959	29,827	4,601	2,448
New York	2,413	385	440	4,228	3,522	11,559	–	14,091	229,311	91,635	4,766
North Carolina . . .	935	448	129	740	447	20	–	3,913	65,592	12,142	1,442
North Dakota	43	121	16	107	85	–	–	224	6,905	1,599	2,526
Ohio	1,541	345	67	1,777	1,147	–	350	11,429	143,620	21,054	1,842
Oklahoma	470	176	72	550	287	298	–	1,521	24,654	6,747	1,925
Oregon	434	370	54	909	285	7	135	3,734	50,893	7,464	2,095
Pennsylvania	1,306	524	154	2,082	1,087	41	949	8,186	93,430	24,330	1,968
Rhode Island	159	42	24	271	251	100	–	850	10,762	6,189	5,754
South Carolina . . .	425	183	66	663	333	1,193	–	2,162	28,498	10,990	2,650
South Dakota	71	103	27	115	113	–	–	235	8,593	2,567	3,357
Tennessee	412	205	101	446	187	5	–	1,630	28,066	3,496	598
Texas	3,079	721	72	1,518	951	–	–	9,582	181,581	14,616	661
Utah	261	189	37	557	190	–	100	976	16,919	5,064	2,129
Vermont	81	90	12	195	142	10	33	222	4,917	2,532	4,090
Virginia	933	171	74	880	647	14	322	2,504	50,836	13,530	1,833
Washington	786	623	82	585	727	22	335	6,222	59,772	14,621	2,385
West Virginia	182	183	68	479	207	7	48	1,950	10,381	4,260	2,353
Wisconsin	812	396	51	538	806	–	–	3,845	69,017	14,801	2,705
Wyoming	89	172	25	108	65	–	46	337	10,480	1,111	2,214

– Represents or rounds to zero. [1] Includes items not shown separately. [2] Based on estimated resident population as of July 1.

Source: U.S. Census Bureau; "Federal, State and Local Governments, State Government Finances," <http://www.census.gov/govs/www/state03.html> (accessed 21 June 2005).

U.S. Census Bureau, Statistical Abstract of the United States: 2007

Table 444. **Local Governments—Revenue by State: 2002**

[In millions of dollars (1,083,129 represents $1,083,129,000,000), except as noted. For fiscal year ending in year shown; see text, this section. Minus sign (–) indicates net loss]

State	Total revenue [1]	General revenue Total	Per capita [2] (dol.)	Intergovernmental revenue Total	From federal govern- ment	From state govern- ments	Taxes Total [1]	Prop- erty	Sales and gross receipts	In- come [3]	Motor licenses
United States...	1,083,129	995,856	3,458	398,497	42,953	355,544	369,730	269,419	61,679	20,190	1,303
Alabama	14,528	12,486	2,788	4,719	468	4,250	3,209	1,278	1,417	96	24
Alaska	2,866	2,678	4,178	1,125	238	887	980	780	169	–	10
Arizona	19,578	16,455	3,024	7,251	844	6,407	5,943	3,925	1,729	–	1
Arkansas	6,282	5,690	2,103	3,180	235	2,944	1,235	517	691	3	–
California	174,136	159,820	4,566	79,046	7,406	71,639	42,669	28,291	10,858	–	–
Colorado	17,835	16,154	3,589	4,390	462	3,928	6,977	4,162	2,467	–	32
Connecticut	11,094	10,679	3,087	3,526	354	3,172	6,092	5,995	–	–	–
Delaware	2,052	1,889	2,343	959	68	891	513	400	3	47	–
District of Columbia	7,352	6,922	12,166	2,840	2,840	–	3,228	803	936	1,160	19
Florida	60,028	54,956	3,292	17,103	2,171	14,932	19,488	15,327	3,480	–	17
Georgia	29,982	26,908	3,149	9,409	816	8,593	10,286	6,586	3,377	–	–
Hawaii	1,739	1,543	1,243	337	183	154	819	615	126	–	54
Idaho	3,839	3,699	2,754	1,539	91	1,448	1,020	959	19	–	4
Illinois	46,218	42,484	3,375	15,007	2,268	12,739	19,095	15,816	2,620	–	116
Indiana	20,291	18,539	3,011	6,441	397	6,044	6,786	5,970	98	580	3
Iowa	9,743	9,118	3,105	3,453	306	3,147	3,324	2,878	348	45	15
Kansas	9,304	8,469	3,123	3,120	135	2,985	3,167	2,470	634	–	3
Kentucky	9,712	8,732	2,135	3,603	312	3,291	2,806	1,539	201	818	24
Louisiana	13,554	12,648	2,826	4,696	490	4,205	4,825	1,906	2,757	–	4
Maine	3,623	3,531	2,727	1,125	84	1,041	1,914	1,864	5	–	26
Maryland	17,927	17,657	3,239	5,721	668	5,054	9,053	5,139	275	2,940	–
Massachusetts	23,427	20,913	3,256	9,132	1,115	8,017	9,073	8,719	152	–	–
Michigan	36,228	34,134	3,399	18,115	1,302	16,813	8,780	7,903	169	472	–
Minnesota	21,133	19,724	3,925	9,101	806	8,296	5,232	4,909	150	–	3
Mississippi	7,998	7,394	2,579	3,236	251	2,985	1,795	1,645	72	–	–
Missouri	16,310	15,183	2,678	5,285	635	4,650	6,395	3,859	1,904	313	12
Montana	2,296	2,219	2,439	982	172	810	692	671	3	–	–
Nebraska	7,587	5,392	3,121	1,709	193	1,515	2,324	1,742	314	–	19
Nevada	8,670	7,998	3,691	3,043	352	2,691	2,487	1,590	502	–	–
New Hampshire	3,518	3,441	2,701	1,332	107	1,225	1,702	1,668	–	–	–
New Jersey	32,488	31,721	3,699	10,635	714	9,921	16,300	16,046	26	30	–
New Mexico	5,530	5,163	2,788	3,042	364	2,678	1,250	703	497	–	2
New York	108,836	105,032	5,489	40,843	3,989	36,855	45,616	26,826	9,370	7,452	147
North Carolina	27,473	24,592	2,961	10,439	775	9,664	7,039	5,422	1,287	–	27
North Dakota	1,767	1,683	2,654	670	134	536	611	531	69	–	–
Ohio	42,138	40,285	3,531	16,158	1,535	14,623	16,035	10,625	1,438	3,458	100
Oklahoma	9,182	8,455	2,423	3,448	369	3,079	2,729	1,482	1,174	–	1
Oregon	13,183	12,118	3,443	5,525	812	4,713	3,840	3,115	239	–	9
Pennsylvania	40,614	38,501	3,123	15,377	2,341	13,036	15,491	10,860	343	2,775	–
Rhode Island	2,877	2,707	2,535	953	129	824	1,495	1,461	4	–	19
South Carolina	12,136	10,991	2,659	4,046	305	3,742	3,664	3,084	267	–	–
South Dakota	1,987	1,812	2,384	601	105	496	865	668	153	–	25
Tennessee	20,001	14,333	2,476	4,757	526	4,231	5,176	3,453	1,415	–	105
Texas	71,362	64,879	2,985	19,462	2,242	17,219	30,318	24,521	5,062	–	306
Utah	7,462	6,017	2,595	2,476	347	2,129	2,101	1,420	596	–	–
Vermont	1,668	1,511	2,452	883	46	837	447	433	3	–	–
Virginia	22,755	21,735	2,982	8,255	857	7,397	9,350	6,690	1,760	–	134
Washington	26,003	21,262	3,504	8,385	826	7,559	6,885	4,333	2,026	–	29
West Virginia	3,939	3,783	2,096	1,824	152	1,672	1,090	897	59	–	–
Wisconsin	20,376	19,507	3,586	9,251	543	8,708	6,796	6,374	270	–	1
Wyoming	2,502	2,394	4,798	944	74	870	724	548	148	–	11

See footnote at end of table.

U.S. Census Bureau, Statistical Abstract of the United States: 2007

Table 444. **Local Governments—Revenue by State: 2002**—Con.

[See headnote, page 290]

State	Current charges & miscellaneous general revenue	General revenue							Utility revenue	Liquor store revenue	Insurance trust revenue
		Current charges				Miscellaneous general revenue					
		Total [1]	Education	Hospital	Sewerage	Total [1]	Interest earnings	Special assessment			
United States. .	227,629	153,382	17,235	41,502	27,056	74,247	35,211	4,661	90,387	777	-3,891
Alabama	4,558	3,706	287	2,600	257	852	438	3	1,978	–	65
Alaska	573	358	37	65	53	215	123	8	207	–	-20
Arizona	3,262	1,968	330	265	386	1,294	681	73	3,170	–	-48
Arkansas.	1,275	783	138	186	171	493	287	8	595	–	-2
California.	38,105	24,547	1,837	4,840	3,585	13,559	5,933	1,154	16,817	–	-2,500
Colorado.	4,787	3,133	318	811	488	1,654	744	142	1,755	–	-74
Connecticut	1,061	688	98	16	189	373	125	25	486	–	-71
Delaware.	416	285	15	–	113	132	77	1	161	–	3
District of Columbia.	854	302	18	–	92	553	132	1	499	–	-69
Florida	18,365	12,095	1,427	3,479	1,614	6,269	3,310	1,207	5,675	–	-603
Georgia	7,213	5,068	230	2,630	650	2,145	1,017	21	3,109	–	-35
Hawaii	387	271	–	–	145	116	52	8	197	–	–
Idaho	1,140	916	58	497	104	223	96	28	141	–	-1
Illinois.	8,382	5,217	959	610	831	3,165	1,506	145	2,781	–	953
Indiana	5,311	3,475	311	1,767	750	1,836	417	26	1,720	–	33
Iowa.	2,340	1,836	479	708	255	504	221	17	615	–	11
Kansas	2,183	1,415	254	530	190	768	441	67	864	–	-29
Kentucky.	2,322	1,203	91	242	282	1,120	883	34	951	–	29
Louisiana	3,127	2,223	68	1,336	235	905	584	5	895	–	10
Maine.	492	364	40	61	116	128	53	2	92	–	–
Maryland.	2,882	1,953	544	–	588	929	353	108	443	162	-335
Massachusetts . . .	2,708	1,962	196	310	682	746	261	32	2,175	–	339
Michigan.	7,239	4,704	767	436	1,118	2,535	940	182	1,634	–	459
Minnesota	5,390	3,335	249	866	613	2,055	922	276	1,369	213	-173
Mississippi.	2,364	1,873	247	1,223	139	491	234	8	604	–	–
Missouri	3,504	2,438	482	756	395	1,066	532	18	1,240	–	-112
Montana	545	360	58	35	50	184	78	45	76	–	–
Nebraska	1,360	876	176	259	102	483	198	37	2,348	–	-154
Nevada	2,469	1,683	98	489	235	786	386	35	671	–	–
New Hampshire . .	407	299	44	–	76	108	38	1	77	–	–
New Jersey	4,787	3,119	599	214	1,113	1,667	541	21	767	–	–
New Mexico	871	534	81	63	114	337	176	20	367	–	–
New York	18,573	12,982	998	3,251	1,453	5,591	1,947	97	4,081	–	-277
North Carolina . . .	7,114	5,822	501	2,925	962	1,292	588	14	2,505	386	-10
North Dakota	401	200	42	–	30	201	63	46	76	–	8
Ohio.	8,092	4,973	831	925	1,360	3,119	1,819	157	1,954	–	-101
Oklahoma	2,278	1,682	253	660	231	597	278	5	729	–	-2
Oregon	2,754	2,016	354	208	525	738	316	46	1,064	–	1
Pennsylvania . . .	7,633	4,775	584	36	1,488	2,858	1,998	83	2,225	–	-112
Rhode Island . . .	260	170	20	1	58	90	21	4	122	–	47
South Carolina . . .	3,201	2,443	201	1,436	262	758	409	26	1,226	–	-1
South Dakota . . .	346	247	48	29	45	99	57	4	160	16	–
Tennessee.	4,400	3,427	267	1,789	417	973	451	17	5,670	–	-2
Texas	15,099	10,045	1,452	2,817	1,959	5,054	3,184	93	7,220	–	-737
Utah.	1,441	829	66	39	163	612	216	22	1,445	–	–
Vermont	181	113	18	–	36	68	17	3	167	–	-10
Virginia	4,130	2,817	309	294	741	1,313	581	73	1,258	–	-238
Washington	5,992	4,246	269	1,088	907	1,746	726	104	4,798	–	-57
West Virginia	869	539	34	198	123	330	231	10	142	–	14
Wisconsin	3,460	2,483	406	102	532	977	448	91	957	–	-88
Wyoming	726	584	47	409	33	142	82	11	106	–	2

– Represents or rounds to zero.   [1] Includes items not shown separately.   [2] Based on estimated resident population as of July 1.

Source: U.S. Census Bureau; "Federal, State and Local Governments, State Government Finances," series GF, No. 3 thereafter. See also <http://www.census.gov/govs/www/state02.html> (accessed 21 June 2005).

Table 445. Local Governments—Expenditures and Debt by State: 2002

[In millions of dollars, (1,140,082 represents $1,140,082,000,000), except as indicated. For fiscal year ending in year shown; see text, this section]

State	Total expenditures [1]	General expenditures		Direct general expenditures	Selected functions (direct expenditures)						
		Total amount	Per capita [2] (dol.)		Education	Public welfare	Health	Hospitals	Highways	Police protection	Fire protection
United States . .	1,140,082	997,623	3,959	986,371	432,537	39,695	29,295	50,282	44,219	55,084	25,978
Alabama	14,642	12,552	3,269	12,540	5,089	52	280	1,981	605	610	279
Alaska	3,051	2,797	4,759	2,797	1,225	6	58	63	248	201	85
Arizona	20,404	16,221	3,750	15,975	6,584	506	204	396	786	1,108	485
Arkansas	6,123	5,507	2,263	5,505	2,951	15	22	172	365	331	148
California	181,512	153,282	5,186	152,079	59,538	12,545	7,335	6,791	5,771	9,015	4,170
Colorado	19,363	16,736	4,302	16,732	6,002	540	212	935	1,702	972	424
Connecticut	11,211	10,399	3,241	10,397	5,634	110	129	25	408	617	391
Delaware	2,127	1,950	2,638	1,946	1,204	-	16	-	133	122	24
District of Columbia . . .	7,832	6,180	13,765	6,180	1,175	1,462	378	177	69	385	136
Florida	61,756	54,078	3,700	53,849	20,690	626	526	4,126	2,013	3,968	1,856
Georgia	30,960	26,488	3,624	26,430	12,355	146	873	2,865	949	1,300	636
Hawaii	2,077	1,741	1,674	1,736	-	30	32	-	183	248	104
Idaho	3,743	3,591	2,787	3,586	1,719	32	62	400	235	197	82
Illinois	51,384	44,257	4,083	44,231	19,825	432	558	1,293	2,693	2,867	1,358
Indiana	20,687	18,802	3,360	18,769	8,046	508	195	1,933	776	702	503
Iowa	9,928	9,149	3,382	9,077	4,328	109	293	728	823	373	161
Kansas	9,098	8,230	3,355	8,230	3,923	40	169	520	561	414	189
Kentucky	9,995	8,778	2,444	8,775	3,896	54	343	258	337	379	266
Louisiana	13,523	12,333	3,021	12,327	5,223	51	112	1,577	580	695	359
Maine	3,386	3,288	2,615	3,287	1,792	30	17	70	179	122	84
Maryland	17,682	16,514	3,244	16,327	8,728	112	241	-	659	1,038	523
Massachusetts . . .	25,035	20,794	3,898	20,160	10,255	67	110	665	630	1,155	848
Michigan	39,489	36,094	3,932	35,963	17,155	769	2,589	440	1,969	1,669	681
Minnesota	22,200	19,832	4,418	19,727	7,770	1,402	450	974	1,600	841	265
Mississippi	8,000	7,380	2,790	7,379	3,403	22	45	1,201	460	394	173
Missouri	17,266	15,411	3,045	15,410	8,000	143	230	842	864	846	476
Montana	2,262	2,178	2,485	2,177	1,155	28	53	38	106	142	42
Nebraska	7,769	5,354	4,496	5,346	2,681	56	36	297	397	216	126
Nevada	9,055	7,964	4,178	7,957	2,775	116	78	534	703	586	285
New Hampshire . . .	3,493	3,416	2,741	3,345	1,809	151	22	-	157	175	119
New Jersey	31,826	31,054	3,711	30,772	15,985	945	355	246	986	2,076	700
New Mexico	5,397	5,015	2,914	4,991	2,708	49	28	62	219	321	146
New York	123,857	109,731	6,473	103,583	40,104	9,175	2,456	5,796	3,855	6,151	2,452
North Carolina. . . .	28,577	24,865	3,441	24,453	10,660	1,135	1,367	2,799	443	1,175	573
North Dakota	1,766	1,669	2,785	1,659	749	38	24	-	150	63	26
Ohio	42,720	40,031	3,744	39,737	17,108	2,555	2,112	1,108	1,837	2,180	1,202
Oklahoma	9,384	8,628	2,689	8,627	4,383	36	115	663	534	477	295
Oregon	13,916	12,320	3,953	12,318	5,503	250	559	234	609	631	376
Pennsylvania	43,527	38,958	3,530	38,952	16,992	2,326	2,204	200	1,224	1,554	482
Rhode Island	2,894	2,663	2,709	2,663	1,509	7	3	1	72	191	189
South Carolina . . .	12,374	11,049	3,015	11,013	5,616	14	142	1,459	215	518	232
South Dakota	2,011	1,837	2,646	1,837	983	12	14	31	190	83	36
Tennessee	21,128	14,982	3,649	14,941	6,152	139	239	1,825	567	851	423
Texas	77,108	67,341	3,547	66,514	34,145	296	1,529	4,190	2,416	3,338	1,496
Utah	7,599	5,901	3,277	5,889	2,845	22	137	36	289	337	147
Vermont	1,616	1,433	2,623	1,433	937	1	6	-	123	44	35
Virginia	24,033	22,113	3,298	22,000	10,492	1,052	667	331	515	1,077	623
Washington	26,875	20,319	4,430	20,292	8,041	47	679	1,245	1,122	916	663
West Virginia	3,980	3,748	2,205	3,742	2,338	3	34	183	54	139	66
Wisconsin	22,077	20,449	4,058	20,408	9,367	1,424	919	194	1,714	1,175	490
Wyoming	2,365	2,220	4,739	2,219	991	9	35	378	123	96	42

See footnote at end of table.

U.S. Census Bureau, Statistical Abstract of the United States: 2007

Table 445. **Local Governments—Expenditures and Debt by State: 2002**—Con.

[See headnote, page 292]

State	General expenditures—Con.								Utility expen- ditures	Insur- ance trust expen- ditures	Debt out- standing
	Selected functions (direct expenditures)—Con.										
	Correc- tions	Parks and recre- ation	Hous- ing ³	Sewer- age	Solid waste	Govern- mental admini- stration	Interest on general debt	Other			
United States ..	**18,215**	**25,143**	**27,827**	**30,189**	**16,311**	**52,878**	**43,876**	**94,841**	**119,389**	**22,386**	**1,043,904**
Alabama	135	317	400	612	230	539	578	834	1,999	91	12,652
Alaska	1	91	108	53	49	162	151	294	236	18	3,338
Arizona	480	602	286	547	314	1,185	905	1,588	4,095	89	22,259
Arkansas	85	88	155	177	134	266	278	318	594	22	5,752
California	3,678	3,636	5,220	3,818	1,870	8,824	5,278	14,590	23,303	4,926	138,037
Colorado	217	914	373	512	63	1,039	933	1,896	2,369	257	21,299
Connecticut	–	197	348	268	201	445	291	1,334	519	293	6,984
Delaware	–	26	52	104	9	78	71	108	147	29	1,494
District of Columbia	174	303	88	211	43	383	236	959	1,490	163	5,436
Florida	1,165	1,658	1,112	1,679	1,649	2,972	3,124	6,682	7,103	575	70,010
Georgia	532	584	708	1,081	461	1,740	698	1,502	4,243	229	26,058
Hawaii	–	211	53	167	144	156	111	297	336	–	2,792
Idaho	59	72	27	120	87	197	68	228	150	2	1,440
Illinois	579	2,236	1,738	1,452	417	2,864	2,080	3,839	4,842	2,284	46,176
Indiana	226	428	418	858	213	1,143	779	2,042	1,782	103	14,615
Iowa	97	277	145	299	142	351	253	700	766	14	5,781
Kansas	94	190	134	190	100	447	506	753	834	33	10,025
Kentucky	186	136	160	423	165	374	1,040	756	1,188	29	19,955
Louisiana	295	226	353	349	249	825	549	883	1,043	147	11,753
Maine	40	45	84	117	90	171	91	357	98	–	2,025
Maryland	228	528	565	421	419	805	658	1,402	490	538	13,354
Massachusetts . . .	225	190	1,036	545	341	785	549	2,760	3,162	1,079	20,106
Michigan	496	883	320	1,426	460	2,041	1,318	3,747	2,277	1,118	32,248
Minnesota	313	622	706	613	241	1,085	1,100	1,743	1,813	359	25,602
Mississippi	73	123	141	116	118	432	286	390	618	2	5,774
Missouri	209	382	332	456	117	790	470	1,253	1,518	337	11,552
Montana	16	37	37	51	54	128	67	223	84	–	1,211
Nebraska	81	118	112	114	67	270	147	628	2,306	109	5,691
Nevada	278	364	183	178	13	712	527	622	1,091	–	12,105
New Hampshire . . .	35	59	85	71	71	174	84	334	76	1	1,825
New Jersey	468	456	714	1,088	857	1,456	1,178	3,261	762	10	25,497
New Mexico	130	156	81	108	101	277	186	419	382	–	4,110
New York	2,292	1,577	3,560	2,213	2,180	3,433	4,682	13,658	7,812	6,314	107,339
North Carolina. . . .	258	520	669	650	551	963	760	1,929	3,359	19	22,332
North Dakota	23	82	48	31	34	77	64	251	89	7	1,232
Ohio	518	947	1,209	1,347	431	2,740	1,560	2,883	2,581	108	31,335
Oklahoma	54	236	166	269	157	407	264	571	723	34	6,031
Oregon	333	271	360	602	107	693	486	1,304	1,530	66	11,159
Pennsylvania	995	529	1,616	1,561	545	2,123	2,973	3,628	3,653	915	62,827
Rhode Island	–	38	141	53	39	112	68	240	124	106	1,489
South Carolina . . .	147	201	176	229	231	751	507	575	1,322	3	12,757
South Dakota	26	77	37	44	25	96	53	128	150	9	1,143
Tennessee	299	339	480	366	299	814	723	1,424	5,803	343	17,500
Texas	1,365	1,965	1,245	1,777	764	3,199	4,049	4,739	9,107	659	98,801
Utah	108	264	153	237	98	453	237	527	1,698	–	8,520
Vermont	–	16	34	40	25	62	30	80	178	4	744
Virginia	429	558	588	694	512	1,328	984	2,241	1,518	402	21,637
Washington	411	665	681	911	435	1,203	865	2,407	6,436	121	32,008
West Virginia	31	45	90	124	52	210	208	164	207	26	3,547
Wisconsin	303	601	294	776	305	948	720	1,177	1,239	389	15,457
Wyoming	27	56	4	44	33	150	55	174	142	7	1,090

– Represents or rounds to zero.   ¹ Duplicate intergovernmental transactions are excluded.   ² Based on estimated population as of July 1.   ³ Includes community development.

Source: U.S. Census Bureau, "Federal, State and Local Governments, State Governmental Finances," series GF, No. 3 thereafter. See also <http://www.census.gov/govs/www.state02.html>(accessed 8 April 2005).

Table 446. City Governments—Revenue for Largest Cities: 2003

[In millions of dollars (60,897 represents $60,897,000,000). For fiscal years ending in year shown; see text, this section. Cities ranked by estimated resident population as of July 1. Data reflect inclusion of fiscal activity of dependent school systems where applicable. Regarding intercity comparisons, see text, this section. See Appendix III]

Cities ranked by 2002 population	Total revenue[1]	General revenue — Total	Intergov. Total	Intergov. From federal govt	Intergov. From state/local govt	Intergov. From local govt	Own sources Total	Taxes Total[1]	Taxes Property	Sales & gross receipts Total	Sales General sales	Sales Public utilities	Current charges Total[1]	Current charges Parks and recreation	Current charges Sewerage[2]	Miscellaneous Total[1]	Miscellaneous Interest earnings	Utility revenue[3]	Employee retirement revenue
New York, NY[4]	60,897	54,220	22,502	2,956	19,443	103	31,718	23,954	10,299	4,826	3,551	438	5,481	58	1,047	2,283	508	2,963	3,713
Los Angeles, CA	10,422	6,427	919	319	598	—	5,509	2,551	864	1,015	364	552	2,184	154	469	774	370	2,729	1,266
Chicago, IL	5,610	4,920	1,296	457	839	—	3,624	2,067	663	1,158	190	488	932	22	141	625	229	321	368
Houston, TX	2,954	2,321	204	137	52	14	2,118	1,303	714	550	347	158	617	16	273	197	101	336	297
Philadelphia, PA[4]	5,890	5,050	2,295	686	1,259	350	2,755	2,009	362	196	108	—	581	28	214	165	87	698	142
Phoenix, AZ	2,576	2,272	823	382	412	29	1,448	761	201	511	389	73	510	51	176	177	117	239	65
San Diego, CA	2,452	1,982	504	209	186	109	1,478	718	239	383	208	65	363	27	211	397	117	236	233
Dallas, TX	1,861	1,749	113	62	49	—	1,637	798	449	332	194	108	641	31	201	198	129	187	—
San Antonio, TX	2,426	1,148	159	49	102	28	989	471	230	224	157	22	333	13	212	185	60	1,371	—
Detroit, MI	4,242	3,766	2,298	331	1,939	28	1,468	902	400	187	—	56	364	22	289	202	38	270	205
San Jose, CA	1,659	1,446	301	68	233	—	1,146	649	291	240	127	98	312	31	151	185	92	18	195
Honolulu, HI[4]	1,151	1,012	170	105	65	—	842	542	386	95	—	48	230	22	198	70	23	139	—
Indianapolis, IN[4]	2,182	1,590	458	62	383	13	1,131	647	495	42	—	—	357	16	69	127	44	581	11
San Francisco, CA[4]	5,991	5,028	1,820	138	1,322	359	3,208	1,648	735	526	311	82	1,265	18	137	296	152	354	609
Jacksonville, FL[4]	2,588	1,349	231	74	157	—	1,118	626	372	237	129	97	273	—	140	219	180	1,082	157
Columbus, OH	1,162	1,012	161	58	93	10	851	517	36	17	—	—	257	—	148	77	37	151	—
Louisville, KY	747	648	127	40	71	17	521	370	—	—	—	—	78	—	—	73	21	98	—
Austin, TX	1,744	981	120	51	57	12	861	408	216	178	115	30	333	26	146	119	68	681	82
Memphis, TN	2,952	1,580	1,034	17	530	487	546	342	285	44	—	16	142	22	61	62	29	1,290	117
Baltimore, MD[4]	2,720	2,577	1,449	97	1,282	70	1,128	823	504	65	—	27	147	49	81	158	33	87	56
Milwaukee, WI	928	645	164	79	40	45	481	221	210	—	—	—	177	11	101	83	43	201	82
Boston, MA	2,691	2,578	1,138	105	1,015	18	1,440	1,120	1,052	38	—	—	176	—	115	145	39	55	58
Charlotte, NC	1,086	1,017	242	58	162	22	775	323	238	29	—	—	208	—	64	244	18	66	—
El Paso, TX	588	503	107	90	17	—	396	239	117	114	74	38	114	—	—	43	38	69	16
Seattle, WA	2,080	1,343	142	37	105	—	1,200	705	269	274	127	—	333	44	87	162	39	723	14
Ft. Worth, TX	689	596	40	—	40	—	556	365	192	129	120	16	109	—	64	82	18	74	19
Denver, CO[4]	2,209	2,064	306	21	282	—	1,758	708	164	463	415	—	724	39	94	326	106	63	82
Washington, DC[4]	7,006	6,447	2,207	2,083	—	124	4,240	3,383	509	991	578	220	317	11	77	540	91	207	352
Nashville, TN[4]	2,619	1,628	629	11	576	42	999	603	205	205	—	—	245	12	159	151	23	833	158
Portland, OR	774	704	104	24	37	43	600	348	179	55	—	—	200	25	75	53	19	69	—
Oklahoma City, OK	756	721	148	45	28	75	573	328	55	268	161	41	150	11	61	95	16	35	—
Las Vegas, NV	653	652	272	111	150	11	380	245	91	47	25	10	85	—	10	50	10	—	—
Tucson, AZ	811	666	282	103	179	—	384	249	182	47	25	10	30	17	76	105	43	145	—
New Orleans, LA	1,095	1,012	281	70	196	15	731	405	182	206	52	44	221	—	78	105	16	54	28
Long Beach, CA	1,214	1,065	187	16	171	—	878	248	90	132	—	64	530	53	—	100	37	148	—

— Represents or rounds to zero.
[1] Includes revenue sources not shown separately.
[2] Includes solid waste management.
[3] Includes water, electric, and transit.
[4] Represents, in effect, city-county consolidated government.

Source: U.S. Census Bureau, "Federal, State and Local Governments, Government Finances, 2002–2003;" see also <http://www.census.gov/govs/estimate.html>.

Table 447. City Governments—Expenditures and Debt for Largest Cities: 2003

[In millions of dollars (69,430 represents $69,430,000,000). For fiscal year ending in year shown; see headnote, Table 446].

Cities ranked by 2002 population	Total expendi- tures [1]	Total direct expendi- tures	General expenditures Total [1]	General expenditures Educa- tion	General expenditures Housing and com- munity devel- opment	General expenditures Public welfare	General expenditures Health and hos- pitals	General expenditures Police protec- tion	General expenditures Fire protec- tion	General expenditures Correc- tion	General expenditures High- ways	General expenditures Parks and recre- ation	General expenditures Sewer- age	General expenditures Solid waste man- age- ment	General expenditures Govern- mental admin- istra- tion [2]	General expenditures Interest on general debt	Utility expendi- tures [3]	Employee retire- ment expendi- tures [3]	Debt out- standing
New York, NY [4]	69,430	65,142	56,252	14,889	3,323	9,008	5,957	3,635	1,339	1,342	1,293	667	1,560	1,007	1,082	2,720	6,086	7,092	71,808
Los Angeles, CA	11,057	11,056	6,860	–	210	–	49	1,166	446	–	497	368	602	204	473	311	2,966	1,231	14,324
Chicago, IL	7,018	6,845	5,643	–	258	163	215	1,151	340	17	644	72	127	188	142	591	374	1,001	13,539
Houston, TX	3,120	3,103	2,702	–	41	–	94	494	299	330	195	160	164	62	94	251	181	237	9,477
Philadelphia, PA [4]	6,254	6,170	4,906	22	166	506	1,056	537	163	11	99	89	217	93	351	156	880	468	5,469
Phoenix, AZ	2,179	2,167	1,774	19	99	–	–	320	175	–	52	146	188	76	108	184	333	73	5,415
San Diego, CA	2,308	2,291	1,816	–	269	–	25	242	123	–	118	168	369	54	83	133	336	166	2,766
Dallas, TX	2,792	2,780	2,380	–	55	–	41	249	121	–	89	205	147	47	48	252	223	190	6,210
San Antonio, TX	2,791	2,789	1,259	47	18	59	126	203	130	–	100	116	187	45	54	61	1,469	63	5,327
Detroit, MI	6,024	5,955	4,937	2,074	133	–	25	376	140	–	164	117	495	90	219	202	582	505	6,781
San Jose, CA	1,721	1,660	1,576	–	270	–	20	206	106	–	101	167	128	64	83	157	33	112	3,506
Honolulu, HI [4]	1,454	1,454	1,168	–	36	–	436	170	61	54	130	114	135	130	73	101	286	–	2,471
Indianapolis, IN [4]	2,531	2,525	1,876	–	196	64	60	153	57	143	96	66	164	36	215	165	591	63	3,732
San Francisco, CA [4]	3,452	3,367	4,748	96	187	532	1,085	362	210	50	152	212	106	–	293	408	1,005	460	8,439
Jacksonville, FL [4]	1,214	1,202	1,061	–	16	11	39	182	117	–	103	83	165	66	74	91	1,315	147	7,817
Columbus, OH	1,990	1,990	1,837	–	18	36	–	159	112	13	97	83	103	39	61	77	153	–	1,657
Austin, TX	2,093	2,093	1,128	–	28	11	112	158	117	–	26	150	41	41	24	77	872	93	4,594
Memphis, TN	3,158	3,140	1,648	953	18	–	13	164	78	–	112	84	72	43	119	47	1,354	157	2,480
Baltimore, MD [4]	2,556	2,503	2,243	1,055	43	101	65	259	103	–	83	98	64	51	31	76	94	219	1,708
Milwaukee, WI	1,105	1,080	873	–	115	–	27	206	81	–	39	–	128	62	49	53	46	185	794
Boston, MA	2,955	2,713	2,581	864	101	–	185	249	146	106	95	32	128	54	49	61	94	280	1,598
Charlotte, NC	1,011	1,006	761	–	41	–	16	138	69	–	29	53	44	35	21	60	235	15	2,243
El Paso, TX	621	458	458	–	28	–	17	84	50	–	107	24	42	17	23	27	148	16	870
Seattle, WA	2,550	2,426	1,514	–	59	–	–	167	99	13	47	263	150	106	95	45	955	81	3,645
Ft. Worth, TX	834	582	582	–	10	–	–	137	70	–	84	44	76	27	40	34	180	72	1,155
Denver, CO [4]	2,459	2,401	2,160	–	54	120	54	155	74	65	98	198	68	–	152	294	222	77	5,181
Washington, DC	6,983	6,695	6,736	1,143	79	1,568	756	407	160	142	50	328	104	43	310	262	102	–	5,854
Louisville, KY [4]	893	893	760	–	23	22	35	118	46	40	27	37	–	20	38	120	129	–	2,681
Nashville, TN [4]	2,795	2,794	1,780	613	–	33	176	125	86	49	116	71	33	22	109	180	902	–	3,905
Portland, OR	977	827	827	–	31	–	–	120	73	–	74	63	206	–	47	84	80	112	2,242
Oklahoma City, OK	892	892	777	25	21	–	–	116	90	27	82	59	68	28	98	50	102	71	869
Las Vegas, NV	616	522	615	–	19	–	–	95	47	–	96	60	31	–	68	19	–	13	355
Tucson, AZ	1,012	805	805	–	77	–	23	115	63	–	51	56	93	59	104	49	182	–	1,023
New Orleans, LA	1,064	896	896	–	121	–	47	105	55	29	72	16	14	33	42	61	117	25	1,608
Long Beach, CA	1,271	1,072	1,072	–	90	–	–	160	55	–	–	100	–	65	42	101	198	51	2,217

– Represents or rounds to zero.   [1] Includes expenditure sources not shown separately.   [2] Excludes public buildings.   [3] Includes water, electric, and transit.   [4] Represents, in effect, city-county consolidated government.

Source: U.S. Census Bureau, "Federal, State and Local Governments, Government Finances, 2002–2003;" see also <http://www.census.gov/govs/estimate.html>.

State and Local Government Finances and Employment   295

Table 448. County Governments—Revenue for Largest Counties: 2003

[In millions of dollars (17,263 represents $17,263,000,000). For fiscal year ending in year shown; see text, this section. See Appendix III]

Counties ranked by 2002 population	Total revenue [1]	General revenue — Total	Intergovernmental — Total	From federal government — Total [1]	From federal — Housing [2]	From state government — Total [1]	From state — Public welfare	From state — Health and hospitals	From local government	General revenue from own sources — Total	Taxes — Total [1]	Taxes — Property	Sales and gross receipts — Total	Sales and gross receipts — General sales	Current charges — Total [1]	Current charges — Parks and recreation	Current charges — Sewerage [3]	Current charges — Hospitals	Miscellaneous general revenue — Total [1]	Miscellaneous — Interest earnings
Los Angeles, CA	17,263	16,404	11,290	326	76	10,498	4,816	2,231	466	5,114	2,641	2,377	145	74	1,539	67	42	706	934	132
Cook, IL	3,510	2,453	519	70	60	431	190	–	19	1,934	1,380	798	562	334	438	47	–	219	116	44
Harris, TX	2,584	2,584	453	84	26	281	99	162	88	2,131	1,202	1,069	66	–	564	–	–	231	365	279
Maricopa, AZ	2,355	2,355	1,145	47	–	1,077	506	31	21	1,210	608	475	104	104	396	26	108	327	206	148
Orange, CA	3,021	3,173	1,851	143	96	1,531	539	260	178	1,325	471	418	44	43	461	–	17	–	393	114
San Diego, CA	3,401	3,173	2,320	147	206	2,057	696	511	116	853	506	420	27	20	167	28	437	–	180	38
Dade, FL	5,472	5,243	1,074	607	–	460	–	25	31	4,168	1,458	960	400	102	533	–	–	930	570	315
Dallas, TX	1,452	1,433	244	–	–	205	90	26	390	1,189	600	554	–	–	470	16	82	449	55	20
Wayne, MI	2,809	2,800	1,908	68	17	1,450	152	926	84	892	333	316	10	–	710	9	39	–	89	33
San Bernardino, CA	2,834	2,768	1,672	498	17	1,090	322	159	128	1,096	238	198	27	22	453	–	326	336	148	51
King, WA	2,066	1,958	510	108	–	274	–	173	49	1,448	884	405	454	377	538	17	140	–	112	109
Broward, FL	1,832	1,786	337	110	21	178	–	112	72	1,449	720	592	108	–	514	–	46	–	191	55
Riverside, CA	2,469	2,469	1,420	91	–	1,257	553	159	109	1,049	346	289	28	22	240	–	–	178	189	27
Santa Clara, CA	2,746	2,746	1,749	28	22	1,612	879	70	16	996	669	493	138	136	–	17	–	143	88	84
Tarrant, TX	540	540	161	31	14	113	14	10	37	379	236	204	12	–	49	–	79	–	94	174
Clark, NV	3,217	2,887	616	78	–	501	642	273	94	2,271	898	449	275	83	959	11	–	401	415	57
Alameda, CA	2,135	2,308	1,230	17	–	1,119	260	62	14	1,079	469	314	136	125	490	–	21	388	120	33
Suffolk, NY	2,359	2,219	540	38	–	488	160	35	11	1,679	1,413	491	896	893	154	–	–	–	111	75
Bexar, TX	1,010	1,010	175	–	–	160	96	187	–	835	345	304	24	–	388	20	–	353	102	119
Cuyahoga, OH	1,837	1,837	847	18	17	822	473	86	–	990	491	279	173	158	324	16	9	289	175	35
Nassau, NY	3,450	3,450	779	88	34	691	389	210	70	2,671	1,671	778	878	863	785	–	257	622	215	52
Sacramento, CA	2,589	2,589	1,505	–	–	1,430	702	394	–	1,084	392	199	142	111	515	–	–	–	177	–
Allegheny, PA	(NA)	1,330	899	42	31	389	244	87	149	431	323	272	49	37	63	25	–	–	44	15
Oakland, MI	1,285	915	578	40	10	852	131	–	–	338	220	207	–	–	87	–	82	–	31	109
Palm Beach, FL	907	1,345	184	53	–	129	–	110	12	1,162	665	500	146	–	222	–	57	295	275	49
Hennepin, MN	1,414	1,709	710	134	–	564	310	182	32	999	445	440	–	–	458	66	–	–	95	138
Franklin, OH	1,709	1,038	424	–	19	385	117	–	–	613	394	290	96	79	70	–	66	–	150	114
Hillsborough, FL	1,039	1,448	252	29	11	219	45	75	–	1,197	674	472	189	15	327	34	–	–	197	25
St Louis, MO	1,591	605	58	11	48	47	–	109	16	547	453	117	324	283	56	–	198	–	39	121
Fairfax, VA	580	3,468	840	94	84	730	125	–	68	2,628	2,093	1,668	238	142	348	40	24	345	187	30
Contra Costa, CA	3,824	1,830	827	101	–	659	314	38	–	1,003	338	274	25	11	558	–	49	–	108	150
Orange, NY	1,607	1,343	228	23	–	205	–	–	12	1,115	652	444	191	–	214	28	–	–	249	41
Erie, NY	1,445	1,399	389	–	–	369	202	88	17	1,010	544	160	372	367	384	39	16	235	82	57
Westchester, NY	1,465	2,101	534	34	–	482	275	135	9	1,567	786	457	324	315	699	–	–	514	83	–
Milwaukee, WI	2,114	1,068	515	145	15	361	67	–	–	553	263	202	58	58	256	–	–	55	34	14

– Represents or rounds to zero.   [1] Includes revenue sources not shown separately.   [2] Includes urban development.   [3] Includes solid waste management.

Source: U.S. Census Bureau, "Federal, State and Local Governments, Government Finances, 2002–2003;" see also <http://www.census.gov/govs/estimate.html>.

Table 449. County Governments—Expenditures and Debt for Largest Counties: 2003

[In millions of dollars (16,069 represents $16,069,000,000). For fiscal year ending in year shown; see text, this section. See headnote, Table 448. See Appendix III]

Counties ranked by 2002 population	Total expenditures[1]	Total direct expenditures	General exp. Total[1]	Education	Housing[2]	Public welfare	Health	Hospitals	Police protection	Correction	Highways	Parks and recreation	Natural resources	Sewerage and solid waste management	Governmental administration	Interest on general debt	Utility expenditures[3]	Employee retirement expenditures[3]	Debt outstanding
Los Angeles, CA	16,069	15,477	14,670	544	127	4,568	1,804	1,822	942	925	341	233	195	56	1,657	351	59	1,339	3,945
Cook, IL	3,061	3,051	2,730	1	9	11	50	936	91	373	132	120	–	–	633	98	–	331	2,736
Harris, TX	2,843	2,843	2,843	–	39	15	144	676	177	188	207	430	104	3	333	363	–	–	7,812
Maricopa, AZ	2,286	2,017	2,286	32	9	687	72	350	46	405	104	11	65	76	301	107	–	–	1,734
Orange, CA	3,185	2,919	2,999	257	24	716	375	–	209	258	57	72	42	29	411	189	–	186	2,976
San Diego, CA	3,503	3,260	3,280	333	101	762	509	1,227	186	263	90	19	14	421	489	52	571	224	1,269
Dade, FL	5,841	5,817	5,270	–	305	132	62	863	382	179	67	201	40	1	271	478	–	–	8,671
Dallas, TX	1,381	1,381	1,372	–	25	5	64	62	25	133	30	–	–	–	146	20	–	9	477
Wayne, MI	3,079	3,000	2,979	–	4	214	974	345	24	243	166	223	18	76	344	130	–	100	2,544
San Bernardino, CA	2,905	2,592	2,755	309	114	753	268	23	239	86	47	15	36	38	204	66	431	145	1,696
King, WA	2,201	2,126	1,770	–	19	6	308	–	102	119	124	48	42	386	194	239	180	–	2,697
Broward, FL	1,865	1,810	1,685	–	19	45	102	231	250	172	79	78	23	136	142	152	–	–	3,106
Riverside, CA	2,481	2,388	2,481	310	50	592	192	434	199	143	88	13	72	34	243	80	–	–	878
Santa Clara, CA	3,063	2,856	3,063	210	7	667	344	1	65	222	404	27	5	9	427	25	–	–	609
Tarrant, TX	551	550	551	–	29	7	115	432	31	96	20	–	–	–	111	79	–	–	1,657
Clark, NV	3,073	3,056	2,478	–	11	101	54	545	352	159	369	54	57	37	266	226	595	162	5,206
Alameda, CA	2,604	2,503	2,442	34	26	600	295	–	78	186	53	31	76	–	290	38	–	–	1,183
Suffolk, NY	2,308	2,050	2,125	255	5	476	157	472	395	114	44	36	17	74	116	52	183	–	1,507
Bexar, TX	980	904	980	–	1	85	43	453	31	77	13	–	7	–	89	82	–	–	1,023
Cuyahoga, OH	1,743	1,726	1,743	–	18	353	306	341	23	90	57	65	–	12	225	129	–	–	2,556
Nassau, NY	3,074	3,074	3,073	237	35	574	180	30	568	183	58	31	–	98	121	208	–	–	3,671
Sacramento, CA	2,853	2,724	2,690	155	–	803	233	9	241	192	218	–	–	168	345	108	37	126	2,292
Allegheny, PA	1,348	1,260	1,298	32	50	312	352	–	39	64	30	60	36	–	111	29	–	50	721
Oakland, MI	867	856	834	8	11	5	210	394	68	97	97	16	45	84	128	12	–	27	322
Palm Beach, FL	1,415	1,384	1,298	–	22	43	35	–	179	77	114	62	6	140	115	101	117	–	1,679
Hennepin, MN	1,700	1,695	1,650	–	10	404	259	–	70	91	54	1	–	53	126	22	50	–	497
Franklin, OH	1,077	1,049	1,076	–	7	281	297	–	35	69	42	22	–	4	119	122	–	–	1,778
Hillsborough, FL	1,400	1,373	1,255	–	5	57	22	–	127	94	78	49	33	65	146	112	145	–	2,221
St Louis, MO	606	405	583	–	10	16	50	–	62	21	43	25	–	5	73	24	–	20	436
Fairfax, VA	3,860	3,796	3,415	1,732	68	201	154	392	155	32	34	106	3	198	109	170	209	236	3,363
Contra Costa, CA	1,980	1,930	1,839	107	88	336	176	–	83	99	75	309	21	15	146	41	–	141	1,057
Orange, FL	1,497	1,472	1,435	–	16	29	18	236	129	119	142	–	11	40	138	169	63	–	3,336
Erie, NY	1,610	1,237	1,539	87	5	555	65	586	37	72	73	–	–	27	50	44	71	–	912
Westchester, NY	2,294	2,008	2,253	81	–	441	107	–	40	126	59	62	1	148	98	51	41	–	1,396

– Represents or rounds to zero. [1] Includes expenditure categories not shown separately. [2] Includes community development. [3] Includes water, electric, and transit.

Source: U.S. Census Bureau, "Federal, State and Local Governments, Government Finances, 2002–2003;" see also <http://www.census.gov/govs/estimate.html>.

Table 450. Governmental Employment and Payrolls: 1982 to 2004

[Employees in thousands (15,841 represents 15,841,000), payroll in millions of dollars (23,173 represents $23,173,000,000). Data are for the month of October through 1995. Beginning with the 1997 survey, data are for the month of March. There was no survey between October 1995 and March 1997. Covers both full-time and part-time employees. Local government data are estimates subject to sampling variation; see Appendix III and source]

Type of government	1982	1987	1992	1997	1999	2000	2001	2002	2003	2004
EMPLOYEES (1,000)										
Total	15,841	17,212	18,745	19,540	20,306	20,876	20,970	21,039	21,336	21,494
Federal (civilian) [1]	2,848	3,091	3,047	2,807	2,799	2,899	2,698	2,690	2,717	2,734
State and local	12,993	14,121	15,698	16,733	17,506	17,976	18,272	18,349	18,649	18,760
Percent of total	82	82	84	86	86	86	87	87	87	87
State	3,744	4,116	4,595	4,733	4,818	4,877	4,985	5,072	5,042	5,041
Local	9,249	10,005	11,103	12,000	12,689	13,099	13,288	13,277	13,606	13,719
Counties	1,824	1,963	2,253	2,425	(NA)	(NA)	(NA)	2,729	(NA)	(NA)
Municipalities	2,397	2,493	2,665	2,755	(NA)	(NA)	(NA)	2,972	(NA)	(NA)
School districts	4,194	4,627	5,134	5,675	(NA)	(NA)	(NA)	6,367	(NA)	(NA)
Townships	356	393	424	455	(NA)	(NA)	(NA)	488	(NA)	(NA)
Special districts	478	529	627	691	(NA)	(NA)	(NA)	721	(NA)	(NA)
PAYROLLS (mil. dol.)										
Total	23,173	32,669	43,120	49,156	54,363	58,166	60,632	63,923	67,194	68,760
Federal (civilian) [1]	5,959	7,924	9,937	9,744	10,748	11,485	11,370	11,599	12,672	12,845
State and local	17,214	24,745	33,183	39,412	43,886	46,681	49,262	52,323	54,522	55,915
Percent of total	74	76	77	80	80	80	81	82	81	81
State	5,022	7,263	9,828	11,413	12,565	13,279	14,136	14,838	15,116	15,478
Local	12,192	17,482	23,355	27,999	31,321	33,402	35,126	37,486	39,406	40,437
Counties	2,287	3,270	4,698	5,750	(NA)	(NA)	(NA)	7,902	(NA)	(NA)
Municipalities	3,428	4,770	6,207	7,146	(NA)	(NA)	(NA)	9,714	(NA)	(NA)
School districts	5,442	7,961	10,394	12,579	(NA)	(NA)	(NA)	16,720	(NA)	(NA)
Townships	370	522	685	869	(NA)	(NA)	(NA)	1,124	(NA)	(NA)
Special districts	665	959	1,370	1,654	(NA)	(NA)	(NA)	2,026	(NA)	(NA)

NA Not available.   [1] Includes employees outside the United States.

Source: U.S. Census Bureau, "Federal, State, and Local Governments, Public Employment and Payroll Data;" see also <http://www.census.gov/govs/www/apes.html>; (accessed 21 June 2005).

Table 451. All Governments—Employment and Payroll by Function: 2004

[Employees in thousands (21,494 represents 21,494,000); payroll in millions of dollars (68,760 represents $68,760,000,000). See headnote, Table 450]

Function	Employees (1,000)					Payrolls (mil. dol.)				
			State and local					State and local		
	Total	Federal (civilian) [1]	Total	State	Local	Total	Federal (civilian) [1]	Total	State	Local
Total	21,494	2,734	18,760	5,041	13,719	68,760	12,845	55,915	15,478	40,437
National defense [2]	688	688	(X)	(X)	(X)	2,624	2,624	(X)	(X)	(X)
Postal Service	790	790	(X)	(X)	(X)	3,407	3,407	(X)	(X)	(X)
Space research and technology	20	20	(X)	(X)	(X)	144	144	(X)	(X)	(X)
Elem. and secondary education	7,541	(X)	7,541	63	7,477	21,456	–	21,456	191	21,265
Higher education	2,830	(X)	2,830	2,274	557	7,091	(X)	7,091	5,898	1,194
Other education	107	11	95	95	(X)	385	63	323	323	(X)
Health	602	137	465	180	285	2,206	729	1,477	626	851
Hospitals	1,146	159	987	424	564	3,891	695	3,196	1,353	1,843
Public welfare	532	9	523	229	294	1,653	56	1,597	720	877
Social insurance administration	160	67	93	93	(X)	661	346	315	315	(X)
Police protection	1,120	160	960	105	855	4,626	829	3,797	441	3,356
Fire protection	431	(X)	431	(X)	431	1,485	(X)	1,485	(X)	1,485
Correction	749	35	714	465	249	2,576	170	2,405	1,554	851
Streets & highways	567	3	564	244	320	1,849	21	1,828	851	976
Air transportation	93	47	46	3	43	629	451	178	15	163
Water transport/terminals	18	5	13	5	8	67	14	53	20	33
Solid waste management	118	(X)	118	2	116	353	(X)	353	8	344
Sewerage	136	(X)	136	2	134	471	(X)	471	9	462
Parks & recreation	409	25	384	41	343	841	111	729	100	629
Natural resources	400	192	208	162	47	1,591	952	639	509	130
Housing & community development	137	17	120	–	120	506	98	409	–	409
Water supply	175	–	175	1	175	588	–	588	3	585
Electric power	80	–	80	4	76	392	–	392	23	369
Gas supply	11	–	11	–	11	37	–	37	–	37
Transit	238	(X)	238	34	204	997	(X)	997	160	837
Libraries	186	4	182	1	181	372	25	347	2	345
State liquor stores	9	(X)	9	(X)	(X)	19	(X)	19	19	(X)
Financial administration	541	113	428	173	255	1,981	606	1,376	603	773
Other government administration	484	22	462	58	403	1,144	129	1,015	202	813
Judicial and legal	497	61	436	168	268	2,017	359	1,658	704	954
Other & unallocable	679	170	510	208	302	2,703	1,016	1,687	830	857

– Represents or rounds to zero.   X Not applicable.   [1] Includes employees outside the United States.   [2] Includes international relations.

Source: U.S. Census Bureau, "Federal, State, and Local Governments, Public Employment and Payroll Data;" see also <http://www.census.gov/govs/www/apes.html>; (accessed 21 June 2005).

Table 452. **State and Local Government—Employer Costs per Hour Worked: 2005**

[**In dollars. As of March.** Based on a sample; see source for details. For additional data, see Table 635]

Occupation and industry	Total compensation	Wages and salaries	Benefit cost						
			Total	Paid leave	Supplemental pay	Insurance	Retirement and savings	Legally required benefits	Other [1]
Total workers...................	**35.50**	**24.26**	**11.24**	**2.68**	**0.31**	**3.76**	**2.34**	**2.10**	**0.05**
Occupational group:									
Management, professional, and related. .	43.18	30.85	12.33	2.89	0.19	4.11	2.67	2.41	0.06
Professional and related..........	42.88	30.98	11.91	2.57	0.19	4.07	2.61	2.40	0.06
Teachers [2]...................	47.87	35.55	12.33	2.43	0.11	4.16	3.01	2.55	0.07
Primary, secondary, and special education school teachers........	46.45	34.18	12.27	2.40	0.11	4.42	2.86	2.40	0.09
Sales and office.................	24.26	15.31	8.95	2.29	0.16	3.49	1.43	1.54	0.04
Office and administrative support	24.24	15.30	8.95	2.28	0.16	3.49	1.44	1.53	0.04
Service......................	27.10	16.81	10.29	2.44	0.61	3.08	2.42	1.69	0.05
Industry group:									
Education and health services........	37.20	26.51	10.69	2.44	0.20	3.74	2.17	2.09	0.05
Educational services	37.84	27.18	10.66	2.33	0.13	3.81	2.26	2.08	0.05
Elementary and secondary schools .	37.07	26.65	10.43	2.09	0.11	3.98	2.17	2.00	0.06
Junior colleges, colleges, and universities	40.54	29.06	11.47	3.07	0.17	3.34	2.57	2.32	([3])
Health care and social assistance....	32.89	22.03	10.86	3.16	0.70	3.24	1.59	2.12	0.04
Hospitals...................	30.21	19.82	10.39	3.01	0.71	3.02	1.55	2.03	0.05
Public administration	33.02	20.85	12.18	3.09	0.47	3.79	2.73	2.03	0.06

[1] Includes severance pay and supplemental unemployment benefits. [2] Includes postsecondary teacher; primary, secondary, and special education teachers; and other teachers and instructors. [3] Cost per hour worked is $0.01 or less.

Source: U.S. Bureau of Labor Statistics, *National Compensation Survey, Benefits, Archives, 2005 National Survey Compensation Publications List, Employer Costs for Employee Compensation News Release*, March 2005; <http://www.bls.gov /ncs/ncspubs.htm> (accessed 16 June 2006).

Table 453. **State and Local Government—Full-Time Employment and Salary by Sex and Race/Ethnic Group: 1980 to 2003**

[**(2,350 represents 2,350,000). As of June 30.** Excludes school systems and educational institutions. Based on reports from state governments (42 in 1980; 42 in 1980; 47 in 1983; 49 in 1981 and 1984 through 1987; and 50 in 1989 through 1991) and a sample of county, municipal, township, and special district jurisdictions employing 15 or more nonelected, nonappointed full-time employees. Beginning 1993, only for state and local governments with 100 or more employees. For definition of median, see Guide to Tabular Presentation]

Year and occupation	Employment (1,000)						Median annual salary ($1,000)					
	Male	Female	White [1]	Minority			Male	Female	White [1]	Minority		
				Total [2]	Black [1]	Hispanic [3]				Total [2]	Black [1]	Hispanic [3]
1980	2,350	1,637	3,146	842	619	163	15.2	11.4	13.8	11.8	11.5	12.3
1981	2,740	1,925	3,591	1,074	780	205	17.7	13.1	16.1	13.5	13.3	14.7
1983	2,674	1,818	3,423	1,069	768	219	20.1	15.3	18.5	15.9	15.6	17.3
1984	2,700	1,880	3,458	1,121	799	233	21.4	16.2	19.6	17.4	16.5	18.4
1985	2,789	1,952	3,563	1,179	835	248	22.3	17.3	20.6	18.4	17.5	19.2
1986	2,797	1,982	3,549	1,230	865	259	23.4	18.1	21.5	19.6	18.7	20.2
1987	2,818	2,031	3,600	1,249	872	268	24.2	18.9	22.4	20.9	19.3	21.1
1989	3,030	2,227	3,863	1,394	961	308	26.1	20.6	24.1	22.1	20.7	22.7
1990	3,071	2,302	3,918	1,456	994	327	27.3	21.8	25.2	23.3	22.0	23.8
1991	3,110	2,349	3,965	1,494	1,011	340	28.4	22.7	26.4	23.8	22.7	24.5
1993	2,820	2,204	3,588	1,436	948	341	30.6	24.3	28.5	25.9	24.2	26.8
1995	2,960	2,355	3,781	1,534	993	379	33.5	27.0	31.4	26.3	26.8	28.6
1997	2,898	2,307	3,676	1,529	973	392	34.6	27.9	32.2	30.2	27.4	29.5
1999	2,939	2,393	3,723	1,609	1,012	417	37.0	29.9	34.8	31.1	29.6	31.2
2001	3,080	2,554	3,888	1,746	1,077	471	39.8	32.1	37.5	34.0	31.5	33.8
2003, total	**3,134**	**2,610**	**3,919**	**1,826**	**1,097**	**508**	**42.2**	**34.7**	**40.0**	**35.9**	**33.6**	**36.6**
Officials/administrators ..	215	126	275	65	39	17	66.4	59.2	64.0	63.0	61.5	62.8
Professionals.........	654	819	1,064	409	228	96	52.2	44.9	48.6	46.6	43.1	45.6
Technicians.........	273	204	340	138	75	40	42.2	34.6	39.6	36.3	34.5	37.8
Protective service......	923	209	795	337	205	107	43.0	35.5	42.2	40.1	37.3	44.0
Paraprofessionals......	109	301	238	172	119	39	31.0	28.0	29.8	27.2	25.7	29.8
Admin. support	122	795	593	325	188	102	31.1	29.2	29.4	29.5	28.8	29.5
Skilled craft.........	401	23	308	116	67	37	38.6	32.9	38.4	38.0	36.2	38.2
Service/maintenance....	437	133	306	264	177	71	31.4	24.2	30.4	29.3	28.3	29.9

[1] Non-Hispanic. [2] Includes other minority groups not shown separately [3] Persons of Hispanic origin may be any race.

Source: U.S. Equal Employment Opportunity Commission, 1980-1991, *State and Local Government Information Report*, annual; beginning 1993, biennial.

State and Local Government Finances and Employment **299**

Table. 454. **State and Local Government Full-Time Equivalent Employment, by Selected Function and State: 2004**

[In thousands (1,672.8 represents 1,672,800). For **March.** Local government amounts are estimates subject to sampling variation; see Appendix III and source; see headnote, Table 455]

State	Total [1]		Education				Public welfare		Health		Hospitals	
			Elem. & secondary		Higher education							
	State	Local	State	Local	State	Local	State	Local	State	Local	State	Local
United States ..	1,672.8	6,739.2	50.6	6,422.9	1,532.6	316.4	225.6	272.5	174.3	249.9	399.2	513.3
Alabama	40.7	96.7	–	96.7	38.0	–	4.3	1.3	5.3	4.8	11.4	23.5
Alaska	8.4	16.6	3.2	16.5	4.8	0.1	1.8	0.2	0.7	0.4	0.3	0.7
Arizona	28.8	117.5	–	105.8	25.9	11.7	5.3	2.1	2.4	2.5	0.7	3.7
Arkansas	22.2	64.9	–	64.9	20.9	–	3.7	0.1	4.6	0.3	4.3	1.5
California	150.5	733.5	–	663.8	146.0	69.7	3.7	64.3	11.8	42.7	39.0	62.0
Colorado	38.3	96.8	–	95.6	37.0	1.3	1.9	5.8	1.1	3.4	3.5	8.9
Connecticut	18.0	85.5	–	85.5	15.7	–	4.3	1.8	1.8	1.6	10.6	–
Delaware	7.6	17.2	–	17.2	7.3	–	1.5	0.0	1.9	0.3	1.8	–
District of Columbia	–	11.9	(X)	–	(X)	0.8	(X)	1.5	(X)	2.0	(X)	1.7
Florida	57.5	326.8	–	301.1	54.1	25.7	11.7	6.2	20.1	5.5	4.8	43.3
Georgia	50.8	232.0	–	231.6	47.8	0.4	8.8	1.2	4.4	11.6	8.2	22.4
Hawaii	35.3	–	26.6	–	8.5	–	1.0	0.1	2.5	0.2	4.0	–
Idaho	9.3	32.9	–	31.5	8.7	1.5	1.8	0.1	1.1	1.0	0.9	5.7
Illinois	58.1	291.1	–	268.0	55.7	23.1	10.5	6.4	2.8	7.1	12.0	12.2
Indiana	54.0	134.5	–	134.5	52.8	–	5.5	1.2	1.8	3.6	4.2	24.3
Iowa	27.3	80.8	–	74.6	26.1	6.1	2.8	1.9	0.4	2.8	6.8	10.1
Kansas	19.8	85.3	–	77.6	19.2	7.7	2.7	0.8	1.0	2.9	2.3	7.6
Kentucky	34.0	106.1	–	106.1	31.1	–	6.9	0.6	2.1	5.8	5.6	4.4
Louisiana	33.2	109.3	–	109.3	29.8	–	5.0	0.5	4.0	1.6	17.1	16.2
Maine	7.6	37.9	–	37.9	7.3	–	2.0	0.4	1.3	0.3	0.7	0.7
Maryland	28.4	121.9	–	111.7	26.4	10.2	6.8	3.3	6.8	4.3	5.2	–
Massachusetts . . .	26.7	151.7	0.1	151.7	25.5	0.1	6.6	2.5	7.3	2.7	6.8	–
Michigan	66.9	241.5	0.9	228.6	64.6	12.9	10.5	2.4	1.5	11.9	11.5	8.8
Minnesota	37.6	119.3	–	119.3	33.5	–	2.7	11.5	2.3	3.6	4.7	9.0
Mississippi	20.4	80.4	–	73.8	18.8	6.6	2.8	0.4	3.0	0.2	12.2	17.3
Missouri	30.6	133.1	–	127.2	28.4	5.8	7.8	2.6	3.3	4.3	12.3	10.5
Montana	7.0	23.1	–	22.7	6.6	0.3	1.5	0.5	0.8	0.9	0.6	0.6
Nebraska	12.8	46.5	–	43.7	12.3	2.8	2.8	0.8	0.8	0.6	5.1	4.3
Nevada	8.9	36.6	–	36.6	8.8	–	1.5	0.8	1.2	0.8	1.0	4.4
New Hampshire . . .	7.5	33.2	–	33.2	7.1	–	1.4	2.5	0.9	0.2	0.8	–
New Jersey	53.7	212.7	19.1	201.7	31.4	11.1	6.6	10.8	3.3	4.4	17.2	1.9
New Mexico	18.7	49.2	–	45.7	17.7	3.5	1.6	0.9	2.3	0.4	9.9	0.8
New York	51.7	488.2	–	466.6	47.0	22.2	6.4	47.5	9.3	17.8	42.0	48.4
North Carolina. . . .	52.4	177.8	–	159.9	49.7	17.9	1.9	14.0	4.1	19.6	16.5	25.1
North Dakota	8.3	14.6	–	14.6	8.1	–	0.5	0.9	1.3	0.6	1.0	–
Ohio	69.3	266.9	–	260.8	66.8	6.1	2.8	24.5	3.7	18.1	11.4	12.0
Oklahoma	27.9	84.8	–	84.2	26.0	0.6	5.7	0.3	5.7	1.4	2.4	9.4
Oregon	19.5	70.0	–	61.8	18.6	8.2	6.0	0.8	2.6	4.5	4.8	2.1
Pennsylvania	61.6	250.8	–	241.3	57.8	9.5	12.7	20.5	1.7	5.5	12.6	–
Rhode Island	6.8	20.5	0.6	20.5	5.6	–	1.5	0.1	1.3	0.1	1.2	–
South Carolina . . .	30.3	97.4	–	97.4	27.6	–	4.4	0.3	6.8	2.4	8.0	18.6
South Dakota	5.2	20.3	–	19.9	4.8	0.4	1.0	0.2	0.6	0.3	0.9	0.5
Tennessee	36.5	125.8	–	125.8	34.5	–	6.0	1.6	3.4	3.6	8.1	21.8
Texas	100.4	658.8	–	621.2	95.6	37.6	18.6	3.2	12.4	21.8	30.4	46.7
Utah	24.3	48.4	–	48.4	23.3	–	3.3	0.5	2.0	1.3	5.7	0.5
Vermont	5.2	19.1	–	19.1	4.6	–	1.2	0.0	0.7	0.0	0.2	–
Virginia	51.6	183.0	–	181.7	48.8	1.3	2.4	8.1	5.2	6.4	13.3	1.9
Washington	49.9	97.8	–	97.8	47.8	–	8.7	1.3	5.4	4.1	8.9	12.2
West Virginia	12.4	40.7	–	40.7	11.0	–	3.1	0.0	0.9	1.6	1.7	2.3
Wisconsin.	35.1	129.2	–	119.7	34.0	9.4	1.3	13.1	1.7	5.8	3.8	0.9
Wyoming	3.5	18.4	–	16.5	3.3	1.9	0.8	0.0	0.7	0.4	0.8	4.7

See footnote at end of table.

U.S. Census Bureau, Statistical Abstract of the United States: 2007

Table. 454. State and Local Government Full-Time Equivalent Employment, by Selected Function and State: 2004—Con.

[See headnote, page 300]

State	Highways State	Highways Local	Police protection State	Police protection Local	Fire protection State	Fire protection Local	Corrections State	Corrections Local	Parks and recreation State	Parks and recreation Local	Government administration State	Government administration Local
United States . . .	**239.6**	**303.0**	**103.0**	**789.5**	**(X)**	**319.0**	**460.4**	**241.5**	**35.5**	**227.3**	**384.5**	**690.1**
Alabama.	4.3	7.2	1.2	11.5	(X)	4.8	4.7	3.2	0.7	3.5	6.2	8.1
Alaska	3.0	0.6	0.5	1.2	(X)	0.7	1.8	0.1	0.1	0.5	2.8	1.8
Arizona.	2.9	5.3	2.0	16.4	(X)	7.0	9.9	4.8	0.4	5.8	5.7	19.2
Arkansas	3.6	3.8	1.1	6.5	(X)	2.5	4.5	1.8	0.8	1.0	3.8	5.8
California	20.8	21.8	13.5	85.7	(X)	32.9	49.7	31.7	3.2	35.2	29.6	100.1
Colorado.	3.1	6.1	1.2	12.2	(X)	5.2	6.3	3.7	0.3	6.3	6.1	11.3
Connecticut.	2.8	3.4	2.0	8.9	(X)	4.5	7.5	–	0.1	2.3	7.7	5.3
Delaware	1.6	0.6	0.9	1.5	(X)	0.2	2.8	–	0.2	0.3	2.5	1.3
District of Columbia	(X)	0.4	(X)	4.4	(X)	1.9	(X)	1.1	(X)	1.0	(X)	3.4
Florida	7.8	15.3	4.3	57.6	(X)	25.8	27.4	16.3	1.5	20.0	27.5	41.6
Georgia	5.8	8.0	2.2	23.3	(X)	10.9	19.5	8.0	2.9	6.7	8.0	21.5
Hawaii	0.9	0.8	–	3.7	(X)	1.8	2.4	–	0.2	2.0	3.6	2.6
Idaho	1.8	1.6	0.5	3.3	(X)	1.2	1.7	1.1	0.2	0.8	2.2	3.7
Illinois	7.7	12.4	3.7	42.4	(X)	17.0	14.5	9.9	0.7	15.9	10.3	29.7
Indiana.	4.3	6.3	1.9	15.4	(X)	6.7	8.2	5.3	0.2	3.6	4.5	16.3
Iowa	2.5	7.1	0.9	6.8	(X)	1.9	3.2	1.3	0.1	2.5	4.2	6.6
Kansas.	3.6	5.7	1.1	7.7	(X)	3.1	3.6	2.5	0.5	2.5	4.8	7.3
Kentucky	5.1	3.2	2.2	8.1	(X)	3.8	3.7	4.0	1.6	1.5	9.3	6.2
Louisiana	5.4	5.1	1.7	14.5	(X)	4.8	7.8	5.6	1.2	3.1	5.8	12.5
Maine.	2.5	1.6	0.6	2.5	(X)	2.6	1.3	0.8	0.2	0.8	2.5	3.5
Maryland	4.7	4.7	2.5	14.1	(X)	5.9	11.9	3.2	0.5	5.9	9.7	8.4
Massachusetts.	3.8	6.5	5.6	17.6	(X)	13.0	6.7	2.7	0.8	2.0	15.0	9.8
Michigan.	2.8	9.9	2.7	21.9	(X)	7.7	17.6	5.6	0.3	5.1	8.0	26.3
Minnesota.	4.7	7.5	0.9	9.5	(X)	2.3	3.8	4.9	0.6	4.3	6.4	12.9
Mississippi	3.3	4.8	1.2	7.5	(X)	3.6	4.2	1.8	0.4	1.1	2.3	6.6
Missouri	6.5	7.2	2.2	16.3	(X)	6.3	11.6	3.2	0.7	4.1	7.7	12.0
Montana.	2.2	1.3	0.4	2.0	(X)	0.6	1.1	0.6	0.1	0.4	1.8	2.5
Nebraska	2.2	3.5	0.8	4.0	(X)	1.4	2.5	1.2	0.3	1.1	1.5	4.8
Nevada	1.7	1.3	0.8	6.1	(X)	2.3	3.3	2.4	0.2	3.2	2.9	5.9
New Hampshire	1.9	1.7	0.4	3.2	(X)	1.7	1.4	0.6	0.2	0.4	2.1	2.1
New Jersey.	7.3	11.1	4.1	31.9	(X)	7.9	10.1	6.7	2.2	5.7	22.0	21.5
New Mexico	2.3	1.8	0.6	5.2	(X)	2.1	4.1	1.8	0.7	1.8	4.8	4.3
New York	12.4	28.0	6.3	79.5	(X)	23.4	33.3	25.0	3.3	10.8	40.3	41.4
North Carolina	11.4	4.1	3.3	20.0	(X)	6.8	19.3	4.3	1.0	4.6	10.9	12.9
North Dakota	1.0	1.2	0.2	1.2	(X)	0.3	0.7	0.3	0.1	0.8	1.4	1.3
Ohio	7.1	14.6	2.7	30.9	(X)	17.5	16.1	8.6	0.6	9.6	11.8	35.2
Oklahoma.	2.9	5.9	1.9	9.4	(X)	4.3	5.5	1.0	0.9	2.0	5.1	7.0
Oregon.	3.4	3.8	1.2	7.4	(X)	3.6	4.7	3.7	0.4	2.7	8.4	7.2
Pennsylvania.	13.7	10.5	6.0	25.2	(X)	6.5	17.3	12.2	1.5	3.3	13.9	30.9
Rhode Island.	0.8	0.7	0.3	2.7	(X)	2.1	1.7	–	0.1	0.5	2.8	1.2
South Carolina	4.8	2.7	3.0	10.7	(X)	4.6	7.6	2.7	0.6	3.0	3.4	9.0
South Dakota	1.0	1.6	0.3	1.5	(X)	0.4	0.8	0.5	0.1	0.5	1.3	2.0
Tennessee	4.5	7.0	2.0	16.2	(X)	7.0	7.0	6.0	1.1	3.5	5.6	12.7
Texas.	15.1	20.3	4.0	58.0	(X)	23.4	46.9	23.3	1.1	15.4	16.7	46.1
Utah	1.7	1.7	0.8	4.7	(X)	2.1	3.2	1.8	0.3	2.4	3.5	5.0
Vermont	1.1	1.1	0.4	0.8	(X)	0.4	1.1	–	0.1	0.2	1.8	1.3
Virginia.	10.0	3.4	2.9	17.3	(X)	8.2	14.0	7.0	0.8	7.3	8.8	17.0
Washington	6.9	7.2	2.2	12.0	(X)	8.3	9.1	4.5	0.6	5.9	6.0	16.8
West Virginia.	5.4	1.1	1.0	2.7	(X)	1.0	3.0	0.2	0.6	0.7	4.2	3.8
Wisconsin	1.8	9.7	0.9	14.9	(X)	4.7	9.4	3.9	0.2	3.3	6.1	12.8
Wyoming	1.8	0.7	0.3	1.6	(X)	0.4	0.9	0.6	0.1	0.7	1.2	1.6

– Represents or rounds to zero.   X Not applicable.   [1] Includes other categories not shown separately.

Source: U.S. Census Bureau; Federal, State, and Local Governments; State and Local Government Public Employment and Payroll Data, <http://www.census.gov/govs/www/apesstl.html>; (accessed 21 June 2005).

Table 455. State and Local Government Employment and Average Monthly Earnings by State: 1994 and 2004

[3,917 represents 3,917,000. 1994, as of October; 2004, as of March. Full-time equivalent employment is a derived statistic that provides an estimate of a government's total full-time employment by converting part-time employees to a full-time amount]

State	Full-time equivalent employment (1,000)				Full-time equivalent employment per 10,000 population [2]				Average monthly earnings [3] (dol.)			
	State		Local [1]		State		Local [1]		State		Local [1]	
	1994	2004	1994	2004	1994	2004	1994	2004	1994	2004	1994	2004
United States . . .	3,917	4,188	9,996	11,601	149	143	380	395	2,776	3,845	2,691	3,604
Alabama	84	86	160	185	198	189	376	408	2,422	3,472	1,977	2,751
Alaska	23	25	25	26	380	376	409	400	3,672	4,149	4,002	4,108
Arizona	57	66	156	205	134	115	368	356	2,561	3,446	2,642	3,515
Arkansas	49	54	87	98	196	196	347	356	2,482	3,130	1,798	2,484
California	327	393	1,120	1,383	104	110	356	385	3,534	5,096	3,446	4,803
Colorado	54	66	141	183	145	143	378	397	3,224	4,447	2,539	3,629
Connecticut	63	59	108	123	191	167	325	351	3,306	4,765	3,492	4,276
Delaware	21	24	18	24	287	292	246	285	2,576	3,693	2,886	3,617
District of Columbia . . .	(X)	(X)	51	45	(X)	(X)	858	806	(X)	(X)	3,549	4,732
Florida	171	183	527	641	120	105	370	368	2,277	3,397	2,420	3,364
Georgia	114	122	314	379	160	138	439	429	2,318	3,333	2,126	2,961
Hawaii	53	57	14	14	447	448	121	114	2,598	3,437	2,962	3,819
Idaho	21	23	45	55	184	167	391	396	2,393	3,368	2,091	2,863
Illinois	134	134	442	502	112	105	371	395	2,924	4,093	2,893	3,788
Indiana	90	90	210	239	156	145	363	383	2,781	3,355	2,316	3,099
Iowa	50	53	113	131	177	180	398	444	2,994	4,383	2,300	2,950
Kansas	48	44	120	136	185	160	467	496	2,317	3,490	2,272	2,885
Kentucky	73	79	128	158	190	192	332	380	2,368	3,401	2,118	2,732
Louisiana	92	91	166	192	211	201	382	425	2,282	3,288	1,831	2,538
Maine	21	22	46	55	172	165	367	420	2,567	3,558	2,281	2,823
Maryland	80	91	170	192	160	163	339	345	2,792	3,893	3,091	4,063
Massachusetts	82	88	215	235	135	137	352	366	3,006	4,310	2,933	4,020
Michigan	132	133	329	371	138	131	342	367	3,163	4,282	3,170	3,874
Minnesota	71	75	191	201	153	146	415	393	3,213	4,486	2,813	3,700
Mississippi	49	57	119	131	181	196	442	453	2,257	3,012	1,726	2,471
Missouri	80	91	185	220	150	158	348	383	2,203	2,955	2,227	2,918
Montana	17	19	38	36	195	200	440	385	2,413	3,212	2,266	2,719
Nebraska	29	34	76	81	179	193	462	464	2,255	3,053	2,362	3,196
Nevada	19	25	49	71	129	108	329	304	2,797	3,837	2,970	4,144
New Hampshire	17	20	38	49	150	154	329	373	2,623	3,498	2,568	3,176
New Jersey	108	149	322	346	135	172	401	398	3,546	4,665	3,336	4,527
New Mexico	42	49	66	75	247	259	393	396	2,291	3,011	1,969	2,716
New York	273	246	878	938	148	128	476	488	3,347	4,497	3,368	4,451
North Carolina	112	132	278	322	156	155	386	377	2,482	3,306	2,278	3,082
North Dakota	16	18	22	23	251	280	343	365	2,385	3,149	2,399	3,246
Ohio	141	136	421	487	126	119	378	425	2,866	3,890	2,646	3,456
Oklahoma	68	64	127	137	207	182	387	388	1,931	3,121	2,069	2,518
Oregon	51	57	109	122	163	160	350	340	2,780	3,664	2,772	3,671
Pennsylvania	150	161	371	409	124	130	305	330	2,927	3,887	2,786	3,751
Rhode Island	19	20	29	30	185	186	285	281	3,111	4,213	3,089	4,192
South Carolina	76	76	132	167	206	180	355	399	2,186	3,081	2,080	2,854
South Dakota	14	13	27	30	195	171	374	394	2,307	3,210	1,963	2,696
Tennessee	80	82	185	236	152	139	353	399	2,435	3,106	2,137	2,896
Texas	263	268	829	1,003	141	119	447	446	2,492	3,474	2,150	2,965
Utah	41	49	61	79	209	205	309	329	2,481	3,434	2,315	3,119
Vermont	13	14	21	24	215	224	367	390	2,357	3,701	2,488	2,990
Virginia	119	119	250	292	181	160	379	391	2,448	3,515	2,406	3,255
Washington	96	113	183	210	179	182	340	339	3,007	3,969	3,198	4,405
West Virginia	34	38	59	61	186	207	324	334	2,163	2,993	2,166	2,763
Wisconsin	69	70	199	217	134	127	388	395	3,066	4,239	2,855	3,576
Wyoming	11	12	27	31	232	238	556	621	2,154	3,204	2,286	3,094

X Not applicable.   [1] Estimates subject to sampling variation; see Appendix III and source.   [2] Based on estimated resident population as of July 1.   [3] For full-time employees.

Source: U.S. Census Bureau; *Federal, State, and Local Governments; Public Employment and Payroll; State and Local Government Employment and Payroll Data;* <http://www.census.gov/govs/www/apesstl.html>; (accessed 21 June 2005).

Table 456. City Government Employment and Payroll—Largest Cities: 1994 and 2004

[In thousands, (433.9 represents 433,900). For 1994 as of October; 2004 as of March. See footnote 3, Table 446, for those areas representing city-county consolidated governments. See headnote, page 302 for full-time equivalent employment definition]

Cities ranked by 2004 population [1]	Total employment (1,000)		Full-time equivalent employment				Payroll (mil. dol.)		Average monthly earnings for full-time employees (dol.)	
			Total (1,000)		Per 10,000 population					
	1994	2004	1994	2004	1994	2004	1994	2004	1994	2004
New York, NY [2,3]	433.9	438.6	398.4	407.4	545	504	1,294.2	1,889.5	3,364	4,770
Los Angeles, CA	50.3	52.2	49.7	50.7	142	133	191.1	284.7	3,860	5,639
Chicago, IL	40.9	40.1	40.9	40.1	148	139	148.3	164.7	3,629	4,110
Houston, TX	23.2	22.3	19.9	22.1	118	110	54.9	71.6	2,405	3,255
Philadelphia, PA.	29.8	30.5	29.1	29.5	187	198	88.4	123.4	3,070	4,191
Phoenix, AZ	12.1	13.9	11.6	13.6	114	99	36.0	63.1	3,220	4,703
San Diego, CA.	11.2	12.2	10.5	11.4	92	90	32.8	56.0	3,212	5,084
San Antonio, TX.	13.2	17.2	12.9	16.3	134	136	32.7	58.6	2,558	3,691
Dallas, TX.	14.1	15.4	14.0	14.9	137	123	36.8	60.4	2,707	4,058
San Jose, CA	6.3	8.9	5.8	8.2	72	91	25.3	47.8	4,594	6,046
Detroit, MI.	17.5	38.4	16.9	34.4	167	372	47.6	139.9	2,826	4,093
Honolulu, HI	10.3	9.7	9.6	9.0	110	101	28.7	34.8	3,029	3,922
Indianapolis, IN	12.7	17.1	11.8	15.9	158	203	32.3	50.2	2,438	3,140
Jacksonville, FL.	10.1	10.8	9.7	10.8	147	141	29.2	41.5	3,142	3,993
San Francisco, CA	24.8	28.0	24.7	28.0	340	366	90.8	175.2	3,670	6,260
Columbus, OH.	7.4	8.4	7.1	8.1	110	112	23.1	33.4	3,348	4,135
Louisville, KY.	4.4	8.2	4.2	7.6	153	109	8.8	24.6	2,170	3,272
Austin, TX.	12.8	12.6	12.2	12.0	248	179	32.4	45.5	2,768	3,810
Memphis, TN [2]	21.5	28.8	20.3	26.7	333	411	51.2	86.5	2,562	3,377
Baltimore, MD [2]	28.0	28.4	27.6	27.3	380	427	77.3	102.3	2,867	3,844
Ft. Worth, TX.	5.5	5.9	5.2	5.6	113	99	12.0	21.2	2,404	3,874
Charlotte, NC	4.8	5.9	4.7	5.8	114	99	12.3	22.3	2,607	3,901
El Paso, TX.	5.8	5.8	5.7	5.7	105	99	12.8	16.5	2,260	2,923
Milwaukee, WI.	8.7	8.0	8.4	7.9	136	134	22.4	28.5	2,693	3,604
Seattle, WA.	11.4	11.5	10.5	10.6	202	186	39.6	54.7	3,923	5,374
Boston, MA [2]	21.6	22.5	21.1	20.9	382	354	63.3	92.4	3,021	4,503
Denver, CO. [2,3]	15.4	12.6	13.5	11.9	279	213	40.5	52.5	3,021	4,421
Washington, DC [2,3]	43.6	35.9	42.2	34.8	721	610	142.3	158.5	3,432	4,748
Nashville, TN [2]	20.5	21.8	18.9	20.8	382	381	41.6	75.1	2,232	3,670
Las Vegas, NV	2.1	3.0	2.0	2.8	68	55	7.0	15.5	3,519	5,685
Portland, OR.	5.6	6.2	5.0	5.4	112	100	18.4	26.6	3,757	5,042
Oklahoma City, OK.	5.2	4.8	5.0	4.4	110	86	15.7	19.3	3,355	4,531
Tucson, AZ.	5.5	6.4	5.0	5.9	121	117	13.1	22.9	2,730	4,059
Albuquerque, NM.	7.4	6.5	6.0	6.2	151	134	13.3	20.1	2,255	3,351
Long Beach, CA	5.8	6.3	5.5	5.8	124	123	20.5	27.9	3,895	5,066
New Orleans, LA	11.0	9.5	10.5	9.3	215	195	19.4	24.1	1,861	2,612
Cleveland, OH.	9.3	8.7	8.7	8.3	173	176	25.0	30.5	2,901	3,690
Fresno, CA.	2.7	3.8	2.7	3.7	72	83	9.7	16.0	3,551	4,595
Sacramento, CA.	4.3	4.7	4.0	4.2	103	95	13.6	21.5	3,609	5,414
Kansas City, MO. [2]	6.8	6.4	6.5	6.4	151	144	17.3	24.2	2,685	3,820
Virginia Beach, VA [2]	16.1	23.7	14.9	19.1	357	439	35.1	54.2	2,400	3,031
Mesa, AZ	2.6	3.9	2.6	3.7	87	87	8.3	17.4	3,200	4,787
Atlanta, GA.	8.2	7.5	7.9	7.4	200	173	20.0	25.9	2,552	3,525
Baton Rouge, LA	7.1	7.2	6.0	6.4	268	154	14.2	18.3	2,459	2,988
Omaha, NE.	3.1	3.1	2.9	2.7	85	68	8.9	11.7	3,286	4,385
Oakland, CA	5.0	5.3	4.6	5.3	124	132	18.2	37.6	4,357	7,078
Tulsa, OK.	4.5	4.2	4.3	4.1	114	105	11.3	14.0	2,732	3,418
Miami, FL.	3.9	4.3	3.8	4.2	103	112	13.4	20.4	3,633	5,159
Minneapolis, MN	6.9	5.9	6.2	5.5	170	146	22.0	23.9	3,846	4,393
Colorado Springs, CO.	6.3	7.5	5.8	7.0	197	189	17.4	29.4	3,067	4,268
Arlington, TX.	2.3	2.7	2.1	2.4	75	68	5.9	9.1	2,989	4,029
Wichita, KS.	3.3	3.6	3.0	3.1	97	86	7.7	10.6	2,558	3,564
St. Louis, MO	7.5	6.7	7.2	6.7	189	198	17.2	23.0	2,412	3,428
Santa Ana, CA.	2.2	2.3	1.9	2.0	67	57	8.1	12.2	4,774	6,760
Anaheim, CA.	3.6	3.3	2.5	2.3	92	70	10.1	14.3	4,631	6,402
Raleigh, NC	2.9	3.9	2.7	3.4	120	109	6.8	11.2	2,602	3,510
Pittsburgh, PA.	5.6	3.6	5.4	3.6	147	110	15.7	15.0	3,037	4,294
Tampa, FL	4.1	4.6	4.0	4.5	141	144	12.6	17.1	3,160	3,803
Cincinnati, OH.	8.0	6.4	7.2	6.1	198	187	21.9	25.3	3,377	4,318
Toledo, OH.	3.0	3.0	3.0	3.0	91	96	9.7	12.3	3,231	4,129
Aurora, CO.	2.0	2.6	2.0	2.5	83	89	5.7	11.3	2,869	4,441
Riverside, CA.	2.2	2.3	2.2	2.1	94	77	8.4	11.3	4,010	5,792
Bakersfield, CA.	1.2	1.3	1.1	1.3	60	49	4.0	6.3	3,705	4,916
Buffalo, NY [2]	14.6	11.4	13.4	10.3	415	358	39.2	46.2	3,220	4,736
Corpus Christi, TX	3.3	3.2	3.1	3.0	116	106	7.0	9.4	2,304	3,224
Newark, NJ.	5.5	6.5	5.3	5.6	198	203	17.9	28.0	3,448	5,157
Stockton, CA.	1.8	2.2	1.7	2.0	75	76	5.7	9.3	3,584	5,493
St. Paul, MN.	3.6	3.2	3.3	2.9	124	101	11.5	13.3	3,588	4,799
Anchorage, AK.	9.6	10.6	8.5	9.5	344	351	37.6	40.1	4,592	4,376
Lexington-Fayette, KY.	3.5	4.2	3.4	3.9	144	147	6.9	12.4	2,089	3,282
St. Petersburg, FL	3.6	3.6	3.2	3.2	134	130	8.2	11.8	2,774	3,789
Plano, TX.	1.5	2.4	1.4	2.1	98	90	4.0	8.4	3,003	4,083
Jersey City, NJ	3.6	3.6	3.5	3.3	152	138	11.8	15.8	3,485	5,082
Norfolk, VA [2]	11.5	13.7	10.5	11.8	413	493	25.3	37.5	2,486	3,257
Lincoln, NE.	3.7	3.0	3.3	2.8	167	118	8.7	10.8	2,759	4,087

[1] 2004 based on estimated resident population as of July 1. [2] Includes city-operated elementary and secondary schools.
[3] Includes city-operated university or college.

Source: U.S. Census Bureau, "Federal, State, and Local Governments, Public Employment and Payroll Data;" see also <http://www.census.gov/govs/www/apes.html>; (accessed 21 June 2005).

State and Local Government Finances and Employment   303

Table 457. County Government Employment and Payroll—Largest Counties: 1994 and 2004

[In thousands, (91.9 represents 91,900). For 1994 as of October; 2004 as of March. See text, this section]

Counties ranked by 2004 population [1]	Total employment (1,000)		Full-time equivalent employment				Payroll (mil. dol.)		Average monthly earnings for full-time employees (dol.)	
			Total (1,000)		Per 10,000 population					
	1994	2004	1994	2004	1994	2004	1994	2004	1994	2004
Los Angeles, CA	91.9	99.9	87.3	95.9	101	102	332.3	456.8	3,838	4,834
Cook, IL	27.2	26.4	27.2	26.4	53	49	80.5	116.0	2,959	4,413
Harris, TX	20.2	22.9	19.5	22.3	88	64	49.5	83.5	2,516	3,755
Maricopa, AZ	17.0	14.6	16.3	14.3	77	44	35.6	46.4	2,197	3,234
Orange, CA	17.7	25.4	16.8	23.6	71	86	55.8	101.3	3,406	4,335
San Diego, CA.	18.1	20.7	17.3	19.7	70	71	50.4	83.9	2,935	4,286
Dade, FL	36.4	43.0	35.1	41.7	181	184	107.5	179.7	3,154	4,431
Dallas, TX.	11.9	14.8	11.2	14.1	62	65	26.0	55.2	2,244	3,937
Wayne, MI	5.7	6.0	5.6	5.9	27	29	16.9	26.2	3,140	4,458
San Bernardino, CA	14.8	19.5	14.0	18.2	96	108	42.0	81.0	3,085	4,481
Riverside, CA	13.2	20.3	12.5	19.0	102	119	41.7	85.4	3,411	4,491
King, WA	14.4	14.6	12.8	13.9	92	83	42.3	63.0	3,338	4,756
Broward, FL	9.9	13.2	9.6	12.8	76	77	25.1	50.7	2,660	3,986
Santa Clara, CA.	18.5	18.5	16.5	17.6	121	110	58.8	100.8	3,664	5,807
Clark, NV	10.7	18.3	10.1	16.9	127	120	32.7	81.4	3,315	4,921
Tarrant, TX	3.8	8.7	3.7	8.4	31	57	8.2	28.8	2,255	3,459
Bexar, TX	8.3	9.9	7.9	9.7	67	69	16.6	30.8	2,091	3,193
Suffolk, NY	13.5	14.1	12.2	12.6	101	97	45.8	65.7	3,788	5,245
Alameda, CA.	11.3	12.5	10.3	12.0	86	85	36.6	67.3	3,507	5,677
Sacramento, CA.	14.5	14.8	14.1	14.0	133	114	44.8	68.2	3,219	4,894
Cuyahoga, OH.	16.0	15.7	16.0	15.1	113	114	41.2	56.0	2,576	3,655
Nassau, NY.	18.5	16.3	16.9	14.7	142	121	59.0	73.4	3,635	5,329
Allegheny, PA	8.2	7.2	8.0	7.0	62	57	18.5	20.5	2,341	2,951
Palm Beach, FL.	8.3	10.2	8.0	10.0	92	86	23.0	40.9	2,872	4,129
Oakland, MI	4.7	4.4	4.5	4.1	42	37	14.1	17.0	3,330	4,189
Hennepin, MN	12.4	11.1	10.4	10.5	119	99	31.4	44.5	3,006	4,214
Franklin, OH	6.5	6.7	6.2	6.4	65	61	15.0	21.0	2,452	3,340
Hillsborough, FL.	13.2	13.8	8.1	11.2	154	131	29.9	37.0	2,450	3,544
St. Louis, MO	4.0	4.1	1.8	4.0	40	40	10.6	14.3	2,784	3,626
Contra Costa, CA.	8.8	9.8	3.4	8.8	104	98	29.3	39.2	3,694	4,501
Fairfax, VA	39.0	44.0	8.1	37.8	477	441	94.0	156.7	2,689	4,212
Orange, FL	8.9	10.9	11.2	10.2	124	115	20.4	34.9	2,565	3,489
Westchester, NY	12.1	7.3	1.4	6.3	137	78	38.5	28.6	3,577	4,495
Erie, NY	11.1	11.4	4.4	10.0	114	121	25.0	36.3	2,551	3,701
Salt Lake, UT	4.5	6.4	1.0	4.8	58	69	9.3	15.4	2,829	3,576
Du Page, IL	3.0	4.0	27.2	3.7	37	43	7.4	14.8	2,700	4,023
Pinellas, FL.	5.6	6.9	1.7	6.7	66	74	13.4	25.4	2,399	3,791
Milwaukee, WI.	10.6	9.1	1.1	8.8	111	97	26.9	33.9	2,550	3,879
Montgomery, MD	33.8	40.3	29.8	29.7	433	443	92.9	167.2	3,668	5,431
Shelby, TN	11.1	15.0	10.4	14.1	131	166	24.0	45.0	2,347	3,181
Pima, AZ	7.0	7.7	6.3	7.1	101	87	14.8	23.4	2,448	3,444
Bergen, NJ	8.5	5.7	7.5	4.9	101	64	22.1	22.5	2,957	4,684
Travis, TX	3.4	4.6	3.3	4.5	55	54	7.6	14.7	2,362	3,297
Fresno, CA	8.8	9.2	8.6	8.6	125	110	23.6	31.4	2,771	3,727
Prince George's, MD. . . .	24.2	33.6	21.9	29.9	323	404	69.0	109.7	3,252	3,852
Macomb, MI	2.8	3.2	2.6	3.0	39	39	6.6	11.3	2,643	3,961
Hamilton, OH.	5.9	6.1	5.8	5.9	68	73	14.0	20.4	2,439	3,444
Fulton, GA	6.1	7.4	5.9	7.2	92	90	14.8	27.4	2,567	3,954
Ventura, CA	8.6	9.1	8.3	8.8	125	117	25.1	41.0	3,046	4,732
Essex, NJ.	8.5	5.1	8.0	4.8	110	64	22.6	22.0	2,838	4,735
Middlesex, NJ	7.1	4.7	6.2	4.2	104	60	19.0	18.1	3,145	4,746
Baltimore, MD	27.3	28.3	22.4	24.0	368	367	65.6	89.5	3,091	3,995
Montgomery, PA.	3.4	3.9	3.2	3.5	49	51	7.2	11.7	2,256	3,209
Mecklenburg, NC	18.8	26.8	16.9	23.4	349	363	40.8	77.3	2,489	3,319
Pierce, WA	3.0	3.6	2.7	3.4	48	49	8.7	16.9	3,220	4,987
Monroe, NY.	7.1	6.8	6.4	5.9	98	92	18.4	22.6	3,035	3,886
Kern, CA	8.5	10.5	8.3	9.9	145	151	23.5	39.5	2,886	4,033
Wake, NC.	15.0	20.7	13.2	18.3	328	306	30.2	61.3	2,314	3,328
El Paso, TX.	3.6	4.4	3.3	4.2	57	63	7.4	13.8	2,270	3,328
Gwinnett, GA.	3.2	4.5	3.1	4.3	82	69	7.5	15.9	2,492	3,833
Jefferson, AL.	4.8	4.8	4.8	4.7	75	72	12.0	16.7	2,488	3,547
San Mateo, CA	5.8	7.2	5.5	6.8	87	102	20.0	34.4	3,771	5,662
Lake, IL	2.5	3.2	2.3	2.9	45	47	6.1	12.3	2,654	4,166
Oklahoma City, OK.	1.7	2.2	1.6	2.1	28	33	3.0	5.3	1,894	2,611
Dekalb, GA	5.4	7.1	5.4	6.9	95	105	14.2	24.1	2,650	3,549
Multnomah, OR	4.5	4.7	4.0	4.4	76	69	10.4	16.8	2,737	3,820
Jackson, MO.	1.8	2.0	1.8	2.0	28	30	3.5	5.7	1,938	2,860
Cobb, GA	3.8	4.5	3.4	4.3	80	70	8.8	15.2	2,619	3,684
San Joaquin, CA	6.5	8.1	6.1	7.2	128	132	17.3	29.8	2,921	4,179
Snohomish, WA.	2.0	2.9	2.0	2.6	40	45	6.2	12.0	3,072	4,626
Monmouth, NJ	7.8	6.2	6.5	5.4	139	99	17.3	22.2	2,707	4,202
Collin, TX	1.0	1.4	0.9	1.3	33	24	2.1	4.8	2,285	3,556
Will, IL	1.4	2.1	1.4	2.0	38	38	3.4	7.7	2,440	3,766
Bernalillo, NM	1.2	1.9	1.2	1.7	23	33	2.7	5.3	2,343	3,119
Montgomery, OH	4.9	5.1	4.8	4.8	84	93	11.9	16.5	2,515	3,409

[1] 2004 based on estimated resident population as of July 1.

Source: U.S. Census Bureau, "Federal, State, and Local Governments, Public Employment and Payroll Data;" see also <http://www.census.gov/govs/www/apes.html>; (accessed 21 June 2005).

Federal Government Finances and Employment

This section presents statistics relating to the financial structure and the civilian employment of the federal government. The fiscal data cover taxes, other receipts, outlays, and debt. The principal sources of fiscal data are the *Budget of the United States Government* and related documents, published annually by the Office of Management and Budget (OMB), and the U.S. Department of the Treasury's *United States Government Annual Report* and its *Appendix.* Detailed data on tax returns and collections are published annually by the Internal Revenue Service. The personnel data relate to staffing and payrolls. They are published by the Office of Personnel Management and the Bureau of Labor Statistics. The primary source for data on public lands is *Public Land Statistics,* published annually by the Bureau of Land Management, Department of the Interior. Data on federally owned land and real property are collected by the General Services Administration and presented in its annual *Inventory Report on Real Property Owned by the United States Throughout the World.*

Budget concept—Under the unified budget concept, all federal monies are included in one comprehensive budget. These monies comprise both federal funds and trust funds. Federal funds are derived mainly from taxes and borrowing and are not restricted by law to any specific government purpose. Trust funds, such as the Unemployment Trust Fund, collect certain taxes and other receipts for use in carrying out specific purposes or programs in accordance with the terms of the trust agreement or statute. Fund balances include both cash balances with the Treasury and investments in U.S. securities. Part of the balance is obligated, part unobligated. Prior to 1985, the budget totals, under provisions of law, excluded some federal activities—including the Federal Financing Bank, the Postal Service, the Synthetic Fuels Corporation, and the lending activities of the Rural Electrification Administration. The Balanced Budget and Emergency Deficit Control Act of 1985 (P.L.99-177) repealed the off-budget status of these entities and placed social security (federal old-age and survivors insurance and the federal disability insurance trust funds) off-budget. Though social security is now off-budget and, by law, excluded from coverage of the congressional budget resolutions, it continues to be a federal program.

Receipts arising from the government's sovereign powers are reported as governmental receipts; all other receipts; i.e., from business-type or market-oriented activities, are offset against outlays. Outlays are reported on a checks-issued (net) basis (i.e., outlays are recorded at the time the checks to pay bills are issued).

Debt concept—For most of U.S. history, the total debt consisted of debt borrowed by the Treasury (i.e., public debt). The present debt series, includes both public debt and agency debt. The *gross federal debt* includes money borrowed by the Treasury and by various federal agencies; it is the broadest generally used measure of the federal debt. *Total public debt* is covered by a statutory debt limitation and includes only borrowing by the Treasury.

Treasury receipts and outlays—All receipts of the government, with a few exceptions, are deposited to the credit of the U.S. Treasury regardless of ultimate disposition. Under the Constitution, no money may be withdrawn from the Treasury unless appropriated by the Congress.

The day-to-day cash operations of the federal government clearing through the accounts of the U.S. Treasury are reported in the *Daily Treasury Statement.* Extensive detail on the public debt is published in the *Monthly Statement of the Public Debt of the United States.*

Budget receipts such as taxes, customs duties, and miscellaneous receipts, which are collected by government agencies, and outlays represented by checks issued and cash payments made by disbursing officers as well as government agencies are reported in the *Daily Treasury Statement of Receipts and Outlays of the United States Government* and in the Treasury's *United States Government Annual Report* and its *Appendix*. These deposits in and payments from accounts maintained by government agencies are on the same basis as the unified budget.

The quarterly *Treasury Bulletin* contains data on fiscal operations and related Treasury activities, including financial statements of government corporations and other business-type activities.

Income tax returns and tax collections—Tax data are compiled by the Internal Revenue Service of the Treasury Department. The annual *Internal Revenue Service Data Book* gives a detailed account of tax collections by kind of tax. The agency's annual *Statistics of Income* reports present detailed data from individual income tax returns and corporation income tax returns. The quarterly *Statistics of Income Bulletin* presents data on such diverse subjects as tax-exempt organizations, unincorporated businesses, fiduciary income tax and estate tax returns, sales of capital assets by individuals, international income and taxes reported by corporations and individuals, and estate tax wealth.

Employment and payrolls—The Office of Personnel Management collects employment and payroll data from all departments and agencies of the federal government, except the Central Intelligence Agency, the National Security Agency, and the Defense Intelligence Agency. Employment figures represent the number of persons who occupied civilian positions at the end of the report month

shown and who are paid for personal services rendered for the federal government, regardless of the nature of appointment or method of payment. Federal payrolls include all payments for personal services rendered during the report month and payments for accumulated annual leave of employees who separate from the service. Since most federal employees are paid on a biweekly basis, the calendar month earnings are partially estimated on the basis of the number of work days in each month where payroll periods overlap.

Federal employment and payroll figures are published by the Office of Personnel Management in its *Federal Civilian Workforce Statistics—Employment and Trends.* It also publishes biennial employment data for minority groups, data on occupations of white- and blue-collar workers, and data on employment by geographic area; reports on salary and wage distribution of federal employees are published annually. General schedule is primarily white-collar; wage system primarily blue-collar. Data on federal employment are also issued by the Bureau of Labor Statistics in its *Monthly Labor Review* and in Employment and Earnings and by the U.S. Census Bureau in its annual publication *Public Employment.*

Public lands—The data on applications, entries, selections, patents, and certifications refer to transactions that involve the disposal, under the public land laws (including the homestead laws), of federal public lands to nonfederal owners. In general, original entries and selections are applications to secure title to public lands that have been accepted as properly filed (i.e., allowed). Some types of applications, however, are not reported until issuance of the final certificate, which passes equitable title to the land to the applicant.

Table 458. Federal Budget—Receipts and Outlays: 1960 to 2006

[In billions of dollars (92.5 represents 92,500,000,000) except percent. For fiscal years ending in year shown; see text, Section 8. See also headnote, Table 460]

Fiscal year	In curent dollars			In constant (2000) dollars			As percentage of GDP [1]		
	Receipts	Outlays	Surplus or deficit (−)	Receipts	Outlays	Surplus or deficit (−)	Receipts	Outlays	Surplus or deficit (−)
1960	92.5	92.2	0.3	528.5	526.8	1.7	17.9	17.8	0.1
1970	192.8	195.6	−2.8	815.9	828.0	−12.0	19.0	19.3	−0.3
1980	517.1	590.9	−73.8	1,028.3	1,175.1	−146.8	19.0	21.7	−2.7
1985	734.1	946.4	−212.3	1,082.6	1,395.7	−313.1	17.7	22.9	−5.1
1986	769.2	990.4	−221.2	1,107.3	1,425.7	−318.4	17.4	22.4	−5.0
1987	854.4	1,004.1	−149.7	1,196.1	1,405.7	−209.6	18.4	21.6	−3.2
1988	909.3	1,064.5	−155.2	1,235.6	1,446.5	−210.9	18.2	21.3	−3.1
1989	991.2	1,143.8	−152.6	1,298.9	1,498.9	−200.0	18.4	21.2	−2.8
1990	1,032.1	1,253.1	−221.0	1,309.4	1,589.9	−280.4	18.0	21.8	−3.9
1991	1,055.1	1,324.3	−269.2	1,282.6	1,609.9	−327.3	17.8	22.3	−4.5
1992	1,091.3	1,381.6	−290.3	1,282.7	1,623.9	−341.2	17.5	22.1	−4.7
1993	1,154.5	1,409.5	−255.1	1,323.2	1,615.5	−292.3	17.6	21.4	−3.9
1994	1,258.7	1,461.9	−203.2	1,414.0	1,642.2	−228.2	18.1	21.0	−2.9
1995	1,351.9	1,515.9	−164.0	1,482.4	1,662.2	−179.8	18.5	20.7	−2.2
1996	1,453.2	1,560.6	−107.4	1,557.9	1,673.0	−115.2	18.9	20.3	−1.4
1997	1,579.4	1,601.3	−21.9	1,661.2	1,684.2	−23.0	19.3	19.6	−0.3
1998	1,722.0	1,652.7	69.3	1,793.1	1,721.0	72.1	20.0	19.2	0.8
1999	1,827.6	1,702.0	125.6	1,874.9	1,746.0	128.9	20.0	18.7	1.4
2000	2,025.5	1,789.2	236.2	2,025.5	1,789.2	236.2	20.9	18.4	2.4
2001	1,991.4	1,863.2	128.2	1,946.1	1,820.8	125.3	19.8	18.5	1.3
2002	1,853.4	2,011.2	−157.8	1,777.8	1,929.2	−151.3	17.9	19.4	−1.5
2003	1,782.5	2,160.1	−377.6	1,667.0	2,020.1	−353.1	16.5	20.0	−3.5
2004	1,880.3	2,293.0	−412.7	1,712.5	2,088.3	−375.9	16.3	19.9	−3.6
2005	2,153.9	2,472.2	−318.3	1,898.3	2,178.9	−280.6	17.5	20.1	−2.6
2006 est.. . . .	2,285.5	2,708.7	−423.2	1,951.1	2,312.3	−361.3	17.5	20.8	−3.2

[1] Gross domestic product; see text, Section 13.

Source: U.S. Office of Management and Budget, *Budget of the United States Government, Historical Tables*, annual. See Internet site <http://www.whitehouse.gov/omb/budget/fy2007/>.

Table 459. Federal Budget Debt: 1960 to 2006

[In billions of dollars (290.5 represents 290,500,000,000, except as indicated. As of the end of the fiscal year]

Fiscal year	Total					As percentage of GDP [1]				
			Held by the public					Held by the public		
	Gross federal debt	Federal govern−ment accounts	Total	Federal Reserve System	Other	Gross federal debt	Federal govern−ment accounts	Total	Federal Reserve System	Other
1960	290.5	53.7	236.8	26.5	210.3	56.1	10.4	45.7	5.1	40.6
1970	380.9	97.7	283.2	57.7	225.5	37.6	9.7	28.0	5.7	22.3
1980	909.0	197.1	711.9	120.8	591.1	33.3	7.2	26.1	4.4	21.7
1985	1,817.4	310.2	1,507.3	169.8	1,337.5	43.9	7.5	36.4	4.1	32.3
1986	2,120.5	379.9	1,740.6	190.9	1,549.8	48.1	8.6	39.4	4.3	35.1
1987	2,346.0	456.2	1,889.8	212.0	1,677.7	50.5	9.8	40.7	4.6	36.1
1988	2,601.1	549.5	2,051.6	229.2	1,822.4	51.9	11.0	41.0	4.6	36.4
1989	2,867.8	677.1	2,190.7	220.1	1,970.6	53.1	12.5	40.6	4.1	36.5
1990	3,206.3	794.7	2,411.6	234.4	2,177.1	55.9	13.9	42.0	4.1	38.0
1991	3,598.2	909.2	2,689.0	258.6	2,430.4	60.6	15.3	45.3	4.4	40.9
1992	4,001.8	1,002.1	2,999.7	296.4	2,703.3	64.1	16.1	48.1	4.8	43.3
1993	4,351.0	1,102.6	3,248.4	325.7	2,922.7	66.2	16.8	49.4	5.0	44.4
1994	4,643.3	1,210.2	3,433.1	355.2	3,077.9	66.7	17.4	49.3	5.1	44.2
1995	4,920.6	1,316.2	3,604.4	374.1	3,230.3	67.2	18.0	49.2	5.1	44.1
1996	5,181.5	1,447.4	3,734.1	390.9	3,343.1	67.3	18.8	48.5	5.1	43.5
1997	5,369.2	1,596.9	3,772.3	424.5	3,347.8	65.6	19.5	46.1	5.2	40.9
1998	5,478.2	1,757.1	3,721.1	458.2	3,262.9	63.5	20.4	43.1	5.3	37.8
1999	5,605.5	1,973.2	3,632.4	496.6	3,135.7	61.4	21.6	39.8	5.4	34.4
2000	5,628.7	2,218.9	3,409.8	511.4	2,898.4	58.0	22.9	35.1	5.3	29.9
2001	5,769.9	2,450.3	3,319.6	534.1	2,785.5	57.4	24.4	33.0	5.3	27.7
2002	6,198.4	2,658.0	3,540.4	604.2	2,936.2	59.7	25.6	34.1	5.8	28.3
2003	6,760.0	2,846.6	3,913.4	656.1	3,257.3	62.6	26.3	36.2	6.1	30.1
2004	7,354.7	3,059.1	4,295.5	700.3	3,595.2	63.7	26.5	37.2	6.1	31.1
2005	7,905.3	3,313.1	4,592.2	736.4	3,855.9	64.3	27.0	37.4	6.0	31.4
2006 est.. . . .	8,611.5	3,592.6	5,018.9	(NA)	(NA)	66.1	27.6	38.5	(NA)	(NA)

NA not available. [1] Gross domestic product; see text, Section 13.

Source: U.S. Office of Management and Budget, *Budget of the United States Government, Historical Tables*, annual. See Internet site <http://www.whitehouse.gov/omb/budget/fy2007/>.

Federal Government Finances and Employment 307

Table 460. **Federal Budget Outlays by Type: 1990 to 2006**

[In billions of dollars (1,253.1 represents $1,253,100,000,000), except percent. **For fiscal year ending in year shown;** see text, Section 8. Given the inherent imprecision in deflating outlays, the data shown in constant dollars present a reasonable perspective—not precision. The deflators and the categories that are deflated are as comparable over time as feasible. Minus sign (–) indicates offset]

Type	1990	1995	2000	2002	2003	2004	2005	2006, est.
Current dollar outlays	**1,253.1**	**1,515.9**	**1,789.2**	**2,011.2**	**2,160.1**	**2,293.0**	**2,472.2**	**2,708.7**
National defense [1]	299.3	272.1	294.5	348.6	404.9	455.9	495.3	535.9
Nondefense, total	953.8	1,243.8	1,494.7	1,662.6	1,755.2	1,837.1	1,976.9	2,172.7
Payments for individuals	585.7	877.5	1,054.5	1,241.5	1,331.7	1,397.4	1,490.0	1,614.6
Direct payments [2]	507.0	728.4	867.7	1,009.9	1,080.9	1,131.2	1,212.4	1,322.8
Grants to state and local governments .	78.7	149.0	186.8	231.6	250.8	266.2	277.6	291.8
All other grants	56.4	75.9	97.9	119.8	136.6	140.1	148.6	157.4
Net interest [2]	184.3	232.1	222.9	170.9	153.1	160.2	184.0	220.1
All other [2]	164.0	102.8	162.0	177.7	188.3	197.9	219.5	253.0
Undistributed offsetting receipts [2]	–36.6	–44.5	–42.6	–47.4	–54.4	–58.5	–65.2	–72.4
Constant (2000) dollar outlay	**1,589.9**	**1,662.2**	**1,789.2**	**1,929.2**	**2,020.1**	**2,088.3**	**2,178.9**	**2,312.3**
National defense [1]	382.7	305.9	294.5	329.4	365.3	397.3	419.8	443.1
Nondefense, total	1,207.0	1,356.3	1,494.7	1,599.7	1,654.8	1,691.0	1,759.1	1,869.2
Payments for individuals	732.5	957.1	1,054.5	1,197.1	1,260.6	1,293.5	1,333.8	1,396.5
Direct payments [2]	634.0	794.5	867.7	974.2	1,023.2	1,047.1	1,085.4	1,144.2
Grants to state and local governments .	98.4	162.6	186.8	223.4	237.4	246.4	248.5	252.3
All other grants	73.3	85.1	97.9	113.7	125.2	124.4	125.7	127.2
Net interest [2]	226.9	251.8	222.9	163.9	143.9	147.1	164.4	191.8
All other [2]	228.0	114.8	162.0	168.7	174.0	176.0	189.4	212.4
Undistributed offsetting receipts [2]	–53.5	–52.6	–42.6	–44.2	–48.9	–50.0	–54.2	–58.7
Outlays as percent of GDP [3]	**21.8**	**20.7**	**18.4**	**19.4**	**20.0**	**19.9**	**20.1**	**20.8**
National defense [1]	5.2	3.7	3.0	3.4	3.7	3.9	4.0	4.1
Nondefense, total	16.6	17.0	15.4	16.0	16.2	15.9	16.1	16.7
Payments for individuals	10.2	12.0	10.9	12.0	12.3	12.1	12.1	12.4
Direct payments [2]	8.8	9.9	8.9	9.7	10.0	9.8	9.9	10.2
Grants to state and local governments .	1.4	2.0	1.9	2.2	2.3	2.3	2.3	2.2
All other grants	1.0	1.0	1.0	1.2	1.3	1.2	1.2	1.2
Net interest [2]	3.2	3.2	2.3	1.6	1.4	1.4	1.5	1.7
All other [2]	2.9	1.4	1.7	1.7	1.7	1.7	1.8	1.9
Undistributed offsetting receipts [2]	–0.6	–0.6	–0.4	–0.5	–0.5	–0.5	–0.5	–0.6

[1] Includes a small amount of grants to state and local governments and direct payments for individuals. [2] Includes some off-budget amounts; most of the off-budget amounts are direct payments for individuals (social security benefits). [3] Gross domestic product; see text, Section 13.

Source: U.S. Office of Management and Budget, *Budget of the United States Government, Historical Tables*, annual. See Internet site <http://www.whitehouse.gov/omb/budget/fy2007/>.

Table 461. **Federal Budget Outlays by Agency: 1990 to 2006**

[In billions of dollars (1,253.1 represents $1,253,100,000,000). For fiscal year ending in year shown]

Department or other unit	1990	1995	2000	2003	2004	2005	2006, est.
Outlays, total [1]	**1,253.1**	**1,515.9**	**1,789.2**	**2,160.1**	**2,293.0**	**2,472.2**	**2,708.7**
Legislative Branch	2.2	2.6	2.9	3.4	3.9	4.0	4.4
The Judiciary Branch	1.6	2.9	4.1	5.1	5.4	5.6	6.1
Agriculture	45.9	56.6	75.5	72.4	71.8	85.3	95.7
Commerce	3.7	3.4	7.8	5.7	5.9	6.2	6.5
Defense-Military	289.7	259.5	281.2	388.9	437.1	474.4	512.1
Education	23.0	31.2	33.9	57.4	62.8	72.9	84.0
Energy	12.1	17.6	15.0	19.4	20.0	21.3	21.7
Health and Human Services	175.5	303.1	382.6	505.3	543.4	581.5	641.5
Homeland Security	7.2	9.4	13.1	32.0	26.5	39.3	66.8
Housing and Urban Development	20.2	29.0	30.8	37.5	45.0	42.5	46.8
Interior	5.8	7.5	8.0	9.2	8.9	9.1	9.1
Justice	5.9	10.1	17.3	21.5	29.0	22.7	22.3
Labor	26.1	32.8	31.9	69.6	56.7	47.0	51.4
State	4.8	6.3	6.9	9.3	10.9	12.8	13.6
Transportation	25.6	35.1	41.5	50.8	54.5	56.9	61.3
Treasury	253.9	346.9	388.6	367.0	375.4	408.7	452.1
Veterans Affairs	29.0	37.8	47.1	56.9	59.6	70.0	70.4
Corps of Engineers	3.3	3.7	4.3	4.8	4.8	4.8	7.4
Other Defense-civil programs	21.7	28.0	32.9	39.9	41.7	43.5	45.7
Environmental Protection Agency	5.1	6.4	7.2	8.1	8.3	7.9	7.9
Executive Office of the President	0.2	0.2	0.3	0.4	3.3	7.7	7.4
General Services Administration	–0.2	0.7	0.1	0.6	–0.4	0.1	0.4
International Assistance Programs	10.1	11.1	12.1	13.5	13.7	15.0	16.3
National Aeronautics and Space Administration . . .	12.4	13.4	13.4	14.6	15.2	15.6	15.6
National Science Foundation	1.8	2.8	3.5	4.7	5.1	5.4	5.8
Office of Personnel Management	31.9	41.3	48.7	54.1	56.5	59.5	63.5
Social Security Administration (on-budget)	17.3	31.0	45.1	46.3	49.0	54.5	53.7
Social Security Administration (off-budget)	245.0	330.4	396.2	461.4	481.2	506.8	538.7
Undistributed offsetting receipts	–98.9	–137.6	–173.0	–210.5	–212.5	–226.2	–241.6

[1] Includes agencies and allowances not shown separately.

Source: U.S. Office of Management and Budget, *Budget of the United States Government, Historical Tables*, annual. See Internet site <http://www.whitehouse.gov/omb/budget/fy2007/>.

Table 462. **Federal Outlays by Detailed Function: 1990 to 2006**

[In billions of dollars (1,253.1 represents $1,253,100,000,000). For fiscal year ending in year shown]

Superfunction and function	1990	1995	2000	2002	2003	2004	2005	2006, est.
Total outlays	1,253.1	1,515.9	1,789.2	2,011.2	2,160.1	2,293.0	2,472.2	2,708.7
National defense [1]	299.3	272.1	294.5	348.6	404.9	455.9	495.3	535.9
Department of Defense-Military	289.7	259.4	281.2	332.0	387.3	436.5	474.2	512.1
Military personnel	75.6	70.8	76.0	86.8	106.7	113.6	127.5	116.3
Operation and maintenance.	88.3	91.0	105.8	130.0	151.4	174.0	188.1	192.6
Procurement.	81.0	55.0	51.7	62.5	67.9	76.2	82.3	88.8
Research, development, test, and evaluation	37.5	34.6	37.6	44.4	53.1	60.8	65.7	70.8
Military construction	5.1	6.8	5.1	5.1	5.9	6.3	5.3	7.3
Anticipated funding for Global War on Terror.	(X)	(X)	(X)	(X)	(X)	(X)	(X)	30.1
Atomic energy defense activities	9.0	11.8	12.1	14.8	16.0	16.6	18.0	18.7
International affairs [1]	13.8	16.4	17.2	22.4	21.2	26.9	34.6	34.8
International development and humanitarian assistance	5.5	7.6	6.5	7.8	10.3	13.8	17.7	19.6
International security assistance	8.7	5.3	6.4	7.9	8.6	8.4	7.9	8.2
Conduct of foreign affairs	3.1	4.2	4.7	7.1	6.7	7.9	9.1	8.6
General science, space and technology	14.4	16.7	18.6	20.8	20.9	23.1	23.7	24.0
General science and basic research.	2.8	4.1	6.2	7.3	8.0	8.4	8.9	9.3
Space flight, research, and supporting activities	11.6	12.6	12.4	13.5	12.9	14.6	14.8	14.7
Energy.	3.3	4.9	-0.8	0.5	-0.7	-0.2	0.4	2.6
Energy supply	2.0	3.6	-1.8	-0.8	-2.1	-1.6	-0.9	1.3
Natural resources and environment [1]	17.1	21.9	25.0	29.5	29.7	30.7	28.0	32.7
Water resources	4.4	4.6	5.1	5.6	5.5	5.6	5.7	8.9
Conservation and land management	4.0	6.0	6.8	9.8	9.7	9.8	6.2	7.6
Recreational resources	1.4	2.0	2.6	2.8	2.9	3.0	3.0	3.1
Pollution control and abatement.	5.2	6.5	7.4	7.6	8.2	8.5	8.1	8.2
Agriculture	11.8	9.7	36.5	22.0	22.5	15.4	26.6	26.8
Farm income stabilization	9.7	7.0	33.4	18.4	18.3	11.2	22.0	22.2
Agricultural research and services	2.1	2.6	3.0	3.6	4.2	4.3	4.5	4.6
Commerce and housing credit [1]	67.6	-17.8	3.2	-0.4	0.7	5.3	7.6	9.1
Mortgage credit	3.8	-1.0	-3.3	-7.0	-4.6	2.7	-0.9	0.9
Postal Service	2.1	-1.8	2.1	0.2	-5.2	-4.1	-1.2	-0.2
Deposit insurance	57.9	-17.8	-3.1	-1.0	-1.4	-2.0	-1.4	-1.3
Transportation [1]	29.5	39.4	46.9	61.8	67.1	64.6	67.9	71.6
Ground transportation	19.0	25.3	31.7	40.2	37.5	40.7	42.3	45.8
Air transportation	7.2	10.0	10.6	16.5	23.3	16.7	18.8	18.6
Water transportation	3.2	3.7	4.4	5.0	5.9	6.9	6.4	6.8
Community and regional development [1]	8.5	10.7	10.6	13.0	18.9	15.8	26.3	52.0
Community development	3.5	4.7	5.5	6.0	6.3	6.2	5.9	7.7
Disaster relief and insurance.	2.1	3.3	2.6	4.4	10.1	7.3	17.7	41.4
Education, training, employment, and social services [1]	37.2	51.0	53.8	70.5	82.6	87.9	97.5	109.7
Elementary, secondary, and vocational education	9.9	14.7	20.6	25.9	31.5	34.4	38.3	40.2
Higher education	11.1	14.2	10.1	17.0	22.7	25.3	31.4	39.8
Research and general education aids	1.6	2.1	2.5	2.9	3.0	3.0	3.1	3.4
Training and employment	5.6	7.4	6.8	8.4	8.4	7.9	6.9	5.9
Social services	8.1	11.6	12.6	14.9	15.6	15.9	16.3	17.1
Health	57.7	115.4	154.5	196.5	219.6	240.1	250.6	268.8
Health care services	47.6	101.9	136.2	172.6	192.6	210.1	219.6	237.1
Health research and training	8.6	11.6	16.0	21.4	24.0	27.1	28.1	28.6
Consumer and occupational health and safety	1.5	1.9	2.3	2.6	2.9	2.9	2.9	3.1
Medicare	98.1	159.9	197.1	230.9	249.4	269.4	298.6	343.0
Income security [1]	148.7	223.8	253.7	312.7	334.6	333.1	345.8	360.6
General retirement and disability insurance (excluding social security).	5.1	5.1	5.2	5.7	7.0	6.6	7.0	7.2
Federal employee retirement and disability	52.0	65.9	77.2	83.4	85.2	88.7	93.4	99.2
Unemployment compensation	18.9	23.6	23.0	53.3	57.1	45.0	35.4	38.6
Housing assistance	15.9	27.6	28.9	33.3	35.5	36.8	37.9	38.9
Food and nutrition assistance	24.0	37.6	32.5	38.2	42.5	46.0	50.8	55.3
Social security	248.6	335.8	409.4	456.0	474.7	495.5	523.3	554.7
Veterans' benefits and services [1]	29.1	37.9	47.1	51.0	57.0	59.8	70.2	70.4
Income security for veterans	15.3	19.0	24.9	26.7	29.1	30.8	35.8	36.1
Veterans' education, training, and rehabilitation	0.2	1.1	1.3	1.7	2.1	2.6	2.8	3.0
Hospital and medical care for veterans	12.1	16.4	19.5	22.3	24.1	26.9	28.8	30.1
Veterans' housing	0.5	0.3	0.4	-1.0	0.5	-2.0	0.9	-1.3
Administration of justice.	10.2	16.5	28.5	35.1	35.3	45.6	40.0	41.3
Federal law enforcement activities	4.8	6.6	12.1	15.4	15.7	19.1	19.9	21.4
Federal litigative and judicial activities	3.6	6.1	7.8	9.1	9.1	9.7	9.6	10.4
Federal correctional activities	1.3	2.7	3.7	4.7	5.4	5.5	5.9	5.9
Criminal justice assistance	0.5	1.0	4.9	5.8	5.1	11.3	4.6	3.7
General government.	10.5	13.8	13.0	16.9	23.1	22.3	17.0	19.1
Net interest [1]	184.3	232.1	222.9	170.9	153.1	160.2	184.0	220.1
Interest on Treasury debt securities (gross)	264.7	332.4	361.9	332.5	318.1	321.7	352.3	398.7
Interest received by on-budget trust funds	-46.3	-59.9	-69.3	-76.5	-72.5	-67.8	-69.2	-71.8
Interest received by off-budget trust funds	-16.0	-33.3	-59.8	-76.8	-83.5	-86.2	-91.8	-97.4
Allowances	–	–	–	–	–	–	–	3.7
Undistributed offsetting receipts	-36.6	-44.5	-42.6	-47.4	-54.4	-54.4	-58.5	-72.4

– Represents or rounds to zero.   X Not applicable.   [1] Includes functions not shown separately.

Source: U.S. Office of Management and Budget, *Budget of the United States Government, Historical Tables*, annual. See Internet site <http://www.whitehouse.gov/omb/budget/fy2007/>.

Table 463. **Outlays for Payments for Individuals by Category and Major Program: 1990 to 2006**

[In billions of dollars (585.7 represents 585,700,000,000). For fiscal years ending in year shown; see text, Section 8]

Category and Program	1990	1995	2000	2002	2003	2004	2005	2006, est.
Total, payments for individuals	585.7	877.5	1,054.5	1,242.1	1,332.2	1,397.8	1,490.7	1,616.2
Social security and railroad retirement	250.5	337.0	410.5	457.0	476.8	496.4	523.4	555.3
Social security:								
Old age and survivors insurance	221.9	292.7	351.4	387.5	400.2	414.8	434.0	458.4
Disability insurance	24.4	40.3	54.4	70.0	70.0	76.5	84.2	91.1
Railroad retirement (excl. social security). . . .	4.1	4.0	4.6	5.1	6.6	5.2	5.3	5.8
Federal employees retirement and insurance. . .	64.1	82.2	100.3	108.2	112.3	117.4	126.7	133.1
Military retirement	21.5	27.8	32.8	35.1	35.6	37.0	39.0	41.2
Civil service retirement.	31.0	38.3	45.1	48.8	50.2	52.1	54.7	58.1
Veterans service-connected compensation . .	10.7	14.8	20.8	22.4	24.7	26.3	30.9	31.3
Other	0.8	1.3	1.7	1.9	1.8	2.0	2.2	2.4
Unemployment assistance	17.4	21.9	21.1	51.2	55.0	43.1	33.1	36.7
Medical care	164.3	289.3	362.7	437.2	478.5	515.4	562.5	633.4
Medicare:								
Hospital insurance	65.9	113.6	127.9	145.6	151.3	164.1	182.8	186.2
Supplementary medical insurance	41.5	63.5	87.2	107.1	121.8	131.8	151.0	204.3
State children's health insurance	–	–	1.2	3.7	4.4	4.6	5.1	5.8
Medicaid	41.1	89.1	117.9	147.5	160.7	176.2	181.7	192.3
Indian health	1.1	2.0	2.4	2.8	2.9	3.1	3.1	3.1
Hospital and medical care for veterans	12.0	16.2	19.3	22.4	24.5	21.6	23.1	25.5
Health resources and services.	1.4	2.2	3.9	5.0	5.3	5.5	5.9	5.8
Substance abuse and mental health								
services.	1.2	2.4	2.5	2.9	3.0	3.1	3.2	3.2
Health care tax credit.	–	–	–	–	(Z)	0.1	0.1	0.1
Uniformed Services retiree health								
care fund.	–	–	–	–	4.3	5.2	6.3	7.0
Other	(Z)	0.3	0.3	0.2	0.2	0.1	0.2	0.2
Assistance to students	11.2	14.8	10.9	16.9	22.8	25.7	32.1	40.6
Veterans education benefits	0.8	1.4	1.6	1.7	2.0	2.4	3.2	3.7
Student assistance, Department of								
Education and other	10.4	13.4	9.2	15.2	20.7	23.3	28.9	36.9
Housing assistance	15.9	25.6	24.1	27.6	29.7	30.8	31.8	32.6
Food and nutrition assistance	23.9	37.5	32.4	38.0	42.4	45.9	50.7	55.1
Food stamp program (including								
Puerto Rico).	15.9	25.6	18.3	22.1	25.3	28.6	32.6	35.2
Child nutrition and special milk programs. . . .	5.0	7.5	9.2	10.3	10.8	11.2	11.9	12.9
Supplemental feeding programs								
(WIC [1] and CSFP [2])	2.1	3.4	4.0	4.3	4.5	4.9	5.0	5.2
Commodity donations and other	0.8	1.0	0.9	1.4	1.7	1.2	1.2	1.8
Public assistance and related programs	34.9	65.0	88.3	100.7	108.9	111.5	123.3	123.1
Supplemental security income program.	11.5	23.6	29.5	29.4	30.4	31.2	35.3	34.9
Family support payments to states and								
TANF [3]	12.2	17.1	18.4	22.7	23.1	21.5	21.3	21.3
Low income home energy assistance	1.3	1.4	1.5	1.8	2.0	1.9	2.1	2.2
Earned income tax credit	4.4	15.2	26.1	27.8	32.0	33.1	34.6	35.1
Legal services	0.3	0.4	0.3	0.3	0.3	0.3	0.3	0.3
Payments to states for daycare								
assistance	–	0.9	3.3	4.5	5.2	4.8	4.9	4.9
Veterans non-service connected								
pensions	3.6	3.0	3.0	3.2	3.2	3.3	3.7	3.5
Payments to states for foster care/adoption								
assistance	1.6	3.2	5.5	5.9	6.1	6.3	6.4	6.6
Payment where child credit exceeds tax								
liability.	–	–	0.8	5.1	6.4	8.9	14.6	14.1
Other public assistance	–	–	–	–	–	–	(Z)	0.1
All other payments for individuals	3.5	4.2	4.3	5.3	5.8	11.5	7.1	6.3
Coal miners and black lung benefits	1.5	1.3	1.0	0.9	0.8	0.8	0.7	0.7
Veterans insurance and burial benefits	1.4	1.4	1.4	1.3	1.3	1.4	1.4	1.4
D.C. employee retirement.	–	–	0.4	0.5	0.5	0.5	2.2	0.5
Aging services programs	–	1.0	0.9	1.1	1.3	1.3	1.4	1.4
Energy employees compensation fund	–	–	–	0.3	0.3	0.3	0.6	1.6
September 11th victim compensation	–	–	–	(Z)	0.7	6.3	(Z)	–
Refugee assistance and other	0.6	0.6	0.6	1.2	0.9	0.9	0.8	0.8

– Represents zero.   Z Less than $50,000,000.   [1] WIC means Women, Infants, and Children.   [2] CSFP means Commodity Supplemental Food Program.   [3] TANF means Temporary Assistance for Needy Families.

Source: U.S. Office of Management and Budget, *Budget of the United States Government, Historical Tables*, annual. See Internet site <http://www.whitehouse.gov/omb/budget/fy2007/>.

310   Federal Government Finances and Employment

Table 464. **Federal Budget Receipts by Source: 1990 to 2006**

[In billions of dollars (1,032.1 represents $1,032,100,000,000). For fiscal years ending in year shown; see text, Section 8. Receipts reflect collections. Covers both federal funds and trust funds; see text, this section]

Source	1990	1995	2000	2002	2003	2004	2005	2006, est.
Total federal receipts	1,032.1	1,351.9	2,025.5	1,853.4	1,782.5	1,880.3	2,153.9	2,285.5
Individual income taxes.	466.9	590.2	1,004.5	858.3	793.7	809.0	927.2	997.6
Corporation income taxes	93.5	157.0	207.3	148.0	131.8	189.4	278.3	277.1
Social insurance and retirement receipts . . .	380.0	484.5	652.9	700.8	713.0	733.4	794.1	841.1
Excise taxes	35.3	57.5	68.9	67.0	67.5	69.9	73.1	73.5
Other.	56.3	62.7	92.0	79.3	76.6	78.7	81.1	96.2
Social insurance and retirement receipts	**380.0**	**484.5**	**652.9**	**700.8**	**713.0**	**733.4**	**794.1**	**841.1**
Employment and general retirement	353.9	451.0	620.5	668.5	675.0	689.4	747.7	791.8
Old-age and survivors' insurance (off-budget)	255.0	284.1	411.7	440.5	447.8	457.1	493.6	521.4
Disability insurance (off-budget)	26.6	67.0	68.9	74.8	76.0	77.6	83.8	88.5
Hospital insurance	68.6	96.0	135.5	149.0	147.2	150.6	166.1	177.6
Railroad retirement/pension fund	2.3	2.4	2.7	2.5	2.3	2.3	2.3	2.4
Unemployment insurance trust funds	21.6	28.9	27.6	27.6	33.4	39.5	42.0	44.8
Other retirement	4.5	4.6	4.8	4.6	4.6	4.6	4.5	4.5
Federal employees' retirement-employee share	4.4	4.5	4.7	4.5	4.6	4.5	4.4	4.4
Excise taxes, total	**35.3**	**57.5**	**68.9**	**67.0**	**67.5**	**69.9**	**73.1**	**73.5**
Federal funds [1]	15.6	26.9	22.7	24.0	23.8	24.6	22.5	21.1
Alcohol	5.7	7.2	8.1	7.8	7.9	8.1	8.1	8.1
Tobacco	4.1	5.9	7.2	8.3	7.9	7.9	7.9	7.7
Telephone	3.0	3.8	5.7	5.8	5.8	6.0	6.0	6.1
Ozone-depleting chemicals/products	0.4	0.6	0.1	–	–	–	–	–
Transportation fuels	–	8.5	0.8	0.8	0.9	1.4	-0.8	-1.9
Trust funds [1]	19.8	30.5	46.2	43.0	43.7	45.3	50.5	52.4
Highway	13.9	22.6	35.0	32.6	33.7	34.7	37.9	39.1
Airport and airway	3.7	5.5	9.7	9.0	8.7	9.2	10.3	10.7
Black lung disability	0.7	0.6	0.5	0.6	0.5	0.6	0.6	0.6
Inland waterway	0.1	0.1	0.1	0.1	0.1	0.1	0.1	0.1
Oil spill liability	0.1	0.2	0.2	–	–	–	–	0.1
Aquatic resources	0.2	0.3	0.3	0.4	0.4	0.4	0.4	0.5
Vaccine injury compensation	0.2	0.1	0.1	0.1	0.1	0.1	0.1	0.2

– Represents zero.   [1] Includes other funds, not shown separately.

Source: U.S. Office of Management and Budget, *Budget of the United States Government, Historical Tables*, annual. See Internet site <http://www.whitehouse.gov/omb/budget/fy2007/>.

Table 465. **Federal Trust Fund Income, Outlays, and Balances: 2005 to 2007**

[In billions of dollars (10.8 represents $10,800,000,000). For years ending September 30. Receipts deposited. Outlays on a checks-issued basis less refunds collected. Balances: That which have not been spent. See text, this section, for discussion of the budget concept and trust funds]

Description	Income			Outlays			Balances [1]		
	2005	2006, est.	2007, est.	2005	2006, est.	2007, est.	2005	2006, est.	2007, est.
Airport and airway trust fund.	10.8	11.2	12.0	11.2	12.3	12.2	11.3	10.2	10.0
Federal civilian employees' retirement funds	85.0	89.6	93.0	55.5	59.1	62.0	674.8	705.3	736.3
Federal employees' health benefits fund . . .	31.3	33.6	36.1	29.6	32.0	35.0	12.5	14.1	15.1
Foreign military sales trust fund	11.1	11.1	11.0	11.5	11.1	11.0	6.7	6.7	6.7
Highway trust fund	38.0	39.3	39.9	40.0	35.7	41.6	12.5	16.1	14.4
Medicare:									
Hospital insurance (HI) trust fund	198.5	209.6	222.1	185.7	189.4	206.0	277.7	297.9	314.0
Supplemental medical insurance trust fund	153.5	219.2	258.6	153.7	207.5	249.1	16.9	28.6	38.1
Military retirement fund	49.5	50.1	50.8	39.0	41.2	43.4	194.7	203.6	211.0
Railroad retirement trust funds	12.7	10.5	12.7	10.2	10.9	12.7	25.6	25.3	25.3
Social security: old-age, survivors' and disability insurance trust funds	696.8	735.5	778.6	523.3	555.1	586.0	1,809.0	1,989.3	2,181.9
Unemployment trust funds	45.3	48.3	49.2	36.2	39.8	41.0	54.8	63.3	71.4
Veterans' life insurance trust funds	1.4	1.3	1.2	1.7	1.7	1.7	12.6	12.2	11.7
Other trust funds	21.7	23.0	26.3	21.3	20.8	23.6	39.4	41.6	44.3

[1] Balances available on a cash basis (rather than an authorization basis) at the end of the year. Balances are primarily invested in federal debt securities.

Source: U.S. Office of Management and Budget, *Budget of the United States Government, Analytical Perspectives*, annual. See Internet site <http://www.whitehouse.gov/omb/budget/fy2007/>.

Table 466. **United States Government Ledger Balance Sheet—Assets and Liabilities: 2004 and 2005**

[In millions of dollars (237,425 represents $237,425,000,000). As of September 30]

Item	2004	2005	Net change
Assets, total	**237,425**	**222,560**	**−14,866**
Cash and monetary assets, total.	87,254	75,782	−11,472
U.S. Treasury operating cash:			
Federal Reserve account	5,987	4,381	−1,606
Tax and loan note accounts.	30,362	31,300	937
Special drawing rights (SDR):			
Total holdings	12,782	8,245	−4,537
SDR's certificates issued to Federal Reserve banks	−2,200	−2,200	−
Monetary assets with IMF [1]	19,442	13,247	−6,195
Other cash and monetary assets	20,880	20,810	−70
Investments in nonfed securities, NRRIT, RRB [2]	24,079	26,135	2,056
Loan financing accounts:			
Guaranteed loans	−24,998	−35,723	−10,725
Direct loans	150,657	155,616	4,958
Miscellaneous asset accounts	433	750	317
Liabilities, total	**4,355,067**	**4,657,891**	**302,825**
Federal securites, total	7,352,017	7,902,800	550,783
Treasury debt securities, total	7,327,834	7,879,163	551,329
Agency securities outstanding	24,183	23,637	−547
Deduct: Net federal securities held as			
investments by government accounts.	3,075,687	3,331,333	255,645
Equals: Borrowing from the public, total	4,292,926	4,589,612	296,687
Accrued interest payable	32,734	34,965	2,231
Special drawing rights allocated by IMF [1]	7,197	7,102	−96
Deposit fund liabilities	13,397	15,399	2,001
Miscellaneous liability accounts			
(checks outstanding, etc.)	8,812	10,813	2,001

– Represents zero. [1] IMF = International Monetary Funds [2] RRB = Railroad Retirement Board; NRRIT = National Railroad Retirement Investment Trust.

Source: U.S. Department of Treasury, Combined Statement of Receipts, Outlays, and Balances of the United States 2005. See Internet site <http://fms.treas.gov/annualreport/index.html>.

Table 467. **U.S. Savings Bonds: 1990 to 2005**

[In billions of dollars (122.5 represents $122,500,000,000), except percent. As of end of fiscal year, see text, Section 8]

Item	1990	1995	1997	1998	1999	2000	2001	2002	2003	2004	2005
Amounts outstanding, total [1]	122.5	181.5	182.6	180.7	166.5	177.7	179.5	185.5	192.6	194.1	189.9
Sales	7.8	7.2	5.3	4.8	6.5	5.6	8.0	12.5	13.2	10.3	6.5
Accrued discounts	8.0	9.5	9.1	9.1	8.4	6.9	8.4	7.7	7.3	6.9	6.7
Redemptions [2]	7.5	11.8	2.1	14.3	16.6	14.5	13.8	12.5	12.2	14.6	13.8
Percent of total outstanding . . .	6.1	6.5	1.1	7.9	10.0	8.2	7.7	6.7	6.3	7.5	7.3

[1] Interest-bearing debt only for amounts at end of year. [2] Matured and unmatured bonds.

Source: U.S. Department of the Treasury, *Treasury Bulletin*, quarterly. See Internet site <http://www.fms.treas.gov/bulletin/>.

Table 468. Tax Expenditures Estimates Relating to Individual and Corporate Income Taxes by Selected Function: 2005 to 2008

[In millions of dollars (2,990 represents $2,990,000,000). For years ending September 30. Tax expenditures are defined as revenue losses attributable to provisions of the federal tax laws which allow a special exclusion, exemption, or deduction from gross income or which provide a special credit, a preferential rate of tax, or a deferral of liability]

Function and provision	2005	2006	2007	2008
National Defense:				
Exclusion of benefits and allowances to armed forces personnel	2,990	3,020	3,050	3,070
International affairs:				
Exclusion of income earned abroad by U.S. citizens	2,750	2,810	2,940	3,100
Extraterritorial income exclusion.	5,220	4,370	1,720	110
Deferral of income from controlled foreign corporations (normal tax method)	10,500	11,160	11,940	12,770
Deferred taxes for financial firms on certain income earned overseas	2,190	2,260	960	–
General science, space, and technology:				
Expensing of research and experimentation expenditures (normal tax method)	4,110	7,920	6,990	6,260
Credit for increasing research activities	5,160	2,160	920	390
Energy:				
Alternative fuel production credit.	2,320	2,390	2,460	990
Commerce and housing:				
Financial institutions insurance:				
Exclusion of interest on life insurance savings.	19,200	19,970	20,770	22,600
Housing:				
Deductibility of mortgage interest on owner-occupied homes	62,160	72,060	79,860	87,820
Deductibility of state and local property tax on owner-occupied homes	19,110	15,020	12,810	12,910
Capital gains exclusion on home sales	35,990	39,750	43,900	48,490
Exclusion of net imputed rental income	28,600	29,720	33,210	36,860
Exception from passive loss rules for $25,000 of rental loss	6,470	6,370	6,230	6,060
Credit for low-income housing investments.	3,880	4,060	4,250	4,460
Accelerated depreciation on rental housing (normal tax method)	9,610	10,630	11,470	12,660
Commerce:				
Capital gains (except agriculture, timber, iron ore, and coal)	26,170	25,990	26,760	31,280
Step-up basis of capital gains at death	26,820	29,510	32,460	35,700
Accelerated depreciation of machinery and equipment (normal tax method)	20,220	40,520	52,230	61,940
Expensing of certain small investments (normal tax method)	5,390	4,720	4,360	350
Graduated corporation income tax rate (normal tax method)	3,160	3,450	3,590	3,940
Deduction for U.S. production activities	6,220	5,150	10,670	12,190
Transportation:				
Exclusion of reimbursed employee parking expenses.	2,590	2,730	2,880	3,030
Education, training, employment, and social services:				
Education:				
HOPE tax credit.	3,710	3,650	3,060	3,090
Lifetime learning tax credit.	2,330	2,340	2,020	2,030
Parental personal exemption for students age 19 or over	3,760	2,500	1,760	1,650
Deductibility of charitable contributions (education).	3,420	3,680	4,030	4,260
Training, employment, and social services:				
Child credit.	41,790	42,090	42,120	42,070
Credit for child and dependent care expenses.	3,060	2,740	2,270	1,750
Deductibility of charitable contributions, other than education and health	29,670	32,550	34,500	36,790
Health:				
Exclusion of employer contributions for medical insurance premiums [1]	118,420	132,730	146,780	161,120
Self-employed medical insurance premiums.	3,790	4,240	4,630	5,080
Deductibility of medical expenses.	6,110	4,410	5,310	6,490
Deductibility of charitable contributions (health).	3,350	3,670	3,890	4,150
Income security:				
Exclusion of workers compensation benefits.	5,770	6,000	6,180	6,390
Net exclusion of pension contributions and earnings:				
Employer plans	50,630	50,360	52,470	48,100
401(k) plans	37,440	37,330	39,800	43,100
Individual Retirement Accounts.	3,100	4,230	5,970	7,180
Keogh plans	9,400	9,990	10,670	11,630
Premiums on group term life insurance	2,020	2,070	2,180	2,250
Earned income tax credit.	4,925	5,050	5,150	5,445
Social Security:				
Exclusion of social security benefits:				
Social security benefits for retired workers	19,110	19,350	19,590	20,250
Social security benefits for disabled.	3,600	3,810	4,110	4,330
Social security benefits for dependents and survivors	3,940	3,980	4,040	4,070
Veterans' benefits and services:				
Exclusion of veterans' death benefits and disability compensation	3,320	3,600	3,770	3,900
General purpose fiscal assistance:				
Exclusion of interest on public purpose state and local bonds	26,360	28,180	29,640	32,330
Deductibility of nonbusiness state and local taxes other than				
on owner-occupied homes.	36,460	30,310	27,210	27,730
Addendum: Aid to state and local governments:				
Deductibility of:				
Property taxes on owner-occupied homes	19,110	15,020	12,810	12,910
Nonbusiness state and local taxes other than on owner-occupied homes	36,460	30,310	27,210	27,730
Exclusion of interest on state and local bonds for				
Public purposes.	26,360	28,180	29,640	32,330

– Represents zero.   [1] Includes medical care.

Source: U.S. Office of Management and Budget, *Budget of the United States Government, Analytical Perspectives*, annual. See Internet site <http://www.whitehouse.gov/omb/budget/fy2007/>.

Table 469. **Federal Funds—Summary Distribution by State and Island Areas: 2004**

[In millions of dollars (2,161,948 represents $2,161,948,000,000), except as indicated. For year ending Sept. 30. Data for grants, salaries and wages and direct payments to individuals are on an expenditures basis; procurement is on an obligation basis]

State and island areas	Federal funds Total	Per capita [1] (dol.)	Agency Defense	Agency Non-defense	Object category Direct payments	Object category Procurement	Object category Grants	Object category Salaries and wages
United States [2]	**2,161,948**	**7,222**	**347,689**	**1,814,259**	**1,136,514**	**339,681**	**460,152**	**225,601**
Alabama............	39,047	8,619	8,725	30,323	20,947	7,600	7,008	3,492
Alaska.............	8,445	12,885	2,522	5,924	1,800	1,700	3,217	1,728
Arizona............	41,979	7,309	11,135	30,844	20,211	9,797	8,364	3,608
Arkansas	19,489	7,080	1,596	17,893	12,449	848	4,683	1,509
California	232,387	6,474	42,723	189,664	115,570	40,254	54,534	22,029
Colorado...........	30,060	6,533	6,182	23,878	14,212	5,747	5,643	4,457
Connecticut.........	30,304	8,649	9,735	20,569	13,637	9,509	5,556	1,602
Delaware	5,253	6,326	629	4,624	3,253	265	1,241	494
District of Columbia	37,630	67,982	5,264	32,366	4,552	13,347	4,205	15,526
Florida	121,934	7,009	17,419	104,514	80,482	11,447	19,610	10,395
Georgia	55,153	6,247	10,175	44,978	29,257	5,813	11,759	8,324
Hawaii	12,187	9,651	4,772	7,415	4,809	2,066	2,158	3,154
Idaho.............	8,968	6,437	744	8,225	4,702	1,373	1,995	898
Illinois	76,828	6,043	5,918	70,910	46,708	6,583	16,531	7,007
Indiana............	37,918	6,079	4,465	33,453	24,023	4,002	7,436	2,457
Iowa [2]	19,218	6,505	1,262	17,956	12,331	1,599	4,039	1,249
Kansas............	19,131	6,993	2,948	16,183	11,213	2,242	3,469	2,208
Kentucky	31,714	7,649	5,132	26,582	17,102	4,637	6,743	3,231
Louisiana	32,954	7,298	4,433	28,521	18,931	3,418	7,787	2,818
Maine.............	10,865	8,248	2,297	8,568	5,438	1,711	2,758	957
Maryland	64,726	11,645	13,796	50,930	24,562	20,804	8,837	10,523
Massachusetts........	53,120	8,279	8,240	44,881	26,560	9,127	13,876	3,557
Michigan...........	60,488	5,981	3,783	56,706	39,532	4,119	13,227	3,610
Minnesota..........	28,791	5,644	2,112	26,679	16,950	2,329	7,209	2,302
Mississippi	22,338	7,695	3,624	18,713	12,493	2,372	5,379	2,094
Missouri	45,730	7,947	8,585	37,145	24,963	7,991	8,734	4,042
Montana...........	7,494	8,085	658	6,836	4,023	587	1,997	886
Nebraska	11,795	6,751	1,321	10,474	7,268	697	2,531	1,298
Nevada	12,769	5,469	1,612	11,158	7,501	1,600	2,322	1,347
New Hampshire.......	7,959	6,124	1,125	6,833	4,440	985	1,879	654
New Jersey..........	55,264	6,353	5,843	49,421	33,471	6,132	11,333	4,328
New Mexico	19,864	10,437	2,471	17,393	7,157	5,973	4,663	2,072
New York	143,903	7,484	7,555	136,348	75,935	8,889	50,009	9,070
North Carolina	55,233	6,467	8,679	46,554	31,529	3,933	12,574	7,197
North Dakota........	6,035	9,513	833	5,202	3,230	503	1,515	787
Ohio	73,195	6,388	7,539	65,656	44,170	6,936	16,514	5,576
Oklahoma...........	26,644	7,562	4,279	22,365	15,107	2,804	5,271	3,463
Oregon............	21,871	6,084	1,311	20,560	13,500	1,283	5,185	1,903
Pennsylvania.........	94,900	7,649	9,037	85,864	59,064	9,311	19,916	6,609
Rhode Island........	8,245	7,630	1,022	7,223	4,529	559	2,329	829
South Carolina	30,051	7,158	4,881	25,170	16,557	4,193	6,145	3,156
South Dakota	6,602	8,564	658	5,944	3,779	438	1,620	765
Tennessee	45,441	7,701	3,770	41,670	23,983	8,118	9,863	3,476
Texas.............	141,858	6,308	31,895	109,963	72,407	26,969	27,792	14,690
Utah	13,684	5,728	3,305	10,378	6,282	2,304	2,948	2,150
Vermont	4,633	7,456	623	4,010	2,264	541	1,423	405
Virginia............	90,638	12,150	38,533	52,105	30,979	35,325	7,991	16,342
Washington.........	44,841	7,228	8,321	36,520	22,754	6,946	9,083	6,058
West Virginia........	15,183	8,364	734	14,449	9,084	1,041	3,701	1,358
Wisconsin..........	31,554	5,728	2,414	29,140	19,534	2,641	7,484	1,895
Wyoming	4,393	8,673	412	3,981	1,834	403	1,636	521
Island areas:								
American Samoa	262	4,528	10	252	58	17	178	9
Federated States of Micronesia	103	954	–	103	9	–	94	–
Guam............	1,249	7,637	660	590	306	355	269	320
Marshall Islands	218	3,860	158	60	3	158	56	–
Northern Marianas ...	213	2,801	5	208	42	9	156	6
Palau	51	2,567	–	51	3	–	47	–
Puerto Rico	15,479	3,991	732	14,746	8,667	462	5,324	1,026
Virgin Islands.......	592	5,438	26	565	241	21	263	66
Undistributed........	23,075	(X)	9,055	14,020	115	18,851	44	4,065

– Represents zero.   X Not applicable.   [1] Based on U.S. Census Bureau estimated resident population as of July 1.
[2] Revised since originally published.

Source: U.S. Census Bureau, *Consolidated Federal Federal Funds Report, 2004*. See Internet site <http://www.census.gov/govs/www/cffr.html>.

314   Federal Government Finances and Employment

Table 470. **Internal Revenue Gross Collections by Type of Tax: 2001 to 2005**

[2,129 represents $2,129,000,000,000. For fiscal year ending in year shown; see text, Section 8. See also text, this section for information on taxes]

Type of tax	Gross collection (bil. dol.)					Percent of total				
	2001	2002	2003	2004	2005	2001	2002	2003	2004	2005
United States, total.	2,129	2,017	1,953	2,019	2,269	100.0	100.0	100.0	100.0	100.0
Individual income taxes	1,178	1,038	987	990	1,108	55.3	51.5	50.5	49.1	48.8
Withheld by employers	795	751	735	747	787	37.3	37.2	37.6	37.0	34.7
Employment taxes [1]	682	688	696	717	771	32.0	34.1	35.6	35.5	34.0
Old-age and disability insurance . . .	670	677	685	706	760	31.5	33.6	35.1	35.0	33.5
Unemployment insurance	7	7	7	7	7	0.3	0.3	0.3	0.3	0.3
Corporation income taxes	187	211	194	231	307	8.8	10.5	9.9	11.4	13.5
Estate and gift taxes	29	27	23	26	26	1.4	1.4	1.2	1.3	1.1
Excise taxes	52	52	53	55	57	2.5	2.6	2.7	2.7	2.5

[1] Includes railroad retirement tax, not shown separately.

Source: U.S. Internal Revenue Service, *IRS Data Book*, annual, Publication 55B. See Internet site <http://www.irs.gov/taxstats/article/0,,id=102174,00.html>.

Table 471. **Taxable Returns Filed—Examination Coverage: 2005**

[130,577 represents 130,577,000. See the annual *IRS Data Book* (Publication 55B) for a detailed explanation]

Type and size of return	Returns filed [1] (1,000)	Returns examined			Total recommended additional tax ($1,000)	Average recommended additional tax per return (dollars)
		Total [2] (1,000)	Percent coverage			
Individual returns, total	130,577	1,215	0.93		13,365,587	10,998
Nonbusiness returns:						
Form 1040A, with TPI under $25,000 [3]	32,913	170	0.52		413,712	2,429
All other returns by size of TPI [3]:						
Under $25,000.	19,795	292	1.48		1,019,639	3,492
$25,000 under $50,000	30,870	186	0.60		1,171,130	6,298
$50,000 under $100,000	25,746	146	0.57		431,144	2,960
$100,000 or more.	11,562	138	1.19		7,371,402	53,383
Business returns:						
Schedule C returns by size of TGR [4]:						
Under $25,000.	3,204	118	3.68		273,794	2,320
$25,000 under $100,000	3,742	83	2.21		594,874	7,207
$100,000 and more	2,149	78	3.65		2,042,322	26,018
Schedule F returns by size of TGR [4]:						
Under $100,000.	337	2	0.48		3,248	2,026
$100,000 or more.	259	3	1.01		44,322	16,878
Corporation (except S corporation)	2,329	29	1.24		32,216,498	1,111,757
Fiduciary.	3,722	7	0.18		307,010	46,580
Estate	74	6	8.20		970,096	159,529
Gift	262	2	0.81		670,901	315,718
Employment	30,494	34	0.11		756,562	22,418
Excise	835	17	1.98		140,355	8,474
Other taxable returns	(NA)	(Z)	(NA)		195,789	475,216

NA Not available.   Z Less than 500.

[1] Returns filed in previous calendar year. [2] Includes taxpayer examinations by correspondence and activities to protect release of funds from the U.S. Treasury in response to taxpayer efforts to recoup tax previously assessed and paid. [3] TPI = Total positive income, i.e., excludes losses. [4] TGR = Total gross receipts.

Source: U.S. Internal Revenue Service, *IRS Data Book,* annual, Publication 55B. See Internet site <http://www.irs.gov/taxstats/article/0,,id=102174,00.html>.

Table 472. **Individual Income Tax Returns Filed—Examination Coverage: 1990 to 2005**

[109,868 represents 109,868,000. See the annual *IRS Data Book* (Publication 55B) for a detailed explanation]

Year	Returns filed [1] (1,000)	Returns examined		Total recommended additional tax [3] ($1,000)	Average recommended additional tax per return (dollars)[3]
		Total [2] (1,000)	Percent coverage		
1990	109,868	1,145	1.04	5,336,063	4,660
1995	114,683	1,919	1.67	7,756,954	4,041
1996	116,060	1,942	1.67	7,600,191	3,915
1997	118,363	1,519	1.28	8,363,918	5,505
1998	120,342	1,193	0.99	6,095,698	5,110
1999	122,547	1,100	0.90	4,458,474	4,052
2000	124,887	618	0.49	3,388,905	5,486
2001	127,097	732	0.58	3,301,860	4,512
2003	130,341	849	0.65	4,559,902	5,369
2004	130,134	1,008	0.77	6,203,236	6,155
2005	130,577	1,215	0.93	13,365,587	10,998

[1] Returns filed in previous calendar year. [2] Includes taxpayer examinations by correspondence and activities to protect release of funds from the U.S. Treasury in response to taxpayer efforts to recoup tax previously assessed and paid. [3] For 1990–1997, amount includes associated penalties.

Source: U.S. Internal Revenue Service, *IRS Data Book*, annual, Publication 55B. See Internet site <http://www.irs.gov/taxstats/article/0,,id=102174,00.html>.

Federal Government Finances and Employment   315

Table 473. **Federal Individual Income Tax Returns With Adjusted Gross Income (AGI)—Summary: 2000 and 2003**

[129,374 represents 129,374,000. Includes Puerto Rico and Virgin Islands. Includes returns of resident aliens, based on a sample of unaudited returns as filed. Data are not comparable for all years because of tax changes and other changes. See *Statistics of Income, Individual Income Tax Returns* publications for a detailed explanation. See Appendix III]

Item	Number of returns (1,000)		Amount (mil. dol.)		Average amount (dollars)	
	2000	2003	2000	2003	2000	2003
Total returns	129,374	130,424	6,365,377	6,207,109	49,201	47,592
Adjusted gross income (AGI).	129,374	130,424	6,365,377	6,207,109	49,201	47,592
Salaries and wages	110,169	110,890	4,456,167	4,649,900	40,448	41,933
Taxable interest received.	68,046	59,459	199,322	127,160	2,929	2,139
Tax-exempt interest	4,658	4,525	53,952	53,750	11,583	11,878
Dividends in AGI	34,141	30,475	146,988	115,141	4,305	3,778
Business or profession net income	13,313	14,442	244,598	268,582	18,373	18,597
Business or profession net loss	4,287	4,973	30,733	38,527	7,169	7,747
Net capital gain in AGI	22,646	9,081	644,285	322,974	28,450	35,566
Net capital loss in AGI	6,875	12,808	13,742	28,952	1,999	2,260
Sales of property other than capital assets, net gain. . .	827	799	7,445	8,139	9,002	10,186
Sales of property other than capital assets, net loss. . .	873	955	8,364	8,469	9,581	8,868
Pensions and annuities in AGI	21,765	22,823	325,828	372,931	14,970	16,340
Unemployment compensation in AGI.	6,478	10,065	16,913	44,036	2,611	4,375
Social security benefits in AGI	10,609	10,975	89,964	97,707	8,480	8,903
Rent net income	4,201	4,086	45,099	49,236	10,735	12,050
Rent net loss	4,520	4,529	30,309	37,558	6,706	8,293
Royalty net income.	1,104	1,243	7,998	10,730	7,245	8,632
Royalty net loss.	36	33	101	124	2,806	3,758
Partnerships and S Corporations net income [1]	4,180	4,454	285,425	333,029	68,283	74,771
Partnerships and S Corporations net loss [1].	2,121	2,553	72,511	78,972	34,187	30,933
Estate or trust net income	557	499	12,134	13,499	21,785	27,052
Estate or trust net loss	39	33	1,128	1,084	28,923	32,848
Farm net income	703	592	8,270	7,473	11,764	12,623
Farm net loss	1,359	1,405	17,305	19,844	12,734	14,124
Statutory adjustments, total [2].	23,197	30,382	58,610	87,576	2,527	2,882
Educator expenses	(X)	3,241	(X)	806	(X)	249
Individual retirement arrangements	3,505	3,418	7,477	10,006	2,133	2,927
Student loan interest deduction	4,478	6,953	2,639	4,410	589	634
Tuition and fees deduction.	(X)	3,571	(X)	6,684	(X)	1,872
Medical savings accounts	65	67	120	129	1,846	1,925
Deduction for self-employment tax	14,300	15,373	17,393	19,791	1,216	1,287
Self-employment health insurance.	3,565	3,802	7,569	16,454	2,123	4,328
Keogh and self-employed retirement plans	1,288	1,209	12,475	17,796	9,686	14,720
Exemptions, total [3]	252,332	261,126	690,109	781,305	2,735	2,992
Deductions, total	128,205	128,593	1,293,181	1,457,645	10,087	11,335
Standard deductions.	85,671	84,643	470,821	539,921	5,496	6,379
Returns with additional standard deductions for age 65 or older or for blindness	11,331	11,201	14,736	15,859	1,301	1,416
Itemized deductions, total [2]	42,534	43,950	822,361	901,865	19,334	20,520
Medical and dental expenses	6,513	8,678	39,251	56,007	6,027	6,454
Taxes paid	41,824	43,062	294,712	310,897	7,046	7,220
Interest paid	35,405	36,212	322,932	340,319	9,121	9,398
Home mortgage interest paid	34,914	35,797	299,963	325,192	8,591	9,084
Charitable contributions	37,525	38,627	140,682	145,702	3,749	3,772
Taxable income.	105,259	101,393	4,544,242	4,200,218	43,172	41,425
Income tax before credits	105,278	101,413	1,018,219	790,006	9,672	7,790
Tax credits, total [2]	37,736	39,247	37,722	41,069	1,000	1,046
Child care credit	6,368	6,313	2,794	3,207	439	508
Elderly and disabled credit.	156	123	33	20	212	163
Child tax credit	26,405	25,672	19,689	22,788	746	888
Education credit.	6,815	7,298	4,851	5,843	712	801
Retirement savings contributions.	(X)	5,297	(X)	1,034	X	195
Foreign tax credit.	3,936	4,145	5,990	5,806	1,522	1,401
General business credit	275	263	764	613	2,778	2,331
Income tax after credits	96,816	88,922	980,497	748,010	10,127	8,412
Income tax, total	96,818	88,922	980,645	748,017	10,129	8,412
Alternative minimum tax	1,304	2,358	9,601	9,470	7,363	4,016
Earned income credit	19,277	22,024	32,296	38,657	1,675	1,755
Used to offset income tax before credits.	5,416	3,606	1,969	926	364	257
Used to offset other taxes	3,148	4,401	2,524	3,718	802	845
Excess earned income credit (refundable)	16,126	19,162	27,804	34,012	1,724	1,775
Tax payments, total	122,244	123,462	1,084,868	974,543	8,875	7,893
Income tax withheld	113,733	114,862	763,901	703,758	6,717	6,127
Excess social security tax withheld	1,641	1,121	2,185	1,566	1,332	1,397
Estimated tax payments	13,327	11,576	221,622	182,907	16,630	15,801
Payments with requests for extension of filing time. . . .	1,611	1,334	63,397	38,303	39,353	28,713
Taxes due at time of filing	30,624	21,072	134,944	73,741	4,406	3,499
Tax overpayments, total	95,921	105,362	196,199	254,554	2,045	2,416
Overpayment refunds	93,000	102,005	167,577	219,752	1,802	2,154

X Not applicable.   [1] S Corporations are certain small corporations with up to 35 shareholders.   [2] Includes items not shown separately.   [3] Total exemptions amount is after limitation.

Source: U.S. Internal Revenue Service, *Statistics of Income Bulletin*, quarterly, and *Statistics of Income, Individual Income Tax Returns*, annual.

Table 474. Individual Income Tax Returns—Number, Income Tax, and Average Tax by Size of Adjusted Gross Income: 2000 and 2003

[129,374 represents 129,374,000. Based on sample of returns; see Appendix III]

Size of adjusted gross income	Number of returns (1,000) 2000	2003	Adjusted gross income (AGI) (bil. dol.) 2000	2003	Income tax total [1] (bil. dol.) 2000	2003	Tax as percent of AGI (for taxable returns only) 2000	2003	Average tax (for taxable returns only) (dol.) 2000	2003
Total	129,374	130,424	6,365	6,207	981	748	16	13	10,129	8,412
Less than $1,000 [2]	2,966	3,525	-58	-80	–	–	2	(NA)	648	(NA)
$1,000 to $2,999	5,385	4,900	11	10	–	–	7	4	134	72
$3,000 to $4,999	5,599	5,087	22	20	–	–	4	2	179	76
$5,000 to $6,999	5,183	5,065	31	30	1	–	5	2	297	134
$7,000 to $8,999	4,972	5,104	40	41	1	–	4	3	331	223
$9,000 to $10,999	5,089	4,973	51	50	1	1	5	3	470	253
$11,000 to $12,999....	4,859	4,644	58	56	2	1	6	4	704	415
$13,000 to $14,999 ...	4,810	4,720	67	66	3	1	6	4	883	582
$15,000 to $16,999 ...	4,785	4,655	76	74	3	2	7	4	1,052	733
$17,000 to $18,999 ...	4,633	4,460	83	80	4	2	7	5	1,279	884
$19,000 to $21,999 ...	6,502	6,318	133	129	7	4	8	5	1,565	1,149
$22,000 to $24,999 ...	5,735	5,692	135	134	8	5	8	6	1,815	1,457
$25,000 to $29,999 ...	8,369	8,542	229	235	16	11	8	6	2,248	1,812
$30,000 to $39,999 ...	13,548	13,957	471	485	40	30	9	7	3,094	2,508
$40,000 to $49,999 ...	10,412	10,452	466	468	46	35	10	7	4,462	3,582
$50,000 to $74,999 ...	17,076	17,372	1,045	1,066	116	94	11	8	6,824	5,536
$75,000 to $99,999 ...	8,597	9,543	738	821	100	84	14	9	11,631	8,882
$100,000 to $199,999...	8,083	8,879	1,066	1,170	184	163	17	10	22,783	18,432
$200,000 to $499,999...	2,136	1,999	614	576	146	121	24	14	68,628	60,453
$500,000 to $999,999...	396	356	269	241	76	60	28	21	192,092	169,166
$1,000,000 or more	240	181	817	535	226	133	28	25	945,172	731,738

– Represents or rounds to zero.   NA Not available.   [1] Consists of income after credits, and alternative minimum tax.
[2] In addition to low income taxpayers, this size class (and others) includes taxpayers with "tax preferences," not reflected in adjusted gross income or taxable income which are subject to the "alternative minimum tax" (included in total income tax).

Source: U.S. Internal Revenue Service, *Statistics of Income Bulletin*, quarterly, and *Statistics of Income, Individual Income Tax Returns*, annual.

Table 475. Individual Income Tax Returns—Itemized Deductions and Statutory Adjustments by Size of Adjusted Gross Income: 2003

[43,950 represents 43,950,000. Based on a sample of returns; see Appendix III]

Item	Unit	Total	Under $10,000	$10,000 to $19,999	$20,000 to $29,999	$30,000 to $39,999	$40,000 to $49,999	$50,000 to $99,999	$100,000 and over
Returns with itemized deductions:									
Number of returns [1,2]	1,000 ..	43,950	989	2,367	3,459	4,449	4,502	17,797	10,388
Amount [1,2]	Mil. dol..	901,864	14,284	29,929	44,766	58,796	63,813	311,412	378,865
Medical and dental expenses:									
Returns	1,000 ..	8,678	676	1,394	1,415	1,304	1,097	2,377	416
Amount	Mil. dol..	56,007	5,916	9,683	8,826	7,404	5,628	13,524	5,026
Taxes paid:									
Returns [2]	1,000 ..	43,062	865	2,179	3,271	4,338	4,420	17,642	10,347
Amount, total [2]	Mil. dol..	310,897	2,433	5,060	8,233	13,067	16,113	96,473	169,519
State and local income taxes:									
Returns	1,000 ..	35,945	395	1,389	2,449	3,583	3,726	15,361	9,043
Amount	Mil. dol..	183,079	501	1,050	2,547	5,316	7,352	50,435	115,879
Real estate taxes:									
Returns	1,000 ..	38,319	734	1,779	2,603	3,554	3,821	16,066	9,762
Amount	Mil. dol..	117,954	1,843	3,716	5,112	7,010	7,883	42,158	50,232
Interest paid:									
Returns	1,000 ..	36,212	584	1,434	2,431	3,409	3,705	15,537	9,112
Amount	Mil. dol..	340,319	4,471	9,508	16,965	23,669	26,118	132,327	127,261
Home mortgage interest:									
Returns	1,000 ..	35,797	570	1,407	2,408	3,378	3,679	15,432	8,923
Amount	Mil. dol..	325,192	4,389	9,318	16,728	23,360	25,736	129,931	115,730
Charitable contributions:									
Returns	1,000 ..	38,627	626	1,799	2,728	3,694	3,860	16,044	9,876
Amount	Mil. dol..	145,702	774	3,119	5,730	7,269	8,358	42,704	77,749
Returns with statutory adjustments:									
Number of returns [2]	1,000 ..	30,382	3,904	3,965	3,454	3,094	2,869	8,561	4,535
Amount of adjustments	Mil. dol..	87,576	4,735	5,700	6,031	5,946	5,973	22,133	37,058
Payments to IRAs: [3]									
Returns	1,000 ..	3,418	110	274	501	440	486	1,062	546
Amount	Mil. dol..	10,007	257	595	1,228	1,170	1,364	3,216	2,178
Student loan interest deduction ...	1,000 ..	6,953	308	748	1,016	1,007	896	2,520	458
Amount	Mil. dol..	4,410	166	371	568	645	635	1,806	218
Deduction for self-employment tax .	1,000 ..	15,373	2,996	2,566	1,662	1,305	1,105	3,377	2,362
Amount	Mil. dol..	19,791	1,232	1,962	1,646	1,453	1,266	4,900	7,332
Payments to Keogh plans	1,000 ..	1,209	18	25	46	57	49	321	692
Amount	Mil. dol..	17,796	86	141	181	357	338	2,703	13,990

[1] After limitations.   [2] Includes other deductions and adjustments, not shown separately.   [3] Individual Retirement Account.

Source: U.S. Internal Revenue Service, *Statistics of Income, Individual Income Tax Returns*, annual.

Table 476. Federal Individual Income Tax Returns—Adjusted Gross Income (AGI) by Source of Income and Income Class for Taxable Returns: 2003

[In millions of dollars (5,746,569 represents $5,764,569,000,000), except as indicated. Minus sign (–) indicates net loss was greater than net income. See headnote, Table 473. Based on sample; see Appendix III]

Item	Total [1]	Under $10,000	$10,000 to $19,999	$20,000 to $29,999	$30,000 to $39,999	$40,000 to $49,999	$50,000 to $99,999	$100,000 and over
Number of taxable returns (1,000). . .	88,922	4,957	12,347	12,187	11,856	9,668	26,511	11,395
Source of income:								
Adjusted gross income (AGI)	5,746,569	29,395	186,019	304,724	413,146	432,976	1,861,718	2,518,591
Salaries and wages	4,198,637	29,336	135,158	238,566	337,402	353,839	1,522,538	1,581,798
Percent of AGI	73.1	99.8	72.7	78.3	81.7	81.7	81.8	62.8
Interest received	111,026	1,577	6,182	6,987	6,306	5,999	24,484	59,491
Dividends in AGI	105,301	936	3,050	3,583	3,667	4,102	19,149	70,814
Business; profession, net profit less loss.	193,396	1,104	7,078	7,776	10,668	10,298	50,153	106,318
Sales of property, [2] net gain less loss	291,382	1,647	321	1,045	726	1,402	14,310	271,931
Pensions and annuities in AGI . . .	342,185	1,610	24,619	34,978	36,068	36,280	131,923	76,707
Rents and royalties, net income less loss	15,563	7	261	131	–248	–449	–105	15,967
Other sources, [3] net	489,078	–6,822	9,349	11,658	18,556	21,505	99,267	335,565
Taxable returns as a percent of all returns: [4]								
Number of returns	68.2	19.1	53.0	66.3	84.9	92.5	98.5	99.8
Adjusted gross income (AGI)	92.6	67.2	53.7	67.0	85.2	92.6	98.7	99.8
Salaries and wages.	90.3	25.8	52.9	64.2	84.2	92.2	98.8	99.9
Interest received.	87.3	16.5	61.7	83.7	88.7	91.6	97.1	98.5
Dividends in AGI	91.5	17.6	59.0	77.6	87.8	89.3	96.6	99.1
Business; profession, net profit less loss	84.2	19.3	31.5	47.6	72.8	84.8	96.5	99.9
Sales of property, [2] net gain less loss	99.1	159.7	102.6	73.6	61.7	95.2	91.5	99.6
Pensions and annuities in AGI . . .	91.8	15.2	62.7	90.1	95.6	98.0	99.4	99.8
Rents and royalties, net income less loss	133.3	–0.3	–334.6	–52.6	41.2	70.5	36.1	99.5

[1] Includes a small number of taxable returns with no adjusted gross income. [2] Includes sales of capital assets and other property; net gain less loss. [3] Excludes rental passive losses disallowed in the computation of AGI; net income less loss. [4] Without regard to taxability.

Source: U.S. Internal Revenue Service, *Statistics of Income, Individual Income Tax Returns,* annual.

Table 477. Federal Individual Income Tax Returns by State: 2003

[130,424 represents 130,424,000. Based on sample; see Appendix III]

State	Number of returns [1] (1,000)	Adjusted gross income (AGI) [2] (mil. dol.)	Income tax Total [3] (mil. dol.)	Income tax Per capita [4] (dol.)	State	Number of returns [1] (1,000)	Adjusted gross income (AGI) [2] (mil. dol.)	Income tax Total [3] (mil. dol.)	Income tax Per capita [4] (dol.)
U.S.. . . .	130,424	6,207,109	748,017	5,735	MT	472	14,943	1,384	2,932
AL	1,957	79,219	8,066	4,122	NE	824	32,924	3,571	4,334
AK	306	12,954	1,644	5,373	NV	1,089	54,267	6,792	6,237
AZ	2,392	105,291	11,358	4,748	NH	665	32,824	3,958	5,952
AR	1,113	41,199	3,930	3,531	NJ	4,012	248,508	35,074	8,742
CA	15,269	811,726	101,990	6,680	NM	788	28,771	2,919	3,704
CO	2,037	105,998	12,654	6,212	NY	8,612	476,008	65,340	7,587
CT	1,599	112,509	17,043	10,659	NC	3,630	157,943	16,545	4,558
DE	347	17,556	2,205	6,354	ND	269	10,388	1,134	4,216
DC	278	16,610	2,368	8,518	OH	5,291	221,703	23,957	4,528
FL	7,834	354,248	44,544	5,686	OK	1,498	56,961	5,914	3,948
GA	3,777	171,514	19,055	5,045	OR	1,617	67,678	6,959	4,304
HI	589	26,266	2,739	4,650	PA	5,761	260,340	31,268	5,428
ID	609	22,706	2,126	3,491	RI	539	28,081	3,480	6,456
IL	5,743	287,391	36,663	6,384	SC	1,841	68,831	6,671	3,624
IN	2,790	120,378	13,019	4,666	SD	324	12,077	1,377	4,250
IA	1,330	52,571	5,239	3,939	TN	2,544	107,860	12,300	4,835
KS	1,173	52,267	5,808	4,951	TX	9,313	421,479	52,570	5,645
KY	1,784	70,981	7,379	4,136	UT	977	41,701	4,005	4,099
LA	1,950	71,688	7,436	3,813	VT	344	15,231	1,483	4,311
ME	589	23,024	2,313	3,927	VA	3,489	187,344	22,900	6,563
MD	2,611	143,565	17,325	6,635	WA	2,751	143,532	18,537	6,738
MA	3,025	173,473	23,636	7,814	WV	697	24,727	2,369	3,399
MI	4,599	204,793	23,463	5,102	WI	2,514	112,638	12,398	4,932
MN	2,413	123,784	14,488	6,004	WY	223	11,175	1,441	6,462
MS	1,042	35,099	3,286	3,154					
MO	2,514	106,856	11,421	4,543	Other [5]	671	25,504	2,471	3,683

[1] Includes returns constructed by Internal Revenue Service for certain self-employment tax returns. [2] Less deficit. [3] Includes additional tax for tax preferences, self-employment tax, tax from investment credit recapture and other income-related taxes. Total is before earned income credit. [4] Based on resident population as of July 1. [5] Includes returns filed from Army Post Office and Fleet Post Office addresses by members of the armed forces stationed overseas; returns by other U.S. citizens abroad; and returns filed by residents of Puerto Rico with income from sources outside of Puerto Rico or with income earned as U.S. Government employees.

Source: U.S. Internal Revenue Service, *Statistics of Income Bulletin,* quarterly.

Table 478. Federal Individual Income Tax—Tax Liability and Effective and Marginal Tax Rates for Selected Income Groups: 2000 to 2005

[Refers to income after exclusions but before deductions for itemized or standard deductions and for pesonal exemptions. Tax liability is after reductions for tax credits. As the result of tax credits, tax liability can be negative, which means that the taxpayer receives a payment from the government. The effective rate represents tax liability, which may be negative as the result of tax credits, divided by stated income. The marginal tax rate is the percentage of the first additional dollar of income which would be paid in income tax. Tax credits which increase with income can result in negative marginal income tax rates. Computations assume itemized deductions (in excess of floors) of 18 percent of adjusted gross income or the standard deduction, whichever is greater. All income is assumed to be from wages and salaries. Does not include social security and Medicare taxes imposed on most wages and salaries]

Adjusted gross income	2000	2001	2002	2003	2004	2005
TAX LIABILITY (dol.)						
Single person, no dependents						
$5,000	[1]–353	[1]–364	[1]–376	[1]–382	[1]–383	[1]–383
$10,000	[1]391	[1,2]201	[1]149	[1]126	[1]91	[1]46
$20,000	1,920	[2]1,583	1,545	1,480	1,450	1,405
$30,000	3,270	[2]2,955	2,940	2,883	2,868	2,845
$40,000	4,988	[2]4,541	4,392	4,248	4,163	4,075
$50,000	7,284	[2]6,796	6,606	6,298	6,213	6,115
$75,000	13,024	[2]12,434	12,141	11,423	11,338	11,240
$100,000	19,233	[2]18,478	18,015	16,852	16,719	16,571
Married couple, two dependents, with one spouse working:						
$5,000	[1]–2,000	[1]–2,000	[1]–2,000	[1]–2,000	[1]–2,000	[1]–2,000
$10,000	[1]–3,888	[1]–4,000	[1]–4,000	[1]–4,000	[1]–4,000	[1]–4,000
$20,000	[1,3]–2,349	[1,2,3,4]–3,553	[1,3,4]–3,951	[1,4]–4,044	[1,4]–4,643	[1,4]–4,986
$30,000	[1,3]475	[1,2,3,4]–567	[1,3,4]–1,065	[1,3,4]–2,158	[1,3,4]–2,359	[1,3,4]–2,810
$40,000	[3]2,218	[2,3]1,320	[3]1,223	[3]45	[3,4]–30	[3,4]–150
$50,000	[3]3,470	[2,3]2,610	[3]2,550	[3]1,545	[3]1,470	[3]1,350
$75,000	[3]7,384	[2,3]6,273	[3]5,961	[3]4,695	[3]4,650	[3]4,575
$100,000	[3]13,124	[2,3]11,910	[3]11,496	[3]9,070	[3]8,875	[3]8,630
EFFECTIVE RATE (percent)						
Single person, no dependents:						
$5,000	[1]–7.1	[1]–7.3	[1]–7.5	[1]–7.6	[1]–7.7	[1]–7.7
$10,000	[1]3.9	[1,2]2.0	[1]1.5	[1]1.3	[1]0.9	[1]0.5
$20,000	9.6	[2]7.9	7.7	7.4	7.3	7.0
$30,000	10.9	[2]9.9	9.8	9.6	9.6	9.5
$40,000	12.5	[2]11.4	11.0	10.6	10.4	10.2
$50,000	14.6	[2]13.6	13.2	12.6	12.4	12.2
$75,000	17.4	[2]16.6	16.2	15.2	15.1	15.0
$100,000	19.2	[2]18.5	18.0	16.9	16.7	16.6
Married couple, two dependents, with one spouse working:						
$5,000	[1]–40.0	[1]–40.0	[1]–40.0	[1]–40.0	[1]–40.0	[1]–40.0
$10,000	[1]–38.9	[1]–40.0	[1]–40.0	[1]–40.0	[1]–40.0	[1]–40.0
$20,000	[1,3]–11.7	[1,2,3,4]–17.8	[1,3,4]–19.8	[1,4]–20.2	[1,4]–23.2	[1,4]–24.9
$30,000	[1,3]1.6	[1,2,3,4]–1.9	[1,3,4]–3.5	[1,3,4]–7.2	[1,3,4]–7.9	[1,3,4]–9.4
$40,000	[3]5.5	[2,3]3.3	[3]3.1	[3]0.1	[3,4]–0.1	[3,4]–0.4
$50,000	[3]6.9	[2,3]5.2	[3]5.1	[3]3.1	[3]2.9	[3]2.7
$75,000	[3]9.8	[2,3]8.4	[3]7.9	[3]6.3	[3]6.2	[3]6.1
$100,000	[3]13.1	[2,3]11.9	[3]11.5	[3]9.1	[3]8.9	[3]8.6
MARGINAL TAX RATE (percent)						
Single person, no dependents:						
$5,000	–	–	–	–	[1]–7.7	[1]–7.7
$10,000	[1]22.7	[1,2]17.7	[1]17.7	[1]17.7	[1]17.7	[1]17.7
$20,000	15.0	15.0	15.0	15.0	15.0	15.0
$30,000	15.0	15.0	15.0	15.0	15.0	15.0
$40,000	28.0	27.5	27.0	25.0	25.0	15.0
$50,000	28.0	27.5	27.0	25.0	25.0	25.0
$75,000	28.0	27.5	27.0	25.0	25.0	25.0
$100,000	31.0	30.5	30.0	28.0	28.0	28.0
Married couple, two dependents, with one spouse working:						
$5,000	[1]–40.0	[1]–40.0	[1]–40.0	[1]–40.0	[1]–40.0	[1]–40.0
$10,000		[1]–40.0	[1]–40.0	[1]–40.0	[1]–40.0	[1]–40.0
$20,000	[1,3]21.1	[1,2,3,4]11.1	[1,3,4]11.1	[1,4]11.1	[1,4]6.1	[1,4]6.1
$30,000	[1]36.1	[1,2,3,4]31.1	[1,3,4]31.1	[1,3,4]31.1	[1,3,4]36.1	[1,3,4]36.1
$40,000	15.0	15.0	15.0	15.0	[3,4]15.0	[3,4]15.0
$50,000	15.0	15.0	15.0	15.0	15.0	15.0
$75,000	28.0	27.5	27.0	15.0	15.0	15.0
$100,000	28.0	27.5	27.0	25.0	25.0	25.0

– Represents zero. [1] Includes affect from the refundable earned income credit. [2] Includes affect from the rate reduction credit. [3] Includes affect from the child credit. [4] Includes affect from the additional (refundable) child tax credit.

Source: U.S. Department of the Treasury, Office of Tax Analysis, unpublished data.

Table 479. Federal Individual Income Tax—Current Income Equivalent to 2000 Constant Income for Selected Income Groups: 2000 to 2005

[Constant 2000 incomes calculated by using the U.S. Bureau of Labor Statistics Consumer Price Index for Urban Consumers (CPI–U); see Table 706, section 14. See also headnote, Table 478]

Adjusted gross income Constant 2000 dollars	2000	2001	2002	2003	2004	2005
REAL INCOME EQUIVALENT (dol.)						
$5,000	5,000	5,140	5,220	5,340	5,480	5,670
$10,000	10,000	10,280	10,450	10,690	10,970	11,340
$20,000	20,000	20,570	20,890	21,370	21,940	22,680
$30,000	30,000	30,850	31,340	32,060	32,910	34,020
$40,000	40,000	41,140	41,790	42,740	43,880	45,370
$50,000	50,000	51,420	52,240	53,430	54,850	56,710
$75,000	75,000	77,130	78,350	80,140	82,270	85,060
$100,000	100,000	102,850	104,470	106,850	109,700	113,410
TAX LIABILITY (dol.) Single person, no dependents:						
$5,000	[1]-353	[1]-364	[1]-376	[1]-382	[1]-390	[1]-399
$10,000	[1]391	[1,2]250	[1]228	[1]248	[1]262	[1]283
$20,000	1,920	[2]1,668	1,679	1,686	1,741	1,807
$30,000	3,270	[2]3,060	3,105	3,136	3,225	3,339
$40,000	4,988	[2]4,798	4,788	4,809	4,958	5,166
$50,000	7,284	[2]7,116	7,102	7,001	7,207	7,491
$75,000	13,024	[2]12,914	12,883	12,476	12,828	13,302
$100,000	19,233	[2]19,191	19,115	18,425	18,946	19,649
Married couple, 2 dependents with one spouse working:						
$5,000	[1]-2,000	[1]-2,056	[1]-2,088	[1]-2,136	[1]-2,192	[1]-2,268
$10,000	[1,3]-3,888	[1,3]-4,036	[1,3]-4,150	[1,3]-4,223	[1,3]-4,333	[1,3]-4,451
$20,000	[1,4]-2,349	[1,2,3,4]-3,490	[1,3,4]-3,852	[1,3]-3,893	[1,3]-4,525	[1,3]-4,823
$30,000	[1,4]475	[1,2,3,4]-303	[1,3,4]-649	[1,3,4]-1,518	[1,3,4]-1,456	[1,3,4]-1,561
$40,000	[4]2,218	[2,4]1,491	[4]1,491	[4]456	[4]552	[4]656
$50,000	[4]3,470	[2,4]2,785	[4]2,826	[4]2,042	[4]2,172	[4]2,325
$75,000	[4]7,384	[2,4]6,753	[4]6,703	[4]5,327	[4]5,544	[4]5,812
$100,000	[4]13,124	[2,4]12,553	[4]12,486	[4]10,474	[4]10,864	[4]11,579
EFFECTIVE TAX RATE (percent) Single person, no dependents:						
$5,000	[1]-7.1	[1]-7.1	[1]-7.2	[1]-7.1	[1]-7.1	[1]-7.0
$10,000	[1]3.9	[1,2]2.4	[1]2.2	[1]2.3	[1]2.4	[1]2.5
$20,000	9.6	[2]8.1	8.0	7.9	7.9	8.0
$30,000	10.9	[2]9.9	9.9	9.8	9.8	9.8
$40,000	12.5	[2]11.7	11.5	11.3	11.3	11.4
$50,000	14.6	[2]13.8	13.6	13.1	13.1	13.2
$75,000	17.4	[2]16.7	16.4	15.6	15.6	15.6
$100,000	19.2	[2]18.7	18.3	17.2	17.3	17.3
Married couple, 2 dependents with one spouse working:						
$5,000	[1]-40.0	[1]-40.0	[1]-40.0	[1]-40.0	[1]-40.0	[1]-40.0
$10,000	[1]-38.9	[1,3]-39.3	[1,3]-39.7	[1,3]-39.5	[1,3]-39.5	[1,3]-39.3
$20,000	[1,4]-11.7	[1,2,3,4]-17.0	[1,3,4]-18.4	[1,3]-18.2	[1,3]-20.6	[1,3]-21.3
$30,000	[1,4]1.6	[1,2,3,4]-1.0	[1,3,4]-2.1	[1,3,4]-4.7	[1,3,4]-4.4	[1,3,4]-4.6
$40,000	[4]5.5	[2,4]3.6	[4]3.6	[4]1.1	[4]1.3	[4]1.4
$50,000	[4]6.9	[2,4]5.4	[4]5.4	[4]3.8	[4]4.0	[4]4.1
$75,000	[4]9.8	[2,4]8.8	[4]8.6	[4]6.6	[4]6.7	[4]6.8
$100,000	[4]13.1	[2,4]12.2	[4]12.0	[4]9.8	[4]9.9	[4]10.2
MARGINAL TAX RATE (percent) Single person, no dependents:						
$5,000	–	–	–	–	–	–
$10,000	[1]22.7	[1,2]17.7	[1]17.7	[1]17.7	[1]17.7	[1]17.7
$20,000	15.0	15.0	15.0	15.0	15.0	15.0
$30,000	15.0	15.0	15.0	15.0	15.0	15.0
$40,000	28.0	27.5	27.0	25.0	25.0	25.0
$50,000	28.0	27.5	27.0	25.0	25.0	25.0
$75,000	28.0	27.5	27.0	25.0	25.0	25.0
$100,000	31.0	30.5	30.0	28.0	28.0	28.0
Married couple, 2 dependents with one spouse working:						
$5,000	[1]-40.0	[1]-40.0	[1]-40.0	[1]-40.0	[1]-40.0	[1]-40.0
$10,000	–	[3]-10.0	[3]-10.0	[3]-10.0	[3]-15.0	[3]-15.0
$20,000	[1,4]21.1	[1,2,3,4]11.1	[1,3,4]11.1	[1,3]11.1	[1,3]36.1	[1,3]36.1
$30,000	[1]36.1	[1,2,3,4]31.1	[1,3,4]31.1	[1,3,4]31.1	[1,3,4]36.1	[1,3,4]36.1
$40,000	15.0	15.0	15.0	15.0	15.0	15.0
$50,000	15.0	15.0	15.0	15.0	15.0	15.0
$75,000	28.0	27.5	27.0	15.0	15.0	15.0
$100,000	28.0	27.5	27.0	25.0	25.0	[4]30.1

– Represents zero.   [1] Includes affect from the refundable earned income credit.   [2] Includes affect from the rate reduction tax credit.   [3] Includes affect from the additional (refundable) child tax credit.   [4] Includes affect from the child tax credit.

Source: U.S. Department of the Treasury, Office of Tax Analysis, unpublished data.

320   Federal Government Finances and Employment

Table 480. Federal Civilian Employment and Annual Payroll by Branch: 1970 to 2005

[2,997 represents 2,997,000. For fiscal year ending in year shown. See text, Section 8. Includes employees in U.S. territories and foreign countries. Data represent employees in active-duty status, including intermittent employees. Annual employment figures are averages of monthly figures. Excludes Central Intelligence Agency, National Security Agency, and, as of November 1984, the Defense Intelligence Agency; and as of October 1996, the National Imagery and Mapping Agency]

Year	Employment					Payroll (mil. dol.)				
	Total (1,000)	Percent of U.S. emp-loyed [1]	Executive (1,000)		Legis-lative (1,000)	Judicial (1,000)	Total	Executive		Legis-lative	Judicial
			Total	Defense				Total	Defense		
1970 . . .	[2]2,997	3.81	2,961	1,263	29	7	27,322	26,894	11,264	338	89
1975 . . .	2,877	3.35	2,830	1,044	37	10	39,126	38,423	13,418	549	154
1980 . . .	[2]2,987	3.01	2,933	971	40	14	58,012	56,841	18,795	883	288
1985 . . .	3,001	2.80	2,944	1,080	39	18	80,599	78,992	28,330	1,098	509
1990 . . .	[2]3,233	2.72	3,173	1,060	38	23	99,138	97,022	31,990	1,329	787
1995 . . .	2,943	2.36	2,880	852	34	28	118,304	115,328	31,753	1,598	1,379
2000 . . .	[2]2,879	2.10	2,816	681	31	32	130,832	127,472	29,607	1,619	1,741
2001 . . .	2,704	1.97	2,641	672	30	33	131,964	128,502	28,594	1,682	1,780
2002 . . .	2,699	1.98	2,635	671	31	34	136,611	132,893	28,845	1,781	1,938
2003 . . .	2,743	1.99	2,677	669	31	34	143,380	139,506	29,029	1,908	1,966
2004 . . .	2,714	1.95	2,649	668	30	34	148,037	144,134	29,128	1,977	1,927
2005 . . .	2,709	1.91	2,645	671	30	34	152,222	148,275	29,331	2,048	1,900

[1] Civilian employed only. See Table 573, Section 12.   [2] Includes temporary census workers.

Source: U.S. Office of Personnel Management, *Federal Civilian Workforce Statistics—Employment and Trends*, bimonthly; and unpublished data.

Table 481. Full-Time Federal Civilian Employment—Employees and Average Pay-by-Pay System: 1990 to 2005

[As of March 31 (2,036 represents 2,036,000). Excludes employees of Congress and federal courts, maritime seamen of Department of Commerce, and small number for whom rates were not reported. See text, this section, for explanation of general schedule and wage system]

Pay system	Employees (1,000)				Average pay (dol.)			
	1990	2000	2004	2005	1990	2000	2004	2005
Total, excluding postal. . .	2,036	1,671	1,744	1,754	31,174	50,429	60,517	63,058
General Schedule	1,506	1,216	1,244	1,248	31,239	49,428	59,593	62,076
Wage System	369	205	184	186	26,565	37,082	42,096	43,907
Other.	161	250	316	320	41,149	66,248	74,876	78,003
Postal pay system [1]	753	788	707	705	29,264	37,627	43,606	45,123

[1] Source: Career employees—U.S. Postal Service, *Annual Report of the Postmaster General*. See also <http://www.usps.com/financials/cspo/welcome.htm>; Average pay—U.S. Postal Service, *Comprehensive Statement of Postal Operations*, annual.

Source: Except as noted, U.S. Office of Personnel Management, *Pay Structure of the Federal Civil Service*, annual.

Table 482. Paid Civilian Employment in the Federal Government by State: 2000 and 2004

[As of December 31. In thousands (2,766 represents 2,766,000). Excludes Central Intelligence Agency, Defense Intelligence Agency, seasonal and on-call employees, and National Security Agency]

State	2000	2004	State	2000	2004	State	2000	2004
U.S. [1]	2,766	2,759	KY	30	31	OH	84	77
AL	48	49	LA	33	32	OK	43	43
AK	14	14	ME	13	14	OR	29	28
AZ	43	47	MD	130	130	PA	107	103
AR	20	20	MA	53	50	RI	10	10
CA	248	239	MI	58	55	SC	26	26
CO	51	51	MN	34	33	SD	9	10
CT	21	19	MS	24	23	TN	50	49
DE	5	5	MO	54	53	TX	162	168
DC	181	187	MT	11	12	UT	30	32
FL	113	123	NE	15	15	VT	6	6
GA	89	90	NV	13	15	VA	145	146
HI	23	25	NH	8	8	WA	62	64
ID	11	11	NJ	62	61	WV	18	19
IL	94	87	NM	25	26	WI	30	29
IN	37	35	NY	134	126	WY	6	6
IA	18	18	NC	57	57			
KS	25	25	ND	8	8			

[1] Includes employees outside the United States and in states not specified, not shown separately.

Source: U.S. Office of Personnel Management, *Biennial Report of Employment by Geographic Area, 2002;* and unpublished data.

Federal Government Finances and Employment   321

Table 483. Federal Civilian Employment by Branch and Agency: 1990 to 2005

[For years ending September 30. Excludes Central Intelligence Agency, National Security Agency; the Defense Intelligence Agency; and, as of October 1996, the National Imagery and Mapping Agency. Minus sign (–) indicates decrease]

Agency	1990	1995	2000	2004	2005	Percent change 1990–2005
Total, all agencies	3,128,267	2,920,277	2,708,101	2,714,140	2,708,753	–13.4
Legislative Branch	37,495	33,367	31,157	30,420	30,303	–19.2
Judicial Branch	23,605	28,993	32,186	34,224	33,690	42.7
Executive Branch......................	3,067,167	2,857,917	2,644,758	2,649,496	2,644,764	–13.8
Executive Office of the President..........	1,731	1,573	1,658	1,732	1,736	0.3
Executive Departments	2,065,542	1,782,834	1,592,200	1,688,152	1,689,914	–18.2
State.............................	25,288	24,859	27,983	33,013	33,808	33.7
Treasury	158,655	155,951	143,508	117,344	114,194	–28.0
Defense...........................	1,034,152	832,352	676,268	668,009	670,790	–35.1
Justice............................	83,932	103,262	125,970	103,536	105,102	25.2
Interior...........................	77,679	76,439	73,818	74,500	73,599	–5.3
Agriculture [1]......................	122,594	113,321	104,466	106,186	104,989	–14.4
Commerce [1].......................	69,920	36,803	47,652	37,641	38,927	–44.3
Labor	17,727	16,204	16,040	16,095	15,599	–12.0
Health & Human Services [2]...........	123,959	59,788	62,605	61,495	60,944	–50.8
Housing & Urban Development	13,596	11,822	10,319	10,411	10,086	–25.8
Transportation [2]...................	67,364	63,552	63,598	57,748	55,975	–16.9
Energy	17,731	19,589	15,692	15,265	15,050	–15.1
Education..........................	4,771	4,988	4,734	4,482	4,429	–7.2
Veterans Affairs.....................	248,174	263,904	219,547	233,501	236,363	–4.8
Homeland Security [3]................	(X)	(X)	(X)	148,927	149,977	(X)
Independent agencies [4]..............	999,894	1,073,510	1,050,900	959,612	953,113	–4.7
Board of Governors Federal Reserve System .	1,525	1,704	2,372	1,820	1,851	21.4
Environmental Protection Agency........	17,123	17,910	18,036	17,975	17,964	4.9
Equal Employment Opportunity Commission..	2,880	2,796	2,780	2,513	2,421	–15.9
Federal Communications Commission......	1,778	2,116	1,965	2,024	1,936	8.9
Federal Deposit Insurance Corporation	17,641	14,765	6,958	5,416	4,998	–71.7
Federal Trade Commission	988	996	1,019	1,081	1,046	5.9
General Services Administration..........	20,277	16,500	14,334	12,764	12,685	–37.4
National Archives & Records Administration ..	3,120	2,833	2,702	3,029	3,048	–2.3
National Aeronautics & Space Administration .	24,872	21,635	18,819	19,105	19,105	–23.2
National Labor Relations Board	2,263	2,050	2,054	1,934	1,822	–19.5
National Science Foundation	1,318	1,292	1,247	1,327	1,325	0.5
Nuclear Regulatory Commission.........	3,353	3,212	2,858	3,124	3,230	–3.7
Office of Personnel Management.........	6,636	4,354	3,780	3,409	4,333	–34.7
Peace Corps	1,178	1,179	1,065	1,105	1,064	–9.7
Railroad Retirement Board	1,772	1,544	1,176	1,110	1,010	–43.0
Securities & Exchange Commission	2,302	2,852	2,955	3,632	3,933	70.9
Small Business Administration	5,128	5,085	4,150	3,520	4,288	–16.4
Smithsonian Institution [2].............	5,092	5,444	5,065	5,034	4,981	–2.2
Social Security Administration	(X)	66,850	64,474	65,215	65,861	(X)
Tennessee Valley Authority	28,392	16,545	13,145	13,078	12,721	–55.2
U.S. Information Agency	8,555	7,480	2,436	2,303	2,212	–74.1
U.S. International Development Cooperation Agency..................	4,698	3,755	2,552	2,547	2,644	–43.7
U.S. Postal Service	816,886	845,393	860,726	775,834	767,972	–6.0

X Not applicable. [1] Includes enumerators for the 1990 and 2000 census. [2] Sizeable changes in 1995 due to the Social Security Administration which was separated from the Department of Health and Human Services to become an independent agency effective April 1995. [3] See text, Section 10, concerning the development of the Department of Homeland Security. [4] Includes agencies with fewer than 1,000 employees in 2005, not shown separately.

Source: U.S. Office of Personnel Management, *Federal Civilian Workforce Statistics—Employment and Trends*, bimonthly. See Internet site <http://www.opm.gov/feddata/index.htm>.

Table 484. Federal Employees—Summary Characteristics: 1990 to 2004

[As of September 30. In percent, except as indicated. For civilian employees, excluding U.S. Postal Service employees]

Characteristics	1990	1995	1998	1999	2000	2001	2002	2003	2004
Average age (years) [1]................	42.3	44.3	45.6	45.9	46.3	46.5	46.5	46.7	46.8
Average length of service (years) [1].......	13.4	15.5	16.6	16.9	17.1	17.1	16.8	16.8	16.6
Retirement eligible: [2]									
Civil Service Retirement System	8	10	13	15	17	19	23	27	30
Federal Employees Retirement System...	3	5	8	10	11	10	11	12	13
Bachelor's degree or higher............	35	39	40	40	41	41	41	41	42
Sex: Male..........................	57	56	56	55	55	55	55	55	56
Female	43	44	44	45	45	45	45	45	44
Race and national origin:									
Total minorities.....................	27.4	28.9	29.7	30.0	30.4	30.6	30.8	31.1	31.4
Black.............................	16.7	16.8	16.7	17.0	17.1	17.1	17.0	17.0	17.0
Hispanic	5.4	5.9	6.4	6.5	6.6	6.7	6.9	7.1	7.3
Asian/Pacific Islander	3.5	4.2	4.5	4.5	4.5	4.6	4.7	4.8	5.0
American Indian/Alaska native	1.8	2.0	2.1	2.2	2.2	2.2	2.2	2.1	2.1
Disabled...........................	7.0	7.0	7.0	7.0	7.0	7.0	7.0	7.0	7.0
Veterans preference	30.0	26.0	25.0	25.0	24.0	24.0	23.0	22.0	22.0
Vietnam Era veterans	17.0	17.0	14.0	14.0	14.0	13.0	13.0	13.0	12.0
Retired military.....................	4.9	4.2	3.9	3.9	3.9	4.2	4.4	4.6	4.9
Retired officers.....................	0.5	0.5	0.5	0.5	0.5	0.6	0.7	0.8	0.9

[1] For full-time permanent employees. [2] Represents full-time permanent employees under the Civil Service Retirement System (excluding hires since January 1984), and the Federal Employees Retirement System (since January 1984).

Source: U.S. Office of Personnel Management, Office of Workforce Information, *The Fact Book, Federal Civilian Workforce Statistics*, annual. See Internet site <http://www.opm.gov/feddata/factbook/index.asp>.

Table 485. **Federal Executive Branch (Nonpostal) Employment by Race and National Origin: 1990 to 2005**

[As of Sept. 30. Covers total employment for only Executive branch agencies participating in OPMs Central Personnel Data File (CPDF). For information on the CPDF, see <http://www.opm.gov/feddata/acpdf.pdf>]

Pay system	1990	1995	2000	2004	2005
All personnel	2,150,359	1,960,577	1,755,689	1,851,349	1,856,966
White, non-Hispanic	1,562,846	1,394,690	1,224,836	1,270,366	1,267,922
General schedule and related	1,218,188	1,101,108	961,261	972,737	973,767
Grades 1 to 4	132,028	79,195	55,067	48,798	46,671
Grades 5 to 8	337,453	288,755	239,128	231,765	227,387
Grades 9 to 12	510,261	465,908	404,649	405,825	408,111
Grades 13 to 15	238,446	267,250	262,417	286,349	291,598
Total executives/senior pay levels	9,337	13,307	14,332	16,337	16,409
Wage pay system	244,220	186,184	146,075	134,821	135,383
Other pay systems	91,101	94,091	103,168	146,471	142,363
Black	356,867	327,302	298,701	313,099	315,644
General schedule and related	272,657	258,586	241,135	244,736	246,691
Grades 1 to 4	65,077	41,381	26,895	20,797	19,774
Grades 5 to 8	114,993	112,962	99,937	95,798	94,655
Grades 9 to 12	74,985	79,795	82,809	88,813	90,809
Grades 13 to 15	17,602	24,448	31,494	39,328	41,453
Total executives/senior pay levels	479	942	1,180	1,238	1,270
Wage pay system	72,755	55,637	42,590	37,798	37,666
Other pay systems	10,976	12,137	13,796	29,327	30,017
Hispanic	115,170	115,964	115,247	135,533	138,507
General schedule and related	83,218	86,762	89,911	102,612	104,927
Grades 1 to 4	15,738	11,081	8,526	7,969	7,768
Grades 5 to 8	28,727	31,152	31,703	34,380	33,653
Grades 9 to 12	31,615	34,056	36,813	43,868	46,268
Grades 13 to 15	7,138	10,473	12,869	16,395	17,238
Total executives/senior pay levels	154	382	547	656	682
Wage pay system	26,947	22,128	16,926	15,915	15,945
Other pay systems	4,851	6,692	7,863	16,350	16,953
American Indian, Alaska Native, Asian, and Pacific Islander	115,476	122,621	116,905	132,351	134,893
General schedule and related	81,499	86,768	86,074	96,014	97,866
Grades 1 to 4	15,286	11,854	9,340	8,528	8,357
Grades 5 to 8	24,960	26,580	25,691	27,601	27,417
Grades 9 to 12	31,346	33,810	33,167	37,172	38,276
Grades 13 to 15	9,907	14,524	17,876	22,713	23,816
Total executives/senior pay levels	148	331	504	760	804
Wage pay system	24,927	21,553	17,613	16,760	16,938
Other pay systems	8,902	13,969	12,714	18,817	19,285

Source: Office of Personnel Management, Central Personnel Data File.

Table 486. **Federal General Schedule Employee Pay Increases: 1980 to 2006**

[Represents legislated pay increases as percent changes from immediate prior year. For some years data based on range. For details see source]

Date	Pay increase	Date	Pay increase	Date	Pay increase
1980	9.1	1995	2.0	2001	2.7
1985	3.5	1996	2.0	2002	3.6
1990	3.6	1997	2.3	2003	3.1
1992	4.2	1998	2.3	2004	2.7
1993	3.7	1999	3.1	2005	2.5
1994	–	2000	3.8	2006	2.1

– Represents zero.
Source: U.S. Office of Personnel Management, *Pay Structure of the Federal Civil Service,* annual.

Table 487. **Turnover Data for the Executive Branch—All Areas: 1990 to 2005**
[For fiscal years. Data exclude Legislative and Judicial branches, U.S. Postal Service, Postal Rate Commission]

Year	Accessions [1]		Separations		Total employment		
	Total	New hires	Total	Quits	Average	Change from prior year	Percent change [2]
1990 [3]	819,554	716,066	799,237	165,099	2,348,458	114,477	5.1
1994	317,509	219,026	398,134	111,096	2,114,387	–75,029	–3.4
1995	345,166	222,025	457,246	91,909	2,037,890	–76,542	–3.6
1996	266,473	199,463	356,566	80,922	1,960,892	–76,953	–3.8
1997	283,517	208,725	333,431	81,574	1,895,295	–65,597	–3.3
1998	320,830	242,637	321,292	84,124	1,855,112	–40,183	–2.1
1999	423,500	346,988	372,778	129,196	1,846,170	–8,942	–0.5
2000 [3]	1,168,783	1,092,888	1,027,653	801,684	1,946,684	100,514	5.4
2001 [3]	308,877	233,034	301,659	82,495	1,783,239	–163,445	–8.4
2002	316,837	242,280	280,714	55,167	1,808,634	25,395	1.4
2003	508,160	254,030	461,171	53,187	1,875,696	67,062	3.7
2004	313,684	223,294	310,776	60,857	1,873,614	–2,081	–0.1
2005	306,731	223,011	317,060	61,503	1,876,747	3,133	0.2

[1] Accessions are employees who have been added to federal employment. These would include temporary and permanent new hires and those who returned to duty.   [2] Percent change from immediate prior year.   [3] Includes hiring for census enumerators.
Source: U.S. Office of Personnel Management, *The Fact Book, Federal Civilian Workforce Statistics,* annual. See Internet site <http://www.opm.gov/feddata/factbook/index.asp>.

Federal Government Finances and Employment   323

Table 488. **Federal Land and Buildings Owned and Leased: 1990 to 2004**

[**For years ending September 30.** Covers federal real property throughout the world, except as noted. Cost of land figures represent total cost of property owned in year shown. For further details, see source. For data on federal land by state, see Table 346]

Item	Unit	1990	1995	2000	2002	2003	2004
Federally owned:							
Land, worldwide.	1,000 acres . . .	650,014	549,670	635,824	675,864	673,207	654,719
United States.	1,000 acres . . .	649,802	549,474	635,355	674,100	671,759	653,299
Buildings [1]	1,000	(NA)	(NA)	435	446	437	416
United States.	1,000	446	424	430	441	433	411
Buildings, floor area [1]	Mil. sq./ft.	(NA)	(NA)	3,003	3,009	3,066	2,875
United States.	Mil. sq./ft.	2,859	2,793	2,968	2,975	3,032	2,840
Costs.	Mil. dol.	187,865	199,387	260,069	334,708	312,415	331,451
Land	Mil. dol.	(NA)	18,972	21,008	53,930	(NA)	(NA)
Buildings.	Mil. dol.	(NA)	113,018	139,291	174,929	(NA)	(NA)
Structures and facilities . . .	Mil. dol.	(NA)	67,398	99,770	105,849	(NA)	(NA)
Federally leased:							
Land, worldwide.	1,000 acres . . .	994	1,385	1,670	894	373	2,453
United States.	1,000 acres . . .	938	1,351	1,611	842	309	2,391
Buildings [1]	1,000	(NA)	(NA)	84	57	54	58
United States.	1,000	47	78	73	46	42	45
Buildings, floor area [1]	Mil. sq./ft.	(NA)	(NA)	347	374	370	381
United States.	Mil. sq./ft.	234	275	313	339	334	344
Annual rental	Mil. dol.	2,590	3,633	3,394	5,111	6,135	6,702
United States.	Mil. dol.	2,125	3,174	2,931	4,588	5,656	6,179

NA Not available.   [1] Excludes data for Department of Defense military functions outside of the United States.

Source: U.S. General Services Administration, *Federal Real Property Profile*, September 2004; and earlier reports.

Table 489. **Federally Owned Property in the United States by State: 2004**

[As of **September 30.** Excludes data for Department of Defense military functions outside of the United States. For data on federal land by state, see Table 346]

State	Number of owned buildings	Owned building area (mil. sq. ft)	Leased building area (mil. sq. ft.)	State	Number of owned buildings	Owned building area (mil. sq. ft)	Leased building area (mil. sq. ft.)
U.S. . .	**411,406**	**2,839.9**	**343.7**	MO	6,689	50.6	8.4
				MT.	6,944	15.7	2.4
AL	8,142	52.7	5.4	NE.	3,281	18.9	2.2
AK.	9,283	55.1	2.3	NV.	7,527	32.9	1.8
AZ	13,869	53.7	4.9	NH.	735	3.4	1.2
AR	4,803	21.6	2.8	NJ	5,461	46.7	9.6
CA	54,463	344.3	27.5	NM.	14,190	61.1	3.1
CO.	9,226	60.5	7.4	NY.	10,808	100.9	15.2
CT.	2,054	15.4	1.8	NC.	14,499	87.0	6.7
DE.	896	7.5	0.5	ND.	3,374	20.3	1.1
DC.	1,596	66.6	22.3	OH.	5,135	70.1	8.5
FL	13,640	110.0	16.1	OK.	8,990	57.0	7.5
GA.	12,216	111.5	18.5	OR.	8,690	23.1	4.1
HI	13,642	74.6	1.2	PA	7,227	77.4	11.9
ID	6,822	18.1	2.1	RI	1,321	12.7	0.8
IL.	6,754	76.2	8.3	SC.	8,098	61.5	3.0
IN	4,827	33.0	4.6	SD	3,159	17.4	1.5
IA	2,326	12.4	3.2	TN	7,063	68.7	4.9
KS	6,059	42.8	3.5	TX	23,548	198.5	18.7
KY	6,180	52.0	4.2	UT	7,390	31.0	3.5
LA	5,329	41.4	4.3	VT	535	2.6	1.3
ME	2,024	13.4	1.3	VA	17,532	152.1	28.0
MD.	9,882	110.5	22.4	WA	14,839	86.9	6.4
MA	4,268	35.0	5.7	WV	1,878	15.4	3.2
MI	5,520	31.3	7.0	WI	4,896	21.9	4.5
MN	3,078	19.7	3.3	WY	5,228	12.6	0.9
MS.	5,470	34.1	2.9				

Source: U.S. General Services Administration, *Federal Real Property Profile*, September 2004.

Section 10
National Security and Veterans Affairs

This section displays data for national security (national defense and homeland security) and benefits for veterans. Data are presented on national defense and its human and financial costs; active and reserve military personnel; and federally sponsored programs and benefits for veterans, and funding, budget and selected agencies for homeland security. The principal sources of these data are the annual *Selected Manpower Statistics* and the *Atlas/Data Abstract for the United States and Selected Areas* issued by the Office of the Secretary of Defense; *Annual Report of Secretary of Veterans Affairs*, Department of Veterans Affairs, *Budget in Brief*, Department of Homeland Security; and *The Budget of the United States Government*, Office of Management and Budget. For more data on expenditures and personnel, see Section 30.

Department of Defense (DoD)—The Department of Defense is responsible for providing the military forces of the United States. It includes the Office of the Secretary of Defense, the Joint Chiefs of Staff, the Army, the Navy, the Air Force, and the defense agencies. The President serves as Commander-in-Chief of the Armed Forces; from him, the authority flows to the Secretary of Defense and through the Joint Chiefs of Staff to the commanders of unified and specified commands (e.g., U.S. Strategic Command).

Reserve components—The Reserve Components of the Armed Forces consist of the Army National Guard of the United States, Army Reserve, Naval Reserve, Marine Corps Reserve, Air National Guard, Air Force Reserve, and Coast Guard Reserve. They provide trained personnel and units available for active duty in the Armed Forces during times of war or national emergency, and at such other times as national security may require. The National Guard has dual federal/state responsibilities and uses jointly provided equipment, facilities, and budget support. The President is empowered to mobilize the National Guard and to use such of the

Armed Forces as he considers necessary to enforce federal authority in any state. There is in each Armed Force a ready reserve, a standby reserve, and a retired reserve. The Ready Reserve includes the Selected Reserve, which provides trained and ready units and individuals to augment the active forces during times of war or national emergency, or at other times when required; and the Individual Ready Reserve, which is a manpower pool that can be called to active duty during times of war or national emergency and would normally be used as individual fillers for active, guard and reserve units, and as a source of combat replacements. Most of the Ready Reserve serves in an active status. See Table 504 for Standby Reserve and Retired Reserve detail.

Department of Veterans Affairs (VA)—A veteran is someone 18 and older (there are a few 17-year-old veterans) who is not currently on active duty, but who once served on active duty in the United States Army, Navy, Air Force, Marine Corps, or Coast Guard, or who served in the Merchant Marine during World War II. There are many groups whose active service makes them veterans including: those who incurred a service-connected disability during active duty for training in the Reserves or National Guard, even though that service would not otherwise have counted for veteran status; members of a national guard or reserve component who have been ordered to active duty by order of the President or who have a full-time military job. The latter are called AGRs (Active Guard and Reserve). No one who has received a dishonorable discharge is a veteran.

The Department of Veterans Affairs administers laws authorizing benefits for eligible former and present members of the Armed Forces and for the beneficiaries of deceased members. Veterans' benefits available under various acts of Congress include compensation for service-connected disability or death; pensions

U.S. Census Bureau, Statistical Abstract of the United States: 2007

for non-service-connected disability or death; vocational rehabilitation, education and training; home loan insurance; life insurance; health care; special housing and automobiles or other conveyances for certain disabled veterans; burial and plot allowances; and educational assistance to families of deceased or totally disabled veterans, servicemen missing in action, or prisoners of war. Since these benefits are legislated by Congress, the dates they were enacted and the dates they apply to veterans may be different from the actual dates the conflicts occurred. VA estimates of veterans cover all persons discharged from active U.S. military service under conditions other than dishonorable.

Homeland Security—In an effort to increase homeland security following the September 11, 2001, terrorist attacks on the United States, President George W. Bush issued the *National Strategy for Homeland Security* in July 2002 and signed legislation creating the Department of Homeland Security (DHS) in November 2002.

The *National Strategy* sets forth a plan to improve homeland security through 43 initiatives that fall within six critical mission areas. These mission areas are intelligence and warning, border and transportation security, domestic counterterrorism, protection of critical infrastructure, defense against catastrophic terrorism, and emergency preparedness and response.

The funding and activities of homeland security are not only carried out by DHS, but also by other federal agencies, state, and local entities. In addition to DHS, there are 32 other federal agencies that comprise federal homeland security funding. DHS, along with four other agencies—Department of Defense (DoD), Energy (DoE), Health and Human Services (HHS), and Justice (DoJ)—account for most of the federal spending for homeland security.

Department of Homeland Security (DHS)—The mission of DHS is to lead a unified effort to secure the United States. This effort is to prevent and deter terrorist attacks and to protect against and respond to threats and hazards to the nation. This effort is to ensure safe and secure borders, to welcome lawful immigrants and visitors, and to promote the free flow of commerce.

The creation of the Department of Homeland Security, which began operations in March 2003, represents a fusion of 22 federal agencies (legacy agencies) to coordinate and centralize the leadership of many homeland security activities under a single department. Out of these agencies, the Secret Service and Coast Guard remain intact and report directly to the Secretary. Immigration and Naturalization Services (INS) adjudications and benefits programs report directly to the Deputy Secretary as the U.S. Citizenship and Immigration Services (USCIS).

The Customs and Border Protection (CBP) is responsible for managing, securing, and controlling U.S. borders. This includes carrying out traditional border-related responsibilities, such as stemming the tide of illegal drugs and illegal aliens; securing and facilitating legitimate global trade and travel; and protecting the food supply and agriculture industry from pests and disease. CBP is composed of the Border Patrol and Inspections (both moved from INS) along with Customs (absorbed from the Department of Treasury) and Animal and Plant Health Inspections Services (absorbed from the Department of Agriculture).

Immigration and Customs Enforcement (ICE) is the largest investigation arm of DHS. ICE is composed of four law enforcement divisions: Investigations, Intelligence, Federal Protective Service, and Apprehension, Detention, and Removal. ICE investigates a wide range of national security, financial and smuggling violations including drug smuggling, human trafficking, illegal arms exports, financial crimes, commercial fraud, human smuggling, document fraud, money laundering, child pornography/exploitation, and immigration fraud.

The Transportation Security Administration (TSA) was created as part of the Aviation and Transportation Security Act on November 19, 2001. TSA was originally part of the Department of Transportation, but was moved to Department of Homeland Security. TSA's mission is to provide security to our nation's transportation systems with a primary focus on aviation security.

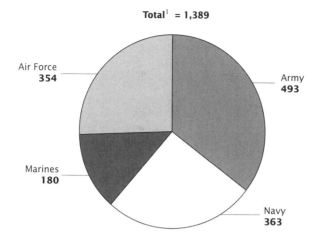

Figure 10.1
Department of Defense Manpower: 2005
(In thousands)

Total[1] = 1,389

Air Force
354

Army
493

Marines
180

Navy
363

[1]Includes National Guard, Reserve, and retired regular personnel on extended or continuous active duty.
Excludes Coast Guard.

Source: Chart prepared by U.S. Census Bureau. For data, see Table 500.

Figure 10.2
Living Veterans by Age: 2005
(In thousands)

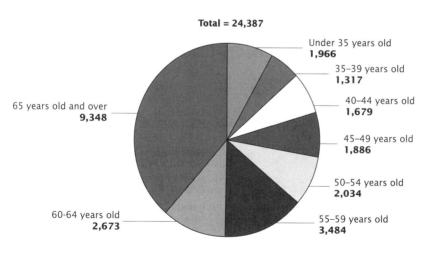

Total = 24,387

Under 35 years old
1,966

35–39 years old
1,317

40–44 years old
1,679

45–49 years old
1,886

50–54 years old
2,034

55–59 years old
3,484

60-64 years old
2,673

65 years old and over
9,348

Source: Chart prepared by U.S. Census Bureau. For data, see Table 508.

Table 490. National Defense Outlays and Veterans Benefits: 1960 to 2007

[In billions of dollars (53.5 represents $53,500,000,000) except percent. For fiscal year ending in year shown, see text, section 8. Includes outlays of Department of Defense, Department of Veterans Affairs, and other agencies for activities primarily related to national defense and veterans programs. For explanation of average annual percent change, see Guide to Tabular Presentation. Minus sign (–) indicates decrease]

Year	National defense and veterans outlays (bil. dol.)				Annual percent change [1]			Defense outlays percent of—	
		Defense outlays							
	Total outlays	Current dollars	Constant (FY2000) dollars	Veterans outlays	Total outlays	Defense outlays	Veterans outlays	Federal outlays	Gross domestic product [2]
1960	53.5	48.1	300.2	5.4	2.5	2.4	3.1	52.2	9.3
1970	90.4	81.7	375.1	8.7	0.3	–1.0	13.6	41.8	8.1
1980	155.1	134.0	267.1	21.1	13.9	15.2	6.3	22.7	4.9
1985	279.0	252.7	356.5	26.3	10.3	11.1	2.7	26.7	6.1
1990	328.4	299.3	382.7	29.1	–1.6	–1.4	–3.2	23.9	5.2
1994	319.2	281.6	322.8	37.6	–2.3	–3.2	5.4	19.3	4.1
1995	310.0	272.1	305.9	37.9	–2.9	–3.4	0.8	17.9	3.7
1996	302.7	265.8	289.2	37.0	–2.3	–2.3	–2.4	17.0	3.5
1997	309.8	270.5	288.4	39.3	2.3	1.8	6.3	16.9	3.3
1998	310.2	268.5	282.6	41.8	0.1	–0.8	6.3	16.2	3.1
1999	320.2	274.9	283.7	43.2	3.2	2.4	3.4	16.1	3.0
2000	341.6	294.5	294.5	47.1	6.7	7.1	9.0	16.5	3.0
2001	350.5	305.5	297.2	45.0	2.6	3.7	–4.3	16.4	3.0
2002	399.5	348.6	329.4	51.0	14.0	14.1	13.2	17.3	3.4
2003	461.9	404.9	365.3	57.0	15.6	16.2	11.8	18.7	3.7
2004	515.7	455.9	397.3	59.8	11.6	12.6	4.8	19.9	3.9
2005	565.5	495.3	419.8	70.2	9.7	8.6	17.4	20.0	4.0
2006, est	606.4	535.9	443.1	70.4	7.2	8.2	0.4	19.8	4.1
2007, est	601.4	527.4	427.4	73.5	–0.8	–1.6	4.4	19.0	3.8

[1] Change from immediate prior year; for 1960, change from 1955. [2] Represents fiscal year GDP; for definition, see text, Section 13.

Source: U.S. Office of Management and Budget, *Budget of the United States Government, Historical Tables*, annual. See also <http://www.whitehouse.gov/omb>.

Table 491. National Defense Budget Authority and Outlays for Defense Functions: 1990 to 2006

[In billions of dollars (303.3 represents $303,300,000,000), except percent. For year ending September 30. Minus sign (–) indicates decrease]

Function	1990	1995	1998	1999	2000	2001	2002	2003	2004	2005	2006, est.
Total budget authority [1]	303.3	266.4	271.3	292.3	304.1	335.5	362.1	456.2	490.6	505.8	561.8
Department of Defense-Military. . . .	293.0	255.7	258.5	278.5	290.4	319.4	345.0	437.9	471.0	483.9	538.2
Military Personnel	78.9	71.6	69.8	70.6	73.8	76.9	87.0	109.1	116.1	121.3	115.8
Operation and Maintenance	88.4	93.7	97.2	104.9	108.7	115.7	133.2	178.3	189.8	179.2	178.3
Procurement	81.4	43.6	44.8	51.1	55.0	62.6	62.7	78.5	83.1	96.6	86.2
Research, Development, Test, and Evaluation	36.5	34.5	37.1	38.3	38.7	41.6	48.7	58.1	64.6	68.8	71.0
Military Construction	5.1	5.4	5.5	5.4	5.1	5.4	6.6	6.7	6.1	7.3	8.9
Family Housing.	3.1	3.4	3.8	3.6	3.5	3.7	4.0	4.2	3.8	4.1	4.4
Other	–0.4	3.4	0.3	4.6	5.6	13.5	2.7	3.0	7.5	6.6	3.4
Atomic energy defense activities . . .	9.7	10.1	11.7	12.4	12.4	14.3	15.2	16.6	16.8	17.9	18.1
Defense-related activities.	0.7	1.0	1.1	1.4	1.3	1.7	1.9	2.0	2.8	4.0	5.6
Total outlays [1]	299.3	272.1	268.5	274.9	294.5	305.5	348.6	404.9	455.9	495.3	535.9
Department of Defense-Military. . . .	289.8	259.4	256.1	261.3	281.2	291.0	332.0	387.3	436.5	474.2	512.1
Military personnel	75.6	70.8	69.0	69.5	76.0	74.0	86.8	106.7	113.6	127.5	116.3
Operation, maintenance	88.3	91.0	93.4	96.3	105.9	112.0	130.0	151.4	174.0	188.1	192.6
Procurement	81.0	55.0	48.2	48.8	51.7	55.0	62.5	67.9	76.2	82.3	88.8
Research, Development, Test, and Evaluation	37.5	34.6	37.4	37.4	37.6	40.5	44.4	53.1	60.8	65.7	70.8
Military construction.	5.1	6.8	6.0	5.5	5.1	5.0	5.1	5.9	6.3	5.3	7.3
Family housing	3.5	3.6	3.9	3.7	3.4	3.5	3.7	3.8	3.9	3.7	3.8
Anticipated funding for Global . . . War on Terror.	(X)	(X)	(X)	(X)	(X)	(X)	(X)	(X)	(X)	(X)	30.1
Other	–1.2	–2.4	–1.9	0.1	1.6	1.1	–0.5	–1.5	1.7	1.5	2.4
Atomic energy activities.	9.0	11.8	11.3	12.2	12.1	12.9	14.8	16.0	16.6	18.0	18.7
Defense-related activities.	0.6	0.9	1.1	1.4	1.2	1.6	1.8	1.6	2.8	3.1	5.1

X Not Applicable. [1] Includes defense budget authority, balances, and outlays by other departments.

Source: U.S. Office of Management and Budget, *Budget of the United States Government, Historical Tables, Budget Authority by Function and Subfunction, Outlay by Function and Subfunction*, annual. See also <http://www.whitehouse.gov/budget>.

Table 492. Military Prime Contract Awards to All Businesses by Program: 1990 to 2005

[In billions of dollars (144.7 represents $144,700,000,000). Net values for year ending September 30. Includes all new prime contracts; debit or credit changes in contracts are also included. Actions cover official awards, amendments, or other changes in prime contracts to obtain military supplies, services, or construction. Excludes term contracts and contracts which do not obligate a firm total dollar amount or fixed quantity, but includes job orders, task orders, and delivery orders against such contracts]

DoD procurement program	1990	1995	1999	2000	2001	2002	2003	2004	2005
Total.	144.7	131.4	135.2	143.0	154.1	180.6	219.5	241.0	269.2
Intragovernmental [1]	10.0	12.3	11.6	14.8	13.4	17.0	19.5	19.8	18.5
For work outside the U.S [2]	7.1	5.6	7.4	7.5	7.1	9.3	16.2	25.5	30.4
Educ. and nonprofit institutions	3.5	3.3	3.9	4.3	4.5	5.5	6.2	6.4	6.6
With business firms for work in the U.S [3] . . .	123.8	110.0	112.2	116.4	129.2	148.8	177.7	189.3	213.7
Major hard goods	79.1	56.0	57.5	59.8	67.9	76.1	90.6	99.0	109.0
Aircraft	24.0	18.8	23.3	28.8	30.5	30.6	41.1	40.4	40.9
Electronics and communication equip. . .	18.5	12.3	10.7	9.5	10.9	13.0	14.9	18.5	21.8
Missiles and space systems	17.1	10.6	9.5	8.2	8.2	11.2	13.3	14.6	14.7
Ships	10.3	9.1	7.8	8.3	12.0	11.4	10.2	12.3	11.8
Tanks, ammo. and weapons	9.2	5.3	6.2	5.0	6.3	9.8	11.0	13.3	19.8
Services	14.6	18.6	23.7	24.0	25.9	33.2	43.1	45.4	54.4

[1] Covers only purchases from other federal agencies and reimbursable purchases on behalf of foreign governments.
[2] Includes foreign firms for perfomance in U.S.   [3] Includes Department of Defense. Includes other business not shown separately. Contracts awarded for work in U.S. possessions, and other areas subject to complete sovereignty of United States; contracts in a classified location; and any intragovernmental contracts entered into overseas.

Source: U.S. Department of Defense, *DoD Personnel and Procurement Statistics, Procurement, DoD Procurement,* annual; <http://siadapp.dior.whs.mil/index.html>.

Table 493. U.S. Military Sales and Assistance to Foreign Governments: 1995 to 2004

[In millions of dollars (8,495 represents $8,495,000,000). For year ending September 30. Department of Defense (DoD) sales deliveries cover deliveries against sales orders authorized under Arms Export Control Act, as well as earlier and applicable legislation. For details regarding individual programs, see source. Table data has been updated throughout]

Item	1995	1997	1998	1999	2000	2001	2002	2003	2004
Military sales agreements	8,495	8,852	9,229	11,755	11,528	13,628	12,906	13,682	13,183
Military construction sales agreements	24	29	474	301	283	124	72	221	675
Military sales deliveries [1]	12,100	15,663	13,179	16,888	10,436	12,001	10,240	9,315	10,681
Military sales financing . . . . [2] . .	3,712	3,530	3,420	3,370	4,333	3,535	4,032	5,955	4,584
Military assistance programs [2] . . .	117	91	95	268	86	41	46	257	135
Military assistance program delivery [3]	20	112	113	37	13	23	35	106	29
IMET program/deliveries [4]	26	43	50	49	50	54	70	79	89

[1] Includes military construction sales deliveries.   [2] Also includes Military Assistance Service Funded (MASF) program data, Section 506(a) drawdown authority, and MAP Merger Funds.   [3] Includes Military Assistance Service Funded (MASF) program data and Section 506(a) drawdown authority.   [4] International Military Education & Training. Includes military assistance service funded and emergency draw downs.

Source: U.S. Department of Defense, Defense Security Cooperation Agency, DSCA Data and Statistics; see also <http://www.dsca.osd.mil/data_stats.htm>.

Table 494. U.S. Military Sales Deliveries by Selected Country: 1995 to 2004

[In millions of dollars (12,100 represents $12,100,000,000). For year ending September 30. Represents Department of Defense military sales. Table has been updated throughout]

Country	1995	1997	1998	1999	2000	2001	2002	2003	2004
Total [1]	12,100	15,663	13,179	16,888	10,436	12,001	10,240	9,315	10,681
Australia.	303	196	207	269	330	245	155	193	186
Bahrain	40	61	62	48	54	336	82	97	78
Belgium	8	107	194	250	58	170	68	71	42
Canada	127	83	111	96	84	110	85	155	147
China: Taiwan	1,332	2,370	1,420	2,504	784	1,160	1,410	593	962
Denmark	54	48	159	157	46	112	23	14	23
Egypt.	1,479	892	551	448	805	862	1,883	878	1,328
France	64	57	35	248	217	142	206	169	251
Germany	257	208	190	251	131	330	222	243	267
Greece	220	691	397	463	315	448	454	1,325	1,158
Israel	327	456	1,195	1,213	562	741	632	825	891
Italy	54	51	43	106	41	97	103	185	283
Japan	693	488	409	439	460	494	470	404	397
Jordan	47	42	47	49	52	80	57	69	107
Korea, South	442	478	836	585	1,400	735	526	493	600
Kuwait	471	1,209	323	316	321	552	131	143	213
Netherlands	153	168	344	321	161	412	242	225	272
Norway.	25	98	119	220	64	192	88	123	80
Portugal.	88	70	21	12	20	42	28	116	31
Saudi Arabia	3,567	4,639	3,800	4,686	2,000	1,940	1,312	1,133	1,136
Singapore.	59	133	232	549	131	244	421	169	208
Spain	193	216	133	324	141	267	178	159	188
Thailand	356	151	144	133	113	118	168	132	188
Turkey	368	1,153	532	854	216	466	280	483	291
United Arab Emirates	345	91	26	95	70	24	92	85	139
United Kingdom	419	425	430	365	347	525	386	350	454

[1] Includes countries not shown.

Source: U.S. Department of Defense, Defense Security Cooperation Agency, DSCA Data and Statistics; see also <http://www.dsca.osd.mil/data_stats.htm>.

National Security and Veterans Affairs   329

Table 495. Military and Civilian Personnel and Expenditures: 1990 to 2004

[Personnel in thousands (3,693 represents 3,693,000); expenditures in millions of dollars (209,904 represents 209,904,000,000). For year ending September 30. For definitions, see headnote, tables 496 and 498]

Item	1990	1995	2000	2001	2002	2003	2004
Personnel, total [1] (1,000).	3,693	3,391	2,791	2,781	2,811	2,806	2,764
Active duty military	1,185	1,085	984	991	1,045	1,071	1,055
Civilian.	931	768	634	628	628	631	634
Reserve and National Guard [2].	1,577	1,538	1,173	1,163	1,138	1,105	1,074
Expenditures, total [2]	209,904	209,695	229,072	243,778	276,281	316,648	345,891
Payroll outlays.	88,650	98,396	103,447	106,013	114,950	122,270	139,490
Active duty military pay	33,705	35,188	36,872	37,873	40,945	46,614	50,489
Civilian pay	28,230	29,932	29,935	29,879	32,805	35,041	36,234
Reserve and National Guard pay . . .	5,556	5,681	4,646	5,066	7,523	7,306	10,303
Retired military pay	21,159	27,595	31,994	33,196	33,677	33,309	42,465
Prime contract awards [3]	121,254	109,005	123,295	135,225	158,737	191,222	203,389
Grants	6,329	7,543	2,330	2,540	2,594	3,156	3,012

[1] Includes those based ashore and excludes those temporarily shore-based, in a transient status, or afloat. [2] Includes expenditures not shown separately. [3] Represents contract awards over $25,000.

Source: U.S. Department of Defense, *DoD Personnel and Procurement Statistics, Personnel, Publications, Atlas/Data Abstract for the United States and Selected Areas,* annual; <http://siadapp.dior.whs.mil/index.html>.

Table 496. Department of Defense Payroll and Contract Awards—States: 2004

[In millions of dollars ($139,490 represents $139,490,000,000); For year ending September 30. *Payroll outlays include the gross earnings of civilian and active duty military personnel for services rendered to the government and for cash allowances for benefits. Excludes employer's share of employee benefits, accrued military retirement benefits and most permanent change of station costs. Contracts refers to awards made in year specified; expenditures relating to awards may extend over several years]*

State	Payroll Total	Payroll Retired military	Contract awards [1]	Grants	State	Payroll Total	Payroll Retired military	Contract awards [1]	Grants
U.S. . . .	139,490	42,465	203,389	3,012	MO	2,112	678	6,502	48
AL	3,284	1,109	5,849	39	MT	404	153	207	34
AK	1,282	174	1,262	38	NE	925	285	401	23
AZ	2,678	1,205	8,430	91	NV	1,168	617	439	14
AR	1,128	492	494	37	NH	384	215	716	23
CA	15,017	4,347	27,875	384	NJ	1,860	397	4,196	61
CO	3,025	1,183	3,151	49	NM	1,447	485	1,071	33
CT	717	218	8,959	43	NY	2,443	601	5,244	139
DE	417	153	194	17	NC	6,569	1,654	2,213	82
DC	1,983	69	3,515	36	ND	498	73	310	33
FL	9,334	4,511	8,386	83	OH	2,894	828	4,637	69
GA	6,633	1,780	3,905	48	OK	2,976	652	1,524	33
HI	3,374	358	1,714	47	OR	805	434	530	11
ID	535	240	187	29	PA	2,912	912	6,203	154
IL	3,025	677	3,004	69	RI	621	130	418	13
IN	1,299	404	3,173	49	SC	3,306	1,125	1,599	45
IA	481	185	734	31	SD	397	119	236	17
KS	1,529	426	1,412	26	TN	1,614	943	2,116	35
KY	2,432	474	4,119	18	TX	11,082	4,113	21,044	127
LA	1,871	541	2,544	82	UT	1,548	281	1,878	25
ME	805	229	1,556	32	VT	140	65	452	11
MD	4,999	1,170	9,206	162	VA	15,992	4,017	23,543	69
MA	1,103	375	6,961	144	WA	5,301	1,540	3,325	51
MI	1,241	461	2,612	120	WV	411	178	280	38
MN	708	285	1,337	63	WI	648	304	1,746	41
MS	1,828	508	1,867	45	WY	302	92	115	1

[1] Military awards for supplies, services, and construction. Net value of contracts of over $25,000 for work in each state and DC. Figures reflect impact of prime contracting on state distribution of defense work. Often the state in which a prime contractor is located is not the state where the subcontracted work is done. See also headnote, Table 492. Undistributed civilians and military personnel, their payrolls, and prime contract awards for performance in classified locations are excluded.

Source: U.S. Department of Defense, *DoD Personnel and Procurement Statistics, Personnel, Publications, Atlas/Data Abstract for the United States and Selected Areas,* annual; <http://siadapp.dior.whs.mil/index.html>.

Table 497. Expenditures and Personnel by Selected Major Locations: 2004

[In thousands of dollars (9,187,656 represents $9,187,656,000), except for personnel. For year ending September 30. See headnote, Table 496]

Major locations	Expenditures Total	Expenditures Payroll outlays	Expenditures Grants/ contracts	Major locations	Military and civilian personnel Total	Military and civilian personnel Active duty military	Military and civilian personnel Civilian
Fort Worth, TX.	9,187,656	278,516	8,909,140	Fort Bragg, NC	48,386	42,768	5,618
San Diego, CA.	7,354,895	3,456,175	3,898,720	Fort Hood, TX.	47,095	42,742	4,353
Washington, DC. . . .	5,227,865	1,676,618	3,551,247	Camp Pendleton, CA. . .	39,515	37,443	2,072
St. Louis, MO	5,101,117	200,776	4,900,341	Camp Lejeune, NC	34,764	31,948	2,816
Huntsville, AL	4,633,003	270,866	4,362,137	San Diego, CA	30,735	17,801	12,934
Norfolk, VA	4,546,509	3,241,181	1,305,328	Fort Campbell, KY.	28,585	26,306	2,279
Arlington, VA	4,517,336	2,227,846	2,289,490	Arlington, VA	26,865	11,742	15,123
Long Beach, CA	3,954,051	68,299	3,885,752	Norfolk, VA.	24,197	15,382	8,815
Groton, CT	3,590,117	298,806	3,291,311	Fort Benning, GA	23,520	20,493	3,027
Tucson, AZ	3,333,045	366,551	2,966,494	Washington, DC	23,289	9,625	13,664

Source: U.S. Department of Defense, *DoD Personnel and Procurement Statistics, Personnel, Publications, Atlas/Data Abstract for the United States and Selected Areas,* annual; <http://siadapp.dior.whs.mil/index.html>.

Table 498. Military and Civilian Personnel in Installations: 2004

[As of September 30. *Civilian personnel* includes United States citizens and foreign national direct-hire civilians subject to Office of Management and Budget (OMB) ceiling controls and civilian personnel involved in civil functions in the United States. Excludes indirect-hire civilians and those direct-hire civilians not subject to OMB ceiling controls. Military personnel include active duty personnel based ashore, excludes personnel temporarily shore-based in a transient status, or afloat]

State	Active military personnel				Reserve and National Guard, total	Civilian personnel			
	Total [1]	Army	Navy/ Marine Corps	Air Force		Total [1]	Army	Navy/ Marine Corps	Air Force
United States.....	**1,055,314**	**395,842**	**346,970**	**312,502**	**1,074,324**	**634,185**	**220,558**	**175,696**	**154,151**
Alabama.........	10,276	5,843	618	3,815	31,912	21,155	17,348	48	2,332
Alaska..........	17,385	7,604	112	9,669	5,681	4,536	2,527	17	1,637
Arizona.........	22,793	5,371	4,826	12,596	17,654	9,002	3,898	474	3,552
Arkansas........	5,257	243	43	4,971	15,460	3,933	2,877	6	903
California........	128,277	7,828	99,536	20,913	88,885	58,062	7,333	33,167	10,125
Colorado........	29,790	14,904	859	14,027	19,630	10,345	2,767	40	5,240
Connecticut......	3,467	30	3,403	34	9,034	2,452	478	1,030	262
Delaware........	3,949	7	17	3,925	5,748	1,448	254	1	1,117
District of Columbia...	12,266	5,830	3,299	3,137	8,674	15,174	4,468	9,496	928
Florida..........	52,300	3,101	22,880	26,319	47,270	27,076	3,260	11,947	8,982
Georgia.........	67,642	52,639	4,292	10,711	35,995	30,623	10,802	3,997	13,640
Hawaii..........	35,061	17,068	13,235	4,758	11,335	16,576	4,302	9,230	1,966
Idaho..........	4,619	37	87	4,495	6,756	1,532	740	46	686
Illinois.........	26,650	614	20,291	5,745	34,214	13,111	6,626	1,870	3,235
Indiana.........	988	478	394	116	23,141	9,088	1,952	3,225	1,062
Iowa...........	364	183	130	51	15,346	1,522	960	5	510
Kansas.........	16,294	13,041	156	3,097	14,701	6,048	4,570	1	1,123
Kentucky........	35,162	34,714	231	217	15,763	8,314	6,811	206	254
Louisiana........	17,380	9,556	1,401	6,423	25,452	7,093	3,762	1,170	1,765
Maine..........	2,350	192	2,133	25	6,323	6,290	314	5,289	278
Maryland........	29,531	7,072	14,711	7,748	22,864	31,611	12,125	15,377	2,255
Massachusetts.....	2,468	255	576	1,637	19,359	6,707	2,350	228	2,980
Michigan........	1,140	448	561	131	24,308	8,110	5,164	24	1,146
Minnesota.......	667	261	311	95	22,765	2,544	1,467	17	838
Mississippi.......	14,483	392	5,623	8,468	19,446	9,088	3,525	2,396	2,878
Missouri........	15,302	9,297	1,830	4,175	27,029	9,208	5,999	255	1,207
Montana........	3,789	27	16	3,746	5,775	1,274	512	–	713
Nebraska.......	7,332	152	583	6,597	8,931	3,769	1,413	16	1,996
Nevada........	9,251	97	1,000	8,154	6,376	2,089	343	298	1,250
New Hampshire....	218	8	152	58	5,028	1,059	545	46	303
New Jersey.......	6,392	928	493	4,971	21,745	13,628	9,270	2,032	1,526
New Mexico......	11,994	259	187	11,548	7,388	6,805	2,935	39	3,327
New York.......	22,714	19,873	2,416	425	43,474	11,409	7,178	146	2,547
North Carolina.....	101,033	42,860	47,757	10,416	29,070	16,942	6,225	7,418	1,296
North Dakota.....	7,840	22	10	7,808	5,368	1,706	491	2	1,125
Ohio...........	7,211	450	642	6,119	37,829	21,704	1,336	73	12,357
Oklahoma........	23,476	12,475	1,506	9,495	19,194	21,860	4,544	84	15,887
Oregon.........	667	212	398	57	13,566	3,276	2,324	20	899
Pennsylvania......	2,837	1,088	1,493	256	45,257	25,079	8,529	7,302	1,605
Rhode Island......	2,336	103	2,154	79	5,887	4,370	303	3,744	230
South Carolina.....	38,213	10,705	17,512	9,996	22,489	9,382	2,839	3,582	1,804
South Dakota.....	3,698	43	15	3,640	5,762	1,161	471	1	637
Tennessee........	2,430	321	1,875	234	23,953	5,390	2,654	928	974
Texas..........	109,760	62,473	6,877	40,410	76,101	39,385	19,588	1,434	14,431
Utah...........	5,756	296	156	5,304	13,404	14,715	2,323	26	11,564
Vermont........	60	20	28	12	4,487	613	312	1	263
Virginia.........	90,088	25,908	49,538	14,642	36,722	78,792	20,388	34,482	4,452
Washington.......	37,906	20,100	10,143	7,663	26,973	23,433	6,013	14,354	1,985
West Virginia......	503	168	288	47	10,585	1,810	1,249	95	445
Wisconsin.......	502	242	175	85	20,788	2,847	1,859	11	873
Wyoming........	3,447	4	1	3,442	3,427	1,039	235	–	761

– Represents zero. [1] Includes Other Defense Activities (ODA) not shown separately.

Source: U.S. Department of Defense, Directorate for Information Operations and Reports, *Atlas/Data Abstract for the United States and Selected Areas*, annual. <http://www.siadapp.dior.whs.mil/index.htm>.

Table 499. Military Personnel on Active Duty by Location: 1980 to 2005

[In thousands (2,051 represents 2,051,000). As of September 30]

Location	1980	1985	1990	1995	2000	2001	2002	2003	2004	2005
Total...........	**2,051**	**2,151**	**2,046**	**1,518**	**1,384**	**1,385**	**1,412**	**1,434**	**1,427**	**1,389**
Shore-based [1]......	1,840	1,920	1,794	1,351	1,237	1,244	1,262	1,287	1,291	1,262
Afloat [2]........	211	231	252	167	147	141	150	148	136	127
United States [3]......	1,562	1,636	1,437	1,280	1,127	1,130	1,181	1,182	1,139	1,098
Foreign countries.....	489	515	609	238	258	255	230	253	288	291

[1] Includes Navy personnel temporarily on shore. [2] Includes Marine Corps. [3] Includes Puerto Rico and Island areas.

Source: U.S. Department of Defense, *DoD Personnel and Procurement Statistics, Personnel, Military, Military Personnel Statistics*, annual; <http://siadapp.dior.whs.mil/index.htm>.

National Security and Veterans Affairs 331

Table 500. Department of Defense Personnel: 1960 to 2005

[In thousands (2,475 represents 2,475,000.) As of end of fiscal year, see text, section 8. Includes National Guard, Reserve, and retired regular personnel on extended or continuous active duty. Excludes Coast Guard. Other officer candidates are included under enlisted personnel]

Year	Total [1,2]	Army Total [1]	Army Male Officers	Army Male Enlisted	Army Female Officers	Army Female Enlisted	Navy [2] Total [1]	Navy Male Officers	Navy Male Enlisted	Navy Female Officers	Navy Female Enlisted	Marine Corps Total [1]	MC Male Officers	MC Male Enlisted	MC Female Officers	MC Female Enlisted	Air Force Total [1]	AF Male Officers	AF Male Enlisted	AF Female Officers	AF Female Enlisted
1960	2,475	873	97	762	4.3	8.3	617	67	540	2.7	5.4	171	16	153	0.1	1.5	815	126	677	3.7	5.7
1965	2,654	969	108	846	3.8	8.5	670	75	583	2.6	5.3	190	17	172	0.1	1.4	825	128	685	4.1	4.7
1970	3,065	1,323	162	1,142	5.2	11.5	691	78	600	2.9	5.8	260	25	233	0.3	2.1	791	125	648	4.7	9.0
1975	2,128	784	98	640	4.6	37.7	535	62	449	3.7	17.5	196	19	174	0.3	2.8	613	100	478	5.0	25.2
1976	2,082	779	94	634	4.8	41.6	525	60	439	3.5	19.3	192	19	171	0.4	3.1	585	95	452	5.0	29.2
1977	2,075	782	92	634	5.7	46.1	530	59	443	3.8	19.5	192	19	169	0.4	3.5	571	91	435	5.4	34.6
1978	2,062	772	92	619	6.3	50.5	530	59	442	4.0	21.3	191	18	167	0.4	4.7	570	89	429	6.0	41.1
1979	2,027	759	90	602	6.9	55.2	523	58	432	4.4	25.0	185	18	161	0.5	5.5	560	89	413	7.3	46.4
1980	2,051	777	91	612	7.6	61.7	527	58	430	4.9	30.1	189	18	164	0.5	6.2	558	90	404	8.5	51.9
1981	2,083	781	94	610	8.3	65.3	540	60	435	5.3	34.6	191	17	165	0.5	7.1	570	90	413	9.1	54.4
1982	2,109	780	94	609	9.0	64.1	553	61	444	5.7	37.3	192	18	165	0.6	7.9	583	92	421	9.9	54.5
1983	2,123	780	97	602	9.5	66.5	558	62	444	6.3	40.8	194	18	166	0.6	8.3	592	94	428	10.6	55.3
1984	2,138	780	98	601	10.2	67.1	565	62	448	6.6	42.6	196	19	167	0.6	8.6	597	95	430	11.2	55.9
1985	2,151	781	99	599	10.8	68.4	571	64	449	6.9	45.7	198	19	169	0.7	9.0	602	96	431	11.9	58.1
1986	2,169	781	99	597	11.3	69.7	581	65	457	7.3	47.2	200	19	170	0.6	9.2	608	97	434	12.4	61.2
1987	2,174	781	96	596	11.6	71.6	587	65	462	7.2	47.7	200	19	170	0.6	9.1	607	94	432	12.6	63.2
1988	2,138	772	95	588	11.8	72.0	593	65	466	7.3	49.7	197	19	168	0.7	9.0	576	92	405	12.9	61.5
1989	2,130	770	95	584	12.2	74.3	593	65	464	7.5	52.1	197	19	168	0.7	9.0	571	91	399	13.4	63.7
1990	2,044	732	92	553	12.4	71.2	579	64	451	7.8	52.1	197	19	168	0.7	8.7	535	87	370	13.3	60.8
1991	1,986	711	91	535	12.5	67.8	570	63	444	8.0	51.4	194	19	166	0.7	8.3	510	84	350	13.3	56.1
1992	1,807	610	83	449	11.7	61.7	542	61	417	8.3	51.0	185	18	157	0.6	7.9	470	77	320	12.7	56.1
1993	1,705	572	77	420	11.1	60.2	510	58	390	8.3	49.3	178	17	153	0.6	7.2	444	72	302	12.3	54.5
1994	1,610	541	74	394	10.9	59.0	469	54	355	8.0	47.9	174	17	149	0.6	7.0	426	69	287	12.3	54.0
1995	1,518	509	72	365	10.8	57.3	435	51	324	7.9	47.9	175	17	150	0.7	7.4	400	66	266	12.1	52.1
1996	1,472	491	70	347	10.6	59.0	417	50	308	7.8	46.9	175	17	149	0.8	7.8	389	64	256	12.0	52.8
1997	1,439	492	69	346	10.4	62.4	396	48	290	7.8	44.8	174	17	148	0.8	8.5	377	62	246	12.0	53.8
1998	1,407	484	68	340	10.4	61.4	382	47	280	7.8	42.9	173	17	146	0.9	8.9	368	60	237	12.0	54.2
1999	1,386	479	67	337	10.5	61.5	373	46	271	7.7	43.9	173	17	145	0.9	9.3	361	58	232	11.8	54.6
2000	1,384	482	66	339	10.8	62.9	373	46	272	7.8	43.8	173	17	146	0.9	9.5	356	57	227	11.8	55.0
2001	1,385	481	65	337	11.0	63.4	378	46	273	8.0	46.6	173	17	145	1.0	9.6	354	57	224	12.0	55.6
2002	1,414	487	66	341	11.5	63.2	385	47	279	8.2	47.3	174	17	146	1.0	9.5	368	59	233	12.9	58.6
2003	1,434	499	68	352	12.0	63.5	382	47	276	8.2	47.3	178	18	149	1.1	9.6	375	61	237	13.5	60.0
2004	1,427	500	69	358	12.3	61.0	373	46	273	8.1	46.1	178	18	149	1.1	9.7	377	61	242	13.6	60.2
2005	1,389	493	69	353	12.4	57.9	363	45	266	7.8	44.5	180	18	151	1.0	9.8	354	60	225	13.4	55.6

[1] Includes cadets, midshipmen, and others not shown separately.   [2] Beginning 1980, excludes Navy Reserve personnel on active duty for Training and Administration of Reserves (TARS).

Source: U.S. Department of Defense, Personnel, Publications, Selected Manpower Statistics, annual. See also <http://siadapp.dior.whs.mil/personnel/Pubs.htm>.

Table 501. **U.S. Military Personnel on Active Duty in Selected Foreign Countries: 1995 to 2005**

[As of September 30]

Country	1995	1999	2000	2001	2002	2003	2004	2005
In foreign countries [1] . . .	**238,064**	**252,763**	**257,817**	**254,788**	**230,484**	**252,764**	**287,802**	**290,997**
Ashore	208,836	207,131	212,858	211,947	208,479	226,570	265,594	268,214
Afloat	29,228	45,632	44,959	42,841	22,005	26,194	20,208	22,783
Argentina	26	24	26	22	28	28	29	28
Australia	314	323	175	803	171	574	196	196
Austria	35	31	18	24	20	24	21	23
Bahamas, The	36	23	24	64	22	25	41	41
Bahrain.	618	1,511	949	2,065	1,560	1,514	1,712	1,641
Belgium	1,689	1,649	1,554	1,578	1,458	1,526	1,474	1,366
Bosnia and Herzegovina	1	5,800	5,708	3,116	3,082	3,041	951	263
Brazil	50	43	38	39	27	34	37	39
Canada.	214	150	156	163	148	141	156	150
Chile	28	30	26	337	28	25	23	29
China (includes Hong Kong) . . .	30	57	74	57	61	53	63	67
Colombia.	44	41	224	63	39	54	55	52
Cuba (Guantanamo)	5,129	1,030	688	557	549	697	682	950
Cyprus	24	38	41	30	28	34	20	43
Denmark.	37	32	26	28	22	21	22	19
Diego Garcia [2]	897	670	625	590	548	528	816	683
Dominican Republic	13	11	12	14	55	14	14	11
Ecuador	86	21	20	22	35	33	32	32
Egypt	1,123	892	499	500	433	385	348	410
El Salvador	25	30	27	26	23	21	23	22
France	67	73	67	71	74	93	77	58
Germany.	73,280	65,538	69,203	70,998	68,701	74,796	76,058	66,418
Greece	489	652	678	506	593	583	473	428
Greenland	131	129	125	153	88	139	133	146
Haiti	1,616	59	21	13	15	13	26	14
Honduras	193	513	351	394	402	414	448	438
Hungary	16	87	375	29	19	15	18	16
Iceland	1,982	1,681	1,636	1,743	1,665	1,747	1,491	1,270
India.	27	25	20	18	19	26	30	31
Indonesia (includes Timor)	46	50	51	43	28	21	24	23
Israel	46	35	36	35	36	36	34	42
Italy	12,007	11,530	11,190	11,704	12,466	13,152	12,606	11,841
Japan.	39,134	40,338	40,159	40,217	41,848	40,519	36,365	35,571
Jordan	24	27	29	18	32	24	25	25
Kenya	40	95	21	62	43	33	32	32
Korea, South	36,016	35,913	36,565	37,605	37,743	41,145	40,840	30,983
Kuwait	771	4,011	4,602	4,208	567	([4])	([4])	([4])
Macedonia	591	1,100	347	351	146	41	40	37
Mexico	36	33	29	27	31	30	32	30
Netherlands	687	673	659	676	629	703	701	583
Norway.	57	95	81	83	123	86	84	77
Oman.	27	101	251	673	31	32	34	36
Pakistan	28	26	22	21	31	33	33	35
Peru.	26	50	425	43	41	33	35	37
Philippines	126	84	79	35	86	107	47	55
Portugal	1,066	1,024	1,005	1,005	992	1,094	1,006	970
Qatar	2	39	52	116	71	2,997	273	463
Russia	60	88	101	20	78	78	84	44
Saudi Arabia	1,077	5,552	7,053	4,805	776	953	235	258
Serbia (includes Kosovo)	13	6,410	5,427	5,679	2,804	319	1,814	1,801
Singapore	166	167	411	160	167	171	237	169
South Africa.	24	32	34	31	32	31	31	33
Spain	2,799	2,127	2,007	1,990	2,621	1,893	2,012	1,660
Switzerland	26	18	19	18	19	18	18	17
Thailand	99	120	526	113	125	132	122	114
Tunisia	20	13	12	15	17	15	15	14
Turkey	3,111	2,312	2,006	2,153	1,587	2,021	1,762	1,780
Ukraine	5	18	16	10	13	13	14	11
United Arab Emirates.	30	679	402	204	21	73	149	71
United Kingdom	12,131	11,311	11,207	11,318	10,258	11,616	11,469	10,752
Venezuela	35	30	28	31	27	21	28	21
DEPLOYMENTS								
Operation Enduring Freedom (OEF)[3]	(X)	(X)	(X)	(X)	(X)	(NA)	(NA)	19,500
Operation Iraqi Freedom (OIF)[4]	(X)	(X)	(X)	(X)	(X)	183,002	170,647	192,600

NA Not available. X Not applicable. [1] Includes areas not shown separately. [2] British Indian Ocean Territory. [3] Total (in/around Afghanistan as of September 30)—includes deployed Reserve/National Guard. [4] Total (in/around Iraq as of September 30)—includes deployed Reserve/National Guard.

Source: U.S. Department of Defense, *DoD Personnel and Procurement Statistics, Personnel, Military, Military Personnel Statistics*, annual; <http://siadapp.dior.whs.mil/index.html>

National Security and Veterans Affairs 333

[As of December 31. Table reflects addition of calendar year 2005 data and updates to death figures throughout]

Manner of death	1980–2005	1980	1990	1995	1998	1999	2000	2001	2002	2003	2004	2005
Deaths, total.......	40,282	2,392	1,507	1,040	827	796	758	891	999	1,228	1,897	1,951
Accident	22,318	1,556	880	538	445	436	398	437	547	440	617	629
Hostile action	2,071	–	–	–	–	–	–	3	18	344	739	738
Homicide............	2,042	174	74	67	26	37	34	49	51	36	47	45
Illness..............	7,229	419	277	174	168	150	138	185	190	207	270	280
Pending.............	166	–	–	–	10	13	–	1	6	16	25	95
Self-inflicted	5,536	231	232	250	161	145	151	140	160	167	192	147
Terrorist attack	426	1	1	7	3	–	17	55	–	–	–	–
Undetermined........	494	11	43	4	14	15	20	21	27	18	7	17
Deaths per 100,000 of personnel strength												
Accident	(X)	72.0	39.0	32.4	28.9	28.6	26.0	28.2	33.6	25.4	36.0	37.8
Hostile action	(X)	–	–	–	–	–	–	0.2	1.1	19.9	43.2	44.4
Homicide............	(X)	8.1	3.3	4.0	1.7	2.4	2.2	3.2	3.1	2.1	2.7	2.7
Illness..............	(X)	19.4	12.3	10.5	10.9	9.8	9.0	11.9	11.7	11.9	15.8	16.8
Pending.............	(X)	–	–	–	0.6	0.9	–	0.1	0.4	0.9	1.5	5.7
Self-inflicted	(X)	10.7	10.3	15.0	10.5	9.5	9.9	9.0	9.8	9.6	11.2	8.8
Terrorist attack	(X)	–	–	0.4	0.2	–	1.1	3.5	–	–	–	–
Undetermined........	(X)	0.5	1.9	0.2	0.9	1.0	1.3	1.4	1.7	1.0	0.4	1.0

– Represents zero.   X Not applicable.

Source: U.S. Department of Defense, Directorate for Information Operations and Reports, Statistical Information Analysis Division, Personnel; <http://www.dior.whs.mil/mmid/casualty/castop.htm>.

Table 503. **Military Personnel on Active Duty by Rank or Grade: 1990 to 2005**

[In thousands (2,043.7 represents 2,043,700). As of Sept. 30]

Rank/grade	1990	1995	2000	2002	2003	2004	2005
Total..................	**2,043.7**	**1,518.2**	**1,384.3**	**1,411.6**	**1,434.4**	**1,426.8**	**1,389.4**
General-Admiral................	(Z)	(Z)	(Z)	(Z)	(Z)	(Z)	(Z)
Lieutenant General-Vice Admiral.....	0.1	0.1	0.1	0.1	0.1	0.1	0.1
Major General-Rear Admiral (U)	0.4	0.3	0.3	0.3	0.3	0.3	0.3
Brigadier General-Rear Admiral (L) ...	0.5	0.4	0.4	0.4	0.4	0.4	0.4
Colonel-Captain..............	14.0	11.7	11.3	11.4	11.6	11.5	11.4
Lieutenant Colonel-Commander	32.3	28.7	27.5	28.2	28.5	28.4	28.1
Major-Lt Commander	53.2	43.9	43.2	43.6	44.1	44.0	44.4
Captain-Lieutenant	106.6	84.3	68.1	66.5	68.1	69.5	72.5
1st Lieutenant-Lieutenant (JG)	37.9	26.1	24.7	28.1	29.9	31.1	27.5
2nd Lieutenant-Ensign	31.9	25.6	26.4	29.0	29.1	26.9	25.9
Chief Warrant Officer W-5	(Z)	(Z)	0.1	0.1	0.1	0.1	0.5
Chief Warrant Officer W-4	3.0	2.2	2.0	2.0	2.1	1.9	2.2
Chief Warrant Officer W-3	5.0	4.5	3.8	4.3	4.6	4.1	4.6
Chief Warrant Officer W-2	8.4	7.4	6.7	6.2	6.2	6.0	6.2
Warrant Officer W-1	3.2	2.0	2.1	2.3	2.4	3.1	2.5
Total Officers................	**296.6**	**237.6**	**217.2**	**223.0**	**227.9**	**226.7**	**226.6**
E-9	15.3	11.1	10.2	10.6	10.8	10.7	10.5
E-8	38.0	28.8	26.0	27.0	27.7	27.1	27.1
E-7	134.1	109.3	97.7	101.9	101.4	99.6	97.8
E-6	239.1	180.5	164.9	170.0	172.4	173.1	172.4
E-5	361.5	261.4	229.5	242.5	250.7	251.1	248.5
E-4	427.8	317.2	251.0	248.1	264.5	264.1	261.7
E-3	280.1	197.1	196.3	219.6	222.1	220.1	201.7
E-2	140.3	99.7	99.0	91.8	85.1	84.3	70.8
E-1	97.6	63.4	80.0	64.7	59.2	55.8	59.5
Total Enlisted................	**1,733.8**	**1,268.5**	**1,154.6**	**1,176.2**	**1,193.9**	**1,172.0**	**1,149.9**
Cadets and Midshipmen	13.3	12.1	12.5	12.5	12.6	12.6	12.9

Z Fewer than 50.

Source: U.S. Department of Defense, DoD Personnel and Procurement Statistics, Personnel, Military, Military Personnel Statistics, annual; <http://siadapp.dior.whs.mil/index.htm>.

Table 504. Military Reserve Personnel: 1990 to 2005

[As of September 30. The Ready Reserve includes the Selected Reserve which is scheduled to augment active forces during times of war or national emergency, and the Individual Ready Reserve which, during times of war or national emergency, would be used to fill out Active, Guard, and Reserve units, and which would also be a source for casualty replacements; Ready Reservists serve in an active status (except for the Inactive National Guard—a very small pool within the Army National Guard). The Standby Reserve cannot be called to active duty, other than for training, unless authorized by Congress under "full mobilization," and a determination is made that there are not enough qualified members in the Ready Reserve in the required categories who are readily available. The Retired Reserve represents a lower potential for involuntary mobilization]

Reserve status and branch of service	1990	1995	2000	2002	2003	2004	2005
Total reserves [1]	1,688,674	1,674,164	1,276,843	1,222,337	1,188,851	1,166,937	1,136,200
Ready reserve	1,658,707	1,648,388	1,251,452	1,199,321	1,167,101	1,145,035	1,113,427
Army [2]	1,049,579	999,462	725,771	699,548	682,522	663,209	636,355
Navy	240,228	267,356	184,080	159,098	152,855	148,643	140,821
Marine Corps..........	81,355	103,668	99,855	97,944	98,868	101,443	99,820
Air Force [3]...........	270,313	263,011	229,009	229,798	219,895	219,159	223,551
Coast Guard	17,232	14,891	12,737	12,933	12,961	12,581	12,880
Standby reserve	29,967	25,776	25,391	23,016	21,750	21,902	22,773
Army	788	1,128	701	726	744	715	1,668
Navy	11,791	12,707	7,213	4,051	2,520	2,502	4,038
Marine Corps..........	1,424	216	895	605	685	992	1,129
Air Force.............	15,369	11,453	16,429	17,430	17,578	17,340	15,897
Coast Guard	595	272	153	204	223	353	41
Retired reserve	462,371	505,905	573,305	590,018	601,611	614,904	627,424
Army	223,919	259,553	296,004	304,524	308,820	315,477	321,312
Navy	111,961	97,532	109,531	112,374	113,485	115,210	117,093
Marine Corps..........	9,101	11,319	12,937	13,672	13,926	14,319	14,693
Air Force.............	117,390	137,501	154,833	159,448	165,380	169,898	174,326

[1] Less retired reserves.   [2] Includes Army National Guard and Army Reserve.   [3] Includes Air National Guard and Air Force Reserve.

Source: U.S. Department of Defense, *Official Guard and Reserve Manpower Strengths and Statistics*, quarterly. See also <http://siadapp.dior.whs.mil/index.html>.

Table 505. Ready Reserve Personnel Profile—Race and Sex: 1990 to 2005

[In thousands (1,658.7 represents 1,658,700). As of September 30]

Year	Race						Sex			
							Officer		Enlisted	
	Total [1]	White	Black	Asian	American Indian	Hispanic [2]	Male	Female	Male	Female
1990 ...	1,658.7	1,304.6	272.3	14.9	7.8	83.1	226.8	40.5	1,204.7	186.7
1993 ...	1,858.1	1,440.7	310.5	21.3	9.2	98.2	232.5	46.3	1,365.6	213.7
1994 ...	1,795.8	1,380.9	298.3	22.4	9.0	99.1	223.9	46.2	1,315.8	210.0
1995 ...	1,648.4	1,267.7	274.5	22.0	8.8	96.2	209.9	44.7	1,196.8	196.9
1996 ...	1,536.6	1,179.0	249.8	21.5	8.6	93.1	196.9	43.6	1,108.8	187.4
1997 ...	1,451.0	1,113.7	230.6	21.7	8.4	91.5	188.7	43.2	1,037.6	181.5
1998 ...	1,353.4	1,033.9	210.4	21.7	7.8	88.2	175.9	40.3	964.1	173.1
1999 ...	1,288.8	980.0	202.6	22.6	7.6	88.9	166.2	38.4	911.2	173.1
2000 ...	1,251.5	942.0	199.6	26.7	8.4	91.8	159.4	36.9	879.9	175.3
2001 ...	1,224.1	912.7	198.4	27.9	8.5	94.3	158.0	36.6	852.2	177.3
2002 ...	1,199.3	891.1	193.2	27.9	8.8	96.0	152.1	35.6	835.2	176.4
2003 ...	1,167.1	865.7	187.5	25.4	8.5	98.0	145.1	34.0	813.7	174.3
2004 ...	1,145.0	845.3	181.3	26.2	9.1	100.2	141.9	33.6	799.7	169.8
2005 ...	1,113.4	825.4	169.9	26.9	9.5	99.8	139.2	33.3	778.0	162.9

[1] Race subgroups do not sum to equal the total. "Pacific Islanders, Other, and Unknowns" are not listed.   [2] Persons of Hispanic origin may be any race.

Source: U.S. Department of Defense, *Official Guard and Reserve Manpower Strengths and Statistics*, annual. See also <http://siadapp.dior.whs.mil/index.html>.

Table 506. National Guard—Summary: 1980 to 2005

[In thousands (368 represents 368,000). As of September 30]

Item	Unit	1980	1990	1995	2000	2001	2002	2003	2004	2005
Army National Guard:										
Units	Number. . .	3,379	4,055	5,872	5,300	5,200	5,150	5,100	[1]5,100	[1]5,000
Personnel [2].	1,000	368	444	375	353	352	352	351	343	334
Females	1,000	17	31	31	38	42	44	44	43	43
Funds obligated [3].	Bil. dol. . . .	1.8	5.2	6.0	6.9	7.7	8.0	10.0	[4]8.3	10.6
Value of equipment.	Bil. dol. . . .	7.6	29.0	33.0	35.0	35.0	35.0	36.0	[5]26.0	[5]25.0
Air National Guard:										
Units	Number. . .	1,054	1,339	1,604	1,550	1,500	1,500	1,500	[1]1,500	[1]1,400
Personnel [2].	1,000	96	118	110	106	109	112	108	108	106
Funds obligated [3].	Bil. dol. . . .	1.7	3.2	4.2	5.6	5.8	6.8	6.4	7.6	7.9

NA Not available.   [1] Includes units on active duty.   [2] Officers and enlisted personnel.   [3] Federal funds; includes personnel, operations, maintenance, and military construction.   [4] Dollar amounts allocated to the National Guard in the states and territories has declined due to large numbers of Army National Guard personnel on active federal service for the war in Iraq and Afghanistan.   [5] Decreased due to equipment left overseas by mobilized units.

Source: National Guard Bureau, *Annual Review of the Chief, National Guard Bureau;* and unpublished data. See also <http://www.ang.af.mil> and <http://www.arng.army.mil>.

Table 507. Veterans by Sex, Period of Service, and State: 2005

[In thousands (24,128 represents 24,128,000). **As of September 30.** VetPop 2004 Version 1.0 is the Department of Veterans Affairs (VA) latest official estimate and projection of the veteran population. It is based on published Census 2000 data supplemented by special extracts prepared for VA Office of the Actuary by the Census Bureau. This estimate and projection also uses administrative data and projections of service member separations from active duty provided by the Department of Defense (the Defense Manpower Data Center and the Office of the Actuary), as well as VA administrative data on veterans benefits]

State	Total veterans [1,2]			Gulf War [3]	Vietnam era	Korean conflict	World War II	Peace-time
	Total	Male	Female					
United States [4]	24,128	22,434	1,695	4,336	7,975	3,212	3,492	6,162
Alabama	422	391	31	86	142	59	53	107
Alaska	67	60	7	19	26	5	4	17
Arizona	553	510	43	99	177	84	89	135
Arkansas	266	248	18	49	89	36	38	68
California	2,257	2,092	165	382	761	313	344	568
Colorado	424	388	36	94	153	48	45	107
Connecticut	260	246	15	30	84	38	47	68
Delaware	80	74	6	14	26	11	11	21
District of Columbia	36	33	3	6	11	5	6	9
Florida	1,768	1,637	131	296	530	283	338	433
Georgia	759	691	68	190	256	80	70	201
Hawaii	105	96	8	20	38	14	14	25
Idaho	133	123	9	30	43	16	17	32
Illinois	874	821	53	143	278	116	135	223
Indiana	543	510	32	90	176	67	72	150
Iowa	260	247	14	39	87	38	40	63
Kansas	242	226	16	45	83	31	35	58
Kentucky	356	334	22	66	120	45	46	91
Louisiana	362	335	27	77	119	45	49	88
Maine	141	132	9	21	49	20	20	38
Maryland	479	435	44	101	156	56	59	130
Massachusetts	476	448	28	58	148	72	88	124
Michigan	820	773	48	124	271	104	118	220
Minnesota	418	396	23	59	145	55	57	112
Mississippi	238	220	18	53	76	33	31	60
Missouri	546	512	35	92	180	74	77	143
Montana	101	94	7	17	36	13	14	25
Nebraska	157	146	11	30	53	22	22	36
Nevada	244	225	19	45	87	34	30	64
New Hampshire	129	121	8	20	45	17	17	36
New Jersey	564	533	30	66	172	86	106	148
New Mexico	178	163	15	34	64	24	23	43
New York	1,133	1,066	67	146	343	166	200	302
North Carolina	762	702	60	164	252	94	92	197
North Dakota	54	51	4	10	19	7	7	13
Ohio	1,032	970	62	166	331	131	153	277
Oklahoma	351	327	24	69	125	46	47	82
Oregon	362	337	25	57	129	45	52	93
Pennsylvania	1,117	1,054	63	144	347	162	204	291
Rhode Island	89	83	5	12	28	13	16	23
South Carolina	412	380	32	91	142	52	48	105
South Dakota	72	67	5	14	24	11	10	17
Tennessee	537	500	37	103	186	66	63	142
Texas	1,667	1,535	133	377	577	199	203	404
Utah	149	140	9	31	49	20	22	35
Vermont	57	53	4	8	19	8	8	16
Virginia	744	670	74	206	259	83	77	178
Washington	625	575	50	130	228	72	74	158
West Virginia	185	175	10	29	64	26	27	46
Wisconsin	466	439	27	70	151	62	67	127
Wyoming	54	51	4	12	20	6	6	12

[1] Veterans serving in more than one period of service are counted only once in the total. [2] Current civilians discharged from active duty, other than for training only without service-connected disability. [3] Service from August 2, 1990, to the present. [4] Totals may not add due to rounding of numbers.

Source: U.S. Department of Veterans Affairs, Office of Policy, Planning & Preparedness; VetPop 2004, Version 1.0, VA Office of the Actuary <http://www1.va.gov/vetdata>.

Table 508. Veterans Living by Age and Period of Service: 2005

[In thousands (24,387 represents 24,387,000). **As of September 30.** Includes those living outside U.S. See headnote, Table 507]

Age	Total veterans	Wartime veterans					Peacetime veterans
		Total [1]	Gulf War [2]	Vietnam era	Korean conflict	World War II	
Total	24,387	18,156	4,378	8,055	3,257	3,526	6,231
Under 35 years old	1,966	1,940	1,940	–	–	–	27
35–39 years old	1,317	886	886	–	–	–	431
40–44 years old	1,679	573	573	–	–	–	1,106
45–49 years old	1,886	595	422	191	–	–	1,291
50–54 years old	2,034	1,609	294	1,448	–	–	425
55–59 years old	3,484	3,360	178	3,309	–	–	124
60–64 years old	2,673	2,102	59	2,091	–	–	571
65 years old and over	9,348	7,091	27	1,015	3,257	3,526	2,257
Female, total	1,712	1,153	688	260	77	164	559

– Represents or rounds to zero. [1] Veterans who served in more than one wartime period are counted only once in the total. [2] Service from August 2, 1990 to the present.

Source: U.S. Department of Veterans Affairs, Office of Policy, Planning and Preparedness; VetPop 2004, Ver 1.0, VA Office of the Actuary <http://www1.va.gov/vetdata>.

Table 509. Veterans by Sex, Race, and Hispanic or Latino Origin: 2004

[In thousands (23,756.3 represents 23,756,300). Data are based on the American Community Survey (ACS). The survey universe is limited to the household population and excludes the population living in institutions, college dormitories, and other group quarters. Based on a sample and subject to sampling variability; see text of this section and Appendix III]

Characteristics	Total number	18 to 64 years	65 years and over
Total	**23,756.3**	**14,694.0**	**9,062.2**
Sex:			
Male	22,147.0	13,419.2	8,727.8
Female	1,609.3	1,274.9	334.4
White alone	20,299.8	11,995.3	8,304.5
Male	19,087.7	11,094.7	7,993.0
Female	1,212.1	900.7	311.5
Black or African American alone	2,381.1	1,870.5	510.6
Male	2,096.5	1,600.2	496.3
Female	284.6	270.3	14.3
American Indian/Alaska Native alone	164.2	129.5	34.7
Male	145.2	111.3	33.8
Female	19.0	18.2	0.8
Asian alone	282.2	195.965	86.2
Male	253.8	169.2	84.6
Female	28.4	26.8	1.6
Native Hawaiian and Other Pacific Islander alone	30.7	24.6	6.1
Male	26.8	22.0	4.9
Female	3.8	2.6	1.2
Some other race alone	329.1	273.1	55.9
Male	296.1	242.6	53.6
Female	32.9	30.6	2.4
Hispanic or Latino origin [1]	1,086.9	834.6	252.4
Male	988.2	744.7	243.5
Female	98.7	89.9	8.8

[1] Persons of Hispanic or Latino origin may be any race.
Source: U.S. Census Bureau, 2000 Census of Population and Housing, Summary File 3, using American FactFinder, tables B21001, B21001A, B21001B, B21001C, B21001D, B21001E, B21001F, and B21001I; <http://www.census.gov/prod/2003pubs /c2kbr-22.pdf> (accessed 15 May 2006).

Table 510. Veterans Benefits—Expenditures by Program and Compensation for Service-Connected Disabilities: 1980 to 2005

[In millions of dollars (23,187 represents $23,187,000,000). For years ending September 30]

Program	1980	1990	1995	2000	2001	2002	2003	2004	2005
Total expenditures	23,187	28,998	37,775	47,086	45,037	50,882	56,892	59,555	69,564
Medical programs	6,042	11,582	16,255	19,637	21,330	23,049	25,188	28,158	29,191
Construction	300	661	641	466	421	449	411	318	480
General operating expenses	605	811	954	1,016	1,222	1,318	1,399	1,252	1,285
Compensation and pension	11,044	14,674	17,765	22,012	23,276	25,573	27,937	29,937	32,131
Vocational rehabilitation and education	2,350	452	1,317	1,610	1,786	2,170	2,565	2,827	3,033
All other [1]	2,846	818	844	2,345	-2,999	-1,676	-666	-2,937	3,445
Compensation for service-connected disabilities [2]	6,104	9,284	11,644	15,511	16,593	18,584	20,855	22,387	24,515

[1] Includes insurance, indemnities and miscellaneous funds and expenditures. (Excludes expenditures from personal funds of patients.)   [2] Represents veterans receiving compensation for service-connected disabilities.
Source: U.S. Department of Veterans Affairs, *Expenditures and Workload*, annual and unpublished data. See also <http://www1.va.gov/vetdata>.

Table 511. Veterans Compensation and Pension Benefits—Number on Rolls by Period of Service and Status: 1980 to 2005

[In thousands (4,646 represents 4,646,000), except as indicated. As of September 30. Living refers to veterans receiving compensation for disability incurred or aggravated while on active duty and low-income wartime veterans receiving pension who have permanent and total mostly non-service connected disabilities or are age 65 or older. Deceased refers to deceased veterans whose dependents were receiving pensions and compensation benefits]

Period of service and veteran status	1980	1990	1995	2000	2002	2003	2004	2005
Total	4,646	3,584	3,330	3,236	3,285	3,369	3,432	3,503
Living veterans	3,195	2,746	2,669	2,672	2,745	2,832	2,899	2,973
Service-connected	2,273	2,184	2,236	2,308	2,398	2,485	2,556	2,637
Nonservice-connected	922	562	433	364	347	347	343	336
Deceased veterans	1,451	838	662	564	540	538	533	530
Service-connected	358	320	307	307	310	314	318	323
Nonservice-connected	1,093	518	355	257	230	224	215	207
Prior to World War I	14	4	2	1	1	1	(Z)	(Z)
Living	(Z)	(Z)	(Z)	(Z)	(Z)	(Z)	(Z)	(Z)
World War I	692	198	89	34	23	19	16	13
Living	198	18	3	(Z)	(Z)	(Z)	(Z)	(Z)
World War II	2,520	1,723	1,307	968	856	813	766	718
Living	1,849	1,294	961	676	583	546	506	466
Korean conflict [1]	446	390	368	323	308	306	302	295
Living	317	305	290	255	243	241	237	231
Vietnam era [2]	662	774	868	969	1,052	1,120	1,172	1,218
Living	569	685	766	848	922	983	1,028	1,068
Gulf War [3]	(X)	(X)	138	334	431	490	552	630
Living	(X)	(X)	134	326	421	479	540	617
Peacetime	312	495	559	607	613	620	624	627
Living	262	444	514	567	575	583	587	591

X Not applicable.   Z Fewer than 500.   [1] Service during period June 27, 1950, to January 31, 1955.   [2] Service from August 5, 1964, to May 7, 1975.   [3] Service from August 2, 1990, to the present.
Source: U.S. Department of Veterans Affairs, 1980 to 1995, *Annual Report of the Secretary of Veterans Affairs*; beginning 2000, *Annual Accountability Report* and unpublished data. See also <http://www1.va.gov/vetdata>.

National Security and Veterans Affairs   337

Table 512. Homeland Security Funding by Agency: 2004 to 2006

[In millions of dollars (41,307.1 represents $41,307,100,000). For year ending September 30. A total of 32 agencies comprise federal homeland security funding for 2006. Department of Homeland Security (DHS) is the designated department to coordinate and centralize the leadership of many homeland security activities under a single department. In addition to DHS, the Departments of Defense (DoD), Energy (DoE), Health and Human Services (HHS), and Justice (DoJ), account for most of the total government-wide homeland security funding]

Agency	2004	2005 [1]	2006 [1]
Total budget authority, excluding BioShield [2, 3, 4]	**41,307.1**	**52,657.2**	**54,852.9**
Department of Agriculture	326.6	595.9	563.0
Department of Commerce	131.2	166.7	181.1
Department of Defense [5]	7,024.0	16,107.7	16,440.4
Department of Education	8.0	23.9	27.5
Department of Energy	1,362.5	1,562.0	1,705.2
Department of Health and Human Services	4,109.0	4,229.4	4,299.1
Department of Homeland Security	23,492.3	23,979.9	25,499.0
Department of Housing and Urban Development	1.8	2.0	1.9
Department of the Interior	67.2	65.0	55.6
Department of Justice	2,165.8	2,690.8	2,975.4
Department of Labor	52.4	56.1	48.3
Department of State	701.3	824.1	1,107.9
Department of Transportation	283.5	219.3	181.0
Department of the Treasury	90.4	101.1	115.8
Department of Veterans Affairs	271.3	249.4	308.8
Corps of Engineers	103.4	89.0	72.0
Environmental Protection Agency	123.3	106.3	129.3
Executive Office of the President	35.0	29.5	20.8
General Services Administration	78.9	65.2	98.6
National Aeronautics and Space Administration	191.0	220.5	212.6
National Science Foundation	327.9	342.2	344.2
Office of Personnel Management	3.0	3.0	2.7
Social Security Administration	143.4	154.7	176.8
District of Columbia	19.0	15.0	13.5
Federal Communications Commission	1.0	1.8	2.3
Intelligence Community Management Account	1.0	72.4	56.0
National Archives and Records Administration	12.0	17.1	18.2
Nuclear Regulatory Commission	66.8	59.2	79.3
Postal Service	(X)	503.0	(X)
Securities and Exchange Commission	5.0	5.0	5.0
Smithsonian Institution	78.3	75.0	83.7
United States Holocaust Memorial Museum	8.0	8.0	7.8
Corporation for National and Community Service	22.8	17.0	20.4

X Not applicable. [1] FY 05 and 06 reflect the adjustments made for the Coast Guard (DHS) and re-estimates for DoD. See "Source" for further details. [2] Enacted Budget. [3] The federal spending estimates are for the Executive Branch's homeland security efforts. These estimates do not include the efforts of the Legislative or Judicial Branches. [4] The Department of Homeland Security Appropriations Act, 2004, provided $5.6 billion for Project BioShield, to remain available through 2008. Including this uneven funding stream can distort year-over-year comparisons. [5] In all tables, classified funds controlled by the Director of National Intelligence are combined with the Department of Defense and titled "Department of Defense."

Source: U.S. Office of Management and Budget, Budget of the United States Government Fiscal Year 2007, The Budget Documents, *Analytical Perspectives, Budget of the United States Government Fiscal Year 2007, Crosscutting Programs, Homeland Security Funding Analysis,* <http://www.whitehouse.gov/omb/budget/fy2007/>.

Table 513. Homeland Security Funding by National Strategy Mission Area: 2004 to 2006

[In millions of dollars. ($41,307.1 represents 41,307,100,000). For Homeland Security funding analysis by OMB, agencies categorize their funding data based on the critical mission areas defined in the *National Strategy*]

Agency	2004	2005 [1]	2006
Total budget authority excluding Bioshield [2, 3]	**41,307.1**	**52,657.2**	**54,852.9**
Intelligence and warning	268.7	349.8	428.2
Border and transportation security	15,322.5	16,652.3	18,348.4
Domestic counterterrorism	2,994.1	3,974.5	4,548.4
Protecting critical infrastructure and key assets	12,571.0	17,835.9	17,851.1
Defending against catastrophic threats	2,827.2	8,146.4	8,639.4
Emergency preparedness and response	7,132.5	5,645.5	4,924.4
Other	191.1	43.8	112.

[1] FY 05 and 06 reflect the adjustments made for the Coast Guard and re-estimates for DoD. See "Source" for further details. [2] Enacted Budget. [3] See footnote 4 in Table 512.

Source: U.S. Office of Management and Budget, Budget of the United States Government Fiscal Year 2007, The Budget Documents, *Analytical Perspectives, Budget of the United States Government Fiscal Year 2007, Crosscutting Programs, Homeland Security Funding Analysis,* <http://www.whitehouse.gov/omb/budget/fy2007/>.

338   National Security and Veterans Affairs

U.S. Census Bureau. Statistical Abstract of the United States: 20

Table 514. Department of Homeland Security Total Budget Authority and Personnel by Organization: 2005 and 2006

[Expenditures in thousands of dollars (38,369,517 represents $38,369,517,000). For the fiscal year ending September 30. Not all activities carried out by DHS constitute homeland security funding (e.g., Coast Guard search and rescue activities]

Organization	Expenditures		Full-time employees	
	2005 [1]	2006 [1]	2005 [1]	2006 [1]
Adjusted Total Budget Authority [2, 3]	38,369,517	40,345,347	179,646	182,131
U.S.—Visitor Immigrant Status Indicator Technology (US—VISIT) .	340,000	336,600	102	102
U.S. Customs & Border Protection.	6,344,398	7,109,875	40,636	41,986
U.S. Immigration & Customs Enforcement	3,127,078	3,866,443	14,600	15,917
Transportation Security Administration	6,068,275	6,167,014	52,615	50,363
Preparedness Directorate [4]	(X)	678,395	(X)	966
Preparedness: Office of Grants and Training	(X)	3,352,437	(X)	233
Analysis and Operations [5]	(X)	252,940	(X)	406
Federal Law Enforcement Training Center	226,807	279,534	982	1,001
U.S. Coast Guard.	7,558,560	8,193,797	46,809	47,121
U.S. Secret Service	1,385,758	1,399,889	6,516	6,564
Federal Emergency Management Agency (FEMA)	5,038,256	4,834,744	4,735	5,708
U.S. Citizenship & Immigration Services	1,775,000	1,887,850	10,052	10,207
Science & Technology Directorate (S&T)	1,115,450	1,487,075	320	387
Office of Screening Coordination and Operation.	(X)	3,960	(X)	17
Departmental Management and Operations	527,257	559,230	687	846
Counter-Terrorism Fund.	8,000	1,980	(X)	(X)
Inspector General.	82,317	82,187	502	540
Legacy DHS Organizations [6]				
BTS Under Secretary	9,617	(X)	67	(X)
IAIP Directorate	887,108	(X)	803	(X)
SLGCP (Formerly ODP)	3,984,846	(X)	220	(X)

X Not applicable. [1] Revised enacted total. [2] Reflects adjustment for recission of prior year carryover funds. [3] Excludes BioShield funding, see footnote 4, table 512. [4] The Preparedness Directorate did not exist for FY 2005. Under the Second Stage Review (2SR) changes, elements of IAIP, SLGCP, and EP&R were combined to the Preparedness Directorate. [5] The Analysis and Operations did not exist for FY 2005. Under the Second Stage Review (2SR) changes, the appropriation provides resources for the support of the Office of Intelligence and Analysis and the Directorate of Operations. [6] For FY 2006, BTS Under Secretary, IAIP Directorate and SLGCP, have become legacy DHS components.

Source: U.S. Department of Homeland Security, "Budget-in-Brief, Fiscal Year 2007." <http://www.dhs.gov/interweb/assetlibrary/Budget_BIB-FY2007.pdf\> (accessed 7 February 2006)

Table 515. Homeland Security Grants by State/Territories: 2004 and 2005

[In thousands of dollars (3,115,550 represents 3,115,550,000). For fiscal years ending September 30. Grants consist of the following programs: Citizen Corps Program (CCP), Law Enforcement Terrorism Prevention Program (LETPP), Emergency Management Performance Grant (EMPG), State Homeland Security Program (SHSP), Metropolitan Medical Response System (MMRS), and Urban Areas Security Initiative (UASI). Urban Areas Security Initiative program includes the Urban Areas Program, Transit Security Program, Port Security Grant Program and the Intercity Bus Program. 2005 grants include all the programs as in 2004 except for Port Security Grant Program and the Intercity Bus Program. These programs have not yet been awarded as of May 2005]

State/Territory	2004	2005	State/Territory	2004	2005	State/Territory	2004	2005
Total . .	3,115,550	2,518,763	KY	45,537	31,419	PA	109,866	87,671
			LA	76,005	42,670	RI.	23,485	16,074
U.S.	3,050,076	2,475,564	ME	23,776	16,609	SC	40,643	26,284
			MD	64,014	42,250	SD	19,996	14,809
AL	38,723	28,153	MA	69,288	62,436	TN	54,157	32,605
AK	21,218	14,879	MI	76,981	64,075	TX	195,671	138,570
AZ	53,371	41,705	MN	60,236	35,311	UT	27,033	20,308
AR	28,815	21,561	MS	31,795	22,081	VT	19,594	14,326
CA	349,894	282,622	MO	66,618	46,952	VA	61,902	38,185
CO	45,583	36,799	MT	20,689	15,318	WA	73,593	45,330
CT	46,523	24,080	NE	24,376	23,656	WV	25,270	18,289
DE	20,206	14,984	NV	37,196	28,386	WI	51,343	37,251
DC	49,231	96,144	NH	24,110	16,776	WY	18,809	13,934
FL	142,667	101,285	NJ	95,795	60,811			
GA	70,815	54,918	NM	24,946	18,499	PR [1]	37,864	25,169
HI.	26,865	23,130	NY	178,492	298,351	VI	6,918	4,612
ID.	22,621	16,805	NC	65,392	46,609	AS	5,776	4,279
IL	114,925	102,593	ND	19,421	14,376	GU	7,016	4,706
IN.	55,534	38,996	OH	103,582	77,823	NM	7,960	4,333
IA.	29,918	22,291	OK	32,824	29,974	RM	–	50
KS	29,064	21,784	OR	41,665	34,820	FM	–	50

– Represents zero. [1] PR—Puerto Rico, VI—Virgin Islands, AS—America Samoa, GU—Guam, NM—Northern Mariana Islands, MH—Marshall Islands, and FM—Micronesia.
Source: U.S. Department of Homeland Security, State and Local Government Coordination and Preparedness, unpublished data. See also <http://www.ojp.gov/odp>.

Table 516. Coast Guard Migrant Interdictions by Nationality of Alien: 2000 to 2005

[For the year ending September 30]

Year	Total	Haiti	Dominican Republic	China	Cuba	Mexico	Ecuador	Other
2000	4,210	1,113	499	261	1,000	49	1,244	44
2001	3,948	1,391	659	53	777	17	1,020	31
2002	4,104	1,486	177	80	666	32	1,608	55
2003	6,068	2,013	1,748	15	1,555	–	703	34
2004	10,899	3,229	5,014	68	1,225	86	1,189	88
2005	9,455	1,850	3,612	32	2,712	55	1,149	45

– Represents zero.
Source: U.S. Department of Homeland Security, United States Coast Guard, "Fact File, Migrants Statistics, Statistics." <http://www.uscg.mil/hq/g-cp/comrel/factfile/index.htm> (accessed 22 March 2006).

National Security and Veterans Affairs **339**

Table 517. Customs and Border Protection (CBP)—Processed and Cleared Passengers, Planes, Vehicles, and Containers: 2000 to 2005

[In thousands (80,519.3 represents 80,519,300). For year ending September 30]

Characteristic	2000	2001	2002	2003	2004	2005
Air						
Passenger	80,519.3	79,675.8	71,607.9	72,959.3	80,866.4	86,123.4
Commercial plane [1]	829.3	839.2	768.9	789.8	823.8	866.3
Private plane.	145.6	125.7	729.2	132.1	140.0	135.4
Land						
Passenger [2, 3]	397,312.2	381,477.3	333,651.7	329,998.2	326,692.7	317,765.2
Auto [2]	127,094.7	129,603.2	118,306.8	120,376.5	121,418.9	121,654.0
Rail containers.	2,156.5	2,257.1	2,430.1	2,471.9	2,587.6	2,655.4
Truck containers [4]	10,396.6	11,001.5	11,129.4	11,163.1	11,252.2	11,308.5
Sea						
Passenger [5]	10,990.1	11,290.9	12,224.4	15,127.5	22,234.2	26,228.2
Vessel [6]	211.2	215.4	211.6	203.6	142.2	113.2
Vessel containers [7].	5,813.2	5,944.0	7,247.6	9,092.3	9,796.3	11,340.8

[1] A commercial aircraft is any aircraft transporting passengers and/or cargo for some payment or other consideration, including money or services rendered. [2] See Table 1251 for more details. [3] Includes pedestrians. [4] Trucks-containers—number of trucks entering the U.S. [5] Does not include passengers on ferries. [6] Number of vessels. Includes every description of water craft or other contrivance used or capable of being used as a means of transportation on water; does not include aircraft. [7] Number of vessel containers.

Source: U.S. Department of Homeland Security, Customs and Border Protection, *About CBP, Statistics and Accomplishments, National Workload Statistics, 2000–2005.* See also <http://www.cbp.gov/xp/cgov/toolbox/about/accomplish/> (Data as of 25 May 2006).

Table 518. Deportable Aliens Located by Border Patrol Sector: 2000 to 2004

[As of the end of September. Excludes Immigration and Customs Enforcement (ICE) Investigations' data. Data for this table comes from the Performance Analysis System (PAS). This system aggregated data updated once a month by DHS offices]

Border Patrol Sector	2000	2001	2002	2003	2004
Total	**1,676,438**	**1,266,214**	**955,310**	**931,557**	**1,160,395**
All southwest sectors	**1,643,679**	**1,235,718**	**929,809**	**905,065**	**1,139,282**
San Diego, CA	151,681	110,075	100,681	111,515	138,608
El Centro, CA.	238,126	172,852	108,273	92,099	74,467
Yuma, AZ	108,747	78,385	42,654	56,638	98,060
Tucson, AZ	616,346	449,675	333,648	347,263	491,771
El Paso, TX	115,696	112,857	94,154	88,816	104,399
Marfa, TX	13,689	12,087	11,392	10,319	10,530
Del Rio, TX	157,178	104,875	66,985	50,145	53,794
Laredo, TX	108,973	87,068	82,095	70,521	74,706
McAllen, TX.	133,243	107,844	89,927	77,749	92,947
All other sectors.	**32,759**	**30,496**	**25,501**	**26,492**	**21,113**
Blaine, WA	2,581	2,089	1,732	1,380	1,354
Buffalo, NY	1,570	1,434	1,102	564	671
Detroit, MI	2,057	2,106	1,511	2,345	1,912
Grand Forks, ND	562	921	1,369	1,223	1,225
Havre, MT	1,568	1,305	1,463	1,406	986
Houlton, ME.	489	685	432	292	263
Livermore, CA [1]	6,205	5,211	4,371	3,565	1,850
Miami, FL	6,237	5,962	5,143	5,931	4,602
New Orleans, LA	6,478	5,033	4,665	5,151	2,889
Ramey, PR	1,731	1,952	835	1,688	1,813
Spokane, WA.	1,324	1,335	1,142	992	847
Swanton, VT	1,957	2,463	1,736	1,955	2,701

[1] Livermore sector closed July 30, 2004.

Source: U.S. Department of Homeland Security, Office of Immigration Statistics, *Yearbook of Immigration Statistics, 2004.* See also <http://uscis.gov/graphics/shared/aboutus/statistics/ybpage.htm>. (accessed 8 May 2006).

Table 519. Border Patrol Enforcement Activities: 2000 to 2004

[See headnote Table 518]

Activities	2000	2001	2002	2003	2004
Persons processed by the Border Patrol [1]	**1,689,195**	**1,277,577**	**967,044**	**946,684**	**1,179,296**
Deportable aliens located by the Border Patrol . . .	**1,676,438**	**1,266,214**	**955,310**	**931,557**	**1,160,395**
Mexican aliens	1,636,883	1,224,046	917,994	882,012	1,085,006
Working in agriculture	1,330	1,248	1,821	1,908	1,647
Working in trades, crafts, industry, and service . . .	2,167	2,678	2,897	3,856	3,634
Seeking employment	1,525,422	1,107,550	822,161	810,671	997,986
Canadian aliens	2,211	2,539	1,836	1,611	1,497
All others.	37,344	39,629	35,480	47,934	73,892
Smugglers of aliens located	14,406	8,720	8,701	11,128	16,074
Aliens located who were smuggled					
into the United States	236,782	112,927	68,192	110,575	193,122
Seizures (conveyances).	17,269	5,892	7,250	9,355	18,024
Value of seizures (mil. dol.)	**1,945**	**1,581**	**1,564**	**1,680**	**1,696**
Narcotics	1,848	1,519	1,499	1,608	1,620
Other	97	62	65	72	75

[1] Includes deportable aliens located and nondeportable (e.g., U.S. citizens).

Source: U.S. Department of Homeland Security, Office of Immigration Statistics, *Yearbook of Immigration Statistics, 2004.* See also <http://uscis.gov/graphics/shared/aboutus/statistics/ybpage.htm>. (accessed 8 May 2006).

Table 520. Immigration and Customs Enforcement (ICE) Investigations Activities: 2004

[Data refer to criminal cases only; administrative cases are not included due to changes in reporting. Data in this table are not comparable with data reported in this table for previous years]

Activities	Cases initiated	Cases closed	Criminal arrests	Criminal indictments	Criminal convictions	Number seizures	Dollar value seizures
Total, all immigration-related categories	**58,727**	**46,656**	**9,455**	**5,363**	**4,007**	**1,782**	**10,105,566**
Human trafficking investigations [1]	3,017	2,860	250	89	70	102	312,259
Criminal alien investigations [2]	10,908	6,262	4,851	2,902	2,308	188	2,277,995
Employers of unauthorized alien investigations [3]	3,258	3,064	159	66	46	54	486,313
Identity and benefit fraud (IBF) investigations [4]	5,351	3,872	1,310	709	533	660	1,497,285
Alien smuggling organizations investigations [5]	3,984	3,141	1,121	689	408	498	4,123,440
Alien smuggling individuals/groups investigations [5]	3,958	3,281	1,295	759	491	234	1,053,737
Alien absconder investigations	2,911	2,866	19	(D)	(D)	(D)	103
Compliance enforcement investigations	9,622	6,458	40	(D)	(D)	(D)	–
Alien Present Without Authorization (PWA) (EWI) status violation investigations [6]	3,521	3,332	260	93	102	11	139,154
Non-Identification and Authentication (I&A) Act related activities requiring investigation	2,811	2,809	(NA)	(NA)	(NA)	(NA)	(NA)
Alien investigative support functions—limited inquiry investigations	2,835	2,815	10	4	3	(D)	–
Alien asset forfeiture investigations	2,840	2,826	10	9	8	6	98,200
Joint Terrorism Task Force (JTTF) [7]	3,711	3,070	130	40	36	25	117,079

– Represents zero. NA Not available. D Figure withheld to avoid disclosure pertaining to a specific organization or individual. [1] Human trafficking cases include investigations into alleged violations of severe forms of human trafficking which is defined by the Trafficking Victims Protection Act of 2000. [2] Criminal alien cases include large-scale organizations engaged in ongoing criminal activity and individual aliens convicted of crimes such as terrorism or drug trafficking. [3] Employer investigations target employers of unauthorized aliens and include criminal investigations, administrative investigations, auxiliary investigations, ICE Headquarters Investigation National Interest Investigations, and Department of Labor ESA-91. Starting in FY 2003, also includes statistics pertaining to Work Site Enforcement National Interest Investigations. [4] Fraud investigations seek to penetrate fraud schemes of all sizes and degrees of complexity which are used to violate immigration and related laws or to shield the true status of illegal aliens in order to obtain entitlement benefits. The fraud schemes may be related to marriage fraud, immigration benefit fraud, employer sanctions document fraud, other document fraud, and entitlement fraud. [5] Smuggling cases involve those which target persons or entities who bring, transport, harbor or smuggle illegal aliens into or within the United States. [6] Includes Entry Without Inspection (EWI). [7] FBI Joint Terrorism Task Forces (JTTF) include ICE Special Agents who perform counter-terrorism investigations and provide actionable proactive counter-terrorism lead information, in efforts to prevent and disrupt alien terrorist cells domestically and abroad.

Source: U.S. Department of Homeland Security, Office of Immigration Statistics, *2004 Yearbook of Immigration Statistics*. See also <http://uscis.gov/graphics/shared/statistics/yearbook/index.htm> (accessed 8 May 2005).

Table 521. Aliens Expelled and Aliens Removed by Administrative Reason for Removal: 2000 to 2004

[**As of the end of September.** The administrative reason for formal removal is the legal basis for removal. Some aliens who are criminals may be removed under a different administrative reason (or charge) for the convenience of the government]

Violations	2000	2001	2002	2003	2004
Total Aliens Expelled:	**1,861,933**	**1,432,061**	**1,084,661**	**1,076,483**	**1,238,319**
Voluntary departures [1]	1,675,711	1,254,035	934,119	887,115	1,035,477
Formal removals [2]	186,222	178,026	150,542	189,368	202,842
Administrative reason for forced removal:					
Attempted entry without proper documents or through fraud or misrepresentation	89,912	76,254	41,347	52,670	50,420
Criminal	41,127	40,170	37,785	40,266	42,510
Failed to maintain status	740	720	1,248	1,309	1,104
Previously removed, ineligible for reentry [3]	11,659	10,677	12,838	17,950	19,773
Present without authorization	40,396	48,053	55,603	75,052	85,659
Security	13	12	11	14	11
Smuggling or aiding illegal entry	492	509	579	619	722
Other	1,877	1,625	1,106	1,482	2,636
Unknown	6	6	25	6	7

[1] Voluntary departures verified includes aliens under docket control required to depart and voluntary departures not under docket control; first recorded in 1927. Beginning FY 2004, voluntary departures verified include both Deportable Alien Control System (DACS) cases under docket control and Performance Analysis System (PAS) Border Patrol voluntary departures verified-cases not under docket or aliens processed for removal under safeguard. The latter is used as a measure of border patrol voluntary departures verified-cases not under docket. In FY 2004, complete Detention and Removal Office district level figures for voluntary departures-cases not under docket are unavailable in PAS and as a result are excluded for that year. Prior to FY 2004, the reporting of voluntary departures verified included all locations, Border Patrol Sectors and districts. [2] Formal removals include deportations, exclusions, and removals. [3] Includes those aliens charged under the statutes previous to April 1, 1997, as "entered without inspection" (EWI).

Source: U.S. Department of Homeland Security, Office of Immigration Statistics, *2004 Yearbook of Immigration Statistics*. See also <http://uscis.gov/graphics/shared/statistics/yearbook/index.htm>. (accessed 8 May 2005).

Table 522. Department Participation in the Control of Marijuana, Narcotics, and Dangerous Drug Traffic: 2000 to 2004

[As of the end of September. Department participation includes Border Patrol, Inspections and Investigations through 2003. For fiscal year 2004, includes narcotic seizure data reported by Customs and Border Protection inspectors and Border Patrol only. Excludes Immigration and Customs Enforcement (ICE) investigations data]

Year and seizure	Total	Type of contraband				
		Marijuana (lbs.)	Heroin (ozs.)	Cocaine (ozs.)	Dangerous drug pills (units)	Other
2000						
Number of seizures...............	12,143	9,914	225	1,020	470	514
Amount seized...................	(X)	1,597,395	5,487	567,341	1,426,547	(X)
Estimated value of seizures (mil. dol.)	2,314	1,289	32	946	5	41
2002						
Number of seizures...............	10,231	8,289	160	991	250	541
Amount seized...................	(X)	1,440,488	6,887	489,491	619,004	(X)
Estimated value of seizures (mil. dol.)	1,980	1,177	32	736	2	32
2003						
Number of seizures...............	10,284	8,528	119	742	362	533
Amount seized...................	(X)	1,562,368	6,624	336,493	395,714	(X)
Estimated value of seizures (mil. dol.)	2,107	1,434	42	598	9	24
2004						
Number of seizures...............	10,897	9,289	71	727	331	479
Amount seized...................	(X)	1,552,906	3,069	350,584	345,776	(X)
Estimated value of seizures (mil. dol.)	2,008	1,278	14	670	3	42

X Not applicable.

Source: U.S. Department of Homeland Security, Office of Immigration Statistics, *2004 Yearbook of Immigration Statistics*. Data as of 3 May 2006. See also <http://uscis.gov/graphics/shared/aboutus/statistics/ybpage.htm>.

Table 523. Prohibited Items Intercepted at U.S. Airport Screening Checkpoints: 2002 to 2005

[Passengers boarding aircraft in thousands (612,876 represents 612,876,000). For the calendar year. Transportation Security Administration (TSA) assumed responsibility for airport security on February 17, 2002, and by November 19, 2002, TSA assumed control over all passenger screenings from private contractors. TSA data are incomplete for 2002]

Year	2002	2003	2004	2005
Passengers boarding aircraft total (1,000) [1].....	**612,876**	**646,275**	**702,921**	**738,568**
Domestic..............................	560,107	592,412	640,698	670,360
International...........................	52,769	53,863	62,222	68,208
Total prohibited items...................	**4,185,916**	**6,167,497**	**7,103,560**	**15,886,014**
Knife [2]..............................	1,147,843	1,969,003	2,055,306	1,822,846
Other cutting items [3]...................	2,063,729	3,029,318	3,409,724	3,276,936
Club [4]...............................	13,134	25,578	28,998	20,531
Box cutter [5].........................	37,504	21,396	22,428	21,319
Firearm [6]............................	983	638	254	(NA)
Incendiary [7].........................	83,086	485,792	697,242	371,711
Lighters [8]...........................	(X)	(X)	(X)	9,420,653
Other [9].............................	839,637	635,772	889,608	952,018

NA Not Available. X Not applicable. [1] Data comes from the Air Transport Association. Data are for U.S. passenger and cargo airlines only. [2] Knife includes any length and type except round-bladed, butter, and plastic cutlery. [3] Other cutting instruments refers to, e.g., scissors, screwdrivers, swords, sabers, and ice picks. [4] Club refers to baseball bats, night sticks, billy clubs, bludgeons; etc. [5] Box cutter. [6] Firearm refers to items like pistols, revolvers, rifles, automatic weapons, shotguns, parts of guns and firearms. [7] Incendiaries refer to categories of ammunition and gunpowder, flammables/irritants, and explosives. [8] As of April 14, 2005, passengers are prohibited from carrying all lighters on their person or in carry-on luggage or onboard an airplane. [9] Other refers to tools, self-defense items, and sporting goods (excluding baseball bats).

Source: U.S. Department of Homeland Security, Transportation Security Administration, unpublished data; 13 April 2006 <http://www.tsa.gov>. Air Transport Association of America, Washington, DC. annual operations, traffic, and capacity. See also <http://www.airlines.org/home/default.aspx>.

Table 524. Seizure Statistics for Intellectual Property Rights (IPR): 2000 to 2005

[Customs and Border Protection (CBP) is dedicated to protecting against the importation of goods which infringe/violate Intellectual Property Rights (IPR) by devoting substantial resources toward identifying and seizing shipments of infringing articles]

Item	2000	2001	2002	2003	2004	2005
Number of IPR Seizures	3,244	3,586	5,793	6,500	7,255	8,022
Total domestic value in U.S. dollars of IPR seizures (1,000) [1]................................	45,328	57,439	98,990	94,019	138,768	93,235
Selected IPR commodities seized by value (1,000): ...						
Wearing apparel	4,329	7,833	9,295	13,889	51,737	16,100
Handbags/wallets/backpacks...................	1,729	3,164	2,927	11,458	23,190	14,955
Cigarettes	4,223	4,550	37,580	41,720	24,161	9,649
Consumer electronics [2]	1,463	(NA)	5,307	3,780	8,880	8,794
Toys/electronic games	5,996	4,355	2,151	1,511	3,971	8,569
Watches/parts...........................	3,993	5,632	3,919	3,384	2,543	3,071
Media [3]	7,851	7,324	28,396	7,358	5,050	(NA)
All others.............................	8,801	8,623	6,154	5,697	13,184	13,550

[1] Domestic value is the cost of the seized goods, plus the costs of shipping and importing the goods into the U.S. and an amount for profit. [2] Consumer electronics includes cell phones and accessories, radios, power strips, electrical tools and appliances. [3] Media includes motion pictures on tape, laser disc, and DVD; interactive and computer software on CD-ROM, CD-R, and floppy discs; and music on CD or tape.

U.S. Department of Homeland Security, Customs and Border Protection, Import, Commercial Enforcement, Intellectual Property Rights, Seizure Statistics for Intellectual Property Rights; <www.cbp.gov/xp/cgov/import/commercial_enforcement/ipr /seizure/>.

Section 11
Social Insurance and Human Services

This section presents data related to governmental expenditures for social insurance and human services; governmental programs for old-age, survivors, disability, and health insurance (OASDHI); governmental employee retirement; private pension plans; government unemployment and temporary disability insurance; federal supplemental security income payments and aid to the needy; child and other welfare services; and federal food programs. Also included here are selected data on workers' compensation and vocational rehabilitation, child support, child care, charity contributions, and philanthropic trusts and foundations.

The principal source for these data is the Social Security Administration's *Annual Statistical Supplement to the Social Security Bulletin* which presents current data on many of the programs.

Social insurance under the Social Security Act—Programs established by the Social Security Act provide protection against wage loss resulting from retirement, prolonged disability, death, or unemployment, and protection against the cost of medical care during old age and disability. The federal OASDI program provides monthly benefits to retired or disabled insured workers and their dependents and to survivors of insured workers. To be eligible, a worker must have had a specified period of employment in which OASDI taxes were paid. The age of eligibility for full retirement benefits had been 65 years old for many years. However, for persons born in 1938 or later that age gradually increases until it reaches age 67 for those born after 1959. Reduced benefits may be obtained as early as age 62. The worker's spouse is under the same limitations. Survivor benefits are payable to dependents of deceased insured workers. Disability benefits are payable to an insured worker under full retirement age with a prolonged disability and to the disabled worker's dependents on the same basis as

dependents of retired workers. Disability benefits are provided at age 50 to the disabled widow or widower of a deceased worker who was fully insured at the time of death. Disabled children, aged 18 or older, of retired, disabled, or deceased workers are also eligible for benefits. A lump sum benefit is generally payable on the death of an insured worker to a spouse or minor children. For information on the medicare program, see Section 3, Health and Nutrition.

Retirement, survivors, disability, and hospital insurance benefits are funded by a payroll tax on annual earnings (up to a maximum of earnings set by law) of workers, employers, and the self-employed. The maximum taxable earnings are adjusted annually to reflect increasing wage levels (see Table 531). Effective January 1994, there is no dollar limit on wages and self-employment income subject to the hospital insurance tax. Tax receipts and benefit payments are administered through federal trust funds. Special benefits for uninsured persons; hospital benefits for persons aged 65 and over with specified amounts of social security coverage less than that required for cash benefit eligibility; and that part of the cost of supplementary medical insurance not financed by contributions from participants are financed from federal general revenues.

Unemployment insurance is presently administered by the U.S. Employment and Training Administration and each state's employment security agency. By agreement with the U.S. Secretary of Labor, state agencies also administer unemployment compensation for eligible ex-military personnel and federal employees. Under state unemployment insurance laws, benefits related to the individual's past earnings are paid to unemployed eligible workers. State laws vary concerning the length of time benefits are paid and their amount. In most states, benefits are payable for 26 weeks and, during periods of high unemployment, extended benefits are payable under a federal-state program to those who have exhausted their regular state benefits. Some states also supplement the basic benefit with allowances for dependents.

Unemployment insurance is funded by a federal unemployment tax levied on the taxable payrolls of most employers. Taxable payroll under the federal act and 12 state laws is the first $7,000 in wages paid each worker during a year. Forty-one states have taxable payrolls above $7,000. Employers are allowed a percentage credit of taxable payroll for contributions paid to states under state unemployment insurance laws. The remaining percent of the federal tax finances administrative costs, the federal share of extended benefits, and advances to states. About 97 percent of wage and salary workers are covered by unemployment insurance.

Retirement programs for government employees—The Civil Service Retirement System (CSRS) and the Federal Employees' Retirement System (FERS) are the two major programs providing age and service, disability, and survivor annuities for federal civilian employees. In general, employees hired after December 31, 1983, are covered under FERS and the social security program (OASDHI), and employees on staff prior to that date are members of CSRS and are covered under Medicare. CSRS employees were offered the option of transferring to FERS during 1987 and 1998. There are separate retirement systems for the uniformed services (supplementing OASDHI) and for certain special groups of federal employees. State and local government employees are covered for the most part by state and local retirement systems similar to the federal programs. In many jurisdictions these benefits supplement OASDHI coverage.

Workers' compensation—All states provide protection against work-connected injuries and deaths, although some states exclude certain workers (e.g., domestic workers). Federal laws cover federal employees, private employees in the District of Columbia, and longshoremen and harbor workers. In addition, the Department of Labor administers "black lung"

benefits programs for coal miners disabled by pneumoconiosis and for specified dependents and survivors. Specified occupational diseases are compensable to some extent. In most states, benefits are related to the worker's salary. The benefits may or may not be augmented by dependents' allowances or automatically adjusted to prevailing wage levels.

Income support—Income support programs are designed to provide benefits for persons with limited income and resources. The Supplemental Security Income (SSI) program and Temporary Assistance for Needy Families (TANF) program are the major programs providing monthly payments. In addition, a number of programs provide money payments or in-kind benefits for special needs or purposes. Several programs offer food and nutritional services. Also, various federal-state programs provide energy assistance, public housing, and subsidized housing to individuals and families with low incomes. General assistance may also be available at the state or local level.

The SSI program, administered by the Social Security Administration, provides income support to persons aged 65 or older and blind or disabled adults and children. Eligibility requirements and federal payment standards are nationally uniform. Most states supplement the basic SSI payment for all or selected categories of persons.

The Personal Responsibility and Work Opportunity Reconciliation Act of 1996 contained provisions that replaced the Aid to Families With Dependent Children (AFDC), Job Opportunities and Basic Skills (JOBS), and Emergency Assistance programs with the Temporary Assistance for Needy Families block grant program. This law contains strong work requirements, comprehensive child support enforcement, support for families moving from welfare to work, and other features. The TANF became effective as soon as each state submitted a complete plan implementing TANF, but no later than July 1, 1997. The AFDC program provided cash assistance based on need, income, resources, and family size.

Federal food stamp program—Under the food stamp program, single persons and those living in households meeting nationwide standards for income and assets may receive coupons redeemable for food at most retail food stores or provides benefits through electronic benefit transfer. The monthly amount of benefits or allotments a unit receives is determined by household size and income. Households without income receive the determined monthly cost of a nutritionally adequate diet for their household size. This amount is updated to account for food price increases. Households with income receive the difference between the amount of a nutritionally adequate diet and 30 percent of their income, after certain allowable deductions.

To qualify for the program, a household must have less than $2,000 in disposable assets ($3,000 if one member is aged 60 or older), gross income below 130 percent of the official poverty guidelines for the household size, and net income below 100 percent of the poverty guidelines. Households with a person aged 60 or older or a disabled person receiving SSI, social security, state general assistance, or veterans' disability benefits may have gross income exceeding 130 percent of the poverty guidelines. All households in which all members receive TANF or SSI are categorically eligible for food stamps without meeting these income or resource criteria. Households are certified for varying lengths of time, depending on their income sources and individual circumstances.

Health and welfare services— Programs providing health and welfare services are aided through federal grants to states for child welfare services, vocational rehabilitation, activities for the aged, maternal and child health services, maternity and infant care projects, comprehensive health services, and a variety of public health activities. For information about the Medicaid program, see Section 3, Health and Nutrition.

Noncash benefits—The U.S. Census Bureau annually collects data on the characteristics of recipients of noncash (in-kind) benefits to supplement the collection of annual money income data in the Current Population Survey (see text, Section 1, Population, and Section 14, Prices). Noncash benefits are those benefits received in a form other than money which serve to enhance or improve the economic well-being of the recipient. As for money income, the data for noncash benefits are for the calendar year prior to the date of the interview. The major categories of noncash benefits covered are public transfers (e.g., food stamps, school lunch, public housing, and Medicaid) and employer or union-provided benefits to employees.

Statistical reliability—For discussion of statistical collection, estimation, and sampling procedures and measures of statistical reliability applicable to HHS and Census Bureau data, see Appendix III.

U.S. Census Bureau, Statistical Abstract of the United States: 2007

Table 525. **Government Transfer Payments to Individuals—Summary: 1980 to 2004**

[In billions of dollars (263.4 represents $263,400,000,000)]

Year	Total	Retirement & disability insurance benefits	Medical payments	Income maintenance benefits	Unemployment insurance benefits	Veterans benefits	Federal education & training assistance payments [1]	Other [2]
1980	263.4	128.8	62.6	34.3	18.7	14.7	4.1	0.2
1990	561.5	264.2	188.8	63.5	18.2	17.7	7.3	1.8
1994	795.2	335.1	310.7	95.6	24.0	19.7	8.6	1.5
1995	840.0	350.3	336.5	100.4	21.8	20.5	9.0	1.4
1996	883.1	364.9	361.7	102.6	22.4	21.4	8.6	1.6
1997	912.8	379.3	377.3	100.5	20.3	22.2	11.5	1.6
1998	932.6	391.8	383.7	101.1	19.9	23.2	11.2	1.8
1999	966.5	402.5	401.1	104.8	20.8	24.1	11.4	1.9
2000	1,018.1	424.8	427.7	106.6	20.7	24.9	11.0	2.4
2001	1,117.2	450.4	482.5	109.4	32.2	26.5	13.1	3.1
2002	1,220.0	474.9	525.4	119.7	53.7	29.3	14.5	2.4
2003	1,282.5	493.9	555.3	131.2	53.6	31.6	13.9	3.0
2004	1,361.7	517.8	609.0	141.5	37.1	33.8	14.8	7.5

[1] See footnote 9, Table 526.   [2] See footnote 10, Table 526.

Source: U.S. Bureau of Economic Analysis, "Regional Accounts Data, Annual State Personal Income"; <http://www.bea.gov /bea/regional/spi/>; (accessed 31 January 2006).

Table 526. **Government Transfer Payments to Individuals by Type: 1990 to 2004**

[In millions of dollars (561,484 represents $561,484,000,000)]

Item	1990	1995	2000	2001	2002	2003	2004
Total	561,484	840,034	1,018,106	1,117,218	1,219,954	1,282,540	1,361,666
Retirement & disability insurance benefit payments	264,230	350,310	424,810	450,415	474,863	493,894	517,840
Old age, survivors', & disability insurance . . .	244,135	327,667	401,218	425,081	446,690	463,406	485,932
Railroad retirement and disability	7,221	8,028	8,265	8,411	8,700	8,855	9,009
Workers' compensation payments (federal & state)	8,618	10,530	10,845	11,673	13,318	14,189	14,801
Other government disability insurance & retirement [1]	4,256	4,085	4,482	5,250	6,155	7,444	8,098
Medical payments	188,808	336,506	427,689	482,527	525,387	555,259	609,035
Medicare	107,638	179,147	219,612	243,462	260,777	275,875	303,322
Public assistance medical care [2]	78,176	155,007	205,021	234,644	258,560	274,272	299,667
Military medical insurance [3]	2,994	2,352	3,056	4,421	6,050	5,112	6,046
Income maintenance benefit payments	63,481	100,443	106,616	109,403	119,718	131,225	141,490
Supplemental security income (SSI)	16,670	27,726	31,675	33,162	34,664	35,703	37,299
Family assistance [4]	19,187	22,637	18,440	18,106	17,684	18,367	18,492
Food stamps	14,741	22,447	14,896	16,000	18,612	22,127	25,779
Other income maintenance [5]	12,883	27,633	41,605	42,135	48,758	55,028	59,920
Unemployment insurance benefit payments . . .	18,208	21,838	20,680	32,155	53,742	53,583	37,119
State unemployment insurance compensation	17,644	20,937	19,913	31,383	52,751	52,365	35,605
Unemployment compensation for federal civilian employees	215	339	226	209	331	333	281
Unemployment compensation for railroad employees	89	62	81	98	96	95	79
Unemployment compensation for veterans . .	144	320	182	183	281	365	431
Other unemployment compensation [6]	116	180	278	282	283	425	723
Veterans' benefit payments	17,687	20,546	24,935	26,500	29,333	31,607	33,806
Veterans' pension and disability	15,550	17,565	21,895	23,287	25,933	27,955	29,956
Veterans' readjustment [7]	257	1,086	1,323	1,510	1,666	1,934	2,159
Veterans' life insurance benefits	1,868	1,884	1,707	1,693	1,723	1,706	1,678
Other assistance to veterans [8]	12	11	10	10	11	12	13
Federal education & training assistance payments [9]	7,300	9,007	10,985	13,129	14,523	13,947	14,833
Other payments to individuals [10]	1,770	1,384	2,391	3,089	2,388	3,025	7,543

[1] Consists largely of temporary disability payments, pension benefit guaranty payments, and black lung payments. [2] Consists of medicaid and other medical vendor payments. [3] Consists of payments made under the TriCare Management Program (formerly called CHAMPUS) for the medical care of dependents of active duty military personnel and of retired military personnel and their dependents at nonmilitary medical facilities. [4] Through 1995, consists of emergency assistance and aid to families with dependent children. Beginning with 1998, consists of benefits—generally known as temporary assistance for needy families—provided under the Personal Responsibility and Work Opportunity Reconciliation Act of 1996. [5] Consists largely of general assistance, expenditures for food under the supplemental program for women, infants, and children; refugee assistance; foster home care and adoption assistance; earned income tax credits; and energy assistance. [6] Consists of trade readjustment allowance payments, Redwood Park benefit payments, public service employment benefit payments, and transitional benefit payments. [7] Consists largely of veterans' readjustment benefit payments, educational assistance to spouses and children of disabled or deceased veterans, payments to paraplegics, and payments for autos and conveyances for disabled veterans. [8] Consists largely of state and local government payments to veterans. [9] Excludes veterans. Consists largely of federal fellowship payments (National Science Foundation fellowships and traineeships, subsistence payments to state maritime academy cadets, and other federal fellowships), interest subsidy on higher education loans, basic educational opportunity grants, and Job Corps payments. [10] Consists largely of Bureau of Indian Affairs payments, education exchange payments, Alaska Permanent Fund dividend payments, compensation of survivors of public safety officers, compensation of victims of crime, disaster relief payments, compensation for Japanese internment, and other special payments to individuals.

Source: U.S. Bureau of Economic Analysis, "Regional Accounts Data, Annual State Personal Income"; <http://www.bea.gov/bea /regional/spi/>; (accessed 31 January 2006).

Table 527. **Government Transfer Payments to Individuals by State: 2000 to 2004**

[In millions of dollars (1,018,106 represents $1,018,106,000,000)]

State	2000, total	2003, total	2004							
			Total	Retirement & disability insurance benefits	Medical payments	Income maintenance benefits	Unemployment insurance benefits	Veterans' benefits	Federal education & training assistance payments [1]	Other [2]
U.S.	1,018,106	1,282,540	1,361,666	517,840	609,035	141,490	37,119	33,806	14,833	7,543
AL......	16,643	20,758	21,950	8,891	9,094	2,584	285	792	289	15
AK......	2,966	3,164	3,113	637	1,317	342	124	124	16	554
AZ......	15,959	22,383	24,320	9,752	10,625	2,288	359	797	369	130
AR......	10,006	12,652	13,593	5,374	5,719	1,469	296	547	181	6
CA......	114,559	147,326	156,745	53,003	71,071	22,582	5,221	2,890	1,788	190
CO.....	11,169	14,680	15,387	6,465	6,294	1,368	419	604	196	40
CT.....	14,086	16,599	17,738	6,864	8,483	1,293	598	259	105	137
DE.....	2,857	3,661	3,915	1,653	1,721	299	116	88	30	8
DC.....	2,709	3,271	3,362	683	1,893	500	73	130	52	32
FL......	64,208	81,297	87,150	36,080	38,886	7,626	1,175	2,548	799	38
GA.....	23,696	30,899	33,272	12,352	14,450	4,202	674	1,157	401	35
HI......	3,844	4,689	5,072	2,086	1,992	640	121	182	44	6
ID......	3,804	4,997	5,381	2,384	2,082	443	177	191	95	9
IL......	41,726	51,500	53,598	21,500	22,842	5,621	2,165	791	623	55
IN......	20,081	24,684	26,316	11,723	10,637	2,337	746	505	355	13
IA......	10,046	12,173	12,730	5,901	5,089	938	334	270	187	12
KS......	8,908	10,790	11,264	5,008	4,566	887	333	308	152	11
KY......	15,778	19,060	20,546	8,045	8,764	2,399	499	571	258	11
LA......	16,582	20,796	22,933	7,275	11,312	3,101	321	608	302	14
ME	5,307	6,757	7,234	2,610	3,487	614	139	314	59	11
MD	16,981	21,663	22,778	8,592	10,862	1,901	529	573	210	111
MA	26,471	32,815	34,226	11,515	17,395	2,643	1,517	704	260	194
MI	36,675	45,147	47,080	19,490	19,614	4,781	1,992	726	455	22
MN	15,748	20,441	21,633	8,523	10,008	1,601	730	523	233	14
MS	10,803	13,836	14,902	5,170	6,869	1,982	191	428	247	14
MO	20,904	26,186	27,778	11,113	12,602	2,512	579	674	278	20
MT	3,127	3,717	4,008	1,872	1,476	343	82	166	60	9
NE	5,694	7,033	7,397	3,150	3,071	665	133	280	93	5
NV	5,588	7,751	8,440	3,723	3,390	654	285	307	63	18
NH	3,918	4,816	5,301	2,340	2,316	303	97	179	43	22
NJ......	33,092	41,282	42,896	17,103	18,736	2,725	1,978	613	322	1,418
NM.....	6,014	7,974	8,601	2,973	3,839	1,023	146	409	127	83
NY......	95,735	118,430	128,601	36,495	69,215	14,020	2,641	1,408	1,222	3,600
NC.....	28,108	36,004	38,907	14,980	16,634	4,497	1,020	1,302	443	31
ND.....	2,322	2,616	2,732	1,239	1,094	206	45	85	45	17
OH	43,149	53,463	56,357	23,700	24,313	5,384	1,332	1,058	541	29
OK	11,999	15,104	15,880	6,381	6,444	1,728	246	831	229	22
OR	12,243	15,429	15,942	7,115	5,904	1,443	723	551	187	19
PA.....	54,928	66,462	69,725	27,424	32,409	5,517	2,482	1,250	556	87
RI......	4,748	5,873	6,352	2,317	3,082	522	214	137	65	16
SC.....	14,340	18,338	19,898	7,807	8,450	2,335	404	655	231	16
SD.....	2,490	3,013	3,197	1,369	1,312	263	33	131	52	36
TN.....	21,864	27,454	29,290	10,925	13,410	3,301	546	805	285	19
TX.....	59,911	78,473	82,867	29,457	36,625	10,649	1,919	2,949	1,149	120
UT.....	4,962	6,414	6,806	3,052	2,580	598	176	178	188	34
VT......	2,245	2,843	2,991	1,142	1,374	281	84	82	27	1
VA......	19,916	25,222	26,858	11,839	10,499	2,513	448	1,086	298	174
WA.....	20,817	26,512	27,061	11,621	10,527	2,331	1,243	1,032	271	36
WV.....	8,894	11,575	12,130	5,845	4,492	1,099	187	386	114	6
WI	17,902	22,492	23,249	10,260	9,341	1,971	899	552	210	18
WY	1,583	2,025	2,162	1,022	827	165	47	70	27	3

[1] Excludes veterans. Consists largely of federal fellowship payments (National Science Foundation, fellowships and traineeships, subsistence payments to state maritime academy cadets, and other federal fellowships), interest subsidy on higher education loans, basic educational opportunity grants, and Job Corps payments.   [2] Consists largely of Bureau of Indian Affairs payments, education exchange payments, Alaska Permanent Fund dividend payments, compensation of survivors of public safety officers, compensation of victims of crime, disaster relief payments, compensation for Japanese internment, and other special payments to individuals.

Source: U.S. Bureau of Economic Analysis, "Regional Accounts Data, Annual State Personal Income"; <http://www.bea.gov/bea/regional/spi/>; (accessed 31 January 2006).

Social Insurance and Human Services 347

Table 528. **Number of Persons With Income by Specified Sources of Income: 2004**

[In thousands (205,146 represents 205,146,000). Persons 15 years old and over as of March of the following year. Based on Current Population Survey; see text, Sections 1 and 13, and Appendix III]

Source of income	Total persons with income	Under 65 years old	65 years old and over	White [1]	Black [2]	Hispanic origin [3]
Total	205,146	170,959	34,187	169,478	22,695	23,644
Earnings	153,355	147,007	6,348	126,255	16,893	19,660
Wages and salary	143,905	138,584	5,321	117,989	16,315	18,703
Nonfarm self-employment	12,858	11,851	1,007	11,182	841	1,192
Farm self-employment	2,625	2,313	312	2,357	148	162
Unemployment compensation	6,354	6,180	174	5,046	894	705
State or local only	6,030	5,862	168	4,793	842	663
Combinations	324	319	6	253	52	42
Workers' compensation	2,087	1,971	116	1,666	269	292
State payments	746	725	21	592	84	142
Employment insurance	894	848	45	736	103	110
Own insurance	41	36	6	33	8	1
Other	442	396	46	330	82	45
Social security, railroad retirement	41,089	10,044	31,045	35,585	3,928	2,495
Supplemental security income (SSI)	5,334	4,155	1,179	3,645	1,281	806
Public assistance [4]	2,080	2,030	49	1,218	714	421
TANF/Welfare (AFDC) only [4]	1,591	1,565	25	887	588	321
Other assistance only	434	411	23	300	104	85
Both	55	54	1	32	21	15
Veterans' payments	2,575	1,458	1,117	2,211	261	117
Disability only	1,409	900	509	1,221	139	65
Survivors only	306	98	208	249	43	9
Pension only	554	245	309	479	50	26
Education only	60	60	–	50	6	8
Other only	114	57	57	102	6	6
Combinations	132	97	35	110	16	2
Means-tested	411	231	180	328	64	21
Nonmeans-tested	2,164	1,227	937	1,884	197	97
Survivors' benefits	2,743	977	1,767	2,483	179	121
Company or union	1,282	285	996	1,177	72	57
Federal government	278	61	217	251	18	22
Military retirement	136	46	90	119	8	6
State or local government	220	80	141	188	25	10
Disability benefits	1,738	1,588	149	1,349	277	192
Workers' compensation	62	50	12	43	15	5
Company or union	447	418	29	368	51	40
Federal government	135	120	15	107	21	9
Military retirement	44	32	12	35	6	1
State or local government	356	314	42	275	55	56
Pensions	15,901	5,077	10,825	14,213	1,174	568
Company or union	11,264	3,378	7,885	10,116	802	475
Federal government	1,772	562	1,210	1,523	169	81
Military retirement	1,095	654	441	951	99	37
State or local government	3,896	1,584	2,313	3,436	315	155
Property income [5]	103,705	84,113	19,592	91,541	6,251	6,039
Interest	97,651	79,392	18,259	86,292	5,822	5,628
Dividends	36,262	29,192	7,070	32,893	1,391	1,144
Rents, royalties, estates or trusts	11,409	8,460	2,949	10,262	546	646
Education	8,011	7,988	23	6,188	1,202	799
Pell grant only	1,725	1,721	4	1,197	405	222
Other government only	1,109	1,103	6	848	179	144
Scholarships only	2,359	2,357	2	1,913	242	171
Child support	5,621	5,595	26	4,432	944	616
Alimony	505	450	55	449	31	41
Financial assistance from outside the household	2,133	1,968	164	1,656	267	148
Other income	596	520	76	465	63	59
Combinations of income types:						
Government transfer payments	59,033	26,703	32,330	49,103	7,138	4,681
Public assistance or SSI	7,172	5,948	1,225	4,707	1,930	1,189

– Represents or rounds to zero. [1] Beginning with the 2003 CPS respondents could choose one or more races. For example "White" refers to people who reported White and did not report any other race category. The use of this single-race population does not imply that it is the preferred method of presenting or analyzing data. Information on people who reported more than one race such as "Asian and Black or African American," is available from Census 2000 through American FactFinder. [2] "Black" refers to people who reported Black and did not report any other race category. [3] Persons of Hispanic origin may be any race. [4] TANF—Temporary Assistance for Needy Families program; AFDC—Aid to Families with Dependent Children program. [5] Includes estates and trusts reported as survivor benefits.

Source: U.S. Census Bureau, "Table PINC-09. Source of Income in 2004—Number With Income and Mean Income of Specified Type in 2004 of People 15 Years Old and Over, by Race, Hispanic Origin and Sex." See also <http://pubdb .census.gov/macro/032005/perinc/new09_000.htm>.

Table 529. Households Receiving Means-Tested Noncash Benefits: 1980 to 2002

[In thousands (82,368 represents 82,368,000), except percent. Households as of March of following year. Covers civilian noninstitutional population, including persons in the Armed Forces living off post or with their families on post. A means-tested benefit program requires that the household's income and/or assets fall below specified guidelines in order to qualify for benefits. There are general trends toward underestimation of noncash beneficiaries. Households are classified according to poverty status of family or nonfamily householder; for explanation of poverty level, see text, Section 13. Data for 1980 and 1990 based on 1980 census population controls; 1995 and 2000 based on 1990 census population controls; beginning 2002, based on Census 2000 population controls and a 28,000 household sample expansion to 78,000 households. Based on Current Population Survey; see text, Section 1 and Appendix III]

Type of benefit received	1980	1990	1995	2001	2002 Total	2002 Below poverty level Number	2002 Below poverty level Percent of total	2002 Above poverty level
Total households	82,368	94,312	99,627	109,297	111,278	13,505	100	97,773
Receiving at least one noncash benefit . . .	14,266	16,098	21,148	21,870	22,478	7,806	58	14,672
Not receiving cash public assistance . . .	7,860	8,819	13,335	16,234	16,890	5,003	37	11,887
Receiving cash public assistance [1]	6,407	7,279	7,813	5,636	5,588	2,803	21	2,785
Total households receiving—								
Food stamps	6,769	7,163	8,388	5,905	6,245	3,834	28	2,411
School lunch	5,532	6,252	8,607	7,942	7,930	3,092	23	4,838
Public housing	2,777	4,339	4,846	5,006	5,125	2,593	19	2,532
Medicaid	8,287	10,321	14,111	15,832	16,765	6,182	46	10,583

[1] Households receiving money from aid to families with dependent children program (beginning 2000, temporary assistance for needy families program), supplemental security income program or other public assistance programs.

Source: U.S. Census Bureau, "Table NC1. Means-Tested Noncash Benefits Received by Households, by Selected Household Characteristics, Race and Hispanic Origin, and Poverty Status: 2002"; May 2004; <http://pubdb3.census.gov/macro/032003/noncash/toc.htm> and Current Population Reports, P-60 reports.

Table 530. Persons Living in Households Receiving Selected Noncash Benefits: 2004

[In thousands (290,605 represents 290,605,000), except percent. Persons, as of March 2005, who lived with someone (a nonrelative or a relative) who received aid. Not every person tallied here received the aid themselves. Excludes members of the Armed Forces except those living off post or with their families on post. Population controls for 2005 based on Census 2000 and an expanded sample of households. Based on Current Population Survey, see text of section 1 and Appendix III]

Age, Sex, and Race	Total [1]	In household that received means-tested assistance [2] Number	In household that received means-tested assistance [2] Per-cent	In household that received means-tested cash assistance Number	In household that received means-tested cash assistance Per-cent	In household that received food stamps Number	In household that received food stamps Per-cent	In household in which one or more persons were covered by Medicaid Number	In household in which one or more persons were covered by Medicaid Per-cent	Lived in public or authorized housing Number	Lived in public or authorized housing Per-cent
Total	290,605	76,745	26.4	18,484	6.4	21,905	7.5	59,107	20.3	10,618	3.7
Under 18 years	73,271	28,986	39.6	5,553	7.6	9,573	13.1	22,250	30.4	3,995	5.5
18 to 24 years	27,972	8,025	28.7	1,986	7.1	2,289	8.2	6,434	23.0	1,238	4.4
25 to 34 years	39,307	10,968	27.9	2,147	5.5	3,248	8.3	8,522	21.7	1,331	3.4
35 to 44 years	43,350	10,337	23.8	2,280	5.3	2,589	6.0	7,748	17.9	1,073	2.5
45 to 54 years	41,960	7,591	18.1	2,489	5.9	1,824	4.3	5,831	13.9	918	2.2
55 to 59 years	16,763	2,690	16.0	1096	6.5	623	3.7	2,104	12.5	347	2.1
60 to 64 years	12,769	1,958	15.3	826	6.5	472	3.7	1,551	12.1	318	2.5
65 years and over . . .	35,213	6,189	17.6	2,107	6.0	1,286	3.7	4,669	13.3	1,399	4.0
65 to 74 years	18,388	3,178	17.3	1,114	6.1	722	3.9	2,469	13.4	665	3.6
75 years and over. . .	16,825	3,011	17.9	993	5.9	564	3.4	2,200	13.1	733	4.4
Male	142,426	35,906	25.2	8,555	6.0	9,549	6.7	27,759	19.5	4,285	3.0
Female	148,179	40,840	27.6	9,929	6.7	12,355	8.3	31,348	21.2	6,333	4.3
White alone	233,702	53,522	22.9	11,746	5.0	13,716	5.9	41,128	17.6	5,340	2.3
Black alone	36,423	17,017	46.7	5,187	14.2	6,557	18.0	13,086	35.9	4,310	11.8
Asian alone	12,301	2,886	23.5	651	5.3	453	3.7	2,313	18.8	324	2.6
Hispanic	41,688	20,678	49.6	3,360	8.1	5,134	12.3	15,061	36.1	2,147	5.2
White alone, Non-Hispanic	195,054	34,338	17.6	8,748	4.5	9,021	4.6	27,242	14.0	3,471	1.8

[1] Number of persons living in households. [2] Means-tested assistance includes means-tested cash assistance, food stamps, Medicaid, and public or authorized housing.

Source: U.S. Census Bureau, Current Population Reports, P60-226. See also <http://pubdb3.census.gov/macro/032005/pov/new26_001_01.htm>.

Table 531. **Social Security—Covered Employment, Earnings, and Contribution Rates: 1990 to 2005**

[164.0 represents 164,000,000. Includes Puerto Rico, Virgin Islands, American Samoa, and Guam. Represents all reported employment. Data are estimated. OASDHI = Old-age, survivors, disability, and health insurance; SMI = Supplementary medical insurance]

Item	Unit	1990	1995	1998	1999	2000	2001	2002	2003	2004	2005
Workers with insured status [1]	Million. . .	164.0	173.2	180.4	182.9	185.5	187.7	189.6	191.5	193.7	195.8
Male.	Million. . .	86.5	90.2	93.2	94.3	95.6	96.6	97.4	98.4	99.4	100.4
Female	Million. . .	77.5	83.0	87.1	88.6	89.8	91.1	92.2	93.1	94.3	95.4
Under 25 years old	Million. . .	21.3	18.8	19.7	20.3	20.8	21.1	21.0	20.8	20.7	20.5
25 to 34 years old.	Million. . .	41.6	39.4	37.5	37.0	36.6	36.4	36.3	36.2	36.2	36.2
35 to 44 years old.	Million. . .	36.5	40.6	42.3	42.5	42.5	42.3	41.8	41.5	41.2	40.8
45 to 54 years old.	Million. . .	22.8	29.5	33.1	34.5	35.9	36.8	37.6	38.5	39.3	40.2
55 to 59 years old.	Million. . .	8.8	9.7	11.3	11.8	12.2	13.0	13.8	14.5	15.4	16.1
60 to 64 years old.	Million. . .	8.7	8.5	9.1	9.2	9.5	10.0	10.5	11.1	11.5	12.0
65 to 69 years old.	Million. . .	8.2	8.1	8.0	8.0	8.1	8.2	8.3	8.6	8.9	9.2
70 years old and over	Million. . .	16.3	18.5	19.4	19.6	19.9	20.0	20.2	20.4	20.7	20.9
Workers reported with—											
Taxable earnings [2]	Million. . .	134	141	149	151	155	155	155	155	157	159
Maximum earnings [2]	Million. . .	8	8	9	9	10	9	8	8	9	10
Earnings in covered											
employment [2]	Bil. dol . .	2,704	3,402	4,194	4,478	4,839	4,939	4,950	5,082	5,378	5,693
Reported taxable [2]	Bil. dol . .	2,358	2,919	3,528	3,749	4,009	4,168	4,248	4,364	4,543	4,770
Percent of total	Percent. .	87.2	85.8	84.1	83.7	82.8	84.4	85.8	85.9	84.5	83.8
Average per worker:											
Total earnings [2]	Dollars . .	20,238	24,126	28,069	29,428	31,209	31,781	31,976	32,799	34,256	35,772
Taxable earnings [2]	Dollars . .	17,650	20,703	23,612	24,640	25,854	26,818	27,441	28,164	28,940	29,973
Annual maximum taxable											
earnings [3]	Dollars . .	51,300	61,200	68,400	72,600	76,200	80,400	84,900	87,000	87,900	90,000
Contribution rates for OASDHI: [4]											
Each employer and employee . .	Percent. .	7.65	7.65	7.65	7.65	7.65	7.65	7.65	7.65	7.65	7.65
Self-employed [5]	Percent. .	15.30	15.30	15.30	15.30	15.30	15.30	15.30	15.30	15.30	15.30
SMI, monthly premium [6]	Dollars . .	28.60	46.10	43.80	45.50	45.50	50.00	54.00	58.70	66.60	78.20

[1] Estimated number fully insured for retirement and/or survivor benefits as of end of year. [2] Includes self-employment. [3] Beginning 1995 upper limit on earnings subject to HI taxes was repealed. [4] As of January 1, 2006, each employee and employer pays 7.65 percent and the self-employed pay 15.3 percent. [5] Self-employed pays 15.3 percent, and half of the tax is deductible for income tax purposes and for computing self-employment income subject to social security tax. [6] As of January 1.

Source: U.S. Social Security Administration, *Annual Statistical Supplement* to the *Social Security Bulletin;* and unpublished data. See also <http://www.ssa.gov/policy/docs/statcomps/supplement/2005/>.

Table 532. **Social Security Trust Funds: 1990 to 2005**

[In billions of dollars (272.4 represents $272,400,000,000)]

Type of trust fund	1990	1995	1999	2000	2001	2002	2003	2004	2005
Old-age and survivors' insurance (OASI):									
Net contribution income [1]	272.4	310.1	407.3	433.0	453.4	468.1	468.6	487.4	520.7
Interest received [2]	16.4	32.8	49.8	57.5	64.7	71.2	75.2	79.0	84.0
Benefit payments [3]	223.0	291.6	334.4	352.7	372.3	388.1	399.8	415.0	435.4
Assets, end of year	214.2	458.5	798.8	931.0	1,071.5	1,217.5	1,355.3	1,500.6	1,663.0
Disability insurance (DI):									
Net contribution income [1]	28.7	54.7	63.9	71.8	75.7	78.2	78.4	81.4	87.2
Interest received [2]	0.9	2.2	5.7	6.9	8.2	9.2	9.7	10.0	10.3
Benefit payments [3]	24.8	40.9	51.4	55.0	59.6	65.7	70.9	78.2	85.4
Assets, end of year	11.1	37.6	97.3	118.5	141.0	160.5	175.4	186.2	195.6

[1] Includes deposits by states and deductions for refund of estimated employee-tax overpayment. Includes government contributions on deemed wage credits for military service in 1957–2001. Includes taxation of benefits. [2] In 1990, includes interest on advance tax transfers. Includes interest on reimbursement for unnegotiated checks. [3] Includes payments for vocational rehabilitation services furnished to disabled persons receiving benefits because of their disabilities. Amounts reflect deductions for unnegotiated benefit checks.

Source: U.S. Social Security Administration, *Annual Report of Board of Trustees, OASI, DI, HI, and SMI Trust Funds.* Also published in *Social Security Bulletin,* quarterly.

Table 533. Social Security (OASDI)—Benefits by Type of Beneficiary: 1990 to 2005

[39,832 represents 39,832,000. A person eligible to receive more than one type of benefit is generally classified or counted only once as a retired-worker beneficiary. OASDI = Old-age, survivors, and disability insurance. See also headnote, Table 531 and Appendix III]

Type of beneficiary	1990	1995	1998	1999	2000	2001	2002	2003	2004	2005
Number of benefits [1] (1,000) . .	39,832	43,387	44,246	44,596	45,415	45,878	46,444	47,038	47,688	48,434
Retired workers [2] (1,000)	24,838	26,673	27,511	27,775	28,499	28,837	29,190	29,532	29,953	30,461
Disabled workers [3] (1,000)	3,011	4,185	4,698	4,879	5,042	5,274	5,544	5,874	6,198	6,519
Wives and husbands [2,4] (1,000) . . .	3,367	3,290	3,054	2,987	2,963	2,899	2,833	2,773	2,722	2,680
Children (1,000)	3,187	3,734	3,769	3,795	3,803	3,839	3,910	3,961	3,986	4,025
Under age 18	2,497	2,956	2,963	2,970	2,976	2,994	3,043	3,080	3,097	3,130
Disabled children [5]	600	686	713	721	729	737	745	753	759	769
Students [6]	89	92	93	104	98	109	123	128	130	127
Of retired workers	422	442	439	442	459	467	477	480	483	488
Of deceased workers	1,776	1,884	1,884	1,885	1,878	1,890	1,908	1,910	1,905	1,903
Of disabled workers	989	1,409	1,446	1,468	1,466	1,482	1,526	1,571	1,599	1,633
Widowed mothers [7] (1,000)	304	275	221	212	203	197	194	190	184	178
Widows and widowers [2,8] (1,000) . .	5,111	5,226	4,990	4,944	4,901	4,828	4,771	4,707	4,643	4,569
Parents [2] (1,000)	6	4	3	3	3	3	2	2	2	2
Special benefits [9] (1,000)	7	1	(Z)	(Z)	(Z)	(Z)	(Z)	(Z)	(Z)	(Z)
AVERAGE MONTHLY BENEFIT, CURRENT DOLLARS										
Retired workers [2]	603	720	780	804	844	874	895	922	955	1,002
Retired worker and wife [2]	1,027	1,221	1,318	1,357	1,420	1,466	1,494	1,535	1,586	1,660
Disabled workers [3]	587	682	733	754	786	814	834	862	894	938
Wives and husbands [2,4]	298	354	386	398	416	430	439	450	464	485
Children of retired workers	259	322	358	373	395	413	426	444	465	493
Children of deceased workers	406	469	510	526	550	571	585	603	625	656
Children of disabled workers	164	183	208	216	228	238	245	254	265	279
Widowed mothers [7]	409	478	545	566	595	621	640	664	689	725
Widows and widowers, nondisabled [2]	556	680	749	775	810	841	861	888	920	967
Parents [2]	482	591	651	674	704	729	753	779	810	851
Special benefits [9]	167	192	204	209	217	224	227	232	238	247
AVERAGE MONTHLY BENEFIT, CONSTANT (2005) DOLLARS [10]										
Retired workers [2]	887	923	936	940	955	974	974	985	988	1,002
Retired worker and wife [2]	1,511	1,565	1,583	1,587	1,606	1,632	1,625	1,639	1,640	1,660
Disabled workers [3]	863	874	880	882	889	907	907	920	925	938
Wives and husbands [2,4]	438	454	464	465	471	479	478	480	480	485
Children of deceased workers	597	601	612	615	622	636	636	644	647	656
Widowed mothers [7]	602	613	654	662	673	691	696	709	713	725
Widows and widowers, nondisabled [2]	818	872	899	906	916	936	937	948	952	967
Number of benefits awarded (1,000)	3,717	3,882	3,800	3,917	4,290	4,162	4,336	4,322	4,459	4,672
Retired workers [2]	1,665	1,609	1,631	1,690	1,961	1,779	1,813	1,791	1,883	2,000
Disabled workers [3]	468	646	608	620	622	691	750	777	796	830
Wives and husbands [2,4]	379	322	311	322	385	358	363	353	367	379
Children	695	809	763	773	777	796	846	852	859	908
Widowed mothers [7]	58	52	42	42	40	41	41	39	40	38
Widows and widowers [2,8]	452	445	444	470	505	496	523	508	514	517
Parents [2]	(Z)	(Z)	(Z)	(Z)	(Z)	(Z)	(Z)	(Z)	(Z)	(Z)
Special benefits [9]	(Z)	(Z)	(Z)	(Z)	(Z)	(Z)	(Z)	(Z)	(Z)	(Z)
BENEFIT PAYMENTS DURING YEAR (bil. dol.)										
Total [11]	247.8	332.6	375.0	385.8	407.6	431.9	453.8	470.8	493.3	520.8
Monthly benefits [12]	247.6	332.4	374.8	385.6	407.4	431.7	453.6	470.6	493.1	520.6
Retired workers [2]	156.8	205.3	232.3	238.5	253.5	269.0	281.6	291.5	304.3	321.7
Disabled workers [3] [2,4]	22.1	36.6	43.5	46.5	49.8	54.2	59.9	64.8	71.7	78.4
Wives and husbands [2,4]	14.5	17.9	18.9	18.8	19.4	19.9	20.3	20.4	20.6	20.5
Children	12.0	16.1	18.1	18.6	19.3	20.4	21.5	22.3	23.3	24.5
Under age 18	9.0	11.9	13.3	13.6	14.1	14.8	15.7	16.2	17.0	17.9
Disabled children [5]	2.5	3.6	4.2	4.4	4.6	4.8	5.1	5.2	5.5	5.8
Students [6]	0.5	0.6	0.7	0.7	0.7	0.7	0.8	0.8	0.9	0.8
Of retired workers	1.3	1.7	1.9	2.0	2.1	2.3	2.5	2.6	2.7	2.9
Of deceased workers	8.6	10.7	11.9	12.1	12.5	13.1	13.7	14.1	14.5	15.1
Of disabled workers	2.2	3.7	4.2	4.4	4.7	4.9	5.3	5.7	6.1	6.5
Widowed mothers [7]	1.4	1.6	1.4	1.4	1.4	1.4	1.5	1.5	1.5	1.5
Widows and widowers [2,8]	40.7	54.8	60.5	61.8	63.9	66.8	68.8	70.1	71.7	73.4
Parents [2]	(Z)	(Z)	(Z)	(Z)	(Z)	(Z)	(Z)	(Z)	(Z)	(Z)
Special benefits [9]	(Z)	(Z)	(Z)	(Z)	(Z)	(Z)	(Z)	(Z)	(Z)	(Z)
Lump sum	0.2	0.2	0.2	0.2	0.2	0.2	0.2	0.2	0.2	0.2

Z Fewer than 500 or less than $50 million. [1] Number of benefit payments in current-payment status, i.e., actually being made at a specified time with no deductions or with deductions amounting to less than a month's benefit. [2] 62 years and over. [3] Disabled workers under age 65. [4] Includes wife beneficiaries with entitled children in their care and entitled divorced wives. [5] 18 years old and over. Disability began before age 18. [6] Full-time students aged 18 and 19. [7] Includes surviving divorced mothers with entitled children in their care and widowed fathers with entitled children in their care. [8] Includes widows aged 60–61, surviving divorced wives aged 60 and over, disabled widows and widowers aged 50 and over; and widowers aged 60–61. [9] Benefits for persons aged 72 and over not insured under regular or transitional provisions of Social Security Act. [10] Constant dollar figures are based on the consumer price index (CPI-U) for December as published by the U.S. Bureau of Labor Statistics. [11] Represents total disbursements of benefit checks by the U.S. Department of the Treasury during the years specified. [12] Distribution by type estimated.

Source: U.S. Social Security Administration, *Annual Statistical Supplement* to the *Social Security Bulletin;* and unpublished data.

Social Insurance and Human Services 351

Table 534. **Social Security—Beneficiaries, Annual Payments, and Average Monthly Benefit, 1990 to 2005, and by State and Other Areas, 2005**

[Number of beneficiaries in current-payment status (**39,832 represents 39,832,000**) and average monthly benefit as of **December**. Data based on 10-percent sample of administrative records. See also headnote, Table 533, and Appendix III]

Year, state, and other area	Number of beneficiaries (1,000)				Annual payments[2] (mil. dol.)				Average monthly benefit (dol.)		
	Total	Retired workers and dependents[1]	Survivors	Disabled workers and dependents	Total	Retired workers and dependents[1]	Survivors	Disabled workers and dependents	Retired workers[3]	Disabled workers	Widows and widowers[4]
1990	39,832	28,369	7,197	4,266	247,796	172,042	50,951	24,803	603	587	557
1995	43,380	30,139	7,379	5,862	332,581	224,381	67,302	40,898	720	682	680
2000	45,417	31,761	6,981	6,675	407,431	274,645	77,848	54,938	845	787	810
2003	46,448	32,360	6,870	7,220	470,546	314,024	85,621	70,899	922	862	888
2004	47,707	33,025	6,730	7,952	493,078	327,139	87,737	78,202	955	894	920
2005, total[5]	48,446	33,488	6,650	8,307	520,561	345,094	90,073	85,394	1,002	938	967
United States	47,255	32,727	6,431	8,097	512,221	340,499	88,098	83,623	(NA)	(NA)	(NA)
Alabama	904	546	140	218	9,259	5,370	1,741	2,149	960	907	897
Alaska	65	42	10	13	659	415	120	124	962	912	913
Arizona	919	654	110	155	10,030	6,887	1,505	1,638	1,023	970	1,002
Arkansas	558	346	80	132	5,564	3,332	961	1,271	935	887	868
California	4,460	3,193	571	697	48,106	32,751	7,946	7,409	1,003	955	995
Colorado	588	419	77	92	6,227	4,206	1,065	955	982	934	977
Connecticut	585	435	68	82	6,917	4,994	1,029	894	1,096	981	1,072
Delaware	152	108	19	26	1,725	1,173	268	284	1,054	984	1,040
District of Columbia . . .	71	49	11	11	674	446	116	112	862	857	806
Florida	3,424	2,526	401	497	36,891	26,145	5,567	5,178	999	943	993
Georgia	1,231	799	182	250	12,846	8,048	2,261	2,537	978	924	913
Hawaii	203	157	23	23	2,162	1,607	302	253	990	964	945
Idaho	228	162	28	37	2,379	1,618	388	373	980	913	985
Illinois	1,898	1,347	271	281	21,364	14,497	3,899	2,967	1,040	966	1,031
Indiana	1,055	728	145	182	11,872	7,937	2,083	1,852	1,053	938	1,030
Iowa	548	397	76	75	5,946	4,102	1,087	757	1,000	896	992
Kansas	451	320	61	70	4,974	3,406	879	690	1,027	909	1,025
Kentucky	799	468	123	207	8,129	4,509	1,547	2,073	949	924	881
Louisiana	716	429	140	146	7,378	4,109	1,782	1,488	937	937	891
Maine	269	178	33	59	2,686	1,702	435	549	926	863	924
Maryland	772	549	110	113	8,512	5,766	1,516	1,231	1,012	967	986
Massachusetts	1,072	748	128	196	11,691	7,865	1,829	1,997	1,009	924	1,001
Michigan	1,743	1,189	247	306	20,106	13,193	3,599	3,315	1,080	994	1,043
Minnesota	786	575	100	112	8,525	5,959	1,425	1,140	1,004	922	988
Mississippi	552	322	88	142	5,395	3,052	998	1,344	920	880	838
Missouri	1,064	712	144	207	11,281	7,289	1,929	2,063	990	913	968
Montana	169	122	23	25	1,748	1,193	305	250	959	903	955
Nebraska	294	212	39	43	3,120	2,153	549	418	985	889	994
Nevada	348	254	38	55	3,830	2,666	538	626	1,008	1,008	1,012
New Hampshire	226	157	26	42	2,485	1,686	369	430	1,028	943	1,023
New Jersey	1,379	1,012	169	197	16,474	11,675	2,565	2,234	1,105	1,023	1,065
New Mexico	311	209	44	58	3,079	1,983	526	570	935	902	895
New York	3,064	2,170	378	516	34,797	23,800	5,427	5,570	1,059	989	1,020
North Carolina	1,511	1,006	192	313	15,856	10,269	2,400	3,187	984	921	907
North Dakota	115	82	19	14	1,174	780	257	137	935	873	927
Ohio	1,965	1,352	308	305	21,546	14,077	4,377	3,091	1,016	914	1,000
Oklahoma	635	427	94	114	6,606	4,226	1,227	1,152	962	924	939
Oregon	625	455	76	94	6,837	4,741	1,095	1,001	1,011	939	1,017
Pennsylvania	2,425	1,708	341	375	27,012	18,227	4,953	3,892	1,030	954	1,014
Rhode Island	192	134	21	36	2,089	1,418	302	368	1,006	913	1,013
South Carolina	774	505	104	164	8,100	5,139	1,283	1,677	982	932	904
South Dakota	142	103	21	19	1,415	966	269	180	920	877	916
Tennessee	1,098	708	159	231	11,406	7,109	2,010	2,288	978	904	923
Texas	2,955	1,990	475	490	30,684	19,643	6,178	4,864	975	924	940
Utah	272	198	36	39	2,913	2,037	495	380	1,009	928	1,033
Vermont	112	78	14	20	1,184	802	184	198	995	889	964
Virginia	1,139	772	155	212	12,115	7,883	2,045	2,187	989	945	930
Washington	937	674	113	150	10,474	7,218	1,646	1,611	1,042	952	1,032
West Virginia	413	239	70	104	4,417	2,377	932	1,108	988	981	927
Wisconsin	952	694	120	138	10,551	7,395	1,733	1,423	1,028	939	1,020
Wyoming	84	61	11	13	908	629	149	130	999	936	1,009
Puerto Rico	713	405	119	189	5,234	2,641	1,010	1,583	669	806	594
Guam	13	9	2	2	93	56	22	15	672	809	687
American Samoa . . .	6	2	2	2	38	12	12	14	584	701	576
Virgin Islands	16	12	2	2	145	104	23	19	866	945	752
Northern Mariana Islands	2	1	1	(Z)	13	7	5	1	563	441	391
Abroad	442	332	94	16	2,817	1,775	903	139	565	819	627

NA Not available.   Z Less than 500. [1] Includes special benefits for persons aged 72 and over not insured under regular or transitional provisions of Social Security Act.   [2] Unnegotiated checks not deducted. 1990 and 1995 include lump-sum payments to survivors of deceased workers.   [3] Excludes persons with special benefits.   [4] Nondisabled only.   [5] Includes those with state or area unknown.

Source: U.S. Social Security Administration, *Annual Statistical Supplement to the Social Security Bulletin.*

Table 535. Public Employee Retirement Systems—Participants and Finances: 1980 to 2004

[For fiscal year of retirement system, except data for the Thrift Savings Plan are for calendar year (4,629 represents 4,629,000)]

Retirement plan	Unit	1980	1990	1995	1999	2000	2001	2002	2003, proj.	2004, proj.
TOTAL PARTICIPANTS [1]										
Federal retirement systems:										
Defined benefit:										
Civil Service Retirement System	1,000	4,629	4,167	3,731	3,362	3,256	(NA)	3,201	(NA)	(NA)
Federal Employees Retirement System [2]	1,000	(X)	1,180	1,512	1,879	1,935	(NA)	2,019	(NA)	(NA)
Military Service Retirement System [3]	1,000	3,380	3,763	3,387	3,374	3,397	3,418	3,453	3,457	(NA)
Thrift Savings Plan [4]	1,000	(X)	1,625	2,195	2,400	2,500	2,600	3,000	3,200	(NA)
State and local retirement systems [5],[6]	1,000	(NA)	16,858	14,734	16,195	16,834	17,021	17,264	17,650	17,891
ACTIVE PARTICIPANTS										
Federal retirement systems:										
Defined benefit:										
Civil Service Retirement System	1,000	2,700	1,826	1,525	1,042	978	(NA)	906	(NA)	(NA)
Federal Employees Retirement System [2]	1,000	(X)	1,136	1,318	1,640	1,668	(NA)	1,717	(NA)	(NA)
Military Service Retirement System [3]	1,000	2,050	2,130	1,572	1,438	1,437	1,438	1,465	1,468	(NA)
Thrift Savings Plan [4]	1,000	(X)	1,419	1,930	1,900	1,900	1,900	2,300	2,400	(NA)
State and local retirement systems [5],[6]	1,000	(NA)	11,345	12,524	13,472	13,917	13,977	14,123	14,249	14,181
ASSETS										
Total	Bil. dol.	258	1,047	1,655	2,644	2,943	2,803	3,013	3,086	3,498
Federal retirement systems	Bil. dol.	73	326	537	738	774	645	855	914	1,003
Defined benefit	Bil. dol.	73	318	502	643	679	544	753	785	815
Civil Service Retirement System	Bil. dol.	73	220	311	376	390	414	416	428	435
Federal Employees Retirement System [2]	Bil. dol.	(X)	18	60	111	126	157	161	174	192
Military Service Retirement System [3]	Bil. dol.	([7])	80	131	156	163	174	177	183	188
Thrift Savings Plan [4]	Bil. dol.	(X)	8	35	95	98	102	102	129	152
State and local retirement systems [5]	Bil. dol.	185	721	1,118	1,906	2,169	2,158	2,158	2,172	2,495
CONTRIBUTIONS										
Total	Bil. dol.	83	103	127	142	143	145	151	164	184
Federal retirement systems	Bil. dol.	19	61	67	75	78	80	85	89	92
Defined benefit	Bil. dol.	19	59	61	67	69	70	73	75	76
Civil Service Retirement System	Bil. dol.	19	28	31	33	33	33	34	33	33
Federal Employees Retirement System [2]	Bil. dol.	(X)	4	6	8	8	9	9	10	11
Military Service Retirement System [3]	Bil. dol.	([7])	27	24	26	28	28	30	32	32
Thrift Savings Plan [4]	Bil. dol.	(X)	2	6	8	9	10	12	14	16
State and local retirement systems [5]	Bil. dol.	64	42	60	67	65	65	66	75	92
BENEFITS										
Total	Bil. dol.	39	89	125	160	172	185	196	213	228
Federal retirement systems	Bil. dol.	27	53	66	78	81	84	86	91	95
Defined benefit	Bil. dol.	27	53	65	76	78	81	84	88	91
Civil Service Retirement System	Bil. dol.	15	31	37	43	44	46	48	50	52
Federal Employees Retirement System [2]	Bil. dol.	(X)	(Z)	1	1	1	1	1	2	2
Military Service Retirement System [3]	Bil. dol.	12	22	28	32	33	34	35	36	37
Thrift Savings Plan [4]	Bil. dol.	(X)	(Z)	1	2	3	3	2	3	4
State and local retirement systems [5]	Bil. dol.	12	36	59	82	91	101	110	122	133

NA Not available.   X Not applicable.   Z Less than $500 million.   [1] Includes active, separated vested, retired employees, and survivors.   [2] The Federal Employees Retirement System was established June 6, 1986.   [3] Includes nondisability and disability retirees, surviving families, and all active personnel with the exception of active reserves.   [4] The Thrift Savings Plan (a defined contribution plan) was established April 1, 1987.   [5] Excludes state and local plans that are fully supported by employee contributions.   [6] Not adjusted for double counting of individuals participating in more than one plan.   [7] The Military Retirement System was unfunded until October 1, 1984.

Source: Employee Benefit Research Institute, Washington, DC, *EBRI Databook on Employee Benefits, Twelfth Edition*, and unpublished data (copyright). See also <http://www.ebri.org/>.

Table 536. Federal Civil Service Retirement: 1980 to 2004

[As of September 30 or for year ending September 30 (2,720 represents 2,720,000). Covers both Civil Service Retirement System and Federal Employees Retirement System]

Item	Unit	1980	1990	1995	1999	2000	2001	2002	2003	2004
Employees covered [1]	1,000.	2,720	2,945	2,668	2,668	2,764	2,655	2,654	2,662	2,670
Annuitants, total	1,000.	1,675	2,143	2,311	2,368	2,376	2,383	2,383	2,389	2,404
Age and service	1,000.	905	1,288	1,441	1,491	1,501	1,509	1,513	1,523	1,544
Disability	1,000.	343	297	263	246	242	239	236	234	231
Survivors	1,000.	427	558	607	631	633	635	634	632	629
Receipts, total [2]	Mil. dol.	24,389	52,689	65,684	74,522	75,967	77,949	80,069	78,366	82,414
Employee contributions	Mil. dol.	3,686	4,501	4,498	4,381	4,637	4,593	4,475	4,522	4,482
Federal government contributions	Mil. dol.	15,562	27,368	33,130	36,561	37,722	38,442	39,692	36,583	42,290
Disbursements, total [3]	Mil. dol.	14,977	31,416	38,435	43,932	45,194	47,356	48,970	50,368	52,277
Age and service annuitants [4]	Mil. dol.	12,639	26,495	32,070	36,492	37,546	39,397	40,758	42,018	43,727
Survivors	Mil. dol.	1,912	4,366	5,864	6,978	7,210	7,533	7,790	7,951	8,127
Average monthly benefit:										
Age and service	Dollars	992	1,369	1,643	1,830	1,885	1,967	2,031	2,085	2,154
Disability	Dollars	723	1,008	1,164	1,221	1,240	1,269	1,286	1,291	1,305
Survivors	Dollars	392	653	819	923	952	992	1,024	1,044	1,073
Cash and security holdings	Bil. dol.	73.7	238.0	366.2	481.3	508.1	542.6	573.7	601.7	631.8

[1] Excludes employees in leave-without-pay status.   [2] Includes interest on investments.   [3] Includes refunds, death claims, and administration.   [4] Includes disability annuitants.

Source: U.S. Office of Personnel Management, *Civil Service Retirement and Disability Trust Fund Annual Report*.

Social Insurance and Human Services   353

Table 537. State and Local Government Retirement Systems—Beneficiaries and Finances: 1990 to 2004

[In billions of dollars, except as indicated (111.3 represents 111,300,000,000). For fiscal years closed during the 12 months ending June 30]

Year and level of government	Number of benefi- ciaries (1,000)	Receipts					Benefits and withdrawals			Cash and security holdings
		Total	Employee contribu- tions	Government contributions		Earn- ings on invest- ments	Total	Ben- efits	With- drawals	
				State	Local					
1990: All systems	4,026	111.3	13.9	14.0	18.6	64.9	38.4	36.0	2.4	721
State-administered	3,232	89.2	11.6	14.0	11.5	52.0	29.6	27.6	2.0	575
Locally administered	794	22.2	2.2	(Z)	7.0	12.9	8.8	8.4	0.4	145
1995: All systems	4,979	148.8	18.6	16.6	24.4	89.2	61.5	58.8	2.7	1,118
State-administered	4,025	123.3	15.7	16.2	15.4	76.0	48.0	45.8	2.2	914
Locally administered	954	25.5	2.9	0.4	9.0	13.3	13.5	13.0	0.5	204
2000: All systems	6,292	297.0	25.0	17.5	22.6	231.9	95.7	91.3	4.4	2,169
State-administered	4,786	247.4	20.7	17.2	16.7	192.8	76.0	72.2	3.8	1,798
Locally administered	1,506	49.7	4.3	0.4	5.9	39.1	19.8	19.1	0.7	371
2003: All systems	6,448	147.7	28.8	19.5	26.6	72.6	134.8	122.3	4.8	2,172
State-administered	5,420	130.0	24.4	19.1	18.2	68.1	109.0	98.8	4.2	1,802
Locally administered	1,027	17.7	4.4	(Z)	8.4	4.5	25.8	23.5	0.1	369
2004: All systems	6,703	407.3	30.7	31.1	29.8	315.5	145.4	133.1	4.4	2,495
State-administered	5,631	339.6	26.3	30.7	18.5	264.1	117.6	107.7	3.6	2,078
Locally administered	1,072	67.7	4.4	(Z)	11.3	51.4	27.8	25.4	0.8	417

Z Less than $50 million.

Source: U.S. Census Bureau, through 1995, *Finances of Employee-Retirement Systems of State and Local Governments*, Series GF, No. 2, annual; beginning 2000, Federal, State, and Local Governments, State and Local Government Public Employee Retirement Systems"; <http://www.census.gov/govs/www/retire.html>.

Table 538. Private Pension Plans—Summary by Type of Plan: 1990 to 2001

[712.3 represents 712,300. "Pension plan" is defined by the Employee Retirement Income Security Act (ERISA) as "any plan, fund, or program which was heretofore or is hereafter established or maintained by an employer or an employee organization, or by both, to the extent that such plan (a) provides retirement income to employees, or (b) results in a deferral of income by employees for periods extending to the termination of covered employment or beyond, regardless of the method of calculating the contributions made to the plan, the method of calculating the benefits under the plan, or the method of distributing benefits from the plan." A defined benefit plan provides a definite benefit formula for calculating benefit amounts—such as a flat amount per year of service or a percentage of salary times years of service. A defined contribution plan is a pension plan in which the contributions are made to an individual account for each employee. The retirement benefit is dependent upon the account balance at retirement. The balance depends upon amounts contributed, investment experience, and, in the case of profit sharing plans, amounts which may be allocated to the account due to forfeitures by terminating employees. Employee Stock Ownership Plans (ESOP) and 401(k) plans are included among defined contribution plans. Data are based on Form 5500 series reports filed with the Department of Labor]

Item	Unit	Total				Defined contribution plan				Defined benefit plan			
		1990	1995	2000	2001	1990	1995	2000	2001	1990	1995	2000	2001
Number of plans [1]	1,000	712.3	693.4	736.0	733.5	599.2	623.9	686.9	686.6	113.1	69.5	48.7	46.9
Total participants [2,3]	Million	76.9	87.5	103.3	106.6	38.1	47.7	61.7	64.5	38.8	39.7	41.6	42.1
Active participants [2,4]	Million	61.8	66.2	73.1	74.4	35.5	42.7	50.9	52.3	26.3	23.5	22.2	22.1
Assets [5]	Bil. dol	1,674	2,724	4,203	3,941	712	1,322	2,216	2,116	962	1,402	1,986	1,825
Contributions [6]	Bil. dol	98.8	158.8	231.9	253.8	75.8	117.4	198.5	204.0	23.0	41.4	33.4	49.7
Benefits [7]	Bil. dol	129.4	183.0	341.0	311.6	63.0	97.9	213.5	182.2	66.4	85.1	127.5	129.4

[1] Excludes all plans covering only one participant. [2] Includes double counting of workers in more than one plan. [3] Total participants include active participants, vested separated workers, and retirees. [4] Any workers currently in employment covered by a plan and who are earning or retaining credited service under a plan. Includes any nonvested former employees who have not yet incurred breaks in service. [5] Asset amounts shown exclude funds held by life insurance companies under allocated group insurance contracts for payment of retirement benefits. These excluded funds make up roughly 10 to 15 percent of total private fund assets. [6] Includes both employer and employee contributions. [7] Benefits paid directly from trust and premium payments made from plan to insurance carriers. Excludes benefits paid directly by insurance carriers.

Source: U.S. Department of Labor, Employee Benefits Security Administration, *Private Pension Plan Bulletin* (Plan Year 2001, Preliminary), Spring 2006.

Table 539. Percent of Workers Participating In Retirement Benefits by Worker Characteristics: 2005

[Based on National Compensation Survey, a sample survey of 4,703 private industry establishments of all sizes, representing over 102.3 million workers; see Appendix III. Survey covers all 50 States and the District of Columbia. See also Table 637]

Characteristic	Total [1]	Defined benefit	Defined contri- bution	Characteristic	Total [1]	Defined benefit	Defined contri- bution
Total	50	21	42	Full time	60	25	50
White-collar occupations	61	24	53	Part time	19	9	14
Blue-collar occupations	51	26	38	Union	85	72	43
Service occupations	22	7	18	Nonunion	46	15	41

[1] Total is less than the sum of the individual retirement items because many employees participated in both types of plans.

Source: U.S. Bureau of Labor Statistics, *Employee Benefits in Private Industry in the United States, March 2005*, Summary 05-01, August 2005. See also <http://www.bls.gov/ncs/ebs/sp/ebsm0003.pdf>.

Table. 540. Defined Benefit Retirement Plans—Selected Features: 2003

[In percent. Covers full-time employees in private industry. Based on National Compensation Survey, a sample survey of 1,436 private industry establishments of all sizes, representing over 107 million workers; see Appendix III. See also Table 637]

Feature	All workers	White collar	Blue collar	Service	Goods pro-ducing	Service pro-ducing	1–99 workers	100 workers or more	Union	Non-union
Plan provisions:										
Benefits based on earnings	52	58	43	57	46	55	32	59	37	60
Early retirement benefits available . . .	84	78	91	95	93	80	76	86	93	79
Availability of lump sum benefits at retirement	48	59	31	43	29	57	48	48	31	57
Benefit formula:										
Percent of terminal earnings	43	47	35	49	40	44	27	48	25	52
Percent of career earnings	10	11	8	8	6	11	6	11	12	9
Dollar amount formula	17	8	30	19	33	9	25	14	34	8
Percent of contribution formula	8	2	16	11	12	6	15	5	21	1
Cash balance	21	30	9	12	8	28	24	20	8	29
Pension equity	2	2	2	1	1	2	3	2	(Z)	3
Requirements for normal retirement [1]:										
No age requirement	6	9	3	1	2	8	10	5	4	7
Less than 30 years of service	5	8	1	1	1	7	8	4	(Z)	7
30 years of service	1	1	2	-	1	2	2	1	4	(Z)
At age 55	1	1	1	2	1	1	1	1	1	1
At age 60	7	7	5	7	3	8	5	7	9	5
At age 62	9	6	13	20	11	8	23	5	15	6
At age 65	73	76	68	71	75	71	61	77	59	80
Sum of age plus service [2]	5	4	8	(S)	9	4	(S)	7	8	4

S Represents no employees in this category or data do not meet publication criteria.   Z Less than 0.5 percent.   [1] Normal retirement is defined as the point at which the participant could retire and immediately receive all accrued benefits by virtue of service and earnings, without reduction due to age. If a plan had alternative age and service requirements, the earliest age and associated service were tabulated; if one alternative did not specify an age, it was the requirement tabulated. Some age and service requirements are not shown separately.   [2] In some plans, participants must also satisfy a minimum age or service requirement.

Source: U.S. Bureau of Labor Statistics, *National Compensation Survey: Employee Benefits in Private Industry in the United States, 2003*, Bulletin 2577. See also <http://bls.gov/ncs/ebs/sp/ebbl0021.pdf>.

Table 541. Pension Plan Coverage of Workers by Selected Characteristics: 2002

[63,767 represents 63,767,000. Covers workers as of March 2003 who had earnings in 2002. Based on Current Population Survey; see text, Section 1, Population and Appendix III]

Sex and age	Number with coverage (1,000)				Percent of total workers			
	Total [1]	White [2]	Black [2]	Hispanic [3]	Total [1]	White [2]	Black [2]	Hispanic [3]
Total	**63,767**	**53,514**	**6,648**	**4,803**	**41.9**	**42.5**	**40.0**	**25.6**
Male	34,602	29,637	3,046	2,757	43.0	43.7	40.0	43.7
Under 65 years old	33,808	28,942	2,999	2,726	43.7	44.6	40.4	24.9
15 to 24 years old	1,630	1,363	190	224	13.2	13.2	15.0	10.1
25 to 44 years old	17,251	14,593	1,589	1,643	45.6	46.7	41.3	25.2
45 to 64 years old	14,926	12,986	1,220	859	55.0	55.6	52.9	38.3
65 years old and over	794	694	46	32	24.9	24.4	24.2	17.6
Female	29,165	23,878	3,602	2,046	40.8	41.2	40.0	26.9
Under 65 years old	28,508	23,312	3,548	2,019	41.3	41.8	40.3	26.9
15 to 24 years old	1,377	1,115	184	149	12.1	12.0	13.2	10.3
25 to 44 years old	14,282	11,414	1,930	1,241	43.7	44.3	41.6	29.2
45 to 64 years old	12,850	10,783	1,433	629	51.7	52.0	51.9	35.1
65 years old and over	656	565	55	27	26.2	25.6	27.9	25.2

[1] Includes other races, not shown separately.   [2] Beginning with the 2003 CPS, respondents could choose one or more races. For example, White refers to people who reported White and did not report any other race category; Black refers to people who reported Black and did not report any other race category. The use of this single-race population does not imply that it is the preferred method of presenting or analyzing data. The Census Bureau uses a variety of approaches. Information on people who reported more than one race, such as "White and American Indian and Alaska Native" or "Asian and Black or African American," is available from Census 2000 through American FactFinder®. About 2.6 percent of people reported more than one race in Census 2000.   [3] Hispanic persons may be of any race.

Source: U.S. Census Bureau, Table NC8, Pension Plan Coverage of Workers by Selected Characteristics, Gender, Race and Hispanic Origin, and Poverty Status: 2002"; published May 2004; <http://pubdb3.census.gov/macro/032003/noncash/toc.htm>.

Table 542. U.S. Households Owning IRAs: 2002 to 2005

[**43.2 represents 43,200,000.** Incidence of IRA ownership is based on an annual tracking survey of 3,000 randomly selected, representative U.S. households; see source for details]

Type of IRA	Number (mil.) [1]				Percent of U.S. households			
	2002	2003	2004	2005	2002	2003	2004	2005
Any type of IRA [2]	43.2	46.1	45.2	46.8	39.5	41.4	40.4	41.4
Traditional IRA...................	35.7	37.1	36.7	37.6	32.7	33.3	32.8	33.2
Roth IRA........................	13.2	16.2	14.3	16.1	12.1	14.6	12.8	14.2
SIMPLE IRA, SEP-IRA, or SAR-SEP IRA ...	8.5	8.3	9.6	8.8	7.8	7.5	8.6	7.8

[1] The number of U.S. households owning IRAs in 2002 through 2005 is based on the following U.S. Census Bureau's total U.S. household estimates: 109.3 million in 2002, 111.3 million in 2003, 112.0 million in 2004, and 116.5 million in 2005 (U.S. Bureau of the Census, Current Population Reports, P60-226, August 2004). [2] Excludes ownership of Coverdell Education Savings Accounts, which were referred to as Education IRAs before July 2001.

Source: Investment Company Institute, Washington, DC, *Fundamentals, Investment Company Institute Research in Brief*, "IRA Ownership in 2005"; Vol 15, No. 1A, January 2006 (copyright). See also <http://www.ici.org/statements/fundamentals/fm-v15n1_appendix.pdf>.

Table 543. 401(k) Plans—Selected Features: 2003

[**In percent.** Covers full-time employees in private industry. Based on National Compensation Survey, a sample survey of private industry establishments of all sizes, representing millions of workers; see Appendix III. See also Table 637]

Feature	All employees	White Collar	Blue Collar	Service
MAXIMUM PRETAX EMPLOYEE CONTRIBUTIONS [1]				
Percent of employee earnings	59	57	63	66
Specified dollar amount........................	1	1	1	(Z)
Up to the Internal Revenue code limit	39	41	37	31
Average maximum pretax contribution [2]	17.2	17.2	17.4	16.9
INVESTMENT CHOICES				
Employee permitted to choose investments............	86	88	81	80
Employee not permitted to choose investments	2	2	2	4

Z Less than 0.5 percent. [1] Includes contributions that are not matched by the employer. If maximum contributions vary, such as by length of service, the highest possible contribution was tabulated. [2] The average is presented for all covered workers; averages exclude workers without the plan provision.

Source: U.S. Bureau of Labor Statistics, National Compensation Survey: Employee Benefits in Private Industry in the United States, 2003, Bulletin 2577. See also <http://stats.bls.gov/ncs/home.htm>.

Table 544. State Unemployment Insurance—Summary: 1990 to 2005

[**2,522 represents 2,522,000.** Includes unemployment compensation for state and local government employees where covered by state law]

Item	Unit	1990	1995	1998	1999	2000	2001	2002	2003	2004	2005
Insured unemployment, avg. weekly	1,000 ...	2,522	2,572	2,222	2,188	2,110	2,974	3,585	3,531	2,950	2,662
Percent of covered employment [1]	Percent ..	2.4	2.3	1.9	1.8	1.7	2.3	2.8	2.8	2.3	2.1
Percent of civilian unemployed	Percent ..	35.8	34.7	35.8	38.0	37.6	44.2	43.2	40.7	36.8	35.7
Unemployment benefits, avg. weekly	Dollars ..	161	187	200	212	221	238	257	262	263	267
Percent of weekly wage	Percent ..	36.0	35.5	32.9	33.1	32.9	34.6	36.8	36.5	35.2	35.5
Weeks compensated	Million ...	116.2	118.3	101.4	100.6	96.0	136.3	166.3	163.2	135.1	121.1
Beneficiaries, first payments [2] ...	1,000 ...	8,629	8,035	7,332	6,951	7,033	9,877	10,088	9,935	8,369	7,922
Average duration of benefits [2] ..	Weeks...	13.4	14.7	13.8	14.5	13.7	13.8	16.5	16.4	16.1	15.3
Claimants exhausting benefits...	1,000 ...	2,323	2,662	2,266	2,300	2,144	2,827	4,416	4,417	3,532	2,856
Percent of first payment [3] ...	Percent ..	29.4	34.3	31.8	31.4	31.8	34.1	42.5	43.4	39.0	35.9
Contributions collected [4]	Bil. dol. .	15.2	22.0	19.8	19.2	19.9	19.7	19.7	25.3	31.2	34.8
Benefits paid	Bil. dol. .	18.1	21.2	19.4	20.3	20.5	31.6	42.0	41.4	34.4	31.2
Funds available for benefits [5] ...	Bil. dol. .	37.9	35.4	48.0	50.3	53.4	45.6	35.2	23.4	23.0	28.6
Average employer contribution rate [6]	Percent ..	1.95	2.44	1.92	1.77	1.75	1.71	1.80	2.20	2.68	2.92

NA Not available. [1] Insured unemployment as percent of average covered employment in preceding year. [2] Weeks compensated divided by first payment. [3] Based on first payments for 12-month period ending June 30. [4] Contributions from employers; also employees in states which tax workers. [5] End of year. Sum of balances in state clearing accounts, benefit-payment accounts, and state accounts in federal unemployment trust funds. [6] As percent of taxable wages.

Source: U.S. Employment and Training Administration, *Unemployment Insurance Financial Data Handbook*.

Table 545. State Unemployment Insurance by State and Other Area: 2005

[7,922 represents 7,922,000. See headnote, Table 544. For state data on insured unemployment, see Table 615]

State or other area	Beneficiaries, first payments (1,000)	Benefits paid (mil. dol.)	Avg. weekly unemploy-ment benefits (dol.)	State or other area	Beneficiaries, first payments (1,000)	Benefits paid (mil. dol.)	Avg. weekly unemploy-ment benefits (dol.)
Total	7,922	31,234	267	MT	21	63	221
AL	107	215	182	NE	39	117	225
AK	44	117	194	NV	59	223	258
AZ	76	243	195	NH	24	75	252
AR	79	227	230	NJ	315	1,822	336
CA	975	4,618	277	NM	29	114	218
CO	74	310	302	NY	488	2,452	276
CT	122	558	295	NC	250	694	258
DE	24	100	247	ND	13	40	238
DC	17	87	267	OH	286	1,108	261
FL	244	886	226	OK	47	154	221
GA	194	524	245	OR	133	528	261
HI.	20	89	337	PA	461	2,038	292
ID.	44	120	235	RI.	38	201	336
IL.	352	1,800	285	SC	116	335	217
IN.	186	666	278	SD	9	27	211
IA.	92	293	271	TN	154	436	212
KS	61	245	278	TX	357	1,241	261
KY	111	377	260	UT	36	117	263
LA	303	706	192	VT	23	79	267
ME	32	112	240	VA	110	339	246
MD.	99	396	257	WA	184	756	297
MA	218	1,297	357	WV	41	141	225
MI	450	1,820	290	WI	263	790	253
MN	144	635	322	WY.	12	35	242
MS	103	212	186	PR	106	206	108
MO.	137	444	206	VI.	2	6	237

Source: U.S. Employment and Training Administration, *Unemployment Insurance Financial Data Handbook.*

Table 546. Persons With Work Disability by Selected Characteristics: 2004

[In thousands, except percent (19,016 represents 19,016,000). As of March. Covers civilian noninstitutional population and members of Armed Forces living off post or with their families on post. Persons are classified as having a work disability if they (1) have a health problem or disability which prevents them from working or which limits the kind or amount of work they can do; (2) have a service-connected disability or ever retired or left a job for health reasons; (3) did not work in survey reference week or previous year because of long-term illness or disability; or (4) are under age 65, and are covered by medicare or receive supplemental security income. Based on Current Population Survey; see text, Section 1, Population, and Appendix III]

Age and participation status in assistance programs	Total [1]	Male	Female	White [2]	Black [3]	Hispanic [4]
Persons with work disability	**19,016**	**9,381**	**9,634**	**14,354**	**3,625**	**1,961**
16 to 24 years old.	1,504	812	692	1,045	374	178
25 to 34 years old.	2,331	1,138	1,193	1,642	527	304
35 to 44 years old.	3,741	1,892	1,849	2,801	721	434
45 to 54 years old.	5,320	2,642	2,678	4,001	1,064	550
55 to 64 years old.	6,120	2,898	3,222	4,866	938	495
Percent work disabled of total population.						
16 to 24 years old.	4.1	4.4	3.8	3.7	7.2	2.9
25 to 34 years old.	6.0	5.9	6.1	5.4	10.6	4.1
35 to 44 years old.	8.7	8.9	8.4	8.0	13.5	7.3
45 to 54 years old.	13.0	13.2	12.8	11.8	22.6	14.0
55 to 64 years old.	21.6	21.4	21.7	20.2	33.8	22.9
Percent work disabled—						
Receiving social security income	33.7	34.4	33.0	34.4	32.8	26.0
Receiving food stamps	18.7	15.8	21.6	15.8	30.2	25.8
Covered by medicaid.	65.3	67.6	63.1	68.6	52.3	56.5
Residing in public housing	6.6	5.8	7.5	4.8	13.7	9.1
Residing in subsidized housing	3.7	3.0	4.5	2.9	6.7	5.8

[1] Includes other races not shown separately. [2] The 2003 Current Population Survey asked respondents to choose one or more races. White alone refers to people who reported White and did not report any other race category. The use of this single-race population does not imply that it is the preferred method of presenting or analyzing data. The Census Bureau uses a variety of approaches. Information on people who reported more than one race, such as "White and American Indian and Alaska Native" or "Asian and Black or African American," is available from Census 2001 through American FactFinder®. About 2.6 percent of people reported more than one race in 2000. [3] Black alone refers to people who reported Black and did not report any other race category. [4] Hispanic persons may be of any race.

Source: U.S. Census Bureau, unpublished data.

Social Insurance and Human Services   357

Table 547. Workers' Compensation Payments: 1990 to 2003

[In billions of dollars, except as indicated (53.1 represents $53,100,000,000). See headnote, Table 548]

Item	1990	1995	1996	1997	1998	1999	2000	2001	2002	2003
Workers covered (mil.)	106	113	115	118	122	124	127	127	126	125
Premium amounts paid [1]	**53.1**	**57.1**	**55.3**	**53.5**	**53.4**	**55.4**	**59.5**	**65.4**	**73.7**	**81.6**
Private carriers [1]	35.1	31.6	30.5	29.9	30.4	32.6	35.0	37.1	41.7	45.5
State funds . . . . [2]	8.0	10.5	10.2	8.0	8.0	7.6	8.9	11.4	14.5	17.4
Federal programs [2]	2.2	2.6	2.6	3.4	3.5	3.5	3.6	3.8	3.9	4.0
Self-insurers	7.9	12.5	12.1	12.3	11.7	11.7	11.9	13.1	13.6	14.7
Annual benefits paid [1]	**38.2**	**43.5**	**41.8**	**42.4**	**43.9**	**45.6**	**46.9**	**49.5**	**53.2**	**54.9**
By private carriers [1]	22.2	21.4	20.4	21.6	23.0	25.7	26.2	27.1	28.9	28.7
From state funds [3]	8.8	10.9	7.6	7.3	7.2	6.9	7.3	7.9	9.2	10.4
Employers' self-insurance [4]	7.2	11.2	10.8	10.6	10.2	10.1	10.5	11.4	11.9	12.6
Type of benefit:										
Medical/hospitalization	15.1	16.6	16.5	17.2	17.9	19.1	20.4	22.1	24.3	25.6
Compensation payments	21.7	25.7	24.2	24.3	24.5	23.3	24.2	25.1	26.5	26.9
Percent of covered payroll: [1]										
Workers' compensation costs [5, 6] . . .	2.18	1.82	1.66	1.49	1.38	1.33	1.32	1.42	1.59	1.72
Benefits [6]	1.57	1.38	1.26	1.18	1.11	1.10	1.04	1.07	1.15	1.16

[1] Premium and benefit amounts include estimated payments under insurance policy deductible provisions. Deductible benefits are allocated to private carriers and state funds.   [2] Years 1990–1996 include federal employer compensation program and that portion of federal black lung benefits program financed from employer contributions. Years 1997–2002 include federal employer compensation program only due to changes in reporting methods.   [3] Net cash and medical benefits paid by competitive and exclusive state funds and by federal workers' compensation programs.   [4] Cash and medical benefits paid by self-insurers, plus value of medical benefits paid by employers carrying workers' compensation policies that exclude standard medical coverage.   [5] Premiums written by private carriers and state funds, and benefits paid by self-insurers increased by 5–10 prior to 1992 and by 11 percent for 1992–2002 for administrative costs. Also includes benefits paid and administrative costs of federal system for government employees.   [6] Excludes programs financed from general revenue—black lung benefits and supplemental pensions in some states.

Source: National Academy of Social Insurance, Washington, DC, *Workers' Compensation: Benefits, Coverage, and Costs,* annual.

Table 548. Workers' Compensation Payments by State: 1999 to 2003

[In millions of dollars (44,563 represents $44,563,000,000). Calendar-year data. Payments represent compensation and medical benefits and include insurance losses paid by private insurance carriers (compiled from state workers' compensation agencies and A.M. Best Co.); disbursements of state funds (compiled from the A.M. Best Co. and state workers' compensation agencies); and self-insurance payments (compiled from state workers' compensation agencies and authors' estimates)]

State	1999	2000	2001	2002	2003	State	1999	2000	2001	2002	2003
Total	44,563	46,908	49,485	53,167	54,871	Montana	146	170	173	191	205
						Nebraska.	196	207	237	288	291
Alabama	623	600	640	657	623	Nevada	471	425	446	404	370
Alaska.	130	146	171	188	199	New Hampshire	188	177	216	218	224
Arizona	384	424	394	417	459	New Jersey	1,244	1,294	1,371	1,471	1,543
Arkansas	152	146	160	180	198	New Mexico	138	149	165	184	197
California.	7,852	9,451	10,082	11,883	13,022	New York.	2,796	2,909	2,978	3,142	3,220
Colorado	725	808	569	777	693	North Carolina	840	847	885	995	1,060
Connecticut	737	667	661	748	754	North Dakota	69	73	74	76	78
Delaware	132	145	145	166	169	Ohio	2,039	2,099	2,248	2,388	2,442
District of Columbia . .	89	87	93	100	94	Oklahoma	491	474	497	521	562
Florida.	2,296	2,057	2,379	2,129	2,201						
Georgia.	896	996	1,067	1,083	1,121	Oregon	384	412	456	448	447
Hawaii.	222	231	252	268	275	Pennsylvania	2,467	2,403	2,440	2,532	2,626
Idaho	121	114	132	152	181	Rhode Island	112	111	118	118	107
Illinois	1,928	1,993	2,127	2,173	2,100	South Carolina	445	515	532	593	657
Indiana	504	531	529	567	568	South Dakota	86	81	82	94	95
Iowa	256	295	331	321	320	Tennessee	580	627	688	668	710
Kansas	319	319	342	351	294	Texas	1,741	1,744	1,781	2,040	1,920
Kentucky	626	593	660	688	717	Utah	193	183	210	231	202
						Vermont	105	109	120	132	141
Louisiana.	510	606	630	652	660	Virginia	667	602	604	625	701
Maine	264	262	264	289	261	Washington	1,395	1,528	1,638	1,714	1,800
Maryland	558	546	575	574	629	West Virginia	696	693	713	833	829
Massachusetts	725	809	771	794	890	Wisconsin	724	768	924	894	840
Michigan	1,393	1,474	1,478	1,512	1,477	Wyoming	75	83	98	104	103
Minnesota	744	798	904	921	884	Federal total [1].	2,862	2,957	3,069	3,154	3,185
Missouri.	972	903	1,093	1,235	1,258	Federal employees. .	2,000	2,119	2,223	2,317	2,368

[1] Federal benefits include: those paid under the Federal Employees' Compensation Act for civilian employees; the portion of the black lung benefit program that is financed by employers; and a portion of benefits under the Longshore and Harbor Workers' Compensation Act that are not reflected in state data, namely, benefits paid by self-insured employers and by special funds under the LHWCA. See Appendix H of source for more information about federal programs.

Source: National Academy of Social Insurance, Washington, DC, *Workers' Compensation: Benefits, Coverage, and Costs,* annual. See also <http://www.nasi.org/>.

Table 549. **Supplemental Security Income—Recipients and Payments: 1990 to 2004**

[In thousands (4,817 represents 4,817,000), except as noted. Recipients and monthly payment as of December. Payments for calendar year. See also Appendix III]

Program	Unit	1990	1995	1999	2000	2001	2002	2003	2004
Recipients, total [1]	1,000....	4,817	6,514	6,557	6,602	6,688	6,787	6,902	6,987
Aged	1,000....	1,454	1,446	1,308	1,289	1,264	1,251	1,233	1,211
Blind	1,000....	84	84	79	79	78	77	77	76
Disabled	1,000....	3,279	4,984	5,169	5,234	5,345	5,459	5,593	5,701
Payments, total [2]	Mil. dol...	16,133	27,037	30,106	30,672	32,166	33,719	34,696	36,065
Aged	Mil. dol..	3,559	4,239	4,454	4,540	4,664	4,803	4,857	4,907
Blind	Mil. dol..	329	367	383	386	399	416	509	412
Disabled	Mil. dol..	12,245	22,431	25,270	25,746	27,126	28,500	29,429	30,745
Average monthly payment, total [1]	Dollars...	299	358	368	378	393	407	417	428
Aged	Dollars...	213	251	289	299	314	330	342	351
Blind	Dollars...	342	370	401	413	428	445	455	463
Disabled	Dollars...	337	389	388	397	412	425	433	444

[1] Persons with a federal SSI payment and/or federally administered state supplementation. [2] Includes payments not distributed by reason for eligibility.

Source: U.S. Social Security Administration, *Social Security Bulletin*, quarterly and *Annual Statistical Supplement to the Social Security Bulletin.*

Table 550. **Supplemental Security Income (SSI)—Recipients and Payments by State and Other Area: 2000 to 2004**

[Recipients as of December; payments for calendar year (6,602 represents 6,602,000). Data cover federal SSI payments and/or federally administered state supplementation. For explanation of methodology, see Appendix III]

State and other area	Recipients (1,000) 2000	2004	Payments for year (mil. dol.) 2000	2003	2004	State and other area	Recipients (1,000) 2000	2004	Payments for year (mil. dol.) 2000	2003	2004
Total ...	6,602	6,989	30,672	34,700	36,066	MO	112	116	471	528	553
U.S.	6,601	6,987	30,669	34,696	36,065	MT	14	15	57	64	66
AL	159	163	659	738	761	NE	21	22	85	95	101
AK	9	11	37	47	51	NV	25	32	108	144	154
AZ	81	94	355	429	458	NH	12	13	49	58	61
AR	85	88	333	361	383	NJ	146	150	672	732	750
CA	1,088	1,138	6,386	7,573	7,906	NM	47	52	193	223	234
CO	54	54	228	246	253	NY	617	627	3,197	3,400	3,502
CT	49	52	216	244	253	NC	191	196	732	825	858
DE	12	13	50	59	63	ND	8	8	30	32	33
DC	20	21	93	105	106	OH	240	245	1,114	1,204	1,231
FL	377	413	1,621	1,908	1,953	OK	72	77	302	339	359
GA	197	200	785	888	916	OR	52	59	228	271	280
HI	21	22	104	113	118	PA	284	317	1,367	1,599	1,672
ID	18	21	76	91	97	RI	28	30	130	150	156
IL	249	256	1,174	1,267	1,298	SC	107	105	429	461	474
IN	88	96	382	441	463	SD	13	12	48	52	53
IA	40	43	158	176	186	TN	164	161	664	719	741
KS	36	38	151	170	181	TX	409	472	1,575	1,901	2,031
KY	174	179	741	819	847	UT	20	22	87	99	103
LA	166	170	715	769	798	VT	13	13	51	57	60
ME	30	32	116	136	141	VA	132	135	535	587	608
MD	88	93	400	441	463	WA	101	112	484	546	582
MA	168	169	807	855	878	WV	71	76	318	357	366
MI	210	219	988	1,086	1,123	WI	85	90	357	398	417
MN	64	71	272	316	334	WY	6	6	23	25	26
MS	129	125	512	550	561	N. Mariana	1	1	3	4	4

Source: U.S. Social Security Administration, *Annual Statistical Supplement* to the *Social Security Bulletin.*

Table 551. **Temporary Assistance for Needy Families (TANF)—Families and Recipients: 1980 to 2005**

[In thousands (3,712 represents 3,712,000). Average monthly families and recipients for calendar year. Prior to TANF, the cash assistance program to families was called Aid to Families with Dependent Children (1980–1996). Under the new welfare law (Personal Responsibility and Work Opportunity Reconciliation Act of 1996), the program became TANF. See text, this section. Includes Puerto Rico, Guam, and Virgin Islands]

Year	Families	Recipients	Year	Families	Recipients	Year	Families	Recipients
1980	3,712	10,774	1990	4,057	11,695	1998	3,050	8,347
1983	3,686	10,761	1991	4,497	12,930	1999	2,554	6,824
1984	3,714	10,831	1992	4,829	13,773	2000	2,215	5,778
1985	3,701	10,855	1993	5,012	14,205	2001	2,104	5,359
1986	3,763	11,038	1994	5,033	14,161	2002	2,047	5,064
1987	3,776	11,027	1995	4,791	13,418	2003	2,024	4,929
1988	3,749	10,915	1996	4,434	12,321	2004	1,981	4,745
1989	3,799	10,993	1997	3,740	10,376	2005	1,909	4,492

Source: U.S. Administration for Children and Families, unpublished data.

Social Insurance and Human Services **359**

Table 552. Temporary Assistance for Needy Families (TANF)—Recipients by State and Other Areas: 2000 to 2005

[In thousands (2,215 represents 2,215,000). Average monthly families and recipients for calendar year. See headnote, Table 551]

State or other area	Families			Recipients			State or other area	Families			Recipients		
	2000	2004	2005	2000	2004	2005		2000	2004	2005	2000	2004	2005
Total...	2,215	1,980	1,908	5,778	4,745	4,491	MT	5	5	4	13	14	12
U.S	2,181	1,960	1,891	5,678	4,686	4,442	NE	9	11	10	24	26	28
AL	19	19	20	45	43	48	NV	6	8	6	16	20	15
AK	7	5	4	21	14	11	NH	6	6	6	14	14	14
AZ	33	48	43	84	111	96	NJ	50	45	45	125	109	107
AR	12	10	8	29	21	18	NM	23	18	18	69	46	45
CA	489	461	461	1,262	1,105	1,078	NY	250	146	140	695	335	321
CO	11	15	15	28	38	39	NC	45	37	33	98	76	64
CT	27	21	19	64	42	39	ND	3	3	3	7	8	7
DE	6	6	6	12	13	13	OH	95	85	82	235	186	177
DC	17	17	17	45	44	41	OK	14	14	14	35	33	31
FL	65	59	58	142	116	101	OR	17	19	19	38	43	44
GA	52	51	39	125	117	82	PA	88	91	97	241	239	254
HI	14	9	10	46	22	24	RI	16	12	10	44	31	26
ID	1	2	5	2	3	9	SC	18	16	16	42	37	36
IL	78	37	38	234	91	96	SD	3	3	3	7	6	6
IN	37	50	48	101	129	124	TN	57	72	70	147	190	184
IA	20	18	17	53	45	42	TX	129	100	82	347	237	189
KS	13	17	18	32	45	46	UT	8	9	9	21	23	22
KY	38	36	34	87	78	74	VT	6	5	5	16	12	11
LA	27	18	16	71	42	36	VA	31	10	10	69	28	28
ME	11	10	9	28	27	25	WA	56	56	57	148	138	136
MD	29	25	23	71	59	53	WV	13	14	12	33	33	26
MA	43	50	48	100	107	102	WI	17	22	19	38	54	44
MI	72	80	81	198	213	215	WY	1	–	–	1	1	1
MN	39	33	28	114	85	71	PR	30	17	15	88	47	41
MS	15	18	15	34	41	33	GU	3	3	2	10	11	8
MO	47	41	40	125	99	96	VI	1	1	–	3	2	1

– Represents or rounds to zero.

Source: U.S. Administration for Children and Families, unpublished data.

Table 553. Temporary Assistance for Needy Families (TANF)—Expenditures by State: 2000 to 2004

[In millions of dollars (24,781 represents $24,781,000,000). Represents federal and state funds expended in fiscal year. Negative values occur when contracted obligations are fulfilled or terminated and the actual cost for the service is less than the obligated amount]

State			2004		State			2004	
	2000, total	2003, total	Total [1]	Expendi- tures on assistance		2000, total	2003, total	Total [1]	Expendi- tures on assistance
U.S. ...	24,781	26,340	25,823	12,029	MO	321	299	300	138
AL	96	171	114	49	MT	44	56	45	25
AK	93	88	76	51	NE	79	79	89	64
AZ	261	342	305	183	NV	69	85	68	39
AR	139	54	42	17	NH	73	72	60	34
CA	6,481	5,851	6,178	3,923	NJ	321	842	889	314
CO	205	236	212	68	NM	149	123	133	74
CT	436	450	435	143	NY	3,512	4,463	4,196	2,063
DE	55	56	54	33	NC	440	457	438	122
DC	157	166	169	70	ND	33	42	34	22
FL	781	852	877	268	OH	995	1,007	834	325
GA	386	501	535	197	OK	130	203	195	155
HI	162	134	128	87	OR	169	226	243	128
ID	43	43	41	7	PA	1,327	1,109	1,192	412
IL	879	989	981	114	RI	172	162	155	84
IN	342	313	314	126	SC	245	148	38	18
IA	163	156	163	82	SD	21	26	29	22
KS	151	150	156	101	TN	293	274	236	138
KY	203	191	196	124	TX	727	911	768	268
LA	118	267	252	71	UT	100	131	114	53
ME	108	100	102	86	VT	62	67	69	43
MD	336	366	350	110	VA	418	273	279	112
MA	690	697	681	361	WA	535	572	589	322
MI	1,264	1,205	1,281	382	WV	134	157	150	87
MN	381	498	402	167	WI	382	489	493	136
MS	62	120	103	-7	WY	34	71	40	18

[1] Includes other items not shown separately.

Source: U.S. Administration for Children and Families, Temporary Assistance for Needy Families (TANF) Program, Annual Report to Congress.

Table 554. Child Support—Award and Recipiency Status of Custodial Parent: 2001

[In thousands except as noted (13,383 represents 13,383,000). Custodial parents 15 years and older with own children under 21 years of age present from absent parents as of spring 2002. Covers civilian noninstitutional population. Based on Current Population Survey; see text, section 1 and Appendix III. For definition of mean, see Guide to Tabular Presentation]

Award and recipiency status	All custodial parents				Custodial parents below the poverty level			
	Total		Mothers	Fathers	Total		Mothers	Fathers
	Number	Percent distri-bution			Number	Percent distri-bution		
Total	13,383	(X)	11,291	2,092	3,131	(X)	2,823	308
With child support agreement or award	7,916	(X)	7,110	807	1,706	(X)	1,571	135
Supposed to receive payments in 2001. . .	6,924	100.0	6,212	712	1,469	100.0	1,339	130
Actually received payments in 2001 . . .	5,119	73.9	4,639	480	963	65.6	885	77
Received full amount	3,099	44.8	2,821	278	453	30.8	423	30
Received partial payments.	2,020	29.2	1,818	202	510	34.7	463	47
Did not receive payments in 2001.	1,804	26.1	1,573	232	507	34.5	454	53
Child support not awarded	5,466	(X)	4,181	1,285	1,425	(X)	1,253	172
MEAN INCOME AND CHILD SUPPORT								
Received child support payments in 2001:								
Mean total money income (dol.).	29,008	(X)	28,258	36,255	7,571	(X)	7,604	7,189
Mean child support received (dol.)	4,274	(X)	4,274	4,273	3,041	(X)	3,078	2,622
Received the full amount due:								
Mean total money income (dol.)	32,338	(X)	31,734	38,479	7,963	(X)	7,958	8,032
Mean child support received (dol.). . .	5,665	(X)	5,655	5,768	4,576	(X)	4,701	2,831
Received partial payments:								
Mean total money income (dol.)	23,899	(X)	22,865	33,199	7,223	(X)	7,281	6,647
Mean child support received (dol.). . .	2,141	(X)	2,132	2,219	1,677	(X)	1,595	2,487
Received no payments in 2001:								
Mean total money income (dol.).	23,571	(X)	21,835	35,348	6,832	(X)	6,755	7,492
Without child support agreement or award:								
Mean total money income (dol.).	24,055	(X)	19,339	39,396	6,113	(X)	6,089	6,287

X Not applicable.

Source: U.S. Census Bureau, unpublished data.

Table 555. Child Support Enforcement Program—Caseload and Collections: 1990 to 2005

[For years ending Sept. 30 (12,796 represents 12,796,000). Includes Puerto Rico, Guam, and the Virgin Islands. The child support enforcement program locates absent parents, establishes paternity of children born out of wedlock, and establishes and enforces support orders. By law, these services are available to all families that need them. The program is operated at the state and local government level, but 66 percent of administrative costs are paid by the federal government. Child support collected for families not receiving Temporary Assistance for Needy Families (TANF) goes to the family to help it remain self-sufficient. Most of the child support collected on behalf of TANF families goes to federal and state governments to offset TANF payments. Some states pass-through a portion of the CS collections to help families become self-sufficient. Based on data reported by state agencies. Minus sign (–) indicates net outlay]

Item	Unit	1990	1995	2000	2001	2002	2003	2004	2005, prel.
Total cases [1]	1,000	12,796	19,162	17,334	17,061	16,066	15,923	15,854	15,861
Paternities established, total [2].	1,000	393	659	867	777	697	663	692	680
Support orders established, total [3]	1,000	1,022	1,051	1,175	1,181	1,220	1,161	1,181	1,180
FINANCES									
Collections, total	Mil. dol. . .	6,010	10,827	17,854	18,958	20,137	21,176	21,861	23,006
TANF/FC collections [4]	Mil. dol. . . .	1,750	2,689	2,593	2,592	2,893	2,972	2,221	2,191
State share	Mil. dol. . . .	620	939	1,080	1,004	947	947	927	911
Estimated Incentive payments to									
states	Mil. dol. . . .	264	400	353	337	338	356	361	365
Federal share [5]	Mil. dol. . . .	533	822	968	895	1,183	1,167	1,147	1,129
Non-TANF collections	Mil. dol. . . .	4,260	8,138	15,261	16,366	17,244	18,204	19,641	20,815
Administrative expenditures, total .	Mil. dol. . . .	1,606	3,012	4,526	4,835	5,183	5,216	5,322	5,353
State share	Mil. dol. . . .	545	918	1,519	1,613	1,752	1,765	1,803	1,813
Federal share	Mil. dol. . . .	1,061	2,095	3,006	3,222	3,432	3,450	3,519	3,540
Program savings, total	Mil. dol. . . .	–190	–852	–2,125	–2,599	–3,053	–3,101	–3,249	–3,312
State share	Mil. dol. . . .	338	421	–87	–272	–466	–462	–515	–537
Federal share	Mil. dol. . . .	–528	–1,273	–2,038	–2,327	–2,587	–2,639	–2,734	–2,776

[1] Passage of the Personal Responsibility and Work Opportunity Reconciliation Act of 1996 (PRWORA) mandated new categories in 1999 and cases were no longer double counted resulting in a 2 million case reduction. [2] Does not include in-hospital paternities. [3] Includes modifications to orders. [4] Collections for current assistance cases where the children are: (1) recipients of TANF under title IV-A of the Social Security Act or (2) entitled to Foster Care (FC) maintenance under title IV-E of the Social Security Act plus collections distributed as assistance reimbursements. Includes medical support and payments to families of current assistance not shown separately. Assistance reimbursements are collections that will be divided between the state and federal goverrments to reimburse their respective shares of either Title IV-A assistance payments or Title IV-E Foster Care maintenance payments. [5] Prior to fiscal year 2002, incentives were paid out of the federal share of collections and the net federal share was reported.

Source: U.S. Department of Health and Human Services, Office of Child Support Enforcement, *Annual Report to Congress.*

Social Insurance and Human Services **361**

Table 556. Federal Food Programs: 1990 to 2005

[20.0 represents 20,000,000, except as noted. For years ending September 30. Program data include Puerto Rico, Virgin Islands, Guam, American Samoa, Northern Marianas, and the former Trust Territory when a federal food program was operated in these areas. Participation data are average monthly figures except as noted. Participants are not reported for the commodity distribution programs. Cost data are direct federal benefits to recipients; they exclude federal administrative payments and applicable state and local contributions. Federal costs for commodities and cash-in-lieu of commodities are shown separately from direct cash benefits for those programs receiving both]

Program	Unit	1990	1995	2000	2001	2002	2003	2004	2005
Food Stamp:									
Participants	Million . . .	20.0	26.6	17.2	17.3	19.1	21.3	23.9	25.7
Federal cost	Mil. dol. . .	14,186	22,764	14,983	15,547	18,256	21,404	24,622	28,567
Monthly average coupon value per recipient	Dollars	58.96	71.27	72.62	74.81	79.67	83.90	86.00	92.69
Nutrition assistance program for Puerto Rico:									
Federal cost	Mil. dol. . .	937	1,131	1,268	1,296	1,351	1,395	1,413	1,495
National school lunch program (NSLP):									
Free lunches served	Million . . .	1,662	2,090	2,205	2,182	2,277	2,335	2,397	2,475
Reduced-price lunches served	Million . . .	273	308	409	425	441	453	462	479
Children participating [1]	Million . . .	24.1	25.7	27.3	27.5	28.0	28.4	29.0	29.6
Federal cost	Mil. dol. . .	3,214	4,466	5,494	5,612	6,050	6,341	6,662	7,050
School breakfast (SB):									
Children participating [1]	Million . . .	4.1	6.3	7.6	7.8	8.1	8.4	8.9	9.4
Federal cost	Mil. dol. . .	596	1,048	1,393	1,450	1,567	1,652	1,775	1,925
Special supplemental food program (WIC): [2]									
Participants	Million . . .	4.5	6.9	7.2	7.3	7.5	7.6	7.9	8.0
Federal cost	Mil. dol. . .	1,637	2,512	2,853	3,008	3,130	3,230	3,562	3,604
Child and adult care (CAC): [3]									
Participants [4]	Million . . .	1.5	2.3	2.7	2.7	2.8	2.9	3.0	3.1
Federal cost	Mil. dol. . .	719	1,296	1,500	1,548	1,657	1,726	1,812	1,905
Federal cost of commodities donated to— [5]									
Child nutrition (NSLP, CACFP, SFS, and SBP)	Mil. dol. . .	644	733	704	917	860	907	1,030	1,048
Emergency feeding [6]	Mil. dol. . .	282	100	182	333	380	396	363	322

[1] Average monthly participation (excluding summer months of June through August). Includes children in public and private elementary and secondary schools and in residential child care institutes. [2] WIC serves pregnant and postpartum women, infants, and children up to age five. [3] CACFP provides year-round subsidies to feed preschool children in child care centers and family day care homes. Certain care centers serving disabled or elderly adults also receive meal subsidies. [4] Average quarterly daily attendance at participating institutions. [5] Includes the federal cost of commodity entitlements, cash-in-lieu of commodities, and bonus foods. [6] Provides free commodities to needy persons for home consumption through food banks, hunger centers, soup kitchens, and similar nonprofit agencies. Includes the Emergency Food Assistance Program, the commodity purchases for soup kitchens/food banks program (FY 1989–96), and commodity disaster relief.

Source: U.S. Department of Agriculture, Food and Nutrition Service, "Food and Nutrition Service, Program Data"; <http://www.fns.usda.gov/pd/>; updated monthly.

Table 557. Federal Food Stamp Program by State: 2000 to 2005

[Participation data are average monthly numbers (17,194 represents 17,194,000). For years ending September 30. Food stamp costs are for benefits only and exclude administrative expenditures]

State	Persons (1,000) 2000	2004	2005	Benefits (mil. dol.) 2000	2004	2005	State	Persons (1,000) 2000	2004	2005	Benefits (mil. dol.) 2000	2004	2005
Total [1]	17,194	23,858	25,682	14,983	24,622	28,567	MS	276	377	391	226	361	463
U.S.	17,156	23,819	25,642	14,927	24,555	28,492	MO	423	700	766	358	663	736
AL	396	498	559	344	513	616	MT	59	77	81	51	79	89
AK	38	49	56	46	64	80	NE	82	114	117	61	109	120
AZ	259	530	550	240	578	634	NV	61	120	122	57	120	129
AR	247	346	374	206	347	401	NH	36	48	52	28	44	51
CA	1,831	1,859	1,991	1,639	1,984	2,312	NJ	345	369	392	304	378	437
CO	156	242	246	127	253	313	NM	169	223	241	140	217	251
CT	165	196	204	138	198	223	NY	1,439	1,598	1,755	1,361	1,876	2,136
DE	32	56	62	31	57	65	NC	488	747	800	403	753	856
DC	81	89	89	77	98	103	ND	32	41	42	25	40	45
FL	882	1,202	1,382	771	1,269	1,598	OH	610	945	1,007	520	1,009	1,157
							OK	253	412	424	208	398	440
GA	559	867	921	489	924	1,048	OR	234	420	429	198	415	456
HI	118	99	94	166	152	156	PA	777	961	1,043	656	933	1,105
ID	58	91	93	46	91	103	RI	74	78	76	59	74	79
IL	817	1,070	1,158	777	1,211	1,400							
IN	300	526	556	268	550	627	SC	295	497	521	249	501	566
IA	123	179	207	100	176	220	SD	43	53	56	37	54	61
KS	117	170	178	83	158	180	TN	496	806	850	415	812	942
KY	403	545	570	337	543	611	TX	1,333	2,259	2,451	1,215	2,307	2,659
LA	500	706	808	448	754	979	UT	82	123	133	68	123	141
ME	102	142	153	81	140	162	VT	41	43	45	32	40	45
							VA	336	486	488	263	476	500
MD	219	274	289	199	287	320	WA	295	453	508	241	455	539
MA	232	335	368	182	304	363	WV	227	256	262	185	232	258
MI	603	944	1,048	457	896	1,099	WI	193	324	346	129	269	317
MN	196	247	260	165	247	275	WY	22	26	25	19	25	27

[1] Includes Guam and the Virgin Islands, American Samoa, and the Northern Marianas.

Source: U.S. Department of Agriculture, Food and Nutrition Service."Food and Nutrition Service, Program Data";<http://www.fns.usda.gov/pd/>; updated monthly.

U.S. Census Bureau. Statistical Abstract of the United States: 2007

Table 558. Selected Characteristics of Food Stamp Households and Participants: 1990 to 2004

[7,811 represents 7,811,000. For years ending September 30. Data for 1990 exclude Guam and the Virgin Islands. Based on a sample of households from the Food Stamp Quality Control System]

Year	Households				Participants		
	Total (1,000)	Percent of total			Total (1,000)	Percent of total	
		With children	With elderly [1]	With disabled [2]		Children	Elderly [1]
1990	7,811	60.3	18.1	8.9	20,440	49.6	7.7
1995	10,883	59.7	16.0	18.9	26,955	51.5	7.1
1999	7,670	55.7	20.1	26.4	18,149	51.5	9.4
2000	7,335	53.9	21.0	27.5	17,091	51.3	10.0
2001	7,450	53.6	20.4	27.7	17,297	51.1	9.6
2002	8,201	54.1	18.7	27.0	19,041	51.0	8.9
2003	8,971	54.7	18.0	23.3	20,934	50.8	8.5
2004	10,070	54.3	17.3	22.9	23,486	50.2	8.2

[1] Persons 60 years old and over. [2] Beginning 1995, disabled households are defined as households with at least one member under age 65 who received SSI, or at least one member age 18 to 61 who received social security, veterans benefits, or other government benefits as a result of a disability. For 1990, disabled households are defined as households with SSI but no members over age 59. The substantial increase in the percentage of households with a disabled member between 1994 and 1995 is due in part to the change in the definition of disabled households. Using the previous definition, 13.3 percent of households included a disabled person in fiscal year 1995.

Source: U.S. Department of Agriculture, Food and Nutrition Service, *Characteristics of Food Stamp Households: Fiscal Year 2004*, November 2005.

Table 559. Food Stamp Households and Participants—Summary: 2004

[10,070 represents 10,070,000. For year ending September 30. Based on a sample of 46,963 households from the Food Stamp Quality Control System]

Household type and income source	Households		Age, sex, race, and Hispanic origin	Participants	
	Number (1,000)	Percent		Number (1,000)	Percent
Total	**10,070**	**100.0**	**Total**	**23,486**	**100.0**
With children	5,472	54.3	Children	11,797	50.2
Single-parent households	3,450	34.3	Under 5 years old	3,967	16.9
Married-couple households	1,004	10.0	5 to 17 years old	7,830	33.3
Other	1,019	10.1	Adults	11,684	49.7
With elderly	1,741	17.3	18 to 35 years old	5,134	21.9
Living alone	1,357	13.5	36 to 59 years old	4,631	19.7
Not living alone	385	3.8	60 years old and over	1,919	8.2
Disabled	2,310	22.9			
Living alone	1,243	12.3	Male	9,668	41.2
Not living alone	1,067	10.6	Female	13,809	58.8
Earned income	2,896	28.8	White, non-Hispanic	10,148	43.2
Wages and salaries	2,589	25.7	Black, non-Hispanic	7,773	33.1
Unearned income	7,027	69.8	Hispanic	4,507	19.2
TANF [1]	1,626	16.1	Asian	586	2.5
Supplemental security income	2,713	26.9	Native American	359	1.5
Social security	2,313	23.0	Other	113	0.5
No income	1,308	13.0			

[1] Temporary Assistance for Needy Families (TANF) program.

Source: U.S. Department of Agriculture, Food and Nutrition Service, *Characteristics of Food Stamp Households: Fiscal Year 2004*, September 2005.

Table 560. Head Start—Summary: 1980 to 2005

[For years ending September 30 (376 represents 376,000)]

Year	Enrollment (1,000)	Appropriation (mil. dol.)	Age and race	Enrollment, 2005 (percent)	Item	Number
1980	376	735	Under 3 years old	10	Average cost per child:	
1990	541	1,552	3 years old	34	1995	$4,534
1995	751	3,534	4 years old	52	2000	$5,951
1996	752	3,569	5 years old and over	4	2005	$7,287
1997	794	3,981				
1998	822	4,347			Paid staff (1,000):	
1999	826	4,658	White	35	1995	147
2000	858	5,267	Black	31	2000	180
2001	905	6,200	Hispanic	33	2005	213
2002	912	6,537	American Indian	5	Volunteers (1,000):	
2003	910	6,668	Asian	2	1995	1,235
2004	906	6,775	Hawaiian/		2000	1,252
2005	907	6,843	Pacific Islander	1	2005	1,360

Source: U.S. Administration for Children and Families, "Head Start Statistical Fact Sheet"; <http://www2.acf.dhhs.gov/programs/hsb/research/2006.htm>.

Table 561. **Social Assistance—Establishments, Receipts, Payroll, and Employees by Kind of Business (NAICS 1997 Basis): 1997 and 2002**

[57,355 represents $57,355,000,000. Data are based on the 1997 and 2002 economic censuses which are subject to nonsampling error. Data for the construction sector are also subject to samping errors. For details on survey methodology and nonsampling and sampling errors, see Appendix III]

Kind of business	NAICS code [1]	Establishments (number)		Sales, receipts or shipments (mil. dol.)		Annual payroll (mil. dol.)		Paid employees [2] (1,000)	
		1997	2002	1997	2002	1997	2002	1997	2002
Social assistance	624	126,428	138,971	57,355	91,412	24,394	36,091	1,744	2,106
Individual & family services	6241	46,207	49,216	29,089	45,546	11,894	17,556	711	897
Child and youth services	62411	12,734	9,415	8,258	9,486	3,381	3,346	184	150
Services for elderly and disabled persons	62412	12,936	15,051	9,025	15,317	3,654	6,152	259	370
Other individual & family services . . .	62419	20,537	24,750	11,806	20,744	4,858	8,058	269	377
Community/emergency and other relief services	6242	9,950	12,436	6,197	12,930	1,768	3,215	102	144
Community food services.	62421	3,083	3,893	1,616	2,864	328	534	23	30
Community housing services	62422	4,904	6,726	3,028	5,629	1,100	2,051	61	92
Emergency & other relief services . . .	62423	1,963	1,817	1,553	4,437	340	630	18	22
Vocational rehabilitation services	6243	8,217	8,485	7,894	11,186	3,769	4,815	302	315
Child day care services.	6244	62,054	68,834	14,175	21,750	6,963	10,506	629	750

[1] North American Industry Classification System, 1997; see text, Section 15.   [2] For pay period including March 12.

Source: U.S. Census Bureau, *2002 Economic Census, Health Care and Social Assistance*, Series EC02-621-04, issued July 2004; <http://www.census.gov/prod/ec02/ec0262i04t.pdf>.

Table 562. **Social Assistance Services—Revenue for Employer Firms: 2000 to 2004**

[In millions of dollars (80,019 represents $80,019,000,000). Based on the North American Industry Classification System, 1997, (NAICS), see text, Section 15, Business Enterprise. See Appendix III]

Kind of business	NAICS code	2000, total	2003, total	2004		
				Total	Taxable firms	Tax-exempt firms
Social assistance.	624	80,019	100,843	107,629	22,383	85,246
Individual and family services	6241	40,298	50,934	54,062	6,295	47,767
Child and youth services	62411	10,503	13,515	13,640	799	12,841
Services for elderly and disabled persons . . .	62412	12,804	16,300	17,711	3,000	14,711
Other individual and family services	62419	16,990	21,119	22,711	2,496	20,215
Community, emergency and other relief services	6242	12,281	15,000	16,593	100	16,492
Community food services	62421	2,835	3,326	3,505	(S)	3,484
Community housing services.	62422	4,888	6,067	6,396	59	6,337
Emergency and other relief services.	62423	4,558	5,607	6,692	(S)	6,671
Vocational rehabilitation services	6243	9,458	12,094	13,025	2,250	10,775
Child day care services	6244	17,982	22,815	23,949	13,738	10,212

S Figure does not meet publication standards.

Source: U.S. Census Bureau, *Service Annual Survey*, 2004. See also <http://www.census.gov/svsd/www/services/sas/sas_summary/62summary.htm>.

Table 563. **Social Assistance—Nonemployer Establishments and Receipts: 1997 to 2003**

[Receipts in millions of dollars (5,451 represents $5,451,000,000). Includes only firms subject to federal income tax. Nonemployers are businesses with no paid employees. Based on the North American Industry Classification System 1997 (NAICS), see text, Section 15]

Kind of business	NAICS code	Establishments			Receipts		
		1997	2000	2003	1997	2000	2003
Social assistance, total	624	526,512	642,946	756,100	5,451	7,539	9,305
Individual & family services	6241	33,227	72,433	96,405	592	1,106	1,578
Community/emergency & other relief services. . .	6242	1,338	3,560	4,643	24	54	67
Vocational rehabilitation services	6243	3,213	7,314	9,653	82	151	204
Child day care services	6244	488,734	559,639	645,399	4,754	6,228	7,456

Source: U.S. Census Bureau, "Nonemployer Statistics"; <http://www.census.gov/epcd/nonemployer/>.

Table 564. Child Care Arrangements of Preschool Children by Type of Arrangement: 1991 to 2005

[In percent, except as indicated (8,428 represents 8,428,000). Estimates are based on children 3 to 5 years old who have not entered kindergarten. Based on interviews from a sample survey of the civilian, noninstitutional population in households with telephones; see source for details. See also Appendix III]

Characteristic	Children		Type of nonparental arrangement [1]			
	Number (1,000)	Percent distribution	In relative care	In nonrelative care	In center-based program [2]	With parental care only
1991, total	8,428	100.0	16.9	14.8	52.8	31.0
1995, total	9,232	100.0	19.4	16.9	55.1	25.9
2005, total	**9,066**	**100.0**	**22.6**	**11.6**	**57.2**	**26.3**
Age:						
3 years old.	4,070	44.9	24.0	14.4	42.5	33.4
4 years old.	3,873	42.7	20.8	9.2	69.2	20.6
5 years old.	1,123	12.4	23.8	9.9	68.7	20.4
Race-ethnicity:						
White, non-Hispanic.	5,177	57.1	21.4	15.0	59.1	24.1
Black, non-Hispanic.	1,233	13.6	25.0	5.2	66.5	19.5
Hispanic	1,822	20.1	22.7	8.1	43.4	38.0
Other	834	9.2	26.4	8.1	61.5	24.7
Household income:						
Less than $10,001.	795	8.8	25.1	8.6	53.4	33.4
$10,001 to $20,000	978	10.8	26.0	7.8	49.2	27.2
$20,001 to $30,000	1,183	13.1	25.4	6.3	43.9	38.5
$30,001 to $40,000	1,124	12.4	23.8	6.9	48.7	33.4
$40,001 to $50,000	808	8.9	21.8	11.6	50.0	35.4
$50,001 to $75,000	1,849	20.4	21.1	13.3	57.1	25.5
$75,001 or more	2,329	25.7	19.8	18.0	75.1	11.4

[1] Columns do not add to 100.0 because some children participated in more than one type of nonparental arrangement. [2] Center-based programs include day care centers, Head Start programs, preschools, prekindergarten, and nursery schools.

Source: U.S. Department of Education, National Center for Education Statistics, Early Childhood Program Participation Survey of the National Household Education Surveys Program (NHES), 2005.

Table 565. Licensed Child Care Centers and Family Child Care Providers by State and Other Areas: 2005

[Centers as of February; family child care providers as of August. Licensed programs are required to have permission from the state to operate and must meet specified family child care or center standards. Some states may call their regulatory processes certification or registration. Family child care providers are programs that operate in the licensee's residence with at least one provider]

State	Licensed child care centers	Licensed family child care providers	State	Licensed child care centers	Licensed family child care providers	State	Licensed child care centers	Licensed family child care providers
US, total . . .	**105,444**	**213,966**	KS	1,270	7,316	ND.	167	1,315
			KY [4]	2,256	1,029	OH.	3,876	154
AL	1,372	1,722	LA [5]	1,993	(5)	OK.	1,526	4,325
AK [1]	107	324	ME.	707	1,789	OR [6]	976	4,692
AZ [1]	2,182	371	MD.	2,672	9,775	PA	3,989	5,197
AR [2]	1,762	987	MA.	2,263	9,403	RI	460	1,314
CA.	14,841	44,494	MI	4,588	13,715	SC	1,339	303
CO.	1,282	4,281	MN.	1,577	13,085	SD [7]	298	92
CT	1,560	3,078	MS.	1,588	126	TN.	2,304	1,468
DE.	409	1,614	MO	1,938	2,069	TX	8,889	10,154
DC.	360	237	MT.	271	1,141	UT.	268	2,342
FL	4,248	2,409	NE.	854	3,066	VT [8]	640	1,244
GA.	3,019	6,736	NV.	447	524	VA.	2,700	1,678
HI	543	462	NH	798	359	WA	2,114	6,280
ID [3]	(3)	(3)	NJ [5]	4,262	(5)	WV	432	2,427
IL.	2,898	10,643	NM.	636	420	WI [9]	2,418	3,192
IN	617	3,111	NY.	3,626	12,093	WY	207	546
IA	1,495	6,193	NC.	4,400	4,671			

[1] Voluntary licensing for family child care homes caring for four or fewer children. [2] Voluntary registration for family child care homes caring for five or fewer children. [3] Voluntary licensing for centers and family child care homes. [4] The state also has certified family child care homes. Information reported was only for licensed family child care homes. [5] Voluntary registration for family child care homes. [6] Voluntary licensing for public assistance reimbursement programs and programs caring for three or fewer children. [7] The state also has voluntarily registered family day care homes. [8] The state also has legally exempt child care. [9] The state also certifies small family care homes that wish to receive state subsidy reimbursement.

Source: National Association for Regulatory Administration, Conyers, GA, *Child Care Center Licensing Study*, 2005 (copyright). See also <http://www.nara.affiniscape.com/displaycommon.cfm?an=1&subarticlenbr=99>.

U.S. Census Bureau, Statistical Abstract of the United States: 2007

Table 566. **Foster Care and Adoption: 2002 to 2003**

[Data are for October 1 of prior year through September 30 of year shown]

Characteristic	In foster care 2002	2003	Entered foster care 2002	2003	Exited foster care 2002	2003	Waiting to be adopted 2002	2003	Adopted from foster care 2002	2003
Total	532,000	523,000	303,000	297,000	281,000	281,000	126,000	119,000	53,000	50,000
AGE										
Under 1 year.	24,290	25,070	41,874	42,910	12,059	12,630	4,224	3,850	984	920
1–5 years.	128,946	129,470	77,623	77,820	76,998	79,790	40,204	38,200	24,412	23,630
6–10 years	116,801	108,500	61,555	58,490	61,089	59,540	37,740	33,430	16,916	15,270
11–15 years	158,290	154,970	87,416	85,310	67,388	66,790	36,310	35,770	9,313	8,900
16 or more years [1] . . .	102,412	103,500	34,254	32,490	62,725	61,990	6,393	7,510	1,351	1,410
RACE										
White.	205,478	203,920	139,861	137,340	125,114	127,680	45,410	43,820	20,833	20,940
Black.	195,040	184,480	83,585	80,300	84,366	82,420	52,935	47,630	18,828	16,570
Asian.	3,423	3,280	2,855	2,640	2,739	2,620	533	510	309	320
Hispanic.	89,177	91,040	51,330	51,180	44,931	45,890	16,324	16,210	8,586	7,900
SEX										
Male	278,916	274,820	(NA)	(NA)	(NA)	(NA)	66,472	63,120	26,587	25,170
Female	252,932	248,150	(NA)	(NA)	(NA)	(NA)	59,509	55,620	26,401	24,960

NA Not available.   [1] For children waiting to be adopted, includes ages 16–18 only.

Source: U.S. Administration for Children and Families, Adoption and Foster Care Analysis and Reporting System Reports, annual. See also <http://www.acf.hhs.gov/programs/cb/stats_research/index.htm#afcars>.

Table 567. **Private Philanthropy Funds by Source and Allocation: 1990 to 2004**

[In billions of dollars (101.4 represents $101,400,000,000). Estimates for sources of funds based on U.S. Internal Revenue Service reports of individual charitable deductions and household surveys of giving by Independent Sector and the Center on Philanthropy at Indiana University. For corporate giving, data are corporate charitable deductions from the U.S. Internal Revenue Service and the contributions made by corporate foundations as reported by the Foundation Center. Data about foundation donations are based upon surveys of foundations and data provided by the Foundation Center. Estimates of the allocation of funds were derived from surveys of nonprofits conducted by various sources]

Source and allocation	1990	1994	1995	1996	1997	1998	1999	2000	2001	2002	2003	2004
Total funds	101.4	119.2	124.0	138.6	159.4	177.4	201.0	227.7	229.0	234.1	236.7	248.5
Individuals.	81.0	92.5	95.4	107.6	124.2	138.4	154.6	174.5	172.4	175.0	180.6	187.9
Foundations [1]	7.2	9.7	10.6	12.0	13.9	17.0	20.5	24.6	27.2	26.8	26.8	28.8
Corporations	5.5	7.0	7.4	7.5	8.6	8.5	10.2	10.7	11.7	12.9	11.2	12.0
Charitable bequests	7.6	10.0	10.7	11.5	12.6	13.6	15.6	17.9	17.7	19.2	18.1	19.8
Allocation:												
Religion.	49.8	56.4	58.1	61.9	64.7	68.3	71.3	77.0	79.9	82.8	84.6	88.3
Health.	9.9	11.5	12.6	13.9	14.0	16.9	18.0	18.8	19.3	18.9	20.9	22.0
Education	12.4	16.6	17.6	19.2	22.0	25.3	27.5	31.7	32.0	31.8	32.1	33.8
Human service	11.8	11.7	11.7	12.2	12.7	16.1	17.4	18.0	20.7	18.7	18.9	19.2
Arts, culture, and humanities . .	7.9	9.7	10.0	10.9	10.6	10.5	11.1	11.5	12.1	12.2	13.1	14.0
Public/societal benefit.	4.9	6.1	7.1	7.6	8.4	10.9	11.0	11.6	11.8	11.6	12.1	13.0
Environment/wildlife	2.5	3.3	3.8	3.8	4.1	5.3	5.8	6.2	6.4	6.6	7.1	7.6
International	1.3	2.4	2.9	2.8	2.6	2.9	3.6	3.7	4.1	4.6	5.3	5.3
Gifts to foundations [1, 2]	3.8	6.3	8.5	12.6	14.0	19.9	28.8	24.7	25.7	19.2	21.6	24.0
Unallocated [3]	-3.0	-4.9	-8.2	-6.3	6.3	1.5	6.8	24.6	17.0	27.7	21.0	21.4

[1] Data are from the Foundation Center through 2001.   [2] Estimate for gifts to foundations in 2002-2004 is from Giving USA.
[3] Money deducted as a charitable contribution by donors but not allocated to sources. May include gifts to governmental entities, in-kind giving, gifts to new charities.

Source: The Giving Institute, Indianapolis, IN, researched and written by the Center on Philanthropy at Indiana University, Giving USA, annual (copyright).

Table 568. **Foundations—Number and Finances: 1990 to 2004**

[142.5 represents $142,500,000,000. Covers nongovernmental nonprofit organizations with funds and programs managed by their own trustees or directors, whose goals were to maintain or aid social, educational, religious, or other activities deemed to serve the common good. Excludes organizations that make general appeals to the public for funds, act as trade associations for industrial or other special groups, or do not currently award grants. Constant dollar figures based on Consumer Price Index, all urban consumers, supplied by U.S. Bureau of Labor Statistics. Minus sign (–) indicates decrease]

Year	Number of founda- tions	Assets Current dollars Amt. (bil. dol.)	Percent change [1]	Constant (1975) dollars Amt. (bil. dol.)	Percent change [1]	Total giving [2] Current dollars Amt. (bil. dol.)	Percent change [1]	Constant (1975) dollars Amt. (bil. dol.)	Percent change [1]	Gifts received Current dollars Amt. (bil. dol.)	Percent change [1]	Constant (1978) dollars Amt. (bil. dol.)	Percent change [1]
1990 .	32,401	142.5	3.6	58.7	-1.7	8.7	9.7	3.6	4.1	5.0	-10.0	2.5	-14.6
1995 .	40,140	226.7	15.8	80.1	12.6	12.3	8.6	4.3	5.6	10.3	26.9	4.4	23.5
2000 .	56,582	486.1	8.4	154.9	4.8	27.6	18.2	8.6	14.3	27.6	-13.9	10.5	-16.7
2004 .	67,736	510.5	7.1	145.4	4.3	31.8	5.1	9.1	2.3	24.0	-3.5	8.3	-6.0

[1] Percent change from immediate preceding year.   [2] Includes grants, scholarships, and employee matching gifts.

Source: The Foundation Center, New York, NY, FC Stats; <http://fdncenter.org/fc_stats/index.html>; (copyright).

Table 569. Foundations—Number and Finances by Asset Size: 2004

[Figures are for latest year reported by foundations (510,481 represents $510,481,000,000). See headnote, Table 568]

Asset size	Number	Assets (mil. dol.)	Gifts received (mil. dol.)	Expenditures (mil. dol.)	Grants (mil. dol.)	Percent distribution				
						Number	Assets	Gifts received	Expenditures	Grants
Total	**67,736**	**510,481**	**23,989**	**39,003**	**31,844**	**100.0**	**100.0**	**100.0**	**100.0**	**100.0**
Under $50,000.	11,413	182	1,348	1,568	1,492	16.8	–	5.6	4.0	4.7
$50,000-$99,999	4,794	353	187	267	238	7.1	0.1	0.8	0.7	0.7
$100,000-$249,999.	9,194	1,539	351	511	429	13.6	0.3	1.5	1.3	1.3
$250,000-$499,999.	8,561	3,116	446	618	522	12.6	0.6	1.9	1.6	1.6
$500,000-$999,999.	9,280	6,695	688	963	813	13.7	1.3	2.9	2.5	2.6
$1,000,000-$4,999,999	15,787	35,527	3,384	4,236	3,599	23.3	7.0	14.1	10.9	11.3
$5,000,000-$9,999,999	3,582	24,990	2,256	2,791	2,349	5.3	4.9	9.4	7.2	7.4
$10,000,000-$49,999,999	3,895	82,226	5,535	6,595	5,363	5.8	16.1	23.1	16.9	16.8
$50,000,000-$99,999,999	603	41,992	2,113	3,227	2,500	0.9	8.2	8.8	8.3	7.9
$100,000,000-$249,999,999 . . .	394	58,950	2,515	4,043	3,232	0.6	11.5	10.5	10.4	10.1
$250,000,000 or more.	233	254,909	5,166	14,185	11,307	0.3	49.9	21.5	36.4	35.5

– Represents zero.

Source: The Foundation Center, New York, NY, *Foundation Yearbook*, annual (copyright).

Table 570. Domestic Private Foundations—Information Returns: 1990 to 2002

[Money amounts in billions of dollars (122.4 represents $122,400,000,000)]

Item	1990	1994	1995	1996	1997	1998	1999	2000	2001	2002
Number of returns.	40,105	45,801	47,917	50,774	55,113	56,658	62,694	66,738	70,787	73,255
Nonoperating foundations . . .	36,880	41,983	43,966	46,066	50,541	52,460	58,840	61,501	63,650	67,101
Operating foundations	3,226	3,818	3,951	4,708	4,572	4,198	3,854	5,238	7,137	6,154
Total assets, book value. .	122.4	169.3	195.6	232.6	280.9	325.7	384.6	409.5	413.6	383.5
Total assets, fair market value. .	151.0	203.6	242.9	288.6	342.7	397.1	466.9	471.6	455.4	413.0
Investments in securities. . . .	115.0	158.9	190.7	225.1	272.4	317.9	363.4	361.4	329.4	294.4
Total revenue.	19.0	26.5	30.8	48.2	55.5	59.7	83.3	72.8	45.3	27.8
Total expenses.	11.3	15.7	17.2	19.9	22.4	25.9	33.9	37.4	36.7	34.4
Contributions, gifts, and grants paid.	8.6	11.8	12.3	14.5	16.4	19.4	22.8	27.6	27.4	26.3
Excess of revenue over expenses (net).	7.7	10.8	13.6	28.4	33.0	33.8	49.4	35.3	8.6	-6.6
Net investment income [1]	11.9	15.0	20.4	26.2	34.8	39.3	57.1	48.8	25.7	17.6

[1] Represents income not considered related to a foundation's charitable purpose, e.g., interest, dividends, and capital gains. Foundations could be subject to an excise tax on such income.

Source: Internal Revenue Service, Statistics of Income, SOI Tax Stats—Charities & Other Tax-Exempt <http://www.irs.gov/taxstats/charitablestats/article/0,,id=97176,00.html>(accessed 17 March 2006).

Table 571. Nonprofit Charitable Organizations—Information Returns: 1990 to 2002

[In billions of dollars (697.3 represents $697,300,000,000), except as indicated. Categories based on The National Taxonomy of Exempt Entities (NTEE), a classification system that uses 26 major field areas that are aggregated into 10 categories. Includes data reported by organizations described in Internal Revenue Code section 501(3), excluding private foundations and most religious organizations. Organizations with receipts under $25,000 were not required to file]

Year and category	Number of returns (1,000)	Total assets	Total fund balance or net worth	Revenue			Total expenses	Excess of revenue over expenses (net)
				Total	Program service revenue [1]	Contributions, gifts, and grants		
1990	141.8	697.3	375.3	435.6	306.9	85.3	409.4	26.1
2000	230.2	1,562.5	1,023.2	866.2	579.1	199.1	796.4	69.8
2002, total	251.7	1,733.9	1,040.3	955.3	691.8	214.5	934.7	20.6
Arts, culture, and humanities .	27.1	68.8	56.1	22.3	6.3	12.8	21.6	0.7
Education.	45.2	563.8	392.2	170.7	101.8	54.7	164.3	6.4
Environment, animals	9.7	25.5	20.9	8.7	2.1	5.6	7.8	0.9
Health	34.1	678.5	341.6	550.5	492.6	40.6	541.2	9.3
Human services.	94.7	201.1	95.9	141.7	74.0	58.8	140.0	1.7
International, foreign affairs . .	3.5	12.3	9.4	12.6	1.0	11.4	12.2	0.4
Mutual, membership benefit . .	0.6	10.8	8.4	1.7	1.5	0.2	1.9	-0.2
Public, societal benefit.	21.4	156.8	102.7	40.4	11.6	25.3	39.0	1.3
Religion related	15.3	16.1	13.1	6.7	1.1	5.0	6.7	0.1

[1] Represents fees collected by organizations in support of their tax-exempt purposes, and income such as tuition and fees at educational institutions, hospital patient charges, and admission and activity fees collected by museums and other nonprofit organizations or institutions.

Source: Internal Revenue Service, Statistics of Income, SOI Tax Stats—Charities & Other Tax-Exempt Organizations Statistics. See also <http://www.irs.gov/taxstats/charitablestats/article/0,,id=97176,00.html> (accessed 26 May 2005).

Table 572. **Volunteers by Selected Characteristics and Type of Main Organization: 2005**

[In percent, except as noted. Data on volunteers relate to persons who performed unpaid volunteer activities for an organization at any point from September 1, 2004, through September 2005. Data represents the percent of the population involved in the activity]

Total and type of main organization [1]	Total, both sexes	Sex		Age						Race and Hispanic or Latino origin				Educational attainment [4]				Employment status			
																		Civilian labor force			Not in labor force
		Men	Women	16 to 24 years	25 to 34 years	35 to 44 years	45 to 54 years	55 to 64 years	65 years and over	White [2]	Black [2]	Asian [2]	Hispanic or Latino [3]	Less than a high school diploma	High school graduate, no college [5]	Less than a bachelor's degree [6]	College graduates	Total	Employed	Unemployed	
Total volunteers (1,000)	65,357	27,370	37,987	8,955	9,881	14,809	13,826	9,173	8,712	56,170	5,879	2,055	4,511	2,837	12,594	16,452	24,517	46,872	44,894	1,978	18,485
Percent of population [7]	28.8	25.0	32.4	24.4	25.3	34.5	32.7	30.2	24.8	30.4	22.1	20.7	15.4	10.0	21.2	33.7	45.8	31.1	31.3	26.4	24.4
Median annual hours	50	52	50	36	36	48	50	56	96	50	52	40	40	48	48	50	55	48	48	42	62
Civic and political [8]	6.4	8.2	5.0	4.2	6.8	4.8	6.8	8.0	8.2	6.5	5.2	6.0	5.8	5.2	6.3	6.5	7.3	6.6	6.7	4.4	5.9
Educational or youth service	26.2	24.4	27.6	32.4	33.6	37.9	25.6	13.5	6.2	26.3	23.8	28.6	31.9	20.9	23.7	26.1	26.0	27.7	27.4	34.0	22.6
Environmental or animal care	1.8	1.8	1.8	2.5	2.1	1.3	2.1	2.1	0.9	2.0	0.5	0.5	0.9	0.4	1.3	1.8	2.0	1.9	1.9	1.5	1.5
Hospital or other health	7.7	5.5	9.2	8.2	6.6	5.8	7.7	8.9	10.1	8.0	4.8	8.8	5.7	5.7	7.9	7.9	7.4	7.5	7.6	5.8	8.0
Public safety	1.3	2.4	0.5	1.5	1.7	1.1	1.3	1.4	0.8	1.4	0.5	0.5	1.0	1.5	2.1	1.3	0.7	1.5	1.5	1.6	0.6
Religious	34.8	34.0	35.4	27.5	29.1	31.2	36.8	41.2	45.0	33.8	45.5	33.6	37.1	45.5	38.9	35.8	33.5	33.5	33.6	29.3	38.2
Social or community service	13.4	14.2	12.8	14.9	13.1	10.5	11.4	15.5	18.0	13.5	12.3	13.3	9.5	13.5	12.2	12.6	13.9	13.1	12.9	16.7	14.2
Sport and hobby [9]	3.3	4.1	2.7	2.8	3.0	3.0	3.6	3.8	3.7	3.4	2.0	3.8	2.3	1.2	2.9	3.3	3.9	3.4	3.4	2.5	3.1
Other	3.5	3.8	3.3	3.6	3.1	3.1	3.1	4.0	4.7	3.6	2.9	2.5	3.9	5.0	3.3	3.4	3.5	3.4	3.4	3.4	3.9
Not determined	1.7	1.6	1.7	2.3	1.0	1.3	1.7	1.7	2.3	1.5	2.5	2.4	1.9	1.0	1.4	1.3	1.8	1.5	1.6	0.8	2.0

[1] Main organization is defined as the organization for which the volunteer worked the most hours during the year. See headnote for more details. [2] Persons who selected this race group only; persons who selected more than one race group are not included. [3] Persons of Hispanic origin may be of any race. [4] Data refer to persons 25 years and over. [5] Includes high school diploma or equivalent. [6] Includes the categories, some college, no degree; and associate's degree. [7] For those reporting annual hours. [8] Includes professional and/or international. [9] Includes cultural and/or arts.

Source: U.S. Bureau of Labor Statistics, News, USDL 05-2278, December 9, 2005. See also <http://www.bls.gov/news.release/pdf/volun.pdf>.

Section 12
Labor Force, Employment, and Earnings

This section presents statistics on the labor force; its distribution by occupation and industry affiliation; and the supply of, demand for, and conditions of labor. The chief source of these data is the Current Population Survey (CPS) conducted by the U.S. Census Bureau for the Bureau of Labor Statistics (BLS). Comprehensive historical and current data are available from the BLS Internet site <http://www .bls.gov/cps/>. These data are published on a current basis in the BLS monthly publication *Employment and Earnings*. Detailed data on the labor force are also available from the Census Bureau's decennial census of population.

Types of data—Most statistics in this section are obtained by two methods: household interviews or questionnaires and reports of establishment payroll records. Each method provides data that the other cannot suitably supply. Population characteristics, for example, are readily obtainable only from the household survey, while detailed industrial classifications can be readily derived only from establishment records.

Household data are obtained from a monthly sample survey of the population. The CPS is used to gather data for the calendar week including the 12th of the month and provides current comprehensive data on the labor force (see text, Section 1, Population). The CPS provides information on the work status of the population without duplication since each person is classified as employed, unemployed, or not in the labor force. Employed persons holding more than one job are counted only once, according to the job at which they worked the most hours during the survey week.

Monthly, quarterly, and annual data from the CPS are published by the Bureau of Labor Statistics in *Employment and Earnings*. Data presented include national totals of the number of persons in the civilian labor force by sex, race, Hispanic or Latino origin, and age; the number employed; hours of work; industry and occupational groups; and the number unemployed, reasons for, and duration of unemployment. Annual data shown in this section are averages of monthly figures for each calendar year, unless otherwise specified. Historical national CPS data are available on the Web site <http://www.bls .gov/cps/>.

The CPS also produces annual estimates of employment and unemployment for each state, 50 large metropolitan statistical areas, and selected cities. These estimates are published by BLS in its annual *Geographic Profile of Employment and Unemployment* available at <http://www .bls.gov/opub/gp/laugp.htm>. More detailed geographic data (e.g., for counties and cities) are provided by the decennial population censuses.

Data based on establishment records are compiled by BLS and cooperating state agencies as part of an ongoing Current Employment Statistics program. Survey data, gathered monthly from a sample of employers through electronic interviewing (including electronic data interchange, touchtone data entry, and computer-assisted telephone interviewing) or by mail, fax, on magnetic tape or computer diskette, are supplemented by data from other government agencies and adjusted at intervals to data from government social insurance program reports. The estimates exclude self-employed persons, private household workers, unpaid family workers, agricultural workers, and the Armed Forces. In March 2005, reporting establishments employed 4.3 million manufacturing workers (30 percent of the total manufacturing employment at the time), 21.0 million workers in private nonmanufacturing industries (22 percent of the total in private nonmanufacturing), and 15.6 million federal, state, and local government employees (70 percent of total government).

Labor Force, Employment, and Earnings   369

The establishment survey counts workers each time they appear on a payroll during the reference period (the payroll period that includes the 12th of the month). Thus, unlike the CPS, a person with two jobs is counted twice. The establishment survey is designed to provide detailed industry information for the nation, states, and metropolitan areas on non-farm wage and salary employment, average weekly hours, and average hourly and weekly earnings. Establishment survey data also are published in *Employment and Earnings*. Historical national data are available on the Web site <http://www.bls.gov/ces/>. Historical data for states and metropolitan areas are available on the Web site <http://www.bls.gov/sae/>.

In June 2003, BLS completed a comprehensive sample redesign of the establishment survey begun in June 2000, changing from a quota-based sample to a probability-based sample. Also in June 2003, all establishment survey employment, hours, and earnings series were converted from being classified by the 1987 Standard Industrial Classification (SIC) system to being classified by the 2002 North American Industry Classification System (NAICS). The NAICS conversion resulted in major definitional changes to many of the previously published SIC-based series. All establishment survey historical time series were reconstructed as part of the NAICS conversion process and all published series have a NAICS-based history extending back to at least 1990. For total nonfarm industries and other high-level aggregates, NAICS history was reconstructed back to the previously existing start date for the series, 1939 in most cases. More information on the sample redesign, the conversion to NAICS, and other changes to the establishment survey implemented in June 2003 appears in "Revisions to the Current Employment Statistics National Estimates Effective May 2003" in the June 2003 issue of *Employment and Earnings,* as well as the Establishment Data portion of the Explanatory Notes and Estimates of Error section of *Employment and Earnings.*

The completion of the sample redesign and the conversion to NAICS for state and metropolitan area establishment survey data was implemented in March 2003 with the release of January 2003 estimates. For a discussion of the changes to the state and area establishment survey data, see "Revisions to the Current Employment Statistics State and Area Estimates Effective January 2003" in the March 2003 issue of *Employment and Earnings.*

Labor force—According to the CPS definitions, the civilian labor force comprises all civilians in the noninstitutionalized population 16 years and over classified as "employed" or "unemployed" according to the following criteria: Employed civilians comprise (a) all civilians, who, during the reference week, did any work for pay or profit (minimum of an hour's work) or worked 15 hours or more as unpaid workers in a family enterprise and (b) all civilians who were not working but who had jobs or businesses from which they were temporarily absent for noneconomic reasons (illness, weather conditions, vacation, labor-management dispute, etc.) whether they were paid for the time off or were seeking other jobs. Unemployed persons comprise all civilians who had no employment during the reference week, who made specific efforts to find a job within the previous 4 weeks (such as applying directly to an employer or to a public employment service or checking with friends) and who were available for work during that week, except for temporary illness. Persons on layoff from a job and expecting recall also are classified as unemployed. All other civilian persons, 16 years old and over, are classified as "not in the labor force."

Various breaks in the CPS data series have occurred over time due to the introduction of population adjustments and other changes. For details on these breaks in series and the effect that they had on the CPS data, see the section on noncomparability of labor force levels in the Household Data portion of the Explanatory Notes and Estimates of Error section of *Employment and Earnings* available on the site <http://www.bls.gov/cps/eetech_methods.pdf>.

Beginning in January 2005, the CPS data reflect the introduction of revised population controls. The effect of the revised population controls on the monthly CPS estimates was to decrease the December 2004 employment level by 45,000 and the civilian noninstitutional population by 49,000. The updated controls had little or no effect on unemployment rates and other ratios. For additional information on the effects of the revised population controls on estimates from the CPS, see "Adjustments to Household Survey Population Estimates in January 2005" in the February 2005 issue of *Employment and Earnings*, available on the Internet at <http://www.bls.gov/cps/cps05adj.pdf>.

Hours and earnings—Average hourly earnings, based on establishment data, are gross earnings (i.e., earnings before payroll deductions) and include overtime premiums; they exclude irregular bonuses and value of payments in kind. Hours are those for which pay was received. Wages and salaries from the CPS consist of total monies received for work performed by an employee during the income year. It includes wages, salaries, commissions, tips, piece-rate payments, and cash bonuses earned before deductions were made for taxes, bonds, union dues, etc. Persons who worked 35 hours or more are classified as working full-time.

Industry and occupational groups— Industry data derived from the CPS for 1983–91 utilize the 1980 census industrial classification developed from the 1972 SIC. CPS data from 1971 to 1982 were based on the 1970 census classification system, which was developed from the 1967 SIC. Most of the industry categories were not affected by the change in classification.

The occupational classification system used in the 1980 census and in the CPS for 1983–91, evolved from the 1980 Standard Occupational Classification (SOC) system, first introduced in 1977. Occupational categories used in the 1980 census classification system are so radically different from the 1970 census system used in the CPS through 1982, that their implementation represented a break in historical data series. In cases where data have not yet been converted to the 1980 classifications and still reflect the 1970 classifications (e.g., Table 634), comparisons between the two systems should not be made.

Beginning in January 1992, the occupational and industrial classification systems used in the 1990 census were introduced into the CPS. (These systems were largely based on the 1980 Standard Occupational Classification and the 1987 Standard Industrial Classification Systems, respectively.)

Beginning in 2003, the 2002 Census Bureau occupational and industrial classification systems were introduced into the CPS. These systems were derived from the 2000 Standard Occupational Classification (SOC) and the 2002 North American Industry Classification System (NAICS). The composition of detailed occupational and industrial classifications in the new classification systems was substantially changed from the previous systems in use, as was the structure for aggregating them into broad groups. Consequently, the use of the new classification systems created breaks in existing data series at all levels of aggregation. CPS data using the new classification systems are available beginning 2000. Additional information on the 2002 Census Bureau occupational and industrial classifications systems appears in "Revisions to the Current Population Survey Effective in January 2003" in the February 2003 issue of *Employment and Earnings*, available on the BLS Web site <http://www.bls.gov /cps/rvcps03.pdf>.

For details on the changes over time in the industrial and occupational classification systems used in the CPS, see the section on changes in the occupational and industrial classification systems in the Household Data portion of the Explanatory Notes and Estimates of Error section of *Employment and Earnings* available on the site <http://www.bls.gov/cps /eetech_methods.pdf>.

Establishments responding to the establishment survey are classified according to the 2002 North American Industrial Classification System (NAICS). Previously they were classified according to the Standard Industrial Classification Manual (SIC). See text, Section 15, Business Enterprise, for information about the SIC manual and NAICS.

Labor Force, Employment, and Earnings   371

Productivity—BLS publishes data on productivity as measured by output per hour (labor productivity), output per combined unit of labor and capital input (multifactor productivity), and, for manufacturing industries, output per combined unit of capital, labor, energy, materials, and purchased service inputs. Labor productivity and related indexes are published for the business sector as a whole and its major subsectors: nonfarm business, manufacturing, and nonfinancial corporations, and for over 200 detailed industries. Labor productivity data have been converted to a NAICS classification from the SIC classification. Data for the business and nonfarm business sectors were reconstructed back to 1947; data for nonfinancial corporations back to 1958, and data for the detailed industry measures and the manufacturing sectors were reconstructed back to 1987. Multifactor productivity and related measures for the private business sector and its major subsectors are also available on a NAICS basis. Productivity indexes that take into account capital, labor, energy, materials, and service inputs are published for the 20 major industry groups that comprise the manufacturing sector, the utility services industry group, for 140 3-digit SIC manufacturing industries, and railroad transportation and air transportation. The major sector data are published in the BLS quarterly news release, *Productivity and Costs* and in the annual *Multifactor Productivity Trends* release. Industry productivity measures are updated and published annually in the news releases *Productivity and Costs by Industry*. The latest data are available at the BLS productivity and costs Web site <http://www.bls.gov/lpc/home .htm>. Detailed information on methods, limitations, and data sources appears in the BLS *Handbook of Methods,* BLS Bulletin 2490 (1997), Chapters 10 and 11.

Unions—As defined here, unions include traditional labor unions and employee associations similar to labor unions. Data on union membership status provided by BLS are for employed wage and salary workers and relate to their principal job. Earnings by union membership status are usual weekly earnings of full-time wage and salary workers. The information is collected through the Current Population Survey.

Work stoppages—Work stoppages include all strikes and lockouts known to BLS that last for at least 1 full day or shift and involve 1,000 or more workers. All stoppages, whether or not authorized by a union, legal or illegal, are counted. Excluded are work slowdowns and instances where employees report to work late or leave early to attend mass meetings or mass rallies.

Seasonal adjustment—Many economic statistics reflect a regularly recurring seasonal movement that can be estimated on the basis of past experience. By eliminating that part of the change which can be ascribed to usual seasonal variation (e.g., climate or school openings and closings), it is possible to observe the cyclical and other nonseasonal movements in the series. However, in evaluating deviations from the seasonal pattern—that is, changes in a seasonally adjusted series—it is important to note that seasonal adjustment is merely an approximation based on past experience. Seasonally adjusted estimates have a broader margin of possible error than the original data on which they are based, since they are subject not only to sampling and other errors, but also are affected by the uncertainties of the adjustment process itself.

Statistical reliability—For discussion of statistical collection, estimation, sampling procedures, and measures of statistical reliability applicable to Census Bureau and BLS data, see Appendix III.

Table 573. Civilian Population—Employment Status: 1970 to 2005

[In thousands (137,085 represents 137,085,000), except as indicated. For the civilian noninstitutional population 16 years old and over. Annual averages of monthly figures. Based on Current Population Survey; see text, Section 1, and Appendix III]

Year	Civilian noninstitutional population	Civilian labor force			Employment/population ratio[1]	Unemployed		Not in labor force	
		Total	Percent of population	Employed		Number	Percent of labor force	Number	Percent of population
1970	137,085	82,771	60.4	78,678	57.4	4,093	4.9	54,315	39.6
1980	167,745	106,940	63.8	99,303	59.2	7,637	7.1	60,806	36.2
1985	178,206	115,461	64.8	107,150	60.1	8,312	7.2	62,744	35.2
1988	184,613	121,669	65.9	114,968	62.3	6,701	5.5	62,944	34.1
1989	186,393	123,869	66.5	117,342	63.0	6,528	5.3	62,523	33.5
1990 [2] . . .	189,164	125,840	66.5	118,793	62.8	7,047	5.6	63,324	33.5
1991	190,925	126,346	66.2	117,718	61.7	8,628	6.8	64,578	33.8
1992	192,805	128,105	66.4	118,492	61.5	9,613	7.5	64,700	33.6
1993	194,838	129,200	66.3	120,259	61.7	8,940	6.9	65,638	33.7
1994 [2] . . .	196,814	131,056	66.6	123,060	62.5	7,996	6.1	65,758	33.4
1995	198,584	132,304	66.6	124,900	62.9	7,404	5.6	66,280	33.4
1996	200,591	133,943	66.8	126,708	63.2	7,236	5.4	66,647	33.2
1997 [2] . . .	203,133	136,297	67.1	129,558	63.8	6,739	4.9	66,837	32.9
1998 [2] . . .	205,220	137,673	67.1	131,463	64.1	6,210	4.5	67,547	32.9
1999 [2] . . .	207,753	139,368	67.1	133,488	64.3	5,880	4.2	68,385	32.9
2000 [2] . . .	212,577	142,583	67.1	136,891	64.4	5,692	4.0	69,994	32.9
2001	215,092	143,734	66.8	136,933	63.7	6,801	4.7	71,359	33.3
2002	217,570	144,863	66.6	136,485	62.7	8,378	5.8	72,707	33.4
2003 [2] . . .	221,168	146,510	66.2	137,736	62.3	8,774	6.0	74,658	33.8
2004 [2] . . .	223,357	147,401	66.0	139,252	62.3	8,149	5.5	75,956	34.0
2005 [2] . . .	226,082	149,320	66.0	141,730	62.7	7,591	5.1	76,762	34.0

[1] Civilian employed as a percent of the civilian noninstitutional population. [2] Data not strictly comparable with data for earlier years. See text, this section, and February 1994, March 1996, February 1997–99, and February 2003–05 issues of *Employment and Earnings*.

Source: U.S. Bureau of Labor Statistics, Bulletin 2307; and *Employment and Earnings,* monthly, January 2006 issue. See Internet site <http://www.bls.gov/cps/home.htm>.

Table 574. Civilian Labor Force and Participation Rates With Projections: 1980 to 2014

[106.9 represents 106,900,000. For civilian noninstitutional population 16 years old and over. Annual averages of monthly figures. Rates are based on annual average civilian noninstitutional population of each specified group and represent proportion of each specified group in the civilian labor force. Based on Current Population Survey; see text, Section 1, and Appendix III]

Race, Hispanic origin, sex, and age	Civilian labor force (millions)						Participation rate (percent)					
	1980	1990[1]	2000[1]	2004[1]	2005[1]	2014, proj.	1980	1990[1]	2000[1]	2004[1]	2005[1]	2014, proj.
Total [2]	106.9	125.8	142.6	147.4	149.3	162.1	63.8	66.5	67.1	66.0	66.0	65.6
White [3]	93.6	107.4	118.5	121.1	122.3	129.9	64.1	66.9	67.3	66.3	66.3	65.9
Male	54.5	59.6	64.5	66.0	66.7	70.3	78.2	77.1	75.5	74.1	74.1	72.7
Female	39.1	47.8	54.1	55.1	55.6	59.6	51.2	57.4	59.5	58.9	58.9	59.3
Black [3]	10.9	13.7	16.4	16.6	17.0	19.4	61.0	64.0	65.8	63.8	64.2	63.4
Male	5.6	6.8	7.7	7.8	8.0	9.1	70.3	71.0	69.2	66.7	67.3	64.7
Female	5.3	6.9	8.7	8.9	9.0	10.4	53.1	58.3	63.1	61.5	61.6	62.3
Asian [3,4]	(NA)	(NA)	6.3	6.3	6.5	8.3	(NA)	(NA)	67.2	65.9	66.1	65.7
Male	(NA)	(NA)	3.4	3.4	3.5	4.4	(NA)	(NA)	76.1	75.0	74.8	74.4
Female	(NA)	(NA)	2.9	2.9	3.0	3.9	(NA)	(NA)	59.2	57.6	58.2	58.1
Hispanic [5]	6.1	10.7	16.7	19.3	19.8	25.8	64.0	67.4	69.7	68.6	68.0	69.2
Male	3.8	6.5	9.9	11.6	12.0	14.9	81.4	81.4	81.5	80.4	80.1	78.6
Female	2.3	4.2	6.8	7.7	7.8	10.8	47.4	53.1	57.5	56.1	55.3	59.3
Male	61.5	69.0	76.3	79.0	80.0	86.2	77.4	76.4	74.8	73.3	73.3	71.8
16 to 19 years	5.0	4.1	4.3	3.6	3.6	3.1	60.5	55.7	52.8	43.9	43.2	38.1
20 to 24 years	8.6	7.9	7.5	8.1	8.1	8.3	85.9	84.4	82.6	79.6	79.1	77.0
25 to 34 years	17.0	19.9	17.8	17.8	17.8	20.6	95.2	94.1	93.4	91.9	91.7	95.3
35 to 44 years	11.8	17.5	20.1	19.5	19.5	18.1	95.5	94.3	92.7	91.9	92.1	90.7
45 to 54 years	9.9	11.1	16.3	17.6	18.1	18.4	91.2	90.7	88.6	87.5	87.7	86.6
55 to 64 years	7.2	6.6	7.8	9.5	10.0	13.0	72.1	67.8	67.3	68.7	69.3	68.7
65 years and over . . .	1.9	2.0	2.5	2.8	3.0	4.8	19.0	16.3	17.7	19.0	19.8	24.6
Female	45.5	56.8	66.3	68.4	69.3	75.9	51.5	57.5	59.9	59.2	59.3	59.7
16 to 19 years	4.4	3.7	4.0	3.5	3.6	3.2	52.9	51.6	51.2	43.8	44.2	40.4
20 to 24 years	7.3	6.8	6.7	7.1	7.1	7.6	68.9	71.3	73.1	70.5	70.1	70.6
25 to 34 years	12.3	16.1	14.9	14.4	14.5	16.2	65.5	73.5	76.1	73.6	73.9	75.4
35 to 44 years	8.6	14.7	17.5	16.6	16.5	15.3	65.5	76.4	77.2	75.6	75.8	75.4
45 to 54 years	7.0	9.1	14.8	16.1	16.3	17.2	59.9	71.2	76.8	76.5	76.0	78.1
55 to 64 years	4.7	4.9	6.6	8.5	8.9	12.6	41.3	45.2	51.9	56.3	57.0	61.9
65 years and over . . .	1.2	1.5	1.8	2.2	2.3	3.9	8.1	8.6	9.4	11.1	11.5	15.9

NA Not available. [1] See footnote 2, Table 573. [2] Includes other races, not shown separately. [3] The 2003 Current Population Survey (CPS) allowed respondents to choose more than one race. Beginning 2003, data represent persons who selected this race group only and exclude persons reporting more than one race. The CPS in prior years only allowed respondents to report one race group. See also comments on the race in the text for Section 1. [4] Prior to 2004, includes Pacific Islanders. [5] Persons of Hispanic or Latino origin may be any race.

Source: U.S. Bureau of Labor Statistics, *Employment and Earnings,* monthly, January 2006 issue; *Monthly Labor Review,* November 2005; and unpublished data. See Internet site <http://www.bls.gov/cps/home.htm>.

Labor Force, Employment, and Earnings   373

Table 575. **Civilian Population—Employment Status by Sex, Race, and Ethnicity: 1970 to 2005**

[In thousands (64,304 represents 64,304,000), except as indicated. Annual averages of monthly figures. See table 573 for U.S. totals and coverage]

Year, sex, race, and Hispanic origin	Civilian noninstitutional population	Civilian labor force				Unemployed		Not in labor force	
		Total	Percent of population	Employed	Employment/population ratio[1]	Number	Percent of labor force	Number	Percent of population
Male:									
1970	64,304	51,228	79.7	48,990	76.2	2,238	4.4	13,076	20.3
1980	79,398	61,453	77.4	57,186	72.0	4,267	6.9	17,945	22.6
1990 [2]	90,377	69,011	76.4	65,104	72.0	3,906	5.7	21,367	23.6
1995	95,178	71,360	75.0	67,377	70.8	3,983	5.6	23,818	25.0
2000 [2]	101,964	76,280	74.8	73,305	71.9	2,975	3.9	25,684	25.2
2003 [2]	106,435	78,238	73.5	73,332	68.9	4,906	6.3	28,197	26.5
2004 [2]	107,710	78,980	73.3	74,524	69.2	4,456	5.6	28,730	26.7
2005 [2]	109,151	80,033	73.3	75,973	69.6	4,059	5.1	29,119	26.7
Female:									
1970	72,782	31,543	43.3	29,688	40.8	1,855	5.9	41,239	56.7
1980	88,348	45,487	51.5	42,117	47.7	3,370	7.4	42,861	48.5
1990 [2]	98,787	56,829	57.5	53,689	54.3	3,140	5.5	41,957	42.5
1995	103,406	60,944	58.9	57,523	55.6	3,421	5.6	42,462	41.1
2000 [2]	110,613	66,303	59.9	63,586	57.5	2,717	4.1	44,310	40.1
2003 [2]	114,733	68,272	59.5	64,404	56.1	3,868	5.7	46,461	40.5
2004 [2]	115,647	68,421	59.2	64,728	56.0	3,694	5.4	47,225	40.8
2005 [3]	116,931	69,288	59.3	65,757	56.2	3,531	5.1	47,643	40.7
White: [3]									
1970	122,174	73,556	60.2	70,217	57.5	3,339	4.5	48,618	39.8
1980	146,122	93,600	64.1	87,715	60.0	5,884	6.3	52,523	35.9
1990 [2]	160,625	107,447	66.9	102,261	63.7	5,186	4.8	53,178	33.1
1995	166,914	111,950	67.1	106,490	63.8	5,459	4.9	54,965	32.9
2000 [2]	176,220	118,545	67.3	114,424	64.9	4,121	3.5	57,675	32.7
2003 [2]	181,292	120,546	66.5	114,235	63.0	6,311	5.2	60,746	33.5
2004 [2]	182,643	121,086	66.3	115,239	63.1	5,847	4.8	61,558	33.7
2005 [2]	184,446	122,299	66.3	116,949	63.4	5,350	4.4	62,148	33.7
Black: [3]									
1973	14,917	8,976	60.2	8,128	54.5	846	9.4	5,941	39.8
1980	17,824	10,865	61.0	9,313	52.2	1,553	14.3	6,959	39.0
1985	19,664	12,364	62.9	10,501	53.4	1,864	15.1	7,299	37.1
1990 [2]	21,477	13,740	64.0	12,175	56.7	1,565	11.4	7,737	36.0
1995	23,246	14,817	63.7	13,279	57.1	1,538	10.4	8,429	36.3
2000 [2]	24,902	16,397	65.8	15,156	60.9	1,241	7.6	8,505	34.2
2003 [2]	25,686	16,526	64.3	14,739	57.4	1,787	10.8	9,161	35.7
2004 [2]	26,065	16,638	63.8	14,909	57.2	1,729	10.4	9,428	36.2
2005 [2]	26,517	17,013	64.2	15,313	57.7	1,700	10.0	9,504	35.8
Asian: [3, 4]									
2000 [2]	9,330	6,270	67.2	6,043	64.8	227	3.6	3,060	32.8
2003 [2]	9,220	6,122	66.4	5,756	62.4	366	6.0	3,098	33.6
2004 [2]	9,519	6,271	65.9	5,994	63.0	277	4.4	3,248	34.1
2005 [2]	9,842	6,503	66.1	6,244	63.4	259	4.0	3,339	33.9
Hispanic: [5]									
1980	9,598	6,146	64.0	5,527	57.6	620	10.1	3,451	36.0
1985	11,915	7,698	64.6	6,888	57.8	811	10.5	4,217	35.4
1986	12,344	8,076	65.4	7,219	58.5	857	10.6	4,268	34.6
1990 [2]	15,904	10,720	67.4	9,845	61.9	876	8.2	5,184	32.6
1995	18,629	12,267	65.8	11,127	59.7	1,140	9.3	6,362	34.2
2000 [2]	23,938	16,689	69.7	15,735	65.7	954	5.7	7,249	30.3
2003 [2]	27,551	18,813	68.3	17,372	63.1	1,441	7.7	8,738	31.7
2004 [2]	28,109	19,272	68.6	17,930	63.8	1,342	7.0	8,837	31.4
2005 [2]	29,133	19,824	68.0	18,632	64.0	1,191	6.0	9,310	32.0
Mexican:									
1986	7,377	4,941	67.0	4,387	59.5	555	11.2	2,436	33.0
1990 [2]	9,752	6,707	68.8	6,146	63.0	561	8.4	3,045	31.2
1995	11,609	7,765	66.9	7,016	60.4	750	9.7	3,844	33.1
2000 [2]	15,333	10,783	70.3	10,144	66.2	639	5.9	4,550	29.7
2003 [2]	17,464	12,081	69.2	11,151	63.9	930	7.7	5,383	30.8
2004 [2]	17,900	12,340	68.9	11,449	64.0	892	7.2	5,559	31.1
2005 [2]	18,523	12,671	68.4	11,887	64.2	784	6.2	5,851	31.6
Puerto Rican:									
1986	1,494	804	53.8	691	46.3	113	14.0	690	46.2
1990 [2]	1,718	960	55.9	870	50.6	91	9.5	758	44.1
1995	1,896	1,098	57.9	974	51.4	123	11.2	798	42.1
2000 [2]	2,193	1,411	64.3	1,318	60.1	92	6.6	783	35.7
2003 [2]	2,652	1,649	62.2	1,495	56.4	154	9.3	1,003	37.8
2004 [2]	2,547	1,610	63.2	1,481	58.1	130	8.1	936	36.7
2005 [2]	2,654	1,619	61.0	1,492	56.2	126	7.8	1,035	39.0
Cuban:									
1986	842	570	67.7	533	63.3	36	6.4	272	32.3
1990 [2]	918	603	65.7	559	60.9	44	7.2	315	34.3
1995	1,019	613	60.2	568	55.7	45	7.4	406	39.8
2000 [2]	1,174	740	63.1	707	60.3	33	4.5	434	37.0
2003 [2]	1,191	679	57.0	638	53.6	41	6.0	512	43.0
2004 [2]	1,264	769	60.9	735	58.1	34	4.5	495	39.2
2005 [2]	1,259	755	60.0	730	58.0	25	3.3	503	40.0

[1] Civilian employed as a percent of the civilian noninstitutional population.   [2] See footnote 2, Table 573.   [3] Beginning 2003, for persons in this race group only. See footnote 3, Table 574.   [4] Prior to 2003, includes Pacific Islanders.   [5] Persons of Hispanic or Latino ethnicity may be of any race. Includes persons of other Hispanic or Latino ethnicity, not shown separately.
Source: U.S. Bureau of Labor Statistics, Bulletin 2307; and *Employment and Earnings*, monthly. January 2006 issue. See Internet site <http://www.bls.gov/cps/home.htm>.

Table 576. **Foreign-Born and Native-Born Populations—Employment Status by Selected Characteristics: 2005**

[226,082 represents 226,082,000. For civilian noninstitutional population 16 years old and over, except as indicated. Annual averages of monthly figures. Based on Current Population Survey; see text, Section 1, and Appendix III]

Characteristics	Civilian noninstitutional population (1,000)	Civilian labor force			Unemployed (1,000)	
		Total (1,000)	Partici-pation rate [1]	Employed (1,000)	Number (1,000)	Unemploy-ment rate
Total.	**226,082**	**149,320**	**66.0**	**141,730**	**7,591**	**5.1**
Male.	109,151	80,033	73.3	75,973	4,059	5.1
Female	116,931	69,288	59.3	65,757	3,531	5.1
FOREIGN BORN						
Total [2].	**32,558**	**22,042**	**67.7**	**21,022**	**1,020**	**4.6**
Sex:						
Male	16,321	13,263	81.3	12,720	544	4.1
Female	16,236	8,779	54.1	8,302	477	5.4
Age:						
16 to 24 years old	4,168	2,469	59.2	2,277	192	7.8
25 to 34 years old	7,902	6,094	77.1	5,824	270	4.4
35 to 44 years old	7,620	6,162	80.9	5,930	232	3.8
45 to 54 years old	5,578	4,473	80.2	4,285	188	4.2
55 to 64 years old	3,499	2,278	65.1	2,163	115	5.1
65 years old and over	3,791	566	14.9	542	24	4.2
Race and Hispanic ethnicity:						
White, non-Hispanic.	7,239	4,351	60.1	4,187	165	3.8
Black, non-Hispanic.	2,360	1,746	74.0	1,631	115	6.6
Asian, non-Hispanic.	7,289	4,922	67.5	4,728	194	3.9
Hispanic [3]	15,360	10,794	70.3	10,252	541	5.0
Educational attainment:						
Total 25 years and over.	28,389	19,573	68.9	18,745	828	4.2
Less than a high school diploma.	9,053	5,545	61.2	5,227	318	5.7
High school graduates, no college [4] . . .	7,106	4,804	67.6	4,599	205	4.3
Some college or associate's degree . . .	4,354	3,181	73.1	3,064	118	3.7
Bachelor's degree and higher [5].	7,876	6,043	76.7	5,856	188	3.1
NATIVE BORN						
Total [2].	**193,525**	**127,278**	**65.8**	**120,708**	**6,570**	**5.2**
Sex:						
Male	92,830	66,769	71.9	63,254	3,516	5.3
Female	100,695	60,509	60.1	57,454	3,055	5.0
Age:						
16 to 24 years old	32,505	19,821	61.0	17,493	2,328	11.7
25 to 34 years old	31,162	26,247	84.2	24,856	1,391	5.3
35 to 44 years old	35,385	29,868	84.4	28,699	1,168	3.9
45 to 54 years old	36,529	29,930	81.9	28,922	1,008	3.4
55 to 64 years old	26,666	16,701	62.6	16,186	515	3.1
Race and Hispanic ethnicity:						
White, non-Hispanic.	150,155	99,539	66.3	95,430	4,109	4.1
Black, non-Hispanic.	23,283	14,694	63.1	13,155	1,538	10.5
Asian, non-Hispanic.	2,444	1,496	61.2	1,434	62	4.2
Hispanic [3]	13,773	9,030	65.6	8,380	650	7.2
Educational attainment:						
Total, 25 years and over	161,019	107,457	66.7	103,215	4,242	3.9
Less than a high school diploma.	18,818	7,135	37.9	6,485	649	9.1
High school graduates, no college [4] . . .	53,302	33,392	62.6	31,799	1,593	4.8
Some college or associate's degree	43,915	31,793	72.4	30,561	1,232	3.9
Bachelor's degree and higher [5].	44,984	35,137	78.1	34,369	768	2.2

[1] Civilian labor force as a percent of the civilian noninstitutional population. [2] Includes other races not shown separately. [3] Persons of hispanic origin may be of any race. [4] Includes persons with a high school diploma or equivalent. [5] Includes persons with bachelor's, master's, professional, and doctoral degrees.

Source: U.S. Bureau of Labor Statistics, *Foreign-Born Workers: Labor Force Characteristics in 2005*, News, USDL 06-640, April 14, 2006. See Internet site <http://www.bls.gov/bls/newsrels.htm#OEUS>.

Table 577. **Civilian Labor Force—Percent Distribution by Sex and Age: 1980 to 2005**

[**106,940 represents 106,940,000.** For civilian noninstitutional population 16 years old and over. Annual averages of monthly figures. Based on Current Population Survey; see text, Section 1, and Appendix III]

Year and sex	Civilian labor force (1,000)	Percent distribution						
		16 to 19 years	20 to 24 years	25 to 34 years	35 to 44 years	45 to 54 years	55 to 64 years	65 yrs. and over
Total: 1980	106,940	8.8	14.9	27.3	19.1	15.8	11.2	2.9
1990 [1]	125,840	6.2	11.7	28.6	25.5	16.1	9.2	2.7
1995.	132,304	5.9	10.3	25.8	27.0	19.1	9.0	2.9
2000 [1]	142,583	5.8	10.0	23.0	26.3	21.8	10.1	3.0
2005 [1]	149,320	4.8	10.1	21.7	24.1	23.0	12.7	3.5
Male: 1980	61,453	8.1	14.0	27.6	19.3	16.1	11.8	3.1
1990 [1]	69,011	5.9	11.4	28.8	25.3	16.1	9.6	2.9
1995	71,360	5.7	10.3	26.2	26.9	18.8	9.1	3.1
2000 [1]	76,280	5.6	9.9	23.4	26.3	21.3	10.2	3.3
2005 [1]	80,033	4.5	10.1	22.3	24.4	22.6	12.6	3.7
Female: 1980	45,487	9.6	16.1	26.9	19.0	15.4	10.4	2.6
1990 [1]	56,829	6.5	12.0	28.3	25.8	16.1	8.7	2.6
1995	60,944	6.1	10.4	25.5	27.2	19.4	8.8	2.7
2000 [1]	66,303	6.0	10.2	22.5	26.4	22.3	9.9	2.7
2005 [1]	69,288	5.2	10.2	20.9	23.9	23.6	12.9	3.3

[1] See footnote 2, Table 573.

Source: U.S. Bureau of Labor Statistics, Bulletin 2307, and *Employment and Earnings*, monthly, January 2006 issue. See Internet site <http://www.bls.gov/cps/home.htm>.

Table 578. **Civilian Labor Force and Participation Rates by Educational Attainment, Sex, Race, and Hispanic Origin: 1992 to 2005**

[**106,490 represents 106,490,000.** For the civilian noninstitutional population 25 years of age and older. Annual averages of monthly figures. See Table 613 for unemployment data. Based on Current Population Survey; see text, Section 1, and Appendix III]

Year, sex, and race	Civilian labor force					Participation rate [1]				
		Percent distribution								
	Total (1,000)	Less than high school diploma	High school graduate, no degree	Less than a bachelor's degree	College graduate	Total	Less than high school diploma	High school gradu-ates, no degree	Less than a bach-elor's degree	College graduate
Total: [2]										
1992	106,490	12.6	35.6	25.4	26.4	66.5	41.2	66.4	75.3	81.3
1995	110,851	10.8	33.1	27.9	28.1	66.7	39.9	65.4	74.5	81.0
2000 [3]	120,061	10.4	31.4	27.7	30.5	67.3	43.5	64.4	73.9	79.4
2004 [3]	125,133	10.0	30.2	27.5	32.3	66.9	45.1	63.2	72.4	77.9
2005 [3]	127,030	10.0	30.1	27.5	32.4	67.1	45.5	63.2	72.5	77.9
Male:										
1992 . . .	58,439	14.1	34.0	24.0	27.9	77.0	54.7	78.3	83.9	86.9
1995 . .	59,986	12.2	32.3	26.1	29.4	76.0	52.1	76.5	82.1	85.8
2000 [3] . .	64,490	11.8	31.1	25.9	31.2	76.1	56.0	75.1	80.9	84.4
2004 [3] . .	67,306	11.7	30.6	25.3	32.4	75.3	58.3	73.5	79.2	82.8
2005 [3] . .	68,389	11.7	30.9	25.4	32.1	75.4	58.6	73.6	79.3	82.9
Female:										
1992 . . .	48,051	10.7	37.5	27.1	24.7	57.1	29.5	56.8	67.8	74.8
1995 . .	50,865	9.2	34.2	30.0	26.6	58.3	29.2	56.4	68.1	75.4
2000 [3] . .	55,572	8.8	31.8	29.7	29.7	59.4	32.3	55.5	68.0	74.0
2004 [3] . .	57,826	7.9	29.8	30.1	32.2	59.3	32.5	54.1	66.8	72.8
2005 [3] . .	58,641	8.0	29.2	30.0	32.8	59.4	32.9	53.8	66.8	72.9
White: [4]										
1992 . . .	90,627	11.8	35.5	25.5	27.2	66.3	41.1	65.4	74.6	81.0
1995 . .	94,139	10.1	33.0	27.8	29.1	66.7	40.0	64.8	73.8	80.6
2000 [3] . .	99,964	10.1	31.4	27.5	31.0	67.0	44.1	63.6	73.1	79.0
2004 [3] . .	102,965	9.8	30.0	27.5	32.7	66.8	46.0	62.4	72.0	77.5
2005 [3] . .	104,240	9.8	29.9	27.6	32.7	66.9	46.4	62.5	72.0	77.5
Black: [4]										
1992 . . .	11,583	18.2	39.5	26.4	15.9	66.7	40.6	72.9	80.9	86.2
1995 . .	12,152	13.9	37.1	30.7	18.3	66.0	36.2	69.7	79.8	85.6
2000 [3] . .	13,582	12.4	36.0	31.2	20.5	68.2	39.3	69.9	79.3	84.4
2004 [3] . .	13,951	11.2	36.2	30.3	22.3	67.0	39.6	67.6	74.9	82.9
2005 [3] . .	14,252	11.2	36.4	30.2	22.2	67.2	39.8	67.9	75.6	82.0
Asian: [4, 5]										
2000 [3] . .	5,402	9.1	20.7	20.2	50.1	70.9	46.0	65.6	76.4	79.1
2005 [3] . .	5,805	8.0	17.7	17.3	57.0	69.4	45.3	61.8	71.6	77.5
Hispanic: [6]										
1992 . . .	8,728	38.9	29.6	20.0	11.5	68.3	56.3	75.5	82.2	83.2
1995 . .	9,599	37.2	29.3	21.7	11.7	67.5	55.3	74.3	79.7	83.1
2000 [3] . .	12,975	36.7	29.3	20.6	13.4	71.5	61.9	75.0	80.8	83.5
2004 [3] . .	15,545	35.7	29.4	20.7	14.2	71.2	62.3	74.0	79.3	82.1
2005 [3] . .	16,135	35.5	29.4	20.9	14.2	70.8	61.4	74.3	78.8	81.7

[1] See headnote, Table 574.   [2] Includes other races, not shown separately.   [3] See footnote 2, Table 573.   [4] Beginning 2004, for persons in this race group only. See footnote 3, Table 574.   [5] 2000 data include Pacific Islanders.   [6] Persons of Hispanic or Latino origin may be any race.

Source: U.S. Bureau of Labor Statistics, *Employment and Earnings*, monthly, January 2006 issue. See Internet site <http://www.bls.gov/cps/home.htm>.

376   Labor Force, Employment, and Earnings

Table 579. Characteristics of the Civilian Labor Force by State: 2004

[In thousands (147,401 represents 147,401,000), except ratio and rate. For civilian noninstitutional population, 16 years old and over. Annual averages of monthly figures. Because of separate processing and weighting procedures, the totals for the United States may differ from results obtained by aggregating totals for states]

State	Total		Employed		Employed popu-lation ratio [1]	Unemployed		Rate [2]			Participation rate [3]	
	Number	Female	Total	Female		Number	Female	Total	Male	Female	Male	Female
United States..	147,401	68,421	139,252	64,728	62.3	8,149	3,694	5.5	5.6	5.4	73.3	59.2
Alabama..........	2,179	1,023	2,053	957	58.9	126	66	5.8	5.3	6.4	70.0	55.8
Alaska	331	152	306	141	65.8	25	11	7.5	7.9	7.2	76.6	65.6
Arizona	2,778	1,242	2,637	1,179	61.8	141	63	5.1	5.0	5.1	73.1	57.4
Arkansas	1,308	601	1,231	562	58.5	77	38	5.9	5.5	6.4	70.1	54.9
California	17,551	7,860	16,466	7,390	61.5	1,084	470	6.2	6.3	6.0	73.9	57.6
Colorado.........	2,525	1,142	2,389	1,084	68.9	137	58	5.4	5.7	5.1	80.5	65.3
Connecticut.......	1,790	848	1,702	807	63.0	88	40	4.9	5.1	4.7	73.3	60.0
Delaware	426	206	409	198	63.7	17	8	3.9	3.9	4.0	72.0	61.1
District of Columbia .	299	149	275	138	62.0	25	11	8.2	9.0	7.4	73.9	62.3
Florida	8,411	3,904	8,021	3,719	59.3	390	185	4.6	4.5	4.7	69.6	55.4
Georgia	4,399	2,010	4,194	1,914	64.2	205	96	4.7	4.6	4.8	76.0	59.2
Hawaii	612	295	591	287	62.5	21	8	3.4	4.1	2.7	69.7	60.1
Idaho	706	323	669	307	64.4	37	15	5.3	5.8	4.7	74.8	61.3
Illinois	6,386	2,979	5,997	2,794	62.2	389	185	6.1	6.0	6.2	73.3	59.7
Indiana..........	3,160	1,486	2,993	1,406	63.4	167	80	5.3	5.2	5.4	73.1	61.0
Iowa	1,620	774	1,545	736	67.0	75	38	4.6	4.4	4.9	75.3	65.4
Kansas..........	1,480	685	1,398	644	67.6	82	40	5.5	5.2	5.9	78.9	64.5
Kentucky........	1,977	920	1,874	876	58.7	103	44	5.2	5.6	4.8	68.9	55.4
Louisiana........	2,058	982	1,934	926	57.3	124	56	6.0	6.3	5.7	67.7	54.9
Maine...........	696	334	664	320	63.0	32	14	4.7	5.1	4.2	71.4	61.0
Maryland	2,883	1,394	2,762	1,331	65.4	121	64	4.2	3.9	4.6	75.0	62.3
Massachusetts.....	3,399	1,629	3,226	1,562	64.1	172	68	5.1	5.9	4.2	73.7	61.9
Michigan.........	5,114	2,394	4,758	2,241	61.4	356	153	7.0	7.5	6.4	72.8	59.7
Minnesota........	2,941	1,384	2,800	1,330	71.0	140	54	4.8	5.5	3.9	80.3	69.0
Mississippi	1,335	637	1,252	593	57.7	83	43	6.2	5.6	6.8	68.4	55.5
Missouri	3,017	1,445	2,844	1,365	64.3	173	80	5.7	5.9	5.6	74.1	62.7
Montana.........	486	230	462	220	63.2	24	10	4.9	5.6	4.3	71.2	62.0
Nebraska........	990	467	953	449	71.6	37	18	3.8	3.7	3.8	80.7	68.5
Nevada	1,175	518	1125	496	64.0	50	22	4.2	4.2	4.2	74.2	59.3
New Hampshire	724	337	698	326	68.5	27	11	3.7	4.0	3.3	77.9	64.7
New Jersey.......	4,388	2,032	4,178	1,933	62.7	210	99	4.8	4.7	4.9	74.0	58.4
New Mexico.......	911	427	860	403	59.9	51	25	5.6	5.4	5.8	69.9	57.5
New York	9,370	4,406	8,823	4,151	59.2	548	254	5.8	5.9	5.8	69.9	56.2
North Carolina.....	4,243	1,973	4,016	1,862	62.4	227	111	5.4	5.1	5.6	73.6	58.8
North Dakota......	359	170	347	166	69.8	12	4	3.4	4.2	2.5	77.1	67.6
Ohio	5,884	2,778	5,514	2,613	62.5	370	165	6.3	6.6	5.9	73.5	60.4
Oklahoma........	1,714	798	1,630	756	61.0	84	42	4.9	4.5	5.3	71.3	57.6
Oregon..........	1,850	840	1,710	780	61.1	140	60	7.6	8.0	7.1	73.5	59.0
Pennsylvania......	6,260	2,950	5,911	2,808	60.9	350	143	5.6	6.3	4.8	71.6	58.1
Rhode Island......	562	275	532	261	62.8	30	14	5.4	5.5	5.2	71.5	61.7
South Carolina.....	2,077	1002	1,935	931	60.6	142	71	6.9	6.7	7.1	71.2	59.5
South Dakota.....	431	207	416	200	71.0	16	8	3.7	3.5	3.8	78.1	69.4
Tennessee	2,894	1,365	2,747	1,295	60.2	147	70	5.1	5.1	5.1	69.9	57.4
Texas...........	10,989	4,901	10,332	4,614	63.0	657	287	6.0	6.1	5.9	76.4	58.2
Utah	1,206	538	1,142	509	67.3	64	29	5.3	5.2	5.4	79.5	62.7
Vermont	353	169	340	163	68.1	13	6	3.7	4.0	3.4	75.9	65.8
Virginia..........	3,766	1,791	3,619	1,718	64.6	147	72	3.9	3.8	4.0	74.3	60.8
Washington.......	3,240	1,494	3,037	1,400	63.6	202	94	6.2	6.2	6.3	74.7	61.2
West Virginia......	795	369	753	352	51.8	42	18	5.3	5.8	4.7	60.8	49.1
Wisconsin........	3,071	1,456	2,917	1,391	68.1	155	65	5.0	5.6	4.4	77.2	66.6
Wyoming	282	130	271	125	68.6	11	5	3.8	3.4	4.2	77.3	65.3

[1] Civilian employment as a percent of civilian noninstitutional population. [2] Percent unemployed of the civilian labor force.
[3] Percent of civilian noninstitutional population of each specified group in the civilian labor force.

Source: U.S. Bureau of Labor Statistics, Local Area Unemployment Statistics, *Geographic Profile of Employment and Unemployment, 2004 Annual Averages.* See Internet site <http://www.bls.gov/gps/> (accessed July 2005).

Labor Force, Employment, and Earnings   377

Table 580. Civilian Labor Force by Selected Metropolitan Area: 2005

[149,320 represents 149,320,000. For the civilian noninstitutional population 16 years old and over. Annual averages of monthly figures. Data are derived from the Local Area Unemployment Statistics Program. For metro areas with a 2000 Census population of one million or more. For definition of metropolitan areas, see Appendix II. Metropolitan areas defined as of December 2005]

Metropolitan areas ranked by population, 2000	Civilian labor force (1,000)	Unemployment rate [1]	Metropolitan areas ranked by population, 2000	Civilian labor force (1,000)	Unemployment rate [1]
United States	149,320	5.1	Portland-Vancouver-Beaverton, OR-WA	1,100	5.8
New York-Northern New Jersey-Long Island, NY-NJ-PA	9,151	4.9	Kansas City, MO-KS	1,038	5.6
Los Angeles-Long Beach-Santa Ana, CA	6,423	4.9	Sacramento-Arden-Arcade-Roseville, CA	1,020	4.7
Chicago-Naperville-Joliet, IL-IN-WI	4,738	5.9	San Jose-Sunnyvale-Santa Clara, CA	849	5.5
Philadelphia-Camden-Wilmington, PA-NJ-DE-MD	2,938	4.8	San Antonio, TX	900	4.9
Dallas-Fort Worth-Arlington, TX	3,026	5.1	Orlando-Kissimmee, FL	1,010	3.5
Miami-Fort Lauderdale-Miami Beach, FL	2,681	4.0	Columbus, OH	923	5.3
Washington-Arlington-Alexandria, DC-VA-MD-WV	2,878	3.4	Virginia Beach-Norfolk-Newport News, VA-NC	800	4.0
Houston-Sugar Land-Baytown, TX	2,629	5.5	Indianapolis-Carmel, IN	878	4.9
Boston-Cambridge-Quincy, MA-NH NECTA	2,441	4.5	Milwaukee-Waukesha-West Allis, WI	787	5.0
Detroit-Warren-Livonia, MI	2,195	7.2	Las Vegas-Paradise, NV	863	4.0
Atlanta-Sandy Springs-Marietta, GA	2,573	5.2	Charlotte-Gastonia-Concord, NC-SC	796	5.2
San Francisco-Oakland-Fremont, CA	2,174	4.9	New Orleans-Metairie-Kenner, LA	578	8.0
Riverside-San Bernardino-Ontario, CA	1,712	5.0	Nashville-Davidson-Murfreesboro, TN	743	4.4
Phoenix-Mesa-Scottsdale, AZ	1,916	4.1	Providence-Fall River-Warwick, RI-MA NECTA	704	5.2
Seattle-Tacoma-Bellevue, WA	1,736	5.1	Austin-Round Rock, TX	806	4.3
Minneapolis-St. Paul-Bloomington, MN-WI	1,851	3.8	Memphis, TN-MS-AR	600	6.2
San Diego-Carlsbad-San Marcos, CA	1,505	4.3	Buffalo-Niagara Falls, NY	587	5.3
St. Louis, MO-IL	1,461	5.5	Louisville-Jefferson County, KY-IN	612	5.9
Baltimore-Towson, MD	1,370	4.4	Jacksonville, FL	625	3.9
Pittsburgh, PA	1,209	5.2	Richmond, VA	621	3.7
Tampa-St. Petersburg-Clearwater, FL	1,295	3.7	Oklahoma City, OK	586	4.3
Denver-Aurora, CO	1,306	5.2	Hartford-West Hartford-East Hartford, CT NECTA	569	5.1
Cleveland-Elyria-Mentor, OH	1,094	5.7	Birmingham-Hoover, AL	534	3.6
Cincinnati-Middletown, OH-KY-IN	1,097	5.4	Rochester, NY	535	4.7

[1] Percent unemployed of the civilian labor force.

Source: U.S. Bureau of Labor Statistics, Local Area Unemployment Statistics program. See Internet site <http://www.bls.gov/lau/>

Table 581. School Enrollment and Labor Force Status: 1990 and 2005

[In thousands (31,421 represents 31,421,000), except percent. As of October. For the civilian noninstitutional population 16 to 24 years old. Based on Current Population Survey; see text, Section 1, and Appendix III]

Characteristic	Population 1990	Population 2005	Civilian labor force 1990	Civilian labor force 2005	Employed 1990	Employed 2005	Unemployed 1990, total	Unemployed 2005 Total	Unemployed 2005 Rate [1]
Total, 16 to 24 years [2]	31,421	36,761	20,679	22,338	18,317	20,032	2,363	2,306	10.3
Enrolled in school [2]	15,210	20,905	7,301	9,442	6,527	8,528	774	914	9.7
16 to 19 years	10,118	13,582	4,244	4,937	3,645	4,267	599	670	13.6
20 to 24 years	5,092	7,323	3,057	4,505	2,882	4,261	174	244	5.4
Sex:									
Male	7,704	10,269	3,635	4,344	3,215	3,912	420	432	9.9
Female	7,507	10,636	3,666	5,098	3,312	4,616	353	482	9.5
College level	8,139	11,000	4,542	6,367	4,231	5,976	311	391	6.1
Full-time	6,810	9,396	3,376	4,952	3,117	4,612	259	340	6.9
Race:									
White [3]	12,308	16,199	6,294	7,756	5,705	7,077	588	679	8.8
Below college	5,535	7,597	2,374	2,587	2,021	2,200	354	387	14.9
College level	6,772	8,603	3,919	5,169	3,685	4,877	234	292	5.7
Black [3]	2,129	2,893	718	948	576	777	142	171	18.1
Below college	1,207	1,565	306	292	212	190	94	102	35.0
College level	922	1,328	411	656	364	587	47	69	10.5
Asian [3]	(NA)	1,058	(NA)	400	(NA)	381	(NA)	19	4.8
Below college	(NA)	343	(NA)	74	(NA)	70	(NA)	4	(4)
College level	(NA)	715	(NA)	326	(NA)	311	(NA)	15	4.6
Not enrolled [2]	16,210	15,856	13,379	12,896	11,789	11,504	1,589	1,392	10.8
White [3]	13,317	12,412	11,276	10,285	10,193	9,323	1,083	962	9.4
Black [3]	2,441	2,448	1,752	1,843	1,298	1,506	454	338	18.3
Asian [3]	(NA)	419	(NA)	339	(NA)	314	(NA)	25	7.5

NA Not available. [1] Percent unemployed of civilian labor force in each category. [2] Includes other races, not shown separately. [3] 2005 data for persons in this race group only. See footnote 3, Table 574. [4] Data not shown where base is less than 75,000.

Source: U.S. Bureau of Labor Statistics, Bulletin 2307; College Enrollment and Work Activity of High School Graduates, News USDL 06-514, March 24, 2006; and unpublished data. See Internet site <http://www.bls.gov/bls/newsrels.htm#OEUS>.

Table 582. Labor Force Participation Rates by Marital Status, Sex, and Age: 1970 to 2005

[For the civilian noninstitutional population 16 years old and over. Annual averages of monthly figures. See Table 579 for definition of participation rate. Based on Current Population Survey; see text, Section 1, and Appendix III]

Marital status and year	Male participation rate Total	16–19 years	20–24 years	25–34 years	35–44 years	45–64 years	65 years and over	Female participation rate Total	16–19 years	20–24 years	25–34 years	35–44 years	45–64 years	65 years and over
Single:														
1970.....	65.5	54.6	73.8	87.9	86.2	75.7	25.2	56.8	44.7	73.0	81.4	78.6	73.0	19.7
1980.....	72.6	59.9	81.3	89.2	82.2	66.9	16.8	64.4	53.6	75.2	83.3	76.9	65.6	13.9
1985.....	73.8	56.3	81.5	89.4	84.6	65.5	15.6	66.6	52.3	76.3	82.4	80.8	67.9	9.8
1990 [1] ...	74.8	55.1	81.6	89.9	84.5	67.3	15.7	66.7	51.7	74.5	80.9	80.8	66.2	12.1
1995.....	73.7	54.4	80.3	88.7	81.4	67.0	17.9	66.8	52.2	72.9	80.2	79.5	67.3	11.6
2000 [1] ...	73.6	52.5	80.5	89.4	82.9	69.7	17.3	68.9	51.1	76.1	83.9	80.9	69.9	10.8
2001.....	72.7	50.0	79.6	89.0	83.2	69.8	15.4	68.1	49.1	75.3	83.2	81.3	69.9	12.1
2002.....	71.7	47.2	78.7	88.7	83.1	69.6	16.9	67.4	47.3	74.5	83.3	79.9	69.6	14.3
2003 [1] ...	70.4	44.0	77.9	87.7	82.9	67.6	19.4	66.2	44.8	72.9	82.2	79.8	69.9	15.2
2004 [1] ...	70.2	43.6	77.7	87.9	82.7	67.8	20.3	65.9	43.8	73.1	81.8	80.5	70.9	14.7
2005 [1] ...	70.1	42.9	77.0	87.9	82.9	68.6	18.8	66.0	44.2	72.6	81.4	80.7	70.9	15.5
Married: [2]														
1970.....	86.1	92.3	94.7	98.0	98.1	91.2	29.9	40.5	37.8	47.9	38.8	46.8	44.0	7.3
1980.....	80.9	91.3	96.9	97.5	97.2	84.3	20.5	49.8	49.3	61.4	58.8	61.8	46.9	7.3
1985.....	78.7	91.0	95.6	97.4	96.8	81.7	16.8	53.8	49.6	65.7	65.8	68.1	49.4	6.6
1990 [1] ...	78.6	92.1	95.6	96.9	96.7	82.6	17.5	58.4	49.5	66.1	69.6	74.0	56.5	8.5
1995.....	77.5	89.2	94.9	96.3	95.4	82.4	18.0	61.0	51.6	64.7	72.0	75.7	62.7	9.1
2000 [1] ...	77.3	79.5	94.1	96.7	95.8	83.0	19.2	61.1	53.2	63.8	70.3	74.8	65.4	10.1
2001.....	77.4	77.7	94.2	95.9	95.6	83.7	19.1	61.2	45.1	63.9	69.9	74.5	66.1	10.3
2002.....	77.4	81.1	93.3	95.7	95.1	83.8	19.4	61.0	49.6	63.4	69.3	73.8	66.5	10.7
2003 [1] ...	77.3	76.6	93.2	95.3	95.1	83.5	19.9	61.0	46.7	62.6	68.5	73.3	67.4	11.3
2004 [1] ...	77.1	77.4	92.4	95.6	95.1	83.1	20.4	60.5	41.1	60.9	67.6	72.7	67.0	11.6
2005 [1] ...	77.2	71.4	93.4	95.3	95.2	83.6	21.4	60.7	44.1	61.1	68.4	73.0	67.0	12.5
Other: [3]														
1970.....	60.7	(B)	90.4	93.7	91.1	78.5	19.3	40.3	48.6	60.3	64.6	68.8	61.9	10.0
1980.....	67.5	(B)	92.6	94.1	91.9	73.3	13.7	43.6	50.0	68.4	76.5	77.1	60.2	8.2
1985.....	68.7	(B)	95.1	93.7	91.8	72.8	11.4	45.1	51.9	66.2	76.9	81.6	61.0	7.5
1990 [1] ...	68.9	(B)	93.1	93.0	90.7	74.9	12.0	47.2	53.9	65.4	77.0	82.1	65.0	8.4
1995.....	66.2	(B)	92.7	90.9	88.2	72.4	12.1	47.4	55.8	67.2	77.1	80.7	67.2	8.4
2000 [1] ...	66.8	60.5	88.1	93.2	89.9	73.9	12.9	49.0	46.0	74.0	83.1	82.9	69.8	8.7
2001.....	66.0	57.3	85.4	92.4	89.4	73.5	13.9	49.0	47.2	75.5	81.6	82.6	69.3	8.9
2002.....	65.5	57.5	87.4	91.2	89.6	74.1	13.2	49.2	46.2	74.7	80.7	82.7	69.7	8.9
2003 [1] ...	65.0	45.6	88.0	91.4	89.3	72.4	14.3	49.6	44.1	71.4	79.1	81.9	70.7	9.8
2004 [1] ...	64.9	53.1	87.2	90.6	88.6	72.8	14.3	49.6	48.7	70.0	79.4	81.7	69.8	10.4
2005 [1] ...	64.9	54.9	86.4	90.4	89.4	72.7	15.1	49.4	46.8	67.4	78.1	80.9	69.4	10.5

B Percentage not shown where base is less than 35,000.   [1] See footnote 2, Table 573.   [2] Spouse present.   [3] Widowed, divorced, and married (spouse absent).

Source: U.S. Bureau of Labor Statistics, Bulletins 2217 and 2340; and unpublished data.

Table 583. Marital Status of Women in the Civilian Labor Force: 1970 to 2005

[31,543 represents 31,543,000. For civilian noninstitutional population 16 years old and over. Annual averages of monthly figures. Based on the Current Population Survey; see text, Section 1, and Appendix III]

Year	Female civilian labor force (1,000) Total	Single	Married [1]	Other [2]	Female participation rate [3] Total	Single	Married [1]	Other [2]
1970	31,543	7,265	18,475	5,804	43.3	56.8	40.5	40.3
1975	37,475	9,125	21,484	6,866	46.3	59.8	44.3	40.1
1980	45,487	11,865	24,980	8,643	51.5	64.4	49.8	43.6
1985	51,050	13,163	27,894	9,993	54.5	66.6	53.8	45.1
1988	54,742	14,194	29,921	10,627	56.6	67.7	56.7	46.2
1989	56,030	14,377	30,548	11,104	57.4	68.0	57.8	47.0
1990 [4]	56,829	14,612	30,901	11,315	57.5	66.7	58.4	47.2
1991	57,178	14,681	31,112	11,385	57.4	66.2	58.5	46.8
1992	58,141	14,872	31,700	11,570	57.8	66.2	59.3	47.1
1993	58,795	15,031	31,980	11,784	57.9	66.2	59.4	47.2
1994 [4]	60,239	15,333	32,888	12,018	58.8	66.7	60.7	47.5
1995	60,944	15,467	33,359	12,118	58.9	66.8	61.0	47.4
1996	61,857	15,842	33,618	12,397	59.3	67.1	61.2	48.1
1997 [4]	63,036	16,492	33,802	12,742	59.8	67.9	61.6	48.6
1998 [4]	63,714	17,087	33,857	12,771	59.8	68.5	61.2	48.8
1999 [4]	64,855	17,575	34,372	12,909	60.0	68.7	61.2	49.1
2000 [4]	66,303	17,849	35,146	13,308	59.9	68.9	61.1	49.0
2001	66,848	18,021	35,236	13,592	59.8	68.1	61.2	49.0
2002	67,363	18,203	35,477	13,683	59.6	67.4	61.0	49.2
2003 [4]	68,272	18,397	36,046	13,828	59.5	66.2	61.0	49.6
2004 [4]	68,421	18,616	35,845	13,961	59.2	65.9	60.5	49.6
2005 [4]	69,288	19,183	35,941	14,163	59.3	66.0	60.7	49.4

[1] Husband present.   [2] Widowed, divorced, or separated.   [3] See footnote 3, Table 579 for definition of participation rate.   [4] See footnote 2, Table 573.

Source: U.S. Bureau of Labor Statistics, Bulletin 2307; and unpublished data.

Labor Force, Employment, and Earnings   379

Table 584. Employment Status of Women by Marital Status and Presence and Age of Children: 1970 to 2005

[As of March (7.0 represents 7,000,000). For the civilian noninstitutional persons 16 years and over. Based on the Current Population Survey; see text, Section 1, and Appendix III]

Item	Total			With any children								
				Total			Children 6 to 17 only			Children under 6		
	Single	Mar-ried[1]	Other[2]	Single	Mar-ried[1]	Other[2]	Single	Mar-ried[1]	Other[2]	Single	Mar-ried[1]	Other[2]
IN LABOR FORCE (mil.)												
1970	7.0	18.4	5.9	(NA)	10.2	1.9	(NA)	6.3	1.3	(NA)	3.9	0.6
1980	11.2	24.9	8.8	0.6	13.7	3.6	0.2	8.4	2.6	0.3	5.2	1.0
1990	14.0	31.0	11.2	1.5	16.5	4.2	0.6	9.3	3.0	0.9	7.2	1.2
1995	15.0	33.6	12.0	2.1	18.0	4.6	0.8	10.2	3.3	1.3	7.8	1.3
2000	17.8	35.0	13.2	3.1	18.2	4.5	1.2	10.8	3.4	1.8	7.3	1.1
2003 [3]	17.9	36.2	14.2	3.2	18.3	4.7	1.3	11.1	3.6	1.9	7.2	1.1
2004 [3]	18.1	35.9	14.2	3.3	18.0	4.7	1.4	10.8	3.6	1.9	7.1	1.1
2005 [3]	18.6	35.8	14.2	3.4	18.2	4.6	1.4	10.9	3.4	1.9	7.3	1.2
PARTICIPATION RATE [4]												
1970	53.0	40.8	39.1	(NA)	39.7	60.7	(NA)	49.2	66.9	(NA)	30.3	52.2
1980	61.5	50.1	44.0	52.0	54.1	69.4	67.6	61.7	74.6	44.1	45.1	60.3
1990	66.4	58.2	46.8	55.2	66.3	74.2	69.7	73.6	79.7	48.7	58.9	63.6
1995	65.5	61.1	47.3	57.5	70.2	75.3	67.0	76.2	79.5	53.0	63.5	66.3
2000	68.6	62.0	50.2	73.9	70.6	82.7	79.7	77.2	85.0	70.5	62.8	76.6
2003 [3]	65.0	61.8	50.1	73.1	69.2	82.0	77.6	77.0	84.8	70.2	59.8	74.3
2004 [3]	64.5	60.9	50.3	72.6	68.2	80.7	79.2	75.6	83.0	68.4	59.3	74.4
2005 [3]	65.1	60.2	49.8	72.9	68.1	79.8	79.8	75.0	82.2	68.4	59.8	73.6
EMPLOYMENT (mil.)												
1970	6.5	17.5	5.6	(NA)	9.6	1.8	(NA)	6.0	1.2	(NA)	3.6	0.6
1980	10.1	23.6	8.2	0.4	12.8	3.3	0.2	8.1	2.4	0.2	4.8	0.9
1990	12.9	29.9	10.5	1.2	15.8	3.8	0.5	8.9	2.7	0.7	6.9	1.1
1995	13.7	32.3	11.3	1.8	17.2	4.2	0.7	9.8	3.1	1.1	7.3	1.2
2000	16.4	34.0	12.7	2.7	17.6	4.3	1.1	10.6	3.2	1.6	7.1	1.1
2003 [3]	16.2	34.8	13.2	2.8	17.5	4.3	1.2	10.7	3.3	1.6	6.8	1.0
2004 [3]	16.5	34.6	13.3	2.8	17.2	4.4	1.2	10.4	3.3	1.6	6.8	1.0
2005 [3]	16.9	34.7	13.5	2.9	17.6	4.3	1.3	10.6	3.2	1.6	7.1	1.1
UNEMPLOYMENT RATE [5]												
1970	7.1	4.8	4.8	(NA)	6.0	7.2	(NA)	4.8	5.9	(NA)	7.9	9.8
1980	10.3	5.3	6.4	23.2	5.9	9.2	15.6	4.4	7.9	29.2	8.3	12.8
1990	8.2	3.5	5.7	18.4	4.2	8.5	14.5	3.8	7.7	20.8	4.8	10.2
1995	8.7	3.9	5.8	16.6	4.3	8.1	11.8	3.6	7.1	19.5	5.3	10.8
2000	7.3	2.7	4.3	11.0	2.9	5.1	8.7	2.6	4.8	14.7	3.5	5.9
2003 [3]	9.4	3.8	6.5	13.4	4.1	8.9	11.6	3.6	7.7	14.7	4.9	13.0
2004 [3]	8.8	3.7	6.1	13.1	4.1	7.2	10.6	3.7	6.3	14.8	4.7	9.9
2005 [3]	8.9	3.0	5.3	15.0	3.1	6.9	10.7	2.9	5.9	14.8	3.4	9.9

NA Not available. [1] Husband present. [2] Widowed, divorced, or separated. [3] See footnote 2, Table 573. [4] Percent of women in each specific category in the labor force. [5] Unemployed as a percent of civilian labor force in specified group.

Source: U.S. Bureau of Labor Statistics, Bulletin 2307; and unpublished data.

Table 585. Labor Force Participation Rates for Wives, Husband Present by Age of Own Youngest Child: 1975 to 2005

[As of March. For civilian noninstitutional population, 16 years old and over. For definition of participation rate, see Table 584. Based on Current Population Survey; see text, Section 1, and Appendix III]

Presence and age of child	Total			White [1]			Black [1]		
	1975	1990	2005	1975	1990	2005	1975	1990	2005
Wives, total	44.4	58.2	60.2	43.6	57.6	59.8	54.1	64.7	66.3
No children under 18	43.8	51.1	53.8	43.6	50.8	53.5	47.6	52.9	57.0
With children under 18	44.9	66.3	68.1	43.6	65.6	67.8	58.4	75.6	76.4
Under 6, total	36.7	58.9	59.8	34.7	57.8	59.3	54.9	73.1	72.8
Under 3	32.7	55.5	57.0	30.7	54.9	56.7	50.1	67.5	68.7
1 year or under	30.8	53.9	55.8	29.2	53.3	55.5	50.0	64.4	65.5
2 years	37.1	60.9	61.0	35.1	60.3	61.0	56.4	75.4	72.6
3 to 5 years	42.2	64.1	64.2	40.1	62.5	63.2	61.2	80.4	77.7
3 years	41.2	63.1	62.7	39.0	62.3	62.1	62.7	74.5	80.3
4 years	41.2	65.1	64.8	38.7	63.2	64.5	64.9	80.6	74.8
5 years	44.4	64.5	67.4	43.8	62.0	65.4	56.3	86.2	84.4
6 to 13 years	51.8	73.0	73.0	50.7	72.6	72.8	65.7	77.6	78.7
14 to 17 years	53.5	75.1	79.6	53.4	74.9	80.1	52.3	78.8	80.4

[1] 2005 for persons in this race group only. See footnote 3, Table 574.

Source: U.S. Bureau of Labor Statistics, Bulletin 2340; and unpublished data.

Table 586. Married Couples by Labor Force Status of Spouse: 1986 to 2005

[50,933 represents 50,933,000. Based on the Current Population Survey and subject to sampling error; for details see source and Appendix III]

Year	Number (1,000)					Percent distribution			
	All married couples	In labor force		Wife only	Husband and wife not in labor force	In labor force		Wife only	Husband and wife not in labor force
		Husband and wife	Husband only			Husband and wife	Husband only		
TOTAL									
1986	50,933	25,428	14,675	2,362	8,468	49.9	28.8	4.6	16.6
1990	52,317	28,056	13,013	2,453	8,794	53.6	24.9	4.7	16.8
1995	53,858	29,999	11,777	3,043	9,039	55.7	21.9	5.7	16.8
1999	54,770	30,635	11,704	3,185	9,245	55.9	21.4	5.8	16.9
2000	55,311	31,095	11,815	3,301	9,098	56.2	21.4	6.0	16.4
2001	56,592	31,794	12,213	3,274	9,311	56.2	21.6	5.8	16.5
2002	56,747	31,637	12,327	3,388	9,395	55.8	21.7	6.0	16.6
2003	57,320	31,951	12,443	3,553	9,373	55.7	21.7	6.2	16.4
2004	57,719	31,536	12,980	3,684	9,519	54.6	22.5	6.4	16.5
2005	58,109	31,476	13,434	3,648	9,551	54.2	23.1	6.3	16.4
WITH CHILDREN UNDER 18									
1986	24,630	14,606	8,916	518	590	59.3	36.2	2.1	2.4
1990	24,537	15,768	7,667	558	544	64.3	31.2	2.3	2.2
1995	25,241	17,024	6,863	756	598	67.4	27.2	3.0	2.4
1999	25,066	16,887	6,998	765	418	67.4	27.9	3.1	1.7
2000	25,248	17,116	6,950	795	387	67.8	27.5	3.1	1.5
2001	25,980	17,563	7,210	784	422	67.6	27.8	3.0	1.6
2002	25,792	17,233	7,301	777	482	66.8	28.3	3.0	1.9
2003	25,914	17,065	7,499	893	457	65.9	28.9	3.4	1.8
2004	25,793	16,691	7,715	952	433	64.7	29.9	3.7	1.7
2005	26,180	16,964	7,877	935	402	64.8	30.1	3.6	1.5
WITH CHILDREN UNDER 6									
1986	11,924	6,271	5,284	155	215	52.6	44.3	1.3	1.8
1990	12,051	6,932	4,692	192	235	57.5	38.9	1.6	2.0
1995	11,951	7,406	4,059	233	253	62.0	34.0	1.9	2.1
1999	11,461	6,878	4,182	257	144	60.0	36.5	2.2	1.3
2000	11,393	6,984	4,077	211	121	61.3	35.8	1.9	1.1
2001	11,732	7,054	4,296	247	134	60.1	36.6	2.1	1.1
2002	11,531	6,796	4,311	250	175	58.9	37.4	2.2	1.5
2003	11,743	6,747	4,507	298	191	57.5	38.4	2.5	1.6
2004	11,711	6,657	4,579	317	158	56.8	39.1	2.7	1.3
2005	11,905	6,876	4,591	300	137	57.8	38.6	2.5	1.2

Source: U.S. Bureau of the Census, Table MC-1, Married Couples by Labor Force Status of Spouses: 1986 to Present; released 25 May 2006. See Internet site <http://www.census.gov/population/www/socdemo/hh-fam.html>.

Table 587. Employed Civilians and Weekly Hours: 1980 to 2005

[In thousands (99,303 represents 99,303,000), except as indicated. For civilian noninstitutional population 16 years old and over. Annual averages of monthly figures. Based on Current Population Survey; see text, Section 1, and Appendix III]

Item	1980	1990 [1]	1995	2000 [1]	2003 [1]	2004 [1]	2005 [1]
Total employed	99,303	118,793	124,900	136,891	137,736	139,252	141,730
Age:							
16 to 19 years old	7,710	6,581	6,419	7,189	5,919	5,907	5,978
20 to 24 years old	14,087	13,401	12,443	13,229	13,433	13,723	13,792
25 to 34 years old	27,204	33,935	32,356	31,549	30,383	30,423	30,680
35 to 44 years old	19,523	30,817	34,202	36,433	34,881	34,580	34,630
45 to 54 years old	16,234	19,525	24,378	30,310	31,914	32,469	33,207
55 to 64 years old	11,586	11,189	11,435	14,002	16,598	17,331	18,349
65 years old and over.	2,960	3,346	3,666	4,179	4,608	4,819	5,094
Class of worker:							
Nonagricultural industries	95,938	115,570	121,460	134,427	135,461	137,020	139,532
Wage and salary worker [2]	88,525	106,598	112,448	125,114	126,015	127,463	129,931
Self-employed	7,000	8,719	8,902	9,205	9,344	9,467	9,509
Unpaid family workers	413	253	110	108	101	90	93
Agriculture and related industries	3,364	3,223	3,440	2,464	2,275	2,232	2,197
Wage and salary worker [2]	1,425	1,740	1,814	1,421	1,299	1,242	1,212
Self-employed	1,642	1,378	1,580	1,010	951	964	955
Unpaid family workers	297	105	45	33	25	27	30
Weekly hours:							
Nonagricultural industries:							
Wage and salary workers [2].	38.1	39.2	39.2	39.6	39.0	39.0	39.1
Self-employed	41.2	40.8	39.4	39.7	38.4	38.4	38.4
Unpaid family workers	34.7	34.0	33.5	32.5	31.7	31.3	32.2
Agriculture and related industries:							
Wage and salary workers [2].	41.6	41.2	41.1	43.2	42.6	42.7	43.7
Self-employed	49.3	46.8	43.5	45.3	45.1	44.4	43.6
Unpaid family workers	38.6	38.5	42.0	38.3	33.4	37.3	44.0

[1] See footnote 2, Table 573.   [2] Includes the incorporated self-employed.

Source: U.S. Bureau of Labor Statistics, *Employment and Earnings*, monthly, January issues; and unpublished data. See Internet site <http://www.bls.gov/cps/home.htm>.

Labor Force, Employment, and Earnings   381

Table 588. **Persons at Work by Hours Worked: 2005**

[136,218 represents 136,218,000. For civilian noninstitutional population 16 years old and over. Annual averages of monthly figures. Based on Current Population Survey; see text, Section 1, and Appendix III. See headnote, Table 591 regarding industries]

Hours of work	Persons at work (1,000) Total	Agriculture and related industries	Non-agricultural industries	Percent distribution Total	Agriculture and related industries	Non-agricultural industries
Total....................	136,218	2,103	134,115	100.0	100.0	100.0
1 to 34 hours................	32,268	550	31,717	23.7	26.2	23.6
1 to 4 hours................	1,385	54	1,330	1.0	2.6	1.0
5 to 14 hours................	4,990	138	4,852	3.7	6.6	3.6
15 to 29 hours................	16,008	246	15,762	11.8	11.7	11.8
30 to 34 hours................	9,885	112	9,773	7.3	5.3	7.3
35 hours and over................	103,950	1,553	102,397	76.3	73.8	76.4
35 to 39 hours................	9,371	103	9,269	6.9	4.9	6.9
40 hours................	56,179	520	55,659	41.2	24.7	41.5
41 hours and over................	38,400	930	37,470	28.2	44.2	27.9
41 to 48 hours................	13,609	147	13,463	10.0	7.0	10.0
49 to 59 hours................	14,569	256	14,313	10.7	12.2	10.7
60 hours and over................	10,222	528	9,694	7.5	25.1	7.2
Average weekly hours: Persons at work......	39.2	43.7	39.1	(X)	(X)	(X)
Persons usually working full-time........	42.9	49.9	42.8	(X)	(X)	(X)

X Not applicable.

Source: U.S. Bureau of Labor Statistics, *Employment and Earnings*, monthly, January 2006 issue. See Internet site <http://www.bls.gov/cps/home.htm>.

Table 589. **Persons With a Job, But Not at Work: 1980 to 2005**

[In thousands (5,881 represents 5,881,000), except percent. For civilian noninstitutional population 16 years old and over. Annual averages of monthly figures. Based on Current Population Survey; see text, Section 1 and Appendix III]

Reason for not working	1980	1990 [1]	1995	1998 [1]	1999 [1]	2000 [1]	2001	2002	2003 [1]	2004 [1]	2005 [1]
All industries, number......	5,881	6,160	5,582	5,586	5,407	5,681	5,631	5,394	5,469	5,482	5,511
Percent of employed.....	5.9	5.2	4.5	4.2	4.1	4.2	4.1	4.0	4.0	3.9	3.9
Reason for not working:											
Vacation..............	3,320	3,529	2,982	3,033	2,899	3,109	3,039	2,929	2,922	2,923	2,892
Illness...............	1,426	1,341	1,084	1,095	1,096	1,156	1,095	1,072	1,090	1,058	1,088
Bad weather...........	155	90	122	130	104	89	100	97	123	133	145
Industrial dispute........	105	24	21	10	7	14	9	7	18	10	6
All other..............	876	1,177	1,373	1,318	1,300	1,313	1,388	1,289	1,316	1,358	1,381

[1] See footnote 2, Table 573.

Source: U.S. Bureau of Labor Statistics, *Employment and Earnings*, monthly, January issues; and unpublished data. See Internet site <http://www.bls.gov/cps/home.htm>.

Table 590. **Class of Worker by Sex and Selected Characteristic: 2005**

[In percent, except as indicated (10,464 represents 10,464,000). For the civilian noninstitutional population 16 years old and over. Annual averages of monthly figures. Based on Current Population Survey; see text, Section 1, and Appendix III]

Characteristic	Unincorporated self-employed Total	Male	Female	Incorporated self-employed Total	Male	Female	Wage and salary workers [1] Total	Male	Female
Total (1,000)..............	10,464	6,632	3,832	5,254	3,828	1,425	125,889	65,467	60,423
PERCENT DISTRIBUTION	100.0	100.0	100.0	100.0	100.0	100.0	100.0	100.0	100.0
Age: 16 to 19 years old.........	0.8	0.8	0.6	0.1	0.1	0.1	4.7	4.4	5.0
20 to 24 years old............	3.0	3.3	2.4	1.1	1.0	1.4	10.7	10.7	10.6
25 to 34 years old............	15.4	14.9	16.2	11.6	11.5	11.8	22.6	23.8	21.3
35 to 44 years old............	24.4	23.7	25.7	26.6	26.3	27.3	24.4	24.7	23.9
45 to 54 years old............	26.9	27.2	26.5	31.4	31.4	31.6	22.8	22.0	23.6
55 to 64 years old............	19.8	19.5	20.3	20.9	21.2	20.1	12.0	11.6	12.5
65 years old and over	9.7	10.6	8.2	8.2	8.4	7.6	2.9	2.8	3.0
Race/ethnicity: White [2]...........	87.6	87.9	87.2	89.7	90.3	88.0	81.8	83.2	80.3
Black [2]................	6.3	6.3	6.1	3.7	3.4	4.6	11.5	10.1	13.0
Asian [2]	4.1	3.8	4.6	5.3	5.0	6.0	4.4	4.4	4.3
Hispanic [3]	9.9	11.2	7.6	6.2	6.2	6.2	13.7	15.8	11.4
Country of birth: U.S.-born	86.6	85.5	88.3	86.6	86.8	86.2	85.0	82.8	87.4
Foreign-born...............	13.7	14.7	12.0	13.4	13.2	13.9	15.0	17.2	12.6
U.S. citizen...............	6.2	6.2	6.1	8.7	8.7	8.8	5.9	5.8	5.9
Not a U.S. citizen...........	7.5	8.5	5.8	4.6	4.5	5.0	9.1	11.3	6.7

[1] Excludes the incorporated self-employed.   [2] For persons in this race group only. See footnote 3, Table 574.   [3] Persons of Hispanic or Latino origin may be of any race.

Source: U.S. Bureau of Labor Statistics, Current Population Survey, unpublished data.

Table 591. Self-Employed Workers by Industry and Occupation: 2000 to 2005

[In thousands (10,214 represents 10,214,000). For civilian noninstitutional population 16 years old and over. Annual averages of monthly figures. Data represent the unincorporated self-employed; the incorporated self-employed are considered wage and salary workers. Based on the occupational and industrial classification derived from those used in the 2000 census and are not comparable to those used in the 1990 census. See text, this section. Based on the Current Population Survey; see text, Section 1, and Appendix III]

Item	2000	2002	2003 [1]	2004 [1]	2005 [1]
Total self-employed	10,214	9,926	10,295	10,431	10,464
Industry:					
Agriculture and related industries	1,010	1,003	951	964	955
Mining	12	13	9	13	11
Construction	1,728	1,598	1,717	1,848	1,830
Manufacturing	334	312	325	316	327
Wholesale and retail trade	1,221	1,163	1,247	1,153	1,251
Transportation and utilities	348	369	357	410	442
Information . . . . . [2]	139	145	152	146	126
Financial activities [2]	735	675	736	792	785
Professional and business services [2]	1,927	1,863	1,908	1,993	1,957
Education and health services [2]	1,107	1,119	1,138	1,105	1,071
Leisure and hospitality [2]	660	627	686	660	674
Other services [3]	993	1,041	1,071	1,031	1,036
Occupation:					
Management, professional, and related occupations	4,169	4,064	4,176	4,179	4,085
Service occupations	1,775	1,786	1,690	1,757	1,774
Sales and office occupations	1,982	1,883	1,945	1,909	1,986
Natural resources, construction, and maintenance occupations	1,591	1,503	1,795	1,847	1,864
Production, transportation, and material-moving occupations	698	690	689	739	756

[1] See footnote 2, Table 573.   [2] For composition of industries, see Table 611.   [3] Includes private households.

Source: U.S. Bureau of Labor Statistics, *Employment and Earnings*, monthly, January issues. See Internet site <http://www.bls.gov/cps/home.htm>.

Table 592. Persons Doing Job-Related Work at Home: 2004

[136,602 represents 136,602,000. As of May. For persons at work 16 years and over in nonagricultural industries doing job-related work at home at least once a week as part of their primary job. Based on the Current Population Survey; see text, Section 1, and Appendix III. Industry and occupational classifications are those based on the 2000 census. See text, this section]

Characteristic	Total employed [1] (1,000)	Persons who usually worked at home [2]					
				Percent distribution by class of worker			
					Wage and salary workers		
		Total (1,000)	Percent of employed	Total [3]	Paid work at home	Unpaid work at home	Self-employed [4]
Total [5]	136,602	20,673	15.1	100.0	16.2	49.3	33.7
SEX							
Male	72,417	10,780	14.9	100.0	14.7	47.3	37.6
Female	64,185	9,893	15.4	100.0	17.8	51.4	29.4
RACE AND HISPANIC ORIGIN							
White [6]	111,756	18,255	16.3	100.0	16.4	49.0	33.8
Black [6]	15,800	1,245	7.9	100.0	14.2	53.0	31.0
Asian [6]	5,630	718	12.7	100.0	14.2	52.1	33.7
Hispanic origin [7]	17,577	1,255	7.1	100.0	19.1	45.0	34.4
OCCUPATION							
Management, professional, and related occupations	47,829	13,445	28.1	100.0	13.9	59.9	25.7
Management, business, and financial operations occupations . . .	19,205	5,602	29.2	100.0	16.2	46.6	36.9
Professional & related occupations . .	28,623	7,842	27.4	100.0	12.2	69.5	17.7
Service occupations	22,752	1,414	6.2	100.0	20.6	20.9	54.8
Sales and office occupations	35,133	4,291	12.2	100.0	24.1	36.1	38.6
Sales and related occupations	15,886	3,137	19.7	100.0	21.8	35.4	42.2
Office and administrative support occupations	19,247	1,154	6.0	100.0	30.5	38.0	28.9
Natural resources, construction, and maintenance occupations	13,111	1,036	7.9	100.0	10.2	15.1	73.8
Farming, fishing, and forestry occupations	195	3	1.5	100.0	(B)	(B)	(B)
Construction and extraction occupations	7,927	705	8.9	100.0	6.1	13.3	80.6
Installation, maintenance, and repair occupations	4,989	329	6.6	100.0	18.4	19.1	59.6
Production, transportation, and material-moving occupations	17,777	488	2.7	100.0	10.6	26.6	62.8
Production occupations	9,240	276	3.0	100.0	12.8	22.1	65.0
Transportation and material-moving occupations	8,538	212	2.5	100.0	7.7	32.5	59.8

B Data not shown where the base is less than 75,000.   [1] Includes persons who did not report information on work at home.   [2] Persons who worked at home at least once per week as part of their primary job.   [3] Unpaid familiy workers and wage and salary workers who did not report pay status are included in the total but not shown separately.   [4] Includes the incorporated and unincorporated self-employed.   [5] Includes other races, not shown separately.   [6] For persons in this race group only. See footnote 2, Table 574.   [7] Persons of Hispanic origin may be any race.

Source: U.S. Bureau of Labor Statistics, *Work at Home in 2004*, News, USDL 05-1768, September 22, 2005. See Internet site <http://www.bls.gov/bls/newsrels.htm#OEUS>.

Table 593. **Persons on Flexible Schedules: 2004**

[In thousands, except percent. (99,778 represents 99,778,000) As of May. For employed full-time wage and salary workers 16 years old and over. Excludes all self-employed persons, regardless of whether or not their businesses were incorporated. Data related to the primary job. Based on the Current Population Survey; see text, Section 1, and Appendix III]

Item	Total	With flexible schedules		Male Total [1]	With flexible schedules		Female Total [1]	With flexible schedules	
	Total [1]	Number	Percent	Total [1]	Number	Percent	Total [1]	Number	Percent
Total	**99,778**	**27,411**	**27.5**	**56,412**	**15,853**	**28.1**	**43,366**	**11,558**	**26.7**
AGE									
16 to 19 years old.	1,427	336	23.6	903	185	20.5	524	151	28.9
20 years and over.	98,351	27,075	27.5	55,509	15,668	28.2	42,842	11,406	26.6
20 to 24 years old	9,004	2,058	22.9	5,147	1,065	20.7	3,856	993	25.8
25 to 34 years old	24,640	6,902	28.0	14,358	4,051	28.2	10,283	2,851	27.7
35 to 44 years old	26,766	7,807	29.2	15,424	4,605	29.9	11,342	3,202	28.2
45 to 54 years old	24,855	6,651	26.8	13,440	3,769	28.0	11,415	2,882	25.2
55 to 64 years old	11,745	3,181	27.1	6,383	1,865	29.2	5,361	1,316	24.5
65 years old and over	1,341	475	35.4	757	314	41.4	585	161	27.6
RACE AND HISPANIC ORIGIN									
White [2]	80,498	23,121	28.7	46,222	13,582	29.4	34,276	9,539	27.8
Black [2]	12,578	2,476	19.7	6,447	1,193	18.5	6,131	1,283	20.9
Asian [2]	4,136	1,132	27.4	2,300	720	31.3	1,836	412	22.4
Hispanic origin [3]	14,110	2,596	18.4	8,621	1,430	16.6	5,489	1,166	21.2
MARITAL STATUS									
Married, spouse present.	57,630	16,270	28.2	34,926	10,382	29.7	22,704	5,888	25.9
Not married	42,148	11,141	26.4	21,486	5,471	25.5	20,662	5,670	27.4
Never married.	25,144	6,693	26.6	14,469	3,605	24.9	10,676	3,088	28.9
Other marital status	17,004	4,448	26.2	7,018	1,866	26.6	9,986	2,582	25.9
PRESENCE AND AGE OF CHILDREN									
Without own children under 18	61,761	16,759	27.1	34,680	9,410	27.1	27,081	7,349	27.1
With own children under 18	38,018	10,652	28.0	21,733	6,443	29.6	16,285	4,209	25.8
With youngest child 6 to 17.	21,739	5,960	27.4	11,477	3,341	29.1	10,262	2,619	25.5
With youngest child under 6	16,279	4,692	28.8	10,256	3,102	30.2	6,023	1,590	26.4

[1] Includes persons who did not provide information on flexible schedules. [2] For persons in the race group only. See footnote 3, Table 574. [3] Persons of Hispanic origin may be of any race.

Source: U.S. Bureau of Labor Statistics, *Workers on Flexible and Shift Schedules in May 2004, News*, USDL 05-1198, July 1, 2005. See Internet site <http://www.bls.gov/bls/newsrels.htm#OEUS>.

Table 594. **Employed Workers With Alternative and Traditional Work Arrangements: 2005**

[In thousands (138,952 represents 138,952,000). As of February. For employed workers 16 years old and over. Based on the Current Population Survey; see text, Section 1, and Appendix III]

Characteristic	Total employed [1]	Workers with alternative arrangements				Workers with traditional arrangements
		Independent contractors	On-call workers	Temporary help agency workers	Workers provided by contract firms	Workers with traditional arrangements
Total employed.	**138,952**	**10,342**	**2,454**	**1,217**	**813**	**123,843**
16 to 19 years	5,510	89	133	33	7	5,194
20 to 24 years	13,114	356	355	202	87	12,055
25 to 34 years	30,103	1,520	535	362	205	27,427
35 to 44 years	34,481	2,754	571	253	196	30,646
45 to 54 years	32,947	2,799	417	200	186	29,324
55 to 64 years	17,980	1,943	267	135	114	15,496
65 years and over.	4,817	881	175	33	18	3,701
Male	73,946	6,696	1,241	574	561	64,673
16 to 19 years	2,579	32	82	24	7	2,389
20 to 24 years	6,928	194	200	107	61	6,331
25 to 34 years	16,624	1,006	299	185	138	14,950
35 to 44 years	18,523	1,824	252	120	140	16,130
45 to 54 years	17,193	1,764	209	71	143	15,003
55 to 64 years	9,485	1,287	108	52	70	7,954
65 years and over	2,615	589	91	16	3	1,917
Female	65,006	3,647	1,212	643	252	59,170
16 to 19 years	2,931	57	52	9	–	2,805
20 to 24 years	6,186	162	155	95	27	5,724
25 to 34 years	13,480	514	236	177	67	12,477
35 to 44 years	15,958	930	319	133	57	14,516
45 to 54 years	15,754	1,035	208	129	43	14,322
55 to 64 years	8,495	656	158	83	44	7,542
65 years and over	2,202	292	84	17	15	1,785
Full-time workers	113,798	7,732	1,370	979	695	102,889
Part-time workers	25,154	2,611	1,084	238	119	20,954

– Represents zero. [1] Includes day laborers (an alternative arrangement) and a small number of workers who were both "on call" and "provided by contract firms," not shown separately.

Source: U.S. Bureau of Labor Statistics, *Contingent and Alternative Employment Arrangements, February 2005, News*, USDL 05-1443, July 27, 2005. See Internet site <http://www.bls.gov/bls/newsrels.htm#OEUS>.

Table 595. **Multiple Jobholders: 2005**

[Annual average of monthly figures (7,546 represents 7,546,000). For the civilian noninstitutional population 16 years old and over. Multiple jobholders are employed persons who, either 1) had jobs as wage or salary workers with two employers or more; 2) were self-employed and also held a wage and salary job; or 3) were unpaid family workers on their primary jobs but also held a wage and salary job. Based on the Current Population Survey; see text, Section 1, and Appendix III]

Characteristic	Total		Male		Female	
	Number (1,000)	Percent of employed	Number (1,000)	Percent of employed	Number (1,000)	Percent of employed
Total [1]	7,546	5.3	3,855	5.1	3,691	5.6
Age:						
16 to 19 years old	298	5.0	118	4.0	180	5.9
20 to 24 years old	798	5.8	373	5.1	425	6.5
25 to 54 years old	5,361	5.4	2,782	5.2	2,579	5.7
55 to 64 years old	900	4.9	473	4.9	426	4.9
65 years old and over	189	3.7	109	3.8	80	3.6
Race and Hispanic ethnicity:						
White [2]	6,342	5.4	3,268	5.1	3,074	5.8
Black [2]	763	5.0	363	5.1	400	4.9
Asian [2]	257	4.1	128	3.8	128	4.4
Hispanic [3]	582	3.1	333	2.9	248	3.4
Marital status:						
Married, spouse present	4,109	5.1	2,416	5.3	1,693	4.9
Widowed, divorced, or separated	1,324	5.8	452	4.8	872	6.5
Single, never married	2,113	5.5	987	4.7	1,125	6.4
Full- or part-time status:						
Primary job full-time, secondary job part-time	3,942	(X)	2,219	(X)	1,724	(X)
Both jobs part-time	1,708	(X)	570	(X)	1,138	(X)
Both jobs full-time	294	(X)	188	(X)	105	(X)
Hours vary on primary or secondary job	1,558	(X)	859	(X)	698	(X)

X Not applicable.   [1] Includes a small number of persons who work part-time on their primary job and full-time on their secondary job(s), not shown separately. Includes other races, not shown separately.   [2] For persons who selected this race group only. See footnote 3, Table 574.   [3] Persons of Hispanic or Latino ethnicity may be of any race.

Source: U.S. Bureau of Labor Statistics, *Employment and Earnings*, January 2006. See Internet site <http://www.bls.gov/cps/home.htm>.

Table 596. **Average Number of Jobs Held from Ages 18 to 38: 1978 to 2002**

[For persons 37 to 45 in 2002. A job is an uninterrupted period of work with a particular employer. Educational attainment as of 2002. Based on the National Longitudinal Survey of Youth 1979; see source for details]

Sex and educational attainment	Total [1]	Number of jobs held by age			
		Age 18 to 22 years old	Age 23 to 27 years old	Age 28 to 32 years old	Age 33 to 38 years old
Total [2]	10.2	4.4	3.3	2.6	2.5
Less than a high school diploma	10.3	3.9	3.2	2.6	2.5
High school graduates, no college	9.7	4.2	3.0	2.6	2.5
Less than a bachelor's degree	10.5	4.6	3.7	2.7	2.6
Bachelor's degree or more	10.6	5.0	3.5	2.6	2.3
Male	10.4	4.5	3.5	2.8	2.5
Less than a high school diploma	11.6	4.6	3.8	3.0	2.7
High school graduates, no college	10.2	4.5	3.4	2.8	2.4
Less than a bachelor's degree	10.6	4.6	3.4	2.9	2.7
Bachelor's degree or more	10.0	4.6	3.4	2.6	2.4
Female	9.9	4.3	3.1	2.4	2.4
Less than a high school diploma	8.5	3.0	2.4	2.1	2.2
High school graduates, no college	9.2	3.8	2.7	2.3	2.5
Less than a bachelor's degree	10.4	4.6	3.3	2.5	2.5
Bachelor's degree or more	11.1	5.4	3.7	2.7	2.2
White, non-Hispanic	10.3	4.6	3.3	2.6	2.5
Less than a high school diploma	10.8	4.3	3.3	2.7	2.6
High school graduates, no college	9.7	4.3	3.1	2.6	2.5
Less than a bachelor's degree	10.8	4.8	3.5	2.7	2.6
Bachelor's degree or more	10.6	5.1	3.5	2.6	2.3
Black, non-Hispanic	9.6	3.6	3.1	2.7	2.6
Less than a high school diploma	9.1	2.9	2.9	2.6	2.3
High school graduates, no college	9.7	3.5	3.0	2.7	2.5
Less than a bachelor's degree	9.7	3.8	3.1	2.6	2.7
Bachelor's degree or more	9.9	4.2	3.6	2.8	2.7
Hispanic or Latino [3]	9.6	4.0	3.0	2.5	2.4
Less than a high school diploma	9.6	3.9	3.0	2.4	2.3
High school graduates, no college	9.5	3.9	2.9	2.5	2.4
Less than a bachelor's degree	9.5	4.2	3.0	2.5	2.4
Bachelor's degree or more	10.5	4.5	3.4	2.8	2.5

[1] Jobs held in more than one age category were counted in each category, but only once in the total.   [2] Includes other races, not shown separately.   [3] Persons of Hispanic or Latino origin may be of any race.

Source: U.S. Bureau of Labor Statistics, Number of Jobs Held, Labor Market Activity, and *Earnings Growth Among Younger Baby Boomers: Recent Results from a Longitudinal Survey*, USDL 04-1678, August 25, 2004. See Internet site <http://www.bls.gov/nls/home.htm>.

Labor Force, Employment, and Earnings   385

Table 597. **Distribution of Workers by Tenure With Current Employer: 2004**

[**121,753 represents 121,753,000. As of January.** For employed wage and salary workers 16 years old and over. Data exclude the incorporated and unincorporated self-employed. Based on the Current Population Survey and subject to sampling error; see source and Appendix III]

Characteristic	Number employed (1,000)	Percent distribution by tenure with current employer								Median years [1]
		12 months or less	13 to 23 months	2 years	3 to 4 years	5 to 9 years	10 to 14 years	15 to 19 years	20 years or more	
Total [2]	121,753	23.0	7.0	5.7	18.5	19.8	9.9	6.4	9.7	4.0
AGE AND SEX										
16 to 19 years old	5,433	73.2	11.2	7.5	7.8	0.3	–	–	–	0.7
20 to 24 years old	13,028	49.6	12.6	10.2	20.8	6.6	0.1	–	–	1.3
25 to 34 years old	27,877	26.9	9.4	7.4	25.9	23.7	5.9	0.9	–	2.9
35 to 44 years old	30,314	17.4	5.7	4.8	19.1	25.1	13.7	9.3	5.0	4.9
45 to 54 years old	27,713	11.0	4.7	3.7	14.8	20.7	13.6	10.5	20.9	7.7
55 to 64 years old	13,983	10.4	4.0	3.4	12.8	18.8	13.9	10.6	26.0	9.6
65 years old and over	3,405	9.9	3.1	4.1	14.0	20.2	14.0	9.2	25.5	9.0
Male	63,146	22.4	6.6	5.6	18.3	19.6	10.1	6.5	10.9	4.1
16 to 19 years old	2,683	70.9	9.9	9.3	9.5	0.4	–	–	–	0.8
20 to 24 years old	6,798	50.0	11.4	9.6	21.5	7.4	0.1	–	–	1.3
25 to 34 years old	15,209	26.0	9.1	6.9	26.4	24.1	6.6	0.9	–	3.0
35 to 44 years old	15,885	16.4	5.0	4.7	18.1	25.1	14.6	10.4	5.6	5.2
45 to 54 years old	13,785	9.6	4.7	3.5	12.8	19.1	13.7	11.3	25.3	9.6
55 to 64 years old	7,026	11.4	3.9	3.5	12.0	17.5	12.9	9.1	29.7	9.8
65 years old and over	1,761	8.7	3.3	4.4	16.8	20.1	13.4	8.4	24.9	8.2
Female	58,608	23.7	7.4	5.8	18.7	20.1	9.6	6.2	8.4	3.8
16 to 19 years old	2,750	75.5	12.3	5.8	6.1	0.3	–	–	–	0.7
20 to 24 years old	6,230	49.2	13.8	10.9	20.1	5.8	0.1	–	–	1.3
25 to 34 years old	12,668	27.9	9.7	7.9	25.2	23.3	5.2	0.8	–	2.8
35 to 44 years old	14,429	18.4	6.5	4.9	20.1	25.0	12.6	8.1	4.3	4.5
45 to 54 years old	13,929	12.4	4.8	3.9	16.8	22.3	13.4	9.8	16.6	6.4
55 to 64 years old	6,957	9.4	4.1	3.3	13.6	20.2	15.0	12.1	22.2	9.2
65 years old and over	1,644	11.2	3.0	3.7	11.0	20.3	14.6	10.1	26.1	9.6
RACE AND HISPANIC ORIGIN										
White [3]	100,243	22.7	7.1	5.4	18.2	19.6	10.2	6.6	10.2	4.0
Male	52,758	22.3	6.7	5.3	17.9	19.3	10.3	6.7	11.5	4.2
Female	47,485	23.2	7.6	5.5	18.5	20.0	10.1	6.4	8.7	3.9
Black [3]	13,401	24.5	5.8	6.6	19.2	20.5	8.4	5.9	9.1	3.7
Male	6,097	23.4	5.4	7.0	18.7	20.6	9.3	5.8	9.8	3.8
Female	7,304	25.4	6.1	6.2	19.6	20.4	7.6	6.1	8.5	3.6
Asian [3]	5,131	22.3	7.2	7.5	21.5	22.8	8.6	5.3	4.9	3.6
Male	2,678	20.3	7.2	6.8	22.4	23.5	9.5	4.8	5.4	3.9
Female	2,453	24.3	7.2	8.2	20.6	21.9	7.6	5.8	4.3	3.3
Hispanic origin [4]	16,338	26.9	7.4	7.8	22.8	18.2	8.0	4.4	4.4	3.1
Male	9,778	26.4	7.5	7.4	23.2	17.9	8.2	4.5	4.7	3.1
Female	6,560	27.6	7.3	8.5	22.2	18.7	7.7	4.3	3.8	3.0

– Represents or rounds to zero. [1] For definition of median, see Guide to Tabular Presentation. [2] Includes other races, not shown separately. [3] For persons in this race group only. See footnote 3, Table 574. [4] Persons of Hispanic or Latino origin may be any race.
Source: U. S. Bureau of Labor Statistics, news, *Employee Tenure in 2004*, USDL 04-1829, September 21, 2004; and unpublished data. See Internet site <http://www.bls.gov/bls/newsrels.htm#OEUS>.

Table 598. **Part-Time Workers by Reason: 2005**

[**In thousands (32,268 represents 32,268,000), except hours.** For persons working 1 to 34 hours per week. For civilian noninstitutional population 16 years old and over. Annual average of monthly figures. Based on the Current Population Survey and subject to sampling error; see text, Section 1, and Appendix III]

Reason	All industries			Nonagriculture industries		
		Usually work—			Usually work—	
	Total	Full-time	Part-time	Total	Full-time	Part-time
Total working fewer than 35 hours	32,268	9,983	22,285	31,717	9,818	21,900
Economic reasons	4,350	1,556	2,794	4,271	1,504	2,766
Slack work or business conditions	2,684	1,294	1,390	2,636	1,260	1,376
Could find only part-time work	1,341	–	1,341	1,330	–	1,330
Seasonal work	188	125	63	169	109	60
Job started or ended during the week	137	137	–	136	136	–
Noneconomic reasons	27,918	8,427	19,491	27,447	8,313	19,134
Child–care problems	791	72	719	787	72	715
Other family or personal obligations	5,558	745	4,813	5,469	734	4,735
Health or medical limitations	806	–	806	784	–	784
In school or training	6,237	98	6,138	6,180	97	6,083
Retired or social security limit on earnings	2,095	–	2,095	1,980	–	1,980
Vacation or personal day	3,431	3,431	–	3,395	3,395	–
Holiday, legal, or religious	901	901	–	895	895	–
Weather-related curtailment	513	513	–	485	485	–
Average hours per week:						
Economic reasons	23.0	23.8	22.5	23.0	23.8	22.5
Noneconomic reasons	21.5	25.2	19.8	21.5	25.3	19.9

– Represents or rounds to zero.
Source: U.S. Bureau of Labor Statistics, *Employment and Earnings*, monthly, January 2006. See Internet site <http://www.bls.gov /cps/home.htm>.

Table 599. Displaced Workers by Selected Characteristics: 2004

[In percent, except total (5,329 represents 5,329,000). As of January. For persons 20 years old and over with tenure of 3 years or more who lost or left a job between January 2001 and December 2003 because of plant closings or moves, slack work, or the abolishment of their positions. Based on Current Population Survey and subject to sampling error; see source and Appendix III]

Characteristic	Total (1,000)	Employment status			Reason for job loss		
		Employed	Unem- ployed	Not in the labor force	Plant or company closed down or moved	Slack/ insufficient work	Position or shift abolished
Total [1]	5,329	64.8	20.2	15.0	43.1	28.3	28.6
20 to 24 years old	149	65.0	19.6	15.3	52.6	28.7	18.7
25 to 54 years old	4,087	68.9	19.5	11.6	42.2	29.3	28.5
55 to 64 years old	887	55.5	24.9	19.6	45.2	22.1	32.7
65 years old and over . . .	206	23.8	12.9	63.3	45.2	34.9	19.9
Males	3,010	67.7	20.8	11.5	40.7	31.9	27.5
20 to 24 years old	96	59.8	24.5	15.7	44.4	33.7	21.9
25 to 54 years old	2,372	71.0	20.8	8.1	39.8	33.3	27.0
55 to 64 years old	461	58.1	22.3	19.6	44.0	23.8	32.3
65 years old and over . . .	81	33.5	8.5	57.9	44.0	34.4	21.6
Females	2,319	61.1	19.3	19.6	46.3	23.7	30.1
20 to 24 years old	53	(2)	(2)	(2)	(2)	(2)	(2)
25 to 54 years old	1,715	65.9	17.7	16.4	45.6	23.8	30.7
55 to 64 years old	426	52.7	27.7	19.6	46.4	20.3	33.3
65 years old and over . . .	125	17.5	15.8	66.7	46.0	35.3	18.8
White [3]	4,273	65.6	18.9	15.5	42.7	27.4	29.9
Black [3]	695	61.6	27.1	11.2	47.1	28.9	24.1
Asian [3]	215	63.2	22.6	14.2	44.8	36.7	18.5
Hispanic origin [4]	608	64.6	20.8	14.6	41.5	36.1	22.4

[1] Includes other races, not shown separately.   [2] Data not shown where base is less than 75,000.   [3] For persons in this race group only. See footnote 3, Table 574.   [4] Persons of Hispanic or Latino origin may be of any race.

Source: U.S. Bureau of Labor Statistics, News, *Worker Displacement, 1999–2001*, USDL 04-1381, July 30, 2004. See Internet site <http://www.bls.gov/bls/newsrels.htm#OEUS>.

Table 600. Labor Force Status of Persons With a Work Disability by Age: 2005

[In percent, except as indicated (23,848 represents 23,848,000). As of March. For civilians 16 to 74 who have a condition which prevents them from working or limits the amount of work they can do. Data from the Current Population Survey and subject to sampling error; see text, Section 1, and Appendix III]

Labor force status	Total	Age						
		16 to 24 years old	25 to 34 years old	35 to 44 years old	45 to 54 years old	55 to 64 years old	65 to 69 years old	70 to 74 years old
Number (1,000)	23,848	1,709	2,475	3,764	5,382	6,327	2,310	1,882
In labor force	22.4	30.2	33.4	30.1	25.2	18.0	9.4	7.7
Employed	19.2	20.4	27.7	26.6	22.0	16.3	8.7	7.1
Full-time	11.3	7.2	18.1	17.3	14.1	9.3	3.5	1.8
Not in labor force	77.6	69.8	66.6	69.9	74.8	82.0	90.6	92.3
Unemployment rate	14.1	32.3	17.3	11.8	12.7	9.6	7.7	7.3

Source: U.S. Census Bureau, "Disability Data from the March Current Population Survey"; <http://www.census.gov/hhes/www /disability/disabcps.html>; (accessed 03 July 2006).

Table 601. Persons Not in the Labor Force: 2005

[In thousands (76,762 represents 76,762,000). Annual average of monthly figures. For the civilian noninstitutional population 16 years old and over. Based on the Current Population Survey; see text, Section 1, and Appendix III]

Status and reason	Total	Age			Sex	
		16 to 24 years old	25 to 54 years old	55 years old and over	Male	Female
Total not in the labor force	76,762	14,383	21,403	40,976	29,119	47,643
Do not want a job now [1]	71,777	12,585	19,238	39,954	26,926	44,851
Want a job now	4,985	1,798	2,165	1,022	2,193	2,792
In the previous year—						
Did not search for a job.	2,841	963	1,163	715	1,173	1,668
Did search for a job [2]	2,144	836	1,002	307	1,020	1,124
Not available for work now	599	285	260	54	231	368
Available for work now, not looking for work. . .	1,545	551	742	252	789	756
Reason for not currently looking for work:						
Discouraged over job prospects [3]	436	141	217	78	260	176
Family responsibilities	159	32	105	22	36	123
In school or training	217	179	35	2	118	99
Ill health or disability	119	16	69	34	64	55
Other [4]	614	182	316	116	311	302

[1] Includes some persons who are not asked if they want a job.   [2] Persons who had a job in the prior 12 months must have searched since the end of that job.   [3] Includes such things as believes no work available, could not find work, lacks necessary schooling or training, employer thinks too young or old, and other types of discrimination.   [4] Includes such things as child care and transportation problems.

Source: U.S. Bureau of Labor Statistics, *Employment and Earnings*, monthly, January 2006 issue. See Internet site <http://www.bls.gov/cps/home.htm>.

Labor Force, Employment, and Earnings   387

Table 602. Employed Civilians by Occupation, Sex, Race, and Hispanic Origin: 2005

[141,730 represents 141,730,000. For civilian noninstitutional population 16 years old and over. Annual average of monthly figures. Based on Current Population Survey; see text, Section 1, and Appendix III. Occupational classifications are those used in the 2000 Census and are not comparable to those used in the 1990 census]

Occupation	Total employed (1,000)	Percent of total			
		Female	Black [1]	Asian [1]	Hispanic [2]
Total, 16 years and over	**141,730**	**46.4**	**10.8**	**4.4**	**13.1**
Management, professional, and related occupations	**49,245**	**50.6**	**8.1**	**5.9**	**6.4**
Management, business, and financial operations occupations	20,450	42.5	7.1	4.8	6.5
Management occupations [3]	14,685	37.2	6.0	4.2	6.3
Chief executives	1,644	23.8	3.0	3.9	3.8
General and operations managers	872	29.9	6.8	3.6	6.2
Marketing and sales managers	798	41.0	3.8	4.2	6.0
Administrative services managers	80	30.2	6.2	2.3	6.4
Computer and information systems managers	351	32.3	5.9	6.3	3.0
Financial managers	1,045	51.7	7.4	6.3	6.0
Human resources managers	272	72.7	8.5	2.9	9.4
Industrial production managers	310	17.2	6.7	2.4	6.5
Purchasing managers	183	39.7	5.7	2.1	5.5
Transportation, storage, and distribution managers	244	11.7	9.1	2.6	8.7
Farm, ranch, and other agricultural managers	195	19.3	1.4	0.2	8.9
Farmers and ranchers	827	25.6	0.6	0.9	1.1
Construction managers	881	6.3	2.7	2.3	5.8
Education administrators	805	63.4	13.4	2.4	5.4
Engineering managers	97	9.5	1.7	10.0	3.8
Food service managers	929	44.2	6.0	10.6	12.0
Lodging managers	159	49.8	5.5	12.2	4.6
Medical and health services managers	470	71.2	9.0	2.7	5.5
Property, real estate, and community association managers	626	48.7	8.0	2.6	13.0
Social and community service managers	307	69.3	11.7	2.0	6.2
Business and financial operations occupations [3]	5,765	55.9	9.8	6.5	7.0
Wholesale and retail buyers, except farm products	213	50.7	7.5	1.9	7.9
Purchasing agents, except wholesale, retail, and farm products	281	55.0	8.2	3.3	7.8
Claims adjusters, appraisers, examiners, and investigators	303	61.6	13.8	3.7	6.8
Compliance officers, except agriculture, construction, health and safety, and transportation	139	47.2	15.8	3.6	12.5
Cost estimators	112	17.4	3.0	1.1	4.0
Human resources, training, and labor relations specialists	660	70.9	13.1	5.2	7.8
Management analysts	549	40.9	8.4	7.6	3.4
Accountants and auditors	1,683	61.9	8.4	9.8	6.4
Appraisers and assessors of real estate	125	34.7	2.2	1.9	4.0
Financial analysts	96	39.0	7.3	13.8	3.7
Personal financial advisors	380	30.8	5.1	6.2	4.4
Insurance underwriters	110	71.9	12.0	2.6	5.8
Loan counselors and officers	439	54.1	11.9	3.8	12.7
Tax examiners, collectors, and revenue agents	76	58.4	20.7	4.9	10.4
Tax preparers	93	68.2	13.6	6.3	14.9
Professional and related occupations	28,795	56.3	8.8	6.6	6.4
Computer and mathematical occupations [3]	3,246	27.0	6.9	14.7	5.3
Computer scientists and systems analysts	745	30.3	8.3	11.4	4.8
Computer programmers	581	26.0	4.6	18.0	5.7
Computer software engineers	832	21.9	5.0	24.6	3.9
Computer support specialists	334	33.2	9.1	5.5	9.7
Database administrators	89	32.3	13.1	6.3	5.1
Network and computer systems administrators	200	18.4	4.9	10.4	4.8
Network systems and data communications analysts	322	24.6	9.3	9.4	6.6
Operations research analysts	86	50.5	10.1	6.2	2.3
Architecture and engineering occupations [3]	2,793	13.8	5.1	9.9	6.1
Architects, except naval	235	24.4	3.2	11.0	8.9
Aerospace engineers	90	13.3	4.3	6.7	8.2
Civil engineers	319	13.2	6.1	10.3	3.5
Computer hardware engineers	81	10.8	8.4	23.1	5.5
Electrical and electronics engineers	352	7.1	5.6	15.6	3.4
Industrial engineers, including health and safety	189	14.9	5.5	7.0	3.8
Mechanical engineers	318	5.8	2.5	8.7	4.0
Drafters	212	21.6	4.2	6.5	10.1
Engineering technicians, except drafters	410	20.2	8.9	7.0	10.1
Surveying and mapping technicians	95	2.7	3.5	2.1	11.8
Life, physical, and social science occupations [3]	1,406	42.5	5.0	10.1	4.5
Biological scientists	119	48.7	2.9	10.2	4.2
Medical scientists	125	45.9	3.0	29.6	2.6
Chemists and materials scientists	116	35.3	5.6	14.0	2.7
Environmental scientists and geoscientists	99	22.5	3.2	1.9	3.0
Market and survey researchers	131	55.3	5.1	7.3	4.3
Psychologists	188	67.3	2.8	0.3	4.7
Chemical technicians	86	28.1	18.8	6.7	7.9
Community and social services occupations [3]	2,138	61.3	17.1	2.8	9.8
Counselors	626	69.8	18.6	1.5	10.1
Social workers	670	80.1	19.0	3.3	9.6
Miscellaneous community and social service specialists	276	67.0	24.3	2.4	16.2
Clergy	435	15.5	9.7	4.4	5.8
Legal occupations	1,614	49.4	6.0	2.6	6.9
Lawyers	961	30.2	4.7	2.0	3.8
Judges, magistrates, and other judicial workers	70	41.2	7.0	4.6	5.9
Paralegals and legal assistants	353	86.4	8.2	2.5	11.5
Miscellaneous legal support workers	229	75.3	7.6	4.3	14.2

See footnotes at end of table.

[141,730 **represents** 141,730,000. For civilian noninstitutional population 16 years old and over. Annual average of monthly figures. Based on Current Population Survey; see text, Section 1, and Appendix III. Occupational classifications are those used in the 2000 Census and are not comparable to those used in the 1990 census]

Occupation	Total employed (1,000)	Percent of total			
		Female	Black [1]	Asian [1]	Hispanic [2]
Professional and related occupations—Con.					
Education, training, and library occupations [3]	8,114	73.8	9.9	3.7	6.9
Postsecondary teachers	1,185	44.4	6.7	11.2	4.1
Preschool and kindergarten teachers	719	97.7	14.7	3.0	10.4
Elementary and middle school teachers	2,616	82.2	9.6	2.4	5.9
Secondary school teachers	1,136	56.8	7.3	1.1	5.2
Special education teachers	421	85.3	10.8	2.5	5.7
Other teachers and instructors	709	65.9	11.0	5.3	6.5
Librarians	214	84.9	5.8	2.5	4.6
Teacher assistants	947	90.9	14.1	1.8	14.0
Arts, design, entertainment, sports, and media occupations [3]	2,736	47.8	5.9	4.3	7.1
Artists and related workers	234	52.6	2.4	5.3	6.7
Designers	774	55.0	2.1	6.8	6.6
Producers and directors	124	35.1	7.5	0.7	7.4
Athletes, coaches, umpires, and related workers	273	30.8	10.2	2.3	6.3
Musicians, singers, and related workers	213	37.6	8.2	3.8	7.8
News analysts, reporters and correspondents	89	56.5	6.3	3.3	6.0
Public relations specialists	154	61.4	6.5	2.9	4.7
Editors	150	58.1	5.8	2.3	5.8
Writers and authors	178	62.8	5.6	0.5	2.2
Broadcast and sound engineering technicians and radio operators	92	13.6	8.5	1.8	11.2
Photographers	150	39.0	8.0	3.9	9.2
Healthcare practitioner and technical occupations [3]	6,748	73.2	9.9	7.4	5.4
Chiropractors	82	21.8	1.4	4.0	2.5
Dentists	164	22.5	3.6	14.1	4.4
Dietitians and nutritionists	68	95.3	18.4	6.0	5.9
Pharmacists	248	48.3	6.3	10.4	5.5
Physicians and surgeons	830	32.3	5.3	17.3	5.2
Physician assistants	74	62.1	9.0	7.5	11.1
Registered nurses	2,416	92.3	10.0	6.4	4.3
Occupational therapists	85	92.9	3.6	12.0	1.4
Physical therapists	177	68.9	4.6	6.0	5.1
Respiratory therapists	94	58.6	11.4	2.6	6.0
Speech-language pathologists	98	92.0	5.0	0.8	2.8
Clinical laboratory technologists and technicians	334	74.2	11.4	12.1	7.5
Dental hygienists	132	97.1	1.0	3.3	8.5
Diagnostic-related technologists and technicians	276	72.0	12.5	1.3	5.5
Emergency medical technicians and paramedics	155	31.3	8.1	1.5	10.1
Health diagnosing and treating practitioner support technicians	390	81.8	11.8	5.7	8.5
Licensed practical and licensed vocational nurses	510	93.4	21.6	2.6	5.5
Medical records and health information technicians	121	86.6	19.0	2.3	9.0
Service occupations	**23,133**	**57.3**	**15.8**	**4.2**	**19.2**
Healthcare support occupations [3]	3,092	89.0	24.8	4.1	13.8
Nursing, psychiatric, and home health aides	1,900	88.7	32.5	4.6	15.0
Massage therapists	111	82.0	5.5	4.3	3.1
Dental assistants	259	96.1	6.3	3.3	13.5
Protective service occupations [3]	2,894	22.4	19.3	1.6	10.4
First-line supervisors/managers of police and detectives	122	12.5	8.2	0.2	6.3
Fire-fighters	243	3.3	10.6	1.4	7.9
Bailiffs, correctional officers, and jailers	424	29.1	23.7	1.3	10.8
Detectives and criminal investigators	123	24.0	13.8	1.4	8.9
Police and sheriff's patrol officers	677	14.3	13.7	1.1	11.3
Private detectives and investigators	89	37.7	12.8	2.8	6.4
Security guards and gaming surveillance officers	814	24.7	31.3	2.5	12.1
Food preparation and serving-related occupations	7,374	56.6	11.6	5.4	20.6
Chefs and head cooks	317	20.4	11.8	19.3	18.1
First-line supervisors/managers of food preparation and serving workers	574	58.5	14.9	3.6	15.5
Cooks	1,838	42.3	16.5	5.0	29.3
Food preparation workers	664	61.2	12.2	6.8	24.4
Bartenders	384	56.8	3.2	1.7	8.6
Combined food preparation and serving workers, including fast food	305	71.5	12.5	3.5	13.0
Counter attendants, cafeteria, food concession, and coffee shop	321	65.7	10.3	4.4	11.4
Waiters and waitresses	1,927	71.8	7.1	5.2	15.3
Food servers, nonrestaurant	147	69.1	23.4	6.4	19.4
Dining room and cafeteria attendants and bartender helpers	373	46.6	9.6	6.7	30.4
Dishwashers	264	23.8	15.4	1.5	35.4
Hosts and hostesses, restaurant, lounge, and coffee shop	256	84.6	6.5	3.3	12.8
Building and grounds cleaning and maintenance occupations	5,241	40.6	15.8	2.7	30.6
First-line supervisors/managers of housekeeping and janitorial workers	291	36.3	15.4	2.8	20.0
First-line supervisors/managers of landscaping, lawn service, and groundskeeping workers	238	6.2	6.3	0.3	13.2
Janitors and building cleaners	2,074	32.8	18.3	2.8	27.3
Maids and housekeeping cleaners	1,382	89.5	20.1	4.2	35.2
Grounds maintenance workers	1,187	7.5	9.0	1.3	37.4

See footnotes at end of table.

Table 602. **Employed Civilians by Occupation, Sex, Race, and Hispanic Origin: 2005**—Con.

[141,730 **represents** 141,730,000. For civilian noninstitutional population 16 years old and over. Annual average of monthly figures. Based on Current Population Survey; see text, Section 1, and Appendix III. Occupational classifications are those used in the 2000 Census and are not comparable to those used in the 1990 census]

Occupation	Total employed (1,000)	Percent of total			
		Female	Black [1]	Asian [1]	Hispanic [2]
Service occupations—Con.					
Personal care and service occupations [3]	4,531	78.3	14.2	6.0	12.9
First-line supervisors/managers of gaming workers	128	48.3	3.7	3.1	5.3
First-line supervisors/managers of personal service workers	152	64.4	7.8	15.0	4.3
Nonfarm animal caretakers	146	69.8	1.4	1.0	10.3
Gaming services workers	98	49.8	6.6	20.0	9.8
Barbers	106	19.2	31.5	4.9	12.3
Hairdressers, hairstylists, and cosmetologists	738	92.0	11.3	4.0	10.3
Miscellaneous personal appearance workers	216	85.1	7.4	43.2	8.9
Transportation attendants	103	74.5	14.0	3.3	9.4
Child care workers	1,329	94.8	15.5	2.5	18.1
Personal and home care aides	668	85.9	24.1	5.3	15.6
Recreation and fitness workers	337	67.0	11.3	1.9	7.5
Sales and office occupations	35,962	63.3	11.2	4.0	11.1
Sales and related occupations [3]	16,433	49.1	9.2	4.4	10.6
First-line supervisors/managers of retail sales workers	3,523	41.5	7.5	5.2	9.0
First-line supervisors/managers of nonretail sales workers	1,414	25.5	5.4	5.1	9.8
Cashiers	3,075	75.9	15.5	5.4	16.2
Counter and rental clerks	159	51.9	12.5	1.9	9.8
Parts salespersons	139	12.0	5.9	1.7	10.3
Retail salespersons	3,248	51.9	10.5	4.2	11.8
Advertising sales agents	235	50.2	7.6	2.9	5.9
Insurance sales agents	531	45.2	7.9	2.6	6.2
Securities, commodities, and financial services sales agents	392	28.7	6.2	5.0	7.6
Travel agents	91	76.3	7.8	11.3	7.5
Sales representatives, services, all other	474	32.9	9.3	1.6	7.3
Sales representatives, wholesale and manufacturing	1,379	27.2	3.4	2.7	7.0
Real estate brokers and sales agents	995	57.1	5.9	4.7	7.4
Telemarketers	179	64.4	21.0	1.4	15.5
Door-to-door sales workers, news and street vendors, and related workers	279	62.7	6.6	3.3	13.3
Office and administrative support occupations [3]	19,529	75.3	12.9	3.8	11.6
First-line supervisors/managers of office and administrative support workers	1,598	69.8	9.8	3.4	9.0
Bill and account collectors	207	72.2	22.7	3.0	14.1
Billing and posting clerks and machine operators	427	89.0	15.9	3.8	9.0
Bookkeeping, accounting, and auditing clerks	1,456	91.3	6.9	3.4	8.4
Payroll and timekeeping clerks	164	91.4	10.7	3.7	11.2
Tellers	418	87.3	12.8	5.9	11.0
Court, municipal, and license clerks	106	81.4	11.3	4.6	7.8
Customer service representatives	1,833	68.7	16.2	3.6	13.1
File clerks	376	81.4	16.2	4.6	13.7
Hotel, motel, and resort desk clerks	138	65.9	15.4	6.9	14.0
Interviewers, except eligibility and loan	167	79.4	17.0	2.6	15.3
Library assistants, clerical	130	85.4	11.0	7.1	13.4
Loan interviewers and clerks	198	77.0	11.4	4.8	12.9
Order clerks	143	67.2	11.4	4.2	13.2
Receptionists and information clerks	1,376	92.4	11.4	3.8	12.2
Reservation and transportation ticket agents and travel clerks	169	64.0	18.7	4.4	13.9
Couriers and messengers	309	15.8	13.3	3.5	14.7
Dispatchers	291	59.1	13.6	1.2	9.4
Postal service clerks	146	41.7	20.1	12.1	11.9
Postal service mail carriers	348	39.1	15.2	5.4	9.9
Postal service mail sorters, processors, and processing machine operators	111	45.1	30.8	14.8	11.1
Production, planning, and expediting clerks	294	57.1	7.1	2.2	10.3
Shipping, receiving, and traffic clerks	543	31.9	15.2	3.1	20.7
Stock clerks and order fillers	1,461	37.1	15.3	3.4	17.0
Weighers, measurers, checkers, and samplers, recordkeeping	71	52.6	15.6	1.9	16.3
Secretaries and administrative assistants	3,499	97.3	9.2	2.0	8.6
Computer operators	184	55.3	14.5	6.2	11.0
Data entry keyers	495	82.2	16.8	5.8	14.2
Word processors and typists	295	95.0	20.0	2.7	12.5
Insurance claims and policy processing clerks	263	86.9	19.4	4.4	8.6
Mail clerks and mail machine operators, except postal service	132	55.5	26.3	6.5	9.5
Office clerks, general	965	84.5	13.8	6.4	13.1
Natural resources, construction, and maintenance occupations	15,348	4.6	7.1	1.8	23.1
Farming, fishing, and forestry occupations	976	22.5	5.1	1.6	40.3
Logging workers	85	1.7	9.2	–	10.7
Construction and extraction occupations [3]	9,145	3.0	7.0	1.2	26.8
First-line supervisors/managers of construction trades and extraction workers	1,012	2.9	5.2	0.7	12.6
Brickmasons, blockmasons, and stonemasons	245	0.9	8.7	0.6	33.7
Carpenters	1,797	1.9	4.8	1.1	24.4
Carpet, floor, and tile installers and finishers	297	2.3	4.5	1.4	40.0

See footnotes at end of table.

Table 602. Employed Civilians by Occupation, Sex, Race, and Hispanic Origin: 2005—Con.

[141,730 represents 141,730,000. For civilian noninstitutional population 16 years old and over. Annual average of monthly figures. Based on Current Population Survey; see text, Section 1, and Appendix III. Occupational classifications are those used in the 2000 Census and are not comparable to those used in the 1990 census]

Occupation	Total employed (1,000)	Percent of total			
		Female	Black[1]	Asian[1]	Hispanic[2]
Construction and extraction occupations[3]—con.					
Cement masons, concrete finishers, and terrazzo workers	119	1.7	7.5	0.4	54.4
Construction laborers	1,491	3.6	10.5	1.2	40.8
Operating engineers and other construction equipment operators	414	2.7	6.2	1.1	10.1
Drywall installers, ceiling tile installers, and tapers	252	0.8	3.2	1.1	46.8
Electricians	852	2.6	8.1	1.7	15.1
Painters, construction and maintenance	689	7.5	7.4	1.8	35.0
Pipelayers, plumbers, pipefitters, and steamfitters	661	1.2	8.9	0.4	18.1
Roofers	274	2.4	7.2	0.7	42.0
Sheet metal workers	147	3.6	3.5	2.4	17.2
Helpers, construction trades	113	3.2	8.9	0.9	38.6
Construction and building inspectors	107	8.5	12.6	3.8	8.1
Highway maintenance workers	94	4.6	10.9	0.1	13.6
Installation, maintenance, and repair occupations[3]	5,226	4.2	7.5	3.0	13.6
First-line supervisors/managers of mechanics, installers, and repairers	314	5.7	7.8	1.1	7.2
Computer, automated teller, and office machine repairers	384	13.7	9.2	5.3	10.4
Radio and telecommunications equipment installers and repairers	214	13.5	15.1	3.8	9.3
Aircraft mechanics and service technicians	140	4.5	7.0	5.4	9.0
Automotive body and related repairers	168	1.9	3.2	3.2	18.5
Automotive service technicians and mechanics	954	1.8	7.3	4.2	17.7
Bus and truck mechanics and diesel engine specialists	365	0.5	4.9	2.3	13.3
Heavy vehicle and mobile equipment service technicians and mechanics	224	1.0	3.6	1.3	14.3
Heating, air conditioning, and refrigeration mechanics and installers	393	1.4	5.0	2.0	12.9
Industrial and refractory machinery mechanics	444	2.6	7.1	3.1	13.8
Maintenance and repair workers, general	344	4.1	10.7	1.7	14.9
Electrical power-line installers and repairers	110	3.5	9.8	0.7	11.1
Telecommunications line installers and repairers	152	6.0	12.1	1.0	13.5
Production, transportation, and material occupations					
Production occupations[3]	**18,041**	**22.9**	**14.1**	**3.5**	**19.2**
First-line supervisors/managers of production and operating workers	9,378	30.3	12.4	4.9	20.0
Electrical, electronics, and electromechanical assemblers	868	20.9	10.4	2.9	12.5
Bakers	209	58.7	10.6	16.1	21.1
Butchers and other meat, poultry, and fish processing workers	183	54.0	9.8	8.1	24.6
Food batchmakers	292	22.3	9.2	3.3	42.0
Cutting, punching, and press machine setters, operators, and tenders, metal and plastic	85	46.4	10.2	4.6	21.5
Grinding, lapping, polishing, and buffing machine tool setters, operators, and tenders, metal and plastic	123	22.8	15.7	1.1	11.0
Lathe and turning machine tool setters, operators, and tenders, metal and plastic	60	10.3	13.6	1.9	18.9
Machinists	420	6.8	7.6	3.6	11.7
Molders and molding machine setters, operators, and tenders, metal and plastic	60	20.3	14.3	0.9	20.4
Tool and die makers	90	1.1	2.1	–	2.6
Welding, soldering, and brazing workers	576	5.8	8.1	2.7	20.0
Printing machine operators	218	15.6	10.8	3.3	16.7
Laundry and dry-cleaning workers	178	62.8	20.3	7.0	29.4
Pressers, textile, garment, and related materials	70	76.0	29.3	8.5	35.7
Sewing machine operators	269	77.4	13.8	14.7	33.6
Tailors, dressmakers, and sewers	91	79.3	5.0	9.3	24.3
Cabinetmakers and bench carpenters	82	4.9	2.5	0.5	7.7
Stationary engineers and boiler operators	116	3.0	16.2	3.1	11.0
Water and liquid waste treatment plant and system operators	79	4.6	4.2	–	9.3
Crushing, grinding, polishing, mixing, and blending workers	93	10.8	12.8	4.4	24.1
Cutting workers	100	21.2	10.7	1.8	28.6
Inspectors, testers, sorters, samplers, and weighers	684	38.5	12.0	6.2	13.7
Medical, dental, and ophthalmic laboratory technicians	103	46.7	9.3	13.8	9.3
Packaging and filling machine operators and tenders	303	55.6	21.6	4.3	37.6
Painting workers	198	15.0	9.5	2.0	25.7
Photographic process workers and processing machine operators	76	62.9	8.1	1.1	10.5
Transportation and material-moving occupations[3]	**8,664**	**14.8**	**16.1**	**2.0**	**18.4**
Supervisors, transportation and material-moving workers	202	18.1	14.7	1.9	8.6
Aircraft pilots and flight engineers	121	5.2	2.5	0.3	5.7
Bus drivers	591	48.7	23.1	1.4	12.7
Driver/sales workers and truck drivers	3,409	4.5	14.5	1.1	16.4
Taxi drivers and chauffeurs	291	15.5	28.7	9.7	16.6
Service station attendants	100	14.2	6.7	7.1	11.3
Crane and tower operators	72	2.8	9.0	1.4	7.8
Dredge, excavating, and loading machine operators	86	0.2	3.7	–	11.4
Industrial truck and tractor operators	541	6.3	12.0	0.8	23.8
Cleaners of vehicles and equipment	347	14.1	14.0	1.2	33.5
Laborers and freight, stock, and material movers, hand	1,806	17.3	15.7	2.4	19.6
Packers and packagers, hand	452	61.1	16.8	4.8	41.6
Refuse and recyclable material collectors	73	8.7	27.4	1.4	19.1

– Represents or rounds to zero. [1] The 2003 Current Population Survey (CPS) allowed respondents to choose more than one race. Data represent persons who selected this race group only and exclude persons reporting more than one race. The CPS in prior years allowed respondents to report one race group. See also comments on race in the text for Section 1. [2] Persons of Hispanic or Latino ethnicity may be of any race. [3] Includes other occupations, not shown separately.

Source: U.S. Bureau of Labor Statistics, *Employment and Earnings*, monthy, January 2006 issue. See Internet site <http://www.bls.gov/cps/home.htm>

Table 603. **Employed Civilians by Occupation—States: 2004**

[In thousands (139,252 represents 139,252,000). Occupation classifications are those used in the 2000 Census and are not comparable to those in other tables using 1990 Census classifications. Based on the Current Population Survey and subject to sampling error; see text, Section 1, and Appendix III]

State	Total	Management, professional, and related occupations			Sales and office occupations		Natural resources, construction, and maintenance occupations			Production, transportation, and material-moving occupations	
		Management, business, and financial operations	Professional and related occupations	Service occupations	Sales and related occupations	Office and administrative support occupations	Farming, fishing, and forestry occupations	Construction and extraction occupations	Installation, maintenance, and repair occupations	Production occupations	Transportation and material-moving occupations
Total.....	139,252	20,235	28,297	22,720	15,983	19,481	991	8,522	5,069	9,462	8,491
AL........	2,053	249	394	326	211	278	23	136	84	199	153
AK........	306	39	64	50	30	47	6	22	14	11	22
AZ........	2,637	369	493	489	347	357	12	198	112	121	140
AR........	1,231	177	213	178	120	164	22	78	58	126	96
CA........	16,466	2,536	3,416	2,614	1,988	2,401	183	997	519	958	853
CO........	2,389	392	531	388	278	311	16	159	74	105	135
CT........	1,702	290	393	260	203	231	3	92	52	105	74
DE........	409	64	77	67	45	65	2	27	16	22	25
DC........	275	62	92	44	17	35	(Z)	8	4	3	10
FL........	8,021	1,205	1,439	1,465	1,096	1,151	40	557	315	316	437
GA........	4,194	669	779	599	485	563	15	336	165	297	286
HI........	591	81	110	130	70	86	7	34	20	19	33
ID........	669	96	116	116	74	97	20	48	26	33	44
IL........	5,997	878	1,170	990	673	893	11	343	189	461	388
IN........	2,993	406	522	443	329	386	16	165	144	348	235
IA........	1,545	221	284	246	169	209	18	76	57	154	112
KS........	1,398	204	278	221	170	190	15	74	62	101	83
KY........	1,874	238	353	294	202	268	17	119	68	191	124
LA........	1,934	237	393	333	232	243	14	150	82	120	129
ME........	664	81	128	117	75	91	8	44	30	50	42
MD........	2,762	462	701	431	306	365	8	172	80	103	134
MA........	3,226	485	824	526	355	450	7	186	98	168	128
MI........	4,758	659	932	775	515	657	25	233	176	510	275
MN........	2,800	478	616	412	325	375	21	149	88	198	137
MS........	1,252	138	242	186	136	156	15	86	50	139	105
MO	2,844	386	579	423	335	455	10	185	114	167	190
MT........	462	77	80	79	52	60	12	35	20	21	26
NE........	953	157	182	146	108	134	16	56	40	60	55
NV........	1,125	134	164	275	163	151	1	94	41	42	60
NH........	698	105	164	93	87	92	3	42	28	52	31
NJ	4,178	649	962	638	492	658	11	190	109	195	275
NM........	860	121	193	157	97	103	7	66	32	35	50
NY........	8,823	1,180	2,001	1,669	967	1,269	21	458	304	477	478
NC........	4,016	544	790	622	441	508	37	297	158	363	255
ND........	347	61	62	61	37	45	7	22	13	17	22
OH........	5,514	764	1,060	951	621	763	15	274	188	487	392
OK........	1,630	243	293	285	181	232	10	104	73	112	95
OR........	1,710	266	334	267	198	237	31	91	59	115	111
PA	5,911	798	1,285	876	583	895	53	327	204	458	432
RI	532	71	111	100	58	75	2	25	15	46	28
SC........	1,935	259	325	314	252	257	17	100	87	194	130
SD........	416	68	71	70	54	58	6	23	13	32	21
TN........	2,747	379	511	393	308	399	17	175	93	265	207
TX........	10,332	1,460	2,022	1,708	1,186	1,391	88	724	421	652	679
UT........	1,142	153	235	170	132	172	7	79	46	73	74
VT........	340	53	81	51	38	40	4	25	12	21	14
VA	3,619	587	846	515	404	479	13	230	139	190	217
WA	3,037	472	653	516	323	390	45	170	115	171	182
WV	753	79	143	132	89	105	3	63	31	51	58
WI	2,917	409	540	467	303	403	24	156	119	302	193
WY	271	42	43	42	29	37	5	25	16	12	20

Z Less than 500.

Source: U.S. Bureau of Labor Statistics, Local Area Unemployment Statistics, *Geographic Profile of Employment and Unemployment, 2004*. See Internet site <http://www.bls.gov/gps/>.

Table 604. Employment Projections by Occupation: 2004 and 2014

[In thousands (624 represents 624,000), except percent and rank. Estimates based on the Current Employment Statistics Program; the Occupational Employment Statistics Survey; and the Current Population Survey. See source for methodological assumptions. Occupations based on the 2000 Standard Occupational Classification system]

Occupation	Employment (1,000) 2004	Employment (1,000) 2014	Change 2002–2014 Number (1,000)	Change 2002–2014 Per-cent	Quartile rank by 2004 median annual earnings [1]	Most significant source of postsecondary education or training
FASTEST GROWING						
Home health aides	624	974	350	56.0	VL	Short-term on-the-job training
Network systems and data communications analysts	231	357	126	54.6	VH	Bachelor's degree
Medical assistants	387	589	202	52.1	L	Moderate-term on-the-job training
Physician assistants	62	93	31	49.6	VH	Bachelor's degree
Computer software engineers, applications .	460	682	222	48.4	VH	Bachelor's degree
Physical therapist assistants.	59	85	26	44.2	H	Associate's degree
Dental hygienists	158	226	68	43.3	VH	Associate's degree
Computer software engineers, systems software	340	486	146	43.0	VH	Bachelor's degree
Dental assistants	267	382	114	42.7	L	Moderate-term on-the-job training
Personal and home care aides	701	988	287	41.0	VL	Short-term on-the-job training
Network and computer systems administrators	278	385	107	38.4	VH	Bachelor's degree
Database administrators	104	144	40	38.2	VH	Bachelor's degree
Physical therapists	155	211	57	36.7	VH	Master's degree
Forensic science technicians	10	13	4	36.4	VH	Associate's degree
Veterinary technologists and technicians. . .	60	81	21	35.3	L	Associate's degree
Diagnostic medical sonographers	42	57	15	34.8	VH	Associate's degree
Physical therapist aides.	43	57	15	34.4	L	Short-term on-the-job training
Occupational therapist assistants	21	29	7	34.1	H	Associate's degree
Medical scientists, except epidemiologists	72	97	25	34.1	VH	Doctoral degree
Occupational therapists	92	123	31	33.6	VH	Master's degree
Preschool teachers, except special education	431	573	143	33.1	L	Postsecondary vocational award
Cardiovascular technologists and technicians	45	60	15	32.6	H	Associate's degree
Postsecondary teachers	1,628	2,153	524	32.2	VH	Doctoral degree
Hydrologists	8	11	3	31.6	VH	Master's degree
Computer systems analysts	487	640	153	31.4	VH	Bachelor's degree
Hazardous materials removal workers	38	50	12	31.2	H	Moderate-term on-the-job training
LARGEST JOB GROWTH						
Retail salespersons	4,256	4,992	736	17.3	VL	Short-term on-the-job training
Registered nurses	2,394	3,096	703	29.4	VH	Associate's degree
Postsecondary teachers	1,628	2,153	524	32.2	VH	Doctoral degree
Customer service representatives	2,063	2,534	471	22.8	L	Moderate-term on-the-job training
Janitors and cleaners, except maids and housekeeping cleaners	2,374	2,813	440	18.5	VL	Short-term on-the-job training
Waiters and waitresses	2,252	2,627	376	16.7	VL	Short-term on-the-job training
Combined food preparation and serving workers, including fast food	2,150	2,516	367	17.1	VL	Short-term on-the-job training
Home health aides	624	974	350	56.0	VL	Short-term on-the-job training
Nursing aides, orderlies, and attendants. . .	1,455	1,781	325	22.3	L	Postsecondary vocational award
General and operations managers.	1,807	2,115	308	17.0	VH	Bachelor's or higher degree, plus work experience
Personal and home care aides	701	988	287	41.0	VL	Short-term on-the-job training
Elementary school teachers, except special education	1,457	1,722	265	18.2	H	Bachelor's degree
Accountants and auditors	1,176	1,440	264	22.4	VH	Bachelor's degree
Office clerks, general	3,138	3,401	263	8.4	L	Short-term on-the-job training
Laborers and freight, stock, and material movers, hand.	2,430	2,678	248	10.2	VL	Short-term on-the-job training
Receptionists and information clerks	1,133	1,379	246	21.7	L	Short-term on-the-job training
Landscaping and groundskeeping workers . .	1,177	1,407	230	19.5	L	Short-term on-the-job training
Truck drivers, heavy and tractor-trailer	1,738	1,962	223	12.9	H	Moderate-term on-the-job training
Computer software engineers, applications . .	460	682	222	48.4	VH	Bachelor's degree
Maintenance and repair workers, general . .	1,332	1,533	202	15.2	H	Moderate-term on-the-job training
Medical assistants	387	589	202	52.1	L	Moderate-term on-the-job training
Executive secretaries and administrative assistants	1,547	1,739	192	12.4	H	Moderate-term on-the-job training
Sales representatives, wholesale and manufacturing, except technical and scientific products	1,454	1,641	187	12.9	VH	Moderate-term on-the-job training
Carpenters	1,349	1,535	186	13.8	H	Long-term on-the-job training
Teacher assistants	1,296	1,478	183	14.1	VL	Short-term on-the-job training
Child care workers	1,280	1,456	176	13.8	VL	Short-term on-the-job training
Food preparation workers	889	1,064	175	19.7	VL	Short-term on-the-job training

[1] Quartile ranks based on the Occupational Employment Statistics annual earnings. VH = very high ($43,600 and over), H = high ($28,580 to $43,590), L = low ($20,190 to $28,570), and VL = very low (up to $20,180). The rankings were based on quartiles using one-fourth of total employment to define each quartile. Earnings are for wage and salary workers.

Source: U.S. Bureau of Labor Statistics "Occupational employment projections to 2014", *Monthly Labor Review*, November 2005. See Internet site <http://www.bls.gov/emp/home.htm>.

Table 605. **Occupations of the Employed by Selected Characteristic: 2005**

[In thousands (121,960 represents 121,960,000). Annual averages of monthly figures. For civilian noninstitutional population 25 years old and over. Based on Current Population Survey; see text, Section 1, and Appendix III. See headnote Table 591 regarding occupations]

Sex, race, and educational attainment	Total employed	Managerial, professional, and related	Service	Sales and office	Natural resources, construction, and maintenance	Production, transportation, and material moving
Total [1]	121,960	46,303	17,448	29,322	13,173	15,714
Less than a high school diploma	11,712	749	3,336	1,557	2,899	3,171
High school graduates, no college	36,398	5,832	6,957	10,213	5,731	7,664
Less than a bachelor's degree	33,625	10,975	5,003	10,403	3,550	3,694
College graduates	40,225	28,748	2,151	7,150	992	1,184
White [2]	100,613	39,019	13,117	24,372	11,607	12,497
Less than a high school diploma	9,579	626	2,500	1,262	2,595	2,596
High school graduates, no college	29,911	5,038	5,067	8,649	5,076	6,081
Less than a bachelor's degree	27,771	9,321	3,868	8,574	3,099	2,909
College graduates	33,352	24,034	1,682	5,887	838	911
Black [2]	13,177	3,730	3,036	3,159	983	2,268
Less than a high school diploma	1,369	65	578	183	185	358
High school graduates, no college	4,742	564	1,408	1,114	439	1,217
Less than a bachelor's degree	4,008	1,082	812	1,267	281	566
College graduates	3,057	2,019	238	596	77	128
Asian [2]	5,601	2,753	818	1,198	249	583
Less than a high school diploma	440	36	165	70	40	130
High school graduates, no college	980	120	301	261	79	220
Less than a bachelor's degree	972	304	178	304	71	115
College graduates	3,208	2,293	174	563	59	119
Hispanic [3]	15,362	2,880	3,553	3,008	2,953	2,968
Less than a high school diploma	5,367	180	1,623	536	1,600	1,427
High school graduates, no college	4,535	500	1,094	1,070	866	1,004
Less than a bachelor's degree	3,228	861	591	1,012	368	396
College graduates	2,232	1,339	245	390	118	140

[1] Includes other races, not shown separately. [2] For persons in this race group only. See footnote 3, Table 574. [3] Persons of Hispanic or Latino ethnicity may be any race.

Source: U.S. Bureau of Labor Statistics, unpublished data.

Table 606. **Employment by Industry: 2000 to 2005**

[In thousands (136,891 represents 136,891,000), except percent. See Table 588 regarding coverage and Table 591 regarding industries]

Industry	2000	2003 [1]	2004 [1]	2005 [1]	2005, percent [1] Female	Black [2]	Asian [2]	Hispanic [3]
Total employed	136,891	137,736	139,252	141,730	46.4	10.8	4.4	13.1
Agriculture and related industries	2,464	2,275	2,232	2,197	24.7	2.3	1.0	19.3
Mining	475	525	539	624	12.8	4.9	1.3	14.0
Construction	9,931	10,138	10,768	11,197	9.6	5.9	1.4	23.0
Manufacturing	19,644	16,902	16,484	16,253	30.0	10.0	5.1	14.2
Durable goods	12,519	10,520	10,329	10,333	26.1	8.6	5.7	12.0
Nondurable goods	7,125	6,382	6,155	5,919	36.9	12.5	4.1	18.1
Wholesale trade	4,216	4,486	4,640	4,579	28.7	6.8	4.3	13.7
Retail trade	15,763	16,220	16,269	16,825	48.7	9.8	4.3	12.4
Transportation and utilities	7,380	6,950	7,013	7,360	23.5	15.6	3.6	12.6
Transportation and warehousing	6,096	5,758	5,844	6,184	23.9	16.7	4.0	13.7
Utilities	1,284	1,193	1,168	1,176	21.3	9.7	1.5	7.4
Information	4,059	3,687	3,463	3,402	44.2	11.3	4.8	9.1
Financial activities	9,374	9,748	9,969	10,203	55.3	9.8	4.8	9.7
Finance and insurance	6,641	6,834	6,940	7,035	58.5	10.3	5.5	8.2
Real estate and rental and leasing	2,734	2,914	3,029	3,168	48.1	8.8	3.3	13.2
Professional and business services	13,649	13,879	14,108	14,294	42.9	9.4	5.6	12.5
Professional and technical services	8,266	8,243	8,386	8,584	44.5	5.9	7.4	6.1
Management, administrative, and waste services	5,383	5,636	5,722	5,709	40.5	14.5	2.9	22.3
Education and health services	26,188	28,260	28,719	29,174	75.0	13.9	4.5	9.0
Educational services	11,255	11,826	12,058	12,264	69.0	11.0	3.6	8.2
Health care and social assistance	14,933	16,434	16,661	16,910	79.3	16.1	5.2	9.6
Hospitals	5,202	5,652	5,700	5,719	76.5	15.7	6.8	7.5
Health services, except hospitals	7,009	7,964	8,118	8,332	79.0	15.4	4.7	9.6
Social assistance	2,722	2,818	2,844	2,860	85.9	18.8	3.1	14.0
Leisure and hospitality	11,186	11,607	11,820	12,071	51.4	10.7	5.8	18.3
Arts, entertainment, and recreation	2,539	2,587	2,690	2,765	45.2	8.2	3.5	10.2
Accommodation and food services	8,647	9,021	9,131	9,306	53.3	11.4	6.5	20.7
Other services	6,450	6,815	6,903	7,020	51.5	10.2	5.2	15.5
Other services, except private households	5,731	6,050	6,124	6,208	46.2	10.1	5.5	13.1
Private households	718	764	779	812	91.7	11.3	2.8	33.9
Government workers	6,113	6,243	6,365	6,530	45.5	15.9	3.3	8.7

[1] See footnote 2, Table 573. [2] Persons in this race group only. See footnote 3, Table 574. [3] Persons of Hispanic or Latino origin may be any race.
Source: U.S. Bureau of Labor Statistics, *Employment and Earnings*, monthly, January 2006 issue. See Internet site <http://www.bls.gov/cps/home.htm>.

Table 607. **Employment Projections by Industry: 2004 to 2014**

[**15,034.5 represents 15,034,500.** Estimates based on the Current Employment Statistics estimates. See source for methodological assumptions. Minus sign (–) indicates decline]

Industry	2002 NAICS code [1]	Employment (1,000)		Change, 2004–2014 (1,000)	Average annual rate of change 2004–2014
		2004	2014		
LARGEST GROWTH					
Retail trade	44,45	15,034.5	16,683.2	1,648.7	1.0
Employment services.	5613	3,470.3	5,050.2	1,579.9	3.8
Food services and drinking places	722	8,850.0	10,300.8	1,450.8	1.5
Offices of health practitioners	6211,6212,6213	3,337.0	4,560.7	1,223.7	3.2
Construction	23	6,964.5	7,756.9	792.4	1.1
Local government educational services.	(X)	7,762.5	8,545.5	783.0	1.0
Hospitals, private	622	4,293.6	4,981.9	688.3	1.5
Residential care facilities	6232,6233,6239	1,239.6	1,840.3	600.7	4.0
Home health care services	6216	773.2	1,310.3	537.1	5.4
Junior colleges, colleges, universities, and professional schools	6112,6113	1,461.8	1,964.8	503.0	3.0
Local government enterprises except passenger transit.	(X)	4,216.0	4,699.3	483.3	1.1
Wholesale trade	42	5,654.9	6,130.8	475.9	0.8
Management, scientific, and technical consulting services.	5416	779.0	1,250.2	471.2	4.8
Computer systems design and related services	5415	1,147.4	1,600.3	452.9	3.4
Individual, family, community, and vocational rehabilitation services.	6241,6242,6243	1,365.3	1,810.0	444.7	2.9
State government educational services.	(X)	2,249.2	2,691.0	441.8	1.8
Amusement, gambling, and recreation industries	713	1,351.3	1,709.7	358.4	2.4
Services to buildings and dwellings	5617	1,694.1	2,049.7	355.6	1.9
MOST RAPID GROWTH					
Home health care services	6216	773.2	1,310.3	537.1	5.4
Software publishers.	5112	238.7	400.0	161.3	5.3
Management, scientific, and technical consulting services.	5416	779.0	1,250.2	471.2	4.8
Residential care facilities	6232,6233,6239	1,239.6	1,840.3	600.7	4.0
Facilities support services.	5612	115.6	170.0	54.4	3.9
Employment services.	5613	3,470.3	5,050.2	1,579.9	3.8
Independent artists, writers, and performers.	7115	41.9	60.8	18.9	3.8
Office administrative services	5611	319.4	449.9	130.5	3.5
Computer systems design and related services	5415	1,147.4	1,600.3	452.9	3.4
Outpatient, laboratory, and other ambulatory care services	6214,6215,6219	836.1	1,160.4	324.3	3.3
Child day care services	6244	767.1	1,061.9	294.8	3.3
Other educational services	6114–17	475.3	649.9	174.6	3.2
Offices of health practitioners	6211,6212,6213	3,337.0	4,560.7	1,223.7	3.2
Accounting, tax preparation, bookkeeping, and payroll services.	5412	816.0	1,099.9	283.9	3.0
Junior colleges, colleges, universities, and professional schools	6112,6113	1,461.8	1,964.8	503.0	3.0
Individual, family, community, and vocational rehabilitation services.	6241,6242,6243	1,365.3	1,810.0	444.7	2.9
Scenic and sightseeing transportation.	487	26.8	35.2	8.4	2.8
Waste treatment and disposal and waste management services	5622,5629	206.3	267.9	61.6	2.6
MOST RAPID DECLINE					
Cut-and-sew apparel manufacturing	3152	219.9	80.0	–139.9	–9.6
Fiber, yarn, and thread mills	3131	54.4	25.0	–29.4	–7.5
Apparel knitting mills	3151	42.0	20.0	–22.0	–7.2
Textile and fabric finishing and fabric coating mills . . .	3133	68.5	35.0	–33.5	–6.5
Fabric mills	3132	115.7	60.0	–55.7	–6.4
Tobacco manufacturing	3122	29.4	16.6	–12.8	–5.6
Footwear manufacturing	3162	19.4	12.5	–6.9	–4.3
Apparel accessories & other apparel manufacturing . .	3159	23.0	15.0	–8.0	–4.2
Basic chemical manufacturing.	3251	156.1	110.0	–46.1	–3.4
Metal ore mining.	2122	27.3	19.3	–8.0	–3.4
Other textile product mills.	3149	75.1	55.0	–20.1	–3.1
Household appliance manufacturing.	3352	90.1	66.0	–24.1	–3.1
Commercial and service industry machinery manufacturing	3333	114.9	85.0	–29.9	–3.0
Federal enterprises, except the Postal Service and electric utilities	(X)	70.5	53.0	–17.5	–2.8
Electrical equipment manufacturing	3353	153.1	117.0	–36.1	–2.7

X Not applicable.   [1] Based on the North American Industry Classification System, 2002; see text, this section.

Source: U.S. Bureau of Labor Statistics, "Industry output and employment projections to 2014" *Monthly Labor Review*, November 2005. See Internet site <http://www.bls.gov/emp/home.htm>.

Labor Force, Employment, and Earnings   **395**

Table 608. **Unemployed Workers—Summary: 1980 to 2005**

[In thousands (7,637 represents 7,637,000), except as indicated. For civilian noninstitutional population 16 years old and over. Annual averages of monthly figures. Based on the Current Populatin Survey; see text Section 1 and Appendix III. For data on unemployment insurance, see Table 544]

Age, sex, race, Hispanic origin	1980	1985	1990 [1]	1995	2000 [1]	2003 [1]	2004 [1]	2005 [1]
UNEMPLOYED								
Total [2]	7,637	8,312	7,047	7,404	5,692	8,774	8,149	7,591
16 to 19 years old	1,669	1,468	1,212	1,346	1,081	1,251	1,208	1,186
20 to 24 years old	1,835	1,738	1,299	1,244	1,022	1,495	1,431	1,335
25 to 44 years old	2,964	3,681	3,323	3,390	2,340	3,775	3,362	3,061
45 to 64 years old	1,075	1,331	1,109	1,269	1,117	2,069	1,970	1,825
65 years and over	94	93	105	153	132	183	179	184
Male	4,267	4,521	3,906	3,983	2,975	4,906	4,456	4,059
16 to 19 years old	913	806	667	744	599	697	664	667
20 to 24 years old	1,076	944	715	673	547	841	811	775
25 to 44 years old	1,619	1,950	1,803	1,776	1,159	2,085	1,819	1,559
45 to 64 years old	600	766	662	697	587	1,176	1,057	955
65 years and over	58	55	59	94	83	107	104	102
Female	3,370	3,791	3,140	3,421	2,717	3,868	3,694	3,531
16 to 19 years old	755	661	544	602	483	554	543	519
20 to 24 years old	760	794	584	571	475	654	619	560
25 to 44 years old	1,345	1,732	1,519	1,615	1,181	1,690	1,543	1,502
45 to 64 years old	473	566	447	574	529	894	914	870
65 years and over	36	39	46	60	50	76	75	82
White [3]	5,884	6,191	5,186	5,459	4,121	6,311	5,847	5,350
16 to 19 years old	1,291	1,074	903	952	795	909	890	845
20 to 24 years old	1,364	1,235	899	866	682	1,012	959	878
Black [3]	1,553	1,864	1,565	1,538	1,241	1,787	1,729	1,700
16 to 19 years old	343	357	268	325	230	255	241	267
20 to 24 years old	426	455	349	311	281	375	353	358
Asian [3, 4]	(NA)	(NA)	(NA)	(NA)	227	366	277	259
16 to 19 years old	(NA)	(NA)	(NA)	(NA)	40	31	20	20
20 to 24 years old	(NA)	(NA)	(NA)	(NA)	41	47	46	35
Hispanic [5]	620	811	876	1,140	954	1,441	1,342	1,191
16 to 19 years old	145	141	161	205	194	192	203	191
20 to 24 years old	138	171	167	209	190	273	255	227
Full-time workers	6,269	6,793	5,677	5,909	4,538	7,361	6,762	6,175
Part-time workers	1,369	1,519	1,369	1,495	1,154	1,413	1,388	1,415
UNEMPLOYMENT RATE (percent) [6]								
Total [2]	7.1	7.2	5.6	5.6	4.0	6.0	5.5	5.1
16 to 19 years old	17.8	18.6	15.5	17.3	13.1	17.5	17.0	16.6
20 to 24 years old	11.5	11.1	8.8	9.1	7.2	10.0	9.4	8.8
25 to 44 years old	6.0	6.2	4.9	4.8	3.3	5.5	4.9	4.5
45 to 64 years old	3.7	4.5	3.5	3.4	2.5	4.1	3.8	3.4
65 years and over	3.1	3.2	3.0	4.0	3.1	3.8	3.6	3.5
Male	6.9	7.0	5.7	5.6	3.9	6.3	5.6	5.1
16 to 19 years old	18.3	19.5	16.3	18.4	14.0	19.3	18.4	18.6
20 to 24 years old	12.5	11.4	9.1	9.2	7.3	10.6	10.1	9.6
25 to 44 years old	5.6	5.9	4.8	4.7	3.1	5.6	4.9	4.2
45 to 64 years old	3.5	4.5	3.7	3.5	2.4	4.4	3.9	3.4
65 years and over	3.1	3.1	3.0	4.3	3.3	4.0	3.7	3.4
Female	7.4	7.4	5.5	5.6	4.1	5.7	5.4	5.1
16 to 19 years old	17.2	17.6	14.7	16.1	12.1	15.6	15.5	14.5
20 to 24 years old	10.4	10.7	8.5	9.0	7.1	9.3	8.7	7.9
25 to 44 years old	6.4	6.6	4.9	5.0	3.6	5.4	5.0	4.8
45 to 64 years old	4.0	4.6	3.2	3.3	2.5	3.7	3.7	3.4
65 years and over	3.1	3.3	3.1	3.7	2.7	3.6	3.4	3.5
White [3]	6.3	6.2	4.8	4.9	3.5	5.2	4.8	4.4
16 to 19 years old	15.5	15.7	13.5	14.5	11.4	15.2	15.0	14.2
20 to 24 years old	9.9	9.2	7.3	7.7	5.9	8.4	7.9	7.2
Black [3]	14.3	15.1	11.4	10.4	7.6	10.8	10.4	10.0
16 to 19 years old	38.5	40.2	30.9	35.7	24.5	33.0	31.7	33.3
20 to 24 years old	23.6	24.5	19.9	17.7	15.0	19.8	18.4	18.3
Asian [3, 4]	(NA)	(NA)	(NA)	(NA)	3.6	6.0	4.4	4.0
16 to 19 years old	(NA)	(NA)	(NA)	(NA)	14.2	17.5	11.5	12.4
20 to 24 years old	(NA)	(NA)	(NA)	(NA)	6.9	9.0	8.6	6.5
Hispanic [5]	10.1	10.5	8.2	9.3	5.7	7.7	7.0	6.0
16 to 19 years old	22.5	24.3	19.5	24.1	16.6	20.0	20.4	18.4
20 to 24 years old	12.1	12.6	9.1	11.5	7.5	10.2	9.3	8.6
Experienced workers [7]	6.9	6.8	5.3	5.4	3.8	5.8	5.3	4.8
Women maintaining families	9.2	10.4	8.3	8.0	5.9	8.5	8.0	7.8
Married men, wife present	4.2	4.3	3.4	3.3	2.0	3.8	3.1	2.8
Percent without work for—								
Fewer than 5 weeks	43.2	42.1	46.3	36.5	44.9	31.7	33.1	35.1
5 to 10 weeks	23.4	22.2	23.5	22.0	23.0	19.8	19.6	20.7
11 to 14 weeks	9.0	8.0	8.5	9.6	8.9	10.0	9.7	9.7
15 to 26 weeks	13.8	12.3	11.7	14.6	11.8	16.4	15.9	14.9
27 weeks and over	10.7	15.4	10.0	17.3	11.4	22.1	21.8	19.6
Unemployment duration, average (weeks)	11.9	15.6	12.0	16.6	12.6	19.2	19.6	18.4

NA Not available.   [1] See footnote 2, Table 573.   [2] Includes other races, not shown separately.   [3] Includes other ages, not shown separately. Also beginning 2003, for this race group only. See footnote 3, Table 574.   [4] Prior to 2003, includes Pacific Islanders.   [5] Persons of Hispanic or Latino origin may be of any race. Also includes ages not shown separately.   [6] Unemployed as percent of civilian labor force in specified group.   [7] Wage and salary workers.

Source: U.S. Bureau of Labor Statistics, *Employment and Earnings*, monthly, January 2006 issue; and unpublished data. See Internet site <http://www.bls.gov/cps/>.

Table 609. **Unemployed Jobseekers Job Search Activities: 2005**

[7,591 represents 7,591,000. For the civilian noninstitutional population 16 years old and over. Annual average of monthly data. Based on the Current Population Survey; see text, Section 1 and Appendix III]

Characteristic	Population (1,000)		Jobseekers job search methods (percent)						Average number of methods used
	Total unemployed	Total jobseekers [1]	Employer directly	Sent out a resume or filled out applications	Placed or answered ads	Friends or relatives	Public employment agency	Private employment agency	
Total, 16 years and over [2] ...	**7,591**	**6,657**	**60.6**	**55.4**	**14.8**	**17.7**	**18.3**	**6.7**	**1.85**
16 to 19 years old	1,186	1,127	57.8	60.2	8.5	13.3	8.5	2.4	1.56
20 to 24 years old	1,335	1,230	61.5	56.1	13.8	16.3	16.7	5.9	1.80
25 to 34 years old	1,661	1,444	61.9	56.0	16.1	17.6	21.0	7.5	1.93
35 to 44 years old	1,400	1,186	60.9	53.8	18.1	20.3	23.3	8.3	1.98
45 to 54 years old	1,195	1,021	62.6	53.4	16.8	19.3	22.0	9.0	1.97
55 to 64 years old	630	507	58.7	52.3	16.6	20.9	19.4	8.5	1.92
65 years old and over	184	143	53.9	41.6	14.5	19.3	12.9	3.7	1.58
Male	4,059	3,467	61.4	53.2	14.7	19.4	18.4	6.8	1.86
16 to 19 years old	667	632	56.9	59.1	8.9	14.7	9.0	2.6	1.57
20 to 24 years old	775	699	61.4	53.7	12.7	18.5	17.5	6.3	1.80
25 to 34 years old	844	704	63.3	54.1	16.7	19.4	20.3	7.6	1.96
35 to 44 years old	715	579	63.9	50.3	18.2	22.8	23.5	8.0	2.01
45 to 54 years old	624	515	63.1	51.0	16.5	21.5	23.0	9.8	2.00
55 to 64 years old	331	260	60.7	50.1	17.4	21.7	19.0	8.4	1.94
65 years old and over....	102	77	54.7	40.1	13.1	18.5	13.9	2.5	1.56
Female	3,531	3,190	59.8	57.7	15.0	15.8	18.3	6.6	1.84
16 to 19 years old	519	495	58.9	61.7	7.9	11.6	7.8	2.0	1.56
20 to 24 years old	560	531	61.5	59.3	15.2	13.3	15.6	5.4	1.80
25 to 34 years old	817	740	60.6	57.8	15.6	16.0	21.7	7.4	1.90
35 to 44 years old	685	607	58.1	57.2	18.0	18.0	23.0	8.5	1.96
45 to 54 years old	571	506	62.0	55.9	17.1	17.0	20.9	8.3	1.94
55 to 64 years old	299	247	56.7	54.6	15.6	20.2	19.9	8.6	1.89
65 years old and over....	82	65	53.0	43.4	16.3	20.3	11.8	5.2	1.60
White [3]	5,350	4,595	61.1	55.6	15.2	17.7	17.2	6.6	1.85
Male	2,931	2,440	62.1	53.4	15.0	19.5	17.5	6.9	1.87
Female	2,419	2,154	59.9	58.2	15.5	15.6	16.8	6.2	1.83
Black [3]	1,700	1,563	60.3	55.6	14.3	17.1	22.0	6.5	1.85
Male	844	766	60.6	53.6	14.3	19.1	21.1	6.1	1.84
Female	856	798	59.9	57.5	14.4	15.1	22.9	6.9	1.86
Asian [3]	259	245	59.1	47.1	13.2	23.6	16.7	9.5	1.86
Male	141	134	60.3	45.6	12.6	22.2	15.9	8.3	1.81
Female	118	110	57.7	49.0	13.9	25.3	17.6	10.9	1.92
Hispanic [4]	1,191	1,142	61.1	48.6	10.4	22.3	18.0	6.1	1.80
Male	647	619	63.7	45.4	10.5	25.3	19.0	5.9	1.82
Female	544	524	58.2	52.2	10.4	18.9	17.0	6.2	1.76

[1] Excludes persons on temporary layoff. [2] Includes other races, not shown separately. [3] Data for this race group only. See footnote 3, Table 574. [4] Persons of Hispanic or Latino origin may be of any race.

Source: U.S. Bureau of Labor Statistics, *Employment and Earnings,* monthly, January 2006 issue. See Internet site <http://www.bls.gov/cps/home.htm>.

Table 610. **Unemployed Persons by Sex and Reason: 1980 to 2005**

[In thousands (4,267 represents 4,267,000). For civilian noninstitutional population 16 years old and over. Annual averages of monthly figures. Based on Current Population Survey; see text, Section 1, and Appendix III]

Sex and reason	1980	1985	1990 [1]	1995	1998 [1]	1999 [1]	2000 [1]	2001	2002	2003 [1]	2004 [1]	2005 [1]
Male, total ...	4,267	4,521	3,906	3,983	3,266	3,066	2,975	3,690	4,597	4,906	4,456	4,059
Job losers [2]	2,649	2,749	2,257	2,190	1,703	1,563	1,516	2,119	2,820	3,024	2,603	2,188
Job leavers	438	409	528	407	368	389	387	422	434	422	437	445
Reentrants	776	876	806	1,113	931	895	854	925	1,068	1,141	1,070	1,067
New entrants...	405	487	315	273	264	219	217	223	274	320	346	359
Female, total .	3,370	3,791	3,140	3,421	2,944	2,814	2,717	3,111	3,781	3,868	3,694	3,531
Job losers [2]	1,297	1,390	1,130	1,286	1,119	1,059	1,001	1,356	1,787	1,814	1,595	1,479
Job leavers	453	468	513	417	366	394	393	413	432	397	421	427
Reentrants	1,152	1,380	1,124	1,412	1,201	1,111	1,107	1,105	1,300	1,336	1,338	1,319
New entrants...	468	552	373	306	257	250	217	237	262	321	340	306

[1] See footnote 2, Table 573. [2] Beginning 1995, persons who completed temporary jobs are identified separately and are included as job losers.

Source: U.S. Bureau of Labor Statistics, *Employment and Earnings,* monthly, January issues; Bulletin 2307; and unpublished data. See Internet site <http://www.bls.gov/cps/home.htm>.

Labor Force, Employment, and Earnings   397

Table 611. **Unemployment Rates by Industry, 2000 to 2005, and by Sex, 2000 and 2005**

[In percent. For civilian noninstitutional population 16 years old and over. Annual averages of monthly figures. Rate represents unemployment as a percent of labor force in each specified group. Based on Current Population Survey; see text, Section 1, and Appendix III. See headnote, Table 591 regarding industries]

Industry	2000	2003 [1]	2004 [1]	2005 [1]	Male 2000	Male 2005 [1]	Female 2000	Female 2005 [1]
All unemployed [2]	4.0	6.0	5.5	5.1	3.9	5.1	4.1	5.1
Industry: [3]								
Agriculture and related industries	9.0	10.2	9.9	8.3	8.3	7.4	11.5	11.4
Mining	4.4	6.7	3.9	3.1	4.6	3.4	2.8	1.5
Construction	6.2	9.3	8.4	7.4	6.4	7.6	5.1	6.0
Manufacturing	3.5	6.6	5.7	4.9	3.0	4.4	4.5	6.0
Wholesale trade	3.3	5.1	4.6	4.0	2.8	3.6	4.4	5.1
Retail trade	4.6	6.3	6.1	5.7	4.0	5.2	5.1	6.3
Transportation and utilities.................	3.4	5.3	4.4	4.1	3.2	4.0	4.2	4.8
Transportation and warehousing	3.8	5.7	4.9	4.5	1.9	4.3	4.6	5.4
Utilities..............................	1.9	3.1	1.9	1.9	2.8	1.9	2.1	1.7
Information	3.2	6.8	5.7	5.0	2.7	4.8	3.7	5.3
Telecommunications	2.3	7.5	6.0	5.2	1.5	4.6	3.3	6.2
Financial activities	2.4	3.5	3.6	2.9	2.1	2.5	2.6	3.1
Finance and insurance	2.2	3.3	3.4	2.7	1.7	2.2	2.5	3.0
Real estate and rental and leasing.........	3.1	4.1	4.1	3.3	2.9	3.2	3.2	3.4
Professional and business services	4.8	8.2	6.8	6.2	4.4	5.8	5.2	6.8
Professional and technical services	2.5	5.4	4.1	3.5	2.2	2.9	2.9	4.2
Management, administrative, and waste services	8.1	12.1	10.6	10.2	7.6	9.5	8.8	11.0
Education and health services	2.5	3.6	3.4	3.4	2.2	2.9	2.5	3.6
Educational services	2.4	4.5	3.7	3.7	2.1	3.1	2.5	4.0
Health care and social assistance	2.5	3.4	3.4	3.3	2.3	2.8	2.5	3.5
Leisure and hospitality	6.6	8.7	8.3	7.8	6.2	7.3	7.0	8.2
Arts, entertainment, and recreation	5.9	7.8	7.2	6.9	6.1	7.3	5.7	6.5
Accommodation and food services.........	6.8	8.9	8.6	8.0	6.2	7.3	7.3	8.5
Other services [4]........................	3.9	5.7	5.3	4.8	3.7	4.9	4.0	4.8
Government workers	2.1	2.8	2.7	2.6	2.1	2.6	2.2	2.5

[1] See footnote 2, Table 573.   [2] Includes the self-employed, unpaid family workers, and persons with no previous work experience, not shown separately.   [3] Covers unemployed wage and salary workers.   [4] Includes private household workers.

Source: U.S. Bureau of Labor Statistics, *Employment and Earnings*, monthly, January issues; and unpublished data. See Internet site <http://www.bls.gov/cps/home.htm>.

Table 612. **Unemployment by Occupation, 2000 to 2005, and by Sex, 2005**

[**5,692 represents 5,692,000.** For civilian noninstitutional population 16 years old and over. Annual averages of monthly data. Rate represents unemployment as a percent of the labor force for each specified group. Based on Current Population Survey; see text, Section 1, and Appendix III. See also headnote, Table 591 regarding occupations]

Occupation	Number (1,000) 2000	Number (1,000) 2004 [1]	Number (1,000) 2005 [1]	Unemployment rate 2000	Unemployment rate 2004 [1]	Unemployment rate 2005 [1]	2005 [1], by sex Male	2005 [1], by sex Female
Total [2]............................	5,692	8,149	7,591	4.0	5.5	5.1	5.1	5.1
Management, professional, and related occupations. . .	827	1,346	1,172	1.8	2.7	2.3	2.2	2.4
Management, business, and financial operations . . .	320	544	464	1.6	2.6	2.2	2.1	2.4
Management	214	369	322	1.5	2.5	2.1	2.0	2.4
Business and financial operations	106	175	142	2.0	3.0	2.4	2.3	2.5
Professional and related occupations	507	801	708	1.9	2.8	2.4	2.4	2.4
Computer and mathematical	74	136	96	2.2	4.2	2.9	2.7	3.3
Architecture and engineering..............	51	80	60	1.7	2.8	2.1	2.0	2.7
Life, physical, and social science	18	35	39	1.4	2.5	2.7	2.3	3.2
Community and social services	40	65	52	2.0	2.9	2.4	2.4	2.3
Legal	18	31	27	1.2	1.9	1.6	1.1	2.2
Education, training, and library	136	207	210	1.8	2.5	2.5	2.6	2.5
Arts, design, entertainment, sports, and media . . .	97	157	135	3.5	5.5	4.7	5.0	4.4
Healthcare practitioner and technical	73	90	90	1.2	1.3	1.3	0.8	1.5
Service occupations	1,132	1,617	1,587	5.2	6.6	6.4	6.3	6.5
Healthcare support	101	169	154	4.0	5.5	4.7	4.4	4.8
Protective service......................	70	113	121	2.7	3.8	4.0	3.4	6.1
Food preparation and serving-related........	469	656	615	6.6	8.3	7.7	7.7	7.7
Building and grounds cleaning and maintenance . . .	301	421	429	5.8	7.5	7.6	7.2	8.1
Personal care and service	190	257	268	4.4	5.4	5.6	6.0	5.5
Sales and office occupations	1,446	1,937	1,820	3.8	5.2	4.8	4.4	5.0
Sales and related......................	673	912	874	4.1	5.4	5.0	3.9	6.2
Office and administrative support...........	773	1,025	946	3.6	5.0	4.6	5.4	4.4
Natural resources, construction, and maintenance	758	1,140	1,069	5.3	7.3	6.5	6.3	10.6
Farming, fishing, and forestry	133	132	103	10.2	11.8	9.6	8.4	13.6
Construction and extraction	507	786	751	6.2	8.4	7.6	7.5	11.4
Installation, maintenance, and repair	119	222	214	2.4	4.2	3.9	3.8	6.4
Production, transportation, and material moving.	1,081	1,393	1,245	5.1	7.2	6.5	5.8	8.7
Production	575	714	677	4.8	7.0	6.7	5.9	8.6
Transportation and material moving	505	679	568	5.6	7.4	6.2	5.7	8.9

[1] See footnote 2, Table 573.   [2] Includes persons with no previous work experience and those whose last job was in the Armed Forces.

Source: U.S. Bureau of Labor Statistics, *Employment and Earnings*, monthly, January issues; and unpublished data. See Internet site<http://www.bls.gov/cps/home.htm>.

398   Labor Force, Employment, and Earnings

Table 613. Unemployed and Unemployment Rates by Educational Attainment, Sex, Race, and Hispanic Origin: 1992 to 2005

[6,543 represents 6,543,000. Annual averages of monthly figures. For the civilian noninstitutional population 25 years old and over. See Table 578 for civilian labor force and participation rate data. Based on Current Population Survey; see text, Section 1, and Appendix III]

Year, sex, and race	Unemployed (1,000)					Unemployment rate [1]				
	Total	Less than high school diploma	High school gradu-ates, no degree	Less than a bach-elor's degree	BA degree or more	Total	Less than high school diploma	High school gradu-ates, no degree	Less than a bach-elor's degree	BA degree or more
Total: [2]										
1992 . . .	6,543	1,533	2,590	1,527	893	6.1	11.5	6.8	5.6	3.2
2000 [3] . .	3,589	791	1,298	890	610	3.0	6.3	3.4	2.7	1.7
2005 [3] . .	5,070	967	1,798	1,349	955	4.0	7.6	4.7	3.9	2.3
Male:										
1992	3,767	942	1,462	829	533	6.4	11.4	7.4	5.9	3.3
2000 [3] . . .	1,829	411	682	427	309	2.8	5.4	3.4	2.6	1.5
2005 [3] . . .	2,617	514	973	636	494	3.8	6.4	4.6	3.7	2.3
Female:										
1992	2,776	591	1,128	697	361	5.8	11.5	6.3	5.4	3.0
2000 [3] . . .	1,760	380	616	463	301	3.2	7.8	3.5	2.8	1.8
2005 [3] . . .	2,453	453	826	713	461	4.2	9.7	4.8	4.0	2.4
White: [4]										
1992	4,978	1,145	1,928	1,162	743	5.5	10.7	6.0	5.0	3.0
2000 [3] . . .	2,644	564	924	667	489	2.6	5.6	2.9	2.4	1.6
2005 [3] . . .	3,627	669	1,257	973	729	3.5	6.5	4.0	3.4	2.1
Black: [4]										
1992	1,269	322	565	301	81	11.0	15.3	12.3	9.8	4.4
2000 [3] . . .	731	179	315	169	68	5.4	10.7	6.4	4.0	2.5
2005 [3] . . .	1,075	231	440	295	110	7.5	14.4	8.5	6.9	3.5
Asian: [4,5]										
2000 [3] . . .	146	28	34	35	49	2.7	5.7	3.0	3.2	1.8
2005 [3] . . .	203	26	47	32	99	3.5	5.5	4.6	3.2	3.0
Hispanic: [6]										
1992	853	434	235	134	50	9.8	12.8	9.1	7.7	5.0
2000 [3] . . .	569	297	150	85	38	4.4	6.2	3.9	3.2	2.2
2005 [3] . . .	773	354	216	138	66	4.8	6.2	4.5	4.1	2.9

[1] Percent unemployed of the civilian labor force.   [2] Includes other races, not shown separately.   [3] See footnote 2, Table 573.   [4] 2005 data are for persons in this race group only. See footnote 3, Table 574.   [5] 2000 data include Pacific Islanders.   [6] Persons of Hispanic or Latino origin may be of any race.

Source: U.S. Bureau of Labor Statistics, *Employment and Earnings*, monthly, January issues.

Table 614. Unemployed Persons by Reason of Unemployment: 2005

[7,591 represents 7,591,000. Annual averages of monthly data. Based on Current Population Survey; see text, Section 1, and Appendix III]

Age, sex, and reason	Total unem-ployed (1,000)	Percent distribution by duration				
		Less than 5 weeks	5 to 14 weeks	15 weeks and over		
				Total	15 to 26 weeks	27 weeks or longer
Total 16 years old and over	7,591	35.1	30.4	34.5	14.9	19.6
16 to 19 years old	1,186	46.4	32.2	21.3	11.2	10.1
Total 20 years old and over	6,405	33.0	30.0	36.9	15.6	21.4
Males	3,392	32.7	29.3	38.0	15.6	22.5
Job losers and persons who completed temporary jobs	2,095	34.7	29.6	35.7	16.0	19.6
On temporary layoff	557	53.3	31.0	15.6	11.0	4.6
Not on temporary layoff	1,538	27.9	29.1	42.9	17.8	25.1
Permanent job losers	1,068	25.8	28.4	45.8	18.2	27.6
Persons who completed temporary jobs	470	32.7	30.8	36.5	17.0	19.4
Job leavers	405	37.6	30.0	32.4	13.4	19.0
Reentrants	793	26.6	28.3	45.1	15.4	29.7
New entrants	99	18.0	27.7	54.3	15.3	39.0
Females	3,013	33.5	30.8	35.7	15.6	20.2
Job losers and persons who completed temporary jobs	1,417	33.2	30.9	35.8	17.2	18.6
On temporary layoff	317	54.6	31.0	14.4	9.7	4.7
Not on temporary layoff	1,100	27.1	30.9	42.0	19.4	22.6
Permanent job losers	831	24.9	30.8	44.3	19.9	24.4
Persons who completed temporary jobs	269	33.8	31.3	34.9	17.6	17.3
Job leavers	391	41.0	31.1	27.9	12.9	15.0
Reentrants	1,103	31.4	30.7	37.9	14.5	23.3
New entrants	101	30.4	28.3	41.4	14.4	26.9

Source: U.S. Bureau of Labor Statistics, *Employment and Earnings,* January 2006 issue. See Internet site <http://www.bls.gov/cps/home.htm>.

Table 615. **Total Unemployed and Insured Unemployed by State: 1980 to 2005**

[**7,637 represents 7,637,000.** For civilian noninstitutional population 16 years old and over. Annual averages of monthly figures. Total unemployment estimates based on the Current Population Survey; see text, Section 1, and Appendix III. U.S. totals derived by independent population controls; therefore state data may not add to U.S. totals]

State	Total unemployed								Insured unemployed [3]			
	Number (1,000)				Percent [1]				Number (1,000)		Percent [4]	
	1980	1990 [2]	2000 [2]	2005 [2]	1980	1990 [2]	2000 [2]	2005 [2]	2000	2004	2000	2004
United States . . .	7,637	7,047	5,692	7,591	7.1	5.6	4.0	5.1	[5]2,110	[5]2,950	[5]1.7	[5]2.3
Alabama	142	121	87	86	8.8	6.9	4.5	4.0	29.0	31.6	1.6	1.8
Alaska	18	19	20	23	9.7	7.0	6.7	6.8	12.3	13.5	4.9	4.9
Arizona	82	94	100	134	6.7	5.5	4.0	4.7	20.5	37.8	1.0	1.7
Arkansas	74	76	53	67	7.6	7.0	4.4	4.9	23.9	29.7	2.2	2.7
California	796	874	833	949	6.8	5.8	4.9	5.4	338.5	427.8	2.4	2.9
Colorado	88	91	65	129	5.9	5.0	2.8	5.0	15.0	31.3	0.7	1.5
Connecticut	93	90	39	89	5.9	5.2	2.2	4.9	28.3	43.7	1.7	2.7
Delaware	21	15	14	18	7.7	5.2	3.9	4.2	5.9	9.2	1.5	2.3
District of Columbia .	23	20	18	19	7.3	6.6	5.7	6.5	5.7	5.6	1.3	1.2
Florida	262	405	300	325	5.9	6.0	3.6	3.8	70.8	109.6	1.1	1.5
Georgia	158	171	148	242	6.4	5.5	3.7	5.3	34.5	57.6	0.9	1.6
Hawaii	21	13	24	18	4.9	2.9	4.3	2.8	8.4	8.2	1.7	1.5
Idaho	30	27	31	28	7.9	5.9	4.9	3.8	12.1	15.4	2.3	2.7
Illinois	452	371	291	369	8.3	6.2	4.3	5.7	103.8	155.5	1.8	2.8
Indiana	253	142	92	174	9.6	5.3	3.2	5.4	31.8	56.0	1.1	2.0
Iowa	81	66	45	76	5.8	4.3	2.6	4.6	19.4	26.5	1.4	1.9
Kansas	54	55	53	75	4.5	4.5	3.7	5.1	15.6	23.6	1.2	1.9
Kentucky	134	107	83	121	8.0	5.9	4.1	6.1	25.4	33.4	1.5	2.0
Louisiana	123	110	101	148	6.7	6.3	5.4	7.1	24.0	34.1	1.3	1.9
Maine	38	33	22	34	7.8	5.2	3.5	4.8	8.9	11.4	1.6	2.0
Maryland	142	118	100	121	6.5	4.7	3.8	4.1	28.9	40.4	0.3	1.8
Massachusetts	164	204	92	162	5.6	6.0	2.6	4.8	60.1	92.4	1.9	3.0
Michigan	524	358	190	344	12.4	7.6	3.5	6.7	81.6	144.4	1.8	3.4
Minnesota	124	114	87	119	5.9	4.9	3.3	4.0	31.4	49.8	1.2	2.0
Mississippi	81	90	74	106	7.5	7.6	5.6	7.9	19.7	22.3	1.8	2.1
Missouri	167	151	98	162	7.2	5.8	3.4	5.4	41.8	59.3	1.6	2.3
Montana	23	25	22	20	6.1	6.0	5.0	4.0	7.8	8.3	2.2	2.2
Nebraska	30	19	27	37	4.1	2.2	3.0	3.8	7.3	12.9	0.9	1.5
Nevada	28	33	48	49	6.2	4.9	4.0	4.1	19.5	22.5	2.0	2.1
New Hampshire	21	35	19	26	4.7	5.7	2.8	3.6	3.1	7.5	0.5	1.3
New Jersey	261	208	157	194	7.2	5.1	3.7	4.4	84.8	124.0	2.3	3.3
New Mexico	43	48	42	49	7.5	6.5	5.0	5.3	9.5	13.5	1.4	1.9
New York	601	469	416	472	7.5	5.3	4.6	5.0	146.2	204.6	1.8	2.5
North Carolina	182	145	155	227	6.6	4.2	3.6	5.2	54.3	83.2	1.5	2.3
North Dakota	15	13	10	12	5.0	4.0	3.0	3.4	3.9	3.7	1.3	1.2
Ohio	432	310	234	350	8.4	5.7	4.0	5.9	71.6	109.9	1.3	2.1
Oklahoma	61	86	52	76	4.8	5.7	3.1	4.4	12.2	22.1	0.9	1.6
Oregon	110	81	93	114	8.3	5.6	4.9	6.1	41.2	52.6	2.7	3.4
Pennsylvania	428	317	255	312	7.8	5.4	4.1	5.0	132.4	183.0	2.5	3.4
Rhode Island	33	32	23	29	7.2	6.8	4.1	5.0	12.2	13.4	2.7	2.9
South Carolina	93	84	71	142	6.9	4.8	3.8	6.8	27.1	40.9	1.5	2.3
South Dakota	16	13	11	17	4.9	3.9	2.3	3.9	2.0	3.0	0.6	0.9
Tennessee	151	132	115	162	7.3	5.3	3.9	5.6	42.2	46.8	1.6	1.8
Texas	350	552	452	596	5.2	6.3	4.2	5.3	107.9	155.5	1.2	1.7
Utah	41	36	38	54	6.3	4.3	3.3	4.3	10.5	13.5	1.1	1.3
Vermont	16	15	9	12	6.4	5.0	2.9	3.5	4.8	6.6	1.7	2.3
Virginia	133	143	82	136	5.0	4.3	2.2	3.5	22.2	36.3	0.7	1.1
Washington	157	131	151	182	7.9	4.9	5.2	5.5	70.6	76.8	2.7	3.0
West Virginia	75	65	44	40	9.4	8.4	5.5	5.0	14.1	15.4	2.1	2.3
Wisconsin	172	113	101	144	7.2	4.4	3.6	4.7	53.1	78.3	2.0	2.9
Wyoming	9	13	10	10	4.0	5.5	3.9	3.6	2.9	3.4	1.3	1.5

[1] Total unemployment as percent of civilian labor force. [2] See footnote 2, Table 573. [3] Source: U.S. Employment and Training Administration, *Unemployment Insurance, Financial Handbook,* annual updates. [4] Insured unemployment as percent of average covered employment in the previous year. [5] Includes 49,800 in Puerto Rico and the Virgin Islands in 2000; and 41,900 in 2004.

Source: Except as noted, U.S. Bureau of Labor Statistics, *Geographic Profile of Employment and Unemployment,* annual. See Internet site <http://www.bls.gov/gps/>.

Table 616. Nonfarm Establishments—Employees, Hours, and Earnings by Industry: 1990 to 2005

[Annual averages of monthly data. (109,487 represents 109,487,000). Based on data from establishment reports. Includes all full- and part-time employees who worked during, or received pay for, any part of the pay period reported. Excludes proprietors, the self-employed, farm workers, unpaid family workers, private household workers, and Armed Forces. Establishment data shown here conform to industry definitions in the 2002 North American Industry Classification System (NAICS) and are adjusted to March 2005 employment benchmarks. Based on the Current Employment Statistics Program; see source and Appendix III]

Item and year	Total nonfarm	Private industry																Government
		Total [1]	Construction	Manufacturing	Wholesale trade	Retail trade	Transportation and warehousing	Utilities	Information	Finance and insurance	Real estate and rental and leasing	Professional and technical services	Administrative and waste services	Educational services	Health care and social insurance	Arts, entertainment, and recreation	Accommodations and food services	
EMPLOYEES (1,000)																		
1990	(NA)	91,072	5,263	17,695	5,268	13,182	3,476	740	2,688	4,979	1,635	4,557	4,624	1,688	9,296	1,132	8,156	18,415
1995	(NA)	97,866	5,274	17,241	5,433	13,897	3,838	666	2,843	5,072	1,755	5,101	6,057	2,010	11,278	1,459	9,042	19,432
2000	(NA)	110,996	6,787	17,263	5,933	15,280	4,410	601	3,631	5,680	2,007	6,734	8,136	2,390	12,718	1,788	10,074	20,790
2002	(NA)	108,828	6,716	15,259	5,652	15,025	4,224	596	3,395	5,817	2,030	6,676	7,670	2,643	13,556	1,783	10,203	21,513
2003	(NA)	108,416	6,735	14,510	5,608	14,917	4,185	577	3,188	5,923	2,054	6,630	7,595	2,695	13,893	1,813	10,360	21,583
2004	(NA)	109,814	6,976	14,315	5,663	15,058	4,249	564	3,118	5,949	2,082	6,774	7,896	2,763	14,190	1,850	10,643	21,621
2005	(NA)	111,660	7,277	14,232	5,750	15,255	4,347	558	3,066	6,012	2,129	7,013	8,117	2,819	14,523	1,891	10,911	21,803
WEEKLY EARNINGS [2] (dol.)																		
1990	(NA)	349.29	513.43	436.16	444.48	235.62	471.72	670.40	479.50	378.21	286.81	504.87	272.70	(NA)	319.80	219.02	143.52	(NA)
1995	(NA)	399.53	571.57	509.26	515.14	272.56	513.37	811.52	564.98	477.39	321.69	583.41	306.54	(NA)	379.66	240.57	160.46	(NA)
2000	(NA)	480.41	685.78	590.65	631.40	333.38	562.31	955.66	700.89	589.64	395.85	745.83	386.33	(NA)	449.17	273.79	201.09	(NA)
2002	(NA)	506.07	711.82	618.75	644.38	360.81	579.75	979.09	738.17	632.34	419.76	784.51	417.44	(NA)	495.17	301.84	207.67	(NA)
2003	(NA)	517.30	726.83	635.99	657.09	367.15	598.41	1,017.27	760.81	670.86	437.20	801.82	427.02	(NA)	516.03	305.85	210.35	(NA)
2004	(NA)	528.36	735.55	658.59	667.09	371.13	614.82	1,048.44	777.05	683.78	455.16	828.71	424.27	(NA)	537.87	313.01	214.42	(NA)
2005	(NA)	543.65	750.63	673.61	684.91	377.68	618.64	1,097.16	805.89	703.56	486.89	862.67	430.76	(NA)	560.76	329.48	219.53	(NA)
WEEKLY HOURS [2]																		
1990	(NA)	34.3	38.3	40.5	38.4	30.6	37.7	41.5	35.8	36.4	33.1	36.1	32.3	(NA)	31.8	26.1	25.9	(NA)
1995	(NA)	34.3	38.8	41.3	38.6	30.8	38.9	42.3	36.0	36.5	32.7	35.8	32.5	(NA)	31.9	26.3	25.8	(NA)
2000	(NA)	34.3	39.2	41.3	38.8	30.7	37.4	42.0	36.8	37.1	32.6	36.2	33.1	(NA)	32.1	25.6	26.2	(NA)
2002	(NA)	33.9	38.4	40.5	38.0	30.9	36.8	40.9	36.5	36.6	32.8	35.6	33.0	(NA)	32.3	25.7	25.8	(NA)
2003	(NA)	33.7	38.4	40.4	37.9	30.9	36.8	41.1	36.2	36.5	32.8	35.6	32.9	(NA)	32.5	25.7	25.6	(NA)
2004	(NA)	33.7	38.0	40.8	37.8	30.7	37.2	40.9	36.3	36.6	32.8	35.7	32.9	(NA)	32.7	25.7	25.6	(NA)
2005	(NA)	33.8	38.6	40.7	37.7	30.6	37.0	41.1	36.5	36.8	33.5	35.7	32.8	(NA)	32.9	25.7	25.7	(NA)
HOURLY EARNINGS [2] (dol.)																		
1990	(NA)	10.19	13.42	10.78	11.58	7.71	12.50	16.14	13.40	10.40	8.66	13.99	8.45	(NA)	10.05	8.41	5.53	(NA)
1995	(NA)	11.64	14.73	12.34	13.34	8.85	13.18	19.19	15.68	13.07	9.85	16.32	9.43	(NA)	11.89	9.14	6.22	(NA)
2000	(NA)	14.00	17.48	14.32	16.28	10.86	15.05	22.75	19.07	15.90	12.14	20.61	11.66	(NA)	13.98	10.68	7.68	(NA)
2002	(NA)	14.95	18.52	15.29	16.98	11.67	15.76	23.96	20.20	17.28	12.79	22.02	12.66	(NA)	15.32	11.75	8.04	(NA)
2003	(NA)	15.35	18.95	15.74	17.36	11.90	16.25	24.77	21.01	18.37	13.32	22.54	13.00	(NA)	15.88	11.99	8.22	(NA)
2004	(NA)	15.67	19.23	16.15	17.65	12.08	16.52	25.61	21.40	18.70	13.88	23.24	12.90	(NA)	16.45	12.17	8.36	(NA)
2005	(NA)	16.11	19.46	16.56	18.16	12.36	16.71	26.70	22.07	19.09	14.55	24.14	13.13	(NA)	17.05	12.81	8.53	(NA)

NA Not available. [1] Includes other industries, not shown separately. [2] Average hours and earnings of production workers for natural resources and mining, manufacturing, and construction; average hours and earnings of nonsupervisory workers for the service-providing industries.

Source: U.S. Bureau of Labor Statistics, the Current Employment Statistics program Internet site <http://www.bls.gov/ces/home.htm>.

Table 617. **Employees in Nonfarm Establishments—States: 2005**

[In thousands (**133,463 represents 133,463,000**). For coverage, see headnote, Table 616. National totals differ from the sum of the state figures because of differing benchmarks among states and differing industrial and geographic stratification. Based on North American Industry Classification System, 2002; see text, this section]

State	Total [1]	Construction	Manufacturing	Trade, transportation, and utilities	Information	Financial activities [2]	Professional and business services [3]	Education and health services [4]	Leisure and hospitality [5]	Other services [6]	Government
U.S. . .	**133,463**	**7,277**	**14,232**	**25,909**	**3,066**	**8,141**	**16,882**	**17,342**	**12,802**	**5,386**	**21,803**
AL. . . .	1,943	106	298	381	31	98	208	200	165	82	363
AK. . . .	310	19	12	63	7	15	24	36	31	11	81
AZ. . . .	2,507	218	181	487	45	174	369	274	254	93	403
AR. . . .	1,178	54	201	246	20	52	112	147	94	42	205
CA. . . .	14,785	902	1,513	2,814	475	927	2,148	1,585	1,474	511	2,414
CO . . .	2,226	160	151	413	77	158	316	225	257	89	363
CT . . .	1,663	66	195	311	38	142	200	273	130	63	244
DE. . . .	430	[7] 28	33	82	7	45	62	54	41	20	59
DC . . .	682	[7] 13	2	28	23	30	148	92	54	59	233
FL. . . .	7,810	576	400	1,565	169	526	1,324	940	889	335	1,081
GA . . .	4,000	209	449	852	116	225	535	423	371	158	650
HI	602	[7] 34	15	118	11	29	74	70	107	25	120
ID	613	45	63	123	11	30	77	68	58	18	115
IL	5,865	269	689	1,186	119	403	824	746	514	259	846
IN	2,956	148	571	583	41	139	274	377	278	111	427
IA	1,481	71	230	307	33	98	113	195	[8] 130	56	246
KS. . . .	1,335	63	180	261	40	70	132	165	111	53	252
KY. . . .	1,825	85	262	378	29	88	172	235	165	77	314
LA. . . .	1,870	112	151	371	30	97	181	240	196	67	379
ME . . .	612	31	61	125	11	34	50	112	59	20	105
MD . . .	2,555	[7] 185	141	471	50	158	384	354	230	118	464
MA . . .	3,196	140	306	570	87	221	461	589	292	118	411
MI	4,384	191	679	804	68	219	591	568	405	179	674
MN . . .	2,709	129	346	527	59	178	303	387	240	118	417
MS . . .	1,130	52	178	221	14	46	87	121	124	37	242
MO . . .	2,728	141	308	540	63	165	320	367	273	119	429
MT . . .	421	28	19	88	8	21	35	56	55	17	86
NE. . . .	936	[7] 48	102	200	20	65	97	128	79	37	161
NV. . . .	1,224	135	48	215	15	65	145	85	328	34	144
NH . . .	635	30	80	141	13	39	59	98	64	21	90
NJ. . . .	4,043	169	329	882	97	280	593	558	334	158	642
NM . . .	809	54	36	140	15	35	93	105	84	29	202
NY. . . .	8,528	324	580	1,500	270	714	1,081	1,541	669	356	1,488
NC . . .	3,912	231	567	735	76	198	443	464	355	173	664
ND . . .	345	17	26	75	8	19	26	49	31	15	75
OH . . .	5,429	233	813	1,044	90	309	642	761	501	225	799
OK . . .	1,511	66	145	279	30	84	170	183	133	74	312
OR . . .	1,658	91	205	329	34	102	185	200	160	58	286
PA. . . .	5,704	254	682	1,125	109	336	656	1,028	485	265	745
RI	492	22	55	80	11	35	55	95	50	23	65
SC. . . .	1,860	117	262	359	27	98	204	185	201	74	328
SD. . . .	390	21	40	79	7	28	24	58	42	16	75
TN. . . .	2,744	120	409	598	50	144	311	330	263	102	414
TX. . . .	9,735	567	899	1,992	224	610	1,154	1,184	908	349	1,683
UT. . . .	1,150	82	118	226	32	68	147	129	104	34	203
VT. . . .	305	17	37	59	6	13	22	54	33	10	53
VA. . . .	3,668	245	296	656	93	193	607	394	329	181	663
WA . . .	2,779	177	272	532	95	155	318	330	263	103	527
WV . . .	747	37	62	139	12	30	59	114	70	56	144
WI. . . .	2,840	129	507	540	50	159	261	386	257	135	413
WY . . .	263	20	10	51	4	11	16	22	32	10	65

[1] Includes natural resources and mining, not shown separately. [2] Finance and insurance; real estate and rental and leasing. [3] Professional, scientific, and technical services; management of companies and enterprises; administrative and support and waste management and remediation services. [4] Education services; health care and social assistance. [5] Arts, entertainment, and recreation; accommodations and food services. [6] Includes repair and maintenance; personal and laundry services; and membership associations and organizations. [7] Natural resources and mining included with construction. [8] Excludes Arts, entertainment, and recreation.

Source: U.S. Bureau of Labor Statistics, the Current Employment Statistics program Internet site <http://www.bls.gov/ces/home.htm> Compiled from data supplied by cooperating state agencies.

Table 618. **Nonfarm Industries—Employees and Earnings: 1990 to 2005**

[Annual averages of monthly figures (109,487 represents 109,487,000). Covers all full- and part-time employees who worked during, or received pay for, any part of the pay period including the 12th of the month. See also headnote, Table 616]

Industry	2002 NAICS [1] code	All employees (1,000)					Average hourly earnings [2] (dollars)		
		1990	2000	2003	2004	2005	2000	2004	2005
Total nonfarm	(X)	109,487	131,785	129,999	131,435	133,463	(NA)	(NA)	(NA)
Goods-producing [3]	(X)	23,723	24,649	21,816	21,882	22,133	15.27	17.19	17.60
Service-providing [4]	(X)	85,764	107,136	108,182	109,553	111,330	(NA)	(NA)	(NA)
Total private	(X)	91,072	110,996	108,416	109,814	111,660	14.00	15.67	16.11
Natural resources and mining	(X)	765	599	572	591	625	16.55	18.07	18.73
Mining	21	680	520	503	523	561	16.94	18.44	19.05
Oil and gas extraction	211	190	125	120	123	126	19.43	18.58	19.34
Mining, except oil and gas	212	302	225	203	205	212	18.07	19.86	20.20
Support activities for mining	213	188	171	180	195	223	14.55	16.92	17.89
Construction	23	5,263	6,787	6,735	6,976	7,277	17.48	19.23	19.46
Construction of buildings	236	1,413	1,633	1,576	1,630	1,695	16.74	18.73	19.06
Residential building	2361	673	823	838	896	949	15.18	17.38	17.72
Nonresidential building	2362	741	809	738	734	746	18.18	20.19	20.55
Heavy and civil engineering construction . . .	237	813	937	903	907	953	16.80	19.21	19.60
Highway, street, and bridge construction . .	2373	289	340	340	347	352	18.17	19.87	20.14
Specialty trade contractors [5]	238	3,037	4,217	4,256	4,439	4,629	17.91	19.39	19.55
Building foundation and exterior contractors	2381	703	919	951	1,010	1,075	16.93	18.28	18.42
Building equipment contractors	2382	1,282	1,897	1,822	1,861	1,898	19.52	20.90	21.04
Building finishing contractors	2383	665	857	884	932	982	16.44	18.64	18.80
Manufacturing	31-33	17,695	17,263	14,510	14,315	14,232	14.32	16.15	16.56
Durable goods	(X)	10,736	10,876	8,963	8,924	8,953	14.93	16.82	17.34
Wood products	321	541	613	538	550	555	11.63	13.03	13.16
Nonmetallic mineral products	327	528	554	494	506	503	14.53	16.25	16.61
Cement and concrete products	3273	195	234	224	235	239	14.64	16.37	16.68
Primary metals	331	689	622	477	467	469	16.64	18.57	18.94
Foundries	3315	214	217	166	165	167	14.72	16.93	17.50
Fabricated metal products [5]	332	1,610	1,753	1,479	1,497	1,519	13.77	15.31	15.80
Architectural and structural metals	3323	357	428	380	389	396	13.43	14.71	15.10
Machine shops and threaded products . . .	3327	309	365	311	327	344	14.53	15.91	16.42
Machinery [5]	333	1,408	1,455	1,149	1,143	1,162	15.22	16.68	17.03
Agricultural, construction, and mining machinery	3331	229	222	188	195	209	14.21	15.16	15.90
HVAC and commercial refrig. equip.	3334	165	194	157	153	153	13.10	14.82	14.60
Metalworking machinery	3335	267	274	205	202	202	16.66	17.80	17.86
Computer and electronic products [5]	334	1,903	1,820	1,355	1,323	1,320	14.73	17.27	18.40
Computer and peripheral equipment	3341	367	302	224	210	207	18.39	20.55	22.75
Communications equipment	3342	232	248	155	148	148	14.39	16.86	18.05
Semiconductors and electronic components	3344	574	676	461	454	451	13.46	16.22	17.04
Electronic instruments	3345	626	479	430	431	438	15.83	17.38	17.70
Electrical equipment and appliances	335	633	591	460	445	436	13.23	14.90	15.25
Electrical equipment	3353	244	210	160	154	152	13.28	14.85	15.32
Transportation equipment [5]	336	2,133	2,056	1,774	1,766	1,772	18.89	21.49	22.10
Motor vehicles	3361	271	291	265	256	250	24.45	28.35	29.03
Motor vehicle parts	3363	653	840	708	692	678	17.95	20.43	21.09
Aerospace products and parts	3364	841	517	442	442	456	20.52	23.93	24.80
Furniture and related products	337	601	680	573	573	563	11.72	13.16	13.44
Household and institutional furniture	3371	398	440	382	385	380	11.39	12.81	13.14
Miscellaneous manufacturing	339	690	733	663	656	654	11.93	13.84	14.08
Medical equipment and supplies	3391	288	310	304	301	306	12.70	14.32	14.71
Nondurable goods	(X)	6,959	6,388	5,547	5,391	5,278	13.31	15.05	15.27
Food manufacturing [5]	311	1,507	1,553	1,518	1,494	1,472	11.77	12.98	13.04
Fruit and vegetable preserving and specialty	3114	218	197	185	181	174	11.90	12.86	12.80
Animal slaughtering and processing	3116	427	507	516	505	502	10.27	11.53	11.48
Bakeries and tortilla manufacturing	3118	292	306	292	285	280	11.45	12.64	12.56
Beverages and tobacco products	312	218	207	200	195	192	17.40	19.14	18.79
Beverages	3121	173	175	169	166	167	17.19	18.73	18.32
Textile mills	313	492	378	261	237	218	11.23	12.13	12.38
Textile product mills	314	209	216	179	176	172	10.43	11.39	11.66
Apparel	315	929	497	312	286	260	8.60	9.75	10.24
Cut-and-sew apparel	3152	776	394	243	221	203	8.40	9.62	10.05
Leather and allied products	316	133	69	45	42	40	10.35	11.63	11.50
Paper and paper products	322	647	605	516	496	484	15.91	17.91	18.04
Pulp, paper, and paperboard mills	3221	238	191	151	146	141	20.62	23.00	22.99
Converted paper products	3222	409	413	365	350	343	13.58	15.71	15.71
Printing and related support activities	323	809	807	681	663	648	14.09	15.71	15.75
Petroleum and coal products	324	153	123	114	112	113	22.80	24.39	24.54
Chemicals [5]	325	1,036	980	906	887	879	17.09	19.17	19.67
Basic chemicals	3251	249	188	162	156	151	21.06	23.15	23.83
Pharmaceuticals and medicines	3254	207	274	292	290	289	20.90	21.31
Plastics and rubber products	326	826	952	815	806	800	12.69	14.59	14.82
Plastics products	3261	619	738	639	633	631	12.04	13.83	14.01
Rubber products	3262	207	214	177	172	169	14.82	17.13	17.62

See footnotes at end of table.

Table 618. **Nonfarm Industries—Employees and Earnings: 1990 to 2005**—Con.

[Annual averages of monthly figures (109,487 represents 109,487,000). Covers all full- and part-time employees who worked during, or received pay for, any part of the pay period including the 12th of the month. See also headnote, Table 616]

Industry	2002 NAICS [1] code	All employees (1,000)					Average hourly earnings [2] (dollars)		
		1990	2000	2003	2004	2005	2000	2004	2005
Trade, transportation, and utilities	(X)	**22,666**	**26,225**	**25,287**	**25,533**	**25,909**	**13.31**	**14.58**	**14.93**
Wholesale trade.	42	**5,268**	**5,933**	**5,608**	**5,663**	**5,750**	**16.28**	**17.65**	**18.16**
Durable goods [5].	423	2,834	3,251	2,941	2,951	2,992	16.71	18.29	18.89
Motor vehicles and parts	4231	309	356	342	341	344	14.27	16.08	16.18
Lumber and construction supplies	4233	181	227	229	240	252	13.61	16.03	16.78
Commercial equipment	4234	597	722	653	640	636	20.29	22.85	23.68
Electric goods	4236	357	425	346	341	345	19.43	20.61	21.79
Hardware and plumbing	4237	216	247	231	236	242	15.07	16.22	16.48
Machinery and supplies	4238	690	725	644	650	659	16.47	17.76	18.71
Nondurable goods [5]	424	1,900	2,065	2,005	2,010	2,022	14.33	15.88	16.16
Paper and paper products	4241	162	177	152	151	151	15.65	17.34	17.23
Druggists' goods.	4242	136	192	211	218	215	18.98	18.89	19.20
Grocery and related products	4244	623	689	685	691	699	13.57	15.29	15.38
Electronic markets and agents and brokers. .	425	535	618	662	702	735	20.79	20.16	20.70
Retail trade.	44,45	**13,182**	**15,280**	**14,917**	**15,058**	**15,255**	**10.86**	**12.08**	**12.36**
Motor vehicle and parts dealers [5]	441	1,494	1,847	1,883	1,902	1,919	14.94	16.10	16.33
Automobile dealers	4411	983	1,217	1,254	1,257	1,261	16.95	17.68	17.85
Auto parts, accessories, and tire stores	4413	418	499	480	487	491	11.04	12.28	12.74
Furniture and home furnishings stores	442	432	544	547	563	578	12.33	13.47	14.24
Furniture stores	4421	244	289	284	292	302	13.37	14.44	14.87
Home furnishings stores	4422	188	254	263	272	276	11.06	12.36	13.46
Electronics and appliance stores.	443	382	564	512	516	533	13.67	16.95	17.73
Building material and garden supply stores.	444	891	1,142	1,185	1,227	1,272	11.25	12.80	13.14
Building material and supplies dealers . . .	4441	753	982	1,038	1,083	1,130	11.30	12.92	13.24
Food and beverage stores.	445	2,779	2,993	2,838	2,822	2,814	9.76	10.86	10.85
Grocery stores	4451	2,406	2,582	2,453	2,444	2,442	9.71	10.79	10.80
Specialty food stores.	4452	232	270	247	242	238	9.97	11.13	11.05
Beer, wine, and liquor stores.	4453	141	141	138	136	135	10.40	11.87	11.48
Health and personal care stores	446	792	928	938	941	955	11.68	13.72	14.03
Gasoline stations	447	910	936	882	876	871	8.05	8.84	8.92
Clothing & clothing accessories stores	448	1,313	1,322	1,305	1,364	1,414	9.96	10.55	11.07
Clothing stores	4481	930	954	956	1,014	1,066	9.88	10.25	10.63
Shoe stores	4482	216	193	179	182	178	8.96	9.46	10.05
Jewelry, luggage, and leather goods stores	4483	167	175	169	169	170	11.48	12.94	14.10
Sporting goods, hobby, book, and music stores.	451	532	686	647	641	642	9.33	10.41	10.34
Sporting goods and musical instrument stores	4511	352	437	428	432	443	9.55	10.82	10.68
Book, periodical, and music stores.	4512	180	249	219	209	200	8.91	9.53	9.58
General merchandise stores	452	2,500	2,820	2,822	2,863	2,919	9.22	10.32	10.54
Department stores	4521	1,494	1,755	1,621	1,605	1,603	9.59	10.67	10.84
Miscellaneous store retailers [5]	453	738	1,007	931	914	903	10.20	10.98	11.22
Florists	4531	121	130	113	107	102	8.95	9.71	9.88
Office supplies, stationery, and gift stores	4532	358	471	416	402	394	10.46	11.39	11.67
Nonstore retailers.	454	419	492	427	429	435	13.22	13.86	14.55
Electronic shopping and mail-order houses	4541	157	257	218	228	241	13.38	13.34	14.52
Transportation and warehousing.	48,49	**3,476**	**4,410**	**4,185**	**4,249**	**4,347**	**15.05**	**16.52**	**16.71**
Air transportation	481	529	614	528	515	501	(NA)	(NA)	(NA)
Scheduled air transportation	4811	503	570	485	472	457	(NA)	(NA)	(NA)
Rail transportation	482	272	232	218	226	228	(NA)	(NA)	(NA)
Water transportation	483	57	56	55	56	61	(NA)	(NA)	(NA)
Truck transportation	484	1,122	1,406	1,326	1,352	1,393	15.86	16.61	16.73
General freight trucking	4841	807	1,013	935	950	977	16.37	17.13	17.20
Specialized freight trucking.	4842	315	393	390	402	416	14.51	15.28	15.60
Transit and ground passenger transportation	485	274	372	382	385	389	11.88	12.83	13.03
Pipeline transportation	486	60	46	40	38	38	19.86	23.94	24.33
Scenic and sightseeing transportation	487	16	28	27	27	30	12.49	13.68	13.77
Support activities for transportation	488	364	537	520	535	551	14.57	17.67	17.67
Freight transportation arrangement	4885	111	178	167	171	175	13.46	16.87	16.94
Couriers and messengers	492	375	605	562	557	572	13.51	15.45	15.34
Couriers	4921	340	546	510	507	523	13.92	16.09	15.76
Warehousing and storage	493	407	514	528	558	585	14.46	14.90	15.05
Utilities.	22	**740**	**601**	**577**	**564**	**558**	**22.75**	**25.61**	**26.70**
Power generation and supply	2211	550	434	418	409	405	23.13	26.48	27.64
Natural gas distribution	2212	155	121	113	109	107	23.41	25.32	26.86
Water, sewage and other systems.	2213	35	46	47	46	45	16.93	18.30	17.69

See footnotes at end of table.

U.S. Census Bureau, Statistical Abstract of the United States: 2007

Table 618. **Nonfarm Industries—Employees and Earnings: 1990 to 2005**—Con.

[Annual averages of monthly figures (109,487 represents 109,487,000). Covers all full- and part-time employees who worked during, or received pay for, any part of the pay period including the 12th of the month. See also headnote, Table 616]

Industry	2002 NAICS [1] code	All employees (1,000)					Average hourly earnings [2] (dollars)		
		1990	2000	2003	2004	2005	2000	2004	2005
Information.	51	2,688	3,631	3,188	3,118	3,066	19.07	21.40	22.07
Publishing industries, except Internet	511	871	1,035	925	909	904	20.18	23.36	24.22
Newspaper, book, and directory publishers.	5111	773	774	686	673	665	15.06	17.77	18.57
Software publishers	5112	98	261	239	236	239	28.48	36.89	38.11
Motion picture and sound recording industries.	512	255	383	376	385	379	21.25	19.96	18.83
Motion picture and video industries	5121	232	352	352	363	359	21.33	20.09	18.95
Broadcasting, except Internet	515	284	344	324	325	327	16.74	19.74	21.23
Radio and television broadcasting.	5151	232	253	238	240	238	17.13	20.49	22.16
Cable and other subscription programming.	5152	52	91	86	86	88	(NA)	(NA)	(NA)
Internet publishing and broadcasting.	516	17	51	29	30	30	(NA)	(NA)	(NA)
Telecommunications [5]	517	980	1,263	1,082	1,035	999	17.81	21.25	22.10
Wired telecommunications carriers	5171	673	719	579	543	514	18.52	23.09	23.78
Wireless telecommunications carriers.	5172	36	186	190	190	192	14.41	18.35	20.39
Telecommunications resellers.	5173	180	214	155	147	135	19.99	21.93	22.28
Cable and other program distribution	5175	70	123	133	130	134	14.67	16.80	17.23
ISPs, search portals, and data processing	518	252	510	402	384	377	20.57	20.43	20.83
ISPs and Web search portals	5181	41	194	122	117	114	25.60	21.58	22.78
Data processing and related services	5182	211	316	280	267	263	16.97	19.93	19.97
Other information services.	519	30	46	49	51	50	10.68	16.00	16.32
Financial activities	**(X)**	**6,614**	**7,687**	**7,977**	**8,031**	**8,141**	**14.98**	**17.52**	**17.94**
Finance and insurance [5].	**52**	**4,979**	**5,680**	**5,923**	**5,949**	**6,012**	**15.90**	**18.70**	**19.09**
Credit intermediation and related activities.	522	2,425	2,548	2,792	2,817	2,866	13.14	15.60	15.86
Depository credit intermediation.	5221	1,909	1,681	1,749	1,752	1,774	11.97	13.80	14.13
Commercial banking	52211	1,362	1,251	1,280	1,281	1,298	11.83	13.48	13.79
Nondepository credit intermediation	5222	398	644	750	757	766	15.30	19.27	19.26
Activities related to credit intermediation.	5223	119	222	294	309	325	15.39	16.29	16.50
Securities, commodity contracts, investments.	523	458	805	758	766	783	20.20	25.14	26.61
Securities and commodity contracts brokerage and exchanges	5232	338	566	493	493	500	20.07	25.74	27.68
Other financial investment activities	5239	120	239	264	274	284	20.48	24.09	24.70
Insurance carriers and related activities	524	2,016	2,221	2,266	2,259	2,255	17.37	20.38	20.66
Insurance carriers.	5241	1,338	1,433	1,429	1,399	1,384	17.92	21.17	21.67
Insurance agencies, brokerages, and related services	5242	678	788	837	860	872	16.28	18.96	18.88
Funds, trusts, and other financial vehicles	525	56	85	84	85	87	17.66	21.96	21.12
Real estate and rental and leasing [5]	**53**	**1,635**	**2,007**	**2,054**	**2,082**	**2,129**	**12.14**	**13.88**	**14.55**
Real estate	531	1,107	1,312	1,384	1,415	1,456	12.24	14.20	14.67
Lessors of real estate	5311	564	607	604	600	600	11.16	13.09	13.75
Offices of real estate agents and brokers	5312	217	281	310	331	355	12.57	14.35	14.90
Activities related to real estate	5313	327	424	470	484	502	13.60	15.55	15.64
Rental and leasing services [5].	532	514	667	643	641	646	11.69	13.01	14.03
Automotive equipment rental and leasing	5321	163	208	193	197	199	10.70	12.57	13.65
Consumer goods rental	5322	220	292	288	279	275	9.53	10.73	12.35
Professional and business services	**(X)**	**10,848**	**16,666**	**15,987**	**16,395**	**16,882**	**15.52**	**17.48**	**18.07**
Professional and technical services [5]	**54**	**4,557**	**6,734**	**6,630**	**6,774**	**7,013**	**20.61**	**23.24**	**24.14**
Legal services.	5411	944	1,066	1,142	1,163	1,164	21.38	22.91	23.97
Accounting and bookkeeping services	5412	664	866	815	806	840	14.42	16.91	17.49
Architectural and engineering services	5413	942	1,238	1,227	1,258	1,307	20.49	23.25	23.93
Computer systems design and related services	5415	410	1,254	1,117	1,149	1,189	27.13	30.15	31.62
Management and technical consulting services	5416	324	705	745	790	844	20.86	23.59	23.99
Scientific research and development services	5417	494	515	539	550	572	21.39	26.89	28.32
Advertising and related services	5418	382	497	430	429	444	16.99	18.70	19.48
Other professional and technical services. . .	5419	317	462	494	507	523	13.55	15.47	15.52
Management of companies and enterprises .	**55**	**1,667**	**1,796**	**1,687**	**1,724**	**1,752**	**15.28**	**17.19**	**18.08**
Administrative and waste services	**56**	**4,624**	**8,136**	**7,670**	**7,896**	**8,117**	**11.66**	**12.90**	**13.13**
Administrative and support services [5]	561	4,395	7,823	7,348	7,567	7,783	11.49	12.67	12.89
Office administrative services	5611	211	264	308	323	343	14.68	16.93	17.82
Employment services	5613	1,494	3,817	3,300	3,429	3,575	11.83	12.92	12.96
Temporary help services.	56132	1,156	2,636	2,224	2,387	2,539	11.79	12.07	12.00
Business support services	5614	505	787	750	758	760	11.08	12.51	13.16
Travel arrangement and reservation services	5615	250	299	235	226	224	12.72	14.05	14.55
Investigation and security services.	5616	507	689	712	724	737	9.78	11.27	11.63
Services to buildings and dwellings	5617	1,175	1,571	1,636	1,694	1,730	10.02	11.16	11.44
Waste management and remediation services	562	229	313	322	329	334	15.29	17.32	17.70

See footnotes at end of table.

Table 618. Nonfarm Industries—Employees and Earnings: 1990 to 2005—Con.

[Annual averages of monthly figures (109,487 represents 109,487,000). Covers all full- and part-time employees who worked during, or received pay for, any part of the pay period including the 12th of the month. See also headnote, Table 616]

Industry	2002 NAICS [1] code	All employees (1,000)					Average hourly earnings [2] (dollars)		
		1990	2000	2003	2004	2005	2000	2004	2005
Education and health services	(X)	10,984	15,109	16,588	16,953	17,342	13.95	16.15	16.72
Educational services	61	1,688	2,390	2,695	2,763	2,819	(NA)	(NA)	(NA)
Elementary and secondary schools	6111	461	716	801	824	838	(NA)	(NA)	(NA)
Junior colleges	6112	44	79	79	89	103	(NA)	(NA)	(NA)
Colleges and universities.	6113	939	1,196	1,361	1,374	1,377	(NA)	(NA)	(NA)
Business, computer, and management training.	6114	60	86	81	79	77	(NA)	(NA)	(NA)
Technical and trade schools.	6115	72	91	96	99	101	(NA)	(NA)	(NA)
Other schools and instruction	6116	96	184	221	231	248	(NA)	(NA)	(NA)
Educational support services	6117	17	39	56	67	75	(NA)	(NA)	(NA)
Health care and social assistance	62	9,296	12,718	13,893	14,190	14,523	13.98	16.45	17.05
Ambulatory health care services [5]	621	2,842	4,320	4,786	4,952	5,110	14.99	17.44	17.87
Offices of physicians	6211	1,278	1,840	2,003	2,048	2,101	15.65	18.41	18.95
Offices of dentists	6212	513	688	744	760	771	15.96	18.96	19.40
Offices of other health practitioners	6213	276	438	503	527	545	14.24	16.02	16.67
Outpatient care centers	6214	261	386	427	451	474	15.29	18.58	18.95
Medical and diagnostic laboratories	6215	129	162	182	190	199	15.74	18.15	18.65
Home health care services	6216	288	633	733	777	814	12.86	14.41	14.42
Hospitals [5]	622	3,513	3,954	4,245	4,285	4,347	16.71	20.31	21.30
General medical and surgical hospitals. . .	6221	3,305	3,745	4,005	4,042	4,099	16.75	20.41	21.40
Psychiatric and substance abuse hospitals	6222	113	86	92	92	92	14.97	17.04	17.79
Nursing and residential care facilities [5]	623	1,856	2,583	2,786	2,818	2,856	10.67	12.06	12.37
Nursing care facilities	6231	1,170	1,514	1,580	1,577	1,579	11.08	12.75	13.04
Residential mental health facilities	6232	269	437	484	490	499	9.96	11.11	11.30
Community care facilities for the elderly.	6233	330	478	558	586	612	9.83	10.90	11.33
Social assistance	624	1,085	1,860	2,075	2,135	2,210	9.78	11.06	11.35
Individual and family services	6241	389	678	813	862	916	10.57	12.12	12.44
Emergency and other relief services.	6242	67	117	128	131	129	10.95	12.80	13.49
Vocational rehabilitation services	6243	242	370	379	378	381	9.57	10.78	10.67
Child day care services	6244	388	696	755	765	785	8.88	9.76	10.14
Leisure and hospitality	(X)	9,288	11,862	12,173	12,493	12,802	8.11	8.91	9.14
Arts, entertainment, and recreation	71	1,132	1,788	1,813	1,850	1,891	10.68	12.17	12.81
Performing arts and spectator sports	711	273	382	372	368	369	13.11	17.36	18.67
Museums, historical sites, zoos, and parks	712	68	110	115	118	121	12.21	12.94	13.67
Amusements, gambling, and recreation	713	791	1,296	1,327	1,364	1,401	9.86	10.71	11.07
Accommodations and food services	72	8,156	10,074	10,360	10,643	10,911	7.68	8.36	8.53
Accommodations	721	1,616	1,884	1,775	1,790	1,812	9.48	10.58	10.75
Traveler and other longer-term accommodations	7211	1,582	1,837	1,724	1,737	1,760	9.49	10.62	10.78
RV parks and recreational camps	7212	34	47	52	52	53	9.03	9.2	9.77
Food services and drinking places	722	6,540	8,189	8,584	8,854	9,099	7.18	7.84	8.01
Full-service restaurants	7221	3,070	3,845	4,089	4,212	4,315	7.15	7.95	8.17
Limited-service eating places	7222	2,765	3,462	3,602	3,748	3,889	6.85	7.36	7.48
Special food services	7223	392	491	516	523	534	9.45	10.42	10.48
Drinking places, alcoholic beverages	7224	312	391	378	371	361	7.24	7.77	7.89
Other services	81	4,261	5,168	5,401	5,409	5,386	12.73	13.98	14.33
Repair and maintenance.	811	1,009	1,242	1,234	1,229	1,236	13.28	14.39	14.81
Automotive repair and maintenance.	8111	659	888	894	891	888	12.45	13.68	14.09
Personal and laundry services	812	1,120	1,243	1,264	1,273	1,273	10.18	11.67	11.80
Personal care services	8121	430	490	542	563	576	10.18	12.07	12.43
Death care services	8122	123	136	140	137	135	13.04	15.03	15.35
Dry-cleaning and laundry services.	8123	371	388	358	352	346	9.17	10.04	10.19
Dry-cleaning and laundry services, except coin-operated	81232	215	211	190	185	180	8.14	8.99	9.14
Other personal services	8129	196	229	223	221	215	10.52	11.73	11.28
Pet care services, except veterinary	81291	23	31	38	41	43	(NA)	(NA)	(NA)
Membership associations & organizations [5] . .	813	2,132	2,683	2,904	2,908	2,877	13.66	14.78	15.18
Social advocacy organizations	8133	126	143	175	175	174	12.08	13.75	13.89
Civic and social organizations.	8134	377	404	413	409	410	9.85	10.86	11.16
Professional and similar organizations	8139	379	473	503	506	487	15.98	17.83	18.59
Government.	92	18,415	20,790	21,583	21,621	21,803	(NA)	(NA)	(NA)
Federal.	(X)	3,196	2,865	2,761	2,730	2,724	(NA)	(NA)	(NA)
State government	(X)	4,305	4,786	5,002	4,982	5,021	(NA)	(NA)	(NA)
Local government	(X)	10,914	13,139	13,820	13,909	14,058	(NA)	(NA)	(NA)

NA Not available.   X Not applicable.   [1] Based on the North American Industry Classification System, 2002 (NAICS). See text, this section.   [2] Production workers in the goods-producing industries and non-supervisory workers in service-producing industries. See footnotes 3 and 4.   [3] Natural resources and mining, construction, and manufacturing.   [4] Trade, transportation and utilities, information, financial activities, professional and business services, education and health services, leisure and hospitality, other services, and government.   [5] Includes other industries not shown separately.

Source: U.S. Bureau of Labor Statistics, the Current Employment Statistics program Internet site <http://www.bls.gov/ces /home.htm>.

406   Labor Force, Employment, and Earnings

Table 619. **Private Sector Job Gains and Losses: 1992 to 2005**

[In thousands (455 represents 455,000). For the three months ending in month shown. Data are for establishments and are seasonally adjusted. Based on the Quarterly Census of Employment and Wages; for details see source. Minus sign (–) indicates loss]

Year and month ending	Net change [1]	Gross job gains			Gross job losses		
		Total	Expanding establish-ments	Opening establish-ments	Total	Contracting establish-ments	Closing establish-ments
1992:							
September	455	7,377	5,632	1,745	6,922	5,351	1,571
December	216	7,101	5,465	1,636	6,885	5,487	1,398
1993:							
March	313	7,309	5,410	1,899	6,996	5,354	1,642
June	786	7,330	5,794	1,536	6,544	5,136	1,408
September	874	7,523	5,881	1,642	6,649	5,316	1,333
December	641	7,436	5,840	1,596	6,795	5,420	1,375
1994:							
March	517	7,400	5,807	1,593	6,883	5,435	1,448
June	1,021	7,807	6,060	1,747	6,786	5,295	1,491
September	1,175	7,972	6,227	1,745	6,797	5,493	1,304
December	507	7,630	5,998	1,632	7,123	5,647	1,476
1995:							
March	746	7,782	6,129	1,653	7,036	5,660	1,376
June	402	7,714	6,017	1,697	7,312	5,839	1,473
September	771	7,970	6,291	1,679	7,199	5,680	1,519
December	407	7,877	6,153	1,724	7,470	5,934	1,536
1996:							
March	460	7,943	6,190	1,753	7,483	5,957	1,526
June	642	8,080	6,302	1,778	7,438	5,894	1,544
September	632	8,189	6,326	1,863	7,557	5,998	1,559
December	861	8,278	6,409	1,869	7,417	5,889	1,528
1997:							
March	799	8,292	6,448	1,844	7,493	5,900	1,593
June	594	8,098	6,342	1,756	7,504	5,925	1,579
September	854	8,593	6,680	1,913	7,739	5,981	1,758
December	702	8,731	6,727	2,004	8,029	6,068	1,961
1998:							
March	747	8,788	6,633	2,155	8,041	6,107	1,934
June	666	8,722	6,569	2,153	8,056	6,218	1,838
September	659	8,539	6,574	1,965	7,880	6,161	1,719
December	759	8,576	6,778	1,798	7,817	6,060	1,757
1999:							
March	380	8,744	6,733	2,011	8,364	6,466	1,898
June	569	8,800	6,788	2,012	8,231	6,419	1,812
September	548	8,817	6,871	1,946	8,269	6,397	1,872
December	1,105	9,144	7,112	2,032	8,039	6,264	1,775
2000:							
March	818	8,906	6,988	1,918	8,088	6,361	1,727
June	541	8,764	6,975	1,789	8,223	6,509	1,714
September	146	8,724	6,834	1,890	8,578	6,719	1,859
December	336	8,690	6,862	1,828	8,354	6,582	1,772
2001:							
March	–101	8,555	6,768	1,787	8,656	6,756	1,900
June	–771	8,254	6,439	1,815	9,025	7,149	1,876
September	–1,380	7,749	5,990	1,759	9,129	7,174	1,955
December	–871	7,893	6,055	1,838	8,764	6,995	1,769
2002:							
March	–1	8,128	6,324	1,804	8,129	6,400	1,729
June	–80	8,050	6,246	1,804	8,130	6,411	1,719
September	–211	7,763	6,083	1,680	7,974	6,345	1,629
December	–175	7,702	6,059	1,643	7,877	6,267	1,610
2003:							
March	–404	7,472	5,932	1,540	7,876	6,321	1,555
June	–142	7,560	6,033	1,527	7,702	6,138	1,564
September	72	7,396	5,897	1,499	7,324	5,893	1,431
December	344	7,646	6,063	1,583	7,302	5,816	1,486
2004:							
March	435	7,745	6,231	1,514	7,310	5,871	1,439
June	594	7,857	6,292	1,565	7,263	5,726	1,537
September	191	7,789	6,123	1,666	7,598	5,953	1,645
December	869	8,081	6,365	1,716	7,212	5,727	1,485
2005:							
March	325	7,635	6,171	1,464	7,310	5,852	1,458
June	574	7,932	6,311	1,621	7,358	5,873	1,485
September	628	8,055	6,423	1,632	7,427	5,915	1,512
December	551	7,818	6,293	1,525	7,267	5,888	1,379

[1] Difference between the total gross job gains and total gross job losses.

Source: U.S. Bureau of Labor Statistics, *Business Employment Dynamics: Fourth Quarter* 2005, USDL 06-1562, September 7, 2006. See Internet site: <http://www.bls.gov/bdm/home.htm>.

Labor Force, Employment, and Earnings   407

Table 620. **Annual Indexes of Output Per Hour for Selected NAICS Industries: 1987 to 2004**

[For a discussion of productivity measures, see text, this section. Minus sign (–) indicates decrease]

Industry	2002 NAICS code [1]	Indexes (1997 = 100)						Average annual percent change [2]
		1987	1990	1995	2000	2003	2004	
Mining	21	85.5	85.1	101.7	111.2	116.2	107.2	1.3
Oil and gas extraction	211	80.1	75.7	95.3	119.4	130.3	112.4	2.0
Mining, except oil and gas	212	69.8	79.3	94.0	106.8	114.0	115.4	3.0
Utilities:								
Power generation and supply	2211	65.6	71.1	88.5	107.0	105.1	107.5	2.9
Natural gas distribution	2212	67.8	71.4	89.0	113.2	114.1	118.6	3.3
Manufacturing:								
Fruit and vegetable preserving and specialty	3114	92.4	87.6	98.3	111.8	122.6	126.0	1.8
Dairy products	3115	82.7	91.1	97.6	95.9	110.6	106.8	1.5
Animal slaughtering and processing	3116	97.4	94.3	99.0	102.6	106.8	108.9	0.7
Bakeries and tortilla manufacturing.	3118	100.9	94.5	100.7	108.3	111.1	114.3	0.7
Other food products	3119	97.5	92.5	104.1	112.6	118.7	118.5	1.2
Beverages	3121	77.1	87.6	103.2	90.8	107.9	111.5	2.2
Fabric mills	3132	68.0	75.3	95.5	110.1	136.8	139.1	4.3
Textile furnishings mills	3141	91.2	88.0	92.3	104.5	114.4	120.7	1.7
Cut-and-sew apparel	3152	69.8	70.1	85.2	119.8	117.3	110.9	2.8
Sawmills and wood preservation	3211	77.6	79.4	90.4	105.4	121.3	117.3	2.5
Plywood and engineered wood products	3212	99.8	102.9	101.5	98.9	107.3	101.8	0.1
Other wood products	3219	103.2	105.5	99.8	103.1	114.4	119.4	0.9
Pulp, paper, and paperboard mills	3221	81.7	84.0	98.4	116.3	141.4	145.4	3.4
Converted paper products	3222	89.0	90.1	97.2	101.1	109.6	112.5	1.4
Printing and related support activities	3231	97.7	97.6	98.8	104.6	111.2	114.0	0.9
Petroleum and coal products.	3241	72.1	76.1	89.9	113.5	119.3	123.2	3.2
Basic chemicals	3251	94.6	93.4	91.3	117.5	136.1	148.7	2.7
Resin, rubber, and artificial fibers	3252	77.4	76.4	95.4	109.8	122.2	123.3	2.8
Pharmaceuticals and medicines.	3254	87.3	91.3	95.9	95.6	100.6	104.2	1.0
Soap, cleaning compounds, and toiletries	3256	84.4	84.8	96.1	102.8	118.0	127.7	2.5
Other chemical products and preparations	3259	75.4	77.8	93.5	119.7	123.1	118.8	2.7
Plastics products	3261	83.1	85.2	94.5	112.3	129.4	130.6	2.7
Rubber products	3262	75.5	83.5	92.9	101.7	110.9	112.0	2.3
Glass and glass products	3272	82.3	79.1	87.5	108.2	114.9	113.7	1.9
Cement and concrete products	3273	93.6	96.6	99.7	101.6	108.2	102.0	0.5
Iron and steel mills and ferralloy production	3311	64.8	70.2	90.0	106.0	130.3	157.7	5.4
Foundries	3315	81.8	86.6	93.1	103.6	116.3	123.7	2.5
Forging and stamping	3321	85.4	89.0	93.9	121.1	133.2	140.1	2.9
Architectural and structural metals	3323	88.7	87.9	93.3	100.7	109.0	103.7	0.9
Boilers, tanks, and shipping containers	3324	86.0	90.1	97.3	94.2	94.2	99.9	0.9
Machine shops and threaded products	3327	76.9	79.2	98.3	108.2	115.9	113.0	2.3
Coating, engraving, and heat treating metals	3328	75.5	81.3	102.2	105.5	118.5	125.5	3.0
Other fabricated metal products.	3329	91.0	86.5	96.3	99.9	111.6	111.4	1.2
Agriculture, construction, and mining machinery	3331	74.6	83.3	95.4	100.3	116.1	126.7	3.2
Industrial machinery	3332	75.1	81.6	97.1	130.0	117.0	125.0	3.0
Commercial and service industry machinery.	3333	86.9	95.6	103.6	100.9	104.5	106.1	1.2
HVAC and commercial refrigeration equipment.	3334	84.0	90.6	96.4	107.9	130.0	130.4	2.6
Metalworking machinery	3335	85.1	86.5	99.2	106.1	115.4	117.1	1.9
Turbine and power transmission equipment	3336	80.2	85.9	91.3	114.9	143.0	124.0	2.6
Other general purpose machinery	3339	83.5	86.8	94.0	113.7	128.3	124.0	2.4
Computer and peripheral equipment.	3341	11.0	14.7	49.9	234.9	375.4	431.7	24.1
Communications equipment	3342	39.8	48.4	74.4	164.1	143.2	143.5	7.8
Semiconductors and electronic components.	3344	17.0	21.9	63.8	232.4	324.4	362.4	19.7
Electronic instruments	3345	70.2	78.5	97.9	116.7	125.7	141.7	4.2
Electrical equipment	3353	68.7	73.6	98.0	99.4	103.2	110.2	2.8
Other electrical equipment and components.	3359	78.7	76.0	92.0	119.1	116.5	116.2	2.3
Motor vehicles	3361	75.4	85.6	88.5	109.7	140.7	142.0	3.8
Motor vehicle bodies and trailers	3362	85.0	75.9	97.4	98.8	109.8	108.2	1.4
Motor vehicle parts	3363	78.7	76.0	92.3	112.3	136.9	138.3	3.4
Aerospace products and parts.	3364	86.5	89.1	94.9	103.2	124.3	116.8	1.8
Ship and boat building	3366	95.5	99.6	93.1	121.9	133.9	136.8	2.1
Household and institutional furniture	3371	85.2	88.2	97.2	101.9	115.1	118.2	1.9
Office furniture and fixtures	3372	85.8	82.2	84.9	100.2	126.6	129.5	2.4
Medical equipment and supplies	3391	76.3	82.9	96.6	114.6	141.1	143.4	3.8
Other miscellaneous manufacturing	3399	85.4	90.5	95.9	113.6	124.6	125.8	2.3
Wholesale trade.	42	73.0	79.6	93.5	116.8	130.7	140.8	3.9
Durable goods	423	62.2	67.4	89.7	123.5	143.2	161.6	5.8
Nondurable goods.	424	90.9	98.6	97.9	107.6	119.5	124.8	1.9
Electronic markets and agents and brokers	425	64.3	74.3	95.4	119.9	112.7	112.1	3.3
Retail trade.	44-45	79.1	81.3	94.1	116.4	132.6	140.7	3.4
Motor vehicle and parts dealers.	441	78.1	82.2	95.7	114.4	124.2	129.2	3.0
Automobile dealers	4411	79.1	83.7	96.1	113.9	119.6	127.4	2.8
Other motor vehicle dealers.	4412	73.5	73.3	90.9	116.7	131.1	138.8	3.8
Auto parts, accessories, and tire stores	4413	67.0	73.8	92.6	110.2	119.3	113.7	3.2
Furniture and home furnishings stores	442	71.9	75.4	92.5	120.1	141.6	153.5	4.6
Furniture stores.	4421	73.5	80.2	92.1	116.5	135.9	149.3	4.3
Home furnishings stores	4422	69.4	68.8	92.7	124.7	149.2	159.2	5.0
Electronics and appliance stores	443	38.6	47.3	89.7	174.2	287.2	320.5	13.3
Building material and garden supply stores	444	76.2	80.2	92.6	115.0	129.8	142.6	3.7
Building material and supplies dealers.	4441	77.1	81.8	93.7	115.5	130.0	142.9	3.7
Lawn and garden equipment and supplies stores . .	4442	71.7	72.3	86.2	112.0	128.7	140.7	4.0

See footnotes at end of table.

408   Labor Force, Employment, and Earnings

Table 620. **Annual Indexes of Output Per Hour for Selected NAICS Industries: 1987 to 2004**—Con.

[For a discussion of productivity measures, see text, this section. Minus sign (–) indicates decrease]

Industry	2002 NAICS code [1]	Indexes (1997 = 100) 1987	1990	1995	2000	2003	2004	Average annual percent change [2]
Retail trade—Con.								
Food and beverage stores	445	109.7	106.6	101.9	101.5	107.9	114.1	0.2
Grocery stores.	4451	110.6	106.5	102.8	101.5	107.4	113.6	0.2
Specialty food stores	4452	127.5	120.1	97.6	97.9	111.2	121.7	–0.3
Beer, wine, and liquor stores	4453	95.6	98.7	95.1	109.9	121.0	129.0	1.8
Health and personal care stores.	446	85.2	92.1	91.2	110.4	130.9	139.1	2.9
Gasoline stations.	447	83.0	83.7	99.7	108.3	120.0	121.6	2.3
Clothing and clothing accessories stores	448	65.8	69.2	92.9	123.3	139.1	138.9	4.5
Clothing stores	4481	66.6	69.1	91.5	125.0	142.5	142.5	4.6
Shoe stores	4482	65.1	71.1	96.8	111.9	132.0	120.7	3.7
Jewelry, luggage, and leather goods stores.	4483	63.6	67.8	95.7	127.3	131.5	139.9	4.7
Sporting goods, hobby, book, and music stores. . . .	451	73.7	81.1	94.3	119.7	127.7	147.5	4.2
Sporting goods and musical instrument stores. . .	4511	69.5	78.3	94.0	126.4	133.2	157.3	4.9
Book, periodical, and music stores	4512	84.4	87.2	95.0	107.4	118.0	129.7	2.6
General merchandise stores	452	73.7	75.3	92.0	119.6	134.9	140.5	3.9
Department stores.	4521	87.7	84.2	94.7	106.3	107.0	108.6	1.3
Other general merchandise stores.	4529	54.8	61.4	87.2	145.0	183.3	192.0	7.6
Miscellaneous store retailers	453	65.9	69.5	88.7	110.4	119.1	124.0	3.8
Florists.	4531	77.9	73.3	82.5	112.5	107.4	101.2	1.5
Office supplies, stationery, and gift stores	4532	56.6	61.0	91.5	124.6	144.4	153.4	6.0
Used merchandise stores	4533	78.5	82.2	86.2	115.5	116.3	116.3	2.3
Other miscellaneous store retailers	4539	75.2	81.9	88.8	97.3	102.9	105.6	2.0
Nonstore retailers	454	53.9	58.2	81.5	159.8	233.0	267.0	9.9
Electronic shopping and mail-order houses	4541	44.0	48.3	74.1	172.9	288.9	338.7	12.7
Vending machine operators	4542	98.7	97.2	88.5	113.2	100.9	100.0	0.1
Direct selling establishments	4543	71.2	74.7	92.9	123.6	149.2	164.0	5.0
Transportation and warehousing:								
Air transportation.	481	81.1	77.5	95.3	98.2	112.7	125.6	2.6
Line-haul railroads	482111	58.9	69.8	92.0	114.3	142.0	146.4	5.5
General freight trucking, long-distance.	48412	85.7	89.2	95.8	101.9	110.7	109.8	1.5
Used household and office goods moving	48421	106.7	112.6	101.4	94.8	86.2	88.7	–1.1
Postal service.	491	90.9	94.2	97.7	105.5	107.8	110.1	1.1
Couriers and messengers	492	148.3	138.5	101.5	121.9	134.1	126.5	–0.9
Information:								
Newspaper, book, and directory publishers	5111	105.9	96.3	92.7	107.7	109.6	107.0	0.1
Software publishers	5112	10.2	18.4	73.2	119.2	138.1	161.6	17.7
Motion picture and video exhibition	51213	90.7	109.2	99.4	106.5	100.6	103.9	0.8
Broadcasting, except Internet	515	99.5	98.2	102.5	103.6	106.7	108.2	0.5
Radio and television broadcasting	5151	98.1	97.7	104.8	92.1	94.4	91.4	–0.4
Cable and other subscription programming	5152	105.6	100.3	92.8	141.2	145.9	158.4	2.4
Wired telecommunications carriers	5171	56.9	66.0	87.6	122.7	130.2	131.3	5.0
Wireless telecommunications carriers	5172	75.6	70.4	90.0	152.8	242.5	288.7	8.2
Cable and other program distribution.	5175	105.2	100.0	92.6	91.6	101.2	113.7	0.5
Finance and insurance:								
Commercial banking	52211	72.8	80.7	95.6	101.7	102.6	108.1	2.4
Real estate and rental leasing:								
Passenger car rental	532111	90.5	88.5	100.2	111.9	120.4	118.3	1.6
Truck, trailer, and RV rental and leasing	53212	60.6	68.8	88.7	119.9	113.7	134.5	4.8
Video tape and disc rental.	53223	77.0	97.1	119.5	134.9	148.5	154.7	4.2
Professional and technical services:								
Tax preparation services	541213	82.9	76.2	90.6	100.9	110.0	101.3	1.2
Architectural services	54131	90.0	93.8	106.5	107.8	112.6	118.4	1.6
Engineering services	54133	90.2	99.4	94.4	102.0	100.5	108.0	1.1
Advertising agencies	54181	95.9	107.9	102.5	107.5	120.7	133.0	1.9
Photography studios, portrait	541921	98.1	95.9	107.3	108.9	104.2	92.1	–0.4
Administrative and waste management:								
Travel agencies	56151	89.3	94.6	93.0	119.4	147.3	167.7	3.8
Janitorial services	56172	70.1	87.0	90.4	101.4	119.2	117.5	3.1
Health care and social assistance:								
Medical and diagnostic laboratories	6215	(NA)	(NA)	90.8	131.9	141.0	141.1	5.0
Medical laboratories	621511	(NA)	(NA)	91.3	127.4	128.7	130.8	4.1
Diagnostic imaging centers	621512	(NA)	(NA)	89.8	139.9	160.3	154.3	6.2
Accommodation and food services:								
Traveler accommodations	7211	82.9	80.0	97.7	112.9	115.6	122.2	2.3
Food services and drinking places	722	96.5	102.7	100.4	103.6	106.0	108.6	0.7
Full-service restaurants	7221	91.9	99.1	96.3	102.0	102.5	104.8	0.8
Limited-service eating places	7222	96.0	103.1	104.4	102.8	106.0	109.5	0.8
Special food services	7223	100.0	108.1	98.8	117.8	121.7	121.5	1.2
Drinking places, alcoholic beverages	7224	136.2	123.0	104.8	100.8	121.8	122.5	–0.6
Other services:								
Automotive repair and maintenance	8111	85.9	89.9	103.2	109.4	104.0	112.1	1.6
Hair, nail, and skin care services	81211	83.4	82.1	93.3	108.1	119.4	126.2	2.5
Funeral homes and funeral services	81221	103.7	98.4	102.4	94.8	95.7	93.3	–0.6
Drycleaning and laundry services	8123	97.1	94.8	99.2	107.6	103.8	111.5	0.8
Photofinishing.	81292	95.8	107.7	108.0	73.8	100.4	102.9	0.4

NA Not available.　　[1] North American Industry Classification System, 2002 (NAICS); see text, this section.　　[2] Average annual percent change, 1987 to 2004, based on compound rate formula. For NAICS industries 6215, 621511, and 621512, annual percent changes are for 1995–2004.

Source: U.S. Bureau of Labor Statistics. Latest data available at: <http://www.bls.gov/lpc/home.htm> (accessed July 2006).

Table 621. **Employed Persons Using Computers at Work by Sex and Occupation: 2003**

[In percent, except as indicated (76,986 represents 76,986,000). As of October. For persons 16 years old and over. Refers to computer use on the sole or primary job. Based on the Current Population Survey and subject to sampling error; see Appendix III and source]

Characterisic	Total using a computer at work (1,000)	Percent of employed	Percent who used a computer at work for—					
			Word process-ing [1]	Internet or e-mail	Calen-dar or sched-uling	Spread-sheets or data-bases	Graph-ics or design	Pro-gram-ming
Total, 16 years and over	76,986	55.5	67.6	75.2	56.8	64.2	29.7	16.4
Sex: Male	37,124	49.9	65.5	77.5	58.5	67.1	33.8	21.4
Female	39,862	61.8	69.6	73.0	55.3	61.5	25.9	11.8
Occupation:								
Management, professional, and related occupations	38,398	79.6	76.9	84.4	63.0	70.7	37.6	20.6
Management, business, and financial operations	15,842	80.8	79.9	88.0	69.1	79.8	35.8	18.4
Professional and related occupations	22,556	78.7	74.8	81.8	58.7	64.4	38.9	22.1
Service occupations	6,025	27.5	55.0	57.9	48.5	48.5	19.9	11.9
Sales and office occupations	23,874	67.3	63.8	71.2	53.9	62.3	22.1	11.6
Sales and related occupations	9,577	59.7	60.6	72.6	53.3	61.0	26.2	11.6
Office and administrative support...	14,297	73.5	66.0	70.2	54.3	63.1	19.4	11.6
Natural resources, construction, and maintenance occupations	3,965	26.4	51.4	63.0	44.0	53.3	23.0	15.7
Farming, fishing, and forestry	140	11.0	54.6	56.9	39.7	54.8	19.5	6.1
Construction and extraction	1,589	18.9	60.9	65.8	43.9	56.6	25.9	12.8
Installation, maintenance, and repair occupations............	2,237	41.9	44.4	61.3	44.3	50.8	21.1	18.3
Production, transportation, and material moving	4,723	26.0	41.3	53.5	43.1	49.9	21.4	13.4
Production occupations	2,878	29.6	42.0	54.8	43.0	52.4	25.9	14.9
Transportation and material moving occupations..........	1,845	21.8	40.3	51.4	43.3	46.0	14.4	11.1

[1] Or desktop publishing.

Source: U.S. Bureau of Labor Statistics, *Computer and Internet Use at Work, 2003, News,* USDL 05-1457, August 2, 2005. See Internet site <http://www.bls.gov/bls/newsrels.htm#OEUS>.

Table 622. **Adults in Selected Work-Related Informal Learning Activities: 2002–2003**

[(206,533 represents 206,533,000). For the civilian noninstitutional population 16 years old and over not enrolled in elementary or secondary school. Based on the Adult Education for Work-Related Reasons Survey of the National Household Education Survey Program and subject to sampling error; see source and Appendix III for details]

Characteristic	Total adults (1,000)	Adults participating in work-related informal learning activities (percent)						
		Any activities	Self-paced study with books [1]	Attended confer-ences [2]	Informal presen-tations [3]	Self-paced study with soft-ware [4]	On the job pre-senta-tions [5]	Received super-vised train-ing [5, 6]
Total	206,533	58	31	23	21	21	56	43
Age:								
24 years or younger............	24,053	73	36	20	18	19	69	58
25 to 44 years old	82,223	70	37	28	26	26	57	45
45 to 64 years old	66,447	59	32	27	26	24	50	37
65 years old and over...........	33,810	17	10	7	5	6	39	21
Sex:								
Male	98,793	62	33	27	23	23	55	42
Female	107,740	55	28	20	20	19	57	45
Race/ethnicity:								
White, non-Hispanic.............	149,135	59	30	24	23	21	57	45
Black, non-Hispanic	23,145	56	34	21	19	20	57	44
Asian or Pacific Islander, non-Hispanic.	6,330	67	44	34	32	39	51	40
Other, non-Hispanic	3,675	55	29	21	18	24	44	41
Hispanic [7]...................	24,248	57	33	20	14	17	46	35
Educational attainment:								
Less than high school...........	32,357	31	17	8	5	7	43	25
High school diploma or equivalent....	61,194	50	26	15	13	14	53	40
Some college	58,055	65	35	24	23	24	58	48
BA degree of higher	32,122	75	38	35	34	34	61	51
Graduate degree or higher	22,804	78	43	51	46	37	59	47
Household income:								
$25,000 or less	53,796	40	22	12	9	10	50	35
$25,001 to 50,000	55,435	58	32	20	19	19	55	43
$50,001 to 75,000	43,189	64	32	24	24	24	56	46
$75,001 to 100,000	24,286	73	36	33	32	30	60	47
$100,001 or more	29,826	73	38	41	36	34	59	47

[1] Includes manuals and audio/video tapes. [2] Includes trade shows and conventions. [3] Such as "brown bag" events. [4] Includes from the Internet. [5] For adults employed in the past 12 months. [6] Or mentoring. [7] Persons of hispanic or latino origin may be of any race.

Source: U.S. National Center for Education Statistics, *Participation in Adult Education for Work-Related Reasons,* NCES 2006-040, November 2005.

Table 623. **Adults in Selected Work-Related Formal Learning Activities: 2004–2005**

[(**211,607 represents 211,607,000**). For the civilian noninstitutional population 16 years old and over not enrolled in elementary or secondary school. Based on the Adult Education Survey of the National Household Education Survey Program and subject to sampling error; see source and Appendix III for details]

Characteristic	Total adults (1,000)	Adults participating in work-related formal learning activities (percent)				
		Any activities	College degree program	Vocational degree/ diploma program	Appren- ticeship	Work- related courses
Total	211,607	33	7	1	1	27
Age:						
24 years old or younger	25,104	46	28	3	3	21
25 to 44 years old	81,674	39	7	2	2	33
45 to 64 years old	70,908	34	2	1	–	33
65 years old and over	33,922	5	–	–	–	5
Sex:						
Male	101,596	31	6	2	2	24
Female	110,011	35	8	1	1	29
Race/ethnicity:						
White, non-Hispanic	146,614	34	7	1	1	29
Black, non-Hispanic	23,467	34	6	2	2	27
Asian or Pacific Islander, non-Hispanic	7,080	35	12	1	1	24
Other, non-Hispanic	8,346	34	11	2	2	23
Hispanic [1]	26,101	23	4	2	2	17
Educational attainment:						
Less than high school	38,538	8	1	1	2	6
High school diploma or equivalent	63,701	23	2	2	1	18
Some college	51,657	43	14	2	2	32
BA degree	37,244	49	9	1	–	44
Graduate degree or higher	20,466	55	8	1	1	51

– Represents or rounds to zero.   [1] Persons of hispanic origin may be of any race.

Source: U.S. National Center for Education Statistics, Adult Education Survey of the National Household Education Surveys Program 2005, unpublished data.

Table 624. **Average Hours Per Day Worked by Employed Persons: 2004**

[(**145,279 represents 145,279,000**). For the civilian noninstitutional population 15 years old and over, except as indicated. Based on the American Time Use Survey, a survey conducted continuously throughout the year, and subject to sampling error; see source for details]

Characteristic	Total employed (1,000)	Employed persons who worked on their diary day						
		Number (1,000)	Percent of employed	Hours of work	Worked at workplace		Worked at home [1]	
					Percent of employed [2]	Hours of work	Percent of employed [2]	Hours of work
Total	145,279	98,665	67.9	7.63	87.0	7.86	19.4	2.83
Work status:								
Full-time workers [3]	112,274	80,678	71.9	8.08	88.6	8.22	19.0	2.99
Part-time workers [3]	33,005	17,987	54.5	5.58	79.8	6.06	21.5	2.20
Male	76,709	54,106	70.5	8.02	87.7	8.16	19.2	3.17
Full-time workers [3]	66,283	47,978	72.4	8.28	88.6	8.38	19.3	3.20
Part-time workers [3]	10,426	6,128	58.8	6.02	81.3	6.30	17.9	2.92
Female	68,570	44,560	65.0	7.15	86.1	7.49	19.7	2.43
Full-time workers [3]	45,991	32,701	71.1	7.80	88.6	7.99	18.4	2.68
Part-time workers [3]	22,579	11,859	52.5	5.35	79.0	5.94	23.3	1.91
Jobholding status:								
Single jobholders	131,273	87,166	66.4	7.58	87.5	7.82	17.9	2.86
Multiple jobholders	14,005	11,499	82.1	8.02	83.3	8.17	31.1	2.69
Educational attainment: [4]								
Less than high school [5]	10,212	6,936	67.9	8.03	94.7	8.11	(B)	(B)
High school diploma	37,091	25,716	69.3	7.86	91.2	7.97	12.6	2.81
Some college	32,455	22,203	68.4	7.70	87.7	7.99	19.1	2.85
BA degree or higher	43,193	31,290	72.4	7.60	78.9	7.98	33.2	2.86

B Percent not shown where base is less than 800,000.   [1] Represents doing activities that were "part of one's job."   [2] Percent of employed who worked on their diary day.   [3] Full-time workers usually worked 35 or more hours per week at all jobs combined; part-time workers fewer than 35 hours per week.   [4] For those 25 years old and over.   [5] Or equivalent.

Source: U.S. Bureau of Labor Statistics, *Time Use Survey—2004 Results Announced by BLS*, News, USDL 05-1766, September 20, 2005. See Internet site <http://www.bls.gov/tus/home.htm>.

Table 625. Annual Total Compensation and Wages and Salary Accruals Per Full-Time Equivalent Employee by Industry: 2000 to 2004

[In dollars. Wage and salary accruals include executives' compensation, bonuses, tips, and payments-in-kind; total compensation includes in addition to wages and salaries, employer contributions for social insurance, employer contributions to private and welfare funds, director's fees, jury and witness fees, etc. Based on the 1997 North American Industry Classification System (NAICS); see text, this section]

Industry	Annual total compensation				Annual wages and salary			
	2000	2002	2003	2004	2000	2001	2002	2004
Domestic industries	46,407	49,229	51,274	53,752	38,762	40,263	41,468	43,327
Private industries	45,240	47,658	49,490	51,876	38,446	39,610	40,742	42,635
Agriculture, forestry, fishing, and hunting	29,332	26,956	26,367	29,778	25,847	23,700	23,078	26,371
Mining.	70,413	74,873	78,555	84,551	58,291	61,069	63,379	67,782
Utilities	78,147	87,398	93,030	98,633	64,271	68,268	69,704	73,040
Construction	44,764	49,330	50,145	51,628	37,196	40,394	40,976	41,945
Manufacturing	54,219	58,071	62,861	64,854	44,216	44,864	46,762	48,731
Wholesale trade	56,264	61,167	63,286	66,508	48,017	51,506	52,953	55,325
Retail trade	30,225	31,275	32,322	33,490	26,307	26,675	27,412	28,216
Transportation and warehousing.	48,336	50,505	51,612	54,241	39,463	40,116	40,848	42,505
Information.	74,196	71,761	75,245	80,785	63,217	59,681	61,909	65,708
Finance and insurance	74,821	79,542	82,028	88,286	64,049	65,721	67,821	73,010
Real estate and rental and leasing . . .	41,906	43,801	45,300	48,328	36,178	37,389	38,670	41,116
Professional, scientific, and technical services	68,436	73,007	74,769	78,575	58,886	62,038	63,614	66,439
Management of companies and enterprises [1].	89,496	86,677	88,456	98,270	75,984	72,971	74,153	82,539
Administrative and waste management services.	28,540	31,901	33,185	34,596	25,181	27,654	28,557	29,664
Educational services	32,736	35,658	37,492	38,849	28,974	31,259	32,682	33,740
Health care and social assistance. . . .	40,897	43,830	45,553	47,695	35,127	37,374	38,642	40,328
Arts, entertainment, and recreation . . .	35,898	37,340	39,903	41,024	31,259	32,154	34,178	34,921
Accommodation and food services . . .	19,092	21,279	21,883	23,266	16,830	18,419	18,816	19,934
Other services, except government. . .	28,630	30,637	31,910	33,196	25,495	27,062	28,040	29,000
Government.	52,845	57,475	60,512	63,548	40,501	43,694	45,228	46,941
Federal	70,004	79,824	84,928	92,619	46,646	52,820	56,253	60,046
State and local	48,020	51,582	54,052	55,987	38,773	41,288	42,312	43,533

[1] Consists of offices of bank and other holding companies and of corporate, subsidiary, and regional managing offices.

Source: U.S. Bureau of Economic Analysis, *Survey of Current Business,* May 2006; and Internet site <http://www.bea.gov /bea/dn/nipaweb/SelectTable.asp?Selected=N>.

Table 626. Average Hourly Earnings by Private Industry Group: 1990 to 2005

[In dollars. Average earnings include overtime. Data are for production workers in natural resources and mining, manufacturing, and construction, and nonsupervisory employees in other industries. See headnote, Table 616]

Private industry group	Current dollars					Constant (1982) dollars [1]				
	1990	2000	2003	2004	2005	1990	2000	2003	2004	2005
AVERAGE HOURLY EARNINGS										
Total private.	10.19	14.00	15.35	15.67	16.11	7.66	8.03	8.27	8.23	8.17
Natural resources and mining	13.40	16.55	17.56	18.07	18.73	10.07	9.50	9.46	9.49	9.50
Construction	13.42	17.48	18.95	19.23	19.46	10.08	10.03	10.21	10.10	9.87
Manufacturing	10.78	14.32	15.74	16.15	16.56	8.10	8.22	8.48	8.48	8.40
Trade, transportation and utilities	9.83	13.31	14.34	14.58	14.93	7.39	7.64	7.73	7.66	7.57
Information	13.40	19.07	21.01	21.40	22.07	10.07	10.94	11.32	11.24	11.20
Financial activities [2]	9.99	14.98	17.14	17.52	17.94	7.51	8.59	9.23	9.20	9.10
Professional and business services [2] . .	11.14	15.52	17.21	17.48	18.07	8.37	8.90	9.27	9.18	9.17
Education and health services [2]	10.00	13.95	15.64	16.15	16.72	7.51	8.00	8.43	8.48	8.48
Leisure and hospitality [2].	5.88	8.11	8.76	8.91	9.14	4.42	4.65	4.72	4.68	4.64
Other services	9.08	12.73	13.84	13.98	14.33	6.82	7.30	7.46	7.34	7.27
AVERAGE WEEKLY EARNINGS										
Total private.	349	480	517	528	544	262	276	279	278	276
Natural resources and mining	603	735	766	804	854	453	422	413	422	433
Construction	513	686	727	736	751	386	393	392	386	381
Manufacturing	436	591	636	659	674	328	339	343	346	342
Trade, transportation, and utilities	332	450	481	488	499	249	258	259	257	253
Information	480	701	761	777	806	360	402	410	408	409
Financial activities [2]	355	537	609	623	645	266	308	328	327	327
Professional and business services [2] . .	381	535	587	598	618	286	307	316	314	314
Education and health services [2]	319	449	506	524	545	240	258	272	275	276
Leisure and hospitality [2].	152	212	224	229	235	115	122	121	120	119
Other services	298	413	434	433	443	224	237	234	227	225

[1] Earnings in current dollars divided by the Consumer Price Index (CPI-W) on a 1982 base; see text, Section 14, Prices.
[2] For composition of industries, see Table 617.

Source: U.S. Bureau of Labor Statistics, the Current Employment Statistics program Internet site <http://www.bls.gov/ces/home.htm>.

Table 627. **Mean Hourly Earnings and Weekly Hours by Selected Characteristics: 2004**

[Covers civilian workers in private industry establishments and state and local governments in the 50 states and DC. Excludes private households, federal government and agriculture. Based on establishment survey; see source and Appendix III for details]

Item	Mean hourly earnings (dol.) [1]			Mean weekly hours		
	Total	Private industry	State and local government	Total	Private industry	State and local government
Total	**18.09**	**17.25**	**22.77**	**35.7**	**35.6**	**36.8**
WORKER CHARACTERISTIC						
White-collar occupations	22.34	21.53	25.73	36.1	36.0	36.5
Professional specialty and technical	29.40	28.87	30.50	36.3	36.4	36.1
Executive, administrative, and managerial	32.43	32.84	30.48	39.9	40.2	38.4
Sales	15.20	15.21	14.22	32.3	32.3	34.1
Administrative support	14.21	14.13	14.57	36.6	36.6	36.5
Blue-collar occupations	15.46	15.34	17.59	38.0	38.1	37.6
Precision production, craft, and repair	19.46	19.41	20.05	39.5	39.5	39.8
Machine operators, assemblers, and inspectors	13.70	13.69	16.70	39.1	39.1	38.4
Transportation and material moving	15.01	14.83	16.64	37.7	38.1	34.4
Handlers, equipment cleaners, helpers, and laborers	11.61	11.42	14.45	35.0	34.8	38.6
Service occupations.	10.65	9.12	17.06	31.8	30.7	37.1
Full-time [2]	19.14	18.36	23.17	39.6	39.7	38.8
Part-time [2]	10.01	9.59	15.57	20.5	20.6	19.2
Union [3]	22.18	20.32	24.80	36.8	36.9	36.7
Nonunion	17.21	16.83	20.82	35.5	35.4	36.8
Time [4]	17.86	16.93	22.77	35.6	35.4	36.8
Incentive [4]	22.45	22.45	(NA)	38.3	38.3	(NA)
ESTABLISHMENT CHARACTERISTIC						
Goods producing [5]	(X)	18.96	(X)	(X)	39.5	(X)
Service producing [5]	(X)	16.63	(X)	(X)	34.3	(X)
1 to 99 workers [6]	15.39	15.35	18.23	34.5	34.5	36.1
100 to 499 workers	17.23	16.73	21.18	36.3	36.4	35.6
500 to 999 workers.	19.94	19.05	23.00	37.0	37.3	36.1
1,000 to 2,499 workers	21.65	21.27	22.64	36.7	36.7	36.6
2,500 workers or more.	24.72	25.93	23.69	37.4	37.3	37.6
GEOGRAPHIC REGION [7]						
New England.	20.12	19.20	26.10	34.5	34.4	35.8
Middle Atlantic	20.59	19.62	26.15	35.0	35.0	35.5
East North Central	18.21	17.38	23.57	35.3	35.2	36.0
West North Central	16.84	16.02	21.40	35.3	35.0	37.2
South Atlantic.	16.71	16.05	19.94	36.2	35.7	38.4
East South Central	14.49	13.87	18.99	37.4	37.4	37.4
West South Central.	16.07	15.47	19.10	36.6	36.3	38.2
Mountain.	16.90	15.80	23.00	35.8	35.6	37.2
Pacific	20.70	19.63	26.45	35.7	35.8	35.4

NA Not available. X Not applicable. [1] Earnings are straight time hourly wages or salary, including incentive pay, cost-of-living adjustments, and hazard pay. Excludes premium pay for overtime, vacations and holidays, nonproduction bonuses and tips. [2] Based on definition used by each establishment. [3] Workers whose wages are determined through collective bargaining. [4] Time worker wages are based solely on an hourly rate or salary. Incentive workers wages are based at least in part on productivity payments such as piece rates or commissions. [5] For private industry only. [6] Private establishments employing 1 to 99 workers and state and local government establishments employing 50 to 99 workers. [7] Composition of regions: NEW ENGLAND: Maine, New Hampshire, Vermont, Massachusetts, Rhode Island, Connecticut. MIDDLE ATLANTIC: New York, New Jersey, and Pennsylvania. EAST NORTH CENTRAL: Ohio, Indiana, Illinois, Michigan, Wisconsin. WEST NORTH CENTRAL: Minnesota, Iowa, Missouri, North Dakota, South Dakota, Nebraska, and Kansas. SOUTH ATLANTIC: Delaware, Maryland, District of Columbia, Virginia, West Virginia. North Carolina, South Carolina, Georgia, Florida. EAST SOUTH CENTRAL: Kentucky, Tennessee, Alabama, Mississippi. WEST SOUTH CENTRAL: Arkansas, Louisiana, Oklahoma, and Texas. MOUNTAIN: Montana, Idaho, Wyoming, Colorado, New Mexico, Arizona, Utah, Nevada. PACIFIC: Washington, Oregon, California, Alaska, and Hawaii.

Source: U.S. Bureau of Labor Statistics, *National Compensation Survey: Occupational Wages in the United States, July 2004,* Summary 05-02, August 2005. See Internet site <http://www.bls.gov/ncs/home.htm>.

Table 628. Employment and Wages: 1995 to 2004

[(115,488 represents 115,488,000). See headnote, Table 629]

Employment and wages	Unit	1995	1999	2000	2001	2002	2003	2004
Average annual employment:								
Total	1,000	115,488	127,042	129,877	129,636	128,234	127,796	129,278
Excluding federal	1,000	112,540	124,256	127,006	126,883	125,475	125,032	126,539
Private	1,000	96,895	107,619	110,015	109,305	107,577	107,066	108,490
State government	1,000	4,202	4,297	4,370	4,452	4,485	4,482	4,485
Local governments	1,000	11,442	12,340	12,620	13,126	13,413	13,484	13,564
Federal government	1,000	2,948	2,787	2,871	2,753	2,759	2,764	2,740
Annual wages:								
Total	Bil. dol.	3,216	4,236	4,588	4,695	4,714	4,826	5,088
Excluding federal	Bil. dol.	3,102	4,112	4,455	4,561	4,571	4,676	4,929
Private	Bil. dol.	2,659	3,578	3,888	3,952	3,931	4,016	4,246
State government	Bil. dol.	128	149	159	168	176	180	184
Local governments	Bil. dol.	315	385	409	440	464	481	499
Federal government	Bil. dol.	114	123	133	135	144	150	158
Annual wage per employee:								
Total	Dol.	27,846	33,340	35,323	36,219	36,764	37,765	39,354
Excluding federal	Dol.	27,567	33,094	35,077	35,943	36,428	37,401	38,955
Private	Dol.	27,441	33,244	35,337	36,157	36,539	37,508	39,134
State government	Dol.	30,497	34,681	36,296	37,814	39,212	40,057	41,118
Local governments	Dol.	27,552	31,234	32,387	33,521	34,605	35,669	36,805
Federal government	Dol.	38,523	44,287	46,228	48,940	52,050	54,239	57,782
Average weekly wage per employee:								
Total	Dol.	536	641	679	697	707	726	757
Excluding federal	Dol.	530	636	675	691	701	719	749
Private	Dol.	528	639	680	695	703	721	753
State government	Dol.	586	667	698	727	754	770	791
Local governments	Dol.	530	601	623	645	665	686	708
Federal government	Dol.	741	852	889	941	1,001	1,043	1,111

Source: U.S. Bureau of Labor Statistics. "Employment and Wages, Annual Averages, 2004". See Internet site <http://www.bls.gov/cew/home.htm>.

Table 629. Average Annual Wage by State: 2003 and 2004

[In dollars, except percent change. For workers covered by state unemployment insurance laws and for federal civilian workers covered by unemployment compensation for federal employees, approximately 97 percent of employees on nonfarm payrolls in 2004. Excludes most agricultural workers on small farms, all Armed Forces, elected officials in most states, railroad employees, most domestic workers, most student workers at school, employees of certain nonprofit organizations, and most self-employed individuals. Pay includes bonuses, stock options, cash value of meals and lodging, and tips and other gratuities]

State	Average annual pay 2003	Average annual pay 2004	Percent change, 2003–04	State	Average annual pay 2003	Average annual pay 2004	Percent change, 2003–04
United States	37,765	39,354	4.2	Missouri	33,788	34,845	3.1
Alabama	32,236	33,414	3.7	Montana	26,907	27,830	3.4
Alaska	37,804	39,062	3.3	Nebraska	30,382	31,507	3.7
Arizona	35,056	36,646	4.5	Nevada	35,329	37,106	5.0
Arkansas	28,893	30,245	4.7	New Hampshire	37,321	39,176	5.0
California	42,592	44,641	4.8	New Jersey	46,351	48,064	3.7
Colorado	38,942	40,276	3.4	New Mexico	30,202	31,411	4.0
Connecticut	48,328	51,007	5.5	New York	47,247	49,941	5.7
Delaware	40,954	42,487	3.7	North Carolina	33,532	34,791	3.8
District of Columbia	60,417	63,887	5.7	North Dakota	27,628	28,987	4.9
Florida	33,544	35,186	4.9	Ohio	35,153	36,441	3.7
Georgia	36,626	37,866	3.4	Oklahoma	29,699	30,743	3.5
Hawaii	33,742	35,198	4.3	Oregon	34,450	35,630	3.4
Idaho	28,677	29,871	4.2	Pennsylvania	36,995	38,555	4.2
Illinois	40,540	42,277	4.3	Rhode Island	36,415	37,651	3.4
Indiana	33,379	34,694	3.9	South Carolina	30,750	31,839	3.5
Iowa	30,708	32,097	4.5	South Dakota	27,210	28,281	3.9
Kansas	31,489	32,738	4.0	Tennessee	33,581	34,925	4.0
Kentucky	31,855	33,165	4.1	Texas	36,968	38,511	4.2
Louisiana	30,782	31,880	3.6	Utah	31,106	32,171	3.4
Maine	30,750	31,906	3.8	Vermont	32,086	33,274	3.7
Maryland	40,686	42,579	4.7	Virginia	38,585	40,534	5.1
Massachusetts	46,323	48,916	5.6	Washington	39,021	39,361	0.9
Michigan	39,433	40,373	2.4	West Virginia	29,284	30,382	3.7
Minnesota	38,610	40,398	4.6	Wisconsin	33,425	34,743	3.9
Mississippi	27,591	28,535	3.4	Wyoming	29,924	31,210	3.3

Source: U.S. Bureau of Labor Statistics. "Employment and Wages, Annual Averages", 2003 and 2004. See Internet site <http://www.bls.gov/cew/home.htm>.

U.S. Census Bureau, Statistical Abstract of the United States: 2007

[In current dollars of usual weekly earnings. Data represent annual averages (101,210 represents 101,210,000). Occupational classifications are those used in the 2000 census; see text this section. Based on the Current Population Survey; see text, Section 1, and Appendix III. For definition of median, see Guide to Tabular Presentation]

Characteristic	Number of workers (1,000)			Median weekly earnings (dol.)		
	2000	2004 [1]	2005 [1]	2000	2004 [1]	2005 [1]
All workers [2]	101,210	101,224	103,560	576	638	651
SEX						
Male	57,107	57,001	58,406	641	713	722
16 to 24 years old	6,770	6,243	6,396	375	400	409
25 years old and over	50,337	50,758	52,010	693	762	771
Female	44,103	44,223	45,154	493	573	585
16 to 24 years old	5,094	4,633	4,711	344	375	381
25 years old and over	39,009	39,590	40,443	516	599	612
RACE/ETHNICITY						
White [3]	83,228	82,468	84,110	590	657	672
Male	48,085	47,495	48,572	662	732	743
Female	35,143	34,972	35,538	502	584	596
Black [3]	12,410	12,032	12,388	474	525	520
Male	5,911	5,706	5,916	510	569	559
Female	6,500	6,326	6,472	429	505	499
Asian [3, 4]	4,598	4,457	4,651	615	708	753
Male	2,538	2,504	2,597	685	802	825
Female	2,060	1,953	2,054	547	613	665
Hispanic origin [5]	12,761	14,061	14,673	399	456	471
Male	8,077	8,996	9,433	417	480	489
Female	4,684	5,065	5,241	366	419	429
OCCUPATION						
Management, professional, and related occupations	34,831	36,149	36,908	810	918	937
Management, business, and financial operations	14,240	14,778	14,977	877	965	997
Management occupations	9,952	10,221	10,340	937	1,052	1,083
Business and financial operations occupations	4,288	4,558	4,637	760	847	871
Professional and related occupations	20,590	21,371	21,931	770	883	902
Computer and mathematical occupations	3,051	2,793	2,924	938	1,114	1,132
Architecture and engineering occupations	2,781	2,500	2,509	949	1,098	1,105
Life, physical, and social science occupations	989	1,073	1,164	811	957	965
Community and social services occupations	1,641	1,846	1,797	629	707	725
Legal occupations	1,039	1,111	1,162	919	1,070	1,052
Education, training, and library occupations	5,467	5,941	6,066	704	781	798
Arts, design, entertainment, sports, and media	1,488	1,426	1,488	724	768	819
Healthcare practitioner and technical occupations	4,134	4,680	4,821	727	852	878
Service occupations	12,595	13,763	14,123	365	411	413
Healthcare support occupations	1,731	1,985	2,085	358	407	410
Protective service occupations	2,281	2,509	2,549	591	700	678
Food preparation and serving-related occupations	3,483	3,863	4,007	317	360	356
Building and grounds cleaning and maintenance	3,354	3,436	3,425	351	385	394
Personal care and service occupations	1,746	1,969	2,057	351	402	409
Sales and office occupations	25,606	24,950	25,193	492	558	575
Sales and related occupations	9,650	9,984	10,031	525	604	622
Office and administrative support occupations	15,956	14,966	15,161	480	535	550
Natural resources, construction, and maintenance occupations	10,958	11,280	12,086	582	621	623
Farming, fishing, and forestry occupations	842	718	755	310	356	372
Construction and extraction occupations	5,852	6,232	6,826	580	604	604
Installation, maintenance, and repair occupations	4,263	4,330	4,504	628	704	705
Production, transportation, and material-moving occupations	17,221	15,082	15,251	475	523	540
Production occupations	10,378	8,478	8,403	471	526	538
Transportation and material-moving occupations	6,843	6,604	6,848	481	520	543

[1] See footnote 2, Table 573. [2] Includes other races, not shown separately. [3] Beginning 2004, for persons in this race group only. See footnote 3, table 574. [4] Prior to 2004, includes Pacific Islanders. [5] Persons of Hispanic or Latino origin may be of any race.

Source: U.S. Bureau of Labor Statistics, Bulletin 2307, and *Employment and Earnings*, monthly, January issues and unpublished data.

Table. 631. Workers With Earnings by Occupation of Longest Held Job and Sex: 2004

[Covers persons 15 years old and over as of March 2005. (71,907, represents 71,907,000). Based on Current Population Survey; see text, Section 1, and Appendix III. For definition of median, see Guide to Tabular Presentation. Occupational classifications are those used in the 2000 Census and are not comparable to those used in the 1990 Census]

Major occupation of longest job held in 2004	All workers				Full-time, year-round			
	Women		Men		Women		Men	
	Number (1,000)	Median earnings (dol.)	Number (1,000)	Median earnings (dol.)	Number (1,000)	Median earnings (dol.)	Number (1,000)	Median earnings (dol.)
Total	71,907	22,224	81,448	32,486	42,307	31,223	60,093	40,798
Management, business, and financial occupations	8,982	39,714	11,635	57,739	7,081	42,342	10,081	61,982
Professional and related occupations . . .	17,127	34,506	12,951	51,236	10,420	41,367	10,058	57,833
Service occupations	14,952	11,987	11,271	17,407	6,751	30,113	6,689	26,226
Sales and office occupations.	25,158	21,116	14,069	30,986	14,676	28,115	10,117	40,301
Natural resources, construction, and maintenance	865	16,880	15,687	29,706	434	28,942	11,327	34,672
Production, transportation, and material moving occupations.	4,757	17,982	15,167	28,971	2,892	23,203	11,241	32,677
Armed Forces	66	(B)	666	37,401	52	(B)	580	40,815

B Data not shown where base is less than 75,000.

Source: U.S. Census Bureau Internet site <http://pubdb3.census.gov/macro/032005/perinc/toc.htm>, Table PINC-06, "Occupation of Longest Job in 2004—People 15 years Old and Over, by Total Money Earnings in 2004, Work Experience in 2004, Race, Hispanic Origin, and Sex" (accessed 7 July 2006).

Table. 632. Employment Cost Index (ECI), Total Compensation by Occupation and Industry: 1985 to 2005

[As of December. The ECI is a measure of the rate of change in employee compensation (wages, salaries, and employer costs for employee benefits). Data are not seasonally adjusted: 1985 based on fixed employment counts from 1970 Census of Population; 1990 based on fixed employment counts from the 1980 Census of Population; beginning 1995 based primarily on 1990 Occupational Employment Survey]

Item	Indexes (June 1989 = 100)						Percent change for 12 months ending Dec.—				
	1985	1990	1995	2000	2004	2005	1985	1990	1995	2000	2005
Civilian workers [1]	86.8	107.6	127.2	150.6	174.7	180.2	4.3	4.9	2.7	4.1	3.1
Workers, by occupational group:											
White-collar occupations	85.8	108.3	128.0	152.5	176.6	182.5	4.9	5.2	2.9	4.2	3.3
Blue-collar occupations	88.4	106.5	125.8	146.5	170.9	175.4	3.3	4.4	2.5	4.2	2.6
Service occupations	87.2	108.0	127.4	150.0	173.6	179.2	3.9	5.1	2.5	3.6	3.2
Workers, by industry division:											
Manufacturing	87.8	107.2	128.3	149.3	175.4	181.3	3.3	5.1	2.6	4.0	3.4
Nonmanufacturing [2]	86.4	107.8	126.8	150.7	174.4	179.8	4.7	4.9	2.8	4.1	3.1
Service industries	84.1	110.2	129.4	152.4	175.5	180.7	4.7	6.3	2.4	4.0	3.0
Public administration [3]	85.4	108.7	128.3	148.3	175.4	183.1	4.9	5.3	3.3	2.7	4.4
State and local government. . .	84.6	110.4	129.3	148.9	172.6	179.6	5.6	5.8	2.9	3.0	4.1
Workers, by occupational group:											
White-collar occupations	84.2	110.9	129.1	148.3	171.2	177.8	5.8	6.0	2.9	3.0	3.9
Blue-collar occupations	86.7	108.7	128.0	147.2	171.0	178.3	5.3	4.8	2.6	3.3	4.3
Workers, by industry division:											
Service industries	84.0	111.3	129.6	148.9	170.8	177.5	5.9	6.3	2.8	3.0	3.9
Schools	83.6	111.6	129.8	149.0	170.3	177.1	6.2	6.0	2.8	3.0	4.0
Elementary and secondary	83.6	112.1	130.1	148.1	169.2	176.0	6.4	6.3	2.8	2.8	4.0
Colleges and universities [4]	(NA)	110.2	128.7	151.7	173.2	179.8	(NA)	5.3	2.5	3.5	3.8
Services, excluding schools [4]	85.2	110.2	129.4	148.8	173.8	180.0	4.7	6.8	3.0	3.5	3.6
Public administration [3]	85.4	108.7	128.3	148.3	175.4	183.1	4.9	5.3	3.3	2.7	4.4
Private industry workers [5]	87.3	107.0	126.7	150.9	175.2	180.4	3.9	4.6	2.6	4.4	3.0
Workers, by occupational group:											
White-collar occupations	86.4	107.4	127.6	153.6	178.1	183.8	4.9	4.9	2.8	4.6	3.2
Blue-collar occupations	88.5	106.4	125.6	146.4	170.8	175.2	3.1	4.4	2.4	4.2	2.6
Service occupations	88.4	107.3	125.2	148.1	169.7	173.7	3.0	4.7	1.9	3.9	2.4
Workers, by industry division:											
Manufacturing	87.8	107.2	128.3	149.3	175.4	181.3	3.3	5.1	2.6	4.0	3.4
Nonmanufacturing [2]	87.0	106.9	125.9	151.1	174.7	179.7	4.3	4.5	2.7	4.6	2.9
Service industries [2]	84.1	109.3	129.4	154.1	177.9	182.4	(NA)	6.2	2.2	4.4	2.5
Business services	(NA)	107.4	126.3	158.4	179.1	181.3	(NA)	6.0	2.7	4.3	1.2
Health services	83.7	110.8	132.2	150.6	178.0	184.3	(NA)	6.8	2.7	4.4	3.5
Hospitals	(NA)	110.7	131.3	151.1	183.2	190.7	(NA)	7.0	2.1	4.5	4.1
Workers by bargaining status:											
Union	90.1	106.2	127.7	146.9	176.2	181.1	2.6	4.3	2.8	4.0	2.8
Nonunion	86.3	107.3	126.5	151.6	174.9	180.2	4.6	4.8	2.7	4.4	3.0

NA Not available. [1] Includes private industry and state and local government workers and excludes farm, household, and federal government workers. [2] Includes other industries, not shown separately. [3] Consists of executive, legislative, judicial, administrative, and regulatory activities. [4] Includes library, social, and health services. Formerly called hospitals and other services. [5] Excludes farm and household workers.

Source: U.S. Bureau of Labor Statistics, News, Employment Cost Index, quarterly; and Internet site <http://www.bls.gov/ncs/ect/home.htm> (accessed June 2006).

Table 633. **Federal Minimum Wage Rates: 1950 to 2000**

Year	Current dollars	Year	Current dollars
1950	0.75	1976	2.30
1951	0.75	1977	2.30
1952	0.75	1978	2.65
1953	0.75	1979	2.90
1954	0.75	1980	3.10
1955	0.75	1981	3.35
1956	1.00	1982	3.35
1957	1.00	1983	3.35
1958	1.00	1984	3.35
1959	1.00	1985	3.35
1960	1.00	1986	3.35
1961	1.15	1987	3.35
1962	1.15	1988	3.35
1963	1.25	1989	3.35
1964	1.25	1990	3.80
1965	1.25	1991	4.25
1966	1.25	1992	4.25
1967	1.40	1993	4.25
1968	1.60	1994	4.25
1969	1.60	1995	4.25
1970	1.60	1996	4.75
1971	1.60	1997	5.15
1972	1.60	1998	5.15
1973	1.60	1999	5.15
1974	2.00	2000	5.15
1975	2.10		

Source: U.S. Employment Standards Administration, Internet site: <http://www.dol.gov/esa/whd/flsa/>.

Table 634. **Workers Paid Hourly Rates by Selected Characteristics: 2005**

[Data are annual averages (75,609 represents 75,609,000). For employed wage and salary workers, excluding the incorporated self-employed. Based on the Current Population Survey; see text, Section 1, and Appendix III]

Characteristic	Number of workers (1,000)			Percent of all workers paid hourly rates			Median hourly earnings of workers paid hourly rates [1]
	Total paid hourly rates	At or below $5.15			At or below $5.15		
		Total	At $5.15	Below $5.15	Total	At $5.15	Below $5.15	
Total, 16 years and over [2]	**75,609**	**1,882**	**479**	**1,403**	**2.5**	**0.6**	**1.9**	**11.19**
16 to 24 years	16,374	1,002	283	720	6.1	1.7	4.4	8.07
16 to 19 years	5,528	491	179	312	8.9	3.2	5.6	7.05
25 years and over	59,235	880	196	683	1.5	0.3	1.2	12.48
Male, 16 years and over	37,652	648	189	459	1.7	0.5	1.2	12.16
16 to 24 years	8,288	353	130	223	4.3	1.6	2.7	8.42
16 to 19 years	2,654	172	86	86	6.5	3.2	3.2	7.21
25 years and over	29,364	296	60	236	1.0	0.2	0.8	13.91
Women, 16 years and over...	37,957	1,234	290	944	3.3	0.8	2.5	10.31
16 to 24 years	8,086	650	153	496	8.0	1.9	6.1	7.80
16 to 19 years	2,874	318	93	225	11.1	3.2	7.8	6.92
25 years and over	29,871	584	137	447	2.0	0.5	1.5	11.58
White [3]	60,978	1,537	349	1,188	2.5	0.6	1.9	11.48
Black [3]	9,793	215	96	119	2.2	1.0	1.2	10.17
Asian [3]	2,720	65	14	51	2.4	0.5	1.9	12.01
Hispanic origin [4]	12,527	282	71	210	2.2	0.6	1.7	9.95
Full-time workers [5]	57,385	752	143	608	1.3	0.2	1.1	12.23
Part-time workers [5]	18,084	1,126	336	790	6.2	1.9	4.4	8.17
Private sector industries	66,135	1,782	438	1,344	2.7	0.7	2.0	10.95

[1] For definition of median, see Guide to Tabular Presentation.   [2] Includes races not shown separately. Also includes a small number of multiple jobholders whose full- or part-time status can not be determined for their principal job.   [3] For persons in this race group only. See footnote 3, Table 574.   [4] Persons of Hispanic or Latino origin may be any race.   [5] Working fewer than 35 hours per week.

Source: U.S. Bureau of Labor Statistics, *Employment and Earnings,* January 2006 and unpublished data. See Internet site <http://www.bls.gov/cps/home.htm>.

Labor Force, Employment, and Earnings   417

Table 635. **Employer Costs for Employee Compensation Per Hour Worked: 2005**

[In dollars. As of December, for civilian workers. Based on a sample of establishments from the National Compensation Survey; see source for details. See also Appendix III]

Compensation component	Total civilian workers	State and local govern- ment workers	Private industry workers Total	Goods produc- ing[1]	Service produc- ing[2]	Union workers	Non- union workers	Full- time workers	Part- time workers
Total compensation	26.46	36.55	24.71	29.37	23.58	33.66	23.64	28.17	13.50
Wages and salaries	18.59	24.83	17.51	19.27	17.08	21.24	17.06	19.63	10.63
Total benefits	7.87	11.72	7.20	10.10	6.50	12.41	6.58	8.54	2.87
Paid leave.	1.77	2.72	1.61	1.84	1.55	2.26	1.53	1.98	0.40
Vacation	0.81	0.94	0.79	0.92	0.76	1.13	0.75	(NA)	(NA)
Holiday	0.60	0.90	0.55	0.65	0.52	0.75	0.52	(NA)	(NA)
Sick	0.26	0.67	0.19	0.14	0.21	0.27	0.18	(NA)	(NA)
Other	0.10	0.21	0.08	0.13	0.07	0.11	0.07	(NA)	(NA)
Supplemental pay.	0.66	0.31	0.72	1.24	0.59	1.12	0.67	0.87	0.21
Insurance	2.13	3.98	1.81	2.59	1.63	3.67	1.59	2.20	0.55
Health insurance	2.01	3.86	1.69	2.42	1.51	3.45	1.48	(NA)	(NA)
Retirement and savings	1.13	2.51	0.89	1.59	0.72	2.28	0.72	1.10	0.20
Defined benefit	0.70	2.24	0.43	1.07	0.28	1.74	0.28	(NA)	(NA)
Defined contributions. . . .	0.43	0.27	0.46	0.52	0.44	0.54	0.45	(NA)	(NA)
Legally required	2.15	2.15	2.14	2.77	1.99	2.98	2.04	2.34	1.51
Social security and Medicare	1.49	1.62	1.47	1.64	1.42	1.84	1.42	(NA)	(NA)
Social security.	1.19	1.25	1.18	1.32	1.14	1.48	1.14	(NA)	(NA)
Medicare	0.30	0.38	0.29	0.32	0.28	0.35	0.28	(NA)	(NA)
Federal unemployment. . .	0.03	–	0.03	0.03	0.03	0.03	0.03	(NA)	(NA)
State unemployment	0.15	0.06	0.16	0.22	0.15	0.24	0.16	(NA)	(NA)
Workers compensation. . .	0.48	0.47	0.48	0.88	0.38	0.87	0.43	(NA)	(NA)
Other benefits [3]	0.04	0.05	0.04	0.08	0.02	0.11	0.03	0.04	–

– Represents or rounds to zero.   NA Not available.   [1] Based on the North American Industry Classification System, 2002 (NAICS). See text, this section. Includes mining, construction, and manufacturing. The agriculture, forestry, farming and hunting sector is excluded.   [2] Based on the 2002 NAICS. Includes utilities; wholesale and retail trade; transportation and warehousing; information; finance and insurance; real estate and rental and leasing; professional and technical services; management of companies and enterprises, administrative and waste services; education services; health care and social assistance; arts, entertainment, and recreation; accommodations and food services; and other services, except public administration.   [3] Includes severance pay, and supplemental unemployment benefits.

Source: U.S. Bureau of Labor Statistics, *Employer Costs for Employee Compensation, News,* USDL 06-456, March 14, 2006. See Intenet site <http://www.bls.gov/ncs/ect/home.htm>.

Table 636. **Workers With Access to Retirement and Health Care Benefits by Selected Characteristics: 2005**

[As of March. Based on National Compensation Survey, a sample survey of 4,560 private industry establishments of all sizes, representing over 103 million workers; see Appendix III. See also Tables 147 and 148]

Characteristic	Retirement benefits All plans[1]	Defined benefit	Defined contri- bution	Healthcare benefits Medical care	Dental care	Vision care	Outpatient prescrip- tion drug coverage
Total	60	22	53	70	46	29	64
WORKER CHARACTERISTICS							
White-collar occupations	70	25	64	77	54	33	69
Blue-collar occupations	60	26	50	77	47	30	71
Service occupations	32	7	28	44	25	19	41
Full-time [2].	69	25	62	85	56	35	78
Part-time [2]	27	10	23	22	14	9	20
Union [3].	88	73	49	92	73	57	87
Nonunion [3]	56	16	54	68	43	26	61
Average wage less than $15 per hour	46	12	41	58	34	21	53
Average wage $15 per hour or more	78	35	69	87	62	40	80
ESTABLISHMENT CHARACTERISTICS							
Goods producing [4].	71	33	61	85	56	36	80
Service producing [4]	56	19	51	66	43	27	59
1 to 99 workers	44	10	40	59	31	19	52
100 or more workers.	78	37	69	84	65	41	79

[1] Employees may have access to both defined benefit and defined contribution plans. Total excludes duplication.   [2] Employees are classified as working either a full-time or part-time schedule based on the definition used by each establishment.   [3] Union workers are those whose wages are determined through collective bargaining.   [4] Based on the Standard Industrial Classification Manual, 1987.

Source: U.S. Bureau of Labor Statistics, *Employee Benefits in Private Industry in the United States, March 2005,* Summary 05-01, August 2005. See Internet site <http://www.bls.gov/ncs/ebs/home.htm>.

Table 637. Percent of Workers With Access to Selected Employee Benefits in Private Industry: 2005

[As of March. Based on National Compensation Survey, a sample survey of 4,560 private industry establishments of all sizes, representing over 103 million workers; see Appendix III. See also Tables 147 and 148]

Characteristic	Paid holidays	Paid vacation	Paid military leave	Family leave Paid	Family leave Unpaid	Employer assistance for child care Total	Employer-provided funds	On-site and off-site child care	Child care resource and referral services	Adoption assistance	Long-term care insurance	Flexible work plans[1]	Subsidized commuting[2]
Total	77	77	48	7	81	14	3	5	10	9	11	4	5
WORKER CHARACTERISTICS													
White-collar occupations	85	83	57	10	86	19	5	7	14	14	17	7	7
Blue-collar occupations	81	80	43	4	79	8	2	2	6	7	6	2	3
Service occupations	49	59	33	5	72	9	2	4	5	2	4	1	2
Full-time[3]	89	90	54	9	85	16	4	6	11	11	13	5	6
Part-time[3]	37	36	30	3	68	8	1	3	5	4	6	2	2
Union[4]	87	86	55	6	89	18	3	7	16	13	15	2	6
Nonunion[4]	75	77	47	8	80	14	3	5	9	9	11	4	5
Average wage less than $15 per hour	68	70	40	5	77	9	2	3	5	5	7	2	2
Average wage $15 per hour or more	88	88	60	11	87	21	5	8	16	15	18	7	8
ESTABLISHMENT CHARACTERISTICS													
Goods producing	85	86	54	5	84	13	3	4	11	10	10	3	4
Service producing	74	75	46	8	80	14	3	6	10	9	12	4	5
1 to 99 workers	68	70	36	6	71	5	1	2	3	3	4	3	2
100 or more workers	87	87	64	9	93	26	5	9	19	17	21	5	8
GEOGRAPHIC AREAS[5]													
New England division	80	76	59	9	79	16	2	7	13	12	12	3	8
Middle Atlantic division	81	82	53	6	82	16	4	6	11	13	13	6	7
East North Central division	77	77	50	8	80	16	4	7	11	10	11	3	3
West North Central division	73	73	45	5	81	15	2	7	8	10	9	2	4
South Atlantic division	77	79	49	8	83	11	4	4	8	9	12	3	2
East South Central division	76	77	43	7	87	11	4	5	7	9	7	3	3
West South Central division	77	77	48	7	77	15	3	5	10	9	13	5	3
Mountain division	70	73	44	8	77	15	4	5	12	7	10	6	7
Pacific division	74	78	41	8	82	12	2	3	6	7	13	4	8

[1] Arrangements permitting employees to work at home several days of the workweek. [2] Employers subsidize employees' cost of commuting to and from work via public transportation, company-sponsored van pool, discounted subway fares, etc. [3] Employees are classified as working either a full-time or part-time schedule based on the definition used by each establishment. [4] Union workers are those whose wages are determined through collective bargaining. [5] For composition of divisions, see map, inside front cover.

Source: U.S. Bureau of Labor Statistics, Employee Benefits in Private Industry in the United States, March 2005, Summary 05-01, August 2005. See Internet site <http://www.bls.gov/ncs/ebs/home.htm>.

Labor Force, Employment, and Earnings 419

Table 638. **Workers Killed or Disabled on the Job: 1970 to 2004**

[Data for 2004 are preliminary estimates (1.7 represents 1,700). Excludes homicides and suicides. Estimates based on data from the U.S. National Center for Health Statistics, state vital statistics departments, state industrial commissions and beginning 1995, Bureau of Labor Statistics, Census of Occupational Fatalities. Numbers of workers based on data from the U.S. Bureau of Labor Statistics]

Year	Manufacturing Number (1,000)	Manufacturing Rate [1]	Nonmanufacturing Number (1,000)	Nonmanufacturing Rate [1]	Dis- abling injuries [2] (mil.)	Year and industry group	Deaths, 2004 Number	Rate [1]	Dis- abling injuries 2004 [2] (1,000)
1970 . . .	1.7	9	12.1	21	2.2	**Total, 2004** [3]	**4,952**	**3.5**	**3,700**
1975 . . .	1.6	9	11.4	17	2.2	Agriculture [4]	642	29.2	90
1980 . . .	1.7	8	11.5	15	2.2	Mining [5]	152	28.3	20
1985 . . .	1.2	6	10.3	12	2.0	Construction	1,194	11.6	460
1990 . . .	1.0	5	9.1	9	3.9	Manufacturing	418	2.5	490
1995 . . .	0.6	3	4.4	4	3.6	Wholesale trade	186	4.1	130
1996 . . .	0.7	3	4.4	4	3.9	Retail trade	187	1.2	450
1997 . . .	0.7	3	4.5	4	3.8	Transportation and warehousing	770	16.5	270
1998 . . .	0.6	3	4.5	4	3.8	Utilities	51	6.1	20
1999 . . .	0.6	3	4.6	4	3.8	Information	49	1.5	50
2000 . . .	0.6	3	4.4	4	3.9	Financial activities [6]	68	0.7	90
2001 . . .	0.5	3	4.5	4	3.9	Professional & business services [6] . . .	398	2.9	200
2002 . . .	0.5	3	4.2	3	3.7	Educational & health services	124	0.7	510
2003 . . .	0.4	2	4.3	4	3.4	Leisure & hospitality [6]	143	1.3	230
2004 . . .	0.4	3	4.5	4	3.7	Other services [7]	142	2.1	140
						Government	427	2.0	550

[1] Per 100,000 workers. [2] Disabling injury defined as one which results in death, some degree of physical impairment, or renders the person unable to perform regular activities for a full day beyond the day of the injury. Due to change in methodology, data beginning 1990 not comparable with prior years. [3] Includes deaths where industry is not known. [4] Includes forestry, fishing, and hunting. [5] Includes oil and gas extraction. [6] For composition of industry, see Table 617. [7] Excludes public service administration.
Source: National Safety Council, Itasca, IL, *Accident Facts*, annual through 1998 edition; thereafter, *Injury Facts*, annual (copyright).

Table 639. **Worker Deaths, Injuries, and Production Time Lost: 1995 to 2004**

[45.7 represents 45,700. Data may not agree with Table 638 because data here are not revised]

Item	Deaths 1,000) 1995	2000	2004	Disabling injuries [1] (mil.) 1995	2000	2004	Production time lost (mil. days) In the current year 1995	2000	2004	In future years [2] 1995	2000	2004
All accidents	**45.7**	**47.0**	**49.1**	**9.9**	**10.5**	**10.5**	**225**	**240**	**245**	**455**	**460**	**485**
On the job	5.3	5.2	5.0	3.6	3.9	3.7	75	80	80	65	60	65
Off the job	40.4	41.8	44.1	6.3	6.6	6.8	150	160	165	390	400	420
Motor vehicle	22.9	22.8	23.9	1.2	1.2	1.3	(NA)	(NA)	(NA)	(NA)	(NA)	(NA)
Public nonmotor vehicle .	7.5	8.3	7.6	2.3	2.8	2.5	(NA)	(NA)	(NA)	(NA)	(NA)	(NA)
Home	10.0	10.7	12.6	2.8	2.6	3.0	(NA)	(NA)	(NA)	(NA)	(NA)	(NA)

NA Not available. [1] See footnote 2, Table 638 for a definition of disabling injuries. [2] Based on an average of 5,850 days lost in future years per fatality and 565 days lost in future years per permanent injury.
Source: National Safety Council, Itasca, IL, *Accident Facts*, annual through 1998 edition; thereafter, *Injury Facts*, annual (copyright).

Table 640. **Industries With the Highest Total Case Incidence Rates for Nonfatal Injuries and Illnesses: 2004**

[Rates per 100 full-time employees. Rates refer to any Occupational Safety and Health Administration recordable occupational injury or illness, whether or not it resulted in days away from work, job transfer, or restriction. Incidence rates were calculated as: Number of injuries and illnesses divided by total hours worked by all employees during the year multiplied by 200,000 as base for 100 full-time equivalent workers (working 40 hours per week, 50 weeks per year)]

Industry	2002 NAICS [1] code	Rate	Industry	2002 NAICS [1] code	Rate
Private industry [2]	**(X)**	**4.8**	Couriers	4921	13.1
Iron foundries	331511	17.0	Copper rolling, drawing, and extruding	331421	13.0
Steel foundries (except investment)	331513	17.0	Travel trailer and camper mfg	336214	12.6
Hog and pig farming [2]	1122	16.9	Truck trailer manufacturing	336212	12.4
Light truck and utility vehicle mfg	336112	16.3	Iron and steel pipe and tube mfg		
Manufactured home (mobile home) mfg. . . .	321991	15.4	from purchased steel	33121	12.1
Truss manufacturing	321214	14.3	Motor vehicle metal stamping	33637	12.1
Amusement parks and arcades	7131	14.1	Boat building	336612	11.9
Motor vehicle air-conditioning mfg	336391	13.9	Other concrete product manufacturing.	32739	11.7
Ship building and repairing	336611	13.5	Sugarcane mills	311311	11.6
Animal (except poultry) slaughtering	311611	13.3	Motor vehicle body manufacturing	336211	11.6
Aluminum foundries (except die-casting) . . .	331524	13.2	Fluid power cylinder and actuator mfg.	333995	11.5
Cut stock, resawing lumber, and planing . . .	321912	13.1	Iron and steel forging.	332111	11.3

X Not applicable. [1] Based on the North American Industry Classification System, 2002 (NAICS). See text, this section. [2] Excludes farms with fewer than 11 employees.
Source: U.S. Bureau of Labor Statistics, *Workplace Injuries and Illnesses in 2004*. See Internet site <http://www.bls.gov/iif/>.

Table 641. Nonfatal Occupational Injury and Illness Incidence Rates: 2004

[Rates per 100 full-time employees. Except as noted, data refer to any Occupational Safety and Health Administration (OSHA) recordable occupational injury or illness, whether or not it resulted in days away from work, job transfer, or restriction. Incidence rates were calculated as: Number of injuries and illnesses divided by total hours worked by all employees during the year multiplied by 200,000 as base for 100 full-time equivalent workers (working 40 hours per week, 50 weeks per year)]

Industry	2002 NAICS code [1]	Rate	Industry	2002 NAICS code [1]	Rate
Private industry [2]	(X)	4.8	General merchandise stores	452	7.0
Agriculture, forestry, fishing			Miscellaneous store retailers	453	3.2
hunting [2]	11	6.4	**Transportation and warehousing [4, 5]**	48-49	7.3
Crop production [2]	111	5.6	Air transportation	481	10.1
Mining [3]	21	3.8	Truck transportation	484	6.1
Construction	23	6.4	Support activities for transportation	488	5.3
Construction of buildings	236	5.6	Couriers and messengers	492	12.4
Heavy and civil engineering			Warehousing and storage	493	9.3
construction	237	5.9	**Utilities**	22	5.2
Specialty trade contractors	238	6.8	**Information**	51	2.0
Manufacturing [4]	31-33	6.6	Telecommunications	517	2.2
Food manufacturing	311	8.2	**Finance and insurance [4]**	52	0.9
Wood product manufacturing	321	10.0	Credit intermediation and related		
Paper manufacturing	322	4.9	activities	522	1.0
Printing and related support activities	323	4.5	Insurance carriers and related activities	524	1.1
Chemical manufacturing	325	3.5	**Real estate and rental and leasing**	53	3.7
Plastics and rubber products mfg	326	7.7	Real estate	531	3.3
Nonmetallic mineral product mfg	327	8.0	Rental and leasing services	532	4.7
Primary metal manufacturing	331	10.0	Professional, scientific, and technical		
Fabricated metal product mfg	332	8.0	services	54	1.3
Machinery manufacturing	333	6.7	**Management of companies and**		
Computer and electronic product mfg	334	2.3	**enterprises**	55	2.7
Electrical equipment, appliance, and			**Administrative and support and**		
component manufacturing	335	5.5	**waste management and**		
Transportation equipment			**remediation services**	56	3.7
manufacturing	336	8.5	Administrative and support services	561	3.4
Furniture and related product mfg.	337	8.3	Waste management and remediation		
Miscellaneous manufacturing	339	4.5	services	562	7.6
Wholesale trade [4]	42	4.5	**Educational services**	61	2.5
Merchant wholesalers, durable goods	423	4.1	Health care and social assistance	62	6.2
Merchant wholesalers, nondurable			Ambulatory health care services	621	3.3
goods	424	5.6	Hospitals	622	8.3
Retail trade [4]	44-45	5.3	Nursing and residential care facilities	623	9.7
Motor vehicle and parts dealers	441	5.1	Social assistance	624	3.9
Furniture and home furnishings stores	442	5.7	**Arts, entertainment, and recreation**	71	5.9
Building material and garden equip.			Amusement, gambling, and recreation		
and supplies dealers	444	8.1	industries	713	6.0
Food and beverage stores	445	6.4	**Accommodation and food services**	72	4.5
Gasoline stations	447	3.4	Accommodation	721	5.8
Clothing and clothing accessories			Food services and drinking places	722	4.2
stores	448	2.6	**Other services, except public admin**	81	3.2

X Not applicable.   [1] North American Industry Classification System, 2002; see text, this section.   [2] Excludes farms with fewer than 11 employees.   [3] Data for mining operators in coal, metal, and nonmetal mining are provided to BLS by the Mine Safety and Health Administration (MHSA), U.S. Department of Labor. Independent mining contractors are excluded. Data provided by MSHA do not reflect 2002 OSHA recordkeeping requirements; therefore, estimates for these industries are not comparable with estimates for other industries.   [4] Includes other industries, not shown separately.   [5] Data for employers in railroad transportation are provided to BLS by the Federal Railroad Administration, U.S. Department of Transportation.

Source: U.S. Bureau of Labor Statistics, *Workplace Injuries and Illnesses in 2004.* See Internet site <http://www.bls.gov/iif/>

Table 642. Fatal Work Injuries by Event or Exposure: 2004

Cause	Number of fatalities	Percent distri- bution	Cause	Number of fatalities	Percent distri- bution
Total	**5,764**	**100**	Contacts with objects and equipment [1]	1,009	18
			Struck by object [1]	602	10
Transportation accidents [1]	2,490	43	Struck by falling objects	373	6
Highway accidents [1]	1,398	24	Struck by flying object [1]	42	1
Collision between vehicles,			Caught in or compressed by—		
mobile equipment	702	12	equipment or objects	269	5
Noncollision accidents	323	6	Caught in or crushed in		
Nonhighway accident (farm,			collapsing materials	117	2
industrial premises)	338	6	Falls	822	14
Aircraft accidents	231	4	Exposure to harmful substances or		
Workers struck by a vehicle	378	7	environments [1]	464	8
Water vehicle accidents	91	2	Contact with electric current	254	4
Railway accidents	50	1	Exposure to caustic, noxious		
			or allergenic substances	116	2
Assaults and violent acts [1]	809	14	Oxygen deficiency	65	1
Homicides [1]	559	10	Drowning, submersion	51	1
Shooting	421	7	Fires and explosions	159	3
Stabbing	68	1	Other events and exposures	11	(Z)
Self-inflicted injury	206	4			

Z Less than 0.5 percent.   [1] Includes other causes, not shown separately.

Source: U.S. Bureau of Labor Statistics, Census of Fatal Occupational Injuries (CFOI)—Current and Revised Data. See Internet site <http://www.bls.gov/iif/oshcfoi1.htm>.

Labor Force, Employment, and Earnings   421

Table 643. **Fatal Occupational Injuries by Industry and Event or Exposure: 2004**

[For the 50 states and DC. Based on the Census of Fatal Occupational Injuries. For details, see source. Due to methodological differences, data differ from National Safety Council data]

Industry	2002 NAICS [1] code	Fatalities [2]	Event or exposure—Percent distribution					Rate [5]
			Transportation incidents	Assaults/violent acts	Contact with objects [3]	Falls	Exposure [4]	
Total.	(X)	**5,764**	**43**	**14**	**18**	**14**	**8**	**4**
Private industry	(X)	5,229	42	14	19	15	8	4
Goods producing	(X)	2,518	33	5	27	21	10	9
Natural resources and mining	11,21	821	49	6	32	5	5	30
Construction	23	1,234	23	3	22	36	14	12
Manufacturing.	31-33	463	31	9	35	10	8	3
Service providing	(X)	2,711	50	22	10	9	7	3
Trade, transportation, and utilities.	42, 44-45,48-49, 22	1,473	59	18	10	6	4	6
Wholesale trade	42	205	58	9	17	6	3	5
Retail trade.	44-45	377	28	50	6	10	4	2
Transportation and warehousing	48-49	840	76	7	10	4	3	18
Utilities	22	51	25	–	8	18	27	6
Information.	51	55	67	11	–	5	15	2
Financial activities	52, 53	116	32	41	3	13	6	1
Finance and insurance	52	46	35	48	–	9	–	1
Real estate and renting and leasing	53	70	30	37	6	16	7	2
Professional and business services [6]	54, 55, 56	452	42	12	16	17	12	3
Professional and technical services . .	54	77	64	16	–	10	5	1
Administration and waste management service.	56	373	38	11	19	18	14	7
Education and health services	61, 62	157	59	22	2	9	8	1
Education services	61	44	73	16	–	11	–	1
Health and social assistance	62	113	53	24	3	8	11	1
Leisure and hospitality	71, 72	247	29	45	9	9	6	2
Arts, entertainment, and recreation	71	99	48	24	11	11	5	4
Accommodation and food services . .	72	148	16	59	7	8	7	2
Other	81	207	25	30	17	11	12	3
Government	92	535	57	19	7	7	6	3

– No data reported or data do not meet publication standards. X Not applicable. [1] North American Industry Classification System, 2002. See text, this section. [2] Includes 4 fatalities in service-producing private industries in 2004 for which there was insufficient information to determine industry classification. Includes fatalities caused by other events and exposures, not shown separately. [3] Includes equipment. [4] Exposure to harmful substances or environments. [5] Rate per 100,000 employed civilians 16 years old and over. [6] Includes other industries, not shown separately.

Source: U.S. Bureau of Labor Statistics, "Census of Fatal Occupational Injuries (CFOI)—Current and Revised Data." See Internet site <http://www.bls.gov/iif/oshcfoi1.htm>.

Table 644. **Work Stoppages: 1960 to 2005**

[896 represents 896,000. Excludes work stoppages involving fewer than 1,000 workers and lasting less than 1 day. Information is based on reports of labor disputes appearing in daily newspapers, trade journals, and other public sources. The parties to the disputes are contacted by telephone, when necessary, to clarify details of the stoppages]

Year	Number of stoppages [1]	Workers involved [2] (1,000)	Days idle		Year	Number of stoppages [1]	Workers involved [2] (1,000)	Days idle	
			Number [3] (1,000)	Percent estimated working time [4]				Number [3] (1,000)	Percent estimated working time [4]
1960	222	896	13,260	0.09	1988	40	118	[5]4,381	0.02
1965	268	999	15,140	0.10	1989	51	452	16,996	0.07
1970	381	2,468	52,761	0.29	1990	44	185	5,926	0.02
1973	317	1,400	16,260	0.08	1991	40	392	4,584	0.02
1974	424	1,796	31,809	0.16	1992	35	364	3,989	0.01
1975	235	965	17,563	0.09	1993	35	182	3,981	0.01
1976	231	1,519	23,962	0.12	1994	45	322	5,021	0.02
1977	298	1,212	21,258	0.10	1995	31	192	5,771	0.02
1978	219	1,006	23,774	0.11	1996	37	273	4,889	0.02
1979	235	1,021	20,409	0.09	1997	29	339	4,497	0.01
1980	187	795	20,844	0.09	1998	34	387	5,116	0.02
1981	145	729	16,908	0.07	1999	17	73	1,996	0.01
1982	96	656	9,061	0.04	2000	39	394	20,419	0.06
1983	81	909	17,461	0.08	2001	29	99	1,151	(Z)
1984	62	376	8,499	0.04	2002	19	46	660	(Z)
1985	54	324	7,079	0.03	2003	14	129	4,091	0.01
1986	69	533	11,861	0.05	2004	17	171	3,344	0.01
1987	46	174	[5]4,481	0.02	2005	22	100	1,736	0.01

Z Less than 0.005 percent. [1] Beginning in year indicated. [2] Workers counted more than once if involved in more than one stoppage during the year. [3] Resulting from all stoppages in effect in a year, including those that began in an earlier year. [4] Agricultural and government employees are included in the total working time; private household and forestry and fishery employees are excluded. [5] Revised since originally published.

Source: U.S. Bureau of Labor Statistics, *Major Work Stoppages in 2005*, News, USDL 06-363, March 2, 2006. See Internet site <http://www.bls.gov/cba/>.

Table 645. **Labor Union Membership by Sector: 1983 to 2005**

[See headnote, Table 647. **(17,717.4 represents 17,717,400)**]

Sector	1983	1985	1990	1995	2000	2002	2003	2004	2005
TOTAL (1,000)									
Wage and salary workers:									
Union members	17,717.4	16,996.1	16,739.8	16,359.6	16,258.2	15,978.7	15,776.0	15,471.6	15,685.4
Covered by unions	20,532.1	19,358.1	19,057.8	18,346.3	17,944.1	17,501.6	17,448.4	17,087.3	17,223.4
Public sector workers:									
Union members.	5,737.2	5,743.1	6,485.0	6,927.4	7,110.5	7,327.2	7,324.1	7,267.1	7,430.4
Covered by unions. . . .	7,112.2	6,920.6	7,691.4	7,986.6	7,975.6	8,131.9	8,184.7	8,131.1	8,261.8
Private sector workers:									
Union members.	11,980.2	11,253.0	10,254.8	9,432.1	9,147.7	8,651.5	8,451.8	8,204.5	8,255.0
Covered by unions. . . .	13,419.9	12,437.5	11,366.4	10,359.8	9,968.5	9,369.7	9,263.7	8,956.2	8,961.6
PERCENT									
Wage and salary workers:									
Union members	20.1	18.0	16.1	14.9	13.5	13.3	12.9	12.5	12.5
Covered by unions	23.3	20.5	18.3	16.7	14.9	14.6	14.3	13.8	13.7
Public sector workers:									
Union members.	36.7	35.7	36.5	37.7	37.5	37.8	37.2	36.4	36.5
Covered by unions. . . .	45.5	43.1	43.3	43.5	42.0	41.9	41.5	40.7	40.5
Private sector workers:									
Union members.	16.5	14.3	11.9	10.3	9.0	8.6	8.2	7.9	7.8
Covered by unions. . . .	18.5	15.9	13.2	11.3	9.8	9.3	9.0	8.6	8.5

Source: The Bureau of National Affairs, Inc., Washington, DC, *Union Membership and Earnings Data Book: Compilations from the Current Population Survey (2006 edition)*, (copyright by BNA PLUS); authored by Barry Hirsch of Trinity University, San Antonio, TX, and David Macpherson of Florida State University. Internet sites <http://www.bna.com/bnaplus/labor/laborrpts.html> and <http://www.unionstats.com>.

Table 646. **Union Members by Selected Characteristics: 2005**

[**Annual averages of monthly data (125,889 represents 125,889,000).** Covers employed wage and salary workers 16 years old and over. Excludes self-employed workers whose businesses are incorporated although they technically qualify as wage and salary workers. Based on Current Population Survey, see text, Section 1, and Appendix III]

Characteristic	Employed wage and salary workers			Median usual weekly earnings [3] (dol.)			
	Total (1,000)	Percent		Total	Union members [1]	Repre-sented by unions [2]	Not repre-sented by unions
		Union members [1]	Repre-sented by unions [2]				
Total [4]	**125,889**	**12.5**	**13.7**	**651**	**801**	**795**	**622**
16 to 24 years old	19,283	4.6	5.3	397	502	502	392
25 to 34 years old	28,450	10.7	11.8	610	735	729	595
35 to 44 years old	30,654	13.7	14.9	731	844	837	708
45 to 54 years old	28,714	16.5	18.0	748	854	851	722
55 to 64 years old	15,158	16.5	18.0	742	852	851	716
65 years and over	3,631	8.9	10.1	569	679	683	551
Men	65,466	13.5	14.7	722	857	855	692
Women	60,423	11.3	12.6	585	731	726	559
White [5]	**102,967**	**12.2**	**13.4**	**672**	**830**	**824**	**641**
Men	54,462	13.4	14.4	743	884	884	714
Women	48,505	10.8	12.2	596	749	743	576
Black [5]	**14,459**	**15.1**	**16.5**	**520**	**656**	**653**	**500**
Men	6,603	16.1	17.7	559	689	682	523
Women	7,857	14.2	15.6	499	632	630	478
Asian [5]	**5,479**	**11.2**	**12.2**	**753**	**809**	**805**	**744**
Men	2,881	10.9	11.7	825	819	817	827
Women	2,598	11.5	12.7	665	789	785	643
Hispanic [6]	**17,191**	**10.4**	**11.5**	**471**	**673**	**661**	**449**
Men	10,324	10.6	11.5	489	713	704	473
Women	6,866	10.2	11.6	429	609	606	414
Private sector industry.	105,508	7.8	8.5	625	757	752	615
Agriculture and related industries	1,021	2.7	3.0	402	(B)	(B)	402
Mining.	600	8.0	9.5	885	(B)	989	870
Construction	8,053	13.1	13.8	619	933	926	590
Manufacturing	15,518	13.0	13.7	676	722	719	667
Wholesale and retail trade	18,989	5.4	5.9	566	615	610	562
Transportation and utilities	5,212	24.0	25.1	726	864	860	676
Information	2,934	13.6	14.4	832	931	925	810
Financial activities [7]	8,619	2.3	2.8	741	698	696	743
Professional and business services [7] . . .	10,951	2.7	3.1	739	663	673	743
Education and health services [7]	17,357	8.3	9.4	627	731	736	617
Leisure and hospitality [7]	10,658	3.1	3.5	409	513	510	405
Other services	5,596	3.2	3.5	535	694	698	524
Public sector.	20,381	36.5	40.5	758	850	842	692

B Data not shown where base is less than 50,000.   [1] Members of a labor union or an employee association similar to a labor union.   [2] Members of a labor union or an employee association similar to a union as well as workers who report no union affiliation but whose jobs are covered by a union or an employee association contract.   [3] For full-time employed wage and salary workers.   [4] Includes races not shown separately. Also includes a small number of multiple jobholders whose full- and part-time status can not be determined for their principal job.   [5] For persons in this race group only. See footnote 3, Table 574.   [6] Persons of Hispanic or Latino ethnicity may be of any race.   [7] For composition of industries, see Table 611.

Source: U.S. Bureau of Labor Statistics, *Employment and Earnings*, January 2006. See Internet site <http://www.bls.gov/cps/home.htm>.

Labor Force, Employment, and Earnings   423

Table 647. Labor Union Membership by State: 1983 and 2005

[Annual averages of monthly figures (17,717.4 represents 17,717,400). For wage and salary workers in agriculture and non-agriculture. Data represent union members by place of residence. Based on the Current Population Survey and subject to sampling error. For methodological details, see source]

State	Union members (1,000) 1983	2005	Workers covered by unions (1,000) 1983	2005	Percent of workers — Union members 1983	2005	Covered by unions 1983	2005	Private sector union members 1983	2005
United States.	17,717.4	15,685.4	20,532.1	17,223.4	20.1	12.5	23.3	13.7	16.5	7.8
Alabama [1].	228.2	195.2	268.2	223.3	16.9	10.2	19.8	11.7	15.3	6.0
Alaska	41.7	62.6	49.2	66.2	24.9	22.8	29.3	24.1	17.3	13.1
Arizona [1]	125.0	144.7	156.4	181.5	11.4	6.1	14.3	7.7	8.6	3.9
Arkansas [1]	82.2	54.5	103.2	68.5	11.0	4.8	13.8	6.0	10.2	3.1
California	2,118.9	2,423.9	2,505.2	2,610.2	21.9	16.5	25.9	17.8	17.7	9.7
Colorado.	177.9	170.0	209.6	192.7	13.6	8.3	16.0	9.4	11.2	5.3
Connecticut.	314.0	246.7	345.1	262.8	22.7	15.9	25.0	17.0	16.7	7.6
Delaware	49.2	45.7	54.1	49.7	20.1	11.8	22.1	12.9	15.9	7.0
District of Columbia	52.4	29.3	69.4	33.3	19.5	11.3	25.9	12.8	15.2	7.6
Florida [1]	393.7	401.0	532.9	531.6	10.2	5.4	13.8	7.2	7.1	2.5
Georgia [1]	267.0	190.0	345.1	226.1	11.9	5.0	15.3	6.0	11.1	3.7
Hawaii	112.6	140.6	124.9	145.3	29.2	25.8	32.4	26.7	21.9	16.9
Idaho [1]	41.3	31.3	53.7	38.1	12.5	5.2	16.2	6.3	10.3	3.3
Illinois	1,063.8	926.8	1,205.1	964.6	24.2	16.9	27.4	17.6	21.5	11.8
Indiana.	503.3	345.7	544.5	367.8	24.9	12.4	27.0	13.2	25.0	10.0
Iowa [1]	185.9	157.1	231.3	185.4	17.2	11.5	21.5	13.5	14.6	7.3
Kansas [1]	125.2	85.2	170.4	115.1	13.7	7.0	18.7	9.5	12.2	5.1
Kentucky	223.7	164.0	259.8	183.9	17.9	9.7	20.8	10.8	18.2	7.6
Louisiana [1]	204.2	114.3	267.8	131.6	13.8	6.4	18.1	7.4	11.0	4.8
Maine.	88.0	69.0	100.4	78.8	21.0	11.9	24.0	13.6	14.2	5.6
Maryland	346.5	336.7	423.1	379.3	18.5	13.3	22.6	15.0	14.4	7.4
Massachusetts.	603.2	402.2	661.4	431.4	23.7	13.9	26.0	14.9	17.6	7.4
Michigan.	1,005.4	880.1	1,084.6	916.4	30.4	20.5	32.8	21.4	25.3	14.4
Minnesota	393.9	392.2	439.4	409.9	23.2	15.7	25.9	16.4	17.1	9.7
Mississippi [1]	79.4	77.2	99.7	105.3	9.9	7.1	12.5	9.7	9.0	5.1
Missouri	374.4	290.0	416.7	318.6	20.8	11.5	23.2	12.6	21.5	9.8
Montana	49.5	41.7	55.5	47.8	18.3	10.7	20.5	12.2	14.8	5.7
Nebraska [1]	80.6	69.3	94.8	78.5	13.6	8.3	16.0	9.5	9.7	4.5
Nevada [1]	90.0	145.3	106.7	158.3	22.4	13.8	26.6	15.1	19.6	12.0
New Hampshire	48.5	65.0	60.8	72.1	11.5	10.4	14.4	11.5	7.5	4.0
New Jersey	822.1	791.3	918.2	837.7	26.9	20.5	30.0	21.7	21.1	11.8
New Mexico	52.6	62.8	70.6	83.3	11.8	8.1	15.8	10.7	10.1	3.4
New York	2,155.6	2,089.7	2,385.9	2,201.2	32.5	26.1	36.0	27.5	24.0	16.1
North Carolina [1]	178.7	107.0	238.1	142.6	7.6	2.9	10.2	3.9	5.4	1.8
North Dakota [1]	28.4	21.0	35.1	26.4	13.2	7.3	16.3	9.2	9.5	3.6
Ohio	1,011.0	804.3	1,125.0	866.3	25.1	16.0	27.9	17.2	22.5	10.8
Oklahoma [2].	131.5	76.7	168.2	91.0	11.5	5.4	14.7	6.4	9.1	2.9
Oregon.	222.9	212.8	261.9	231.4	22.3	14.5	26.2	15.7	16.4	7.7
Pennsylvania	1,195.7	752.5	1,350.0	817.5	27.5	13.8	31.1	15.0	23.2	8.5
Rhode Island.	85.8	78.8	93.7	83.1	21.5	15.9	23.5	16.8	13.7	8.4
South Carolina [1]	69.6	40.0	100.6	57.9	5.9	2.3	8.6	3.3	3.9	1.1
South Dakota [1]	26.8	20.5	34.8	28.7	11.5	5.9	14.9	8.2	8.0	2.7
Tennessee [1]	252.4	128.1	300.9	155.5	15.1	5.4	18.0	6.6	12.4	3.3
Texas [1]	583.7	506.2	712.8	590.3	9.7	5.3	11.9	6.2	8.1	3.1
Utah [1]	81.6	50.5	100.9	63.2	15.2	4.9	18.9	6.1	11.3	2.7
Vermont.	25.9	31.1	31.5	37.3	12.6	10.8	15.3	13.0	6.7	5.1
Virginia [1]	268.3	164.6	346.1	210.5	11.7	4.8	15.1	6.2	10.2	3.4
Washington.	419.9	523.3	499.7	558.9	27.1	19.1	32.3	20.4	22.0	11.4
West Virginia	142.7	99.1	160.6	106.7	25.3	14.4	28.5	15.5	26.1	10.6
Wisconsin.	465.5	410.1	526.7	438.1	23.8	16.1	26.9	17.2	19.8	11.1
Wyoming [1]	27.1	18.0	31.8	21.6	13.9	7.9	16.2	9.5	10.4	5.6

[1] Right to work state.   [2] Passed right to work law in 2001.

Source: The Bureau of National Affairs, Inc., Washington, DC, *Union Membership and Earnings Data Book: Compilations from the Current Population Survey (2005 edition)*, (copyright by BNA PLUS); authored by Barry Hirsch of Trinity University, San Antonio, TX, and David Macpherson of Florida State University. Internet sites <http://www.bna.com/bnaplus/labor/laborrpts.html> and <http://www.unionstats.com>.

Section 13
Income, Expenditures, and Wealth

This section presents data on gross domestic product (GDP), gross national product (GNP), national and personal income, saving and investment, money income, poverty, and national and personal wealth. The data on income and expenditures measure two aspects of the U.S. economy. One aspect relates to the National Income and Product Accounts (NIPA), a summation reflecting the entire complex of the nation's economic income and output and the interaction of its major components; the other relates to the distribution of money income to families and individuals or consumer income. New information on personal income, alternative poverty definitions, wealth, and millionaires may be found in Tables 663 and 698–700.

The primary source for data on GDP, GNP, national and personal income, gross saving and investment, and fixed reproducible tangible wealth is the *Survey of Current Business*, published monthly by the Bureau of Economic Analysis (BEA). A comprehensive revision to the NIPA was released beginning in October 1999. Discussions of the revision appeared in the January, June, August, September, and the December 2003 issues of the *Survey of Current Business*. Summary historical estimates appeared in the February 2004 issue of the *Survey of Current Business*. Detailed historical data on the NIPA are available on an interactive Web site at <http://www.bea.doc.gov/bea/dn/nipaweb/index.asp>.

Sources of income distribution data are the decennial censuses of population and the Current Population Survey (CPS), both products of the U.S. Census Bureau (see text, Section 1 and Section 4). Annual data on income of families, individuals, and households are presented in *Current Population Reports, Consumer Income*, P60 Series, in print, and many data series found on the Census Web site at <http://www.census.gov/hhes/www/income.html>. Data on the household

sector's saving and assets are published by the Board of Governors of the Federal Reserve System in the quarterly *Flow of Funds Accounts*. The Board also periodically conducts the *Survey of Consumer Finances*, which presents financial information on family assets and net worth. Detailed information on personal wealth is published periodically by the Internal Revenue Service (IRS) in *SOI Bulletin*.

National income and product—Gross domestic product is the total output of goods and services produced by labor and property located in the United States, valued at market prices. GDP can be viewed in terms of the expenditure categories that comprise its major components purchases of goods and services by consumers and government, gross private domestic investment, and net exports of goods and services. The goods and services included are largely those bought for final use (excluding illegal transactions) in the market economy. A number of inclusions, however, represent imputed values, the most important of which is rental value of owner-occupied housing. GDP, in this broad context, measures the output attributable to the factors of production located in the United States. Gross state product (GSP) is the gross market value of the goods and services attributable to labor and property located in a state. It is the state counterpart of the nation's gross domestic product.

In January 1996, BEA replaced its fixed weighted index as the featured measure of real GDP with an index based on chain-type annual weights. Changes in this measure of real output and prices are calculated as the average of changes based on weights for the current and preceding years. (Components of real output are weighted by price, and components of prices are weighted by output.) These annual changes are "chained" (multiplied) together to form a time series that allows for the effects of changes in relative prices and changes in the composition of output over time. Quarterly and monthly changes are also based on annual weights. The new output indexes are expressed as 2000 = 100, and for recent years, in 2000 dollars; the new price indexes are based to 2000 = 100. For more information on chain-dollar indexes, see the article on this subject in the November 2003 issue of the *Survey of Current Business.*

Chained (2000) dollar estimates of most components of GDP are not published for periods prior to 1990, because during periods far from the base period, the levels of the components may provide misleading information about their contributions to an aggregate. Values are published in index form (2000 = 100) for 1929 to the present to allow users to calculate the percent changes for all components, changes that are accurate for all periods.

Gross national product measures the output attributable to all labor and property supplied by United States residents. GNP differs from "national income" mainly in that GNP includes allowances for depreciation consumption of fixed capital.

National Income includes all net incomes (net of CFC) earned in production. National income is the sum of compensation of employees, proprietors' income with inventory valuation adjustment (IVA) and capital consumption adjustment (CCAdj), rental income of persons with CCAdj, corporate profits with IVA and CCAdj, net interest and miscellaneous payments, taxes on production and imports, business current transfer payments, current surplus of government enterprises, less subsidies.

Capital consumption adjustment for corporations and for nonfarm sole proprietorships and partnerships is the difference between capital consumption based on income tax returns and capital consumption measured using empirical evidence on prices of used equipment and structures in resale markets, which have shown that depreciation for most types of assets approximates a geometric pattern. The tax return data are valued at historical costs and reflect changes over time in service lives and depreciation patterns as

permitted by tax regulations. *Inventory valuation adjustment* represents the difference between the book value of inventories used up in production and the cost of replacing them.

Personal income is the current income received by persons from all sources minus their personal contributions for government social insurance. Classified as "persons" are individuals (including owners of unincorporated firms), non-profit institutions that primarily serve individuals, private trust funds, and private noninsured welfare funds. Personal income includes personal current transfer receipts (payments not resulting from current production) from government and business such as social security benefits, public assistance, etc., but excludes transfers among persons. Also included are certain nonmonetary types of income chiefly, estimated net rental value to owner-occupants of their homes and the value of services furnished without payment by financial intermediaries. Capital gains (net losses) are excluded.

Disposable personal income is personal income less personal current taxes. It is the income available to persons for spending or saving. Personal current taxes are tax payments (net of refunds) by persons (except personal contributions for government social insurance) that are not chargeable to business expense and certain personal payments to general government that are treated like taxes. Personal taxes include income, estate and gift, and personal property taxes and motor vehicle licenses. Nontax payments include passport fees, fines and forfeitures, and donations.

Gross domestic product by industry—The BEA also prepares estimates of value added by industry. *Value added* is a measure of the contribution of each private industry and of government to the nation's GDP. It is defined as an industry's gross output (which consists of sales or receipts and other operating income, commodity taxes, and inventory change) minus its intermediate inputs (which consists of energy, raw materials, semi-finished goods, and services that are purchased from domestic industries or from foreign sources). These estimates of value added are produced for 61 private industries and for 4 government classifications—federal general government and government enterprises and state and local general government and government enterprises.

The estimates by industry are available in current dollars and are derived from the estimates of gross domestic income, which consists of three components—the compensation of employees, gross operating surplus, and taxes on production and imports, less subsidies. Real, or inflation-adjusted, estimates are also prepared.

Regional Economic Accounts—These accounts consist of estimates of state and local area personal income and of gross state product and are consistent with estimates of personal income and gross domestic product in the Bureau's national economic accounts. BEA's estimates of state and local area personal income provide a framework for analyzing individual state and local economies, and they show how the economies compare with each other. The *personal income* of a state and/or local area is the income received by, or on behalf of, the residents of that state or area. Estimates of labor and proprietors' earnings by place of work indicate the economic activity of business and government within that area, and estimates of personal income by place of residence indicate the income within the area that is available for spending. BEA prepares estimates for states, counties, metropolitan areas, and BEA economic areas.

Gross state product estimates measure the value added to the nation's production by the labor and property in each state. GSP is often considered the state counterpart of the nation's GDP. The GSP estimates provide the basis for analyzing the regional impacts of national economic trends. GSP is measured as the sum of the distributions by industry and state of the components of gross domestic income; that is, the sum of the costs incurred and incomes earned in the production of GDP. The GSP estimates are presented in current dollars and in real (chained dollars) for 63 industries.

Consumer Expenditure Survey—The Consumer Expenditure Survey program was begun in late 1979. The principal objective of the survey is to collect current consumer expenditure data, which provide a continuous flow of data on the buying habits of American consumers. The data are necessary for future revisions of the Consumer Price Index.

The survey conducted by the Census Bureau for the Bureau of Labor Statistics consists of two components: (1) an interview panel survey in which the expenditures of consumer units are obtained in five interviews conducted every 3 months, and (2) a diary or recordkeeping survey completed by participating households for two consecutive 1-week periods.

Each component of the survey queries an independent sample of consumer units representative of the U.S. total population. Over 52 weeks of the year, 5,000 consumer units are sampled for the diary survey. Each consumer unit keeps a diary for two 1-week periods yielding approximately 10,000 diaries a year. The interview sample is selected on a rotating panel basis, targeted at 5,000 consumer units per quarter. Data are collected in 88 urban and 16 rural areas of the country that are representative of the U.S. total population. The survey includes students in student housing. Data from the two surveys are combined; integration is necessary to permit analysis of total family expenditures because neither the diary nor quarterly interview survey was designed to collect a complete account of consumer spending.

Distribution of money income to families and individuals—Money income statistics are based on data collected in various field surveys of income conducted since 1936. Since 1947, the Census Bureau has collected the data on an annual basis and published them in *Current Population Reports*, P60 Series. In each of the surveys, field representatives interview samples of the population with respect to income received during the previous year. *Money income* as defined by the Census Bureau differs from the BEA concept of "personal income." Data on consumer income collected in the CPS by

Income, Expenditures, and Wealth   427

the Census Bureau cover money income received (exclusive of certain money receipts such as capital gains) before payments for personal income taxes, social security, union dues, medicare deductions, etc. Therefore, money income does not reflect the fact that some families receive part of their income in the form of noncash benefits (see Section 11) such as food stamps, health benefits, and subsidized housing; that some farm families receive noncash benefits in the form of rent-free housing and goods produced and consumed on the farm; or that noncash benefits are also received by some nonfarm residents which often take the form of the use of business transportation and facilities, full or partial payments by business for retirement programs, medical and educational expenses, etc. These elements should be considered when comparing income levels. None of the aggregate income concepts (GDP, national income, or personal income) is exactly comparable with money income, although personal income is the closest.

Poverty—Families and unrelated individuals are classified as being above or below the poverty level using the poverty index originated at the Social Security Administration in 1964 and revised by Federal Interagency Committees in 1969 and 1980.

The poverty index is based solely on money income and does not reflect the fact that many low-income persons receive noncash benefits such as food stamps, medicaid, and public housing. The index is based on the Department of Agriculture's 1961 Economy Food Plan and reflects the different consumption

requirements of families based on their size and composition. The poverty thresholds are updated every year to reflect changes in the Consumer Price Index. The following technical changes to the thresholds were made in 1981: (1) distinctions based on sex of householder have been eliminated, (2) separate thresholds for farm families have been dropped, and (3) the matrix has been expanded to families of nine or more persons from the old cutoff of seven or more persons. These changes have been incorporated in the calculation of poverty data beginning with 1981. Besides the Census Bureau Web site at <http://www.census.gov/hhes/www /poverty.html>, information on poverty guidelines and research may be found at the U.S. Department of Human Services Web site at <http://aspe.hhs.gov /poverty/poverty.shtml>.

In the recent past, the Census Bureau has published a number of technical papers that presented experimental poverty estimates based on income definitions that counted the value of selected government noncash benefits. The Census Bureau has also published annual reports on aftertax income. In addition, in July 1999, the Census Bureau released a report (P60-205) that showed the effect of using experimental poverty following the recommendations of a National Academy of Sciences panel on redefining our nation's poverty measure and recently published a report entitled *Alternative Poverty Estimates in the United States: 2004.*

Statistical reliability—For a discussion of statistical collection and estimation, sampling procedures, and measures of statistical reliability pertaining to Census Bureau data, see Appendix III.

Table 648. Gross Domestic Product in Current and Real (2000) Dollars: 1960 to 2005

[In billions of dollars (526.4 represents $526,400,000,000). For explanation of gross domestic product and chained dollars, see text, this section]

Item	1960	1970	1980	1990	1993	1994	1995	1996	1997	1998	1999	2000	2001	2002	2003	2004	2005
CURRENT DOLLARS																	
Gross domestic product	526.4	1,038.5	2,789.5	5,803.1	6,657.4	7,072.2	7,397.7	7,816.9	8,304.3	8,747.0	9,268.4	9,817.0	10,128.0	10,469.6	10,971.2	11,734.3	12,487.1
Personal consumption expenditures	331.7	648.5	1,757.1	3,839.9	4,477.9	4,743.3	4,975.8	5,256.8	5,547.4	5,879.5	6,282.5	6,739.4	7,055.0	7,350.7	7,709.9	8,214.3	8,745.7
Durable goods	43.3	85.0	214.2	474.2	526.7	582.2	611.6	652.6	692.7	750.2	817.6	863.3	883.7	923.9	950.1	987.8	1,026.5
Nondurable goods	152.8	272.0	696.1	1,249.9	1,379.4	1,437.2	1,485.1	1,555.5	1,619.0	1,683.6	1,804.8	1,947.2	2,017.1	2,079.6	2,189.0	2,368.3	2,564.4
Services	135.6	291.5	846.9	2,115.9	2,571.8	2,723.9	2,879.1	3,048.7	3,235.8	3,445.7	3,660.0	3,928.8	4,154.3	4,347.2	4,570.8	4,858.2	5,154.9
Gross private domestic investment	78.9	152.4	479.3	861.0	953.4	1,097.1	1,144.0	1,240.3	1,389.8	1,509.1	1,625.7	1,735.5	1,614.3	1,582.1	1,670.4	1,928.1	2,105.0
Fixed investment	75.7	150.4	485.6	846.4	932.5	1,033.3	1,112.9	1,209.5	1,317.8	1,438.4	1,558.8	1,679.0	1,646.1	1,570.2	1,654.9	1,872.6	2,086.1
Change in business inventories	3.2	2.0	-6.3	14.5	20.8	63.8	31.1	30.8	72.0	70.8	66.9	56.5	-31.7	11.9	15.4	55.4	18.9
Net exports of goods and services	4.2	4.0	-13.1	-78.0	-65.0	-93.6	-91.4	-96.2	-101.6	-159.9	-260.5	-379.5	-367.0	-424.4	-500.9	-624.0	-726.5
Exports	27.0	59.7	280.8	552.4	655.8	720.9	812.2	868.6	955.3	955.9	991.2	1,096.3	1,032.8	1,005.9	1,045.6	1,173.8	1,301.2
Imports	22.8	55.8	293.8	630.3	720.9	814.5	903.6	964.8	1,056.9	1,115.9	1,251.7	1,475.8	1,399.8	1,430.3	1,546.5	1,797.8	2,027.7
Government consumption expenditures and gross investment	111.6	233.8	566.2	1,180.2	1,291.2	1,325.5	1,369.2	1,416.0	1,468.7	1,518.3	1,620.8	1,721.6	1,825.6	1,961.1	2,091.9	2,215.9	2,362.9
Federal	64.1	113.5	243.8	508.3	525.2	519.1	519.2	527.4	530.9	530.4	555.8	578.8	612.9	679.7	754.8	827.6	877.7
National defense	53.4	87.6	168.0	374.0	362.9	353.7	348.7	354.6	349.6	345.7	360.6	370.3	392.6	437.1	496.7	552.7	587.1
Nondefense	10.7	25.8	75.8	134.3	162.4	165.5	170.5	172.8	181.3	184.7	195.2	208.5	220.3	242.5	258.2	274.9	290.6
State and local	47.5	120.3	322.4	671.9	766.0	806.3	850.0	888.6	937.8	987.9	1,065.0	1,142.8	1,212.8	1,281.5	1,337.1	1,388.3	1,485.2
CHAINED (2000) DOLLARS																	
Gross domestic product	2,501.8	3,771.9	5,161.7	7,112.5	7,532.7	7,835.5	8,031.7	8,328.9	8,703.5	9,066.9	9,470.3	9,817.0	9,890.7	10,048.8	10,320.6	10,755.7	11,134.8
Personal consumption expenditures	1,597.4	2,451.9	3,374.1	4,770.3	5,099.8	5,290.7	5,433.5	5,619.4	5,831.8	6,125.8	6,438.6	6,739.4	6,910.4	7,099.3	7,306.6	7,588.6	7,856.9
Durable goods	(NA)	(NA)	(NA)	453.5	488.4	529.4	552.6	595.9	646.9	720.4	804.6	863.3	900.7	964.8	1,028.5	1,089.9	1,138.4
Nondurable goods	(NA)	(NA)	(NA)	1,484.0	1,550.4	1,603.9	1,638.6	1,680.4	1,725.3	1,794.4	1,876.6	1,947.2	1,986.7	2,037.1	2,101.8	2,200.4	2,297.9
Services	(NA)	(NA)	(NA)	2,851.7	3,085.7	3,176.6	3,259.9	3,356.0	3,468.0	3,615.0	3,758.0	3,928.8	4,023.2	4,100.4	4,183.9	4,310.9	4,436.4
Gross private domestic investment	266.6	427.1	645.3	895.1	968.3	1,099.6	1,134.0	1,234.3	1,387.7	1,524.1	1,642.6	1,735.5	1,598.4	1,557.1	1,617.4	1,809.8	1,919.8
Fixed investment	(NA)	(NA)	(NA)	886.6	953.5	1,042.3	1,109.6	1,209.2	1,320.6	1,455.0	1,576.3	1,679.0	1,629.4	1,544.6	1,600.0	1,755.1	1,897.1
Change in business inventories	(NA)	(NA)	(NA)	15.4	20.6	63.6	29.9	28.7	71.2	72.6	68.9	56.5	-31.7	12.5	15.5	52.0	20.3
Net exports of goods and services	(NA)	(NA)	(NA)	-54.7	-52.1	-79.4	-71.0	-79.6	-104.6	-203.7	-296.2	-379.5	-399.1	-471.3	-521.4	-601.3	-633.1
Exports	90.6	161.4	323.5	552.5	650.0	706.5	778.2	843.4	943.7	966.5	1,008.2	1,096.3	1,036.7	1,013.3	1,031.2	1,117.9	1,195.3
Imports	103.3	213.4	310.9	607.1	702.1	785.9	849.1	923.0	1,048.3	1,170.3	1,304.4	1,475.8	1,435.8	1,484.6	1,552.6	1,719.2	1,828.3
Government consumption expenditures and gross investment	715.4	1,012.9	1,115.4	1,530.0	1,541.1	1,541.3	1,549.7	1,564.9	1,594.0	1,624.4	1,686.9	1,721.6	1,780.3	1,858.8	1,911.1	1,952.3	1,987.1
Federal	(NA)	(NA)	(NA)	659.1	619.6	596.4	580.3	573.5	567.6	561.2	573.7	578.8	601.6	643.4	687.8	723.7	740.5
National defense	(NA)	(NA)	(NA)	479.4	425.3	404.6	389.2	383.8	373.0	365.3	372.2	370.3	384.9	413.2	449.7	481.3	493.6
Nondefense	(NA)	(NA)	(NA)	178.6	191.7	191.1	191.0	189.6	194.5	195.9	201.5	208.5	216.5	230.2	238.0	242.2	246.6
State and local	(NA)	(NA)	(NA)	868.4	919.5	943.3	968.3	990.5	1,025.9	1,063.0	1,113.2	1,142.8	1,179.0	1,215.4	1,223.3	1,228.4	1,246.3
Residual	-64.9	-68.0	14.3	-91.1	-78.6	-63.7	-51.1	-38.5	-23.8	-14.6	-5.8	0.2	1.6	3.0	2.6	-5.1	-16.3

NA Not available.

Source: U.S. Bureau of Economic Analysis, *Survey of Current Business*, May 2006. See also <http://www.bea.gov/bea/dn/nipaweb/SelectTable.asp?Selected=N> (released 28 April 2006).

Table 649. Gross Domestic Product in Current and Real (2000) Dollars by Industry: 2000 to 2005

[In billions of dollars (9,817 represents $9,817,000,000,000). Data are based on the 1997 North American Industry Classification System (NAICS); see text, Section 15. Data include nonfactor charges (capital consumption allowances, indirect business taxes, etc.) as well as factor charges against gross product; corporate profits and capital consumption allowances have been shifted from a company to an establishment basis]

Industry	Current dollars				Chained (2000) dollars			
	2000	2003	2004	2005	2000	2003	2004	2005
Gross domestic product [1]	9,817	10,971	11,734	12,487	9,817	10,321	10,756	11,135
Private industries	8,614	9,557	10,251	10,935	8,614	9,060	9,482	9,839
Agriculture, forestry, and fishing	98	114	142	119	98	104	106	101
Farms	72	88	112	(NA)	72	76	76	(NA)
Agricultural services	27	26	29	(NA)	27	28	31	(NA)
Mining	121	142	172	214	121	106	108	106
Metal mining	81	93	115	(NA)	81	77	77	(NA)
Coal mining	27	27	31	(NA)	27	24	25	(NA)
Oil and gas extraction	13	22	26	(NA)	13	8	9	(NA)
Utilities	189	223	235	239	189	202	205	205
Construction	436	501	550	594	436	422	433	445
Manufacturing	1,426	1,369	1,420	1,497	1,426	1,410	1,478	1,537
Durable goods	865	786	824	868	865	863	918	970
Wood products	31	33	39	(NA)	31	31	32	(NA)
Nonmetallic mineral products	46	46	50	(NA)	46	47	49	(NA)
Primary metals	48	39	51	(NA)	48	43	47	(NA)
Fabricated metal products	122	109	115	(NA)	122	108	111	(NA)
Machinery	109	95	100	(NA)	109	92	101	(NA)
Computer and electronic products	186	126	133	(NA)	186	215	260	(NA)
Electronic equipment, appliances, and components	51	49	48	(NA)	51	50	49	(NA)
Motor vehicles, bodies & trailers, & parts	118	130	120	(NA)	118	143	139	(NA)
Other transportation equipment	64	65	67	(NA)	64	58	58	(NA)
Furniture and related products	33	31	31	(NA)	33	29	31	(NA)
Miscellaneous manufacturing	58	64	69	(NA)	58	60	66	(NA)
Nondurable goods	561	584	596	628	561	549	564	573
Food & beverage & tobacco	155	171	168	(NA)	155	153	156	(NA)
Textile mills and textile product mills	27	23	23	(NA)	27	23	23	(NA)
Apparel and leather and allied products	25	18	19	(NA)	25	19	20	(NA)
Paper products	56	46	49	(NA)	56	49	54	(NA)
Printing and related support activities	49	45	46	(NA)	49	43	44	(NA)
Petroleum and coal products	26	34	35	(NA)	26	26	25	(NA)
Chemical products	157	182	186	(NA)	157	173	174	(NA)
Plastics and rubber products	67	66	70	(NA)	67	64	71	(NA)
Wholesale trade	592	633	695	733	592	654	684	692
Retail trade	662	751	790	829	662	750	798	821
Transportation and warehousing	302	322	333	362	302	311	324	336
Air transportation	58	55	53	(NA)	58	71	80	(NA)
Rail transportation	26	27	29	(NA)	26	25	26	(NA)
Water transportation	7	9	8	(NA)	7	6	5	(NA)
Truck transportation	93	99	105	(NA)	93	89	91	(NA)
Transit & ground passenger transport	15	16	17	(NA)	15	14	14	(NA)
Pipeline transportation	9	11	11	(NA)	9	10	10	(NA)
Other transportation & support	70	76	83	(NA)	70	72	76	(NA)
Warehousing and storage	25	28	27	(NA)	25	27	26	(NA)
Information	458	492	539	578	458	500	564	606
Publishing industries (includes software)	117	119	125	(NA)	117	119	131	(NA)
Motion picture and sound recording	33	42	47	(NA)	33	37	40	(NA)
Broadcasting and telecommunications	271	280	312	(NA)	271	297	340	(NA)
Information and data processing services	38	50	54	(NA)	38	47	53	(NA)
Finance and insurance	741	885	927	1,012	741	837	845	902
Real estate and rental and leasing	1,191	1,375	1,486	1,563	1,191	1,257	1,328	1,361
Professional, scientific, and technical services	675	727	784	862	675	684	733	784
Legal services	136	156	164	(NA)	136	137	136	(NA)
Computer systems design, related services	126	126	133	(NA)	126	129	140	(NA)
Miscellaneous services	413	445	487	(NA)	413	419	459	(NA)
Management of companies & enterprises	183	192	221	231	183	192	203	204
Administrative and waste management	282	317	347	376	282	292	308	329
Educational services	79	100	106	113	79	82	83	83
Health care and social assistance	599	751	803	864	599	668	691	724
Ambulatory health care services	308	385	413	(NA)	308	358	375	(NA)
Hospitals, nursing, residential care	239	299	319	(NA)	239	248	251	(NA)
Social assistance	53	67	71	(NA)	53	63	67	(NA)
Arts, entertainment, and recreation	89	106	112	118	89	95	97	99
Performing arts, spectator sports, museums, and related activities	40	50	50	(NA)	40	44	43	(NA)
Amusements, gambling, & recreation	49	57	61	(NA)	49	52	55	(NA)
Accommodation and food services	261	293	313	338	261	269	278	291
Accommodation	91	94	101	(NA)	91	90	91	(NA)
Food services and drinking places	171	199	212	(NA)	171	179	186	(NA)
Government	1,203	1,415	1,483	1,552	1,203	1,248	1,260	1,274
Federal	379	447	476	495	379	387	393	397
State and local	824	967	1,007	1,058	824	861	867	877

NA Not available. [1] Includes industries, not shown separately.

Source: U.S. Bureau of Economic Analysis, *Survey of Current Business*, May 2006. See also <http://www.bea.gov/bea /newsrelarchive/2006/gdpind05.pdf> (released 27 April 2006).

Table 650. **Gross Domestic Product in Current and Real (2000) Dollars by Type of Product and Sector: 1990 to 2005**

[In billions of dollars (5,803.1 represents $5,803,100,000,000). For explanation of chained dollars, see text, this section]

Type of product and sector	1990	1995	1999	2000	2001	2002	2003	2004	2005
CURRENT DOLLARS									
Gross domestic product	5,803.1	7,397.7	9,268.4	9,817.0	10,128.0	10,469.6	10,971.2	11,734.3	12,487.1
PRODUCT									
Goods	2,155.8	2,661.1	3,311.3	3,449.3	3,412.6	3,442.4	3,536.7	3,783.0	3,967.3
Durable goods	957.9	1,235.7	1,616.5	1,689.4	1,588.6	1,575.0	1,599.1	1,705.7	1,800.0
Nondurable goods	1,198.0	1,425.4	1,694.8	1,760.0	1,824.0	1,867.4	1,937.6	2,077.4	2,167.3
Services	3,113.7	4,098.4	5,081.8	5,425.6	5,725.6	6,031.4	6,366.1	6,755.4	7,186.1
Structures	533.5	638.1	875.3	942.1	989.8	995.8	1,068.4	1,195.8	1,333.7
SECTOR									
Business	4,462.6	5,700.6	7,243.4	7,666.7	7,841.2	8,040.5	8,427.8	9,041.2	9,647.6
Nonfarm	4,386.0	5,632.0	7,174.7	7,595.1	7,768.0	7,969.7	8,339.8	8,928.9	9,560.5
Farm	76.6	68.5	68.8	71.5	73.1	70.8	88.0	112.2	87.2
Households and institutions	618.9	815.5	1,012.3	1,080.7	1,160.4	1,227.3	1,267.1	1,353.5	1,436.5
General government	721.6	881.6	1,012.7	1,069.6	1,126.4	1,201.8	1,276.3	1,339.7	1,403.0
Federal	258.9	284.7	300.9	315.4	325.7	352.9	382.6	408.2	424.3
State and local	462.6	596.9	711.8	754.2	800.8	848.9	893.7	931.4	978.7
CHAINED (2000) DOLLARS									
Gross domestic product	7,112.5	8,031.7	9,470.3	9,817.0	9,890.7	10,048.8	10,320.6	10,755.7	11,134.8
PRODUCT									
Goods	2,252.7	2,639.0	3,312.6	3,449.3	3,390.9	3,432.5	3,549.0	3,778.2	3,954.9
Durable goods	877.2	1,124.5	1,594.1	1,689.4	1,613.0	1,626.5	1,694.2	1,837.5	1,947.4
Nondurable goods	1,407.1	1,531.6	1,718.9	1,760.0	1,776.9	1,804.7	1,854.5	1,944.2	2,014.6
Services	4,170.0	4,654.7	5,245.1	5,425.6	5,553.2	5,693.4	5,820.7	5,979.6	6,138.9
Structures	718.3	753.5	913.0	942.1	945.6	922.1	951.6	1,006.1	1,054.2
SECTOR									
Business	5,287.0	6,076.8	7,376.8	7,666.7	7,691.0	7,806.9	8,070.6	8,454.4	8,794.9
Nonfarm	5,237.9	6,030.2	7,314.2	7,595.1	7,625.7	7,736.9	7,994.6	8,379.5	8,729.6
Farm	49.3	49.6	62.9	71.5	65.6	70.1	76.0	75.9	69.8
Households and institutions	841.2	945.1	1,042.3	1,080.7	1,110.0	1,130.9	1,126.3	1,172.0	1,203.6
General government	1,003.9	1,020.6	1,051.4	1,069.6	1,089.3	1,110.4	1,126.3	1,135.7	1,146.9
Federal	371.6	334.1	312.7	315.4	317.0	323.3	331.8	334.9	336.8
State and local	633.6	686.5	738.7	754.2	772.3	787.1	794.4	800.7	810.1

Source: U.S. Bureau of Economic Analysis, *Survey of Current Business,* May 2006. See also <http://www.bea.gov/bea/dn /nipaweb/SelectTable.asp?Selected=N> (released 28 April 2006).

Table 651. **GDP Components in Real (2000) Dollars—Annual Percent Change: 1990 to 2005**

[Change from previous year; for 1990, change from 1989 and for 1997, change from 1996. Minus sign (–) indicates decrease]

Component	1990	1997	1998	1999	2000	2001	2002	2003	2004	2005
Gross domestic product (GDP). . .	1.9	4.5	4.2	4.5	3.7	0.8	1.6	2.7	4.2	3.5
Personal consumption expenditures	2.0	3.8	5.0	5.1	4.7	2.5	2.7	2.9	3.9	3.5
Durable goods.	(NA)	8.6	11.3	11.7	7.3	4.3	7.1	6.6	6.0	4.5
Nondurable goods	(NA)	2.7	4.0	4.6	3.8	2.0	2.5	3.2	4.7	4.4
Services.	(NA)	3.3	4.2	4.0	4.5	2.4	1.9	2.0	3.0	2.9
Gross private domestic investment	–3.4	12.4	9.8	7.8	5.7	–7.9	–2.6	3.9	11.9	6.1
Fixed investment	(NA)	9.2	10.2	8.3	6.5	–3.0	–5.2	3.6	9.7	8.1
Nonresidential	(NA)	12.1	11.1	9.2	8.7	–4.2	–9.2	1.3	9.4	8.6
Structures	(NA)	7.3	5.1	–0.4	6.8	–2.3	–17.1	–4.2	2.2	2.0
Equipment and software	(NA)	13.8	13.3	12.7	9.4	–4.9	–6.2	3.2	11.9	10.9
Residential	(NA)	1.9	7.6	6.0	0.8	0.4	4.8	8.4	10.3	7.1
Exports	9.0	11.9	2.4	4.3	8.7	–5.4	–2.3	1.8	8.4	6.9
Goods	(NA)	14.4	2.2	3.8	11.2	–6.1	–4.0	1.8	8.9	7.0
Services.	(NA)	6.0	2.9	5.6	2.9	–3.7	1.9	1.7	7.4	6.0
Imports	3.6	13.6	11.6	11.5	13.1	–2.7	3.4	4.6	10.7	6.3
Goods	(NA)	14.4	11.7	12.4	13.5	–3.2	3.7	4.9	11.0	6.9
Services.	(NA)	9.4	11.4	6.9	11.1	–0.3	2.1	3.0	9.6	3.6
Government consumption expenditures and gross investment	3.2	1.9	1.9	3.9	2.1	3.4	4.4	2.8	2.2	1.8
Federal	(NA)	–1.0	–1.1	2.2	0.9	3.9	7.0	6.9	5.2	2.3
National defense	(NA)	–2.8	–2.1	1.9	–0.5	3.9	7.4	8.8	7.0	2.6
Nondefense	(NA)	2.6	0.7	2.8	3.5	3.9	6.3	3.4	1.8	1.8
State and local	(NA)	3.6	3.6	4.7	2.7	3.2	3.1	0.6	0.4	1.5

NA Not available.

Source: U.S. Bureau of Economic Analysis, *Survey of Current Business,* May 2006. See also <http://www.bea.gov/bea/dn /nipaweb/SelectTable.asp?Selected=N> (released 28 April 2006).

Income, Expenditures, and Wealth　431

Table 652. **Gross State Product in Current and Real (2000) Dollars by State: 2000 to 2005**

[In billions of dollars (9,749.1 represents $9,749,100,000,000). For definition of gross state product or chained dollars, see text, this section]

State	Current dollars					Chained (2000) dollars				
	2000	2002	2003	2004	2005, prel.	2000	2002	2003	2004	2005, prel.
United States [1]	9,749.1	10,398.4	10,896.4	11,655.3	12,403.0	9,749.1	9,981.9	10,237.2	10,662.2	11,035.6
Alabama	114.6	123.8	130.5	141.4	149.8	114.6	118.2	122.0	128.3	132.2
Alaska	27.0	29.2	31.5	36.0	39.9	27.0	28.0	27.7	29.7	29.9
Arizona	158.5	171.9	182.4	194.2	215.8	158.5	166.9	174.7	182.0	197.8
Arkansas	66.8	72.2	75.6	82.7	86.8	66.8	68.9	70.7	75.0	76.9
California	1,287.1	1,340.4	1,410.5	1,519.2	1,621.8	1,287.1	1,298.8	1,340.2	1,409.2	1,471.0
Colorado	171.9	182.2	188.9	201.4	216.1	171.9	175.5	177.9	184.9	192.6
Connecticut	160.4	166.1	170.2	182.5	194.5	160.4	158.6	159.8	166.9	173.1
Delaware	41.5	45.3	48.1	52.3	54.4	41.5	42.9	44.7	47.0	47.6
District of Columbia	58.7	67.7	71.3	77.5	82.8	58.7	62.8	64.3	67.3	70.3
Florida	471.3	522.7	556.7	609.4	674.0	471.3	497.3	518.8	552.7	595.8
Georgia	290.9	306.7	317.5	339.7	364.3	290.9	294.1	299.5	313.1	327.5
Hawaii	40.2	43.5	46.4	50.2	53.7	40.2	41.1	42.6	44.7	46.8
Idaho	35.0	36.7	38.5	43.5	47.2	35.0	35.7	36.8	40.5	43.5
Illinois	464.2	487.1	509.2	533.7	560.2	464.2	466.2	478.4	489.0	499.5
Indiana	194.4	205.0	216.7	229.4	238.6	194.4	196.8	204.8	211.7	214.1
Iowa	90.2	97.4	102.4	110.2	114.3	90.2	92.8	95.6	99.8	101.5
Kansas	82.8	89.6	93.1	98.9	105.4	82.8	85.3	86.4	89.1	92.7
Kentucky	111.9	120.7	125.8	133.0	140.4	111.9	115.5	118.2	121.7	124.5
Louisiana	131.5	134.3	146.1	160.2	166.3	131.5	129.7	131.6	137.5	135.4
Maine	35.5	38.6	40.2	43.3	45.1	35.5	36.7	37.4	39.2	39.7
Maryland	180.4	204.1	214.5	230.7	244.9	180.4	193.5	199.1	208.5	216.2
Massachusetts	274.9	284.4	295.9	312.7	328.5	274.9	275.0	282.4	292.4	300.0
Michigan	337.2	349.8	362.8	366.6	377.9	337.2	336.9	344.9	342.4	342.7
Minnesota	185.1	198.6	209.3	224.6	233.3	185.1	191.1	198.0	207.2	209.9
Mississippi	64.3	68.1	72.5	77.1	80.2	64.3	64.6	66.9	68.8	69.7
Missouri	176.7	188.4	195.6	205.8	216.1	176.7	179.9	183.5	188.2	192.2
Montana	21.4	23.6	25.5	27.6	29.9	21.4	22.2	23.3	24.2	25.5
Nebraska	55.5	59.9	64.8	68.0	70.3	55.5	56.9	60.1	60.8	61.8
Nevada	73.7	81.3	89.0	99.1	110.5	73.7	77.1	82.8	89.3	96.6
New Hampshire	43.5	46.2	48.4	52.1	55.7	43.5	44.6	46.1	48.5	50.7
New Jersey	344.8	372.8	388.6	410.3	430.8	344.8	357.9	366.3	377.6	385.5
New Mexico	50.7	52.5	57.5	63.6	69.3	50.7	51.6	53.7	57.2	59.9
New York	777.2	821.6	847.1	906.8	963.5	777.2	791.7	802.8	839.3	867.1
North Carolina	273.7	296.4	307.9	324.0	344.6	273.7	282.4	288.6	296.7	308.4
North Dakota	17.8	19.9	21.7	22.7	24.2	17.8	18.8	19.9	20.0	20.9
Ohio	372.0	389.8	402.6	425.2	442.4	372.0	373.5	379.4	390.9	394.9
Oklahoma	89.8	97.2	103.8	111.8	120.5	89.8	92.9	94.8	97.9	100.8
Oregon	112.4	117.1	120.5	134.6	145.4	112.4	115.0	116.9	128.1	136.6
Pennsylvania	389.6	423.1	439.2	463.8	487.2	389.6	403.0	410.4	421.4	430.3
Rhode Island	33.6	36.9	39.3	41.8	43.8	33.6	34.9	36.4	37.8	38.6
South Carolina	112.5	121.6	127.5	131.5	139.8	112.5	115.7	119.3	120.1	124.3
South Dakota	23.1	26.4	27.4	29.7	31.1	23.1	25.3	25.7	26.7	27.7
Tennessee	174.9	191.5	201.5	216.8	226.5	174.9	183.2	189.8	199.8	203.1
Texas	727.2	783.5	828.5	903.2	982.4	727.2	760.6	771.1	810.5	845.5
Utah	67.6	72.7	76.2	82.5	89.8	67.6	69.1	70.9	74.8	79.2
Vermont	17.8	19.6	20.6	22.0	23.1	17.8	18.9	19.6	20.5	21.1
Virginia	260.7	285.8	301.9	327.0	352.7	260.7	271.2	281.1	297.5	314.1
Washington	222.0	231.5	240.0	253.1	268.5	222.0	221.1	224.4	230.7	239.3
West Virginia	41.5	45.0	46.6	49.9	53.8	41.5	42.5	42.9	44.3	45.7
Wisconsin	175.7	188.6	196.3	207.7	217.5	175.7	180.3	184.8	190.6	194.5
Wyoming	17.3	19.6	21.8	24.1	27.4	17.3	18.4	19.0	19.7	20.7

[1] For chained (2000) dollar estimates, states will not add to U.S. total.

Source: U.S. Bureau of Economic Analysis, *Survey of Current Business*, July 2006; and "Gross State Product"; published 6 June 2006; <http://www.bea.gov/bea/regional/gsp/default.cfm?series=NAICS>.

432   Income, Expenditures, and Wealth

Table 653. **Gross State Product by Selected Industries and State: 2004**

[In billions of dollars (11,655.3 represents $11,655,300,000,000). For definition of gross state product, see text, this section. Industries based on 1997 North American Industry Classification System; see text, Section 15]

State	Total [1]	Construction	Manufacturing	Wholesale trade	Retail trade	Finance and insurance	Information	Professional and technical services	Health care and social assistance	Government [2]
United States.	11,655.3	549.5	1,420.1	694.7	790.4	927.4	538.7	784.3	802.7	1,404.3
Alabama.	141.4	6.8	25.1	8.1	11.3	7.3	4.6	8.0	9.8	21.7
Alaska	36.0	1.8	0.8	0.7	1.7	1.1	0.9	1.2	2.0	6.6
Arizona.	194.2	13.2	17.9	11.6	16.3	16.3	6.3	10.8	13.4	24.3
Arkansas	82.7	3.5	16.2	5.4	6.0	3.6	2.9	3.0	6.1	10.7
California	1,519.2	69.8	145.2	86.2	108.3	108.8	99.3	120.4	89.4	171.1
Colorado.	201.4	12.6	13.2	11.0	12.8	12.8	17.9	16.8	11.7	24.2
Connecticut.	182.5	6.5	21.0	9.9	11.1	29.1	7.2	13.2	13.7	16.5
Delaware	52.3	2.0	4.2	1.9	2.3	16.5	1.1	3.4	2.7	4.6
District of Columbia	77.5	1.1	0.2	0.7	1.0	4.0	5.0	15.2	3.5	26.8
Florida	609.4	41.1	31.1	40.3	49.2	44.0	26.6	36.9	44.8	71.6
Georgia	339.7	17.4	43.9	26.6	23.0	20.7	21.6	20.8	19.5	44.0
Hawaii	50.2	2.7	0.8	1.8	3.8	2.4	1.3	2.2	3.4	11.3
Idaho	43.5	2.5	5.8	2.3	3.6	2.1	1.0	3.0	2.9	6.1
Illinois	533.7	25.0	70.9	37.5	31.8	50.9	19.6	42.3	34.0	52.7
Indiana.	229.4	10.2	65.1	12.2	14.8	13.3	5.2	8.4	16.2	22.3
Iowa	110.2	4.4	23.2	6.2	7.0	10.1	3.3	3.2	7.4	12.9
Kansas.	98.9	3.9	14.5	6.2	7.0	6.0	6.6	5.2	7.0	13.9
Kentucky	133.0	5.7	26.3	8.3	9.4	6.5	3.5	5.1	10.6	19.2
Louisiana.	160.2	6.9	24.7	7.9	11.1	6.3	3.9	6.8	10.4	20.1
Maine.	43.3	2.3	4.8	2.4	4.0	2.9	1.2	2.0	4.5	6.2
Maryland	230.7	14.0	13.1	12.1	15.3	15.7	9.3	22.8	16.7	38.8
Massachusetts.	312.7	13.6	31.8	18.6	17.4	35.0	14.2	32.2	26.4	27.8
Michigan.	366.6	15.9	71.0	21.7	25.1	21.4	10.1	27.8	26.3	39.5
Minnesota.	224.6	11.1	30.8	15.3	14.3	22.2	8.1	12.8	17.6	22.9
Mississippi	77.1	3.1	12.0	4.0	6.4	3.4	1.9	2.5	5.4	13.6
Missouri	205.8	9.6	31.2	13.2	14.4	12.4	9.5	11.4	15.2	24.3
Montana	27.6	1.7	1.3	1.5	2.1	1.4	0.8	1.3	2.5	4.6
Nebraska	68.0	2.9	7.2	4.1	4.4	5.3	2.4	2.9	4.9	10.1
Nevada	99.1	9.0	3.7	3.9	7.7	8.8	2.1	4.9	5.0	9.9
New Hampshire	52.1	2.6	6.3	3.3	4.5	4.3	1.8	3.1	4.2	4.8
New Jersey	410.3	17.1	39.3	33.9	27.0	33.6	19.4	33.0	28.5	42.4
New Mexico	63.6	2.8	6.2	2.2	4.4	2.3	1.6	4.2	4.1	12.2
New York	906.8	29.4	59.2	48.0	50.1	135.7	68.6	73.1	68.8	92.2
North Carolina	324.0	15.3	64.2	18.3	21.7	32.5	10.7	14.9	20.3	41.7
North Dakota	22.7	1.1	2.0	1.8	1.7	1.4	0.9	0.7	2.0	3.6
Ohio	425.2	17.2	83.8	25.7	30.3	30.9	11.9	21.9	33.2	47.5
Oklahoma.	111.8	4.4	11.3	5.6	8.2	5.6	4.0	4.8	7.6	18.3
Oregon.	134.6	5.6	25.3	8.9	7.8	7.2	4.3	6.2	9.7	18.4
Pennsylvania.	463.8	20.6	70.1	27.4	30.9	35.5	16.7	31.9	42.3	46.0
Rhode Island.	41.8	2.0	4.1	2.1	2.7	5.4	1.6	2.1	3.8	5.1
South Carolina	131.5	7.5	23.9	7.5	10.8	6.6	3.5	5.5	7.6	21.1
South Dakota	29.7	1.2	2.8	1.6	2.1	5.0	0.8	0.7	2.5	3.9
Tennessee	216.8	9.0	39.7	14.6	17.8	12.9	7.1	10.8	17.9	24.0
Texas.	903.2	46.3	110.2	61.0	61.2	54.9	38.3	56.7	53.7	101.9
Utah	82.5	4.6	9.0	4.2	6.3	7.4	3.1	5.5	4.6	11.9
Vermont	22.0	1.2	2.8	1.2	1.9	1.3	0.9	1.2	2.0	2.9
Virginia.	327.0	16.8	31.0	14.3	20.4	22.1	18.5	35.5	17.2	57.0
Washington	253.1	11.8	22.8	16.1	18.6	15.0	19.8	15.5	17.1	36.3
West Virginia	49.9	2.0	5.4	2.4	4.1	2.0	1.4	1.9	4.7	8.6
Wisconsin	207.7	9.6	43.1	11.9	13.6	14.9	6.0	8.2	16.8	23.5
Wyoming	24.1	1.3	1.0	0.9	1.4	0.7	0.4	0.7	1.0	3.4

[1] Includes industries not shown separately.   [2] Includes federal civilian and military and state and local government.

Source: U.S. Bureau of Economic Analysis, *Survey of Current Business,* July 2006; and "Gross State Product"; published 6 June 2006; <http://www.bea.gov/bea/regional/gsp/>.

Income, Expenditures, and Wealth   433

Table 654. Relation of GDP, GNP, Net National Product, National Income, Personal Income, Disposable Personal Income, and Personal Saving: 1990 to 2005

[In billions of dollars (5,803.1 represents $5,803,100,000,000). For definitions, see text, this section]

Item	1990	1995	2000	2001	2002	2003	2004	2005
Gross domestic product.	5,803.1	7,397.7	9,817.0	10,128.0	10,469.6	10,971.2	11,734.3	12,487.1
Plus: Income receipts from the rest of the world	189.1	233.9	382.7	322.4	305.7	343.7	415.4	507.6
Less: Income payments to the rest of the world	154.3	198.1	343.7	278.8	275.0	275.6	361.7	474.0
Equals: Gross national product.	5,837.9	7,433.4	9,855.9	10,171.6	10,500.2	11,039.3	11,788.0	12,520.8
Less: Consumption of fixed capital	682.5	878.4	1,187.8	1,281.5	1,292.0	1,331.3	1,435.3	1,574.1
Equals: Net national product	5,155.4	6,555.1	8,668.1	8,890.2	9,208.3	9,708.0	10,352.8	10,946.7
Less: Statistical discrepancy	66.2	101.2	-127.2	-89.6	-21.0	47.1	76.8	42.8
Equals: National income.	5,089.1	6,453.9	8,795.2	8,979.8	9,229.3	9,660.9	10,275.9	10,903.9
Less: Corporate profits [1]	437.8	696.7	817.9	767.3	886.3	1,031.8	1,161.5	1,351.9
Taxes on production and imports less subsidies	398.7	524.2	664.6	673.3	724.4	754.8	809.4	848.0
Contributions for government social insurance	410.1	532.8	702.7	731.1	750.0	776.6	822.2	871.2
Net interest and miscellaneous payments on assets	442.2	367.1	559.0	566.3	520.9	528.5	505.5	498.3
Business current transfer payments (net)	39.4	46.9	87.1	92.8	84.3	81.6	91.1	80.2
Current surplus of government enterprises	1.6	11.4	5.3	-1.4	0.9	1.3	-3.0	-11.3
Wage accruals less disbursements . . .	0.1	16.4	–	–	–	–	–	–
Plus: Personal income receipts on assets.	924.0	1,016.4	1,387.0	1,380.0	1,333.2	1,338.7	1,396.5	1,457.4
Personal current transfer receipts	595.2	877.4	1,084.0	1,193.9	1,286.2	1,344.0	1,427.5	1,525.3
Equals: Personal income	4,878.6	6,152.3	8,429.7	8,724.1	8,881.9	9,169.1	9,713.3	10,248.3
Less: Personal current taxes	592.8	744.1	1,235.7	1,237.3	1,051.8	999.9	1,049.1	1,209.7
Equals: Disposable personal income. .	4,285.8	5,408.2	7,194.0	7,486.8	7,830.1	8,169.2	8,664.2	9,038.6
Less: Personal outlays	3,986.4	5,157.3	7,025.6	7,354.5	7,645.3	7,996.3	8,512.5	9,072.1
Equals: Personal saving.	299.4	250.9	168.5	132.3	184.7	172.8	151.8	-33.5

– Represents or rounds to zero. [1] Corporate profits with inventory valuation and capital consumption adjustments.

Source: U.S. Bureau of Economic Analysis, *Survey of Current Business*, June 2006. See also <http://www.bea.gov/bea/dn/nipaweb/SelectTable.asp?Selected=N> (released 28 April 2006).

Table 655. Selected Per Capita Income and Product Measures in Current and Real (2000) Dollars: 1960 to 2005

[In dollars. Based on U.S. Census Bureau estimated population including Armed Forces abroad; based on quarterly averages. For explanation of chained dollars, see text, this section]

Year	Current dollars					Chained (2000) dollars			
	Gross domestic product	Gross national product	Personal income	Disposable personal income	Personal consumption expenditures	Gross domestic product	Gross national product	Disposable personal income	Personal consumption expenditures
1960	2,912	2,929	2,277	2,022	1,835	13,840	13,938	9,735	8,837
1965	3,700	3,727	2,860	2,563	2,283	16,420	16,554	11,594	10,331
1970	5,064	5,095	4,090	3,587	3,162	18,391	18,520	13,563	11,955
1975	7,586	7,646	6,181	5,498	4,789	19,961	20,133	15,291	13,320
1980	12,249	12,400	10,134	8,822	7,716	22,666	22,956	16,940	14,816
1981	13,601	13,745	11,266	9,765	8,439	23,007	23,259	17,217	14,879
1982	14,017	14,174	11,951	10,426	8,945	22,346	22,607	17,418	14,944
1983	15,092	15,251	12,635	11,131	9,775	23,146	23,396	17,828	15,656
1984	16,638	16,792	13,915	12,319	10,589	24,593	24,828	19,011	16,343
1985	17,695	17,806	14,787	13,037	11,406	25,382	25,548	19,476	17,040
1986	18,542	18,616	15,466	13,649	12,048	26,024	26,137	19,906	17,570
1987	19,517	19,590	16,255	14,241	12,766	26,664	26,770	20,072	17,994
1988	20,827	20,923	17,358	15,297	13,685	27,514	27,647	20,740	18,554
1989	22,169	22,275	18,545	16,257	14,546	28,221	28,358	21,120	18,898
1990	23,195	23,335	19,500	17,131	15,349	28,429	28,600	21,281	19,067
1991	23,650	23,770	19,923	17,609	15,722	28,007	28,150	21,109	18,848
1992	24,668	24,783	20,870	18,494	16,485	28,556	28,693	21,548	19,208
1993	25,578	25,700	21,356	18,872	17,204	28,940	29,079	21,493	19,593
1994	26,844	26,944	22,176	19,555	18,004	29,741	29,850	21,812	20,082
1995	27,749	27,884	23,078	20,287	18,665	30,128	30,271	22,153	20,382
1996	28,982	29,112	24,176	21,091	19,490	30,881	31,015	22,546	20,835
1997	30,424	30,544	25,334	21,940	20,323	31,886	32,010	23,065	21,365
1998	31,674	31,752	26,880	23,161	21,291	32,833	32,912	24,131	22,183
1999	33,181	33,302	27,933	23,968	22,491	33,904	34,027	24,564	23,050
2000	34,759	34,897	29,847	25,472	23,862	34,759	34,897	25,472	23,862
2001	35,491	35,643	30,571	26,235	24,722	34,659	34,809	25,697	24,215
2002	36,321	36,427	30,813	27,164	25,501	34,861	34,966	26,235	24,629
2003	37,687	37,921	31,497	28,062	26,484	35,452	35,674	26,594	25,099
2004	39,922	40,105	33,046	29,477	27,946	36,592	36,763	27,232	25,817
2005	42,090	42,203	34,544	30,466	29,479	37,532	37,638	27,370	26,483

Source: U.S. Bureau of Economic Analysis, *Survey of Current Business*, May 2006. See also <http://www.bea.gov/bea/dn/nipaweb/SelectTable.asp?Selected=N> (released 04 May 2006).

434 Income, Expenditures, and Wealth

Table 656. **Personal Consumption Expenditures in Current and Real (2000) Dollars by Type: 1990 to 2004**

[In billions of dollars (3,839.9 represents $3,839,900,000,000). For definition of "chained" dollars, see text, this section]

Expenditure	Current dollars				Chained (2000) dollars			
	1990	2000	2003	2004	1990	2000	2003	2004
Total expenditures [1]	**3,839.9**	**6,739.4**	**7,709.9**	**8,214.3**	**4,770.3**	**6,739.4**	**7,306.6**	**7,588.6**
Food and tobacco [1]	677.8	1,003.7	1,136.5	1,222.3	867.1	1,003.7	1,053.4	1,100.2
Food purchased for off-premise consumption [2]	401.6	566.7	638.4	688.4	485.7	566.7	601.0	628.7
Purchased meals and beverages [2]	227.7	348.8	399.1	434.9	289.6	348.8	368.9	390.0
Tobacco products	41.0	78.5	87.9	87.6	87.7	78.5	74.0	72.4
Clothing, accessories, and jewelry [1]	261.5	397.0	419.7	445.5	247.7	397.0	441.4	467.5
Shoes	31.5	47.0	51.3	54.2	30.4	47.0	53.1	56.3
Clothing	172.4	250.4	259.0	274.4	157.7	250.4	280.4	298.4
Jewelry and watches	30.3	50.6	53.9	57.2	26.5	50.6	57.4	60.5
Personal care	56.9	93.4	98.5	103.1	68.5	93.4	95.2	98.6
Housing [1]	597.9	1,006.5	1,158.0	1,221.1	802.2	1,006.5	1,048.4	1,078.4
Owner-occupied nonfarm dwellings-space rent	412.8	712.2	842.9	897.0	551.6	712.2	761.7	792.5
Tenant-occupied nonfarm dwellings-space rent	150.7	227.5	245.3	248.2	199.9	227.5	220.4	217.5
Household operation [1]	433.3	719.3	779.2	821.0	485.0	719.3	763.8	798.2
Furniture [3]	38.4	67.6	70.0	75.5	41.8	67.6	73.6	79.7
Semidurable house furnishings [4]	22.5	36.5	38.6	40.3	20.1	36.5	43.9	48.1
Cleaning and polishing preparations	38.9	61.6	68.7	73.4	46.2	61.6	66.8	71.1
Household utilities	141.1	209.9	241.4	256.0	174.5	209.9	214.8	216.7
Electricity	74.2	102.3	115.4	120.5	81.1	102.3	105.6	108.2
Gas	26.8	41.0	51.1	55.4	36.6	41.0	41.2	41.1
Water and other sanitary services	27.1	50.8	57.8	60.6	41.1	50.8	52.5	52.0
Fuel oil and coal	12.9	15.8	17.0	19.5	16.7	15.8	15.5	15.5
Telephone and telegraph	60.5	125.1	129.9	132.1	58.3	125.1	133.6	138.6
Medical care [1]	635.1	1,218.3	1,555.6	1,677.2	905.9	1,218.3	1,415.3	1,475.3
Drug preparations and sundries [5]	65.4	169.4	234.1	253.3	90.1	169.4	209.0	220.0
Physicians	138.6	236.8	301.1	323.3	194.7	236.8	288.6	303.6
Dentists	32.4	61.8	74.6	80.0	53.5	61.8	65.9	67.4
Hospitals and nursing homes [6]	270.9	482.6	612.6	657.4	386.4	482.6	542.9	558.4
Health insurance [7]	43.4	84.0	107.7	120.5	70.1	84.0	99.7	106.6
Medical care [7]	31.8	68.4	89.6	100.6	52.8	68.4	80.2	86.3
Personal business [1]	250.9	539.1	568.5	612.2	330.0	539.1	536.8	554.7
Expense of handling life insurance [8]	53.2	96.1	92.6	98.4	86.2	96.1	83.1	81.7
Legal services	40.9	63.9	78.1	81.0	62.2	63.9	66.7	66.1
Funeral and burial expenses	9.5	14.0	15.9	16.4	15.0	14.0	14.1	14.0
Transportation	471.7	853.4	928.5	979.1	590.1	853.4	912.3	925.6
User-operated transportation [1]	434.7	793.8	873.1	920.4	546.6	793.8	853.3	863.4
New autos	89.7	103.6	98.0	97.5	102.5	103.6	101.5	101.6
Net purchases of used autos	29.3	60.7	54.8	53.1	42.4	60.7	56.2	55.6
Tires, tubes, accessories, etc.	29.9	49.0	51.8	54.3	29.3	49.0	49.2	51.4
Repair, greasing, washing, parking, storage, rental, and leasing	84.9	183.5	186.8	189.0	109.4	183.5	173.0	172.5
Gasoline and oil	111.2	175.7	192.6	230.4	141.8	175.7	183.2	185.9
Purchased local transportation	8.4	12.2	13.1	14.1	10.9	12.2	11.6	11.8
Mass transit systems	5.8	9.1	9.5	10.3	7.5	9.1	8.4	8.6
Taxicab	2.6	3.1	3.6	3.8	3.4	3.1	3.2	3.2
Purchased intercity transportation [1]	28.6	47.4	42.2	44.6	32.5	47.4	47.5	51.0
Railway (commutation)	0.6	0.5	0.6	0.6	0.8	0.5	0.5	0.6
Bus	1.3	2.4	2.3	2.1	1.5	2.4	2.1	1.9
Airline	22.7	36.7	31.2	33.1	24.8	36.7	36.8	39.9
Recreation [1,9]	290.2	585.7	658.8	702.4	276.5	585.7	687.8	738.0
Magazines, newspapers, and sheet music	21.6	35.0	35.9	38.7	29.3	35.0	33.9	35.5
Nondurable toys and sport supplies	32.8	56.6	60.1	64.0	28.3	56.6	70.1	77.6
Video and audio products, including musical instruments and computer goods	53.0	116.6	122.3	130.8	18.6	116.6	178.1	208.0
Computers, peripherals, and software	8.9	43.8	46.5	51.0	(NA)	(NA)	(NA)	(NA)
Education and research	83.7	163.8	200.4	211.3	125.6	163.8	173.7	173.1
Higher education	43.8	86.4	110.0	117.7	69.6	86.4	94.0	94.3
Religious and welfare activities	88.7	172.3	206.7	219.0	121.2	172.3	189.1	194.4
Foreign travel and other, net [1]	-7.7	-13.0	-0.5	0.1	-13.1	-13.0	-6.5	-7.3
Foreign travel by U.S. residents	42.7	84.4	80.5	91.6	53.3	84.4	72.1	78.3
Expenditures abroad by U.S. residents	3.6	4.6	6.6	7.0	3.6	4.6	5.2	5.0
Less: Expenditures in the United States by nonresidents	53.0	100.7	85.8	96.6	68.8	100.7	82.1	88.6

NA Not available. [1] Includes other expenditures not shown separately. [2] Consists of purchases (including tips) of meals and beverages from retail, service, and amusement establishments; hotels; dining and buffet cars; schools; school fraternities; institutions; clubs; and industrial lunch rooms. Includes meals and beverages consumed both on- and off-premise. [3] Includes mattresses and bedsprings. [4] Consists largely of textile house furnishings including piece goods allocated to house furnishing use. Also includes lamp shades, brooms, and brushes. [5] Excludes drug preparations and related products dispensed by physicians, hospitals, and other medical services. [6] Consists of (1) current expenditures (including consumption of fixed capital) of nonprofit hospitals and nursing homes and (2) payments by patients to proprietary and government hospitals and nursing homes. [7] Consists of (1) premiums, less benefits and dividends, for health hospitalization and accidental death and dismemberment insurance provided by commercial insurance carriers and (2) administrative expenses (including consumption of fixed capital) of Blue Cross and Blue Shield plans and of other independent prepaid and self-insured health plans. [8] Consists of (1) operating expenses of life insurance carriers and private noninsured pension plans and (2) premiums less benefits and dividends of fraternal benefit societies. Excludes expenses allocated by commercial carriers to accident and health insurance. [9] For additional items, see Table 1222.

Source: U.S. Bureau of Economic Analysis, *Survey of Current Business*, August 2005. See also <http://www.bea.gov /bea/dn/nipaweb/SelectTable.asp?Selected=N> (released as 04 August 2005).

Income, Expenditures, and Wealth   435

Table 657. **Personal Income and Its Disposition: 1990 to 2005**

[In billions of dollars (4,878.6 represents $4,878,600,000,000), except as indicated. For definition of personal income and chained dollars, see text, this section]

Item	1990	1995	2000	2001	2002	2003	2004	2005
Personal income	**4,878.6**	**6,152.3**	**8,429.7**	**8,724.1**	**8,881.9**	**9,169.1**	**9,713.3**	**10,248.3**
Compensation of employees, received.	3,338.2	4,177.0	5,782.7	5,942.1	6,091.2	6,321.1	6,687.6	7,125.3
Wage and salary disbursements . . .	2,754.0	3,419.3	4,829.2	4,942.8	4,980.9	5,111.1	5,389.4	5,723.7
Supplements to wages and salaries .	584.2	757.7	953.4	999.3	1,110.3	1,210.0	1,298.1	1,401.6
Proprietors' income [1]	380.6	492.1	728.4	771.9	768.4	810.2	889.6	938.7
Farm	31.9	22.7	22.7	19.7	10.6	27.7	35.8	20.8
Nonfarm	348.7	469.5	705.7	752.2	757.8	782.4	853.8	917.8
Rental income of persons [1]	50.7	122.1	150.3	167.4	152.9	131.7	134.2	72.9
Personal income receipts on assets . .	924.0	1,016.4	1,387.0	1,380.0	1,333.2	1,338.7	1,396.5	1,457.4
Personal interest income	755.2	763.2	1,011.0	1,011.0	936.1	917.6	905.9	945.7
Personal dividend income	168.8	253.2	376.1	369.0	397.2	421.1	490.6	511.7
Personal current transfer receipts	595.2	877.4	1,084.0	1,193.9	1,286.2	1,344.0	1,427.5	1,525.3
Government social benefits to persons.	573.1	858.4	1,041.6	1,143.9	1,248.9	1,313.5	1,394.5	1,483.7
Old-age, survivors', disability, and health insurance benefits.	351.8	506.8	620.8	668.5	707.5	739.3	789.3	844.7
Other current transfer receipts, from business (net)	22.2	19.0	42.4	50.0	37.3	30.5	33.0	41.6
Less: Contributions for government social insurance.	410.1	532.8	702.7	731.1	750.0	776.6	822.2	871.2
Less: Personal current taxes	592.8	744.1	1,235.7	1,237.3	1,051.8	999.9	1,049.1	1,209.7
Equals: Disposable personal income. .	**4,285.8**	**5,408.2**	**7,194.0**	**7,486.8**	**7,830.1**	**8,169.2**	**8,664.2**	**9,038.6**
Less: Personal outlays	3,986.4	5,157.3	7,025.6	7,354.5	7,645.3	7,996.3	8,512.5	9,072.1
Personal consumption expenditures . .	3,839.9	4,975.8	6,739.4	7,055.0	7,350.7	7,709.9	8,214.3	8,745.7
Personal interest payments	116.1	132.7	204.7	212.2	196.4	183.2	186.7	205.9
Personal current transfer payments . . .	30.4	48.9	81.5	87.2	98.2	103.3	111.5	120.4
Equals: Personal saving.	**299.4**	**250.9**	**168.5**	**132.3**	**184.7**	**172.8**	**151.8**	**-33.5**
Personal saving as a percentage of disposable personal income	7.0	4.6	2.3	1.8	2.4	2.1	1.8	-0.4
Addenda:								
Disposable personal income:								
Total, billions of chained (**2000**) dollars.	5,324.2	5,905.7	7,194.0	7,333.3	7,562.2	7,741.8	8,004.3	8,120.0
Per capita:								
Current dollars	17,131	20,287	25,472	26,235	27,164	28,062	29,477	30,466
Chained (**2000**) dollars	21,281	22,153	25,472	25,697	26,235	26,594	27,232	27,370

[1] With inventory valuation adjustments and capital consumption adjustment.

Source: U.S. Bureau of Economic Analysis, *Survey of Current Business,* June 2006. See also <http://www.bea.gov/bea/dn /nipaweb/SelectTable.asp?Selected=N> (released 25 May 2006).

Table 658. **Gross Saving and Investment: 1990 to 2005**

[In billions of dollars (940.4 represents $940,400,000,000)]

Item	1990	1995	2000	2001	2002	2003	2004	2005
Gross saving.	**940.4**	**1,184.5**	**1,770.5**	**1,657.6**	**1,489.1**	**1,474.1**	**1,572.0**	**1,680.2**
Net saving	258.0	306.2	582.7	376.1	197.1	142.7	136.8	106.1
Net private saving.	422.7	491.1	343.3	324.6	479.2	549.3	549.1	426.2
Personal saving	299.4	250.9	168.5	132.3	184.7	172.8	151.8	-33.5
Undistributed corporate profits with IVA and CCA [1]	123.3	223.8	174.8	192.3	294.5	376.5	397.3	459.6
Wage accruals less disbursements . . .	–	16.4	–	–	–	–	–	–
Net government saving	-164.8	-184.9	239.4	51.5	-282.1	-406.5	-412.3	-320.0
Federal	-172.0	-197.0	189.5	46.7	-247.9	-382.7	-406.5	-323.0
State and local	7.2	12.0	50.0	4.8	-34.2	-23.8	-5.9	3.0
Consumption of fixed capital.	682.5	878.4	1,187.8	1,281.5	1,292.0	1,331.3	1,435.3	1,574.1
Private	551.6	713.4	990.8	1,075.5	1,080.3	1,112.8	1,206.2	1,327.0
Domestic business.	466.4	600.2	836.1	903.7	893.6	911.5	973.3	1,041.8
Households and institutions	85.1	113.2	154.8	171.7	186.8	201.3	232.8	285.2
Government.	130.9	165.0	197.0	206.0	211.6	218.5	229.1	247.0
Federal	67.9	81.9	87.2	88.2	88.9	90.3	93.8	98.3
State and local	63.0	83.1	109.8	117.8	122.7	128.3	135.3	148.7
Gross domestic investment, capital acct. transactions, & net lending . .	**1,006.7**	**1,285.7**	**1,643.3**	**1,567.9**	**1,468.1**	**1,521.1**	**1,648.9**	**1,723.0**
Gross domestic investment	1,076.7	1,376.7	2,040.0	1,938.3	1,926.4	2,025.6	2,300.6	2,505.3
Gross private domestic investment. . . .	861.0	1,144.0	1,735.5	1,614.3	1,582.1	1,670.4	1,928.1	2,105.0
Gross government investment	215.7	232.7	304.5	324.0	344.3	355.3	372.5	400.3
Capital account transactions (net)	6.6	0.9	0.8	1.1	1.4	3.2	1.6	4.7
Net lending or net borrowing	-76.6	-91.9	-397.4	-371.5	-459.7	-507.7	-653.4	-787.0
Statistical discrepancy	66.2	101.2	-127.2	-89.6	-21.0	47.1	76.8	42.8
Addenda:								
Gross private saving	974.3	1,204.5	1,334.1	1,400.1	1,559.6	1,662.1	1,755.3	1,753.2
Gross government saving.	-33.8	-19.9	436.4	257.5	-70.5	-188.0	-183.2	-73.0
Federal	-104.1	-115.1	276.6	134.9	-159.1	-292.5	-312.7	-224.7
State and local	70.3	95.2	159.8	122.6	88.6	104.5	129.4	151.7
Net domestic investment	394.2	498.4	852.1	656.9	634.4	694.3	865.3	931.2
Gross saving as a percentage of gross national income	16.3	16.2	17.7	16.2	14.2	13.4	13.4	13.5
Net saving as a percentage of gross national income	4.5	4.2	5.8	3.7	1.9	1.3	1.2	0.9

- Represents or rounds to zero.   [1] IVA and CCA=Inventory valuation adjustment and capital consumption adjustment.

Source: U.S. Bureau of Economic Analysis, *Survey of Current Business,* May 2006. See also <http://www.bea.gov/dn/nipaweb/SelectTable.asp?Selected=N> (released 4 May 2006).

Table 659. **Personal Income in Current and Constant (2000) Dollars by State: 1990 to 2005**

[In billions of dollars (4,861.9 represents $4,861,900,000,000). Represents a measure of income received from all sources during the calendar year by residents of each state. Data exclude federal employees overseas and U.S. residents employed by private U.S. firms on temporary foreign assignment. Totals may differ from those in Tables 654, 655, and 657]

State	Current dollars					Constant (2000) dollars [1]				
	1990	2000	2003	2004	2005, prel.	1990	2000	2003	2004	2005, prel.
United States ..	4,861.9	8,422.1	9,157.3	9,705.5	10,251.6	6,039.9	8,422.1	8,679.0	8,966.2	9,209.7
Alabama..........	63.7	105.8	118.5	125.3	132.8	79.1	105.8	112.3	115.8	119.3
Alaska	12.6	18.7	21.4	22.4	23.6	15.7	18.7	20.3	20.7	21.2
Arizona...........	62.6	132.6	151.7	164.5	179.8	77.8	132.6	143.8	152.0	161.5
Arkansas	34.1	58.7	66.3	71.0	74.7	42.3	58.7	62.9	65.6	67.1
California	648.3	1,103.8	1,184.3	1,262.3	1,338.2	805.3	1,103.8	1,122.4	1,166.2	1,202.2
Colorado..........	64.7	144.4	157.0	166.2	177.0	80.4	144.4	148.8	153.5	159.0
Connecticut........	87.3	141.6	148.8	158.6	167.9	108.4	141.6	141.0	146.5	150.8
Delaware	14.3	24.3	27.6	29.7	31.3	17.8	24.3	26.2	27.4	28.1
District of Columbia ...	16.0	23.1	26.6	28.4	30.3	19.9	23.1	25.2	26.2	27.2
Florida	255.0	457.5	512.0	547.1	591.0	316.8	457.5	485.2	505.4	530.9
Georgia	114.6	230.4	250.7	265.6	282.3	142.4	230.4	237.6	245.4	253.7
Hawaii	24.7	34.5	38.1	41.2	44.0	30.7	34.5	36.1	38.0	39.6
Idaho	15.9	31.3	34.7	37.5	40.2	19.8	31.3	32.9	34.6	36.2
Illinois	238.5	400.4	427.0	441.4	461.0	296.3	400.4	404.7	407.8	414.2
Indiana...........	97.2	165.3	178.9	188.1	196.2	120.8	165.3	169.6	173.7	176.2
Iowa	48.4	77.8	84.1	91.7	95.9	60.1	77.8	79.7	84.7	86.1
Kansas...........	44.9	74.6	80.9	85.0	90.1	55.7	74.6	76.7	78.5	81.0
Kentucky	57.0	98.8	106.8	112.9	119.0	70.8	98.8	101.3	104.3	106.9
Louisiana	64.1	103.2	116.2	123.0	112.3	79.6	103.2	110.1	113.7	100.9
Maine............	21.4	33.2	37.3	39.5	41.3	26.6	33.2	35.3	36.5	37.1
Maryland	109.7	182.0	206.3	220.4	233.9	136.3	182.0	195.5	203.6	210.1
Massachusetts.......	138.8	240.2	255.4	270.2	283.4	172.4	240.2	242.1	249.7	254.6
Michigan..........	176.2	294.2	318.3	324.1	335.2	218.9	294.2	301.7	299.4	301.1
Minnesota.........	87.3	158.0	173.4	184.4	191.8	108.5	158.0	164.3	170.4	172.3
Mississippi	33.8	59.8	67.0	71.1	74.0	41.9	59.8	63.5	65.7	66.4
Missouri	90.4	152.7	167.0	175.5	185.0	112.3	152.7	158.3	162.2	166.2
Montana..........	12.4	20.7	24.0	25.6	27.5	15.4	20.7	22.8	23.7	24.7
Nebraska	28.4	47.3	53.4	56.5	59.1	35.3	47.3	50.6	52.2	53.1
Nevada	24.8	61.4	71.6	78.8	86.7	30.9	61.4	67.9	72.8	77.8
New Hampshire	22.8	41.4	44.4	47.6	50.3	28.3	41.4	42.1	43.9	45.2
New Jersey.........	190.8	323.6	342.4	361.5	381.6	237.0	323.6	324.5	334.0	342.8
New Mexico	22.7	40.3	46.8	49.8	53.3	28.2	40.3	44.3	46.0	47.9
New York	423.9	663.0	691.1	737.8	779.9	526.6	663.0	655.0	681.6	700.7
North Carolina......	114.9	218.7	234.6	250.4	265.3	142.8	218.7	222.4	231.4	238.3
North Dakota........	10.2	16.1	18.2	18.8	20.0	12.6	16.1	17.3	17.3	18.0
Ohio	203.6	320.5	342.4	356.8	372.3	253.0	320.5	324.5	329.6	334.5
Oklahoma..........	51.0	84.3	93.1	98.1	104.1	63.3	84.3	88.2	90.6	93.5
Oregon............	51.5	96.4	103.9	109.8	116.9	64.0	96.4	98.5	101.4	105.0
Pennsylvania	234.3	364.8	392.8	412.9	433.8	291.1	364.8	372.3	381.4	389.7
Rhode Island........	20.1	30.7	34.9	36.9	38.9	25.0	30.7	33.1	34.1	35.0
South Carolina.......	55.6	98.3	107.7	114.1	120.6	69.1	98.3	102.1	105.4	108.4
South Dakota	11.3	19.4	22.3	23.3	24.5	14.0	19.4	21.1	21.5	22.0
Tennessee	81.7	148.8	166.1	175.9	185.5	101.5	148.8	157.5	162.5	166.6
Texas............	297.1	593.1	650.9	690.6	742.1	369.1	593.1	616.9	638.0	666.7
Utah	25.8	53.6	60.3	64.4	69.3	32.1	53.6	57.1	59.5	62.3
Vermont	10.1	16.9	18.7	19.7	20.8	12.5	16.9	17.7	18.2	18.7
Virginia...........	127.1	220.8	251.1	270.5	290.5	157.9	220.8	238.0	249.9	261.0
Washington	97.4	187.9	201.6	217.5	222.6	121.0	187.9	191.1	200.9	200.0
West Virginia........	26.0	39.6	44.4	46.7	49.4	32.3	39.6	42.1	43.2	44.4
Wisconsin..........	88.6	153.5	167.8	177.0	185.8	110.1	153.5	159.0	163.5	166.9
Wyoming	8.2	14.1	16.2	17.3	18.7	10.1	14.1	15.4	16.0	16.8

[1] Constant dollar estimates are computed by the U.S. Census Bureau using the national implicit price deflator for personal consumption expenditures from the Bureau of Economic Analysis. Any regional differences in the rate of inflation are not reflected in these constant dollar estimates.

Source: Except as noted, U.S. Bureau of Economic Analysis, Survey of Current Business, April 2006. See also <http://www.bea.gov/bea/regional/statelocal.htm>.

Income, Expenditures, and Wealth 437

Table 660. Personal Income Per Capita in Current and Constant (2000) Dollars by State: 1990 to 2005

[In dollars, except as indicated. 2005 preliminary. See headnote, Table 659]

State	Current dollars 1990	2000	2004	2005	Constant (2000) dollars [1] 1990	2000	2004	2005	Income rank 2000	2005
United States	19,477	29,845	33,050	34,586	24,196	29,845	30,533	31,071	(X)	(X)
Alabama	15,723	23,764	27,695	29,136	19,532	23,764	25,585	26,175	44	41
Alaska.	22,804	29,867	34,000	35,612	28,329	29,867	31,410	31,993	15	16
Arizona	17,005	25,660	28,658	30,267	21,125	25,660	26,475	27,191	37	38
Arkansas	14,460	21,925	25,814	26,874	17,963	21,925	23,848	24,143	48	48
California	21,638	32,463	35,219	37,036	26,881	32,463	32,536	33,272	8	11
Colorado	19,575	33,371	36,113	37,946	24,318	33,371	33,362	34,089	7	8
Connecticut	26,504	41,489	45,318	47,819	32,925	41,489	41,866	42,959	1	1
Delaware	21,422	30,869	35,728	37,065	26,612	30,869	33,007	33,298	13	10
District of Columbia	26,473	40,456	51,155	54,985	32,887	40,456	47,259	49,397	(X)	(X)
Florida	19,564	28,509	31,469	33,219	24,304	28,509	29,072	29,843	20	23
Georgia	17,603	27,989	29,782	31,121	21,868	27,989	27,514	27,958	26	35
Hawaii	22,186	28,422	32,625	34,539	27,561	28,422	30,140	31,029	22	19
Idaho	15,724	24,075	26,877	28,158	19,534	24,075	24,830	25,296	42	44
Illinois	20,824	32,185	34,721	36,120	25,869	32,185	32,076	32,449	9	14
Indiana	17,491	27,132	30,204	31,276	21,729	27,132	27,903	28,097	31	33
Iowa	17,389	26,554	31,058	32,315	21,602	26,554	28,692	29,031	33	28
Kansas	18,085	27,694	31,078	32,836	22,467	27,694	28,711	29,499	27	25
Kentucky	15,437	24,412	27,265	28,513	19,177	24,412	25,188	25,615	40	42
Louisiana	15,173	23,079	27,297	24,820	18,849	23,079	25,218	22,297	45	50
Maine	17,376	25,969	30,046	31,252	21,586	25,969	27,757	28,076	35	34
Maryland	22,852	34,257	39,631	41,760	28,389	34,257	36,612	37,516	5	4
Massachusetts	23,043	37,756	42,176	44,289	28,626	37,756	38,963	39,788	3	2
Michigan	18,922	29,552	32,079	33,116	23,506	29,552	29,636	29,750	17	24
Minnesota	19,891	32,017	36,184	37,373	24,710	32,017	33,428	33,575	10	9
Mississippi	13,089	21,005	24,518	25,318	16,260	21,005	22,650	22,745	50	49
Missouri	17,627	27,241	30,475	31,899	21,898	27,241	28,154	28,657	30	30
Montana	15,448	22,929	27,657	29,387	19,191	22,929	25,550	26,400	46	39
Nebraska	17,983	27,625	32,341	33,616	22,340	27,625	29,878	30,200	29	20
Nevada	20,346	30,437	33,787	35,883	25,275	30,437	31,213	32,236	14	15
New Hampshire	20,512	33,396	36,616	38,408	25,482	33,396	33,827	34,505	6	6
New Jersey	24,572	38,364	41,626	43,771	30,525	38,364	38,455	39,322	2	3
New Mexico	14,924	22,134	26,184	27,644	18,540	22,134	24,190	24,834	47	46
New York	23,523	34,897	38,264	40,507	29,222	34,897	35,349	36,390	4	5
North Carolina	17,246	27,068	29,322	30,553	21,424	27,068	27,089	27,448	32	37
North Dakota	15,943	25,106	29,494	31,395	19,806	25,106	27,247	28,204	38	32
Ohio	18,743	28,207	31,161	32,478	23,284	28,207	28,787	29,177	24	26
Oklahoma	16,187	24,407	27,840	29,330	20,109	24,407	25,719	26,349	41	40
Oregon	18,010	28,097	30,561	32,103	22,374	28,097	28,233	28,840	25	29
Pennsylvania	19,687	29,695	33,312	34,897	24,457	29,695	30,775	31,350	16	18
Rhode Island	20,006	29,214	34,207	36,153	24,853	29,214	31,601	32,479	18	13
South Carolina	15,894	24,424	27,185	28,352	19,745	24,424	25,114	25,471	39	43
South Dakota	16,172	25,720	30,209	31,614	20,090	25,720	27,908	28,401	36	31
Tennessee	16,692	26,097	29,844	31,107	20,736	26,097	27,571	27,946	34	36
Texas	17,421	28,313	30,732	32,462	21,642	28,313	28,391	29,163	23	27
Utah	14,913	23,878	26,603	28,061	18,526	23,878	24,577	25,209	43	45
Vermont	17,876	27,680	31,780	33,327	22,207	27,680	29,359	29,940	28	22
Virginia	20,449	31,087	36,160	38,390	25,403	31,087	33,406	34,488	12	7
Washington	19,865	31,779	34,541	35,409	24,678	31,779	32,372	31,810	11	17
West Virginia	14,493	21,899	25,792	27,215	18,004	21,899	23,827	24,449	49	47
Wisconsin	18,072	28,570	32,166	33,565	22,451	28,570	29,716	30,154	19	21
Wyoming	18,002	28,460	34,279	36,778	22,364	28,460	31,668	33,040	21	12

X Not applicable.   [1] Constant dollar estimates are computed by the U.S. Census Bureau using the national implicit price deflator for personal consumption expenditures. Any regional differences in the rate of inflation are not reflected in these constant dollar estimates.

Source: Except as noted, U.S. Bureau of Economic Analysis, *Survey of Current Business*, April 2006. See also <http://www.bea.gov/bea/regional/statelocal.htm>.

Table 661. **Disposable Personal Income Per Capita in Current and Constant (2000) Dollars by State: 1990 to 2005**

[In dollars, except percent. 2005 preliminary. Disposable personal income is the income available to persons for spending or saving; it is calculated as personal income less personal tax and nontax payments]

State	Current dollars				Constant (2000) dollars [1]				Percent of U.S. average	
	1990	2000	2004	2005	1990	2000	2004	2005	1990	2005
United States . . .	17,108	25,471	29,404	30,509	21,253	25,471	27,164	27,408	100.0	100.0
Alabama.	14,047	21,046	25,416	26,348	17,450	21,046	23,480	23,670	82.1	86.4
Alaska	20,147	26,425	31,454	32,268	25,028	26,425	29,058	28,989	117.8	105.8
Arizona.	15,131	22,326	25,770	27,185	18,797	22,326	23,807	24,422	88.4	89.1
Arkansas	12,987	19,375	23,453	24,264	16,134	19,375	21,667	21,798	75.9	79.5
California	18,871	26,716	30,964	32,188	23,443	26,716	28,605	28,917	110.3	105.5
Colorado.	17,201	28,235	32,207	33,499	21,368	28,235	29,754	30,094	100.5	109.8
Connecticut.	23,121	33,383	38,559	39,974	28,723	33,383	35,622	35,911	135.1	131.0
Delaware	18,474	26,278	31,900	32,549	22,950	26,278	29,470	29,241	108.0	106.7
District of Columbia	22,858	33,408	45,213	47,265	28,396	33,408	41,769	42,461	133.6	154.9
Florida	17,525	24,810	28,515	29,813	21,771	24,810	26,343	26,783	102.4	97.7
Georgia	15,464	24,054	26,891	27,573	19,211	24,054	24,843	24,771	90.4	90.4
Hawaii	19,269	24,842	28,808	30,569	23,938	24,842	26,614	27,462	112.6	100.2
Idaho	13,988	20,959	24,692	25,354	17,377	20,959	22,811	22,777	81.8	83.1
Illinois	18,168	27,412	30,616	31,737	22,570	27,412	28,284	28,511	106.2	104.0
Indiana	15,368	23,647	27,125	27,918	19,091	23,647	25,059	25,081	89.8	91.5
Iowa	15,369	23,390	27,794	29,127	19,093	23,390	25,677	26,167	89.8	95.5
Kansas.	15,971	24,047	27,799	29,375	19,840	24,047	25,682	26,390	93.4	96.3
Kentucky	13,621	21,344	24,929	25,429	16,921	21,344	23,030	22,845	79.6	83.3
Louisiana	13,689	20,574	25,256	22,813	17,006	20,574	23,332	20,494	80.0	74.8
Maine.	15,387	22,489	27,512	27,791	19,115	22,489	25,416	24,967	89.9	91.1
Maryland	19,591	28,800	34,282	35,986	24,338	28,800	31,671	32,329	114.5	118.0
Massachusetts.	19,795	30,310	36,169	37,711	24,591	30,310	33,414	33,878	115.7	123.6
Michigan.	16,571	25,435	28,719	29,553	20,586	25,435	26,531	26,549	96.9	96.9
Minnesota.	17,304	27,187	31,702	32,511	21,496	27,187	29,287	29,207	101.1	106.6
Mississippi	11,910	18,935	22,823	23,246	14,796	18,935	21,085	20,883	69.6	76.2
Missouri	15,536	23,676	27,614	28,570	19,300	23,676	25,511	25,666	90.8	93.6
Montana.	13,795	20,233	24,334	26,378	17,137	20,233	22,480	23,697	80.6	86.5
Nebraska	16,031	24,090	28,316	30,158	19,915	24,090	26,159	27,093	93.7	98.8
Nevada	17,866	26,322	30,177	31,841	22,195	26,322	27,878	28,605	104.4	104.4
New Hampshire	18,292	28,566	33,453	34,339	22,724	28,566	30,905	30,849	106.9	112.6
New Jersey.	21,381	32,010	36,223	37,817	26,561	32,010	33,464	33,974	125.0	124.0
New Mexico	13,413	19,578	23,929	25,045	16,663	19,578	22,106	22,500	78.4	82.1
New York	20,183	28,881	32,743	34,208	25,073	28,881	30,249	30,731	118.0	112.1
North Carolina	15,196	23,396	26,232	27,086	18,878	23,396	24,234	24,333	88.8	88.8
North Dakota	14,457	22,596	29,041	28,674	17,960	22,596	26,829	25,760	84.5	94.0
Ohio	16,446	24,263	27,981	28,636	20,431	24,263	25,850	25,726	96.1	93.9
Oklahoma.	14,280	21,517	25,496	26,449	17,740	21,517	23,554	23,761	83.5	86.7
Oregon.	15,823	23,905	26,580	28,153	19,657	23,905	24,555	25,292	92.5	92.3
Pennsylvania.	17,344	25,573	29,789	30,831	21,546	25,573	27,520	27,698	101.4	101.1
Rhode Island.	17,639	25,059	29,996	31,897	21,913	25,059	27,711	28,655	103.1	104.5
South Carolina.	14,095	21,501	24,712	25,562	17,510	21,501	22,830	22,964	82.4	83.8
South Dakota	14,822	23,163	28,711	29,130	18,413	23,163	26,524	26,169	86.6	95.5
Tennessee	15,122	23,409	27,794	28,498	18,786	23,409	25,677	25,602	88.4	93.4
Texas.	15,623	24,965	27,722	29,600	19,408	24,965	25,610	26,592	91.3	97.0
Utah	13,197	20,801	24,122	25,169	16,394	20,801	22,285	22,611	77.1	82.5
Vermont	15,759	24,010	29,640	29,677	19,577	24,010	27,382	26,661	92.1	97.3
Virginia	17,872	26,215	31,277	33,418	22,202	26,215	28,895	30,022	104.5	109.5
Washington.	17,676	27,300	32,219	31,769	21,959	27,309	29,765	28,540	103.3	104.1
West Virginia	12,965	19,535	23,676	24,761	16,106	19,535	21,873	22,244	75.8	81.2
Wisconsin	15,801	24,498	28,645	29,527	19,629	24,498	26,463	26,526	92.4	96.8
Wyoming	16,149	24,497	30,972	32,768	20,062	24,497	28,613	29,438	94.4	107.4

[1] Constant dollar estimates are computed by the Census Bureau using the national implicit price deflator for personal consumption expenditures from the Bureau of Economic Analysis. Any regional differences in the rate of inflation are not reflected in these constant dollar estimates.

Source: Except as noted, U.S. Bureau of Economic Analysis, *Survey of Current Business*, April 2006. See also <http://www.bea.gov/bea/regional/statelocal.htm>.

Table 662. Personal Income by Selected Large Metropolitan Area: 2000 to 2004

[8,422,074 represents $8,422,074,000,000. Metropolitan areas as defined December 2005. See Appendix II]

Metropolitan area ranked by 2004 population	Personal income				Per capita personal income			
	2000 (mil. dol.)	2003 (mil. dol.)	2004 (mil. dol.)	Annual percent change, 2003– 2004	2000 (dol.)	2003 (dol.)	2004 (dol.)	Percent of national aver- age, 2004
United States.................	8,422,074	9,157,257	9,705,504	6.0	29,845	31,484	33,050	100.0
New York-Northern New Jersey-Long Island, NY-NJ-PA MSA.............	732,799	760,159	811,644	6.8	39,915	40,679	43,277	130.9
Los Angeles-Long Beach-Santa Ana, CA MSA........................	385,053	427,041	453,902	6.3	31,045	33,318	35,188	106.5
Chicago-Naperville-Joliet, IL-IN-WI MSA.....	318,439	335,618	349,141	4.0	34,918	35,967	37,169	112.5
Philadelphia-Camden-Wilmington, PA-NJ-DE-MD MSA.................	193,919	213,362	224,811	5.4	34,059	36,971	38,768	117.3
Dallas-Fort Worth-Arlington, TX MSA ...	176,530	190,517	202,219	6.1	33,972	34,109	35,502	107.4
Miami-Fort Lauderdale-Miami Beach, FL MSA .	157,015	172,864	183,587	6.2	31,223	32,762	34,278	103.7
Houston-Sugar Land-Baytown,TX MSA......	161,398	179,138	190,771	6.5	34,040	35,304	36,852	111.5
Washington-Arlington-Alexandria, DC-VA-MD-WV MSA.............	196,093	223,286	241,286	8.1	40,672	43,913	46,782	141.5
Atlanta-Sandy Springs-Marietta, GA MSA ...	141,817	153,070	162,297	6.0	33,122	32,739	33,838	102.4
Detroit-Warren-Livonia, MI MSA........	151,793	162,957	164,543	1.0	34,047	36,330	36,650	110.9
Boston-Cambridge-Quincy, MA-NH MSA....	182,380	191,958	203,527	6.0	41,436	43,345	46,060	139.4
San Francisco-Oakland-Fremont, CA MSA . .	199,989	193,833	204,346	5.4	48,343	46,652	49,276	149.1
Riverside-San Bernardino-Ontario, CA MSA. . .	74,787	89,307	97,560	9.2	22,808	24,499	25,769	78.0
Phoenix-Mesa-Scottsdale, AZ MSA	92,975	106,385	115,604	8.7	28,363	29,609	31,133	94.2
Seattle-Tacoma-Bellevue, WA MSA	115,203	120,821	131,886	9.2	37,746	38,447	41,634	126.0
Minneapolis-St. Paul-Bloomington, MN-WI MSA........................	109,818	119,741	127,365	6.4	36,838	38,836	40,915	123.8
San Diego-Carlsbad-San Marcos, CA MSA ..	92,654	104,050	111,435	7.1	32,803	35,620	37,965	114.9
St. Louis, MO-IL MSA...............	84,222	92,668	96,170	3.8	31,172	33,667	34,735	105.1
Baltimore-Towson, MD MSA..........	85,144	96,583	102,650	6.3	33,293	36,757	38,813	117.4
Tampa-St. Petersburg-Clearwater, FL MSA . .	68,891	76,757	81,929	6.7	28,653	30,341	31,677	95.8
Pittsburgh, PA MSA................	74,361	79,442	83,168	4.7	30,610	32,987	34,685	104.9
Denver-Aurora, CO MSA............	82,196	90,184	95,238	5.6	37,848	39,212	40,939	123.9
Cleveland-Elyria-Mentor, OH MSA......	67,935	69,859	73,111	4.7	31,625	32,651	34,264	103.7
Portland-Vancouver-Beaverton, OR-WA MSA. .	62,190	65,959	69,853	5.9	32,122	32,328	33,875	102.5
Cincinnati-Middletown, OH-KY-IN MSA.....	61,393	66,984	70,689	5.5	30,476	32,738	34,368	104.0
Sacramento-Arden-Arcade-Roseville, CA MSA. .	54,236	62,857	67,162	6.8	29,989	31,829	33,338	100.9
Kansas City, MO-KS MSA............	58,247	63,337	66,654	5.2	31,607	33,191	34,585	104.6
Orlando-Kissimmee, FL MSA..........	44,751	50,821	55,103	8.4	27,017	28,206	29,576	89.5
San Antonio, TX MSA..............	45,997	50,418	53,622	6.4	26,751	27,773	28,946	87.6
San Jose-Sunnyvale-Santa Clara, CA MSA ...	92,947	79,313	84,343	6.3	53,415	45,803	48,530	146.8
Columbus, OH MSA................	49,770	54,931	57,700	5.0	30,743	32,794	34,128	103.3
Las Vegas-Paradise, NV MSA.........	41,239	48,916	54,340	11.1	29,601	31,054	32,963	99.7
Virginia Beach-Norfolk-Newport News, VA-NC MSA......................	41,659	48,892	52,222	6.8	26,364	30,090	31,811	96.3
Providence-New Bedford-Fall River, RI-MA MSA.....................	45,976	52,205	55,181	5.7	28,973	32,176	33,912	102.6
Indianapolis-Carmel, IN MSA.........	48,862	53,807	57,040	6.0	31,916	33,631	35,266	106.7
Milwaukee-Waukesha-West Allis, WI MSA...	49,151	52,865	55,217	4.4	32,717	34,949	36,488	110.4
Charlotte-Gastonia-Concord, NC-SC MSA....	43,120	47,998	51,349	7.0	32,182	33,363	34,816	105.3
Austin-Round Rock, TX MSA	41,157	43,142	45,855	6.3	32,548	31,353	32,494	98.3
Nashville-Davidson-Murfreesboro, TN MSA ...	40,309	45,742	48,690	6.4	30,601	33,354	34,904	105.6
New Orleans-Metairie-Kenner, LA MSA.....	34,606	38,591	40,889	6.0	26,301	29,342	31,024	93.9
Memphis, TN-MS-AR MSA............	34,459	38,592	40,877	5.9	28,518	31,172	32,741	99.1
Jacksonville, FL MSA...............	33,151	36,882	39,505	7.1	29,436	30,826	32,283	97.7
Louisville-Jefferson County, KY-IN MSA....	34,250	37,575	39,650	5.5	29,395	31,580	33,058	100.0
Hartford-West Hartford-East Hartford, CT MSA......................	42,568	45,274	48,353	6.8	36,981	38,389	40,880	123.7
Richmond, VA MSA................	33,603	38,013	40,978	7.8	30,546	33,316	35,422	107.2
Buffalo-Niagara Falls, NY MSA........	31,806	34,135	35,773	4.8	27,210	29,477	31,006	93.8
Oklahoma City, OK MSA............	29,092	33,053	34,785	5.2	26,501	29,202	30,449	92.1
Birmingham-Hoover, AL MSA.........	29,898	33,658	35,770	6.3	28,383	31,348	33,067	100.1
Rochester, NY MSA................	30,455	32,082	33,630	4.8	29,327	30,814	32,303	97.7
Salt Lake City, UT MSA.............	27,081	30,071	32,001	6.4	27,852	29,897	31,419	95.1
Raleigh-Cary, NC MSA.............	27,062	29,407	31,564	7.3	33,654	33,122	34,498	104.4
Tucson, AZ MSA..................	20,514	22,953	24,697	7.6	24,175	25,777	27,244	82.4
Bridgeport-Stamford-Norwalk, CT MSA....	52,190	53,174	56,796	6.8	58,986	59,108	62,979	190.6
Honolulu, HI MSA................	26,605	29,090	31,404	8.0	30,392	32,573	34,911	105.6
Tulsa, OK MSA...................	24,984	26,841	28,315	5.5	29,004	30,523	32,150	97.3
Fresno, CA MSA..................	17,628	20,637	22,136	7.3	21,975	24,267	25,573	77.4
Albany-Schenectady-Troy, NY MSA	25,168	27,278	28,686	5.2	30,444	32,453	33,950	102.7
Dayton, OH MSA.................	24,210	25,681	26,518	3.3	28,549	30,385	31,387	95.0
New Haven-Milford, CT MSA.........	28,379	30,326	32,300	6.5	34,396	36,046	38,254	115.7
Omaha-Council Bluffs, NE-IA MSA......	24,230	27,215	28,980	6.5	31,506	34,363	36,124	109.3
Oxnard-Thousand Oaks-Ventura, CA MSA	25,364	27,980	30,047	7.4	33,521	35,407	37,740	114.2
Albuquerque, NM MSA	18,910	21,731	23,014	5.9	25,848	28,339	29,453	89.1
Allentown-Bethlehem-Easton, PA-NJ MSA...	22,220	24,309	25,589	5.3	29,945	31,606	32,817	99.3
Worcester, MA MSA...............	24,539	26,034	27,550	5.8	32,602	33,576	35,384	107.1
Grand Rapids-Wyoming, MI MSA.......	20,818	22,810	23,553	3.3	28,123	29,926	30,739	93.0
Bakersfield, CA MSA...............	13,891	16,558	17,864	7.9	20,927	23,215	24,335	73.6
Baton Rouge, LA MSA..............	17,206	19,131	20,208	5.6	24,243	26,531	27,780	84.1
El Paso, TX MSA..................	12,650	14,641	15,556	6.2	18,562	20,841	21,829	66.0
Akron, OH MSA..................	20,593	21,756	22,783	4.7	29,590	31,017	32,462	98.2
Springfield, MA MSA...............	18,766	20,415	21,406	4.9	27,576	29,717	31,146	94.2

Source: U.S. Bureau of Economic Analysis, *Survey of Current Business*, May 2006. See also <http://www.bea.gov/bea/regional /statelocal.htm>.

Table 663. **Personal Income and Its Disposition by Households and by Nonprofit Institutions Serving Households: 1995 to 2004**

[Billions of dollars. CCA = Capital consumption adjustment]

Item	1995	1998	1999	2000	2001	2002	2003	2004
Personal income.	6,152	7,423	7,802	8,430	8,724	8,882	9,169	9,713
Compensation of employees, received	4,177	5,020	5,352	5,783	5,942	6,091	6,321	6,688
Proprietors' income with inventory valuation and capital consumption adjustments . . .	492	628	678	728	772	768	810	890
Rental income of persons with capital consumption adjustment.	122	138	147	150	167	153	132	134
Personal income receipts on assets	1,016	1,283	1,264	1,387	1,380	1,333	1,339	1,397
Personal current transfer receipts.	877	979	1,022	1,084	1,194	1,286	1,344	1,428
Less: Contributions for government social insurance . . .	533	624	661	703	731	750	777	822
Less: Personal current taxes	744	1,027	1,108	1,236	1,237	1,052	1,000	1,049
Equals: Disposable personal income	5,408	6,396	6,695	7,194	7,487	7,830	8,169	8,664
Less: Personal outlays	5,157	6,119	6,536	7,026	7,355	7,645	7,996	8,513
Equals: Personal saving	251	277	159	169	132	185	173	152
Personal saving as a percentage of disposable personal income	4.6	4.3	2.4	2.3	1.8	2.4	2.1	1.8
Household income	6,122	7,399	7,777	8,402	8,708	8,874	9,160	9,710
Compensation of employees, received	4,177	5,020	5,352	5,783	5,942	6,091	6,321	6,688
Proprietors' income with inventory valuation and CCA . .	492	628	678	728	772	768	810	890
Rental income of households with CCA.	120	135	145	148	165	151	130	132
Household income receipts on assets.	976	1,244	1,222	1,341	1,341	1,300	1,303	1,365
Household current transfer receipts	889	996	1,041	1,104	1,218	1,314	1,373	1,459
Less: Contributions for government social insurance . . .	533	624	661	703	731	750	777	822
Less: Household current taxes	744	1,027	1,108	1,236	1,237	1,052	1,000	1,049
Equals: Disposable household income	5,378	6,372	6,669	7,167	7,471	7,822	8,160	8,661
Less: Household outlays	5,142	6,131	6,555	7,050	7,363	7,653	7,998	8,526
Household consumption expenditures.	4,872	5,760	6,154	6,594	6,899	7,188	7,543	8,045
Household interest payments [1]	133	175	181	205	212	196	183	187
Household transfer payments	137	197	220	252	251	269	272	294
Equals: Household saving.	236	240	114	117	108	169	162	135
Household saving as a percentage of household disposable income	4.4	3.8	1.7	1.6	1.4	2.2	2.0	1.6
Nonprofit institution income	148	201	223	250	240	242	244	256
Less: Nonprofit institution outlays.	133	164	178	198	215	225	234	239
Equals: Nonprofit institution saving	15	37	45	52	25	16	11	17

[1] Consists of nonmortgage interest paid by households.

Source: U.S. Bureau of Economic Analysis *Survey of Current Business,* November 2005, and http://www.bea.gov/bea /dn/nipaweb/SelectTable.asp?Selected=N (released 10 November 2005).

Table 664. **Flow of Funds Accounts—Composition of Individuals' Savings: 1990 to 2005**

[In billions of dollars (518.3 represents $518,300,000,000). Combined statement for households, farm business, and nonfarm noncorporate business. Minus sign (–) indicates decrease]

Composition of savings	1990	1995	2000	2001	2002	2003	2004	2005
Increase in financial assets	518.3	516.2	396.9	678.5	579.7	984.5	1,042.7	907.7
Foreign deposits.	1.4	4.6	7.6	0.4	1.3	1.3	6.7	5.9
Checkable deposits and currency	-9.5	-43.2	-82.0	68.9	-2.8	-51.2	-25.1	1.5
Time and savings deposits	33.8	147.0	312.0	233.4	328.1	384.8	373.0	466.4
Money market fund shares	31.4	102.4	152.4	163.0	-40.9	-118.3	-47.6	58.6
Securities	210.7	20.3	-497.8	-279.5	-10.9	327.0	122.6	-153.4
Open market paper	5.8	2.0	12.4	–	13.1	-4.5	30.2	28.1
U.S. savings bonds	8.5	5.1	-1.7	5.6	4.5	8.9	0.6	0.7
Other Treasury securities	89.3	-17.5	-208.0	-88.1	-119.9	24.3	58.3	-85.6
Agency and GSE-backed securities [1]	36.3	27.2	33.9	-120.0	-191.1	173.4	95.6	201.8
Municipal securities	35.4	-59.0	4.8	50.6	101.3	33.9	37.3	84.0
Corporate and foreign bonds	52.3	77.5	63.0	-27.5	163.3	-60.1	-114.4	-106.7
Corporate equities [2]	-48.4	-101.2	-486.6	-241.9	-93.3	-77.5	-242.4	-501.1
Mutual fund shares	31.5	86.2	84.4	141.7	111.3	228.6	257.3	225.3
Life insurance reserves	26.5	45.8	50.2	77.2	60.1	66.8	33.1	52.2
Pension fund reserves	191.0	160.1	189.8	213.2	181.4	213.9	230.8	204.4
Miscellaneous and other assets	33.0	79.2	264.6	202.0	63.5	160.3	349.2	272.1
Gross investment in tangible assets.	808.0	1,012.5	1,487.1	1,515.2	1,571.9	1,686.1	1,839.5	1,979.1
Minus: Consumption of fixed capital.	558.8	712.1	940.9	971.4	1,007.9	1,056.9	1,139.3	1,256.7
Equals: Net investment in tangible assets. . .	249.2	300.3	546.3	543.8	564.0	629.2	700.2	722.4
Net increase in liabilities	233.4	410.7	915.9	787.5	899.1	1,093.1	1,501.1	1,609.0
Mortgage debt on nonfarm homes	206.0	168.1	399.0	494.0	672.1	778.2	973.3	1,126.1
Other mortgage debt [3]	-0.3	5.8	117.4	104.8	95.3	160.2	171.9	240.4
Consumer credit	15.1	147.4	168.1	132.3	87.1	88.4	88.8	62.5
Policy loans	4.1	10.5	2.8	2.2	1.1	-0.6	1.7	-0.2
Security credit	-3.7	3.5	7.2	-38.8	-48.2	34.3	81.5	-31.7
Other liabilities [3]	12.2	75.4	221.2	92.9	91.7	32.7	184.0	211.9
Personal saving with consumer durables [4] . .	549.3	426.6	633.7	471.6	274.9	535.1	257.4	37.3
Personal saving without consumer durable [4] . . .	473.3	330.9	-142.2	277.3	69.7	325.8	41.1	-181.9
Personal saving (NIPA, excludes consumer durables) [5] . .	299.4	250.9	168.5	132.3	184.7	172.8	151.8	-33.9

– Represents or rounds to zero.   [1] GSE = government-sponsored enterprises.   [2] Only directly held and those in closed-end funds. Other equities are included in mutual funds, life insurance and pension reserves, and bank personal trusts.   [3] Includes corporate farms.   [4] Flow of Funds measure.   [5] National Income and Product Accounts measure.

Source: Board of Governors of the Federal Reserve System, Federal Reserve Statistical Release, Z.1, Flow of Funds Accounts of the United States; published: 9 March 2006; <http://www.federalreserve.gov/releases/z1/20060309/>.

Income, Expenditures and Wealth   441

Table 665. Average Annual Expenditures of All Consumer Units by Selected Major Types of Expenditure: 1990 to 2004

[In dollars, except as indicated (96,968 represents 96,968,000). Based on Consumer Expenditure Survey. Data are averages for the noninstitutional population. Expenditures reported here are out-of-pocket]

Type	1990	1995	1999	2000	2001	2002	2003	2004
Number of consumer units (1,000)......	96,968	103,123	108,465	109,367	110,339	112,108	115,356	116,282
Expenditures, total............	**$28,381**	**$32,264**	**$36,995**	**$38,045**	**$39,518**	**$40,677**	**$40,817**	**$43,395**
Food....................	4,296	4,505	5,031	5,158	5,321	5,375	5,340	5,781
Food at home [1]..........	2,485	2,803	2,915	3,021	3,086	3,099	3,129	3,347
Meats, poultry, fish, and eggs	668	752	749	795	828	798	825	880
Dairy products	295	297	322	325	332	328	328	371
Fruits and vegetables...........	408	457	500	521	522	552	535	561
Other food at home...........	746	856	896	927	952	970	999	1,075
Food away from home..........	1,811	1,702	2,116	2,137	2,235	2,276	2,211	2,434
Alcoholic beverages	293	277	318	372	349	376	391	459
Housing [1]...................	8,703	10,458	12,057	12,319	13,011	13,283	13,432	13,918
Shelter................	4,836	5,928	7,016	7,114	7,602	7,829	7,887	7,998
Fuels, utilities, public services	1,890	2,191	2,377	2,489	2,767	2,684	2,811	2,927
Apparel and services	1,618	1,704	1,743	1,856	1,743	1,749	1,640	1,816
Transportation [1]..............	5,120	6,014	7,011	7,417	7,633	7,759	7,781	7,801
Vehicle purchases............	2,129	2,638	3,305	3,418	3,579	3,665	3,732	3,397
Gasoline and motor oil..........	1,047	1,006	1,055	1,291	1,279	1,235	1,333	1,598
Other vehicle expenses..........	1,642	2,015	2,254	2,281	2,375	2,471	2,331	2,365
Health care.................	1,480	1,732	1,959	2,066	2,182	2,350	2,416	2,574
Entertainment................	1,422	1,612	1,891	1,863	1,953	2,079	2,060	2,218
Reading..................	153	162	159	146	141	139	127	130
Tobacco products, smoking supplies	274	269	300	319	308	320	290	288
Personal insurance and pensions	2,592	2,964	3,436	3,365	3,737	3,899	4,055	4,823
Life and other personal insurance	345	373	394	399	410	406	397	390
Pensions and Social Security	2,248	2,591	3,042	2,966	3,326	3,493	3,658	4,433

[1] Includes expenditures not shown separately.

Source: U.S. Bureau of Labor Statistics, *Consumer Expenditures in 2004;* and earlier reports. See also <http://stats.bls.gov/cex/home.htm>.

Table 666. Average Annual Expenditures of All Consumer Units by Metropolitan Area: 2003–2004

[In dollars. Metropolitan areas defined June 30, 1983, CMSA = Consolidated Metropolitan Statistical Area; MSA = Metropolitan Statistical Area; PMSA = Primary Metropolitan Statistical Area. See text, Section 1, and Appendix II. See headnote, Table 665]

Metropolitan area	Total expendi- tures [1]	Housing				Transportation			Health care
		Food	Total [1]	Shel- ter	Utility, fuels [2]	Total [1]	Vehicle pur- chases	Gaso- line and motor oil	
Anchorage, AK MSA.............	53,520	6,585	17,438	10,811	2,824	10,493	5,129	1,622	2,858
Atlanta, GA MSA	37,130	5,241	13,711	8,233	3,372	5,794	2,320	1,295	1,760
Baltimore, MD MSA..............	37,681	4,688	13,640	8,584	2,846	5,970	2,290	1,257	2,077
Boston-Lawrence-Salem, MA-NH CMSA..............	46,444	6,578	16,337	10,556	2,822	7,400	3,443	1,299	2,274
Chicago-Gary-Lake County, IL-IN-WI CMSA..............	50,627	6,023	18,114	10,737	3,383	8,179	3,618	1,449	2,704
Cincinnati-Hamilton, OH-KY-IN CMSA.	40,594	5,333	13,573	8,046	2,685	7,268	3,317	1,400	2,341
Cleveland-Akron-Lorain, OH CMSA ..	37,070	4,589	12,616	7,237	3,287	6,753	2,744	1,244	2,161
Dallas-Fort Worth, TX CMSA	50,304	6,111	15,891	9,050	3,604	9,574	4,624	1,640	3,063
Denver-Boulder-Greeley, CO CMSA..	48,719	6,263	15,762	9,790	2,878	8,610	3,583	1,447	2,647
Detroit-Ann Arbor, MI CMSA.......	46,731	5,726	15,011	8,930	3,070	8,974	3,473	1,639	2,005
Honolulu, HI MSA.............	48,339	6,666	15,874	10,324	2,606	8,778	4,356	1,277	2,668
Houston-Galveston-Brazoria, TX CMSA..............	48,063	5,737	15,512	8,706	3,594	9,126	4,250	1,686	2,642
Kansas City, MO-Kansas City, KS CMSA..............	46,308	6,092	15,129	7,626	3,419	8,518	3,996	1,689	2,813
Los Angeles-Long Beach, CA PMSA.	52,652	7,194	18,714	12,054	2,713	9,733	4,096	1,938	2,309
Miami-Fort Lauderdale, FL CMSA ...	39,875	5,758	15,907	10,086	3,109	6,791	2,386	1,397	1,924
Milwaukee, WI PMSA	42,111	5,189	14,575	8,993	2,790	7,145	3,261	1,444	2,643
Minneapolis-St. Paul, MN-WI MSA...	55,951	6,549	18,282	10,697	2,928	9,202	3,878	1,610	2,928
New York-Northern New Jersey- Long Island, NY-NJ-CT CMSA....	51,979	7,054	19,708	13,047	3,248	7,599	2,672	1,198	2,224
Philadelphia-Wilmington-Trenton, PA-NJ-DE-MD CMSA..........	44,484	5,622	15,200	9,015	3,312	7,678	3,623	1,243	2,126
Phoenix-Mesa, AZ MSA...........	46,628	5,698	14,524	8,374	2,851	10,529	5,612	1,455	2,609
Pittsburgh-Beaver Valley, PA CMSA ..	40,604	5,527	12,021	6,322	2,964	6,488	2,483	1,266	2,527
Portland-Vancouver, OR-WA CMSA ..	47,762	6,276	15,655	9,363	2,794	7,276	2,845	1,433	2,972
San Diego, CA MSA	53,949	6,545	19,365	13,041	2,633	9,871	4,532	1,733	2,605
San Francisco-Oakland-San Jose, CA CMSA..............	56,162	7,108	21,075	14,527	2,670	8,878	3,441	1,590	2,775
Seattle-Tacoma, WA CMSA	52,843	6,854	16,703	10,381	2,631	9,345	4,204	1,528	2,992
St. Louis-East St. Louis-Alton, MO-IL CMSA	47,793	5,976	14,330	7,904	3,178	8,978	4,737	1,450	2,837
Tampa-St. Petersburg-Clearwater, FL MSA..............	35,911	4,750	13,123	7,512	3,008	6,855	3,078	1,191	2,241
Washington, DC-MD-VA MSA	53,251	6,049	19,461	12,685	3,361	8,086	3,280	1,496	2,419

[1] Includes expenditures not shown separately.   [2] Includes public services.

Source: U.S. Bureau of Labor Statistics, "Consumer Expenditures"; and earlier reports. See also <http://stats.bls.gov/cex/home.htm>.

442   Income, Expenditures, and Wealth

Table 667. Average Annual Expenditures of All Consumer Units by Race, Hispanic Origin, and Age of Householder: 2004

[**In dollars.** Based on Consumer Expenditure Survey. Data are averages for the noninstitutional population. Expenditures reported here are out-of-pocket]

Type	All consumer units [1]	White and all other races	Asian	Black or African American	Hispanic or Latino	Age of householder Under 25 yrs.	65 yrs. and over
Expenditures, total	**43,395**	**44,962**	**49,459**	**30,286**	**37,578**	**24,535**	**31,104**
Food	5,781	5,958	6,742	4,265	5,911	3,715	4,206
Food at home	3,347	3,418	3,689	2,749	3,883	1,853	2,722
Cereals and bakery products	461	469	527	388	517	265	394
Cereals and cereal products	154	151	243	152	202	99	118
Bakery products	307	318	284	236	315	166	276
Meats, poultry, fish, and eggs	880	872	1,021	898	1,175	480	694
Beef	265	274	231	216	367	148	205
Pork	181	177	183	208	236	95	148
Other meats	108	113	64	87	113	53	91
Poultry	156	150	192	186	231	101	108
Fish and seafood	128	117	305	157	159	57	103
Eggs	42	41	46	44	68	26	38
Dairy products	371	391	286	249	425	205	313
Fresh milk and cream	144	151	135	100	201	86	118
Other dairy products	226	240	151	149	224	119	195
Fruits and vegetables	561	566	870	442	712	285	510
Fresh fruits	187	189	329	130	249	92	174
Fresh vegetables	183	185	359	120	250	86	167
Processed fruits	110	110	118	107	127	64	99
Processed vegetables	82	82	63	86	86	44	70
Other food at home	1,075	1,121	985	772	1,054	618	812
Nonalcoholic beverages	290	300	245	227	328	171	201
Food away from home	2,434	2,539	3,053	1,516	2,027	1,862	1,484
Alcoholic beverages	459	505	325	171	320	503	261
Housing	13,918	14,181	17,418	11,043	12,884	7,649	10,259
Shelter	7,998	8,071	11,728	6,411	7,833	4,901	5,329
Owned dwellings [2]	5,324	5,530	7,734	3,165	4,107	1,009	3,523
Mortgage interest and charges	2,936	3,001	4,810	1,936	2,589	615	863
Property taxes	1,391	1,461	1,900	743	866	236	1,416
Rented dwellings	2,201	2,022	3,537	3,097	3,501	3,647	1,393
Other lodging	473	519	458	149	226	244	414
Utilities, fuels, and public services	2,927	2,938	2,781	2,884	2,671	1,413	2,580
Natural gas	424	419	442	452	337	135	442
Electricity	1,064	1,069	876	1,088	909	507	957
Fuel oil and other fuels	121	133	40	52	73	28	163
Telephone	990	982	1,078	1,025	1,031	642	695
Water and other public services	327	335	345	267	320	101	323
Household operations	753	788	885	466	574	270	694
Personal services	300	302	450	241	331	159	201
Other household expenses	453	486	435	225	243	110	493
Housekeeping supplies	594	630	472	374	503	253	509
Household furnishings and equipment [2] . .	1,646	1,754	1,552	907	1,303	812	1,147
Household textiles	158	167	96	107	110	55	154
Furniture	417	426	513	326	351	261	236
Floor coverings	52	55	64	25	22	7	44
Major appliances	204	220	139	109	205	72	175
Miscellaneous household equipment . . .	711	775	573	294	536	355	448
Apparel and services	1,816	1,821	1,885	1,765	1,817	1,371	907
Men and boys	406	411	548	334	413	235	204
Women and girls	739	750	718	665	586	587	431
Children under 2 years old	79	82	82	50	144	102	20
Footwear	329	304	313	508	424	258	123
Other apparel products and services	264	273	224	208	250	188	129
Transportation . . . . [2] .	7,801	8,166	8,556	4,976	7,497	4,704	4,875
Vehicle purchases (net outlay) [2] . .	3,397	3,615	3,676	1,759	3,445	2,035	1,966
Cars and trucks, new	1,748	1,860	2,307	786	1,604	542	1,089
Cars and trucks, used	1,582	1,678	1,354	960	1,833	1,430	872
Gasoline and motor oil	1,598	1,647	1,637	1,231	1,650	1,130	963
Other vehicle expenses [2]	2,365	2,460	2,330	1,696	2,048	1,326	1,546
Vehicle finance charges	323	338	260	240	285	147	115
Maintenance and repair	652	681	701	427	574	400	490
Vehicle insurance	964	995	954	745	865	535	711
Public transportation	441	443	913	290	355	214	400
Health care [3]	2,574	2,762	2,101	1,368	1,588	654	3,899
Entertainment [4]	2,218	2,401	1,789	1,040	1,443	1,166	1,429
Personal care products and services	581	595	506	503	519	334	468
Reading	130	142	112	53	53	51	146
Education	905	904	2,087	573	438	1,821	274
Tobacco products and smoking supplies	288	308	103	200	155	236	147
Miscellaneous	690	728	569	457	477	297	641
Cash contributions	1,408	1,501	1,089	835	710	310	2,000
Personal insurance and pensions	4,823	4,991	6,176	3,230	3,765	1,726	1,592
Life and other personal insurance	390	408	306	292	155	31	372
Pensions and social security	4,433	4,584	5,871	2,938	3,610	1,695	1,220
Personal taxes	**2,166**	**2,399**	**2,131**	**507**	**895**	**333**	**948**

[1] Includes other householders not shown separately. [2] Includes other types not shown separately. [3] For additional health care expenditures, see Table 131. [4] For additional recreation expenditures, see Section 26.

Source: U.S. Bureau of Labor Statistics, *Consumer Expenditures in 2004.* See also <http://www.bls.gov/cex/2004/Standard/race.pdf> and <http://www.bls.gov/cex/2004/Standard/hispanic.pdf> and <http://www.bls.gov/cex/2004/Standard/age.pdf> (released 29 November 2005).

Income, Expenditures, and Wealth   443

[**In dollars.** For composition of regions, see map, inside front cover. See headnote, Table 665]

Type	Region				Size of consumer unit				
	North-east	Mid-west	South	West	One person	Two per-sons	Three per-sons	Four per-sons	Five or more
Expenditures, total	**46,115**	**43,371**	**39,174**	**47,922**	**25,423**	**45,855**	**51,503**	**57,866**	**55,468**
Food	6,368	5,592	5,318	6,224	3,095	5,808	6,930	8,171	8,516
Food at home	3,634	3,189	3,119	3,634	1,681	3,288	4,007	4,809	5,416
Cereals and bakery products	521	446	427	480	229	435	556	673	791
Cereals and cereal products	176	141	143	165	73	135	190	224	303
Bakery products	346	305	284	314	156	300	366	449	489
Meats, poultry, fish, and eggs	1,008	781	849	922	411	864	1,097	1,252	1,464
Beef	279	242	263	283	117	251	342	394	455
Pork	189	170	189	172	83	182	229	252	295
Other meats	135	119	92	100	49	108	124	160	188
Poultry	194	127	149	163	75	146	200	215	274
Fish and seafood	164	91	117	154	63	138	152	176	180
Eggs	47	32	40	51	24	40	49	55	71
Dairy products	417	358	329	411	183	358	442	548	608
Fresh milk and cream	156	137	133	161	69	127	177	218	273
Other dairy products	261	221	197	249	114	231	265	330	335
Fruits and vegetables	638	510	501	645	298	576	643	745	908
Fresh fruits	213	171	161	222	101	198	204	243	299
Fresh vegetables	208	148	166	225	93	194	216	231	291
Processed fruits	127	112	93	120	62	105	129	154	177
Processed vegetables	89	78	82	78	42	79	94	117	141
Other food at home	1,050	1,094	1,013	1,177	560	1,055	1,269	1,590	1,644
Nonalcoholic beverages	279	278	286	316	155	286	349	427	415
Food away from home	2,733	2,403	2,199	2,590	1,414	2,520	2,924	3,362	3,100
Alcoholic beverages	625	427	348	532	359	569	468	478	345
Housing	15,734	13,438	12,250	15,557	9,244	14,036	16,177	18,360	17,593
Shelter	9,626	7,339	6,621	9,513	5,841	7,866	9,036	10,382	9,849
Owned dwellings [1]	6,387	5,260	4,456	5,887	2,916	5,311	6,263	7,977	7,299
Mortgage interest and charges . . .	3,057	2,750	2,531	3,678	1,360	2,566	3,712	5,023	4,683
Property taxes	2,131	1,530	1,046	1,176	832	1,552	1,515	1,864	1,654
Rented dwellings	2,674	1,556	1,826	3,066	2,659	1,930	2,213	1,921	2,121
Other lodging	565	523	339	560	265	625	561	484	429
Utilities, fuels, and public services	3,098	2,957	2,975	2,672	1,830	3,004	3,470	3,757	3,917
Natural gas	564	631	255	365	274	429	498	538	580
Electricity	985	958	1,288	880	649	1,101	1,256	1,379	1,440
Fuel oil and other fuels	322	105	69	48	84	138	132	138	126
Telephone	988	946	1,031	971	634	997	1,207	1,270	1,293
Water and other public services	240	317	331	407	188	339	377	432	479
Household operations	793	707	673	894	443	595	980	1,346	993
Personal services	352	301	257	323	125	55	516	808	565
Other household expenses	442	406	417	571	318	540	464	537	427
Housekeeping supplies	586	661	549	606	315	661	713	802	720
Household furnishings and equipment [1]	1,630	1,775	1,432	1,871	816	1,909	1,977	2,073	2,114
Household textiles	209	126	151	158	87	199	167	173	195
Furniture	381	438	356	523	174	487	488	568	585
Floor coverings	44	57	35	81	24	67	70	64	43
Major appliances	216	234	161	232	88	245	232	244	314
Miscellaneous household equipment	685	822	630	748	385	790	878	914	866
Apparel and services	2,176	1,672	1,643	1,936	949	1,758	2,266	2,601	2,784
Men and boys	460	407	377	406	169	374	497	642	746
Women and girls	933	661	662	777	416	751	922	1,034	951
Children under 2 years old	69	79	73	95	12	42	137	170	178
Footwear	427	271	312	332	186	271	435	480	570
Other apparel products and services . . .	287	254	220	325	166	319	275	276	339
Transportation	7,622	7,710	7,233	8,966	3,941	8,151	9,790	11,148	10,258
Vehicle purchases (net outlay) [1]	3,196	3,315	3,195	3,979	1,600	3,412	4,297	5,298	4,575
Cars and trucks, new	1,590	1,610	1,627	2,221	796	1,921	2,154	2,726	1,966
Cars and trucks, used	1,512	1,621	1,520	1,703	776	1,373	2,094	2,506	2,573
Gasoline and motor oil	1,386	1,620	1,598	1,755	806	1,634	1,994	2,250	2,293
Other vehicle expenses [1]	2,396	2,413	2,160	2,622	1,281	2,543	2,976	3,136	2,951
Vehicle finance charges	256	331	357	318	127	342	420	479	477
Maintenance and repair	590	654	578	821	404	699	794	804	793
Vehicle insurance	991	924	944	1,017	537	1,019	1,218	1,285	1,200
Public transportation	644	363	280	609	254	561	523	464	439
Health care [2]	2,371	2,861	2,508	2,560	1,697	3,212	2,865	2,635	2,520
Entertainment [3]	2,017	2,208	2,134	2,538	1,162	2,618	2,417	2,910	2,743
Personal care products and services	631	563	542	620	355	631	650	740	753
Reading	145	150	98	150	97	161	129	138	118
Education	1,152	928	631	1,115	629	793	1,019	1,417	1,190
Tobacco products and smoking supplies . .	296	340	291	223	167	309	374	346	365
Miscellaneous	760	797	512	809	517	780	763	745	714
Cash contributions	1,108	1,790	1,252	1,525	1,027	1,888	1,393	1,162	1,327
Personal insurance and pensions	5,110	4,895	4,414	5,167	2,184	5,141	6,263	7,014	6,242
Life and other personal insurance	364	439	394	357	146	486	479	496	513
Pensions and Social Security	4,746	4,456	4,020	4,809	2,039	4,655	5,783	6,518	5,729
Personal taxes	**2,377**	**2,445**	**1,695**	**2,460**	**1,383**	**2,914**	**2,541**	**2,343**	**1,127**

[1] Includes other types not shown separately.   [2] For additional health care expenditures, see Table 131.   [3] For additional recreation expenditures, see Section 26.

Source: U.S. Bureau of Labor Statistics, *Consumer Expenditures in 2004.* See also <http://www.bls.gov/cex/2004/Standard/race.pdf> and <http://www.bls.gov/cex/2004/Standard/hispanic.pdf> and <http://www.bls.gov/cex/2004/Standard/age.pdf> (released 29 November 2005).

Table 669. **Average Annual Expenditures of All Consumer Units by Income Level: 2004**

[**In dollars.** Based on Consumer Expenditure Survey. Data are averages for the noninstitutional population. Expenditures reported here are out-of-pocket]

Income level	Total expendi-tures [1]	Food	Housing			Transportation			Health care
			Total [1]	Shelter	Utility, fuels [2]	Total [1]	Vehicle pur-chases	Gaso-line and motor oil	
All consumer units	**43,395**	**5,781**	**13,918**	**7,998**	**2,927**	**7,801**	**3,397**	**1,598**	**2,574**
Consumer units with complete reporting:									
Less than $70,000	31,280	4,562	10,456	6,004	2,498	5,756	2,459	1,307	2,195
$70,000 to $79,999	55,012	7,337	17,422	10,213	3,552	9,965	4,218	2,131	3,029
$80,000 to $99,999	65,446	7,467	20,397	11,761	3,903	12,446	5,516	2,366	3,384
$100,000 and over	93,526	10,733	28,140	16,143	4,511	15,707	7,106	2,559	4,042
$100,000 to $119,999	75,213	9,444	22,273	12,871	3,977	13,520	6,013	2,452	3,732
$120,000 to $149,999	87,299	10,419	26,339	14,869	4,446	15,515	7,028	2,686	3,812
$150,000 and over	119,449	12,555	36,246	20,843	5,159	18,308	8,364	2,573	4,581

[1] Includes expenditures not shown separately.   [2] Includes public service.

Source: U.S. Bureau of Labor Statistics, *Consumer Expenditures in 2004*. See also <http://www.bls.gov/cex/2004/share /higherincome.pdf> (released 29 November 2005).

Table 670. **Annual Expenditure Per Child by Husband-Wife Families by Family Income and Expenditure Type: 2005**

[**In dollars**. Expenditures based on data from the 1990–92 Consumer Expenditure Survey updated to 2004 dollars using the Consumer Price Index. Excludes expenses for college. For more on the methodology, see report cited below]

Family income and age of child	Total	Expenditure type							
		Housing	Food	Trans-por-tation	Clothing	Health care	Child care and educa-tion	Miscel-lan-eous [1]	
INCOME: LESS THAN $43,200									
Less than 2 years old	7,300	2,770	1,000	880	350	550	1,080	670	
3 to 5 years old.	7,480	2,740	1,120	850	340	520	1,220	690	
6 to 8 years old.	7,510	2,640	1,440	990	380	600	730	730	
9 to 11 years old.	7,480	2,390	1,720	1,080	420	660	440	770	
12 to 14 years old.	8,310	2,660	1,810	1,210	700	660	310	960	
15 to 17 years old.	8,290	2,150	1,960	1,630	620	710	510	710	
INCOME: $43,200 to $72,600									
Less than 2 years old	10,220	3,750	1,200	1,310	410	720	1,780	1,050	
3 to 5 years old.	10,500	3,710	1,390	1,280	400	690	1,970	1,060	
6 to 8 years old.	10,410	3,620	1,770	1,420	440	790	1,270	1,100	
9 to 11 years old.	10,250	3,360	2,080	1,500	490	850	830	1,140	
12 to 14 years old.	10,990	3,640	2,090	1,640	820	860	610	1,330	
15 to 17 years old.	11,290	3,120	2,330	2,080	730	910	1,040	1,080	
INCOME: MORE THAN $72,600									
Less than 2 years old	15,190	5,960	1,590	1,830	540	830	2,690	1,750	
3 to 5 years old.	15,550	5,920	1,800	1,800	530	800	2,930	1,770	
6 to 8 years old.	15,250	5,830	2,170	1,940	570	910	2,020	1,810	
9 to 11 years old.	14,970	5,570	2,520	2,030	620	980	1,400	1,850	
12 to 14 years old.	15,800	5,850	2,650	2,160	1,040	980	1,080	2,040	
15 to 17 years old.	16,390	5,330	2,790	2,620	940	1,040	1,890	1,780	

[1] Expenses include personal care items, entertainment, and reading materials.

Source: Dept. of Agriculture, Center for Nutrition Policy and Promotion, *Expenditures on Children by Families*, 2005 Annual Report. See also <http://www.cnpp.usda.gov/Crc/crc2005.pdf> (released April 2006).

Income, Expenditures, and Wealth   445

Table 671. **Money Income of Households—Percent Distribution by Income Level, Race, and Hispanic Origin, in Constant (2004) Dollars: 1980 to 2004**

[Constant dollars based on CPI-U-RS deflator. Households as of **March of following year. (82,368 represents 82,368,000).** Based on Current Population Survey; see text, Sections 1 and 13, and Appendix III. For data collection changes over time, see <http://www.census.gov/hhes/income/histinc/hstchg.html>. For definition of median, see Guide to Tabular Presentation]

Year	Number of house- holds (1,000)	Percent distribution							Median income (dollars)
		Under $15,000	$15,000– $24,999	$25,000– $34,999	$35,000– $49,999	$50,000– $74,999	$75,000– $99,999	$100,000 and over	
ALL HOUSEHOLDS [1]									
1980	82,368	18.1	14.3	13.6	17.7	20.3	9.1	6.9	38,453
1990 [2]	94,312	16.6	13.0	12.5	17.1	19.5	10.3	11.1	41,963
2000 [2]	108,209	14.2	12.2	12.1	15.2	18.5	11.7	16.0	46,058
2002	111,278	15.3	12.5	12.2	14.8	18.2	11.5	15.6	44,546
2003	112,000	15.6	12.7	11.9	14.7	18.0	11.2	15.9	44,482
2004	113,146	15.4	12.9	11.9	14.8	18.3	11.0	15.7	44,389
WHITE									
1980	71,872	16.1	13.8	13.6	18.1	21.3	9.7	7.5	40,568
1990 [2]	80,968	14.4	12.8	12.5	17.4	20.1	11.0	11.8	43,768
2000 [2]	90,030	13.0	11.8	12.0	15.2	19.0	12.3	16.9	48,171
2003 [3, 4]	91,962	13.8	12.4	11.8	14.8	18.5	11.7	16.9	46,857
2004 [3, 4]	92,702	13.8	12.6	11.7	14.8	18.8	11.5	16.8	46,697
BLACK									
1980	8,847	34.7	18.2	14.0	14.5	12.2	4.4	2.0	23,372
1990 [2]	10,671	33.2	15.3	12.9	14.7	14.1	5.2	4.6	26,173
2000 [2]	13,174	23.8	15.9	13.7	15.9	15.6	7.5	7.6	32,541
2003 [3, 5]	13,629	27.0	15.6	13.6	14.6	14.8	7.3	7.1	30,442
2004 [3, 5]	13,792	26.6	16.0	14.1	14.8	14.6	7.2	6.6	30,134
ASIAN AND PACIFIC ISLANDER									
1990 [2]	1,958	12.7	9.7	8.8	14.8	22.6	12.8	18.6	53,885
2000 [2]	3,963	10.7	8.4	9.6	13.6	18.1	14.8	24.9	61,159
2003 [3, 6]	4,040	15.1	9.4	7.1	13.3	17.9	12.9	24.3	57,196
2004 [3, 6]	4,140	11.6	9.0	8.9	13.5	19.2	12.4	25.4	57,518
HISPANIC [7]									
1980	3,906	23.3	19.4	15.8	17.3	15.9	5.3	3.0	29,640
1990 [2]	6,220	23.6	17.0	14.5	17.8	15.7	6.2	5.2	31,294
2000 [2]	10,034	16.9	16.4	14.8	17.8	17.3	9.1	7.6	36,382
2003	11,693	18.6	17.2	15.9	16.5	15.9	8.2	7.8	33,884
2004	12,181	18.5	17.4	14.9	17.0	16.5	7.7	8.0	34,241

[1] Includes other races not shown separately. [2] Data reflect implementation of Census 2000-based population controls and a 28,000 household sample expansion to 78,000 households. [3] Beginning with the 2003 Current Population Survey (CPS), the questionnaire allowed respondents to choose more than one race. For 2002 and later, data represent persons who selected this race group only and excludes persons reporting more than one race. The CPS in prior years allowed respondents to report only one race group. See also comments on race in the text for Section 1. [4] Data represents White alone, which refers to people who reported White and did not report any other race category. [5] Data represents Black alone, which refers to people who reported Black and did not report any other race category. [6] Data represents Asian alone, which refers to people who reported Asian and did not report any other race category. [7] People of Hispanic origin may be of any race.

Source: U.S. Census Bureau, *Current Population Reports,* P60-229; and Internet sites <http://www.census.gov/prod/2005pubs/p60-229.pdf> (released 30 August 2005) and <http://www.census.gov/hhes/www/income/histinc/inchhtoc.html>.

Table 672. **Money Income of Households—Median Income by Race and Hispanic Origin, in Current and Constant (2004) Dollars: 1980 to 2004**

[**In dollars.** See headnote, Table 671]

Year	Median income in current dollars					Median income in constant (2004) dollars				
	All house- holds [1]	White [2]	Black [3]	Asian, Pacific Islander [4]	His- panic [5]	All house- holds [1]	White [2]	Black [3]	Asian, Pacific Islander [4]	His- panic [5]
1980	17,710	18,684	10,764	(NA)	13,651	38,453	40,568	23,372	(NA)	29,640
1990	29,943	31,231	18,676	38,450	22,330	41,963	43,768	26,173	53,885	31,294
1995	34,076	35,766	22,393	40,614	22,860	41,943	44,023	27,563	49,991	28,138
1996	35,492	37,161	23,482	43,276	24,906	42,544	44,545	28,148	51,875	29,855
1997	37,005	38,972	25,050	45,249	26,628	43,430	45,739	29,400	53,106	31,252
1998	38,885	40,912	25,351	46,637	28,330	45,003	47,349	29,340	53,975	32,787
1999	40,696	42,325	27,910	50,960	30,746	46,129	47,975	31,636	57,763	34,851
2000 [6]	41,990	43,916	29,667	55,757	33,168	46,058	48,171	32,541	61,159	36,382
2001 [7]	42,228	44,517	29,470	53,635	33,565	45,062	47,504	31,448	57,234	35,817
2002 [7]	42,409	45,086	29,026	52,626	33,103	44,546	47,358	30,489	55,278	34,771
2003	43,318	45,631	29,645	55,699	32,997	44,482	46,857	30,442	57,196	33,884
2004	44,389	46,697	30,134	57,518	34,241	44,389	46,697	30,134	57,518	34,241

NA Not available. [1] Includes other races not shown separately. [2] Beginning with 2002, data represents White alone, which refers to people who reported White and did not report any other race category. [3] Beginning with 2002, data represents Black alone, which refers to people who reported Black and did not report any other race category. [4] Beginning with 2002, data represents Asian alone, which refers to people who reported Asian and did not report any other race category. [5] People of Hispanic origin may be of any race. [6] Implementation of Census 2000-based population controls and sample expanded by 28,000 households. [7] See footnote 2, Table 671. See also comments on race in the text for Section 1.

Source: U.S. Census Bureau, *Current Population Reports,* P60-229; and Internet sites <http://www.census.gov/prod/2004pubs/p60-229.pdf> (released 30 August 2005) and <http://www.census.gov/hhes/www/income/histinc/inchhtoc.html>.

446 Income, Expenditures, and Wealth

Table 673. Money Income of Households—Distribution by Income Level and Selected Characteristics: 2004

[113,146 represents 113,146,000. Households as of **March of the following year**. Based on Current Population Survey; see text, Sections 1 and 13, and Appendix III. For definition of median, see Guide to Tabular Presentation]

Characteristic	Total	Under $15,000	$15,000– $24,999	$25,000– $34,999	$35,000– $49,999	$50,000– $74,999	$75,000– $99,999	$100,000 and over	Median income (dollars)
Total	113,146	17,361	14,634	13,475	16,736	20,698	12,428	17,814	44,389
Age of householder:									
15 to 24 years	6,686	1,714	1,283	1,037	1,207	859	298	288	27,586
25 to 34 years	19,255	2,196	2,215	2,617	3,602	4,148	2,235	2,238	45,485
35 to 44 years	23,226	2,192	2,043	2,384	3,435	5,015	3,386	4,768	56,785
45 to 54 years	23,370	2,379	1,909	2,121	3,023	4,811	3,362	5,765	61,111
55 to 64 years	17,476	2,365	1,900	1,983	2,409	3,315	2,132	3,370	50,400
65 years and over	23,135	6,513	5,283	3,335	3,060	2,543	1,016	1,385	24,509
Region: [1] Northeast	21,137	3,335	2,541	2,183	2,835	3,787	2,437	4,018	47,994
Midwest	25,911	3,847	3,342	3,094	3,915	4,898	3,131	3,684	44,657
South	41,159	6,953	5,681	5,231	6,267	7,255	4,098	5,673	40,773
West	24,939	3,223	3,068	2,968	3,719	4,757	2,761	4,439	47,680
Size of household:									
One person	29,859	10,131	6,005	4,397	4,024	3,088	1,140	1,073	22,480
Two people	37,247	3,732	4,889	4,895	6,182	7,469	4,202	5,878	47,031
Three people	18,347	1,676	1,588	1,724	2,759	4,034	2,700	3,865	57,876
Four people	16,506	1,066	1,219	1,370	2,129	3,650	2,713	4,358	65,869
Five people	7,230	488	555	694	998	1,620	1,120	1,754	62,475
Six people	2,522	166	251	255	419	524	342	566	57,087
Seven or more people	1,435	104	123	139	227	314	208	319	58,688
Type of household:									
Family households	77,010	6,695	8,002	8,311	11,471	16,168	10,551	15,815	55,327
Married-couple	58,109	2,826	4,871	5,515	8,132	12,971	9,224	14,573	63,813
Male householder, wife absent	4,893	517	563	674	994	1,044	533	568	44,923
Female householder, husband absent	14,009	3,351	2,569	2,120	2,345	2,154	796	675	29,826
Nonfamily households	36,136	10,667	6,631	5,166	5,265	4,532	1,877	1,998	26,176
Male householder	16,344	3,659	2,700	2,355	2,738	2,497	1,111	1,284	31,967
Female householder	19,792	7,007	3,930	2,809	2,527	2,036	765	714	21,797
Educational attainment of householder: [2]									
Total	106,461	15,647	13,350	12,437	15,529	19,840	12,131	17,526	45,996
Less than 9th grade	6,355	2,443	1,539	833	747	505	191	98	19,541
9th to 12th grade (no diploma)	9,217	3,120	1,899	1,363	1,171	958	398	306	22,476
High school graduate	32,206	5,373	5,164	4,546	5,233	6,252	3,051	2,588	37,378
Some college, no degree	18,744	2,181	2,204	2,406	3,043	4,004	2,340	2,566	47,390
Associate degree	9,405	799	901	1,109	1,516	2,146	1,419	1,512	54,004
Bachelor's degree or more	30,535	1,732	1,644	2,180	3,822	5,971	4,731	10,455	74,527
Bachelor's degree	19,595	1,216	1,168	1,608	2,676	4,040	3,056	5,833	68,626
Master's degree	7,714	388	372	443	862	1,497	1,230	2,921	80,282
Professional degree	1,767	62	65	70	152	221	241	954	100,000
Doctoral degree	1,459	62	40	60	134	213	202	747	100,000
Number of earners:									
No earners	23,891	11,191	5,567	2,913	2,101	1,298	400	422	16,151
One earner	41,622	5,425	7,219	7,334	7,872	7,175	2,991	3,606	36,149
Two earners and more	47,633	745	1,848	3,228	6,763	12,225	9,039	13,785	72,590
2 earners	38,120	705	1,729	2,876	5,890	10,083	6,946	9,889	68,892
3 earners	7,227	32	110	308	764	1,767	1,570	2,676	83,877
4 earners or more	2,287	7	9	45	108	377	524	1,220	100,000
Work experience of householder:									
Total	113,146	17,361	14,634	13,475	16,736	20,698	12,428	17,814	44,389
Worked	78,345	5,304	7,614	9,052	12,489	17,137	10,859	15,887	55,900
Worked at full-time jobs	66,278	3,127	5,787	7,665	10,714	15,066	9,744	14,173	58,760
50 weeks or more	56,497	1,711	4,389	6,238	9,100	13,347	8,770	12,945	61,601
27 to 49 weeks	6,212	549	870	915	1,075	1,183	712	907	45,575
26 weeks or less	3,568	867	528	513	542	538	262	321	32,129
Worked at part-time jobs	12,068	2,177	1,829	1,388	1,773	2,072	1,116	1,713	39,817
50 weeks or more	6,700	894	1,064	807	976	1,216	677	1,069	43,026
27 to 49 weeks	2,478	441	333	279	351	459	228	387	42,476
26 weeks or less	2,890	842	432	301	448	396	212	257	30,249
Did not work	34,801	12,056	7,018	4,423	4,247	3,560	1,567	1,927	22,243
Tenure:									
Owner-occupied	78,574	8,219	8,318	7,995	11,293	15,983	10,628	16,137	54,614
Renter-occupied	33,090	8,625	6,069	5,293	5,239	4,524	1,736	1,604	27,898
Occupier paid no cash rent	1,482	518	247	187	203	192	63	73	23,341

[1] For composition of regions, see map inside front cover.　　[2] People 25 years old and over.

Source: U.S. Census Bureau, *Income, Poverty, and Health Insurance Coverage in the United States: 2004,* Current Population Reports, P60-229; and Internet sites <http://www.census.gov/prod/2005pubs/p60-229.pdf> (released 30 August 2005) and <http://pubdb3.census.gov/macro/032005/hhinc/toc.htm> (released 26 July 2005).

Income, Expenditures, and Wealth   447

Table 674. Money Income of Households—Number and Distribution by Race and Hispanic Origin: 2004

[Households as of **March of the following year. (113,146 represents 113,146,000).** Based on Current Population Survey (CPS); see text, Sections 1 and 13, and Appendix III. The 2005 CPS allowed respondents to choose more than one race. Data represent persons who selected this race group only and excludes persons reporting more than one race. See also comments on race in the text for Section 1]

Income interval	Number (1,000)					Percent distribution				
	All races	White	Black	Asian	Hispanic [1]	All races	White	Black	Asian	Hispanic [1]
All households.....	**113,146**	**92,702**	**13,792**	**4,140**	**12,181**	**100.0**	**100.0**	**100.0**	**100.0**	**100.0**
Under $10,000.........	9,805	6,771	2,450	310	1,303	8.7	7.3	17.8	7.5	10.7
$10,000 to $14,999......	7,556	6,000	1,227	170	945	6.7	6.5	8.9	4.1	7.8
$15,000 to $19,999......	7,198	5,740	1,064	186	1,012	6.4	6.2	7.7	4.5	8.3
$20,000 to $24,999......	7,436	5,952	1,146	187	1,110	6.6	6.4	8.3	4.5	9.1
$25,000 to $29,999......	6,827	5,487	978	199	930	6.0	5.9	7.1	4.8	7.6
$30,000 to $34,999......	6,648	5,328	970	168	889	5.9	5.7	7.0	4.1	7.3
$35,000 to $39,999......	5,993	4,888	799	168	742	5.3	5.3	5.8	4.1	6.1
$40,000 to $44,999......	5,672	4,676	665	199	721	5.0	5.0	4.8	4.8	5.9
$45,000 to $49,999......	5,071	4,176	574	191	605	4.5	4.5	4.2	4.6	5.0
$50,000 to $59,999......	9,229	7,783	896	354	1,018	8.2	8.4	6.5	8.6	8.4
$60,000 to $74,999......	11,469	9,630	1,122	440	991	10.1	10.4	8.1	10.6	8.1
$75,000 to $84,999......	5,958	5,111	509	231	479	5.3	5.5	3.7	5.6	3.9
$85,000 to $99,999......	6,470	5,592	482	279	457	5.7	6.0	3.5	6.7	3.8
$100,000 to $149,999	11,194	9,745	639	626	672	9.9	10.5	4.6	15.1	5.5
$150,000 to $199,999	3,595	3,147	156	227	172	3.2	3.4	1.1	5.5	1.4
$200,000 to $249,999	1,325	1,176	58	79	70	1.2	1.3	0.4	1.9	0.6
$250,000 and above	1,699	1,499	61	118	66	1.5	1.6	0.4	2.9	0.5

[1] Persons of Hispanic origin may be of any race.

Source: U.S. Census Bureau, *Income, Poverty, and Health Insurance 2004,* Current Population Reports, P60-229; and Internet site at <http://pubdb3.census.gov/macro/032005/hhinc/new06000.htm> (revised 24 June 2005).

Table 675. Money Income of Families—Number and Distribution by Race and Hispanic Origin: 2004

[Households as of **March of the following year. (77,019 represents 77,019,000).** Based on Current Population Survey (CPS); see text, Sections 1 and 13, and Appendix III. The 2005 CPS allowed respondents to choose more than one race. Data represent persons who selected this race group only and excludes persons reporting more than one race. See also comments on race in the text for Section 1]

Income interval	Number (1,000)					Percent distribution				
	All races	White	Black	Asian	Hispanic [1]	All races	White	Black	Asian	Hispanic [1]
All families	**77,019**	**63,227**	**8,908**	**3,155**	**9,537**	**100.0**	**100.0**	**100.0**	**100.0**	**100.0**
Under $10,000.........	4,257	2,736	1,260	121	837	5.5	4.3	14.1	3.8	8.8
$10,000 to $14,999......	3,060	2,270	620	77	673	4.0	3.6	7.0	2.4	7.1
$15,000 to $19,999......	3,762	2,894	625	108	801	4.9	4.6	7.0	3.4	8.4
$20,000 to $24,999......	4,479	3,513	732	136	913	5.8	5.6	8.2	4.3	9.6
$25,000 to $29,999......	4,140	3,318	579	149	753	5.4	5.2	6.5	4.7	7.9
$30,000 to $34,999......	4,238	3,364	620	121	738	5.5	5.3	7.0	3.8	7.7
$35,000 to $39,999......	4,013	3,260	527	126	579	5.2	5.2	5.9	4.0	6.1
$40,000 to $44,999......	3,771	3,094	429	163	546	4.9	4.9	4.8	5.2	5.7
$45,000 to $49,999......	3,623	2,938	429	158	455	4.7	4.6	4.8	5.0	4.8
$50,000 to $59,999......	6,977	5,892	653	279	850	9.1	9.3	7.3	8.8	8.9
$60,000 to $74,999......	8,859	7,461	856	356	810	11.5	11.8	9.6	11.3	8.5
$75,000 to $84,999......	4,872	4,189	420	181	389	6.3	6.6	4.7	5.7	4.1
$85,000 to $99,999......	5,466	4,730	387	248	366	7.1	7.5	4.3	7.9	3.8
$100,000 to $149,999	9,599	8,374	535	545	563	12.5	13.2	6.0	17.3	5.9
$150,000 to $199,999	3,213	2,815	137	207	153	4.2	4.5	1.5	6.6	1.6
$200,000 to $249,999	1,173	1,038	51	74	51	1.5	1.6	0.6	2.3	0.5
$250,000 and above	1,517	1,342	47	108	62	2.0	2.1	0.5	3.4	0.7

[1] Persons of Hispanic origin may be of any race.

Source: U.S. Census Bureau, *Income, Poverty, and Health Insurance 2004,* Current Population Report, P60-229; and Internet site at <http://pubdb3.census.gov/macro/032005/faminc/new07000.htm> (revised 31 January 2006).

Table 676. Money Income of Families—Percent Distribution by Income Level in Constant (2004) Dollars: 1980 to 2004

[Constant dollars based on CPI-U-RS deflator. Families as of March of the following year (60,309 represents 60,309,000). Based on Current Population Survey; see text, Sections 1 and 13, and Appendix III. For data collection changes over time, see <http://www.census.gov/hhes/income/histinc/hstchg.html>. For definition of median, see Guide to Tabular Presentation]

Year	Number of families (1,000)	Percent distribution							Median income (dollars)
		Under $15,000	$15,000– $24,999	$25,000– $34,999	$35,000– $49,999	$50,000– $74,999	$75,000– $99,999	$100,000 and over	
ALL FAMILIES [1]									
1980	60,309	10.9	12.4	13.3	19.2	24.2	11.4	8.6	45,647
1990	66,322	10.6	11.0	11.7	17.5	22.5	12.8	13.9	49,545
2000 [2]	73,778	8.4	10.0	11.3	15.3	20.6	14.2	20.1	55,647
2003	76,232	9.5	10.8	11.3	14.7	20.0	13.5	20.3	54,096
2004	77,019	9.5	10.7	10.9	14.8	20.6	13.4	20.1	54,061
WHITE									
1980	52,710	8.8	11.6	13.2	19.7	25.3	12.0	9.3	47,560
1990	56,803	8.3	10.4	11.6	17.9	23.4	13.6	14.9	51,734
2000 [2]	61,330	6.9	9.3	11.1	15.3	21.2	14.9	21.3	58,167
2003 [3, 4]	62,620	7.6	10.2	11.1	14.7	20.5	14.2	21.7	57,267
2004 [3, 4]	63,227	7.9	10.1	10.6	14.7	21.1	14.1	21.5	56,700
BLACK									
1980	6,317	27.2	18.7	14.7	16.0	15.1	5.7	2.6	27,519
1990	7,471	28.1	15.1	13.1	15.2	16.3	6.5	5.7	30,023
2000 [2]	8,731	18.3	15.6	14.1	16.2	17.4	9.1	9.4	36,939
2003 [3, 5]	8,914	21.1	15.4	13.6	15.2	16.6	8.9	9.2	35,293
2004 [3, 5]	8,908	21.1	15.2	13.5	15.5	17.0	9.1	8.7	35,158
ASIAN AND PACIFIC ISLANDER									
1990	1,536	9.2	9.2	8.3	14.4	22.5	15.1	21.2	59,205
2000 [2]	2,982	7.1	7.4	8.7	12.9	18.8	16.3	28.9	68,684
2003 [3, 6]	3,064	9.6	8.3	6.8	13.3	19.8	13.8	28.3	64,951
2004 [3, 6]	3,155	6.3	7.7	8.6	14.2	20.1	13.5	29.6	65,482
HISPANIC ORIGIN [7]									
1980	3,235	19.3	19.3	16.5	18.6	17.3	5.8	3.3	31,952
1990	4,981	20.9	17.4	14.6	17.9	16.6	6.8	5.8	32,837
2000 [2]	8,017	15.0	16.3	15.2	18.0	17.9	9.5	8.1	37,779
2003	9,274	16.2	17.8	16.2	16.5	16.6	8.4	8.4	35,193
2004	9,537	15.9	18.0	15.6	16.6	17.4	7.9	8.7	35,401

[1] Includes other races not shown separately. [2] Data reflect implementation of Census 2000-based population controls and a 28,000 household sample expansion to 78,000 households. [3] Beginning with the 2003 Current Population Survey (CPS), the questionnaire allowed respondents to choose more than one race. For 2003 and later, data represent persons who selected this race group only and exclude persons reporting more than one race. The CPS in prior years allowed respondents to report only one race group. See also comments on race in the text for Section 1, Population. [4] Data represent White alone, which refers to people who reported White and did not report any other race category. [5] Data represent Black alone, which refers to people who reported Black and did not report any other race category. [6] Data represent Asian alone, which refers to people who reported Asian and did not report any other race category. [7] People of Hispanic origin may be of any race.

Source: U.S. Census Bureau, Current Population Reports, P60-229, Income, Poverty, and Health Insurance Coverage in the United States: 2004; and Internet site (released 30 August 2005) and <http://www.census.gov/hhes/www/income/histinc/f23.html> (released 04 November 2005).

Table 677. Money Income of Families—Median Income by Race and Hispanic Origin in Current and Constant (2004) Dollars: 1980 to 2004

[See headnote, Table 676]

Year	Median income in current dollars					Median income in constant (**2004**) dollars				
	All families [1]	White [2]	Black [3]	Asian, Pacific Islander [4]	His- panic [5]	All families [1]	White [2]	Black [3]	Asian, Pacific Islander [4]	His- panic [5]
1980	21,023	21,904	12,674	(NA)	14,716	45,647	47,560	27,519	(NA)	31,952
1985	27,735	29,152	16,786	(NA)	19,027	46,439	48,811	28,106	(NA)	31,858
1990	35,353	36,915	21,423	42,246	23,431	49,545	51,734	30,023	59,205	32,837
1995	40,611	42,646	25,970	46,356	24,570	49,987	52,492	31,966	57,058	30,243
1996	42,300	44,756	26,522	49,105	26,179	50,705	53,649	31,792	58,862	31,381
1997	44,568	46,754	28,602	51,850	28,142	52,307	54,872	33,568	60,853	33,028
1998	46,737	49,023	29,404	52,826	29,608	54,091	56,736	34,030	61,138	34,267
1999	48,831	51,079	31,850	56,127	31,523	55,350	57,898	36,102	63,620	35,731
2000 [6]	50,732	53,029	33,676	62,617	34,442	55,647	58,167	36,939	68,684	37,779
2001 [7]	51,407	54,067	33,598	60,158	34,490	54,857	57,695	35,853	64,195	36,804
2002 [7]	51,680	54,633	33,525	60,984	34,185	54,285	57,387	35,215	64,058	35,908
2003	52,680	55,768	34,369	63,251	34,272	54,096	57,267	35,293	64,951	35,193
2004	54,061	56,700	35,158	65,482	35,401	54,061	56,700	35,158	65,482	35,401

NA Not available. [1] Includes other races not shown separately. [2] Beginning with 2002, data represent White alone, which refers to people who reported White and did not report any other race category. [3] Beginning with 2002, data represent Black alone, which refers to people who reported Black and did not report any other race category. [4] Beginning with 2002, data represent Asian alone, which refers to people who reported Asian and did not report any other race category. [5] People of Hispanic origin may be of any race. [6] Implementation of Census 2000-based population controls and sample expanded by 28,000 households. [7] See footnote 3, table 676.

Source: U.S. Census Bureau, Current Population Reports, P60-229; and Internet sites <http://www.census.gov/prod/2005pubs/p60-229.pdf> (released 30 August 2005) and <http://www.census.gov/hhes/www/income/histinc/F05.HTML> (revised 20 December 2005).

Income, Expenditures, and Wealth   449

Table 678. **Share of Aggregate Income Received by Each Fifth and Top 5 Percent of Families: 1980 to 2004**

[**Families as of March of the following year (60,309 represents 60,309,000).** Income in constant 2004 CPI-U-RS adjusted dollars. Based on the Current Population Survey; see text, Sections 1 and 13, and Appendix III. For data collection changes over time, see <http://www.census.gov/hhes/income/histinc/hstchg.html>]

Year	Number of families (1,000)	Income at selected positions (dollars)					Percent distribution of aggregate income					
		Upper limit of each fifth				Top 5 percent	Lowest 5th	Second 5th	Third 5th	Fourth 5th	Highest 5th	Top 5 percent
		Lowest	Second	Third	Fourth							
1980 . . .	60,309	22,581	38,019	53,848	75,560	119,420	5.3	11.6	17.6	24.4	41.1	14.6
1985 . . .	63,558	22,244	38,320	55,509	80,753	132,217	4.8	11.0	16.9	24.3	43.1	16.1
1990 . . .	66,322	23,608	40,703	58,916	86,174	143,447	4.6	10.8	16.6	23.8	44.3	17.4
1991 . . .	67,173	22,993	39,373	58,158	85,196	139,070	4.5	10.7	16.6	24.1	44.2	17.1
1992 . . .	68,216	22,052	39,153	58,055	84,509	139,875	4.3	10.5	16.5	24.0	44.7	17.6
1993 . . .	68,506	21,846	38,620	57,968	85,985	145,701	4.1	9.9	15.7	23.3	47.0	20.3
1994 . . .	69,313	22,618	39,462	59,256	88,251	151,347	4.2	10.0	15.7	23.3	46.9	20.1
1995 . . .	69,597	23,473	40,600	60,294	88,943	152,205	4.4	10.1	15.8	23.2	46.5	20.0
1996 . . .	70,241	23,590	41,133	61,236	90,281	153,433	4.2	10.0	15.8	23.1	46.8	20.3
1997 . . .	70,884	24,160	42,251	62,926	93,891	160,882	4.2	9.9	15.7	23.0	47.2	20.7
1998 . . .	71,551	24,999	43,623	64,834	96,861	168,045	4.2	9.9	15.7	23.0	47.3	20.7
1999 . . .	73,206	25,839	44,764	67,182	99,785	175,715	4.3	9.9	15.6	23.0	47.2	20.3
2000 [1] . .	73,778	26,325	44,797	67,267	100,227	175,634	4.3	9.8	15.4	22.7	47.7	21.1
2001 . . .	74,340	25,611	43,887	66,694	100,468	175,116	4.2	9.7	15.4	22.9	47.7	21.0
2002 . . .	75,616	25,210	43,529	66,175	99,230	172,605	4.2	9.7	15.5	23.0	47.6	20.8
2003 . . .	76,232	24,765	43,187	66,747	100,839	174,653	4.1	9.6	15.5	23.2	47.6	20.5
2004 . . .	77,019	24,780	43,400	65,832	100,000	173,640	4.0	9.6	15.4	23.0	47.9	20.9

[1] Data reflect implementation of Census 2000-based population controls and a 28,000 household sample expansion to 78,000 households.

Source: U.S. Census Bureau, *Income, Poverty, and Health Insurance Coverage in the United States: 2004*, Current Population Reports, P60-229, and Internet sites at <http://www.census.gov/prod/2004pubs/p60-229.pdf> (released 30 August 2005). and <http://www.census.gov/hhes/income/histinc/f01.html> and <http://www.census.gov/hhes/income/histinc/f02.html> (revised 20 December 2005).

Table 679. **Money Income of Families—Distribution by Family Characteristics and Income Level: 2003**

[(**76,232 represents 76,232,000).** See headnote, Table 676. For composition of regions, see map inside front cover]

Characteristic	Number of families (1,000)								Median income (dollars)
	Total	Under $15,000	$15,000 to $24,999	$25,000 to $34,999	$35,000 to $49,999	$50,000 to $74,999	$75,000 to $99,999	$100,000 and over	
All families	**76,232**	**7,366**	**8,489**	**8,657**	**11,443**	**15,352**	**10,157**	**14,768**	**52,680**
Age of householder:									
15 to 24 years old	3,592	1,027	696	571	545	450	163	139	26,198
25 to 34 years old	13,561	1,808	1,560	1,668	2,186	2,942	1,698	1,701	46,554
35 to 44 years old	18,329	1,493	1,585	1,784	2,655	4,081	2,799	3,927	59,122
45 to 54 years old	17,137	956	1,097	1,336	2,242	3,619	2,942	4,946	70,149
55 to 64 years old	11,621	891	988	1,106	1,661	2,391	1,667	2,916	60,976
65 years old and over	11,991	1,191	2,563	2,192	2,153	1,871	883	1,139	35,310
Region:									
Northeast	13,994	1,222	1,368	1,378	1,926	2,774	1,977	3,350	59,874
Midwest	17,378	1,342	1,710	2,003	2,650	3,804	2,658	3,214	55,613
South	28,000	3,217	3,537	3,475	4,476	5,378	3,326	4,591	47,322
West	16,860	1,584	1,875	1,801	2,392	3,397	2,198	3,613	55,095
Type of family:									
Married-couple families	57,725	2,873	5,107	5,661	8,505	12,721	9,058	13,802	62,281
Male householder, no spouse present.	4,717	632	755	768	813	875	416	458	38,032
Female householder, no spouse present.	13,791	3,861	2,628	2,227	2,125	1,759	684	508	26,550
Unrelated subfamilies	509	199	92	115	53	29	3	20	20,160
Education attainment of house-holder: [1]									
Total	**72,640**	**6,337**	**7,793**	**8,087**	**10,896**	**14,901**	**9,993**	**14,629**	**54,739**
Less than 9th grade	4,056	922	1,072	729	619	448	160	106	25,313
9th to 12th grade (no diploma) . . .	5,996	1,250	1,281	1,108	966	841	322	230	28,848
High school graduate (includes equivalency)	21,966	2,171	2,843	3,138	4,110	4,723	2,682	2,297	44,620
Some college, no degree.	13,145	996	1,366	1,489	2,111	3,133	2,007	2,045	54,255
Associate's degree	6,537	375	461	597	1,033	1,685	1,100	1,289	61,208
Bachelor's degree or more.	20,940	624	771	1,029	2,056	4,075	3,724	8,662	86,921
Bachelor's degree.	13,497	418	569	731	1,455	2,871	2,524	4,927	81,094
Master's degree	5,080	130	136	193	458	915	927	2,319	93,867
Professional degree	1,274	31	39	77	67	141	131	787	100,000
Doctoral degree	1,089	46	28	28	75	146	136	629	100,000

[1] Persons 25 years old and over.

Source: U.S. Census Bureau, Current Population Reports, *Income, Poverty, and Health Insurance Coverage in the United States*, 2003, and Internet sites <http://www.census.gov/prod/2004pubs/p60-226.pdf> (released 26 August 2004) and <http://pubdb3.census.gov/macro/032004/faminc/new01000.htm> (accessed 13 June 2005).

Table 680. Median Income of Families by Type of Family in Current and Constant (2004) Dollars: 1980 to 2004

[In dollars. See headnote, Table 676. For definition of median, see Guide to Tabular Presentation]

| Year | Current dollars | | | | | | Constant (2004) dollars | | | | | |
| | Married-couple families | | | | Male house-holder, no spouse present | Female house-holder, no spouse present | Married-couple families | | | | Male house-holder, no spouse present | Female house-holder, no spouse present |
	Total	Total	Wife in paid labor force	Wife not in paid labor force			Total	Total	Wife in paid labor force	Wife not in paid labor force		
1980 . . .	21,023	23,141	26,879	18,972	17,519	10,408	45,647	50,245	58,362	41,193	38,038	22,599
1990 . . .	35,353	39,895	46,777	30,265	29,046	16,932	49,545	55,910	65,555	42,414	40,706	23,729
1995 . . .	40,611	47,062	55,823	32,375	30,358	19,691	49,987	57,927	68,711	39,849	37,367	24,237
1996 . . .	42,300	49,707	58,381	33,748	31,600	19,911	50,705	59,583	69,981	40,453	37,879	23,867
1997 . . .	44,568	51,591	60,669	36,027	32,960	21,023	52,307	60,549	71,203	42,283	38,683	24,673
1998 . . .	46,737	54,180	63,751	37,161	35,681	22,163	54,091	62,705	73,782	43,008	41,295	25,650
1999 . . .	48,831	56,501	66,478	38,480	37,339	23,762	55,350	64,044	75,353	43,617	42,324	26,934
2000 . . .	50,732	59,099	69,235	39,982	37,727	25,716	55,647	64,825	75,943	43,856	41,382	28,208
2001 . . .	51,407	60,335	70,834	40,782	36,590	25,745	54,857	64,384	75,587	43,519	39,045	27,473
2002 . . .	51,680	61,130	72,806	40,102	37,739	26,423	54,285	64,211	76,475	42,123	39,641	27,755
2003 . . .	52,680	62,281	75,170	41,122	38,032	26,550	54,096	63,955	77,190	42,227	39,054	27,264
2004 . . .	54,061	63,630	76,814	42,221	40,293	26,964	54,061	63,630	76,814	42,221	40,293	26,964

Source: U.S. Census Bureau, *Income, Poverty, and Health Insurance Coverage in the United States: 2004*, Current Population Reports, P60-229, and Internet sites at <http://www.census.gov/prod/2004pubs/p60-229.pdf> (released 30 August 2005) and Table F-7 Type of Family, All Races by Median and Mean Income: 1953 to 2004 at <http://www.census.gov/hhes/income/histinc/f07.html> (revised 20 December 2005).

Table 681. Married-Couple Families—Number and Median Income by Work Experience of Husbands and Wives and Presence of Children: 2003

[(57,725 represents 57,725,000). See headnote, Table 678. For definition of median, see Guide to Tabular Presentaton]

| Work experience of husband or wife | Number (1,000) | | One or more related children under 18 years old | | | Median income (dollars) | | One or more related children under 18 years old | | |
	All married-couple families	No related chil-dren	Total	One child	Two or more	All married-couple families	No related chil-dren	Total	One child	Two or more
All married-couple families	57,725	30,766	26,959	10,261	16,698	62,281	58,514	66,419	68,427	65,091
Husband worked	45,446	20,170	25,277	9,470	15,807	71,685	75,766	68,712	71,119	66,991
Wife worked	33,256	15,292	17,963	7,213	10,750	77,899	81,422	75,396	77,319	74,119
Wife did not work	12,191	4,877	7,314	2,257	5,057	51,303	53,533	50,422	50,333	50,450
Husband year-round, full-time worker	37,582	15,749	21,833	8,129	13,704	75,644	80,987	71,702	74,212	70,526
Wife worked	27,801	12,342	15,459	6,194	9,265	81,255	85,293	77,808	80,259	76,488
Wife did not work	9,781	3,407	6,374	1,935	4,439	55,616	60,189	53,406	53,406	52,509
Husband did not work	12,279	10,596	1,682	792	891	31,042	31,205	29,935	30,917	29,020
Wife worked	3,568	2,502	1,066	469	597	37,693	46,680	37,693	40,027	36,392
Wife did not work	8,711	8,094	616	322	294	27,130	27,589	17,943	20,518	14,826

Source: U.S. Census Bureau, Current Population Reports, P60-226; and <http://www.census.gov/prod/2004pubs/p60-226.pdf> (released 26 August 2004) and <http://pubdb3.census.gov/macro/032004/faminc/toc.htm> (accessed June 13 2005).

Table 682. Median Income of People With Income in Constant (2004) Dollars by Sex, Race, and Hispanic Origin: 1990 to 2004

[In dollars (28,439 represents $28,439). People as of March of following year. People 15 years old and over. Constant dollars based on CPI-U-RS deflator. Based on the Current Population Survey; see text, Sections 1 and 13, and Appendix III. For data collection changes over time, see <http://www.census.gov/hhes/income/histinc/hstchg.html>]

| Race and Hispanic origin | Male | | | | | Female | | | | |
	1990	2000 [1]	2002 [2]	2003	2004	1990	2000 [1]	2002 [2]	2003	2004
All races [3]	28,439	31,089	30,712	30,735	30,513	14,112	17,619	17,659	17,723	17,629
White [4]	29,668	32,684	31,914	31,558	31,335	14,459	17,637	17,687	17,890	17,648
Black [5]	18,034	23,411	22,648	22,577	22,714	11,671	17,420	16,920	17,572	17,027
Asian [6]	(NA)	(NA)	32,652	33,159	32,886	(NA)	(NA)	18,999	18,154	20,533
Hispanic [7]	18,877	21,387	21,745	21,619	21,559	10,556	13,435	14,038	14,009	14,425
White, non-Hispanic	30,773	34,561	33,649	33,200	33,652	14,828	18,280	18,265	18,793	18,379

NA Not available. [1] Implementation of Census 2000-based population controls and sample expanded by 28,000 households. [2] Beginning with the 2003 Current Population Survey (CPS), the questionnaire allowed respondents to choose more than one race. For 2002 and later, data represent persons who selected this race group only and excludes persons reporting more than one race. The CPS in prior years allowed respondents to report only one race group. See also comments on race in the text for Section 1. [3] Includes other races not shown separately. [4] Beginning with 2002, data represents White alone, which refers to people who reported White and did not report any other race category. [5] Beginning with 2002, data represents Black alone, which refers to people who reported Black and did not report any other race category. [6] Beginning with 2002, data represents Asian alone, which refers to people who reported Asian and did not report any other race category. [7] People of Hispanic origin may be of any race.

Source: U.S. Census Bureau, *Income, Poverty, and Health Insurance Coverage in the United States: 2004*, Current Population Reports, P60-229; and Internet site <http://www.census.gov/hhes/www/income/histinc/p02.html> (released 13 January 2006).

Table 683. **Money Income of People—Selected Characteristics by Income Level: 2003**

[People as of March 2004 (110,257 represents 110,257,000). Covers people 15 years old and over. For definition of median, see Guide to Tabular Presentation. For composition of regions, see map, inside front cover. Based on the Current Population Survey (CPS), see Appendix III]

| Characteristic | All persons (1,000) | Persons with income | | | | | | | | | Median income (dollars) |
| | | Number (1,000) | | | | | | | | | |
		Total (1,000)	Under $5,000[1]	$5,000 to $9,999	$10,000 to $14,999	$15,000 to $24,999	$25,000 to $34,999	$35,000 to $49,999	$50,000 to $74,999	$75,000 and over	
MALE											
Total	110,257	100,769	8,169	7,848	9,654	17,566	14,458	15,746	14,394	12,934	29,931
15 to 24 years old	20,699	14,237	4,742	2,394	1,990	2,832	1,315	656	222	86	9,961
25 to 34 years old	19,598	18,684	860	1,110	1,608	3,772	3,524	3,749	2,543	1,518	30,562
35 to 44 years old	21,530	20,781	843	941	1,081	2,989	3,268	4,055	3,994	3,610	39,195
45 to 54 years old	20,082	19,417	725	959	1,068	2,389	2,561	3,628	4,069	4,018	42,079
55 to 64 years old	13,551	13,097	505	760	1,001	1,906	1,744	2,186	2,357	2,638	38,915
65 yrs. old and over	14,797	14,554	496	1,682	2,907	3,679	2,045	1,474	1,208	1,063	20,363
Region:											
Northeast	20,589	18,834	1,589	1,415	1,792	2,860	2,516	2,972	2,807	2,883	31,412
Midwest	24,977	23,231	2,011	1,748	2,017	3,925	3,426	3,846	3,541	2,717	30,289
South	39,272	35,654	2,733	2,967	3,589	6,761	5,437	5,426	4,665	4,076	27,613
West	25,418	23,050	1,835	1,718	2,255	4,022	3,081	3,502	3,380	3,257	30,426
Education attainment of householder:[2]											
Total	89,558	86,532	3,432	5,454	7,663	14,733	13,144	15,091	14,169	12,846	33,517
Less than 9th grade	5,804	5,405	349	1,042	1,209	1,628	634	345	151	47	15,461
9th to 12th grade[3]	7,766	7,245	497	944	1,311	1,938	1,226	772	410	147	18,990
High school graduate[4]	27,889	26,800	1,174	1,849	2,575	5,699	5,154	5,209	3,578	1,562	28,763
Some college, no degree	15,012	14,586	548	721	1,205	2,288	2,510	3,060	2,729	1,525	35,073
Associate's degree	6,751	6,618	181	264	383	909	1,152	1,532	1,403	794	39,015
Bachelor's degree or more	26,336	25,879	687	634	980	2,273	2,468	4,170	5,898	8,769	55,751
Bachelor's degree	16,632	16,295	450	464	680	1,584	1,803	2,909	3,877	4,528	50,916
Master's degree	6,157	6,076	141	129	184	451	480	904	1,434	2,353	61,698
Professional degree	1,925	1,901	36	29	68	121	112	161	271	1,103	88,530
Doctoral degree	1,621	1,606	57	12	49	117	74	195	315	787	73,853
Tenure:											
Owner-occupied	80,538	74,163	5,894	4,822	6,047	11,193	10,233	12,314	12,171	11,489	33,218
Renter-occupied	28,429	25,437	2,172	2,910	3,442	6,070	4,024	3,283	2,139	1,397	21,403
Occupier paid no cash rent	1,290	1,169	100	118	164	303	204	150	83	47	21,580
FEMALE											
Total	117,327	102,713	16,335	16,155	13,409	19,291	13,859	12,037	7,462	4,165	17,259
15 to 24 years old	20,009	13,594	5,189	2,687	1,841	2,436	965	384	72	20	7,435
25 to 34 years old	19,603	17,156	2,511	1,695	1,886	3,446	3,124	2,628	1,255	611	21,992
35 to 44 years old	22,043	20,010	2,877	1,884	1,969	3,739	3,160	3,151	2,051	1,179	23,472
45 to 54 years old	20,987	19,303	2,121	1,772	1,738	3,627	3,244	3,207	2,297	1,297	25,866
55 to 64 years old	14,824	13,424	1,950	2,065	1,439	2,336	1,907	1,689	1,263	775	20,368
65 yrs. old and over	19,862	19,225	1,681	6,051	4,536	3,708	1,461	982	525	281	11,845
Region:											
Northeast	22,599	20,104	3,206	3,122	2,510	3,554	2,675	2,482	1,527	1,028	17,951
Midwest	26,353	23,897	3,765	3,681	3,070	4,696	3,429	2,744	1,675	837	17,498
South	42,226	36,262	5,753	6,019	4,914	6,894	4,897	4,108	2,432	1,245	16,663
West	26,149	22,449	3,617	3,332	2,915	4,147	2,858	2,701	1,831	1,048	17,499
Education attainment of householder:[2]											
Total	97,319	89,118	11,142	13,468	11,567	16,857	12,895	11,654	7,391	4,144	19,679
Less than 9th grade	5,943	4,734	833	1,795	1,053	759	177	69	33	15	9,296
9th to 12th grade[3]	8,233	6,965	1,087	2,096	1,566	1,470	449	184	65	48	10,786
High school graduate[4]	31,921	28,976	3,899	5,158	4,622	6,703	4,400	2,757	1,036	401	15,962
Some college, no degree	16,796	15,691	1,828	2,044	1,978	3,294	2,798	2,207	1,157	385	21,007
Associate's degree	9,013	8,523	904	804	923	1,661	1,571	1,458	890	312	24,808
Bachelor's degree or more	25,413	24,229	2,596	1,570	1,426	2,968	3,496	4,980	4,208	2,985	35,125
Bachelor's degree	17,134	16,198	1,942	1,142	1,023	2,289	2,614	3,272	2,424	1,492	31,309
Master's degree	6,451	6,268	527	334	345	525	693	1,473	1,428	943	41,334
Professional degree	1,027	990	81	52	37	109	98	122	183	308	48,536
Doctoral degree	801	773	44	43	23	46	93	108	174	242	53,003
Tenure:											
Owner-occupied	84,718	75,289	12,241	10,874	8,982	13,345	10,331	9,574	6,305	3,637	18,777
Renter-occupied	31,221	26,255	3,818	5,023	4,238	5,735	3,416	2,395	1,119	511	15,068
Occupier paid no cash rent	1,389	1,169	279	258	188	212	112	67	38	15	11,089

[1] Includes persons with income deficit. [2] Persons 25 years and over. [3] No diploma attained. [4] Includes high school equivalency.

Source: U.S. Census Bureau, *Income, Poverty, and Health Insurance Coverage in the United States, 2003,* Current Population Reports, series P60-226. See also <http://www.census.gov/prod/2004pubs/p60-226.pdf> (released 26 August 2004) and <http://pubdb3.census.gov/macro/032004/perinc/toc.htm> (accessed 10 June 2005).

Table 684. Average Earnings of Year-Round, Full-Time Workers by Educational Attainment: 2003

[In dollars. For people 18 years old and over as of March 2004. See headnote, Table 682]

Sex and Age	All workers	Less than 9th grade	High school 9th to 12th grade (no diploma)	High school High school graduate[1]	College Some college, no degree	College Associate's degree	College Bachelor's degree or more
Male, total	**53,039**	**23,972**	**29,100**	**38,331**	**46,332**	**48,683**	**81,007**
18 to 24 years old	23,785	16,805	20,156	23,119	23,872	26,554	33,952
25 to 34 years old	41,993	20,977	26,797	33,509	40,417	42,200	58,500
35 to 44 years old	56,515	25,733	30,968	40,885	49,498	50,832	85,368
45 to 54 years old	61,291	26,139	33,781	43,638	52,314	53,701	89,499
55 to 64 years old	65,765	29,067	34,341	44,619	54,630	55,888	95,568
65 years old and over . . .	58,398	23,499	32,695	38,108	59,160	(B)	86,713
Female, total	**37,197**	**20,979**	**21,426**	**27,956**	**31,655**	**36,528**	**53,215**
18 to 24 years old	20,812	(B)	16,698	18,915	19,727	23,070	27,650
25 to 34 years old	35,845	23,142	19,646	26,132	27,927	32,145	49,339
35 to 44 years old	39,234	17,401	23,908	28,975	33,814	38,078	57,208
45 to 54 years old	40,335	21,853	22,076	29,729	36,008	40,785	56,596
55 to 64 years old	39,448	20,496	22,625	30,590	36,032	37,467	55,511
65 years old and over . . .	30,927	28,687	(B)	27,955	31,018	(B)	44,576

B Base figure too small to meet statistical standards for reliability of derived figure.   [1] Includes equivalency.

Source: U.S. Census Bureau, *Income, Poverty, and Health Insurance Coverage in the United States, 2003,* Current Population Reports, series P60-226. See also <http://www.census.gov/prod/2004pubs/p60-226.pdf> (released 26 August 2004) and <http://pubdb3.census.gov/macro/032004/perinc/toc.htm> (accessed 10 June 2005).

Table 685. Per Capita Money Income in Current and Constant (2004) Dollars by Race and Hispanic Origin: 1990 to 2004

[In dollars. Constant dollars based on CPI-U-RS deflator. People as of March of following year. Based on the Current Population Survey; see text, Sections 1 and 13, and Appendix III. For data collection changes over time, see<http://www.census.gov/hhes/income/histinc/hstchg.html]

Year	Current dollars All races[1]	Current dollars White[2]	Current dollars Black[3]	Current dollars Asian, Pacific Islander[4]	Current dollars His- panic[5]	Constant (2004) dollars All races[1]	Constant (2004) dollars White[2]	Constant (2004) dollars Black[3]	Constant (2004) dollars Asian, Pacific Islander[4]	Constant (2004) dollars His- panic[5]
1990 . . .	14,387	15,265	9,017	(NA)	8,424	20,162	21,393	12,637	(NA)	11,806
1995 . . .	17,227	18,304	10,982	20,392	9,300	21,204	22,530	13,517	20,392	11,447
1996 . . .	18,136	19,181	11,899	21,482	10,048	21,739	22,992	14,263	21,482	12,044
1997 . . .	19,241	20,425	12,351	21,391	10,772	22,582	23,971	14,496	21,391	12,642
1998 . . .	20,120	21,394	12,957	18,709	11,434	23,286	24,760	14,996	21,653	13,233
1999 . . .	21,239	22,451	14,362	21,454	11,621	24,074	25,448	16,279	24,318	13,110
2000 . . .	22,346	23,582	14,796	23,350	12,651	24,511	25,867	16,230	25,612	13,877
2001 . . .	22,851	24,127	14,953	24,277	13,003	24,384	25,746	15,956	25,906	13,876
2002 [6] . .	22,794	24,142	15,441	24,131	13,487	23,943	25,359	16,219	25,347	14,167
2003 . . .	23,276	24,626	15,775	24,604	13,492	23,902	25,288	16,199	25,265	13,855
2004 . . .	23,848	25,203	16,035	26,217	14,106	23,848	25,203	16,035	26,217	14,106

NA Not available.   [1] Includes other races not shown separately.   [2] White alone, which refers to people who reported White and did not report any other race category.   [3] Beginning with 2002, data represents Black alone, which refers to people who reported Black and did not report any other race category.   [4] Beginning with 2002, data represents Asian alone, which refers to people who reported Asian and did not report any other race category.   [5] People of Hispanic origin may be of any race.   [6] Beginning with the 2003 Current Population Survey (CPS), the questionnaire allowed respondents to choose more than one race. For 2002 and later, data represent persons who selected this race group only and excludes persons reporting more than one race. The CPS in prior years allowed respondents to report only one race group. See also comments on race in the text for Section 1.

Source: U.S. Census Bureau, *Income, Poverty, and Health Insurance Coverage in the United States: 2004,* Current Population Reports, P60-229; and Internet site <http://www.census.gov/hhes/www/income/histinc/incpertoc.html> (revised 13 January 2006).

Table 686. Money Income of People—Number by Income Level and by Sex, Race, and Hispanic Origin: 2003

[In thousands (110,257 represents 110,257,000). People as of March of the following year. Based on Current Population Survey (CPS); see text, Sections 1 and 13, and Appendix III]

Income interval	Male All races[1]	Male White[2]	Male Black[3]	Male Asian[4]	Male His- panic[5]	Female All races[1]	Female White[2]	Female Black[3]	Female Asian[4]	Female His- panic[5]
All households	**110,257**	**90,980**	**12,008**	**4,617**	**14,664**	**117,327**	**94,958**	**14,671**	**4,982**	**13,902**
Under $10,000 [6]	25,505	18,906	4,456	1,300	4,196	47,104	37,362	6,132	2,296	7,562
$10,000 to $19,999	18,662	15,492	2,070	643	3,660	23,652	19,238	3,108	783	2,879
$20,000 to $29,999	15,777	13,099	1,761	513	2,694	16,526	13,394	2,270	563	1,567
$30,000 to $39,999	13,043	11,077	1,251	451	1,644	11,444	9,437	1,370	410	844
$40,000 to $49,999	9,942	8,411	920	391	932	6,974	5,791	770	267	460
$50,000 to $59,999	7,280	6,318	565	254	542	3,984	3,312	405	191	209
$60,000 to $74,999	7,114	6,205	429	346	442	3,478	2,894	325	190	193
$75,000 to $84,999	3,139	2,755	169	175	136	1,241	1,014	111	103	48
$85,000 to $99,999	2,751	2,401	168	127	136	960	821	59	61	51
$100,000 to $149,999	4,260	3,772	144	291	181	1,317	1,147	78	73	56
$150,000 to $199,999	1,362	1,231	40	68	49	337	297	21	17	15
$200,000 to $249,999	526	482	17	20	15	136	110	7	12	8
$250,000 and above	897	832	16	36	37	174	140	16	15	12

[1] Includes races not shown separately.   [2] White alone refers to people who reported White and did not report any other race category.   [3] Black alone refers to people who reported Black and did not report any other race category.   [4] Asian alone refers to people who reported Asian and did not report any other race category.   [5] Persons of Hispanic origin may be of any race.   [6] Includes persons without income.

Source: U.S. Census Bureau, Current Population Reports, P60-226; and Internet site at <http://www.census.gov/hhes /www/income/histinc/histinctb.html> and <http://pubdb3.census.gov/macro/032004/perinc/toc.htm> (released 13 May 2005).

Income, Expenditures, and Wealth   453

Table 687. **Household Income—Distribution by Income Level and State: 2004**

[In thousands (109,902 represents 109,902,000), except as indicated. The American Community Survey universe is limited to the household population and excludes the population living in institutions, college dormitories, and other group quarters. Based on a sample and subject to sampling variability; see Appendix III. For definition of median, see Guide to Tabular Presentation]

State	Number of house-holds (1,000)	Number of households by income level (1,000)							Median income (dol.)
		Under $25,000	$25,000–$49,999	$50,000–$74,999	$75,000–$99,999	$100,000–$149,999	$150,000–$199,999	$200,000 and over	
United States. .	**109,902**	**30,218**	**30,184**	**20,897**	**12,162**	**10,354**	**3,136**	**2,953**	**44,684**
Alabama.	1,755	616	491	316	159	115	30	28	36,709
Alaska	228	41	57	50	34	33	9	6	57,027
Arizona.	2,132	607	636	393	226	172	50	48	41,995
Arkansas	1,099	416	341	184	82	51	12	12	32,983
California	11,972	2,820	3,017	2,202	1,465	1,449	528	491	51,185
Colorado.	1,850	443	513	366	225	198	52	54	48,198
Connecticut.	1,330	262	293	252	185	204	64	69	60,528
Delaware	311	71	83	65	42	31	11	8	50,315
District of Columbia .	249	70	62	40	25	25	11	16	46,574
Florida	6,819	1,962	2,058	1,280	654	534	170	162	41,236
Georgia	3,210	913	914	602	345	269	85	83	43,037
Hawaii	428	94	105	88	56	55	18	13	53,554
Idaho	515	152	166	101	46	35	9	6	39,934
Illinois	4,660	1,182	1,191	918	580	496	157	136	48,953
Indiana	2,413	646	748	502	263	178	42	35	42,195
Iowa	1,176	334	374	236	122	78	19	13	41,350
Kansas	1,076	309	318	221	106	82	21	20	41,638
Kentucky	1,647	600	475	282	146	96	25	24	35,269
Louisiana	1,714	635	476	276	156	114	29	27	35,110
Maine	534	155	159	105	58	40	8	10	42,163
Maryland	2,078	392	503	404	287	286	112	93	57,424
Massachusetts.	2,435	546	548	467	319	338	109	109	55,658
Michigan.	3,923	1,047	1,094	780	447	386	95	75	44,905
Minnesota	2,055	443	564	448	278	219	56	48	50,860
Mississippi	1,075	436	298	173	83	56	14	14	31,642
Missouri	2,309	678	695	452	225	180	39	39	41,473
Montana	369	128	116	67	30	19	4	4	35,239
Nebraska	687	194	212	137	69	53	12	9	41,657
Nevada	872	207	280	169	99	78	21	18	44,646
New Hampshire	492	98	121	109	74	59	18	13	55,580
New Jersey.	3,134	619	676	567	434	493	176	170	61,359
New Mexico	712	249	215	121	60	40	14	12	36,043
New York	7,088	1,943	1,744	1,290	806	771	250	284	47,349
North Carolina	3,340	1,082	959	608	326	241	60	63	39,428
North Dakota.	263	84	79	55	25	15	3	2	39,447
Ohio	4,515	1,293	1,312	914	482	347	87	80	42,240
Oklahoma	1,360	472	417	231	120	83	22	14	35,357
Oregon.	1,428	412	419	296	145	101	30	25	41,794
Pennsylvania	4,818	1,386	1,340	924	517	420	120	111	42,941
Rhode Island.	410	113	97	83	54	42	12	10	48,722
South Carolina.	1,611	512	458	288	173	122	29	30	39,837
South Dakota	301	94	95	59	29	16	3	5	38,472
Tennessee	2,315	751	683	446	206	150	39	41	38,794
Texas.	7,791	2,322	2,179	1,404	790	699	203	195	41,759
Utah	780	174	240	177	94	62	16	16	47,074
Vermont	250	61	73	56	29	21	5	5	46,543
Virginia.	2,846	647	728	559	353	329	121	109	51,689
Washington	2,416	600	655	488	302	249	69	53	47,659
West Virginia.	737	297	217	117	57	38	7	5	31,504
Wisconsin	2,173	559	632	485	252	171	39	34	45,315
Wyoming	202	53	60	43	25	15	3	3	44,275

Source: U.S. Census Bureau, *Income, Earnings, and Poverty From the 2004 American Community Survey,* series ACS-01; and 2004 American Community Survey; B19001. Household Income in the Past 12 Months; B19013. Median Household Income in the Past 12 Months (In 2004 Inflation-Adjusted Dollars) using American FactFinder®; <http://factfinder.census.gov/; (accessed: 25 January 2006).

Table 688. Family Income—Distribution by Income Level and State: 2004

[In thousands (73,886 represents 73,886,000), except as indicated. The American Community Survey universe is limited to the household population and excludes the population living in institutions, college dormitories, and other group quarters. Based on a sample and subject to sampling variability; see Appendix III. For definition of median, see Guide to Tabular Presentation]

State	Number of families (1,000)	Number of families by income level (1,000)							Median income (dol.)
		Under $25,000	$25,000– $49,999	$50,000– $74,999	$75,000– $99,999	$100,000– $149,999	$150,000– $199,999	$200,000 and over	
United States. .	73,886	14,472	19,625	15,727	9,967	8,829	2,709	2,557	53,692
Alabama.	1,220	319	345	260	140	103	28	25	45,768
Alaska	156	19	37	34	27	27	7	5	66,254
Arizona.	1,435	309	424	295	180	143	44	41	48,995
Arkansas	746	214	245	148	73	44	10	11	39,945
California	8,193	1,502	2,001	1,576	1,118	1,157	428	410	58,327
Colorado.	1,187	195	299	257	180	163	45	49	58,849
Connecticut.	899	106	176	176	152	169	58	62	73,458
Delaware	208	34	50	46	34	27	9	7	60,352
District of Columbia .	110	28	24	15	13	13	7	10	54,193
Florida	4,475	934	1,325	955	525	454	147	135	49,461
Georgia	2,217	499	616	439	284	235	73	72	49,745
Hawaii	295	42	65	66	48	48	15	11	63,813
Idaho	367	76	120	86	41	30	7	6	46,586
Illinois	3,096	519	739	677	474	434	136	117	60,387
Indiana.	1,622	273	492	401	228	160	38	31	52,267
Iowa	774	127	246	191	109	70	18	12	51,505
Kansas.	708	115	210	176	93	76	18	19	53,541
Kentucky	1,142	305	338	238	129	89	23	21	43,953
Louisiana	1,171	323	337	224	138	99	25	24	42,886
Maine.	350	69	100	80	52	34	7	8	51,372
Maryland	1,383	166	288	289	218	241	102	80	69,695
Massachusetts.	1,566	218	322	315	246	276	93	96	68,701
Michigan.	2,629	464	690	605	377	339	85	69	55,778
Minnesota.	1,363	165	339	336	230	197	52	45	62,538
Mississippi	756	243	219	146	73	50	13	13	39,319
Missouri	1,537	297	458	356	197	158	37	35	50,819
Montana.	239	57	76	56	26	17	4	4	44,958
Nebraska	450	78	134	114	58	46	11	8	52,472
Nevada	560	104	166	122	72	64	17	15	51,722
New Hampshire	332	40	69	81	62	51	16	12	67,848
New Jersey.	2,200	287	426	400	350	427	155	154	73,973
New Mexico	460	137	132	88	48	33	11	10	42,240
New York	4,615	927	1,102	896	625	629	203	233	56,556
North Carolina	2,280	561	645	474	278	214	52	56	47,112
North Dakota.	166	29	51	46	21	14	3	2	51,020
Ohio	3,004	584	843	708	412	307	77	72	51,966
Oklahoma.	913	221	291	185	108	75	20	12	44,508
Oregon.	919	186	262	221	116	85	26	23	51,011
Pennsylvania.	3,217	596	884	727	437	366	109	97	53,680
Rhode Island.	268	51	60	60	42	36	10	9	58,978
South Carolina.	1,102	256	319	222	140	112	25	27	47,680
South Dakota	196	39	61	50	25	14	3	5	49,380
Tennessee	1,556	372	448	355	180	131	34	36	47,530
Texas.	5,483	1,296	1,488	1,067	659	617	183	173	49,086
Utah	595	92	185	150	83	55	15	14	52,286
Vermont	162	23	46	43	23	18	4	4	55,819
Virginia.	1,953	309	465	417	281	277	105	97	61,309
Washington.	1,566	272	385	352	245	209	58	46	57,478
West Virginia.	494	140	157	99	52	34	6	5	40,827
Wisconsin.	1,418	227	386	371	220	148	36	29	55,780
Wyoming	131	22	37	33	20	13	3	3	54,935

Source: U.S. Census Bureau, *Income, Earnings, and Poverty From the 2004 American Community Survey,* series ACS-01; and 2004 American Community Survey; B19101. Family Income in the Past 12 Months using American FactFinder® and B19113. Median Family Income in the Past 12 Months (In 2004 Inflation-Adjusted Dollars); <http://factfinder.census.gov/; (accessed: 25 January 2006).

Income, Expenditures, and Wealth   455

Table 689. **Household Income, Family Income, and Per Capita Income and Individual and Family Below Poverty Level by City: 2004**

[For number and percent below poverty, see headnote, Table 690. The American Community Survey universe is limited to the household population and excludes the population living in institutions, college dormitories, and other group quarters. Based on a sample and subject to sampling variability; see Appendix III. For definition of median, see Guide to Tabular Presentation]

City	Median household income (dol.)	Median family income (dol.)	Per capita income (dol.)	Number below poverty level Individuals	Number below poverty level Families	Percent below poverty level Individuals	Percent below poverty level Families
Albuquerque, NM	40,527	44,944	23,235	73,596	15,035	14.9	12.6
Anaheim, CA	49,622	52,524	20,868	26,447	5,009	8.2	6.4
Anchorage municipality, AK	61,595	73,840	28,371	19,490	3,232	7.4	4.9
Arlington, TX	45,712	58,924	23,943	30,539	5,544	10.2	7.5
Atlanta, GA	37,385	40,173	34,304	97,158	18,845	27.8	23.9
Aurora, CO	44,480	50,522	20,891	31,736	6,900	11.2	9.9
Austin, TX	45,508	55,488	26,513	100,489	16,894	15.4	11.8
Bakersfield, CA	42,891	48,746	20,124	37,136	7,340	13.0	10.7
Baltimore, MD	34,055	38,706	19,921	144,893	25,375	23.9	19.3
Boston, MA	45,892	50,495	30,456	98,989	17,855	19.0	16.5
Buffalo, NY	28,544	36,845	17,095	68,806	14,528	25.9	22.9
Charlotte, NC	46,082	58,116	28,731	75,062	13,280	13.0	9.4
Chicago, IL	40,656	47,186	23,162	571,727	106,333	21.1	18.1
Cincinnati, OH	31,960	38,737	21,707	56,702	12,189	19.6	18.9
Cleveland, OH	27,688	31,064	15,493	96,895	20,420	23.2	20.6
Colorado Springs, CO	45,388	55,554	24,262	49,890	12,620	13.4	12.7
Columbus, OH	40,437	48,567	21,982	116,668	21,768	16.7	13.3
Corpus Christi, TX	37,794	43,468	21,404	45,010	10,160	16.8	14.0
Dallas, TX	38,125	42,218	23,205	247,222	49,360	20.8	18.7
Denver, CO	43,777	53,616	27,676	81,948	12,389	15.1	10.6
Detroit, MI	27,871	32,314	14,573	280,948	54,317	33.6	29.1
El Paso, TX	31,764	35,097	15,630	166,433	35,521	28.8	24.6
Fort Worth, TX	37,601	44,611	19,546	109,843	21,376	17.6	14.0
Fresno, CA	38,842	46,389	17,901	99,263	21,107	21.2	19.3
Honolulu, HI [1]	46,500	60,618	27,532	44,797	8,345	12.4	9.6
Houston, TX	37,483	41,229	21,854	379,562	77,422	19.6	16.7
Indianapolis, IN [2]	39,815	47,621	22,945	99,701	22,176	13.1	11.4
Jacksonville, FL	41,894	52,049	21,796	102,499	20,721	13.5	10.3
Kansas City, MO	38,414	47,631	22,405	73,663	14,406	17.6	14.2
Las Vegas, NV	44,737	52,997	24,787	61,932	11,558	11.6	8.8
Lexington-Fayette, KY	38,322	53,627	29,549	45,513	10,678	18.1	15.6
Long Beach, CA	37,497	38,024	20,987	121,883	23,685	26.4	23.9
Los Angeles, CA	40,682	43,703	22,466	672,763	127,264	18.0	15.8
Memphis, TN	32,399	39,160	20,036	153,761	32,484	24.6	21.5
Mesa, AZ	42,371	51,374	21,938	54,154	10,610	12.1	9.1
Miami, FL	24,031	26,824	17,165	91,542	19,830	28.3	26.4
Milwaukee, WI	31,231	39,419	18,119	143,358	27,739	26.0	21.8
Minneapolis, MN	44,116	57,164	25,309	66,194	6,970	19.1	10.0
Nashville-Davidson, TN [2]	42,298	47,847	24,561	87,669	18,825	16.8	14.3
New Orleans, LA	31,369	36,465	19,711	102,636	14,879	23.2	14.5
New York, NY	41,509	46,717	25,751	1,600,574	313,142	20.3	17.4
Newark, NJ	26,309	27,124	13,914	70,073	15,830	28.1	26.7
Oakland, CA	46,190	54,333	28,409	71,469	11,892	19.7	15.0
Oklahoma City, OK	36,347	50,186	21,687	65,671	12,389	12.7	9.2
Omaha, NE	40,983	51,690	23,019	51,567	10,211	13.9	11.2
Philadelphia, PA	30,631	35,547	17,867	351,305	75,568	24.9	22.0
Phoenix, AZ	41,025	45,867	22,039	210,457	40,189	15.9	12.8
Pittsburgh, PA	31,910	41,886	21,509	55,638	8,875	18.8	12.2
Portland, OR	41,128	53,073	24,751	86,065	12,748	16.5	11.2
Raleigh, NC	47,878	64,908	28,854	46,848	7,289	14.7	9.6
Riverside, CA	44,866	50,387	20,370	35,413	5,236	12.2	7.2
Sacramento, CA	39,381	43,175	20,304	81,619	14,975	17.8	15.2
San Antonio, TX	36,598	42,423	19,319	235,657	50,013	19.8	17.0
San Diego, CA	51,382	59,818	27,741	161,755	24,755	13.0	8.8
San Francisco, CA	60,031	68,667	39,929	73,845	11,327	10.2	7.7
San Jose, CA	71,765	77,232	30,290	99,216	17,636	11.4	9.0
Santa Ana, CA	43,525	40,475	15,772	48,074	7,543	15.0	12.1
Seattle, WA	46,650	65,080	33,061	95,837	13,598	17.3	12.2
St. Louis, MO	30,389	42,323	20,436	71,649	12,397	21.6	17.1
St. Paul, MN	38,731	53,834	22,553	35,750	4,741	13.9	8.3
St. Petersburg, FL	38,079	45,856	23,958	32,693	6,884	14.2	11.8
Stockton, CA	37,322	42,225	16,796	62,958	12,578	23.0	19.8
Tampa, FL	39,231	44,127	26,168	53,754	10,689	17.7	14.2
Toledo, OH	35,239	42,920	18,437	50,207	9,709	16.5	12.8
Tucson, AZ	31,901	39,707	17,612	95,898	17,812	19.5	15.7
Tulsa, OK	36,255	47,433	23,457	69,888	15,271	18.5	16.3
Virginia Beach, VA	55,781	60,926	27,042	33,084	6,834	7.7	6.0
Washington, DC	46,574	54,193	36,893	97,525	18,591	18.9	16.9
Wichita, KS	38,811	50,146	21,910	41,842	6,511	12.2	7.5

[1] Data shown for census designated place (CDP).   [2] Represents the portion of a consolidated city that is not within one or more separately incorporated places.

Source: U.S. Census Bureau, *Income, Earnings, and Poverty From the 2004 American Community Survey,* series ACS-01; and 2004 American Community Survey; using American FactFinder; <http://factfinder.census.gov/>; (25 January 2006).

Table 690. **Individuals and Families Below Poverty Level—Number and Rate by State: 2000 and 2004**

[In thousands (33,311 represents 33,311,000), except as indicated. Represents number and percent below poverty in the past 12 months. The American Community Survey universe is limited to the household population and excludes the population living in institutions, college dormitories, and other group quarters. Based on a sample and subject to sampling variability; see Appendix III]

State	Number below poverty level (1,000)				Percent below poverty level			
	Individuals		Families		Individuals		Families	
	2000	2004	2000	2004	2000	2004	2000	2004
United States	33,311	37,162	6,615	7,444	12.2	13.1	9.3	10.1
Alabama	672	706	146	160	15.6	16.1	12.4	13.1
Alaska	55	52	11	9	9.1	8.2	6.8	5.5
Arizona	780	798	150	156	15.6	14.2	11.6	10.9
Arkansas	439	476	96	105	17.0	17.9	13.0	14.1
California	4,520	4,661	832	863	13.7	13.3	10.7	10.5
Colorado	363	498	64	102	8.7	11.1	5.7	8.6
Connecticut	254	257	51	56	7.7	7.6	5.8	6.2
Delaware	70	80	14	16	9.3	9.9	6.7	7.6
District of Columbia	94	98	17	19	17.5	18.9	15.4	16.9
Florida	1,987	2,062	387	409	12.8	12.2	9.3	9.1
Georgia	999	1,266	206	266	12.6	14.8	10.0	12.0
Hawaii	103	129	19	23	8.8	10.6	6.8	7.9
Idaho	144	196	26	41	11.4	14.5	7.7	11.1
Illinois	1,335	1,474	262	279	11.1	11.9	8.6	9.0
Indiana	592	652	113	128	10.1	10.8	7.1	7.9
Iowa	281	282	53	52	10.0	9.9	7.0	6.8
Kansas	247	279	43	48	9.5	10.5	6.2	6.8
Kentucky	640	700	148	158	16.4	17.4	13.5	13.9
Louisiana	862	845	182	175	20.0	19.4	16.0	14.9
Maine	124	157	22	33	10.1	12.3	6.6	9.5
Maryland	477	473	89	81	9.3	8.8	6.6	5.8
Massachusetts	586	570	110	112	9.6	9.2	7.1	7.1
Michigan	975	1,210	196	237	10.1	12.3	7.7	9.0
Minnesota	328	412	66	72	6.9	8.3	5.1	5.3
Mississippi	498	604	104	133	18.2	21.6	14.2	17.6
Missouri	606	659	118	134	11.2	11.8	7.7	8.7
Montana	117	127	23	25	13.4	14.2	9.5	10.5
Nebraska	158	186	28	35	9.6	11.0	6.5	7.7
Nevada	194	288	34	56	9.9	12.6	6.9	10.0
New Hampshire	63	95	11	18	5.3	7.6	3.5	5.5
New Jersey	651	722	126	143	7.9	8.5	6.0	6.5
New Mexico	320	358	64	73	18.0	19.3	14.2	15.9
New York	2,391	2,641	491	511	13.1	14.2	10.7	11.1
North Carolina	1,018	1,256	203	276	13.1	15.2	9.6	12.1
North Dakota	71	73	14	13	11.6	12.1	8.1	8.0
Ohio	1,216	1,388	246	301	11.1	12.5	8.4	10.0
Oklahoma	459	520	100	110	13.8	15.3	11.0	12.0
Oregon	439	493	84	95	13.2	14.1	9.5	10.4
Pennsylvania	1,240	1,389	247	285	10.5	11.7	7.8	8.9
Rhode Island	108	132	23	28	10.7	12.8	8.5	10.4
South Carolina	557	635	123	137	14.4	15.7	11.7	12.5
South Dakota	83	81	16	16	11.5	11.0	8.4	8.4
Tennessee	745	830	158	181	13.5	14.5	10.5	11.6
Texas	3,056	3,625	639	741	15.1	16.6	12.3	13.5
Utah	192	256	40	49	8.8	10.9	7.2	8.2
Vermont	63	54	12	9	10.7	9.0	7.5	5.6
Virginia	630	682	124	140	9.2	9.5	6.8	7.2
Washington	667	794	127	147	11.6	13.1	8.6	9.4
West Virginia	327	317	72	70	18.6	17.9	14.7	14.1
Wisconsin	461	571	75	107	8.9	10.7	5.6	7.6
Wyoming	55	50	10	10	11.4	10.3	7.9	7.7

Source: U.S. Census Bureau, *Income, Earnings, and Poverty From the 2004 American Community Survey*, series ACS-01; and 2004 American Community Survey; B17001. Poverty Status in the Past 12 Months by Sex and Age, and B17010. Poverty Status in the Past 12 Months of Families by Family Type by Presence of Related Children under 18 Years by Age of Related Children; using American FactFinder®; <http://factfinder.census.gov/; (accessed: 25 January 2006).

Income, Expenditures, and Wealth   457

Table 691. Weighted Average Poverty Thresholds by Size of Unit: 1980 to 2004

[In dollars. For information on the official poverty thresholds; see text, this section]

Size of family unit	1980[1]	1990	1995	1999	2000	2001	2002	2003	2004
One person (unrelated individual) ...	4,190	6,652	7,763	8,499	8,791	9,039	9,183	9,393	9,645
Under 65 years	4,290	6,800	7,929	8,667	8,959	9,214	9,359	9,573	9,827
65 years and over	3,949	6,268	7,309	7,990	8,259	8,494	8,628	8,825	9,060
Two persons	5,363	8,509	9,933	10,864	11,235	11,569	11,756	12,015	12,334
Householder under 65 years ...	5,537	8,794	10,259	11,213	11,589	11,920	12,110	12,384	12,649
Householder 65 years and over ...	4,983	7,905	9,219	10,075	10,418	10,715	10,885	11,133	11,418
Three persons	6,565	10,419	12,158	13,289	13,740	14,128	14,348	14,680	15,067
Four persons	8,414	13,359	15,569	17,030	17,604	18,104	18,392	18,810	19,307
Five persons	9,966	15,792	18,408	20,128	20,815	21,405	21,744	22,245	22,831
Six persons	11,269	17,839	20,804	22,730	23,533	24,195	24,576	25,122	25,788
Seven persons	13,955	20,241	23,552	25,918	26,750	27,517	28,001	28,544	29,236
Eight persons	14,199	22,582	26,237	28,970	29,701	30,627	30,907	31,589	32,641
Nine or more persons	16,896	26,848	31,280	34,436	35,150	36,286	37,062	37,656	39,048

[1] Poverty levels for nonfarm families.

Source: U.S. Census Bureau, *Income, Poverty, and Health Insurance Coverage*, Current Population Reports, P60-229. See also <http://www.census.gov/prod/2005pubs/p60-229.pdf> (released 30 August 2005).

Table 692. People Below Poverty Level and Below 125 Percent of Poverty Level by Race and Hispanic Origin: 1980 to 2004

[(29,272 represents 29,272,000.) People as of March of the following year. Based on Current Population Survey; See text, this section 1, and Appendix III. For data collection changes over time, see <http://www.census.gov/hhes/income/histinc/hstchg.html>]

Year	Number below poverty level (1,000)					Percent below poverty level					Below 125 percent of poverty level	
	All races[1]	White[2]	Black[3]	Asian and Pacific Islander[4]	His-panic[5]	All races[1]	White[2]	Black[3]	Asian and Pacific Islander[4]	His-panic[5]	Num-ber (1,000)	Percent of total popu-lation
1980	29,272	19,699	8,579	(NA)	3,491	13.0	10.2	32.5	(NA)	25.7	40,658	18.1
1985	33,064	22,860	8,926	(NA)	5,236	14.0	11.4	31.3	(NA)	29.0	44,146	18.7
1986	32,370	22,183	8,983	(NA)	5,117	13.6	11.0	31.1	(NA)	27.3	43,486	18.2
1987	32,221	21,195	9,520	1,021	5,422	13.4	10.4	32.4	16.1	28.0	43,032	17.9
1988	31,745	20,715	9,356	1,117	5,357	13.0	10.1	31.3	17.3	26.7	42,551	17.5
1989	31,528	20,785	9,302	939	5,430	12.8	10.0	30.7	14.1	26.2	42,653	17.3
1990	33,585	22,326	9,837	858	6,006	13.5	10.7	31.9	12.2	28.1	44,837	18.0
1991	35,708	23,747	10,242	996	6,339	14.2	11.3	32.7	13.8	28.7	47,527	18.9
1992	38,014	25,259	10,827	985	7,592	14.8	11.9	33.4	12.7	29.6	50,592	19.7
1993	39,265	26,226	10,877	1,134	8,126	15.1	12.2	33.1	15.3	30.6	51,801	20.0
1994	38,059	25,379	10,196	974	8,416	14.5	11.7	30.6	14.6	30.7	50,401	19.3
1995	36,425	24,423	9,872	1,411	8,574	13.8	11.2	29.3	14.6	30.3	48,761	18.5
1996	36,529	24,650	9,694	1,454	8,697	13.7	11.2	28.4	14.5	29.4	49,310	18.5
1997	35,574	24,396	9,116	1,468	8,308	13.3	11.0	26.5	14.0	27.1	46,036	17.0
1998	34,476	23,454	9,091	1,360	8,070	12.7	10.5	26.1	12.5	25.6	44,286	16.2
1999	32,791	22,169	8,441	1,285	7,876	11.9	9.8	23.6	10.7	22.7	43,612	15.6
2000[6]	31,581	21,645	7,982	1,258	7,747	11.3	9.5	22.5	9.9	21.5	45,320	16.1
2001	32,907	22,739	8,136	1,275	7,997	11.7	9.9	22.7	10.2	21.4	47,084	16.5
2002[7]	34,570	23,466	8,602	1,161	8,555	12.1	10.2	24.1	10.1	21.8	48,687	16.9
2003	35,861	24,272	8,781	1,401	9,051	12.5	10.5	24.4	11.8	22.5	49,666	17.1
2004	36,997	25,301	9,000	1,209	9,132	12.7	10.8	24.7	9.8	21.9		

NA Not available. [1] Includes other races not shown separately. [2] Beginning 2002, data represents White alone, which refers to people who reported White and did not report any other race category. [3] Beginning 2002, data represents Black alone, which refers to people who reported Black and did not report any other race category. [4] Beginning 2002, data represents Asian alone, which refers to people who reported Asian and did not report any other race category. [5] People of Hispanic origin may be of any race. [6] Implementation of Census 2000-based population controls and sample expanded by 28,000 households. [7] Beginning with the 2003 Current Population Survey (CPS), the questionnaire allowed respondents to choose more than one race. For 2002 and later, data represent persons who selected this race group only and excludes persons reporting more than one race. The CPS in prior years allowed respondents to report only one race group. See also comments on race in the text for Section 1, Population.

Source: U.S. Census Bureau, *Income, Poverty, and Health Insurance Coverage in the United States: 2004*, Current Population Reports, P60-229; and Internet sites <http://www.census.gov/prod/2005pubs/p60-229.pdf> (released 30 August 2005) and <http://www.census.gov/hhes/poverty/histpov/hstpov6.html> (revised 14 December 2005).

Table 693. Children Below Poverty Level by Race and Hispanic Origin: 1980 to 2004

[(11,114 represents 11,114,000.) Persons as of March of the following year. Covers only related children in families under 18 years old. Based on Current Population Survey; see text, this section and Section 1, and Appendix III. For data collection changes over time, see <http://www.census.gov/hhes/income/histinc/hstchg.html>]

Year	Number below poverty level (1,000)					Percent below poverty level				
	All races [1]	White [2]	Black [3]	Asian and Pacific Islander [4]	His-panic [5]	All races [1]	White [2]	Black [3]	Asian and Pacific Islander [4]	His-panic [5]
1980	11,114	6,817	3,906	(NA)	1,718	17.9	13.4	42.1	(NA)	33.0
1985	12,483	7,838	4,057	(NA)	2,512	20.1	15.6	43.1	(NA)	39.6
1986	12,257	7,714	4,037	(NA)	2,413	19.8	15.3	42.7	(NA)	37.1
1987	12,275	7,398	4,234	432	2,606	19.7	14.7	44.4	22.7	38.9
1988	11,935	7,095	4,148	458	2,576	19.0	14.0	42.8	23.5	37.3
1989	12,001	7,164	4,257	368	2,496	19.0	14.1	43.2	18.9	35.5
1990	12,715	7,696	4,412	356	2,750	19.9	15.1	44.2	17.0	37.7
1991	13,658	8,316	4,637	348	2,977	21.1	16.1	45.6	17.1	39.8
1992	14,521	8,752	5,015	352	3,440	21.6	16.5	46.3	16.0	39.0
1993	14,961	9,123	5,030	358	3,666	22.0	17.0	45.9	17.6	39.9
1994	14,610	8,826	4,787	308	3,956	21.2	16.3	43.3	17.9	41.1
1995	13,999	8,474	4,644	532	3,938	20.2	15.5	41.5	18.6	39.3
1996	13,764	8,488	4,411	553	4,090	19.8	15.5	39.5	19.1	39.9
1997	13,422	8,441	4,116	608	3,865	19.2	15.4	36.8	19.9	36.4
1998	12,845	7,935	4,073	542	3,670	18.3	14.4	36.4	17.5	33.6
1999	11,678	7,194	3,698	367	3,561	16.6	13.1	32.8	11.5	29.9
2000 [6]	11,005	6,834	3,495	407	3,342	15.6	12.4	30.9	12.5	27.6
2001	11,175	7,086	3,423	353	3,433	15.8	12.8	30.0	11.1	27.4
2002 [7]	11,646	7,203	3,570	302	3,653	16.3	13.1	32.1	11.4	28.2
2003	12,340	7,624	3,750	331	3,982	17.2	13.9	33.6	12.1	29.5
2004	12,460	7,868	3,694	269	3,989	17.3	14.2	33.3	9.5	28.6

NA Not available. [1] Includes other races not shown separately. [2] Beginning 2002, data represents White, which refers to people who reported White and did not report any other race category. [3] Beginning 2002, data represents Black alone, which refers to people who reported Black and did not report any other race category. [4] Beginning 2002, data represents Asian alone, which refers to people who reported Asian and did not report any other race category. [5] People of Hispanic origin may be of any race. [6] Implementation of Census 2000-based population controls and sample expanded by 28,000 households. [7] Beginning with the 2003 Current Population Survey (CPS), the questionnaire allowed respondents to choose more than one race. For 2002 and later, data represent persons who selected this race group only and excludes persons reporting more than one race. The CPS in prior years allowed respondents to report only one race group. See also comments on race in the text for Section 1.

Source: U.S. Census Bureau, *Income, Poverty, and Health Insurance Coverage in the United States: 2004*, Current Population Reports, P60-229; and Internet sites <http://www.census.gov/prod/2005pubs/p60-229.pdf> (released 30 August 2005), and <http://www.census.gov/hhes/poverty/histpov/hstpov3.html> (revised 14 December 2005).

Table 694. Persons Below Poverty Level by Selected Characteristics: 2004

[(36,997 represents 36,997,000.) People as of March 2005. Based on Current Population Survey (CPS); see text, this section and Section 1, and Appendix III. The 2005 CPS allowed respondents to choose more than one race. For 2004, data represent persons who selected this race group only and excludes persons reporting more than one race. The CPS in prior years allowed respondents to report only one race group. See also comments on race in the text for Section 1. For composition of regions, see map, inside front cover]

Characteristic	Number below poverty level (1,000)					Percent below poverty level				
	All races [1]	White alone	Black alone	Asian alone	His-panic [2]	All races [1]	White alone	Black alone	Asian alone	His-panic [2]
Total	36,997	25,301	9,000	1,209	9,132	12.7	10.8	24.7	9.8	21.9
Male	16,381	11,331	3,833	554	4,250	11.5	9.8	22.6	9.3	19.9
Female	20,617	13,970	5,167	655	4,882	13.9	11.8	26.5	10.3	24.0
Under 18 years old	13,027	8,299	3,780	286	4,102	17.8	14.8	33.6	10.0	28.9
18 to 24 years old	5,068	3,536	1,116	199	1,120	18.1	16.2	28.1	17.9	22.6
25 to 34 years old	4,924	3,415	1,123	178	1,492	12.5	11.1	22.0	7.9	19.5
35 to 44 years old	4,272	2,986	991	178	1,075	9.9	8.6	18.4	8.2	17.2
45 to 54 years old	3,507	2,460	778	129	591	8.4	7.1	16.0	7.5	14.2
55 to 59 years old	1,416	1,056	267	53	170	8.4	7.5	15.9	8.1	12.7
60 to 64 years old	1,326	1,013	241	39	171	10.4	9.3	19.7	8.7	17.6
65 years old and over	3,457	2,537	705	148	410	9.8	8.3	23.9	13.6	18.7
65 to 74 years old	1,721	1,213	381	85	250	9.4	7.7	22.2	13.2	19.0
75 years old and over	1,736	1,324	325	63	159	10.3	8.9	26.1	14.0	18.2
Northeast	6,233	4,135	1,666	271	1,355	11.6	9.4	25.2	10.9	23.9
Midwest	7,538	5,072	1,965	168	682	11.6	9.2	29.9	11.0	19.6
South	14,798	9,401	4,674	265	3,406	14.1	11.8	23.4	10.4	23.3
West	8,429	6,692	696	505	3,689	12.6	12.3	21.0	8.8	20.6
Native	30,991	20,845	8,438	401	5,266	12.1	9.9	25.2	9.1	21.2
Foreign born	6,006	4,456	563	807	3,866	17.1	19.0	18.9	10.3	23.0
Naturalized citizen	1,328	844	195	271	551	17.1	19.0	18.9	10.3	23.0
Not a citizen	4,678	3,612	368	536	3,315	21.6	23.1	22.1	14.1	26.1

[1] Includes other races not shown separately. [2] Persons of Hispanic origin may be any race.

Source: U.S. Census Bureau, *Income, Poverty, and Health Insurance Coverage in the United States, 2004*, Current Population Reports, P60-229. See also <http://www.census.gov/prod/2005pubs/p60-229.pdf> (released 30 August 2005), and <http://pubdb3.census.gov/macro/032004/pov/toc.htm> (revised 19 May and 16 June 2005).

Income, Expenditures, and Wealth **459**

Table 695. **Work Experience During 2004 by Poverty Status, Sex, and Age: 2004**

[(**102,427 represents 102,427,000**). Covers only persons 16 years old and over. Based on Current Population Survey; see text, this section and Section 1, and Appendix III]

Sex and age	Worked full-time year-round Number (1,000)	Below poverty level Number (1,000)	Percent	Did not work full-time year-round Number (1,000)	Below poverty level Number (1,000)	Percent	Did not work Number (1,000)	Below poverty level Number (1,000)	Percent
BOTH SEXES									
Total.	102,427	2,896	2.8	50,598	6,487	12.8	73,081	15,845	21.7
16 to 17 years old	94	7	7.5	2,764	204	7.4	5,913	1,046	17.7
18 to 64 years old	99,829	2,842	2.8	43,976	6,189	14.1	38,316	11,482	30.0
18 to 24 years old	7,791	453	5.8	12,435	2,111	17.0	7,745	2,504	32.3
25 to 34 years old	23,345	867	3.7	9,411	1,707	18.1	6,551	2,350	35.9
35 to 54 years old	54,672	1,295	2.4	16,485	1,956	11.9	14,153	4,529	32.0
55 to 64 years old	14,021	227	1.6	5,645	416	7.4	9,866	2,099	21.3
65 years old and over.	2,503	47	1.9	3,858	93	2.4	28,852	3,317	11.5
MALE									
Total.	60,096	1,681	2.8	21,106	2,672	12.6	28,217	6,004	21.3
16 to 17 years old	60	2	(B)	1,394	101	7.3	3,079	539	17.5
18 to 64 years old	58,503	1,637	2.8	17,799	2,535	14.2	13,492	4,483	33.2
18 to 24 years old	4,567	236	5.2	5,897	821	13.9	3,585	1,101	30.7
25 to 34 years old	14,111	518	3.7	3,795	669	17.6	1,769	720	40.7
35 to 54 years old	31,803	739	2.3	5,819	874	15.0	4,402	1,806	41.0
55 to 64 years old	8,023	145	1.8	2,289	172	7.5	3,736	856	22.9
65 years old and over.	1,533	42	2.7	1,972	35	1.8	11,646	981	8.4
FEMALE									
Total.	42,331	1,215	2.9	29,432	3,815	13.0	44,864	9,842	21.9
16 to 17 years old	34	5	(B)	1,370	103	7.5	2,834	507	17.9
18 to 64 years old	41,326	1,205	2.9	26,177	3,654	14.0	24,824	6,999	28.2
18 to 24 years old	3,225	217	6.7	6,539	1,290	19.7	4,160	1,403	33.7
25 to 34 years old	9,234	349	3.8	5,616	1,038	18.5	4,782	1,630	34.1
35 to 54 years old	22,869	556	2.4	10,666	1,082	10.1	9,751	2,722	27.9
55 to 64 years old	5,998	83	1.4	3,356	243	7.3	6,130	1,243	20.3
65 years old and over. . . .	971	5	0.5	1,885	58	3.1	17,207	2,336	13.6

B Base figure too small to meet statistical standards for reliability of a derived figure.
Source: U.S. Census Bureau, *Income, Poverty, and Health Insurance Coverage in the United States: 2004,* Current Population Reports, series P60-229; and <http://www.census.gov/prod/2005pubs/p60-229.pdf> (released 30 August 2005) and <http://pubdb3.census.gov/macro/032005/pov/toc.htm> (released 10 June 2005).

Table 696. **Families Below Poverty Level and Below 125 Percent of Poverty by Race and Hispanic Origin: 1980 to 2004**

[(**6,217 represents 6,217,000.**) **Families as of March of the following year**). Based on Current Population Survey; see text, this section, Section 1, and Appendix III. For data collection changes over time, see <http://www.census.gov/hhes/income/histinc/hstchg.html>]

Year	Number below poverty level (1,000) All races [1]	White [2]	Black [3]	Asian and Pacific Islander [4]	His-panic [5]	Percent below poverty level All races [1]	White [2]	Black [3]	Asian and Pacific Islander [4]	His-panic [5]	Below 125 percent of poverty level Num-ber (1,000)	Percent
1980 . . .	6,217	4,195	1,826	(NA)	751	10.3	8.0	28.9	(NA)	23.2	8,764	14.5
1985 . . .	7,647	5,220	2,161	(NA)	981	12.3	9.7	32.3	(NA)	25.9	9,753	15.3
1986 . . .	7,023	4,811	1,987	(NA)	1,085	10.9	8.6	28.0	(NA)	24.7	9,476	14.7
1987 . . .	7,005	4,567	2,117	199	1,168	10.7	8.1	29.4	13.5	25.5	9,338	14.3
1988 . . .	6,874	4,471	2,089	201	1,141	10.4	7.9	28.2	13.6	23.7	9,284	14.1
1989 . . .	6,784	4,409	2,077	182	1,133	10.3	7.8	27.8	11.9	23.4	9,267	14.0
1990 . . .	7,098	4,622	2,193	169	1,244	10.7	8.1	29.3	11.0	25.0	9,564	14.4
1991 . . .	7,712	5,022	2,343	210	1,372	11.5	8.8	30.4	13.0	26.5	10,244	15.3
1992 . . .	8,144	5,255	2,484	215	1,529	11.9	9.1	31.1	12.2	26.7	10,959	16.1
1993 . . .	8,393	5,452	2,499	235	1,625	12.3	9.4	31.3	13.5	27.3	11,203	16.4
1994 . . .	8,053	5,312	2,212	208	1,724	11.6	9.1	27.3	13.1	27.8	10,771	15.5
1995 . . .	7,532	4,994	2,127	264	1,695	10.8	8.5	26.4	12.4	27.0	10,223	14.7
1996 . . .	7,708	5,059	2,206	284	1,748	11.0	8.6	26.1	12.7	26.4	10,476	14.9
1997 . . .	7,324	4,990	1,985	244	1,721	10.3	8.4	23.6	10.2	24.7	9,714	13.6
1998 . . .	7,186	4,829	1,981	270	1,648	10.0	8.0	23.4	11.0	22.7	9,320	12.9
1999 . . .	6,792	4,447	1,887	258	1,593	9.3	7.3	21.8	10.3	20.5	9,032	12.2
2000 [6] . .	6,400	4,333	1,686	233	1,540	8.7	7.1	19.3	7.8	19.2	8,530	—
2001 . . .	6,813	4,579	1,829	234	1,649	9.2	7.4	20.7	7.8	19.4	9,525	12.8
2002 [7] . .	7,229	4,862	1,923	210	1,792	9.6	7.8	21.5	7.4	19.7	9,998	13.2
2003 . . .	7,607	5,058	1,986	311	1,925	10.0	8.1	22.3	10.2	20.8	10,360	13.6
2004 . . .	7,854	5,315	2,034	232	1,958	10.2	8.4	22.8	7.4	20.5	10,530	13.7

NA Not available. [1] Includes other races not shown separately. [2] Beginning 2002, data represents White alone, which refers to people who reported White and did not report any other race category. [3] Beginning 2002, data represents Black alone, which refers to people who reported Black and did not report any other race category. [4] Beginning 2002, data represents Asian alone, which refers to people who reported Asian and did not report any other race category. [5] People of Hispanic origin may be of any race. [6] Implementation of Census 2000-based population controls and sample expanded by 28,000 households. [7] Beginning with the 2003 Current Population Survey (CPS), the questionnaire allowed respondents to choose more than one race. For 2002 and later, data represent persons who selected this race group only and excludes persons reporting more than one race. The CPS in prior years allowed respondents to report only one race group. See also comments on race in the text for Section 1.
Source: U.S. Census Bureau, Current Population Reports, P60-226; and Internet site <http://www.census.gov/prod/2005pubs /p60-229.pdf> (released 30 August 2005) and <http://www.census.gov/hhes/www/poverty/histpov/hstpov4.html> (revised 14 December 2005).

Table 697. Families Below Poverty Level by Selected Characteristics: 2004

[(7,854 represents 7,854,000.) Families as of March 2005. Based on Current Population Survey (CPS); see text, this section, Section 1, and Appendix III. The 2005 CPS allowed respondents to choose more than one race. For 2004, data represent persons who selected this race group only and exclude persons reporting more than one race. See also comments on race in the text for Section 1. For composition of regions, see map inside front cover]

Characteristic	Number below poverty level (1,000)					Percent below poverty level				
	All races [1]	White alone	Black alone	Asian alone	His-panic [2]	All races [1]	White alone	Black alone	Asian alone	His-panic [2]
Total families	7,854	5,315	2,034	232	1,958	10.2	8.4	22.8	7.4	20.5
Age of householder:										
15 to 24 years old	1,045	658	319	11	258	30.3	25.8	49.8	9.8	31.0
25 to 34 years old	2,155	1,429	594	40	672	15.7	13.3	31.1	6.2	24.9
35 to 44 years old	1,844	1,258	477	61	518	10.1	8.6	21.4	6.5	20.0
45 to 54 years old	1,150	791	267	56	263	6.6	5.5	13.9	8.2	15.3
55 to 64 years old	829	604	184	17	131	6.9	5.9	15.7	4.0	13.9
65 years old and over	792	556	186	35	106	6.5	5.2	18.7	10.5	15.0
Region:										
Northeast.	1,281	824	368	62	305	9.1	7.1	23.4	9.4	23.4
Midwest.	1,607	1,073	450	26	146	9.2	7.0	28.1	6.9	19.5
South	3,242	2,043	1,056	56	726	11.4	9.2	21.4	8.7	20.7
West	1,723	1,375	159	89	781	10.1	9.8	19.9	6.0	19.7
Type of family:										
Married couple	3,222	2,591	380	147	939	5.5	5.2	9.1	5.7	14.7
Male householder, no spouse present	658	435	154	38	148	13.5	11.7	21.0	15.2	15.9
Female householder, no spouse present	3,973	2,288	1,500	48	871	28.4	24.8	37.6	13.8	38.9
Education of householder: [3]										
No high school diploma	2,473	1,793	550	43	1,086	24.5	22.2	37.4	15.5	30.8
High school diploma, no college. . . .	2,325	1,513	685	57	358	10.4	8.2	23.6	10.0	15.6
Some college, less than bachelor's degree	1,361	893	375	44	171	6.8	5.4	15.5	8.8	9.4
Bachelor's degree or more	612	439	98	65	74	2.9	2.5	6.8	3.9	7.4

[1] Includes other races not shown separately.   [2] Hispanic persons may be of any race.   [3] Householder 25 years old and over.

Source: U.S. Census Bureau, *Income, Poverty, and Health Insurance Coverage in the United States, 2004,* Current Population Reports, P60-229. See also <http://www.census.gov/prod/2005pubs/p60-229.pdf> (released 30 August 2005) and <http://pubdb3.census.gov/macro/032005/pov/toc.htm> (revised 10 June 2005).

Table 698. People and Families With Alternative Definitions of Income Below Poverty: 2004

[290,605 represents 290,605,000. People and families as of March 2005]

Race and Hispanic origin	Number (1,000)	Alternative definitions of income, percent below poverty			
		Money income [1]	Market income [2]	Post-social insurance income [3]	Disposable income [4]
PEOPLE					
Total [5]	290,605	12.6	19.4	12.9	10.4
White alone or in combination.	238,453	10.8	17.6	11.0	9.0
White alone [6]	233,702	10.7	17.5	10.9	8.9
White alone, not Hispanic.	195,054	8.6	15.7	8.5	7.2
Black alone or in combination.	38,016	24.6	32.1	25.6	19.6
Black alone [7]	36,423	24.6	32.2	25.5	19.7
Asian alone or in combination.	13,356	9.9	13.9	10.8	9.1
Asian alone [8]	12,301	10.0	14.0	10.9	9.3
Hispanic [9]	41,688	21.8	26.9	23.0	17.9
FAMILIES					
Total [5]	77,019	10.5	17.4	10.8	8.5
White alone or in combination.	64,128	8.8	15.7	8.9	7.1
White alone [6]	63,227	8.7	15.6	8.8	7.0
White alone, not Hispanic.	54,388	6.7	13.9	6.7	5.4
Black alone or in combination.	9,113	23.4	30.6	24.1	18.7
Black alone [7]	8,908	23.4	30.6	24.1	18.7
Asian alone or in combination.	3,295	7.8	12.1	8.4	7.1
Asian alone [8]	3,155	7.8	12.0	8.4	7.0
Hispanic [9]	9,537	21.1	26.9	22.2	17.1

[1] Money income concept includes all money income received by individuals who are 15 years or older. It consists of income before deductions for taxes and other expenses and does not include lump-sum payments or capital gains. It also does not include the value of noncash benefits such as food stamps. This income concept is the basis for the official U.S. poverty measure.   [2] Market income concept includes money income except government cash transfers; includes imputed realized capital gains and losses; includes imputed rate of return on home equity; and subtracts imputed work expenses.   [3] Post-Social insurance income concept includes money income except government means-tested cash transfers; includes imputed realized capital gains and losses; includes imputed rate of return on home equity; and subtracts imputed work expenses.   [4] Disposable income concept includes money income; includes the value of noncash transfers (food stamps, public or subsidized housing, and free or reduced-price school lunches); includes imputed realized capital gains and losses; includes imputed rate of return on home equity; and subtracts imputed work expenses, federal payroll taxes, federal and state income taxes, and property taxes on owner-occupied homes.   [5] Data for American Indians and Alaska Natives, Asian, and Native Hawaiian and Other Pacific Islanders are not shown separately.   [6] White alone refers to people who reported White and did not report any other race category.   [7] Black alone refers to people who reported Black and did not report any other race category.   [8] Asian alone refers to people who reported Asian and did not report any other race category.   [9] Persons of Hispanic origin may be of any race.

Source: U.S. Census Bureau, *The Effects of Government Taxes and Transfers on Income and Poverty: 2004.* See also <http://www.census.gov/hhes/www/poverty/effect2004/effectofgovtandt2004.pdf> (released 14 February 2006).

Income, Expenditures, and Wealth   461

Table 699. Top Wealth Holders With Gross Assets of $675,000 or More by Type of Property, Sex, and Size of Net Worth: 2001

[7,357 represents 7,357,000. Net worth is defined as assets minus liabilities. Based on a sample of federal estate tax returns (Form 706). Based on the estate multiplier technique; for more information on this methodology, see source]

Sex and net worth	Number of top wealth holders (1,000)	Assets (mil. dol.)				
		Total[1]	Personal residences	Other real estate	Closely held stock	Publicly traded stock
Both sexes, total	7,357	15,181,904	1,790,586	1,483,808	1,228,657	3,492,512
Size of net worth:						
Negative net worth[2]	32	34,900	6,897	4,116	2,209	8,058
$1 under $600,000	1,508	980,726	282,507	140,049	29,826	68,119
$600,000 under $1,000,000	2,307	2,080,347	411,849	221,197	49,671	333,887
$1,000,000 under $2,500,000	2,569	4,127,949	585,453	451,974	203,716	814,725
$2,500,000 under $5,000,000	573	2,106,827	211,564	259,276	165,506	487,587
$5,000,000 under $10,000,000	243	1,771,701	143,179	175,206	173,792	450,143
$10,000,000 under $20,000,000 ...	77	1,128,102	74,680	96,322	154,327	300,377
$20,000,000 or more	46	2,951,351	74,457	135,669	449,612	1,029,617
Males, total	3,953	8,890,276	887,979	848,748	883,579	1,946,329
Size of net worth:						
Negative net worth[2]	26	32,272	5,907	3,400	2,209	8,026
$1 under $600,000	919	562,062	158,339	74,712	23,875	38,808
$600,000 under $1,000,000	1,083	984,350	162,180	114,128	35,262	141,310
$1,000,000 under $2,500,000	1,363	2,243,244	284,976	247,600	145,384	385,646
$2,500,000 under $5,000,000	333	1,222,038	110,947	143,503	121,794	253,438
$5,000,000 under $10,000,000	155	1,148,462	83,846	115,265	150,390	269,144
$10,000,000 under $20,000,000 ...	42	624,240	30,216	50,809	77,985	159,053
$20,000,000 or more	31	2,073,608	51,568	99,331	326,681	690,904
Females, total	3,404	6,291,628	902,607	635,060	345,078	1,546,183
Size of net worth:						
Negative net worth[2]	6	2,628	990	716	(Z)	32
$1 under $600,000	589	418,664	124,168	65,337	5,951	29,311
$600,000 under $1,000,000	1,224	1,095,997	249,669	107,069	14,409	192,577
$1,000,000 under $2,500,000	1,206	1,884,705	300,477	204,374	58,332	429,079
$2,500,000 under $5,000,000	240	884,789	100,617	115,773	43,712	234,149
$5,000,000 under $10,000,000	88	623,239	59,333	59,941	23,402	180,999
$10,000,000 under $20,000,000 ...	35	503,862	44,464	45,513	76,342	141,324
$20,000,000 or more	15	877,743	22,889	36,338	122,931	338,713

Z Less than $500,000.   [1] Includes other types of assets not shown separately.   [2] Includes individuals with zero net worth.

Source: Internal Revenue Service, *Statistics of Income Bulletin*, Winter 2005–2006, volume 25, no. 3. See also <http://www.irs.gov/pub/irs-soi/01pwart.pdf> and <http://www.irs.gov/taxstats/indtaxstats/article/0,,id=96426,00.html>

Table 700. Top Wealth Holders With Net Worth of $1 Million or More—Number and Net Worth by State: 2001

[3,510 represents 3,510,000. Millionaire is defined as those adults with net worth (assets minus liabilities) of $1 million or more. Based on a sample of federal estate tax returns (Form 706). Estimates of wealth by state can be subject to significant year-to-year fluctuations and this is especially true for individuals at the extreme tail of the net worth distribution and for states with relatively small decedent populations. Based on the estate multiplier technique; for more information on this methodology, see source]

State	Number of millionaires (1,000)	Net worth (mil. dol.)	State	Number of millionaires (1,000)	Net worth (mil. dol.)
Total	3,510	11,275,755	Montana	11	29,836
Alabama	35	88,579	Nebraska	14	66,470
Alaska	6	15,689	Nevada.............	26	97,954
Arizona.............	45	152,533	New Hampshire	17	42,208
Arkansas............	22	58,856	New Jersey	178	579,085
California............	572	1,940,734	New Mexico.........	18	47,827
Colorado............	59	267,715	New York	317	1,315,450
Connecticut	83	322,668	North Carolina	83	266,524
Delaware............	11	30,846	North Dakota	5	8,831
District of Columbia....	11	38,063	Ohio..............	114	328,870
Florida	249	837,498	Oklahoma	22	106,653
Georgia	86	220,277	Oregon	41	111,321
Hawaii	13	29,387	Pennsylvania	135	372,109
Idaho	13	34,559	Rhode Island	13	28,121
Illinois.............	185	522,196	South Carolina	40	110,356
Indiana	53	128,883	South Dakota	10	20,185
Iowa..............	32	60,127	Tennessee	49	141,637
Kansas	28	62,142	Texas	182	577,967
Kentucky	26	65,622	Utah..............	14	38,342
Louisiana	34	89,790	Vermont	3	9,355
Maine	12	26,130	Virginia	94	229,300
Maryland............	69	186,861	Washington	73	257,268
Massachusetts	105	455,761	West Virginia	10	29,580
Michigan	88	237,762	Wisconsin	54	165,763
Minnesota...........	60	180,335	Wyoming	7	24,221
Mississippi..........	11	32,457			
Missouri	58	155,805	Other areas[1]	9	29,251

[1] Includes U.S. territories and possessions.

Source: Internal Revenue Service, *Statistics of Income Bulletin*, Winter 2005–2006, volume 25, no. 3. See also <http://www.irs.gov/pub/irs-soi/01pwart.pdf> and <http://www.irs.gov/taxstats/indtaxstats/article/0,,id=96426,00.html>

Table 701. **Nonfinancial Assets Held by Families by Type of Asset: 2004**

[(172.9 represents $172,900.) **Median value in thousands of dollars**. Constant dollar figures are based on consumer price index for all urban consumers published by U.S. Bureau of Labor Statistics. Families include one-person units and, as used in this table, are comparable to the U.S. Census Bureau household concept. For definition of family, see text, Section 1. Based on Survey of Consumer Finance; see Appendix III. For data on financial assets, see Section 25. For definition of median, see Guide to Tabular Presentation]

Family Characteristic	Total [1]	Vehicles	Primary residence	Other residential property	Equity in nonresidential property	Business equity	Other	Any nonfinancial asset
PERCENT OF FAMILIES HOLDING ASSET								
All families, total	97.9	86.3	69.1	12.5	8.3	11.5	7.8	92.5
Age of family head:								
Under 35 years old	96.5	82.9	41.6	5.1	3.3	6.9	5.5	88.6
35 to 44 years old	97.7	89.4	68.3	9.4	6.4	13.9	6.0	93.0
45 to 54 years old	98.3	88.8	77.3	16.3	11.4	15.7	9.7	94.7
55 to 64 years old	97.5	88.6	79.1	19.5	12.8	15.8	9.2	92.6
65 to 74 years old	99.5	89.1	81.3	19.9	10.6	8.0	9.0	95.6
75 years old and over	99.6	76.9	85.2	9.7	7.7	5.3	8.5	92.5
Race or ethnicity of respondent:								
White non-Hispanic	99.3	90.3	76.1	14.0	9.2	13.6	9.3	95.8
Non-White or Hispanic	94.4	76.1	50.8	8.9	5.8	5.9	3.8	84.0
Tenure:								
Owner-occupied	100.0	92.3	100.0	15.7	11.0	14.7	9.2	100.0
Renter-occupied or other	93.3	73.0	(X)	5.4	2.4	4.3	4.6	75.9
MEDIAN VALUE [2] ($1,000)								
All families, total	172.9	14.2	160.0	100.0	60.0	100.0	15.0	147.8
Age of family head:								
Under 35 years old	39.2	11.3	135.0	82.5	55.0	50.0	5.0	32.3
35 to 44 years old	173.4	15.6	160.0	80.0	42.2	100.0	10.0	151.3
45 to 54 years old	234.9	18.8	170.0	90.0	43.0	144.0	20.0	184.5
55 to 64 years old	351.2	18.6	200.0	135.0	75.0	190.9	25.0	226.3
65 to 74 years old	233.2	12.4	150.0	80.0	78.0	100.0	30.0	161.1
75 years old and over	185.2	8.4	125.0	150.0	85.8	80.3	11.0	137.1
Race or ethnicity of respondent:								
White non-Hispanic	224.5	15.7	165.0	105.0	66.0	135.0	16.5	164.8
Non-White or Hispanic	59.6	9.8	130.0	80.0	30.0	66.7	10.0	64.1
Tenure:								
Owner-occupied	289.9	17.5	160.0	100.0	62.0	122.8	17.5	201.6
Renter-occupied or other	12.2	7.2	(X)	80.0	56.0	50.0	8.0	8.4

X Not applicable.   [1] Any financial or nonfinancial asset.   [2] Median value of asset for families holding such assets.

Source: Board of Governors of the Federal Reserve System, "2004 Survey of Consumer Finances"; published 28 February 2006; <http://www.federalreserve.gov/pubs/oss/oss2/2004/scf2004home.html>.

Table 702. **Family Net Worth—Mean and Median Net Worth in Constant (2004) Dollars by Selected Family Characteristics: 1995 to 2004**

[**Net worth in thousands of constant (2004) dollars (260.8 represents $260,800).** Constant dollar figures are based on consumer price index for all urban consumers published by U.S. Bureau of Labor Statistics. Families include one-person units and as used in this table are comparable to the U.S. Census Bureau household concept. Based on Survey of Consumer Finance; see Appendix III. For definition of median, see Guide to Tabular Presentation]

Family characteristic	1995		1998		2001		2004	
	Mean	Median	Mean	Median	Mean	Median	Mean	Median
All families	260.8	70.8	327.5	83.1	421.5	91.7	448.2	93.1
Age of family head:								
Under 35 years old	53.2	14.8	74.0	10.6	96.6	12.3	73.5	14.2
35 to 44 years old	176.8	64.2	227.6	73.5	276.4	82.6	299.2	69.4
45 to 54 years old	364.8	116.8	420.2	122.3	517.6	141.6	542.7	144.7
55 to 64 years old	471.1	141.9	617.0	148.2	775.4	193.3	843.8	248.7
65 to 74 years old	429.3	136.6	541.1	169.8	717.9	187.8	690.9	190.1
75 years old and over	317.9	114.5	360.3	145.6	496.2	161.2	528.1	163.1
Race or ethnicity of respondent:								
White, non-Hispanic	308.7	94.3	391.1	111.0	518.7	129.6	561.8	140.7
Non-White or Hispanic	94.9	19.5	116.5	19.3	123.8	19.1	153.1	24.8
Tenure:								
Owner-occupied	373.7	128.1	468.7	153.2	594.8	182.9	624.9	184.4
Renter-occupied or other	53.8	6.0	50.4	4.9	58.5	5.1	54.1	4.0

Source: Board of Governors of the Federal Reserve System, "2004 Survey of Consumer Finances"; published 28 February 2006; <http://www.federalreseve.gov/pubs/oss/oss2/2004/scf2004home.html>.

Income, Expenditures, and Wealth   463

Table 703. **Household and Nonprofit Organization Sector Balance Sheet: 1980 to 2005**

[In billions of dollars (10,872 represents $10,872,000,000,000). **As of December 31**. For details of financial assets and liabilities, see Table 1151]

Item	1980	1990	1995	1999	2000	2001	2002	2003	2004	2005
Assets	10,872	23,953	32,731	48,896	48,944	48,610	47,679	53,732	58,985	64,023
Tangible assets [1]	4,272	9,351	11,248	14,488	15,793	17,028	18,424	20,040	22,556	25,558
Real estate	3,338	7,377	8,772	11,519	12,633	13,730	14,982	16,472	18,776	21,580
Consumer durable goods	910	1,899	2,371	2,835	3,015	3,144	3,273	3,383	3,578	3,761
Financial assets [1]	6,555	14,602	21,483	34,408	33,151	31,582	29,255	33,692	36,429	38,465
Deposits [1]	1,531	3,304	3,336	4,031	4,312	4,760	5,026	5,202	5,455	5,888
Checkable deposits and currency .	221	413	525	371	280	348	342	286	242	219
Time and savings deposits	1,245	2,485	2,310	2,803	3,024	3,250	3,564	3,905	4,251	4,654
Money market fund shares	64	392	478	816	960	1,113	1,070	960	903	951
Credit market instruments [1]	504	1,793	2,285	2,547	2,399	2,174	2,220	2,557	2,681	2,733
Open market paper	52	94	72	85	97	97	110	106	136	164
Treasury	174	509	834	848	619	471	304	452	495	401
Savings bonds	73	126	185	186	185	190	195	204	204	205
Corporate equities	1,010	1,960	4,348	9,596	8,091	6,721	4,997	6,216	6,406	6,089
Mutual fund shares	52	512	1,344	3,226	3,041	2,835	2,500	3,188	3,726	4,208
Pension fund reserves	970	3,306	5,695	9,192	9,000	8,572	7,815	9,214	10,150	10,647
Equity in noncorporate business	2,172	3,032	3,465	4,344	4,705	4,797	4,943	5,365	5,869	6,677
Liabilities [1]	1,449	3,715	5,055	6,777	7,350	7,909	8,605	9,605	10,735	11,916
Credit market instruments [1]	1,397	3,593	4,858	6,398	6,961	7,561	8,297	9,254	10,292	11,497
Home mortgages	928	2,500	3,326	4,411	4,770	5,221	5,844	6,680	7,593	8,660
Consumer credit	358	824	1,168	1,551	1,730	1,862	1,949	2,038	2,126	2,189
Net worth	9,378	20,238	27,676	42,119	41,594	40,701	39,074	44,127	48,250	52,107
Replacement cost value of structures: . . .										
Residential	2,553	4,624	6,105	7,887	8,468	9,142	9,766	10,535	11,708	12,722
Households	2,449	4,367	5,817	7,542	8,106	8,761	9,369	10,121	11,261	12,252
Farm households	35	149	171	211	223	235	245	257	278	293
Nonprofit organizations	70	108	117	134	140	146	151	157	169	177
Nonresidential (nonprofits)	263	472	591	760	813	867	907	952	1,042	1,221
Disposable personal income	2,115	4,351	5,479	6,846	7,309	7,525	7,882	8,321	8,930	9,246
Owners' equity in household real estate . .	1,940	4,076	4,664	5,984	6,629	7,269	7,830	8,382	9,628	11,157
Owners' equity as percentage of										
household real estate	67.6	62.0	58.4	57.6	58.2	58.2	57.3	55.7	55.9	56.3

[1] Includes types of assets and/or liabilities not shown separately.

Source: Board of Governors of the Federal Reserve System, "Federal Reserve Statistical Release, Z.1, Flow of Funds Accounts of the United States"; published: 9 March 2006; <http://www.federalreserve.gov/releases/z1/20060309/>.

Table 704. **Net Stock of Fixed Reproducible Tangible Wealth in Current and Real (2000) Dollars: 1980 to 2003**

[In billions of dollars (10,108 represents $10,108,000,000,000). As of December 31]

Item	1980	1990	1995	1999	2000	2001	2002	2003	2004
CURRENT DOLLARS									
Net stock, total	10,108	18,111	22,670	28,081	29,917	31,609	33,061	34,673	37,610
Fixed assets	9,198	16,212	20,299	25,246	26,902	28,465	29,788	31,290	34,032
Private	7,049	12,611	15,794	19,847	21,190	22,485	23,523	24,763	27,043
Nonresidential	3,545	6,500	7,954	9,860	10,514	11,020	11,330	11,675	12,569
Equipment and software	1,396	2,469	3,067	3,822	4,077	4,203	4,271	4,391	4,616
Information processing									
equipment and software	(NA)	622	811	1,109	1,238	1,294	1,319	1,349	1,414
Structures	2,149	4,031	4,887	6,038	6,437	6,817	7,059	7,283	7,953
Residential	3,505	6,111	7,840	9,987	10,676	11,465	12,193	13,088	14,473
Housing units	(NA)	4,955	6,354	8,106	8,663	9,320	9,922	10,645	11,785
Government	2,149	3,601	4,505	5,399	5,713	5,980	6,266	6,527	6,990
Nonresidential	2,071	3,452	4,317	5,179	5,481	5,733	6,002	6,244	6,690
Equipment and software	252	551	675	698	703	711	723	739	791
Structures	1,820	2,900	3,642	4,481	4,778	5,022	5,279	5,505	5,899
Residential	78	149	188	220	232	247	264	283	300
Federal	(NA)	1,079	1,291	1,399	1,425	1,447	1,470	1,500	1,595
Defense	(NA)	735	865	891	896	904	914	929	987
State and local	(NA)	2,522	3,213	4,000	4,288	4,533	4,796	5,028	5,395
Consumer durable goods	910	1,899	2,371	2,835	3,015	3,144	3,273	3,383	3,578
Motor vehicles and parts	(NA)	670	842	1,021	1,092	1,156	1,214	1,259	1,341
Furniture and household equipment . . .	(NA)	814	1,011	1,196	1,260	1,292	1,335	1,364	1,436
Other	(NA)	415	518	618	662	696	725	760	801
CHAINED (2000) DOLLARS									
Net stock, total	(NA)	22,580	25,156	28,524	29,528	30,393	31,189	32,022	32,961
Fixed assets	(NA)	20,726	22,939	25,700	26,498	27,170	27,759	28,382	29,107
Private	(NA)	16,029	17,804	20,190	20,880	21,438	21,901	22,400	22,996
Nonresidential	(NA)	7,809	8,638	9,986	10,392	10,669	10,841	11,010	11,249
Equipment and software	(NA)	2,532	2,972	3,823	4,091	4,249	4,343	4,444	4,623
Structures	(NA)	5,347	5,702	6,163	6,302	6,422	6,499	6,569	6,635
Residential	(NA)	8,223	9,174	10,203	10,488	10,769	11,068	11,404	11,775
Government	(NA)	4,700	5,137	5,510	5,618	5,731	5,857	5,982	6,110
Nonresidential	(NA)	4,507	4,926	5,285	5,390	5,501	5,623	5,745	5,871
Equipment and software	(NA)	631	686	699	706	714	727	739	761
Structures	(NA)	3,872	4,237	4,587	4,684	4,786	4,896	5,005	5,110
Residential	(NA)	201	220	225	227	231	234	237	240
Consumer durable goods	(NA)	1,903	2,242	2,824	3,030	3,228	3,441	3,666	3,901

NA Not available.

Source: U.S. Bureau of Economic Analysis, *Survey of Current Business,* periodic articles, and <http://www.bea.gov/bea/dn/FA2004 /SelectTable.asp> (released 15 March 2006).

Section 14
Prices

This section presents indexes of producer and consumer prices, actual prices for selected commodities, and energy prices. The primary sources of these data are monthly publications of the Department of Labor, Bureau of Labor Statistics (BLS), which include *Monthly Labor Review, Consumer Price Index, Detailed Report, Producer Price Indexes,* and *U.S. Import and Export Price Indexes.* The Department of Commerce, Bureau of Economic Analysis is the source for gross domestic product measures. Cost of living data for many urban and metropolitan areas are provided by the ACCRA, a private organization in Alexandria, VA. Table 710 on housing price indexes appears in this edition from the Office of Federal Housing Enterprise *Oversight, Housing Price Index.* Other commodity, housing, and energy prices may be found in the Energy and Utilities, Natural Resources, and Construction and Housing sections.

Consumer price indexes (CPI)—The CPI is a measure of the average change in prices over time in a "market basket" of goods and services purchased either by urban wage earners and clerical workers or by all urban consumers. In 1919, BLS began to publish complete indexes at semiannual intervals, using a weighting structure based on data collected in the expenditure survey of wage-earner and clerical-worker families in 1917–19 (BLS Bulletin 357, 1924). The first major revision of the CPI occurred in 1940, with subsequent revisions in 1953, 1964, 1978, 1987, and 1998.

Beginning with the release of data for January 1988 in February 1988, most consumer price indexes shifted to a new reference base year. All indexes previously expressed on a base of 1967 = 100, or any other base through December 1981, have been rebased to 1982–84 = 100. The expenditure weights are based upon data tabulated from the Consumer Expenditure Surveys.

BLS publishes CPIs for two population groups: (1) a CPI for all urban consumers (CPI-U), which covers approximately 80 percent of the total population; and (2) a CPI for urban wage earners and clerical workers (CPI-W), which covers 32 percent of the total population. The CPI-U . includes, in addition to wage earners and clerical workers, groups which historically have been excluded from CPI coverage, such as professional, managerial, and technical workers; the self-employed; short-term workers; the unemployed; and retirees and others not in the labor force.

The current CPI is based on prices of food, clothing, shelter, fuels, transportation fares, charges for doctors' and dentists' services, drugs, etc. purchased for day-to-day living. Prices are collected in 87 areas across the country from over 50,000 housing units and 23,000 establishments. Area selection was based on the 1990 census. All taxes directly associated with the purchase and use of items are included in the index. Prices of food, fuels, and a few other items are obtained every month in all 87 locations. Prices of most other commodities and services are collected monthly in the three largest geographic areas and every other month in other areas.

In calculating the index, each item is assigned a weight to account for its relative importance in consumers' budgets. Price changes for the various items in each location are then averaged. Local data are then combined to obtain a U.S. city average. Separate indexes are also published for regions, area size-classes, cross-classifications of regions and size-classes, and for 26 local areas, usually consisting of the Metropolitan Statistical Area (MSA); see Appendix II. Area definitions are those established by the Office of Management and Budget in 1983. Definitions do not include revisions made since 1992. Area indexes do not measure differences in the level of prices among cities; they only measure the average change in prices for each area since the base period. For further detail regarding the CPI, see the BLS *Handbook of Methods*, Bulletin 2490, Chapter 17; the *Consumer Price Index*, and the CPI home page: <http://www.bls.gov/cpi/>. In January 1983, the method of measuring home-ownership costs in the CPI-U was changed to a rental equivalence approach. This treatment calculates homeowner costs of shelter based on the implicit rent owners would pay to rent the homes they own. The rental equivalence approach was introduced into the CPI-W in 1985. The CPI-U was used to prepare the consumer price tables in this section.

Producer price index (PPI)—This index, dating from 1890, is the oldest continuous statistical series published by BLS. It is designed to measure average changes in prices received by producers of all commodities, at all stages of processing, produced in the United States.

The index has undergone several revisions (see *Monthly Labor Review*, February 1962, April 1978, and August 1988). It is now based on approximately 10,000 individual products and groups of products along with about 100,000 quotations per month. Indexes for the net output of manufacturing and mining industries have been added in recent years. Prices used in constructing the index are collected from sellers and generally apply to the first significant large-volume commercial transaction for each commodity—i.e., the manufacturer's or other producer's selling price or the selling price on an organized exchange or at a central market.

The weights used in the index represent the total net selling value of commodities produced or processed in this country. Values are f.o.b. (free on board) production point and are exclusive of excise taxes. Effective with the release of data for January 1988, many important producer price indexes were changed to a new reference base year, 1982 = 100, from 1967 = 100. The reference year of the PPI shipment weights has been taken primarily from the 1987 Census of Manufactures. For further detail regarding the PPI, see the BLS *Handbook of Methods*, Bulletin 2490 (April 1997), Chapter 16. The PPI Web page is <http://www.bls.gov/ppi/>.

BEA price indexes—Chain-weighted price indexes, produced by the Bureau of Economic Analysis (BEA), are weighted averages of the detailed price indexes used in the deflation of the goods and services that make up the gross domestic product (GDP) and its major components. Growth rates are constructed for years and quarters using quantity weights for the current and preceding year or quarter; these growth rates are used to move the index for the preceding period forward a year or quarter at a time. All chain-weighted price indexes are expressed in terms of the reference year value 2000 = 100.

Personal consumption expenditures (PCE) price and quantity indexes are based on market transactions for which there are corresponding price measures. The price index provides a measure of the prices paid by persons for domestic purchases of goods and services, which may be a useful measure of consumer prices for some analytical purposes. PCEs are defined as market value of spending by individuals and not-for-profit institutions on all goods and services. Personal consumption expenditures also include the value of certain imputed goods and services—such as the rental value of owner-occupied homes and compensation paid in kind—such as employer-paid health and life insurance premiums. More information on this index may be found at <http://www.bea.gov/bea/mp_National.htm>.

Measures of inflation—Inflation is defined as a time of generally rising prices for goods and factors of production. The Bureau of Labor Statistics samples prices of items in a representative market basket and publishes the result as the CPI. The media invariably announce the inflation rate as the percent change in the CPI from month to month. A much more meaningful indicator of inflation is the percent change from the same month of the prior year. The producer price index measures prices at the producer level only. The PPI shows the same general pattern of inflation as does the CPI but is more volatile. The PPI can be roughly viewed as a leading indicator. It often tends to foreshadow trends that later occur in the CPI.

Other measures of inflation include the gross domestic purchases chain-weighted price index, the index of industrial materials prices; the Futures Price and Spot Market prices from the Commodity Research Bureau; the Employment Cost Index, the Hourly Compensation Index, or the Unit Labor Cost Index found in Section 12 on Labor Force, Employment, and Earnings, as a measure of the change in cost of the labor factor of production; and changes in long-term interest rates that are often used to measure changes in the cost of the capital factor of production.

International price indexes—The BLS International Price Program produces export and import price indexes for non-military goods traded between the United States and the rest of the world.

The export price index provides a measure of price change for all products sold by U.S. residents to foreign buyers. The

import price index provides a measure of price change for goods purchased from other countries by U.S. residents. The reference period for the indexes is 2000 = 100, unless otherwise indicated. The product universe for both the import and export indexes includes raw materials, agricultural products, semifinished manufactures, and finished manufactures, including both capital and consumer goods. Price data for these items are collected primarily by mail questionnaire. In nearly all cases, the data are collected directly from the exporter or importer, although in a few cases, prices are obtained from other sources.

To the extent possible, the data gathered refer to prices at the U.S. border for exports and at either the foreign border or the U.S. border for imports. For nearly all products, the prices refer to transactions completed during the first week of the month. Survey respondents are asked to indicate all discounts, allowances, and rebates applicable to the reported prices, so that the price used in the calculation of the indexes is the actual price for which the product was bought or sold.

Table 705. **Purchasing Power of the Dollar: 1950 to 2005**

[Indexes: PPI, 1982 = $1.00; CPI, 1982–84 = $1.00. Producer prices prior to 1961, and consumer prices prior to 1964, exclude Alaska and Hawaii. Producer prices based on finished goods index. Obtained by dividing the average price index for the 1982 = 100, PPI; 1982–84 = 100, CPI base periods (100.0) by the price index for a given period and expressing the result in dollars and cents. Annual figures are based on average of monthly data]

Year	Annual average as measured by—		Year	Annual average as measured by—	
	Producer prices	Consumer prices		Producer prices	Consumer prices
1950	3.546	4.151	1978	1.433	1.532
1951	3.247	3.846	1979	1.289	1.380
1952	3.268	3.765	1980	1.136	1.215
1953	3.300	3.735	1981	1.041	1.098
1954	3.289	3.717	1982	1.000	1.035
			1983	0.984	1.003
1955	3.279	3.732	1984	0.964	0.961
1956	3.195	3.678			
1957	3.077	3.549	1985	0.955	0.928
1958	3.012	3.457	1986	0.969	0.913
1959	3.021	3.427	1987	0.949	0.880
			1988	0.926	0.846
1960	2.994	3.373	1989	0.880	0.807
1961	2.994	3.340			
1962	2.985	3.304	1990	0.839	0.766
1963	2.994	3.265	1991	0.822	0.734
1964	2.985	3.220	1992	0.812	0.713
			1993	0.802	0.692
1965	2.933	3.166	1994	0.797	0.675
1966	2.841	3.080			
1967	2.809	2.993	1995	0.782	0.656
1968	2.732	2.873	1996	0.762	0.638
1969	2.632	2.726	1997	0.759	0.623
			1998	0.765	0.614
1970	2.545	2.574	1999	0.752	0.600
1971	2.469	2.466			
1972	2.392	2.391	2000	0.725	0.581
1973	2.193	2.251	2001	0.711	0.565
1974	1.901	2.029	2002	0.720	0.556
			2003	0.698	0.544
1975	1.718	1.859	2004	0.673	0.530
1976	1.645	1.757			
1977	1.546	1.649	2005	0.642	0.512

Source: U.S. Bureau of Labor Statistics. *CPI Detailed Report,* monthly, and at <http://www.bls.gov/cpi/cpi_dr.htm>. See also *Monthly Labor Review* at <http://www.bls.gov/opub/mlr/welcome.htm> and *Producer Price Indexes,* monthly and annual.

Prices   467

Figure 14.1
Annual Percent Change in Consumer Price Indexes: 1990 to 2005

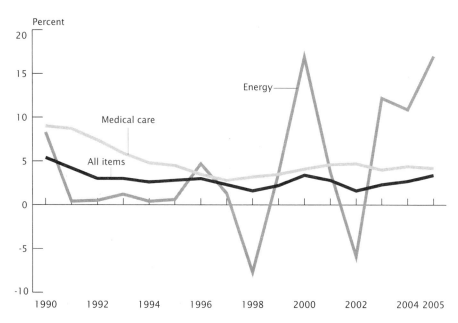

Source: Chart prepared by U.S. Census Bureau. For data, see Table 706.

Figure 14.2
Percent Change in Single-Family Housing Price Indexes: 2004 to 2005

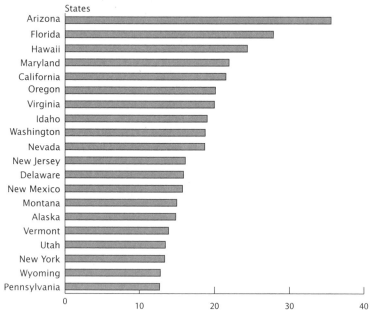

Source: Chart prepared by U.S. Census Bureau. For data, see Table 710.

Table 706. Consumer Price Indexes (CPI-U) by Major Groups: 1990 to 2005

[1982–84 = 100, except as indicated. Represents annual averages of monthly figures. Reflects buying patterns of all urban consumers. Minus sign (–) indicates decrease. See text, this section]

Year	All items	Com- modities	Ser- vices	Food	Energy	All items less food and energy	Food and bever- ages	Shel- ter	Transpor- tation	Medi- cal care	Apparel	Education and communi- cation [1]
1990	130.7	122.8	139.2	132.4	102.1	135.5	132.1	140.0	120.5	162.8	124.1	(NA)
1991	136.2	126.6	146.3	136.3	102.5	142.1	136.8	146.3	123.8	177.0	128.7	(NA)
1992	140.3	129.1	152.0	137.9	103.0	147.3	138.7	151.2	126.5	190.1	131.9	(NA)
1993	144.5	131.5	157.9	140.9	104.2	152.2	141.6	155.7	130.4	201.4	133.7	85.5
1994	148.2	133.8	163.1	144.3	104.6	156.5	144.9	160.5	134.3	211.0	133.4	88.8
1995	152.4	136.4	168.7	148.4	105.2	161.2	148.9	165.7	139.1	220.5	132.0	92.2
1996	156.9	139.9	174.1	153.3	110.1	165.6	153.7	171.0	143.0	228.2	131.7	95.3
1997	160.5	141.8	179.4	157.3	111.5	169.5	157.7	176.3	144.3	234.6	132.9	98.4
1998	163.0	141.9	184.2	160.7	102.9	173.4	161.1	182.1	141.6	242.1	133.0	100.3
1999	166.6	144.4	188.8	164.1	106.6	177.0	164.6	187.3	144.4	250.6	131.3	101.2
2000	172.2	149.2	195.3	167.8	124.6	181.3	168.4	193.4	153.3	260.8	129.6	102.5
2001	177.1	150.7	203.4	173.1	129.3	186.1	173.6	200.6	154.3	272.8	127.3	105.2
2002	179.9	149.7	209.8	176.2	121.7	190.5	176.8	208.1	152.9	285.6	124.0	107.9
2003	184.0	151.2	216.5	180.0	136.5	193.2	180.5	213.1	157.6	297.1	120.9	109.8
2004	188.9	154.7	222.8	186.2	151.4	196.6	186.6	218.8	163.1	310.1	120.4	111.6
2005	195.3	160.2	230.1	190.7	177.1	200.9	191.2	224.4	173.9	323.2	119.5	113.7
PERCENT CHANGE [2]												
1990	5.4	5.2	5.5	5.8	8.3	5.0	5.8	5.4	5.6	9.0	4.6	(NA)
1991	4.2	3.1	5.1	2.9	0.4	4.9	3.6	4.5	2.7	8.7	3.7	(NA)
1992	3.0	2.0	3.9	1.2	0.5	3.7	1.4	3.3	2.2	7.4	2.5	(NA)
1993	3.0	1.9	3.9	2.2	1.2	3.3	2.1	3.0	3.1	5.9	1.4	(NA)
1994	2.6	1.7	3.3	2.4	0.4	2.8	2.3	3.1	3.0	4.8	–0.2	3.9
1995	2.8	1.9	3.4	2.8	0.6	3.0	2.8	3.2	3.6	4.5	–1.0	3.8
1996	3.0	2.6	3.2	3.3	4.7	2.7	3.2	3.2	2.8	3.5	–0.2	3.4
1997	2.3	1.4	3.0	2.6	1.3	2.4	2.6	3.1	0.9	2.8	0.9	3.3
1998	1.6	0.1	2.7	2.2	–7.7	2.3	2.2	3.3	–1.9	3.2	0.1	1.9
1999	2.2	1.8	2.5	2.1	3.6	2.1	2.2	2.9	2.0	3.5	–1.3	0.9
2000	3.4	3.3	3.4	2.3	16.9	2.4	2.3	3.3	6.2	4.1	–1.3	1.3
2001	2.8	1.0	4.1	3.2	3.8	2.6	3.1	3.7	0.7	4.6	–1.8	2.6
2002	1.6	–0.7	3.1	1.8	–5.9	2.4	1.8	3.7	–0.9	4.7	–2.6	2.6
2003	2.3	1.0	3.2	2.2	12.2	1.4	2.1	2.4	3.1	4.0	–2.5	1.8
2004	2.7	2.3	2.9	3.4	10.9	1.8	3.4	2.7	3.5	4.4	–0.4	1.6
2005	3.4	3.6	3.3	2.4	17.0	2.2	2.5	2.6	6.6	4.2	–0.7	1.9

NA Not available. [1] Dec. 1997 = 100. [2] Change from immediate prior year. 1990 change from 1989.
Source: Bureau of Labor Statistics, *CPI Detailed Report*, monthly, and at <http://www.bls.gov/cpi/cpi_dr.htm>. See also *Monthly Labor Review* at <http://www.bls.gov/opub/mlr/welcome.htm>.

Table 707. Annual Percent Changes From Prior Year in Consumer Price Indexes (CPI-U)—Selected Areas: 2005

[Represents percent changes of annual averages of monthly figures. Local area CPI indexes are by-products of the national CPI program. Each local index has a smaller sample size than the national index and is therefore subject to substantially more sampling and other measurement error. As a result, local area indexes show greater volatility than the national index, although their long-term trends are similar. Area definitions are those established by the Office of Management and Budget in 1983. For further detail, see the U.S. Bureau of Labor Statistics Handbook of Methods, Bulletin 2285, Chapter 19, the Consumer Price Index, and Report 736, the CPI: 1987 Revision. Minus sign (–) indicates decrease. See also text, this section and Appendix III]

Area	All items	Food and bever- ages	Food	Hous- ing	Apparel	Trans- porta- tion	Medi- cal care	Fuel and other utilities
U.S. city average	3.4	2.5	2.4	3.3	–0.7	6.6	4.2	10.6
Anchorage, AK MSA	3.1	2.5	2.7	2.7	–2.1	5.5	(NA)	8.2
Atlanta, GA MSA	3.1	1.7	1.7	1.9	–1.5	8.8	4.5	14.0
Boston, MA MSA	3.3	2.5	2.6	2.7	–1.1	7.6	5.0	18.1
Chicago-Gary, IL-IN CMSA	3.0	2.1	2.1	3.0	2.3	4.7	5.6	11.0
Cincinnati-Hamilton, OH-KY-IN CMSA	2.9	2.3	2.4	2.3	–3.4	6.4	4.8	6.9
Cleveland-Akron-Lorain, OH CMSA	3.5	2.7	2.7	2.5	1.5	6.9	6.6	14.2
Dallas-Fort Worth, TX CMSA	3.4	2.1	1.9	3.2	–3.0	7.2	3.8	15.2
Denver-Boulder-Greely, CO CMSA	2.1	1.7	1.9	–0.5	1.2	7.6	3.7	12.6
Detroit-Ann Arbor-Flint, MI CMSA	2.9	1.9	1.9	3.1	–5.7	6.7	3.6	14.5
Honolulu, HI MSA.	3.8	3.2	3.3	5.6	1.3	5.0	(NA)	11.6
Houston-Galveston-Brazoria, TX CMSA	3.6	2.1	1.9	3.6	5.1	7.6	3.0	14.5
Kansas City, MO-KS CMSA	2.5	3.3	3.7	1.2	2.1	6.9	2.3	6.7
Los Angeles-Anaheim-Riverside, CA CMSA . . .	4.5	2.2	2.2	5.9	0.4	5.0	5.1	9.5
Miami-Fort Lauderdale, FL CMSA	4.7	2.6	2.7	6.3	4.0	6.6	5.5	5.1
Milwaukee, WI PMSA	2.8	2.3	2.6	1.3	2.8	8.2	5.3	11.2
Minneapolis-St. Paul, MN-WI MSA	2.8	3.4	3.6	2.0	0.2	4.4	0.0	12.5
New York-Northern New Jersey-Long Island, NY-NJ-CT CMSA	3.9	2.8	2.8	4.5	6.1	5.3	3.0	14.8
Philadelphia-Wilmington-Trenton, PA-NJ-DE-MD CMSA. .	3.9	2.9	2.8	4.0	0.7	7.1	5.4	6.9
Pittsburgh, PA MSA	3.7	2.2	2.1	4.4	–1.3	6.3	4.6	10.9
Portland, OR MSA	2.6	1.7	1.6	2.0	–3.4	6.7	5.5	5.7
San Diego, CA MSA	3.7	2.4	2.1	3.9	–2.8	5.6	6.3	8.4
San Francisco-Oakland-San Jose, CA CMSA . . .	2.0	1.7	1.6	1.0	–0.9	4.3	2.9	10.3
Seattle-Tacoma, WA CMSA	2.8	2.8	2.6	2.3	–2.5	7.1	3.8	6.8
St. Louis-East St. Louis, MO-IL CMSA	3.3	2.8	3.0	3.6	–1.5	6.4	4.2	6.3
Tampa-St. Petersburg-Clearwater, FL MSA	4.0	2.9	3.0	4.2	3.6	6.1	3.7	5.8
Washington-Baltimore, DC-MD-VA-WV CMSA . . .	4.0	2.4	2.4	3.8	5.7	7.8	3.9	9.3

NA Not available.
Source: Bureau of Labor Statistics, *CPI Detailed Report*, monthly, and at <http://www.bls.gov/cpi/cpi_dr.htm>. See also *Monthly Labor Review* at <http://www.bls.gov/opub/mlr/welcome.htm>.

Prices   469

Table 708. Consumer Price Indexes for All Urban Consumers (CPI-U) for Selected Items and Groups: 1990 to 2005

[1982–84 = 100, except as noted. Annual averages of monthly figures. See headnote, Table 706]

Item	1990	2000	2001	2002	2003	2004	2005	Annual percentage change, 2004–2005
All items	130.7	172.2	177.1	179.9	184.0	188.9	195.3	3.4
Food and beverages.	132.1	168.4	173.6	176.8	180.5	186.6	191.2	2.5
Food	132.4	167.8	173.1	176.2	180.0	186.2	190.7	2.4
Food at home	132.3	167.9	173.4	175.6	179.4	186.2	189.8	1.9
Cereals and bakery products	140.0	188.3	193.8	198.0	202.8	206.0	209.0	1.5
Cereals and cereal products	141.1	175.9	178.7	181.8	185.2	186.2	186.7	0.3
Breakfast cereal	158.6	198.0	199.7	203.0	204.3	203.5	203.6	0.0
Rice, pasta, and cornmeal	122.0	150.7	154.6	155.8	160.3	164.5	165.3	0.5
Rice [1]	(NA)	99.3	98.2	98.3	100.8	108.0	108.8	0.7
Bakery products	139.2	194.1	201.3	206.1	211.7	216.2	220.5	2.0
Bread [1]	(NA)	107.4	112.5	115.4	118.5	121.1	126.2	4.2
White bread	136.4	199.1	208.3	213.4	218.6	223.3	232.1	3.9
Bread other than white	(NA)	202.6	213.2	219.3	224.2	227.8	238.6	4.7
Cookies	(NA)	187.6	190.7	196.2	202.6	205.2	206.4	0.6
Other bakery products	(NA)	191.5	199.1	203.0	207.3	211.8	211.4	-0.2
Meats, poultry, fish and eggs	130.0	154.5	161.3	162.1	169.3	181.7	184.7	1.7
Meats	128.5	150.7	159.3	160.3	169.0	183.2	187.5	2.3
Beef and veal	128.8	148.1	160.5	160.6	175.1	193.5	200.4	2.6
Uncooked ground beef	(NA)	125.2	135.5	138.1	149.2	166.3	175.1	5.3
Uncooked beef roasts [1]	(NA)	108.1	118.7	117.6	129.3	142.3	146.5	3.0
Uncooked beef steaks [1]	(NA)	109.1	118.1	116.6	127.6	144.7	145.1	0.3
Pork	129.8	156.5	162.4	161.8	164.9	174.2	177.7	2.0
Bacon, breakfast sausage, and related products [1]	(NA)	108.2	112.0	112.9	116.1	123.1	122.7	-0.3
Ham	132.4	152.7	157.3	160.0	161.9	166.0	175.9	6.0
Pork chops	140.2	152.2	159.0	156.0	160.9	170.4	170.2	-0.1
Poultry [1]	132.5	159.8	164.9	167.0	169.1	181.7	185.3	2.0
Chicken [1]	(NA)	102.5	105.5	107.6	108.9	118.2	120.6	2.0
Fresh whole chicken	134.9	162.9	168.0	169.1	165.8	182.4	186.7	2.4
Fish and seafood	146.7	190.4	191.1	188.1	190.0	194.3	200.1	3.0
Eggs	124.1	131.9	136.4	138.2	157.3	167.0	144.1	-13.7
Dairy products	126.5	160.7	167.1	168.1	167.1	167.9	180.2	1.2
Milk [1]	(NA)	107.8	112.7	110.6	111.5	125.0	127.0	1.6
Fresh whole milk	126.7	156.9	165.9	162.1	162.5	183.4	184.9	0.8
Other dairy and related products [1]	(NA)	109.4	112.5	114.5	115.0	120.2	122.1	1.6
Fruits and vegetables	149.0	204.6	212.2	220.9	225.9	232.7	241.4	3.7
Fresh fruits and vegetables	(NA)	238.8	247.9	258.4	265.3	274.7	285.3	3.9
Fresh fruits	170.9	258.3	265.1	270.2	279.1	286.8	297.4	3.7
Apples	147.5	212.6	213.9	230.7	244.4	251.7	246.0	-2.3
Bananas	138.2	162.5	166.6	166.5	164.8	164.8	167.1	2.5
Citrus fruits [1]	(NA)	135.7	142.0	150.3	152.5	162.1	178.7	10.2
Oranges, tangerines	160.6	257.0	271.7	294.6	302.0	330.8	354.7	7.2
Fresh vegetables	151.1	219.4	230.6	245.4	250.5	261.2	271.7	4.0
Potatoes	162.6	196.3	202.3	238.5	228.1	231.1	247.7	7.2
Lettuce	150.3	228.1	233.8	252.1	246.2	239.8	257.3	7.3
Tomatoes	160.8	234.7	250.0	251.0	271.0	296.8	298.8	0.7
Processed fruits and vegetables [1] . . .	(NA)	105.6	109.0	113.1	114.1	115.5	119.3	3.3
Nonalcoholic beverages	113.5	137.8	139.2	139.2	139.8	140.4	144.4	2.8
Juices and nonalcoholic drinks [1]	(NA)	105.6	107.5	107.8	108.0	108.5	110.6	1.9
Carbonated drinks	112.1	123.4	125.4	125.6	125.6	127.9	131.9	3.1
Coffee	117.5	154.0	146.7	142.6	144.9	145.3	161.2	10.9
Snacks	129.6	166.3	169.0	168.7	176.3	173.7	178.5	2.8
Food away from home	(NA)	169.0	173.9	178.3	182.1	187.5	193.4	3.1
Alcoholic beverages	129.3	174.7	179.3	183.6	187.2	192.1	195.9	2.0
Alcoholic beverages at home	123.0	158.1	161.1	164.0	166.5	170.2	172.3	1.2
Beer, ale, and other malt beverages at home . . .	123.6	156.8	160.7	164.7	168.5	174.6	176.4	1.0
Distilled spirits at home	(NA)	162.3	168.0	171.4	173.1	175.3	177.4	1.2
Wine at home	114.4	151.6	151.5	152.3	153.1	153.8	156.2	1.6
Alcoholic beverages away from home	144.4	207.1	215.2	222.5	228.6	236.6	244.5	3.3
Beer, ale, and other malt beverages away from home [1]	(NA)	107.3	110.2	113.4	117.0	121.1	124.1	2.5
Wine away from home [1]	(NA)	108.1	114.5	122.6	124.3	128.0	133.7	4.5
Distilled spirits away from home [1]	(NA)	107.6	112.5	115.9	117.9	120.0	124.8	3.4
Housing	128.5	169.6	176.4	180.3	184.8	189.5	195.7	3.3
Shelter	140.0	193.4	200.6	208.1	213.1	218.8	224.4	2.6
Owners' equivalent rent of primary residence [2] . . .	144.8	198.7	206.3	214.7	219.9	224.9	230.2	2.4
Fuels and utilities	111.6	137.9	150.2	143.6	154.5	161.9	179.0	10.6
Fuels	104.5	122.8	135.4	127.2	138.2	144.4	161.6	11.9
Fuel oil and other	99.3	129.7	129.3	115.5	139.5	160.5	208.6	30.0
Gas (piped) and electricity	109.3	128.0	142.4	134.4	145.0	150.6	166.5	10.6
Electricity	117.4	128.5	137.8	136.2	139.5	142.1	150.8	6.1
Utility (piped) gas	97.3	132.0	158.3	135.3	166.3	180.1	215.4	19.6
Water and sewer and trash collection services [1] . . .	(NA)	106.5	109.0	113.0	117.2	124.0	130.3	5.1
Water and sewerage maintenance	150.2	227.5	234.6	242.5	251.7	268.1	283.4	5.7
Garbage and trash collection [3]	171.2	269.8	275.5	283.0	291.9	303.3	314.0	3.5

See footnotes at end of table.

U.S. Census Bureau, Statistical Abstract of the United States: 2007

[1982-84 = 100, except as noted. Annual averages of monthly figures. See headnote, Table 706]

Item	1990	2000	2001	2002	2003	2004	2005	Annual percentage change, 2004–2005
Household furnishings and operations	113.3	128.2	129.1	128.3	126.1	125.5	126.1	0.5
Furniture and bedding	115.7	134.4	132.2	129.4	127.7	127.3	125.9	-1.1
Appliances [1]	(NA)	96.3	94.7	92.7	89.5	85.9	86.9	1.2
Housekeeping supplies	125.2	153.4	158.4	159.8	157.5	157.4	159.9	1.6
Apparel	124.1	129.6	127.3	124.0	120.9	120.4	119.5	-0.7
Men's and boy's apparel	120.4	129.7	125.7	121.7	118.0	117.5	116.1	-1.2
Women's and girl's apparel	122.6	121.5	119.3	115.8	113.1	113.0	110.8	-1.9
Footwear	117.4	123.8	123.0	121.4	119.6	119.3	122.6	2.8
Infants' and toddlers' apparel	125.8	130.6	129.2	126.4	122.1	118.5	116.7	-1.5
Jewelry and watches [4]	(NA)	137.0	136.9	133.2	128.7	129.5	127.6	-1.5
Transportation	120.5	153.3	154.3	152.9	157.6	163.1	173.9	6.6
Private transportation [1]	118.8	149.1	150.0	148.8	153.6	159.4	170.2	6.8
New and used motor vehicles [1]	(NA)	100.8	101.3	99.2	96.5	94.2	95.6	1.5
New vehicles	121.4	142.8	142.1	140.0	137.9	137.1	137.9	0.6
New cars and trucks	(NA)	99.0	98.6	97.1	95.6	95.1	95.6	0.5
New cars [2]	121.0	139.6	138.9	137.3	134.7	133.9	135.2	1.0
New trucks [2]	121.6	151.7	150.7	147.8	146.1	145.0	145.3	0.2
Used cars and trucks	117.6	155.8	158.7	152.0	142.9	133.3	139.4	4.6
Motor fuel	101.2	129.3	124.7	116.6	135.8	160.4	195.7	22.0
Gasoline (all types)	(NA)	128.6	124.0	116.0	135.1	159.7	194.7	21.9
Gasoline, unleaded regular	(NA)	127.3	122.6	114.4	134.0	158.9	194.4	22.3
Gasoline, unleaded midgrade [5]	(NA)	133.0	127.9	120.2	139.2	163.8	199.1	21.6
Gasoline, unleaded premium [1]	(NA)	127.7	123.4	116.3	133.8	156.4	188.7	20.7
Motor vehicle parts and equipment	(NA)	101.5	104.8	106.9	107.8	108.7	111.9	2.9
Tires	(NA)	97.5	100.5	101.8	101.7	101.8	104.5	2.7
Vehicle accessories other than tires [2]	(NA)	101.6	105.0	107.9	110.1	112.0	115.9	3.5
Motor vehicle maintenance and repair	130.1	177.3	183.5	190.2	195.6	200.2	206.9	3.3
Motor vehicle insurance	177.9	256.7	268.1	291.6	314.4	323.2	329.9	2.1
Motor vehicle fees	(NA)	107.3	109.3	112.5	116.5	131.0	134.7	2.8
Public transportation	142.6	209.6	210.6	207.4	209.3	209.1	217.3	3.9
Airline fares	148.4	239.4	239.4	231.6	231.3	227.2	236.6	4.1
Medical care	162.8	260.8	272.8	285.6	297.1	310.1	323.2	4.2
Medical care commodities	163.4	238.1	247.6	256.4	262.8	269.3	276.0	2.5
Prescription drugs and medical supplies	181.7	285.4	300.9	316.5	326.3	337.1	349.0	3.5
Nonprescription drugs and medical supplies [4]	120.6	149.5	150.6	150.4	152.0	152.3	151.7	-0.4
Medical care services	162.7	266.0	278.8	292.9	306.0	321.3	336.7	4.8
Professional medical services	156.1	237.7	246.5	253.9	261.2	271.5	281.7	3.8
Physicians' services	160.8	244.7	253.6	260.6	267.7	278.3	287.5	3.3
Dental services	155.8	258.5	269.0	281.0	292.5	306.9	324.0	5.6
Eyeglasses and eye care [4]	117.3	149.7	154.5	155.5	155.9	159.3	163.2	2.4
Services by other medical professionals [4] . . .	(NA)	161.9	167.3	171.8	177.1	181.9	186.8	2.7
Hospital and related services	178.0	317.3	338.3	367.8	394.8	417.9	439.9	5.3
Hospital services [1]	(NA)	115.9	123.6	134.7	144.7	153.4	161.6	5.3
Nursing homes and adult daycare	(NA)	117.0	121.8	127.9	135.2	140.4	145.0	3.3
Recreation [1]	(NA)	103.3	104.9	106.2	107.5	108.6	109.4	0.7
Video and audio	80.8	101.0	101.5	102.8	103.6	104.2	104.2	0.0
Televisions	74.6	49.9	44.8	40.1	34.9	30.0	26.6	-11.3
Cable and satellite television and radio service [2] . . .	158.4	266.8	278.4	295.0	309.5	322.4	331.9	2.9
Pets, pet products, and services [1]	(NA)	106.1	109.7	113.2	115.7	120.1	123.6	2.9
Sporting goods	114.9	119.0	118.5	116.4	115.3	115.0	115.5	0.4
Photography	(NA)	99.2	99.0	97.9	96.0	92.9	90.4	-2.7
Other recreational goods [1]	(NA)	87.8	84.6	80.5	76.1	73.3	69.5	-5.2
Recreation services [1]	(NA)	111.7	116.1	119.6	124.5	127.5	130.5	2.4
Club membership dues & fees for participant sports [1]	117.0	108.9	111.7	112.9	116.1	116.7	117.4	0.6
Admissions	151.2	230.5	242.4	251.4	263.2	272.9	282.3	3.4
Recreational reading materials	(NA)	188.3	191.4	195.8	197.5	201.2	203.9	1.3
Newspapers and magazines [1]	(NA)	106.4	108.5	110.5	112.7	116.0	119.0	2.6
Recreational books [1]	(NA)	100.7	101.9	105.0	104.1	104.3	103.9	-0.4
Education and communication [1]	(NA)	102.5	105.2	107.9	109.8	111.6	113.7	1.9
Education [1]	(NA)	112.5	118.5	126.0	134.4	143.7	152.7	6.3
Educational books and supplies	171.3	279.9	295.9	317.6	335.4	351.0	365.6	4.2
Tuition/child care fees and other school fees	175.7	324.0	341.1	362.1	386.7	414.3	440.9	6.4
College tuition and fees	175.0	331.9	348.8	372.6	403.9	442.1	475.1	7.5
Communication	(NA)	93.6	93.3	92.3	89.7	86.7	84.7	-2.3
Postage and delivery services [1]	(NA)	103.2	107.3	113.7	119.4	119.8	120.2	0.3
Postage	125.1	165.1	171.5	181.8	190.9	190.9	190.9	0.0
Delivery services [1]	(NA)	114.5	123.0	127.9	134.9	150.1	160.2	6.7
Information and information processing [1]	(NA)	92.8	92.3	90.8	87.8	84.6	82.6	-2.4
Telephone services [1]	(NA)	98.5	99.3	99.7	98.3	95.8	94.9	-0.9
Wireless telephone services [1]	(NA)	76.0	68.1	67.4	66.8	66.2	65.0	-1.8
Information technology, hardware, and services [6] . . .	(NA)	25.9	21.3	18.3	16.1	14.8	13.6	-8.1
Personal computers and peripheral equipment [1] . . .	(NA)	41.1	29.5	22.2	17.6	15.3	12.8	-16.3
Computer software and accessories [1]	(NA)	85.4	79.1	74.0	67.4	62.4	58.9	-5.6
Internet services & electronic information providers [1] .	(NA)	96.4	98.1	98.9	99.8	97.4	95.7	-1.7
Other goods and services	(NA)	271.1	282.6	293.2	298.7	304.7	313.4	2.9
Tobacco and smoking products	181.5	394.9	425.2	461.5	469.0	478.0	502.8	5.2
Personal care	130.4	165.6	170.5	174.7	178.0	181.7	185.6	2.1

NA Not available. [1] December 1997 = 100. [2] December 1982 = 100. [3] December 1983 = 100. [4] December 1986 = 100. [5] December 1993 = 100. [6] December 1988 = 100.

Source: Bureau of Labor Statistics, *CPI Detailed Report*, monthly, and at <http://www.bls.gov/cpi/cpi_dr.htm> See also *Monthly Labor Review* at <http://www.bls.gov/opub/mlr/welcome.htm>.

Prices   471

Table 709. Cost of Living Index—Selected Metropolitan Areas: Fourth Quarter 2005

[Measures relative price levels for consumer goods and services in participating areas for a mid-management standard of living. The nationwide average equals 100 and each index is read as a percent of the national average. The index does not measure inflation, but compares prices at a single point in time. Excludes taxes. Metropolitan areas as defined by the Office of Management and Budget. For definitions and components of metropolitan areas, see source for details on coverage]

Metropolitan areas and metropolitan divisions	Com- posite index (100%)	Grocery items (13%)	Housing (29%)	Utilities (10%)	Transpor- tation (10%)	Health care (4%)	Misc. goods and services (35%)
Birmingham-Hoover, AL	95.4	111.6	81.0	114.9	99.5	99.2	94.3
Huntsville, AL	89.9	93.3	76.0	84.0	105.9	90.6	97.6
Mobile, AL	88.8	96.2	75.7	93.3	97.4	81.5	94.3
Montgomery, AL	97.3	98.1	95.6	98.8	102.1	85.7	98.0
Anchorage, AK	117.9	125.8	125.3	75.8	106.5	133.2	122.1
Phoenix-Mesa-Scottsdale, AZ	100.4	98.4	101.8	91.0	103.8	101.8	101.5
Tucson, AZ	97.3	97.8	90.5	89.6	105.5	97.4	102.9
Fayetteville-Springdale-Rogers, AR-MO	89.6	90.6	81.0	91.8	93.3	94.3	94.2
Fort Smith, AR-OK	85.3	87.9	69.0	86.0	95.0	88.7	94.7
Little Rock-North Little Rock, AR	88.6	93.2	75.2	86.4	92.5	95.1	96.8
Fresno, CA	119.9	114.2	149.7	110.4	111.4	105.9	103.7
Los Angeles-Long Beach-Glendale, CA metro. div.	159.0	136.6	266.1	108.8	105.1	118.9	111.3
Oakland-Fremont-Hayward, CA metro. div.	147.5	139.3	219.1	81.4	110.8	117.3	122.9
Riverside-San Bernardino-Ontario, CA:							
Riverside City, CA	115.8	102.3	150.9	89.5	108.9	104.3	102.4
San Bernardino, CA	128.1	125.6	167.7	112.3	128.9	113.5	102.3
San Diego-Carlsbad-San Marcos, CA	150.3	113.6	232.7	93.8	110.7	118.6	125.6
San Francisco-San Mateo-Redwood City, CA metro. div.:							
San Francisco, CA	171.4	142.1	286.8	94.6	107.8	118.2	130.9
San Jose, CA	158.1	146.0	257.1	101.4	107.2	117.0	114.7
Santa Ana-Anaheim-Irvine, CA metro. div.	156.1	130.9	258.4	109.8	106.5	115.4	111.4
Colorado Springs, CO	94.7	98.5	84.4	103.4	109.5	109.9	93.8
Denver-Aurora, CO	100.6	104.5	101.8	91.6	99.0	109.1	100.2
Fort, Collins-Loveland, CO	97.2	107.8	93.5	99.9	104.9	100.9	93.2
Greeley, CO	95.4	94.9	104.5	87.2	97.5	100.6	89.3
Bridgeport-Stamford-Norwalk, CT	150.6	117.5	236.3	111.1	107.4	119.2	117.8
Hartford-West Hartford-East Hartford, CT	115.7	111.8	127.9	118.2	103.5	117.1	109.3
New Haven-Milford, CT	121.3	115.2	145.5	111.4	100.6	123.0	111.4
Norwich-New London, CT	114.4	110.5	126.7	101.9	97.7	126.6	112.3
Dover, DE	98.3	96.7	91.7	103.9	101.2	102.1	101.5
Wilmington, DE-MD-NJ metro. div.	103.2	112.6	101.9	103.6	102.7	109.2	100.1
Washington-Arlington-Alexandria, DC-VA-MD-WV metro. div.	142.4	108.5	220.6	113.9	112.3	112.3	110.5
Cape Coral-Fort Myers, FL	104.3	92.9	112.7	106.4	111.4	97.3	99.9
Fort Lauderdale-Pompano Beach-Deerfield Beach, FL metro. div.	117.2	105.0	155.1	101.4	106.3	110.9	98.5
Gainesville, FL	92.6	95.9	86.2	86.1	105.0	95.6	95.2
Jacksonville, FL	95.5	97.6	84.3	91.4	110.2	100.7	100.9
Miami-Miami Beach-Kendall, FL metro. div.	116.2	101.5	144.6	101.4	107.2	119.5	104.3
Orlando-Kissimmee, FL	107.3	96.9	115.6	94.3	108.3	91.2	109.5
Pensacola-Ferry Pass-Brent, FL	94.3	100.9	87.4	90.8	105.3	87.4	96.4
Sarasota-Bradenton-Venice, FL:							
Bradenton, FL	98.5	100.5	100.9	96.5	108.8	102.0	93.3
Sarasota, FL	107.9	101.7	118.8	98.8	111.7	109.6	102.7
Tampa-St. Petersburg-Clearwater, FL;							
St. Petersburg-Clearwater, FL	99.9	96.6	107.8	96.4	102.5	86.5	96.4
Tampa, FL	96.0	102.0	89.1	88.9	105.4	98.3	98.9
West Palm Beach-Boca Raton-Boynton Beach, FL metro. div.	116.6	108.1	137.9	102.8	108.1	112.0	108.8
Atlanta-Sandy Springs-Marietta, GA:							
Atlanta, GA	97.4	94.9	94.3	87.3	109.7	100.4	100.2
Douglas County, GA	98.4	94.8	88.9	102.2	119.7	100.6	100.9
Honolulu, HI	163.2	152.4	251.4	111.1	126.6	111.4	124.3
Boise City-Nampa, ID	97.9	98.7	86.1	92.8	103.8	101.7	107.0
Champaign-Urbana, IL	95.9	96.6	83.1	101.9	98.4	100.7	103.2
Chicago-Naperville-Joliet, IL metro. div.:							
Chicago, IL	117.4	119.0	133.5	110.9	112.1	108.2	107.6
Joliet-Will County, IL	102.8	105.7	107.2	103.3	103.8	100.1	98.0
Peoria, IL	94.7	98.6	87.7	104.0	115.5	84.5	92.1
Springfield, IL	92.9	92.9	87.5	89.8	104.2	108.0	93.6
Fort Wayne, IN	92.7	95.6	81.9	116.4	94.0	88.3	94.0
Indianapolis, IN	95.0	99.5	94.0	97.0	101.4	93.8	92.2
South Bend-Mishawaka, IN-MI	95.1	90.7	88.5	117.7	97.9	94.7	95.0
Cedar Rapids, IA	92.5	92.6	76.9	110.2	97.6	105.2	97.5
Davenport-Moline-Rock Island, IA-IL	96.0	104.9	83.6	107.7	99.6	91.5	99.2
Des Moines, IA	93.9	88.1	88.6	111.3	91.6	90.6	96.3
Lawrence, KS	96.1	86.8	95.1	108.7	94.9	94.3	97.3
Clarksville TN-KY	87.0	85.3	74.2	95.1	97.8	82.2	93.8
Lexington-Fayette, KY	94.9	96.5	85.2	105.8	94.4	99.2	98.7
Louisville, KY-IN	93.9	92.4	81.3	93.9	111.0	97.2	100.1
Lafayette, LA	96.3	92.8	91.4	89.4	105.0	103.5	100.7
New Orleans-Metairie-Kenner, LA:							
Slidell - Saint Tammany Parish, LA	95.6	105.6	90.1	80.2	102.4	94.3	99.3
Shreveport-Bossier City, LA	92.9	91.2	84.7	82.9	100.0	104.9	100.1

See source at end of table.

U.S. Census Bureau, Statistical Abstract of the United States: 2007

Table 709. Cost of Living Index—Selected Metropolitan Areas: Fourth Quarter 2005—Con.

[Measures relative price levels for consumer goods and services in participating areas for a mid-management standard of living. The nationwide average equals 100 and each index is read as a percent of the national average. The index does not measure inflation, but compares prices at a single point in time. Excludes taxes. Metropolitan areas as defined by the Office of Management and Budget. For definitions and components of metropolitan areas, see source for details on coverage]

Metropolitan areas and metropolitan divisions	Composite index (100%)	Grocery items (13%)	Housing (29%)	Utilities (10%)	Transportation (10%)	Health care (4%)	Misc. goods and services (35%)
Baltimore-Towson, MD	118.6	102.3	149.4	120.0	111.7	105.9	102.0
Bethesda-Gaithersburg-Frederick, MD metro. div.	133.1	105.4	183.6	123.9	120.1	112.1	109.9
Boston-Quincy, MA metro. div.	135.4	123.1	170.1	122.7	108.7	131.3	122.3
Cambridge-Newton-Framingham, MA metro. div.	137.1	112.0	182.4	133.0	109.2	112.8	120.0
Worcester, MA	118.2	103.8	134.9	127.0	106.9	99.8	112.1
Grand Rapids-Wyoming, MI	101.8	107.7	87.5	128.3	106.0	98.6	103.3
Kalamazoo-Portage, MI	96.2	104.8	96.6	90.2	89.9	99.2	95.6
Rochester, MN	98.6	87.8	88.8	125.7	95.4	102.6	103.4
St. Cloud, MN	100.8	96.6	95.2	115.1	94.6	98.1	104.8
Jackson, MS	91.6	88.4	83.3	102.8	97.7	106.0	93.3
Kansas City, MO-KS	94.2	93.1	87.0	92.6	96.8	96.0	100.3
St. Louis, MO-IL	94.3	105.8	90.9	100.4	95.8	92.9	90.8
Springfield, MO	92.0	92.2	78.5	99.7	92.2	88.1	101.3
Missoula, MT	101.1	112.3	94.5	115.5	90.4	104.4	100.8
Omaha-Council Bluffs, NE-IA	89.0	88.3	78.7	102.4	94.8	95.8	91.5
Las Vegas-Paradise, NV	109.9	99.7	134.8	108.0	103.9	112.7	95.0
Reno-Sparks, NV	112.1	109.7	126.9	90.1	102.2	111.6	109.6
Edison, NJ metro. div.	129.4	117.3	173.5	110.0	107.5	107.0	111.1
Newark-Union, NJ-PA metro. div.	133.0	119.3	179.8	110.6	112.9	106.9	113.9
New York-White Plains-Wayne NY-NJ metro. div.	134.4	119.6	183.0	110.2	113.0	107.4	115.0
Albuquerque, NM	100.7	106.4	105.8	95.2	104.3	98.9	95.2
Nassau-Suffolk, NY metro. div.	146.9	131.6	204.2	124.6	104.9	109.1	126.7
New York-White Plains-Wayne, NY-NJ metro. div.:							
New York (Manhattan), NY	204.3	139.6	375.4	139.6	110.5	128.0	138.0
New York (Queens), NY	146.6	129.1	196.4	125.8	104.9	119.9	131.6
Rochester, NY	98.7	96.0	90.4	109.8	107.3	94.8	101.6
Syracuse, NY	100.4	103.6	84.3	136.6	110.9	93.9	100.3
Asheville, NC	99.4	95.9	104.4	80.0	96.7	99.8	102.7
Charlotte-Gastonia-Concord, NC-SC:							
Charlotte, NC	92.4	101.8	77.7	74.8	108.6	108.0	100.3
Gastonia, NC	88.8	98.3	72.9	82.6	104.4	100.7	94.7
Durham, NC	91.8	101.5	77.3	92.6	105.1	100.4	95.6
Fayetteville, NC	97.1	108.6	82.1	99.1	100.7	114.5	101.8
Greenville, NC	95.2	100.5	83.3	108.2	98.4	103.9	97.6
Hickory-Lenoir-Morganton, NC	98.6	96.0	98.0	90.9	96.7	105.5	101.9
Raleigh-Cary, NC	91.6	100.4	74.9	97.5	92.8	118.1	97.2
Wilmington, NC	97.2	102.2	88.2	90.3	108.8	107.5	100.6
Winston-Salem, NC.	89.6	97.2	74.9	88.3	96.7	106.0	95.7
Bismarck, ND.	93.0	101.3	76.6	118.0	99.8	91.3	95.0
Fargo, ND-MN	92.7	93.0	80.7	131.2	90.8	96.5	91.6
Akron, OH.	93.1	105.8	82.9	102.8	98.0	97.4	92.3
Cincinnati-Middletown, OH-KY-IN	93.0	94.1	82.3	110.0	88.9	95.5	97.3
Cleveland-Elyria-Mentor, OH	99.2	107.2	93.3	115.4	97.0	101.0	97.0
Columbus, OH	102.3	99.5	104.4	114.6	98.9	107.6	98.4
Dayton, OH	92.6	94.9	81.0	104.6	94.1	91.7	97.6
Toledo, OH	96.9	100.3	84.6	123.4	98.3	89.5	98.8
Oklahoma City, OK	88.0	84.4	77.3	93.0	91.7	96.2	95.0
Tulsa, OK	90.1	90.8	74.2	93.8	97.3	95.7	99.5
Portland-Vancouver-Beaverton, OR-WA	115.5	115.9	121.2	119.6	102.4	112.2	113.3
Erie, PA	95.7	94.9	85.1	100.4	102.4	92.1	102.1
Lancaster, PA	105.1	102.0	103.8	102.6	97.5	95.5	111.2
Philadelphia, PA metro. div.	123.9	121.5	144.6	111.4	103.4	114.9	117.5
Pittsburgh, PA	93.0	96.5	88.7	96.6	91.3	91.2	94.9
York-Hanover, PA	98.9	91.2	96.8	117.3	92.6	91.4	100.8
Providence-New Bedford-Fall River, RI-MA	124.6	116.8	149.6	113.9	99.8	114.4	117.5
Charleston-North Charleston, SC.	97.9	104.9	90.7	91.7	104.4	112.1	99.7
Camden, SC	95.7	97.6	82.8	113.1	96.0	90.6	101.0
Columbia, SC.	96.4	98.9	84.7	113.7	94.3	108.6	99.3
Myrtle Beach-Conway-North Myrtle Beach, SC.	93.4	101.1	79.8	91.6	105.0	102.3	98.2
Spartanburg, SC.	90.9	95.1	77.2	83.7	106.6	94.7	98.4
Kingsport-Bristol-Bristol, TN-VA	89.5	103.4	77.3	78.6	96.0	91.0	95.7
Knoxville, TN.	87.5	88.7	78.3	90.1	90.1	90.4	93.1
Memphis, TN-MS-AR.	94.4	96.8	85.2	83.5	99.6	100.6	102.2
Nashville-Davidson-Murfreesboro, TN:							
Hendersonville-Sumner County, TN	92.4	95.7	80.8	100.5	98.7	92.5	96.9
Murfreesboro-Smyrna, TN.	94.7	103.0	77.8	106.0	116.0	97.8	96.5
Amarillo, TX.	86.2	88.5	80.6	96.0	95.0	92.5	84.3
Austin-Round Rock, TX:							
Austin, TX.	96.1	91.9	84.0	91.8	99.1	101.9	107.4
Round Rock , TX.	91.4	80.7	78.0	103.1	99.2	96.5	100.5
Brownsville-Harlingen, TX:							
Brownsville, TX.	86.3	81.0	71.2	103.3	103.7	90.4	90.9
Harlingen, TX.	87.6	88.1	69.8	100.0	110.0	101.8	91.2
Corpus Christi, TX	88.3	79.3	78.1	93.6	98.4	90.7	95.6

See source at end of table.

U.S. Census Bureau, Statistical Abstract of the United States: 2007

Table 709. Cost of Living Index—Selected Metropolitan Areas: Fourth Quarter 2005—Con.

[Measures relative price levels for consumer goods and services in participating areas for a mid-management standard of living. The nationwide average equals 100 and each index is read as a percent of the national average. The index does not measure inflation, but compares prices at a single point in time. Excludes taxes. Metropolitan areas as defined by the Office of Management and Budget. For definitions and components of metropolitan areas, see source for details on coverage]

Metropolitan areas and metropolitan divisions	Composite index (100%)	Grocery items (13%)	Housing (29%)	Utilities (10%)	Transportation (10%)	Health care (4%)	Misc. goods and services (35%)
Dallas-Plano-Irving, TX metro. div.:							
Dallas, TX	94.6	99.2	76.7	117.7	108.0	105.1	96.3
Plano, TX	95.0	86.4	83.4	104.7	100.9	107.4	102.0
El Paso, TX	91.1	106.0	72.2	96.3	98.6	99.0	96.8
Fort Worth-Arlington, TX metro. div.:							
Arlington, TX	91.1	91.7	76.9	100.6	103.1	104.3	95.3
Fort Worth, TX	88.6	91.7	77.5	93.7	102.7	93.8	91.1
Houston-Sugar Land-Baytown, TX:	88.9	84.7	72.9	103.3	103.8	98.5	94.8
Killeen-Temple-Fort Hood, TX	91.8	82.0	79.0	109.8	112.1	95.3	95.2
Lubbock, TX	84.8	86.2	72.3	75.4	89.6	98.3	94.6
McAllen-Edinburg-Mission, TX	84.8	80.9	69.8	80.2	94.3	105.3	95.3
San Antonio, TX	91.6	82.9	84.5	84.2	89.1	100.8	102.3
Waco, TX	89.7	83.6	74.9	105.3	98.0	94.7	97.0
Salt Lake City, UT	95.9	102.9	83.4	89.3	100.8	97.9	104.1
Burlington-South Burlington, VT	117.1	105.4	137.5	108.8	104.3	107.1	111.3
Richmond, VA	105.9	97.7	109.8	106.4	117.0	95.9	103.8
Roanoke, VA	90.7	93.9	84.9	77.2	96.7	94.4	96.2
Virginia Beach-Norfolk-Newport News, VA-NC	104.5	101.1	100.2	125.4	106.5	112.3	101.8
Washington-Arlington-Alexandria, DC-VA-MD-WV metro. div.:							
Prince William County, VA	129.4	101.3	179.3	121.5	112.1	106.2	107.9
Richland-Kennewick-Pasco, WA	96.5	93.6	88.7	85.9	108.5	112.4	102.1
Olympia, WA	104.8	115.0	98.4	82.0	104.6	118.1	111.3
Portland-Vancouver-Beaverton OR-WA	98.5	93.3	97.2	88.7	102.5	115.6	101.3
Seattle-Bellevue-Everett, WA metro. div.	115.3	106.7	134.2	98.6	109.3	118.3	108.7
Spokane, WA	97.4	101.6	91.4	79.0	102.6	110.0	103.3
Tacoma, WA metro. div.	109.9	120.8	118.8	94.3	100.5	120.9	104.2
Charleston, WV	92.6	92.9	88.0	94.8	100.0	92.5	93.9
Washington-Arlington-Alexandria, DC-VA-MD-WV metro. div.:							
Martinsburg-Berkeley County, WV	89.8	88.4	93.0	77.6	87.5	95.1	91.2
Appleton, WI	95.4	91.8	87.3	101.2	108.4	102.9	97.5
Green Bay, WI	92.3	86.9	87.9	100.5	97.6	93.8	94.2
Cheyenne, WY	107.3	108.8	119.6	111.4	96.1	95.1	99.6

Source: ACCRA, 4232 King St., Alexandria, VA 22302-1507, *ACCRA Cost of Living Index*, Fourth Quarter 2005 (copyright).

Table 710. Single-Family Housing Price Indexes by State

[Index 1980, 1st quarter = 100. The index reflects average price changes in repeat sales or refinancings on the same properties. The information is obtained by reviewing repeat mortgage transactions on single-family properties whose mortages have been purchased or securitized by either Fannie Mae or Freddie Mac; for more information on methodology, see Appendix III]

State	1990	2000	2003	2004	2005	State	1990	2000	2003	2004	2005
United States....	170	244	304	341	386	Montana	124	220	266	295	339
Alabama	140	204	230	242	265	Nebraska	127	205	228	241	251
Alaska	115	170	204	225	258	Nevada	146	194	251	335	398
Arizona	132	207	250	291	395	New Hampshire	216	296	407	452	497
Arkansas	129	186	212	226	244	New Jersey	230	295	413	475	552
California	228	284	407	509	618	New Mexico	137	204	236	255	295
Colorado	130	280	324	338	359	New York	278	362	494	560	635
Connecticut	241	279	367	414	465	North Carolina	164	242	271	286	310
Delaware	226	277	358	412	477	North Dakota	114	167	196	214	233
District of Columbia	194	266	401	494	610	Ohio	145	223	251	261	271
Florida	152	213	290	348	445	Oklahoma	102	151	172	181	193
Georgia	162	248	286	303	323	Oregon	135	255	299	334	401
Hawaii	251	238	321	402	499	Pennsylvania	198	246	304	340	383
Idaho	128	204	232	257	306	Rhode Island	254	299	457	537	596
Illinois	170	251	302	328	360	South Carolina	150	223	254	269	294
Indiana	140	211	234	243	254	South Dakota	123	203	236	249	270
Iowa	120	193	220	230	245	Tennessee	147	221	247	260	281
Kansas	120	186	213	224	235	Texas	117	166	187	194	205
Kentucky	142	220	249	263	278	Utah	119	241	257	271	307
Louisiana	104	164	190	201	221	Vermont	214	261	335	379	432
Maine	236	297	398	450	498	Virginia	184	239	312	366	439
Maryland	201	247	339	405	494	Washington	178	279	325	362	430
Massachusetts	291	441	608	675	732	West Virginia	111	162	186	200	224
Michigan	147	262	298	311	323	Wisconsin	137	233	275	298	323
Minnesota	139	240	313	340	367	Wyoming	91	156	187	208	235
Mississippi	122	182	202	212	229						
Missouri	145	215	254	271	291						

Source: Office of Federal Housing Enterprise Oversight, *Housing Price Index, 4th quarter 2005*, at <http://www.ofheo.gov/media/pdf/4q05hpi.pdf> (released 01 March 2006). For most recent release, see <http://www.ofheo.gov/HPIHistData.asp>.

Table 711. **Weekly Food Cost by Type of Family: 2000 and 2005**

[**In dollars**. Assumes that food for all meals and snacks is purchased at the store and prepared at home. See source for details on estimation procedures]

Family type	December **2000**				December **2005**			
	Thrifty plan	Low-cost plan	Moderate-cost plan	Liberal plan	Thrifty plan	Low-cost plan	Moderate-cost plan	Liberal plan
FAMILIES								
Family of two:								
20–50 years	60.60	78.20	96.40	120.00	70.90	89.80	111.00	139.10
51 years and over	57.60	75.20	93.10	111.50	67.20	86.40	107.10	128.90
Family of four:								
Couple, 20–50 years and children—								
1–2 and 3–5 years	88.40	112.60	137.60	169.40	102.50	128.80	158.30	195.60
6–8 and 9–11 years	101.90	132.60	165.30	199.20	119.00	152.40	190.00	230.30
INDIVIDUALS [1]								
Child:								
1 year	16.10	19.80	23.20	28.20	18.10	22.80	26.60	32.20
2 years.	16.00	19.80	23.20	28.20	18.10	22.50	26.90	32.40
3–5 years	17.30	21.70	26.80	32.10	19.90	24.70	30.50	36.80
6–8 years.	21.50	28.80	35.90	41.70	25.10	33.30	41.10	48.00
9–11 years	25.30	32.70	41.80	48.40	29.40	37.40	48.00	55.80
Male:								
12–14 years	26.20	36.90	45.70	53.80	30.60	42.30	52.30	61.90
15–19 years	27.00	38.00	47.40	54.70	31.70	43.70	54.50	63.40
20–50 years	28.90	37.90	47.20	57.20	33.90	43.60	54.40	66.50
51 years and over	26.40	36.10	44.50	53.40	30.90	41.60	51.30	61.70
Female:								
12–19 years	26.30	31.80	38.60	46.70	30.50	36.70	44.50	53.70
20–50 years	26.20	33.20	40.40	51.90	30.60	38.00	46.50	60.00
51 years and over	26.00	32.30	40.10	48.00	30.20	37.00	46.10	55.40

[1] The costs given are for individuals in 4-person families. For individuals in other size families, the following adjustments are suggested: 1-person, add 20 percent; 2-person, add 10 percent; 3-person, add 5 percent; 5- or 6-person, subtract 5 percent; 7- (or more) person, subtract 10 percent.

Source: U.S. Department of Agriculture, *Official USDA Food Plans: Cost of Food at Home at Four Levels,* monthly. See also <http://www.usda.gov/cnpp/FoodPlans/Updates/fooddec05.pdf>.

Table 712. **Food—Retail Prices of Selected Items: 2000 to 2005**

[**In dollars per pound, except as indicated. As of December.** See Appendix III]

Food	2000	2004	2005	Food	2000	2004	2005
Cereals and bakery products:				Fresh fruits and vegetables:			
Flour, white, all purpose	0.28	0.29	0.30	Apples, red Delicious	0.82	0.95	0.97
Rice, white, lg. grain, raw	(NA)	0.57	0.52	Bananas	0.49	0.47	0.48
Spaghetti and macaroni	0.88	0.95	0.87	Oranges, navel	0.62	0.87	0.89
Bread, white, pan	0.99	0.97	1.05	Grapefruit	0.58	0.95	1.10
Bread, whole wheat	1.36	1.30	1.29	Grapes, Thompson seedless	2.36	3.09	2.76
Meats, poultry, fish and eggs:				Lemons	1.11	1.16	1.51
Ground beef, 100% beef.	1.63	2.14	2.30	Pears, Anjou.	(NA)	1.17	0.99
Ground chuck, 100% beef.	1.98	2.47	2.61	Potatoes, white	0.35	0.51	0.50
Ground beef, lean and extra lean	2.33	2.99	2.91	Lettuce, iceberg	0.85	0.99	0.85
Round steak, USDA Choice.	3.28	4.26	4.12	Tomatoes, field grown	1.57	2.46	1.85
Sirloin steak, boneless	4.81	6.09	5.93	Processed fruits and vegetables:			
Pork:				Orange juice, frozen concentrate, ...			
Bacon, sliced	3.03	3.37	3.33	12 oz. can, per 16 oz.	1.88	1.96	1.78
Chops, center cut, bone-in	3.46	2.89	3.28	Potatoes, frozen, french-fried.	1.09	0.93	(NA)
Ham, boneless, excluding canned	2.75	3.25	3.09	Sugar and sweets:			
Poultry:				Sugar, white, all sizes.	0.41	0.43	0.45
Chicken, fresh, whole.	1.08	1.03	1.06	Sugar, white, 33–80 oz. pkg.	0.40	0.42	0.43
Chicken legs, bone-in.	1.26	1.37	1.33	Fats and oils:			
Turkey, frozen, whole	0.99	1.00	1.07	Margarine, stick.	(NA)	0.91	0.84
Tuna, light, chunk, canned	1.92	1.78	(NA)	Margarine, tubs, soft	0.84	1.13	0.91
Eggs, Grade A, large, (dozen)	0.96	1.20	1.35	Shortening, vegetable oil blends.	1.07	1.29	(NA)
Dairy products:				Peanut butter, creamy, all sizes	1.96	1.76	1.70
Milk, fresh, whole, fortified (per gal.) . . .	2.79	3.23	3.24	Nonalcoholic beverages:			
Butter, salted, grade AA, stick	2.80	3.46	2.98	Coffee, 100% ground roast, all sizes . . .	3.21	2.78	3.24
American processed cheese	3.69	3.94	3.92	Other prepared foods:			
Cheddar cheese, natural.	3.76	4.16	4.43	Potato chips, per 16 oz.	3.44	3.35	3.46
Ice cream, prepkgd., bulk, reg.(1/2 gal.).	3.66	3.85	3.69				

NA Not available.

Source: Bureau of Labor Statistics, *CPI Detailed Report,* monthly, and at <http://www.bls.gov/cpi/cpi_dr.htm> See also *Monthly Labor Review* at <http://www.bls.gov/opub/mlr/welcome.htm>.

Table 713. **Average Prices of Selected Fuels and Electricity: 1990 to 2005**

[In dollars per unit, except electricity, in cents per kWh. Represents price to end-users, except as noted]

Type	Unit [1]	1990	1995	1998	1999	2000	2001	2002	2003	2004	2005
Crude oil, composite [2]	Barrel	22.22	17.23	12.52	17.51	28.26	22.95	24.10	28.53	36.98	50.23
Motor gasoline: [3]											
Unleaded regular	Gallon	1.16	1.15	1.06	1.17	1.51	1.46	1.36	1.59	1.88	2.30
Unleaded premium	Gallon	1.35	1.34	1.25	1.36	1.69	1.66	1.56	1.78	2.07	2.49
Propane, consumer grade	Gallon	.75	.49	.41	.46	.60	.51	.42	.58	.84	1.18
No. 2 diesel fuel	Gallon	0.73	0.56	0.49	0.58	0.94	0.84	0.76	0.94	1.24	1.78
No. 2 heating oil	Gallon	.73	.56	.48	.56	.93	.83	.74	.93	1.17	1.71
Residual fuel oil	Gallon	0.44	0.39	0.31	0.37	0.60	0.53	0.57	0.70	0.74	1.05
Natural gas, residential	1,000 cu/ft	5.80	6.06	6.82	6.69	7.76	9.63	7.89	9.63	10.75	12.81
Electricity, residential	kWh	7.83	8.40	8.26	8.16	8.24	8.62	8.46	8.70	8.97	9.43

[1] See headnote.   [2] Refiner acquisition cost.   [3] Average, all service.

Source: U.S. Energy Information Administration, *Monthly Energy Review.* For most current issue, see <http://www.eia.doe.gov/emeu/mer /contents.html>.

Table 714. **Retail Gasoline Prices—Selected Areas: 2003 to 2005**

[In cents per gallon. Prices are annual averages.]

Area	Regular			Midgrade			Premium		
	2003	2004	2005	2003	2004	2005	2003	2004	2005
Boston, MA	158.9	185.8	225.6	168.9	195.8	236.2	178.5	205.6	246.4
Chicago, IL	161.9	190.0	231.8	171.9	200.1	241.9	181.8	209.9	251.9
Cleveland, OH	151.8	180.2	221.9	161.7	190.2	232.1	172.1	200.4	242.9
Denver,CO	151.9	180.4	223.8	163.4	191.9	235.3	173.7	201.8	245.3
Houston, TX	143.3	171.2	216.8	153.3	181.0	226.7	163.3	190.7	236.5
Los Angeles, CA	181.9	214.7	249.0	192.6	224.8	258.6	202.3	234.6	268.0
Miami, FL	219.3	191.3	238.8	234.7	202.0	249.2	246.1	210.5	258.4
New York, NY	163.1	190.4	229.9	173.1	201.0	241.4	181.2	209.2	251.3
San Francisco, CA	189.8	214.8	248.0	200.7	225.9	259.4	210.5	235.7	269.3
Seattle, WA	162.5	194.9	236.3	173.1	205.9	247.3	183.1	216.0	257.5

Source: U.S. Energy Information Administration, *Weekly U.S. Retail Gasoline Prices,* Gasoline Historical Data. See also <http://www.eia.doe.gov/oil_gas/petroleum/data_publications/wrgp/mogas_history.html>.

Table 715. **Producer Price Indexes by Stage of Processing: 1990 to 2005**

[1982 = 100, except as indicated. See Appendix III]

Year	Crude materials			Inter-mediate materials, supplies, and components	Finished goods		Finished consumer foods		Finished consumer goods excl. food
	Total	Food-stuffs and feed-stuffs	Fuel	Crude nonfood materials except fuel		Con-sumer goods	Capital equip-ment	Crude	Pro-cessed	
1990	108.9	113.1	84.8	107.3	114.5	118.2	122.9	123.0	124.4	115.3
1991	101.2	105.5	82.9	97.5	114.4	120.5	126.7	119.3	124.4	118.7
1992	100.4	105.1	84.0	94.2	114.7	121.7	129.1	107.6	124.4	120.8
1993	102.4	108.4	87.1	94.1	116.2	123.0	131.4	114.4	126.5	121.7
1994	101.8	106.5	82.4	97.0	118.5	123.3	134.1	111.3	127.9	121.6
1995	102.7	105.8	72.1	105.8	124.9	125.6	136.7	118.8	129.8	124.0
1996	113.8	121.5	92.6	105.7	125.7	129.5	138.3	129.2	133.8	127.6
1997	111.1	112.2	101.3	103.5	125.6	130.2	138.2	126.6	135.1	128.2
1998	96.8	103.9	86.7	84.5	123.0	128.9	137.6	127.2	134.8	126.4
1999	98.2	98.7	91.2	91.1	123.2	132.0	137.6	125.5	135.9	130.5
2000	120.6	100.2	136.9	118.0	129.2	138.2	138.8	123.5	138.3	138.4
2001	121.0	106.1	151.4	101.5	129.7	141.5	139.7	127.7	142.4	141.4
2002	108.1	99.5	117.3	101.0	127.8	139.4	139.1	128.5	141.0	138.8
2003	135.3	113.5	185.7	116.9	133.7	145.3	139.5	130.0	147.2	144.7
2004	159.0	127.0	211.4	149.2	142.6	151.7	141.4	138.2	153.9	150.9
2005	182.1	122.6	279.1	176.8	153.9	160.5	144.7	139.4	156.9	162.0
PERCENT CHANGE [1]										
1990	5.6	1.7	−0.6	12.0	2.2	5.4	3.5	2.8	4.9	5.9
1991	−7.1	−6.7	−2.2	−9.1	−0.1	1.9	3.1	−3.0	–	2.9
1992	−0.8	−0.4	1.3	−3.4	0.3	1.0	1.9	−9.8	–	1.8
1993	2.0	3.1	3.7	−0.1	1.3	1.1	1.8	6.3	1.7	0.7
1994	−0.6	−1.8	−5.4	3.1	2.0	0.2	2.1	−2.7	1.1	−0.1
1995	0.9	−0.7	−12.5	9.1	5.4	1.9	1.9	6.7	1.5	2.0
1996	10.8	14.8	28.4	−0.1	0.6	3.1	1.2	8.8	3.1	2.9
1997	−2.4	−7.7	9.4	−2.1	−0.1	0.5	−0.1	−2.0	1.0	0.5
1998	−12.9	−7.4	−14.4	−18.4	−2.1	−1.0	−0.4	0.5	−0.2	−1.4
1999	1.4	−5.0	5.2	7.8	0.2	2.4	0.0	−1.3	0.8	3.2
2000	22.8	1.5	50.1	29.5	4.9	4.7	0.9	−1.6	1.8	6.1
2001	0.3	5.9	10.6	−14.0	0.4	2.4	0.6	3.4	3.0	2.2
2002	−10.7	−6.2	−22.5	−0.5	−1.5	−1.5	−0.4	0.6	−1.0	−1.8
2003	25.2	14.1	58.3	15.7	4.6	4.2	0.3	1.2	4.4	4.3
2004	17.5	11.9	13.8	27.6	6.7	4.4	1.4	6.3	4.6	4.3
2005	14.5	−3.5	32.0	18.5	7.9	5.8	2.3	0.9	1.9	7.4

– Represents or rounds to zero.   [1] Change from immediate prior year. 1990, change from 1989.

Source: U.S. Bureau of Labor Statistics, *Producer Price Indexes,* monthly and annual. See also *Monthly Labor Review* at <http://www.bls.gov/opub/mlr/welcome.htm>.

Table 716. **Producer Price Indexes by Stage of Processing: 1990 to 2005**

[1982 = 100, **except as indicated.** See Appendix III]

Stage of processing	1990	1995	2000	2001	2002	2003	2004	2005 [1]
Finished goods	**119.2**	**127.9**	**138.0**	**140.7**	**138.9**	**143.3**	**148.5**	**155.7**
Finished consumer goods	**118.2**	**125.6**	**138.2**	**141.5**	**139.4**	**145.3**	**151.7**	**160.5**
Finished consumer foods.	**124.4**	**129.0**	**137.2**	**141.3**	**140.1**	**145.9**	**152.7**	**155.6**
Fresh fruits and melons.	118.1	85.8	91.4	97.7	91.5	84.1	104.9	102.3
Fresh and dry vegetables	118.1	144.4	126.7	124.7	136.5	135.7	129.4	141.5
Eggs for fresh use (Dec. 1991 = 100)	(NA)	86.3	84.9	81.8	82.9	106.6	100.0	79.6
Bakery products.	141.0	164.3	182.3	187.7	189.9	195.0	196.3	201.0
Milled rice.	102.5	113.1	101.2	87.3	80.3	102.5	135.5	120.1
Pasta products (June 1985 = 100).	114.1	125.0	121.6	122.1	121.7	126.4	127.3	127.9
Beef and veal	116.0	100.9	113.7	120.6	114.7	137.9	141.2	147.6
Pork.	119.8	101.5	113.4	120.3	109.0	115.7	132.7	131.9
Processed young chickens.	111.0	113.5	110.4	117.2	109.7	119.7	138.9	136.2
Processed turkeys	107.6	104.9	98.7	98.9	95.3	92.5	107.8	104.1
Finfish and shellfish	147.2	170.8	198.1	190.8	191.2	195.3	206.3	221.0
Dairy products	117.2	119.7	133.7	145.2	136.2	139.4	155.9	154.6
Processed fruits and vegetables	124.7	122.4	128.6	129.6	132.6	133.8	135.2	140.4
Confectionery end products	140.0	160.7	170.6	171.4	175.6	183.7	189.9	205.0
Soft drinks	122.3	133.1	144.1	148.2	151.3	153.0	156.5	158.9
Roasted coffee	113.0	146.5	133.5	124.2	121.5	127.3	130.1	151.3
Shortening and cooking oils	123.2	142.5	132.4	132.9	140.8	160.8	193.7	176.9
Finished consumer goods excluding foods . . .	**115.3**	**124.0**	**138.4**	**141.4**	**138.8**	**144.7**	**150.9**	**162.0**
Alcoholic beverages	117.2	128.5	140.6	145.4	147.0	148.9	152.8	158.5
Apparel	117.5	124.2	127.4	126.8	125.5	125.7	125.6	125.6
Women's apparel	116.1	119.6	124.6	123.7	122.7	124.4	(NA)	(NA)
Men's and boy's apparel	120.2	130.3	133.2	132.4	129.0	127.2	(NA)	(NA)
Girls', children's, and infants' apparel	115.3	121.6	117.4	116.6	118.4	119.5	(NA)	(NA)
Textile house furnishings	109.5	119.5	122.0	122.5	122.3	122.4	123.4	123.0
Footwear	125.6	139.2	144.9	145.8	146.0	147.1	146.2	148.2
Residential electric power (Dec. 1990 = 100).	(NA)	111.8	110.8	116.6	115.4	118.8	121.4	126.3
Residential gas (Dec. 1990 = 100)	(NA)	104.4	135.5	158.7	131.9	167.6	183.2	217.3
Gasoline.	78.7	63.7	94.6	90.5	83.3	102.7	128.1	168.9
Fuel oil No. 2.	73.3	56.6	93.5	84.3	75.0	95.3	120.7	178.2
Soaps and synthetic detergents	117.7	122.9	128.2	130.6	130.0	130.9	132.9	134.5
Cosmetics and other toilet preparations	121.6	129.0	137.4	138.5	139.4	140.4	140.6	143.0
Tires, tubes, and tread	96.8	100.2	93.0	94.1	95.2	97.9	102.5	108.2
Sanitary papers and health products	135.3	144.4	146.7	147.3	149.3	150.5	148.5	154.7
Newspaper circulation.	144.1	185.6	210.0	219.5	225.6	230.5	234.7	241.5
Periodical circulation.	150.3	176.6	198.9	200.7	210.0	219.9	223.2	225.7
Book publishing	153.4	185.0	218.2	225.5	234.8	243.1	253.1	263.8
Household furniture	125.1	141.8	152.7	154.9	157.1	158.2	160.5	166.5
Floor coverings	119.0	123.7	129.6	130.2	130.5	133.6	136.7	146.5
Household appliances	110.8	112.4	107.3	105.3	104.6	102.4	101.5	103.3
Home electronic equipment	82.7	78.9	71.8	70.4	69.0	67.7	65.2	63.2
Household glassware	132.5	153.2	166.0	169.6	169.9	168.9	171.4	174.7
Household flatware.	122.1	138.3	142.6	142.8	144.7	145.2	144.5	147.7
Lawn and garden equipment, except tractors	123.0	130.4	132.0	132.8	133.9	133.5	134.5	134.4
Passenger cars	118.3	134.1	132.8	132.0	129.5	129.5	131.7	131.7
Toys, games, and children's vehicles	118.1	124.3	121.9	123.4	124.8	124.9	125.1	127.0
Sporting and athletic goods	112.6	122.0	126.1	126.3	125.5	124.0	123.4	124.9
Tobacco products.	221.4	231.3	397.2	441.9	459.4	431.6	434.0	458.2
Mobile homes	117.5	145.6	161.3	164.1	166.6	169.6	186.6	201.0
Jewelry, platinum, and karat gold	122.8	127.8	127.2	128.5	130.0	132.4	135.3	138.7
Costume jewelry and novelties	125.3	135.1	141.6	144.0	144.2	144.9	147.9	153.5
Capital Equipment	**122.9**	**136.7**	**138.8**	**139.7**	**139.1**	**139.5**	**141.4**	**144.7**
Agricultural machinery and equipment	121.7	142.9	153.7	156.1	158.5	160.9	165.9	174.8
Construction machinery and equipment	121.6	136.7	148.6	149.1	151.1	153.2	158.5	168.4
Metal cutting machine tools	129.8	148.0	161.9	158.8	152.4	150.6	151.4	155.6
Metal forming machine tools.	128.7	145.7	161.8	164.8	166.8	167.6	171.6	179.1
Tools, dies, jigs, fixtures, and industrial molds	117.2	133.8	141.1	141.3	140.6	139.5	139.4	142.0
Pumps, compressors, and equipment	119.2	139.4	154.1	157.6	161.0	162.9	167.5	178.4
Industrial material handling equipment	115.0	125.3	134.7	136.8	136.9	137.9	143.4	150.6

See footnote at end of table.

U.S. Census Bureau, Statistical Abstract of the United States: 2007

[1982 = 100, except as indicated]

Stage of processing	1990	1995	2000	2001	2002	2003	2004	2005 [1]
Capital Equipment—Continued								
Electronic computers (Dec. 1990 = 100)	(NA)	850.1	261.6	203.4	153.5	122.3	107.3	85.6
Textile machinery	128.8	146.7	156.2	158.0	157.0	157.6	158.1	160.7
Paper industries machinery (June 1982 = 100)	134.8	151.0	164.7	166.8	168.9	170.3	173.7	178.0
Printing trades machinery	124.9	133.6	142.1	143.3	143.7	143.1	143.4	144.5
Transformers and power regulators	120.9	128.9	135.8	134.4	131.7	131.9	135.7	150.8
Communication/related equip. (Dec. 1985 = 100) . . .	106.1	112.1	110.6	109.5	107.6	105.5	103.3	102.5
X-ray and electromedical equipment	109.8	111.8	101.5	100.2	100.9	100.5	97.5	95.6
Oil field and gas field machinery	102.4	114.1	128.2	134.3	135.8	139.6	143.6	156.1
Mining machinery and equipment	121.0	135.6	146.1	148.5	151.8	155.2	163.4	175.4
Office and store machines and equipment	109.5	111.5	112.7	112.7	112.5	112.3	113.2	115.2
Commercial furniture	133.4	148.2	158.4	160.3	160.9	162.3	165.6	172.7
Light motor trucks	130.0	159.0	157.6	155.0	150.5	150.2	151.3	148.4
Heavy motor trucks	120.3	144.1	148.0	147.7	152.2	154.2	155.7	162.5
Truck trailers	110.8	131.7	139.4	138.8	138.1	139.4	148.1	157.2
Civilian aircraft (Dec. 1985 = 100)	115.3	141.8	159.6	168.5	171.3	179.9	190.5	202.2
Ships (Dec. 1985 = 100)	110.1	132.8	146.9	148.9	150.6	159.4	171.4	176.9
Railroad equipment	118.6	134.8	135.7	135.2	134.9	136.3	143.9	160.6
Intermediate materials, supplies, and components	**114.5**	**124.9**	**129.2**	**129.7**	**127.8**	**133.7**	**142.6**	**153.9**
Intermediate foods and feeds	**113.3**	**114.8**	**111.7**	**115.9**	**115.5**	**125.9**	**137.1**	**133.8**
Flour	103.6	123.0	103.8	109.9	116.2	123.6	129.0	133.6
Refined sugar	122.7	119.3	110.6	109.9	117.7	121.8	120.7	124.8
Confectionery materials	101.2	109.1	94.2	105.8	117.4	125.1	125.3	125.2
Crude vegetable oils	115.8	130.0	73.6	70.1	77.6	87.6	(NA)	(NA)
Soft drink beverage bases (Dec. 1985 = 100)	126.2	148.3	167.1	170.6	172.6	174.3	176.2	180.8
Prepared animal feeds	107.4	109.1	102.9	105.1	105.7	112.8	124.8	115.3
Intermediate materials less foods and feed. .	**114.5**	**125.5**	**130.1**	**130.5**	**128.5**	**134.2**	**143.0**	**155.0**
Synthetic fibers	106.7	109.4	107.2	108.6	106.2	106.4	106.6	112.1
Processed yarns and threads	112.6	112.8	107.9	105.6	102.6	103.6	108.7	111.8
Gray fabrics	117.2	121.2	113.2	114.0	112.6	111.1	112.6	115.0
Leather	177.5	191.4	182.2	200.9	202.5	214.0	220.6	219.5
Liquefied petroleum gas	77.4	65.1	127.1	119.0	104.5	150.9	193.3	244.5
Commercial electric power	115.3	131.7	131.5	139.6	137.5	140.9	142.8	150.1
Industrial electric power	119.6	130.8	131.5	141.1	139.9	145.8	147.2	156.1
Commercial natural gas (Dec. 1990 = 100)	(NA)	96.5	134.7	168.3	135.0	173.6	194.9	232.6
Industrial natural gas (Dec. 1990 = 100)	(NA)	90.9	139.0	177.3	136.5	180.5	201.7	247.8
Natural gas to electric utilities (Dec. 1990 = 100) . . .	(NA)	87.7	120.7	146.5	103.9	158.2	171.6	202.5
Jet fuels	76.0	55.0	88.5	77.4	71.6	86.3	112.6	169.6
No. 2 diesel fuel	74.1	57.0	93.3	83.4	77.9	100.5	128.2	189.1
Residual fuel	57.7	52.6	84.7	74.6	75.4	101.2	100.2	148.4
Industrial chemicals	113.2	128.4	129.1	128.4	127.3	141.7	162.8	186.0
Prepared paint	124.8	142.1	160.8	164.4	166.9	170.8	175.7	187.9
Paint materials	136.3	139.4	148.5	149.8	165.9	172.9	179.7	190.5
Medicinal and botanical chemicals	102.2	128.3	146.2	141.2	132.6	135.3	135.0	136.2
Fats and oils, inedible	88.1	126.9	70.1	77.6	90.3	123.4	153.6	146.2
Mixed fertilizers	103.3	111.1	112.4	116.6	113.9	119.1	127.8	138.9
Nitrogenates	92.3	129.4	118.2	143.0	106.0	146.5	168.8	195.1
Phosphates	96.5	109.1	96.9	95.2	99.8	109.6	120.9	129.2
Other agricultural chemicals	119.9	144.3	146.1	148.3	148.5	148.8	149.4	151.3
Plastic resins and materials	124.1	143.5	141.6	134.2	130.7	146.1	163.1	193.5
Synthetic rubber	111.9	126.3	119.1	122.9	119.3	125.7	132.4	151.3
Plastic construction products	117.2	133.8	135.8	132.9	136.1	138.6	144.6	159.0
Unsupported plastic film, sheet, and shapes	119.0	135.6	133.2	138.0	136.5	142.8	149.1	166.3
Plastic parts and components for manufacturing . . .	112.9	115.9	117.3	116.9	116.2	116.3	116.5	120.2
Softwood lumber	123.8	178.5	178.6	170.1	170.8	170.8	209.8	203.5
Hardwood lumber	131.0	167.0	185.9	181.3	178.3	188.8	199.3	196.5
Millwork	130.4	163.8	176.4	179.2	179.8	181.8	191.9	197.2
Plywood	114.2	165.3	157.6	154.3	151.7	167.0	198.5	187.0
Woodpile	151.3	183.2	145.5	125.8	116.2	121.4	132.2	138.0
Paper	128.8	159.0	149.8	150.6	144.7	146.1	149.4	159.5
Paperboard	135.7	183.1	176.7	172.1	164.3	162.7	170.2	175.2
Paper boxes and containers	129.9	163.8	172.6	175.2	172.8	172.9	177.6	183.5
Building paper and board	112.2	144.9	138.8	129.3	129.3	159.9	192.4	184.8

See footnotes at end of table.

Table 716. **Producer Price Indexes by Stage of Processing: 1990 to 2005**—Con.

[1982 = 100, except as indicated]

Stage of processing	1990	1995	2000	2001	2002	2003	2004	2005 [1]
Intermediate materials less foods and feeds—Con.								
Commercial printing (June 1982 = 100)	128.0	144.5	155.2	157.6	157.0	158.3	159.4	161.7
Foundry and forge shop products	117.2	129.3	136.5	136.9	136.8	137.4	144.0	156.3
Steel mill products	112.1	120.1	108.4	101.3	104.8	109.5	147.2	159.7
Primary nonferrous metals	133.4	146.8	113.6	105.2	100.8	104.8	133.6	157.9
Aluminum mill shapes	127.9	160.4	149.0	148.7	143.3	143.3	150.0	161.7
Copper and brass mill shapes	174.6	195.2	162.3	155.0	149.6	152.3	199.9	235.6
Nonferrous wire and cable	142.6	151.5	143.7	140.4	134.3	134.5	152.5	169.0
Metal containers	114.0	117.2	106.8	106.3	107.8	109.2	116.2	123.9
Hardware	125.9	141.1	151.2	154.4	156.0	156.5	161.6	167.7
Plumbing fixtures and brass fittings	144.3	166.0	180.4	180.8	181.9	183.4	188.3	197.6
Heating equipment	131.6	147.5	155.6	157.1	157.9	163.2	169.5	179.9
Fabricated structural metal products	121.8	135.1	144.9	144.6	145.0	145.5	163.4	175.1
Fabricated ferrous wire products (June 1982 = 100)	114.6	125.7	130.0	129.8	129.7	131.3	149.3	157.0
Other miscellaneous metal products	120.7	124.9	126.0	127.0	126.8	127.4	131.9	136.7
Mechanical power transmission equipment	125.3	146.9	163.9	167.0	169.5	171.7	179.3	189.5
Air conditioning and refrigeration equipment	122.1	130.2	135.3	136.0	136.9	137.2	139.4	146.1
Metal valves, excluding fluid power (Dec. 1982 = 100)	125.3	145.3	162.1	164.7	167.2	169.4	176.4	189.0
Ball and roller bearings	130.6	152.0	168.8	169.5	170.0	170.6	177.1	187.1
Wiring devices	132.2	147.2	152.9	153.5	153.8	152.9	169.0	177.1
Motors, generators, motor generator sets	132.9	143.9	146.2	146.8	146.8	147.4	149.8	157.8
Switchgear and switchboard equipment	124.4	140.3	153.0	156.9	158.4	159.9	163.8	170.4
Electronic components and accessories	118.4	113.6	97.1	93.9	92.4	90.8	88.8	87.1
Internal combustion engines	120.2	135.6	143.8	143.9	144.4	144.6	145.8	147.6
Machine shop products	124.3	131.3	138.0	140.1	140.0	140.7	144.7	150.9
Flat glass	107.5	113.2	109.7	112.0	111.2	111.0	108.6	110.9
Cement	103.7	128.1	150.1	150.2	152.6	152.0	156.8	176.2
Concrete products	113.5	129.4	147.8	151.7	152.7	153.6	161.2	177.2
Asphalt felts and coatings	97.1	100.0	104.1	107.5	110.9	114.6	117.7	131.2
Gypsum products	105.2	154.5	201.4	156.4	168.9	171.5	198.8	229.5
Glass containers	120.4	130.5	127.4	132.9	135.6	140.2	144.4	146.0
Motor vehicle parts	111.2	116.0	113.6	113.3	112.9	111.8	112.0	113.1
Aircraft engines and engine parts (Dec. 1985 = 100) [2]	113.5	132.8	141.0	145.1	145.7	153.8	163.0	166.0
Aircraft parts and auxiliary equipment, n.e.c. (June 1985 = 100)	117.7	135.7	145.7	149.2	151.1	150.6	152.0	155.3
Photographic supplies	127.6	126.8	125.2	128.5	121.6	117.5	115.1	120.1
Medical/surgical/personal aid devices	127.3	141.3	146.0	148.3	150.9	154.7	157.8	159.1
Crude materials for further processing	108.9	102.7	120.6	121.0	108.1	135.3	159.0	182.1
Crude foodstuffs and feedstuffs	113.1	105.8	100.2	106.1	99.5	113.5	127.0	122.6
Wheat	87.6	118.6	80.3	85.5	97.9	98.5	106.0	102.7
Corn	100.9	109.0	76.4	78.8	89.4	93.8	97.5	75.9
Slaughter cattle	122.5	99.5	104.1	108.4	100.8	124.3	126.2	131.5
Slaughter hogs	94.1	70.2	72.7	73.4	55.4	66.1	87.8	82.7
Slaughter broilers/fryers	119.5	129.1	127.6	138.4	125.9	149.8	188.5	181.0
Slaughter turkeys	116.9	120.3	120.7	110.3	104.3	102.8	122.0	131.1
Fluid milk	100.8	93.6	92.0	111.8	90.0	93.8	120.1	113.3
Soybeans	100.8	102.2	83.4	78.6	87.7	108.8	130.0	102.6
Cane sugar, raw	119.2	119.7	101.8	111.4	110.9	114.0	(NA)	(NA)
Crude nonfood materials	101.5	96.8	130.4	126.8	111.4	148.2	179.2	223.2
Raw cotton	118.2	156.2	95.2	67.2	61.5	92.9	85.6	79.3
Leaf tobacco	95.8	102.5	(NA)	105.2	(NA)	102.0	92.4	(NA)
Cattle hides	217.8	209.9	169.4	(NA)	(NA)	(NA)	(NA)	(NA)
Coal	97.5	95.0	87.9	96.2	99.8	99.9	109.2	115.8
Natural gas	80.4	66.6	155.5	171.8	122.5	214.5	245.9	335.0
Crude petroleum	71.0	51.1	85.2	69.2	67.9	83.0	108.2	150.2
Logs and timber	142.8	220.4	196.4	182.8	180.1	181.8	193.3	197.5
Wastepaper	138.9	371.1	282.5	148.6	173.1	197.3	231.4	230.2
Iron ore	83.3	91.8	94.8	96.2	95.2	95.9	98.2	116.9
Iron and steel scrap	166.0	202.7	142.1	120.0	141.4	182.6	323.7	290.8
Nonferrous metal ores (Dec. 1983 = 100)	98.3	101.6	68.0	63.7	68.1	78.5	113.7	148.6
Copper base scrap	181.3	193.5	123.7	114.8	111.4	128.4	186.5	262.0
Aluminum base scrap	172.6	209.4	177.0	156.5	158.0	168.7	194.1	209.2
Construction sand, gravel, and crushed stone	125.4	142.3	163.1	168.8	173.0	177.1	183.3	195.7

NA Not available. [1] Preliminary data. [2] n.e.c. Not elsewhere classified.

Source: U.S. Bureau of Labor Statistics, *Producer Price Indexes*, monthly and annual. See also *Monthly Labor Review* at <http://www.bls.gov/opub/mlr/welcome.htm>.

Prices 479

Table 717. Producer Price Indexes for the Net Output of Selected Industries: 2001 to 2005

[Indexes are based on selling prices reported by establishments of all sizes by probability sampling. Manufacturing industries selected by shipment value. n.e.c. = Not elsewhere classified. See text, Section 22. See Appendix III]

Industry	NAICS code [1]	Index base [2]	2001	2002	2003	2004	2005 [3]
Logging	113310	12/81	167.6	165.1	168.8	175.3	179.5
Total mining industries	21	12/84	114.3	96.6	131.3	153.4	200.9
Crude petroleum & natural gas extraction	211111	06/02	(NA)	(NA)	152.3	183.4	253.5
Natural gas liquid extraction	211112	06/02	(NA)	(NA)	181.2	216.5	284.9
Bituminous coal & lignite surface mining	212111	12/01	(NA)	101.9	101.5	107.1	111.3
Anthracite mining	212113	12/79	161.0	163.0	168.4	180.9	205.2
Iron ore mining	212210	12/84	95.2	94.2	95.0	97.2	115.7
Gold ore mining	212221	06/85	81.5	92.4	107.6	121.6	131.7
Copper ore & nickel ore mining	212234	06/88	81.7	80.1	90.1	150.1	197.0
Dimension stone mining and quarrying	212311	06/85	156.9	164.0	169.9	173.4	182.0
Crushed and broken limestone mining and quarrying	212312	12/83	150.9	154.7	159.2	165.4	174.4
Crushed and broken granite mining and quarrying.	212313	12/83	188.3	193.2	197.5	203.7	217.2
Other crushed and broken stone mining and quarrying. ..	212319	12/83	156.8	160.8	164.0	170.3	187.1
Construction sand and gravel mining	212321	06/82	181.6	185.8	188.9	195.0	209.7
Industrial sand mining	212322	06/82	154.3	157.1	162.1	167.1	176.8
Kaolin and ball clay mining	212324	06/84	119.6	118.8	121.0	122.7	126.2
Clay and ceramic and refractory minerals mining	212325	06/84	140.3	140.9	142.5	144.4	148.3
Potash, soda, and borate mineral mining.	212391	12/84	110.0	107.7	106.1	110.8	130.2
Drilling oil and gas wells.	213111	12/85	173.9	153.5	153.5	168.0	257.5
Oil & gas operations support activities.	213112	12/85	142.4	137.4	135.6	141.8	164.6
Nonmetallic minerals support activity (except fuel)	213115	06/85	109.3	110.5	114.6	119.6	127.6
Total manufacturing industries	31-33	12/84	134.6	133.7	137.1	142.9	150.8
Dog & cat food mfg..	311111	12/85	134.7	135.7	136.2	144.0	145.7
Flour milling	311211	06/83	101.9	107.6	113.7	117.4	117.5
Rice milling	311212	06/84	81.9	72.2	87.6	113.1	102.1
Soybean processing	311222	12/79	67.3	72.1	87.1	102.3	91.1
Fats and oils refining and blending	311225	12/81	131.5	138.1	158.1	186.8	171.8
Chocolate & confectionery mfg. from cacao beans	311320	06/83	138.6	148.1	156.2	155.0	157.0
Confectionery mfg. (purchased chocolate)	311330	12/03	(NA)	(NA)	(NA)	100.1	102.3
Frozen fruit, juice, & vegetable mfg.	311411	06/81	140.2	144.1	147.8	149.3	156.2
Frozen specialty food mfg.	311412	12/82	138.8	139.0	139.2	142.1	143.6
Fruit and vegetable canning	311421	06/81	142.2	143.7	144.8	146.5	151.3
Specialty canning	311422	12/82	173.8	174.6	176.1	177.5	184.0
Fluid milk.	311511	12/82	153.6	146.4	147.7	162.5	165.3
Ice cream and frozen dessert mfg..	311520	06/83	157.1	158.8	160.4	166.0	168.2
Animal (except poultry) slaughtering.	311611	12/80	120.3	113.1	130.1	137.8	141.1
Meat processed from carcasses.	311612	12/82	125.8	121.1	129.7	132.9	136.7
Poultry processing.	311615	12/81	121.5	115.9	121.5	137.5	135.2
Seafood canning.	311711	12/84	108.9	110.3	110.2	114.5	114.0
Fresh & frozen seafood processing	311712	12/82	161.7	157.2	161.5	164.1	170.9
Frozen cakes, pies, & other pastries mfg.	311813	06/91	119.5	120.9	124.8	127.5	129.1
Cookie and cracker manufacturing	311821	06/83	173.3	175.0	181.6	183.4	184.4
Flour mixes & dough mfg. from purchased flour	311822	06/85	124.6	126.4	131.9	134.0	135.8
Dry pasta manufacturing.	311823	06/85	122.4	122.0	126.3	127.1	127.9
Coffee and tea manufacturing	311920	06/81	136.4	133.8	139.4	142.2	161.3
Mayonnaise, dressing, & other sauces mfg.	311941	12/03	(NA)	(NA)	(NA)	101.6	103.0
Spice and extracts manufacturing.	311942	12/03	(NA)	(NA)	(NA)	100.3	99.1
Soft drinks manufacturing	312111	06/81	156.5	159.5	161.5	165.3	168.3
Bottled water manufacturing	312112	12/03	(NA)	(NA)	(NA)	100.7	101.6
Breweries	312120	06/82	140.5	142.7	145.8	151.9	158.4
Wineries	312130	12/83	141.3	141.7	140.8	140.0	144.9
Distilleries	312140	06/83	165.1	164.9	165.1	164.7	165.5
Tobacco stemming & redrying	312210	06/84	112.3	114.7	117.5	119.4	119.9
Cigarettes	312221	12/82	425.8	442.8	411.7	412.6	437.5
Other tobacco product mfg..	312229	12/03	(NA)	(NA)	(NA)	99.6	103.0
Broadwoven fabric finishing mills	313311	12/03	(NA)	(NA)	(NA)	99.9	103.1
Textile/fabric finishing (exc. broadwoven) mills	313312	12/03	(NA)	(NA)	(NA)	99.6	100.8
Underwear & nightwear knitting mills.	315192	06/82	131.5	130.1	129.1	128.6	128.6
Men's/boys' cut & sew trouser/slack/jean mfg.	315224	12/81	135.1	132.2	128.4	126.6	123.2
Women's/girls' cut & sew dress mfg.	315233	12/80	123.6	122.1	122.8	124.9	123.6
Women's/girls' cut & sew other outerwear mfg.	315239	06/83	111.7	111.5	112.9	112.8	113.6
Sawmills	321113	12/80	141.2	139.1	141.1	163.4	162.0
Wood preservation	321114	06/85	152.7	151.6	154.0	167.7	175.6
Hardwood veneer & plywood manufacturing.	321211	06/85	142.5	142.3	138.6	143.6	146.2
Softwood veneer or plywood mfg..	321212	12/80	135.8	131.8	154.4	189.0	173.0
Engineered wood member (exc truss) mfg.	321213	12/03	(NA)	(NA)	(NA)	110.1	121.6
Truss mfg.	321214	12/03	(NA)	(NA)	(NA)	112.5	119.6
Reconstituted wood product mfg.	321219	06/91	112.5	112.3	139.1	168.2	162.1
Wood window & door mfg.	321911	12/03	(NA)	(NA)	(NA)	101.9	103.1
Manufactured homes (mobile homes) mfg..	321991	06/81	170.0	172.6	175.8	190.0	204.5
Pulp mills.	322110	12/82	122.9	116.5	120.9	131.3	137.4
Paper (except newsprint) mills.	322121	12/03	(NA)	(NA)	(NA)	102.4	108.4
Newsprint mills	322122	12/03	(NA)	(NA)	(NA)	104.0	115.6
Paperboard mills	322130	12/82	187.4	179.7	180.4	190.1	196.0
Digital printing.	323115	12/03	(NA)	(NA)	(NA)	99.3	98.3
Book printing.	323117	12/83	154.1	150.7	150.2	151.5	154.7
Petroleum refineries.	324110	06/85	103.1	96.3	121.2	151.5	205.5
Petroleum lubricating oils and greases	324191	12/80	183.3	185.5	191.5	199.4	230.8
Industrial gas manufacturing	325120	12/03	(NA)	(NA)	(NA)	108.3	118.6

See footnotes at end of table.

U.S. Census Bureau, Statistical Abstract of the United States: 2007

[See headnote, page 480]

Industry	NAICS code [1]	Index base [2]	2001	2002	2003	2004	2005 [3]
Plastics material and resins manufacturing............	325211	12/80	159.9	148.9	167.8	192.0	228.8
Synthetic rubber manufacturing..................	325212	06/81	122.5	119.1	125.2	131.6	150.6
Nitrogenous fertilizer manufacturing	325311	12/79	171.7	131.6	177.0	203.9	235.2
Phosphatic fertilizer manufacturing...............	325312	12/79	129.4	132.8	145.4	161.3	174.5
Fertilizer (mixing only) manufacturing	325314	12/79	147.0	143.3	149.2	156.7	169.0
Pesticide and other agricultural chemical manufacturing..	325320	06/82	138.0	138.2	138.1	138.6	140.9
Pharmaceutical preparation mfg..................	325412	06/81	314.5	326.7	343.3	360.1	378.7
Photo film, paper, plate, & chemical mfg...........	325992	12/03	(NA)	(NA)	(NA)	99.1	102.6
Plastics pipe and pipe fitting manufacturing	326122	06/93	107.8	114.6	124.7	140.8	171.7
Cement manufacturing.......................	327310	06/82	148.7	151.1	150.5	155.4	175.0
Lime.................................	327410	12/85	122.7	126.1	128.1	133.1	144.1
Cut stone and stone products	327991	12/84	147.9	149.3	149.7	149.5	151.6
Steel investment foundries	331512	06/81	205.0	205.6	199.8	197.7	204.9
Steel foundries (except investment)	331513	06/81	136.7	135.3	137.5	146.2	160.7
Aluminum die-casting foundries	331521	06/91	110.0	109.6	111.5	114.1	116.5
Iron & steel forging	332111	12/83	114.7	112.9	112.8	117.5	128.5
Hand and edge tools, except machine tools and handsaws	332212	06/83	162.5	164.7	165.1	168.8	176.1
Saw blade & handsaw mfg.....................	332213	06/83	139.9	142.0	142.9	142.9	146.0
Metal window and door manufacturing	332321	06/83	158.1	159.2	161.0	166.5	175.2
Sheetmetal work mfg........................	332322	12/82	141.5	142.9	144.4	159.4	165.5
Heating equipment (except warm air furnaces) mfg.....	333414	06/80	195.0	196.3	199.8	206.2	215.4
Electronic computer mfg......................	334111	12/98	71.3	61.1	49.1	107.4	92.5
Computer storage device mfg...................	334112	12/98	78.2	64.2	55.4	105.7	98.9
Computer terminal mfg.......................	334113	12/93	90.7	88.5	86.4	85.3	85.9
Telephone apparatus mfg......................	334210	12/85	108.8	104.6	100.9	95.8	93.8
Radio/TV broadcast & wireless comm. equip mfg.......	334220	12/91	101.7	98.2	95.1	93.3	92.5
Audio & video equipment mfg..................	334310	03/80	74.6	74.0	72.8	71.1	69.6
Laboratory apparatus and furniture...............	339111	12/91	129.4	132.7	137.3	141.2	148.0
Surgical and medical instrument mfg.	339112	06/82	128.7	130.8	133.1	134.6	135.2
Services industries							
Recyclable materials wholesalers.................	421930	12/86	123.9	129.3	151.6	220.7	220.1
New car dealers	441110	12/99	103.1	108.7	111.5	113.5	116.1
Recreational vehicle dealers	441210	06/01	(NA)	112.2	109.7	121.4	137.0
Boat dealers.............................	441222	06/01	(NA)	107.9	113.8	116.4	121.7
Automotive parts and accessories stores............	441310	12/03	(NA)	(NA)	(NA)	106.8	111.5
Household appliance stores	443111	06/03	(NA)	(NA)	(NA)	93.3	100.8
Radio, TV, and other electronics stores	443112	06/03	(NA)	(NA)	(NA)	100.4	101.1
Computer and software stores	443120	06/03	(NA)	(NA)	(NA)	92.7	90.5
Hardware stores	444130	06/03	(NA)	(NA)	(NA)	103.5	108.6
Nursery, garden, and farm supply stores	444220	12/02	(NA)	(NA)	102.1	112.4	117.2
Grocery (except convenience) stores	445110	12/99	109.9	113.6	117.9	123.6	131.3
Specialty food stores	445200	12/03	(NA)	(NA)	(NA)	107.1	110.2
Beer, wine, and liquor stores	445310	06/00	102.9	103.5	106.9	110.7	110.8
Food (health) supplement stores	446191	12/99	123.5	130.6	139.1	144.9	147.8
Gasoline stations with convenience stores	447110	12/03	(NA)	(NA)	(NA)	102.5	103.8
Men's clothing stores	448110	06/02	(NA)	(NA)	102.2	103.8	106.0
Women's clothing stores......................	448120	06/03	(NA)	(NA)	(NA)	105.1	105.6
Family clothing stores	448140	06/03	(NA)	(NA)	(NA)	103.7	108.2
Luggage and leather goods stores	448320	06/00	103.6	93.6	94.7	98.5	103.4
Sporting goods stores	451110	06/00	103.6	107.2	104.4	99.1	100.4
Book stores	451211	06/00	108.0	106.9	113.7	118.2	114.7
Discount department stores....................	452112	12/03	(NA)	(NA)	(NA)	106.1	106.7
Office supplies and stationery stores..............	453210	06/00	107.3	114.8	124.3	127.1	130.5
Manufactured (mobile) home dealers..............	453930	12/02	(NA)	(NA)	103.6	113.8	123.5
Mail-order houses	454113	06/00	90.9	93.5	92.8	94.2	105.4
Scheduled passenger air transportation.............	481111	12/89	200.6	200.4	205.7	205.8	216.8
Scheduled freight air transportation	481112	12/03	(NA)	(NA)	(NA)	100.2	105.2
General freight trucking, local..................	484110	12/03	(NA)	(NA)	(NA)	105.2	111.5
General freight trucking, long-distance.............	484121	12/03	(NA)	(NA)	(NA)	102.7	108.8
Used household and office goods moving	484210	12/03	(NA)	(NA)	(NA)	102.6	106.0
Marine cargo handling	488320	12/91	111.4	110.9	111.5	113.2	115.1
Navigational services to shipping	488330	12/92	125.4	127.4	129.3	133.1	138.7
Freight transportation arrangement...............	488510	12/94	100.3	99.5	99.9	100.9	101.2
United States Postal Service	491110	06/89	143.4	150.2	155.0	155.0	155.0
Couriers	492110	12/03	(NA)	(NA)	(NA)	106.6	115.0
Newspaper publishers	511110	12/79	367.9	381.8	395.6	409.7	426.3
Periodical publishers	511120	12/79	305.9	320.4	332.3	339.1	347.5
Software publishers	511210	12/97	101.4	98.0	96.9	94.3	94.4
Commercial banking	522110	12/03	(NA)	(NA)	(NA)	102.8	105.6
Savings institutions	522120	12/03	(NA)	(NA)	(NA)	100.9	99.0
Direct life insurance carriers	524113	12/98	100.1	101.6	103.4	105.2	106.4
Direct health and medical insurance carriers	524114	12/02	(NA)	(NA)	106.2	111.8	116.6
Direct property and casualty insurance carriers........	524126	06/98	104.4	108.8	115.1	118.8	121.0
Insurance agencies and brokerages	524210	12/02	(NA)	(NA)	102.3	104.4	105.4
Nursing care facilities.......................	623110	12/94	139.3	144.6	149.4	155.6	161.3
Hotels (except casino hotels) and motels..........	721110	12/03	(NA)	(NA)	(NA)	103.5	110.1
Casino hotels	721120	12/03	(NA)	(NA)	(NA)	105.0	107.7

NA Not available.   [1] North American Industry Classification System, 1997.   [2] Index base year equals 100.   [3] Preliminary data.

Source: U.S. Bureau of Labor Statistics, *Producer Price Indexes,* monthly.

Table 718. Commodity Research Bureau Futures Price Index: 1990 to 2005

[**1967 = 100**. Index computed daily. Represents unweighted geometric average of commodity futures prices (through 6 months forward) of 17 major commodity futures markets. Represents end of year index]

Item	1990	1995	1996	1997	1998	1999	2000	2001	2002	2003	2004	2005
All commodities	**222.6**	**243.2**	**239.6**	**229.1**	**191.2**	**205.1**	**227.8**	**190.6**	**234.5**	**255.3**	**283.9**	**347.9**
Softs [1]	276.0	354.4	322.2	408.7	344.8	280.9	254.4	252.8	303.7	250.5	343.5	420.5
Industrials	245.5	272.5	266.3	210.9	185.3	192.9	211.0	141.8	176.6	256.6	232.1	302.5
Grains and oilseeds [2]	171.2	218.6	284.7	210.7	172.8	156.6	174.9	159.0	188.2	225.8	177.0	193.8
Energy	246.0	180.0	224.0	180.4	135.0	221.0	355.8	204.9	320.7	358.7	457.3	705.3
Oilseeds [3]	223.6	277.5	307.9	[3]	[3]	[3]	[3]	[3]	[3]	[3]	[3]	[3]
Livestock and meats	226.2	192.4	241.7	238.1	186.7	239.6	253.6	247.4	251.0	237.8	303.6	300.3
Metals (precious)	257.8	276.0	271.3	249.3	234.3	253.4	265.7	246.8	289.1	364.1	396.6	478.1

[1] Prior to 1997, reported as Imported. Softs include commodities that are grown and not mined such as coffee, cocoa, lumber, cotton, and sugar. [2] Prior to 1997, reported as Grains. [3] Incorporated into Grains and Oilseeds beginning 1997.

Source: Commodity Research Bureau (CRB), Chicago, IL, *CRB Commodity Index Report,* weekly (copyright).

Table 719. Indexes of Spot Primary Market Prices: 1990 to 2005

[**1967 = 100**. Computed weekly for 1980; daily thereafter. Represents unweighted geometric average of price quotations of 23 commodities; much more sensitive to changes in market conditions than is a monthly producer price index]

Items and number of commodities	1990	1995	1996	1997	1998	1999	2000	2001	2002	2003	2004	2005
All commodities (23)	**258.1**	**289.1**	**288.2**	**271.8**	**235.2**	**227.3**	**224.0**	**212.1**	**244.3**	**283.6**	**293.0**	**303.3**
Foodstuffs (10).	206.4	236.4	231.8	227.3	197.5	178.1	184.7	201.6	238.1	250.2	256.0	241.7
Raw industrials (13)	301.2	332.2	334.9	307.5	265.3	268.9	255.8	217.3	248.6	309.1	321.5	354.7
Livestock and products (5)	292.7	307.4	363.0	306.1	232.3	265.7	265.5	257.2	317.8	365.9	365.0	326.6
Metals (5)	283.2	300.6	289.9	269.8	218.5	261.6	214.0	172.5	184.5	276.7	357.7	440.9
Textiles and fibers (4)	257.6	274.3	267.4	261.5	237.5	223.8	245.7	217.4	230.2	255.2	237.9	252.5
Fats and oils (4)	188.7	226.7	246.4	257.1	236.0	174.8	163.6	175.8	234.0	297.2	262.6	223.4

Source: Commodity Research Bureau, Chicago, IL, *CRB Commodity Index Report,* weekly (copyright).

Table 720. Chain-Type Price Indexes for Gross Domestic Product: 1990 to 2005

[**2000 = 100**. For explanation of "chain-type," see text, Section 13.]

Component	1990	1995	2000	2001	2002	2003	2004	2005
Gross domestic product	**81.6**	**92.1**	**100.0**	**102.4**	**104.2**	**106.3**	**109.1**	**112.2**
Personal consumption expenditures. . . .	**80.5**	**91.6**	**100.0**	**102.1**	**103.5**	**105.5**	**108.2**	**111.3**
Durable goods	104.6	110.7	100.0	98.1	95.8	92.4	90.6	90.2
Nondurable goods.	84.2	90.6	100.0	101.5	102.1	104.2	107.6	111.6
Services	74.2	88.3	100.0	103.3	106.0	109.2	112.7	116.2
Gross private domestic investment	**96.4**	**100.9**	**100.0**	**101.0**	**101.6**	**103.3**	**106.6**	**109.8**
Fixed investment	95.5	100.3	100.0	101.0	101.7	103.4	106.7	110.0
Nonresidential.	104.7	106.2	100.0	99.7	99.5	99.8	101.0	103.2
Structures.	74.0	83.9	100.0	105.4	110.0	113.9	120.1	132.2
Equipment and software	118.2	115.2	100.0	97.7	96.0	95.1	95.0	94.7
Residential	74.9	85.8	100.0	104.6	107.2	112.4	119.9	125.7
Change in private inventories								
Net exports of goods and services:								
Exports	100.0	104.4	100.0	99.6	99.3	101.4	105.0	108.9
Goods	108.0	109.2	100.0	99.3	98.7	100.6	104.4	107.7
Services	82.5	93.1	100.0	100.4	100.8	103.2	106.4	111.7
Imports	103.8	106.4	100.0	97.5	96.3	99.6	104.6	110.9
Goods	108.2	108.6	100.0	97.0	95.3	98.1	103.0	109.5
Services	85.7	96.1	100.0	100.1	101.9	107.8	113.0	118.2
Government consumption expenditures and gross investment	**77.1**	**88.4**	**100.0**	**102.5**	**105.5**	**109.5**	**113.5**	**118.9**
Federal	77.1	89.5	100.0	101.9	105.6	109.7	114.4	118.5
National defense	78.0	89.6	100.0	102.0	105.8	110.4	114.8	118.9
Nondefense	75.3	89.4	100.0	101.7	105.3	108.5	113.5	117.8
State and local	77.4	87.8	100.0	102.9	105.4	109.3	113.0	119.2

Source: U.S. Bureau of Economic Analysis, *Survey of Current Business,* May 2006. See also <http://www.bea.gov /bea/dn/nipaweb/SelectTable.asp?Selected=N> (released 28 April 2006).

Table 721. Price Indexes For Personal Consumption Expenditures by Type of Expenditure: 1990 to 2004

[2000 = 100. See also Table 656]

Type of expenditure	1990	1995	2000	2001	2002	2003	2004
Total expenditures [1]	**80.5**	**91.6**	**100.0**	**102.1**	**103.5**	**105.5**	**108.2**
Food and tobacco [1]	78.2	86.8	100.0	103.3	105.9	107.9	111.1
Food purchased for off-premise consumption	82.7	90.4	100.0	102.9	104.4	106.2	109.5
Purchased meals and beverages [2]	78.6	88.2	100.0	103.1	105.9	108.2	111.5
Tobacco products	46.7	57.6	100.0	107.7	116.8	118.8	121.0
Clothing, accessories, and jewelry [1]	105.6	105.7	100.0	99.0	97.0	95.1	95.3
Shoes	103.7	106.2	100.0	99.4	98.0	96.6	96.3
Clothing	109.4	106.3	100.0	97.8	94.9	92.4	92.0
Jewelry and watches	114.4	117.9	100.0	99.9	97.3	93.9	94.5
Personal care	83.1	91.8	100.0	102.0	102.9	103.5	104.6
Housing [1]	74.5	86.1	100.0	103.9	107.8	110.5	113.2
Owner-occupied nonfarm dwellings-space rent. . .	74.8	86.2	100.0	103.9	108.0	110.7	113.2
Tenant-occupied nonfarm dwellings-space rent. . .	75.4	86.2	100.0	104.3	108.3	111.3	114.1
Household operation [1]	89.3	96.6	100.0	102.3	100.9	102.0	102.9
Furniture [3]	91.9	99.6	100.0	98.3	96.3	95.0	94.7
Semidurable house furnishings [4]	112.0	111.0	100.0	97.7	94.8	87.8	83.9
Cleaning and polishing preparations	84.2	89.5	100.0	103.6	104.4	102.8	103.3
Household utilities.	80.9	90.3	100.0	108.5	104.5	112.4	118.2
Electricity	91.5	100.9	100.0	108.0	106.8	109.3	111.4
Gas	73.2	77.3	100.0	119.1	101.2	124.1	134.7
Water and other sanitary services.	66.1	87.1	100.0	102.9	106.2	110.1	116.7
Fuel oil and coal	76.9	69.9	100.0	101.7	91.7	109.7	125.8
Telephone and telegraph	103.8	107.0	100.0	98.0	98.1	97.2	95.3
Medical care [1]	70.1	88.0	100.0	103.7	106.5	109.9	113.7
Drug preparations and sundries [5].	72.7	87.2	100.0	104.6	109.0	112.0	115.1
Physicians	71.2	92.3	100.0	102.8	102.8	104.3	106.5
Dentists	60.6	80.1	100.0	104.1	108.7	113.2	118.8
Hospitals and nursing homes [6]	70.1	87.7	100.0	104.2	108.1	112.8	117.7
Health insurance	62.0	82.4	100.0	102.3	103.5	108.0	113.1
Medical care [7]	60.3	84.2	100.0	103.7	107.1	111.7	116.6
Personal business [1]	76.0	90.3	100.0	100.7	103.9	105.9	110.4
Expense of handling life insurance [8]	61.7	75.2	100.0	102.0	106.7	111.4	120.4
Legal services	65.7	80.5	100.0	105.3	111.5	117.1	122.7
Funeral and burial expenses.	63.7	82.1	100.0	103.6	108.6	112.9	117.8
Transportation	79.9	90.8	100.0	100.0	99.0	101.8	105.8
User-operated transportation [1].	79.5	90.8	100.0	100.3	99.6	102.3	106.6
New autos	87.5	99.9	100.0	99.5	98.4	96.5	96.0
Net purchases of used autos	69.1	95.6	100.0	101.6	103.9	97.5	95.5
Tires, tubes, accessories, etc.	102.2	101.8	100.0	102.5	104.3	105.2	105.7
Repair, greasing, washing, parking, storage,							
rental, and leasing	77.6	90.4	100.0	103.4	106.1	108.0	109.6
Gasoline and oil	78.4	77.8	100.0	96.3	90.4	105.2	123.9
Purchased local transportation	77.0	90.2	100.0	103.0	105.3	112.8	119.5
Mass transit systems	77.9	90.9	100.0	103.0	105.3	112.8	119.5
Taxicab	75.0	88.7	100.0	103.0	105.3	112.9	119.5
Purchased intercity transportation [1]	87.9	91.4	100.0	94.3	87.1	88.9	87.5
Railway (commutation)	76.2	85.7	100.0	104.9	108.7	107.6	98.4
Bus.	86.8	86.6	100.0	103.3	106.6	110.5	114.8
Airline	91.5	93.0	100.0	92.2	82.9	84.8	83.0
Recreation [1]	104.9	109.0	100.0	98.7	97.2	95.8	95.2
Magazines, newspapers, and sheet music.	73.9	89.4	100.0	102.0	103.8	105.9	109.0
Nondurable toys and sport supplies	115.9	118.4	100.0	95.9	90.6	85.8	82.5
Video and audio products, including musical							
instruments and computer goods	284.8	205.9	100.0	87.3	77.1	68.7	62.9
Computers, peripherals, and software	1,516.2	516.5	100.0	75.7	60.2	49.2	43.6
Education and research.	66.6	82.6	100.0	104.7	109.6	115.4	122.1
Higher education	62.9	82.8	100.0	105.0	110.7	117.1	124.9
Religious and welfare activities	73.1	84.5	100.0	102.9	105.9	109.3	112.6
Foreign travel and other, net:							
Foreign travel by U.S. residents.	80.1	95.1	100.0	101.4	105.0	111.6	117.1
Expenditures abroad by U.S. residents	102.0	124.1	100.0	99.9	105.9	125.5	140.2
Less: Expenditures in the United States by							
nonresidents	76.9	87.3	100.0	101.1	101.4	104.5	109.0

[1] Includes other expenditures not shown separately.   [2] Consists of purchases (including tips) of meals and beverages from retail, service, and amusement establishments; hotels; dining and buffet cars; schools; school fraternities; institutions; clubs; and industrial lunch rooms. Includes meals and beverages consumed both on- and off-premise.   [3] Includes mattresses and bedsprings.   [4] Consists largely of textile house furnishings including piece goods allocated to house furnishing use. Also includes lamp shades, brooms, and brushes.   [5] Excludes drug preparations and related products dispensed by physicians, hospitals, and other medical services.   [6] Consists of (1) current expenditures (including consumption of fixed capital) of nonprofit hospitals and nursing homes and (2) payments by patients to proprietary and government hospitals and nursing homes.   [7] Consists of (1) premiums, less benefits and dividends, for health hospitalization and accidental death and dismemberment insurance provided by commercial insurance carriers and (2) administrative expenses (including consumption of fixed capital) of Blue Cross and Blue Shield plans and of other independent prepaid and self-insured health plans.   [8] Consists of (1) operating expenses of life insurance carriers and private noninsured pension plans and (2) premiums less benefits and dividends of fraternal benefit societies. Excludes expenses allocated by commercial carriers to accident and health insurance.

Source: U.S. Bureau of Economic Analysis, *Survey of Current Business,* August 2006. See also <http://www.bea.gov /bea/dn/nipaweb/SelectTable.asp?Selected=N> (released as 04 August 2005).

Table 722. **Export Price Indexes—Selected Commodities: 1990 to 2005**

[2000 = 100. Indexes are weighted by 2000 export values according to the Schedule B classification system of the U.S. Census Bureau. Prices used in these indexes were collected from a sample of U.S. manufacturers of exports and are factory transaction prices, except as noted. n.e.s. = not elsewhere specified.]

Commodities	1990	1995	2000 [1]	2001	2002	2003	2004	2005
All commodities	95.1	104.5	100.1	99.4	98.0	99.5	103.4	106.7
Food and live animals	102.4	112.1	100.6	101.1	99.8	107.5	123.9	124.3
Meat	81.4	95.7	104.8	106.1	90.0	102.9	127.3	140.2
Fish	86.8	107.1	100.6	90.8	97.9	108.2	108.6	110.1
Cereals and cereal preparations	126.5	133.2	100.0	102.6	106.5	118.5	141.2	118.7
Fruits and vegetables	93.2	107.2	97.9	98.6	99.0	99.6	111.1	133.6
Feeding stuff for animals	99.5	104.9	100.4	101.1	101.2	108.8	131.9	118.1
Miscellaneous food products	94.0	94.8	100.0	100.1	100.7	101.5	101.6	108.1
Beverages and tobacco	84.9	98.2	100.0	98.4	98.2	98.2	101.6	103.3
Tobacco and tobacco manufactures	85.0	98.1	99.9	98.2	97.6	96.6	100.0	101.6
Crude materials	96.7	125.4	101.6	92.6	95.3	103.9	125.7	130.3
Oil seeds and oleaginous fruits	116.1	115.6	103.3	95.6	102.9	122.7	168.5	136.5
Cork and wood	76.5	117.5	99.8	92.8	87.1	90.4	98.3	97.6
Pulp and waste paper	70.9	122.2	106.9	80.6	89.3	90.1	100.8	101.5
Textile fibers	118.2	154.3	100.5	90.9	88.6	103.2	108.7	103.1
Metalliferous ores and metal scrap	105.9	132.2	99.2	91.0	99.8	109.0	167.5	212.9
Mineral fuels and related materials	67.2	68.5	97.4	103.2	93.9	107.6	131.8	181.0
Coal, coke and briquettes	109.5	106.4	99.5	106.9	110.9	(NA)	(NA)	(NA)
Crude petroleum and petroleum products	57.5	59.6	96.8	101.8	87.9	102.7	129.7	188.7
Chemicals and related products	90.4	108.4	100.9	96.2	95.8	100.8	105.8	115.7
Organic chemicals	93.9	122.8	102.1	90.6	90.8	103.1	114.6	128.6
Chemical materials and products, n.e.s	86.4	100.7	99.7	99.1	97.5	101.6	104.9	106.1
Intermediate manufactured products	86.8	100.6	100.2	99.5	98.1	100.0	107.0	113.9
Rubber manufactures	81.4	95.7	100.1	99.8	102.7	110.1	111.2	115.5
Paper and paperboard products	90.8	115.6	100.5	97.4	94.8	98.3	99.2	103.9
Textiles	91.2	102.8	100.2	98.5	100.0	102.7	105.4	111.7
Nonmetallic mineral manufactures	85.8	94.3	100.4	100.8	102.2	100.4	99.9	103.5
Nonferrous metals	87.1	98.2	98.5	98.0	85.3	80.3	95.4	106.1
Manufactures of metals, n.e.s	81.2	92.3	100.9	101.5	102.5	104.8	108.4	118.3
Machinery and transport equipment [2]	97.9	102.8	100.0	100.3	98.9	97.8	98.2	98.7
Power generating machinery [3]	77.0	88.5	99.7	102.3	104.5	107.2	108.7	111.3
Machinery specialized for particular industries	82.7	94.0	100.2	100.3	101.8	102.6	105.4	110.7
Metalworking machinery	82.1	92.3	99.3	101.0	99.9	101.0	100.0	103.7
General industrial machines, parts, n.e.s	82.5	92.0	100.1	101.3	102.3	102.4	104.9	109.3
Computer equipment and office machines	193.2	147.5	99.9	95.6	90.4	88.1	87.2	80.9
Computer equipment	234.5	160.7	99.7	96.0	92.1	88.1	83.9	77.5
Telecommunications [4]	97.3	103.8	100.3	99.8	97.7	93.8	91.8	89.7
Electrical machinery and equipment	112.7	117.2	99.8	98.3	93.9	89.7	88.2	87.4
Road vehicles	88.7	96.1	100.0	100.2	100.5	101.1	102.4	103.0
Miscellaneous manufactured articles	90.5	98.6	99.7	100.1	100.4	101.2	100.9	102.1

NA Not available.   [1] June 2000 may not equal 100 because indexes were reweighted to an "average" trade value in 2000.   [2] Excludes military and commercial aircraft.   [3] Includes equipment.   [4] Includes sound recording and reproducing equipment.

Source: U.S. Bureau of Labor Statistics, *U.S. Import and Export Price Indexes*, monthly.

Table 723. **Import Price Indexes—Selected Commodities: 1990 to 2005**

[2000 = 100. As of June. Indexes are weighted by the 2000 Tariff Schedule of the United States Annotated, a scheme for describing and reporting product composition and value of U.S. imports. Import prices are based on U.S. dollar prices paid by importer]

Commodity	1990	1995	2000 [1]	2001	2002	2003	2004	2005
All commodities	90.8	101.4	100.2	97.6	94.1	96.2	101.7	109.2
Food and live animals	92.1	108.6	99.0	96.0	94.5	99.4	106.9	113.9
Meat	118.4	100.8	100.8	106.2	104.0	102.9	128.9	138.5
Fish	70.9	92.5	99.3	90.0	79.8	81.3	84.1	87.8
Beverages and tobacco	76.5	88.6	100.4	101.7	103.0	103.9	105.3	108.5
Crude materials	90.4	109.5	99.4	102.8	96.4	99.5	125.8	130.5
Mineral fuels and related products	54.7	61.9	101.3	90.4	86.1	101.7	131.5	179.0
Crude petroleum and petroleum products	54.8	63.0	102.2	89.3	85.9	97.6	130.0	182.4
Natural gas	54.9	49.3	95.2	97.4	83.6	130.1	140.0	148.5
Chemicals and related products	93.7	106.8	99.8	100.5	97.0	100.1	103.8	112.4
Intermediate manufactured products	91.3	102.7	100.4	98.0	92.8	94.4	106.1	112.8
Machinery and transport equipment	100.8	112.4	100.1	98.5	97.1	95.8	95.1	95.0
Computer equipment and office machines	198.5	167.2	99.9	93.6	87.8	81.8	75.5	70.5
Computer equipment	284.6	198.4	100.4	89.3	80.3	71.9	64.9	58.2
Telecommunications [2]	120.9	119.1	100.2	97.2	94.4	89.3	84.7	82.1
Electrical machinery and equipment	111.3	122.9	100.7	98.8	97.1	95.4	94.7	94.4
Road vehicles	82.0	97.3	100.1	99.8	100.2	100.7	102.4	103.8
Miscellaneous manufactured articles	94.7	103.2	99.7	99.8	98.6	99.7	99.9	101.0
Plumbing, heating & lighting fixtures	102.0	107.4	99.2	99.2	98.8	96.9	96.5	96.4
Furniture and parts	96.0	103.1	99.6	98.5	98.8	100.2	102.3	106.4
Articles of apparel and clothing	96.5	99.0	99.6	100.6	99.7	100.6	100.7	100.6
Footwear	96.5	99.3	99.6	100.1	99.2	100.0	100.4	100.5

[1] June 1995 and 2000 may not equal 100 because indexes were reweighted to an "average" trade value in 1995 and 2000.   [2] Includes sound recording and reproducing equipment.

Source: U.S. Bureau of Labor Statistics, *U.S. Import and Export Price Indexes*, monthly.

Section 15
Business Enterprise

This section relates to the place and behavior of the business firm and to business initiative in the American economy. It includes data on the number, type, and size of businesses; financial data of domestic and multinational U.S. corporations; business investments, expenditures, and profits; and sales and inventories.

The principal sources of these data are the *Survey of Current Business,* published by the Bureau of Economic Analysis (BEA), the *Statistical Supplement to the Federal Reserve Bulletin,* issued by the Board of Governors of the Federal Reserve System, the annual *Statistics of Income (SOI)* reports of the Internal Revenue Service (IRS), and the Census Bureau's Economic Census, *County Business Patterns, Quarterly Financial Report for Manufacturing, Mining, and Trade Corporations (QFR), Survey of Business Owners,* and *Annual Capital Expenditures Survey.*

Business firms—A firm is generally defined as a business organization under a single management and may include one or more establishments. The terms firm, business, company, and enterprise are used interchangeably throughout this section. A firm doing business in more than one industry is classified by industry according to the major activity of the firm as a whole.

The IRS concept of a business firm relates primarily to the legal entity used for tax reporting purposes. A sole proprietorship is an unincorporated business owned by one person and may include large enterprises with many employees and hired managers and part-time operators. A partnership is an unincorporated business owned by two or more persons, each of whom has a financial interest in the business. A corporation is a business that is legally incorporated under state laws. While many corporations file consolidated tax returns, most corporate tax returns represent individual corporations, some of which are affiliated through common ownership or control with other corporations filing separate returns.

Economic census—The economic census is the major source of facts about the structure and functioning of the nation's economy. It provides essential information for government, business, industry, and the general public. It furnishes an important part of the framework for such composite measures as the gross domestic product estimates, input/output measures, production and price indexes, and other statistical series that measure short-term changes in economic conditions. The Census Bureau takes the economic census every 5 years, covering years ending in "2" and "7."

The economic census is collected on an establishment basis. A company operating at more than one location is required to file a separate report for each store, factory, shop, or other location. Each establishment is assigned a separate industry classification based on its primary activity and not that of its parent company. Establishments responding to the establishment survey are classified into industries on the basis of their principal product or activity (determined by annual sales volume). The statistics issued by industry in the 2002 Economic Census are classified primarily on the 2002 North American Industry Classification System (NAICS), and, to a lesser extent, on the 1997 NAICS used in the previous census (see below).

More detailed information about the scope, coverage, methodology, classification system, data items, and publications for each of the economic censuses and related surveys is published in the *Guide to the 2002 Economic Census* at <http://www.census.gov/econ/census02/guide/index.html>.

Data from the 2002 Economic Census were released through the Census Bureau's American FactFinder service, on

CD-ROM, in Adobe Acrobat PDF reports and in hypertext "drill-down" tables available on the Census Bureau Web site. For more information on these various media of release, see the following page on the Census Bureau Web site <http://www.census.gov/econ/census02/>.

Survey of Business Owners—The Survey of Business Owners (SBO), formerly known as the Surveys of Minority- and Women-Owned Business Enterprises (SMOBE/SWOBE), provides statistics that describe the composition of U.S. businesses by gender, Hispanic or Latino origin, and race. Data from SBO are published in a series of reports: *American Indian- and Alaska Native-Owned Firms, Asian-Owned Firms, Black-Owned Firms, Hispanic-Owned Firms, Native Hawaiian- and Other Pacific Islander-Owned Firms* and *Women-Owned Firms*. Data are presented by industry classifications and/or geographic area and size of firm (employment and receipts). The reports include totals for all U.S. businesses based on the 2002 Economic Census and estimates of business ownership by gender, Hispanic or Latino origin, and race based on the 2002 SBO. Each owner had the option of selecting more than one race and therefore is included in each race selected. For information on confidentiality protection and survey methodology, see Appendix III and the SBO Web site <http://www.census.gov/csd/sbo/>.

North American Industry Classification System (NAICS)—NAICS has replaced the previous Standard Industrial Classification (SIC) system.

NAICS 2002 is the same as NAICS 1997 for 14 of the 20 sectors. Construction and wholesale trade are substantially changed, but the revisions also modify a number of retail classifications and the organization of the information sector. Very minor boundary adjustments affect administrative and support services and mining. NAICS also reflects, in a much more explicit way, the enormous changes in technology and in the growth and

diversification of services that have marked recent decades. A key feature of NAICS is the revision for the Information sector. A few of the new and important industries created in this section include: Internet service providers and Web search portals, and Internet publishing and broadcasting. Also included in the Information sector is electronic shopping and electronic auctions.

Quarterly Financial Report—The Quarterly Financial Report (QFR) program publishes quarterly aggregate statistics on the financial conditions of U.S. corporations. The QFR requests companies to report estimates from their statements of income and retained earnings, and balance sheets. The statistical data are classified and aggregated by type of industry and asset size. The QFR sample includes manufacturing companies with assets of $250 thousand and above, and mining, wholesale, and retail companies with assets of $50 million and above. The data are available quarterly in the *Quarterly Financial Report for Manufacturing, Mining, and Trade Corporations* on the Internet at <http://www.census.gov/csd/qfr/>.

Multinational Companies—BEA collects data on financial and operating data on U.S. multinational companies. These data provide a picture of the overall activities of foreign affiliates and U.S. parent companies, using a variety of indicators of their financial structure and operations. The data on foreign affiliates cover the entire operations of the affiliate, irrespective of the percentage of U.S. ownership. These data cover items that are needed in analyzing the characteristics, performance, and economic impact of multinational companies, such as sales, value added, employment and compensation of employees, capital expenditures, exports and imports, and research and development expenditures. Separate tabulations are available for all affiliates and for affiliates that are majority-owned by their U.S. parent(s).

Table 724. **Number of Returns, Receipts, and Net Income by Type of Business: 1980 to 2003**

[8,932 represents 8,932,000. Covers active enterprises only. Figures are estimates based on sample of unaudited tax returns; see Appendix III. Minus sign (−) indicates net loss]

Item	Number of returns (1,000)			Business receipts [2] (bil. dol.)			Net income (less loss) [3] (bil. dol.)		
	Nonfarm propri- etor- ships [1]	Partner- ships	Corpora- tions	Nonfarm propri- etor- ships [1]	Partner- ships	Corpora- tions	Nonfarm propri- etor- ships [1]	Partner- ships	Corpora- tions
1980	8,932	1,380	2,711	411	286	6,172	55	8	239
1985	11,929	1,714	3,277	540	349	8,050	79	−9	240
1990	14,783	1,554	3,717	731	541	10,914	141	17	371
1991	15,181	1,515	3,803	713	539	10,963	142	21	345
1992	15,495	1,485	3,869	737	571	11,272	154	43	402
1993	15,848	1,468	3,965	757	627	11,814	156	67	498
1994	16,154	1,494	4,342	791	732	12,858	167	82	577
1995	16,424	1,581	4,474	807	854	13,969	169	107	714
1996	16,955	1,654	4,631	843	1,042	14,890	177	145	806
1997	17,176	1,759	4,710	870	1,297	15,890	187	168	915
1998	17,409	1,855	4,849	918	1,534	16,543	202	187	838
1999	17,576	1,937	4,936	969	1,829	18,009	208	228	929
2000	17,905	2,058	5,045	1,021	2,316	19,593	215	269	928
2001	18,338	2,132	5,136	1,017	2,569	19,308	217	276	604
2002	18,926	2,242	5,267	1,030	2,669	18,849	221	271	564
2003	19,710	2,375	5,401	1,050	2,818	19,755	230	301	780

[1] In 1980, represents individually-owned businesses, including farms; thereafter, represents only nonfarm proprietors, i.e., business owners. [2] Excludes investment income except for partnerships and corporations in finance, insurance, and real estate before 1998. Beginning 1998, finance and insurance, real estate, and management of companies included investment income for partnerships and corporations. Starting 1985, investment income no longer included for S corporations. [3] Net income (less loss) is defined differently by form of organization, basically as follows: (a) Proprietorships: Total taxable receipts less total business deductions, including cost of sales and operations, depletion, and certain capital expensing, excluding charitable contributions and owners' salaries; (b) Partnerships: Total taxable receipts (including investment income except capital gains) less deductions, including cost of sales and operations and certain payments to partners, excluding charitable contributions, oil and gas depletion, and certain capital expensing; (c) Corporations: Total taxable receipts (including investment income, capital gains, and income from foreign subsidiaries deemed received for tax purposes, except for S corporations beginning 1985) less business deductions, including cost of sales and operations, depletion, certain capital expensing, and officers' compensation excluding S corporation charitable contributions and investment expenses starting 1985; net income is before income tax.

Source: U.S. Internal Revenue Service, *Statistics of Income*, various publications.

Table 725. **Number of Returns and Business Receipts by Size of Receipts: 1990 to 2003**

[3,717 represents 3,717,000. Covers active enterprises only. Figures are estimates based on sample of unaudited tax returns; see Appendix III]

Size-class of receipts	Returns (1,000)					Business receipts [1] (bil. dol.)				
	1990	2000	2001	2002	2003	1990	2000	2001	2002	2003
Corporations	3,717	5,045	5,136	5,267	5,401	10,914	19,593	19,308	18,849	19,755
Under $25,000 [2]	879	1,220	1,248	1,283	1,280	5	4	3	4	3
$25,000 to $49,999	252	302	296	314	346	9	10	11	12	13
$50,000 to $99,999	359	477	485	514	522	26	35	36	38	39
$100,000 to $499,999	1,162	1,515	1,550	1,583	1,649	291	397	388	395	412
$500,000 to $999,999	416	582	601	611	623	294	407	428	434	441
$1,000,000 or more	649	946	956	962	981	10,289	18,738	18,442	17,967	18,848
Partnerships	1,554	2,058	2,132	2,242	2,375	541	2,316	2,569	2,669	2,818
Under $25,000 [2]	963	1,105	1,130	1,204	1,284	4	5	5	5	5
$25,000 to $49,999	126	183	183	185	192	5	7	7	7	7
$50,000 to $99,999	133	187	192	195	206	10	13	14	14	15
$100,000 to $499,999	222	353	373	394	410	51	82	88	92	95
$500,000 to $999,999	52	92	103	105	111	36	66	73	74	78
$1,000,000 or more	57	137	151	159	172	435	2,143	2,383	2,478	2,619
Nonfarm proprietorships	14,783	17,905	18,338	18,926	19,710	731	1,021	1,017	1,030	1,050
Under $25,000 [2]	10,196	11,997	12,345	12,716	13,308	69	82	86	87	93
$25,000 to $49,999	1,660	2,247	2,239	2,358	2,450	58	80	79	83	87
$50,000 to $99,999	1,282	1,645	1,704	1,752	1,805	91	117	121	124	128
$100,000 to $499,999	1,444	1,733	1,759	1,803	1,851	296	355	353	362	373
$500,000 to $999,999	143	190	197	203	200	97	126	133	138	135
$1,000,000 or more	57	92	93	93	96	119	261	245	234	235

[1] Excludes investment income except for partnerships and corporations in finance, insurance, and real estate before 1998. Beginning 1998, finance and insurance, real estate, and management of companies included investment income for partnerships and corporations. [2] Includes firms with no receipts.

Source: U.S. Internal Revenue Service, *Statistics of Income Bulletin*; and unpublished data.

Table 726. Number of Returns, Receipts, and Net Income by Type of Business and Industry: 2003

[**19,710 represents 19,710,000**. Covers active enterprises only. Figures are estimates based on sample of unaudited tax returns; see Appendix III. Based on the North American Industry Classification System (NAICS), 2002; see text, this section. Minus sign (–) indicates net loss]

Industry	NAICS code	Number of returns (1,000)			Business receipts [1] (bil. dol.)			Net income (less loss) (bil. dol.)		
		Non-farm propri-etor-ships	Partner-ships	Corpo-rations	Non-farm propri-etor-ships	Partner-ships	Corpo-rations	Non-farm propri-etor-ships	Partner-ships	Corpo-rations
Total [2]	(X)	19,710	2,375	5,401	1,050	2,818	19,755	230	301	780
Agriculture, forestry, fishing, and hunting [3]	11	264	122	143	15	23	114	1	(–Z)	1
Mining	21	127	28	30	8	69	178	1	19	11
Utilities	22	10	2	9	(Z)	152	522	(Z)	2	–5
Construction	23	2,491	140	676	176	192	1,129	29	14	29
Special trade contractors	238	1,998	54	405	120	32	460	23	2	9
Manufacturing	31-33	309	40	281	22	509	5,195	2	24	186
Wholesale and retail trade [4]	(X)	2,705	171	975	215	568	5,601	12	12	108
Wholesale trade	42	289	44	366	38	293	2,570	4	8	47
Retail trade [5]	44-45	2,416	127	605	177	274	3,030	8	3	62
Motor vehicle and parts dealers	441	141	15	91	34	87	785	1	1	8
Food and beverage stores	445	105	16	91	29	44	469	1	(Z)	5
Gasoline stations	447	24	6	35	20	31	159	(Z)	(Z)	1
Transportation and warehousing	48-49	945	30	183	58	70	548	8	2	2
Information	51	267	32	120	7	162	822	2	1	–4
Broadcasting (except Internet)	515	[6]38	2	(NA)	[6]1	33	(NA)	[6](Z)	(Z)	(NA)
Telecommunications	517	([6])	5	(NA)	([6])	83	(NA)	([6])	–3	(NA)
Finance and insurance	52	659	259	235	64	324	2,575	16	106	303
Real estate and rental and leasing	53	1,074	1,081	577	63	192	207	26	51	6
Professional, scientific, and technical services [5]	54	2,753	151	760	129	212	692	52	51	9
Legal services	5411	345	28	97	34	101	72	15	36	6
Accounting, tax preparation, bookkeeping, and payroll services	5412	381	22	62	12	34	27	4	6	2
Management, scientific, and technical consulting services.	5416	659	33	212	28	27	151	14	5	4
Management of companies and enterprises	55	(NA)	22	47	(NA)	25	677	(NA)	8	93
Administrative and support and waste management and remediation services	56	1,881	44	243	47	51	360	13	3	7
Educational services	61	452	9	44	5	3	30	2	(–Z)	1
Health care and social assistance	62	1,763	54	355	99	106	488	40	14	19
Arts, entertainment and recreation	71	1,098	43	110	24	47	70	5	–2	1
Accommodation and food services	72	395	81	279	40	97	382	1	–1	7
Accommodation	721	53	26	36	5	45	107	(Z)	–2	–
Food services and drinking places	722	342	55	243	35	52	276	1	1	7
Other services [5]	81	2,263	63	329	74	18	165	18	(Z)	4
Auto repair and maintenance	8111	358	21	103	23	6	59	3	(Z)	1
Personal and laundry services.	812	1,239	30	135	32	7	67	10	(–Z)	2
Religious, grantmaking, civic, professional, and similar organizations	813	268	1	36	3	(Z)	9	2	(Z)	–
Unclassified.	(X)	254	2	5	3	(Z)	–	(Z)	1	–

– Represents zero.   NA Not available.   Z Less than $500 million.   [1] Includes investment income for partnerships and corporations in finance and insurance, real estate, and management of companies industries.   Excludes investment income for S corporations.   [2] For corporations, includes businesses not allocable to individual industries.   [3] For corporations, represents agricultural services only.   [4] For corporations, includes trade business not identified as wholesale or retail.   [5] Includes other industries not shown separately.   [6] Broadcasting includes telecommunications.

Source: U.S. Internal Revenue Service, *Statistics of Income,* various publications.

488   Business Enterprise

Table 727. Nonfarm Sole Proprietorships—Selected Income and Deduction Items: 1990 to 2003

[In billions of dollars (731 represents $731,000,000,000) except as indicated. All figures are estimates based on samples. Tax law changes have affected the comparability of the data over time; see *Statistics of Income* reports for a description. See Appendix III]

Item	1990	1995	1997	1998	1999	2000	2001	2002	2003
Number of returns (1,000)	14,783	16,424	17,176	17,409	17,576	17,905	18,338	18,926	19,710
Returns with net income (1,000).	11,222	12,213	12,703	13,080	13,159	13,308	13,604	13,751	14,448
Business receipts	731	807	870	918	969	1,021	1,017	1,030	1,050
Income from sales and operations . . .	719	797	858	905	955	1,008	1,002	1,015	1,034
Business deductions [1]	589	638	684	716	761	806	800	809	820
Cost of goods sold/operations [1]	291	307	320	341	370	387	363	352	338
Purchases	210	219	224	231	256	269	247	227	218
Labor costs.	23	24	25	27	29	29	28	30	28
Materials and supplies	30	34	38	42	42	43	44	46	47
Advertising.	(NA)	(NA)	9	9	9	10	11	11	12
Car and truck expenses	22	33	39	40	41	46	47	50	53
Commissions	9	10	11	11	11	12	12	14	14
Depreciation.	24	27	29	29	31	32	33	37	42
Insurance.	13	13	13	13	13	14	14	16	17
Interest paid	13	10	11	11	11	12	13	11	11
Office expenses	(NA)	(NA)	9	10	10	10	11	11	12
Rent paid.	23	28	29	30	31	33	34	35	36
Repairs	9	10	11	11	12	12	12	13	13
Salaries and wages (net)	47	54	58	59	61	63	64	66	68
Supplies	(NA)	(NA)	20	20	22	22	23	25	26
Taxes paid	10	13	14	14	14	14	14	15	15
Utilities	14	17	19	18	18	19	20	21	22
Net income (less loss) [2].	141	169	187	202	208	215	217	221	230
Net income [2]	162	192	210	226	233	245	250	257	269
Constant (2000) Dollars [3]									
Business receipts	896	877	912	952	991	1,021	993	991	991
Business deductions	722	693	717	742	778	806	781	778	774
Net income (less loss)	173	184	196	210	213	215	212	213	217
Net income.	198	208	221	235	239	245	244	248	254

NA Not available. [1] Includes other amounts not shown separately. [2] After adjustment for the passive loss carryover from prior years. Therefore, "business receipts" minus "total deductions" do not equal "net income." [3] Based on the overall implicit price deflator for gross domestic product.

Source: U.S. Internal Revenue Service, *Statistics of Income Bulletin.*

Table 728. Partnerships—Selected Income and Balance Sheet Items: 1990 to 2003

[In billions of dollars (1,735 represents $1,735,000,000,000), except as indicated. Covers active partnerships only. All figures are estimates based on samples. See Appendix III]

Item	1990	1995	1997	1998	1999	2000	2001	2002	2003
Number of returns (1,000)	1,554	1,581	1,759	1,855	1,937	2,058	2,132	2,242	2,375
Returns with net income (1,000).	854	955	1,092	1,171	1,226	1,261	1,301	1,325	1,357
Number of partners (1,000).	17,095	15,606	16,184	15,663	15,924	13,660	14,232	14,328	14,108
Assets [1, 2]	1,735	2,719	4,171	5,127	5,999	6,694	8,428	8,867	9,675
Depreciable assets (net)	681	767	980	1,153	1,314	1,487	1,646	1,792	1,846
Inventories, end of year	57	88	147	176	174	150	208	203	214
Land	215	221	257	291	326	359	392	423	455
Liabilities [1, 2]	1,415	1,886	2,658	3,151	3,453	3,696	4,835	4,972	5,303
Accounts payable	67	91	159	191	244	230	362	346	276
Short-term debt [3].	88	124	127	230	232	252	289	283	274
Long-term debt [4].	498	544	706	884	989	1,132	1,286	1,375	1,389
Nonrecourse loans	470	466	492	523	582	639	700	770	800
Partners' capital accounts [2]	320	832	1,513	1,976	2,546	2,999	3,593	3,895	4,372
Receipts [1]	566	890	1,354	1,603	1,907	2,405	2,665	2,773	2,923
Business receipts [5]	483	854	1,297	1,534	1,829	2,316	2,569	2,669	2,818
Interest received	21	31	41	51	62	82	85	70	71
Deductions [1]	550	784	1,186	1,416	1,679	2,136	2,389	2,502	2,621
Cost of goods sold/operations	243	395	625	737	902	1,226	1,338	1,430	1,523
Salaries and wages	56	80	115	143	170	201	231	238	245
Taxes paid	9	13	18	24	27	31	35	36	39
Interest paid	30	43	60	73	74	93	97	68	65
Depreciation.	60	23	38	43	52	59	72	83	84
Net income (less loss)	17	107	168	187	228	269	276	271	301
Net income.	116	179	262	298	298	410	446	440	469

[1] Includes items not shown separately. [2] Assets, liabilities, and partners' capital accounts are understated because not all partnerships file complete balance sheets. [3] Mortgages, notes, and bonds payable in less than 1 year. [4] Mortgages, notes, and bonds payable in 1 year or more. [5] Excludes investment income except for partnerships in finance, insurance, and real estate from 1995 to 1997. Beginning 1998, finance and insurance, real estate, and management of companies included investment income for partnerships.

Source: U.S. Internal Revenue Service, *Statistics of Income,* various issues.

Business Enterprise 489

Table 729. Partnerships—Selected Items by Industry: 2003

[In billions of dollars (9,675 represents $9,675,000,000,000), except as indicated. Covers active partnerships only. Figures are estimates based on samples. Based on the North American Industry Classification System (NAICS), 2002; see text, this section. See Appendix III]

Industry	NAICS code	Number of partnerships (1,000)			Total assets [1]	Business receipts [2]	Total deductions	Net income less loss	Net income	Net loss
		Total	With net income	With net loss						
Total [3]	(X)	2,375	1,357	1,018	9,675	2,818	2,621	301.4	468.6	167.2
Agriculture, forestry, fishing and hunting	11	122	64	58	84	23	29	−0.3	5.2	5.5
Mining	21	28	17	11	140	69	58	18.6	23.0	4.4
Utilities	22	2	1	1	145	152	153	1.6	5.7	4.1
Construction	23	140	82	59	155	192	183	13.6	18.5	4.9
Manufacturing	31-33	40	19	22	373	509	499	24.2	37.2	13.1
Wholesale trade	42	44	22	22	84	293	290	8.3	10.9	2.6
Retail trade	44-45	127	58	69	90	274	277	3.5	7.9	4.4
Transportation and warehousing	48-49	30	15	15	104	70	71	1.9	5.8	3.9
Information	51	32	10	21	391	162	172	1.2	19.9	18.7
Finance and insurance	52	259	189	70	5,007	324	219	105.6	125.5	19.9
Real estate and rental and leasing	53	1,081	618	463	2,393	192	150	51.4	106.2	54.8
Professional, scientific, and technical services	54	151	96	55	100	212	175	50.8	55.9	5.1
Management of companies and enterprises	55	22	11	10	308	25	17	7.9	13.5	5.6
Admin/support waste mgt./remediation services	56	44	27	17	27	51	50	3.0	4.3	1.3
Educational services	61	9	3	6	3	3	3	−0.1	0.4	0.4
Health care and social assistance	62	54	33	21	64	106	101	13.6	17.2	3.6
Arts, entertainment and recreation	71	43	14	30	55	47	54	−2.3	4.1	6.4
Accommodation and food services	72	81	39	42	140	97	103	−1.4	5.6	7.0
Other services	81	63	37	25	13	18	18	0.3	1.7	1.4

X Not applicable.   [1] Total assets are understated because not all partnerships file complete balance sheets.   [2] Finance and insurance, real estate, and management of companies includes investment income for partnerships.   [3] Includes businesses not allocable to individual industries.

Source: U.S. Internal Revenue Service, *Statistics of Income*, various issues.

Table 730. Nonfarm Noncorporate Business-Sector Balance Sheet: 1990 to 2005

[In billions of dollars (3,712 represents $3,712,000,000,000), except as noted. Represents year-end outstandings]

Item	1990	1995	1999	2000	2001	2002	2003	2004	2005
Assets	**3,712**	**4,092**	**5,767**	**6,422**	**6,705**	**6,997**	**7,441**	**8,214**	**9,342**
Tangible assets	3,356	3,544	4,591	5,000	5,126	5,340	5,700	6,196	6,980
Real estate [1]	3,045	3,194	4,177	4,562	4,682	4,882	5,224	5,688	6,434
Residential	2,126	2,349	3,096	3,375	3,516	3,688	3,983	4,375	4,990
Nonresidential	919	845	1,081	1,187	1,166	1,193	1,241	1,313	1,444
Equipment and software [2]	263	294	348	367	377	390	406	430	462
Residential [3]	32	36	37	39	40	40	40	42	46
Nonresidential	232	259	311	329	338	350	365	388	416
Inventories [2]	47	56	66	70	67	69	71	78	83
Financial assets	356	548	1,176	1,423	1,579	1,657	1,741	2,018	2,363
Checkable deposits and currency	71	105	156	164	165	167	171	189	214
Time and savings deposits	51	71	180	248	255	269	313	365	429
Money market fund shares	7	17	41	49	59	61	53	62	73
Treasury securities	13	24	37	40	43	43	45	52	61
Municipal securities	–	2	3	2	4	3	3	3	4
Mortgages	31	22	24	23	27	26	26	30	35
Trade receivables	98	140	273	342	344	363	339	394	464
Miscellaneous assets	86	167	464	554	684	724	792	922	1,084
Insurance receivables	39	44	46	46	48	52	57	60	65
Equity investment in GSEs [4]	1	1	2	2	2	2	2	2	3
Other	47	122	416	506	634	670	733	859	1,016
Liabilities	**1,349**	**1,396**	**2,332**	**2,674**	**2,890**	**3,085**	**3,180**	**3,554**	**3,965**
Credit market instruments	1,093	1,062	1,600	1,797	1,959	2,108	2,205	2,448	2,749
Bank loans n.e.c. [5]	136	165	313	361	405	430	442	465	504
Other loans and advances	94	92	117	128	125	128	133	135	138
Mortgages	863	805	1,170	1,308	1,429	1,550	1,630	1,848	2,107
Trade payables	60	86	213	260	255	281	257	286	322
Taxes payable	32	33	53	65	69	70	70	78	87
Miscellaneous liabilities	164	215	467	553	607	626	649	743	808
Net worth	**2,363**	**2,696**	**3,435**	**3,749**	**3,814**	**3,912**	**4,261**	**4,660**	**5,377**
Debt/net worth (percent)	46.3	39.4	46.6	47.9	51.4	53.9	51.7	52.5	51.1

– Represents or rounds to zero.   [1] At market value.   [2] At replacement (current) cost.   [3] Durable goods in rental properties.   [4] GSEs = government-sponsored enterprises. Equity in the Farm Credit System.   [5] Not elsewhere classified.

Source: Board of Governors of the Federal Reserve System, "Federal Reserve Statistical Release, Z.1, Flow of Funds Accounts of the United States"; published 9 March 2006; <http://www.federalreserve.gov/releases/Z1/20060309/data.htm>.

Table 731. **Nonfinancial Corporate Business-Sector Balance Sheet: 1990 to 2005**

[In billions of dollars (9,683 represents $9,683,000,000,000). Represents year-end outstandings]

Item	1990	1995	1999	2000	2001	2002	2003	2004	2005
Assets.	9,683	11,460	16,647	19,016	19,124	19,457	20,068	21,386	22,731
Tangible assets	6,108	6,501	8,553	9,243	9,225	9,516	9,959	10,736	11,754
Real estate [1]	3,388	3,145	4,437	4,843	4,792	5,019	5,355	5,852	6,594
Equipment and software [2]	1,819	2,287	2,864	3,067	3,167	3,193	3,257	3,403	3,579
Inventories [2]	901	1,070	1,252	1,334	1,266	1,303	1,347	1,481	1,581
Financial assets [3]	3,575	4,959	8,094	9,772	9,899	9,942	10,109	10,650	10,977
Foreign deposits	15	17	31	24	16	20	38	45	79
Checkable deposits and currency	166	205	231	246	182	149	200	252	227
Time and savings deposits	75	100	237	272	281	291	363	426	452
Money market fund shares	20	60	155	191	302	328	290	278	286
Commercial paper	14	20	48	58	60	65	76	96	104
Consumer credit	67	85	79	84	76	78	63	65	63
Trade receivables	967	1,185	1,655	1,937	1,815	1,717	1,698	1,822	1,985
Mutual fund shares [1]	10	46	127	124	113	95	125	143	165
Liabilities [3]	4,729	6,010	8,407	9,611	9,809	9,923	9,867	10,120	10,122
Credit market instruments.	2,533	2,910	4,190	4,536	4,758	4,783	4,890	5,065	5,354
Commercial paper	117	157	230	278	190	126	86	102	94
Municipal securities [4]	115	135	153	154	158	161	164	169	176
Corporate bonds [5]	1,008	1,344	2,068	2,230	2,578	2,710	2,869	2,946	3,007
Bank loans n.e.c. [6]	545	602	809	853	744	636	562	564	635
Other loans and advances	473	454	585	651	659	675	681	702	777
Mortgages	274	218	345	369	430	476	529	581	665
Trade payables	626	878	1,228	1,541	1,438	1,457	1,403	1,509	1,626
Taxes payable	38	40	71	78	81	93	81	88	90
Net worth (market value)	4,954	5,450	8,240	9,404	9,315	9,535	10,201	11,266	12,608
Debt/net worth (percent).	51.1	53.4	50.9	48.2	51.1	50.2	47.9	45.0	42.5

[1] At market value.   [2] At replacement (current) cost.   [3] Includes items not shown separately.   [4] Industrial revenue bonds. Issued by state and local governments to finance private investment and secured in interest and principal by the industrial user of the funds.   [5] Through 1992, corporate bonds include net issues by Netherlands Antillean financial subsidiaries.   [6] Not elsewhere classified.

Source: Board of Governors of the Federal Reserve System, "Federal Reserve Statistical Release, Z.1, Flow of Funds Accounts of the United States"; published 9 March 2006; <http://www.federalreserve.gov/releases/Z1/20060309/data.htm>.

Table 732. **Corporate Funds—Sources and Uses: 1990 to 2005**

[In billions of dollars (238 represents $238,000,000,000). Covers nonfarm nonfinancial corporate business]

Item	1990	1995	1999	2000	2001	2002	2003	2004	2005
Profits before tax (book)	238	419	457	422	310	336	448	574	867
– Taxes on corporate income	98	141	171	170	111	97	126	165	249
– Net dividends	117	177	223	250	243	253	293	359	235
+ Capital consumption allowance [1]	365	463	598	629	678	734	737	804	668
= U.S. internal funds, book	388	564	661	632	633	721	765	854	1,051
+ Foreign earnings retained abroad	45	53	69	100	111	93	123	125	–9
+ Inventory valuation adjustment (IVA)	–13	–18	3	–14	11	–2	–13	–40	–24
= Internal funds + IVA	420	598	731	718	755	811	876	939	1,019
Gross investment	369	653	846	900	883	782	821	984	1,077
Capital expenditures	429	618	864	929	800	737	751	861	925
Fixed investment [2]	422	577	806	882	839	734	748	823	915
Inventory change + IVA	12	40	66	55	–30	14	14	50	24
Nonproduced nonfinancial assets	–5	1	–8	–9	–9	–11	–11	–12	–13
Net financial investment	–59	36	–18	–28	82	45	69	123	151
Net acquisition of financial assets [3]	124	426	970	1,209	178	130	83	501	307
Foreign deposits	(Z)	2	1	–7	–9	4	18	6	34
Checkable deposits and currency	6	4	36	15	–65	–32	50	52	–25
Time and savings deposits.	–6	3	44	35	9	10	71	63	26
Commercial paper	(Z)	1	8	10	2	5	11	20	8
Municipal securities	–8	–20	–1	7	–3	3	3	5	10
Trade receivables	29	78	207	282	–122	–99	–19	125	163
Miscellaneous assets [3]	114	320	666	811	254	192	–10	234	74
U.S. direct investment abroad [4]	36	90	194	128	119	138	109	233	–31
Insurance receivables	13	8	1	(Z)	10	17	18	19	23
Net increase in liabilities [3]	184	391	988	1,237	95	85	13	379	156
Net funds raised in markets	71	169	262	228	173	–17	27	33	–73
Net new equity issues	–63	–58	–110	–118	–48	–42	–58	–141	–366
Credit market instruments [3]	134	227	373	346	221	25	85	174	293
Corporate bonds [4]	47	91	222	163	348	132	158	78	61
Bank loans n.e.c [5]	3	75	40	44	–110	–108	–86	3	71
Other loans and advances [3]	56	32	23	66	8	16	6	21	75
Finance companies	16	24	49	57	–10	7	2	13	29
Rest of the world	50	(Z)	–23	–2	–2	10	–1	6	61
Asset-backed securities issuers .	4	6	–3	7	18	–3	–1	–1	–19
Mortgages	19	8	45	24	60	46	43	52	84
Trade payables	28	81	178	313	–104	20	–55	106	117
Miscellaneous liabilities [3]	84	141	540	689	23	70	53	233	110
Foreign direct investment in U.S.	59	54	179	192	85	28	24	25	43

Z Less than $500 million.   [1] Consumption of fixed capital plus capital consumption adjustment.   [2] Nonresidential fixed investment plus residential fixed investment.   [3] Includes other items not shown separately.   [4] 1990, corporate bonds include net issues by Netherlands Antillean financial subsidiaries, and U.S. direct investment abroad excludes net inflows from those bond issues.   [5] Not elsewhere classified.

Source: Board of Governors of the Federal Reserve System, "Federal Reserve Statistical Release, Z.1, Flow of Funds Accounts of the United States"; published 9 March 2006; <http://www.federalreserve.gov/releases/Z1/20060309/data.htm>.

Table 733. **Corporations—Selected Financial Items: 1990 to 2003**

[In billions of dollars (18,190 represents $18,190,000,000,000), except as noted. Covers active corporations only. All corporations are required to file returns except those specifically exempt. See source for changes in law affecting comparability of historical data. Based on samples; see Appendix III]

Item	1990	1995	1997	1998	1999	2000	2001	2002	2003
Number of returns (1,000)	3,717	4,474	4,710	4,849	4,936	5,045	5,136	5,267	5,401
Number with net income (1,000) . . .	1,911	2,455	2,647	2,761	2,812	2,819	2,822	2,801	2,932
S Corporation returns [1] (1,000)	1,575	2,153	2,452	2,588	2,726	2,860	2,986	3,154	3,342
Assets [2]	18,190	26,014	33,030	37,347	41,464	47,027	49,154	50,414	53,645
Cash	771	962	1,299	1,336	1,597	1,820	1,926	1,923	2,120
Notes and accounts receivable	4,198	5,307	6,632	7,062	7,745	8,754	8,756	8,886	8,995
Inventories.	894	1,045	1,114	1,139	1,198	1,272	1,208	1,221	1,267
Investments in government obligations	921	1,363	1,343	1,366	1,340	1,236	1,392	1,527	1,656
Mortgage and real estate	1,538	1,713	2,029	2,414	2,555	2,822	3,229	3,687	4,073
Other investments.	4,137	7,429	10,756	13,201	15,799	17,874	18,344	18,728	20,536
Depreciable assets	4,318	5,571	6,208	6,541	6,936	7,292	7,614	7,678	7,805
Depletable assets	129	154	177	193	184	191	199	226	237
Land.	210	242	262	271	286	303	320	326	342
Liabilities [2]	18,190	26,014	33,030	37,347	41,464	47,027	49,154	50,414	53,645
Accounts payable	1,094	1,750	2,111	2,501	2,792	3,758	3,927	4,074	4,338
Short-term debt [3]	1,803	2,034	2,582	3,216	3,658	4,020	4,132	3,814	4,002
Long-term debt [4].	2,665	3,335	4,072	4,813	5,448	6,184	6,782	7,185	7,384
Net worth	4,739	8,132	11,353	13,108	15,363	17,349	17,615	17,545	18,819
Capital stock.	1,585	2,194	2,951	3,244	3,522	3,966	4,253	4,000	3,151
Paid-in or capital surplus.	2,814	5,446	7,253	8,610	10,186	12,265	13,920	15,287	15,258
Retained earnings [5]	1,410	2,191	3,113	3,373	3,970	3,627	2,132	1,111	2,282
Receipts [2, 6]	11,410	14,539	16,610	17,324	18,892	20,606	20,273	19,749	20,690
Business receipts [6, 7]	9,860	12,786	14,461	15,010	16,314	17,637	17,504	17,297	18,264
Interest [8]	977	1,039	1,140	1,277	1,354	1,628	1,549	1,282	1,182
Rents and royalties	133	145	176	200	223	254	251	252	270
Deductions [2, 6].	11,033	13,821	15,704	16,489	17,967	19,692	19,683	19,199	19,941
Cost of sales and operations [7]	6,611	8,206	9,114	9,362	10,284	11,135	11,042	10,607	11,319
Compensation of officers	205	304	336	357	374	401	383	381	389
Rent paid on business property	185	232	265	308	347	380	398	411	407
Taxes paid.	251	326	350	355	371	390	392	397	417
Interest paid.	825	744	866	967	1,019	1,272	1,203	913	818
Depreciation	333	437	513	542	584	614	650	711	692
Advertising	126	163	188	198	216	234	220	218	225
Net income (less loss) [6, 9]	371	714	915	838	929	928	604	564	780
Net income	553	881	1,118	1,091	1,229	1,337	1,112	1,053	1,176
Deficit.	182	166	202	253	300	409	509	489	396
Income subject to tax	366	565	684	663	694	760	635	601	699
Income tax before credits [10]	119	194	235	231	242	266	221	210	244
Tax credits	32	42	55	50	49	62	54	56	66
Foreign tax credit	25	30	42	37	38	49	41	42	50
Income tax after credits [11]	96	156	184	182	193	204	167	154	178

[1] Represents certain small corporations with up to 75 shareholders (35 for 1990 and 1995), mostly individuals, electing to be taxed at the shareholder level.   [2] Includes items not shown separately.   [3] Payable in less than 1 year.   [4] Payable in 1 year or more.   [5] Appropriated and unappropriated and "adjustments to shareholders' equity."   [6] Receipts, deductions and net income of S corporations are limited to those from trade or business. Those from investments are excluded.   [7] Includes gross sales and cost of sales of securities, commodities, and real estate by exchanges, brokers, or dealers selling on their own accounts. Excludes investment income.   [8] Includes tax-exempt interest in state and local government obligations.   [9] Excludes regulated investment companies.   [10] Consists of regular (and alternative tax) only.   [11] Includes minimum tax, alternative minimum tax, adjustments for prior year credits, and other income-related taxes.

Source: U.S. Internal Revenue Service, *Statistics of Income, Corporation Income Tax Returns*, annual.

492 Business Enterprise

Table 734. Corporations by Receipt-Size Class and Industry: 2003

[**Number of returns in thousands (5,401 represents 5,401,000); receipts and net income in billions of dollars (19,755 represents $19,755,000,000,000).** Covers active enterprises only. Figures are estimates based on a sample of unaudited tax returns; see Appendix III. Numbers in parentheses represent North American Industry Classification System 2002 codes, see text, this section]

Industry	Total	Under $1 mil. [1]	$1 mil.– $4.9 mil.	$5 mil.– $9.9 mil.	$10 mil.– $49.9 mil.	$50 mil. or more
Total: [2]						
Number of returns [3]	5,401	4,420	733	119	104	26
Business receipts [3]	19,755	907	1,553	823	2,139	14,333
Net income (less loss)	780	3	34	18	67	658
Agriculture, forestry, fishing, and hunting (11):						
Number	143	127	13	2	1	–
Business receipts [3]	114	21	25	11	22	36
Mining (21):						
Number	30	24	5	–	1	–
Business receipts [3]	178	4	10	2	14	149
Utilities (22):						
Number	9	8	–	–	–	–
Business receipts [3]	522	1	1	1	2	517
Construction (23):						
Number	676	521	120	19	14	2
Business receipts [3]	1,129	131	258	127	261	353
Manufacturing (31-33):						
Number	281	179	65	15	16	6
Business receipts [3]	5,195	47	147	109	333	4,558
Wholesale and retail trade (42,44-45):						
Number	975	671	211	42	41	10
Business receipts [3]	5,601	180	469	288	892	3,773
Transportation and warehousing (48-49):						
Number	183	146	27	6	4	1
Business receipts [3]	548	26	55	40	73	353
Information (51):						
Number	120	103	11	2	2	1
Business receipts [3]	822	14	24	15	46	723
Finance and insurance (52):						
Number	235	195	25	6	6	3
Business receipts [3]	2,575	36	57	39	129	2,314
Real estate and rental and leasing (53):						
Number	577	552	22	2	2	–
Business receipts [3]	207	51	46	11	28	71
Professional, scientific, and technical services (54):						
Number	760	675	68	9	6	1
Business receipts [3]	692	114	133	66	136	241
Management of companies & enterprises (55):						
Number	47	41	3	1	2	–
Business receipts [3]	677	–	7	10	35	625
Administrative and support and waste management and remediation services (56):						
Number	243	206	31	3	2	1
Business receipts [3]	360	43	66	24	44	182
Educational services (61):						
Number	44	41	3	–	–	–
Business receipts [3]	30	5	6	1	5	12
Health care and social assistance (62):						
Number	355	286	58	6	4	1
Business receipts [3]	488	87	114	38	67	182
Arts, entertainment, and recreation (71):						
Number	110	101	8	1	1	–
Business receipts [3]	70	17	15	4	10	24
Accommodation and food services (72):						
Number	279	235	39	4	1	–
Business receipts [3]	382	65	75	25	26	191
Other services (81):						
Number	329	301	25	2	1	–
Business receipts [3]	165	63	45	13	17	27

– Represents or rounds to zero.   [1] Includes businesses without receipts.   [2] Includes businesses not allocable to individual industries.   [3] Includes investment income for corporations in finance and insurance and management of companies industries. Excludes investment income for S corporations (certain small corporations with up to 75 shareholders, mostly individuals, electing to be taxed at the shareholder level).

Source: U.S. Internal Revenue Service, Statistics of Income, Corporation Income Tax Returns, annual.

Table 735. Corporations by Asset-Size Class and Industry: 2003

[In billions of dollars (126 represents $126,000,000,000), except number of returns. Covers active corporations only. Excludes corporations not allocable by industry. Numbers in parentheses represent North American Industry Classification System 2002 codes, see text, this section]

Industry	Total	Under $10 mil. [1]	$10–$24.9 mil.	$25–$49.9 mil.	$50–$99.9 mil.	$100–$249.9 mil.	$250 mil. and over
Agriculture, forestry, fishing, and hunting (11):							
Returns	143,019	142,112	583	168	86	49	21
Total receipts	126	79	11	7	7	10	12
Mining (21):							
Returns	30,252	29,128	519	226	121	94	163
Total receipts	194	21	6	5	6	9	147
Utilities (22):							
Returns	8,504	8,125	101	60	30	42	146
Total receipts	561	9	2	2	4	4	539
Construction (23):							
Returns	676,120	670,251	4,093	1,005	448	195	128
Total receipts	1,148	699	117	60	51	48	173
Manufacturing (31-33):							
Returns	281,239	267,134	7,054	2,754	1,586	1,228	1,483
Total receipts	5,643	476	187	144	153	240	4,442
Wholesale and retail trade (42, 44-45):							
Returns	975,011	958,482	10,821	2,966	1,260	741	741
Total receipts	5,736	1,799	524	301	224	260	2,628
Transportation and warehousing (48-49):							
Returns	182,881	181,253	925	286	157	121	137
Total receipts	571	185	27	16	16	22	305
Information (51):							
Returns	119,875	117,163	1,260	517	288	257	391
Total receipts	939	76	20	16	17	29	782
Finance and insurance (52):							
Returns	234,746	215,985	3,514	2,593	2,745	3,545	6,365
Total receipts	2,575	172	26	23	30	64	2,261
Real estate and rental and leasing (53):							
Returns	577,400	572,098	3,515	1,000	429	220	138
Total receipts	233	128	16	9	9	13	59
Professional, scientific, and technical services (54):							
Returns	760,087	756,933	1,736	639	328	250	201
Total receipts	720	437	43	28	24	37	151
Management of companies and enterprises (55):							
Returns	46,887	40,291	1,117	1,014	1,355	1,639	1,471
Total receipts	677	6	1	2	6	16	646
Administrative and support and waste management and remediation services (56):							
Returns	242,904	241,891	522	198	114	81	98
Total receipts	378	189	23	14	15	15	122
Educational services (61):							
Returns	44,059	43,909	72	28	23	14	13
Total receipts	31	16	2	1	2	2	7
Health care and social assistance (62):							
Returns	354,603	353,613	517	206	104	92	71
Total receipts	503	325	17	13	11	22	116
Arts, entertainment, and recreation (71):							
Returns	110,119	109,449	399	145	44	52	30
Total receipts	77	43	5	3	2	7	16
Accommodation and food services (72):							
Returns	278,722	277,468	718	214	112	88	122
Total receipts	407	181	14	9	10	20	173
Other services (81):							
Returns	329,336	328,899	276	66	46	24	24
Total receipts	171	136	5	3	4	6	16

[1] Includes returns with zero assets.

Source: U.S. Internal Revenue Service, *Statistics of Income, Corporation Income Tax Returns*, annual.

Table 736. **Economic Census Summary (NAICS 1997 Basis): 1997 and 2002**

[**25 represents 25,000**. Data for 2002 are preliminary. Covers establishments with payroll. Data are based on the 1997 and 2002 economic censuses which are subject to nonsampling error. Data for the construction sector are also subject to sampling errors. For details on survey methodology and nonsampling and sampling errors, see Appendix III]

Kind of business	NAICS code [1]	Establishments (1,000)		Sales, receipts or shipments (bil. dol.)		Annual payroll (bil. dol.)		Paid employees [2] (1,000)	
		1997	2002	1997	2002	1997	2002	1997	2002
Mining	21	25	(S)	174	(S)	20.8	(S)	509	(S)
Oil & gas extraction.	211	8	8	103	107	5.5	5.4	111	100
Mining (except oil & gas)	212	7	7	51	54	9.4	8.9	229	200
Mining support activities	213	9	(S)	20	(S)	5.9	(S)	169	(S)
Utilities . . . . ₄	22	16	19	412	478	36.6	45.1	703	739
Construction [3]	23	656	698	859	1,140	174.2	235.5	5,665	6,944
Manufacturing	31-33	363	344	3,835	3,833	569.8	568.4	16,805	14,543
Wholesale trade.	42	453	442	4,060	4,379	214.9	255.6	5,797	6,035
Wholesale trade, durable goods	421	291	288	2,180	2,354	133.2	159.0	3,398	3,565
Wholesale trade, nondurable goods	422	163	154	1,880	2,025	81.7	96.6	2,398	2,470
Retail trade	44-45	1,118	1,112	2,461	3,171	237.2	306.0	13,991	15,029
Motor vehicle & parts dealers	441	123	123	645	812	50.2	64.3	1,719	1,884
Furniture & home furnishings stores	442	65	65	72	94	10.0	13.0	483	554
Electronics & appliance stores.	443	43	47	69	88	7.1	10.0	345	418
Bldg. material & garden equipment & supplies dealers.	444	93	(S)	228	(S)	25.6	(S)	1,118	(S)
Food & beverage stores.	445	149	150	402	488	40.6	49.1	2,893	2,896
Health & personal care stores	446	83	79	118	183	15.2	20.6	904	1,043
Gasoline stations	447	127	(S)	198	(S)	11.5	(S)	922	(S)
Clothing & clothing accessories stores . .	448	157	149	136	170	16.6	21.2	1,280	1,425
Sporting goods, hobby, book, & music stores	451	69	63	62	78	7.1	9.0	561	633
General merchandise stores	452	36	40	330	451	30.9	42.6	2,508	2,549
Miscellaneous store retailers	453	130	129	78	95	10.2	13.7	753	849
Nonstore retailers . . . . . . ₄, ₅	454	44	56	123	171	12.3	17.6	506	587
Transportation & warehousing [4, 5]	48-49	178	201	318	(S)	82.3	116.8	2,921	3,751
Information [4]	51	114	137	623	905	129.5	189.7	3,066	3,846
Publishing industries	511	34	32	179	235	43.4	64.1	1,006	1,132
Motion picture & sound recording industries.	512	22	23	56	77	9.4	11.7	276	334
Broadcasting & telecommunications . . . ₄	513	43	57	346	499	63.5	83.7	1,434	1,740
Information & data processing services [4] .	514	15	25	42	94	13.3	30.2	350	638
Finance & insurance [6]	52	395	449	2,198	2,616	264.6	343.5	5,835	6,664
Real estate & rental & leasing [6]	53	288	326	241	348	41.6	61.8	1,702	2,136
Professional, scientific, & technical services [4]	54	621	747	595	896	231.4	374.5	5,361	7,509
Management of companies & enterprises . .	55	47	(S)	92	(S)	154.2	(S)	2,618	(S)
Admin/support waste management/ remediation services [4]	56	276	276	296	414	137.3	193.5	7,347	8,345
Administrative & support services [4]	561	260	258	257	362	128.4	181.4	7,067	8,003
Waste management & remediation services [4]	562	16	18	39	51	8.9	12.1	281	342
Educational services [4].	61	41	50	20	32	6.4	10.2	321	452
Health care and social assistance	62	646	712	885	1,234	378.2	497.8	13,562	15,347
Ambulatory health care services	621	455	492	355	500	155.9	204.3	4,414	5,071
Hospitals.	622	7	7	379	511	155.8	196.2	4,933	5,165
Nursing & residential care facilities.	623	57	70	93	130	42.2	59.8	2,471	2,878
Social assistance	624	126	144	57	93	24.4	37.6	1,744	2,233
Arts, entertainment, & recreation	71	99	111	105	138	32.8	43.1	1,588	1,896
Performance arts, spectator sports, & related industries.	711	31	39	38	55	14.5	19.6	327	438
Museums, historical sites, & like institutions	712	6	7	7	9	1.8	2.9	92	124
Amusement, gambling, & recreation industries	713	63	66	60	74	16.5	20.6	1,169	1,334
Accommodation & food services	72	545	565	350	452	97.0	127.5	9,451	10,836
Accommodation	721	58	(S)	98	(S)	26.7	(S)	1,697	(S)
Food services & drinking places	722	487	(S)	252	(S)	70.3	(S)	7,755	(S)
Other services (except public administration) [4]	81	520	528	266	315	65.5	82.7	3,256	3,528
Repair & maintenance [4].	811	235	233	105	120	29.9	35.5	1,276	1,367
Personal and laundry services [4]	812	185	192	58	73	18.6	22.6	1,217	1,311
Religious/grantmaking/prof/like organizations	813	99	102	103	122	17.1	24.6	763	849

S Estimates did not meet publication standards.   [1] Based on North American Industry Classification System, 1997; see text this section.   [2] For pay period including March 12.   [3] For detailed industries, see Table 927.   [4] Enterprise support establishments are included in the 2002 data but not in the 1997 data affecting comparability for this industry.   [5] For detailed industries, see Table 1044.   [6] For detailed industries, see Table 1145.

Source: U.S. Census Bureau, "2002 Economic Census Advance Report;" published 29 March 2004; <http://www.census.gov/econ /census02/>.

Business Enterprise   495

Table 737. **Nonemployer Establishments and Receipts by Industry: 2000 to 2003**

[**Establishments: 16,530 represents 16,530,000.** Includes only firms subject to federal income tax. Nonemployers are businesses with no paid employees. Data originate chiefly from administrative records of the Internal Revenue Service; see Appendix III. Data for 2000 based on the North American Industry Classification System (NAICS), 1997; beginning 2002 based on NAICS 2002, see text, this section]

Kind of business	NAICS code	Establishments (1,000)			Receipts (mil. dol.)		
		2000	2002	2003	2000	2002	2003
All industries	(X)	**16,530**	**17,646**	**18,649**	**709,379**	**770,032**	**829,819**
Forestry, fishing & hunting, & ag support services	113-115	223	220	226	9,196	8,994	9,558
Mining	21	86	83	88	5,227	4,924	6,278
Utilities	22	14	13	14	504	549	600
Construction	23	2,014	2,071	2,239	107,538	115,269	126,479
Manufacturing	31-33	285	290	300	13,022	13,402	14,105
Wholesale trade	42	388	364	376	31,684	30,022	31,400
Retail trade	44-45	1,743	1,839	1,880	73,810	77,896	80,548
Transportation & warehousing.	48-49	747	809	859	37,824	40,698	44,953
Information	51	238	233	260	7,620	7,550	8,518
Finance & insurance	52	692	660	695	49,058	44,139	47,345
Real estate & rental & leasing.	53	1,696	1,880	2,046	133,398	161,790	176,079
Professional, scientific, & technical services .	54	2,420	2,553	2,648	90,272	96,395	102,911
Admin/support waste mgt/ remediation services	56	1,032	1,263	1,294	23,754	26,910	28,885
Educational services	61	283	345	374	3,736	4,581	5,002
Health care & social assistance.	62	1,317	1,457	1,543	36,550	42,268	45,500
Arts, entertainment, & recreation	71	782	866	888	17,713	20,000	21,010
Accommodation & food services	72	218	242	260	13,418	14,178	15,271
Other services (except public administration) .	81	2,350	2,459	2,660	55,056	60,468	65,377

X Not applicable.

Source: U.S. Census Bureau, "Nonemployer Statistics"; <http://www.census.gov/epcd/nonemployer/>.

Table 738. **Establishments, Employees, and Payroll by Employment-Size Class: 1990 to 2003**

[**6,176 represents 6,176,000.** Excludes most government employees, railroad employees, self-employed persons. Employees are for the week including March 12. Covers establishments with payroll. An *establishment* is a single physical location where business is conducted or where services or industrial operations are performed. For statement on methodology, see Appendix III]

Employment-size class	Unit	1990	1995	1998	1999	2000	2001	2002	2003
Establishments, total	1,000 . . .	**6,176**	**6,613**	**6,942**	**7,008**	**7,070**	**7,095**	**7,201**	**7,255**
Under 20 employees	1,000 . . .	5,354	5,733	5,991	6,036	6,069	6,083	6,199	6,240
20 to 99 employees	1,000 . . .	684	730	786	802	826	836	835	845
100 to 499 employees	1,000 . . .	122	135	147	152	157	157	149	151
500 to 999 employees	1,000 . . .	10	10	11	12	12	12	11	11
1,000 or more employees . . .	1,000 . . .	6	6	6	7	7	7	7	7
Employees, total	1,000 . . .	**93,476**	**100,335**	**108,118**	**110,706**	**114,065**	**115,061**	**112,401**	**113,398**
Under 20 employees	1,000 . . .	24,373	25,785	27,131	27,289	27,569	27,681	28,116	28,313
20 to 99 employees	1,000 . . .	27,414	29,202	31,464	32,193	33,147	33,555	33,335	33,760
100 to 499 employees	1,000 . . .	22,926	25,364	27,842	28,707	29,736	29,692	28,101	28,549
500 to 999 employees	1,000 . . .	6,551	7,021	7,689	7,923	8,291	8,357	7,743	7,638
1,000 or more employees . . .	1,000 . . .	12,212	12,962	13,991	14,594	15,322	15,776	15,105	15,138
Annual payroll, total	Bil. dol. .	**2,104**	**2,666**	**3,309**	**3,555**	**3,879**	**3,989**	**3,943**	**4,041**
Under 20 employees	Bil. dol. .	485	608	734	773	818	839	866	885
20 to 99 employees	Bil. dol. .	547	696	866	925	1,006	1,037	1,041	1,068
100 to 499 employees	Bil. dol. .	518	675	858	931	1,031	1,052	1,021	1,054
500 to 999 employees	Bil. dol. .	174	219	277	298	336	342	329	334
1,000 or more employees . . .	Bil. dol. .	381	467	575	628	690	719	685	700

Source: U.S. Census Bureau, "County Business Patterns;" <http://www.census.gov/epcd/cbp/view/cbpview.html>.

496 Business Enterprise

Table 739. **Establishments, Employees, and Payroll by Employment-Size Class and Industry: 2000 to 2003**

[Establishments and employees in thousands (7,070.0 represents 7,070,000); payroll in billions of dollars. See headnote, Table 738. Data for 2000 and 2002 based on the North American Industry Classification System (NAICS), 1997; 2003 data based on NAICS 2002. See text, this section.]

Industry	NAICS code	2000, total	2002, total	2003					
				Total	Under 20 employ-ees	20 to 99 employ-ees	100 to 499 employ-ees	500 to 999 employ-ees	1,000 or more employ-ees
Establishments, total [1]	(X)	7,070.0	7,200.8	7,254.7	6,240.4	845.0	151.5	11.2	6.7
Agriculture, forestry, fishing & hunting. . .	11	26.1	26.6	25.9	24.2	1.5	0.2	(Z)	(Z)
Mining	21	23.7	23.9	23.6	19.3	3.5	0.7	0.1	(Z)
Utilities	22	17.3	18.4	18.4	13.1	3.9	1.2	0.1	0.1
Construction	23	709.6	710.3	732.2	667.8	57.0	6.9	0.3	0.1
Manufacturing	31-33	354.5	344.3	341.8	234.5	77.6	26.1	2.5	1.1
Wholesale trade	42	446.2	436.9	432.5	371.1	53.5	7.3	0.5	0.2
Retail trade	44-45	1,113.6	1,125.7	1,115.9	965.0	125.9	24.5	0.5	(Z)
Transportation and warehousing	48-49	190.0	195.1	202.7	168.6	27.6	5.7	0.5	0.3
Information	51	133.6	138.6	140.0	110.9	22.3	5.9	0.6	0.3
Finance and insurance	52	423.7	450.4	460.6	413.5	38.7	6.9	0.9	0.6
Real estate and rental and leasing.	53	300.2	323.0	333.6	317.6	14.2	1.6	0.1	(Z)
Professional, scientific, and technical services.	54	722.7	772.4	780.9	720.7	51.2	8.0	0.6	0.3
Management of companies and enterprises.	55	47.4	49.4	47.4	31.3	10.9	4.2	0.6	0.4
Admin/support waste mgt/remediation services.	56	351.5	343.5	348.7	288.7	44.3	13.8	1.1	0.7
Educational services	61	68.0	73.7	76.4	58.0	14.6	3.0	0.4	0.4
Health care and social assistance	62	658.6	703.5	716.4	608.4	84.6	19.9	1.7	1.8
Arts, entertainment, and recreation	71	103.8	110.4	114.0	95.3	15.7	2.7	0.2	0.1
Accommodation and food services.	72	542.4	565.1	575.3	412.7	153.0	9.2	0.3	0.2
Other services [2]	81	723.3	740.1	732.0	683.2	44.8	3.8	0.1	(Z)
Unclassified establishments	99	99.0	35.7	36.5	36.4	0.1	–	–	–
Employees, total [1]	(X)	114,065	112,401	113,398	28,313	33,760	28,549	7,638	15,138
Agriculture, forestry, fishing & hunting. . .	11	184	181	181	87	56	28	6	4
Mining	21	456	466	455	91	141	131	41	51
Utilities	22	655	648	676	68	174	239	93	101
Construction	23	6,573	6,307	6,381	2,517	2,182	1,237	210	236
Manufacturing	31-33	16,474	14,394	14,132	1,364	3,393	5,266	1,713	2,395
Wholesale trade	42	6,112	5,860	5,864	1,792	2,083	1,352	307	330
Retail trade	44-45	14,841	14,820	14,868	5,128	5,077	4,313	270	80
Transportation and warehousing	48-49	3,790	3,581	4,068	705	1,144	1,098	350	770
Information	51	3,546	3,536	3,600	506	947	1,163	429	555
Finance and insurance	52	5,963	6,415	6,464	1,830	1,494	1,405	638	1,096
Real estate and rental and leasing.	53	1,942	2,017	2,045	1,102	519	298	76	49
Professional, scientific, and technical services.	54	6,816	7,046	7,340	2,498	1,972	1,536	438	897
Management of companies and enterprises.	55	2,874	2,914	2,879	173	490	903	431	883
Admin/support waste mgt/remediation services.	56	9,138	8,299	8,511	1,142	1,947	2,694	755	1,973
Educational services	61	2,532	2,702	2,777	279	612	587	271	1,027
Health care and social assistance	62	14,109	14,900	15,472	3,214	3,382	3,697	1,195	3,984
Arts, entertainment, and recreation	71	1,741	1,801	1,833	357	661	498	104	213
Accommodation and food services.	72	9,881	10,049	10,440	2,518	5,851	1,453	227	391
Other services [2]	81	5,293	5,420	5,367	2,899	1,630	651	85	102
Unclassified establishments	99	144	33	46	42	4	–	–	–
Annual payroll, total [1]	(X)	3,879	3,943	4,041	885	1,068	1,054	334	700
Agriculture, forestry, fishing & hunting. . .	11	5	5	5	2	2	1	(Z)	(Z)
Mining	21	22	24	25	4	7	8	2	3
Utilities	22	41	42	45	4	10	16	7	8
Construction	23	240	247	253	86	91	57	9	10
Manufacturing	31-33	644	580	576	45	122	206	74	130
Wholesale trade	42	270	263	272	75	93	66	18	20
Retail trade	44-45	303	321	319	103	113	94	7	3
Transportation and warehousing	48-49	126	127	143	23	38	38	12	32
Information	51	209	188	204	26	47	68	25	37
Finance and insurance	52	347	373	393	88	93	93	42	77
Real estate and rental and leasing.	53	59	65	69	34	19	11	3	2
Professional, scientific, and technical services.	54	362	369	398	114	113	96	28	47
Management of companies and enterprises.	55	211	205	212	15	33	65	31	68
Admin/support waste mgt/remediation services.	56	210	212	219	36	53	62	18	50
Educational services	61	62	72	75	6	14	16	6	33
Health care and social assistance	62	431	499	526	120	104	101	42	160
Arts, entertainment, and recreation	71	43	48	48	12	13	16	3	4
Accommodation and food services.	72	126	131	139	33	68	23	5	11
Other services [2]	81	110	119	118	59	36	17	2	3
Unclassified establishments	99	4	1	1	1	(Z)	–	–	–

– Represents zero.   X Not applicable.   Z Less than 50 establishments or 500 million dollars.   [1] Totals for 2000 and 2002 include auxiliaries. Beginning 2003, cases previously classified under NAICS code 95 (auxiliaries) are coded in the operating NAICS sector of the establishment.   [2] Except public administration.

Source: U.S. Census Bureau, "County Business Patterns;" <http://www.census.gov/epcd/cbp/view/cbpview.html>.

Business Enterprise   497

Table 740. **Employer Firms, Establishments, Employment, and Annual Payroll by Enterprise Size: 1990 to 2003**

[In thousands except as noted (5,074 represents 5,074,000). Firms are an aggregation of all establishments owned by a parent company with some annual payroll. Establishments are locations with active payroll in any quarter. Employment is measured in March and payroll is annual leading to some enterprises with zero employment. This table illustrates the changing importance of enterprise sizes over time, not job growth, as enterprises can grow or decline and change enterprise size cells over time]

Item		All industries—employment size of enterprise						
	Total	0 to 4 [1]	5 to 9	10 to 19	20 to 99	100 to 499	Less than 500	500 or more
Firms:								
1990............	5,074	3,021	952	563	454	70	5,060	14
1995............	5,369	3,250	981	577	470	76	5,354	15
1998............	5,579	3,376	1,012	600	494	80	5,563	16
1999............	5,608	3,389	1,013	606	502	81	5,591	17
2000............	5,653	3,397	1,021	617	516	84	5,635	17
2001............	5,658	3,402	1,019	616	518	85	5,640	17
2002............	5,698	3,466	1,011	614	508	82	5,681	17
2003............	5,767	3,504	1,025	620	515	85	5,750	17
Establishments:								
1990............	6,176	3,032	971	600	590	255	5,448	728
1995............	6,613	3,260	998	618	639	284	5,799	814
1998............	6,942	3,383	1,026	640	675	307	6,030	911
1999............	7,008	3,398	1,027	643	671	309	6,048	960
2000............	7,070	3,406	1,035	652	674	312	6,080	990
2001............	7,095	3,410	1,034	650	670	316	6,080	1,015
2002............	7,201	3,471	1,024	653	693	333	6,173	1,028
2003............	7,255	3,510	1,038	655	687	331	6,222	1,033
Employment:								
1990............	93,469	5,117	6,252	7,543	17,710	13,545	50,167	43,302
1995............	100,315	5,395	6,440	7,734	18,422	14,660	52,653	47,662
1998............	108,118	5,584	6,643	8,048	19,378	15,411	55,064	53,053
1999............	110,706	5,606	6,652	8,130	19,703	15,638	55,729	54,977
2000............	114,065	5,593	6,709	8,286	20,277	16,260	57,124	56,941
2001............	115,061	5,630	6,698	8,275	20,370	16,410	57,383	57,678
2002............	112,401	5,698	6,640	8,246	19,874	15,909	56,366	56,034
2003............	113,398	5,768	6,732	8,330	20,187	16,430	57,448	55,950
Annual payroll (bil. dol.):								
1990............	2,104	117	114	144	352	279	1,007	1,097
1995............	2,666	142	137	175	437	361	1,252	1,414
1998............	3,309	168	160	207	531	446	1,513	1,797
1999............	3,555	177	167	218	565	475	1,601	1,954
2000............	3,879	186	174	231	608	528	1,727	2,152
2001............	3,989	188	179	237	624	539	1,768	2,222
2002............	3,943	194	182	241	624	536	1,777	2,166
2003............	4,041	197	187	247	635	552	1,818	2,222

[1] Employment is measured in March, thus some firms (start-ups after March, closures before March, and seasonal firms) will have zero employment and some annual payroll.

Source: U.S. Small Business Administration, Office of Advocacy, "Firm Size Data, Statistics of U.S. Businesses and Nonemployer Statistics"; <http://www.sba.gov/advo/research/data.html>; accessed 26 April 2006.

Table 741. **Firm Births and Deaths by Employment Size of Enterprise: 1990 to 2003**

[In thousands (541.1 represents 541,100). Data represent activity from March of the beginning year to March of the ending year. Establishments with no employment in the first quarter of the beginning year were excluded. This table provides the number of births and deaths of initial establishments (based on plant number) as an approximation of firm births and deaths]

Item	Births (initial locations)				Deaths (initial locations)			
	Total	Less than 20	Less than 500	500 or more	Total	Less than 20	Less than 500	500 or more
Firms:								
1990 to 1991	541.1	515.9	540.9	0.3	546.5	517.0	546.1	0.4
1995 to 1996	597.8	572.4	597.5	0.3	512.4	485.5	512.0	0.4
1997 to 1998	590.0	564.8	589.7	0.3	540.6	511.6	540.1	0.5
1998 to 1999	579.6	554.3	579.3	0.3	544.5	514.3	544.0	0.4
1999 to 2000	574.3	548.0	574.0	0.3	542.8	514.2	542.4	0.5
2000 to 2001	585.1	558.0	584.8	0.3	553.3	524.0	552.8	0.5
2001 to 2002 [1]	569.8	541.5	568.3	1.5	586.9	557.1	586.5	0.4
2002 to 2003	612.3	585.6	612.0	0.3	540.7	514.6	540.3	0.3
Employment:								
1990 to 1991	3,105	1,713	2,907	198	3,208	1,723	3,044	164
1995 to 1996	3,256	1,845	3,056	200	3,100	1,560	2,808	291
1997 to 1998	3,205	1,812	3,002	203	3,233	1,662	2,992	242
1998 to 1999	3,225	1,670	2,991	235	3,180	1,645	2,969	210
1999 to 2000	3,229	1,793	3,031	198	3,177	1,654	2,946	230
2000 to 2001	3,418	1,821	3,109	310	3,262	1,701	3,050	212
2001 to 2002	3,370	1,748	3,034	336	3,660	1,755	3,257	403
2002 to 2003	3,667	1,856	3,174	493	3,324	1,608	2,880	445

[1] A change in methodology has affected the allocation of firms by employment size.

Source: U.S. Small Business Administration, Office of Advocacy, "Firm Size Data, Statistics of U.S. Businesses and Nonemployer Statistics"; <http://www.sba.gov/advo/research/data.html>; accessed 26 April 2006.

Table 742. Employer Firms, Employment, and Annual Payroll by Enterprise Size and Industry: 2003

[5,767 represents 5,767,000. A firm is an aggregation of all establishments owned by a parent company (within a geographic location and/or industry) with some annual payroll. A firm may be a single location or it can include multiple locations. Employment is measured in March and payroll is annual leading to some firms with zero employment. Numbers in parentheses represent North American Industry Classification System codes, 2002; see text, this section]

Industry and data type	Unit	Total	All industries—employment size of enterprise							
			0	1 to 4	5 to 9	10 to 19	20 to 99	100 to 499	Less than 500	500 or more
Total [1]:										
Firms	1,000	5,767	770	2,734	1,025	620	515	85	5,750	17
Employment	1,000	113,398	–	5,768	6,732	8,330	20,187	16,430	57,448	55,950
Annual payroll	Bil. dol.	4,041	38	159	187	247	635	552	1,818	2,222
Construction (23):										
Firms	1,000	723	122	349	121	71	53	6	722	1
Employment	1,000	6,381	–	734	792	949	1,988	1,024	5,487	894
Annual payroll	Bil. dol.	253	5	21	24	33	80	45	209	44
Manufacturing (31-33):										
Firms	1,000	296	21	96	55	47	58	14	291	4
Employment	1,000	14,132	–	217	369	640	2,381	2,494	6,102	8,030
Annual payroll	Bil. dol.	576	2	6	11	20	82	92	213	363
Wholesale trade (42):										
Firms	1,000	342	36	157	60	41	38	8	339	3
Employment	1,000	5,864	–	329	396	547	1,386	982	3,640	2,223
Annual payroll	Bil. dol.	272	2	12	15	22	58	43	151	121
Retail trade (44-45):										
Firms	1,000	733	84	343	150	84	60	9	731	2
Employment	1,000	14,868	–	769	985	1,111	2,220	1,320	6,405	8,463
Annual payroll	Bil. dol.	319	3	14	19	24	60	38	156	163
Transportation & warehousing (48-49):										
Firms	1,000	162	24	79	23	16	15	3	160	2
Employment	1,000	4,068	–	152	153	213	562	472	1,552	2,516
Annual payroll	Bil. dol.	143	1	4	4	6	17	15	46	96
Information (51):										
Firms	1,000	76	12	32	12	8	9	2	75	1
Employment	1,000	3,600	–	65	77	113	334	334	922	2,678
Annual payroll	Bil. dol.	204	2	3	3	5	16	18	45	159
Finance & insurance (52):										
Firms	1,000	245	30	141	35	17	16	4	243	2
Employment	1,000	6,464	–	288	225	225	629	698	2,065	4,399
Annual payroll	Bil. dol.	393	2	10	10	12	35	40	110	283
Professional, scientific & technical services (54):										
Firms	1,000	715	113	399	101	55	38	6	712	3
Employment	1,000	7,340	–	768	658	731	1,389	1,001	4,547	2,794
Annual payroll	Bil. dol.	398	6	29	27	34	76	58	231	167
Management of companies & enterprises (55):										
Firms	1,000	28	1	3	1	1	6	8	21	7
Employment	1,000	2,879	–	6	4	8	74	256	348	2,531
Annual payroll	Bil. dol.	212	1	(Z)	(Z)	1	4	14	20	193
Admin/support waste mgt/ remediation services (56):										
Firms	1,000	299	53	134	45	28	27	8	296	3
Employment	1,000	8,511	–	279	297	378	1,088	1,424	3,465	5,046
Annual payroll	Bil. dol.	219	3	7	8	10	29	32	89	130
Educational services (61):										
Firms	1,000	69	9	24	10	9	13	3	68	1
Employment	1,000	2,777	–	51	69	119	525	541	1,305	1,471
Annual payroll	Bil. dol.	75	(Z)	1	1	2	12	14	31	44
Health care and social assistance (62):										
Firms	1,000	575	52	241	134	76	55	15	571	4
Employment	1,000	15,472	–	543	886	1,003	2,163	2,863	7,459	8,013
Annual payroll	Bil. dol.	526	4	21	32	38	72	77	243	283
Accommodation & food services (72):										
Firms	1,000	438	63	129	85	73	78	9	436	2
Employment	1,000	10,440	–	307	568	1,001	2,926	1,548	6,349	4,090
Annual payroll	Bil. dol.	139	3	4	6	11	34	19	76	63
Other services (except public administration) (81):										
Firms	1,000	670	58	365	135	66	41	4	668	1
Employment	1,000	5,367	–	790	872	870	1,469	634	4,636	731
Annual payroll	Bil. dol.	118	1	14	17	18	31	16	98	20

– Represents zero.   Z Less than $500 million.   [1] Includes other industries not shown separately.

Source: U.S. Small Business Administration, Office of Advocacy, "Firm Size Data, Statistics of U.S. Businesses and Nonemployer Statistics"; <http://www.sba.gov/advo/research/data.html>; accessed 26 April 2006.

Table 743. **Employer Firms, Employment, and Payroll by Employment Size of Enterprise and State: 2000 and 2003**

[5,652.5 represents 5,652,500. A firm is an aggregation of all establishments owned by a parent company (within a state) with some annual payroll. A firm may be a single location or it can include multiple locations. Employment is measured in March and payroll is annual leading to some firms with zero employment]

| State | Employer firms (1,000) | | | | | Employment, 2003 (mil.) | | | Annual payroll, 2003 (bil. dol.) | | |
| | 2000 | | 2003 | | | | | | | | |
	Total	Less than 20 employees	Total	Less than 20 employees	Less than 500 employees	Total	Less than 20 employees	Less than 500 employees	Total	Less than 20 employees	Less than 500 employees
U.S	5,652.5	5,035.0	5,767.1	5,150.3	5,750.2	113.4	20.8	57.4	4,040.9	631.2	1,818.5
AL.......	79.9	68.2	78.6	67.0	76.5	1.6	0.3	0.8	47.1	7.4	21.3
AK.......	15.9	14.0	16.3	14.4	15.8	0.2	0.1	0.1	8.7	2.0	4.7
AZ.......	93.0	79.3	97.8	83.4	95.0	2.0	0.3	1.0	64.4	9.9	28.1
AR.......	52.4	45.4	52.3	45.1	50.8	1.0	0.2	0.5	27.0	4.3	11.6
CA.......	664.6	581.1	682.9	598.9	677.4	13.0	2.4	6.9	520.6	84.6	245.9
CO	116.2	101.5	121.3	106.8	118.6	1.9	0.4	1.0	67.9	12.1	31.8
CT.......	78.5	67.2	77.1	65.9	75.1	1.6	0.3	0.8	69.7	10.6	30.1
DE.......	20.2	16.6	20.5	16.6	19.1	0.4	0.1	0.2	15.1	2.0	5.7
DC	16.3	12.4	15.9	11.9	14.8	0.4	0.1	0.2	22.5	2.7	10.1
FL.......	354.0	319.3	381.7	345.0	377.5	6.5	1.2	3.0	202.4	35.9	89.5
GA	160.4	138.3	167.5	144.8	163.7	3.4	0.6	1.5	116.3	16.9	47.4
HI	24.3	20.8	25.4	21.6	24.6	0.5	0.1	0.3	14.1	2.6	7.4
ID	32.2	28.0	34.2	29.9	33.2	0.5	0.1	0.3	13.1	2.9	6.8
IL	254.1	218.1	255.8	220.5	251.6	5.2	0.9	2.6	201.0	29.6	89.9
IN	116.3	98.1	116.5	98.8	113.7	2.5	0.4	1.3	81.4	11.4	35.8
IA	65.6	56.2	65.4	56.2	63.8	1.2	0.2	0.6	36.0	5.5	16.8
KS.......	61.6	52.4	61.1	52.1	59.3	1.1	0.2	0.6	34.0	5.4	15.9
KY.......	72.3	61.0	72.0	60.9	69.9	1.5	0.3	0.7	43.8	6.5	19.4
LA.......	81.7	69.5	82.3	69.8	80.3	1.6	0.3	0.9	47.1	7.8	22.8
ME	34.1	30.1	34.8	30.7	33.9	0.5	0.1	0.3	14.8	3.1	8.3
MD	106.0	90.4	109.8	93.9	107.2	2.1	0.4	1.1	78.9	13.0	38.7
MA	148.2	127.8	149.3	129.2	146.4	3.0	0.5	1.5	127.1	19.0	58.0
MI	193.9	167.2	192.3	166.5	189.3	3.9	0.7	2.0	144.0	21.4	63.5
MN	116.2	99.4	120.8	103.9	118.4	2.4	0.4	1.2	87.3	12.3	38.8
MS	48.3	41.5	47.9	40.9	46.4	0.9	0.2	0.5	23.6	4.0	10.8
MO	118.1	101.1	122.4	105.3	119.7	2.4	0.4	1.2	75.6	11.2	33.7
MT.......	28.0	25.0	29.7	26.5	29.0	0.3	0.1	0.2	7.7	2.2	5.0
NE.......	41.4	35.5	41.6	35.7	40.4	0.8	0.1	0.4	23.1	3.4	10.2
NV.......	40.3	33.4	44.3	36.8	42.4	1.0	0.1	0.4	31.3	4.9	13.6
NH	32.1	27.3	32.7	27.8	31.6	0.5	0.1	0.3	18.8	3.7	10.2
NJ.......	202.2	178.4	204.2	180.4	201.1	3.6	0.7	1.8	154.5	25.3	68.8
NM	35.5	30.1	36.0	30.5	34.7	0.6	0.1	0.3	15.8	3.2	8.3
NY.......	424.8	379.2	433.9	388.8	429.8	7.4	1.4	3.8	332.6	50.9	146.4
NC	163.6	142.0	166.1	143.9	162.8	3.3	0.6	1.6	104.6	15.8	44.3
ND	17.2	14.7	17.2	14.7	16.6	0.3	0.1	0.2	6.9	1.4	3.9
OH	212.5	180.5	210.8	179.7	207.1	4.8	0.8	2.4	157.5	22.3	69.2
OK	70.2	61.0	70.4	61.1	68.6	1.2	0.2	0.6	33.6	6.0	16.3
OR	85.1	74.2	86.3	75.6	84.4	1.3	0.3	0.8	44.3	7.9	21.8
PA	237.5	204.6	238.4	205.9	234.5	5.0	0.9	2.5	174.5	25.1	77.4
RI	25.2	21.5	26.0	22.2	25.1	0.4	0.1	0.2	14.5	2.7	7.7
SC.......	78.4	67.2	79.5	68.2	77.4	1.6	0.3	0.8	44.6	7.2	19.6
SD.......	20.6	17.7	21.0	18.1	20.4	0.3	0.1	0.2	8.0	1.6	4.7
TN.......	102.4	86.7	100.6	85.1	97.8	2.3	0.4	1.1	73.2	10.1	30.8
TX.......	369.0	321.3	375.9	327.1	371.0	8.1	1.4	3.8	281.6	41.5	116.9
UT.......	46.2	39.3	50.9	43.9	49.3	0.9	0.2	0.4	26.8	4.4	12.6
VT.......	19.1	16.7	19.2	16.7	18.6	0.3	0.1	0.2	7.7	1.8	4.5
VA	139.7	120.3	145.6	125.5	142.5	2.9	0.5	1.4	106.1	15.7	46.9
WA	138.2	120.9	140.0	123.1	137.4	2.3	0.5	1.2	90.6	14.1	39.3
WV	33.5	28.8	32.5	27.9	31.5	0.6	0.1	0.3	15.2	2.6	7.1
WI	115.6	98.2	116.2	98.9	113.9	2.4	0.4	1.3	78.3	11.8	37.0
WY	15.9	13.9	16.7	14.5	16.1	0.2	0.1	0.1	5.4	1.4	3.3

Source: U.S. Small Business Administration, Office of Advocacy, "Firm Size Data, Statistics of U.S. Businesses and Nonemployer Statistics"; <http://www.sba.gov/advo/research/data.html>; accessed 26 April 2006.

Table 744. Employer Firm Births and Deaths and Business Bankruptcies by State: 2000 to 2005

[2004 and 2005 births and deaths data are estimated. At the state level, births represent requests for new employer codes, deaths represent the elimination of all employees, and a third category, successor firms or the rebirth of terminated firms, is not listed; so state deaths greater than state births does not necessarily indicate a loss of state employer firms]

State	Births			Deaths			Business bankruptcies		
	2000	2004	2005	2000	2004	2005	2000	2004	2005
United States [1]	574,300	642,600	671,800	542,831	544,300	544,800	35,219	34,019	38,711
Alabama	10,067	9,413	10,575	9,302	10,104	10,168	445	325	331
Alaska	2,333	1,848	1,982	2,671	2,650	2,294	118	64	83
Arizona	15,175	12,421	21,339	11,984	17,553	18,249	765	480	525
Arkansas	4,680	7,852	7,591	5,581	6,481	7,021	261	376	426
California	167,047	117,016	121,482	134,541	143,115	151,944	4,595	3,748	4,236
Colorado	25,462	23,694	26,610	7,561	9,734	14,035	373	786	1,120
Connecticut	9,910	9,064	9,220	11,528	11,018	11,131	139	132	156
Delaware	3,682	3,270	3,299	3,052	3,362	3,355	2,320	276	218
District of Columbia	4,472	4,393	4,316	4,996	3,440	3,952	58	41	46
Florida	59,912	77,754	84,890	55,186	54,498	58,737	1,447	1,183	1,622
Georgia	28,925	29,547	29,804	26,754	27,835	29,315	1,012	2,090	2,232
Hawaii	3,745	3,698	3,763	3,521	3,754	3,794	63	47	81
Idaho	5,829	7,814	9,312	6,249	5,716	6,334	269	160	141
Illinois	28,875	28,453	30,445	31,361	33,472	32,846	1,270	912	1,042
Indiana	14,112	13,906	14,545	15,738	15,282	16,504	398	524	758
Iowa	5,668	5,954	6,004	7,485	7,391	6,802	214	360	455
Kansas	6,483	6,742	7,095	6,981	7,250	7,330	169	268	410
Kentucky	8,637	8,807	9,617	7,508	8,597	8,515	355	319	409
Louisiana	10,468	9,875	9,393	13,708	9,668	9,123	619	622	718
Maine	5,135	4,300	4,251	4,906	4,987	4,711	162	138	144
Maryland	20,539	21,751	22,083	19,563	20,636	21,769	677	417	760
Massachusetts	18,640	18,822	19,723	18,164	20,270	18,878	393	315	406
Michigan	23,760	24,625	24,642	30,240	24,584	26,971	577	681	1,071
Minnesota	13,906	15,167	12,555	4,829	15,209	15,302	1,492	1,374	1,721
Mississippi	6,439	6,141	6,071	7,555	7,380	6,823	203	170	200
Missouri	13,996	16,155	17,239	17,580	17,924	20,109	369	354	438
Montana	4,418	4,588	4,768	2,435	4,896	4,394	141	109	129
Nebraska	4,441	4,849	5,127	5,234	5,051	4,982	115	207	296
Nevada	8,587	10,483	10,487	7,761	9,012	3,674	332	257	333
New Hampshire	4,677	4,865	4,758	7,341	5,401	5,406	302	158	586
New Jersey	27,885	35,895	33,022	23,950	50,034	32,751	660	684	765
New Mexico	5,836	5,683	10,648	6,451	5,592	5,670	513	727	828
New York	61,507	62,854	62,045	57,423	64,013	62,667	1,960	4,070	2,112
North Carolina	23,310	23,387	25,906	23,467	22,055	22,867	445	486	612
North Dakota	1,493	1,747	1,893	2,191	2,621	2,512	92	85	95
Ohio	22,290	22,725	22,542	24,276	21,328	23,429	1,471	1,432	2,099
Oklahoma	8,979	9,263	8,609	8,848	8,018	7,231	876	659	944
Oregon	14,729	13,481	14,445	16,102	14,407	14,804	1,453	852	1,160
Pennsylvania	35,104	33,188	38,368	34,893	34,507	38,113	1,455	1,138	1,356
Rhode Island	3,675	3,932	3,677	4,170	4,250	4,164	74	74	136
South Carolina	11,114	11,745	12,341	11,721	10,975	10,681	138	175	176
South Dakota	2,138	1,691	2,102	1,809	2,251	2,354	133	108	196
Tennessee	15,793	17,415	17,484	17,563	16,520	17,135	641	548	574
Texas	54,330	54,098	55,858	57,300	55,792	55,039	2,592	3,094	3,590
Utah	9,875	11,357	11,536	10,135	11,597	11,871	451	440	449
Vermont	2,511	2,322	1,911	2,653	2,578	2,346	71	85	78
Virginia	22,219	24,134	25,061	20,569	19,919	21,359	815	750	476
Washington	40,357	31,955	30,353	41,793	47,141	40,944	717	665	786
West Virginia	4,177	3,937	3,493	5,542	5,136	4,869	277	247	282
Wisconsin	12,436	13,093	13,656	15,151	12,711	13,397	685	742	820
Wyoming	2,314	2,519	2,632	2,908	2,737	2,689	47	65	84

[1] State births and deaths do not necessarily add to the U.S. as firms enter and exit multiple states and the U.S. data is based upon a different data source.

Source: U.S. Small Business Administration, Office of Advocacy, "Small Business Economy", forthcoming; based on data provided by U.S. Employment and Training Administration, U.S. Census Bureau, and Administrative Office of the U.S. Courts.

Table 745. Small Business Administration Loans to Minority-Owned Small Businesses: 2000 to 2005

[3,634 represents $3,634,000,000. For year ending September 30. A small business must be independently owned and operated, must not be dominant in its particular industry, and must meet standards set by the Small Business Administration as to its annual receipts or number of employees]

Minority group	Number of loans					Amount (mil. dol.)				
	2000	2002	2003	2004	2005	2000	2002	2003	2004	2005
Total minority loans	11,999	14,304	20,183	25,413	29,717	3,634	4,228	4,215	5,144	6,133
Percent of all loans	24.8	25.0	27.2	28.4	28.3	29.4	28.8	29.2	29.3	30.2
African American	2,120	2,148	3,769	4,827	6,632	388	419	399	481	627
Asian American	5,838	7,248	9,507	12,100	13,455	2,383	2,799	2,756	3,400	4,056
Hispanic American	3,500	4,272	6,112	7,686	8,795	761	885	942	1,151	1,325
Native American	541	636	795	800	835	101	126	118	113	125

Source: U.S. Small Business Administration, Management Information Summary, unpublished data.

Table 746. U.S. Firms—Ownership by Women, Race, and Hispanic or Latino Origin Groups: 2002

[**22,975 represents 22,975,000**. A Hispanic firm may be of any race and, therefore may be included in more than one race group. See text, this section and Appendix III]

Group	All firms [1] — Firms (1,000)	All firms [1] — Sales and receipts (bil. dol.)	Firms with paid employees — Firms (1,000)	Firms with paid employees — Sales and receipts (bil. dol.)	Firms with paid employees — Employees (1,000)	Firms with paid employees — Annual payroll (bil. dol.)
All firms [2]	**22,975**	**22,604**	**5,525**	**21,836**	**110,767**	**3,812**
Female-owned.	6,489	940	917	803	7,141	174
Male-owned	13,184	7,061	3,525	6,564	42,429	1,320
Equally male-/female-owned.	2,693	732	718	627	5,665	130
Publicly held and other firms [3]	494	13,820	353	13,797	55,398	2,186
Hispanic or Latino origin	1,573	222	200	180	1,537	37
Mexican, Mexican American,						
Chicano.	701	97	89	77	720	16
Puerto Rican	109	12	12	10	77	2
Cuban	152	35	28	31	206	6
Other Spanish/Hispanic/Latino.	596	74	67	59	504	12
Black	1,198	89	95	66	754	18
American Indian and Alaska Native . . .	201	27	24	22	191	5
Asian	1,104	327	319	291	2,214	56
Asian Indian.	223	88	82	80	610	18
Chinese	286	105	89	96	649	15
Filipino	125	14	20	11	132	4
Japanese	87	31	22	28	205	6
Korean	158	47	57	41	321	7
Vietnamese	147	16	26	12	126	3
Other Asian	89	24	25	22	161	4
Native Hawaiian and Other Pacific						
Islander	29	4	4	4	29	1
Native Hawaiian	17	3	2	2	20	1
Samoan	2	(Z)	(Z)	(Z)	2	(Z)
Guamanian or Chamorro	4	1	(S)	(S)	(S)	(S)
Other Pacific Islander	6	(Z)	1	(Z)	4	(Z)

S Does not meet publication standards.   Z Less than 500 or $500 million.   [1] Both firms with paid employees and firms with no paid employees.   [2] U.S. totals are based on the 2002 Economic Census, whereas the gender, Hispanic or Latino origin, and race estimates are based on the 2002 Survey of Business Owners.   [3] Publicly held and other firms not classifiable by gender, Hispanic or Latino origin, and race.

Source: U.S. Census Bureau, *2002 Economic Census, Survey of Business Owners, Women-Owned Firms: 2002* (SB02-00CS-WMN)(RV); *Hispanic-Owned Firms: 2002* (SB02-00CS-HISP)(RV); *Black-Owned Firms: 2002* (SB02-00CS-BLK)(RV); *American Indian- and Alaska Native-Owned Firms: 2002* (SB02-00CS-AIAN)(RV); *Asian-Owned Firms: 2002* (SB02-00CS-ASIAN)(RV); and *Native Hawaiian- and Other Pacific Islander-Owned Firms: 2002* (SB02-00CS-NHPI)(RV).

Table 747. Women-Owned Firms by Kind of Business and Receipts Size: 2002

[**6,489 represents 6,489,000**. Based on the 2002 Survey of Business Owners; see text, this section and Appendix III]

Kind of business and receipts size	2002 NAICS code [1]	All firms [2] — Firms (1,000)	All firms [2] — Sales and receipts (mil. dol.)	Firms with paid employees — Firms (1,000)	Firms with paid employees — Sales and receipts (mil. dol.)	Firms with paid employees — Employees (1,000)	Firms with paid employees — Annual payroll (mil. dol.)
Total [3]	**(X)**	**6,489**	**939,538**	**917**	**802,851**	**7,141**	**173,529**
Construction	23	202	68,423	52	62,366	456	15,977
Manufacturing	31-33	110	93,168	40	91,286	636	20,386
Wholesale trade.	42	121	210,405	42	206,290	378	12,812
Retail trade	44-45	945	148,947	146	131,483	851	15,293
Real estate and rental and leasing	53	504	48,318	50	24,247	170	4,797
Professional, scientific, and technical services	54	935	79,133	133	57,176	573	21,288
Admin./support waste mgt./ remediation services	56	569	48,062	61	40,567	1,004	19,589
Health care and social assistance	62	1,036	68,383	116	51,519	961	21,819
Accommodation and food services	72	167	38,688	87	35,980	909	10,276
Other services (except public administration) [4] . .	81	1,016	36,216	86	19,622	386	6,559
Less than $5,000	(X)	1,831	4,372	13	32	31	1,112
$5,000 to $9,999	(X)	1,168	7,876	16	112	6	63
$10,000 to $24,999	(X)	1,405	21,642	51	876	34	281
$25,000 to $49,999	(X)	731	25,408	80	2,953	86	869
$50,000 to $99,999	(X)	496	34,580	141	10,330	238	2,898
$100,000 to $249,999	(X)	423	66,287	240	39,208	710	10,775
$250,000 to $499,999	(X)	197	68,982	154	54,463	838	15,125
$500,000 to $999,999	(X)	122	84,729	106	73,701	986	20,913
$1,000,000 or more	(X)	117	625,662	114	621,175	4,213	121,492

X Not applicable.   [1] Based on the 2002 North American Industry Classification System (NAICS); see text, this section.   [2] Both firms with paid employees and firms with no paid employees.   [3] Firms with more than one establishment are counted in each industry in which they operate, but only once in the total. Includes other kinds of businesses not shown separately.   [4] Excludes religious, grantmaking, civic, professional, and similar organizations (NAICS 813) and private households (NAICS 814).

Source: U.S. Census Bureau, *2002 Economic Census, Survey of Business Owners, Women-Owned Firms: 2002* (SB02-00CS-WMN)(RV).

U.S. Census Bureau, Statistical Abstract of the United States: 2007

Table 748.

Table 748. **Hispanic- or Latino-Owned Firms by Kind of Business and Receipts Size: 2002**

[1,573 represents 1,573,000. Based on the 2002 Survey of Business Owners; see text, this section and Appendix III]

Kind of business and receipts size	2002 NAICS code [1]	All firms [2]		Firms with paid employees			
		Firms (1,000)	Sales and receipts (mil. dol.)	Firms (1,000)	Sales and receipts (mil. dol.)	Employees (1,000)	Annual payroll (mil. dol.)
Total [3]	(X)	1,573	221,927	200	179,508	1,537	36,712
Construction	23	213	31,446	25	22,662	190	5,280
Manufacturing	31-33	31	17,965	10	17,245	125	3,739
Wholesale trade..................	42	34	39,323	12	37,503	86	2,831
Retail trade......................	44-45	151	40,424	26	35,511	156	3,271
Transportation and warehousing [4]	48-49	126	10,671	9	5,622	54	1,341
Professional, scientific, and technical services............	54	138	15,017	19	11,529	98	4,167
Admin./support waste mgt./ remediation services	56	208	12,206	16	9,087	243	4,099
Health care and social assistance	62	182	13,758	20	11,208	140	4,237
Accommodation and food services	72	48	11,265	22	10,384	237	2,812
Other services (except public administration) [5]..	81	249	10,082	19	5,329	74	1,486
Less than $5,000	(X)	328	814	2	5	2	79
$5,000 to $9,999	(X)	301	2,065	3	21	2	28
$10,000 to $24,999	(X)	391	5,865	9	156	6	57
$25,000 to $49,999	(X)	190	6,550	15	571	16	160
$50,000 to $99,999	(X)	138	9,726	29	2,109	40	534
$100,000 to $249,999	(X)	112	17,481	51	8,341	129	2,072
$250,000 to $499,999	(X)	51	17,894	36	12,892	176	3,323
$500,000 to $999,999	(X)	33	22,825	26	18,461	229	4,901
$1,000,000 or more	(X)	29	138,708	28	136,953	938	25,559

X Not applicable. [1] Based on the 2002 North American Industry Classification System (NAICS); see text, this section. [2] Both firms with paid employees and firms with no paid employees. [3] Firms with more than one establishment are counted in each industry in which they operate, but only once in the total. Includes other kinds of businesses not shown separately. [4] Excludes large certificated passenger carriers that report to the Office of Airline Information, U.S. Department of Transportation. Also excludes railroad transportation and U.S. Postal Service. [5] Excludes religious, grantmaking, civic, professional, and similar organizations (NAICS 813) and private households (NAICS 814).

Source: U.S. Census Bureau, *2002 Economic Census, Survey of Business Owners, Hispanic-Owned Firms: 2002* (SB02-00CS-HISP)(RV).

Table 749. **Women-Owned and Minority-Owned Firms With Paid Employees by Employment Size: 2002**

[917 represents 917,000. Employment reflects number of paid employees during the March 12 pay period. Based on the 2002 Survey of Business Owners; see text, this section and Appendix III]

Item	Unit				Number of employees				
		Total	None [1]	1 to 4	5 to 9	10 to 19	20 to 49	50 to 99	100 to 499	500 or more
WOMEN-OWNED									
Firms	1,000 .	917	161	462	149	83	43	11	7	1
Sales and receipts............	Mil. dol.	802,851	23,539	113,447	96,282	103,160	117,875	74,053	114,484	160,012
Employees..................	1,000 .	7,141	–	939	971	1,105	1,269	750	1,194	913
Annual payroll	Mil. dol..	173,529	3,953	20,483	21,360	25,946	31,578	19,316	30,015	20,877
HISPANIC-OWNED									
Firms	1,000 .	200	37	100	31	18	9	3	1	(Z)
Sales and receipts............	Mil. dol.	179,508	6,703	28,292	26,627	26,945	29,496	19,447	27,206	14,792
Employees..................	1,000 .	1,537	–	202	205	248	267	185	244	186
Annual payroll	Mil. dol..	36,712	1,153	4,568	4,958	5,705	6,393	4,817	5,900	3,217
BLACK-OWNED									
Firms	1,000 .	95	19	47	14	7	4	1	1	(Z)
Sales and receipts............	Mil. dol.	65,799	2,986	10,679	7,773	7,769	10,912	9,697	11,193	4,790
Employees..................	1,000 .	754	–	96	92	100	133	87	162	82
Annual payroll	Mil. dol..	17,550	541	2,251	2,133	2,279	3,034	2,154	3,623	1,535
AMERICAN INDIAN- AND ALASKA NATIVE-OWNED									
Firms	1,000 .	24	5	12	4	2	1	(Z)	(Z)	(Z)
Sales and receipts............	Mil. dol..	21,987	1,021	3,378	2,411	2,996	3,814	3,092	2,842	2,433
Employees..................	1,000 .	191	–	26	23	28	36	23	26	29
Annual payroll	Mil. dol..	5,135	137	578	528	706	945	675	773	793
ASIAN-OWNED									
Firms	1,000 .	319	54	161	55	30	15	3	2	(Z)
Sales and receipts............	Mil. dol..	291,163	10,287	56,967	46,155	44,109	50,950	30,759	32,955	18,980
Employees..................	1,000 .	2,214	–	347	353	393	437	226	302	155
Annual payroll	Mil. dol..	56,045	1,616	7,946	7,992	9,130	10,947	6,048	8,211	4,154
NATIVE HAWAIIAN- AND OTHER PACIFIC ISLANDER-OWNED									
Firms	1,000 .	4	1	2	1	(Z)	(Z)	(Z)	(Z)	–
Sales and receipts............	Mil. dol..	3,502	73	520	413	574	805	420	698	–
Employees..................	1,000 .	29	–	4	4	5	7	4	5	–
Annual payroll	Mil. dol..	826	12	133	99	123	228	100	132	–

– Represents zero. Z Less than 500. [1] Firms reported annual payroll, but did not report any employees on their payroll during specified period in 2002.

Source: U.S. Census Bureau, *2002 Economic Census, Survey of Business Owners, Women-Owned Firms: 2002* (SB02-00CS-WMN)(RV). *Hispanic-Owned Firms: 2002* (SB02-00CS-HISP)(RV); *Black-Owned Firms: 2002* (SB02-00CS-BLK)(RV); *American Indian- and Alaska Native-Owned Firms: 2002* (SB02-00CS-AIAN)(RV); *Asian-Owned Firms: 2002* (SB02-00CS-ASIAN)(RV); and *Native Hawaiian- and Other Pacific Islander-Owned Firms: 2002* (SB02-00CS-NHPI)(RV).

Business Enterprise 503

Table 750. Black-Owned Firms by Kind of Business and Receipts Size: 2002

[1,198 represents 1,198,000. Based on the 2002 Survey of Business Owners; see text, this section and Appendix III]

Kind of business and receipts size	2002 NAICS code [1]	All firms [2]		Firms with paid employees			
		Firms (1,000)	Sales and receipts (mil. dol.)	Firms (1,000)	Sales and receipts (mil. dol.)	Employ-ees (1,000)	Annual payroll (mil. dol.)
Total [3]	(X)	1,198	88,642	95	65,799	754	17,550
Construction	23	75	9,632	9	7,504	55	1,718
Manufacturing	31-33	10	4,647	2	4,456	31	1,022
Wholesale trade.	42	12	5,604	2	5,136	11	392
Retail trade	44-45	102	13,587	9	11,550	45	982
Transportation and warehousing [4]	48-49	99	5,445	5	2,160	26	555
Professional, scientific, and technical services	54	116	9,395	11	7,097	71	2,879
Admin./support waste mgt./ remediation services	56	121	6,416	10	4,908	134	2,316
Health care and social assistance	62	246	11,828	20	8,415	164	3,495
Accommodation and food services . . .	72	25	5,033	7	4,416	115	1,171
Other services (except public administration) [5]	81	210	5,178	9	2,092	32	571
Less than $5,000	(X)	360	863	1	4	3	163
$5,000 to $9,999	(X)	249	1,688	2	14	1	6
$10,000 to $24,999	(X)	295	4,453	6	101	5	45
$25,000 to $49,999	(X)	125	4,286	9	342	10	103
$50,000 to $99,999	(X)	74	5,159	15	1,122	26	325
$100,000 to $249,999	(X)	52	7,912	25	4,094	77	1,158
$250,000 to $499,999	(X)	21	7,233	15	5,359	86	1,580
$500,000 to $999,999	(X)	12	8,295	10	6,927	99	2,218
$1,000,000 or more	(X)	11	48,753	10	47,835	447	11,951

X Not applicable.   [1] Based on the 2002 North American Industry Classification System (NAICS); see text, this section.
[2] Both firms with paid employees and firms with no paid employees.   [3] Firms with more than one establishment are counted in each industry in which they operate, but only once in the total. Includes other kinds of businesses not shown separately.
[4] Excludes large certificated passenger carriers that report to the Office of Airline Information, U.S. Department of Transportation. Also excludes railroad transportation and U.S. Postal Service.   [5] Excludes religious, grantmaking, civic, professional, and similar organizations (NAICS 813) and private households (NAICS 814).

Source: U.S. Census Bureau, *2002 Economic Census, Survey of Business Owners, Black-Owned Firms: 2002* (SB02-00CS-BLK)(RV).

Table 751. American Indian- and Alaska Native-Owned Firms by Kind of Business and Receipts Size: 2002

[201.4 represents 201,400. Based on the 2002 Survey of Business Owners; see text, this section and Appendix III]

Kind of business and receipts size	2002 NAICS code [1]	All firms [2]		Firms with paid employees			
		Firms (1,000)	Sales and receipts (mil. dol.)	Firms (1,000)	Sales and receipts (mil. dol.)	Employ-ees (1,000)	Annual payroll (mil. dol.)
Total [3]	(X)	201.4	26,873	24.5	21,987	191.3	5,135
Construction	23	32.3	6,055	4.8	4,866	31.3	1,072
Manufacturing	31-33	6.0	3,125	1.4	3,016	20.0	657
Wholesale trade.	42	4.3	2,162	0.8	2,048	5.7	191
Retail trade	44-45	20.5	4,967	3.0	4,382	21.1	437
Transportation and warehousing [4]	48-49	10.0	942	0.9	501	4.8	129
Real estate and rental and leasing . . .	53	9.3	715	0.6	342	2.3	69
Professional, scientific, and technical services	54	22.5	2,091	3.3	1,570	15.3	641
Admin./support waste mgt./ remediation services	56	15.7	1,699	1.8	1,505	31.2	638
Health care and social assistance	62	24.4	1,234	2.1	920	17.5	369
Other services (except public administration) [5]	81	26.7	935	1.7	447	6.3	116
Less than $5,000	(X)	54.2	130	0.4	1	0.3	4
$5,000 to $9,999	(X)	36.4	245	0.5	3	0.2	5
$10,000 to $24,999	(X)	43.3	662	1.1	17	0.9	7
$25,000 to $49,999	(X)	24.2	841	1.9	71	2.0	18
$50,000 to $99,999	(X)	16.9	1,188	3.4	252	4.2	63
$100,000 to $249,999	(X)	13.3	2,086	6.4	1,064	17.4	277
$250,000 to $499,999	(X)	6.1	2,141	4.4	1,534	19.8	391
$500,000 to $999,999	(X)	3.5	2,338	2.9	1,975	22.9	530
$1,000,000 or more	(X)	3.6	17,242	3.5	17,069	123.5	3,840

X Not applicable.   [1] Based on the 2002 North American Industry Classification System (NAICS); see text, this section.
[2] Both firms with paid employees and firms with no paid employees.   [3] Firms with more than one establishment are counted in each industry in which they operate, but only once in the total. Includes other kinds of businesses not shown separately.
[4] Excludes large certificated passenger carriers that report to the Office of Airline Information, U.S. Department of Transportation. Also excludes railroad transportation and U.S. Postal Service.   [5] Excludes religious, grantmaking, civic, professional, and similar organizations (NAICS 813) and private households (NAICS 814).

Source: U.S. Census Bureau, *2002 Economic Census, Survey of Business Owners, American Indian- and Alaska Native-Owned Firms: 2002* (SB02-00CS-AIAN).

Table 752. Asian-Owned Firms by Kind of Business and Receipts Size: 2002

[**1,104 represents 1,104,000**. Based on the 2002 Survey of Business Owners; see text, this section and Appendix III]

Kind of business and receipts size	2002 NAICS code [1]	All firms [2]		Firms with paid employees			
		Firms (1,000)	Sales and receipts (mil. dol.)	Firms (1,000)	Sales and receipts (mil. dol.)	Employees (1,000)	Annual payroll (mil. dol.)
Total [3]	(X)	1,104	326,663	319	291,163	2,214	56,045
Construction	23	39	9,715	7	8,129	47	1,665
Manufacturing	31-33	24	26,434	12	25,924	170	5,115
Wholesale trade	42	47	87,083	25	83,924	155	5,590
Retail trade	44-45	152	65,143	62	58,564	292	5,004
Finance and insurance [4]	52	30	6,970	5	5,169	26	1,357
Real estate and rental and leasing	53	75	9,759	9	4,778	35	1,032
Professional, scientific, and technical services	54	154	27,234	30	23,360	196	9,963
Health care and social assistance	62	123	29,951	45	26,689	280	10,315
Accommodation and food services	72	105	32,830	75	31,094	671	7,697
Other services (except public administration) [5]	81	189	11,266	31	7,184	113	2,004
Less than $5,000	(X)	175	437	2	6	17	638
$5,000 to $9,999	(X)	143	960	4	28	1	14
$10,000 to $24,999	(X)	200	3,129	12	201	7	65
$25,000 to $49,999	(X)	140	4,923	20	738	19	204
$50,000 to $99,999	(X)	122	8,651	38	2,785	56	716
$100,000 to $249,999	(X)	141	22,424	84	13,874	228	3,305
$250,000 to $499,999	(X)	82	28,992	65	23,266	303	5,561
$500,000 to $999,999	(X)	52	36,158	46	31,787	369	7,753
$1,000,000 or more	(X)	50	220,991	49	218,477	1,214	37,790

X Not applicable.   [1] Based on the 2002 North American Industry Classification System (NAICS); see text, this section.   [2] Both firms with paid employees and firms with no paid employees.   [3] Firms with more than one establishment are counted in each industry in which they operate, but only once in the total. Includes other kinds of businesses not shown separately.   [4] Excludes funds, trusts, and other financial vehicles (NAICS 525), except real estate investment trusts (NAICS 525930).   [5] Excludes religious, grantmaking, civic, professional, and similar organizations (NAICS 813) and private households (NAICS 814).

Source: U.S. Census Bureau, *2002 Economic Census, Survey of Business Owners, Asian-Owned Firms: 2002* (SB02-00CS-ASIAN)(RV).

Table 753. Native Hawaiian- and Other Pacific Islander-Owned Firms by Kind of Business and Receipts Size: 2002

[**4,279.6 represents $4,279,600,000**. Based on the 2002 Survey of Business Owners; see text, this section and Appendix III]

Kind of business and receipts size	2002 NAICS code [1]	All firms [2]		Firms with paid employees			
		Firms	Sales and receipts (mil. dol.)	Firms	Sales and receipts (mil. dol.)	Employ- ees	Annual payroll (mil. dol.)
Total [3]	(X)	28,948	4,279.6	3,693	3,502.2	29,319	826.2
Construction	23	2,853	906.3	(S)	(S)	(S)	(S)
Manufacturing	31-33	324	184.1	84	177.0	1,478	45.4
Wholesale trade	42	377	482.2	146	469.1	1,078	35.9
Retail trade	44-45	3,601	645.5	459	552.7	2,492	56.6
Transportation and warehousing [4]	48-49	1,412	190.3	243	140.4	2,758	46.6
Information	51	311	144.6	58	135.3	427	27.1
Real estate and rental and leasing	53	1,851	153.2	266	80.5	732	21.7
Professional, scientific, and technical services	54	3,239	267.3	321	172.7	1,351	53.4
Admin./support waste mgt./ remediation services	56	3,362	451.6	(S)	(S)	(S)	(S)
Accommodation and food services	72	511	137.7	193	130.0	2,645	33.2
Less than $5,000	(X)	7,316	17.5	(S)	(S)	(S)	(S)
$5,000 to $9,999	(X)	6,164	42.3	(S)	(S)	(S)	(S)
$10,000 to $24,999	(X)	5,951	89.0	221	3.5	131	1.1
$25,000 to $49,999	(X)	2,933	101.9	166	5.9	161	1.5
$50,000 to $99,999	(X)	2,173	150.5	343	24.6	495	4.9
$100,000 to $249,999	(X)	2,241	338.3	857	139.5	2,094	44.1
$250,000 to $499,999	(X)	962	347.6	804	295.7	3,847	80.3
$500,000 to $999,999	(X)	480	335.2	452	315.3	4,444	99.7
$1,000,000 or more	(X)	727	2,857.3	(S)	(S)	(S)	(S)

S Data do not meet publication standards.   X Not applicable.   [1] Based on the 2002 North American Industry Classification System (NAICS); see text, this section.   [2] Both firms with paid employees and firms with no paid employees.   [3] Firms with more than one establishment are counted in each industry in which they operate, but only once in the total. Includes other kinds of businesses not shown separately.   [4] Excludes large certificated passenger carriers that report to the Office of Airline Information, U.S. Department of Transportation. Also excludes railroad transportation and U.S. Postal Service.

Source: U.S. Census Bureau, *2002 Economic Census, Survey of Business Owners, Native Hawaiian- and Other Pacific Islander-Owned Firms: 2002* (SB02-00CS-NHPI)(RV).

U.S. Census Bureau, Statistical Abstract of the United States: 2007

Table 754. **Bankruptcy Petitions Filed and Pending by Type and Chapter: 1990 to 2005**

[For years ending June 30. Covers only bankruptcy cases filed under the Bankruptcy Reform Act of 1978. *Bankruptcy:* legal recognition that a company or individual is insolvent and must restructure or liquidate. Petitions "filed" means the commencement of a proceeding through the presentation of a petition to the clerk of the court; "pending" is a proceeding in which the administration has not been completed]

Item	1990	1995	1999	2000	2001	2002	2003	2004	2005
Total filed	**725,484**	**858,104**	**1,391,964**	**1,276,922**	**1,386,606**	**1,505,306**	**1,650,279**	**1,635,725**	**1,637,254**
Business [1]	64,688	51,288	39,934	36,910	37,135	39,201	37,182	35,739	32,406
Nonbusiness [2]	660,796	806,816	1,352,030	1,240,012	1,349,471	1,466,105	1,613,097	1,599,986	1,604,848
Chapter 7 [3]	468,171	552,244	968,807	864,183	950,724	1,030,372	1,144,658	1,146,761	1,174,681
Chapter 11 [4]	2,116	1,755	731	722	745	894	966	935	847
Chapter 13 [5]	190,509	252,817	382,492	375,107	397,996	434,835	467,466	452,286	429,315
Voluntary	723,886	856,991	1,391,130	1,276,146	1,385,840	1,504,500	1,649,543	1,635,099	1,636,678
Involuntary	1,598	1,113	834	776	766	806	736	626	576
Chapter 7 [3]	505,337	581,390	993,414	885,447	972,659	1,053,230	1,165,993	1,167,101	1,196,212
Chapter 9 [6]	7	12	3	8	10	8	7	7	6
Chapter 11 [4]	19,591	13,221	8,684	9,947	10,272	11,401	10,602	11,048	6,703
Chapter 12 [7]	1,351	904	829	732	206	367	775	302	290
Chapter 13 [5]	199,186	262,551	389,004	380,770	403,418	440,231	472,811	457,171	433,945
Section 304 [8]	12	26	30	18	41	69	91	96	98
Total pending . .	**961,919**	**1,090,446**	**1,394,794**	**1,400,416**	**1,535,903**	**1,613,742**	**1,729,139**	**1,697,267**	**1,750,562**

[1] Business bankruptcies include those filed under chapters 7, 9, 11, or 12.   [2] Includes Section 304 petitions not shown separately.   [3] Chapter 7, liquidation of non-exempt assets of businesses or individuals.   [4] Chapter 11, individual or business reorganization.   [5] Chapter 13, adjustment of debts of an individual with regular income.   [6] Chapter 9, adjustment of debts of a municipality.   [7] Chapter 12, adjustment of debts of a family farmer with regular income, effective November 26, 1986.   [8] Chapter 11 U.S.C., Section 304, cases ancillary to foreign proceedings.

Source: Administrative Office of the U.S. Courts, *Statistical Tables for the Federal Judiciary* and "Bankruptcy Statistics"; <http://www.uscourts.gov/bnkrpctystats/statistics.htm>.

Table 755. **Bankruptcy Cases Filed by State: 2000 to 2005**

[In thousands (1,276.9 represents 1,276,900). For years ending June 30. Covers only bankruptcy cases filed under the Bankruptcy Reform Act of 1978. *Bankruptcy:* legal recognition that a company or individual is insolvent and must restructure or liquidate. Petitions "filed" means the commencement of a proceeding through the presentation of a petition to the clerk of the court]

State	2000	2003	2004	2005	State	2000	2003	2004	2005
Total [1]	**1,276.9**	**1,650.3**	**1,635.7**	**1,637.3**	Missouri	26.3	37.3	38.0	39.2
					Montana	3.3	4.3	4.4	4.4
Alabama	31.4	42.0	42.4	42.6	Nebraska	5.6	8.3	8.8	9.6
Alaska	1.4	1.6	1.5	1.6	Nevada.	14.3	20.7	19.4	16.3
Arizona	21.7	31.7	31.8	32.4	New Hampshire	3.9	4.3	4.5	4.9
Arkansas.	16.3	24.5	24.2	25.5					
California.	160.6	148.6	132.5	122.6	New Jersey	38.7	42.0	42.5	40.7
					New Mexico	7.1	10.0	9.4	10.1
Colorado	15.6	24.2	27.4	30.2	New York	61.7	75.0	80.2	81.7
Connecticut	11.4	12.2	11.8	11.8	North Carolina	25.8	38.6	37.7	37.5
Delaware.	4.9	3.9	3.8	3.6	North Dakota	2.0	2.3	2.3	2.5
District of Columbia. .	2.6	2.5	2.1	1.9	Ohio.	53.6	85.4	90.9	95.8
Florida	74.0	94.9	92.2	85.8	Oklahoma	19.3	26.1	27.2	28.2
Georgia	57.9	80.2	79.8	77.3	Oregon	18.1	25.5	24.9	25.3
Hawaii	5.0	4.1	3.5	3.2	Pennsylvania	43.8	57.9	59.1	62.3
Idaho	7.3	9.3	9.7	9.7	Rhode Island	4.8	4.8	4.3	4.4
Illinois.	62.3	86.9	81.3	83.6					
Indiana	37.5	55.3	55.7	55.9	South Carolina	11.7	15.9	15.9	15.2
					South Dakota	2.1	2.8	2.9	2.9
Iowa	8.2	12.4	13.0	14.3	Tennessee.	47.1	65.9	62.9	60.8
Kansas	11.4	16.0	16.3	17.3	Texas	62.9	88.4	92.2	97.5
Kentucky	20.8	28.7	29.3	29.2	Utah	14.4	22.8	21.3	20.5
Louisiana	23.1	28.4	30.2	31.1					
Maine	4.1	4.6	4.6	4.7	Vermont	1.6	1.9	1.8	1.7
					Virginia	37.1	44.1	42.1	38.8
Maryland.	31.1	35.8	32.0	28.5	West Virginia	8.2	11.0	11.4	12.6
Massachusetts	16.7	18.0	18.2	19.6	Wisconsin	18.0	27.7	27.7	29.0
Michigan	36.4	60.8	63.0	68.5	Wyoming.	2.0	2.5	2.4	2.5
Minnesota	15.4	20.6	19.1	19.4					
Mississippi.	17.9	23.0	21.2	21.8					

[1] Includes island areas not shown separately.

Source: Administrative Office of the U.S. Courts, *Statistical Tables for the Federal Judiciary* and "Bankruptcy Statistics"; <http://www.uscourts.gov/bnkrpctystats/statistics.htm>.

U.S. Census Bureau, *Statistical Abstract of the United States: 2007*

Table 756. **Patents and Trademarks: 1990 to 2005**

[In thousands (99.2 represents 99,200). Calendar year data. Covers U.S. patents issued to citizens of the United States and residents of foreign countries. For data on foreign countries, see Table 1323]

Type	1990	1995	1999	2000	2001	2002	2003	2004	2005
Patents issued	**99.2**	**113.8**	**169.1**	**176.0**	**184.0**	**184.4**	**187.0**	**181.3**	**157.7**
Inventions	90.4	101.4	153.5	157.5	166.0	167.3	169.0	164.3	143.8
Individuals	17.3	17.4	22.8	22.4	21.7	20.5	19.6	17.6	14.7
Corporations:									
United States	36.1	44.0	69.4	70.9	74.3	74.2	75.3	73.0	65.2
Foreign [1]	36.0	39.1	60.3	63.3	69.0	71.8	73.2	72.9	63.2
U.S. government	1.0	1.0	1.0	0.9	1.0	0.9	0.9	0.8	0.7
Designs	8.0	11.7	14.7	17.4	16.9	15.5	16.6	15.7	13.0
Botanical plants	0.3	0.4	0.4	0.5	0.6	1.1	1.0	1.0	0.7
Reissues.	0.4	0.3	0.4	0.5	0.5	0.5	0.4	0.3	0.2
U.S. residents	52.8	64.4	94.0	96.9	98.6	97.1	98.6	94.1	82.6
Foreign country residents	46.2	49.4	75.1	79.1	85.4	87.3	88.5	87.2	75.2
Percent of total	46.7	43.4	44.4	44.9	46.4	47.3	47.3	48.1	47.6
Trademarks:									
Applications filed.	127.3	181.0	328.6	361.8	277.3	264.1	271.7	304.5	334.7
Issued	60.8	92.5	191.9	115.2	142.9	176.0	166.6	146.0	154.8
Trademarks	53.6	85.6	184.9	106.4	109.6	146.9	130.9	113.7	121.6
Trademark renewals.	7.2	6.9	7.0	8.8	33.3	29.2	35.6	32.3	33.3

[1] Includes patents to foreign governments.

Source: U.S. Patent and Trademark Office, "Statistical Reports Available For Viewing, Calendar Year Patent Statistics"; <http://www.uspto.gov/web/offices/ac/ido/oeip/taf/reports.htm> and unpublished data.

Table 757. **Patents by State and Island Areas: 2005**

[Includes only U.S. patents granted to residents of the United States and territories]

State	Total	Inventions	Designs	Botanical plants	Reissues	State	Total	Inventions	Designs	Botanical plants	Reissues
Total	**82,562**	**74,637**	**7,553**	**236**	**136**	Missouri	732	628	96	7	1
Alabama.	359	318	37	4	–	Montana.	119	101	18	–	–
Alaska	36	35	1	–	–	Nebraska	205	182	23	–	–
Arizona.	1,598	1,457	137	–	4	Nevada	443	383	58	–	2
Arkansas	153	126	26	1	–	New Hampshire . .	538	498	39	–	1
California	19,656	17,989	1,532	106	29	New Jersey.	2,868	2,557	307	1	3
Colorado.	1,972	1,854	113	1	4	New Mexico	272	265	5	–	2
Connecticut.	1,677	1,520	149	4	4	New York	5,305	4,703	592	2	8
Delaware	341	318	23	–	–	North Carolina . . .	1,839	1,610	219	5	5
District of						North Dakota. . . .	81	74	4	3	–
Columbia	59	55	4	–	–	Ohio	2,727	2,319	404	1	3
Florida	2,707	2,291	387	26	3	Oklahoma	429	403	25	1	–
Georgia	1,358	1,214	136	3	5	Oregon	1,849	1,618	198	28	5
Hawaii	58	50	7	1	–	Pennsylvania. . . .	2,546	2,298	240	4	4
Idaho	1,549	1,529	16	1	3	Rhode Island	312	263	48	–	1
Illinois	3,297	2,752	533	5	7	South Carolina . . .	539	460	76	–	3
Indiana.	1,246	1,108	133	4	1	South Dakota . . .	68	66	2	–	–
Iowa	629	560	68	–	1	Tennessee	712	584	128	–	–
Kansas.	455	380	74	–	1	Texas.	5,524	5,260	257	1	6
Kentucky	377	346	30	–	1	Utah	644	554	87	–	3
Louisiana	298	271	25	–	1	Vermont	411	367	44	–	–
Maine.	159	151	6	1	1	Virginia.	1,027	946	80	–	1
Maryland	1,283	1,191	85	3	4	Washington.	2,482	2,291	187	2	3
Massachusetts. . .	3,301	3,114	177	4	6	West Virginia. . . .	98	91	6	1	–
Michigan.	3,664	3,367	283	11	3	Wisconsin	1,756	1,489	261	3	3
Minnesota.	2,582	2,431	146	1	4	Wyoming	55	53	2	–	–
Mississippi	127	114	12	–	1	Island areas	40	33	7	–	–

– Represents zero.

Source: U.S. Patent and Trademark Office, unpublished data.

Table 758. **Copyright Registration by Subject Matter: 1990 to 2005**

[In thousands (590.7 represents 590,700). For years ending September 30. Comprises claims to copyrights registered for both U.S. and foreign works. Semiconductor chips and renewals are not considered copyright registration claims]

Subject matter	1990	2000	2004	2005	Subject matter	1990	2000	2004	2005
Total copyright claims . . .	**590.7**	**497.6**	**642.0**	**515.2**	Works of the visual arts [3]	76.7	85.8	107.8	82.5
Monographs [1]	179.7	169.7	227.5	191.4					
Serials.	111.5	69.0	68.2	57.7	Semiconductor chip				
Sound recordings	37.5	34.2	68.0	49.9	products	1.0	0.7	0.3	0.5
Musical works [2]	185.3	138.9	170.5	133.7	Renewals	51.8	16.8	18.9	15.8

[1] Includes computer software and machine readable works. [2] Includes dramatic works, accompanying music, choreography, pantomimes, motion pictures, and filmstrips. [3] Two-dimensional works of fine and graphic art, including prints and art reproductions; sculptural works; technical drawings and models; photographs; commercial prints and labels; works of applied arts, cartographic works, and multimedia works.

Source: The Library of Congress, Copyright Office, *Annual Report.*

Business Enterprise 507

Table 759. **Net Stock of Private Fixed Assets by Industry: 2000 to 2004**

[In billions of dollars (21,190 represents $21,190,000,000,000). **Estimates as of Dec. 31.** Net stock estimates are presented in terms of current cost and cover equipment, software, and structures]

Industry	NAICS code [1]	2000	2002	2003	2004
Private fixed assets	(X)	21,190	23,523	24,763	27,043
Agriculture, forestry, fishing, and hunting.	11	406	434	452	489
Farms [2]	111, 112	379	407	423	458
Forestry, fishing, and related activities.	113-115	27	28	28	31
Mining	21	580	639	650	757
Oil and gas extraction	211	442	498	509	606
Mining, except oil and gas	212	92	93	94	101
Support activites for mining.	213	46	48	47	50
Utilities.	22	1,039	1,138	1,180	1,308
Construction	23	173	187	191	205
Manufacturing	31-33	1,759	1,813	1,815	1,892
Durable goods	(X)	996	1,033	1,033	1,075
Wood products	321	31	32	31	32
Nonmetallic mineral products.	327	55	58	59	62
Primary metals	331	124	122	120	123
Fabricated metal products.	332	112	115	116	121
Machinery	333	140	150	150	157
Computer and electronic products	334	245	257	253	259
Electrical equipment, appliances, and components	335	45	46	46	48
Motor vehicles, bodies and trailers, and parts	3361-3363	105	108	111	118
Other transportation equipment	3364, 3365, 3369	79	83	84	89
Furniture and related products	337	16	17	18	19
Miscellaneous manufacturing.	339	43	45	45	47
Nondurable goods.	(X)	763	779	782	817
Food and beverage and tobacco products	311, 312	182	186	188	198
Textile mills and textile product mills	313, 314	44	42	41	42
Apparel and leather and allied products.	315, 316	17	17	16	17
Paper products	322	100	98	97	99
Printing and related support activities	323	41	42	43	45
Petroleum and coal products	324	92	96	99	105
Chemical products.	325	220	228	228	239
Plastics and rubber products	326	67	70	70	73
Wholesale trade.	42	348	363	373	393
Retail trade.	44-45	641	704	730	790
Transportation and warehousing	48-49	805	850	872	919
Air transportation	481	196	224	233	248
Railroad transportation.	482	267	273	280	285
Water transportation	483	39	42	44	47
Truck transportation.	484	68	66	65	67
Transit and ground passenger transportation	485	34	35	36	38
Pipeline transportation	486	74	82	86	102
Other transportation and support activites [3]	487, 488, 492	105	104	103	105
Warehousing and storage.	493	22	24	25	27
Information	51	817	869	879	923
Publishing industries (includes software)	511	50	50	51	54
Motion picture and sound recording industries	512	32	32	32	33
Broadcasting and telecommunications	513	716	764	771	807
Information and data processing services	514	19	23	26	29
Finance and insurance	52	822	877	906	964
Federal Reserve banks	521	11	12	13	14
Credit intermediation and related activities.	522	465	494	512	544
Securities, commodity contracts, and investments.	523	86	91	93	99
Insurance carriers and related activities.	524	165	173	179	190
Funds, trusts, and other financial vehicles	525	95	107	109	117
Real estate and rental and leasing	53	11,476	13,058	13,974	15,412
Real estate	531	11,233	12,792	13,696	15,122
Rental and leasing services and lessors of intangible assets [4] .	532, 533	243	266	279	290
Professional, scientific, and technical services	54	205	236	257	283
Legal services	5411	20	21	22	23
Computer systems design and related services	5415	50	57	60	65
Miscellaneous professional, scientific, and technical services [5] .	([5])	135	158	175	195
Management of companies and enterprises [6]	551111, 551112	269	295	309	336
Administrative and waste management services.	56	153	167	176	190
Administrative and support services	561	84	97	103	113
Waste management and remediation services	562	68	71	72	77
Educational services.	61	213	251	269	299
Health care and social assistance	62	693	777	827	906
Ambulatory health care services	621	190	210	222	240
Hospitals.	622	449	508	542	597
Nursing and residential care facilities	623	29	33	35	38
Social assistance	624	24	27	28	30
Arts, entertainment, and recreation	71	128	149	158	174
Performing arts, spectator sports, museums, and related activities	711, 712	48	56	60	68
Amusements, gambling, and recreation industries.	713	80	93	97	106
Accommodation and food services	72	336	361	374	403
Accommodation	721	177	186	189	201
Food services and drinking places	722	160	175	185	203
Other services, except government	81	329	357	371	401

X Not applicable.　[1] Based on North American Industry Classification System, 1997; see text this section.　[2] NAICS crop and animal production.　[3] Consists of scenic and sightseeing transportation; transportation support activities; and couriers and messengers.　[4] Intangible assets include patents, trademarks, and franchise agreements, but not copyrights.　[5] Consists of accounting, tax preparation, bookkeeping, and payroll services (NAICS code 5412); architectural, engineering, and related services (5413); specialized design services (5414); management, scientific, and technical consulting services (5416); scientific research and development services (5417); advertising and related services (5418); and other professional, scientific, and technical services (5419).　[6] Consists of bank and other holding companies.

Source: U.S. Bureau of Economic Analysis, "Table 3.1ES. Current-Cost Net Stock of Private Fixed Assets by Industry"; <http://www.bea.gov/bea/dn/FA2004/SelectTable.asp#S3>; accessed 26 April 2006.

Table 760. **Gross Private Domestic Investment in Current and Real (2000) Dollars: 1990 to 2004**

[In billions of dollars (861 represents $861,000,000,000). Covers equipment, software, and structures]

Item	1990	1995	1999	2000	2001	2002	2003	2004
CURRENT DOLLARS								
Gross private domestic investment . . .	861	1,144	1,626	1,736	1,614	1,582	1,670	1,928
Less: Consumption of fixed capital	552	713	914	991	1,076	1,080	1,113	1,206
Equals: Net private domestic investment	309	431	711	745	539	502	558	722
Fixed investment	846	1,113	1,559	1,679	1,646	1,570	1,655	1,873
Less: Consumption of fixed capital . . .	552	713	914	991	1,076	1,080	1,113	1,206
Equals: Net fixed investment	295	400	644	688	571	490	542	667
Nonresidential	622	810	1,134	1,232	1,177	1,066	1,082	1,199
Residential	224	303	425	447	469	504	573	674
Change in private inventories	15	31	67	57	-32	12	15	55
CHAINED (2000) DOLLARS								
Gross private domestic investment . . .	895	1,134	1,643	1,736	1,598	1,557	1,617	1,810
Less: Consumption of fixed capital	572	707	922	991	1,072	1,080	1,108	1,174
Equals: Net private domestic investment	323	427	721	745	527	477	510	636
Fixed investment	887	1,110	1,576	1,679	1,629	1,545	1,600	1,755
Nonresidential	595	763	1,133	1,232	1,181	1,072	1,085	1,187
Residential	299	353	444	447	449	470	509	562
Change in private inventories	15	30	69	57	-32	13	16	52

Source: U.S. Bureau of Economic Analysis, *Survey of Current Business*, May 2006. See also <http://www.bea.gov/bea/dn/nipaweb/selecttable.asp>.

Table 761. **Information and Communications Technology (ICT) Equipment and Computer Software Expenditures: 2003 and 2004**

[In millions of dollars (91,320 represents $91,320,000,000). Covers companies with employees. Supplemental to the Annual Capital Expenditure Survey, the Information and Communication Technology Survey collects investment figures related to technology falling below a company's capitalization threshold. This survey is sent to a sample of approximately 46,000 private nonfarm employer businesses operating in the United States]

Type of expenditure and industry	NAICS code [1]	Noncapitalized expenditures [2]		Capitalized expenditures [3]	
		2003	2004	2003	2004
Total expenditures for ICT equipment and computer software	(X)	91,320	92,608	132,086	139,335
Total equipment expenditures	(X)	39,569	38,871	(NA)	(NA)
Purchases	(X)	19,924	17,780	87,794	86,445
Computer and peripheral equipment	(X)	13,469	11,899	55,847	52,690
Information and communication technology equipment	(X)	6,043	5,538	28,894	29,225
Electromedical and electrotherapeutic apparatus	(X)	413	344	3,052	4,530
Operating leases and rental payments	(X)	19,645	21,091	(NA)	(NA)
Computer and peripheral equipment	(X)	12,337	13,813	(NA)	(NA)
Information and communication technology equipment	(X)	6,588	5,724	(NA)	(NA)
Electromedical and electrotherapeutic apparatus	(X)	720	1,555	(NA)	(NA)
Total computer software expenditures	(X)	51,750	53,737	(NA)	(NA)
Purchases and payroll for developing software	(X)	32,379	31,948	44,292	52,890
Software licensing and service/maintenance agreements	(X)	19,372	21,789	(NA)	(NA)
Forestry, fishing, and agricultural services	113-115	34	83	53	81
Mining	21	530	624	421	717
Utilities	22	1,251	1,403	2,271	2,347
Construction	23	1,109	1,163	1,043	1,576
Manufacturing	31-33	16,174	16,359	14,014	17,386
Durable goods industries	321, 327, 33	10,827	11,031	7,863	10,613
Nondurable goods industries	31, 322-326	5,347	5,328	6,150	6,772
Wholesale trade	42	3,932	3,761	5,790	5,492
Retail trade	44-45	4,108	4,177	9,129	10,028
Transportation and warehousing	48-49	1,711	1,473	2,054	3,018
Information	51	18,294	17,977	37,088	36,509
Finance and insurance	52	18,363	18,900	23,857	24,210
Real estate and rental and leasing	53	852	908	3,043	2,333
Professional, scientific, and technical services	54	12,759	12,104	11,409	10,492
Management of companies and enterprises	55	552	716	1,258	1,634
Administrative and support and waste management	56	2,502	2,626	4,602	3,261
Educational services	61	1,584	1,522	2,255	2,113
Health care and social assistance	62	4,954	6,009	8,928	12,991
Arts, entertainment, and recreation	71	349	392	976	1,108
Accommodation and food services	72	611	674	1,338	1,297
Other services (except public administration)	81	1,322	1,287	1,980	2,238
Equipment expenditures serving multiple industry codes	(X)	327	452	575	506

NA Not available.   X Not applicable.   [1] Based on North American Industry Classification System, 2002; see text, this section.   [2] Expenses for ICT equipment including computer software not charged to asset accounts for which depreciation or amortization accounts are ordinarily maintained.   [3] Expenses for ICT equipment including computer software chargeable to asset accounts for which depreciation or amortization accounts are ordinarily maintained.

Source: U.S. Census Bureau, *Information and Communication Technology: 2004*, ICT/04, March 2006.

Business Enterprise 509

Table 762. **Capital Expenditures: 2000 to 2004**

[In billions of dollars (1,161 represents $1,161,000,000,000). Based on a sample survey and subject to sampling error; see source for details]

Item	All companies				Companies with employees				Companies without employees			
	2000	2002	2003	2004	2000	2002	2003	2004	2000	2002	2003	2004
Capital expenditures, total.............	1,161	997	975	1,047	1,090	917	887	959	71	80	88	89
Structures.............	364	358	345	372	338	325	314	339	26	33	31	33
New................	329	321	305	327	309	300	282	303	20	21	23	24
Used................	35	37	39	45	29	25	32	36	6	12	7	9
Equipment and software.....	797	639	630	676	752	592	573	620	45	47	58	56
New................	751	598	579	630	718	564	541	589	32	34	39	40
Used................	46	41	51	46	34	28	32	31	12	13	19	15
Capital leases..........	20	15	16	18	19	15	15	18	(Z)	(Z)	(Z)	(Z)

Z Less than $500 million.

Source: U.S. Census Bureau, *Annual Capital Expenditures, 2004*, Series ACE.

Table 763. **Capital Expenditures by Industry: 2000 and 2004**

[In billions of dollars (1,090 represents $1,090,000,000,000). Covers only companies with employees. Based on the North American Industry Classification System (NAICS), 2002; see text, this section. Based on a sample survey and subject to sampling error; see source for details]

Industry	NAICS code	2000	2004	Industry	NAICS code	2000	2004
Total expenditures.....	(X)	1,090	959	Professional, scientific, and technical services.........	54	34	27
Forestry, fishing, and agricultural services.......	113-115	1	2	Management of companies and enterprises..........	55	5	4
Mining................	21	43	54	Admin/support waste mgt/ remediation services.......	56	18	18
Utilities...............	22	61	50	Educational services........	61	18	19
Construction............	23	25	29	Health care and social assistance	62	52	65
Manufacturing...........	31-33	215	157	Arts, entertainment, and recreation..............	71	19	12
Durable goods..........	321, 327, 33	134	85	Accommodation and food services...........	72	26	21
Nondurable goods	31, 322-326	81	72	Other services (except public administration)........	81	21	20
Wholesale trade	42	34	32	Structure and equipment expenditures serving multiple industry categories ..	(X)	2	1
Retail trade.............	44-45	70	72				
Transportation and warehousing	48-49	60	48				
Information.............	51	160	83				
Finance and insurance......	52	134	153				
Real estate and rental and leasing...............	53	92	92				

X Not applicable.

Source: U.S. Census Bureau, *Annual Capital Expenditures, 2004* Series ACE.

Table 764. **Business Cycle Expansions and Contractions—Months of Duration: 1945 to 2001**

[A trough is the low point of a business cycle; a peak is the high point. Contraction, or recession, is the period from peak to subsequent trough; expansion is the period from trough to subsequent peak. Business cycle reference dates are determined by the National Bureau of Economic Research, Inc.]

Business cycle reference date				Contraction (peak to trough)	Expansion (previous trough to this peak)	Length of cycle	
Peak		Trough				Trough from previous trough	Peak from previous peak
Month	Year	Month	Year				
February.............	1945	October	1945	8	[1]80	[1]88	[2]93
November............	1948	October	1949	11	37	48	45
July	1953	May..........	1954	10	45	55	56
August	1957	April	1958	8	39	47	49
April................	1960	February	1961	10	24	34	32
December............	1969	November	1970	11	106	117	116
November............	1973	March	1975	16	36	52	47
January	1980	July..........	1980	6	58	64	74
July	1981	November	1982	16	12	28	18
July	1990	March	1991	8	92	100	108
March...............	2001	November	2001	8	120	128	128
Average, all cycles: 1945 to 2001 (10 cycles).				10	57	67	67
Average, peacetime cycles: 1945 to 2001 (8 cycles) .				10	52	63	63

[1] Previous trough: June 1938. [2] Previous peak: May 1937.

Source: National Bureau of Economic Research, Inc., Cambridge, MA, "Business Cycle Expansions and Contractions"; <http://www.nber.org/cycles.html>; (accessed: 19 June 2006).

Table 765. Composite Indexes of Leading, Coincident, and Lagging Economic Indicators: 2000 to 2005

[299.3 represents 299,300]

Item	Unit	2000	2001	2002	2003	2004	2005
Leading index, composite	1996 = 100	115.0	112.9	118.4	124.3	133.5	136.6
Average weekly hours, manufacturing . . .	Hours........	41.2	40.4	40.5	40.4	40.8	40.6
Average weekly initial claims for unemployment insurance	1,000........	299.3	406.2	403.9	401.8	342.9	331.8
Manufacturers' new orders, consumer goods and materials (1982 dol.)	Mil. dol.	152,031	144,733	143,867	143,459	147,231	146,839
Vendor performance, slower deliveries diffusion index [1]................	Percent	53.3	48.0	53.3	53.0	62.6	54.1
Manufacturers' new orders, nondefense capital goods (1982 dol.)...........	Mil. dol.	49,780	41,707	37,792	39,282	43,014	50,368
Building permits, new private housing units	1,000........	1,598	1,637	1,749	1,888	2,058	2,122
Stock prices, 500 common stocks [1]	1941-43 = 10. ..	1,426.8	1,192.1	995.6	963.7	1,130.6	1,207.1
Money supply, M2 (chain 2000 dol.)	Bil. dol.......	4,798	5,113	5,423	5,691	5,799	5,880
Interest rate spread, 10-year Treasury bonds less federal funds	Percent	-0.20	1.10	2.90	2.90	2.90	1.10
Index of consumer expectations [1]......	1966:1 = 100. ..	102.7	82.3	84.6	81.4	88.5	77.4
Coincident index, composite	1996 = 100	115.4	114.7	114.1	114.5	117.5	120.0
Employees on nonagricultural payrolls...	1,000........	131,792	131,832	130,342	129,993	131,424	133,458
Personal income less transfer payments (chain 2000 dol.)	Bil. dol........	7,345	7,376	7,336	7,415	7,654	7,828
Industrial production.	2002 = 100	103.5	99.9	100.0	100.6	104.7	108.1
Manufacturing and trade sales (chain 2000 dol.)	Mil. dol.	844,794	834,827	844,978	861,783	913,141	944,066
Lagging index, composite	1996 = 100	116.7	117.2	116.4	116.4	116.4	120.5
Average duration of unemployment.....	Weeks	12.7	13.1	16.7	19.2	19.6	18.4
Inventories to sales ratio, manufacturing and trade (chain 2000 dol.)	Ratio........	1.40	1.40	1.40	1.40	1.30	1.30
Change in labor cost per unit of output, manufacturing..................	Percent	2.3	-11.2	0.6	2.7	-2.1	1.0
Average prime rate	Percent	9.2	6.9	4.7	4.1	4.3	6.2
Commercial and industrial loans outstanding (chain 2000 dol.)........	Mil. dol.	953,143	846,293	686,318	588,372	536,711	568,032
Consumer installment credit to personal income ratio.............	Percent	19.2	20.3	21.2	21.5	21.2	20.9
Change in consumer price index for services....................	Percent	3.8	3.9	3.2	3.0	3.0	3.5

[1] Data are from private sources and provided through the courtesy of the compilers and are subject to their copyrights: stock prices, Standard & Poors Corporation; index of consumer expectations, University of Michigan's Survey Research Center; vendor perfomance, Institute for Supply Management.

Source: The Conference Board, New York, NY 10022-6601, *Business Cycle Indicators*, monthly, <http://www.conferenceboard.org/economics/bci/> (copyright).

Table 766. Manufacturing and Trade—Sales and Inventories: 1992 to 2005

[In billions of dollars (541 represents $541,000,000,000), except ratios. Based on North American Industry Classification System (NAICS) 2002; see text, this section]

Year	Sales, average monthly [1]				Inventories [2]				Inventory-sales ratios [3]			
	Total	Manu-factur-ing	Retail trade	Mer-chant whole-salers	Total	Manu-factur-ing	Retail trade	Mer-chant whole-salers	Total	Manu-factur-ing	Retail trade	Mer-chant whole-salers
1992 ..	541	242	151	147	837	379	261	197	1.52	1.57	1.67	1.31
1993 ..	568	252	162	154	864	380	280	205	1.50	1.51	1.68	1.30
1994 ..	610	270	176	165	928	400	305	222	1.46	1.44	1.66	1.29
1995 ..	655	290	185	180	986	425	323	238	1.48	1.44	1.72	1.29
1996 ..	687	300	197	190	1,006	431	334	241	1.46	1.43	1.67	1.27
1997 ..	724	320	206	198	1,047	444	345	258	1.42	1.37	1.64	1.26
1998 ..	743	325	216	202	1,079	449	357	272	1.43	1.38	1.62	1.32
1999 ..	787	336	234	217	1,139	464	385	290	1.40	1.35	1.59	1.30
2000 ..	834	351	249	235	1,199	482	407	310	1.41	1.35	1.59	1.29
2001 ..	823	335	256	232	1,141	448	395	298	1.43	1.39	1.58	1.32
2002 ..	828	330	261	236	1,158	439	416	302	1.38	1.32	1.55	1.26
2003 ..	850	331	272	247	1,147	407	432	308	1.35	1.27	1.56	1.23
2004 ..	919	355	290	275	1,234	435	461	338	1.30	1.19	1.56	1.18
2005 ..	985	379	310	296	1,288	452	474	362	1.28	1.18	1.50	1.19

[1] Averages of monthly not-seasonally-adjusted figures. [2] Seasonally adjusted end-of-year data. [3] Averages of seasonally adjusted monthly ratios.

Source: U.S. Council of Economic Advisors, *Economic Indicators*, May 2006.

Business Enterprise 511

Table 767. **Industrial Production Indexes by Industry and Major Market Groups: 1990 to 2005**

[2002 = 100. Except as noted, based on the North American Industry Classification System (NAICS); 2002; see text, this section.

Industry and market group	NAICS code	1990	1995	2000	2001	2002	2003	2004	2005
Total index	(X)	69.4	80.2	103.5	99.9	100.0	100.6	104.7	108.2
INDUSTRY GROUP									
Manufacturing (SIC) [1]	(X)	66.6	78.3	104.3	99.9	100.0	100.5	105.4	109.6
Manufacturing (NAICS).	31-33	65.3	77.6	104.0	99.7	100.0	100.7	105.8	110.0
Durable goods.	(X)	52.5	66.8	105.3	100.2	100.0	102.3	109.8	117.0
Wood products.	321	83.9	90.8	103.6	97.0	100.0	98.8	104.9	107.6
Nonmetallic mineral products	327	83.4	89.1	103.8	99.9	100.0	100.1	105.4	107.2
Primary metals.	331	95.4	104.5	109.5	99.1	100.0	97.6	103.4	100.7
Fabricated metal products	332	80.7	95.1	111.3	103.2	100.0	98.6	103.2	106.7
Machinery.	333	87.1	102.7	118.4	104.8	100.0	99.0	110.7	115.7
Computers and electronic products . .	334	13.2	26.4	102.5	103.6	100.0	112.6	130.7	156.7
Electrical equipment, appliances, and components.	335	86.7	101.7	120.6	108.3	100.0	97.8	101.5	106.9
Motor vehicles and parts	3361-3	55.5	79.0	99.5	90.6	100.0	104.0	108.0	112.1
Aerospace and other misc. transportation equipment	3364-9	123.2	87.5	99.7	105.9	100.0	97.3	100.7	109.8
Furniture and related products	337	73.2	80.0	100.4	94.0	100.0	98.3	101.4	100.7
Miscellaneous products	339	65.7	77.2	94.9	93.7	100.0	102.0	105.5	110.3
Nondurable goods	(X)	87.8	95.8	102.4	99.0	100.0	98.9	101.0	101.8
Food, beverage and tobacco products	311,2	89.7	97.1	100.9	100.7	100.0	100.5	102.3	104.4
Textile and product mills.	313,4	100.2	113.1	113.3	101.6	100.0	95.9	93.1	91.4
Apparel and leather.	315,6	162.0	169.3	141.7	120.4	100.0	92.1	88.4	86.0
Paper	322	97.0	106.7	105.0	99.0	100.0	95.9	98.0	98.0
Printing and related support	323	101.9	107.1	113.0	106.0	100.0	95.8	96.0	97.7
Petroleum and coal products	324	86.6	89.5	96.6	96.0	100.0	98.3	103.7	103.8
Chemical.	325	79.1	84.4	96.0	94.3	100.0	99.7	102.8	102.6
Plastics and rubber products.	326	67.7	85.7	103.6	97.6	100.0	99.4	102.5	104.8
Other manufacturing (non-NAICS) [2].	1133, 5111	96.7	90.9	109.5	103.1	100.0	97.0	98.8	101.9
Mining	21	106.9	104.4	103.5	104.5	100.0	99.8	99.5	97.4
Utilities	2211,2	77.9	87.2	97.4	97.0	100.0	102.0	103.1	105.7
Electric power generation, transmission and distribution	2211	76.7	85.7	97.2	96.9	100.0	102.1	104.1	107.4
Natural gas distribution.	2212	85.6	96.9	98.6	97.2	100.0	101.2	98.2	97.2
MAJOR MARKETS									
Final products and nonindustrial supplies.	(X)	73.6	83.2	103.4	100.5	100.0	100.8	104.8	109.3
Consumer goods.	(X)	75.8	86.9	99.0	97.8	100.0	101.0	103.1	105.5
Durable	(X)	56.4	75.0	98.3	94.1	100.0	104.0	106.9	109.3
Automotive products	(X)	50.5	70.4	93.4	90.5	100.0	107.1	109.3	112.6
Home electronics	(X)	7.2	32.5	98.7	98.8	100.0	112.1	113.6	120.0
Appliances, furniture, carpeting	(X)	75.8	84.0	100.5	96.2	100.0	99.6	103.9	105.4
Miscellaneous goods	(X)	81.8	92.4	106.3	98.8	100.0	99.4	103.2	103.9
Nondurable.	(X)	84.8	92.2	99.2	99.3	100.0	99.8	101.6	104.0
Nonenergy	(X)	86.3	93.5	100.2	100.0	100.0	99.7	101.5	103.8
Foods and tobacco	(X)	91.2	98.3	101.6	101.5	100.0	100.6	102.7	104.4
Clothing.	(X)	161.3	169.5	141.2	120.5	100.0	92.2	88.2	85.3
Chemical products.	(X)	64.0	72.2	88.2	92.9	100.0	100.3	102.2	104.8
Paper products	(X)	84.6	87.7	103.7	100.9	100.0	96.7	99.6	105.4
Energy	(X)	78.3	86.4	94.9	96.0	100.0	100.6	101.9	104.6
Business equipment.	(X)	61.0	73.8	116.6	108.4	100.0	100.0	109.4	119.5
Transit	(X)	110.3	90.8	117.5	111.9	100.0	96.6	105.6	117.5
Information processing	(X)	29.5	47.0	123.2	117.7	100.0	103.4	113.8	134.0
Industrial and other	(X)	82.4	96.1	112.6	101.7	100.0	99.3	108.2	112.8
Defense and space equipment.	(X)	145.8	108.2	92.2	100.1	100.0	105.0	113.1	125.7
Construction supplies.	(X)	77.3	87.0	105.0	100.2	100.0	99.1	104.6	108.7
Business supplies	(X)	71.3	80.7	104.0	99.8	100.0	100.7	103.9	107.7
Materials.	(X)	64.2	76.3	103.7	99.0	100.0	100.4	104.6	106.7
Nonenergy.	(X)	57.3	71.4	104.5	98.6	100.0	100.6	106.5	110.2
Durable	(X)	44.0	60.3	104.5	99.0	100.0	102.3	110.4	117.1
Consumer parts	(X)	59.7	86.6	108.8	95.9	100.0	97.7	99.9	102.0
Equipment parts	(X)	20.8	33.1	100.1	99.6	100.0	109.6	125.8	143.9
Other	(X)	80.8	94.2	107.4	99.9	100.0	98.7	103.7	105.2
Nondurable.	(X)	92.1	98.2	104.7	98.1	100.0	97.8	100.1	99.2
Textile.	(X)	103.9	119.3	112.6	99.6	100.0	94.4	89.2	84.5
Paper	(X)	102.0	108.8	108.3	101.8	100.0	95.0	96.7	97.1
Chemical.	(X)	86.3	91.1	102.4	95.4	100.0	99.4	104.2	100.8
Energy	(X)	95.7	98.1	101.1	100.0	100.0	99.6	99.6	97.9

X Not applicable. [1] Standard Industrial Classification (SIC); see text, this section. [2] Those industries—logging and newspaper, periodical, book, and directory publishing— that have traditionally been considered to be manufacturing.

Source: Board of Governors of the Federal Reserve System, *Statistical Supplement to the Federal Reserve Bulletin*, monthly; and *Industrial Production and Capacity Utilization*, Statistical Release G.17, monthly.

512 Business Enterprise

Table 768. **Index of Industrial Capacity: 1990 to 2005**

[**2002 output = 100**. Annual figures are averages of monthly data. Capacity represents estimated quantity of output relative to output in 2002 which the current stock of plant and equipment was capable of producing]

Year	Index of capacity		Relation of output to capacity (percent)				
			Total industry	Stage of process			
	Total industry	Manufacturing		Crude [1]	Primary and semifinished [2]	Finished [3]	Manufacturing
1990	84.2	81.7	82.4	88.2	82.6	80.3	81.6
1995	95.6	94.3	83.9	88.5	86.7	79.4	83.0
1996	100.7	100.1	83.0	88.2	85.6	78.7	81.8
1997	106.9	107.0	83.9	89.7	85.8	80.2	83.0
1998	114.8	116.1	82.7	87.0	83.9	80.4	81.7
1999	121.1	123.4	81.9	86.6	84.1	78.5	80.8
2000	126.6	129.9	81.8	88.4	84.4	77.3	80.3
2001	131.0	134.9	76.3	85.6	77.5	72.8	74.1
2002	133.1	136.4	75.1	84.0	77.1	71.2	73.3
2003	133.0	136.4	75.7	84.9	77.4	71.7	73.7
2004	133.3	136.6	78.6	86.8	80.6	74.3	77.1
2005	135.0	138.7	80.0	85.5	81.8	76.9	78.9

[1] Crude processing, covers a relatively small portion of total industrial capacity and consists of logging (NAICS 1133), much of mining (excluding stone, sand, and gravel mining and oil and gas drilling, which are NAICS 21231, 21221-2, and 213111) and some basic manufacturing industries, including basic chemicals (NAICS 3251); fertilizers, pesticides, and other agricultural chemicals (NAICS 32531,2); pulp, paper, and paperboard mills (NAICS 3221); and alumina, aluminum, and other nonferrous production and processing mills (NAICS 3313,4).   [2] Primary and semifinished processing loosely corresponds to the previously published aggregate, primary processing. Includes utilities and portions of several 2-digit SIC industries included in the former advanced processing group. These include printing and related support activities (NAICS 3231); paints and adhesives (NAICS 3255); and newspaper, periodical, book, and directory publishers (NAICS 5111).   [3] Finished processing generally corresponds to the previously published aggregate, advanced processing. Includes oil and gas well drilling and carpet and rug mills.

Source: Board of Governors of the Federal Reserve System, *Industrial Production and Capacity Utilization*, Statistical Release G.17, monthly. (Based on data from Federal Reserve Board, U.S. Department of Commerce, U.S. Bureau of Labor Statistics, and McGraw-Hill Information Systems Company, New York, NY; and other sources.)

Table 769. **Productivity and Related Measures: 1980 to 2005**

[See text, this section. Minus sign (–) indicates decrease]

Item	1980	1990	1995	2000	2001	2002	2003	2004	2005
INDEXES (1992 = 100)									
Output per hour, business sector	79.2	94.4	101.5	115.9	118.8	123.6	128.6	133.1	136.6
Nonfarm business	80.6	94.5	102.0	115.5	118.3	123.1	128.0	132.4	136.0
Manufacturing	(NA)	92.9	110.0	134.4	137.1	146.2	154.4	163.0	171.2
Output, [1] business sector	68.8	96.9	111.4	140.5	141.0	143.1	147.9	154.9	161.2
Nonfarm business	69.2	97.1	111.8	140.8	141.3	143.4	148.2	155.3	161.8
Manufacturing	(NA)	97.6	115.0	138.9	132.5	131.2	131.8	138.4	143.8
Hours, [2] business sector.	87.0	102.7	109.7	121.2	118.6	115.7	115.0	116.4	118.0
Nonfarm business	85.9	102.7	109.6	121.9	119.5	116.5	115.8	117.3	119.0
Manufacturing	(NA)	105.0	104.6	103.4	96.6	89.8	85.4	84.9	84.0
Compensation per hour, [3] business sector	54.1	90.6	105.8	134.4	140.0	144.9	150.7	157.8	165.8
Nonfarm business	54.4	90.4	105.9	133.9	139.2	144.2	149.9	156.7	164.7
Manufacturing	(NA)	90.5	107.3	134.7	137.9	147.8	160.1	163.8	174.9
Real hourly compensation, [3] business sector . . .	89.1	96.2	98.7	111.8	113.3	115.4	117.3	119.6	121.6
Nonfarm business	89.5	96.1	98.8	111.3	112.6	114.8	116.6	118.8	120.8
Manufacturing	(NA)	96.1	100.1	112.0	111.5	117.7	124.6	124.1	128.2
Unit labor costs, [4] business sector	68.4	96.0	104.2	116.0	117.8	117.2	117.1	118.5	121.4
Nonfarm business	67.5	95.7	103.8	115.9	117.6	117.1	117.1	118.4	121.1
Manufacturing	(NA)	97.4	97.6	100.3	100.6	101.1	103.7	100.5	102.2
ANNUAL PERCENT CHANGE [5]									
Output per hour, business sector	–0.2	2.1	0.1	2.8	2.5	4.0	4.1	3.5	2.6
Nonfarm business	–0.2	1.9	0.5	2.8	2.4	4.1	3.9	3.4	2.7
Manufacturing	(NA)	2.9	3.6	4.8	2.0	6.6	5.6	5.5	5.0
Output, [1] business sector	–1.1	1.5	2.9	3.9	0.3	1.5	3.4	4.8	4.0
Nonfarm business	–1.0	1.5	3.2	3.8	0.4	1.5	3.3	4.8	4.2
Manufacturing	(NA)	0.3	4.5	3.1	–4.7	–0.9	0.5	5.0	3.9
Hours, [2] business sector.	–0.9	–0.6	2.8	1.1	–2.1	–2.4	–0.7	1.3	1.4
Nonfarm business	–0.8	–0.4	2.7	1.1	–2.0	–2.5	–0.6	1.3	1.4
Manufacturing	(NA)	–2.5	0.8	–1.6	–6.5	–7.1	–4.9	–0.5	–1.1
Compensation per hour, [3] business sector	10.8	6.3	2.1	7.0	4.2	3.5	4.0	4.7	5.1
Nonfarm business	10.8	6.1	2.1	7.1	3.9	3.6	4.0	4.6	5.1
Manufacturing	(NA)	4.4	1.9	9.2	2.3	7.3	8.3	2.3	6.8
Real hourly compensation, [3] business sector . . .	–0.2	1.3	–0.4	3.5	1.3	1.9	1.7	2.0	1.7
Nonfarm business	–0.2	1.0	–0.3	3.6	1.1	2.0	1.6	1.8	1.7
Manufacturing	(NA)	–0.5	–0.5	5.6	–0.5	5.6	5.9	–0.4	3.3
Unit labor costs, [4] business sector	11.0	4.1	1.9	4.0	1.6	–0.5	–0.1	1.2	2.4
Nonfarm business	11.0	4.1	1.6	4.2	1.4	–0.5	(Z)	1.1	2.3
Manufacturing	(NA)	1.5	–1.7	4.2	0.3	0.6	2.5	–3.1	1.7

NA Not available.   Less than 0.05 percent.   [1] Refers to gross sectoral product, annual weighted.   [2] Hours at work of all persons engaged in the business and nonfarm business sectors (employees, proprietors, and unpaid family workers); employees' and proprietors' hours in manufacturing.   [3] Wages and salaries of employees plus employers' contributions for social insurance and private benefit plans. Also includes an estimate of same for self-employed. Real compensation deflated by the consumer price index for all urban consumers, see text, Section 14.   [4] Hourly compensation divided by output per hour.   [5] All changes are from the immediate prior year.

Source: U.S. Bureau of Labor Statistics, *Productivity and Costs*, News USDL 06-941, June 1, 2006; and Internet site <http://www.bls.gov/lpc/home.htm>.

Business Enterprise   513

Table 770. **Corporate Profits, Taxes, and Dividends: 1990 to 2005**

[In billions of dollars (438 represents $438,000,000,000). Covers corporations organized for profit and other entities treated as corporations. Represents profits to U.S. residents, without deduction of depletion charges and exclusive of capital gains and losses; intercorporate dividends from profits of domestic corporations are eliminated; net receipts of dividends, reinvested earnings of incorporated foreign affiliates, and earnings of unincorporated foreign affiliates are added. CCA = capital consumption adjustment]

Item	1990	2000	2001	2002	2003	2004	2005
Corporate profits with IVA and CCA	438	818	767	886	1,032	1,162	1,352
Taxes on corporate income	145	265	204	193	232	271	378
Profits after tax with IVA and CCA	292	553	563	694	800	890	974
Net dividends	169	378	371	399	423	493	514
Undistributed profits with IVA and CCA. . .	123	175	192	295	377	397	460
Cash flow:							
Net cash flow with IVA and CCA	491	865	945	1,037	1,131	1,197	1,303
Undistributed profits with IVA and CCA. . .	123	175	192	295	377	397	460
Consumption of fixed capital	368	690	753	742	754	800	844
Less: Inventory valuation adjustment							
(IVA)	-13	-14	11	-2	-13	-40	-32
Equals: Net cash flow.	504	879	934	1,039	1,144	1,237	1,335

Source: U.S. Bureau of Economic Analysis, *Survey of Current Business,* monthly. See also <http://www.bea.gov/bea/dn/nipaweb/selecttable.asp>.

Table 771. **Corporate Profits With Inventory Valuation and Capital Consumption Adjustments—Financial and Nonfinancial Industries: 2000 to 2005**

[In billions of dollars (818 represents $818,000,000,000). Based on the North American Industry Classification System 1997; see text, this section. Minus sign (–) indicates loss. See headnote, Table 770]

Item	2000	2001	2002	2003	2004	2005
Corporate profits with IVA/CCA [1] . . .	**818**	**767**	**886**	**1,032**	**1,162**	**1,352**
Domestic industries	672	598	731	856	977	1,146
Rest of the world	146	170	156	176	185	206
Corporate profits with IVA [1]	**759**	**719**	**766**	**924**	**1,020**	**1,407**
Domestic industries	614	550	610	748	835	1,201
Financial [2]	200	228	276	313	301	347
Nonfinancial.	413	322	334	435	534	854
Utilities	24	25	11	11	12	27
Manufacturing.	144	53	48	81	119	208
Wholesale trade	60	52	49	56	64	94
Retail trade	60	71	79	88	90	115
Transportation and warehousing.	15	1	–1	8	8	28
Information.	–18	–26	–9	–2	17	51
Other nonfinancial [3]	128	146	156	192	224	330
Rest of the world	146	170	156	176	185	206

[1] Inventory valuation adjustment and capital consumption adjustment. [2] Consists of finance and insurance and bank and other holding companies. [3] Consists of agriculture, forestry, fishing, and hunting; mining; construction; real estate and rental and leasing; professional, scientific, and technical services; administrative and waste management services; educational services; health care and social assistance; arts, entertainment, and recreation; accommodation and food services; and other services, except government.
Source: U.S. Bureau of Economic Analysis, *Survey of Current Business,* August 2005. See also <http://www.bea.gov/bea/dn/nipaweb/selecttable.asp>.

Table 772. **Corporate Profits Before Taxes by Industry: 2000 to 2004**

[In billions of dollars (773 represents $773,000,000,000). Profits are without inventory valuation and capital consumption adjustments. Minus sign (–) indicates loss. See headnote, Table 770]

Industry	NAICS code [1]	2000	2001	2002	2003	2004
Corporate profits before tax	(X)	773	708	768	937	1,059
Domestic industries	(X)	628	538	613	761	874
Agriculture, forestry, fishing, and hunting	11	2	1	(Z)	2	3
Mining.	21	15	16	5	17	30
Utilities	221	25	24	11	12	12
Construction	23	42	44	47	48	56
Manufacturing	31-33	153	48	48	88	140
Wholesale trade	42	62	48	52	61	73
Retail trade	44-45	61	70	79	88	95
Transportation and warehousing	48-49	15	1	–1	8	9
Information	51	–18	–26	–9	–2	16
Finance and insurance.	52	113	126	158	189	185
Real estate and rental and leasing.	53	9	10	10	13	16
Professional, scientific, and technical services . . .	54	1	9	20	28	34
Management of companies and enterprises [2]	551111,551112	87	102	119	124	116
Admin/support waste mgt/remediation services. . .	56	9	10	10	14	16
Educational services	61	2	2	3	3	4
Health care and social assistance	62	25	32	37	43	43
Arts, entertainment, and recreation.	71	2	3	4	4	6
Accommodation and food services	72	14	11	13	14	12
Other services, except public administration.	81	8	9	7	8	8
Rest of the world [3]	(X)	146	170	156	176	185

X Not applicable. Z Less than $500 million. [1] Based on North American Industry Classification System, 1997; see text, this section. [2] Consists of bank and other holding companies. [3] Consists of receipts by all U.S. residents, including both corporations and persons, of dividends from foreign corporations and, for U.S. corporations, their share of reinvested earnings of their incorporated foreign affiliates, and earnings of unincorporated foreign affiliates, net of corresponding payments.
Source: U.S. Bureau of Economic Analysis, *Survey of Current Business,* August 2005. See also <http://www.bea.gov/bea/dn/nipaweb/selecttable.asp>.

514 Business Enterprise

Table 773. Manufacturing, Mining, and Trade Corporations—Profits and Stockholders' Equity by Industry: 2004 and 2005

[Averages of quarterly figures at annual rates. Manufacturing data exclude estimates for corporations with less than $250,000 in assets at time of sample selection. Based on sample; see source for discussion of methodology. Based on North American Industry Classification System (NAICS), 1997; see text, this section]

Industry	NAICS code	Ratio of profits after taxes to stockholders' equity (percent)		Profits after taxes per dollar of sales (cents)		Ratio of stockholders' equity to debt	
		2004	2005	2004	2005	2004	2005
Manufacturing	**31-33**	**15.8**	**16.9**	**7.1**	**7.4**	**1.7**	**1.9**
Nondurable manufacturing	(X)	19.3	22.4	8.0	9.0	1.4	1.6
Food	311	18.0	17.6	4.9	4.9	1.0	1.1
Beverage and tobacco products	312	28.4	25.3	16.4	16.3	1.0	1.2
Textile mills and textile product mills	313, 314	5.8	10.4	1.7	3.2	1.3	1.5
Apparel and leather products	315, 316	20.9	20.7	6.7	7.2	2.0	2.1
Paper	322	8.1	8.3	3.1	3.2	0.8	0.9
Printing and related support activities	323	17.8	15.2	3.5	3.2	0.8	0.8
Petroleum and coal products	324	26.3	30.2	9.3	9.3	2.6	3.1
Chemicals	325	15.4	20.7	10.3	13.8	1.5	1.6
Plastics and rubber products	326	12.9	15.8	2.9	3.6	0.1	0.7
Durable manufacturing	(X)	12.9	12.2	6.2	5.9	2.1	2.2
Wood products	321	22.8	17.2	6.0	4.4	1.5	1.3
Nonmetallic mineral products	327	2.7	2.6	1.3	0.1	1.1	1.1
Primary metals	331	21.2	19.5	7.2	7.3	1.4	1.8
Fabricated metal products	332	17.2	20.3	5.7	6.4	1.4	1.4
Machinery	333	11.8	14.1	5.1	6.0	1.7	1.8
Computer and electronic products	334	10.3	10.4	9.3	9.5	4.1	4.4
Electrical equipment, appliances, & components	335	16.5	15.3	12.0	12.5	3.6	3.9
Transportation equipment	336	13.2	6.8	3.4	1.8	1.3	1.3
Furniture and related products	337	12.2	16.5	3.4	4.4	1.8	1.8
Miscellaneous manufacturing	339	15.5	15.9	9.6	10.5	1.9	2.2
All mining	**21**	**14.6**	**20.5**	**18.7**	**24.8**	**2.0**	**2.2**
All wholesale trade	**42**	**15.3**	**14.8**	**2.3**	**2.2**	**1.6**	**1.8**
Durable goods	421	14.1	12.4	2.7	2.4	1.8	1.9
Nondurable goods	422	17.2	18.9	1.9	2.0	1.4	1.5
All retail trade	**44-45**	**16.8**	**16.0**	**3.2**	**3.1**	**1.6**	**1.8**
Food and beverage stores	445	11.7	12.5	1.3	1.5	0.8	1.0
Clothing and general merchandise stores	448, 452	17.4	15.5	4.0	3.9	1.9	2.0
All other retail trade	(X)	17.8	17.6	3.4	3.3	2.0	2.0

X Not applicable.

Source: U.S. Census Bureau, *Quarterly Financial Report for Manufacturing, Mining, and Trade Corporations.*

Table 774. Value Added, Employment, and Capital Expenditures of Nonbank U.S. Multinational Companies: 1990 to 2003

[Value added and capital expenditures in billions of dollars (1,717 represents $1,717,000,000,000); employees in thousands. See headnote, Table 775. MNC = Multinational company. MOFA = Majority-owned foreign affiliate. Minus sign (–) indicates decrease]

Item	1990 [1]	1994 [1]	1999	2000	2001	2002	2003	Percent change at annual rates 1994–2002	2002–2003
VALUE ADDED									
MNCs worldwide:									
Parents and all affiliates	(NA)	(NA)	(NA)	(NA)	(NA)	(NA)	(NA)	(NA)	(NA)
Parents and MOFAs	(NA)	1,717	2,481	2,748	2,478	2,460	2,688	4.6	9.3
Parents	(NA)	1,314	1,914	2,141	1,892	1,859	1,983	4.4	6.7
Affiliates, total	(NA)	(NA)	(NA)	(NA)	(NA)	(NA)	(NA)	(NA)	(NA)
MOFAs	356	404	566	607	586	602	705	5.1	17.1
Other	(NA)	(NA)	(NA)	(NA)	(NA)	(NA)	(NA)	(NA)	(NA)
EMPLOYEES									
MNCs worldwide:									
Parents and all affiliates	25,264	25,670	32,227	33,598	32,539	31,894	31,580	2.8	–1.0
Parents and MOFAs	23,786	24,273	30,773	32,057	30,929	30,373	30,065	2.8	–1.0
Parents	18,430	18,565	23,007	23,885	22,735	22,118	21,701	2.2	–1.9
Affiliates, total	6,834	7,105	9,220	9,713	9,804	9,776	9,879	4.1	1.1
MOFAs	5,356	5,707	7,766	8,171	8,194	8,256	8,364	4.7	1.3
Other	1,478	1,398	1,454	1,542	1,610	1,520	1,515	1.1	–0.4
CAPITAL EXPENDITURES									
MNCs worldwide:									
Parents and all affiliates	(NA)	328	514	(NA)	(NA)	(NA)	(NA)	(NA)	(NA)
Parents and MOFAs	275	303	483	507	524	443	436	4.9	–1.6
Parents	213	232	370	396	413	333	321	4.6	–3.5
Affiliates, total	(NA)	96	144	(NA)	(NA)	(NA)	(NA)	(NA)	(NA)
MOFAs	62	71	113	111	111	110	115	5.6	4.3
Other	(NA)	25	31	(NA)	(NA)	(NA)	(NA)	(NA)	(NA)

NA Not available.   [1] Data for 1990 and 1994 are not strictly comparable with data beginning 1999; see source.

Source: U.S. Bureau of Economic Analysis, *Survey of Current Business*, July 2005.

Business Enterprise   515

Table 775. U.S. Multinational Companies—Selected Characteristics: 2003

[Preliminary. In billions of dollars (15,911 represents $15,911,000,000,000), except as indicated. Consists of nonbank U.S. parent companies and their nonbank foreign affiliates. U.S. parent comprises the domestic operations of a multinational and is a U.S. person that owns or controls directly or indirectly, 10 percent or more of the voting securities of an incorporated foreign business enterprise, or an equivalent interest in an unincorporated foreign business enterprise. A U.S. person can be an incorporated business enterprise. A majority-owned foreign affiliate (MOFA) is a foreign business enterprise in which a U.S. parent company owns or controls more than 50 percent of the voting securities]

| Industry [1] | NAICS code | U.S. parents | | | MOFAs | | |
		Total assets	Capital expendi-tures	Value added	Employ-ment (1,000)	Capital expendi-tures	Value added	Employ-ment (1,000)
All industries	(X)	15,911	321.4	1,983	21,701	115.0	705	8,364
Mining	21	194	13.3	31	144	29.3	71	160
Utilities.	22	707	31.1	88	347	3.5	12	70
Manufacturing [2]	31-33	4,603	126.6	866	8,153	45.0	347	4,262
Petroleum and coal products.	324	418	17.2	95	218	3.0	51	39
Chemicals	325	665	18.9	138	915	9.3	74	604
Computers and electronic products . . .	334	501	16.1	111	981	6.3	35	606
Transportation equipment	336	1,221	29.2	144	1,697	9.9	49	926
Wholesale trade.	42	418	18.3	94	781	6.4	110	792
Information [2]	51	1,384	54.3	263	1,855	6.0	29	344
Broadcasting & telecommunications . . .	513	940	44.9	169	1,120	4.3	8	101
Finance (except depository institutions) and insurance	52 exc. 521, 522	7,311	18.4	155	1,384	10.0	32	297
Professional, scientific, and technical services	54	256	8.3	102	946	2.6	37	437
Other industries [2]	(X)	1,039	51.1	385	8,091	12.2	67	2,003
Retail trade	44-45	364	25.0	171	3,819	3.0	27	659

X Not applicable.   [1] Represents North American Industry Classification System 1997 based industry of U.S. parent or industry of foreign affiliate.   [2] Includes other industries not shown separately.

Source: U.S. Bureau of Economic Analysis, *Survey of Current Business*, July 2005 and unpublished data.

Table 776. U.S. Multinational Companies—Value Added: 2000 and 2003

[In billions of dollars (2,748 represents $2,748,000,000,000). See headnote, Table 775. Data are by industry of U.S. parent. Based on the North American Industry Classification System, 1997 (NAICS); see text this section]

| Industry | NAICS code | U.S. multinationals | | U.S. parents | | Majority-owned foreign affiliates | |
		2000	2003	2000	2003	2000	2003
All industries	(X)	2,748	2,688	2,141	1,983	607	705
Mining	21	39	50	28	31	11	19
Utilities	22	86	98	81	88	5	10
Manufacturing [1]	31-33	1,410	1,341	995	866	415	474
Petroleum and coal products	324	232	226	112	95	120	132
Chemicals	325	212	226	141	138	71	88
Computers and electronic products.	334	188	159	142	111	46	48
Transportation equipment	336	271	202	209	144	62	58
Wholesale trade	42	133	118	99	94	34	24
Information [1]	51	325	292	302	263	22	29
Broadcasting & telecommunications	513	226	177	218	169	8	8
Finance (except depository institutions) and insurance	52 exc. 521, 522	181	189	157	155	24	34
Professional, scientific, and technical services . . .	54	141	147	101	102	41	46
Other industries [1]	(X)	433	453	379	385	54	68
Retail trade	44-45	166	197	149	171	18	26

X Not applicable.   [1] Includes other industries not shown separately.

Source: U.S. Bureau of Economic Analysis, *Survey of Current Business*, November 2003 and July 2005.

Table 777. U.S. Multinational Companies—Value Added by Industry of Affiliate and Country: 2003

[In millions of dollars (704,653 represents $704,653,000,000. See headnote, Table 775. Numbers in parentheses represent North American Industry Classification System 1997 codes; see text, this section. Minus sign (–) represents loss]

| Country | All industries [1] | Mining (21) | Manufacturing (31-33) | | | | Wholesale trade (42) | Professional, scientific, and technical services (54) |
			Total [1]	Chemicals (325)	Transporta-tion equip-ment (336)		
All countries [2]	704,653	70,899	346,669	74,343	49,292	110,414	36,572
United Kingdom	117,516	9,084	47,730	7,903	5,233	14,876	9,935
Canada	83,514	12,266	43,983	4,931	10,870	6,179	1,466
Germany	66,861	1,275	36,094	5,262	8,828	17,241	3,059
France	41,764	74	23,201	6,078	2,806	7,136	2,004
Japan	38,930	4	18,606	3,825	457	6,762	5,198
Ireland	28,287	6	22,409	13,808	111	2,445	567
Italy	25,252	–16	18,412	3,304	1,053	3,363	925
Netherlands	25,027	932	12,465	3,499	1,490	6,253	1,075
Australia	23,865	3,361	8,928	1,583	1,583	4,139	2,304
Mexico	22,897	561	15,965	3,263	5,400	1,012	409

[1] Includes other industries not shown separately.   [2] Includes other countries not shown separately.

Source: U.S. Bureau of Economic Analysis, *Survey of Current Business*, July 2005.

Science and Technology

This section presents statistics on scientific, engineering, and technological resources, with emphasis on patterns of research and development (R&D) funding and on scientific, engineering, and technical personnel; education; and employment. Also included are statistics on space program outlays and accomplishments. Principal sources of these data are the National Science Foundation (NSF) and the National Aeronautics and Space Administration (NASA).

NSF gathers data chiefly through recurring surveys. Current NSF publications containing data on funds for research and development and on scientific and engineering personnel include detailed statistical tables; issue briefs; and annual, biennial, triennial, and special reports. Titles or the areas of coverage of these reports include the following: *Science and Engineering Indicators; National Patterns of R&D Resources; Women, Minorities, and Persons with Disabilities in Science and Engineering*—science and technology data presented in chart and tabular form in a pocket-sized publication—*Federal Funds for Research and Development; Federal R&D Funding by Budget Function; Federal Support to Universities, Colleges, and Selected Nonprofit Institutions; Research and Development in Industry;* R&D expenditures and graduate enrollment and support in academic science and engineering; and characteristics of doctoral scientists and engineers and of recent graduates in the United States. Statistical surveys in these areas pose problems of concept and definition and the data should therefore be regarded as broad estimates rather than precise, quantitative statements. See sources for methodological and technical details.

The National Science Board's biennial *Science and Engineering Indicators* contains data and analysis of international and domestic science and technology, including measures of inputs and outputs.

The *Budget of the United States Government,* published by the U.S. Office of Management and Budget, contains summary financial data on federal R&D programs.

Research and development outlays— NSF defines research as "systematic study directed toward fuller scientific knowledge of the subject studied" and development as "the systematic use of scientific knowledge directed toward the production of useful materials, devices, systems, or methods, including design and development of prototypes and processes."

National coverage of R&D expenditures is developed primarily from periodic surveys in four principal economic sectors: (1) *Government,* made up primarily of federal executive agencies; (2) *industry,* consisting of manufacturing and nonmanufacturing firms and the federally funded research and development centers (FFRDCs) they administer; (3) *universities and colleges,* composed of universities, colleges, and their affiliated institutions, agricultural experiment stations, and associated schools of agriculture and of medicine, and FFRDCs administered by educational institutions; and (4) *other nonprofit institutions,* consisting of such organizations as private philanthropic foundations, nonprofit research institutes, voluntary health agencies, and FFRDCs administered by nonprofit organizations.

The R&D funds reported consist of current operating costs, including planning and administration costs, except as otherwise noted. They exclude funds for routine testing, mapping and surveying, collection of general-purpose data, dissemination of scientific information, and training of scientific personnel.

Scientists, engineers, and technicians—Scientists and engineers are defined as persons engaged in scientific and engineering work at a level requiring a knowledge of sciences equivalent at least to that acquired through completion of a 4-year college course. Technicians are defined as persons engaged in technical work at a level requiring knowledge acquired through a technical institute, junior college, or other type of training less extensive than 4-year college training. Craftsmen and skilled workers are excluded.

Table 778. **Research and Development (R&D) Expenditures by Source and Objective: 1970 to 2004**

[In millions of dollars (26,271 represents $26,271,000,000), except as indicated. For calendar years]

| Year | Total | Sources of funds | | | | | Objective (percent of total) | | | Character of work | | |
		Federal govern-ment	Indus-try	Univer-sities/col-leges	Non-profit	Non-federal govern-ment [1]	Defense related [2]	Space re-lated [3]	Other	Basic research	Applied research	Devel-opment
1970...	26,271	14,984	10,449	259	343	237	33	10	56	3,594	5,752	16,925
1971...	26,952	15,210	10,824	290	366	262	33	10	58	3,720	5,833	17,399
1972...	28,740	16,039	11,715	312	393	282	33	8	59	3,850	6,147	18,743
1973...	30,952	16,587	13,299	343	422	302	32	7	61	4,099	6,655	20,197
1974...	33,359	17,287	14,885	393	474	320	29	7	64	4,511	7,344	21,504
1975...	35,671	18,533	15,824	432	534	348	28	8	65	4,875	8,091	22,706
1976...	39,435	20,292	17,702	480	592	369	27	8	65	5,373	8,976	25,085
1977...	43,338	22,071	19,642	569	663	394	27	7	66	6,008	9,662	27,667
1978...	48,719	24,414	22,457	679	727	443	26	6	68	6,959	10,704	31,056
1979...	55,379	27,225	26,097	785	791	482	25	6	70	7,836	12,097	35,445
1980...	63,213	29,975	30,929	920	871	519	24	5	70	8,790	13,745	40,678
1981...	72,269	33,715	35,948	1,058	967	581	24	5	70	9,830	16,391	46,047
1982...	80,783	37,168	40,692	1,207	1,095	621	26	5	69	10,824	18,280	51,679
1983...	89,971	41,472	45,264	1,357	1,221	658	28	4	68	12,059	20,373	57,540
1984...	102,251	46,477	52,187	1,514	1,352	721	29	3	68	13,484	22,505	66,261
1985...	114,685	52,655	57,962	1,743	1,491	834	30	3	67	14,857	25,410	74,417
1986...	120,259	54,633	60,991	2,019	1,647	969	31	3	66	17,247	27,259	75,754
1987...	126,344	58,593	62,576	2,262	1,849	1,065	32	3	65	18,498	27,915	79,804
1988...	133,880	60,130	67,977	2,527	2,081	1,165	30	4	66	19,786	29,528	84,566
1989...	141,889	60,463	74,966	2,852	2,333	1,274	28	4	69	21,889	32,277	87,723
1990...	151,990	61,607	83,208	3,187	2,589	1,399	25	4	71	23,028	34,896	94,067
1991...	160,872	60,780	92,300	3,457	2,852	1,483	22	4	73	27,139	38,629	95,104
1992...	165,347	60,912	96,229	3,568	3,114	1,525	22	4	74	27,604	37,933	99,810
1993...	165,724	60,524	96,549	3,708	3,387	1,557	21	4	74	28,741	37,279	99,704
1994...	169,198	60,772	99,203	3,937	3,665	1,622	20	5	76	29,648	36,614	102,936
1995...	183,616	62,963	110,870	4,109	3,924	1,750	19	4	77	29,607	40,931	113,077
1996...	197,336	63,387	123,416	4,434	4,240	1,860	18	4	78	32,796	43,165	121,375
1997...	212,140	64,566	136,227	4,837	4,590	1,921	17	4	79	36,910	46,553	128,677
1998...	227,651	66,373	149,160	5,161	4,986	1,971	16	4	80	35,268	46,361	146,023
1999...	244,970	67,043	164,660	5,617	5,552	2,098	15	3	82	38,830	52,083	154,055
2000...	267,207	66,400	186,136	6,227	6,198	2,247	13	2	84	42,567	56,844	167,792
2001...	277,326	72,819	188,438	6,820	6,853	2,397	14	2	84	47,553	64,605	165,168
2002...	275,797	77,685	180,709	7,350	7,492	2,560	15	2	82	51,033	50,787	173,977
2003 [4]..	291,864	86,742	186,568	7,820	8,016	2,717	17	3	81	55,104	62,084	174,677
2004 [4]..	312,068	93,384	199,025	8,205	8,565	2,890	17	3	80	58,356	66,364	187,349

[1] Nonfederal R&D expenditures to university and college performers. [2] R&D spending by the Department of Defense, including space activities, and a portion of the Department of Energy funds. [3] For the National Aeronautics and Space Administration only. [4] Preliminary.

Source: U.S. National Science Foundation, *National Patterns of R&D Resources*, annual. See also <http://www.nsf.gov/statistics/>.

Table 779. Performance Sector of Research and Development (R&D) Expenditures: 1995 to 2004

[In millions of dollars (183,616 represents $183,616,000,000). For calendar year. FFRDCs are federally funded research and development centers. For most academic institutions and the federal government before 1997, began on July 1 instead of October 1]

Year	Total	Federal government	Industry Total	Industry: Funded by—Federal government	Industry: Funded by—Industry[1]	Industry FFRDCs	Universities and colleges Total	Univ: Funded by—Federal government	Univ: Funded by—Nonfederal government[2]	Univ: Funded by—Industry	Univ: Funded by—Universities & colleges	Univ: Funded by—Nonprofits	University & college FFRDCs[3]	Other nonprofit institutions Total	Other: Funded by—Federal government	Other: Funded by—Industry	Other: Nonprofits
RESEARCH AND DEVELOPMENT TOTAL																	
1995	183,616	16,904	129,830	21,178	108,652	2,273	22,608	13,586	1,750	1,547	4,109	1,616	5,367	5,827	2,847	671	2,308
2000	267,326	17,917	200,007	17,163	182,844	1,955	30,683	17,710	2,247	2,175	6,227	2,326	5,742	9,437	4,447	1,118	3,872
2001	277,326	20,426	202,017	16,899	185,118	2,020	33,712	19,767	2,397	2,188	6,820	2,540	6,225	10,734	5,289	1,132	4,313
2002	275,977	21,499	193,868	16,401	177,467	2,263	37,185	22,370	2,560	2,158	7,350	2,746	7,102	11,561	5,731	1,084	4,746
2003, prel.	291,864	23,326	204,004	20,699	183,305	2,486	40,173	24,580	2,717	2,142	7,820	2,913	7,275	11,531	5,807	1,121	5,103
2004, prel.	312,068	24,742	219,226	23,535	195,691	2,584	42,431	26,115	2,890	2,135	8,205	3,087	7,500	12,750	6,072	1,199	5,478
BASIC RESEARCH																	
1995	29,607	2,689	5,569	190	5,379	530	15,144	9,633	1,069	945	2,510	987	2,702	2,899	1,170	390	1,338
2000	42,567	3,765	7,053	938	6,115	534	22,856	13,904	1,550	1,500	4,296	1,605	2,874	4,870	2,099	621	2,150
2001	47,553	4,260	8,053	754	7,299	552	25,181	15,507	1,663	1,518	4,731	1,762	3,104	5,488	2,464	629	2,395
2002	51,033	4,511	7,547	888	6,659	619	27,853	17,616	1,769	1,492	5,078	1,898	3,714	5,812	2,575	602	2,635
2003, prel.	55,104	4,700	8,585	1,628	6,957	679	30,047	19,379	1,859	1,466	5,351	1,993	3,799	6,222	2,766	622	2,834
2004, prel.	58,356	4,887	9,278	1,851	7,427	706	31,735	20,589	1,974	1,458	5,605	2,109	3,917	6,651	2,944	666	3,042
APPLIED RESEARCH																	
1995	40,931	4,952	26,919	3,164	23,755	535	5,654	2,775	558	494	1,311	516	1,050	1,692	934	170	589
2000	56,844	6,105	39,170	2,676	36,494	275	6,652	3,354	571	553	1,583	591	1,329	3,096	1,831	283	981
2001	64,605	7,052	44,012	3,603	40,409	935	7,260	3,757	602	550	1,713	638	1,485	3,530	2,150	287	1,093
2002	50,787	7,487	28,533	2,452	26,081	1,048	7,980	4,227	649	547	1,863	696	1,685	3,744	2,267	275	1,203
2003, prel.	62,084	7,939	38,076	5,182	32,894	1,200	8,686	4,648	704	555	2,025	754	1,721	4,095	2,518	284	1,293
2004, prel.	66,364	8,407	41,009	5,892	35,117	1,268	9,223	4,983	751	555	2,132	802	1,806	4,287	2,595	304	1,388
DEVELOPMENT																	
1995	113,077	9,262	97,342	17,824	79,518	1,208	1,810	1,178	123	108	288	113	1,616	1,236	744	111	381
2000	167,792	8,047	153,784	13,549	140,235	1,146	1,176	452	125	121	347	130	1,539	1,468	513	214	741
2001	165,168	9,114	149,952	12,542	137,410	534	1,271	502	132	121	376	140	1,637	1,716	675	217	825
2002	173,997	9,501	157,788	13,061	144,727	597	1,351	527	142	120	409	153	1,703	2,005	890	207	908
2003, prel.	174,677	10,686	157,343	13,889	143,454	607	1,440	553	154	122	445	166	1,754	1,714	523	214	976
2004, prel.	187,349	11,447	168,939	15,792	153,147	610	1,474	543	165	122	468	176	1,778	1,812	534	229	1,048

[1] Includes all nonfederal sources of industry R&D expenditures. [2] Includes all nonfederal sources. [3] Includes all R&D expenditures of FFRDCs administered by academic institutions and funded by the federal government.

Source: National Science Foundation. Data derived from: Research and Development in Industry, annual; Academic Research and Development Expenditures, annual; and Federal Funds For Research and Development, annual. See also <http://www.nsf.gov/statistics/>.

Table 780. **National Research and Development (R&D) Expenditures as a Percent of Gross Domestic Product by Country: 1985 to 2004**

| Year | Total R&D | | | | | | | Nondefense R&D [1] | |
	United States	Japan [2]	Unified Germany [3]	France	United Kingdom	Italy	Canada	Russia	Total OECD [4]
1985	2.75	2.56	2.68	2.15	2.24	1.12	1.44	(NA)	2.23
1990	2.65	2.79	2.67	2.33	2.15	1.29	1.53	2.03	2.27
1995	2.51	2.69	2.19	2.29	1.95	1.00	1.72	0.85	2.08
2000	2.74	2.99	2.45	2.15	1.86	1.07	1.93	1.05	2.23
2001	2.76	3.07	2.46	2.20	1.87	1.11	2.08	1.18	2.28
2002	2.65	3.12	2.49	2.23	1.89	1.16	1.97	1.25	2.24
2003	2.68	3.15	2.52	2.18	1.88	–	1.95	1.29	2.26
2004	2.68	(NA)	2.49	2.16	(NA)	(NA)	1.93	1.17	(NA)

– Represents or rounds to zero.   NA Not available.   [1] Estimated.   [2] Data on Japanese research and development in 2000 and later years may not be consistent with data in earlier years because of changes in methodology.   [3] Data for 1985–90 are for West Germany only.   [4] Organization for Economic Cooperation and Development.

Source: National Science Foundation, *National Patterns of R&D Resources*, annual; and Organization for Economic Cooperation and Development.

Table 781. **Federal Obligations for Research in Current and Constant (2000) Dollars by Field of Science: 1980 to 2005**

[In millions of dollars (11,597 represents $11,597,000,000). For fiscal years ending in year shown; see text, Section 8. Excludes R&D plant]

Field of science	1980	1990	1995	2000	2001	2002	2003	2004, prel.	2005, prel.
CURRENT DOLLARS									
Research, total	11,597	21,622	28,434	38,471	44,714	48,007	51,072	54,450	54,698
Basic	4,674	11,286	13,877	19,570	21,958	23,668	24,751	26,436	26,860
Applied	6,923	10,337	14,557	18,901	22,756	24,338	26,320	28,013	27,838
Life sciences	4,192	8,830	11,811	17,965	23,057	25,477	27,772	29,746	29,781
Psychology	199	449	623	1,627	742	906	1,104	1,150	1,157
Physical sciences	2,001	3,809	4,278	4,788	4,601	4,983	5,022	5,384	5,373
Environmental sciences	1,261	2,174	2,854	3,329	3,252	3,418	3,741	3,957	3,916
Mathematics and computer sciences . . .	241	841	1,579	2,206	2,611	2,631	2,672	2,806	2,841
Engineering	2,830	4,227	5,708	6,346	8,197	8,275	8,405	9,044	9,147
Social sciences	524	630	679	1,050	1,009	983	1,026	1,067	1,081
Other sciences, n.e.c. [1]	350	664	902	1,160	1,246	1,334	1,329	1,296	1,391
CONSTANT (2000) DOLLARS [2]									
Research, total	21,840	26,612	30,846	38,471	43,683	46,019	48,009	49,986	48,868
Basic	8,802	13,890	15,054	19,570	21,452	22,688	23,267	24,269	23,997
Applied	13,038	12,722	15,792	18,901	22,231	23,330	24,742	25,717	24,871
Life sciences	7,895	10,868	12,813	17,965	22,525	24,422	26,107	27,307	26,606
Psychology	375	553	676	1,627	725	868	1,038	1,056	1,034
Physical sciences	3,768	4,688	4,641	4,788	4,495	4,777	4,777	4,943	4,801
Environmental sciences	2,375	2,676	3,096	3,329	3,177	3,277	3,517	3,633	3,499
Mathematics and computer sciences . . .	454	1,035	1,713	2,206	2,551	2,522	2,512	2,576	2,539
Engineering	5,330	5,202	6,192	6,346	8,008	7,932	7,901	8,302	8,172
Social sciences	987	775	737	1,050	986	942	964	980	966
Other sciences, n.e.c. [1]	659	817	979	1,160	1,217	1,279	1,250	1,190	1,243

[1] Not elsewhere classified.   [2] Based on gross domestic product implicit price deflator.

Source: U.S. National Science Foundation, *Federal Funds for Research and Development*, annual. See also <http://www.nsf.gov/statistics/>.

Table 782. **Federal Budget Authority for Research and Development (R&D) in Current and Constant (2000) Dollars by Selected Budget Functions: 2003 to 2006**

[In millions of dollars (112,544 represents $112,544,000,000). For year ending September 30. Excludes R&D plant. Represents budget authority. Functions shown are those for which $1 billion or more was authorized since 1995]

| Function | Current dollars | | | | Constant (2000) dollars [1] | | | |
	2003	2004	2005, prel.	2006, prel.	2003	2004	2005, prel.	2006, prel.
Total [2]	112,544	121,867	127,336	127,621	105,794	111,876	113,764	111,217
National defense	63,048	69,593	74,668	74,759	59,267	63,888	66,710	65,149
Health	26,517	28,251	28,746	28,984	24,927	25,935	25,682	25,258
Space research and technology	7,355	7,612	7,686	8,089	6,914	6,988	6,867	7,049
Energy	1,403	1,343	1,194	1,210	1,319	1,233	1,067	1,054
General science	6,129	6,466	6,482	6,423	5,761	5,936	5,791	5,597
Natural resources and environment	2,151	2,168	2,108	1,990	2,022	1,990	1,883	1,734
Transportation	1,869	1,863	1,828	1,640	1,757	1,710	1,633	1,429
Agriculture	1,708	1,750	1,803	1,575	1,606	1,607	1,611	1,373

[1] Based on gross domestic product implicit price deflator.   [2] Includes other functions, not shown separately.

Source: U.S. National Science Foundation, *Federal R&D Funding by Budget Function*, annual. See also <http://www.nsf.gov/statistics/> (released October 2005).

520   Science and Technology

Table 783. **Research and Development (R&D) Expenditures in Science and Engineering at Universities and Colleges in Current and Constant (2000) Dollars: 1990 to 2003**

[In millions of dollars (16,286 represents $16,286,000,000). Totals may not add due to rounding]

Characteristic	Current dollars				Constant (2000) dollars [1]			
	1990	1995	2000	2003	1990	1995	2000	2003
Total	16,286	22,170	30,063	40,077	20,052	24,053	30,063	37,681
Basic research [2]	10,643	14,808	22,243	29,981	13,104	16,066	22,243	28,188
Applied R&D [2]	5,643	7,362	7,820	10,096	6,948	7,987	7,820	9,492
Source of funds:								
All governments	9,638	13,331	17,518	24,734	11,867	14,463	17,518	23,255
Institutions' own funds	1,324	1,689	2,198	2,653	1,630	1,832	2,198	2,494
Industry.	3,006	4,047	5,940	7,683	3,701	4,391	5,940	7,224
Other	1,127	1,489	2,153	2,162	1,388	1,615	2,153	2,033
Fields:								
Physical sciences	1,807	2,256	2,711	3,273	2,225	2,448	2,711	3,077
Environmental sciences . . .	1,069	1,434	1,764	2,188	1,316	1,556	1,764	2,057
Mathematical sciences. . . .	222	279	341	429	273	303	341	403
Computer sciences	515	682	876	1,304	634	740	876	1,226
Life sciences	8,726	12,188	17,468	23,764	10,744	13,223	17,468	22,343
Psychology	253	371	516	769	311	403	516	723
Social sciences.	703	1,019	1,298	1,661	866	1,106	1,298	1,562
Other sciences	336	427	535	691	414	463	535	650
Engineering	2,656	3,515	4,554	5,999	3,270	3,814	4,554	5,640

[1] Based on gross domestic product implicit price deflator. [2] Basic research and applied R&D statistics were re-estimated for FY 2001 and forward. These data are not directly comparable to those from earlier years.
Source: U.S. National Science Foundation, *Survey of Research and Development Expenditures at Universities and Colleges,* annual.

Table 784. **Federal Research and Development (R&D) Obligations to Selected Universities and Colleges: 2001 and 2002**

[In millions of dollars (19,390.2 represents $19,390,200,000). For years ending September 30. For the top 40 institutions receiving federal R&D funds in 2002. Awards to the administrative offices of university systems are excluded from totals for individual institutions because that allocation of funds is unknown, but those awards are included in "total all institutions"]

Major institution ranked by total 2002 federal R&D obligations	2001	2002	Major institution ranked by total 2002 federal R&D obligations	2001	2002
Total, all institutions [1]	19,390.2	21,117.9	Massachusetts Institute of Technology . .	252.5	268.8
Johns Hopkins University	838.0	974.7	Baylor College of Medicine	231.7	266.8
University of Washington	474.5	525.6	University Southern California	232.5	254.3
University of Pennsylvania	412.0	447.2	University of Alabama—Birmingham. . . .	201.6	224.2
University of Michigan	403.4	419.7	Vanderbilt University	166.1	215.5
University of California—Los Angeles . . .	363.9	415.7	Case Western Reserve University	200.0	213.4
Stanford University	351.1	381.0	University of Illinois—Urbana		
University of California—San Diego	333.9	373.6	Champaign	186.9	194.0
University of California—San Francisco. . .	344.9	361.0	The Scripps Research Institute	157.4	193.6
Washington University	314.7	348.0	University of Rochester	171.2	189.2
University of Pittsburgh	300.8	335.8	University of California—Berkeley	210.6	187.3
Columbia University—City of NY	305.8	330.2	University of California—Davis	166.2	185.3
University of Wisconsin—Madison	290.2	327.9	Boston University	154.4	182.9
Duke University	274.1	327.5	Emory University	161.9	180.6
Harvard University	321.7	313.4	Ohio State University.	156.6	174.7
University of Colorado	290.7	308.3	Northwestern University	164.0	174.0
Yale University	276.2	306.9	University of Iowa	163.9	172.7
University of North Carolina at			University of Arizona	166.9	168.5
Chapel Hill.	275.9	297.9	University of Florida	157.4	167.1
University of Minnesota	273.1	291.9	University of Texas SW Medical		
Pennsylvania State University	253.6	287.1	Center Dallas.	146.9	162.3
Cornell University	271.9	283.1	University of Chicago.	160.1	161.5

[1] Includes other institutions, not shown separately.
Source: U.S. National Science Foundation, *Federal S&E Support to Universities and Colleges and Nonprofit Institutions,* annual.

Table 785. **Graduate Science/Engineering Students in Doctorate-Granting Colleges by Characteristic and Field: 1990 to 2003**

[In thousands (397.8 represents 397,800). As of fall. Includes outlying areas]

Field of science or engineering	Characteristic										
	Total			Female			Foreign		Part-time		
	1990	2000	2003	1990	2000	2003	2000	2003	1990	2000	2003
Total, all surveyed fields .	397.8	433.3	507.2	149.7	195.3	233.4	122.3	148.0	123.2	118.2	135.5
Science/engineering	350.6	366.7	428.0	113.4	145.6	174.2	116.9	141.0	100.7	94.7	107.8
Engineering, total	99.9	98.4	119.3	13.6	19.6	25.5	46.1	58.2	35.9	27.8	31.6
Sciences, total	250.7	268.3	308.7	99.8	126.0	148.7	70.8	82.7	64.8	66.9	76.2
Physical sciences	32.5	29.3	33.3	7.6	8.7	10.4	11.5	13.9	3.6	3.2	3.3
Environmental.	12.9	12.7	13.5	3.8	5.2	6.0	2.6	2.7	3.0	2.6	2.5
Mathematical sciences . .	17.3	13.8	17.4	5.3	4.9	6.3	5.7	7.1	4.0	2.7	3.5
Computer sciences	27.7	39.5	46.7	6.4	11.4	12.5	19.3	21.6	12.9	16.3	18.4
Agricultural sciences . . .	10.9	11.2	12.4	3.2	4.7	5.6	2.4	2.5	2.0	2.3	2.9
Biological sciences.	46.0	52.3	60.6	21.0	27.4	33.4	11.5	14.5	6.8	7.2	8.2
Psychology.	35.8	37.7	41.8	23.6	27.0	30.8	2.1	2.8	10.3	9.5	11.6
Social sciences	67.7	71.8	82.8	29.0	36.8	43.8	15.7	17.6	22.1	23.0	25.9
Health fields, total	47.2	66.6	79.3	36.3	49.6	59.2	5.4	7.0	22.5	23.5	27.6

Source: U.S. National Science Foundation, *Survey of Graduate Science Engineering Students and Postdoctorates,* annual.

U.S. Census Bureau, Statistical Abstract of the United States: 2007

Table 786. **College Graduates by Education and Occupation: 1993 and 2003**

[**In percent, except as noted.** S&E stands for science and engineering. College graduates includes individuals with degrees at the bachelor level or higher]

Field and occupation	1993	2003	Field and occupation	1993	2003
All college graduates (1,000) ...	**29,021**	**40,621**	S&E-related or non-S&E occupations.	78	77
S&E occupations ...	11	12	Not employed ...	16	17
S&E-related or non-S&E occupations ..	71	69			
Not employed ...	18	20	Non-S&E degrees only (1,000)...	15,723	21,395
			S&E occupations ...	3	3
S&E degrees only (1,000) ...	7,153	10,118	S&E-related or non-S&E occupations.	78	75
S&E occupations ...	30	31	Not employed ...	19	21
S&E-related or non-S&E occupations.	52	50	Degrees in more than one broad		
Not employed ...	18	19	field [1] (1,000) ...	3,676	5,568
			S&E occupations ...	11	12
S&E-related degrees only (1,000) ...	2,469	3,540	S&E-related or non-S&E occupations.	76	72
S&E occupations ...	6	6	Not employed ...	13	16

[1] S&E, S&E-related, and non-S&E.

Source: U.S. National Science Foundation, National Survey of College Graduates: 1993 and 2003.

Table 787. **Profile of Employed College Graduates by Employment Sector and Occupation Group: 2003**

[**32,575 represents 32,575,000,000.** S&E stands for science and engineering. Includes individuals with degrees at the bachelor's level or higher]

Characteristic	All employed graduates (1,000)	Occupation (percent)			Median annual salary (dollars)			
		S&E	S&E-related	Non-S&E	All employed graduates	S&E	S&E-related	Non-S&E
HIGHEST LEVEL OF DEGREE ATTAINMENT								
All degree levels ...	32,575	14	15	70	50,000	69,000	55,000	47,000
Bachelor's ...	20,359	12	14	74	47,000	67,000	48,000	43,000
Master's ...	8,675	17	14	70	54,000	70,000	55,000	50,000
Doctorate ...	1,271	50	7	43	70,000	71,000	77,000	65,000
Professional ...	2,270	4	44	52	95,000	80,000	112,000	80,000
EMPLOYMENT SECTOR								
Educational institutions ...	7,156	11	17	71	42,000	49,000	44,000	40,000
4-year colleges, medical schools, university-affiliated research institutes ..	2,003	32	22	46	47,000	50,000	50,000	44,000
2-year colleges ...	295	31	2	67	40,000	40,000	40,000	40,000
Precollege and other institutions ...	4,857	1	16	82	41,000	50,000	42,000	40,000
Government ...	3,527	16	13	71	53,000	64,000	56,000	50,000
Federal ...	1,232	23	13	65	66,000	75,000	65,000	62,000
State ...	1,044	16	13	71	43,000	50,000	45,000	42,000
Local ...	1,251	10	13	77	45,000	54,000	44,000	44,000
Business/industry ...	21,893	15	15	70	56,000	73,000	60,000	50,000
For-profit ...	13,771	19	13	68	61,000	75,000	67,000	55,000
Self-employed, incorporated ...	3,403	11	18	71	60,000	72,000	85,000	50,000
Self-employed, not incorporated ...	2,583	7	14	78	40,000	50,000	65,000	35,000
Nonprofit ...	2,534	7	28	65	42,000	53,000	50,000	35,000

Source: U.S. National Science Foundation, National Survey of College Graduates: 2003.

522   Science and Technology

Table 788. Science and Engineering Degree Recipients, 2001 and 2002, and Post-Graduate Employment Status, 2003

[In thousands (937.7 represents 937,700). FT represents full-time. Based on a survey and subject to sampling error; see source for details]

Degree and field	Graduates 2001 and 2002 (1,000)	2003[1]				
		In school[2]	Employed		Not employed or not FT students	Median salary[4] ($1,000)
			In S&E[3]	In other		
Bachelor's recipients[5]	937.7	222.0	287.2	358.7	69.8	36
All science fields	682.2	185.1	114.9	327.4	54.7	32
Computer and information sciences	84.8	6.4	38.6	33.6	5.7	45
Mathematical sciences	25.6	6.0	4.1	13.7	1.5	36
Life and related sciences	150.7	61.4	35.2	44.4	9.8	29
Physical and related sciences	35.7	15.5	9.5	8.8	1.9	35
Psychology	153.0	44.6	10.7	82.7	15.2	28
Social and related sciences	232.3	51.0	16.3	144.4	20.6	30
All engineering fields	112.3	19.1	67.5	17.7	7.3	50
Aerospace and related engineering	3.1	0.6	1.8	0.7	(B)	48
Chemical engineering	10.6	2.7	6.0	1.4	(B)	53
Civil and architectural engineering	16.3	1.1	12.5	1.9	(B)	44
Electrical, electronics, computer, and communications engineering	35.8	5.5	21.6	5.5	2.8	53
Industrial engineering	6.6	0.7	3.4	2.1	(B)	47
Mechanical engineering	24.8	4.7	14.5	4.2	1.5	50
Other engineering	15.1	3.8	7.7	2.0	1.4	43
All health fields	143.0	17.7	103.7	13.6	(B)	43
Master's recipients[5]	246.7	40.9	134.7	51.6	19.4	52
All science fields	117.0	27.9	44.0	36.2	9.0	45
Computer and mathematical sciences	27.2	4.8	13.6	4.9	4.0	60
Mathematical sciences	5.9	1.8	2.7	1.0	(B)	54
Life and related sciences	16.8	4.5	8.6	2.8	(B)	40
Physical and related sciences	9.6	3.1	4.8	1.3	(B)	49
Psychology	32.0	6.8	9.2	14.4	(B)	38
Social and related sciences	25.5	6.8	4.4	11.7	2.4	42
All engineering fields	47.0	10.8	29.9	3.6	2.6	65
Aerospace and related engineering	1.1	(B)	0.8	(B)	(B)	60
Chemical engineering	1.9	0.7	0.9	(B)	(B)	63
Civil and architectural engineering	6.0	0.9	4.7	(B)	(B)	54
Electrical, electronics, computer, and communications engineering	16.1	4.4	9.9	(B)	(B)	70
Industrial engineering	3.7	(B)	2.3	(B)	(B)	(B)
Mechanical engineering	6.0	1.2	4.0	(B)	(B)	59
Other engineering	12.2	2.3	7.4	1.2	(B)	65
All health fields	82.7	(B)	56.8	11.8	(B)	53

B Base figure too small to meet statistical standards of reliability of a derived figure. [1] As of April. [2] Full-time students. [3] In science and engineering or related occupation. [4] For the principal job. Excludes full-time students, the self-employed, and persons whose principal job is less than 35 hours per week. For definition of median, see Guide to Tabular Presentation. [5] Includes health degrees beginning in 2003.

Source: National Science Foundation, *National Survey of Recent College Graduates: 2003.*

Table 789. Doctorates Conferred by Characteristics of Recipients: 2000 and 2004

[In percent, except as indicated. Based on the Survey of Earned Doctorate Awards; for description of methodology, see <http://www.nsf.gov/sbe/srs/ssed/sedmeth.htm>]

Characteristic	2000 total[1]	2004									
		All fields[1]	Engineering	Physical sciences[2]	Earth sciences	Mathematics	Computer sciences	Biological sciences[3]	Agricultural	Social sciences[4]	Psychology
Total conferred (number)	41,368	42,155	5,776	3,353	672	1,075	949	5,937	1,046	4,131	3,336
Male	56.0	54.5	82.2	74.1	66.1	71.6	78.9	53.6	62.0	56.0	32.6
Female	43.8	45.3	17.6	25.9	33.9	28.4	20.5	46.3	38.0	44.0	67.3
Median age[5]	33.6	33.3	31.4	30.0	32.4	32.3	30.3	33.5	34.1	32.3	(NA)
CITIZENSHIP[6]											
Total conferred (number)	39,485	39,544	5,484	3,198	662	1,036	907	5,649	1,078	3,302	2,977
U.S. citizen	75.6	70.7	39.8	58.0	66.2	49.2	49.4	74.1	56.1	69.7	93.7
Foreign citizen	24.4	29.3	60.2	42.0	33.8	50.8	50.6	25.9	43.9	30.3	6.3
RACE/ETHNICITY[7]											
Total conferred (number)	29,837	27,959	2,182	1,854	438	510	448	4,187	605	2,303	2,789
White[8]	79.3	76.5	70.7	79.1	86.5	78.0	71.7	76.0	82.3	77.9	76.8
Black[8]	5.9	7.0	4.3	3.2	1.6	2.0	3.8	3.5	3.8	6.6	7.3
Asian/Pacific[8]	7.8	7.3	16.2	8.7	2.5	10.6	16.1	11.7	5.6	6.1	5.5
Indian/Alaskan[8]	0.6	0.5	0.3	0.3	0.9	0.0	0.4	0.3	0.7	0.3	0.5
Hispanic	4.3	4.6	4.0	3.3	2.5	5.1	2.9	4.6	2.8	4.7	6.1
Other/unknown[9]	2.2	4.0	4.5	5.2	5.9	4.3	5.1	3.9	4.8	4.4	3.9

NA Not available. [1] Includes other fields, not shown separately. [2] Astronomy, physics, and chemistry. [3] Biochemistry, botany, microbiology, physiology, zoology, and related fields. [4] Anthropology, sociology, political science, economics, international relations, and related fields. [5] For definition of median, see Guide to Tabular Presentation. [6] For those with known citizenship. [7] Excludes those with temporary visas. [8] Non-Hispanic. [9] For the year 2004, includes Native Hawaiians and Other Pacific Islanders, respondents choosing multiple races (excluding those selecting an Hispanic ethnicity), and respondents with unknown race/ethnicity.

Source: U.S. National Science Foundation, *Science and Engineering Doctorate Awards*, annual. See also <http://www.nsf.gov/statistics/pubseri.cfm?TopID=2&SubID=5&SeriID=11> (released February 2006).

Table 790. **Doctorates Awarded, by Field of Study and Year of Doctorate: 1995 to 2004**

Field of study	1995	1999	2000	2001	2002	2003	2004
Grand total, all fields	41,748	41,090	41,357	40,808	39,964	40,710	42,155
Science and engineering, total	26,535	25,932	25,966	25,540	24,571	25,258	26,275
Engineering, total	6,008	5,330	5,321	5,502	5,071	5,265	5,776
Aeronautical/astronautical	252	206	214	203	208	199	201
Chemical	708	674	725	728	705	643	723
Civil	656	584	556	594	625	672	675
Electrical	1,731	1,478	1,544	1,576	1,392	1,463	1,649
Industrial/manufacturing	284	211	176	205	230	211	217
Materials/metallurgical	588	469	451	497	396	473	509
Mechanical.	1,025	855	864	953	827	814	853
Other	764	853	791	746	688	790	949
Science, total	20,527	20,602	20,645	20,038	19,500	19,993	20,499
Biological/agricultural sciences	6,412	6,548	6,797	6,543	6,580	6,616	6,983
Agricultural sciences	1,036	966	943	853	893	922	1,046
Biological sciences	5,376	5,582	5,854	5,690	5,687	5,694	5,937
Earth, atmospheric, and ocean. sciences, total	780	805	758	749	785	783	672
Atmospheric	130	124	143	116	117	139	126
Earth	454	452	386	393	428	373	420
Oceanography.	115	130	134	121	128	133	126
Other environmental sciences	81	99	95	119	112	138	(NA)
Mathematical/computer sciences, total. . . .	2,187	1,938	1,909	1,833	1,725	1,860	2,024
Computer sciences	997	855	859	826	807	866	949
Mathematics	1,190	1,083	1,050	1,007	918	994	1,075
Physical sciences, total.	3,841	3,579	3,407	3,393	3,209	3,320	3,353
Astronomy	173	159	185	186	144	167	165
Chemistry.	2,162	2,132	1,989	1,980	1,923	2,037	1,987
Physics	1,479	1,271	1,204	1,197	1,124	1,080	1,186
Other	27	17	29	30	18	36	(NA)
Psychology.	3,429	3,668	3,618	3,442	3,198	3,275	3,336
Social sciences, total	3,878	4,064	4,156	4,078	4,003	4,139	4,131
Economics	1,152	1,075	1,086	1,081	1,023	1,051	1,066
Political science	894	1,016	987	984	938	1,026	946
Sociology	555	572	637	577	565	612	598
Other social sciences	1,277	1,401	1,446	1,436	1,477	1,450	1,521
Non-science and engineering, total	15,213	15,158	15,391	15,268	15,393	15,452	15,880
Education	6,650	6,546	6,429	6,337	6,487	6,627	6,635
Health.	1,329	1,407	1,591	1,620	1,655	1,633	1,730
Humanities	4,691	5,034	5,213	5,160	5,009	5,015	5,017
Professional/other/unknown	2,543	2,171	2,158	2,151	2,242	2,177	2,498

NA Not available.

Source: U.S. National Science Foundation, *Science and Engineering Doctorate Awards*, annual. See also <http://www.nsf.gov/statistics/nsf06308/> (released February 2006).

Table 791. **Non-U.S. Citizens Awarded Doctorates in Science and Engineering, by Visa Type and Country of Citizenship: 1995 to 2004**

Visa and country/economy	1995	1996	1997	1998	1999	2000	2001	2002	2003	2004
All non-U.S. citizens.	10,516	10,845	9,790	9,795	8,891	9,069	9,242	8,857	9,507	10,121
Canada.	274	278	263	288	289	294	307	314	325	381
Mexico.	130	162	148	179	172	209	207	182	219	180
Brazil.	137	207	151	164	164	131	143	126	107	136
United Kingdom	132	117	92	124	142	100	138	134	110	110
Germany.	208	170	181	210	183	229	220	197	189	184
China	2,781	3,022	2,395	2,510	2,233	2,378	2,418	2,401	2,501	2,869
Japan	155	169	155	156	158	201	150	158	202	186
Korea	1,009	985	901	823	760	753	867	855	961	1,053
Taiwan	1,249	1,162	1,093	913	746	676	541	469	442	394
Thailand	114	119	97	123	134	153	236	264	311	271
India	1,212	1,271	1,281	1,142	915	834	815	679	771	857
Iran	173	150	113	93	92	80	100	57	68	59
Turkey	167	151	170	172	192	275	309	342	374	344
Science	7,033	7,318	6,642	6,734	6,296	6,267	6,152	5,937	6,325	6,578
Engineering.	3,483	3,527	3,148	3,061	2,595	2,802	3,090	2,920	3,182	3,543
Permanent visa	3,509	3,009	2,281	2,019	1,653	1,409	1,278	1,167	1,100	999
Temporary visa.	7,007	7,836	7,509	7,776	7,238	7,660	7,964	7,690	8,407	9,122

Source: U.S. National Science Foundation, *Science and Engineering Doctorate Awards*, annual. See also <http://www.nsf.gov/statistics/nsf06308/> (released February 2006)

Table 792. Research and Development (R&D) Funds in R&D-Performing Manufacturing and Nonmanufacturing Companies by Industry: 2001 to 2003

Industry	NAICS [1] code	Total R&D funds as a percent of net sales			Company R&D funds as a percent of net sales		
		2001	2002	2003	2001	2002	2003
All industries, total	(X)	4.2	3.9	3.5	3.8	3.6	3.2
All manufacturing industries, total	(X)	4.1	3.7	3.5	3.7	3.3	3.1
Food	311	0.5	(D)	(D)	0.5	0.6	0.6
Paper, printing, and support activities	322, 326	(D)	(D)	(D)	2.1	1.3	1.1
Petroleum and coal products	324	(D)	(D)	(D)	0.3	0.4	0.3
Chemicals.	325	4.9	6.0	5.7	4.8	5.9	5.6
Plastic and rubber products	326	(D)	(D)	(D)	2.9	1.8	2.1
Nonmetallic mineral products	327	2.4	(D)	2.1	2.3	1.2	1.0
Primary metals.	331	0.7	0.7	1.0	0.7	0.7	0.7
Fabricated metal products	332	1.7	1.5	0.7	1.6	1.4	1.5
Machinery.	333	4.3	4.4	1.6	4.2	4.3	4.2
Navigational, measuring, electromedical, and control instruments	3345	12.6	8.7	4.2	7.3	5.4	7.2
Electrical equipment, appliances, and components . .	335	3.1	2.8	12.9	2.9	2.7	2.2
Motor vehicles, trailers, and parts	3361-3363	(D)	(D)	2.2	3.5	3.1	2.4
Aerospace products and parts	3364	5.7	4.1	(D)	3.0	2.3	3.5
All nonmanufacturing industries, total	(X)	4.3	4.4	6.8	4.0	4.1	3.3
Transportation and warehousing services	48, 49	2.5	(D)	3.6	2.4	0.5	0.4
Software publishing	5112	19.4	21.5	0.4	19.3	21.4	23.4
Architectural, engineering, and related services	5413	7.5	7.8	(D)	5.2	5.3	7.8
Computer systems design and related services	5415	17.4	16.5	12.3	16.5	14.3	9.8
Scientific R&D services	5417	47.7	21.3	11.1	36.5	17.6	16.5
Management of companies and enterprises	55	7.8	7.6	19.4	7.8	7.6	4.1

X Not applicable. D Figure withheld to avoid disclosure of information pertaining to a specific organization or individual.
[1] North American Industry Classification System 1997 (NAICS); see text, Section 15.

Source: U.S. National Science Foundation, *Research and Development in Industry*, annual. See also <http://www.nsf.gov/statistics/pubseri.cfm?TopID=2&SubID=5&SeriID=26>.

Table 793. Civilian Employment of Scientists, Engineers, and Technicians by Occupation and Industry: 2004

[In thousands (6,834.8 represents 6,834,800). Based on sample and subject to sampling error. For details, see source]

Occupation		Wage and salary workers							
	Total [1]	Mining [2]	Construction	Manufacturing	Information	Professional, scientific and technical services	Government	Other service-providing industries	Self employed [3]
Scientists, engineers, and technicians, total	6,834.8	45.6	76.4	1,251.2	516.7	1,874.7	1,118.8	1,603.4	336.2
Scientists	1,080.8	7.8	2.5	104.6	31.1	225.8	331.3	252.4	118.4
Physical scientists.	250.4	7.4	0.5	43.8	0.8	82.8	84.2	22.9	6.5
Life scientists.	231.7	(NA)	(NA)	28.8	0.1	44.8	96.2	41.4	16.2
Mathematical science occupations . .	107.0	0.1	0.1	7.2	8.3	23.2	20.5	45.9	1.7
Social scientists and related occupations	491.7	0.3	2.0	24.9	21.9	75.0	130.3	142.3	94.0
Computer specialists	3,045.8	6.0	9.0	272.5	411.0	868.8	332.2	996.3	150.1
Engineers [4]	1,448.9	19.1	36.6	554.7	49.7	378.1	194.2	174.9	40.9
Civil engineers	237.3	0.4	19.6	3.3	1.2	115.1	75.6	9.5	12.7
Electrical/electronics engineers	298.8	0.5	4.5	103.4	33.6	69.5	31.5	45.1	10.6
Mechanical engineers	225.9	0.7	4.1	122.1	0.4	55.8	13.5	23.5	5.7
Drafters, engineering, and mapping technicians [5]	850.9	3.9	24.2	260.9	24.2	281.2	122.1	113.8	19.8
Electrical/electronics engineering technicians.	181.6	1.1	2.3	64.8	17.3	26.8	24.8	43.5	0.6
Other engineering technicians	350.3	1.7	4.2	128.2	4.0	91.3	78.5	41.0	1.1
Drafters.	254.0	0.5	16.9	67.6	2.5	119.3	7.2	25.1	14.9
Surveying and mapping technicians	65.0	0.7	0.9	0.3	0.4	43.8	11.6	4.2	3.1
Life, physical, and social science technicians.	341.9	8.2	0.3	58.3	0.5	73.2	129.4	64.0	4.3
Surveyors, cartographers, and photogrammetrists	66.5	0.5	3.7	0.1	0.2	47.7	9.6	1.9	2.7

NA Not available. [1] Includes agriculture, forestry, and fishing not shown separately. [2] Includes oil and gas extraction. [3] Includes secondary jobs. [4] Includes kinds of engineers and technicians not shown separately. [5] Includes other drafters, technicians, and mapping technnicians, not shown separately.

Source: U.S. Bureau of Labor Statistics, *National Industry-Occupation Employment Matrix*, February 2006 (Data collected biennially).

Science and Technology   525

Table 794. Funds for Performance of Industrial Research and Development (R&D) by Selected Industries: 2000 to 2003

[In millions of dollars (201,962 represents $201,962,000,000). For calendar years. Covers basic research, applied research, and development. Based on the Survey of Industry Research and Development]

Industry	NAICS[1] code	2000	2001	2002	2003
CURRENT DOLLARS					
Total funds[2]	(X)	201,962	202,017	193,868	204,004
Petroleum and coal products	324	(D)	(D)	(D)	(D)
Chemicals and allied products	325	20,918	17,892	20,641	23,001
Machinery	333	6,580	6,404	6,429	6,304
Navigational, measuring, electromedical, and control instruments . . .	3345	15,116	12,947	13,729	14,014
Electrical equipment, appliances, and components	335	(D)	4,980	2,039	2,073
Motor vehicles, trailers, and parts	3361-3363	(D)	(D)	(D)	(D)
Aerospace products and parts	3364	10,319	7,868	9,654	15,731
All other[2]	(X)	(D)	(D)	(D)	(D)
CONSTANT (1996) DOLLARS[3]					
Total funds[2]	(X)	201,962	197,282	186,072	191,913
Petroleum and coal products	324	(D)	(D)	(D)	(D)
Chemicals	325	20,918	17,473	19,811	21,638
Machinery	333	6,580	6,254	6,170	5,930
Navigational, measuring, electromedical, and control instruments . . .	3345	15,116	12,644	13,177	13,183
Electrical equipment, appliances, and components	335	(D)	4,863	1,957	1,950
Motor vehicles, trailers, and parts	3361-3363	(D)	(D)	(D)	(D)
Aerospace products and parts	3364	10,319	7,684	9,266	14,799
All other[2]	(X)	(D)	(D)	(D)	(D)

D Figure withheld to avoid disclosure of information pertaining to a specific organization or individual.   X Not applicable.
[1] North American Industry Classification System, 1997; see text, Section 15.   [2] Includes other industries not shown separately.
[3] Based on gross domestic product implicit price deflator.

Source: U.S. National Science Foundation, *Research and Development in Industry,* annual.

Table 795. Research and Development (R&D) Scientists and Engineers— Employment and Cost, by Industry: 2001 to 2003

[1,059.6 represents 1,059,600]

Industry	NAICS[1] code	Employed scientists and engineers[2] (1,000)			Cost per scientist or engineer, Constant (1996) dollars[3, 4] ($1,000)		
		2001	2002	2003	2001	2002	2003
All industries[5]	(X)	1,059.6	1,073.3	1,115.8	184.5	181.5	180.8
Chemicals	325	82.4	84.2	89.1	214.6	239.2	245.1
Machinery	333	54.9	56.2	55.9	116.3	115.4	111.5
Electrical equipment, appliances, and components . . .	335	29.0	23.8	15.2	(D)	149.8	(D)
Motor vehicles, trailers, and parts	3361-3363	65.8	69.6	41.6	(D)	(D)	(D)
Aerospace products and parts	3364	22.1	25.8	36.6	348.2	(D)	405.9
Transportation and warehousing services	48, 49	1.3	0.4	—	(D)	(D)	(D)
Software publishing	5112	82.6	81.0	93.6	155.8	163.0	155.3
Architectural, engineering, and related services	5413	30.3	28.0	35.3	114.6	152.7	141.9
Computer systems design and related services	5415	62.5	76.8	77.8	163.7	133.2	152.7
Scientific R&D services	5417	62.1	55.0	48.5	238.3	260.2	258.1
Management of companies and enterprises	55	0.9	1.5	1.0	412.5	167.6	162.2

– Represents or rounds to zero.   D Withheld to avoid disclosure.   X Not applicable.   [1] North American Industry Classification System 1997 (NAICS); see text, Section 15.   [2] The mean number of full-time equivalent R&D scientists and engineers employed in January of the year shown and the following January.   [3] Based on gross domestic product implicit price deflator.   [4] Represents the arithmetic mean of the numbers of R&D scientists and engineers reported in each industry for January in 2 consecutive years divided into total R&D expenditures in each industry.   [5] Includes other industries not shown separately.

Source: U.S. National Science Foundation, *Research and Development in Industry,* annual.

Table 796. Space Vehicle Systems—Net Sales and Backlog Orders: 1970 to 2004

[In millions of dollars (1,956 represents $1,956,000,000). Backlog orders as of Dec. 31. Based on data from major companies engaged in manufacture of aerospace products. Includes parts but excludes engines and propulsion units, except where noted]

Year	Net sales			Backlog orders			Year	Net sales			Backlog orders		
	Total	Military	Non-military	Total	Military	Non-military		Total	Military	Non-military	Total	Military	Non-military
1970 . .	1,956	1,025	931	1,184	786	398	2001[1]	9,032	(D)	(D)	24,425	(D)	(D)
1980 . .	3,483	1,461	2,022	1,814	951	863	2002[1]	7,946	(D)	(D)	21,968	(D)	(D)
1990 . .	9,691	6,556	3,135	12,462	8,130	4,332	2003[1]	7,325	(D)	(D)	14,037	(D)	(D)
2000 . .	8,164	3,723	4,441	21,395	8,942	12,453	2004[1]	7,335	(D)	(D)	16,346	(D)	(D)

D Withheld to avoid disclosing data for individual companies.   [1] Includes engines and/or propulsion units for space vehicles, including parts.

Source: U.S. Census Bureau, *Current Industrial Reports,* M336G, *Civil Aircraft and Aircraft Engines,* annual. See also <http://www.census.gov/industry/1/m336g0413.pdf>.

Table 797. Federal Outlays for General Science, Space, and Other Technology, 1970 to 2005, and Projections, 2006 and 2007

[In billions of dollars (4.5 represents $4,500,000,000). For fiscal years ending in year shown; see text, Section 8]

Year	Current dollars			Constant (**2000**) dollars		
	Total	General science/basic research	Space and other technologies	Total	General science/basic research	Space and other technologies
1970	4.5	0.9	3.6	19.3	4.0	15.2
1980	5.8	1.4	4.5	12.0	2.8	9.1
1985	8.6	2.0	6.6	13.7	3.2	10.5
1990	14.4	2.8	11.6	20.0	3.9	16.1
1995	16.7	4.1	12.6	18.7	4.6	14.1
2000	18.6	6.2	12.4	18.6	6.2	12.4
2001	19.7	6.5	13.2	19.3	6.4	12.9
2002	20.7	7.2	13.5	19.7	6.9	12.8
2003	20.8	7.9	12.9	19.2	7.3	11.9
2004	23.0	8.3	14.6	20.4	7.4	13.0
2005	23.6	8.8	14.8	20.4	7.6	12.7
2006, proj.	23.9	9.1	14.7	20.0	7.7	12.4
2007, proj.	25.3	9.8	15.6	20.9	8.1	12.8

Source: U.S. Office of Management and Budget, *Budget of the United States, Historical Tables, Fiscal Year 2007*, annual. See also <http://www.gpoaccess.gov/usbudget/fy07/hist.html>.

Table 798. U.S. and Worldwide Commercial Space Industry Revenue by Type: 2001 to 2004

[In billions of dollars (20.8 represents $20,800,000,000). For calendar years]

Industry	U.S.				World			
	2001	2002	2003	2004	2001	2002	2003	2004
Revenue, total	20.8	22.7	24.9	26.1	78.6	86.1	91.1	97.2
Satellite manufacturing [1]	3.8	4.4	4.6	3.9	9.5	12.1	9.8	10.2
Launch industry	1.1	1.0	2.1	1.4	3.0	3.7	3.2	2.8
Satellite services [2]	15.9	16.6	18.2	20.8	46.5	49.1	56.0	60.9
Ground equipment manufacturing [3]	(NA)	(NA)	(NA)	(NA)	19.6	21.2	22.1	23.3

NA Not available. [1] Includes revenues from the construction and sale of satellites to both commercial and government. [2] Includes revenues derived from transponder leasing and subscription/retail services such as direct-to-home television and satellite mobile and data communications. [3] Includes revenues from the manufacture of gateways and satellite control stations, satellite news-gathering trucks, very small aperture terminals, direct-to-home television equipment and mobile satellite phones.

Source: Satellite Industry Association/Futron Corporation, Bethesda, MD, *2004–2005 Satellite Industry Indicators Survey* (copyright). See also <http://www.sia.org/>.

Table 799. Worldwide Successful Space Launches: 1957 to 2005

[Criterion of success is attainment of Earth orbit or Earth escape]

Country	Total, 1957–05	1957–64	1965–69	1970–74	1975–79	1980–84	1985–89	1990–94	1995–2003	2004	2005
Total	4,410	289	586	555	607	605	550	466	647	53	52
Soviet Union/Russia [1] . . .	2,746	82	302	405	461	483	447	283	238	22	23
United States	1,305	207	279	139	126	93	61	122	250	16	12
Japan	62	–	–	5	10	12	11	9	13	–	2
ESA [2]	160	–	–	–	1	8	21	33	89	3	5
China	88	–	–	2	6	6	9	15	37	8	5
France	10	–	4	3	3	–	–	–	–	–	–
India	16	–	–	–	–	3	–	3	8	1	1
Israel	4	–	–	–	–	–	1	1	2	–	–
Ukraine [1]	17	–	–	–	–	–	–	–	10	3	4
Australia	1	–	1	–	–	–	–	–	–	–	–
United Kingdom	1	–	–	1	–	–	–	–	–	–	–

– Represents zero. [1] Launches conducted by the former Soviet Union are listed separately as Russia or Ukraine. [2] European Space Agency. Includes launches by Arianespace.

Source: Library of Congress, Congressional Research Service, Science Policy Research Division, *Space Activities of the United States, CIS, and Other Launching Countries/Organizations 1957–1999*; thereafter, Resources, Science, and Industry Division, 2005.

Table 800. National Aeronautics and Space Administration—Budget Appropriations, 2006, and Projections, 2007 to 2011

[In millions of dollars (16,623.0 represents $16,623,000,000). Figures may not add due to rounding]

Item	2006	2007	2008	2009	2010	2011
Appropriations, total	**16,623.0**	**16,792.3**	**17,309.4**	**17,614.2**	**18,026.3**	**18,460.4**
Science, exploration, & aeronautics	9,721.3	10,524.4	10,594.4	11,136.4	11,747.0	15,526.4
Science	5,253.7	5,330.0	5,383.1	5,437.1	5,491.5	5,546.4
Solar system exploration.	1,582.3	1,610.2	1,598.6	1,840.4	1,899.6	1,846.7
The universe	1,507.9	1,509.2	1,500.9	1,307.9	1,276.1	1,309.7
Earth-sun system	2,163.5	2,210.6	2,283.7	2,288.9	2,315.8	2,390.0
Exploration systems	3,050.1	3,978.3	3,981.6	4,499.8	5,055.9	8,775.1
Constellation systems	1,733.5	3,057.6	3,067.6	3,612.9	4,083.8	7,698.4
Exploration systems research & technology . . .	692.5	646.1	632.2	605.1	679.2	764.6
Human systems research & technology.	624.1	274.6	281.8	281.8	292.8	312.1
Aeronautics research & technology	884.1	724.4	731.8	732.4	722.8	722.7
Cross-agency support programs	533.5	491.7	497.9	467.1	476.8	482.2
Education	162.4	153.3	152.4	153.1	154.0	153.3
Advanced business systems	156.3	108.2	106.9	73.8	78.5	80.6
Innovative partnerships program	214.8	197.9	205.5	206.2	209.7	212.9
Shared capabilities	–	32.2	33.1	33.9	34.7	35.5
Exploration capabilities	6,869.7	6,234.4	6,680.4	6,442.3	6,242.9	2,896.7
Space operations	6,869.7	6,234.4	6,680.4	6,442.3	6,242.9	2,896.7
International space station	1,753.4	1,811.3	2,200.3	2,255.6	2,197.1	2,360.8
Space shuttle	4,777.5	4,056.7	4,087.3	3,794.8	3,651.1	146.7
Space & flight support	338.8	366.5	392.8	392.0	394.7	398.2
Inspector General.	32.0	33.5	34.6	35.5	36.4	37.3

– Represents or rounds to zero.

Source: U.S. National Aeronautics and Space Administration, *Fiscal Year 2007 Budget* <http://www.nasa.gov/pdf/142458mainFY07budgetfull.pdf> (accessed April 2006).

Table 801. Nobel Prize Laureates in Selected Sciences: 1901 to 2004

[Presented by location of award-winning research and by date of award]

Country	1901-2004				1901–1930	1931–1945	1946–1960	1961–1975	1976–1990	1991–2003	2004
	Total	Physics	Chemistry	Physiology/ Medicine							
Total	**502**	**174**	**146**	**182**	**93**	**49**	**74**	**92**	**98**	**82**	**8**
United States	225	80	54	91	6	14	38	41	63	59	6
United Kingdom	76	21	27	28	15	11	14	20	9	6	–
Germany [1]	63	19	29	15	27	11	4	8	7	4	–
France	25	11	7	7	13	2	–	5	2	3	–
Soviet Union/Russia. . .	12	9	1	2	2	–	4	3	1	2	–
Japan	8	4	4	–	–	–	1	2	1	4	–
Other countries	93	30	24	39	30	11	13	13	15	4	2

– Represents zero. [1] Between 1946 and 1991, data are for the former West Germany only.

Source: U.S. National Science Foundation, unpublished data.

U.S. Census Bureau, Statistical Abstract of the United States: 2007

Agriculture

This section presents statistics on farms and farm operators; land use; farm income, expenditures, and debt; farm output, productivity, and marketings; foreign trade in agricultural products; specific crops; and livestock, poultry, and their products.

The principal sources are the reports issued by the National Agricultural Statistics Service (NASS) and the Economic Research Service (ERS) of the U.S. Department of Agriculture. The information from the 2002 Census of Agriculture is available in printed form in the Volume 1, Geographic Area Series; in electronic format on CD-ROM; and on the Internet site <http://www.nass.usda.gov/Census_of _Agriculture/index.asp>. The Department of Agriculture publishes annually *Agricultural Statistics*, a general reference book on agricultural production, supplies, consumption, facilities, costs, and returns. The ERS publishes data on farm assets, debt, and income on the Internet site <http://www.ers.usda .gov/briefing /farmincome/>. Sources of current data on agricultural exports and imports include *Outlook for U.S. Agricultural Trade,* published by the ERS; the ERS Internet site <http://www.ers.usda.gov /briefing/AgTrade/>; and the reports of the U.S. Census Bureau, particularly *U.S. Imports of Merchandise on CD-ROM,* and *U.S. Exports of Merchandise on CD-ROM.*

The 45 field offices of the NASS collect data on crops, livestock and products, agricultural prices, farm employment, and other related subjects mainly through sample surveys. Information is obtained on some 75 crops and 50 livestock items as well as scores of items pertaining to agricultural production and marketing. State estimates and supporting information are sent to the Agricultural Statistics Board of NASS, which reviews the estimates and issues reports containing state and national data. Among these reports are annual summaries such as *Crop Production, Crop Values, Agricultural Prices,* and *Livestock Production, Disposition and Income.* For more information about concepts and methods underlying USDA's statistical series, see *Major Statistical Series of the U.S. Department of Agriculture* (Agricultural Handbook No. 671), a 12-volume set of publications.

Farms and farmland—The definitions of a farm have varied through time. Since 1850, when minimum criteria defining a farm for census purposes first were established, the farm definition has changed nine times. The current definition, first used for the 1974 census, is any place from which $1,000 or more of agricultural products were produced and sold, or normally would have been sold, during the census year.

Acreage designated as "land in farms" consists primarily of agricultural land used for crops, pasture, or grazing. It also includes woodland and wasteland not actually under cultivation or used for pasture or grazing, provided it was part of the farm operator's total operation. Land in farms includes acres set aside under annual commodity acreage programs as well as acres in the Conservation Reserve and Wetlands Reserve Programs for places meeting the farm definition. Land in farms is an operating unit concept and includes land owned and operated as well as land rented from others. All grazing land, except land used under government permits on a per-head basis, was included as "land in farms" provided it was part of a farm or ranch.

An evaluation of coverage has been conducted for each census of agriculture since 1945 to provide estimates of the completeness of census farm counts. The 2002 coverage evaluation shows the census covered 96 percent of the farms with $50,000 or more in sales, but only 78 percent of farms with less than $50,000 in sales. The overall coverage of all farms was 82 percent. The census covered nearly 98 percent of all land in farms and

97 percent of the market value of agricultural products sold. In 2002, census farm counts and totals were statistically adjusted for coverage and reported at the county level. The size of the adjustments varies considerably by state. In general, farms not on the census mail list tended to be small in acreage, production, and sales of farm products. For more explanation about census mail list compilation, collection methods, coverage measurement, and adjustments, see Appendixes A and C, 2002 Census of Agriculture, Volume 1 reports.

Farm income—The final agricultural sector output comprises cash receipts from farm marketings of crops and livestock, federal government payments made directly to farmers for farm-related activities, rental value of farm homes, value of farm products consumed in farm homes, and other farm-related income such as machine hire and custom work. Farm marketings represent quantities of agricultural products sold by farmers multiplied by prices received per unit of production at the local market. Information on prices received for farm products is generally obtained by the NASS Agricultural Statistics Board from surveys of firms (such as grain elevators, packers, and processors) purchasing agricultural commodities directly from producers. In some cases, the price information is obtained directly from the producers.

Crops—Estimates of crop acreage and production by the NASS are based on current sample survey data obtained from individual producers and objective yield counts, reports of carlot shipments, market records, personal field observations by field statisticians, and reports from

other sources. Prices received by farmers are marketing year averages. These averages are based on U.S. monthly prices weighted by monthly marketings during specific periods. U.S. monthly prices are state average prices weighted by marketings during the month. Marketing year average prices do not include allowances for outstanding loans, government purchases, deficiency payments or disaster payments.

All state prices are based on individual state marketing years, while U.S. marketing year averages are based on standard marketing years for each crop. For a listing of the crop marketing years and the participating states in the monthly program, see *Crop Values*. Value of production is computed by multiplying state prices by each state's production. The U.S. value of production is the sum of state values for all states. Value of production figures shown in Tables 831–834, 838, and 839 should not be confused with cash receipts from farm marketings which relate to sales during a calendar year, irrespective of the year of production.

Livestock—Annual inventory numbers of livestock and estimates of livestock, dairy, and poultry production prepared by the Department of Agriculture are based on information from farmers and ranchers obtained by probability survey sampling methods.

Statistical reliability—For a discussion of statistical collection and estimation, sampling procedures, and measures of statistical reliability pertaining to Department of Agriculture data, see Appendix III.

Table 802. Farms by Size and Type of Organization: 1974 to 2002

[2,314 represents 2,314,000. For comments on adjustment, see text, this section. See also Appendix III]

Size and type of organization	Unit	Not adjusted for coverage						1997 [1]	2002 [1]
		1974	1978	1982	1987	1992	1997		
Farms.	1,000	2,314	2,258	2,241	2,088	1,925	1,912	2,216	2,129
Land in farms.	Mil. acres. .	1,017	1,015	987	964	946	932	955	938
Average size of farm	Acres	440	449	440	462	491	487	431	441
Farms by size:									
Under 10 acres.	1,000	128	151	188	183	166	154	205	179
10 to 49 acres	1,000	380	392	449	412	388	411	531	564
50 to 179 acres.	1,000	828	759	712	645	584	593	694	659
180 to 499 acres.	1,000	616	582	527	478	428	403	428	389
500 to 999 acres.	1,000	207	213	204	200	186	176	179	162
1,000 to 1,999 acres	1,000	93	98	97	102	102	101	103	99
2,000 acres or more	1,000	62	63	65	67	71	75	74	78
Farms by type of organization:									
Family or individual	1,000	(NA)	1,966	1,946	1,809	1,653	1,643	1,923	1,910
Partnership	1,000	(NA)	233	223	200	187	169	186	130
Corporation	1,000	(NA)	50	60	67	73	84	90	74
Other [2]	1,000	(NA)	9	12	12	12	15	17	16

NA Not available. [1] Data have been adjusted for coverage; see text, this section. [2] Cooperative, estate or trust, institutional, etc.

Source: U.S. Department of Agriculture, National Agricultural Statistics Service, *2002 Census of Agriculture*, Vol. 1.

Table 803. Farm Operators—Tenure and Characteristics: 1997 and 2002

[In thousands, except as indicated (2,216 represents 2,216,000). An "operator" is a person who operates a farm, either doing the work or making day-to-day decisions. A family operation may have more than one operator. A principal operator is the person primarily responsible for the on-site, day-to-day operation of the farm or ranch business. Data on operator characteristics were collected up to a maximum of three operators per farm, though operations were asked to report the total number of operators. Data have been adjusted for coverage; see text, this section and Appendix III]

Characteristic	Princi-pal opera-tors, 1997	2002			Characteristic	Princi-pal opera-tors, 1997	2002		
		Total opera-tors	Princi-pal opera-tors	Other opera-tors			Total opera-tors	Princi-pal opera-tors	Other opera-tors
Total	2,216	3,054	2,129	925	Full owner.	1,385	(NA)	1,428	(NA)
					Part owner.	616	(NA)	551	(NA)
White	2,154	2,966	2,067	899	Tenant	215	(NA)	150	(NA)
Black or									
African American.	27	36	29	7	Principal occupation:				
American Indian or					Farming.	1,044	1,658	1,224	434
Alaska Native.	13	24	15	9	Other	1,171	1,396	905	491
Native Hawaiian or									
Other Pacific Islander [1] . .	(NA)	2	1	1	Place of residence: [3]				
Asian [1]	10	13	8	5	On farm operated	1,577	2,391	1,680	711
More than one race					Not on farm operated. . .	475	662	449	214
reported	(NA)	12	8	4					
Other	12	(NA)	(NA)	(NA)	Years on present farm: [3]				
					2 years or less	115	143	75	68
Operators of Hispanic					3 to 4 years	157	251	144	108
origin [2]	33	72	51	22	5 to 9 years	318	587	375	212
Female.	210	822	238	585	10 years or more.	1,253	2,073	1,536	537
Under 25 years old	24	60	17	43	Average years on				
25 to 34 years old	155	201	106	95	present farm	19.4	(NA)	20.7	(NA)
35 to 44 years old.	444	590	366	224	Days worked off farm: [3]				
45 to 54 years old.	552	838	573	265	None.	833	1,354	962	392
55 to 64 years old.	481	690	509	181	1 to 49 days.	121	183	122	61
65 to 74 years old.	(NA)	439	354	85	50 to 99 days	65	102	66	36
75 years old and over	(NA)	236	203	32	100 to 199 days	(NA)	224	146	78
Average age (years)	54.0	53.2	55.3	(NA)	200 days or more	871	1,190	832	358

NA Not available. [1] In 1997, Asians and Native Hawaiians or Other Pacific Islanders were tabulated in one group. [2] Operators of Hispanic origin may be any race. [3] Data for 1997 exclude "not reported."

Source: U.S. Department of Agriculture, National Agricultural Statistics Service, *2002 Census of Agriculture*, Vol. 1.

Agriculture   531

Table 804. **Farms—Number and Acreage by Size of Farm: 1997 and 2002**

[2,216 represents 2,216,000. Data have been adjusted for coverage; see text, this section and Appendix III]

Size of farm	Number of farms (1,000) 1997	Number of farms (1,000) 2002	Land in farms (mil. acres) 1997	Land in farms (mil. acres) 2002	Cropland harvested (mil. acres) 1997	Cropland harvested (mil. acres) 2002	Percent distribution, 2002 Number of farms	Percent distribution, 2002 All land in farms	Percent distribution, 2002 Cropland harvested
Total	2,216	2,129	954.8	938.3	318.9	302.7	100.0	100.0	100.0
Under 10 acres	205	179	0.9	0.8	0.3	0.2	8.4	0.1	0.1
10 to 49 acres	531	564	14.0	14.7	4.3	4.1	26.5	1.6	1.4
50 to 69 acres	154	152	9.0	8.8	2.7	2.5	7.1	0.9	0.8
70 to 99 acres	200	191	16.5	15.7	5.2	4.7	9.0	1.7	1.5
100 to 139 acres	187	175	21.7	20.2	7.0	6.1	8.2	2.2	2.0
140 to 179 acres	153	142	24.1	22.3	8.4	7.3	6.7	2.4	2.4
180 to 219 acres	100	91	19.8	18.0	7.2	6.2	4.3	1.9	2.1
220 to 259 acres	79	72	18.8	17.1	7.5	6.5	3.4	1.8	2.1
260 to 499 acres	249	226	89.2	80.6	40.1	34.1	10.6	8.6	11.3
500 to 999 acres	179	162	124.6	112.4	66.5	56.7	7.6	12.0	18.7
1,000 to 1,999 acres. . .	103	99	140.7	135.7	75.9	72.8	4.7	14.5	24.0
2,000 acres or more . . .	74	78	475.6	491.9	94.1	101.6	3.7	52.4	33.6

Source: U.S. Department of Agriculture, National Agricultural Statistics Service, *2002 Census of Agriculture*, Vol. 1.

Table 805. **Farms—Number, Acreage, and Value by Tenure of Principal Operator and Type of Organization: 1997 and 2002**

[2,216 represents 2,216,000. Full owners own all the land they operate. Part owners own a part and rent from others the rest of the land they operate. A principal operator is the person primarily responsible for the on-site, day-to-day operation of the farm or ranch business. Data have been adjusted for coverage; see text, this section and Appendix III]

Item and year	Unit	Total [1]	Tenure of operator Full owner	Tenure of operator Part owner	Tenure of operator Tenant	Type of organization Family or indi-vidual	Type of organization Partner-ship	Type of organization Corpora-tion
NUMBER OF FARMS								
1997.	1,000	2,216	1,385	616	215	1,923	186	90
2002, total	1,000	2,129	1,428	551	150	1,910	130	74
Under 50 acres	1,000	743	639	64	41	697	24	18
50 to 179 acres.	1,000	659	487	131	41	611	31	12
180 to 499 acres	1,000	389	203	153	33	344	29	12
500 to 999 acres	1,000	162	54	91	17	133	17	10
1,000 acres or more.	1,000	177	46	112	18	125	29	21
LAND IN FARMS								
1997.	Mil. acres. . .	955	332	512	111	605	151	133
2002.	Mil. acres. . .	938	357	495	87	622	146	108
Value of land and buildings, 2002 [2] . . .	Bil. dol.	1,145	495	551	99	836	158	129
Value of farm products sold, 2002	Bil. dol.	201	88	91	22	104	37	57

[1] Includes other types, not shown separately. [2] Based on a sample of farms.

Source: U.S. Department of Agriculture, National Agricultural Statistics Service, *2002 Census of Agriculture*, Vol. 1.

Table 806. **Farms—Number, Acreage, and Value of Sales by Size of Sales: 2002**

[2,129 represents 2,129,000. Data have been adjusted for coverage; see text, this section and Appendix III]

Market value of agricultural products sold	Farms (1,000)	Acreage Total (mil.)	Acreage Average per farm	Value of sales Total (mil. dol.)	Value of sales Average per farm (dol.)	Percent distribution Farms	Percent distribution Acreage	Percent distribution Value of sales
Total	2,129	938.3	441	200,646	94,244	100.0	100.0	100.0
Less than $2,500	827	107.0	129	485	586	38.8	11.4	0.2
$2,500 to $4,999	213	23.1	108	763	3,582	10.0	2.5	0.4
$5,000 to $9,999	223	34.8	156	1,577	7,072	10.5	3.7	0.8
$10,000 to $24,999	256	69.5	271	4,068	15,891	12.0	7.4	2.0
$25,000 to $49,999	158	77.9	494	5,594	35,405	7.4	8.3	2.8
$50,000 to $99,999	140	110.1	784	10,024	71,600	6.6	11.7	5.0
$100,000 to $249,999.	159	189.4	1,191	25,401	159,755	7.5	20.2	12.7
$250,000 to $499,999.	82	140.8	1,723	28,530	347,927	3.9	15.0	14.2
$500,000 to $999,999.	42	94.0	2,241	28,944	689,143	2.0	10.0	14.4
$1,000,000 or more	29	91.7	3,198	95,259	3,284,793	1.4	9.8	47.5

Source: U.S. Department of Agriculture, National Agricultural Statistics Service, *2002 Census of Agriculture*, Vol. 1.

Table 807. Farms—Number and Acreage: 1980 to 2005

[As of June 1 (2,440 represents 2,440,000). Based on 1974 census definition; for definition of farms and farmland, see text of this section. Activities included as agriculture have undergone changes in recent years. Data for period 1995 to 2004 are not directly comparable with data for 1980 to 1990. Data for 2002 have been adjusted for underenumeration. Minus sign (–) indicates decrease]

Year	Unit	1980	1990	1995	2000	2001	2002	2003	2004	2005
Number of farms	1,000.	2,440	2,146	2,196	2,167	2,149	2,135	2,127	2,113	2,101
Annual change [1] . . .	1,000. . .	3	–29	–1	–21	–18	–13	–9	–14	–12
Land in farms	Mil. acres . . .	1,039	987	963	945	942	940	939	936	933
Average per farm . . .	Acres.	426	460	438	436	438	440	441	443	444

[1] Annual change from immediate preceding year.

Source: U.S. Dept. of Agriculture, National Agricultural Statistics Service, *Farms and Land in Farms, Final Estimates by States, 1979–1987; Farms and Land in Farms, Final Estimates, 1988–1992; Farms and Land in Farms, Final Estimates, 1993–1997; Farm Numbers and Land in Farms, Final Estimates, 1998–2002;* and *Farms, Land in Farms, and Livestock Operations,* annual.

Table 808. Farms—Number and Acreage by State: 2000 and 2005

[2,167 represents 2,167,000. See headnote, Table 807]

State	Farms (1,000)		Acreage (mil.)		Acreage per farm		State	Farms (1,000)		Acreage (mil.)		Acreage per farm	
	2000	2005	2000	2005	2000	2005		2000	2005	2000	2005	2000	2005
U.S	2,167	2,101	945	933	436	444	Montana	28	28	59	60	2,133	2,146
Alabama.	47	44	9	9	191	198	Nebraska	52	48	46	46	887	952
Alaska	1	1	1	1	1,569	1,406	Nevada	3	3	6	6	2,065	2,100
Arizona.	11	10	27	26	2,514	2,594	New						
Arkansas	48	47	15	14	304	306	Hampshire. . .	3	3	(Z)	(Z)	133	132
California	83	77	28	26	337	345	New Jersey.	10	10	1	1	86	81
Colorado.	30	31	32	31	1,053	1,007	New Mexico	18	18	45	45	2,494	2,543
Connecticut.	4	4	(Z)	(Z)	86	86	New York	38	36	8	8	205	212
Delaware	3	2	1	1	215	226	North Carolina . . .	56	50	9	9	166	178
Florida	44	43	10	10	236	235	North Dakota. . . .	31	30	39	39	1,279	1,300
Georgia	49	49	11	11	222	214	Ohio	79	77	15	14	187	187
Hawaii	6	6	1	1	251	236	Oklahoma	85	83	34	34	400	406
Idaho	25	25	12	12	486	472	Oregon.	40	40	17	17	433	428
Illinois	77	73	28	27	357	377	Pennsylvania. . . .	59	58	8	8	130	132
Indiana.	63	59	15	15	240	254	Rhode Island. . . .	1	1	(Z)	(Z)	75	71
Iowa	94	89	33	32	346	355	South Carolina. . .	24	24	5	5	203	199
Kansas	65	65	48	47	736	732	South Dakota. . .	32	31	44	44	1,358	1,392
Kentucky	90	84	14	14	152	164	Tennessee	88	84	12	12	134	138
Louisiana	29	27	8	8	277	291	Texas.	228	230	131	130	573	564
Maine.	7	7	1	1	190	193	Utah	16	15	12	12	748	763
Maryland	12	12	2	2	172	169	Vermont	7	6	1	1	192	198
Massachusetts. . .	6	6	1	1	89	85	Virginia.	49	47	9	9	180	181
Michigan.	53	53	10	10	192	191	Washington.	37	35	16	15	420	438
Minnesota	81	80	28	28	344	345	West Virginia. . . .	21	21	4	4	173	173
Mississippi	42	42	11	11	266	262	Wisconsin.	78	77	16	15	206	201
Missouri	109	105	30	30	277	287	Wyoming	9	9	35	34	3,750	3,739

Z Less than 500,000 acres.

Source: U.S. Department of Agriculture, National Agricultural Statistics Service, *Farm Numbers and Land in Farms, Final Estimates, 1998–2002* and *Farms, Land in Farms, and Livestock Operations,* annual.

Table 809. Certified Organic Farmland Acreage and Livestock: 2000 to 2003

Item	Unit	2000	2002	2003	Crop	Certified organic acreage (1,000)	
						2000	2003
Certified growers	Number. . .	6,592	7,323	8,035	Corn	78	106
					Wheat.	181	234
Certified organic acreage,					Oats	30	46
total	1,000	1,776	1,926	2,197	Barley	42	30
Pastureland and rangeland . . .	1,000	557	626	745	Rice	27	20
Cropland	1,000	1,219	1,300	1,452	Millet.	15	27
					Rye	7	12
Certified animals:					Soybeans	136	122
Beef cows	1,000	13.8	23.4	27.3	Dry beans	14	10
Milk cows	1,000	38.2	67.2	74.4	Dry peas and lentils.	10	16
Hogs and pigs	1,000	1.7	2.8	6.6	Hay and silage	231	328
Sheep and lambs	1,000	2.3	4.9	4.6	Lettuce	11	12
Layer hens	1,000	1,114	1,052	1,591	Tree nuts	4	10
Broilers	1,000	1,925	3,032	6,301	Citrus	7	12
Turkeys	1,000	9	306	217	Apples	9	14
Unclassified/other	1,000	111	1,880	671	Grapes	13	21

Source: U.S. Department of Agriculture, Economic Research Service, "Organic Production"; <http://www.ers.usda.gov/data/organic>.

Table 810. **Balance Sheet of the Farming Sector: 1990 to 2004**

[In billions of dollars, except as indicated (841 represents $841,000,000,000). As of December 31]

Item	1990	1995	1996	1997	1998	1999	2000	2001	2002	2003	2004
Assets	**841**	**966**	**1,003**	**1,051**	**1,083**	**1,139**	**1,203**	**1,256**	**1,304**	**1,379**	**1,501**
Real estate	619	740	770	808	840	887	946	996	1,046	1,112	1,227
Livestock and poultry [1]	71	58	60	67	63	73	77	79	76	79	79
Machinery, motor vehicles [2]	86	88	88	89	90	90	90	93	94	96	99
Crops [3]	23	27	32	33	30	28	28	25	23	24	24
Purchased inputs	3	3	4	5	5	4	5	4	6	6	6
Financial assets	38	49	49	50	55	57	57	59	60	62	66
Claims	841	966	1,003	1,051	1,083	1,139	1,203	1,256	1,304	1,379	1,501
Debt [4]	131	143	149	157	165	168	178	186	193	198	207
Real estate debt	68	72	74	79	83	87	91	96	103	108	114
Non-real estate debt	63	71	74	78	82	80	87	90	90	90	93
Equity	**709**	**823**	**854**	**894**	**919**	**971**	**1,026**	**1,070**	**1,111**	**1,181**	**1,294**
FINANCIAL RATIOS (percent)											
Farm debt/equity ratio	18.5	17.4	17.4	17.5	17.9	17.3	17.3	17.4	17.4	16.8	16.0
Farm debt/asset ratio	15.6	14.8	14.8	14.9	15.2	14.7	14.8	14.8	14.8	14.4	13.8
Rate of return on assets from:											
Total	3.5	4.3	5.8	5.7	5.1	5.3	5.1	4.6	3.2	6.6	11.4
Current income [5]	4.1	2.2	4.1	3.0	2.4	1.8	2.0	2.0	0.7	2.2	3.4
Real capital gains [6]	-0.7	2.1	1.7	2.7	2.7	3.4	3.1	2.6	2.5	4.4	8.0
Rate of return on equity from:											
Total	3.0	3.9	5.6	5.5	4.8	5.1	5.0	4.4	2.8	6.8	13.4
Current income [7]	3.0	1.1	3.3	2.0	1.4	0.7	0.9	1.1	-0.4	1.5	3.1
Real capital gains [8]	0.1	2.8	2.3	3.5	3.4	4.3	4.1	3.4	3.2	5.2	10.4

[1] Excludes horses, mules, and broilers. [2] Includes only farm share value for trucks and autos. [3] All non-CCC crops held on farms plus the value above loan rate for crops held under Commodity Credit Corporation. [4] Excludes debt for nonfarm purposes. [5] Returns to farm assets from current income/farm business assets. Measures how efficiently the farm business uses its assets; the per dollar return on farm assets from current income only. [6] Real capital gains on farm business assets/farm business assets. The per dollar return on farm assets from real capital gains. [7] Returns to farm assets from current income minus interest/farm business equity. Measures the returns to equity capital employed in farm business from current income less interest. [8] Real capital gains on farm business assets/farm business equity. The per dollar return on farm equity from real capital gains.

Source: U.S. Department of Agriculture, Economic Research Service, "Farm Balance Sheet"; published 10 February 2006; <http://www.ers.usda.gov/Data/FarmBalanceSheet/FBSDMU.HTM>.

Table 811. **Farm Sector Output and Value Added: 1990 to 2004**

[In billions of dollars (180.1 represents $180,100,000,000). For definition of value added, see text, Section 13. Minus sign (–) indicates decrease]

Item	1990	1995	1996	1997	1998	1999	2000	2001	2002	2003	2004
CURRENT DOLLARS											
Farm output, total	**180.1**	**192.0**	**215.9**	**222.0**	**208.9**	**198.5**	**203.6**	**210.8**	**202.1**	**225.8**	**258.0**
Cash receipts from farm marketings	172.1	194.3	201.6	211.2	199.0	190.2	196.6	200.1	194.6	213.3	242.9
Farm products consumed on farms	0.7	0.5	0.5	0.5	0.5	0.5	0.6	0.5	0.5	0.5	0.5
Other farm income	4.9	6.3	6.1	7.4	8.5	9.4	8.4	9.5	10.6	11.6	11.1
Change in farm finished goods											
inventories	2.4	–9.2	7.8	2.8	0.8	–1.6	–2.0	0.6	–3.7	0.4	3.4
Less: Intermediate goods and services											
consumed [1]	103.5	123.5	125.2	133.9	130.0	129.8	132.1	137.7	131.2	137.8	145.8
Equals: **Gross farm value added**	**76.6**	**68.5**	**90.7**	**88.1**	**78.9**	**68.8**	**71.5**	**73.1**	**70.8**	**88.0**	**112.2**
Less: Consumption of fixed capital	18.6	19.6	19.9	20.3	20.9	21.2	21.3	27.4	27.0	27.9	30.1
Equals: Net farm value added	58.0	48.9	70.8	67.8	58.0	47.6	50.2	45.7	43.9	60.1	82.2
Compensation of employees	13.4	15.4	16.0	17.1	18.2	18.9	19.7	20.9	20.8	20.0	22.5
Taxes on production and imports	3.8	4.2	4.2	4.4	4.3	4.9	4.7	4.8	5.0	5.2	5.4
Less: Subsidies to operators	7.6	6.1	6.2	6.4	10.5	18.6	19.6	18.3	9.6	13.7	10.7
Net operating surplus	48.5	35.4	56.7	52.6	46.0	42.4	45.4	38.3	27.7	48.5	64.9
CHAINED (**2000**) DOLLARS [2]											
Farm output, total	**164.5**	**179.6**	**183.3**	**198.4**	**198.4**	**200.5**	**203.6**	**200.7**	**201.4**	**206.3**	**206.1**
Cash receipts from farm marketings	159.0	183.5	172.1	189.2	189.2	192.0	196.6	190.1	194.1	194.3	192.8
Farm products consumed on farms	0.7	0.5	0.5	0.5	0.6	0.6	0.6	0.5	0.5	0.5	0.4
Other farm income	4.8	5.8	5.2	6.5	7.9	9.5	8.4	9.4	10.1	10.4	9.4
Change in farm finished goods											
inventories	2.1	–8.8	6.0	2.5	0.9	–1.8	–2.0	0.6	–3.6	0.4	2.5
Less: Intermediate goods and services											
consumed [1]	117.5	134.4	128.5	133.7	137.5	138.1	132.1	135.3	131.3	130.1	130.0
Equals: **Gross farm value added**	**49.3**	**49.6**	**56.1**	**64.4**	**61.6**	**62.9**	**71.5**	**65.6**	**70.1**	**76.0**	**75.9**
Less: Consumption of fixed capital	23.0	21.3	21.1	21.3	21.6	21.6	21.3	27.0	26.2	26.7	27.6
Equals: Net farm value added	29.4	30.4	36.0	42.9	40.2	40.2	50.2	39.0	44.2	49.5	48.8

[1] Includes rent paid to nonoperator landlords. [2] See text, Section 13.

Source: U.S. Bureau of Economic Analysis, *Survey of Current Business,* August 2005. See also <http://www.bea.gov/bea /dn/nipaweb/selecttable.asp>.

Table 812. Value Added to Economy by Agricultural Sector: 1990 to 2004

[In billions of dollars (188.5 represents $188,500,000,000). Data are consistent with the net farm income accounts and include income and expenses related to the farm operator dwellings. The concept presented is consistent with that employed by the Organization for Economic Co-operation and Development]

Item	1990	1995	1996	1997	1998	1999	2000	2001	2002	2003	2004
Value of agricultural sector production	188.5	203.6	228.5	230.5	220.2	213.5	219.1	228.0	218.7	242.6	279.0
Value of crop production	83.2	95.9	115.7	112.5	102.1	92.8	94.9	95.0	98.3	109.4	124.0
Food grains	7.5	10.4	10.8	10.4	8.8	6.9	6.5	6.4	6.8	8.0	9.1
Feed crops	18.7	24.5	27.2	27.1	22.6	19.5	20.5	21.5	24.0	24.7	28.2
Cotton	5.5	6.9	7.0	6.3	6.1	4.6	2.9	3.6	3.4	6.5	5.4
Oil crops	12.3	15.5	16.3	19.8	17.4	13.4	13.5	13.3	15.0	18.7	19.8
Tobacco	2.7	2.5	2.8	2.9	2.8	2.3	2.3	1.9	1.7	1.6	1.5
Fruits and tree nuts	9.4	11.0	11.8	13.0	12.0	12.0	12.5	12.0	12.6	13.4	15.5
Vegetables	11.3	15.0	14.4	14.7	15.0	15.0	15.6	15.5	17.2	17.4	17.3
All other crops	12.9	15.3	16.1	17.2	17.6	18.4	18.7	19.2	20.2	20.7	21.0
Home consumption	0.1	0.2	0.2	0.2	0.2	0.2	0.2	0.2	0.2	0.2	0.1
Value of inventory adjustment	2.8	-5.3	9.0	1.0	-0.3	0.5	2.2	1.5	-2.9	-1.7	6.1
Value of livestock production	90.0	87.8	92.1	96.3	94.2	95.2	99.1	106.4	93.5	104.9	124.6
Meat animals	51.1	44.9	44.2	49.7	43.4	45.7	53.0	53.3	48.1	56.2	62.2
Dairy products	20.2	19.9	22.8	20.9	24.1	23.2	20.6	24.7	20.6	21.2	27.4
Poultry and eggs	15.3	19.1	22.5	22.3	23.0	23.0	21.8	24.6	21.2	23.9	29.5
Miscellaneous livestock	2.5	3.4	3.6	3.6	3.8	3.9	4.2	4.1	4.1	4.3	4.4
Home consumption	0.5	0.3	0.3	0.2	0.2	0.1	0.1	0.1	0.1	0.1	0.2
Value of inventory adjustment	0.4	0.2	-1.1	-0.4	-0.3	-0.7	-0.6	-0.4	-0.6	-0.8	0.9
Services and forestry	15.3	19.9	20.7	21.7	23.9	25.4	25.0	26.5	26.9	28.3	30.5
Machine hire and customwork	1.8	1.9	2.2	2.4	2.2	2.0	2.2	2.1	2.2	3.0	3.5
Forest products sold	1.8	2.8	2.6	2.8	3.0	2.7	2.8	2.6	2.5	2.2	2.4
Other farm income	4.5	5.8	6.2	6.9	8.7	10.1	8.7	10.1	10.2	10.5	11.3
Gross imputed rental value of farm dwellings	7.2	9.4	9.8	9.6	10.0	10.6	11.3	11.7	12.0	12.6	13.3
Less: Purchased inputs	92.2	108.8	112.2	120.0	117.7	118.7	121.8	125.7	123.1	130.0	136.5
Farm origin	39.5	41.8	42.7	46.9	44.8	45.5	47.9	48.2	48.3	53.7	57.1
Feed purchased	20.4	23.8	25.2	26.3	25.0	24.5	24.5	24.8	25.0	27.5	30.0
Livestock and poultry purchased	14.6	12.5	11.3	13.8	12.6	13.8	15.9	15.2	14.4	16.8	17.6
Seed purchased	4.5	5.5	6.2	6.7	7.2	7.2	7.5	8.2	8.9	9.4	9.5
Manufactured inputs	22.0	26.1	28.6	29.2	28.1	27.1	28.7	29.4	28.5	28.6	31.4
Fertilizers and lime	8.2	10.0	10.9	10.9	10.6	9.9	10.0	10.3	9.6	10.0	11.4
Pesticides	5.4	7.7	8.5	9.0	9.0	8.6	8.5	8.6	8.3	8.4	8.5
Petroleum fuel and oils	5.8	5.4	6.0	6.2	5.6	5.6	7.2	6.9	6.6	6.8	8.2
Electricity	2.6	3.0	3.2	3.0	2.9	3.0	3.0	3.6	3.9	3.3	3.2
Other purchased inputs	30.7	40.9	40.8	43.9	44.8	46.1	45.2	48.1	46.4	47.7	48.0
Repair and maintenance of capital items	8.6	9.6	10.4	10.6	10.5	10.7	10.9	11.2	10.4	10.3	13.1
Machine hire and custom work	3.0	3.9	3.7	4.0	4.6	4.4	4.1	4.0	4.0	3.5	3.7
Marketing, storage, and transportation expenses	4.2	7.2	6.9	7.1	6.9	7.3	7.5	7.8	7.5	7.4	7.1
Contract labor	1.6	2.0	2.1	2.5	2.4	2.5	2.7	3.1	2.7	3.2	2.6
Miscellaneous expenses	13.4	18.2	17.7	19.7	20.4	21.3	19.9	21.9	21.7	23.3	21.5
Plus: Net government transactions [1]	3.1	0.4	0.4	0.4	5.3	14.3	15.5	13.3	4.0	9.9	5.8
Direct government payments	9.3	7.3	7.3	7.5	12.4	21.5	22.9	20.7	11.2	17.2	13.3
Motor vehicle registration and licensing fees	0.4	0.4	0.4	0.5	0.5	0.4	0.5	0.5	0.4	0.5	0.5
Property taxes	5.8	6.4	6.6	6.7	6.6	6.8	6.9	6.9	6.8	6.8	7.0
Equals: Gross value added	99.3	95.2	116.7	110.9	107.8	109.0	112.8	115.6	99.6	122.5	148.3
Less: Capital consumption	18.1	18.9	19.1	19.3	19.6	19.8	20.1	20.6	21.0	21.3	22.3
Equals: Net value added	81.2	76.3	97.6	91.7	88.2	89.3	92.7	95.0	78.6	101.2	125.9
Less: Employee compensation	12.4	14.3	15.1	15.9	16.8	17.4	17.9	18.8	19.1	18.8	20.6
Less: Net rent received by nonoperator landlords	9.0	9.6	10.5	11.2	10.9	10.4	11.2	11.1	9.8	10.3	9.7
Less: Real estate and nonreal estate interest	13.5	12.6	13.1	13.2	13.5	13.8	14.7	13.6	13.1	12.7	13.1
Equals: Net farm income	46.3	39.8	59.0	51.3	47.1	47.7	48.9	51.5	36.6	59.5	82.5

[1] Direct government payments minus motor vehicle registration and licensing fees and property taxes.

Source: U.S. Dept. of Agriculture, Economic Research Service, "United States and State Farm Income Data"; <http://www.ers.usda.gov/Data/farmincome/finfidmu.htm>; accessed 3 October 2005.

Table 813. Cash Receipts for Selected Commodities—Leading States: 2004

[In millions of dollars (47,296 represents $47,296,000,000). See headnote, Table 814]

State	Value	State	Value	State	Value	State	Value
Cattle and calves	**47,296**	**Dairy products**	**27,368**	**Corn**	**22,199**	**Broilers**	**20,446**
Texas	7,990	California	5,366	Iowa	4,220	Georgia	2,858
Nebraska	6,197	Wisconsin	3,688	Illinois	4,121	Arkansas	2,731
Kansas	5,644	New York	1,950	Nebraska	2,544	Alabama	2,407
Colorado	3,343	Pennsylvania	1,769	Minnesota	1,828	North Carolina	2,042
Oklahoma	2,362	Idaho	1,358	Indiana	1,786	Mississippi	1,930

Source: U.S. Department of Agriculture, Economic Research Service, "Farm Income"; published 12 September 2005; <http://www.ers.usda.gov/Data/farmincome/firkdmu.htm>.

Agriculture 535

Table 814. Farm Income—Cash Receipts From Farm Marketings: 2000 to 2004

[In millions of dollars (192,113 represents $192,113,000,000). Represents gross receipts from commercial market sales as well as net Commodity Credit Corporation loans. The source estimates and publishes individual cash receipt values only for major commodities and major producing states. The U.S. receipts for individual commodities, computed as the sum of the reported states, may understate the value of sales for some commodities. The degree of underestimation in some of the minor commodities can be substantial]

Commodity	2000	2002	2003	2004	Commodity	2000	2002	2003	2004
Total	192,113	194,984	216,592	241,241	Corn, sweet	709	718	780	833
Livestock and					Cucumbers	382	377	366	370
products [1]	99,624	93,981	105,594	123,481	Lettuce [1]	1,863	2,358	2,302	2,069
Cattle and calves	40,783	38,095	45,092	47,296	Head	1,202	1,429	1,233	1,171
Hogs	11,758	9,602	10,618	14,348	Romaine	299	469	624	514
Sheep and lambs	470	421	502	514	Leaf	312	454	442	380
Dairy products	20,587	20,582	21,239	27,368	Onions	713	758	1,034	1,024
Broilers	13,989	13,438	15,215	20,446	Peppers, green	531	464	495	576
Chicken eggs	4,335	4,302	5,263	5,303	Tomatoes	1,845	1,934	1,910	2,063
Turkeys	2,771	2,643	2,632	2,996	Fresh	1,195	1,254	1,333	1,344
Horses/mules	1,239	982	1,018	1,161	Processing	650	680	577	720
Aquaculture [1, 2]	798	783	828	893	Fruits/nuts [1]	12,458	12,618	13,419	15,463
Catfish	501	410	425	480	Oranges	1,775	1,417	1,431	1,570
					Apples	1,482	1,442	1,641	1,785
Crops [1]	92,489	101,004	110,998	117,760	Avocados	353	346	380	380
Rice	837	882	1,225	1,728	Cherries	327	302	422	507
Wheat	5,654	5,894	6,783	7,381	Grapes [1]	3,100	2,838	2,617	3,015
Barley	556	514	676	678	Wine	1,909	1,683	1,543	1,605
Corn	15,162	17,867	18,993	22,199	Table	437	456	408	536
Hay	3,844	4,612	4,125	4,405	Raisins	487	424	374	617
Sorghum grain	864	915	823	838	Peaches	470	488	454	462
Cotton	2,950	3,418	6,527	5,405	Strawberries	1,045	1,162	1,375	1,472
Tobacco	2,316	1,743	1,553	1,519	Almonds	666	1,201	1,600	2,200
Peanuts	897	600	799	834	Walnuts	296	330	375	439
Soybeans	12,047	13,847	17,285	18,375	Pistachios	245	333	145	444
Vegetables [1]	15,554	17,177	17,401	17,256	Sugarbeets	1,113	1,097	1,270	1,270
Beans, dry	436	464	472	492	Cane for sugar	881	931	1,004	998
Potatoes	2,376	2,902	2,561	2,373	Greenhouse/nursery [1]	13,796	15,181	15,492	15,697
Beans, snap	393	404	396	400	Floriculture	4,576	5,090	5,082	5,180
Broccoli	622	568	616	677	Christmas trees	502	517	506	506
Cabbage	321	309	295	347	Mushrooms	867	907	914	893

[1] Includes other commodities not shown separately.   [2] See also Table 868.

Source: U.S. Department of Agriculture, Economic Research Service, "United States and State Farm Income Data"; published 11 October 2005; <http://www.ers.usda.gov/Data/farmincome/finfidmu.htm>.

Table 815. Farm Output, Income, and Government Payments by State: 2003 and 2004

[In millions of dollars (242,624 represents $242,624,000,000). Farm income data are after inventory adjustment and include income and expenses related to the farm operator's dwelling]

State	Final agricultural sector output		Net farm income		Government payments,	State	Final agricultural sector output		Net farm income		Government payments,
	2003	2004	2003	2004	2004		2003	2004	2003	2004	2004
U.S.	242,624	279,014	59,500	82,540	13,304	MT	2,338	2,608	479	722	282
AL	4,193	4,825	1,685	2,034	156	NE	12,117	13,378	2,807	3,459	728
AK	59	62	10	16	6	NV	456	505	89	128	7
AZ	2,963	3,476	882	1,399	100	NH	195	213	32	37	5
AR	6,080	7,458	2,500	3,243	599	NJ	997	1,027	159	158	10
CA	30,206	34,294	8,426	12,250	507	NM	2,270	2,714	523	862	81
CO	5,426	6,213	849	1,299	221	NY	3,611	4,064	556	638	82
CT	563	614	82	102	7	NC	8,615	9,978	1,793	2,990	213
DE	857	1,030	271	350	16	ND	4,363	4,319	1,528	971	467
FL	6,921	7,238	2,063	2,373	214	OH	6,207	6,801	1,176	1,417	333
GA	6,221	7,000	2,468	2,845	344	OK	5,085	5,993	1,224	1,452	220
HI	616	622	135	122	2	OR	3,971	4,412	767	1,293	81
ID	4,281	4,871	838	1,536	153	PA	5,076	5,563	1,186	1,273	91
IL	9,348	11,635	1,689	4,022	1,163	RI	74	79	16	18	1
IN	5,924	7,320	1,222	2,360	530	SC	1,967	2,224	673	773	81
IA	12,970	17,177	2,021	5,683	1,264	SD	4,819	5,813	1,621	2,012	399
KS	10,463	10,800	1,959	1,466	645	TN	2,961	3,243	469	458	153
KY	4,440	5,159	661	1,083	147	TX	17,899	20,096	6,043	6,722	1,152
LA	2,281	2,574	793	822	320	UT	1,338	1,463	264	382	37
ME	616	639	114	111	11	VT	557	645	93	118	18
MD	1,764	2,059	453	588	52	VA	2,804	3,337	471	628	68
MA	503	538	72	76	7	WA	6,091	6,784	1,537	2,012	197
MI	4,510	5,067	743	1,057	215	WV	499	579	18	38	8
MN	9,418	11,143	1,692	2,645	704	WI	6,808	7,950	1,639	1,979	298
MS	3,966	4,831	1,439	1,802	401	WY	1,143	1,215	190	223	36
MO	5,774	7,366	1,078	2,492	470						

Source: U.S. Department of Agriculture, Economic Research Service, "Farm Income Summary Totals for 50 States"; <http://www.ers.usda.gov/Data/FarmIncome/50State/50stmenu.htm>; accessed 28 September 2005.

536   Agriculture

Table 816. Farm Income—Farm Marketings, 2003 and 2004, and Principal Commodities, 2004, by State

[In millions of dollars (216,592 represents $216,592,000,000). Livestock includes products; cattle include calves; and greenhouse includes nursery]

State	2003			2004			State rank for total farm marketings and four principal commodities in order of marketing receipts
	Total	Crops	Live-stock	Total	Crops	Live-stock	
U.S. ...	216,592	110,998	105,594	241,241	117,760	123,481	Cattle, dairy products, corn, broilers
AL	3,636	897	2,739	4,103	735	3,369	24-Broilers, cattle, chicken eggs, greenhouse
AK	51	23	27	53	24	29	50-Greenhouse, hay, dairy products, potatoes
AZ	2,645	1,384	1,260	3,066	1,629	1,437	29-Cattle, lettuce, dairy products, cotton
AR	5,586	2,337	3,250	6,604	2,432	4,173	12-Broilers, rice,soybeans, cattle
CA	28,926	21,883	7,043	31,835	23,212	8,623	1-Dairy products, greenhouse, grapes, almonds
CO	4,922	1,278	3,644	5,501	1,345	4,156	16-Cattle, dairy products, corn, greenhouse
CT	486	320	166	527	349	178	44-Greenhouse, dairy products, chicken eggs, aquaculture
DE	760	168	592	934	191	743	39-Broilers, soybeans, corn, greenhouse
FL	6,561	5,321	1,240	6,844	5,360	1,484	10-Greenhouse, oranges, sugar cane, tomatoes
GA	5,376	2,153	3,224	6,107	2,036	4,071	12-Broilers, cotton, cattle, chicken eggs
HI	547	461	86	550	457	93	43-Greenhouse, pineapples, sugar cane, macadamia nuts
ID	3,920	1,738	2,183	4,349	1,819	2,531	21-Dairy products, cattle, potatoes, wheat
IL	8,630	6,832	1,798	9,708	7,769	1,939	6-Corn, soybeans, hogs, cattle
IN	4,999	3,270	1,729	6,043	3,978	2,065	13-Corn, soybeans, hogs, dairy products
IA	12,942	6,855	6,087	14,653	7,369	7,284	3-Corn, hogs, soybeans, cattle
KS	9,140	2,960	6,180	9,503	3,083	6,420	7-Cattle, wheat, corn, soybeans
KY	3,463	1,230	2,233	4,126	1,388	2,739	23-Horses/mules, broilers, cattle, tobacco
LA	2,126	1,428	697	2,226	1,348	878	34-Sugar cane, rice, cattle, soybeans
ME	550	241	309	554	223	331	42-Dairy products, potatoes, chicken eggs, greenhouse
MD	1,467	622	845	1,743	733	1,011	36-Broilers, greenhouse, dairy products, corn
MA	392	304	89	414	320	94	47-Greenhouse, cranberries, dairy products, sweet corn
MI	3,882	2,480	1,402	4,312	2,566	1,746	22-Dairy products, greenhouse, corn, soybeans
MN	8,807	4,727	4,080	9,795	4,861	4,934	5-Corn, hogs, soybeans, dairy products
MS	3,752	1,588	2,164	4,089	1,377	2,712	26-Broilers, cotton, soybeans, aquaculture
MO	5,169	2,572	2,596	5,819	2,756	3,063	15-Soybeans, cattle, corn, hogs
MT	1,908	799	1,109	2,239	961	1,278	33-Cattle, wheat, barley, hay
NE	11,028	4,159	6,868	11,780	4,442	7,338	4-Cattle, corn, soybeans, hogs
NV	389	134	254	454	147	307	45-Cattle, hay, dairy products, onions
NH	156	93	63	169	95	74	48-Greenhouse, dairy products, apples, cattle
NJ	852	664	188	867	680	187	40-Greenhouse, horses/mules, blueberries, dairy products
NM	2,150	552	1,597	2,565	565	2,000	31-Dairy products, cattle, hay, pecans
NY	3,169	1,226	1,943	3,653	1,351	2,302	28-Dairy products, greenhouse, apples, cattle
NC	7,008	2,850	4,158	8,210	2,859	5,351	8-Hogs, broilers, greenhouse, tobacco
ND	3,910	3,041	869	4,091	3,153	938	25-Wheat, cattle, soybeans, corn
OH	4,853	3,043	1,810	5,459	3,387	2,072	17-Soybeans, corn, dairy products, greenhouse
OK	4,527	1,021	3,506	5,055	1,173	3,882	18-Cattle, hogs, broilers, wheat
OR	3,265	2,459	806	3,692	2,648	1,044	27-Greenhouse, cattle, dairy products, hay
PA	4,308	1,449	2,859	4,859	1,545	3,315	20-Dairy products, cattle, greenhouse, mushrooms
RI	61	51	9	64	54	10	49-Greenhouse, sweet corn, dairy products, potatoes
SC	1,655	783	872	1,909	833	1,076	35-Broilers, greenhouse, turkeys, cattle
SD	4,228	2,097	2,130	4,877	2,455	2,422	19-Cattle, corn, soybeans, wheat
TN	2,500	1,440	1,060	2,562	1,263	1,299	32-Cattle, broilers, soybeans, greenhouse
TX	15,268	4,955	10,313	16,498	5,391	11,107	2-Cattle, cotton, broilers, greenhouse
UT	1,132	253	879	1,253	270	983	37-Cattle, dairy products, hogs, hay
VT	486	83	402	582	85	497	41-Dairy products, cattle, greenhouse, hay
VA	2,326	755	1,571	2,684	902	1,782	30-Broilers, cattle, dairy products, greenhouse
WA	5,514	3,987	1,527	5,868	4,132	1,736	14-Apples, dairy products, cattle, wheat
WV	390	74	316	423	74	349	46-Broilers, cattle, chicken eggs, dairy products
WI	5,906	1,812	4,094	6,864	1,782	5,082	9-Dairy products, cattle, corn, greenhouse
WY	870	146	724	1,105	154	951	38-Cattle, hay, sugar beets, hogs

Source: U.S. Department of Agriculture, Economic Research Service, "United States and State Farm Income Data"; <http://www.ers.usda.gov/Data/farmincome/finfidmu.htm>; accessed 3 October 2005.

Table 817. Indexes of Prices Received and Paid by Farmers: 2000 to 2005

[1990–1992 = 100, except as noted]

Item	2000	2003	2004	2005	Item	2000	2003	2004	2005
Prices received, all products	96	107	119	116	Prices paid, total [2]	118	126	132	140
					Production	116	124	131	139
					Feed	102	114	121	117
Crops	96	111	117	112	Livestock & poultry	110	109	128	140
Food grains	85	109	120	111	Seed	124	154	158	168
Feed grains and hay......	86	104	110	95	Fertilizer	110	124	140	162
Cotton	82	85	90	70	Agricultural chemicals	120	121	120	120
Tobacco	107	107	94	91	Fuels	134	140	162	224
Oil-bearing crops	85	107	134	105	Supplies & repairs	124	134	137	144
Fruits and nuts	98	107	124	133	Autos and trucks	119	115	114	114
Commercial vegetables [1]...	121	137	131	134	Farm machinery..........	139	151	162	171
Potatoes & dry beans	93	104	102	114	Building materials........	121	124	134	142
All other crops	110	114	115	117	Farm services	119	123	124	128
					Rent	110	120	120	125
Livestock and products......	97	103	122	120	Interest	113	102	104	109
Meat animals	94	103	116	121	Taxes	123	126	125	126
Dairy products..........	94	96	123	116	Wage rates	140	157	160	165
Poultry and eggs	106	111	132	124	Parity ratio (1910–14 = 100) [3] ..	38	40	43	39

[1] Excludes potatoes and dry beans. [2] Includes production items, interest, taxes, wage rates, and a family living component. The family living component is the Consumer Price Index for all urban consumers from the Bureau of Labor Statistics. See text, Section 14, and Table 706. [3] Ratio of prices received by farmers to prices paid.

Source: U.S. Department of Agriculture, National Agricultural Statistics Service, Agricultural Prices: Annual Summary.

Agriculture   537

Table 818. Civilian Consumer Expenditures for Farm Foods: 1990 to 2004

[In billions of dollars, except percent (449.8 represents $449,800,000,000). Excludes imported and nonfarm foods, such as coffee and seafood, as well as food consumed by the military, or exported]

Item	1990	1995	1996	1997	1998	1999	2000	2001	2002	2003	2004
Consumer expenditures, total...	**449.8**	**529.5**	**546.7**	**566.5**	**585.0**	**625.3**	**661.1**	**687.5**	**709.4**	**744.2**	**788.9**
Farm value, total	106.2	113.8	122.2	121.9	119.6	122.2	123.3	130.0	132.5	140.2	155.5
Marketing bill, total [1]	343.6	415.7	424.5	444.6	465.4	503.1	537.8	557.5	576.9	604.0	633.4
Percent of total consumer expenditures	76.4	78.5	77.6	78.5	79.6	80.5	81.3	81.1	81.3	81.2	80.3
At-home expenditures [2]	276.2	316.9	328.0	339.2	346.8	370.7	390.2	403.9	416.8	437.2	463.5
Farm value	80.2	76.1	81.6	79.0	77.0	78.7	79.6	83.9	85.7	91.4	101.3
Marketing bill [1]	196.0	240.8	246.4	260.2	269.8	292.0	310.6	320.0	331.1	345.8	362.2
Away-from-home expenditures	173.6	212.6	218.7	227.3	238.2	254.6	270.9	283.6	292.6	307.0	325.4
Farm value	26.0	37.7	40.6	42.9	42.6	43.5	43.7	46.1	46.8	48.8	54.2
Marketing bill [1]	147.6	174.9	178.1	184.4	195.6	211.1	227.2	237.5	245.8	258.2	271.2
Marketing bill cost components:											
Labor cost	154.0	196.6	204.6	216.9	229.9	241.5	252.9	263.8	273.1	285.9	303.7
Packaging materials	36.5	48.2	47.7	48.7	50.4	50.9	53.5	55.0	56.8	59.5	63.1
Rail and truck transport	19.8	22.3	22.9	23.6	24.4	25.2	26.4	27.5	28.4	29.7	31.6
Corporate profits before taxes	13.2	19.5	20.7	22.3	25.5	29.2	31.1	32.0	33.0	34.6	35.5
Fuels and electricity.	15.2	18.6	19.6	20.2	20.7	22.0	23.1	24.1	24.9	26.1	27.6
Advertising	17.1	19.8	20.9	22.1	23.4	24.8	26.1	27.5	28.1	29.4	30.8
Depreciation	16.3	18.9	20.1	21.0	21.6	23.0	24.2	24.5	25.3	26.5	27.8
Net interest	13.5	11.6	11.4	12.5	12.9	14.4	16.9	18.6	19.2	20.1	21.1
Net rent	13.9	19.8	21.0	21.8	23.7	25.3	26.7	29.4	30.3	31.7	33.2
Repairs..................	6.2	7.9	8.5	8.8	9.0	9.6	10.1	10.6	10.9	11.4	12.0
Taxes	15.7	19.1	19.4	19.8	20.9	22.2	23.5	24.1	24.9	26.1	27.4
Other	22.2	13.4	7.7	6.9	3.0	15.0	23.3	20.4	22.0	23.0	19.6

[1] The difference between expenditures for domestic farm-originated food products and the farm value or payment farmers received for the equivalent farm products. [2] Food primarily purchased from retail food stores for use at home.

Source: U.S. Department of Agriculture, Economic Research Service, *Food Cost Review, 1950–97*, ERS Agricultural Economic Report No. AER780, June 1999; and "ERS/USDA Briefing Room—Food marketing and price spreads: USDA marketing bill"; <http://www.ers.usda.gov/Briefing/FoodPriceSpreads/bill/>.

Table 819. Agricultural Exports and Imports—Volume by Principal Commodities: 1990 to 2005

[In thousands of metric tons, except fruit juices, wine and malt beverages in thousands of hectoliters (7,703 represents 7,703,000). Includes Puerto Rico, U.S. territories, and shipments under foreign aid programs]

Commodity	1990	1995	2000	2002	2003	2004	2005
EXPORTS							
Fruit juices and wine	7,703	10,688	14,356	15,118	13,714	15,383	13,966
Beef, pork, lamb, and poultry meats [1]...	1,451	3,723	4,935	5,074	5,127	4,033	4,588
Wheat, unmilled	27,384	32,317	27,568	24,159	25,117	31,044	26,857
Wheat products	863	1,142	844	707	420	381	307
Rice, paddy, milled	2,534	3,275	3,241	3,808	4,469	3,518	4,428
Feed grains	61,066	66,795	54,946	53,218	48,428	53,324	50,495
Feed grain products.............	1,430	2,018	2,062	3,153	4,353	4,519	5,575
Feeds and fodders [2]	10,974	13,338	13,065	12,677	11,839	11,393	11,339
Fresh fruits and nuts	2,648	3,323	3,450	3,493	3,490	3,450	3,595
Fruit products................	390	462	471	475	502	529	479
Vegetables, fresh	1,297	1,708	2,029	2,059	1,997	1,967	2,013
Vegetables, frozen and canned	529	892	1,112	1,065	1,010	1,048	1,083
Oilcake and meal	5,079	6,404	6,462	6,672	5,661	4,752	5,615
Oilseeds	15,820	23,596	28,017	29,139	32,083	26,870	27,826
Vegetable oils	1,226	2,532	2,043	2,682	2,251	1,939	1,936
Tobacco, unmanufactured	223	209	180	153	156	164	152
Cotton, excluding linters...........	1,696	2,039	1,485	2,108	2,674	2,885	3,397
IMPORTS							
Fruit juices..................	33,116	21,922	31,154	29,047	35,488	33,651	42,939
Wine	2,510	2,781	4,584	5,655	6,214	6,549	7,262
Malt beverages	10,382	13,251	23,464	27,087	27,618	27,946	29,747
Coffee, including products	1,214	989	1,370	1,238	1,302	1,323	1,307
Rubber and allied gums, crude	840	1,044	1,232	1,213	1,120	1,158	1,169
Beef, pork, lamb, and poultry meats [1]...	1,169	1,050	1,579	1,704	1,665	1,876	1,804
Grains	2,071	4,553	4,622	4,472	3,484	3,701	3,715
Biscuits, pasta, and noodles	300	489	711	834	904	934	1,001
Feeds and fodders [2]	959	1,247	1,224	1,266	1,160	1,067	967
Fruits, nuts, and preparations [3]	5,401	6,530	8,354	8,711	9,052	9,171	9,557
Vegetables, fresh or frozen.........	1,898	2,777	3,763	4,457	4,765	5,004	5,043
Tobacco, unmanufactured	173	190	216	260	288	254	224
Oilseeds and oilnuts	509	713	1,056	825	622	897	922
Vegetable oils and waxes..........	1,204	1,509	1,846	1,931	1,841	2,274	2,364
Oilcake and meal	316	805	1,254	1,008	1,314	1,779	1,541

[1] Includes variety meats. [2] Excluding oil meal. [3] Includes bananas and plantains.

Source: U.S. Department of Agriculture, Economic Research Service, "Foreign Agricultural Trade of the United States (FATUS)"; <http://www.ers.usda.gov/data/fatus/> and "U.S. Trade Internet System"; <http://www.fas.usda.gov/ustrade>.

Table 820. **Agricultural Exports and Imports—Value: 1990 to 2005**

[In billions of dollars, except percent (16.6 represents $16,600,000,000). Includes Puerto Rico, U.S. territories, and shipments under foreign aid programs. Excludes fish, forest products, distilled liquors, manufactured tobacco, and products made from cotton; but includes raw tobacco, raw cotton, rubber, beer and wine, and processed agricultural products]

Year	Trade balance	Exports, domestic products	Percent of all exports	Imports for consumption	Percent of all imports	Year	Trade balance	Exports, domestic products	Percent of all exports	Imports for consumption	Percent of all imports
1990...	16.6	39.5	11	22.9	5	1999...	10.7	48.4	8	37.7	4
1993...	17.7	42.9	10	25.1	4	2000...	12.3	51.2	7	39.0	3
1994...	19.2	46.2	10	27.0	4	2001...	14.3	53.7	8	39.4	3
1995...	26.0	56.3	10	30.3	4	2002...	11.2	53.1	8	41.9	4
1996...	26.8	60.3	10	33.5	4	2003...	12.0	59.4	8	47.4	4
1997...	21.0	57.2	9	36.1	4	2004...	7.4	61.4	8	54.0	4
1998...	14.9	51.8	8	36.9	4	2005...	3.7	63.0	7	59.3	4

Source: U.S. Department of Agriculture, Economic Research Service, *U.S. Agricultural Trade Update*, February 13, 2006; and "Foreign Agricultural Trade of the United States (FATUS)"; <http://www.ers.usda.gov/data/fatus/> and U.S. Department of Agriculture, Foreign Agricultural Service, "U.S. Trade Internet System"; <http://www.fas.usda.gov/ustrade>.

Table 821. **Agricultural Imports—Value by Selected Commodity: 1990 to 2005**

[22,918 represents $22,918,000,000. See headnote, Table 820]

Commodity	Value (mil. dol.)							Percent distribution		
	1990	2000	2001	2002	2003	2004	2005	1990	2000	2005
Total [1]............	22,918	38,974	39,366	41,909	47,376	53,977	59,282	100.0	100.0	100.0
Cattle, live...........	978	1,152	1,461	1,446	867	543	1,039	4.3	3.0	1.8
Beef and veal	1,872	2,399	2,712	2,741	2,623	3,626	3,651	8.2	6.2	6.2
Pork................	938	997	1,048	1,001	1,190	1,367	1,281	4.1	2.6	2.2
Dairy products	891	1,671	1,789	1,783	1,978	2,424	2,686	3.9	4.3	4.5
Grains and feeds	1,188	3,076	3,320	3,666	3,910	4,292	4,526	5.2	7.9	7.6
Fruits and preparations ...	2,167	3,846	3,977	4,351	4,715	5,068	5,830	9.5	9.9	9.8
Vegetables and preparations...........	2,317	4,740	5,252	5,614	6,394	7,165	7,612	10.1	12.2	12.8
Sugar and related products	1,213	1,555	1,600	1,854	2,129	2,107	2,492	5.3	4.0	4.2
Wine	917	2,207	2,250	2,671	3,268	3,416	3,763	4.0	5.7	6.3
Malt beverages	923	2,179	2,348	2,581	2,681	2,767	3,096	4.0	5.6	5.2
Oilseeds and products....	952	1,847	1,630	1,789	2,072	3,026	3,057	4.2	4.7	5.2
Coffee and products	1,915	2,700	1,677	1,693	1,958	2,263	2,976	8.4	6.9	5.0
Cocoa and products	1,072	1,404	1,536	1,761	2,439	2,484	2,751	4.7	3.6	4.6
Rubber, crude natural	707	842	613	751	1,047	1,466	1,552	3.1	2.2	2.6

[1] Includes other commodities not shown separately.

Source: U.S. Department of Agriculture, Economic Research Service, "Foreign Agricultural Trade of the United States (FATUS)"; <http://www.ers.usda.gov/data/fatus/> and U.S. Department of Agriculture, Foreign Agricultural Service, "U.S. Trade Internet System"; <http://www.fas.usda.gov/ustrade>.

Table 822. **Agricultural Imports—Value by Selected Countries of Origin: 1990 to 2005**

[22,918 represents $22,918,000,000. See headnote, Table 820]

Commodity	Value (mil. dol.)							Percent distribution		
	1990	2000	2001	2002	2003	2004	2005	1990	2000	2005
Total [1]..............	22,918	38,974	39,366	41,909	47,376	53,977	59,282	100.0	100.0	100.0
European Union [2].......	4,991	8,276	8,178	8,911	10,956	12,331	13,334	21.8	21.2	22.5
Canada..............	3,171	8,661	9,863	10,350	10,286	11,453	12,267	13.8	22.2	20.7
Mexico..............	3,614	5,077	5,265	5,518	6,301	7,262	8,333	15.8	13.0	14.1
Australia.............	1,174	1,592	1,757	1,894	2,120	2,486	2,421	5.1	4.1	4.1
Brazil	1,563	1,144	999	1,154	1,550	1,662	1,966	6.8	2.9	3.3
China [3]..............	273	812	816	1,002	1,288	1,615	1,873	1.2	2.1	3.2
New Zealand..........	855	1,132	1,261	1,199	1,317	1,597	1,711	3.7	2.9	2.9
Indonesia	638	998	833	931	1,227	1,490	1,702	2.8	2.6	2.9
Chile	481	1,026	1,023	1,154	1,216	1,342	1,521	2.1	2.6	2.6
Colombia............	790	1,123	926	929	1,031	1,162	1,436	3.4	2.9	2.4
Thailand	470	779	695	733	926	1,083	1,089	2.0	2.0	1.8
India...............	285	826	687	671	687	858	922	1.2	2.1	1.6
Guatemala	497	710	609	685	764	784	918	2.2	1.8	1.5
Costa Rica	400	812	804	803	869	899	916	1.7	2.1	1.5
Argentina	389	672	610	602	572	616	816	1.7	1.7	1.4

[1] Includes other countries not shown separately.   [2] For consistency, data for all years are shown on the basis of 25 countries in the European Union; see footnote 1, Table 1346.   [3] See footnote 2, Table 1308.

Source: U.S. Department of Agriculture, Foreign Agricultural Service, "U.S. Trade Internet System"; <http://www.fas.usda.gov/ustrade>; (accessed 10 April, 2006).

Agriculture **539**

Table 823. Selected Farm Products—United States and World Production and Exports: 2000 to 2005

[In metric tons, except as indicated (61 represents 61,000,000). Metric ton = 1.102 short tons or .984 long tons]

Commodity	Unit	Amount						United States as percent of world		
		United States			World					
		2000	2004	2005	2000	2004	2005	2000	2004	2005
PRODUCTION [1]										
Wheat	Million	61	59	57	581	629	620	10.4	9.3	9.2
Corn for grain	Million	252	300	282	590	712	686	42.7	42.1	41.1
Soybeans	Million	75	85	84	176	216	222	42.6	39.4	37.9
Rice, milled	Million	5.9	7.5	7.1	398	403	412	1.5	1.9	1.7
Cotton [2]	Million bales [3] . . .	17.0	18.3	23.3	87.7	95.3	120.5	19.3	19.2	19.3
EXPORTS [4]										
Wheat [5]	Million	28.0	28.5	27.5	104.0	113.0	110.8	26.9	25.2	24.8
Corn	Million	48.3	45.2	52.0	76.4	76.2	76.2	63.3	59.3	68.2
Soybeans	Million	27.1	30.0	24.5	53.9	64.8	66.4	50.3	46.3	36.9
Rice, milled basis	Million	2.8	3.1	3.8	22.8	27.2	28.6	12.5	11.4	13.4
Cotton [2]	Million bales [3] . . .	6.8	13.8	14.4	27.1	33.3	34.8	24.9	41.4	41.4

[1] Production years vary by commodity. In most cases, includes harvests from July 1 of the year shown through June 30 of the following year. [2] For production and trade years ending in year shown. [3] Bales of 480 lb. net weight. [4] Trade years may vary by commodity. Wheat, corn, and soybean data are for trade year beginning in year shown. Rice data are for calendar year. [5] Includes wheat flour on a grain equivalent.

Source: U.S. Department of Agriculture, Foreign Agricultural Service, *Foreign Agricultural Commodity Circular Series*, periodic.

Table 824. Percent of U.S. Agricultural Commodity Output Exported: 1990 to 2004

[All export shares are estimated from export and production weights]

Commodity group	1990–94, average	1995–99, average	2000–04, average	2000	2001	2002	2003	2004
Total agriculture	18.2	18.2	17.2	17.6	17.6	16.7	17.9	16.3
Livestock [1]	4.1	4.5	4.3	4.5	4.6	4.3	4.5	3.8
Red meat.	4.1	7.1	8.0	8.1	8.3	8.5	9.0	6.1
Poultry meat.	7.4	15.5	14.6	15.5	16.4	13.9	14.0	13.2
Dairy products [2]	3.4	1.4	1.0	1.0	1.0	1.0	1.2	1.0
Crops	24.4	24.2	22.9	23.3	23.3	22.3	23.9	21.8
Wheat and rice	51.3	49.3	47.5	44.7	47.1	45.7	51.7	48.5
Coarse grains [3]	21.2	21.5	19.3	21.0	20.0	18.0	19.5	17.8
Oilseeds/meal/oil	25.0	26.8	27.2	27.2	27.6	28.0	28.1	25.3
Fruits and nuts [4]	13.4	14.2	15.0	13.7	15.2	15.4	15.2	15.7
Vegetables [5]	5.7	6.4	6.5	6.6	6.8	6.7	6.3	6.1
Cotton and tobacco	40.7	38.1	59.1	43.7	57.1	60.3	66.7	67.6

[1] Excludes hides, animal fats, and live animals. [2] Includes butter, cheese, and nonfat dried milk. [3] Includes corn, barley, sorghum, oats, and rye. [4] Includes fruit juices and wine, whose volumes are converted to weight units using 8 pounds per gallon. [5] Total vegetable production is estimated from U.S. per capita use of major fresh and processing vegetables.

Source: U.S. Department of Agriculture, Economic Research Service, USDA's commodity yearbooks, "Foreign Agricultural Trade of the U.S."; <http://www.ers.usda.gov/data/fatus/>, and "Production, Supply, and Distribution database"; <http://www.fas.usda.gov/psd/>.

Table 825. Top 10 U.S. Export Markets for Selected Commodities: 2005

[In thousands of metric tons (45,134 represents 45,134,000)]

Corn		Wheat [1]		Soybeans		Cotton [2]	
Country	Amount	Country	Amount	Country	Amount	Country	Amount
World, total	45,134	World, total. . .	26,857	World, total. . .	25,603	World, total. . .	3,397
Japan	14,841	Nigeria	3,168	China [3]	9,395	China [3]	1,234
Mexico	5,799	Japan	2,977	Mexico	3,399	Turkey	478
Taiwan [3]	4,810	Mexico	2,692	Japan	2,837	Mexico	329
Egypt	3,650	Philippines	1,643	Taiwan [3]	1,684	Indonesia	231
Colombia.	2,271	Egypt	1,359	Indonesia	1,163	Thailand	160
Korea, South	2,175	Iraq	1,305	Germany	865	Taiwan [3]	156
Canada	2,109	Korea, South	1,157	Korea, South	760	Korea, South	127
Syria	1,083	Taiwan [3]	970	Netherlands	521	Pakistan	121
Algeria	997	Venezuela.	943	Turkey	477	Hong Kong	59
Dominican Republic. .	969	Colombia	802	Egypt	415	Japan	59
Rest of world	6,431	Rest of world. . . .	9,841	Rest of world. . . .	4,087	Rest of world. . . .	442

[1] Unmilled. [2] Excluding linters. [3] See footnote 2, Table 1308.

Source: U.S. Department of Agriculture, Foreign Agricultural Service, "FAS Online, U.S. Trade Exports—FATUS Commodity Aggregations"; <http://www.fas.usda.gov/ustrade/USTExFatus.asp>; (accessed 18 May 2006).

Table 826. Agricultural Exports—Value by Principal Commodities: 1990 to 2005

[(39,492 represents $39,492,000,000) Includes Puerto Rico, U.S. territories, and shipments under foreign aid programs. Excludes fish, forest products, distilled liquors, manufactured tobacco, and products made from cotton; but includes raw tobacco, raw cotton, rubber, beer and wine, and processed agricultural products]

Commodity	Value (mil. dol.)							Percent distribution		
	1990	2000	2001	2002	2003	2004	2005	1990	2000	2005
Total agricultural exports	39,492	51,246	53,659	53,115	59,364	61,383	62,958	100.0	100.0	100.0
Animals and animal products [1]	6,648	11,600	12,431	11,087	12,161	10,369	12,183	16.8	22.6	19.4
Meat and meat products	2,558	5,276	5,284	5,042	5,741	3,240	4,280	6.5	10.3	6.8
Beef and veal	1,580	2,986	2,632	2,585	3,145	550	919	4.0	5.8	1.5
Poultry and poultry products	910	2,235	2,636	2,064	2,287	2,577	3,117	2.3	4.4	5.0
Dairy products	353	1,018	1,130	993	1,048	1,505	1,681	0.9	2.0	2.7
Fats, oils, and greases.	424	383	334	461	538	575	463	1.1	0.7	0.7
Hides and skins, including furskins. . .	1,751	1,562	1,963	1,745	1,782	1,745	1,775	4.4	3.0	2.8
Bovine hides, whole.	1,337	1,193	1,471	1,042	1,062	1,075	1,119	3.4	2.3	1.8
Grains and feeds [1]	14,409	13,687	13,923	14,459	15,129	17,775	16,458	36.5	26.7	26.1
Wheat and products	4,035	3,578	3,560	3,845	4,099	5,273	4,486	10.2	7.0	7.1
Rice	801	855	692	769	1,024	1,161	1,288	2.0	1.7	2.0
Feed grains and products.	7,150	5,372	5,503	5,875	5,815	6,920	5,886	18.1	10.5	9.3
Corn	6,026	4,469	4,502	4,845	4,724	5,875	4,755	15.3	8.7	7.6
Fruits and preparations	2,009	2,742	2,768	2,775	2,968	3,156	3,452	5.1	5.4	5.5
Fresh fruits	1,486	2,080	2,125	2,134	2,273	2,394	2,692	3.8	4.1	4.3
Nuts and preparations.	976	1,319	1,292	1,525	1,762	2,220	2,903	2.5	2.6	4.6
Vegetables and preparations	2,225	4,457	4,483	4,554	4,813	5,307	5,775	5.6	8.7	9.2
Fresh vegetables	696	1,207	1,180	1,232	1,293	1,353	1,507	1.8	2.4	2.4
Oilseeds and products [1]	5,728	8,586	9,219	9,632	11,655	10,443	10,256	14.5	16.8	16.3
Soybeans	3,548	5,258	5,403	5,677	7,960	6,668	6,306	9.0	10.3	10.0
Soybean meal	979	1,169	1,386	1,216	1,183	1,064	1,131	2.5	2.3	1.8
Vegetable oils and waxes.	832	1,259	1,250	1,634	1,691	1,677	1,654	2.1	2.5	2.6
Tobacco, unmanufactured	1,441	1,204	1,269	1,050	1,038	1,044	983	3.6	2.3	1.6
Cotton, excluding linters	2,783	1,873	2,162	2,015	3,361	4,226	3,920	7.0	3.7	6.2
Other	3,273	5,777	6,112	6,017	6,477	6,843	7,027	8.3	11.3	11.2

[1] Includes commodities not shown separately.

Source: U.S. Department of Agriculture, Economic Research Service, U.S. Agricultural Trade Update, February 13, 2006; and "Foreign Agricultural Trade of the United States (FATUS)"; <http://www.ers.usda.gov/data/fatus/> and U.S. Department of Agriculture, Foreign Agricultural Service, "U.S. Trade Internet System"; <http://www.fas.usda.gov/ustrade>.

Table 827. Agricultural Exports—Value by Selected Countries of Destination: 1990 to 2005

[(39,492 represents $39,492,000,000). See headnote, Table 826]

Country	Value (mil. dol.)							Percent distribution		
	1990	2000	2001	2002	2003	2004	2005	1990	2000	2005
Total agricultural exports [1] . . .	39,492	51,246	53,659	53,115	59,364	61,383	62,958	100.0	100.0	100.0
Canada	4,217	7,640	8,121	8,660	9,313	9,741	10,570	10.7	14.9	16.8
Mexico	2,561	6,410	7,404	7,226	7,879	8,494	9,362	6.5	12.5	14.9
Caribbean.	1,016	1,408	1,399	1,518	1,589	1,850	1,892	2.6	2.7	3.0
Central America	482	1,120	1,233	1,250	1,337	1,428	1,572	1.2	2.2	2.5
South America [2]	1,063	1,701	1,703	1,788	1,909	1,951	1,933	2.7	3.3	3.1
Brazil	177	263	221	329	383	278	226	0.4	0.5	0.4
Colombia.	119	415	452	520	512	593	677	0.3	0.8	1.1
Asia, excluding Middle East [2]	15,862	19,872	20,312	19,724	23,681	22,996	22,477	40.2	38.8	35.7
Japan	8,146	9,290	8,883	8,382	8,903	8,139	7,874	20.6	18.1	12.5
Korea, South	2,650	2,546	2,588	2,672	2,884	2,488	2,226	6.7	5.0	3.5
Taiwan [3]	1,663	1,996	2,009	1,966	2,025	2,064	2,300	4.2	3.9	3.7
China [3] [4]	818	1,716	1,939	2,067	5,016	5,541	5,225	2.1	3.3	8.3
Hong Kong	704	1,262	1,227	1,091	1,113	912	868	1.8	2.5	1.4
India.	108	210	353	274	317	256	293	0.3	0.4	0.5
Indonesia	274	668	907	810	996	925	957	0.7	1.3	1.5
Philippines	381	901	794	776	625	695	797	1.0	1.8	1.3
Thailand	275	493	570	611	684	685	661	0.7	1.0	1.0
Australia	226	317	290	338	412	410	460	0.6	0.6	0.7
Europe/Eurasia [2]	7,751	7,669	8,425	7,692	7,812	8,316	8,533	19.6	15.0	13.6
European Union [5]	7,244	6,483	6,626	6,335	6,661	6,786	6,837	18.3	12.7	10.9
Former Soviet Union [6]	(X)	670	1,060	695	739	1,112	1,206	(X)	1.3	1.9
Russia.	(X)	580	917	551	578	802	955	(X)	1.1	1.5
Middle East [2]	1,816	2,322	2,223	2,259	2,547	2,830	2,861	4.6	4.5	4.5
Saudi Arabia	564	477	429	342	331	363	353	1.4	0.9	0.6
Turkey	226	658	571	675	921	943	1,079	0.6	1.3	1.7
Africa [2]	1,935	2,308	2,105	2,297	2,489	2,953	2,785	4.9	4.5	4.4
Egypt	692	1,050	1,022	862	966	935	837	1.8	2.0	1.3
South Africa.	81	134	99	148	148	168	147	0.2	0.3	0.2
Oceania	343	489	471	511	621	601	751	0.9	1.0	1.2

X Not applicable. [1] Totals include transshipments through Canada, but transshipments are not distributed by country after 1998. [2] Includes areas not shown separately. [3] See footnote 2, Table 1308. [4] China includes Macao. However Hong Kong remains separate economically until 2050 and is not included. [5] For consistency, data for all years are shown on the basis of 25 countries in the European Union; see footnote 1, Table 1346. [6] Includes the 12 member states of the Former Soviet Union.

Source: U.S. Department of Agriculture, Economic Research Service, U.S. Agricultural Trade Update, February 13, 2006; and "Foreign Agricultural Trade of the United States (FATUS)"; <http://www.ers.usda.gov/data/fatus/> and U.S. Department of Agriculture, Foreign Agricultural Service, "U.S. Trade Internet System"; <http://www.fas.usda.gov/ustrade>.

Agriculture 541

Table 828. Cropland Used for Crops and Acreages of Crops Harvested: 1990 to 2005

[In millions of acres, except as indicated (341 represents 341,000,000)]

Item	1990	1995	1998	1999	2000	2001	2002	2003	2004	2005
Cropland used for crops.....	341	332	345	344	345	340	340	342	336	337
Index (1977 = 100)........	90	88	91	91	91	90	90	90	89	89
Cropland harvested [1].........	310	302	315	316	314	311	307	316	312	314
Crop failure...............	6	8	10	8	11	10	17	10	9	7
Cultivated summer fallow......	25	22	20	20	20	19	16	16	16	16
Cropland idled by all federal programs................	62	55	30	30	31	32	34	34	34	36
Acres of crops harvested [2]...	322	314	326	327	325	321	316	324	321	321

[1] Land supporting one or more harvested crops.   [2] Area in principal crops harvested as reported by Crop Reporting Board plus acreages in fruits, vegetables for sale, tree nuts, and other minor crops.

Source: U.S. Department of Agriculture, Economic Research Service, *Major Uses of Land in the United States, 2002*, 2006; Also in *Agricultural Statistics*, annual. Beginning 1995 *Agricultural Resources and Environmental Indicators*, periodic, and *AREI Updates: Cropland Use*. See also ERS Briefing Room at <http://www.ers.usda.gov/Briefing/LandUse/majorlandusechapter.htm#trends>.

Table 829. Percent of Corn, Soybean, and Cotton Acreage Planted With Genetically Modified Seed: 2000 and 2005

[In percent. Based on the June Agricultural Survey. Randomly selected farmers across the United States were asked if they planted corn, soybeans, or upland cotton seed that, through biotechnology, is resistant to herbicides, insects, or both. The states published individually below represent 82 percent of all corn planted acres, 89 percent of all soybean planted acres, and 81 percent of all upland cotton planted acres. Conventionally bred herbicide resistant varieties were excluded. Insect resistant varieties include only those containing bacillus thuringiensis (Bt). The acreage estimates are subject to sampling variability because all operations planting biotech varieties are not included in the sample]

State	Corn 2000	Corn 2005	State	Soybeans 2000	Soybeans 2005	State	Cotton 2000	Cotton 2005
US, total..............	25	52	US, total......	54	87	US, total......	61	79
IL....................	17	36	AR...........	43	92	AR...........	70	96
IN	11	26	IL............	44	81	CA...........	24	53
IA	30	60	IN............	63	89	GA...........	82	95
KS...................	33	63	IA............	59	91	LA...........	80	95
MI...................	12	40	KS...........	66	90	MS...........	78	96
MN	37	66	MI	50	76	NC...........	76	95
MO...................	28	55	MN...........	46	83	TX...........	46	63
NE...................	34	69	MS...........	48	96	Other states [1]....	74	91
OH...................	9	18	MO...........	62	89			
SD...................	48	83	NE	72	91			
WI...................	18	46	ND...........	22	89			
Other states [1]	17	52	OH...........	48	77			
			SD	68	95			
			WI	51	84			
			Other states [1]....	54	84			

[1] Includes all other states in the specified commodity estimating program.

Source: U.S. Department of Agriculture, National Agricultural Statistics Service, *Acreage*, annual.

Table 830. Quantity of Pesticides Applied to Selected Crops: 1990 to 2004

[In million pounds of active ingredients, except as indicated (497.7 represents 497,700,000)]

Type of pesticide and commodity	1990	1995	1999	2000	2001	2002	2003	2004
Total......................	497.7	543.3	553.7	539.4	511.1	486.0	499.0	494.5
Herbicides....................	344.6	324.9	316.8	308.6	307.6	285.5	300.5	311.0
Insecticides...................	57.4	69.9	75.4	77.4	62.0	55.6	40.8	40.7
Fungicides....................	27.8	47.5	42.3	36.6	33.3	33.6	35.7	29.8
Other	67.9	101.0	119.1	116.8	108.3	111.3	122.1	112.9
Corn	240.7	201.3	186.0	176.1	187.3	153.5	169.6	174.6
Cotton.......................	50.9	83.7	90.6	94.5	72.8	64.5	55.9	56.7
Wheat.......................	17.8	21.5	21.4	19.2	18.3	13.9	14.8	22.3
Soybeans	74.4	68.7	77.3	79.1	72.2	90.7	90.6	87.8
Potatoes	43.8	53.1	64.6	61.8	60.5	55.3	66.3	62.1
Other vegetables...............	39.8	78.0	70.5	70.1	66.5	75.4	75.3	65.1
Citrus fruit	11.0	14.0	13.3	13.0	12.8	12.4	7.5	7.2
Apples	8.3	9.0	7.9	7.6	7.6	7.2	8.6	8.5
Other deciduous fruit	10.9	14.1	22.2	18.1	13.1	13.1	10.4	10.3
POUNDS OF ACTIVE INGREDIENT PER PLANTED ACRE								
Total......................	2.2	2.4	2.3	2.2	2.2	2.1	2.1	2.1
Herbicides....................	1.5	1.4	1.3	1.3	1.3	1.2	1.3	1.3
Insecticides...................	0.3	0.3	0.3	0.3	0.3	0.2	0.2	0.2
Fungicides....................	0.1	0.2	0.2	0.2	0.1	0.1	0.2	0.1
Other	0.3	0.4	0.5	0.5	0.5	0.5	0.5	0.5

Source: U.S. Department of Agriculture, Economic Research Service, *Production Practices for Major Crops in U.S. Agriculture, 1990-97*, Statistical Bulletin No. 969, August 2000 and unpublished data.

Table 831. **Principal Crops—Production, Supply, and Disappearance: 1990 to 2005**

[**67.0 represents 67,000,000.** Marketing year beginning January 1 for potatoes, May 1 for hay, June 1 for wheat, August 1 for cotton, September 1 for soybeans and corn. Acreage, production, and yield of all crops periodically revised on basis of census data]

Item	Unit	1990	2000	2001	2002	2003	2004	2005
CORN FOR GRAIN								
Acreage harvested	Million	67.0	72.4	68.8	69.3	70.9	73.6	75.1
Yield per acre	Bushel.	119	137	138	129	142	160	148
Production	Mil. bu.	7,934	9,915	9,503	8,967	10,089	11,807	11,112
Farm price [1]	Dol./bu.	2.28	1.85	1.97	2.32	2.42	2.06	1.90
Farm value	Mil. dol.	18,192	18,499	18,888	20,882	24,477	24,381	21,041
Total supply [2]	Mil. bu.	9,282	11,639	11,412	10,578	11,190	12,776	13,236
Total disappearance [3] . . .	Mil. bu.	7,761	9,740	9,815	9,491	10,232	10,662	10,885
Ethanol	Mil. bu.	(NA)	(NA)	(NA)	996	1,168	1,323	1,600
Exports	Mil. bu.	1,725	1,941	1,905	1,588	1,900	1,814	1,900
Ending stocks	Mil. bu.	1,521	1,899	1,596	1,087	958	2,114	2,351
SOYBEANS								
Acreage harvested	Million	56.5	72.4	73.0	72.5	72.5	74.0	71.4
Yield per acre	Bushel.	34.1	38.1	39.6	38.0	33.9	42.2	43.3
Production	Mil. bu.	1,926	2,758	2,891	2,756	2,454	3,124	3,086
Farm price [1]	Dol./bu.	5.74	4.54	4.38	5.53	7.34	5.74	5.50
Farm value	Mil. dol.	11,042	12,467	12,606	15,253	18,014	17,895	16,928
Total supply [2]	Mil. bu.	2,169	3,052	3,141	2,969	2,638	3,242	3,346
Total disappearance [3] . . .	Mil. bu.	1,840	2,804	2,933	2,791	2,525	2,986	2,781
Exports	Mil. bu.	557	996	1,064	1,044	887	1,103	900
Ending stocks	Mil. bu.	329	248	208	178	112	256	565
HAY								
Acreage harvested	Million	61.0	59.9	63.5	63.9	63.4	62.0	61.6
Yield per acre	Sh. tons.	2.40	2.54	2.46	2.34	2.49	2.55	2.44
Production	Mil. sh. tons . . .	146	152	156	149	158	158	151
Farm price [4, 5]	Dol./ton	80.60	84.60	96.50	92.40	85.50	92.00	98.00
Farm value	Mil. dol.	10,462	11,417	12,597	12,338	12,007	12,212	12,491
WHEAT								
Acreage harvested	Million	69.1	53.1	48.5	45.8	53.1	50.0	50.1
Yield per acre	Bushel.	39.5	42.0	40.2	35.0	44.2	43.2	42.0
Production	Mil. bu.	2,730	2,228	1,947	1,606	2,345	2,158	2,105
Farm price [1]	Dol./bu.	2.61	2.62	2.78	3.56	3.40	3.40	3.40
Farm value	Mil. dol.	7,184	5,782	5,440	5,637	7,929	7,283	7,140
Total supply [2]	Mil. bu.	3,303	3,268	2,931	2,460	2,899	2,775	2,730
Total disappearance [3] . . .	Mil. bu.	2,435	2,392	2,154	1,969	2,353	2,235	2,188
Exports	Mil. bu.	1,069	1,062	962	850	1,158	1,063	1,000
Ending stocks	Mil. bu.	868	876	777	491	546	540	542
COTTON								
Acreage harvested	Million	11.7	13.1	13.8	12.4	12.0	13.1	13.7
Yield per acre	Pounds	634	632	705	665	730	855	831
Production [6]	Mil. bales [7]	15.5	17.2	20.3	17.2	18.3	23.3	23.7
Farm price [1]	Cents/lb.	68.2	51.6	32.0	45.7	63.0	43.5	49.0
Farm value	Mil. dol.	5,076	4,260	3,122	3,777	5,517	4,854	5,574
Total supply [2]	Mil. bales [7]	18.5	21.1	26.3	24.7	23.7	26.8	29.3
Total disappearance [3] . . .	Mil. bales [7]	16.5	15.6	18.7	19.2	20.0	21.1	22.7
Exports	Mil. bales [7]	7.8	6.7	11.0	11.9	13.8	14.4	16.8
Ending stocks [8]	Mil. bales [7]	2.3	6.0	7.4	5.4	3.5	5.5	6.6
POTATOES								
Acreage harvested	Million	1.4	1.3	1.2	1.3	1.2	1.2	1.1
Yield per acre	Cwt.	293	381	358	362	367	391	388
Production	Mil. cwt.	402	514	458	458	458	456	421
Farm price [1]	Dol./cwt.	6.08	5.08	6.99	6.67	5.89	5.67	6.90
Farm value	Mil. dol.	2,431	2,591	3,058	3,045	2,686	2,575	2,903

NA Not available. [1] Marketing year average price. U.S. prices are computed by weighting U.S. monthly prices by estimated monthly marketings and do not include an allowance for outstanding loans and government purchases and payments. [2] Comprises production, imports, and beginning stocks. [3] Includes feed, residual, and other domestic uses not shown separately. [4] Prices are for hay sold baled. [5] Season average prices received by farmers. U.S. prices are computed by weighting state prices by estimated sales. [6] State production figures, which conform with annual ginning enumeration with allowance for cross-state ginnings, rounded to thousands and added for U.S. totals. [7] Bales of 480 pounds, net weight. [8] Stock estimates based on Census Bureau data which results in an unaccounted difference between supply and use estimates and changes in ending stocks.

Source: Production—U.S. Department of Agriculture, National Agricultural Statistics Service. In *Crop Production*, annual; and *Crop Values*, annual. Supply and disappearance—U.S. Department of Agriculture, Economic Research Service, *Feed Situation*, quarterly; *Fats and Oils Situation*, quarterly; *Wheat Situation*, quarterly; *Cotton and Wool Outlook Statistics*, periodic; and *Agricultural Supply and Demand Estimates*, periodic. Data are also in *Agricultural Statistics*, annual; and "Agricultural Outlook: Statistical Indicators"; <http://www.ers.usda.gov/publications/agoutlook/aotables/>.

Agriculture   543

Table 832. Corn—Acreage, Production, and Value by Leading States: 2003 to 2005

[70,944 represents 70,944,000. One bushel of corn = 56 pounds]

State	Acreage harvested (1,000 acres) 2003	2004	2005	Yield per acre (bu.) 2003	2004	2005	Production (mil. bu.) 2003	2004	2005	Price ($/bu.) 2003	2004	2005	Farm value (mil. dol.) 2003	2004	2005
U.S.[1]	70,944	73,631	75,107	142	160	148	10,089	11,807	11,112	2.42	2.06	1.90	24,477	24,381	21,041
IA	11,900	12,400	12,500	157	181	173	1,868	2,244	2,163	2.37	1.99	1.85	4,428	4,466	4,001
IL	11,050	11,600	11,950	164	180	143	1,812	2,088	1,709	2.42	2.14	1.95	4,386	4,468	3,332
NE	7,700	7,950	8,250	146	166	154	1,124	1,320	1,271	2.39	2.02	1.85	2,687	2,666	2,350
MN	6,650	7,050	6,850	146	159	174	971	1,121	1,192	2.35	1.94	1.75	2,282	2,175	2,086
IN	5,390	5,530	5,770	146	168	154	787	929	889	2.53	1.99	1.80	1,991	1,849	1,599
SD	3,850	4,150	3,950	111	130	119	427	540	470	2.28	1.82	1.70	974	982	799
KS	2,500	2,880	3,450	120	150	135	300	432	466	2.51	2.12	2.10	753	916	978
OH	3,070	3,110	3,250	156	158	143	479	491	465	2.45	2.04	1.80	1,173	1,002	837
WI	2,850	2,600	2,900	129	136	148	368	354	429	2.35	2.15	1.85	864	760	794
MO	2,800	2,880	2,970	108	162	111	302	467	330	2.46	2.03	1.90	744	947	626
MI	2,030	1,920	2,020	128	134	143	260	257	289	2.37	1.97	1.70	616	507	491
TX	1,650	1,680	1,850	118	139	114	195	234	211	2.59	2.60	2.50	504	607	527
KY	1,080	1,140	1,180	137	152	132	148	173	156	2.53	2.24	2.05	374	388	319
ND	1,170	1,150	1,200	112	105	129	131	121	155	2.37	1.88	1.80	311	227	279
CO	890	1,040	950	135	135	148	120	140	141	2.49	2.23	2.25	299	313	316
PA	890	980	960	115	140	122	102	137	117	2.96	2.25	2.20	303	309	258
NC	680	740	700	106	117	120	72	87	84	2.68	2.44	2.25	193	211	189
TN	620	615	595	131	140	130	81	86	77	2.37	2.17	1.95	192	187	151
NY	440	500	460	121	122	124	53	61	57	2.82	2.37	2.05	150	145	117
MD	410	425	400	123	153	135	50	65	54	2.83	2.17	2.00	143	141	108
MS	530	440	365	135	136	129	72	60	47	2.28	2.43	2.15	163	145	101

[1] Includes other states, not shown separately.

Source: U.S. Department of Agriculture, National Agricultural Statistics Service, *Crop Production*, annual; and *Crop Values*, annual.

Table 833. Soybeans—Acreage, Production, and Value by Leading States: 2003 to 2005

[72,476 represents 72,476,000. One bushel of soybeans = 60 pounds]

State	Acreage harvested (1,000 acres) 2003	2004	2005	Yield per acre (bu.) 2003	2004	2005	Production (mil. bu.) 2003	2004	2005	Price ($/bu.) 2003	2004	2005	Farm value (mil. dol.) 2003	2004	2005
U.S.[1]	72,476	73,958	71,361	34	42	43	2,454	3,124	3,086	7.34	5.74	5.50	18,014	17,895	16,928
IA	10,550	10,150	10,050	33	49	53	343	497	533	7.70	5.76	5.45	2,640	2,865	2,903
IL	10,260	9,900	9,450	37	50	47	380	495	444	7.51	5.84	5.50	2,851	2,891	2,443
MN	7,450	7,050	6,800	32	33	45	238	233	306	7.26	5.90	5.45	1,731	1,373	1,668
IN	5,370	5,520	5,380	38	52	49	204	284	264	7.67	5.66	5.50	1,565	1,609	1,450
NE	4,500	4,750	4,660	41	46	51	182	219	235	7.02	5.54	5.50	1,279	1,210	1,294
OH	4,280	4,420	4,480	39	47	45	165	208	202	7.20	5.74	5.55	1,186	1,192	1,119
MO	4,950	4,960	4,960	30	45	37	146	223	184	7.52	5.62	5.45	1,098	1,254	1,000
SD	4,200	4,120	3,850	28	34	36	116	140	139	6.96	5.58	5.30	804	782	735
ND	3,050	3,570	2,900	29	23	37	88	82	107	6.62	5.75	5.30	586	472	569
KS	2,480	2,710	2,850	23	41	37	57	111	105	7.68	5.39	5.30	438	599	559
AR	2,890	3,150	3,000	39	39	34	111	123	102	7.11	5.88	5.80	791	722	592
MI	1,990	1,980	1,990	28	38	39	55	75	78	7.30	5.72	5.55	399	430	431
WI	1,670	1,550	1,580	28	35	44	47	53	70	7.11	5.70	5.50	332	305	382
MS	1,430	1,640	1,590	39	38	37	56	62	59	6.61	6.20	5.80	369	381	341

[1] Includes other states, not shown separately.

Source: U.S. Department of Agriculture, National Agricultural Statistics Service, *Crop Production*, annual; and *Crop Values*, annual.

Table 834. Wheat—Acreage, Production, and Value by Leading States: 2003 to 2005

[53,063 represents 53,063,000. One bushel of wheat = 60 pounds]

State	Acreage harvested (1,000 acres) 2003	2004	2005	Yield per acre (bu.) 2003	2004	2005	Production (mil. bu.) 2003	2004	2005	Price ($/bu.) 2003	2004	2005	Farm value (mil. dol.) 2003	2004	2005
U.S.[1]	53,063	49,999	50,119	44.2	43.2	42.0	2,345	2,158	2,105	3.40	3.40	3.40	7,929	7,283	7,140
KS	10,000	8,500	9,500	48.0	37.0	40.0	480	315	380	3.15	3.25	3.30	1,512	1,022	1,254
ND	8,500	7,775	8,835	37.3	39.4	34.4	317	307	304	3.63	3.40	3.55	1,150	1,043	1,075
MT	5,200	5,025	5,235	27.4	34.5	36.8	142	173	192	3.73	3.61	3.60	527	623	697
WA	2,345	2,275	2,225	59.4	63.1	62.6	139	144	139	3.75	3.68	3.45	521	524	476
SD	2,797	2,798	3,193	42.3	46.0	41.8	118	129	133	3.46	3.37	3.60	408	432	481
OK	4,600	4,700	4,000	39.0	35.0	32.0	179	165	128	3.31	3.32	3.35	594	546	429
ID	1,130	1,190	1,200	74.9	85.5	83.8	85	102	101	3.49	3.61	3.40	294	365	338
TX	3,450	3,500	3,000	28.0	31.0	32.0	97	109	96	3.06	3.34	3.30	296	362	317

[1] Includes other states, not shown separately.

Source: U.S. Department of Agriculture, National Agricultural Statistics Service, *Crop Production*, annual; and *Crop Values*, annual.

Table 835. **Greenhouse and Nursery Crops—Value of Production, Trade, and Consumption: 1990 to 2004**

[In millions of dollars, except as noted (8,764 represents $8,764,000,000). Includes all floriculture and nursery crops except cut Christmas trees, seeds, and food crops grown under cover. Domestic production based on grower wholesale receipts. Domestic consumption equals supply minus exports. Supply equals domestic production plus imports]

Year	Production and trade				Consumption				
	Domestic production	Imports	Supply	Exports	Domestic consump-tion	Per household (dol.)	Per capita (dol.)	Import share (percent)
1990	8,764	536	9,300	204	9,096	99	36	5.9
1995	10,800	855	11,655	241	11,413	117	43	7.5
2000	13,796	1,159	14,955	279	14,676	139	52	7.9
2001	14,396	1,150	15,546	264	15,282	143	54	7.5
2002	15,181	1,132	16,313	250	16,063	149	56	7.0
2003	15,492	1,249	16,741	272	16,469	151	57	7.6
2004, total	**15,697**	**1,378**	**17,075**	**293**	**16,782**	**153**	**57**	**8.2**
Nursery and other greenhouse crops	10,517	356	10,874	176	10,697	97	36	3.3
Floriculture crops	5,180	1,022	6,201	117	6,084	55	21	16.8
Flowering plants and other floriculture crops [1] . .	4,758	316	5,074	90	4,983	45	17	6.3
Cut flowers.	422	706	1,127	27	1,101	10	4	64.1

[1] Includes potted flowering plants, foliage plants for indoor or patio use, bedding and garden plants, cut cultivated greens, and propagative material.

Source: U.S. Department of Agriculture, Economic Research Service, *Floriculture and Nursery Crops Yearbook.*

Table 836. **Fresh Fruits and Vegetables—Supply and Use: 2000 to 2005**

[In millions of pounds, except per capita in pounds (8,355 represents 8,355,000,000)]

Year	Utilized production [1]	Imports [2]	Supply, [1] total	Exports [2]	Consumption	
					Total	Per capita
FRUITS						
Citrus:						
2000.	8,355	720	9,075	2,445	6,630	23.5
2001.	8,331	871	9,202	2,392	6,810	23.9
2002.	8,256	707	8,962	2,245	6,718	23.4
2003.	8,442	969	9,411	2,456	6,955	23.9
2004.	8,156	993	9,149	2,495	6,654	22.7
2005.	7,366	1,001	8,367	1,937	6,430	21.7
Noncitrus: [3]						
2000.	13,850	11,225	25,074	3,389	21,685	76.6
2001.	12,781	10,911	23,692	3,104	20,588	72.0
2002.	12,833	11,552	24,385	2,902	21,483	74.4
2003.	13,386	12,164	25,550	2,835	22,716	77.9
2004.	14,407	12,300	26,708	3,067	23,641	80.3
VEGETABLES AND MELONS						
2000.	46,922	6,719	54,986	4,197	48,566	172.0
2001.	46,377	7,304	54,947	4,115	48,602	170.3
2002.	46,736	7,691	55,768	4,265	49,394	171.4
2003.	46,919	8,037	56,206	4,249	49,925	171.5
2004.	48,878	8,197	58,328	4,344	51,340	174.8
2005.	47,703	8,708	57,918	4,269	51,572	174.0
POTATOES						
2000.	13,185	806	13,990	677	13,313	47.1
2001.	13,252	671	13,923	636	13,287	46.6
2002.	12,567	883	13,450	693	12,757	44.3
2003.	13,349	872	14,221	590	13,631	46.8
2004.	13,181	755	13,936	479	13,457	45.8
2005.	12,435	788	13,223	635	12,588	42.5

[1] Crop-year basis for fruits. Supply data for vegetables include ending stocks of previous year.   [2] Fiscal year for fruits; calendar year for vegetables and potatoes.   [3] Includes bananas.

Source: U.S. Department of Agriculture, Economic Research Service, *Fruit and Tree Nuts Situation and Outlook Yearbook*, and *Vegetables and Melons Situation and Outlook Yearbook.*

Table 837. **Nuts—Supply and Use: 2000 to 2004**

[In millions of pounds (shelled) (366 represents 366,000,000)]

Year	Beginning stocks	Marketable production [1]	Imports	Supply, total	Consumption	Exports	Ending stocks
2000	366	1,110	297	1,773	647	851	275
2001	274	1,335	322	1,931	805	845	281
2002	281	1,562	361	2,204	929	912	362
2003	363	1,504	428	2,295	1,000	946	350
2004	350	1,523	490	2,363	1,043	998	322

[1] Utilized production minus inedibles and noncommercial usage.

Source: U.S. Department of Agriculture, Economic Research Service, *Fruit and Tree Nuts Situation and Outlook Yearbook.*

Agriculture   545

Table 838. Commercial Vegetable and Other Specified Crops—Area, Production, and Value, 2003 to 2005, and Leading Producing States, 2005

[283 represents 283,000. Except as noted, relates to commercial production for fresh market and processing combined. Includes market garden areas but excludes minor producing acreage in minor producing states. Excludes production for home use in farm and nonfarm gardens. Value is for season or crop year and should not be confused with calendar-year income]

Crop	Area [1] (1,000 acres)			Production [2] (1,000 short tons)			Value [3] (mil. dol.)			Leading states in order of production, 2005
	2003	2004	2005	2003	2004	2005	2003	2004	2005	
Beans, snap	283	294	208	1,012	1,126	1,095	395	393	403	WI, OR, NY [4]
Beans, dry edible	1,347	1,219	1,563	1,125	889	1,361	423	453	526	NC, MI, NE
Broccoli [5]	132	134	134	973	992	990	616	638	564	CA, AZ
Cabbage [5]	75	76	74	1,132	1,249	1,212	295	345	325	CA, NY, GA
Cantaloupes [5]	86	87	89	1,105	1,094	1,106	372	322	300	CA, AZ, TX
Carrots	102	99	109	1,805	1,764	1,751	549	573	587	AZ, MI [5]
Cauliflower	39	38	38	327	321	326	226	196	197	CA, AZ
Celery	28	28	28	963	974	959	259	289	274	CA, MI
Corn, sweet.	673	649	643	4,691	4,362	4,537	780	794	819	(NA)
Fresh market	247	243	239	1,425	1,394	1,363	550	580	602	FL, CA, GA
Processed	427	406	404	3,266	2,968	3,174	230	214	217	MN, WA, WI
Cucumbers	174	170	171	1,120	1,096	1,083	366	383	383	MI, NC, FL [4]
Garlic	35	32	29	312	261	232	160	139	190	CA
Lettuce, head [5]	185	181	180	3,412	3,311	3,180	1,235	1,119	991	CA, AZ
Lettuce, leaf [5]	56	62	63	675	740	770	424	455	533	CA, AZ
Lettuce, Romaine [5] . . .	77	75	82	1,135	1,158	1,186	625	443	458	CA, AZ
Mushrooms [6]	30	32	29	418	441	419	856	878	862	PA, CA
Onions	166	169	162	3,668	4,150	3,688	929	777	922	CA, WA
Peppers, bell	54	53	57	806	820	725	495	559	483	CA, FL
Potatoes	1,249	1,167	1,085	22,891	22,802	21,044	2,686	2,575	2,903	ID, WA, WI
Squash	51	53	55	384	388	407	197	223	210	CA, MI, GA
Sweet potatoes	93	93	88	795	806	787	305	282	309	NC, CA, MS
Tomatoes	416	432	412	11,599	14,072	12,173	1,908	2,158	2,259	(NA)
Fresh market	122	131	130	1,779	1,917	1,973	1,332	1,439	1,637	FL, CA, OH
Processed	294	301	282	9,820	12,266	10,200	576	719	622	CA, IN
Watermelons	150	142	136	1,910	1,844	1,895	343	313	410	FL, CA, TX

NA Not available.   [1] Area of crops for harvest for fresh market, including any partially harvested or not harvested because of low prices or other factors, plus area harvested for processing.   [2] Excludes some quantities not marketed.   [3] Fresh market vegetables valued at f.o.b. shipping point. Processing vegetables are equivalent returns at packinghouse door.   [4] Processed only.   [5] Fresh market only.   [6] Area is shown in million square feet. All data are for marketing year ending June 30.

Source: U.S. Department of Agriculture, National Agricultural Statistics Service, *Vegetables, 2005 Summary*, January 2006. Also in *Agricultural Statistics*, annual.

Table 839. Fruits and Nuts—Utilized Production and Value, 2003 to 2005, and Leading Producing States, 2005

[4,397 represents 4,397,000]

Fruit or nut	Unit	Utilized production [1]			Farm value (mil. dol.)			Leading states in order of production, 2005
		2003	2004	2005	2003	2004	2005	
Apples [2]	1,000 tons . . .	4,397	5,225	4,935	1,817	1,648	1,787	WA, NY, MI
Apricots	1,000 tons . . .	98	101	91	35	35	41	CA, WA
Avocados	1,000 tons . . .	233	179	(NA)	394	293	(NA)	(NA)
Blueberries	1,000 tons . . .	135	137	146	248	297	359	MI, NJ, OR
Cherries, sweet	1,000 tons . . .	246	283	251	342	437	484	WA, CA, OR
Cherries, tart	1,000 tons . . .	113	107	135	80	70	65	MI, UT, WA
Cranberries	1,000 tons . . .	310	309	311	210	199	212	WI, MA, NJ
Grapefruit	1,000 tons . . .	2,063	2,165	1,008	269	317	398	FL, TX, CA
Grapes (13 states)	1,000 tons . . .	6,644	6,240	6,975	2,609	3,011	3,013	CA, WA, NY
Lemons	1,000 tons . . .	1,026	798	813	291	270	352	CA, AZ
Nectarines	1,000 tons . . .	273	269	249	119	86	130	CA, WA
Olives (CA)	1,000 tons . . .	118	104	139	48	59	76	CA
Oranges	1,000 tons . . .	11,545	12,872	9,112	1,565	1,782	1,498	FL, CA
Peaches	1,000 tons . . .	1,260	1,307	1,183	454	462	510	CA, SC, GA
Pears	1,000 tons . . .	934	872	812	273	296	315	WA, CA, OR
Pineapples	1,000 tons . . .	300	220	212	101	83	79	HI
Plums (CA)	1,000 tons . . .	209	156	171	87	74	94	CA
Prunes (dried basis) (CA)	1,000 tons . . .	181	49	90	130	72	131	CA
Raspberries	1,000 tons . . .	69	79	82	172	245	220	CA, WA
Strawberries	1,000 tons . . .	1,078	1,107	1,161	1,375	1,460	1,383	CA, FL
Tangerines	1,000 tons . . .	382	417	331	117	130	130	FL, CA, AZ
Almonds (shelled basis) (CA)	Mil. lb	1,040	1,005	900	1,600	2,189	2,725	CA
Hazelnuts (in the shell)	1,000 tons . . .	38	38	28	39	54	57	OR
Macadamia nuts	1,000 tons . . .	27	28	30	32	41	47	HI
Pecans (in the shell) (11 states) . . .	1,000 tons . . .	141	93	130	278	327	400	GA, TX, NM
Pistachios	1,000 tons . . .	60	174	142	145	465	574	CA
Walnuts, English (in the shell)	1,000 tons . . .	326	325	355	378	452	(NA)	CA

NA Not available.   [1] Excludes quantities not harvested or not marketed.   [2] Production in commercial orchards with 100 or more bearing age trees.

Source: U.S. Department of Agriculture, National Agricultural Statistics Service, *Noncitrus Fruits and Nuts, 2005 Preliminary Summary*, January 2006; and *Citrus Fruits, 2005 Summary*, September 2005.

546   Agriculture

Table 840. **Meat Supply and Use: 1990 to 2005**

[**In millions of pounds** (carcass weight equivalent) (**62,255 represents 62,255,000,000**). Carcass weight equivalent is the weight of the animal minus entrails, head, hide, and internal organs; includes fat and bone. Covers federal and state inspected, and farm slaughter]

Year and type of meat	Production	Imports	Supply [1]	Exports	Consumption [2]	Ending stocks
RED MEAT AND POULTRY						
1990	62,255	3,295	66,673	2,472	62,937	1,263
1995	74,068	2,838	78,636	6,956	69,911	1,768
2000	82,372	4,136	88,480	9,344	77,068	2,069
2003	85,187	4,376	91,902	9,740	80,138	2,025
2004	85,140	4,992	92,157	8,090	81,875	2,192
2005	86,780	4,846	93,818	9,205	82,401	2,212
ALL RED MEATS						
1990	38,787	3,295	42,742	1,250	40,784	707
1995	43,675	2,832	47,511	2,614	43,967	929
2000	46,299	4,127	51,340	3,760	46,559	1,021
2003	46,710	4,359	52,307	4,242	47,006	1,059
2004	45,555	4,959	51,573	2,650	47,735	1,187
2005	45,845	4,803	51,835	3,358	47,397	1,080
Beef:						
1990.	22,743	2,356	25,434	1,006	24,031	397
1995.	25,222	2,104	27,874	1,821	25,534	519
2000.	26,888	3,032	30,332	2,468	27,338	525
2003.	26,339	3,006	30,036	2,518	27,000	518
2004.	24,650	3,679	28,847	460	27,750	637
2005.	24,784	3,599	29,020	689	27,760	571
Pork:						
1990.	15,354	898	16,565	238	16,031	296
1995.	17,849	664	18,952	787	17,768	396
2000.	18,952	965	20,406	1,287	18,642	478
2003.	19,966	1,185	21,684	1,717	19,436	532
2004.	20,529	1,099	22,160	2,181	19,437	543
2005.	20,705	1,024	22,272	2,660	19,118	494
Veal:						
1990.	327	(NA)	331	(NA)	325	6
1995.	319	(NA)	326	(NA)	319	7
2000.	225	(NA)	230	(NA)	225	5
2003.	202	(NA)	209	(NA)	204	5
2004.	176	(NA)	181	(NA)	177	5
2005.	165	(NA)	169	(NA)	164	5
Lamb and mutton:						
1990.	363	41	412	6	397	8
1995.	285	64	359	6	346	8
2000.	234	130	372	5	354	13
2003.	203	168	378	7	367	4
2004.	200	180	384	9	372	3
2005.	191	180	374	9	355	10
POULTRY, TOTAL						
1990	23,468	–	23,931	1,222	22,153	556
1995	30,393	6	31,125	4,342	25,944	839
2000	36,073	9	37,140	5,584	30,508	1,048
2003	38,477	17	39,595	5,498	33,131	966
2004	39,585	33	40,584	5,440	34,139	1,005
2005	40,935	43	41,982	5,847	35,004	1,132
Broilers:						
1990.	18,430	–	18,651	1,143	17,266	242
1995.	24,827	1	25,286	3,894	20,832	560
2000.	30,209	6	31,011	4,918	25,295	798
2003.	32,399	12	33,173	4,920	27,645	608
2004.	33,699	27	34,334	4,784	28,837	713
2005.	34,987	34	35,734	5,147	29,662	924
Mature chicken:						
1990.	523	–	530	25	496	9
1995.	496	3	513	99	406	7
2000.	531	2	540	220	311	9
2003.	502	3	510	95	413	9
2004.	504	2	509	214	292	3
2005.	516	1	519	131	387	2
Turkeys:						
1990.	4,514	–	4,750	54	4,390	306
1995.	5,069	2	5,326	348	4,706	271
2000.	5,333	1	5,589	445	4,902	241
2003.	5,576	2	5,911	484	5,074	354
2004.	5,383	5	5,741	442	5,010	288
2005.	5,433	8	5,729	569	4,954	206

– Represents zero.   NA Not available.   [1] Total supply equals production plus imports plus ending stocks of previous year.
[2] Includes shipments to territories.

Source: U.S. Department of Agriculture, Economic Research Service, *Food Consumption, Prices, and Expenditures, 1970–1997*; and "Agricultural Outlook: Statistical Indicators"; <http://www.ers.usda.gov/publications/agoutlook/aotables/>.

Table 841. Livestock Inventory and Production: 1990 to 2006

[95.8 represents 95,800,000. **Production in live weight**; includes animals-for-slaughter market, younger animals shipped to other states for feeding or breeding purposes, farm slaughter and custom slaughter consumed on farms where produced, minus livestock shipped into states for feeding or breeding with an adjustment for changes in inventory]

Type of livestock	Unit	1990	1995	1999	2000	2001	2002	2003	2004	2005	2006
ALL CATTLE [1]											
Inventory: [2] Number on farms	Mil.	95.8	102.8	99.1	98.2	97.3	96.7	96.1	94.9	95.4	97.1
Total value.	Bil. dol. . . .	59.0	63.2	58.8	67.1	70.5	72.3	69.9	77.6	87.4	97.9
Value per head.	Dol.	616	615	594	683	725	747	728	818	916	1,008
Production: Quantity	Bil. lb.	39.2	42.5	42.6	43.0	42.6	42.4	42.2	41.5	41.6	(NA)
Beef, price per 100 lb.	Dol.	74.60	61.80	63.40	68.60	71.30	66.50	79.70	85.80	89.70	(NA)
Calves, price per 100 lb. . .	Dol.	95.60	73.10	87.70	104.00	106.00	96.40	102.00	119.00	135.00	(NA)
Value of production	Bil. dol. . . .	29.3	24.7	26.1	28.5	29.4	27.1	32.1	34.8	36.7	(NA)
HOGS AND PIGS											
Inventory: [3] Number on farms	Mil.	53.8	59.7	62.2	59.3	59.1	59.7	59.6	60.4	61.0	61.3
Total value.	Bil. dol. . . .	4.3	3.2	2.8	4.3	4.5	4.6	4.2	4.0	6.3	5.7
Value per head.	Dol.	79	53	44	72	77	77	71	67	103	92
Production: Quantity	Bil. lb.	21.3	24.4	25.9	25.7	25.9	26.3	26.3	26.7	27.5	(NA)
Price per 100 lb.	Dol.	53.70	40.50	30.30	42.30	44.40	33.40	37.20	49.30	50.20	(NA)
Value of production	Bil. dol. . . .	11.3	9.8	7.8	10.8	11.4	8.7	9.7	13.1	13.6	(NA)
SHEEP AND LAMBS											
Inventory: [2] Number on farms	Mil.	11.4	9.0	7.2	7.0	6.9	6.6	6.3	6.1	6.1	6.2
Total value.	Mil. dol. . . .	901	663	641	670	690	614	657	724	799	875
Value per head.	Dol.	79	75	88	95	100	92	104	119	130	141
Production: Quantity	Mil. lb.	781	602	537	512	501	485	470	464	476	(NA)
Sheep, price per 100 lb. . .	Dol.	23.20	28.00	31.10	34.30	34.60	28.20	34.90	38.80	45.10	(NA)
Lambs, price per 100 lb. . .	Dol.	55.50	78.20	74.50	79.80	66.90	74.10	94.40	101.00	110.00	(NA)
Value of production	Mil. dol. . . .	374	414	352	365	303	314	392	411	456	(NA)

NA Not available.   [1] Includes milk cows.   [2] As of January 1.   [3] As of December 1 of preceding year.
Source: U.S. Department of Agriculture, National Agricultural Statistics Service, *Meat Animals—Production, Disposition, and Income Final Estimates 1998–2002*, May 2004; *Meat Animals Production, Disposition, and Income*, annual; and annual livestock summaries. Also in *Agricultural Statistics*, annual.

Table 842. Livestock Operations by Size of Herd: 2000 to 2005

[In thousands (1,076 represents 1,076,000). An operation is any place having one or more head on hand at any time during the year]

Size of herd	2000	2004	2005	Size of herd	2000	2004	2005
CATTLE [1]				MILK COWS [2]			
Total operations	1,076	989	983	Total operations	105	82	78
1 to 49 head.	671	619	612	1 to 49 head.	53	39	37
50 to 99 head	186	164	164	50 to 99 head.	31	24	23
100 to 499 head	192	179	178	100 head or more	21	18	18
500 to 999 head	19	18	19				
1,000 head or more	10	10	10	HOGS AND PIGS			
				Total operations	87	70	67
BEEF COWS [2]				1 to 99 head.	50	42	41
Total operations	831	775	770	100 to 499 head	17	10	10
1 to 49 head.	655	602	597	500 to 999 head	8	5	5
50 to 99 head	100	96	95	1,000 to 1,999 head	6	4	4
100 to 499 head	71	72	73	2,000 to 4,999 head.	5	5	5
500 head or more	6	5	5	5,000 head or more	2	2	2

[1] Includes calves.   [2] Included in operations with cattle.

Source: U.S. Department of Agriculture, National Agricultural Statistics Service, *Livestock Operations Final Estimates 1998–2002*, April 2004; *Farms, Land in Farms, and Livestock Operations 2005 Summary*, January 2006; and *Agricultural Statistics*, annual.

Table 843. Hogs and Pigs—Number, Production, and Value by State: 2003 to 2005

[60,444 represents 60,444,000. See headnote, Table 841]

State	Number on farms [1] (1,000)			Quantity produced (mil. lb.)			Value of production (mil. dol.)			Commercial slaughter [2] (mil. lb.)	
	2003	2004	2005	2003	2004	2005	2003	2004	2005	2004	2005
U.S. [3]	60,444	60,975	61,327	26,260	26,689	27,489	9,663	13,072	13,644	27,588	27,828
IA.	15,900	16,300	16,500	6,799	7,196	7,811	2,198	3,265	3,648	8,012	8,079
NC	10,000	9,900	9,800	3,772	3,852	3,840	1,532	2,067	2,089	2,728	2,847
MN	6,500	6,500	6,600	3,016	3,110	3,238	1,127	1,511	1,570	2,398	2,443
IL	4,000	4,100	4,000	1,828	1,733	1,614	752	938	902	2,544	2,611
IN	3,100	3,200	3,250	1,568	1,426	1,487	560	679	704	1,870	1,873
NE	2,900	2,850	2,850	1,429	1,374	1,368	584	717	730	1,846	1,934
OK	2,380	2,390	2,370	1,169	1,230	1,285	415	578	604	1,362	1,400

[1] As of December 1.   [2] Includes slaughter in federally inspected and other slaughter plants; excludes animals slaughtered on farms.   [3] Includes other states not shown separately.
Source: U.S. Department of Agriculture, National Agricultural Statistics Service, *Meat Animals—Production, Disposition and Income*, annual; and *Livestock Slaughter*, annual.

548   Agriculture

Table 844. Cattle and Calves—Number, Production, and Value by State: 2003 to 2006

[94,888 represents 94,888,000. Includes milk cows. See headnote, Table 841]

State	Number on farms [1] (1,000)			Quantity produced (mil. lb.)			Value of production (mil. dol.)			Commercial slaughter [2] (mil. lb.)	
	2004	2005	2006	2003	2004	2005	2003	2004	2005	2004	2005
U.S. [3]	94,888	95,438	97,102	42,243	41,497	41,578	32,113	34,831	36,739	40,589	40,689
TX	13,900	13,700	14,100	7,767	7,402	7,328	6,029	6,187	6,459	7,343	7,483
NE	6,250	6,350	6,550	4,401	4,392	4,510	3,380	3,605	3,836	8,822	9,078
KS	6,650	6,600	6,650	4,025	3,862	3,994	3,033	2,796	2,978	8,752	9,097
OK	5,100	5,350	5,450	2,044	1,968	2,066	1,671	1,942	2,189	32	28
CA	5,200	5,400	5,500	1,987	1,983	1,940	1,148	1,267	1,213	1,731	1,813
CO	2,400	2,500	2,650	1,865	1,915	1,798	1,522	1,849	1,817	3,001	2,655
IA	3,450	3,600	3,800	1,797	1,611	1,725	1,420	1,329	1,407	(4)	(4)
SD	3,650	3,700	3,750	1,482	1,546	1,501	1,220	1,446	1,528	(4)	(4)
MO	4,350	4,400	4,550	1,155	1,170	1,234	991	1,191	1,335	(4)	(4)
MN	2,400	2,400	2,350	1,096	1,053	1,076	789	799	851	973	901
WI	3,350	3,350	3,400	1,058	1,055	1,075	682	801	858	1,939	1,948

[1] As of January 1. [2] Data cover cattle only. Includes slaughter in federally inspected and other slaughter plants; excludes animals slaughtered on farms. [3] Includes other states not shown separately. [4] Included in U.S. total. Not printed to avoid disclosing individual operation.

Source: U.S. Department of Agriculture, National Agricultural Statistics Service, *Meat Animals—Production, Disposition and Income*, annual; and *Livestock Slaughter*, annual.

Table 845. Milk Cows—Number, Production, and Value by State: 2003 to 2005

[9,083 represents 9,083,000]

State	Number on farms [1] (1,000)			Milk produced on farms (mil. lb.)			Value of production [2] (mil. dol.)		
	2003	2004	2005	2003	2004	2005	2003	2004	2005
United States [3] . . .	9,083	9,012	9,041	170,394	170,934	176,989	21,381	27,568	26,904
California	1,688	1,725	1,755	35,437	36,465	37,564	4,033	5,371	5,229
Wisconsin	1,256	1,241	1,236	22,266	22,085	22,866	2,872	3,732	3,567
New York	671	655	648	11,952	11,650	12,078	1,566	1,957	1,920
Pennsylvania	575	562	561	10,338	10,062	10,503	1,447	1,771	1,775
Idaho	404	424	455	8,774	9,093	10,161	1,009	1,364	1,423
Minnesota	473	463	453	8,258	8,102	8,195	1,057	1,353	1,262
New Mexico	317	326	328	6,666	6,737	6,951	800	1,017	994
Michigan	302	303	311	6,375	6,330	6,735	803	1,032	1,037
Texas	319	319	320	5,630	6,009	6,442	732	979	986

[1] Average number during year. Represents cows and heifers that have calved, kept for milk; excluding heifers not yet fresh. [2] Valued at average returns per 100 pounds of milk in combined marketings of milk and cream. Includes value of milk fed to calves. [3] Includes other states not shown separately.

Source: U.S. Department of Agriculture, National Agricultural Statistics Service, *Dairy Products*, annual; and *Milk: Production, Disposition, and Income*, annual.

Table 846. Milk Production and Manufactured Dairy Products: 1990 to 2005

[193 represents 193,000]

Item	Unit	1990	1995	1999	2000	2001	2002	2003	2004	2005
Number of farms with milk cows	1,000	193	140	111	105	97	91	86	82	78
Cows and heifers that have calved, kept for milk . .	Mil. head. . .	10.0	9.5	9.2	9.2	9.1	9.1	9.1	9.0	9.0
Milk produced on farms	Bil. lb	148	155	163	167	165	170	170	171	177
Production per cow	1,000 lb . . .	14.8	16.4	17.8	18.2	18.2	18.6	18.8	19.0	20.0
Milk marketed by producers [1]	Bil. lb	146	154	161	166	164	169	169	170	176
Value of milk produced	Bil. dol	20.4	20.1	23.4	20.8	24.9	20.7	21.4	27.6	26.9
Cash receipts from marketing of milk and cream [1]	Bil. dol	20.1	19.9	23.2	20.6	24.7	20.6	21.2	27.4	26.7
Number of dairy manufacturing plants	Number. . . .	1,723	1,495	1,192	1,164	1,179	1,149	1,119	1,093	1,081
Manufactured dairy products:										
Butter (incl. whey butter)	Mil. lb	1,302	1,264	1,277	1,256	1,232	1,355	1,242	1,247	1,347
Cheese, total [2]	Mil. lb	6,059	6,917	7,941	8,258	8,261	8,547	8,557	8,873	9,127
American (excl. full-skim American). .	Mil. lb	2,894	3,131	3,568	3,642	3,544	3,691	3,622	3,739	3,813
Cream and Neufchatel	Mil. lb	431	544	639	687	645	686	677	699	693
All Italian varieties	Mil. lb	2,207	2,674	3,152	3,289	3,426	3,470	3,524	3,662	3,805
Cottage cheese: creamed [3]	Mil. lb	832	711	720	735	742	748	769	788	764
Curd, pot, and bakers.	Mil. lb	493	459	465	461	453	437	448	464	368
Condensed bulk milk	Mil. lb	1,426	1,372	1,365	1,202	1,110	1,191	1,047	1,021	1,144
Nonfat dry milk [4]	Mil. lb	902	1,243	1,364	1,457	1,419	1,596	1,589	1,418	1,509
Dry whey [5]	Mil. lb	1,143	1,147	1,147	1,188	1,046	1,115	1,085	1,035	1,046
Yogurt, plain and fruit-flavored	Mil. lb	(NA)	1,646	1,717	1,837	2,003	2,311	2,507	2,707	2,990
Ice cream, regular.	Mil. gal	824	862	972	980	970	1,005	993	920	953
Ice cream, lowfat [6]	Mil. gal	352	357	381	373	380	373	339	387	364

NA Not available. [1] Comprises sales to plants and dealers, and retail sales by farmers direct to consumers. [2] Includes varieties not shown separately. [3] Includes partially creamed (low fat). [4] Includes dry skim milk for animal feed. [5] Includes animal but excludes modified whey production. [6] Includes freezer-made milkshake in most states.

Source: U.S. Department of Agriculture, National Agricultural Statistics Service, *Dairy Products*, annual; and *Milk: Production, Disposition, and Income*, annual.

Agriculture 549

Table 847. **Milk Production and Commercial Use: 1990 to 2005**

[In billions of pounds milkfat basis (147.7 represents 147,700,000,000) except as noted]

Year	Production	Farm use	Commercial Farm marketings	Commercial Beginning stock	Imports	Commercial supply, total	CCC net removals [1]	Commercial Ending stock	Disappearance	Milk price per 100 lb. [2] (dol.)
1990	147.7	2.0	145.7	4.1	2.7	152.5	8.5	5.1	138.8	13.68
1995	155.3	1.6	153.7	4.3	2.9	160.9	2.1	4.1	154.7	12.78
2000	167.4	1.3	166.1	6.1	4.4	176.7	0.8	6.8	169.0	12.40
2001	165.3	1.2	164.1	6.8	5.7	176.7	0.1	7.0	169.5	15.04
2002	170.1	1.1	168.9	7.0	5.1	181.1	0.3	9.9	170.9	12.19
2003	170.4	1.1	169.3	9.9	5.0	184.2	1.2	8.3	174.7	12.52
2004	170.9	1.1	169.8	8.3	5.3	183.4	-0.1	7.2	176.3	16.04
2005	177.0	1.1	175.9	7.2	4.6	187.7	–	8.0	179.7	15.15

– Represents zero. [1] Removals from commercial supply by Commodity Credit Corporation (CCC). [2] Wholesale price received by farmers for all milk delivered to plants and dealers.

Source: U.S. Department of Agriculture, Economic Research Service, "Agricultural Outlook: Statistical Indicators"; <http://www.ers.usda.gov/publications/agoutlook/aotables/>.

Table 848. **Broiler, Turkey, and Egg Production: 1990 to 2005**

[For year ending November 30 (353 represents 353,000,000)]

Item	Unit	1990	1995	1998	1999	2000	2001	2002	2003	2004	2005
Chickens:[1]											
Number [2]	Million	353	388	425	437	437	444	444	450	454	453
Value per head [2] . . .	Dollars . . .	2.29	2.41	2.69	2.64	2.44	2.41	2.38	2.48	2.48	2.50
Value, total [2]	Mil. dol. . . .	808	935	1,143	1,156	1,064	1,069	1,055	1,116	1,123	1,134
Number sold	Million . . .	208	180	200	214	218	202	200	190	192	193
Price per lb.	Cents . . .	9.6	6.5	8.1	7.1	5.7	4.5	4.8	4.9	5.8	6.5
Value of sales	Mil. dol. . . .	94	60	80	75	64	47	50	48	58	65
PRODUCTION											
Broilers: [3]											
Number.	Million	5,864	7,326	7,934	8,146	8,284	8,390	8,591	8,493	8,741	8,870
Weight	Bil. lb.	25.6	34.2	38.6	40.8	41.6	42.5	44.1	44.0	45.8	47.9
Price per lb.	Cents . . .	32.6	34.2	39.3	37.1	33.6	39.3	30.5	34.6	44.6	43.6
Production value. . . .	Mil. dol. . . .	8,366	11,762	15,147	15,129	13,989	16,696	13,437	15,215	20,446	20,902
Turkeys:											
Number.	Million	282	292	286	270	270	273	275	274	264	256
Weight	Bil. lb.	6.0	6.8	7.1	6.9	7.0	7.2	7.5	7.5	7.3	7.2
Price per lb	Cents . . .	39.6	41.0	38.0	40.8	40.6	39.0	36.5	36.1	42.0	44.9
Production value. . . .	Mil. dol. . . .	2,393	2,769	2,683	2,807	2,828	2,797	2,732	2,700	3,065	3,233
Eggs:											
Number.	Billion	68.1	74.8	79.8	82.9	84.7	86.1	87.3	87.5	89.1	90.0
Price per dozen	Cents	70.8	62.5	66.8	62.0	61.6	62.0	58.9	73.2	71.4	53.4
Production value. . . .	Mil. dol. . . .	4,021	3,893	4,439	4,287	4,346	4,446	4,281	5,333	5,299	4,042

[1] Excludes commercial broilers. [2] As of December 1. [3] Young chickens of the heavy breeds and other meat-type birds, to be marketed at 2-5 lbs. live weight and from which no pullets are kept for egg production.

Source: U.S. Department of Agriculture, National Agricultural Statistics Service, *Poultry Production and Value Final Estimates 1998–2002*, April 2004; *Turkeys Final Estimates 1998–2002*, April 2004; *Chickens and Eggs Final Estimates 1998–2002*, April 2004; *Poultry—Production and Value*, annual; *Turkeys*, annual; and *Chickens and Eggs*, annual.

Table 849. **Broiler and Turkey Production by State: 2003 to 2005**

[In millions of pounds, live weight production (43,958 represents 43,958,000,000)]

State	Broilers 2003	Broilers 2004	Broilers 2005	Turkeys 2003	Turkeys 2004	Turkeys 2005	State	Broilers 2003	Broilers 2004	Broilers 2005	Turkeys 2003	Turkeys 2004	Turkeys 2005
U.S. [1]. . .	43,958	45,796	47,908	7,487	7,305	7,207	MS	4,189	4,387	4,779	(NA)	(NA)	(NA)
AL	5,405	5,470	5,604	(NA)	(NA)	(NA)	MO	(NA)	(NA)	(NA)	724	667	644
AR	5,843	6,208	6,314	540	527	566	NY	15	15	16	13	14	14
CA	(NA)	(NA)	(NA)	419	414	407	NC	4,320	4,537	4,852	1,105	1,069	1,069
DE	1,507	1,492	1,835	(NA)	(NA)	(NA)	OH	226	225	228	212	220	213
FL.	511	463	463	(NA)	(NA)	(NA)	OK	1,115	1,243	1,325	(NA)	(NA)	(NA)
GA	6,303	6,495	6,738	(NA)	(NA)	(NA)	PA	687	708	795	216	234	227
IL	(NA)	(NA)	(NA)	90	89	93	SC	1,145	1,186	1,280	456	463	310
IN	(NA)	(NA)	(NA)	397	410	429	SD	(NA)	(NA)	(NA)	153	151	141
IA	(NA)	(NA)	(NA)	268	324	326	TN	948	999	1,003	(NA)	(NA)	(NA)
KY	1,490	1,570	1,638	(NA)	(NA)	(NA)	TX	2,947	3,166	3,265	(NA)	(NA)	(NA)
MD	1,374	1,366	1,228	15	13	15	VA	1,299	1,341	1,326	492	435	527
MI	(NA)	(NA)	(NA)	191	188	176	WV	358	354	363	92	71	60
MN	229	232	230	1,215	1,228	1,202	WI	155	152	161	(NA)	(NA)	(NA)

NA Not available. [1] Includes other states not shown separately.

Source: U.S. Department of Agriculture, National Agricultural Statistics Service, *Poultry—Production and Value*, annual.

550 Agriculture

Section 18
Natural Resources

This section presents data on the area, ownership, production, trade, reserves, and disposition of natural resources. Natural resources is defined here as including forestry, fisheries, and mining and mineral products.

Forestry—Presents data on the area, ownership, and timber resource of commercial timberland; forestry statistics covering the National Forests and Forest Service cooperative programs; product data for lumber, pulpwood, woodpulp, paper and paperboard, and similar data.

The principal sources of data relating to forests and forest products are *Forest Resources of the United States, 1991; Timber Demand and Technology Assessment, 2003; U.S. Timber Production, Trade, Consumption, and Price Statistics; Land Areas of the National Forest System,* issued annually by the Forest Service of the Department of Agriculture; *Agricultural Statistics* issued by the Department of Agriculture; and reports of the annual survey of manufactures, and the annual *Current Industrial Reports,* issued by the Census Bureau on the Internet and in print in the annual *Manufacturing Profiles.* Additional information is published in the monthly *Survey of Current Business* of the Bureau of Economic Analysis, and the annual *Wood Pulp* and *Fiber Statistics* and *The Statistics of Paper, Paperboard, and Wood Pulp* of the American Forest and Paper Association, Washington, DC.

The completeness and reliability of statistics on forests and forest products vary considerably. The data for forest land area and stand volumes are much more reliable for areas that have been recently surveyed than for those for which only estimates are available. In general, more data are available for lumber and other manufactured products such as particle board and softwood panels, etc., than for the primary forest products such as poles and piling and fuelwood.

Fisheries—The principal source of data relating to fisheries is *Fisheries of the United States,* issued annually by the National Marine Fisheries Service (NMFS), National Oceanic and Atmospheric Administration (NOAA). The NMFS collects and disseminates data on commercial landings of fish and shellfish. Annual reports include quantity and value of commercial landings of fish and shellfish disposition of landings and number and kinds of fishing vessels and fishing gear. Reports for the fish-processing industry include annual output for the wholesaling and fish processing establishments, annual and seasonal employment. The principal source for these data is the annual *Fisheries of the United States.*

Mining and mineral products—Presents data relating to mineral industries and their products, general summary measures of production and employment, and more detailed data on production, prices, imports and exports, consumption, and distribution for specific industries and products. Data on mining and mineral products may also be found in Sections 19, 21, and 28 of this *Abstract;* data on mining employment may be found in Section 12.

Mining comprises the extraction of minerals occurring naturally (coal, ores, crude petroleum, natural gas) and quarrying, well operation, milling, refining and processing, and other preparation customarily done at the mine or well site or as a part of extraction activity. (Mineral preparation plants are usually operated together with mines or quarries.) Exploration for minerals is included as is the development of mineral properties.

The principal governmental sources of these data are the *Minerals Yearbook* and *Mineral Commodity Summaries,* published by the U.S. Geological Survey, Department of the Interior, and various monthly and annual publications of the Energy Information Administration, Department of

Energy. See text, Section 19, for a list of Department of Energy publications. In addition, the Census Bureau conducts a census of mineral industries every 5 years.

Nongovernment sources include the *Annual Statistical Report* of the American Iron and Steel Institute, Washington, DC; *Metals Week* and the monthly *Engineering and Mining Journal,* issued by the McGraw-Hill Publishing Co., New York, NY; *The Iron Age,* issued weekly by the Chilton Co., Philadelphia, PA; and the *Joint Association Survey of the U.S. Oil and Gas Industry,* conducted jointly by the American Petroleum Institute, Independent Petroleum Association of America, and Mid-Continent Oil and Gas Association.

Mineral statistics, with principal emphasis on commodity detail, have been collected by the U.S. Geological Survey and the former Bureau of Mines since 1880. Current data in U.S. Geological Survey publications include quantity and value of non-fuel minerals produced, sold, or used by producers, or shipped; quantity of minerals stocked; crude materials treated and prepared minerals recovered; and consumption of mineral raw materials.

Censuses of mineral industries have been conducted by the Census Bureau at various intervals since 1840. Beginning with the 1967 census, legislation provides for a census to be conducted every 5 years for years ending in "2" and "7." The most recent results, published for 2002, are based on the North American Industry Classification System (NAICS). The censuses provide, for the various types of mineral establishments, information on operating costs, capital expenditures, labor, equipment, and energy requirements in relation to their value of shipments and other receipts. Commodity statistics on many manufactured mineral products are also collected by the Census Bureau at monthly, quarterly, or annual intervals and issued in its *Current Industrial Reports* series.

In general, figures shown in the individual commodity tables include data for outlying areas and may therefore not agree with summary tables. Except for crude petroleum and refined products, the export and import figures include foreign trade passing through the customs districts of United States and Puerto Rico but exclude shipments between U.S. territories and the customs districts.

Table 850. **Gross Domestic Product of Natural Resource-Related Industries in Current and Real (2000) Dollars by Industry: 2000 to 2005**

[In billions of dollars (9,817.0 represents $9,817,000,000,000). Data are based on the 2002 NAICS Codes. Data include nonfactor charges (capital consumption allowances, indirect business taxes, etc.) as well as factor charges against gross product; corporate profits and capital consumption allowances have been shifted from a company to an establishment basis]

Industry	Current dollars				Chained (2000) dollars			
	2000	2003	2004	2005	2000	2003	2004	2005
All industries, total	9,817.0	10,971.2	11,734.3	12,487.1	9,817.0	10,320.6	10,755.7	11,134.8
Industries covered	306.3	335.9	401.6	(NA)	306.3	290.5	300.3	(NA)
Percent of all industries	3.1	3.1	3.4	(NA)	3.1	2.8	2.8	(NA)
Agriculture, forestry, fishing, and hunting .	98.0	114.2	141.6	119.1	98.0	104.2	106.0	101.3
Farms	71.5	88.0	112.2	(NA)	71.5	76.0	75.9	(NA)
Forestry, fishing and related activities .	26.5	26.2	29.4	(NA)	26.5	28.1	30.5	(NA)
Mining	121.3	142.3	171.9	213.6	121.3	106.0	108.4	105.6
Oil and gas extraction	81.0	93.1	115.2	(NA)	81.0	77.4	76.6	(NA)
Mining, except oil and gas	27.0	27.4	30.6	(NA)	27.0	24.3	25.1	(NA)
Support activities for mining	13.4	21.7	26.1	(NA)	13.4	7.8	9.1	(NA)
Timber-related manufacturing	87.0	79.4	88.1	(NA)	87.0	80.3	85.9	(NA)
Wood products	31.4	33.0	39.2	(NA)	31.4	31.4	32.4	(NA)
Paper products	55.6	46.4	48.9	(NA)	55.6	48.9	53.5	(NA)

NA Not available.

Source: U.S. Bureau of Economic Analysis, *Survey of Current Business,* May 2006. See also <http://www.bea.gov /bea/newsrelarchive/2006/gdpind05.pdf> (released 27 April 2006).

Table 851. Natural Resource-Related Industries—Establishments, Sales, Payroll, and Employees by Industry: 1997 and 2002

[174 represents $174,000,000,000. Includes only establishments of firms with payroll. Data are based on the 1997 and 2002 econoomic censuses, which are subject to nonsampling error. For details on methodology and nonsampling and sampling errors, see Appendix III]

Industry	NAICS code [1]	Establishments (number)		Sales, receipts, revenue, or shipments (bil. dol.)		Annual payroll (bil. dol.)		Paid employees [2] (1,000)	
		1997	2002	1997	2002	1997	2002	1997	2002
Mining	21	25,000	(S)	174	(S)	21	(S)	509	(S)
Oil & gas extraction	211	8,312	7,514	103	107	6	5	111	100
Mining (except oil & gas) . . .	212	7,348	7,173	51	54	9	9	229	200
Mining support activities	213	9,340	(S)	20	(S)	6	(S)	169	(S)
Manufacturing [3]	31-33	362,829	344,259	3,835	3,833	570	568	16,805	14,543
Wood product mfg	321	17,367	16,912	88	89	14	16	570	535
Paper mfg	322	5,868	5,463	150	151	22	21	574	476
Petroleum & coal products manufacturing	324	2,146	2,278	177	212	6	6	108	106

S Estimates did not meet publication standards.   [1] North American Industry Classification System, 1997.   [2] For pay period including March 12.   [3] Includes other industries not shown separately.

Source: U.S. Census Bureau, 2002 Economic Census Advance Report; published 29 March 2004; <http://www.census.gov/econ/census02>.

Table 852. Natural Resource-Related Industries—Establishments, Employees, and Annual Payroll by Industry: 2000 and 2003

[1,791.3 represents 1,791,300. Excludes government employees, railroad employees, self-employed persons, etc. See "General Explanation" in source for definitions and statement on reliability of data. An establishment is a single physical location where business is conducted or where services or industrial operations are performed]

Industry	NAICS code [1]	Establishments (number)		Number of employees [2] (1,000)		Annual payroll (bil. dol.)	
		2000	2003	2000	2003	2000	2003
Natural resource-related industries, total	(X)	72,932	71,724	1,791.3	1,641.4	66.58	67.31
Forestry, fishing, hunting and agriculture support	11	26,076	25,861	183.6	180.7	4.68	5.10
Forestry and logging	113	13,347	11,914	83.1	75.8	2.26	2.26
Timber tract operations	1131	469	621	3.3	5.5	0.13	0.22
Forest nurseries & gathering forest products	1132	258	316	1.7	2.3	0.07	0.07
Logging	1133	12,620	10,977	78.1	68.0	2.06	1.97
Fishing, hunting & trapping	114	2,671	2,474	10.0	8.9	0.34	0.34
Fishing	1141	2,308	2,042	7.5	6.2	0.27	0.26
Hunting & trapping	1142	363	432	2.5	2.7	0.08	0.09
Agriculture & forestry support activities.	115	10,058	11,473	90.4	95.9	2.08	2.49
Crop production support activities	1151	5,061	5,357	57.6	58.8	1.35	1.57
Animal production support activities	1152	3,450	4,354	18.2	22.1	0.38	0.50
Forestry support activities.	1153	1,547	1,762	14.7	15.0	0.35	0.42
Mining.	21	23,738	23,599	456.1	454.6	22.09	24.66
Oil & gas extraction	211	7,740	7,493	83.0	83.4	5.39	6.16
Mining (except oil & gas).	212	7,231	6,982	204.3	184.4	9.34	9.14
Coal mining	2121	1,253	1,144	70.7	68.7	3.54	3.71
Metal ore mining.	2122	522	309	34.8	24.9	1.72	1.37
Nonmetallic mineral mining & quarrying . . .	2123	5,456	5,529	98.8	90.9	4.08	4.07
Mining support activities	213	8,767	9,124	168.8	186.7	7.35	9.35
Timber-related manufacturing	(X)	23,118	22,264	1,151.6	1,006.2	39.80	37.56
Wood product manufacturing	321	17,328	16,808	597.7	524.0	16.51	15.89
Sawmills & wood preservation.	3211	4,695	4,229	131.4	112.3	3.78	3.50
Veneer, plywood & engineered wood product manufacturing	3212	1,904	1,906	120.6	111.0	3.75	3.75
Other wood product manufacturing	3219	10,729	10,673	345.8	300.7	8.95	8.64
Paper manufacturing	322	5,790	5,456	553.9	482.2	23.29	21.67
Pulp, paper & paperboard mills	3221	597	635	177.1	154.9	9.48	8.94
Converted paper product manufacturing . . .	3222	5,193	4,821	376.8	327.3	13.82	12.73

X Not applicable.   [1] North American Industry Classification System, 2002.   [2] Covers full- and part-time employees who are on the payroll in the pay period including March 12.

Source: U.S. Census Bureau, County Business Patterns; annual. See also <http://www.census.gov/epcd/cbp/view/cbpview.html>.

Table 853. Timber-Based Manufacturing Industries—Establishments, Shipments, Payroll, and Employees: 2002

[88,294,243 represents $88,294,243,000. Data based on the 2002 Economic Census. See Appendix III]

Industry	NAICS code [1]	Estab-lishments	Value of shipments ($1,000)	Annual payroll ($1,000)	Paid employees
Wood product manufacturing	**321**	**17,178**	**88,294,243**	**15,909,908**	**539,784**
Sawmills and wood preservation	3211	4,322	25,761,530	3,490,857	107,728
Saw mills	321113	3,807	21,339,251	3,118,252	95,452
Wood preservation	321114	515	4,422,279	372,605	12,276
Veneer, plywood, and engineered wood product manufacturing	3212	1,916	20,093,795	3,659,563	113,589
Other wood product manufacturing.	3219	10,940	42,438,918	8,759,488	318,467
Millwork	32191	4,717	22,353,587	4,386,903	150,073
Wood container and pallet manufacturing.	32192	2,946	5,075,309	1,152,608	50,896
All other wood product manufacturing	32199	3,277	15,010,022	3,219,977	117,498
Paper manufacturing.	**322**	**5,501**	**152,651,488**	**21,336,257**	**487,906**
Pulp, paper, and paperboard mills	3221	560	70,483,801	8,879,983	158,857
Pulp mills	32211	32	3,531,242	469,688	7,730
Paper mills	32212	329	46,098,951	5,849,652	104,938
Paperboard mills	32213	199	20,853,608	2,560,643	46,189
Converted paper product manufacturing	3222	4,941	82,167,687	12,456,274	329,049
Paperboard container manufacturing	32221	2,664	43,271,298	7,033,538	184,008
Paper bag and coated and treated paper manufacturing	32222	924	17,658,326	2,551,871	64,520
Stationery product manufacturing	32223	636	7,903,016	1,302,387	38,647
Other converted paper product manufacturing	32229	717	13,335,047	1,568,478	41,874

[1] North American Industry Classification System, 2002.

Source: U.S. Census Bureau, 2002 Economic Census, *Manufacturing Series*, issued July 2004. See <http://www.census.gov/econ /census02>.

Table 854. Timber-Based Manufacturing Industries—Employees, Payroll, and Shipments: 2004

[In thousands (13,404 represents 13,404,000). Based on the Annual Survey of Manufactures; see Appendix III]

Selected industries	2002 NAICS code [1]	All employees			Produc-tion workers, total (1,000)	Value added by manufactures		Value of ship-ments (mil. dol.)
		Number (1,000)	Payroll			Total (mil. dol.)	Per produc-tion worker (dol.)	
			Total (mil. dol.)	Per employee (dol.)				
Manufacturing, all industries [2] . . .	**31-33**	**13,404**	**569,414**	**42,480**	**9,357**	**2,031,439**	**217,101**	**4,265,784**
Timber-based manufacturing, total	**321-322**	**975**	**37,600**	**38,555**	**769**	**117,678**	**153,108**	**257,389**
Percent of total manufacturing .	(X)	7	6.60	(X)	8.21	5.79	(X)	6.03
Wood product manufacturing	321	535	17,039	31,834	428	43,662	101,960	103,420
Sawmills & wood preservation	3211	106	3,683	34,897	88	10,861	123,011	30,227
Veneer, plywood, & engineered wood product	3212	111	3,870	34,913	89	10,783	121,070	24,581
Other wood product.	3219	319	9,486	29,749	251	22,018	87,765	48,612
Millwork	32191	158	4,927	31,224	125	11,706	93,784	27,190
Wood container & pallet	32192	50	1,203	23,974	40	2,505	63,358	5,378
All other wood product	32199	111	3,357	30,263	87	7,807	90,238	16,044
Paper manufacturing.	322	440	20,561	46,731	340	74,016	217,460	153,969
Pulp, paper, & paperboard mills	3221	137	8,121	59,257	109	37,026	339,443	70,505
Pulp mills	32211	8	492	63,949	6	1,869	314,551	4,099
Paper mills	32212	90	5,290	58,968	72	24,817	345,298	45,434
Paperboard mills	32213	40	2,339	59,002	31	10,340	330,705	20,972
Converted paper product	3222	303	12,440	41,064	231	36,990	159,930	83,464
Paperboard container.	32221	169	7,027	41,499	129	18,086	140,282	44,444
Paper bag & coated & treated paper.	32222	61	2,619	42,901	45	8,377	184,546	18,401
Stationery product	32223	36	1,295	36,320	28	3,233	116,471	7,677
Other converted paper product. . .	32229	37	1,499	40,618	29	7,295	249,668	12,942

X Not applicable.   [1] North American Industry Classification System, 2002; see text, Section 15.   [2] Includes other industries not shown separately.

Source: U.S. Census Bureau, *Annual Survey of Manufactures, 2004*, Series M04(AS)-1. See also <http://www.census.gov/prod/2005pubs/am0431gs1.pdf> (issued December 2005).

Table 855. Forest Land and Timberland by Type of Owner and Region: 2003

[In thousands of acres (748,920 represents 748,920,000). As of January 1. Forest land is land at least 10 percent stocked by forest trees of any size, including land that formerly had such tree cover and that will be naturally or artificially regenerated. The minimum area for classification of forest land is 1 acre or strips of timber with a crown width of at least 120 feet wide. Timberland is forest land that is producing or is capable of producing crops of industrial wood and that is not withdrawn from timber utilization by statute or administrative regulation]

Region	Forest land, total	Timberland							
		Total	Federal			State, county, and municipal	Private		
			Total	National forest	Other		Total	National forest	Farmer and other private [1]
Total	748,920	541,098	147,278	96,644	50,634	37,559	356,261	65,595	290,666
North	169,684	179,998	32,547	9,840	22,707	21,285	126,166	14,648	111,518
Northeast	85,031	85,834	10,085	2,164	7,921	7,464	68,285	10,855	57,430
North Central	84,653	94,164	22,462	7,676	14,786	13,821	57,881	3,793	54,088
South	214,605	208,051	21,227	11,246	9,981	5,378	181,446	35,915	145,531
Southeast	88,561	87,429	9,609	4,710	4,899	2,655	75,165	14,180	60,985
South Central	126,044	120,622	11,618	6,536	5,082	2,723	106,281	21,735	84,546
Rocky Mountains	144,343	73,467	50,268	43,959	6,309	2,839	20,360	2,926	17,434
Great Plains	4,783	4,521	1,277	1,020	257	180	3,064	–	3,064
Intermountain	139,560	68,946	48,991	42,939	6,052	2,659	17,296	2,926	14,370
Pacific Coast	220,290	79,582	43,236	31,599	11,637	8,057	28,289	12,106	16,183
Alaska	126,860	16,209	9,094	3,772	5,322	4,344	2,771	–	2,771
Pacific Northwest	51,440	44,386	23,505	17,911	5,594	3,207	17,674	9,174	8,500
Pacific Southwest [2] . . .	41,980	18,987	10,637	9,916	721	506	7,844	2,932	4,912

– Represents or rounds to zero.   [1] Includes Indian lands.   [2] Includes Hawaii.

Source: U.S. Department of Agriculture, National Agricultural Statistics Service, *Agricultural Statistics, 2005*. See also <http://www.nass.usda.gov/Publications/AgStatistics/index.asp>.

Table 856. Timber Volume, Growth, and Removal on Timberland by Species Group and Region: 2003

[856,061 represents 856,061,000,000]

Region	Net volume [1]						Timber growth [4] (mil. cu. ft.)			Timber removals [5] (mil. cu. ft.)		
	Growing stock [2] (mil. cu. ft.)			Sawtimber [3] (bil. board ft.)								
	All species	Soft-woods	Hard-woods	All species	Soft-woods	Hard-woods	All species	Soft-woods	Hard-woods	All species	Soft-woods	Hard-woods
Total	856,061	491,803	364,258	3,317	2,270	1,047	23,689	13,651	9,971	16,012	10,064	5,948
North	217,624	49,878	167,746	598	149	449	5,418	1,167	4,184	2,865	680	2,185
Northeast	123,667	31,476	92,191	334	94	239	2,833	658	2,175	1,275	414	861
North Central	93,957	18,402	75,555	264	55	209	2,585	525	2,061	1,590	266	1,324
South	267,965	108,018	159,947	895	400	495	11,522	6,467	5,055	10,126	6,506	3,620
Southeast	124,004	52,758	71,244	396	177	219	5,157	3,097	2,059	4,363	2,881	1,482
South Central	143,963	55,260	88,703	499	223	276	6,365	3,370	2,995	5,763	3,625	2,138
Rocky Mountains	131,659	120,837	10,822	516	492	24	2,062	1,858	204	532	502	30
Great Plains	4,260	1,880	2,380	15	7	8	87	42	45	37	21	16
Intermountain	127,399	118,957	8,442	501	485	16	1,975	1,816	159	495	481	14
Pacific Coast	238,813	213,070	25,743	1,308	1,229	79	4,687	4,159	528	2,489	2,376	113
Alaska	31,997	29,124	2,873	146	142	4,611	207	122	85	140	137	3
Pacific Northwest	148,635	135,591	13,044	843	795	47	3,154	2,841	313	1,721	1,621	99
Pacific Southwest [6] . .	58,181	48,355	9,826	319	292	28	1,326	1,196	131	628	618	10

[1] As of January 1.   [2] Live trees of commercial species meeting specified standards of quality or vigor. Cull trees are excluded. Includes only trees 5.0-inches in diameter or larger at 4 1/2 feet above ground.   [3] Live trees of commercial species containing at least one 12-foot sawlog or two noncontiguous 8-foot logs, and meeting regional specifications for freedom from defect. Softwood trees must be at least 9.0-inches in diameter and hardwood trees must be at least 11.0-inches in diameter at 4 1/2 feet above ground.   [4] The net increase in the volume of trees during a specified year. Components include the increment in net volume of trees at the beginning of the specific year surviving to its end, plus the net volume of trees reaching the minimum size class during the year, minus the volume of trees that died during the year, and minus the net volume of trees that became cull trees during the year.   [5] The net volume of trees removed from the inventory during a specified year by harvesting, cultural operations such as timber stand improvement, or land clearing.   [6] Includes Hawaii.

Source: U.S. Department of Agriculture, National Agricultural Statistics Service, *Agricultural Statistics, 2005*. See also <http://www.nass.usda.gov/Publications/Ag_Statistics/index.asp>.

Natural Resources   555

Table 857. Timber Removals—Roundwood Product Output by Source and Species Group: 2003

[In million cubic feet (16,001 represents 16,001,000,000)]

Source and species group	Total	Sawlogs	Pulpwood	Veneer logs	Other products[1]	Fuelwood[2]
Total	**16,001**	**7,237**	**4,977**	**1,353**	**814**	**1,621**
Softwoods	10,107	5,218	2,865	1,183	444	397
Hardwoods	5,894	2,019	2,112	170	370	1,224
Growing stock[3]	13,750	6,793	4,352	1,285	728	592
Softwoods	9,167	4,962	2,528	1,124	396	156
Hardwoods	4,583	1,831	1,824	160	331	436
Other sources[4]	2,251	444	625	68	86	1,029
Softwoods	941	256	337	58	48	241
Hardwoods	1,310	187	288	9	38	788

[1] Includes such items as cooperage, pilings, poles, posts, shakes, shingles, board mills, charcoal, and export logs. [2] Downed and dead wood volume left on the ground after trees have been cut on timberland. [3] Includes live trees of commercial species meeting specified standards of quality or vigor. Cull trees are excluded. Includes only trees 5.0-inches in diameter or larger at 4 1/2 feet above the ground. [4] Includes salvable dead trees, rough and rotten trees, trees of noncommercial species, trees less than 5.0-inches in diameter at 4 1/2 feet above the ground, tops, and roundwood harvested from nonforest land (for example, fence rows).

Source: U.S. Department of Agriculture, National Agricultural Statistics Service, *Agricultural Statistics, 2005*. See also <http://www.nass.usda.gov/Publications/Ag_Statistics/index.asp>.

Table 858. Timber Products—Production, Foreign Trade, and Consumption by Type of Product: 1990 to 2005

[In millions of cubic feet, roundwood equivalent (15,577 represents 15,577,000,000)]

Type of product	1990	1995	1997	1998	1999	2000	2001	2002	2003	2004	2005
Industrial roundwood:											
Domestic production	15,577	15,537	15,703	15,620	15,632	15,436	14,634	14,902	14,571	15,139	14,142
Softwoods	10,968	10,191	10,180	10,097	10,381	10,201	9,859	10,124	10,290	10,710	10,376
Hardwoods	4,609	5,347	5,523	5,523	5,251	5,235	4,775	4,778	4,282	4,428	3,766
Imports	3,091	3,907	4,008	4,157	4,370	4,529	4,605	4,505	5,096	5,805	5,417
Exports	2,307	2,282	2,290	1,951	1,964	1,996	1,759	1,769	1,535	1,604	1,450
Consumption	16,361	17,161	17,421	17,827	18,038	17,969	17,481	17,637	18,132	19,339	18,110
Softwoods	11,779	11,961	12,072	12,339	12,754	12,659	12,552	12,790	13,398	14,357	13,828
Hardwoods	4,582	5,200	5,349	5,488	5,284	5,310	4,929	4,847	4,734	4,983	4,282
Lumber:											
Domestic production . . .	7,317	6,815	7,103	7,093	7,379	7,199	6,820	7,060	7,131	7,510	7,633
Imports	1,909	2,522	2,619	2,721	2,807	2,845	2,903	3,036	3,193	3,704	3,582
Exports	589	460	452	350	404	428	354	353	347	348	353
Consumption	8,637	8,877	9,270	9,463	9,782	9,616	9,369	9,744	9,977	10,866	10,862
Plywood and veneer:											
Domestic production . . .	1,423	1,303	1,213	1,201	1,208	1,187	1,067	1,074	1,054	1,086	1,089
Imports	97	107	114	131	160	155	173	205	240	354	356
Exports	109	89	103	55	45	42	32	31	35	43	38
Consumption	1,410	1,321	1,224	1,277	1,323	1,300	1,208	1,249	1,259	1,397	1,407
Pulp products:											
Domestic production . . .	5,313	6,079	6,097	6,114	5,813	5,881	5,691	5,708	5,557	5,692	4,591
Imports	1,038	1,248	1,249	1,269	1,355	1,459	1,458	1,180	1,579	1,669	1,356
Exports	646	905	929	818	768	842	801	810	643	680	547
Consumption	5,704	6,422	6,417	6,565	6,400	6,498	6,348	6,078	6,493	6,680	5,400
Logs:											
Imports	4	13	20	30	47	68	70	81	80	73	114
Exports	674	451	384	316	326	331	307	309	356	366	345
Pulpwood chips, exports	288	377	422	412	422	353	265	265	155	168	166
Fuelwood consumption	3,019	2,937	2,542	2,523	2,542	2,561	2,571	2,581	1,515	1,540	2,611

Source: U.S. Forest Service, *U.S. Timber Production, Trade, Consumption, and Price Statistics, 1965–1999*, Research Paper FPL-RP-595; and unpublished data. See also <http://www.fpl.fs.fed.us/documnts/fplrp/fplrp595.pdf>.

Table 859. **Selected Timber Products—Imports and Exports: 1990 to 2005**

[In million board feet (13,063 represents 13,063,000,000) except as indicated]

Product	Unit	1990	1995	1999	2000	2001	2002	2003	2004	2005
IMPORTS [1]										
Lumber, total [2]	Mil. bd. ft. . .	13,063	17,524	19,576	19,906	20,443	21,434	21,981	25,493	25,738
From Canada	Percent. . . .	91.3	97.1	93.0	92.0	93.0	90.4	90.0	83.3	85.3
Logs, total	Mil. bd. ft.[3] . .	23	80	294	435	452	525	497	454	710
From Canada	Percent. . . .	84	70	95	96	97	97	98	97	90
Paper and board [4]	1,000 tons . .	12,195	14,292	16,917	17,555	18,513	19,433	20,034	21,146	20,534
Woodpulp	1,000 tons . .	4,893	5,969	6,660	7,227	7,348	7,247	6,691	6,726	6,683
Plywood	Mil. sq. ft.[5] . .	1,687	1,951	2,987	2,917	3,246	3,868	4,489	5,896	8,975
EXPORTS										
Lumber, total [2]	Mil. bd. ft. . .	4,623	2,958	2,549	2,700	2,190	2,186	2,193	3,842	2,682
To: Canada	Percent. . . .	14	22	26	26	26	27	29	12	27
Japan	Percent. . . .	28	33	14	12	10	7	7	11	3
Europe	Percent. . . .	15	17	21	19	18	16	16	9	13
Logs, total	Mil. bd. ft.[3] . .	4,213	2,820	2,038	2,068	1,918	1,934	2,224	2,287	2,157
To: Canada	Percent. . . .	9	25	39	41	46	50	54	49	49
Japan	Percent. . . .	62	61	49	45	39	34	29	28	27
China	Percent. . . .	9	1	–	–	1	2	2	3	4
Paper and board [4] . . .	1,000 tons . .	5,163	7,621	9,477	10,003	11,504	11,564	11,868	12,566	13,480
Woodpulp	1,000 tons . .	5,905	8,261	5,936	6,409	6,167	6,254	5,847	6,225	6,391
Plywood	Mil. sq. ft.[5] . .	1,766	1,517	797	754	580	563	640	783	482

– Represents zero.   [1] Customs value of imports; see text, Section 28.   [2] Includes railroad ties.   [3] Log scale.   [4] Includes paper and board products. Excludes hardboard.   [5] 3/8 inch basis.

Source: U.S. Forest Service, *U.S. Timber Production, Trade, Consumption, and Price Statistics, 1965–1999*, Research Paper FPL-RP-595; and unpublished data. See also <http://www.fpl.fs.fed.us/documnts/fplrp/fplrp595.pdf>.

Table 860. **Pulpwood Consumption, Woodpulp Production, and Paper and Board Production and Consumption: 1994 to 2002**

Item	Unit	1994	1995	1996	1997	1998	1999	2000	2001	2002
Pulpwood consumption [1] . .	1,000 cords [2] .	98,142	97,052	90,190	95,247	96,305	94,265	95,904	92,181	90,500
Woodpulp production [3] . . .	1,000 tons . . .	65,920	67,103	65,503	66,650	65,163	62,914	62,758	58,198	58,069
Paper and board [4]:										
Production	1,000 tons . . .	89,080	89,509	90,381	95,029	94,510	97,020	94,491	88,913	89,636
Consumption or										
new supply	1,000 tons . . .	95,195	96,126	94,287	99,175	100,978	104,873	103,147	97,303	97,227
Per capita	Pounds	730	731	710	740	747	768	731	683	676

[1] Revised to match data from American Forest and Paper Association and American Pulpwood Association.   [2] One cord equals 128 cubic feet.   [3] Includes changes in stocks.   [4] Excludes defibrated and exploded woodpulp used for hard pressed board.

Source: U.S. Department of Agriculture, National Agricultural Statistics Service, *Agricultural Statistics, 2005*. See also <http://www.nass.usda.gov/Publications/Ag_Statistics/index.asp>.

Table 861. **Paper and Paperboard—Production and New Supply: 1990 to 2004**

[In millions of short tons (80.45 represents 80,450,000]

Item	1990	1995	1998	1999	2000	2001	2002	2003	2004
Production, total.	**80.45**	**91.33**	**96.40**	**98.65**	**96.05**	**90.38**	**91.11**	**89.81**	**93.41**
Paper, total	39.36	42.87	44.76	45.98	45.52	42.10	41.56	40.37	41.82
Paperboard, total	39.32	46.64	49.83	51.04	48.97	46.81	48.13	48.02	50.09
Unbleached kraft	20.36	22.70	23.20	23.11	21.80	20.44	21.09	21.73	22.67
Semichemical	5.64	5.66	5.89	6.01	5.95	5.58	5.84	6.10	6.53
Bleached kraft.	4.40	5.30	5.49	5.71	5.44	5.30	5.30	5.36	5.65
Recycled	8.92	12.98	15.25	16.21	15.79	15.50	15.91	14.83	15.24
Wet machine board	0.15	0.15	0.10	0.06	0.06	0.05	0.05	0.05	0.05
Building paper	0.81	0.81	0.79	0.66	0.64	0.58	0.55	0.55	0.58
Insulating board	0.86	0.86	0.93	0.91	0.86	0.85	0.83	0.83	0.88
New supply, all grades,									
excluding products	**87.68**	**98.16**	**103.01**	**106.90**	**105.02**	**99.19**	**100.43**	**99.74**	**103.73**
Paper, total	49.49	52.77	55.13	57.30	57.13	53.23	53.52	53.20	54.87
Newsprint.	13.41	12.76	12.80	13.09	12.92	11.47	11.18	11.05	10.84
Printing/writing papers	25.46	29.55	31.38	32.53	32.99	30.38	30.94	31.01	32.67
Packaging and ind. conv. papers	4.72	4.24	4.29	4.71	4.27	4.31	4.20	3.96	4.14
Tissue	5.90	6.22	6.66	6.98	6.95	7.07	7.20	7.18	7.22
Paperboard, total	36.30	43.45	45.67	47.59	46.02	44.09	45.29	44.95	47.20
Construction and other.	1.90	1.95	2.20	2.00	1.88	1.80	1.62	1.59	1.66

Source: American Forest and Paper Association, Washington, DC, *Monthly Statistical Summary of Paper, Paperboard and Woodpulp.*

Table 862. **Lumber Consumption by Species Group and End Use: 1995 to 2005**

[In billion board feet (59.3 represents 59,300,000,000), except per capita in board feet. Per capita consumption based on estimated resident population as of **July 1**]

Item	1995	1996	1997	1998	1999	2000	2001	2002	2003	2004	2005
Consumption, total . . .	**59.3**	**62.2**	**63.0**	**65.1**	**68.3**	**66.1**	**64.6**	**67.5**	**67.0**	**73.1**	**75.8**
Per capita	225	234	235	241	250	240	227	235	230	249	255
SPECIES GROUP											
Softwoods.	47.6	50.2	50.9	52.1	54.5	54.0	53.7	56.4	56.5	62.0	64.4
Hardwoods	11.7	12.0	12.1	13.0	13.8	12.2	11.0	11.1	10.5	11.1	11.4
END USE											
New housing	15.9	19.0	19.2	20.6	22.1	20.6	20.1	23.4	24.0	26.1	28.6
Residential upkeep and improvements	14.3	17.7	15.1	14.7	15.1	16.4	17.0	17.8	18.3	20.0	20.6
New nonresidential construction [1]	5.8	4.6	7.5	7.8	7.6	5.1	5.6	4.5	4.4	4.4	4.3
Manufacturing	5.5	7.6	8.4	8.4	(NA)	(NA)	(NA)	(NA)	8.1	7.9	7.7
Shipping	8.5	6.3	6.9	7.2	7.4	7.7	8.1	8.0	7.5	7.8	7.6
Other [2]	9.3	(NA)	(NA)	(NA)	16.1	16.3	13.8	13.8	4.7	6.9	7.0

NA Not available.   [1] In addition to new construction, includes railroad ties laid as replacements in existing track and lumber used by railroads for railcar repair.   [2] Includes upkeep and improvement of nonresidential buildings and structures; made-at-home projects, such as furniture, boats, and picnic tables; made-on-the-job items such as advertising and display structures; and miscellaneous products and uses.

Source: U.S. Forest Service, *U.S. Timber Production, Trade, Consumption, and Price Statistics, 1965–1999*, Research Paper FPL-RP-595; and unpublished data. See also <http://www.fpl.fs.fed.us/documnts/fplrp/fplrp595.pdf>.

Table 863. **Selected Timber Products—Producer Price Indexes: 1990 to 2005**

[**1982 = 100.** For information about producer prices, see text, Section 14]

Product	1990	1995	1999	2000	2001	2002	2003	2004	2005
Lumber and wood products [1]	**129.7**	**178.1**	**183.6**	**178.2**	**174.4**	**173.3**	**177.4**	**195.6**	**196.4**
Lumber	124.6	173.4	188.2	178.8	171.6	170.6	174.3	203.6	198.5
Softwood lumber.	123.8	178.5	196.0	178.6	170.1	170.8	170.8	209.8	203.5
Hardwood lumber	131.0	167.0	177.3	185.9	181.3	178.3	188.8	199.3	196.5
Millwork [1]	130.4	163.8	174.7	176.4	179.2	179.8	181.8	191.9	197.2
General millwork.	132.0	165.4	175.6	178.0	181.8	183.3	185.4	193.1	196.1
Prefabricated structural members.	122.3	163.5	178.1	175.1	173.5	168.5	171.0	193.7	206.9
Plywood	114.2	165.3	176.4	157.6	154.3	151.7	167.0	198.5	187.0
Softwood plywood.	119.6	188.1	207.0	173.3	167.8	164.1	195.9	250.9	224.1
Hardwood plywood and related products.	102.7	122.2	128.6	130.2	130.4	131.5	129.0	134.4	138.0
Other wood products [1]	114.7	143.7	131.1	130.5	130.5	127.2	129.9	134.3	139.3
Boxes.	119.1	145.0	152.3	155.2	154.5	154.3	157.6	163.1	165.0
Pulp, paper, and allied products [1]	**141.2**	**172.2**	**174.1**	**183.7**	**184.8**	**185.9**	**190.0**	**195.7**	**202.5**
Pulp, paper, and prod, ex. bldg. paper [1]	132.9	163.4	147.9	161.4	157.7	155.3	157.1	162.1	169.7
Woodpulp	151.3	183.2	119.7	145.3	125.8	116.2	121.4	132.2	138.0
Wastepaper.	138.9	371.1	183.6	282.5	148.6	173.1	197.3	231.4	230.2
Paper [1]	128.8	159.0	141.8	149.8	150.6	144.7	146.1	149.4	159.5
Writing and printing papers	129.1	164.4	146.6	146.4	146.4	143.8	144.7	146.0	156.1
Newsprint.	119.6	161.8	(NA)	127.5	138.6	105.7	112.1	124.5	138.2
Paperboard	135.7	183.1	153.2	176.7	172.1	164.3	162.7	170.2	175.2
Converted paper and paperboard products [1] . .	135.2	157.0	153.5	162.7	164.5	163.8	165.3	168.3	176.1
Office supplies and accessories	121.4	134.9	129.5	133.8	136.9	135.7	137.4	137.6	143.1
Building paper & building board mill prods	112.2	144.9	141.6	138.8	129.3	129.3	159.9	192.4	184.8

NA Not available.   [1] Includes other products not shown separately.

Source: U.S. Bureau of Labor Statistics, *Producer Price Indexes*, monthly.

Table 864. **Selected Species—Stumpage Prices in Current and Constant (1996) Dollars: 2000 to 2005**

[**In dollars per 1,000 board feet.** Stumpage prices are based on sales of sawtimber from National Forests]

Species	Current dollars				Constant (1996) dollars [1]			
	2000	2003	2004	2005	2000	2003	2004	2005
Softwoods:								
Douglas fir [2]	433	193	93	321	397	140	64	204
Southern pine [3]	258	164	183	193	237	119	125	123
Sugar pine [4]	187	95	94	114	172	69	64	73
Ponderosa pine [4, 5]	155	111	65	103	142	81	44	66
Western hemlock [6]	46	86	63	70	42	62	43	45
Hardwoods:								
All eastern hardwoods [7]	341	284	427	415	313	206	292	264
Oak, white, red, and black [7]	258	304	291	329	237	221	199	210
Maple, sugar [8]	314	560	618	648	288	406	422	413

[1] Deflated by the producer price index, all commodities.   [2] Western Washington and western Oregon.   [3] Southern region.   [4] Pacific Southwest region (formerly California region).   [5] Includes Jeffrey pine.   [6] Pacific Northwest region.   [7] Eastern and Southern regions.   [8] Eastern region.

Source: U.S. Forest Service, *Timber Demand and Technology Assessment*, RWU-4851. Also in *Agricultural Statistics*, annual.

Table 865. **Fishery Products—Domestic Catch, Imports, and Disposition: 1990 to 2004**

[Live weight, in millions of pounds (16,349 represents 16,349,000,000). For data on commercial catch for selected countries, see Table 1344, Section 30]

Item	1990	1995	1998	1999	2000	2001	2002	2003	2004
Total................	16,349	16,484	16,897	17,378	17,338	18,115	19,028	19,850	20,373
For human food..............	12,662	13,584	14,175	14,462	14,738	15,303	16,007	17,187	17,622
For industrial use.............	3,687	2,900	2,722	2,916	2,599	2,812	3,021	2,663	2,751
Domestic catch	9,404	9,788	9,194	9,339	9,069	9,489	9,397	9,507	9,643
For human food...........	7,041	7,667	7,174	6,832	6,912	7,311	7,205	7,521	7,768
For industrial use...........	2,363	2,121	2,020	2,507	2,157	2,178	2,192	1,986	1,875
Imports [1]..................	6,945	6,696	7,703	8,039	8,269	8,626	9,631	10,343	10,730
For human food...........	5,621	5,917	7,001	7,630	7,827	7,992	8,802	9,666	9,854
For industrial use [2].......	1,324	779	702	409	442	634	829	677	876
Exports [1]..................	4,627	5,166	4,889	5,208	5,757	7,107	6,979	6,756	8,203
For human food...........	3,832	4,175	3,709	4,130	4,586	5,774	5,587	5,392	6,462
For industrial use [2].......	795	991	1,180	1,078	1,171	1,333	1,392	1,364	1,741
Disposition of domestic catch ..	9,404	9,788	9,194	9,339	9,069	9,489	9,397	9,507	9,643
Fresh and frozen.................	6,501	7,099	6,870	6,416	6,657	7,082	6,826	7,266	7,448
Canned......................	751	769	516	712	530	536	652	498	552
Cured	126	90	129	133	119	123	117	119	137
Reduced to meal, oil, etc.	2,026	1,830	1,679	2,078	1,763	1,748	1,802	1,624	1,506

[1] Excludes imports of edible fishery products consumed in Puerto Rico; includes landings of tuna caught by foreign vessels in American Samoa. [2] Fish meal and sea herring.

Source: U.S. National Oceanic and Atmospheric Administration, National Marine Fisheries Service, *Fisheries of the United States,* annual. See also <http://www.st.nmfs.gov/st1/fus/fus04/fus_2004.pdf> (released November 2005).

Table 866. **Fisheries—Quantity and Value of Domestic Catch: 1980 to 2004**

Year	Quantity (mil. lb. [1])			Value (mil. dol.)	Average price per lb. (cents)	Year	Quantity (mil. lb. [1])			Value (mil. dol.)	Average price per lb. (cents)
	Total	For human food	For industrial products [2]				Total	For human food	For industrial products [2]		
1980	6,482	3,654	2,828	2,237	34.5	1997	9,846	7,248	2,597	3,447	35.0
1985	6,258	3,294	2,964	2,326	37.2	1998	9,194	7,174	2,020	3,128	34.0
1990	9,404	7,041	2,363	3,522	37.5	1999	9,339	6,832	2,507	3,464	37.1
1992	9,637	7,618	2,019	3,678	38.2	2000	9,069	6,912	2,157	3,549	39.1
1993	[3]10,467	8,214	2,253	3,471	33.2	2001	9,489	7,311	2,178	3,218	34.0
1994	10,461	7,936	2,525	3,807	36.8	2002	9,397	7,205	2,192	3,092	32.9
1995	9,788	7,667	2,121	3,770	38.5	2003	9,507	7,521	1,986	3,347	35.2
1996	9,565	7,474	2,091	3,487	36.5	2004	9,643	7,768	1,875	3,652	37.9

[1] Live weight. [2] Meal, oil, fish solubles, homogenized condensed fish, shell products, bait, and animal food. [3] Represents record year.

Source: U.S. National Oceanic and Atmospheric Administration, National Marine Fisheries Service, *Fisheries of the United States,* annual. See also <http://www.st.nmfs.gov/st1/fus/fus04/fus_2004.pdf> (released November 2005).

Table 867. **Domestic Fish and Shellfish Catch and Value by Major Species Caught: 1990 to 2004**

Species	Quantity (1,000 lb.)				Value ($1,000)			
	1990	2000	2003	2004	1990	2000	2003	2004
Total	9,403,571	9,068,985	9,506,986	9,643,291	3,521,995	3,549,481	3,347,530	3,652,281
Fish, total [1].........	8,091,068	7,689,661	8,251,711	8,398,010	1,900,097	1,594,815	1,519,537	1,714,395
Cod: Atlantic	95,881	25,060	23,628	16,071	61,329	26,384	27,559	21,666
Pacific...........	526,396	530,505	567,544	586,661	91,384	142,330	159,619	147,981
Flounder...............	254,519	412,723	364,600	361,510	112,921	109,910	94,454	123,984
Halibut...............	70,454	75,190	79,515	79,189	96,700	143,826	172,191	176,912
Herring, sea; Atlantic.....	113,095	160,269	212,520	180,653	5,746	9,972	15,554	14,286
Herring, sea; Pacific	108,120	74,835	74,332	75,278	32,178	12,043	10,456	14,869
Menhaden...............	1,962,160	1,760,498	1,599,344	1,497,610	93,896	112,403	96,080	72,448
Pollock, Alaska...........	3,108,031	2,606,802	3,361,802	3,350,832	268,344	160,525	203,183	271,424
Salmon...............	733,146	628,638	674,120	737,935	612,367	270,213	200,892	272,730
Tuna	62,393	50,779	61,886	56,503	105,040	95,176	86,882	90,957
Whiting (Atlantic, silver)	44,500	26,855	19,066	18,684	11,281	11,370	9,330	9,873
Whiting (Pacific, hake)....	21,232	452,718	309,363	474,528	1,229	18,809	17,153	21,823
Shellfish, total [1]......	1,312,503	1,379,324	1,255,275	1,245,281	1,621,898	1,954,666	1,827,993	1,937,886
Clams...................	139,198	118,482	127,806	118,519	130,194	153,973	162,490	158,782
Crabs...................	499,416	299,006	332,069	314,428	483,387	405,006	480,844	447,978
Lobsters: American	61,017	83,180	73,657	75,328	154,677	301,300	292,146	315,361
Oysters..............	29,193	41,146	37,103	38,506	93,718	90,667	103,603	111,125
Scallops, sea...........	39,917	32,747	56,023	64,757	153,696	164,609	229,167	312,909
Shrimp...............	346,494	332,486	315,273	308,275	491,433	690,453	420,705	425,605
Squid, Pacific...........	36,082	259,508	100,709	88,532	2,636	27,077	25,433	19,536

[1] Includes other types of fish and shellfish, not shown separately.

Source: U.S. National Oceanic and Atmospheric Administration, National Marine Fisheries Service, *Fisheries of the United States,* annual. See also <http://www.st.nmfs.gov/st1/fus/fus04/fus_2004.pdf> (released November 2005).

Natural Resources **559**

Table 868. U.S. Private Aquaculture—Trout and Catfish Production and Value: 1990 to 2005

[67.8 represents 67,800,000. Data are for calendar year and foodsize fish (those over 12 inches long)]

Item	Unit	1990	1995	2000	2001	2002	2003	2004	2005
TROUT FOODSIZE									
Number sold..................	Millions ...	67.8	60.2	58.5	54.5	50.2	46.1	49.6	55.5
Total weight	Mil. lb.....	56.8	55.6	59.2	56.9	54.4	50.8	57.6	59.7
Total value of sales	Mil. dol....	64.6	60.8	63.7	64.4	58.5	52.9	59.4	62.6
Avg. price received by processors. . .	Dol./lb....	1.14	1.09	1.08	1.13	1.08	1.04	1.03	1.05
Percent sold to processors	Percent ...	58	68	70	68	69	68	73	66
CATFISH FOODSIZE									
Number sold..................	Millions ...	272.9	321.8	420.1	406.9	407.0	381.7	389.3	405.4
Total weight	Mil. lb.....	392.4	481.5	633.8	647.5	675.8	699.3	682.2	638.4
Total value of sales	Mil. dol....	305.1	378.1	468.8	410.7	380.0	397.1	450.9	449.9
Avg. price received by processors. . .	Cents/lb. . .	0.78	0.79	0.74	0.63	0.56	0.57	0.66	0.70
Fish sold to processors..........	Mil. lb.....	360.4	446.9	593.6	597.1	630.6	661.5	630.5	600.7
Avg. price paid by processors	Cents/lb. . .	75.8	78.6	75.1	64.7	56.8	58.1	69.7	72.5
Processor sales...............	Mil. lb.....	183.1	227.0	297.2	296.4	317.6	319.3	306.8	300.0
Avg. price received by processors. . .	Dol./lb....	224.1	240.3	236.0	226.0	207.0	205.0	223.0	229.0
Inventory (Jan. 1)	Mil. lb....	9.4	10.9	13.6	15.0	12.3	13.6	15.2	13.7

Source: U.S. Department of Agriculture, National Agricultural Statistics Service, *Trout Production*, released September; *Catfish Production*, released February; and *Catfish Processing*, released February. Also in *Agricultural Statistics*, annual.

Table 869. Supply of Selected Fishery Items: 1990 to 2004

[In millions of pounds (734 represents 734,000,000). Totals available for U.S. consumption are supply minus exports plus imports. Round weight is the complete or full weight as caught]

Species	Unit	1990	1995	1998	1999	2000	2001	2002	2003	2004
Shrimp...................	Heads-off weight...	734	832	1,002	1,084	1,172	1,312	1,430	1,608	1,669
Tuna, canned	Canned weight	856	875	912	1,020	980	796	922	982	874
Snow crab	Round weight....	37	42	254	216	122	171	172	198	168
Clams	Meat weight	152	144	119	125	133	139	144	143	131
Salmon, canned..........	Canned weight	148	147	83	123	95	81	135	111	98
American lobster	Round weight.....	95	94	110	122	124	125	135	128	125
Spiny lobster	Round weight.....	89	89	100	91	99	79	87	93	93
Scallops	Meat weight	74	62	58	64	78	76	91	94	94
Sardines, canned........	Canned weight	61	44	50	57	(NA)	(NA)	(NA)	(NA)	(NA)
Oysters	Meat weight	56	63	61	55	71	58	62	69	53
King crab	Round weight.....	19	21	62	52	41	38	47	47	52
Crab meat, canned.......	Canned weight	9	12	22	26	29	35	44	47	56

NA Not available.

Source: U.S. National Oceanic and Atmospheric Administration, National Marine Fisheries Service, *Fisheries of the United States*, annual. See also <http://www.st.nmfs.gov/st1/fus/fus04/fus_2004.pdf> (released November 2005).

Table 870. Canned, Fresh, and Frozen Fishery Products—Production and Value: 1990 to 2004

[In millions of pounds (1,178 represents 1,178,000,000). Fresh fishery products exclude Alaska and Hawaii. Canned fishery products data are for natural pack only]

Product	Production (mil. lb.)					Value (mil. dol.)				
	1990	1995	2000	2003	2004	1990	1995	2000	2003	2004
Canned, total [1]	1,178	1,927	1,747	1,295	1,106	1,562	1,887	1,626	1,239	1,099
Tuna	581	667	671	529	434	902	939	856	669	569
Salmon...............	196	244	171	188	199	366	419	288	242	251
Clam products..........	110	129	127	123	109	76	110	120	132	113
Sardines, Maine	13	14	(Z)	(NA)	(NA)	17	24	(Z)	(NA)	(NA)
Shrimp	1	1	2	1	1	3	7	11	5	5
Crabs................	1	(Z)	(Z)	(Z)	(Z)	4	(Z)	(Z)	(Z)	(Z)
Oysters [2]	1	(Z)	(Z)	(Z)	(Z)	1	(Z)	1	1	1
Fish fillets and steaks [3] ..	441	385	368	612	590	843	841	823	1,133	969
Cod.................	65	65	56	56	37	132	152	167	171	81
Flounder..............	54	35	27	21	20	154	86	71	62	66
Haddock..............	7	3	6	8	10	24	11	24	35	44
Ocean perch, Atlantic	1	(Z)	(Z)	1	1	1	1	1	3	3
Rockfish	33	25	11	5	4	53	38	25	12	9
Pollock, Atlantic	12	4	2	4	4	21	10	4	10	6
Pollock, Alaska	164	135	160	367	384	174	184	178	395	366
Other................	105	118	106	147	130	284	359	353	445	394

NA Not available. Z Less than 500,000 pounds or $500,000. [1] Includes other products, not shown separately. [2] Includes oyster specialties. [3] Fresh and frozen.

Source: U.S. National Oceanic and Atmospheric Administration, National Marine Fisheries Service, *Fisheries of the United States*, annual. See also <http://www.st.nmfs.gov/st1/fus/fus04/fus_2004.pdf> (released November 2005).

Table 871. Mineral Industries—Employment, Hours, and Earnings: 1990 to 2005

[In thousands (680 represents 680,000). Based on the Current Employment Statistics Program, see Appendix III]

Industry and item	Unit	1990	1995	2000	2001	2002	2003	2004	2005
All mining:									
All employees.	1,000. . .	680	558	520	533	512	503	523	561
Production workers	1,000. . .	469	391	383	398	378	364	384	418
Avg. weekly hours	Number .	46.1	46.8	45.5	45.5	43.9	44.4	45.4	46.4
Avg. weekly earnings . . .	Dollars. .	630	711	771	789	769	796	837	884
Coal mining:									
All employees.	1,000. . .	136	97	72	74	74	70	71	74
Production workers	1,000. . .	110	78	59	63	63	59	59	61
Avg. weekly hours	Number .	44.7	45.7	45.6	47.0	45.4	46.2	47.7	48.5
Avg. weekly earnings . . .	Dollars. .	822	929	945	957	934	963	1,029	1,071
Oil and gas extraction:									
All employees.	1,000. . .	190	152	125	124	122	120	123	126
Production workers	1,000. . .	84	73	67	68	68	67	70	72
Avg. weekly hours	Number .	44.4	43.6	41.3	41.3	39.5	41.1	43.5	44.3
Avg. weekly earnings . . .	Dollars. .	591	677	802	825	761	778	808	856
Metal mining:									
All employees.	1,000. . .	53	48	38	33	29	27	28	29
Production workers	1,000. . .	43	39	29	25	22	20	20	22
Avg. weekly hours	Number .	42.5	43.4	43.4	43.4	42.8	43.7	45.2	44.2
Avg. weekly earnings . . .	Dollars. .	646	788	871	866	878	957	1,035	1,001
Nonmetallic minerals, except fuels:									
All employees.	1,000. . .	113	108	115	111	107	106	107	109
Production workers	1,000. . .	85	81	87	83	80	78	81	83
Avg. weekly hours	Number .	45.0	46.3	46.1	46.3	45.2	45.1	44.6	45.8
Avg. weekly earnings . . .	Dollars. .	532	632	722	745	749	773	791	830

Source: U.S. Bureau of Labor Statistics, the Current Employment Statistics program Internet site <http://www.bls.gov/ces/home.htm>.

Table 872. Mine Safety: 1995 to 2004

[Reported injury rates per 200,000 employee hours]

Item	All mines			Coal			Metal and nonmetal		
	1995	2000	2004	1995	2000	2004	1995	2000	2004
Number of mines	13,859	14,413	14,478	2,946	2,124	2,011	10,913	12,289	12,467
Number of miners	361,647	348,548	329,008	132,111	108,098	108,734	229,536	240,450	220,274
Fatalities	100	85	55	47	38	28	53	47	27
Fatal injury rate	0.03	0.03	0.02	0.04	0.04	0.03	0.03	0.02	0.01
All injury rate	6.30	5.13	4.05	8.22	6.64	5.00	5.24	4.45	3.55
Small mines [1]	5,923	6,592	6,918	885	571	560	5,038	6,021	6,358
Coal production (mil. tons)	1,030	1,078	1,111	1,030	1,078	1,111	(X)	(X)	(X)
On-site inspection hours/mine	41.1	52.8	51.1	175.1	212.5	218.0	24.7	24.3	24.8
Hazard complaints	632	968	1,150	332	300	402	300	468	748
Citations and orders	123,147	120,053	120,849	82,121	58,305	64,484	41,026	61,748	56,365
S&S [2] citations and orders (percent). .	42	36	33	49	42	41	28	30	24
Amount assessed [3] (mil.dol.).	25.1	24.7	26.8	18.4	12.0	17.0	6.7	12.7	9.8

X Not applicable. [1] Five or fewer operator employees. [2] A violation that "significantly and substantially" contributes to the cause and effect of a coal or other mine safety or health hazard. [3] Government penalties or fines.

Source: U.S. Mine Safety and Health Administration, Office of Program Education and Outreach Services, "Mine Safety and Health At a Glance" (accessed 11 May 2006); <http://www.msha.gov/MSHAINFO/FactSheets/MSHAFCT10.HTM>.

Table 873. Mining and Primary Metal Production Indexes: 1990 to 2005

[Index 2002 = 100]

Industry group	NAICS code [1]	1990	1995	1999	2000	2001	2002	2003	2004	2005
Mining [2]	21	106.9	104.4	101.2	103.5	104.5	100.0	99.8	99.5	97.4
Oil and gas extraction [2]	211	107.3	104.0	100.4	101.0	102.0	100.0	98.8	96.7	92.3
Crude oil and natural gas	211111	109.2	104.8	100.6	100.9	102.2	100.0	99.5	96.7	92.3
Coal	2121	98.3	96.8	101.1	99.2	103.9	100.0	97.5	101.0	100.4
Metal ore mining	2122	112.1	122.6	120.7	120.2	109.2	100.0	94.3	94.0	100.2
Iron ore mining	21221	109.8	121.8	111.4	122.2	90.1	100.0	90.3	102.1	102.0
Gold ore and silver ore mining .	21222	99.6	106.6	115.1	118.8	112.7	100.0	92.8	82.9	87.4
Copper, nickel, lead, and zinc mining	21223	120.2	137.7	132.1	121.8	114.6	100.0	97.8	100.9	100.3
Oil and gas drilling.	213111	102.3	89.5	80.7	114.4	138.6	100.0	116.2	126.9	142.5
Primary metal manufacturing [2] . . .	331	95.4	104.5	113.2	109.5	99.1	100.0	97.6	103.4	100.7
Iron and steel products.	3311	94.7	105.2	111.6	110.5	99.9	100.0	99.0	108.4	101.8
Alumina and aluminum production and processing.	3313	101.0	96.6	109.9	102.0	91.0	100.0	95.2	100.1	99.3
Nonferrous metals (excludes aluminum) [2]	3314	107.9	119.3	117.4	107.7	97.9	100.0	99.8	101.4	100.4
Copper.	33142	142.4	263.0	209.5	133.8	112.1	100.0	90.0	89.9	87.1

[1] Based on the 2002 North American Industry Classification (NAICS) System. [2] Includes other industries not shown separately.

Source: Board of Governors of the Federal Reserve System, Statistical Supplement to the *Federal Reserve Bulletin*, monthly; and *Industrial Production and Capacity Utilization*, Statistical Release G.17, monthly.

Natural Resources   561

Table 874. **Mineral Production: 1990 to 2005**

[**In millions of short tons (1,029.1 represents 1,029,100,000).** Data represent production as measured by mine shipments, mine sales, or marketable production]

Minerals and Metals	Unit	1990	1995	2000	2004	2005, est.
FUEL MINERALS						
Coal, total	Mil. sh. tons	1,029.1	1,033.0	1,073.6	1,111.5	1,133.3
Bituminous	Mil. sh. tons	693.2	613.8	574.3	546.6	(NA)
Subbituminous	Mil. sh. tons	244.3	328.0	409.2	479.6	(NA)
Lignite	Mil. sh. tons	88.1	86.5	85.6	83.5	(NA)
Anthracite	Mil. sh. tons	3.5	4.7	4.6	1.7	(NA)
Natural gas (marketed production)	Tril. cu. ft.	18.59	19.51	20.20	19.64	19.11
Petroleum (crude)	Mil. bbl. [1]	2,685	2,394	2,131	1,988	1,869
Uranium (recoverable content)	Mil. lb.	8.9	6.0	4.0	2.3	(NA)
NONFUEL MINERALS						
Asbestos (sales)	1,000 metric tons . .	(D)	9	5	–	–
Barite, primary, sold/used by producers . .	1,000 metric tons . .	430	543	392	532	500
Boron minerals, sold or used by producers	1,000 metric tons . .	1,090	1,190	1,070	1,210	1,230
Bromine, sold or used by producers	1,000 metric tons . .	177	218	228	222	212
Cement:						
Portland	Mil. metric tons	67	73	84	92	94
Masonry	Mil. metric tons	3	4	4	5	5
Clays	1,000 metric tons . .	42,900	43,000	40,800	41,200	41,900
Diatomite	1,000 metric tons . .	631	722	677	620	635
Feldspar [2]	1,000 metric tons . .	630	880	790	770	760
Fluorspar, finished shipments	1,000 metric tons . .	64	51	–	–	–
Garnet (industrial)	1,000 metric tons . .	47	46	60	28	28
Gypsum, crude	Mil. metric tons	15	17	20	17	18
Helium [3]	Mil. cu. meters	85	101	98	86	84
Lime, sold or used by producers	Mil. metric tons	16	19	20	20	20
Mica, scrap & flake, sold/used by producers	1,000 metric tons . .	109	108	101	99	78
Peat, sales by producers	1,000 metric tons . .	721	660	847	741	827
Perlite, processed, sold or used	1,000 metric tons . .	576	700	672	508	506
Phosphate rock (marketable)	Mil. metric tons	46	44	39	36	38
Potash (K_2O equivalent) sales	1,000 metric tons . .	1,710	1,480	1,300	1,300	1,200
Pumice & pumicite, producer sales	1,000 metric tons . .	443	529	1,050	1,490	1,360
Salt, common, sold/used by producers . .	Mil. metric tons	37	41	46	47	46
Sand & gravel, sold/used by producer . .	Mil. metric tons	855	935	1,148	1,270	1,291
Construction	Mil. metric tons	829	907	1,120	1,240	1,260
Industrial	Mil. metric tons	26	28	28	30	31
Sodium carbonate (natural) (soda ash) .	1,000 metric tons . .	9,100	10,100	10,200	11,000	11,100
Sodium sulfate (natural)	1,000 metric tons . .	349	327	(NA)	467	480
Stone [4]	Mil. metric tons	1,110	2,420	2,810	3,050	3,110
Crushed and broken	Mil. metric tons	1,110	1,260	1,560	1,590	1,650
Dimension [5]	1,000 metric tons . .	1,120	1,160	1,250	1,460	1,460
Sulfur: Total shipments	1,000 metric tons . .	11,500	12,100	10,700	10,100	9,400
Sulfur: Frasch mines (shipments)	1,000 metric tons . .	3,680	3,150	900	–	–
Talc, and pyrophyllite, crude	1,000 metric tons . .	1,270	1,060	851	833	856
Vermiculite concentrate	1,000 metric tons . .	209	171	150	(NA)	(NA)
METALS						
Antimony ore and concentrate	Metric tons	(D)	262	(D)	–	–
Aluminum	1,000 metric tons . .	4,048	3,375	3,668	2,516	2,500
Bauxite (dried)	1,000 metric tons . .	(D)	(D)	(NA)	(NA)	(NA)
Copper (recoverable content)	1,000 metric tons . .	1,590	1,850	1,450	1,160	1,140
Gold (recoverable content)	Metric tons	294	317	353	258	250
Iron ore (gross weight) [6]	Mil. metric tons	57	61	61	56	52
Lead (recoverable content)	1,000 metric tons . .	484	386	449	430	427
Magnesium metal	1,000 metric tons . .	139	142	(D)	(D)	(D)
Manganiferous ore (gross weight) [7]	1,000 metric ton . . .	(D)	(D)	–	(NA)	(NA)
Mercury [8]	Metric tons	(NA)	(D)	(NA)	(NA)	(NA)
Molybdenum (concentrate)	1,000 metric tons . .	62	61	41	42	58
Nickel	1,000 metric tons . .	(Z)	2	–	–	–
Palladium metal	Kilograms	5,930	5,260	10,300	13,700	14,200
Platinum metal	Kilograms	1,810	1,590	4,390	4,040	4,200
Silicon (silicon content)	1,000 metric tons . .	418	396	367	275	276
Silver (recoverable content)	Metric tons	2,120	1,560	1,860	1,250	1,300
Titanium concentrate: Ilmenite (gross weight)	1,000 metric tons . .	(D)	(D)	300	300	300
Tungsten ore and concentrate [9]	Metric tons	(D)	–	–	–	–
Zinc (recoverable content)	1,000 metric tons . .	515	603	805	715	719

– Represents zero.   D Withheld to avoid disclosing individual company data.   NA Not available.   Z Less than half of the unit of measure.   [1] 42 gal. bbl.   [2] Beginning 1995, includes aplite.   [3] Refined.   [4] Excludes abrasive stone, bituminous limestone and sandstone, and ground soapstone, all included elsewhere in table.   Includes calcareous marl and slate.   [5] Includes Puerto Rico.   [6] Represents shipments; includes by-product ores.   [7] 5- to 35-percent manganiferous ore.   [8] Covers mercury recovered as a by-product of gold ores only.   [9] Content of ore and concentrate.

Source: Nonfuels, through 1995, U.S. Bureau of Mines, thereafter, U.S. Geological Survey, *Minerals Yearbook* and *Mineral Commodities Summaries*, annual; fuels, U.S. Energy Information Administration, *Annual Energy Review*, 2004; most recent year from *Monthly Energy Review* and *Quarterly Coal Report.*

562   Natural Resources

Table 875. Nonfuel Mineral Commodities—Summary: 2005

[In thousands of metric tons (2,500 represents 2,500,000) except as indicated. Preliminary estimates. Average price in dollars per metric tons except as noted]

Mineral	Unit	Mineral disposition				Average price per unit (dollars)	Employment (number)
		Production	Exports	Net import reliance [1] (percent)	Consumption, apparent		
Aluminum	1,000 metric tons.	2,500	2,300	47	6,800	[2]0.91	56,000
Antimony (contained)	Metric tons	[3]6,110	3,200	82	34,100	[2]1.45	10
Asbestos	1,000 metric tons.	–	2	100	3	255.00	–
Barite	1,000 metric tons.	500	90	82	2,790	[4]35.60	340
Bauxite and alumina	1,000 metric tons.	(NA)	642	100	2,800	[4]25.00	(NA)
Beryllium (contained)	Metric tons	90	210	[5]	70	(NA)	(NA)
Bismuth (contained)	Metric tons	–	100	95	(NA)	[2]3.83	(NA)
Boron (B_2O_3 content)	1,000 metric tons.	562	192	[5]	(NA)	[4,6]400–425	1,300
Bromine (contained)	1,000 metric tons.	212	9	[5]	509	[7,8]81.00	1,200
Cadmium (contained)	Metric tons	[3]550	686	[5]	224	[2,9]1.50	(NA)
Cement	1,000 metric tons.	99,800	425	23	129,800	[4]90.00	18,100
Chromium	1,000 metric tons.	[10]170	40	69	550	(NA)	(NA)
Clays	1,000 metric tons.	41,900	5,340	[5]	36,900	(NA)	670
Cobalt (contained)	Metric tons	[10]2,400	2,700	78	11,000	[2]15.80	(NA)
Columbium (contained)	Metric tons	–	300	100	11,000	[2,11](NA)	(NA)
Copper (Mine, contained)	1,000 metric tons.	1,140	825	43	2,400	(NA)	7.4
Diamond (industrial)	Million carats	257	95	43	454	[12]1.00	(NA)
Diatomite	1,000 metric tons.	653	142	[5]	515	[4]268.00	1,000
Feldspar	1,000 metric tons.	760	12	2	773	[4]58.00	400
Fluorspar	1,000 metric tons.	–	36	100	616	(NA)	–
Garnet (industrial)	Metric tons	28,400	13,300	40	50,300	[4]50–2,000	160
Gemstones	Million dollars	58	8,580	99	8,380	(NA)	1,200
Germanium (contained)	Kilograms	4,500	26,500	(NA)	(NA)	610.00	65
Gold (contained)	Metric tons	250	315	8	(NA)	[13]446.00	7,600
Graphite (crude)	1,000 metric tons.	–	23	100	37	[4,14]578.00	(NA)
Gypsum (crude)	1,000 metric tons.	18,000	150	29	37,900	[4]7.31	5,900
Iodine	Metric tons	1,240	979	82	7,080	[7,15]16.11	30
Iron ore (usable)	Million metric tons	55	12	2	54	[4,16]39.88	4,400
Iron and steel scrap (metal)	Million metric tons	76	14	[5]	54	[4,17]90.00	30,000
Iron and steel slag (metal)	1,000 metric tons.	21,000	–	8	21,000	[4]15.50	2,600
Lead (contained)	1,000 metric tons.	427	390	[5]	1,510	[2]0.61	2,720
Lime	1,000 metric tons.	20,000	133	1	20,200	75.00	5,300
Magnesium compounds	1,000 metric tons.	300	52	55	660	(NA)	370
Magnesium metal	1,000 metric tons.	(D)	10	68	110	[2]1.46	400
Manganese (gross weight)	1,000 metric tons.	–	12	100	760	[18]4.71	(NA)
Mercury	Metric tons	[10](NA)	300	(NA)	(NA)	[19]750.00	(NA)
Mica, scrap and flake	1,000 metric tons.	78	9	27	106	[4]247.00	(NA)
Molybdenum (contained)	Metric tons	58,000	45,900	[5]	35,300	[7]70.67	568
Nickel (contained)	Metric tons	–	63,200	[20]52	134,000	[21]14,738.00	–
Nitrogen (fixed)-ammonia	1,000 metric tons.	8,040	525	43	14,100	[4,22]314.00	1,300
Peat	1,000 metric tons.	690	30	55	1,540	[4]29.00	700
Perlite	1,000 metric tons.	506	37	24	665	[4]42.08	131
Phosphate rock	1,000 metric tons.	38,300	–	7	(NA)	[4]27.89	2,900
Platinum-group metals	Kilograms	18,400	47,000	91	(NA)	[13,23](NA)	1,600
Potash (K_2O equivalent)	1,000 metric tons.	1,200	200	80	6,100	[4,24]270.00	1,130
Pumice and pumicite	1,000 metric tons.	1,268	21	[5]	1,490	[4]31.00	100
Salt	1,000 metric tons.	45,900	1,000	21	53,600	[4,25]130.00	4,100
Silicon (contained)	1,000 metric tons.	276	23	52	577	[4,26]56.00	(NA)
Silver (contained)	Metric tons	1,200	390	57	7,700	[13]7.15	900
Sodium carbonate (soda ash)	1,000 metric tons.	11,100	4,600	[5]	6,500	[27]155.00	2,500
Sodium sulfate	1,000 metric tons.	480	140	[5]	385	[28]134.00	225
Stone (crushed)	Million metric tons	1,650	1	[5]	1,660	[4]6.17	79,700
Sulfur (all forms)	1,000 metric tons.	9,460	791	23	12,300	[4,29]35.00	2,700
Talc	1,000 metric tons.	856	198	4	895	[4]29.00	470
Thallium (contained)	Kilograms	–	263	100	(NA)	[7]1,900.00	(NA)
Tin (contained)	Metric tons	[10]5,000	4,600	93	65,800	[2]3.69	–
Titanium dioxide	1,000 metric tons.	1,420	524	[5]	1,240	[2,30]0.98	4,300
Tungsten (contained)	Metric tons	[10]4,600	6,140	70	11,600	[31]140.00	(NA)
Vermiculite	1,000 metric tons.	105	10	35	165	[4]125.00	100
Zinc (contained)	Metric tons	719	901	52	1,370	[2]0.67	1,200
Zirconium (ZrO_2) content	Metric tons	(D)	65,600	52	(D)	[4,32]415.00	(NA)

– Represents or rounds to zero. D Withheld to avoid disclosure. NA Not available. [1] Calculated as a percent of apparent consumption. [2] Dollars per pound. [3] Refinery production. [4] Dollars per metric ton. [5] Net exporter. [6] Granulated pentahydrate borax in bulk, f.o.b. mine. [7] Dollars per kilogram. [8] Bulk, purified bromine. [9] 1- to 5-short ton lots. [10] Secondary production. [11] Columbite price. [12] Value of imports, dollars per carat. [13] Dollars per troy ounce. [14] Price of flake imports. [15] C.i.f. value, crude, per kilogram. [16] Price of eastern Canadian ore. [17] Delivered, No. 1 Heavy Melting composite price. [18] 46%–48% Mn metallurgical ore, per unit contained Mn, c.i.f. U.S. ports. [19] Dollars per 76-pound flask. [20] Exports include both primary and secondary materials. [21] London Metal Exchange cash price. [22] F.o.b. gulf coast. [23] Dealer price of platinum. [24] Price of K_2O, muriate. [25] Vacuum and open pan, bulk, pellets and packaged, f.o.b. mine and plant. [26] Ferrosilicon, 50% Si. [27] Quoted year-end price, dense, bulk, f.o.b. Green River, WY, dollars per short ton. [28] Quoted price, bulk, f.o.b. works, East, dollars per short ton. [29] Elemental sulfur, f.o.b. mine and/or plant. [30] Rutile, list, year-end. [31] Dollars per metric ton unit WO_3 (7.93 kilograms of contained tungsten per metric ton unit). [32] Price for imported zircon, f.o.b. U.S. east coast.

Source: U.S. Geological Survey, *Mineral Commodity Summaries*, annual. See also <http://minerals.er.usgs.gov/minerals/pubs/mcs /2006/mcs2006.pdf> (released 13 January 2006).

Table 876. Selected Mineral Products—Average Prices: 1990 to 2005

[Excludes Alaska and Hawaii, except as noted]

	Nonfuels								Fuels		
Year	Copper, cathode (cents per lb.)	Platinum[1] (dol./ troy oz.)	Gold (dol./ fine oz.)	Silver (dol./ fine oz.)	Lead (cents per lb.)	Tin (New York) (cents per lb.)	Zinc (cents per lb.)	Sulfur, crude[2] (dol./ metric ton)	Bituminous coal[3,4] (dol./ short ton)	Crude petroleum[3] (dol./ bbl.)	Natural gas[3] (dol./ 1,000 cu. ft.)
1990	123	467	385	4.82	46	386	75	80.14	27.43	20.03	1.71
1992	107	356	345	3.94	35	402	58	48.14	26.78	15.99	1.74
1993	92	370	361	4.30	32	350	46	31.86	26.15	14.25	2.04
1994	111	411	385	5.29	37	369	49	30.08	25.68	13.19	1.85
1995	138	425	386	5.15	42	416	56	44.46	25.56	14.62	1.55
1996	109	398	389	5.19	49	412	51	34.11	25.17	18.46	2.17
1997	107	397	332	4.89	47	381	65	36.06	24.64	17.23	2.32
1998	79	375	295	5.54	45	373	51	29.14	24.87	10.87	1.96
1999	76	379	280	5.25	44	366	53	37.81	23.92	15.56	2.19
2000	88	549	280	5.00	44	370	56	24.73	24.15	26.72	3.68
2001	77	533	272	4.39	44	315	44	10.01	25.36	21.84	4.00
2002	76	543	311	4.62	44	292	39	11.84	26.57	22.51	2.95
2003	85	694	365	4.91	44	340	41	28.71	26.73	27.56	4.88
2004	134	849	411	6.69	55	555	52	32.50	30.47	36.77	5.49
2005	173	900	446	7.34	61	534	67	35.00	(NA)	50.26	7.51

NA Not available. [1] Average annual dealer prices. [2] F.o.b. (Free on Board) works. [3] Average value at the point of production or domestic first purchase price. [4] Includes lignite.

Source: Nonfuels, through 1994, U.S. Bureau of Mines, thereafter, U.S. Geological Survey, *Minerals Yearbook* and *Mineral Commodities Summaries,* annual; fuels, U.S. Energy Information Administration, *Annual Energy Review* and most recent year from *Monthly Energy Review.*

Table 877. Value of Domestic Nonfuel Mineral Production by State: 2000 to 2005

[In millions of dollars (39,400 represents $39,400,000,000), except as indicated. For similar data on fuels, see table 882]

State	2000	2004	2005	State	2000	2004	2005
United States .	[1]39,400	45,700	51,600	Montana	596	624	866
Alabama	930	972	1,010	Nebraska	[2]84	106	116
Alaska	1,140	1,270	1,370	Nevada	2,980	3,470	3,640
Arizona	2,510	3,330	4,730	New Hampshire	[2]57	71	75
Arkansas	484	518	523	New Jersey	[2]291	341	365
California	3,270	3,760	3,530	New Mexico	786	866	1,120
Colorado	592	1,010	1,770	New York	1,020	1,110	1,080
Connecticut	[2]112	131	140	North Carolina	744	805	846
Delaware	[2]14	22	22	North Dakota	35	45	51
Florida	1,820	2,320	2,590	Ohio	999	1,120	1,080
Georgia	1,620	1,800	1,790	Oklahoma	473	507	555
Hawaii	[2]92	71	71	Oregon	299	367	398
Idaho.	358	446	893	Pennsylvania	[2]1,250	1,410	1,410
Illinois	913	1,050	1,140	Rhode Island	[2]20	34	37
Indiana	695	772	789	South Carolina	[2]551	532	580
Iowa	503	529	604	South Dakota	233	210	216
Kansas	629	754	822	Tennessee	737	653	696
Kentucky	501	648	645	Texas	1,950	2,290	2,610
Louisiana	325	366	356	Utah	1,430	1,950	2,870
Maine	96	118	124	Vermont	[2]67	85	88
Maryland	[2]358	481	507	Virginia	710	894	962
Massachusetts	[2]200	210	208	Washington	607	507	562
Michigan	1,640	1,670	1,690	West Virginia	[2]172	167	170
Minnesota	1,460	1,890	2,070	Wisconsin.	[2]372	470	472
Mississippi	149	194	202	Wyoming	978	1,040	1,200
Missouri	1,370	1,470	1,680				

[1] Includes undistributed not shown separately. [2] Partial data only; excludes values withheld to avoid disclosing individual company data.

Source: U.S. Geological Survey, *Minerals Yearbook,* annual, and *Mineral Commodities Summaries,* annual. See also <http://minerals.er.usgs.gov/minerals/pubs/mcs/2006/mcs2006.pdf> (released 13 January 2006).

U.S. Census Bureau, Statistical Abstract of the United States: 2007

Table 878. **Principal Fuels, Nonmetals, and Metals—World Production and the U.S. Share: 1990 to 2005**
[In millions of short tons (5,348 represents 5,348,000,000), except as indicated]

Mineral	Unit	World production 1990	1995	2000	2005	Percent U.S. of world 1990	1995	2000	2005
Fuels: [1]									
Coal	Mil. sh. ton	5,348	5,096	4,931	(NA)	19	20	22	(NA)
Petroleum (crude)	Bil. bbl	22.1	22.8	25.0	(NA)	12	11	9	(NA)
Natural gas (dry, marketable).	Tril. cu. ft	73.6	78.0	88.3	(NA)	24	24	22	(NA)
Natural gas plant liquids	Bil. bbl	1.7	2.1	2.4	(NA)	34	31	29	(NA)
Nonmetals:									
Asbestos	1,000 metric tons.	4,010	2,180	2,110	2,400	(D)	(Z)	(Z)	–
Barite	1,000 metric tons.	5,770	4,870	6,470	7,620	7	11	6	7
Feldspar	1,000 metric tons.	5,990	7,910	9,580	11,500	11	11	8	7
Fluorspar	1,000 metric tons.	5,120	4,170	4,470	5,080	1	1	(NA)	–
Gypsum.	Mil. metric tons .	104	98	106	110	15	17	19	16
Mica (incl. scrap).	1,000 metric tons.	217	328	328	290	51	43	31	27
Nitrogen, (fixed)—ammonia. .	Mil. metric tons .	98	100	108	115	13	13	11	7
Phosphate rock, gross wt.. . .	Mil. metric tons .	162	130	132	148	29	33	30	26
Potash (K₂O equivalent). . . .	Mil. metric tons .	28	25	27	31	6	6	4	4
Sulfur, elemental	Mil. metric tons .	58	54	58	64	20	22	19	15
Metals, mine basis:									
Bauxite	Mil. metric tons .	113	112	136	165	(D)	(D)	(NA)	NA
Columbian concentrates									
(Nb content)	1,000 metric tons.	12	18	33	34	–	–	–	–
Copper	1,000 metric tons.	8,950	10,100	13,200	14,900	18	18	11	8
Gold	Metric tons	2,180	2,230	2,590	2,450	14	14	14	10
Iron ore	Mil. metric tons .	983	1,030	1,070	1,520	6	6	6	4
Lead [2]	1,000 metric tons.	3,370	2,830	3,184	3,300	15	14	15	13
Mercury	Metric tons	4,523	3,160	1,350	1,100	12	(D)	(NA)	(D)
Molybdenum.	1,000 metric tons.	111	126	133	187	55	48	31	31
Nickel [2]	1,000 metric tons.	974	1,040	1,270	1,500	(Z)	(Z)	(Z)	–
Silver	1,000 metric tons.	16	15	18	20	13	10	11	6
Tantalum concentrates	Metric tons	344	356	1,040	1,910	–	–	–	–
Titanium concentrates:									
Ilmenite	1,000 metric tons.	4,070	4,010	5,010	4,800	(D)	(D)	7	6
Rutile.	1,000 metric tons.	481	416	387	360	(D)	(D)	(D)	(D)
Tungsten [2]	1,000 metric tons.	52	39	44	77	(D)	–	(NA)	–
Vanadium [2]	1,000 metric tons.	33	34	56	43	6	6	–	–
Zinc [2]	1,000 metric tons.	7,180	7,280	8,788	10,100	7	9	10	8
Metals, smelter basis:									
Aluminum.	1,000 metric tons.	19,300	19,700	24,400	31,200	21	17	15	8
Cadmium	1,000 metric tons.	20	20	20	19	8	7	10	3
Copper	1,000 metric tons.	9,472	10,400	11,000	13,300	15	15	9	4
Iron, pig.	Mil. metric tons .	551	536	573	747	9	10	8	4
Lead [3]	1,000 metric tons.	5,950	5,590	6,580	7,400	22	25	22	17
Magnesium [4]	1,000 metric tons.	354	395	428	610	39	36	(D)	(D)
Raw Steel	Mil. metric tons .	771	752	845	1,129	12	13	12	9
Tin [7]	1,000 metric tons.	220	189	271	280	–	–	2	–
Zinc	1,000 metric tons.	7,180	7,370	9,137	10,300	5	5	4	4

– Represents or rounds to zero.   D Withheld to avoid disclosing company data.   NA Not available.   Z Less than half the unit of measure.   [1] Source: Energy Information Administration, *International Energy Annual.*   [2] Content of ore and concentrate.   [3] Refinery production.   [4] Primary production; no smelter processing necessary.   [5] Production from primary sources only.

Source: Nonfuels, through 1990, U.S. Bureau of Mines; thereafter, U.S. Geological Survey, *Minerals Yearbook*, annual, and *Mineral Commodities Summaries*, annual; fuels, U.S. Energy Information Administration, *International Energy Annual*. See also <http://minerals.er.usgs.gov/minerals/pubs/mcs/2006/mcs2006.pdf> (published 13 January 2006).

Table 879. **Net U.S. Imports of Selected Minerals and Metals as Percent of Apparent Consumption: 1980 to 2005**
[In percent. Based on net imports which equal the difference between imports and exports plus or minus government stockpile and industry stock changes]

Minerals in rank of net imports	1980	1990	1995	2000	2001	2002	2003	2004	2005 [1]
Bauxite [2]	94	98	99	100	100	100	100	100	100
Columbium	100	100	100	100	100	100	100	100	100
Fluorspar	87	91	92	100	100	100	100	100	100
Manganese. . . .	98	100	100	100	100	100	100	100	100
Mica (sheet) . . .	100	100	100	100	100	100	100	100	100
Strontium	100	100	100	100	100	100	100	100	100
Vanadium	35	(D)	84	100	100	100	100	100	100
Tin.	79	71	84	88	86	88	89	88	93
Platinum.	87	78	(NA)	78	92	91	91	92	91
Tantalum	90	86	80	80	81	82	79	88	91
Barite.	44	71	65	84	86	78	77	79	82
Potash	65	68	75	80	80	80	80	70	80
Cobalt	93	84	79	78	76	72	79	77	78
Tungsten	53	81	90	66	64	69	63	73	70
Chromium.	67	80	75	77	60	61	67	70	69
Zinc.	60	64	71	72	73	75	72	73	64
Titanium	(NA)	(NA)	70	79	78	74	68	58	63
Silver	7	(NA)	(NA)	43	49	60	65	53	57
Nickel.	76	64	60	55	52	52	50	55	52
Iron and steel . .	25	13	21	18	16	15	10	14	15
Iron ore	25	21	14	10	26	10	12	6	2

D Withheld to avoid disclosure.   NA Not available.   [1] Preliminary.   [2] Includes alumina.
Source: Through 1994, U.S. Bureau of Mines; thereafter, U.S. Geological Survey, *Mineral Commodity Summaries and Minerals Yearbook*, annual and *Historical Statistics for Mineral and Material Commodities in the United States*; import and export data from U.S. Census Bureau.

Natural Resources   565

Table 880. **Petroleum Industry—Summary: 1980 to 2004**

[548 represents 548,000. Includes all costs incurred for drilling and equipping wells to point of completion as productive wells or abandonment after drilling becomes unproductive. Based on sample of operators of different size drilling establishments]

Item	Unit	1980	1990	1995	1999	2000	2001	2002	2003	2004
Crude oil producing wells (Dec. 31). . .	1,000	548	602	574	546	534	530	529	513	510
Daily output per well	Bbl.	15.7	12.2	11.4	10.8	10.9	10.9	10.9	11.1	10.7
Completed wells drilled, total	1,000	57.73	26.50	17.75	16.57	25.68	31.25	23.64	28.31	32.23
Crude oil	1,000	30.88	11.54	7.09	4.02	7.09	7.74	5.83	6.97	6.62
Gas	1,000	15.25	10.36	7.78	10.34	15.85	21.10	15.49	18.94	22.74
Dry.	1,000	11.60	4.60	2.88	2.22	2.74	2.42	2.33	2.40	2.88
Average depth per well [1]	Feet . . .	4,172	4,649	5,500	5,236	4,882	5,289	5,213	5,647	5,678
Average cost per well [1]	$1,000 . .	368	384	513	856	755	943	1,054	1,200	(NA)
Average cost per foot [1]	Dollars . .	77.02	76.07	87.22	142.52	142.16	181.94	195.31	216.27	(NA)
Crude oil production, total	Mil. bbl. . .	3,146	2,685	2,394	2,147	2,131	2,118	2,097	2,073	1,988
Value at wells	Bil. dol. . . .	67.93	53.77	35.00	33.40	56.93	46.25	47.21	57.14	73.08
Average price per barrel.	Dollars . .	21.59	20.03	14.62	15.56	26.72	21.84	22.51	27.56	36.77
Lower 48 states	Mil. bbl. . .	2,555	2,037	1,853	1,764	1,776	1,766	1,738	1,718	1,655
Alaska	Mil. bbl. . .	592	647	542	383	355	351	359	356	332
Onshore	Mil. bbl. . .	2,768	2,290	1,838	1,508	1,482	1,416	1,366	1,339	1,305
Offshore	Mil. bbl. . .	379	395	557	640	649	702	731	735	683
Imports: Crude oil.	Mil. bbl. . .	1,926	2,151	2,639	3,187	3,320	3,405	3,336	3,528	3,674
Refined petroleum products	Mil. bbl. . .	603	775	586	774	874	928	872	949	1,047
Exports: Crude oil.	Mil. bbl. . .	104.9	39.7	34.5	43.0	18.4	7.4	4.5	9.8	9.8
Proved reserves.	Bil. bbl. . .	29.8	26.3	22.4	21.8	22.0	22.4	22.7	21.9	21.4
Operable refineries	Number . . .	319	205	175	159	158	155	153	149	149
Capacity (Jan. 1)	Mil. bbl. . .	6,566	5,684	5,634	5,935	6,027	6,057	6,127	6,116	6,166
Refinery input, total	Mil. bbl. . .	5,133	5,325	5,555	5,878	5,964	5,979	5,955	6,027	6,130
Crude oil	Mil. bbl. . .	4,934	4,894	5,100	5,403	5,514	5,522	5,456	5,586	5,665
Natural gas plant liquids	Mil. bbl. . .	169	171	172	136	139	156	156	153	151
Other liquids	Mil. bbl. . .	30	260	283	338	311	301	344	289	314
Refinery output, total [2]	Mil. bbl. . .	5,352	5,574	5,838	6,201	6,311	6,309	6,305	6,383	6,505
Motor gasoline	Mil. bbl. . .	2,376	2,540	2,722	2,896	2,910	2,928	2,987	2,991	3,013
Jet fuel	Mil. bbl. . .	366	543	517	571	588	558	553	543	566
Distillate fuel oil.	Mil. bbl. . .	974	1,067	1,152	1,241	1,310	1,349	1,311	1,353	1,398
Residual fuel oil.	Mil. bbl. . .	578	347	288	255	255	263	219	241	238
Liquefied petroleum gases	Mil. bbl. . .	121	182	239	250	258	243	245	240	236
Utilization rate	Percent . . .	75.4	87.1	92.0	92.6	92.6	92.6	90.7	92.6	92.8

NA Not available.   [1] Source: American Petroleum Institute, *Joint Association Survey on Drilling Costs*, annual.   [2] Includes other products not shown separately.

Source: Except as noted, U.S. Energy Information Administration, *Annual Energy Review; Petroleum Supply Annual; U.S. Crude Oil, Natural Gas, and Natural Gas Liquids Reserves*; and *Monthly Energy Review*.

Table 881. **U.S. Petroleum Balance: 1980 to 2004**

[In millions of barrels (6,242 represents 6,242,000,000). Minus sign (–) indicates decrease]

Item	1980	1990	1995	1999	2000	2001	2002	2003	2004
Petroleum products supplied for domestic use	6,242	6,201	7,087	7,125	7,211	7,172	7,213	7,312	7,588
Production of products	5,765	5,934	6,940	6,774	6,903	6,942	6,925	6,979	7,198
Crude input to refineries	4,934	4,894	5,718	5,403	5,514	5,522	5,456	5,586	5,664
Oil, field production [1]	3,138	2,685	2,406	2,147	2,125	2,118	2,097	2,073	1,983
Alaska.	592	647	542	383	354	351	359	356	332
Lower 48 States	2,555	2,037	1,853	1,764	1,771	1,766	1,738	1,718	1,651
Net imports	1,821	2,112	2,604	3,144	3,301	3,398	3,333	3,523	3,682
Imports (gross excluding SPR) [2]	1,910	2,142	2,639	3,184	3,317	3,401	3,330	3,528	3,692
SPR [2] imports	16	10	–	3	3	4	6	–	–
Exports	–105	40	35	43	18	7	3	5	10
Other sources	33	98	102	113	82	7	26	–11	2
Natural gas liquids (NGL), supply	577	574	708	757	799	801	798	756	844
Other liquids	253	465	514	614	589	619	671	637	691
Net imports of refined products	484	326	101	252	305	303	249	312	392
Imports	578	598	407	537	648	636	581	660	742
Exports	94	272	307	284	343	333	332	348	350
Stock withdrawal, refined products	–7	–59	46	98	2	–73	39	21	–2
TYPE OF PRODUCT SUPPLIED									
Total products supplied for domestic use	6,242	6,201	6,469	7,125	7,211	7,172	7,213	7,312	7,588
Finished motor gasoline	2,407	2,641	2,843	3,077	3,101	3,143	3,229	3,261	3,333
Distillate fuel oil.	1,049	1,103	1,170	1,304	1,362	1,404	1,378	1,433	1,485
Residual fuel oil	918	449	311	303	333	296	255	282	316
Liquified petroleum gases [3]	414	568	693	801	816	746	789	757	780
Other	1,454	1,440	1,452	1,639	1,598	1,583	1,561	1,579	1,673
ENDING STOCKS									
Ending stocks, all oils	1,392	1,621	1,563	1,493	1,468	1,586	1,548	1,568	1,645
Crude oil and lease condensate	358	323	303	284	286	312	278	269	286
Strategic Petroleum Reserve (SPR) [1]	108	586	592	567	541	550	599	638	676
Other	926	712	668	641	641	724	671	661	683

– Represents zero.   [1] See footnote 2, Table 882.   [2] SPR = Strategic petroleum reserve.   [3] Includes ethane.

Source: U.S. Energy Information Administration, *Petroleum Supply Annual*, volume 1. See also <http://www.eia.doe.gov/pub /oil_gas/petroleum/data_publications/petroleum_supply_annual/psa_volume1/current/pdf/volume1_all.pdf> (released June 2005).

Figure 18.1
Crude Oil Production and Imports: 1990 to 2004

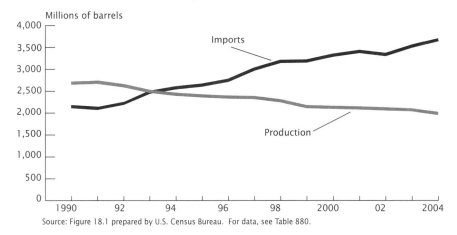

Source: Figure 18.1 prepared by U.S. Census Bureau. For data, see Table 880.

Figure 18.2
Natural Gas Marketed Production and Imports: 1990 to 2004

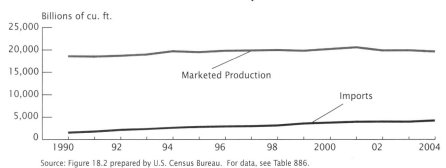

Source: Figure 18.2 prepared by U.S. Census Bureau. For data, see Table 886.

Figure 18.3
Coal Production and Imports: 1990 to 2004

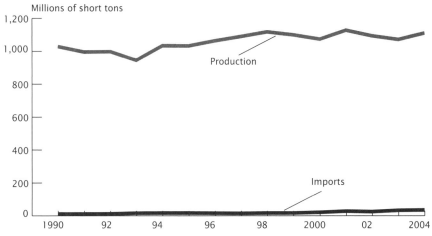

Source: Figure 18.3 prepared by U.S. Census Bureau. For data, see Table 890.

Natural Resources 567

Table 882. **Crude Petroleum and Natural Gas—Production and Value by Major Producing States: 2002 to 2004**

[2,097 represents 2,097,000,000 barrels]

State	Crude petroleum Quantity (mil. bbl.) 2002	2003	2004	Value (mil. dol.) 2002	2003	2004	Natural gas marketed production [1] Quantity (bil. cu. ft.) 2002	2003	2004	Value (mil. dol.) 2002	2003	2004
Total [2]	2,097	2,073	1,983	47,206	57,144	72,926	19,885	19,974	19,684	58,597	97,555	107,431
AL	9	8	7	202	228	289	356	346	316	1,238	2,051	2,103
AK	359	356	332	8,793	10,127	12,886	463	490	472	(NA)	1,179	1,612
AR	7	7	7	158	192	247	162	170	(NA)	(NA)	877	1,063
CA	258	250	240	5,643	6,608	8,280	360	337	320	1,052	1,698	1,808
CO	18	21	22	448	648	892	937	1,011	1,079	2,261	4,591	5,622
FL	4	3	3	(NA)	(NA)	(NA)	3	3	3	(NA)	(NA)	(NA)
IL	12	12	11	287	340	426	(Z)	(Z)	(NA)	(Z)	(Z)	(Z)
IN	2	2	2	46	53	67	1	1	(NA)	4	8	21
KS	33	34	34	773	974	1,327	455	419	397	1,187	1,815	1,961
KY	3	3	3	60	69	94	88	88	(NA)	(NA)	398	495
LA	93	90	83	2,322	2,750	3,376	1,362	1,350	1,357	4,363	7,614	8,095
MI	7	7	6	171	190	251	274	237	260	594	950	1,000
MS	18	17	17	398	456	635	113	134	146	(NA)	688	849
MT	17	19	25	384	554	953	86	86	97	206	321	437
NE	3	3	3	66	79	96	1	1	(NA)	2	5	5
NM	67	66	64	1,616	1,952	2,521	1,632	1,604	1,633	4,380	7,307	8,119
NY	(Z)	(Z)	(Z)	(NA)	(NA)	(NA)	37	36	(NA)	(NA)	209	321
ND	31	29	31	748	861	1,224	57	56	55	156	197	315
OH	6	6	6	136	159	221	103	94	(NA)	466	552	602
OK	67	65	63	1,632	1,942	2,497	1,582	1,558	1,663	4,657	7,737	9,187
PA	2	2	3	56	72	100	158	160	(NA)	(NA)	(NA)	(NA)
TX	412	406	393	9,793	11,821	15,239	5,141	5,244	5,067	16,258	27,171	29,561
UT	14	13	15	326	378	576	275	268	278	(NA)	1,103	1,458
WV	1	1	1	31	37	51	190	188	(NA)	(NA)	(NA)	(NA)
WY	55	52	52	1,202	1,396	1,812	1,454	1,539	1,592	(NA)	6,362	7,893
Federal offshore	(NA)	(NA)	(NA)	26,687	32,434	40,652	(NA)	(NA)	(NA)	(NA)	(NA)	(NA)
Lower 48 states	1,738	1,718	1,651	38,413	47,017	60,040	19,421	19,484	19,212	(NA)	(NA)	(NA)

NA Not available. Z Less than 500,000 barrels or 500 million cubic feet. [1] Excludes nonhydrocarbon gases. [2] Includes other states not shown separately. State production does not include state offshore production. U.S. level totals shown in Tables 880 and 886 may contain revisions not carried to state level.

Source: U.S. Energy Information Administration, *Petroleum Supply Annual*, Vol. 2, and *Petroleum Marketing Annual*; and *Natural Gas Annual*, and *Natural Gas Monthly*.

Table 883. **Crude Oil, Natural Gas, and Natural Gas Liquids—Reserves by State: 2002 to 2004**

[22,677 mil. bbl. represents 22,677,000,000 bbl. As of **December 31**. Proved reserves are estimated quantities of the mineral, which geological and engineering data demonstrate with reasonable certainty, to be recoverable in future years from known reservoirs under existing economic and operating conditions. Based on a sample of operators of oil and gas wells]

Area	2002 Crude oil proved reserves (mil. bbl.)	Natural gas (bil. cu. ft.)	Natural gas liquids (mil. bbl.)	2003 Crude oil proved reserves (mil. bbl.)	Natural gas (bil. cu. ft.)	Natural gas liquids (mil. bbl.)	2004 Crude oil proved reserves (mil. bbl.)	Natural gas (bil. cu. ft.)	Natural gas liquids (mil. bbl.)
United States [1]	22,677	186,946	7,994	21,891	189,044	7,459	21,371	192,513	7,928
Alabama	51	3,884	57	52	4,301	60	53	4,120	50
Alaska	4,678	8,468	405	4,446	8,285	387	4,327	8,407	369
Arkansas	49	1,650	4	50	1,663	3	51	1,835	3
California	3,633	2,951	95	3,452	2,450	101	3,376	2,634	122
Colorado	214	13,888	396	217	15,436	395	225	14,743	465
Florida	73	91	14	68	79	17	65	78	12
Illinois	107	(NA)	(NA)	125	(NA)	(NA)	92	(NA)	(NA)
Indiana	15	(NA)	(NA)	19	(NA)	(NA)	11	(NA)	(NA)
Kansas	237	4,983	263	243	4,819	248	245	4,652	271
Kentucky	27	1,907	66	25	1,889	66	27	1,880	72
Louisiana	501	8,960	323	452	9,325	295	427	9,588	263
Michigan	61	3,254	47	75	3,428	48	53	3,091	48
Mississippi	179	744	47	169	746	7	178	691	6
Montana	288	906	6	315	1,059	8	364	995	6
Nebraska	18	(NA)	(NA)	16	(NA)	(NA)	15	(NA)	(NA)
New Mexico	710	17,320	838	677	17,020	875	669	18,512	864
New York	(NA)	315	(NA)	(NA)	365	(NA)	(NA)	324	(NA)
North Dakota	342	471	47	353	448	45	389	417	43
Ohio	67	1,117	(NA)	66	1,126	(NA)	49	974	(NA)
Oklahoma	598	14,886	695	588	15,401	686	570	16,238	790
Pennsylvania	12	2,216	(NA)	13	2,487	(NA)	12	2,361	(NA)
Texas	5,015	44,297	2,711	4,583	45,730	2,517 [2]	4,613	49,955	2,801 [2]
Utah	241	4,135	[2]	221	3,516	[2]	215	3,866	[2]
Virginia	(NA)	1,673	(NA)	(NA)	1,717	(NA)	(NA)	1,742	(NA)
West Virginia	13	3,360	99	13	3,306	68	11	3,397	85
Wyoming	524	20,527	938	517	21,744	[3]898	628	22,632	[3]927
Federal offshore	5,009	25,204	973	5,120	22,570	725	4,691	19,271	721
Lower 48 states	17,999	178,478	7,589	17,445	180,759	7,072	17,044	184,106	7,559

NA Not available. [1] Includes miscellaneous not shown separately. [2] Included with Wyoming. [3] Includes Utah.
Source: Energy Information Administration, *U.S. Crude Oil, Natural Gas, and Natural Gas Liquids Reserves, 2004 Annual Report*, December 2005.

568 Natural Resources

Table 884. **Federal Offshore Leasing, Exploration, Production, and Revenue: 1990 to 2005**

[In millions (56.79 represents 56,790,000), except as indicated. See source for explanation of terms and for reliability statement]

Item	Unit	1990	1995	2000	2001	2002	2003	2004	2005
Tracts offered.	Number. .	10,459	10,995	7,992	8,790	8,548	10,349	8,676	11,447
Tracts leased	Number. .	825	835	553	942	804	923	888	989
Acres offered	Millions . .	56.79	59.70	42.89	49.15	45.69	55.31	46.14	61.08
Acres leased	Millions . .	4.30	4.34	2.92	5.00	4.20	4.85	4.69	5.24
Bonus paid for leased tracts	Bil. dol. . .	0.6	0.4	0.3	1.0	0.1	0.4	0.6	0.7
New wells being drilled:									
Active	Number. .	120	124	224	213	119	135	156	242
Suspended.	Number. .	266	247	146	97	72	48	56	67
Cumulative wells (since 1953):									
Wells completed	Number. .	13,167	13,475	13,718	13,921	13,282	18,424	18,260	18,001
Wells plugged and abandoned. .	Number. .	14,677	18,008	22,814	24,218	25,232	32,251	33,746	34,878
Revenue, total [1]	Bil. dol. . .	3.4	2.7	5.2	[2]5.8	5.0	5.9	5.3	6.3
Bonuses	Bil. dol. . .	0.8	0.4	0.4	[2]0.5	0.1	1.1	0.5	0.6
Oil and gas royalties [1]	Bil. dol. . .	2.6	2.1	4.1	[2]4.8	4.7	4.4	4.5	5.5
Rentals	Bil. dol. . .	0.09	0.09	0.21	[2]0.13	0.44	0.25	0.21	0.22
Sales value [3]	Bil. dol. . .	17.0	13.8	27.4	[2]31.4	31.0	29.0	30.6	37.2
Oil	Bil. dol. . .	7.0	6.3	11.5	[2]11.3	12.1	8.3	8.4	15.4
Natural gas	Bil. dol. . .	9.5	7.5	15.9	[2]20.1	18.9	20.7	22.2	21.8
Sales volume: [4]									
Oil	Mil. bbls. .	324	409	566	[2]463	612	310	248	332
Natural gas	Bil. cu. ft .	5,093	4,692	4,723	[2]3,470	4,971	3,501	3,941	3,504

[1] Includes condensate royalties.   [2] Covers January through September 2001 only.   [3] Production value is value at time of production, not current value.   [4] Excludes sales volumes for gas lost, gas plant products or sulfur.

Source: U.S. Dept. of the Interior, Minerals Management Service, *Federal Offshore Statistics*, annual.

Table 885. **Oil and Gas Extraction Industry—Establishments, Employees, and Payroll by State: 2002**

[5,036,621 represents $5,036,621,000. Covers establishments with payroll. Employees are for the week including March 12. Data based on the 2002 Economic Census. Offshore areas refer to those areas not associated with a state. For statement on methodology, see Appendix III]

State	Crude petroleum and natural gas extraction (211111) [1]			State	Natural gas liquid extraction (211112)[1]		
	Establish-ments	Paid employees	Annual payroll ($1,000)		Establish-ments	Paid employees	Annual payroll ($1,000)
United States . . .	7,178	94,886	5,036,621	United States . . .	511	9,693	528,190
Alabama	37	1,042	64,411	Alabama	10	204	11,004
California.	215	3,666	224,144	California	18	708	38,567
Colorado.	344	4,057	254,900	Colorado	21	401	22,276
Illinois	175	899	32,210	Illinois	9	281	15,946
Kansas	375	2,325	104,281	Kansas	10	126	6,526
Louisiana	425	11,270	634,319	Louisiana	76	1,341	72,969
Michigan	88	926	41,363	Michigan	11	156	7,920
New Mexico.	167	2,097	118,118	New Mexico	39	840	47,263
Oklahoma	1,039	9,382	438,850	Oklahoma	35	581	30,090
Pennsylvania	145	1,629	81,514	Texas	180	3,631	200,008
Texas	2,794	40,408	2,172,312	Wyoming	35	583	35,671
Utah.	55	1,860	56,946				
West Virginia	210	1,720	71,397				
Wyoming.	180	2,553	127,296				
Offshore areas	5	501	36,626				

[1] Based on North American Industry Classification System, 2002.

Source: U.S. Census Bureau, 2002 Economic Census, issued October 2004. See also <http://www.census.gov/econ/census02>.

Natural Resources   569

Table 886. Natural Gas—Supply, Consumption, Reserves, and Marketed Production: 1980 to 2004

[182 represents 182,000)]

Item	Unit	1980	1990	1995	1999	2000	2001	2002	2003	2004
Producing wells (year-end)	1,000	182	269	299	302	342	373	388	393	385
Production value at wells	Bil. dol.	32.1	31.8	30.2	43.4	74.3	82.3	58.7	97.2	107.2
Avg. per 1,000 cu. ft.	Dollars	1.59	1.71	1.55	2.19	3.68	4.00	2.95	4.88	5.46
Proved reserves [1]	Tril. cu. ft.	199	169	165	167	177	183	187	189	193
Marketed production [2]	Bil. cu. ft.	20,180	18,594	19,506	19,805	20,198	20,570	19,885	19,912	19,640
Minus: Extraction losses [3]	Bil. cu. ft.	777	784	908	973	1,016	954	957	876	864
Equals: Dry production	Bil. cu. ft.	19,403	17,810	18,599	18,832	19,182	19,616	18,928	19,036	18,776
Plus: Supplemental gas supplies	Bil. cu. ft.	155	123	110	98	90	86	68	68	55
Equals: Dry production with supplemental gas	Bil. cu. ft.	19,558	17,932	18,709	18,931	19,272	19,703	18,996	19,104	18,831
Plus: Withdrawals from storage	Bil. cu. ft.	1,972	1,986	3,025	2,808	3,550	2,344	3,180	3,166	3,003
Plus: Imports [4]	Bil. cu. ft.	985	1,532	2,841	3,586	3,782	3,977	4,015	3,996	4,259
Plus: Balancing item	Bil. cu. ft.	-640	307	396	-119	-306	99	45	161	196
Equals: Total supply	Bil. cu. ft.	21,875	21,758	24,971	25,205	26,298	26,122	26,237	26,427	26,288
Minus: Exports	Bil. cu. ft.	49	86	154	163	244	373	516	692	854
Minus: Additions to storage [5]	Bil. cu. ft.	1,949	2,499	2,610	2,636	2,721	3,510	2,713	3,360	3,113
Equals: Consumption, total	Bil. cu. ft.	19,877	19,174	22,207	22,405	23,333	22,239	23,007	22,375	22,321
Lease and plant fuel	Bil. cu. ft.	1,026	1,236	1,220	1,079	1,151	1,119	1,113	1,123	1,107
Pipeline fuel	Bil. cu. ft.	635	660	700	645	642	625	667	665	663
Residential	Bil. cu. ft.	4,752	4,391	4,850	4,726	4,996	4,771	4,889	5,078	4,881
Commercial [6]	Bil. cu. ft.	2,611	2,623	3,031	3,045	3,182	3,023	3,144	3,217	3,000
Industrial	Bil. cu. ft.	8,198	8,255	9,384	9,158	9,293	8,463	8,620	8,262	8,405
Vehicle fuel	Bil. cu. ft.	(NA)	–	5	12	13	15	15	18	20
Electric utilities	Bil. cu. ft.	3,682	3,245	4,237	4,820	5,206	5,342	5,672	5,135	5,352
World production (dry)	Tril. cu. ft.	53.4	73.6	78.0	84.9	88.3	90.4	92.2	95.2	(NA)
U.S. production (dry)	Tril. cu. ft.	19.4	17.8	18.6	18.8	19.2	19.2	18.9	19.0	(NA)
Percent U.S. of world	Percent	36.4	24.2	23.9	22.2	21.7	21.7	20.5	20.0	(NA)

– Represents zero. NA Not available. [1] Estimated, end of year. Source: U.S. Energy Information Administration, U.S. Crude Oil, Natural Gas, and Natural Gas Liquids Reserves, annual. [2] Marketed production includes gross withdrawals from reservoirs less quantities used for reservoir repressuring and quantities vented or flared. Excludes nonhydrocarbon gases subsequently removed. [3] Volumetric reduction in natural gas resulting from the extraction of natural gas constituents at natural gas processing plants. [4] Includes imports of liquefied natural gas. [5] Includes liquefied natural gas (LNG) storage in above ground tanks. [6] Includes deliveries to municipalities and public authorities for institutional heating and other purposes.

Source: Except as noted, U.S. Energy Information Administration, Annual Energy Review, International Energy Annual, and Natural Gas Annual, Volume I and II.

Table 887. Liquefied Petroleum Gases—Summary: 1980 to 2005

[In millions of 42-gallon barrels (561 barrels represents 561,000,000 barrels). Includes ethane, propane, normal butane, and isobutane]

Item	1980	1990	1995	2000	2001	2002	2003	2004	2005
Production	561	638	760	843	813	822	767	795	(NA)
At natural gas plants	441	456	521	587	570	577	527	559	527
At refineries	121	182	234	258	243	245	240	235	210
Imports	79	68	53	79	75	67	82	96	116
Refinery input	85	107	105	87	88	90	83	87	91
Exports	9	14	21	27	16	24	20	16	19
Stocks, Dec. 31	116	98	93	83	121	106	94	104	110

NA Not available.

Source: U.S. Energy Information Administration, Petroleum Supply Annual, volume I.

Table 888. Natural Gas Plant Liquids—Production and Value: 1980 to 2004

[Barrels of 42 gallons (567 represents 567,000,000)]

Item	Unit	1980	1990	1995	1999	2000	2001	2002	2003	2004
Field production [1]	Mil. bbl.	567	566	643	675	699	682	686	686	662
Pentanes plus	Mil. bbl.	126	112	122	111	112	112	109	109	101
Liquefied petroleum gases	Mil. bbl.	441	454	521	564	587	570	577	577	561
Natural gas processed	Tril. cu. ft.	15	15	17	17	17	17	16	15	15

[1] Includes other finished petroleum products, not shown separately.

Source: U.S. Energy Information Administration, Petroleum Supply Annual and Natural Gas Annual.

Table 889. **Coal Supply, Disposition, and Prices: 1999 to 2005**

[In millions of short tons (1,100.4 represents 1,100,400,000)]

Item	1999	2000	2001	2002	2003	2004	2005
United States, total supply	**1,100.4**	**1,073.6**	**1,127.7**	**1,094.3**	**1,071.8**	**1,112.1**	**1,133.3**
Consumption by sector:							
Total	1,045.3	1,084.1	1,060.1	1,066.4	1,094.9	1,107.3	1,128.3
Electric power	946.8	985.8	964.4	977.5	1,005.1	1,016.3	1,039.0
Coke plants	28.1	28.9	26.1	23.7	24.2	23.7	23.4
Other industrial plants	65.5	65.2	65.3	60.7	61.3	62.2	60.8
Combined heat and power (CHP)	(NA)	(NA)	25.8	26.2	24.8	26.6	20.6
Noncombined heat and power	(NA)	(NA)	39.5	34.5	36.4	35.6	40.2
Residential/commercial users	4.9	4.1	4.4	4.4	4.2	5.1	5.1
Year-end coal stocks:							
Total	183.0	140.0	181.9	192.1	165.5	154.0	144.0
Electric power	136.0	102.0	138.5	141.7	121.6	106.7	101.2
Coke plants	1.9	1.5	1.5	1.4	0.9	1.3	2.6
Other industrial plants	5.6	4.6	6.0	5.8	4.7	4.8	5.6
Producers/distributors	39.5	31.9	35.9	43.3	38.3	41.2	34.6
U.S. coal trade:							
Net exports	49.4	46.0	28.9	22.7	18.0	20.7	19.5
Exports	58.5	58.5	48.7	39.6	43.0	48.0	49.9
Steam coal	26.3	25.7	23.3	18.1	20.9	21.2	21.3
Metallurgical coal	32.1	32.8	25.4	21.5	22.1	26.8	28.7
Imports	9.1	12.5	19.8	16.9	25.0	27.3	30.5
Average delivered price (dollars per short ton):							
Electric utilities	24.72	24.28	24.68	24.74	25.82	27.30	30.91
Coke plants	45.85	44.38	46.42	50.67	50.63	61.50	83.79
Other industrial plants	31.59	31.46	32.26	35.49	34.70	39.30	47.63
Average free alongside ship (f.a.s.):							
Exports	36.50	34.90	36.97	40.44	35.98	54.11	67.10
Steam Coal	29.91	29.67	31.88	34.51	26.94	42.03	47.64
Metallurgical Coal	41.91	38.99	41.63	45.41	44.55	63.63	81.56
Imports	30.77	30.10	34.00	35.51	31.45	37.52	46.71

NA Not available.

Source: U.S. Energy Information Administration, *U.S. Coal Supply and Demand: 2005 Review*, annual. See also <http://www.eia.doe.gov/cneaf/coal/page/special/feature.html>.

Table 890. **Coal and Coke—Summary: 1980 to 2004**

[(830 represents 830,000,000.) Includes coal consumed at mines. Recoverability varies between 40 and 90 percent for individual deposits; 50 percent or more of overall U.S. coal reserve base is believed to be recoverable]

Item	Unit	1980	1990	1995	2000	2001	2002	2003	2004
COAL									
Coal production, total [1] . .	Mil. sh. tons . . .	830	1,029	1,033	1,074	1,128	1,094	1,072	1,111
Value	Bil. dol.	20.45	22.39	19.45	18.02	19.60	19.68	19.13	22.06
Anthracite production	Mil. sh. tons . . .	6.1	3.5	4.7	4.6	1.9	1.4	1.3	1.7
Bituminous coal and lignite	Mil. sh. tons . . .	824	1,026	1,028	1,069	1,126	1,093	1,070	1,110
Underground	Mil. sh. tons . . .	338	425	396	374	381	357	353	368
Surface	Mil. sh. tons . . .	492	605	637	700	747	737	719	744
Exports	Mil. sh. tons . . .	92	106	89	58	49	40	43	48
Imports	Mil. sh. tons . . .	1	3	9	13	20	17	25	27
Consumption [2]	Mil. sh. tons . . .	703	904	962	1,084	1,060	1,066	1,095	1,104
Electric power utilities	Mil. sh. tons . . .	569	783	850	986	964	978	1,005	1,015
Industrial	Mil. sh. tons . . .	127	115	106	94	91	84	86	85
Number of mines	Number	5,598	3,243	2,104	1,453	1,512	1,426	1,316	1,379
Daily employment	1,000	225	131	90	72	77	75	71	74
Production, by state:									
Alabama	Mil. sh. tons . . .	26	29	25	19	19	19	20	22
Illinois	Mil. sh. tons . . .	63	60	48	33	34	33	32	32
Indiana	Mil. sh. tons . . .	31	36	26	28	37	35	35	35
Kentucky	Mil. sh. tons . . .	150	173	154	131	134	124	113	114
Montana	Mil. sh. tons . . .	30	38	39	38	39	37	37	40
Ohio	Mil. sh. tons . . .	39	35	26	22	25	21	22	23
Pennsylvania	Mil. sh. tons . . .	93	71	62	75	74	68	64	66
Virginia	Mil. sh. tons . . .	41	47	34	33	33	30	32	31
West Virginia	Mil. sh. tons . . .	122	169	163	158	162	150	140	148
Wyoming	Mil. sh. tons . . .	95	184	264	339	369	373	376	396
Other states	Mil. sh. tons . . .	140	187	192	197	201	202	202	203
World production	Mil. sh. tons . . .	4,182	5,348	5,096	4,931	5,225	5,259	5,406	(NA)
Percent U.S. of world	Percent	19.8	19.2	20.3	21.8	21.6	20.8	19.8	(NA)
COKE									
Coke production [3]	Mil. sh. tons . . .	46.1	27.6	23.7	20.8	18.9	16.8	17.2	16.9
Imports	Mil. sh. tons . . .	0.7	0.8	3.8	3.8	2.5	3.2	2.8	6.9
Exports	Mil. sh. tons . . .	2.1	0.6	1.4	1.1	1.3	0.8	0.7	1.3
Consumption	Mil. sh. tons . . .	41.3	27.8	25.8	23.2	20.2	19.6	19.4	22.5

NA Not available.　　1 Includes bituminous coal, subbituminous coal, lignite, and anthracite.　　2 Includes some categories not shown separately.　　3 Includes beehive coke.

Source: U.S. Energy Information Administration, *Annual Energy Review, International Energy Annual*, and *Annual Coal Report*.

Natural Resources　571

Table 891. **Demonstrated Coal Reserves by Major Producing State: 2003 and 2004**

[In millions of short tons (496,092 represents 496,092,000,000). As of January 1. The demonstrated reserve base represents the sum of coal in both measured and indicated resource categories of reliability. Measured resources of coal are estimates that have a high degree of geologic assurance from sample analyses and measurements from closely spaced and geological well known sample sites. Indicated resources are estimates based partly from sample and analyses and measurements and partly from reasonable geologic projections]

State	2003			2004		
		Method of mining			Method of mining	
	Total reserves	Under-ground	Surface	Total reserves	Under-ground	Surface
United States [1]	**496,092**	**336,199**	**159,893**	**494,450**	**335,468**	**158,982**
Alabama	4,282	1,066	3,215	4,242	1,034	3,208
Alaska	6,114	5,423	691	6,112	5,423	689
Colorado	16,365	11,599	4,766	16,293	11,529	4,764
Illinois	104,589	88,025	16,563	104,529	87,972	16,557
Indiana	9,586	8,784	802	9,534	8,764	771
Iowa	2,189	1,732	457	2,189	1,732	457
Kentucky	30,422	17,346	13,076	30,225	17,202	13,023
Kentucky, Eastern	10,824	1,387	9,437	10,671	1,282	9,389
Kentucky, Western	19,597	15,959	3,639	19,554	15,920	3,634
Missouri	5,991	1,479	4,512	5,990	1,479	4,511
Montana	119,330	70,958	48,372	119,280	70,958	48,322
New Mexico	12,212	6,187	6,025	12,172	6,171	6,001
North Dakota	9,128	(NA)	9,128	9,090	–	9,090
Ohio	23,382	17,606	5,777	23,342	17,577	5,765
Oklahoma	1,559	1,233	327	1,557	1,232	325
Pennsylvania	27,719	23,437	4,283	27,597	23,330	4,267
Anthracite	7,203	3,845	3,358	7,200	3,844	3,356
Bituminous	20,517	19,592	925	20,397	19,486	911
Texas	12,500	(NA)	12,500	12,442	–	12,442
Utah	5,488	5,221	268	5,445	5,177	268
Virginia	1,794	1,204	590	1,740	1,163	576
Washington	1,348	1,332	16	1,341	1,332	8
West Virginia	33,473	29,548	3,925	33,220	29,366	3,854
Wyoming	64,821	42,501	22,320	64,325	42,501	21,824

– Represents or rounds to zero.   NA Not available.   [1] Includes other states not shown separately.

Source: U.S. Energy Information Administration, *Annual Coal Report*, 2004. See also <http://www.eia.doe.gov/cneaf/coal/page/acr/acr_sum.html>.

Table 892. **Uranium Concentrate (U_3O_8) Industry—Summary: 1990 to 2005**

[In millions of feet (1.7 represents 1,700,000), except as indicated. See also Table 916 in Section 19]

Item	Unit	1990	1995	1999	2000	2001	2002	2003	2004	2005 [1]
Exploration and development, surface drilling	Mil. ft	1.7	1.3	2.5	1.0	0.7	(D)	(D)	1.2	1.7
Expenditures	Mil. dol	(NA)	2.6	7.9	5.6	2.7	(D)	(D)	10.6	16.4
Number of mines operated	Number	39	12	14	10	7	6	4	6	10
Underground	Number	27	–	3	1	–	–	1	2	4
Openpit	Number	2	–	–	–	–	–	–	–	–
In situ leaching	Number	7	5	6	4	3	3	3	3	4
Other sources	Number	3	7	5	5	4	3	1	1	2
Mine production	1,000 pounds [1]	5,876	3,528	4,548	3,123	2,647	2,405	2,200	2,452	3,045
Underground	1,000 pounds [1]	(D)	–	(D)	(D)	(D)	(D)	(D)	(D)	(D)
Openpit	1,000 pounds [1]	1,881	–	–	–	–	–	–	–	–
In situ leaching	1,000 pounds [1]	(D)	3,372	3,830	2,995	(D)	(D)	(D)	(D)	2,681
Other sources	1,000 pounds [1]	3,995	156	718	128	(D)	(D)	(D)	(D)	(D)
Uranium concentrate production	1,000 pounds [1]	8,886	6,043	4,611	3,958	2,639	2,344	2,000	2,282	2,689
Concentrate shipments from mills and plants	1,000 pounds [1]	12,957	5,500	5,527	3,187	2,203	3,810	1,600	2,280	2,702
Employment	Person-years	1,335	1,107	848	627	423	426	321	420	638

– Represents zero.   D Data withheld to avoid disclosing figures for individual companies.   NA Not available.   [1] Preliminary.

Source: U.S. Department of Energy, through 2002, *Uranium Industry*, annual. Thereafter, *Domestic Uranium Production Report*, annual. See also <http://www.eia.doe.gov/cneaf/nuclear/dupr/dupr.html>.

Energy and Utilities

This section presents statistics on fuel resources, energy production and consumption, electric energy, hydroelectric power, nuclear power, solar energy, wood energy, and the electric and gas utility industries. The principal sources are the U.S. Department of Energy's Energy Information Administration (EIA), the Edison Electric Institute, Washington, DC, and the American Gas Association, Arlington, VA. The Department of Energy was created in October 1977 and assumed and centralized the responsibilities of all or part of several agencies including the Federal Power Commission (FPC), the U.S. Bureau of Mines, the Federal Energy Administration, and the U.S. Energy Research and Development Administration. For additional data on transportation, see Section 23; on fuels, see Section 18; and on energy-related housing characteristics, see Section 20.

The EIA, in its *Annual Energy Review,* provides statistics and trend data on energy supply, demand, and prices. Information is included on petroleum and natural gas, coal, electricity, hydroelectric power, nuclear power, solar, wood, and geothermal energy. Among its annual reports are *Annual Energy Review, Electric Power Annual, Natural Gas Annual, Petroleum Supply Annual, State Energy Data Report, State Energy Price and Expenditure Report, Performance Profiles of Major Energy Producers, Annual Energy Outlook,* and *International Energy Annual.* These various publications contain state, national, and international data on production of electricity, net summer capability of generating plants, fuels used in energy production, energy sales and consumption, and hydroelectric power. The EIA also issues the *Monthly Energy Review,* which presents current supply, disposition, and price data and monthly publications on petroleum, coal, natural

gas, and electric power. Data on residential energy consumption, expenditures, and conservation activities are available from EIA's Residential Energy Consumption Survey and are published every 4 years.

The Edison Electric Institute's monthly bulletin and annual *Statistical Year Book of the Electric Utility Industry for the Year* contain data on the distribution of electric energy by public utilities; information on the electric power supply, expansion of electric generating facilities, and the manufacture of heavy electric power equipment is presented in the annual *Year-End Summary of the Electric Power Situation in the United States.* The American Gas Association, in its monthly and quarterly bulletins and its yearbook, *Gas Facts,* presents data on gas utilities and financial and operating statistics.

Btu conversion factors—Various energy sources are converted from original units to the thermal equivalent using British thermal units (Btu). A Btu is the amount of energy required to raise the temperature of 1 pound of water 1 degree Fahrenheit (F) at or near 39.2 degrees F. Factors are calculated annually from the latest final annual data available; some are revised as a result. The following list provides conversion factors used in 2002 for production and consumption, in that order, for various fuels: Petroleum, 5.800 and 5.324 mil. Btu per barrel; total coal, 20.620 and 20.814 mil. Btu per short ton; and natural gas (dry), 1,027 Btu per cubic foot for both. The factors for the production of nuclear power and geothermal power were 10,442 and 21,017 Btu per kilowatt-hour, respectively. The fossil fuel steam-electric power plant generation factor of 10,119 Btu per kilowatt-hour was used for hydroelectric power generation and for wood and waste, wind, photovoltaic, and solar thermal energy consumed at electric utilities.

U.S. Census Bureau, Statistical Abstract of the United States: 2007

In the past few years, EIA has restructured the industry categories it once used to gather and report electricity statistics. The electric power industry, previously divided into electric utilities and non-utilities, now consists of the Electric Power Sector, the Commercial Sector, and the Industrial Sector (see Table 909).

The Electric Power Sector is composed of electricity-only and combined-heat-and-power (CHP) plants whose primary business is to sell electricity, or electricity and heat to the public.

Electricity-only plants are composed of traditional electric utilities, and nontraditional participants, including energy service providers, power marketers, independent power producers (IPPs), and the portion of combined-heat-and-power plants (CHPs) that produce only electricity.

A utility is defined as a corporation, person, agency, authority, or other legal entity or instrumentality aligned with distribution facilities for delivery of electric energy for use primarily by the public. Electric utilities include investor-owned electric utilities, municipal and state utilities, federal electric utilities, and rural electric cooperatives. In total, there are more than 3,100 electric utilities in the United States.

An independent power producer is an entity defined as a corporation, person, agency, authority, or other legal entity or instrumentality that owns or operates facilities whose primary business is to produce electricity for use by the public. They are not generally aligned with distribution facilities and are not considered electric utilities.

Combined-heat-and-power producers are plants designed to produce both heat and electricity from a single heat source. These types of electricity producers can be independent power producers or industrial or commercial establishments. As some independent power producers are combined-heat-and-power producers, their information is included in the data for the combined-heat-and-power sector. There are approximately 2,800 unregulated independent power producers and combined-heat-and-power plants in the United States.

The Commercial Sector consists of commercial CHP and commercial electricity-only plants. Industrial CHP and industrial electricity-only plants make up the Industrial Sector. For more information, please refer to the *Electric Power Annual 2004* Web site located at <http://www.eia.doe.gov/cneaf/electricity/epa/epa_sum.html>.

U.S. Census Bureau, Statistical Abstract of the United States: 2007

Table 893. Utilities—Establishments, Revenue, Payroll, and Employees by Kind of Business: 2002

[478,268 represents $478,268,000,000. See headnote, Table 736 and Appendix III]

Kind of business	2002 NAICS code [1]	Estab-lish-ments (number)	Revenue		Annual payroll		Paid employ-ees for pay period including March 12 (number)
			Total (mil. dol.)	Per paid employee (dol.)	Total (mil. dol.)	Per paid employee (dol.)	
Utilities.................	22	18,594	478,268	647,524	45,111	61,076	738,611
Electric power generation, transmission, & distribution....................	2211	9,676	337,033	625,827	35,921	66,701	538,540
Electric power generation	22111	2,138	78,163	641,913	9,195	75,513	121,766
Hydroelectric power generation......	221111	416	3,260	425,084	483	62,952	7,668
Fossil fuel electric power generation...	221112	1,233	53,329	792,480	4,945	73,484	67,294
Nuclear electric power generation	221113	78	11,909	375,696	2,507	79,094	31,698
Other electric power generation......	221119	411	9,666	639,857	1,260	83,415	15,106
Electric power transmission, control, & distribution..................	22112	7,538	258,870	621,128	26,726	64,126	416,774
Electric bulk power transmission & control...........	221121	158	12,738	847,369	1,173	78,021	15,032
Electric power distribution..........	221122	7,380	246,132	612,662	25,553	63,606	401,742
Natural gas distribution...............	2212	2,431	71,827	771,772	5,973	64,179	93,068
Water, sewage, & other systems	2213	5,780	7,594	166,333	1,600	35,040	45,654
Water supply & irrigation systems......	22131	4,830	5,860	162,575	1,252	34,731	36,046
Sewage treatment facilities	22132	866	1,051	137,443	241	31,472	7,647
Steam & air-conditioning supply	22133	84	683	348,056	107	54,628	1,961

[1] North American Industry Classification System, 2002; see text, Section 15.

Source: U.S. Census Bureau, *2002 Economic Census*, Series EC02-221-US, issued December 2004. See also <http://www.census.gov/econ/census02/>.

Table 894. Private Utilities—Employees, Annual Payroll, and Establishments by Industry: 2003

[44,568 represents 44,568,000,000. Excludes government employees, railroad employees, self-employed persons, etc. An establishment is a single physical location where business is conducted or where services or industrial operations are performed. See Appendix III]

Year and industry	2002 NAICS code [1]	Number of employ-ees [2]	Annual payroll (mil. dol.)	Aver-age payroll per em-ployee (dol.)	Establishment by employment size-class				
					Total	Under 20 em-ployees	20 to 99 em-ployees	100 to 499 em-ployees	500 and over employ-ees
Utilities, total..............	22	675,938	44,568	65,935	18,413	13,125	3,875	1,218	195
Electric power generation, transmission and distribution.......	2211	543,782	37,438	68,847	9,986	5,834	2,991	986	175
Electric power generation........	22111	132,930	9,686	72,867	2,347	1,477	591	228	51
Hydroelectric power generation ..	221111	5,966	358	59,977	416	347	57	12	–
Fossil fuel electric power generation	221112	77,377	5,399	69,769	1,430	814	414	192	10
Nuclear electric power generation	221113	33,583	2,801	83,405	75	19	13	11	32
Other electric power generation ..	221119	16,004	1,129	70,533	426	297	107	13	9
Electric power transmission, control & distribution..........	22112	410,852	27,751	67,546	7,639	4,357	2,400	758	124
Electric bulk power transmission & control.................	221121	4,348	309	71,157	102	67	21	13	1
Electric power distribution......	221122	406,504	27,442	67,507	7,537	4,290	2,379	745	123
Natural gas distribution...........	2212	87,452	5,430	62,086	2,626	1,855	569	184	18
Water, sewage, & other systems.....	2213	44,704	1,701	38,042	5,801	5,436	315	48	2
Water supply & irrigation systems ..	22131	36,520	1,404	38,458	4,867	4,588	235	43	1
Sewage treatment facilities.......	22132	6,627	215	32,414	840	779	56	4	1
Steam & air-conditioning supply....	22133	1,557	81	52,240	94	69	24	1	–

– Represents zero. [1] North American Industry Classification System, 2002. [2] Covers full- and part-time employees who are on the payroll in the pay period including March 12.

Source: U.S. Census Bureau, "County Business Patterns"; <http://censtats.census.gov/cgi-bin/cbpnaic/cbpdetl.pl> (accessed December 2005).

Energy and Utilities 575

Table 895. **Energy Supply and Disposition by Type of Fuel: 1960 to 2004**

[In quadrillion British thermal units (Btu) (42.80 represents 42,800,000,000,000,000). For Btu conversion factors, see source and text, this section]

Year	Production									Net imports[5], total	Consumption					
	Total[1]	Crude oil[2]	Natural gas	Coal	Nuclear power	Renewable energy[3] Total[1]	Hydro-electric power	Biofuel[4]	Solar energy		Total[1]	Petro-leum[6,7]	Natural gas[8]	Coal	Nuclear power	Renewable energy[3] total
1960	42.80	14.93	12.66	10.82	(Z)	2.93	1.61	1.32	(NA)	2.71	45.09	19.92	12.39	9.84	(Z)	2.93
1970	63.50	20.40	21.67	14.61	0.24	4.08	2.63	1.43	(NA)	5.71	67.84	29.52	21.79	12.26	0.24	4.08
1974	62.37	18.57	21.21	14.07	1.27	4.77	3.18	1.54	(NA)	12.10	73.99	33.45	21.73	12.66	1.27	4.77
1975	61.36	17.73	19.64	14.99	1.90	4.72	3.15	1.50	(NA)	11.71	72.00	32.73	19.95	12.66	1.90	4.72
1976	61.60	17.26	19.48	15.65	2.11	4.77	2.98	1.71	(NA)	14.59	76.01	35.17	20.35	13.58	2.11	4.77
1977	62.05	17.45	19.57	15.75	2.70	4.25	2.33	1.84	(NA)	17.90	78.00	37.12	19.93	13.92	2.70	4.25
1978	63.14	18.43	19.49	14.91	3.02	5.04	2.94	2.04	(NA)	17.19	79.99	37.97	20.00	13.77	3.02	5.04
1979	65.95	18.10	20.08	17.54	2.78	5.17	2.93	2.15	(NA)	16.60	80.90	37.12	20.67	15.04	2.78	5.17
1980	67.24	18.25	19.91	18.60	2.74	5.49	2.90	2.48	(NA)	12.10	78.29	34.20	20.39	15.42	2.74	5.49
1981	67.01	18.15	19.70	18.38	3.01	5.47	2.76	2.59	(NA)	9.41	76.34	31.93	19.93	15.91	3.01	5.47
1982	66.57	18.31	18.32	18.64	3.13	5.99	3.27	2.62	(NA)	7.25	73.25	30.23	18.51	15.32	3.13	5.99
1983	64.11	18.39	16.59	17.25	3.20	6.49	3.53	2.83	(NA)	8.06	73.10	30.05	17.36	15.89	3.20	6.49
1984	68.83	18.85	18.01	19.72	3.55	6.43	3.39	2.88	(Z)	8.68	76.74	31.05	18.51	17.07	3.55	6.43
1985	67.65	18.99	16.98	19.33	4.08	6.03	2.97	2.86	(Z)	7.58	76.47	30.92	17.83	17.48	4.08	6.03
1986	67.09	18.38	16.54	19.51	4.38	6.13	3.07	2.84	(Z)	10.13	76.78	32.20	16.71	17.26	4.38	6.13
1987	67.61	17.67	17.14	20.14	4.75	5.69	2.63	2.82	(Z)	11.59	79.23	32.87	17.74	18.01	4.75	5.69
1988	68.95	17.28	17.60	20.74	5.59	5.49	2.33	2.94	(Z)	12.93	82.84	34.22	18.55	18.85	5.59	5.49
1989 [9]	69.36	16.12	17.85	21.35	5.60	6.29	2.84	3.06	0.06	14.11	84.96	34.21	19.71	19.07	5.60	6.29
1990	70.77	15.57	18.33	22.46	6.10	6.13	3.05	2.66	0.06	14.06	84.70	33.55	19.73	19.17	6.10	6.13
1991	70.41	15.70	18.23	21.59	6.42	6.16	3.02	2.70	0.06	13.19	84.64	32.85	20.15	18.99	6.42	6.16
1992	69.98	15.22	18.38	21.63	6.48	5.91	2.62	2.85	0.06	14.44	85.99	33.53	20.84	19.12	6.48	5.91
1993	68.30	14.49	18.58	20.25	6.41	6.16	2.89	2.80	0.07	17.01	87.62	33.84	21.35	19.84	6.41	6.16
1994	70.71	14.10	19.35	22.11	6.69	6.06	2.68	2.94	0.07	18.33	89.28	34.67	21.84	19.91	6.69	6.06
1995	71.18	13.89	19.08	22.03	7.08	6.67	3.21	3.07	0.07	17.75	91.25	34.55	22.78	20.09	7.08	6.67
1996	72.50	13.72	19.34	22.68	7.09	7.14	3.59	3.13	0.07	19.07	94.26	35.76	23.20	21.00	7.09	7.14
1997	72.43	13.66	19.39	23.21	6.60	7.08	3.64	3.01	0.07	20.70	94.77	36.27	23.33	21.45	6.60	7.08
1998	72.83	13.24	19.61	23.94	7.07	6.56	3.30	2.83	0.07	22.28	95.19	36.93	22.94	21.66	6.56	6.56
1999	71.71	12.45	19.34	23.19	7.61	6.60	3.27	2.89	0.07	23.54	96.84	37.96	23.01	21.62	7.61	6.60
2000	71.27	12.36	19.66	22.62	7.86	6.16	2.81	2.91	0.07	24.97	98.96	38.40	23.92	22.58	7.86	6.16
2001	71.88	12.28	20.20	23.49	8.03	5.33	2.24	2.64	0.07	26.39	96.47	38.33	22.91	21.91	8.03	5.33
2002	70.76	12.16	19.44	22.62	8.14	5.84	2.69	2.65	0.06	25.74	97.88	38.40	23.63	21.90	8.14	5.84
2003	70.01	12.03	19.63	21.97	7.96	6.08	2.82	2.74	0.06	27.05	98.31	39.05	23.07	22.32	7.96	6.08
2004 [10]	70.37	11.53	19.34	22.69	8.23	6.12	2.73	2.85	0.06	28.57	99.74	40.13	22.99	22.39	8.23	6.12

NA Not available. Z Less than 5 trillion. [1] Includes types of fuel not shown separately. [2] Includes lease condensate. [3] Electricity net generation from conventional hydroelectric power, geothermal, solar, and wind; consumption of wood, waste, and alcohol fuels; geothermal heat pump and direct use energy; and solar thermal direct use energy. [4] Wood, waste, and alcohol (ethanol blended into motor gasoline). [5] Imports minus exports. [6] Beginning in 1993, ethanol blended into motor gasoline is included in Petroleum. [7] Petroleum products supplied, including natural gas plant liquids and crude oil burned as fuel. [8] Includes supplemental gaseous fuels. [9] There is a discontinuity in this time series between 1989 and 1990. [10] Preliminary.

Source: U.S. Energy Information Administration, Annual Energy Review 2004. See also <http://www.eia.doe.gov/emeu/aer/overview.html> (released August 2005).

Table 896. Energy Supply and Disposition by Type of Fuel—Estimates, 2003 and 2004, and Projections, 2005 to 2020

[Quadrillion Btu (70.52 represents 70,520,000,000,000,000) per year. Btu = British thermal unit. Projections are "reference" or mid-level forecasts. See report for methodology and assumptions used in generating projections]

Type of fuel	2003	2004	Projections			
			2005	2010	2015	2020
Production, total	**70.52**	**70.42**	**70.72**	**77.42**	**80.58**	**84.05**
Crude oil and lease condensate	12.05	11.47	11.27	12.45	12.37	11.75
Natural gas plant liquids	2.34	2.46	2.42	2.39	2.57	2.67
Natural gas, dry	19.63	19.02	18.68	19.13	20.97	22.09
Coal	22.12	22.86	23.41	25.78	25.73	27.30
Nuclear power	7.96	8.23	8.08	8.44	8.66	9.09
Renewable energy [1]	5.69	5.74	5.88	7.08	7.43	8.00
Other [2]	0.72	0.64	0.97	2.16	2.85	3.16
Imports, total	**30.98**	**33.14**	**34.01**	**33.83**	**36.75**	**39.83**
Crude oil [3]	21.06	22.02	22.34	22.01	22.91	24.63
Petroleum products [4]	5.16	5.93	6.40	6.36	7.29	8.01
Natural gas	4.10	4.36	4.34	5.01	5.81	5.83
Other imports [5]	0.67	0.83	0.93	0.45	0.74	1.36
Exports, total	**3.86**	**4.18**	**4.15**	**3.74**	**3.30**	**3.39**
Petroleum [6]	2.03	2.07	2.07	2.15	2.18	2.24
Natural gas	0.71	0.86	0.86	0.55	0.58	0.68
Coal	1.12	1.25	1.22	1.03	0.54	0.46
Consumption, total	**98.05**	**99.68**	**100.49**	**107.87**	**114.18**	**120.63**
Petroleum products [7]	38.96	40.08	40.22	43.14	45.69	48.14
Natural gas	23.04	23.07	22.86	24.04	26.67	27.70
Coal	22.38	22.53	23.37	25.09	25.66	27.65
Nuclear power	7.96	8.23	8.08	8.44	8.66	9.09
Renewable energy [1], other [8]	5.72	5.77	5.96	7.15	7.51	8.05
Net imports of petroleum	**24.19**	**25.88**	**26.67**	**26.22**	**28.02**	**30.39**
Prices (1999 dollars per unit):						
Imported crude oil price [9]	28.46	35.99	49.70	43.99	43.00	44.99
Gas wellhead price (dol. per mcf) [10]	5.08	5.49	7.62	5.03	4.52	4.90
Coal minemouth price (dol. per ton)	18.40	20.07	21.20	22.23	20.39	20.20
Average electric price (cents per kWh)	7.6	7.6	8.3	7.3	7.1	7.2

[1] Includes grid-connected electricity from conventional hydroelectric; wood and wood waste; landfill gas; municipal solid waste; other biomass; wind; photovoltaic and solar thermal sources; non-electric energy from renewable sources, such as active and passive solar systems, and wood; and both the ethanol and gasoline components of E85, but not the ethanol components of blends less than 85 percent. Excludes electricity imports using renewable sources and nonmarketed renewable energy. See Table A18 of source for selected nonmarketed residential and commercial renewable energy. [2] Includes liquid hydrogen, methanol, supplemental natural gas, and some domestic inputs to refineries. [3] Includes imports of crude oil for the Strategic Petroleum Reserve. [4] Includes imports of finished petroleum products, imports of unfinished oils, alcohols, ethers, and blending components. [5] Includes coal, coal coke (net), and electricity (net). [6] Includes crude oil and petroleum products. [7] Includes natural gas plant liquids, crude oil consumed as a fuel, and nonpetroleum-based liquids for blending, such as ethanol. [8] Includes net electricity imports, methanol, and liquid hydrogen. [9] Weighted average price delivered to U.S. refiners. [10] Represents lower 48 onshore and offshore supplies.

Source: U.S. Energy Information Administration, *Annual Energy Outlook 2006*, DOE/EIA-0383(2006). See also <http://www.eia.doe.gov/oiaf/aeo/excel/aeotab_1.xls>.

Table 897. Energy Consumption by End-Use Sector: 1970 to 2004

[67.84 represents 67,840,000,000,000,000 Btu. Btu = British thermal units. For Btu conversion factors, see source and text, this section. See Appendix III]

Year	Total (quad. Btu)	Residential and commercial [1] (quad. Btu)	Industrial [2] (quad. Btu)	Transportation (quad. Btu)	Percent of total		
					Residential and commercial [1]	Industrial [2]	Transportation
1970	67.84	22.11	29.64	16.10	32.6	43.7	23.7
1975	72.00	24.31	29.45	18.24	33.8	40.9	25.3
1980	78.29	26.44	32.15	19.70	33.8	41.1	25.2
1985	76.47	27.49	28.89	20.09	36.0	37.8	26.3
1990	84.70	30.39	31.90	22.42	35.9	37.7	26.5
1995	91.25	33.38	34.01	23.85	36.6	37.3	26.1
1996	94.26	34.83	34.98	24.44	37.0	37.1	25.9
1997	94.77	34.75	35.26	24.75	36.7	37.2	26.1
1998	95.19	35.05	34.89	25.26	36.8	36.7	26.5
1999	96.84	36.07	34.81	25.95	37.2	35.9	26.8
2000	98.96	37.71	34.70	26.55	38.1	35.1	26.8
2001	96.47	37.66	32.53	26.28	39.0	33.7	27.2
2002	97.88	38.49	32.53	26.85	39.3	33.2	27.4
2003	98.31	38.65	32.56	27.10	39.3	33.1	27.6
2004 [3]	99.74	38.69	33.25	27.79	38.8	33.3	27.9

[1] Commercial sector fuel use, including that at commercial combined-heat-and-power (CHP) and industrial electricity-only plants. [2] Industrial sector fuel use, including that at industrial combined-heat-and-power (CHP) and industrial electricity-only plants. [3] Preliminary.

Source: U.S. Energy Information Administration, *Annual Energy Review 2004*. See also <http://www.eia.doe.gov/emeu/aer/pdf/pages/sec_24.pdf> (released August 2005).

Table 898. **Renewable Energy Consumption Estimates by Source: 1995 to 2004**

[In quadrillion Btu (6.67 represents 6,670,000,000,000,000). Renewable energy is obtained from sources that are essentially inexhaustible unlike fossil fuels of which there is a finite supply]

Source and sector	1995	1999	2000	2001	2002	2003	2004[1]
Consumption, total	6.67	6.60	6.16	5.33	5.84	6.08	6.12
Conventional hydroelectric power[2]	3.21	3.27	2.81	2.24	2.69	2.83	2.73
Geothermal energy[3]	0.29	0.33	0.32	0.31	0.33	0.34	0.34
Biomass[4]	3.07	2.89	2.91	2.64	2.65	2.74	2.85
Solar energy[5]	0.07	0.07	0.07	0.07	0.06	0.06	0.06
Wind energy[6]	0.03	0.05	0.06	0.07	0.11	0.12	0.14
Residential[7]	0.67	0.49	0.50	0.44	0.38	0.43	0.41
Biomass[4]	0.60	0.41	0.43	0.37	0.31	0.36	0.33
Geothermal[3]	0.01	0.01	0.01	0.01	0.01	0.02	0.02
Solar[5,8]	0.07	0.06	0.06	0.06	0.06	0.06	0.06
Commercial[9]	0.09	0.11	0.11	0.09	0.09	0.10	0.11
Biomass[4]	0.09	0.11	0.10	0.08	0.08	0.09	0.09
Geothermal[3]	0.01	0.01	0.01	0.01	0.01	0.01	0.02
Hydroelectric[2]	(Z)	(Z)	(Z)	(Z)	(Z)	(Z)	(Z)
Industrial[10]	1.91	1.84	1.83	1.63	1.61	1.58	1.68
Biomass[4]	1.85	1.79	1.78	1.59	1.57	1.53	1.62
Geothermal[3]	(Z)	(Z)	(Z)	0.01	0.01	0.01	0.01
Hydroelectric[2]	0.06	0.05	0.04	0.03	0.04	0.04	0.05
Transportation: Alcohol fuels[11]	0.12	0.12	0.14	0.15	0.17	0.24	0.30
Electric power[12]	3.89	4.03	3.58	3.02	3.58	3.73	3.63
Biomass[4]	0.42	0.45	0.45	0.45	0.52	0.52	0.51
Geothermal[3]	0.28	0.31	0.30	0.29	0.31	0.30	0.30
Hydroelectric[2]	3.15	3.22	2.77	2.21	2.65	2.78	2.67
Solar[5]	0.01	0.01	0.01	0.01	0.01	0.01	0.01
Wind[6]	0.03	0.05	0.06	0.07	0.11	0.12	0.14

Z Less than 5 trillion Btu.   [1] Preliminary.   [2] Power produced from natural streamflow as regulated by available storage. [3] As used at electric power plants, hot water or steam extracted from geothermal reservoirs in the Earth's crust that is supplied to steam turbines at electric power plants that drive generators to produce electricity.   [4] Organic nonfossil material of biological origin constituting a renewable energy source.   [5] Includes small amounts of distributed solar thermal and photovoltaic energy. [6] Energy present in wind motion that can be converted to mechanical energy for driving pumps, mills, and electric power generators. Wind pushes against sails, vanes, or blades radiating from a central rotating shaft.   [7] Consists of living quarters for private households, but excludes institutional living quarters.   [8] The radiant energy of the sun, which can be converted into other forms of energy, such as heat or electricity.   [9] Consists of service-providing facilities and equipment of businesses, governments, and other private and public organizations. Includes institutional living quarters and sewage treatment facilities.   [10] Consists of all facilities and equipment used for producing, processing, or assembling goods.   [11] Ethanol primarily derived from corn. [12] Consists of electricity only and combined heat and power plants who sell electricity and heat to the public.

Source: U.S. Energy Information Administration, *Renewable Energy Annual 2004.* See also <http://www.eia.doe.gov /cneaf/solar.renewables/page/trends/table05.pdf> (issued June 2006).

Table 899. **Energy Expenditures and Average Fuel Prices by Source and Sector: 1970 to 2002**

[In millions of dollars (82,911 represents $82,911,000,000), except as indicated. For definition of Btu, see text, this section. End-use sector and electric utilities exclude expenditures and prices on energy sources such as hydropower, solar, wind, and geothermal. Also excludes expenditures for reported amounts of energy consumed by the energy industry for production, transportation, and processing operations]

Source and sector	1970	1980	1985	1990	1995	1998	1999	2000	2001	2002
EXPENDITURES (mil. dol.)										
Total[1]	82,911	374,346	438,184	472,539	514,049	525,737	556,538	689,199	694,078	661,659
Natural gas	10,891	51,061	72,938	65,278	75,020	83,620	84,960	119,092	139,296	111,366
Petroleum products	47,955	237,676	223,928	235,368	236,905	231,898	262,820	360,751	336,389	320,028
Motor gasoline	31,596	124,408	118,048	126,558	136,647	132,730	149,260	193,947	185,892	179,508
Coal	4,630	22,607	29,678	28,602	27,431	27,888	27,310	28,080	28,139	28,511
Electricity sales	23,345	98,095	149,233	176,691	205,876	218,361	218,413	231,577	245,449	248,357
Residential sector[2]	20,213	69,418	99,772	111,097	128,388	135,101	137,573	156,089	168,550	161,505
Commercial sector[3]	10,628	46,932	70,396	79,284	91,788	99,138	99,290	112,870	125,921	119,924
Industrial sector[4]	16,691	94,316	106,518	[5]102,402	107,060	107,723	111,833	141,536	138,285	128,528
Transportation sector	35,379	163,680	161,498	179,757	186,813	183,775	207,843	278,703	261,322	251,702
Motor gasoline	30,525	121,809	115,205	123,845	134,641	130,709	147,592	191,620	182,122	175,726
Electric utilities[2]	4,329	37,788	43,421	40,155	38,728	42,650	43,932	57,597	61,902	53,182
AVERAGE FUEL PRICES (dol. per mil. Btu)										
All sectors	1.65	6.89	8.37	8.25	8.28	8.20	8.53	10.33	10.73	10.07
Residential sector[2]	2.10	7.46	10.91	11.88	12.63	13.48	13.19	14.27	15.72	14.75
Commercial sector[3]	1.98	7.85	11.65	11.89	12.64	13.07	12.87	13.93	15.63	14.70
Industrial sector[4]	0.84	4.71	6.03	[4]5.23	4.97	4.91	5.12	6.49	6.80	6.29
Transportation sector	2.31	8.61	8.27	8.28	8.09	7.48	8.23	10.78	10.21	9.64
Electric utilities[2]	0.32	1.76	1.88	1.47	1.28	1.30	1.31	1.64	1.78	1.51

[1] Includes other sources not shown separately.   [2] There are no direct fuel costs for geothermal, photovoltaic, or solar thermal energy.   [3] There are no direct fuel costs for hydroelectric, geothermal, photovoltaic, or solar thermal energy.   [4] There are no direct fuel costs for hydroelectric, geothermal, wind, photovoltaic, or solar thermal energy.   [5] There is a discontinuity in the total time series and the industrial time series between 1988 and 1989 due to the expanded coverage of nonelectric utility use of wood and waste beginning in 1989.

Source: U.S. Energy Information Administration, *State Energy Price and Expenditure Report,* 2002. See also <http://www.eia.doe.gov/emeu/states/state.html?q_state_a=us&q_state=UNITED%20STATES> (published 30 June 2006).

Table 900. Residential Energy Consumption, Expenditures, and Average Price: 1980 to 2001

[9.32 represents 9,320,000,000,000,000 Btu. For period April to March for 1980; January to December for 1987 to 2001. Excludes Alaska and Hawaii in 1980. Covers occupied units only. Excludes household usage of gasoline for transportation and the use of wood or coal. Based on Residential Energy Consumption Survey; see source. Btu = British thermal unit; see text, this section]

Type of fuel	Unit	1980	1987	1990	1993	1997	2001
CONSUMPTION							
Total.	Quad. Btu	9.32	9.13	9.22	10.01	10.25	9.86
Average per household . . .	Mil. Btu	114	101	98	104	101	92
Natural gas	Quad. Btu	4.97	4.83	4.86	5.27	5.28	4.84
Electricity, site	Quad. Btu	2.48	2.76	3.03	3.28	3.54	3.89
Fuel oil, kerosene	Quad. Btu	1.52	1.22	1.04	1.07	1.07	0.76
Liquid petroleum gas	Quad. Btu	0.35	0.32	0.28	0.38	0.36	0.38
EXPENDITURES							
Total	Bil. dol..	75.6	97.8	110.2	123.9	135.8	159.7
Average per household . . .	Dollars	926	1,080	1,172	1,282	1,338	1,493
Natural gas	Bil. dol.	19.8	26.2	27.3	32.0	35.8	47.0
Electricity	Bil. dol.	40.8	61.6	71.5	81.1	88.3	100.3
Fuel oil, kerosene	Bil. dol.	12.2	7.2	8.3	7.0	7.6	6.8
Liquid petroleum gas	Bil. dol.	2.8	2.8	3.1	3.8	4.0	5.6
AVERAGE PRICE							
Total	Dol./mil. Btu . .	8.12	10.71	11.95	12.38	13.25	16.19
Natural gas	Dol./mil. Btu . . .	3.98	5.41	5.61	6.07	6.78	9.70
Electricity	Dol./mil. Btu . . .	16.46	22.34	23.60	24.69	24.97	25.80
Fuel oil, kerosene	Dol./mil. Btu . . .	8.03	5.89	7.92	6.53	7.13	9.05
Liquid petroleum gas	Dol./mil. Btu . . .	8.00	8.91	11.18	10.04	11.23	14.87

Source: U.S. Energy Information Administration, *Residential Energy Consumption Survey: Household Energy Consumption and Expenditures*, 1980, 1987, 1990, 1993, 1997, and 2001. See also <http://www.eia.doe.gov/emeu/recs/contents.html>.

Table 901. Residential Energy Consumption and Expenditures, by Type of Fuel and Selected Household Characteristic: 2001

[Quad. = quadrillion. (9.86 represents 9,860,000,000,000,000 Btu). See headnote, Table 900]

Characteristic	Consumption (Btu's)					Expenditures				
	Total [1] (quad.)	Avg. per house-hold [1, 2] (mil.)	Natural gas (quad.)	Electric-ity (quad.)	Fuel oil [3] (quad.)	Total [1] (bil. dol.)	Avg. per house-hold [1, 2] (dol.)	Natural gas (bil. dol.)	Electric-ity (bil. dol.)	Fuel oil [3] (bil. dol.)
Total households . . .	9.86	92.2	4.84	3.89	0.71	159.74	1,493	46.98	100.34	6.83
Single family.	7.91	107.3	3.98	3.01	0.59	125.02	1,697	38.04	76.69	5.32
Two-to-four unit building . . .	0.74	78.1	0.45	0.23	0.06	11.97	1,261	4.70	6.68	0.54
Five-or-more unit building . .	0.70	41.0	0.28	0.36	0.05	13.66	803	2.98	10.29	0.37
Mobile home	0.52	75.9	0.14	0.29	0.01	9.09	1,336	1.26	6.68	0.08
Year house built:										
1949 or earlier.	2.92	109.8	1.68	0.76	0.34	42.18	1,586	16.47	20.65	3.04
1950 to 1959	1.39	97.9	0.75	0.46	0.14	21.25	1,500	7.15	12.34	1.29
1960 to 1969	1.19	86.5	0.61	0.45	0.09	19.48	1,414	6.00	12.09	0.77
1970 to 1979	1.48	79.0	0.57	0.77	0.07	26.03	1,388	5.28	18.99	0.61
1980 to 1989	1.45	79.7	0.57	0.78	0.04	26.22	1,438	5.53	19.37	0.40
1990 to 2001 [4]	1.43	92.5	0.66	0.68	0.02	24.59	1,591	6.54	16.90	0.21

[1] Includes liquid petroleum gas, not shown separately. [2] The averages are over the set of all households; otherwise the averages are over the set of households using a given fuel or enduse. [3] Includes kerosene. [4] New construction for 2001 includes only those housing units built and occupied between January and the April–August period when the household interviews were conducted.

Source: U.S. Energy Information Administration, *Residential Energy Consumption Survey: Household Energy Consumption and Expenditures*, 2001. See also <http://www.eia.doe.gov/emeu/recs/contents.html>.

Table 902. Fossil Fuel Prices by Type of Fuel: 1990 to 2004

[In dollars per million British thermal units (Btu), except as indicated. All fuel prices taken as close to the point of production as possible. See text, this section, for explanation of Btu conversions from mineral fuels]

Fuel	Current dollars					Constant (2000) dollars				
	1990	1995	2000	2003	2004 [1]	1990	1995	2000	2003	2004 [1]
Composite [2]	1.84	1.47	2.60	3.10	3.63	2.26	1.60	2.60	2.92	3.35
Crude oil [3]	3.45	2.52	4.61	4.75	6.34	4.23	2.74	4.61	4.48	5.86
Natural gas [4]	1.55	1.40	3.32	4.41	4.96	1.90	1.52	3.32	4.16	4.59
Bituminous coal [5]	1.00	0.88	0.80	0.87	0.97	1.22	0.96	0.80	0.82	0.90

[1] Preliminary. [2] Derived by multiplying the price per Btu of each fossil fuel by the total Btu content of the production of each fossil fuel and dividing this accumulated value of total fossil fuel production by the accumulated Btu content of total fossil fuel production. [3] Domestic first purchase prices. [4] Wellhead prices. [5] Includes bituminous coal, subbituminous coal, and lignite.

Source: U.S. Energy Information Administration, *Annual Energy Review 2004*. See also <http://www.eia.doe.gov/emeu/aer/pdf/pages/sec3_3.pdf> (released August 2005).

Energy and Utilities   579

Table 903. Energy Imports and Exports by Type of Fuel: 1980 to 2004

[In quadrillion of Btu. (12.10 represents 12,100,000,000,000,000 Btu). For definition of Btu, see text, this section]

Type of fuel	1980	1985	1990	1995	1998	1999	2000	2001	2002	2003	2004 [1]
Net imports, total [2]	12.10	7.58	14.06	17.75	22.28	23.54	24.97	26.39	25.74	27.05	28.57
Coal	-2.39	-2.39	-2.70	-2.08	-1.87	-1.30	-1.21	-0.77	-0.61	-0.49	-0.57
Natural gas (dry).	0.96	0.90	1.46	2.74	3.06	3.50	3.62	3.69	3.58	3.40	3.49
Petroleum [3]	13.50	8.95	15.29	16.89	20.94	21.18	22.38	23.36	22.63	24.07	25.47
Other [4]	0.04	0.13	0.01	0.19	0.16	0.16	0.18	0.10	0.14	0.07	0.18
Imports, total	15.80	11.78	18.82	22.26	26.58	27.25	28.97	30.16	29.41	31.11	33.00
Coal	0.03	0.05	0.07	0.24	0.22	0.23	0.31	0.49	0.42	0.63	0.68
Natural gas (dry).	1.01	0.95	1.55	2.90	3.22	3.66	3.87	4.07	4.10	4.10	4.36
Petroleum [3]	14.66	10.61	17.12	18.88	22.91	23.13	24.53	25.40	24.68	26.22	27.68
Other [4]	0.10	0.17	0.08	0.24	0.23	0.23	0.26	0.19	0.20	0.17	0.29
Exports, total	3.69	4.20	4.75	4.51	4.30	3.71	4.01	3.77	3.66	4.07	4.43
Coal	2.42	2.44	2.77	2.32	2.09	1.53	1.53	1.27	1.03	1.12	1.25
Natural gas (dry).	0.05	0.06	0.09	0.16	0.16	0.16	0.25	0.38	0.52	0.70	0.86
Petroleum	1.16	1.66	1.82	1.99	1.97	1.95	2.15	2.04	2.04	2.15	2.21
Other [4]	0.07	0.04	0.07	0.05	0.07	0.07	0.08	0.09	0.07	0.10	0.11

[1] Preliminary.   [2] Net imports equals imports minus exports. Minus sign (–) denotes an excess of exports over imports.
[3] Includes imports into the Strategic Petroleum Reserve, which began in 1977.   [4] Coal coke and small amounts of electricity transmitted across U.S. borders with Canada and Mexico.

Source: U.S. Energy Information Administration, *Annual Energy Review, 2004*. See also <http://www.eia.doe.gov/emeu/aer /pdf/pages/sec1_11.pdf> (released August 2005).

Table 904. U.S. Foreign Trade in Selected Mineral Fuels: 1980 to 2004

[985 represents 985,000,000,000 cu. ft. Minus sign (–) indicates an excess of imports over exports]

Mineral fuel	Unit	1980	1985	1990	1995	2000	2001	2002	2003	2004 [1]
Natural gas:										
Imports	Bil. cu. ft.	985	950	1,532	2,841	3,782	3,977	4,015	3,996	4,259
Exports	Bil. cu. ft.	49	55	86	154	244	373	516	692	854
Net trade	Bil. cu. ft.	-936	-894	-1,447	-2,687	-3,538	-3,604	-3,499	-3,305	-3,404
Crude oil:										
Imports [2]	Mil. bbl.	1,926	1,168	2,151	2,639	3,320	3,405	3,336	3,528	3,674
Exports	Mil. bbl.	105	75	40	35	18	7	3	5	10
Net trade	Mil. bbl.	-1,821	-1,094	-2,112	-2,604	-3,301	-3,398	-3,333	-3,523	-3,664
Petroleum products:										
Imports	Mil. bbl.	603	681	775	586	874	928	872	949	1,047
Exports	Mil. bbl.	94	211	273	312	362	347	356	370	374
Net trade	Mil. bbl.	-508	-471	-502	-274	-512	-581	-517	-579	-673
Coal:										
Imports	Mil. sh. tons . . .	1.2	2.0	2.7	9.5	12.5	19.8	16.9	25.0	27.3
Exports	Mil. sh. tons . . .	91.7	92.7	105.8	88.5	58.5	48.7	39.6	43.0	48.0
Net trade	Mil. sh. tons . . .	90.5	90.7	103.1	79.1	46.0	28.9	22.7	18.0	20.7

[1] Preliminary.   [2] Includes strategic petroleum reserve imports.

Source: U.S. Energy Information Administration, *Annual Energy Review 2004*. See also <http://www.eia.doe.gov/emeu /aer/contents.html> (released August 2005).

Table 905. Crude Oil Imports Into the U.S. by Country of Origin: 1980 to 2005

[In millions of barrels (1,921 represents 1,921,000,000). Barrels contain 42 gallons. Total OPEC excludes, and Non-OPEC includes, petroleum imported into the United States indirectly from members of OPEC, primarily from Caribbean and West European areas, as petroleum products that were refined from crude oil produced by OPEC]

Country of origin	1980	1985	1990	1995	1999	2000	2001	2002	2003	2004	2005
Total imports . . .	1,921	1,168	2,151	2,639	3,187	3,311	3,405	3,336	3,521	3,674	3,670
OPEC, [1, 2, 3] total	1,410	479	1,283	1,219	1,543	1,659	1,770	1,490	1,671	1,836	1,738
Algeria	166	31	23	10	9	(Z)	4	11	41	79	83
Iraq	10	17	188	–	265	226	290	168	171	238	190
Kuwait [4]	10	1	29	78	90	96	87	79	75	88	79
Libya	200	–	–	–	–	–	–	–	–	7	16
Saudi Arabia [4]	456	48	436	460	506	556	588	554	629	547	525
Indonesia	115	107	36	23	26	13	15	18	10	12	7
Nigeria	307	102	286	227	227	319	307	215	306	389	387
Venezuela	57	112	243	420	420	446	471	438	436	473	449
Non-OPEC, total [5]	511	689	869	1,419	1,643	1,652	1,635	1,846	1,850	1,838	1,932
Angola	(NA)	(NA)	86	131	130	108	117	117	132	112	164
Canada.	73	171	235	380	430	492	495	527	565	590	600
Colombia	(NA)	(NA)	51	76	165	116	95	86	59	51	57
Ecuador [2]	6	20	(NA)	35	42	46	41	37	50	83	101
Gabon [3]	9	19	(NA)	84	61	52	51	52	48	52	47
Mexico	185	261	251	375	458	479	509	548	580	584	566
Norway	53	11	35	94	96	110	103	31	60	54	43
Russia	(NA)	(NA)	(Z)	5	8	3	–	31	54	55	70
United Kingdom	63	101	57	124	104	106	89	148	127	86	80

– Represents zero.   NA Not available.   Z Represents less than 500,000 barrels.   [1] OPEC (Organization of Petroleum Exporting Countries) includes the Persian Gulf nations shown below, except Bahrain, which is not a member of OPEC, and also includes Iran, Qatar, and United Arab Emirates.   [2] Ecuador withdrew from OPEC on Dec. 31, 1992; therefore, it is included under OPEC for the period 1973 to 1992.   [3] Gabon withdrew from OPEC on Dec. 31, 1994; therefore, it is included under OPEC for the period 1973 to 1994.   [4] Imports from the Neutral Zone between Kuwait and Saudi Arabia are included in Saudi Arabia. [5] Non-OPEC total includes nations not shown.

Source: U.S. Energy Information Administration, *Petroleum Supply Monthly*, February 2006. See also <http://www.eia.doe.gov /pub/oil_gas/petroleum/data_publications/petroleum_supply_monthly/historical/2006/2006_02/pdf/table38.pdf>.

Table 906. Crude Oil and Refined Products—Summary: 1980 to 2005

[13,481 represents 13,481,000 bbl. Barrels (bbl.) of 42 gallons. Data are averages]

Year	Crude oil (1,000 bbl. per day)					Refined oil products (1,000 bbl. per day)			Total oil imports [3] (1,000 bbl. per day)	Crude oil stocks [4] (mil. bbl.)	
	Input to refineries	Domestic production	Imports			Domestic demand	Imports	Exports		Total	Strategic reserve [5]
			Total [1]	Strategic reserve [2]	Exports						
1980	13,481	8,597	5,263	44	287	17,056	1,646	258	6,909	[6]466	108
1985	12,002	8,971	3,201	118	204	15,726	1,866	577	5,067	814	493
1990	13,409	7,355	5,894	27	109	16,988	2,123	748	8,018	908	586
1995	13,973	6,560	7,230	–	95	17,725	1,605	855	8,835	895	592
1996	14,195	6,465	7,508	–	110	18,309	1,971	871	9,478	850	566
1997	14,662	6,452	8,225	–	108	18,620	1,936	896	10,162	868	563
1998	14,889	6,252	8,706	–	110	18,917	2,002	835	10,708	895	571
1999	14,804	5,881	8,731	8	118	19,519	2,122	822	10,852	852	567
2000	15,067	5,822	9,071	8	50	19,701	2,389	990	11,459	826	541
2001	15,128	5,801	9,328	11	20	19,649	2,543	951	11,871	862	550
2002	14,947	5,746	9,140	16	9	19,761	2,390	975	11,530	877	599
2003	15,304	5,681	9,665	–	12	20,034	2,599	1,014	12,264	907	638
2004	15,475	5,419	10,088	77	27	20,731	3,057	1,021	13,145	961	676
2005	15,204	5,121	10,056	38	41	20,656	3,471	1,133	13,527	1,008	685

– Represents zero.   [1] Includes Strategic Petroleum Reserve.   [2] SPR is the Strategic Petroleum Reserve. Through 2003, includes imports by SPR only; beginning in 2004, includes imports by SPR, and imports into SPR by others.   [3] Crude oil (including Strategic Petroleum Reserve imports) plus refined products.   [4] Crude oil at end of period. Includes commercial and Strategic Petroleum Reserve stocks.   [5] Crude oil stocks in the Strategic Petroleum Reserve include non-U.S. stocks held under foreign or commercial storage agreements.   [6] Stocks of Alaskan crude oil in transit are included from January 1985 forward.

Source: U.S. Energy Information Administration, *Monthly Energy Review*, February 2006 issue.

Table 907. Petroleum and Coal Products Corporations—Sales, Net Profit, and Profit Per Dollar of Sales: 1990 to 2005

[318.5 represents $318,500,000,000. Represents SIC group 29 (NAICS group 324). Through 2000 based on Standard Industrial Classification code; beginning 2001 based on North American Industry Classification System, 1997 (NAICS). Profit rates are averages of quarterly figures at annual rates. Beginning 1990, excludes estimates for corporations with less than $250,000 in assets]

Item	Unit	1990	1995	1997	1998	1999	2000	2001	2002	2003	2004	2005
Sales..................	Bil. dol. . .	318.5	283.1	320.0	250.4	277.0	455.2	472.5	474.9	597.8	767.7	1,019.2
Net profit:												
Before income taxes	Bil. dol. . .	23.1	16.5	36.8	9.7	20.3	55.5	47.2	22.4	52.8	89.7	118.6
After income taxes	Bil. dol. . .	17.8	13.9	29.4	8.3	17.2	42.6	35.8	19.5	43.6	71.8	94.5
Depreciation[1].	Bil. dol. . .	18.7	16.7	15.6	14.7	13.5	15.5	17.2	17.8	19.4	18.5	18.0
Profits per dollar of sales:												
Before income taxes	Cents . . .	7.3	5.8	11.5	3.5	7.1	12.2	9.7	4.6	10.4	15.5	18.0
After income taxes	Cents . . .	5.6	4.9	9.2	3.1	6.0	9.4	7.4	4.2	8.6	12.4	14.3
Profits on stockholders' equity:												
Before income taxes	Percent . .	16.4	12.6	23.5	6.0	13.0	29.4	21.8	9.7	20.8	32.9	37.9
After income taxes	Percent . .	12.7	10.6	18.9	5.2	11.0	22.6	16.5	8.4	17.1	26.3	30.2

[1] Includes depletion and accelerated amortization of emergency facilities.
Source: U.S. Census Bureau, *Quarterly Financial Report for Manufacturing, Mining and Trade Corporations.*

Table 908. Major Petroleum Companies—Financial Summary: 1980 to 2005

[32.9 represents $32,900,000,000. Data represent a composite of approximately 42 major worldwide petroleum companies aggregated on a consolidated total company basis]

Item	1980	1990	1995	1999	2000	2001	2002	2003	2004	2005
FINANCIAL DATA (bil. dol.)										
Net income.	32.9	26.8	24.3	35.3	76.4	62.0	44.3	85.5	120.5	170.6
Depreciation, depletion, etc.	32.5	38.7	43.1	45.0	53.3	63.4	61.2	68.0	76.9	76.5
Cash flow [1].	65.4	65.5	67.4	75.3	129.7	140.0	118.0	157.7	205.1	239.9
Dividends paid.	9.3	15.9	17.6	21.7	23.0	29.7	27.3	27.5	33.5	37.5
Net internal funds available for investment or debt repayment [2]	56.1	49.6	49.8	54.1	106.7	110.4	90.7	130.3	171.5	202.4
Capital and exploratory expenditures	62.1	59.6	59.8	67.7	72.8	99.9	88.7	90.7	112.4	140.4
Long-term capitalization.	211.4	300.0	304.3	456.2	516.9	543.8	548.1	606.1	700.1	800.4
Long-term debt.	49.8	90.4	85.4	105.4	112.8	143.2	153.5	142.1	161.0	165.2
Preferred stock.	2.0	5.2	5.7	4.8	5.4	6.7	2.5	2.2	1.3	3.5
Common stock and retained earnings [3] . .	159.6	204.4	213.2	346.0	398.7	393.9	392.1	461.8	537.8	631.7
Excess of expenditures over cash income [4]	6.0	10.0	10.0	13.6	-33.9	-10.5	-2.0	-39.5	-59.2	-62.0
RATIOS [5] (percent)										
Long-term debt to long-term capitalization	23.6	30.1	28.1	23.1	21.8	26.7	28.3	26.5	24.1	23.5
Net income to total average capital	17.0	9.1	8.1	8.9	15.7	12.3	8.7	15.2	18.9	23.0
Net income to average common equity. . . .	22.5	13.5	11.6	12.4	20.5	20.5	11.5	20.1	24.2	29.3

[1] Generally represents internally-generated funds from operations. Sum of net income and noncash charges such as depreciation, depletion, and amortization.   [2] Cash flow minus dividends paid.   [3] Includes common stock, capital surplus, and earned surplus accounts after adjustments.   [4] Capital and exploratory expenditures plus dividends paid minus cash flow.   [5] Represents approximate year-to-year comparisons because of changes in the makeup of the group due to mergers and other corporate changes.

Source: Carl H. Pforzheimer & Co., New York, NY, *Comparative Oil Company Statements,* annual.

Energy and Utilities   581

Table 909. **Electric Power Industry—Sales, Prices, Net Generation, Net Summer Capacity, and Consumption of Fuels: 1990 to 2004**

[2,837.1 represents 2,837,100,000,000 kWh. Net generation for calendar years; capacity as of December 31]

Item	Unit	1990	2000	2001	2002	2003	2004 [1]
ELECTRIC POWER INDUSTRY, ALL SECTORS							
Consumption, total.	Bil. kWh . .	2,837.1	3,592.4	3,532.4	3,628.7	3,656.5	3,716.5
Net generation, total	Bil. kWh. .	3,038.0	3,802.1	3,736.6	3,858.5	3,883.2	[2]3,970.6
Electric power sector	Bil. kWh. .	2,901.3	3,637.5	3,580.1	3,698.5	3,721.2	3,793.6
Commercial sector	Bil. kWh. .	5.8	7.9	7.4	7.4	7.5	7.4
Industrial sector	Bil. kWh. .	130.8	156.7	149.2	152.6	154.5	152.4
Electricity imports.	Bil. kWh. .	18.4	48.6	38.5	36.4	30.4	34.2
Electricity exports.	Bil. kWh. .	16.1	14.8	16.5	13.6	24.0	22.9
Electricity losses and unaccounted for	Bil. kWh. .	203.2	243.5	226.2	252.6	233.1	248.2
Retail sales of electricity	Bil. kWh. .	2,712.6	3,421.4	3,369.8	3,462.5	3,488.2	3,550.5
Direct use of electricity	Bil. kWh. .	124.5	170.9	162.6	166.2	168.3	166.0
Electricity retail prices per kWh:							
All sectors, current dollars	Cents	6.57	6.81	7.32	7.21	7.42	7.57
All sectors, real (**2000**) dollars.	Cents	8.05	6.81	7.15	6.93	7.00	6.99
Residential, current dollars.	Cents	7.83	8.24	8.62	8.46	8.70	8.94
Residential, real (**2000**) dollars	Cents	9.60	8.24	8.42	8.13	8.21	8.26
Commercial, current dollars	Cents	7.34	7.43	7.93	7.86	7.98	8.17
Commercial, real (**2000**) dollars	Cents	9.00	7.43	7.74	7.55	7.53	7.55
Industrial, current dollars	Cents	4.74	4.64	5.04	4.88	5.13	5.11
Industrial, real (**2000**) dollars.	Cents	5.81	4.64	4.92	4.69	4.84	4.72
Transportation, current dollars	Cents	(NA)	(NA)	(NA)	(NA)	7.58	6.48
Transportation, real (**2000**) dollars.	Cents	(NA)	(NA)	(NA)	(NA)	7.15	5.99
Other users, current dollars	Cents	6.40	6.56	7.03	6.73	(NA)	(NA)
Other users, real (**2000**) dollars.	Cents	7.84	6.56	6.87	6.47	(NA)	(NA)
Net generation, total [3] **. . . . .**	**Bil. kWh .**	**3,038.0**	**3,802.1**	**3,736.6**	**3,858.5**	**3,883.2**	[2]**3,970.6**
Coal	Bil. kWh. .	1,594.0	1,966.3	1,904.0	1,933.1	1,973.7	[2]1,978.6
Petroleum	Bil. kWh. .	126.6	111.2	124.9	94.6	119.4	[2]120.6
Natural gas	Bil. kWh. .	372.8	601.0	639.1	691.0	649.9	[2]709.0
Nuclear	Bil. kWh. .	576.9	753.9	768.8	780.1	763.7	[2]788.5
Hydroelectric pumped storage plants . . .	Bil. kWh. .	-3.5	-5.5	-8.8	-8.7	-8.5	[2]-8.5
Conventional hydroelectric power plants .	Bil. kWh. .	292.9	275.6	217.0	264.3	275.8	[2]268.4
Geothermal	Bil. kWh. .	15.4	14.1	13.7	14.5	14.4	14.4
Net summer capacity, total [3] **. . . . .**	**Mil. kW .**	**734.1**	**811.7**	**848.3**	**905.3**	**948.4**	[2]**962.9**
Coal-fired plants	Mil. kW . .	307.4	315.1	314.2	315.4	313.0	[2]313.0
Petroleum-fired plants	Mil. kW . .	49.0	35.9	39.7	38.2	36.4	[2]33.7
Natural gas-fired plants	Mil. kW . .	56.2	95.7	125.8	171.7	208.4	[2]224.3
Dual-fired plants	Mil. kW . .	113.6	149.8	153.5	162.3	171.3	[2]172.2
Nuclear electric power plants	Mil. kW . .	99.6	97.9	98.2	98.7	99.2	[2]99.6
Hydroelectric pumped storage plants . . .	Mil. kW . .	19.5	19.5	19.1	20.4	20.5	[2]20.8
Conventional hydroelectric power plants .	Mil. kW . .	73.9	79.4	79.5	79.4	78.7	[2]77.6
Geothermal energy plants	Mil. kW . . .	2.7	2.8	2.2	2.3	2.1	2.1
Fuel consumption:							
Petroleum	Mil. bbl . .	219.0	195.2	216.7	168.6	206.7	[2]209.5
Coal	Mil. sh. tons.	792.5	994.9	972.7	987.6	1,014.1	[2]1,026.0
Petroleum coke	Mil. sh. tons.	1.9	3.7	3.9	6.8	6.3	7.5
Natural gas	Bil. cu. ft. .	3,691.6	5,691.5	5,832.3	6,126.1	5,616.1	[2]6,111.3
ELECTRIC POWER SECTOR							
Net generation, total [3] **. . . . .**	**Bil. kWh .**	**2,901.3**	**3,637.5**	**3,580.1**	**3,698.5**	**3,721.2**	**3,793.6**
Coal	Bil. kWh. .	1,572.1	1,943.1	1,882.8	1,910.6	1,952.7	1,954.0
Petroleum	Bil. kWh. .	118.9	105.2	119.1	89.7	113.7	112.5
Natural gas	Bil. kWh. .	309.5	518.0	554.9	607.7	567.3	618.6
Nuclear	Bil. kWh. .	576.9	753.9	768.8	780.1	763.7	788.6
Net summer capacity, total [3] **. . . . .**	**Mil. kW .**	**709.9**	**782.1**	**818.8**	**875.8**	**918.6**	**938.3**
Coal-fired plants	Mil. kW . .	302.3	310.2	309.8	311.0	308.5	308.9
Petroleum-fired plants	Mil. kW . .	48.0	34.9	38.4	37.3	35.5	35.6
Natural gas-fired plants	Mil. kW . .	47.9	82.6	111.1	157.4	193.9	208.3
Dual-fired plants	Mil. kW . .	110.8	147.9	152.0	160.4	169.4	173.6
Nuclear electric power plants	Mil. kW . .	99.6	97.9	98.2	98.7	99.2	99.6
COMBINED-HEAT-AND-POWER PLANTS							
Commercial:							
Net generation, total [3]	Bil. kWh. .	5.8	7.9	7.4	7.4	7.5	[2]8.3
Coal	Bil. kWh. .	0.8	1.1	1.0	1.0	1.2	[2]1.3
Petroleum	Bil. kWh. .	0.6	0.4	0.4	0.4	0.4	[2]0.5
Natural gas	Bil. kWh. .	3.3	4.3	4.4	4.3	3.9	[2]4.1
Net summer capacity, total [3].	Mil. kW . .	1.4	2.2	2.9	2.2	2.1	[2]2.2
Coal-fired plants	Mil. kW . .	0.3	0.3	0.3	0.3	0.3	[2]0.4
Petroleum-fired plants	Mil. kW . .	0.2	0.3	0.3	0.3	0.3	[2]0.3
Natural gas-fired plants	Mil. kW . .	0.2	0.6	1.4	0.5	0.5	[2]0.5
Dual-fired plants	Mil. kW . .	0.6	0.6	0.6	0.7	0.6	[2]0.6
Industrial:							
Net generation, total [3]	Bil. kWh. .	130.8	156.7	149.2	152.6	154.5	[2]153.9
Coal.	Bil. kWh. .	21.1	22.1	20.1	21.5	19.8	[2]20.1
Petroleum	Bil. kWh. .	7.2	5.6	5.3	4.4	5.3	[2]5.6
Natural gas	Bil. kWh. .	60.0	78.8	79.8	79.0	78.7	[2]77.4
Net summer capacity, total [3].	Mil. kW . .	22.9	27.3	26.6	27.3	27.7	[2]27.4
Coal-fired plants	Mil. kW . .	4.8	4.6	4.2	4.0	4.1	[2]3.8
Petroleum-fired plants	Mil. kW . .	0.9	0.8	1.0	0.6	0.7	[2]0.7
Natural gas-fired plants	Mil. kW . .	8.1	12.5	13.3	13.7	14.1	[2]13.6
Dual-fired plants	Mil. kW . .	2.2	1.3	0.9	1.1	1.3	[2]1.3

NA Not available.   [1] Preliminary.   [2] Final 2004 values. Source: U.S. Energy Information Administration, *Electric Power Annual 2004*. See also <http://www.eia.doe.gov/cneaf/electricity/epa/epa_sum.html>.   [3] Includes types not shown separately.

Source: Except as noted, U.S. Energy Information Administration, *Annual Energy Review 2004*. See also <http://www.eia.doe.gov /emeu/aer/elect.html>.

Table 910. Electric Power Industry—Net Generation and Net Summer Capacity by State: 2000 to 2004

[Capacity as of December 31. (3,802.1 represents 3,802,100,000,000). Covers utilities for public use]

State	Net generation (bil. kWh)					Net summer capacity (mil. kW)			
				2004					
	2000	2002	2003	Total	Percent from coal	2000	2002	2003	2004
United States	3,802.1	3,858.5	3,883.2	3,970.6	49.8	811.7	905.3	948.4	962.9
Alabama	124.4	132.9	137.5	137.4	54.5	23.5	26.6	30.2	30.6
Alaska	6.2	6.8	6.3	6.5	9.9	2.1	2.0	1.9	1.9
Arizona	88.9	94.1	94.4	104.6	38.1	15.3	19.4	23.5	24.3
Arkansas	43.9	47.6	50.4	51.9	48.8	9.7	11.3	13.5	13.5
California	208.1	184.2	192.8	194.8	1.2	51.9	56.7	57.9	58.3
Colorado	44.2	45.6	46.6	47.9	74.9	8.4	9.4	10.4	11.1
Connecticut	33.0	31.3	29.5	32.6	13.0	6.4	7.4	7.6	7.9
Delaware	6.0	6.0	7.4	7.9	60.5	2.1	3.4	3.4	3.4
District of Columbia	0.1	0.3	0.1	(Z)	–	0.8	0.8	0.8	0.8
Florida	191.8	203.4	212.6	218.1	29.7	41.5	47.1	49.4	50.7
Georgia	123.9	126.5	124.1	126.8	63.1	27.8	34.6	34.8	35.3
Hawaii	10.6	11.7	11.0	11.4	14.1	2.4	2.3	2.3	2.3
Idaho	11.9	9.8	10.4	10.9	0.9	3.0	3.3	3.0	3.0
Illinois	178.5	188.1	189.1	192.0	49.2	36.3	44.7	45.5	42.0
Indiana	127.8	125.6	124.9	127.8	94.4	23.3	25.3	25.6	26.7
Iowa	41.5	42.5	42.1	43.2	81.6	9.1	9.3	10.1	10.9
Kansas	44.8	47.2	46.6	46.8	73.9	10.1	10.4	10.9	10.9
Kentucky	93.0	92.1	91.7	94.5	91.1	16.8	19.1	19.1	19.6
Louisiana	92.9	95.0	94.9	98.2	24.1	21.0	25.6	25.7	26.5
Maine	14.0	22.5	19.0	19.1	1.9	4.2	4.3	4.3	4.2
Maryland	51.1	48.3	52.2	52.1	56.1	10.4	11.9	12.5	12.5
Massachusetts	38.7	42.0	48.4	47.5	22.2	12.4	12.2	13.9	14.0
Michigan	104.2	117.9	111.3	118.5	57.9	25.8	29.3	30.4	30.4
Minnesota	51.4	52.8	55.1	52.4	65.0	10.3	11.3	11.5	11.6
Mississippi	37.6	42.9	40.1	43.7	40.0	9.0	13.7	17.3	17.0
Missouri	76.6	81.2	87.2	87.6	85.6	17.3	19.8	20.0	20.2
Montana	26.5	25.5	26.3	26.8	64.9	5.2	5.2	5.2	5.1
Nebraska	29.1	31.6	30.5	32.0	63.9	6.0	6.1	6.7	6.7
Nevada	35.5	32.1	33.2	37.7	48.5	6.7	6.9	7.5	8.7
New Hampshire	15.0	16.0	21.6	23.9	17.1	2.9	3.4	4.2	4.3
New Jersey	58.1	61.6	57.4	55.9	18.5	16.5	18.4	18.6	18.2
New Mexico	34.0	30.7	32.7	32.9	88.8	5.6	5.9	6.3	6.3
New York	138.1	139.6	137.6	138.0	16.6	35.6	36.0	36.7	37.8
North Carolina	122.3	124.5	127.6	126.3	59.8	24.5	26.7	27.3	27.1
North Dakota	31.3	31.3	31.3	29.9	93.7	4.7	4.7	4.7	4.8
Ohio	149.1	147.1	146.6	148.3	86.4	28.4	31.5	34.1	34.1
Oklahoma	55.6	59.2	60.6	60.7	55.7	14.1	16.2	18.2	19.4
Oregon	51.8	47.1	49.0	51.4	6.9	11.3	12.5	12.9	12.1
Pennsylvania	201.7	204.3	206.3	214.7	54.6	36.7	39.8	42.4	45.1
Rhode Island	6.0	7.1	5.6	4.9	–	1.2	1.7	1.7	1.7
South Carolina	93.3	96.6	93.8	97.9	39.7	18.7	20.4	20.7	22.2
South Dakota	9.7	7.7	7.9	7.5	48.2	2.8	2.9	2.7	2.7
Tennessee	95.8	96.1	92.2	97.6	59.8	19.5	20.7	20.9	20.9
Texas	377.7	385.6	379.2	390.3	38.1	81.7	94.5	99.6	101.1
Utah	36.6	36.6	38.0	38.2	95.8	5.2	5.8	5.8	6.2
Vermont	6.3	5.5	6.0	5.5	–	1.0	1.0	1.0	1.0
Virginia	77.2	75.0	75.3	78.9	45.2	19.4	20.2	21.3	22.5
Washington	108.2	102.8	100.1	102.2	10.2	26.1	27.1	27.7	27.6
West Virginia	92.9	94.8	94.7	89.7	97.6	15.0	16.2	16.1	16.4
Wisconsin	59.6	58.4	60.1	60.4	69.7	13.6	14.2	14.3	14.7
Wyoming	45.5	43.8	43.6	44.8	96.7	6.2	6.3	6.6	6.6

– Represents or rounds to zero. Z Represents less than 50 million kWh or 50,000 kW.

Source: U.S. Energy Information Administration, *Electric Power Annual 2004.* See also <http://www.eia.doe.gov/cneaf/electricity /epa/epa_sprdshts.html> (accessed June 12, 2006).

Table 911. **Electric Power Industry—Capability, Peak Load, and Capacity Margin: 1980 to 2005**

[558,237 represents 558,237,000 kW. Excludes Alaska and Hawaii. Capability represents the maximum kilowatt output with all power sources available and with hydraulic equipment under actual water conditions, allowing for maintenance, emergency outages, and system operating requirements. Capacity margin is the difference between capability and peak load]

Year	Capability at the time of— Summer peak load (1,000 kW) Amount	Change from prior year	Winter peak load (1,000 kW) Amount	Change from prior year	Noncoincident peak load Summer (1,000 kW)	Winter (1,000 kW)	Capacity margin Summer Amount (1,000 kW)	Percent of capability	Winter Amount (1,000 kW)	Percent of capability
1980	558,237	13,731	572,195	17,670	427,058	384,567	131,179	23.5	187,628	32.8
1985	621,597	17,357	636,475	14,350	460,503	423,660	161,094	25.9	212,815	33.4
1986	633,291	11,694	646,721	10,246	476,320	422,857	156,971	24.8	223,864	34.6
1987	648,118	14,827	662,977	16,256	496,185	448,277	151,933	23.4	214,700	32.4
1988	661,580	13,462	676,940	13,963	529,460	466,533	132,120	20.0	210,407	31.1
1989	673,316	11,736	685,249	8,309	524,110	496,378	149,206	22.2	188,871	27.6
1990	685,091	11,775	696,757	11,508	546,331	484,231	138,760	20.3	212,526	30.5
1991	690,915	5,824	703,212	6,455	551,418	485,761	139,497	20.2	217,451	30.9
1992	695,436	4,521	707,752	4,540	548,707	492,983	146,729	21.1	214,769	30.4
1993	694,250	-1,186	711,957	4,205	575,356	521,733	118,894	17.1	190,224	26.7
1994	702,985	8,735	715,090	3,133	585,320	518,253	117,665	16.7	196,837	27.5
1995	714,222	11,237	727,679	12,589	620,249	544,684	93,973	13.2	182,995	25.2
1996	724,728	10,506	737,637	9,958	616,790	554,081	107,938	14.9	183,556	24.9
1997	725,829	1,101	736,666	-971	637,677	529,874	88,152	12.1	206,792	28.1
1998	724,193	-1,636	735,090	-1,576	660,293	567,558	63,900	8.8	167,532	22.8
1999	733,481	9,288	748,271	13,181	682,122	570,915	51,359	7.0	177,356	23.7
2000	750,771	17,290	767,505	19,234	678,413	588,426	72,358	9.6	179,079	23.3
2001	783,737	32,966	806,598	39,093	687,812	576,312	95,925	12.2	230,286	28.6
2002	825,145	41,408	850,984	44,386	714,565	604,986	110,580	13.4	245,998	28.9
2003	853,649	28,504	882,120	31,136	709,375	593,874	144,274	16.9	288,246	32.7
2004	851,766	-1,883	864,849	-17,271	704,459	618,701	147,307	17.3	246,148	28.5
2005 [1]	860,137	8,371	878,110	13,261	747,332	625,233	112,805	13.1	252,877	28.8

[1] Preliminary.

Source: Edison Electric Institute, Washington, DC, *Statistical Yearbook of the Electric Power Industry*, annual.

Table 912. **Electric Energy Retail Sales by Class of Service and State: 2004**

[In billions of kilowatt-hours (3,548.2 represents 3,548,200,000,000)]

State	Total [1]	Residential	Commercial	Industrial	State	Total [1]	Residential	Commercial	Industrial
United States. . .	3,548.2	1,293.6	1,229.0	1,018.5	Missouri	74.1	31.4	28.4	14.3
					Montana.	13.0	4.1	4.3	4.6
Alabama.	86.9	30.1	21.2	35.6	Nebraska	25.9	8.8	8.5	8.6
Alaska	5.8	2.1	2.6	1.1	Nevada	31.3	10.7	8.3	12.4
Arizona.	66.9	28.9	26.1	11.9	New Hampshire	11.0	4.3	4.4	2.3
Arkansas	43.7	15.6	10.7	17.3					
California	252.8	85.0	117.6	49.5	New Jersey.	77.6	28.0	38.1	11.2
					New Mexico	19.8	5.6	8.2	6.0
Colorado.	46.7	15.5	19.5	11.7	New York	145.1	47.4	74.4	20.7
Connecticut.	32.2	13.2	13.5	5.4	North Carolina	125.7	51.7	42.9	31.1
Delaware	11.8	4.3	4.0	3.4	North Dakota.	10.5	3.7	3.8	3.0
District of Columbia . .	11.4	1.8	9.0	0.3					
Florida	218.6	112.2	86.8	19.5	Ohio	154.2	50.3	45.3	58.6
					Oklahoma.	50.9	19.7	17.0	14.2
Georgia	129.5	51.1	42.3	35.8	Oregon.	45.6	18.0	15.7	12.0
Hawaii	10.7	3.2	3.6	3.9	Pennsylvania.	143.5	50.7	44.4	47.7
Idaho	21.8	7.3	5.5	9.0	Rhode Island.	7.9	3.0	3.5	1.3
Illinois	139.3	43.4	47.4	48.0					
Indiana.	103.1	31.2	23.0	48.9	South Carolina.	79.9	27.9	20.1	31.9
					South Dakota	9.2	3.7	3.6	1.9
Iowa	40.9	12.6	10.8	17.4	Tennessee	99.7	38.5	28.2	32.9
Kansas	37.1	12.4	13.8	10.9	Texas.	320.6	120.3	99.6	100.6
Kentucky	86.5	25.2	18.4	42.9	Utah	24.5	7.3	9.3	7.8
Louisiana	79.7	28.9	22.6	28.3					
Maine.	12.4	4.3	4.3	3.7	Vermont	5.7	2.1	2.0	1.6
					Virginia.	105.4	42.5	43.0	19.7
Maryland	66.9	28.0	17.3	21.2	Washington	80.0	32.5	28.2	19.3
Massachusetts.	56.1	19.8	26.0	9.9	West Virginia.	28.9	10.8	7.2	10.9
Michigan.	106.6	33.1	38.6	34.9	Wisconsin	68.0	21.2	19.3	27.4
Minnesota	63.3	20.5	20.4	22.4	Wyoming	13.5	2.3	3.4	7.9
Mississippi	46.0	17.6	12.8	15.7					

[1] Includes transportation, not shown separately.

Source: U.S. Energy Information Administration, *Electric Sales and Revenue 2004*. See also <http://www.eia.doe.gov/cneaf/electricity/esr/esr_sum.html> (released December 2005).

Table 913. Electric Energy Price by Class of Service and State: 2004

[Revenue (in cents) per kilowatthour (kWh). Data include both bundled and unbundled consumers]

State	Total [1]	Resi-dential	Com-mercial	Indus-trial	State	Total [1]	Resi-dential	Com-mercial	Indus-trial
United States	7.62	8.97	8.16	5.27	Missouri	6.07	6.97	5.80	4.62
Alabama	6.08	7.62	7.12	4.15	Montana	6.40	7.86	7.42	4.15
Alaska	10.99	12.44	10.99	8.33	Nebraska	5.70	6.96	5.84	4.28
Arizona	7.45	8.46	7.28	5.35	Nevada	8.56	9.69	9.08	7.24
Arkansas	5.67	7.36	5.64	4.16	New Hampshire	11.37	12.49	10.99	10.01
California	11.45	12.51	11.53	9.52					
					New Jersey	10.29	11.23	9.96	9.03
Colorado	6.95	8.42	6.89	5.11	New Mexico	7.10	8.67	7.39	5.22
Connecticut	10.26	11.63	9.90	7.89	New York	12.55	14.54	12.98	7.04
Delaware	7.53	8.78	7.44	6.06	North Carolina	6.97	8.45	6.70	4.88
District of Columbia	7.47	8.00	7.45	4.74	North Dakota	5.69	6.79	5.86	4.13
Florida	8.16	8.99	7.61	5.84					
					Ohio	6.89	8.45	7.75	4.89
Georgia	6.58	7.86	6.88	4.43	Oklahoma	6.50	7.72	6.55	4.76
Hawaii	15.70	18.06	16.19	13.35	Oregon	6.21	7.18	6.45	4.43
Idaho	4.97	6.10	5.37	3.82	Pennsylvania	8.00	9.58	8.51	5.87
Illinois	6.80	8.37	7.54	4.65	Rhode Island	10.96	12.19	10.53	9.37
Indiana	5.58	7.30	6.31	4.13					
					South Carolina	6.22	8.12	6.91	4.13
Iowa	6.40	8.96	6.75	4.33	South Dakota	6.44	7.65	6.18	4.59
Kansas	6.37	7.74	6.45	4.69	Tennessee	6.14	6.90	7.05	4.46
Kentucky	4.63	6.11	5.60	3.34	Texas	7.95	9.73	7.90	5.87
Louisiana	7.13	8.05	7.58	5.82	Utah	5.69	7.21	5.90	4.01
Maine	9.69	12.16	9.89	6.56					
					Vermont	11.02	12.94	11.42	7.96
Maryland	7.15	7.80	7.56	5.99	Virginia	6.43	7.99	5.88	4.27
Massachusetts	10.77	11.75	10.99	8.48	Washington	5.80	6.37	6.17	4.28
Michigan	6.94	8.33	7.57	4.92	West Virginia	5.13	6.23	5.46	3.83
Minnesota	6.24	7.92	6.31	4.63	Wisconsin	6.88	9.07	7.24	4.93
Mississippi	7.00	8.21	7.99	4.83	Wyoming	4.98	7.21	5.98	3.91

[1] Includes transportation, not shown separately.

Source: U.S. Energy Information Administration, *Electric Sales and Revenue 2004*. See also <http://www.eia.doe.gov/cneaf/electricity /esr/esr_sum.html> (released December 2005).

Table 914. Total Electric Power Industry—Generation, Sales, Revenue, and Customers: 1990 to 2005

[2,808 represents 2,808,000,000,000 kWh. Sales and revenue are to and from ultimate customers. Commercial and Industrial are not wholly comparable on a year-to-year basis due to changes from one classification to another. For the 2003 period forward, the Energy Information Administration replaced the "Other" sector with the Transportation sector. The Transportation sector consists entirely of electrified rail and urban transit systems. Data previously reported in "Other" have been relocated to the Commercial sector, except for Agriculture (i.e., irrigation load), which have been relocated to the Industrial sector]

Class	Unit	1990	1995	1999	2000	2001	2002	2003	2004	2005 [1]
Generation [2]	Bil. kWh . .	2,808	3,353	3,695	3,802	3,737	3,858	3,883	3,971	4,038
Sales [3]	Bil. kWh .	2,713	3,013	3,312	3,421	3,382	3,466	3,489	3,548	3,648
Residential or domestic . . .	Bil. kWh . .	924	1,043	1,145	1,192	1,201	1,265	1,274	1,294	1,362
Percent of total	Percent . .	34.1	34.6	34.6	34.9	35.5	36.5	36.5	36.5	37.3
Commercial [4]	Bil. kWh . .	751	863	1,002	1,055	1,088	1,105	1,197	1,229	1,269
Industrial [5]	Bil. kWh . .	946	1,013	1,058	1,064	985	990	1,012	1,019	1,017
Revenue [3]	Bil. dol . . .	178.2	207.7	219.9	233.2	247.3	250.2	258.9	270.5	295.7
Residential or domestic . . .	Bil. dol . . .	72.4	87.6	93.5	98.2	103.7	107.1	110.8	116.0	128.3
Percent of total	Percent . .	40.6	42.2	42.5	42.1	41.9	42.8	42.8	42.9	43.4
Commercial [4]	Bil. dol . . .	55.1	66.4	72.8	78.4	86.5	87.3	95.8	100.3	110.1
Industrial [5]	Bil. dol . . .	44.9	47.2	46.8	49.4	49.1	48.6	51.8	53.7	56.7
Ultimate customers, Dec. 31 [3]	Million . . .	110.6	118.3	125.9	127.6	131.4	133.6	134.5	136.1	136.4
Residential or domestic . . .	Million . . .	97.1	103.9	110.4	111.7	114.9	116.6	117.3	118.8	119.0
Commercial [4]	Million . . .	12.1	12.9	14.1	14.3	14.9	15.3	16.5	16.6	16.6
Industrial [5]	Million . . .	0.5	0.6	0.6	0.5	0.6	0.6	0.7	0.7	0.8
Avg. kWh used per customer	1,000	24.5	25.5	26.3	26.8	25.7	25.9	25.9	26.1	26.8
Residential	1,000	9.5	10.0	10.4	10.7	10.5	10.9	10.9	10.9	11.4
Commercial [4]	1,000	62.2	66.6	71.2	73.5	73.2	72.0	72.3	74.0	76.3
Avg. annual bill per customer	Dollar . . .	1,612	1,756	1,746	1,828	1,883	1,872	1,924	1,987	2,168
Residential	Dollar . . .	745	843	847	879	902	918	945	977	1,079
Commercial [4]	Dollar . . .	4,562	5,124	5,171	5,464	5,821	5,693	5,786	6,037	6,622
Avg. revenue per kWh sold	Cents . . .	6.57	6.89	6.64	6.81	7.31	7.22	7.42	7.62	8.11
Residential	Cents . . .	7.83	8.40	8.17	8.24	8.63	8.46	8.70	8.97	9.42
Commercial [4]	Cents . . .	7.34	7.69	7.26	7.43	7.95	7.90	8.00	8.16	8.68
Industrial [5]	Cents . . .	4.74	4.66	4.43	4.64	4.98	4.91	5.12	5.27	5.57

[1] Preliminary. [2] "Generation" includes batteries, chemicals, hydrogen, pitch, sulfur, and purchased steam. [3] Includes other types not shown separately. [4] Small light and power. [5] Large light and power.

Source: Edison Electric Institute, Washington, DC, *Statistical Yearbook of the Electric Power Industry*, annual.

Energy and Utilities 585

Table 915. Revenue and Expense Statistics for Major U.S. Investor-Owned Electric Utilities: 1995 to 2004

[In millions of nominal dollars (199,967 represents $199,967,000,000). Covers approximately 180 investor-owned electric utilities that during each of the last 3 years met any one or more of the following conditions—1 mil. megawatt-hours of total sales; 100 megawatt-hours of sales for resale, 500 megawatt-hours of gross interchange out, and 500 megawatt-hours of wheeling for other]

Item	1995	1999	2000	2001	2002	2003	2004
Utility operating revenues.	199,967	214,160	235,336	267,525	219,389	226,227	240,318
Electric utility	183,655	197,578	214,707	244,219	200,135	202,369	213,539
Other utility	16,312	16,583	20,630	23,306	19,254	23,858	26,779
Utility operating expenses	165,321	182,258	210,324	235,198	188,745	197,459	207,161
Electric utility	150,599	167,266	191,329	213,733	171,291	175,473	182,337
Operation.	91,881	108,461	132,662	159,929	116,374	122,723	131,962
Production	68,983	83,555	107,352	136,089	90,649	96,181	104,287
Cost of fuel	29,122	29,826	32,555	29,490	24,132	26,476	28,678
Purchased power	29,981	43,258	61,969	98,231	58,828	62,173	67,354
Other	9,880	10,470	12,828	8,368	7,688	7,532	8,256
Transmission.	1,425	2,423	2,699	2,365	3,494	3,585	4,519
Distribution	2,561	2,956	3,115	3,217	3,113	3,185	3,301
Customer accounts.	3,613	4,195	4,246	4,434	4,165	4,180	4,087
Customer service	1,922	1,889	1,839	1,856	1,821	1,893	2,012
Sales	348	492	403	282	261	234	238
Administrative and general.	13,028	12,951	13,009	11,686	12,872	13,466	13,519
Maintenance.	11,767	12,276	12,185	11,167	10,843	11,141	11,774
Depreciation.	19,885	23,968	22,761	20,845	17,319	16,962	16,373
Taxes and other	27,065	22,561	23,721	21,792	26,755	24,648	22,228
Other utility	14,722	14,992	18,995	21,465	17,454	21,986	24,823
Net utility operating income	34,646	31,902	25,012	32,327	30,644	28,768	33,158

Source: U.S. Energy Information Administration, *Electric Power Annual 2004*. See also <http://www.eia.doe.gov/cneaf/electricity/epa/epat8p1.html> (released November 2005).

Table 916. Uranium Concentrate—Supply, Inventories, and Average Prices: 1980 to 2004

[43.70 represents 43,700,000 pounds (lbs.). Years ending December 31. For additional data on uranium, see Section 18]

Item	Unit	1980	1990	1995	1999	2000	2001	2002	2003	2004
Production [1].	Mil. lb. . . .	43.70	8.89	6.04	4.61	3.96	2.64	2.34	2.00	2.28
Exports [2].	Mil. lb. . . .	5.8	2.0	9.8	8.5	13.6	11.7	15.4	13.2	13.2
Imports [2].	Mil. lb. . . .	3.6	23.7	41.3	47.6	44.9	46.7	52.7	53.0	66.1
Electric plant purchases from										
domestic suppliers.	Mil. lb. . . .	(NA)	20.5	22.3	21.4	24.3	27.5	22.7	21.7	28.2
Loaded into U.S. nuclear reactors [3] . . .	Mil. lb. . . .	(NA)	(NA)	51.1	58.8	51.5	52.7	57.2	62.3	50.8
Inventories, total.	Mil. lb. . . .	(NA)	129.1	72.5	127.1	111.3	103.8	102.1	85.5	94.3
At domestic suppliers.	Mil. lb. . . .	(NA)	26.4	13.7	68.8	56.5	48.1	48.7	39.9	38.0
At electric utilities	Mil. lb. . . .	(NA)	102.7	58.7	58.3	54.8	55.6	53.5	45.6	56.4
Average price per pound:										
Purchased imports.	Dollars. . .	(NA)	12.55	10.20	10.55	9.84	9.51	10.05	10.59	12.25
Domestic purchases	Dollars. . .	(NA)	15.70	11.11	11.88	11.45	10.45	10.35	10.84	11.91

NA Not available. [1] Data are for uranium concentrate, a yellow or brown powder obtained by the milling of uranium ore, processing of in situ leach mining solutions, or as a byproduct of phosphoric acid production. [2] Trade data prior to 1982 were for transactions conducted by uranium suppliers only. For 1982 forward, transactions by uranium buyers (consumers) have been included. Buyer imports and exports prior to 1982 are believed to be small. [3] Does not include any fuel rods removed from reactors and later reloaded into the reactor.

Source: U.S. Energy Information Administration, *Annual Energy Review 2004*. Also see <http://www.eia.doe.gov/emeu/aer/pdf/pages/sec9_7.pdf> (released August 2005).

Table 917. Nuclear Power Plants—Number, Capacity, and Generation: 1980 to 2005

[51.8 represents 51,800,000 kW]

Item	1980	1985	1990	1995	1998	1999	2000	2001	2002	2003	2004	2005
Operable generating units [1, 2] . . .	71	96	112	109	104	104	104	104	104	104	104	104
Net summer capacity [2, 3] (mil. kW)	51.8	79.4	99.6	99.5	97.1	97.4	97.9	98.2	98.7	99.2	99.6	99.6
Net generation (bil. kWh)	251.1	383.7	576.9	673.4	673.7	728.3	753.9	768.8	780.1	763.7	788.5	780.5
Percent of total electricity net generation	11.0	15.5	19.0	20.1	18.6	19.7	19.8	20.6	20.2	19.7	19.9	19.3
Capacity factor [4] (percent)	56.3	58.0	66.0	77.4	78.2	85.3	88.1	89.4	90.3	87.9	90.1	89.4

[1] Total of nuclear generating units holding full-power licenses, or equivalent permission to operate, at the end of the year. Although Browns Ferry 1 was shut down in 1985, the unit has remained fully licensed and thus has continued to be counted as operable during the shutdown. [2] As of year-end. [3] Net summer capacity is the peak steady hourly output that generating equipment is expected to supply to system load, exclusive of auxiliary and other power plant, as demonstrated by test at the time of summer peak demand. [4] Weighted average of monthly capacity factors. Monthly factors are derived by dividing actual monthly generation by the maximum possible generation for the month (number of hours in the month multiplied by the net summer capacity at the end of the month).

Source: U.S. Energy Information Administration, *Monthly Energy Review*, May 2006. See also <http://www.eia.doe.gov/emeu/mer/nuclear.html> (accessed June 6, 2006).

Table 918. Nuclear Power Plants—Number of Units, Net Generation, and Net Summer Capacity by State: 2004

[788,528 represents 788,528,000,000 kWh]

State	Number of units	Net generation Total (mil. kWh)	Percent of total [1]	Net summer capacity Total (mil. kW)	Percent of total [1]	State	Number of units	Net generation Total (mil. kWh)	Percent of total [1]	Net summer capacity Total (mil. kW)	Percent of total [1]
U.S.	104	788,528	19.9	99.63	10.3	MS	1	10,233	23.4	1.27	7.5
AL	5	31,636	23.0	5.01	16.3	MO	1	7,831	8.9	1.14	5.6
AZ	3	28,113	26.9	3.80	15.7	NE	2	10,241	32.0	1.23	18.3
AR	2	15,450	29.8	1.84	13.6	NH	1	10,178	42.6	1.16	27.1
CA	4	30,268	15.5	4.32	7.4	NJ	4	27,082	48.5	3.97	21.9
CT	2	16,539	50.7	2.04	25.7	NY	6	40,640	29.5	5.07	13.4
FL	5	31,216	14.3	3.90	7.7	NC	5	40,091	31.7	4.94	18.2
GA	4	33,748	26.6	4.05	11.5	OH	2	15,950	10.8	2.11	6.2
IL	11	92,047	48.0	11.38	27.1	PA	9	77,459	36.1	9.23	20.4
IA	1	4,929	11.4	0.56	5.2	SC	7	51,201	52.3	6.47	29.2
KS	1	10,133	21.7	1.17	10.7	TN	3	28,612	29.3	3.40	16.2
LA	2	17,080	17.4	2.06	7.8	TX	4	40,435	10.4	4.86	4.8
MD	2	14,580	28.0	1.74	13.9	VT	1	3,858	70.5	0.51	50.7
MA	1	5,939	12.5	0.69	4.9	VA	4	28,315	35.9	3.44	15.3
MI	4	30,562	25.8	3.97	13.0	WA	1	8,982	8.8	1.12	4.1
MN	3	13,296	25.4	1.61	14.0	WI	3	11,888	19.7	1.59	10.8

[1] For total generation and capacity, see Table 910.

Source: U.S. Energy Information Administration, *Electric Power Annual 2004*. See also <http://www.eia.doe.gov/cneaf/electricity/epa/epa_sprdshts.html>.

Table 919. Solar Collector Shipments by Type, End Use, and Market Sector: 1980 to 2004

[Shipments in thousands of square feet (19,398 represents 19,398,000). Solar collector is a device for intercepting sunlight, converting the light to heat, and carrying the heat to where it will be either used or stored. 1985 data are not available. Based on the Annual Solar Thermal Collector Manufacturers Survey]

Year	Number of manufac- turers	Total ship- ments [1, 2, 3]	Collector type Low tempera- ture [1, 2]	Medium tempera- ture, spe- cial, other [2]	End use Pool heating	Hot water	Space heating	Market sector Resi- dential	Com- mercial	Industrial
1980	233	19,398	12,233	7,165	12,029	4,790	1,688	16,077	2,417	488
1986 [4] . . .	98	9,360	3,751	1,111	3,494	1,181	127	4,131	703	13
1990 [4] . . .	51	11,409	3,645	2,527	5,016	1,091	2	5,835	294	22
1995	36	7,666	6,813	840	6,763	755	132	6,966	604	82
2000	26	8,354	7,948	400	7,863	367	99	7,473	810	57
2002	27	11,663	11,126	535	11,073	423	146	11,000	595	62
2003	26	11,444	10,877	560	10,800	511	76	10,506	864	71
2004 [5] . . .	24	14,114	13,608	506	13,634	452	13	12,864	1,178	70

[1] Includes shipments of high temperature collectors to the government, including some military, but excluding space applications. Also includes end uses such as process heating, utility, and other market sectors not shown separately. [2] Includes imputation of shipment data to account for nonrespondents. [3] Total shipments include all domestic and export shipments and may include imported collectors that subsequently were shipped to domestic or foreign customers. [4] Declines between 1986 and 1990 are primarily due to the expiration of the federal energy tax credit and industry consolidation. [5] Preliminary.

Source: U.S. Energy Information Administration, 1980–1990, *Solar Collector Manufacturing Activity*, annual reports; 1995–2002, *Renewable Energy Annual*; thereafter, *Solar Thermal and Photovoltaic Collector Manufacturing Activities 2004*. See also <http://www.eia.doe.gov/cneaf/solar.renewables/page/solarreport/table38.html> (released November 2005).

Energy and Utilities   587

Table 920. **Total Renewable Energy Net Generation by Source and State: 2002**

[In millions of kilowatthours (351,251 represents 351,251,000,000). MSW = municipal solid waste]

State	Total [1]	Hydro-electric	MSW/ landfill gas	Other Bio-mass [2]	Wood/ Wood Waste	State	Total [1]	Hydro-electric	MSW/ landfill gas	Other Bio-mass [2]	Wood/ Wood Waste
U.S. ..	**351,251**	**264,329**	**20,185**	**2,672**	**38,665**	MO	1,423	1,357	(NA)	66	(Z)
AL	12,575	8,825	(NA)	23	3,727	MT......	9,630	9,567	(NA)	(NA)	63
AK......	1,452	1,439	(NA)	11	1	NE.....	1,119	1,097	(NA)	13	(NA)
AZ......	7,569	7,427	50	91	(NA)	NV.....	3,395	2,268	(NA)	(NA)	(NA)
AR......	5,021	3,436	(NA)	5	1,581	NH.....	2,066	1,141	225	(NA)	700
CA......	54,821	31,141	1,858	434	3,958	NJ.....	1,342	12	1,315	16	(NA)
CO......	1,378	1,209	(NA)	30	(NA)	NM.....	284	265	(NA)	19	(NA)
CT......	1,961	335	1,437	188	(NA)	NY.....	27,671	25,048	2,129	(NA)	412
DE......	(NA)	(NA)	(NA)	(NA)	(NA)	NC.....	5,310	3,492	106	30	1,683
DC......	(NA)	(NA)	(NA)	(NA)	(NA)	ND.....	1,593	1,593	(NA)	(Z)	(NA)
FL......	5,328	184	3,309	282	1,553	OH.....	640	488	23	2	126
GA......	9,131	2,716	28	168	6,219	OK.....	2,227	1,988	(NA)	(NA)	239
HI	609	95	301	139	(NA)	OR.....	35,500	34,413	87	(NA)	624
ID	9,278	8,769	(NA)	(NA)	508	PA.....	4,968	2,211	1,925	9	766
IL......	974	129	592	254	(NA)	RI.....	101	4	98	(NA)	(NA)
IN	543	411	124	7	(NA)	SC.....	2,634	1,390	16	(NA)	1,229
IA	1,964	946	78	21	(Z)	SD.....	4,360	4,354	(NA)	(NA)	4,360
KS......	479	13	(NA)	(NA)	(NA)	TN.....	8,776	7,974	38	10	751
KY......	4,390	4,025	(NA)	(NA)	365	TX.....	5,117	1,123	53	211	1,073
LA	3,754	891	(NA)	114	2,749	UT.....	687	458	11	(NA)	(NA)
ME......	7,198	2,768	408	298	3,724	VT.....	1,481	1,115	(NA)	(NA)	356
MD......	2,438	1,661	594	(Z)	183	VA.....	3,386	868	1,106	4	1,408
MA......	2,914	863	1,918	27	107	WA	79,955	78,167	225	21	1,126
MI	4,171	1,669	945	81	1,475	WV.....	1,097	1,066	(NA)	22	(Z)
MN......	2,886	809	791	3	377	WI.....	3,676	2,515	396	74	645
MS......	949	12	(NA)	(Z)	937	WY.....	1,031	584	(NA)	(NA)	(NA)

NA Not available. Z Less than 500,000 million kilowatt hours. [1] Includes types not shown separately. [2] Agriculture byproducts/crops, sludge waste, tires, and other biomass solids, liquids and gases.

Source: Energy Information Administration, *Renewable Energy Trends 2004*. See also <http://www.eia.doe.gov /cneaf/solar.renewables/page/trends/table17.pdf> (released August 2005).

Table 921. **Privately Owned Gas Utility Industry—Balance Sheet and Income Account: 1990 to 2004**

[In millions of dollars (121,686 represents $121,686,000,000). The gas utility industry consists of pipeline and distribution companies. Excludes operations of companies distributing gas in bottles or tanks]

Item	1990	1995	1998	1999	2000	2001	2002	2003	2004
COMPOSITE BALANCE SHEET									
Assets, total	**121,686**	**141,965**	**119,715**	**155,413**	**165,709**	**171,681**	**185,064**	**174,756**	**168,306**
Total utility plant.............	112,863	143,636	135,092	166,134	162,206	175,530	197,717	188,807	180,884
Depreciation and amortization. . . .	49,483	62,723	61,226	73,823	69,366	73,753	85,038	76,642	79,889
Utility plant (net)............	63,380	80,912	73,866	92,311	92,839	101,777	112,679	112,165	100,996
Investment and fund accounts ...	23,872	26,489	12,337	17,344	10,846	10,237	13,000	13,430	12,716
Current and accrued assets	23,268	18,564	17,348	22,443	35,691	29,345	25,786	22,905	22,107
Deferred debits [1]	9,576	13,923	13,721	20,922	24,279	28,553	31,928	24,663	31,033
Liabilities, total	**121,686**	**141,965**	**119,715**	**155,413**	**165,709**	**171,681**	**185,064**	**174,756**	**168,306**
Capitalization, total...........	74,958	90,581	71,718	95,244	96,079	107,310	117,362	112,089	105,799
Capital stock	43,810	54,402	37,977	[2]859	760	701	333	305	220
Long-term debts	31,148	35,548	33,386	46,906	48,267	49,739	58,962	54,179	51,327
Current and accrued liabilities...	29,550	28,272	26,953	32,683	42,312	34,962	30,856	28,599	25,515
Deferred income taxes [3]	11,360	14,393	13,239	17,120	17,157	20,445	24,612	23,888	23,944
Other liabilities and credits	5,818	8,715	7,806	10,365	10,161	8,964	12,235	10,179	13,048
COMPOSITE INCOME ACCOUNT									
Operating revenues, total ..	**66,027**	**58,390**	**57,117**	**59,142**	**72,042**	**79,276**	**68,352**	**75,527**	**79,167**
Minus: Operating expenses [4]	60,137	50,760	50,896	38,752	64,988	71,209	60,041	66,677	70,887
Operation and maintenance ...	51,627	37,966	41,026	41,415	54,602	58,873	48,521	55,036	59,283
Federal, state, and local taxes..	4,957	6,182	5,429	5,605	6,163	7,394	6,249	6,581	6,368
Equals: Operating income	5,890	7,630	6,220	20,390	7,053	8,068	8,310	8,852	8,280
Utility operating income	6,077	7,848	6,361	16,614	7,166	8,192	8,564	9,198	8,417
Income before interest charges...	8,081	9,484	7,779	17,531	7,589	8,266	9,305	10,053	9,414
Net income	4,410	5,139	4,379	10,420	4,245	4,038	4,792	6,198	5,815
Dividends	3,191	4,037	2,263	5,595	3,239	3,560	3,887	3,765	2,005

[1] Includes capital stock discount and expense and reacquired securities. [2] Data not comparable to earlier years. [3] Includes reserves for deferred income taxes. [4] Includes expenses not shown separately.

Source: American Gas Association, Arlington, VA, *Gas Facts*, annual (copyright).

Table 922. Gas Utility Industry—Summary: 1990 to 2004

[54,261 represents 54,261,000. Covers natural, manufactured, mixed, and liquid petroleum gas. Based on a questionnaire mailed to all privately and municipally owned gas utilities in United States, except those with annual revenues less than $25,000]

Item	Unit	1990	1995	1999	2000	2001	2002	2003	2004
End users [1]	1,000	54,261	58,728	60,778	61,262	61,385	62,034	62,610	63,297
Residential	1,000	49,802	53,955	56,017	56,494	56,680	57,293	57,802	58,501
Commercial	1,000	4,246	4,530	4,599	4,610	4,546	4,590	4,661	4,641
Industrial and other	1,000	166	181	159	157	159	149	145	152
Sales [2]	Tril. Btu [3]	9,842	9,221	8,975	9,232	8,667	8,864	8,927	8,766
Residential	Tril. Btu	4,468	4,803	4,622	4,741	4,525	4,589	4,722	4,566
Percent of total	Percent	45	52	51	51	52	52	53	52
Commercial	Tril. Btu	2,192	2,281	2,067	2,077	2,053	2,055	2,125	2,075
Industrial	Tril. Btu	3,010	1,919	1,553	1,698	1,461	1,748	1,672	1,763
Other	Tril. Btu	171	218	734	715	627	472	408	353
Revenues [2]	Mil. dol.	45,153	46,436	47,202	59,243	69,150	57,112	72,606	79,929
Residential	Mil. dol.	25,000	28,742	30,095	35,828	42,454	35,062	43,664	47,275
Percent of total	Percent	55	62	64	60	61	61	60	59
Commercial	Mil. dol.	10,604	11,573	10,731	13,339	16,848	13,512	17,349	18,689
Industrial	Mil. dol.	8,996	5,571	4,715	7,432	7,513	6,841	11,525	11,230
Other	Mil. dol.	553	549	1,662	2,645	2,335	1,698	2,115	2,735
Prices per mil. Btu [3]	Dollars	4.59	5.05	5.26	6.42	7.98	6.44	8.13	9.13
Residential	Dollars	5.60	6.00	6.51	7.56	9.38	7.64	9.25	10.37
Commercial	Dollars	4.84	5.07	5.19	6.42	8.20	6.57	8.17	9.01
Industrial	Dollars	2.99	2.98	3.04	4.38	5.14	3.84	5.67	6.37
Gas mains mileage	1,000	1,189	1,278	1,340	1,369	1,374	1,411	1,424	1,462
Field and gathering	1,000	32	31	32	27	20	22	22	24
Transmission	1,000	292	297	301	297	287	310	304	299
Distribution	1,000	865	950	1,008	1,046	1,066	1,080	1,098	1,140
Construction expenditures [4]	Mil. dol.	7,899	10,760	8,320	8,624	9,516	11,552	13,034	16,567
Transmission	Mil. dol.	2,886	3,380	1,785	1,590	3,212	5,184	7,317	3,205
Distribution	Mil. dol.	3,714	5,394	4,180	5,437	4,546	4,890	3,870	11,636
Production and storage	Mil. dol.	309	367	161	138	113	73	258	181
General	Mil. dol.	770	1,441	1,974	1,273	1,457	1,156	1,350	1,271
Underground storage	Mil. dol.	219	177	220	185	187	249	239	274

[1] Annual average. [2] Excludes sales for resale. [3] For definition of Btu, see text, this section. [4] Includes general.

Source: American Gas Association, Arlington, VA, *Gas Facts*, annual (copyright).

Table 923. Gas Utility Industry—Customers, Sales, and Revenues by State: 2004

[63,296 represents 63,296,000. See headnote, Table 922. For definition of Btu, see text, this section]

State	Customers [1] (1,000) Total	Resi-dential	Sales [2] (tril. Btu) Total	Resi-dential	Revenues [2] (mil. dol.) Total	Resi-dential	State	Customers [1] (1,000) Total	Resi-dential	Sales [2] (tril. Btu) Total	Resi-dential	Revenues [2] (mil. dol.) Total	Resi-dential
U.S.	63,296	58,501	8,766	4,565	79,929	47,275	MS	500	445	88	25	709	255
							MO	1,490	1,347	172	113	1,768	1,209
AL	873	806	103	45	1,075	585	MT	268	237	31	21	278	183
AK	117	104	94	19	333	89	NE	462	423	62	35	498	306
AZ	1,050	994	91	39	859	464	NV	684	649	85	38	728	367
AR	626	555	67	36	668	408	NH	104	89	15	7	200	103
CA	10,387	9,921	750	525	6,863	5,030	NJ	2,679	2,468	368	228	3,897	2,556
							NM	551	506	56	35	483	327
CO	1,634	1,496	193	124	1,505	1,021	NY	4,210	3,899	548	355	6,002	4,317
CT	518	469	84	45	999	612	NC	1,056	948	136	65	1,411	798
DE	145	133	20	11	213	126	ND	129	112	30	11	228	101
DC	128	121	15	11	209	154	OH	2,261	2,095	273	199	2,820	2,093
FL	669	627	44	16	569	277	OK	950	871	94	61	886	606
GA	350	317	56	19	515	213	OR	668	595	85	40	782	428
HI	29	26	3	1	59	14	PA	2,610	2,398	338	232	3,919	2,779
ID	322	288	33	21	284	187	RI	246	224	29	20	364	258
IL	3,828	3,593	522	410	4,707	3,742	SC	584	527	119	30	1,075	352
IN	1,688	1,541	239	148	2,177	1,434	SD	169	148	24	13	203	117
IA	937	839	116	70	1,063	693	TN	1,165	1,037	160	67	1,465	692
KS	939	855	96	67	956	697	TX	4,268	3,939	1,419	197	9,937	1,986
KY	811	731	105	55	1,021	582	UT	753	701	95	62	701	492
LA	997	935	287	44	2,097	476	VT	37	32	8	3	71	34
ME	26	19	5	1	58	17	VA	1,041	958	129	75	1,459	952
MD	910	854	94	69	1,116	857	WA	1,024	927	131	73	1,211	703
MA	1,431	1,306	176	116	2,340	1,624	WV	393	358	52	31	518	331
MI	3,299	3,056	497	355	4,010	2,936	WI	1,729	1,570	243	139	2,209	1,373
MN	1,465	1,338	275	137	2,309	1,262	WY	84	75	13	7	100	57

[1] Averages for the year. [2] Excludes sales for resale.

Source: American Gas Association, Arlington, VA, *Gas Facts*, annual (copyright).

Table 924. Public Drinking Water Systems by Size of Community Served and Source of Water: 2004

[As of **September**. Covers systems that provide water for human consumption through pipes and other constructed conveyances to a least 15 service connections or serve an average of at least 25 persons for at least 60 days a year. Based on reported data in the Safe Drinking Water Information System maintained by the Environmental Protection Agency]

Type of system	Total	Size of community served					Water source	
		500 or fewer persons	501 to 3,300 persons	3,301 to 10,000 persons	10,001 to 100,000	100,001 persons or more	Ground water	Surface water
Total systems.............	159,796	131,291	19,632	4,913	3,584	376	145,498	14,298
COMMUNITY WATER SYSTEMS [1]								
Number of systems.............	52,838	30,006	14,212	4,707	3,541	372	41,264	11,574
Percent of systems	100	57	27	9	7	1	78	22
Population served (1,000)...........	272,496	4,957	20,138	27,346	99,809	120,246	90,500	181,996
Percent of population	100	2	7	10	37	44	33	67
NONTRANSIENT, NONCOMMUNITY WATER SYSTEM [2]								
Number of systems.............	19,375	16,545	2,720	96	14	(NA)	18,647	728
Percent of systems	100	85	14	–	–	(NA)	96	4
Population served (1,000)...........	5,933	2,302	2,713	517	402	(NA)	5,357	577
Percent of population	100	39	46	9	7	(NA)	90	10
TRANSIENT, NONCOMMUNITY WATER SYSTEM [3]								
Number of systems.............	87,583	84,740	2,700	110	29	4	85,587	1,996
Percent of systems	100	97	3	–	–	–	98	2
Population served (1,000)...........	18,485	7,318	2,668	612	618	7,269	15,691	2,793
Percent of population	100	40	14	3	3	39	85	15

NA Not available. – Represents zero. [1] A public water system that supplies water to the same population year-round. [2] A public water system that regularly supplies water to at least 25 of the same people at least 6 months per year, but not year-round. Some examples are schools, factories, and office buildings which have their own water systems. [3] A public water system that provides water in a place such as a gas station or campground where people do not remain for long periods of time.

Source: U.S. Environmental Protection Agency, *Factoids: Drinking Water and Ground Water Statistics for 2004*, annual reports. See also <http://www.epa.gov/safewater/data/getdata.html> (accessed June 2005).

Table 925. Sewage Treatment Facilities: 2003

[Based on the North American Industry Classification System (NAICS), 2002; see text, Section 15]

State	Sewage Treatment Facilities (NAICS 22132)		State	Sewage Treatment Facilities (NAICS 22132)	
	Number of establishments	Paid employees		Number of establishments	Paid employees
U.S.	840	6,627	MO	25	(2)
AL	11	(1)	MT	8	(3)
AK	6	(3)	NE	2	(3)
AZ	16	(1)	NV	2	(1)
AR	7	36	NH	2	(4)
CA	22	(2)	NJ	13	(4)
CO	15	50	NM	6	(1)
CT	8	117	NY	32	(2)
DE	1	(3)	NC	27	(1)
DC	(NA)	(NA)	ND	(NA)	(NA)
FL	84	608	OH	14	83
GA	5	(3)	OK	8	(1)
HI	14	74	OR	4	(3)
ID	8	(1)	PA	100	562
IL	51	(4)	RI	3	(1)
IN	54	(5)	SC	10	52
IA	6	(1)	SD	4	(3)
KS	6	28	TN	10	(6)
KY	10	105	TX	73	(6)
LA	24	(2)	UT	4	(3)
ME	5	(3)	VT	4	(3)
MD	3	(3)	VA	14	(2)
MA	14	(2)	WA	5	(1)
MI	24	(1)	WV	20	91
MN	14	53	WI	16	51
MS	24	127	WY	3	(1)

NA Not available. [1] 20–99 employees. [2] 100–249 employees. [3] 0–19 employees. [4] 250–499 employees. [5] 500–999 employees. [6] 1,000–2,499 employees.

Source: U.S. Census Bureau, County Business Patterns; annual. See <http://www.census.gov/epcd/cbp/view/cbpview.html>.

This section presents data on the construction industry and on various indicators of its activity and costs; on housing units and their characteristics and occupants; and on the characteristics and vacancy rates for commercial buildings. This edition contains data from the 2005 American Housing Survey.

The principal source of these data is the U.S. Census Bureau, which issues a variety of current publications, as well as data from the decennial census. Current construction statistics compiled by the Census Bureau appear in its *New Residential Construction* and *New Residential Sales* press releases and Web site <http://www.census.gov/const/www/>. Statistics on expenditures by owners of residential properties are issued quarterly and annually in *Expenditures for Residential Improvements and Repairs. Value of New Construction Put in Place* presents data on all types of construction. Reports of the censuses of construction industries (see below) are also issued on various topics.

Other Census Bureau publications include the *Current Housing Reports* series, which comprise the quarterly *Housing Vacancies*, the quarterly *Market Absorption of Apartments*, the biennial *American Housing Survey* (formerly *Annual Housing Survey*), and reports of the censuses of housing and of construction industries.

Other sources include the monthly *Dodge Construction Potentials* of McGraw-Hill Construction, New York, NY, which present national and state data on construction contracts; the National Association of Home Builders with state-level data on housing starts; the NATIONAL ASSOCIATION OF REALTORS®, which presents data on existing home sales; the Bureau of Economic Analysis, which presents data on residential capital and gross housing product; and the U.S. Energy Information Administration, which provides data on commercial buildings through its periodic sample surveys.

Censuses and surveys—Censuses of the construction industry were first conducted by the Census Bureau for 1929, 1935, and 1939; beginning in 1967, a census has been taken every 5 years (through 2002, for years ending in "2" and "7"). The latest reports are part of the 2002 Economic Census. See text, Section 15, Business Enterprise.

The construction sector of the economic census, covers all employer establishments primarily engaged in (1) building construction by general contractors or operative builders; (2) heavy (nonbuilding) construction by general contractors; and (3) construction by special trade contractors. This sector includes construction management and land subdividers and developers. The 2002 census was conducted in accordance with the 2002 North American Industrial Classification System (NAICS). See text, Section 15, Business Enterprise, for general information on the SIC and NAICS.

From 1850 through 1930, the Census Bureau collected some housing data as part of its censuses of population and agriculture. Beginning in 1940, separate censuses of housing have been taken at 10-year intervals. For the 1970 and 1980 censuses, data on year-round housing units were collected and issued on occupancy and structural characteristics, plumbing facilities, value, and rent; for 1990 such characteristics were presented for all housing units.

The American Housing Survey (*Current Housing Reports* Series H-150 and H-170), which began in 1973, provided an annual and ongoing series of data on selected housing and demographic characteristics until 1983. In 1984, the name of the survey was changed from the Annual Housing Survey. Currently, national data are collected every other year, and data for selected metropolitan areas are collected on a rotating basis. All samples represent a cross section of the housing stock in their respective areas. Estimates are subject to both sampling and nonsampling errors; caution should therefore be used in making comparisons between years.

Data on residential mortgages were collected continuously from 1890 to 1970, except 1930, as part of the decennial census by the Census Bureau. Since 1973, mortgage status data, limited to single family homes on less than 10 acres with no business on the property, have been presented in the American Housing Survey. Data on mortgage activity are covered in Section 25, Banking and Finance.

Housing units—In general, a housing unit is a house, an apartment, a group of rooms or a single room occupied or intended for occupancy as separate living quarters; that is, the occupants live separately from any other individual in the building, and there is direct access from the outside or through a common hall. Transient accommodations, barracks for workers, and institutional-type quarters are not counted as housing units.

Statistical reliability—For a discussion of statistical collection and estimation, sampling procedures, and measures of statistical reliability applicable to Census Bureau data, see Appendix III.

Figure 20.1
New and Existing Homes Sold: 1990 to 2005

In thousands

Existing homes sold

New homes sold

Source: Chart prepared by U.S. Census Bureau. For data, see Tables 940 and 943.

Median Sales Price of Homes: 1990 to 2005

In dollars

New homes

Existing homes

Source: Chart prepared by U.S. Census Bureau. For data, see Tables 941 and 943.

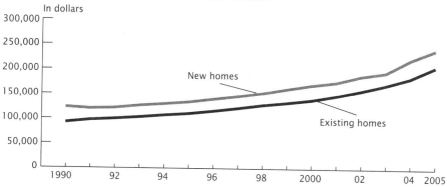

Figure 20.2
House Remodeling: 2005

Millions of households

Remodel bathroom
Carpeting
Remodel kitchen
Roofing
Ceramic tile floors
Remodel bedroom
Exterior doors
Add deck/porch/patio
Kitchen counter tops
Hardwood floors
Laminate flooring
Concrete or masonry work
Vinyl windows

Source: Chart prepared by U.S. Census Bureau. For data, see Table 969.

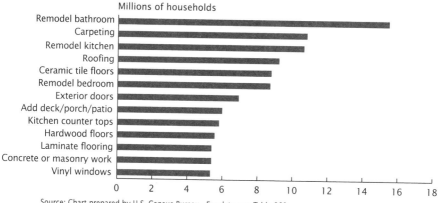

U.S. Census Bureau, Statistical Abstract of the United States: 2007

Table 926. **Construction—Establishments, Employees, and Payroll by Kind of Business (NAICS Basis): 2000 and 2003**

[6,573 represents 6,573,000. Covers establishments with payroll. Employees are for the week including March 12. Excludes most government employees, railroad employees, and self-employed persons. Kind-of-business classification for 2000 based on North American Industry Classification System (NAICS) 1997; data for 2003 based on NAICS 2002. See text, Section 15. For statement on methodology, see Appendix III]

Industry	NAICS code [1]	Establishments		Paid employees [2] (1,000)		Annual payroll (mil. dol.)	
		2000	2003	2000	2003	2000	2003
Construction	23	709,590	732,175	6,573	6,381	239,910	252,940
1997 NAICS							
Building, developing, & general contracting	233	216,354	(NA)	1,605	(NA)	60,798	(NA)
Heavy construction.	234	39,516	(NA)	901	(NA)	38,628	(NA)
Special trade contractors.	235	453,720	(NA)	4,067	(NA)	140,484	(NA)
2002 NAICS							
Construction of buildings	236	(NA)	219,899	(NA)	1,492	(NA)	62,827
Residential building construction	2361	(NA)	176,600	(NA)	789	(NA)	30,252
New single-family housing construction (except operative builders).	236115	(NA)	105,329	(NA)	400	(NA)	13,346
New multifamily housing construction (except operative builders).	236116	(NA)	4,878	(NA)	46	(NA)	1,958
New housing operative builders	236117	(NA)	10,959	(NA)	140	(NA)	8,428
Residential remodelers.	236118	(NA)	55,434	(NA)	204	(NA)	6,521
Nonresidential building construction	2362	(NA)	43,299	(NA)	702	(NA)	32,575
Industrial building construction	23621	(NA)	1,773	(NA)	71	(NA)	2,900
Commercial and institutional building construction . .	23622	(NA)	41,526	(NA)	631	(NA)	29,674
Heavy and civil engineering construction	237	(NA)	50,905	(NA)	911	(NA)	42,678
Utility system construction	2371	(NA)	21,166	(NA)	462	(NA)	20,138
Water and sewer line and related structures.	23711	(NA)	14,105	(NA)	185	(NA)	7,917
Oil and gas pipeline and related structures.	23712	(NA)	1,751	(NA)	85	(NA)	3,959
Power and communication line and related structures.	23713	(NA)	5,310	(NA)	192	(NA)	8,262
Land subdivision.	2372	(NA)	11,986	(NA)	61	(NA)	2,717
Highway, street, and bridge construction	2373	(NA)	12,446	(NA)	309	(NA)	16,109
Other heavy and civil engineering construction.	2379	(NA)	5,307	(NA)	80	(NA)	3,715
Specialty trade contractors.	238	(NA)	461,371	(NA)	3,979	(NA)	147,434
Foundation, structure, and building exterior contractors.	2381	(NA)	112,299	(NA)	984	(NA)	32,913
Poured concrete foundation and structures contractors	23811	(NA)	27,517	(NA)	265	(NA)	9,463
Structural steel and precast concrete contractors. . .	23812	(NA)	3,547	(NA)	63	(NA)	2,556
Framing contractors.	23813	(NA)	18,456	(NA)	149	(NA)	4,266
Masonry contractors.	23814	(NA)	24,723	(NA)	208	(NA)	6,679
Glass and glazing contractors	23815	(NA)	5,163	(NA)	46	(NA)	1,702
Roofing contractors.	23816	(NA)	18,999	(NA)	172	(NA)	5,644
Siding contractors	23817	(NA)	10,082	(NA)	50	(NA)	1,428
Other foundation, structure, and building exterior contractors.	23819	(NA)	3,812	(NA)	31	(NA)	1,176
Building equipment contractors	2382	(NA)	165,428	(NA)	1,746	(NA)	70,976
Electrical contractors	23821	(NA)	68,211	(NA)	725	(NA)	29,929
Plumbing, heating, and air-conditioning contractors .	23822	(NA)	91,111	(NA)	912	(NA)	35,907
Other building equipment contractors	23829	(NA)	6,106	(NA)	109	(NA)	5,140
Building finishing contractors.	2383	(NA)	115,155	(NA)	802	(NA)	26,294
Drywall and insulation contractors.	23831	(NA)	18,773	(NA)	273	(NA)	9,590
Drywall and insulation contractors	23832	(NA)	39,174	(NA)	208	(NA)	6,052
Painting and wall covering contractors	23833	(NA)	14,088	(NA)	75	(NA)	2,606
Flooring contractors	23834	(NA)	8,737	(NA)	55	(NA)	1,805
Tile and terrazzo contractors	23835	(NA)	28,639	(NA)	135	(NA)	4,284
Finish carpentry contractors.		(NA)	5,744	(NA)	56	(NA)	1,958
Other building finishing contractors	23839	(NA)	68,489	(NA)	447	(NA)	17,251
Other specialty trade contractors	2389	(NA)	36,198	(NA)	257	(NA)	10,352
Site preparation contractors.	23891	(NA)	32,291	(NA)	190	(NA)	6,899
All other specialty trade contractors.	23899						

NA Not available. [1] North American Industry Classification System code; see text, Section 15, Business Enterprise.
[2] Employees on the payroll for the pay period including March 12.

Source: U.S. Census Bureau, "County Business Patterns"; annual. See <http://www.census.gov/epcd/cbp/view/cbpview.html>.

Table 927. Construction—Establishments, Employees, Payroll, Value of Construction, Costs, and Capital Expenditures by Kind of Business (NAICS Basis): 2002

[Preliminary. For establishments with payroll. (8,263 represents $8,263,000,000). Based on the 2002 Economic Censuses; See Appendix III]

Kind of business	2002 NAICS code [1]	Number of establishments	Number of employees	Total payroll (mil. dol.)	Average number of construction workers	Total payroll construction workers (mil. dol.)	Value of construction work (mil. dol.)	Net value of construction work (mil. dol.)	Value added (mil. dol.)	Cost of materials, components, and supplies (mil. dol.)	Capital expenditures, excluding land (mil. dol.)
New single-family general contractors	236115	58,472	273,055	8,263	179,390	4,482	61,781	38,573	19,678	18,612	621
New multifamily general contractors	236116	4,397	44,384	1,731	27,856	935	16,673	7,638	4,411	3,429	191
New housing operative builders	236117	26,043	240,292	10,458	119,509	4,087	139,021	87,134	51,361	35,738	904
Industrial building construction	236210	2,777	93,931	3,827	70,567	2,535	17,029	9,581	6,252	3,320	164
Commercial building construction	236220	37,208	715,896	29,210	478,923	16,517	241,065	108,229	71,882	36,592	1,441
Water and sewer system construction	237110	12,357	204,085	7,381	162,096	5,312	32,501	26,838	16,022	10,336	1,201
Oil and gas pipeline construction	237120	1,403	93,176	3,985	78,317	3,172	11,459	10,224	7,663	(D)	303
Power and communication system construction	237130	6,034	253,506	10,601	192,704	7,743	34,810	30,475	23,045	7,760	786
Land subdivision	237210	8,403	66,105	2,396	25,630	699	20,481	16,044	14,374	(D)	395
Highway, street, and bridge construction	237310	11,239	434,714	15,791	339,437	11,487	81,660	62,319	36,211	26,278	2,903
Other heavy construction	237990	10,502	154,071	4,997	119,355	3,531	21,801	18,108	12,042	5,796	1,134
Poured concrete structure contractors	238110	27,151	309,955	9,203	261,917	7,187	33,982	30,665	18,211	12,057	819
Steel and precast concrete contractors	238120	4,321	78,286	2,900	63,625	2,214	8,722	7,985	5,823	2,067	199
Framing contractors	238130	14,455	158,003	4,410	134,663	3,515	14,432	12,651	8,587	4,085	195
Masonry contractors	238140	25,720	260,703	7,173	221,790	5,801	20,274	19,212	13,174	5,833	426
Glass and glazing contractors	238150	5,294	50,800	1,764	34,086	1,092	6,285	6,017	3,513	2,551	75
Roofing contractors	238160	23,192	226,203	6,019	176,512	4,100	22,991	21,100	12,801	8,016	450
Siding contractors	238170	6,632	43,042	1,185	30,284	797	4,253	3,810	2,262	1,550	67
Other building exterior contractors	238190	2,786	31,972	1,153	23,444	773	3,494	3,246	2,046	1,189	52
Electrical contractors	238210	62,586	771,184	29,324	606,403	22,228	82,141	77,672	51,677	25,662	1,188
Plumbing and HVAC contractors	238220	87,501	974,368	35,942	712,452	25,620	117,786	105,323	66,878	37,813	1,838
Other building equipment contractors	238290	6,087	126,559	4,941	90,504	3,587	14,503	13,680	10,093	3,631	286
Drywall and insulation contractors	238310	19,598	311,077	9,767	261,239	7,593	30,822	27,046	18,042	8,725	349
Painting and wall covering contractors	238320	38,943	234,562	6,005	184,328	4,448	16,853	15,317	11,516	3,620	326
Flooring contractors	238330	12,865	79,813	2,421	51,933	1,446	9,775	8,623	4,869	3,746	138
Tile and terrazzo contractors	238340	8,950	60,001	1,835	44,729	1,260	5,858	5,640	3,754	1,872	96
Finish carpentry contractors	238350	35,087	179,476	4,712	129,888	3,240	18,154	15,641	9,762	5,905	322
Other building finishing contractors	238390	3,729	50,617	1,719	37,353	1,167	4,862	4,560	3,404	1,133	75
Site preparation contractors	238910	30,496	285,430	9,702	223,045	7,112	37,442	32,286	23,115	8,457	2,325
All other specialty trade contractors	238990	33,452	248,065	6,965	178,700	4,669	27,072	23,833	15,339	8,664	949

D Withheld to avoid disclosing data of individual companies.   [1] North American Industry Classification System, 2002; see text, this section and Section 15.

Source: U.S. Census Bureau, "2002 Economic Census Industry Series Reports, Construction"; using American Factfinder®. See Internet site: <http://www.census.gov/econ/census02/guide/INDRPT23.HTM>; (accessed 17 November 2005).

Construction and Housing   595

Table 928. **Construction Materials—Producer Price Indexes: 1990 to 2005**

[1982 = 100, except as noted. Data for 2005 are preliminary. For discussion of producer price indexes, see text, Section 14. This index, more formally known as the special commodity grouping index for construction materials, covers materials incorporated as integral part of a building or normally installed during construction and not readily removable. Excludes consumer durables such as kitchen ranges, refrigerators, etc. This index is not the same as the stage-of-processing index of intermediate materials and components for construction]

Commodity	1990	1995	1999	2000	2001	2002	2003	2004	2005
Construction materials	**119.6**	**138.8**	**142.8**	**144.1**	**142.8**	**144.0**	**147.1**	**161.5**	**169.6**
Interior solvent-based paint	133.0	164.5	188.0	191.1	190.2	190.5	198.0	(NA)	(NA)
Construction products from plastics	117.2	133.8	128.0	135.8	132.9	136.1	138.6	144.6	159.0
Douglas fir, dressed	138.4	198.8	212.1	185.2	178.1	178.5	176.7	(NA)	(NA)
Southern pine, dressed	111.2	166.9	185.7	161.0	152.5	145.2	145.4	(NA)	(NA)
Millwork	130.4	163.8	174.7	176.4	179.2	179.8	181.8	191.9	197.2
Softwood plywood	119.6	188.1	207.0	173.3	167.8	164.1	195.9	250.9	224.1
Hardwood plywood and related products	102.7	122.2	128.6	130.2	130.4	131.5	129.0	134.4	138.0
Softwood plywood veneer, ex. reinforced/backed . . .	142.3	203.5	197.4	182.2	175.5	172.8	184.1	209.5	206.0
Building paper and building board mill products	112.2	144.9	141.6	138.8	129.3	129.3	159.9	192.4	184.8
Steel pipe and tubes [1]	102.6	104.4	102.5	106.6	104.0	106.7	113.3	166.3	193.2
Builders' hardware	133.0	153.2	161.9	163.8	166.4	169.3	170.3	172.9	179.0
Plumbing fixtures and brass fittings	144.3	166.0	176.7	180.4	180.8	181.9	183.4	188.3	197.6
Heating equipment	131.6	147.5	154.0	155.6	157.1	157.9	163.2	169.5	179.9
Metal doors, sash, and trim	131.4	156.5	162.2	165.1	167.1	168.0	169.9	175.8	184.9
Siding, aluminum [2]	(NA)	132.4	135.4	142.2	141.5	141.0	152.6	(NA)	(NA)
Outdoor lighting equipment, including parts [3]	113.0	120.8	122.3	124.7	125.7	126.2	126.9	129.4	131.8
Commercial fluorescent fixtures [4]	113.0	121.0	118.7	117.7	113.6	114.0	115.2	113.6	(NA)
Architectural and ornamental metalwork [5]	118.7	128.0	136.2	139.8	141.7	144.2	147.2	172.5	185.8
Fabricated ferrous wire products [1]	114.6	125.7	130.6	130.0	129.8	129.7	131.3	149.3	157.0
Elevators, escalators, and other lifts.	110.1	113.0	117.5	118.7	119.4	120.0	118.7	120.5	123.5
Stamped metal switch and receptacle box	158.0	183.5	192.8	183.0	195.4	195.4	196.1	205.2	(NA)
Concrete ingredients and related products	115.3	134.7	152.1	155.6	159.1	162.6	164.8	170.4	185.2
Concrete products	113.5	129.4	143.7	147.8	151.7	152.7	153.6	161.2	177.2
Clay construction products exc. refractories.	129.9	141.3	148.3	152.8	155.7	152.8	154.2	156.6	165.3
Prep. asphalt and tar roofing and siding products. . .	95.8	97.8	95.2	100.0	103.3	106.6	110.6	111.3	125.5
Gypsum products.	105.2	154.5	208.0	201.4	156.4	168.9	171.5	198.8	229.5
Insulation materials.	108.4	118.8	131.7	128.6	127.6	128.3	128.8	137.2	142.2
Paving mixtures and blocks	101.2	105.8	112.9	130.4	134.6	136.2	142.6	144.9	156.9

NA Not available. [1] June 1982 = 100. [2] December 1982 = 100. [3] June 1985 = 100. [4] Recessed nonair. [5] December 1983 = 100.

Source: U.S. Bureau of Labor Statistics, *Producer Price Indexes*, monthly and annual. See Internet site <http://www.bls.gov/ppi/home.htm>.

Table 929. **Value of New Construction Put in Place: 1980 to 2005**

[In millions of dollars (273,936 represents $273,936,000,000)]. Represents value of construction put in place during year; differs from building permit and construction contract data in timing and coverage. Includes installed cost of normal building service equipment and selected types of industrial production equipment (largely site fabricated). Excludes cost of shipbuilding, land, and most types of machinery and equipment. For methodology, see Appendix III]

Year		Private			Public		
	Total	Total	Residential buildings	Non-residential	Total	Federal	State and local
1980	273,936	210,290	100,381	109,909	63,646	9,642	54,004
1981	289,070	224,378	99,241	125,137	64,691	10,413	54,278
1982	279,332	216,268	84,676	131,592	63,064	10,008	53,056
1983	311,887	248,437	125,833	122,604	63,450	10,557	52,893
1984	370,190	299,952	155,015	144,937	70,238	11,240	58,998
1985	403,416	325,601	160,520	165,081	77,815	12,004	65,811
1986	433,454	348,872	190,677	158,195	84,582	12,412	72,170
1987	446,643	355,994	199,652	156,342	90,648	14,052	76,596
1988	462,012	367,277	204,496	162,781	94,735	12,264	82,471
1989	477,502	379,328	204,255	175,073	98,174	12,155	86,018
1990	476,778	369,300	191,103	178,197	107,478	12,099	95,379
1991	432,592	322,483	166,251	156,232	110,109	12,845	97,264
1992	463,661	347,814	199,393	148,421	115,847	14,376	101,471
1993	491,033	375,073	225,067	150,006	115,960	14,424	101,535
1994	539,193	418,999	258,561	160,438	120,193	14,440	105,753
1995	557,818	427,885	247,351	180,534	129,933	15,751	114,181
1996	615,900	476,638	281,115	195,523	139,263	15,325	123,938
1997	653,429	502,734	289,014	213,720	150,695	14,087	136,608
1998	706,303	552,001	314,607	237,394	154,302	14,318	139,984
1999	769,461	599,729	350,562	249,167	169,732	14,025	155,706
2000	835,279	649,750	374,457	275,293	185,529	14,166	171,362
2001	868,310	662,247	388,324	273,922	206,063	15,081	190,981
2002	876,802	659,651	421,912	237,739	217,150	16,578	200,572
2003	926,870	702,887	475,941	226,946	223,983	17,913	206,071
2004	1,034,729	804,235	564,827	239,408	230,494	18,342	212,152
2005	1,143,655	898,970	642,276	256,694	244,686	17,732	226,954

Source: U.S. Census Bureau, "Construction Spending," Internet site <http://www.census.gov/const/www/c30index.html>.

Table 930. **Value of Private Construction Put in Place: 1995 to 2005**

[In millions of dollars (427,885 represents $427,885,000,000). Represents value of construction put in place during year; differs from building permit and construction contract data in timing and coverage. See Appendix III]

Type of construction	1995	1998	1999	2000	2001	2002	2003	2004	2005
Total construction [1]	427,885	552,001	599,729	649,750	662,247	659,651	702,887	804,235	898,970
Residential	247,351	314,607	350,562	374,457	388,324	421,912	475,941	564,827	642,276
New single family	153,515	199,409	223,837	236,788	249,086	265,889	310,575	377,557	433,510
New multifamily	17,889	24,574	27,434	28,259	30,305	32,952	35,116	39,944	48,228
Improvements	75,947	90,624	99,290	109,410	108,933	123,071	130,250	147,326	160,538
Nonresidential	180,534	237,394	249,167	275,293	273,922	237,739	226,946	239,408	256,694
Lodging	7,131	14,818	15,955	16,304	14,519	10,467	9,930	11,982	12,809
Office [1]	22,996	40,394	45,052	52,407	49,745	35,296	30,579	32,879	36,823
General	20,569	37,615	41,745	49,637	47,136	32,356	27,380	28,679	32,358
Financial	2,339	2,636	3,125	2,689	2,586	2,857	3,174	4,186	4,434
Commercial [1]	44,096	55,681	59,376	64,055	63,606	59,008	57,505	64,110	69,143
Automotive [1]	4,191	5,270	5,904	5,967	5,650	5,807	5,039	5,235	5,859
Sales	883	1,542	1,573	1,629	2,014	2,235	2,099	2,443	2,936
Service/parts	2,448	2,527	3,270	3,009	2,394	2,308	1,866	1,978	1,887
Parking	860	1,200	1,062	1,330	1,242	1,265	1,074	814	1,036
Food/beverage [1]	7,169	9,118	8,277	8,786	8,765	7,914	8,369	8,232	8,106
Food	3,062	4,665	4,610	4,792	4,300	4,207	4,234	3,590	3,290
Dining/drinking	3,408	3,817	2,874	2,935	3,441	2,916	3,321	3,937	4,224
Fast food	699	636	793	1,058	1,024	792	813	705	592
Multiretail [1]	11,976	13,254	15,234	14,911	16,373	15,581	15,400	18,828	23,037
General merchandise	5,339	3,778	4,668	5,100	5,066	6,009	5,341	6,416	6,981
Shopping center	4,086	6,045	7,187	6,803	7,769	6,605	6,867	9,256	12,416
Shopping mall	2,175	2,917	2,873	2,523	2,701	2,108	2,231	2,138	2,667
Other commercial [1]	8,432	11,050	11,179	13,537	11,945	12,083	11,249	13,341	11,689
Drug store	536	1,409	1,645	1,682	1,185	1,644	1,790	1,427	1,319
Building supply store	1,372	1,742	1,588	2,592	3,016	2,471	2,268	2,521	2,517
Other stores	5,653	7,025	6,849	8,136	6,995	7,145	6,214	8,229	6,864
Warehouse	9,299	12,698	13,702	14,822	15,691	11,908	12,345	12,074	13,219
General commercial	8,944	11,732	12,756	13,511	14,440	10,934	11,004	10,830	11,825
Farm	3,014	4,284	5,059	5,988	5,135	5,611	5,103	6,400	7,232
Health care	15,259	17,737	18,388	19,455	19,506	22,438	24,217	26,272	27,723
Hospital	8,807	9,469	9,491	10,183	11,313	13,925	15,234	16,147	17,963
Medical building	4,064	4,070	4,910	5,066	4,638	4,924	6,068	7,615	7,621
Special care	2,388	4,197	3,987	4,206	3,555	3,538	2,915	2,510	2,139
Educational [1]	5,699	9,829	9,756	11,683	12,846	13,109	13,424	12,701	12,787
Preschool	326	619	663	770	874	593	711	674	526
Primary/secondary	1,245	2,174	2,420	2,948	3,536	3,605	3,204	3,202	2,706
Higher education [1]	3,055	4,945	5,204	6,333	6,597	6,875	7,259	6,496	7,065
Instructional	1,712	2,469	2,258	3,058	3,210	3,619	3,701	3,200	3,643
Dormitory	483	955	1,274	1,356	1,555	1,528	1,761	1,669	1,549
Sports/recreation	192	403	515	645	755	772	677	739	821
Other educational	817	1,798	1,232	1,318	1,421	1,651	1,785	1,998	2,184
Gallery/museum	571	1,127	778	920	990	1,312	1,371	1,335	1,629
Religious	4,348	6,604	7,371	8,030	8,393	8,335	8,559	8,153	7,772
House of worship	2,951	4,549	5,057	5,656	6,040	6,021	6,238	6,015	6,064
Other religious	1,389	2,054	2,314	2,347	2,330	2,312	2,322	2,138	1,709
Auxiliary building	619	992	1,252	1,280	1,247	1,358	1,296	1,258	1,273
Public safety	185	586	465	423	274	217	185	289	380
Amusement and recreation [1]	5,886	8,589	9,550	8,768	7,828	7,478	7,781	8,432	7,693
Theme/amusement park	563	866	919	747	462	230	270	198	190
Sports	910	1,136	1,495	1,068	1,067	1,427	1,306	900	928
Fitness	637	889	1,137	1,152	1,294	1,286	1,262	1,141	1,391
Performance/meeting center	365	603	546	732	977	900	844	1,054	1,435
Social center	1,558	2,093	2,006	2,368	2,337	2,285	1,996	2,594	1,607
Movie theater/studio	848	2,441	2,376	1,461	792	568	855	1,218	1,250
Transportation [1]	4,759	7,290	6,525	6,879	7,058	6,773	6,568	6,841	7,347
Air	666	1,093	1,106	1,804	1,993	1,281	1,012	869	826
Land	4,008	6,112	5,164	4,907	4,883	5,325	5,462	5,800	6,347
Railroad	3,509	5,736	4,670	4,263	4,456	4,584	4,851	5,392	5,928
Communication	11,112	12,473	18,405	18,799	19,596	18,384	12,067	12,440	13,346
Power [1]	22,006	21,690	22,040	29,344	31,499	32,608	33,619	30,404	28,958
Electricity	14,274	12,993	15,489	23,374	25,270	24,998	25,592	20,431	19,526
Gas	6,279	7,372	4,918	4,891	5,078	6,080	6,358	8,140	7,420
Oil	929	1,265	1,489	1,003	943	1,193	1,068	1,579	1,415
Sewage and waste disposal	576	339	516	508	402	246	278	331	271
Water supply	670	543	413	714	563	397	393	405	261
Manufacturing [1]	35,364	40,485	35,126	37,583	37,815	22,744	21,434	23,667	30,914
Food/beverage/tobacco	4,525	3,536	3,654	3,985	4,088	2,817	2,695	3,157	4,828
Textile/apparel/leather & allied	824	713	490	413	307	284	218	188	423
Wood	616	492	460	483	343	477	376	485	1,006
Paper	1,448	1,232	896	479	1,265	584	818	548	394
Print/publishing	1,197	1,103	924	848	1,232	666	630	654	795
Petroleum/coal	4,741	1,064	1,004	1,255	1,171	887	717	1,204	743
Chemical	5,531	8,266	6,632	3,798	4,896	5,625	5,368	5,507	6,811
Plastic/rubber	1,475	2,139	2,388	1,645	1,379	776	659	936	882
Nonmetallic mineral	856	1,481	1,282	1,898	2,216	536	865	896	1,226
Primary metal	2,533	2,606	2,137	1,976	773	241	436	312	771
Fabricated metal	808	2,037	2,046	2,148	1,447	833	662	595	735
Machinery	1,275	1,256	1,040	864	863	797	707	645	991
Computer/electronic/electrical	6,332	7,552	4,748	6,392	6,029	1,918	1,444	2,835	4,502
Transportation equipment	2,382	3,498	3,683	6,318	6,901	3,832	3,314	2,610	3,852
Furniture	213	413	232	148	232	148	278	217	95

[1] Includes other types of construction, not shown separately.

Source: U.S. Census Bureau, "Construction Spending", Internet site <http://www.census.gov/const/www/c30index.html>.

Table 931. **Value of State and Local Government Construction Put in Place: 1995 to 2005**

[In millions of dollars (114,181 represents $114,181,000,000). See headnote, Table 930]

Type of construction	1995	1998	1999	2000	2001	2002	2003	2004	2005
Total construction [1]	114,181	139,984	155,706	171,362	190,981	200,572	206,071	212,152	226,954
Residential	4,043	4,340	4,603	4,200	5,005	5,320	5,434	6,319	6,749
Multifamily	3,976	4,242	4,584	4,175	4,929	5,204	5,243	6,082	6,272
Nonresidential	110,138	135,644	151,103	167,163	185,976	195,252	200,637	205,833	220,205
Office	3,914	4,605	4,521	6,256	7,196	8,156	8,208	8,232	7,365
Commercial [1]	1,329	1,993	2,519	2,543	3,189	3,149	2,958	2,704	2,734
Automotive	965	1,603	1,915	1,719	2,486	2,224	2,143	2,052	2,139
Parking	794	1,549	1,703	1,596	2,467	2,198	2,092	1,853	1,947
Warehouse	231	258	342	464	394	384	428	377	350
Health care	3,156	2,884	3,166	3,944	3,805	4,541	5,378	6,865	8,019
Hospital	1,960	1,980	2,220	2,716	2,749	3,303	3,607	4,542	5,452
Medical building	801	515	494	684	630	664	1,173	1,655	1,839
Special care	395	389	452	545	427	575	598	668	729
Educational [1]	25,743	35,015	41,117	45,616	51,289	54,571	56,761	60,149	64,666
Primary/secondary [1]	17,545	26,064	30,494	32,888	35,621	38,498	38,580	41,267	44,115
Elementary	5,242	9,492	10,314	11,939	13,697	13,893	12,824	14,405	14,163
Middle/junior high	3,745	3,930	5,992	5,676	6,727	7,735	7,599	8,187	9,101
High	4,833	7,627	11,053	12,998	13,673	15,711	17,771	18,072	19,790
Higher education [1]	6,883	7,721	8,914	10,483	12,974	13,120	14,764	15,976	17,019
Instructional	4,277	4,307	5,272	6,163	7,646	7,332	8,630	8,759	8,942
Parking	158	331	369	498	545	398	487	769	1,001
Administration	128	179	270	287	192	418	227	306	260
Dormitory	324	548	802	1,051	1,386	1,489	1,987	2,692	2,494
Library	300	368	327	300	363	402	518	528	589
Student union/cafeteria	238	318	298	314	601	947	670	637	867
Sports/recreation	625	795	767	942	1,250	1,425	1,271	1,380	1,683
Infrastructure	788	780	701	814	808	501	590	873	1,118
Other educational	1,110	1,128	1,372	1,602	2,100	2,420	2,570	2,371	2,744
Library/archive	704	566	945	948	1,625	1,947	1,732	1,510	2,094
Public safety [1]	5,928	7,575	7,858	8,146	7,845	7,747	7,843	7,495	8,544
Correctional	4,854	6,588	6,575	6,611	6,342	5,909	5,642	5,159	5,678
Detention	4,049	5,618	5,338	5,431	4,977	4,440	4,224	3,811	4,189
Police/sheriff	804	970	1,237	1,180	1,366	1,469	1,418	1,348	1,488
Other public safety	1,025	988	1,284	1,534	1,503	1,838	2,201	2,335	2,867
Fire/rescue	652	795	1,095	1,387	1,284	1,606	1,826	1,973	2,320
Amusement and recreation [1]	6,142	7,666	9,159	10,563	11,834	11,978	11,223	10,643	10,452
Sports	1,637	3,173	3,402	3,181	3,516	3,339	2,776	2,385	2,243
Performance/meeting center	1,751	1,343	1,572	2,905	3,779	3,784	3,039	2,813	2,761
Convention center	1,224	835	1,099	1,957	2,933	2,760	2,079	1,842	1,941
Social center	772	947	1,399	1,605	1,846	1,881	2,155	2,010	1,443
Neighborhood center	581	622	1,059	1,234	1,375	1,216	1,638	1,788	1,240
Park/camp	1,696	2,020	2,584	2,681	2,386	2,512	2,684	3,149	3,861
Transportation	8,967	10,197	11,296	14,231	16,076	17,678	17,351	17,640	17,876
Air [1]	3,855	5,594	5,960	7,347	7,940	8,308	8,571	9,360	9,810
Passenger terminal	1,209	2,196	2,217	3,198	2,815	3,113	3,976	4,259	3,550
Runway	2,176	2,563	3,100	3,520	4,391	4,403	3,990	4,355	5,392
Land [1]	4,009	3,823	4,275	5,649	6,340	7,447	7,589	6,877	6,601
Passenger terminal	1,147	1,222	1,249	1,366	1,580	1,905	2,210	1,470	1,008
Mass transit	1,734	1,548	1,347	1,624	2,519	3,442	3,327	3,287	3,582
Railroad	462	564	1,033	1,607	1,121	684	474	374	615
Water [1]	1,103	780	1,061	1,236	1,796	1,923	1,191	1,404	1,465
Dock/marina	690	421	657	940	1,286	1,222	941	1,102	1,039
Dry dock/marine terminal	204	352	404	257	484	702	250	302	427
Power	2,879	2,495	3,228	3,891	3,995	4,365	6,553	6,048	7,095
Electrical	2,231	2,052	2,538	3,714	3,751	3,738	5,844	5,019	5,991
Distribution	733	1,511	1,494	1,479	1,038	1,349	2,078	1,590	1,572
Highway and street [1]	37,616	44,782	49,174	53,081	59,125	58,286	57,977	58,996	64,750
Pavement	29,164	33,180	36,464	39,048	43,095	42,130	40,501	41,428	46,360
Lighting	659	1,180	910	878	1,286	913	1,192	1,179	1,231
Retaining wall	187	711	816	1,133	653	764	583	568	710
Tunnel	346	862	926	919	1,120	676	639	536	387
Bridge	6,615	7,229	8,479	9,568	11,429	12,084	13,375	13,528	14,562
Toll/weigh	152	247	277	331	109	222	186	239	332
Maintenance building	53	362	354	302	426	306	251	174	100
Rest facility/streetscape	167	838	940	901	1,008	1,189	1,250	1,344	1,069
Sewage and waste disposal [1]	8,419	9,943	10,524	10,249	11,084	12,919	13,684	14,434	14,950
Sewage/dry waste [1]	4,825	6,589	7,082	6,836	7,079	8,386	8,594	9,156	9,548
Plant	1,641	1,925	2,178	2,025	1,879	2,259	2,396	2,614	2,735
Line/pump station	2,960	4,422	4,612	4,629	4,996	5,963	6,072	6,401	6,728
Waste water	3,522	3,317	3,436	3,413	4,005	4,533	5,090	5,279	5,401
Plant	2,467	2,276	2,613	2,363	2,987	3,561	3,855	3,932	4,267
Line/drain	1,055	1,041	823	1,050	1,018	972	1,235	1,347	1,135
Water supply [1]	4,713	6,678	6,967	6,972	8,972	9,835	10,249	10,127	10,924
Plant	1,204	1,912	2,154	2,246	3,185	3,221	3,770	3,733	4,014
Well	212	247	254	277	308	467	319	270	286
Line	2,516	3,106	3,089	3,395	4,156	4,378	4,328	4,485	5,063
Pump station	286	418	571	458	536	717	670	595	617
Reservoir	208	429	409	195	325	390	395	426	400
Tank/tower	246	565	491	402	462	662	767	616	545
Conservation and development [1]	1,265	1,444	1,346	1,304	1,396	1,316	1,371	2,010	2,456
Dam/levee	329	597	525	425	316	363	311	408	570
Breakwater/jetty	358	456	382	377	635	510	691	899	1,031

[1] Includes other types of construction, not shown separately.

Source: U.S. Census Bureau, "Construction Spending", Internet site <http://www.census.gov/const/www/c30index.html>.

Table 932. Construction Contracts—Value of Construction and Floor Space of Buildings by Class of Construction: 1980 to 2005

[151.8 reresents $151,800,000,000. Building construction includes new structures and additions; nonbuilding construction includes major alterations to existing structures which affect only valuation, since no additional floor area is created by "alteration"]

Year	Total	Residential buildings	Nonresidential buildings Total	Commercial [1]	Manu-facturing	Educa-tional [2]	Health	Public buildings	Religious	Social and recrea-tional	Mis-cella-neous	Nonbuild-ing construc-tion
VALUE (bil. dol.)												
1980	151.8	60.4	56.9	27.7	9.2	7.4	5.4	1.6	1.2	2.7	1.7	34.5
1985	235.6	102.1	92.1	54.6	8.1	10.0	7.8	3.1	2.0	4.0	2.5	41.4
1990	246.0	100.9	95.4	44.8	8.4	16.6	9.2	5.7	2.2	5.3	3.1	49.7
1995	306.5	127.9	114.2	46.6	13.8	22.9	10.8	6.3	2.8	7.1	3.8	64.4
1997	362.4	153.6	138.9	59.8	14.0	28.4	11.9	7.0	3.8	10.0	4.0	69.8
1998	405.6	179.8	154.5	74.0	12.1	30.1	12.9	6.6	4.3	10.8	3.6	71.3
1999	447.2	195.0	168.7	77.2	11.3	37.1	13.6	8.2	4.5	11.6	5.1	83.5
2000	472.9	208.3	173.3	80.9	8.9	40.9	12.4	7.5	4.6	13.8	4.4	91.3
2001	496.5	219.7	169.1	70.2	8.0	47.0	14.4	7.8	4.8	12.0	4.8	107.7
2002	504.2	248.7	155.2	59.7	5.5	45.3	16.1	7.3	5.1	11.5	4.7	100.3
2003	531.9	283.4	156.0	58.9	6.8	47.8	15.7	7.1	4.5	10.9	4.3	92.6
2004	591.2	332.8	163.6	66.8	7.9	43.9	17.5	7.1	4.5	11.5	4.4	94.8
2005	659.0	380.9	176.2	69.9	8.5	48.4	21.3	7.8	4.1	11.4	4.9	101.9
FLOOR SPACE (mil. sq. ft.)												
1980	3,102	1,839	1,263	738	220	103	55	18	28	49	52	(X)
1985	3,853	2,324	1,529	1,039	165	111	73	28	32	44	38	(X)
1990	3,020	1,817	1,203	694	128	152	69	47	29	51	32	(X)
1995	3,454	2,172	1,281	700	163	186	70	40	33	56	33	(X)
1997	4,126	2,586	1,540	855	191	204	89	48	42	77	35	(X)
1998	4,812	3,015	1,797	1,107	166	219	96	42	47	85	34	(X)
1999	5,091	3,253	1,838	1,115	141	261	98	49	48	87	39	(X)
2000	4,982	3,113	1,869	1,180	111	273	88	44	49	94	29	(X)
2001	4,828	3,159	1,669	988	93	295	92	44	50	81	27	(X)
2002	4,793	3,355	1,438	811	68	277	97	37	52	71	26	(X)
2003	5,093	3,689	1,404	795	75	270	92	35	45	67	26	(X)
2004	5,504	4,056	1,448	869	84	230	93	34	43	68	27	(X)
2005	5,799	4,315	1,484	897	74	245	106	33	36	65	28	(X)

X Not applicable. [1] Includes nonindustrial warehouses. [2] Includes science.

Source: McGraw-Hill Construction, a Division of the McGraw-Hill Companies, New York, NY (copyright).

Table 933. Construction Contracts—Value by State: 2000 to 2005

[In millions of dollars (472,930 represents $472,930,000,000). Represents value of construction in states in which work was actually done. See headnote, Table 932]

State	2000	2004	2005 Total [1]	2005 Resi-den-tial	2005 Non-resi-den-tial	State	2000	2004	2005 Total [1]	2005 Resi-den-tial	2005 Non-resi-den-tial
U.S.	472,930	591,203	658,984	380,867	176,236	MO	7,498	10,177	12,024	6,481	3,872
AL	7,225	8,354	9,533	5,325	2,409	MT	1,004	1,205	1,547	688	323
AK	1,327	1,937	1,804	538	506	NE	2,646	3,391	4,472	1,685	1,020
AZ	13,966	21,174	23,995	16,445	5,090	NV	6,978	11,223	12,547	7,705	3,064
AR	3,739	4,415	4,838	2,793	1,356	NH	2,514	2,594	2,686	1,425	894
CA	52,858	67,242	71,768	43,053	18,856	NJ	10,940	11,180	14,016	5,856	5,523
CO	12,491	13,986	15,834	9,981	4,084	NM	3,140	3,946	4,169	2,291	1,017
CT	5,181	5,028	5,861	2,691	2,316	NY	20,756	23,250	26,630	10,763	9,450
DE	1,350	1,479	1,921	1,059	636	NC	17,258	21,469	23,957	16,427	5,173
DC	1,763	1,763	1,454	467	802	ND	854	1,146	1,129	465	294
FL	35,079	58,809	69,928	51,938	11,203	OH	16,270	18,603	19,312	8,579	7,290
GA	20,419	23,819	26,740	16,472	6,817	OK	5,330	5,443	6,273	3,422	1,864
HI	1,409	2,492	3,037	2,025	573	OR	6,020	7,694	10,069	6,232	2,436
ID	2,521	3,908	4,926	3,795	694	PA	14,861	15,742	16,522	7,570	5,801
IL	17,167	21,561	24,589	13,889	7,276	RI	1,063	1,303	1,749	569	634
IN	11,011	13,202	14,175	7,026	5,129	SC	7,759	11,758	12,785	8,770	2,796
IA	3,776	5,842	6,353	2,626	2,232	SD	1,221	1,544	1,564	724	369
KS	4,463	4,950	5,050	2,456	1,378	TN	10,108	12,035	13,501	8,128	3,283
KY	6,625	7,521	7,417	3,852	2,050	TX	41,124	48,936	56,243	32,854	13,913
LA	5,528	6,276	6,549	3,216	1,820	UT	4,420	6,510	8,198	4,762	1,915
ME	1,710	2,245	2,408	1,394	598	VT	602	1,178	1,239	649	383
MD	7,836	9,548	10,041	5,247	3,358	VA	13,634	16,005	18,448	11,105	5,445
MA	11,983	10,067	11,162	5,220	4,204	WA	10,332	14,107	16,258	9,280	4,013
MI	14,735	14,476	14,178	7,064	4,534	WV	1,856	2,039	2,818	1,121	692
MN	8,838	11,066	10,007	5,964	2,016	WI	8,044	12,388	11,008	5,827	3,175
MS	2,917	4,052	4,183	2,117	1,367	WY	778	1,125	1,616	834	293

[1] Includes nonbuilding construction, not shown separately.

Source: McGraw-Hill Construction, a Division of the McGraw-Hill Companies, New York, NY, (copyright).

Construction and Housing 599

Table 934. **New Privately Owned Housing Units Authorized by State: 2000 and 2005**

[1,592.3 represents 1,592,300. Based on about 19,000 places in United States having building permit systems in 2000 and 20,000 in 2005]

State	Housing units (1,000) 2000	2005 Total	2005 1 unit	Valuation (mil. dol.) 2000	2005 Total	2005 1 unit
U.S..	1,592.3	2,155.3	1,682.0	185,744	329,255	284,452
AL ...	17.4	30.6	24.7	1,718	4,110	3,453
AK ...	2.1	2.9	1.7	333	525	355
AZ ...	61.5	90.9	80.8	7,158	14,487	13,724
AR ...	9.2	17.9	13.2	859	2,257	1,949
CA ...	145.6	205.0	154.7	23,344	38,370	32,774
CO ...	54.6	45.9	40.1	6,822	8,803	8,157
CT ...	9.4	11.9	8.8	1,425	2,201	1,912
DE ...	4.6	8.2	6.7	414	988	850
DC ...	0.8	2.9	0.1	54	228	18
FL. ...	155.3	287.3	209.2	17,462	46,803	36,301
GA ...	91.8	109.3	94.5	8,722	14,074	12,961
HI ...	4.9	9.8	6.6	823	2,050	1,511
ID. ...	10.9	21.6	19.2	1,359	3,512	3,317
IL. ...	51.9	66.9	47.7	6,528	10,964	9,297
IN ...	37.9	38.5	32.1	4,414	5,807	5,376
IA. ...	12.5	16.8	12.8	1,333	2,383	2,068
KS ...	12.5	14.0	11.6	1,397	2,043	1,874
KY ...	18.5	21.2	17.9	1,767	2,629	2,460
LA ...	14.7	22.8	20.2	1,553	2,744	2,556
ME ...	6.2	9.0	7.8	723	1,362	1,252
MD ...	30.4	30.2	22.9	3,232	4,688	4,064
MA ...	18.0	24.5	14.6	2,741	4,050	3,140
MI. ...	52.5	45.3	38.9	6,256	6,642	6,102
MN ...	32.8	36.5	29.6	4,204	6,291	5,386
MS ...	11.3	13.4	11.7	918	1,594	1,502

State	Housing units (1,000) 2000	2005 Total	2005 1 unit	Valuation (mil. dol.) 2000	2005 Total	2005 1 unit
MO ...	24.3	33.1	25.9	2,569	4,702	4,137
MT ...	2.6	4.8	3.5	235	691	552
NE ...	9.1	9.9	8.7	830	1,277	1,200
NV ...	32.3	47.7	37.5	3,312	6,547	5,254
NH ...	6.7	7.6	6.4	937	1,352	1,221
NJ. ...	34.6	38.6	22.3	3,376	4,993	3,655
NM ...	8.9	14.2	13.4	1,073	2,169	2,123
NY ...	44.1	61.9	25.2	4,992	7,828	4,973
NC ...	78.4	97.9	85.0	8,643	14,814	13,849
ND ...	2.1	4.0	2.4	190	458	350
OH ...	49.7	47.7	38.3	6,154	7,870	7,211
OK ...	11.1	18.4	15.7	1,204	2,490	2,336
OR ...	19.9	31.0	23.8	2,533	5,483	4,798
PA ...	41.1	44.5	37.3	4,616	6,776	6,255
RI ...	2.6	2.8	1.8	296	384	328
SC ...	32.8	54.2	43.3	3,533	7,761	6,579
SD ...	4.2	5.7	4.7	369	693	631
TN ...	32.2	46.6	40.2	3,378	6,601	6,132
TX ...	141.2	210.6	166.2	15,418	26,830	23,970
UT ...	17.6	27.8	24.0	2,138	4,553	4,210
VT ...	2.5	2.9	2.4	319	441	387
VA ...	48.4	61.5	50.0	5,052	8,989	8,074
WA ...	39.0	53.0	41.4	4,426	8,742	7,627
WV ...	3.8	6.1	5.5	360	996	949
WI. ...	34.2	35.3	26.0	3,917	5,554	4,697
WY ...	1.6	4.0	3.2	314	657	596

Source: U.S. Census Bureau, Construction Reports, "New Residential Construction". See Internet site <http://www.census.gov/const/www/newresconstindex.html>.

Table 935. **New Privately Owned Housing Units Started—Selected Characteristics: 1970 to 2005**

[In thousands (1,434 represents 1,434,000). For composition of regions, see map inside front cover]

Year	Total units	Structures with— 1 unit	2 to 4 units	5 or more units	Region North-east	Mid-west	South	West	Units for sale Total	Single-family	Multi-family
1970	1,434	813	85	536	218	294	612	311	(NA)	(NA)	(NA)
1975	1,160	892	64	204	149	294	442	275	576	531	45
1979	1,745	1,194	122	429	178	349	748	470	915	742	173
1980	1,292	852	110	331	125	218	643	306	689	526	163
1981	1,084	705	91	288	117	165	562	240	584	426	158
1982	1,062	663	80	320	117	149	591	205	549	409	140
1983	1,703	1,068	113	522	168	218	935	382	923	713	210
1984	1,750	1,084	121	544	204	243	866	436	934	728	206
1985	1,742	1,072	93	576	252	240	782	468	867	713	154
1986	1,805	1,179	84	542	294	296	733	483	925	782	143
1987	1,621	1,146	65	409	269	298	634	420	862	732	130
1988	1,488	1,081	59	348	235	274	575	404	808	709	99
1989	1,376	1,003	55	318	179	266	536	396	735	648	87
1990	1,193	895	38	260	131	253	479	329	585	529	56
1991	1,014	840	36	138	113	233	414	254	531	490	41
1992	1,200	1,030	31	139	127	288	497	288	659	618	41
1993	1,288	1,126	29	133	127	298	562	302	760	716	44
1994	1,457	1,198	35	224	138	329	639	351	815	763	52
1995	1,354	1,076	34	244	118	290	615	331	763	712	51
1996	1,477	1,161	45	271	132	322	662	361	833	774	59
1997	1,474	1,134	45	296	137	304	670	363	843	784	59
1998	1,617	1,271	43	303	149	331	743	395	941	882	59
1999	1,641	1,302	32	307	156	347	746	392	981	912	69
2000	1,569	1,231	39	299	155	318	714	383	946	871	75
2001	1,603	1,273	37	293	149	330	732	391	990	919	71
2002	1,705	1,359	39	308	158	350	782	416	1,070	999	71
2003	1,848	1,499	34	315	163	374	839	472	1,207	1,120	87
2004	1,956	1,611	42	303	175	356	909	516	1,360	1,240	120
2005	2,068	1,716	41	311	190	357	996	525	1,508	1,358	150

NA Not available.

Source: U.S. Census Bureau,Current Construction Reports, "New Residential Construction." See Internet site <http://www.census.gov/const/www/newresconstindex.html>

U.S. Census Bureau, Statistical Abstract of the United States: 2007

Table 936. New Privately Owned Housing Units Started by State: 2000 to 2006

[In thousands of units (1,573 represents 1,573,000)]

State	2000	2004, est.	2005, est.	2006, est. Total units	2006, est. Single-family units	State	2000	2004, est.	2005, est.	2006, est. Total units	2006, est. Single-family units
U.S.	1,573	1,724	1,658	1,614	1,319	MO	27.4	27.7	27.5	27.5	24.3
AL......	21.2	20.8	20.9	21.1	18.2	MT......	2.4	2.9	2.9	2.8	2.0
AK......	2.0	2.3	2.3	2.3	1.6	NE......	9.2	10.5	10.0	9.7	8.5
AZ......	59.4	64.4	61.9	60.1	53.2	NV......	31.0	37.8	36.1	35.0	27.9
AR......	12.5	13.8	13.6	13.6	10.4	NH......	6.4	7.4	7.0	6.6	5.6
CA......	137.1	177.7	165.0	154.2	120.3	NJ......	31.4	27.2	26.5	26.1	20.7
CO......	52.5	35.9	36.8	37.7	31.7	NM......	7.3	10.6	10.3	10.1	8.9
CT......	8.9	8.6	8.5	8.5	7.7	NY......	41.1	41.0	38.8	37.5	22.0
DE......	4.4	6.2	5.9	5.7	5.4	NC......	76.1	72.8	71.1	70.2	59.3
DC......	0.4	0.4	0.4	0.4	0.1	ND......	2.4	3.6	3.4	3.3	2.3
FL......	147.9	185.7	173.6	165.4	123.7	OH......	47.8	51.2	49.7	48.8	41.7
GA......	90.4	89.3	86.1	84.1	71.0	OK......	14.1	14.6	14.3	14.2	12.6
HI	4.7	6.8	6.5	6.2	5.1	OR......	18.8	19.2	19.6	20.0	15.6
ID......	11.3	13.5	13.1	12.8	11.1	PA......	39.2	40.4	39.4	39.0	34.6
IL.......	51.3	61.5	58.5	56.6	45.2	RI	2.6	2.4	2.4	2.4	2.0
IN......	38.2	40.4	39.4	38.8	33.5	SC......	31.6	35.1	33.4	32.3	27.2
IA......	12.8	15.3	14.6	14.1	11.5	SD......	4.4	5.2	4.9	4.8	4.0
KS......	13.4	14.0	13.8	13.8	11.7	TN......	34.6	34.3	34.2	34.3	30.4
KY......	21.8	20.4	20.4	20.5	17.9	TX......	145.0	163.3	154.9	149.1	117.8
LA......	15.5	18.7	18.0	17.7	15.2	UT......	18.1	20.2	19.9	19.8	16.7
ME......	6.3	7.3	6.8	6.5	6.0	VT......	2.6	2.8	2.7	2.6	2.4
MD......	28.7	27.4	27.1	27.0	22.5	VA	47.5	53.4	51.8	50.6	43.2
MA......	17.1	16.2	16.0	16.0	12.8	WA......	36.9	38.8	38.3	38.2	29.9
MI......	50.4	53.4	51.7	50.7	45.2	WV......	5.3	5.4	5.4	5.4	5.1
MN......	32.9	41.7	39.0	37.1	31.9	WI	32.6	38.1	36.7	35.8	27.9
MS......	14.1	12.8	12.8	12.9	11.1	WY	1.9	2.2	2.2	2.3	2.1

Source: National Association of Home Builders, Economics Division, Washington, DC. Data provided by the Econometric Forecasting Service.

Table 937. Characteristics of New Privately Owned One-Family Houses Completed: 1990 to 2005

[Percent distribution, except as indicated. (966 represents 966,000). Data are percent distribution of characteristics for all houses completed (includes new houses completed, houses built for sale completed, contractor-built and owner-built houses completed, and houses completed for rent). Percents exclude houses for which characteristics specified were not reported]

Characteristic	1990	1995	2000	2005	Characteristic	1990	1995	2000	2005
Total houses (1,000)	966	1,066	1,242	1,636	Bedrooms.............	100	100	100	100
					2 or less.............	15	13	11	12
Construction type	100	100	100	100	3.................	57	57	54	49
Site built.............	(NA)	94	94	96	4 or more	29	30	35	39
Modular	(NA)	3	3	3					
Other	(NA)	3	3	2	Bathrooms	100	100	100	100
					1 1/2 or less	13	11	7	4
Exterior wall material	100	100	100	100	2.................	42	41	39	36
Brick	18	20	20	20	2 1/2 or more	45	48	54	59
Wood................	39	25	14	7					
Stucco	18	16	17	22	Heating fuel...........	100	100	100	100
Vinyl siding [1].........	(NA)	30	39	34	Gas................	59	67	70	66
Aluminum siding	5	3	1	1	Electricity	33	28	27	31
Other [1]..............	20	6	7	16	Oil.................	5	3	3	2
					Other...............	3	1	1	1
Floor area	100	100	100	100					
Under 1,200 sq. ft	11	10	6	4	Heating system	100	100	100	100
1,200 to 1,599 sq. ft.....	22	22	18	16	Warm air furnace	65	67	71	67
1,600 to 1,999 sq. ft.....	22	23	23	20	Electric heat pump	23	25	23	29
2,000 to 2,399 sq. ft	17	17	18	18	Other	12	9	6	4
2,400 sq. ft. and over	29	28	35	42					
Average (sq. ft.)........	2,080	2,095	2,266	2,434	Central air-conditioning ...	100	100	100	100
Median (sq. ft.)	1,905	1,920	2,057	2,227	With................	76	80	85	89
					Without	24	20	15	11
Number of stories	100	100	100	100					
1.................	46	49	47	44	Fireplaces.............	100	100	100	100
2 or more	49	48	52	55	No fireplace	34	37	40	45
Split level	4	3	1	(Z)	1 or more	66	63	60	55
Foundation	100	100	100	100	Parking facilities	100	100	100	100
Full or partial basement. . .	38	39	37	31	Garage..............	82	84	89	91
Slab.................	40	42	46	53	Carport..............	2	2	1	1
Crawl space	21	19	17	16	No garage or carport	16	14	11	8

NA Not available.   Z Less than 0.5 percent.   [1] Prior to 1995 "other" includes vinyl siding.

Source: U.S. Census Bureau, "Characteristics of New Housing," see Internet site <http://www.census.gov/const/www/charindex.html>.

Construction and Housing   601

Table 938. **Housing Starts and Average Length of Time From Start to Completion of New Privately Owned One-Unit Residential Buildings: 1980 to 2005**

[For buildings started in permit issuing places]

Year		Purpose of construction			Region [2]			
	Total [1]	Built for sale	Contractor built	Owner built	North-east	Midwest	South	West
STARTS (1,000)								
1980	852	526	149	164	87	142	428	196
1985	1,072	713	177	157	182	148	504	239
1990	895	529	196	147	104	193	371	226
1995	1,076	712	199	133	102	234	485	256
1996	1,161	774	218	144	112	254	524	271
1997	1,134	784	189	131	111	238	507	278
1998	1,271	882	209	144	122	273	574	303
1999	1,302	912	208	142	126	289	580	308
2000	1,231	871	195	128	118	260	556	297
2001	1,273	919	186	129	111	269	590	303
2002	1,359	999	198	125	118	277	628	336
2003	1,499	1120	205	127	116	309	686	388
2004	1,611	1240	198	130	128	306	743	433
2005	1,716	1358	197	129	138	306	831	441
COMPLETION (months)								
1980	6.9	6.2	5.5	10.1	7.7	8.0	6.1	7.4
1985	6.2	5.4	4.9	10.6	7.2	6.0	5.7	6.7
1990	6.4	5.9	5.3	10.3	9.3	5.6	5.7	6.9
1995	5.9	5.2	5.8	9.5	7.4	6.0	5.4	6.0
1996	6.0	5.2	5.8	9.9	8.2	6.1	5.6	5.6
1997	6.0	5.2	5.9	9.8	7.3	6.2	5.6	5.8
1998	6.0	5.4	6.0	9.5	7.1	6.2	5.5	6.1
1999	6.1	5.5	6.4	9.2	7.0	6.4	5.7	6.3
2000	6.2	5.6	6.5	9.2	7.5	6.4	5.9	6.0
2001	6.2	5.6	7.0	9.2	7.6	6.5	5.8	6.3
2002	6.1	5.5	6.6	9.6	7.3	6.4	5.6	6.2
2003	6.2	5.5	6.8	9.9	7.5	6.7	5.7	6.2
2004	6.2	5.7	7.0	9.1	7.3	6.7	5.8	6.3
2005	6.4	5.9	7.6	9.8	7.7	6.6	6.0	6.8

[1] Includes units built for rent, not shown separately. [2] For composition of regions, see map inside front cover.

Source: U.S. Census Bureau, "New Residential Construction." See Internet site <http://www.census.gov/const/www/newresconstindex.html>.

Table 939. **Price Indexes of New One-Family Houses Sold by Region: 1980 to 2005**

[**1996 = 100.** Based on kinds of homes sold in 1996. Includes value of the lot. For composition of regions, see map, inside front cover]

Year	Total	Northeast	Midwest	South	West
1980	59.5	48.0	56.8	63.2	58.4
1981	64.2	52.1	62.1	68.7	62.0
1982	65.7	54.0	63.9	70.9	62.8
1983	67.1	57.3	63.7	72.8	64.0
1984	69.8	62.2	67.5	75.2	66.3
1985	70.7	68.5	66.4	76.7	66.7
1986	73.4	78.6	70.2	79.0	68.4
1987	77.4	89.2	74.9	81.9	72.0
1988	80.3	91.5	78.2	83.7	75.9
1989	83.5	94.1	80.0	86.1	80.7
1990	85.1	92.2	80.7	86.3	84.6
1991	86.2	89.2	82.8	87.9	85.1
1992	87.3	96.1	84.3	88.8	85.6
1993	91.1	93.3	90.0	93.0	88.7
1994	95.5	94.5	94.4	96.4	94.9
1995	98.2	96.7	98.1	99.4	96.5
1996	100.0	100.0	100.0	100.0	100.0
1997	102.9	102.8	103.3	102.8	102.9
1998	105.5	104.5	105.3	106.0	105.1
1999	110.7	108.8	110.3	110.5	111.7
2000	115.4	114.6	114.4	114.7	117.3
2001	119.5	122.6	115.8	117.8	123.9
2002	124.8	127.5	120.7	121.2	132.5
2003	131.9	137.5	124.7	126.5	144.3
2004	141.9	149.1	132.6	133.0	161.5
2005	153.1	152.9	139.2	140.8	185.5

Source: U.S. Census Bureau, "Construction Price Indexes". See Internet site <http://www.census.gov/const/www/constpriceindex.html>.

602   Construction and Housing

Table 940. New Privately Owned One-Family Houses Sold by Region and Type of Financing, 1980 to 2005, and by Sales-Price Group, 2005

[In thousands (545 represents 545,000). Based on a national probability sample of monthly interviews with builders or owners of one-family houses for which building permits have been issued or, for nonpermit areas, on which construction has started. For details, see source and Appendix III. For composition of regions, see map inside front cover]

Year and sales-price group	Total sales	Region				Financing type			
		North-east	Midwest	South	West	Conven-tional [1]	FHA and VA	Rural Housing Service [2]	Cash
1980	545	50	81	267	145	302	196	14	32
1985	688	112	82	323	170	403	208	11	64
1990	534	71	89	225	149	337	138	10	50
1995	667	55	125	300	187	490	129	9	39
1998	886	81	164	398	243	693	136	9	48
1999	880	76	168	395	242	689	143	6	41
2000	877	71	155	406	244	695	138	4	40
2001	908	66	164	439	239	726	141	2	39
2002	973	65	185	450	273	788	140	4	42
2003	1,086	79	189	511	307	911	130	4	41
2004	1,203	83	210	562	348	1,047	105	6	46
2005	**1,283**	**81**	**205**	**638**	**358**	**1,150**	**79**	**1**	**52**
Under $200,000	472	11	87	325	49	(NA)	(NA)	(NA)	(NA)
$200,000 to $299,999	352	21	69	162	99	(NA)	(NA)	(NA)	(NA)
$300,000 to $499,999	314	32	40	106	137	(NA)	(NA)	(NA)	(NA)
$500,000 and over	144	17	9	45	73	(NA)	(NA)	(NA)	(NA)

NA Not available.   [1] Includes all other types of financing.   [2] Prior to 1998, the Farmers Home Administration.

Source: U.S. Census Bureau and U.S. Dept. of Housing and Urban Development, Current Construction Reports, Series C25, *Characteristics of New Housing*, annual; and *New One-Family Houses Sold*, monthly; publications discontinued in 2001. See "New Residential Sales" at Internet site <http://www.census.gov/const/www/newressalesindex.html>.

Table 941. Median Sales Price of New Privately Owned One-Family Houses Sold by Region: 1980 to 2005

[In dollars. For definition of median, see Guide to Tabular Presentation. For composition of regions, see map inside front cover. See Appendix III. See also headnote, table 940]

Year	U.S.	North-east	Mid-west	South	West	Year	U.S.	North-east	Mid-west	South	West
1980	64,600	69,500	63,400	59,600	72,300	2000	169,000	227,400	169,700	148,000	196,400
1985	84,300	103,300	80,300	75,000	92,600	2001	175,200	246,400	172,600	155,400	213,600
1990	122,900	159,000	107,900	99,000	147,500	2002	187,600	264,300	178,000	163,400	238,500
1995	133,900	180,000	134,000	124,500	141,400	2003	195,000	264,500	184,300	168,100	260,900
1998	152,500	200,000	157,500	135,800	163,500	2004	221,000	315,800	205,000	181,100	283,100
1999	161,000	210,500	164,000	145,900	173,700	2005	240,900	343,800	216,900	197,300	332,600

Source: U.S. Census Bureau and U.S. Department of Housing and Urban Development, Current Construction Reports, Series C25, *Characteristics of New Housing*, annual; and *New One-Family Houses Sold*, monthly; publications discontinued in 2001. See "New Residential Sales" at Internet site <http://www.census.gov/const/www/newressalesindex.html>.

Table 942. New Manufactured (Mobile) Homes Placed for Residential Use and Average Sales Price by Region: 1980 to 2005

[233.7 represents 233,700. A mobile home is a moveable dwelling, 8 feet or more wide and 40 feet or more long, designed to be towed on its own chassis, with transportation gear integral to the unit when it leaves the factory, and without need of permanent foundation. Excluded are travel trailers, motor homes, and modular housing. Data are based on a probability sample and subject to sampling variability; see source. For composition of regions, see map inside front cover]

Year	Units placed (1,000)					Average sales price (dol.)				
	Total	North-east	Mid-west	South	West	U.S.	North-east	Mid-west	South	West
1980	233.7	12.3	32.3	140.3	48.7	19,800	18,500	18,600	18,200	25,400
1985	283.4	20.2	38.6	187.6	36.9	21,800	22,700	21,500	20,400	28,700
1990	195.4	18.8	37.7	108.4	30.6	27,800	30,000	27,000	24,500	39,300
1995	319.4	15.0	57.5	203.2	43.7	35,300	35,800	35,700	33,300	44,100
1996	337.7	16.2	58.8	218.2	44.4	37,200	37,300	38,000	35,500	45,000
1997	336.3	14.3	55.3	219.4	47.3	39,800	41,300	40,300	38,000	47,300
1998	373.7	14.7	58.3	250.3	50.4	41,600	42,200	42,400	40,000	48,400
1999	338.3	14.1	53.6	227.2	43.5	43,300	44,000	44,400	41,900	49,600
2000	280.9	14.9	48.7	178.7	38.6	46,400	47,000	47,900	44,300	54,100
2001	196.2	12.2	37.6	116.4	30.0	48,900	50,000	49,100	46,500	58,000
2002	174.3	11.8	34.2	101.0	27.2	51,300	53,200	51,700	48,000	62,600
2003	139.8	11.2	25.2	77.2	26.1	54,900	57,300	55,100	50,500	67,700
2004	124.4	11.0	20.6	67.4	25.5	58,200	60,200	58,800	52,300	73,200
2005	122.8	9.2	17.3	67.9	28.4	62,300	66,500	60,500	55,500	79,500

Source: U.S. Census Bureau, "Manufactured Housing". See Internet site <http://www.census.gov/const/www/mhsindex.html>.

Construction and Housing   603

Table 943. Existing One-Family Homes Sold and Price by Region: 1980 to 2005

[2,973 represents 2,973,000. Includes existing detached single-family homes and townhomes; excludes condos and co-ops. Data shown here reflect revisions to previous estimates. Based on data (adjusted and aggregated to regional and national totals) reported by participating real estate multiple listing services. For definition of median, see Guide to Tabular Presentation. See Table 946 for data on condos and co-ops. For composition of regions, see map inside front cover]

Year	Homes sold (1,000)					Median sales price (dol.)				
	Total	North-east	Mid-west	South	West	Total	North-east	Mid-west	South	West
1980	2,973	403	806	1,092	672	62,200	60,800	51,900	58,300	89,300
1985	3,134	561	806	1,063	704	75,500	88,900	58,900	75,200	95,400
1988	3,513	606	865	1,224	817	89,300	143,000	68,400	82,200	124,900
1989 [1]	3,010	545	829	1,003	633	89,500	127,700	71,800	84,400	127,100
1990	2,914	510	806	1,010	587	92,000	126,400	75,300	85,100	129,600
1991	2,885	515	808	992	569	97,100	129,100	79,500	88,500	135,300
1992	3,150	578	906	1,049	618	99,700	128,900	83,000	91,500	131,500
1993	3,427	611	961	1,173	681	103,100	129,100	86,000	94,300	132,500
1994	3,544	615	963	1,220	746	107,200	129,100	89,300	95,700	139,400
1995	3,519	609	944	1,219	747	110,500	126,700	94,800	97,700	141,000
1996	3,797	652	988	1,289	868	115,800	127,800	101,000	103,400	147,100
1997	3,964	678	1,009	1,363	914	121,800	131,800	107,000	109,600	155,200
1998	4,495	741	1,136	1,598	1,020	128,400	135,900	114,300	116,200	164,800
1999	4,649	728	1,144	1,705	1,072	133,300	139,000	119,600	120,300	173,900
2000	4,603	714	1,116	1,706	1,066	139,000	139,400	123,600	128,300	183,000
2001	4,734	709	1,155	1,793	1,076	147,800	146,500	130,200	137,400	194,500
2002	4,975	731	1,217	1,871	1,155	158,100	164,300	136,000	147,300	215,400
2003	5,443	769	1,322	2,072	1,280	170,000	190,500	141,300	157,100	234,200
2004	5,959	821	1,389	2,312	1,437	184,100	220,000	149,000	169,000	265,800
2005	6,179	839	1,410	2,458	1,472	206,600	243,500	165,600	178,100	312,900

[1] Beginning 1989 data not comparable to earlier years due to rebenchmarking.

Source: NATIONAL ASSOCIATION OF REALTORS®, Washington, DC, prior to 1990, *Home Sales*, monthly, and *Home Sales Yearbook: 1990*; (copyright); thereafter, *Real Estate Outlook; Market Trends & Insights*, monthly, (copyright). See Internet site <http://www.realtor.org/research>.

Table 944. Median Sales Price of Existing One-Family Homes by Selected Metropolitan Area: 2004 and 2005

[In thousands of dollars (184.1 represents $184,100). Includes existing detached single family homes and townhouses. Areas are metropolitan statistical areas defined by Office of Management and Budget as of 2004, except as noted]

Metropolitan area	2004	2005, prel.	Metropolitan area	2004	2005, prel.
United States, total	**184.1**	**207.3**	New York-Wayne-White Plains, NY-NJ . . .	436.6	497.0
			Norwich-New London, CT.	231.5	256.0
Albany-Schenectady-Troy, NY.	161.3	183.6	NY: Edison, NJ.	328.1	377.8
Allentown-Bethlehem-Easton, PA-NJ	207.3	244.4	NY: Nassau-Suffolk, NY.	413.5	465.2
Anaheim-Santa Ana-Irvine, CA [1]	627.3	691.9	NY: Newark-Union, NJ-PA	375.8	415.8
Atlantic City, NJ	197.9	251.7			
Baltimore-Towson, MD.	217.0	262.3	Orlando, FL	169.6	243.6
Barnstable Town, MA.	377.2	396.5	Palm Bay-Melbourne-Titusville, FL.	153.4	209.0
Boston-Cambridge-Quincy, MA-NH	389.7	414.0	Philadelphia-Camden-		
Boulder, CO.	325.3	348.4	Wilmington, PA-NJ-DE-MD	185.1	215.3
Bridgeport-Stamford-Norwalk, CT.	441.3	482.4	Phoenix-Mesa-Scottsdale, AZ	169.4	247.4
Cape Coral-Fort Myers, FL.	187.2	269.2	Pittsfield, MA	192.8	206.6
Charleston-North Charleston, SC.	183.5	197.0	Portland-South Portland-Biddeford, ME. . .	224.8	245.1
Charlotte-Gastonia-Concord, NC-SC	168.0	180.9	Portland-Vancouver-Beaverton, OR-WA . .	206.5	244.9
Chicago-Naperville-Joliet, IL	240.1	263.7	Providence-New Bedford-Fall		
Colordo Springs, CO	187.6	204.4	River, RI-MA	276.9	293.5
Deltona-Daytona Beach-Ormond			Raleigh-Cary, NC	169.9	194.5
Beach, FL	148.6	194.0	Reno-Sparks, NV	284.3	349.9
Denver-Aurora, CO	239.1	247.1	Richmond, VA	170.7	199.6
Eugene-Springfield, OR	164.9	197.6	Riverside-San Bernardino-Ontario, CA [1] . .	296.4	374.2
Gainesville, FL	159.0	184.0	Sacramento-Arden-Arcade-		
Hagerstown-Martinsburg, MD-WV	165.9	209.3	Roseville, CA [1]	317.0	375.9
Hartford-West Hartford-East			San Diego-Carlsbad-San Marcos, CA [1] . .	551.6	604.3
Hartford, CT.	231.6	252.9	San Francisco-Oakland-Fremont, CA [1] . . .	641.7	715.7
Honolulu, HI.	460.0	590.0	San Jose-Sunnyvale-Santa Clara, CA [1] . .	698.5	744.5
Kingston, NY	216.8	251.0	Sarasota-Bradenton-Venice, FL.	255.7	354.2
Las Vegas-Paradise, NV	266.4	304.7	Seattle-Tacoma-Bellevue, WA	284.6	316.8
Los Angeles-Long Beach-Santa Ana,			Springfield, MA.	180.3	201.8
CA [1]	446.4	529.0			
Madison, WI	200.8	218.3	Tampa-St.Petersburg-Clearwater, FL	159.7	205.3
Miami-Fort Lauderdale-			Trenton-Ewing, NJ	234.2	261.1
Miami Beach, FL.	286.4	371.1	Tucson, AZ	177.3	231.0
Milwaukee-Waukesha-West Allis, WI	197.1	213.4	Virginia Beach-Norfolk-		
Minneapolis-St. Paul-			Newport News, VA-NC.	163.0	197.2
Bloomington, MN-WI	217.4	234.8	Washington-Arlington-		
New Haven-Milford, CT	249.2	278.9	Alexandria, DC-VA-MD-WV	339.8	424.7
New York-Northern New			Worcester, MA.	275.9	290.7
Jersey-Long Island, NY-NJ-PA	385.9	446.5			

[1] California data supplied by the California Association of REALTORS.

Source: NATIONAL ASSOCIATION OF REALTORS®, Washington, DC, *Real Estate Outlook: Market Trends & Insights*, monthly, (copyright). See Internet site <http://www.realtor.org/research>.

Table 945. **Existing Home Sales by State: 2000 to 2005**

[In thousands (5,171 represents 5,171,000). Includes condos and co-ops as well as single-family homes. Data shown here reflect revisions from prior estimates]

State	2000	2003	2004	2005, prel.	State	2000	2003	2004	2005, prel.
United States ..	5,171	6,183	6,784	7,073.0	Missouri..........	110.2	131.1	141.8	143.2
Alabama	67.0	93.7	112.0	128.0	Montana	17.4	23.2	24.2	25.7
Alaska...........	14.3	18.4	23.0	25.6	Nebraska.........	32.3	38.0	39.8	41.2
Arizona	104.8	149.6	186.8	199.0	Nevada	44.6	80.9	99.8	98.0
Arkansas	45.0	53.8	60.9	75.3	New Hampshire.....	26.7	25.4	27.2	(NA)
California	573.5	577.6	610.1	599.6	New Jersey	160.8	174.1	188.7	184.6
Colorado	111.5	112.4	126.0	130.4	New Mexico	29.9	43.3	50.6	57.5
Connecticut	61.5	63.5	72.5	77.7	New York	273.3	282.6	307.5	319.8
Delaware	12.9	15.8	18.9	19.3	North Carolina.....	134.2	156.3	192.6	215.7
District of Columbia ..	10.6	12.1	13.4	12.1	North Dakota	10.8	12.9	14.5	15.8
Florida...........	393.6	476.1	526.5	546.1	Ohio	216.4	253.1	275.7	286.9
Georgia	143.6	174.0	215.8	242.1	Oklahoma	67.3	85.1	93.6	104.6
Hawaii...........	22.1	34.4	35.5	36.8	Oregon	62.6	78.3	90.7	100.5
Idaho............	24.1	27.6	32.0	(NA)	Pennsylvania	194.0	218.8	247.3	254.5
Illinois	246.8	275.1	307.5	315.3	Rhode Island	17.0	16.9	19.2	19.8
Indiana	111.0	120.4	130.5	138.3	South Carolina	64.3	83.0	99.3	114.6
Iowa	53.3	62.4	71.1	75.0	South Dakota	12.6	15.6	17.3	18.3
Kansas	52.6	65.3	73.4	77.9	Tennessee	100.4	128.8	156.1	170.9
Kentucky	66.0	81.1	89.3	96.2	Texas	381.8	425.4	485.5	531.6
Louisiana	66.8	76.2	79.6	87.2	Utah	35.5	43.9	43.6	51.7
Maine	27.6	30.7	33.6	33.3	Vermont	12.1	14.5	14.2	(NA)
Maryland	100.5	120.8	140.6	135.5	Virginia	130.0	158.3	186.0	181.8
Massachusetts	112.3	118.3	141.7	148.6	Washington	112.4	132.3	147.6	167.7
Michigan	185.0	207.4	213.4	208.1	West Virginia	22.9	28.9	36.0	38.4
Minnesota	96.3	126.7	137.4	134.9	Wisconsin.........	91.6	105.9	116.8	123.0
Mississippi	38.7	51.5	58.1	61.4	Wyoming	9.6	11.4	13.2	14.3

NA Not available.

Source: NATIONAL ASSOCIATION OF REALTORS®, Washington, DC, *Real Estate Outlook: Market Trends & Insights,* monthly (copyright). See Internet site <http://www.realtor.org/research>.

Table 946. **Existing Apartment Condos and Co-ops—Units Sold and Median Sales Price by Region: 1990 to 2005**

[272 represents 272,000. Data shown here reflect revisions from prior estimates. For definition of median, see Guide to Tabular Presentation. For composition of regions, see map inside front cover]

Year	Units sold (1,000)					Median sales price (dol.)				
	U.S.	North-east	Mid-west	South	West	U.S.	North-east	Mid-west	South	West
1990	272	73	55	80	64	85,200	110,200	70,200	66,800	105,200
1995	333	108	66	96	63	87,400	94,800	90,700	70,600	105,300
1997	407	134	79	111	83	95,500	101,100	99,100	76,300	118,300
1998	471	157	92	126	95	100,600	103,400	106,400	80,000	126,400
1999	534	182	102	145	105	108,000	112,500	114,600	84,100	132,100
2000	571	197	106	160	108	111,800	111,200	121,700	87,700	136,800
2001	601	203	116	174	108	123,200	124,200	134,900	97,100	147,200
2002	657	221	129	193	114	142,200	147,000	148,600	114,500	171,600
2003	732	250	146	211	125	165,400	182,400	162,600	132,200	204,000
2004	820	292	161	230	137	193,600	219,300	181,000	163,200	236,700
2005	896	331	177	245	143	220,000	251,100	189,200	195,200	260,400

Source: NATIONAL ASSOCIATION OF REALTORS®, Washington, DC, *Real Estate Outlook: Market Trends & Insights,* monthly (copyright). See Internet site <http://www.realtor.org/research>.

Table 947. **New Unfurnished Apartments Completed and Rented in 3 Months by Region: 2000 to 2005**

[226.2 represents 226,200. Structures with five or more units, privately financed, nonsubsidized, unfurnished rental apartments. Based on sample and subject to sampling variability; see source for details. For composition of regions, see map, inside front cover]

Year and rent	Number (1,000)					Percent rented in 3 months				
	U.S.	North-east	Mid-west	South	West	U.S.	North-east	Mid-west	South	West
2000	226.2	14.8	39.5	125.9	45.9	72	85	76	67	77
2003	166.5	19.8	35.5	72.0	39.2	61	72	62	56	63
2004	153.8	13.1	31.7	72.7	36.3	62	75	59	60	65
2005, prel...................	**111.9**	**4.8**	**19.5**	**57.4**	**30.3**	**64**	**75**	**63**	**63**	**65**
Less than $750	28.6	(Z)	11.9	14.3	2.4	71	(Z)	70	72	71
$750 to $849.................	13.8	–	2.6	8.0	3.1	61	(X)	57	63	62
$850 to $949.................	14.5	(Z)	2.0	8.9	3.5	58	(Z)	46	60	59
$950 to $1,049	10.5	0.1	0.6	6.5	3.3	63	80	47	62	69
$1,050 to $1,149	8.1	0.1	0.5	4.7	2.7	58	96	62	59	55
$1,150 or more	36.5	4.6	1.8	14.9	15.2	63	74	55	57	66
Median monthly asking rent (dollars) ..	$943	(¹)	(²)	$921	(¹)	(X)	(X)	(X)	(X)	(X)

– Represents zero. X Not applicable. Z Fewer than 50 units or less than one-half of 1 percent. ¹ Over $1,150.
² Under $750.

Source: U.S. Census Bureau, *Current Housing Reports,* Series H130, *Market Absorption of Apartments,* and unpublished data. See Internet site: <http://www.census.gov/prod/www/abs/apart.html>.

Construction and Housing 605

Table 948. Total Housing Inventory for the United States: 1980 to 2005

[In thousands (87,739 represents 87,739,000), except percent. Based on the Current Population Survey and the Housing Vacancy Survey and subject to sampling error; see source and Appendix III for details]

Item	1980	1985	1990	1995	2000	2001	2002 [1]	2003	2004	2005
All housing units	87,739	97,333	106,283	112,655	119,628	121,480	119,297	120,834	122,187	123,925
Vacant	8,101	9,446	12,059	12,669	13,908	14,470	14,332	15,274	15,599	15,694
Year-round vacant.	5,996	7,400	9,128	9,570	10,439	10,916	10,771	11,631	11,884	11,916
For rent	1,575	2,221	2,662	2,946	3,024	3,203	3,347	3,676	3,802	3,721
For sale only.	734	1,006	1,064	1,022	1,148	1,301	1,220	1,308	1,307	1,451
Rented or sold	623	664	660	810	856	882	842	976	991	1,060
Held off market	3,064	3,510	4,742	4,793	5,411	5,530	5,362	5,671	5,784	5,684
Occasional use	814	977	1,485	1,667	1,892	1,887	1,819	1,989	1,967	1,884
Usual residence elsewhere	568	659	1,068	801	1,037	1,064	995	994	1,068	1,128
Other.	1,683	1,875	2,189	2,325	2,482	2,579	2,548	2,688	2,749	2,672
Seasonal [2].	2,106	2,046	2,931	3,099	3,469	3,554	3,561	3,643	3,715	3,778
Total occupied	79,638	87,887	94,224	99,985	105,720	107,010	104,965	105,560	106,588	108,231
Owner	52,223	56,152	60,248	64,739	71,250	72,593	71,278	72,054	73,575	74,553
Renter	27,415	31,736	33,976	35,246	34,470	34,417	33,687	33,506	33,013	33,678
PERCENT DISTRIBUTION										
All housing units	100.0	100.0	100.0	100.0	100.0	100.0	100.0	100.0	100.0	100.0
Vacant	9.2	9.7	11.3	11.2	11.6	11.9	12.0	12.6	12.8	12.7
Total occupied	90.8	90.3	88.7	88.8	88.4	88.1	88.0	87.4	87.2	87.3
Owner	59.5	57.7	56.7	57.5	59.6	59.8	59.7	59.6	60.2	60.2
Renter	31.2	32.6	32.0	31.3	28.8	28.3	28.2	27.7	27.0	27.2

[1] Revised. Based on 2000 census controls. [2] Beginning 1990, includes vacant seasonal mobile homes. For years shown, seasonal vacant housing units were underreported prior to 1990.

Source: U.S. Census Bureau, "Housing Vacancies and Home Ownership," <http://www.census.gov/hhes/www/housing/hvs/hvs.html>.

Table 949. Occupied Housing Inventory by Age of Householder: 1985 to 2005

[In thousands (87,887 represents 87,887,000). Based on the Current Population Survey/Housing Vacancy Survey; See source for details]

Age of householder	1985	1990	1995	1999	2000	2001	2002 [1]	2003	2004	2005
Total [2]	87,887	94,224	99,986	104,929	105,719	107,009	104,965	105,560	106,588	108,231
Less than 25 years old	5,483	5,143	5,502	6,000	6,221	6,460	6,372	6,441	6,538	6,536
25 to 29 years old.	9,543	9,508	8,662	8,661	8,482	8,358	8,231	8,213	8,491	8,790
30 to 34 years old.	10,288	11,213	11,206	10,400	10,219	10,301	10,176	10,084	9,865	9,583
35 to 39 years old.	9,615	10,914	11,993	11,950	11,834	11,587	10,924	10,777	10,438	10,526
40 to 44 years old.	7,919	9,893	11,151	12,206	12,377	12,504	11,839	11,748	11,768	11,722
45 to 49 years old.	6,517	8,038	10,080	10,973	11,164	11,529	11,204	11,341	11,583	11,780
50 to 54 years old.	6,157	6,532	7,882	9,412	9,834	10,288	10,123	10,194	10,316	10,595
55 to 59 years old.	6,558	6,182	6,355	7,389	7,602	7,827	8,261	8,550	8,928	9,504
60 to 64 years old.	6,567	6,446	5,860	6,183	6,215	6,345	6,422	6,776	7,112	7,336
65 to 69 years old.	5,976	6,407	6,088	5,845	5,816	5,749	5,644	5,570	5,656	5,900
70 to 74 years old.	5,003	5,397	5,693	5,621	5,567	5,496	5,137	5,163	5,065	5,016
75 years old and over	7,517	8,546	9,514	10,289	10,388	10,546	10,632	10,703	10,827	10,943

[1] Revised. Based on 2000 census controls. [2] 1985 total includes ages not reported. Thereafter cases allocated by age.

Source: U.S. Census Bureau, "Housing Vacancies and Home Ownership," <http://www.census.gov/hhes/www/housing/hvs/hvs.html>.

Table 950. Vacancy Rates for Housing Units—Characteristics: 2000 to 2005

[In percent. Rate is relationship between vacant housing for rent or for sale and the total rental and homeowner supply, which comprises occupied units, units rented or sold and awaiting occupancy, and vacant units available for rent or sale. Based on the Current Population/Housing Vacancy Survey; see source for details. For composition of regions, see map, inside front cover]

Characteristic	Rental units				Homeowner units			
	2000	2003	2004 [1]	2005	2000	2003	2004 [1]	2005
Total units	8.0	9.8	10.2	9.8	1.6	1.8	1.7	1.9
Northeast.	5.6	6.6	7.3	6.5	1.2	1.2	1.1	1.5
Midwest.	8.8	10.8	12.2	12.6	1.3	1.7	2.0	2.2
South	10.5	12.5	12.6	11.8	1.9	2.1	2.0	2.1
West.	5.8	7.7	7.5	7.3	1.5	1.6	1.4	1.4
Units in structure:								
1 unit.	7.0	8.4	9.3	9.9	1.5	1.6	1.6	1.7
2 units or more	8.7	10.7	10.9	10.0	4.7	5.5	5.2	6.2
5 units or more	9.2	11.4	11.5	10.4	5.8	5.3	4.8	6.6
Units with—								
3 rooms or less	10.3	12.2	12.4	12.1	10.4	8.1	9.5	12.0
4 rooms	8.2	10.0	10.4	9.6	2.9	3.4	3.3	3.3
5 rooms	6.9	8.9	9.3	9.3	2.0	2.1	2.0	2.2
6 rooms or more	5.2	7.0	8.2	8.1	1.1	1.3	1.2	1.4

[1] Revised.

Source: U.S. Census Bureau, "Housing Vacancies and Home Ownership," <http://www.census.gov/hhes/www/housing/hvs/hvs.html>.

Table 951. **Housing Units and Tenure—States: 2004**

[122,672 represents 122,672,000. The American Community Survey universe is limited to the household population and excludes the population living in institutions, college dormitories, and other group quarters. Based on a sample and subject to sampling variability; see Appendix III]

State	Housing units						Housing tenure			
			Vacant (1,000)		Vacancy rate		Owner-occupied units		Renter-occupied units	
	Total (1,000)	Occu-pied (1,000)	Total	For sea-sonal use [1]	Home-owner [2]	Renter [3]	Total (1,000)	Average house-hold size	Total (1,000)	Average house-hold size
United States . . .	122,672	109,902	12,770	3,719	1.7	8.1	73,754	2.70	36,148	2.39
Alabama	2,059	1,755	304	59	1.9	10.6	1,263	2.58	493	2.35
Alaska.	272	228	43	23	1.0	7.6	150	2.91	79	2.54
Arizona	2,458	2,132	327	149	1.8	9.9	1,464	2.69	668	2.53
Arkansas	1,233	1,099	134	16	1.0	8.5	720	2.50	379	2.30
California	12,805	11,972	833	232	1.2	4.8	7,012	3.01	4,960	2.81
Colorado	2,011	1,850	161	34	1.9	9.2	1,269	2.55	582	2.18
Connecticut	1,414	1,330	84	17	0.9	6.8	928	2.68	402	2.25
Delaware	367	311	57	27	2.2	12.3	226	2.67	84	2.38
District of Columbia . . .	277	249	28	1	1.4	5.3	108	2.20	140	2.00
Florida	8,009	6,819	1,190	586	1.6	9.9	4,808	2.52	2,011	2.42
Georgia	3,673	3,210	463	101	2.7	11.1	2,172	2.76	1,038	2.48
Hawaii.	483	428	55	30	0.6	4.1	252	3.09	176	2.56
Idaho	579	515	64	25	2.9	7.9	373	2.74	142	2.38
Illinois	5,094	4,660	434	30	1.9	10.1	3,227	2.78	1,433	2.39
Indiana	2,691	2,413	278	52	2.2	9.4	1,733	2.61	679	2.25
Iowa	1,293	1,176	117	15	1.5	10.0	868	2.55	308	2.07
Kansas	1,185	1,076	109	10	1.9	8.8	748	2.64	328	2.07
Kentucky	1,843	1,647	196	29	1.6	8.5	1,156	2.52	492	2.28
Louisiana	1,920	1,714	206	30	1.3	7.4	1,135	2.67	579	2.34
Maine	677	534	142	101	1.7	7.4	390	2.51	145	2.07
Maryland	2,250	2,078	172	40	1.0	6.4	1,444	2.72	634	2.35
Massachusetts	2,672	2,435	237	97	0.9	5.5	1,572	2.79	863	2.11
Michigan	4,433	3,923	510	214	1.7	9.1	2,929	2.62	994	2.21
Minnesota	2,213	2,055	158	54	0.8	7.5	1,547	2.56	507	1.97
Mississippi	1,221	1,075	147	21	1.7	9.9	748	2.66	326	2.49
Missouri.	2,564	2,309	255	18	1.8	8.8	1,635	2.55	674	2.09
Montana	423	369	55	24	1.4	4.8	253	2.54	116	2.25
Nebraska.	758	687	70	17	1.6	7.6	470	2.62	217	2.13
Nevada.	976	872	105	28	1.9	8.1	534	2.73	338	2.50
New Hampshire	576	492	84	57	0.8	6.3	357	2.73	135	2.12
New Jersey	3,415	3,134	280	111	0.9	5.7	2,134	2.86	1,000	2.41
New Mexico	826	712	114	36	1.9	6.7	493	2.70	219	2.43
New York.	7,819	7,088	732	230	1.4	5.2	3,941	2.80	3,146	2.42
North Carolina	3,860	3,340	520	162	2.5	11.1	2,305	2.54	1,035	2.33
North Dakota	301	263	38	13	1.0	7.8	179	2.49	84	1.96
Ohio	4,967	4,515	452	39	2.3	9.8	3,150	2.61	1,365	2.15
Oklahoma	1,573	1,360	213	34	3.0	10.4	928	2.59	432	2.33
Oregon	1,535	1,428	108	17	1.5	6.0	899	2.54	529	2.32
Pennsylvania	5,386	4,818	568	170	1.6	7.2	3,506	2.62	1,311	2.12
Rhode Island	446	410	37	13	0.5	5.3	253	2.72	157	2.23
South Carolina	1,891	1,611	279	99	2.4	10.5	1,124	2.57	488	2.41
South Dakota	343	301	42	13	0.9	8.3	208	2.65	93	2.07
Tennessee	2,595	2,315	280	60	1.9	9.0	1,620	2.57	695	2.29
Texas	8,847	7,791	1,056	200	2.3	11.9	5,075	2.96	2,716	2.53
Utah	849	780	69	18	1.8	6.9	544	3.16	236	2.67
Vermont	304	250	55	42	0.7	5.5	183	2.52	67	2.11
Virginia	3,117	2,846	270	56	1.0	8.4	1,969	2.63	878	2.32
Washington	2,607	2,416	190	52	1.1	6.1	1,548	2.66	868	2.24
West Virginia	867	737	130	43	2.4	7.3	545	2.51	192	2.08
Wisconsin	2,464	2,173	291	156	1.7	8.8	1,519	2.62	654	2.11
Wyoming	233	202	30	14	1.4	5.8	142	2.53	61	2.22

[1] For seasonal, recreational, or occasional use.   [2] Proportion of the homeowner housing inventory which is vacant for sale.
[3] Proportion of the rental inventory which is vacant for rent.

Source: U.S. Census Bureau, 2004 American Community Survey Tables B25002. Occupancy Status; B25003. Tenure; B25004. Vacancy Status; and B25010. Average Household Size of Units by Tenure; using American FactFinder®. See Internet site <http://factfinder.census.gov/>; (accessed 31 January 2006).

Construction and Housing   607

Table 952. **Housing Units—Characteristics by Tenure and Region: 2005**

[In thousands of units (124,377 represents 124,377,000), except as indicated. As of fall. Based on the American Housing Survey; see Appendix III. For composition of regions, see map, inside front cover]

Characteristic	Total housing units	Sea-sonal	Total	Owner	Renter	North-east	Mid-west	South	West	Vacant
			Year-round units / Occupied							
Total units	**124,377**	**3,845**	**108,871**	**74,931**	**33,940**	**20,337**	**24,955**	**39,722**	**23,858**	**11,660**
Percent distribution	100.0	3.1	87.5	68.8	31.2	18.7	22.9	36.5	21.9	9.4
Units in structure:										
Single family detached	77,703	2,287	69,996	61,699	8,297	11,044	17,707	26,254	14,992	5,420
Single family attached	7,046	197	6,158	3,976	2,182	1,825	1,042	2,035	1,256	691
2 to 4 units.	10,071	188	8,379	1,550	6,829	2,604	1,863	2,073	1,840	1,504
5 to 9 units.	6,073	125	5,109	502	4,607	917	1,004	1,824	1,364	840
10 to 19 units	5,696	94	4,739	563	4,175	817	902	1,830	1,190	863
20 to 49 units	4,402	125	3,639	436	3,203	1,041	601	964	1,033	638
50 or more units	4,757	186	3,912	689	3,222	1,589	682	809	831	659
Manufactured/mobile home [1]	8,630	644	6,940	5,516	1,424	500	1,155	3,932	1,352	1,047
Single-wide.	5,584	457	4,257	3,093	1,164	371	843	2,443	600	869
Double-wide.	2,897	174	2,558	2,302	255	126	312	1,435	685	165
Triple-wide or larger	118	7	107	103	4	–	–	44	64	4
Year structure built:										
Median year.	1973	1972	1973	1974	1970	1956	1968	1978	1976	1971
1980 or later.	42,502	1,284	37,543	28,249	9,293	3,866	7,096	17,426	9,154	3,672
1970 to 1979	25,091	831	21,858	13,860	7,998	2,907	4,854	8,695	5,403	2,401
1960 to 1969	15,192	486	13,499	9,217	4,282	2,467	3,019	4,876	3,136	1,207
1950 to 1959	13,003	366	11,555	8,469	3,086	2,527	3,025	3,490	2,513	1,082
1940 to 1949	7,904	279	6,821	4,458	2,363	1,654	1,497	2,156	1,513	805
1939 and earlier	20,686	598	17,595	10,677	6,919	6,915	5,463	3,079	2,139	2,493
Stories in structure: [2]										
1 story.	39,963	1,553	34,814	26,278	8,537	1,139	4,031	19,192	10,453	3,596
2 stories	41,189	984	36,283	24,026	12,257	6,187	10,111	11,154	8,832	3,922
3 stories	26,287	393	23,714	16,375	7,340	8,482	8,342	4,353	2,537	2,180
4 to 6 stories	5,819	137	5,128	2,248	2,880	2,932	999	719	478	554
7 or more stories.	2,488	135	1,992	488	1,504	1,097	317	372	206	362
Foundation: [3]										
Full basement.	26,882	350	24,984	22,612	2,372	8,586	10,745	3,793	1,860	1,547
Partial building	9,431	153	8,735	7,840	894	2,378	3,626	1,590	1,140	544
Crawlspace	22,292	1,151	19,038	15,646	3,392	732	2,575	10,037	5,694	2,103
Concrete slab	25,514	660	23,012	19,317	3,695	1,129	1,720	12,675	7,488	1,843
Other	629	169	384	259	125	44	82	192	66	75
Equipment:										
Lacking complete facilities.	5,345	462	1,695	257	1,438	298	345	536	515	3,188
With complete facilities.	119,032	3,384	107,177	74,674	32,502	20,038	24,610	39,186	23,343	8,472
Kitchen sink	123,262	3,644	108,656	74,889	33,767	20,296	24,923	39,663	23,775	10,962
Refrigerator	121,035	3,466	108,673	74,856	33,818	20,311	24,909	39,640	23,814	8,895
Cooking stove or range	121,208	3,475	108,140	74,718	33,422	20,179	24,812	39,506	23,642	9,593
Burners only, no stove or range . .	189	32	131	60	71	31	19	37	43	26
Microwave oven only	481	23	397	106	291	104	68	98	126	61
Dishwasher	75,239	1,677	68,508	54,060	14,448	11,132	14,491	26,271	16,614	5,055
Washing machine	95,272	1,979	89,287	71,997	17,290	15,039	20,969	34,138	19,141	4,006
Clothes dryer	92,179	1,949	86,169	70,348	15,821	13,976	20,765	32,893	18,534	4,062
Disposal in kitchen sink	58,906	1,217	53,299	38,595	14,704	5,107	12,423	18,584	17,185	4,390
Trash compactor	4,513	125	4,077	3,343	734	601	659	1,638	1,179	311
Main heating equipment:										
Warm-air furnace.	76,665	1,727	68,275	50,459	17,817	8,546	20,331	23,735	15,664	6,662
Steam or hot water system	14,074	176	12,880	7,719	5,161	9,496	1,996	588	800	1,018
Electric heat pump.	14,551	605	12,484	9,074	3,411	344	664	9,993	1,483	1,462
Built-in electric units.	5,607	310	4,699	2,116	2,583	1,065	1,116	918	1,600	598
Floor, wall, or pipeless furnace. . .	5,916	149	5,102	2,172	2,930	443	399	1,300	2,961	664
Room heaters with flue.	1,615	111	1,294	752	542	165	172	646	310	211
Room heaters without flue.	1,627	76	1,327	881	447	18	42	1,222	45	224
Portable electric heaters	1,127	73	907	441	467	29	20	642	216	146
Stoves.	1,171	183	896	742	155	150	143	304	299	93
Fireplaces [4]	251	47	190	166	24	24	22	69	74	15
Other	505	65	298	167	131	18	31	159	90	142
Cooking stoves	148	–	120	50	70	34	–	50	36	28
None.	1,120	324	399	194	205	4	20	96	279	397
Air conditioning: central	80,511	1,662	72,629	55,849	16,780	6,535	17,401	36,249	12,443	6,220
One or more room units	27,124	579	24,863	14,326	10,537	10,132	5,707	5,697	3,326	1,681
Source of water:										
Public system or private company	108,210	2,638	95,313	62,991	32,322	17,168	20,874	34,871	22,401	10,260
Well serving 1 to 5 units	15,372	1,014	13,132	11,607	1,525	3,079	4,008	4,648	1,396	1,227
Other	795	194	427	334	93	90	73	203	61	174
Means of sewage disposal:										
Public sewer.	98,013	1,976	86,850	55,496	31,355	16,107	20,053	29,617	21,093	9,187
Septic tank, cesspool, chemical toilet.	25,976	1,685	21,967	19,403	2,564	4,229	4,888	10,067	2,783	2,323
Other	388	184	54	32	22	–	13	38	2	151

– Represents or rounds to zero.   [1] Includes trailers. Includes width not reported, not shown separately.   [2] Excludes mobile homes; includes basements and finished attics.   [3] Limited to single-family units.   [4] With and without inserts.

Source: U.S. Census Bureau, Current Housing Reports, Series H150/05, *American Housing Survey for the United States*. See Internet site <http://www.census.gov/hhes/www/housing/ahs/nationaldata.html>.

608 Construction and Housing

Table 953. **Housing Units by Units in Structure and State: 2004**

[In percent, except as indicated (122,672 represents 122,672,000). The American Community Survey universe is limited to the household population and excludes the population living in institutions, college dormitories, and other group quarters. Based on a sample and subject to sampling variability; see Appendix III]

State	Total housing units (1,000)	Percent of units by units in structure—								
		1-unit detached	1-unit attached	2 units	3 or 4 units	5 to 9 units	10 to 19 units	20 or more units	Mobile homes	Boat, RV, van, etc.
U.S.....	**122,672**	**61.2**	**5.6**	**4.1**	**4.7**	**5.0**	**4.5**	**7.8**	**7.1**	**0.1**
AL	2,059	67.4	2.0	2.4	2.9	5.0	3.0	2.6	14.7	(Z)
AK	272	61.1	6.9	4.9	7.4	5.0	2.8	5.0	6.9	0.3
AZ	2,458	59.1	5.1	1.4	3.6	4.5	6.2	6.3	13.3	0.6
AR	1,233	69.0	1.7	3.9	3.5	3.9	2.9	2.2	12.8	(Z)
CA	12,805	57.5	7.4	2.5	5.6	6.4	5.1	11.0	4.4	0.2
CO	2,011	63.4	6.7	2.0	3.8	4.7	5.8	8.7	4.9	(Z)
CT	1,414	59.5	5.4	8.3	9.9	5.0	3.3	7.5	1.2	(Z)
DE	367	55.4	13.7	2.1	2.5	4.3	5.5	4.7	11.7	(Z)
DC	277	13.5	26.5	3.3	6.8	6.1	12.5	31.3	–	–
FL	8,009	53.4	5.9	2.4	4.3	5.1	6.0	12.3	10.4	0.1
GA	3,673	66.0	2.8	2.3	3.5	5.3	5.2	4.0	11.0	(Z)
HI	483	51.4	6.0	3.6	4.3	6.8	5.3	22.2	0.2	0.1
ID	579	71.2	2.9	2.7	3.6	3.1	2.4	3.3	10.9	(Z)
IL	5,094	58.9	5.5	6.1	6.7	6.4	4.3	9.3	2.8	(Z)
IN	2,691	71.5	3.4	2.8	3.8	4.6	3.3	4.2	6.5	–
IA	1,293	74.7	2.9	2.5	3.8	4.2	3.3	4.4	4.2	(Z)
KS	1,185	73.9	3.6	2.8	3.4	4.3	3.2	3.7	5.2	–
KY	1,843	67.2	2.1	3.1	3.5	4.5	3.1	2.6	13.9	0.1
LA	1,920	65.8	4.0	3.7	4.6	3.6	3.1	3.5	11.7	(Z)
ME	677	69.0	2.0	5.7	5.8	4.2	1.6	2.7	8.9	(Z)
MD	2,250	52.0	21.3	2.2	2.3	4.8	8.8	6.7	2.0	(Z)
MA	2,672	52.6	4.6	11.5	11.5	6.1	4.3	8.5	1.0	–
MI	4,433	70.5	4.7	3.2	2.8	4.5	3.5	4.8	6.0	(Z)
MN	2,213	68.0	6.4	3.0	2.4	2.6	3.5	10.3	3.9	–
MS	1,221	69.4	1.5	2.7	3.8	5.3	1.7	1.6	13.8	0.1
MO	2,564	69.3	3.6	3.3	5.6	4.1	3.1	3.5	7.3	0.1
MT	423	69.9	2.1	3.3	4.2	3.2	1.8	2.6	12.8	0.1
NE	758	73.9	3.3	2.0	2.4	3.6	4.7	5.7	4.5	(Z)
NV	976	54.6	5.6	2.0	7.8	10.9	5.0	6.1	7.9	0.2
NH	576	62.9	4.7	6.1	6.2	5.0	3.7	4.8	6.5	(Z)
NJ	3,415	54.6	8.4	10.6	6.2	4.5	5.1	9.7	0.9	(Z)
NM	826	62.6	4.2	2.3	4.2	3.2	2.4	4.3	16.6	0.3
NY	7,819	42.3	4.8	11.2	7.3	5.2	4.0	22.6	2.6	(Z)
NC	3,860	64.8	2.8	2.3	2.9	4.6	3.5	2.3	16.8	(Z)
ND	301	63.3	3.8	2.4	4.7	4.3	4.8	8.0	8.6	(Z)
OH	4,967	68.1	4.6	4.4	4.7	4.7	4.1	4.9	4.4	(Z)
OK	1,573	72.6	2.0	2.1	3.1	3.9	3.3	3.6	9.5	(Z)
OR	1,535	62.5	3.4	3.6	5.1	4.2	3.6	7.4	9.9	0.2
PA	5,386	57.7	17.6	5.0	4.2	3.2	2.2	5.4	4.6	(Z)
RI	446	55.9	3.0	11.9	12.5	5.0	3.2	7.5	1.0	–
SC	1,891	60.6	2.9	2.4	3.4	4.7	3.7	3.3	18.8	(Z)
SD	343	65.8	3.2	2.8	3.9	3.5	3.8	5.0	12.1	–
TN	2,595	68.4	2.7	3.2	3.7	5.1	3.8	3.2	9.9	(Z)
TX	8,847	64.6	2.7	2.1	3.5	5.5	7.5	6.1	8.0	0.1
UT	849	67.4	5.6	3.7	5.4	2.9	3.5	7.1	4.2	0.1
VT	304	66.4	3.3	6.8	6.9	5.1	1.6	2.8	7.2	(Z)
VA	3,117	62.8	10.0	1.7	2.8	5.2	5.7	5.7	6.1	(Z)
WA	2,607	62.2	3.1	3.0	3.8	5.1	5.9	9.1	7.5	0.2
WV	867	70.3	1.4	2.9	2.6	3.1	1.9	1.7	16.0	(Z)
WI	2,464	65.2	3.7	7.5	3.7	4.8	3.2	5.8	6.0	–
WY	233	65.4	3.6	2.8	4.8	3.5	2.1	2.9	14.5	0.3

– Represents zero.   Z Less than .05 percent.

Source: U.S. Census Bureau, 2004 American Community Survey Table B25024. Units in Structure; using American FactFinder®. See Internet site <http://factfinder.census.gov/>; (accessed 31 January 2006).

Construction and Housing   609

Table 954. Housing Units—Size of Units and Lot: 2005

[In thousands (124,377 represents 124,377,000), except as indicated. As of fall. Based on the American Housing Survey; see Appendix III. For composition of regions, see map inside front cover]

Item	Total housing units	Sea-sonal	Year-round units — Occupied — Total	Owner	Renter	North-east	Mid-west	South	West	Vacant
Total units	124,377	3,845	108,871	74,931	33,940	20,337	24,955	39,722	23,858	11,660
Rooms:										
1 room	637	80	379	9	370	128	50	40	160	177
2 rooms	1,399	106	989	46	943	338	141	185	325	303
3 rooms	10,941	622	8,692	1,043	7,649	2,173	1,815	2,489	2,215	1,627
4 rooms	22,774	1,175	18,141	6,829	11,312	3,316	3,964	6,571	4,290	3,458
5 rooms	28,619	932	24,763	16,949	7,814	3,713	5,831	10,007	5,211	2,924
6 rooms	25,325	516	23,096	19,493	3,603	4,343	5,103	8,822	4,828	1,714
7 rooms	15,284	226	14,332	13,086	1,247	2,677	3,468	5,268	2,920	725
8 rooms or more	19,399	187	18,480	17,477	1,003	3,649	4,582	6,340	3,908	732
Complete bathrooms:										
No bathrooms	2,115	497	554	224	330	157	89	198	110	1,063
1 bathroom	47,221	1,591	39,920	16,983	22,937	9,754	9,992	12,253	7,922	5,710
1 and one-half bathrooms	17,205	346	15,876	12,362	3,514	3,871	5,129	4,256	2,621	982
2 or more bathrooms	57,837	1,412	52,520	45,361	7,159	6,555	9,745	23,015	13,205	3,905
Square footage of unit:										
Single detached and mobile homes	86,333	2,931	76,936	67,215	9,720	11,544	18,862	30,186	16,344	6,467
Less than 500	1,037	215	622	395	227	104	112	248	158	200
500 to 749	2,652	454	1,775	1,092	683	235	373	822	345	423
750 to 999	6,211	463	4,959	3,597	1,362	579	1,358	2,020	1,002	789
1,000 to 1,499	20,301	610	18,135	15,144	2,991	2,035	4,284	7,588	4,228	1,556
1,500 to 1,999	19,546	375	18,035	16,161	1,875	2,415	4,190	7,056	4,374	1,135
2,000 to 2,499	13,465	240	12,559	11,732	827	2,096	3,234	4,624	2,605	666
2,500 to 2,999	6,964	95	6,565	6,255	310	1,187	1,600	2,496	1,281	304
3,000 to 3,999	6,446	112	5,932	5,745	187	1,119	1,631	2,024	1,157	403
4,000 or more	3,952	58	3,662	3,468	193	817	901	1,313	631	232
Other [1]	5,759	308	4,691	3,626	1,066	957	1,179	1,992	563	759
Median square footage	1,758	1,146	1,795	1,858	1,344	1,985	1,824	1,742	1,747	1,463
Lot size:										
Single detached and attached units and mobile homes	90,932	2,913	81,115	69,484	11,631	12,959	19,456	31,669	17,032	6,903
Less than one-eighth acre	12,409	555	10,402	8,139	2,263	2,005	2,429	2,849	3,119	1,451
One-eighth to one-quarter acre	25,467	747	22,916	18,910	4,005	2,916	5,686	7,473	6,840	1,804
One-quarter to one-half acre	17,808	432	16,203	14,359	1,844	2,464	3,929	6,461	3,349	1,172
One-half up to one acre	11,757	307	10,650	9,492	1,159	1,983	2,183	5,164	1,319	800
1 up to 5 acres	16,318	481	14,809	13,037	1,772	2,662	3,216	7,299	1,631	1,029
5 up to 10 acres	2,628	94	2,367	2,204	163	326	685	982	374	167
10 acres or more	4,545	297	3,767	3,343	424	602	1,328	1,440	398	480
Median acreage	0.36	0.34	0.36	0.38	0.24	0.41	0.35	0.46	0.22	0.29

[1] Represents units not reported or size unknown.

Source: U.S. Census Bureau, Current Housing Reports, Series H150/05, *American Housing Survey for the United States.* See Internet site <http://www.census.gov/hhes/www/housing/ahs/nationaldata.html>.

Table 955. Occupied Housing Units—Tenure by Race of Householder: 1991 to 2005

[In thousands (93,147 represents 93,147,000), except percent. As of fall. Based on the American Housing Survey; see Appendix III]

Race of householder and tenure	1991	1993	1995	1997	1999	2001	2003 [1]	2005
ALL RACES [2]								
Occupied units, total	93,147	94,724	97,693	99,487	102,803	106,261	105,842	108,871
Owner-occupied	59,796	61,252	63,544	65,487	68,796	72,265	72,238	74,931
Percent of occupied	64.2	64.7	65.0	65.8	66.9	68.0	68.3	68.8
Renter-occupied	33,351	33,472	34,150	34,000	34,007	33,996	33,604	33,940
WHITE [3]								
Occupied units, total	79,140	80,029	81,611	82,154	83,624	85,292	87,483	89,449
Owner-occupied	53,749	54,878	56,507	57,781	60,041	62,465	63,126	65,023
Percent of occupied	67.9	68.6	69.2	70.3	71.8	73.2	72.2	72.7
Renter-occupied	25,391	25,151	25,104	24,372	23,583	22,826	24,357	24,426
BLACK [3]								
Occupied units, total	10,832	11,128	11,773	12,085	12,936	13,292	13,004	13,447
Owner-occupied	4,635	4,788	5,137	5,457	6,013	6,318	6,193	6,471
Percent of occupied	42.8	43.0	43.6	45.2	46.5	47.5	47.6	48.1
Renter-occupied	6,197	6,340	6,637	6,628	6,923	6,974	6,811	6,975
HISPANIC ORIGIN [4]								
Occupied units, total	6,239	6,614	7,757	8,513	9,041	9,814	11,038	11,651
Owner-occupied	2,423	2,788	3,245	3,646	4,087	4,731	5,106	5,752
Percent of occupied	38.8	42.2	41.8	42.8	45.2	48.2	46.3	49.4
Renter-occupied	3,816	3,826	4,512	4,867	4,955	5,083	5,931	5,899

[1] Based on 2000 census controls. [2] Includes other races, not shown separately. [3] The 2003 American Housing Survey (AHS) allowed respondents to choose more than one race. Beginning in 2003, data represent householders who selected this race group only and exclude householders reporting more than one race. The AHS in prior years only allowed respondents to report one race group. See also comments on race in the text for Section 1 and the below cited source. [4] Persons of Hispanic origin may be of any race.

Source: U.S. Census Bureau, Current Housing Reports, Series H150/91, H150/93, H150/95RV, H150/97, H150/99, H150/01, H150/03, and H150/05, *American Housing Survey for the United States.* See Internet site <http://www.census.gov/hhes/www/housing/ahs/nationaldata.html>.

U.S. Census Bureau, Statistical Abstract of the United States: 2007

Table 956. **Homeownership Rates by Age of Householder and Household Type: 1985 to 2005**

[In percent. Represents the proportion of owner households to the total number of occupied households. Based on the Current Population Survey/Housing Vacancy Survey; see source and Appendix III for details]

Age of householder and household type	1985	1990	1995	1999	2000	2001	2002	2003	2004	2005
United States.	**63.9**	**63.9**	**64.7**	**66.8**	**67.4**	**67.8**	**67.9**	**68.3**	**69.0**	**68.9**
AGE OF HOUSEHOLDER										
Less than 25 years old	17.2	15.7	15.9	19.9	21.7	22.5	22.9	22.8	25.2	25.7
25 to 29 years old	37.7	35.2	34.4	36.5	38.1	38.9	38.8	39.8	40.2	40.9
30 to 34 years old	54.0	51.8	53.1	53.8	54.6	54.8	54.9	56.5	57.4	56.8
35 to 39 years old	65.4	63.0	62.1	64.4	65.0	65.5	65.2	65.1	66.2	66.6
40 to 44 years old	71.4	69.8	68.6	69.9	70.6	70.8	71.7	71.3	71.9	71.7
45 to 49 years old	74.3	73.9	73.7	74.5	74.7	75.4	74.8	75.4	76.3	75.0
50 to 54 years old	77.5	76.8	77.0	77.8	78.5	78.2	77.9	77.9	78.2	78.3
55 to 59 years old	79.2	78.8	78.8	80.7	80.4	81.0	80.8	80.9	81.2	80.6
60 to 64 years old	79.9	79.8	80.3	81.3	80.3	81.8	81.6	81.9	82.4	81.9
65 to 69 years old	79.5	80.0	81.0	82.9	83.0	82.4	82.9	82.5	83.2	82.8
70 to 74 years old	76.8	78.4	80.9	82.8	82.6	82.5	82.5	82.0	84.4	82.9
75 years old and over	69.8	72.3	74.6	77.1	77.7	78.1	78.4	78.7	78.8	78.4
Less than 35 years old	39.9	38.5	38.6	39.7	40.8	41.2	41.3	42.2	43.1	43.0
35 to 44 years old	68.1	66.3	65.2	67.2	67.9	68.2	68.6	68.3	69.2	69.3
45 to 54 years old	75.9	75.2	75.2	76.0	76.5	76.7	76.3	76.6	77.2	76.6
55 to 64 years old	79.5	79.3	79.5	81.0	80.3	81.3	81.1	81.4	81.9	81.2
65 years and over	74.8	76.3	78.1	80.1	80.4	80.3	80.6	80.5	81.1	80.6
TYPE OF HOUSEHOLD										
Family households:										
Married-couple families . . .	78.2	78.1	79.6	81.8	82.4	82.9	82.9	83.3	84.0	84.2
Male householder, no spouse present.	57.8	55.2	55.3	56.1	57.5	57.9	57.3	57.9	59.6	59.1
Female householder, no spouse present.	45.8	44.0	45.1	48.2	49.1	49.9	49.2	49.6	50.9	51.0
Nonfamily households:										
One-person	45.8	49.0	50.5	52.7	53.6	54.4	54.9	55.2	55.8	55.6
Male householder	38.8	42.4	43.8	46.3	47.4	48.2	48.6	50.0	50.5	50.3
Female householder . . .	51.3	53.6	55.4	57.6	58.1	59.0	59.6	59.1	59.9	59.6
Other:										
Male householder	30.1	31.7	34.2	37.2	38.0	38.6	38.7	40.0	41.7	41.7
Female householder . . .	30.6	32.5	33.0	41.5	40.6	41.0	41.9	43.1	43.5	44.8

Source: U.S. Census Bureau, "Housing Vacancies and Home Ownership." See Internet site <http://www.census.gov/hhes/www/hvs.html>.

Table 957. **Homeownership Rates by State: 1985 to 2005**

[In percent. See headnote, Table 956]

State	1985	1990	1995	2000	2004	2005	State	1985	1990	1995	2000	2004	2005
United States .	**63.9**	**63.9**	**64.7**	**67.4**	**69.0**	**68.9**	Missouri	69.2	64.0	69.4	74.2	72.4	72.3
Alabama	70.4	68.4	70.1	73.2	78.0	76.6	Montana	66.5	69.1	68.7	70.2	72.4	70.4
Alaska	61.2	58.4	60.9	66.4	67.2	66.0	Nebraska	68.5	67.3	67.1	70.2	71.2	70.2
Arizona	64.7	64.5	62.9	68.0	68.7	71.1	Nevada	57.0	55.8	58.6	64.0	65.7	63.4
Arkansas.	66.6	67.8	67.2	68.9	69.1	69.2	New Hampshire . . .	65.5	65.0	66.0	69.2	73.3	74.0
California.	54.2	53.8	55.4	57.1	59.7	59.7	New Jersey	62.3	65.0	64.9	66.2	68.8	70.1
Colorado	63.6	59.0	64.6	68.3	71.1	71.0	New Mexico	68.2	68.6	67.0	73.7	71.5	71.4
Connecticut	69.0	67.9	68.2	70.0	71.7	70.5	New York	50.3	53.3	52.7	53.4	54.8	55.9
Delaware.	70.3	67.7	71.7	72.0	77.3	75.8	North Carolina	68.0	69.0	70.1	71.1	69.8	70.9
Dist. of Columbia . .	37.4	36.4	39.2	41.9	45.6	45.8	North Dakota	69.9	67.2	67.3	70.7	70.0	68.5
Florida	67.2	65.1	66.6	68.4	72.2	72.4	Ohio.	67.9	68.7	67.9	71.3	73.1	73.3
Georgia	62.7	64.3	66.6	69.8	70.9	67.9	Oklahoma	70.5	70.3	69.8	72.7	71.1	72.9
Hawaii	51.0	55.5	50.2	55.2	60.9	59.8	Oregon	61.5	64.4	63.2	65.3	69.0	68.3
Idaho	71.0	69.4	72.0	70.5	73.7	74.2	Pennsylvania	71.6	73.8	71.5	74.7	74.9	73.3
Illinois	60.6	63.0	66.4	67.9	72.7	70.9	Rhode Island	61.4	58.5	57.9	61.5	61.5	63.1
Indiana	67.6	67.0	71.0	74.9	75.8	75.0	South Carolina	72.0	71.4	71.3	76.5	76.2	73.9
Iowa	69.9	70.7	71.4	75.2	73.2	73.9	South Dakota	67.6	66.2	67.5	71.2	68.5	68.4
Kansas	68.3	69.0	67.5	69.3	69.9	69.5	Tennessee	67.6	68.3	67.0	70.9	71.6	72.4
Kentucky	68.5	65.8	71.2	73.4	74.3	71.6	Texas	60.5	59.7	61.4	63.8	65.6	65.9
Louisiana	70.2	67.8	65.3	68.1	70.6	72.5	Utah	71.5	70.1	71.5	72.7	74.9	73.9
Maine	73.7	74.2	76.7	76.5	74.7	73.9	Vermont	69.5	72.6	70.4	68.7	72.0	74.2
Maryland	65.6	64.9	65.8	69.9	72.1	71.2	Virginia	68.5	69.8	68.1	73.9	73.4	71.2
Massachusetts	60.5	58.6	60.2	59.9	63.8	63.4	Washington	66.8	61.8	61.6	63.6	66.0	67.6
Michigan	70.7	72.3	72.2	77.2	77.1	76.4	West Virginia	75.9	72.0	73.1	75.9	80.3	81.3
Minnesota	70.0	68.0	73.3	76.1	76.4	76.5	Wisconsin	63.8	68.3	67.5	71.8	73.3	71.1
Mississippi.	69.6	69.4	71.1	75.2	74.0	78.8	Wyoming.	73.2	68.9	69.0	71.0	72.8	72.8

Source: U.S. Census Bureau, "Housing Vacancies and Home Ownership." See Internet site <http://www.census.gov/hhes/www/hvs.html>.

Construction and Housing   611

Table 958. Occupied Housing Units—Costs by Region: 2005

[74,931 represents 74,931,000. As of fall. See headnote, Table 959, for an explanation of housing costs. Based on the American Housing Survey; see Appendix III. For composition of regions, see map inside front cover]

Category	Number (1,000)					Percent distribution				
	Total units	North-east	Mid-west	South	West	Total units	North-east	Mid-west	South	West
OWNER-OCCUPIED UNITS										
Total	74,931	13,217	18,360	28,003	15,350	100.0	100.0	100.0	100.0	100.0
Monthly housing costs:										
Less than $300	12,426	1,027	2,652	6,942	1,804	16.6	7.8	14.4	24.8	11.8
$300 to $399	6,763	997	2,008	2,538	1,220	9.0	7.5	10.9	9.1	7.9
$400 to $499	5,096	977	1,456	1,844	819	6.8	7.4	7.9	6.6	5.3
$500 to $599	4,704	1,059	1,235	1,756	654	6.3	8.0	6.7	6.3	4.3
$600 to $699	4,192	847	1,118	1,636	591	5.6	6.4	6.1	5.8	3.9
$700 to $799	3,933	763	1,105	1,436	629	5.2	5.8	6.0	5.1	4.1
$800 to $999	7,632	1,336	2,089	2,885	1,322	10.2	10.1	11.4	10.3	8.6
$1,000 to $1,249	8,031	1,249	2,272	2,821	1,689	10.7	9.4	12.4	10.1	11.0
$1,250 to $1,499	6,184	1,213	1,595	1,884	1,492	8.3	9.2	8.7	6.7	9.7
$1,500 or more	15,971	3,749	2,830	4,261	5,130	21.3	28.4	15.4	15.2	33.4
Median (dol.) [1]	809	941	764	656	1,094	(X)	(X)	(X)	(X)	(X)
RENTER-OCCUPIED UNITS										
Total	33,940	7,120	6,595	11,719	8,507	100.0	100.0	100.0	100.0	100.0
Monthly housing costs:										
Less than $300	2,922	736	637	1,036	514	8.6	10.3	9.7	8.8	6.0
$300 to $399	1,859	316	493	765	285	5.5	4.4	7.5	6.5	3.4
$400 to $499	3,353	515	890	1,380	568	9.9	7.2	13.5	11.8	6.7
$500 to $599	3,897	625	927	1,648	698	11.5	8.8	14.1	14.1	8.2
$600 to $699	4,099	723	952	1,488	936	12.1	10.2	14.4	12.7	11.0
$700 to $799	3,694	703	721	1,317	953	10.9	9.9	10.9	11.2	11.2
$800 to $999	5,273	1,274	817	1,643	1,540	15.5	17.9	12.4	14.0	18.1
$1,000 to $1,249	3,178	816	360	847	1,154	9.4	11.5	5.5	7.2	13.6
$1,250 to $1,499	1,644	421	146	343	733	4.8	5.9	2.2	2.9	8.6
$1,500 or more	1,886	576	201	350	760	5.6	8.1	3.0	3.0	8.9
No cash rent	2,134	415	449	904	366	6.3	5.8	6.8	7.7	4.3
Median (dol.) [1]	694	762	613	639	915	(X)	(X)	(X)	(X)	(X)

X Not applicable.　　[1] For explanation of median, see Guide to Tabular Presentation.

Source: U.S. Census Bureau, Current Housing Reports, Series H150/05, *American Housing Survey for the United States*. See Internet site <http://www.census.gov/hhes/www/housing/ahs/nationaldata.html>.

Table 959. Occupied Housing Units—Financial Summary by Selected Characteristics of the Householder: 2005

[In thousands of units (108,871 represents 108,871,000), except as indicated. As of fall. Housing costs include real estate taxes, property insurance, utilities, fuel, water, garbage collection, and mortgage. Based on the American Housing Survey; see Appendix III]

Characteristic	Total occu-pied units	Tenure		Black [1]		Hispanic origin [2]		Elderly [3]		Households below poverty level	
		Owner	Renter	Owner	Renter	Owner	Renter	Owner	Renter	Owner	Renter
Total units [4]	108,871	74,931	33,940	6,471	6,975	5,752	5,899	17,818	4,379	6,450	8,674
Monthly housing costs:											
Less than $300	15,348	12,426	2,922	1,272	879	861	343	5,695	818	2,412	1,844
$300 to $399	8,622	6,763	1,859	613	426	399	225	3,008	366	850	736
$400 to $499	8,449	5,096	3,353	466	760	292	509	1,963	427	614	1,037
$500 to $599	8,601	4,704	3,897	474	880	284	735	1,562	386	480	1,052
$600 to $699	8,291	4,192	4,099	402	768	306	797	1,069	400	367	864
$700 to $799	7,627	3,933	3,694	404	899	309	687	735	340	282	708
$800 to $999	12,905	7,632	5,273	733	1,067	674	1,115	1,125	498	414	802
$1,000 or more.	36,893	30,186	6,708	2,107	916	2,627	1,271	2,661	666	1,032	828
Median amount (dol.) [5]	753	809	694	702	646	926	734	409	588	395	530
Monthly housing costs as percent of income: [6]											
Less than 5 percent	4,304	4,051	253	300	42	217	35	732	10	20	12
5 to 9 percent	11,687	10,761	925	790	178	626	87	2,858	57	69	48
10 to 14 percent	13,771	11,412	2,359	873	373	625	338	2,989	140	172	68
15 to 19 percent	14,960	11,499	3,462	898	620	716	507	2,294	172	243	140
20 to 24 percent	12,605	8,947	3,658	746	725	627	565	1,693	297	269	215
25 to 29 percent	10,394	6,788	3,607	586	678	570	692	1,265	459	267	453
30 to 34 percent	7,652	4,658	2,994	367	613	484	659	922	355	238	449
35 to 39 percent	5,561	3,344	2,217	334	495	376	368	773	266	355	312
40 percent or more . . . . [5] . .	23,967	12,628	11,339	1,469	2,617	1,463	2,288	4,182	2,062	4,041	5,278
Median amount (percent) [5] . .	23	20	32	22	35	25	34	20	44	75	77

[1] For persons who selected this race group only. See footnote 3, Table 955.　　[2] Persons of Hispanic origin may be of any race.　　[3] Householders 65 years old and over.　　[4] Includes units with no cash rent not shown separately.　　[5] For explanation of median, see Guide to Tabular Presentation.　　[6] Money income before taxes.

Source: U.S. Census Bureau, Current Housing Reports, Series H150/05, *American Housing Survey for the United States*. See Internet site <http://www.census.gov/hhes/www/housing/ahs/nationaldata.html>.

Table 960. Owner-Occupied Housing Units—Value and Costs by State: 2004

[In percent, except as indicated (73,754 represents 73,754,000). The American Community Survey universe is limited to the household population and excludes the population living in institutions, college dormitories, and other group quarters. Based on a sample and subject to sampling variability; see Appendix III. For definition of median, see Guide to Tabular Presentation]

State	Total (1,000)	Percent of units with value of—			Median value (dol.)	Median selected monthly owner costs [1] (dol.)	Selected monthly owner costs as a percent of household income in the past 12 months [1]			
		$99,999 or less	$100,000 to $199,999	$200,000 or more			Less than 20 percent	20.0 to 24.9 percent	25.0 to 34.9 percent	35 percent or more
U.S.	**73,754**	**30.6**	**33.1**	**36.3**	**151,366**	**1,212**	**38.0**	**16.9**	**21.0**	**24.1**
AL	1,263	53.6	31.8	14.6	94,671	872	49.2	15.0	16.6	19.3
AK	150	17.3	41.6	41.1	179,304	1,421	42.1	17.7	22.2	18.0
AZ	1,464	25.6	46.2	28.2	145,741	1,130	37.8	16.4	21.2	24.6
AR	720	63.9	27.8	8.2	79,006	773	51.4	16.6	15.3	16.7
CA	7,012	7.3	11.9	80.8	391,102	1,733	27.4	14.7	23.9	33.9
CO	1,269	7.7	37.3	55.0	211,740	1,355	32.7	17.4	23.0	26.8
CT	928	5.7	32.9	61.4	236,559	1,603	37.0	17.5	22.9	22.6
DE	226	19.1	41.1	39.7	171,589	1,191	43.6	18.5	19.7	18.2
DC	108	5.7	21.2	73.1	334,702	1,612	38.1	15.3	22.3	24.3
FL	4,808	28.7	39.0	32.3	149,291	1,143	33.6	16.0	21.2	29.2
GA	2,172	32.0	41.4	26.6	136,912	1,126	40.1	17.6	19.5	22.8
HI	252	4.8	16.1	79.1	364,840	1,648	32.1	16.1	24.4	27.3
ID	373	36.3	46.2	17.5	120,825	953	40.7	18.8	19.2	21.3
IL	3,227	27.4	32.5	40.1	167,711	1,370	36.7	16.5	21.4	25.4
IN	1,733	43.9	41.7	14.4	110,020	963	46.3	18.1	17.7	17.9
IA	868	52.9	34.0	13.1	95,901	942	45.8	19.6	18.6	16.0
KS	748	48.9	35.9	15.2	102,458	1,013	45.1	18.0	20.5	16.4
KY	1,156	51.1	35.4	13.5	98,438	888	46.9	16.6	17.1	19.3
LA	1,135	52.2	34.8	13.0	95,910	902	47.5	15.1	16.4	21.1
ME	390	32.7	37.6	29.7	143,182	1,020	44.3	15.9	19.3	20.5
MD	1,444	16.2	29.3	54.6	216,529	1,406	41.2	17.9	21.1	19.8
MA	1,572	3.7	16.1	80.1	331,200	1,645	34.5	16.9	22.4	26.2
MI	2,929	28.8	43.4	27.8	145,177	1,137	40.3	17.4	21.1	21.2
MN	1,547	19.5	38.2	42.3	181,135	1,260	40.0	17.9	20.8	21.3
MS	748	64.1	26.7	9.2	79,023	843	42.1	16.3	17.9	23.7
MO	1,635	41.0	40.0	19.0	117,033	954	47.2	16.5	18.9	17.4
MT	253	40.6	39.1	20.3	119,319	974	37.1	16.8	21.5	24.6
NE	470	46.0	41.6	12.4	106,656	1,051	44.2	19.7	19.3	16.8
NV	534	15.5	33.7	50.8	202,937	1,274	29.3	20.2	21.1	29.3
NH	357	12.8	31.1	56.1	216,639	1,472	33.1	19.6	23.8	23.5
NJ	2,134	7.0	22.0	71.0	291,294	1,847	29.9	16.9	24.4	28.9
NM	493	44.1	39.2	16.7	110,788	935	40.2	16.5	19.8	23.6
NY	3,941	26.3	20.4	53.3	220,981	1,525	35.8	14.8	20.2	29.2
NC	2,305	40.6	39.3	20.1	117,771	1,028	40.2	17.5	20.5	21.9
ND	179	61.5	31.4	7.2	84,354	902	50.9	16.8	17.9	14.4
OH	3,150	36.4	45.0	18.6	122,384	1,090	40.4	18.7	20.9	20.0
OK	928	60.6	29.3	10.0	85,060	871	47.1	16.9	16.6	19.4
OR	899	15.4	42.7	41.9	181,544	1,217	33.9	17.2	23.6	25.4
PA	3,506	42.5	34.8	22.7	116,520	1,114	41.1	17.2	20.5	21.1
RI	253	3.8	27.9	68.3	240,150	1,469	31.9	17.3	24.1	26.7
SC	1,124	43.4	36.0	20.6	113,910	987	41.9	17.0	20.8	20.3
SD	208	53.0	34.9	12.1	95,523	952	42.3	18.3	20.2	19.2
TN	1,620	44.1	38.1	17.9	110,198	954	41.2	18.4	19.2	21.2
TX	5,075	50.1	34.5	15.4	99,858	1,166	40.4	17.6	19.5	22.5
UT	544	14.0	57.4	28.7	157,275	164	36.1	17.3	23.1	23.5
VT	183	24.7	43.1	32.2	154,318	1,174	35.8	17.9	23.6	22.6
VA	1,969	24.4	30.9	44.7	179,191	1,323	40.6	18.2	20.4	20.8
WA	1,548	12.0	36.4	51.6	204,719	1,389	31.9	17.9	25.2	24.9
WV	545	62.0	27.7	10.2	81,826	769	47.7	16.1	17.2	19.0
WI	1,519	29.0	47.2	23.8	137,727	1,155	37.2	19.0	23.2	20.5
WY	142	38.2	41.1	20.7	119,654	954	46.4	17.2	18.8	17.6

[1] For homes with a mortgage. Includes all forms of debt where the property is pledged as security for repayment of the debt, including deeds of trust, land contracts, home equity loans, etc.

Source: U.S. Census Bureau, 2004 American Community Survey Tables B25075. Value for Owner-Occupied Housing Units; B25077. Median Value for Owner-Occupied Housing Units; B25088. Median Selected Monthly Owner Costs by Mortgage Status; B25091. Mortgage Status by Selected Monthly Owner Cost as a Percentage of Household Income; using American FactFinder®. See Internet site <http://factfinder.census.gov/> (accessed May 2006).

Construction and Housing 613

Table 961. Renter-Occupied Housing Units—Gross Rent by State: 2004

[In percent, except as indicated (36,148 represents 36,148,000. The American Community Survey universe is limited to the household population and excludes the population living in institutions, college dormitories, and other group quarters. Based on a sample and subject to sampling variability; see Appendix III]

State	Total[1] (1,000)	Percent of units with gross rent of— $299 or less	$300 to $499	$500 to $749	$750 to $999	$1,000 or more	Median gross rent (dol.)	Gross rent as a percent of household income in the past 12 months Less than 15 percent	15 to 24 percent	25 to 34 percent	35 percent or more
U.S. ...	36,148	7.6	15.4	30.7	21.3	18.9	694	12.9	24.2	19.1	35.9
AL	493	11.8	29.1	32.0	11.9	3.2	519	13.9	24.0	13.6	33.9
AK	79	3.0	6.0	26.5	30.9	21.2	808	12.6	27.8	19.0	28.2
AZ	668	4.3	13.1	40.1	20.8	15.4	691	11.3	22.3	19.3	38.9
AR	379	11.5	29.9	34.9	9.2	3.3	517	15.5	22.6	17.9	31.6
CA	4,960	3.8	6.7	20.9	25.2	40.1	914	10.1	23.2	20.3	41.2
CO	582	4.6	10.8	35.7	22.3	21.0	724	10.3	22.9	21.0	38.1
CT	402	7.7	8.5	22.9	31.0	25.3	811	13.5	26.2	19.2	35.2
DE	84	7.2	9.0	30.9	28.0	16.5	743	12.1	27.6	19.4	31.1
DC	140	10.4	8.1	25.1	21.1	31.8	799	12.9	24.5	22.3	34.3
FL	2,011	4.8	9.2	31.4	28.9	21.0	766	8.9	22.7	21.1	40.8
GA	1,038	8.5	15.8	32.6	25.8	10.8	677	14.5	21.9	18.9	35.9
HI	176	5.2	8.6	19.8	19.6	34.4	871	10.3	23.2	19.5	33.6
ID	142	8.2	26.7	36.8	13.0	7.4	566	14.6	22.0	20.0	35.1
IL	1,433	7.3	15.2	32.2	23.6	16.9	698	13.7	25.7	17.7	35.6
IN	679	8.9	22.1	41.3	15.3	6.1	589	14.6	28.1	19.4	30.0
IA	308	12.2	27.1	33.2	12.4	4.8	533	14.4	26.5	17.7	30.5
KS	328	11.2	24.3	33.0	15.5	7.4	567	13.4	27.6	19.6	30.0
KY	492	14.9	28.8	31.4	10.0	3.3	503	15.5	22.7	16.1	33.1
LA	579	10.8	26.0	34.7	11.6	5.1	540	14.2	20.7	15.0	35.4
ME	145	12.2	22.2	33.1	16.3	8.7	582	11.5	28.4	20.0	31.6
MD	634	7.2	8.2	22.2	28.1	29.9	837	14.0	26.4	22.1	31.4
MA	863	11.0	9.9	18.2	21.2	35.3	852	12.5	25.7	22.1	33.3
MI	994	7.8	18.1	38.1	20.0	10.9	628	13.4	24.8	19.0	35.4
MN	507	10.7	13.6	33.2	21.4	14.9	673	13.3	25.3	21.1	33.7
MS	326	12.7	25.7	31.4	13.0	3.3	529	11.3	21.4	16.5	35.2
MO	674	10.2	24.4	36.9	15.1	5.1	567	13.9	25.9	18.7	31.7
MT	116	13.9	26.8	31.8	11.0	5.7	520	15.7	24.4	16.8	32.2
NE	217	11.2	27.1	35.1	11.0	6.1	547	16.7	25.7	18.7	28.9
NV	338	2.0	7.7	32.9	31.8	22.0	787	11.7	27.4	19.6	35.3
NH	135	7.2	8.5	24.1	28.7	27.3	810	11.2	28.9	22.0	33.3
NJ	1,000	6.4	6.3	19.0	31.4	32.9	877	13.3	25.1	19.6	36.6
NM	219	11.3	26.7	32.8	13.7	7.0	546	15.5	24.2	19.9	31.0
NY	3,146	7.7	10.8	24.8	24.3	28.8	796	15.0	21.7	18.8	38.9
NC	1,035	8.2	20.5	37.8	16.6	7.3	610	13.5	23.8	17.7	33.5
ND	84	15.7	36.0	28.8	5.6	2.7	466	19.4	28.8	14.1	25.6
OH	1,365	9.5	22.0	40.0	16.2	6.8	587	13.8	26.7	17.3	33.9
OK	432	7.8	32.9	32.8	11.2	5.5	525	14.6	24.1	16.5	32.6
OR	529	5.6	15.2	37.9	22.7	14.4	681	11.0	24.4	19.8	38.5
PA	1,311	10.1	21.5	32.9	18.5	10.6	611	14.3	24.1	19.6	33.9
RI	157	12.1	9.5	28.1	28.3	18.4	740	14.5	22.1	22.7	35.8
SC	488	9.0	18.8	35.0	16.5	8.2	610	15.9	22.3	15.0	32.6
SD	93	15.6	28.7	29.0	8.7	4.2	493	15.1	24.8	18.6	26.5
TN	695	10.2	23.9	37.8	14.3	5.8	564	14.4	24.7	18.0	33.3
TX	2,716	6.2	17.8	37.0	20.2	12.2	648	13.5	24.7	18.6	34.3
UT	236	5.5	15.8	40.7	22.4	11.1	662	13.9	27.1	18.7	35.1
VT	67	8.7	14.2	34.2	22.8	13.5	674	13.2	27.1	20.7	31.6
VA	878	7.4	13.4	25.2	22.3	25.2	757	13.0	27.2	19.2	32.6
WA	868	6.2	11.4	33.4	25.3	19.0	727	9.8	24.5	20.6	39.0
WV	192	14.8	32.4	28.3	6.5	1.7	461	14.9	19.5	16.0	31.2
WI	654	8.1	19.2	43.4	16.9	7.9	609	15.1	27.1	18.4	33.3
WY	61	10.2	27.9	28.9	10.0	9.4	534	18.4	26.4	17.3	23.8

[1] Includes units with no cash rent.

Source: U.S. Census Bureau, 2004 American Community Survey Tables B25063. Gross Rent; B25064. Median Gross Rent; B25070. Gross Rent as a Percentage of Household Income; using American FactFinder®. See Internet site <http://factfinder.census.gov/> (accessd May 2006).

Table 962. Mortgage Characteristics—Owner-Occupied Units: 2005

[In thousands (74,931 represents 74,931). **As of fall.** Based on the American Housing Survey; see Appendix III]

Mortgage characteristic	Total owner-occupied units	New construction [1]	Mobile homes	Black [2]	Hispanic [3]	Elderly [4]	Moved in past year	Below poverty level
ALL OWNERS								
Total	74,931	4,919	5,516	6,471	5,752	17,818	6,591	6,450
Mortgages currently on property:								
None, owned free and clear	24,776	839	3,066	2,078	1,539	12,139	1,258	3,690
Regular and home equity mortgages	48,394	3,987	2,352	4,190	4,098	5,224	5,192	2,512
Regular mortgage	44,652	3,843	2,233	3,971	3,964	4,115	5,064	2,338
Home equity lump sum mortage	4,385	269	87	264	253	527	269	164
Home equity line of credit	10,044	712	132	438	476	1,320	652	297
Not reported	1,694	87	96	201	115	391	139	243
Number of regular and home equity mortgages: [5]								
1 mortgage	33,409	2,815	2,053	3,208	3,085	3,878	3,634	1,824
2 mortgages	10,877	921	108	558	719	688	1,149	259
3 mortgages or more	1,164	100	5	56	90	77	146	40
Type of mortgage:								
Regular and home equity lump sum [5]	2,958	224	15	157	183	162	208	96
With home equity line of credit	587	38	–	23	44	45	54	27
No home equity line of credit	2,348	183	15	131	137	115	151	69
Regular no home equity lump sum [5]	41,694	3,619	2,218	3,814	3,781	3,953	4,855	2,242
With home equity line of credit	6,835	572	70	290	366	455	509	144
No home equity line of credit	31,992	2,899	1,962	3,162	3,223	2,936	4,089	1,714
Home equity lump sum no regular [5]	1,427	45	73	107	70	365	61	68
With home equity line of credit	307	3	15	14	3	76	22	19
No home equity line of credit	1,099	42	57	91	66	280	40	46
No regular or home equity lump sum [5]	28,851	1,031	3,210	2,393	1,718	13,338	1,466	4,045
With home equity line of credit	2,315	99	46	112	64	744	67	107
No home equity line of credit	24,842	845	3,068	2,081	1,539	12,203	1,260	3,695
OWNERS WITH ONE OR MORE REGULAR OR LUMP SUM HOME EQUITY MORTGAGES, 2003								
Total [5]	46,079	3,888	2,306	4,078	4,034	4,480	5,125	2,405
Type of primary mortgage:								
FHA	4,689	450	111	820	615	298	551	238
VA	1,809	160	37	231	115	150	203	66
RHS/RD [6]	364	41	13	44	31	23	50	29
Other types	35,908	3,087	1,894	2,561	3,049	3,332	4,059	1,621
Mortgage origination:								
Placed new mortgage(s)	45,798	3,879	2,264	4,032	3,977	4,448	5,077	2,371
Primary obtained when property acquired	27,592	3,401	1,872	2,844	2,771	2,304	4,940	1,718
Obtained later	18,206	478	392	1,188	1,206	2,144	138	653
Assumed	231	3	40	41	47	27	43	32
Wrap-around	11	6	2	–	3	3	5	–
Combination of the above	40	–	–	5	8	2	–	2
Payment plan of primary mortgage:								
Fixed payment, self amortizing	37,392	3,187	1,853	3,227	3,284	3,297	3,955	1,677
Adjustable rate mortgage	2,441	235	92	194	253	178	404	98
Adjustable term mortgage	160	–	15	13	7	43	7	14
Graduated payment mortgage	517	71	19	49	47	36	133	26
Balloon	518	76	45	22	51	37	102	32
Combination of the above	474	67	5	26	28	59	91	14
Payment plan of secondary mortgage:								
Units with two or more mortgages [5]	5,286	494	27	339	478	260	834	143
Fixed payment, self amortizing	3,897	334	25	287	344	171	571	108
Adjustable rate mortgage	460	67	–	11	37	21	110	3
Adjustable term mortgage	156	13	–	3	27	29	13	5
Graduated payment mortgage	70	13	–	5	16	–	35	2
Balloon	106	11	3	5	11	3	15	5
Other	5	–	–	–	–	–	–	–
Combination of the above	174	31	–	2	5	4	29	–
Reason primary refinanced:								
Units with a refinanced primary mortgage [7]	17,685	535	302	1,102	1,192	1,502	133	513
To get a lower interest rate	15,322	453	195	851	978	1,186	80	369
To increase payment period	568	10	13	31	57	45	10	12
To reduce payment period	2,007	29	13	68	126	111	2	128
To renew or extend a loan that has fallen due	178	–	3	20	12	17	–	12
To receive cash	2,375	60	36	169	230	261	25	70
Other reason	1,646	42	95	137	116	185	23	67
Cash received in primary mortgage refinance:								
Units receiving refinance cash	2,375	60	36	169	230	261	25	70
Median amount received (dol.)	28,084	–	–	19,690	31,701	33,553	–	21,390

– Represents or rounds to zero. [1] Constructed in the past 4 years. [2] For persons who selected this race group only. See footnote 3, Table 955. [3] Persons of Hispanic origin may be of any race. [4] 65 years old and over. [5] Includes "don't know" and "not reported." [6] Rural Housing Service/Rural Development Mortgage, formerly Farmers Home Adminsitration [7] Persons reporting more than one reason are counted once in the total.

Source: U.S. Census Bureau, *Current Housing Reports*, Series H150/05, *American Housing Survey for the United States*. See Internet site <http://www.census.gov/hhes/www/housing/ahs/nationaldata.html>.

Construction and Housing **615**

Table 963. **Occupied Housing Units—Neighborhood Indicators by Selected Characteristics of the Householder: 2005**

[In thousands (108,871 represents 108,871,000). **As of fall.** Based on the American Housing Survey; see Appendix III]

Characteristic	Total occupied units	Tenure		Black [1]		Hispanic origin [2]		Elderly [3]		Households below poverty level	
		Owner	Renter	Owner	Renter	Owner	Renter	Owner	Renter	Owner	Renter
Total units	108,871	74,931	33,940	6,471	6,975	5,752	5,899	17,818	4,379	6,450	8,674
Street noise or traffic present [4] . .	28,436	16,918	11,519	1,797	2,565	1,363	1,757	4,188	1,221	1,609	2,978
Condition not bothersome	16,866	9,988	6,878	1,078	1,510	731	973	2,869	880	942	1,720
Condition bothersome	11,522	6,906	4,616	719	1,048	633	782	1,314	340	664	1,252
So bothersome they want to move	4,370	2,314	2,056	274	596	230	365	311	126	241	658
Neighborhood crime present [4] . . .	16,419	9,203	7,215	1,340	1,968	885	1,351	1,825	566	920	2,115
Condition not bothersome	6,944	4,025	2,920	587	777	339	439	936	312	359	808
Condition bothersome	9,447	5,166	4,280	748	1,179	546	912	881	255	558	1,302
So bothersome they want to move	4,003	1,646	2,357	288	724	253	562	216	80	191	806
Odors present [4]	5,991	3,445	2,546	362	685	330	495	644	207	366	797
Condition not bothersome	2,279	1,397	882	160	211	113	119	293	76	131	246
Condition bothersome	3,708	2,048	1,660	202	474	217	374	351	129	235	550
So bothersome they want to move	1,415	617	799	87	283	72	196	95	49	69	312
Other problems:											
Noise	2,552	1,458	1,094	155	260	137	224	314	91	144	318
Litter or housing deterioration . .	1,918	1,226	691	168	237	130	138	289	37	80	209
Poor city or county services. . .	844	513	330	102	128	84	59	106	18	41	85
People	4,057	2,530	1,527	283	381	249	272	456	67	247	505
With public transportation [4]. . . .	58,623	35,092	23,531	3,888	5,455	3,584	4,542	8,315	3,063	2,768	6,000
Household uses it at least weekly.	11,219	4,148	7,071	902	2,218	616	1,838	771	859	454	2,285
Household uses it less than weekly.	8,641	5,095	3,545	592	803	430	642	1,007	483	321	999
Household does not use.	37,978	25,425	12,553	2,329	2,362	2,498	2,019	6,440	1,679	1,958	2,627
No public transportation	46,499	37,361	9,138	2,392	1,268	1,958	1,196	8,956	1,188	3,422	2,393
Not reported	3,750	2,478	1,271	192	251	210	161	548	128	261	280
Police protection:											
Satisfactory	96,834	66,895	29,939	5,543	5,923	4,948	5,149	16,024	4,000	5,449	7,390
Unsatisfacory	8,391	5,714	2,676	693	781	633	572	1,195	183	726	923
Secured communities [5]:											
Community access secured with walls or fences	6,925	3,150	3,775	223	846	357	893	974	543	221	844
Community access not secured	101,136	71,201	29,935	6,163	6,069	5,353	4,977	16,690	3,803	6,137	7,754
Secured multiunits: [5]											
Multiunit access secured.	5,841	1,061	4,781	81	1,029	99	694	389	1,306	154	1,308
Multiunit access not secured . .	19,792	2,645	17,147	269	3,824	277	3,339	774	1,926	252	4,416
Senior citizen communities:											
Households with persons 55 years old and over.	42,934	34,557	8,377	2,865	1,533	1,945	1,086	17,818	4,379	3,902	2,537
Community age restricted [6] . .	2,834	1,435	1,399	47	198	45	106	1,118	1,228	222	536
Access to structure:											
Enter building from outside [4, 7].	25,778	3,740	22,038	349	4,882	380	4,053	1,179	3,248	411	5,757
Use of steps not required . .	10,049	1,498	8,550	97	1,738	165	1,634	556	1,777	165	2,517
Use of steps required	15,692	2,229	13,463	252	3,139	214	2,412	621	1,460	241	3,238
Enter home from outside [4, 8]. .	83,093	71,191	11,903	6,122	2,093	5,372	1,845	16,639	1,131	6,039	2,916
Use of steps not required . .	39,953	34,712	5,241	2,869	903	3,197	945	8,271	527	2,689	1,228
Use of steps required	43,043	36,393	6,650	3,247	1,187	2,167	900	8,340	604	3,341	1,688
Community quality:											
Some or all activities present. .	38,786	25,667	13,119	2,219	2,632	1,783	1,836	6,522	2,210	1,815	3,281
Community center or clubhouse	23,287	14,379	8,908	1,243	1,782	961	1,172	4,111	1,696	982	2,094
Golf in the community	6,236	4,678	1,558	306	200	233	184	1,159	209	255	338
Trails in the community	18,641	13,581	5,061	1,012	733	801	630	2,955	767	738	1,091
Shuttle bus	9,565	5,831	3,734	429	542	411	500	2,084	1,142	474	1,145
Daycare	14,531	9,883	4,648	1,111	1,209	691	722	2,212	533	736	1,319
Private or restricted beach, park, or shoreline	6,556	4,937	1,620	244	278	267	194	1,190	193	316	368
Trash, litter, or junk on street: [9]											
None.	96,984	68,345	28,639	5,503	5,451	5,077	4,824	16,494	4,011	5,601	6,969
Minor accumulation	6,578	3,273	3,305	479	889	373	637	617	225	406	1,036
Major accumulation	2,757	1,450	1,308	216	414	148	322	336	70	198	467

[1] For persons who selected this race group only. See footnote 3, Table 955. [2] Persons of Hispanic origin may be of any race. [3] Householders 65 years old and over. [4] Includes those not reporting. [5] Public access is restricted (walls, gates, private security). Includes high rise apartments, retirement communities, resorts, etc. [6] At least one family member must be aged 55 years old or older. [7] Restricted to multiunits. [8] Restricted to single units. [9] Or on any properties within 300 feet.

Source: U.S. Census Bureau, *Current Housing Reports,* Series H150/05, *American Housing Survey for the United States.*

Table 964. **Heating Equipment and Fuels for Occupied Units: 1995 to 2005**

[97,693 represents 97,693,000. As of fall.Based on American Housing Survey. See Appendix III]

Type of equipment or fuel	Number (1,000)					Percent distribution	
	1995	1999	2001	2003 [1]	2005	1995	2005
Occupied units, total.	97,693	102,803	106,261	105,842	108,871	100.0	100.0
Heating equipment:							
Warm air furnace.	53,165	62,018	65,262	65,380	68,275	54.4	62.7
Steam or hot water	13,669	13,153	13,441	13,257	12,880	14.0	11.8
Heat pumps	9,406	10,992	11,080	11,347	12,484	9.6	11.5
Built-in electric units.	7,035	4,939	5,063	4,760	4,699	7.2	4.3
Floor, wall, or pipeless furnace. . .	4,963	5,310	5,343	5,322	5,102	5.1	4.7
Room heaters with flue.	1,620	1,624	1,542	1,432	1,294	1.7	1.2
Room heaters without flue.	1,642	1,790	1,558	1,509	1,327	1.7	1.2
Fireplaces, stoves, portable							
heaters or other.	5,150	2,434	2,571	2,396	2,411	5.3	2.2
None.	1,044	544	401	439	399	1.1	0.4
House main heating fuel:							
Electricity.	26,771	31,142	32,590	32,341	34,263	27.4	31.5
Utility gas.	49,203	52,366	54,689	54,928	56,317	50.4	51.7
Bottled, tank, or LP gas	4,251	5,905	6,079	6,134	6,228	4.4	5.7
Fuel oil, kerosene, etc.	12,029	10,750	10,473	10,136	9,929	12.3	9.1
Coal or coke.	210	168	128	126	95	0.2	0.1
Wood and other fuel	4,186	1,927	1,902	1,735	1,640	4.3	1.5
None.	1,042	545	400	441	398	1.1	0.4
Cooking fuel:							
Electricity.	57,621	61,315	63,685	62,859	65,297	59.0	60.0
Gas [2]	39,218	41,051	42,161	42,612	43,316	40.1	39.8
Other fuel	566	69	66	62	51	0.6	0.0
None.	287	368	349	309	206	0.3	0.2

[1] Based on 2000 census controls.   [2] Includes utility, bottled, tank, and LP gas.

Source: U.S. Census Bureau, Current Housing Reports, Series H150/95RV, H150/99, H150/01, H150/03, and H150/05, *American Housing Survey for the United States.* See Internet site <http://www.census.gov/hhes/www/housing/ahs/nationaldata.html>.

Table 965. **Occupied Housing Units—Housing Indicators by Selected Characteristics of the Householder: 2005**

[In thousands of units (108,871 represents 108,871,000). As of fall. Based on the American Housing Survey; see Appendix III]

Characteristic	Total occupied units	Tenure		Black [1]		Hispanic origin [2]		Elderly [3]		Households below poverty level	
		Owner	Renter	Owner	Renter	Owner	Renter	Owner	Renter	Owner	Renter
Total units	108,871	74,931	33,940	6,471	6,975	5,752	5,899	17,818	4,379	6,450	8,674
Amenities:											
Porch, deck, balcony or											
patio	92,659	68,940	23,719	5,633	4,651	5,118	3,932	16,276	2,605	5,661	5,586
Telephone available.	105,741	73,152	32,589	6,265	6,671	5,599	5,672	17,486	4,209	6,218	8,232
Usable fireplace	37,804	33,757	4,047	2,123	559	1,900	567	6,879	304	1,736	571
Separate dining room	52,782	43,119	9,663	3,833	2,197	3,074	1,574	9,842	929	3,176	2,122
With 2 or more living rooms											
or recreation rooms	32,544	30,183	2,360	2,128	327	1,572	203	6,431	204	1,468	371
Garage or carport with											
home	68,238	57,322	10,917	3,785	1,364	4,266	1,969	13,917	1,238	3,895	1,873
Cars and trucks available:											
No cars, trucks, or vans . . .	9,227	2,462	6,765	526	2,186	158	1,224	1,528	1,938	794	3,232
Other households without											
cars	13,794	9,614	4,180	625	556	881	864	1,760	269	904	921
1 car with or without trucks											
or vans	51,687	34,948	16,740	3,090	3,328	2,449	2,687	10,216	1,945	3,379	3,774
2 cars.	26,066	20,773	5,294	1,685	791	1,653	944	3,695	199	1,082	645
3 or more cars	8,097	7,134	962	544	113	612	180	621	28	290	102
Selected deficiencies:											
Signs of rats in last 3											
months	880	464	416	48	131	102	156	57	25	50	154
Signs of mice in last 3											
months	6,140	3,917	2,223	366	669	233	520	737	180	420	669
Holes in floors	981	489	492	46	139	47	115	77	20	119	184
Open cracks or holes	5,241	2,797	2,445	279	620	259	415	448	143	404	737
Broken plaster or peeling											
paint (interior of unit)	2,218	1,059	1,159	147	320	118	216	215	87	174	359
No electrical wiring	50	40	10	–	–	3	–	10	2	15	2
Exposed wiring	700	459	240	55	46	32	29	100	30	71	90
Rooms without electric											
outlet	1,543	898	645	113	160	88	119	196	60	161	180
Water leakage from inside											
structure [4]	9,049	5,210	3,840	494	876	422	665	825	286	422	1,003
Water leakage from outside											
structure [4]	11,701	8,391	3,310	784	719	498	493	1,562	244	668	853

– Represents or rounds to zero.   [1] For persons who selected this race group only. See footnote 3, Table 955.   [2] Persons of Hispanic origin may be of any race.   [3] Householders 65 years old and over.   [4] During the 12 months prior to the survey.

Source: U.S. Census Bureau, Current Housing Reports, Series H150/05, *American Housing Survey for the United States.* See Internet site <http://www.census.gov/hhes/www/housing/ahs/nationaldata.html>

Construction and Housing 617

Table 966.

Table 966. **Appliances and Office Equipment Used by Households by Region and Household Income: 2001**

[In millions (107.0 represents 107,000,000). Represents appliances possessed and generally used by the household. Based on Residential Energy Consumption Survey; see source. For composition of regions, see map, inside front cover]

Type of appliance	Households using appliance	Region				Household income in 2001			
		North-east	Midwest	South	West	Under $15,000	$15,000– $29,999	$30,000– $49,999	$50,000 and over
Total households	**107.0**	**20.3**	**24.5**	**38.9**	**23.3**	**18.7**	**22.9**	**27.1**	**38.3**
Oven [1]	101.7	19.6	23.8	36.2	22.1	18.0	22.0	26.1	35.6
Electric	63.0	9.9	14.0	26.0	13.1	10.1	12.9	16.2	23.8
Natural gas	34.3	8.6	8.7	8.8	8.2	7.1	7.8	8.6	10.9
Self-cleaning oven	48.2	10.2	12.3	16.1	9.6	4.1	8.5	12.4	23.2
Range [1]	105.7	20.1	24.1	38.6	22.9	18.5	22.5	26.9	37.7
Electric	64.2	10.0	13.9	27.2	13.2	10.4	13.2	16.5	24.2
Natural gas	36.7	8.9	9.1	9.8	8.9	7.3	8.0	9.1	12.4
Refrigerator	106.8	20.2	24.5	38.9	23.2	18.6	22.8	27.1	38.3
Frost-free	96.9	18.3	21.7	36.3	20.7	15.5	19.9	25.0	36.5
Freezer	34.2	4.9	9.6	13.6	6.2	4.4	6.9	9.2	13.7
1	30.8	4.5	8.6	12.2	5.6	3.9	6.1	8.4	12.4
2 or more	3.4	0.4	1.0	1.4	0.6	0.4	0.9	0.8	1.3
Most used defrost method:									
Frost-free	12.2	1.8	2.8	5.7	1.8	1.3	2.0	3.2	5.7
Manual	22.0	3.1	6.7	7.9	4.4	3.0	4.9	6.0	8.1
Dishwasher	56.7	9.2	12.1	22.1	13.2	3.3	9.1	14.9	29.3
Electric coffee maker	65.5	12.4	16.1	23.0	14.0	8.7	12.8	16.7	27.3
Electric toaster oven	36.1	8.5	5.5	14.7	7.4	5.1	7.7	8.9	14.3
Microwave oven	92.1	15.2	22.3	34.7	19.9	14.0	19.4	23.8	35.0
Air conditioning	80.8	14.2	20.2	36.9	9.6	11.9	16.7	21.0	31.2
Central system	57.5	5.7	14.3	30.4	7.1	6.2	10.7	15.2	25.3
Room	23.3	8.5	5.8	6.4	2.5	5.7	6.0	5.8	5.9
Color TV	105.8	20.0	24.4	38.4	22.9	18.1	22.7	26.9	38.0
1	29.3	5.8	6.4	9.8	7.3	8.5	8.6	6.5	5.7
2	38.4	8.1	8.2	13.7	8.4	6.4	8.5	10.7	12.8
3	23.3	3.8	5.9	9.2	4.3	2.5	3.8	6.1	10.9
4	10.2	1.6	2.7	3.9	2.0	0.6	1.4	2.6	5.7
5 or more	4.5	0.7	1.1	1.8	0.9	(S)	0.4	1.1	2.9
Large screen TV [2]	36.6	7.1	8.1	13.3	8.0	4.7	6.7	9.8	15.3
1	27.3	5.3	5.9	9.7	6.5	3.7	5.1	7.0	11.4
2	7.9	1.4	1.8	3.3	1.4	0.9	1.5	2.2	3.2
Three or more	1.4	(S)	(S)	0.4	(S)	(S)	(S)	0.5	0.7
Cable/satellite dish antenna	82.2	16.3	19.1	30.2	16.6	12.1	16.2	20.9	33.0
VCR and DVD players	96.1	18.0	22.5	34.6	21.0	13.9	19.8	25.3	37.0
Stereo equipment	80.3	15.1	18.2	28.5	18.5	10.2	15.4	20.9	33.8
Clothes washer	84.1	14.7	19.8	32.7	16.9	10.7	16.4	22.1	34.9
Clothes dryer [1]	78.8	13.3	19.2	30.3	16.0	8.4	15.0	21.3	34.1
Electric	61.1	9.2	13.4	26.6	11.9	6.9	12.2	16.8	25.1
Natural gas	16.9	4.0	5.4	3.4	4.1	1.4	2.6	4.2	8.7
Water heater [1]	107.0	20.3	24.5	38.9	23.3	18.7	22.9	27.1	38.3
Electric	40.8	4.7	6.3	22.4	7.3	8.3	9.5	10.6	12.4
Natural gas	58.0	10.8	16.9	15.4	14.9	9.3	11.7	14.1	23.0
Personal computers	60.0	10.9	14.1	20.7	14.3	3.7	8.7	16.0	31.6
Access to Internet	50.7	9.7	11.8	16.9	12.2	2.8	6.6	13.1	28.3
Cell/mobile telephone	56.8	10.3	12.8	21.4	12.3	4.4	8.6	14.7	29.1

S Figure does not meet publication standards.   [1] Includes other types, not shown separately.   [2] Determined by respondent.

Source: U.S. Energy Information Administration. See Internet site <http://www.eia.doe.gov/emeu/recs/contents.html> (accessed 04 May 2004).

Table 967. **Net Stock of Residential Fixed Assets: 1990 to 2004**

[In billions of dollars (6,260.2 represents $6,260,200,000,000). End of year estimates]

Item	1990	1995	1998	1999	2000	2001	2002	2003	2004
Total residential fixed assets	6,260.2	8,028.0	9,507.0	10,206.7	10,907.4	11,711.5	12,456.7	13,371.0	14,773.0
By type of owner and legal form of organization:									
Private	6,111.0	7,839.8	9,300.1	9,986.7	10,675.7	11,464.8	12,193.1	13,088.1	14,473.3
Corporate	65.7	76.6	90.0	94.5	99.5	105.0	110.1	115.9	126.0
Noncorporate	6,045.3	7,763.3	9,210.1	9,892.2	10,576.1	11,359.8	12,083.0	12,972.2	14,347.3
Government	149.2	188.2	206.9	219.9	231.7	246.7	263.6	282.9	299.7
Federal	51.8	61.6	68.7	72.2	75.4	79.2	82.9	87.9	93.9
State and local	97.3	126.6	138.2	147.7	156.4	167.5	180.7	195.0	205.8
By tenure group: [1]									
Owner-occupied	4,515.6	5,987.9	7,174.7	7,752.3	8,328.7	8,996.0	9,614.3	10,377.7	11,538.7
Farm	48.7	51.3	62.0	67.0	72.2	77.2	80.6	85.5	92.8
Nonfarm	4,467.0	5,936.7	7,112.7	7,685.3	8,256.4	8,918.8	9,533.7	10,292.2	11,445.9
Tenant-occupied	1,718.8	2,011.3	2,300.6	2,420.6	2,543.0	2,677.2	2,802.0	2,950.4	3,187.7

[1] Excludes stocks of other nonfarm residential assets, which consists primarily of dormitories, and of fraternity and sorority houses.

Source: U.S. Bureau of Economic Analysis, Internet site <http://www.bea.gov/bea/dn/FA2004/SelectTable.asp> (accessed April 2006).

Table 968. Expenditures by Residential Property Owners for Improvements and Maintenance and Repairs by Type of Payment and Year Structure Built: 1995 to 2005

[In millions of dollars (124,971 represents $124,971,000,000). Based on personal interviews and mail surveys; see source for details]

Type of expenditure	All residen-tial proper-ties	Owner-occupied one-unit properties							
				Materials pruchased by owners			Year structure built		
		Total[1]	Pay-ments to contrac-tors	Total	For jobs done by owners	For jobs done under contract	Before 1960	1960 to 1979	1980 to 2005
Total:									
1995	124,971	79,003	63,017	15,987	12,305	3,682	30,080	28,157	14,718
2000	152,975	100,161	84,778	15,382	11,682	3,700	30,451	27,872	32,717
2002	173,324	116,193	99,190	17,002	13,017	3,985	42,798	25,597	47,051
2003	176,899	115,876	101,207	14,669	11,750	2,920	40,497	29,498	45,881
2004	198,556	136,080	114,197	21,883	17,213	4,670	39,452	36,035	60,594
2005	215,030	159,458	133,684	25,774	20,365	5,409	40,821	45,505	73,132
Maintenance and repairs:									
1995	47,032	25,460	19,487	5,973	5,498	476	9,979	8,388	5,511
2000	42,236	22,411	18,260	4,151	3,384	767	8,074	5,226	6,788
2002	47,379	21,885	18,279	3,607	3,048	559	7,734	5,232	8,867
2003	44,094	18,381	15,714	2,667	2,387	279	5,583	4,545	8,253
2004	50,611	26,575	20,655	5,920	5,356	564	8,197	6,401	11,977
2005	53,293	32,888	24,574	8,314	7,869	444	9,315	8,022	15,551
Improvements:									
1995	77,940	53,543	43,530	10,013	6,807	3,206	20,101	19,768	9,208
2000	110,739	77,750	66,517	11,232	8,298	2,934	22,377	22,646	25,929
2002	125,946	94,308	80,911	13,395	9,969	3,426	35,064	20,363	38,184
2003	132,805	97,495	85,494	12,003	9,362	2,640	34,914	24,953	37,628
2004	147,945	109,506	93,542	15,962	11,857	4,106	31,254	29,634	48,617
2005	161,737	126,570	109,110	17,460	12,496	4,964	31,507	37,483	57,581

[1] Includes year built not reported, not shown separately.

Source: U.S. Census Bureau, Residential Improvement and Repair Statistics. See Internet site <http://www.census.gov/const/www/c50index.html>.

Table 969. Home Remodeling—Work Done and Amount Spent: 2005

[In thousands, except percent (4,401 represents 4,401,000). As of fall 2005. For work done in the prior 12 months. Based on household survey and subject to sampling error; see source]

Remodeling project	Households with work done [1]			Amount spent (dol.)		
	Number	Percent of house-holds	Done by outside contractor	Under $1,000	$1,000 to $2,999	Over $3,000
Conversion of garage/attic/basement into living space	4,401	2.0	1,191	991	863	1,440
Remodel bathroom	15,475	7.2	4,040	6,942	3,195	2,349
Remodel kitchen	10,638	4.9	3,249	2,856	1,980	3,430
Remodel bedroom	8,702	4.0	1,254	4,828	1,244	796
Remodel/convert room to home office	2,718	1.3	220	1,612	356	112
Remodel other rooms	8,563	4.0	1,240	3,511	1,568	1,384
Add bathroom	1,939	0.9	523	427	483	504
Add/extend garage	983	0.5	309	207	93	403
Add other rooms—exterior addition	1,804	0.8	790	199	303	983
Add deck/porch/patio	5,978	2.8	2,048	1,527	1,578	1,672
Roofing	9,206	4.3	5,915	1,477	2,163	4,163
Siding—vinyl/metal	3,294	1.5	1,757	400	694	1,429
Aluminum windows	1,525	0.7	640	318	407	244
Clad-wood/wood windows	1,390	0.6	702	256	538	437
Vinyl windows	5,324	2.5	2,854	1,170	1,158	1,907
Ceramic tile floors	8,760	4.1	3,812	4,103	2,163	908
Hardwood floors	5,562	2.6	2,376	1,672	1,603	1,169
Laminate flooring	5,391	2.5	1,482	2,361	1,413	468
Vinyl flooring	4,132	1.9	1,040	2,272	558	215
Carpeting	10,808	5.0	6,894	3,943	3,534	1,279
Kitchen cabinets	4,881	2.3	1,829	903	997	1,414
Kitchen counter tops	5,805	2.7	2,924	1,578	1,334	1,284
Skylights	1,089	0.5	451	548	159	42
Exterior doors	6,914	3.2	2,894	3,922	1,227	375
Interior doors	5,143	2.4	1,292	2,801	454	374
Garage doors	4,210	2.0	2,443	1,746	1,194	214
Concrete or masonry work	5,382	2.5	2,506	1,966	1,142	1155
Swimming pool—in-ground	886	0.4	490	82	36	473
Wall paneling	1,394	0.7	159	672	143	4
Ceramic wall tile	2,728	1.3	941	1,348	518	204

[1] Includes no response and amount unknown.

Source: Mediamark Research Inc., New York, NY, *Top-Line Reports,* (copyright) Internet site <http://www.mediamark.com/>.

Construction and Housing   619

Table 970. **Commercial Buildings—Summary: 2003**

[**4,645 represents 4,645,000.** Excludes mall buildings. Building type based on predominant activity in which the occupants were engaged. Based on a sample survey of building representatives conducted in 2003, therefore subject to sampling variability]

Characteristic	All buildings (1,000)	Total floor space (mil. sq. ft.)	Total workers in all buildings (1,000)	Mean square foot per building [1]	Mean square foot per worker [1]	Mean operating hours per week [1]
All buildings	**4,645**	**64,783**	**72,807**	**13.9**	**890**	**61**
Building floorspace (sq. ft.):						
1,001 to 5,000	2,552	6,789	9,936	2.7	683	57
5,001 to 10,000	889	6,585	7,512	7.4	877	61
10,001 to 25,000	738	11,535	10,787	15.6	1,069	67
25,001 to 50,000	241	8,668	8,881	35.9	976	72
50,001 to 100,000	129	9,057	8,432	70.4	1,074	80
100,001 to 200,000	65	9,064	11,632	138.8	779	89
200,001 to 500,000	25	7,176	6,883	289.0	1,043	100
Over 500,000	7	5,908	8,744	896.1	676	115
Principal activity within building:						
Education	386	9,874	12,489	25.6	791	50
Food sales	226	1,255	1,430	5.6	877	107
Food service	297	1,654	3,129	5.6	528	86
Health care	129	3,163	6,317	24.6	501	59
Inpatient	8	1,905	3,716	241.4	513	168
Outpatient	121	1,258	2,600	10.4	484	52
Lodging	142	5,096	2,457	35.8	2,074	167
Retail (other than mall)	443	4,317	3,463	9.7	1,246	59
Office	824	12,208	28,154	14.8	434	55
Public assembly	277	3,939	2,395	14.2	1,645	50
Public order and safety	71	1,090	1,347	15.5	809	103
Religious worship	370	3,754	1,706	10.1	2,200	32
Service	622	4,050	3,667	6.5	1,105	55
Warehouse and storage	597	10,078	4,369	16.9	2,306	66
Other	79	1,738	1,819	21.9	956	63
Vacant	182	2,567	(NA)	14.1	(NA)	(NA)
Census region: [2]						
Northeast	726	12,905	14,908	17.8	866	67
Midwest	1,266	17,080	16,373	13.5	1,043	59
South	1,775	23,489	27,078	13.2	867	60
West	878	11,310	14,448	12.9	783	62
Year constructed:						
1919 or before	330	3,769	3,045	11.4	1,238	48
1920 to 1945	527	6,871	6,122	13.0	1,122	51
1946 to 1959	562	7,045	6,646	12.5	1,060	52
1960 to 1969	579	8,101	8,708	14.0	930	63
1970 to 1979	731	10,772	12,597	14.7	855	65
1980 to 1989	707	10,332	15,032	14.6	687	62
1990 to 1999	876	12,360	16,181	14.1	764	71
2000 to 2003	334	5,533	4,476	16.6	1,236	68
Workers (main shift):						
Fewer than 5	2,653	15,492	4,633	5.8	3,344	56
5 to 9	778	6,166	5,080	7.9	1,214	63
10 to 19	563	7,803	7,305	13.9	1,068	66
20 to 49	398	10,989	11,780	27.6	933	73
50 to 99	147	7,934	9,545	53.8	831	75
100 to 249	77	6,871	11,093	89.7	619	90
250 or more	30	9,528	23,371	320.4	408	99
Energy sources: [3]						
Electricity	4,404	63,307	72,708	14.4	871	62
Natural gas	2,391	43,468	51,956	18.2	837	65
Fuel oil	451	15,157	19,625	33.6	772	68
District heat	67	5,443	10,190	81.4	534	79
District chilled water	33	2,853	7,189	86.7	397	79
Propane	502	7,076	5,858	14.1	1,208	60
Wood	62	289	262	4.6	1,105	46
Heating equipment: [3]						
Heat pumps	476	8,814	10,754	18.5	820	64
Furnaces	1,864	19,615	18,616	10.5	1,054	57
Individual space heaters	819	12,545	12,878	15.3	974	61
District heat	65	5,166	9,838	79.7	525	78
Boilers	579	20,423	23,472	35.3	870	70
Packaged heating units	953	18,021	22,588	18.9	798	69
Other	205	3,262	3,475	15.9	939	63
Cooling equipment: [3]						
Residential-type central A/C	1,006	11,035	11,438	11.0	965	57
Heat pumps	492	9,041	10,961	18.4	825	63
Individual A/C	742	12,558	11,477	16.9	1,094	66
District chilled water	33	2,853	7,189	86.7	397	79
Central chillers	111	11,636	17,545	105.1	663	81
Packaged A/C units	1,613	29,969	35,810	18.6	837	69
Swamp coolers	122	1,561	1,655	12.8	943	71
Other	40	1,232	1,682	31.1	732	75

NA Not available. [1] For explanation of mean, see Guide to Tabular Presentation. [2] For composition of regions, see map inside front cover. [3] More than one type may apply.

Source: U.S. Energy Information Administration, 2003 Commercial Buildings Energy Consumption Buildings (CBECS) Detailed Tables; Table B1. See Internet site <http://www.eia.doe.gov/emeu/cbecs/cbecs2003/detailed_tables_2003/detailed_tables_2003.html> (accessed 11 July 2006).

Manufactures

This section presents summary data for manufacturing as a whole and more detailed information for major industry groups and selected products. The types of measures shown at the different levels include data for establishments, employment and payroll, plant and equipment expenditures, value and quantity of production and shipments, value added by manufacture, inventories, and various indicators of financial status.

The principal sources of these data are U.S. Census Bureau reports of the censuses of manufactures conducted every 5 years, the *Annual Survey of Manufactures,* and *Current Industrial Reports.* Reports on current activities of industries or current movements of individual commodities are compiled by such government agencies as the Bureau of Labor Statistics; the Economic Research Service of the Department of Agriculture; the International Trade Administration; and by private research or trade associations.

Data on financial aspects of manufacturing industries are collected by the U.S. Census Bureau (see especially Tables 987–989) as part of the Quarterly Financial Report. Industry aggregates in the form of balance sheets, profit and loss statements, analyses of sales and expenses, lists of subsidiaries, and types and amounts of security issues are published for leading manufacturing corporations registered with the Securities and Exchange Commission. The BEA issues data on capital in manufacturing industries and capacity utilization rates in manufacturing. See also Section 15, Business Enterprise.

Several private trade associations provide industry coverage for certain sections of the economy. They include the Aluminum Association (Table 996), American Iron and Steel Institute (Tables 997 and 998), Consumer Electronics Association (Table 1004), and the Aerospace Industries Association (Tables 1009 and 1011). Machine tool consumption data (Table 1000) is

produced jointly by the Association for Manufacturing Technology and American Machine Tool Distributors Association.

Censuses and annual surveys—The first census of manufactures covered the year 1809. Between 1809 and 1963, a census was conducted at periodic intervals. Since 1967, it has been taken every 5 years (for years ending in "2" and "7"). Results from the 2002 census are presented in this section utilizing the NAICS (North American Industry Classification System). For additional information see text, Section 15, Business Enterprise, and the Census Bureau Web site at <http://www.census.gov/econ/census02/>. Census data, either directly reported or estimated from administrative records, are obtained for every manufacturing plant with one or more paid employees.

The *Annual Survey of Manufactures* (ASM), conducted for the first time in 1949, collects data for the years between censuses for the more general measure of manufacturing activity covered in detail by the censuses. The annual survey data are estimates derived from a scientifically selected sample of establishments. The 2004 annual survey is based on a sample of about 50,000 from a universe of 346,000 establishments. These establishments represent all manufacturing establishments of multiunit companies and all single-establishment manufacturing companies mailed schedules in the 2002 Census of Manufactures. For the current panel of the ASM sample, all establishments of companies with 2002 shipments in manufacturing in excess of $500 million were included in the survey with certainty. For the remaining portion of the mail survey, the establishment was defined as the sampling unit. For this portion, all establishments with 500 employees or more and establishments with a very large value of shipments also were included. Therefore, of the 50,000 establishments included in the ASM panel, approximately

U.S. Census Bureau, Statistical Abstract of the United States: 2007

24,000 are selected with certainty. Smaller establishments in the remaining portion of the mail survey were selected by sample.

Establishments and classification—Each of the establishments covered in the 2002 Economic Census—Manufacturing was classified in 1 of 480 industries (473 manufacturing industries and 7 former manufacturing industries) in accordance with the industry definitions in the 2002 NAICS Manual. In the NAICS system, an industry is generally defined as a group of establishments that have similar production processes. To the extent practical, the system uses supply-based or production-oriented concepts in defining industries. The resulting group of establishments must be significant in terms of number, value added by manufacture, value of shipments, and number of employees.

Establishments frequently make products classified both in their industry (primary products) and other industries (secondary products). Industry statistics (employment, payroll, value added by manufacture, value of shipments, etc.) reflect the activities of the establishments, which may make both primary and secondary products. Product statistics, however, represent the output of all establishments without regard for the classification of the producing establishment. For this reason, when relating the industry statistics, especially the value of shipments, to the product statistics, the composition of the industry's output should be considered.

The censuses of manufactures for 1947 through 1992 cover operating manufacturing establishments as defined in the Standard Industrial Classification Manual

(SIC), issued by the U.S. Office of Management and Budget (see text, Section 12). The Manual was also used for classifying establishments in the annual surveys. The comparability of manufactures data over time is affected by changes in the official definitions of industries as presented in the Manual. It is important to note, therefore, that the 1987 edition of the Manual was used for the 1987 and 1992 censuses; and the 1972 edition of the Manual and the 1977 Supplement were used for the 1972 through 1982 censuses.

Establishment—Establishment signifies a single physical plant site or factory. It is not necessarily identical to the business unit or company, which may consist of one or more establishments. A company operating establishments at more than one location is required to submit a separate report for each location and include establishments with payroll at any time during the year. An establishment engaged in distinctly different lines of activity and maintaining separate payroll and inventory records is also required to submit separate reports.

Durable goods—Items with a normal life expectancy of 3 years or more. Automobiles, furniture, household appliances, and mobile homes are common examples.

Nondurable goods—Items which generally last for only a short time (3 years or less). Food, beverages, clothing, shoes, and gasoline are common examples.

Statistical reliability—For a discussion of statistical collection and estimation, sampling procedures, and measures of statistical reliability applicable to Census Bureau data, see Appendix III.

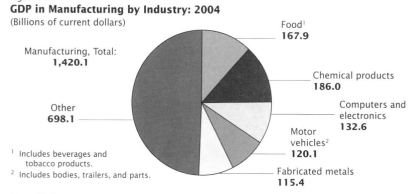

Figure 21.1
GDP in Manufacturing by Industry: 2004
(Billions of current dollars)

Manufacturing, Total:
1,420.1

Other
698.1

Food[1]
167.9

Chemical products
186.0

Computers and electronics
132.6

Motor vehicles[2]
120.1

Fabricated metals
115.4

[1] Includes beverages and tobacco products.
[2] Includes bodies, trailers, and parts.

Figure 21.2
Manufacturing as a Percent of Total Gross Domestic Product (GDP): 1998 to 2005

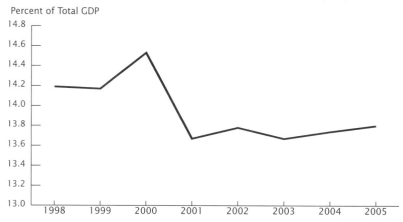

Percent of Total GDP

Source: Figure 21.1 and 21.2 charts prepared by U.S. Census Bureau. For data, see Table 971.

Figure 21.3
Employment in Top Five Manufacturing Industries: 1990 to 2005

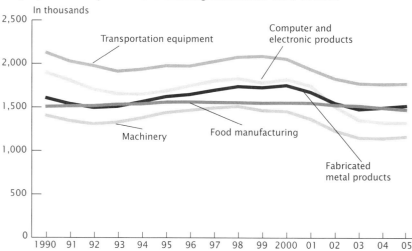

In thousands

Transportation equipment

Computer and electronic products

Machinery

Food manufacturing

Fabricated metal products

Source: Chart prepared by U.S. Census Bureau. For data, see Table 980.

Manufactures 623

Table 971. Gross Domestic Product in Manufacturing in Current and Real (2000) Dollars by Industry: 2000 to 2005

[In billions of dollars (9,817.0 represents $9,817,000,000,000), except as indicated. Data are based on the 1997 North American Industry Classification System (NAICS) codes 31-33. Data include nonfactor charges (capital consumption allowances, indirect business taxes, etc.) as well as factor charges against gross product; corporate profits and capital consumption allowances have been shifted from a company to an establishment basis]

Industry	2000	2001	2002	2003	2004	2005
CURRENT DOLLARS						
Gross domestic product, total [1]	9,817.0	10,128.0	10,469.6	10,971.3	11,734.3	12,487.1
Manufacturing, total	1,426.2	1,341.3	1,352.6	1,369.2	1,420.1	1,496.5
Percent of total..	14.53	13.24	12.92	12.48	12.10	11.98
Durable goods	865.3	778.9	774.8	785.5	824.1	868.4
Wood products	31.4	31.3	30.4	33.0	39.2	(NA)
Nonmetallic mineral products.	45.7	44.9	45.9	46.2	49.7	(NA)
Primary metals	48.2	41.1	41.9	38.7	50.9	(NA)
Fabricated metal products.	121.7	112.0	107.4	109.1	115.4	(NA)
Machinery	109.3	103.2	96.5	95.1	100.2	(NA)
Computer and electronic products	185.6	136.9	124.2	125.6	132.6	(NA)
Electrical equipment, appliances, and						
components	50.6	49.2	48.8	48.6	48.2	(NA)
Motor vehicles, bodies and trailers, and parts . .	118.1	103.7	118.9	129.9	120.1	(NA)
Other transportation equipment	64.4	69.2	69.6	65.0	66.9	(NA)
Furniture and related products	32.7	30.2	31.1	30.7	31.4	(NA)
Miscellaneous manufacturing.	57.5	57.2	60.0	63.7	69.4	(NA)
Nondurable goods.	561.0	562.5	577.9	583.7	596.1	628.1
Food and beverage and tobacco products	154.8	167.1	172.9	170.6	167.9	(NA)
Textile mills and textile product mills	26.5	22.7	21.9	22.7	23.3	(NA)
Apparel and leather and allied products.	25.1	22.8	20.9	18.4	18.9	(NA)
Paper products	55.6	48.9	50.3	46.4	48.9	(NA)
Printing and related support activities	49.0	46.9	45.7	44.5	45.9	(NA)
Petroleum and coal products	26.2	33.4	26.2	33.5	34.8	(NA)
Chemical products.	157.1	157.2	174.4	181.8	186.0	(NA)
Plastics and rubber products	66.7	63.4	65.5	65.6	70.3	(NA)
CHAINED (2000) DOLLARS						
Gross domestic product, total [1]	9,817.0	9,890.6	10,048.8	10,320.6	10,755.7	11,134.8
Manufacturing, total	1,426.2	1,346.9	1,384.4	1,410.4	1,478.1	1,536.6
Percent of total..	14.53	13.62	13.78	13.67	13.74	13.80
Durable goods	865.3	813.6	827.7	863.2	917.8	970.1
Wood products	31.4	30.9	30.3	31.4	32.4	(NA)
Nonmetallic mineral products.	45.7	45.2	45.5	46.6	49.0	(NA)
Primary metals	48.2	43.2	44.1	42.6	46.5	(NA)
Fabricated metal products.	121.7	109.4	104.4	107.5	110.7	(NA)
Machinery	109.3	100.4	93.3	92.3	100.7	(NA)
Computer and electronic products	185.6	181.9	185.8	215.0	260.3	(NA)
Electrical equipment, appliances, and						
components	50.6	48.5	48.8	49.9	49.3	(NA)
Motor vehicles, bodies and trailers, and parts . .	118.1	104.6	127.5	143.2	139.2	(NA)
Other transportation equipment	64.4	65.2	64.2	57.9	58.0	(NA)
Furniture and related products	32.7	29.1	29.2	28.9	31.0	(NA)
Miscellaneous manufacturing.	57.5	55.3	56.4	59.6	66.3	(NA)
Nondurable goods.	561.0	533.1	555.7	548.8	563.8	572.8
Food and beverage and tobacco products	154.8	156.0	153.7	153.3	155.8	(NA)
Textile mills and textile product mills	26.5	21.5	21.4	23.1	23.2	(NA)
Apparel and leather and allied products.	25.1	22.7	21.1	18.7	19.7	(NA)
Paper products	55.6	48.8	50.8	48.9	53.5	(NA)
Printing and related support activities	49.0	45.3	43.5	42.5	44.4	(NA)
Petroleum and coal products	26.2	23.9	32.5	26.1	24.7	(NA)
Chemical products.	157.1	153.1	170.5	172.9	173.6	(NA)
Plastics and rubber products	66.7	61.4	62.9	64.0	70.8	(NA)

NA Not available.   [1] For additional industry detail, see Table 649.

Source: U.S. Bureau of Economic Analysis, *Survey of Current Business*, May 2006. See also <http://www.bea.gov /bea/newsrelarchive/2006/gdpind05.pdf> (released 27 April 2006).

624   Manufactures

Table 972. **Manufacturing—Establishments, Employees, and Annual Payroll by Industry: 2003 and 2004**

[(113,398 represents 113,398,000). Excludes government employees, railroad employees, self-employed persons, etc. See "General Explanation" in source for definitions and statement on reliability of data. An *establishment* is a single physical location where business is conducted or where services or industrial operations are performed. See Appendix III]

Industry	2002 NAICS code [1]	2003 Estab-lishments, number	2003 Employees [2] (1,000)	2003 Annual payroll (mil. dol.)	2004 Estab-lishments, number	2004 Employees [2] (1,000)	2004 Annual payroll (mil. dol.)
All industries, total	(X)	7,254,745	113,398	4,040,889	7,387,724	115,075	4,253,996
Manufacturing, total	31-33	341,849	14,132	576,058	339,083	13,822	592,830
Percent of all industries	(X)	4.7	12.5	14.3	4.6	12.0	14.0
Food manufacturing.	311	27,274	1,496	46,593	26,767	1,482	47,540
Beverage & tobacco product	312	3,212	155	7,111	3,359	155	7,211
Textile mills	313	3,840	255	7,366	3,638	224	6,875
Textile product mills.	314	7,289	188	4,997	7,117	171	4,905
Apparel manufacturing	315	13,376	304	7,065	12,314	280	6,804
Leather & allied product	316	1,519	44	1,265	1,475	43	1,307
Wood product.	321	16,808	524	15,891	16,783	535	17,194
Paper	322	5,456	482	21,668	5,422	465	21,590
Printing & related support activities.	323	36,024	700	25,033	35,321	673	24,997
Petroleum & coal products	324	2,299	98	6,487	2,457	104	7,776
Chemical.	325	13,247	841	48,532	13,364	823	48,816
Plastics & rubber products	326	15,019	921	32,126	14,886	908	33,160
Nonmetallic mineral product	327	16,446	468	18,087	16,714	472	18,963
Primary metal.	331	5,725	480	20,863	5,426	451	21,486
Fabricated metal product	332	59,407	1,518	55,778	59,373	1,515	58,581
Machinery	333	27,459	1,129	48,994	27,037	1,088	50,459
Computer & electronic product.	334	15,426	1,189	66,583	15,097	1,108	66,318
Electrical equip, appliance & component	335	6,383	460	17,617	6,294	439	17,797
Transportation equipment	336	12,503	1,607	79,967	12,705	1,626	85,128
Furniture & related product	337	21,716	564	16,796	21,735	555	17,221
Miscellaneous.	339	31,421	708	27,239	31,799	703	28,702

X Not applicable.   [1] North American Industry Classification System, 2002; see text, Section 15.   [2] Covers full- and part-time employees who are on the payroll in the pay period including March 12.

Source: U.S. Census Bureau, "County Business Patterns"; annual. See <http://www.census.gov/epcd/cbp/view/cbpview.html>.

Table 973. **Manufacturing Establishments, Employees, and Annual Payroll by State: 2004**

[13,822 represents 13,822,000.) Data are for North American Industry Classification System (NAICS) 2002 codes 31-33. Excludes government employees, railroad employees, self-employed persons, etc. See "General Explanation" in source for definitions and statement on reliability of data. An *establishment* is a single physical location where business is conducted or where services or industrial operations are performed]

State	Establish-ments	Employees (1,000) [1]	Annual payroll (mil. dol.)	State	Establish-ments	Employees (1,000) [1]	Annual payroll (mil. dol.)
United States . . .	**339,083**	**13,822**	**592,830**	Missouri	7,019	303	11,703
Alabama	4,964	274	10,068	Montana	1,267	18	688
Alaska	501	10	396	Nebraska	1,998	104	3,633
Arizona	4,818	167	7,493	Nevada	1,844	43	1,789
Arkansas	3,144	201	6,551	New Hampshire	2,191	76	3,529
California.	46,110	1,476	70,372	New Jersey	9,962	326	17,001
Colorado	5,235	138	6,275	New Mexico.	1,549	33	1,297
Connecticut	5,174	188	9,579	New York	19,994	599	25,307
Delaware.	696	36	1,645	North Carolina	10,327	571	20,691
District of Columbia. . .	147	2	74	North Dakota	741	24	780
Florida	14,433	372	14,653	Ohio	16,887	815	35,719
Georgia	8,709	433	15,894	Oklahoma	3,941	141	5,371
Hawaii	928	15	479	Oregon	5,541	177	7,532
Idaho	1,805	60	2,415	Pennsylvania	15,915	668	27,931
Illinois.	16,363	685	29,467	Rhode Island	2,024	58	2,261
Indiana	9,068	544	23,739	South Carolina	4,270	275	10,796
Iowa.	3,811	219	8,644	South Dakota	923	40	1,274
Kansas	3,179	173	6,986	Tennessee	6,804	392	15,268
Kentucky	4,174	258	10,716	Texas	20,780	829	36,255
Louisiana	3,416	149	6,980	Utah.	3,113	111	4,321
Maine	1,845	63	2,526	Vermont	1,152	39	1,638
Maryland.	3,813	141	6,747	Virginia	5,817	295	12,026
Massachusetts	8,263	294	15,590	Washington	7,401	254	12,232
Michigan	14,447	662	32,391	West Virginia	1,453	67	2,598
Minnesota	8,067	333	15,026	Wisconsin	9,804	489	20,479
Mississippi.	2,710	174	5,594	Wyoming	546	10	432

[1] Covers full- and part-time employees who are on the payroll in the pay period including March 12.

Source: U.S. Census Bureau, "County Business Patterns"; annual. See <http://www.census.gov/epcd/cbp/view/cbpview.html>.

Table 974. **Manufactures—Summary by Selected Industry: 2004**

[**13,404.3 represents** 13,404,300. Based on the Annual Survey of Manufactures; see Appendix III]

| Industry based on shipments | 2002 NAICS code [1] | All employees [2] | | | Produc-tion workers (1,000) [2] | Value added by manufac-tures [3] (mil.dol.) | Value of ship-ments [4] (mil. dol.) |
| | | Number (1,000) | Payroll | | | | |
			Total (mil. dol.)	Per employee (dol.)			
Manufacturing, total	**31-33**	**13,404.3**	**569,414**	**42,480**	**9,357.1**	**2,031,439**	**4,265,784**
Food [5]	311	1,448.1	46,563	32,154	1,097.5	223,433	511,450
Grain and oilseed milling	3112	51.8	2,512	48,501	38.3	21,703	58,791
Sugar and confectionery product	3113	70.0	2,676	38,259	54.3	14,183	26,684
Fruit and vegetable preserving and specialty food	3114	164.1	5,209	31,745	135.6	27,838	53,083
Dairy product	3115	125.6	5,063	40,312	86.9	24,422	73,038
Meat product	3116	493.4	13,176	26,706	422.4	47,811	143,147
Bakeries and tortilla	3118	286.8	8,993	31,354	174.7	34,098	51,633
Other food	3119	174.4	6,113	35,060	124.7	37,392	64,199
Beverage and tobacco product	312	144.9	6,879	47,474	80.7	71,700	112,270
Beverage	3121	123.0	5,589	45,454	64.3	38,259	73,457
Tobacco	3122	21.9	1,290	58,793	16.3	33,441	38,813
Wood product [5]	321	535.2	17,039	31,834	428.2	43,662	103,420
Other wood product	3219	318.9	9,486	29,749	250.9	22,018	48,612
Paper	322	440.0	20,561	46,731	340.4	74,016	153,969
Pulp, paper, and paperboard mills	3221	137.0	8,121	59,257	109.1	37,026	70,505
Converted paper product	3222	302.9	12,440	41,064	231.3	36,990	83,464
Printing and related support activities	323	658.9	24,789	37,623	465.2	57,250	93,193
Petroleum and coal products	324	96.7	7,017	72,583	61.4	61,830	312,885
Chemical	325	768.5	43,664	56,813	435.5	295,328	528,215
Basic chemical	3251	161.3	10,430	64,653	93.1	58,589	139,431
Resin, syn. rubber, and artificial and syn. fibers and filaments	3252	84.7	4,873	57,562	57.6	28,555	72,919
Pharmaceutical and medicine	3254	231.0	14,209	61,500	112.9	120,870	157,479
Soap, cleaning compound, and toilet preparation	3256	100.7	4,808	47,747	62.4	40,459	66,053
Other chemical product	3259	100.4	4,825	48,060	56.4	19,007	38,026
Plastics and rubber products	326	882.7	32,121	36,390	685.0	91,517	182,547
Plastics product	3261	724.9	25,517	35,203	561.7	74,396	148,492
Nonmetallic mineral product [5]	327	455.1	18,107	39,782	351.4	58,800	101,870
Cement and concrete product	3273	211.6	8,418	39,773	161.0	26,460	48,201
Primary metal [5]	331	435.2	21,159	48,625	342.3	73,011	178,996
Iron and steel mills and ferroalloy	3311	109.3	6,758	61,816	87.2	31,445	73,855
Fabricated metal product [5]	332	1,469.6	57,426	39,076	1,084.5	143,899	259,875
Architectural and structural metals	3323	362.1	13,392	36,984	259.5	32,004	63,682
Machine shops, turned product and screw, nut, and bolt	3327	349.8	13,973	39,948	261.8	28,749	45,564
Other fabricated metal product	3329	262.9	10,944	41,630	190.3	31,938	52,769
Machinery [5]	333	1,054.0	48,225	45,756	666.4	133,826	269,203
Agriculture, construction, and mining machinery	3331	167.2	7,265	43,456	110.4	26,918	60,210
Other general-purpose machinery	3339	268.3	12,386	46,157	155.5	30,831	61,864
Computer and electronic product [5]	334	1,060.8	61,152	57,646	473.1	214,650	361,938
Computer and peripheral equipment	3341	118.5	7,383	62,332	35.6	32,344	64,894
Communications equipment	3342	143.1	8,417	58,823	53.3	30,347	58,213
Semiconductor and other electronic components	3344	354.8	17,815	50,219	201.1	77,874	116,660
Navigational, measuring, medical, control instruments	3345	389.2	25,061	64,386	146.8	66,470	103,509
Electrical equipment, appliance, and component [5]	335	432.2	17,166	39,714	304.0	52,723	104,245
Transportation equipment [5]	336	1,585.2	83,848	52,895	1,138.8	255,974	666,503
Motor vehicle	3361	216.0	14,906	69,017	189.1	70,796	261,716
Motor vehicle parts	3363	644.0	31,422	48,788	505.3	84,807	203,591
Aerospace product and parts	3364	384.6	24,550	63,832	189.9	67,594	126,129
Furniture and related product [5]	337	560.6	17,499	31,215	430.1	45,441	80,153
Household and institutional furniture and kitchen cabinet	3371	367.6	10,653	28,982	291.1	26,505	47,356
Miscellaneous manufacturing [5]	339	701.8	27,840	39,669	438.7	84,083	132,287
Medical equipment and supplies	3391	312.5	13,865	44,366	180.6	47,779	68,262
Other miscellaneous	3399	389.3	13,976	35,898	258.2	36,305	64,026

[1] North American Industry Classification System, 2002; see text, Section 15.   [2] Includes employment and payroll at administrative offices and auxiliary units. All employees represents the average of production workers plus all other employees for the payroll period ended nearest the 12th of March. Production workers represents the average of the employment for the payroll periods ended nearest the 12th of March, May, August, and November.   [3] Adjusted value added; takes into account (a) value added by merchandising operations (that is, difference between the sales value and cost of merchandise sold without further manufacture, processing, or assembly), plus (b) net change in finished goods and work-in-process inventories between beginning and end of year.   [4] Includes extensive and unmeasurable duplication from shipments between establishments in the same industry classification.   [5] Includes industries not shown separately.

Source: U.S. Census Bureau, *Annual Survey of Manufactures, Statistics for Industry Groups and Industries,* Series M04(AS)-1. See also <http://www.census.gov/prod/2005pubs/am0431gs1.pdf> (issued December 2005).

Table 975. Manufactures—Summary by State: 2004

[13,381.2 represents 13,381,200. Data are for North American Industry Classification System (NAICS) 2002 codes 31-33. Sum of state totals may not add to U.S. total because U.S. and state figures were independently derived. See Appendix III]

State	All employees [1]			Production workers [1]		Value added by manufactures [2]		Value of ship-ments [3] (mil. dol.)
	Number (1,000)	Payroll		Total (1,000)	Wages (mil. dol.)	Total (mil. dol.)	Per production worker (dol.)	
		Total (mil. dol.)	Per employee (dol.)					
United States.	13,381.2	569,203	42,537	9,339.6	331,658	2,025,957	216,922	4,259,366
Alabama	259.1	9,358	36,122	200.6	6,393	34,002	169,464	76,096
Alaska	10.3	352	34,257	8.7	268	1,736	199,668	4,753
Arizona	158.0	7,240	45,823	96.9	3,485	24,096	248,609	41,644
Arkansas.	193.7	6,392	32,991	155.9	4,565	25,655	164,614	54,547
California.	1,440.9	65,249	45,284	895.2	29,858	202,312	226,008	388,332
Colorado	132.9	5,950	44,765	87.4	3,139	16,965	194,004	33,594
Connecticut	191.9	9,632	50,191	111.3	4,535	28,745	258,285	45,105
Delaware	36.4	1,624	44,630	25.7	991	7,660	298,433	17,488
District of Columbia. . .	1.9	71	37,830	1.2	37	164	141,966	271
Florida	354.2	13,967	39,435	232.1	7,161	44,926	193,531	84,301
Georgia	419.6	15,518	36,986	318.4	10,139	59,477	186,791	131,455
Hawaii	14.0	522	37,215	8.9	322	1,489	167,313	4,561
Idaho	56.5	2,108	37,318	36.6	1,104	9,605	262,189	16,583
Illinois.	676.1	29,166	43,142	466.3	16,846	102,971	220,848	210,043
Indiana	534.9	23,343	43,637	403.8	15,917	86,549	214,346	183,564
Iowa.	217.2	8,496	39,112	157.7	5,379	36,688	232,679	79,470
Kansas	168.0	6,937	41,296	117.3	4,165	22,108	188,464	56,465
Kentucky	246.7	10,345	41,925	187.6	6,939	36,519	194,640	97,254
Louisiana	141.0	6,705	47,558	103.2	4,367	43,393	420,643	124,305
Maine.	58.0	2,317	39,948	42.5	1,521	7,248	170,661	13,657
Maryland	135.8	6,309	46,471	85.7	3,143	19,131	223,314	36,490
Massachusetts	302.3	14,895	49,280	179.7	6,561	45,010	250,405	76,538
Michigan	651.9	32,548	49,924	478.5	21,733	93,659	195,749	220,455
Minnesota	325.6	14,211	43,645	214.8	7,631	43,707	203,489	88,472
Mississippi.	169.9	5,546	32,632	134.2	3,836	18,201	135,639	43,862
Missouri	302.9	12,707	41,949	228.9	8,333	44,783	195,680	102,804
Montana	17.3	665	38,407	12.7	423	2,386	187,776	6,469
Nebraska	99.7	3,533	35,434	76.6	2,393	12,477	162,932	34,434
Nevada	44.0	1,850	42,073	28.9	976	5,251	181,840	9,551
New Hampshire	72.5	3,333	45,970	45.6	1,598	8,466	185,698	15,439
New Jersey	308.6	14,448	46,822	201.4	7,494	49,127	243,907	94,125
New Mexico.	32.9	1,343	40,793	22.8	766	11,708	513,043	17,393
New York	569.6	24,146	42,387	370.7	12,921	83,146	224,311	146,692
North Carolina	550.2	19,861	36,097	411.1	12,508	90,231	219,494	163,838
North Dakota	22.0	764	34,702	16.5	508	2,913	176,729	7,372
Ohio.	782.6	34,503	44,087	570.1	22,613	117,751	206,527	258,799
Oklahoma	132.5	5,241	39,545	96.3	3,330	17,933	186,261	45,710
Oregon	174.2	7,277	41,770	124.2	4,378	33,773	271,687	54,836
Pennsylvania	645.8	26,816	41,524	457.0	16,274	96,329	210,785	190,371
Rhode Island	55.4	2,236	40,377	35.5	1,120	6,322	177,874	11,173
South Carolina	258.2	10,293	39,863	194.7	6,608	35,663	183,157	81,630
South Dakota	37.5	1,222	32,617	28.6	824	4,500	157,189	12,084
Tennessee	384.2	14,808	38,548	286.8	9,679	58,678	204,591	125,531
Texas	773.5	33,559	43,386	525.3	18,583	150,698	286,862	385,534
Utah.	107.4	4,202	39,142	72.8	2,299	14,015	192,481	29,589
Vermont	38.3	1,687	44,009	24.4	893	5,019	205,863	9,911
Virginia	284.1	11,915	41,944	206.1	7,158	49,715	241,263	87,843
Washington	242.5	11,179	46,103	153.8	5,599	36,834	239,453	77,665
West Virginia	63.1	2,652	42,032	47.5	1,792	8,846	186,039	20,579
Wisconsin	476.8	19,808	41,545	344.7	12,307	65,693	190,592	135,676
Wyoming	8.7	352	40,624	6.5	243	1,684	260,123	5,010

[1] Includes employment and payroll at administrative offices and auxiliary units. All employees represents the average of production workers plus all other employees for the payroll period ended nearest the 12th of March. Production workers represents the average of employment for the payroll periods ended nearest the 12th of March, May, August, and November. [2] Adjusted value added; takes into account (a) value added by merchandising operations (that is, difference between the sales value and cost of merchandise sold without further manufacture, processing, or assembly), plus (b) net change in finished goods and work-in-process inventories between beginning and end of year. [3] Includes extensive and unmeasurable duplication from shipments between establishments in the same industry classification.

Source: U.S. Census Bureau, Annual Survey of Manufactures, Geographic Area Statistics, Series M01(AS)-4. See also <http://www.census.gov/prod/ec02/am0431as1.pdf> (issued January 2006).

Table 976. **Manufacturing Industries—Export-Related Shipments and Employment by Industry: 2002**

[3,915,599 represents $3,915,599,000,000. Exports include both "direct" exports (exports manufactured in the U.S. and consumed in foreign markets and "indirect" exports (intermediate goods and services required to manufacture export goods). For methodology, see report]

Industry	2002 NAICS code [1]	Value of manfacturers' shipments (mil. dol.)	Export-related shipments (mil. dol.)	All manufac-turing employ-ment (1,000)	Export-related manufac-turing employ-ment (1,000)	Export-related as percent of all manufacturers Ship-ments	Export-related as percent of all manufacturers Employ-ment
Manufacturing, total	31-33	3,915,599	687,748	14,745	2,568	17.6	17.4
Food manufacturing	311	458,128	26,864	1,509	74	5.9	4.9
Beverage and tobacco products	312	104,871	3,143	162	4	3.0	2.6
Textile mills	313	45,637	10,780	268	68	23.6	25.4
Textile products	314	32,226	2,532	184	16	7.9	8.8
Apparel.	315	44,793	4,916	342	32	11.0	9.3
Leather and allied products	316	6,336	2,476	45	14	39.1	31.0
Wood products	321	88,398	5,615	541	31	6.4	5.8
Paper.	322	154,468	20,553	493	62	13.3	12.7
Printing and related support activities. .	323	95,618	7,303	718	57	7.6	8.0
Petroleum and coal products.	324	215,473	16,046	103	7	7.4	6.5
Chemicals.	325	455,932	91,978	854	173	20.2	20.3
Plastics and rubber products.	326	172,931	25,233	983	143	14.6	14.5
Nonmetallic mineral products	327	94,982	8,242	484	45	8.7	9.4
Primary metals.	331	140,312	39,776	496	138	28.3	27.9
Fabricated metal products	332	248,369	42,437	1,576	275	17.1	17.5
Machinery.	333	252,257	68,386	1,170	316	27.1	27.0
Computers and electronic products . . .	334	361,961	121,731	1,277	445	33.6	34.9
Electrical equipment, appliances, and components.	335	104,623	21,626	494	106	20.7	21.5
Transportation equipment	336	636,400	146,223	1,697	435	23.0	25.6
Furniture and related products.	337	75,913	2,395	597	18	3.2	3.1
Miscellaneous	339	125,972	19,493	754	106	15.5	14.0

[1] North American Industry Classification System, 2002; see text, Section 15.

Source: U.S. Census Bureau, *Exports from Manufacturing Establishments: 2002*, series AR(02)-1. See also <http://www.census.gov /mcd/exports/ar02.pdf> (released May 2006); and unpublished data.

Table 977. **Manufacturing Industries—Export-Related Shipments and Employment by State: 2002**

[687,748 represents $687,748,000,000. Exports include both "direct" exports (exports manufactured in the U.S. and consumed in foreign markets and "indirect" exports (intermediate goods and services required to manufacture export goods). For methodology, see report]

State	Export-related ship-ments (mil. dol.)	Export-related manu-facturing employ-ment (1,000)	Export-related as percent of all manufacturers Ship-ments	Export-related as percent of all manufacturers Employ-ment	State	Export-related ship-ments (mil. dol.)	Export-related manu-facturing employ-ment (1,000)	Export-related as percent of all manufacturers Ship-ments	Export-related as percent of all manufacturers Employ-ment
U.S.	687,748	2,568	17.6	17.4	Mississippi	4,128	15	10.7	8.4
					Missouri	10,665	41	11.6	12.8
Alabama.	10,557	35	15.9	12.2	Montana.	306	1	6.1	6.4
Alaska	327	1	8.6	7.3	Nebraska	4,724	17	16.0	16.6
Arizona.	14,783	51	34.3	30.5	Nevada	751	4	9.2	9.6
Arkansas	5,197	20	11.2	9.6	New Hampshire. .	2,977	16	19.5	19.6
California	77,158	311	20.2	19.0	New Jersey.	12,988	48	13.4	13.1
Colorado.	5,134	22	14.8	14.5	New Mexico	3,220	9	31.9	27.9
Connecticut	10,836	50	25.5	23.5	New York	22,932	97	15.5	15.2
Delaware	1,335	4	8.2	11.7	North Carolina. . .	20,963	92	13.4	14.8
District					North Dakota . . .	1,226	4	17.9	16.7
of Columbia	8	(D)	3.2	(D)	Ohio	48,749	186	20.1	21.3
Florida	9,253	39	11.7	10.4	Oklahoma.	5,658	24	14.3	15.8
Georgia	17,693	62	14.0	13.8	Oregon.	6,539	27	14.2	14.9
Hawaii	242	–	6.9	2.3	Pennsylva nia . . .	31,469	116	17.4	16.2
Idaho	2,223	8	14.3	12.4	Rhode Island . . .	1,899	10	17.6	16.7
Illinois	30,891	122	16.4	16.5	South Carolina . .	18,399	66	22.7	22.8
Indiana.	25,923	100	16.1	17.5	South Dakota . . .	899	3	8.4	8.9
Iowa	9,384	36	14.6	16.1	Tennessee	17,538	66	16.1	16.0
Kansas.	8,302	30	16.5	16.8	Texas.	61,382	170	20.1	19.9
Kentucky	15,820	50	18.1	19.2	Utah	5,852	21	23.5	19.4
Louisiana	11,090	22	12.4	14.6	Vermont	2,078	8	21.5	18.9
Maine.	2,116	8	15.1	11.9	Virginia.	11,030	42	13.1	13.4
Maryland	3,754	16	10.3	10.8	Washington	37,460	117	46.6	42.2
Massachusetts. . .	19,705	84	25.2	24.2	West Virginia . . .	3,098	10	16.6	15.0
Michigan.	38,528	149	17.4	19.9	Wisconsin	17,362	74	13.5	14.5
Minnesota.	12,786	59	15.9	16.8	Wyoming	414	1	10.5	10.5

D Data withheld to avoid disclosure of individual companies.   – Represents or rounds to zero.

Source: U.S. Census Bureau, *Exports from Manufacturing Establishments: 2002*, series AR(02)-1. See also <http://www.census.gov /mcd/exports/ar02.pdf> (released May 2006); and unpublished data.

Table 978. Manufacturers' E-Commerce Shipments by Industry: 2003 and 2004

[(4,015,081 represents $4,015,081,000,000). Based on the Annual Survey of Manufactures; subject to sampling variability. E-commerce is the value of goods and services sold over computer-mediated networks (open or proprietary)]

Industry	2002 NAICS code [1]	2003				2004			
		Ship-ments, total (mil. dol.)	E-commerce			Ship-ments, total (mil.dol.)	E-commerce		
			Ship-ments, total (mil.dol.)	Percent of total ship-ments	Percent distri-bution		Ship-ments, total (mil.dol.)	Percent of total ship-ments	Percent distri-bution
Manufacturing, total	**31-33**	**4,015,081**	**842,666**	**21.0**	**100.0**	**4,259,366**	**996,174**	**23.4**	**100.0**
Food products	311	483,226	59,576	12.3	7.1	509,500	64,121	12.6	6.4
Beverage and tobacco.	312	108,806	46,998	43.2	5.6	111,891	52,783	47.2	5.3
Textile mills	313	42,588	3,639	8.5	0.4	40,144	4,416	11.0	0.5
Textile product mills.	314	31,261	7,244	23.2	0.9	33,394	8,472	25.4	0.0
Apparel.	315	38,668	9,137	23.6	1.1	33,364	8,694	26.1	0.9
Leather and allied products . . .	316	5,784	653	11.3	0.1	5,745	611	10.6	0.1
Wood products.	321	92,119	5,753	6.2	0.7	103,211	7,974	7.7	0.8
Paper.	322	151,094	18,683	12.4	2.2	154,208	19,631	12.7	2.0
Printing and related support activities	323	92,663	4,452	4.8	0.5	93,495	8,259	8.8	0.8
Petroleum and coal products . .	324	247,316	51,586	20.9	6.1	312,940	77,527	24.8	7.8
Chemicals	325	486,563	85,186	17.5	10.1	527,930	102,967	19.5	10.3
Plastics and rubber products. . .	326	178,328	26,954	15.1	3.2	182,948	33,220	18.2	3.3
Nonmetallic mineral products . .	327	96,923	8,631	8.9	1.0	102,040	10,850	10.6	1.1
Primary metals	331	138,142	12,578	9.1	1.5	179,241	33,410	18.6	3.4
Fabricated metal products	332	245,550	23,735	9.7	2.8	259,772	33,992	13.1	3.4
Machinery	333	257,375	34,797	13.5	4.1	269,321	52,292	19.4	5.2
Computer and electronic products	334	352,636	67,476	19.1	8.0	362,492	76,197	21.0	7.6
Electrical equipment, appliances, and components. .	335	100,140	23,722	23.7	2.8	103,892	25,177	24.2	2.5
Transportation equipment.	336	661,142	327,401	49.5	38.9	663,352	346,473	52.2	34.8
Furniture and related products .	337	75,423	9,983	13.2	1.2	78,099	11,264	14.4	1.1
Miscellaneous	339	129,334	14,482	11.2	1.7	132,387	17,844	13.5	1.8

[1] North American Industry Classification System, 2002; see text, Section 15.

Source: U.S. Census Bureau, Internet site <http://www.census.gov/eos/www/papers/2004/2004reportfinal.pdf> (released 25 May 2006).

Table 979. Manufacturing Employer Costs for Employee Compensation Per Hour Worked: 1990 to 2005

[As of March, for private industry workers. Based on a sample of establishments in the National Compensation Survey; see Appendix III and source for details. See also Table 635, Section 12]

Compensation component	Cost (dol.)					Percent distribution				
	1990	2000	2003	2004	2005	1990	2000	2003	2004	2005
Total compensation	**17.33**	**23.41**	**26.02**	**28.10**	**29.47**	**100.0**	**100.0**	**100.0**	**100.0**	**100.0**
Wages and salaries.	11.86	16.01	17.43	18.14	18.98	68.4	68.4	67.0	64.6	64.4
Total benefits	5.47	7.40	8.59	9.96	10.49	31.6	31.6	33.0	35.4	35.6
Paid leave	1.31	1.74	1.97	2.05	2.17	7.6	7.4	7.6	7.3	7.4
Vacation.	0.67	0.86	1.00	1.03	1.10	3.9	3.7	3.8	3.7	3.7
Holiday	0.48	0.65	0.73	0.76	0.80	2.8	2.8	2.8	2.7	2.7
Sick.	0.12	0.13	0.16	0.16	0.17	0.7	0.6	0.6	0.6	0.6
Other.	0.05	0.10	0.10	0.10	0.10	0.3	0.4	0.4	0.4	0.3
Supplemental pay	0.65	1.04	1.23	1.20	1.25	3.8	4.4	4.7	4.3	4.2
Premium pay.	0.34	0.58	0.60	0.60	0.62	2.0	2.5	2.3	2.1	2.1
Nonproduction bonuses. . .	0.22	0.36	0.51	0.48	0.50	1.3	1.5	2.0	1.7	1.7
Shift pay.	0.09	0.10	0.11	0.12	0.13	0.5	0.4	0.4	0.4	0.4
Insurance.	1.37	1.85	2.27	2.59	2.81	7.9	7.9	8.7	9.2	9.5
Health insurance	(NA)	1.69	2.08	2.40	2.60	(NA)	7.2	8.0	8.5	8.8
Retirement and savings	0.56	0.75	0.86	1.56	1.65	3.2	3.2	3.3	5.6	5.6
Defined benefit	(NA)	0.34	0.41	1.06	1.12	(NA)	1.5	1.6	3.8	3.8
Defined contributions	(NA)	0.41	0.45	0.50	0.53	(NA)	1.8	1.7	1.8	1.8
Legally required	1.54	1.92	2.18	2.43	2.50	8.9	8.2	8.4	8.6	8.5
Social security	1.02	1.38	1.51	1.57	1.32	5.9	5.9	5.8	5.6	4.5
Federal unemployment . . .	0.03	0.03	0.03	0.03	0.03	0.2	0.1	0.1	0.1	0.1
State unemployment.	0.12	0.11	0.13	0.18	0.20	0.7	0.5	0.5	0.6	0.7
Workers compensation . . .	0.36	0.40	0.51	0.64	0.63	2.1	1.7	2.0	2.3	2.1
Other benefits [1]	0.04	0.09	0.08	0.13	0.11	0.2	0.4	0.3	0.5	0.4

NA Not available.   [1] Includes severance pay, and supplemental unemployment benefits.

Source: U.S. Bureau of Labor Statistics, *Employer Costs for Employee Compensation Historical Listing, annual, 1986–2001*, and *Employer Costs for Employee Compensation, March 2005*. See also <http://ftp.bls.gov/pub/special.requests/ocwc/ect/ecechist.pdf> (issued 19 June 2002) and <http://www.bls.gov/ncs/ect/sp/ecnr0058.pdf> (released 16 June 2005).

Manufactures   629

Table 980. **Manufacturing Industries—Employment by Industry: 1990 to 2005**

[Annual averages of monthly figures (109,487 represents 109,487,000). Covers all full- and part-time employees who worked during, or received pay for, any part of the pay period including the 12th of the month. Minus sign (–) indicates decrease. See also headnote, Table 618]

Industry	2002 NAICS code[1]	All employees (1,000)						Percent change	
		1990	2000	2002	2003	2004	2005	1990– 2000	2000– 2005
All industries	(X)	109,487	131,785	130,341	129,999	131,435	133,463	20.4	1.3
Manufacturing	31-33	17,695	17,263	15,259	14,510	14,315	14,232	–2.4	–17.6
Percent of all industries	(X)	16.2	13.1	11.7	11.2	10.9	10.7	(X)	(X)
Durable goods	(X)	10,736	10,876	9,483	8,963	8,924	8,953	1.3	–17.7
Wood products	321	541	613	555	538	550	555	13.4	–9.5
Sawmills & wood preservation	3211	148	134	121	117	119	119	–9.6	–10.9
Plywood & engineered wood products	3212	96	122	116	114	118	123	28.2	0.4
Other wood products	3219	297	357	318	306	313	313	20.1	–12.3
Nonmetallic mineral products	327	528	554	516	494	506	503	4.9	–9.2
Clay products & refractories	3271	84	82	72	66	65	61	–1.9	–25.1
Glass & glass products	3272	152	141	124	115	113	108	–7.6	–23.1
Cement & concrete products	3273	195	234	230	224	235	239	20.1	2.2
Lime, gypsum, & other nonmetallic mineral products	3279	98	97	91	89	94	94	–0.3	–3.1
Primary metals	331	689	622	509	477	467	469	–9.7	–24.6
Iron & steel mills & ferroalloy production	3311	187	135	107	102	95	96	–27.7	–29.0
Steel products from purchased steel . .	3312	70	73	63	61	61	60	4.0	–17.9
Alumina & aluminum production	3313	108	101	80	75	74	74	–7.3	–26.2
Other nonferrous metal production . . .	3314	109	96	81	74	71	72	–11.7	–25.4
Foundries	3315	214	217	178	166	165	167	1.4	–23.1
Fabricated metal products	332	1,610	1,753	1,549	1,479	1,497	1,519	8.9	–13.3
Forging & stamping	3321	128	138	113	109	110	111	7.9	–19.8
Cutlery & hand tools	3322	79	79	64	61	59	56	0.3	–29.2
Architectural & structural metals	3323	357	428	399	380	389	396	20.0	–7.5
Boilers, tanks, & shipping containers . .	3324	117	107	96	91	92	90	–9.1	–15.4
Hardware	3325	57	50	42	40	38	35	–12.8	–29.9
Spring & wire products	3326	78	81	70	64	62	59	4.3	–26.5
Machine shops & threaded products . .	3327	309	365	318	311	327	344	18.4	–5.9
Coating, engraving, & heat treating metals	3328	143	175	149	143	143	144	22.7	–17.8
Other fabricated metal products	3329	344	330	296	281	278	284	–4.0	–13.8
Machinery	333	1,408	1,455	1,230	1,149	1,143	1,162	3.3	–20.1
Agricultural, construction, & mining machinery	3331	229	222	200	188	195	209	–2.8	–5.8
Industrial machinery	3332	152	163	131	123	121	124	7.5	–23.8
Commercial & service industry machinery	3333	147	147	130	118	115	111	0.3	–24.7
HVAC & commercial refrigeration equipment	3334	165	194	167	157	153	153	17.8	–21.2
Metalworking machinery	3335	267	274	217	205	202	202	2.5	–26.1
Turbine & power transmission equipment	3336	114	111	101	94	93	97	–2.4	–12.8
Other general purpose machinery	3339	335	343	285	265	265	265	2.4	–22.8
Computer & electronic products	334	1,903	1,820	1,507	1,355	1,323	1,320	–4.3	–27.5
Computer & peripheral equipment . . .	3341	367	302	250	224	210	207	–17.8	–31.6
Communications equipment	3342	232	248	186	155	148	148	7.0	–40.2
Audio & video equipment	3343	60	52	42	37	33	32	–13.3	–38.0
Semiconductors & electronic components	3344	574	676	525	461	454	451	17.8	–33.3
Electronic instruments	3345	626	479	450	430	431	438	–23.6	–8.5
Magnetic media manufacturing & reproduction	3346	43	63	55	48	46	44	46.4	–30.1
Electrical equipment & appliances	335	633	591	497	460	445	436	–6.7	–26.3
Electric lighting equipment	3351	81	85	72	67	65	61	5.0	–27.9
Household appliances	3352	114	106	98	93	90	86	–7.0	–18.5
Electrical equipment	3353	244	210	175	160	154	152	–13.9	–27.5
Other electrical equipment & components	3359	195	191	152	140	137	136	–2.3	–28.4
Transportation equipment [2]	336	2,133	2,056	1,829	1,774	1,766	1,772	–3.6	–13.8
Motor vehicles	3361	271	291	265	265	256	250	7.4	–14.3
Motor vehicle bodies & trailers	3362	130	183	152	153	165	171	40.8	–6.6
Motor vehicle parts	3363	653	840	734	708	692	678	28.6	–19.2
Aerospace products & parts	3364	841	517	470	442	442	456	–38.5	–11.8
Ship & boat building	3366	173	153	146	146	148	153	–11.4	–0.1
Other transportation equipment	3369	35	40	39	38	38	39	14.0	–3.3

See footnotes at end of table.

U.S. Census Bureau, Statistical Abstract of the United States: 2007

Table. 980. **Manufacturing Industries—Employment by Industry: 1990 to 2005**—Con.

[Annual averages of monthly figures (109,487 represents 109,487,000). Covers all full- and part-time employees who worked during, or received pay for, any part of the pay period including the 12th of the month. See also headnote, Table 618]

Industry	2002 NAICS code [1]	All employees (1,000)						Percent change	
		1990	2000	2002	2003	2004	2005	1990– 2000	2000– 2005
Furniture & related products	337	601	680	604	573	573	563	13.0	−17.1
Household & institutional furniture. . . .	3371	398	440	400	382	385	380	10.6	−13.7
Office furniture & fixtures.	3372	156	181	151	139	135	130	16.0	−28.1
Other furniture-related products	3379	47	58	54	52	53	53	23.1	−9.1
Miscellaneous manufacturing	339	690	733	688	663	656	654	6.2	−10.8
Medical equipment & supplies	3391	288	310	308	304	301	306	7.7	−1.4
Other miscellaneous manufacturing . .	3399	403	423	380	359	354	348	5.1	−17.7
Nondurable goods	(X)	6,959	6,388	5,775	5,547	5,391	5,278	−8.2	−17.4
Food manufacturing	311	1,507	1,553	1,526	1,518	1,494	1,472	3.0	−5.2
Animal food	3111	57	55	51	50	50	48	−4.2	−12.1
Grain & oilseed milling	3112	71	65	62	62	60	60	−9.1	−7.6
Sugar & confectionery products	3113	99	92	84	85	83	78	−7.3	−15.3
Fruit & vegetable preserving & specialty.	3114	218	197	183	185	181	174	−9.5	−12.0
Dairy products	3115	145	136	137	135	131	132	−5.9	−3.2
Animal slaughtering & processing. . . .	3116	427	507	517	516	505	502	18.6	−1.1
Seafood product preparation & packaging.	3117	54	45	44	42	42	42	−17.2	−7.6
Bakeries & tortilla manufacturing	3118	292	306	297	292	285	280	4.9	−8.8
Other food products	3119	143	150	151	152	156	158	5.0	5.3
Beverages & tobacco products	312	218	207	207	200	195	192	−4.9	−7.3
Beverages	3121	173	175	174	169	166	167	1.2	−4.6
Textile mills	313	492	378	291	261	237	218	−23.1	−42.4
Fiber, yarn, & thread mills	3131	102	81	63	57	54	50	−20.5	−38.1
Fabric mills.	3132	270	192	145	130	115	104	−29.0	−45.6
Textile & fabric finishing mills	3133	120	105	83	74	68	64	−12.1	−39.8
Textile product mills.	314	209	216	195	179	176	172	3.3	−20.3
Textile furnishings mills.	3141	127	129	116	105	101	98	1.3	−24.1
Other textile product mills	3149	82	88	78	74	75	75	6.4	−14.7
Apparel.	315	929	497	360	312	286	260	−46.5	−47.6
Apparel knitting mills	3151	112	69	50	45	42	37	−38.4	−46.9
Cut & sew apparel.	3152	776	394	283	243	221	203	−49.3	−48.5
Accessories & other apparel	3159	41	34	27	24	23	21	−16.9	−39.5
Leather & allied products	316	133	69	50	45	42	40	−48.3	−42.6
Footwear	3162	83	31	22	20	19	18	−62.8	−41.7
Leather & hide tanning & finishing & other leather products.	3169	51	38	28	25	23	22	−25.0	−43.2
Paper & paper products	322	647	605	547	516	496	484	−6.6	−19.9
Pulp, paper, & paperboard mills	3221	238	191	165	151	146	141	−19.7	−26.3
Converted paper products.	3222	409	413	382	365	350	343	1.1	−16.9
Printing & related support activities.	323	809	807	707	681	663	648	−0.2	−19.7
Petroleum & coal products	324	153	123	118	114	112	113	−19.4	−8.5
Chemicals	325	1,036	980	928	906	887	879	−5.3	−10.3
Basic chemicals	3251	249	188	170	162	156	151	−24.4	−19.8
Resin, rubber, & artificial fibers.	3252	158	136	115	112	110	110	−14.2	−18.6
Agricultural chemicals.	3253	52	48	45	42	42	41	−8.8	−15.1
Pharmaceuticals & medicines	3254	207	274	291	292	290	289	32.4	5.1
Paints, coatings, & adhesives	3255	85	79	72	69	68	68	−6.6	−13.7
Soaps, cleaning compounds, and toiletries.	3256	132	129	121	119	115	116	−2.4	−10.1
Other chemical products and preparations	3259	153	127	114	111	107	105	−17.1	−17.1
Plastics & rubber products	326	826	952	848	815	806	800	15.3	−16.0
Plastics products.	3261	619	738	664	639	633	631	19.3	−14.5
Rubber products	3262	207	214	184	177	172	169	3.5	−21.0

X Not applicable. [1] Based on the North American Industry Classification System, 2002 (NAICS). See text, this section.
[2] Includes railroad rolling stock manufacturing not shown separately.

Source: U.S. Bureau of Labor Statistics, the Current Employment Statistics program Internet site <http://www.bls.gov/ces/home.htm>.

Manufactures 631

Table 981. **Average Hourly Earnings of Production Workers in Manufacturing Industries by State: 2002 to 2005**

[In dollars. Data are based on the North American Industry Classification System (NAICS) 2002 basis]

State	2002	2003	2004	2005	State	2002	2003	2004	2005
United States	15.29	15.74	16.15	16.56	Missouri	16.80	18.22	17.92	17.43
					Montana	14.43	14.02	14.87	15.61
Alabama	13.10	13.56	14.33	14.93	Nebraska	14.05	14.86	15.19	15.44
Alaska	13.24	12.18	12.01	14.22	Nevada.	14.62	14.63	14.60	14.98
Arizona	14.16	14.38	14.20	14.55	New Hampshire	14.21	14.85	15.48	15.87
Arkansas.	13.30	13.55	13.49	13.71	New Jersey	15.19	15.45	15.89	16.33
California.	14.89	15.04	15.36	15.70	New Mexico	13.41	13.19	13.13	13.66
Colorado.	15.44	16.89	16.46	15.91	New York	16.75	16.78	17.29	17.77
Connecticut	17.24	17.74	18.35	18.96	North Carolina	13.18	13.66	14.25	14.38
Delaware. . . . . . .·. . .	16.60	16.91	17.66	17.72	North Dakota	13.17	14.04	14.35	15.29
District of Columbia [1] . . .	(NA)	15.76	16.73	16.80	Ohio.	17.49	17.99	18.47	19.07
Florida	13.30	14.09	13.84	13.89	Oklahoma	14.11	14.13	14.24	14.65
Georgia	13.38	14.08	14.54	14.56	Oregon	15.06	15.20	15.34	15.49
Hawaii	13.07	12.90	13.50	14.35	Pennsylvania	14.75	14.99	15.16	15.26
Idaho	13.80	13.72	14.15	14.96	Rhode Island	12.75	12.88	13.03	13.12
Illinois.	14.99	15.20	15.61	15.84	South Carolina	14.00	14.19	14.73	15.23
Indiana	17.15	17.84	17.92	18.14	South Dakota.	12.60	13.13	13.37	13.47
Iowa.	15.32	15.70	16.17	16.25	Tennessee.	13.15	13.56	13.84	14.03
Kansas	15.98	15.83	16.57	17.14	Texas	13.93	13.94	13.98	14.03
Kentucky.	15.73	16.01	16.50	16.64	Utah.	14.12	14.90	15.38	14.71
Louisiana	17.03	16.86	16.40	17.30	Vermont	14.33	14.54	14.60	15.06
Maine.	15.55	16.28	16.97	17.28	Virginia	15.20	15.90	16.11	16.40
Maryland	15.21	15.74	16.47	16.98	Washington	18.15	18.02	18.28	18.83
Massachusetts	16.25	16.53	16.89	17.67	West Virginia	15.40	16.05	16.57	17.14
Michigan	20.51	21.20	21.51	21.50	Wisconsin	15.86	16.12	16.19	16.29
Minnesota	15.06	15.43	16.04	16.63	Wyoming	17.72	16.75	16.58	17.07
Mississippi.	12.32	12.89	13.12	13.53					

[1] Represents the Washington-Arlington-Alexandria Metropolitan Division.

Source: U.S. Bureau of Labor Statistics, the Current Employment Statistics program Internet site <http://www.bls.gov/ces/home.htm>.

Table 982. **Manufacturing Full-Time Equivalent Employees and Wages by Industry: 2000 to 2004**

[124,707 represents 124,707,000. Full-time equivalent employees equals the number of employees on full-time schedules plus the number of employees for part-time schedules converted to full-time basis]

Industry	1997 NAICS code [1]	Full-time equivalent (FTE) employees (1,000)				Wage and salary accruals per FTE worker (dol.)			
		2000	2002	2003	2004	2000	2002	2003	2004
All industries, total	(X)	124,707	123,843	123,389	124,523	38,762	40,263	41,468	43,327
Manufacturing.	31-33	16,947	15,056	14,301	14,112	44,216	44,864	46,762	48,731
Percent of all industries.	(X)	13.6	12.2	11.6	11.3	114.1	111.4	112.8	112.5
Durable goods.	(X)	10,713	9,374	8,851	8,807	47,007	47,047	49,061	51,125
Wood products.	321	606	566	544	556	30,360	31,058	32,130	33,710
Nonmetallic mineral products	327	545	511	491	495	38,879	40,481	41,676	43,002
Primary metals.	331	611	498	466	458	45,745	46,575	48,500	51,710
Fabricated metal products	332	1,738	1,527	1,458	1,469	37,688	39,147	40,340	41,967
Machinery	333	1,420	1,209	1,135	1,125	46,882	47,117	49,009	51,589
Computer and electronic products	334	1,813	1,479	1,336	1,300	71,372	66,344	70,702	74,649
Electrical equipment, appliances, and components	335	568	491	456	440	42,732	42,051	43,976	46,741
Motor vehicles, bodies and trailers, and parts	3361-3363 3364-	1,283	1,143	1,103	1,104	49,727	51,390	54,249	54,728
Other transportation equipment . . .	3365	736	673	639	647	52,612	57,952	59,946	62,546
Furniture and related products	337	664	593	560	560	29,660	30,823	32,087	33,090
Miscellaneous manufacturing	339	728	685	663	652	38,504	40,973	43,171	45,672
Nondurable goods	(X)	6,235	5,681	5,449	5,305	39,420	41,264	43,028	44,758
Food and beverage and tobacco products	311-312	1,719	1,702	1,670	1,650	34,110	35,482	36,778	37,656
Textile mills and textile product mills	313-314	584	474	436	405	29,018	30,632	31,189	32,845
Apparel and leather and allied products	315	538	408	360	332	24,769	26,365	27,988	29,790
Paper products	322	596	528	501	484	45,578	48,497	50,169	51,420
Printing and related support activities	323	767	705	671	662	38,966	38,384	39,345	40,619
Petroleum and coal products	324	120	116	114	109	62,310	65,972	68,847	76,067
Chemical products	325	968	913	893	870	60,928	62,782	66,146	69,382
Plastics and rubber products	326	942	835	805	793	35,375	37,212	38,445	39,961

[1] North American Industry Classification System, 1997; see text, this section.

Source: U.S. Bureau of Economic Analysis, *Survey of Current Business*, monthly. See also <http://www.bea.gov/bea/dn /nipaweb/SelectTable.asp?Selected=N> (released 04 August 2005).

U.S. Census Bureau, *Statistical Abstract of the United States: 2007*

Table 983. Manufactures' Shipments, Inventories, and New Orders: 1992 to 2005

[In billions of dollars (2,904 represents $2,904,000,000,000), except ratio. Based on a sample survey; for methodology, see source]

Year	Shipments	Inventories (Dec. 31)[1]	Ratio of inventories to shipments [2]	New orders	Unfilled orders (Dec. 31)
1992	2,904	370	1.57	(NA)	448
1993	3,020	371	1.51	2,960	422
1994	3,238	391	1.48	3,200	431
1995	3,480	415	1.47	3,427	443
1996	3,597	421	1.44	3,567	485
1997	3,835	433	1.39	3,780	508
1998	3,900	439	1.38	3,808	492
1999	4,032	453	1.38	3,957	501
2000	4,209	470	1.37	4,161	545
2001	4,023	437	1.34	3,917	507
2002	3,965	428	1.33	3,867	474
2003	3,972	396	1.23	3,901	470
2004	4,259	423	1.23	4,208	491
2005	4,545	440	1.19	4,550	572

NA Not available.   [1] Inventories are stated at current cost.   [2] Ratio based on December seasonally adjusted data.

Source: U.S. Census Bureau, *Current Industrial Reports, Manufacturers' Shipments, Inventories, and Orders: 1992–2005,* Series M3-1(05). See also <http://www.census.gov/prod/2006pubs/m3-05.pdf> (released May 2006) and <http://www.census.gov /indicator/www/m3/PastPressReleases/Prel/2005/dec05prel.pdf> (released 03 February 2006).

Table 984. Ratios of Manufacturers' Inventories to Shipments and Unfilled Orders to Shipments by Industry Group: 1999 to 2005

[Based on a sample survey; for methodology, see source]

Industry	1999	2000	2001	2002	2003	2004	2005
INVENTORIES-TO-SHIPMENTS RATIO							
All manufacturing industries	**1.38**	**1.37**	**1.34**	**1.33**	**1.23**	**1.23**	**1.19**
Durable goods	1.53	1.55	1.52	1.51	1.39	1.41	1.37
Wood products	1.26	1.32	1.24	1.23	1.25	1.25	1.35
Nonmetallic mineral products.	1.17	1.23	1.17	1.15	1.17	1.16	1.09
Primary metals	1.69	1.69	1.73	1.70	1.63	1.64	1.56
Fabricated metals	1.56	1.56	1.47	1.50	1.50	1.57	1.50
Machinery	2.05	2.08	2.12	2.13	1.83	1.84	1.76
Computers and electronic products.	1.42	1.54	1.49	1.52	1.39	1.41	1.30
Electrical equipment, appliances, and components	1.42	1.44	1.42	1.43	1.35	1.40	1.38
Transportation equipment	1.42	1.35	1.35	1.29	1.15	1.13	1.17
Furniture and related products.	1.35	1.35	1.25	1.25	1.17	1.21	1.15
Miscellaneous products	1.89	1.90	1.80	1.77	1.70	1.72	1.60
Nondurable goods	1.18	1.14	1.11	1.12	1.04	1.02	0.99
Food products	0.86	0.88	0.87	0.87	0.78	0.75	0.73
Beverages and tobacco products	1.55	1.51	1.48	1.63	1.65	1.59	1.65
Textile mills	1.52	1.49	1.54	1.42	1.21	1.19	1.20
Textile product mills	1.62	1.75	1.61	1.59	1.29	1.09	1.09
Apparel	1.89	1.89	1.74	1.72	1.42	1.60	1.64
Leather and allied products.	2.18	2.12	2.47	2.59	1.57	1.63	1.71
Paper products	1.16	1.11	1.11	1.11	1.10	1.11	1.08
Printing	0.81	0.80	0.75	0.77	0.76	0.79	0.79
Petroleum and coal products.	0.90	0.71	0.65	0.71	0.85	0.77	0.74
Basic chemicals	1.38	1.40	1.37	1.38	1.23	1.23	1.19
Plastics and rubber products	1.20	1.21	1.12	1.07	1.07	1.14	1.12
UNFILLED ORDERS-TO- SHIPMENTS RATIO							
All manufacturing industries	**1.51**	**1.57**	**1.53**	**1.45**	**1.43**	**1.40**	**1.52**
Durable goods	2.61	2.78	2.79	2.65	2.67	2.64	2.90
Primary metals	1.69	1.45	1.51	1.37	1.57	1.49	1.58
Fabricated metals	2.02	2.02	1.92	1.75	1.83	1.94	2.12
Machinery	2.50	2.51	2.50	2.16	2.39	2.37	2.56
Computers and electronic products.	2.93	3.07	3.22	3.29	3.45	3.38	3.29
Electrical equipment, appliances, and components	1.78	1.76	1.57	1.68	1.68	1.77	1.96
Transportation equipment	4.24	4.92	4.97	4.67	4.46	4.50	5.41
Furniture and related products.	1.27	1.14	1.10	0.93	0.99	1.04	1.02
Miscellaneous products	0.49	0.62	0.41	0.42	0.52	0.53	0.40

Source: U.S. Census Bureau, *Current Industrial Reports, Manufacturers' Shipments, Inventories, and Orders: 1992–2005,* Series M3-1(05). See also <http://www.census.gov/prod/2006pubs/m3-05.pdf> (released May 2006) and <http://www.census.gov /indicator/www/m3/PastPressReleases/Prel/2005/dec05prel.pdf> (released 03 February 2006).

Manufactures   633

Table 985. Value of Manufacturers' Shipments, Inventories, and New Orders by Industry: 1999 to 2005

[In millions of dollars (4,031,887 represents $4,031,887,000,000). Based on a sample survey; for methodology, see source. These data are on a North American Industry Classification System (NAICS) 2002 basis and not comparable to previous data, which were based on the Standard Industrial Classification system]

Industry	1999	2000	2001	2002	2003	2004	2005
SHIPMENTS							
All manufacturing industries	4,031,887	4,208,584	4,022,901	3,965,245	3,972,114	4,259,207	4,544,839
Durable goods	2,326,736	2,373,688	2,203,102	2,168,434	2,130,238	2,251,915	2,385,367
Wood products	97,311	93,669	88,550	90,120	91,240	103,420	105,030
Nonmetallic mineral products	96,153	97,329	94,460	93,755	96,349	101,870	112,321
Primary metals	156,648	156,598	137,469	137,789	136,839	178,996	194,247
Fabricated metals	257,071	268,213	258,918	257,475	244,662	259,874	275,301
Machinery	276,904	291,548	268,457	256,215	253,600	269,203	295,315
Computers and electronic products . . .	467,059	510,639	434,427	391,274	353,667	361,938	394,644
Electrical equipment, appliances, and components	118,313	125,443	116,919	105,393	101,770	104,244	112,096
Transportation equipment	676,328	639,861	613,837	634,614	645,759	659,930	666,790
Furniture and related products	72,659	75,107	70,885	72,898	76,621	80,153	87,079
Miscellaneous products	108,290	115,281	119,180	128,901	129,731	132,287	142,544
Nondurable goods	1,705,151	1,834,896	1,819,799	1,796,811	1,841,876	2,007,292	2,159,472
Food products	426,001	435,229	456,692	467,353	482,815	511,450	532,496
Beverages and tobacco products	106,920	111,692	117,422	104,579	106,873	112,270	114,800
Textile mills	54,306	52,112	45,141	43,152	42,557	40,258	36,012
Textile product mills	32,689	33,654	34,165	34,933	30,827	33,254	34,326
Apparel	62,305	60,339	56,545	53,201	40,624	33,495	33,879
Leather and allied products	9,653	9,647	8,108	8,718	6,003	5,757	5,630
Paper products	156,915	165,298	159,150	157,834	149,271	153,969	158,053
Printing	101,536	104,396	99,303	96,045	92,191	93,193	89,822
Petroleum and coal products	162,620	235,134	222,356	211,910	237,010	312,884	404,591
Basic chemicals	420,321	449,159	442,790	441,494	477,360	528,215	553,657
Plastics and rubber products	171,885	178,236	178,127	177,592	176,345	182,547	196,206
INVENTORIES (Dec. 31)							
All manufacturing industries	452,803	470,084	436,622	428,086	395,920	423,197	439,763
Durable goods	288,362	298,232	271,597	264,010	239,411	256,144	264,976
Wood products	10,289	10,329	9,146	9,150	9,398	10,663	11,776
Nonmetallic mineral products	9,279	9,799	9,009	8,746	9,114	9,570	9,925
Primary metals	22,309	22,199	19,887	19,603	18,622	24,410	25,295
Fabricated metals	32,800	34,085	31,070	31,368	29,844	33,087	33,631
Machinery	46,050	49,151	45,966	43,964	37,467	39,914	42,026
Computers and electronic products . . .	52,838	63,024	52,001	47,614	39,309	41,073	41,131
Electrical equipment, appliances, and components	13,510	14,505	13,307	12,112	11,027	11,694	12,354
Transportation equipment	76,781	69,199	66,633	65,631	59,490	59,488	62,280
Furniture and related products	7,983	8,261	7,216	7,399	7,316	7,878	8,111
Miscellaneous products	16,523	17,680	17,362	18,423	17,824	18,367	18,447
Nondurable goods	164,441	171,852	165,025	164,076	156,509	167,053	174,787
Food products	30,650	31,882	33,273	34,061	31,223	31,680	32,479
Beverages and tobacco products	14,167	14,831	14,696	14,335	14,765	14,961	15,779
Textile mills	6,648	6,243	5,586	4,906	4,147	3,854	3,473
Textile product mills	4,219	4,698	4,401	4,441	3,185	2,886	2,991
Apparel	9,454	9,170	7,889	7,322	4,596	4,261	4,406
Leather and allied products	1,675	1,634	1,603	1,814	759	757	780
Paper products	15,034	15,205	14,604	14,414	13,448	14,083	14,008
Printing	6,394	6,445	5,811	5,737	5,508	5,765	5,550
Petroleum and coal products	11,375	12,840	11,179	11,614	15,466	18,675	23,303
Basic chemicals	47,806	51,623	49,567	49,768	47,902	53,052	53,916
Plastics and rubber products	17,019	17,781	16,416	15,664	15,510	17,079	18,102
NEW ORDERS							
All manufacturing industries	3,957,242	4,161,472	3,917,225	3,866,899	3,900,807	4,208,065	4,549,636
Durable goods	2,252,091	2,326,576	2,097,426	2,070,088	2,058,931	2,200,773	2,390,164
Wood products	97,311	93,669	88,550	90,120	91,240	103,420	105,030
Nonmetallic mineral products	96,153	97,329	94,460	93,755	96,349	101,870	112,321
Primary metals	156,968	153,625	135,902	136,421	139,030	183,267	197,739
Fabricated metals	258,116	270,021	255,179	253,809	244,335	264,364	281,683
Machinery	278,277	294,608	263,754	246,231	258,145	271,736	304,955
Computers and electronic products . . .	402,216	436,415	352,220	316,275	281,435	289,773	324,505
Electrical equipment, appliances, and components	120,774	126,196	113,930	104,845	101,309	105,329	114,951
Transportation equipment	660,215	663,326	605,854	627,219	639,000	667,728	720,083
Furniture and related products	73,393	74,532	70,270	72,102	77,255	80,770	87,452
Miscellaneous products	108,668	116,855	117,307	129,311	130,833	132,516	141,445
Nondurable goods	1,705,151	1,834,896	1,819,799	1,796,811	1,841,876	2,007,292	2,159,472

Source: U.S. Census Bureau, Current Industrial Reports, Manufacturers' Shipments, Inventories, and Orders: 1992–2005, Series M3-1(05). See also <http://www.census.gov/prod/2006pubs/m3-05.pdf> (released May 2006) and <http://www.census.gov /indicator/www/m3/PastPressReleases/Prel/2005/dec05prel.pdf> (released 03 February 2006).

634   Manufactures

Table 986. Value of Manufactures' Shipments, Inventories, and New Orders by Market Grouping: 1999 to 2005

[In millions of dollars (4,031,887 represents $4,031,887,000,000). Based on a sample survey; for methodology, see source]

Market grouping	1999	2000	2001	2002	2003	2004	2005
SHIPMENTS							
All manufacturing industries	4,031,887	4,208,584	4,022,901	3,965,245	3,972,114	4,259,207	4,544,839
Consumer goods	1,438,519	1,500,532	1,499,818	1,499,041	1,560,671	1,679,985	1,793,004
Consumer durable goods	426,337	391,463	377,514	395,817	416,418	419,372	422,668
Consumer nondurable goods.	1,012,182	1,109,069	1,122,304	1,103,224	1,144,253	1,260,613	1,370,336
Aircraft and parts	120,242	111,658	118,333	110,504	99,477	102,780	119,883
Defense aircraft and parts.	27,719	24,560	27,848	34,538	37,584	40,084	39,897
Nondefense aircraft and parts	92,523	87,098	90,485	75,966	61,893	62,696	79,986
Construction materials and supplies.	434,138	444,812	430,226	432,419	426,625	459,478	488,096
Motor vehicles and parts	498,716	471,180	439,905	463,808	485,921	494,622	481,835
Computers and related products	113,162	110,242	92,595	84,835	68,768	64,894	78,405
Information technology industries.	374,384	399,751	357,327	314,988	277,281	283,889	307,279
Nondefense capital goods	768,799	808,345	731,280	674,464	631,666	654,931	730,842
Excluding aircraft	713,042	757,617	680,413	633,454	600,469	624,559	683,934
Defense capital goods.	70,955	67,051	72,946	78,434	83,825	91,107	90,677
Durables excluding capital goods	1,486,982	1,498,292	1,398,876	1,415,536	1,414,747	1,505,877	1,563,848
INVENTORIES (Dec. 31)							
All manufacturing industries	452,803	470,084	436,622	428,086	395,920	423,197	439,763
Consumer goods	123,218	128,148	124,225	126,144	120,753	126,882	131,725
Consumer durable goods	26,307	26,108	23,506	24,805	23,824	25,010	25,384
Consumer nondurable goods.	96,911	102,040	100,719	101,339	96,929	101,872	106,341
Aircraft and parts	42,599	36,091	35,347	34,220	31,790	30,317	31,922
Defense aircraft and parts.	11,052	9,423	9,153	9,387	10,227	10,580	11,405
Nondefense aircraft and parts	31,547	26,668	26,194	24,833	21,563	19,737	20,517
Construction materials and supplies.	47,510	49,389	45,034	46,201	44,546	48,890	51,168
Motor vehicles and parts	22,102	22,283	19,773	20,428	20,686	21,837	22,445
Computers and related products	7,963	8,350	7,035	6,126	3,662	3,971	3,974
Information technology industries.	44,375	50,795	42,259	37,905	33,715	35,553	34,758
Nondefense capital goods	121,653	127,162	115,012	105,939	95,757	98,275	102,346
Excluding aircraft	96,254	106,669	95,193	88,050	78,880	83,672	86,644
Defense capital goods.	19,754	17,153	17,788	17,940	15,054	14,966	14,861
Durables excluding capital goods	146,955	153,917	138,797	140,131	128,600	142,903	147,769
NEW ORDERS							
All manufacturing industries	3,957,242	4,161,472	3,917,225	3,866,899	3,900,807	4,208,065	4,549,636
Consumer goods	1,440,903	1,501,810	1,498,197	1,498,851	1,561,641	1,680,496	1,791,838
Consumer durable goods	428,721	392,741	375,893	395,627	417,388	419,883	421,502
Consumer nondurable goods.	1,012,182	1,109,069	1,122,304	1,103,224	1,144,253	1,260,613	1,370,336
Aircraft and parts	107,336	130,575	111,611	103,304	90,126	102,561	175,721
Defense aircraft and parts.	25,717	31,326	36,587	39,414	40,274	30,988	36,575
Nondefense aircraft and parts	81,619	99,249	75,024	63,890	49,852	71,573	139,146
Construction materials and supplies.	435,034	446,792	426,392	431,760	425,288	462,478	494,225
Motor vehicles and parts	499,527	468,470	438,837	464,201	487,464	495,364	483,467
Computers and related products	114,481	107,656	92,137	85,740	67,235	63,530	78,173
Information technology industries.	389,160	409,500	347,051	308,181	272,614	286,039	314,559
Nondefense capital goods	772,703	831,335	698,785	647,124	627,150	664,570	805,784
Excluding aircraft	728,089	767,754	663,396	615,525	604,513	623,449	698,118
Defense capital goods.	67,900	79,598	82,723	78,180	87,295	97,156	82,560
Durables excluding capital goods	1,411,488	1,415,643	1,315,918	1,344,784	1,344,486	1,439,047	1,501,820

Source: U.S. Census Bureau, *Current Industrial Reports, Manufacturers' Shipments, Inventories, and Orders: 1992–2005,* Series M3-1(05). See also <http://www.census.gov/prod/2006pubs/m3-05.pdf> (released May 2006) and <http://www.census.gov /indicator/www/m3/PastPressReleases/Prel/2005/dec05prel.pdf> (released 03 February 2006).

Table 987. Finances and Profits of Manufacturing Corporations: 1990 to 2005

[In billions of dollars (2,811 represents $2,811,000,000,000). Data exclude estimates for corporations with less than $250,000 in assets at time of sample selection. For 1990–2001, based on Standard Industrial Classification system; thereafter, based on North American Industry Classification System (NAICS). See text, Section 15. See Table 773 for individual industry data]

Item	1990	1995	1999	2000	2001 [1]	2001 [2]	2002 [2]	2003 [2]	2004 [2]	2005 [2]
Net sales.	2,811	3,528	4,149	4,548	4,308	4,295	4,217	4,397	4,934	5,466
Net operating profit	173	268	317	348	185	186	225	237	320	353
Net profit:										
Before taxes	160	274	355	381	82	83	196	306	447	524
After taxes	112	198	258	275	36	36	135	237	348	406
Cash dividends.	62	81	104	132	102	103	106	115	143	173
Net income retained in business . .	49	117	154	143	-67	-66	28	122	205	233

[1] Based on Standard Industrial Classification system. [2] Based on the North American Industry Classification System; see Text, Section 15.

Source: U.S. Census Bureau, *Quarterly Financial Report for Manufacturing, Mining, and Trade Corporations.* See also <http://www.census.gov/prod/2006pubs/qfr05q4.pdf> (released April 2006).

Manufactures 635

Table 988. **Manufacturing Corporations—Assets and Profits by Asset Size: 1990 to 2005**

[In millions of dollars (2,629,458 represents $2,629,458,000,000). Corporations and assets as of end of 4th quarter; profits for entire year. Through 2000, based on Standard Industrial Classification (SIC) code; beginning 2001, based on North American Industry Classification System (NAICS). For corporations above a certain asset value based on complete canvass. The asset value for complete canvass was raised in 1988 to $50 million and in 1995 to $250 million. Asset sizes less than these values are sampled, except as noted. For details regarding methodology, see source for first quarter, 1988. Minus sign (–) indicates loss]

Year	Total [1]	Asset-size class						
		Under $10 mil. [1]	$10– $25 mil.	$25– $50 mil.	$50– $100 mil.	$100– $250 mil.	$250– $1 bil.	$1 bil. and over
Assets:								
1990......	2,629,458	142,498	74,477	55,914	72,554	123,967	287,512	1,872,536
1991......	2,688,422	140,056	70,567	58,549	72,694	127,748	295,743	1,923,066
1992......	2,798,625	143,766	70,446	65,718	75,967	132,742	302,287	2,007,698
1993......	2,904,869	149,763	72,854	61,243	81,389	134,388	317,774	2,087,457
1994......	3,080,231	148,751	81,505	66,405	82,116	138,950	358,100	2,204,404
1995......	3,345,229	155,618	87,011	68,538	87,262	159,133	370,263	2,417,403
1996......	3,574,407	163,928	87,096	69,722	93,205	156,702	398,651	2,605,102
1997......	3,746,797	167,921	87,398	76,034	85,186	157,130	397,559	2,775,570
1998......	3,967,309	170,068	87,937	69,627	86,816	148,060	419,153	2,985,647
1999......	4,382,814	170,058	85,200	67,352	97,810	138,143	398,881	3,425,370
2000......	4,852,106	171,666	85,482	72,122	90,866	149,714	389,537	3,892,720
2001 [2].....	4,747,789	169,701	84,664	67,493	88,088	131,617	393,752	3,812,474
2002......	4,823,219	166,191	82,369	62,654	81,667	134,821	407,423	3,888,095
2003......	5,162,852	161,462	80,681	62,592	77,205	126,826	392,192	4,261,894
2004......	5,538,113	163,070	80,085	71,674	81,741	126,950	414,144	4,600,447
Net profit: [3]								
1990......	110,128	8,527	5,160	2,769	2,661	3,525	7,110	80,377
1991......	66,407	6,820	4,271	2,564	1,704	1,707	5,027	44,316
1992......	22,085	9,567	4,748	3,245	3,034	4,553	5,919	–8,979
1993......	83,156	11,195	5,415	3,439	3,218	3,584	4,555	51,750
1994......	174,874	14,131	7,057	4,072	4,996	6,745	14,626	123,250
1995......	198,151	13,224	5,668	3,767	5,771	7,000	16,549	146,172
1996......	224,869	15,802	6,872	4,266	5,664	7,935	16,059	168,271
1997......	244,505	17,948	8,383	4,153	4,675	7,074	18,433	183,836
1998......	234,386	18,350	6,421	3,790	4,681	5,610	14,364	181,170
1999......	257,805	17,398	7,618	3,504	4,798	4,795	12,756	206,934
2000......	275,313	16,578	6,820	3,403	2,742	3,510	15,121	227,136
2001 [2].....	36,168	8,387	3,366	–408	403	–543	–6,782	31,746
2002......	134,686	10,003	2,784	807	1,699	3,356	–1,227	117,262
2003......	237,041	9,821	3,374	2,005	2,256	2,973	4,115	212,497
2004......	348,160	14,973	5,745	3,828	3,080	5,140	12,787	302,571
2005......	406,359	17,436	6,464	3,995	3,928	8,087	16,737	349,711

[1] Excludes estimates for corporations with less than $250,000 in assets at time of sample selection.   [2] Beginning 2001, data reported on a NAICS basis.   [3] After taxes.

Source: U.S. Census Bureau, *Quarterly Financial Report for Manufacturing, Mining, and Trade Corporations.* See also <http://www.census.gov/prod/2006pubs/qfr05q4.pdf> (released April 2006).

Table 989. **Manufacturing Corporations—Selected Finances: 1990 to 2005**

[In billions of dollars (2,811 represents $2,811,000,000,000). Data are not necessarily comparable from year to year due to changes in accounting procedures, industry classifications, sampling procedures, etc.; for detail, see source. Through 2000, based on Standard Industrial Classification code; beginning 2001, based on North American Industry Classification System (NAICS)]

Year	All manufacturing corps.			Durable goods industries			Nondurable goods industries		
		Profits [1]			Profits [1]			Profits [1]	
	Sales	Before taxes	After taxes	Sales	Before taxes	After taxes	Sales	Before taxes	After taxes
1990	2,811	158	110	1,357	57	41	1,454	101	69
1991	2,761	99	66	1,304	14	7	1,457	85	59
1992 [2]	2,890	31	22	1,390	–34	–24	1,500	65	46
1993	3,015	118	83	1,490	39	27	1,525	79	56
1994	3,256	244	175	1,658	121	87	1,598	123	88
1995	3,528	275	198	1,808	131	94	1,721	144	104
1996	3,758	307	225	1,942	147	106	1,816	160	119
1997	3,922	331	244	2,076	167	121	1,847	164	123
1998	3,949	315	234	2,169	175	128	1,781	140	107
1999	4,149	355	258	2,314	199	140	1,835	157	117
2000	4,548	381	275	2,457	191	132	2,091	190	144
2001 [3]	4,295	83	36	2,321	–69	–76	1,974	152	112
2002	4,217	196	135	2,261	45	21	1,955	149	113
2003	4,397	306	237	2,283	118	88	2,114	188	149
2004	4,934	447	348	2,537	200	157	2,397	248	192
2005	5,466	524	406	2,722	209	160	2,744	315	246

[1] Beginning 1998, profits before and after income taxes reflect inclusion of minority stockholders' interest in net income before and after income taxes.   [2] Data for 1992 (most significantly 1992: I qtr.) reflect the early adoption of Financial Accounting Standards Board Statement 106 (Employer's Accounting for Post-Retirement Benefits Other Than Pensions) by a large number of companies during the fourth quarter of 1992. Data for 1993: I qtr. also reflect adoption of Statement 106. Corporations must show the cumulative effect of a change in accounting principle in the first quarter of the year in which the change is adopted.   [3] Beginning 2001, data reported on a NAICS basis.

Source: U.S. Census Bureau, *Quarterly Financial Report for Manufacturing, Mining and Trade Corporations.* See also <http://www.census.gov/prod/2006pubs/qfr05q4.pdf> (released April 2006).

Table 990. **Tobacco Products—Summary: 1990 to 2005**

[(**710 represents 710,000,000,000**). Production data are for calendar years. Excludes cigars produced in customs bonded manufacturing warehouses. 2005 data are preliminary]

Item	Unit	1990	1995	1999	2000	2001	2002	2003	2004	2005
PRODUCTION										
Cigarettes, total	Billions	710	747	607	565	562	532	499	494	489
Nonfilter tip	Billions	23	15	8	7	6	5	6	5	(NA)
Filter tip	Billions	687	732	599	558	556	527	494	488	(NA)
Cigars	Billions	1.9	2.1	2.9	2.8	3.7	3.8	4.0	4.4	3.7
Tobacco [1]	Mil. lb..	142	131	133	133	130	133	137	135	143
Smoking	Mil. lb..	16	12	15	14	13	16	18	16	17
Chewing tobacco	Mil. lb..	73	63	51	49	47	45	43	39	39
Snuff	Mil. lb..	53	60	67	70	70	73	76	79	87
EXPORTS										
Cigarettes.	Bil. cigarettes . .	164.3	231.1	151.4	147.9	133.9	127.4	121.5	118.7	113.1
Cigars	Bil. cigars.	72.0	94.0	84.0	113.0	124.0	122.7	130.2	171.5	183.4
Smoking tobacco	Bil. lb.	0.8	0.3	1.6	0.5	11.0	7.9	0.7	1.3	1.2
IMPORTS										
Cigarettes.	Bil. cigarettes . .	1.4	3.0	8.7	11.3	14.7	20.8	23.1	22.7	18.1
Cigars	Bil. cigars.	111.0	195.0	463.4	497.0	543.4	413.5	508.0	615.6	651.7
Smoking tobacco	Bil. lb.	2.9	4.2	4.3	4.2	1.9	2.1	2.1	1.5	3.0
CONSUMPTION										
Tobacco products per person [2]	Lb. [3]	5.6	4.8	4.2	4.1	4.3	4.2	4.0	3.9	3.7
Cigarettes per person [2]	1,000	2.8	2.5	2.1	2.1	2.1	2.0	1.9	1.8	1.7
EXPENDITURES										
Consumer expenditures, total	Bil. dol.	43.8	48.7	72.1	77.5	82.9	88.2	86.8	86.3	88.9
Cigarettes	Bil. dol.	41.6	45.8	68.3	72.9	77.8	82.8	81.1	80.0	82.0
Cigars	Bil. dol.	0.7	1.0	1.8	1.8	2.1	2.2	2.5	2.9	3.2
Other	Bil. dol.	1.5	2.5	2.7	2.7	3.0	3.1	3.2	3.2	3.7

NA Not available.   [1] Smoking and chewing tobaccos and snuff output.   [2] Based on estimated population, 18 years old and over, as of July 1, including Armed Forces abroad.   [3] Unstemmed processing weight equivalent.
Source: U.S. Dept. of Agriculture, Economic Research Service, *Tobacco Situation and Outlook*, quarterly. See also <http://usda.mannlib.cornell.edu/usda/ers/TBS/2000s/2006/TBS-04-28-2006.pdf> (released 25 April 2006).

Table 991. **Cotton, Wool, and Manmade Fibers—Consumption by End-Use: 1990 to 2004**

[**14,011 represents 14,011,000,000**. Represents products manufactured by U.S. mills. Excludes glass fiber]

Year	Cotton			Wool			Manufactured fibers					
										Artificial		Synthetic	
	Total (mil. lb.)	Total (mil. lb.)	Percent of end-use	Total (mil. lb.)	Total (mil. lb.)	Percent of end-use	Total (mil. lb.)	Total (mil. lb.)	Percent of end-use	Total (mil. lb.)	Percent of end-use	Total (mil. lb.)	Percent of end-use
Total:												
1990.	14,011	4,699	33.5	185	1.3	9,127	65.1	599	4.3	8,528	60.9
2000.	17,904	5,128	28.6	132	0.7	12,645	70.6	305	1.7	12,340	68.9
2001.	16,231	4,619	28.5	116	0.7	11,496	70.8	282	1.7	11,214	69.1
2002.	15,715	4,102	26.1	96	0.6	11,518	73.3	250	1.6	11,268	71.7
2003.	14,816	3,512	23.7	99	0.7	11,205	75.6	225	1.5	10,980	74.1
2004.	13,948	2,726	19.5	93	0.7	11,129	79.8	228	1.6	10,911	78.2
Apparel:												
1990.	5,204	2,897	55.7	118	2.3	2,189	42.1	287	5.5	1,902	36.5
2000.	6,039	3,089	51.2	79	1.3	2,871	47.5	154	2.5	2,717	45.0
2001.	5,335	2,648	49.6	73	1.4	2,613	49.0	135	2.5	2,479	46.5
2002.	4,733	2,232	47.2	64	1.4	2,437	51.5	113	2.4	2,325	49.1
2003.	4,133	1,912	46.3	65	1.6	2,157	52.2	93	2.3	2,064	49.9
2004.	3,447	1,420	41.2	62	1.8	1,965	57.0	76	2.2	1,889	54.8
Home textiles:												
1990.	2,235	1,325	59.3	14	0.6	896	40.1	104	4.7	792	35.4
2000.	2,862	1,644	57.4	15	0.5	1,203	42.0	61	2.1	1,142	39.9
2001.	2,678	1,587	59.3	13	0.5	1,079	40.3	56	2.1	1,022	38.2
2002.	2,504	1,492	59.6	10	0.4	1,002	40.0	49	2.0	953	38.0
2003.	2,173	1,278	58.8	12	0.6	883	40.6	43	2.0	840	38.7
2004.	1,778	974	54.8	10	0.6	794	44.7	40	2.3	753	42.4
Floor coverings:												
1990.	3,075	18	0.6	21	0.7	3,036	98.7	–	–	3,036	98.7
2000.	4,519	31	0.7	25	0.6	4,464	98.8	–	–	4,463	98.8
2001.	4,059	30	0.7	20	0.5	4,009	98.8	–	–	4,009	98.8
2002.	4,261	30	0.7	14	0.3	4,218	99.0	–	–	4,218	99.0
2003.	4,377	29	0.7	14	0.3	4,334	99.0	–	–	4,334	99.0
2004.	4,481	29	0.6	14	0.3	4,438	99.0	–	–	4,438	99.0
Industrial: [1]												
1990.	2,965	313	10.6	10	0.3	2,642	89.1	179	6.0	2,463	83.1
2000.	4,484	364	8.1	13	0.3	4,107	91.6	90	2.0	4,017	89.6
2001.	4,160	354	8.5	10	0.2	3,796	91.3	91	2.2	3,705	89.1
2002.	4,216	347	8.2	8	0.2	3,861	91.6	88	2.1	3,773	89.5
2003.	4,133	293	7.1	8	0.2	3,832	92.7	89	2.1	3,743	90.6
2004.	4,242	303	7.1	7	0.2	3,932	92.7	112	2.6	3,831	90.3

– Represents or rounds to zero.   [1] Includes consumer-type products.
Source: Fiber Economics Bureau, Inc., Arlington, VA, *Fiber Organon*, monthly (copyright).

Manufactures   637

Table 992. Broadwoven and Knit Fabrics—Shipments and Foreign Trade: 2004

[2,106,257 represents 2,106,257,000. Fabric blends as shown in the report are reported based on the chief weight of the fiber; whereas, fabrics blends as shown for imports are based on the chief value of the fiber]

Product description	Manufac-turers' ship-ments (quantity) (1,000 sq. meters)	Imports for consumption Quantity (1,000 sq. meters)	Imports for consumption Value [1] ($1,000)	Percent imports to manufac-turers' ship-ments	Exports of domestic merchandise Quantity (1,000 sq. meters)	Exports of domestic merchandise Value ($1,000)	Percent exports to manufac-turers' ship-ments
BROADWOVEN FABRICS							
Cotton fabrics [2]	2,106,257	1,463,642	1,651,717	69.5	567,112	1,095,264	26.9
Manmade fiber fabrics	7,076,464	1,156,673	1,364,501	16.3	629,473	1,237,438	8.9
Silk fabrics	(D)	40,462	298,456	(D)	4,379	21,006	(D)
Wool fabrics	15,910	21,662	199,852	136.2	8,998	47,047	56.6
KNIT FABRICS							
Total	**432,333**	**182,681**	**1,120,374**	**42.3**	**272,322**	**1,625,238**	**63.0**
Pile fabrics	35,885	31,421	190,124	87.6	17,472	162,083	48.7
Elastic fabric	26,413	34,527	345,550	(S)	41,070	389,721	(S)
Other warp knit fabrics	50,017	28,242	173,883	56.5	11,849	104,934	23.7
Other narrow knit fabrics	9,890	1,058	11,744	10.7	3,649	30,150	36.9
Other knit fabrics	310,128	87,434	399,072	28.2	198,282	938,350	63.9

D Data withheld to avoid disclosing figures for individual companies.   S Does not meet publication standards.

Source: U.S. Census Bureau, *Current Industrial Reports*, Series MQ313 and MA313K, annual. See also<http://www.census.gov/industry/1/mq313t045.pdf> (issued June 2005)<http://www.census.gov/industry/1/ma313k04.pdf> (issued May 2005).

Table 993. Footwear—Consumption, Production, and Imports: 1990 to 2004

[In millions of pairs of shoes (1,305.2 represents 1,305,200,000), except as indicated]

Item	1990	2000	2003	2004	Item	1990	2000	2003	2004
CONSUMPTION					Other.	(NA)	2.0	0.2	0.2
					Rubber or fabric	(NA)	20.6	11.3	8.5
Consumption, total .	**1,305.2**	**1,851.5**	**2,007.9**	**2,159.0**	Plastic or protective	(NA)	7.2	6.2	6.8
Production	184.6	86.6	39.8	35.2	IMPORTS				
Imports	1,120.7	1,764.9	1,968.1	2,123.8	Men's	102.1	200.5	213.3	220.5
Percent of consumption. .	85.9	95.3	98.0	98.4	Men's work	13.2	24.1	26.5	27.8
PRODUCTION					Women's	415.2	587.2	730.5	814.4
Men's	(NA)	24.0	12.7	12.1	Juveniles'.	132.8	228.3	251.5	259.8
Men's work	(NA)	9.2	8.1	8.9	Athletic	212.3	288.1	345.2	361.8
Women's	(NA)	9.8	5.2	4.7	Slippers	17.9	76.3	84.5	124.9
Juveniles'.	(NA)	1.4	0.3	0.2	Other.	3.9	9.9	9.6	9.6
Athletic	(NA)	0.3	0.1	0.1	Rubber or fabric	199.2	317.3	225.7	188.4
Slippers	(NA)	31.2	3.9	2.7	Plastic or protective	23.9	10.4	18.3	19.2

NA Not available.

Source: American Apparel and Footwear Association, Arlington, VA, *Shoe Stats*, annual. See also <http://www.apparelandfootwear.org/>.

Table 994. Pharmaceutical Preparations—Value of Shipments: 1990 to 2005

[In millions of dollars (33,954 represents 33,954,000,000]

Product description	NAICS product code[1]	1990	2000	2002	2003	2004	2005
Pharmaceutical preparations, except biologicals	(X)	**33,954**	**79,262**	**100,741**	**107,561**	**109,852**	**116,301**
Affecting neoplasms, endocrine systems, and metabolic disease.	3254121100	2,743	9,784	17,499	20,065	20,789	23,341
Acting on the central nervous system and sense organs.	3254124100	7,219	18,508	24,345	24,759	25,001	25,044
Acting on the cardiovascular system	3254127100	4,815	8,993	10,339	9,671	10,224	10,246
Acting on the respiratory system	325412A100	3,724	10,179	12,504	13,758	15,148	16,216
Acting on the digestive system	325412D100	4,840	10,046	13,373	15,052	15,252	16,776
Acting on the skin.	325412G100	1,558	2,941	2,844	3,083	3,283	3,245
Vitamin, nutrient, and hematinic preps.	325412L100	2,588	5,676	6,029	6,877	6,683	6,827
Affecting parasitic and infective disease . . .	325412P100	5,411	11,037	11,337	11,848	10,819	11,244
Pharmaceutical preps. for veterinary use . .	325412T100	1,057	2,096	2,471	2,449	2,653	3,362

X Not applicable.   [1] Based on the North American Industry Classification System, 1997; see text Section 15.

Source: U.S. Census Bureau, 1990, *Current Industrial Reports*, Series MA28G; thereafter, MA325G(01)-1. See also <http://www.census.gov/industry/1/ma325g05.pdf> (released June 2006).

Table 995. Inorganic Chemicals and Fertilizers—Production: 1995 to 2004

[17,402 represents 17,402,000]

Product description	Unit	1995	2000	2001	2002	2003	2004
INORGANIC FERTILIZERS							
Ammonia, synthetic anhydrous	1,000 sh. tons	17,402	15,809	12,227	13,863	11,130	12,058
Ammonium nitrate, original solution	1,000 sh. tons	8,489	7,979	6,431	7,096	6,328	7,229
Ammonium sulfate	1,000 sh. tons	2,647	2,808	2,588	2,945	2,871	3,005
Urea (100%)	1,000 sh. tons	8,117	7,682	6,702	7,758	6,375	6,344
Nitric acid (100%)	1,000 sh. tons	8,839	8,708	7,074	7,651	7,189	7,129
Phosphoric acid (100% P2O5)	1,000 sh. tons	13,134	12,492	11,546	12,289	12,537	12,693
Sulfuric acid, gross (100%)	1,000 sh. tons	47,519	43,643	40,064	39,760	41,144	41,920
Superphosphates and other fertilizer materials (100% P2O5)	1,000 sh. tons	10,364	8,899	8,109	8,756	8,837	8,737
INORGANIC CHEMICALS							
Chlorine gas	1,000 metric tons . .	12,395	14,000	11,489	11,438	10,361	12,329
Sodium hydroxide, total liquid	1,000 metric tons . . .	11,408	11,523	9,813	9,461	8,796	9,620
Potassium hydroxide liquid	1,000 metric tons . . .	(D)	539	465	470	471	525
Finished sodium bicarbonate	1,000 metric tons . . .	520	536	513	535	540	579
Titanium dioxide, composite and pure	1,000 metric tons . . .	1,382	1,547	1,327	1,409	1,422	(NA)
Hydrochloric acid	1,000 metric tons . . .	3,904	4,717	3,970	4,028	(S)	5,302
Aluminum oxide	1,000 metric tons . . .	4,764	(D)	2,863	(D)	(D)	(D)
Aluminum sulfate (commercial)	1,000 metric tons . . .	1,144	1,076	1,020	1,054	965	992
Sodium chlorate	1,000 metric tons . . .	617	940	792	721	669	677
Sodium phosphate tripoly	1,000 metric tons . . .	(D)	(D)	(D)	(D)	(D)	(D)
Sodium silicates [1]	1,000 metric tons . . .	1,203	1,136	1,070	1,054	1,074	1,114
Sodium metasilicates	1,000 metric tons . . .	93	72	63	58	61	58
Sodium sulfate	1,000 metric tons . . .	(D)	509	76	74	89	86
Carbon activated [2]	1,000 metric tons . . .	156	166	(S)	(D)	112	(D)
Hydrogen peroxide	1,000 metric tons . . .	355	1,083	(S)	(S)	340	357
Phosphorous, oxychloride, and trichlorde	1,000 metric tons . . .	226	(D)	(D)	(D)	(D)	(D)

D Withheld to avoid disclosing data for individual companies.   NA Not available.   S Does not meet publication standards.
[1] Other than metasilicates.   [2] Granular and pulverized.

Source: U.S. Census Bureau, Current Industrial Reports, Series MAQ325A, and MA325B, annual. See also <http://www.census.gov/industry/1/mq325a045.pdf> (released September 2005) and <http://www.census.gov/industry/1/mq325b045.pdf> (released September 2005).

Table 996. Aluminum—Supply, Shipments, and Foreign Trade: 1990 to 2005

[In millions of pounds (17,334 represents 17,334,000,000)]

Item	1990	1995	2000	2001	2002	2003	2004	2005
SUPPLY								
Aluminum supply, total	**17,334**	**20,425**	**23,586**	**20,071**	**21,118**	**21,146**	**22,282**	**23,571**
Primary production	8,925	7,441	8,087	5,812	5,964	5,962	5,549	5,468
Recovery from scrap	5,276	7,030	7,606	6,543	6,453	6,215	6,669	6,592
Imports of ingot and mill products	3,133	5,956	7,893	7,687	8,702	8,969	10,064	11,510
Aluminum net shipments, total [1] . . .	**17,188**	**21,019**	**24,496**	**22,802**	**23,607**	**23,391**	**24,952**	**25,595**
PRODUCT								
Mill products, total	13,013	15,716	17,676	15,434	15,700	15,691	17,123	17,784
Sheet, plate, and foil	9,297	11,168	12,116	10,376	10,569	10,561	11,461	11,817
Rod, bar, and wire	370	534	690	571	591	576	631	660
Electrical conductor	542	566	681	675	708	693	766	807
Extruded shapes and tube	2,546	3,102	3,792	3,447	3,457	3,468	3,821	4,048
Powder and paste	106	108	142	142	142	146	155	144
Forgings and impacts	152	238	255	223	233	247	289	308
Ingot for castings and other [2]	4,175	5,303	6,820	7,368	7,907	7,700	7,829	7,811
MARKET								
Domestic, total	14,637	18,152	21,680	20,506	21,211	21,403	22,904	23,113
Building and construction	2,663	2,679	3,204	3,288	3,437	3,432	3,692	3,693
Transportation	3,205	5,749	7,947	7,033	7,523	7,804	8,509	8,683
Consumer durables	1,122	1,369	1,692	1,421	1,504	1,498	1,585	1,561
Electrical	1,309	1,395	1,704	1,507	1,491	1,433	1,583	1,657
Machinery and equipment	992	1,257	1,496	1,476	1,427	1,452	1,610	1,664
Containers and packaging	4,772	5,088	4,992	4,961	4,979	4,941	5,098	5,115
Other	574	615	645	820	850	843	827	740
Exports	2,551	2,867	2,816	2,296	2,396	1,988	2,048	2,482
FOREIGN TRADE [3]								
Exports	3,753	3,846	4,100	3,734	3,746	3,662	4,416	5,629
Imports	3,718	6,899	9,358	8,828	9,679	9,884	11,221	12,607

[1] Statistics on shipments and markets for 1990–2000 represent total U.S. producer's shipments plus imports by consumers. Figures for 2001–2005 include Canada.   [2] Net ingot for foundry castings, export and destructive uses.   [3] U.S. imports and exports of aluminum ingot, mill products, and scrap.

Source: The Aluminum Association, Inc., Washington, DC, *Aluminum Statistical Review*, annual.

Manufactures   639

Table 997. Iron and Steel Industry—Summary: 1990 to 2005

[95.5 represents 95,500,000 tons. For financial data, the universe in 1992 consists of the companies that produced 68 percent of the total reported raw steel production. The financial data represent the operations of the steel segment of the companies. Minus sign (−) indicates net loss]

Item	Unit	1990	1995	2000	2001	2002	2003	2004	2005, prel.
Steel mill products, apparent supply	Mil. tons [1]	95.5	109.6	131.9	116.4	117.8	116.1	131.8	119.3
Net shipments	Mil. tons [1]	85.0	97.5	109.1	98.9	100.0	106.0	111.4	103.5
Exports	Mil. tons [1]	4.3	7.1	6.5	6.1	6.0	8.2	7.9	9.4
Imports	Mil. tons [1]	17.2	24.4	29.4	30.1	32.6	23.1	35.8	32.1
Scrap consumed	Mil. tons [1]	50.1	62.0	65.0	63.0	62.0	61.8	57.3	(NA)
Scrap inventory	Mil. tons [1]	3.6	4.1	5.3	4.9	4.2	4.5	4.8	(NA)
Iron and steel products: Exports	Mil. tons [1]	5.3	8.2	7.7	7.2	7.0	9.3	9.6	11.3
Imports	Mil. tons [1]	21.9	27.3	42.6	34.4	37.3	27.9	41.2	37.8
Capacity by steelmaking process	Mil. net tons	116.7	112.4	130.3	125.5	113.7	121.6	116.1	119.5
Revenue	Bil. dol.	30.9	35.1	38.8	31.0	31.6	34.3	53.1	(NA)
Net income	Bil. dol.	0.1	1.5	−1.1	−3.9	−1.3	−6.9	4.4	(NA)
Stockholders' equity	Bil. dol.	4.3	8.6	9.9	5.5	1.4	−5.0	11.2	(NA)
Total assets	Bil. dol.	28.3	35.1	43.9	38.1	34.1	29.8	37.3	(NA)
Capital expenditures [2]	Bil. dol.	2.6	2.5	2.1	1.1	1.1	2.1	1.6	(NA)
Working capital ratio [2]	Ratio	1.6	1.5	1.7	1.6	1.3	0.9	2.1	(NA)
Inventories	Bil. dol.	4.7	5.1	6.8	5.7	5.5	4.9	6.5	(NA)
Average employment	1,000	169.0	122.6	99.5	88.0	74.4	42.5	39.7	(NA)
Hours worked	Million	350.0	269.2	219.7	186.4	157.1	90.6	87.8	(NA)
Index of output, all employees [3]	1997 = 100	70.2	90.0	106.0	104.4	124.9	130.3	157.7	(NA)

NA Not available. [1] In millions of short tons. [2] Current assets to current liabilities. [3] NAICS code 3311. Output per hour.
Source: U.S. Bureau of Labor Statistics, Internet site <http://stats.bls.gov/iprhome.htm>.
Source: Except as noted, American Iron and Steel Institute, Washington, DC, *Annual Statistical Report* (copyright).

Table 998. Steel Products—Net Shipments by Market Classes: 1990 to 2005

[In thousands of short tons (84,981 represents 84,981,000). Comprises carbon, alloy, and stainless steel]

Market class	1990	1995	2000	2001	2002	2003	2004	2005
Net shipments, total [1]	84,981	97,494	109,050	99,448	99,191	105,974	111,385	103,474
Automotive	11,100	14,622	16,063	14,059	12,562	15,883	13,858	13,031
Steel service centers, distributors	21,111	23,751	30,108	27,072	22,828	28,551	34,667	23,213
Construction, incl. maintenance [2]	9,245	14,892	20,290	21,543	15,729	23,787	23,810	15,858
Containers, packaging, shipping	4,474	4,139	3,708	3,232	3,251	3,028	2,592	2,504
Machinery, industrial equipment, tools	2,388	2,310	1,784	1,456	1,137	1,178	1,853	1,300
Steel for converting and processing	9,441	10,440	12,708	10,311	7,201	9,448	8,151	7,559
Rail transportation	1,080	1,373	1,307	981	751	938	1,185	1,019
Contractors' products	2,870	(2)	(2)	(2)	(2)	(2)	(2)	(2)
Oil and gas industries	1,892	2,643	2,885	2,953	1,658	2,112	2,487	2,056
Electrical equipment	2,453	2,397	2,055	1,684	1,336	1,099	2,026	1,088
Appliances, utensils, and cutlery	1,540	1,589	1,907	1,820	1,734	2,018	919	1,895

[1] Includes nonclassified shipments and other classes not shown separately. [2] Beginning 1994, contractors' products included with construction.
Source: American Iron and Steel Institute, Washington, DC, *Annual Statistical Report* (copyright).

Table 999. Metalworking Machinery—Value of Shipments: 1990 to 2004

[In millions of dollars (3,426 represents $3,426,000,000)]

Product	2000 NAICS code [1]	1990	1995	2000	2001	2002	2003	2004
Metalworking machinery	(X)	3,426	4,547	3,632	2,988	2,002	1,966	2,492
Metal cutting type [2]	(X)	2,371	3,037	2,552	2,164	1,419	1,399	1,839
Boring machines [3]	333512A1	(3)	172	87	125	128	77	91
Drilling machines [3]	333512A1	184	79	24	23	17	53	53
Gear cutting machines	33351211	103	137	181	137	111	287	342
Grinding and polishing machines	33351221	434	550	454	368	211	169	196
Lathes [4]	33351231	356	478	287	262	132	119	232
Milling machines [5]	33351241	214	195	151	138	56	39	35
Machining centers [6]	33351271	437	699	630	435	274	318	475
Station type machines	33351281	502	477	402	348	170	(D)	(D)
Other metal cutting machine tools [7]	33351291	142	246	333	276	238	250	365
Remanufactured metal cutting machine tools	3335126111	(NA)	(NA)	(NA)	49	50	42	46
Metal forming type	(X)	1,080	1,511	1,080	824	583	567	653
Punching and shearing machines	33351311 pt.	200	326	204	155	106	103	148
Bending and forming machines	33351311 pt.	223	257	262	203	141	133	175
Presses, except forging	33351331	308	379	303	180	140	121	123
Forging machines [8]	33351351 pt.	74	(D)	(D)	(D)	(D)	(D)	(D)
Other metal forming [8]	33351351 pt.	275	548	311	276	187	169	150

D Data withheld to avoid disclosure. NA Not available. X Not applicable. [1] Based on the North American Industry Classification System, 2000; see text Section 15. [2] Beginning 1995, data for "All lathes (turning machines)" and "All milling machines," valued at under $3,025 each are included in total "Metal cutting type" for 1995 through 2000. [3] For 1990, data for "Boring machines" were combined with "Drilling machines" to avoid disclosing individual company data. [4] Beginning 1995, product code 33351230, "Lathes," excludes the value for product code 3335123031. All lathes valued under $3,025 each. [5] Beginning 1995, product code 33351240, "Milling machines," excludes the value for product code 33351240001. "All milling machines valued under $3,025 each." [6] Multiplication numerically controlled machines. [7] Excludes those designed primarily for home workshops, labs, etc. [8] For 1995 through 2003, data for "Forging machines" have been combined with "Other metal forming machines" to avoid disclosing individual company data.
Source: U.S. Census Bureau, 1990, *Current Industrial Reports*, Series MQ35W; and thereafter, MQ333W. See also <http://www.census.gov/industry/1/mq333w045.pdf> (released July 2005).

Table 1000. **U.S. Machine Tool Consumption—Gross New Orders and Exports: 2004 and 2005**

[Value in millions of dollars (3,244 represents $3,244,000,000)]

Item	2004				2005			
	Total	Metal cutting machines	Metal forming machines	Other manufac- turing technology	Total	Metal cutting machines	Metal forming machines	Other manufac- turing technology
New order units, total . .	**21,015**	**18,434**	**1,184**	**1,397**	**22,943**	**19,324**	**1,103**	**2,516**
Northeast [1]	3,509	3,121	157	231	3,605	3,077	165	363
South [2]	3,460	2,898	270	292	3,892	3,198	209	485
Midwest [3]	6,331	5,422	369	540	6,837	5,545	289	1,003
Central [4]	4,429	3,960	249	220	4,993	4,252	297	445
West [5]	3,287	3,034	139	114	3,615	3,252	143	221
New order value, total .	**3,244**	**2,658**	**185**	**401**	**3,606**	**2,887**	**194**	**526**
Northeast [1]	479	402	18	59	480	404	24	52
South [2]	495	376	57	62	596	452	45	99
Midwest [3]	1,267	1,040	59	169	1,254	992	66	196
Central [4]	610	495	34	81	803	633	42	128
West [5]	392	345	18	29	473	406	16	51
Export order units [6]	1,763	1,425	159	179	1,943	1,461	206	276
Export order value [6]	447	345	35	67	565	424	48	93

[1] Covers Maine, New Hampshire, Vermont, New York, Massachusetts, Connecticut, Rhode Island, New Jersey, and Pennsylvania. [2] Covers Delaware, Maryland, Virginia, West Virginia, Kentucky, North Carolina, South Carolina, Tennessee, Mississippi, Alabama, Georgia, and Florida. [3] Covers Wisconsin, Michigan, Ohio, Illinois, and Indiana. [4] Covers Minnesota, North Dakota, South Dakota, Montana, Wyoming, Idaho, Iowa, Nebraska, Kansas, Missouri, Oklahoma, Arkansas, Louisiana, Texas, New Mexico, Colorado, and Utah. [5] Covers Washington, Oregon, California, Nevada, and Arizona. [6] Represents orders placed with U.S. builders.

Source: The Association for Manufacturing Technology, McLean, VA, (copyright); and American Machine Tool Distributors Association, Rockville, MD, *U.S. Machine Tool Consumption Report*, monthly.

Table 1001. **Semiconductors, Printed Circuit Boards, and Other Electronic Components—Value of Shipments by Class of Product: 1990 to 2004**

[In millions of dollars (56,301 represents $56,301,000,000). N.e.c. = not elsewhere classified]

Product	2000 NAICS code [1]	1990	2000	2001	2002	2003	2004
Total	(X)	**56,301**	**164,854**	**118,868**	**104,897**	**103,438**	**115,340**
Transmittal, industrial, and special-purpose electron tubes (except x-ray)	3344111	1,097	703	700	584	629	638
Electron tubes, receiving type	(X)	24	([2])	([2])	([2])	([2])	([2])
Receiving type electron tubes and cathode ray picture tubes	3344114	1,344	[2]3,458	[2]2,847	[2]2,486	[2]1,508	[2]1,049
Electron tube parts	3344117	143	144	125	91	63	68
Printed circuit boards	3344120	7,175	11,892	8,911	5,764	4,871	4,965
Integrated microcircuits (semiconductor networks)	3344131	16,623	73,664	46,337	49,726	54,830	65,950
Transistors	3344134	682	1,569	913	818	608	656
Diodes and rectifiers	3344137	668	621	403	370	391	407
Other semiconductor devices	334413A	5,741	9,757	7,632	6,632	6,519	7,176
Capacitors for electronic applications	3344140	1,392	2,786	1,734	1,338	1,192	1,170
Resistors	3344150	800	982	776	653	636	714
Coils, transformers, reactors, and chokes for electronic applications	3344160	976	1,719	1,362	1,154	957	1,048
Coaxial connectors	3344171	420	805	506	464	402	400
Cylindrical connectors	3344174	514	725	688	528	563	631
Rack and panel connectors	3344177	500	532	359	264	268	290
Printed circuit connectors	334417A	805	1,811	1,147	776	834	1,015
Other connectors including parts	334417D	1,085	2,059	2,052	1,436	1,418	1,101
Filters (except microwave) and piezoelectric devices	3344191	457	1,168	984	726	601	619
Transducers, electrical/electronic input or output . .	3344194	741	1,519	1,331	1,203	1,219	1,464
Switches, mechanical types for electronic circuitry .	3344197	579	903	828	836	739	729
Printed circuit assemblies	334418B	8,269	37,273	31,214	23,171	19,775	19,838
Microwave components and devices	334419A	1,369	2,435	1,848	1,511	1,415	1,303
All other electronic components n.e.c	334419E	4,898	8,332	6,173	4,366	4,060	4,110

X Not applicable. [1] North American Industry Classification System, 2000; see text, Section 15. [2] Product codes combined to avoid disclosing figures for individual companies.

Source: U.S. Census Bureau, 1990, Current Industrial Reports, Series MA36Q; thereafter, MA334Q. See also <http://www.census.gov/industry/1/ma334q04.pdf> (released August 2005).

Manufactures 641

Table 1002. Computers and Office and Accounting Machines—Value of Shipments: 1990 to 2004

[In millions of dollars (25,630 represents $25,630,000,000)]

Selected products	1990	1995	2000	2001	2002	2003	2004
Electronic computers [1]	25,630	49,038	62,857	48,541	40,448	38,271	39,540
Host computers (multiusers)	(NA)	(NA)	22,877	16,469	13,053	12,237	12,786
Single user computers	(NA)	(NA)	38,981	31,492	26,586	25,164	26,164
Other computers	(NA)	(NA)	998	581	809	870	590
Loaded computer processor boards and board subassemblies [2]	2,247	24,448	37,273	31,214	23,171	19,715	19,838
Computer storage devices & equipment	7,488	7,903	8,995	7,319	5,027	5,101	5,065
Parts for computer storage devices & subassemblies	955	2,236	1,692	1,699	1,578	1,130	991
Computer terminals.	2,067	1,086	415	361	266	258	299
Computer peripheral equipment, n.e.c. [3]	7,697	12,331	12,434	10,637	10,460	9,483	9,373
Parts for input/output equipment	3,706	2,391	2,766	2,360	1,905	1,849	2,593
Calculating and accounting machines.	(D)	1,279	1,210	1,191	845	923	735
Magnetic and optical recording media	3,695	5,106	3,206	2,228	2,207	2,271	1,882

NA Not available.   D Withheld to avoid disclosing data for individual companies.   [1] Beginning 2000, computer industry data are not entirely comparable to previous years.   [2] These data are collected on two Current Industrial Report forms, MA35R, Computers and Office and Accounting Machines (Shipments) and MA36Q, Semiconductors, Printed Circuit Boards, and Other Electronic Components.   [3] n.e.c. = not elsewhere classified.

Source: U.S. Census Bureau, *Current Industrial Reports,* Series MA334R. See also <http://www.census.gov/industry/1/ma334r04.pdf> (released August 2005).

Table 1003. Computers and Office and Accounting Machines—Shipments: 2003 and 2004

[Quantity in thousands of units (23,029 represents 23,029,000, value in millions of dollars (38,271 represents $38,271,000,000)]

Product	Number of companies, 2004	Quantity (1,000)		Value (mil. dol.)	
		2003	2004	2003	2004
Electronic computers (automatic data processors). .	109	23,029	24,492	38,271	39,540
Host computers (multiusers):					
Large scale systems and unix servers	13	175	94	3,184	2,463
Medium-scale systems and unix servers.	17	(D)	(D)	(D)	(D)
PC servers	21	(D)	(D)	(D)	(D)
Other host computers	7	(D)	(D)	(D)	(D)
Single-user computers:					
Personal computers	29	14,950	15,790	14,709	15,272
Workstations	33	1,168	1,027	1,991	1,912
Laptops (AC/DC)	8	9	42	25	72
Notebooks, subnotebooks (battery operated).	12	5,107	5,641	8,161	8,604
Personal digital assistants	5	(D)	(D)	(D)	(D)
Other portable computers	4	(D)	(D)	(D)	(D)
Other single-user computers	4	315	416	278	304
Other computers	26	164	184	870	590
Computer storage devices and equipment.	51	(X)	(X)	5,101	5,065
Parts for computer storage devices and subassemblies	16	(X)	(X)	1,129	991
Computer terminals.	25	(X)	(X)	258	299
Computer peripheral equipment, n.e.c. [1]	185	(X)	(X)	9,483	9,373
Keyboards	19	1,100	195	47	34
Computer printers:					
Laser.	20	2,040	2,694	1,998	1,293
Inkjet	8	(D)	(D)	(D)	(D)
Calculating and accounting machines.	34	(X)	(X)	923	735
Printed circuit assemblies.	615	(X)	(X)	19,715	19,838
Magnetic and optical recording media.	34	(X)	(X)	2,271	1,882

X Not applicable.   D Withheld to avoid disclosure of individual companies.   [1] n.e.c. = not elsewhere classsified.

Source: U.S. Census Bureau, *Current Industrial Reports,* Series MA334R. See also <http://www.census.gov/industry/1/ma334r04.pdf> (released August 2005).

Table 1004. Consumer Electronics and Electronic Components—Factory Sales by Product Category: 1990 to 2005

[In millions of dollars (43,033 representes $43,033,000,000). Factory sales include imports]

Product category	1990	1995	2000	2001	2002	2003	2004	2005
Total [1]	43,033	67,905	96,943	94,211	95,793	102,611	113,090	125,910
Video products, total [1]	12,440	15,376	17,927	16,607	18,506	19,267	20,999	22,552
Analog direct-view color TV	6,197	6,798	6,503	5,130	5,782	4,756	3,526	2,734
Analog projection TV	626	1,417	1,481	1,060	733	293	85	15
Monochrome TV	99	34	15	15	12	9	5	4
Digital direct-view and projection TV	(NA)	(NA)	1,355	2,485	3,574	4,351	6,271	5,320
LCD TV	83	75	64	62	246	664	1,579	3,295
Plasma TV	(NA)	(NA)	(NA)	116	515	1,590	2,347	4,012
TV Combinations	178	723	1,292	790	733	778	867	1569
Videocassette players	65	59	14	5	4	2	2	(NA)
VCR decks	2,439	2,767	1,869	1,058	826	407	130	71
Camcorders	2,260	2,130	2,838	2,236	2,361	2,002	1,651	1,466
Direct-to-home satellite	421	1,265	790	1,175	1,116	1,476	1,886	1,358
Personal video recorders	(NA)	(NA)	77	144	57	178	460	718
Digital versatile disc players (DVD)	(NA)	(NA)	1,717	2,097	2,427	3,050	2,183	1,679
Home and portable products,total [1]	5,210	6,378	6,323	5,726	5,111	4,779	5,671	7,266
Compact audio systems	1,270	1,162	1,776	1,357	965	731	900	627
Separate audio components	1,935	1,911	1,545	1,261	1,202	981	1,325	1,211
Home radios	360	284	351	326	300	318	232	202
Portable audio equipment	1,645	2,506	2,156	1,846	1,526	1,355	992	777
Portable MP3 players	(NA)	(NA)	80	100	205	424	1,289	3,754
Mobile electronics, total [1]	5,733	11,422	17,071	16,799	16,189	17,184	18,984	22,367
Aftermarket autosound equipment	1,192	1,931	2,169	2,098	2,211	2,090	2,124	2,230
Mobile video and navigation	(NA)	(NA)	386	436	586	580	782	951
Factory installed autosound	3,100	3,100	2,700	2,850	2,950	3,245	3,569	3,855
Wireless (cellular) telephones	1,133	2,574	8,995	8,651	8,106	9,163	10,538	13,585
Pagers	118	300	750	790	810	729	675	525
Family Radio Services (FRS)	(NA)	(NA)	418	461	251	235	201	168
Vehicle security	190	142	218	266	265	260	255	253
PDAs	(NA)	(NA)	1,265	1,077	875	759	720	680
Home office products, total [1]	11,021	24,140	36,854	34,924	33,505	38,282	41,770	45,032
Cordless telephones	842	1,141	1,562	1,960	1,261	1,268	1,134	1,017
Corded telephones	638	557	386	294	266	256	259	261
Telephone answering devices	827	1,077	984	1,062	1,060	1,210	1,247	1,426
Caller ID devices	(NA)	(NA)	54	35	20	17	13	9
Home computers	4,187	12,600	16,400	12,960	12,609	15,584	18,233	18,215
Computer printers	(NA)	2,430	5,116	5,245	4,829	4,734	4,053	3,858
Modems/fax modems	(NA)	770	1,564	1,564	1,445	1,419	1,465	1,525
Computer peripherals	1,980	816	1,950	2,150	2,256	2,707	3,032	3,575
Computer software (incl. CDROM)	971	2,500	4,480	5,062	4,961	5,060	5,162	5,250
Home fax machines	920	919	386	349	297	242	186	128
Digital cameras	(NA)	(NA)	1,825	1,972	2,794	3,921	4,739	7,468
Electronic gaming, total	3,375	4,500	8,550	9,689	10,848	10,253	10,512	11,635
Electronic gaming hardware	975	1,500	2,700	3,250	3,750	3,188	3,162	3,594
Electronic gaming software	2,400	3,000	5,850	6,439	7,098	7,065	7,350	8,041
Blank media, total	1,638	1,415	2,169	2,679	3,210	3,750	5,458	6,373
Blank audio cassettes	376	334	162	129	98	77	65	57
Blank videocassettes	948	708	351	357	602	527	450	422
Blank computer media	314	373	1,200	1,550	1,600	1,800	1,841	2,294
Flash media	(NA)	(NA)	456	643	910	1,346	3,102	3,600
Accessories and batteries, total	2,176	3,544	6,299	5,968	6,460	7,041	7,545	8,435
Electronic accessories	793	944	1,356	1,378	1,500	1,635	1,815	2,175
Batteries	1,383	2,600	4,943	4,590	4,960	5,406	5,730	6,260
Home security systems	1,440	1,130	1,750	1,820	1,965	2,055	2,150	2,250

NA Not available. [1] Includes categories, not shown separately.

Source: Consumer Electronics Association, Washington, DC, *Electronic Market Data Book,* annual (copyright).

Table 1005. Communication Equipment—Value of Shipments: 1990 to 2004

[In millions of dollars (36,990 represents $36,990,000,000]

Product description	1997 NAICS code [1]	1990	2000	2001	2002	2003	2004
Total	(X)	36,990	104,389	93,803	62,212	56,587	61,672
Telephone switching and switchboard equipment	3342101	7,537	15,174	12,118	7,437	4,900	6,161
Carrier line equipment and modems	3342104	5,014	13,112	10,943	4,488	3,045	3,227
Other telephone and telegraph equipment and components	3342107	3,181	28,971	22,841	13,886	12,272	12,139
Communication systems and equipment (except broadcast)	3342201	14,768	36,357	36,501	25,104	25,805	28,535
Broadcast, studio, and related electronic equipment	3342202	1,856	4,029	3,491	3,304	2,932	2,898
Intercommunications systems, including inductive paging systems (selective calling)	3342903	346	447	451	385	428	462
Alarm systems	3342901	1,027	2,755	2,374	2,440	2,258	2,370
Vehicular and pedestrian traffic control equipment and electrical railway signals and attachments	3342902	471	838	806	928	945	910
Electronic teaching machines, teaching aids, trainers and simulators [2]	3333197	1,209	782	1,172	1,168	1,223	1,460
Laser sources [2]	3359997	(NA)	(S)	1,051	929	833	983
Ultrasonic equipment	335999A	109	272	233	174	196	255
Other electronic systems and equipment, n.e.c.	335999F	1,473	1,652	1,752	1,971	1,760	2,273

NA Not available. S Does not meet publication standards. [1] North American Industry Classification System, 1997; see text, Section 15. [2] Beginning in 1995, data for laser equipment, instrumentation, and components were eliminated from this survey. Only laser sources are being collected.

Source: U.S. Census Bureau, *Current Industrial Reports,* Series MA334P. See also <http://www.census.gov/industry/1/ma334p04.pdf> (released August 2005).

Manufactures   643

Table 1006. **Motor Vehicle Manufactures—Summary by Selected Industry: 2004**

[51,123 represents $51,123,000,000. Based on the Annual Survey of Manufactures; see Appendix III]

Industry	2002 NAICS code [1]	All employees [2]			Production workers [2]	Value of shipments [3] (mil. dol.)
		Number	Payroll			
			Total (mil. dol.)	Per employee (dol.)		
Motor vehicle manufacturing, total	3361-3363	1,016,713	51,123	50,283	803,098	494,623
Motor vehicle, total	3361	215,974	14,906	69,017	189,101	261,716
Automobile & light duty motor vehicle	33611	186,912	13,589	72,703	165,854	241,294
Automobile	336111	74,305	5,305	71,400	64,074	86,818
Light truck & utility vehicle	336112	112,607	8,284	73,563	101,780	154,475
Heavy duty truck	33612	29,062	1,317	45,311	23,247	20,422
Motor vehicle body & trailer	3362	136,694	4,796	35,084	108,660	29,316
Motor vehicle body & trailer	33621	136,694	4,796	35,084	108,660	29,316
Motor vehicle body	336211	39,052	1,460	37,383	29,852	8,861
Truck trailer	336212	27,133	875	32,249	22,477	5,695
Motor home	336213	22,557	828	36,719	18,662	6,357
Travel trailer & camper	336214	47,952	1,633	34,048	37,670	8,404
Motor vehicle parts	3363	664,045	31,422	47,318	505,337	203,591
Motor vehicle gasoline engine & engine parts	33631	81,082	4,501	55,508	63,348	36,258
Motor vehicle electrical and electronic equipment	33632	77,496	3,320	42,844	55,861	22,275
Motor vehicle steering and suspension	33633	38,856	1,918	49,364	30,904	10,982
Motor vehicle brake system	33634	39,727	1,587	39,958	31,463	13,494
Motor vehicle transmission & power train parts	33635	89,183	5,864	65,751	72,192	35,240
Motor vehicle seating & interior trim	33636	49,968	2,029	40,599	36,854	16,104
Motor vehicle metal stamping	33637	107,521	5,930	55,157	88,877	26,451
Other motor vehicle parts	33639	160,212	6,272	39,149	125,839	42,788

[1] North American Industry Classification System, 2002; see text, Section 15. [2] Includes employment and payroll at administrative offices and auxiliary units. All employees represents the average of production workers plus all other employees for the payroll period ended nearest the 12th of March. Production workers represents the average of the employment for the payroll periods ended nearest the 12th of March and May. [3] Includes extensive and unmeasurable duplication from shipments between establishments in the same industry classification.

Source: U.S. Census Bureau, *Annual Survey of Manufactures, Statistics for Industry Groups and Industries*, Series M03(AS)-1. See also <http://www.census.gov/MCD/ASM-AS1.html>.

Table 1007. **Motor Vehicle Manufactures—Employees, Payroll, and Shipments by Major State: 2003**

[14,314 represents $14,314,000,000. Industry based on the North American Industry Classification System (NAICS), 2002; see text, Section 15]

Major state based on employment	Motor vehicle manufacturing (NAICS 3361)			Motor vehicle body and trailer manufacturing (NAICS 3362)			Motor vehicle parts manufacturing (NAICS 3363)		
	Employees, total	Payroll (mil. dol.)	Shipments (mil. dol.)	Employees, total	Payroll (mil. dol.)	Shipments (mil. dol.)	Employees, total	Payroll (mil. dol.)	Shipments (mil. dol.)
United States . . .	211,423	14,314	259,588	127,157	4,325	25,868	670,428	31,398	200,681
Alabama	5,231	317	5,820	3,221	105	721	11,111	538	3,621
Arkansas	(1)	(D)	(D)	1,353	34	227	6,603	192	1,000
California	6,877	475	7,068	10,116	296	1,811	26,337	942	4,903
Florida	(NA)	(NA)	(NA)	3,300	116	604	5,640	171	892
Georgia	6,649	402	7,378	3,054	95	661	9,960	367	2,173
Illinois	7,580	407	6,540	2,837	100	533	26,511	1,066	6,218
Indiana	12,575	784	20,165	31,254	1,209	7,864	78,215	3,980	23,449
Iowa	(NA)	(NA)	(NA)	7,855	262	1,455	6,342	238	1,511
Kansas	(1)	(D)	(D)	2,680	82	448	2,982	105	662
Kentucky	17,825	1,322	22,992	(NA)	(NA)	(NA)	26,253	1,003	8,222
Michigan	43,782	3,322	62,323	2,217	81	428	164,474	9,247	55,281
Minnesota	2,333	155	2,401	2,833	100	773	3,585	133	629
Mississippi	(2)	(D)	(D)	(3)	(D)	(D)	5,940	201	1,224
Missouri	17,014	1,256	22,172	(D)	(D)	(D)	13,118	508	3,486
New York	(NA)	(NA)	(NA)	1,382	46	253	27,280	1,594	8,994
North Carolina	4,405	173	3,092	2,784	114	883	18,223	672	5,817
Ohio	27,210	1,925	34,278	4,155	131	702	95,587	4,888	30,391
Oklahoma	(2)	(D)	(D)	(2)	(D)	(D)	5,590	181	1,189
Oregon	1,202	45	319	6,257	194	1,264	1,374	60	313
Pennsylvania	(NA)	(NA)	(NA)	(D)	(D)	(D)	12,961	488	2,686
South Carolina	(4)	(D)	(D)	(1)	(D)	(D)	16,920	673	5,781
Tennessee	(5)	(D)	(D)	2,458	69	415	32,415	1,165	11,530
Texas	5,683	352	11,797	6,302	211	1,048	13,777	516	3,722
Virginia	(2)	(D)	(D)	1,526	41	255	6,231	247	1,796
Wisconsin	(4)	(D)	(D)	(2)	(D)	(D)	17,383	827	5,184

NA Not available. D Withheld to avoid disclosing data on individual companies. [1] Employee size class of 1,000 to 2,499 employees. [2] Employee size class of 2,500 to 4,999 employees. [3] Employee size class of 950 to 999 employees. [4] Employee size class of 5,000 to 9,999 employees. [5] Employee size class of 10,000 to 24,999 employees.

Source: U.S. Census Bureau, Annual Survey of Manufactures, *Geographic Area Statistics*, Series M01(AS)-3. See also <http://www.census.gov/MCD/ASM-AS3.html>.

Table 1008. Aerospace—Sales, New Orders, and Backlog: 1990 to 2005

[In billions of dollars (136.6 represents $136,600,000,000), except as indicated. Reported by establishments in which the principal business is the development and/or production of aerospace products]

Item	1990	2000	2001	2002	2003	2004	2005
Net sales	**136.6**	**109.3**	**117.1**	**115.2**	**116.2**	**116.4**	**125.2**
Percent U.S. government	53.8	37.5	38.6	46.1	52.9	52.9	52.0
Complete aircraft and parts [1]	49.9	57.2	58.7	53.9	49.0	49.6	49.6
Aircraft engines and parts	16.4	12.5	15.9	14.8	13.9	13.8	16.1
Missiles and space vehicles, parts . . .	22.0	15.6	15.5	15.6	16.0	15.6	14.4
Other products, services	48.3	24.0	26.9	30.9	37.3	37.4	45.2
Net, new orders	146.0	140.1	122.3	114.8	116.7	117.7	132.6
Backlog, Dec. 31	250.1	215.0	220.1	222.5	222.9	226.9	234.3

[1] Except engines sold separately.

Source: U.S. Census Bureau, 1990, *Current Industrial Reports,* Series M37G; thereafter M336G. See also <http://www.census.gov/industry/1/m336g0413.pdf> (released August 2005).

Table 1009. Net Orders for U.S. Civil Jet Transport Aircraft: 1990 to 2005

[1990 data are net new firm orders; beginning 1995, net announced orders. Minus sign (–) indicates net cancellations. In 1997, Boeing acquired McDonnell Douglas]

Type of aircraft and customer	1990	1995	2000	2001	2002	2003	2004	2005
Total number [1]	**670**	**421**	**585**	**271**	**174**	**237**	**267**	**1,004**
U.S. customers	259	138	412	49	89	84	23	220
Foreign customers	411	283	193	130	172	185	204	811
Boeing 737, total	189	189	378	184	117	204	142	571
U.S. customers	38	85	302	51	64	74	16	152
Foreign customers	151	104	86	73	127	145	92	439
Boeing 747, total	153	35	24	16	17	4	10	43
U.S. customers	24	2	1	7	–	–	1	13
Foreign customers	129	33	18	13	13	9	10	30
Boeing 757, total	66	–7	43	23	–	–1	–	–
U.S. customers	33	–6	38	15	2	–7	–	–
Foreign customers	33	–1	14	6	–	6	–	–
Boeing 767, total	60	26	6	32	–2	10	9	15
U.S. customers	23	4	–2	–1	1	–	–	–
Foreign customers	37	22	14	9	12	15	1	20
Boeing 777, total	34	83	113	30	26	12	42	154
U.S. customers	34	–	60	–	–1	11	–	10
Foreign customers	–	83	53	20	27	8	43	146
Boeing 787, total	–	–	–	–	–	–	56	235
U.S. customers	–	–	–	–	–	–	–	45
Foreign customers	–	–	–	–	–	–	56	190
Unidentified	–	–	–	–	–	–	–	–
McDonnell Douglas MD-11, total	52	–6	–	–	–	–	–	–
U.S. customers	16	3	–	–	–	–	–	–
Foreign customers	36	–9	–	–	–	–	–	–
McDonnell Douglas MD-80/90, total	116	51	–	–	–	–	–	–
U.S. customers	91	–	–	–	–	–	–	–
Foreign customers	25	51	–	–	–	–	–	–
McDonnell Douglas MD-95, total	–	50	21	–14	16	8	8	–14
U.S. customers	–	50	13	–23	23	6	6	–
Foreign customers	–	–	8	9	–7	2	2	–14

– Represents zero. [1] Includes types of aircraft not shown separately. Beginning 1999, includes unidentified customers.

Source: Aerospace Industries Association of America, Washington, DC, Research Center, Statistical Series 23, Internet site at <http://www.aia-aerospace.org/stats/aerostats/aerostats.cfm>.

Table 1010. U.S. Aircraft Shipments, 1990 to 2004, and Projections, 2005

[Value in millions of dollars (64,567 represents $64,567,000,000)]

Year	Total		Civil						Military	
			Large transports		General aviation [1]		Helicopters			
	Units	Value	Units	Value	Units	Value	Units	Value	Units	Value
1990	3,321	64,567	521	22,215	1,144	2,007	603	254	1,053	40,091
1991	3,092	67,510	589	26,856	1,021	1,968	571	211	911	38,475
1992	2,585	64,740	567	28,750	941	1,840	324	142	753	34,008
1993	2,585	59,103	408	24,133	964	2,144	258	113	955	32,713
1994	2,309	52,718	309	18,124	928	2,357	308	185	764	32,052
1995	2,436	49,381	256	15,263	1,077	2,842	292	194	811	31,082
1996	2,220	55,583	269	18,915	1,115	3,048	278	193	558	33,427
1997	2,757	65,129	374	26,929	1,549	4,593	346	231	488	33,376
1998	3,533	75,724	559	35,663	2,193	5,534	363	252	418	34,275
1999	3,799	80,974	620	38,171	2,475	6,803	345	200	359	35,800
2000	4,113	72,669	485	30,327	2,802	8,040	493	270	333	34,032
2001	3,902	77,608	526	34,155	2,616	7,991	415	247	345	35,215
2002	3,251	73,112	379	27,547	2,196	7,261	318	157	358	38,147
2003	3,221	68,006	281	21,033	2,080	6,205	517	366	343	40,402
2004	3,804	74,526	283	20,484	2,296	6,918	805	515	420	46,609
2005	4,518	81,498	290	22,116	2,853	8,632	925	750	450	50,000

[1] Excludes off-the-shelf military aircraft.

Source: U.S. Department of Commerce, International Trade Administration, Internet site <http://www.ita.doc.gov/td/aerospace/inform/>.

Manufactures   645

Table 1011. Aerospace Industry Sales by Product Group and Customer: 1990 to 2006

[In billions of dollars (134.4 represents $134,400,000,000). Due to reporting practices and tabulating methods, figures may differ from those in Table 1008]

Product group and customer	1990	1995	2000	2001	2002	2003	2004	2005 [1]	2006 [2]
CURRENT DOLLARS									
Total sales.	134.4	107.8	144.7	151.6	152.3	146.6	155.7	170.1	184.0
Product group:									
Aircraft, total	71.4	55.0	81.6	86.5	79.5	72.8	79.1	89.1	100.4
Civil [4]	31.3	24.0	47.6	51.3	41.3	32.4	32.5	39.2	49.5
Military.	40.1	31.1	34.0	35.2	38.1	40.4	46.6	50.0	50.8
Missiles.	14.2	7.4	9.3	10.4	12.8	3.5	14.7	15.3	14.4
Space. . . . .; . . .	26.4	27.4	29.7	29.5	34.6	35.9	35.9	37.3	38.5
Related products and services [5] . . .	22.4	18.0	24.1	25.3	25.4	24.4	26.0	28.3	30.7
Customer group:									
Aerospace, total	112.0	89.8	120.6	126.4	127.0	122.2	129.8	141.7	153.3
DOD [6]	60.5	42.4	47.5	50.1	57.7	64.0	70.1	74.3	74.9
NASA [7] and other agencies.	11.1	11.4	13.4	14.5	16.4	15.5	16.0	17.4	17.8
Other customers [8]	40.4	36.0	59.7	61.8	52.9	42.7	43.8	50.1	60.6
Related products and services [5] . . .	22.4	18.0	24.1	25.3	25.4	24.4	26.0	28.3	30.7
CONSTANT (1987) DOLLARS [3]									
Total sales.	123.5	86.1	108.2	110.6	109.4	102.3	105.1	110.4	114.8
Product group:									
Aircraft, total	65.6	44.0	61.0	63.1	57.1	50.8	53.4	57.8	62.6
Civil [4]	28.7	19.1	35.6	37.4	29.7	22.6	22.0	25.4	30.9
Military.	36.8	24.8	25.4	25.7	27.4	28.2	31.5	32.4	31.7
Missiles.	31.0	5.9	6.9	7.6	9.2	9.4	9.9	9.9	9.0
Space.	24.3	21.9	22.2	21.5	24.9	25.0	24.3	24.2	24.0
Related products and services [5] . . .	20.6	14.3	18.0	18.4	18.2	17.1	17.5	18.4	19.1
Customer group:									
Aerospace, total	102.9	71.7	90.1	92.2	91.2	85.3	87.6	92.0	95.7
DOD [6]	55.6	33.9	35.5	36.6	41.5	44.7	47.3	48.2	46.7
NASA [7] and other agencies.	10.2	9.1	10.0	10.6	11.8	10.8	10.8	11.3	11.1
Other customers [8]	37.1	28.8	44.6	45.0	38.0	29.8	29.5	32.5	37.8
Related products and services [5] . . .	20.6	14.3	18.0	18.4	18.2	17.1	17.5	18.4	19.1

[1] Preliminary.   [2] Estimate.   [3] Based on AIA's aerospace composite price deflator.   [4] All civil sales of aircraft (domestic and export sales of jet transports, commuters, business, and personal aircraft and helicopters).   [5] Electronics, software, and ground support equipment, plus sales of nonaerospace products which are produced by aerospace-manufacturing use technology, processes, and materials derived from aerospace products.   [6] Department of Defense.   [7] National Aeronautics and Space Administration.   [8] Includes civil aircraft sales (see footnote 4), commercial space sales, all exports of military aircraft and missiles, and related propulsion and parts.

Source: Aerospace Industries Association of America, Inc., Washington, DC, *2005 Year-end Review and Forecast*; and Internet site <http://www.aia-aerospace.org>.

Table 1012. Major Household Appliances—Value of Shipments: 1990 to 2005

[In millions of dollars (11,670.0 represents $11,670,000,000). For North American Industry Classification System (NAICS) 2000 based codes]

Product	2000 NAICS code	1990	2000	2001	2002	2003	2004	2005
Total	33522	11,670.0	17,125.2	16,710.6	16,835.8	18,119.3	18,721.3	20,230.5
Electric household ranges, ovens, and surface cooking units, equipment, and parts.	3352211	1,659.8	2,170.3	2,004.5	1,823.5	2,176.1	2,284.7	2,554.7
Gas household ranges, ovens, and surface cooking units, equipment, and parts.	3352213	739.4	779.1	902.0	929.4	1,017.9	1,119.8	1,390.2
Other household ranges, cooking equipment, outdoor cooking equipment incl. parts and accessories	3352215	581.1	1,251.1	1,027.0	1,050.8	966.7	913.6	964.0
Household refrigerators [1], [2].	3352221	3,208.1	5,395.8	5,227.1	5,080.3	4,993.3	5,001.5	5,404.9
Food freezers, complete units, for freezing and/or storing frozen food— (household type) [2]	3352222	226.6	(D)	(D)	(D)	(D)	(D)	(D)
Parts and attachments for household refrigerators and freezers	3352223	134.0	(D)	(D)	(D)	(D)	(D)	(D)
Household laundry machines and parts.	3352240	2,924.5	4,046.6	4,162.0	4,446.5	4,769.5	5,129.6	5,236.3
Water heaters, electric	3352281	433.8	572.7	555.7	576.0	569.5	545.3	638.4
Water heaters, except electric	3352283	577.2	843.6	799.3	842.0	985.6	884.1	973.8
Household appliances, n.e.c. and parts [3]	3352285	1,185.5	2,066.1	2,033.1	2,008.9	2,055.9	2,296.8	2,480.7

D Withheld to avoid disclosing data for individual companies.   [1] Includes combination refrigerator-freezers.   [2] Product code 33522210000 and 3352222000 are combined to avoid disclosing data for individual companies.   [3] n.e.c. = not elsewhere classified.

Source: U.S. Census Bureau, 1990, Current Industrial Reports, Series MA36F; thereafter Series MA335F. See also <http://www.census.gov/industry/1/ma335f05.pdf> (released July 2006).

Section 22
Wholesale and Retail Trade

This section presents statistics relating to the distributive trades, specifically wholesale trade and retail trade. Data shown for the trades are classified by kind of business and cover sales, establishments, employees, payrolls, and other items. The principal sources of these data are from the Census Bureau and include the *2002 Economic Census*, annual surveys, and the *County Business Patterns* program. These data are supplemented by several tables from trade associations, such as the National Automobile Dealers Association (Table 1027). Several notable research groups are also represented, such as Claritas (Table 1022), National Research Bureau (Tables 1035 and 1036), Jupiter Research, Inc. (Table 1024), and Forrester Research, Inc. (Table 1023).

Data on wholesale and retail trade also appear in several other sections. For instance, labor force employment and earnings data appear in Section 12, Labor Force, Employment, and Earnings; gross domestic product of the industry (Table 651) appear in Section 13, Income, Expenditures, and Wealth; financial data (several tables) from the quarterly *Statistics of Income Bulletin*, published by the Internal Revenue Service, appear in Section 15, Business Enterprise.

Censuses—Censuses of wholesale trade and retail trade have been taken at various intervals since 1929. Beginning with the 1967 census, legislation provides for a census of each area to be conducted every 5 years (for years ending in "2" and "7"). For more information on these censuses, see the *History of the 1997 Economic Census* found at <http://www.census.gov/prod/ec97/pol00-hec.pdf>. The industries covered in the censuses and surveys of business are those classified in 13 sectors defined in the *North American Industry Classification System,* called NAICS (see below). *Retail trade* refers to places of business primarily engaged in retailing merchandise to the general public; and *wholesale trade,* to

establishments primarily engaged in selling goods to other businesses and normally operating from a warehouse or office that have little or no display of merchandise. All Census Bureau tables in this section are utilizing the 2002 NAICS codes, which replaced the Standard Industrial Classification (SIC) system. NAICS makes substantial structural improvements and identifies over 350 new industries. At the same time, it causes breaks in time series far more profound than any prior revision of the previously used SIC system. For information on this system and how it affects the comparability of wholesale and retail statistics historically, see text, Section 15, Business Enterprise, and especially the Census Bureau Web site at <http://www.census .gov/epcd/www /naics.html>. In general, the 2002 Economic Census has two series of publications for these two sectors: 1) subject series with reports such as product lines and establishment and firm sizes, and 2) geographic reports with individual reports for each state. For information on these series, see the Census Bureau Web site at <http://www.census.gov/econ/census02/>.

Current surveys—Current sample surveys conducted by the Census Bureau cover various aspects of wholesale and retail trade. Its *Monthly Retail Trade and Food Services* release <http://www.census .gov/mrts/www/mrts.html> contains monthly estimates of sales, inventories, and inventory/sales ratios for the United States, by kind of business. Annual figures on sales, year-end inventories, and inventory/sales ratios, purchases, accounts receivable, and gross margins by kind of business, appear in the *Annual Revision of Monthly Retail and Food Services: Sales and Inventories*. Statistics from the Bureau's monthly wholesale trade survey include national estimates of sales, inventories, and inventory/sales ratios for merchant wholesalers excluding manufacturers' sales branches and offices. Data are presented by major summary groups "durable and nondurable," and 4-digit NAICS industry groups. Merchant wholesalers excluding manufacturers' sales branches and offices are those wholesalers who take title to the goods they sell (e.g., jobbers, exporters, importers, industrial distributors). These data, based on reports submitted by a sample of firms, appear in the *Monthly Wholesale Trade Report* <http://www.census.gov /mwts/www/mwts/html>. Annual figures on sales, inventory/sales ratios, year-end inventories, purchases, and gross margins appear in the *Annual Revision of Monthly Wholesale Distributors: Sales and Inventories* . Data on manufacturers' sales branches and offices were collected for the first time in the 2003 *Annual Trade Survey* and appear in the *Annual Report for Wholesale Trade*. Data are presented by major summary groups "durable and nondurable" and 4-digit NAICS industry groups for sales, end-of-year inventories, and operating expenses. The reports just mentioned may appear in print in some cases, but principally are available as documents on the Census Bureau Web site at <http://www.census .gov/econ/www /retmenu.html>.

E-commerce—Electronic commerce (or e-commerce) are sales of goods and services over the Internet and extranet, electronic data interchange (EDI), or other online systems. Payment may or may not be made online. This edition has several tables on e-commerce sales, such as Tables 1021 and 1023 to 1025 in this section, 978 in Section 21, Manufactures, and 1257 in Section 27, Accommodation, Food Services, and Other Services. Also, there are several private sources for similar data such as Forrester Research Inc., Cambridge MA; and Jupiter Research, Inc., New York, NY. These sources show estimated and projected online retail sales by key categories from business to consumers or to other businesses. Their methods of collecting the data vary widely between the sources and consequently these estimates of this activity vary also. Users of these estimates may want to contact the sources for descriptions of their methodology. Methodology for Census Bureau estimates can be found at <www.census.gov/eos/www /ebusiness614.htm>.

Statistical reliability—For a discussion of statistical collection and estimation, sampling procedures, and measures of statistical reliability applicable to Census Bureau data, see Appendix III.

U.S. Census Bureau, *Statistical Abstract of the United States: 2007*

Table 1013. Wholesale and Retail Trade—Establishments, Sales, Payroll, and Employees: 2002

[4,635 represents $4,635,000,000,000. Covers establishments with payroll. For statement on methodology, see Appendix III]

Kind of business	2002 NAICS code [1]	Estab-lishments	Sales (bil. dol.)	Annual payroll (bil. dol.)	Paid employees (1,000)
Wholesale trade	42	435,521	4,635	260	5,878
Durable goods wholesalers (except agents, brokers, and electronic markets)	423	260,445	2,171	157	3,357
Nondurable goods wholesalers (except agents, brokers, and electronic markets)	424	142,661	1,980	93	2,273
Wholesale electronic market and agents and brokers.	425	32,415	483	10	249
Retail trade.	44-45	1,114,637	3,056	302	14,648
Motor vehicle and parts dealers	441	125,139	802	65	1,845
Furniture and home furnishings stores	442	65,204	92	13	535
Electronics and appliance stores.	443	46,779	82	9	391
Building material and garden equipment and supplies dealers.	444	88,314	247	30	1,160
Food and beverage stores.	445	148,804	457	49	2,839
Health and personal care stores	446	81,797	178	20	1,024
Gasoline stations	447	121,446	249	14	927
Clothing and clothing accessories stores	448	149,810	168	21	1,427
Sporting goods, hobby, book, and music stores	451	62,236	73	9	611
General merchandise stores.	452	40,723	445	43	2,525
Miscellaneous store retailers	453	129,464	91	13	792
Nonstore retailers.	454	54,921	173	17	571

[1] North American Industry Classification System; see text, Section 15.

Source: U.S. Census Bureau, 2002 Economic Census, *Wholesale Trade, Geographic Area Series, United States: 2002* (EC02-42A-1US) and *Retail Trade, Geographic Area Series, United States: 2002* (EC02-44A-1US).

Table 1014. Wholesale and Retail Trade—Establishments, Sales, Payroll, and Employees: 1997 and 2002

[4,060 represents $4,060,000,000,000. Covers establishments with payroll. These data are preliminary and are subject to change. For statement on methodology, see Appendix III]

Kind of business	1997 NAICS code [1]	Establishments		Sales (bil. dol.)		Annual payroll (bil. dol.)		Paid employees (1,000)	
		1997	2002	1997	2002	1997	2002	1997	2002
Wholesale trade.	42	453,470	441,810	4,060	4,379	215	256	5,797	6,035
Wholesale trade, durable goods	421	290,629	288,286	2,180	2,354	133	159	3,398	3,565
Wholesale trade, nondurable goods	422	162,841	153,524	1,880	2,025	82	97	2,398	2,470
Retail trade	44-45	1,118,447	1,111,583	2,461	3,171	237	306	13,991	15,029
Motor vehicle and parts dealers.	441	122,633	122,692	645	812	50	64	1,719	1,884
Furniture and home furnishings stores . . .	442	64,725	65,088	72	94	10	13	483	554
Electronics and appliance stores	443	43,373	46,724	69	88	7	10	345	418
Building material and garden equipment and supplies dealers	444	93,117	(S)	228	(S)	26	(S)	1,118	(S)
Food and beverage stores	445	148,528	149,802	402	488	41	49	2,893	2,896
Health and personal care stores	446	82,941	79,360	118	183	15	21	904	1,043
Gasoline stations	447	126,889	(S)	198	(S)	11	(S)	922	(S)
Clothing and clothing accessories stores.	448	156,601	149,318	136	170	17	21	1,280	1,425
Sporting goods, hobby, book, and music stores.	451	69,149	63,033	62	78	7	9	561	633
General merchandise stores	452	36,171	39,846	330	451	31	43	2,508	2,549
Miscellaneous store retailers.	453	129,838	129,070	78	95	10	14	753	849
Nonstore retailers	454	44,482	55,764	123	171	12	18	506	587

S Figure does not meet publication standards.   [1] North American Industry Classification System; see text, Section 15, Business Enterprise.

Source: U.S. Census Bureau, 2002 Economic Census, *Advance Report,* published 29 March 2004; <http://www.census.gov/econ/census02/>.

Table 1015. Wholesale and Retail Trade—Establishments, Employees, and Payroll by State: 2000 and 2003

[6,112 represents 6,112,000. Covers establishments with payroll. Employees are for the week including March 12. Excludes most government employees, railroad employees, and self-employed persons. Kind-of-business classification for 2000 based on North American Industry Classification System (NAICS) 1997; data for 2003 based on NAICS 2002. See text, Section 15. For statement on methodology, see Appendix III]

State	Wholesale trade (NAICS 42)						Retail trade (NAICS 44, 45)					
	Number of establishments		Number of employees (1,000)		Annual payroll (mil. dol.)		Number of establishments		Number of employees (1,000)		Annual payroll (mil. dol.)	
	2000	2003	2000	2003	2000	2003	2000	2003	2000	2003	2000	2003
U.S....	446,237	432,537	6,112	5,864	270,122	272,156	1,113,573	1,115,906	14,841	14,868	302,553	319,469
AL	6,132	5,651	82	76	2,892	2,785	19,723	19,455	230	229	4,074	4,479
AK	752	758	7	7	281	326	2,733	2,668	33	34	790	853
AZ	6,731	6,576	86	90	3,627	3,842	16,911	17,503	255	280	5,694	6,321
AR	3,505	3,459	45	44	1,402	1,570	12,211	11,921	135	135	2,268	2,501
CA	58,326	59,137	808	794	40,011	40,649	107,987	110,506	1,491	1,592	36,073	39,385
CO	7,452	7,362	97	97	4,906	4,800	18,748	18,954	252	246	5,883	5,704
CT	5,076	4,668	77	73	4,481	4,329	14,111	13,786	191	196	4,540	4,889
DE	1,009	999	19	23	1,117	1,354	3,742	3,785	52	53	1,048	1,195
DC	372	367	5	6	282	298	1,945	1,813	19	19	431	416
FL......	30,671	31,820	315	305	12,536	12,370	67,396	70,306	903	920	18,044	19,663
GA	13,892	13,713	199	198	9,064	9,362	33,788	34,012	464	449	9,365	9,259
HI......	1,809	1,895	19	20	627	699	4,924	4,893	63	64	1,313	1,451
ID......	2,012	2,001	24	23	845	829	5,871	5,915	70	71	1,347	1,444
IL	21,509	20,228	344	326	16,683	16,447	43,800	43,303	637	598	12,992	13,821
IN	8,642	8,122	120	112	4,607	4,505	24,261	23,994	354	339	6,332	6,559
IA	5,155	4,821	65	60	2,173	2,216	14,382	13,828	184	177	3,169	3,300
KS	4,876	4,590	62	64	2,333	2,623	12,261	11,834	153	149	2,747	2,774
KY	4,939	4,583	74	71	2,536	2,668	16,988	16,672	221	214	3,804	4,030
LA	6,192	5,763	79	73	2,723	2,697	17,755	17,671	232	228	4,032	4,326
ME	1,740	1,690	22	19	744	714	7,015	7,019	77	79	1,436	1,685
MD	6,098	6,062	95	99	4,526	4,570	19,539	19,461	285	287	6,062	6,597
MA	9,735	9,066	156	146	9,114	8,633	25,813	25,755	353	365	7,729	8,429
MI.....	13,576	12,507	191	174	8,887	8,559	38,862	38,620	545	521	10,667	10,712
MN	9,294	8,770	137	131	6,399	6,903	20,862	21,086	304	309	5,980	6,657
MS	3,116	2,950	40	36	1,222	1,211	12,794	12,387	141	136	2,384	2,472
MO	9,072	8,412	146	126	5,458	4,896	23,911	23,778	318	316	6,258	6,369
MT	1,537	1,500	15	14	433	441	5,101	5,196	52	53	920	1,064
NE	3,061	2,866	41	36	1,346	1,337	8,248	8,102	110	105	1,895	2,005
NV	2,556	2,702	31	33	1,238	1,410	6,940	7,599	108	121	2,533	2,852
NH	2,105	2,012	25	23	1,184	1,259	6,545	6,657	93	95	1,930	2,185
NJ.....	17,157	16,709	279	272	14,724	15,397	34,841	34,782	439	450	9,897	10,569
NM.....	2,162	2,044	22	21	753	729	7,249	7,241	91	91	1,745	1,884
NY	36,606	35,966	422	407	20,941	20,895	75,500	76,777	844	863	18,116	19,295
NC	12,364	11,724	173	166	7,153	7,130	35,785	35,744	450	442	8,739	8,781
ND	1,543	1,445	18	16	532	551	3,435	3,460	42	42	719	789
OH	16,646	15,629	261	237	10,437	9,927	42,708	41,702	644	615	11,903	12,061
OK	5,005	4,673	62	55	2,126	1,966	14,147	13,856	168	168	2,913	3,165
OR	5,836	5,650	79	76	3,266	3,357	14,256	14,308	193	190	4,126	4,141
PA	16,796	15,848	243	242	10,287	11,282	48,518	47,589	668	660	12,556	13,377
RI......	1,530	1,464	21	18	768	752	4,342	4,204	53	53	1,149	1,209
SC	5,091	4,830	65	63	2,353	2,500	18,619	18,379	224	215	4,083	4,112
SD	1,390	1,295	16	15	472	484	4,181	4,240	50	48	879	908
TN	8,006	7,439	127	118	4,848	5,055	24,624	23,729	311	304	5,908	6,244
TX	32,631	31,460	458	431	20,176	19,568	74,758	75,745	1,021	1,036	21,846	21,878
UT	3,294	3,382	44	44	1,583	1,726	7,952	8,280	124	123	2,455	2,458
VT	889	873	11	10	401	425	3,974	3,948	38	40	750	863
VA	7,893	7,688	110	106	4,651	4,790	28,794	29,183	399	405	7,949	8,528
WA	9,869	9,546	125	121	5,412	5,507	22,700	22,650	313	310	7,181	7,335
WV	1,869	1,669	22	21	698	720	7,788	7,348	92	89	1,493	1,552
WI.....	7,928	7,377	119	116	4,636	4,840	21,354	21,372	322	312	5,891	6,268
WY	790	776	7	6	229	251	2,881	2,890	28	29	515	654

Source: U.S. Census Bureau, "County Business Patterns"; <http://www.census.gov/epcd/cbp/view/cbpview.html>.

U.S. Census Bureau, Statistical Abstract of the United States: 2007

Table 1016. **Retail Trade—Establishments, Employees, and Payroll: 2000 and 2003**

[1,113.6 represents 1,113,600. Covers establishments with payroll. Employees are for the week including March 12. Most government employees are excluded. For statement on methodology, see Appendix III]

Kind of business	NAICS code [1]	Establishments (1,000)		Employees (1,000)		Payroll (bil. dol.)	
		2000	2003	2000	2003	2000	2003
Retail trade, total	44-45	1,113.6	1,115.9	14,841	14,868	302.6	319.5
Motor vehicle & parts dealers	441	124.5	127.0	1,866	1,921	63.9	69.4
Automobile dealers	4411	50.9	52.3	1,222	1,290	47.8	52.4
New car dealers	44111	26.2	26.7	1,112	1,175	44.8	49.2
Used car dealers	44112	24.7	25.6	110	115	3.1	3.2
Other motor vehicle dealers	4412	14.5	16.2	127	148	3.8	4.9
Automotive parts, accessories & tire stores	4413	59.1	58.5	517	483	12.2	12.1
Furniture & home furnishings stores	442	64.8	65.4	549	561	13.4	13.7
Furniture stores	4421	29.7	28.3	284	265	7.5	7.4
Home furnishings stores	4422	35.1	37.1	265	296	5.9	6.3
Electronics & appliance stores	443	45.6	47.7	407	419	11.2	10.3
Appliance, television & other electronics stores	44311	29.6	34.7	279	324	6.6	7.9
Computer & software stores	44312	12.9	10.5	106	77	4.2	2.0
Camera & photographic supplies stores	44313	3.1	2.6	22	19	0.4	0.4
Bldg. material & garden equip. & supp. dealers	444	91.9	87.7	1,235	1,190	32.5	31.8
Building material & supplies dealers	4441	70.9	66.9	1,055	1,014	28.4	27.8
Lawn & garden equip. & supplies stores	4442	21.0	20.9	180	175	4.0	4.0
Food & beverage stores	445	154.5	152.6	3,004	2,884	48.4	50.4
Grocery stores	4451	98.3	97.0	2,717	2,595	44.0	45.7
Supermarkets & other grocery (except convenience) stores	44511	68.8	67.0	2,544	2,444	41.8	43.7
Convenience stores	44512	29.5	29.9	173	150	2.2	2.0
Specialty food stores	4452	27.8	26.5	154	150	2.4	2.4
Meat markets	44521	6.5	5.9	41	41	0.6	0.6
Fish & seafood markets	44522	1.9	2.1	8	10	0.1	0.2
Fruit & vegetable markets	44523	3.2	3.3	18	20	0.3	0.3
Other specialty food stores	44529	16.2	15.2	86	79	1.3	1.2
Beer, wine & liquor stores [2]	4453	28.5	29.1	134	139	2.1	2.2
Health & personal care stores	446	81.2	82.4	914	970	19.3	21.5
Pharmacies & drug stores	44611	40.6	39.4	680	700	14.5	16.0
Cosmetics, beauty supplies & perfume stores	44612	9.6	11.9	61	95	0.8	1.3
Optical goods stores	44613	14.3	12.9	74	74	1.7	1.7
Other health & personal care stores	44619	16.7	18.2	98	101	2.2	2.6
Food (health) supplement stores	446191	8.7	9.5	49	50	0.7	0.8
All other health & personal care stores	446199	8.0	8.6	49	52	1.5	1.8
Gasoline stations	447	119.6	119.5	937	936	13.3	14.3
Gasoline stations with convenience stores	44711	80.5	92.7	653	733	8.9	10.6
Other gasoline stations	44719	39.1	26.8	284	203	4.4	3.7
Clothing & clothing accessories stores	448	150.9	148.0	1,369	1,467	20.2	22.6
Clothing stores	4481	90.0	90.5	1,015	1,116	13.7	15.9
Men's clothing stores	44811	10.7	9.2	85	65	1.6	1.3
Women's clothing stores	44812	35.6	32.6	302	296	3.9	4.0
Children's & infants' clothing stores	44813	5.6	6.5	59	70	0.7	0.8
Family clothing stores	44814	20.6	24.1	453	557	5.9	7.7
Clothing accessories stores	44815	5.7	6.2	28	29	0.4	0.6
Other clothing stores	44819	11.8	12.1	88	99	1.2	1.5
Shoe stores	4482	29.7	27.4	185	188	2.6	2.8
Jewelry, luggage & leather goods stores	4483	31.3	30.2	168	163	3.9	3.9
Jewelry stores	44831	29.3	28.5	156	154	3.6	3.7
Luggage & leather goods stores	44832	2.0	1.6	12	9	0.2	0.2
Sporting goods, hobby, book & music stores	451	65.0	61.8	616	603	8.8	8.9
Sporting goods, hobby & musical instrument stores [3]	4511	43.6	42.6	389	402	6.0	6.3
Sporting goods stores	45111	22.6	22.4	185	192	2.9	3.2
Book, periodical & music stores [3]	4512	21.4	19.2	228	201	2.8	2.6
Book stores	451211	11.7	11.0	142	135	1.7	1.7
Prerecorded tape, compact disc & record stores	45122	7.7	6.4	76	57	0.9	0.7
General merchandise stores	452	39.6	42.0	2,526	2,525	39.8	44.6
Department stores	4521	10.4	9.4	1,766	1,369	27.2	23.5
Other general merchandise stores	4529	29.2	32.6	760	1,157	12.6	21.1
Warehouse clubs & superstores	45291	2.0	3.0	478	890	8.7	17.3
All other general merchandise stores	45299	27.2	29.5	283	267	3.8	3.8
Miscellaneous store retailers [3]	453	131.0	127.6	850	819	13.8	13.5
Used merchandise stores	4533	17.5	17.9	114	129	1.6	1.9
Other miscellaneous store retailers	4539	46.4	44.6	264	254	5.4	5.3
Nonstore retailers	454	44.8	54.1	567	572	18.1	18.5
Electronic shopping & mail-order houses	4541	11.8	16.0	277	265	10.4	9.7
Vending machine operators	4542	6.2	5.6	67	63	1.5	1.4
Direct selling establishments	4543	26.8	32.4	223	244	6.1	7.3
Fuel dealers	45431	11.8	10.7	106	99	3.1	3.3
Other direct selling establishments	45439	15.0	21.7	117	145	3.0	4.1

[1] Data for 2000 based on North American Industry Classification System 1997; 2003 data based on NAICS 2002. See text, Section 15.   [2] Includes government employees.   [3] Includes other kinds of business not shown separately.

Source: U.S. Census Bureau, County Business Patterns; <http://www.census.gov/epcd/cbp/view/cbpview.html>.

Table 1017. **Retail Trade and Food Services—Sales by Kind of Business: 1995 to 2005**

[In billions of dollars (2,456.1 represents $2,456,100,000,000)]

Kind of business	2002 NAICS code[1]	1995	1999	2000	2001	2002	2003	2004	2005
Retail & food services sales, total ...	44, 45, 72	2,456.1	3,093.6	3,294.2	3,385.6	3,466.1	3,615.2	3,849.7	4,115.8
Retail sales, total	44, 45	2,222.5	2,808.6	2,988.8	3,067.7	3,134.3	3,265.5	3,477.3	3,719.2
GAFO, total[2]		651.1	816.8	863.9	883.9	913.9	948.2	1,007.9	1,061.8
Motor vehicle and parts dealers	441	580.8	765.5	797.6	816.9	820.3	841.2	864.8	895.3
Automobile and other motor vehicle dealers	4411, 4412	528.7	702.7	733.9	755.6	757.4	776.6	797.5	822.3
Automobile dealers	4411	502.5	662.8	688.7	708.6	707.7	721.0	735.1	747.2
New car dealers	44111	464.6	606.2	630.1	649.4	645.8	656.9	665.9	670.0
Used car dealers	44112	37.8	56.6	58.6	59.2	61.9	64.1	69.2	77.2
Automotive parts, accessories, and tire stores	4413	52.1	62.9	63.7	61.3	62.9	64.6	67.4	73.0
Furniture, home furnishings, electronics and appliance stores	442, 443	128.5	163.6	173.7	172.0	178.5	184.5	200.5	211.7
Furniture and home furnishings stores	442	63.6	84.5	91.3	91.6	94.6	97.5	105.5	111.3
Furniture stores	4421	37.0	47.1	50.7	50.6	51.3	52.1	56.6	58.9
Home furnishings stores	4422	26.6	37.4	40.6	41.0	43.3	45.5	48.9	52.4
Electronics and appliance stores[3]	443	64.9	79.1	82.4	80.4	83.9	87.0	95.0	100.4
Appliance, television, and other electronics stores	44311	42.1	52.2	58.3	60.2	63.3	66.1	72.3	77.2
Household appliance stores	443111	10.0	12.1	12.6	13.5	14.2	14.5	15.7	17.4
Radio, television, and other electronics stores	443112	32.2	40.1	45.6	46.8	49.1	51.6	56.6	59.8
Computer and software stores	44312	20.5	23.9	20.7	16.9	17.3	17.5	19.2	19.7
Building materials, garden equipment & supply stores	444	164.8	218.6	229.3	239.7	248.9	265.1	298.9	327.0
Building materials & supply dealers	4441	141.2	188.2	197.9	207.3	217.4	232.0	263.7	288.7
Hardware stores	44413	13.8	15.6	16.2	16.6	17.0	17.6	18.1	18.9
Food and beverage stores[3]	445	391.3	434.6	445.7	463.3	465.8	477.1	495.7	519.3
Grocery stores	4451	356.9	394.7	403.0	418.6	420.3	430.0	445.1	463.9
Beer, wine and liquor stores	4453	22.1	26.6	28.7	29.8	30.1	30.7	32.6	35.0
Health and personal care stores	446	101.7	142.8	155.4	166.7	180.1	192.2	198.6	208.4
Pharmacies and drug stores	44611	85.9	121.3	130.9	141.8	153.9	164.6	167.2	174.2
Gasoline stations	447	181.3	212.7	250.0	251.5	250.8	273.6	320.8	388.3
Clothing & clothing accessories stores[3]	448	131.6	160.0	168.0	167.6	172.6	178.8	190.2	201.7
Clothing stores[3]	4481	90.8	111.8	118.2	119.3	123.0	128.3	137.1	147.0
Women's clothing stores	44812	28.7	29.6	31.5	31.5	31.3	32.5	34.7	36.7
Family clothing stores	44814	40.0	55.3	58.9	60.2	64.3	67.3	72.0	77.3
Shoe stores	4482	20.4	22.7	22.9	22.9	23.2	23.2	23.8	24.6
Jewelry stores	44831	19.2	23.9	25.0	23.7	24.8	25.5	27.6	28.3
Sporting goods, hobby, book & music stores[3]	451	60.9	72.8	76.1	77.1	77.0	77.3	80.2	81.9
Sporting goods stores	45111	20.0	23.8	25.4	26.3	26.3	27.2	28.9	31.0
Book stores	451211	11.2	14.2	14.9	15.5	15.5	16.2	16.8	16.6
General merchandise stores	452	300.6	380.3	404.3	427.6	446.6	468.7	497.2	525.7
Department stores (excl. L.D.)[4]	4521	205.9	230.3	232.5	228.4	220.7	214.4	215.7	214.7
Department stores (incl. L.D.)[4]	4521	210.9	236.8	239.9	235.6	227.8	221.0	222.0	220.3
Other general merchandise stores	4529	94.7	150.0	171.9	199.2	225.9	253.4	281.6	311.1
Warehouse clubs and superstores	45291	65.1	118.8	139.6	164.7	191.3	216.3	242.4	270.8
Miscellaneous store retailers[3]	453	77.2	105.6	108.1	104.4	104.2	103.1	105.6	111.0
Nonstore retailers[3]	454	103.7	152.0	180.7	180.8	189.5	203.9	224.7	249.9
Electronic shopping & mail order houses	4541	52.7	94.4	113.9	114.8	122.3	131.2	147.1	161.6
Fuel dealers	45431	19.8	19.9	26.7	26.1	24.0	29.0	32.0	38.3
Food services and drinking places[5]	722	233.6	285.0	305.5	317.9	331.8	349.7	372.4	396.6

[1] North American Industry Classification System, 2002; see text, Section 15. [2] GAFO (General Merchandise, Apparel, Furniture, and Office Supplies) represents stores classified in the following NAICS codes: 442, 443, 448, 451, 452, and 4532. [3] Includes other kinds of business not shown separately. [4] L.D. represents leased departments. [5] See also Table 1263.
Source: U.S. Census Bureau, *Current Business Reports, Annual Revision of Monthly Retail and Food Services: Sales and Inventories—January 1992 Through February 2006*, Series BR/05-A.

Table 1018. **Retail Trade Corporations—Sales, Net Profit, and Profit Per Dollar of Sales: 2004 and 2005**

[Represents North American Industry Classification System, 1997 (NAICS) groups 44 and 45. Profit rates are averages of quarterly figures at annual rates. Covers corporations with assets of $50,000,000 or more]

Item	Unit	Total retail trade		Food and beverage stores (NAICS 445)		Clothing and general merchandise stores (NAICS 448 and 452)		All other retail stores	
		2004	2005	2004	2005	2004	2005	2004	2005
Sales	Bil. dol.	1,666	1,780	360	374	637	638	669	768
Net profit:									
Before income taxes	Bil. dol.	80.5	82.5	7.4	8.5	39.2	36.6	33.9	37.4
After income taxes	Bil. dol.	53.2	55.5	4.7	5.4	25.6	24.8	22.9	25.3
Profits per dollar of sales:									
Before income taxes	Cents	4.8	4.6	2.1	2.3	6.1	5.7	5.1	4.9
After income taxes	Cents	3.2	3.1	1.3	1.5	4.0	3.9	3.4	3.3
Profits on stockholders' equity:									
Before income taxes	Percent	25.5	23.8	18.4	19.6	26.6	22.9	26.5	26.1
After income taxes	Percent	16.8	16.0	11.7	12.5	17.4	15.5	17.8	17.6

Source: U.S. Census Bureau, *Quarterly Financial Report for Manufacturing, Mining and Trade Corporations*; <http://www.census.gov/csd/qfr/>.

652   Wholesale and Retail Trade

Table 1019. **Retail Trade and Food Services—Estimated Per Capita Sales by Selected Kinds of Business: 1995 to 2005**

[In dollars. **As of December 31.** Based on estimated resident population estimates as of July. For statement on methodology, see Appendix III]

Kind of business	2002 NAICS code [1]	1995	1999	2000	2001	2002	2003	2004	2005
Retail and food service sales	44-45,72	9,346	11,344	11,673	11,875	12,036	12,429	13,109	13,885
Retail sales, total	44-45	8,457	10,299	10,591	10,760	10,884	11,227	11,841	12,547
Total (excluding motor vehicle and parts dealers)	44-45 ex 441	6,247	7,492	7,765	7,894	8,035	8,335	8,896	9,527
Motor vehicle and parts dealers . . .	441	2,210	2,807	2,826	2,865	2,848	2,892	2,945	3,020
Furniture and home furnishings stores	442	242	310	324	321	329	335	359	375
Electronics and appliance stores	443	247	290	292	282	291	299	323	339
Building material and garden equipment and supplies dealers	444	627	802	813	841	864	911	1,018	1,103
Food and beverage stores	445	1,489	1,594	1,579	1,625	1,617	1,640	1,688	1,752
Health and personal care stores	446	387	524	551	585	626	661	676	703
Gasoline stations	447	690	780	886	882	871	941	1,092	1,310
Clothing and clothing accessories stores . .	448	501	587	595	588	599	615	648	680
Sporting goods, hobby, book, and music stores	451	232	267	270	271	267	266	273	276
General merchandise stores	452	1,144	1,395	1,433	1,500	1,551	1,612	1,693	1,774
Miscellaneous store retailers	453	294	387	383	366	362	354	360	374
Nonstore retailers	454	395	557	640	634	658	701	765	840
Food services and drinking places . . .	722	889	1,045	1,082	1,115	1,152	1,202	1,268	1,338

[1] North American Industry Classification System, 2002; see text, Section 15.

Source: U.S. Census Bureau, *Current Business Reports, Annual Revision of Monthly Retail and Food Services: Sales and Inventories—January 1992 Through February 2006*, Series BR/05-A.

Table 1020. **Retail Trade—Merchandise Inventories and Inventory/Sales Ratio by Kind of Business: 2000 to 2005**

[**Inventories in billions of dollars (407.0 represents $407,000,000,000).** As of December 31. Estimates exclude food services. Includes warehouses. Adjusted for seasonal variations. Sales data also adjusted for holiday and trading-day differences. Based on data from the Monthly Retail Trade Survey, Annual Retail Trade Survey, and administrative records; see Appendix III. Data have been adjusted using results of the 2002 Economic Census]

Kind of business	2002 NAICS code [1]	Inventories				Inventory/sales ratio			
		2000	2003	2004	2005	2000	2003	2004	2005
Total [2]	44-45	407.0	432.3	461.2	473.9	1.62	1.56	1.54	1.50
Excluding motor vehicle and parts dealers	44-45 ex 441	278.4	286.0	306.3	320.0	1.49	1.38	1.36	1.32
Motor vehicle and parts dealers	441	128.6	146.3	154.9	153.8	2.01	2.09	2.05	2.07
Furniture, home furnishings, electronics, and appliance stores	442,443	25.4	26.4	29.2	30.3	1.83	1.65	1.71	1.70
Building material and garden equipment and supplies dealers	444	34.6	38.3	42.8	46.2	1.77	1.67	1.65	1.61
Food and beverage stores	445	32.0	32.3	33.2	33.6	0.84	0.81	0.79	0.76
Clothing and clothing accessories stores	448	36.5	37.6	40.3	42.4	2.59	2.44	2.51	2.48
General merchandise stores	452	64.9	66.6	71.0	74.2	1.87	1.66	1.67	1.66
Department stores	4521	42.7	37.0	37.6	37.8	2.17	2.08	2.07	2.13

[1] North American Industry Classification System, 2002; see text, Section 15. [2] Includes kind of business not shown separately.

Source: U.S. Census Bureau, *Current Business Reports, Annual Revision of Monthly Retail and Food Services: Sales and Inventories—January 1992 Through February 2006*, Series BR/05-A.

Table 1021. **Retail Trade Sales—Total and E-Commerce by Kind of Business: 2004**

[**3,477,308 represents $3,477,308,000,000.** Covers retailers with and without payroll. Based on the Annual Retail Trade Survey; see Appendix III]

Kind of business	2002 NAICS code [1]	Value of sales (mil. dol.)		E-commerce as percent of total sales	Percent distribution of E-commerce sales
		Total	E-commerce		
Retail trade, total [2]	44-45	3,477,308	70,906	2.0	100.0
Motor vehicle and parts dealers	441	864,848	11,450	1.3	16.1
Electronics and appliance stores	443	94,989	1,097	1.2	1.5
Building material and garden equipment and supplies stores	444	298,935	269	0.1	0.4
Clothing and clothing accessories stores	448	190,204	820	0.4	1.2
Sporting goods, hobby, book, and music stores	451	80,211	1,363	1.7	1.9
Miscellaneous store retailers	453	105,616	1,249	1.2	1.8
Nonstore retailers	454	224,699	53,630	23.9	75.6
Electronic shopping and mail-order houses	454110	147,123	52,217	35.5	73.6

[1] North American Industry Classification System, 2002; see text, Section 15. [2] Includes other kinds of business not shown separately.

Source: U.S. Census Bureau, "E-Stats, 2004 E-commerce Multi-sector Report"; published 25 May 2006; <http://www.census.gov/eos/www/ebusiness614.htm>.

Wholesale and Retail Trade 653

Table 1022. **Retail Trade and Food Services—Sales by Type of Store and State: 2004**

[In millions of dollars (3,906,482 represents $3,906,482,000,000). Kind-of-business classification based on North American Industry Classification System (NAICS), 1997; see text, Section 15. Data are estimates]

State	Total retail sales and food and drink (NAICS 44-45, 722)	All retail stores [1] (NAICS 44-45)	Motor vehicle and parts dealers (NAICS 441)	Furniture and home furnishings (NAICS 442)	Electronics and appliances (NAICS 443)	Building material & garden equip. & supplies dealers (NAICS 444)	Food and beverage stores (NAICS 445)	Health and personal care (NAICS 446)
U.S....	3,906,482	3,522,754	906,076	104,986	98,252	355,220	526,194	215,424
AL	50,618	45,859	12,200	1,185	744	4,581	6,090	2,745
AK	9,076	8,028	1,697	132	172	1,100	1,353	133
AZ	74,855	67,909	18,436	2,203	1,867	5,930	9,388	3,887
AR	31,464	28,926	8,170	663	482	3,041	3,234	1,305
CA	481,895	428,851	111,604	13,186	19,075	41,457	70,435	27,118
CO	68,426	61,285	15,999	2,429	1,942	7,262	9,272	2,021
CT	53,814	48,829	11,560	1,508	1,414	5,180	8,685	3,299
DE	13,236	11,909	3,122	585	376	1,425	1,472	812
DC	4,681	2,783	122	119	100	277	668	417
FL......	229,956	209,355	63,010	6,348	5,704	17,747	32,838	14,234
GA	115,211	103,516	28,583	3,446	2,334	12,945	15,870	4,688
HI	16,685	14,260	2,306	253	215	954	2,854	1,245
ID......	19,564	18,211	4,881	505	442	2,463	2,456	557
IL......	162,211	144,755	35,026	4,167	4,054	13,950	23,488	11,044
IN......	79,750	72,222	18,839	1,726	1,584	8,049	8,808	4,489
IA......	40,101	37,089	9,436	943	920	5,254	5,229	1,956
KS	37,215	34,263	8,615	982	994	3,512	4,878	1,534
KY	46,500	41,326	10,182	860	661	4,835	5,589	2,765
LA	52,810	47,385	12,409	1,074	744	4,835	6,663	3,106
ME	20,547	19,001	4,138	368	229	1,967	3,742	756
MD	76,380	69,072	17,301	2,165	2,253	6,545	13,341	4,287
MA	94,893	83,465	20,257	2,274	1,812	7,592	14,953	5,702
MI......	135,626	123,244	33,550	3,501	2,783	11,169	15,785	10,038
MN	80,931	74,127	17,209	2,607	2,197	9,594	9,642	3,494
MS	30,884	28,192	7,499	822	426	3,260	3,875	1,534
MO	76,046	68,687	17,963	1,704	1,494	6,778	8,553	3,592
MT	10,723	9,577	2,280	235	187	1,358	1,691	312
NE	23,563	21,486	4,802	1,090	437	2,819	2,997	1,040
NV	33,846	29,721	6,762	1,064	787	2,871	4,367	1,456
NH	27,265	25,328	7,184	707	876	2,142	3,651	1,014
NJ......	126,940	116,147	29,067	4,232	3,696	9,324	19,018	9,965
NM	23,040	20,859	4,883	635	393	1,802	2,614	1,129
NY	229,401	205,165	44,139	6,255	5,602	18,477	33,300	18,133
NC	104,764	94,049	25,471	3,516	2,032	11,885	13,074	5,228
ND	9,097	8,374	1,855	219	117	1,719	841	498
OH	154,089	139,302	35,807	4,081	3,924	13,955	18,683	10,483
OK	42,369	38,292	11,229	922	1,009	3,196	4,470	2,170
OR	49,091	44,357	11,312	1,161	1,057	5,150	6,722	1,407
PA	155,423	140,302	35,614	3,544	2,710	12,925	22,867	10,891
RI......	12,911	10,990	2,547	311	233	824	1,941	1,161
SC	51,079	45,705	11,995	1,202	71	6,204	6,785	2,332
SD	16,433	15,516	2,379	218	17	1,476	1,356	409
TN	81,572	73,920	19,586	2,033	1,283	7,066	12,338	4,127
TX	319,203	288,967	82,487	8,650	9,148	25,172	35,674	12,671
UT	29,708	27,310	7,122	1,015	876	3,464	4,428	460
VT	8,905	8,175	2,104	190	186	1,045	1,459	404
VA	101,475	92,453	22,821	3,436	3,548	9,889	12,960	4,384
WA	84,161	74,935	16,493	2,106	1,906	8,671	11,178	3,720
WV	19,875	18,126	4,561	343	204	1,828	2,573	1,685
WI......	80,444	74,044	17,837	1,931	1,864	9,522	10,892	3,446
WY	7,727	7,109	1,626	135	100	736	1,151	143

See footnotes at end of table.

Table 1022. **Retail Trade and Food Services—Sales by Type of Store and State: 2004**—Con.

[See headnote, page 654]

State	Gasoline stations (NAICS 447)	Clothing and clothing accessories (NAICS 448)	Sporting goods, hobby, book & music stores (NAICS 451)	General merchandise (NAICS 452)	Miscellaneous stores (NAICS 453)	Nonstore retailers (NAICS 454)	Food services & drinking places (NAICS 722)
U.S....	249,258	184,752	81,733	504,356	99,566	196,938	383,728
AL	4,232	2,086	771	8,820	1,323	1,082	4,759
AK	503	353	192	1,826	192	374	1,048
AZ	5,438	2,493	1,561	10,189	2,715	3,802	6,946
AR	2,794	1,107	495	6,099	829	708	2,538
CA	27,174	25,282	11,937	56,316	12,122	13,146	53,044
CO	4,097	2,562	2,183	8,703	2,082	2,733	7,141
CT	2,481	2,846	1,204	3,986	1,240	5,426	4,985
DE	591	681	361	1,590	378	514	1,327
DC	234	390	167	87	136	66	1,897
FL......	12,323	11,736	4,037	25,911	5,734	9,733	20,601
GA	9,024	5,095	1,815	14,283	2,761	2,672	11,695
HI......	1,029	1,584	357	2,769	561	134	2,425
ID......	1,289	532	514	2,884	560	1,127	1,354
IL......	8,719	8,824	3,019	17,734	3,574	11,155	17,456
IN......	5,970	2,468	1,231	12,109	1,708	5,242	7,527
IA......	4,007	1,238	661	5,341	769	1,334	3,013
KS	2,900	1,563	775	6,777	915	819	2,952
KY	4,286	1,456	689	7,683	1,340	978	5,174
LA	4,646	2,150	745	8,906	1,180	927	5,425
ME	1,540	809	370	2,119	465	2,497	1,547
MD	4,049	4,398	2,033	8,518	1,860	2,321	7,308
MA	4,683	5,663	2,351	9,090	2,341	6,747	11,428
MI......	7,465	5,245	3,697	21,820	4,299	3,891	12,382
MN	5,847	2,792	2,170	9,493	2,003	7,080	6,805
MS	2,992	1,012	338	5,150	720	564	2,692
MO	6,875	2,457	1,406	11,597	1,930	4,337	7,359
MT	749	273	292	1,704	262	234	1,147
NE	1,792	863	391	2,939	421	1,895	2,077
NV	1,759	2,260	639	3,667	1,366	2,724	4,125
NH	1,420	1,091	676	3,345	588	2,635	1,937
NJ......	5,462	7,484	3,512	12,708	3,143	8,535	10,793
NM	1,944	855	514	3,660	1,101	1,329	2,182
NY	10,471	20,293	5,868	23,525	7,154	11,948	24,236
NC	7,220	4,310	1,609	13,057	3,251	3,366	10,715
ND	660	242	248	1,279	203	424	723
OH	9,720	6,089	2,719	22,837	3,299	7,719	14,786
OK	3,833	1,060	763	7,553	1,089	987	4,077
OR	2,465	1,703	1,241	8,074	1,514	2,550	4,734
PA	8,919	7,648	2,817	15,694	3,118	13,484	15,121
RI......	702	683	271	1,105	283	921	1,921
SC	4,332	2,280	628	6,893	1,562	782	5,375
SD	916	302	210	1,396	235	6,446	917
TN	6,251	3,664	1,324	12,532	2,034	1,680	7,653
TX	21,918	14,367	5,830	45,371	7,862	19,816	30,236
UT	1,952	1,151	775	4,341	504	1,222	2,398
VT	711	309	203	537	190	837	730
VA	7,894	4,890	2,072	13,634	2,051	4,873	9,022
WA	4,094	3,043	2,317	13,368	2,538	5,500	9,226
WV	1,888	712	268	3,217	456	391	1,750
WI......	5,913	2,176	1,326	10,870	1,386	6,881	6,400
WY	1,084	179	137	1,250	217	351	618

[1] Includes other types of stores, not shown separately.

Source: Market Statistics, a division of Claritas Inc., Arlington, VA, *The Survey of Buying Power Data Service*, annual (copyright).

U.S. Census Bureau, Statistical Abstract of the United States: 2007

Table 1023. U.S. Projected Online Retail Sales: 2005 to 2010

[In billions of dollars (172.4 represents $172,400,000,000)]

Online product or service	2005	2006	2007	2008	2009	2010
Retail trade, total [1]	172.4	201.7	233.4	265.8	298.2	328.6
Apparel [1]	12.5	15.2	17.8	20.5	23.2	25.9
General apparel	8.0	9.6	11.3	13.2	15.2	17.4
Computer hardware/software [1]	13.9	14.9	15.6	16.2	16.6	17.0
Computer hardware	11.3	12.1	12.7	13.1	13.5	13.8
Consumer electronics	8.5	10.0	11.8	13.5	15.2	16.8
Home products	19.1	23.5	27.9	32.2	36.5	40.6
Tickets	5.4	6.3	7.1	7.9	8.7	9.4
Auto/auto parts	9.3	9.3	11.4	13.8	16.5	19.4
Food/beverage	5.8	7.4	9.3	11.5	14.1	16.9
Travel	62.8	73.4	84.6	96.5	108.7	119.1

[1] Includes other products/services not shown separately.
Source: Forrester Research, Inc., Cambridge, MA, "US eCommerce: 2005 to 2010", September 14, 2005 (copyright).

Table 1024. Online Retail Spending, 2000 to 2005, and Projections, 2006

[24.1 represents $24,100,000,000]

Category	Online retail spending (bil.dol.)					Percentage of total retail spending by category				
	2000	2003	2004	2005	2006, proj.	2000	2003	2004	2005	2006, proj.
Total [1]	24.1	53.9	67.3	80.9	95.3	(X)	(X)	(X)	(X)	(X)
Personal computers	6.1	8.9	9.9	10.9	12.2	25.3	36.0	37.3	39.7	42.7
Peripherals	1.8	2.6	2.9	3.2	3.4	18.7	24.9	24.2	25.6	26.1
Software	1.4	3.0	3.3	3.6	3.8	17.4	36.1	37.8	39.2	40.9
Consumer electronics	1.1	2.6	3.4	4.2	5.0	2.4	5.5	6.3	7.3	8.2
Books	2.2	3.2	3.6	3.9	4.2	9.5	13.0	14.4	15.4	16.1
Music	0.7	0.9	1.2	1.8	2.2	4.6	7.4	9.8	14.7	17.9
Videos	0.5	1.2	1.5	1.8	2.1	3.9	7.5	7.7	8.1	8.4
Event tickets	1.0	2.7	3.3	3.8	4.3	6.4	14.6	17.2	19.3	20.9
Personal care	0.1	0.4	0.7	1.0	1.6	0.3	0.9	1.5	2.0	3.2
Apparel	2.3	6.2	7.7	9.1	10.6	1.2	2.9	3.4	3.8	4.3
Footwear	0.3	1.1	1.4	1.6	1.8	0.6	1.9	2.4	2.7	2.9
Jewelry	0.8	1.4	1.7	1.9	2.2	2.6	4.2	4.7	5.4	5.9
Grocery	0.6	1.7	2.5	3.3	4.2	0.1	0.3	0.4	0.5	0.7
Pets	0.1	0.4	0.5	0.7	0.9	0.3	1.6	2.4	3.1	3.8
Toys	0.8	0.8	0.8	0.9	0.9	2.9	3.7	4.2	4.5	4.8
Video games	–	1.4	1.6	2.0	2.6	(NA)	5.8	6.8	7.9	10.0
Sporting goods	0.5	1.3	1.6	2.0	2.2	2.1	5.4	6.7	7.8	8.6
Flowers	0.4	1.0	1.3	1.4	1.6	2.9	6.3	7.4	8.2	8.9
Specialty gifts	0.4	1.1	1.4	1.7	2.0	1.2	2.8	3.6	4.3	4.9
Furniture	0.1	0.5	0.7	0.9	1.1	0.1	0.7	0.9	1.2	1.4
Large appliances	0.1	0.7	0.9	1.1	1.3	0.7	3.0	3.9	4.8	5.6
Housewares/small appliances	0.3	2.0	3.0	4.1	5.7	0.5	2.7	3.9	5.3	7.1
Art and collectibles	0.2	0.6	0.8	1.1	1.4	0.8	2.2	2.9	3.6	4.4
Home improvement	0.1	1.0	1.5	2.0	2.7	0.1	0.5	0.7	0.8	1.1
Garden supplies	0.1	0.3	0.5	0.7	0.9	0.2	0.9	1.4	1.9	2.3
Office products	0.3	1.8	2.6	3.2	3.8	1.1	5.2	7.3	9.0	10.2
Auto parts	–	0.3	0.5	0.8	1.1	–	0.9	1.5	2.2	2.9

– Represents or rounds to zero. NA Not available. X Not applicable. [1] Includes other categories not shown separately.
Source: Jupiter Research, Inc., New York, NY, unpublished data (copyright).

Table 1025. Electronic Shopping and Mail-Order Houses—Total and E-Commerce Sales by Merchandise Line: 2003 and 2004

[131,171 represents $131,171,000,000 in sales. Represents NAICS code 454110 which comprises establishments primarily engaged in retailing all types of merchandise using non-store means, such as catalogs, toll free telephone numbers, or electronic media, such as interactive television or computer. Covers businesses with or without paid employees. Based on the Annual Retail Survey; see Appendix III]

Merchandise line	Value of sales, total, 2003 (mil. dol.)	2004				
		Value of sales (mil. dol.)		E-commerce as percent of total sales	Percent distribution	
		Total	E-commerce		Total	E-commerce
Total	131,171	147,123	52,217	35.5	100.0	100.0
Books and magazines	4,106	4,457	2,466	55.3	3.0	4.7
Clothing & clothing accessories (includes footwear)	15,064	16,364	7,152	43.7	11.1	13.7
Computer hardware	23,423	26,854	9,410	35.0	18.3	18.0
Computer software	3,878	4,332	1,515	35.0	2.9	2.9
Drugs, health aids, beauty aids	27,250	31,663	2,266	7.2	21.5	4.3
Electronics and appliances	6,274	7,857	4,653	59.2	5.3	8.9
Food, beer and wine	2,199	2,549	1,114	43.7	1.7	2.1
Furniture and home furnishings	8,251	8,752	4,289	49.0	5.9	8.2
Music and videos	3,730	3,901	1,960	50.2	2.7	3.8
Office equipment and supplies	7,001	7,634	4,084	53.5	5.2	7.8
Sporting goods	2,615	2,914	1,415	48.6	2.0	2.7
Toys, hobby goods, and games	3,870	3,889	1,753	45.1	2.6	3.4
Other merchandise [1]	17,659	19,170	6,572	34.3	13.0	12.6
Nonmerchandise receipts [2]	5,851	6,783	3,568	52.6	4.6	6.8

[1] Includes other merchandise such as jewelry, collectibles, souvenirs, auto parts and accessories, hardware, and lawn and garden equipment and supplies. [2] Includes nonmerchandise receipts such as auction commissions, shipping and handling, customer training, customer support, and advertising.
Source: U.S. Census Bureau, "E-Stats, 2004 E-commerce Multi-sector Report"; published 25 May 2006; <http://www.census.gov/eos/www/ebusiness614.htm>.

656   Wholesale and Retail Trade

Table 1026. Retail Trade—Nonemployer Establishments and Receipts by Kind of Business: 2000 to 2003

[**1,743 represents** 1,743,000. Includes only firms subject to federal income tax. Nonemployers are businesses with no paid employees. Data for 2000 based on the North American Industry Classification System (NAICS), 1997; beginning 2002 based on NAICS 2002, see text, Section 15]

Kind of business	NAICS code	Establishments (1,000)			Receipts (mil. dol.)		
		2000	2002	2003	2000	2002	2003
Retail trade, total	44-45	1,743	1,839	1,880	73,810	77,896	80,548
Motor vehicle & parts dealers [1]	441	122	138	143	17,355	18,529	19,482
Used car dealers	44112	74	83	84	13,255	13,835	14,429
Motorcycle & boat & other MV dealers	44122	21	24	26	1,969	2,217	2,440
Automotive parts, accessories, & tire stores. . . .	4413	25	28	29	1,872	2,150	2,280
Furniture & home furnishings stores.	442	37	41	42	2,574	2,794	2,962
Furniture stores	4421	14	14	15	1,034	1,120	1,188
Home furnishings stores.	4422	23	26	27	1,540	1,674	1,774
Electronics & appliance stores	443	29	29	29	1,688	1,669	1,674
Bldg. material & garden equip. & supp. dealers [1] . .	444	28	30	31	2,182	2,326	2,427
Building material & supplies dealers	4441	20	22	23	1,677	1,803	1,883
Food & beverage stores	445	82	88	90	8,493	8,851	8,983
Grocery stores	4451	39	41	41	4,609	4,673	4,644
Specialty food stores	4452	33	36	38	2,135	2,362	2,474
Beer, wine, & liquor stores	4453	10	10	10	1,749	1,815	1,866
Health & personal care stores.	446	92	104	115	1,915	2,196	2,349
Gasoline stations	447	10	9	9	1,721	1,628	1,659
Clothing & clothing accessories stores [1]	448	89	96	102	4,464	4,683	4,808
Clothing stores	4481	60	62	67	2,718	2,823	2,930
Jewelry stores	44831	23	29	29	1,416	1,512	1,519
Sporting goods, hobby, book, & music stores [1] . . .	451	96	94	96	3,761	3,776	3,815
Sporting goods stores	45111	23	23	23	1,340	1,340	1,357
Book, periodical, & music stores	4512	32	31	31	1,007	973	973
General merchandise stores.	452	28	30	33	1,291	1,423	1,497
Miscellaneous store retailers [1]	453	339	338	334	12,963	13,350	13,467
Gift, novelty, & souvenir stores	45322	73	76	75	2,104	2,161	2,166
Used merchandise stores	4533	76	73	69	2,115	1,953	1,860
Nonstore retailers [1].	454	792	843	857	15,401	16,670	17,425
Electronic shopping & mail-order houses.	4541	49	48	58	1,391	1,584	1,941
Direct selling establishments	4543	708	761	767	13,047	14,138	14,562

[1] Includes other kinds of business not shown separately.

Source: U.S. Census Bureau, "Nonemployer Statistics"; <http://www.census.gov/epcd/nonemployer/>.

Table 1027. Franchised New Car Dealerships—Summary: 1990 to 2005

[**316 represents** $316,000,000,000]

Item	Unit	1990	1995	1998	1999	2000	2001	2002	2003	2004	2005
Dealerships [1]	Number .	24,825	22,800	22,600	22,400	22,250	21,800	21,725	21,650	21,640	21,495
Sales	Bil. dol. .	316	456	546	607	650	690	680	699	714	699
New cars sold [2]	Millions .	9.3	8.6	8.1	8.7	8.8	8.4	8.1	7.6	7.5	7.7
Used vehicles sold	Millions .	14.2	18.5	19.3	20.1	20.5	21.4	19.4	19.5	19.7	19.7
Employment	1,000 .	924	996	1,048	1,081	1,114	1,130	1,130	1,130	1,130	1,138
Annual payroll	Bil. dol. .	24.0	33.1	39.8	42.5	46.1	48.0	48.8	50.0	50.5	51.5
Advertising expenses	Bil. dol. .	3.7	4.6	5.3	5.6	6.4	6.6	7.5	8.5	8.3	7.7
Dealer pretax profits as a percentage of sales . . .	Percent .	1.0	1.4	1.7	1.8	1.6	2.0	1.9	1.7	1.7	1.6
Inventory: [3]											
Domestic: [4]											
Total	1,000. . .	2,537	2,974	2,732	2,901	3,183	2,824	2,727	3,085	3,267	2,991
Days' supply	Days . . .	73	71	63	62	68	63	63	63	75	70
Imported: [4]											
Total	1,000. . .	707	445	350	378	468	508	521	618	646	566
Days' supply	Days . . .	72	72	54	47	50	51	49	49	59	52

[1] At beginning of year.   [2] Data provided by "Ward's Automotive Reports."   [3] Annual average. Includes light trucks. [4] Classification based on where automobiles are produced (i.e., automobiles manufactured by foreign companies but produced in the U.S. are classified as domestic).

Source: National Automobile Dealers Association, McLean, VA, *NADA Data*, annual.

Table 1028. Retail Sales—New Passenger Cars: 1990 to 2004

[In thousands (**9,303 represents** 9,303,000). Retail new car sales include both sales to individuals and to corporate fleets. It also includes leased cars]

Item	1990	1995	1998	1999	2000	2001	2002	2003	2004
Total retail sales	9,303	8,635	8,142	8,698	8,847	8,423	8,103	7,610	7,506
Domestic [1]	6,919	7,129	6,762	6,979	6,831	6,325	5,878	5,527	5,357
Imports	2,384	1,506	1,380	1,719	2,016	2,098	2,226	2,083	2,149
Japan	1,719	982	691	758	863	837	923	817	798
Germany	263	207	367	467	517	523	547	544	542
Other	402	317	322	494	637	738	756	722	809

[1] Includes cars produced in Canada and Mexico.

Source: U.S. Bureau of Transportation Statistics, *National Transportation Statistics*, annual. See Internet site <http://www.bts.gov/publications/nationaltransportationstatistics/>. Data supplied by *Ward's Motor Vehicle Facts & Figures 2005*.

Wholesale and Retail Trade   **657**

Table 1029. Retail Sales and Leases of New Cars by Sector: 1990 to 2004

[In thousands (9,300 represents 9,300,000), **except as indicated**. Includes imported cars, but not vans, trucks, or sport utility vehicles]

Sector	1990	1995	1998	1999	2000	2001	2002	2003	2004
Total	**9,300**	**8,636**	**8,142**	**8,697**	**8,852**	**8,422**	**8,102**	**7,615**	**7,505**
Consumer	5,677	4,326	3,980	4,389	4,680	4,632	4,523	4,328	4,186
Business	3,477	4,070	3,943	4,076	3,949	3,568	3,374	3,087	3,112
Government	147	241	218	232	224	223	205	200	207
PERCENT DISTRIBUTION									
Total	100.0	100.0	100.0	100.0	100.0	100.0	100.0	100.0	100.0
Consumer	61.0	50.1	48.9	50.5	52.9	55.0	55.8	56.8	55.8
Business	37.4	47.1	48.4	46.9	44.6	42.4	41.6	40.5	41.5
Government	1.6	2.8	2.7	2.7	2.5	2.6	2.5	2.6	2.8

Source: U.S. Bureau of Transportation Statistics, *National Transportation Statistics*, annual. See Internet site <http://www.bts.gov/publications/nationaltransportationstatistics/>. Data supplied by U.S. Department of Commerce, Bureau of Economic Analysis.

Table 1030. New and Used Vehicle Sales and Leases: 1990 to 2004

[In thousands (51,390 represents 51,390,000), **except as indicated**. Vehicle sales, value of sales, and average prices are from different sources and cannot be calculated from the data presented in this table]

Item	1990	1995	1998	1999	2000	2001	2002	2003	2004
Vehicle sales and leases, total . .	**51,390**	**56,476**	**56,375**	**57,618**	**58,964**	**59,742**	**59,835**	**60,215**	**59,410**
New vehicle sales and leases.	13,860	14,718	15,534	16,879	17,344	17,118	16,810	16,643	16,865
Passenger cars	9,300	8,636	8,142	8,697	8,852	8,422	8,102	7,615	7,505
Light trucks	4,560	6,081	7,392	8,183	8,492	8,696	8,708	9,029	9,360
New vehicle sales [1].	13,285	12,070	11,947	12,468	13,181	13,510	13,639	13,594	13,608
Passenger cars.	8,766	6,841	5,968	6,396	6,580	6,407	6,370	5,932	5,737
Light trucks	4,519	5,228	5,979	6,073	6,601	7,103	7,269	7,663	7,871
New vehicle leases [2].	575	2,648	3,587	4,411	4,163	3,608	3,171	3,049	3,257
Passenger cars.	534	1,795	2,174	2,301	2,272	2,015	1,732	1,683	1,768
Light trucks	41	853	1,413	2,110	1,891	1,593	1,439	1,366	1,489
Used vehicle sales [3].	37,530	41,758	40,841	40,739	41,620	42,624	43,025	43,572	42,545
New and used vehicle sales, total value (bil. dol.) [4]	**446**	**611**	**651**	**698**	**737**	**737**	**721**	**738**	**759**
New vehicle sales (bil. dol.)	227	292	316	348	380	369	371	382	392
Used vehicle sales (bil. dol.).	219	319	335	350	357	367	350	356	367
Average price (current dollars): [4]									
New and used vehicle sales	8,672	10,818	11,545	12,098	12,491	12,321	12,034	12,253	12,774
New vehicle sales	16,350	19,819	20,276	20,534	21,850	21,507	22,005	22,894	23,200
Used vehicle sales	5,830	7,644	8,211	8,587	8,578	8,619	8,130	8,180	8,629

[1] New vehicle sales data is calculated by subtracting CNW Marketing's vehicle leasing data from BEA's data which combines sales and leases. [2] Consumer leases only. [3] Used car sales include sales from franchised dealers, independent dealers, and casual sales. [4] Includes leased vehicles.

Source: U.S. Bureau of Transportation Statistics, *National Transportation Statistics*, annual. See Internet site <http://www.bts.gov/publications/nationaltransportationstatistics/>. Data supplied by following sources: New vehicle sales and leases—U.S. Bureau of Economic Analysis; New vehicle leases—CNW Marketing/Research; Used vehicle sales, value, and average price—Manheim, Used Car Market Report, Atlanta, GA.

Table 1031. New Motor Vehicle Sales and Expenditures: 1990 to 2005

[In thousands (14,137 represents 14,137,000), **except as indicated**. Includes leases]

Type of vehicle	1990	1995	2000	2001	2002	2003	2004	2005
New motor vehicle sales	**14,137**	**15,106**	**17,806**	**17,468**	**17,137**	**16,971**	**17,298**	**17,445**
New-car sales.	9,300	8,636	8,852	8,422	8,102	7,615	7,505	7,667
Domestic	6,897	7,129	6,833	6,323	5,871	5,527	5,350	5,480
Import	2,403	1,507	2,019	2,099	2,231	2,087	2,155	2,187
New-truck sales	4,838	6,469	8,954	9,046	9,035	9,356	9,793	9,778
Light	4,560	6,081	8,492	8,696	8,713	9,028	9,361	9,281
Domestic	3,957	5,691	7,651	7,718	7,647	7,801	8,115	8,065
Import	603	391	841	978	1,066	1,227	1,246	1,216
Other	278	388	462	350	322	328	432	497
Domestic-car production.	6,231	6,340	5,542	4,878	5,019	4,510	4,230	4,321
Avg. expenditure per new car [1] (dollar) . .	14,371	17,959	20,600	20,945	21,248	21,336	21,627	22,021
Domestic (dollar)	13,936	16,864	18,577	18,755	18,897	18,875	19,022	19,433
Import (dollar)	15,510	23,202	27,447	27,539	27,436	27,851	28,095	28,529

[1] BEA estimate based on the manufacturer's suggested retail price.

Source: U.S. Bureau of Economic Analysis, *Survey of Current Business*, February 2001 and unpublished data. Data on unit sales and production are mainly from "Ward's Automotive Reports" published by Ward's Communications, Southfield, MI.

Table 1032. **Annual U.S. Motor Vehicle Production and Factory (Wholesale) Sales: 1990 to 2004**

[In thousands (9,767 represents 9,767,000) except as indicated. Factory sales can be greater than production total because of sales from previous year's inventory]

Item	1990	1995	1998	1999	2000	2001	2002	2003	2004
Production, total	9,767	11,995	12,003	13,025	12,774	11,425	12,280	12,087	11,960
Passenger cars	6,078	6,340	5,554	5,638	5,542	4,879	5,019	4,510	4,230
Commercial vehicles [1]	3,690	5,655	6,448	7,387	7,231	6,546	7,261	7,577	7,731
Factory sales, commercial vehicles [1] . .	3,725	5,713	6,435	6,699	7,022	6,224	6,964	7,143	7,467

[1] Includes trucks under 10,000 pounds gross vehicle weight rating (GVWR), such as compact and conventional pickups, sport utility vehicles, minivans and vans, and trucks and buses.

Source: U.S. Bureau of Transportation Statistics, *National Transportation Statistics*, annual. See Internet site <http://www.bts.gov/publications/nationaltransportationstatistics/>. Data supplied by *Ward's Motor Vehicle Facts & Figures 2005*.

Table 1033. **Retail Foodstores—Number and Sales by Type: 1990 to 2004**

[133.6 represents 133,600. Beginning 2000 data based on North American Industry Classification System (NAICS), 2002; 1990 based on Standard Industrial Classification (SIC) codes]

Type of foodstore	Number [1] (1,000)					Sales [2] (bil. dol.)					Percent distribution			
											Number		Sales	
	1990	2000	2002	2003	2004	1990	2000	2002	2003	2004	2000	2004	2000	2004
Total.	133.6	119.6	120.0	120.2	120.5	335.8	417.3	435.7	446.4	463.1	100.0	100.0	100.0	100.0
Grocery stores	109.1	95.9	95.5	95.3	95.1	324.6	403.1	420.3	430.0	445.1	80.2	78.9	96.6	96.1
Supermarkets [3]	24.5	21.9	20.3	21.1	21.0	261.7	310.3	336.3	310.4	318.0	18.3	17.4	74.4	68.7
Conventional	13.2	7.2	4.4	4.1	3.6	92.3	58.3	62.4	57.6	59.0	6.0	3.0	14.0	12.7
Superstore [4]	5.8	7.9	7.9	8.1	8.2	87.6	131.0	144.2	133.1	136.3	6.6	6.8	31.4	29.4
Warehouse [5]	3.4	2.4	2.7	3.2	3.2	33.1	20.2	23.0	21.2	21.7	2.0	2.6	4.8	4.7
Combination food and drug [6]	1.6	3.7	4.5	5.0	5.2	29.3	75.3	79.5	73.4	75.2	3.1	4.3	18.0	16.2
Super warehouse [7] . . .	0.3	0.5	0.5	0.5	0.5	12.6	16.0	16.8	15.5	15.9	0.4	0.4	3.8	3.4
Hypermarket [8]	0.1	0.2	0.3	0.2	0.3	6.8	9.5	10.4	9.6	9.9	0.2	0.2	2.3	2.1
Convenience stores [9] . .	28.0	28.2	29.4	29.4	30.4	20.3	19.2	20.9	21.0	22.6	23.6	25.2	4.6	4.9
Superette [10] . .	56.6	45.8	45.8	44.8	43.8	42.5	73.6	63.1	98.6	104.5	38.3	36.3	17.6	22.6
Specialized food stores [11] .	24.5	23.7	24.5	24.9	25.4	11.2	14.2	15.4	16.4	18.0	19.8	21.1	3.4	3.9

[1] Estimated. [2] Includes nonfood items. [3] A grocery store, primarily self-service in operation, providing a full range of departments, and having at least $2.5 million in annual sales in 1985 dollars. [4] Contains greater variety of products than conventional supermarkets, including specialty and service departments, and considerable nonfood (general merchandise) products. [5] Contains limited product variety and fewer services provided, incorporating case lot stocking and shelving practices. [6] Contains a pharmacy, a nonprescription drug department, and a greater variety of health and beauty aids than that carried by conventional supermarkets. [7] A larger warehouse store that offers expanded product variety and often service meat, deli, or seafood departments. [8] A very large store offering a greater variety of general merchandise—like clothes, hardware, and seasonal goods—and personal care products than other grocery stores. [9] A small grocery store selling a limited variety of food and nonfood products, typically open extended hours. [10] A grocery store, primarily self-service in operation, selling a wide variety of food and nonfood products with annual sales below $2.5 million (1985 dollars). [11] Primarily engaged in the retail sale of a single food category such as meat and seafood stores and retail bakeries.

Source: U.S. Department of Agriculture, Economic Research Service, *The U.S. Food Marketing System, 2002*, Agricultural Economic Report 811, August 2002; and unpublished data.

Table 1034. **Food and Alcoholic Beverage Sales by Sales Outlet: 1990 to 2004**

[In billions of dollars (554.0 represents $554,000,000,000)]

Sales outlet	1990	1995	1997	1998	1999	2000	2001	2002	2003	2004
Food sales, total [1]	554.0	653.6	714.3	742.2	779.5	808.7	838.5	851.7	886.8	943.0
Food at home [2]	305.3	350.7	382.0	391.9	413.2	418.4	433.4	432.5	446.3	468.2
Food stores [2]	256.4	276.2	289.9	292.4	301.9	306.3	316.3	315.7	326.1	340.2
Other stores [3]	32.3	54.8	62.8	70.8	81.5	82.0	88.5	87.7	90.1	94.7
Home-delivered, mail order	5.3	8.6	18.9	18.1	18.7	19.0	17.8	18.1	18.5	21.2
Farmers, manufacturers, wholesalers	3.5	4.1	4.6	4.5	4.5	4.5	4.3	4.3	4.5	4.6
Home production and donations	7.7	7.0	5.9	6.2	6.7	6.6	6.4	6.7	7.0	7.4
Food away from home [4]	248.8	303.0	332.3	350.3	366.3	390.2	405.1	419.2	440.6	474.8
Alcoholic beverage sales, total . .	72.6	80.3	87.4	96.3	105.7	113.9	122.3	130.2	135.9	143.0
Packaged alcoholic beverages	38.0	41.5	44.7	48.5	52.2	53.6	55.9	58.5	59.0	61.4
Liquor stores	18.6	19.0	20.9	22.4	23.8	26.0	26.9	28.2	28.6	30.1
Food stores	10.8	12.3	12.8	14.1	15.1	15.6	16.6	17.0	17.6	18.5
All other.	8.6	10.3	11.0	12.0	13.3	12.0	12.4	13.3	12.8	12.8
Alcoholic drinks	34.5	38.8	42.7	47.7	53.4	60.3	66.4	71.8	77.0	81.6
Eating and drinking places [5]	26.6	30.3	33.5	36.1	38.8	42.7	45.6	48.5	51.4	55.8
Hotels and motels [5]	3.8	3.9	4.2	6.4	8.9	11.8	14.9	17.4	19.5	19.6
All other.	4.1	4.6	5.1	5.2	5.7	5.8	5.8	5.8	6.1	6.2

[1] Includes taxes and tips. [2] Excludes sales to restaurants and institutions. [3] Includes eating and drinking establishments, trailer parks, commissary stores, and military exchanges. [4] Includes food furnished and donations. [5] Includes tips.

Source: U.S. Department of Agriculture, Economic Research Service, "food cpi, prices, and expenditures: food expenditure tables"; published 15 November 2005; <http://www.ers.usda.gov/briefing/CPIFoodAndExpenditures/Data/>.

Wholesale and Retail Trade   659

Table 1035. **Shopping Centers—Number, Gross Leasable Area, and Retail Sales by Gross Leasable Area: 1990 to 2005**

[4,390 represents 4,390,000,000. As of December 31. A shopping center is a group of architecturally unified commercial establishments built on a site that is planned, developed, owned, and managed as an operating unit related in its location, size, and type of shops to the trade area that the unit serves. The unit provides on-site parking in definite relationship to the types and total size of the stores. The data base attempts to include all centers with three or more stores. Estimates are based on a sample of data available on shopping center properties; for details, contact source]

Year	Total	Gross leasable area (square feet)					
		Less than 100,001	100,001– 200,000	200,001– 400,000	400,001– 800,000	800,001– 1,000,000	More than 1 million
NUMBER							
1990	36,515	23,231	8,756	2,781	1,102	288	357
1995	41,235	26,001	9,974	3,345	1,234	301	380
2000	45,115	28,062	10,958	3,935	1,424	326	410
2003	47,104	29,234	11,336	4,233	1,540	334	427
2004	47,835	29,710	11,471	4,315	1,573	335	430
2005	48,695	30,270	11,617	4,405	1,628	338	437
Percent distribution	100.0	62.2	23.9	9.0	3.3	0.7	0.9
Percent change, 2004–2005 . . .	1.8	1.9	1.3	2.1	3.5	0.9	1.6
GROSS LEASABLE AREA							
1990 (mil. sq. ft.)	4,390	1,125	1,197	734	618	259	457
1995 (mil. sq. ft.)	4,967	1,267	1,368	886	689	271	486
2000 (mil. sq. ft.)	5,566	1,383	1,514	1,059	790	294	526
2003 (mil. sq. ft.)	5,865	1,446	1,569	1,147	854	301	548
2004 (mil. sq. ft.)	5,953	1,469	1,588	1,171	872	302	552
2005 (mil. sq. ft.)	6,060	1,486	1,608	1,196	903	305	561
Percent distribution	100.0	24.5	26.5	19.7	14.9	5.0	9.3
Percent change, 2004–2005 . . .	1.8	1.2	1.3	2.2	3.6	0.9	1.6
RETAIL SALES							
1990 (bil. dol.)	706.4	205.1	179.5	108.0	91.7	45.1	77.0
1995 (bil. dol.)	893.8	259.6	227.1	136.4	115.8	57.0	97.8
2000 (bil. dol.)	1,181.1	342.8	300.0	180.5	152.8	75.2	129.8
2003 (bil. dol.)	1,339.2	388.5	340.1	204.8	173.1	85.2	147.5
2004 (bil. dol.)	1,432.6	415.5	363.8	219.2	185.1	91.1	158.0
2005 (bil. dol.)	1,530.4	443.8	388.6	234.2	197.6	97.3	168.9
Percent distribution	100.0	29.0	25.4	15.3	12.9	6.4	11.0
Percent change, 2004–2005 . . .	6.8	6.8	6.8	6.9	6.8	6.8	6.9

Source: National Research Bureau, Chicago, IL (copyright, 2006). Data published by International Council of Shopping Centers, <http://www.icsc.org/>.

Table 1036. **Shopping Centers—Gross Leasable Area and Retail Sales by State: 2005**

[6,060 represents 6,060,000,000. See headnote, Table 1035]

State	Gross leasable area, (mil. sq. ft.)	Retail sales (bil. dol.)	Retail sales per sq. ft. (dol.)	Percent change, 2004–2005		State	Gross leasable area, (mil. sq. ft.)	Retail sales (bil. dol.)	Retail sales per sq. ft. (dol.)	Percent change, 2004–2005	
				Gross leasable area	Retail sales					Gross leasable area	Retail sales
U.S. . . .	**6,060**	**1,530.4**	**253**	**1.8**	**6.8**						
AL	84	21.7	258	0.8	5.8	MO	129	33.0	255	1.9	6.5
AK	8	3.3	429	–	8.5	MT	10	3.0	293	–	6.8
AZ	150	36.8	245	3.2	7.0	NE	40	8.3	207	1.7	6.3
AR	41	10.2	252	5.7	5.4	NV	64	10.2	158	3.3	7.4
CA	755	182.8	242	1.6	6.7	NH	27	7.6	283	0.1	9.9
CO	125	35.3	282	4.9	7.6	NJ	191	43.9	230	1.8	7.7
CT	102	29.8	293	0.7	8.3	NM	32	9.1	281	–	6.0
DE	25	6.9	280	4.0	8.2	NY	266	65.2	245	0.3	6.6
DC	11	2.5	237	–	6.7	NC	207	42.1	203	3.6	6.5
FL	488	144.5	296	2.3	7.6	ND	10	3.2	313	–	9.4
GA	205	45.5	222	1.9	6.4	OH	270	59.9	222	1.1	6.3
HI	21	7.4	346	2.0	10.1	OK	63	17.8	284	1.3	5.1
ID	20	4.6	228	0.1	5.7	OR	63	14.3	227	1.5	7.4
IL	282	63.4	225	1.3	7.2	PA	270	59.8	221	1.3	6.9
IN	132	30.7	232	1.2	6.2	RI	24	5.6	237	2.8	6.9
IA	52	10.9	208	2.9	6.4	SC	95	22.3	235	2.8	6.2
KS	62	16.7	268	1.1	6.3	SD	8	1.9	244	9.0	6.3
KY	71	19.8	279	1.0	6.1	TN	142	33.5	237	1.3	6.6
LA	92	26.9	291	2.4	6.3	TX	410	127.0	310	2.8	6.5
ME	19	6.8	351	–	8.6	UT	41	9.0	219	1.5	5.7
MD	136	36.8	271	1.1	6.8	VT	9	2.8	318	–	8.2
MA	123	35.7	291	1.8	7.4	VA	187	47.9	256	1.4	7.2
MI	155	37.0	238	0.9	6.6	WA	107	26.7	249	0.8	7.1
MN	76	20.7	272	1.7	6.8	WV	23	5.1	216	–	5.2
MS	48	11.0	230	4.5	4.9	WI	82	21.7	264	0.7	6.9
						WY	6	1.9	308	–	5.8

– Represents zero.
Source: National Research Bureau, Chicago, IL (copyright, 2006). Data published by International Council of Shopping Centers, <http://www.icsc.org/>.

660 Wholesale and Retail Trade

Table 1037. **Wholesale Trade—Establishments, Employees, and Payroll: 2003**

[432.5 represents 432,500. Covers establishments with payroll. Employees are for the week including March 12. Excludes most government employees, railroad employees, and self-employed persons. Kind-of-business classification based on North American Industry Classification System (NAICS), 2002; see text, Section 15. For statement on methodology, see Appendix III]

Kind of business	2002 NAICS code	Establishments (1,000)	Employees (1,000)	Payroll (bil. dol.)
Wholesale trade	42	432.5	5,864	272.2
Merchant wholesalers, durable goods.	**423**	**254.0**	**3,313**	**162.0**
Motor vehicle/motor vehicle parts & supplies wholesale	4231	26.0	364	14.1
Furniture & home furnishings wholesale	4232	13.8	162	6.6
Lumber & other construction materials wholesale	4233	18.0	236	10.0
Professional & commercial equipment & supplies wholesale	4234	36.4	703	42.6
Metal & mineral (except petroleum) wholesale	4235	10.7	147	6.7
Electrical goods wholesale	4236	31.4	469	29.1
Hardware, & plumbing & heating equipment & supplies wholesale . .	4237	19.0	212	9.3
Machinery, equipment & supplies wholesale.	4238	62.2	688	30.8
Miscellaneous durable goods wholesale	4239	36.6	330	12.8
Merchant wholesalers, nondurable goods.	**424**	**138.9**	**2,288**	**99.3**
Paper & paper products wholesale.	4241	12.9	215	8.8
Drugs & druggists' sundries wholesale	4242	7.7	252	16.6
Apparel, piece goods, & notions wholesale	4243	17.3	197	9.1
Grocery & related products wholesale.	4244	35.2	757	29.3
Farm product raw materials wholesale	4245	7.3	65	2.2
Chemical & allied products wholesale.	4246	13.1	146	7.6
Petroleum & petroleum products wholesale	4247	7.7	105	4.7
Beer/wine/distilled alcoholic beverages wholesale	4248	4.3	169	7.7
Miscellaneous nondurable goods wholesale.	4249	33.4	383	13.4
Wholesale electronic markets and agents and brokers	**425**	**39.7**	**264**	**10.8**

Source: U.S. Census Bureau, "County Business Patterns"; <http://www.census.gov/epcd/cbp/view/cbpview.html>.

Table 1038. **Merchant Wholesale Trade Sales—Total and E-Commerce: 2004**

[3,296,520 represents $3,296,520,000,000. Covers only businesses with paid employees. Excludes manufacturers' sales branches and offices. Based on the Annual Trade Survey, see Appendix III]

Kind of business	2002 NAICS code [1]	Value of sales (mil. dol.)		E-commerce as percent of total sales	Percent distribution of E-commerce sales
		Total	E-commerce		
Merchant wholesale trade, total	42	3,296,520	451,574	13.7	100.0
Durable goods	423	1,654,621	198,597	12.0	44.0
Motor vehicles, parts and supplies.	4231	277,765	74,832	26.9	16.6
Furniture and home furnishings.	4232	58,298	7,340	12.6	1.6
Lumber and other construction materials	4233	128,624	5,517	4.3	1.2
Professional & commercial equipment & supplies . . .	4234	296,276	43,669	14.7	9.7
Computer, peripheral equipment, and software . . .	42343	157,547	23,246	14.8	5.1
Metals and minerals, excluding petroleum.	4235	121,160	(S)	(S)	(S)
Electrical goods	4236	253,761	23,699	9.3	5.2
Hardware, and plumbing and heating equipment and supplies	4237	77,524	9,993	12.9	2.2
Machinery, equipment and supplies	4238	260,190	13,418	5.2	3.0
Miscellaneous durable goods	4239	181,023	18,767	10.4	4.2
Nondurable goods	424	1,641,899	252,977	15.4	56.0
Paper and paper products	4241	81,584	6,474	7.9	1.4
Drugs and druggists' sundries.	4242	296,556	155,170	52.3	34.4
Apparel, piece goods, and notions.	4243	108,432	23,092	21.3	5.1
Groceries and related products	4244	409,743	38,582	9.4	8.5
Farm product raw materials	4245	122,997	4,138	3.4	0.9
Chemical and allied products	4246	76,369	(D)	(D)	(D)
Petroleum and petroleum products	4247	274,942	10,496	3.8	2.3
Beer, wine, and distilled alcoholic beverages	4248	85,607	(D)	(D)	(D)
Miscellaneous nondurable goods.	4249	185,669	9,011	4.9	2.0

D Data withheld to avoid disclosing data of individual companies. S Figure does not meet publication standards. [1] North American Industry Classification System, 2002; see text, Section 15.

Source: U.S. Census Bureau, "E-Stats, 2004 E-commerce Multi-sector Report"; published 25 May 2006; <http://www.census.gov /eos/www/ebusiness614.htm>.

Table 1039. Merchant Wholesalers—Summary: 1995 to 2005

[In billions of dollars (2,159.0 represents $2,159,000,000,000), except ratios. Inventories and inventories/sales ratios, as of December, seasonally adjusted. Excludes manufacturers' sales branches and offices. Data reflect latest revision. Based on data from the Annual Wholesale Trade Survey and the Monthly Wholesale Trade Survey; see Appendix III]

Kind of business	2002 NAICS code [1]	1995	2000	2001	2002	2003	2004	2005
SALES								
Merchant wholesalers	42	2,159.0	2,814.6	2,785.2	2,835.5	2,962.3	3,296.5	3,550.1
Durable goods	423	1,141.7	1,486.7	1,422.2	1,421.5	1,448.9	1,654.6	1,760.7
Motor vehicles, parts, and supplies	4231	169.7	222.2	234.9	251.9	257.3	277.8	293.8
Furniture and home furnishings.	4232	36.6	52.7	52.4	53.5	54.8	58.3	61.1
Lumber and construction materials	4233	66.3	87.2	89.7	95.1	105.7	128.6	132.3
Professional and commercial equipment.........	4234	197.9	282.2	267.8	272.5	272.6	296.3	306.2
Computer, peripheral equipment, and software...	42343	(NA)	174.8	153.8	150.6	144.3	157.5	159.5
Metals and minerals, except petroleum.	4235	87.0	93.8	84.8	81.7	81.4	121.2	133.2
Electrical and electronic goods	4236	186.6	260.0	231.9	223.0	227.1	253.8	264.3
Hardware, plumbing and heating equipment	4237	56.4	72.1	69.0	70.4	71.2	77.5	84.1
Machinery, equipment and supplies	4238	191.3	256.1	247.2	227.8	230.8	260.2	292.0
Miscellaneous durable goods	4239	149.9	160.3	144.4	145.6	148.0	181.0	193.8
Nondurable goods.....................	424	1,017.3	1,327.9	1,363.0	1,414.0	1,513.3	1,641.9	1,789.4
Paper and paper products	4241	66.1	77.8	76.2	72.6	73.9	81.6	88.8
Drugs and druggists' sundries.	4242	83.7	176.0	210.7	245.6	273.5	296.6	326.9
Apparel, piece goods, and notions.............	4243	67.6	96.5	99.0	105.8	104.4	108.4	115.8
Grocery and related products	4244	309.0	374.7	377.2	385.9	405.3	409.7	424.2
Farm-product raw materials	4245	125.5	102.7	100.9	103.4	115.1	123.0	107.8
Chemicals and allied products	4246	50.3	62.3	64.2	67.7	69.7	76.4	87.4
Petroleum and petroleum products	4247	126.5	195.8	191.5	192.7	225.7	274.9	342.1
Beer, wine, and distilled beverages	4248	52.5	71.3	74.9	79.2	82.2	85.6	94.5
Miscellaneous nondurable goods	4249	136.0	170.9	168.5	161.1	163.4	185.7	202.0
INVENTORIES								
Merchant wholesalers	42	238.4	309.8	298.4	302.5	308.0	338.2	362.1
Durable goods	423	154.1	202.0	185.7	185.4	187.8	213.0	228.9
Motor vehicles, parts, and supplies	4231	23.0	28.9	27.4	29.7	30.9	32.5	35.1
Furniture and home furnishings.	4232	4.9	6.6	6.3	6.7	7.1	7.5	7.9
Lumber and construction materials	4233	6.7	8.8	8.8	9.2	10.9	14.0	15.5
Professional and commercial equipment.........	4234	23.6	28.5	25.2	26.0	26.3	28.6	29.2
Computer, peripheral equipment and software ...	42343	(NA)	12.3	9.6	9.4	10.0	10.8	10.6
Metals and minerals, except petroleum.	4235	11.0	13.5	12.1	12.3	12.5	19.7	18.7
Electrical and electronic goods	4236	23.9	31.6	26.8	25.5	24.8	27.0	28.3
Hardware, plumbing and heating equipment	4237	8.7	11.6	11.0	11.0	11.1	12.2	13.7
Machinery, equipment and supplies	4238	36.1	52.0	50.0	47.2	45.4	50.6	57.9
Miscellaneous durable goods	4239	16.2	20.5	18.2	17.7	18.9	21.0	22.6
Nondurable goods.....................	424	84.3	107.8	112.6	117.1	120.2	125.2	133.1
Paper and paper products	4241	5.3	6.8	6.1	5.8	5.9	6.8	7.4
Drugs and druggists' sundries.	4242	10.4	23.2	29.7	31.0	31.2	31.0	29.0
Apparel, piece goods, and notions.............	4243	11.6	14.1	14.4	14.9	14.2	14.7	15.7
Grocery and related products	4244	18.1	20.8	19.9	21.3	21.6	22.6	24.6
Farm-product raw materials	4245	10.6	9.4	9.4	9.8	12.2	9.5	11.4
Chemicals and allied products	4246	4.9	6.1	6.3	6.8	6.9	7.5	8.2
Petroleum and petroleum products	4247	4.3	4.6	4.4	4.8	5.0	7.0	9.0
Beer, wine, and distilled beverages	4248	5.1	7.1	6.9	7.6	7.8	8.3	9.1
Miscellaneous nondurable goods	4249	13.9	15.7	15.6	15.2	15.5	17.8	18.7
INVENTORIES/SALES RATIO								
Merchant wholesalers	42	1.28	1.29	1.31	1.26	1.20	1.18	1.17
Durable goods	423	1.55	1.65	1.61	1.59	1.49	1.47	1.49
Motor vehicles, parts, and supplies	4231	1.60	1.53	1.39	1.40	1.35	1.38	1.36
Furniture and home furnishings.	4232	1.60	1.49	1.46	1.57	1.53	1.51	1.47
Lumber and construction materials	4233	1.21	1.21	1.12	1.19	1.17	1.27	1.29
Professional and commercial equipment.........	4234	1.33	1.28	1.16	1.15	1.12	1.12	1.10
Computer, peripheral equipment and software ...	42343	(NA)	0.93	0.79	0.76	0.80	0.77	0.78
Metals and minerals, except petroleum.	4235	1.53	1.73	1.87	1.92	1.69	1.77	1.59
Electrical and electronic goods	4236	1.47	1.44	1.45	1.38	1.27	1.24	1.25
Hardware, plumbing and heating equipment	4237	1.73	1.93	1.87	1.95	1.85	1.85	1.84
Machinery, equipment and supplies	4238	2.06	2.49	2.59	2.54	2.31	2.13	2.24
Miscellaneous durable goods	4239	1.27	1.55	1.59	1.49	1.43	1.26	1.36
Nondurable goods.....................	424	0.96	0.92	1.01	0.95	0.92	0.89	0.85
Paper and paper products	4241	0.96	1.02	1.01	0.95	0.93	0.95	0.95
Drugs and druggists' sundries.	4242	1.40	1.46	1.54	1.46	1.32	1.23	1.01
Apparel, piece goods, and notions.............	4243	1.98	1.69	1.72	1.75	1.58	1.54	1.52
Grocery and related products	4244	0.68	0.64	0.63	0.65	0.65	0.65	0.68
Farm-product raw materials	4245	1.02	1.05	1.23	0.98	1.13	1.01	1.33
Chemicals and allied products	4246	1.12	1.12	1.18	1.23	1.16	1.10	1.07
Petroleum and petroleum products	4247	0.40	0.24	0.32	0.26	0.25	0.29	0.28
Beer, wine, and distilled beverages	4248	1.14	1.17	1.06	1.09	1.11	1.11	1.14
Miscellaneous nondurable goods	4249	1.16	1.07	1.11	1.07	1.07	1.09	1.10

NA Not available.   [1] North American Industry Classification System, 2002; see text, Section 15.

Source: U.S. Census Bureau, *Current Business Reports, Series (BW/05-A), Annual Revision of Monthly Wholesale Distributors: Sales and Inventories: January 1992 Through January 2006.* See also <http://www.census.gov/svsd/www/whltable.html>.

662   Wholesale and Retail Trade

Section 23
Transportation

This section presents data on civil air transportation, both passenger and cargo, and on water transportation, including inland waterways, oceanborne commerce, the merchant marine, cargo, and vessel tonnages.

This section also presents statistics on revenues, passenger and freight traffic volume, and employment in various revenue-producing modes of the transportation industry, including motor vehicles, trains, and pipelines. Data are also presented on highway mileage and finances, motor vehicle travel, accidents, and registrations; and characteristics of public transit, railroads, and pipelines. Data from the 2001 National Household Travel Survey are now included in Section 26.

Principal sources of air and water transportation data are the annual *National Transportation Statistics*, issued by the U.S. Bureau of Transportation Statistics; the *Annual Report* issued by the Air Transport Association of America, Washington, DC; and the annual *Waterborne Commerce of the United States* issued by the Corps of Engineers of the Department of the Army. In addition, the U.S. Census Bureau in its commodity flow survey (part of the census of transportation, taken every 5 years through 2002, for years ending in "2" and "7") provides data on the type, weight, and value of commodities shipped by manufacturing establishments in the United States, by means of transportation, origin, and destination. The latest reports for 2002 are part of the 2002 Economic Census. This census was conducted in accordance with the 2002 North American Industry Classification System (NAICS). See text, Section 15, Business Enterprise, for a discussion of the 2002 Economic Census and NAICS.

The principal compiler of data on public roads and on operation of motor vehicles is the U.S. Department of Transportation's

(DOT) Federal Highway Administration (FHWA). These data appear in FHWA's annual *Highway Statistics* and other publications.

The U.S. National Highway Traffic Safety Administration issues data on traffic accident deaths and death rates in two annual reports: the *Fact Book* and the *Fatal Accident Reporting System Annual Report*. DOT's Federal Railroad Administration presents data on accidents involving railroads in its annual *Accident/Incident Bulletin*, and the *Rail-Highway Crossing Accident/Incident and Inventory Bulletin*.

Data are also presented in many nongovernment publications. Among them are the weekly and annual *Cars of Revenue Freight Loaded* and the annual *Yearbook of Railroad Facts*, both published by the Association of American Railroads, Washington, DC; *Transit Fact Book*, containing electric railway and motorbus statistics, published annually by the American Public Transit Association, Washington, DC; and *Injury Facts*, issued by the National Safety Council, Chicago, IL.

Civil aviation—Federal promotion and regulation of civil aviation have been carried out by the FAA and the Civil Aeronautics Board (CAB). The CAB promoted and regulated the civil air transportation industry within the United States and between the United States and foreign countries. The Board granted licenses to provide air transportation service, approved or disapproved proposed rates and fares, and approved or disapproved proposed agreements and corporate relationships involving air carriers. In December 1984, the CAB ceased to exist as an agency. Some of its functions were transferred to the Department of Transportation (DOT), as outlined below. The responsibility for investigation of aviation accidents resides with the National Transportation Safety Board.

U.S. Census Bureau, Statistical Abstract of the United States: 2007

The Office of the Secretary, DOT aviation activities include: negotiation of international air transportation rights, selection of U.S. air carriers to serve capacity-controlled international markets, oversight of international rates and fares, maintenance of essential air service to small communities, and consumer affairs. DOT's Bureau of Transportation Statistics (BTS) handles aviation information functions formerly assigned to CAB. Prior to BTS, the Research and Special Programs Administration handled these functions.

The principal activities of the FAA include: the promotion of air safety; controlling the use of navigable airspace; prescribing regulations dealing with the competency of airmen, airworthiness of aircraft and air traffic control; operation of air route traffic control centers, airport traffic control towers, and flight service stations; the design, construction, maintenance, and inspection of navigation, traffic control, and communications equipment; and the development of general aviation.

The CAB published monthly and quarterly financial and traffic statistical data for the certificated route air carriers. BTS continues these publications, including both certificated and noncertificated (commuter) air carriers. The FAA annually publishes data on the use of airway facilities; data related to the location of airmen, aircraft, and airports; the volume of activity in the field of nonair carrier (general aviation) flying; and aircraft production and registration.

General aviation comprises all civil flying (including such commercial operations as small demand air taxis, agriculture application, powerline patrol, etc.) but excludes certificated route air carriers, supplemental operators, large-aircraft commercial operators, and commuter airlines.

Air carriers and service—The CAB previously issued "certificates of public convenience and necessity" under Section 401 of the Federal Aviation Act of 1958 for scheduled and nonscheduled (charter) passenger services and cargo services. It also issued certificates under Section 418 of the Act to cargo air carriers for domestic all-cargo service only. The DOT Office of the Secretary now issues the certificates under a "fit, willing, and able" test of air carrier operations. Carriers operating only a 60-seat-or-less aircraft are given exemption authority to carry passengers, cargo, and mail in scheduled and nonscheduled service under Part 298 of the DOT (formerly CAB) regulations. Exemption authority carriers who offer scheduled passenger service to an essential air service point must meet the "fit, willing, and able" test.

Vessel shipments, entrances, and clearances—Shipments by dry cargo vessels comprise shipments on all types of watercraft, except tanker vessels; shipments by tanker vessels comprise all types of cargo, liquid and dry, carried by tanker vessels.

A vessel is reported as entered only at the first port which it enters in the United States, whether or not cargo is unloaded at that port. A vessel is reported as cleared only at the last port at which clearance is made to a foreign port, whether or not it takes on cargo. Army and Navy vessels entering or clearing without commercial cargo are not included in the figures.

Units of measurement—Cargo (or freight) tonnage and shipping weight both represent the gross weight of the cargo including the weight of containers, wrappings, crates, etc. However, shipping weight excludes lift and cargo vans and similar substantial outer containers. Other tonnage figures generally refer to stowing capacity of vessels, 100 cubic feet being called 1 ton. Gross tonnage comprises the space within the frames and the ceiling of the hull, together with those closed-in spaces above deck available for cargo, stores, passengers, or crew, with certain minor exceptions. Net or registered tonnage is the gross tonnage less the spaces occupied by the propelling machinery, fuel, crew quarters, master's cabin, and navigation spaces. Substantially, it represents space available for cargo and passengers. The net tonnage capacity of a ship may bear little relation to weight of cargo. Deadweight tonnage is the weight in long tons required to depress a vessel from light water line (that is, with only the machinery and equipment on board) to load line. It is, therefore, the weight of the cargo, fuel, etc., which a vessel is designed to carry with safety.

Federal-aid highway systems—The Intermodal Surface Transportation Efficiency Act (ISTEA) of 1991 eliminated the historical Federal-Aid Highway Systems and created the National Highway System (NHS) and other federal-aid highway categories. The final NHS was approved by Congress in December of 1995 under the National Highway System Designation Act.

Functional systems—Roads and streets are assigned to groups according to the character of service intended. The functional systems are (1) arterial highways that generally handle the long trips, (2) collector facilities that collect and disperse traffic between the arterials and the lower systems, and (3) local roads and streets that primarily serve direct access to residential areas, farms, and other local areas.

Regulatory bodies—The ICC, created by the U.S. Congress to regulate transportation in interstate commerce, has jurisdiction over railroads, trucking companies, bus lines, freight forwarders, water carriers, coal slurry pipelines, and transportation brokers. The Federal Energy Regulatory Commission is responsible for setting rates and charges for transportation and sale of natural gas and for establishing rates or charges for transportation.

Motor carriers—For 1960–73, Class I for-hire motor carriers of freight were classified by the ICC as those with $1 million or more of gross annual operating revenue; 1974–79, the class minimum was $3 million. Effective January 1, 1980, Class I carriers are those with $5 million or more in revenue. For 1960–68, Class I motor carriers of passengers were classified by the ICC as those with $200,000 or more of gross annual operating revenue; for 1969–76, as those with revenues of $1 million or more; and since 1977, as those with $3 million or more. Effective January 1, 1988, Class I motor carriers of passengers are those with $5 million or more in operating revenues; Class II less than $5 million in operating revenues.

Railroads—Railroad companies reporting to the ICC are divided into specific groups as follows: (1) regular line-haul (interstate) railroads (and their nonoperating subsidiaries), (2) switching and terminal railroads, (3) private railroads prior to 1964 (identified by ICC as "circular" because they reported on brief circulars), and (4) unofficial railroads, so designated when their reports are received too late for tabulation. For the most part, the last three groups are not included in the statistics shown here.

For years prior to 1978, Class I railroads were those with annual revenues of $1 million or more for 1950–55; $3 million or more for 1956–64; $5 million or more for 1965–75; and $10 million or more for 1976–77. In 1978, the classification became Class I, those having more than $50 million gross annual operating revenue; Class II, from $10 million to $50 million; and Class III, less than $10 million. Effective January 1, 1982, the ICC adopted a procedure to adjust the threshold for inflation by restating current revenues in constant 1978 dollars. In 1988, the criteria for Class I and Class II railroads were $92.0 million and $18.4 million, respectively. Also effective January 1, 1982, the ICC adopted a Carrier Classification Index Survey Form for carriers not filing annual report Form R-1 with the commission. Class II and Class III railroads are currently exempted from filing any financial report with the Commission. The form is used for reclassifying carriers.

The Surface Transportation Board (STB) was established pursuant to the ICC Termination Act of 1995, Pub. L. No. 104-88, 109 Stat. 803 (1995) (ICCTA), to assume certain of the regulatory functions that had been administered by the Interstate Commerce Commission. The Board has broad economic regulatory oversight of railroads, addressing such matters as rate reasonableness, car service and interchange, mergers and line acquisitions, line construction, and line abandonments (49 U.S.C. 10101-11908). Other ICC regulatory functions were either eliminated or transferred to the Federal Highway Administration or the Bureau of Transportation Statistics within DOT.

Transportation   665

Class I Railroads are regulated by the STB and subject to the Uniform System of Accounts and required to file annual and periodic reports. Railroads are classified based on their annual operating revenues. The class to which a carrier belongs is determined by comparing its adjusted operating revenues for 3 consecutive years to the following scale: Class I, $250 million or more; Class II, $20 million to $250 million; and Class III, $0 to $20 million.

Postal Service—The Postal Service provides mail processing and delivery services within the United States. The Postal Reorganization Act of 1970 created the Postal Service, effective July 1971, as an independent establishment of the Federal Executive Branch.

Revenue and cost analysis describes the Postal Service's system of attributing revenues and costs to classes of mail and service. This system draws primarily upon probability sampling techniques to develop estimates of revenues, volumes, and weights, as well as costs by class of mail and special service. The costs attributed to classes of mail and special services are primarily incremental costs which vary in response to changes in volume; they account for roughly 60 percent of the total costs of the Postal Service. The balance represents "institutional costs." Statistics on revenues, volume of mail, and distribution of expenditures are presented in the Postal Service's annual report, *Cost and Revenue Analysis,* and its *Annual Report of the Postmaster General* and its annual *Comprehensive Statement on Postal Operations.*

Statistical reliability—For a discussion of statistical collection and estimation, sampling procedures, and measures of statistical reliability applicable to Census Bureau data, see Appendix III.

U.S. Census Bureau, Statistical Abstract of the United States: 2007

Table 1040. **Transportation-Related Components of U.S. Gross Domestic Product: 1995 to 2004**

[In billions dollars (7,397.7 represents $7,397,700,000,000), except percent]

Item	1995	2000	2001	2002	2003	2004
CURRENT DOLLARS						
Total transportation-related final demand [1] ...	(NA)	1,089.5	1,103.9	1,106.4	1,156.9	1,227.7
Total gross domestic product (GDP)	7,397.7	9,817.0	10,128.0	10,649.6	10,971.2	11,734.3
Transportation as a percent of GDP.......	(NA)	11.1	10.9	10.4	10.5	10.5
Personal consumption of transportation	594.6	853.5	872.3	882.2	928.5	979.1
Motor vehicles and parts	266.7	386.5	407.9	429.3	439.1	441.8
Gasoline and oil	120.2	175.7	171.6	164.5	192.6	230.4
Transportation services	207.7	291.3	292.8	288.4	296.8	306.9
Gross private domestic investment	(NA)	167.4	148.6	132.8	133.9	158.4
Transportation structures	(NA)	6.6	6.9	6.5	6.0	6.5
Transportation equipment	116.1	160.8	141.7	126.3	127.9	151.9
Net exports of transportation-related goods and service [2]	–43.6	–109.0	–108.2	–112.1	–125.6	–135.3
Exports (+)	132.4	179.0	174.3	175.5	174.4	195.1
Civilian aircraft, engines,and parts	26.1	48.1	52.6	50.4	46.7	50.0
Automotive vehicles, engines, and parts	61.3	80.4	75.4	78.9	80.7	89.3
Passenger fares	18.9	20.7	17.9	17.0	15.7	18.9
Other transportation..................	26.1	29.8	28.4	29.2	31.3	36.9
Imports (–)..........................	176.0	288.0	282.5	287.6	300.0	330.4
Civilian aircraft, engines,and parts	10.7	26.4	31.4	25.5	24.1	24.3
Automotive vehicles, engines, and parts	123.6	195.9	189.8	203.7	210.2	228.2
Passenger fares	14.7	24.3	22.6	20.0	21.0	23.7
Other transportation..................	27.0	41.4	38.7	38.4	44.7	54.2
Government transportation-related purchases	133.8	177.6	191.2	203.5	220.1	225.5
Federal purchases [3]	16.1	19.2	21.1	26.4	30.6	29.7
State and local purchases [3].............	109.3	149.4	160.3	166.6	173.3	179.2
Defense-related purchases [4].............	8.4	9.0	9.8	10.5	16.2	16.6
CHAINED (2000) DOLLARS						
Total transportation-related final demand [1] ...	(NA)	1,089.5	1,098.7	1,100.7	1,117.1	1,139.8
Total gross domestic product (GDP)	8,031.7	9,817.0	9,890.7	10,048.8	10,320.6	10,755.7
Transportation as a percent of GDP.......	(NA)	11.1	11.1	11.0	10.8	10.6
Personal consumption of transportation	658.6	853.5	872.1	891.1	913.0	926.3
Motor vehicles and parts	272.3	386.5	405.8	429.0	449.7	457.0
Gasoline and oil	154.5	175.7	178.3	181.9	183.2	185.9
Transportation services	231.8	291.3	288.0	280.2	280.1	283.4
Gross private domestic investment	(NA)	167.4	149.4	132.1	128.6	144.4
Transportation structures	(NA)	6.6	6.6	6.1	5.5	5.7
Transportation equipment	120.6	160.8	142.8	126.0	123.1	138.7
Net exports of transportation-related goods and service [2]	–46.9	–109.0	–108.5	–114.5	–126.6	–132.9
Exports (+)	142.1	179.0	171.6	170.7	164.2	178.6
Civilian aircraft, engines,and parts	30.3	48.1	49.9	46.5	41.5	42.6
Automotive vehicles, engines, and parts	63.4	80.4	75.2	78.3	79.4	87.2
Passenger fares	19.6	20.7	17.8	16.5	13.5	14.8
Other transportation..................	28.8	29.8	28.7	29.4	29.8	34.0
Imports (–)..........................	189.0	288.0	280.1	285.2	290.8	311.5
Civilian aircraft, engines,and parts	12.4	26.4	30.2	24.2	22.8	22.2
Automotive vehicles, engines, and parts	126.6	195.9	189.9	203.3	208.6	222.7
Passenger fares	17.3	24.3	20.7	17.4	17.9	20.6
Other transportation..................	32.7	41.4	39.3	40.3	41.5	46.0
Government transportation-related purchases	156.5	177.6	185.7	192.0	202.1	202.0
Federal purchases [3]	18.0	19.2	20.6	25.0	28.2	26.2
State and local purchases [3].............	128.8	149.4	155.8	157.3	159.9	161.9
Defense-related purchases [4].............	9.7	9.0	9.3	9.7	14.0	13.9

NA Not available. [1] Sum of total personal consumption of transportation, total gross private domestic investment, net exports of transportation-related goods and services, and total government transportation-related purchases. [2] Sum of exports and imports. [3] Federal purchases and state and local purchases are the sum of consumption expenditures and gross investment. [4] Defense-related purchases are the sum of transportation of material and travel.

Source: U.S. Bureau of Transportation Statistics, *National Transportation Statistics,* annual. See Internet site <http://www.bts.gov /publications/national_transportation_statistics/>.

Transportation   667

Table 1041. **Transportation System Mileage Within the U.S.: 1980 to 2004**

[3,860 represents 3,860,000]

System	1980	1985	1990	1995	2000	2001	2002	2003	2004
Highway (1,000)........	3,860	3,864	3,867	3,912	3,936	3,948	3,966	3,974	3,982
Class 1 rail..........	164,822	145,764	119,758	108,264	99,250	97,817	100,125	99,126	97,662
Amtrak.............	24,000	24,000	24,000	24,000	23,000	23,000	23,000	22,675	22,256
Transit:									
Commuter rail [1]	(X)	3,574	4,132	4,160	5,209	5,209	6,831	6,809	6,875
Heavy rail [2]	(X)	1,293	1,351	1,458	1,558	1,572	1,572	1,597	1,596
Light rail [3]	(X)	384	483	568	834	897	960	996	1,187
Navigable channels	26,000	26,000	26,000	26,000	26,000	26,000	26,000	26,000	(NA)
Oil pipeline [4]	218,393	213,605	208,752	181,912	176,996	158,489	161,189	160,868	(NA)
Gas pipeline [5] (1,000)...	1,052	1,119	1,189	1,278	1,369	1,374	1,411	1,424	1,462

NA Not available.   X Not applicable.   [1] Also called metropolitan rail or regional rail.   [2] Also called metro, subway, rapid transit, or rapid rail.   [3] Also called streetcar, tramway, or trolley.   [4] Includes trunk and gathering lines for crude-oil pipeline.   [5] Excludes service pipelines.

Source: U.S. Bureau of Transportation Statistics, *National Transportation Statistics*, annual. See Internet site <http://www.bts.gov/publications/national_transportation_statistics/>.

Table 1042. **U.S. Aircraft, Vehicles, and Other Conveyances: 1980 to 2004**

[121,601 represents 121,601,000]

System	1980	1990	1995	1999	2000	2001	2002	2003	2004
Air:									
Air carrier [1]................	3,808	6,083	7,411	8,228	8,055	8,497	8,194	8,176	8,186
General aviation [2] (active fleet) ...	211,045	198,000	188,089	219,464	217,533	211,446	211,244	209,708	(NA)
Highway, registered vehicles (1,000):									
Passenger car	121,601	133,700	128,387	132,432	133,621	137,633	135,921	135,670	136,431
Motorcycle	5,694	4,259	3,897	4,152	4,346	4,903	5,004	5,370	5,781
Vans, pick-ups, SUVs..........	27,876	48,275	65,738	75,356	79,085	84,188	85,011	87,187	91,845
Trucks....................	5,791	6,196	6,719	7,791	8,023	7,858	7,927	7,757	8,171
Bus.....................	529	627	686	729	746	750	761	777	795
Transit: [3]									
Motor bus	59,411	58,714	67,107	74,228	75,013	76,075	76,190	77,328	(NA)
Light rail cars [4]	1,013	913	999	1,297	1,577	1,366	1,445	1,482	(NA)
Heavy rail cars [5]	9,641	10,419	10,157	10,306	10,591	10,718	10,718	10,754	(NA)
Trolley bus	823	832	885	859	951	600	600	672	(NA)
Commuter rail cars and									
locomotives	4,500	4,415	4,565	4,883	5,073	5,124	5,300	5,959	(NA)
Demand response	(X)	16,471	29,352	31,884	33,080	34,661	34,699	35,954	(NA)
Other [6]	(NA)	1,197	2,809	5,059	5,208	5,727	6,330	6,990	(NA)
Rail:									
Class I, freight cars (1,000)	1,168	659	583	579	560	500	478	467	474
Class I, locomotive	28,094	18,835	18,812	20,256	20,028	19,745	20,506	20,774	22,015
Nonclass I freight cars	102,161	103,527	84,724	126,762	132,448	125,470	130,590	124,580	120,169
Car companies and shippers									
freight cars	440,552	449,832	550,717	662,934	688,194	688,806	691,329	687,337	693,978
Amtrak, passenger train car......	2,128	1,863	1,722	1,992	1,894	2,084	2,896	1,623	1,211
Amtrak, locomotive	419	318	313	329	378	401	372	442	276
Water:									
Non-self-propelled vessels [7]	31,662	31,209	31,360	33,387	33,152	33,042	32,381	31,335	(NA)
Self-propelled vessels [8]	7,126	8,236	8,281	8,379	8,202	8,546	8,621	8,648	(NA)
Oceangoing steam and motor ships									
(1,000 gross tons and over).....	849	635	512	470	461	454	443	416	412
Recreational boats (1,000)	8,578	10,997	11,735	12,738	12,782	12,876	12,854	12,795	12,781

NA Not available.   X Not applicable.   [1] Air carrier aircraft are those carrying passengers or cargo for hire under 14 CFR 121 and 14 CFR 135.   [2] Includes air taxi aircraft.   [3] 2003 data are preliminary.   [4] Fixed rail streetcar or trolley, for example.   [5] Metro, subway, or rapid transit, for example.   [6] Includes aerial tramway, automated guideway transit, cablecar, ferry boat, inclined plane, monorail, and vanpool.   [7] Includes dry-cargo barges, tank barges, and railroad-car floats.   [8] Includes dry-cargo and/or passenger, offshore supply vessels, railroad-car ferries, tankers, and towboats.

Source: U.S. Bureau of Transportation Statistics, *National Transportation Statistics*, annual. See Internet site <http://www.bts.gov /publications/national_transportation_statistics/>.

668   Transportation

Table 1043. **U.S. Freight Gateways: 2004**

[In billions of dollars, except as indicated (2,286 represents $2,286,000,000,000). For the top 50 gateways ranked by value of shipments. Excludes imports of less than $1,250, exports less than $2,500, and intransit shipments]

Port	Mode	Rank	Total trade	Exports	Imports	Exports as a percent of total
Total U.S. merchandise trade	**(X)**	**(X)**	**2,286**	**817**	**1,470**	**35.7**
Top 50 gateways	(X)	(X)	1,821	646	1,176	35.5
As a percent of total	(X)	(X)	79.7	79.1	80.0	(X)
JFK International Airport, NY	Air	1	125	53	73	42.0
Port of Los Angeles, CA	Water	2	121	16	105	13.5
Port of Long Beach, CA	Water	3	121	19	103	15.3
Port of Detroit, MI	Land	4	114	58	56	51.1
Port of New York, NY and NJ	Water	5	114	23	90	20.4
Port of Laredo, TX	Land	6	90	38	51	42.9
Los Angeles International Airport, CA	Air	7	69	34	35	49.3
Port of Buffalo-Niagara Falls, NY	Land	8	68	32	37	46.4
Port of Houston, TX	Water	9	66	29	37	44.0
Port of Huron, MI	Land	10	66	24	42	35.8
Chicago, IL	Air	11	65	25	40	38.6
San Francisco International Airport, CA	Air	12	55	24	30	44.5
Port of Charleston, SC	Water	13	47	15	31	32.9
Port of El Paso, TX	Land	14	43	18	24	42.9
Port of Norfolk Harbor, VA	Water	15	33	12	21	35.8
Port of Baltimore, MD	Water	16	31	7	24	22.0
Dallas-Fort Worth, TX	Air	17	31	15	17	46.7
New Orleans, LA	Air	18	30	15	15	50.6
Port of Seattle, WA	Water	19	30	7	23	22.6
Port of Tacoma, WA	Water	20	29	5	24	18.3
Port of Oakland, CA	Water	21	27	8	19	31.1
Port of Savannah, GA	Water	22	26	10	17	36.9
Anchorage, AK	Air	23	26	6	21	21.8
Miami International Airport, FL	Air	24	25	16	9	64.0
Atlanta, GA	Air	25	25	10	15	41.6
Cleveland, OH	Air	26	23	13	10	55.6
Port of Otay Mesa Station, CA	Land	27	22	9	13	40.2
Port of New Orleans, LA	Water	28	20	8	12	40.1
Port of Miami, FL	Water	29	18	8	11	41.5
Port of Beaumont, TX	Water	30	16	1	15	8.2
Port of Champlain-Rouses Pt., NY	Land	31	16	6	10	37.0
Port of Hidalgo, TX	Land	32	16	7	9	41.9
Newark, NJ	Air	33	15	3	12	22.3
Port of Blaine, WA	Land	34	14	6	8	44.3
Port of Morgan City, LA	Water	35	14	(Z)	14	1.1
Port of Jacksonville, FL	Water	36	14	5	9	33.0
Boston Logan Airport, MA	Air	37	13	8	5	61.3
Port of Portland, OR	Water	38	12	3	9	24.7
Port of Nogales, AZ	Land	39	12	4	8	35.2
Port of Corpus Christi, TX	Water	40	12	2	10	16.6
San Juan International Airport, PR	Air	41	12	6	6	51.3
Port of Port Everglades, FL	Water	42	12	5	7	41.2
Port of Philadelphia, PA	Water	43	11	1	10	12.1
Port of Alexandria Bay, NY	Land	44	11	4	7	39.2
Port of Pembina, ND	Land	45	11	6	5	54.2
Port of Brownsville-Cameron, TX	Land	46	11	6	5	51.8
Port of Calexico-East, CA	Land	47	10	4	6	43.4
Texas City, TX	Water	48	10	1	8	13.8
Philadelphia International Airport, PA	Air	49	9	5	4	55.6
Port of Sweetgrass, MT	Land	50	9	4	5	46.1

Z Less than $500,000,000.   X Not applicable.

Source: U.S. Bureau of Transportation Statistics, *National Transportation Statistics*, annual. See Internet site <http://www.bts.gov /publications/national_transportation_statistics/>.

Transportation   669

Table 1044. **Transportation and Warehousing—Establishments, Revenue, Payroll, and Employees by Industry: 2002**

[17,973 represents $17,973,000,000. Data are preliminary. For establishments with payroll. Based on the 2002 Economic Censuses; See Appendix III]

Kind of business	2002 NAICS code [1]	Number of establish- ments	Revenue (mil. dol.)	Annual payroll (mil. dol.)	Paid employees (1,000)
Air transportation [2]	481	3,847	17,973	3,549	85.9
Scheduled air transportation [2]	4811	1,674	10,532	2,028	54.6
Nonscheduled air transportation	4812	2,173	7,441	1,522	31.3
Water transportation	483	1,924	23,124	3,032	65.3
Deep sea, coastal, and Great Lakes water transportation	4831	1,334	20,631	2,438	52.0
Inland water transportation	4832	590	2,493	594	13.3
Truck transportation	484	112,698	165,561	47,834	1,437.3
General freight trucking	4841	59,120	111,550	34,230	992.9
Specialized freight trucking	4842	53,578	54,011	13,603	444.3
Transit and ground passenger transportation [3]	485	17,333	18,770	7,575	404.8
Urban transit systems	4851	1,234	3,603	2,047	65.6
Interurban and rural bus transportation	4852	360	769	231	9.2
Taxi and limousine service	4853	6,998	4,160	1,146	67.5
School and employee bus transportation	4854	4,407	5,901	2,570	175.7
Charter bus industry	4855	1,222	1,700	532	28.8
Pipeline transportation [3]	486	2,512	27,641	3,083	46.6
Pipeline transportation of crude oil	4861	271	3,334	506	6.9
Pipeline transportation of natural gas	4862	1,701	19,968	2,120	32.5
Scenic and sightseeing transportation [3]	487	2,493	1,773	500	22.1
Scenic and sightseeing transportation, land	4871	590	645	200	9.3
Scenic and sightseeing transportation, water	4872	1,726	964	267	11.6
Support activities for transportation [3]	488	34,223	62,316	16,558	478.2
Support activities for air transportation	4881	4,972	13,151	3,961	132.7
Support activities for rail transportation	4882	840	2,068	745	21.6
Support activities for water transportation	4883	2,502	9,801	2,764	69.6
Support activities for road transportation	4884	8,000	4,153	1,360	56.3
Freight transportation arrangement	4885	16,570	31,040	7,086	175.9
Couriers and messengers	492	12,754	59,373	17,432	578.3
Couriers	4921	7,485	56,028	16,296	523.0
Local messengers and local delivery	4922	5,269	3,345	1,136	55.2
Warehousing and storage	493	12,637	17,925	18,689	639.2

[1] North American Industry Classification System, 2002; see text, Section 15. [2] Excludes large certificated passenger carriers that do not report to the Office of Airline Information, U.S. Department of Transportation. [3] Includes other industries, not shown separately.

Source: U.S. Bureau of the Census, 2002 Economic Census Industry Series Reports, "Transporation and Warehousing." See Internet site <http://www.census.gov/econ/census02/guide/INDRPT48.HTM> (accessed 2 May 2005).

Table 1045. **Employment and Earnings in Transportation and Warehousing by Industry: 1990 to 2005**

[3,476 represents 3,476,000. Annual average of monthly figures. Earnings data for air, rail, and water transportation are not available. Based on Current Employment Statistics program; see Appendix III]

Industry	2002 NAICS code [1]	1990	1995	2000	2002	2003	2004	2005
EMPLOYEES (1,000)								
Transportation and warehousing	48,49	3,476	3,838	4,410	4,224	4,185	4,249	4,347
Air transportation	481	529	511	614	564	528	515	501
Rail transportation	482	272	233	232	218	218	226	228
Water transportation	483	57	51	56	53	55	56	61
Truck transportation	484	1,122	1,249	1,406	1,339	1,326	1,352	1,393
Transit and ground	485	274	328	372	381	382	385	389
Pipeline transportation	486	60	54	46	42	40	38	38
Scenic and sightseeing	487	16	22	28	26	27	27	30
Support activities	488	364	430	537	525	520	535	551
Couriers and messengers	492	375	517	605	561	562	557	572
Warehousing and storage	493	407	444	514	517	528	558	585
AVG. WEEKLY EARNINGS [2] (dol.)								
Transportation and warehousing	48,49	472	513	562	580	598	615	619
Truck transportation	484	490	554	635	626	652	686	690
Transit and ground	485	316	356	400	422	426	415	412
Pipeline transportation	486	610	751	826	937	1,078	1,100	1,114
Scenic and sightseeing	487	289	303	360	361	369	352	384
Support activities	488	437	491	549	616	658	657	647
Couriers and messengers	492	236	343	384	398	404	415	408
Warehousing and storage	493	405	463	558	572	567	558	557

[1] North American Industry Classification System 2002, see text, sections 12 and 15. [2] For nonsupervisory workers.

Source: U.S. Bureau of Labor Statistics, the Current Employment Statistics program Internet site <http://www.bls.gov/ces/home.htm>.

U.S. Census Bureau, Statistical Abstract of the United States: 2007

Table 1046. Transportation and Warehousing—Establishments, Employees, and Payroll by Kind of Business (NAICS Basis): 2000 and 2003

[3,790.0 represents 3,790,000. Covers establishments with payroll. Employees are for the week including March 12. Excludes most government employees, railroad employees, and self-employed persons. NAICS 2002. See text, Section 15. For statement on methodology, see Appendix III. County Business Patterns excludes rail transportation (NAICS 482) and the National Postal Service (NAICS 491)]

Industry	NAICS code [1]	Establishments		Paid employees [2] (1,000)		Annual payroll (mil. dol.)	
		2000	2003	2000	2003	2000	2003
Transportation & warehousing	**48-49**	**190,044**	**202,673**	**3,790.0**	**4,067.9**	**125,592**	**142,749**
Air transportation	481	5,429	5,478	615.6	533.8	26,569	25,360
Scheduled air transportation	4811	3,324	3,169	570.9	498.4	24,485	23,649
Scheduled passenger air transportation . .	481111	2,740	2,679	536.2	477.0	23,471	22,918
Scheduled freight air transportation	481112	584	490	34.7	21.4	1,014	731
Nonscheduled air transportation	4812	2,105	2,309	44.7	35.4	2,085	1,711
Water transportation	483	1,900	1,930	67.6	67.3	3,003	3,397
Deep sea, coastal, & Great Lakes water transportation	4831	1,254	1,310	47.8	48.7	2,214	2,538
Inland water transportation	4832	646	620	19.7	18.6	789	860
Inland water freight transportation	483211	402	342	16.3	12.6	674	630
Inland water passenger transportation . . .	483212	244	278	3.5	6.0	115	229
Truck transportation	484	110,416	111,581	1,415.8	1,423.3	46,451	48,495
General freight trucking	4841	55,874	60,227	922.7	986.7	31,614	34,679
General freight trucking, local.	48411	20,329	23,323	153.3	187.8	4,530	5,874
General freight trucking, long distance. . .	48412	35,545	36,904	769.5	798.9	27,084	28,805
Specialized freight trucking	4842	54,542	51,354	493.1	436.6	14,838	13,816
Used household & office goods moving . .	48421	9,147	8,358	128.9	109.4	3,661	3,077
Specialized freight (except used goods) trucking, local.	48422	32,493	31,656	200.4	192.6	5,692	6,042
Specialized freight (except used goods) trucking, long distance	48423	12,902	11,340	163.7	134.6	5,484	4,697
Transit & ground passenger transportation . . .	485	16,383	17,257	386.9	397.9	7,215	7,655
Urban transit systems	4851	705	971	43.1	48.2	1,296	1,408
Mixed mode systems	485111	152	49	6.2	1.6	147	43
Commuter rail	485112	15	19	(D)	0.7	(D)	32
Bus and other motor vehicle mode systems	485113	505	864	31.4	45.1	925	1,305
Other	485119	33	39	(D)	0.9	(D)	28
Interurban & rural bus transportation	4852	444	486	26.8	17.9	710	475
Taxi & limousine service.	4853	6,806	6,962	67.8	64.5	1,244	1,225
Taxi service	48531	3,116	3,079	30.4	29.3	485	500
Limousine service	48532	3,690	3,883	37.5	35.2	759	725
School & employee bus transportation	4854	4,217	4,464	162.9	183.7	2,323	2,872
Charter bus industry	4855	1,451	1,246	34.1	28.5	669	578
Other transit & ground passenger transportation	4859	2,760	3,128	52.2	55.0	974	1,098
Special needs transportation	485991	1,914	2,108	34.8	40.5	649	841
Pipeline transportation.	486	2,802	2,733	53.0	41.0	3,829	2,893
Pipeline transportation of crude oil	4861	307	307	6.7	7.4	426	562
Pipeline transportation of natural gas	4862	1,938	1,912	39.2	27.7	2,961	1,928
Other pipeline transportation	4869	557	514	7.0	5.9	442	403
Scenic & sightseeing transportation	487	2,254	2,532	23.6	22.5	583	553
Scenic & sightseeing transportation, land . .	4871	454	615	8.7	9.6	193	211
Scenic & sightseeing transportation, water. .	4872	1,642	1,745	13.0	11.2	331	287
Scenic & sightseeing transportation, other . .	4879	158	172	2.0	1.7	59	55
Support activities for transportation	488	31,440	34,481	472.4	504.6	16,507	19,295
Support activities for air transportation	4881	4,368	5,052	126.7	140.6	3,634	4,746
Airport operations	48811	1,834	1,593	67.9	57.9	1,569	1,425
Air traffic control.	488111	137	153	0.8	1.5	30	77
Other support activities for air transportation	48819	2,534	3,459	58.8	82.7	2,065	3,322
Support activities for rail transportation	4882	821	904	21.4	25.2	714	843
Support activities for water transportation . . .	4883	2,543	2,353	81.6	82.5	3,251	3,952
Port and harbor operations	48831	196	223	7.4	6.4	266	280
Marine cargo handling	48832	607	542	53.5	50.6	2,195	2,423
Navigational services to shipping	48833	863	782	11.8	11.8	479	630
Other	48839	877	806	8.9	13.6	312	620
Support activities for road transportation . . .	4884	7,010	8,277	56.2	61.1	1,309	1,549
Motor vehicle towing	48841	6,078	7,072	41.8	45.7	962	1,121
Freight transportation arrangement.	4885	15,177	16,481	161.7	173.2	6,620	7,446
Other support activities for transportation . . .	4889	1,521	1,414	24.7	21.9	979	759
Couriers & messengers.	492	12,297	14,163	619.3	534.1	17,399	17,305
Couriers	4921	6,667	9,090	548.9	489.3	15,891	16,320
Local messengers & local delivery	4922	5,630	5,073	70.5	44.9	1,509	985
Warehousing & storage	493	7,123	12,518	135.9	543.3	4,035	17,795

D Figure withheld to avoid disclosure pertaining to individual companies.   [1] For 2000, North American Industry Classification System (NAICS), 1997; beginning 2003, based on NAICS 2002; see text, Section 15.   [2] For employees on the payroll for the pay period including March 12.

Source: U.S. Census Bureau, "County Business Patterns." See <http://www.census.gov/epcd/cbp/view/cbpview.html>.

Transportation **671**

Table 1047. **Transportation Accidents, Deaths, and Injuries: 1980 to 2004**

[6,216 represents 6,216,000]

Year and casualty	Land surface			Air				Water		Pipeline [9]		Haz-ardous materi-als [10]
	High way [1] (1,000)	Rail road [2]	Rail rapid transit [3]	U.S. air carrier [4]	Com-muter air carriers [5]	On demand air carriers [6]	Gen-eral avia-tion	Recre-ational boat-ing [7]	Water-borne (vessel-related) [8]	Gas	Hazard-ous liquid	
Accidents:												
1980 ..	6,216	8,205	6,789	19	38	171	3,590	5,513	4,624	1,524	246	15,719
1990 ..	6,471	2,879	12,178	24	15	107	2,242	6,411	3,613	198	180	8,879
2000 ..	6,394	2,983	12,782	56	12	80	1,837	7,740	5,403	234	146	17,557
2003 ..	6,328	2,997	5,554	54	2	74	1,739	5,438	5,163	244	128	15,162
2004 ..	6,181	3,296	6,222	30	4	66	1,617	4,904	4,962	286	138	14,740
Deaths:												
1980 ..	51.1	584	83	1	37	105	1,239	1,360	206	15	4	19
1990 ..	44.6	599	117	39	6	51	770	865	85	6	3	8
2000 ..	41.9	512	80	92	5	71	596	701	53	37	1	16
2003 ..	42.9	533	49	22	2	42	632	703	53	12	–	15
2004 ..	42.6	530	59	14	–	64	558	676	36	18	5	13
Injuries:												
1980 ..	2,848	58,696	6,801	19	14	43	681	2,650	180	177	15	626
1990 ..	3,231	22,736	10,036	29	11	36	409	3,822	175	69	7	423
2000 ..	3,189	10,424	10,848	29	7	12	309	4,355	150	77	4	251
2003 ..	2,889	8,149	4,158	30	1	15	322	3,888	227	66	5	119
2004 ..	2,788	7,790	4,738	19	1	18	266	3,363	198	42	13	289

– Represents zero. [1] Data on deaths are from U.S. National Highway Traffic Safety Administration and are based on 30-day definition. Includes only police reported crashes. For more detail, see Table 1090. [2] Accidents which result in damages to railroad property. Grade crossing accidents are also included when classified as a train accident. Deaths exclude fatalities in railroad-highway grade crossing accidents. [3] Reporting criteria and source of data changed between 1989 and 1990; these data from 1990 to present are not comparable to earlier years. [4] Includes scheduled and nonscheduled (charter) air carriers. Represents serious injuries. [5] All scheduled service. Represents serious injuries. [6] All nonscheduled service. Represents serious injuries. [7] Accidents resulting in death; injury or requiring medical treatment beyond first aid; damages exceeding $500; or a person's disappearance. [8] Covers accidents involving commercial vessels which must be reported to U.S. Coast Guard if there is property damage exceeding $25,000; material damage affecting the seaworthiness or efficiency of a vessel; stranding or grounding; loss of life; or injury causing a person's incapacity for more than 3 days. [9] Beginning 1990, pipeline accidents/incidents are credited to year of occurrence; 1980 data are credited to the year filed. [10] Incidents, deaths, and injuries involving hazardous materials cover all types of transport; excludes pipelines and bulk, nonpackaged water incidents.

Source: U.S. Bureau of Transportation Statistics, *National Transportation Statistics*, annual. See Internet site <http://www.bts.gov/publications/national_transportation_statistics/>

Table 1048. **U.S. Scheduled Airline Industry—Summary: 1995 to 2005**

[For calendar years or Dec. 31 (547.8 represents 547,800,000). For domestic and international operations. Covers carriers certificated under Section 401 of the Federal Aviation Act. Minus sign (–) indicates loss]

Item	Unit	1995	1999	2000	2001 [1]	2002 [1]	2003 [2]	2004	2005
SCHEDULED SERVICE									
Revenue passengers enplaned...	Mil.	547.8	636.0	666.2	622.1	612.9	646.3	702.9	738.4
Revenue passenger miles	Bil.	540.7	652.0	692.8	651.7	641.1	656.9	733.6	778.9
Available seat miles	Bil.	807.1	918.4	957.0	930.5	892.6	893.8	971.4	1,003.2
Revenue passenger load factor ..	Percent ..	67.0	71.0	72.4	70.0	71.8	73.5	75.5	77.6
Mean passenger trip length [3] ...	Miles.....	987	1,025	1,040	1,048	1,046	1,016	1,044	1,055
Cargo ton miles	Mil.	16,921	21,613	23,888	22,003	24,591	26,735	27,978	28,007
Aircraft departures	1,000	8,062	8,627	9,035	8,788	9,187	10,839	11,398	11,475
FINANCES [4]									
Total operating revenue [5]....	**Mil. dol. ..**	**95,117**	**119,455**	**130,839**	**115,526**	**106,985**	**117,920**	**134,300**	**147,504**
Passenger revenue	Mil. dol....	69,835	84,383	93,622	80,947	73,577	77,379	85,669	91,861
Freight and express revenue	Mil. dol....	8,616	11,415	12,486	12,066	12,865	14,101	16,445	18,728
Mail revenue	Mil. dol....	1,266	1,739	1,970	1,063	660	902	701	661
Charter revenue	Mil. dol....	3,742	4,284	4,913	4,449	4,225	5,589	5,503	5,637
Total operating expense	Mil. dol....	89,266	111,119	123,840	125,852	115,552	120,028	135,782	147,413
Operating profit (or loss)	Mil. dol....	5,852	8,337	6,999	–10,326	–8,566	–2,108	–1,482	91
Interest income (or expense)	Mil. dol....	–2,426	–1,833	–2,193	–2,500	–3,263	–3,442	–5,645	–25,394
Net profit (or loss)	Mil. dol....	2,283	5,277	2,486	–8,275	–11,312	–3,658	–9,060	–27,402
Revenue per passenger mile	Cents ...	12.9	12.9	13.5	12.4	11.5	11.8	11.7	11.8
Operating profit margin	Percent ...	6.2	7.0	5.3	–8.9	–8.0	–1.8	–1.1	0.1
Net profit margin	Percent ...	2.4	4.4	1.9	–7.2	–10.6	–3.1	–6.7	–18.6
EMPLOYEES [6]									
Total	1,000	547.0	646.4	680.0	672.0	601.4	569.8	569.5	552.9
Average annual compensation per employee [7]	$1,000 ...	59.1	62.9	66.0	70.7	74.8	78.6	77.8	73.1

[1] Includes cash compensation remitted to carriers under the Air Transportation Safety and System Stabilization Act (P.L. 107-42). [2] Includes security costs reimbursements remitted to carriers under the Emergency Wartime Supplemental Appropriations Act (P.L. 108-11). [3] For definition of mean, see Guide to Tabular Presentation. [4] 2005 data are preliminary. [5] Includes other types of revenues, not shown separately. [6] Average full-time equivalents. [7] For majors and nationals, passenger carriers only.

Source: Air Transport Association of America, Washington, DC, *Air Transport Annual Report*.

Table 1049. **Airline Cost Indexes: 1980 to 2005**

[**1982 = 100.** Covers U.S. major and national passenger carriers. Major carriers have operating revenues of $1 billion or more; nationals have operating revenues from $100 million to $1 billion]

Index	1980	1985	1990	1995	1999	2000	2001	2002	2003	2004	2005
Composite index [1]	87.5	109.1	141.5	160.3	173.1	175.9	182.0	187.6	187.6	183.5	182.5
Labor costs	84.7	109.6	121.1	152.2	162.0	169.9	182.0	193.6	202.4	200.2	188.0
Fuel.	92.0	91.0	77.4	54.9	52.2	77.2	76.7	71.5	85.4	113.2	165.4
Aircraft ownership [2]	91.7	138.6	207.3	247.2	277.5	296.8	298.6	309.3	312.9	332.0	311.8
Nonaircraft ownership	79.9	111.7	184.0	212.3	202.4	206.4	230.2	226.3	227.6	212.3	219.3
Professional services	83.2	134.9	196.8	248.0	282.6	285.6	290.9	279.7	285.2	293.9	301.4
Food and beverage	93.4	99.5	128.8	109.7	104.8	102.4	102.5	89.1	77.0	70.8	64.6
Landing fees	90.1	98.7	141.2	171.1	178.3	174.3	180.6	201.9	217.5	221.4	218.2
Maintenance material	108.3	127.3	191.5	147.2	163.3	168.8	148.2	127.1	106.5	103.5	94.9
Aircraft insurance	93.4	150.7	56.8	119.5	36.0	36.0	50.9	94.7	61.4	62.7	54.4
Nonaircraft insurance	91.6	160.4	84.0	266.0	124.7	120.7	218.0	686.1	539.2	454.9	382.7
Passenger commissions	83.6	117.7	156.3	126.9	88.7	68.6	59.5	39.8	28.8	26.4	22.8
Communication	70.3	98.4	114.2	115.0	134.8	131.4	144.5	133.2	109.9	103.3	100.8
Advertising and promotion . . .	69.8	95.1	96.8	64.0	61.0	59.7	55.1	44.6	41.7	47.4	45.8
Utilities and office supplies . . .	88.8	113.2	128.4	115.4	128.1	137.8	143.2	120.2	105.9	105.4	110.9
Other operating expenses . . .	86.2	111.1	130.1	146.8	156.0	159.4	163.2	165.9	169.0	173.6	178.8
Interest [3]	87.9	98.5	97.9	94.7	53.8	54.4	50.6	53.6	50.6	52.6	65.7

[1] Weighted average of all components, including interest. [2] Includes lease, aircraft and engine rentals, depreciation and amortization. [3] Interest on long-term debt and capital and other interest expense

Source: Air Transport Association of America, Washington, DC, *Airline Cost Index, Major and National Carriers, Fourth Quarter 2005.* See Internet site <http://www.airlines.org/econ/econ.aspx> (accessed 10 August 2006).

Table 1050. **Top 40 Airports in 2004—Passengers Enplaned: 1994 and 2004**

[**In thousands (501,197 represents 501,197,000), except rank. For calendar year.** Airports ranked by total passengers enplaned by large certificated air carriers on scheduled and nonscheduled operations]

Airport	1994 Total	1994 Rank	2004 Total	2004 Rank	Airport	1994 Total	1994 Rank	2004 Total	2004 Rank
All airports	501,197	(X)	652,712	(X)	Baltimore, MD (BWI)	5,481	27	9,735	22
					Washington, DC (Dulles				
Total, top 40.	382,759	(X)	502,609	(X)	Intl)	4,218	35	9,389	23
Atlanta, GA (Hartsfield Intl). .	25,630	2	40,399	1	Chicago, IL (Midway)	4,049	36	9,236	24
Chicago, IL (O'Hare Intl) . . .	29,700	1	33,653	2	Fort Lauderdale-Hollywood				
Dallas/Ft.Worth Intl, TX	25,117	3	27,563	3	Intl, FL	4,500	32	9,173	25
Los Angeles Intl, CA	19,721	4	22,892	4	Salt Lake City Intl, UT	7,825	23	8,868	26
Denver Intl, CO	14,640	5	19,856	5	San Diego, CA (Lindbergh				
Las Vegas, NV (McCarran					Field)	6,160	26	8,089	27
Intl)	10,435	14	19,413	6	Tampa Intl, FL	5,416	29	8,065	28
Phoenix Sky Harbor Intl, AZ.	12,427	7	19,123	7	Honolulu Intl, HI.	8,494	22	7,830	29
Minneapolis/St. Paul Intl,					Wash, DC (Ronald Reagan				
MN	10,456	13	17,282	8	Washington National	6,975	25	7,184	30
Detroit, MI (Wayne County) .	11,822	8	16,784	9	Metropolitan Oakland Intl,				
Houston Intercontinental,					CA.	3,992	38	6,825	31
TX	9,626	17	16,707	10	Portland Intl, OR	4,826	30	6,267	32
Newark Intl, NJ	11,782	9	14,026	11	St. Louis, MO (Lambert-				
Orlando Intl, FL	8,863	21	13,752	12	St. Louis Intl)	11,453	10	5,880	33
Seattle-Tacoma Intl, WA . . .	9,936	15	13,744	13	Pittsburgh Intl, PA.	8,928	19	5,704	34
San Francisco Intl, CA	14,309	6	13,504	14	Memphis Intl, TN	3,454	43	5,285	35
New York, NY (JFK Intl). . . .	8,894	20	13,222	15	San Jose Intl, CA	4,016	37	5,190	36
Philadelphia Intl, PA	7,537	24	12,480	16	Cleveland, OH (Cleveland-				
Miami Intl, FL	10,810	11	11,521	17	Hopkins Intl)	4,665	31	5,151	37
Charlotte-Douglas Intl, NC . .	9,370	18	11,306	18	San Juan, PR (Luis Munoz				
Boston, MA (Logan Intl). . . .	10,609	12	11,094	19	Marin Intl)	4,377	33	5,074	38
New York, NY (La Guardia) . .	9,780	16	10,980	20	Kansas City Intl, MO.	4,236	34	5,003	39
Greater Cincinnati, OH	5,441	28	10,594	21	Sacramento Intl, CA	2,791	50	4,768	40

X Not applicable.

Source: U.S. Bureau of Transportation Statisics, Office of Airline Information, BTS Form 41, Schedule T-3, unpublished data.

Table 1051. **Domestic Airline Markets: 2005**

[**In thousands (4,160 represents 4,160,000). For calendar year.** Data are for the 25 top markets and include all commercial airports in each metro area. Data represent origin and final destination of travel]

Market	Passengers	Market	Passengers
New York to—from Fort Lauderdale	4,160	Chicago to—from Los Angeles	1,607
New York to—from Orlando	3,589	Dallas/Fort Worth to—from Houston	1,568
New York to—from Chicago	2,991	Honolulu to—from Kahului, Maui	1,534
New York to—from Los Angeles	2,736	Chicago to—from Orlando	1,498
New York to—from Atlanta	2,621	New York to—from Miami	1,472
New York to—from West Palm Beach. . . .	2,007	Chicago to—from Washington.	1,443
New York to—from Las Vegas.	1,829	Atlanta to—from Washington.	1,418
New York to—from Washington	1,792	Chicago to—from Phoenix	1,404
New York to—from Tampa	1,780	New York to—from Dallas/Fort Worth	1,397
New York to—from San Juan	1,771	Los Angeles to—from Las Vegas	1,369
New York to—from San Francisco	1,767	Orlando to—from Philadelphia/Camden. . .	1,279
New York to—from Boston	1,662	Los Angeles to—from Oakland	1,264
Chicago to—from Las Vegas	1,651		

Source: Air Transport Association of America, Washington, DC, *Annual Report.*

Table 1052. **Worldwide Airline Fatalities: 1986 to 2005**

[For scheduled air transport operations. Excludes accidents due to acts of unlawful interference]

Year	Fatal accidents	Passenger deaths	Death rate [1]	Death rate [2]	Year	Fatal accidents	Passenger deaths	Death rate [1]	Death rate [2]
1986	24	641	0.07	0.04	1996	24	1,146	0.07	0.05
1987	25	900	0.09	0.06	1997	25	921	0.06	0.04
1988	29	742	0.07	0.04	1998	20	904	0.05	0.03
1989	29	879	0.08	0.05	1999	21	499	0.03	0.02
1990	27	544	0.05	0.03	2000	18	757	0.04	0.03
1991	29	638	0.06	0.03	2001	13	577	0.03	0.02
1992	28	1,070	0.09	0.06	2002	14	791	0.04	0.03
1993	33	864	0.07	0.04	2003	7	466	0.02	0.02
1994	27	1,170	0.09	0.05	2004	9	203	0.01	0.01
1995	25	711	0.05	0.03	2005	18	713	0.03	0.02

[1] Rate per 100 million passenger miles flown.   [2] Rate per 100 million passenger kilometers flown.

Source: International Civil Aviation Organization, Montreal, Canada, *Civil Aviation Statistics of the World*, annual.

Table 1053. **Aircraft Accidents: 1990 to 2005**

[**For years ending December 31**]

Item	Unit	1990	1995	2000	2002	2003	2004	2005, prel.
Air carrier accidents, all services [1].......	Number...	24	36	56	41	54	30	39
Fatal accidents..................	Number...	6	3	3	–	2	2	3
Fatalities	Number...	39	168	92	–	22	14	22
Aboard..................	Number...	12	162	92	–	21	14	20
Rates per 100,000 flight hours:								
Accidents..................	Rate.....	0.198	0.267	0.306	0.237	0.309	0.159	0.200
Fatal accidents	Rate.....	0.049	0.022	0.016	–	0.011	0.011	0.015
Commuter air carrier accidents [2]........	Number...	15	12	12	7	2	4	6
Fatal accidents..................	Number...	3	2	1	–	1	–	–
Fatalities	Number...	6	9	5	–	2	–	–
Aboard..................	Number...	4	9	5	–	2	–	–
Rates per 100,000 flight hours:								
Accidents..................	Rate.....	0.641	0.457	3.247	2.559	0.627	1.324	2.000
Fatal accidents	Rate.....	0.128	0.076	0.271	–	0.313	–	–
On-demand air taxi accidents [3]........	Number...	107	75	80	60	74	66	66
Fatal accidents..................	Number...	29	24	22	18	18	23	11
Fatalities	Number...	51	52	71	35	42	64	18
Aboard..................	Number...	49	52	68	35	40	63	16
Rates per 100,000 flight hours:								
Accidents..................	Rate.....	4.76	3.02	2.04	2.06	2.53	2.04	2.02
Fatal accidents	Rate.....	1.29	0.97	0.56	0.62	0.61	0.71	0.34
General aviation accidents [4]........	Number...	2,242	2,056	1,837	1,715	1,739	1,617	1,669
Fatal accidents..................	Number...	444	413	345	345	352	314	321
Fatalities	Number...	770	735	596	581	632	558	562
Aboard..................	Number...	765	728	585	575	629	558	557
Rates per 100,000 flight hours:								
Accidents..................	Rate.....	7.85	8.21	6.57	6.69	6.75	6.49	6.83
Fatal accidents	Rate.....	1.55	1.63	1.21	1.33	1.36	1.26	1.31

– Represents zero.   [1] U.S. air carriers operating under 14 CFR 121. Beginning 2000, includes aircraft with 10 or more seats, previously operating under 14 CFR 135.   [2] All scheduled service of U.S. air carriers operating under 14 CFR 135. Beginning 2000, only aircraft with fewer than 10 seats.   [3] All nonscheduled service of U.S. air carriers operating under 14 CFR 135.   [4] U.S. civil registered aircraft not operated under 14 CFR 121 or 135.

Source: U.S. National Transportation Safety Board, "Aviation Accident Statistics", Internet site <http://www.ntsb.gov/aviation/stats.htm> (accessed 31 July 2006).

Table 1054. **U.S. Carrier Delays, Cancellations, and Diversions: 1995 to 2005**

[**In thousands (5,327.4 represents 5,327,400). For calendar year.** See headnote, table 1055]

Item	1995	1997	1998	1999	2000	2001	2002	2003	2004	2005
Total operations...........	5,327.4	5,411.8	5,384.7	5,527.9	5,683.0	5,967.8	5,271.4	6,488.5	7,129.3	7,140.6
Delays:										
Late departures [1]...........	827.9	846.9	870.4	937.3	1,131.7	953.8	717.4	834.4	1,187.6	1,279.4
Late arrivals [2]............	1,039.3	1,083.8	1,070.1	1,152.7	1,356.0	1,104.4	868.2	1,057.8	1,421.4	1,466.1
Cancellations [3]..............	91.9	97.8	144.5	154.3	187.5	231.2	65.1	101.5	127.8	133.7
Diversions [4]................	10.5	12.1	13.2	13.6	14.3	12.9	8.4	11.4	13.8	14.0

[1] Late departures comprise flights departing 15 minutes or more after the scheduled departure time.   [2] Late arrivals comprise flights arriving 15 minutes or more after the scheduled arrival time.   [3] A cancelled flight is one that was not operated, but was listed in a carrier's computer reservation system within seven days of the scheduled departure.   [4] A diverted flight is one that left from the scheduled departure airport but flew to a destination point other than the scheduled destination point.

Source: U.S. Bureau of Transportation Statistics, *National Transportation Statistics*, annual. See Internet site <http://www.bts.gov/publications/national_transportation_statistics/>

Table 1055. **On-Time Flight Arrivals and Departures at Major U.S. Airports: 2005**

[In percent. Quarterly, based on gate arrival and departure times for domestic scheduled operations of U.S. major airlines. All U.S. airlines with 1 percent or more of total U.S. domestic scheduled airline passenger revenues are required to report on-time data. A flight is considered on time if it operated less than 15 minutes after the scheduled time shown in the carrier's computerized reservation system. See source for data on individual airlines]

Airport	On-time arrivals				On-time departures			
	1st qtr.	2d qtr.	3d qtr.	4th qtr.	1st qtr.	2d qtr.	3d qtr.	4th qtr.
Total, all airports	**75.3**	**80.8**	**76.1**	**77.5**	**78.6**	**83.2**	**78.7**	**80.2**
Total major airports	74.6	80.4	76.0	77.1	77.3	82.0	77.5	79.2
Atlanta, Hartsfield	70.0	77.2	66.3	73.9	72.9	77.6	67.6	74.7
Boston, Logan International	69.6	77.5	69.9	72.9	74.7	83.0	77.4	79.1
Baltimore/Washington International	78.4	83.0	78.0	81.4	78.2	82.1	77.6	78.6
Charlotte, Douglas	79.0	81.1	78.9	80.4	77.8	81.5	79.3	82.9
Cincinnati, Greater Cincinnati	77.6	86.0	82.9	84.3	78.6	87.2	84.1	85.2
Washington, Reagan National.	74.9	81.6	77.7	80.5	78.5	84.7	82.4	84.7
Denver International	79.8	82.8	84.3	82.2	80.0	81.3	82.9	81.5
Dallas-Fort Worth International	82.5	84.7	76.2	81.9	81.3	82.5	74.7	80.4
Detroit, Metro Wayne County	76.9	82.9	75.5	76.6	79.3	82.9	71.8	76.9
Newark International	65.7	69.5	63.3	58.1	76.2	79.7	72.6	71.2
Fort Lauderdale-Hollywood International . . .	64.1	75.3	74.3	71.4	69.5	79.9	79.0	75.3
Washington/Dulles	79.0	78.6	77.0	82.5	79.1	79.9	79.3	84.5
Houston, George Bush	80.3	87.2	76.8	81.7	85.7	89.4	79.3	85.5
New York, JFK International	68.9	74.0	67.7	70.5	73.6	81.5	74.2	77.7
Las Vegas, McCarran International	73.9	81.5	77.6	78.1	74.1	80.4	75.6	76.3
Los Angeles International.	75.9	82.7	80.9	80.8	80.5	85.6	83.4	83.3
New York, La Guardia.	62.7	72.8	68.4	62.8	74.6	82.3	78.7	75.9
Orlando International	74.9	80.9	77.6	76.8	78.0	82.9	79.6	80.0
Chicago, Midway	79.2	86.2	82.2	81.5	76.9	82.2	76.1	74.1
Miami International	76.1	77.1	72.9	70.2	77.9	78.0	72.7	76.1
Minneapolis-St. Paul International	78.7	82.2	75.2	76.6	82.5	84.6	72.7	78.1
Oakland International	78.1	81.3	79.8	79.0	78.6	81.2	79.4	77.3
Chicago, O'Hare	70.2	78.0	76.4	75.0	70.9	76.5	75.0	72.5
Philadelphia International.	65.7	74.7	72.2	75.0	63.9	75.8	72.6	75.9
Phoenix, Sky Harbor International	75.2	84.1	81.6	83.2	75.7	82.3	79.3	81.3
Pittsburgh, Greater International	75.6	80.6	77.4	80.4	81.5	84.4	81.7	84.3
San Diego, Lindbergh Field	75.5	81.8	79.0	80.2	80.2	86.1	83.4	83.8
Seattle-Tacoma International	77.3	72.5	74.4	74.2	79.1	73.6	77.6	79.5
San Francisco International	74.5	78.3	77.1	70.5	81.4	84.7	84.1	78.3
Salt Lake City International	79.7	86.0	84.7	83.1	81.0	86.8	86.0	86.3
Tampa, Tampa International	74.5	80.2	76.0	77.4	78.9	83.7	80.0	82.1
Portland International	78.9	78.0	79.5	74.1	83.4	83.5	84.3	80.8
St. Louis, Lambert	79.7	82.9	78.4	81.3	82.1	85.1	81.0	82.7

Source: U.S. Department of Transportation, Aviation Consumer Protection Division, *Air Travel Consumer Report*, monthly. See Internet site <http://airconsumer.ost.dot.gov>.

Table 1056. **Consumer Complaints Against U.S. Airlines: 1990 to 2005**

[Calendar year data. Represents complaints filed by consumers to the U.S. Department of Transportation, Aviation Consumer Protection Division, regarding service problems with air carrier personnel. See source for data on individual airlines]

Complaint category	1990	1995	1999	2000	2001	2002	2003	2004	2005
Total	**7,703**	**4,629**	**17,345**	**20,564**	**14,076**	**7,697**	**4,601**	**5,839**	**6,894**
Flight problems [1]	3,034	1,133	6,449	8,698	5,048	1,808	1,049	1,462	1,942
Customer service [2]	758	667	3,657	4,074	2,531	1,478	584	742	800
Baggage	1,329	628	2,351	2,753	1,965	1,082	802	1,085	1,586
Ticketing/boarding [3]	624	666	1,329	1,405	1,310	898	643	637	679
Refunds	701	576	935	803	942	737	428	376	529
Fares [4]	312	185	584	708	568	436	243	180	219
Disability [5]	(NA)	(NA)	520	612	457	420	325	467	427
Oversales [6]	399	263	673	759	539	364	223	263	283
Discrimination [7]	(NA)	(NA)	(NA)	(NA)	164	176	71	96	99
Advertising	96	66	57	42	42	43	13	41	45
Tours	29	18	28	25	11	(8)	(8)	(8)	(8)
Animals	(NA)	(NA)	(NA)	6	–	2	3	3	3
Smoking	74	15	(9)	(9)	(9)	(9)	(9)	(9)	(9)
Credit	5	4	(9)	(9)	(9)	(9)	(9)	(9)	(9)
Other	342	408	762	684	493	255	218	487	282

– Represents zero. NA Not available. [1] Cancellations, delays, etc. from schedule. [2] Unhelpful employees, inadequate meals or cabin service, treatment of delayed passengers. [3] Errors in reservations and ticketing; problems in making reservations and obtaining tickets. [4] Incorrect or incomplete information about fares, discount fare conditions, and availability, etc. [5] Prior to 1999, included in ticketing/boarding. [6] All bumping problems, whether or not airline complied with DOT regulations. [7] Allegations of discrimination by airlines due to factors other than disability, such as race, religion, national origin or sex. [8] Included in "Other" beginning 2002. [9] Included in "Other" beginning 1999.

Source: U.S. Department of Transportation, Aviation Consumer Protection Division, *Air Travel Consumer Report*, monthly. See Internet site <http://airconsumer.ost.dot.gov>.

Transportation   **675**

Table 1057. Commuter/Regional Airline Operations—Summary: 1990 to 2005

[Calendar year data (42.1 represents 42,100,000). Commuter/regional airlines operate primarily aircraft of predominately 75 passengers or less and 18,000 pounds of payload capacity serving short haul and small community markets. Represents operations within all North America by U.S. Regional Carriers. Averages are means. For definition of mean, see Guide to Tabular Presentation]

Item	Unit	1990	1995	2000	2002	2003	2004	2005
Passenger carriers operating	Number.	150	124	94	91	82	74	80
Passengers enplaned	Millions .	42.1	57.2	84.6	98.4	113.0	134.7	150.8
Average passengers enplaned per carrier. .	1,000 . .	277.5	461.4	830.4	1,080.9	1,379.3	1,820.0	1,876.0
Revenue passenger miles (RPMs).	Billions .	7.61	12.75	25.27	32.77	43.34	56.21	65.52
Average RPMs per carrier	Millions .	50.75	102.80	268.83	360.11	528.51	759.54	819.05
Airports served	Number.	811	780	729	707	709	735	750
Average trip length	Miles. . .	183	223	299	333	384	417	437
Passenger aircraft operated	Number.	1,917	2,138	2,271	2,385	2,569	2,757	2,676
Average seating capacity (seats).	Number.	22.1	24.6	31.7	35.1	37.7	39.9	40.4
Fleet flying hours [1]	1,000 . .	3,447	4,659	5,362	5,248	6,088	6,587	7,177
Average annual utilization per aircraft.	Hours . .	1,798	2,179	2,368	2,201	2,370	2,389	2,682

[1] Prior to 1995, utilization results reflected airborne rather than block hours.

Source: Regional Airline Association and AvStat Associates, Washington, DC, *Annual Report of the Regional Airline Industry* (copyright).

Table 1058. Airports, Aircraft, and Airmen: 1980 to 2004

[As of December 31 or for years ending December 31]

Item	1980	1985	1990	1995	2000	2002	2003	2004
Airports, total [1]	15,161	16,319	17,490	18,224	19,281	19,572	19,581	19,820
Public	4,814	5,858	5,589	5,415	5,317	5,286	5,286	5,288
Percent—with lighted runways	66.2	68.1	71.4	74.3	75.9	76.1	76.2	76.3
With paved runways	72.3	66.7	70.7	73.3	74.3	74.5	74.5	74.5
Private.	10,347	10,461	11,901	12,809	13,964	14,286	14,295	14,532
Percent—with lighted runways	15.2	9.1	7.0	6.4	7.2	8.3	8.6	9.0
With paved runways	13.3	17.4	31.5	33.0	32.0	32.4	32.7	32.8
Certificated [2].	730	700	680	667	651	633	628	599
Civil	(X)	(X)	(X)	572	563	558	555	542
Civil military.	(X)	(X)	(X)	95	88	75	73	57
General aviation	14,431	15,619	16,810	17,557	18,630	18,939	18,953	19,221
Active air carrier fleet [3].	3,805	4,678	6,083	7,411	8,055	8,194	8,176	8,186
Fixed wing	3,803	4,673	6,072	7,293	8,016	8,161	8,144	8,150
Helicopter.	2	5	11	118	39	33	32	36
General aviation fleet [4].	211,043	196,500	198,000	188,089	217,533	211,244	209,708	219,426
Fixed-wing	200,094	184,700	184,500	162,342	183,276	176,283	176,624	182,867
Turbojet	2,992	4,100	4,100	4,559	7,001	8,355	7,997	9,298
Turboprop	4,089	5,000	5,300	4,995	5,762	6,841	7,689	8,379
Piston.	193,013	175,600	175,200	152,788	170,513	161,087	160,938	165,189
Rotorcraft	6,001	6,000	6,900	5,830	7,150	6,648	6,525	7,821
Other.	4,945	5,800	6,600	4,741	6,700	6,377	6,008	5,939
Gliders	(X)	(X)	(X)	2,182	2,041	1,951	2,002	2,116
Lighter than air.	(X)	(X)	(X)	2,559	4,660	4,426	4,006	3,823
Experimental.	(X)	(X)	(X)	15,176	20,407	21,936	20,550	22,800
Airman certificates held: [5]								
Pilot, total	827,071	709,540	702,659	639,184	625,581	631,762	625,011	618,633
Women	52,902	43,082	40,515	38,030	36,757	38,257	37,694	37,243
Student.	199,833	146,652	128,663	101,279	93,064	85,991	87,296	87,910
Recreational	(X)	(X)	87	232	340	317	310	291
Airplane:								
Private	357,479	311,086	299,111	261,399	251,561	245,230	241,045	235,994
Commercial	183,442	151,632	149,666	133,980	121,858	125,920	123,990	122,592
Air transport.	69,569	82,740	107,732	123,877	141,596	144,708	143,504	142,160
Rotorcraft only [6]	6,030	8,123	9,567	7,183	7,775	7,770	7,916	8,586
Glider only	7,039	8,168	7,833	11,234	9,387	21,826	20,950	21,100
Flight instructor certificates	60,440	58,940	63,775	77,613	80,931	86,089	87,816	89,596
Instrument ratings	260,462	258,559	297,073	298,798	311,944	317,389	315,413	313,546
Nonpilot [7]	368,356	395,139	492,237	651,341	547,453	515,570	509,835	515,293
Mechanic	250,157	274,100	344,282	405,294	344,434	315,928	313,032	317,111
Repairmen	(X)	(X)	(X)	61,233	38,208	37,114	37,248	39,231
Parachute rigger	9,547	9,395	10,094	11,824	10,477	8,063	7,883	8,011
Ground instructor	61,550	58,214	66,882	96,165	72,326	73,658	72,692	73,735
Dispatcher.	6,799	8,511	11,002	15,642	16,340	16,695	16,955	17,493
Flight navigator	1,936	1,542	1,290	916	570	431	382	336
Flight engineer.	38,367	43,377	58,687	60,267	65,098	63,681	61,643	59,376

X Not applicable. [1] Existing airports, heliports, seaplane bases, etc. recorded with FAA. Includes military airports with joint civil and military use. Includes U.S. outlying areas. Airport-type definitions: Public—publicly owned and under control of a public agency; private—owned by a private individual or corporation. May or may not be open for public use. [2] Certificated airports serve air-carriers with aircraft seating more than 30 passengers. [3] Air-carrier aircraft are aircraft carrying passengers or cargo for hire under 14 CFR 121 (large aircraft—more than 30 seats) and 14 CFR 135 (small aircraft— 30 seats or fewer). [4] Beginning 1995 excludes commuters. [5] Source: U.S. Federal Aviation Administration. See Internet site <http://www.faa.gov/data_statistics/>. Prior years in the *Statistical Handbook of Aviation*, annual. [6] Data for 1980 and 1985 are for helicopters only. [7] All certificates on record. No medical examination required.

Source: Except as noted, U.S. Bureau of Transportation Statistics, *National Transportation Statistics, annual*. See Internet site <http://www.bts.gov/publications/national_transportation_statistics/>.

Table 1059. **Freight Carried on Major U.S. Waterways: 1980 to 2004**

[In millions of tons (4.0 represents 4,000,000)]

Item	1980	1985	1990	1995	2000	2001	2002	2003	2004
Atlantic intracoastal waterway	4.0	3.1	4.2	3.5	3.1	2.5	1.9	1.9	2.3
Great Lakes.	183.5	148.1	167.1	177.8	187.5	171.4	167.2	156.5	178.4
Gulf intracoastal waterway	94.5	102.5	115.4	118.0	113.8	112.2	107.7	117.8	123.3
Mississippi River system [1]	584.2	527.8	659.1	707.2	715.5	714.8	712.8	676.8	699.8
Mississippi River mainstem	441.5	384.0	475.3	520.3	515.6	504.2	501.7	478.0	496.9
Ohio River system [2]	179.3	203.9	260.0	267.6	274.4	281.8	280.9	261.3	271.5
Columbia River.	49.2	42.4	51.4	57.1	55.2	50.3	45.0	47.2	53.5
Snake River.	5.1	3.5	4.8	6.8	6.7	5.6	4.3	5.3	5.7

[1] Main channels and all tributaries of the Mississippi, Illinois, Missouri, and Ohio Rivers.   [2] Main channels and all navigable tributaries and embayments of the Ohio, Tennessee, and Cumberland Rivers.

Source: U.S. Army Corps of Engineers, *Waterborne Commerce of the United States*, annual. See Internet site <http://www.iwr.usace.army.mil/ndc/wcsc/wcsc.htm>.

Table 1060. **Waterborne Commerce by Type of Commodity: 1995 to 2004**

[In millions of short tons (2,240.4 represents 2,240,400,000). Domestic trade includes all commercial movements between United States ports and on inland rivers, Great Lakes, canals, and connecting channels of the United States, Puerto Rico, and Virgin Islands]

Commodity	1995	2000	2003	2004 Total	2004 Domestic	2004 Foreign imports	2004 Foreign exports
Total	2,240.4	2,424.6	2,394.3	2,551.9	1,047.1	1,089.1	415.8
Coal.	324.5	297.0	281.2	306.1	222.9	29.4	53.7
Petroleum and petroleum products	907.1	1,044.0	1,080.5	1,127.1	365.4	697.8	63.8
Crude petroleum	504.6	571.4	604.5	616.2	84.4	531.6	0.1
Petroleum products [1]	402.5	472.4	476.1	510.9	281.0	166.3	63.7
Gasoline	114.4	125.2	126.4	149.1	87.3	50.7	11.1
Distillate fuel oil	76.7	91.7	101.7	139.1	69.0	53.9	16.2
Residual fuel oil	111.9	131.6	116.7	92.9	77.7	14.0	1.3
Chemicals and related products	153.7	172.4	171.3	180.3	75.8	43.8	60.7
Fertilizers.	35.7	35.1	35.2	34.3	13.4	7.5	13.4
Other chemicals and related products	118.0	137.3	136.1	146.0	62.4	36.3	47.3
Crude material, inedible.	381.7	380.3	358.0	390.3	229.4	108.6	52.3
Forest products, wood and chips	47.2	33.1	23.6	27.8	9.7	9.7	8.4
Pulp and waste paper	14.9	13.6	16.1	17.5	0.1	2.0	15.4
Soil, sand, gravel, rock, and stone [1]	152.5	165.0	170.8	179.8	134.3	41.5	3.9
Limestone	54.0	67.4	64.7	73.2	54.9	15.5	2.8
Phosphate rock	10.7	3.4	5.7	6.4	3.6	2.8	0.0
Sand & gravel	77.0	79.0	85.3	83.6	72.2	10.5	0.9
Iron ore and scrap.	104.9	97.9	80.9	94.8	63.1	16.2	15.4
Marine shells	0.5	0.3	0.1	–	–	–	–
Nonferrous ores and scrap	27.9	29.2	26.2	25.4	7.1	15.4	2.9
Sulphur, clay, and salt	23.4	11.3	8.4	8.3	1.0	2.6	4.8
Slag	1.9	4.0	3.6	6.2	3.0	3.1	0.0
Other nonmetal minerals	8.4	25.9	28.3	30.5	11.0	18.1	1.4
Primary manufactured goods	106.3	153.0	134.7	159.6	43.0	98.4	18.2
Papers products	13.1	12.1	11.8	13.1	0.3	6.4	6.5
Lime, cement, and glass.	33.9	55.9	49.1	55.3	18.6	35.1	1.6
Primary iron and steel products	44.1	57.1	41.7	54.0	15.9	36.6	1.5
Primary nonferrous metal products	12.3	25.5	28.6	32.6	8.1	16.2	8.3
Primary wood products.	2.9	2.5	3.3	4.6	0.1	4.2	0.3
Food and farm products.	303.2	283.3	265.7	271.3	86.9	35.2	149.2
Fish	3.6	2.4	2.6	2.9	0.1	1.7	1.1
Grain [1]	167.9	145.2	130.1	141.8	53.1	1.3	87.4
Wheat	48.5	43.4	37.3	44.8	12.4	0.1	32.3
Corn	105.0	88.2	78.2	86.4	37.6	0.1	48.7
Oilseeds	46.1	57.6	56.9	48.4	19.4	0.5	28.5
Soybeans.	42.0	47.3	49.7	42.7	17.2	0.1	25.4
Vegetables products	9.0	8.9	8.3	9.1	0.9	4.1	4.1
Processed grain and animal feed	33.0	23.1	20.3	19.3	6.7	0.8	11.8
Other agricultural products	43.5	46.1	47.5	49.7	6.7	26.8	16.2
All manufactured equipment, machinery and product	57.0	83.6	90.0	102.7	20.6	67.2	15.0
Waste and scrap, n.e.c.[2]	5.4	4.3	3.1	3.0	3.0	–	–
Unknown or not elsewhere classified	1.6	6.8	9.7	11.6	0.1	8.6	2.9

– Represents or rounds to zero.   [1] Includes commodities not shown separately.   [2] N.e.c. means not elsewhere classified.

Source: U.S. Army Corps of Engineers, *Waterborne Commerce of the United States*, annual. See Internet site <http://www.iwr.usace.army.mil/ndc/wcsc/wcsc.htm>

Transportation   677

Table 1061. **Selected U.S. Ports by Tons of Traffic: 2004**

[In thousands of short tons (7,541 represents 7,541,000), except rank. For calendar year for the top 70 ports. Represents tons of cargo shipped from or received by the specified port. Excludes cargo carried on general ferries; coal and petroleum products loaded from shore facilities directly onto bunkers of vessels for fuel; and owned equipment in support of Corps projects]

Port name	Rank	Total	Foreign Total	Foreign Inbound	Foreign Outbound	Domestic
Albany, NY	67	7,541	1,168	916	252	6,372
Anacortes, WA.	43	16,305	2,246	1,076	1,170	14,059
Ashtabula, OH.	51	10,938	5,377	450	4,927	5,562
Baltimore, MD	16	47,399	32,780	24,950	7,830	14,619
Baton Rouge, LA	10	57,083	21,939	18,156	3,783	35,144
Beaumont, TX	4	91,698	70,874	65,316	5,558	20,824
Boston, MA.	31	25,797	17,806	16,826	979	7,991
Burns Waterway Harbor, IN	56	9,802	1,854	1,407	447	7,948
Calcite, MI	59	8,949	944	88	856	8,005
Camden-Gloucester, NJ.	69	7,189	4,750	4,436	314	2,439
Charleston, SC	34	24,739	20,816	14,643	6,173	3,923
Chicago, IL.	35	24,602	3,828	2,550	1,278	20,774
Cincinnati, OH.	48	13,898	–	–	–	13,898
Cleveland, OH.	44	15,775	3,919	3,568	351	11,855
Conneaut, OH	63	8,027	3,210	258	2,952	4,817
Corpus Christi, TX	6	78,925	53,795	44,990	8,805	25,130
Detroit, MI.	42	16,858	4,282	4,021	261	12,577
Duluth-Superior, MN and WI.	18	45,393	13,720	489	13,231	31,672
Freeport, TX	23	33,908	28,138	25,157	2,981	5,770
Galveston, TX	62	8,113	3,372	538	2,834	4,741
Gary, IN	60	8,531	569	310	259	7,962
Honolulu, HI	39	19,085	5,884	5,316	569	13,201
Houston, TX	2	202,047	137,537	97,713	39,823	64,511
Huntington–Tristate.	8	77,308	–	–	–	77,308
Indiana Harbor, IN	40	18,228	890	818	72	17,338
Jacksonville, FL.	38	21,451	11,429	10,198	1,231	10,022
Kalama, WA	54	10,116	9,072	435	8,637	1,044
Lake Charles, LA	12	54,768	31,693	27,036	4,657	23,075
Long Beach, CA	5	79,708	62,515	44,620	17,896	17,193
Los Angeles, CA	14	51,363	43,872	32,420	11,452	7,491
Louisville, KY.	65	7,799	–	–	–	7,799
Marcus Hook, PA.	36	24,569	14,117	14,117	–	10,452
Matagorda Ship Channel, TX	50	12,524	8,908	7,401	1,507	3,616
Memphis, TN.	41	17,520	–	–	–	17,520
Miami, FL.	57	9,755	8,332	5,201	3,131	1,423
Mobile, AL.	11	56,212	29,318	19,916	9,402	26,894
New Castle, DE	61	8,170	2,346	2,207	140	5,824
New Haven, CT	52	10,856	3,067	2,704	363	7,789
New Orleans, LA	7	78,085	40,423	24,135	16,288	37,662
New York, NY and NJ	3	152,378	82,200	70,749	11,451	70,178
Newport News, VA	46	14,280	8,481	1,050	7,431	5,799
Nikishka, AK	68	7,505	3,430	396	3,034	4,076
Norfolk Harbor, VA	21	34,166	26,192	8,572	17,620	7,974
Oakland, CA	45	15,541	12,725	5,748	6,977	2,817
Pascagoula, MS.	22	34,100	23,410	19,476	3,933	10,690
Paulsboro, NJ	25	30,486	18,602	18,117	485	11,884
Philadelphia, PA.	20	35,220	21,437	21,123	314	13,782
Pittsburgh, PA	19	41,032	–	–	–	41,032
Plaquemines, LA, Port of	13	54,405	17,694	9,308	8,386	36,710
Port Arthur, TX.	29	27,570	18,954	13,594	5,360	8,616
Port Everglades, FL	32	24,900	13,388	11,091	2,296	11,512
Portland, ME.	27	29,709	27,834	27,615	219	1,875
Portland, OR	26	29,993	17,658	4,434	13,224	12,335
Presque Isle, MI.	53	10,134	2,071	–	2,071	8,064
Providence, RI.	58	9,559	4,825	4,537	288	4,734
Richmond, CA.	33	24,744	12,893	11,440	1,453	11,850
San Juan, PR	47	14,179	6,207	5,746	461	7,972
Savannah, GA.	28	28,177	26,078	16,535	9,544	2,098
Seattle, WA.	37	23,501	17,612	9,134	8,478	5,889
South Louisiana, LA, Port of.	1	224,187	104,771	40,087	64,683	119,417
St. Louis, MO and IL.	24	33,387	–	–	–	33,387
Stoneport, MI	66	7,754	76	–	76	7,678
Tacoma, WA	30	26,282	18,608	6,225	12,383	7,674
Tampa, FL	15	48,289	18,605	9,551	9,054	29,684
Texas City, TX	9	68,283	50,806	46,385	4,421	17,477
Toledo, OH	55	9,862	7,398	4,226	3,172	2,464
Two Harbors, MN	49	13,473	109	–	109	13,364
Valdez, AK	17	46,758	3	1	3	46,755
Vancouver, WA	70	6,973	5,211	860	4,350	1,762
Wilmington, NC	64	7,888	4,347	3,488	859	3,541

– Represents zero.

Source: U.S. Army Corps of Engineers, *Waterborne Commerce of the United States, 2004.* See Internet site <http://www.iwr.usace.army.mil/ndc/>.

Table 1062. **Leading U.S. Ports/Waterways by Container Traffic: 2004**

[In thousands of twenty-foot equivalent units (TEUS). 29,926.9 represents 29,926,900. For calendar year. For the 70 leading ports/waterways in total TEUS. A TEUS is a measure of containerized cargo capacity equal to 1 standard 20 foot length by 8-foot width by 8-foot 6-inch height container]

Port/waterway name	Total loaded	Domestic			Foreign loaded	
		Total [1]	Inbound loaded	Outbound loaded	Total	Inbound
Total [2]	29,926.9	7,336.3	3,089.3	3,089.4	23,748.2	15,794.5
Albany, NY	2.5	4.8	1.2	1.3	–	–
Anchorage, AK	604.3	663.5	440.6	161.3	2.4	1.9
Apra Harbor, GU	125.1	128.8	121.8	3.4	–	–
Baltimore, MD	443.8	120.8	55.1	42.3	346.4	228.3
Boston, MA	135.4	19.7	9.4	5.8	120.1	73.1
Camden-Gloucester, NJ.	27.9	12.2	7.2	0.5	20.1	18.5
Cedar Bayou, TX	3.9	3.9	–	3.9	–	–
Charleston, SC	1,422.9	30.4	6.7	8.9	1,407.4	823.9
Chatham Strait, AK.	2.8	4.7	2.1	0.7	–	–
Chester, PA.	84.8	–	–	–	84.8	48.3
Clarence Strait, AK.	3.6	5.2	2.3	1.2	(Z)	(Z)
Clearwater River, ID	10.0	16.7	0.3	9.7	–	–
Columbia River, Dalles—McNary, OR. .	26.8	32.6	16.5	10.3	–	–
Cordova, AK	4.3	6.2	2.0	2.3	–	–
East Pearl River, MS.	43.2	–	–	–	43.2	19.4
Fernandina Beach, FL.	12.5	-	–	–	12.5	4.3
Freeport, TX	51.7	0.1	–	0.1	51.5	28.5
Galveston, TX	9.2	–	–	–	9.2	6.4
GIWW, Morgan City—Port Allen, LA . .	6.8	10.0	1.7	5.2	–	–
Gulfport, MS	183.5	–	–	–	183.5	100.6
Haines, AK	2.9	4.7	2.0	0.8	–	–
Hilo, HI	36.4	52.4	26.7	7.8	1.9	1.5
Honolulu, HI	1,150.2	1,434.7	741.5	371.7	37.0	19.5
Houston, TX	1,235.7	156.3	58.5	87.1	1,090.1	532.2
Jacksonville, FL	748.9	635.0	232.7	384.5	131.7	39.1
Juneau, AK	35.3	57.0	24.7	10.6	–	–
Kahului, Maui, HI	83.5	112.3	64.4	19.1	–	–
Kawaihae Harbor, HI.	59.3	82.2	48.2	11.1	–	–
Ketchikan, AK	33.9	53.3	19.8	13.8	0.4	0.4
Kodiak, AK	29.2	29.2	14.9	14.3	(Z)	0.0
Lake Charles, LA	7.3	8.3	2.1	4.3	0.8	0.0
Long Beach, CA	5,184.9	553.8	47.3	390.6	4,747.1	3,706.9
Los Angeles, CA	3,900.6	13.4	2.7	9.0	3,888.9	3,109.7
Mayaguez, PR	24.3	–	–	–	24.3	12.7
Memphis, TN.	2.7	5.4	0.1	2.7	–	–
Miami, FL	817.6	28.0	5.7	4.4	807.5	459.1
Mobile, AL.	22.0	0.3	–	0.2	21.8	9.3
Morehead City, NC	7.2	–	–	–	7.2	4.2
Nawiliwili, Kauai, HI	32.2	49.6	26.4	5.8	–	–
New Orleans, LA	274.7	37.2	13.0	18.2	243.5	99.9
New York, NY and NJ	3,409.1	287.1	128.0	127.5	3,153.6	2,236.7
Newport News, VA	96.3	–	–	–	96.3	58.2
Norfolk Harbor, VA	1,308.0	130.5	49.0	58.0	1,201.0	716.0
Oakland, CA	1,509.9	406.4	89.5	247.5	1,173.0	610.6
Pacific Islands excl. Hawaii, OT	3.5	5.8	2.8	0.6	–	–
Palm Beach, FL	131.4	–	–	–	131.4	35.3
Petersburg, AK	27.6	43.4	13.6	14.0	–	–
Philadelphia, PA.	114.6	–	–	–	114.6	96.4
Port Everglades, FL	501.6	15.7	1.1	14.6	485.9	230.8
Port Hueneme, CA	13.6	–	–	–	13.6	12.6
Port Manatee, FL.	6.0	–	–	–	6.0	4.7
Portland, ME	2.0	–	–	–	2.0	1.2
Portland, OR	229.3	36.9	17.8	0.3	211.2	72.6
Richmond, VA	38.9	–	–	–	38.9	21.6
Salem River, NJ	6.9	–	–	–	6.9	0.3
San Diego, CA.	49.7	–	–	–	49.7	44.7
San Francisco, CA	20.8	–	–	–	20.8	16.1
San Juan, PR	1,037.6	870.0	522.3	326.3	189.0	152.2
Savannah, GA	1,308.5	32.4	6.4	3.8	1,298.3	665.7
Seattle, WA.	1,198.5	276.6	43.2	136.8	1,018.5	656.0
Sitka, AK	12.0	19.6	7.3	4.8	–	–
Skagway, AK	3.0	5.4	2.6	0.4	–	–
Tacoma, WA	1,626.1	709.9	154.9	493.4	977.8	630.8
Tampa, FL	11.7	0.1	(Z)	–	11.6	7.4
Unalaska Bay and Island, AK	74.2	47.7	25.7	21.7	26.8	0.1
Vancouver, WA	21.1	21.7	3.2	17.2	0.7	0.7
Whittier, AK.	12.9	15.2	11.1	1.8	–	–
Wilmington, DE	150.2	–	–	–	150.2	121.0
Wilmington, NC	73.9	–	–	–	73.9	47.6
Wrangell, AK	2.7	4.3	1.8	0.9	–	–

– Represents zero.   Z Less than 50.   [1] Includes empty TEUS.   [2] Includes other ports/waterways not shown separately.

Source: U.S. Army Corps of Engineers, "2004 Waterborne Container Traffic for U.S. Ports and all 50 States and U.S. Territories." See Internet site <http://www.iwr.usace.army.mil/ndc/wcsc/wcsc.htm> (accessed 1 August 2006).

Transportation   679

Table 1063. **Highway Mileage—Urban and Rural by Ownership: 1980 to 2004**

[In thousands (3,955 represents 3,955,000). As of Dec. 31. Includes Puerto Rico beginning 2000]

Type and control	1980	1985	1990	1995	2000	2001	2002	2003	2004
Total mileage [1]	[2]3,955	3,862	3,880	3,912	3,951	3,963	3,982	3,991	3,997
Urban mileage [3]	624	691	757	819	859	884	902	954	994
Under state control	79	111	96	112	112	110	112	127	130
Under local control	543	578	661	706	746	771	787	828	862
Rural mileage	[2]3,331	3,171	3,123	3,093	3,092	3,079	3,080	3,036	3,003
Under state control	702	773	703	691	664	665	665	653	650
Under local control	2,270	2,173	2,242	2,231	2,311	2,295	2,297	2,263	2,236
Under federal control.	262	225	178	170	117	119	118	120	118

[1] Beginning 1985, includes only public road mileage as defined 23 USC 402.   [2] Includes 98,000 miles of nonpublic road mileage previously contained in other rural categories.   [3] Includes a small amount of road owned by the federal government, such as roads in federal parks that are not part of a state or local highway system.

Source: U.S. Federal Highway Administration, *Highway Statistics*, annual. See Internet site <http://www.fhwa.dot.gov/policy/ohpi/hss /hsspubs.htm>.

Table 1064. **Highway Mileage by State—Functional Systems and Urban/Rural: 2004**

[**As of Dec. 31.** Excludes Puerto Rico. For definition of fuctional systems see text, this section]

State		Functional systems						
	Total	Interstate	Other free- ways and expressways	Arterial	Collector	Local	Urban	Rural
U.S.	**3,981,512**	**46,572**	**10,246**	**388,523**	**790,038**	**2,746,133**	**981,276**	**3,000,236**
AL.	95,483	904	33	8,946	20,416	65,184	21,521	73,962
AK.	14,107	1,082	–	1,512	2,825	8,688	2,095	12,012
AZ.	58,112	1,168	149	4,944	8,620	43,231	22,055	36,057
AR.	98,606	656	95	6,887	20,269	70,699	10,863	87,743
CA.	169,791	2,458	1,452	27,128	31,878	106,875	86,137	83,654
CO	87,096	956	315	8,915	16,271	60,639	18,465	68,631
CT.	21,143	346	236	2,773	3,144	14,644	15,006	6,137
DE.	6,043	41	14	632	936	4,420	2,860	3,183
DC	1,500	13	22	264	152	1,049	1,500	–
FL.	119,529	1,471	549	12,844	14,384	90,281	78,272	41,257
GA	116,916	1,244	117	14,094	22,812	78,649	36,413	80,503
HI	4,318	55	34	753	834	2,642	2,136	2,182
ID	47,100	612	–	3,916	10,009	32,563	4,620	42,480
IL	138,624	2,169	92	14,183	21,762	100,418	37,550	101,074
IN	94,597	1,169	136	7,963	22,663	62,666	20,600	73,997
IA	113,835	782	–	9,680	31,522	71,851	10,961	102,874
KS.	135,016	874	141	9,209	33,322	91,470	10,859	124,157
KY.	77,363	762	65	5,856	16,063	54,617	11,977	65,386
LA	60,942	903	45	5,542	9,947	44,505	14,814	46,128
ME	22,749	367	19	2,249	5,979	14,135	2,641	20,108
MD	30,808	481	285	3,710	4,871	21,461	16,893	13,915
MA	35,783	573	296	6,186	4,825	23,903	27,856	7,927
MI	122,382	1,243	321	12,104	25,771	82,943	35,561	86,821
MN	131,937	914	148	12,770	29,457	88,648	16,293	115,644
MS	74,129	685	66	7,365	15,440	50,573	10,621	63,508
MO	125,923	1,181	342	9,982	24,819	89,599	18,331	107,592
MT	69,452	1,192	–	6,039	16,367	45,854	2,754	66,698
NE.	93,245	482	21	8,027	20,747	63,968	5,922	87,323
NV.	33,977	560	52	2,875	5,210	25,280	5,727	28,250
NH	15,630	235	37	1,609	2,789	10,960	3,036	12,594
NJ	38,122	431	402	5,761	4,156	27,372	31,151	6,971
NM	64,004	1,000	5	5,084	8,483	49,432	7,958	56,046
NY	113,341	1,674	798	13,502	20,557	76,810	41,224	72,117
NC	102,666	1,046	307	8,934	17,659	74,720	24,680	77,986
ND	86,782	571	–	5,881	11,741	68,589	1,846	84,936
OH	124,752	1,574	485	10,887	22,556	89,250	44,479	80,273
OK	112,713	931	186	8,197	25,307	78,092	15,113	97,600
OR	65,861	728	55	6,995	17,761	40,322	12,358	53,503
PA	120,623	1,757	534	13,187	19,807	85,338	44,416	76,207
RI	6,419	71	85	833	880	4,550	5,193	1,226
SC.	66,250	844	71	6,884	13,377	45,074	10,688	55,562
SD	83,547	678	–	6,362	19,224	57,283	2,443	81,104
TN.	88,988	1,105	137	8,979	17,861	60,906	21,060	67,928
TX.	303,176	3,233	1,182	28,534	63,559	206,668	83,447	219,729
UT.	42,710	940	17	3,333	7,849	30,571	10,416	32,294
VT.	14,368	320	20	1,303	3,133	9,592	1,396	12,972
VA	71,534	1,116	233	8,255	14,080	47,850	21,226	50,308
WA	81,216	764	366	7,456	16,876	55,754	20,124	61,092
WV	37,011	555	9	3,241	8,776	24,430	3,191	33,820
WI	113,699	743	269	12,323	21,306	79,058	21,980	91,719
WY	27,594	913	3	3,635	10,986	12,057	2,548	25,046

– Represents zero.

Source: U.S. Federal Highway Administration, *Highway Statistics*, annual. See Internet site <http://www.fhwa.dot.gov/policy/ohpi/hss /hsspubs.htm>.

Table 1065. **Commodity Shipments—Value, Tons, and Ton-Miles: 1997 and 2002**

[6,859,805 represents $6,859,805,000,000. For business establishments in mining, manufacturing, wholesale trade, and selected retail industries. 2002 industries classified by the 1997 North American Classification System (NAICS); 1997 classified by the Standard Industry Classification (SIC) Manual. Selected auxiliary establishments are also included. See source for details. Based on the Economic Census; see Appendix III]

Mode of transportation	Value (mil. dol.)		Tons (1,000)		Ton-miles (mil.)	
	1997	2002	1997	2002	1997	2002
All modes	6,859,805	8,397,210	10,566,330	11,667,919	2,592,590	3,137,898
Single modes	5,673,920	7,049,383	9,928,296	11,086,660	2,317,973	2,867,938
Truck [1]	4,936,491	6,235,001	7,292,256	7,842,836	998,035	1,255,908
Rail	318,915	310,884	1,543,727	1,873,884	1,021,250	1,261,612
Water	75,765	89,344	535,558	681,227	240,572	282,659
Air (includes truck and air)	229,272	264,959	4,378	3,760	6,124	5,835
Pipeline [2]	113,476	149,195	552,377	684,953	(S)	(S)
Multiple modes	913,164	1,079,185	212,981	216,686	202,602	225,715
Parcel, U.S. Postal Service or courier . .	823,311	987,746	22,100	25,513	16,729	19,004
Truck and rail	75,566	69,929	53,730	42,984	55,371	45,525
Other multiple modes	14,287	21,510	137,151	148,189	130,503	161,187
Other and unknown modes	272,722	268,642	425,053	364,573	72,015	44,245

S Data do not meet publication standards due to high sampling variability or other reasons. [1] Truck as a single mode includes shipments that went by private truck only, for-hire truck only, or a combination of private truck and for-hire truck. [2] Commodity Flow Survey data exclude shipments of crude oil.

Source: U.S. Bureau of Transportation Statistics and U.S. Census Bureau, 2002 Economic Census, Transportation, 2002 "Commodity Flow Survey," Series EC02TCF-US, issued December 2004. See Internet site <http://www.census.gov/svsd/www /cfsmain.html>.

Table 1066. **Hazardous Shipments—Value, Tons, and Ton-Miles: 2002**

[660,181 represents $660,181,000,000. Based on the Economic Census; see Appendix III. See also headnote, table 1065]

Mode of transportation	Value (mil. dol.)		Tons (1,000)		Ton-miles (mil.)		Average miles per shipment
	Total	Percent	Total	Percent	Total	Percent	
All modes	660,181	100.0	2,191,519	100.0	326,727	100.0	136
Single modes	644,489	97.6	2,158,533	98.5	311,897	95.5	105
Truck [1]	419,630	63.6	1,159,514	52.9	110,163	33.7	86
For-hire truck	189,803	28.8	449,503	20.5	65,112	19.9	285
Private truck	226,660	34.3	702,186	32.0	44,087	13.5	38
Rail	31,339	4.7	109,369	5.0	72,087	22.1	695
Water	46,856	7.1	228,197	10.4	70,649	21.6	(S)
Air (includes truck and air)	1,643	0.2	64	–	85	–	2,080
Pipeline [2]	145,021	22.0	661,390	30.2	(S)	(S)	(S)
Multiple modes	9,631	1.5	18,745	0.9	12,488	3.8	849
Parcel, U.S. Postal Service or courier .	4,268	0.6	245	–	119	–	837
Other multiple modes	5,363	0.8	18,500	0.8	12,369	3.8	1,371
Other and unknown modes	6,061	0.9	14,241	0.6	2,342	0.7	57
Class of material	660,181	100.0	2,191,519	100.0	326,727	100.0	136
Class 1, explosives	7,901	1.2	5,000	0.2	1,568	0.5	651
Class 2, gasses	73,932	11.2	213,358	9.7	37,262	11.4	95
Class 3, flammable liquids	490,238	74.3	1,788,986	81.6	218,574	66.9	106
Class 4, flammable solids.	6,566	1.0	11,300	0.5	4,391	1.3	158
Class 5, oxidizers and organic peroxides.	5,471	0.8	12,670	0.6	4,221	1.3	407
Class 6, toxic (poison)	8,275	1.3	8,459	0.4	4,254	1.3	626
Class 7, radioactive materials	5,850	0.9	57	–	44	–	(S)
Class 8, corrosive materials	38,324	5.8	90,671	4.1	36,260	11.1	301
Class 9, miscellaneous dangerous goods	23,625	3.6	61,018	2.8	20,153	6.2	368

– Rounds to zero. S Data do not meet publication standards due to high sampling variability or other reasons. [1] Truck as a single mode includes shipments that went by private truck only, for-hire truck only, or a combination of private truck and for-hire truck. [2] Commodity Flow Survey data exclude shipments of crude oil.

Source: U.S. Bureau of Transportation Statistics and U.S. Census Bureau, 2002 Economic Census, Transportation, 2002 "Commodity Flow Survey," Hazardous Shipments Series EC02TCF-US(HM), issued December 2004. See Internet site <http://www.census .gov/svsd/www/cfsmain.html>

Transportation 681

Table 1067. **Shipments by Commodity: 2002**

[8,397,210 represents $8,397,210,000,000. Based on the Economic Census; see Appendix III. See also headnote, table 1065]

Mode of transportation	Value (mil. dol.)		Tons (1,000)		Ton-miles (mil.)		Average miles per shipment
	Total	Percent	Total	Percent	Total	Percent	
Total	8,397,210	100.0	11,667,919	100.0	3,137,898	100.0	546
Live animals and live fish	7,410	–	6,118	–	1,586	–	530
Cereal grains	53,835	0.6	561,089	4.8	264,239	8.4	138
Other agricultural products	129,471	1.5	259,178	2.2	109,362	3.5	481
Animal feed and products of animal origin, n.e.c.[1]	52,142	0.6	227,991	2.0	51,158	1.6	167
Meat, fish, seafood, and their preparations	201,304	2.4	84,506	0.7	41,352	1.3	162
Milled grain products and preparations, and bakery products	113,379	1.4	109,311	0.9	49,001	1.6	189
Other prepared foodstuffs and fats and oils	355,561	4.2	448,924	3.8	161,565	5.1	179
Alcoholic beverages	108,991	1.3	89,434	0.8	25,735	0.8	55
Tobacco products	69,868	0.8	4,370	–	983	–	334
Monumental or building stone	3,039	–	22,451	0.2	1,571	–	170
Natural sands	3,644	–	472,975	4.1	29,990	1.0	45
Gravel and crushed stone	12,850	0.2	1,866,487	16.0	105,826	3.4	30
Nonmetallic minerals n.e.c.[1]	10,066	0.1	184,632	1.6	56,630	1.8	185
Metallic ores and concentrates	14,027	0.2	98,267	0.8	63,028	2.0	474
Coal	22,875	0.3	1,239,862	10.6	686,279	21.9	120
Gasoline and aviation turbine fuel	279,407	3.3	1,063,569	9.1	117,219	3.7	52
Fuel oils	116,119	1.4	549,007	4.7	55,464	1.8	32
Coal and petroleum products, n.e.c.[1]	82,130	1.0	447,975	3.8	93,001	3.0	102
Basic chemicals	153,656	1.8	347,670	3.0	115,961	3.7	417
Pharmaceutical products	479,117	5.7	24,270	0.2	11,337	0.4	693
Fertilizers	34,049	0.4	264,319	2.3	87,605	2.8	157
Chemical products and preparations, n.e.c.[1]	226,598	2.7	105,962	0.9	53,657	1.7	385
Plastics and rubber	325,673	3.9	139,973	1.2	80,827	2.6	424
Logs and other wood in the rough	5,756	–	(S)	(S)	7,790	0.2	(S)
Wood products	158,586	1.9	345,940	3.0	120,151	3.8	242
Pulp, newsprint, paper, and paperboard	102,495	1.2	137,053	1.2	78,160	2.5	206
Paper or paperboard articles	103,713	1.2	69,211	0.6	23,360	0.7	282
Printed products	134,452	1.6	34,015	0.3	17,037	0.5	816
Textiles, leather, and articles of textiles or leather	466,429	5.6	51,232	0.4	31,787	1.0	940
Nonmetallic mineral products	149,951	1.8	967,978	8.3	135,937	4.3	357
Base metal in primary or semi-finished forms and in finished basic shapes	259,834	3.1	328,053	2.8	121,330	3.9	270
Articles of base metal	234,571	2.8	116,447	1.0	42,680	1.4	392
Machinery	484,152	5.8	63,390	0.5	34,535	1.1	377
Electronic and other electrical equip. and components and office equip.	890,803	10.6	49,592	0.4	30,269	1.0	713
Motorized and other vehicles (including parts)	748,550	8.9	133,088	1.1	59,029	1.9	395
Transportation equipment, n.e.c.[1]	155,013	1.8	18,352	0.2	10,649	0.3	1,074
Precision instruments and apparatus	225,070	2.7	18,352	0.2	3,912	0.1	922
Furniture, mattresses and mattress supports, lamps, lighting fittings, and illuminated signs	139,727	1.7	32,546	0.3	13,705	0.4	515
Miscellaneous manufactured products	387,426	4.6	79,208	0.7	34,467	1.1	995
Waste and scrap	37,896	0.5	217,234	1.9	48,000	1.5	166
Mixed freight	840,346	10.0	299,926	2.6	52,823	1.7	329
Commodity unknown	17,229	0.2	24,266	0.2	8,889	0.3	485

– Rounds to zero.   S Data do not meet publication standards due to high sampling variability or other reasons.   [1] N.e.c. means not elsewhere classified.

Source: U.S. Bureau of Transportation Statistics and U.S. Census Bureau, "2002 Economic Census, Transportation, 2002 Commodity Flow Survey", Series EC02TCF-US, issued December 2004. See Internet site <http://www.census.gov/svsd/www /cfsmain.html>.

Table 1068. **Bridge Inventory—Total and Deficient, 1996 to 2005, and by State, 2005**

[Based on the National Bridge Inventory program; for details, see source]

State and year	Number of bridges	Deficient and obsolete					
		Total number	Percent	Structurally deficient [1]		Functionally obsolete [2]	
				Number	Percent	Number	Percent
1996, total	581,862	182,726	31.4	101,518	17.4	81,208	14.0
1997, total	582,751	175,885	30.2	98,475	16.9	77,410	13.3
1998, total	582,984	172,582	29.6	93,076	16.0	79,506	13.6
1999, total	585,542	170,050	29.0	88,150	15.1	81,900	14.0
2000, total	587,755	167,993	28.6	87,106	14.8	80,887	13.8
2001, total	590,066	165,099	28.0	83,630	14.2	81,469	13.8
2002, total	591,220	163,010	27.6	81,437	13.8	81,573	13.8
2003, total	592,246	160,819	27.2	79,811	13.5	81,008	13.7
2004, total	593,885	158,318	26.7	77,758	13.1	80,560	13.6
U.S. total, 2005	**594,616**	**156,177**	**26.3**	**75,871**	**12.8**	**80,306**	**13.5**
Alabama	15,703	4,488	28.6	2,248	14.3	2,240	14.3
Alaska	1,172	358	30.5	158	13.5	200	17.1
Arizona	7,173	720	10.0	162	2.3	558	7.8
Arkansas	12,477	3,019	24.2	1,143	9.2	1,876	15.0
California	23,171	6,531	28.2	2,876	12.4	3,655	15.8
Colorado	8,253	1,404	17.0	571	6.9	833	10.1
Connecticut	4,168	1,388	33.3	340	8.2	1,048	25.1
Delaware	849	130	15.3	42	4.9	88	10.4
District of Columbia	245	155	63.3	23	9.4	132	53.9
Florida	11,527	2,076	18.0	327	2.8	1,749	15.2
Georgia	14,490	2,970	20.5	1,179	8.1	1,791	12.4
Hawaii	1,104	514	46.6	160	14.5	354	32.1
Idaho	4,060	753	18.5	318	7.8	435	10.7
Illinois	25,803	4,346	16.8	2,456	9.5	1,890	7.3
Indiana	18,273	4,045	22.1	2,007	11.0	2,038	11.2
Iowa	24,846	6,839	27.5	5,232	21.1	1,607	6.5
Kansas	25,511	5,663	22.2	3,137	12.3	2,526	9.9
Kentucky	13,501	4,104	30.4	1,282	9.5	2,822	20.9
Louisiana	13,344	4,200	31.5	1,947	14.6	2,253	16.9
Maine	2,370	822	34.7	347	14.6	475	20.0
Maryland	5,021	1,403	27.9	406	8.1	997	19.9
Massachusetts	4,919	2,572	52.3	599	12.2	1,973	40.1
Michigan	10,872	3,030	27.9	1,772	16.3	1,258	11.6
Minnesota	12,989	1,586	12.2	1,140	8.8	446	3.4
Mississippi	16,900	4,509	26.7	3,220	19.1	1,289	7.6
Missouri	23,883	7,965	33.4	4,826	20.2	3,139	13.1
Montana	4,922	1,018	20.7	511	10.4	507	10.3
Nebraska	15,457	3,864	25.0	2,488	16.1	1,376	8.9
Nevada	1,632	196	12.0	50	3.1	146	8.9
New Hampshire	2,361	744	31.5	320	13.6	424	18.0
New Jersey	6,445	2,341	36.3	838	13.0	1,503	23.3
New Mexico	3,836	724	18.9	407	10.6	317	8.3
New York	17,338	6,510	37.5	2,114	12.2	4,396	25.4
North Carolina	17,512	5,125	29.3	2,301	13.1	2,824	16.1
North Dakota	4,477	1,023	22.9	771	17.2	252	5.6
Ohio	28,058	7,006	25.0	2,987	10.6	4,019	14.3
Oklahoma	23,383	8,400	35.9	6,938	29.7	1,462	6.3
Oregon	7,238	1,872	25.9	697	9.6	1,175	16.2
Pennsylvania	22,291	9,560	42.9	5,532	24.8	4,028	18.1
Rhode Island	749	413	55.1	194	25.9	219	29.2
South Carolina	9,202	2,101	22.8	1,274	13.8	827	9.0
South Dakota	5,961	1,575	26.4	1,229	20.6	346	5.8
Tennessee	19,763	4,452	22.5	1,407	7.1	3,045	15.4
Texas	49,226	10,264	20.9	2,385	4.8	7,879	16.0
Utah	2,821	502	17.8	246	8.7	256	9.1
Vermont	2,701	929	34.4	455	16.8	474	17.5
Virginia	13,248	3,390	25.6	1,192	9.0	2,198	16.6
Washington	7,600	2,080	27.4	434	5.7	1,646	21.7
West Virginia	6,913	2,576	37.3	1,073	15.5	1,503	21.7
Wisconsin	13,687	2,262	16.5	1,460	10.7	802	5.9
Wyoming	3,028	627	20.7	400	13.2	227	7.5
Puerto Rico	2,143	1,033	48.2	250	11.7	783	36.5

[1] Bridges are structurally deficient if they have been restricted to light vehicles, require immediate rehabilitation to remain open, or are closed.   [2] Bridges are functionally obsolete if they have deck geometry, load carrying capacity, clearance or approach roadway alignment that no longer meet the criteria for the system of which the bridge is carrying a part.

Source: U.S. Federal Highway Administration, Office of Bridge Technology; <http://www.fhwa.dot.gov/bridge/britab.htm>.

Transportation   683

Table 1069. Funding for Highways and Disposition of Highway-User Revenue: 1990 to 2004

[In millions of dollars (75,444 represents $75,444,000,0000. Data compiled from reports of state and local authorities]

Type	1990	1995	1999	2000	2001	2002	2003	2004
Total receipts	75,444	96,269	121,650	131,115	132,324	138,878	139,246	145,315
Current income.	69,880	87,620	110,376	119,815	119,659	123,802	124,593	129,521
Highway-user revenues	44,346	59,331	74,222	81,335	77,719	79,487	79,280	83,006
Other taxes and fees	19,827	21,732	29,380	31,137	34,190	36,168	37,783	38,956
Investment income, other receipts . . .	5,707	6,557	6,774	7,342	7,749	8,147	7,530	7,560
Bond issue proceeds [1]	5,564	8,649	11,274	11,301	12,665	15,076	14,654	15,794
Funds from (+) or to (–) reserves	-36	-2,791	-5,639	-8,418	-2,423	-239	4,359	2,174
Total funds available	75,408	93,478	116,011	122,697	129,900	138,639	143,605	147,489
Total disbursements	75,408	93,478	116,011	122,697	129,900	138,639	143,605	147,489
Current disbursements.	72,457	88,994	111,097	117,592	124,815	131,694	136,213	139,478
Capital outlay	35,151	44,228	57,227	61,323	65,968	68,794	70,004	70,274
Maintenance and traffic services.	20,365	24,319	29,997	30,636	31,677	33,893	35,011	36,327
Administration and research	6,501	8,419	9,130	10,020	10,423	10,934	11,986	12,737
Law enforcement and safety	7,235	8,218	10,393	11,031	11,977	12,548	13,501	14,322
Interest on debt.	3,205	3,810	4,350	4,583	4,770	5,526	5,711	5,819
Bond retirement [1]	2,951	4,484	4,914	5,105	5,086	6,945	7,393	8,011

[1] Excludes issue and redemption of short-term notes or refunding bonds.
Source: U.S. Federal Highway Administration, *Highway Statistics*, annual. See Internet site <http://www.fhwa.dot.gov/policy/ohpi/hss /hsspubs.htm>.

Table 1070. Federal Aid to State and Local Governments for Highway Trust Fund and Federal Transit Administration (FTA) by State: 2004

[Year ending Sept. 30. (28,881 represents $28,881,000,000]

State	Highway trust fund Total (mil. dol.)	Highway trust fund Per capita (dol.)[1]	FTA Total (mil. dol.)	FTA Per capita (dol.)[1]	State	Highway trust fund Total (mil. dol.)	Highway trust fund Per capita (dol.)[1]	FTA Total (mil. dol.)	FTA Per capita (dol.)[1]	State	Highway trust fund Total (mil. dol.)	Highway trust fund Per capita (dol.)[1]	FTA Total (mil. dol.)	FTA Per capita (dol.)[1]
U.S.[2] . .	28,881	97	6,818	23	KS	369	135	13	5	ND	181	285	3	5
U.S.[3] . .	28,813	98	6,689	23	KY	435	105	38	9	OH	958	84	152	13
AL	491	108	19	4	LA	501	111	60	13	OK	487	138	19	6
AK	373	569	18	27	ME	177	134	11	8	OR	355	99	131	37
AZ	450	78	165	29	MD	426	77	74	13	PA	1,224	99	448	36
AR	375	136	17	6	MA	604	94	192	30	RI	157	145	12	11
CA	2,365	66	1,080	30	MI	799	79	88	9	SC	670	160	24	6
CO	434	94	125	27	MN	453	89	139	27	SD	182	236	2	3
CT	460	131	60	17	MS	362	125	12	4	TN	622	105	57	10
DE	91	110	4	5	MO	723	126	93	16	TX	2,827	126	255	11
DC	131	237	237	428	MT	314	339	1	2	UT	245	103	50	21
FL	1,563	90	262	15	NE	257	147	10	6	VT	122	197	11	18
GA	788	89	127	14	NV	199	85	53	23	VA	588	79	162	22
HI	97	77	38	30	NH	128	99	4	3	WA	486	78	264	43
ID	231	166	8	6	NJ	752	87	537	62	WV	331	182	8	4
IL	611	48	341	27	NM	281	147	25	13	WI	518	94	75	14
IN	607	97	54	9	NY	1,470	76	1,011	53	WY	225	444	3	5
IA	339	115	23	8	NC	977	114	73	9					

[1] Based on estimated population as of July 1.   [2] Includes outlying areas and undistributed funds, not shown separately.
[3] For the 50 states and D.C.
Source: U.S. Census Bureau, *Federal Aid to States for Fiscal Year, 2004*. See Inernet site <http://www.census.gov/prod/www/abs /fas.html>.

Table 1071. State Motor Fuel Tax Receipts, 2003 and 2004, and Gasoline Tax Rates, 2004

[566 represents $566,000,000]

State	Net receipts (mil. dol.) 2003	Net receipts (mil. dol.) 2004	Tax rate,[1] 2004	State	Net receipts (mil. dol.) 2003	Net receipts (mil. dol.) 2004	Tax rate,[1] 2004	State	Net receipts (mil. dol.) 2003	Net receipts (mil. dol.) 2004	Tax rate,[1] 2004
AL	566	550	18.00	KY	499	461	16.40	ND	104	100	21.00
AK	28	29	8.00	LA	573	558	20.00	OH	1,432	1,615	26.00
AZ	656	651	18.00	ME	217	211	25.20	OK	407	415	17.00
AR	436	438	21.70	MD	709	742	23.50	OR	404	396	24.00
CA	3,248	3,532	18.00	MA	676	683	21.00	PA	1,754	1,800	25.90
CO	544	554	22.00	MI	1,093	1,055	19.00	RI	135	147	30.00
CT	447	465	25.00	MN	639	672	20.00	SC	463	500	16.00
DE	107	117	23.00	MS	391	408	18.40	SD	127	128	22.00
DC	30	27	20.00	MO	680	700	17.00	TN	752	812	21.40
FL	1,841	1,891	13.90	MT	184	188	27.00	TX	2,863	2,912	20.00
GA	465	502	7.50	NE	305	311	24.60	UT	330	328	24.50
HI	75	79	16.00	NV	401	449	24.80	VT	86	89	20.00
ID	209	211	25.00	NH	157	153	19.50	VA	849	876	17.50
IL	1,310	1,274	19.00	NJ	554	618	10.50	WA	750	889	28.00
IN	1,047	867	18.00	NM	253	254	18.50	WV	290	309	25.35
IA	413	418	20.30	NY	1,499	1,587	24.55	WI	902	900	28.50
KS	407	422	24.00	NC	1,160	1,311	24.60	WY	89	100	14.00

[1] State gasoline tax rates in cents per gallon. In effect December 31.
Source: U.S. Federal Highway Administration, *Highway Statistics*, annual. See Internet site <http://www.fhwa.dot.gov/policy/ohpi/hss /hsspubs.htm>.

Table 1072. **Public Highway Debt—State and Local Governments: 1980 to 2004**

[In millions of dollars (2,381 represents $2,381,000,000). Long-term obligations. Data are for varying calendar and fiscal years. Excludes duplicated and interunit obligations]

Item	1980	1985	1990	1995	2000	2001	2002	2003	2004
Total debt issued.	2,381	8,194	5,708	11,305	14,513	15,697	19,089	22,127	(NA)
State [1].	1,160	5,397	3,147	4,718	9,067	11,012	13,250	16,618	13,344
Local [1].	1,221	2,797	2,561	6,587	5,446	4,685	5,839	5,509	(NA)
Total debt redeemed	1,987	5,294	3,120	5,634	8,623	7,230	13,537	15,171	(NA)
State [1].	1,114	3,835	1,648	2,939	3,897	4,660	9,988	11,550	8,292
Local [1].	873	1,459	1,472	2,695	4,726	2,570	3,549	3,621	(NA)
Total debt outstanding [2].	27,616	32,690	46,586	68,733	96,383	103,342	111,226	119,571	(NA)
State [1].	20,210	21,277	28,362	39,228	61,434	66,256	70,826	77,592	85,565
Local [1].	7,406	11,413	18,224	29,505	34,949	37,086	40,400	41,979	(NA)

NA Not available.   [1] Local data estimated.   [2] End-of-year.

Source: U.S. Federal Highway Administration, *Highway Statistics,* annual. See Internet site <http://www.fhwa.dot.gov/policy/ohpi/hss/hsspubs.htm>.

Table 1073. **State Disbursements for Highways by State: 1995 to 2004**

[In millions of dollars (67,615 represents $67,615,000,000). Comprises disbursements from current revenues or loans for construction, maintenance, interest and principal payments on highway bonds, transfers to local units, and miscellaneous. Includes transactions by state toll authorities. Excludes amounts allocated for collection expenses and nonhighway purposes, and mass transit]

State	1995	1998	1999	2000	2001	2002	2003	2004
United States	67,615	80,518	83,675	89,832	94,513	104,977	109,403	104,677
Alabama	1,002	1,053	1,085	1,246	1,433	1,575	1,572	1,562
Alaska	438	404	416	501	482	541	618	623
Arizona	1,199	1,430	1,860	2,040	2,149	2,445	2,453	2,569
Arkansas	666	815	736	817	976	1,161	1,176	1,219
California	5,966	6,574	6,876	6,750	6,795	8,570	9,349	7,967
Colorado	922	1,166	1,260	1,392	1,616	2,195	1,788	1,870
Connecticut	1,153	1,427	1,094	1,304	1,236	1,848	1,743	1,677
Delaware	441	647	507	595	647	738	929	798
District of Columbia	140	259	242	244	406	336	368	369
Florida	3,421	4,024	3,992	4,208	4,348	4,985	6,664	5,804
Georgia	1,437	1,613	1,763	1,567	1,748	1,945	1,756	1,935
Hawaii	360	326	355	272	263	275	375	314
Idaho	350	414	445	492	480	508	547	568
Illinois	3,006	3,306	2,957	3,447	3,788	4,286	4,595	4,289
Indiana	1,433	1,652	1,522	1,932	3,202	1,975	2,445	2,578
Iowa	1,078	1,177	1,253	1,494	1,388	1,405	1,419	1,401
Kansas	1,019	1,306	1,155	1,206	1,271	1,951	1,891	1,387
Kentucky	1,397	1,481	1,578	1,651	1,612	1,776	2,152	1,907
Louisiana	1,198	1,400	1,237	1,301	1,154	1,287	1,498	1,576
Maine	379	485	458	488	505	744	579	702
Maryland	1,289	1,492	1,554	1,599	1,673	1,803	1,885	1,831
Massachusetts	2,501	3,351	4,407	3,524	3,965	3,783	3,547	3,612
Michigan	1,974	2,745	2,629	2,748	2,920	2,859	2,799	2,930
Minnesota	1,210	1,377	1,534	1,692	1,683	1,866	1,969	1,995
Mississippi	662	843	968	1,039	911	1,040	1,014	1,087
Missouri	1,313	1,438	1,600	1,818	2,044	2,110	2,120	2,135
Montana	388	378	434	474	469	535	578	657
Nebraska	578	589	681	745	661	867	839	859
Nevada	484	446	557	651	668	631	807	1,045
New Hampshire	328	371	416	387	445	522	453	389
New Jersey	2,102	2,513	2,905	4,503	4,276	4,863	6,364	3,849
New Mexico	535	570	753	1,162	1,119	983	862	1,164
New York	4,584	6,051	5,347	5,307	5,301	7,161	6,592	6,094
North Carolina	1,871	2,352	2,441	2,621	2,868	3,001	3,013	3,557
North Dakota	270	306	413	385	358	385	379	388
Ohio	2,637	3,327	3,158	3,351	3,493	3,580	3,660	3,657
Oklahoma	828	944	1,322	1,417	1,443	1,839	1,379	1,175
Oregon	888	1,051	1,009	1,010	984	1,029	1,183	1,000
Pennsylvania	3,153	3,902	4,143	4,517	4,875	5,365	5,258	4,283
Rhode Island	290	339	316	256	380	380	299	373
South Carolina	668	766	885	970	1,104	1,201	1,191	1,254
South Dakota	286	305	371	466	463	437	441	455
Tennessee	1,230	1,420	1,398	1,440	1,563	1,622	1,661	1,549
Texas	3,593	4,295	4,840	5,665	5,716	6,019	6,758	7,134
Utah	431	1,129	1,072	1,072	941	956	879	1,871
Vermont	194	222	252	287	297	265	312	297
Virginia	2,107	2,619	2,771	2,678	2,909	3,185	3,419	3,002
Washington	1,909	1,805	1,780	1,871	2,042	2,276	2,288	2,469
West Virginia	781	893	930	1,170	1,289	1,210	1,169	1,056
Wisconsin	1,252	1,398	1,614	1,663	1,793	2,204	1,904	1,942
Wyoming	272	321	386	396	360	460	468	458

Source: U.S. Federal Highway Administration, *Highway Statistics,* annual. See Internet site <http://www.fhwa.dot.gov/policy/ohpi/hss/hsspubs.htm>.

Transportation   685

Table 1074. State Motor Vehicle Registrations: 1980 to 2004

[In thousands (155,796 represents 155,796,000). Compiled principally from information obtained from state authorities, but it was necessary to draw on other sources and to make numerous estimates in order to complete series. See also Table 1077]

Item	1980	1990	1995	2000	2002	2003	2004
All motor vehicles	155,796	188,798	201,530	221,475	229,620	231,390	237,243
Private and commercial	153,265	185,541	197,941	217,567	225,772	227,476	233,266
Publicly owned	2,531	3,257	3,589	3,908	3,848	3,914	3,977
Automobiles [1]	121,601	133,700	128,387	133,621	135,921	135,670	136,431
Private and commercial	120,743	132,164	126,900	132,247	134,605	134,337	135,077
Publicly owned	857	1,536	1,487	1,374	1,316	1,333	1,354
Buses	529	627	686	746	761	777	795
Private and commercial	254	275	288	314	320	325	330
Publicly owned	275	351	398	432	441	452	465
Trucks [1]	33,667	54,470	72,458	87,108	92,939	94,943	100,017
Private and commercial	32,268	53,101	70,754	85,005	90,847	92,814	97,860
Publicly owned	1,399	1,369	1,704	2,103	2,091	2,129	2,157

[1] Trucks include pickups, panels and delivery vans. Beginning 1990, personal passenger vans, passenger minivans and utility-type vehicles are no longer included in automobiles but are included in trucks.

Source: U.S. Federal Highway Administration, *Highway Statistics*, annual. See Internet site <http://www.fhwa.dot.gov/policy/ohpi/hss/hsspubs.htm>.

Table 1075. Alternative Fueled Vehicles in Use by Fuel Type: 2002 to 2004

[2004 data are projections. 378,589 represents 378,589,000]

Fuel type	Alternative fueled vehicles			Fuel consumption (1,000 gasoline-equivalent gallons)		
	2002	2003	2004	2002	2003	2004
Total	471,098	510,805	547,904	378,589	412,725	447,198
Liquified petroleum gases (LPG)	187,680	190,438	194,389	223,143	230,486	242,368
Compressed natural gas (CNG)	120,839	132,988	143,742	120,670	141,726	159,464
Liquified natural gas (LNG)	2,708	3,030	3,134	9,382	10,514	10,868
Methanol, 85 percent (M85) [1]	5,873	4,917	4,592	337	274	257
Ethanol, 85 percent (E85) [1]	120,951	133,776	146,195	17,783	20,092	22,405
Electricity [2]	33,047	45,656	55,852	7,274	9,633	11,836

[1] The remaining portion is gasoline. [2] Excludes gasoline-electric hybrids.

Source: U.S. Energy Information Administration, *Alternatives to Traditional Transportation Fuels*. See Internet site <http://www.eia.doe.gov/fuelalternate.html> (released February 2004)

Table 1076. Onroad Alternative Fuel and Hybrid Vehicles Made Available, by Supplier Type and Vehicle Type: 2000 to 2004

Item	2000	2001	2002	2003	2004
Total made available.	633,351	623,043	895,984	930,538	775,638
Automobiles [1]	130,680	87,367	156,434	126,951	242,130
Vans & minivans	176,859	271,731	262,842	108,329	6,946
Pickup trucks.	304,030	98,419	81,323	29,633	60,428
Light duty trucks & SUVs [1, 2]	13,588	157,852	377,121	651,379	461,803
Medium duty trucks [3, 4]	709	353	345	511	278
Heavy duty trucks [5]	795	1,017	724	217	285
Buses [3]	1,745	2,184	2,370	1,519	1,816
Other	4,945	4,120	14,825	11,999	1,952
Original Equipment Manufacturer	630,894	621,680	894,594	929,441	774,290
Automobiles [1]	130,316	87,218	156,354	126,872	241,444
Vans & minivans	176,793	271,627	262,786	108,270	6,896
Pickup trucks	302,865	97,840	80,910	29,392	60,323
Light duty trucks & SUVs [1, 2]	13,214	157,759	377,096	651,302	461,604
Medium duty trucks [3, 4]	539	332	43	107	163
Heavy duty trucks [5]	573	684	402	188	258
Buses [3]	1,649	2,101	2,178	1,311	1,650
Other	4,945	4,119	14,825	11,999	1,952
Converter	2,457	1,363	1,390	1,097	1,348
Automobiles	364	149	80	79	686
Vans & minivans	66	104	56	59	50
Pickup trucks	1,165	579	413	241	105
Light duty trucks & SUVs [2]	374	93	25	77	199
Medium duty trucks [4]	170	21	302	404	115
Heavy duty trucks [5]	222	333	322	29	27
Buses	96	83	192	208	166
Other	–	1	–	–	–

– Represents zero. [1] Includes gasoline-electric hybrid vehicles. [2] Light Duty includes vehicles less than or equal to 8,500 gross vehicle weight rating (GVWR). [3] Includes diesel-electric hybrid vehicles. [4] Medium Duty includes vehicles 8,501 to 26,000 GVWR.

Source: U.S. Energy Informstion Administration, Annual Survey of Alternative Fuel Vehicle Suppliers. See Internet site <http://www.eia.doe.gov/fuelrenewable.html>

Table 1077. **State Motor Vehicle Registrations, 1980 to 2004, and Licensed Drivers, and Motorcycle Registrations by State: 2004**

[In thousands (155,796 represents 155,796,000). Motor vehicle registrations cover publicly, privately, and commercially owned vehicles. For uniformity, data have been adjusted to a calendar-year basis as registration years in states differ; figures represent net numbers where possible, excluding reregistrations and nonresident registrations. See also Table 1074]

| State | Motor vehicle registrations [1] | | | | | | 2004 | | Motor-cycle registra-tion [2] 2004 | Licensed drivers, 2004 |
	1980	1985	1990	1995	2000	2003	Total	Auto-mobiles (incl. taxis)		
U.S.	155,796	171,689	188,798	201,530	221,475	231,390	237,243	136,431	5,738	198,889
AL.	2,938	3,383	3,744	3,553	3,960	4,329	4,508	1,694	81	3,613
AK.	262	353	477	542	594	637	660	255	21	483
AZ.	1,917	2,235	2,825	2,873	3,795	3,574	3,776	2,055	208	3,784
AR.	1,574	1,384	1,448	1,613	1,840	1,889	1,918	960	44	1,862
CA.	16,873	18,899	21,926	22,432	27,698	30,248	31,400	19,256	611	22,761
CO	2,342	2,759	3,155	2,812	3,626	2,027	2,023	895	8	3,205
CT.	2,147	2,465	2,623	2,622	2,853	2,964	3,042	2,047	64	2,695
DE.	397	465	526	592	630	687	711	423	17	534
DC	268	306	262	243	242	228	239	189	1	349
FL.	7,614	9,865	10,950	10,369	11,781	14,526	15,057	8,441	456	13,146
GA	3,818	4,580	5,489	6,120	7,155	7,730	7,882	4,222	128	5,793
HI	570	651	771	802	738	903	947	540	23	844
ID	834	854	1,054	1,043	1,178	1,301	1,344	575	49	943
IL	7,477	7,527	7,873	8,973	8,973	9,250	9,232	5,652	276	8,058
IN	3,826	3,824	4,366	5,072	5,571	5,739	5,525	3,067	153	4,521
IA	2,329	2,696	2,632	2,814	3,106	3,369	3,369	1,882	140	2,004
KS.	2,007	2,148	2,012	2,085	2,296	2,314	2,347	853	61	1,980
KY.	2,593	2,615	2,909	2,631	2,826	3,389	3,319	1,881	53	2,823
LA	2,779	3,012	2,995	3,286	3,557	3,714	3,767	1,973	55	3,170
ME	724	840	977	967	1,024	1,052	1,068	609	39	985
MD	2,803	3,276	3,607	3,654	3,848	3,877	4,120	2,548	73	3,594
MA	3,749	3,738	3,726	4,502	5,265	5,479	5,456	3,505	137	4,646
MI	6,488	6,727	7,209	7,674	8,436	8,540	8,399	4,681	227	7,103
MN	3,091	3,385	3,508	3,882	4,630	4,525	4,593	2,502	189	3,083
MS	1,577	1,746	1,875	2,144	2,289	1,951	1,964	1,123	27	1,896
MO	3,271	3,558	3,905	4,255	4,580	4,460	4,812	2,698	77	4,048
MT	680	652	783	968	1,026	1,010	1,009	433	48	713
NE.	1,254	1,258	1,384	1,467	1,619	1,677	1,689	842	28	1,316
NV.	655	709	853	1,047	1,220	1,222	1,281	643	44	1,548
NH	704	974	946	1,122	1,052	1,145	1,178	673	66	986
NJ.	4,761	5,164	5,652	5,906	6,390	6,712	6,224	4,016	149	5,800
NM	1,068	1,226	1,301	1,484	1,529	1,509	1,543	696	36	1,271
NY.	8,002	9,042	10,196	10,274	10,235	10,802	11,099	8,549	169	11,247
NC	4,532	4,501	5,162	5,682	6,223	6,119	6,198	3,658	100	6,122
ND	627	655	630	695	694	694	701	347	21	462
OH	7,771	8,102	8,410	9,810	10,467	10,536	10,636	6,452	298	7,675
OK	2,583	2,911	2,649	2,856	3,014	3,074	3,151	1,634	84	2,370
OR	2,081	2,204	2,445	2,785	3,022	3,061	3,003	1,475	75	2,626
PA.	6,926	7,209	7,971	8,481	9,260	9,724	9,821	6,001	291	8,430
RI	623	610	672	699	760	806	808	532	26	742
SC.	1,996	2,222	2,521	2,833	3,095	3,162	3,257	1,923	60	2,972
SD.	601	657	704	709	793	827	841	396	42	563
TN.	3,271	3,754	4,444	5,400	4,820	4,796	5,035	2,889	108	4,248
TX.	10,475	12,444	12,800	13,682	14,070	14,889	16,907	8,736	284	14,544
UT.	992	1,099	1,206	1,447	1,628	2,006	2,084	1,037	44	1,583
VT.	347	398	462	492	515	516	523	280	28	550
VA.	3,626	4,253	4,938	5,613	6,046	6,346	6,497	4,091	75	5,113
WA	3,225	3,526	4,257	4,503	5,116	5,379	5,535	3,034	159	4,505
WV	1,320	1,143	1,225	1,425	1,442	1,409	1,396	741	19	1,292
WI	2,941	3,187	3,815	3,993	4,366	4,647	4,705	2,592	232	3,910
WY	467	500	528	601	586	620	641	234	31	380

[1] Automobiles, trucks, and buses (excludes motorcycles). Excludes vehicles owned by military services. [2] Private and commercial.

Source: U.S. Federal Highway Administration, *Highway Statistics*, annual. See Internet site <http://www.fhwa.dot.gov/policy/ohpi/hss/hsspubs.htm>.

Transportation 687

Table 1078. **Roadway Congestion: 2003**

[**15,919 represents 15,919,000.** Various federal, state, and local information sources were used to develop the data base with the primary source being the Federal Highway Administration's Highway Performance Monitoring System. Areas shown are rated the top 73 in annual per-person hours of delay]

Urbanized areas	Freeway daily vehicle miles of travel		Annual person hours of delay		Annual congestion cost		
	Total miles (1,000)	Per lane-mile of freeway	Total hours (1,000)	Per person	Per person (dol.)	Delay and fuel cost (mil. dol.)	Fuel wasted (gal. per person)
Total, average	**15,919**	**16,206**	**43,802**	**25**	**422**	**742**	**15**
Akron, OH	5,435	12,494	3,672	6	105	62	4
Albany-Schenectady, NY	5,820	10,582	3,784	7	122	64	4
Albuquerque, NM	4,285	12,985	9,258	16	269	156	9
Allentown-Bethlehem, PA-NJ	4,600	11,646	5,618	9	151	95	6
Atlanta, GA	43,590	19,077	103,618	34	584	1,754	24
Austin, TX	9,200	15,726	23,201	27	457	391	16
Baltimore, MD	26,050	17,026	62,436	27	458	1,057	17
Beaumont, TX	1,685	12,481	1,101	8	127	18	4
Birmingham, AL	9,020	13,363	9,705	14	242	165	10
Boston, MA-NH-RI	37,300	15,738	100,237	25	424	1,692	15
Bridgeport-Stamford, CT-NY	10,000	16,667	14,550	17	291	250	13
Buffalo, NY	6,720	10,500	6,981	6	104	118	3
Cape Coral, FL	435	9,667	2,712	8	141	46	5
Charleston-North Charleston, SC	3,130	12,275	6,364	14	228	107	8
Charlotte, NC-SC	7,755	15,990	16,692	23	389	282	15
Chicago, IL-IN	52,010	19,516	252,822	31	526	4,274	19
Cincinnati, OH-KY-IN	17,635	15,203	27,288	17	287	461	10
Cleveland, OH	17,390	12,647	10,709	6	97	182	5
Colorado Springs, CO	3,435	11,845	6,953	14	243	117	8
Columbus, OH	14,665	15,356	18,550	16	264	314	10
Dallas-Fort Worth-Arlington, TX	51,870	16,705	151,840	35	592	2,545	19
Dayton, OH	6,870	12,491	4,438	6	102	75	4
Denver-Aurora, CO	17,960	15,754	64,506	31	530	1,087	18
Detroit, MI	33,465	17,521	119,581	30	499	2,019	18
El Paso, TX-NM	4,030	14,393	6,491	10	164	110	6
Fresno, CA	3,280	12,377	4,180	7	120	72	5
Grand Rapids, MI	4,515	12,203	5,852	10	169	99	6
Hartford, CT	10,425	13,196	7,434	8	144	127	6
Honolulu, HI	5,930	14,289	7,476	11	184	129	6
Houston, TX	46,665	18,970	135,652	36	609	2,283	22
Indianapolis, IN	11,290	15,466	21,358	21	350	362	14
Jacksonville, FL	10,275	13,980	16,850	18	308	285	11
Kansas City, MO-KS	20,185	11,404	13,874	9	156	235	6
Las Vegas, NV	8,275	17,062	22,245	16	279	380	11
Los Angeles-Long Beach-Santa Ana, CA	136,000	23,248	623,796	50	855	10,686	33
Louisville, KY-IN	11,500	15,972	19,916	22	377	336	14
Memphis, TN-MS-AR	7,815	14,081	17,465	18	295	294	10
Miami, FL	36,685	19,057	147,294	29	487	2,486	17
Milwaukee, WI	10,465	14,950	18,249	13	214	310	8
Minneapolis-St. Paul, MN	27,580	17,346	57,537	23	394	975	15
Nashville-Davidson, TN	13,085	13,702	18,890	20	331	318	11
New Haven, CT	7,450	14,327	5,848	11	181	100	7
New Orleans, LA	5,960	14,024	10,853	10	167	183	6
New York-Newark, NY-NJ-CT	112,555	15,698	404,480	23	383	6,780	11
Oklahoma City, OK	9,500	12,102	7,218	7	112	122	4
Omaha, NE-IA	3,600	12,000	7,984	13	211	134	7
Orlando, FL	10,570	13,551	38,157	30	510	643	18
Oxnard-Ventura, CA	6,700	18,873	10,249	18	307	176	12
Pensacola, FL-AL	1,200	10,909	2,977	10	162	50	5
Philadelphia, PA-NJ-DE-MD	33,875	14,728	112,309	21	357	1,884	11
Phoenix, AZ	23,610	17,819	76,662	26	431	1,294	15
Pittsburgh, PA	12,210	9,768	14,530	8	135	243	4
Portland, OR-WA	12,945	18,105	33,387	20	341	569	13
Providence, RI-MA	11,095	12,328	21,668	18	295	363	9
Raleigh-Durham, NC	8,145	13,352	11,481	15	248	194	10
Richmond, VA	10,830	10,995	8,305	9	153	140	5
Riverside-San Bernardino, CA	19,500	21,429	50,155	30	517	863	21
Sacramento, CA	13,705	19,303	35,929	22	374	619	15
Salem, OR	1,245	12,450	1,714	8	135	29	5
Salt Lake City, UT	8,300	15,660	15,094	16	279	257	11
San Antonio, TX	16,100	14,977	23,788	18	301	401	11
San Diego, CA	36,195	19,460	81,756	28	492	1,411	21
San Francisco-Oakland, CA	48,985	20,242	152,352	37	631	2,605	23
San Jose, CA	16,565	18,508	48,134	29	492	823	18
Sarasota-Bradenton, FL	825	12,692	5,772	10	170	97	6
Seattle, WA	30,700	17,593	72,461	25	427	1,237	17
St. Louis, MO-IL	26,145	14,647	39,936	19	326	675	13
Tampa-St. Petersburg, FL	9,855	14,600	51,360	25	422	865	14
Toledo, OH-MI	4,115	12,470	3,391	7	110	57	4
Tucson, AZ	3,285	13,408	13,767	19	324	233	12
Tulsa, OK	7,025	10,036	5,419	7	113	91	4
Virginia Beach, VA	12,875	13,697	21,746	14	239	367	9
Washington, DC-VA-MD	37,815	18,537	145,484	34	577	2,465	21

Source: Texas Transportation Institute, College Station, Texas; *2005 Urban Mobility Study* (issued May 2005). (Copyright). See <http://mobility.tamu.edu/ums/>.

U.S. Census Bureau, Statistical Abstract of the United States: 2007

Table 1079. Commuting to Work by State: 2004

[In percent, except as indicated (130,831 represents 130,831,000). For workers 16 years old and over. The American Community Survey universe is limited to the household population and excludes the population living in institutions, college dormitories, and other group quarters. Based on a sample and subject to sampling variability; see Appendix III]

State	Total workers (1,000)	Commuted by car, truck, or van		Used public transportation [1]	Walked	Used other means	Worked at home	Mean travel time to work (min.)
		Drove alone	Car-pooled					
U.S.	130,831	77.7	10.1	4.6	2.4	1.4	3.8	24.7
AL	1,931	85.4	9.7	0.5	1.0	1.1	2.3	23.8
AK	295	68.8	13.8	1.0	6.7	4.9	4.7	18.0
AZ	2,427	76.0	14.4	1.8	2.0	2.2	3.6	23.4
AR	1,176	83.4	10.9	0.4	1.7	1.3	2.4	20.8
CA	15,441	75.4	11.3	4.8	2.3	1.8	4.4	27.1
CO	2,206	77.5	9.9	2.5	2.5	1.6	6.1	23.5
CT	1,645	81.6	7.8	3.9	1.8	1.2	3.7	24.0
DE	383	82.0	9.2	2.1	1.6	1.3	3.8	23.2
DC	254	40.5	8.7	33.6	11.4	2.0	3.8	28.0
FL	7,490	81.0	10.1	1.7	1.5	1.7	4.0	25.4
GA	3,981	79.9	11.7	2.1	1.2	1.6	3.6	26.8
HI	575	68.4	16.4	5.5	3.0	2.6	4.2	25.8
ID	620	75.6	12.5	1.2	3.7	2.0	5.0	19.7
IL	5,694	74.8	9.7	8.0	2.6	1.3	3.7	27.7
IN	2,835	82.6	10.0	0.8	1.8	1.7	3.1	21.8
IA	1,438	80.3	9.6	1.0	2.7	1.3	5.2	18.2
KS	1,325	83.6	8.6	0.2	2.2	1.2	4.2	18.0
KY	1,752	83.1	10.7	1.0	1.3	0.8	3.0	22.7
LA	1,875	82.3	9.9	1.8	1.3	2.2	2.4	23.9
ME	630	80.5	9.1	0.6	3.7	1.1	5.1	21.9
MD	2,666	74.3	10.3	8.3	2.1	1.4	3.6	29.7
MA	3,059	75.9	7.2	8.3	3.5	1.3	3.8	26.4
MI	4,348	84.6	8.6	0.9	1.9	0.7	3.2	22.9
MN	2,562	79.2	9.2	2.9	2.8	1.2	4.7	22.3
MS	1,176	82.5	11.3	0.2	1.6	1.5	2.9	21.7
MO	2,671	82.2	9.0	1.4	1.9	1.1	4.5	23.3
MT	444	74.9	10.3	0.5	5.7	2.1	6.4	16.3
NE	875	81.0	8.6	0.6	2.8	1.5	5.5	16.5
NV	1,073	77.5	11.2	3.8	2.7	1.7	3.1	22.6
NH	651	83.2	8.1	0.7	2.4	1.3	4.2	24.6
NJ	3,916	73.5	8.5	10.7	2.7	1.2	3.4	29.4
NM	824	80.6	11.2	1.2	1.8	1.4	3.9	20.1
NY	8,309	56.3	7.8	25.1	5.3	1.8	3.7	30.6
NC	3,777	81.7	11.5	0.9	1.7	1.1	3.1	23.9
ND	323	78.3	8.8	0.4	4.1	1.4	6.9	15.4
OH	5,129	84.5	7.9	1.5	1.8	1.0	3.2	21.9
OK	1,528	83.3	9.2	0.4	1.9	1.7	3.4	19.5
OR	1,603	73.8	11.3	3.7	2.9	2.3	5.9	21.4
PA	5,441	78.5	9.4	5.0	3.1	0.9	3.2	25.1
RI	493	82.7	9.4	2.2	1.7	1.1	2.9	23.1
SC	1,846	82.6	10.7	0.5	1.6	1.3	3.3	22.4
SD	382	77.5	10.0	0.2	3.8	1.1	7.5	15.8
TN	2,656	83.9	10.2	0.7	1.2	0.9	3.1	23.2
TX	9,763	80.5	11.5	1.5	1.4	1.5	3.6	23.8
UT	1,077	73.8	13.6	2.6	2.3	1.7	6.0	20.7
VT	315	76.5	10.0	1.1	5.3	1.2	5.9	21.4
VA	3,514	78.7	11.2	3.5	1.7	1.2	3.6	26.5
WA	2,800	75.3	10.3	4.3	3.2	1.7	5.2	24.8
WV	719	81.7	10.3	1.1	3.0	1.4	2.5	25.6
WI	2,663	80.7	8.3	1.9	3.4	1.4	4.3	20.6
WY	254	75.5	12.4	1.5	4.1	1.3	5.2	17.3

[1] Including taxicabs.

Source: U.S. Census Bureau; 2004 American Community Survey; B08006. Sex of Worker by Means of Transportation to Work; and Multi-Year Profile—Selected Economic Characteristics: 2004; using American FactFinder®; <http://factfinder.census.gov/>; (accessed 31 January 2006).

Transportation 689

Table 1080. Motor Vehicle Distance Traveled by Type of Vehicle: 1970 to 2004

[**1,110 represents 1,110,000,000,000.** Travel estimates based on automatic vehicle classification data]

| Year | Vehicle-miles of travel (bil.) | | | | | Average miles per vehicle (1,000) | | | | |
| | Total [1] | Passenger vehicles | | Vans, pickups, SUVs | Trucks [3] | Total | Passenger vehicles | | Vans, pickups, SUVs | Trucks [3] |
		Cars [1]	Buses [2]				Cars [1]	Buses [2]		
1970	1,110	920	4.5	123	62	10.0	10.0	12.0	8.7	13.6
1980	1,527	1,122	6.1	291	108	9.5	8.8	11.5	10.4	18.7
1983	1,653	1,204	5.2	328	116	9.8	9.1	8.9	10.5	21.1
1984	1,720	1,236	4.6	358	122	10.0	9.2	8.0	11.2	22.6
1985	1,775	1,256	4.5	391	124	10.0	9.4	7.5	10.5	20.6
1986	1,835	1,280	4.7	424	127	10.1	9.5	7.9	10.8	22.1
1987	1,921	1,325	5.3	457	134	10.5	9.7	8.9	11.1	23.3
1988	2,026	1,380	5.5	502	138	10.7	10.0	8.9	11.5	22.5
1989	2,096	1,412	5.7	536	143	10.9	10.2	9.1	11.7	22.9
1990	2,144	1,418	5.7	575	146	11.1	10.3	9.1	11.9	23.6
1991	2,172	1,367	5.8	649	150	11.3	10.3	9.1	12.2	24.2
1992	2,247	1,381	5.8	707	153	11.6	10.6	9.0	12.4	25.4
1993	2,296	1,385	6.1	746	160	11.6	10.5	9.4	12.4	26.3
1994	2,358	1,416	6.4	765	170	11.7	10.8	9.6	12.2	25.8
1995	2,423	1,438	6.4	790	178	11.8	11.2	9.4	12.0	26.5
1996	2,486	1,470	6.6	817	183	11.8	11.3	9.4	11.8	26.1
1997	2,562	1,503	6.8	851	191	12.1	11.6	9.8	12.1	27.0
1998	2,632	1,550	7.0	868	196	12.2	11.8	9.8	12.2	25.4
1999	2,691	1,569	7.7	901	203	12.2	11.9	10.5	12.0	26.0
2000	2,747	1,600	7.6	923	206	12.2	11.9	10.2	11.7	25.7
2001	2,797	1,628	7.1	943	209	11.9	11.8	9.4	11.2	26.6
2002	2,856	1,658	6.8	966	215	12.2	12.2	9.0	11.4	27.1
2003	2,890	1,672	6.8	984	218	12.2	12.3	8.7	11.3	28.1
2004	2,963	1,705	6.6	1,014	227	12.2	12.5	8.3	11.0	27.7

[1] Motorcycles included with cars through 1994; thereafter in total, not shown separately.   [2] Includes school buses.
[3] Includes combinations.

Source: U.S. Federal Highway Administration, *Highway Statistics,* annual. See Internet site <http://www.fhwa.dot.gov/policy/ohpi /hss/hsspubs.htm>.

Table 1081. Domestic Motor Fuel Consumption by Type of Vehicle: 1970 to 2004

[**92.3 represents 92,300,000,000.** Comprises all fuel types used for propulsion of vehicles under state motor fuels laws. Excludes federal purchases for military use. Minus sign (–) indicates decrease]

| Year | Annual fuel consumption (bil. gal.) | | | | | Average miles per gallon | | | | |
	All vehicles [1]	Avg. annual percent change [2]	Cars [1]	Buses [3]	Vans, pickups, SUVs	Trucks [4]	All vehicles [1]	Cars [1]	Buses [3]	Vans, pickups, SUVs	Trucks [4]
1970 . . .	92.3	4.8	67.8	0.8	12.3	11.3	830	737	2,172	866	2,467
1980 . . .	115.0	–5.9	70.2	1.0	23.8	20.0	712	551	1,926	854	3,447
1983 . . .	116.1	2.4	70.5	0.9	23.9	20.8	686	534	1,507	767	3,769
1984 . . .	118.7	2.2	70.8	0.8	25.6	21.4	691	530	1,398	797	3,967
1985 . . .	121.3	2.2	71.7	0.8	27.4	21.4	685	538	1,405	735	3,570
1986 . . .	125.2	3.2	73.4	0.9	29.1	21.9	692	543	1,496	738	3,821
1987 . . .	127.5	1.8	73.5	0.9	30.6	22.5	694	539	1,527	744	3,937
1988 . . .	130.1	2.0	73.5	0.9	32.7	22.9	688	531	1,523	745	3,736
1989 . . .	131.9	1.4	74.1	0.9	33.3	23.5	688	533	1,519	724	3,776
1990 . . .	130.8	–0.8	69.8	0.9	35.6	24.5	677	506	1,428	738	3,953
1991 . . .	128.6	–1.7	64.5	0.9	38.2	25.0	669	487	1,369	721	4,047
1992 . . .	132.9	3.3	65.6	0.9	40.9	25.5	683	502	1,362	717	4,210
1993 . . .	137.3	3.3	67.2	0.9	42.9	26.2	693	512	1,420	714	4,309
1994 . . .	140.8	2.5	68.1	1.0	44.1	27.7	698	517	1,438	701	4,202
1995 . . .	143.8	2.1	68.1	1.0	45.6	29.0	700	530	1,412	694	4,315
1996 . . .	147.4	2.5	69.2	1.0	47.4	29.6	700	534	1,425	685	4,221
1997 . . .	150.4	2.0	69.9	1.0	49.4	29.9	711	539	1,472	703	4,218
1998 . . .	155.4	3.3	71.7	1.1	50.5	32.0	721	544	1,454	707	4,135
1999 . . .	161.4	3.9	73.2	1.1	52.8	33.9	732	552	1,576	701	4,352
2000 . . .	162.5	0.7	73.1	1.1	52.9	35.2	720	547	1,490	668	4,391
2001 . . .	163.5	0.6	73.6	1.0	53.5	35.2	695	534	1,369	636	4,477
2002 . . .	168.7	3.2	75.5	1.0	55.2	36.8	719	555	1,314	650	4,642
2003 . . .	170.0	0.8	75.5	1.0	60.7	32.7	718	556	1,248	697	4,215
2004 . . .	173.7	2.2	76.0	1.0	62.6	33.9	715	557	1,192	682	4,157

[1] Motorcycles included with cars through 1994; thereafter in total, not shown separately.   [2] Change from immediate prior year.   [3] Includes school buses.   [4] Includes combinations.

Source: U.S. Federal Highway Administration, *Highway Statistics,* annual. See Internet site <http://www.fhwa.dot.gov/policy/ohpi /hss/hsspubs.htm>.

Table 1082. **Motor Vehicle Accidents—Number and Deaths: 1980 to 2004**

[17.9 represents 17,900,000]

Item	Unit	1980	1985	1990	1995	2000	2001	2002	2003	2004
ACCIDENTS										
Motor vehicle accidents [1]	Million . . .	17.9	19.3	11.5	10.7	13.4	12.5	18.3	11.8	10.9
Vehicles involved:										
Cars	Million . . .	22.8	25.6	14.3	12.3	15.9	13.6	18.1	11.5	10.8
Trucks	Million . . .	5.5	6.1	4.4	4.5	8.8	7.4	12.2	8.2	8.1
Motorcycles	1,000 . . .	560	480	180	152	130	119	190	150	150
DEATHS										
Motor vehicle deaths within 1 yr. [2] . . .	1,000 . . .	53.2	45.9	46.8	43.4	43.4	43.8	45.4	44.1	46.2
Noncollision accidents	1,000 . . .	(NA)	(NA)	4.9	4.4	4.8	4.9	5.3	5.1	5.2
Collision accidents:										
With other motor vehicles	1,000 . . .	23.0	19.9	19.9	19.0	19.1	18.8	19.2	19.8	20.6
With pedestrians	1,000 . . .	9.7	8.5	7.3	6.4	5.9	6.1	6.1	5.7	5.9
With fixed objects.	1,000 . . .	(NA)	(NA)	13.1	12.1	12.3	12.8	13.6	12.4	13.3
Deaths within 30 days [3]	1,000 . . .	51.1	43.8	44.6	41.8	41.9	42.2	43.0	42.9	42.6
Occupants	1,000 . . .	36.8	31.5	33.9	33.1	33.5	33.2	34.1	33.6	33.1
Passenger cars	1,000 . . .	27.4	23.2	24.1	22.4	20.7	20.3	20.6	19.7	19.1
Light trucks [4]	1,000 . . .	7.5	6.7	8.6	9.6	11.5	11.7	12.3	12.5	12.6
Large trucks [4]	1,000 . . .	1.3	1.0	0.7	0.6	0.8	0.7	0.7	0.7	0.8
Buses	1,000 . . .	(Z)	0.1	(Z)	(Z)	(Z)	(Z)	(Z)	(Z)	(Z)
Other/unknown	1,000 . . .	0.5	0.5	0.5	0.4	0.5	0.5	0.5	0.6	0.6
Motorcycle riders [5].	1,000 . . .	5.1	4.6	3.2	2.2	2.9	3.2	3.3	3.7	4.0
Nonoccupants.	1,000 . . .	9.2	7.8	7.5	6.5	5.6	5.8	5.6	5.5	5.5
Pedestrians.	1,000 . . .	8.1	6.8	6.5	5.6	4.8	4.9	4.9	4.8	4.6
Pedalcyclist.	1,000 . . .	1.0	0.9	0.9	0.8	0.7	0.7	0.7	0.6	0.7
Other/unknown	1,000 . . .	0.1	0.1	0.1	0.1	0.1	0.1	0.1	0.1	0.1
Traffic death rates: [3, 6]										
Per 100 million vehicle miles	Rate	3.3	2.5	2.1	1.7	1.5	1.5	1.5	1.5	1.4
Per 100,000 licensed drivers	Rate	35.2	27.9	26.7	23.7	22.0	22.1	22.1	21.9	21.4
Per 100,000 registered vehicles . . .	Rate	34.8	26.4	24.2	21.2	19.3	19.1	19.1	18.6	17.9
Per 100,000 resident population . . .	Rate	22.5	18.4	17.9	15.9	14.9	14.8	14.9	14.8	14.5

NA Not available. Z Fewer than 50. [1] Covers only accidents occurring on the road. Data are estimated. Year-to-year comparisons should be made with caution. [2] Deaths that occur within 1 year of accident. Includes collision categories not shown separately. [3] Within 30 days of accident. Source: U.S. National Highway Traffic Safety Administration, *Traffic Safety Facts*, annual; and unpublished data. See Internet site <http://www.nhtsa.dot.gov/people/Crash/Index.html>. [4] See footnotes 1 and 2 in Table 1084. [5] Includes motorized cycles. [6] Based on 30-day definition of traffic deaths.

Source: Except as noted, National Safety Council, Itasca, IL, *Injury Facts*, annual (copyright). See Internet site <http://www.nsc.org/>.

Table 1083. **Traffic Fatalities by State: 1980 to 2004**

[For deaths within 30 days of the accident]

State	1980	1990	2000	2004	Fatality rate [1] 1980	Fatality rate [1] 2004	State	1980	1990	2000	2004	Fatality rate [1] 1980	Fatality rate [1] 2004
U.S. . . .	51,091	44,599	41,945	42,636	3.3	1.4	MO	1,175	1,097	1,157	1,130	3.4	1.6
							MT.	325	212	237	229	4.9	2.0
AL	940	1,121	996	1,154	3.2	2.0	NE.	396	262	276	254	3.5	1.3
AK	88	98	106	101	3.3	2.0	NV	346	343	323	395	5.7	2.0
AZ	947	869	1,036	1,150	5.3	2.0	NH	194	158	126	171	3.0	1.3
AR	588	604	652	704	3.6	2.2	NJ	1,120	886	731	731	2.2	1.0
CA	5,496	5,192	3,753	4,120	3.5	1.3	NM	606	499	432	521	5.4	2.2
CO	709	544	681	665	3.2	1.5	NY	2,610	2,217	1,460	1,493	3.4	1.1
CT	575	385	341	291	3.0	0.9	NC	1,503	1,385	1,557	1,557	3.6	1.6
DE	153	138	123	134	3.6	1.4	ND	151	112	86	100	2.9	1.3
DC	41	48	48	43	1.2	1.2	OH	2,033	1,638	1,366	1,286	2.8	1.2
FL	2,825	2,891	2,999	3,244	3.6	1.7	OK	959	641	650	774	3.5	1.7
GA	1,508	1,562	1,541	1,634	3.5	1.5	OR	646	579	451	456	3.4	1.3
HI	186	177	132	142	3.3	1.5	PA	2,089	1,646	1,520	1,490	2.9	1.4
ID	331	244	276	260	4.8	1.8	RI	129	84	80	83	2.4	1.0
IL	1,975	1,589	1,418	1,356	3.0	1.2	SC	852	979	1,065	1,046	3.8	2.1
IN	1,166	1,049	886	947	3.0	1.3	SD	228	153	173	197	3.7	2.2
IA	626	465	445	390	3.3	1.2	TN	1,153	1,177	1,307	1,288	3.4	1.8
KS	595	444	461	461	3.4	1.6	TX	4,366	3,250	3,779	3,583	3.8	1.6
KY	820	849	820	964	3.2	2.0	UT	334	272	373	296	3.1	1.2
LA	1,219	959	938	904	5.0	2.0	VT	137	90	76	98	3.7	1.3
ME	265	213	169	194	3.5	1.3	VA	1,045	1,079	929	925	2.7	1.2
MD	756	707	588	643	2.6	1.2	WA	971	825	631	563	3.4	1.0
MA	881	605	433	476	2.5	0.9	WV	523	481	411	411	4.9	2.0
MI	1,750	1,571	1,382	1,159	2.8	1.1	WI	972	769	799	792	3.1	1.3
MN	848	566	625	567	3.0	1.0	WY	245	125	152	164	4.9	1.8
MS	695	750	949	900	4.2	2.3							

[1] Deaths per 100 million vehicle miles traveled.

Source: U.S. National Highway Safety Traffic Administration, *Traffic Safety Facts*, annual. See Internet site <http://www.nhtsa.dot.gov /people/Crash/Index.html>.

Transportation 691

Table 1084. **Fatal Motor Vehicle Accidents—National Summary: 1990 to 2004**

[Based on data from the Fatality Analysis Reporting System (FARS). FARS gathers data on accidents that result in loss of human life. FARS is operated and maintained by National Highway Traffic Safety Administration's (NHTSA) National Center for Statistics and Analysis (NCSA). FARS data are gathered on motor vehicle accidents that occurred on a roadway customarily open to the public, resulting in the death of a person within 30 days of the accident. Collection of these data depend on the use of police, hospital, medical examiner/coroner, and Emergency Medical Services reports; State vehicle registration, driver licensing, and highway department files; and vital statistics documents and death certificates. See source for further detail]

Item	1990	1995	1999	2000	2001	2002	2003	2004
Fatal crashes, total	**39,836**	**37,241**	**37,140**	**37,526**	**37,862**	**38,491**	**38,477**	**38,253**
One vehicle involved	23,445	21,250	20,911	21,117	21,510	22,164	21,775	21,739
Two or more vehicles involved.	16,391	15,991	16,229	16,409	16,352	16,327	16,702	16,514
Persons killed in fatal crashes	**44,599**	**41,817**	**41,717**	**41,945**	**42,196**	**43,005**	**42,884**	**42,636**
Occupants	37,134	35,291	35,875	36,348	36,440	37,375	37,341	37,142
Drivers.	25,750	24,390	25,257	25,567	25,869	26,659	26,779	26,756
Passengers	11,276	10,782	10,521	10,695	10,469	10,604	10,458	10,304
Other	108	119	97	86	102	112	104	82
Nonoccupants	7,465	6,526	5,842	5,597	5,756	5,630	5,543	5,494
Pedestrians	6,482	5,584	4,939	4,763	4,901	4,851	4,774	4,641
Pedalcyclists.	859	833	754	693	732	665	629	725
Other	124	109	149	141	123	114	140	128
Occupants killed by vehicle type:								
Passenger cars	24,092	22,423	20,862	20,699	20,320	20,569	19,725	19,091
Mini-compact (95 inches)	3,556	2,207	1,224	1,113	887	813	636	594
Subcompact (95 to 99 inches)	4,753	4,584	3,663	3,660	3,571	3,435	3,081	2,701
Compact (100 to 104 inches).	5,310	6,899	6,942	7,022	6,731	7,061	6,769	6,604
Intermediate (105 to 109) inches	4,849	4,666	4,721	5,204	5,402	5,514	5,583	5,613
Full-size (110 to 114) inches	2,386	2,116	2,179	2,287	2,344	2,434	2,451	2,336
Largest (115 inches and over)	2,249	1,297	708	897	864	828	782	796
Unknown	989	654	1,425	516	521	484	423	447
Motorcycles	3,129	2,114	2,374	2,783	3,077	3,150	3,583	3,812
Other motorized cycles	115	113	109	114	120	120	131	196
Light trucks [1]	8,601	9,568	11,265	11,526	11,723	12,274	12,546	12,602
Pickup.	5,979	5,938	6,127	6,003	6,139	6,100	5,957	5,801
Utility.	1,214	1,935	3,026	3,358	3,530	4,031	4,483	4,735
Van.	1,154	1,639	2,088	2,129	2,019	2,109	2,080	2,036
Other	254	56	24	36	35	34	26	30
Large trucks [2]	705	648	759	754	702	689	726	761
Medium trucks	134	96	90	106	82	87	82	99
Heavy trucks	571	552	669	648	620	602	644	662
Buses.	32	33	59	22	34	45	41	41
Other vehicles	296	307	355	401	401	424	477	515
Unknown.	164	85	92	49	63	104	112	124
Persons involved in fatal crashes.	**107,777**	**102,102**	**100,666**	**100,716**	**101,175**	**101,784**	**101,862**	**100,227**
Occupants	99,297	94,621	93,959	94,325	94,706	95,403	95,470	94,086
Drivers.	58,893	56,164	56,502	57,280	57,586	58,113	58,517	58,080
Passengers	40,229	38,252	37,280	36,889	36,892	37,080	36,743	35,809
Other	175	205	177	156	228	210	210	197
Nonoccupants	8,480	7,481	6,707	6,391	6,469	6,381	6,392	6,141
Vehicle miles traveled (VMT) (100 mil.) . . .	21,444	24,227	26,911	27,469	27,973	28,556	28,900	29,630
Licensed drivers (1,000)	167,015	176,628	187,170	190,625	191,276	194,602	196,166	198,889
Registered vehicles (1,000)	184,275	197,065	212,685	217,028	221,230	225,685	230,788	230,633
Percent distribution of fatal accidents by the highest blood alcohol concentration (BAC) in accident:								
0.00 percent	49.5	57.7	60.2	58.7	58.9	59.2	60.2	60.9
0.01 to 0.07 percent	6.5	5.7	5.5	5.9	5.9	5.6	5.6	5.3
0.08 percent and over	44.0	36.7	34.3	35.4	35.2	35.3	34.3	33.9
Fatalities per 100,000 resident population:								
Under 5 years old	4.9	4.3	3.9	3.7	3.4	3.1	3.1	3.1
5 to 15 years old	6.4	6.0	5.1	4.7	4.3	4.3	4.4	4.4
16 to 24 years old	35.2	30.7	28.9	28.5	28.6	29.3	28.1	27.6
25 to 44 years old	19.7	17.2	16.4	16.1	16.2	16.2	16.0	15.7
45 to 64 years old	14.9	13.6	13.8	13.8	13.5	13.8	14.0	13.9
65 to 79 years old	18.8	18.5	18.3	17.1	17.1	17.0	16.3	16.2
80 years old and over	26.8	28.0	27.3	25.0	24.5	23.3	24.5	22.2
Fatalities per 100 million VMT [3]	2.1	1.7	1.6	1.5	1.5	1.5	1.5	1.4
Fatalities per 100,000 licensed drivers	26.7	23.7	22.3	22.0	22.1	22.1	21.9	21.4
Licensed driver per person.	0.7	0.7	0.7	0.7	0.7	0.7	0.7	0.7
VMT [3] per registered vehicle	11,637	12,294	12,653	12,657	12,644	12,653	12,522	12,847
Fatalities per 100,000 registered vehicles . .	24.2	21.2	19.6	19.3	19.1	19.1	18.6	17.9
Fatal crashes per 100 million VMT [3]	1.9	1.5	1.4	1.4	1.4	1.3	1.3	1.3
Involved vehicles per fatal crash	1.5	1.5	1.5	1.5	1.5	1.5	1.5	1.5
Fatalities per fatal crash	1.1	1.1	1.1	1.1	1.1	1.1	1.1	1.1
Average occupants per fatal crash.	2.5	2.5	2.5	2.5	2.5	2.5	2.5	2.5
Fatalities per 100,000 resident population	17.9	15.9	15.3	14.9	14.8	14.9	14.8	14.5

[1] Trucks with a gross vehicle weight rating of 10,000 pounds or less, including pickups, vans, truck-based station wagons, and utility vehicles. [2] Trucks with a gross vehicle weight rating of over 10,000 pounds. [3] VMT = vehicle miles of travel.

Source: U.S. National Highway Traffic Safety Administration, *Fatality Analysis Reporting System,* annual. See Internet site <http://www.nhtsa.dot.gov/people/Crash/Index.html>.

Table 1085. Motor Vehicle Occupants and Nonoccupants Killed and Injured: 1980 to 2004

[For deaths within 30 days of the accident. (3,416 represents 3,416,000)]

Year	Occupants							Motor-cycle riders[2]	Nonoccupants			
	Total	Total	Passenger cars	Light trucks[1]	Large trucks[1]	Buses	Other/unknown[3]		Total	Pedestrian	Pedal-cyclist	Other/unknown
KILLED												
1980	51,091	36,783	27,449	7,486	1,262	46	540	5,144	9,164	8,070	965	129
1985	43,825	31,479	23,212	6,689	977	57	544	4,564	7,782	6,808	890	84
1990	44,599	33,890	24,092	8,601	705	32	460	3,244	7,465	6,482	859	124
1992	39,250	30,485	21,387	8,098	585	28	387	2,395	6,370	5,549	723	98
1993	40,150	31,125	21,566	8,511	605	18	425	2,449	6,576	5,649	816	111
1994	40,716	31,998	21,997	8,904	670	18	409	2,320	6,398	5,489	802	107
1995	41,817	33,064	22,423	9,568	648	33	392	2,227	6,526	5,584	833	109
1996 [4]	42,065	33,534	22,505	9,932	621	21	455	2,161	6,368	5,449	765	154
1997	42,013	33,609	22,199	10,249	723	18	420	2,116	6,288	5,321	814	153
1998	41,501	33,088	21,194	10,705	742	38	409	2,294	6,119	5,228	760	131
1999	41,717	33,392	20,862	11,265	759	59	447	2,483	5,842	4,939	754	149
2000	41,945	33,451	20,699	11,526	754	22	450	2,897	5,597	4,763	693	141
2001	42,196	33,243	20,320	11,723	708	34	458	3,197	5,756	4,901	732	123
2002	43,005	34,105	20,569	12,274	689	45	528	3,270	5,630	4,851	665	114
2003	42,884	33,627	19,725	12,546	726	41	589	3,714	5,543	4,774	629	140
2004	42,636	33,134	19,091	12,602	761	41	639	4,008	5,494	4,641	725	128
INJURED (1,000)												
1988	3,416	3,119	2,585	478	37	15	4	105	192	110	75	8
1990	3,231	2,960	2,376	505	42	33	4	84	187	105	75	7
1992	3,070	2,843	2,232	545	34	20	12	65	162	89	63	10
1993	3,149	2,919	2,265	601	32	17	4	59	171	94	68	9
1994	3,266	3,045	2,364	631	30	16	4	57	164	92	62	9
1995	3,465	3,246	2,469	722	30	19	4	57	162	86	67	10
1996	3,483	3,277	2,458	761	33	20	4	55	151	82	58	11
1997	3,348	3,149	2,341	755	31	17	6	53	146	77	58	11
1998	3,192	3,012	2,201	763	29	16	4	49	131	69	53	8
1999	3,236	3,047	2,138	847	33	22	7	50	140	85	51	3
2000	3,189	2,997	2,052	887	31	18	10	58	134	78	51	5
2001	3,033	2,841	1,927	861	29	15	9	60	131	78	45	7
2002	2,926	2,735	1,805	879	26	19	6	65	126	71	48	7
2003	2,889	2,697	1,756	889	27	18	7	67	124	70	46	8
2004	2,788	2,594	1,643	900	27	16	7	76	118	68	41	9

[1] See footnotes 2 and 3 in Table 1086. [2] Includes motorized cycles. [3] Includes combination trucks. [4] Includes two fatalities of unknown person type.

Source: U.S. National Highway Traffic Safety Administration, *Traffic Safety Facts*, annual; and unpublished data. See Internet site <http://www.nhtsa.dot.gov/people/Crash/Index.html>

Table 1086. Vehicles Involved in Crashes by Vehicle Type, Rollover Occurrence, and Crash Severity: 2004

[Numbers in thousands (10,874.2 represents 10,874,200). Excludes motorcycles]

Vehicle type	Total		Rollover occurrence			
			Yes		No	
	Number	Percent	Number	Percent	Number	Percent
Vehicles involved in all crashes [1]	10,874.2	100.0	279.2	2.6	10,595.0	97.4
Passenger cars	6,231.6	100.0	108.3	1.7	6,123.3	98.3
Light trucks: [2]						
Pickup	1,654.6	100.0	59.2	3.6	1,595.4	96.4
Utility	1,568.6	100.0	74.9	4.8	1,493.7	95.2
Van	826.9	100.0	16.4	2.0	810.5	98.0
Other	103.7	100.0	3.0	2.9	100.7	97.1
Large truck [3]	416.0	100.0	15.3	3.7	400.7	96.3
Bus	52.4	100.0	0.1	0.2	52.3	99.8
Other/unknown	20.4	100.0	2.0	9.8	18.4	90.2
Fatal crashes	54.3	100.0	11.1	20.5	43.2	79.5
Passenger cars	25.5	100.0	4.1	16.0	21.4	84.0
Light trucks: [2]						
Pickup	10.8	100.0	2.7	25.3	8.1	74.7
Utility	7.8	100.0	2.8	36.2	5.0	63.8
Van	3.7	100.0	0.6	17.2	3.0	82.8
Other	0.1	100.0	(Z)	17.9	0.1	82.1
Large truck [3]	4.9	100.0	0.6	13.1	4.2	86.9
Bus	0.3	100.0	(Z)	2.9	0.3	97.1
Other/unknown	1.3	100.0	0.2	16.1	1.1	83.9

Z Less than 500. [1] Includes injury and property only crashes, not shown separately. [2] Trucks of 10,000 pounds gross vehicle weight rating or less, including pickups, vans, truck-based station wagons and utility vehicles. [3] Trucks over 10,000 pounds gross vehicle weight rating.

Source: U.S. National Highway Safety Traffic Administration, *Traffic Safety Facts*, annual. See Internet site <http://www.nhtsa.dot.gov /people/Crash/Index.html>.

Transportation 693

Table 1087. Speeding-Related Traffic Fatalities by State and Road Type and Speed Limit: 2004

[Speeding consists of exceeding the posted speed limit or driving too fast for the road conditions or any speed-related violation charged (racing, driving above speed limit, speed greater than reasonable, exceeding special speed limit)]

State	Traffic fatalities, total	Total [1]	Interstate Over 55 mph	Interstate At or under 55 mph	Noninterstate 55 mph	Noninterstate 50 mph	Noninterstate 45 mph	Noninterstate 40 mph	Noninterstate 35 mph	Noninterstate Under 35 mph
United States	**42,636**	**13,192**	**1,407**	**371**	**3,662**	**525**	**1,717**	**905**	**1,425**	**1,391**
Alabama	1,154	508	49	4	113	15	164	50	46	36
Alaska	101	38	5	10	6	4	5	1	3	1
Arizona	1,150	406	75	9	52	29	58	42	40	31
Arkansas	704	104	9	–	51	2	9	2	15	6
California	4,120	1,333	186	29	330	56	127	94	158	134
Colorado	665	255	30	8	32	14	35	27	28	37
Connecticut	291	98	5	7	6	2	12	16	8	36
Delaware	134	42	–	4	6	15	4	4	2	6
District of Columbia	43	20	–	1	–	–	2	–	3	14
Florida	3,244	550	54	16	81	10	131	45	74	84
Georgia	1,634	335	28	6	125	10	64	21	55	17
Hawaii	142	67	–	10	15	1	4	–	17	19
Idaho	260	73	17	2	5	3	6	2	9	5
Illinois	1,356	589	62	38	229	4	51	44	74	62
Indiana	947	267	15	21	83	17	30	23	26	48
Iowa	390	32	2	1	10	1	1	–	4	10
Kansas	461	123	14	–	43	1	9	4	7	14
Kentucky	964	196	14	5	124	1	15	1	23	7
Louisiana	904	217	18	3	81	11	48	8	26	16
Maine	194	90	8	1	5	14	35	5	13	9
Maryland	643	243	14	16	34	26	15	51	42	37
Massachusetts	476	158	16	5	8	11	10	27	21	50
Michigan	1,159	249	20	10	147	2	18	5	10	16
Minnesota	567	144	14	3	87	4	4	1	4	15
Mississippi	900	173	21	1	66	8	32	9	17	10
Missouri	1,130	494	54	11	180	4	37	27	48	45
Montana	229	101	13	–	9	–	2	3	15	10
Nebraska	254	42	14	1	5	8	1	–	1	8
Nevada	395	135	20	8	4	7	4	–	5	1
New Hampshire	171	41	1	3	4	10	1	6	5	6
New Jersey	731	64	3	5	7	10	4	10	4	16
New Mexico	521	195	41	2	23	7	16	7	13	15
New York	1,493	465	21	11	173	15	35	29	28	81
North Carolina	1,557	561	42	7	307	13	106	2	60	8
North Dakota	100	23	3	–	7	–	1	2	1	3
Ohio	1,286	272	21	5	141	7	15	9	39	27
Oklahoma	774	315	33	4	50	18	74	19	25	19
Oregon	456	145	11	4	70	3	18	6	8	12
Pennsylvania	1,490	661	40	24	189	13	105	79	113	67
Rhode Island	83	45	1	6	2	1	5	6	6	18
South Carolina	1,046	463	53	4	156	15	96	18	47	30
South Dakota	197	71	11	–	34	2	1	1	1	8
Tennessee	1,288	269	21	10	50	12	63	33	27	39
Texas	3,583	1,425	187	32	188	40	128	101	123	152
Utah	296	92	34	–	5	8	9	11	3	1
Vermont	98	46	5	–	1	23	–	5	9	3
Virginia	925	253	18	19	99	6	44	16	29	14
Washington	563	226	27	–	14	40	15	18	55	32
West Virginia	411	119	18	1	48	–	13	8	14	14
Wisconsin	792	295	17	4	155	–	31	5	19	40
Wyoming	164	64	22	–	2	2	4	2	4	2

– Represents zero. [1] Includes fatalities that occurred on roads for which the speed limit was unknown.

Source: U.S. National Highway Traffic Safety Administration, *Traffic Safety Facts, Speeding*, annual. See Internet site <http://www.nhtsa.dot.gov/people/Crash/Index.html>.

694 Transportation

Table 1088. Fatalities by Highest Blood Alcohol Concentration in the Crash: 1985 to 2004

[BAC means blood alcohol concentration; g/dl means grams per deciliter]

Item	1985	1990	1995	2000	2001	2002	2003	2004
Total fatalities	43,825	44,599	41,817	41,945	42,196	43,005	42,884	42,636
Fatalities in alcohol-related crashes . . .	23,167	22,587	17,732	17,380	17,400	17,524	17,105	16,694
Percent	52.9	50.6	42.4	41.4	41.2	40.7	40.0	39.0
BAC = 0.01-0.07 g/dl:								
Number	3,081	2,980	2,490	2,511	2,542	2,432	2,427	2,285
Percent	7.0	6.7	6.0	6.0	6.0	5.7	6.0	5.0
BAC = 0.08 g/dl or more:								
Number	20,086	19,607	15,242	14,870	14,858	15,093	14,678	14,409
Percent	45.8	44.0	36.5	35.5	35.2	35.1	34.0	34.0
Fatalities with BAC = 0.00 g/dl:								
Number.	20,659	22,012	24,085	24,565	24,796	25,481	25,779	25,942
Percent.	47.1	49.4	57.6	58.6	58.8	59.3	60.0	61.0

Source: U.S. National Highway Traffic Safety Administration, *Traffic Safety Facts*, annual; and unpublished data. See Internet site <http://www.nhtsa.dot.gov/people/Crash/Index.html>.

Table 1089. Traffic Fatalities by State and Highest Blood Alcohol Concentration (BAC) in the Crash: 2004

[BAC means blood alcohol concentration; g/dl means grams per deciliter]

State	Traffic fatalities, total	No alcohol (BAC = 0.00 g/dl) Number	Percent	Any alcohol (BAC=0.01 g/dl or more) Number	Percent	Low alcohol (BAC = 0.01-0.07 g/dl) Number	Percent	High alcohol (BAC = 0.08 g/dl or more) Number	Percent
United States . . .	42,636	25,942	61	16,694	39	2,285	5	14,409	34
Alabama	1,154	713	62	442	38	48	4	394	34
Alaska.	101	70	69	31	31	1	1	30	30
Arizona	1,150	715	62	435	38	60	5	376	33
Arkansas	704	428	61	276	39	40	6	236	33
California	4,120	2,477	60	1,643	40	276	7	1,367	33
Colorado	665	406	61	259	39	34	5	225	34
Connecticut	291	164	56	127	44	15	5	112	38
Delaware	134	83	62	51	38	3	2	48	36
District of Columbia . . .	43	26	59	18	41	5	12	12	28
Florida	3,244	2,023	62	1,222	38	169	5	1,053	32
Georgia	1,634	1,109	68	525	32	75	5	450	28
Hawaii.	142	77	54	65	46	13	9	52	37
Idaho	260	167	64	93	36	12	5	81	31
Illinois	1,356	752	55	604	45	87	6	517	38
Indiana	947	648	68	299	32	45	5	254	27
Iowa	390	280	72	110	28	19	5	91	23
Kansas	461	313	68	148	32	27	6	121	26
Kentucky	964	656	68	308	32	39	4	269	28
Louisiana.	904	490	54	414	46	69	8	345	38
Maine	194	124	64	70	36	11	6	58	30
Maryland	643	357	55	286	45	55	9	231	36
Massachusetts	476	274	57	203	43	22	5	181	38
Michigan	1,159	729	63	430	37	64	6	367	32
Minnesota	567	383	68	184	32	14	2	170	30
Mississippi	900	559	62	341	38	23	3	317	35
Missouri.	1,130	681	60	449	40	62	5	388	34
Montana	229	124	54	106	46	6	3	100	43
Nebraska.	254	162	64	92	36	14	5	78	31
Nevada	395	243	61	152	39	20	5	133	34
New Hampshire	171	112	65	59	35	8	5	51	30
New Jersey	731	461	63	270	37	42	6	227	31
New Mexico.	521	310	60	211	40	26	5	185	36
New York	1,493	906	61	587	39	93	6	494	33
North Carolina	1,557	1,005	65	553	35	57	4	496	32
North Dakota	100	61	61	39	39	5	5	35	35
Ohio	1,286	794	62	492	38	75	6	418	32
Oklahoma	774	496	64	278	36	34	4	245	32
Oregon	456	257	56	199	44	40	9	159	35
Pennsylvania	1,490	877	59	614	41	72	5	541	36
Rhode Island	83	41	50	42	50	1	2	41	49
South Carolina	1,046	583	56	464	44	51	5	413	39
South Dakota	197	111	56	86	44	10	5	76	39
Tennessee	1,288	769	60	519	40	65	5	454	35
Texas	3,583	1,941	54	1,642	46	225	6	1,417	40
Utah	296	224	76	72	24	1	-	70	24
Vermont	98	66	68	32	32	12	12	20	20
Virginia	925	567	61	359	39	52	6	307	33
Washington	563	317	56	246	44	23	4	223	40
West Virginia	411	275	67	136	33	22	5	114	28
Wisconsin	792	434	55	358	45	40	5	318	40
Wyoming	164	105	64	59	36	5	3	54	33

Source: U.S. National Highway Traffic Safety Administration, *Traffic Safety Facts*, annual. See Internet site <http://www.nhtsa.dot.gov/people/Crash/Index.html>.

U.S. Census Bureau, Statistical Abstract of the United States: 2007

Table 1090. Crashes by Crash Severity: 1990 to 2004

[6,471 represents 6,471,000. A crash is a police-reported event that produces injury and/or property damage, involves a vehicle in transport and occurs on a trafficway or while the vehicle is in motion after running off the trafficway]

Item	1990	1995	1998	1999	2000	2001	2002	2003	2004
Crashes (1,000)..............	**6,471**	**6,699**	**6,335**	**6,279**	**6,394**	**6,323**	**6,316**	**6,328**	**6,181**
Fatal.....................	39.8	37.2	37.1	37.1	37.5	37.9	38.5	38.5	38.3
Nonfatal injury...............	2,122	2,217	2,029	2,054	2,070	2,003	1,929	1,925	1,862
Property damage only	4,309	4,446	4,269	4,188	4,286	4,282	4,348	4,365	4,281
Percent of total crashes:									
Fatal.....................	0.6	0.6	0.6	0.6	0.6	0.6	0.6	0.6	0.6
Nonfatal injury...............	32.8	33.1	32.0	32.7	32.4	31.7	30.5	30.4	30.1
Property damage only	66.6	66.4	67.4	66.7	67.0	67.7	68.8	69.0	69.3

Source: U.S. National Highway Safety Traffic Administration, *Traffic Safety Facts, annual.* See Internet site <http://www.nhtsa.dot.gov/people/Crash/Index.html>.

Table 1091. Alcohol Involvement for Drivers in Fatal Crashes: 1994 and 2004

[BAC = blood alcohol concentration]

Age, sex, and vehicle type	1994		2004	
	Number of drivers	Percentage with BAC of .08% or greater	Number of drivers	Percentage with BAC of .08% or greater
Total drivers involved in fatal crashes [1]	**54,549**	**23**	**58,080**	**20**
Drivers by age group:				
Under 16 years old	397	12	344	10
16 to 20 years old......................	7,723	18	7,709	17
21 to 24 years old......................	6,291	33	6,382	32
25 to 34 years old......................	12,891	31	11,179	27
35 to 44 years old......................	9,951	26	10,682	23
45 to 54 years old......................	6,493	18	9,102	19
55 to 64 years old......................	3,828	12	5,573	12
65 to 74 years old......................	3,194	9	3,057	7
75 years old and over	2,867	4	3,142	5
Drivers by sex:				
Male...............................	40,233	26	42,045	23
Female.............................	13,567	14	15,268	12
Drivers by vehicle type:				
Passenger cars	30,103	24	25,393	22
Light trucks [2].......................	16,235	25	22,217	21
Large trucks [3]	4,592	2	4,799	1
Motorcycles.........................	2,330	33	4,095	27
Buses..............................	255	4	273	3

[1] Includes age and sex unknown, and other and unknown types of vehicles. [2] Trucks of 10,000 pounds gross vehicle weight rating or less, including pickups, vans, truck-based station wagons, and utility vehicles. [3] Trucks over 10,000 pounds gross vehicle weight rating.

Source: U.S. National Highway Safety Traffic Administration, *Traffic Safety Facts,* annual. See Internet site <http://www.nhtsa.dot.gov/people/Crash/Index.html>.

Table 1092. Licensed Drivers and Number in Accidents by Age: 2004

[198,100 represents 198,100,000]

Age group	Licensed drivers		Drivers in accidents				Accident rates per number of drivers	
			Fatal		All			
	Number (1,000)	Percent	Number	Percent	Number (1,000)	Percent	Fatal [1]	All [2]
Total..............	**198,100**	**100.0**	**63,000**	**100.0**	**19,200**	**100.0**	**32**	**10**
19 years old and under	9,369	4.7	6,900	11.0	2,690	14.0	74	29
Under 16 years old	77	(Z)	500	0.8	70	0.4	([3])	([3])
16 years old.	1,274	0.6	1,000	1.6	660	3.4	78	52
17 years old.	2,176	1.1	1,500	2.4	580	3.0	69	27
18 years old.	2,778	1.4	2,000	3.2	730	3.8	72	26
19 years old.	3,064	1.6	1,900	3.0	650	3.4	62	21
20 to 24 years old	16,907	8.5	9,000	14.3	2,940	15.3	53	17
20 years old.	3,136	1.6	1,900	3.0	830	4.3	61	26
21 years old.	3,300	1.7	2,100	3.3	560	2.9	64	17
22 years old.	3,357	1.7	1,800	2.9	530	2.8	54	16
23 years old.	3,484	1.8	1,700	2.7	490	2.6	49	14
24 years old.	3,630	1.8	1,500	2.4	530	2.8	41	15
25 to 34 years old	36,040	18.2	11,400	18.1	3,950	20.6	32	11
35 to 44 years old	40,609	20.5	10,400	16.5	3,580	18.6	26	9
45 to 54 years old	38,944	19.7	9,800	15.6	2,980	15.5	25	8
55 to 64 years old	27,424	13.8	6,200	9.8	1,650	8.6	23	6
65 to 74 years old	16,226	8.2	4,000	6.3	820	4.3	25	5
75 years old and over......	12,581	6.4	5,300	8.4	590	3.1	42	5

Z Less than 0.05. [1] Per 100,000 licensed drivers. [2] Per 100 licensed drivers. [3] Rates for drivers under age 16 are substantially overstated due to the high proportion of unlicensed drivers involved.
Source: National Safety Council, Itasca, IL, *Injury Facts, 2005,* (copyright). See Internet site <http://www.nsc.org/>.

696   Transportation

Table 1093. Passenger Transit Industry—Summary: 1980 to 2004

[**6,510 represents $6,510,000,000.** Includes Puerto Rico. Includes aggregate information for all transit systems in the United States. Excludes nontransit services such as taxicab, school bus, unregulated jitney, sightseeing bus, intercity bus, and special application mass transportation systems (e.g., amusement parks, airports, island, and urban park ferries). Includes active vehicles only]

Item	Unit	1980	1985	1990	1995	2000	2003	2004
Motor bus systems	Number. . .	1,040	2,631	2,688	2,250	2,262	1,982	1,500
Recreational vehicles, active	Number. . .	75,388	94,368	93,553	116,473	131,918	138,290	143,822
Motor bus	Number. . .	59,411	64,258	58,714	67,107	75,013	77,328	81,033
Commuter rail	Number. . .	4,500	4,035	5,007	5,164	5,498	5,959	6,228
Demand response	Number. . .	(NA)	14,490	16,471	29,352	33,080	35,954	37,078
Heavy rail	Number. . .	9,641	9,326	10,419	10,157	10,591	10,754	10,858
Light rail	Number. . .	1,013	717	913	999	1,577	1,482	1,622
Trolley bus	Number. . .	823	676	832	885	951	672	597
Other	Number. . .	(NA)	867	1,197	2,809	5,208	6,141	6,406
Operating funding, total.	Mil. dol. . . .	6,510	12,195	16,053	18,241	24,243	28,021	29,718
Passenger funding	Mil. dol. . . .	2,557	4,575	5,891	6,801	8,746	9,149	9,775
Other operating funding [1]	Mil. dol. . . .	248	702	895	2,812	4,217	5,065	4,960
Operating assistance.	Mil. dol. . . .	3,705	6,918	9,267	8,628	11,280	13,807	14,983
Federal	Mil. dol. . . .	1,094	940	970	817	994	1,616	2,086
Local [2]	Mil. dol. . . .	2,611	5,979	5,327	3,981	5,319	5,558	6,184
State [2]	Mil. dol. . . .	(NA)	(NA)	2,970	3,830	4,967	6,633	6,713
Total expense	Mil. dol. . . .	6,711	14,077	17,979	21,540	28,194	33,431	35,490
Operating expense	Mil. dol. . . .	6,247	12,381	15,742	17,849	22,646	26,852	28,506
Vehicle operations	Mil. dol. . . .	3,248	5,655	6,654	8,282	10,111	11,936	12,866
Maintenance	Mil. dol. . . .	1,774	3,672	4,631	5,047	6,445	7,368	7,833
General administration	Mil. dol. . . .	1,224	2,505	3,450	2,590	3,329	3,962	3,974
Purchased transportation	Mil. dol. . . .	(NA)	549	1,008	1,930	2,761	3,586	3,833
Reconciling expense	Mil. dol. . . .	464	1,696	2,237	3,691	5,548	6,579	6,984
Capital and planning grants, federal [3] . .	Mil. dol. . . .	2,787	2,559	2,428	5,534	7,366	7,390	7,913
Capital expenditures.	Mil. dol. . . .	(NA)	(NA)	(NA)	7,230	9,587	13,241	13,246
Vehicle-miles operated	Million	2,287	2,791	3,242	3,550	4,081	4,363	4,471
Motor bus	Million	1,677	1,863	2,130	2,184	2,315	2,421	2,471
Trolley bus	Million	13	16	14	14	14	14	13
Heavy rail	Million	385	451	537	537	595	630	642
Light rail	Million	18	17	24	35	53	64	67
Commuter rail	Million	179	183	213	238	271	286	295
Demand response	Million	(NA)	247	306	507	759	864	890
Other	Million	15	15	18	37	74	85	92
Passengers carried	Million	8,567	8,636	8,799	7,763	9,363	9,434	9,575
Motor bus	Million	5,837	5,675	5,677	4,848	5,678	5,692	5,731
Trolley bus	Million	142	142	126	119	122	109	106
Heavy rail	Million	2,108	2,290	2,346	2,033	2,632	2,667	2,748
Light rail	Million	133	132	175	251	320	338	350
Commuter rail	Million	280	275	328	344	413	410	414
Demand response	Million	(NA)	59	68	88	105	111	114
Other	Million	67	63	79	80	93	109	112
Avg. funding per passenger, ...	Cents	29.8	53.0	66.9	87.6	93.4	97.0	102
Employees, number (avg.) [4]	1,000	187	270	273	311	360	351	359
Payroll, employee	Mil. dol. . . .	3,281	5,843	7,226	8,213	10,400	11,634	12,487
Fringe benefits, employee	Mil. dol. . . .	1,353	2,868	3,986	4,484	5,413	6,913	8,172

NA Not available. [1] Beginning 1995, includes taxes levied directly by transit agency and other dedicated funds, formerly included in Local. [2] Includes other operating revenue, nonoperating revenue, and auxiliary income. Data for 1985 are state and local combined. [3] 1980, capital grants only. [4] Through 1990, represents employee equivalents of 2,080 hours = one employee; beginning 1995, equals actual employees.

Source: American Public Transportation Association, Washington, DC, *Public Transportation Fact Book,* annual. See Internet site <http://www.apta.com/>.

Table 1094. Transit Buses Equipped for Disabilities: 1995 to 2004

[Represents ADA (Americans with Disabilities Act of 1992) lift- or ramp-equipped buses. Includes buses of transit agencies receiving federal funding for bus purchases and buses of agencies not receiving federal funds that voluntarily report data to the Federal Transit Administration]

Item	1995	1998	1999	2000	2001	2002	2003	2004
Transit buses, total	57,322	60,830	63,618	65,324	67,379	68,418	68,596	68,789
Percent ADA equipped	61.7	76.1	80.5	83.6	87.2	94.1	95.3	98.1
Small buses, total [1]	5,372	7,147	8,265	8,850	9,622	9,822	10,084	10,248
Percent ADA equipped	84.5	91.6	93.4	94.5	95.4	99.2	99.2	98.5
Medium buses, total [1]	3,879	5,929	6,613	7,455	7,830	8,693	9,346	10,031
Percent ADA equipped	66.0	86.9	90.1	92.9	93.7	98.4	97.7	100.0
Large buses, total [1]	46,355	46,188	46,891	47,017	47,925	47,764	46,608	45,919
Percent ADA equipped	59.2	72.6	76.8	79.9	84.5	92.2	93.9	97.4
Articulated buses, total [1]	1,716	1,566	1,849	2,002	2,002	2,139	2,558	2,591
Percent ADA equipped	50.2	68.4	81.3	85.5	88.5	97.2	96.4	99.8

[1] Small buses have fewer than 25 seats; medium buses have 25 to 35 seats; large ones have more than 35 seats; articulated buses are extra long and measure between 54 and 60 feet.

Source: U.S. Bureau of Transportation Statistics, *National Transportation Statistics,* annual. See Internet site <http://www.bts.gov /publications/nts/index.html>.

U.S. Census Bureau, Statistical Abstract of the United States: 2007

Table 1095. **Characteristics of Rail Transit by Transit Authority: 2003**

Mode and transit agency	Primary city served	States served	Directional route-miles [1]	Number of highway-rail crossings	Number of stations	Number of ADA-accessible stations [2]
Total [3]	33	28	9,522.5	6,015	2,816	1,554
Heavy rail.	11	12	1,597.3	27	1,023	416
Chicago Transit Authority.	Chicago	IL	206.3	25	144	66
Greater Cleveland Regional Transit Authority.	Cleveland	OH	38.1	–	18	9
L.A. County Metropolitan Transportation Authority	Los Angeles	CA	31.9	–	16	16
Maryland Transit Administration.	Baltimore	MD	29.4	–	14	14
Massachusetts Bay Transportation Authority	Boston	MA	76.3	–	53	42
Metropolitan Atlanta Rapid Transit Authority	Atlanta	GA	96.1	–	38	38
Miami-Dade Transit Agency	Miami	FL	45.0	–	22	22
MTA New York City Transit.	New York	NY	493.8	–	468	50
MTA Staten Island Railway.	New York	NY	28.6	–	23	4
Port Authority Trans-Hudson Corp.	New York	NY, NJ	28.6	2	13	7
Port Authority Transit Corporation	Philadelphia	PA, NJ	31.5	–	13	5
San Francisco Bay Area Rapid Transit District	San Francisco	CA	209.0	–	43	43
Southeastern Pennsylvania Transportation Authority	Philadelphia	PA	76.1	–	75	17
Washington Metropolitan Area Transit Authority	Washington	DC, MD, VA	206.6	–	83	83
Commuter rail [4].	16	18	6,905.2	2,531	1,163	656
Alaska Railroad Corporation.	Anchorage	AK	92.4	27	10	10
Altamont Commuter Express Authority . . .	San Jose	CA	172.0	127	10	10
Central Puget Sound Regional Transit Authority	Seattle	WA	78.6	35	9	9
Connecticut Department of Transportation	New Haven	CT	101.2	3	8	8
Maryland Transit Administration.	Baltimore	MD, DC, WV	400.4	40	42	22
Massachusetts Bay Transportation Authority	Boston	MA, RI	702.1	–	125	81
MTA Long Island Rail Road	New York	NY	638.2	402	124	99
MTA Metro-North Railroad	New York	NY, NJ, CT	545.7	161	109	32
New Jersey Transit Corporation	New York	NY, NJ, PA	1,070.2	329	168	52
North San Diego County Transit Development Board	San Diego	CA	82.2	34	8	8
NE Illinois Regional Commuter Rail Corporation	Chicago	IL, WI	940.4	512	227	134
Northern Indiana Commuter Trans District	Chicago	IL, IN	179.8	117	20	11
ON TRACK.	Syracuse	NY	3.5	(NA)	3	3
Peninsula Corridor Joint Powers Board.	San Francisco	CA	153.7	49	34	24
Pennsylvania Department of Transportation	Philadelphia	PA	144.4	7	12	4
South Florida Regional Transportation Authority	Miami	FL	142.2	72	18	18
Southeastern Pennsylvania Transportation Authority	Philadelphia	PA	449.2	116	156	51
Southern California Regional Rail Authority	Los Angeles	CA	778.0	443	53	53
Trinity Railway Express	Dallas	TX	69.5	34	9	9
Virginia Railway Express	Washington	DC, VA	161.5	23	18	18

– Represents zero.   NA Not available.   [1] The mileage in each direction over which public transportation vehicles travel while in revenue service. The mileage is computed without regard to the number of traffic lanes or rail tracks existing in the right-of-way.   [2] Number of stations that comply with the American with Disabilities Act of 1992 (ADA). Additional stations may be wheelchair accessible but not comply with other provisions of the ADA.   [3] Includes light rail, not shown separately.   [4] Excludes commuter-type services operated independently by AMTRAK.

Source: U.S. Bureau of Transportation Statistics, *State Transportation Statistics, 2005* See Internet site <http://www.bts.gov/publications /state_transportation_profiles/>.

Table 1096. **Transit Ridership in 50 Largest Urbanized Areas: 2003**

[Areas ranked by 2000 population size]

Urbanized area	2000 Population [1] Total (1,000)	Rank	Annual unlinked passenger trips [2] (mil.)	Percent distribution Motor bus	Heavy rail [3]	Light rail [4]	Com- muter rail [5]	Other [6]
U.S. urbanized area total [7] . . .	195,984	(X)	8,809.9	58.0	30.3	3.8	4.7	3.2
Top 50, total	127,900	(X)	8,160.0	55.2	32.7	4.1	5.0	3.0
Atlanta, GA	3,500	11	149.0	51.3	48.2	–	–	0.5
Austin,TX	902	40	37.2	98.3	–	–	–	1.7
Baltimore, MD	2,076	18	110.1	77.9	12.0	6.6	2.9	0.6
Boston, MA-NH-RI	4,032	7	394.1	31.7	38.1	18.4	10.1	1.7
Bridgeport-Stamford, CT-NY	889	41	24.7	39.9	–	–	58.8	1.4
Buffalo, NY	977	38	24.1	75.4	–	24.3	–	0.3
Charlotte, NC-SC	759	47	18.9	97.4	–	–	–	2.6
Chicago, IL-IN	8,308	3	582.0	55.8	31.1	0.0	12.3	0.8
Cincinnati, OH-KY-IN	1,503	26	28.1	98.4	–	–	–	1.6
Cleveland, OH	1,787	21	60.6	81.5	12.2	5.2	0.0	1.1
Columbus, OH	1,133	36	15.8	99.0	–	–	–	1.0
Dallas-Fort Worth-Arlington, TX . . .	4,146	6	85.8	74.5	–	19.8	2.8	2.9
Denver-Aurora, CO	1,985	20	78.6	85.4	–	13.5	0.0	1.1
Detroit, MI	3,903	9	48.5	95.3	–	0.1	0.0	4.6
Hartford, CT.	852	45	15.0	94.0	–	–	2.5	3.5
Houston, TX.	3,823	10	93.0	97.6	–	–	–	2.4
Indianapolis, IN	1,219	33	11.3	97.3	–	–	–	2.7
Jacksonville, FL	882	43	9.8	87.0	–	–	–	13.0
Kansas City, MO-KS	1,362	29	14.0	96.2	–	–	–	3.8
Las Vegas, NV	1,314	31	47.9	98.5	–	–	–	1.5
Los Angeles-Long Beach- Santa Ana, C	11,789	2	635.0	88.0	5.0	5.0	1.0	1.0
Louisville, KY-IN	864	44	13.3	97.3	–	–	–	2.7
Memphis, TN-MS-AR.	972	39	13.0	82.0	–	16.4	–	1.6
Miami, FL	4,919	5	133.8	80.4	10.7	–	2.0	6.8
Milwaukee, WI	1,309	32	59.8	97.9	–	–	–	2.1
Minneapolis-St. Paul, MN	2,389	16	73.3	97.3	–	–	–	2.7
Nashville-Davidson, TN	750	48	6.8	96.0	–	–	–	4.0
New Orleans, LA	1,009	37	60.6	83.8	–	10.5	–	5.8
New York-Newark, NY-NJ-CT	17,800	1	3,315.2	38.9	53.3	0.3	6.6	0.9
Oklahoma City, OK	747	49	4.1	96.1	–	–	–	3.9
Orlando, FL	1,157	35	22.7	96.3	–	–	–	3.7
Philadelphia, PA-NJ-DE-MD	5,149	4	338.8	54.2	27.9	7.3	9.2	1.3
Phoenix-Mesa, AZ.	2,907	13	54.4	96.8	–	–	–	3.2
Pittsburgh, PA	1,753	22	71.4	85.2	–	10.0	–	4.8
Portland, OR-WA	1,583	23	105.6	69.4	–	29.5	–	1.1
Providence, RI-MA	1,175	34	18.8	90.6	–	–	4.3	5.0
Richmond, VA	819	46	12.6	97.4	–	–	–	2.6
Riverside-San Bernardino, CA. . . .	1,507	25	25.8	90.1	–	–	6.1	3.8
Sacramento, CA	1,393	28	30.5	69.9	–	29.0	–	1.1
Salt Lake City, UT.	888	42	31.7	65.2	–	31.0	–	3.9
San Antonio, TX	1,328	30	40.3	97.5	–	0.0	–	2.5
San Diego, CA.	2,674	15	93.5	69.7	–	26.9	1.7	1.7
San Francisco-Oakland, CA	3,229	12	407.7	44.4	23.0	10.5	0.9	21.2
San Jose, CA.	1,538	24	50.6	78.6	–	12.0	7.4	2.0
Seattle, WA	2,712	14	151.8	62.2	–	0.4	0.5	36.8
St. Louis, MO-IL	2,078	17	48.1	67.3	–	30.9	–	1.8
Tampa-St. Petersburg, FL.	2,062	19	20.1	95.3	–	2.5	–	2.2
Tucson, AZ	720	50	16.9	98.3	–	–	–	1.7
Virginia Beach, VA	1,394	27	17.8	95.4	–	–	–	4.6
Washington, DC-VA-MD	3,934	8	437.5	42.6	55.6	–	1.5	0.4
Top 50 as percent of total	65	(X)	92.6	88.0	100.0	100.0	100.0	87.0

– Represents zero.   X Not applicable.   [1] As of April 1. Based on the 2000 decennial census.   [2] The number of times passengers board public transportation vehicles.   [3] Also called metro, subway, rapid transit, or rapid rail.   [4] Also called streetcar, tramway, or trolley.   [5] Also called metropolitan rail or regional rail.   [6] Includes such modes as trolley bus, ferry, cable car, vanpool, and demand response.   [7] Includes Puerto Rico.

Source: U.S. Bureau of Transportation Statistics, *State Transportation Statistics, 2005.* See Internet site <http://www.bts.gov/publications /state_transportation_profiles/>.

Transportation   699

Table 1097. Truck Transportation, Couriers and Messengers, and Warehousing and Storage—Estimated Revenue: 2000 to 2004

[In millions of dollars (237,811 represents $237,811,000,000). For taxable employer firms. Estimates have been adjusted to the results of the 2002 Economic Census. Based on the North American Industry Classification System, 1997; see text, Section 15]

Kind of business	1997 NAICS code [1]	2000	2003	2004
Selected transportation and warehousing industries	48, 49	237,811	245,767	265,941
Truck transportation	484	165,422	168,487	185,944
General freight trucking	4841	108,051	113,346	124,970
General freight trucking, local.	48411	17,254	18,625	20,112
General freight trucking, long-distance.	48412	90,797	94,721	104,858
General freight trucking, long-distance, truckload	484121	61,562	68,381	75,854
General freight trucking, long-distance, less than truckload	484122	29,235	26,340	29,005
Specialized freight trucking	4842	57,371	55,141	60,974
Used household and office goods moving	48421	14,484	12,839	13,891
Specialized freight (except used goods) trucking, local	48422	21,912	22,865	25,263
Specialized freight (except used goods) trucking, long-distance	48423	20,974	19,438	21,821
Couriers and messengers	492	57,776	59,825	62,246
Couriers	4921	54,114	56,492	58,797
Local messengers and local delivery	4922	3,662	3,333	3,449
Warehousing and storage	493	14,614	17,455	17,751
General warehousing and storage	49311	8,967	11,174	10,930
Refrigerated warehousing and storage	49312	2,859	2,945	3,167
Farm product warehousing and storage	49313	776	748	691
Other warehousing and storage.	49319	2,013	2,588	2,963

[1] Based on the 1997 North American Industry Classification System; see text Section 15.

Source: U.S. Census Bureau, "2004 Service Annual Survey, Truck Transportation, Messenger Services and Warehousing." See <http://www.census.gov/econ/www/servmenu.html> (issued 20 December 2005).

Table 1098. Truck Transportation—Summary: 2000 to 2004

[In millions of dollars (165,422 represents $165,422,000,000). For taxable employer firms. Covers NAICS 484. Estimates have been adjusted to the results of the 2002 Economic Census. Based on the North American Industry Classification System, 1997; see text, Section 15]

Item	2000	2002	2003	2004
Total operating revenue	165,422	164,219	168,487	185,944
Total motor carrier revenue	154,404	153,873	158,336	174,959
Local trucking [1]	49,878	51,319	54,329	58,916
Long-distance trucking [1].	104,526	102,553	104,008	116,044
Size of shipments:				
Less-than-truckload	44,318	45,117	45,613	49,125
Truckload	110,086	108,756	112,724	125,834
Commodities handled:				
Agricultural and fish products.	11,689	10,804	12,454	13,313
Grains, alcohol, and tobacco products	5,636	7,174	6,986	7,178
Stone, nonmetallic minerals, and metallic ores	9,330	10,235	10,774	11,766
Coal and petroleum products.	5,548	5,628	5,950	6,756
Pharmaceutical and chemical products	9,083	7,721	8,160	8,968
Wood products, textiles, and leathers	15,741	15,025	15,645	18,273
Base metal and machinery	12,235	13,063	12,828	14,929
Electronic, motorized vehicles, and precision instruments	9,584	11,134	10,712	11,364
Used household and office goods	9,526	8,025	8,313	9,559
New furniture and miscellaneous manufactured products	15,074	15,844	15,862	17,339
Other goods	50,958	49,219	50,653	55,516
Hazardous materials	9,603	9,352	9,239	10,109
Origin and destination of shipments:				
U.S. to U.S.	148,524	148,896	153,165	169,541
U.S. to Canada	1,709	1,605	1,659	1,730
U.S. to Mexico	1,237	1,071	1,107	1,108
Canada to U.S.	1,186	981	1,036	1,154
Mexico to U.S.	1,072	749	822	846
All other destinations	677	571	548	580
Inventory of revenue generating equipment (1,000):				
Trucks	201	209	210	212
Owned	169	186	184	187
Leased	32	23	26	(S)
Truck-tractors	913	883	868	895
Owned	769	739	727	753
Leased	143	145	141	142
Trailers	1,885	1,877	1,851	1,935
Owned	1,565	1,582	1,576	1,653
Leased	320	295	275	282
Highway miles traveled (mil.):				
Total	84,708	85,281	84,797	87,812
By loaded or partially loaded vehicles	67,390	67,741	68,113	70,895

S Data do not meet publication standards. [1] Local trucking is the carrying of goods within a single metro area and its adjacent nonurban areas; long-distance trucking is the carrying of goods between metro areas.

Source: U.S. Census Bureau, "2004 Service Annual Survey, Truck Transportation, Messenger Services and Warehousing." See <http://www.census.gov/econ/www/servmenu.html> (issued 20 December 2005).

700 Transportation

Table 1099. **Railroads, Class I—Summary: 1990 to 2004**

[As of Dec. 31, or calendar year data, except as noted (216 represents 216,000). Compiled from annual reports of class I railroads only, except where noted. Minus sign (–) indicates deficit]

Item	Unit	1990	1995	1999	2000	2001	2002	2003	2004
Class I line-hauling companies [1]	Number. . .	14	11	9	8	8	7	7	7
Employees [2]	1,000	216	188	178	168	162	157	155	158
Compensation	Mil. dol. . . .	8,654	9,070	9,603	9,623	9,430	9,387	9,576	10,337
Average per hour.	Dollars . . .	15.83	19	21	21.5	22.1	22.7	23.4	24.2
Average per year.	Dollars . . .	39,987	48,188	54,082	57,157	58,153	59,650	61,920	65,550
Mileage:									
Railroad line owned [3]	1,000	146	137	122	121	119	118	117	123
Railroad track owned [4]	1,000	244	228	207	205	204	200	200	211
Equipment:									
Locomotives in service.	Number. . .	18,835	18,812	20,256	20,028	19,745	20,506	20,774	22,015
Average horsepower	1,000 lb. . .	2,665	2,927	3,200	3,261	3,275	3,378	3,415	3,458
Cars in service:									
Freight train [5] [6]	1,000	1,212	1,219	1,369	1,381	1,314	1,300	1,279	1,288
Freight cars [6]	1,000	659	583	579	560	500	478	467	474
Average capacity	Tons	87.5	88.6	92.2	92.3	92.7	93.1	93.7	94.3
Income and expenses:									
Operating revenues.	Mil. dol. . .	28,370	32,279	33,521	34,102	34,576	35,327	36,639	40,517
Operating expenses	Mil. dol. . .	24,652	27,897	28,011	29,040	29,164	29,592	31,440	35,107
Net revenue from operations.	*Mil. dol. . . .*	*3,718*	*4,383*	*5,510*	*5,062*	*5,412*	*5,735*	*5,199*	*5,410*
Income before fixed charges.	Mil. dol. . .	4,627	5,016	6,001	5,361	5,517	6,179	5,220	5,523
Provision for taxes [7]	Mil. dol. . .	1,088	1,556	1,664	1,430	1,614	1,823	1,494	1,543
Ordinary income	Mil. dol. . .	1,961	2,439	2,976	2,501	2,740	3,201	2,683	2,867
Net income	Mil. dol. . .	1,977	2,324	2,971	2,500	2,740	3,201	2,687	2,867
Net railway operating income	Mil. dol. . .	2,648	2,858	4,047	3,924	4,111	4,248	4,078	4,147
Total taxes [8].	Mil. dol. . . .	3,780	4,075	4,459	4,379	4,673	4,724	4,316	4,480
Indus. return on net investment	Percent . . .	8.1	7.0	6.9	6.5	6.9	7.0	6.3	6.1
Gross capital expenditures	Mil. dol. . .	3,591	5,720	6,193	5,290	5,113	5,605	5,989	6,345
Equipment	Mil. dol. . .	996	2,343	2,183	1,508	1,013	1,021	1,300	1,301
Roadway and structures	Mil. dol. . .	2,644	3,651	4,446	4,549	4,421	4,645	4,561	4,941
Other	Mil. dol. . .	–49	–275	–436	–767	–321	–61	128	102
Balance sheet:									
Total property investment	Mil. dol. . . .	70,348	86,186	103,424	106,136	108,588	117,770	122,902	135,941
Accrued depreciation and									
amortization	Mil. dol. . . .	22,222	23,439	23,177	23,989	24,635	26,649	29,215	29,771
Net investment	Mil. dol. . .	48,126	62,746	80,247	82,147	83,953	91,121	93,686	106,170
Shareholder's equity	Mil. dol. . .	23,662	31,419	30,478	32,401	34,822	39,675	41,151	51,955
Net working capital	Mil. dol. . .	–3,505	–2,634	–4,834	–5,783	–6,282	–6,037	–6,750	–5,171
Cash dividends.	Mil. dol. . .	2,074	1,518	2,084	819	2,120	870	1,406	1,888
AMTRAK passenger traffic:									
Passenger revenue	Mil. dol. . .	941.9	734.1	1,067.8	1,201.6	1,299.9	1,304.3	1,421.1	1,432.6
Revenue passengers carried.	1,000	22,382	20,349	21,544	22,985	23,444	23,269	24,595	25,215
Revenue passenger miles	Million . . .	6,125	5,401	5,289	5,574	5,571	5,314	5,680	5,511
Averages:									
Revenue per passenger	Dollars . . .	42.1	36.1	49.6	52.3	55.4	56.1	57.8	56.8
Revenue per passenger mile . . .	Cents . . .	15.4	13.6	20.2	21.6	23.3	24.5	25.0	26.0
Freight service:									
Freight revenue	Mil. dol. . .	24,471	31,356	32,680	33,083	33,533	34,110	35,413	39,131
Per ton-mile	Cents . . .	2.7	2.4	2.3	2.3	2.2	2.3	2.3	2.4
Per ton originated	Dollar . . .	19.3	20.2	19.0	19.0	19.3	19.3	19.7	21.2
Revenue-tons originated	Million . . .	1,425	1,550	1,717	1,738	1,742	1,767	1,799	1,844
Revenue-tons carried	Million . . .	2,024	2,322	2,155	2,179	2,187	2,207	2,240	2,398
Tons carried one mile	Billion . . .	1,034	1,306	1,433	1,466	1,495	1,507	1,551	1,663
Average miles of road operated . .	1,000	133	125	121	121	121	123	122	121
Revenue ton-miles per mile of									
road	1,000	7,763	10,439	11,848	12,156	12,358	12,245	12,686	13,695
Revenue per ton-mile	Cents . . .	3	2	2	2	2	2	2	2
Train miles.	Million . . .	380	458	490	504	500	500	516	535
Net ton-miles per train-mile [9]	Number. . .	2,755	2,870	2,947	2,923	3,005	3,030	3,024	3,126
Net ton-miles per loaded									
car-mile [9].	Number. . .	69.1	73.6	73.8	73.1	72.4	71.5	71.4	78.5
Train-miles per train-hour	Miles.	23.7	21.8	20	21	21	21	20	19
Haul per ton, U.S. as a system . . .	Miles.	726	843	835	843	858	853	862	902
Accidents/incidents:									
Casualties—all railroads:									
Persons killed	Number. . .	1,297	1,146	932	937	971	951	867	895
Persons injured	Number. . .	25,143	14,440	11,700	11,643	10,985	11,103	9,196	8,972
Class I railroads:									
Persons killed	Number. . .	1,166	994	808	778	805	796	739	776
Persons injured	Number. . .	19,284	9,571	7,805	7,655	7,232	7,722	5,909	5,783

[1] See text, this section, for definition of Class I.   [2] Average midmonth count.   [3] Represents the aggregate length of roadway of all line-haul railroads. Excludes yard tracks, sidings, and parallel lines. (Includes estimate for class II and III railroads).   [4] Includes multiple main tracks, yard tracks, and sidings owned by both line-haul and switching and terminal. (Includes estimate for class II and III railroads).   [5] Includes cars owned by all railroads, private car companies, and shippers.   [6] Class I railroads only.   [7] Includes state income taxes.   [8] Includes payroll, income, and other taxes.   [9] Revenue and nonrevenue freight.   [10] Source: Federal Railroad Admin., *Accident Bulletin*, annual. Includes highway grade crossing casualties. See Internet site <http://www.fra.dot.gov/>

Source: Except as noted, Association of American Railroads, Washington, DC, *Railroad Facts, Statistics of Railroads of Class I*, annual, and *Analysis of Class I Railroads*, annual. See Internet site <http://www.aar.org/AboutTheIndustry/AboutTheIndustry.asp>.

Transportation   701

Table 1100. **Railroads, Class-I Cars of Revenue Freight Loaded, 1970 to 2005, and by Commodity Group, 2004 and 2005**

[In thousands (27,160 represents 27,160,000). Figures are 52-week totals]

Year	Car- loads [1]	Commodity group	Carloads 2004 [3]	2005 [3]	Commodity group	Carloads 2004 [3]	2005 [3]
1970....	27,160	Coal	6,823	6,930	Metals and products	644	631
1980....	22,598	Metallic ores...............	257	253	Stone, clay, and glass products. . .	527	525
1990....	16,177	Chemicals, allied products	1,521	1,495	Crushed stone, gravel, sand.....	938	1,011
1995 [2]...	16,706	Grain	1,126	1,130	Nonmetallic minerals..........	391	372
1998 [2]...	16,914	Motor vehicles and equipment...	1,182	1,155	Waste and scrap materials......	515	493
1999 [2]...	16,407	Pulp, paper, allied products.....	446	444	Lumber, wood products	297	309
2000 [3]...	16,354	Primary forest products	173	162	Coke	278	297
2001 [3]...	16,286	Food and kindred products.....	421	432	Petroleum products	298	308
2002 [3]...	16,101	Grain mill products	462	486	All other carloads............	301	306
2003 [3]...	16,159						
2004 [3]...	16,600						
2005 [3]...	16,738						

[1] Beginning 1990 excludes intermodal. [2] Excludes 2 Class I railroads. [3] Excludes 3 Class I railroads. 2005 data preliminary.

Source: Association of American Railroads, Washington, DC, *Weekly Railroad Traffic,* annual. See Internet site <http://www.aar.org/AboutTheIndustry/AboutTheIndustry.asp>.

Table 1101. **Railroads, Class-I Line-Haul-Revenue Freight Originated by Commodity Group: 1990 to 2005**

[21,401 represents 21,401,000]

Commodity group	1990	1995	1999	2000	2001	2002	2003	2004	2005
Carloads (1,000) [1]	21,401	23,726	27,096	27,763	27,205	27,901	28,870	30,095	31,142
Farm products	1,689	1,692	1,477	1,437	1,461	1,471	1,519	1,519	1,512
Metallic ores	508	463	295	322	251	328	331	339	662
Coal......................	5,912	6,095	6,965	6,954	7,295	7,088	7,037	7,102	7,202
Nonmetallic minerals...........	1,202	1,159	1,306	1,309	1,280	1,310	1,370	1,430	1,488
Food and kindred products.......	1,307	1,377	1,354	1,377	1,446	1,472	1,478	1,461	1,448
Lumber and wood products......	780	719	673	648	603	619	612	616	611
Pulp, paper, allied products	611	628	612	633	601	646	667	669	679
Chemicals, allied products	1,531	1,642	1,814	1,820	1,777	1,866	1,913	1,981	1,937
Petroleum and coal products	573	596	543	565	547	533	606	651	689
Stone, clay, and glass products....	539	516	538	541	528	559	581	594	603
Primary metal products	477	575	682	723	642	656	648	701	680
Fabricated metal products	31	32	27	30	51	38	36	39	36
Machinery, exc. electrical........	39	41	34	35	46	38	38	45	42
Transportation equipment........	1,091	1,473	1,896	1,984	1,777	1,831	1,811	1,849	1,923
Waste and scrap materials	439	623	624	619	591	617	651	725	706
Tons (mil.) [1]	1,425	1,550	1,717	1,738	1,742	1,767	1,799	1,844	1,899
Farm products	147	154	139	136	137	138	141	142	140
Metallic ores	47	44	29	32	25	31	33	33	60
Coal......................	579	627	751	758	801	785	784	792	804
Nonmetallic minerals...........	109	110	125	126	123	126	133	140	146
Food and kindred products.......	81	91	92	94	98	102	102	100	102
Lumber and wood products......	53	51	50	49	46	48	47	47	48
Pulp, paper, allied products	33	36	35	36	34	37	39	38	38
Chemicals, allied products	126	138	154	155	150	157	162	167	165
Petroleum and coal products	40	43	40	42	42	42	49	54	57
Stone, clay, and glass products....	44	43	47	48	46	49	51	53	55
Primary metal products	38	47	56	60	53	55	54	59	57
Fabricated metal products	1	1	1	1	1	1	1	1	1
Machinery, exc. electrical........	1	1	1	1	1	1	1	1	1
Transportation equipment........	23	30	40	42	37	38	36	37	38
Waste and scrap materials	28	38	40	40	37	38	41	46	47
Gross revenue (mil. dol.) [1]...	29,775	33,782	35,441	36,331	36,063	36,742	38,434	41,622	46,743
Farm products	2,422	3,020	2,720	2,673	2,741	2,711	2,870	3,176	3,628
Metallic ores	408	394	330	338	288	285	289	317	485
Coal......................	6,954	7,356	7,739	7,794	8,181	7,797	7,890	8,418	9,393
Nonmetallic minerals...........	885	875	955	969	945	967	1,041	1,131	1,293
Food and kindred products.......	2,188	2,464	2,400	2,424	2,579	2,657	2,760	2,892	3,253
Lumber and wood products......	1,390	1,385	1,528	1,524	1,519	1,628	1,745	1,924	2,278
Pulp, paper, allied products	1,486	1,543	1,457	1,526	1,457	1,567	1,646	1,730	1,953
Chemicals, allied products	3,933	4,553	4,616	4,636	4,504	4,658	4,779	5,100	5,432
Petroleum and coal products	918	997	980	1,010	1,014	1,026	1,123	1,268	1,500
Stone, clay, and glass products....	931	1,044	1,089	1,113	1,090	1,149	1,211	1,323	1,505
Primary metal products	979	1,199	1,289	1,371	1,292	1,288	1,349	1,518	1,734
Fabricated metal products	42	44	38	48	65	61	47	50	55
Machinery, exc. electrical........	67	69	61	73	61	60	72	91	
Transportation equipment........	3,100	3,269	3,582	3,843	3,590	3,731	3,707	3,746	3,960
Waste and scrap materials	504	685	689	706	685	717	799	956	1,070

[1] Includes commodity groups and small packaged freight shipments, not shown separately.

Source: Association of American Railroads, Washington, DC, *Freight Commodity Statistics,* annual. See Internet site <http://www.aar.org/AboutTheIndustry/AboutTheIndustry.asp>.

702 Transportation

Table 1102. **Line Haul Railroads—Producer Price Indexes: 1999 to 2005**

[Index base date = 100]

Commodity	Index base date	1999	2000	2001	2002	2003	2004	2005, prel.
Line-haul railroads	Dec. 1984	113.0	114.5	116.6	118.9	121.4	126.5	139.5
Railroad transportation, freight, (carload)	Dec. 1996	100.5	101.9	104.1	106.3	109.0	114.7	128.1
Coal	Dec. 1984	107.3	108.7	110.6	110.1	111.4	114.6	(NA)
Farm products	Dec. 1984	121.7	123.1	124.5	125.5	132.1	146.4	(NA)
Food products	Dec. 1984	99.7	100.4	102.8	102.7	101.7	107.5	(NA)
Metallic ores	Dec. 1984	103.8	105.9	107.0	107.0	105.9	110.0	(NA)
Chemicals and allied products.	Dec. 1984	119.1	121.3	122.3	126.2	131.7	140.7	(NA)
Nonmetallic minerals	Dec. 1984	121.7	122.1	123.0	124.3	125.7	131.1	(NA)
Lumber and wood products	Dec. 1984	109.8	109.0	112.2	120.5	123.3	131.5	(NA)
Transportation equipment	Dec. 1984	113.3	112.6	118.7	130.5	136.6	141.8	(NA)
Pulp, paper, and allied products.	Dec. 1984	115.5	119.0	122.4	122.4	124.4	134.4	(NA)
Primary metal products	Dec. 1984	118.4	124.1	128.8	132.5	136.1	141.1	(NA)
Stone, clay, glass, and concrete products	Dec. 1984	122.6	128.7	129.0	124.3	127.1	132.8	(NA)
Petroleum and coal products.	Dec. 1984	123.0	124.6	126.8	127.5	129.6	132.2	(NA)
Railroad transportation, freight, (intermodal)	Dec. 1996	102.9	102.9	103.2	103.8	106.4	107.6	113.0
Railroad transportation, passenger	Dec. 1996	111.1	116.3	119.1	124.6	115.3	111.1	115.1

NA Not available.

Source: U.S. Bureau of Labor Statistics, *Producer Price Indexes*, monthly and annual. See Internet site <http://www.bls.gov/ppi/>.

Table 1103. **Petroleum Pipeline Companies—Characteristics: 1980 to 2004**

[**173 represents 173,000.** Covers pipeline companies operating in interstate commerce and subject to jurisdiction of the Federal Energy Regulatory Commission]

Item	Unit	1980	1985	1990	1995	2000	2001	2002	2003	2004
Miles of pipeline, total . . .	1,000	173	171	168	177	152	155	150	140	142
Gathering lines	1,000	36	35	32	35	18	17	16	14	15
Trunk lines.	1,000	136	136	136	142	134	138	133	126	127
Total deliveries.	Mil. bbl.	10,600	10,745	11,378	12,862	14,450	13,352	13,343	13,236	13,394
Crude oil	Mil. bbl.	6,405	6,239	6,563	6,952	6,923	7,082	7,019	6,941	6,612
Products	Mil. bbl.	4,195	4,506	4,816	5,910	7,527	6,270	6,324	6,295	6,782
Total trunk line traffic. . . .	Bil. bbl.-miles . .	3,405	3,342	3,500	3,619	3,508	3,505	3,563	3,591	3,652
Crude oil	Bil. bbl.-miles . .	1,948	1,842	1,891	1,899	1,602	1,566	1,620	1,609	1,604
Products	Bil. bbl.-miles . .	1,458	1,500	1,609	1,720	1,906	1,939	1,943	1,982	2,049
Carrier property value . . .	Mil. dol.	19,752	21,605	25,828	27,460	29,648	32,148	32,605	32,018	29,552
Operating revenues	Mil. dol.	6,356	7,461	7,149	7,711	7,483	7,730	7,812	7,704	8,020
Net income	Mil. dol.	1,912	2,431	2,340	2,670	2,705	3,007	3,409	3,470	3,323

Source: PennWell Publishing Co., Houston, Texas, *Oil & Gas Journal*, annual (copyright).

Table 1104. **U.S. Postal Service Rates for Letters and Postcards: 1958 to 2006**

[Domestic airmail letters discontinued in 1973 at 13 cents per ounce; superseded by express mail. Prior to February 3, 1991, international airmail rates were based on international zones which have been discontinued. Rates exclude Canada and Mexico]

Domestic mail date rate of change	Surface mail Letters Each ounce	Surface mail Letters First ounce	Surface mail Letters Each added ounce	Surface mail Post cards	Express mail [1]	International air mail date of rate change	Letters First 1/2 ounce	Letters Second 1/2 ounce	Letters Each added 1/2 ounce	Post-cards	Aero-grammes
1958 (Aug. 1) . .	0.04	(X)	(X)	0.03	(X)	1961 (July 1) . .	(X)	(X)	(X)	0.11	0.11
1963 (Jan. 7). .	0.05	(X)	(X)	0.04	(X)	1967 (May 1) . .	(X)	(X)	(X)	0.13	0.13
1968 (Jan. 7). .	0.06	(X)	(X)	0.05	(X)	1971 (July 1) . .	(X)	(X)	(X)	0.13	0.13
1971 (May 16). .	0.08	(X)	(X)	0.06	(X)	1974 (Mar. 2) . .	(X)	(X)	(X)	0.18	0.18
1974 (Mar. 2). .	0.10	(X)	(X)	0.08	(X)	1976 (Jan. 4) . .	(X)	(X)	(X)	0.21	0.22
1975 (Sept. 14) .	(X)	0.10	0.09	0.07	(X)	1981 (Jan. 1) . .	(X)	(X)	(X)	0.28	0.30
1975 (Dec. 31). .	[2]0.13	[2]0.13	[2]0.11	[2]0.09	(X)	1985 (Feb. 17) .	(X)	(X)	(X)	0.33	0.36
1978 (May 29). .	(X)	0.15	0.13	0.10	(X)	1988 (Apr. 17) . .	(X)	(X)	(X)	0.36	0.39
1981 (Mar. 22). .	(X)	0.18	0.17	0.12	(X)	1991 (Feb. 3) . .	0.50	[3]0.45	[3]0.39	0.40	0.45
1981 (Nov. 1) . .	(X)	0.20	0.17	0.13	9.35	1995 (July 9) . .	0.60	[3]0.40	(X)	0.40	0.45
1985 (Feb.17) . .	(X)	0.22	0.17	0.14	10.75	1999 (Jan. 10) . .	0.60	[3]0.40	(X)	0.50	0.50
1988 (Apr. 3). . .	(X)	0.25	0.20	0.15	[4]12.00	2001 (Jan. 7) . .	[3, 5]0.80	[3, 5]1.70	(X)	0.70	0.70
1991 (Feb. 3) . .	(X)	0.29	0.23	0.19	[4]13.95	2002 (June 30) .	[3, 5]0.80	[3, 5]1.70	(X)	0.70	0.70
1995 (Jan. 1). . .	(X)	0.32	0.23	0.20	[4]15.00	2006 (January 8).	[3, 5]0.84	[3, 5]1.70	(X)	0.75	0.75
1999 (Jan. 10). .	(X)	0.33	0.22	0.20	[4]15.75						
2001 (Jan. 7). . .	(X)	0.34	0.21	0.20	[4]16.00						
2002 (June 30) .	(X)	0.37	0.23	0.23	[4]17.85						
2006 (Jan. 8). . .	(X)	0.39	0.24	0.24	[4]18.80						

X Not applicable. [1] Post Office to addressee rates. Rates shown are for weights up to 2 pounds, all zones. Beginning Feb. 17, 1985, for weights between 2 and 5 pounds, $12.85 is charged. Prior to Nov. 1, 1981, rate varied by weight and distances. Over 5 pounds still varies by distance. [2] As of October 11, 1975, surface mail service upgraded to level of airmail. [3] Up to the limit of 64 ounces. [4] Over 8 ounces and up to 2 pounds. [5] The rate increments changed to 1 ounce.

Source: U.S. Postal Service, "United States Domestic Postage Rate: Recent History," and unpublished data. See Internet site <http://www.usps.com/common/category/postage.htm>.

Table 1105. U.S. Postal Service—Summary: 1980 to 2005

[106,311 represents 106,311,000,000. For years ending September 30. Includes Puerto Rico and all outlying areas. See text, this section]

Item	1980	1990	1995	2000	2003	2004	2005
Offices, stations, and branches	**39,486**	**40,067**	**39,149**	**38,060**	**37,579**	**37,159**	**37,142**
Number of post offices	30,326	28,959	28,392	27,876	27,556	27,505	27,385
Number of stations and branches	9,160	11,108	10,757	10,184	10,023	9,654	9,757
Delivery Points (mil.)	(NA)	(NA)	(NA)	135.9	141.4	142.3	144.3
Residential	(NA)	(NA)	(NA)	123.9	128.7	129.6	131.3
City	(NA)	(NA)	(NA)	76.1	77.5	78.0	78.5
P. O. Box	(NA)	(NA)	(NA)	15.9	15.7	15.6	15.6
Rural/highway contract	(NA)	(NA)	(NA)	31.9	35.5	36.0	37.2
Business	(NA)	(NA)	(NA)	12.1	12.7	12.7	13.0
Pieces of mail handled (mil.)	**106,311**	**166,301**	**180,734**	**207,882**	**202,185**	**206,106**	**211,743**
Domestic [1]	105,348	165,503	179,933	206,782	201,380	205,262	210,891
First class mail [2]	60,276	89,270	96,296	103,526	99,059	97,926	98,071
Express Mail	17	59	57	71	56	54	55
Priority Mail	248	518	869	1,223	860	849	888
Periodicals (formerly 2d class)	10,220	10,680	10,194	10,365	9,320	9,135	9,070
Standard Mail (formerly Standard A)	30,381	63,725	71,112	90,057	90,492	95,564	100,942
Package Services (formerly Standard B)	633	663	936	1,128	1,129	1,132	1,166
Mailgram	39	14	5	4	3	2	2
U.S. Postal Service	(NA)	538	412	363	392	529	621
Free for the blind	28	35	52	47	70	71	76
International economy mail (surface)	450	166	106	79	30	26	23
International airmail	513	632	696	1,021	775	818	829
Employees, total (1,000)	**667**	**843**	**875**	**901**	**827**	**808**	**803**
Career	643	761	753	788	729	708	705
Headquarters	3	2	2	2	2	3	3
Headquarters support	(NA)	6	4	6	4	3	4
Inspection Service	5	4	4	4	4	4	3
Inspector General	(X)	(X)	(X)	1	1	1	1
Field Career	635	747	745	775	719	697	693
Postmasters	29	27	27	26	26	26	25
Supervisors/managers	36	43	35	39	35	34	33
Professional, administrative, and technical	5	10	11	10	9	9	9
Clerks	263	290	274	282	242	226	222
Mail handlers	37	51	57	61	57	55	56
City carriers	187	236	240	241	229	228	228
Motor vehicle operators	6	7	8	9	9	9	9
Rural carriers	33	42	46	57	62	63	64
Special delivery messengers	3	2	2	(X)	(X)	(X)	(X)
Building and equipment maintenance	27	33	38	42	41	40	40
Vehicle maintenance	5	5	5	6	6	6	5
Other [3]	4	1	2	2	2	2	1
Noncareer	25	83	122	114	98	100	98
Casuals	5	27	26	30	17	21	19
Transitional	(X)	(X)	32	13	11	10	8
Rural substitutes	20	43	50	58	56	56	57
Relief/Leave replacements	(X)	12	13	12	12	12	12
Nonbargaining temporary	(X)	(Z)	1	1	1	1	1
Compensation and employee benefits (mil. dol.)	16,541	34,214	41,931	49,532	50,428	52,134	53,932
Avg. salary per employee (dol.) [4]	24,799	37,570	45,001	50,103	57,051	60,261	62,635
Pieces of mail per employee, (1,000)	159	197	207	231	244	255	264
Total revenue (mil. dol.) [5]	**19,253**	**40,074**	**54,509**	**64,540**	**68,529**	**68,996**	**69,907**
Operating postal revenue	17,143	39,201	54,176	64,476	68,498	68,960	69,798
Mail revenue [6]	16,377	37,892	52,490	62,284	65,701	65,869	66,649
First class mail	10,146	24,023	31,955	35,516	37,048	36,377	36,062
Priority mail [7]	612	1,555	3,075	4,837	4,494	4,421	4,637
Express mail [8]	184	630	711	996	888	852	872
Mailgram	15	8	2	2	1	1	1
Periodicals (formerly 2d class)	863	1,509	1,972	2,171	2,235	2,192	2,161
Standard Mail (formerly Standard A)	2,412	8,082	11,792	15,193	17,231	18,123	18,954
Package Services (formerly Standard B)	805	919	1,525	1,912	2,216	2,207	2,201
International economy mail (surface)	154	222	205	180	146	145	134
International airmail	442	941	1,254	1,477	1,441	1,551	1,631
Service revenue	765	1,310	1,687	2,191	2,798	3,091	3,150
Registry [9]	157	174	118	98	82	75	77
Certified [9]	120	310	560	385	624	630	601
Insurance [9]	55	47	52	109	138	128	132
Collect-on-delivery	21	26	21	22	11	11	9
Special delivery [10]	73	6	3	(X)	(X)	(X)	(X)
Money orders	95	155	196	235	231	231	208
Other [9]	244	592	737	1,342	1,711	2,017	2,123
Operating expenses (mil. dol.) [11]	19,413	40,490	50,730	62,992	63,902	65,851	68,283

NA Not available. X Not applicable. Z Fewer than 500. [1] Data for 1980 includes penalty and franked mail, not shown separately. [2] Items mailed at 1st class rates and weighing 11 ounces or less. [3] Includes discontinued operations, area offices, and nurses. [4] For career bargaining unit employees. Includes fringe benefits. [5] Net revenues after refunds of postage. Includes operating reimbursements, stamped envelope purchases, indemnity claims, and miscellaneous revenue and expenditure offsets. Shown in year which gave rise to the earnings. [6] For 1980, includes penalty and franked mail not shown separately. Later years have that mail distributed into the appropriate class. [7] Provides 2- to 3- day delivery service. [8] Overnight delivery of packages weighing up to 70 pounds. [9] Beginning 2000, return receipt revenue broken out from registry, certified, and insurance and included in "other." [10] Special delivery discontinued June 8, 1997. [11] Shown in year in which obligation was incurred.

Source: U.S. Postal Service, *Annual Report of the Postmaster General* and *Comprehensive Statement on Postal Operations,* annual; and unpublished data.

Section 24
Information and Communications

This section presents statistics on the various information and communications media: publishing, including newspapers, periodicals, books, and software; motion pictures, sound recordings, broadcasting, and telecommunications; and information services, such as libraries. Statistics on computer use and Internet access are also included. Data on the usage, finances, and operations of the Postal Service previously shown in this section are now presented in Section 23, Transportation.

Information industry—The U.S. Census Bureau's *Service Annual Survey, Information Services Sector,* provides estimates of operating revenue of taxable firms and revenues and expenses of firms exempt from federal taxes for industries in the information sector of the economy. Similar estimates were previously issued in the *Annual Survey of Communications Services.* Data beginning 1998 are based on the North American Industry Classification System (NAICS), 1997 and the information sector is a newly created economic sector. It comprises establishments engaged in the following processes: (a) producing and distributing information and cultural products, (b) providing the means to transmit or distribute these products as well as data or communications, and (c) processing data. It includes establishments previously classified in the Standard Industrial Classification (SIC) in manufacturing (publishing); transportation, communications, and utilities (telecommunications and broadcasting); and services (software publishing, motion picture production, data processing, online information services, and libraries).

This new sector is comprised of industries which existed previously, were revised from previous industry definitions, or are completely new industries. Among those which existed previously are newspaper publishers, motion picture and video production, and online information services.

Revised industries include book publishers and libraries and archives. Newly created industries include database and directory publishers, record production, music publishers, sound recording studios, cable networks, wired telecommunications carriers, paging, and satellite telecommunications. The following URL contains detailed information about NAICS and provides a comparison of the SIC and NAICS <http://www.census.gov /epcd/www/naics.html>. See also the text in Section 15, Business Enterprise.

Beginning 2001, the Service Annual Survey estimates reflect the introduction of the provisional North American Product Classification System (NAPCS) for the information sector. Data for prior years are not comparable. See <http://www.census.gov/eos/www /napcs/napcs.htm>.

The 1997 Economic Census was the first economic census to cover the new information sector of the economy. The census, conducted every 5 years, for the years ending "2" and "7," provides information on the number of establishments, receipts, payroll, and paid employees for the United States and various geographic levels. The most recent reports are from the 2002 Economic Census. This census was conducted in accordance with the 2002 NAICS.

The Federal Communications Commission (FCC), established in 1934, regulates wire and radio communications. Only the largest carriers and holding companies file annual financial reports which are publically available. The FCC has jurisdiction over interstate and foreign communication services but not over intrastate or local services. The gross operating revenues of the telephone carriers reporting publically available data annually to the FCC, however, are estimated to cover about 90 percent of the revenues of all U.S. telephone companies. Data are not comparable with Census Bureau *Annual*

Information and Communications   705

Survey because of coverage and different accounting practices for those telephone companies which report to the FCC.

Reports filed by the broadcasting industry cover all radio and television stations operating in the United States. The private radio services represent the largest and most diverse group of licensees regulated by the FCC. These services provide voice, data communications, point-to-point, and point-to-multipoint radio communications for fixed and mobile communicators. Major users of these services are small businesses, the aviation industry, the maritime trades, the land transportation industry, the manufacturing industry, state and local public safety and governmental authorities, emergency medical service providers, amateur radio operators, and personal radio operations (CB and the General Mobile Radio Service). The FCC also licenses entities as private and common carriers. Private and common carriers provide fixed and land mobile communications service on a for-profit basis. Principal sources of wire, radio, and television data are the FCC's *Annual Report* and its annual *Statistics of Communications Common Carriers.*

Statistics on publishing are available from the Census Bureau, as well as from various private agencies. Editor & Publisher Co., New York, NY, presents annual data on the number and circulation of daily and Sunday newspapers in its *International Year Book.* The Book Industry Study Group, New York, NY, collects data on books sold and domestic consumer expenditures. Data on academic and public libraries are collected by the U.S. National Center for Education Statistics. Data on Internet use by adults are collected by the Pew Internet and American Life Project, Washington, DC, and Mediamark Research, New York, NY.

Advertising—Data on advertising previously shown in this section are now presented in Section 27, Accommodation, Food Services, and Other Services.

Statistical reliability—For a discussion of statistical collection and estimation, sampling procedures, and measures of statistical reliability applicable to Census Bureau data, see Appendix III.

Table 1106. **Information—Establishments, Receipts, Payroll, and Employees by Kind of Business (NAICS Basis): 2002**

[Preliminary. For establishments with payroll. (45,660 represents $45,660,000,000). Based on the 2002 Economic Censuses; see Appendix III]

Kind of business	2002 NAICS code [1]	Number of establish-ments	Receipts (mil. dol.)	Annual payroll (mil. dol.)	Paid employees (1,000)
Newspaper publishers.	51111	8,574	45,660	13,570	398.8
Periodical publishers.	51112	7,146	39,279	8,131	148.8
Book publishers.	51113	3,570	27,163	4,880	95.2
Directory & mailing list publishers	51114	1,839	16,564	2,465	53.7
Other publishers.	51119	994	7,487	1,074	26.5
Software publishers	51121	9,899	103,737	34,593	353.3
Motion picture & video industries [2]	5121	19,101	62,013	10,236	275.4
Motion picture & video production	51211	11,106	45,019	7,137	110.2
Motion picture & video exhibition	51213	5,268	11,211	1,307	133.1
Postproduction & other motion picture & video industries.	51219	2,207	4,395	1,531	27.3
Sound recording industries.	5122	3,468	15,530	2,280	32.9
Sound recording studios.	51224	1,498	695	241	6.2
Broadcasting (except Internet)	515	9,570	75,326	14,838	295.1
Radio & television broadcasting.	5151	8,856	49,298	11,903	254.5
Radio broadcasting	51511	6,897	15,793	4,825	128.9
Cable & other subscription programming.	5152	714	26,028	2,935	40.6
Internet publishing & broadcasting.	516	2,060	6,427	2,301	39.5
Telecommunications [2].	517	49,055	411,808	71,486	1,428.0
Wired telecommunications carriers.	5171	27,891	238,263	46,949	835.4
Wireless telecommunications carriers (except satellite).	5172	11,175	100,106	13,348	286.1
Cable & other program distribution.	5175	6,118	56,710	8,328	247.1
Internet service providers, Web search portals, & data processing.	518	18,642	79,212	26,048	521.0
Internet service providers & Web search portals.	5181	4,863	23,327	4,540	83.3
Data processing, hosting, & related services	5182	13,779	55,885	21,508	437.7
Other information services.	519	3,476	4,826	1,639	54.3
Libraries & archives.	51912	2,714	1,674	730	34.5

[1] North American Industry Classification System, 2002; see text, this section and Section 15.   [2] Includes other industries, not shown separately.

Source: U.S. Census Bureau, "2002 Economic Census Industry Series Reports, Information." See Internet site: <http://www.census.gov/econ/census02/guide/INDRPT51.HTM> (accessed 16 May 2005).

Table 1107. **Information Sector Services—Estimated Revenue: 2000 to 2004**

[In millions of dollars (863,871 represents $863,871,000,000). For taxable and tax-exempt employer firms. Estimates have been adjusted to the results of the 2002 Economic Census. Based on the Service Annual Survey; see Appendix III]

Industry	1997 NAICS code [1]	2000	2002	2003	2004
Information industries	51	863,871	891,846	908,209	955,084
Publishing industries.	511	246,800	246,043	247,635	260,348
Newspaper, periodical, book, database, and other publishers [2].	5111	144,763	142,537	142,914	148,087
Newspaper publishers	51111	50,290	46,402	47,443	48,599
Periodical publishers	51112	40,770	39,757	39,560	41,760
Book publishers.	51113	24,979	26,926	26,058	26,786
Database and directory publishers	51114	18,180	18,992	19,181	20,249
Software publishers	5112	102,037	103,506	104,721	112,262
Motion picture and sound recording industries.	512	71,560	78,250	83,113	88,267
Motion picture and video [2].	5121	55,978	62,927	67,589	71,772
Motion picture and video production and distribution.	51211,12	41,786	47,924	52,374	56,604
Motion picture and video exhibition	51213	9,689	10,838	11,147	11,180
Sound recording.	5122	15,582	15,324	15,525	16,495
Integrated record production/distribution.	51222	10,963	10,512	10,194	11,021
Broadcasting and telecommunications	513	473,503	485,607	492,997	512,896
Radio and television broadcasting	5131	49,326	48,589	48,708	52,093
Radio broadcasting	51311	15,618	15,603	15,820	16,494
Radio stations	513112	13,723	13,503	13,566	13,817
Television broadcasting.	51312	33,707	32,987	32,888	35,599
Cable networks and program distribution.	5132	70,097	83,082	93,314	104,690
Cable networks.	51321	22,034	25,373	28,463	31,373
Cable and other program distribution.	51322	48,063	57,709	64,851	73,317
Telecommunications [2].	5133	354,080	353,936	350,976	356,113
Wired telecommunications carriers	51331	270,150	237,697	221,231	211,176
Wireless telecommunications carriers (except satellite).	51332	65,846	99,193	112,089	127,602
Cellular and other wireless telecommunications	513322	60,696	96,530	109,933	125,693
Telecommunications resellers.	51333	9,995	9,717	10,320	9,849
Satellite telecommunications	51334	6,007	5,748	5,959	6,030
Information services and data processing services	514	72,009	81,946	84,464	93,572
Information services.	5141	29,925	28,857	31,193	36,242
Online information services	514191	18,384	18,711	19,157	20,202
Data processing services	5142	42,084	53,089	53,271	57,330

[1] North American Industry Classification System, 1997; see text this section and Section 15.   [2] Includes other industries, not shown separately.

Source: U.S. Census Bureau, "2004 Service Annual Survey, Information Sector Services". See <http://www.census.gov/econ/www/servmenu.html>. (released December 2005).

Information and Communications   707

Table 1108. **Information Industries—Establishments, Employees, and Payroll: 2000 and 2003**

[For establishments with payroll (3,545.7 represents 3,545,700). Excludes most government employees, railroad employees, and self-employed persons. Data for 2000 based on North American Industrial Classification, 1997; 2003 based on North Amercian Industrial Classification, 2002. For statement on methodology, see Appendix III]

Industry	NAICS code [1]	Establishments (number) 2000	Establishments (number) 2003	Paid employees [2] (1,000) 2000	Paid employees [2] (1,000) 2003	Annual payroll (mil. dol.) 2000	Annual payroll (mil. dol.) 2003
Information industries.	51	**133,590**	**140,027**	**3,545.7**	**3,599.9**	**209,394**	**204,024**
2002 NAICS							
Publishing industries.	511	32,545	31,336	1,080.7	1,049.6	75,348	66,312
Newspaper, periodical, book, and database publishers.	5111	21,946	22,179	749.2	705.4	31,258	30,842
Newspaper publishers	51111	8,586	8,376	412.6	384.7	14,216	13,735
Periodical publishers	51112	6,252	7,176	135.6	155.8	7,676	8,933
Book publishers	51113	2,661	3,377	87.2	83.6	4,310	4,357
Database and directory publishers	51114	1,370	1,808	46.2	52.0	2,418	2,610
Other publishers	51119	3,077	1,442	67.5	29.3	2,637	1,207
Greeting card publishers	511191	112	114	17.8	14.3	631	617
All other publishers.	511199	2,965	1,328	49.7	15.0	2,006	590
Software publishers	5112	10,599	9,157	331.5	344.2	44,090	35,470
Motion picture and sound recording industries	512	22,899	22,207	304.2	283.8	11,736	13,046
Motion picture and video industries	5121	19,730	18,914	276.6	257.5	9,806	10,999
Motion picture and video production	51211	10,018	11,225	84.5	93.0	5,723	7,723
Motion picture and video distribution	51212	678	449	13.9	3.5	1,119	198
Motion picture and video exhibition	51213	5,884	5,110	144.0	136.0	1,130	1,514
Motion picture theaters (except drive-ins)	512131	5,593	4,834	142.3	134.6	1,107	1,494
Drive-in motion picture theaters.	512132	291	276	1.7	1.4	23	20
Post production and other motion picture and video industries	51219	3,150	2,100	34.2	25.0	1,834	1,564
Teleproduction and other post-production services.	512191	2,816	1,786	29.7	21.0	1,591	1,302
Other motion picture and video industries	512199	334	314	4.5	4.0	243	262
Sound recording industries	5122	3,169	3,293	27.6	26.3	1,930	2,047
Record production	51221	276	328	1.1	1.4	55	72
Integrated record production/distribution.	51222	310	402	9.0	11.0	1,100	1,297
Music publishers	51223	670	612	5.1	4.5	283	305
Sound recording studios	51224	1,516	1,482	8.1	5.4	327	213
Other sound recording industries	51229	397	469	4.3	4.0	166	160
Broadcasting (except Internet)	515	(NA)	10,372	(NA)	286.4	(NA)	16,004
Radio and television broadcasting	5151	(NA)	9,688	(NA)	254.6	(NA)	13,029
Radio broadcasting	51511	(NA)	7,711	(NA)	131.4	(NA)	5,493
Radio networks	515111	(NA)	669	(NA)	10.4	(NA)	611
Radio stations	515112	(NA)	7,042	(NA)	121.0	(NA)	4,882
Television broadcasting.	51512	(NA)	1,977	(NA)	123.2	(NA)	7,535
Cable and other subscription programming	5152	(NA)	684	(NA)	31.8	(NA)	2,976
Internet publishing and broadcasting	516	(NA)	2,038	(NA)	35.6	(NA)	2,324
Telecommunications	517	(NA)	50,142	(NA)	1,415.2	(NA)	77,957
Wired telecommunications carriers.	5171	(NA)	27,607	(NA)	855.2	(NA)	51,445
Wireless telecommunications carriers (except satellite	5172	(NA)	13,020	(NA)	266.3	(NA)	13,500
Paging.	517211	(NA)	1,508	(NA)	17.2	(NA)	684
Cellular and other wireless telecommunications. . . .	517212	(NA)	11,512	(NA)	249.0	(NA)	12,816
Telecommunications resellers	5173	(NA)	2,726	(NA)	36.6	(NA)	1,660
Satellite telecommunications.	5174	(NA)	698	(NA)	14.6	(NA)	890
Cable and other program distribution	5175	(NA)	5,383	(NA)	234.1	(NA)	9,961
Other telecommunications	5179	(NA)	708	(NA)	8.3	(NA)	500
Internet service providers, Web search portals, and data processing service	518	(NA)	19,643	(NA)	473.9	(NA)	26,516
Internet service providers and Web search portals . . .	5181	(NA)	5,365	(NA)	70.9	(NA)	4,803
Internet service providers	518111	(NA)	4,790	(NA)	60.9	(NA)	3,539
Web search portals	518112	(NA)	575	(NA)	10.0	(NA)	1,264
Data processing, hosting, and related services.	5182	(NA)	14,278	(NA)	403.0	(NA)	21,713
Other information services	519	(NA)	4,289	(NA)	55.4	(NA)	1,865
News syndicates.	51911	(NA)	623	(NA)	11.5	(NA)	693
Libraries and archives	51912	(NA)	2,951	(NA)	32.3	(NA)	717
All other information services	51919	(NA)	715	(NA)	11.6	(NA)	455

NA Not available.   [1] North American Industry Classification System; see text, this section and Section 15.   [2] For employees on the payroll for the pay period including March 12.

Source: U.S. Census Bureau, "County Business Patterns"; <http://www.census.gov/epcd/cbp/view/cbpview.html>.

Table 1109. **Information Technologies (IT)—Employment, 2000 to 2004, and Wages, 2000 and 2003**

[110,996 represents 110,996,000]

Industry	2002 NAICS [1] code	Employment (1,000)			Annual wages per worker (dol.)	
		2000	2003	2004	2000	2003
Total private	(X)	110,996	108,416	109,862	35,350	37,510
IT producing industries	**(X)**	**5,381.7**	**4,356.0**	**4,283.0**	**72,330**	**70,100**
Computer hardware [2]	(X)	1,679.8	1,232.2	1,195.4	77,800	73,350
Electronic computers	334111	168.6	123.6	115.5	130,720	101,250
Computer and software wholesalers	423430	299.4	241.1	233.7	92,910	88,160
Computer and software retailers	443120	190.5	140.3	132.4	53,650	52,960
Bare printed circuit boards.	334412	139.5	65.6	62.0	38,810	43,300
Semiconductors and related devices	334413	289.2	225.5	223.1	95,300	82,480
Miscellaneous electronic components	334415,6,7,9	146.0	98.5	97.9	42,320	45,640
Software and computer services [2]	(X)	2,127.4	1,845.6	1,860.0	77,310	74,520
Software publishers	511210	260.6	238.9	238.7	114,410	102,310
Data processing and related services	518210	315.7	280.0	270.5	53,610	58,440
Custom computer programming services	541511	540.0	489.8	505.0	78,070	77,350
Computer systems design services	541512	502.9	456.6	475.1	77,040	74,890
Communications equipment [2]	(X)	322.0	201.7	189.8	66,990	69,110
Telephone apparatus	334210	106.5	50.7	47.2	80,960	80,790
Broadcast and wireless communications equipment.	334220	107.3	77.9	75.7	63,160	68,230
Communications services [2]	(X)	1,252.5	1,076.4	1,037.8	58,810	59,180
Wired telecommunications carriers	517110	719.2	579.2	548.4	62,560	63,870

X Not applicable.   [1] North American Industry Classification System, 2002; see text, this section and Section 15.   [2] Includes other industries, not shown separately.

Source: U.S. Department of Commerce, Economics and Statistics Administration, *The Digital Economy 2006*, forthcoming report. See Internet site <https://www.esa.doc.gov/reports.cfm>.

Table 1110. **Media Usage and Consumer Spending: 2000 to 2009**

[Estimates of time spent were derived using rating data for television, cable and satellite television and radio, survey research and consumer purchase data (units, admissions, access) for books, home video, Internet, interactive TV, magazines, movies in theaters, newspapers, recorded music, and video games. Adults 18 and older were the basis for estimates for television, cable and satellite television, daily newspapers, consumer books, consumer magazines, home video, and interactive TV. Persons 12 and older were the basis for estimates for radio, recorded music, movies in theaters, video games, and consumer Internet]

Item	2000	2002	2003	2004	2005, proj.	2006, proj.	2007, proj.	2008, proj.	2009, proj.
HOURS PER PERSON PER YEAR									
Total	3,333	3,430	3,471	3,480	3,483	3,499	3,518	3,549	3,555
Television.	1,467	1,519	1,543	1,546	1,548	1,555	1,555	1,566	1,562
Broadcast TV	793	719	696	678	679	684	678	675	681
Network stations [1]	700	624	601	583	584	590	585	580	587
Cable & satellite TV	674	800	847	868	869	871	877	891	881
Basic cable and satellite TV [1]	555	664	697	719	733	737	731	742	747
Premium cable and satellite TV [1]	119	136	150	149	136	134	146	149	134
Broadcast and satellite radio [2]	942	991	1,003	986	978	975	974	984	984
Box office	12	14	13	12	12	12	12	12	12
Home video [2, 3].	43	57	60	67	76	84	91	95	99
Interactive TV & wireless content [4]	–	4	7	11	15	19	26	32	42
Recorded music [2]	258	200	184	185	179	175	175	169	165
Videogames [2]	64	70	75	77	78	82	86	93	96
Consumer Internet	104	147	164	176	183	190	195	200	203
Daily newspapers [2]	201	194	192	188	183	179	175	170	165
Consumer books [2]	107	109	109	108	106	106	106	106	106
Consumer magazines [2]	135	125	121	124	124	122	122	122	121
CONSUMER SPENDING PER PERSON PER YEAR (dol.)									
Total	608.31	712.64	757.49	794.78	841.48	888.06	936.75	982.56	1,023.69
Cable and satellite TV [1]	189.45	224.30	240.53	255.36	269.85	282.92	296.02	308.40	320.81
Broadcast and satellite radio [2]	–	0.07	0.04	1.15	2.65	4.68	6.91	9.13	11.16
Box office	32.64	35.99	39.01	38.76	38.82	39.11	39.71	40.17	41.04
Home video [2, 3].	81.49	108.22	122.19	135.31	138.60	151.09	161.14	171.63	180.27
Interactive TV & wireless content [4]	0.10	3.35	7.40	13.31	20.10	26.95	32.96	37.94	42.41
Recorded music [2]	61.04	52.47	48.73	49.39	47.65	45.77	45.35	43.49	42.39
Videogames [2]	27.89	32.34	32.65	32.94	33.49	36.13	38.87	42.63	44.30
Consumer Internet.	49.47	85.84	100.63	113.48	125.43	138.83	151.91	165.60	177.42
Daily newspapers [2]	51.93	53.00	52.68	51.62	50.17	48.97	47.95	47.13	46.47
Consumer books [2]	85.84	87.64	89.69	89.67	91.39	91.27	93.26	93.23	93.90
Consumer magazines [2]	47.54	46.86	46.08	46.88	47.82	47.59	48.50	49.19	49.57

– Represents zero.   [1] UPN, WB, and PAX affiliates included in network-affiliated stations, superstations included in basic cable, and pay-per-view included in premium service. [2] Does not include Internet-related use of traditional media. Some examples include: listening to downloaded music directly on the computer or from a burned disc on an MP3 player, reading a downloaded e-book, listening to a radio station transmitted by a Windows media player, and reading a Web-based newspaper article. Such activities are included in the time spent data under Consumer Internet, although the media content was originally provided on a traditional medium. [3] Playback of prerecorded VHS cassettes and DVDs only. [4] Video-on-demand (VOD) only. Personal video recorders (PVRs) included in total TV.

Source: Veronis Suhler Stevenson, New York, NY, *Communications Industry Forecast & Report,* annual (copyright).

Information and Communications **709**

Table 1111. Utilization of Selected Media: 1980 to 2004

[78.6 represents 78,600,000]

Item	Unit	1980	1990	1995	1998	1999	2000	2001	2002	2003	2004
Households with—											
Telephone service [1]	Percent...	93.0	93.3	93.9	94.1	94.0	94.6	94.6	95.5	95.5	94.2
Radio [2]	Millions...	78.6	94.4	98.0	(NA)	(NA)	100.5	101.9	105.1	106.7	108.3
Percent of total households...	Percent...	99.0	99.0	99.0	99.0	99.0	99.0	99.0	99.0	99.0	99.0
Average number of sets...	Number...	5.5	5.6	5.6	5.6	5.6	5.6	5.6	5.6	8.0	8.0
Television [3]	Millions...	78	94	97	100	101	103	104	107	108	110
Percent of total households...	Percent...	97.9	98.2	98.3	98.3	98.2	98.2	98.2	98.2	98.2	98.2
Television sets in homes...	Millions...	128	193	217	235	240	245	248	254	260	268
Average number of sets per home	Number...	1.7	2.0	2.3	2.4	2.4	2.4	2.4	2.4	2.4	2.5
Color set households...	Millions...	63	90	94	98	99	101	102	105	107	108
Wired cable television [4]...	Millions...	15.2	51.9	60.5	65.8	67.1	68.6	69.5	73.2	74.4	73.8
Percent of TV households...	Percent...	19.9	56.4	63.4	67.2	67.5	68.0	68.0	69.4	69.8	68.1
Alternative delivery system (ADS) households [4]	Millions...	(NA)	(NA)	4.0	9.1	9.4	11.7	14.7	17.4	19.7	21.2
Percent of TV households...	Percent...	(NA)	(NA)	4.2	9.1	9.3	11.4	14.1	16.3	18.2	19.3
VCRs [4]	Millions...	1	63	77	83	84	86	88	96	98	98
Percent of TV households...	Percent...	1.1	68.6	81.0	84.6	84.6	85.1	86.2	91.2	91.5	90.8
Computers [5]	Percent...	(NA)	(NA)	(NA)	42.1	(NA)	51.0	56.2	(NA)	61.8	(NA)
Internet connections [5]	Percent...	(NA)	(NA)	(NA)	26.2	(NA)	41.5	50.3	(NA)	54.6	(NA)
Broadband Internet [5]	Percent...	(NA)	(NA)	(NA)	(NA)	(NA)	4.4	9.1	(NA)	19.9	(NA)
Commercial radio stations: [2]											
AM	Number...	4,589	4,987	4,909	4,793	4,783	4,685	4,727	4,804	4,802	4,770
FM	Number...	3,282	4,392	5,296	5,662	5,766	5,892	6,051	6,161	6,207	6,217
Television stations: [6] Total	Number...	1,011	1,442	1,532	1,589	1,615	1,663	1,686	1,714	1,730	1,748
Commercial	Number...	734	1,092	1,161	1,221	1,243	1,288	1,309	1,333	1,349	1,366
VHF	Number...	516	547	562	561	561	567	572	581	587	589
UHF	Number...	218	545	599	660	682	721	737	752	762	777
Cable television systems [7]	Number...	4,225	9,575	11,218	10,845	10,700	10,243	9,924	9,339	9,038	8,869
Daily newspaper circulation [8]	Millions...	62.2	62.3	58.2	56.2	56.0	55.8	55.6	55.2	55.2	54.6

NA Not available. [1] For occupied housing units. 1980 as of April 1; all other years as of March. Source: U.S. Census Bureau, *1980 Census of Housing*, vol. 1; thereafter Federal Communications Commission, *Trends in Telephone Service*, annual. [2] 1980–1995 as of December 31. Source: M Street Corp. as reported by Radio Advertising Bureau New York, NY, through 1990, Radio Facts, annual (copyright); beginning 1995, Radio Marketing Guide and Fact Book for Advertisers, annual (copyright). Number of stations on the air compiled from Federal Communications Commission reports. Beginning 1997, Federal Communications Commission, unpublished data as of Sept. 30. See Internet site <http://www.fcc.gov/mb/audio/totals>. [3] As of January of year shown. Excludes Alaska and Hawaii. Source: Television Bureau of Advertising, Inc., *Trends in Television*, annual (copyright). [4] Wired cable and VCR as of February; ADS for fourth quarter. Excludes Alaska and Hawaii. Source: See footnote 3. [5] As of December 1998, August 2000, September 2001, and October 2003. Source: U.S. Department of Commerce, National Telecommunications and Information Administration, *A Nation Online: Entering the Broadband Age*, September 2004. See Internet site <http://www.ntia.doc.gov/reports/anol/index.html>. [6] Source: Beginning 1998, Federal Communications Commission, unpublished data. See Internet site <http://www.fcc.gov/mb/audio/totals>. 1998 as of December; beginning 1999, as of September. For prior years data, see footnote 3. [7] As of January 1. Source: Warren Communications News, Washington DC, *Television and Cable Factbook* (copyright). [8] As of September 30. Source: Editor & Publisher, Co., New York, NY, *Editor & Publisher International Year Book*, annual (copyright).

Source: Compiled from sources mentioned in footnotes.

Table 1112. Multimedia Audiences—Summary: 2005

[In percent, except total (215,800 represents 215,800,000). As of fall. For persons 18 years old and over. Represents the percent of persons participating during the prior week, except as indicated. Based on sample and subject to sampling error; see source for details]

Item	Total population (1,000)	Television viewing	Television prime-time viewing	Cable viewing [1]	Radio listening	Newspaper reading	Accessed Internet [2]
Total	**215,800**	**94.3**	**83.2**	**79.1**	**84.1**	**77.1**	**64.0**
18 to 24 years old	27,962	92.0	75.1	73.0	88.7	73.1	74.4
25 to 34 years old	39,399	93.1	81.8	76.7	89.5	72.1	76.1
35 to 44 years old	43,806	93.4	82.7	80.1	90.1	78.0	73.5
45 to 54 years old	41,262	94.4	83.9	82.2	88.6	79.1	69.8
55 to 64 years old	28,516	95.6	86.4	82.0	79.9	81.0	58.9
65 years old and over	34,856	97.3	88.6	79.8	64.8	79.1	27.1
Male	103,951	94.4	82.8	79.1	86.0	77.3	64.2
Female	111,849	94.2	83.6	79.2	82.3	76.8	63.8
Not high school graduate	34,134	94.6	82.8	67.0	74.8	57.8	21.6
High school graduate	68,518	95.0	84.2	79.5	83.3	76.7	50.4
Attended college	58,764	94.8	83.7	82.4	87.7	81.4	79.6
College graduate	54,384	92.6	81.6	82.9	86.9	84.9	90.7
Household income:							
Less than $10,000	13,296	92.4	80.4	59.5	72.6	58.1	28.2
$10,000 to $19,999	22,441	94.8	82.5	63.1	75.5	64.9	27.6
$20,000 to $29,999	23,848	95.4	84.7	71.8	79.6	73.4	42.5
$30,000 to $34,999	11,843	94.1	83.4	75.3	79.9	76.0	48.4
$35,000 to $39,999	11,217	94.5	85.8	76.2	83.3	73.5	54.9
$40,000 to $49,999	20,935	94.7	83.3	78.8	84.3	77.5	62.9
$50,000 to $74,999	42,691	95.2	84.1	84.1	86.8	80.9	74.9
$75,000 to $99,999	28,188	94.0	82.9	87.1	88.7	83.5	83.4
$100,000 or more	41,340	93.1	82.2	90.0	90.3	84.7	90.5

[1] In the past 7 days. [2] In the last 30 days.

Source: Mediamark Research Inc., New York, NY, *Multimedia Audiences*, fall 2005 (copyright).

Table 1113. **Newspaper, Periodical, and Database and Directory Publishers— Estimated Revenue and Inventories: 2002 to 2004**

[In millions of dollars (46,402 represents $46,402,000,000). For taxable and tax-exempt employer firms. Estimates have been adjusted to the results of the 2002 Economic Census. Based on the North American Industry Classification System, 1997; see text, this section and Section 15. See also Appendix III]

Item	Newspaper publishers (NAICS 51111)			Periodical publishers (NAICS 51112)			Database and directory publishers (NAICS 51114)		
	2002	2003	2004	2002	2003	2004	2002	2003	2004
Revenue..............	46,402	47,443	48,599	39,757	39,560	41,760	18,992	19,181	20,249
Source of revenue:									
Print......................	41,105	41,756	42,670	31,119	29,931	31,020	13,471	13,504	14,101
Subscription and sales........	9,213	9,383	9,149	13,276	12,126	12,231	713	745	719
Advertising................	31,892	32,372	33,521	17,844	17,805	18,788	12,758	12,759	13,382
Internet....................	583	718	902	1,329	1,446	1,528	596	760	786
Subscription and sales........	(S)	(S)	(S)	915	1,071	994	(S)	(S)	(S)
Advertising................	455	554	716	(S)	374	(S)	315	479	548
Other media...............	161	149	103	2,405	2,647	2,932	1,809	1,456	1,659
Subscription and sales........	60	(S)	(S)	2,329	2,573	2,863	1,767	1,414	1,617
Advertising................	101	94	67	76	73	(S)	42	42	42
Contract printing..............	1,708	1,628	1,622	706	643	700	(S)	(S)	(S)
Distribution of flyers, inserts, etc.....	996	1,163	1,251	121	(S)	(S)	(NA)	(NA)	(NA)
Graphic design services..........	(S)	(S)	(S)	(S)	(S)	(S)	(NA)	(NA)	(NA)
Market research...............	2	(S)	4	(NA)	(NA)	(NA)	(NA)	(NA)	(NA)
Archival sales services..........	22	25	26	(NA)	(NA)	(NA)	(NA)	(NA)	(NA)
Sales or licensing of rights of content .	44	73	77	281	300	(S)	(S)	(S)	(S)
Rental or sales of mailing lists......	(S)	7	7	172	168	170	1,333	1,344	1,340
Non-newspaper publishing	298	361	200	(NA)	(NA)	(NA)	(NA)	(NA)	(NA)
Publishing services for others	12	19	21	(S)	321	(S)	33	65	71
Other revenue	1,450	1,536	1,705	3,215	3,906	4,485	1,440	1,717	1,962
Breakdown of revenue by type of publication:									
General interest publications.......	40,272	40,926	41,461	16,693	16,396	16,812	(NA)	(NA)	(NA)
Special interest publications	1,141	1,049	1,166	16,695	16,051	17,169	(NA)	(NA)	(NA)
Other publications.............	(S)	647	(S)	(S)	1,576	(S)	(NA)	(NA)	(NA)
Inventories at end of year ..	**700**	**762**	**754**	**1,711**	**1,578**	**1,708**	**(S)**	**(S)**	**(S)**
Finished goods and work-in-process..	78	106	90	1,282	1,183	1,243	(S)	(S)	(S)
Materials, supplies, fuel, etc.......	621	656	664	429	(S)	466	(S)	(S)	(S)

NA Not available.   S Data do not meet publication standards.

Source: U.S. Census Bureau, *"2004 Service Annual Survey, Information Sector Services"*. See <http://www.census.gov/econ/www /servmenu.html> (released December 2005).

Table 1114. **Daily and Sunday Newspapers—Number and Circulation: 1970 to 2005**

[Number of newspapers as of February 1 the following year. Circulation figures as of September 30 of year shown (62.1 represents 62,100,000). For English language newspapers only]

Type	1970	1975	1980	1985	1990	1995	2000	2001	2002	2003	2004	2005
NUMBER												
Daily: Total [1]...............	1,748	1,756	1,745	1,676	1,611	1,533	1,480	1,468	1,457	1,456	1,457	1,452
Morning	334	339	387	482	559	656	766	776	777	787	814	817
Evening	1,429	1,436	1,388	1,220	1,084	891	727	704	692	680	653	645
Sunday	586	639	736	798	863	888	917	913	913	917	915	914
NET PAID CIRCULATION (mil.)												
Daily: Total [1]...............	62.1	60.7	62.2	62.8	62.3	58.2	55.8	55.6	55.2	55.2	54.6	53.3
Morning	25.9	25.5	29.4	36.4	41.3	44.3	46.8	46.8	46.6	46.9	46.9	46.1
Evening	36.2	35.2	32.8	26.4	21.0	13.9	9.0	8.8	8.6	8.3	7.7	7.2
Sunday	49.2	51.1	54.7	58.8	62.6	61.5	59.4	59.1	58.8	58.5	57.8	55.3
PER CAPITA CIRCULATION [2]												
Daily: Total [1]...............	0.30	0.28	0.27	0.26	0.25	0.22	0.20	0.20	0.19	0.19	0.19	0.18
Morning	0.13	0.12	0.13	0.15	0.17	0.17	0.17	0.16	0.16	0.16	0.16	0.16
Evening	0.18	0.16	0.14	0.11	0.08	0.05	0.03	0.03	0.03	0.03	0.03	0.02
Sunday	0.24	0.24	0.24	0.25	0.25	0.23	0.21	0.21	0.20	0.20	0.20	0.18

[1] All-day newspapers are counted in both morning and evening columns but only once in total. Circulation is divided equally between morning and evening.   [2] Based on U.S. Census Bureau estimated resident population as of July 1.

Source: Editor & Publisher Co., New York, NY, *Editor & Publisher International Year Book*, annual (copyright).

Information and Communications   711

[Number of newspapers as of February 1 the following year. Circulation as of September 30 (29,413 represents 29,413,000). For English language newspapers only. See Table 32 for number of cities by population size. All-day newspapers are counted in both morning and evening columns; circulation is divided equally between morning and evening]

Type of daily and population-size class	Number					Net paid circulation (1,000)				
	1980	1990	1995	2000	2005	1980	1990	1995	2000	2005
Morning dailies, total. . .	387	559	656	766	817	29,413	41,311	44,310	46,772	46,123
In cities of—										
1,000,001 or more	20	18	25	26	32	8,795	6,508	10,173	10,820	10,791
500,001 to 1,000,000	27	22	22	25	33	5,705	4,804	5,587	5,412	6,253
100,001 to 500,000	99	138	153	163	166	8,996	20,051	17,214	17,469	16,510
50,001 to 100,000	75	100	138	162	160	2,973	4,373	5,602	5,887	5,439
25,001 to 50,000	64	102	115	141	157	1,701	3,209	3,150	3,899	3,737
Less than 25,000	102	179	203	249	269	1,243	2,365	2,584	3,285	3,392
Evening dailies, total. . .	1,388	1,084	891	727	645	32,788	21,017	13,883	9,000	7,222
In cities of—										
1,000,001 or more	11	7	3	1	1	2,984	1,423	390	1	1
500,001 to 1,000,000	23	12	7	3	5	4,101	1,350	1,017	519	583
100,001 to 500,000	123	71	45	32	23	8,178	4,687	2,529	1,603	1,138
50,001 to 100,000	156	94	72	54	37	4,896	2,941	2,029	1,332	916
25,001 to 50,000	246	204	158	124	110	5,106	4,278	2,819	1,898	1,517
Less than 25,000	829	696	606	513	469	7,523	6,338	5,099	3,648	3,067

Source: Editor & Publisher Co., New York, NY, *Editor & Publisher International Year Book,* annual (copyright).

Table 1116. **Daily and Sunday Newspapers—Number and Circulation, 1991 to 2004, and by State, 2005**

[Number of newspapers as of February 1 the following year. Circulation as of September 30 (60,687 represents 60,687,000). For English language newspapers only. California, New York, Massachusetts, and Virginia Sunday newspapers include national circulation]

State	Daily			Sunday		State	Daily			Sunday	
		Circulation [1]			Net paid circu-lation			Circulation [1]			Net paid circu-lation
	Num-ber	Net paid (1,000)	Per capita [2]	Num-ber	lation (1,000)		Num-ber	Net paid (1,000)	Per capita [2]	Num-ber	lation (1,000)
Total, 1991 . .	1,586	60,687	0.24	875	62,068	LA	26	701	0.15	21	769
Total, 1992 . .	1,570	60,164	0.23	891	62,160	ME	7	223	0.17	4	186
Total, 1993 . .	1,556	59,812	0.23	884	62,566	MD	11	479	0.09	8	646
Total, 1994 . .	1,548	59,305	0.23	886	62,294	MA	32	1,430	0.22	16	1,398
Total, 1995 . .	1,533	58,193	0.22	888	61,529	MI	48	1,600	0.16	27	1,813
Total, 1996 . .	1,520	56,983	0.21	890	60,798	MN	25	847	0.17	15	1,105
Total, 1997 . .	1,509	56,728	0.21	903	60,484	MS	23	354	0.12	19	359
Total, 1998 . .	1,489	56,182	0.20	898	60,066	MO	42	875	0.15	23	1,105
Total, 1999 . .	1,483	55,979	0.20	905	59,894	MT	11	186	0.20	7	186
Total, 2000 . .	1,480	55,773	0.20	917	59,421	NE	17	396	0.23	6	380
Total, 2001 . .	1,468	55,578	0.19	913	59,090	NV	8	283	0.12	4	319
Total, 2002 . .	1,457	55,186	0.19	913	58,780	NH	11	211	0.16	8	215
Total, 2003 . .	1,456	55,185	0.19	917	58,495	NJ	18	1,230	0.14	15	1,522
Total, 2004 . .	1,457	54,626	0.19	915	57,753	NM	18	271	0.14	13	279
						NY	60	6,943	0.36	38	5,154
Total, 2005 . .	1,452	53,345	0.18	914	55,270	NC	47	1,267	0.15	39	1,397
AL	23	611	0.13	20	686	ND	10	155	0.24	7	161
AK	7	105	0.16	5	140	OH	84	2,217	0.19	41	2,458
AZ	16	743	0.13	11	846	OK	42	585	0.16	34	732
AR	28	454	0.16	16	525	OR	19	654	0.18	12	682
CA	88	5,524	0.15	58	5,671	PA	80	2,528	0.20	42	2,958
CO	30	970	0.21	15	1,111	RI	6	202	0.19	3	257
CT	17	653	0.19	13	729	SC	16	604	0.14	14	686
DE	2	130	0.15	2	159	SD	11	153	0.20	4	134
DC	3	840	1.52	3	1,391	TN	26	833	0.14	18	973
FL	40	2,988	0.17	37	3,770	TX	85	2,838	0.12	77	3,494
GA	34	967	0.11	29	1,263	UT	6	326	0.13	6	360
HI	6	267	0.21	6	297	VT	8	113	0.18	3	86
ID	12	209	0.15	8	225	VA	24	3,132	0.41	17	960
IL	67	2,160	0.17	32	2,360	WA	23	1,022	0.16	17	1,160
IN	68	1,246	0.20	25	1,195	WV	20	325	0.18	12	328
IA	37	587	0.20	13	621	WI	35	853	0.15	18	1,019
KS	43	395	0.14	14	353	WY	9	86	0.17	5	69
KY	23	573	0.14	14	603						

[1] Circulation figures based on the principal community served by a newspaper which is not necessarily the same location as the publisher's office. [2] Per capita based on estimated resident population as of July 1, except 2000, enumerated resident population as of April 1.

Source: Editor & Publisher Co., New York, NY, *Editor & Publisher International Year Book,* annual (copyright).

712   Information and Communications

Table 1117. Periodicals—Average Retail Prices: 2002 to 2006

[**In dollars.** Reflects prices for an annual subscription]

Subject	2002	2003	2004	2005	2006
Agriculture	631	686	777	834	890
Anthropology	300	342	372	397	416
Art and architecture	134	144	160	172	185
Astronomy	1,256	1,353	1,500	1,577	1,724
Biology.	1,089	1,206	1,316	1,427	1,548
Botany	880	939	1,036	1,134	1,238
Business and economics	527	582	643	699	746
Chemistry	2,432	2,596	2,845	3,012	1,756
Education	300	328	366	405	442
Engineering.	1,305	1,412	1,523	1,648	1,756
Food science.	897	969	1,085	1,188	1,292
General science.	810	886	954	1,013	1,098
General works	181	197	217	232	241
Geography	746	819	882	937	984
Geology	1,012	1,081	1,171	1,260	1,323
Health sciences	808	881	964	1,046	1,132
History	132	152	171	189	201
Language and literature.	120	135	153	166	176
Law	159	174	192	200	225
Library and information science.	286	316	350	390	437
Math and computer science	981	1,047	1,134	1,205	1,278
Military and naval science	346	400	432	489	538
Music.	96	105	110	127	130
Philosophy and religion	156	174	195	211	226
Physics	2,178	2,333	2,538	2,695	2,850
Political science	288	321	367	399	437
Psychology	358	388	437	471	516
Recreation	146	156	169	195	206
Sociology	332	365	412	452	491
Technology	1,151	1,241	1,360	1,464	1,560
Zoology	973	1,033	1,091	1,161	1,259

Source: Library Journal, New York, NY, *Library Journal*, April 15, 2006. (Copyright 2006, used with permission of Library Journal, a publication of Reed Business Information, a division of Reed Elsevier).

Table 1118. Quantity of Books Sold: 2004 to 2009

[**In millions (2,966.2 represents 2,966,200,000). Represents net publishers' shipments after returns.** Includes all titles released by publishers in the United States and imports which appear under the imprints of American publishers. Multivolume sets, such as encyclopedias, are counted as one unit. Due to changes in methodology and scope, these data are not comparable to those previously published]

Type of publication	2004	2005	2006, proj.	2007, proj.	2008, proj.	2009, proj.
Total	**2,966.2**	**3,078.9**	**3,150.1**	**3,171.2**	**3,183.0**	**3,228.2**
Trade	1,613.1	1,689.8	1,747.3	1,748.1	1,747.5	1,776.1
Adult.	785.8	810.4	828.3	841.8	848.3	861.0
Hardback	396.9	406.4	413.8	419.2	421.0	424.7
Paperback	388.9	404.0	414.5	422.6	427.2	436.3
Juvenile.	827.3	879.4	919.0	906.2	899.3	915.1
Hardback	253.4	273.0	274.7	277.4	302.8	279.5
Paperback	574.0	606.4	644.4	628.9	596.5	635.7
Mass market paperbacks—rack sized.						
Religious.	241.1	255.5	266.9	278.0	288.9	300.0
Hardback.	85.3	91.0	97.1	101.2	105.2	109.2
Paperback	155.8	164.5	169.8	176.9	183.7	190.8
Professional.	274.0	278.9	282.7	286.7	290.9	295.9
Hardback.	97.8	99.2	100.0	101.0	96.9	96.2
Paperback	176.1	179.8	182.7	185.8	194.0	199.7
University press	24.7	24.5	24.6	24.7	24.6	24.7
Hardback.	9.3	9.1	9.2	9.3	9.3	9.3
Paperback	15.4	15.5	15.3	15.4	15.4	15.4
Elementary/High school text	159.5	179.8	181.6	189.6	194.2	199.0
Hardback.	56.1	63.2	64.9	67.7	69.4	71.1
Paperback	103.4	116.6	116.8	121.9	124.9	127.9
College text	77.1	76.5	75.9	75.4	74.4	73.8
Hardback.	34.2	33.8	33.5	33.3	32.8	32.6
Paperback	42.9	42.7	42.4	42.2	41.6	41.3

Source: Book Industry Study Group, Inc., New York, NY, *Book Industry Trends, 2006*, annual (copyright).

Information and Communications   713

Table 1119. Books Sold—Value of U.S. Domestic Consumer Expenditures: 2004 to 2009

[In millions of dollars (49,146.6 represents $49,146,600,000). Includes all titles released by publishers in the United States and imports which appear under the imprints of American publishers. Due to changes in methodology and scope, these data are not comparable to those previously published]

Type of publication	2004	2005	2006, proj.	2007, proj.	2008, proj.	2009, proj.
Total	49,146.6	51,919.8	53,723.8	55,546.9	57,194.3	58,875.2
Trade	23,394.4	24,571.1	25,362.6	25,992.3	26,553.2	27,086.2
Adult	14,952.1	15,532.4	15,937.2	16,370.1	16,670.0	16,985.4
Hardback	9,036.3	9,387.6	9,631.4	9,904.1	10,095.2	10,330.8
Paperback	5,915.8	6,144.8	6,305.8	6,466.0	6,574.8	6,654.6
Juvenile	5,369.3	5,883.0	6,185.9	6,298.4	6,500.5	6,643.7
Hardback	2,489.0	2,727.1	2,755.3	2,831.4	3,122.1	2,927.4
Paperback	2,880.3	3,155.9	3,430.6	3,467.0	3,378.4	3,716.3
Mass market paperbacks—rack sized	3,073.0	3,155.7	3,239.5	3,323.8	3,382.7	3,457.1
Religious	4,104.0	4,436.7	4,725.7	5,013.5	5,322.2	5,628.5
Hardback	2,436.6	2,634.1	2,847.8	3,018.2	3,207.2	3,391.7
Paperback	1,667.4	1,802.6	1,877.9	1,995.3	2,115.0	2,236.8
Professional	10,275.3	10,680.4	11,046.6	11,415.8	11,798.1	12,192.4
Hardback	6,428.0	6,695.8	6,923.4	7,175.8	7,428.8	7,553.5
Paperback	2,791.9	2,908.5	3,017.5	3,112.2	3,218.9	3,465.5
Subscription reference	1,055.4	1,076.1	1,105.7	1,127.8	1,150.4	1,173.4
University press	547.1	582.3	639.9	655.8	667.4	682.0
Hardback	267.4	279.5	305.8	310.9	315.7	320.5
Paperback	279.7	302.8	334.1	344.9	351.7	361.5
Elementary/High school text	4,622.0	5,320.0	5,507.6	5,892.9	6,187.6	6,493.7
Hardback	2,307.3	2,654.6	2,793.4	2,989.0	3,138.5	3,295.4
Paperback	2,314.7	2,665.4	2,714.2	2,903.9	3,049.1	3,198.3
College text	6,203.8	6,329.3	6,441.4	6,576.6	6,665.8	6,792.4
Hardback	4,156.6	4,221.5	4,289.8	4,379.9	4,439.3	4,523.7
Paperback	2,047.2	2,107.8	2,151.6	2,196.7	2,226.5	2,268.7

Source: Book Industry Study Group, Inc., New York, NY, *Book Industry Trends, 2006*, annual (copyright).

Table 1120. Book Publishers—Estimated Revenue and Inventories: 2001 to 2004

[In millions of dollars (25,831 represents $25,831,000,000), except percent. For taxable and tax-exempt employer firms. For NAICS 51113. Estimates have been adjusted to the results of the 2002 Economic Census. Based on the North American Industry Classification System, 1997; see text, this section and Section 15. See also Appendix III. Minus sign (–) indicates decrease]

Item	2001	2002	2003	2004	Percent change, 2003–04
Revenue, total	25,831	26,926	26,058	26,786	2.8
Books, print, total	20,996	22,208	21,600	22,271	3.1
Books, Internet, total	1,484	1,390	1,439	1,497	4.0
Books, other media, total	810	982	808	800	–0.9
Sale or licensing of rights to content	295	272	228	266	16.7
Contract printing services	184	233	(S)	222	(S)
Fulfillment services	140	143	148	169	13.7
Rental or sale of mailing lists	(S)	7	(S)	(S)	(S)
Publishing services for others	37	51	57	(S)	(S)
Other services revenue	1,876	1,640	1,545	1,499	–3.0
Breakdown of revenue:					
Books, print	20,996	22,208	21,600	22,271	3.1
Textbooks	7,196	7,706	7,276	7,349	1.0
Children's books	2,682	2,817	(S)	(S)	(S)
General reference books	1,617	1,698	1,810	(S)	(S)
Professional, technical, and scholarly books	3,051	3,414	3,118	(S)	(S)
Adult trade	5,428	5,502	5,602	5,778	3.1
Other books	1,021	1,071	(S)	(S)	(S)
Books, Internet	1,484	1,390	1,439	1,497	4.0
Textbooks	109	120	(S)	112	(S)
Children's books	(S)	(S)	(S)	(S)	(S)
General reference books	(S)	34	(S)	39	(S)
Professional, technical, and scholarly books	1,258	1,164	1,219	1,269	4.1
Adult trade	60	64	(S)	(S)	(S)
Other books	(S)	(S)	(S)	(S)	(S)
Books, other media	810	982	808	800	–0.9
Textbooks	149	147	(S)	(S)	(S)
Children's books	51	104	(S)	(S)	(S)
General reference books	27	36	44	47	7.1
Professional, technical, and scholarly books	284	435	349	321	–8.1
Adult trade	220	170	(S)	87	(S)
Other books	79	91	(S)	(S)	(S)
Inventories at end of year	4,050	4,281	4,177	3,981	–4.7
Finished goods and work-in-process	3,896	4,112	4,034	3,835	–4.9
Materials, supplies, fuel, etc	154	169	144	146	1.4

S Data do not meet publication standards.

Source: U.S. Census Bureau, "2004 Service Annual Survey, Information Sector Services." See <http://www.census.gov/econ/www/servmenu.html> (released December 2005)

U.S. Census Bureau, *Statistical Abstract of the United States: 2007*

Table 1121. **Software Publishers—Estimated Revenue and Inventories: 2001 to 2004**

[In millions of dollars (105,538 represents $105,538,000,000), except percent. For taxable and tax-exempt employer firms. Covers NAICS 5112. Estimates have been adjusted to the results of the 2002 Economic Census. Based on the North American Industry Classification System, 1997; see text this section, and Section 15. Minus sign (–) indicates decrease]

Item	2001	2002	2003	2004	Percent change, 2003–04
Revenue [1]	105,538	103,506	104,721	112,262	7.2
Source of revenue:					
System software publishing, total	37,096	36,649	36,694	38,438	4.8
Operating system software	10,738	11,661	12,105	13,348	10.3
Network software	8,787	9,277	9,894	9,688	-2.1
Database management software	11,567	10,022	9,409	9,710	3.2
Development tools and programming languages software	4,330	4,118	3,766	3,950	4.9
Other systems software	1,674	1,571	1,520	1,742	14.6
Application software publishing, total	43,451	43,656	44,843	49,261	9.9
General business productivity and home use applications	19,781	20,900	22,267	25,214	13.2
Cross-industry application software	13,490	12,399	12,303	13,437	9.2
Vertical market application software	8,637	8,991	8,970	9,104	1.5
Utilities software	1,099	991	984	1,185	20.4
Other application software	442	(S)	319	321	0.6
Customization and integration of packaged software	4,713	4,693	3,910	3,649	-6.7
Information technology consulting services	6,812	5,829	5,526	5,523	-0.1
Information technology-related training services	1,451	1,366	1,031	1,139	10.4
Other services revenue	8,932	8,690	10,214	11,243	10.1
Breakdown of revenue:					
System software [1]	37,096	36,649	36,694	38,438	4.8
Personal computer software	6,709	7,884	8,571	9,570	11.7
Enterprise software	20,889	19,227	19,171	19,668	2.6
Mainframe computer software	9,498	9,085	8,504	8,762	3.0
Application software [1]	43,451	43,656	44,843	49,261	9.9
Personal computer software	14,234	15,280	16,624	17,940	7.9
Enterprise software	27,216	26,162	25,693	28,772	12.0
Mainframe computer software	2,000	1,663	2,058	2,285	11.0
Inventories at end of year	**1,947**	**2,414**	**2,109**	**1,974**	**-6.4**
Finished goods and work-in-process	1,526	1,970	1,651	1,477	-10.5
Materials, supplies, fuel, etc.	421	444	459	497	8.3

S Data do not meet publication standards.   [1] Includes other sources and types of revenue, not shown separately.

Source: U.S. Census Bureau, "2004 Service Annual Survey, Information Sector Services". See <http://www.census.gov/econ/www/servmenu.html> (released December 2005).

Table 1122. **Motion Picture and Sound Recording Industries—Estimated Revenue and Inventories: 1998 to 2004**

[In millions of dollars (60,389 represents $60,389,000,000). For taxable and tax-exempt employer firms. Estimates have been adjusted to results of the 2002 Economic Census. Based on the North American Industry Classification System, 1997; see text, this section, and Section 15]

Item	1998	1999	2000	2001	2002	2003	2004
Motion picture and recording industries (NAICS 512):							
Operating revenue	**60,389**	**66,720**	**71,560**	**72,904**	**78,250**	**83,113**	**88,267**
Total inventories	13,304	13,993	15,394	15,829	17,276	20,349	24,047
Finished goods and work-in-process	13,118	13,795	15,162	15,578	17,053	20,133	23,808
Materials, supplies, fuel, etc.	187	199	232	(S)	(S)	215	240
Motion picture and video (NAICS 5121):							
Operating revenue	47,238	52,271	55,978	57,886	62,927	67,589	71,772
Total inventories	12,887	13,588	14,908	15,327	16,748	19,824	23,481
Finished goods and work-in-process	12,753	13,445	14,748	15,155	16,598	19,706	23,358
Materials, supplies, fuel, etc.	(S)	(S)	(S)	(S)	(S)	118	123
Sound recording (NAICS 5122):							
Operating revenue	13,151	14,450	15,582	15,018	15,324	15,525	16,495
Total inventories	417	406	486	502	528	525	566
Finished goods and work-in-process	365	350	413	423	455	428	449
Materials, supplies, fuel, etc.	52	56	73	79	73	97	117

S Data do not meet publication standards.

Source: U.S. Census Bureau, "2004 Service Annual Survey, Information Sector Services". See <http://www.census.gov/econ/www/servmenu.html> (released December 2005).

Information and Communications   715

Table 1123. **Recording Media—Manufacturers' Shipments and Value: 1990 to 2005**

[865.7 represents 865,700,000. Based on reports of RIAA member companies who distributed about 84 percent of the prerecorded music in 2005. These data are supplemented by other sources. Minus sign (–) indicates returns greater than shipments]

Medium	1990	1995	2000	2001	2002	2003	2004	2005
UNIT SHIPMENTS [1] (mil.)								
Total [2,3]	865.7	1,112.7	1,079.2	968.5	859.7	798.4	958.0	1,301.8
CDs	286.5	722.9	942.5	881.9	803.3	746.0	767.0	705.4
CD singles	1.1	21.5	34.2	17.3	4.5	8.3	3.1	2.8
Cassettes	442.2	272.6	76.0	45.0	31.1	17.2	5.2	2.5
Cassette singles	87.4	70.7	1.3	–1.5	–0.5	(X)	(X)	(X)
Albums—LPs and EPs	11.7	2.2	2.2	2.3	1.7	1.5	1.4	1.0
Vinyl singles	27.6	10.2	4.8	5.5	4.4	3.8	3.5	2.3
Music video	9.2	12.6	18.2	17.7	14.7	19.9	32.8	33.8
DVD video	(X)	(X)	3.3	7.9	10.7	17.5	29.0	27.8
DVD audio	(X)	(X)	(X)	0.3	0.4	0.4	0.3	0.5
SACD [4]	(X)	(X)	(X)	(X)	(X)	1.3	0.8	0.5
Download single	(X)	(X)	(X)	(X)	(X)	(X)	139.4	366.9
Download album	(X)	(X)	(X)	(X)	(X)	(X)	4.6	13.6
Mobile [5]	(X)	(X)	(X)	(X)	(X)	(X)	(X)	170.0
Subscription	(X)	(X)	(X)	(X)	(X)	(X)	(X)	1.3
VALUE (mil. dol.)								
Total [3]	7,541.1	12,320.3	14,323.7	13,740.9	12,614.2	11,854.4	12,338.1	12,269.5
CDs	3,451.6	9,377.4	13,214.5	12,909.4	12,044.1	11,232.9	11,446.5	10,520.2
CD singles	6.0	110.9	142.7	79.4	19.6	36.0	15.0	10.9
Cassettes	3,472.4	2,303.6	626.0	363.4	209.8	108.1	23.7	13.1
Cassette singles	257.9	236.3	4.6	–5.3	–1.6	(X)	(X)	(X)
Albums—LPs and EPs	86.5	25.1	27.7	27.4	20.5	21.7	19.3	14.2
Vinyl singles	94.4	46.7	26.3	31.4	24.9	21.5	19.9	13.2
Music video	172.3	220.3	281.9	329.2	288.4	399.9	607.2	602.2
DVD video	(X)	(X)	80.3	190.7	236.3	369.6	561.0	539.8
DVD audio	(X)	(X)	(X)	6.0	8.5	8.0	6.5	11.2
SACD	(X)	(X)	(X)	(X)	(X)	26.3	16.6	10.0
Download single	(X)	(X)	(X)	(X)	(X)	(X)	138.0	363.3
Download album	(X)	(X)	(X)	(X)	(X)	(X)	45.5	135.7
Mobile [5]	(X)	(X)	(X)	(X)	(X)	(X)	(X)	421.6
Subscription	(X)	(X)	(X)	(X)	(X)	(X)	(X)	149.2

X Not applicable. [1] Net units, after returns. [2] Total number of units excludes subscriptions. [3] Includes other formats, not shown separately. [4] Super Audio CD. [5] Includes Master Ringtunes, Ringbacks, Full Length Downloads and other mobile.

Source: Recording Industry Association of America, Washington, DC, *2005 Year-end Statistics* and earlier issues (copyright). See Internet site <http://www.riaa.com> (accessed 24 July 2006).

Table 1124. **Profile of Consumer Expenditures for Sound Recordings—Percent Distribution: 1990 to 2003**

[In percent. Based on monthly telephone surveys of the population 10 years old and over]

Item	1990	1995	2000	2001	2002	2003	2004	2005
Total [1]	100.0	100.0	100.0	100.0	100.0	100.0	100.0	100.0
Age: 10 to 14 years	7.6	8.0	8.9	8.5	8.9	8.6	9.4	8.6
15 to 19 years	18.3	17.1	12.9	13.0	13.3	11.4	11.9	11.9
20 to 24 years	16.5	15.3	12.5	12.2	11.5	10.0	9.2	12.7
25 to 29 years	14.6	12.3	10.6	10.9	9.4	10.9	10.0	12.1
30 to 34 years	13.2	12.1	9.8	10.3	10.8	10.1	10.4	11.3
35 to 39 years	10.2	10.8	10.6	10.2	9.8	11.2	10.7	8.8
40 to 44 years	7.8	7.5	9.6	10.3	9.9	10.0	10.9	9.2
45 years and over	11.1	16.1	23.8	23.7	25.5	26.6	26.4	25.5
Sex: Male	54.4	53.0	50.6	48.8	49.4	49.1	49.5	51.8
Female	45.6	47.0	49.4	51.2	50.6	50.9	50.5	48.2
Sales outlet:								
Record store	69.8	52.0	42.4	42.5	36.8	33.2	32.5	39.4
Other store	18.5	28.2	40.8	42.4	50.7	52.8	53.8	32.0
Tape/record club	8.9	14.3	7.6	6.1	4.0	4.1	4.4	8.5
Ad or 800 number	2.5	4.0	2.4	3.0	2.0	1.5	1.7	2.4
Internet [2]	(NA)	(NA)	3.2	2.9	3.4	5.0	5.9	8.2
Digital download	(NA)	(NA)	(NA)	(NA)	(NA)	(NA)	(NA)	6.0
Music type: [3]								
Rock	36.1	33.5	24.8	24.4	24.7	25.2	23.9	31.5
Rap/Hip Hop	8.5	6.7	12.9	11.4	13.8	13.3	12.1	13.3
R&B/Urban	11.6	11.3	9.7	10.6	11.2	10.6	11.3	10.2
Country	9.6	16.7	10.7	10.5	10.7	10.4	13.0	12.5
Pop	13.7	10.1	11.0	12.1	9.0	8.9	10.0	8.1
Religious	2.5	3.1	4.8	6.7	6.7	5.8	6.0	5.3
Media type: CDs	31.1	65.0	89.3	89.2	90.5	87.8	90.3	87.0
Cassettes	54.7	25.1	4.9	3.4	2.4	2.2	1.7	1.1
Singles (all types)	8.7	7.5	2.5	2.4	1.9	2.4	2.4	2.7
Music video [4]	(NA)	0.9	0.8	1.1	0.7	0.6	1.0	0.7
DVD audio	(NA)	(NA)	(NA)	1.1	1.3	2.7	1.7	0.8
Digital download	(NA)	(NA)	(NA)	0.2	0.5	1.3	0.9	5.7
SACD [5]	(NA)	(NA)	(NA)	(NA)	(NA)	0.5	0.8	1.2
Vinyl LPs	4.7	0.5	0.5	0.6	0.7	0.7	0.9	0.7

NA Not available. [1] Percent distributions exclude nonresponses and responses of "Don't know." Some types of music and sales outlets are not shown separately. [2] Excludes record club purchases over the Internet. [3] As classified by respondent. [4] Beginning 2001 includes video DVDs. [5] Super Audio CD.

Source: Recording Industry Association of America, Washington, DC, *2005 Consumer Profile* and earlier issues (copyright). See Internet site <http://www.riaa.com> (accessed 24 July 2006).

716 Information and Communications

Table 1125. **Radio and Television Broadcasting—Estimated Revenue and Expenses: 2002 to 2004**

[In millions of dollars (48,589 represents $48,589,000,000). For taxable and tax-exempt employer firms. Estimates have been adjusted to the results of the 2002 Economic Census. Based on the North American Industry Classification System, 1997; see text, this section, and Section 15]

Item	Total (NAICS 5131)			Radio broadcasting (NAICS 51311)			TV broadcasting (NAICS 51312)		
	2002	2003	2004	2002	2003	2004	2002	2003	2004
Operating revenue	**48,589**	**48,708**	**52,093**	**15,603**	**15,820**	**16,494**	**32,987**	**32,888**	**35,599**
Station time sales.	29,605	29,662	30,999	12,619	12,538	12,803	16,986	17,124	18,196
Network compensation.	448	430	400	101	94	93	347	336	307
National/regional advertising	9,976	9,683	10,209	2,922	2,834	2,879	7,053	6,849	7,330
Local advertising revenue.	19,181	19,549	20,390	9,596	9,610	9,830	9,586	9,939	10,560
Network time sales.	14,250	14,257	15,580	1,310	1,349	1,401	12,940	12,907	14,179
Program rights.	302	278	265	290	268	258	(S)	(S)	(S)
Production and postproduction services . . .	63	81	130	(S)	(S)	(S)	(S)	(S)	(S)
Public and noncommercial programming rights	1,919	2,029	2,099	(S)	(S)	(S)	1,317	1,366	1,405
Other operating services revenue	2,451	2,402	3,021	758	994	1,329	1,693	1,407	1,692
Operating expenses [1]	**38,209**	**38,212**	**40,753**	**11,972**	**12,187**	**13,077**	**26,238**	**26,025**	**27,676**
Annual payroll	11,281	11,587	12,016	4,816	4,780	5,100	6,465	6,807	6,916
Employer contributions to employee benefit plans	1,415	1,517	1,665	621	594	636	795	923	1,029
Contract labor	319	298	251	225	209	162	94	88	88
Total materials and supplies	(NA)	402	497	(NA)	161	283	(NA)	241	214
Total purchased services [1]	(NA)	5,801	6,319	(NA)	2,896	2,979	(NA)	2,905	3,340
Data processing and other computer services.	(NA)	109	95	(NA)	12	19	(NA)	97	76
Communication services.	340	391	372	167	187	175	173	204	196
Advertising and promotional services . . .	1,522	1,787	2,028	690	846	1,089	832	941	939
Electricity.	289	321	313	135	141	135	154	179	178
Prrofessional services [2]	(NA)	573	730	(NA)	269	344	(NA)	304	386
Lease and rental payments.	837	763	808	377	380	408	460	383	400
Broadcast rights and music license fees . . .	11,468	10,929	12,215	701	747	869	10,766	10,182	11,347
Depreciation	2,704	2,647	2,570	967	1,099	1,010	1,737	1,548	1,560
Taxes and license fees	691	759	673	483	513	408	207	246	266
Other	6,193	4,271	4,547	2,280	1,188	1,630	3,913	3,083	2,917

NA Not available.   S Data do not meet publication standards.   [1] Includes other expenses, not shown separately.
[2] Management consulting, administrative, and other.

Source: U.S. Census Bureau, "2004 Service Annual Survey, Information Sector Services." See <http://www.census.gov/econ/www /servmenu.html> (released December 2005).

Table 1126. **Cable and Pay TV—Summary: 1975 to 2005**

[9,800 represents 9,800,000. Cable TV for calendar year. Pay TV as of December 31 of year shown]

Year	Cable TV				Pay TV					
	Avg. basic sub-scribers (1,000)	Avg. monthly basic rate (dol.)	Revenue [1] (mil. dol.)		Units [2] (1,000)			Monthly rate (dol.)		
			Total	Basic	Total pay [3]	Pay cable	Non-cable delivered premium	All pay weighted average [3]	Pay cable	Non-cable delivered premium
1975	9,800	6.50	804	764	194	194	(NA)	(NA)	7.85	(NA)
1980	17,500	7.69	2,609	1,615	8,581	7,336	(NA)	8.91	8.62	(NA)
1985	35,440	9.73	8,831	4,138	29,885	29,418	(NA)	10.29	10.25	(NA)
1990	50,520	16.78	17,582	10,174	39,902	39,751	(NA)	10.35	10.30	(NA)
1992	54,300	19.08	21,079	12,433	40,893	36,879	(NA)	10.29	10.17	(NA)
1993	56,200	[4]19.39	22,809	13,528	42,010	37,113	(NA)	9.27	9.11	(NA)
1994	58,373	21.62	21,531	15,144	47,478	42,528	4,950	8.19	8.33	6.99
1995	60,550	23.07	24,137	16,763	55,723	46,798	8,925	8.29	8.54	6.99
1996	62,300	24.41	26,195	18,249	63,705	49,728	13,977	7.98	8.12	7.50
1997	63,600	26.48	28,931	20,213	72,785	51,933	20,852	8.31	8.43	8.00
1998	64,650	27.81	31,174	21,574	80,605	55,280	25,325	8.58	8.74	8.22
1999	65,500	28.92	34,095	22,732	88,455	59,005	29,450	8.73	8.85	8.50
2000	66,250	30.37	37,070	24,142	102,590	65,918	36,672	8.69	8.81	8.48
2001	66,732	32.87	42,577	26,324	115,325	75,433	39,892	8.95	9.10	8.66
2002	66,472	34.71	48,733	27,690	118,575	77,292	41,283	9.19	9.29	9.00
2003	66,050	36.59	54,352	29,000	119,927	78,939	40,988	9.37	9.45	9.23
2004	65,727	38.14	60,008	30,080	122,248	80,753	41,495	10.03	10.11	9.88
2005, est. . .	65,337	39.63	66,414	31,075	125,662	81,128	44,534	10.08	10.16	9.93

NA Not available.   [1] Includes installation revenue, subscriber revenue, and nonsubscriber revenue; excludes telephony and high-speed access.   [2] Individual program services sold to subscribers.   [3] Includes multipoint distribution service (MDS), satellite TV (STV), multipoint multichannel distribution service (MMDS), satellite master antenna TV (SMATV), C-band satellite, and DBS satellite. Includes average pay unit price based on data for major premium pay movie services.   [4] Weighted average representing 8 months of unregulated basic rate and 4 months of FCC rolled-back rate.

Source: Kagan Research, LLC. From the *Broadband Cable Financial Databook* 2004, 2005 (copyright); *Cable Program Investor,* December 16, 2004, March 30, 2006, and various other publications.

Information and Communications 717

Table 1127. **Cable Networks and Program Distribution Services—Estimated Revenue and Expenses: 2001 to 2004**

[In millions of dollars (76,760 represents $76,760,000,000). For taxable and tax-exempt employer firms. Covers NAICS 5132. Estimates have been adjusted to the results of the 2002 Economic Census. Based on the North American Industry Classification System; see text, this section, and Section 15. Minus sign (–) indicates decrease]

Item	2001	2002	2003	2004	Percent change, 2003–04
Operating revenue [1]	76,760	83,082	93,314	104,690	12.2
Air time (advertising)	12,798	13,441	14,951	16,548	10.7
Specialty programming service	13,121	14,835	16,471	18,090	9.8
Basic programming service	32,839	35,077	38,434	43,699	13.7
Premium cable programming packages	5,327	5,468	5,130	5,548	8.1
Pay-per-view service	1,968	2,178	2,403	2,661	10.7
Program distribution equipment sales and rentals	1,817	1,813	1,948	2,205	13.2
Other program distribution related services	2,404	2,357	2,388	2,577	7.9
Internet access services	2,364	3,743	6,702	8,582	28.0
Basic fixed local telephony	862	891	1,449	1,452	0.3
Operating expenses [1]	72,893	71,750	76,817	83,602	8.8
Annual payroll	10,945	11,011	11,686	12,600	7.8
Employer contributions to employee benefit plans	2,074	1,950	2,304	2,515	9.2
Contract labor	(NA)	983	1,444	1,550	7.4
Total materials and supplies	(NA)	(NA)	721	792	9.9
Total purchased services [1]	(NA)	(NA)	7,554	8,172	8.2
Communication services	(NA)	622	900	863	–4.1
Advertising and promotional services	2,414	2,802	2,990	3,276	9.5
Electricity	(NA)	348	348	363	4.1
Professional services [2]	(NA)	(NA)	670	789	17.8
Lease and rental payments	1,091	1,007	1,157	1,232	6.4
Program and production costs	22,927	25,266	28,909	32,247	11.5
Depreciation	17,257	13,029	14,478	15,341	6.0
Taxes and license fees	(NA)	900	1,104	1,136	3.0
Other	14,465	11,697	8,619	9,249	7.3

NA Not available.   [1] Includes other revenues and expenses, not shown separately.   [2] Management consulting, administration, and other.

Source: U.S. Census Bureau, "2004 Service Annual Survey, Information Sector Services". See <http://www.census.gov/econ/www /servmenu.html> (released December 2005).

Table 1128. **Telecommunications—Estimated Revenue and Expenses: 2002 to 2004**

[In millions of dollars (353,936 represents $353,936,000,000). For taxable and tax-exempt employer firms. Estimates have been adjusted to the results of the 2002 Economic Census. Based on the North American Industry Classification System, 1997; see text, this section, and Section 15. See Table 1129 for cellular and other wireless telecommunications carriers, NAICS 513322]

Item	Telecommunications (NAICS 5133)			Wired telecommunications carriers (NAICS 51331)		
	2002	2003	2004	2002	2003	2004
Operating revenue	353,936	350,976	356,113	237,697	221,231	211,176
Fixed total [1]	162,135	147,534	136,002	153,141	139,100	128,282
Fixed local	80,148	75,021	73,928	78,542	73,432	72,336
Basic service	66,905	62,687	61,093	65,486	61,280	59,684
Fixed long-distance	55,843	48,240	40,280	52,009	44,602	36,841
Outbound service	44,938	39,640	33,987	41,818	36,461	31,017
Dedicated network services	11,702	10,493	9,525	9,261	8,256	7,629
Data transmission services	10,526	9,816	8,835	9,847	9,128	8,204
Mobile total	89,690	99,672	111,450	(S)	(S)	(S)
Mobile telephony services	85,728	96,142	108,401	(X)	(X)	(X)
Local access and use	63,204	73,469	81,273	(X)	(X)	(X)
Carrier services	60,506	59,212	59,792	55,608	54,024	54,617
Network access	54,614	53,349	53,768	51,786	49,917	50,547
Other telecommunications services	14,436	14,448	14,440	8,890	7,587	6,982
Other services revenue	27,169	30,110	34,430	18,251	18,810	19,997
Operating expenses	307,195	302,642	314,103	203,329	193,199	198,315
Annual payroll	56,691	56,874	53,826	42,557	41,380	36,941
Employer contributions to social security and other supplemental benefits	14,964	16,365	18,570	12,139	12,899	14,106
Contract labor	4,614	4,885	4,946	2,636	2,719	2,921
Total materials and supplies	(NA)	6,068	6,158	(NA)	4,364	4,447
Total purchased services [1]	(NA)	45,259	47,930	(NA)	26,881	27,544
Communication services	6,874	6,070	5,903	(S)	3,592	3,055
Advertising and promotional services	8,568	8,686	9,525	3,538	3,210	3,085
Professional services [2]	(NA)	6,303	6,947	(NA)	4,575	5,028
Lease and rental payments	9,306	9,502	9,901	4,752	4,440	4,311
Access charges	44,237	42,205	42,710	35,257	33,379	33,635
Depreciation	60,311	62,234	67,313	41,106	39,881	44,254
Universal service contributions and other similar charges	4,048	3,670	3,945	3,327	2,731	2,677
Taxes and license fees	5,876	6,585	6,597	5,004	5,603	5,318
Other	69,051	58,496	62,108	(S)	23,363	(S)

NA Not available.   S Data do not meet publication standards.   X Not applicable.   [1] Includes other revenue sources and expenses, not shown separately.   [2] Includes management consulting, administration, and other professional services.

Source: U.S. Census Bureau, "2004 Service Annual Survey, Information Sector Services". See <http://www.census.gov/econ /www/servmenu.html> (released December 2005).

718 Information and Communications

Table 1129. Cellular and Other Wireless Telecommunications Carriers—Estimated Revenue and Expenses: 2001 to 2004

[In millions of dollars (82,521 represents $82,521,000,000), except percent. For taxable and tax-exempt employer firms. Covers NAICS 513322. Estimates have been adjusted to the results of the 2002 Economic Census. Based on the North American Industry Classification System, 1997; see text, this section and Section 15. See Table 1128 for telecommunications total and wired carriers (NAICS 5133 and 51331). Minus sign (–) indicates decrease]

Item	2001	2002	2003	2004	Percent change, 2003–04
Operating revenue	82,521	96,530	109,933	125,693	14.3
Mobile total	71,531	83,879	94,818	106,989	12.8
Mobile telephone services [1]	70,903	83,319	94,260	106,232	12.7
Local access and use	52,349	62,489	72,830	80,624	10.7
Mobile long distance	5,127	6,073	5,402	6,972	29.1
Mobile all distance	8,669	10,158	10,799	12,078	11.8
Messaging services	441	351	386	217	–43.6
Mobile dispatch services	187	209	(S)	(S)	(S)
Carrier services	2,868	2,738	2,415	2,340	–3.1
Network access	1,149	1,197	1,334	1,029	–22.9
Other telecommunications services	2,515	3,181	3,890	4,300	10.5
Other services revenue	5,607	6,733	8,810	12,064	36.9
Operating expenses	75,587	86,636	92,018	99,729	8.4
Annual payroll	11,164	10,440	11,967	13,513	12.9
Employer contributions to social security and other supplemental benefits	2,155	2,348	2,930	3,886	32.6
Contract labor	(NA)	1,729	1,822	(S)	(S)
Total materials and supplies	(NA)	(NA)	1,447	1,391	–3.9
Total purchased services [1]	(NA)	(NA)	14,801	16,951	14.5
Data processing and other computer services	(NA)	(NA)	426	481	13.1
Communication services	(NA)	1,335	1,729	2,165	25.2
Advertising and promotional services	4,301	4,727	5,187	6,103	17.7
Electricity	(NA)	246	277	325	17.4
Professional services [2]	(NA)	(NA)	1,197	1,415	18.2
Lease and rental payments	3,137	3,572	4,216	4,887	15.9
Access charges	6,902	6,564	6,795	6,746	–0.7
Depreciation	16,739	16,240	19,313	20,606	6.7
Universal service contributions and other similar charges	651	616	840	1,174	39.6
Taxes and license fees	(NA)	681	769	1,101	43.2
Other	27,739	31,872	31,333	32,582	4.0

NA Not available. S Data do not meet publication standards. [1] Includes other revenue source and expenses, not shown separately. [2] Includes management consulting, administration, and other professional services.

Source: U.S. Census Bureau, "2004 Service Annual Survey, Information Sector Services". See <http://www.census.gov/econ/www/servmenu.html> (released December 2005).

Table 1130. Telecommunications Industry—Carriers and Revenue: 1995 to 2003

[Revenue in millions of dollars (190,076 represents $190,076,000,000). Data based on carrier filings to the FCC. Because of reporting changes, data beginning 2000 are not strictly comparable with previous years; see source for details]

Category	Carriers					Telecommunications revenue				
	1995	2000	2001	2002 [1]	2003	1995	2000	2001	2002	2003
Total [2]	3,058	4,879	5,001	4,390	4,636	190,076	292,762	301,799	292,341	291,123
Local service providers	1,675	2,641	2,755	2,531	2,681	103,792	128,075	133,502	130,941	126,860
Incumbent local exchange carriers (ILECs)	1,347	1,335	1,335	1,310	1,303	102,820	116,158	117,885	114,990	109,480
Pay telephone providers	271	699	751	606	605	349	972	836	641	523
Competitors of ILECs	57	607	669	615	773	623	10,945	14,781	15,310	16,857
CAPs and CLECs [3]	57	479	511	451	601	623	9,814	12,998	13,043	15,509
Local resellers	(4)	105	132	100	100	(4)	879	1,393	1,538	721
Other local exchange carriers	(4)	23	26	64	72	(4)	11	329	406	338
Private carriers	(4)	(4)	(4)	(4)	(4)	(4)	39	15	281	267
Shared tenant service providers	(4)	(4)	(4)	(4)	(4)	(4)	202	46	42	22
Wireless service providers [5]	930	1,430	1,306	927	939	18,627	63,280	74,596	80,467	89,342
Telephony [6]	792	783	670	422	413	17,208	59,823	71,887	78,568	88,168
Paging service providers	138	425	425	346	347	(4)	3,102	2,197	1,473	1,007
Toll service providers	453	808	940	932	1,026	76,447	101,407	93,702	80,934	74,920
Interexchange carriers	130	212	233	229	232	70,938	87,311	81,272	68,146	61,246
Operator service providers	25	20	19	18	17	500	635	611	554	567
Prepaid service providers	8	23	27	27	50	(4)	727	133	460	812
Satellite service carriers	(4)	25	34	33	40	(4)	336	373	406	663
Toll resellers	260	493	558	574	642	4,220	10,641	8,797	9,279	9,294
Other toll carriers	30	35	69	51	45	773	1,758	2,516	2,089	2,339

[1] Counts dropped in 2002 because many affiliated filers were allowed to file consolidated reports. [2] Revenue data include adjustments, not shown separately. For 1995, revenue data include some nontelecommunications revenue, formerly reported as local exchange wireless revenue. [3] Competitive access providers (CAPs) and competitive local exchange carriers (CLECs). [4] Data not available separately. [5] Beginning 2000, includes specialized mobile radio services and other services, not shown separately. [6] Cellular service, personal communications service, and specialized mobile radio.

Source: U.S. Federal Communications Commission, Trends in Telephone Service, annual.

Information and Communications 719

Table 1131. **Telephone Systems—Summary: 1985 to 2003**

[**112 represents 112,000,000.** Covers principal carriers filing annual reports with Federal Communications Commission]

Item	Unit	1985	1990	1995	1998	1999	2000	2001 [1]	2002 [1]	2003 [1]
LOCAL EXCHANGE CARRIERS [2]										
Carriers [3]	Number .	55	51	53	52	52	52	30	29	28
Access lines	Millions .	112	130	166	205	228	245	253	262	268
Business access lines	Millions .	31	36	46	57	57	58	54	54	49
Residential access lines	Millions .	79	89	101	110	115	115	112	103	99
Other access lines (public, mobile, special)	Millions .	2	6	19	38	55	72	87	105	120
Number of local calls (originating) . . .	Billions .	365	402	484	544	554	537	515	459	425
Number of toll calls (originating)	Billions .	(NA)	63	94	97	102	106	98	90	81
Gross book cost of plant	Bil. dol. .	191	240	284	325	342	362	360	367	368
Depreciation and amortization reserves	Bil. dol. .	49	89	127	163	176	190	194	210	222
Net plant	Bil. dol. .	142	151	157	161	166	172	166	157	146
Total assets	Bil. dol. .	162	180	197	200	204	214	208	195	182
Total stockholders equity	Bil. dol. .	63	74	72	70	67	72	66	58	47
Operating revenues	Bil. dol. .	73	84	96	108	113	117	109	103	108
Local revenues	Bil. dol. .	32	37	46	55	58	60	55	51	51
Operating expenses [4]	Bil. dol. .	48	62	72	78	79	81	77	79	83
Net operating income [5]	Bil. dol. .	13	14	14	18	20	20	19	23	9
Net income	Bil. dol. .	9	11	11	12	13	15	11	8	4
Employees	(1,000). .	(NA)	569	447	436	436	434	386	333	303
Compensation of employees	Bil. dol. .	(NA)	23	21	23	24	24	23	23	23
Average monthly residential local telephone rate [6]	Dollars. .	(NA)	19.24	20.01	19.76	19.93	20.78	22.62	23.38	24.31
Average monthly single-line business telephone rate [6]	Dollars. .	(NA)	41.21	41.80	41.29	41.21	41.80	42.43	43.59	43.75
LONG DISTANCE CARRIERS										
Number of carriers with presubscribed lines	Number .	(NA)	325	583	(NA)	(NA)	(NA)	(NA)	(NA)	(NA)
Number of presubscribed lines	Millions .	(NA)	132	153	(NA)	(NA)	(NA)	(NA)	(NA)	(NA)
Total toll service revenues [7]	Bil. dol. .	55	67	90	105	108	110	99	84	77
Interstate switched access minutes . .	Bil. min. .	167	307	432	519	553	567	538	486	444
INTERNATIONAL TELEPHONE SERVICE [8]										
Number of U.S. billed calls	Millions .	425	984	2,830	4,477	5,305	5,742	6,265	5,926	7,350
Number of U.S. billed minutes	Millions .	3,446	8,030	15,889	24,250	28,515	30,135	33,287	35,063	42,664
U.S. billed revenues	Mil. dol. .	3,487	8,059	14,335	14,726	14,980	14,909	11,380	9,773	8,944
U.S. carrier revenue net of settlements with foreign carriers . . .	Mil. dol. .	2,332	5,188	9,397	10,242	10,379	10,982	8,034	6,931	5,964
Revenue from private-line service . . .	Mil. dol. .	172	201	514	921	1,216	1,480	1,467	988	620
Revenue from resale service	Mil. dol. .	(NA)	607	1,756	4,798	4,528	7,600	5,341	4,871	5,420

NA Not available.   [1] Beginning 2001, detailed financial data only filed by regional Bell-operating companies. Access lines and calls reported by 50 reporting companies.   [2] Gross operating revenues, gross plant, and total assets of reporting carriers estimated at more than 90 percent of total industry. New accounting rules became effective in 1990; prior years may not be directly comparable on a one-to-one basis. Includes Virgin Islands, and prior to 1995, Puerto Rico.   [3] The reporting threshold for carriers is $100 million in annual operating revenue.   [4] Excludes taxes.   [5] After tax deductions.   [6] Based on surveys conducted by FCC.   [7] Series revised to include all toll revenues: toll, wireless, ILECs, carriers (ILECs) and competitive local exchange carriers (CLECs).   [8] Beginning 1995, data are for all U.S. points, and include calls to and from Alaska, Hawaii, Puerto Rico, Guam, the U.S. Virgin Islands, and offshore U.S. points. Beginning 1995, carriers first started reporting traffic to and from Canada and Mexico. Data for Canada and Mexico in prior years are staff estimates.

Source: U.S. Federal Communications Commission, *Statistics of Communications Common Carriers,* annual; *Trends in Telephone Service,* annual; and *Trends in the International Telecommunications Industry,* annual.

Table 1132. Cellular Telecommunications Industry: 1990 to 2005

[Calendar year data, except as noted (**5,283 represents 5,283,000**). Based on a survey sent to all facilities-based cellular, personal communications services, and enhanced special mobile radio (ESMR) systems. The number of operational systems beginning 2000 differs from that reported for previous periods as a result of the consolidated operation of ESMR systems in a broader service area instead of by a city-to-city basis]

Item	Unit	1990	1995	2000	2001	2002	2003	2004	2005
Systems	Number. . .	751	1,627	2,440	2,587	2,846	3,123	(NA)	(NA)
Subscribers	1,000	5,283	33,786	109,478	128,375	140,766	158,722	182,140	207,896
Cell sites [1]	Number. . .	5,616	22,663	104,288	127,540	139,338	162,986	175,725	183,689
Employees	Number. . .	21,382	68,165	184,449	203,580	192,410	205,629	226,016	233,067
Service revenue	Mil. dol. . .	4,548	19,081	52,466	65,016	76,508	87,624	102,121	113,538
Roamer revenue [2]	Mil. dol. . .	456	2,542	3,883	3,936	3,896	3,766	4,210	3,786
Capital investment [3]	Mil. dol. . .	6,282	24,080	89,624	105,030	126,922	145,867	173,794	199,025
Average monthly bill [4]	Dollars . . .	80.90	51.00	45.27	47.37	48.40	49.91	50.64	49.98
Average length of call [4] . . .	Minutes . . .	2.20	2.15	2.56	2.74	2.73	2.87	3.05	3.00

[1] The basic geographic unit of a wireless PCS or cellular system. A city or county is divided into smaller "cells," each of which is equipped with a low-powered radio transmitter/receiver. The cells can vary in size depending upon terrain, capacity demands, etc. By controlling the transmission power, the radio frequencies assigned to one cell can be limited to the boundaries of that cell. When a wireless PCS or cellular phone moves from one cell toward another, a computer at the Switching Office monitors the movement and at the proper time, transfers or hands off the phone call to the new cell and another radio frequency.   [2] Service revenue generated by subscribers' calls outside of their system areas.   [3] 2005 Cumulative capital investment figure reached by summing cumulative capital investment through year-end 2004 with reported incremental capital investment for 2005.   [4] As of December 31.

Source: Cellular Telecommunications & Internet Association, Washington, DC, *Semi-annual Wireless Survey* (copyright).

720   Information and Communications

Table 1133. **Information Services and Data Processing Services—Estimated Revenue: 2001 to 2004**

[In millions of dollars (76,531 represents $76,531,000,000), except percent. For taxable and tax-exempt employer firms. Estimates have been adjusted to results of the 2002 Economic Census. Based on the 1997 North American Industry Classification System; see text, this section, and Section 15. Minus sign (–) indicates decrease]

Item	2001	2002	2003	2004	Percent change, 2003–04
Total (NAICS 514)........................	76,531	81,946	84,464	93,572	10.8
News syndicates (NAICS 51411):					
Revenue...........................	1,885	1,844	1,873	1,972	5.3
Fees from supplying information...............	1,768	1,768	1,756	1,883	7.2
Other services revenue.....................	117	76	117	89	–23.7
Libraries and archives (NAICS 51412):					
Revenue [1]...........................	1,518	1,649	1,692	1,879	11.1
Subsidies, contributions, gifts, and grants..........	1,104	1,231	1,204	1,300	7.9
Fees and dues from providing access to collections. . .	67	65	72	87	20.5
Online information services (NAICS 514191):					
Revenue...........................	19,579	18,711	19,157	20,202	5.5
Internet access services....................	10,339	10,596	10,665	10,585	–0.8
Advertising............................	2,846	2,320	2,137	2,425	13.5
Web site hosting........................	679	592	586	512	–12.7
Internet backbone services	(S)	(S)	(S)	(S)	(S)
Internet telecommunications services	(S)	(S)	(S)	(S)	(S)
Information technology consulting services.........	(S)	(S)	(S)	(S)	(S)
Information technology design and development	(S)	(S)	(S)	(S)	(S)
Application service provisioning	(S)	(S)	(S)	(S)	(S)
Business process management	(S)	(S)	(S)	(S)	(S)
Video and audio streaming services	(S)	(S)	(S)	(S)	(S)
Other services revenue.....................	3,585	3,494	3,893	4,706	20.9
All other information services (NAICS 514199):					
Revenue [1]...........................	6,178	6,654	8,472	12,189	43.9
Advertising............................	2,770	2,336	2,221	(S)	(S)
Web hosting and design	(S)	79	81	(S)	(S)
Information search services..................	1,183	1,409	2,262	2,726	20.5
Stock photo services	1,192	1,244	1,308	1,657	26.7
Video and audio streaming services	(S)	55	40	66	64.2
Data processing services (NAICS 5142):					
Revenue............................	47,370	53,089	53,271	57,330	7.6
Business process management	16,004	20,188	20,884	22,908	9.7
Information and document transformation..........	1,187	1,249	(S)	1,510	(S)
Information technology design and development	13,703	13,484	12,774	12,284	–3.8
Data storage services......................	224	215	(S)	84	(S)
Data management services..................	3,248	4,335	3,889	3,830	–1.5
Collocation services	(S)	(S)	(S)	(S)	(S)
Information technology consulting services.........	(S)	(S)	(S)	(S)	(S)
Web site hosting	(S)	(S)	(S)	(S)	(S)
Software publishing	774	746	770	912	18.4
Rental and leasing of computer hardware	(S)	(S)	(S)	(S)	(S)
Application service provisioning	976	1,069	1,179	1,308	10.9
Video and audio streaming services	43	40	(S)	(S)	(S)
Other services revenue....................	8,504	8,741	9,385	11,197	19.3

S Data do not meet publication standards.   [1] Includes other sources of revenue, not shown separately.

Source: U.S. Census Bureau, "2004 Service Annual Survey, Information Sector Services". See <http://www.census.gov/econ/www/servmenu.html> (released December 2005)

Table 1134. **Academic Libraries—Summary: 2000**

[For fiscal year 193,963 represents 193,963,000. For 2- and 4-year degree-granting institutions. Based on the Academic Libraries Survey; see source for details]

Item	Number of libraries	Circulation [1] (1,000)	Gate count [2] (1,000)	Volumes held [3] (1,000)	Staff [4] Total	Staff [4] Librarians (percent)	Expenditures Total (mil. dol.)	Expenditures Salary [5] (percent)	Percent with access from within library to— Electronic catalog	Percent with access from within library to— Internet
Total..............	3,527	193,963	16,457	913,547	95,665	26.3	5,026	50.1	93.7	98.6
Control: Public...........	1,566	127,848	10,890	544,917	58,277	25.6	3,080	51.5	98.9	99.6
Private	1,961	66,115	5,567	368,630	37,388	27.4	1,946	47.9	88.9	97.8
Level: [6]										
4-year degree and above [7].	2,148	166,442	12,563	856,414	81,800	25.9	4,473	48.0	95.6	98.7
Doctorate...........	568	117,186	7,449	605,978	55,090	24.9	3,284	46.6	98.0	98.6
Master's............	884	34,228	3,667	179,758	19,193	27.3	859	52.4	96.1	99.1
Bachelor's	660	12,814	1,278	66,740	6,887	28.8	286	51.7	92.4	98.2
Less than 4-year........	1,379	27,521	3,894	57,133	13,864	28.9	553	66.6	90.6	98.5
Enrollment: [4]										
Less than 1,500	1,910	25,131	2,982	117,713	14,385	30.2	596	53.4	87.9	97.6
1,500 to 4,999	1,051	39,563	4,395	176,512	22,355	27.5	1,041	53.0	99.4	99.8
5,000 or more	566	129,268	9,079	619,323	58,925	24.9	3,389	48.6	99.8	99.6

[1] Includes reserves.   [2] In a typical week.   [3] At end of year.   [4] Full-time equivalent.   [5] Salary and wages.   [6] Level of highest degree offered.   [7] Includes 36 institutions granting "other" degrees, not shown separately.

Source: U.S. National Center for Education Statistics, *Academic Libraries: 2000*, NCES 2004-317, November, 2003.

Information and Communications 721

Table 1135. **Public Libraries by Selected Characteristics: 2003**

[8,741 represents $8,741,000,000. Based on survey of public libraries. Data are for public libraries in the 50 states and the District of Columbia. The response rates for these items are between 98 and 100 percent]

Population of service area	Number of— Public libraries	Number of— Stationary outlets [1]	Operating income— Total (mil. dol.) [2]	Operating income— Source (percent) State govern- ment	Operating income— Source (percent) Local govern- ment	Paid staff [3] Total	Paid staff [3] Librarians with ALA-MLS [4]	Public use Internet terminals, average per stationary outlet
Total	9,211	16,541	8,741	10.9	80.0	136,172	30,479	9.5
1,000,000 or more . . .	25	1,029	1,306	8.4	78.2	16,342	4,580	16.5
500,000 to 999,000. . .	52	1,104	1,342	13.7	78.0	18,549	4,798	16.2
250,000 to 499,999. . .	97	1,108	1,038	10.6	82.5	15,519	3,781	13.7
100,000 to 249,999. . .	329	1,981	1,417	10.2	82.4	22,367	4,881	12.0
50,000 to 99,999 . . .	531	1,602	1,103	12.9	79.8	17,853	3,930	12.1
25,000 to 49,999	935	1,741	1,075	11.1	81.3	17,883	4,042	10.6
10,000 to 24,999	1,772	2,282	906	10.5	79.8	15,782	3,190	8.7
5,000 to 9,999	1,463	1,626	319	10.7	77.3	6,337	914	6.3
2,500 to 4,999	1,326	1,369	134	6.1	76.2	2,932	239	4.8
1,000 to 2,499	1,649	1,664	79	5.4	71.5	1,991	104	3.4
Fewer than 1,000 . . .	1,032	1,035	21	6.2	66.8	618	20	2.5

[1] The sum of central and branch libraries. The total number of central libraries was 9,062; the total of branch libraries was 7,479. [2] Includes income from the federal government (0.5%) and other sources (8.6%), not shown separately. [3] Full-time equivalents. [4] Librarians with master's degrees from a graduate library education program accredited by the American Library Association (ALA). Total librarians, including those without ALA-MLS, were 45,115.

Source: U.S. National Center for Education Statistics, *Public Libraries in the United States: 2003,* NCES 2005-363, September 2005.

Table 1136. **Public Library Use of the Internet: 2004**

[In percent, except number of outlets. As of spring. Based on sample survey; see source for details]

Item	Total	Metropolitan status [1] Urban	Metropolitan status [1] Sub- urban	Metropolitan status [1] Rural	Poverty status [2] Less than 20 percent	Poverty status [2] 20 to 40 percent	Poverty status [2] More than 40 percent
All libraries' outlets [3]	16,192	2,868	5,270	8,054	13,579	2,432	181
Connected to the Internet	99.6	99.7	99.7	99.5	99.7	99.2	100.0
Connected with public access.	98.9	98.5	99.4	98.7	99.0	96.3	98.1
Average number of workstations.	10.4	17.3	13.0	6.7	9.7	12.5	27.2
Speed of access: [4]							
128kbps or less	12.8	5.6	6.5	18.6	12.1	16.6	18.0
129kbps–1.5mbps	45.2	51.7	46.1	42.7	45.1	45.6	49.0
Greater than 1.5mbps	20.3	33.0	25.9	13.2	19.3	25.4	23.5
Public access Internet content or service filtering/blocking:							
The library does not filter.	58.2	68.3	58.1	56.6	58.7	53.8	62.3
Each public access workstation	16.7	10.4	14.1	19.2	16.5	19.5	7.9
Entire network in the library	13.4	16.3	13.1	13.0	12.7	19.3	21.8
All computers due to local community network with a public school.	2.6	0.9	1.6	3.5	2.7	2.6	(NA)
All computers due to library consortium	6.2	5.4	12.3	3.2	6.7	2.2	7.9

NA Not available. [1] Urban = inside central city; Suburban = in metro area, outside of a central city; Rural = outside a metro area. [2] Determined by the 2000 poverty status of the service area of the outlet. [3] Central libraries and branches; excludes bookmobiles. [4] Less than 56kbps accounts for 1.7 percent of public libraries connected to the Internet. "Don't know" responses are 21 percent total.

Source: Information Use Management and Policy Institute, College of Information, Florida State University, Tallahassee, FL, *Public Libraries and the Internet 2004: Survey Results and Findings,* by John Carlo Bertot, Charles R. McClure, and Paul T. Jaeger, Florida State University, Tallahassee, FL.

[For persons 18 years old and over (193,462 represents 193,462,000). As of spring for 1997 and 2000; as of fall beginning 2003. Based on sample and subject to sampling error; see source for details]

Item	Total adults	Any online/ Internet usage in the past 30 days	Have Internet access — Home or work or other	Have Internet access — Home	Have Internet access — Work	Used the Internet in the last 30 days — Home or work or other	Used the Internet in the last 30 days — Home	Used the Internet in the last 30 days — Work
Total adults, 1997 (1,000)	193,462	31,686	46,305	25,500	22,931	29,127	16,640	13,806
Total adults, 2000 (1,000)	199,438	90,458	112,949	77,621	50,476	86,289	65,471	40,449
Total adults, 2003 (1,000)	209,657	131,839	165,898	128,549	73,315	128,417	107,604	62,159
Total adults, 2004 (1,000)	213,454	134,440	168,582	132,395	73,570	130,964	111,052	61,469
Total adults, 2005 [1] (1,000).	**215,800**	**140,507**	**172,050**	**137,866**	**77,044**	**138,037**	**118,047**	**65,252**
PERCENT DISTRIBUTION								
Total	100.0	100.0	100.0	100.0	100.0	100.0	100.0	100.0
Age:								
18 to 34 years old	31.2	36.6	33.6	32.0	33.3	36.8	34.4	33.9
35 to 54 years old	39.4	44.1	42.4	44.6	52.3	44.2	45.5	52.3
55 years old and over	29.4	19.3	24.0	23.4	14.4	19.0	20.1	13.7
Sex:								
Male	48.2	48.4	48.4	49.2	50.3	48.3	48.9	50.2
Female	51.8	51.6	51.6	50.8	49.7	51.7	51.1	49.8
Census region: [2]								
Northeast	19.1	19.8	20.1	20.8	20.5	19.8	20.4	20.3
Midwest	22.5	23.0	23.8	22.6	22.2	23.1	22.6	22.1
South.	36.2	33.6	33.3	33.0	34.0	33.4	33.0	33.7
West	22.2	23.5	22.8	23.6	23.3	23.6	24.0	23.8
Household size:								
1 to 2 persons	46.9	42.2	43.5	41.1	42.4	42.1	41.7	42.7
3 to 4 persons	37.4	42.1	40.6	43.0	43.4	42.3	43.1	43.7
5 or more persons	15.7	15.7	15.8	15.9	14.2	15.6	15.3	13.6
Any child in household	41.7	46.0	44.5	45.6	47.5	46.1	46.1	47.4
Marital status:								
Single	24.8	26.3	25.1	22.6	23.0	26.3	23.9	22.7
Married.	56.5	60.5	59.4	64.5	64.6	60.5	64.0	64.8
Other	18.7	13.2	15.5	12.9	12.4	13.2	12.1	12.5
Educational attainment:								
Graduated college plus	25.2	35.4	30.3	34.5	46.2	35.7	38.0	49.6
Attended college	27.2	33.7	30.7	32.0	32.0	33.9	33.8	31.8
Did not attend college	47.6	31.0	39.0	33.5	21.8	30.4	28.2	18.6
Employed full-time	52.9	63.3	59.0	61.2	87.5	63.6	63.2	88.8
Employed part-time	11.3	12.9	12.2	12.5	12.1	12.9	12.9	10.8
Occupation of the employed:								
Professional	13.3	19.2	16.3	18.5	30.2	19.5	20.6	31.1
Management/business/financial. . .	9.4	13.2	11.4	12.8	20.9	13.4	13.9	22.8
Sales/office	16.0	20.8	18.7	18.8	29.0	21.0	19.9	30.0
Natural resources/construction/ maintenance	6.8	6.1	6.6	6.5	5.6	6.1	5.8	4.8
Other.	18.7	16.8	18.3	17.1	13.8	16.6	15.8	10.9
Type of firm of employed:								
Business.	35.8	41.5	38.7	39.6	52.1	41.7	40.9	53.1
Government	10.2	13.6	12.1	13.2	21.5	13.8	14.1	21.7
Other	18.2	21.1	20.3	20.9	26.0	21.1	21.1	24.8
Household income:								
Less than $50,000	48.0	33.1	38.8	30.9	21.4	32.7	29.1	19.4
$50,000 to $74,999.	19.8	23.2	22.4	23.6	23.2	23.2	23.2	22.5
$75,000 to $149,999	25.0	33.5	29.8	34.7	41.8	33.8	36.3	43.7
$150,000 or more.	7.2	10.2	8.9	10.8	13.6	10.3	11.5	14.4

[1] Includes other labor force status, not shown separately.   [2] For composition of regions, see map inside front cover.

Source: Mediamark Research Inc., New York, NY, *CyberStats*, spring 1997 and 2000, fall 2003, 2004, and 2005 (copyright). See Internet site <http://www.mriplus.com/pocketpiece.html>.

Information and Communications   723

Table 1138. **Adult Computer and Adult Internet Users by Selected Characteristics: 1995 to 2005**

[Percent of persons 18 years old and over. Represents persons who use a computer or the Internet at a workplace, school, home, or anywhere else, on at least an occasional basis. Based on telephone surveys of persons with land-line telephones. In 2005, 5,262 persons were interviewed and the response rate was 30 percent. For 1995, Internet users include those who ever use a home, work, or school computer and modem to connect to information services, bulletin boards or other computers over the Internet. For 2000 and 2004, Internet users include persons who ever go online to access the Internet or World Wide Web or to send and receive e-mail. For 2005, Internet users include those who at least occasionally use the Internet or send and receive e-mail]

Characteristic	Adult computer users				Adult Internet users				All adults by type of home connection, 2005	
	1995	2000	2004	2005	1995	2000	2004	2005	Broadband	Dial-up
Total adults	54	65	68	71	14	53	59	69	36	22
Age:										
18 to 29 years old	70	82	80	83	21	72	72	82	46	22
30 to 49 years old	66	76	79	81	18	62	69	80	45	25
50 to 64 years old	46	61	69	72	9	48	59	68	34	24
65 years old and over	12	21	29	31	2	15	24	28	11	14
Sex:										
Male	58	66	68	72	18	56	61	70	40	22
Female	51	64	68	70	10	51	58	67	33	22
Race/ethnicity:										
White, non-Hispanic	54	66	69	72	14	55	62	70	38	23
Black, non-Hispanic	50	59	58	60	11	42	45	54	23	16
English-speaking Hispanic . . .	64	64	67	75	21	48	52	73	39	20
Educational attainment:										
Less than high school	17	28	28	36	2	19	22	35	14	12
High school graduate [1]	46	56	59	63	8	41	48	59	26	22
Some college	72	80	82	81	20	69	75	80	44	25
College graduate or higher . .	82	88	89	90	29	79	82	88	56	24
Annual household income:										
Less than $30,000	37	48	51	52	8	35	43	50	20	18
$30,000 to $49,000	61	74	72	76	15	61	65	74	30	30
$50,000 to $74,000	(NA)	85	87	88	23	74	80	86	50	29
$75,000 or more	(NA)	90	92	92	32	81	84	91	64	21

NA Not available. [1] Includes those with a GED certificate.

Source: 1995 data based on the Times Mirror Center for the People & the Press survey from May and June of 1995; thereafter Pew Internet & American Life Project Surveys from September–December 2000; November and December of 2004; and September and December of 2005. See Internet site <http://www.pewinternet.org/index.asp>.

Table 1139. **Internet Activities of Adults by Type of Home Internet Connection: 2005**

[For Internet users 18 years old and over (97 represents 97,000,000). For persons who have ever performed the activity. Based on telephone surveys of persons with land-line telephones. In September 2005, 2,251 persons were interviewed and the response rate was 30 percent]

Activity	Survey date (month, year)	Adult Internet users (mil.)	Percent of users performing activity	Percent of home dial-up users performing activity	Percent of home broadband users performing activity
Get news online	Feb–Mar, 05	97	72	70	79
Buy a product online	May–Jun, 05	92	67	59	81
Buy or make a reservation for travel	Sept, 05	91	63	57	72
Do research for school or training	Jan, 05	76	57	53	63
Do work or research for your job	Feb–Mar, 05	69	51	43	59
Send instant messages	Sept, 05	68	47	44	54
Bank online	Feb–Mar, 05	55	41	33	56
Download computer programs	May–Jun, 05	53	39	35	47
Play online games	May–Jun, 05	49	36	33	41
Read someone else's blog	Sept, 05	39	27	20	35
Share files from your own computer	May–Jun, 05	37	27	22	33
Download music	May–Jun, 05	34	25	17	33
Participate in an online auction	Feb–Mar, 05	32	24	18	34
Download video files to your computer . . .	May–Jun, 05	25	18	12	24
Remix material you find online into your own creation	Jan, 05	24	18	14	22
Sell something online	Sept, 05	25	17	13	22
Use an online social or professional networking site	Sept, 05	16	11	8	14
Create a blog	Sept, 05	13	9	6	12

Source: Pew Internet & American Life Project Surveys. See Internet site <http://www.pewinternet.org/index.asp>

U.S. Census Bureau, Statistical Abstract of the United States: 2007

Table 1140. **Typical Daily Internet Activities of Adult Internet Users: 2004 and 2005**

[Percent of Internet users 18 years old and over. Represents persons who report doing the activity "yesterday." Based on telephone surveys persons with land-line telephones. In December 2005, 3,011 persons were interviewed and the response rate was 29 percent]

Activity	Survey date (month, year)	Total	Age				Sex	
			18 to 29 years old	30 to 49 years old	50 to 64 years old	65 years old and over	Male	Female
Use the Internet............	Sept and Dec, 05	64	65	66	64	56	67	61
Send e-mail...............	Sept and Dec, 05	53	49	56	56	48	54	52
Use a search engine to find information	Sept, 05	41	43	44	38	28	43	39
Get news	Feb–Mar, 05	30	26	35	29	24	35	26
Surf the Web for fun	Dec, 05	30	37	31	25	20	34	26
Do research for your job	Feb–Mar, 05	19	14	25	19	4	21	17
Research a product or service before buying it	Feb–Mar, 05	19	18	23	13	11	23	15
Research for school or training...	Jan, 05	16	21	16	12	5	16	15
Look for political news.........	May–Jun, 04	13	7	16	13	11	17	8
Bank online...............	Feb–Mar, 05	12	10	16	10	4	13	11
Send instant messages	Sept, 05	12	23	10	7	3	12	12
Send or receive text messages using a cell phone	Sept, 05	11	24	9	2	2	10	11
Check sports scores or information	Feb, 04	11	14	11	8	5	18	4
Play online games	Jan, 05	9	11	7	8	14	8	9
Read someone else's Web log or "blog"................	Sept, 05	7	12	6	3	2	7	6
Log on to the Internet using a wireless device	Feb, 04	6	6	6	7	1	6	5
Download music files to your computer	Jan, 05	4	8	3	1	2	5	3
Download video files to your computer	Jan, 05	3	4	3	1	1	4	1

Source: Pew Internet & American Life Project Surveys. See Internet site <http://www.pewinternet.org/index.asp>

Table 1141. **Primary News Sources of Adults: 2005**

[Percent of persons 18 years old and over. Represents where people said they got their news "yesterday." Based on December 2005 telephone survey of 3,011 persons with land-line telephones. The response rate was 29 percent]

News source	All adults	All Internet users	All non-Internet users	Home dial-up users	Home broadband users
Local TV.....................	59	60	57	66	57
National TV..................	47	49	43	50	49
Radio.......................	44	49	34	52	49
Local paper..................	38	38	37	41	38
National paper................	12	14	9	12	17
Internet, total................	(X)	35	(X)	26	43
National TV news site	(X)	14	(X)	9	17
Portal	(X)	16	(X)	13	21
Local daily paper site...........	(X)	9	(X)	6	11
Local TV news site	(X)	8	(X)	6	10
National daily paper site.........	(X)	6	(X)	4	8
International news site..........	(X)	3	(X)	2	5
News blogs	(X)	3	(X)	2	5
Radio news organization	(X)	2	(X)	2	3
Alternative news organization	(X)	2	(X)	1	2
Online listervs	(X)	2	(X)	2	2

X Not applicable.

Source: Pew Internet & American Life Project December 2005 Survey. See Internet site <http://www.pewinternet.org/index.asp>

Information and Communications   725

Table 1142. **Households With Computers and Internet Access by Selected Characteristic: 2003**

[Percent of households in specified group. As of October. Based on the Current Population Survey and subject to sampling error; for details, see source. See also text Section 1, and Appendix III]

Characteristic	Households with computers				Households with Internet access			
	Total	Rural [1]	Urban [1]	Central city [1]	Total	Rural [1]	Urban [1]	Central city [1]
All households	**61.8**	**61.9**	**61.7**	**56.9**	**54.6**	**54.1**	**54.8**	**49.3**
Age of householder:								
Under 25 years old	56.5	52.5	57.2	56.6	46.9	43.3	47.5	46.0
25 to 34 years old............	68.6	71.6	67.8	64.3	60.2	62.1	59.7	56.1
35 to 44 years old............	73.2	75.3	72.6	65.8	65.2	66.2	64.9	57.0
45 to 54 years old............	71.9	71.5	72.1	65.3	65.1	63.9	65.6	58.4
55 years old or over	46.6	46.7	46.6	41.5	40.8	40.3	40.9	35.4
Sex:								
Male......................	65.6	64.2	66.2	61.3	58.6	56.3	59.5	54.2
Female	57.4	58.6	57.1	52.5	50.1	51.1	49.8	44.4
Education of householder:								
Elementary	20.6	18.1	21.6	20.7	14.0	12.7	14.5	13.2
Some high school............	32.7	34.7	32.0	28.0	24.3	26.3	23.6	20.1
High school graduate or GED [2]	51.1	56.5	48.7	43.0	43.0	47.5	41.1	34.6
Some college................	70.6	73.3	69.7	65.4	62.4	64.8	61.6	56.7
Bachelor's degree or more	83.3	84.4	83.0	80.1	78.3	79.3	78.1	74.3
Household income:								
Under $5,000................	35.6	29.8	37.0	33.6	26.8	20.0	28.4	24.3
$5,000 to $9,999	26.9	24.4	27.5	27.0	20.0	17.7	20.6	20.4
$10,000 to $14,999............	31.7	31.7	31.7	32.2	23.7	23.6	23.7	23.2
$15,000 to $19,999............	38.2	36.7	38.8	37.8	29.4	26.9	30.3	28.8
$20,000 to $24,999............	46.1	47.7	45.5	45.6	36.7	36.6	36.7	37.8
$25,000 to $34,999............	55.4	55.7	55.4	54.7	45.6	46.3	45.4	44.5
$35,000 to $49,999............	71.1	72.6	70.6	70.0	62.8	62.3	63.0	62.0
$50,000 to $74,999............	81.9	82.4	81.7	81.7	76.0	75.8	76.1	75.1
$75,000 to $99,999............	88.1	87.9	88.2	85.6	84.1	84.1	84.1	81.7
$100,000 to $149,999	92.9	92.2	93.2	89.8	90.4	89.7	90.6	86.0
$150,000 or more	94.7	95.0	94.7	92.3	92.4	91.6	92.5	91.8

[1] The "urban" category includes those areas classified as having a population density of at least 1,000 persons per square mile and a total population of at least 50,000, as well as cities, villages, boroughs (except in Alaska and New York), towns (except in the six New England states, New York, and Wisconsin), and other designated census areas having 2,500 or more persons. A "central city" is the largest city within a "metropolitan" area as defined by the Census Bureau. Additional cities within the metropolitan area can also be classified as central cities if they meet certain employment, population, and employment/residence ratio requirements. All areas not classified by the Census Bureau as urban are defined as rural and generally include communities less than 2,500 persons.   [2] GED = General Equivalency Diploma.

Source: U.S. Department of Commerce, National Telecommunications and Information Administration, *A Nation Online: Entering the Broadband Age,* September 2004; and unpublished data. See Internet site <http://www.ntia.doc.gov/reports/anol/index.html>.

Table 1143. **Households With Computers and Internet Access: 1998 and 2003**

[Percent of all households. As of October. Based on survey and subject to sampling error; for details, see source]

State	1998		2003		State	1998		2003	
	Computers	Internet access	Computers	Internet access		Computers	Internet access	Computers	Internet access
U.S.. .	**42.1**	**26.2**	**61.8**	**54.6**	MO	41.8	24.3	60.7	53.0
AL	34.3	21.6	53.9	45.7	MT......	40.9	21.5	59.5	50.4
AK	62.4	44.1	72.7	67.6	NE......	42.9	22.9	66.1	55.4
AZ	44.3	29.3	64.3	55.2	NV......	41.6	26.5	61.3	55.2
AR	29.8	14.7	50.0	42.4	NH......	54.2	37.1	71.5	65.2
CA......	47.5	30.7	66.3	59.6	NJ	48.1	31.3	65.5	60.5
CO......	55.3	34.5	70.0	63.0	NM......	42.2	25.8	53.9	44.5
CT......	43.8	31.8	69.2	62.9	NY......	37.3	23.7	60.0	53.3
DE......	40.5	25.1	64.3	56.8	NC......	35.0	19.9	57.7	51.1
DC......	41.4	24.2	59.5	53.2	ND......	40.2	20.6	61.2	53.2
FL	39.5	27.8	61.0	55.6	OH......	40.7	24.6	58.8	52.5
GA......	35.8	23.9	60.6	53.5	OK......	37.8	20.4	55.4	48.4
HI	42.3	27.9	63.3	55.0	OR......	51.3	32.7	67.0	61.0
ID	50.0	27.4	69.2	56.4	PA......	39.3	24.9	60.2	54.7
IL	42.7	26.5	60.0	51.1	RI	41.0	27.1	62.3	55.7
IN	43.5	26.1	59.6	51.0	SC......	35.7	21.4	54.9	45.6
IA	41.4	21.8	64.7	57.1	SD......	41.6	23.9	62.1	53.6
KS......	43.7	25.7	63.8	54.3	TN......	37.5	21.3	56.7	48.9
KY......	35.9	21.1	58.1	49.6	TX......	40.9	24.5	59.0	51.8
LA	31.1	17.8	52.3	44.1	UT......	60.1	35.8	74.1	62.6
ME......	43.4	26.0	67.8	57.9	VT	48.7	31.8	65.5	58.1
MD.....	46.3	31.0	66.0	59.2	VA......	46.4	27.9	66.8	60.3
MA.....	43.4	28.1	64.1	58.1	WA.....	56.3	36.6	71.4	62.3
MI	44.0	25.4	59.9	52.0	WV.....	28.3	17.6	55.0	47.6
MN.....	47.6	29.0	67.9	61.6	WI	43.0	25.1	63.8	57.4
MS.....	25.7	13.6	48.3	38.9	WY	46.1	22.7	65.4	57.7

Source: U.S. Department of Commerce, National Telecommunications and Information Administration, *Falling through the Net: Defining the Digital Divide,* July 1999; and *A Nation Online: Entering the Broadband Age,* September 2004; and unpublished data. See Internet site <http://www.ntia.doc.gov/reports/anol/index.html>.

Section 25
Banking, Finance, and Insurance

This section presents data on the nation's finances, various types of financial institutions, money and credit, securities, insurance, and real estate. The primary sources of these data are publications of several departments of the federal government, especially the Treasury Department, and independent agencies such as the Federal Deposit Insurance Corporation, the Federal Reserve Board, and the Securities and Exchange Commission. National data on insurance are available primarily from private organizations, such as the American Council of Life Insurers and the Insurance Information Institute.

Flow of funds—The flow of funds accounts of the Federal Reserve Board bring together statistics on all of the major forms of financial instruments to present an economy-wide view of asset and liability relationships. In flow form, the accounts relate borrowing and lending to one another and to the nonfinancial activities that generate income and production. Each claim outstanding is included simultaneously as an asset of the lender and as a liability of the debtor. The accounts also indicate the balance between asset totals and liability totals over the economy as a whole. Several publications of the Board of Governors of the Federal Reserve System contain information on the flow of funds accounts: Summary data on flows and outstandings, in the *Statistical Supplement to the Federal Reserve Bulletin,* and *Flow of Funds Accounts of the United States* (quarterly); and concepts and organization of the accounts in *Guide to the Flow of Funds Accounts* (2000). Data are also available at the Board's Web site <http://www .federalreserve.gov/releases/>.

Survey of Consumer Finances (SCF)—The Federal Reserve Board in cooperation with the Department of the Treasury sponsors this survey, which is conducted every 3 years to provide detailed information on the finances of U.S. families. Among the topics covered are the balance sheet, pension, income,

and other demographic characteristics of U.S. families. The survey also gathers information on the use of financial institutions. Since 1992, data for the SCF have been collected by the National Organization for Social Science and Survey Research at the University of Chicago. Data and information on the survey are available at the following Web site of the Federal Reserve Board: <http://www .federalreserve.gov/pubs/oss/oss2/ scfindex.html>.

Banking system—Banks in this country are organized under the laws of both the states and the federal government and are regulated by several bank supervisory agencies. National banks are supervised by the Comptroller of the Currency. *Reports of Condition* have been collected from national banks since 1863. Summaries of these reports are published in the Comptroller's *Annual Report,* which also presents data on the structure of the national banking system.

The Federal Reserve System was established in 1913 to exercise central banking functions, some of which are shared with the U.S. Treasury. It includes national banks and such state banks that voluntarily join the system. Statements of state bank members are consolidated by the Board of Governors of the Federal Reserve System with data for national banks collected by the Comptroller of the Currency into totals for all member banks of the system. Balance sheet data for member banks and other commercial banks are published quarterly in the *Statistical Supplement to the Federal Reserve Bulletin.* The Federal Deposit Insurance Corporation (FDIC), established in 1933, insures each depositor up to $100,000. Major item balance sheet and income data for all insured financial institutions are published in the *FDIC Quarterly Banking Profile.* This publication is also available on the Internet at the following address: <http://www.fdic.gov>. Quarterly financial information for individual institutions is available through the FDIC and Federal

Financial Institutions Examination Council Web sites at <http://www.fdic.gov> and <http://www.ffiec.gov>.

Credit unions—Federally chartered credit unions are under the supervision of the National Credit Union Administration. State-chartered credit unions are supervised by the respective state supervisory authorities. The administration publishes comprehensive program and statistical information on all federal and federally insured state credit unions in the *Annual Report of the National Credit Union Administration.* Deposit insurance (up to $100,000 per account) is provided to members of all federal and those state credit unions that are federally insured by the National Credit Union Share Insurance Fund which was established in 1970. Deposit insurance for state chartered credit unions is also available in some states under private or state-administered insurance programs.

Other credit agencies—Insurance companies, finance companies dealing primarily in installment sales financing, and personal loan companies represent important sources of funds for the credit market. Statistics on loans, investments, cash, etc., of life insurance companies are published principally by the American Council of Life Insurers in its *Life Insurers Fact Book.* Consumer credit data are published currently in the *Statistical Supplement to the Federal Reserve Bulletin.*

Government corporations and credit agencies make available credit of specified types or to specified groups of private borrowers, either by lending directly or by insuring or guaranteeing loans made by private lending institutions. Data on operations of government credit agencies, along with other government corporations, are available in reports of individual agencies; data on their debt outstanding are published in the *Statistical Supplement to the Federal Reserve Bulletin.*

Securities—The Securities and Exchange Commission (SEC) was established in 1934 to protect the interests of the public and investors against malpractices in the securities and financial markets and to provide the fullest possible disclosure of information regarding securities to the investing public. Statistical data are published in the *SEC Annual Report.*

Data on the securities industry and securities transactions are also available from a number of private sources. The Securities Industry Association, New York, NY, <http://www.sia.com/>, publishes the *Securities Industry Fact Book, Securities Industry Yearbook,* and the periodic *Securities Industry Trends.* The Investment Company Institute, Washington, DC, <http://www.ici.org/>, publishes a reference book, research newsletters, and a variety of research reports that examine the industry, its shareholders, or industry issues. The annual *Mutual Fund Fact Book* is a guide to trends and statistics observed in the investment company industry. *Fundamentals* is a newsletter summarizing the findings of major Institute research projects. Institute research reports provide a detailed examination of shareholder demographics and other aspects of fund ownership.

Among the many sources of data on stock and bond prices and sales are the New York Stock Exchange, New York, NY, <http://www.nyse.com/>; NASDAQ, Washington, DC, <http://www.nasdaq.com/>; Global Financial Data, Los Angeles, CA, <http://www.globalfindata.com/>; Dow-Jones & Company, Inc., New York, NY, <http://www.djindexes.com/mdsidx/>; and the Bond Market Association, New York, NY, <http://www.bondmarkets.com/>.

Insurance—Insuring companies, which are regulated by the various states or the District of Columbia, are classified as either life or property. Both life and property insurance companies may underwrite health insurance. Insuring companies, other than those classified as life, are permitted to underwrite one or more property lines provided they are so licensed and have the necessary capital or surplus.

There are a number of published sources for statistics on the various classes of insurance—life, health, fire, marine, and casualty. Organizations representing certain classes of insurers publish reports for these classes. The American Council of Life Insurers publishes statistics on life insurance purchases, ownership, benefit payments, and assets in its *Life Insurers Fact Book.*

Figure 25.1
Percent of Families Owning Retirement Accounts¹ by Age of Family Head: 2004

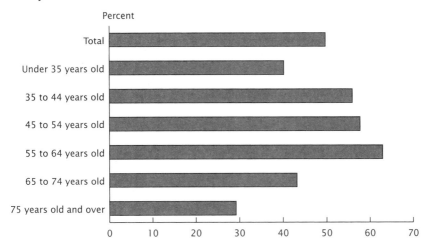

Percent

¹ Tax-deferred retirement accounts consist of IRAs, Keogh accounts, and certain employer-sponsored accounts.
Source: Chart prepared by U.S. Census Bureau. For data, see Table 1152.

Figure 25.2
Interest Rates and Bond Yields: 1990 to 2005
(Percent per year. Annual averages)

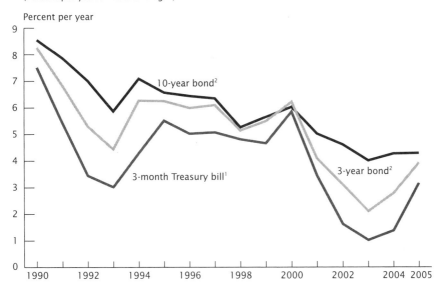

Percent per year

¹New issues.
²U.S. Treasury, constant maturities.
Source: Chart prepared by U.S. Census Bureau. For data, see Tables 1178 and 1179.

Banking, Finance, and Insurance   729

Table 1144. **Gross Domestic Product in Finance and Insurance/Real Estate and Rental and Leasing in Current and Real (2000) Dollars: 2000 to 2005**

[In billions of dollars, except percent (741 represents $741,000,000,000). Represents value added by industry. For definition of gross domestic product and explanation of chained dollars, see text, Section 13]

Industry	1997 NAICS code [1]	Current dollars				Chained (2000) dollars			
		2000	2003	2004	2005	2000	2003	2004	2005
Finance & insurance, total	52	**741**	**885**	**927**	**1,012**	**741**	**837**	**845**	**902**
Percent of gross domestic product ...		7.5	8.1	7.9	8.1	7.5	8.1	7.9	8.1
Monetary authorities—central bank, credit intermediation & related activities	521,522	319	452	465	(NA)	319	410	407	(NA)
Security, commodity contracts & like activity	523	168	153	171	(NA)	168	175	193	(NA)
Insurance carriers & related activities	524	238	260	270	(NA)	238	234	230	(NA)
Funds, trusts, & other financial vehicles (part)	525	16	20	22	(NA)	16	14	15	(NA)
Real estate & rental & leasing, total ..	53	**1,191**	**1,375**	**1,486**	**1,563**	**1,191**	**1,257**	**1,328**	**1,361**
Percent of gross domestic product ...		12.1	12.5	12.7	12.5	12.1	12.2	12.3	12.2
Real estate	531	1,082	1,269	1,375	(NA)	1,082	1,154	1,224	(NA)
Rental & leasing services [2]	532,533	108	107	111	(NA)	108	103	103	(NA)

NA Not available. [1] See footnote 1, Table 1145. [2] Includes lessors of other nonfinancial intangible assets.

Source: U.S. Bureau of Economic Analysis, *Survey of Current Business*, May 2006. See also <http://www.bea.gov /bea/newsrelarchive/2006/gdpind05.pdf> (released 27 April 2006).

Table 1145. **Finance and Insurance/Real Estate and Rental and Leasing— Establishments, Revenue, Payroll, and Employees by Kind of Business (1997 NAICS Basis): 1997 and 2002**

[2,198 represents $2,198,000,000,000. For establishments with payroll. Data for 2002 are preliminary. Based on the 1997 and 2002 Economic Censuses; see Appendix III]

Kind of business	1997 NAICS code [1]	Number of establishments		Revenue (bil. dol.)		Annual payroll (bil. dol.)		Paid employees (1,000)	
		1997	2002	1997	2002	1997	2002	1997	2002
Finance & insurance	52	395,203	449,134	2,198	2,616	264.6	343.5	5,835	6,664
Monetary authorities—central bank	521	42	47	25	29	0.9	1.2	22	22
Credit intermediation & related activities	522	166,882	194,822	809	923	98.7	127.0	2,745	3,055
Security, commodity contracts & like activity	523	54,491	80,493	275	316	71.3	95.6	706	976
Insurance carriers & related activities...	524	172,299	170,795	1,073	1,320	92.2	118.0	2,327	2,579
Funds, trusts, and other financial vehicles (part)	525	1,489	2,977	17	27	1.4	1.6	35	30
Real estate & rental & leasing	53	288,273	325,590	241	348	41.6	61.8	1,702	2,136
Real estate	531	221,650	258,639	153	238	27.9	42.8	1,117	1,450
Rental & leasing services.	532	64,472	64,624	76	95	12.6	17.5	559	658
Lessors of other nonfinancial intangible assets	533	2,151	2,327	11	14	1.1	1.5	26	28

[1] 1997 North American Industry Classification System; see text, Section 15.

Source: U.S. Census Bureau, 2002 Economic Census, *Advance Report*, issued March 2004. See Internet site: <http://www.census.gov /econ/census02/>.

Table 1146. **Finance and Insurance—Nonemployer Establishments and Receipts by Kind of Business: 2000 to 2003**

[691.8 represents 691,800. Includes only firms subject to federal income tax. Nonemployers are businesses with no paid employees. Data originate chiefly from administrative records of the Internal Revenue Service; see Appendix III. Data for 2000 based on the 1997 North American Industry Classification System (NAICS); beginning 2002 based on 2002 NAICS, see text, Section 15]

Kind of business	NAICS code	Establishments (1,000)			Receipts (mil. dol.)		
		2000	2002	2003	2000	2002	2003
Finance and insurance	52	691.8	660.3	695.0	49,058	44,139	47,345
Credit intermediation & related activities	522	165.3	66.0	77.2	4,848	3,796	4,605
Depository credit intermediation.	5221	6.5	6.4	7.0	197	224	248
Nondepository credit intermediation	5222	134.1	22.9	26.4	3,624	1,845	2,138
Activities related to credit intermediation	5223	24.7	36.7	43.8	1,028	1,727	2,219
Security, commodity contracts & like activity	523	181.5	240.5	251.8	29,379	24,172	25,737
Scrty & comdty contracts interm & brokerage	5231	29.6	32.0	32.8	6,395	5,433	5,327
Investment banking and securities dealing	52311	5.6	7.0	7.7	2,043	1,897	1,861
Securities brokerage	52312	19.5	20.3	20.3	3,712	2,833	2,736
Commodity contracts dealing	52313	1.0	1.3	1.2	238	201	143
Commodity contracts brokerage	52314	3.6	3.5	3.7	402	501	588
Securities & commodity exchanges	5232	1.6	1.8	2.0	1,495	867	1,082
Other financial investment activities	5239	150.2	206.7	217.1	21,488	17,872	19,328
Insurance carriers & related activities.	524	345.0	353.8	366.0	14,831	16,171	17,003
Insurance carriers	5241	1.0	0.5	0.6	98	55	50
Agencies & other insurance-related activities	5242	344.0	353.2	365.4	14,733	16,111	16,953
Insurance agencies & brokerages	52421	245.5	246.5	250.8	11,570	12,357	12,880
Other insurance related activities	52429	98.5	106.7	114.6	3,163	3,760	4,073

Source: U.S. Census Bureau, "Nonemployer Statistics"; <http://www.census.gov/epcd/nonemployer/>.

Table 1147. **Finance and Insurance—Establishments, Employees, and Payroll: 2000 and 2003**

[423.7 represents 423,700. Covers establishments with payroll. Kind-of-business classification for 2000 based on North American Industry Classification System (NAICS) 1997; data for 2003 based on NAICS 2002. See text, Section 15. Employees are for the week including March 12. Most government employees are excluded. For statement on methodology, see Appendix III]

Kind of business	NAICS code	Establishments (1,000)		Employees (1,000)		Payroll (bil. dol.)	
		2000	2003	2000	2003	2000	2003
Finance & insurance, total	52	423.7	460.6	5,963	6,464	346.8	392.9
Monetary authorities—central bank	521	0.1	0.1	22	22	1.1	1.2
Credit intermediation & related activities	522	176.3	202.1	2,753	3,114	116.1	154.9
Depository credit intermediation [1]	5221	105.6	114.2	1,935	2,082	78.5	94.0
Commercial banking.	52211	73.9	80.7	1,493	1,596	63.6	74.5
Savings institutions	52212	15.9	17.2	244	259	9.2	11.9
Credit unions	52213	15.6	16.1	192	221	5.4	7.2
Nondepository credit intermediation [1]	5222	49.3	52.6	621	719	29.6	45.2
Real estate credit	522292	19.8	21.5	238	318	10.8	23.4
Activities related to credit intermediation	5223	21.4	35.3	198	313	7.9	15.7
Security, commodity contracts & like activity	523	72.9	85.0	866	902	119.5	106.9
Security & commodity contracts intermediate & brokerage [1]	5231	38.1	45.4	539	530	80.2	67.5
Investment banking & securities dealing	52311	6.3	6.1	138	132	31.2	24.7
Securities brokerage	52312	29.5	36.8	378	376	47.0	40.8
Securities & commodity exchanges	5232	(Z)	0.1	7	7	0.5	0.7
Other financial investment activities [1]	5239	34.8	39.5	320	365	38.8	38.6
Portfolio management	52392	11.6	12.8	156	185	24.9	24.5
Insurance carriers & related activities.	524	172.2	170.2	2,290	2,393	108.1	127.3
Insurance carriers [1]	5241	37.4	31.2	1,489	1,509	74.7	86.1
Direct life/health/medical insurance carriers . . .	52411	13.9	12.3	813	787	40.0	44.5
Direct life insurance carriers	524113	10.7	8.2	491	334	25.7	20.3
Direct health & medical insurance carriers . .	524114	3.1	4.2	322	453	14.3	24.1
Other direct insurance carriers [1]	52412	23.0	18.0	660	696	33.5	39.1
Direct property & casualty insurance carriers.	524126	19.8	12.8	609	612	31.1	34.4
Agencies & other insurance-related activities	5242	134.8	139.0	801	884	33.3	41.3
Insurance agencies & brokerages.	52421	121.5	126.7	596	678	24.7	31.6
Other insurance-related activities	52429	13.3	12.3	205	206	8.6	9.6
Funds, trusts, & other financial vehicles (part)	525	2.3	3.3	32	33	2.1	2.5

Z Less than 50. [1] Includes industries not shown separately.
Source: U.S. Census Bureau, "County Business Patterns"; <http://www.census.gov/epcd/cbp/view/cbpview.html>.

Table 1148. **Flow of Funds Accounts—Financial Assets of Financial and Nonfinancial Institutions by Holder Sector: 1990 to 2005**

[In billions of dollars (35,902 represents $35,902,000,000,000). As of Dec. 31]

Sector	1990	1995	1998	1999	2000	2001	2002	2003	2004	2005
All sectors.	35,902	53,445	75,579	86,362	89,428	90,335	88,880	99,219	108,132	115,961
Households [1]	14,602	21,483	30,110	34,408	33,151	31,582	29,255	33,692	36,429	38,465
Nonfinancial business	3,979	5,568	7,872	9,335	11,260	11,545	11,671	11,927	12,750	13,427
Farm business	47	61	64	65	65	67	72	77	83	88
Nonfarm noncorporate	356	548	992	1,176	1,423	1,579	1,657	1,741	2,018	2,363
Nonfinancial corporations	3,575	4,959	6,816	8,094	9,772	9,899	9,942	10,109	10,650	10,977
State and local government	1,020	1,122	1,475	1,607	1,671	1,755	1,807	1,905	2,007	2,153
U.S. government	442	442	445	561	514	615	611	653	615	603
Monetary authorities	342	472	567	697	636	683	754	797	841	879
Commercial banking	3,337	4,494	5,629	5,986	6,469	6,829	7,329	7,810	8,497	9,236
U.S.-chartered commercial banks. . . .	2,644	3,322	4,081	4,434	4,774	5,015	5,427	5,840	6,398	6,906
Foreign banking offices in U.S.	367	666	806	751	789	792	801	734	570	680
Bank-holding companies.	298	467	686	741	842	942	1,026	1,152	1,429	1,542
Banks in U.S.-affiliated areas.	28	39	56	59	63	80	75	84	100	109
Savings institutions	1,323	1,013	1,089	1,150	1,218	1,291	1,349	1,465	1,649	1,789
Credit unions	217	311	391	415	441	506	561	617	655	686
Life insurance companies.	1,351	2,064	2,770	3,068	3,136	3,225	3,335	3,773	4,130	4,381
Property-casualty insurance companies .	533	740	876	873	862	860	940	1,060	1,166	1,265
Private pension funds [2]	1,627	2,889	4,105	4,571	4,355	3,916	3,309	4,027	4,473	4,613
State and local government employee retirement funds	730	1,327	2,031	2,326	2,293	2,207	1,930	2,344	2,572	2,722
Federal government retirement funds . . .	340	541	716	774	797	860	894	959	1,024	1,075
Money market mutual funds	493	741	1,328	1,580	1,812	2,241	2,224	2,016	1,880	2,007
Mutual funds	608	1,853	3,613	4,538	4,435	4,135	3,638	4,653	5,436	6,045
Closed-end funds	53	136	149	152	142	140	151	206	246	271
Exchange-traded funds	–	1	16	34	66	83	102	151	226	296
Government-sponsored enterprises (GSE).	478	897	1,406	1,723	1,965	2,309	2,549	2,786	2,870	2,805
Agency- and GSE-backed mortgage pools	1,020	1,571	2,019	2,294	2,493	2,832	3,159	3,489	3,542	3,678
Asset-backed securities issuers.	268	662	1,155	1,305	1,469	1,699	1,882	2,088	2,414	3,059
Finance companies.	547	672	853	1,004	1,140	1,159	1,193	1,385	1,456	1,335
Mortgage companies.	49	33	32	32	32	32	32	32	32	32
Real estate investment trusts	28	33	71	69	66	76	102	136	253	355
Security brokers and dealers.	262	568	921	1,001	1,221	1,466	1,335	1,613	1,845	2,144
Funding corporations	251	383	780	1,086	1,200	1,224	1,190	1,252	1,286	1,488
Rest of the world	1,999	3,428	5,162	5,776	6,585	7,066	7,577	8,381	9,836	11,154

– Represents zero. [1] Includes nonprofit organizations. [2] Private defined benefit and defined contribution plans (including 401(k) type plans).
Source: Board of Governors of the Federal Reserve System, "Federal Reserve Statistical Release, Z.1, Flow of Funds Accounts of the United States"; published: 9 March 2006; <http://www.federalreserve.gov/releases/z1/20060309/>.

Banking, Finance, and Insurance **731**

Table 1149. **Flow of Funds Accounts—Credit Market Debt Outstanding: 1990 to 2005**

[In billions of dollars (13,777 represents $13,777,000,000,000). As of December 31]

Item	1990	1995	1998	1999	2000	2001	2002	2003	2004	2005
Credit market debt..........	13,777	18,457	23,250	25,290	26,972	28,904	31,234	34,092	36,963	40,230
Domestic nonfinancial............	10,845	13,657	16,151	17,216	18,053	19,148	20,467	22,149	24,097	26,391
Households [1]................	3,593	4,858	5,910	6,398	6,961	7,561	8,297	9,254	10,292	11,497
Corporations................	2,533	2,910	3,780	4,190	4,536	4,758	4,783	4,890	5,065	5,354
Nonfarm noncorporate business....	1,093	1,062	1,405	1,600	1,797	1,959	2,108	2,205	2,448	2,749
Farm business...............	135	145	165	170	181	192	200	207	219	235
State and local government......	992	1,045	1,138	1,177	1,192	1,298	1,442	1,560	1,678	1,855
U.S. government..............	2,498	3,637	3,752	3,681	3,385	3,379	3,637	4,033	4,395	4,702
Rest of the world..............	318	567	783	748	814	773	961	1,142	1,248	1,343
Financial sectors...............	2,614	4,233	6,315	7,325	8,105	8,982	9,806	10,801	11,619	12,496
Commercial banking...........	198	251	382	449	509	562	612	661	739	824
Savings institutions...........	140	115	212	260	288	286	262	268	333	349
Credit unions................	–	–	1	3	3	5	7	9	11	15
Life insurance companies	–	1	2	3	2	3	3	5	8	11	11
Government-sponsored enterprises (GSE)...................	399	807	1,275	1,594	1,826	2,131	2,350	2,594	2,659	2,575
Agency- and GSE-backed mortgage pools	1,020	1,571	2,019	2,294	2,493	2,832	3,159	3,489	3,542	3,678
Asset-backed securities issuers.....	269	666	1,167	1,314	1,476	1,706	1,888	2,093	2,418	3,063
Finance companies............	374	484	625	696	778	779	821	940	1,057	1,023
Mortgage companies..........	25	17	16	16	16	16	16	16	16	16
Real estate investment trusts	28	45	159	165	168	171	196	228	341	421
Security brokers and dealers	15	29	43	25	41	42	41	47	62	62
Funding corporations	147	249	413	504	504	449	449	447	429	458

– Represents or rounds to zero.   [1] Includes nonprofit organizations.

Source: Board of Governors of the Federal Reserve System, "Federal Reserve Statistical Release, Z.1, Flow of Funds Accounts of the United States"; published 9 March 2006; <http://www.federalreserve.gov/releases/z1/20060309/>.

Table 1150. **Flow of Funds Accounts—Financial Assets and Liabilities of Foreign Sector: 1990 to 2005**

[In billions of dollars (1,999 represents $1,999,000,000,000). As of December 31]

Type of instrument	1990	1995	1998	1999	2000	2001	2002	2003	2004	2005
Total financial assets [1]	1,999	3,428	5,162	5,776	6,585	7,066	7,577	8,381	9,836	11,154
Net interbank assets	53	229	146	140	161	116	120	110	94	74
U.S. checkable deposits and currency ..	108	194	257	279	287	306	327	356	397	441
U.S. time deposits.................	49	50	129	126	109	121	152	140	214	252
Security RPs [2]	20	68	72	80	91	151	190	460	647	701
Credit market instruments...........	890	1,490	2,231	2,316	2,591	2,949	3,424	3,918	4,680	5,576
Open market paper	11	43	87	86	90	87	98	105	135	149
Treasury securities	438	817	1,166	1,058	1,021	1,095	1,285	1,534	1,900	2,198
Official	286	490	623	618	640	720	812	990	1,261	1,344
Private....................	152	327	543	441	382	375	474	543	640	854
Agency- and GSE-backed securities [3]..................	50	146	228	300	441	535	648	658	762	934
Official	5	18	47	76	116	127	158	202	239	337
Private....................	45	129	181	224	325	408	490	456	523	596
U.S. corporate bonds [4]...........	218	361	608	752	921	1,116	1,267	1,497	1,751	2,102
Loans to U.S. corporate business....	172	122	142	120	117	116	126	125	131	192
U.S. corporate equities	244	550	1,250	1,612	1,643	1,573	1,336	1,827	2,071	2,304
Trade receivables	45	53	53	47	47	44	47	49	48	60
Miscellaneous assets.............	591	795	1,024	1,175	1,656	1,808	1,981	1,522	1,685	1,747
Foreign direct investment in U.S [5] ...	505	680	920	1,102	1,421	1,518	1,517	1,586	1,709	1,820
Other	85	115	104	74	235	289	464	-64	-24	-72
Total liabilities [1].........	1,419	2,126	2,908	3,226	3,562	3,747	4,276	4,501	5,334	5,344
U.S. official foreign exchange and net IMF position	61	64	60	50	46	47	56	62	62	46
U.S. private deposits..............	298	419	628	676	803	810	831	853	965	1,063
Credit market instruments [1]	318	567	783	748	814	773	961	1,142	1,248	1,343
Commercial paper..............	75	56	73	89	121	107	143	165	229	299
Bonds	145	413	594	548	573	557	705	874	917	934
Bank loans n.e.c. [6]	19	35	59	59	71	63	69	61	63	76
Miscellaneous liabilities [1]	714	1,030	1,393	1,702	1,849	2,069	2,391	2,396	3,008	2,839
U.S. direct investment abroad [4,5]....	630	886	1,196	1,414	1,532	1,693	1,860	2,063	2,367	2,355

[1] Includes other items not shown separately.   [2] Repurchase agreements.   [3] GSE = Government-sponsored enterprises.
[4] Through 1992, corporate bonds include net issues by Netherlands Antillean financial subsidiaries; U.S. direct investment abroad excludes net inflows from those bond issues.   [5] Direct investment is valued on a current-cost basis.   [6] Not elsewhere classified.

Source: Board of Governors of the Federal Reserve System, "Federal Reserve Statistical Release, Z.1, Flow of Funds Accounts of the United States"; published 9 March 2006; <http://www.federalreserve.gov/releases/z1/20060309/>.

Table 1151. **Flow of Funds Accounts—Assets of Households: 1990 to 2005**

[As of December 31 (14,602 represents $14,602,000,000,000). Includes nonprofit organizations]

Type of instrument	Total (bil. dol.)							Percent distribution		
	1990	1995	2000	2002	2003	2004	2005	1990	2000	2005
Total financial assets	14,602	21,483	33,151	29,255	33,692	36,429	38,465	100.0	100.0	100.0
Deposits	3,304	3,336	4,312	5,026	5,202	5,455	5,888	22.6	13.0	15.3
Foreign deposits	13	23	48	50	51	58	64	0.1	0.1	0.2
Checkable deposits and currency . . .	413	525	280	342	286	242	219	2.8	0.8	0.6
Time and savings deposits	2,485	2,310	3,024	3,564	3,905	4,251	4,654	17.0	9.1	12.1
Money market fund shares	392	478	960	1,070	960	903	951	2.7	2.9	2.5
Credit market instruments	1,793	2,285	2,399	2,220	2,557	2,681	2,733	12.3	7.2	7.1
Open-market paper	94	72	97	110	106	136	164	0.6	0.3	0.4
Treasury securities	509	834	619	304	452	495	401	3.5	1.9	1.0
Agency and GSE-backed securities [1]	119	199	508	206	378	455	656	0.8	1.5	1.7
Municipal securities	656	537	539	690	725	762	845	4.5	1.6	2.2
Corporate and foreign bonds	272	527	518	774	749	672	492	1.9	1.6	1.3
Mortgages	143	116	117	136	148	161	174	1.0	0.4	0.5
Corporate equities [2]	1,960	4,347	8,091	4,997	6,216	6,406	6,089	13.4	24.4	15.8
Mutual fund shares	512	1,344	3,041	2,500	3,188	3,726	4,207	3.5	9.2	10.9
Security credit	62	128	412	413	475	578	567	0.4	1.2	1.5
Life insurance reserves	392	566	819	921	1,013	1,060	1,121	2.7	2.5	2.9
Pension fund reserves	3,306	5,695	9,000	7,815	9,214	10,150	10,647	22.6	27.1	27.7
Equity in noncorporate business	3,032	3,465	4,705	4,943	5,365	5,869	6,677	20.8	14.2	17.4
Miscellaneous assets	243	316	371	420	462	503	535	1.7	1.1	1.4

[1] GSE = government-sponsored enterprises.   [2] Only those directly held and those in closed-end and exchange-traded funds. Other equities are included in mutual funds and life insurance and pension reserves.

Source: Board of Governors of the Federal Reserve System, "Federal Reserve Statistical Release, Z.1, Flow of Funds Accounts of the United States"; published 9 March 2006; <http://www.federalreserve.gov/releases/z1/20060309/>.

Table 1152. **Financial Assets Held by Families by Type of Asset: 2001 and 2004**

[Median value in thousands of constant 2004 dollars (29.8 represents $29,800). All dollar figures are adjusted to 2004 dollars using the "current methods" version of the consumer price index for all urban consumers published by U.S. Bureau of Labor Statistics. Families include one-person units; for definition of family, see text, Section 1. Based on Survey of Consumer Finances; see Appendix III]

Age of family head and family income	Any financial asset [1]	Trans-action accounts [2]	Certifi-cates of deposit	Savings bonds	Stocks [3]	Pooled invest-ment funds [4]	Retirement accounts [5]	Life insur-ance [6]	Other man-aged [7]
PERCENT OF FAMILIES OWNING ASSET									
2001, total	93.4	91.4	15.7	16.7	21.3	17.7	52.2	28.0	6.6
2004, total	**93.8**	**91.3**	**12.7**	**17.6**	**20.7**	**15.0**	**49.7**	**24.2**	**7.3**
Under 35 years old	90.1	86.4	5.6	15.3	13.3	8.3	40.2	11.0	2.9
35 to 44 years old	93.6	90.8	6.7	23.3	18.5	12.3	55.9	20.1	3.7
45 to 54 years old	93.6	91.8	11.9	21.0	23.2	18.2	57.7	26.0	6.2
55 to 64 years old	95.2	93.2	18.1	15.2	29.1	20.6	62.9	32.1	9.4
65 to 74 years old	96.5	93.9	19.9	14.9	25.4	18.6	43.2	34.8	12.8
75 years old and over	97.6	96.4	25.7	11.0	18.4	16.6	29.2	34.0	16.7
Percentiles of income: [8]									
Less than 20	80.1	75.5	5.0	6.2	5.1	3.6	10.1	14.0	3.1
20 to 39.9	91.5	87.3	12.7	8.8	8.2	7.6	30.0	19.2	4.9
40 to 59.9	98.5	95.9	11.8	15.4	16.3	12.7	53.4	24.2	7.9
60 to 79.9	99.1	98.4	14.9	26.6	28.2	18.6	69.7	29.8	7.8
80 to 89.9	99.8	99.1	16.3	32.3	35.8	26.2	81.9	29.5	12.1
90 to 100	100.0	100.0	21.5	29.9	55.0	39.1	88.5	38.1	13.0
MEDIAN VALUE [9]									
2001, total	29.8	4.2	16.0	1.1	21.3	37.3	30.9	10.7	74.6
2004, total	**23.0**	**3.8**	**15.0**	**1.0**	**15.0**	**40.4**	**35.2**	**6.0**	**45.0**
Under 35 years old	5.2	1.8	4.0	0.5	4.4	8.0	11.0	3.0	5.0
35 to 44 years old	19.0	3.0	10.0	0.5	10.0	15.9	27.9	5.0	18.3
45 to 54 years old	38.6	4.8	11.0	1.0	14.5	50.0	55.5	8.0	43.0
55 to 64 years old	78.0	6.7	29.0	2.5	25.0	75.0	83.0	10.0	65.0
65 to 74 years old	36.1	5.5	20.0	3.0	42.0	60.0	80.0	8.0	60.0
75 years old and over	38.8	6.5	22.0	5.0	50.0	60.0	30.0	5.0	50.0

[1] Includes other types of financial assets, not shown separately.   [2] Checking, savings, and money market deposit accounts, money market mutual funds, and call accounts at brokerages.   [3] Covers only those stocks that are directly held by families outside mutual funds, retirement accounts and other managed assets.   [4] Excludes money market mutual funds and indirectly held mutual funds and includes all other types of directly held pooled investment funds, such as traditional open-ended and closed-end mutual funds, real estate investment trusts, and hedge funds.   [5] The tax-deferred retirement accounts consist of IRAs, Keogh accounts, and certain employer-sponsored accounts. Employer-sponsored accounts include 401(k), 403(b), and thrift saving accounts from current or past jobs; other current job plans from which loans or withdrawals can be made; and accounts from past jobs from which the family expects to receive the account balance in the future.   [6] The value of such policies according to their current cash value, not their death benefit.   [7] Includes personal annuities and trusts with an equity interest and managed investment accounts.   [8] Percentiles of income distribution in 2004 dollars: 20th: $18,900; 40th: $33,900; 60th: $53,600; 80th: $89,300; 90th: $129,400. Percentile: A value on a scale of zero to 100 that indicates the percent of a distribution that is equal to or below it. For example, a family with income in the 80th percentile has income equal to or better than 80 percent of all other families.   [9] Median value of financial asset for families holding such assets.

Source: Board of Governors of the Federal Reserve System, "2004 Survey of Consumer Finances"; published 28 February 2006; <http://www.federalreserve.gov/pubs/oss/oss2/2004/scf2004home.html>.

Banking, Finance, and Insurance   733

Table 1153. **Flow of Funds Accounts—Liabilities of Households: 1990 to 2005**

[As of December 31 (3,715 represents $3,715,000,000,000). Includes nonprofit organizations. n.e.c. = Not elsewhere classified]

Type of instrument	Total (bil. dol.)							Percent distribution		
	1990	1995	2000	2002	2003	2004	2005	1990	2000	2005
Total liabilities	3,715	5,055	7,350	8,605	9,605	10,735	11,916	100.0	100.0	100.0
Credit market instruments.	3,593	4,858	6,961	8,297	9,254	10,292	11,497	96.7	94.7	96.5
Home mortgages [1]	2,500	3,326	4,770	5,844	6,680	7,593	8,660	67.3	64.9	72.7
Consumer credit	824	1,168	1,730	1,949	2,038	2,126	2,189	22.2	23.5	18.4
Municipal securities	87	98	143	170	184	194	211	2.3	1.9	1.8
Bank loans, n.e.c.	18	57	77	58	74	79	106	0.5	1.0	0.9
Other loans	82	116	120	121	119	120	119	2.2	1.6	1.0
Commercial mortgages.	83	92	121	156	160	180	212	2.2	1.6	1.8
Security credit	39	79	235	148	183	264	232	1.0	3.2	1.9
Trade payables	67	101	135	140	148	157	164	1.8	1.8	1.4
Unpaid life insurance premiums [2]	16	18	20	20	21	22	23	0.4	0.3	0.2

[1] Includes loans made under home equity lines of credit and home equity loans secured by junior liens.   [2] Includes deferred premiums.

Source: Board of Governors of the Federal Reserve System, "Federal Reserve Statistical Release, Z.1, Flow of Funds Accounts of the United States"; published 9 March 2006; <http://www.federalreserve.gov/releases/z1/20060309/>.

Table 1154. **Financial Debt Held by Families by Type of Debt: 2001 and 2004**

[Median debt in thousands of constant 2004 dollars (41.3 represents $41,300). See headnote, Table 1152]

Age of family head and family income	Any debt	Secured by residential property		Lines of credit not secured by residential property	Installment loans	Credit card balances [2]	Other [3]
		Primary residence [1]	Other				
PERCENT OF FAMILIES HOLDING DEBT							
2001, total	75.1	44.6	4.6	1.5	45.2	44.4	7.2
2004, total	**76.4**	**47.9**	**4.0**	**1.6**	**46.0**	**46.2**	**7.6**
Under 35 years old	79.8	37.7	2.1	2.2	59.4	47.5	6.2
35 to 44 years old	88.6	62.8	4.0	1.5	55.7	58.8	11.3
45 to 54 years old	88.4	64.6	6.3	2.9	50.2	54.0	9.4
55 to 64 years old	76.3	51.0	5.9	0.7	42.8	42.1	8.4
65 to 74 years old	58.8	32.1	3.2	0.4	27.5	31.9	4.0
75 years old and over [4]	40.3	18.7	1.5	(B)	13.9	23.6	2.5
Percentiles of income: [4]							
Less than 20.	52.6	15.9	(B)	(B)	26.9	28.8	4.6
20 to 39.9	69.8	29.5	1.5	1.5	39.9	42.9	5.8
40 to 59.9.	84.0	51.7	2.6	1.8	52.4	55.1	8.0
60 to 79.9	86.6	65.8	4.1	1.8	57.8	56.0	8.3
80 to 89.9	92.0	76.8	7.5	2.6	60.0	57.6	12.3
90 to 100	86.3	76.2	15.4	2.5	45.7	38.5	10.6
MEDIAN DEBT [5]							
2001, total	41.3	74.6	42.6	4.2	10.3	2.0	3.2
2004, total	**55.3**	**95.0**	**87.0**	**3.0**	**11.5**	**2.2**	**4.0**
Under 35 years old	33.6	107.0	62.5	1.0	11.9	1.5	3.0
35 to 44 years old	87.2	110.0	75.0	1.9	12.0	2.5	4.0
45 to 54 years old	83.2	97.0	87.0	7.0	12.0	2.9	4.0
55 to 64 years old	48.0	83.0	108.8	14.0	12.9	2.2	5.5
65 to 74 years old	25.0	51.0	100.0	4.0	8.3	2.2	5.0
75 years old and over	15.4	31.0	39.0	(B)	6.7	1.0	2.0

B Base figure too small.   [1] First and second mortgages and home equity loans and lines of credit secured by the primary residence.   [2] Families that had an outstanding balance on any of their credit cards after paying their most recent bills.   [3] Includes loans on insurance policies, loans against pension accounts, borrowing on margin accounts and unclassified loans.   [4] See footnote 8, Table 1152.   [5] Median amount of financial debt for families holding such debts.

Source: Board of Governors of the Federal Reserve System, "2004 Survey of Consumer Finances"; published 28 February 2006; <http://www.federalreserve.gov/pubs/oss/oss2/2004/scf2004home.html>.

Table 1155. **Percent Distribution of Amount of Debt Held by Families: 2001 and 2004**

[See headnote, Table 1152]

Type of debt	2001	2004	Purpose of debt	2001	2004	Type of lending institution	2001	2004
Total	100.0	100.0	Total	100.0	100.0	Total	100.0	100.0
Secured by residential property:			Primary residence:			Commercial bank	34.1	35.1
Primary residence	75.2	75.2	Purchase	70.9	70.2	Thrift institution	6.1	7.3
Other	6.2	8.5	Improvement.	2.0	1.9	Credit union	5.5	3.6
Lines of credit not			Other residential			Finance or loan company.	4.3	4.1
secured by			property.	6.5	9.5	Brokerage	3.1	2.5
residential property	0.5	0.7	Investments, excluding			Real estate lender [1] . . .	38.0	39.4
Installment loans	12.3	11.0	real estate	2.8	2.2	Individual lender	2.0	1.7
Credit card balances. . . .	3.4	3.0	Vehicles	7.8	6.7	Other nonfinancial	1.4	2.0
Other	2.3	1.6	Goods and services. . . .	5.8	6.0	Government	1.1	0.7
			Education	3.1	3.0	Credit card issuer	3.7	3.0
			Other loans	1.1	0.6	Other loans	0.8	0.5

[1] Includes mortgage lender.

Source: Board of Governors of the Federal Reserve System, "2004 Survey of Consumer Finances"; published 28 February 2006; <http://www.federalreserve.gov/pubs/oss/oss2/2004/scf2004home.html>.

Table 1156. **Ratios of Debt Payments to Family Income: 1995 to 2004**

[In percent. All dollar figures are adjusted to 2004 dollars using the "current methods" version of the consumer price index for all urban consumers published by U.S. Bureau of Labor Statistics. Families include one-person units; for definition of family, see text, Section 1. Based on Survey of Consumer Finance; see Appendix III. For definition of median, see Guide to Tabular Presentation]

Age of family head and family income (constant (2004) dollars)	Ratio of debt payments to family income						Percent of debtors with—					
	Aggregate			Median			Ratios above 40 percent			Any payment 60 days or more past due		
	1995	2001	2004	1995	2001	2004	1995	2001	2004	1995	2001	2004
All families	14.1	12.9	14.4	16.2	16.7	18.0	11.7	11.8	12.2	7.1	7.0	8.9
Under 35 years old	17.8	17.2	17.8	16.8	17.7	18.0	12.1	12.0	12.8	8.7	11.9	13.7
35 to 44 years old	17.2	15.1	18.2	18.3	17.8	20.6	9.9	10.1	12.6	7.7	5.9	11.7
45 to 54 years old	15.1	12.8	15.3	16.6	17.4	18.4	12.3	11.6	13.1	7.4	6.2	7.6
55 to 64 years old	11.8	10.9	11.5	14.2	14.3	15.8	15.1	12.3	10.2	3.2	7.1	4.2
65 to 74 years old	7.2	9.2	8.7	12.3	16.0	15.6	11.3	14.7	11.6	5.3	1.5	3.4
75 years old and over	2.5	3.9	7.1	2.9	8.0	12.8	7.4	14.6	10.7	5.4	0.8	3.9
Percentiles of income: [1]												
Less than 20	19.1	16.1	18.2	13.3	19.2	19.7	27.5	29.3	27.0	10.2	13.4	15.9
20 to 39.9	17.0	15.8	16.7	17.5	16.7	17.4	18.0	16.6	18.6	10.1	11.7	13.8
40 to 59.9	15.6	17.1	19.4	15.7	17.6	19.5	9.9	12.3	13.7	8.7	7.9	10.4
60 to 79.9	17.9	16.8	18.5	18.9	18.1	20.6	7.7	6.5	7.1	6.6	4.0	7.1
80 to 89.9	16.6	17.0	17.3	16.8	17.3	18.1	4.7	3.5	2.4	2.8	2.6	2.3
90 to 100	9.5	8.1	9.3	12.6	11.2	12.7	2.3	2.0	1.8	1.0	1.3	0.3

[1] See footnote 8, Table 1152.

Source: Board of Governors of the Federal Reserve System, "2004 Survey of Consumer Finances"; published 28 February 2006; <http://www.federalreserve.gov/pubs/oss/oss2/2004/scf2004home.html>.

Table 1157. **Household Debt-Service Payments and Financial Obligations as a Percentage of Disposable Personal Income: 1980 to 2005**

[As of end of year, seasonally adjusted. Household debt service ratio is an estimate of the ratio of debt payments to disposable personal income. Debt payments consist of the estimated required payments on outstanding mortgage and consumer debt. The financial obligations ratio adds automobile lease payments, rental payments on tenant-occupied property, homeowners' insurance, and property tax payments to the debt service ratio]

Year	Household debt service ratio	Financial obligations ratio			Year	Household debt service ratio	Financial obligations ratio		
		Total	Home-owner	Renter			Total	Home-owner	Renter
1980 . . .	10.58	15.37	13.31	23.70	2001 . . .	13.20	18.68	16.06	31.73
1990 . . .	11.98	17.37	15.50	24.69	2002 . . .	13.27	18.53	16.10	30.81
1995 . . .	11.84	17.45	15.14	27.00	2003 . . .	13.17	18.18	15.83	30.76
1999 . . .	12.35	17.83	15.41	29.39	2004 . . .	13.17	17.97	15.87	29.22
2000 . . .	12.77	18.14	15.64	30.54	2005 . . .	13.86	18.62	16.77	28.43

Source: Board of Governors of the Federal Reserve System, "Household Debt Service and Financial Obligations Ratios;" <http://www.federalreserve.gov/releases/housedebt/default.htm>.

Table 1158. **Selected Financial Institutions—Number and Assets by Asset Size: 2005**

[As of December. 9,039.7 represents $9,039,700,000,000. FDIC = Federal Deposit Insurance Corporation]

Asset size	Number of institutions			Assets (bil. dol.)		
	F.D.I.C.-insured			F.D.I.C.-insured		
	Commercial banks	Savings institutions	Credit unions [1]	Commercial banks [2]	Savings institutions	Credit unions [1]
Total	7,527	1,305	8,695	9,039.7	1,837.0	678.7
Less than $25.0 million	596	83	5,673	10.1	1.3	41.8
$25.0 million to $49.9 million	1,096	114	1,079	40.7	4.3	38.3
$50.0 million to $99.9 million	1,765	207	756	129.1	15.1	52.9
$100.0 million to $499.9 million . . .	3,137	588	921	688.2	136.1	198.5
$500.0 million to $999.9 million . . .	458	158	160	312.9	110.6	108.7
$1.0 billion to $2.9 billion	272	86	90	436.4	137.3	137.9
$3.0 billion or more	203	69	16	7,422.3	1,432.8	100.4
	Percent distribution					
Total	100.0	100.0	100.0	100.0	100.0	100.0
Less than $25.0 million	7.9	6.4	65.2	0.1	0.1	6.2
$25.0 million to $49.9 million	14.6	8.7	12.4	0.5	0.2	5.6
$50.0 million to $99.9 million	23.4	15.9	8.7	1.4	0.8	7.8
$100.0 million to $499.9 million . . .	41.7	45.1	10.6	7.6	7.4	29.3
$500.0 million to $999.9 million . . .	6.1	12.1	1.8	3.5	6.0	16.0
$1.0 billion to $2.9 billion	3.6	6.6	1.0	4.8	7.5	20.3
$3.0 billion or more	2.7	5.3	0.2	82.1	78.0	14.8

[1] Source: National Credit Union Administration, *National Credit Union Administration Year-end Statistics 2005*. Excludes nonfederally insured state chartered credit unions and federally insured corporate credit unions.   [2] Includes foreign branches of U.S. banks.

Source: Except as noted, U.S. Federal Deposit Insurance Corporation, *Statistics on Banking, 2005.*

Table 1159. **FDIC-Insured Financial Institutions—Number, Assets, and Liabilities: 1990 to 2005**

[In billions of dollars, except as indicated (4,649 represents $4,649,000,000,000). As of Dec. 31. 2005 data preliminary. Includes island areas. Except as noted, includes foreign branches of U.S. banks]

Item	1990	1995	1999	2000	2001	2002	2003	2004	2005
All banking offices	**84,240**	**81,172**	**86,199**	**86,158**	**86,709**	**87,560**	**88,635**	**90,956**	**92,379**
Commercial bank offices, total [1]	62,630	65,711	71,641	72,027	72,569	73,642	74,785	77,239	79,243
Number of main offices	12,376	9,972	8,598	8,331	8,096	7,903	7,783	7,643	7,527
Number of branches	50,254	55,739	63,043	63,696	64,473	65,739	67,002	69,596	71,716
Savings institutions offices, total	21,610	15,461	14,558	14,131	14,140	13,918	13,850	13,717	13,136
Number of main offices	2,815	2,030	1,642	1,589	1,534	1,466	1,411	1,345	1,305
Number of branches	18,795	13,431	12,916	12,542	12,606	12,452	12,439	12,372	11,831
Number of financial institutions reporting	15,158	11,970	10,222	9,905	9,613	9,354	9,181	8,976	8,832
Assets, total [2]	**4,649**	**5,338**	**6,884**	**7,462**	**7,868**	**8,436**	**9,075**	**10,106**	**10,877**
Net loans and leases	2,867	3,198	4,187	4,576	4,687	4,968	5,349	6,037	6,639
Real estate loans	1,586	1,690	2,181	2,396	2,561	2,850	3,144	3,684	4,142
1–4 family residential mortgages . .	859	1,006	1,251	1,340	1,380	1,513	1,611	1,837	2,046
Commercial real estate	328	349	471	525	570	628	682	753	824
Construction and development	171	90	165	197	232	245	272	337	449
Home equity loans [3]	86	98	121	151	184	256	346	491	534
Commercial and industrial loans	646	674	996	1,086	1,020	953	922	968	1,086
Loans to individuals.	451	576	618	672	701	772	848	930	948
Credit cards and related plans	142	224	227	266	250	292	339	399	395
Farm loans	33	40	46	49	48	47	47	49	52
Other loans and leases	245	294	416	448	440	435	478	492	492
Less: Reserve for losses	65	60	66	71	80	85	86	82	77
Less: Unearned income	29	15	4	3	3	4	3	3	3
Securities	890	1,099	1,338	1,361	1,465	1,633	1,771	1,860	1,893
Domestic office assets	4,259	4,753	6,144	6,702	7,119	7,684	8,251	9,160	9,824
Foreign office assets.	390	585	740	760	749	752	824	945	1,053
Liabilities and capital, total	**4,649**	**5,338**	**6,884**	**7,462**	**7,868**	**8,436**	**9,075**	**10,106**	**10,877**
Noninterest-bearing deposits	511	641	745	802	927	1,002	1,028	1,121	1,267
Interest-bearing deposits	3,127	3,129	3,793	4,113	4,262	4,566	4,926	5,463	5,875
Other borrowed funds	569	849	1,376	1,467	1,496	1,571	1,735	1,905	2,063
Subordinated debt	28	46	79	90	99	99	107	119	131
Other liabilities.	128	238	315	356	377	422	450	459	423
Equity capital.	286	436	575	634	707	776	831	1,039	1,119
Domestic office deposits	3,344	3,315	3,882	4,208	4,560	4,911	5,213	5,719	6,221
Foreign office deposits	293	454	656	707	630	658	741	866	921
Estimated insured deposits [4]	2,629	2,662	2,868	3,054	3,210	3,382	3,452	3,621	3,892

[1] Includes insured branches of foreign banks that file a Call Report. [2] Includes other items not shown separately. [3] For one- to four-family residential properties. [4] Excludes foreign office deposits which are uninsured.

Source: U.S. Federal Deposit Insurance Corporation, *The FDIC Quarterly Banking Profile, Annual Report, Statistics on Banking*, annual; and *FDIC Quarterly Banking Profile Graph Book*.

Table 1160. **FDIC-Insured Financial Institutions—Income and Selected Measures of Financial Condition: 1990 to 2005**

[In billions of dollars, except as indicated (437.7 represents $437,700,000,000). 2005 data preliminary. Includes island areas. Includes foreign branches of U.S. banks]

Item	1990	1995	1999	2000	2001	2002	2003	2004	2005
Interest income	437.7	373.4	441.5	512.2	486.8	429.5	404.6	418.7	523.5
Interest expense	295.9	190.7	218.0	276.5	235.0	152.9	122.6	124.0	204.9
Net interest income.	141.8	182.7	223.5	235.7	251.8	276.6	281.9	294.7	318.6
Provisions for loan losses	41.4	14.7	23.4	32.0	46.3	51.5	37.3	28.9	29.6
Noninterest income.	62.2	89.5	154.2	164.8	168.8	183.5	202.7	202.9	222.1
Percent of net operating revenue [1]	30.5	32.9	40.8	41.1	40.1	39.9	41.8	40.8	41.1
Noninterest expense.	144.2	171.6	228.2	241.6	251.1	263.7	279.7	295.5	317.2
Income taxes.	9.1	30.3	45.5	43.7	44.0	51.9	58.9	58.6	64.8
Net income	11.3	56.4	82.4	81.7	87.2	105.0	120.5	122.4	134.2
PERFORMANCE RATIOS									
Return on assets [2] (percent)	0.24	1.10	1.25	1.14	1.14	1.30	1.38	1.28	1.28
Return on equity [3] (percent)	3.95	13.63	14.71	13.55	12.99	14.12	15.04	13.22	12.46
Net interest margin [4] (percent)	3.47	4.05	3.90	3.78	3.78	3.96	3.73	3.53	3.49
Net charge-offs [5]	34.8	14.4	21.6	26.3	38.9	47.0	40.8	32.0	31.6
Net charge-offs to loans and leases, total (percent).	1.19	0.46	0.53	0.59	0.83	0.97	0.78	0.56	0.49
Net charge-off rate, credit card loans (percent). . .	3.39	3.39	4.40	4.37	5.15	5.47	5.75	4.88	6.05
CONDITION RATIOS									
Equity capital to assets (percent).	6.16	8.16	8.35	8.49	8.99	9.20	9.15	10.29	10.29
Noncurrent assets plus other real estate owned to assets [6] (percent)	3.16	0.92	0.63	0.71	0.88	0.90	0.75	0.53	0.50
Percentage of banks losing money	16.5	3.1	7.6	7.5	8.2	6.7	6.0	6.0	6.1
Number of problem institutions	1,492	193	79	94	114	136	116	80	52
Assets of problem institutions	640	31	10	24	40	39	30	28	7
Number of failed/assisted institutions	169	6	8	7	4	11	3	4	–

– Represents zero. [1] Net operating revenue equals net interest income plus noninterest income. [2] Net income (including securities transactions and nonrecurring items) as a percentage of average total assets. [3] Net income as a percentage of average total equity capital. [4] Interest income less interest expense as a percentage of average earning assets (i.e. the profit margin a bank earns on its loans and investments). [5] Total loans and leases charged off (removed from balance sheet because of uncollectibility), less amounts recovered on loans and leases previously charged off. [6] Noncurrent assets: the sum of loans, leases, debt securities and other assets that are 90 days or more past due, or in nonaccrual status. Other real estate owned: primarily foreclosed property.

Source: U.S. Federal Deposit Insurance Corporation, *Annual Report; Statistics on Banking*, annual; and *FDIC Quarterly Banking Profile.*

Table 1161. FDIC-Insured Financial Institutions by Asset Size: 2005

[In percent, except as indicated (9,040 represents $9,040,000,000,000). Preliminary. See headnote, Table 1160]

Item	Total	Less than $100 million	$100 million to $1 billion	$1 billion to $10 billion	Greater than $10 billion
COMMERCIAL BANKS					
Number of institutions reporting.	7,527	3,459	3,593	391	84
Assets, total (bil. dol.).	9,040	180	1,001	1,075	6,784
Deposits (bil. dol.).	6,073	150	814	754	4,356
Net income (bil. dol.).	114	2	12	14	86
Return on assets	1.31	1.01	1.32	1.37	1.31
Return on equity	12.91	8.28	13.03	12.74	13.07
Equity capital to assets	10.10	11.92	10.02	10.69	9.96
Noncurrent assets plus other real estate					
owned to assets.	0.48	0.67	0.54	0.43	0.48
Net charge-offs to loans and leases.	0.56	0.21	0.22	0.29	0.67
Percentage of banks losing money	6.2	10.8	2.4	1.5	–
SAVINGS INSTITUTIONS					
Number of institutions reporting.	1,305	404	746	121	34
Assets, total (bil. dol.).	1,837	20	247	318	1,252
Deposits (bil. dol.).	1,068	16	185	219	648
Net income (bil. dol.).	20	2	2	3	14
Return on assets	1.15	0.96	0.94	1.01	1.24
Return on equity	10.38	6.68	8.61	9.62	11.00
Equity capital to assets	11.23	14.36	10.96	10.64	11.38
Noncurrent assets plus other real estate					
owned to assets.	0.57	0.76	0.47	0.46	0.61
Net charge-offs to loans and leases.	0.25	0.08	0.09	0.09	0.31
Percentage of banks losing money	5.5	11.1	3.1	3.3	–

– Represents zero.

Source: U.S. Federal Deposit Insurance Corporation, *Annual Report; Statistics on Banking*, annual; and *FDIC Quarterly Banking Profile*. See also <http://www.fdic.gov/bank/index.html>.

Table 1162. FDIC-Insured Financial Institutions—Number and Assets by State and Island Areas: 2005

[In billions of dollars, except as indicated (10,877.1 represents $10,877,100,000,000). As of Dec. 31. Information is obtained primarily from the Federal Financial Institutions Examination Council (FFIEC) Call Reports and the Office of Thrift Supervision's Thrift Financial Reports. Data are based on the location of each reporting institution's main office. Reported data may include assets located outside of the reporting institution's home state]

State or island area	Number of insti- tutions	Assets by asset size of bank				State or island area	Number of insti- tutions	Assets by asset size of bank			
		Total	Less than $1 bil.	$1 bil. to $10 bil.	Greater than $10 bil.			Total	Less than $1 bil.	$1 bil. to $10 bil.	Greater than $10 bil.
Total	8,832	10,877.1	1,448.3	1,393.0	8,035.8	NV	40	392.0	6.8	38.0	347.3
						NH	27	19.4	8.0	11.4	–
AL	161	220.2	26.7	7.7	185.8	NJ	136	157.8	31.7	64.7	61.4
AK	7	4.1	1.9	2.2	–	NM	56	16.7	8.6	8.1	–
AZ	52	81.3	7.9	10.4	63.0	NY	205	1,198.7	43.4	112.1	1,043.2
AR	161	44.4	28.8	15.6	–	NC	108	1,707.8	27.5	12.7	1,667.6
CA	303	656.3	60.3	146.0	450.0	ND	99	16.7	10.2	6.5	–
CO	172	43.9	27.6	16.3	–	OH	278	1,633.9	42.3	37.1	1,554.6
CT	58	65.8	16.3	21.0	28.5	OK	273	62.1	31.1	7.9	23.1
DE	35	470.9	5.3	45.6	420.0	OR	40	25.9	8.1	17.8	–
DC	7	1.1	1.1	–	–	PA	254	383.7	59.2	69.0	255.5
FL	300	142.1	62.4	68.5	11.2	RI	13	29.8	1.7	14.6	13.4
GA	349	274.5	64.3	32.9	177.2	SC	95	48.7	17.1	31.7	–
HI	7	36.2	1.1	13.3	21.8	SD	92	471.2	12.5	11.5	447.3
ID	18	6.5	6.5	–	–	TN	204	82.4	36.8	9.3	36.3
IL	707	377.2	111.2	67.6	198.4	TX	661	237.6	87.8	87.4	62.4
IN	186	101.7	36.7	38.8	26.3	UT	69	224.5	12.0	23.2	189.4
IA	411	53.7	46.9	6.9	–	VT	19	8.3	3.8	4.5	–
KS	371	60.5	37.2	23.4	–	VA	144	269.4	32.9	16.1	220.4
KY	227	52.6	33.8	18.8	–	WA	96	57.8	23.4	34.4	–
LA	163	72.6	27.8	5.0	39.8	WV	70	21.0	10.2	10.8	–
ME	37	47.7	11.6	4.0	32.1	WI	302	128.3	48.4	19.2	60.7
MD	113	50.7	24.9	25.8	–	WY	43	6.2	6.2	–	–
MA	194	231.1	54.3	42.3	134.5						
MI	174	212.2	32.6	24.7	154.9						
MN	466	66.5	48.3	4.6	13.5	AS	1	0.1	0.1	–	–
MS	100	47.9	17.6	18.5	11.8	GU	3	1.0	1.0	–	–
MO	373	98.1	52.5	33.1	12.5	FM	1	0.1	0.1	–	–
MT	81	15.9	10.2	5.7	–	PR	10	103.0	–	31.2	71.8
NE	258	36.8	21.4	15.5	–	VI	2	0.2	0.2	–	–

– Represents zero.

Source: U.S. Federal Deposit Insurance Corporation, *Statistics on Banking*, annual.

Table 1163. FDIC-Insured Financial Institutions—Number of Offices and Deposits by State: 2005

[As of June 30 (5,933.8 represents $5,933,800,000,000). Includes insured U.S. branches of foreign banks. The term "offices" includes both main offices and branches. "Banking office" is defined to include all offices and facilities that actually hold deposits, and does not include loan production offices, computer centers, and other nondeposit installations, such as automated teller machines (ATMs). Several institutions have designated home offices that do not accept deposits; these have been included to provide a more complete listing of all offices. The figures for each geographical area only include deposits of offices located within that area. Based on the Summary of Deposits survey]

State	Number of offices	Total deposits (bil. dol.)	State	Number of offices	Total deposits (bil. dol.)	State	Number of offices	Total deposits (bil. dol.)
Total [1] .	92,047	5,933.8	IA.	1,577	51.0	NC	2,544	184.2
			KS	1,505	48.3	ND	422	12.2
U.S.	91,408	5,875.8	KY	1,750	57.2	OH	3,994	201.2
AL	1,454	65.3	LA	1,547	57.1	OK	1,280	48.3
AK	134	6.4	ME	507	18.1	OR	1,044	42.3
AZ	1,140	72.8	MD	1,707	88.9	PA	4,643	225.2
AR	1,370	41.4	MA	2,131	172.2	RI	240	21.8
CA	6,621	753.6	MI	3,057	139.4	SC	1,289	53.8
CO	1,464	70.4	MN	1,763	96.1	SD	459	42.1
CT	1,197	76.9	MS	1,136	35.0	TN	2,113	95.2
DE	263	138.8	MO	2,225	92.8	TX	5,863	356.1
DC	211	22.6	MT	370	12.6	UT	594	118.1
FL	5,081	342.8	NE	1,021	33.4	VT	276	9.5
GA	2,643	149.4	NV	502	48.2	VA	2,438	155.3
HI	285	24.8	NH	427	29.7	WA	1,832	91.5
ID	489	15.1	NJ	3,222	222.6	WV	639	23.3
IL	4,646	303.7	NM	498	19.7	WI	2,298	100.6
IN	2,345	84.5	NY	4,942	695.5	WY	210	8.6

[1] Includes Puerto Rico and other areas, not shown separately.

Source: U.S. Federal Deposit Insurance Corporation, *Bank and Thrift Branch Office Data Book*, annual.

Table 1164. U.S. Banking Offices of Foreign Banks—Summary: 1990 to 2005

[In billions of dollars, except as indicated (791 represents $791,000,000,000). As of December. Data cover foreign-bank branches and agencies in the 50 states and the District of Columbia, New York investment companies (through September 1996); U.S. commercial banks of which more than 25 percent is owned by foreign banks, and International Banking Facilities. Foreign banks are those owned by institutions located outside of the United States and its affiliated insular areas]

Item	1990	1995	2000	2001	2002	2003	2004	2005	Share [1] 1990	Share [1] 1995	Share [1] 2000	Share [1] 2005
Assets	791	984	1,299	1,385	1,338	1,369	1,548	1,845	21.4	21.7	19.9	19.8
Loans, total	398	461	531	523	471	445	503	631	18.0	17.3	13.7	11.8
Business	193	249	296	271	238	192	198	241	30.8	35.1	27.1	22.8
Deposits	384	523	709	743	665	686	808	932	14.5	17.6	17.6	16.2

[1] Percent of "domestically owned" commercial banks plus U.S. offices of foreign banks.

Source: Board of Governors of the Federal Reserve System, "Share Data for U.S. Offices of Foreign Banks"; published 27 March 2006; <http://www.federalreserve.gov/releases/Iba/Share/SHRTBL1.html>.

Table 1165. Federal and State-Chartered Credit Unions—Summary: 1990 to 2005

[Except as noted, as of December 31 (36,241 represents 36,241,000). Federal data include District of Columbia, Puerto Rico, Guam, and Virgin Islands. Excludes state-insured, privately-insured, and noninsured state-chartered credit unions and corporate central credit unions which have mainly other credit unions as members]

Year	Operating credit unions Federal	Operating credit unions State	Number of failed institutions [1]	Members (1,000) Federal	Members (1,000) State	Assets (mil. dol.) Federal	Assets (mil. dol.) State	Loans outstanding (mil. dol.) Federal	Loans outstanding (mil. dol.) State	Savings (mil. dol.) Federal	Savings (mil. dol.) State
1990 . . .	8,511	4,349	164	36,241	19,454	130,073	68,133	83,029	44,102	117,892	62,082
1995 . . .	7,329	4,358	26	42,163	24,927	193,781	112,860	120,514	71,606	170,300	99,838
1998 . . .	6,814	4,181	17	43,865	29,674	231,890	156,811	144,849	100,890	202,651	137,348
1999 . . .	6,566	4,062	23	44,076	31,308	239,316	172,086	155,578	116,366	207,614	149,305
2000 . . .	6,336	3,980	29	43,883	33,705	242,881	195,363	163,851	137,485	210,188	169,053
2001 . . .	6,118	3,866	22	43,817	35,560	270,123	231,432	170,326	152,112	235,201	201,923
2002 . . .	5,953	3,735	15	44,600	36,300	301,238	255,837	181,768	160,881	261,819	222,372
2003 . . .	5,776	3,593	13	46,153	36,287	336,611	273,572	202,898	173,236	291,484	236,856
2004 . . .	5,572	3,442	21	46,858	36,710	358,701	288,294	223,878	190,376	308,317	247,804
2005 . . .	5,393	3,302	22	47,914	36,896	377,827	300,871	249,521	208,734	321,831	255,588

[1] 1990 for year ending September 30; 1995 reflects 15-month period from October 1994 through December 1995; beginning 1998, reflects calendar year. A failed institution is defined as a credit union which has ceased operation because it was involuntarily liquidated or merged with assistance from the National Credit Union Share Insurance Fund.

Source: National Credit Union Administration, *Annual Report of the National Credit Union Administration*, and unpublished data.

U.S. Census Bureau, *Statistical Abstract of the United States: 2007*

Table 1166. **Percentage of Households Using Selected Electronic Banking Technologies: 1995 to 2004**

[Covers only those households that have an account at a bank, thrift institution, or credit union. Based on sample surveys. For details of Survey of Consumer Finances, see Appendix III. For Surveys of Consumers, based on data from approximately 1,000 respondents; for details, see source]

Technology	Survey of Consumer Finances				Surveys of Consumers	
	1995	1998	2001	2004	1999	2003
ELECTRONIC						
Direct deposit of any type.	53	67	71	74	65	70
ATM card	35	55	57	65	59	65
Debit card [1]	20	37	49	61	(NA)	54
Preauthorized debts	25	40	44	50	31	46
Automated phone system.	(NA)	26	22	20	40	44
Computer banking	4	7	20	34	10	32
Smart card [2]	1	2	3	(NA)	(NA)	6
Prepaid card [2]	(NA)	(NA)	(NA)	(NA)	(NA)	73
NON-ELECTRONIC						
In person	87	81	78	78	(NA)	(NA)
Mail	59	55	51	51	(NA)	(NA)
Phone (talk in person)	(NA)	43	42	42	(NA)	(NA)

NA Not available.   [1] A debit card is a card that automatically deducts the amount of a purchase from the money in an account.   [2] A smart card is a type of payment card containing a computer chip which is set to hold a sum of money. As the card is used, purchases are subtracted from that sum. Prepaid cards are cards that contain a stored value, or a value that has been paid up-front, allowing you to use the card much like cash. As you use the card, the prepaid value is drawn down. Examples are phone cards and gift cards. Smart cards are different from prepaid cards in that you can add money to the card at special machines designed for smart cards or sometimes at ATMs.

Source: Board of Governors of the Federal Reserve System, *Federal Reserve Bulletin*, winter 2004 and unpublished data.

Table 1167. **Percent of U.S. Households That Use Selected Payment Instruments: 1995 to 2004**

[**In percent**. Based on Survey of Consumer Finances conducted by the Board of Governors of the Federal Reserve System; see Appendix III]

Age and education of head of household	Any of these instruments		ATM [1]		Debit card		Direct deposit		Automatic bill paying		Software [2]	
	1995	2004	1995	2004	1995	2004	1995	2004	1995	2004	2001	2004
All households	77.7	90.4	62.5	74.4	17.6	59.3	46.7	71.2	21.8	47.4	18.0	19.3
Under 30 years old	76.3	87.3	72.3	83.0	24.4	74.4	31.0	54.0	17.7	36.5	17.0	20.4
30 to 60 years old.	78.7	90.3	68.6	82.3	19.7	67.6	42.8	68.2	24.4	50.3	22.0	21.9
61 years old and over	76.1	91.9	44.2	51.6	9.6	32.5	63.3	87.0	18.2	46.5	9.0	12.8
No college degree.	71.4	86.2	54.7	67.4	14.3	54.9	40.3	64.3	18.1	39.5	10.9	12.4
College degree.	91.8	97.5	80.4	86.4	25.2	67.0	61.0	83.2	30.1	61.1	31.8	31.3

[1] The question on ATMs asked whether any member of the household had an ATM card, not whether the member used it. The other questions asked about usage.   [2] The question on software asked whether the respondent or spouse/partner uses any type of computer software to help in managing their money.

Source: Mester, Loretta J., "Changes in the Use of Electronic Means of Payment: 1995–2004," *Business Review*, Second Quarter 2006, published by Federal Reserve Bank of Philadelphia. See also <http://www.philadelphiafed.org/files/br/br_q2-2006-4_changes-electronic-means.pdf>.

Table 1168. **Debit Cards—Holders, Number, Transactions, and Volume, 2000 and 2004, and Projections, 2009**

[172 represents 172,000,000]

Type of debit card	Cardholders (mil.)		Number of cards (mil.)			Number of transactions (mil.)			Volume (bil. dol.)		
	2004	2009, proj.	2000	2004	2009, proj.	2000	2004	2009, proj.	2000	2004	2009, proj.
Total [1]	172	183	235	278	293	9,797	22,233	38,445	448	1,010	1,886
Bank [2]	189	220	137	229	234	6,797	14,106	22,120	327	692	1,137
EFT systems [3].	171	182	223	267	283	2,979	8,107	16,306	119	317	748
Other [4].	11	10	11	11	10	22	19	19	1	1	1

[1] Cardholders may hold more than one type of card. Bank cards and EFT cards are the same pieces of plastic that carry multiple brands. The total card figure shown does not include any duplication.   [2] Visa and MasterCard debit cards.   [3] Cards issued by financial institution members of regional and national switches such as Star, Interlink, Pulse, NYCE, etc. EFT = Electronic funds transfer.   [4] Retail cards such as those issued by supermarkets.

Source: The Nilson Report, Carpinteria, CA, Twice-monthly newsletter. (Copyright used by permission.)

Banking, Finance, and Insurance   739

Table 1169. **Credit Cards—Holders, Number, Spending, and Debt, 2000 and 2004, and Projections, 2009**

[159 represents 159,000,000]

Type of credit card	Cardholders (mil.)			Number of cards (mil.)			Credit card volume (bil. dol.)			Credit card debt outstanding (bil. dol.)		
	2000	2004	2009, proj.	2000	2004	2009, proj.	2000	2004	2009, proj.	2000	2004	2009, proj.
Total [1]	**159**	**164**	**176**	**1,425**	**1,422**	**1,471**	**1,458**	**1,882**	**2,742**	**680**	**801**	**962**
Bank [2]	(NA)	(NA)	(NA)	455	567	659	938	1,269	1,794	480	596	701
Store	114	114	114	597	503	468	120	123	136	92	84	93
Oil company	76	62	55	98	81	77	50	59	85	5	8	10
Other [3]	132	131	119	275	272	267	350	432	728	103	114	158

NA Not available. [1] Cardholders may hold more than one type of card. [2] Visa and MasterCard credit cards. [3] Includes Universal Air Travel Plan (UATP), phone cards, automobile rental, and miscellaneous cards. Except for data on cardholders, also includes Discover and American Express.

Source: The Nilson Report, Carpinteria, CA, Twice-monthly newsletter. (Copyright used by permission.)

Table 1170. **Usage of General Purpose Credit Cards by Families: 1995 to 2004**

[General purpose credit cards include Mastercard, Visa, Optima, and Discover cards. Excludes cards used only for business purposes. All dollar figures are given in constant 2004 dollars based on consumer price index data as published by U.S. Bureau of Labor Statistics. Families include one-person units; for definition of family, see text, Section 1. Based on Survey of Consumer Finances; see Appendix III. For definition of median, see Guide to Tabular Presentation]

Age of family head and family income	Percent having a general purpose credit card	Median number of cards	Median new charges on last month's bills (dol.)	Percent having a balance after last month's bills	Median balance (dol.) [1]	Percent of cardholding families who—		
						Almost always pay off the balance	Some-times pay off the balance	Hardly ever pay off the balance
1995, total	66.5	2	200	56.0	1,700	52.4	20.1	27.5
1998, total	67.5	2	200	54.7	2,000	53.8	19.3	26.9
2001, total	72.7	2	200	53.7	1,900	55.3	19.1	25.6
2004, total	**71.5**	**2**	**300**	**56.2**	**2,100**	**55.7**	**20.3**	**24.0**
Under 35 years old	60.6	2	200	66.1	1,500	49.0	20.4	30.6
35 to 44 years old.	73.3	2	300	70.8	2,400	41.6	26.2	32.2
45 to 54 years old.	77.5	2	300	61.2	3,000	49.3	23.9	26.8
55 to 64 years old.	78.2	2	400	46.1	2,500	66.8	16.8	16.5
65 to 74 years old.	75.5	2	300	37.7	2,300	70.7	13.4	15.9
75 years old and over	65.4	2	200	32.2	1,100	77.5	12.9	9.7
Less than $10,000	31.5	1	100	59.4	1,200	50.9	17.3	31.9
$10,000 to $24,999	48.6	1	100	59.7	1,200	49.9	17.0	33.1
$25,000 to $49,999	71.2	2	200	64.3	2,000	46.9	20.3	32.8
$50,000 to $99,999	88.2	2	300	56.1	2,800	56.1	22.0	21.8
$100,000 and more.	96.6	2	1,200	42.8	3,400	71.1	20.2	8.7

[1] Among families having a balance.

Source: Board of Governors of the Federal Reserve System, unpublished data.

Table 1171. **Consumer Credit Outstanding and Finance Rates: 1990 to 2005**

[In billions of dollars, except percent (808 represents $808,000,000,000). Covers most short- and intermediate-term credit extended to individuals, excluding loans secured by real estate. Estimated amounts of seasonally adjusted credit outstanding as of end of year; finance rates, annual averages]

Type of credit	1990	1995	1998	1999	2000	2001	2002	2003	2004	2005
Total.	808	1,141	1,416	1,528	1,705	1,836	1,922	2,010	2,097	2,158
Revolving	239	443	576	604	676	713	733	753	781	802
Nonrevolving [1]	570	698	839	924	1,029	1,122	1,189	1,257	1,316	1,356
FINANCE RATES (percent)										
Commercial banks:										
New automobiles (48 months)	11.78	9.57	8.73	8.44	9.34	8.50	7.62	6.93	6.60	7.08
Other consumer goods (24 months)	15.46	13.94	13.76	13.39	13.90	13.22	12.54	11.95	11.89	12.02
Credit-card plans.	18.17	15.99	15.70	15.19	15.78	14.87	13.40	12.30	12.71	12.50
Finance companies:										
New automobiles.	12.54	11.19	6.30	6.66	6.61	5.65	4.29	3.40	4.36	5.46
Used automobiles	15.99	14.48	12.64	12.60	13.55	12.18	10.74	9.72	8.96	9.03

[1] Comprises automobile loans and all other loans not included in revolving credit, such as loans for mobile homes, education, boats, trailers, or vacations. These loans may be secured or unsecured.

Source: Board of Governors of the Federal Reserve System, *Statistical Supplement to the Federal Reserve Bulletin*, monthly.

Table 1172. Consumer Credit by Type of Holder: 1990 to 2005

[In billions of dollars. As of December 31. Not seasonally adjusted]

Type of holder	1990	1995	1998	1999	2000	2001	2002	2003	2004	2005
Total	824	1,168	1,438	1,551	1,730	1,862	1,949	2,038	2,126	2,189
Nonfinancial corporations	67	85	79	79	84	76	78	63	65	63
U.S. government	–	10	37	51	67	80	93	94	98	102
Commercial banking	382	502	512	508	551	568	603	669	704	707
Savings institutions	50	40	52	62	65	71	69	78	91	109
Credit unions	92	132	155	168	184	190	196	206	215	231
Government-sponsored enterprises	19	34	28	34	37	39	37	21	–	–
Asset-backed securities issuers	77	213	389	448	521	600	637	611	585	618
Finance companies	138	152	183	202	221	238	238	295	367	358

– Represents or rounds to zero.

Source: Board of Governors of the Federal Reserve System, "Federal Reserve Statistical Release, Z.1, Flow of Funds Accounts of the United States"; published 9 March 2006; <http://www.federalreserve.gov/releases/z1/20060309/>.

Table 1173. Mortgage Debt Outstanding by Type of Property and Holder: 1990 to 2005

[In billions of dollars (3,803 represents $3,803,000,000,000). As of December 31]

Type of property and holder	1990	1995	1998	1999	2000	2001	2002	2003	2004	2005
Total mortgages [1]	3,803	4,550	5,614	6,216	6,761	7,423	8,244	9,234	10,472	11,942
Home [2]	2,615	3,451	4,259	4,674	5,075	5,571	6,244	7,024	8,016	9,149
Multifamily residential	288	276	334	376	406	448	487	557	612	674
Commercial	821	739	923	1,063	1,170	1,286	1,388	1,520	1,702	1,968
Farm	79	85	97	103	110	118	125	133	142	151
Household sector	143	116	98	106	117	125	136	148	161	174
Commercial banking	849	1,090	1,337	1,495	1,660	1,790	2,058	2,256	2,595	2,958
Savings institutions	802	597	644	668	723	758	781	870	1,057	1,152
Credit unions	50	66	97	111	125	141	159	183	213	246
Life insurance companies	268	213	214	231	236	243	250	261	273	283
Government-sponsored enterprises (GSE)	156	250	247	242	264	297	357	463	478	474
Agency- and GSE-backed mortgage pools	1,020	1,571	2,019	2,294	2,493	2,832	3,159	3,489	3,542	3,678
Asset-backed securities issuers	68	248	479	552	611	712	797	967	1,428	2,144
Finance companies	65	72	121	146	172	161	175	199	243	285
HOME MORTGAGES [2]										
Total [1]	2,615	3,451	4,259	4,674	5,075	5,571	6,244	7,024	8,016	9,149
Commercial banking	430	647	797	880	966	1,024	1,222	1,347	1,568	1,776
Savings institutions	600	482	534	548	594	620	631	703	875	955
Credit unions	50	66	97	111	125	141	159	183	213	246
Government-sponsored enterprises (GSE)	115	205	200	189	205	226	271	363	363	354
Agency- and GSE-backed mortgage pools	991	1,543	1,970	2,235	2,426	2,749	3,064	3,367	3,417	3,547
Asset-backed securities issuers	55	194	321	353	377	433	487	605	1,004	1,592
Finance companies	38	43	90	108	131	120	135	152	190	233

[1] Includes other holders not shown separately.   [2] Mortgages on one- to four-family properties.

Source: Board of Governors of the Federal Reserve System, "Federal Reserve Statistical Release, Z.1, Flow of Funds Accounts of the United States"; published 9 March 2006; <http://www.federalreserve.gov/releases/z1/20060309/>.

Table 1174. Characteristics of Conventional First Mortgage Loans for Purchase of Single-Family Homes: 1990 to 2005

[In percent, except as indicated (154.1 represents $154,100). Annual averages. Covers fully amortized conventional mortgage loans used to purchase single-family nonfarm homes. Excludes refinancing loans, nonamortized and balloon loans, loans insured by the Federal Housing Administration, and loans guaranteed by the Veterans Administration. Based on a sample of mortgage lenders, including savings and loans associations, savings banks, commercial banks, and mortgage companies]

Loan characteristics	New homes						Previously occupied homes					
	1990	1995	2000	2003	2004	2005	1990	1995	2000	2003	2004	2005
Contract interest rate, [1]												
all loans	9.7	7.7	7.4	5.7	5.7	5.9	9.8	7.7	7.9	5.7	5.7	5.8
Fixed-rate loans	10.1	8.0	8.0	5.9	6.0	6.1	10.1	8.0	8.2	5.8	6.0	6.0
Adjustable-rate loans [2]	8.9	7.2	6.5	5.1	5.4	5.3	8.9	7.0	7.2	5.0	5.1	5.6
Initial fees, charges [3]	1.98	1.20	0.69	0.63	0.50	0.54	1.74	0.93	0.66	0.32	0.37	0.33
Effective interest rate, [4]												
all loans	10.1	7.9	7.5	5.8	5.8	5.9	10.1	7.8	8.1	5.7	5.7	5.9
Fixed-rate loans	10.4	8.2	8.2	6.0	6.0	6.2	10.4	8.2	8.3	5.9	6.0	6.0
Adjustable-rate loans [2]	9.2	7.4	6.5	5.2	5.4	5.3	9.2	7.1	7.2	5.0	5.2	5.6
Term to maturity (years)	27.3	27.7	29.2	28.7	28.8	29.2	27.0	27.4	28.6	26.5	27.7	28.3
Purchase price ($1,000)	154.1	175.4	234.9	275.3	293.6	328.5	140.3	137.3	191.8	237.0	253.2	291.3
Loan-to-price ratio	74.9	78.6	77.4	77.9	76.0	75.2	74.9	80.1	77.9	72.6	74.6	74.6
Percent of number of loans with adjustable rates	31	37	40	21	42	29	27	31	17	17	33	30

[1] Initial interest rate paid by the borrower as specified in the loan contract.   [2] Loans with a contractual provision for periodic adjustments in the contract interest rate.   [3] Includes all fees, commissions, discounts and "points" paid by the borrower, or seller, in order to obtain the loan. Excludes those charges for mortgage, credit, life or property insurance; for property transfer; and for title search and insurance.   [4] Contract interest rate plus fees and charges amortized over a 10-year period.

Source: U.S. Federal Housing Finance Board, Rates & Terms on Conventional Home Mortgages, Annual Summary.

Banking, Finance, and Insurance   741

Table 1175. **Mortgage Originations and Delinquency and Foreclosure Rates: 1990 to 2005**

[In percent, except as indicated (459 represents $459,000,000,000). Covers one- to four-family residential nonfarm mortgage loans]

Item	1990	1995	1999	2000	2001	2002	2003	2004	2005
MORTGAGE ORIGINATIONS									
Total (bil. dol.)	459	640	1,379	1,139	2,243	2,854	3,812	2,773	2,908
Purchase (bil. dol.)	389	494	878	905	960	1,097	1,280	1,309	1,512
Refinance (bil. dol.)	70	145	500	234	1,283	1,757	2,532	1,463	1,397
DELINQUENCY RATES [1]									
Total	4.7	4.2	4.3	4.4	5.1	5.1	4.7	4.5	4.5
Prime conventional loans	(NA)	(NA)	2.3	2.3	2.7	2.6	2.5	2.3	2.3
Subprime conventional loans.	(NA)	(NA)	11.4	11.9	14.0	14.3	12.2	10.8	10.8
FHA loans	6.7	7.6	8.6	9.1	10.8	11.5	12.2	12.2	12.5
VA loans	6.3	6.4	6.8	6.8	7.7	7.9	8.0	7.3	7.0
FORECLOSURE RATES [2]									
Total	0.9	0.9	1.2	1.2	1.5	1.5	1.3	1.2	1.0
Prime conventional loans	(NA)	(NA)	0.5	0.4	0.5	0.5	0.6	0.5	0.4
Subprime conventional loans.	(NA)	(NA)	6.3	9.4	9.4	8.0	5.6	3.8	3.3
FHA loans	1.3	1.3	2.0	1.7	2.2	2.8	2.9	2.7	2.3
VA loans	1.2	1.3	1.7	1.2	1.3	1.6	1.6	1.5	1.1

NA Not available.   [1] Number of loans delinquent 30 days or more as percentage of mortgage loans serviced in survey. Annual average of quarterly figures.   [2] Percentage of loans in the foreclosure process at yearend, not seasonally adjusted.

Source: Mortgage Bankers Association of America, Washington, DC, "1–4 Family Mortgage Originations 1990-2005"; <http://www.mbaa.org/ResearchandForecasts/MarketEnvironment/1-4FamilyMortgageOriginations1990-2005.htm>; accessed 16 June 2006; and *National Delinquency Survey*, quarterly.

Table 1176. **Insured Commercial Banks—Delinquency Rates on Loans: 1990 to 2005**

[In percent. Annual averages of quarterly figures, not seasonally adjusted. Delinquent loans are those past due 30 days or more and still accruing interest as well as those in nonaccrual status. They are measured as a percentage of end-of-period loans]

Type of loan	1990	1995	1999	2000	2001	2002	2003	2004	2005
Total loans.	5.33	2.48	2.13	2.18	2.61	2.69	2.33	1.80	1.57
Real estate	6.10	2.94	1.93	1.89	2.13	1.99	1.76	1.44	1.38
Residential [1]	(NA)	2.20	2.08	2.11	2.29	2.11	1.83	1.55	1.55
Commercial [2]	(NA)	3.94	1.69	1.49	1.79	1.71	1.54	1.20	1.07
Consumer	3.83	3.09	3.61	3.55	3.67	3.51	3.28	3.08	2.81
Credit cards	(NA)	3.74	4.54	4.50	4.86	4.87	4.47	4.11	3.70
Other	(NA)	2.67	3.09	2.98	3.03	2.79	2.67	2.46	2.23
Leases	1.97	0.79	1.28	1.59	2.11	2.24	1.91	1.33	1.28
Commercial and industrial	5.34	1.95	1.91	2.22	3.08	3.84	3.34	2.19	1.51
Agricultural	3.84	2.50	3.00	2.54	2.63	2.51	2.50	1.68	1.30

NA Not available.   [1] Residential real estate loans include loans secured by one- to four-family properties, including home equity lines of credit.   [2] Commercial real estate loans include construction and land development loans, loans secured by multifamily residences, and loans secured by nonfarm, nonresidential real estate.

Source: Federal Financial Institutions Examination Council (FFIEC), *Consolidated Reports of Condition and Income* (1990–2000: FFIEC 031 through 034; beginning 2001: FFIEC 031 & 041).

Table 1177. **Money Stock: 1990 to 2005**

[In billions of dollars (825 represents $825,000,000,000). As of December. Seasonally adjusted averages of daily figures]

Item	1990	1995	1998	1999	2000	2001	2002	2003	2004	2005
M1, total.	825	1,127	1,095	1,123	1,088	1,182	1,219	1,304	1,372	1,369
Currency [1]	246	372	460	518	531	581	626	662	697	724
Travelers' checks [2]	8	9	9	9	8	8	8	8	8	7
Demand deposits [3]	277	389	377	353	310	336	306	325	340	321
Other checkable deposits [4].	294	357	250	243	238	257	279	310	327	317
M2, total.	3,279	3,641	4,384	4,649	4,931	5,451	5,801	6,080	6,422	6,676
M1.	825	1,127	1,095	1,123	1,088	1,182	1,219	1,304	1,372	1,369
Non-M1 components of M2.	2,454	2,514	3,289	3,526	3,844	4,269	4,582	4,775	5,050	5,307
Retail money funds	358	448	732	831	921	982	910	796	713	711
Savings deposits (including MMDAs [5])	923	1,134	1,605	1,740	1,878	2,313	2,779	3,169	3,520	3,622
Commercial banks	581	775	1,188	1,289	1,424	1,739	2,061	2,338	2,632	2,771
Thrift institutions.	342	360	417	452	454	573	718	831	887	851
Small time deposits [6]	1,173	931	952	955	1,045	975	892	810	817	974
Commercial banks	611	575	626	635	700	635	590	536	545	637
Thrift institutions.	563	357	326	320	345	340	302	273	272	336

[1] Currency outside U.S. Treasury, Federal Reserve Banks and the vaults of depository institutions.   [2] Outstanding amount of U.S. dollar-denominated travelers' checks of nonbank issuers. Travelers' checks issued by depository institutions are included in demand deposits.   [3] Demand deposits at domestically chartered commercial banks, U.S. branches and agencies of foreign banks, and Edge Act corporations (excluding those amounts held by depository institutions, the U.S. government, and foreign banks and official institutions) less cash items in the process of collection and Federal Reserve float.   [4] Negotiable order of withdrawal (NOW) and automatic transfer service (ATS) balances at domestically chartered commercial banks, U.S. branches and agencies of foreign banks, Edge Act corporations, and thrift institutions, credit union share draft balances, and demand deposits at thrift institutions.   [5] Money market deposit accounts (MMDA).   [6] Small-denomination time deposits are those issued in amounts of less than $100,000. All Individual Retirement Account (IRA) and Keogh account balances at commercial banks and thrift institutions are subtracted from small time deposits.

Source: Board of Governors of the Federal Reserve System, *Statistical Supplement to the Federal Reserve Bulletin*, monthly, and *Money Stock Measures, Federal Reserve Statistical Release H.6*, weekly.

Table 1178. Money Market Interest Rates and Mortgage Rates: 1980 to 2005

[Percent per year. Annual averages of monthly data, except as indicated]

Type	1980	1985	1990	1993	1994	1995	1996	1997	1998	1999	2000	2001	2002	2003	2004	2005
Federal funds, effective rate	13.35	8.10	8.10	3.02	4.21	5.83	5.30	5.46	5.35	4.97	6.24	3.88	1.67	1.13	1.35	3.22
Prime rate charged by banks [1]	15.26	9.93	10.01	6.00	7.15	8.83	8.27	8.44	8.35	8.00	9.23	6.91	4.67	4.12	4.34	6.19
Discount rate [1]	11.77	7.69	6.98	3.00	3.60	5.21	5.02	5.00	4.92	4.62	5.73	3.40	1.17	2.12	2.34	4.19
Eurodollar deposits, 3-month	14.00	8.27	8.16	3.18	4.63	5.93	5.38	5.61	5.45	5.31	6.45	3.70	1.73	1.14	1.55	3.51
Large negotiable CDs:																
3-month, secondary market	13.02	8.04	8.15	3.17	4.63	5.92	5.39	5.62	5.47	5.33	6.46	3.71	1.73	1.15	1.57	3.51
6-month, secondary market	12.94	8.24	8.17	3.28	4.96	5.98	5.47	5.73	5.44	5.46	6.59	3.66	1.81	1.17	1.74	3.73
Taxable money market funds [2]	12.68	7.71	7.82	2.70	3.75	5.48	4.95	5.10	5.04	4.64	5.89	3.67	1.29	0.64	0.82	2.66
Tax-exempt money market funds [2]	(NA)	4.90	5.45	1.97	2.38	3.39	2.99	3.14	2.94	2.72	3.54	2.24	0.94	0.53	0.66	1.87
Certificates of deposit (CDs): [3]																
6-month	(NA)	8.05	7.79	2.88	3.42	4.92	4.68	4.86	4.58	4.27	5.09	3.43	1.67	1.02	1.14	2.37
1-year	(NA)	8.53	7.92	3.16	4.01	5.39	4.95	5.15	4.81	4.55	5.46	3.60	1.98	1.20	1.45	2.77
2½-year	(NA)	9.32	7.96	3.80	4.58	5.69	5.14	5.40	4.93	4.73	5.64	3.97	2.74	1.77	2.21	3.18
5-year	(NA)	9.99	8.06	4.98	5.42	6.00	6.46	5.66	5.08	4.93	5.97	4.58	3.96	2.93	3.34	3.75
U.S. Government securities:																
Secondary market: [4]																
3-month Treasury bill	11.39	7.47	7.50	3.00	4.25	5.49	5.01	5.06	4.78	4.64	5.82	3.40	1.61	1.01	1.37	3.15
6-month Treasury bill	11.32	7.65	7.46	3.12	4.64	5.56	5.08	5.18	4.83	4.75	5.90	3.34	1.68	1.05	1.58	3.39
Auction average: [5]																
3-month Treasury bill	11.51	7.48	7.51	3.02	4.29	5.51	5.02	5.07	4.81	4.66	5.85	3.45	1.62	1.02	1.38	3.16
Home mortgages:																
New-home mortgage yields [6]	12.66	11.55	10.05	7.20	7.49	7.87	7.80	7.71	7.07	7.04	7.52	7.00	6.43	5.80	5.77	5.94
Conventional, 15 yr. fixed [3]	(NA)	11.48	9.73	6.65	7.77	7.39	7.28	7.16	6.58	7.09	7.76	6.53	6.02	5.25	5.23	5.50
Conventional, 30 yr. fixed [3]	(NA)	11.85	9.97	7.17	8.28	7.86	7.76	7.57	6.91	7.46	8.08	7.01	6.56	5.89	5.86	5.93

NA Not available. [1] Rate for the Federal Reserve Bank of New York. Beginning 2003, the rate charged for discounts made and advances extended under the Federal Reserve's primary credit discount window program, which became effective January 9, 2003. The rate replaced that for adjustment credit, which was discontinued after January 8, 2003. [2] 12 month return for period ending December 31. Source: iMoneyNet, Inc. Westborough, MA, Money Market Insight, monthly, <http://www.imoneynet.com> (copyright). Annual averages. Source: Bankrate, Inc., North Palm Beach, FL, Bank Rate Monitor, weekly (copyright). [4] Averages based on daily closing bid yields in secondary market, bank discount basis. [5] Averages computed on an issue-date basis; bank discount basis. Source: U.S. Council of Economic Advisors, Economic Indicators, monthly. [6] Effective rate (in the primary market) on conventional mortgages, reflecting fees and charges as well as contract rate and assumed, on the average, repayment at end of ten years. Source: U.S. Federal Housing Finance Board, Rates & Terms on Conventional Home Mortgages, Annual Summary.

Source: Except as noted, Board of Governors of the Federal Reserve System, Statistical Supplement to the Federal Reserve Bulletin, monthly.

Banking, Finance, and Insurance 743

Table 1179. Bond Yields: 1980 to 2005

[Percent per year. Annual averages of daily figures, except as indicated]

Type	1980	1985	1990	1995	1999	2000	2001	2002	2003	2004	2005
U.S. Treasury, constant maturities:[1,2]											
1-year	12.00	8.42	7.89	5.94	5.08	6.11	3.49	2.00	1.24	1.89	3.62
2-year	11.73	9.27	8.16	6.15	5.43	6.26	3.83	2.64	1.65	2.38	3.85
3-year	11.51	9.64	8.26	6.25	5.49	6.22	4.09	3.10	2.10	2.78	3.93
5-year	11.45	10.12	8.37	6.38	5.55	6.16	4.56	3.82	2.97	3.43	4.05
7-year	11.40	10.50	8.52	6.50	5.79	6.20	4.88	4.30	3.52	3.87	4.15
10-year	11.43	10.62	8.55	6.57	5.65	6.03	5.02	4.61	4.01	4.27	4.29
20-year	(NA)	(NA)	(NA)	6.95	6.20	6.23	5.63	5.43	4.96	5.04	4.64
State and local govt. bonds, Aaa	7.84	8.60	6.96	5.79	5.29	5.58	5.01	4.87	4.52	4.50	4.28
State and local govt. bonds, Baa	8.99	9.59	7.30	6.05	5.70	5.71	5.75	5.64	5.20	5.09	4.86
Municipal (Bond Buyer, 20 bonds)	8.55	9.11	7.27	5.95	5.43	5.71	5.15	5.04	4.75	4.68	4.40
High-grade municipal bonds (Standard & Poor's)[3]	8.51	9.18	7.25	5.95	5.43	5.77	5.19	5.05	4.73	4.63	4.29
Corporate Aaa seasoned[4]	11.94	11.37	9.32	7.59	7.05	7.62	7.08	6.49	5.66	5.63	5.23
Corporate Baa seasoned[4]	13.67	12.72	10.36	8.20	7.88	8.37	7.95	7.80	6.76	6.39	6.06
Corporate seasoned, all industries[4]	12.75	12.05	9.77	7.83	7.45	7.98	7.49	7.10	6.24	6.00	5.57

NA Not available.   [1] Yields on actively traded non-inflation-indexed issues adjusted to constant maturities. Data from U.S. Treasury.   [2] Through 1995, yields are based on closing bid prices quoted by at least five dealers. Beginning 1999, yields are based on closing indicative prices quoted by secondary market participants.   [3] Source: U.S. Council of Economic Advisors, Economic Indicators, monthly.   [4] Source: Moody's Investors Service, New York, NY.

Source: Except as noted, Board of Governors of the Federal Reserve System, Statistical Supplement to the Federal Reserve Bulletin, monthly.

Table 1180. Volume of Debt Markets by Type of Security: 1990 to 2005

[In billions of dollars (2,780 represents $2,780,000,000,000). Covers debt markets as represented by the source]

Type of security	1990	1995	2000	2002	2003	2004	2005
NEW ISSUE VOLUME							
Total	2,780	6,803	12,638	16,913	19,618	18,922	20,490
U.S. Treasury securities[1]	1,531	2,331	2,038	3,812	4,249	4,690	4,363
Federal agency debt[2]	637	3,531	8,746	9,236	10,496	10,422	11,945
Municipal	163	198	242	430	453	417	458
Mortgage-backed securities[3]	235	269	483	2,296	3,072	1,764	1,920
Asset-backed securities[4]	50	143	387	489	585	902	1,103
Corporate debt[5]	164	331	742	650	763	728	702
DAILY TRADING VOLUME							
Total	111.2	246.3	357.6	632.3	754.5	821.2	923.0
U.S. Treasury securities[1,6]	111.2	193.2	206.6	366.4	433.5	499.0	554.5
Federal agency debt[6]	(NA)	23.7	72.8	81.8	81.7	78.8	78.8
Municipal[7]	(NA)	(NA)	8.8	10.7	12.6	14.8	16.9
Mortgage-backed securities[3,6]	(NA)	29.4	69.5	154.5	206.0	207.4	251.8
Corporate[5]	(NA)	(NA)	(NA)	18.9	20.7	21.2	21.0
VOLUME OF SECURITIES OUTSTANDING							
Total	7,745	11,229	16,969	20,224	22,096	23,594	25,345
U.S. Treasury securities[1]	2,196	3,307	2,967	3,205	3,575	3,944	4,166
Federal agency debt[8]	435	845	1,852	2,359	2,637	2,745	2,604
Municipal	1,184	1,294	1,481	1,765	1,892	2,028	2,216
Mortgage-backed securities[3,8]	1,333	2,352	3,565	4,705	5,309	5,473	5,908
Asset-backed securities[4,8]	90	316	1,072	1,543	1,694	1,828	1,955
Money market instruments[9]	1,157	1,177	2,661	2,551	2,526	2,872	3,469
Corporate debt[5,8]	1,350	1,938	3,372	4,096	4,462	4,705	5,027

NA Not available.   [1] Marketable public debt.   [2] Includes overnight discount notes.   [3] Includes only Government National Mortgage Association (GNMA), Federal National Mortgage Association (FNMA), Federal Home Loan Mortgage Corporation (FHLMC) mortgage-backed securities (MBS) and collateralized mortgage obligations (CMOs) and private-label MBS/CMOs.   [4] Excludes mortgage-backed assets.   [5] Includes non-convertible corporate debt, Yankee bonds, and MTNs (Medium-Term Notes), but excludes all issues with maturities of one year or less, agency debt, and all certificates of deposit.   [6] Primary dealer transactions.   [7] Beginning 2000 includes customer-to-dealer and dealer-to-dealer transactions.   [8] The Bond Market Association estimates.   [9] Commercial paper, bankers acceptances, and large time deposits.

Source: The Bond Market Association, New York, NY. Copyright. Based on data supplied by Board of Governors of the Federal Reserve System, U.S. Department of Treasury, Thompson Financial Securities Data Company, Inside MBS & ABS, FHLMC, FNMA, GNMA, Federal Home Loan Banks, Student Loan Marketing Association, Federal Farm Credit Banks, Tennessee Valley Authority, and Municipal Securities Rulemaking Board.

Table 1181. **Total Returns of Stocks, Bonds, and Treasury Bills: 1980 to 2005**

[**In percent**. Average annual percent change. Stock return data are based on the Standard & Poor's 500 index. Minus sign (−) indicates loss]

Period	Stocks				Treasury bills, total return	Bonds (10-year), total return
	Total return	Capital gains	Dividends and reinvestment	Total return after inflation		
1980 to 1989	17.55	12.59	4.40	11.85	9.13	13.01
1990 to 1999	18.21	15.31	2.51	14.85	4.95	8.02
2000 to 2004	−2.30	−3.38	1.54	−4.67	2.66	8.41
2001	−11.89	−13.04	1.32	−13.68	3.32	5.51
2002	−22.10	−23.37	1.65	−23.91	1.61	15.15
2003	28.68	26.38	1.82	26.31	1.03	0.54
2004	10.88	8.99	1.73	7.38	1.43	4.59
2005	4.91	3.00	1.85	1.45	3.30	3.16

Source: Global Financial Data, Los Angeles, CA, "GFD Guide to Total Returns"; <http://www.globalfindata.com/articles/totalreturnworksheet.xls>; and unpublished data. (copyright).

Table 1182. **Equities, Corporate Bonds, and Municipal Securities—Holdings and Net Purchases by Type of Investor: 1990 to 2005**

[**In billions of dollars (3,531 represents $3,531,000,000,000). Holdings as of Dec. 31**. Minus sign (−) indicates net sales]

Type of investor	Holdings					Net purchases				
	1990	2000	2003	2004	2005	1990	2000	2003	2004	2005
EQUITIES [1]										
Total [2]	3,531	17,627	15,618	17,389	18,199	−45.7	5.3	119.1	50.4	−161.1
Household sector [3]	1,960	8,091	6,216	6,406	6,089	−48.4	−486.6	−77.5	−242.4	−501.1
Rest of the world [4]	244	1,643	1,827	2,071	2,304	−16.0	193.6	35.0	61.9	86.0
Property-casualty insurance companies	80	194	183	202	207	−7.0	0.7	−2.7	−3.5	−4.4
Life insurance companies	82	892	919	1,054	1,154	−5.7	111.3	45.5	51.5	57.3
Private pension funds	606	1,915	1,492	1,691	1,726	0.6	−82.7	−44.8	−44.0	−29.6
State and local retirement funds. . . .	285	1,299	1,422	1,607	1,752	22.5	11.6	−0.6	−22.6	19.5
Mutual funds	233	3,227	3,052	3,694	4,174	14.4	193.1	136.8	158.3	128.6
Exchange-traded funds	−	66	146	218	281	−	42.4	15.1	51.2	47.1
CORPORATE & FOREIGN BONDS										
Total [2]	1,733	4,761	6,714	7,387	8,050	122.9	344.5	664.1	634.9	736.7
Household sector [3]	272	518	749	672	492	52.3	63.0	−60.1	−114.4	−106.7
Rest of the world [4]	218	921	1,497	1,751	2,102	6.0	168.4	230.0	254.4	351.1
Commercial banking	89	266	482	560	688	4.6	56.0	44.6	77.3	127.8
Property-casualty insurance companies	89	188	219	245	274	10.4	6.4	20.0	26.4	28.8
Life insurance companies	567	1,222	1,620	1,768	1,860	56.5	49.0	171.0	147.8	91.8
Private pension funds	158	290	315	331	342	19.8	−57.6	8.2	15.8	10.8
Money market mutual funds	2	180	259	261	258	−1.7	27.3	30.5	2.3	−2.7
Mutual funds	59	362	548	623	699	4.7	−6.2	77.4	74.5	76.3
Government-sponsored enterprises .	−	131	226	337	388	−	19.1	36.6	110.8	50.9
Brokers and dealers.	29	113	228	252	337	−4.0	19.3	36.4	23.9	85.2
MUNICIPAL SECURITIES [5]										
Total [2]	1,184	1,481	1,898	2,031	2,232	49.3	23.6	135.1	133.1	200.8
Household sector [3]	656	539	725	762	845	35.4	5.0	34.6	36.9	83.5
Property-casualty insurance companies	137	184	224	268	301	1.8	−14.9	41.2	43.6	33.4
Money market mutual funds	84	243	292	314	337	13.9	34.1	13.6	21.8	23.2
Mutual funds	113	230	290	294	313	13.9	12.9	4.1	18.9

− Represents or rounds to zero. [1] Excludes mutual fund shares. [2] Includes other types not shown separately. [3] Includes nonprofit organizations. [4] Holdings and net purchases of U.S. issues by foreign residents. [5] Includes loans.

Source: Board of Governors of the Federal Reserve System, "Federal Reserve Statistical Release, Z.1, Flow of Funds Accounts of the United States"; published 9 March 2006; <http://www.federalreserve.gov/releases/z1/20060309/>.

Table 1183. **New Security Issues of Corporations by Type of Offering: 2000 to 2005**

[**In billions of dollars (1,082.2 represents $1,082,200,000,000)**. Represents gross proceed of issues maturing in more than one year. Figures are the principal amount or the number of units multiplied by the offering price. Excludes secondary offerings, employee stock plans, investment companies other than closed-end, intracorporate transactions, and Yankee bonds. Stock data include ownership securities issued by limited partnerships]

Type of offering	2000	2004	2005	Type of offering	2000	2004	2005
Total [1]	1,082.2	2,070.7	2,439.0				
Bonds, total	947.3	1,923.1	2,323.7	Stocks, total	311.9	(NA)	(NA)
Sold in the United States	824.5	1,737.3	2,141.5	Public.	134.9	147.6	115.3
Sold abroad	122.8	185.8	182.2	Nonfinancial.	118.4	64.3	54.7
Nonfinancial	259.2	260.0	216.1	Financial	16.5	83.2	60.5
Financial.	688.1	1,663.1	2,107.7	Private placement.	177.0	(NA)	(NA)

NA Not available. [1] Excludes private placements of stocks.

Source: Board of Governors of the Federal Reserve System, *Statistical Supplement to the Federal Reserve Bulletin*, monthly.

Banking, Finance, and Insurance 745

Table 1184. Purchases and Sales by U.S. Investors of Foreign Bonds and Stocks, 1990 to 2005, and by Selected Country, 2005

[In billions of dollars (31.2 represents $31,200,000,000). Covers transactions in all types of long-term foreign securities as reported by banks, brokers, and other entities in the United States. Data cover new issues of securities, transactions in outstanding issues, and redemptions of securities. Includes transactions executed in the United States for the account of foreigners, and transactions executed abroad for the account of reporting institutions and their domestic customers. Data by country show the country of location of the foreign buyers and sellers who deal directly with reporting institutions in the United States. The data do not necessarily indicate the country of beneficial owner or issuer. The term "foreigner" covers all institutions and individuals domiciled outside the United States, including U.S. citizens domiciled abroad, and the foreign branches, subsidiaries and other affiliates abroad of U.S. banks and businesses; the central governments, central banks, and other official institutions of foreign countries; and international and regional organizations. "Foreigner" also includes persons in the United States to the extent that they are known by reporting institutions to be acting on behalf of foreigners. Minus sign (–) indicates net sales by U.S. investors or a net inflow of capital into the United States]

Year and country	Net purchases			Total transactions [1]			Bonds		Stocks	
	Total	Bonds	Stocks	Total	Bonds	Stocks	Purchases	Sales	Purchases	Sales
1990	31.2	21.9	9.2	907	652	255	337	315	132	123
1993	143.1	80.4	62.7	2,126	1,572	554	826	746	308	245
1994	57.3	9.2	48.1	2,526	1,706	820	858	848	434	386
1995	98.7	48.4	50.3	2,569	1,827	741	938	890	396	346
1996	110.6	51.4	59.3	3,239	2,279	960	1,165	1,114	510	450
1997	89.1	48.1	40.9	4,505	2,952	1,553	1,500	1,452	797	756
1998	11.1	17.3	−6.2	4,527	2,674	1,853	1,346	1,328	923	930
1999	−10.0	5.7	−15.6	3,941	1,602	2,339	804	798	1,162	1,177
2000	17.1	4.1	13.1	5,539	1,922	3,617	963	959	1,815	1,802
2001	19.6	−30.5	50.1	5,135	2,290	2,845	1,130	1,160	1,448	1,398
2002	−27.0	−28.5	1.5	5,253	2,716	2,537	1,344	1,372	1,269	1,268
2003	56.5	−32.0	88.6	5,580	2,883	2,698	1,425	1,457	1,393	1,305
2004	152.8	67.9	85.0	6,399	2,986	3,413	1,527	1,459	1,749	1,664
2005, total [2]	**137.8**	**16.2**	**121.6**	**7,516**	**3,020**	**4,495**	**1,518**	**1,502**	**2,308**	**2,187**
United Kingdom	41.7	14.9	26.8	3,148	1,435	1,713	725	710	870	843
Japan	34.6	−5.2	39.8	739	189	549	92	97	295	255
Cayman Islands	−7.2	−4.2	−3.0	693	293	400	144	149	199	202
Canada	1.2	−2.2	3.4	535	299	236	148	150	120	116
Bermuda	3.9	0.4	3.5	250	51	199	26	25	101	98
Hong Kong	5.7	−1.0	6.7	213	28	185	14	15	96	89
Ireland	−5.6	−3.8	−1.8	188	161	27	79	82	12	14
France	5.4	1.4	4.0	155	36	119	19	17	62	58
Australia	10.8	7.3	3.5	145	34	111	21	13	57	54
Germany	0.7	−1.2	1.9	125	73	51	36	37	27	25
Sweden	7.3	1.2	6.1	88	4	83	3	2	45	39
Singapore	−1.1	−4.0	2.9	80	19	61	7	11	32	29
Switzerland	2.4	(Z)	2.4	80	17	63	9	9	32	30
Bahamas, The	−1.1	0.4	−1.5	64	30	34	15	15	16	18
Mexico	4.6	3.1	1.5	58	32	26	18	15	14	12
Netherlands	0.9	−0.8	1.6	56	12	44	6	6	23	21

Z Less than $50 million.   [1] Total purchases plus total sales.   [2] Includes other countries, not shown separately.
Source: U.S. Dept. of Treasury, *Treasury Bulletin*, quarterly.

Table 1185. U.S. Holdings of Foreign Stocks and Bonds by Country: 2003 to 2005

[In billions of dollars (2,079.4 represents $2,079,400,000,000). See also Table 1271]

Country	Stocks			Country	Bonds		
	2003	2004	2005		2003	2004	2005
Total holdings	**2,079.4**	**2,560.4**	**3,086.5**	**Total holdings**	**874.4**	**993.0**	**987.5**
Europe [1]	1,135.3	1,356.2	1,582.1	Europe [1]	442.4	478.2	487.0
United Kingdom	426.2	461.8	553.7	United Kingdom	148.3	178.6	192.7
France	130.8	164.6	188.5	Germany	71.4	67.9	63.0
Switzerland	117.9	138.2	157.4	Netherlands	58.0	55.1	53.1
Netherlands	115.8	136.5	156.9	France	43.0	41.8	41.5
Germany	103.2	123.7	140.4	Belgium & Luxembourg	20.2	31.8	25.9
Spain	43.8	63.0	71.7	Sweden	12.8	14.6	17.0
Italy	39.0	57.5	65.9	Italy	25.0	17.4	16.2
Sweden	27.5	38.3	49.2	Canada	139.4	151.9	146.8
Finland	35.2	33.9	38.7	Caribbean financial centers [1]	89.8	129.3	126.4
Canada	149.3	180.4	207.0	Cayman Islands	75.7	114.4	110.3
Caribbean financial centers [1]	180.3	257.5	292.3	Latin America, excl. Caribbean financial centers [1]	75.2	83.8	97.0
Bermuda	107.5	153.5	175.8	Mexico	27.6	28.6	29.7
Cayman Islands	45.3	69.7	82.1	Brazil	18.4	19.9	26.6
Latin America, excl. Caribbean financial centers [1]	80.1	105.8	145.9	Asia [1]	69.3	78.9	53.7
Brazil	31.8	43.1	61.4	Japan	37.2	36.4	27.8
Mexico	28.5	37.5	50.8	Africa [1]	6.6	6.3	5.8
Asia [1]	454.4	565.8	739.6	South Africa	2.7	3.0	3.1
Japan	255.5	330.4	411.2	Other countries [1]	51.7	64.6	70.7
Korea, South	49.1	66.6	88.9	Australia	29.2	40.4	47.8
Taiwan [2]	27.0	34.6	54.5				
Hong Kong	36.2	35.4	47.5				
Africa [1]	18.7	28.9	40.0				
South Africa	15.1	21.6	30.2				
Other countries [1]	61.3	65.8	79.6				
Australia	56.5	57.1	68.8				

[1] Includes other countries not shown separately.   [2] See footnote 3, Table 1187.
Source: U.S. Bureau of Economic Analysis, *Survey of Current Business*, July 2006.

Table 1186. **Foreign Purchases and Sales of U.S. Securities by Type of Security, 1990 to 2005, and by Selected Country, 2005**

[In billions of dollars (18.7 represents $18,700,000,000). Covers transactions in all types of long-term domestic securities by foreigners as reported by banks, brokers, and other entities in the United States (except nonmarketable U.S. Treasury notes, foreign series; and nonmarketable U.S. Treasury bonds and notes, foreign currency series). See headnote, Table 1184. Minus sign (–) indicates net sales by foreigners or a net outflow of capital from the United States]

Year and country	Net purchases					Total transactions [4]				
	Total	Treasury bonds and notes [1]	U.S. Govt. corporations [2] bonds	Corporate bonds [3]	Corporate stocks	Total	Treasury bonds and notes [1]	U.S. Govt. corporations [2] bonds	Corporate bonds [3]	Corporate stocks
1990	18.7	17.9	6.3	9.7	–15.1	4,204	3,620	104	117	362
1993	111.1	23.6	35.4	30.6	21.6	6,314	5,195	263	239	618
1994	140.4	78.8	21.7	38.0	1.9	6,562	5,343	297	222	699
1995	231.9	134.1	28.7	57.9	11.2	7,243	5,828	222	278	915
1996	370.2	232.2	41.7	83.7	12.5	8,965	7,134	241	422	1,169
1997	388.0	184.2	49.9	84.4	69.6	12,759	9,546	469	617	2,126
1998	277.8	49.0	56.8	121.9	50.0	14,989	10,259	992	641	3,097
1999	350.2	–10.0	92.2	160.4	107.5	14,617	8,586	880	577	4,574
2000	457.8	–54.0	152.8	184.1	174.9	16,910	7,795	1,305	775	7,036
2001	520.8	18.5	164.0	222.0	116.4	20,003	10,517	2,239	1,260	5,986
2002	547.6	119.9	195.1	182.3	50.2	25,498	14,409	3,261	1,459	6,369
2003	719.9	263.6	155.8	265.7	34.7	26,332	15,739	2,725	1,694	6,174
2004	916.5	352.1	226.4	309.5	28.5	29,441	17,520	2,192	2,033	7,696
2005, total [5]	1,048.5	350.8	226.8	391.7	79.1	33,050	20,013	2,025	2,152	8,859
United Kingdom	368.0	134.3	40.9	172.9	20.0	12,289	8,618	408	1,016	2,246
Cayman Islands	37.9	–13.5	12.3	34.2	4.9	5,245	2,228	475	373	2,169
Bermuda	44.8	33.2	1.3	5.6	4.7	2,613	1,322	73	64	1,154
France	32.1	9.5	0.6	14.8	7.3	2,425	1,600	25	36	764
Japan	81.6	–4.0	59.1	26.3	0.2	1,376	1,005	206	64	100
Canada	55.4	21.5	12.7	4.9	16.3	1,195	861	56	58	220
Ireland	19.6	–0.5	3.7	14.7	1.8	1,003	836	26	49	92
Bahamas, The	31.5	28.1	(Z)	1.2	2.2	793	557	10	14	212
Norway	13.3	6.4	1.2	3.4	2.3	539	444	60	10	25
China [6]	90.4	38.7	24.8	27.3	–0.5	535	362	132	35	6
Germany	23.9	14.6	6.0	7.1	–3.8	431	214	13	29	176
Hong Kong	41.2	11.9	17.0	11.6	0.8	311	211	52	22	26
Switzerland	0.8	–4.1	–0.7	4.4	1.2	257	86	14	24	134
Spain	11.4	4.0	0.2	7.1	0.1	235	61	59	103	12
Singapore	11.7	1.3	1.7	1.6	7.1	214	140	14	19	39

Z Less than $50 million.   [1] Marketable bonds and notes.   [2] Includes federally sponsored agencies.   [3] Includes transactions in directly placed issues abroad by U.S. corporations and issues of states and municipalities.   [4] Total purchases plus total sales.   [5] Includes other countries, not shown separately.   [6] See footnote 3, Table 1187.

Source: U.S. Dept. of Treasury, *Treasury Bulletin*, quarterly.

Table 1187. **Foreign Holdings of U.S. Securities by Country: 2003 to 2005**

[In billions of dollars (1,513.5 represents $1,513,500,000,000). Covers only private holdings of U.S. securities, except as noted. See also Table 1271]

Type of security and country	2003	2004	2005	Type of security and country	2003	2004	2005
U.S. Treasury securities [1,2]	1,513.5	1,803.5	1,993.8	Asia [2]	233.3	308.9	398.5
Japan	551.1	683.1	659.0	Japan	158.9	213.7	264.4
China [3]	176.2	245.3	335.8	Africa	1.6	2.1	2.7
United Kingdom	46.3	60.2	98.5	Other countries	13.4	18.3	24.7
Korea, South	55.5	56.7	67.8				
Taiwan [3]	56.1	66.3	66.9	**Corporate stocks**	1,712.1	1,960.4	2,115.5
OPEC Asia [4]	22.8	48.1	60.7	Europe [2]	948.5	1,098.7	1,174.5
Belgium and Luxembourg	46.1	56.0	51.4	United Kingdom	247.4	292.4	304.1
Germany	49.5	41.6	47.4	Belgium and Luxembourg	140.1	162.6	186.0
Hong Kong	47.6	43.3	39.7	Netherlands	129.8	156.5	167.0
Mexico	24.4	31.5	34.5	Switzerland	123.6	134.4	140.2
				Germany	75.6	81.9	83.7
Corporate and agency bonds	1,710.8	2,035.2	2,275.2	France	57.0	67.4	80.1
Europe [2]	1,139.3	1,295.8	1,393.4	Ireland	48.5	60.6	60.6
United Kingdom	492.9	463.7	522.4	Sweden	43.0	49.9	50.8
Belgium and Luxembourg	413.0	517.3	521.7	Italy	33.6	34.2	31.3
Netherlands	40.0	60.8	72.9	Canada	203.9	220.2	247.5
Germany	44.2	62.5	67.8	Caribbean financial centers [2]	243.3	281.7	322.3
Ireland	47.6	56.2	63.6	Cayman Islands	116.0	139.5	163.7
Switzerland	42.6	60.2	60.6	Bermuda	51.9	56.7	63.7
France	24.7	25.1	30.3	Netherlands Antilles	21.8	23.3	25.4
Canada	47.1	52.0	63.2	Latin America, excluding			
Caribbean financial centers [2]	255.6	329.8	359.3	Caribbean financial centers	29.7	31.8	34.4
Cayman Islands	140.8	197.6	231.1	Asia [2]	230.7	256.1	264.3
Bermuda	78.4	96.0	95.7	Japan	155.8	179.4	186.0
Latin America, excluding				Africa	4.3	4.9	4.9
Caribbean financial centers	20.5	28.3	33.4	Other countries [2]	51.7	67.0	67.6
				Australia	45.1	59.3	60.0

[1] Includes foreign official holdings.   [2] Includes other countries not shown separately.   [3] With the establishment of diplomatic relations with China on January 1, 1979, the U.S. government recognized the People's Republic of China as the sole legal government of China and acknowledged the Chinese position that there is only one China and that Taiwan is part of China.   [4] Comprises Indonesia, Iran, Iraq, Kuwait, Qatar, Saudi Arabia, and the United Arab Emirates.

Source: U.S. Bureau of Economic Analysis, *Survey of Current Business*, July 2006.

Banking, Finance, and Insurance   747

Table 1188. Stock Prices and Yields: 1990 to 2005

[Closing values as of end of December, except as noted]

Index	1990	2000	2001	2002	2003	2004	2005
STOCK PRICES							
Standard & Poor's indices: [1]							
S&P 500 composite (1941–43 = 10)............	330.2	1,320.3	1,148.1	879.8	1,111.9	1,211.9	1,248.3
S&P 400 MidCap Index (1982 = 100)............	100.0	516.7	508.3	429.8	576.0	663.3	738.1
S&P 600 Small Cap Index (Dec. 31, 1993 = 100)....	(NA)	219.6	232.2	196.6	270.4	328.8	350.7
S&P 500/Barra Value Index (Dec. 31, 1974 = 35).	177.7	636.2	552.0	428.0	551.9	625.5	647.5
S&P 500/Barra Growth Index (Dec. 31, 1974 = 35)...	159.9	687.6	594.6	448.8	555.9	582.0	596.5
Russell indices: [2]							
Russell 1000 (Dec. 31, 1986 = 130).............	171.2	700.1	604.9	466.2	594.6	651.0	679.4
Russell 2000 (Dec. 31, 1986 = 135).............	132.2	483.5	488.5	383.1	556.9	651.6	673.2
Russell 3000 (Dec. 31, 1986 = 140).............	180.9	725.8	634.2	489.5	630.1	693.6	723.3
N.Y. Stock Exchange common stock index:							
Composite (Dec. 31, 2002 = 5000)..............	1,908.5	6,945.6	6,236.4	5,000.0	6,440.3	7,250.1	7,754.0
Yearly high	2,126.7	7,164.6	7,048.1	6,445.0	6,469.5	7,373.2	7,867.6
Yearly low	1,715.1	6,094.9	5,331.4	4,452.5	4,418.6	6,211.3	6,902.5
American Stock Exchange Composite Index (Dec. 29, 1995 = 550)	(NA)	897.8	847.6	824.4	1,173.6	1,434.3	1,759.1
NASDAQ composite index (Feb. 5, 1971 = 100)	373.8	2,470.5	1,950.4	1,335.5	2,003.4	2,175.4	2,205.3
Nasdaq-100 (Jan. 31, 1985 = 125).............	200.5	2,341.7	1,577.1	984.4	1,467.9	1,621.1	1,645.2
Industrial (Feb. 5, 1971 = 100)	406.1	1,483.0	1,389.2	1,029.7	1,603.7	1,857.7	1,859.9
Banks (Feb. 5, 1971 = 100)	254.9	1,939.5	2,134.9	2,231.3	2,899.2	3,217.9	3,078.4
Computers (Oct. 29, 1993 = 200).	(NA)	1,295.0	980.5	622.6	934.9	965.3	991.8
Transportation (Feb. 5, 1971 = 100).............	417.1	1,160.4	1,285.0	1,297.6	1,754.4	2,229.5	2,438.2
Telecommunications (October 29, 1993 = 200)....	84.0	463.4	236.6	108.8	183.6	198.3	184.0
Biotech (Oct. 29, 1993 = 200)	(NA)	1,084.5	908.8	496.9	724.1	768.5	790.3
Dow-Jones and Co., Inc.:							
Composite (65 stocks)	920.6	3,317.4	2,892.2	2,375.0	3,000.8	3,395.8	3,638.1
Industrial (30 stocks)	2,633.7	10,786.9	10,021.5	8,341.6	10,453.9	10,783.1	10,717.5
Transportation (20 stocks).	910.2	2,946.6	2,640.0	2,310.0	3,007.1	3,797.5	4,196.0
Utility (15 stocks).	209.7	412.2	293.9	215.2	266.9	335.0	405.1
Dow Jones Wilshire 5000 Composite Index [3] (Dec. 31, 1980 = 1404.596)	3,101.4	12,175.9	10,707.7	8,343.2	10,799.4	11,971.1	12,517.7
COMMON STOCK YIELDS (percent)							
Standard & Poor's composite index (500 stocks): [4]							
Dividend-price ratio [5].....................	3.61	1.15	1.32	1.61	1.77	1.72	1.83
Earnings-price ratio [6].....................	6.47	3.63	2.95	2.92	3.84	4.89	5.36

NA Not available. [1] Standard & Poor's Indices are market-value weighted and are chosen for market size, liquidity, and industry group representation. The S&P 500 index represents 500 large publicly-traded companies. The S&P MidCap Index tracks mid-cap companies. The S&P SmallCap Index consists of 600 domestic small-cap stocks. [2] The Russell 1000 and 3000 indices show respectively the 1000 and 3000 largest capitalization stocks in the United States. The Russell 2000 index shows the 2000 largest capitalization stocks in the United States after the first 1000. [3] The Dow Jones Wilshire 5000 Composite Index measures the performance of all U.S. headquartered equity securities with readily available prices. Source: Dow Jones & Company, Inc., New York, NY, Dow Jones Indexes, (copyright). [4] Source: U.S. Council of Economic Advisors, Economic Indicators, monthly. [5] Aggregate cash dividends (based on latest known annual rate) divided by aggregate market value based on Wednesday closing prices. Averages of monthly figures. [6] Averages of quarterly ratios which are ratio of earnings (after taxes) for 4 quarters ending with particular quarter to price index for last day of that quarter.

Source: Except as noted, Global Financial Data, Los Angeles, CA, <http://www.globalfindata.com/trial/index2.html>; (copyright).

Table 1189. Dow Jones U.S. Total Market Index by Industry: 1995 to 2005

[As of end of year]

Industry	1995	2000	2001	2002	2003	2004	2005
U.S. Total Market Index, total	147.49	306.88	266.71	204.51	262.68	289.38	302.37
Basic materials	139.19	154.49	153.22	136.97	181.10	200.33	205.79
Consumer goods	146.35	219.82	212.88	198.48	240.91	266.44	265.88
Consumer services.................	128.48	279.11	284.94	212.34	280.07	306.85	298.62
Oil and gas	134.54	272.96	236.74	200.29	246.08	319.76	422.12
Financial.......................	176.60	440.91	404.50	346.36	445.96	492.54	510.02
Healthcare	127.77	360.18	310.76	242.87	286.04	295.22	315.50
Industrial.......................	156.39	276.11	245.14	179.78	235.69	272.24	280.72
Technology	229.18	749.01	535.89	327.84	493.02	499.78	513.48
Telecommunications	154.84	210.38	180.62	115.04	119.12	136.84	126.90
Utilities	109.07	177.80	127.04	95.75	114.54	136.79	152.41

Source: Dow Jones & Company, Inc., New York, NY, Dow Jones Indexes, (copyright).

Table 1190. Transaction Activity in Equities, Options, and Security Futures, 1990 to 2005, and by Exchange, 2005

[In billions of dollars (2,229 represents $2,229,000,000,000). Market value of all sales of equities and options listed on an exchange or subject to last-sale reporting. Also reported are the value of such options that were exercised and the value of single-stock futures that were delivered. Excludes options and futures on indexes]

Year and exchange	Total	Equity trading	Option trading	Option exercises and futures deliveries
1990	2,229	2,154	27	48
1995	6,321	6,208	51	63
1996	8,266	8,124	68	75
1997	11,693	11,488	105	100
1998	15,164	14,903	140	121
1999	23,219	22,813	260	145
2000	36,275	35,557	485	233
2001	26,138	25,636	278	224
2002	23,028	22,658	161	209
2003	22,737	22,292	164	282
2004	27,876	27,158	223	495
2005, total [1]	**34,560**	**33,215**	**350**	**995**
American Stock Exchange	725	558	42	124
Boston Stock Exchange	229	160	18	51
Chicago Board Options Exchange	314	13	78	223
Chicago Stock Exchange	397	397	–	–
International Securities Exchange	358	–	92	266
National Association of Securities Dealers	10,440	10,440	–	–
National Stock Exchange	3,489	3,489	–	–
New York Stock Exchange	14,367	14,367	–	–
The Pacific Exchange	3,996	3,742	71	183
Philadelphia Stock Exchange	232	48	49	135

– Represents zero.   [1] Includes other exchanges not shown separately.

Source: U.S. Securities and Exchange Commission, *Annual Report.*

Table 1191. Volume of Trading on New York Stock Exchange: 1990 to 2005

[39,946 represents 39,946,000,000. *Round lot.* A unit of trading or a multiple thereof. On the NYSE the unit of trading is generally 100 shares in stocks. For some inactive stocks, the unit of trading is 10 shares. *Odd lot.* An amount of stock less than the established 100-share unit or 10-share unit of trading]

Item	Unit	1990	1995	1999	2000	2001	2002	2003	2004	2005
Shares traded	Million	39,946	87,873	206,299	265,499	311,290	369,069	356,767	372,718	410,832
Round lots	Million	39,665	87,218	203,914	262,478	307,509	363,136	352,398	367,099	403,764
Average daily shares	Million	157	346	809	1,042	1,240	1,441	1,398	1,457	1,602
High day	Million	292	653	1,350	1,561	2,368	2,813	1,886	2,690	3,116
Low day	Million	57	118	312	403	414	462	360	509	545
Odd lots	Million	282	656	2,384	3,021	3,781	5,933	4,370	5,619	7,068
Value of shares traded	Bil. dol.	1,336	3,110	9,073	11,205	10,645	10,491	9,847	11,841	14,441
Round lots	Bil. dol.	1,325	3,083	8,945	11,060	10,489	10,278	9,692	11,618	14,125
Odd lots	Bil. dol.	11	27	128	145	155	213	154	223	316
Bond volume [1]	Mil. dol.	10,893	6,979	3,221	2,328	2,668	3,646	2,502	1,291	951
Daily average	Mil. dol.	43.1	27.7	12.8	9.2	10.8	14.5	10.0	5.1	3.8

[1] Par value.

Source: New York Stock Exchange, Inc., New York, NY, *Fact Book*, annual (copyright).

Table 1192. Securities Listed on New York Stock Exchange: 1990 to 2005

[As of December 31, except cash dividends are for calendar year (1,689 represents $1,689,000,000,000)]

Item	Unit	1990	1995	1997	1998	1999	2000	2001	2002	2003	2004	2005
BONDS												
Number of issuers	Number	743	564	533	474	416	392	369	343	312	228	211
Number of issues	Number	2,912	2,097	1,965	1,858	1,736	1,627	1,447	1,323	1,273	1,059	971
Face value	Bil. dol.	1,689	2,773	2,625	2,554	2,402	2,125	1,654	1,378	1,355	1,080	968
STOCKS												
Companies	Number	1,774	2,675	3,047	3,114	3,025	2,862	2,798	2,783	2,750	2,768	2,767
Number of issues	Number	2,284	3,126	3,358	3,382	3,286	3,072	2,984	2,959	2,938	3,010	3,052
Shares listed	Billions	90.7	154.7	207.1	239.3	280.9	313.9	341.5	349.9	359.7	380.8	396.8
Market value	Bil. dol.	2,820	6,013	9,413	10,864	12,296	12,372	11,714	9,603	12,158	13,728	14,588
Average price [1]	Dollars	31.08	38.86	45.45	45.40	43.77	42.14	34.11	28.39	33.80	36.05	36.76

[1] This average cannot be used as an index of price trend due to changes in shares listed caused by new listings, suspensions, stock splits and stock dividends.

Source: New York Stock Exchange, Inc., New York, NY, *Fact Book*, annual (copyright).

Table 1193. **Stock Ownership by Age of Head of Family and Family Income: 1995 to 2004**

[Median value in thousands of constant 2004 dollars (18.0 represents $18,000). Constant dollar figures are based on consumer price index data published by U.S. Bureau of Labor Statistics. Families include one-person units; for definition of family, see text, Section 1. Based on Survey of Consumer Finance; see Appendix III. For definition of median, see Guide to Tabular Presentation]

Age of family head and family income (constant (2004) dollars)	Families having direct or indirect stock holdings [1] (percent)			Median value among families with holdings			Stock holdings' share of group's financial assets (percent)		
	1995	2001	2004	1995	2001	2004	1995	2001	2004
All families	**40.4**	**51.9**	**48.6**	**18.0**	**37.7**	**24.3**	**40.1**	**56.0**	**47.4**
Under 35 years old.	36.6	48.9	38.8	6.3	7.5	5.2	27.2	52.5	30.0
35 to 44 years old	46.4	59.5	52.3	12.3	29.3	12.7	39.5	57.3	47.7
45 to 54 years old	48.9	59.2	54.4	31.9	53.3	30.6	43.1	59.1	46.8
55 to 64 years old	40.0	57.1	61.6	38.2	86.5	59.5	44.5	56.2	51.1
65 to 74 years old	34.4	39.2	45.8	41.9	159.8	75.0	35.8	55.2	51.1
75 years old and over	27.9	34.2	34.8	24.6	127.8	85.9	39.8	51.4	39.1
Percentiles of income: [2]									
Less than 20	6.5	12.4	11.7	4.6	7.4	7.0	14.2	36.9	31.3
20 to 39.9	24.7	33.5	28.8	7.8	8.0	8.8	26.7	34.9	29.6
40 to 59.9	41.5	52.1	49.2	7.7	16.0	11.6	28.5	46.5	41.0
60 to 79.9	54.3	75.7	66.5	15.6	30.4	20.0	35.6	51.7	37.5
80 to 89.9	69.7	82.0	82.5	30.8	68.8	34.6	41.3	57.4	43.2
90 to 100	80.0	89.6	91.0	73.9	263.8	169.9	45.7	60.5	53.6

[1] Indirect holdings are those in retirement accounts and other managed assets.   [2] See footnote 8, Table 1152.

Source: Board of Governors of the Federal Reserve System, "2004 Survey of Consumer Finances"; published 28 February 2006; <http://www.federalreserve.gov/pubs/oss/oss2/2004/scf2004home.html>.

Table 1194. **Household Ownership of Equities: 2005**

[56.9 represents 56,900,000. Based on a national probability sample of 4,927 household financial decision-makers. Further questions about equity ownership were asked of those 2,476 decision-makers who indicated they owned equities]

Type of holding	Households owning equities		Number of individual investors (mil.)
	Number (mil.)	Percent of all households	
Any type of equity (net) [1]	56.9	50.3	91.1
Any equity inside employer-sponsored retirement plans	37.6	33.2	48.8
Any equity outside employer-sponsored retirement plans	39.3	34.7	58.9
Individual stock (net) [1]	28.4	25.1	42.6
Individual stock inside employer-sponsored retirement plans.	7.6	6.7	9.9
Individual stock outside employer-sponsored retirement plans.	23.3	20.6	35.0
Stock mutual funds (net) [1]	51.8	45.8	77.7
Stock mutual funds inside employer-sponsored retirement plans	36.0	31.8	46.8
Stock mutual funds outside employer-sponsored retirement plans . . .	31.1	27.5	46.7

[1] Net figure adjusted for multiple responses.

Source: Investment Company Institute, Washington, DC, and Securities Industry Association, New York, NY, Equity Ownership in America, Fall 2005 (copyright).

Table 1195. **Characteristics of Equity Owners: 2005**

[In percent, except as indicated. See headnote, Table 1194. For definition of median, see Guide to Tabular Presentation]

Item	Total	Age					Household income		
		18 to 34 years old	35 to 44 years old	45 to 54 years old	55 to 64 years old	65 years old and over	Less than $50,000	$50,000 to $99,999	$100,000 and over
Median age of owner (years)	51	30	40	50	59	72	52	46	49
Median household income (dol.) . .	65,000	62,000	70,000	70,000	65,000	45,000	30,000	70,000	133,300
Median household financial assets [1] (dol.)	125,000	40,000	80,000	152,700	275,700	350,000	46,500	116,800	367,900
Equity investments owned:									
Individual stock (net) [2]	49	38	46	45	53	63	38	44	61
Inside retirement plans [3]	12	9	14	17	12	8	5	13	20
Outside retirement plans [3] . . .	43	32	41	39	47	57	32	36	55
Stock mutual funds (net) [2]	90	94	92	93	92	81	88	93	92
Inside retirement plans [3]	66	77	77	77	61	32	55	75	79
Outside retirement plans [3] . . .	55	47	52	51	64	60	50	50	60
Have retirement plan coverage [3] . .	78	84	85	84	77	58	68	86	87
Have Individual Retirement Account (IRA)	67	61	64	65	74	70	57	66	76

[1] Includes assets in employer-sponsored retirement plans but excludes value of primary residence.   [2] Net figure adjusted for multiple responses.   [3] Employer-sponsored.

Source: Investment Company Institute, Washington, DC, and Securities Industry Association, New York, NY, Equity Ownership in America, Fall 2005 (copyright).

Table 1196. **Households Owning Mutual Funds by Age and Income: 2000 and 2005**

[In percent. Ownership includes money market, stock, bond and hybrid mutual funds, variable annuities, and mutual funds owned through Individual Retirement Accounts (IRAs), Keoghs, and employer-sponsored retirement plans. In 2005 an estimated 53,700,000 households own mutual funds. Based on a sample survey of 3,000 households; for details, see source]

Age of household head and household income	Percent distribution, 2005	As percent of all households 2000	As percent of all households 2005	Age of household head and household income	Percent distribution, 2005	As percent of all households 2000	As percent of all households 2005
Total	100	49	48	Less than $25,000......	6	17	12
Less than 25 years old...	3	23	24	$25,000 to $34,999	9	37	32
25 to 34 years old	16	49	44	$35,000 to $49,999	16	49	49
35 to 44 years old	24	58	54	$50,000 to $74,999	27	66	61
45 to 54 years old	24	59	53	$75,000 to $99,999	19	77	73
55 to 64 years old	18	54	57	$100,000 and over	23	79	82
65 years old and over ...	15	32	37				

Source: Investment Company Institute, Washington, DC, *Fundamentals, Investment Company Institute Research in Brief*, Vol. 9, No. 4, August 2000; and Vol. 14, No. 5, October 2005 (copyright).

Table 1197. **Characteristics of Mutual Fund Owners: 2004**

[In percent, **except as indicated**. Mutual fund ownership includes holdings of money market, stock, bond, and hybrid mutual funds; and funds owned through variable annuities, Individual Retirement Accounts (IRAs), Keoghs, and employer-sponsored retirement plans. Based on a national probability sample of 3,613 primary financial decision-makers in households with mutual fund investments. For definition of median, see Guide to Tabular Presentation]

Characteristic	Total	Age Under 40 years old	Age 40 to 64 years old	Age 65 years old and over	Household income Less than $50,000	Household income $50,000 to $99,999	Household income $100,000 or more
Median age (years)	48	33	51	71	48	46	46
Median household income (dol.)	68,700	65,000	75,000	45,000	32,500	70,000	130,000
Median household financial assets [1] (dol.)..	125,000	50,000	200,000	207,100	50,000	110,000	350,000
Own an IRA	69	63	72	64	58	65	77
Household has a defined contribution retirement plan(s), net [2]	84	86	87	67	74	89	88
401(k) plan	67	78	71	28	56	72	76
403(b) plan	14	12	15	6	9	13	19
State, local, or federal government plan. . .	35	27	37	46	32	38	31
Median mutual fund assets (dol.)	48,000	20,000	70,000	60,000	17,600	43,800	95,000
Median number of mutual funds owned	4	4	5	4	3	4	6
Own: [2]							
Equity funds	80	79	83	74	70	80	91
Bond funds	44	41	46	39	35	41	50
Own mutual funds bought: [2]							
Outside employer-sponsored retirement plan(s)........................	68	59	69	84	63	60	74
Inside employer-sponsored retirement plan(s)........................	63	69	67	30	55	68	68

[1] Includes assets in employer-sponsored retirement plans but excludes value of primary residence. [2] Net figure adjusted for multiple responses.

Source: Investment Company Institute, Washington, DC, *Profile of Mutual Fund Shareholders, 2004* (copyright).

Table 1198. **Mutual Funds—Summary: 1990 to 2005**

[Number of funds and assets as of December 31 (1,065 represents $1,065,000,000,000). A mutual fund is an open-end investment company that continuously issues and redeems shares that represent an interest in a pool of financial assets. Excludes data for funds that invest in other mutual funds. Minus sign (–) indicates net redemptions]

Type of fund	Unit	1990	1995	1999	2000	2001	2002	2003	2004	2005
Number of funds, total	Number...	3,079	5,725	7,791	8,155	8,305	8,244	8,126	8,041	7,977
Equity funds	Number...	1,099	2,139	3,952	4,385	4,716	4,747	4,599	4,547	4,586
Hybrid funds	Number...	193	412	532	523	483	473	508	510	505
Bond funds	Number...	1,046	2,177	2,262	2,208	2,091	2,035	2,045	2,041	2,015
Money market funds, taxable [1] ...	Number...	506	674	702	703	689	679	662	639	595
Money market funds, tax-exempt [2]..	Number...	235	323	343	336	326	310	312	304	276
Assets, total	Bil. dol....	1,065	2,811	6,846	6,965	6,975	6,390	7,414	8,107	8,905
Equity funds	Bil. dol. ...	239	1,249	4,042	3,962	3,418	2,662	3,684	4,384	4,940
Hybrid funds	Bil. dol. ...	36	210	379	346	346	325	430	519	567
Bond funds	Bil. dol. ...	291	599	812	811	925	1,130	1,248	1,290	1,357
Money market funds, taxable [1] ...	Bil. dol. ...	415	630	1,409	1,607	2,013	1,997	1,764	1,603	1,707
Money market funds, tax-exempt [2]..	Bil. dol. ...	84	123	204	238	272	275	288	310	334
Equity, hybrid and bond funds:										
Sales	Bil. dol. ...	149	475	1,274	1,630	1,383	1,434	1,430	1,471	1,589
Redemptions	Bil. dol. ...	98	313	1,021	1,330	1,177	1,228	1,148	1,178	1,286
Net sales.................	Bil. dol. ...	51	163	252	300	206	206	282	293	303
Money market funds, taxable: [1]										
Sales	Bil. dol. ...	1,219	2,729	7,083	8,691	10,701	11,012	10,150	9,717	11,064
Redemptions	Bil. dol. ...	1,183	2,617	6,866	8,499	10,314	11,075	10,402	9,874	10,998
Net sales.................	Bil. dol. ...	36	112	217	192	386	-63	-252	-157	67
Money market funds, tax-exempt: [2]										
Sales	Bil. dol. ...	197	396	687	788	783	750	873	1,082	1,389
Redemptions	Bil. dol. ...	190	385	675	757	751	736	866	1,066	1,365
Net sales.................	Bil. dol. ...	7	11	12	31	31	14	7	16	24

[1] Funds invest in short-term, high-grade securities sold in the money market. [2] Funds invest in municipal securities with relatively short maturities.

Source: Investment Company Institute, Washington, DC, *Mutual Fund Fact Book*, annual (copyright).

Table 1199. **Mutual Fund Shares—Holdings and Net Purchases by Type of Investor: 1990 to 2005**

[In billions of dollars (608 represents $608,000,000,000). Holdings as of Dec. 31. Minus sign (–) indicates net sales]

Type of investor	Holdings					Net purchases				
	1990	2000	2003	2004	2005	1990	2000	2003	2004	2005
Total	608	3,638	4,653	5,436	6,045	53.7	239.4	288.0	299.1	257.5
Households, nonprofit organizations	512	2,500	3,188	3,726	4,207	31.5	84.4	228.6	257.3	225.3
Nonfinancial corporate business. . .	10	95	125	143	165	–1.0	12.0	11.0	5.0	5.0
State and local governments.	5	24	26	27	28	3.5	1.3	–5.4	–1.5	–0.2
Commercial banking	2	20	17	18	17	–0.3	2.5	–6.2	–0.9	–1.8
Credit unions	1	4	4	3	2	0.2	–0.3	0.5	–0.9	–1.0
Life insurance companies	31	77	92	114	131	12.6	5.6	0.5	12.8	9.0
Private pension funds	40	752	994	1,174	1,252	6.6	84.0	51.7	25.8	18.5
State and local government retirement funds	8	167	208	231	241	0.5	49.9	7.3	1.6	2.7

Source: Board of Governors of the Federal Reserve System, "Federal Reserve Statistical Release, Z.1, Flow of Funds Accounts of the United States"; published: 9 March 2006; <http://www.federalreserve.gov/releases/z1/20060309/>.

Table 1200. **Mutual Fund Retirement Assets: 1990 to 2005**

[In billions of dollars, except percent (205 represents $205,000,000,000). Based on data from the Institute's Annual Questionnaire for Retirement Statistics. The 2005 survey gathered data from 16,089 mutual fund share classes representing approximately 84 percent of mutual fund industry assets. Assets were estimated for all nonreporting funds. Estimates of retirement assets in street name and omnibus accounts were derived from data reported on the Annual Questionnaire for Retirement Statistics and the Annual Institutional Survey]

Type of account	1990	1995	2000	2001	2002	2003	2004	2005
Mutual fund retirement assets . . .	**205**	**913**	**2,492**	**2,360**	**2,105**	**2,682**	**3,084**	**3,444**
Percent of total retirement assets.	5	13	21	21	20	22	23	24
Individual retirement accounts (IRAs) . . .	139	468	1,236	1,173	1,052	1,319	1,497	1,668
Employer-sponsored defined contribution retirement plans	67	445	1,256	1,188	1,053	1,363	1,588	1,776
401(k) plans [1]	35	266	819	798	712	927	1,096	1,238
Percent of total 401(k) assets	9	31	47	47	45	47	48	51
403(b) plans [2]	15	120	265	237	198	262	295	321
457 plans [3]................	2	9	45	43	36	44	51	59
Other defined contribution plans [4]	15	50	127	110	106	130	146	158
Percent of all mutual funds:								
Mutual fund retirement assets	19	32	36	34	33	36	38	39
Individual retirement accounts (IRAs) . . .	13	16	18	17	16	18	18	19
Employer-sponsored retirement plans . .	6	16	18	17	17	18	20	20

[1] A 401(k) plan is a qualified retirement plan that allows participants to have a portion of their compensation (otherwise payable in cash) contributed pretax to a retirement account on their behalf. Predominantly 401(k) assets, but may also include some profit-sharing plan assets that do not have a 401(k) feature. [2] Section 403(b) of the Internal Revenue Code permits employees of certain charitable organizations, nonprofit hospitals, universities, and public schools to establish tax-sheltered retirement programs. These plans may invest in either annuity contracts or mutual fund shares. [3] These plans are deferred compensation arrangements for government employees and employees of certain tax-exempt organizations. [4] Includes Keoghs and defined contribution plans (profit-sharing, thrift-savings, stock bonus, and money purchase) without 401(k)features.

Source: Investment Company Institute, Washington, DC, *Fundamentals, Investment Company Institute Research in Brief, "The U.S. Retirement Market, 2005"*; Vol. 15, No. 5, July 2006; and *"Appendix: Additional Data on the U.S. Retirement Market"*; Vol. 15, No. 5A, July 2006; <http://www.ici.org> (copyright).

Table 1201. **Individual Retirement Accounts (IRA) Plans—Value by Institution: 1990 to 2005**

[As of December 31 (637 represents $637,000,000,000). Estimated]

Institution	Amount (bil. dol.)								Percent distribution		
	1990	1995	2000	2001	2002	2003	2004	2005	1990	2000	2005
Total IRA assets	**637**	**1,288**	**2,629**	**2,619**	**2,533**	**2,991**	**3,336**	**3,667**	**100**	**100**	**100**
Bank and thrift deposits [1]	266	261	252	254	263	268	270	273	42	10	7
Life insurance companies [2]	40	81	203	211	268	285	311	333	6	8	9
Mutual funds.	139	468	1,236	1,173	1,052	1,319	1,497	1,668	22	47	45
Securities held in brokerage accounts [3].	192	479	939	982	949	1,118	1,259	1,393	30	36	38

[1] Includes Keogh deposits. [2] Annuities held by IRAs, excluding variable annuity mutual fund IRA assets. [3] Excludes mutual fund assets held through brokerage accounts, which are included in mutual funds.

Source: Investment Company Institute, Washington, DC, *Fundamentals, Investment Company Institute Research in Brief, "The U.S. Retirement Market, 2005"*; Vol. 15, No. 5, July 2006; and *"Appendix: Additional Data on the U.S. Retirement Market"*; Vol. 15, No. 5A, July 2006; <http://www.ici.org> (copyright).

752   Banking, Finance, and Insurance

Table 1202. **Assets of Private and Public Pension Funds by Type of Fund: 1990 to 2005**

[In billions of dollars (3,267 represents $3,267,000,000,000). As of end of year. Except for corporate equities, represents book value. Excludes social security trust funds, see Table 532]

Type of pension fund	1990	1995	1999	2000	2001	2002	2003	2004	2005
Total, all types	3,267	5,638	9,099	8,911	8,477	7,718	9,117	10,056	10,558
Private funds	2,197	3,769	5,999	5,821	5,411	4,893	5,814	6,460	6,762
Insured [1]	570	881	1,428	1,466	1,495	1,584	1,786	1,987	2,148
Noninsured [2, 3]	1,627	2,889	4,571	4,355	3,916	3,309	4,027	4,473	4,613
Credit market instruments [3]	464	608	720	624	637	663	677	712	735
Agency- and GSE-backed securities [4] . .	133	214	233	207	215	220	227	241	248
Corporate and foreign bonds	158	240	348	290	295	307	315	331	342
Corporate equities	606	1,278	2,081	1,915	1,562	1,097	1,492	1,691	1,726
Mutual fund shares	40	327	898	946	862	752	994	1,174	1,252
Unallocated insurance contracts [5]	215	332	396	369	340	271	334	369	378
State and local pension funds [3]	730	1,327	2,326	2,293	2,207	1,930	2,344	2,572	2,722
Credit market instruments [3]	402	510	707	743	689	639	650	677	667
Agency- and GSE-backed securities [4]	63	63	129	179	181	193	248	293	296
Corporate equities	285	704	1,408	1,299	1,260	1,057	1,422	1,607	1,752
Mutual fund shares	8	63	141	178	184	167	208	231	241
Federal government retirement funds [6]	340	541	774	797	860	894	959	1,024	1,075

[1] Annuity reserves held by life insurance companies, excluding unallocated contracts held by private pension funds. [2] Private defined benefit plans and defined contribution plans (including 401(k) type plans). [3] Includes other types of assets not shown separately. [4] GSE = Government-sponsored enterprises. [5] Assets held at life insurance companies (e.g., guaranteed investment contracts (GICs), variable annuities). [6] Includes the Federal Employees Thrift Savings Plan, the National Railroad Retirement Investment Trust, and nonmarketable government securities held by federal government retirement funds.

Source: Board of Governors of the Federal Reserve System, "Federal Reserve Statistical Release, Z.1, Flow of Funds Accounts of the United States"; published 9 March 2006; <http://www.federalreserve.gov/releases/z1/20060309/>.

Table 1203. **Annual Revenues of Selected Securities Industries: 2000 to 2004**

[In millions of dollars (384,991 represents $384,991,000,000). Covers taxable and tax-exempt employer firms only. Based on the North American Industry Classification System (NAICS), 1997; see text, Section 15. Based on Service Annual Survey. Estimates have been adjusted to the results of the 2002 Economic Census. See Appendix III]

Kind of business	1997 NAICS code	2000	2001	2002	2003	2004
Total	523x	384,991	331,774	292,646	311,525	349,166
Securities and commodity contracts intermediation and brokerage	5231	296,045	248,131	212,236	225,299	250,080
Investment banking & securities dealing	52311	145,416	121,942	98,930	108,306	127,257
Securities brokerage	52312	144,631	120,048	107,199	110,690	115,626
Commodity contracts dealing	52313	2,945	3,037	3,044	3,329	3,858
Commodity contracts brokerage	52314	3,053	3,105	3,064	2,975	3,339
Other financial investment activities [1]	5239x	88,947	83,643	80,410	86,226	99,086
Portfolio management	52392	75,349	71,389	67,370	71,535	80,872
Investment advice	52393	13,598	12,254	13,040	14,691	18,214

[1] Excludes NAICS 52391 (miscellaneous intermediation) and NAICS 52399 (all other financial investment activities).

Source: U.S. Census Bureau, *Service Annual Survey: 2004.*

Table 1204. **Securities Industry—Financial Summary: 1990 to 2004**

[In billions of dollars, except as indicated. (71.4 represents $71,400,000,000)]

Type	1990	1995	1998	1999	2000	2001	2002	2003	2004
Number of firms	8,437	7,722	7,685	7,461	7,258	7,002	6,768	6,565	6,284
Revenues, total	71.4	143.4	235.0	266.8	349.5	280.1	221.8	219.0	242.9
Commissions	12.0	23.2	36.7	45.9	54.1	44.8	45.0	45.5	47.6
Trading/investment gains	15.7	29.0	32.8	55.5	70.8	39.0	24.2	38.8	30.7
Underwriting profits	3.7	8.9	16.2	17.8	18.7	16.9	14.7	17.2	19.1
Margin interest	3.2	6.5	12.7	15.2	24.5	13.9	6.4	5.3	7.0
Mutual fund sales	3.2	7.4	14.8	16.7	19.4	16.4	15.7	16.2	18.5
Other	33.4	68.5	121.7	115.7	161.9	149.1	115.8	96.0	120.1
Expenses, total	70.6	132.1	217.8	237.7	310.4	260.7	206.5	193.3	219.7
Interest expense	28.1	56.9	98.1	87.5	131.9	98.9	56.4	44.4	59.7
Compensation	22.9	41.5	65.0	81.7	95.2	83.5	74.9	77.4	83.5
Commissions/clearance paid	3.0	5.7	10.3	13.5	15.5	14.0	15.0	16.3	17.4
Other	16.6	28.0	44.3	55.0	67.8	64.2	60.3	55.1	59.2
Net income, pretax	0.8	11.3	17.2	29.1	39.1	19.4	15.3	25.7	23.2
Pre-tax profit margin (percent)	1.1	7.9	7.3	10.9	11.2	6.9	6.9	11.7	9.5
Pre-tax return on equity (percent) . .	2.2	20.1	19.4	27.8	31.1	13.8	10.7	17.6	15.0
Assets	657	1,494	2,187	2,537	2,866	3,371	3,261	3,980	4,831
Liabilities	623	1,435	2,092	2,423	2,728	3,227	3,119	3,831	4,671
Ownership equity	34	59	95	114	138	144	142	149	160

Source: U.S. Securities and Exchange Commission, *Annual Report.*

Banking, Finance, and Insurance **753**

Table 1205. Life Insurance in Force and Purchases in the United States— Summary: 1990 to 2004

[As of December 31 or calendar year, as applicable (389 represents 389,000,000). Covers life insurance with life insurance companies only. Represents all life insurance in force on lives of U.S. residents whether issued by U.S. or foreign companies]

Year	Number of policies, total (mil.)	Life insurance in force Value (bil. dol.) Total[1]	Individual	Group	Life insurance purchases[2] Number (1,000) Total	Individual	Group	Amount (bil. dol.) Total	Individual	Group
1990	389	9,393	5,391	3,754	28,791	14,199	14,592	1,529	1,070	459
1995	370	11,696	6,890	4,605	31,999	12,595	19,404	1,577	1,039	538
1997	351	13,364	7,873	5,279	31,707	11,734	19,973	1,892	1,204	689
1998	358	14,471	8,523	5,735	31,891	11,559	20,332	2,064	1,325	740
1999	367	15,496	9,172	6,110	38,584	11,673	26,912	2,367	1,400	967
2000	369	15,953	9,376	6,376	34,882	13,345	21,537	2,515	1,594	921
2001	377	16,290	9,346	6,765	40,095	14,059	26,036	2,773	1,600	1,172
2002	375	16,346	9,312	6,876	38,713	14,692	24,020	2,767	1,753	1,014
2003	379	17,044	9,655	7,236	35,767	13,821	21,946	2,823	1,773	1,050
2004	373	17,508	9,717	7,631	38,453	12,581	25,872	2,948	1,846	1,102

[1] Includes other types of policy not shown separately. [2] Excludes revivals, increases, dividend additions, and reinsurance acquired. Includes long-term credit insurance (life insurance on loans of more than 10 years' duration).

Source: American Council of Life Insurers, Washington, DC, *Life Insurers Fact Book*, annual (copyright).

Table 1206. U.S. Life Insurance Companies—Summary: 1990 to 2004

[As of December 31 or calendar year, as applicable (402.2 represents $402,200,000,000). Covers domestic and foreign business of U.S. companies. Beginning 1995 includes annual statement data that companies that primarily are health insurance companies]

Item	Unit	1990	1995	1997	1998	1999	2000	2001	2002	2003	2004
U.S. companies [1]	Number..	2,195	2,079	1,620	1,563	1,470	1,269	1,225	1,171	1,227	1,179
Income	**Bil. dol.**	**402.2**	**528.1**	**610.6**	**663.4**	**726.9**	**811.5**	**724.4**	**734.0**	**727.0**	**756.8**
Life insurance premiums	Bil. dol.	76.7	102.8	115.0	119.9	120.3	130.6	125.3	134.5	127.3	139.7
Annuity considerations [2]	Bil. dol.	129.1	158.4	197.5	229.5	270.2	306.7	251.3	269.3	268.6	276.7
Health insurance premiums	Bil. dol.	58.3	90.0	92.7	94.9	100.0	105.6	103.4	108.7	115.8	125.8
Investment and other	Bil. dol.	138.2	176.9	205.3	219.1	236.4	268.5	244.5	221.5	215.3	214.7
Payments under life insurance and annuity contracts	Bil. dol.	88.4	227.6	276.6	301.8	355.3	375.2	304.9	301.3	307.1	331.7
Payments to life insurance beneficiaries	Bil. dol.	24.6	34.5	37.5	40.1	41.4	44.1	46.5	48.2	51.7	51.6
Surrender values under life insurance [3]	Bil. dol.	18.0	19.5	24.0	26.8	32.8	27.2	30.7	32.9	35.9	35.5
Surrender values under annuity contracts [3,4]	Bil. dol.	(NA)	105.4	140.8	154.5	198.3	214.0	151.3	142.9	140.3	162.9
Policyholder dividends	Bil. dol.	12.0	17.8	18.0	18.9	19.1	20.0	20.0	21.0	20.8	19.0
Annuity payments	Bil. dol.	32.6	48.5	55.1	60.4	62.5	68.7	55.2	55.0	57.1	61.2
Matured endowments	Bil. dol.	0.7	1.0	0.6	0.6	0.5	0.6	0.5	0.6	0.6	0.6
Other payments	Bil. dol.	0.6	0.9	0.6	0.6	0.6	0.6	0.6	0.6	0.7	0.9
Health insurance benefit payments	Bil. dol.	40.0	64.7	67.4	70.0	74.5	78.8	76.3	78.7	81.9	88.5
BALANCE SHEET											
Assets	**Bil. dol.**	**1,408**	**2,144**	**2,579**	**2,827**	**3,071**	**3,182**	**3,269**	**3,380**	**3,887**	**4,253**
Government bonds	Bil. dol.	211	409	391	379	362	364	377	481	538	563
Corporate securities	Bil. dol.	711	1,241	1,658	1,898	2,180	2,238	2,263	2,266	2,666	2,965
Percent of total assets	Percent..	50	58	64	67	71	70	69	67	69	70
Bonds	Bil. dol.	583	869	1,060	1,140	1,190	1,241	1,354	1,475	1,644	1,785
Stocks	Bil. dol.	128	372	598	758	990	997	909	791	1,022	1,180
Mortgages	Bil. dol.	270	212	210	216	230	237	244	251	269	283
Real estate	Bil. dol.	43	52	46	41	38	36	32	33	31	31
Policy loans	Bil. dol.	63	96	105	105	99	102	104	105	107	109
Other	Bil. dol.	110	133	169	187	163	204	248	244	276	303
Interest earned on assets [5]	Percent..	8.89	7.41	7.35	6.95	6.71	7.05	6.31	5.38	5.03	4.80
Obligations and surplus funds [6]	Bil. dol.	1,408	2,144	2,579	2,826	3,071	3,182	3,269	3,380	3,888	4,253
Policy reserves	**Bil. dol.**	**1,197**	**1,812**	**2,165**	**2,377**	**2,610**	**2,712**	**2,446**	**2,507**	**2,895**	**3,160**
Annuities [7]	Bil. dol.	798	1,213	1,455	1,608	1,781	1,841	1,516	1,550	1,835	2,024
Group	Bil. dol.	516	619	762	845	907	960	571	570	662	712
Individual	Bil. dol.	282	594	693	763	874	881	945	980	1,173	1,312
Supplementary contracts [8]	Bil. dol.	17	25	28	31	32	34	13	14	15	16
Life insurance	Bil. dol.	349	511	606	656	705	742	816	833	921	988
Health insurance	Bil. dol.	33	63	75	82	92	96	101	111	123	134
Liabilities for deposit-type contracts [9]	Bil. dol.	18	20	20	21	21	21	338	364	405	445
Capital and surplus	Bil. dol.	91	151	160	173	181	188	191	202	231	250

NA Not available. [1] Beginning 1995, includes life insurance companies that sell accident and health insurance. [2] Beginning 2001, excludes certain deposit-type funds from income due to codification. [3] Beginning with 1995, "surrender values" include annuity withdrawals of funds, which were not included in prior years. [4] Beginning 2001, excludes payments under deposit-type contracts. [5] Net rate. [6] Includes other obligations not shown separately. [7] Beginning 2001, excludes reserves for guaranteed interest contracts (GICs). [8] Through 2000, includes reserves for contracts with and without life contingencies; beginning 2001, includes only reserves for contracts with life contingencies. [9] Policyholder dividend accumulations for all years. Beginning 2001, also includes liabilities for guaranteed interest contracts, supplementary contracts without life contingencies, and premium and other deposits.

Source: American Council of Life Insurers, Washington, DC, *Life Insurers Fact Book*, annual (copyright).

Table 1207. Property and Casualty Insurance—Summary: 1999 to 2004

[In billions of dollars (293.1 represents $293,100,000,000). Minus sign (–) indicates loss]

Item	1999	2000	2001	2002	2003	2004
Premiums, net written [1]	293.1	305.1	327.8	375.1	409.5	429.0
Automobile, private [2]	122.7	120.0	128.1	139.8	151.3	156.7
Automobile, commercial [2]	18.4	19.8	21.8	24.6	25.5	26.7
Fire	(NA)	(NA)	5.1	7.4	8.4	8.3
Homeowners' multiple peril	30.8	32.7	35.4	40.3	46.1	50.0
Commercial multiple peril	(NA)	(NA)	22.5	25.6	27.5	29.1
Marine, inland and ocean	7.8	8.3	8.7	9.4	10.4	11.0
Accident and health	13.8	14.5	15.6	15.6	12.0	10.0
Workers' compensation	23.1	26.2	27.1	30.9	33.2	36.8
Medical malpractice	(NA)	(NA)	6.3	7.5	8.8	9.1
Other liability [3]	(NA)	(NA)	20.0	29.5	36.4	40.7
Reinsurance	(NA)	(NA)	11.8	15.1	15.5	13.7
Losses and expenses	302.6	321.3	361.8	377.4	389.4	406.0
Underwriting gain/loss	–19.9	–27.3	–50.2	–28.3	–3.2	6.9
Net investment income	40.3	42.0	38.7	39.8	39.8	40.8
Operating earnings after taxes	8.8	4.4	–13.6	4.3	23.5	29.4
Assets	947.3	924.9	952.8	1,014.6	1,194.9	1,310.1
Policyholders' surplus	342.0	124.5	295.4	292.5	359.8	415.0

NA Not available.   [1] Excludes state funds.   [2] Includes premiums for automobile liability and physical damage.   [3] Coverages protecting against legal liability resulting from negligence, carelessness, or failure to act.
Source: Insurance Information Institute, New York, NY, *The III Insurance Fact Book*, annual (copyright). See also <http://www.iii.org>.

Table 1208. Automobile Insurance—Average Expenditures Per Insured Vehicle by State: 2000 to 2003

[In dollars. Average expenditure equals total premiums written divided by liability car-years. A car-year is equal to 365 days of insured coverage for a single vehicle. The average expenditures for automobile insurance in a state are affected by a number of factors, including the underlying rate structure, the coverages purchased, the deductibles and limits selected, the types of vehicles insured, and the distribution of driver characteristics. The NAIC does not rank state average expenditures and does not endorse any conclusions drawn from this data]

State	2000	2002	2003	State	2000	2002	2003	State	2000	2002	2003
U.S.	689	777	821	KS	540	586	610	ND	477	504	536
				KY	616	685	737	OH	579	639	671
AL	594	626	656	LA	806	926	1,014	OK	603	650	689
AK	770	884	938	ME	528	585	631	OR	625	682	735
AZ	792	877	920	MD	757	837	891	PA	699	783	811
AR	606	670	698	MA	946	984	1,052	RI	825	937	992
CA	667	763	821	MI	702	870	931	SC	620	702	745
CO	755	914	923	MN	696	800	836	SD	482	540	563
CT	871	965	983	MS	654	679	709	TN	592	632	650
DE	849	907	973	MO	612	666	702	TX	678	791	837
DC	996	1,040	1,129	MT	530	628	674	UT	620	700	732
FL	781	934	1,015	NE	533	589	624	VT	568	644	683
GA	674	739	759	NV	829	887	913	VA	576	625	657
HI	702	736	774	NH	665	731	776	WA	722	788	824
ID	505	560	585	NJ	977	1,113	1,188	WV	680	776	842
IL	652	726	761	NM	674	699	730	WI	545	609	620
IN	570	646	670	NY	939	1,087	1,161	WY	496	580	617
IA	479	547	580	NC	564	588	605				

Source: National Association of Insurance Commissioners (NAIC), Kansas City, MO, *Auto Insurance Database Report*, annual (copyright). Reprinted with permission of the NAIC. Further reprint or distribution strictly prohibited without prior written permission of the NAIC.

Table 1209. Renters and Homeowners Insurance—Average Premiums by State: 2003

[In dollars. Average premium equals premiums divided by exposure per house-years. A house-year is equal to 365 days of insured coverage for a single dwelling and is the standard measurement for homeowners insurance]

State	Renters [1]	Homeowners [2]	State	Renters [1]	Homeowners [2]	State	Renters [1]	Homeowners [2]
U.S.	192	668	KS	171	772	ND	123	625
			KY	164	559	OH	164	476
AL	213	681	LA	252	975	OK	268	925
AK	173	731	ME	138	462	OR	168	461
AZ	222	614	MD	154	584	PA	145	543
AR	231	721	MA	207	671	RI	185	673
CA	261	753	MI	185	673	SC	183	672
CO	186	762	MN	154	733	SD	121	557
CT	197	714	MS	264	793	TN [3]	204	622
DE	160	442	MO	187	650	TX [3]	277	1,328
DC	175	806	MT	158	628	UT	149	463
FL	206	810	NE	148	690	VT	150	552
GA	215	570	NV	218	582	VA	144	560
HI	213	687	NH	155	539	WA	169	549
ID	153	433	NJ	175	585	WV	171	534
IL	187	610	NM	200	551	WI	124	434
IN	183	594	NY	213	721	WY	154	621
IA	144	542	NC	152	576			

[1] Based on the HO-4 renters insurance policy for tenants. Includes broad named-peril coverage for the personal property of tenants.   [2] Based on the HO-3 homeowner package policy for owner-occupied dwellings, 1–4 family units. Provides "all risks" coverage (except those specifically excluded in the policy) on buildings, broad named-peril coverage on personal property, and is the most common package written.   [3] The Texas Insurance Commissioner promulgates residential policy forms which are similar but not identical to the standard forms.
Source: National Association of Insurance Commissioners (NAIC), Kansas City, MO, *Dwelling Fire, Homeowners Owner-Occupied, and Homeowners Tenant and Condominium/Cooperative Unit Owners Insurance* (copyright). Reprinted with permission of the NAIC. Further reprint or distribution strictly prohibited without prior written permission of the NAIC.

Table 1210. **Real Estate and Rental and Leasing—Nonemployer Establishments and Receipts by Kind of Business: 2000 to 2003**

[1,696 represents 1,696,000. Includes only firms subject to federal income tax. Nonemployers are businesses with no paid employees. Data originate chiefly from administrative records of the Internal Revenue Service; see Appendix III. Data for 2000 based on the North American Industry Classification System (NAICS), 1997; beginning 2002 based on NAICS 2002, see text, Section 15]

Kind of business	NAICS code	Establishments (1,000)			Receipts (mil. dol.)		
		2000	2002	2003	2000	2002	2003
Real estate & rental & leasing, total . . .	53	1,696	1,880	2,046	133,398	161,790	176,079
Real estate	531	1,616	1,799	1,964	127,862	156,150	170,133
Lessors of real estate	5311	714	753	789	86,934	100,504	106,472
Offices of real estate agents & brokers	5312	522	570	629	22,623	26,007	29,442
Activities related to real estate.	5313	380	476	546	18,305	29,640	34,220
Rental & leasing services.	532	79	80	80	5,440	5,519	5,807
Automotive equipment rental & leasing	5321	19	20	20	995	904	950
Consumer goods rental	5322	17	17	17	766	705	764
General rental centers	5323	3	3	3	252	301	316
Commercial/industrial equipment rental & leasing.	5324	41	40	40	3,426	3,610	3,778
Lessors of other nonfinancial intangible assets	533	1	1	1	96	121	138

Source: U.S. Census Bureau, "Nonemployer Statistics"; <http://www.census.gov/epcd/nonemployer/>.

Table 1211. **Real Estate and Rental and Leasing—Establishments, Employees, and Payroll: 2000 and 2003**

[300.2 represents 300,200. Covers establishments with payroll. Kind-of-business classification for 2000 based on North American Industry Classification System (NAICS) 1997; data for 2003 based on NAICS 2002. See text, Section 15. Employees are for the week including March 12. Most government employees are excluded. For statement on methodology, see Appendix III]

Kind of business	NAICS code	Establishments (1,000)		Employees (1,000)		Payroll (bil. dol.)	
		2000	2003	2000	2003	2000	2003
Real estate & rental & leasing, total . . .	53	300.2	333.6	1,942	2,045	59.2	68.6
Real estate	531	234.9	268.0	1,280	1,388	40.4	48.8
Lessors of real estate	5311	108.2	114.3	501	523	12.5	14.6
Offices of real estate agents & brokers	5312	65.1	82.8	271	299	10.6	12.6
Activities related to real estate.	5313	61.6	70.9	507	566	17.3	21.7
Rental & leasing services.	532	63.2	63.2	636	627	17.2	17.7
Automotive equipment rental & leasing	5321	11.1	11.3	182	172	5.1	5.3
Passenger car rental & leasing	53211	5.2	5.3	129	123	3.4	3.5
Truck, utility trailer & RV rental & leasing.	53212	5.8	6.1	53	50	1.7	1.8
Consumer goods rental [1]	5322	33.1	33.4	255	269	4.2	4.9
Video tape & disk rental	53223	19.6	18.5	152	164	1.6	1.9
General rental centers	5323	6.4	5.4	42	34	1.2	1.0
Commercial/industrial equipment rental & leasing.	5324	12.6	13.1	157	152	6.7	6.5
Lessors of other nonfinancial intangible assets	533	2.1	2.4	26	29	1.6	2.0

[1] Includes other kinds of business not shown separately.

Source: U.S. Census Bureau, "County Business Patterns"; <http://www.census.gov/epcd/cbp/view/cbpview.html>.

Table 1212. **Rental and Leasing Services—Revenue by Kind of Business: 1999 to 2004**

[In millions of dollars (91,209 represents $91,209,000,000). Based on the North American Industry Classification System (NAICS) 1997; see text, Section 15. Covers taxable and tax-exempt employer firms. Estimates have been adjusted using the results of the 2002 Economic Census. Based on Service Annual Survey; see Appendix III]

Kind of business	1997 NAICS code	1999	2000	2001	2002	2003	2004
Rental & leasing services	532	91,209	98,505	96,932	95,107	96,387	102,756
Automotive equipment rental & leasing.	5321	34,822	37,231	36,035	35,779	37,007	41,126
Passenger car rental & leasing	53211	21,366	22,949	22,485	22,683	23,007	24,793
Truck, utility trailer, & RV rental & leasing . .	53212	13,455	14,282	13,550	13,096	14,000	16,333
Consumer goods rental [1]	5322	19,399	20,159	20,760	20,700	21,924	23,217
Video tape & disk rental	53223	9,303	9,569	9,584	9,364	10,053	10,604
General rental centers	5323	3,395	3,636	3,337	3,387	3,611	3,799
Commercial/industrial equipment rental & leasing	5324	33,593	37,478	36,800	35,242	33,846	34,614

[1] Includes other kinds of business not shown separately.

Source: U.S. Census Bureau, *Service Annual Survey: 2004*.

Arts, Entertainment, and Recreation

This section presents data on the arts, entertainment, and recreation economic sector of the economy, and personal recreational activities, the arts and humanities, and domestic and foreign travel.

Arts, Entertainment, and Recreation Industry—The U.S. Census Bureau's *Service Annual Survey, Arts, Entertainment, and Recreation Sector,* provides estimates of operation revenue of taxable firms and revenues and expenses of firms exempt from federal taxes for industries in this sector of the economy. Data beginning 1998 are based on the North American Industry Classification System (NAICS). Most establishments were previously classified in the Standard Industrial Classification (SIC) in services, some in retail trade.

This new sector is comprised of industries which existed previously, were revised from previous industry definitions, or are completely new industries. Among those which existed previously are amusement and theme parks. Revised industries include museums. New industries include theater companies and dinner theaters. The following URL contains detailed information about NAICS and provides a comparison of the SIC and NAICS <http://www.census.gov/epcd/www/naics.html>. See also the text in Section 15, Business Enterprise.

The Economic Census, conducted every 5 years, for the years ending "2" and "7," provides information on the number of establishments, receipts, payroll, and paid employees for the U.S. and various geographic levels.

Recreation and leisure activities— Data on the participation in various recreation and leisure time activities are based on several sample surveys. Data on participation in fishing, hunting, and other forms of wildlife-associated recreation are published periodically by the U.S. Department of Interior, Fish and Wildlife Service. The most recent data are from the 2001 survey. Data on participation in various sports recreation activities are published by the National Sporting Goods Association. Mediamark, Inc. also conducts periodic surveys on sports and leisure activities, as well as other topics.

Parks and recreation—The Department of the Interior has responsibility for administering the national parks. The National Park Service publishes information on visits to national park areas in its annual report, *National Park Statistical Abstract. The National Parks: Index (year)* is an annual report which contains brief descriptions, with acreages, of each area administered by the service, plus certain "related" areas. This information can be found at: <http://www2.nature.nps.gov/stats>. Statistics for state parks are compiled by the National Association of State Park Directors.

Travel—Statistics on arrivals and departures to the United States are reported by the International Trade Administration (ITA), Office of Travel & Tourism Industries (OTTI). Data on domestic travel, business receipts and employment of the travel industry, and travel expenditures are published by the research department of the Travel Industry Association (TIA) and the national nonprofit center for travel and tourism research located in Washington, DC. Other data on household transportation characteristics are in Section 23, Transportation.

Statistical reliability—For a discussion of statistical collection and estimation, sampling procedures, and measures of statistical reliability applicable to Census Bureau data, see Appendix III.

Table 1213. **Arts, Entertainment and Recreation Services—Estimated Revenue: 2000 to 2004**

[In millions of dollars (127,400 represents $127,400,000,000), except percent. For taxable and tax-exempt employer firms. Except where indicated, estimates adjusted using the results of the 2002 Economic Census. Minus sign (-) indicates decrease. Based on the Service Annual Survey, see Appendix III]

Industry	1997 NAICS code [1]	2000	2001	2002	2003	2004	Percent change, 2003– 2004
Arts, entertainment, and recreation	71	**127,400**	**133,886**	**141,904**	**149,346**	**158,545**	6.2
Performing arts, spectator sports.	711	51,155	54,155	58,286	60,356	62,783	4.0
Performing arts companies [2].	7111	10,745	10,804	10,864	11,071	11,554	4.4
Spectator sports	7112	19,340	20,392	22,313	22,445	23,659	5.4
Sports teams and clubs	711211	10,739	11,461	13,025	13,257	14,115	6.5
Racetracks.	711212	6,349	6,473	6,703	6,582	7,022	6.7
Other spectator sports	711219	2,251	2,458	2,586	2,606	2,522	-3.2
Promoters of performing arts, sports and similar events	7113	9,688	10,555	11,698	12,390	13,061	5.4
Agents and managers for artists, athletes, entertainers and other public figures	7114	3,600	3,823	4,073	4,075	4,317	6.0
Independent artists, writers, and performers.	7115	7,782	8,581	9,338	10,376	10,193	-1.8
Museums, historical sites, and similar institutions . . .	712	9,350	9,218	8,608	9,081	9,688	6.7
Amusement, gambling, and recreation industries . . .	713	66,895	70,512	75,011	79,909	86,073	7.7
Amusement parks and arcades	7131	9,441	9,813	9,443	9,929	10,561	6.4
Amusement and theme parks	71311	8,245	8,637	8,174	8,737	9,344	6.9
Amusement arcades	71312	1,196	1,176	1,269	1,193	1,217	2.0
Gambling industries.	7132	14,621	16,686	18,893	22,369	25,698	14.9
Casinos (except casino hotels).	71321	9,592	11,148	12,387	14,601	16,664	14.1
Other gambling industries	71329	5,029	5,538	6,506	7,769	9,034	16.3
Other amusement and recreation industries.	7139	42,833	44,013	46,674	47,611	49,814	4.6
Golf courses and country clubs	71391	16,692	16,863	17,534	16,988	17,879	5.2
Skiing facilities	71392	1,551	1,635	1,801	1,839	1,980	7.7
Marinas	71393	3,379	3,389	3,352	3,382	3,393	0.3
Fitness and recreational sports centers	71394	12,543	13,542	14,988	16,130	16,839	4.4
Bowling centers.	71395	2,762	2,882	3,075	3,293	3,505	6.4
All other amusement and recreation	71399	5,906	5,702	5,925	5,980	6,217	4.0

[1] Based on the North American Industry Classification System 1997; see text, this section and Section 15, Business Enterprise. [2] Estimates for NAICS 71113 and 71119, not shown separately, have not been adjusted to the 1997 Economic Census.

Source: U.S. Census Bureau, "2004 Service Annual Survey, Arts, Entertainment, and Recreation Services." See <http://www.census.gov/econ/www/servmenu.html>; issued April 2006.

Table 1214. **Arts, Entertainment and Recreation—Establishments, Revenue, Payroll, and Employees by Kind of Business (1997 NAICS Basis): 1997 and 2002**

[(104,715 represents $104,715,000,000) For establishments with payroll. Data are based on the 1997 and 2002 economic censuses which are subject to nonsampling error. For details on survey methodology, sampling and nonsampling errors, see Appendix III. Numbers in parentheses represent North American Industry Classification System (NAICS) 1997 codes, see text, section 15]

Kind of business	1997 NAICS code	Number of establishments		Revenue (mil. dol.)		Annual payroll (mil. dol.)		Paid employees (1,000)	
		1997	2002	1997	2002	1997	2002	1997	2002
Arts, entertainment and recreation, total.	71	**99,099**	**111,128**	**104,715**	**137,782**	**32,787**	**43,075**	**1,588**	**1,896**
Performing arts, spectator sports, and related industries	711	30,566	38,181	37,619	57,708	14,456	21,145	327	422
Performing arts companies	7111	9,199	9,353	8,570	10,697	2,725	3,206	122	138
Spectator sports	7112	3,881	4,314	13,656	21,933	6,151	10,175	92	107
Promoters of performing arts, sports and similar events	7113	3,941	4,603	6,622	11,612	1,401	2,071	72	100
Agents and managers for artists, athletes, entertainers and others	7114	2,532	4,043	2,410	4,189	911	1,457	13	22
Museums, historical sites, and similar institutions.	712	5,580	6,651	6,764	8,577	1,837	2,912	92	122
Amusement, gambling, and recreation industries	713	62,859	65,462	57,832	76,293	15,776	21,070	1,134	1,303
Amusement parks and arcades	7131	3,344	3,196	8,418	9,622	1,962	2,111	139	123
Gambling industries.	7132	2,005	2,201	13,042	20,181	2,504	3,726	133	162
Other amusement and recreation services.	7139	57,510	60,065	36,372	46,490	11,310	15,233	862	1,018

Source: U.S. Census Bureau, "2002 Economic Census, Industry Series Reports, Arts, Entertainment and Recreation"; published summer 2004; <http://www.census.gov/econ/census02/guide/INDRPT71.HTM>.

758 Arts, Entertainment, and Recreation

Table 1215. Arts, Entertainment, and Recreation—Nonemployer Establishments and Receipts by Kind of Business (NAICS Basis): 2000 to 2003

[(781.7 represents 781,700). Includes only firms subject to federal income tax. Nonemployers are businesses with no paid employees]

Kind of business	2002 NAICS code [1]	Establishments (1,000)			Receipts (mil. dol.)		
		2000	2002	2003	2000	2002	2003
Arts, entertainment, and recreation	71	781.7	866.0	888.1	17,713	20,000	21,010
Performing arts, spectator sports, and related industries	711	645.4	732.9	751.8	13,008	14,808	15,536
Performing arts companies	7111	19.3	26.0	27.4	576	677	700
Spectator sports	7112	67.3	95.7	91.5	1,481	1,774	1,820
Promoters of performing arts, sports, and similar events	7113	23.1	29.3	31.8	851	1,100	1,203
Agents/managers for artists, athletes, and other public figures	7114	27.1	28.1	30.5	857	969	1,051
Independent artists, writers and performers.....................	7115	508.6	553.8	570.6	9,244	10,289	10,763
Museums, historical sites, and similar institutions.....................	712	3.6	4.4	4.7	52	66	68
Amusement, gambling, and recreation industries	713	132.7	128.7	131.7	4,653	5,125	5,406
Amusement parks and arcades	7131	5.4	5.2	5.3	291	322	339
Gambling industries.................	7132	5.9	7.3	7.2	532	875	927
Other amusement and recreation services...	7139	121.3	116.2	119.1	3,830	3,929	4,140

[1] Based on the 2002 North American Industry Classification System (NAICS); see text, Section 15.

Source: U.S. Census Bureau, Nonemployer Statistics; <http://www.census.gov/epcd/nonemployer/index.html> and *2002 Economic Census: Nonemployer Statistics*; published 28 September 2005; <http://www.census.gov/epcd/nonemployer/2003/us/US000.HTM>.

Table 1216. Arts, Entertainment, and Recreation—Establishments, Payroll, and Employees by Kind of Business (NAICS Basis): 2000 and 2003

[(1,741.5 represents 1,741,500). For establishments with payroll. See Appendix III]

Kind of business	NAICS code [1]	Establishments		Paid employees [2] (1,000)		Annual payroll (mil. dol.)	
		2000	2003	2000	2003	2000	2003
Arts, entertainment, & recreation	71	103,816	113,991	1,741.5	1,833.0	43,204	48,147
Performing arts, spectator sports	711	33,859	39,123	351.9	394.6	19,090	22,433
Performing arts companies	7111	9,253	9,138	126.4	131.3	3,251	3,307
Theater companies & dinner theaters......	71111	3,367	3,578	63.4	67.7	1,469	1,603
Dance companies...................	71112	584	563	10.7	9.1	216	201
Musical groups & artists..............	71113	4,497	4,457	44.0	47.4	1,341	1,303
Other performing arts companies........	71119	805	540	8.3	7.1	226	200
Spectator sports	7112	4,461	4,268	100.2	107.8	9,215	10,969
Sports teams & clubs	711211	684	763	36.3	40.3	7,587	9,106
Racetracks	711212	899	750	45.8	50.9	994	1,171
Other spectator sports...............	711219	2,878	2,755	18.1	16.7	633	691
Promoters of performing arts, sports, and similar events	7113	4,394	5,382	71.8	98.7	1,917	2,290
Promoters of performing arts, sports, & similar events with facilities............	71131	1,107	1,914	44.3	73.3	787	1,315
Promoters of performing arts, sports, & similar events without facilities..........	71132	3,287	3,468	27.6	25.4	1,130	975
Agents/managers for artists, athletes, and other public figures....................	7114	3,048	3,376	16.0	15.5	1,117	1,291
Independent artists, writers, & performers.....	7115	12,703	16,959	37.5	41.2	3,589	4,576
Museums, historical sites, & similar institutions ...	712	5,777	6,740	110.4	120.0	2,549	2,984
Museums........................	71211	3,988	4,591	75.4	79.3	1,765	2,004
Historical sites....................	71212	892	974	8.3	9.2	143	189
Zoos & botanical gardens	71213	414	570	20.5	26.2	509	661
Nature parks & other similar institutions	71219	483	605	6.2	5.2	133	130
Amusement, gambling, & recreation industries ...	713	64,180	68,128	1,279.2	1,318.4	21,564	22,730
Amusement parks & arcades	7131	2,879	3,011	124.0	133.4	2,277	2,453
Amusement & theme parks	71311	716	569	102.8	106.0	2,011	2,086
Amusement arcades	71312	2,163	2,442	21.3	27.5	266	368
Gambling industries.................	7132	2,191	2,191	202.6	167.9	4,757	4,194
Casinos (except casino hotels)	71321	537	429	150.2	113.6	3,592	2,956
Other gambling industries	71329	1,654	1,762	52.4	54.2	1,165	1,237
Other amusement & recreation services.....	7139	59,110	62,926	952.6	1,017.1	14,531	16,083
Golf courses & country clubs	71391	11,885	12,027	297.9	302.4	6,243	7,002
Skiing facilities....................	71392	389	387	56.9	71.4	452	523
Marinas	71393	4,126	4,150	24.8	27.9	640	774
Fitness & recreational sports centers	71394	23,003	27,813	382.8	451.8	4,499	5,334
Bowling centers	71395	5,234	4,795	87.9	83.1	888	935
All other amusement & recreation industries	71399	14,473	13,754	102.4	80.5	1,808	1,516

[1] North American Industry Classification System code; see text, this section and Section 15.   [2] For employees on the payroll for the period including March 12.

Source: U.S. Census Bureau, County Business Patterns; annual. See <http://www.census.gov/epcd/cbp/view/cbpview.html>.

Table 1217. **Expenditures Per Consumer Unit for Entertainment and Reading: 1985 to 2004**

[Data are annual averages. In dollars, except as indicated. Based on Consumer Expenditure Survey; see text, Section 13, Income, Expenditures, and Wealth for description of survey. See also headnote, Table 667. Consumer Expenditures Survey (CE) has implemented multiple imputation of income data, starting with the publication of the 2004 tables. Because of income imputation, data for 2004 are not strictly comparable to data from previous years, especially for income tables. Thus with the introduction of income imputation with the publication of the 2004 tables, income data are available for all consumer units and data are no longer shown for complete income reporters. For more information go to <http://www.bls.gov/cex/csxann04.pdf>, page 4. For composition of regions, see map, inside front cover]

Year and characteristic	Entertainment and reading		Entertainment				Reading
	Total	Percent of total expenditures	Total	Fees and admissions	Television, radios, and sound equipment	Other equipment and services [1]	
1985........................	1,311	5.6	1,170	320	371	479	141
1988........................	1,479	5.7	1,329	353	416	560	150
1989........................	1,581	5.7	1,424	377	429	618	157
1990........................	1,575	5.6	1,422	371	454	597	153
1991........................	1,635	5.5	1,472	378	468	627	163
1992........................	1,662	5.6	1,500	379	492	629	162
1993........................	1,792	5.8	1,626	414	590	621	166
1994........................	1,732	5.5	1,567	439	533	595	165
1995........................	1,775	5.5	1,612	433	542	637	163
1996........................	1,993	5.9	1,834	459	561	814	159
1997........................	1,977	5.7	1,813	471	577	766	164
1998........................	1,907	5.4	1,746	449	535	762	161
1999........................	2,050	5.5	1,891	459	608	824	159
2000........................	2,009	5.3	1,863	515	622	727	146
2001........................	2,094	5.3	1,953	526	660	767	141
2002........................	2,218	5.5	2,079	542	692	845	139
2003........................	2,187	5.4	2,060	494	730	835	127
2004, total	**2,348**	**5.4**	**2,218**	**528**	**788**	**903**	**130**
Age of reference person:							
Under 25 years old..........	1,217	5.0	1,166	277	500	390	51
25 to 34 years old	2,216	5.2	2,122	415	843	864	94
35 to 44 years old	2,627	5.2	2,504	666	921	917	123
45 to 54 years old	2,860	5.4	2,711	667	926	1,118	149
55 to 64 years old	3,000	6.3	2,823	618	810	1,395	177
65 to 74 years old	2,037	5.6	1,879	463	628	788	158
75 years old and over........	1,125	4.4	990	262	474	254	135
Hispanic or Latino origin of reference person:							
Hispanic...................	1,496	4.0	1,443	308	656	479	53
Non-Hispanic	2,451	5.6	2,311	554	803	954	140
Race of reference person:							
White, Asian and all other races .	2,518	5.6	2,377	574	805	999	141
Black.....................	1,093	3.6	1,040	185	657	197	53
Region of residence:							
Northeast..................	2,162	4.7	2,017	545	840	632	145
Midwest...................	2,358	5.4	2,208	586	768	854	150
South	2,232	5.7	2,134	398	753	983	98
West	2,688	5.6	2,538	664	818	1,056	150
Size of consumer unit:							
One person	1,259	5.0	1,162	283	516	363	97
Two or more persons	2,793	5.5	2,649	628	898	1,123	144
Two persons	2,779	6.1	2,618	579	795	1,244	161
Three persons	2,546	4.9	2,417	551	973	894	129
Four persons	3,048	5.3	2,910	809	1,023	1,077	138
Five persons or more	2,861	5.2	2,743	650	946	1,147	118
Income before taxes: Quintiles of income:							
Lowest 20 percent	819	4.6	764	131	387	246	55
Second 20 percent	1,459	5.3	1,377	201	566	610	82
Third 20 percent..........	1,840	5.0	1,728	346	732	650	112
Fourth 20 percent	2,880	5.6	2,735	604	963	1,167	145
Highest 20 percent	4,740	5.7	4,484	1,356	1,290	1,838	256
Education:							
Less than a high school graduate .	998	3.9	953	103	505	347	45
High school graduate	1,770	5.0	1,685	270	703	711	85
High school graduate with some college	2,392	5.9	2,276	464	787	1,025	116
Associate's degree...........	2,595	5.4	2,465	535	895	1,035	130
Bachelor's degree	3,238	5.7	3,045	910	966	1,169	193
Master's, professional, doctoral degree	3,931	5.8	3,639	1,278	1,006	1,355	292

[1] Other equipment and services include pets, toys, and playground equipment; sports, exercise, and photographic equipment; and recreational vehicles.

Source: U.S. Bureau of Labor Statistics, *Consumer Expenditure Survey,* annual and Current Standard Tables. See also <http://www.bls.gov/cex/home/htm>.

Table 1218. **Personal Consumption Expenditures for Recreation: 1990 to 2004**

[In billions of dollars (290.2 represents $290,200,000,000), except percent. Represents market value of purchases of goods and services by individuals and nonprofit institutions.]

Type of product or service	1990	1995	2000	2001	2002	2003	2004
Total recreation expenditures	290.2	418.1	585.7	604.0	629.9	658.8	702.4
Percent of total personal consumption [1]	7.6	8.4	8.7	8.6	8.6	8.5	8.6
Books and maps	16.2	23.2	33.7	34.6	37.1	39.0	41.4
Magazines, newspapers, and sheet music	21.6	27.5	35.0	35.0	35.1	35.9	38.7
Nondurable toys and sport supplies	32.8	44.4	56.6	57.6	59.2	60.1	64.0
Wheel goods, sports and photographic equipment [2]	29.7	39.7	57.6	59.2	61.4	65.7	70.4
Video and audio products, computer equipment, and musical instruments	53.0	81.5	116.6	115.5	120.0	122.3	130.8
Video and audio goods, including musical instruments. . . .	44.1	57.2	72.8	73.6	75.4	75.8	79.8
Computers, peripherals, and software	8.9	24.3	43.8	42.0	44.6	46.5	51.0
Radio and television repair.	3.2	3.6	4.2	4.0	4.1	4.1	4.5
Flowers, seeds, and potted plants	10.9	14.0	18.0	18.0	18.0	17.8	18.2
Admissions to specified spectator amusements	15.1	21.1	30.4	32.2	34.8	36.1	37.4
Motion picture theaters	5.1	5.6	8.6	9.0	9.6	9.9	9.9
Legitimate theaters and opera, and entertainments of nonprofit institutions [3]	5.2	8.1	10.3	10.9	11.7	12.1	12.7
Spectator sports [4]	4.8	7.4	11.5	12.4	13.5	14.1	14.8
Clubs and fraternal organizations except insurance [5]	13.5	17.4	19.0	20.0	21.1	22.3	23.2
Commercial participant amusements [6]	25.2	48.8	75.8	79.6	83.7	91.3	99.4
Pari-mutuel net receipts.	3.5	3.7	5.0	5.1	5.3	5.2	5.3
Other [7]	65.4	93.4	133.9	143.2	150.0	159.0	169.0

[1] See Table 656.   [2] Includes boats and pleasure aircraft.   [3] Except athletic.   [4] Consists of admissions to professional and amateur athletic events and to racetracks, including horse, dog, and auto.   [5] Consists of current expenditures (including consumption of fixed capital) of nonprofit clubs and fraternal organizations and dues and fees paid to proprietary clubs.   [6] Consists of billiard parlors; bowling alleys; dancing, riding, shooting, skating, and swimming places; amusement devices and parks; golf courses; sightseeing buses and guides; private flying operations; casino gambling; and other commercial participant amusements.   [7] Consists of net receipts of lotteries and expenditures for purchases of pets and pet care services, cable TV, film processing, photographic studios, sporting and recreation camps, video cassette rentals, and recreational services, not elsewhere classified.

Source: Bureau of Economic Analysis, *Survey of Current Business,* April 2006. See also <http://www.bea.gov/bea/dn/nipaweb /index.asp>.

Table 1219. **Performing Arts—Selected Data: 1990 to 2004**

[Sales, receipts and expenditures in millions of dollars (282 represents $282,000,000). For season ending in year shown, except as indicated]

Item	1990	1995	1997	1998	1999	2000	2001	2002	2003	2004
Legitimate theater: [1]										
Broadway shows:										
New productions	40	33	37	33	39	37	28	37	36	39
Attendance (mil.)	8.0	9.0	10.6	11.5	11.7	11.4	11.9	11.0	11.4	11.6
Playing weeks [2,3]	1,070	1,120	1,349	1,442	1,441	1,464	1,484	1,434	1,544	1,451
Gross ticket sales	282	406	499	558	588	603	666	643	721	771
Broadway road tours:[4]										
Attendance (mil.)	11.1	15.6	17.6	15.2	14.6	11.7	11.0	11.7	12.4	12.9
Playing weeks.	944	1,242	1,334	1,127	1,082	888	823	863	877	1060
Gross ticket sales	367	701	782	721	707	572	541	593	642	714
Nonprofit professional theatres: [5]										
Companies reporting [6]	185	215	197	189	313	262	363	1,146	1,274	1,477
Gross income	307.6	444.4	565.0	570.0	740.0	791.0	961.4	1,436.0	1,481.0	1,570.8
Earned income	188.4	281.2	349.9	342.0	442.0	466.0	554.5	761.0	787.0	856.2
Contributed income	119.2	163.1	215.1	228.0	298.0	325.0	406.6	675.0	694.0	714.6
Gross expenses	306.3	444.9	526.6	518.5	701.0	708.0	923.6	1,405.0	1,476.0	1,464.4
Productions	2,265	2,646	2,295	2,135	3,921	3,241	4,787	10,000	13,000	11,000
Performances.	46,131	56,608	51,453	46,628	64,556	66,123	81,828	157,000	170,000	169,000
Total attendance (mil.)	15.2	18.6	17.2	14.6	18.0	22.0	21.1	32.2	34.3	32.1
OPERA America professional member companies: [7]										
Number of companies reporting [8] . . .	98	88	91	89	95	98	96	86	89	95
Expenses [8]	321.2	435.0	534.1	556.3	591.1	636.7	685.1	684.4	691.6	677.9
Performances [9]	2,336	2,251	2,137	2,222	2,200	2,153	2,031	1,868.0	1,730	1,946
Total attendance (mil.) [9,10]	7.5	6.5	6.9	6.6	6.6	6.7	6.5	4.9	5.9	5.1
Main season attendance (mil.) [9,11] . .	4.1	3.9	4.0	3.7	4.0	4.3	4.2	3.2	3.1	3.4
Symphony orchestras: [12]										
Concerts	18,931	29,328	26,906	31,766	31,549	33,154	36,437	37,118	38,182	37,263
Attendance (mil.).	24.7	30.9	31.9	32.2	30.8	31.7	31.5	30.3	27.8	27.7
Gross revenue	377.5	536.2	575.5	627.6	671.8	730.4	774.7	763.6	781.2	826.8
Operating expenses	621.7	858.8	937.1	1,012.0	1,088.0	1,126.3	1,285.9	1,311.9	1,314.8	1,482.6
Support.	257.8	351.0	401.1	459.7	486.0	521.0	559.6	580.0	575.7	639.4

[1] Source: The League of American Theaters and Producers, Inc, New York, NY. For season ending in year shown.   [2] All shows (new productions and holdovers from previous seasons).   [3] Eight performances constitute one playing week.   [4] North American Tours include U.S. and Canadian companies.   [5] Source: Theatre Communications Group, New York, NY. For years ending on or prior to Aug. 31.   [6] Beginning in 2002, nonprofit theatre data are based on survey responses and extrapolated data from IRS Form 990.   [7] Source: OPERA America, New York, NY. For years ending on or prior to Aug. 31.   [8] U.S. companies.   [9] Prior to 1993, and for 1999, U.S. and Canadian companies; 1993 to 1998 U.S. companies only.   [10] Includes educational performances, outreach, etc.   [11] For paid performances.   [12] Source: American Symphony Orchestra League, Inc., New York, NY. For years ending Aug. 31. Prior to 1995, represents 254 U.S. orchestras; beginning 1995, represents all U.S. orchestras, excluding college/university and youth orchestras. Also, beginning 1995, data based on 1,200 orchestras.

Source: Compiled from sources listed in footnotes. <http://www.broadway.org>; <http://www.tcg.org>; <http://www.operaamerica.org/>; <http://www.symphony.org>.

Arts, Entertainment, and Recreation   761

Table 1220. **Arts and Humanities—Selected Federal Aid Programs: 1990 to 2004**

[In millions of dollars (170.8 represents $170,800,000), except as indicated. For fiscal year ending September 30]

Type of fund and program	1990	1995	1998	1999	2000	2001	2002	2003	2004
National Endowment for the Arts:									
Funds available [1]	170.8	152.1	85.3	85.0	85.2	94.0	98.6	101.0	105.5
Program appropriation	124.3	109.0	64.3	66.0	66.0	86.7	95.8	95.1	99.3
Grants awarded (number)	4,475	3,685	1,459	1,675	1,882	2,093	2,138	1,925	2,150
Funds obligated [2, 3]	157.6	147.9	82.3	82.6	83.5	92.5	96.2	99.3	102.6
National Endowment for the Humanities:									
Funds available [1]	140.6	152.3	94.0	95.5	102.6	106.8	110.1	111.6	127.1
Program appropriation	114.2	125.7	80.0	80.0	82.7	86.4	89.9	89.3	98.7
Matching funds [4]	26.3	25.7	13.9	13.9	15.1	15.6	16.1	16.0	15.9
Grants awarded (number)	2,195	1,871	852	874	1,230	1,290	1,252	963	1,246
Funds obligated [2]	141.0	151.8	92.7	92.1	100.0	105.7	106.1	100.1	125.1
Education programs	16.3	19.2	10.8	10.3	13.0	12.1	12.1	11.3	17.4
State programs	29.6	32.0	29.1	29.3	30.6	32.1	32.8	33.0	36.3
Research grants	22.5	22.2	7.7	6.6	6.9	7.0	7.0	7.9	8.4
Fellowship program	15.3	16.5	5.7	5.6	6.1	7.0	7.7	6.9	8.1
Challenge [5]	14.6	13.8	9.9	9.9	10.8	11.9	13.4	8.3	12.6
Public programs	25.4	25.8	11.1	12.2	11.8	16.3	13.2	12.7	18.3
Preservation and access	17.5	22.2	18.4	18.2	20.7	19.2	19.8	20.7	23.7

[1] Includes other funds, not shown separately. Excludes administrative funds. [2] Includes obligations for new grants, supplemental awards on previous years' grants, and program contracts. [3] Beginning with 1997 data, the grant-making structure changed from discipline-based categories to thematic ones. [4] Represents federal funds obligated only upon receipt or certification by endowment of matching nonfederal gifts. [5] Program designed to stimulate new sources and higher levels of giving to institutions for the purpose of guaranteeing long-term stability and financial independence. Program usually requires a match of at least 3 private dollars to each federal dollar. Funds for challenge grants are not allocated by program area because they are awarded on a grant-by-grant basis.

Source: U.S. National Endowment for the Arts, *Annual Report;* and U.S. National Endowment for the Humanities, *Annual Report.* <http://arts.endow.gov/>and <http://www.neh.gov/>.

Table 1221. **Attendance Rates for Various Arts Activities: 2002**

[In percent. For persons 18 years old and over. Represents attendance at least once in the prior 12 months. Excludes elementary and high school performances. Based on the 2002 household survey Public Participation in the Arts. Data are subject to sampling error; see source. See also Tables 1222 and 1223]

Item	Jazz	Classical music	Musicals	Non-musical plays	Ballet	Art museums/ galleries	Art/craft fairs and festivals	Historic sites [1]	Litera-ture [2]
Total	10.8	11.6	17.1	12.3	3.9	26.5	33.4	31.6	46.7
Sex: Male	10.7	10.3	14.0	10.3	2.5	24.6	27.0	30.5	37.6
Female	10.8	12.7	20.0	14.2	5.1	28.2	39.2	32.5	55.1
Race and ethnicity:									
White alone	11.4	13.7	20.1	14.2	4.7	29.5	38.0	36.0	51.4
African American alone	12.7	4.5	10.3	7.1	1.5	14.8	9.7	17.8	37.1
Other alone	7.3	10.3	11.9	10.0	2.3	32.7	25.8	30.4	43.7
Hispanic	6.2	5.5	6.9	6.2	1.6	16.1	20.3	17.2	26.5
Age:									
18 to 24 years old	10.5	7.8	14.8	11.4	2.6	23.7	29.2	28.3	42.8
25 to 34 years old	10.8	9.0	15.4	10.7	3.5	26.7	33.5	33.3	47.7
35 to 44 years old	13.0	10.7	19.1	13.0	4.9	27.4	37.2	35.8	46.6
45 to 54 years old	13.9	15.2	19.3	15.2	5.1	32.9	38.8	38.0	51.6
55 to 64 years old	8.8	15.6	19.7	13.8	3.3	27.8	35.1	31.6	48.9
65 to 74 years old	7.6	12.5	16.6	13.0	3.3	23.4	31.1	24.2	45.3
75 years old and older	3.9	9.5	10.1	5.4	2.2	13.4	15.7	12.8	36.7
Education:									
Grade school	0.9	1.5	1.6	1.1	–	4.5	8.4	6.3	14.0
Some high school	2.7	1.9	4.1	3.7	0.8	7.7	14.0	11.4	23.4
High school graduate	5.3	4.5	9.1	5.7	1.2	14.2	25.7	20.2	37.7
Some college	12.2	11.5	19.4	12.7	3.9	29.0	38.2	36.5	52.9
College graduate	19.4	21.9	30.2	22.5	7.2	46.6	49.3	51.2	63.1
Graduate school	24.0	34.1	37.6	31.8	12.9	58.6	51.9	56.8	74.3
Income:									
Less than $10,000	5.1	6.7	7.6	5.3	1.5	12.4	19.7	14.1	32.1
$10,000 to $19,999	5.4	5.2	8.2	5.4	1.9	14.0	21.4	14.9	37.5
$20,000 to $29,999	6.3	6.3	8.6	6.0	2.4	16.2	24.5	20.8	37.5
$30,000 to $39,999	10.9	10.3	13.6	10.0	2.8	23.3	33.2	28.6	44.1
$40,000 to $49,999	10.3	12.9	16.1	12.2	3.6	25.3	34.6	32.7	47.9
$50,000 to $74,999	11.2	12.4	21.5	14.0	4.3	30.4	40.3	39.1	52.3
$75,000 or more	18.2	19.9	29.3	21.8	7.2	44.6	46.5	50.9	60.8

– Represents or rounds to zero. [1] Parks, historic buildings, neighborhoods. [2] Read a book (literature) during the previous twelve months. Literature includes novels, short stories, poetry, and/or plays.

Source: U.S. National Endowment for the Arts, *Research Division Report #45, 2002 Survey of Public Participation in the Arts.* See also <http://www.arts.endow.gov/pub/ResearchReportschrono.html>.

762 Arts, Entertainment, and Recreation

Table 1222. **Participation in Various Leisure Activities: 2002**

[In percent, except as indicated (205.9 represents 205,900,000). For persons 18 years old and over. Covers activities engaged in at least once in the prior 12 months. See headnote, Table 1221]

Item	Adult popu-lation (mil.)	Attendance at—			Participation in—				
		Movies	Sports events	Amuse-ment park	Exercise program	Playing sports	Charity work	Home improve-ment/ repair	Garden-ing
Total	205.9	60.0	35.0	41.7	55.1	30.4	29.0	42.4	47.3
Sex:									
Male	98.7	59.5	41.4	40.4	55.0	38.8	25.6	46.3	37.1
Female	107.2	60.5	29.2	42.9	55.1	22.7	32.1	38.9	56.7
Race and ethnicity:									
White alone	150.1	63.0	38.4	42.8	59.1	33.0	32.5	47.7	52.3
African American alone . . .	23.7	49.2	27.0	36.6	46.1	23.1	22.7	26.3	30.3
Other alone	9.5	58.1	22.3	43.9	50.4	26.9	22.5	33.8	41.3
Hispanic	22.7	52.5	26.4	38.9	40.1	22.3	15.3	28.0	34.8
Age:									
18 to 24 years old.	26.8	82.8	46.0	57.6	61.3	49.4	25.3	21.1	20.7
25 to 34 years old.	36.9	73.3	41.8	56.2	60.2	39.6	26.0	41.1	41.4
35 to 44 years old.	44.2	68.0	42.2	53.3	59.5	36.6	33.2	53.0	51.8
45 to 54 years old.	39.0	60.4	35.8	37.1	58.6	28.6	33.4	54.9	55.4
55 to 64 years old.	25.9	46.6	25.5	27.1	48.4	16.0	28.1	44.8	56.6
65 to 74 years old.	17.6	32.2	19.7	18.4	47.0	13.7	28.8	38.4	57.2
75 years old and over	15.5	19.5	11.1	9.6	31.3	6.0	21.3	22.1	47.9
Education:									
Grade school	11.6	19.5	9.4	17.2	21.0	6.9	8.2	19.5	32.5
Some high school	20.1	39.4	17.4	30.6	32.7	17.2	12.5	24.9	31.2
High school graduate.	63.8	51.7	28.3	37.9	45.6	22.6	20.2	35.6	43.8
Some college.	56.9	68.7	39.9	48.9	62.3	35.2	33.1	46.5	49.6
College graduate	36.1	77.1	51.0	50.1	73.2	45.2	42.6	56.0	56.1
Graduate school	17.4	77.5	48.3	44.0	77.3	43.6	53.1	61.6	63.3
Income:									
Less than $10,000	14.4	38.7	16.5	30.4	36.5	15.0	16.2	19.7	32.2
$10,000 to $19,999	22.7	41.8	20.1	30.7	42.0	18.5	18.8	23.5	38.8
$20,000 to $29,999	25.0	48.3	23.0	34.7	45.2	21.4	20.7	28.4	40.9
$30,000 to $39,999	24.2	57.5	30.0	39.3	53.3	26.6	27.4	42.0	46.6
$40,000 to $49,999	17.6	63.1	34.8	42.6	55.0	29.3	29.1	46.0	49.1
$50,000 to $74,999	34.7	69.3	44.8	50.2	63.0	36.0	35.3	53.6	54.4
$75,000 or more.	45.8	79.4	53.3	54.0	72.5	48.0	41.5	61.2	56.3
Not reported	21.5	51.0	28.4	31.4	45.1	22.6	23.2	33.6	42.9

Source: U.S. National Endowment for the Arts, *Research Division Report #45, 2002 Survey of Public Participation in the Arts.* See also <http://www.nea.gov/pub/ResearchReports_chrono.html>.

Table 1223. **Participation in Various Arts Activities: 2002**

[In percent. For persons 18 years old and over. Covers activities engaged in at least once in the prior 12 months. See headnote in Table 1221]

Item	Classical music	Other dance [1]	Painting	Pottery [2]	Sewing	Photo-graphy [3]	Writing	Pur-chased art recently	Choir/ chorale
Total	1.8	4.2	8.6	6.9	16.0	11.5	7.0	29.5	4.8
Sex:									
Male	1.5	3.3	6.4	4.9	2.4	10.8	5.8	29.7	3.8
Female	2.1	4.9	10.6	8.7	28.5	12.1	8.2	29.3	5.7
Race and ethnicity:									
White alone	2.1	4.1	9.4	7.6	17.6	12.8	7.6	28.9	4.5
African American alone. .	0.4	3.5	5.6	4.1	9.4	7.6	7.4	35.9	9.1
Other alone	2.3	5.8	7.4	6.5	14.9	11.9	5.3	26.3	3.5
Hispanic	0.7	4.2	6.8	5.1	12.5	6.7	4.0	37.5	2.9
Age:									
18 to 24 years old	2.5	6.0	15.4	9.3	10.4	12.9	12.7	41.0	4.9
25 to 34 years old	1.4	4.5	10.2	7.8	13.0	12.3	7.9	39.1	3.9
35 to 44 years old	1.8	3.9	8.1	7.4	15.3	14.1	6.7	31.2	4.8
45 to 54 years old	2.5	4.2	8.2	7.5	18.6	12.1	6.8	27.9	5.1
55 to 64 years old	1.5	3.4	6.7	5.6	19.1	10.5	5.0	26.1	5.6
65 to 74 years old	1.4	3.7	4.8	4.6	20.5	8.1	4.1	23.7	5.3
75 years old and older . .	0.7	2.5	3.1	2.4	18.0	3.8	3.7	11.4	3.7
Education:									
Grade school	0.4	0.7	1.7	1.6	12.0	1.7	1.7	22.8	1.1
Some high school	0.4	3.5	5.2	3.9	11.1	4.7	2.8	24.1	2.6
High school graduate . . .	0.6	2.8	6.3	6.1	15.0	8.1	4.1	23.2	3.4
Some college	1.8	5.7	11.6	9.0	18.3	13.4	9.1	28.3	6.0
College graduate	3.6	4.9	11.0	8.0	17.4	17.3	10.6	31.4	6.4
Graduate school	5.4	5.7	11.0	7.3	17.6	20.1	12.7	34.4	7.3
Income:									
$9,999 or less	1.5	3.1	7.3	6.6	15.7	6.7	7.8	23.4	3.3
$10,000 to $19,999	0.8	3.2	7.1	5.5	17.5	7.1	5.5	21.6	4.8
$20,000 to $29,999	0.5	4.5	7.4	5.7	15.9	6.8	5.6	26.5	4.0
$30,000 to $39,999	1.9	4.6	9.7	6.9	16.8	10.5	7.6	26.9	5.5
$40,000 to $49,999	2.9	4.2	9.4	6.8	17.8	13.8	7.4	24.1	5.3
$50,000 to $74,999	2.5	4.6	8.4	8.1	16.9	13.3	7.0	31.0	5.6
$75,000 or More	2.4	4.0	10.6	8.1	15.2	17.2	8.5	33.6	4.6
Not reported	1.2	4.6	6.7	5.4	12.3	9.1	5.9	25.5	4.3

[1] Dancing other than ballet (e.g., folk and tap). [2] Includes ceramics, jewelry, leatherwork, and metalwork. [3] Includes making movies or video as an artistic activity.

Source: U.S. National Endowment for the Arts, *Research Division Report #45, 2002 Survey of Public Participation in the Arts,* <http://www.nea.gov/pub/ResearchReports_chrono.html>.

Arts, Entertainment, and Recreation **763**

Table 1224. **Adult Attendance at Sports Events by Frequency: 2005**
[In thousands (2,664 represents 2,664,000), except percent. For fall 2005. Based on survey and subject to sampling error; see source]

Event	Attend one or more times a month		Attend less than once a month		Event	Attend one or more times a month		Attend less than once a month	
	Number	Percent	Number	Percent		Number	Percent	Number	Percent
Auto racing—NASCAR	2,664	1.2	8,518	4.0	Weekend				
Auto racing—Other	2,440	1.1	6,083	2.8	professional games	3,809	1.8	9,591	4.4
Baseball	8,502	3.9	18,575	8.6	Golf	1,587	0.7	4,636	2.2
Basketball:					High school sports	12,087	5.6	8,363	3.9
College games	4,383	2.0	7,485	3.5	Horse racing:				
Professional games	3,202	1.5	9,168	4.3	Flats, runners	1,281	0.6	3,842	1.8
Bowling	1,749	0.8	3,533	1.6	Trotters/harness	745	0.4	2,747	1.3
Boxing	1,175	0.5	3,240	1.5	Ice hockey	1,973	0.9	6,754	3.1
Equestrian events	574	0.3	3,534	1.6	Motorcycle racing	980	0.5	3,554	1.7
Figure skating	696	0.3	3,330	1.5	Pro beach volleyball	254	0.1	2,731	1.3
Fishing tournaments	716	0.3	3,132	1.5	Rodeo/bull riding	1,190	0.6	4,267	2.0
Football:					Soccer	3,389	1.6	4,429	2.1
College games	6,308	2.9	9,513	4.4	Tennis	903	0.4	3,655	1.7
Monday night					Truck and tractor pull/				
professional games	1,958	0.9	4,493	2.1	mud racing	655	0.3	3,638	1.7
					Wrestling—professional	1,243	0.6	3,604	1.7

Source: Mediamark Research, Inc., New York, NY, *Top-line Reports* (copyright). See also <http://www.mediamark.com/mri/docs/TopLineReports.html>.

Table 1225. Adult Participation in Selected Leisure Activities by Frequency: 2005
[In thousands (13,711 represents 13,711,000), except percent. For fall 2005. Based on sample and subject to sampling error; see source]

Activity	Participated in the last 12 months [1]		Frequency of participation							
			Two or more times a week		Once a week		Two to three times a month		Once a month	
	Number	Percent	Number	Percent	Number	Percent	Number	Percent	Number	Percent
Adult education courses	13,711	6.4	2,551	1.2	2,080	1.0	528	0.2	835	0.4
Attend adult shows	16,421	7.6	161	0.1	219	0.1	662	0.3	912	0.4
Attend country music performances	10,871	5.0	125	0.1	205	0.1	158	0.1	480	0.2
Attend dance performances	7,771	3.6	183	0.1	101	0.1	236	0.1	312	0.1
Attend horse races	6,163	2.9	190	0.1	259	0.1	263	0.1	371	0.2
Attend other music performances [2]	25,743	11.9	214	0.1	416	0.2	905	0.4	2,531	1.2
Attend rock music performances	20,085	9.3	212	0.1	251	0.1	403	0.2	1,060	0.5
Backgammon	4,393	2.0	735	0.3	214	0.1	569	0.3	516	0.2
Baking	39,599	18.4	7,274	3.4	5,797	2.7	8,936	4.1	6,656	3.1
Barbecuing	74,050	34.3	11,499	5.3	12,019	5.6	17,188	8.0	9,421	4.4
Billiards/pool	19,423	9.0	1,588	0.7	1,269	0.6	2,260	1.1	2,311	1.1
Bird watching	10,256	4.8	4,792	2.2	858	0.4	868	0.4	556	0.3
Board games	38,124	17.7	2,936	1.4	3,695	1.7	6,602	3.1	7,416	3.4
Book clubs	6,961	3.2	303	0.1	375	0.2	625	0.3	2,668	1.2
Ceramics/pottery	2,263	1.1	235	0.1	293	0.1	156	0.1	122	0.1
Chess	7,080	3.3	919	0.4	487	0.2	1,021	0.5	678	0.3
Concerts on radio	6,653	3.1	1,386	0.6	1,077	0.5	623	0.3	583	0.3
Cooking for fun	37,667	17.5	13,145	6.1	6,380	3.0	5,949	2.8	3,214	1.5
Crossword puzzles	32,042	14.9	14,216	6.6	4,439	2.1	3,737	1.7	2,211	1.0
Dance/go dancing	19,824	9.2	1,512	0.7	2,072	1.0	2,479	1.2	2,616	1.2
Dining out	104,113	48.3	21,202	9.8	24,446	11.3	23,333	10.8	12,444	5.8
Electronic games (not TV)	17,453	8.1	5,920	2.7	2,180	1.0	2,123	1.0	1,256	0.6
Entertain friends or relatives at home	80,860	37.5	6,928	3.2	9,782	4.5	18,008	8.3	16,860	7.8
Fly kites	5,397	2.5	96	(Z)	138	0.1	240	0.1	233	0.1
Furniture refinishing	7,633	3.5	302	0.1	141	0.1	415	0.2	555	0.3
Go to bars/night clubs	40,114	18.6	3,645	1.7	4,369	2.0	6,533	3.0	6,357	3.0
Go to beach	48,290	22.4	2,115	1.0	2,440	1.1	4,702	2.2	3,703	1.7
Go to live theater	28,566	13.2	223	0.1	316	0.2	1,357	0.6	3,213	1.5
Go to museums	27,135	12.6	280	0.1	194	0.1	752	0.4	2,554	1.2
Model making	3,111	1.4	248	0.1	172	0.1	299	0.1	157	0.1
Painting, drawing	13,746	6.4	2,657	1.2	1,728	0.8	1,847	0.9	1,617	0.8
Photo album/scrap booking	18,490	8.6	958	0.4	1,552	0.7	2,610	1.2	3,284	1.5
Photography	25,561	11.8	3,342	1.6	3,268	1.5	4,508	2.1	4,610	2.1
Picnic	23,572	10.9	314	0.2	718	0.3	1,868	0.9	2,883	1.3
Play bingo	10,159	4.7	718	0.3	1,085	0.5	843	0.4	1,074	0.5
Play cards	54,140	25.1	6,304	2.9	6,227	2.9	8,650	4.0	8,334	3.9
Play musical instrument	15,727	7.3	5,863	2.7	1,685	0.8	1,420	0.7	1,251	0.6
Reading books	76,455	35.4	43,036	19.9	7,805	3.6	6,792	3.2	4,112	1.9
Surf the Net	60,162	27.9	39,182	18.2	6,159	2.9	3,650	1.7	1,861	0.9
Trivia games	14,460	6.7	1,923	0.9	1,518	0.7	1,754	0.8	1,945	0.9
Video games	25,495	11.8	9,432	4.4	3,024	1.4	3,213	1.5	1,835	0.9
Woodworking	11,042	5.1	2,159	1.0	1,433	0.7	1,631	0.8	1,709	0.8
Word games	19,274	8.9	6,832	3.2	2,153	1.0	2,553	1.2	1,822	0.8
Zoo attendance	25,224	11.7	64	(Z)	123	0.1	497	0.2	1,433	0.7

Z represents less than 0.05. [1] Includes those participating less than once a month not shown separately. [2] Excluding country and rock.

Source: Mediamark Research, Inc., New York, NY, *Top-line Reports* (copyright). See also <http://www.mediamark.com/mri/docs/TopLineReports.html>.

Table 1226. Retail Sales and Household Participation in Lawn and Garden Activities: 2000 to 2005

[(33,404 represents $33,404,000,000). For calendar year. Subject to sampling variability; see source]

Activity	Retail sales (mil. dol.)					Percent households engaged in activity				
	2000	2002	2003	2004	2005	2000	2002	2003	2004	2005
Total	33,404	39,635	38,371	36,778	35,208	72	79	78	75	83
Lawn care	9,794	11,963	10,413	8,887	9,657	50	55	54	48	54
Indoor houseplants	1,332	2,128	1,571	1,495	1,464	39	44	41	39	42
Flower gardening	4,167	3,131	3,025	2,735	3,003	45	41	38	36	41
Insect control	1,232	2,281	2,053	1,823	1,869	27	32	30	28	30
Shrub care	1,429	1,072	1,042	1,027	1,109	31	27	27	26	31
Vegetable gardening	2,169	1,270	1,408	1,058	1,154	27	25	24	22	25
Tree care	1,872	2,790	2,359	3,067	2,820	23	26	25	24	26
Landscaping	6,809	8,854	10,507	11,346	9,078	30	34	33	33	31
Flower bulbs	912	1,191	1,036	892	945	28	29	26	26	29
Fruit trees	284	695	635	589	507	13	12	12	11	13
Container gardening	1,257	1,362	1,219	1,196	1,295	18	23	24	21	26
Raising transplants [1]	334	262	230	258	237	11	12	10	9	11
Herb gardening	204	444	345	367	371	12	15	14	14	17
Growing berries	147	171	345	141	151	8	7	6	6	8
Ornamental gardening	519	580	831	769	678	8	8	9	9	12
Water gardening	943	1,441	1,565	1,128	870	10	14	15	13	11

[1] Starting plants in advance of planting in ground.

Source: The National Gardening Association, Burlington, VT, *National Gardening Survey*, annual (copyright). See also <http://www.garden.org/home>.

Table 1227. Household Pet Ownership: 2001

[Based on a sample survey of 80,000 households in 2001; for details, see source]

Item	Unit	Dogs	Cats	Birds	Horses
Percent of households owning companion pets [1]	Percent . . .	36.1	31.6	4.6	1.7
Average number owned	Number . . .	1.6	2.1	2.1	2.9
Households obtaining veterinary care [2]	Percent . . .	83.6	65.3	11.7	54.6
Average visits per household per year	Number . . .	2.7	1.8	0.3	2.1
PERCENT OF HOUSEHOLDS OWNING PETS					
Annual household income:					
Under $20,000	Percent . . .	29.7	28.1	5.1	1.0
$20,000 to $34,999	Percent . . .	33.9	30.9	4.5	1.3
$35,000 to $54,999	Percent . . .	37.9	32.2	4.8	2.0
$55,000 to $84,999	Percent . . .	40.5	34.3	4.4	2.1
$85,000 and over	Percent . . .	39.7	33.7	4.2	2.1
Household size:[1]					
One person	Percent . . .	20.8	23.5	2.8	0.7
Two persons	Percent . . .	34.3	31.3	4.0	1.6
Three persons	Percent . . .	46.2	37.4	5.9	2.2
Four persons	Percent . . .	50.6	38.2	6.3	2.3
Five or more persons.	Percent . . .	53.0	39.7	8.3	3.2
Veterinary Expenditures:					
Per household per year (mean)	Dollars . . .	261	160	18	263
Per animal (mean)	Dollars . . .	179	85	9	112

[1] As of December 31, 2001.   [2] During 2001.

Source: American Veterinary Medical Association, Schaumburg, IL, *U.S. Pet Ownership and Demographics Sourcebook, 2002* (copyright). <http://www.avma.org/>.

Table 1228. College and Professional Football Summary: 1990 to 2005

[35,330 represents 35,330,000. For definition of median, see Guide to Tabular Presentation]

Sport	Unit	1990	1995	2000	2001	2002	2003	2004	2005
Football:									
NCAA college: [1]									
Teams	Number.	533	565	606	608	617	617	612	615
Attendance	1,000 . .	35,330	35,638	39,059	40,481	44,556	46,145	43,106	43,487
National Football League: [2]									
Teams	Number.	28	30	31	31	32	32	32	32
Attendance, total	1,000 . .	17,666	19,203	20,954	20,590	21,505	21,639	21,709	21,792
Regular season	1,000 . .	13,960	15,044	16,387	16,166	16,833	16,914	17,001	17,012
Average per game. . .	Number.	62,321	62,682	66,078	65,187	65,755	66,328	66,409	66,455
Postseason games [3] . . .	1,000 . .	848	(NA)	809	767	782	806	789	802
Players' salaries: [4]									
Average	$1,000 . .	354	584	787	986	1,180	1,259	1,331	1,400
Median base salary	$1,000 .	275	301	441	501	525	534	537	569

NA Not available.   [1] Source: National Collegiate Athletic Assn., Indianapolis, IN; <www.ncaasports.com>(copyright). [2] Source: National Football League, New York, NY; <http://www.nfl.com/>.   [3] Includes Pro Bowl, a nonchampionship game, and Super Bowl.   [4] Source: National Football League Players Association, Washington, DC.; <http://www.nflpa.org/>.

Source: Compiled from sources listed in footnotes.

Table 1229. **Selected Recreational Activities: 1990 to 2005**

[41 represents 41,000,000]

Activity	Unit	1990	1995	2000	2001	2002	2003	2004	2005
Softball, amateur: [1]									
Total participants [2]........	Million..	41	42	31	31	31	30	28	27
Youth participants.......	1,000..	1,100	1,350	1,370	1,355	1,365	1,351	1,356	1,447
Adult teams [3]........	1,000..	188	187	155	149	143	119	132	128
Youth teams [3]..........	1,000..	46	74	81	80	80	79	80	85
Golf facilities [4]...........	Number.	12,846	14,074	15,489	15,689	15,827	15,899	16,057	16,052
Tennis players: [5]..........	1,000..	21,000	17,820	22,900	22,000	23,200	24,100	24,000	24,720
Tenpin bowling: [6]									
Establishments.......	Number.	7,611	7,049	6,247	6,022	5,973	5,811	5,761	5,818
Membership, total [7]......	1,000..	6,588	4,925	3,756	3,553	3,382	3,246	3,112	2,896
Skiing [8]									
Skier visits [9]...........	Million..	50.0	52.7	52.2	57.3	54.4	57.6	57.1	56.9
Operating resorts........	Number.	591	520	503	490	493	490	494	492
Motion picture screens [10].....	1,000..	24	28	38	37	36	37	37	39
Receipts, box office.......	Mil. dol..	5,022	5,494	7,661	8,413	9,520	9,489	9,539	8,991
Attendance............	Million..	1,189	1,263	1,421	1,487	1,639	1,574	1,536	1,403
Boating: [11]									
People participating in recreational boating......	Million..	73.4	76.8	68.9	68.0	71.6	68.7	69.0	71.3
Retail expenditures on boating [12]..........	Mil. dol..	13,731	17,226	27,065	29,710	31,563	30,283	32,953	37,317
Recreational boats in use by boat type [13]..........	Million..	16.0	15.4	16.8	17.0	17.4	17.4	17.6	18.0
Outboard..............	Million..	(NA)	(NA)	8.3	8.3	8.4	8.4	8.5	8.6
Inboard..............	Million..	(NA)	(NA)	1.7	1.7	1.7	1.7	1.8	1.8
Sterndrive.............	Million..	(NA)	(NA)	1.7	1.7	1.8	1.8	1.8	1.9
Personal watercraft.......	Million..	(NA)	(NA)	1.2	1.3	1.4	1.4	1.5	1.6
Sailboats..............	Million..	(NA)	(NA)	1.6	1.6	1.6	1.6	1.6	1.6
Other................	Million..	(NA)	(NA)	2.3	2.4	2.5	2.5	2.5	2.7

NA Not available. [1] Source: Amateur Softball Association, Oklahoma City, OK. [2] Amateur Softball Association teams and other amateur softball teams. [3] Amateur Softball Association teams only. [4] Source: National Golf Foundation, Jupiter, FL. [5] Source: Tennis Industry Association, Hilton Head, SC. Players for persons 12 years old and over who played at least once. [6] Source: Bowling Headquarters, Greendale, WI. [7] Membership totals are for U.S., Canada, and for U.S. military personnel worldwide. [8] Source: National Ski Areas Association, Kottke National End of Season Survey 2004/05-final report (copyright). [9] Represents one person visiting a ski area for all or any part of a day or night, and includes full-and half-day, night, complimentary, adult, child, season, and other types of tickets. Data are estimated and are for the season ending in the year shown. [10] Source: Motion Picture Association of America, Inc., Encino, CA. [11] Source: National Marine Manufacturers Association, Chicago, IL. (copyright). [12] Represents estimated expenditures for new and used boats, motors and engines, accessories, safety equipment, fuel, insurance, docking, maintenance, launching, storage, repairs, and other expenses. [13] 2005 data are estimated.

Source: Compiled from sources listed in footnotes.

Table 1230. **Selected Spectator Sports: 1990 to 2005**

[55,512 represents 55,512,000]

Sport	Unit	1990	1995	2000	2001	2002	2003	2004	2005
Baseball, major leagues: [1]									
Attendance.............	1,000..	55,512	51,288	74,339	73,881	69,428	69,501	74,822	76,286
Regular season........	1,000..	54,824	50,469	72,748	72,267	67,859	67,568	73,023	74,926
National League......	1,000..	24,492	25,110	39,851	39,558	36,949	36,661	40,221	41,644
American League.....	1,000..	30,332	25,359	32,898	32,709	30,910	30,908	32,802	33,282
Playoffs [2].........	1,000..	479	533	1,314	1,247	1,262	1,568	1,625	1,191
World Series.........	1,000..	209	286	277	366	306	365	174	168
Players' salaries: [3]									
Average............	$1,000.	598	1,111	1,896	2,139	2,296	2,372	2,313	2,476
Basketball: [4, 5]									
NCAA—Men's college:									
Teams............	Number.	767	868	932	937	936	967	981	983
Attendance..........	1,000..	28,741	28,548	29,025	28,949	29,395	30,124	30,761	30,569
NCAA—Women's college:									
Teams............	Number.	782	864	956	958	975	1,009	1,008	1,036
Attendance..........	1,000..	2,777	4,962	8,698	8,825	9,533	10,164	10,016	9,940
National Hockey League: [6]									
Regular season attendance..	1,000..	12,580	9,234	18,800	20,373	20,615	20,409	22,065	(7)
Playoffs attendance.......	1,000..	1,356	1,329	1,525	1,584	1,691	1,636	1,709	(7)
Professional rodeo: [8]									
Rodeos..............	Number.	754	739	688	668	666	657	671	662
Performances..........	Number.	2,159	2,217	2,081	2,081	2,015	2,207	1,949	1,940
Members.............	Number.	5,693	6,894	6,255	5,913	6,209	6,158	6,247	6,127
Permit-holders (rookies)....	Number.	3,290	3,835	3,249	2,544	2,543	3,121	2,990	2,701
Total prize money.......	Mil dol.	18.2	24.5	32.3	33.1	33.3	34.3	35.5	36.6

[1] Source: Major League Baseball (previously, The National League of Professional Baseball Clubs), New York, NY, National League Green Book; and The American League of Professional Baseball Clubs, New York, NY, American League Red Book. [2] Beginning 1997, two rounds of playoffs were played. Prior years had one round. [3] Source: Major League Baseball Players Association, New York, NY. [4] Season ending in year shown. [5] Source: National Collegiate Athletic Association, Indianapolis, IN (copyright). For women's attendance total, excludes double-headers with men's teams. [6] For season ending in year shown. Source: National Hockey League, Montreal, Quebec. [7] In September 2004, franchise owners locked out their players upon the expiration of the collective bargaining agreement. The entire season was cancelled in February 2005. [8] Source: Professional Rodeo Cowboys Association, Colorado Springs, CO., Official Professional Rodeo Media Guide, annual(copyright).

Source: Compiled from sources listed in footnotes.

766 Arts, Entertainment, and Recreation

Table 1231. **High School Students Engaged in Organized Physical Activity by Sex, Race and Hispanic Origin: 2005**

[In percent. For students in grades 9 to 12. Based on the Youth Risk Behavior Survey, a school-based survey and subject to sampling error; for details see source]

| Characteristic | Enrolled in physical education class | | | Played on a sports team | Watched three or more hours/day of TV |
	Total	Attended daily	Exercised 20 minutes or more per class [1]		
All students.	**54.2**	**33.0**	**84.0**	**56.0**	**37.2**
Male	60.0	37.1	87.2	61.8	38.0
Grade 9	72.8	46.5	86.3	64.7	42.4
Grade 10.	65.4	39.0	88.0	63.4	42.7
Grade 11.	51.1	33.5	87.5	61.0	34.1
Grade 12.	45.9	26.1	87.3	57.3	30.3
Female.	48.3	29.0	80.3	50.2	36.3
Grade 9	70.3	43.1	80.3	56.1	42.4
Grade 10.	53.0	31.5	81.0	52.3	37.4
Grade 11.	32.9	19.4	79.5	48.9	31.7
Grade 12.	32.0	18.8	79.7	41.3	32.4
White, non-Hispanic	52.1	31.7	86.3	57.8	29.2
Male.	58.1	36.7	89.3	61.5	30.2
Female	46.1	26.6	82.5	53.9	28.1
Black, non-Hispanic	55.8	34.4	78.7	53.7	64.1
Male.	61.7	37.5	83.8	64.6	63.5
Female	50.5	31.6	73.1	43.6	64.5
Hispanic.	61.5	38.3	81.6	53.0	45.8
Male.	65.9	38.1	85.0	62.0	45.8
Female	57.1	38.6	77.5	43.8	45.8

[1] For students enrolled in physical education classes. Source: U.S. Centers for Disease Control and Prevention, Atlanta, GA, Youth Risk Behavior Surveillance—United States, 2005, Morbidity and Mortality Weekly Report, Vol. 55, No. SS-1, June 9, 2006. See also: <http://www.cdc.gov/mmwr/preview/mmwrhtml/ss5505a1.htm>.

Table 1232. **Participation in High School Athletic Programs by Sex: 1973 to 2005**

[Data based on number of state associations reporting and may under represent the number of schools with and participants in athletic programs]

| Year | Participants [1] | | Sex and sport | Most popular sports, 2004–2005 [2] | |
	Males	Females		Schools	Participants
1973–74.	4,070,125	1,300,169	MALE		
1975–76.	4,109,021	1,645,039			
1977–78.	4,367,442	2,083,040	Football (11-player)	13,671	1,045,494
1978–79.	3,709,512	1,854,400	Basketball	17,482	545,497
1979–80.	3,517,829	1,750,264	Track & field (outdoor)	15,294	516,703
1980–81.	3,503,124	1,853,789	Baseball	15,161	459,717
1981–82.	3,409,081	1,810,671	Soccer	10,392	354,587
1982–83.	3,355,558	1,779,972	Wrestling	9,562	243,009
1983–84.	3,303,599	1,747,346	Cross country.	12,727	201,719
1984–85.	3,354,284	1,757,884	Golf	13,152	161,025
			Tennis.	9,426	148,530
1985–86.	3,344,275	1,807,121	Swimming & diving	5,878	103,754
1986–87.	3,364,082	1,836,356			
1987–88.	3,425,777	1,849,684	FEMALE		
1988–89.	3,416,844	1,839,352			
1989–90.	3,398,192	1,858,659	Basketball	17,175	456,543
1990–91.	3,406,355	1,892,316	Track & field (outdoor)	15,213	428,198
1991–92.	3,429,853	1,940,801	Volleyball	14,526	386,022
1992–93.	3,416,389	1,997,489	Softball (fast pitch).	14,493	364,759
1993–94.	3,472,967	2,130,315	Soccer	9,695	316,104
1994–95.	3,536,359	2,240,461	Cross country.	12,345	170,450
			Tennis.	9,646	169,292
1995–96.	3,634,052	2,367,936	Swimming & diving	6,238	148,154
1996–97.	3,706,225	2,474,043	Competitive spirit squads	3,482	84,416
1997–98.	3,763,120	2,570,333	Golf	8,249	64,245
1998–99.	3,832,352	2,652,726			
1999–00.	3,861,749	2,675,874			
2000–01.	3,921,069	2,784,154			
2001–02.	3,960,517	2,806,998			
2002–03.	3,988,738	2,856,358			
2003–04.	4,038,253	2,865,299			
2004–05.	4,110,319	2,908,390			

[1] A participant is counted in the number of sports participated in. [2] Ten most popular sports for each sex in terms of number of participants.

Source: National Federation of State High School Associations, Indianapolis, IN, The 2004–2005 High School Athletics Participation Survey (copyright). <http://www.nfhs.org>.

Arts, Entertainment, and Recreation 767

Table 1233. **Participation in Selected Sports Activities: 2004**

[In thousands (258,533 represents 258,533,000), except rank. For persons 7 years of age or older. Except as indicated, a participant plays a sport more than once in the year]

Activity	All persons Number	All persons Rank	Sex Male	Sex Female	Age 7–11 years	Age 12–17 years	Age 18–24 years	Age 25–34 years	Age 35–44 years	Age 45–54 years	Age 55–64 years	Age 65 years and over	Household income Under 15,000	Household income 15,000–24,999	Household income 25,000–34,999	Household income 35,000–49,000	Household income 50,000–74,999	Household income 75,000 and over
Total	**258,533**	**(X)**	**125,831**	**132,702**	**19,650**	**24,988**	**28,320**	**36,882**	**43,167**	**41,021**	**28,514**	**35,989**	**29,769**	**29,456**	**31,927**	**42,184**	**53,420**	**71,778**
SERIES I SPORTS [1]																		
Number participated in—																		
Aerobic exercising [3]	29,458	10	7,709	21,749	1,158	1,997	4,768	6,921	6,141	4,137	2,471	1,865	1,957	2,060	3,164	4,773	6,464	11,041
Backpacking [3]	17,280	17	9,964	7,316	1,621	2,339	3,128	3,842	3,163	2,397	617	173	1,761	1,694	2,511	2,993	3,520	4,801
Baseball	15,850	18	12,343	3,506	4,333	3,959	1,792	1,810	1,825	1,058	399	672	1,181	1,436	1,596	2,550	3,217	5,869
Basketball	27,847	12	19,150	8,696	5,867	7,175	5,050	3,413	3,562	1,650	456	674	2,117	2,249	3,368	4,568	5,681	9,863
Bicycle riding [2]	40,317	7	21,570	18,747	9,196	7,770	3,098	5,632	6,002	4,402	2,344	1,873	3,083	3,707	4,163	6,262	8,851	14,251
Billiards	34,228	9	20,590	13,638	1,647	3,318	8,833	7,995	6,734	3,878	1,110	712	3,297	3,668	4,852	6,110	6,414	9,887
Bowling [4]	43,832	5	22,498	21,333	5,598	6,852	8,666	8,150	7,367	4,408	1,179	1,611	3,200	4,204	5,841	6,527	10,520	13,540
Camping [4]	55,265	2	28,768	26,497	5,842	7,173	6,976	10,111	10,576	8,522	4,032	2,033	4,968	5,077	6,699	11,100	12,846	14,575
Exercising with equipment [2]	52,169	4	24,163	28,006	1,124	4,599	6,949	10,239	10,604	9,480	5,480	3,693	2,555	3,434	5,094	8,351	11,670	21,064
Exercise walking [2]	84,718	1	32,327	52,391	3,709	5,164	7,813	14,334	16,042	15,385	11,008	11,262	8,637	8,778	9,760	13,538	18,246	25,759
Fishing (net)	41,174	6	28,244	12,929	4,027	4,535	4,977	7,411	8,069	6,110	3,596	2,448	4,172	4,795	5,162	7,817	9,041	10,187
Fishing—fresh water	36,265	8	24,816	11,448	3,583	4,103	4,329	6,642	7,032	5,309	3,144	2,121	3,788	4,535	4,664	6,935	7,908	8,434
Fishing—salt water	10,283	22	7,563	2,720	633	1,104	1,182	1,708	2,395	1,624	807	829	739	880	1,074	2,097	2,140	3,354
Football—tackle	8,195	25	7,216	979	1,350	1,378	1,354	746	580	270	159	359	961	868	1,088	1,066	1,801	2,411
Football—touch	9,569	24	7,395	2,174	2,039	3,175	1,548	1,178	1,041	342	70	174	919	954	1,309	1,040	2,130	3,218
Golf	24,479	15	18,761	5,718	1,027	2,487	2,596	4,374	5,014	4,029	2,517	2,436	699	1,440	1,554	3,165	5,718	11,903
Hiking	28,342	11	14,642	13,699	2,309	3,248	4,045	5,790	5,472	4,607	1,847	1,023	2,217	2,321	2,910	3,501	5,861	9,531
Hunting with firearms	17,711	16	15,726	1,985	864	1,995	2,499	3,429	4,100	2,571	1,455	799	1,690	1,747	2,442	3,752	4,008	4,072
Martial arts	4,657	27	3,014	1,643	1,415	576	596	915	518	437	111	89	433	372	524	767	848	1,712
Running/jogging [2]	24,665	14	13,183	11,483	1,927	4,537	5,188	5,429	3,732	2,440	917	496	1,655	1,785	3,049	4,021	5,210	8,945
Soccer	13,287	19	7,752	5,535	5,411	3,578	1,483	1,113	930	344	195	232	519	893	1,684	1,837	2,567	5,787
Softball	12,501	20	6,029	6,472	2,412	2,610	2,161	1,844	1,975	847	359	292	1,203	1,146	1,550	1,554	2,615	4,432
Swimming [2]	53,449	3	24,809	28,639	8,298	9,650	7,244	7,282	8,532	6,263	3,097	3,083	3,544	4,477	6,608	8,364	11,095	19,361
Tai Chi/Yoga	6,664	26	851	5,813	135	325	1,434	1,754	1,238	928	475	375	365	681	910	1,162	1,443	2,103
Tennis	9,619	23	4,528	5,091	937	2,248	1,311	1,453	1,609	1,210	508	343	550	777	789	1,111	1,623	4,769
Volleyball	10,790	21	4,481	6,309	1,140	3,458	2,294	1,767	1,349	612	125	47	769	617	1,762	1,675	2,494	3,473
Weightlifting	26,237	13	17,359	8,878	285	3,906	5,943	5,515	4,877	3,522	1,392	797	1,148	1,638	3,543	4,057	5,867	9,985

See footnote at end of table.

U.S. Census Bureau, Statistical Abstract of the United States: 2007

Table 1233. **Participation in Selected Sports Activities: 2004**—Con.

[See headnote, page 768]

Activity	All persons Number	Rank	Sex Male	Sex Female	Age 7–11 years	Age 12–17 years	Age 18–24 years	Age 25–34 years	Age 35–44 years	Age 45–54 years	Age 55–64 years	Age 65 years and over	Household income (dol.) Under 15,000	15,000–24,999	25,000–34,999	35,000–49,999	50,000–74,999	75,000 and over
Total	**258,537**	(X)	**125,835**	**132,703**	**19,650**	**24,990**	**28,322**	**36,883**	**43,168**	**41,022**	**28,515**	**35,987**	**28,223**	**29,293**	**31,494**	**43,905**	**55,594**	**70,028**
Number participating in—																		
Archery (target)	5,265	12	3,799	1,466	699	1,581	403	769	697	643	210	262	190	407	815	912	1,131	1,810
Boating—motor/power	22,773	2	12,827	9,946	2,160	2,568	2,821	4,364	4,195	3,348	1,817	1,501	912	1,526	3,073	3,638	5,424	8,200
Cheerleading	4,100	15	200	3,900	1,480	1,481	605	105	63	115	99	152	342	253	319	680	717	1,789
Hockey (ice)	2,423	19	1,823	600	292	544	307	405	453	304	66	53	140	253	272	298	623	1,038
Hunting with bow and arrow .	5,818	11	5,318	499	90	437	860	1,326	1,303	916	512	374	355	464	1,060	1,217	1,473	1,249
In-line roller skating	11,677	5	5,805	5,872	3,313	3,913	1,280	1,368	880	544	118	259	702	703	1,453	1,802	3,458	3,559
Kick boxing	2,785	17	890	1,895	317	269	481	558	580	412	97	71	107	256	219	597	543	1,063
Mountain biking—off road . .	8,019	8	5,306	2,712	754	1,204	1,292	1,697	1,589	1,215	228	40	731	519	886	1,052	1,984	2,848
Muzzleloading	3,810	16	3,396	414	27	315	542	692	792	815	412	215	220	310	637	840	998	804
Paintball games	9,448	7	7,601	1,847	1,063	3,649	2,195	1,136	713	569	98	25	746	704	948	1,837	1,499	3,714
Sailing	2,583	18	1,433	1,150	117	250	314	577	392	483	257	193	103	168	144	441	428	1,299
Scooter riding	12,915	4	7,062	5,853	6,086	3,723	456	712	695	530	307	406	621	486	1,876	2,479	3,234	4,220
Skateboarding	10,338	6	7,718	2,620	3,439	4,262	1,305	397	366	149	137	284	551	510	1,409	2,019	2,376	3,473
Skiing—alpine	5,903	10	3,284	2,620	659	979	686	1,060	1,286	815	212	206	101	208	426	760	1,600	2,808
Skiing—cross country	2,352	20	1,359	994	74	304	408	408	310	466	136	246	268	149	342	329	320	944
Snowboarding	6,572	9	4,825	1,747	971	2,356	1,758	662	211	136	237	241	284	364	599	959	1,633	2,732
Target shoot	19,154	3	14,842	4,312	1,034	2,705	2,311	3,989	3,630	3,058	1,526	901	1,126	1,786	2,566	3,666	4,136	5,873
Target shoot—air gun	5,095	13	3,803	1,292	838	1,783	269	509	571	685	241	199	535	294	593	952	1,053	1,668
Water skiing	4,730	14	2,822	1,908	357	918	986	1,062	723	405	160	118	112	110	327	1,026	1,046	2,109
Work-out at club	31,805	1	14,022	17,784	597	1,880	5,374	7,721	6,091	5,212	2,656	2,274	1,466	1,745	2,181	4,663	7,850	13,900

SERIES II SPORTS [5]

X Not applicable.   [1] Based on a sampling of 15,000 households.   [2] Participant engaged in activity at least six times in the year.   [3] Includes wilderness camping.   [4] Vacation/overnight.   [5] Based on a sampling of 20,000 households.

Source: National Sporting Goods Association, Mt. Prospect, IL, Sports Participation in 2004: Series 1 and Series II (copyright) <http://www.nsga.org/public/pages/index.cfm?pageid=864>.

Arts, Entertainment, and Recreation   769

Table 1234. **Participation in NCAA Sports: 2004 to 2005**

Sport	Males			Females		
	Teams	Athletes	Average squad	Teams	Athletes	Average squad
Total [1]	8,135	222,838	(X)	9,074	166,728	(X)
Baseball	873	28,009	32.1	(X)	(X)	(X)
Basketball	1,000	16,271	16.3	1,025	14,686	14.3
Bowling [2]	1	22	22.0	45	393	8.7
Cross country	865	11,638	13.5	940	12,901	13.7
Equestrian [2]	3	28	9.3	39	1,103	28.3
Fencing [3]	36	623	17.3	45	696	15.5
Field hockey	(X)	(X)	(X)	257	5,505	21.4
Football	614	60,117	97.9	(X)	(X)	(X)
Golf	762	7,953	10.4	483	3,828	7.9
Gymnastics	19	329	17.3	85	1,402	16.5
Ice hockey [4]	133	3,843	28.9	74	1,679	22.7
Lacrosse	214	7,313	34.2	264	5,746	21.8
Rifle [3]	35	241	6.9	36	229	6.4
Rowing [5]	59	2,254	38.2	141	6,987	49.6
Rugby [2]	1	25	25.0	3	76	25.3
Sailing [2]	33	385	11.7	(X)	(X)	(X)
Skiing [3]	35	489	14.0	39	474	12.2
Soccer	737	19,291	26.2	913	21,126	23.1
Softball	(X)	(X)	(X)	911	16,324	17.9
Squash [2]	21	369	17.6	27	380	14.1
Swimming/diving [4]	381	7,650	20.1	489	10,845	22.2
Synchronized swimming [4]	(X)	(X)	(X)	8	104	13.0
Tennis	742	7,386	10.0	876	8,429	9.6
Track, indoor	565	18,866	33.4	621	18,533	29.8
Track, outdoor	656	21,686	33.1	704	20,388	29.0
Volleyball	79	1,161	14.7	982	13,634	13.9
Water polo	46	939	20.4	61	1,193	19.6
Wrestling	224	5,939	26.5	(X)	(X)	(X)

X Not applicable. [1] Includes other sports, not shown separately. [2] Sport recognized by the NCAA but does not have an NCAA championship. [3] Co-ed championship sport. [4] Sport recognized by the NCAA but does not have an NCAA championship for women. [5] Sport recognized by the NCAA but does not have an NCAA championship for men.

Source: The National Collegiate Athletic Association (NCAA), Indianapolis, IN, *2004–05 Participation Study (copyright)*; <http://www.ncaa.org/wps/portal>.

Table 1235. **Sporting Goods Sales by Product Category: 1990 to 2005**

[In millions of dollars (50,725 represents $50,725,000,000), except percent. Based on a sample survey of consumer purchases of 80,000 households, (100,000 beginning 1995), except recreational transport, which was provided by industry associations. Excludes Alaska and Hawaii. Minus sign (–) indicates decrease]

Selected product category	1990	1995	1999	2000	2001	2002	2003	2004	2005, proj.
Sales, all products	50,725	59,794	71,161	74,442	74,337	77,726	79,779	84,684	86,774
Annual percent change [1]	(NA)	6.5	1.9	4.6	–0.1	4.6	2.6	6.1	2.5
Percent of retail sales	(NA)	2.5	2.5	2.5	2.4	2.5	2.4	2.4	2.3
Athletic and sport clothing [2]	10,130	10,311	10,307	11,030	10,217	9,801	10,543	11,201	11,649
Athletic and sport footwear [2]	11,654	11,415	12,546	13,026	13,814	14,144	14,446	14,752	15,002
Aerobic shoes	611	372	275	292	281	239	222	237	239
Basketball shoes	918	999	821	786	761	789	890	877	912
Cross training shoes	679	1,191	1,364	1,528	1,476	1,421	1,407	1,327	1,340
Golf shoes	226	225	208	226	223	243	222	230	235
Gym shoes, sneakers	2,536	1,741	1,936	1,871	2,004	2,042	2,059	2,221	2,265
Jogging and running shoes	1,110	1,043	1,502	1,638	1,670	1,733	1,802	1,989	2,049
Tennis shoes	740	480	505	533	505	503	544	508	498
Walking shoes	2,950	2,841	3,099	3,317	3,280	3,415	3,468	3,496	3,497
Athletic and sport equipment [2]	14,439	18,809	20,343	21,608	21,594	21,699	22,394	22,934	23,390
Archery	265	287	262	259	276	279	320	332	338
Baseball and softball	217	251	329	319	316	334	340	346	356
Billiards and indoor games	192	304	354	516	528	574	625	627	640
Camping	1,072	1,205	1,265	1,354	1,371	1,442	1,487	1,531	1,547
Exercise	1,824	2,960	3,396	3,610	3,889	4,378	4,957	5,012	5,112
Fishing tackle	1,910	2,010	1,917	2,030	2,058	2,024	1,981	2,015	2,035
Golf	2,514	3,194	3,567	3,805	3,871	3,258	3,046	3,148	3,243
Hunting and firearms	2,202	3,003	2,437	2,274	2,206	2,449	2,654	2,870	2,928
Optics	438	655	718	729	783	826	847	859	885
Skin diving and scuba	294	328	363	355	348	348	338	351	365
Skiing, downhill	475	562	648	495	515	527	462	458	468
Tennis	333	297	338	383	371	358	343	362	373
Recreational transport	14,502	19,259	27,965	28,779	28,712	32,083	32,397	35,797	36,733
Bicycles and supplies	2,423	3,390	4,770	5,131	4,725	4,961	4,736	4,898	5,045
Pleasure boats, motors, & accessories	7,644	9,064	11,962	13,224	14,558	15,382	14,705	16,054	17,017
Recreational vehicles	4,113	5,895	10,413	9,529	8,598	10,960	12,058	14,018	13,819
Snowmobiles	322	910	820	894	831	779	898	827	852

NA Not available. [1] Represents change from immediate prior year. [2] Includes other products not shown separately.

Source: National Sporting Goods Association, Mt. Prospect, IL, *The Sporting Goods Market in 2005*; and prior issues (copyright); <http://www.nsga.org/public/pages/index.cfm?pageid=869>.

770 Arts, Entertainment, and Recreation

Table 1236. **Participants in Wildlife-Related Recreation Activities: 2001**

[Preliminary. In thousands (37,805 represents 37,805,000). For persons 16 years old and over engaging in activity at least once in 2001. Based on survey and subject to sampling error; see source for details]

Participant	Number	Days of participa-tion	Trips	Participant	Number	Days of participa-tion
Total sportsmen [1]	**37,805**	**785,762**	**636,787**	**Wildlife watchers** [1]	**66,105**	**(X)**
Total anglers	34,071	557,394	436,662	Nonresidential [2]	21,823	372,006
Freshwater	28,439	466,984	365,076	Observe wildlife	20,080	295,345
Excluding Great Lakes	27,913	443,247	349,188	Photograph wildlife	9,427	76,324
Great Lakes	1,847	23,138	15,888	Feed wildlife	7,077	103,307
Saltwater.	9,051	90,838	71,586			
				Residential [3]	62,928	(X)
Total hunters	13,034	228,368	200,125	Observe wildlife	42,111	(X)
Big game	10,911	153,191	114,445	Photograph wildlife	13,937	(X)
Small game	5,434	60,142	46,450	Feed wildlife	53,988	(X)
Migratory birds	2,956	29,310	24,155	Visit public parks	10,981	(X)
Other animals.	1,047	19,207	15,074	Maintain plantings or. . . natural areas	13,072	(X)

X Not applicable.   [1] Detail does not add to total due to multiple responses and nonresponse.   [2] Persons taking a trip of at least 1 mile for activity.   [3] Activity within 1 mile of home.

Source: U.S. Fish and Wildlife Service, *2001 National Survey of Fishing, Hunting, and Wildlife Associated Recreation,* May 2002. Internet links: <http://www.census.gov/prod/www/abs/fishing.html> <http://federalaid.fws.gov/surveys/surveys.html>.

Table 1237. **Consumer Purchases of Sporting Goods by Consumer Characteristics: 2004**

[**In percent.** Based on sample survey of consumer purchases of 100,000 households. Excludes Alaska and Hawaii]

Characteristic	Total house-holds	Footwear						Equipment				
		Aero-bic shoes	Gym shoes/ sneak-ers	Jog-ging/ run-ning shoes	Skate-board-ing shoes	Walk-ing shoes	Multi-pur-pose home gyms	Rod/ reel combi-nation	Golf club sets	Rifles	Soccer balls
Total.	**100**	**100**	**100**	**100**	**100**	**100**	**100**	**100**	**100**	**100**	**100**
Age of user:											
Under 14 years old	19.4	4.5	45.7	10.9	32.8	5.2	–	7.4	6.4	1.6	76.5
14 to 17 years old	5.7	2.7	9.5	8.4	35.5	2.4	7.2	4.3	8.6	3.6	7.4
18 to 24 years old	9.9	7.0	5.9	9.7	12.3	4.5	5.0	6.5	7.4	6.8	2.2
25 to 34 years old	13.7	26.9	13.3	25.5	13.2	11.5	24.2	26.7	18.2	19.1	2.6
35 to 44 years old	15.3	24.2	11.5	20.8	5.4	14.9	36.1	14.0	13.9	36.2	3.7
45 to 64 years old	23.6	29.0	10.9	22.2	0.8	40.4	20.5	31.8	33.7	25.1	2.9
65 years old and over	12.4	5.7	3.2	2.5	–	21.1	0.4	7.0	11.8	5.9	0.2
Multiple ages	–	–	–	–	–	–	6.6	2.3	–	1.7	4.5
Sex of user:											
Male	49.2	14.9	55.7	51.5	82.4	36.4	47.0	77.5	81.4	92.2	49.9
Female	50.8	85.1	44.3	48.5	17.6	63.6	40.3	15.9	18.6	5.9	45.8
Household use	–	–	–	–	–	–	12.7	6.6	–	1.9	4.3
Annual household income:											
Under $15,000	13.8	4.9	9.4	4.6	8.7	8.5	7.6	8.9	0.7	9.3	3.8
$15,000 to $24,999	13.9	3.8	12.1	7.2	13.3	11.3	10.7	13.2	6.7	5.0	9.9
$25,000 to $34,999	11.7	13.8	9.5	5.6	11.6	10.5	8.2	8.7	3.9	6.3	9.2
$35,000 to $49,999	15.6	15.1	15.1	14.2	11.3	15.4	10.7	16.8	7.3	9.1	20.0
$50,000 to $74,999	18.3	18.2	23.7	20.6	25.7	21.0	23.3	23.8	22.8	20.1	17.8
$75,000 to $99,999	12.5	13.9	13.9	18.4	14.0	14.9	17.8	12.0	28.9	27.6	16.0
$100,000 and over	14.2	30.3	16.3	29.4	15.4	18.4	21.7	16.6	29.7	22.6	23.3

– Represents or rounds to zero.

Source: National Sporting Goods Association, Mt. Prospect, IL, *The Sporting Goods Market in 2005* (copyright). <http://www.nsga.org.public/pages/index.cfm?pageid=869>.

Table 1238. **Tourism Sales by Commodity Group, 2000 to 2005, and Tourism Employment by Industry Group, 2000 to 2005**

[**Sales in billions of dollars,** (517 represents $517,000,000,000). Employment in thousands (5,712 represents 5,712,000). Direct tourism-related sales comprise all output consumed directly by visitors.(e.g., traveler accommodations, passenger air transportation, souvenirs). Direct tourism-related employment comprises all jobs where the workers are engaged in the production of direct tourism-related output (e.g., hotel staff, airline pilots, and souvenir sellers)]

Tourism commodity group	Direct tourism sales (mil. dol.)				Tourism industry group	Direct tourism employment			
	2000	2003	2004	2005		2000	2003	2004	2005
All commodities [1] **. . . . .**	**517**	**523**	**572**	**619**	**All industries. . . . .**	**5,712**	**5,452**	**5,560**	**5,645**
Traveler accommodations . . .	88	86	95	104	Traveler accommodations .	1,408	1,319	1,328	1,348
Passenger air transportation. .	100	86	97	105	Air transportation services .	600	477	496	495
All other transportation-related commodities	102	104	109	121	All other transportation-related industries	702	627	608	608
Food services and drinking places	84	94	103	110	Food and beverage services	1,625	16,198	1,760	1,806
Recreation and entertainment.	60	70	77	80	Recreation and entertainment	589	603	636	649
Shopping (Retailers).	83	82	92	98	Shopping (Retailers).	584	527	532	536
					All other industries	205	201	200	204

[1] Commodities that are typically purchased by visitors from the producer: such as airline passenger fares, meals, or hotel services.

Source: U.S. Bureau of Economic Analysis, Industry Economic Accounts, Satellite Industry Accounts, Travel and Tourism. <http://www.bea.gov/bea/dn2/home/tourism.htm>

Arts, Entertainment and Recreation   771

Table 1239. **National Park System—Summary: 1990 to 2005**

[For year ending September 30, except as noted. (986 represents $986,000,000) Includes data for five areas in Puerto Rico and Virgin Islands, one area in American Samoa, and one area in Guam]

Item	1990	1995	2000	2001	2002	2003	2004	2005
Finances (mil. dol.): [1]								
Expenditures reported	986	1,445	1,833	1,985	2,161	2,315	2,371	2,451
Salaries and wages	459	633	799	840	876	934	956	984
Improvements, maintenance	160	234	299	305	311	344	332	361
Construction	109	192	215	199	296	293	354	381
Other	259	386	520	641	678	744	729	725
Funds available	1,506	2,225	3,316	3,642	3,940	4,099	4,087	4,218
Appropriations	1,053	1,325	1,881	2,241	2,257	3,298	2,388	2,425
Other [2]	453	900	1,435	1,401	1,683	1,801	1,699	1,793
Revenue from operations	79	106	234	246	245	274	264	286
Recreation visits (millions): [3]								
All areas	258.7	269.6	285.9	279.9	277.3	266.1	276.9	273.5
National parks [4]	57.7	64.8	66.1	64.1	64.5	63.4	63.8	63.5
National monuments	23.9	23.5	23.8	21.8	20.3	20.0	19.8	20.9
National historical, commemorative, archaeological [5]	57.5	56.9	72.2	66.7	70.2	66.6	77.0	74.9
National parkways	29.1	31.3	34.0	34.4	35.7	31.1	31.7	31.7
National recreation areas [4]	47.2	53.7	50.0	48.3	48.2	47.7	46.6	46.8
National seashores and lakeshores	23.3	22.5	22.5	22.2	23.3	22.6	21.3	21.7
National Capital Parks	7.5	5.5	5.4	4.6	3.8	3.5	4.7	4.3
Recreation overnight stays (millions)	17.6	16.8	15.4	15.3	14.7	14.2	13.7	13.5
In commercial lodgings	3.9	3.8	3.7	3.6	3.5	3.5	3.5	3.4
In Park Service campgrounds	7.9	7.1	5.9	5.7	5.8	5.7	5.4	5.2
In backcountry	1.7	2.2	1.9	2.0	1.9	1.8	1.7	1.7
Other	4.2	3.7	3.8	3.9	3.5	3.2	3.1	3.2
Land (1,000 acres): [6]								
Total	76,362	77,355	78,153	78,943	78,811	79,006	79,023	79,048
Parks	46,089	49,307	49,785	49,862	49,639	49,823	49,892	49,892
Recreation areas	3,344	3,353	3,388	3,388	3,390	3,391	3,391	3,391
Other	26,929	24,695	24,980	25,693	25,782	25,792	25,740	25,747
Acquisition, net	21	27	186	20	20	60	138	16

[1] Financial data are those associated with the National Park System. Certain other functions of the National Park Service (principally the activities absorbed from the former Heritage Conservation and Recreation Service in 1981) are excluded. [2] Includes funds carried over from prior years. [3] For calendar year. Includes other areas, not shown separately. [4] For 1990, combined data for North Cascades National Park and two adjacent National Recreation Areas are included in National Parks total. [5] Includes military areas. [6] Federal land only, as of Dec. 31. Federal land acreages, in addition to National Park Service administered lands, also include lands within national park system area boundaries but under the administration of other agencies. Year-to-year changes in the federal lands figures include changes in the acreages of these other lands and hence often differ from "net acquisition."

Source: U.S. National Park Service, *National Park Statistical Abstract*, annual; and unpublished data. See also <http://www2.nature.nps.gov/stats/>.

Table 1240. **State Parks and Recreation Areas by State: 2004**

[For year ending June 30 (14,180 represents 14,180,000). Data are shown as reported by state park directors. In some states, park agency has under its control forests, fish and wildlife areas, and/or other areas. In other states, agency is responsible for state parks only]

State	Acreage (1,000)	Visitors (1,000) [1]	Revenue Total ($1,000)	Percent of operating expenditures	State	Acreage (1,000)	Visitors (1,000) [1]	Revenue Total ($1,000)	Percent of operating expenditures
United States...	14,180	697,831	758,049	41.8	Missouri	201	17,318	5,114	17.7
					Montana	62	5,256	1,124	15.1
Alabama	48	2,699	16,607	100.0	Nebraska	135	10,086	11,674	70.2
Alaska	3,353	4,334	1,894	29.6	Nevada	133	(NA)	2,435	25.7
Arizona	64	2,286	10,682	54.1	New Hampshire	232	(NA)	8,948	100.0
Arkansas	53	10,455	13,548	37.7	New Jersey	399	15,945	3,757	10.7
California	1,548	77,049	101,173	34.3	New Mexico	92	(NA)	–	–
Colorado	393	11,204	19,076	65.9	New York	1,549	53,605	–	–
Connecticut	204	6,814	1,004	7.5	North Carolina	183	11,771	4,036	10.2
Delaware	24	3,471	8,515	34.1	North Dakota	17	966	1,067	36.6
Florida	724	17,381	36,766	49.1	Ohio	165	51,440	28,785	42.1
Georgia	84	11,488	29,039	51.9	Oklahoma	72	12,742	21,397	54.0
Hawaii	31	9,221	1,994	26.1	Oregon	101	44,253	16,393	39.6
Idaho	45	(NA)	4,346	31.9	Pennsylvania	291	35,095	16,040	21.3
Illinois	465	44,358	–	–	Rhode Island	9	5,471	–	–
Indiana	181	17,050	34,755	74.7	South Carolina	81	6,508	15,257	64.0
Iowa	67	14,129	3,885	29.4	South Dakota	106	7,148	8,155	61.8
Kansas	33	7,623	6,000	67.8	Tennessee	141	29,228	29,999	47.9
Kentucky	58	7,134	51,709	64.4	Texas	610	9,654	32,202	62.4
Louisiana	41	2,183	337	1.4	Utah	150	4,274	9,272	36.4
Maine	100	2,094	–	–	Vermont	69	694	6,196	91.0
Maryland	268	11,538	14,186	36.2	Virginia	65	6,543	7,827	40.3
Massachusetts	307	9,785	3,170	13.5	Washington	260	40,331	18,165	31.2
Michigan	273	20,447	35,056	75.9	West Virginia	177	7,969	19,539	60.7
Minnesota	237	8,039	9,271	32.2	Wisconsin	134	14,492	14,312	68.7
Mississippi	24	2,942	8,759	83.9	Wyoming	119	3,316	1,282	8.2

– Represents or rounds to zero.   NA Not available.   [1] Includes overnight visitors.

Source: The National Association of State Park Directors, Raleigh, NC, *2006 Annual Information Exchange*. http://www.naspd.org/

772   Arts, Entertainment, and Recreation

Table 1241. **Summary of Travel Trends: 1977 to 2001**

[(108,826 represents 108,826,000,000). Data obtained by collecting information on all trips taken by the respondent on a specific day (known as travel day), combined with longer trips taken over a 4-week period (known as travel period). For comparability with previous survey data, all data are based only on trips taken during travel day. Be aware that terminology changes from survey to survey. See source for details]

Characteristics	Unit	1977	1983	1990	1995	2001
Vehicle trips.	Millions . . .	108,826	126,874	158,927	229,745	233,040
Vehicle miles of travel (VMT)	Millions . . .	907,603	1,002,139	1,409,600	2,068,368	2,274,797
Person trips.	Millions . . .	211,778	224,385	249,562	378,930	407,262
Person miles of travel	Millions . . .	1,879,215	1,946,662	2,315,300	3,411,122	3,972,749
Average annual VMT per household [1]	Miles.	12,036	11,739	15,100	20,895	21,188
To or from work.	Miles.	3,815	3,538	4,853	6,492	5,724
Shopping.	Miles.	1,336	1,567	1,743	2,807	3,062
Other family or personal business.	Miles.	1,444	1,816	3,014	4,307	3,956
Social and recreational.	Miles.	3,286	3,534	4,060	4,764	5,186
Average annual vehicle trips per household [1]. . . .	Number. . .	1,442	1,486	1,702	2,321	2,171
To or from work.	Number. . .	423	414	448	553	479
Shopping.	Number. . .	268	297	345	501	458
Other family or personal business.	Number. . .	215	272	411	626	537
Social and recreational.	Number. . .	320	335	349	427	441
Average vehicle trip length [1]	Miles.	8.35	7.90	8.98	9.06	9.87
To or from work.	Miles.	9.02	8.55	10.97	11.80	12.08
Shopping.	Miles.	4.99	5.28	5.10	5.64	6.74
Other family or personal business.	Miles.	6.72	6.68	7.43	6.93	7.45
Social and recreational.	Miles.	10.27	10.55	11.80	11.24	11.94
Average vehicle occupancy [1]	Persons. . .	1.9	1.8	1.6	1.6	1.6
To or from work.	Persons. . .	1.3	1.3	1.1	1.1	1.1
Shopping.	Persons. . .	2.1	1.8	1.7	1.7	1.8
Other family or personal business.	Persons. . .	2.0	1.8	1.8	1.8	1.8
Social and recreational.	Persons. . .	2.4	2.1	2.1	2.0	2.0
Workers by usual mode to work	Percent . . .	100.0	100.0	100.0	100.0	100.0
Auto	Percent . . .	93.0	92.4	87.8	91.0	91.0
Public transit.	Percent . . .	4.7	5.8	5.3	5.1	5.0
Other	Percent . . .	2.3	1.8	6.9	3.9	4.0

[1] Includes other purposes not shown separately.

Source: 1995 and prior years—U.S. Federal Highway Administration, Summary of Travel Trends, 1995 National Personal Transportation Survey, December 1999; 2001—U.S. Federal Highway Administration and the U.S. Bureau of Transportation Statistics, 2001 National Household Travel Survey, January 2004 Release. See Internet site <http://www.bts.gov/programs/national_household_travel_survey/>.

Table 1242. **Travel in the United States by Selected Trip Characteristics: 2001**

[In millions (2,554 represents 2,554,000,000). Trips of 50 miles or more, one way. U.S. destinations only. Data based on a sample and subject to sampling variability]

Trip characteristics	Person trips		Person miles		Personal use vehicle trips		Personal use vehicle miles	
	Number (1,000)	Percent	Number (1,000)	Percent	Number (1,000)	Percent	Number (1,000)	Percent
Total	2,554	100.0	1,138,323	100.0	1,470,475	100.0	434,764	100.0
Principal means of transportation:								
Personal use vehicles	2,310	90.5	735,882	64.7	1,470,475	100.0	434,764	100.0
Airplane	165	6.5	367,889	32.3	(X)	(X)	(X)	(X)
Commercial airplane	159	6.2	361,717	31.8	(X)	(X)	(X)	(X)
Bus [1]	53	2.1	23,747	2.1	(X)	(X)	(X)	(X)
Intercity bus	3	0.1	1,766	0.2	(X)	(X)	(X)	(X)
Charter, tour, or school bus	46	1.8	21,020	1.9	(X)	(X)	(X)	(X)
Train.	21	0.8	9,266	0.8	(X)	(X)	(X)	(X)
Ship, boat, or ferry	(B)	(B)	(B)	(B)	(X)	(X)	(X)	(X)
Other	(B)	(B)	(B)	(B)	(X)	(X)	(X)	(X)
Round trip distance:								
100 to 300 miles.	1,688	66.1	284,586	25.0	1,086,375	73.9	179,730	41.3
300 to 499 miles.	374	14.6	143,572	12.6	207,377	14.1	79,095	18.2
500 to 999 miles	262	10.3	180,669	15.9	126,324	8.6	85,265	19.6
1,000 to 1,999 miles	126	4.9	178,630	15.7	36,180	2.5	48,308	11.1
2,000 miles or more	105	4.1	350,865	30.8	14,219	1.0	42,366	9.7
Mean (miles).	446	(X)	(X)	(X)	296	(X)	(X)	(X)
Median [2] (miles)	206	(X)	(X)	(X)	180	(X)	(X)	(X)
Main purpose of trip:								
Commuting	329	12.9	65,878	5.8	273,779	18.6	49,069	11.3
Other business.	406	15.9	242,353	21.3	268,688	18.3	82,157	18.9
Personal/leisure	1,406	55.1	667,471	58.7	708,145	48.2	235,475	54.2
Personal business.	323	12.6	130,021	11.4	162,832	11.1	48,761	11.2
Other	88	3.5	32,032	2.8	56,085	3.8	19,062	4.4
Mean travel party size:								
Household members	2.1	(X)	(X)	(X)	1.8	(X)	(X)	(X)
Nonhousehold members	1.0	(X)	(X)	(X)	–	(X)	(X)	(X)
Nights away from home:								
1 to 3 nights	808	31.7	414,219	36.4	406,999	27.7	153,688	35.4
4 to 7 nights	214	8.4	269,266	23.7	82,548	5.6	59,428	13.7
8 or more nights	76	3.0	150,368	13.2	25,793	1.8	36,216	8.3
Mean excluding none (nights).	3.3	(X)	(X)	(X)	2.9	(X)	(X)	(X)

– Represents or rounds to zero. B Base figure too small to meet statistical standards for reliability of a derived figure. X Not applicable. [1] Includes other types of buses. [2] For definition of median, see Guide to Tabular Presentation. Source: U.S. Department of Transportation, Bureau of Transportation Statistics and the Federal Highway Administration, National Household Travel Survey. <http://www.bts.gov/programs/national_household_travel_survey/>.

Arts, Entertainment and Recreation 773

Table 1243. Domestic Travel by U.S. Resident Households—Summary: 1998 to 2004

[In millions (656.3 represents 656,300,000). See headnote, Table 1244]

Type of trip	1998	1999	2000	2001	2002	2003	2004
All travel: [1]							
Household trips	656.3	640.8	637.7	645.6	637.0	643.5	663.5
Person-trips	1,108.0	1,089.5	1,100.8	1,123.1	1,127.0	1,140.0	1,163.9
All overnight travel:							
Household trips	479.4	475.5	477.5	483.7	482.7	491.2	508.4
Person-trips	800.0	804.9	822.4	839.2	855.4	871.6	893.1
Business travel:							
Household trips	195.8	192.9	184.9	179.0	166.6	163.5	168.2
Person-trips	245.4	240.9	235.1	227.6	214.7	210.5	219.0
Leisure travel: [2]							
Household trips	460.5	447.9	452.8	466.6	470.4	480.0	490.1
Person-trips	862.6	848.6	865.7	895.5	912.3	929.5	944.3

[1] Includes personal and other trips (e.g. medical, funerals, weddings), not shown separately. All domestic travel included. 95% of U.S. resident person-trips are domestic. [2] Includes visiting friends/relatives, outdoor recreation, entertainment and travel for other pleasure/personal reasons, etc.

Source: Travel Industry Association of America, Washington, DC, *TravelScope*, annual (copyright). <http://www.tia.org/home.asp>.

Table 1244. Characteristics of Domestic Overnight Leisure Trips by U.S. Resident Households: 1999 to 2004

[In millions except as indicated (331.1 represents 331,100,000). Represents household trips to destinations 50 miles or more, one-way, away from home and including one or more overnights. "Leisure" includes visiting friends/relatives, outdoor recreation, entertainment, and travel for other pleasure/personal reasons etc. Other pleasure/personal trips are trips such as for medical reasons, funerals, weddings, etc. Based on a monthly mail panel survey of 25,000 U.S. households. For details, see source]

Overnight leisure trip characteristics	Unit	1999	2000	2001	2002	2003	2004
Total overnight leisure trips	Millions. . .	331.1	337.1	349.1	354.0	360.3	375.4
Average nights per trip	Number. . .	4.2	4.2	4.2	4.2	4.1	4.1
Traveled primarily by auto, truck, RV, or rental car.	Percent . . .	74	74	74	75	74	73
Traveled primarily by air	Percent . . .	18	18	18	17	17	19
Stayed in a hotel/motel/B&B while on trip . .	Percent . . .	42	43	42	43	44	44
Household income:							
Less than $50,000	Percent . . .	(NA)	48	44	45	43	42
$50,000 or more	Percent . . .	(NA)	52	56	55	57	58

NA Not available.

Source: Travel Industry Association of America, Washington, DC, *TravelScope*, annual (copyright); <http://www.tia.org/home.asp>.

Table 1245. North America Cruise Industry in the United States: 2000 to 2004

[The North American passenger cruise industry is defined as those cruise lines that primarily market their cruises in North America. These cruise lines offer cruises with destinations throughout the globe. While most of these cruises originate in ports throughout North America, cruises also originate at ports in other continents]

Items	Unit	2000	2001	2002	2003	2004
Capacity measures:						
Number of ships.	Number. . .	163	167	176	184	192
Lower berths [1]	Number. . .	165,381	173,846	196,694	215,405	240,401
Passenger embarkations: [2]						
Global	1,000	8,000	8,400	9,220	9,830	10,850
United States	1,000	5,315	5,900	6,500	7,113	8,100
Florida.	1,000	3,723	4,019	4,413	4,676	4,724
California	1,000	705	643	600	807	1,095
New York	1,000	309	238	326	438	547
Other U.S. ports	1,000	682	1,000	1,056	1,192	1,734
Canada.	1,000	473	505	527	482	454
San Juan	1,000	373	300	298	325	450
Rest of world	1,000	1,839	1,695	1,895	1,910	1,846
Direct economic impact in the United States: [3]						
Passenger and cruise line spending [4] .	Bil. dol. . . .	10.30	10.98	11.95	12.92	14.70
Cruise lines	Bil. dol. . . .	8.07	8.14	8.84	9.49	10.70
Passenger and crew	Bil. dol. . . .	1.34	1.85	2.06	2.36	2.88
Wages & taxes paid by cruise lines .	Bil. dol. . . .	0.89	0.99	1.05	1.07	1.12

[1] Single beds. [2] Port of departure. [3] Consist of the expenditures made by the cruise lines and their crew and passengers during the course of providing or taking cruises. These included cruise expenditures for headquarters operations, food and beverages provided aboard cruise ships and businesses services such as advertising and marketing. Additionally, cruise passengers and crew purchase a variety of goods and services including clothing, shore excursions, and lodging as part of their cruise vacation or as part of a pre- or post-cruise stay. [4] Includes wages and salaries paid to U.S. employees of the cruise lines.

Source: Business Research & Economic Advisors (BREA), Exton PA. The Contribution of the North American Cruise Industry to the U.S. Economy in 2005. Prepared for the International Council of Cruise Lines, August 2006. See also <http://www.iccl.org>.

774 Arts, Entertainment, and Recreation

Table 1246. **Top States and Cities Visited by Overseas Travelers: 2000 and 2005**

[26,853 represents 26,853,000. Includes travelers for business and pleasure, international travelers in transit through the United States, and students. Excludes travel by international personnel and international businessmen employed in the United States. **States and Cities are ranked by the latest overseas travelers data**]

State	Overseas visitors [1] (1,000)		Market share (percent)		City	Overseas visitors [1] (1,000)		Market share (percent)	
	2000	2005	2000	2005		2000	2005	2000	2005
Total overseas travelers [2, 3]. .	26,853	21,679	100.0	100.0	New York City, NY.	5,714	5,810	22.0	26.8
New York	5,922	6,092	22.8	28.1	Los Angeles, CA	3,533	2,580	13.6	11.9
California.	6,364	4,791	24.5	22.1	San Francisco, CA	2,831	2,124	10.9	9.8
Florida	6,026	4,379	23.2	20.2	Miami, FL	2,935	2,081	11.3	9.6
Hawaiian Islands	2,727	2,255	10.5	10.4	Orlando, FL	3,013	2,016	11.6	9.3
Nevada.	2,364	1,821	9.1	8.4	Oahu/Honolulu, HI.	2,234	1,821	8.6	8.4
Illinois.	1,377	1,149	5.3	5.3	Las Vegas, NV	2,260	1,778	8.7	8.2
Guam.	1,325	1,127	5.1	5.2	Washington, DC	1,481	1,106	5.7	5.1
New Jersey	909	997	3.5	4.6	Chicago, IL	1,351	1,084	5.2	5.0
Texas	1,169	954	4.5	4.4	Boston, MA	1,325	802	5.1	3.7
Massachusetts.	1,429	867	5.5	4.0	Atlanta, GA	701	564	2.7	2.6
Georgia	805	650	3.1	3.0	San Diego, CA	701	499	2.7	2.3
Pennsylvania	649	629	2.5	2.9	Tampa/St. Petersburg, FL. .	519	455	2.0	2.1
Arizona.	883	564	3.4	2.6	Philadelphia, PA	390	434	1.5	2.0
Ohio.	390	369	1.5	1.7	Anaheim, CA	494	390	1.9	1.8
Washington	468	369	1.8	1.7	Houston, TX.	442	369	1.7	1.7
Michigan	494	325	1.9	1.5	Dallas/Ft. Worth, TX	494	347	1.9	1.6
Colorado.	519	303	2.0	1.4	San Jose, CA.	494	347	1.9	1.6
North Carolina	416	282	1.6	1.3	Seattle, WA	416	347	1.6	1.6
Virginia	364	282	1.4	1.3	Ft. Lauderdale, FL.	468	260	1.8	1.2
Connecticut.	260	260	1.0	1.2	Florida Keys.	286	217	1.1	1.0
Utah.	416	260	1.6	1.2	Denver, CO	286	173	1.1	0.8
Louisiana	390	108	1.5	0.5	New Orleans, LA.	364	108	1.4	0.5

[1] Excludes Canada and Mexico.   [2] A person is counted in each area visited, but only once in the total.   [3] Includes other states and cities, not shown separately.

Source: U.S. Department of Commerce; International Trade Administration; Office of Travel and Tourism Industries and Bureau of Economic Analysis (BEA); released: March 2006 <http://www.tinet.ita.doc.gov>.

Table 1247. **Impact of International Travel on States' Economies: 2004**

[Preliminary. (74,547.0 represents $74,547,000,000)]

State	Travel expenditures (mil. dol.)	Travel generated payroll (mil. dol.)	Travel generated employment (1,000)	Travel generated tax receipts (mil. dol.)	State	Travel expenditures (mil. dol.)	Travel generated payroll (mil. dol.)	Travel generated employment (1,000)	Travel generated tax receipts (mil. dol.)
U.S., total [1] . . .	74,547.0	20,444.3	883.4	11,654.6	MO	134.9	40.0	2.0	24.5
AL	(NA)	(NA)	(NA)	(NA)	MT	(NA)	(NA)	(NA)	(NA)
AK	(NA)	(NA)	(NA)	(NA)	NE	(NA)	(NA)	(NA)	(NA)
AZ	1,525.4	501.2	21.7	243.3	NV	2,596.4	948.4	42.1	372.5
AR	(NA)	(NA)	(NA)	(NA)	NH	125.4	21.5	1.1	12.0
CA	11,605.3	3,312.7	134.7	1,925.3	NJ	723.9	230.0	9.2	132.1
CO	684.5	221.9	10.0	144.1	NM	(NA)	(NA)	(NA)	(NA)
CT	219.3	44.2	1.8	34.8	NY	10,507.8	3,148.3	112.8	2,126.7
DE	(NA)	(NA)	(NA)	(NA)	NC	456.7	141.1	7.1	79.1
DC	1,641.9	386.2	13.7	238.5	ND	(NA)	(NA)	(NA)	(NA)
FL	14,446.1	4,145.4	190.6	2,229.9	OH	509.8	117.3	6.2	87.3
GA	1,249.8	493.1	17.3	275.1	OK	(NA)	(NA)	(NA)	(NA)
HI	6,505.6	1,806.0	71.4	947.4	OR	362.7	92.7	4.9	53.9
ID	(NA)	(NA)	(NA)	(NA)	PA	1,192.6	363.3	15.5	201.1
IL	1,511.1	436.9	18.8	303.5	RI	(NA)	(NA)	(NA)	(NA)
IN	217.3	57.7	3.1	33.7	SC	515.7	114.1	7.4	75.1
IA	(NA)	(NA)	(NA)	(NA)	SD	(NA)	(NA)	(NA)	(NA)
KS	(NA)	(NA)	(NA)	(NA)	TN	311.9	85.5	4.3	65.5
KY	(NA)	(NA)	(NA)	(NA)	TX	3,247.2	1,049.5	46.6	582.8
LA	425.4	93.3	5.2	56.9	UT	357.7	133.3	7.5	72.5
ME	(NA)	(NA)	(NA)	(NA)	VT	(NA)	(NA)	(NA)	(NA)
MD	341.8	106.7	4.5	68.3	VA	471.7	131.6	6.6	73.2
MA	1,432.0	398.8	14.8	245.4	WA	803.5	218.3	10.0	140.2
MI	604.3	167.5	7.2	107.3	WV	(NA)	(NA)	(NA)	(NA)
MN	396.4	153.4	6.5	121.1	WI	257.2	69.4	4.2	43.6
MS	(NA)	(NA)	(NA)	(NA)	WY	(NA)	(NA)	(NA)	(NA)

NA Data not available due to small sample size for international visitors.   [1] Total of states listed with data does not equal U.S. total.

Source: Travel Industry Association of America, Washington, DC, *Impact of Travel on State Economies*, Annual (copyright). <http://www.tia.org/index.html>.

Arts, Entertainment, and Recreation   775

Table 1248. Domestic Travel Expenditures by State: 2004

[532,355 represents $532,355,000,000. Represents U.S. spending on domestic overnight trips and day trips of 50 miles or more, one way, away from home. Excludes spending by foreign visitors and by U.S. residents in U.S. territories and abroad]

State	Total (mil. dol.)	Percent distribution	Rank	State	Total (mil. dol.)	Percent distribution	Rank	State	Total (mil. dol.)	Percent distribution	Rank
U.S., total . . .	532,355	100.0	(X)	IA	5,014	0.9	32	NC	13,253	2.5	11
				KS	4,172	0.8	37	ND	1,340	0.3	50
				KY	5,868	1.1	29	OH	13,171	2.5	12
AL	5,969	1.1	28	LA	9,539	1.8	19	OK	4,456	0.8	34
AK	1,470	0.3	48	ME	2,085	0.4	43	OR	5,835	1.1	30
AZ	9,974	1.9	16	MD	9,734	1.8	18	PA	16,175	3.0	7
AR	4,281	0.8	36	MA	10,975	2.1	15	RI	1,510	0.3	47
CA	65,700	12.3	1	MI	12,751	2.4	13	SC	7,764	1.5	24
CO	9,965	1.9	17	MN	8,494	1.6	22	SD	1,663	0.3	46
CT	7,132	1.3	27	MS	5,697	1.1	31	TN	11,164	2.1	14
DE	1,181	0.2	51	MO	9,465	1.8	20	TX	33,818	6.4	3
DC	4,776	0.9	33	MT	2,184	0.4	42	UT	4,030	0.8	38
FL	46,672	8.8	2	NE	2,982	0.6	39	VT	1,446	0.3	49
GA	15,390	2.9	9	NV	26,250	4.9	5	VA	15,041	2.8	10
HI	8,032	1.5	23	NH	2,860	0.5	40	WA	8,594	1.6	21
ID	2,404	0.5	41	NJ	15,733	3.0	8	WV	1,966	0.4	44
IL	23,010	4.3	6	NM	4,348	0.8	35	WI	7,581	1.4	25
IN	7,143	1.3	26	NY	30,458	5.7	4	WY	1,842	0.3	45

X Not applicable.

Source: Travel Industry Association of America, Washington, DC, *Impact of Travel on State Economies, 2004* (copyright); <http://www.tia.org/index.html>.

Table 1249. International Travelers and Expenditures: 1990 to 2005

[(47,880 represents $47,880,000,000). For coverage, see Table 1250. Some traveler data revised since originally issued]

Year	Payments by U.S. travelers		Receipts from international visitors		U.S. net travel and passenger receipts (mil. dol.)	U.S. travelers to international countries (1,000)	International travelers to the U.S. (1,000)
	Total[1]	Expenditures abroad	Total[1]	Travel receipts			
1990	47,880	37,349	58,305	43,007	10,425	44,623	39,363
1995	59,579	44,916	82,304	63,395	22,725	51,285	43,490
1998	76,454	56,483	91,423	71,325	14,969	55,698	46,377
1999	80,278	58,963	94,586	74,801	14,308	57,222	48,509
2000	88,979	64,705	103,087	82,400	14,108	61,327	51,238
2001	82,833	60,200	89,819	71,893	6,986	59,433	46,927
2002	78,684	58,715	83,651	66,605	4,967	58,065	43,581
2003	78,401	57,444	80,041	64,348	1,640	56,250	41,218
2004	89,336	65,635	93,398	74,547	4,062	61,808	46,084
2005 [2]	95,730	69,529	102,611	81,680	6,881	63,866	49,402

[1] Includes passenger fares not shown separately.   [2] Preliminary estimates for the receipt payment figures and U.S. travelers to international countries.

Source: U.S. Department of Commerce; International Trade Administration; Office of Travel and Tourism Industries and Bureau of Economic Analysis (BEA); released March 2006; <http://www.tinet.ita.doc.gov>.

Table 1250. International Travel: 1990 to 2005

[In thousands (44,623 represents 44,623,000). U.S. travelers cover residents of the United States, its territories and possessions. International travelers to the U.S. include travelers for business and pleasure, excludes travel by international personnel and international businessmen employed in the United States. Some traveler data revised since originally issued]

Item and area	1990	1995	2000	2001	2002	2003	2004	2005
U.S. travelers to international countries [1,2]	44,623	51,285	61,327	59,433	58,065	56,250	61,808	63,866
Canada	12,252	13,005	15,188	15,561	16,167	14,232	15,038	14,416
Mexico	16,381	19,221	19,285	18,623	18,501	17,566	19,369	20,663
Total overseas [3]	15,990	19,059	26,853	25,249	23,397	24,452	27,351	28,787
Europe	8,043	8,596	13,373	11,438	10,131	10,319	11,679	11,976
International travelers to the U.S.	39,363	43,491	51,237	46,927	43,581	41,218	46,084	49,402
Canada	17,263	14,663	14,666	13,527	13,024	12,666	13,856	14,865
Mexico	7,041	8,189	10,596	11,567	11,440	10,526	11,906	12,858
Total overseas	15,059	20,639	25,975	21,833	19,117	18,026	20,322	21,679
Europe	6,659	8,793	11,597	9,496	8,603	8,639	9,686	10,313
South America	4,360	6,616	7,554	6,316	5,689	5,003	5,802	6,198
Central America	1,328	2,449	2,941	2,531	1,815	1,522	1,645	1,820
Caribbean	1,137	1,044	1,331	1,202	1,053	998	1,095	1,135
Far East	412	509	822	771	704	656	692	696
Middle East	662	588	731	586	529	525	660	737
Oceania	365	454	702	644	483	447	502	527
Africa	137	186	295	287	241	236	241	252

[1] A person is counted in each area visited but only once in the total.   [2] 2005 U.S. outbound totals are preliminary estimates.

Source: U.S. Department of Commerce; International Trade Administration; Office of Travel and Tourism Industries and Bureau of Economic Analysis (BEA); released March 2006; <http://www.tinet.ita.doc.gov>.

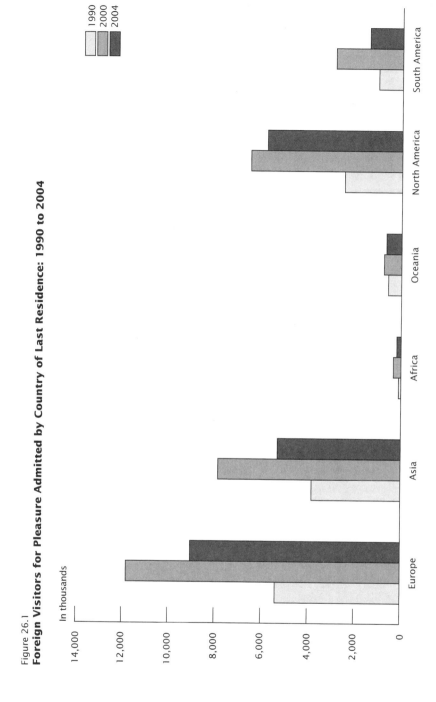

Figure 26.1
Foreign Visitors for Pleasure Admitted by Country of Last Residence: 1990 to 2004

In thousands

1990
2000
2004

Source: Chart prepared by U.S. Census Bureau. For data, see Table 1252.

Arts, Entertainment, and Recreation 777

Table 1251. **Selected U.S.-Canadian and U.S.-Mexican Border Land-Passenger Gateways: 2005**

[(30,353 represents 30,353,000)]

Item and gateway	Entering the U.S. (1,000)	Item and gateway	Entering the U.S. (1,000)
All U.S.-Canadian land gateways [1]		**All U.S.-Mexican land gateways** [1]	
Personal vehicles	30,353	Personal vehicles	91,756
Personal vehicle passengers	62,503	Personal vehicle passengers	185,967
Buses	153	Buses	270
Bus passengers	3,855	Bus passengers	3,150
Train passengers	236	Train passengers	18
Pedestrians	605	Pedestrians	45,830
Selected top 5 gateways:		**Selected top 5 gateways:**	
Personal vehicles		Personal vehicles	
Detroit, MI	6,035	San Ysidro, CA	17,208
Buffalo-Niagara Falls, NY	6,034	El Paso, TX	15,972
Blaine, WA	2,482	Brownsville, TX	7,104
Port Huron, MI	1,953	Hidalgo, TX	6,970
Calais, ME	1,174	Otay Mesa/San Ysidro, CA	6,673
Personal vehicle passengers		Personal vehicle passengers:	
Buffalo-Niagara Falls, NY	13,224	San Ysidro, CA	32,265
Detroit, MI	10,655	El Paso, TX	29,181
Blaine, WA	4,868	Brownsville, TX	14,615
Port Huron, MI	4,002	Laredo, TX	14,017
Champlain-Rouses Point, NY	2,921	Hidalgo, TX	13,989
Pedestrians:		Pedestrians:	
Buffalo-Niagara Falls, NY	370	San Ysidro, CA	8,156
Calais, ME	44	El Paso, TX	7,614
Sumas, WA	34	Nogales, AZ	6,930
International Falls, MN	24	Calexico, CA	4,481
Point Roberts, WA	22	Laredo, TX	4,356

[1] Data reflects all personal vehicles, buses, passengers, and pedestrians entering the U.S.-Canadian border, and U.S.-Mexican border, regardless of nationality. Source: U.S. Department of Transportation, Research and Innovative Technology Administration, Bureau of Transportation Statistics, special tabulations, June 2006. Based on the following primary data.

Source: U.S. Department of Homeland Security, Customs and Border Protection, Office of Field Operations, Operations Management Database (Washington, D.C. 2006) <http://www.bts.gov/programs/international/bordercrossingentrydata/>.

Table 1252. **Foreign Visitors for Pleasure Admitted by Country of Last Residence: 1990 to 2004**

[In thousands (13,418 represents 13,418,000). For years ending September 30. Represents non-U.S. citizens (also known as nonimmigrants) admitted to the country for a temporary period of time]

Country	1990	1995	2000 [1]	2004	Country	1990	1995	2000 [1]	2004
All countries [2]	13,418	17,612	30,511	22,803	United Arab Emirates	7	14	36	14
					Africa [2]	105	137	327	183
Europe [2]	5,383	7,012	11,806	9,029	Egypt	16	16	44	15
Austria	87	146	182	103	Nigeria	11	10	27	33
Belgium	95	153	254	149	South Africa	26	59	114	54
Czech Republic	(X)	12	44	24	Oceania [2]	562	478	748	649
Denmark	75	78	150	120	Australia	380	327	535	458
Finland	83	47	95	59	New Zealand [5]	153	115	170	160
France	566	738	1,113	833	North America [2]	2,463	2,240	6,501	5,793
Germany [3]	969	1,550	1,925	1,139	Canada	119	127	277	347
Greece	43	44	60	33	Mexico	1,061	893	3,972	3,779
Hungary	15	29	58	25	Caribbean [2]	963	831	1,404	1,030
Iceland	10	14	27	23	Aruba	10	19	24	20
Ireland	81	126	325	321	Bahamas, The	332	234	377	295
Italy	308	427	626	487	Barbados	34	36	57	42
Netherlands	214	308	559	387	British Virgin Islands	8	9	31	25
Norway	80	71	144	111	Cayman Islands	31	31	53	47
Poland	55	36	116	102	Dominican Republic	137	138	195	148
Portugal	30	40	86	60	Haiti	57	43	72	53
Russia	(X)	33	74	42	Jamaica	132	130	240	146
Spain	183	248	370	397	Netherlands Antilles	31	32	43	40
Sweden	230	142	321	205	Trinidad and Tobago	81	64	133	105
Switzerland	236	321	400	231	Central America [2]	320	387	792	616
United Kingdom	1,899	2,342	4,671	4,042	Costa Rica	62	91	172	115
Asia [2]	3,830	5,666	7,853	5,303	El Salvador	46	63	175	160
China [4]	187	378	656	279	Guatemala	91	99	177	139
Hong Kong	111	162	195	80	Honduras	52	37	87	73
India	75	75	253	186	Nicaragua	13	28	47	37
Indonesia	28	44	62	35	Panama	43	54	106	73
Israel	128	160	319	218	South America [2]	1,016	1,978	2,867	1,406
Japan	2,846	3,986	4,946	3,649	Argentina	136	320	515	136
Korea	120	427	606	432	Bolivia	14	16	48	20
Malaysia	27	40	64	24	Brazil	300	710	706	337
Pakistan	27	27	47	27	Chile	54	117	194	87
Philippines	76	85	163	123	Colombia	122	174	411	252
Saudi Arabia	33	45	67	11	Ecuador	57	77	122	116
Singapore	32	61	131	58	Peru	97	98	190	143
Thailand	25	59	76	37	Uruguay	16	37	66	26
Turkey	20	27	93	49	Venezuela	199	400	570	263

X Not applicable.   [1] Due to the temporary expiration of the Visa Waiver Program from May through October 2000, data for business and pleasure not available separately for 2000 and 2001.   [2] Includes other countries and countries unknown, not shown separately.   [3] Data for 1990 are for former West Germany.   [4] Includes People's Republic of China and Taiwan.   [5] Prior to fiscal year 1995, data for Niue are included in New Zealand.

Source: U.S. Dept. of Homeland Security, Office of Immigration Statistics, *2004 Yearbook of Immigration Statistics*,. See also <http://www.uscis.gov/graphics/shared/aboutus/statistics/ybpage.htm>.

Accommodation, Food Services, and Other Services

This section presents statistics relating to services other than those covered in the previous few sections (22 to 26) on domestic trade, transportation, communications, financial services, and recreation services. Data shown for services are classified by kind of business and cover sales or receipts, establishments, employees, payrolls, and other items. The principal sources of these data are from the Census Bureau and include the *2002 Economic Census* , annual surveys, and the *County Business Patterns* program. These data are supplemented by data from several sources such as the National Restaurant Association on food and drink sales (Table 1265), the American Hotel & Lodging Association on lodging (Table 1264), and Universal McCann on advertising (Table 1261).

Data on these services also appear in several other sections. For instance, labor force employment and earnings data appear in Section 12, Labor Force, Employment, and Earnings; gross domestic product of the industry (Table 649) appears in Section 13, Income, Expenditures, and Wealth; and financial data (several tables) from the quarterly *Statistics of Income Bulletin,* published by the Internal Revenue Service, appear in Section 15, Business Enterprise.

Censuses—Limited coverage of the service industries started in 1933. Beginning with the 1967 census, legislation provides for a census of each area to be conducted every 5 years (for years ending in "2" and "7"). For more information on the most current census, see the Economic Census, *Guide to Economic Census*, found at <http://www.census.gov/econ /census02/guide/index.html>. The industries covered in the censuses and surveys of business are defined in the *North American Industry Classification System* (NAICS). All Census Bureau tables in this section are utilizing the new NAICS codes, which replaced the Standard Industrial Classification (SIC) system. NAICS makes

substantial structural improvements and identifies over 350 new industries. At the same time, it causes breaks in time series far more profound than any prior revision of the previously used SIC system. For information on this system and how it affects the comparability of statistics historically, see text, Section 15, Business Enterprise, and especially the Census Web site at <http://www.census.gov/epcd /www/naics.html>.

The *Accommodation and Food Services sector* (NAICS sector 72) comprises establishments providing customers with lodging and/or preparing meals, snacks, and beverages for immediate consumption. The *Other Services (Except Public Administration) sector* (NAICS sector 81) comprises establishments with payroll engaged in providing services not specifically provided for elsewhere in the NAICS. Establishments in this sector are primarily engaged in activities such as repair and maintenance of equipment and machinery, personal and laundry services, and religious, grantmaking, civic, professional, and similar organizations. Establishments providing death care services, pet care services, photofinishing services, temporary parking services, and dating services are also included. Private households that employ workers on or about the premises in activities primarily concerned with the operation of the household are included in this sector but are not included in the scope of the census. In general, the 2002 Economic Census has three series of publications for these two sectors: 1) subject series with reports such as product lines, and establishment and firm sizes, 2) geographic reports with individual reports for each state, and 3) industry series with reports on product lines by kind of business. For information on these series, see the Census Bureau Web site at <http://www.census.gov /econ/census02>.

Current surveys—The Service Annual Survey provides annual estimates of nationwide receipts for selected personal, business, leasing and repair, amusement and entertainment, social and health, and other professional service industries in the United States. For selected social, health, and other professional service industries, separate estimates are developed for receipts of taxable firms and revenue and expenses for firms and organizations exempt from federal income taxes. Several service sectors from this survey are covered in other sections of this publication. The estimates for tax exempt firms in these industries are derived from a sample of employer firms only. Estimates obtained from annual and monthly surveys are based on sample data and are not expected to agree exactly with results that would be obtained from a complete census of all establishments. Data include estimates for sampling units not reporting.

Statistical reliability—For a discussion of statistical collection and estimation, sampling procedures, and measures of statistical reliability applicable to Census Bureau data, see Appendix III.

Table 1253. **Service-Related Industries—Establishments, Employees, and Payroll: 2002**

[In thousands (886,801,038 represents $886,801,038,000) except as indicated. Covers establishments with payroll. For statement on methodology, see Appendix III]

Kind of business	NAICS code [1]	Estab- lishments (number)	Sales or receipts ($1,000)	Annual payroll ($1,000)	Paid employees (number) [2]
Professional, scientific, and technical services	54	**771,305**	**886,801,038**	**376,090,052**	**7,243,505**
Professional, scientific, and technical services [3]	541	771,305	886,801,038	376,090,052	7,243,505
Accounting, tax preparation, bookkeeping, and payroll services	5412	112,240	84,072,026	41,271,953	1,317,281
Management, scientific, and technical consulting services	5416	116,159	105,451,814	42,824,709	738,675
Other professional, scientific, and technical services . . .	5419	66,525	41,693,231	13,779,163	508,389
Administrative and support and waste management and remediation services.	56	**350,583**	**432,577,580**	**206,439,329**	**8,741,854**
Administrative and support services [3]	561	331,921	381,268,304	194,207,071	8,410,033
Office administrative services.	5611	22,611	32,080,759	14,577,949	366,019
Business support services.	5614	34,735	43,978,782	17,617,080	769,999
Services to buildings and dwellings.	5617	156,555	75,315,804	29,133,626	1,583,580
Waste management and remediation services	562	18,662	51,309,276	12,232,258	331,821
Accommodation and food services	72	**565,590**	**449,498,718**	**127,554,483**	**10,120,951**
Accommodation	721	60,949	128,098,210	34,955,244	1,813,326
Food services and drinking places [3]	722	504,641	321,400,508	92,599,239	8,307,625
Full-service restaurants.	7221	195,659	144,649,964	46,064,140	3,904,628
Limited-service eating places.	7222	228,789	135,324,135	35,441,793	3,526,264
Special food services	7223	31,337	26,524,822	7,728,973	540,896
Other services (except public administration)	81	**537,576**	**307,049,461**	**82,954,939**	**3,475,310**
Repair and maintenance [3]	811	231,043	118,305,746	35,117,838	1,285,371
Automotive repair and maintenance	8111	166,821	75,219,140	21,592,456	871,040
Personal and household goods repair and maintenance .	8114	25,136	8,618,604	2,669,453	112,626
Personal and laundry services [3]	812	201,019	72,220,404	22,908,300	1,296,540
Personal care services	8121	99,454	20,217,426	8,179,812	535,297
Other personal services	8129	37,182	17,279,219	4,231,539	241,807
Religious, grant making, civic, professional, and similar organizations.	813	105,514	116,523,311	24,928,801	893,399

[1] North American Industry Classification System, 2002; see text, Section 15. [2] Paid employees consists of full- and part-time employees, including salaried officers and executives of corporations, who were on the payroll during the pay period including March 12. [3] Includes other kinds of business not shown separately.

Source: U.S. Census Bureau, *2002 Economic Census, Subject Series;* November 2005. See also <http://www.census.gov/econ/census02/guide/SUBSUMM.HTM>.

Table 1254. **Service-Related Industries—Establishments, Sales, Employees, and Payroll: 1997 and 2002**

[In millions of dollars (595,251 represents $595,251,000,000) except as indicated. Covers establishments with payroll. These data are preliminary and are subject to change. For statement on methodology, see Appendix III]

Kind of business	NAICS code [1]	Establishments (number) 1997	Establishments (number) 2002	Sales or receipts (mil. dol.) 1997	Sales or receipts (mil. dol.) 2002	Annual payroll (mil. dol.) 1997	Annual payroll (mil. dol.) 2002	Paid employees (1,000) [2] 1997	Paid employees (1,000) [2] 2002
Professional, scientific, and technical services	54	621,129	746,964	595,251	896,343	231,399	374,515	5,361	7,509
Professional, scientific, and technical services	541	621,129	746,964	595,251	896,343	231,399	374,515	5,361	7,509
Administrative and support, waste management, and remediation services	56	276,393	276,040	295,936	413,623	137,337	193,517	7,347	8,345
Administrative and support services	561	260,025	257,569	256,591	362,310	128,438	181,411	7,067	8,003
Waste management and remediation services	562	16,368	18,471	39,346	51,313	8,899	12,106	281	342
Accommodation and food services .	72	545,068	562,059	350,399	463,375	97,007	128,683	9,451	10,836
Accommodation	721	58,162	(S)	98,457	(S)	26,674	(S)	1,697	(S)
Food services and drinking places.	722	486,906	(S)	251,942	(S)	70,334	(S)	7,755	(S)
Other services (except public administration)	81	519,715	527,508	265,898	315,049	65,520	82,670	3,256	3,528
Repair and maintenance	811	235,466	232,949	105,154	120,365	29,875	35,459	1,276	1,367
Personal and laundry services.	812	185,484	192,333	57,879	72,893	18,577	22,591	1,217	1,311
Religious, grantmaking, civic, professional, and similar organizations.	813	98,765	102,226	102,864	121,790	17,068	24,619	763	849

S Estimates did not meet publication standards.   [1] North American Industry Classification System, 1997 see text, Section 15.   [2] Paid employees consists of full- and part-time employees, including salaried officers and executives of corporations, who were on the payroll during the pay period including March 12.

Source: U.S. Census Bureau, "2002 Economic Census, Advance Comparative Statistics for the United States," published March 2004; <http://www.census.gov/econ/census02/advance/TABLE2.HTM>.

Table 1255. **Service-Related Industries—Nonemployer Establishments and Receipts by Kind of Business: 2002 to 2004**

[2,553 represents 2,553,000. Nonemployers are businesses with no paid employees, and are subject to federal income taxes. Based on the North American Industry Classification System, 2002 (NAICS), see text, Section 15]

Kind of business	NAICS code	Establishments (1,000) 2002	Establishments (1,000) 2003	Establishments (1,000) 2004 [1]	Receipts (mil. dol.) 2002	Receipts (mil. dol.) 2003	Receipts (mil. dol.) 2004 [1]
Professional, scientific, and technical services	54	2,553	2,648	2,725	96,395	102,911	110,596
Professional, scientific, and technical services [2]	541	2,553	2,648	2,725	96,395	102,911	110,596
Accounting, tax preparation, bookkeeping, and payroll services	5412	325	337	340	6,423	6,830	7,159
Management, scientific, and technical consulting services	5416	465	432	416	18,637	19,148	20,157
Other professional, scientific, and technical services. .	5419	770	816	867	28,018	30,274	33,421
Administrative and support and waste management and remediation services	56	1,263	1,294	1,337	26,910	28,885	30,932
Administrative & support services [2].	561	1,244	1,276	1,319	25,826	27,701	29,685
Office administrative services	5611	127	151	172	1,886	2,206	2,517
Business support services	5614	176	179	183	4,460	4,779	5,102
Services to buildings and dwellings	5617	722	732	750	13,261	14,292	15,189
Waste management and remediation services	562	18	18	18	1,084	1,184	1,247
Accommodation and food services.	72	242	260	275	14,178	15,271	15,510
Accommodation	721	52	54	56	3,766	4,083	3,976
Food services & drinking places [2].	722	190	206	219	10,412	11,188	11,534
Full-service restaurants	7221	34	36	37	3,561	3,922	3,964
Limited-service eating places	7222	43	46	48	2,978	3,162	3,238
Special food services	7223	90	100	109	2,358	2,542	2,755
Other services (except public administration)	81	2,459	2,660	2,800	60,468	65,377	70,299
Repair & maintenance (R&M) [2]	811	643	670	695	22,817	24,130	25,466
Automotive R&M	8111	271	280	287	12,182	12,823	13,266
Personal & household goods R&M	8114	274	290	305	6,831	7,378	7,983
Personal & laundry services [2]	812	1,642	1,814	1,924	35,127	38,648	42,151
Personal care services	8121	666	723	776	13,582	14,914	16,354
Other personal services	8129	925	1,041	1,097	19,057	21,148	23,141
Religious, grantmaking, civic, professional, and similar organizations.	813	174	176	181	2,524	2,600	2,682

[1] Totals may be low due to late tax reporting in hurricane impacted counties/regions.   [2] Includes other kinds of business not shown separately.

Source: U.S. Census Bureau, "Nonemployer Statistics;" <http://www.census.gov/epcd/nonemployer/index.html> (accessed 11 August 2006).

Table 1256. Service-Related Industries—Establishments, Employees, and Payroll by Industry: 2003 and 2004

[7,255 represents 7,255,000. Covers establishments with payroll. Excludes most government employees, railroad employees, and self-employed persons. Kind-of-business classification based on North American Industry Classification System, 2002 (NAICS); see text, Section 15. For statement on methodology, see Appendix III]

Kind of business	NAICS code	Establishments (1,000)		Employees (1,000)[1]		Payroll (bil. dol.)	
		2003	2004	2003	2004	2003	2004
All industries, total	(X)	**7,255**	**7,388**	**113,398**	**115,075**	**4,041**	**4,254**
Professional, scientific, & technical services	54	**781**	**805**	**7,340**	**7,570**	**398**	**427**
Professional, scientific, & technical services	541	781	805	7,340	7,570	398	427
Legal services	5411	182	185	1,183	1,218	74	78
Accounting/tax prep/bookkeeping/payroll services . .	5412	114	117	1,325	1,390	43	47
Architectural, engineering & related services.	5413	106	109	1,235	1,265	71	76
Specialized design services.	5414	30	32	117	119	5	5
Computer systems design & related services	5415	102	106	1,059	1,105	72	78
Management, science & tech consulting services . .	5416	123	129	838	880	49	56
Scientific R&D services.	5417	15	16	616	641	47	51
Advertising & related services	5418	37	39	419	390	21	20
Other professional/scientific/technical services . . .	5419	71	72	547	562	16	17
Management of companies & enterprises	55	**47**	**46**	**2,879**	**2,825**	**212**	**222**
Admin/support waste mgt/remediation services	56	**349**	**359**	**8,511**	**8,708**	**219**	**236**
Administrative & support services[2]	561	330	340	8,171	8,364	206	222
Employment services	5613	41	41	3,902	4,028	97	107
Temporary help services	56132	27	27	2,188	2,326	49	55
Business support services.	5614	35	35	760	774	19	20
Travel arrangement & reservation services.	5615	26	24	284	270	10	10
Waste management & remediation services.	562	18	19	340	344	13	13
Accommodation & food services	72	**575**	**591**	**10,440**	**10,750**	**139**	**147**
Accommodation[2]	721	61	62	1,804	1,845	37	39
Traveler accommodation.	7211	51	52	1,754	1,794	36	38
RV parks & recreational camps	7212	7	7	37	38	1	1
Food services & drinking places	722	514	529	8,636	8,905	102	108
Full-service restaurants.	7221	200	206	4,091	4,263	52	55
Limited-service eating places.	7222	234	242	3,641	3,772	38	40
Special food services	7223	31	32	553	508	9	8
Drinking places (alcoholic beverages)	7224	48	48	351	361	4	4
Other services (except public administration)	81	**732**	**735**	**5,367**	**5,416**	**118**	**123**
Repair & maintenance (R&M)[2]	811	229	229	1,305	1,320	37	38
Automotive R&M.	8111	165	166	892	905	23	23
Electronic & precision equipment R&M	8112	14	14	130	127	6	6
Personal and laundry services.	812	205	208	1,310	1,333	24	25
Religious/grantmaking/prof/like organizations	813	299	297	2,753	2,763	57	59

X Not applicable. [1] Includes employees on the payroll for the pay period including March 12. [2] Includes other kinds of business not shown separately.

Source: U.S. Census Bureau, "County Business Patterns;" <http://www.census.gov/epcd/cbp/view/cbpview.html>.

Table 1257. Selected Service Industries—E-Commerce Revenue: 2003 and 2004

[51,435 represents $51,435,000,000. Includes data only for businesses with paid employees, except for accommodation and food services, which also includes businesses with and without paid employees. Except as noted, based on the Service Annual Survey.]

Kind of business	NAICS code[1]	E-commerce revenue (mil. dol.)		E-commerce as percent of total revenue,	E-commerce revenue, percent distribution,
		2003	2004	2004	2004
Selected service industries, total	(X)	**51,435**	**59,206**	**1.1**	**100.0**
Selected transportation and warehousing[2]	48-49	4,385	4,964	1.9	8.4
Information	51	13,483	15,131	1.6	25.6
Publishing industries	511	6,533	6,355	2.4	10.7
Online information services	51419	2,763	4,393	13.6	7.4
Selected finance[3]	52	6,015	6,963	2.0	11.8
Securities and commodity contracts intermediation and brokerage.	5231	5,934	6,871	2.7	11.6
Rental and leasing services	532	(S)	(S)	(S)	(S)
Selected professional, scientific, and technical services[4] . .	54	8,281	9,569	1.0	16.2
Computer systems design and related services.	5415	5,522	4,834	2.8	8.2
Selected administrative and support and waste management and remediation services[5]	56	10,168	10,385	2.3	17.5
Health care and social assistance services	62	(S)	(S)	(S)	(S)
Arts, entertainment, and recreation services.	71	(S)	(S)	(S)	(S)
Accommodation and food services[6].	72	(S)	(S)	(S)	(S)
Selected other services[7]	81	1,860	2,279	0.7	3.8

S Data do not meet publication standards because of high sampling variability or poor response quality. X Not applicable. [1] North American Industry Classification System, 1997; see text, Section 15. [2] Excludes NAICS 481 (air transportation), 482 (rail transportation), 483 (water transportation), 485 (transit and ground passenger transportation), 487 (scenic and sightseeing transportation), 488 (support activities for transportation) and 491 (postal service). [3] Excludes NAICS 521 (monetary authorities-central bank), 522 (credit intermediation and related activities), 5232 (securities and commodity exchanges), 52391 (miscellaneous intermediation), 52399 (all other financial investment activities), 524 (insurance carriers and related activities) and 525 (funds and trusts). [4] Excludes NAICS 54112 (offices of notaries) and 54132 (landscape architectural services). [5] Excludes NAICS 56173 (landscaping services). [6] Based on Annual Retail Trade Survey. [7] Excludes NAICS 81311 (religious organizations), 81393 (labor and similar organizations), 81394 (political organizations) and 814 (private households).

Source: U.S. Census Bureau, 2004 Service Annual Survey, "E-Stats"; release 25 May 2006 <http://www.census.gov/eos/www /2004tables.html>

782 Accommodation, Food Services, and Other Services

Table 1258. Selected Service-Related Industries—Establishments, Employees, and Annual Payroll by State: 2004

[426,713 represents $426,713,000,000. Covers establishments with payroll. Excludes most government employees, railroad employees, and self-employed persons. Kind-of-business classification based on North American Industry Classification System, 2002 (NAICS); see text, Section 15. For statement on methodology, see Appendix III]

State	Professional, scientific, & technical services (NAICS 54)			Admin./support waste mgt./remediation services (NAICS 56)			Accommodation and food services (NAICS 72)		
	Establishments	Employees [1]	Annual payroll (mil. dol.)	Establishments	Employees [1]	Annual payroll (mil. dol.)	Establishments	Employees [2]	Annual payroll (mil. dol.)
United States. .	804,569	7,569,981	426,713	358,902	8,708,052	235,542	591,022	10,749,811	147,178
Alabama.	9,036	91,498	4,470	3,939	107,523	2,352	7,292	141,442	1,491
Alaska.	1,769	11,867	616	944	12,877	516	1,944	23,382	473
Arizona.	14,672	116,458	5,716	7,234	194,121	5,184	10,412	222,833	2,962
Arkansas	5,321	34,550	1,368	2,357	48,566	910	4,765	82,711	828
California	104,260	1,239,251	70,228	40,132	981,640	28,448	69,774	1,240,070	18,669
Colorado.	20,749	146,891	8,653	7,476	171,198	5,004	11,393	213,648	2,945
Connecticut.	10,250	98,504	6,454	5,368	105,249	3,073	7,414	124,603	2,285
Delaware	2,451	26,500	1,815	1,249	26,200	631	1,670	28,794	420
District of Columbia .	4,278	86,216	8,080	919	29,051	950	1,790	46,570	1,064
Florida	62,597	414,121	20,069	29,653	1,157,253	30,802	32,285	699,500	9,566
Georgia	25,359	200,213	10,873	10,874	298,726	7,940	16,592	329,704	4,126
Hawaii	3,215	23,738	1,087	1,706	36,958	876	3,330	95,337	2,028
Idaho	3,635	31,256	1,242	1,852	40,631	847	3,170	49,916	549
Illinois	37,837	343,894	21,160	15,383	415,654	10,769	25,170	438,895	5,904
Indiana.	12,524	103,265	4,654	6,757	149,017	3,821	12,237	243,887	2,849
Iowa	6,058	41,763	1,677	3,301	59,810	1,283	6,711	107,271	1,091
Kansas.	7,025	60,378	2,531	3,301	60,729	1,544	5,681	98,511	1,047
Kentucky	7,882	59,446	2,260	3,627	72,783	1,562	6,888	143,457	1,613
Louisiana	11,055	81,969	3,316	4,389	104,943	2,351	7,901	177,247	2,191
Maine.	3,438	22,540	975	1,833	25,170	669	3,833	44,769	693
Maryland	18,717	215,303	12,722	7,641	157,969	4,624	9,875	184,041	2,574
Massachusetts.	21,952	236,527	17,984	8,975	180,387	6,024	15,393	245,121	3,978
Michigan.	22,393	294,303	18,042	11,748	317,073	9,359	19,222	335,036	3,775
Minnesota.	16,150	124,194	6,833	6,909	136,635	3,862	10,742	207,157	2,650
Mississippi	4,610	31,651	1,221	2,162	43,179	856	4,591	117,820	1,622
Missouri	13,323	130,591	6,266	6,998	144,410	3,393	11,610	229,914	2,754
Montana.	3,155	16,737	578	1,426	12,123	238	3,343	42,712	457
Nebraska	4,023	40,338	1,773	2,420	57,991	1,454	4,097	66,798	680
Nevada	7,003	53,874	2,687	3,705	86,167	2,487	4,677	280,229	7,094
New Hampshire	4,008	28,418	1,488	1,954	39,686	1,160	3,319	52,975	770
New Jersey.	31,376	293,046	18,556	13,126	294,417	8,394	18,500	270,112	4,781
New Mexico	4,583	34,186	1,571	1,802	32,813	818	3,853	76,578	912
New York	57,075	564,633	36,745	23,214	476,156	15,608	41,383	542,309	9,365
North Carolina	20,319	170,712	8,804	10,400	222,661	5,282	16,601	307,230	3,698
North Dakota.	1,342	11,514	400	818	10,589	195	1,791	27,588	281
Ohio	25,497	237,590	11,772	13,476	318,081	7,711	23,148	426,820	4,673
Oklahoma.	8,731	60,972	2,528	3,842	93,656	2,285	6,555	117,314	1,215
Oregon.	10,650	72,597	3,446	4,896	84,998	2,062	9,329	135,163	1,828
Pennsylvania.	29,279	308,253	17,757	13,822	290,143	7,364	25,774	403,150	4,778
Rhode Island.	3,109	23,564	1,082	1,658	21,556	552	2,865	41,425	597
South Carolina. . . .	8,862	70,666	3,267	5,080	121,168	2,699	8,607	166,575	2,022
South Dakota	1,632	10,447	318	870	9,002	184	2,203	34,028	362
Tennessee	10,950	103,039	4,961	5,977	169,390	4,165	10,571	215,426	2,580
Texas.	54,623	515,243	29,851	22,904	688,558	18,469	38,710	773,538	9,690
Utah	6,996	64,593	2,521	3,305	81,057	2,018	4,344	84,816	946
Vermont	2,076	12,481	514	938	6,944	181	1,975	28,518	387
Virginia.	24,900	341,324	22,020	9,723	231,750	6,530	14,224	280,719	3,719
Washington.	17,791	143,231	8,413	8,124	124,986	4,460	14,551	206,951	2,996
West Virginia.	2,991	23,527	797	1,481	28,357	576	3,452	58,464	633
Wisconsin.	11,374	94,498	4,285	6,405	121,464	2,860	13,722	213,765	2,256
Wyoming	1,668	7,605	269	809	6,587	141	1,768	24,972	313

[1] Includes employees on the payroll for the pay period including March 12.

Source: U.S. Census Bureau, "County Business Patterns;" <http://www.census.gov/epcd/cbp/view/cbpview.html>.

U.S. Census Bureau, Statistical Abstract of the United States: 2007

Table 1259. Professional, Scientific, and Technical Services—Estimated Revenue for Taxable Employer Firms: 2000 to 2004

[In millions of dollars (803,602 represents $803,602,000,000). Estimates are based on data from the 2004 Service Annual Survey (SAS). Estimates for prior years have been revised to reflect historical corrections to individual responses. Estimates have been adjusted using the results of the 2002 Economic Census. Based on North American Industry Classification System, 1997 (NAICS).]

Kind of business	NAICS code	Taxable employer firms					Percent change	
		2000	2001	2002	2003	2004	2002–2003	2003–2004
Professional, scientific, and technical services (except notaries and landscape architectual services)	**54**	**803,602**	**838,402**	**846,054**	**879,763**	**942,784**	**4.0**	**7.2**
Legal services (except notaries)	5411	160,620	171,598	180,042	199,915	209,475	11.0	4.8
Offices of lawyers	54111	152,834	162,958	170,808	187,819	197,385	10.0	5.1
Other legal services	54119	7,785	8,640	9,234	12,096	12,090	31.0	−0.1
Accounting, tax preparation, bookkeeping, and payroll services	5412	79,361	82,845	84,072	87,791	92,884	4.4	5.8
Offices of certified public accountants	541211	45,773	49,635	48,498	47,835	50,679	−1.4	5.9
Tax preparation services	541213	3,347	3,765	4,129	4,468	4,944	8.2	10.6
Payroll services	541214	21,394	20,149	21,418	24,366	25,359	13.8	4.1
Other accounting services	541219	8,847	9,296	10,028	11,122	11,902	10.9	7.0
Architectural, engineering, & related services (except landscape architectural services)	5413	150,269	157,489	158,265	160,915	180,074	1.7	11.9
Architectural services.	54131	25,022	26,719	25,240	26,851	28,609	6.4	6.5
Engineering services	54133	111,929	115,837	116,887	117,509	132,814	0.5	13.0
Testing laboratories	54138	7,128	7,865	8,771	8,849	9,908	0.9	12.0
Other related services [1]	5413x	6,191	7,067	7,367	7,706	8,742	4.6	13.4
Specialized design services	5414	17,889	17,775	17,075	18,090	19,617	5.9	8.4
Interior design services	54141	6,798	6,897	7,018	7,497	8,061	6.8	7.5
All other design services [2]	5414x	11,091	10,878	10,057	10,593	11,556	5.3	9.1
Computer systems design and services	5415	186,401	183,878	173,414	171,394	173,171	−1.2	1.0
Custom computer programming services	541511	70,004	65,578	60,126	58,140	58,303	−3.3	0.3
Computer systems design services	541512	82,763	80,787	78,336	76,992	76,688	−1.7	−0.4
Computer facilities management services . . .	541513	21,816	25,435	22,279	22,518	23,422	1.1	4.0
Other computer-related services	541519	11,819	12,078	12,674	13,743	14,758	8.4	7.4
Management, scientific, and technical consulting services	5416	90,510	99,950	105,912	109,313	122,317	3.2	11.9
Management consulting services	54161	78,250	86,023	90,915	92,129	102,424	1.3	11.2
Environmental consulting services	54162	5,578	6,213	6,933	7,902	8,749	14.0	10.7
Other scientific and technical consulting services	54169	6,682	7,714	8,065	9,282	11,145	15.1	20.1
Scientific research and development services . .	5417	35,587	41,569	45,983	48,142	54,272	4.7	12.7
Research and development in physical, engineering, and life sciences	54171	34,029	39,870	44,089	46,104	51,994	4.6	12.8
Research and development in social sciences and humanities.	54172	1,558	1,698	1,894	2,038	2,278	7.6	11.8
Advertising and related services	5418	59,680	58,634	56,681	58,629	63,583	3.4	8.4
Advertising agencies	54181	21,584	21,268	21,104	22,396	24,551	6.1	9.6
Public relations agencies	54182	6,501	6,156	6,205	6,305	6,954	1.6	10.3
Display advertising	54185	4,752	4,509	4,617	4,925	5,440	6.7	10.5
Direct mail advertising	54186	10,351	10,739	10,545	10,648	11,570	1.0	8.7
All other advertising [3]	5418x	16,491	15,963	14,211	14,355	15,069	1.0	5.0
Other professional, scientific, and technical services (except veterinary services)	5419	23,286	24,664	24,610	25,574	27,391	3.9	7.1
Marketing research and public opinion polling	54191	11,683	11,412	10,890	11,118	11,851	2.1	6.6
Photographic services	54192	6,613	6,761	6,538	6,758	6,984	3.4	3.3
Photography studios, portrait	541921	4,642	4,773	4,752	4,879	5,031	2.7	3.1
Commercial photography	541922	1,971	1,987	1,786	1,880	1,953	5.2	3.9
Translation and interpretation services	54193	810	850	876	968	1,093	10.4	12.9
All other professional, scientific, and technical services	54199	4,180	5,643	6,305	6,730	7,463	6.7	10.9

[1] Includes NAICS 54134 (drafting services), NAICS 54135 (building inspection services), NAICS 54136 (geophysical surveying and mapping services), and NAICS 54137 (surveying and mapping (except geophysical) services).   [2] Includes NAICS 54142 (industrial design services), NAICS 54143 (graphic design services), and NAICS 54149 (other specialized design services).   [3] Includes NAICS 54183 (media buying agencies), NAICS 54184 (media representatives), NAICS 54187 (advertising material distribution services), and NAICS 54189 (other services related to advertising).

Source: U.S. Census Bureau, "Service Annual Survey 2004"; issued April 2006; <http://www.census.gov/prod/2006pubs/sas-04.pdf>.

Table 1260. Computer Systems Design and Related Services—Estimated Revenue for Employer Firms: 2004

[In millions of dollars (173,171 represents $173,171,000,000). Estimates are based on data from the 2004 Service Annual Survey and administrative data. Estimates have been adjusted using the results of the 2002 Economic Census. Based on North American Industry Classification System, 1997 (NAICS)]

Kind of business	Amount	Kind of business	Amount
Computer systems design and related services (NAICS 5415), total [1]	**173,171**	Information technology infrastructure (computer) and network management services	2,616
		Information technology technical support services.	5,672
Information technology design and development, total	68,772	Software publishing	2,934
Custom application design and development. .	28,119	Information technology-related training services .	663
Computer systems design, development, and integration services.	32,959	Other services revenue	2,928
Network design and development services . . .	7,694	**Computer systems design services (NAICS 541512), total**	**76,688**
Information technology infrastructure (computer) and network management services	27,769	Information technology design and development, total	37,946
Information technology technical support services.	21,309	Custom application design and development. .	6,021
Information technology consulting services.	16,328	Computer systems design, development, and integration services.	25,873
Software publishing	7,479	Network design and development services . . .	6,052
Data management services.	2,760	Information technology infrastructure (computer) and network management services	5,860
Information technology related training services .	2,003	Information technology technical support services.	10,911
Internet access services	544	Information technology consulting services.	5,129
Web site hosting services	(S)	Software publishing	2,812
Application service provisioning	2,333	Data storage services	343
Resale of computer hardware and software	7,962	Data management services.	1,313
Other services revenue	8,289	Information technology-related training services .	636
Custom computer programming services (NAICS 541511), total	**58,303**	Internet access services	200
		Web site hosting services	728
Information technology design and development, total	27,138	Application service provisioning	956
Custom application design and development. .	20,268	Business process management services	2,166
Computer systems design, development, and integration services.	5,943	Resale of computer hardware and software	3,977
Network design and development services . . .	(S)	Other services revenue	3,680

S Data do not meet publication standards.   [1] Includes other kinds of business not shown separately.

Source: U.S. Census Bureau, "Service Annual Survey 2004; issued April 2006;" <http://www.census.gov/econ/www/servmenu.html>.

Table 1261. Advertising—Estimated Expenditures by Medium: 1990 to 2005

[In millions of dollars (129,968 represents $129,968,000,000). See source for definitions of types of advertising]

Medium	1990	1995	1999	2000	2001	2002	2003	2004	2005 [1]
Total	**129,968**	**165,147**	**222,308**	**247,472**	**231,287**	**236,875**	**245,477**	**263,766**	**276,009**
National	73,638	96,933	132,170	151,664	141,797	145,429	152,482	167,096	177,147
Local	56,330	68,214	90,138	95,808	89,490	91,446	92,995	96,670	98,862
Newspapers.	32,281	36,317	46,648	49,050	44,255	44,031	44,843	46,614	47,898
National.	3,867	3,996	6,358	7,229	6,615	6,806	7,357	7,629	7,743
Local.	28,414	32,321	40,290	41,821	37,640	37,225	37,486	38,985	40,155
Magazines.	6,803	8,580	11,433	12,370	11,095	10,995	11,435	12,247	12,859
Broadcast TV.	26,616	32,720	40,011	44,802	38,881	42,068	41,932	46,264	45,261
Four TV networks	9,863	11,600	13,961	15,888	14,300	15,000	15,030	16,713	16,880
Syndication	1,109	2,016	2,870	3,108	3,102	3,034	3,434	3,674	3,792
Spot (national)	7,788	9,119	10,500	12,264	9,223	10,920	9,948	11,370	10,517
Spot (local).	7,856	9,985	12,680	13,542	12,256	13,114	13,520	14,507	14,072
Cable TV.	2,631	6,166	12,570	15,455	15,736	16,297	18,814	21,527	24,501
Cable TV networks	2,000	4,500	9,405	11,765	11,777	12,071	13,954	16,424	18,888
Spot (local).	631	1,666	3,165	3,690	3,959	4,226	4,860	5,103	5,613
Radio	8,726	11,338	17,215	19,295	17,861	18,877	19,100	19,581	19,950
Network.	482	480	684	780	711	775	798	836	848
Spot (national)	1,635	1,959	3,275	3,668	2,956	3,340	3,540	3,540	3,593
Spot (local).	6,609	8,899	13,256	14,847	14,194	14,762	14,762	15,205	15,509
Yellow Pages	8,926	10,236	12,652	13,228	13,592	13,776	13,896	14,002	14,272
National.	1,132	1,410	1,986	2,093	2,087	2,087	2,114	2,110	2,142
Local.	7,794	8,826	10,666	11,135	11,505	11,689	11,782	11,892	12,130
Direct mail.	23,370	32,866	41,403	44,591	44,725	46,067	48,370	52,191	56,627
Business papers.	2,875	3,559	4,274	4,915	4,468	3,976	4,004	4,072	4,174
Out-of-home [2]	1,084	1,263	1,725	5,176	5,134	5,175	5,443	5,770	6,149
National.	640	701	925	2,068	2,051	2,061	2,298	2,530	2,682
Local.	444	562	800	3,108	3,083	3,114	3,145	3,240	3,467
Internet.	(NA)	(NA)	2,832	6,507	5,645	4,883	5,650	6,853	7,881
Miscellaneous [3]	16,656	22,102	31,545	32,083	29,895	30,730	31,990	34,645	36,437
National.	12,074	16,147	22,264	24,418	23,042	23,414	24,550	26,907	28,521
Local.	4,582	5,955	9,281	7,665	6,853	7,316	7,440	7,738	7,916

NA Not available.   [1] Preliminary data.   [2] Prior to 2000, represents only "outdoor" billboards. Beginning 2000, includes other forms of outdoor advertising (i.e. transportation vehicles, bus shelters, telephone kiosks, etc.) previously covered under "Miscellaneous."   [3] Beginning 2000, part of miscellaneous now included under Out-of-home advertising. See footnote 2.

Source: Universal McCann, New York, N.Y. (copyright). See also <http://www.universalmccann.com>.

Accommodation, Food Services, and Other Services   785

Table 1262. **Administrative and Support and Waste Management and Remediation Services—Estimated Revenue for Employer Firms: 2000 to 2004**

[In millions of dollars (396,254 represents $396,254,000,000), except percent. Except as indicated, estimates adjusted to the results of the 2002 Economic Census. Based on the Service Annual Survey; see Appendix III]

Kind of business	NAICS code [1]	2000	2003	2004	Percent change, 2003–2004
Administrative & support waste and management and remediation services	56	**396,254**	**414,606**	**443,507**	**7.0**
Administrative & support services	561	345,056	360,050	384,865	6.9
Office administrative services	56111	26,288	34,556	38,014	10.0
Facilities support services.	56121	13,211	12,158	12,520	3.0
Employment services [2]	5613	144,241	133,832	145,717	8.9
Temporary help services	56132	79,622	69,910	77,660	11.1
Employee leasing services	56133	59,635	58,049	61,544	6.0
Business support services [2]	5614	41,202	46,110	48,162	4.5
Telephone call centers	56142	14,805	13,274	13,843	4.3
Business service centers	56143	8,257	8,335	8,469	1.6
Travel arrangement & reservation services	5615	26,118	26,593	28,199	6.0
Travel agencies.	56151	11,639	9,759	10,101	3.5
Other travel arrangement & reservation services	56159	10,916	13,623	14,584	7.1
Investigation and security services [2]	5616	27,594	32,325	33,723	4.3
Investigation, guard, & armored car services	56161	17,581	20,920	21,754	4.0
Security systems services	56162	10,013	11,405	11,969	4.9
Services to buildings & dwellings [2]	5617	35,548	43,317	45,214	4.4
Janitorial services	56172	24,707	29,440	30,428	3.4
Other support services.	5619	30,855	31,159	33,316	6.9
Waste management & remediation services	562	51,198	54,556	58,642	7.5
Waste collection	5621	28,820	30,272	32,430	7.1
Waste treatment & disposal [3]	5622	11,026	11,174	11,398	2.0
Remediation & other waste management services	5629	11,353	13,110	14,815	13.0

[1] North American Industry Classification System, 1997; see text, Section 15.   [2] Includes other kinds of business not shown separately.   [3] Estimates have not been adjusted to the results of the 2002 Economic Census.

Source: U.S. Census Bureau, "Service Annual Survey 2004;" issued April 2006; <http://www.census.gov/econ/www/servmenu.html>

Table 1263. **Estimated Accommodation and Food Services Sales by Kinds of Business: 1995 to 2004**

[In millions of dollars (322,818 represents $322,818,000,000). Estimates are based on data from the Annual Retail Trade Survey and administrative records and have been adjusted to the results of the 2002 Economic Census]

Kind of business	NAICS code	1995	1999	2000	2001	2002	2003	2004
Accommodation and food services, total . .	72	**322,818**	**407,870**	**443,642**	**451,300**	**463,678**	**484,174**	**517,495**
Accommodation [1]	721	89,193	122,857	138,181	133,448	131,864	134,481	145,055
Traveler accommodation.	7211	85,526	118,495	133,582	128,591	127,050	129,610	140,202
RV parks and recreational camps	7212	2,749	3,332	3,608	3,838	3,799	3,884	3,867
Rooming and boarding houses.	7213	918	1,030	991	1,019	1,015	987	986
Food services and drinking places [1]	722	233,625	285,013	305,461	317,852	331,814	349,693	372,440
Full service restaurants.	7221	99,430	125,706	134,204	140,682	148,211	155,085	164,074
Limited service eating places	7222	103,143	119,991	127,879	132,924	138,302	147,087	158,898
Drinking places	7224	12,515	14,610	15,415	15,769	16,417	17,580	18,229

[1] Includes other kinds of business not shown separately.

Source: U.S. Census Bureau, "Estimated Accommodation and Food Service Sales by Kinds of Business: 1992 through 2004;" <http://www.census.gov/svsd/retlann/view/table10.txt>; (accessed 14 August 2006).

Table 1264. Lodging Industry Summary: 1990 to 2004

Year	Average occu-pancy rate (percent)	Average room rate (dol.)	Room size of property	2004 Estab-lish-ments	2004 Rooms (mil.)	Item	2004 Busi-ness traveler	2004 Leisure traveler
1990	63.3	57.96	Total	47,598	4.4	Typical night:		
1995	65.5	66.65				Made reservations		
1999	63.2	81.33	Percent:			(percent)	90	84
2000	63.7	85.89	Under 75 rooms . . .	57.7	26.4	Amount paid	$96.00	$89.00
2001	60.3	88.27	75–149 rooms. . . .	30.1	34.5	Length of stay (percent):		
2002	59.1	83.54	150–299 rooms. . . .	8.9	19.2	One night	39	45
2003	61.6	82.52	300–500 rooms. . . .	2.2	9.0	Two nights	24	28
2004	61.3	86.24	Over 500 rooms . . .	1.1	10.8	Three or more	37	27

Source: American Hotel & Lodging Association, Washington, DC *Lodging Industry Profile*, annual (copyright); <http://www.ahla.com>.

Table 1265. Commercial and Noncommercial Groups—Food and Drink Establishments and Sales: 1990 to 2006

[(238,149 represents $238,149,000,000). Excludes military. Data refer to sales to consumers of food and alcoholic beverages. Sales are estimated. For details, see source]

Type of group	Estab-lish-ments, 2003	Sales (mil. dol.) 1990	1995	2000	2002	2003	2004	2005	2006 [1]
Total	898,746	238,149	294,631	377,652	416,106	434,590	461,476	484,366	509,222
Commercial restaurant services [2, 3]	698,527	211,606	265,910	345,345	379,329	396,433	421,883	443,734	467,607
Eating places [2]	437,882	155,552	198,293	259,743	279,754	292,769	312,060	327,868	345,159
Full-service restaurants	196,461	77,811	96,396	133,834	141,874	148,258	157,005	164,855	173,428
Limited-service restaurants [4, 5]	189,918	[5]69,798	[5]92,901	107,147	115,076	120,484	129,400	135,611	142,392
Snack and nonalcoholic beverage bars [5]	37,189	([5])	([5])	12,867	13,293	14,363	15,716	16,996	18,419
Bars and taverns [6]	48,856	9,533	9,948	12,412	13,414	13,950	14,564	15,132	15,737
Managed services [2]	20,693	14,149	18,186	24,841	26,744	27,964	(NA)	31,942	34,008
Manufacturing and industrial plants .	(NA)	3,856	4,814	6,223	6,118	6,063	(NA)	6,570	6,846
Colleges and universities.	(NA)	2,788	3,989	5,879	7,033	7,776	(NA)	9,207	9,907
Lodging places [2]	14,619	13,568	15,561	19,438	20,829	21,344	(NA)	23,723	24,998
Retail hosts [2, 7]	133,453	9,513	12,589	14,869	18,957	20,297	(NA)	23,527	25,285
Department store restaurants	4,115	876	1,038	903	519	477	(NA)	(NA)	(NA)
Grocery store restaurants [7]	61,318	5,432	6,624	7,116	10,358	11,035	(NA)	(NA)	(NA)
Gasoline service stations.	52,413	1,718	2,520	4,693	5,104	5,441	(NA)	(NA)	(NA)
Recreation and sports . . . . [2]	26,874	2,871	3,866	4,772	9,938	10,169	(NA)	10,882	11,364
Noncommercial restaurant services [2] . . .	200,219	26,543	28,722	32,307	36,777	38,157	39,592	40,632	41,616
Employee restaurant services	3,653	1,864	1,364	986	742	665	(NA)	541	516
Industrial, commercial organizations.	1,241	1,603	1,129	717	475	398	(NA)	(NA)	(NA)
Educational restaurant services	104,063	7,671	9,059	9,977	10,328	10,484	(NA)	10,548	10,444
Elementary and secondary schools . .	99,890	3,700	4,533	5,039	5,111	5,104	(NA)	5,103	5,059
Hospitals . . . . [2].	5,741	8,968	9,219	9,982	10,596	11,213	(NA)	12,041	12,403
Miscellaneous [2].	49,970	2,892	3,673	4,898	8,278	8,700	(NA)	(NA)	(NA)
Clubs.	26,689	1,993	2,278	3,164	6,428	6,751	(NA)	(NA)	(NA)

NA Not available. [1] Projection. [2] Includes other types of groups, not shown separately. [3] Data for establishments with payroll. [4] Fast-food restaurants. [5] Snack and nonalcoholic beverage bars included in limited service restaurants, prior to 1997. [6] For establishments serving food. [7] Includes a portion of delicatessen sales in grocery stores.
Source: National Restaurant Association, Washington, DC, *Restaurant Numbers: 25 Year History, 1970–1995*, 1998; *Restaurant Industry in Review*, annual; and *National Restaurant Association Restaurant Industry Forecast*, December 2005 (copyright).

Table 1266. National Nonprofit Associations—Number by Type: 1980 to 2006

[Data compiled during last few months of year previous to year shown and the beginning months of year shown]

Type	1980	1990	1995	1999	2000	2001	2002	2003	2004	2005	2006 [1]
Total	14,726	22,289	22,663	22,474	21,840	22,449	22,141	22,464	22,659	22,720	23,772
Trade, business, commercial . .	3,118	3,918	3,757	3,815	3,880	3,922	3,883	3,818	3,812	3,789	3,942
Agriculture and environment. .	677	940	1,122	1,113	1,103	1,120	1,125	1,137	1,140	1,170	1,286
Legal, governmental, public admin., military . . .	529	792	776	778	790	807	814	832	839	868	887
Scientific, engineering, tech . .	1,039	1,417	1,355	1,332	1,302	1,317	1,309	1,326	1,354	1,354	1,396
Educational.	[2]2,376	1,291	1,290	1,321	1,297	1,346	1,307	1,301	1,313	1,318	1,365
Cultural	([2])	1,886	1,918	1,876	1,786	1,812	1,766	1,749	1,735	1,733	1,782
Social welfare	994	1,705	1,885	1,913	1,829	1,925	1,917	1,941	1,972	2,072	2,218
Health, medical	1,413	2,227	2,348	2,481	2,495	2,574	2,601	2,808	2,921	2,982	3,089
Public affairs	1,068	2,249	2,148	1,877	1,776	1,857	1,808	1,836	1,881	1,854	1,938
Fraternal, nationality, ethnic .	435	573	552	552	525	537	529	557	547	550	567
Religious	797	1,172	1,230	1,151	1,123	1,160	1,154	1,155	1,157	1,147	1,162
Veteran, hereditary, patriotic. .	208	462	686	877	835	834	785	802	803	774	790
Hobby, avocational	910	1,475	1,549	1,463	1,330	1,408	1,380	1,435	1,449	1,433	1,525
Athletic sports	504	840	838	782	717	762	730	760	755	762	863
Labor unions	235	253	245	235	232	233	218	211	213	208	209
Chambers of Commerce [3] . . .	105	168	168	146	143	142	141	139	136	135	137
Greek and non-Greek letter societies	318	340	336	313	296	312	301	309	305	303	302
Fan clubs	(NA)	581	460	449	381	381	373	348	327	314	314

NA Not available. [1] The increase in the number of associations comes from the increase in newly discovered and established associations. [2] Data for cultural associations included with educational associations. [3] National and binational. Includes trade and tourism organizations.
Source: Gale Group, Farmington Hills, MI. Compiled from *Encyclopedia of Associations*, annual (copyright).

Accommodation, Food Services, and Other Services   787

[In millions of dollars (299,735 represents $299,735,000,000), except percent. Except where indicated, results have been adjusted to the results of the 2002 Economic Census. Based on the Service Annual Survey. See text, this section and Appendix III]

Kind of business	NAICS code [1]	2000	2003	2004	Percent change, 2003– 2004
Other services [2]	81	299,735	313,413	332,170	6.0
Repair & maintenance	811	112,994	123,079	127,824	3.9
Automotive repair & maintenance	8111	73,219	78,565	81,116	3.2
Automotive mechanical and electrical repair and maintenance	81111	37,879	40,445	42,154	4.2
Automotive body, paint, interior, and glass repair	81112	25,766	27,179	27,693	1.9
Other automotive repair and maintenance	81119	9,574	10,942	11,269	3.0
Electronic and precision equipment repair & maintenance	8112	14,420	15,103	16,383	8.5
Commercial equipment (exc. auto. elec.) repair & maintenance	8113	15,232	18,927	19,380	2.4
Personal and household goods repair & maintenance	8114	10,123	10,484	10,945	4.4
Home and garden equipment and appliance repair and maintenance	81141	3,865	4,209	4,285	1.8
Reupholstery and furniture repair	81142	1,229	1,271	1,248	-1.8
Footwear and leather goods repair	81143	190	181	189	4.4
Other personal and household goods repair and maintenance	81149	4,838	4,824	5,223	8.3
Personal & laundry services	812	67,140	72,053	74,480	3.4
Personal care services	8121	18,263	21,094	23,177	9.9
Hair, nail, & skin care services	81211	15,553	17,082	18,932	10.8
Barber shops	812111	479	499	522	4.6
Beauty salons	812112	14,445	15,449	17,191	11.3
Nail salons	812113	629	1,134	1,219	7.5
Other personal care services	81219	2,711	4,012	4,246	5.8
Death care services	8122	13,707	15,334	15,080	-1.7
Funeral homes and funeral services	81221	10,279	12,016	11,705	-2.6
Cemeteries and crematories	81222	3,428	3,318	3,375	1.7
Drycleaning & laundry services	8123	19,950	19,545	20,039	2.5
Coin-operated laundries & drycleaners	81231	3,359	3,238	3,235	-0.1
Drycleaning and laundry services, (excluding coin-op)	81232	7,846	7,282	7,581	4.1
Linen & uniform supply	81233	8,745	9,025	9,224	2.2
Other personal services	8129	15,219	16,081	16,184	0.6
Photofinishing	81292	3,809	3,678	3,173	-13.7
Parking lots and garages	81293	6,390	7,041	7,121	1.1
All other personal services	81299	5,021	5,362	5,890	9.8
Religious/grantmaking/prof./like organizations (except religious, labor, and political organizations)	813	119,601	118,281	129,866	9.8
Grantmaking and giving services	8132	57,465	47,132	56,408	19.7
Social advocacy organizations	8133	10,582	13,359	13,424	0.5
Civic & social organizations	8134	10,381	12,084	12,646	4.7
Business, professional, and other organizations (except labor and political organizations)	8139	40,903	45,706	47,387	3.7

[1] North American Industry Classification System, 1997; see text, Section 15.   [2] Except public administration, religious, labor, and political organizations, and private household.

Source: U.S. Census Bureau, "Service Annual Survey 2004;" issued April 2006; <http://www.census.gov/econ/www/servmenu.html>.

This section presents data on the flow of goods, services, and capital between the United States and other countries; changes in official reserve assets of the United States; international investments; and foreign assistance programs.

The Bureau of Economic Analysis publishes current figures on U.S. international transactions and the U.S. international investment position in its monthly *Survey of Current Business*. Statistics for the foreign aid programs are presented by the Agency for International Development (AID) in its annual *U.S. Overseas Loans and Grants and Assistance from International Organizations* and by the Department of Agriculture in its *Foreign Agricultural Trade of the United States*.

The principal source of merchandise import and export data is the U.S. Census Bureau. Current data are presented monthly in *U.S. International Trade in Goods and Services* report Series FT 900. The *Guide to Foreign Trade Statistics,* found on the Census Bureau Web site at <http://www.census.gov/foreign-trade /guide/index.html>, lists the Bureau's monthly and annual products and services in this field. In addition, the International Trade Administration and the Bureau of Economic Analysis present summary as well as selected commodity and country data for U.S. foreign trade in the *U.S. Foreign Trade Highlights* and the *Survey of Current Business*, respectively. The Web sites for these data are found at <http://ita.doc.gov/td/industry/otea/> and <http://www.bea.doc.gov/bea/di /home/trade.htm>. The merchandise trade data in the latter source include balance of payments adjustments to the Census Bureau data. The Treasury Department's *Monthly Treasury Statement of Receipts and Outlays of the United States Government* contains information on import duties. The International Trade Commission, U.S. Department of Agriculture (agricultural products), U.S. Department of Energy (mineral fuels, like petroleum and coal), and the U.S. Geological Survey (minerals) release various reports and specialized products on U.S. trade.

International accounts—The international transactions tables (Tables 1268 to 1270) show, for given time periods, the transfer of goods, services, grants, and financial assets and liabilities between the United States and the rest of the world. The international investment position table (Table 1271) presents, for specific dates, the value of U.S. investments abroad and of foreign investments in the United States. The movement of foreign and U.S. capital as presented in the balance of payments is not the only factor affecting the total value of foreign investments. Among the other factors are changes in the valuation of assets or liabilities, including changes in prices of securities, defaults, expropriations, and write-offs.

Direct investment abroad means the ownership or control, directly or indirectly, by one person of 10 percent or more of the voting securities of an incorporated business enterprise or an equivalent interest in an unincorporated business enterprise. Direct investment position is the value of U.S. parents' claims on the equity of and receivables due from foreign affiliates, less foreign affiliates' receivables due from their U.S. parents. Income consists of parents' shares in the earnings of their affiliates plus net interest received by parents on intercompany accounts, less withholding taxes on dividends and interest.

Foreign aid—Foreign assistance is divided into three major categories—grants (military supplies and services and other grants), credits, and other assistance (through net accumulation of foreign currency claims from the sale of agricultural commodities). *Grants* are transfers for which no payment is expected (other than a limited percentage of the foreign currency "counterpart" funds generated by the grant), or which at most involve an obligation on the part of the receiver to extend aid to the United States or other countries to achieve a common objective. *Credits* are loan disbursements or transfers under other agreements which give rise to specific obligations to repay, over a period of years, usually with interest. All known returns to the U.S. government stemming from grants and credits (reverse grants, returns of grants, and payments of principal) are taken into account in net grants and net credits, but no allowance is made for interest or commissions. *Other assistance* represents the transfer of U.S. farm products in exchange for foreign currencies (plus, since enactment of Public Law 87-128, currency claims from principal and interest collected on credits extended under the farm products program), less the government's disbursements of the currencies as grants, credits, or for purchases. The net acquisition of currencies represents net transfers of resources to foreign countries under the agricultural programs, in addition to those classified as grants or credits.

The basic instrument for extending military aid to friendly nations has been the Mutual Defense Assistance Program authorized by the Congress in 1949. Prior to 1952, economic and technical aid was authorized in the Foreign Assistance Act of 1948, the 1950 Act for International Development, and other legislation which set up programs for specific countries. In 1952, these economic, technical, and military aid programs were combined under the Mutual Security Act, which in turn was followed by the Foreign Assistance Act passed in 1961. Appropriations to provide military assistance were also made in the Department of Defense Appropriation Act (rather than the Foreign Assistance Appropriation Act) beginning in 1966 for certain countries in Southeast Asia and in other legislation concerning programs for specific countries (such as Israel). Figures on activity under the Foreign Assistance Act as reported in the *Foreign Grants and Credits* series differ from data published by AID or its immediate predecessors, due largely to differences in reporting, timing, and treatment of particular items.

Exports—The Census Bureau compiles export data primarily from Shipper's Export Declarations required to be filed with customs officials for shipments leaving the United States. They include U.S. exports under mutual security programs and exclude shipments to U.S. Armed Forces for their own use.

The value reported in the export statistics is generally equivalent to a free alongside ship (f.a.s.) value at the U.S. port of export, based on the transaction price, including inland freight, insurance, and other charges incurred in placing the merchandise alongside the carrier at the U.S. port of exportation. This value, as defined, excludes the cost of loading merchandise aboard the exporting carrier and also excludes freight, insurance, and any other charges or transportation and other costs beyond the U.S. port of exportation. The country of destination is defined as the country of ultimate destination or country where the merchandise is to be consumed, further processed, or manufactured, as known to the shipper at the time of exportation. When ultimate destination is not known, the shipment is statistically credited to the last country to which the shipper knows the merchandise will be shipped in the same form as exported.

Effective January 1990, the United States began substituting Canadian import statistics for U.S. exports to Canada. As a result of the data exchange between the United States and Canada, the United States has adopted the Canadian import exemption level for its export statistics based on shipments to Canada.

Data are estimated for shipments valued under $2,501 to all countries, except Canada, using factors based on the ratios of low-valued shipments to individual country totals.

Prior to 1989, exports were based on Schedule B, Statistical Classification of Domestic and Foreign Commodities Exported from the United States. These statistics were retabulated and published using Schedule E, Standard International Trade Classification, Revision 2. Beginning in 1989, Schedule B classifications are based on the Harmonized System and coincide with the Standard International

Trade Classification, Revision 3. This revision will affect the comparability of most export series beginning with the 1989 data for commodities.

Imports—The Census Bureau compiles import data from various customs forms required to be filed with customs officials. Data on import values are presented on two valuations bases in this section: The c.i.f. (cost, insurance, and freight) and the customs import value (as appraised by the U.S. Customs Service in accordance with legal requirements of the Tariff Act of 1930, as amended). This latter valuation, primarily used for collection of import duties, frequently does not reflect the actual transaction value. Country of origin is defined as country where the merchandise was grown, mined, or manufactured. If country of origin is unknown, country of shipment is reported.

Imports are classified either as "General imports" or "Imports for consumption." *General imports* are a combination of entries for immediate consumption, entries into customs bonded warehouses, and entries into U.S. Foreign Trade Zones, thus generally reflecting total arrivals of merchandise. *Imports for consumption* are a combination of entries for immediate consumption, withdrawals from warehouses for consumption, and entries of merchandise into U.S. customs territory from U.S. Foreign Trade Zones, thus generally reflecting the total of the commodities entered into U.S. consumption channels.

Prior to 1989, imports were based on the Tariff Schedule of the United States Annotated. The statistics were retabulated and published using Schedule A, Standard International Trade Classification, Revision 2. Beginning in 1989, the statistics are based on the Harmonized Tariff Schedule of the United States, which coincides with the Standard International Trade Classification, Revision 3. This revision will affect the comparability of most import series beginning with the 1989 data.

Area coverage—Except as noted, the geographic area covered by the export and import trade statistics is the United States Customs area (includes the 50 states, the District of Columbia, and Puerto Rico), the U.S. Virgin Islands (effective January 1981), and U.S. Foreign Trade Zones (effective July 1982). Data for selected tables and total values for 1980 have been revised to reflect the U.S. Virgin Islands' trade with foreign countries, where possible.

Statistical reliability—For a discussion of statistical collection and estimation, sampling procedures, and measures of statistical reliability applicable to Census Bureau data, see Appendix III.

U.S. Census Bureau, Statistical Abstract of the United States: 2007

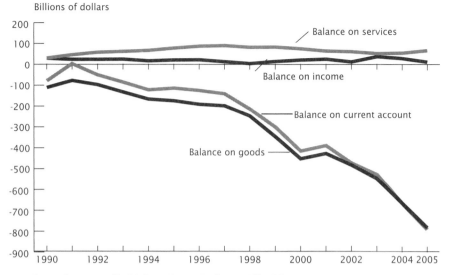

Figure 28.1
U.S. International Transaction Balances: 1990 to 2005

Billions of dollars

Source: Chart prepared by U.S. Census Bureau. For data, see Table 1268.

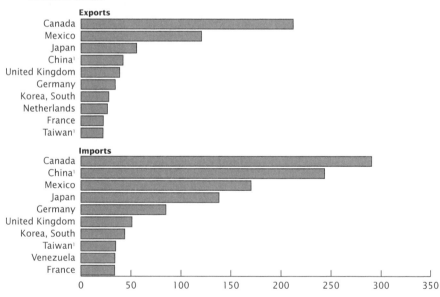

Figure 28.2
Top Purchasers of U.S. Exports and Suppliers of U.S. General Imports: 2005

Billions of dollars

[1] With the establishment of diplomatic relations with China on January 1, 1979, the U.S. government recognized the People's Republic of China as the sole legal government of China and acknowledged the Chinese position that there is only one China and that Taiwan is part of China.

Source: Chart prepared by U.S. Census Bureau. For data, see Table 1288.

[In millions of dollars (706,975 represents $706,975,000,000). Minus sign (–) indicates debits. n.i.e. = Not included elsewhere]

Type of transaction	1990	1995	1997	1998	1999	2000	2001	2002	2003	2004	2005
Exports of goods and services and income receipts.	**706,975**	**1,004,631**	**1,191,257**	**1,194,993**	**1,259,809**	**1,421,515**	**1,293,147**	**1,245,373**	**1,319,158**	**1,526,855**	**1,749,892**
Exports of goods and services	535,233	794,387	934,453	933,174	965,884	1,070,597	1,004,896	974,721	1,016,096	1,151,942	1,275,245
Goods, balance of payments basis [1] . .	387,401	575,204	678,366	670,416	683,965	771,994	718,712	682,422	713,415	807,516	894,631
Services [2]	147,832	219,183	256,087	262,758	281,919	298,603	286,184	292,299	302,681	344,426	380,614
Transfers under U.S. military agency sales contracts [3] .	9,932	14,643	16,675	17,405	15,928	13,790	12,539	11,943	12,769	15,467	19,038
Travel	43,007	63,395	73,426	71,325	74,801	82,400	71,893	66,605	64,348	74,547	81,680
Passenger fares	15,298	18,909	20,868	20,098	19,785	20,687	17,926	17,046	15,693	18,851	20,931
Other transportation	22,042	26,081	27,006	25,604	26,916	29,803	28,442	29,195	31,512	37,436	42,245
Royalties and license fees [4] . .	16,634	30,289	33,228	35,626	39,670	43,233	40,696	44,508	46,988	52,512	57,410
Other private services [4] . .	40,251	65,048	83,929	91,774	103,934	107,904	113,857	122,207	130,561	144,654	158,223
U.S. government miscellaneous services	668	818	955	926	885	786	831	795	810	959	1,087
Income receipts	171,742	210,244	256,804	261,819	293,925	350,918	288,251	270,652	303,062	374,913	474,647
Income receipts on U.S.-owned assets abroad .	170,570	208,065	254,534	259,382	291,177	348,083	285,372	267,841	300,249	372,035	471,722
Direct investment receipts . .	65,973	95,260	115,323	103,963	131,626	151,839	128,665	145,590	186,750	226,224	251,370
Other private receipts . . .	94,072	108,092	135,652	151,818	156,354	192,398	153,146	118,948	108,802	142,813	217,637
U.S. government receipts . .	10,525	4,713	3,559	3,601	3,197	3,846	3,561	3,303	4,697	2,998	2,715
Compensation of employees .	1,172	2,179	2,270	2,437	2,748	2,835	2,879	2,811	2,813	2,878	2,925
Imports of goods and services and income payments	**-759,290**	**-1,080,124**	**-1,286,597**	**-1,355,334**	**-1,509,207**	**-1,778,020**	**-1,630,811**	**-1,654,232**	**-1,777,462**	**-2,110,559**	**-2,455,328**
Imports of goods and services	-616,097	-890,771	-1,042,402	-1,097,780	-1,229,170	-1,448,156	-1,367,691	-1,395,789	-1,510,993	-1,763,238	-1,991,975
Goods, balance of payments basis [1] .	-498,438	-749,374	-876,470	-917,103	-1,029,980	-1,224,408	-1,145,900	-1,164,720	-1,260,717	-1,472,926	-1,677,371
Services [2]	-117,659	-141,397	-165,932	-180,677	-199,190	-223,748	-221,791	-231,069	-250,276	-290,312	-314,604
Direct defense expenditures . .	-17,531	-10,043	-11,707	-12,185	-13,335	-13,473	-14,835	-19,101	-25,296	-29,299	-30,062
Travel	-37,349	-44,916	-52,051	-56,483	-58,963	-64,705	-60,200	-58,715	-57,444	-65,750	-69,175
Passenger fares	-10,531	-14,663	-18,138	-19,971	-21,315	-24,274	-22,633	-19,969	-20,957	-23,723	-26,066
Other transportation	-24,966	-27,034	-28,959	-30,363	-34,139	-41,425	-38,682	-38,407	-44,705	-54,161	-62,107
Royalties and license fees [4] . .	-3,135	-6,919	-9,161	-11,235	-13,107	-16,468	-16,538	-19,353	-19,033	-23,211	-24,501
Other private services [4] . .	-22,229	-35,199	-43,154	-47,591	-55,510	-60,520	-66,021	-72,604	-79,710	-90,390	-98,714
U.S. government miscellaneous services	-1,919	-2,623	-2,762	-2,849	-2,821	-2,883	-2,882	-2,920	-3,131	-3,778	-3,979
Income payments	-143,192	-189,353	-244,195	-257,554	-280,037	-329,864	-263,120	-258,443	-266,469	-347,321	-463,353
Income payments on foreign-owned assets in the U.S. . .	-139,728	-183,090	-237,529	-250,560	-272,082	-322,345	-255,034	-250,063	-257,957	-338,400	-454,124
Direct investment payments . .	-3,450	-30,318	-42,950	-38,418	-53,437	-56,910	-12,783	-43,244	-73,961	-102,357	-116,953
Other private payments . . .	-95,508	-97,149	-112,878	-127,988	-138,120	-180,918	-159,825	-130,177	-110,125	-147,569	-223,612
U.S. government payments . .	-40,770	-55,623	-81,701	-84,154	-80,525	-84,517	-82,426	-76,642	-73,871	-88,474	-113,559
Compensation of employees .	-3,464	-6,263	-6,666	-6,994	-7,955	-7,519	-8,086	-8,380	-8,512	-8,921	-9,229
Unilateral current transfers, net	**-26,654**	**-38,074**	**-45,062**	**-53,187**	**-50,428**	**-58,645**	**-51,295**	**-63,587**	**-69,210**	**-81,582**	**-86,072**
U.S. government grants [3]	-10,359	-11,190	-12,472	-13,270	-13,774	-16,714	-11,517	-17,097	-21,834	-23,317	-31,362
U.S. government pensions and other transfers . .	-3,224	-3,451	-4,191	-4,305	-4,406	-4,705	-5,798	-5,125	-5,341	-6,264	-6,303
Private remittances and other transfers [5] . . .	-13,070	-23,433	-28,399	-35,612	-32,248	-37,226	-33,980	-41,365	-42,035	-52,001	-48,407

See footnotes at end of table.

Foreign Commerce and Aid   793

Table 1268. **U.S. International Transactions by Type of Transaction: 1990 to 2005**—Con.

[See headnote, Page 793]

Type of transaction	1990	1995	1997	1998	1999	2000	2001	2002	2003	2004	2005
Capital account transactions, net	-6,579	-927	-1,027	-766	-4,939	-1,010	-1,270	-1,470	-3,321	-2,261	-4,351
U.S. assets abroad, net (increase/financial outflow (-))	**-81,234**	**-352,264**	**-485,475**	**-353,829**	**-504,062**	**-560,523**	**-382,616**	**-294,646**	**-326,424**	**-867,802**	**-426,801**
U.S. official reserve assets, net	-2,158	-9,742	-1,010	-6,783	8,747	-290	-4,911	-3,681	1,523	2,805	14,096
Gold [6]	–	–	–	–	–	–	–	–	–	–	–
Special drawing rights	-192	-808	-350	-147	10	-722	-630	-475	601	-398	4,511
Reserve position in the International Monetary Fund	731	-2,466	-3,575	-5,119	5,484	2,308	-3,600	-2,632	1,494	3,826	10,200
Foreign currencies	-2,697	-6,468	2,915	-1,517	3,253	-1,876	-681	-574	-572	-623	-615
U.S. government assets, other than official reserve assets, net	2,317	-984	68	-422	2,750	-941	-486	345	537	1,710	5,539
U.S. credits and other long-term assets	-8,410	-4,859	-5,417	-4,678	-6,175	-5,182	-4,431	-5,251	-7,279	-3,044	-2,255
Repayments on U.S. credits and other long-term assets [7]	10,856	4,125	5,438	4,111	9,559	4,265	3,873	5,701	7,981	4,716	5,603
U.S. foreign currency holdings and U.S. short-term assets, net	-130	-250	47	145	-634	-24	72	-105	-165	38	2,191
U.S. private assets, net	-81,393	-341,538	-484,533	-346,624	-515,559	-559,292	-377,219	-291,310	-328,484	-872,317	-446,436
Direct investment	-37,183	-98,750	-104,803	-142,644	-224,934	-159,212	-142,349	-154,460	-149,897	-244,128	-9,072
Foreign securities	-28,765	-122,394	-116,852	-130,204	-122,236	-127,908	-90,644	-48,568	-146,722	-146,549	-180,125
U.S. claims on unaffiliated foreigners reported by U.S. nonbanking concerns	-27,824	-45,286	-121,760	-38,204	-97,704	-138,790	-8,520	-50,022	-18,851	-120,017	-44,221
U.S. claims reported by U.S. banks, n.i.e.	12,379	-75,108	-141,118	-35,572	-70,685	-133,382	-135,706	-38,260	-13,014	-361,623	-213,018
Foreign-owned assets in the United States, net (increase/financial inflow (+))	**141,571**	**438,562**	**706,809**	**423,569**	**740,210**	**1,046,896**	**782,859**	**797,813**	**864,769**	**1,450,221**	**1,212,250**
Foreign official assets in the U.S., net	33,910	109,880	19,036	-19,903	43,543	42,758	28,059	115,945	278,275	387,809	199,495
U.S. government securities	30,243	72,712	-2,161	-3,589	32,527	35,710	54,620	90,971	224,874	305,000	156,450
Other U.S. government liabilities	1,868	-105	-881	-3,326	-2,863	-1,825	-2,309	137	-517	-139	-488
U.S. liabilities reported by U.S. banks, n.i.e.	3,385	34,008	22,286	-9,501	12,964	5,746	-29,978	21,221	48,643	69,245	24,275
Other foreign official assets	-1,586	3,265	-208	-3,487	915	3,127	5,726	3,616	5,275	13,703	19,258
Other foreign assets in the U.S., net	107,661	328,682	687,773	443,472	696,667	1,004,138	754,800	681,868	586,494	1,062,412	1,012,755
Direct investments in U.S.	48,494	57,776	105,603	179,045	289,444	321,274	167,021	84,372	63,961	133,162	109,754
U.S. Treasury securities	-2,534	91,544	130,435	28,581	-44,497	-69,983	-14,378	100,403	91,455	102,940	199,491
U.S. securities other than U.S. Treasury securities	1,592	77,249	161,409	156,315	298,834	459,889	393,885	283,299	220,705	381,493	474,140
U.S. currency flows	18,800	12,300	24,782	16,622	22,407	5,315	23,783	21,513	16,640	14,827	19,416
U.S. liabilities to unaffiliated foreigners reported by U.S. nonbanking concerns	45,133	59,133	116,518	23,140	76,247	170,672	66,110	95,871	96,526	93,250	30,105
U.S. liabilities reported by U.S. banks, n.i.e.	-3,824	30,176	149,026	39,769	54,232	116,971	118,379	96,410	97,207	336,740	179,849
Statistical discrepancy	25,211	28,196	-79,905	144,554	68,617	-70,213	-10,014	-29,257	-7,510	85,128	10,410
Balance on goods	-111,037	-174,170	-198,104	-246,687	-346,015	-452,414	-427,188	-482,298	-547,302	-665,410	-782,740
Balance on services	30,173	77,786	90,155	82,081	82,729	74,855	64,393	61,230	52,405	54,114	66,011
Balance on income	28,550	20,891	12,609	4,265	13,888	21,054	25,131	12,209	36,593	27,592	11,293
Balance on current account [8]	-78,968	-113,567	-140,402	-213,528	-299,826	-415,150	-388,959	-472,446	-527,514	-665,286	-791,508

– Represents or rounds to zero. [1] Excludes exports of goods under U.S. military agency sales contracts identified in census export documents, excludes imports of goods under direct defense expenditures identified in census import documents, and reflects various other adjustments (for valuation, coverage, and timing) of Census statistics to balance of payments basis. [2] Includes some goods: Mainly military equipment; major equipment, other materials, supplies, and petroleum products purchased abroad by U.S. military agencies; and fuels purchased by airline and steamship operators. [3] Includes transfers of goods and services under U.S. military grant programs. [4] These lines are presented on a gross basis. The definition of exports is revised to exclude U.S. parents' payments to foreign affiliates and to include U.S. affiliates' receipts from foreign parents. The definition of imports is revised to include U.S. parents' payments to foreign affiliates and to exclude U.S. affiliates' receipts from foreign parents. [5] The "other transfers" component includes taxes paid by U.S. private residents to foreign governments and taxes paid by private nonresidents to the U.S. government. [6] At the present time, all U.S. Treasury-owned gold is held in the United States. [7] Includes sales of foreign obligations to foreigners. [8] Conceptually, "Balance on current account" is equal to "net foreign investment" in the national income and product accounts (NIPAs). However, the foreign transactions account in the NIPAs (a) includes adjustments to the international transactions accounts for the different geographical treatment of transactions with U.S. territories and Puerto Rico, and (c) includes services furnished without payment by financial pension plans except life insurance carriers and private noninsured pension plans.

Source: U.S. Bureau of Economic Analysis, *Survey of Current Business*, July 2006, and <http://www.bea.gov/international/bpweb/list.cfm?anon=71&registered=0> (released 16 June 2006).

Table 1269. **U.S. Balances on International Transactions by Area and Selected Country: 2004 and 2005**

[In millions of dollars (-665,410 represents -$665,410,000,000). Minus sign (-) indicates debits]

Area or country	2004, balance on—				2005, balance on—			
	Goods [1]	Services	Income	Current account	Goods [1]	Services	Income	Current account
All areas	**-665,410**	**54,114**	**27,592**	**-665,286**	**-782,740**	**66,011**	**11,293**	**-791,508**
Europe	-131,504	14,683	-2,351	-123,328	-146,378	12,196	-16,021	-159,070
European Union	-110,473	12,444	-7,760	-107,036	-124,443	12,212	-25,473	-141,535
Euro Area	(NA)	(NA)	(NA)	(NA)	-92,812	2,438	-3,885	-101,539
Belgium	(NA)	(NA)	(NA)	(NA)	5,545	669	-11,217	-5,140
France	-10,490	1,045	-970	-10,540	-11,512	295	-2,040	-13,481
Germany	-46,287	-5,022	132	-51,444	-51,004	-5,259	-1,733	-58,891
Italy	-17,667	-319	2,226	-14,830	-19,721	-217	3,561	-16,777
Netherlands	11,716	1,380	4,355	17,239	11,486	1,084	1,063	14,019
United Kingdom	-10,908	7,573	-13,641	-14,485	-12,966	8,907	-21,083	-20,936
Canada	-69,053	8,630	17,767	-43,019	-81,122	10,223	19,387	-51,486
Latin America, other West. Hemisphere	-83,872	1,721	12,212	-104,366	-102,606	7,817	16,497	-101,255
Mexico	-46,407	4,191	309	-52,009	-51,846	5,767	641	-56,501
Venezuela	-20,179	1,888	-47	-18,453	-27,568	2,053	603	-25,019
Asia and Pacific	(NA)	(NA)	(NA)	(NA)	-369,633	29,989	-35,864	-389,243
China [2]	(NA)	(NA)	(NA)	(NA)	-201,673	2,568	-19,044	-220,077
Hong Kong	(NA)	(NA)	(NA)	(NA)	7,394	-1,210	1,919	8,006
India	(NA)	(NA)	(NA)	(NA)	-10,831	1,581	964	-10,278
Japan [3]	-77,519	14,750	-31,434	-93,684	-84,744	18,671	-33,334	-98,668
Korea, South	(NA)	(NA)	(NA)	(NA)	-16,646	3,092	-670	-14,802
Taiwan [2]	(NA)	(NA)	(NA)	(NA)	-13,374	1,078	-3,394	-16,133
Middle East	(NA)	(NA)	(NA)	(NA)	-32,677	837	-394	-48,862
Africa	(NA)	(NA)	(NA)	(NA)	-50,324	4,629	5,344	-48,190
International and unallocated	(X)	-325	20,148	9,834	(X)	330	22,345	6,608

NA Not available.   X Not applicable.   [1] Adjusted to balance of payments basis; excludes exports under U.S. military sales contracts and imports under direct defense expenditures.   [2] See footnote 2, Table 1308.   [3] Includes Ryukyu Islands.

Source: U.S. Bureau of Economic Analysis, *Survey of Current Business*, July 2006, and <http://www.bea.gov/bea/international/bpweb/list.cfm?anon=71&registered=0>(released June 16, 2006).

Table 1270. **Private International Service Transactions by Selected Type of Service and Selected Country: 2000 to 2005**

[In millions of dollars (284,027 represents $284,027,000,000). For all transactions, see Table 1268]

Type of service and country	Exports				Imports			
	2000	2003	2004	2005	2000	2003	2004	2005
Private services, total	**284,027**	**289,102**	**328,000**	**360,489**	**207,392**	**221,849**	**257,235**	**280,563**
TYPE OF SERVICE								
Travel	82,400	64,348	74,547	81,680	64,705	57,444	65,750	69,175
Passenger fares	20,687	15,693	18,851	20,957	24,274	20,957	23,723	26,066
Other transportation	29,803	31,512	37,436	42,245	41,425	44,705	54,161	62,107
Freight	12,547	14,037	15,958	17,340	27,388	31,772	39,225	44,156
Port services	17,256	17,475	21,478	24,905	14,037	12,933	14,936	17,951
Royalties and license fees	43,233	46,988	52,512	57,410	16,468	19,033	23,211	24,501
Affiliated	30,479	35,539	39,074	42,106	12,536	15,179	17,946	20,360
Unaffiliated	12,754	11,449	13,438	15,304	3,932	3,854	5,265	4,141
Industrial processes	4,662	4,617	5,660	6,633	1,692	2,358	2,778	2,747
Other	8,093	6,833	7,778	8,671	2,241	1,495	2,487	1,394
Other private services	107,904	130,561	144,654	158,223	60,520	79,710	90,390	98,714
Affiliated	34,970	43,006	45,175	49,389	27,176	31,459	33,915	38,989
Unaffiliated	72,934	87,555	99,479	108,834	33,344	48,251	56,475	59,725
Education	10,348	13,312	13,643	14,123	2,032	3,148	3,556	4,029
Financial services	16,026	18,699	25,185	29,281	4,840	3,996	5,309	6,549
Insurance services	3,631	5,974	6,838	6,831	11,284	25,234	29,038	28,482
Telecommunications	3,884	4,452	4,463	4,724	5,429	4,255	4,542	4,658
Business, professional, & technical services	25,319	30,781	34,523	39,491	9,130	10,915	13,078	14,516
Other unaffiliated services	13,730	14,337	14,827	14,384	632	705	952	1,493
AREA AND COUNTRY								
Europe	107,650	117,851	134,272	145,519	89,825	99,470	110,015	123,144
European Union	94,232	101,962	117,284	127,837	77,876	84,974	95,822	105,899
Belgium	(NA)	(NA)	(NA)	3,128	(NA)	(NA)	(NA)	2,238
Luxembourg	(NA)	(NA)	(NA)	1,625	(NA)	(NA)	(NA)	510
France	10,555	11,049	12,900	13,097	10,644	10,039	11,609	12,507
Germany	15,927	17,120	19,142	20,040	12,401	15,787	17,284	18,660
Italy	5,457	5,638	6,167	6,948	5,062	4,742	5,544	6,215
Netherlands	7,060	7,893	8,246	8,918	5,699	6,479	6,829	7,758
United Kingdom	31,973	34,959	40,878	45,286	28,304	30,516	32,646	35,452
Canada	24,559	27,135	29,475	32,507	17,711	19,217	20,627	22,022
Latin America and Other Western Hemisphere	54,417	49,591	56,026	60,810	38,092	45,449	53,886	53,076
Argentina	(NA)	(NA)	(NA)	1,815	(NA)	(NA)	(NA)	797
Brazil	(NA)	(NA)	(NA)	5,854	(NA)	(NA)	(NA)	2,076
Mexico	14,333	16,216	17,907	20,603	10,798	12,170	13,525	14,674
Venezuela	3,310	2,124	2,416	2,636	610	377	524	581
Australia	5,575	6,030	6,853	7,408	3,494	3,207	3,880	4,657
Japan	33,411	29,589	35,552	41,815	17,405	17,039	19,490	22,286
South Africa	1,423	1,184	1,291	1,417	799	998	1,059	918
International organizations and unallocated	6,206	4,618	4,866	5,249	3,946	3,334	5,183	5,169

NA Not available.

Source: U.S. Bureau of Economic Analysis, *Survey of Current Business*, July 2006.

Foreign Commerce and Aid   795

Table 1271. International Investment Position by Type of Investment: 1990 to 2005

[In millions of dollars (–245,347 represents –$245,347,000,000). Estimates for end of year; subject to considerable error due to nature of basic data. Unless otherwise specified, types below refer to current-cost method. For information on current-cost method and market value, see article cited in source]

Type of investment	1990	1995	2000	2002	2003	2004	2005
U.S. net international investment position:							
Current cost	–245,347	–458,462	–1,381,196	–2,088,008	–2,131,170	–2,360,785	–2,693,799
Market value	–164,495	–305,836	–1,581,007	–2,454,328	–2,339,788	–2,448,744	–2,546,175
U.S.-owned assets abroad:							
Current cost	2,178,978	3,486,272	6,238,785	6,652,248	7,648,880	9,186,661	10,008,676
Market value	2,294,085	3,964,558	7,401,192	6,807,793	8,318,156	10,075,337	11,079,202
U.S. official reserve assets	174,664	176,061	128,400	158,602	183,577	189,591	188,043
Gold	102,406	101,279	71,799	90,806	108,866	113,947	134,175
Special drawing rights	10,989	11,037	10,539	12,166	12,638	13,628	8,210
Reserve position in IMF	9,076	14,649	14,824	21,979	22,535	19,544	8,036
Foreign currencies	52,193	49,096	31,238	33,651	39,538	42,472	37,622
U.S. government assets, other	84,344	85,064	85,168	85,309	84,772	83,062	77,523
U.S. credits, long-term assets . . .	83,716	82,802	82,574	82,682	81,980	80,308	76,960
Repayable in dollars	82,602	82,358	82,293	82,406	81,706	80,035	76,687
Other	1,114	444	281	276	274	273	273
U.S. foreign currency holdings and U.S. short-term assets	628	2,262	2,594	2,627	2,792	2,754	563
U.S. private assets:							
Current cost	1,919,970	3,225,147	6,025,217	6,408,337	7,380,531	8,914,008	9,743,110
Market value	2,035,077	3,703,433	7,187,624	6,563,882	8,049,807	9,802,684	10,813,636
Direct investments abroad:							
Current cost	616,655	885,506	1,531,607	1,867,043	2,059,850	2,399,224	2,453,933
Market value	731,762	1,363,792	2,694,014	2,022,588	2,729,126	3,287,900	3,524,459
Foreign securities	342,313	1,203,925	2,425,534	2,079,891	2,953,778	3,553,387	4,073,997
Bonds	144,717	413,310	572,692	705,226	874,356	992,969	987,543
Corporate stocks	197,596	790,615	1,852,842	1,374,665	2,079,422	2,560,418	3,086,454
U.S. claims on unaffiliated foreigners [1]	265,315	367,567	836,559	901,946	594,004	733,538	784,521
U.S. claims reported by U.S. banks [2]	695,687	768,149	1,231,517	1,559,457	1,772,899	2,227,859	2,430,659
Foreign-owned assets in the U.S.:							
Current cost	2,424,325	3,944,734	7,619,981	8,740,256	9,780,050	11,547,446	12,702,475
Market value	2,458,580	4,270,394	8,982,199	9,262,121	10,657,944	12,524,081	13,625,377
Foreign official assets in the U.S	373,293	682,873	1,030,708	1,250,977	1,562,770	2,001,407	2,216,123
U.S. government securities	291,228	507,460	756,155	970,359	1,186,500	1,499,293	1,649,397
U.S. Treasury securities	285,911	489,952	639,796	811,995	986,301	1,241,250	1,288,881
Other	5,317	17,508	116,359	158,364	200,199	258,043	360,516
Other U.S. government liabilities . .	17,243	23,573	19,316	17,144	16,627	16,488	16,000
U.S. liabilities reported by U.S. banks	39,880	107,394	153,403	155,876	201,054	270,387	294,662
Other foreign official assets	24,942	44,446	101,834	107,598	158,589	215,239	256,064
Other foreign assets in the U.S:							
Current cost	2,051,032	3,261,861	6,589,273	7,489,279	8,217,280	9,546,039	10,486,352
Market value	2,085,287	3,587,521	7,951,491	8,011,144	9,095,174	10,522,674	11,409,254
Direct investments:							
Current cost	505,346	680,066	1,421,017	1,499,952	1,576,983	1,727,062	1,874,263
Market value	539,601	1,005,726	2,783,235	2,021,817	2,454,877	2,703,697	2,797,165
U.S. Treasury securities	152,452	326,995	381,630	473,503	527,223	562,288	704,875
U.S. securities other than							
U.S. Treasury securities	460,644	969,849	2,623,014	2,779,067	3,422,856	3,995,506	4,390,682
Corporate and other bonds . . .	238,903	459,080	1,068,566	1,530,982	1,710,787	2,035,149	2,275,197
Corporate stocks	221,741	510,769	1,554,448	1,248,085	1,712,069	1,960,357	2,115,485
U.S. currency	85,933	169,484	255,972	301,268	317,908	332,735	352,151
U.S. liabilities to unaffiliated foreigners [1]	213,406	300,424	738,904	897,335	450,884	507,668	563,749
U.S. liabilities reported by U.S. banks [2]	633,251	815,043	1,168,736	1,538,154	1,921,426	2,420,780	2,600,632

[1] Reported by U.S. nonbanking concerns.   [2] Not included elsewhere.

Source: U.S. Bureau of Economic Analysis, *Survey of Current Business*, July 2006.

Table 1272. U.S. Reserve Assets: 1990 to 2005

[In billions of dollars ($83.3 represents $83,300,000,000). As of end of year, except as indicated]

Type	1990	1995	1999	2000	2001	2002	2003	2004	2005
Total	83.3	85.8	71.5	67.6	68.7	79.0	85.9	86.8	65.1
Gold stock	11.1	11.1	11.0	11.0	11.0	11.0	11.0	11.0	11.0
Special drawing rights	11.0	11.0	10.3	10.5	10.8	12.2	12.6	13.6	8.2
Foreign currencies	52.2	49.1	32.2	31.2	29.0	33.8	39.7	42.7	37.8
Reserve position in IMF [1]	9.1	14.6	18.0	14.8	17.9	22.0	22.5	19.5	8.0

[1] International Monetary Fund.

U.S. Department of the Treasury, *Treasury Bulletin*, quarterly. For latest issue, see <http://www.fms.treas.gov/bulletin/index.html>.

U.S. Census Bureau, Statistical Abstract of the United States: 2007

ble 1273. **Foreign Direct Investment Position in the United States on a Historical-Cost Basis by Selected Country, 1990 to 2005, and by Industry, 2005**

millions of dollars (394,911 represents $394,911,000,000)]

Country	1990	2000	2003	2004	2005 Total [1]	2005 Manufac-turing	2005 Whole-sale	2005 Infor-mation
All countries	394,911	1,256,867	1,395,159	1,520,729	1,635,291	538,122	230,104	142,556
ada	29,544	114,309	95,707	125,503	144,033	30,588	4,192	6,122
ope	247,320	887,014	1,001,237	1,066,908	1,143,614	414,852	124,349	109,677
ustria	625	3,007	3,606	3,675	2,502	1,242	401	-1
elgium.	3,900	14,787	11,239	11,735	9,712	3,209	1,305	-2
enmark.	819	4,025	4,531	5,454	6,255	4,814	391	-1
inland	1,504	8,875	5,300	5,665	6,205	3,740	2,242	–
rance	18,650	125,740	136,434	143,586	143,378	45,480	13,316	26,202
iermany.	28,232	122,412	160,691	163,981	184,213	70,943	14,972	29,971
eland	1,340	25,523	23,346	20,403	21,898	5,268	402	(D)
aly	1,524	6,576	6,944	6,998	7,716	1,056	991	(D)
uxembourg.	2,195	58,930	109,212	115,688	116,736	26,305	952	5,256
etherlands.	64,671	138,894	146,601	155,452	170,770	72,459	9,691	12,283
lorway.	773	2,665	4,203	3,344	6,144	2,477	556	269
pain	792	5,068	5,670	5,581	7,114	2,410	178	(D)
weden	5,484	21,991	20,156	23,712	24,774	9,236	9,026	(D)
witzerland	17,674	64,719	124,247	121,634	122,399	76,385	7,055	(D)
Jnited Kingdom	98,676	277,613	217,841	251,422	282,457	76,792	62,392	17,918
n America and other estern Hemisphere.	20,168	53,691	84,134	87,259	82,530	21,968	10,936	1,316
outh and Central America. . .	6,140	13,384	22,910	26,088	30,012	806	8,202	(D)
Mexico	575	7,462	9,022	8,167	8,653	1,223	1,400	(D)
Panama.	4,188	3,819	8,874	10,360	11,470	(D)	35	(D)
ther Western Hemisphere. . .	14,028	40,307	61,224	61,170	52,518	21,162	2,734	(D)
Bahamas	1,535	1,254	1,227	1,257	703	207	(D)	(D)
Netherlands Antilles	12,974	3,807	3,597	4,418	4,179	643	354	(D)
U.K.Islands, Caribbean. . . .	-2,979	15,191	26,202	23,777	26,501	(D)	2,602	(D)
ica	505	2,700	2,196	1,671	2,564	721	(D)	(D)
ldle East	4,425	6,506	7,177	7,888	9,965	882	(D)	809
srael	640	3,012	3,316	3,872	4,362	847	427	803
.uwait	1,805	908	(D)	(D)	612	(D)	-1	–
audi Arabia	1,811	(Z)	(Z)	(D)	(D)	(D)	(D)	6
a and Pacific	92,948	192,647	204,708	231,500	252,584	69,112	86,473	(D)
.ustralia	6,542	18,775	37,059	40,884	44,061	4,986	1,722	(D)
China [2]	(NA)	(NA)	284	435	481	15	190	(D)
long Kong	1,511	1,493	1,984	1,437	2,600	448	1,009	(D)
idia.	(NA)	(NA)	342	630	1,355	-39	(D)	72
apan.	83,091	159,690	157,176	175,728	190,279	62,934	76,732	1,880
ingapore	1,289	5,087	2,166	1,954	2,404	-991	425	20
aiwan	836	3,174	2,888	3,191	3,565	1,167	1,065	(D)

– Represents or rounds to zero.   D Suppressed to avoid disclosure of data of individual companies.   Z Less than 0,000.   [1] Includes other industries not shown separately.   [2] See footnote 2, Table 1308.

Source: U.S. Bureau of Economic Analysis, *Survey of Current Business*, July 2006. For most recent copy and historical issues, <http://www.bea.doc.gov/bea/pubs.htm>.

ble 1274. **U.S. Majority-Owned Affiliates of Foreign Companies—Assets, Sales, Employment, Land, Exports, and Imports by Industry: 2003**

093,531 represents $5,093,531,000,000). A U.S. affiliate is a U.S. business enterprise in which one foreign owner (individual, nch, partnership, association, trust, corporation, or government) has a direct or indirect voting interest of 10 percent or more. mates cover the universe of nonbank affiliates. These data are now on a NAICS (North American Industry Classification tem) basis]

Industry	Total assets (mil. dol.)	Sales [1] (mil. dol.)	Employ-ment [2] (1,000)	Employee compen-sation (mil. dol.)	Gross book value (mil. dol.) P & E [3]	Gross book value (mil. dol.) Land	Merchan-dise exports[4] (mil. dol.)	Merchan-dise imports[4] (mil. dol.)
All industries	5,093,531	2,136,617	5,253.0	317,948	1,049,569	52,557	150,829	356,659
nufacturing [5]	1,035,133	854,519	2,138.3	151,447	484,624	15,961	93,260	138,965
etroleum & coal products.	235,676	160,222	(6)	(D)	106,540	2,171	16,071	21,084
hemicals	(D)	(D)	305.4	31,319	(D)	(D)	(D)	(D)
omputers & electronic products .	92,661	91,809	219.8	18,200	34,191	749	13,987	24,218
ransportation equipment	223,885	199,677	377.1	24,196	104,947	1,231	28,713	52,705
olesale trade	453,529	656,019	512.1	37,716	195,086	4,739	53,113	206,503
ail trade	61,254	121,967	564.9	16,687	42,035	2,918	597	3,545
rmation.	265,832	81,471	239.1	17,495	43,063	599	1,014	1,059
ance (except depository stitutions) & insurance	2,710,029	174,766	244.5	33,133	32,537	934	–	–
al estate & rental & leasing	91,170	19,839	36.3	2,305	75,103	9,066	(D)	396
fessional, scientific, & technical rvices	62,246	49,068	167.8	13,107	8,494	185	(D)	366
er industries	414,339	178,969	1,349.9	46,058	168,626	18,155	2,239	5,824

– Represents or rounds to zero   D Withheld to avoid disclosure of data of individual companies.   [1] Excludes returns, counts, allowances, and sales and excise taxes.   [2] Average number of full-time and part-time employees.   [3] Plant and ipment (P & E). Includes mineral rights and minor amounts of property other than land.   [4] F.a.s. value at port of exportation. cludes industries not shown separately.   [6] Employment between 25,000 to 49,999.

Source: U.S. Bureau of Economic Analysis, *Survey of Current Business*, August 2005, and previous issues. For most recent y and historical issues, see <http://www.bea.doc.gov/bea/pubs.htm>. *Foreign Direct Investment in the United States: erations of U.S. Affiliates of Foreign Companies, Preliminary 2003 Estimates*.

Foreign Commerce and Aid   **797**

Table 1275. **Foreign Direct Investment in the United States—Gross Book Value and Employment of U.S. Affiliates of Foreign Companies by State: 1990 to 2003**

[(**578,355 represents $578,355,000,000.** A U.S. affiliate is a U.S. business enterprise in which one foreign owner (individual, branch, partnership, association, trust corporation, or government) has a direct or indirect voting interest of 10 percent or more. Estimates cover the universe of nonbank U.S. affiliates. Data for 2002 and 2003 are on a majority-owned basis and not strictly comparable with earlier data]

State and other area	Gross book value of property, plant, and equipment (mil. dol.)				Total employment (1,000)			2003, prel.	
	1990	2000	2002, prel.	2003, prel.	1990	2000	2002	Total (1,000)	Percent of all businesses
Total	578,355	1,175,628	1,024,364	1,049,569	4,734.5	6,524.6	5,425.4	5,253.0	(X)
United States	552,902	1,070,422	913,611	934,271	4,704.4	6,498.3	5,398.6	5,221.8	4.7
Alabama.	7,300	16,646	15,520	16,102	55.7	77.9	75.1	72.8	4.6
Alaska	19,435	28,964	30,052	(D)	13.2	12.0	12.6	11.7	5.2
Arizona.	7,234	10,716	9,252	10,015	57.1	73.2	57.5	59.8	3.0
Arkansas	2,344	4,613	4,872	4,864	29.2	40.9	35.7	33.7	3.4
California	75,768	121,040	87,509	88,247	555.9	749.4	612.6	561.0	4.5
Colorado.	6,544	15,319	13,026	13,505	56.3	102.6	77.7	73.5	4.0
Connecticut.	5,357	13,604	12,790	12,682	75.9	118.0	111.0	104.9	7.3
Delaware	5,818	6,114	6,211	6,154	43.1	31.8	22.4	26.5	7.3
District of Columbia	3,869	4,247	5,132	4,461	11.4	17.1	17.4	16.5	3.6
Florida	18,659	38,755	28,662	29,452	205.7	312.1	252.1	248.9	3.9
Georgia	16,729	29,510	24,941	26,125	161.0	227.9	191.2	182.8	5.5
Hawaii	11,830	10,369	7,720	7,751	53.0	44.8	36.7	36.1	7.8
Idaho	776	2,749	2,131	2,139	11.7	14.2	12.5	11.2	2.3
Illinois	23,420	48,425	40,300	40,852	245.8	325.8	262.9	254.9	5.0
Indiana.	13,426	30,179	27,985	29,836	126.9	168.2	133.2	134.2	5.3
Iowa	2,712	7,186	5,776	6,028	32.8	40.9	36.6	38.1	3.1
Kansas.	5,134	9,036	5,238	5,726	29.6	61.0	34.9	35.6	3.2
Kentucky	9,229	22,091	24,091	25,575	65.7	106.0	88.4	87.0	5.8
Louisiana	17,432	31,160	26,993	29,200	61.4	61.3	50.5	48.0	3.0
Maine.	2,080	5,087	5,511	5,986	26.6	33.9	31.7	30.1	5.9
Maryland	5,713	13,157	10,339	10,902	79.6	112.9	105.4	104.1	5.0
Massachusetts.	8,890	23,875	24,109	23,088	131.2	226.8	196.9	189.0	6.5
Michigan.	12,012	39,238	37,814	39,009	139.6	249.9	202.9	205.0	5.4
Minnesota.	11,972	13,472	9,805	10,828	89.8	106.2	88.1	84.6	3.6
Mississippi	2,989	4,121	5,097	5,836	23.6	24.2	25.8	22.8	2.5
Missouri	5,757	15,773	14,484	14,438	73.7	107.4	91.5	87.2	3.8
Montana.	2,181	3,099	1,824	2,353	5.1	6.8	5.9	6.6	2.0
Nebraska	776	2,737	1,840	1,986	14.9	21.7	18.7	18.9	2.5
Nevada	5,450	10,128	6,726	6,795	22.7	36.3	25.8	27.2	2.8
New Hampshire	1,446	5,124	4,488	4,613	25.9	46.5	41.1	41.9	7.7
New Jersey.	18,608	35,115	30,866	33,362	227.0	272.2	228.3	223.2	6.5
New Mexico	4,312	5,801	4,557	4,246	17.4	16.7	12.8	12.5	2.1
New York	36,424	68,522	64,016	62,257	347.5	479.1	386.8	382.6	5.4
North Carolina	15,234	29,931	24,045	25,021	181.0	264.8	214.8	204.6	6.3
North Dakota.	1,251	1,824	1,100	1,617	3.1	7.7	7.4	7.9	3.0
Ohio	20,549	37,530	32,124	32,686	219.1	260.3	214.2	208.6	4.4
Oklahoma.	6,049	7,635	7,434	8,100	43.6	41.9	33.9	32.5	2.8
Oregon.	3,427	13,178	10,241	10,314	39.1	62.1	50.9	48.4	3.6
Pennsylvania.	16,587	34,106	29,118	30,245	221.6	283.4	235.8	227.7	4.5
Rhode Island.	1,120	3,394	3,037	(D)	13.3	24.2	27.5	25.9	6.1
South Carolina.	10,067	23,563	21,570	20,533	104.7	138.4	133.0	127.5	8.4
South Dakota	553	1,011	685	777	4.5	6.9	7.6	7.0	2.2
Tennessee	10,280	20,842	16,790	18,002	116.9	153.2	130.1	127.4	5.5
Texas.	57,079	110,032	88,107	85,350	299.5	445.2	352.8	339.3	4.3
Utah	3,918	14,340	10,612	11,933	21.0	38.1	32.3	32.2	3.5
Vermont	631	2,146	1,286	(D)	7.7	11.5	11.1	10.4	4.1
Virginia.	10,702	23,570	17,331	16,733	113.3	181.9	141.9	138.6	4.8
Washington	7,985	22,257	16,414	18,069	77.5	106.8	84.5	82.8	3.7
West Virginia.	7,975	7,061	7,388	6,238	34.9	28.1	22.7	22.2	3.9
Wisconsin	5,088	13,961	16,103	16,463	81.4	110.3	107.1	97.6	4.0
Wyoming	2,782	8,072	10,551	10,946	5.8	7.8	8.5	8.8	4.6
Puerto Rico	1,499	2,169	2,338	2,646	16.1	17.9	16.6	16.4	(NA)
Other territories and offshore.	18,484	34,105	39,746	39,436	9.0	7.9	9.9	14.4	(NA)
Foreign	5,470	2,406	2,328	(D)	5.0	0.5	0.3	0.4	(NA)
Unspecified [1]	(NA)	66,526	66,341	73,216	(NA)	(NA)	(NA)	(NA)	(NA)

D Data withheld to avoid disclosure.   NA Not available.   X Not applicable.   [1] Covers property, plant, and equipment not located in a particular state, including aircraft, railroad rolling stock, satellites, undersea cable, and trucks engaged in interstate transportation.

Source: U.S. Bureau of Economic Analysis, *Survey of Current Business*, August 2005 issue, and *Foreign Direct Investment in the United States, Operations of U.S. Affiliates of Foreign Companies*, annual.

798   Foreign Commerce and Aid

Table 1276. **U.S. Businesses Acquired or Established by Foreign Direct Investors—Investment Outlays by Industry of U.S. Business Enterprise and Country of Ultimate Beneficial Owner: 1990 to 2005**

[In millions of dollars (65,932 represents $65,932,000,000). Foreign direct investment is the ownership or control directly or indirectly, by one foreign individual branch, partnership, association, trust, corporation, or government of 10 percent or more of the voting securities of a U.S. business enterprise or an equivalent interest in an unincorporated one. Data represent number and full cost of acquisitions of existing U.S. business enterprises, including business segments or operating units of existing U.S. business enterprises and establishments of new enterprises. Investments may be made by the foreign direct investor itself, or indirectly by an existing U.S. affiliate of the foreign direct investor. Covers investments in U.S. business enterprises with assets of over $1 million, or ownership of 200 acres of U.S. land]

Industry and country	1990	1995	2000	2001	2002	2003	2004	2005 prel.
Total	65,932	57,195	335,629	147,109	54,519	63,591	86,219	86,823
U.S. businesses acquired	(NA)	47,179	322,703	138,091	43,442	50,212	72,738	79,220
U.S. businesses established	(NA)	10,016	12,926	9,017	11,077	13,379	13,481	7,603
By type of investor:								
Foreign direct investors	(NA)	11,927	105,151	23,134	13,650	27,866	34,184	43,579
U.S. affiliates	(NA)	45,268	230,478	123,975	40,869	35,725	52,035	43,244
INDUSTRY								
Manufacturing	(NA)	(NA)	143,285	37,592	16,446	10,750	18,251	31,286
Wholesale trade	(NA)	(NA)	8,561	3,982	871	1,086	(D)	2,292
Retail trade	(NA)	(NA)	1,672	1,913	551	941	3,073	2,166
Information	(NA)	(NA)	67,932	27,599	14,181	9,236	4,315	9,639
Depository institutions	(NA)	(NA)	2,636	5,709	613	4,864	(D)	9,609
Finance, (except depository institutions) and insurance	(NA)	(NA)	44,420	40,780	4,344	23,511	26,234	6,196
Real estate and rental and leasing	(NA)	(NA)	4,526	3,572	5,266	2,817	6,335	5,532
Professional, scientific, and technical services	(NA)	(NA)	32,332	7,044	4,012	1,955	(D)	6,879
Other industries	(NA)	(NA)	30,264	18,917	8,234	8,429	10,121	13,224
COUNTRY [1]								
Canada	3,430	8,029	28,346	16,646	4,333	9,157	31,502	13,269
Europe	36,011	38,195	249,167	78,328	39,644	39,024	43,815	57,244
France	10,217	1,129	26,149	5,772	15,196	2,955	6,415	6,105
Germany	2,363	13,117	18,452	12,733	3,067	8,830	4,788	7,110
Netherlands	2,247	1,061	47,686	14,879	3,476	1,077	461	3,110
Switzerland	3,905	7,533	22,789	16,468	2,656	649	6,505	2,237
United Kingdom	13,096	9,094	110,208	17,095	12,188	20,373	23,288	30,310
Other Europe	4,183	6,261	23,883	11,381	3,061	5,140	2,358	8,372
Latin America and other Western Hemisphere	796	1,550	15,400	15,274	3,487	1,607	2,629	2,398
South and Central America	399	1,283	5,334	431	373	182	1,382	763
Other Western Hemisphere	397	267	10,066	14,843	3,144	1,425	1,247	1,634
Africa	(D)	472	(D)	(D)	(D)	(D)	(D)	(D)
Middle East	472	447	947	(D)	(D)	(D)	1,738	3,156
Asia and Pacific	23,170	8,688	40,282	11,383	5,131	11,469	6,015	10,655
Australia	1,412	2,270	(D)	4,869	1,565	9,032	3,850	5,148
Japan	19,933	3,602	26,044	5,345	3,275	1,544	1,027	3,565
Other Asia and Pacific	1,825	2,816	(D)	1,169	291	893	1,139	1,942

NA Not available.   D Suppressed to avoid disclosure of data of individual companies.   [1] For investments in which more than one investor participated, each investor and each investor's outlays are classified by country of each ultimate beneficial owner.
Source: U.S. Bureau of Economic Analysis, *Survey of Current Business*, June 2006, and previous issues. For most recent copy and historical issues, see <http://www.bea.gov/bea/pubs.htm>.

Table 1277. **U.S. Direct Investment Position Abroad, Capital Outflows, and Income by Industry of Foreign Affiliates: 2000 to 2005**

[In millions of dollars (1,316,247 represents $1,316,247,000,000). See headnote, table 1278]

Industry	Direct investment position on a historical-cost basis			Capital outflows (inflows (–))			Income		
	2000	2004	2005	2000	2004	2005	2000	2004	2005
All industries, total	1,316,247	2,051,204	2,069,983	142,627	222,437	–12,714	133,692	203,484	227,864
Mining	72,111	102,058	114,386	2,174	14,059	11,378	13,164	16,869	22,225
Utilities	21,964	(NA)	(NA)	2,466	(NA)	(NA)	1,610	(NA)	(NA)
Manufacturing	343,899	414,353	451,402	43,002	53,680	38,765	42,230	47,910	49,782
Food	23,497	29,452	31,524	2,014	1,391	2,921	2,681	3,810	3,956
Chemicals	75,807	99,435	109,354	3,812	11,336	9,078	(D)	12,930	14,403
Primary and fabricated metals	21,644	23,629	21,671	1,233	2,298	–393	1,536	2,485	2,221
Machinery	22,229	25,251	29,224	2,659	3,426	3,831	2,257	2,817	3,279
Computer and electronic products	59,909	54,317	58,785	17,303	6,108	6,094	8,860	6,516	7,174
Electrical equipment, appliances, and components	10,005	11,679	13,079	2,100	941	730	1,079	1,124	1,367
Transportation equipment	49,887	50,732	48,930	7,814	2,313	–667	4,107	4,576	2,531
Wholesale trade	93,936	130,594	142,960	11,938	10,603	17,194	14,198	24,003	27,615
Information	52,345	49,155	55,479	16,531	–3,526	6,932	–964	9,528	9,983
Depository institutions	40,152	64,719	70,331	–1,274	–304	–3,941	2,191	2,657	1,045
Finance and insurance	217,086	369,281	393,723	21,659	24,086	20,242	15,210	24,201	28,162
Professional, scientific, and technical services	32,868	45,167	49,202	5,441	8,389	4,281	3,548	5,394	5,778
Holding companies (nonbank)	(NA)	724,229	623,076	(NA)	101,353	–118,634	(NA)	59,902	69,014
Other industries	441,886	151,647	169,424	40,690	14,096	11,070	42,504	13,021	14,260

NA Not available.   D Withheld to avoid disclosure of individual company data.
Source: U.S. Bureau of Economic Analysis, *Survey of Current Business*, July 2006, and earlier issues. See also <http://www.bea.doc.gov/bea/ARTICLES/2006/07July/0706DIP_Web.pdf>.

Foreign Commerce and Aid   799

Table 1278. U.S. Direct Investment Position Abroad on a Historical-Cost Basis by Selected Country: 1990 to 2005

[In millions of dollars (430,521 represents 430,521,000,000). U.S. investment abroad is the ownership or control by one U.S. person of 10% or more of the voting securities of an incorporated foreign business enterprise or an equivalent interest in a unincorporated foreign business enterprise. Negative position can occur when a U.S. parent company's liabilities to the foreign affiliate are greater than its equity in, and loans to the foreign affiliate]

Country	1990	1995	2000	2001	2002	2003	2004	2005
All countries	430,521	699,015	1,316,247	1,460,352	1,616,548	1,769,613	2,051,204	2,069,983
Canada	69,508	83,498	132,472	152,601	166,473	187,953	212,829	234,831
Europe.................	214,739	344,596	687,320	771,936	859,378	976,889	1,104,886	1,059,443
Austria	1,113	2,829	2,872	3,964	4,011	6,366	6,688	8,762
Belgium................	9,464	18,706	17,973	22,589	25,727	27,415	30,218	36,733
Denmark...............	1,726	2,161	5,270	5,160	6,184	5,597	5,499	5,695
Finland	544	965	1,342	1,686	1,722	1,677	2,089	2,493
France	19,164	33,358	42,628	40,125	43,348	51,229	61,200	60,860
Germany	27,609	44,242	55,508	63,396	61,073	72,262	83,588	86,319
Greece	282	533	795	835	981	1,431	1,681	1,903
Hungary	(NA)	(NA)	1,920	2,033	2,503	2,856	3,317	3,402
Ireland	5,894	7,996	35,903	39,541	51,598	60,604	63,983	61,596
Italy	14,063	17,096	23,484	22,883	23,771	23,092	26,909	25,931
Luxembourg.............	1,697	5,929	27,849	50,771	62,181	68,298	81,129	61,615
Netherlands............	19,120	42,113	115,429	147,687	158,415	186,366	204,319	181,384
Norway	4,209	4,741	4,379	4,446	6,045	7,511	8,418	8,795
Poland	(NA)	(NA)	3,884	4,573	4,231	4,382	5,942	5,736
Portugal	897	1,413	2,664	2,746	3,093	2,402	2,657	2,712
Russia	(NA)	(NA)	1,147	883	1,135	2,511	3,809	5,545
Spain	7,868	10,856	21,236	28,174	38,001	41,119	44,808	43,280
Sweden	1,787	6,816	25,959	26,374	30,114	27,004	32,941	33,398
Switzerland	25,099	31,125	55,377	63,768	74,229	92,750	106,849	83,424
Turkey	522	973	1,826	1,641	1,869	2,213	2,399	2,417
United Kingdom	72,707	106,332	230,762	228,230	247,952	277,246	312,156	323,796
Latin America and other Western Hemisphere........	71,413	131,377	266,576	279,611	289,413	297,222	330,468	353,011
South America	22,933	49,170	84,220	76,809	64,603	66,256	67,568	74,403
Argentina	2,531	7,660	17,488	15,535	11,288	10,663	11,455	13,163
Brazil...............	14,384	25,002	36,717	32,027	27,598	29,553	30,226	32,420
Chile................	1,896	6,216	10,052	10,526	8,928	9,021	9,672	9,811
Colombia............	1,677	3,506	3,693	3,122	2,622	2,773	2,811	3,393
Ecuador.............	280	889	832	579	809	975	720	760
Peru	599	1,335	3,130	3,197	3,310	3,401	3,387	3,900
Venezuela	1,087	3,634	10,531	10,069	8,671	8,438	8,034	9,610
Other	479	928	1,778	1,755	1,377	1,431	1,263	1,347
Central America	20,415	33,493	73,841	60,716	65,395	64,647	72,086	79,924
Costa Rica	251	921	1,716	1,835	1,803	840	1,085	1,277
Honduras............	262	68	399	227	181	272	314	402
Mexico	10,313	16,873	39,352	52,544	56,303	56,851	63,502	71,423
Panama.............	9,289	15,123	30,758	5,141	5,842	5,409	5,631	5,162
Other	299	506	1,618	970	1,267	1,274	1,553	1,660
Other Western Hemisphere....	28,065	48,714	108,515	142,086	159,416	166,319	190,813	198,684
Barbados	252	698	2,141	2,240	1,817	984	2,519	2,940
Bermuda	20,169	28,374	60,114	84,969	89,473	84,508	86,547	90,358
Dominican Republic	529	330	1,143	1,116	983	816	1,076	758
Africa..................	3,650	6,017	11,891	15,574	16,040	19,835	21,414	24,257
Egypt.................	1,231	1,093	1,998	2,557	2,682	3,524	4,125	4,839
Nigeria	-401	629	470	260	901	1,100	1,999	874
South Africa...........	775	1,422	3,562	3,070	3,334	3,580	3,432	3,594
Other	2,045	2,873	5,861	9,687	9,122	11,631	11,857	14,950
Middle East..............	3,959	7,198	10,863	13,212	15,158	16,885	18,775	21,591
Israel	746	1,831	3,735	5,690	5,726	7,020	6,854	7,920
Saudi Arabia	1,899	2,741	3,661	3,570	4,930	3,140	3,202	3,531
United Arab Emirates........	409	500	683	834	1,087	1,934	2,292	2,663
Other	905	2,126	2,784	3,118	3,415	4,790	6,427	7,478
Asia and Pacific..............	64,716	122,712	207,125	227,418	270,086	270,830	362,833	376,849
Australia	15,110	24,328	34,838	27,778	39,074	48,447	(D)	113,385
China	354	2,765	11,140	12,081	10,570	11,261	15,006	16,877
Hong Kong	6,055	11,768	27,447	32,494	40,329	36,426	34,848	37,884
India.................	372	1,105	2,379	2,496	4,232	4,868	7,677	8,456
Indonesia	3,207	6,777	8,904	10,511	(D)	(D)	(D)	9,948
Japan.................	22,599	37,309	57,091	55,651	66,468	57,794	68,071	75,491
Korea, South	2,695	5,557	8,968	9,977	11,856	13,063	16,752	18,759
Malaysia	1,466	4,237	7,910	7,489	7,101	7,057	8,096	9,993
New Zealand	3,156	4,601	4,271	4,273	3,926	3,859	4,668	4,809
Philippines............	1,355	2,719	3,638	5,436	5,964	6,390	6,009	6,649
Singapore	3,975	12,140	24,133	40,764	50,955	51,053	57,075	48,051
Taiwan [1]	2,226	4,293	7,836	9,301	10,144	11,983	(D)	13,374
Thailand	1,790	4,283	5,824	6,176	7,774	6,886	7,582	8,556
Other	356	830	2,746	2,990	(D)	(D)	(D)	4,616

D Suppressed to avoid disclosure of data of individual companies.   NA Not available.   [1] See footnote 2, Table 1308.

Source: U.S. Bureau of Economic Analysis, *Survey of Current Business*, July 2006, and earlier issues. See also <http://www.bea.gov/bea/ARTICLES/2006/07July/0706DIPWEB.pdf> (released July 2006).

Table 1279. **U.S. Government Foreign Grants and Credits by Country: 1990 to 2005**

[In millions of dollars (14,396 represents $14,396,000,000). See text, this section. Negative figures (–) occur when the total of grant returns, principal repayments, and/or foreign currencies disbursed by the U.S. government exceeds new grants and new credits utilized and/or acquisitions of foreign currencies through new sales of farm products]

Country	1990	1995	2000	2001	2002	2003	2004	2005
Total, net	**14,396**	**12,666**	**17,878**	**12,602**	**17,213**	**22,973**	**22,108**	**29,993**
Investment in financial institutions.	1,304	1,517	1,500	1,704	1,486	1,434	1,994	1,263
Western Europe.	**–103**	**177**	**183**	**220**	**104**	**345**	**152**	**139**
Austria	–10	–1	–	–	–	–	–	–
Belgium and Luxembourg	–9	–	–	–	–	–	–	–
Finland	–8	–1	–	–	–	–	–	–
France	–15	–	–	–	–	–	–	–
Germany	–338	(Z)	–	–	–1	–	–	–
Iceland	(Z)	–	–	–	–	–	–	–
Ireland	2	–	–	–	–	44	50	–
Italy	–30	(Z)	–	–	(Z)	–	–	–
Norway	–	–	–	–	–	–	–	–
Portugal	56	–16	–79	–28	–27	–74	1	(Z)
Spain	–122	–59	–19	–19	–19	–19	–19	–19
United Kingdom	–111	–120	–135	–56	–66	–68	–72	–84
Yugoslavia [1]	–39	–	1	–	–51	231	13	4
Former Yugoslavia [1]:								
Bosnia and Herzegovina	(X)	94	52	115	64	47	66	72
Croatia	(X)	9	3	18	36	52	29	29
Macedonia	(X)	1	50	29	15	58	42	67
Slovenia	(X)	–24	2	2	7	8	4	4
Former Yugoslavia - Regional [1]. . . .	(X)	(Z)	74	87	128	66	38	66
Other [2] and unspecified [3]	520	293	234	72	17	(Z)	(Z)	–
Eastern Europe	**973**	**1,979**	**1,830**	**1,300**	**1,464**	**1,291**	**1,186**	**–193**
Albania	–	15	26	38	40	42	43	53
Bulgaria	–	6	46	54	34	48	36	53
Czechoslovakia	(Z)	–2	1	–	–	–	–	–
Czech Republic	(X)	3	11	11	23	10	13	21
Estonia	(X)	2	6	3	–2	20	12	2
Hungary	1	36	12	8	16	9	16	11
Latvia	(X)	2	6	1	11	10	9	1
Lithuania	(X)	28	–16	(Z)	3	13	(Z)	–51
Poland	912	6	40	–1	16	21	–181	–917
Romania	79	9	38	43	48	66	34	57
Slovakia	–	2	7	10	10	14	1	5
Soviet Union	–30	–	–	–	–	–	–	–
Newly independent states:								
Armenia	(X)	102	20	52	54	74	66	85
Azerbaijan	(X)	19	8	15	32	35	47	72
Belarus	(X)	50	1	4	2	(Z)	1	2
Georgia	(X)	89	36	49	97	66	111	169
Kazakhstan	(X)	17	42	58	52	50	56	69
Kyrgyzstan	(X)	33	15	32	36	35	39	54
Moldova	(X)	19	32	60	28	23	27	38
Russia	(X)	465	797	280	266	191	250	–682
Tajikistan	(X)	34	8	34	18	24	34	51
Turkmenistan	(X)	16	4	8	6	6	4	7
Ukraine	(X)	171	138	195	118	96	114	145
Uzbekistan	(X)	1	22	41	39	53	52	52
Former Soviet Union - Regional [3] . .	(X)	613	501	295	510	364	372	456
Other and unspecified [3]	11	241	29	10	7	21	30	54
Near East and South Asia.	**6,656**	**3,025**	**7,658**	**2,520**	**5,656**	**10,024**	**11,791**	**20,158**
Afghanistan	57	10	5	6	140	555	1,141	1,403
Bangladesh	181	87	43	89	45	29	50	48
Cyprus	16	6	–	–	–	(Z)	14	2
Egypt	4,976	1,639	3,091	1,296	1,689	2,024	2,687	2,818
Greece	282	261	–169	–153	–218	–317	–457	–121
India	13	48	–64	–56	–122	–150	–40	–70
Iran [4]	–	–	–	–	–	(Z)	4	–
Iraq [4]	–7	128	(Z)	1	(Z)	3,339	5,011	9,805
Israel	4,380	420	3,932	589	3,061	2,743	2,156	4,936
Jordan	155	129	317	298	483	1,403	798	581
Kuwait	–2,506	–	–	–	–	75	32	–
Lebanon	9	5	22	60	28	24	30	37
Nepal	20	20	15	27	28	43	37	50
Oman	4	4	–6	–10	–8	–2	51	32
Pakistan	531	–187	366	170	445	223	153	461
Saudi Arabia	–1,614	–	–	–	–	–	–	–
Sri Lanka	72	27	–15	–6	–10	–16	–11	36
Syria	(Z)	–	–	–	–	–	(Z)	(Z)
Turkey	367	147	–86	–5	–138	–324	–301	–228
United Arab Emirates	–361	–	–	–	–	–	(Z)	19
Yemen [5]	43	3	16	7	5	17	30	24
UNRWA [5]	7	103	97	77	71	124	27	48
West Bank-Gaza	1	58	64	115	143	195	171	179
Other and unspecified [3]	29	118	30	15	14	39	208	98

See footnotes at end of table.

U.S. Census Bureau, Statistical Abstract of the United States: 2007

[**In millions of dollars.** See headnote, p. 801]

Country	1990	1995	2000	2001	2002	2003	2004	2005
Africa	**1,883**	**2,217**	**1,042**	**1,562**	**2,015**	**2,822**	**2,157**	**1,970**
Algeria	59	755	−53	182	−73	−123	−146	−173
Angola	−15	37	31	43	87	27	−7	18
Benin	5	14	22	38	23	24	22	23
Botswana	17	18	1	1	12	1	(Z)	4
Burkina Faso	15	23	7	9	12	2	5	6
Burundi	18	39	3	6	3	18	27	6
Cameroon	42	4	1	3	6	3	2	7
Cape Verde	8	11	1	2	2	1	4	2
Chad	24	14	2	7	3	1	24	8
Congo (Kinshasa)	242	1	9	16	33	1,078	229	118
Cote d'Ivoire	18	16	9	2	32	52	11	2
Eritrea	–	9	48	45	36	23	42	62
Ethiopia	57	127	142	98	87	138	234	308
Ghana	14	63	40	86	48	50	67	53
Guinea	16	28	19	45	41	30	33	36
Kenya	115	35	44	108	50	58	82	91
Lesotho	16	13	1	1	1	1	1	1
Liberia	32	67	19	19	10	13	50	40
Madagascar	34	33	21	63	36	31	34	35
Malawi	35	64	45	41	46	42	54	46
Mali	31	31	50	9	49	50	45	55
Mauritania	13	2	2	5	4	3	4	13
Morocco	96	−48	−9	−29	760	−57	−49	−46
Mozambique	83	115	119	133	105	107	105	64
Niger	34	31	5	5	9	3	4	4
Nigeria	156	1	−17	17	45	468	41	67
Rwanda	13	138	26	57	32	36	35	47
Senegal	61	24	27	51	42	45	52	38
Sierra Leone	2	11	10	11	29	36	17	10
Somalia	80	26	7	1	6	10	16	7
South Africa	20	112	68	119	98	115	332	103
Sudan	150	11	17	13	11	41	120	130
Swaziland	14	13	–	–	–	–	(Z)	(Z)
Tanzania	51	19	15	50	44	49	66	62
Togo	10	3	2	2	4	5	1	1
Tunisia	44	−4	−19	−18	−12	−15	−3	−10
Uganda	43	56	92	55	71	86	120	148
Zambia	63	27	44	42	34	52	56	90
Zimbabwe	10	29	23	24	21	23	31	27
Other and unspecified [3]	157	246	168	200	168	295	396	467
Far East and Pacific	**39**	**753**	**550**	**725**	**331**	**689**	**−193**	**−18**
Australia	−34	–	–	–	–	–	–	–
Burma	1	−2	–	1	4	5	4	3
Cambodia	5	39	23	42	35	32	44	57
China [6]	71	136	167	132	45	4	2	(Z)
Hong Kong	−8	73	−15	−24	−20	−23	−28	−28
Indonesia	46	25	270	488	221	821	−157	−9
Japan and Ryukyu Islands	−635	(Z)	–	1	–	–	–	–
Korea, South	−192	−49	−132	−215	−134	−137	−110	−43
Laos	(Z)	3	5	6	7	6	5	2
Malaysia	−1	(Z)	134	184	11	1	−46	−46
Mongolia	–	11	9	18	20	15	20	19
New Zealand	−2	–	–	–	–	–	–	–
Pacific Islands, Trust Territory of the [7]	220	209	145	206	193	103	205	190
Philippines	557	56	20	−17	−46	−39	−16	−39
Singapore	(Z)	1	–	–	–	–	–	–
Taiwan [6]	−7	−5	−1	−1	−1	(Z)	(Z)	(Z)
Thailand	−19	205	−102	−118	−27	−48	5	(Z)
Vietnam	1	(Z)	1	10	7	9	24	13
Other and unspecified [3]	38	51	26	12	16	−60	−145	−137
Western Hemisphere	**2,025**	**485**	**1,173**	**1,380**	**710**	**676**	**1,294**	**1,392**
Argentina	64	−26	−73	−55	4	20	150	97
Bolivia	114	101	136	189	152	208	213	153
Brazil	261	−204	195	119	106	−79	−137	−94
Canada	−41	–	–	–	–	–	–	–
Chile	−32	−24	−22	−19	−19	−5	(Z)	−3
Colombia	−30	5	33	71	76	153	284	442
Costa Rica	108	−28	−34	−31	−27	−41	−16	−2
Dominican Republic	28	−15	−58	−41	−65	−60	−25	14
Ecuador	61	5	14	38	75	18	18	38
El Salvador	303	119	27	78	45	55	98	46

See footnotes at end of table.

U.S. Census Bureau, Statistical Abstract of the United States: 2007

No. 1279. **U.S. Government Foreign Grants and Credits by Type and Country: 1990 to 2005**—Con.

[In millions of dollars. See headnote, p. 801]

Country	1990	1995	2000	2001	2002	2003	2004	2005
Western Hemisphere—Con.:								
Guatemala	98	39	49	106	54	41	39	21
Guyana	42	10	5	9	4	4	7	10
Haiti	54	156	63	106	66	64	83	118
Honduras	226	77	100	258	85	50	83	70
Jamaica	108	30	-34	-21	-15	-8	-2	3
Mexico.	140	-198	-123	14	-13	-8	4	30
Nicaragua.	105	41	53	152	60	40	28	35
Panama [8]	102	8	-13	-9	(Z)	3	13	6
Paraguay	(Z)	1	4	9	9	11	10	7
Peru	93	151	87	133	109	84	158	120
Trinidad and Tobago.	5	-14	-19	-21	-26	-31	-108	-5
Uruguay	-3	1	-2	(Z)	-2	(Z)	-2	-2
Venezuela	-18	-2	133	2	-8	-6	(Z)	-6
Other [9] and unspecified [3]	236	251	652	292	40	164	396	294
Other international organizations and unspecified areas [3]	**1,619**	**2,513**	**3,942**	**3,191**	**5,447**	**5,692**	**3,727**	**5,282**

– Represents or rounds to zero. X Not applicable. Z Less than $500,000. [1] In 1992, some successor countries assumed portions of outstanding credits of the former Yugoslavia (assignment of the remaining portions is pending). Subsequent negative totals reflect payments to the United States on these assumed credits which were greater than the extension of new credits and grants to these countries. [2] Includes North Atlantic Treaty Organization and Organization for Economic Cooperation and Development. [3] In recent years, significant amounts of foreign assistance has been reported on a regional, inter-regional, and worldwide basis. Country totals in this table may understate actual assistance to many countries. [4] Foreign assistance to Iraq during the 1991–96 period was direct humanitarian assistance to ethnic minorities of Northern Iraq after the conflict in the Persian Gulf. [5] United Nations Relief and Works Agency for Palestine refugees. [6] See footnote 2, Table 1380. [7] Excludes transactions with Commonwealth of the Northern Mariana Islands after 1990; includes transactions with Federated States of Micronesia, Republic of the Marshall Islands, and Republic of Palau. [8] Includes transfer of Panama Canal to the Republic of Panama on December 1999. [9] Includes Andean Development Corporation, Caribbean Development Bank, Central American Bank for Economic Integration, Eastern Caribbean Central Bank, Inter-American Institute of Agricultural Science, Organizations of American States, and Pan American Health Organization.

Source: U.S. Bureau of Economic Analysis, press releases, and unpublished data.

Table 1280. **U.S. Foreign Economic and Military Aid Programs: 1980 to 2004**

[In millions of dollars (9,694 represents $9,694,000,000). For years ending September 30. Economic aid shown here represents U.S. economic aid—not just aid under the Foreign Assistance Act. Major components in recent years include AID, Food for Peace, Peace Corps, and paid-in subscriptions to international financial institutions, such as IBRD, and IDB. Annual figures are gross unadjusted program figures]

Year and region	Total economic and military aid	Economic aid			Military aid		
		Total	Loans	Grants	Total	Loans	Grants
1980	9,694	7,572	843	6,729	2,122	1,450	672
1981	10,539	7,294	775	6,519	3,245	2,546	699
1982	12,316	8,122	690	7,432	4,195	3,084	1,111
1983	19,314	8,602	773	7,830	10,711	9,044	1,667
1984	15,524	9,038	784	8,255	6,485	4,401	2,084
1985	18,128	12,327	984	11,343	5,801	2,365	3,436
1986	16,620	10,796	890	9,907	5,824	1,980	3,844
1987	14,797	9,705	892	8,813	5,092	953	4,139
1988	13,965	9,135	693	8,442	4,831	763	4,068
1989	14,846	10,018	687	9,331	4,828	410	4,418
1990	16,056	11,044	748	10,296	5,012	404	4,608
1991	17,268	12,099	345	11,754	5,169	478	4,692
1992	16,181	11,564	494	11,070	4,617	345	4,272
1993	17,434	12,611	545	12,066	4,823	855	3,968
1994	16,705	12,355	978	11,377	4,350	770	3,581
1995	15,823	11,894	277	11,617	3,930	558	3,372
1996	14,201	9,898	393	9,505	4,303	544	3,759
1997	13,544	9,588	244	9,344	3,956	298	3,658
1998	14,469	10,827	335	10,492	3,642	100	3,542
1999	15,787	12,023	900	11,123	3,764	–	3,764
2000	16,092	11,474	244	11,229	4,619	–	4,619
2001	16,740	12,986	268	12,718	3,754	–	3,754
2002	20,689	16,166	187	15,979	4,522	–	4,522
2003	27,312	20,807	245	20,562	6,506	–	6,506
2004, total	**33,405**	**26,613**	**216**	**26,397**	**6,791**	**–**	**6,791**
Asia	3,587	2,865	81	2,783	722	–	722
Central Asia	1,942	1,893	18	1,875	49	–	49
Eastern Europe.	715	551	–	551	163	–	163
Latin America and Caribbean	2,362	2,228	37	2,191	134	–	134
Middle East and North Africa	14,118	8,514	58	8,456	5,604	–	5,604
Oceania	146	145	–	145	1	–	1
Sub-Saharan Africa	3,975	3,911	22	3,888	64	–	64
Western Europe	66	25	–	25	41	–	41
World not specified	6,473	6,461	–	6,461	12	–	12

– Represents or rounds to zero.

Source: U.S. Agency for International Development, *U.S. Overseas Loans, Grants, Obligations and Loan Authorizations,* annual. See also <http://qesdb.cdie.org/gbk/index.html> (released 01 March 2006).

Foreign Commerce and Aid   803

Table 1281. **U.S. Foreign Economic and Military Aid by Major Recipient Country: 2000 to 2004**

[In millions of dollars (16,092 represents $16,092,000,000). For years ending Sept. 30]

Recipient country	2000	2001	2002	2003	2004		
					Total	Economic aid	Military aid
Total [1]	16,092	16,740	20,689	27,312	33,405	26,613	6,791
Afghanistan	40	89	556	1,330	2,033	1,463	570
Albania	69	54	53	56	48	42	6
Angola	102	77	121	158	118	118	1
Armenia	104	116	101	74	77	74	3
Azerbaijan	54	40	61	55	57	54	4
Bangladesh	78	154	96	104	92	91	1
Bolivia	240	197	183	210	183	178	5
Bosnia and Herzegovina	164	171	92	89	89	58	31
Bulgaria	49	62	60	58	47	37	10
Burundi	7	23	25	45	47	47	–
Cambodia	24	35	44	61	73	73	–
Chad	4	8	5	8	58	57	1
Colombia	1,158	257	536	678	748	648	100
Congo (Kinshasa)	31	75	80	121	120	119	–
Dominican Republic	21	44	31	40	45	42	3
Ecuador	76	63	86	89	91	91	–
Egypt	2,044	1,708	2,196	1,754	1,958	664	1,294
El Salvador	35	114	114	64	69	62	7
Eritrea	37	69	28	104	88	87	–
Ethiopia	277	198	138	603	436	433	3
Georgia	111	135	184	86	124	108	16
Ghana	66	72	56	78	73	72	2
Guatemala	72	75	82	90	74	73	1
Guinea	33	61	45	50	53	52	1
Haiti	88	86	57	84	158	158	1
Honduras	41	48	45	73	66	63	4
India	185	181	205	183	174	173	1
Indonesia	242	168	194	202	157	157	1
Iraq	5	–	39	3,944	8,263	6,421	1,842
Israel	3,770	2,814	2,760	3,684	2,702	555	2,147
Jordan	400	265	348	1,594	609	401	208
Kazakhstan	53	51	66	56	73	69	4
Kenya	90	142	101	131	186	177	9
Korea, North	139	162	118	41	56	56	–
Kosovo	197	178	141	57	117	110	7
Liberia	14	54	15	41	138	138	–
Macedonia	60	63	86	73	52	44	9
Madagascar	27	33	32	47	45	45	–
Malawi	44	34	51	45	53	52	–
Mali	44	41	42	53	54	54	–
Mexico	44	52	94	69	94	93	1
Micronesia, Federated States of	81	82	100	100	78	78	–
Moldova	49	73	46	40	45	42	2
Mozambique	78	83	62	91	102	101	–
Nepal	22	41	59	56	55	51	5
Nicaragua	34	61	49	68	62	59	2
Nigeria	113	97	105	94	125	125	–
Pakistan	19	187	1,081	370	231	155	76
Peru	203	209	280	232	275	275	–
Philippines	80	137	202	223	220	168	53
Romania	46	64	60	69	53	42	11
Russia	389	508	463	883	1,142	1,142	1
Rwanda	37	31	41	47	60	59	–
Serbia and Montenegro	353	398	340	208	242	235	7
South Africa	55	56	77	92	126	126	–
Sri Lanka	9	26	29	34	37	34	3
Sudan	51	69	121	186	479	474	5
Tajikistan	36	64	89	49	50	47	2
Tanzania	43	81	45	81	101	101	–
Turkey	3	7	257	1,028	50	10	40
Uganda	76	90	94	179	225	222	3
Ukraine	180	209	226	98	135	125	10
West Bank/Gaza	122	135	336	192	137	137	–
Yemen	56	40	23	41	79	58	21
Zambia	35	46	66	66	102	102	1

– Represents zero or rounds to zero.   [1] Includes countries not shown separately.

Source: U.S. Agency for International Development, *U.S. Overseas Loans, Grants, Obligations and Loan Authorizations*, annual. See also <http://qesdb.cdie.org/gbk/index.html>.

804   Foreign Commerce and Aid

Table 1282. U.S. International Trade in Goods and Services: 1998 to 2005

[In millions of dollars (–163,153 represents –$163,153,000,000). Data presented on a balance of payments basis and will not agree with the following merchandise trade Tables 1283 to 1293]

Category	1998	1999	2000	2001	2002	2003	2004	2005
TRADE BALANCE								
Total	–164,606	–263,286	–377,559	–362,795	–421,068	–494,897	–611,296	–716,730
Goods	–246,687	–346,015	–452,414	–427,188	–482,297	–547,302	–665,410	–782,740
Services	82,081	82,729	74,855	64,393	61,230	52,405	54,114	66,010
Travel	14,842	15,838	17,695	11,693	7,890	6,904	8,797	12,505
Passenger fares	127	–1,530	–3,587	–4,707	–2,923	–5,264	–4,872	–5,135
Other transportation	–4,759	–7,223	–11,622	–10,240	–9,212	–13,193	–16,725	–19,862
Royalties, license fees	24,391	26,563	26,765	24,158	25,155	27,955	29,301	32,909
Other private services	44,183	48,424	47,384	47,836	49,603	50,851	54,264	59,509
Other [1]	5,220	2,593	317	–2,296	–7,158	–12,527	–13,832	–11,024
U.S. govt misc. services. . .	–1,923	–1,936	–2,097	–2,051	–2,125	–2,321	–2,819	–2,892
EXPORTS								
Total	933,174	965,884	1,070,597	1,004,896	974,721	1,016,096	1,151,942	1,275,245
Goods	670,416	683,965	771,994	718,712	682,422	713,415	807,516	894,631
Services	262,758	281,919	298,603	286,184	292,299	302,681	344,426	380,614
Travel	71,325	74,801	82,400	71,893	66,605	64,348	74,547	81,680
Passenger fares	20,098	19,785	20,687	17,926	17,046	15,693	18,851	20,931
Other transportation	25,604	26,916	29,803	28,442	29,195	31,512	37,436	42,245
Royalties, license fees	35,626	39,670	43,233	40,696	44,508	46,988	52,512	57,410
Other private services	91,774	103,934	107,904	113,857	122,207	130,561	144,654	158,223
Other [1]	17,405	15,928	13,790	12,539	11,943	12,769	15,467	19,038
U.S. govt misc. services. . .	926	885	786	831	795	810	959	1,087
IMPORTS								
Total	1,097,780	1,229,170	1,448,156	1,367,691	1,395,789	1,510,993	1,763,238	1,991,975
Goods	917,103	1,029,980	1,224,408	1,145,900	1,164,720	1,260,717	1,472,926	1,677,371
Services	180,677	199,190	223,748	221,791	231,069	250,276	290,312	314,604
Travel	56,483	58,963	64,705	60,200	58,715	57,444	65,750	69,175
Passenger fares	19,971	21,315	24,274	22,633	19,969	20,957	23,723	26,066
Other transportation	30,363	34,139	41,425	38,682	38,407	44,705	54,161	62,107
Royalties, license fees	11,235	13,107	16,468	16,538	19,353	19,033	23,211	24,501
Other private services	47,591	55,510	60,520	66,021	72,604	79,710	90,390	98,714
Other [1]	12,185	13,335	13,473	14,835	19,101	25,296	29,299	30,062
U.S. govt misc. services. . .	2,849	2,821	2,883	2,882	2,920	3,131	3,778	3,979

[1] Represents transfers under U.S. military sales contracts for exports and direct defense expenditures for imports.
Source: U.S. Census Bureau, *U.S. International Trade in Goods and Services, Annual Revision for 2005*, Series FT-900(06-04) and previous reports. See also <http://www.census.gov/foreign-trade/Press-Release/2005pr/final_revisions/05final.pdf> (released 09 June 2006).

Table 1283. U.S. Exports, General Imports, and Trade Balance in Goods: 1980 to 2004

[In billions of dollars (225.7 represents $225,700,000,000). Domestic and foreign exports, are f.a.s. value basis; general imports are on customs value basis]

Year	Total goods [1]			Manufactured goods [2, 3]			Agricultural products [4]			Mineral fuels [3, 5]		
	Exports	Imports	Balance	Exports	Imports	Balance	Exports	Imports	Balance	Exports	Imports	Balance
1980 . .	225.7	245.3	–19.5	160.7	133.0	27.7	41.8	17.4	24.3	8.2	78.9	–70.7
1981 . .	238.7	261.0	–22.3	171.7	149.8	22.0	43.8	17.2	26.6	10.3	81.2	–70.9
1982 . .	216.4	244.0	–27.5	155.3	151.7	3.6	37.0	15.7	21.3	12.8	65.3	–52.5
1983 . .	205.6	258.0	–52.4	148.5	171.2	–22.7	36.5	16.5	19.9	9.8	57.8	–48.0
1983 . .	205.6	258.0	–52.4	148.7	170.9	–22.2	36.1	16.0	20.2	9.8	57.8	–48.0
1984 . .	224.0	330.7	–106.7	164.1	230.9	–66.8	37.9	19.3	18.6	9.7	60.8	–51.1
1985 . .	218.8	336.5	–117.7	168.0	257.5	–89.5	29.3	19.5	9.8	10.3	53.7	–43.4
1986 . .	227.2	365.4	–138.3	179.8	296.7	–116.8	26.3	20.9	5.4	8.4	37.2	–28.8
1987 . .	254.1	406.2	–152.1	199.9	324.4	–124.6	28.7	20.3	8.4	8.0	44.1	–36.1
1988 . .	322.4	441.0	–118.5	255.6	361.4	–105.7	37.1	20.7	16.4	8.5	41.0	–32.5
1989 . .	363.8	473.2	–109.4	287.0	379.4	–92.4	41.6	21.1	20.5	9.9	52.6	–42.7
1990 . .	393.6	495.3	–101.7	315.4	388.8	–73.5	39.6	22.3	17.2	12.4	64.7	–52.3
1991 . .	421.7	488.5	–66.7	345.1	392.4	–47.3	39.4	22.1	17.2	12.3	54.1	–41.8
1992 . .	448.2	532.7	–84.5	368.5	434.3	–65.9	43.1	23.4	19.8	11.3	55.3	–43.9
1993 . .	465.1	580.7	–115.6	388.7	479.9	–91.2	42.8	23.6	19.2	9.9	55.9	–46.0
1994 . .	512.6	663.3	–150.6	431.1	557.3	–126.3	45.9	26.0	20.0	9.0	56.4	–47.4
1995 . .	584.7	743.4	–158.7	486.7	629.7	–143.0	56.0	29.3	26.8	10.5	59.1	–48.6
1996 . .	625.1	795.3	–170.2	524.7	658.8	–134.1	60.6	32.6	28.1	12.4	78.1	–65.7
1997 . .	689.2	870.7	–181.5	592.5	728.9	–136.4	57.1	35.2	21.9	13.0	78.3	–65.3
1998 . .	682.1	911.9	–229.8	596.6	790.8	–194.2	52.0	35.7	16.3	10.4	57.3	–47.0
1999 . .	695.8	1,024.6	–328.8	611.6	882.7	–271.1	48.2	36.7	11.5	9.9	75.2	–65.3
2000 . .	781.9	1,218.0	–436.1	691.5	1,012.9	–321.3	53.0	39.2	13.8	13.4	135.4	–122.0
2001 . .	729.1	1,141.0	–411.9	640.2	950.7	–310.4	55.2	39.5	15.7	12.7	121.9	–109.2
2002 . .	693.1	1,164.7	–471.6	606.3	974.6	–368.3	54.8	42.0	12.8	11.7	115.7	–104.0
2003 . .	724.8	1,257.1	–532.4	627.1	1,027.4	–400.3	61.4	47.5	13.9	14.1	153.3	–139.2
2004 . .	818.8	1,469.7	–650.9	710.3	1,174.8	–464.4	63.4	54.2	9.2	19.0	206.7	–187.6

[1] Includes nonmonetary gold, military grant aid, special category shipments, trade between the U.S. Virgin Islands and foreign countries and undocumented exports to Canada. Adjustments were also made for carryover. Import values are based on transaction prices whenever possible. [2] Manufactured goods include commodity sections 5–9 under Schedules A and E for 1980–1982 and SITC Rev. 3 for 1983–forward. Manufactures include undocumented exports to Canada, nonmonetary gold (excluding ore, scrap, and base bullion), and special category shipments. [3] Data for 1980 exclude trade between the U.S. Virgin Islands and foreign countries. Census data concordances link the 1980–92 trade figures into time series that are as consistent as possible. Import values for Customs value; these values are based on transaction prices while maintaining a data series as consistent as possible over time. 1991 Imports include revisions for passenger cars, trucks, petroleum, and petroleum products not included elsewhere. [4] Agricultural products for 1983–forward utilize the latest census definition that excludes manufactured goods that were previously classified as manufactured agricultural products. [5] Mineral fuels include commodity section 3 under SITC Rev. 2 for 1980–1982 and SITC Rev. 3 for 1983–forward.
Source: U.S. International Trade Administration, through 1996, *U.S. Foreign Trade Highlights*, annual; and thereafter, <http://www.ita.doc.gov/td/industry/otea/usfth/aggregate/H04t03.pdf> (released 20 June 2005).

Table 1284. **U.S. Exports and Imports for Consumption of Merchandise by Customs District: 1990 to 2005**

[In billions of dollars (393.0 represents $393,000,000,000). Exports are f.a.s. (free alongside ship) value all years; imports are on customs value basis. These data may differ from those in Tables 1283, 1288, and 1289. For methodology, see Foreign Trade Statistics in Appendix III]

Customs district	Exports					Imports for consumption				
	1990	2000	2003	2004	2005	1990	2000	2003	2004	2005
Total [1]	393.0	780.0	723.7	817.9	904.4	490.6	1,205.6	1,250.1	1,460.2	1,662.4
Anchorage, AK.........	3.7	5.9	8.4	8.7	12.1	0.7	13.4	9.2	10.5	10.2
Baltimore, MD	6.7	6.2	6.0	7.2	9.0	11.2	18.6	22.7	26.7	29.5
Boston, MA	5.6	7.0	7.0	9.7	9.9	12.2	18.7	16.4	19.2	21.4
Buffalo, NY	15.8	38.2	28.8	33.6	34.7	19.2	38.4	35.9	40.9	42.1
Charleston, SC [2]	6.7	12.6	13.6	15.4	16.1	6.8	16.9	21.0	26.0	30.9
Chicago, IL	10.2	21.7	21.3	25.9	30.0	18.3	51.1	58.3	69.1	78.5
Cleveland, OH	4.0	22.7	17.2	19.0	20.8	11.3	36.5	36.1	44.6	51.2
Dallas/Fort Worth, TX	3.4	11.5	12.3	16.4	17.8	4.8	18.8	22.4	27.8	32.0
Detroit, MI	35.6	79.4	87.6	93.4	105.7	37.8	97.6	98.8	112.2	122.8
Duluth, MN	0.8	1.5	1.7	1.8	1.9	3.9	7.0	7.6	9.0	9.4
El Paso, TX	3.9	18.0	17.5	19.3	19.9	5.0	24.1	25.3	27.8	27.7
Great Falls, MT	2.4	5.0	5.4	6.1	9.7	4.7	14.3	17.5	21.5	26.8
Honolulu, HI..........	0.5	0.7	2.5	1.8	2.4	2.1	2.9	2.0	2.2	2.9
Houston/Galveston, TX ...	17.6	29.7	32.1	39.5	46.7	21.6	40.9	48.4	64.4	89.4
Laredo, TX	15.2	57.7	48.6	56.0	60.3	10.0	62.7	66.1	74.4	78.2
Los Angeles, CA........	42.1	77.6	67.7	70.8	78.4	64.1	150.1	165.4	191.0	213.5
Miami, FL	11.2	31.0	26.3	30.0	34.1	7.1	23.3	25.0	27.8	30.4
Milwaukee, WI	0.1	0.1	0.2	0.1	0.2	1.1	1.5	1.8	1.5	1.5
Minneapolis, MN.......	0.9	1.4	1.5	1.7	2.3	2.0	4.3	5.4	5.8	6.9
Mobile, AL [2].........	1.9	4.0	4.6	5.0	4.9	3.4	7.9	8.9	11.0	13.7
New Orleans, LA	18.0	35.9	33.6	36.8	32.4	24.1	54.0	59.2	76.2	94.2
New York, NY	50.9	79.5	71.9	80.8	90.8	68.0	145.6	147.5	163.6	176.3
Nogales, AZ	2.1	7.3	5.0	5.9	6.9	4.2	14.1	11.6	12.5	13.6
Norfolk, VA [2]	11.7	12.4	12.3	13.4	16.7	7.4	13.6	17.7	20.0	23.5
Ogdensburg, NY........	7.9	12.4	10.4	11.9	13.2	9.8	23.7	21.3	24.2	27.8
Pembina, ND.........	3.4	8.7	9.2	11.0	13.6	4.1	11.0	9.6	11.1	12.8
Philadelphia, PA........	4.0	6.0	7.3	9.0	10.1	18.3	28.3	29.8	38.6	47.5
Port Arthur, TX	0.9	1.2	1.4	2.0	2.1	3.2	10.9	13.7	18.0	21.3
Portland, ME	1.7	2.6	2.8	2.8	2.8	4.3	8.7	8.8	9.3	10.9
Portland, OR	5.8	7.2	6.2	6.7	6.3	5.6	12.5	11.8	13.9	14.2
Providence, RI	(Z)	(Z)	0.1	0.1	0.1	1.3	1.3	3.1	3.3	4.4
San Diego, CA........	3.4	12.7	12.7	14.0	15.0	4.3	22.2	22.8	25.4	28.2
San Francisco, CA	23.1	58.3	33.1	38.2	36.6	28.0	68.6	46.2	54.9	61.8
San Juan, PR	2.5	4.8	8.9	9.7	9.7	5.4	11.8	19.0	19.1	19.4
Savannah, GA	7.4	15.9	17.0	21.6	24.6	9.8	26.1	30.8	38.4	47.6
Seattle, WA..........	32.6	40.4	39.8	43.5	48.9	20.9	40.5	35.7	43.2	51.0
St. Albans, VT	4.0	4.5	3.0	3.6	4.2	5.2	9.4	9.8	10.5	12.6
St. Louis, MO.........	0.3	1.3	0.6	0.7	1.3	3.0	7.9	7.9	9.1	10.1
Tampa, FL...........	4.3	4.8	6.2	7.5	10.0	7.0	14.7	14.6	15.4	19.7
Virgin Islands of the U.S. ..	0.2	0.3	0.4	0.5	0.5	2.1	4.8	5.0	6.8	9.0
Washington, DC	1.1	2.8	2.4	2.8	3.7	0.8	2.6	2.4	3.3	3.7
Wilmington, NC	3.0	2.5	1.7	1.9	2.2	3.3	10.6	13.2	13.9	15.5

Z Less than $50 million. [1] Totals shown for exports reflect the value of estimated parcel post and Special Category shipments, and beginning 1990, adjustments for undocumented exports to Canada, which are not distributed by customs district. The value of bituminous coal exported through Norfolk, VA; Charleston, SC; and Mobile, AL is reflected in the total but not distributed by district. [2] Excludes exports of bituminous coal, which are included in the "Total" line.

Source: U.S. Census Bureau, 1990, *U.S. Merchandise Trade: Selected Highlights,* Series FT 920, monthly; 2000–2004, *U.S. Export History* and *U.S. Import History* on compact disc; beginning 2005, *U.S. Merchandise Trade: Selected Highlights,* December 2005, series FT920. See also <http://www.census.gov/foreign-trade/Press-Release/ft920index.html> (released 10 February 2006).

Table 1285. **Export and Import Unit Value Indexes—Selected Countries: 2001 to 2005**

[Indexes in U.S. dollars, 2000 = 100. A unit value is an implicit price derived from value and quantity data]

Country	Export unit value					Import unit value				
	2001	2002	2003	2004	2005	2001	2002	2003	2004	2005
United States	99.2	98.2	99.7	103.6	106.9	96.5	94.1	96.9	102.3	110.0
Australia	98.2	100.0	109.9	129.1	152.9	94.3	94.5	103.8	111.1	116.6
Belgium	99.3	103.5	120.4	134.9	142.0	99.5	102.2	119.8	136.1	142.8
Canada..............	97.8	93.2	103.8	114.8	129.0	98.8	98.2	101.9	107.9	115.9
France	107.7	109.0	130.7	141.4	140.4	99.5	98.9	118.7	127.6	127.0
Germany.............	99.0	100.5	118.3	128.9	129.7	97.1	97.2	110.4	120.3	123.2
Greece..............	104.9	111.5	133.4	154.1	160.1	(NA)	(NA)	(NA)	(NA)	(NA)
Ireland	98.3	103.2	114.7	115.4	119.1	100.0	101.1	111.1	119.5	119.5
Italy	100.6	107.3	129.6	148.6	158.7	99.7	104.4	124.8	143.8	157.0
Japan................	91.4	87.6	90.9	96.0	96.1	90.9	86.8	93.1	103.9	115.4
Korea, South	86.9	83.1	85.1	91.5	92.7	91.0	87.5	95.6	107.3	117.3
Netherlands..........	99.6	99.4	115.9	126.3	131.7	101.2	101.1	117.5	130.9	132.6
Norway..............	93.1	93.3	104.3	126.8	160.9	98.2	102.8	116.1	126.5	132.4
Spain	97.6	101.7	120.1	133.4	139.9	96.2	98.0	115.9	130.6	137.4
Sweden	90.1	93.8	110.3	121.2	124.1	92.7	98.6	116.2	131.2	138.4
Switzerland	101.3	107.1	123.5	137.2	139.4	100.1	104.8	121.5	135.3	142.1
United Kingdom	93.6	97.4	108.0	121.5	125.5	94.3	95.8	103.6	115.6	119.6

NA Not available.

Source: International Monetary Fund, Washington, DC, *International Financial Statistics,* monthly, (copyright).

806   Foreign Commerce and Aid

Table 1286. U.S. Exports by State of Origin: 2000 to 2005

[In millions of dollars (782,429 represents $782,429,000,000) except as indicated. Exports are on a f.a.s. value basis. Exports are based on origin of movement]

State and other area	2000	2004	2005 Total	2005 Rank	State and other area	2000	2004	2005 Total	2005 Rank
Total........	782,429	819,026	904,289	(X)	Montana.........	541	565	711	49
United States ...	712,055	769,332	853,746	(X)	Nebraska........	2,511	2,316	3,004	40
Alabama.........	7,317	9,037	10,796	24	Nevada	1,482	2,907	3,937	35
Alaska..........	2,464	3,157	3,592	37	New Hampshire....	2,373	2,286	2,548	41
Arizona..........	14,334	13,423	14,950	17	New Jersey.......	18,638	19,192	21,080	12
Arkansas........	2,599	3,493	3,862	36	New Mexico......	2,391	2,046	2,540	42
California	119,640	109,968	116,819	2	New York	42,846	44,401	50,492	3
Colorado.........	6,593	6,651	6,784	29	North Carolina....	17,946	18,115	19,463	14
Connecticut.......	8,047	8,559	9,687	26	North Dakota......	626	1,008	1,185	46
Delaware	2,197	2,053	2,525	43	Ohio	26,322	31,208	34,801	7
District of Columbia .	1,003	1,164	825	(X)	Oklahoma........	3,072	3,178	4,314	32
Florida	26,543	28,982	33,377	8	Oregon..........	11,441	11,172	12,381	22
Georgia	14,925	19,633	20,577	13	Pennsylvania......	18,792	18,487	22,271	9
Hawaii	387	405	1,028	47	Rhode Island......	1,186	1,286	1,269	45
Idaho...........	3,559	2,915	3,260	38	South Carolina.....	8,565	13,376	13,944	21
Illinois	31,438	30,214	35,868	6	South Dakota.....	679	826	942	48
Indiana..........	15,386	19,109	21,476	11	Tennessee	11,592	16,123	19,070	16
Iowa	4,466	6,394	7,348	27	Texas...........	103,866	117,245	128,761	1
Kansas..........	5,145	4,931	6,720	30	Utah	3,221	4,718	6,056	31
Kentucky	9,612	12,992	14,899	19	Vermont	4,097	3,283	4,240	33
Louisiana	16,814	19,922	19,232	15	Virginia..........	11,698	11,631	12,216	23
Maine...........	1,779	2,432	2,310	44	Washington.......	32,215	33,793	37,948	4
Maryland	4,593	5,746	7,119	28	West Virginia......	2,219	3,262	3,147	39
Massachusetts.....	20,514	21,837	22,043	10	Wisconsin........	10,508	12,706	14,924	18
Michigan.........	33,845	35,625	37,584	5	Wyoming	503	680	669	50
Minnesota........	10,303	12,678	14,705	20	Puerto Rico	9,735	13,162	13,264	(X)
Mississippi	2,726	3,179	4,008	34	Virgin Islands	174	389	539	(X)
Missouri.........	6,497	8,997	10,462	25	Other [1]	60,464	36,142	36,740	(X)

X Not applicable.　　[1] Includes unreported, not specified, special category, estimated shipments, re-exports, and any timing adjustments.

Source: U.S. Census Bureau, *U.S. International Trade in Goods and Services,* series FT-900, December issues. For most recent release, see <http://www.census.gov/foreign-trade/Press-Release/2005pr/12/> (released 10 February 2006).

Table 1287. U.S. Agricultural Exports by State: 2000 to 2005

[In millions of dollars (50,744 represents $50,744,000,000). Fiscal years]

State	2000	2002	2003	2004	2005	State	2000	2002	2003	2004	2005
U.S...	50,744	53,291	55,987	62,368	62,369	NE......	2,977	3,122	3,128	2,990	2,825
AL.....	393	418	388	513	520	NV......	40	42	35	39	45
AK.....	1	1	1	1	1	NH......	9	9	8	11	10
AZ.....	394	392	454	445	419	NJ......	125	143	147	156	158
AR.....	1,235	1,212	1,445	1,756	1,721	NM......	128	137	137	167	187
CA.....	6,685	7,059	8,150	9,487	10,168	NY......	481	494	451	493	565
CO.....	964	926	869	806	675	NC......	1,294	1,470	1,301	1,644	1,615
CT.....	119	72	50	58	56	ND......	1,121	1,662	1,759	1,942	1,968
DE.....	114	139	115	134	148	OH......	1,160	1,305	1,184	1,526	1,497
FL.....	1,289	1,275	1,287	1,312	1,261	OK......	553	569	614	844	822
GA.....	859	956	924	1,063	1,070	OR......	682	686	722	819	816
HI	73	65	71	74	79	PA......	914	954	1,002	1,043	1,102
ID	772	777	837	802	856	RI......	3	4	3	5	5
IL......	2,843	3,119	3,204	3,724	3,282	SC.....	266	312	251	371	334
IN	1,412	1,698	1,563	1,945	1,847						
IA	3,124	3,162	3,654	3,917	4,017	SD.....	1,065	1,045	900	1,268	1,231
KS.....	3,175	3,030	2,979	3,304	2,773	TN.....	489	617	655	784	761
KY.....	737	886	819	942	1,074	TX.....	3,063	2,851	3,407	3,740	3,526
LA.....	432	397	476	536	550	UT.....	247	248	253	222	221
ME.....	64	62	61	63	68	VT.....	28	26	31	37	38
MD.....	223	249	211	254	244	VA.....	454	475	438	541	552
MA.....	117	114	126	158	150	WA.....	1,557	1,781	1,913	1,861	2,035
MI.....	857	766	889	905	961	WV	33	36	35	36	39
MN.....	2,286	2,229	2,707	2,623	2,869	WI	1,293	1,278	1,409	1,246	1,429
MS.....	617	665	793	1,008	918	WY	52	46	36	41	44
MO.....	1,038	1,140	1,202	1,559	1,317	Unallo-					
MT.....	352	282	394	459	520	cated	2,536	2,887	2,499	2,694	2,980

Source: U.S. Dept. of Agriculture, Economic Research Service, *Foreign Agricultural Trade of the United States (FATUS),* annual; and *U.S. Agricultural Trade Update—State Exports.* See also <http://www.ers.usda.gov/publications/fau/june06/fau11401 /fau11401.pdf> (released 30 June 2006).

Foreign Commerce and Aid　807

Table 1288. U.S. Exports, Imports, and Merchandise Trade Balance by Country: 2001 to 2005

[In millions of dollars (729,100.3 represents $729,100,300,000). Includes silver ore and bullion. Country totals include exports of special category commodities, if any. Data include nonmonetary gold and include trade of Virgin Islands with foreign countries. For methodology, see Foreign Trade Statistics in Appendix III. Minus sign (−) denotes an excess of imports over exports]

Country [1]	Exports, domestic and foreign					General imports					Merchandise trade balance				
	2001	2002	2003	2004	2005	2001	2002	2003	2004	2005	2001	2002	2003	2004	2005
Total [1]	729,100.3	693,103.2	724,006.3	818,774.9	905,977.6	1,140,999.4	1,161,366.0	1,259,705.2	1,469,704.4	1,673,454.5	−411,899.1	−468,262.8	−535,698.9	−650,929.5	−767,476.9
Afghanistan	5.8	80.0	60.7	150.4	262.2	0.8	3.3	56.1	24.9	67.3	5.0	76.7	4.6	125.5	194.9
Albania	15.5	14.8	9.7	20.1	18.5	7.3	5.8	4.4	11.4	37.2	8.2	9.0	5.3	8.7	−18.7
Algeria	1,037.8	984.4	487.3	971.6	1,167.4	2,701.9	2,360.2	4,752.9	7,409.5	10,446.4	−1,664.1	−1,375.8	−4,265.6	−6,437.9	−9,279.0
Andorra	8.2	11.0	8.2	11.6	10.5	0.2	0.8	0.3	0.9	0.7	8.0	10.2	7.9	10.7	9.8
Angola	275.9	374.0	491.9	593.9	929.0	3,095.9	3,122.7	4,264.3	4,521.2	8,484.4	−2,820.0	−2,748.7	−3,772.4	−3,927.3	−7,555.4
Anguilla	20.1	19.9	21.3	20.8	32.2	1.8	1.0	1.3	0.9	3.8	18.3	18.9	20.0	19.9	28.4
Antigua and Barbuda	95.5	81.4	127.3	125.7	190.4	3.7	3.5	12.7	4.4	4.4	91.8	77.9	114.6	121.3	186.0
Argentina	3,920.2	1,585.4	2,435.4	3,388.1	4,121.9	3,013.4	3,187.3	3,169.3	3,745.5	4,583.6	906.8	−1,601.9	−733.9	−357.4	−461.7
Armenia	49.9	111.8	102.8	90.7	65.5	32.9	30.7	37.6	46.1	46.2	17.0	81.1	65.2	44.6	19.3
Aruba	276.5	464.6	355.0	384.4	558.9	1,034.0	773.7	963.9	1,776.4	2,919.7	−757.5	−309.1	−608.9	−1,392.0	−2,360.8
Australia	10,930.5	13,085.0	13,103.8	14,225.3	15,828.2	6,477.9	6,478.8	6,413.9	7,545.5	7,342.2	4,452.6	6,606.2	6,689.9	6,679.8	8,486.0
Austria	2,604.7	2,427.4	1,792.5	1,945.7	2,593.3	3,968.5	3,814.9	4,489.2	5,798.4	6,102.9	−1,363.8	−1,387.5	−2,696.7	−3,852.7	−3,509.6
Azerbaijan	64.3	69.6	121.2	158.8	132.5	20.6	34.4	9.5	38.1	45.4	43.7	35.2	111.7	120.7	87.1
Bahamas, The	1,026.3	975.3	1,084.3	1,185.8	1,786.7	313.9	449.7	479.4	637.7	699.9	712.4	525.6	604.9	548.1	1,086.8
Bahrain	432.7	419.3	508.8	301.8	350.8	424.1	394.9	378.3	405.3	431.6	8.6	24.4	130.5	−103.5	−80.8
Bangladesh	306.9	269.1	226.5	289.3	319.8	2,359.0	2,134.2	2,073.6	2,302.6	2,693.0	−2,052.1	−1,865.1	−1,847.1	−2,013.3	−2,373.2
Barbados	286.6	267.6	301.8	348.4	394.9	39.5	34.4	43.5	36.9	31.9	247.1	233.2	258.3	311.5	363.0
Belarus	34.9	19.1	84.1	32.6	34.9	108.2	125.5	215.4	335.9	345.2	−73.3	−106.4	−131.3	−303.3	−310.3
Belgium	13,502.3	13,325.8	15,217.9	16,871.1	18,690.6	10,158.4	9,806.8	10,140.7	12,446.2	13,022.9	3,343.9	3,519.0	5,077.2	4,424.9	5,667.7
Belize	173.2	137.7	199.4	151.8	217.6	97.4	77.7	101.4	107.0	98.3	75.8	60.0	98.0	44.8	119.3
Benin	32.2	35.2	30.2	45.8	72.3	1.3	0.7	0.6	1.5	0.5	30.9	34.5	29.6	44.3	71.8
Bermuda	371.0	415.1	401.2	472.4	490.5	65.6	22.9	15.2	25.0	87.3	305.4	392.2	386.0	447.4	403.2
Bolivia	215.9	192.1	181.8	193.9	219.5	166.4	160.4	184.8	260.4	293.2	49.5	31.7	−3.0	−66.5	−73.7
Bosnia and Herzegovina	43.1	31.7	21.2	27.8	17.6	11.9	15.1	11.7	11.2	70.5	31.2	16.6	9.5	16.6	−52.9
Brazil	15,879.5	12,376.0	11,218.3	13,897.3	15,371.1	14,466.4	15,780.6	17,884.0	21,159.9	24,435.5	1,413.1	−3,404.6	−6,665.7	−7,262.6	−9,063.8
Brunei	104.0	46.3	35.8	47.9	49.6	398.9	287.1	422.5	405.8	562.7	−294.9	−240.8	−386.7	−357.9	−513.1
Bulgaria	108.4	101.4	155.8	171.9	267.9	337.0	339.7	441.4	507.3	454.3	−228.6	−238.3	−285.6	−335.4	−186.4
Burkina Faso	4.4	18.8	11.0	22.0	25.1	5.0	2.9	0.9	0.6	2.1	−0.6	15.9	10.1	21.4	23.0
Burma	11.4	10.1	6.9	11.7	5.4	469.9	356.4	275.7	220.4	46.3	−458.5	−346.3	−268.8	−208.7	−40.9
Cameroon	184.0	155.8	90.8	99.6	117.3	101.6	172.1	214.0	308.2	290.4	82.4	−16.3	−123.2	−208.6	−173.1
Canada	163,424.1	160,922.6	169,770.0	189,879.9	211,898.7	216,267.8	209,087.6	224,166.1	256,359.8	290,384.3	−52,843.7	−48,165.0	−54,396.1	−66,479.9	−78,485.6
Cayman Islands	261.8	231.6	309.6	399.9	680.7	6.8	8.7	11.8	13.1	53.5	255.0	222.8	297.8	386.8	627.2
Chad	137.0	127.3	64.4	41.4	53.8	5.7	5.7	22.4	756.2	1,498.1	131.3	121.6	42.0	−714.8	−1,444.3
Chile	3,118.4	2,609.0	2,719.3	3,606.0	5,222.6	3,495.3	3,784.5	3,703.1	4,732.3	6,664.3	−376.9	−1,175.5	−983.8	−1,126.3	−1,441.7
China [2]	19,182.3	22,127.8	28,418.5	34,744.1	41,925.3	102,278.3	125,192.5	152,379.2	196,682.0	243,470.1	−83,096.0	−103,064.7	−123,960.7	−161,937.9	−201,544.8
Colombia	3,583.1	3,582.5	3,754.7	4,505.5	5,462.4	5,710.3	6,385.3	6,385.5	7,256.9	8,849.4	−2,127.2	−2,802.8	−2,630.8	−2,751.4	−3,387.0
Congo (Brazzaville)	90.0	52.4	78.8	65.7	104.1	473.8	182.1	432.8	857.5	1,622.9	−383.8	−129.7	−354.0	−791.8	−1,518.8
Congo (Kinshasa)	18.6	20.6	30.6	66.8	65.0	154.0	204.1	174.5	124.2	263.6	−135.4	−183.5	−143.9	−57.4	−198.6
Costa Rica	2,502.3	3,116.5	3,414.2	3,305.9	3,598.6	2,886.1	3,141.8	3,361.6	3,333.3	3,415.3	−383.8	−25.3	52.6	−27.4	183.3
Cote d'Ivoire	96.8	76.2	102.8	118.1	124.2	333.1	376.4	489.7	714.7	1,198.0	−236.3	−300.2	−386.9	−596.6	−1,073.8
Croatia	109.8	78.1	196.8	130.2	158.6	139.0	145.6	180.7	290.9	364.3	−29.2	−67.5	16.1	−160.7	−205.7
Cyprus	267.9	193.4	326.9	96.0	84.2	35.1	25.6	24.8	25.8	30.5	232.8	167.8	302.1	70.2	53.7
Czech Republic	706.1	653.7	672.3	826.6	1,053.6	1,116.2	1,233.4	1,394.3	1,755.9	2,192.9	−410.1	−579.7	−722.0	−929.3	−1,139.3

See footnotes at end of table.

U.S. Census Bureau, Statistical Abstract of the United States: 2007

Table 1288. U.S. Exports, Imports, and Merchandise Trade Balance, by Country: 2001 to 2005—Con.

[See headnote, page 808]

Country	Exports, domestic and foreign					General imports					Merchandise trade balance				
	2001	2002	2003	2004	2005	2001	2002	2003	2004	2005	2001	2002	2003	2004	2005
Denmark	1,609.2	1,495.9	1,548.4	2,146.6	1,918.4	3,406.7	3,237.3	3,718.4	3,876.3	5,144.2	-1,797.5	-1,741.4	-2,170.0	-1,729.7	-3,225.8
Djibouti	18.6	58.6	34.3	43.7	47.6	1.0	1.9	0.6	1.0	1.1	17.6	56.7	33.7	42.7	46.5
Dominica	30.7	45.0	34.4	36.0	61.5	5.3	4.7	5.3	2.9	3.3	25.4	40.3	29.1	33.1	58.2
Dominican Republic	4,397.6	4,250.1	4,213.6	4,358.3	4,718.7	4,183.4	4,168.9	4,455.1	4,527.1	4,603.7	214.2	81.2	-241.5	-168.8	115.0
Ecuador	1,412.1	1,605.7	1,448.4	1,668.6	1,963.8	2,009.7	2,143.4	2,720.9	4,283.4	5,758.7	-597.6	-537.7	-1,272.5	-2,614.8	-3,794.9
Egypt	3,564.4	2,868.4	2,660.2	3,077.8	3,159.3	882.0	1,356.0	1,143.8	1,283.8	2,091.2	2,682.4	1,512.4	1,516.4	1,794.0	1,068.1
El Salvador	1,759.5	1,664.1	1,823.8	1,867.7	1,854.3	1,880.2	1,982.3	2,019.4	2,052.2	1,988.8	-120.7	-318.2	-195.6	-184.5	-134.5
Estonia	57.7	81.5	120.6	134.3	145.4	241.1	163.6	181.6	393.1	511.4	-183.4	-82.1	-61.0	-258.8	-366.0
Ethiopia	61.1	60.5	409.1	354.8	510.1	29.1	25.7	30.5	41.2	61.8	32.0	34.8	378.6	313.6	448.3
Fiji	19.4	16.9	19.6	25.4	28.2	182.3	156.3	175.4	213.5	169.5	-162.9	-139.4	-155.8	-188.1	-141.3
Finland	1,554.0	1,534.9	1,713.8	2,069.0	2,254.1	3,393.8	3,447.0	3,598.0	3,886.9	4,341.7	-1,839.8	-1,912.1	-1,884.2	-1,817.9	-2,087.6
France	19,864.5	19,016.2	17,068.2	21,263.3	22,410.4	30,408.2	28,240.1	29,221.2	31,605.7	33,842.1	-10,543.7	-9,223.9	-12,153.0	-10,342.4	-11,431.7
French Guiana	129.9	249.7	155.7	228.3	27.0	0.4	7.5	3.4	0.2	0.1	129.5	242.2	152.3	228.1	26.9
French Polynesia	83.0	78.9	91.5	93.1	111.8	48.0	44.1	47.9	67.0	60.1	35.0	34.8	43.6	26.1	51.7
Gabon	73.0	65.5	63.0	93.0	99.1	1,659.7	1,587.5	1,969.5	2,466.7	2,815.6	-1,586.7	-1,522.0	-1,906.5	-2,373.7	-2,716.5
Gambia, The	8.4	9.6	26.7	23.1	30.6	0.5	0.3	0.1	0.5	0.4	7.9	9.3	26.6	22.6	30.2
Georgia	105.9	98.8	131.5	227.1	213.9	30.7	17.5	54.0	77.7	194.4	75.2	81.3	77.5	149.4	19.5
Germany	29,995.3	26,629.6	28,847.9	31,415.9	34,183.7	59,076.7	62,505.7	68,047.0	77,265.6	84,750.9	-29,081.4	-35,876.1	-39,199.1	-45,849.7	-50,567.2
Ghana	199.6	192.6	209.4	309.6	337.4	186.9	116.3	81.9	145.4	158.4	12.7	76.3	127.5	164.2	179.0
Gibraltar	10.4	25.7	14.0	137.9	163.3	2.6	1.1	2.9	1.5	4.6	7.8	24.6	11.1	136.4	158.7
Greece	1,293.6	1,151.8	1,191.1	2,063.2	1,192.2	505.2	546.2	616.0	723.6	883.7	788.4	605.6	575.1	1,339.6	308.5
Greenland	4.7	4.0	3.0	3.6	5.1	28.8	22.6	13.9	14.6	17.3	-24.1	-18.6	-10.9	-11.0	-12.2
Grenada	59.9	56.4	68.4	70.1	82.4	24.1	10.5	7.6	5.1	5.9	35.8	45.9	60.8	65.0	76.5
Guadeloupe	58.8	39.7	45.4	38.2	54.5	10.6	10.5	2.8	3.1	2.1	48.2	29.2	42.6	35.1	52.4
Guatemala	1,869.6	2,044.4	2,273.6	2,551.3	2,835.4	2,588.6	2,796.4	2,945.3	3,154.0	3,137.4	-719.0	-752.0	-671.7	-602.7	-302.0
Guinea	73.3	62.9	35.8	58.8	93.6	87.8	71.6	69.2	64.2	74.7	-14.5	-8.7	-33.4	-5.4	18.9
Guyana	141.3	128.2	117.2	138.4	176.7	140.3	115.6	118.3	122.4	119.9	1.0	12.6	-1.1	16.0	56.8
Haiti	550.4	573.2	639.8	673.0	709.6	263.1	255.0	332.3	370.7	447.2	287.3	318.2	307.5	302.3	262.4
Honduras	2,415.9	2,571.1	2,844.9	3,078.4	3,253.4	3,126.5	3,261.0	3,311.5	3,640.0	3,749.2	-710.6	-690.2	-466.6	-561.6	-495.4
Hong Kong	14,027.5	12,594.4	13,542.1	15,827.4	16,351.0	9,646.3	9,328.2	8,850.4	9,313.9	8,891.7	4,381.2	3,266.2	4,691.7	6,513.5	7,459.3
Hungary	685.5	687.9	933.8	1,142.6	1,023.3	2,964.6	2,637.4	2,699.3	2,572.6	2,561.2	-2,279.1	-1,949.5	-1,765.5	-1,430.0	-1,537.9
Iceland	225.4	219.0	242.3	308.6	512.0	232.5	296.9	282.8	273.8	269.0	-7.1	-77.9	-40.5	34.8	243.0
India	3,757.0	4,101.1	4,986.3	6,109.4	7,989.4	9,737.2	11,818.3	13,052.8	15,572.0	18,804.2	-5,980.2	-7,717.2	-8,066.5	-9,462.6	-10,814.8
Indonesia	2,520.6	2,555.8	2,520.1	2,671.4	3,053.9	10,103.6	9,643.3	9,520.0	10,810.5	12,014.3	-7,583.0	-7,087.5	-6,999.9	-8,139.1	-8,960.4
Iran	8.1	31.8	98.8	85.1	95.8	143.4	156.3	161.2	151.6	174.5	-135.3	-124.5	-62.4	-66.5	-78.7
Iraq	46.2	31.6	315.7	856.5	1,374.0	5,820.3	3,548.2	4,573.8	8,513.5	9,053.7	-5,774.1	-3,516.6	-4,258.1	-7,657.0	-7,679.7
Ireland	7,144.0	6,745.1	7,698.5	8,167.2	9,335.7	18,499.3	22,437.7	25,840.8	27,447.9	28,733.1	-11,355.3	-15,692.6	-18,142.3	-19,280.7	-19,397.4
Israel	7,475.3	7,026.7	6,878.4	9,169.1	9,737.3	11,959.0	12,415.7	12,770.2	14,551.5	16,830.5	-4,483.7	-5,389.0	-5,891.8	-5,382.4	-7,093.2
Italy	9,915.6	10,056.8	10,570.1	10,684.7	11,524.3	23,789.9	24,220.3	25,436.7	28,097.3	31,009.3	-13,874.3	-14,163.5	-14,866.6	-17,412.6	-19,485.0
Jamaica	1,405.5	1,420.2	1,469.6	1,430.8	1,700.8	460.6	396.3	494.7	319.7	375.6	944.9	1,023.9	974.9	1,111.1	1,325.2
Japan	57,451.6	51,449.3	52,063.8	54,243.1	55,484.5	126,473.3	121,428.7	118,029.0	129,805.2	138,003.7	-69,021.7	-69,979.4	-65,965.2	-75,562.1	-82,519.2
Jordan	339.0	404.4	492.0	551.5	644.2	229.1	412.3	673.5	1,093.4	1,266.8	109.9	-7.9	-181.5	-541.9	-622.6
Kazakhstan	160.3	604.6	168.3	320.4	538.6	351.8	334.6	392.3	538.6	1,101.1	-191.5	270.0	-224.0	-218.2	-562.5
Kenya	577.7	271.2	196.7	393.9	632.5	128.3	188.6	249.2	352.2	348.0	449.4	82.6	-52.5	41.7	284.5

See footnotes at end of table.

U.S. Census Bureau, Statistical Abstract of the United States: 2007

Table 1288. U.S. Exports, Imports, and Merchandise Trade Balance, by Country: 2001 to 2005—Con.

[See headnote, page 808]

Country	Exports, domestic and foreign					General imports					Merchandise trade balance				
	2001	2002	2003	2004	2005	2001	2002	2003	2004	2005	2001	2002	2003	2004	2005
Korea, South	22,180.6	22,575.8	24,098.6	26,412.5	27,765.0	35,181.4	35,571.8	36,963.3	46,167.9	43,781.4	-13,000.8	-12,996.0	-12,864.7	-19,755.4	-16,016.4
Kuwait	902.4	1,014.7	1,509.1	1,519.3	1,974.9	1,990.7	1,940.4	2,276.8	3,230.8	4,334.8	-1,088.3	-925.7	-767.7	-1,711.5	-2,359.9
Kyrgyzstan	27.7	31.1	39.1	29.4	31.1	3.3	4.8	11.0	10.8	4.6	24.4	26.3	28.1	18.6	26.5
Latvia	110.5	90.8	124.0	121.1	177.5	144.5	197.0	377.4	364.6	362.2	-34.0	-106.2	-253.4	-243.5	-184.7
Lebanon	418.2	317.4	314.3	464.0	465.7	89.6	61.7	92.3	74.5	86.4	328.6	255.7	222.0	389.5	379.3
Lesotho	0.8	2.0	5.1	5.5	4.0	215.3	321.7	393.3	466.9	403.6	-214.5	-319.7	-388.2	-461.4	-399.6
Liberia	36.8	27.7	33.4	60.9	69.3	42.6	45.8	59.5	84.3	90.8	-5.8	-18.1	-26.1	-23.4	-21.5
Liechtenstein	7.1	14.5	15.9	10.8	19.7	224.2	237.7	261.9	286.4	295.7	-217.1	-223.2	-246.0	-275.6	-276.0
Lithuania	99.8	102.8	162.6	295.1	390.0	164.2	299.6	347.3	482.0	633.9	-64.4	-196.8	-184.7	-186.9	-243.9
Luxembourg	548.6	480.1	279.1	704.6	782.4	305.6	300.0	264.9	290.2	388.8	243.0	180.1	14.2	414.4	393.6
Macau	70.1	79.0	54.6	85.5	101.6	1,225.1	1,231.7	1,355.9	1,486.7	1,249.0	-1,155.0	-1,152.7	-1,301.3	-1,401.2	-1,147.4
Macedonia	32.9	18.6	26.3	26.3	31.6	111.6	73.2	60.8	83.3	48.1	-78.7	-54.6	-34.5	-57.0	-16.5
Madagascar	21.0	15.4	46.4	35.6	28.2	271.6	215.8	383.7	469.6	323.6	-250.6	-200.4	-337.3	-434.0	-295.4
Malawi	12.8	30.1	16.6	21.7	28.0	77.9	76.9	76.9	60.6	115.5	-65.1	-46.8	-60.3	-38.9	-87.5
Malaysia	9,357.7	10,343.7	10,920.6	10,921.2	10,460.8	22,340.3	24,008.9	25,437.7	28,178.9	33,685.2	-12,982.6	-13,665.2	-14,517.1	-17,257.7	-23,224.4
Maldives	6.4	4.1	6.6	9.9	9.3	97.7	113.6	94.4	82.7	5.5	-91.3	-109.5	-87.8	-72.8	3.8
Mali	32.7	11.2	31.5	42.9	32.4	6.1	2.6	2.4	3.7	3.6	26.6	8.6	29.1	39.2	28.8
Malta	258.9	210.1	201.6	181.3	193.7	368.9	309.9	372.8	383.0	282.7	-110.0	-99.8	-171.2	-201.7	-89.0
Marshall Islands	26.5	28.7	28.1	18.8	75.5	5.5	9.4	27.1	12.1	17.2	21.0	19.3	1.0	6.7	58.3
Martinique	23.2	23.7	21.7	28.1	35.0	0.6	0.7	0.6	1.7	22.2	22.6	23.0	21.1	26.4	12.8
Mauritania	25.4	22.9	34.9	34.4	86.1	0.3	0.9	0.9	7.3	0.8	25.1	22.0	34.0	27.1	85.3
Mauritius	29.0	27.5	32.0	28.4	30.9	277.9	280.6	298.1	270.4	221.9	-248.9	-253.1	-266.1	-242.0	-191.0
Mexico	101,296.5	97,470.3	97,457.4	110,835.0	120,364.8	131,337.9	134,615.8	138,073.3	155,901.5	170,108.6	-30,041.4	-37,145.5	-40,615.9	-45,066.5	-49,743.8
Micronesia, Federated States of	30.0	27.2	23.6	24.6	25.3	20.8	15.2	14.3	11.4	1.6	9.2	12.0	9.3	13.2	23.7
Moldova	35.5	30.7	25.2	39.5	40.1	68.3	39.1	42.9	49.4	50.2	-32.8	-8.4	-17.7	-9.9	-10.1
Monaco	15.0	11.4	50.3	18.2	16.8	15.1	15.1	21.6	23.0	37.5	-0.1	-3.7	28.7	-4.8	-20.7
Mongolia	12.1	66.3	20.7	28.1	21.9	143.8	161.7	183.4	239.1	143.6	-131.7	-95.4	-162.7	-211.0	-121.7
Morocco	282.2	565.4	465.1	525.7	525.0	434.6	392.4	385.2	515.2	445.8	-152.4	173.0	79.9	10.5	79.2
Mozambique	28.4	94.6	62.5	76.5	62.8	7.1	8.5	8.4	10.8	11.9	21.3	86.1	54.1	65.7	50.9
Namibia	255.6	57.8	74.5	74.5	112.2	37.3	57.4	169.7	238.3	129.6	218.3	0.4	-95.2	-163.8	-17.4
Netherlands	19,484.7	18,310.7	20,702.9	24,289.1	26,484.6	9,515.3	9,848.5	10,971.9	12,450.5	14,862.0	9,969.4	8,462.2	9,731.0	11,838.6	11,622.6
Netherlands Antilles	816.4	741.4	747.1	824.2	1,137.6	484.6	361.7	620.4	434.6	922.4	331.8	379.7	126.7	389.6	215.2
New Caledonia	25.1	36.6	43.2	45.1	38.4	14.6	9.6	12.6	19.4	27.2	10.5	27.0	30.6	25.7	11.2
New Zealand	2,110.5	1,813.1	1,848.8	2,072.9	2,651.8	2,199.2	2,281.6	2,403.4	2,967.9	3,155.2	-88.7	-468.5	-554.6	-895.0	-503.4
Nicaragua	443.1	437.0	502.8	592.4	625.5	603.6	679.6	769.3	990.3	1,180.8	-160.5	-242.6	-266.5	-397.9	-555.3
Niger	63.4	40.9	33.6	34.0	78.5	4.6	0.9	4.0	26.9	65.5	58.8	40.0	29.6	7.1	13.0
Nigeria	955.1	1,057.8	1,029.0	1,554.3	1,621.2	8,774.8	5,945.4	10,393.6	16,248.5	24,239.4	-7,819.7	-4,887.6	-9,364.6	-14,694.2	-22,618.2
Norway	1,834.7	1,406.5	1,467.5	1,604.3	1,941.9	5,202.8	5,842.6	5,212.4	6,508.7	6,776.3	-3,368.1	-4,436.1	-3,744.9	-4,904.4	-4,834.4
Oman	306.2	356.0	323.1	330.1	594.9	420.1	400.6	694.8	418.0	555.0	-113.9	-44.6	-371.7	-87.9	39.9
Pakistan	541.3	693.4	839.6	1,813.6	1,251.6	2,249.4	2,305.0	2,531.5	2,875.0	3,253.2	-1,708.1	-1,611.6	-1,691.9	-1,061.4	-2,001.6
Panama	1,330.5	1,406.7	1,848.0	1,835.3	2,162.0	290.7	302.6	301.2	315.9	327.1	1,039.8	1,104.1	1,546.8	1,519.4	1,834.9
Papua New Guinea	22.2	23.2	30.3	42.6	55.3	39.3	90.2	66.1	54.3	58.5	-17.1	-67.0	-35.8	-11.7	-3.2
Paraguay	388.8	432.9	488.8	622.9	895.8	32.6	43.7	53.3	58.6	51.6	356.2	389.2	435.5	564.3	844.2
Peru	1,564.3	1,562.5	1,706.8	2,101.0	2,309.4	1,843.8	1,939.3	2,406.8	3,701.6	5,119.2	-279.5	-376.8	-700.0	-1,600.6	-2,809.8
Philippines	7,660.0	7,276.0	7,992.2	7,087.0	6,895.4	11,325.4	10,979.9	10,060.9	9,136.7	9,250.4	-3,665.4	-3,703.9	-2,068.7	-2,049.7	-2,355.0
Poland	787.7	686.3	758.7	929.2	1,267.7	952.6	1,108.5	1,325.8	1,821.5	1,948.6	-164.9	-422.2	-567.1	-892.3	-680.9

See footnotes at end of table.

Table 1288. U.S. Exports, Imports, and Merchandise Trade Balance, by Country: 2001 to 2005—Con.

[See headnote, page 808]

Country	Exports, domestic and foreign					General imports					Merchandise trade balance				
	2001	2002	2003	2004	2005	2001	2002	2003	2004	2005	2001	2002	2003	2004	2005
Portugal	1,239.7	861.3	862.8	1,046.1	1,131.9	1,555.4	1,672.6	1,967.3	2,243.3	2,328.7	-315.7	-811.3	-1,104.5	-1,197.2	-1,196.8
Qatar	335.9	313.9	408.5	454.9	986.6	502.2	484.7	331.3	387.4	447.9	-166.3	-170.8	77.2	67.5	538.7
Romania	374.5	248.2	366.9	525.4	608.9	519.9	695.1	730.2	853.0	1,207.6	-145.4	-446.9	-363.3	-327.6	-598.7
Russia	2,716.1	2,397.0	2,450.2	2,961.0	3,962.4	6,264.4	6,870.2	8,598.2	11,891.3	15,306.7	-3,548.3	-4,473.2	-6,148.0	-8,930.3	-11,344.3
Samoa	69.9	7.6	11.1	12.4	14.5	7.3	6.4	4.4	4.7	7.9	62.6	1.2	6.7	7.7	6.6
Saudi Arabia	5,957.5	4,780.7	4,596.0	5,256.7	6,812.8	13,272.2	13,149.9	18,068.9	20,958.7	27,192.6	-7,314.7	-8,369.2	-13,472.9	-15,702.0	-20,379.8
Senegal	79.5	74.6	102.0	89.4	158.5	103.8	3.6	4.5	3.0	3.7	-24.3	71.0	97.5	86.4	154.8
Serbia and Montenegro	66.2	78.1	50.0	142.9	132.5	6.1	9.6	14.6	91.8	54.6	60.1	68.5	35.4	51.1	77.9
Singapore	17,651.7	16,217.9	16,575.7	16,608.5	20,642.2	15,000.0	14,802.2	15,158.2	15,370.4	15,110.1	2,651.7	1,415.7	1,417.5	1,238.1	5,532.1
Slovakia	69.8	92.7	115.2	131.7	154.8	237.6	260.3	1,013.0	1,211.3	960.7	-167.8	-167.6	-897.8	-1,079.6	-810.9
Somalia	6.6	6.2	7.0	9.1	8.8	0.3	0.3	0.2	0.7	0.3	6.3	5.9	6.8	8.4	8.5
South Africa	2,959.6	2,525.5	2,821.2	3,178.5	3,906.9	4,432.6	4,034.1	4,637.6	5,944.8	5,885.6	-1,473.0	-1,508.6	-1,816.4	-2,766.3	-1,978.7
Spain	5,756.0	5,297.9	5,935.3	6,638.3	6,913.6	5,197.3	5,733.0	6,707.8	7,350.2	8,614.6	558.7	-435.1	-772.5	-711.9	-1,701.0
Sri Lanka	183.0	171.9	154.8	164.1	197.6	1,984.2	1,810.4	1,807.4	1,956.7	2,082.9	-1,801.2	-1,638.5	-1,652.6	-1,792.6	-1,885.3
St. Lucia	86.7	99.5	121.2	105.3	135.4	28.9	19.2	13.0	14.3	32.4	57.8	80.3	108.2	91.0	103.0
St. Vincent and the Grenadines	38.8	40.4	46.5	45.5	45.4	22.5	16.5	4.1	4.1	15.7	16.3	23.9	42.4	41.4	29.7
Sudan	17.0	10.8	26.1	68.4	108.1	3.4	1.4	2.8	3.7	13.6	13.6	9.4	23.3	64.7	94.5
Suriname	155.3	124.8	192.9	179.2	245.7	142.9	132.7	140.1	140.8	165.3	12.4	-7.9	52.8	38.4	80.4
Sweden	3,541.0	3,153.0	3,225.5	3,267.3	3,715.4	8,908.5	9,216.3	11,124.6	12,683.0	13,821.0	-5,367.5	-6,063.3	-7,899.1	-9,415.7	-10,105.6
Switzerland	9,807.3	7,782.5	8,660.1	9,279.9	10,719.8	9,669.6	9,382.0	10,667.9	11,627.7	12,999.9	137.7	-1,599.5	-2,007.8	-2,347.8	-2,280.1
Syria[2]	231.4	274.1	214.0	213.0	155.0	158.5	160.8	258.9	267.8	323.6	72.9	113.3	-44.9	-54.8	-168.6
Taiwan[2]	18,121.6	18,381.8	17,487.9	21,744.4	22,069.2	33,374.5	32,147.9	31,599.9	34,623.6	34,825.8	-15,252.9	-13,766.1	-14,112.0	-12,879.2	-12,756.6
Tajikistan	28.6	33.1	50.0	55.7	28.8	5.2	1.1	7.3	7.3	7.9	23.4	32.0	42.7	48.4	20.9
Tanzania	64.0	62.7	66.0	127.6	96.4	27.9	24.8	24.2	24.2	33.7	36.1	37.9	41.8	103.4	62.7
Thailand	5,989.4	4,860.2	5,841.7	6,368.4	7,256.6	14,727.2	14,792.9	15,180.7	17,578.9	19,889.8	-8,737.8	-9,932.7	-9,339.0	-11,210.5	-12,633.2
Togo	16.3	13.8	15.2	23.7	27.9	12.6	2.7	5.6	1.6	6.4	3.7	11.1	9.6	22.1	21.5
Trinidad and Tobago	1,087.1	1,020.2	1,064.0	1,207.6	1,416.7	2,380.0	2,440.3	4,321.7	5,842.1	7,890.9	-1,292.9	-1,420.1	-3,257.7	-4,634.5	-6,474.2
Tunisia	276.0	194.8	170.5	258.2	261.2	121.7	93.2	100.1	209.1	263.8	154.3	101.6	70.4	49.1	-2.6
Turkey	3,094.7	3,113.0	2,904.3	3,362.3	4,269.0	3,054.8	3,516.0	3,787.9	4,933.8	5,182.1	39.9	-403.0	-883.6	-1,571.5	-913.1
Turkmenistan	248.4	47.1	34.2	294.6	237.1	45.5	59.6	76.4	80.7	135.3	202.9	-12.5	-42.2	213.9	101.8
Turks and Caicos Islands	77.1	53.6	71.9	137.4	237.8	8.1	5.1	6.1	7.3	9.4	69.0	48.5	65.8	130.1	228.4
Uganda	31.7	24.0	42.7	63.4	62.6	17.7	15.3	34.9	25.9	25.8	14.0	8.7	7.8	37.5	36.8
Ukraine	200.1	254.8	230.8	399.4	533.0	673.6	362.4	282.0	799.6	1,098.0	-473.5	-107.6	-51.2	-400.2	-565.0
United Arab Emirates	2,637.9	3,593.2	3,510.4	4,085.7	8,482.4	1,194.2	922.9	1,129.0	1,142.7	1,468.3	1,443.7	2,670.3	2,381.4	2,943.0	7,014.1
United Kingdom	40,774.4	33,204.7	33,895.4	36,000.2	38,587.8	41,368.8	40,744.9	42,666.9	46,273.8	51,032.6	-594.4	-7,540.2	-8,771.5	-10,273.6	-12,444.8
Uruguay	406.3	208.6	326.8	326.1	356.7	227.7	193.2	255.8	184.3	732.3	178.6	15.4	71.0	141.8	-375.6
Uzbekistan	144.9	138.5	256.7	229.8	73.8	53.5	77.1	83.7	483.7	95.6	91.4	61.4	173.0	-253.9	-21.8
Venezuela	5,642.1	4,429.7	2,839.5	4,767.4	6,420.9	15,250.5	15,093.5	17,144.2	24,920.6	33,978.1	-9,608.4	-10,663.8	-14,304.7	-20,153.2	-27,557.2
Vietnam	460.3	580.2	1,324.4	1,164.3	1,193.2	1,052.9	2,394.7	4,554.9	5,275.3	6,631.2	-592.6	-1,814.5	-3,230.5	-4,111.0	-5,438.0
Virgin Islands, British	74.7	67.4	70.5	96.7	124.9	11.9	15.4	35.0	17.4	33.6	62.8	52.0	35.5	79.3	91.3
Yemen	185.4	366.1	195.3	232.3	219.0	202.4	246.3	66.1	61.5	278.6	-17.0	119.8	129.2	170.8	-59.6
Zambia	31.2	35.7	19.5	26.4	29.1	15.6	7.9	12.5	32.5	31.7	15.6	27.8	7.0	-6.1	-2.6
Zimbabwe	31.2	49.3	41.7	47.3	45.5	90.8	102.8	56.6	62.5	60.4	-59.6	-53.5	-14.9	-15.2	-14.9

– Represents or rounds to zero.

[1] Includes timing adjustment and unidentified countries, not shown separately. [2] See footnote 2, Table 1308.

Source: U.S. Census Bureau, U.S. International Trade in Goods and Services, Series FT-900(05), and previous final reports. See also <http://www.census.gov/foreign-trade/Press-Release/2005pr/final_revisions/> (released 09 June 2006).

U.S. Census Bureau, Statistical Abstract of the United States: 2007

Table 1289. U.S. Exports and General Imports by Selected SITC Commodity Groups: 2002 to 2005

[In millions of dollars (693,103 represents $693,103,000,000). SITC = Standard International Trade Classification. For methodology, see Foreign Trade Statistics in Appendix III. N.e.s. = not elsewhere specified]

Selected commodities	Exports [1]				General imports [2]			
	2002	2003	2004	2005	2002	2003	2004	2005
Total	693,103	724,006	818,775	905,978	1,161,366	1,259,705	1,469,704	1,673,455
Agricultural commodities [3]	**53,115**	**59,495**	**61,383**	**63,139**	**42,012**	**47,419**	**54,222**	**59,530**
Animal feeds	3,824	3,885	3,808	4,029	605	635	778	699
Coffee	8	5	7	5	1,369	1,612	1,868	2,502
Corn	5,108	4,963	6,132	5,062	137	151	127	125
Cotton, raw and linters	2,031	3,219	4,251	3,929	25	27	18	20
Hides and skins	1,594	1,653	1,581	1,629	84	74	80	79
Meat and preparations	6,356	7,261	5,203	6,669	4,269	4,403	5,707	5,747
Soybeans	5,734	7,935	6,680	6,282	28	47	53	63
Sugar	13	6	4	8	495	535	516	706
Tobacco, unmanufactured	1,050	1,035	1,044	990	701	690	690	750
Vegetables and fruits	7,607	8,123	8,890	10,259	10,194	11,454	12,787	14,082
Wheat	3,630	3,955	5,148	4,410	266	141	162	174
Manufactured goods [3]	**544,913**	**556,800**	**623,961**	**685,398**	**974,576**	**1,027,358**	**1,174,788**	**1,287,376**
ADP equipment, office machinery . .	30,368	28,852	28,241	29,800	76,877	80,826	93,762	98,584
Airplane parts	14,309	14,524	15,295	17,538	4,986	4,474	4,824	5,592
Airplanes	27,115	23,418	24,493	30,291	12,329	12,327	11,389	10,734
Alcoholic beverages, distilled	505	551	684	726	3,273	3,693	4,022	4,360
Aluminum	2,947	2,941	3,807	4,483	6,757	7,238	9,547	11,931
Artwork/antiques	977	1,157	1,322	1,858	5,194	4,398	5,307	5,512
Basketware, etc	3,842	4,692	5,084	5,612	6,564	7,854	8,435	8,585
Chemicals, cosmetics	5,870	6,557	7,441	8,059	4,195	5,611	6,948	7,922
Chemicals, dyeing	3,860	4,137	4,569	4,901	2,357	2,480	2,667	2,971
Chemicals, fertilizers	2,106	2,341	2,595	2,990	1,619	2,130	2,536	3,701
Chemicals, inorganic	5,464	5,577	6,196	7,698	6,018	7,419	8,276	10,165
Chemicals, medicinal	15,732	18,775	23,433	25,012	24,748	31,516	34,937	39,176
Chemicals, n.e.s	12,348	12,986	14,563	15,846	6,168	6,857	7,982	8,939
Chemicals, organic	16,406	20,105	25,852	26,765	30,366	32,876	35,447	38,009
Chemicals, plastics	19,380	21,069	25,202	28,861	10,760	12,161	14,222	17,385
Cigarettes	1,466	1,403	1,294	1,202	316	300	257	208
Clothing	5,485	4,960	4,423	4,129	63,803	68,162	72,316	76,383
Cork, wood, lumber	3,364	3,387	3,857	4,038	7,872	7,276	10,605	10,399
Crude fertilizers	1,520	1,582	1,724	1,702	1,275	1,340	1,471	1,698
Electrical machinery	66,948	69,772	73,320	74,286	81,158	82,433	93,290	99,121
Fish and preparations	2,976	3,084	3,517	3,864	10,000	10,930	11,177	11,915
Footwear	518	495	453	508	15,387	15,603	16,506	17,932
Furniture and parts	3,814	3,608	4,058	4,415	21,577	24,356	27,737	30,653
Gem diamonds	1,182	338	939	2,578	12,088	12,931	14,661	16,238
General industrial machinery	30,075	30,115	34,824	38,902	35,200	38,467	45,632	52,333
Gold, nonmonetary	3,244	4,820	4,430	5,533	2,428	2,932	3,996	4,430
Iron and steel mill products	5,252	6,268	8,022	10,430	12,951	11,112	22,400	24,632
Lighting, plumbing	1,333	1,347	1,476	1,694	5,566	6,003	6,811	7,591
Metal manufactures, n.e.s	11,170	11,218	12,121	13,510	16,681	17,985	21,777	24,777
Metal ores; scrap	4,626	5,646	7,766	11,057	3,101	3,142	4,583	5,335
Metalworking machinery	4,140	4,108	5,983	6,457	5,104	5,335	6,262	7,530
Optical goods	2,132	2,249	2,556	3,076	2,836	2,992	3,534	3,789
Paper and paperboard	9,551	9,814	10,689	11,457	14,435	14,849	16,581	17,561
Photographic equipment	3,529	3,330	3,534	3,343	5,325	5,046	4,905	4,481
Plastic articles, n.e.s	6,820	6,778	7,390	8,036	9,138	10,216	11,776	13,633
Platinum	723	481	548	610	2,830	2,624	3,508	3,916
Power generating machinery	32,430	31,495	36,177	41,296	33,922	32,485	35,981	41,263
Printed materials	4,429	4,607	4,910	5,445	3,960	4,148	4,508	4,917
Pulp and waste paper	3,842	4,096	4,488	5,093	2,363	2,597	2,949	3,049
Records/magnetic media	4,414	4,473	4,757	5,142	5,279	5,852	6,799	7,258
Rubber articles, n.e.s	1,423	1,412	1,520	1,598	2,139	2,358	2,733	2,925
Rubber tires and tubes	2,232	2,200	2,532	2,778	4,765	5,258	6,305	7,725
Scientific instruments	27,087	27,998	33,049	34,544	20,884	23,661	28,449	30,242
Ships, boats	1,200	1,172	1,649	1,913	1,325	1,592	2,084	1,719
Silver and bullion	262	177	275	287	687	801	1,013	1,178
Spacecraft	509	142	467	547	310	188	39	—
Specialized industrial machinery . . .	23,532	23,371	28,842	33,144	18,401	20,841	26,417	31,076
Television, VCR, etc	19,374	16,851	20,072	20,974	66,212	71,137	87,885	104,079
Textile yarn, fabric	10,263	10,457	11,516	11,830	16,097	17,257	19,505	21,249
Toys/games/sporting goods	2,985	3,155	3,403	3,756	22,067	21,566	22,479	25,069
Travel goods	277	291	312	379	4,402	4,842	5,655	6,183
Vehicles	57,698	60,521	65,217	71,747	168,073	172,578	187,723	195,926
Watches/clocks/parts	236	242	272	256	3,203	3,600	3,790	3,939
Wood manufactures	1,564	1,578	1,796	1,818	7,853	9,289	12,309	12,847
Mineral fuel [3]	**11,541**	**13,691**	**18,642**	**26,488**	**115,748**	**155,561**	**206,660**	**289,723**
Coal	1,673	1,621	2,758	3,471	966	1,176	2,416	2,418
Crude oil	92	155	277	595	79,252	101,722	136,030	182,944
Petroleum preparations	6,009	7,057	9,726	14,782	20,748	26,735	37,988	59,698
Natural gas	995	1,300	2,125	3,094	10,974	20,621	23,908	34,911
Reexports	63,792	72,319	89,662	101,125	(X)	(X)	(X)	(X)

– Represents zero.   X Not applicable.   [1] F.a.s. basis. Exports by commodity are only for domestic exports.   [2] Customs value basis.   [3] Includes other commodities not shown separately.

Source: U.S. Census Bureau, *U.S. International Trade in Goods and Services*, Series FT-900(05), and previous final reports. See also <http://www.census.gov/foreign-trade/Press-Release/2005pr/final_revisions/> (released 09 June 2006).

Table 1290. United States Total and Aerospace Foreign Trade: 1990 to 2005

[In millions of dollars (–101,718 represents –$101,718,000,000), except percent. Data are reported as exports of domestic merchandise, including Department of Defense shipments and undocumented exports to Canada, f.a.s. (free alongside ship) basis, and imports for consumption, customs value basis. Minus sign (–) indicates deficit]

Year	Merchandise trade			Aerospace trade						
						Exports				
								Civil		
	Trade balance	Imports	Exports	Trade balance	Imports	Total	Percent of U.S. exports	Total	Transports	Military
1990	–101,718	495,311	393,592	27,282	11,801	39,083	9.9	31,517	16,691	7,566
1991	–66,723	488,453	421,730	30,785	13,003	43,788	10.4	35,548	20,881	8,239
1992	–84,501	532,665	448,164	31,356	13,662	45,018	10.0	36,906	22,379	8,111
1993	–115,568	580,659	465,091	27,235	12,183	39,418	8.5	31,823	18,146	7,596
1994	–150,630	663,256	512,626	25,010	12,363	37,373	7.3	30,050	15,931	7,322
1995	–158,801	743,543	584,742	21,561	11,509	33,071	5.7	25,079	10,606	7,991
1996	–170,214	795,289	625,075	26,602	13,668	40,270	6.4	29,477	13,624	10,792
1997	–180,522	869,704	689,182	32,239	18,134	50,374	7.3	40,075	21,028	10,299
1998	–229,758	911,896	682,138	40,960	23,110	64,071	9.4	51,999	29,168	12,072
1999	–328,821	1,024,618	695,797	37,381	25,063	62,444	9.0	50,624	25,694	11,820
2000	–436,104	1,218,022	781,918	26,734	27,944	54,679	7.0	45,566	19,615	9,113
2001	–411,899	1,140,999	729,100	26,035	32,473	58,508	8.0	49,371	22,151	9,137
2002	–468,263	1,161,366	693,103	29,533	27,242	56,775	8.2	47,348	21,661	9,427
2003	–532,350	1,257,121	724,771	27,111	25,393	52,504	7.2	44,060	19,434	8,445
2004	–650,930	1,469,704	818,775	31,002	25,815	56,817	6.9	47,325	18,577	9,492
2005	–766,367	1,670,751	904,383	39,784	27,649	67,433	7.5	57,225	21,888	10,207

Source: Aerospace Industries Association of America, Washington, DC, *Aerospace Facts and Figures*, annual.

Table 1291. U.S. High Technology Exports by Industry and Selected Major Country: 2003 to 2005

[In billions of dollars (191.4 represents $191,400,000,000)]

Selected industries	Industry			Selected countries	Country		
	2003	2004	2005		2003	2004	2005
Total exports	170.9	191.4	199.1	Total exports	170.9	191.4	199.1
Computers and office equipment. . .	41.5	44.4	47.4	Canada	24.3	27.6	29.6
Consumer electronics	8.1	9.1	10.2	China	7.0	8.8	10.0
Communications equipment	18.8	22.5	24.1	Japan	12.2	13.2	13.1
Electronic components	14.6	15.9	15.6	Korea, South	8.5	9.1	9.9
Semiconductors	46.1	48.0	47.2	Malaysia	8.2	7.6	7.4
Industrial electronics	26.2	33.7	34.7	Mexico	25.0	28.1	27.1
Electromedical equipment	10.9	12.2	13.8	Taiwan	7.3	8.6	8.0
Photonics	4.7	5.6	6.2	European Union 25	37.5	40.9	42.6

Source: AeA (formerly the American Electronics Association), Washington DC, *Cyberstates 2006*, annual (copyright). See <http://aeanet.org>.

Table 1292. U.S. Exporting Companies Profile by Employment-Size Class: 2000 and 2004

[(668,310 represents $668,310,000,000). Data are based on economic census and survey data on file at the Census Bureau, administrative records from other government agencies, and documents filed for export clearances]

Employment-size class	Number of exporters		Known export value [1] (mil. dol.)		Percent of—			
					Number of exporters		Known export value	
	2000	2004	2000	2004	2000	2004	2000	2004
All companies, total . . .	246,452	231,736	668,310	709,495	100.0	100.0	100.0	100.0
No employees	74,772	64,604	47,024	36,589	30.3	27.9	7.0	5.2
1 to 19 employees	96,268	97,876	45,272	50,288	39.1	42.2	6.8	7.1
20 to 49 employees	31,362	30,301	21,262	24,936	12.7	13.1	3.2	3.5
50 to 99 employees	16,988	15,834	19,711	22,334	6.9	6.8	2.9	3.1
100 to 249 employees.	13,685	11,954	32,192	38,420	5.6	5.2	4.8	5.4
250 to 499 employees.	5,454	4,570	27,397	30,438	2.2	2.0	4.1	4.3
500 or more employees.	7,923	6,597	475,453	506,488	3.2	2.8	71.1	71.4

[1] Known value is defined as the value of exports by known exporters, i.e., those export transactions that could be matched to specific companies. Export values are on f.a.s. or "free alongside ship basis."

Source: U.S. Census Bureau, *A Profile of U.S. Exporting Companies, 2000* and *2003–2004*. See also <http://www.census.gov /foreign-trade/aip/edbrel-0304.pdf> (released 09 March 2006).

Foreign Commerce and Aid   813

Table 1293. **Domestic Exports and Imports for Consumption of Merchandise by Selected NAICS Product Category: 2000 to 2005**

[In millions of dollars (712,285 represents $712,285,000,000). Includes nonmonetary gold. For methodology, see Foreign Trade Statistics in Appendix III. NAICS = North American Industry Classification System; see text, Section 15]

Product category	2000	2001	2002	2003	2004	2005
Domestic exports, total.	**712,285**	**666,021**	**629,599**	**651,687**	**729,452**	**803,901**
Agricultural, forestry and fishery products	29,153	29,666	30,068	34,699	37,830	37,013
Agricultural products, total	23,596	24,068	24,827	29,194	31,949	30,611
Livestock and livestock products	1,255	1,309	1,020	1,177	963	1,123
Forestry products, not elsewhere specified	1,644	1,436	1,419	1,462	1,653	1,667
Fish, fresh or chilled; and other marine products. .	2,658	2,854	2,802	2,866	3,265	3,612
Mining, total	6,187	5,403	5,585	6,117	8,677	12,550
Oil and gas	1,706	1,261	1,725	2,143	3,001	4,453
Minerals and ores	4,481	4,141	3,860	3,973	5,676	8,098
Manufacturing, total	644,440	597,101	562,834	577,789	645,104	711,420
Food and kindred products	24,966	26,486	25,175	26,795	25,952	28,849
Beverages and tobacco products	5,568	4,334	3,559	3,648	3,644	3,400
Textiles and fabrics	7,010	7,098	7,397	7,557	8,363	8,471
Textile mill products.	2,236	1,991	1,875	1,881	2,072	2,343
Apparel and accessories	8,104	6,469	5,462	4,923	4,350	4,069
Leather and allied products	2,322	2,285	2,049	2,035	2,190	2,295
Wood products	4,854	3,944	3,777	3,818	4,249	4,445
Paper products	15,539	14,045	13,640	13,965	15,168	16,565
Printed, publishing, & similar products.	4,869	4,867	4,509	4,706	4,983	5,495
Petroleum and coal products.	8,862	8,214	7,897	9,349	12,579	17,788
Chemicals	77,649	76,837	78,049	88,384	105,238	114,214
Plastics and rubber products	16,970	15,745	15,383	15,661	17,316	18,787
Nonmetallic mineral products	7,830	7,378	6,025	6,069	6,596	6,911
Primary metal products	20,126	18,150	15,371	17,877	21,159	27,423
Fabricated metal products	21,737	19,547	18,893	18,848	20,821	23,296
Machinery, except electrical	85,038	76,572	70,178	69,285	86,264	96,760
Computers and electronic products	161,449	134,263	116,243	115,883	122,161	123,926
Electrical equipment, appliances and components	25,401	22,764	20,587	20,632	23,606	26,551
Transportation equipment	121,701	122,877	123,970	122,246	129,907	147,244
Furniture and fixtures.	2,882	2,419	2,158	2,349	2,633	2,829
Miscellaneous manufactured commodities	19,327	20,815	20,640	21,591	24,795	29,831
Special classification provisions	32,505	33,852	31,112	33,109	37,814	42,936
Waste & scrap	4,948	4,738	5,081	6,456	8,548	10,357
Used or second-hand merchandise	1,950	2,169	1,562	1,808	2,108	2,742
Goods returned or reimported	333	310	241	205	152	62
Special classification provision, not elsewhere specified.	25,274	26,635	24,228	24,640	27,006	29,776
Imports for consumption, total	**1,205,339**	**1,132,635**	**1,154,811**	**1,250,097**	**1,460,161**	**1,662,380**
Agricultural, forestry, and fishery products	24,378	23,598	24,327	26,197	27,814	30,751
Agricultural products, total	11,771	11,290	11,773	13,035	14,356	15,803
Livestock and livestock products	3,085	3,445	3,455	2,782	2,498	3,276
Forestry products, not elsewhere specified	1,409	1,158	1,288	1,612	2,019	2,250
Fish, fresh or chilled; and other marine products. .	8,113	7,706	7,811	8,768	8,942	9,422
Mining, total	79,841	76,243	76,288	105,662	138,427	188,942
Oil and gas	76,166	72,690	72,830	101,800	133,606	182,473
Minerals and ores	3,675	3,553	3,458	3,862	4,821	6,469
Manufacturing, total	1,040,329	972,669	995,103	1,060,349	1,231,005	1,373,160
Food and kindred products	18,944	19,646	21,110	23,769	27,740	29,759
Beverages and tobacco products	8,350	8,723	9,772	10,925	11,652	12,845
Textiles and fabrics	7,042	6,336	6,778	6,791	7,387	7,453
Textile mill products.	7,347	7,580	8,643	9,857	11,707	13,508
Apparel and accessories	62,928	62,429	62,313	66,499	70,533	74,473
Leather and allied products	21,463	21,865	22,104	22,627	24,541	26,554
Wood products	15,388	14,968	15,720	16,581	22,869	23,652
Paper products	19,080	18,170	17,528	18,414	20,645	22,120
Printed, publishing, & similar products.	4,197	4,143	4,432	4,699	5,148	5,601
Petroleum and coal products.	40,156	35,222	31,976	39,161	54,544	81,402
Chemicals	76,606	80,681	87,311	102,078	115,246	132,031
Plastics and rubber products	17,362	16,887	18,554	20,504	24,085	28,087
Nonmetallic mineral products	14,740	13,552	13,547	14,428	16,531	18,455
Primary metal products	43,833	36,350	34,356	34,065	56,498	64,642
Fabricated metal products	27,974	26,386	28,607	30,068	35,976	41,065
Machinery, except electrical	79,366	72,124	66,457	77,344	94,402	109,589
Computers and electronic products	250,694	204,950	205,564	212,201	248,033	269,986
Electrical equipment, appliances and components	39,567	38,949	39,707	41,914	48,781	55,179
Transportation equipment	213,110	212,013	219,186	223,304	239,565	252,199
Furniture and fixtures.	15,607	15,266	17,492	19,636	22,560	25,590
Miscellaneous manufactured commodities	56,577	56,427	61,759	65,484	72,563	79,465
Special classification provisions	60,791	60,125	59,093	57,889	62,915	69,526
Waste & scrap	1,875	1,590	1,613	1,808	3,054	3,206
Used or second-hand merchandise	6,345	5,902	5,668	4,752	5,710	6,013
Goods returned or reimported	33,851	34,682	34,981	33,605	34,223	37,057
Special classification provision, not elsewhere specified	18,720	17,951	16,831	17,723	19,928	23,250

Source: U.S. Census Bureau, *U.S. International Trade in Goods and Services*, series FT-900, December issues. For most recent, see <http://www.census.gov/foreign-trade/Press-Release/2005pr/12/> (released 10 February 2006) and previous December or Final reports.

Puerto Rico and the Island Areas

This section presents summary economic and social statistics for Puerto Rico, the U.S. Virgin Islands, Guam, American Samoa, and the Northern Mariana Islands. Primary sources are the decennial censuses of population and housing, county business patterns, and the censuses of agriculture, business, manufactures, and construction (taken every 5 years) conducted by the U.S. Census Bureau; the annual *Vital Statistics of the United States,* issued by the National Center for Health Statistics; and the annual *Income and Product* of the Puerto Rico Planning Board, San Juan.

Jurisdiction—The United States gained jurisdiction over these areas as follows: the islands of *Puerto Rico* and *Guam,* surrendered by Spain to the United States in December 1898, were ceded to the United States by the Treaty of Paris, ratified in 1899. Puerto Rico became a commonwealth on July 25, 1952, thereby achieving a high degree of local autonomy under its own constitution. The *U.S. Virgin Islands,* comprising 50 islands and cays, was purchased by the United States from Denmark in 1917. *American Samoa,* a group of seven islands, was acquired by the United States in accordance with a convention among the United States, Great Britain, and Germany, ratified in 1900 (Swains Island was annexed in 1925). By an agreement approved by the Security Council and the United States, the Northern Mariana Islands, previously under Japanese mandate, was administered by the United States between 1947 and 1986 under the United Nations trusteeship system. The Northern Mariana Islands became a commonwealth in 1986.

Censuses—Because characteristics of the Puerto Rico and the Island Areas differ, the presentation of census data for them is not uniform. The 1960 Census of Population covered all of the places listed above except the Northern Mariana Islands (their census was conducted in April 1958 by the Office of the High Commissioner), while the 1960 Census of Housing also excluded American Samoa. The 1970, 1980, 1990, and 2000 Censuses of Population and Housing covered all five areas. The 1959, 1969, and 1978 Censuses of Agriculture covered Puerto Rico, American Samoa, Guam, and the Virgin Islands; the 1964, 1974, and 1982 censuses covered the same areas except American Samoa; and the 1969, 1978, 1987, 1992, and 1997 censuses included the Northern Mariana Islands. Beginning in 1967, Congress authorized the economic censuses, to be taken at 5-year intervals, for years ending in "2" and "7." Prior economic censuses were conducted in Puerto Rico for 1949, 1954, 1958, and 1963 and in Guam and the U.S. Virgin Islands for 1958 and 1963. In 1967, the census of construction industries was added for the first time in Puerto Rico; in 1972, the U.S. Virgin Islands and Guam were covered. For 1982, 1987, 1992, and 1997 the economic censuses covered the Northern Mariana Islands.

Information in other sections—In addition to the statistics presented in this section, other data are included as integral parts of many tables showing distribution by states in various sections of the *Abstract.* See "Puerto Rico and the Island Areas" in the Index. For definition and explanation of terms used, see Section 1, Population; Section 4, Education; Section 17, Agriculture; Section 20, Construction and Housing; Section 21, Manufactures; and Section 22, Wholesale and Retail Trade.

U.S. Census Bureau, *Statistical Abstract of the United States: 2007*

Fig. 29.1
Selected Island Areas of the United States

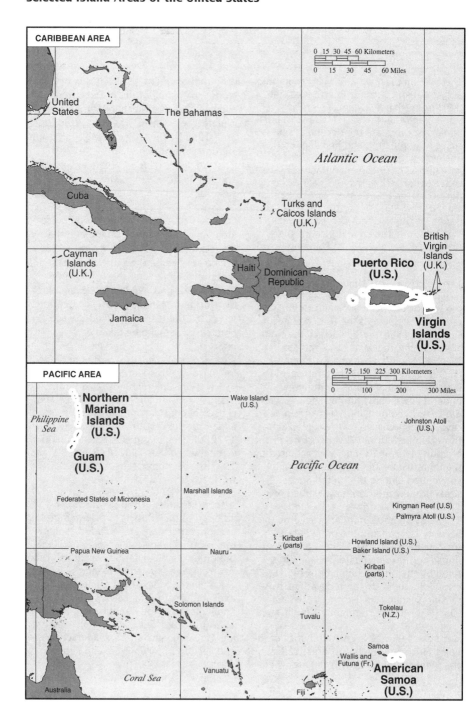

Table 1294. **Estimated Resident Population With Projection: 1970 to 2025**

[In thousands (2,722 represents 2,722,000). Births, deaths, and infant deaths by place of residence. Rates for 1970, 1980, 1990, and 2000 based on population enumerated as of April 1; for other years, on population estimated as of July 1. Population data generally are de-facto figures for the present territory. Data for 1990 to 2000 are adjusted to the 2000 Census of Population for Puerto Rico only. See text, Section 30, for general comments regarding the data. For details of methodology, coverage, and reliability, see source]

Area	1970	1980	1990	1995	2000	2002	2003	2004	2005	2025, proj.
Puerto Rico.	2,722	3,210	3,537	3,683	3,816	3,860	3,878	3,895	3,911	4,086
American Samoa	27	32	47	57	57	58	58	58	58	52
Guam	86	107	134	144	155	161	164	166	169	213
Virgin Islands	63	98	104	114	109	109	109	109	109	108
Northern Mariana Islands	12	17	44	58	70	74	76	78	80	116

Source: U.S. Bureau of the Census, International Data Base. See Internet site: <http://census.gov/ipc/www/idbnew.html>.

Table 1295. **Vital Statistics—Specified Areas: 1980 to 2004**

[Births, deaths, and infant deaths by place of residence. Rates for 1990 and 2000 based on population enumerated as of **April 1**; for other years, on population estimated as of **July 1**]

Area and year	Births		Deaths		Infant deaths	
	Number	Rate [1]	Number	Rate [1]	Number	Rate [2]
Puerto Rico:						
1980.	72,986	22.8	20,413	6.4	1,351	18.5
1990.	66,417	18.8	25,957	7.3	888	13.4
2000.	59,333	15.2	28,369	7.2	574	9.7
2003.	50,696	13.1	28,202	7.3	492	9.7
2004 [3]	51,099	13.1	28,922	7.4	415	(NA)
Guam:						
1980.	2,945	27.8	393	3.7	43	14.6
1990.	3,839	28.6	520	3.9	31	8.1
2000.	3,766	24.4	648	4.2	22	5.8
2003.	3,281	20.1	680	4.2	37	11.3
2004 [3]	3,419	20.6	683	4.1	40	(NA)
Virgin Islands:						
1980.	2,504	25.9	504	5.2	61	24.4
1990.	2,267	21.8	480	4.6	33	14.6
2000.	1,564	12.9	641	5.3	21	13.4
2003.	1,522	14.0	631	5.8	12	(NA)
2004 [3]	1,413	13.0	624	5.8	8	(NA)
American Samoa:						
1997.	1,634	27.1	257	4.3	17	(B)
2002.	1,627	28.2	294	5.1	25	(NA)
2004 [3]	1,714	29.6	286	4.9	26	(NA)
Northern Marianas:						
1998.	1,462	21.9	162	2.4	13	(B)
2002.	1,290	17.4	163	2.2	9	(NA)
2004 [3]	1,358	17.4	165	2.1	12	(NA)

B Base figure too small to meet statistical standards of reliability.   NA Not available.   [1] Per 1,000 population.   [2] Rates are infant deaths (under 1 year) per 1,000 live births.   [3] Data for 2004 is preliminary.

Source: U.S. National Center for Health Statistics, *Vital Statistics of the United States,* annual; and *National Vital Statistics Reports (NSVR)* and unpublished data; <http://www.cdc.gov/nchs/nvss.htm>.

Table 1296. **Public Elementary and Secondary Schools by Area: 2003**

[For school year ending in year shown, unless otherwise indicated. (2,541,385 represents $2,541,385,000)]

Item	Puerto Rico	Guam	Virgin Islands	Amer- ican Samoa	Item	Puerto Rico	Guam	Virgin Islands	Amer- ican Samoa
Enrollment, fall	584,916	31,572	17,716	15,893	Teachers	42,444	1,760	1,512	988
Elementary (kindergarten grade 8)	418,588	22,551	12,738	11,772	Student support staff.	3,899	52	85	84
Secondary (grades 9–12 and post graduates)	166,328	9,021	4,978	4,121	Other support services staff.	17,815	239	481	167
Staff, fall	74,697	3,466	2,896	1,771	Current expendi-				
School district staff . .	2,108	272	217	136	tures [1] ($1,000)	2,541,385	(NA)	125,405	47,566
School staff	50,875	2,903	2,113	1,384	Per pupil [2] (dol).	4,324	(NA)	7,163	3,225

NA Not available   [1] Public elementary and secondary day schools.   [2] Per pupil expenditures include current expenditures, capital expenditures, and interest on school debt and excludes "other current expenditures" such as community services, private school programs, adult education and other programs not allocable to expenditures per pupil in public schools.

Source: U.S. National Center for Education Statistics, *Digest of Education Statistics,* annual; and unpublished data. See Internet site <http://nces.ed.gov/annuals>.

Puerto Rico and the Island Areas   817

Table 1297. **Puerto Rico—Summary: 1980 to 2005**

[3,184.0 represents 3,184,000]

Item	Unit	1980	1990	1995	2000	2002	2003	2004	2005
POPULATION									
Total [1]	1,000	3,184.0	3,512.4	3,641.1	3,808.0	3,849.3	3,869.0	3,887.0	3,903.0
Persons per family	Number...	4.3	3.7	3.5	3.4	3.4	3.3	3.3	3.3
EDUCATION [2]									
Enrollment, total	1,000	941.4	953.0	932.7	971.4	1,067.1	1,172.3	(NA)	(NA)
Public (except public colleges or universities)....	1,000	716.1	651.2	621.4	612.3	603.5	596.3	584.9	575.9
Private schools	1,000	95.2	145.8	145.9	183.7	272.9	376.2	(NA)	(NA)
College and university	1,000	130.1	156.0	165.4	175.4	190.7	199.8	206.8	208.0
Expenses	Mil. dol...	825.0	1,686.4	2,555.8	4,254.1	4,740.6	4,962.3	5,414.9	5,893.2
As percent of GNP	Percent...	7.5	7.8	9.0	10.3	10.5	10.5	10.7	11.0
Public	Mil. dol...	612.2	1,054.2	1,689.4	3,160.4	3,429.6	3,617.0	3,945.5	4,389.5
Private	Mil. dol....	212.8	644.2	866.4	1,093.7	1,311.0	1,345.3	1,469.4	1,503.7
LABOR FORCE [3]									
Total [4]	1,000	907	1,124	1,219	1,303	1,330	1,352	1,360	1,385
Employed [5]	1,000	753	963	1,051	1,159	1,170	1,188	1,206	1,238
Agriculture [6]	1,000	38	36	34	24	23	24	25	26
Manufacturing	1,000	143	168	172	159	139	134	136	138
Trade	1,000	138	185	211	239	240	252	253	261
Government	1,000	184	222	232	249	261	269	268	274
Unemployed	1,000	154	161	168	143	160	164	155	147
Unemployment rate [7]	Rate	17.0	14.0	14.0	11.0	12.0	12.1	11.4	10.6
Compensation of employees...	Mil. dol...	7,200	13,639	17,773	23,504	25,080	26,183	27,836	29,486
Average compensation	Dollar	9,563	14,854	16,911	20,280	21,436	22,039	23,081	23,817
Salary and wages	Mil. dol...	7,200	13,639	17,773	23,504	21,859	22,670	23,959	25,269
INCOME [8]									
Personal income:									
Current dollars	Mil. dol...	11,002	21,105	27,378	38,856	42,039	44,216	45,937	48,802
Constant (1954) dollars	Mil. dol...	3,985	5,551	6,547	8,491	8,852	9,155	9,405	9,643
Disposable personal income:									
Current dollars	Mil. dol...	10,403	19,914	25,591	36,239	39,251	41,120	42,847	45,479
Constant (1954) dollars	Mil. dol...	3,768	5,238	6,119	7,919	8,265	8,514	8,772	8,986
Average family income:									
Current dollars	Dollar	14,858	22,232	26,316	34,693	36,285	37,716	39,003	41,258
Constant (1954) dollars	Dollar	5,381	5,847	6,293	7,581	7,818	7,809	7,985	8,152
BANKING [9]									
Assets	Mil. dol...	10,223	27,902	39,859	58,813	66,294	74,315	94,427	109,292
TOURISM [8]									
Number of visitors	1,000	2,140	3,426	4,087	4,566	4,364	4,402	4,889	5,073
Visitor expenditures	Mil. dol...	619	1,366	1,828	2,388	2,486	2,677	3,024	3,239
Average per visitor	Dollar	289	399	447	523	570	608	619	638
Net income from tourism	Mil. dol...	202	383	499	615	645	678	733	772

NA Not available.   [1] 1980, 1990, and 2000 enumerated as of April 1; all other years estimated as of July 1.   [2] Enrollment for the first school month. Expenses for school year ending in year shown. "Public" includes: Public Preschool, Public Elementary, Public Intermediate, Public High School, Public Post-High School, Public Technological, Public Adult Education, Public Vocational Education, and Public Special Education. "College and university" includes both public and private colleges and universities.
[3] Annual average of monthly figures. For fiscal years.   [4] For population 16 years old and over.   [5] Includes other employment not shown separately.   [6] Includes forestry and fisheries.   [7] Percent unemployed of the labor force.   [8] For fiscal years.   [9] As of June 30. Does not include federal savings banks and international banking entities.

Source: Puerto Rico Planning Board, San Juan, PR, *Economic Report of the Governor,* annual; <http://www.gobierno.pr/gprportal/inicio>.

Table 1298. **Puerto Rico—Agricultural Summary: 1998 and 2002**

[1 cuerda = .97 acre]

All farms	Unit	1998	2002	All farms	Unit	1998	2002
Farms	Number..	19,951	17,659	260 cuerdas or more .	Number..	674	488
Farm land	Cuerdas .	865,478	690,687	Tenure of operator:			
Average size of farm .	Cuerdas .	43.4	39.1	Operators	Number..	19,951	17,659
Approximate land area..	Cuerdas .	2,254,365	2,254,365	Full owners	Number..	15,620	13,693
Proportion in farms...	Percent..	38.4	30.6	Part owners	Number..	2,207	2,330
Farms by size:				Tenants	Number..	2,124	1,636
Less than 10 cuerdas .	Number. .	7,759	7,943	Farms by type of			
10 to 19 cuerdas	Number. .	4,473	3,847	organization:			
20 to 49 cuerdas	Number. .	4,023	3,228	Individual or family . . .	Number..	17,887	15,843
50 to 99 cuerdas	Number. .	1,792	1,282	Partnership	Number..	211	162
100 to 174 cuerdas ..	Number. .	809	590	Corporation	Number..	437	595
175 to 259 cuerdas ..	Number. .	421	281	Other	Number..	1,416	1,059

Source: U.S. Department of Agriculture, National Agricultural Statistics Service, *2002 Census of Agriculture—Geographic Area Series Part 52, Puerto Rico,* Volume 1, Series AC-02-A-52.

818   Puerto Rico and the Island Areas

Table 1299. **Puerto Rico—Gross Product and Net Income: 1990 to 2005**

[In millions of dollars (21,619 represents $21,619,000,000). For fiscal years ending June 30. Data for 2005 are preliminary. Minus sign (–) indicates decrease]

Item	1990	1995	2000	2002	2003	2004	2005
Gross product.	**21,619**	**28,452**	**41,419**	**45,073**	**47,479**	**50,391**	**53,380**
Agriculture	434	318	529	277	333	410	395
Manufacturing	12,126	17,867	24,079	31,243	31,532	32,991	33,132
Contract construction and mining [1]	720	1,006	1,875	1,648	1,772	1,893	1,881
Transportation & other public services [2]	2,468	3,276	4,237	4,948	5,178	5,333	5,474
Trade	4,728	5,989	8,340	8,623	9,150	9,859	10,433
Finance, insurance, real estate	3,896	5,730	9,977	11,212	12,508	12,964	13,633
Services	3,015	4,724	6,603	7,079	7,261	7,744	8,220
Government	3,337	4,440	5,478	6,303	6,948	7,377	8,336
Commonwealth	2,884	3,793	4,601	5,364	5,947	6,350	7,182
Municipalities	453	647	877	939	1,000	1,027	1,154
Rest of the world	–8,985	–14,195	–20,283	–26,552	–27,348	–28,556	–28,653
Statistical discrepancy	–121	–703	585	292	146	378	531
Net income.	**17,941**	**23,653**	**32,610**	**35,852**	**38,045**	**40,323**	**42,786**
Agriculture	486	442	669	544	604	697	714
Manufacturing	11,277	16,685	22,348	29,454	29,761	31,121	31,204
Mining	26	30	41	41	41	40	41
Contract construction	679	903	1,691	1,439	1,593	1,696	1,681
Transportation & other public services [2]	1,778	2,360	2,968	3,389	3,542	3,634	3,771
Trade	3,420	4,108	5,752	5,960	6,289	6,901	7,268
Finance, insurance, and real estate	3,280	4,735	8,264	9,200	10,411	10,792	11,380
Services	2,643	4,146	5,682	6,074	6,208	6,622	7,044
Commonwealth government [3]	3,337	4,440	5,478	6,303	6,948	7,377	8,336
Rest of the world	–8,985	–14,195	–20,283	–26,552	–27,348	–28,556	–28,653

[1] Mining includes only quarries. [2] Includes other public utilities, and radio and television broadcasting. [3] Includes public enterprises not elsewhere classified.

Source: Puerto Rico Planning Board, San Juan, PR, *Economic Report of the Governor,* annual; <http://www.gobierno.pr/gprportal/inicio>.

Table 1300. **Puerto Rico—Transfer Payments: 1990 to 2005**

[In millions of dollars (4,871 represents $4,871,000,000). Data represent transfer payments between federal and state governments and other nonresidents. See headnote, Table 1299]

Item	1990	1995	2000	2002	2003	2004	2005
Total receipts	**4,871**	**6,236**	**8,659**	**9,818**	**10,451**	**10,615**	**10,867**
Federal government	4,649	5,912	7,966	9,041	9,742	9,802	9,989
Transfers to individuals [1]	4,577	5,838	7,868	8,919	9,619	9,690	9,862
Veterans benefits	349	440	491	516	517	520	524
Medicare	368	661	1,196	1,433	1,929	1,998	2,070
Old age, disability, survivors (social security)	2,055	2,912	3,863	4,643	4,739	4,796	4,854
Nutritional assistance	880	1,063	1,193	1,194	1,237	1,241	1,306
Industry subsidies	72	74	98	123	123	112	127
U.S. state governments	18	18	15	17	19	16	15
Other nonresidents	205	307	679	760	690	797	863
Total payments	**1,801**	**2,301**	**2,763**	**3,023**	**3,229**	**3,471**	**3,584**
Federal government	1,756	2,132	2,693	2,919	3,085	3,350	3,517
Transfers from individuals	817	1,052	1,326	1,456	1,548	1,700	1,792
Contribution to Medicare	97	162	191	227	227	258	303
Employee contribution for social security	720	888	1,133	1,227	1,317	1,438	1,483
Transfers from industries	16	49	51	64	58	49	76
Unemployment insurance	247	184	234	228	240	219	221
Employer contribution for social security	675	847	1,081	1,171	1,240	1,382	1,429
Other nonresidents [2]	45	164	70	104	144	121	67
Net balance	**3,070**	**3,935**	**5,897**	**6,796**	**7,222**	**7,144**	**7,282**
Federal government	2,893	3,780	5,273	6,123	6,657	6,452	6,471
U.S. state governments	16	13	10	–32	–56	–21	10
Other nonresidents	162	143	614	705	621	714	801

[1] Includes other receipts and payments not shown separately. [2] Includes U.S. state governments.

Source: Puerto Rico Planning Board, San Juan, PR, *Economic Report of the Governor,* annual; <http://www.gobierno.pr/gprportal/inicio>.

Table 1301. **Puerto Rico—Merchandise Imports and Exports: 1980 to 2005**

[In millions of dollars (9,018 represents $9,018,000,000). Imports are imports for consumption; see text, Section 28]

Item	1980	1985	1990	1995	1998	1999	2000	2001	2002	2003	2004	2005
Imports	9,018	10,162	16,200	18,969	21,706	26,697	27,199	27,690	30,511	35,945	37,252	40,418
From U.S.	5,345	6,130	10,792	12,213	13,318	15,949	14,718	15,675	16,949	16,949	18,124	20,994
From other	3,673	4,032	5,408	6,756	8,388	10,754	11,834	12,972	14,824	18,996	19,128	19,424
Exports	6,576	11,087	20,402	23,573	31,501	37,779	43,191	46,689	50,641	55,814	54,982	56,843
To U.S.	5,643	9,873	17,915	20,986	28,109	33,173	38,335	40,981	44,907	46,880	45,311	47,121
To other	933	1,214	2,487	2,587	3,392	4,785	4,856	5,708	5,734	8,934	9,671	9,722

Source: U.S. Census Bureau, *Foreign Commerce and Navigation of the United States,* annual; *U.S. Trade with Puerto Rico and U.S. Possessions, FT 895;* and, through 1985, *Highlights of U.S. Export and Import Trade, FT990;* thereafter, *FT920;* <http://www.census.gov/foreign-trade/statistics/index.html>.

Table 1302. Puerto Rico—Economic Summary by Industry: 2003

[In thousands of dollars, (14,528,411 represents $14,528,411,000). Covers establishments with payroll. Employees are for the pay period including March 12. See headnote Table 738. Based on the County Business Patterns (CBP). This annual series is used as a benchmark for statistical series, surveys, and databases between economic censuses. For a description of CBP; see Appendix III. Starting with the 2003 CBP series, the data are tabulated using the 2002 North American Industial Classification System (NAICS)]

Industry	2002 NAICS code [1]	Number of employees	Annual payroll (1,000)	Total number of establishments
Establishments, total [2]	(X)	**704,680**	**14,528,411**	**45,890**
Construction	23	57,689	1,089,225	2,738
Manufacturing	31-33	114,681	3,126,193	2,180
Wholesale trade.	42	33,971	1,005,221	2,312
Retail trade.	44-45	124,571	1,769,041	10,979
Transportation and warehousing	48-49	15,101	340,340	1,049
Information	51	21,060	754,573	515
Finance and insurance	52	35,450	1,270,284	1,854
Real estate and rental and leasing	53	13,228	250,379	1,746
Professional, scientific, and technical services	54	24,853	747,835	3,901
Management of companies and enterprises	55	5,576	149,131	84
Admin/support waste mgt/remediation services	56	61,218	928,643	1,711
Educational services.	61	29,201	545,912	718
Health care and social assistance	62	67,882	1,231,688	6,397

X Not Applicable.   [1] See text, Section 12 for more information on NAICS.   [2] Includes other industries not shown separately.

Source: U.S. Census Bureau, County Business Patterns; annual. See <http://www.census.gov/epcd/cbp/view/cbppr.html>.

Table 1303. Guam, Virgin Islands, and Northern Mariana Islands—Economic Summary: 2002

[Sales and payroll in millions of dollars (4,592 represents $4,592,000,000). Based on the 2002 Economic Census; see Appendix III. Selected kinds of businesses displayed]

Selected kinds of business	Guam	Virgin Islands	Northern Mariana Islands	Selected kinds of business	Guam	Virgin Islands	Northern Mariana Islands
Total: Establishments: [1] . .	2,926	2,615	1,276				
Sales.	4,592	3,961	1,832	Paid employees [2].	1,920	1,028	849
Annual payroll	846	669	382	Retail trade:			
Paid employees [2].	43,104	28,660	32,790	Establishments	632	680	297
Construction:				Sales.	1,250	1,217	312
Establishments	244	190	63	Annual payroll	123	128	29
Sales.	262	286	50	Paid employees [2].	7,402	6,653	2,916
Annual payroll	54	91	11	Accommodation & Food			
Paid employees [2].	3,136	3,050	1,013	Service			
Wholesale trade:				Establishments	392	313	151
Establishments	187	74	78	Sales.	630	331	197
Sales.	516	263	123	Annual payroll	169	92	47
Annual payroll	43	28	9	Paid employees [2].	11,199	5,639	4,304

X Not applicable.   [1] Includes other kinds of businesses not shown separately.   [2] For pay period including March 12.

Source: U.S. Census Bureau, *2002 Economic Census of the Island Areas;* IA02-00A-Guam, IA02-00A-VI, and IA02-00A-NMI. (Accessed: 18 July 2005); <http://www.census.gov/econ/census02/guide/islandareas.htm>.

Table 1304. Federal Direct Payments: 2004

[In thousands of dollars (5,667,797 represents $5,667,797,000). For fiscal years ending September 30]

Selected program payments	Puerto Rico	Guam	Virgin Islands	American Samoa	Northern Mariana Islands
Direct payments to individuals for retirement and disability [1]	5,667,797	221,055	155,075	43,973	24,090
Social security:					
Retirement insurance	2,341,320	69,584	89,762	11,191	5,750
Survivors' insurance	1,028,104	29,500	23,803	11,580	4,558
Disability insurance	1,506,016	15,796	18,678	9,905	1,310
Federal retirement and disability:					
Civilian [2]	223,124	56,249	14,908	1,756	5,812
Military	110,554	35,393	4,824	4,022	1,890
Veterans' benefits:					
Service-connected disability.	250,964	11,384	1,698	4,376	606
Other	178,185	2,195	659	1,076	82

[1] Includes other payments, not shown separately.   [2] Includes retirement and disability payments to former U.S. Postal Service employees.

Source: U.S. Census Bureau, *Consolidated Federal Funds Report for Fiscal Year,* 2004 (issued December 2005). See also <http://www.census.gov/govs/www/cffr04.html>.

Comparative International Statistics

This section presents statistics for the world as a whole and for many countries on a comparative basis with the United States. Data are shown for population, births and deaths, social and industrial indicators, finances, agriculture, communication, and military affairs.

Statistics of the individual nations may be found primarily in official national publications, generally in the form of yearbooks, issued by most of the nations at various intervals in their own national languages and expressed in their own or customary units of measure. (For a listing of selected publications, see Guide to Sources.) For handier reference, especially for international comparisons, the United Nations Statistics Division compiles data as submitted by member countries and issues a number of international summary publications, generally in English and French. Among these are the *Statistical Yearbook*; the *Demographic Yearbook; International Trade Statistics Yearbook; National Accounts Statistics: Main Aggregates and Detailed Tables; Population and Vital Statistics Reports* (quarterly); the *Monthly Bulletin of Statistics*; and the *Energy Statistics Yearbook*. Specialized agencies of the United Nations also issue international summary publications on agricultural, labor, health, and education statistics. Among these are the *Production Yearbook* and *Trade Yearbook* issued by the Food and Agriculture Organization, the *Yearbook of Labour Statistics* issued by the International Labour Office, *World Health Statistics* issued by the World Health Organization, and the *Statistical Yearbook* issued by the Educational, Scientific, and Cultural Organization.

The U.S. Census Bureau presents estimates and projections of basic demographic measures for countries and regions of the world in the *World Population Reports* (WP) series. The *International Population Reports* (Series IPC), and *International Briefs* (Series IB) also present population figures for many foreign

countries. Detailed population statistics are also available from the Census Bureau's International Data Base (http://www.census.gov/ipc/www/idbnew.html>.

The International Monetary Fund (IMF) and the Organization for Economic Cooperation and Development (OECD) also compile data on international statistics. The IMF publishes a series of reports relating to financial data. These include *International Financial Statistics, Direction of Trade,* and *Balance of Payments Yearbook,* published in English, French, and Spanish. The OECD publishes a vast number of statistical publications in various fields such as economics, health, and education. Among these are *OECD in Figures, Main Economic Indicators, Economic Outlook, National Accounts, Labour Force Statistics, OECD Health Data,* and *Education at a Glance.*

Statistical coverage, country names, and classifications—Problems of space and availability of data limit the number of countries and the extent of statistical coverage shown. The list of countries included and the spelling of country names are based almost entirely on the list of sovereign nations, dependencies, and areas of special sovereignty provided by the U.S. Department of State.

In recent years, several important changes took place in the status of the world's nations. In 1991, the Soviet Union broke up into 15 independent countries: Armenia, Azerbaijan, Belarus, Estonia, Georgia, Kazakhstan, Kyrgyzstan, Latvia, Lithuania, Moldova, Russia, Tajikistan, Turkmenistan, Ukraine, and Uzbekistan.

In the South Pacific, the Marshall Islands, Micronesia, and Palau gained full independence from the U.S. in 1991.

Following the breakup of the Socialist Federal Republic of Yugoslavia in 1992, the United States recognized Bosnia and

U.S. Census Bureau, Statistical Abstract of the United States: 2007

Herzegovina, Croatia, Slovenia, and The Former Yugoslav Republic of Macedonia as independent countries.

The Treaty of Maastricht created the European Union (EU) in 1992 with 12 member countries. The EU is not a state intended to replace existing states, but it is more than just an international organization. Its member states have set up common institutions to which they delegate some of their sovereignty so that decisions on specific matters of joint interest can be made democratically at a European level. This pooling of sovereignty is also called "European integration." The EU has grown in size with successive waves of accessions in 1995 and 2004. The 25 current members of the EU are: Austria, Belgium, Cyprus, Czech Republic, Denmark, Estonia, Finland, France, Germany, Greece, Hungary, Ireland, Italy, Latvia, Lithuania, Luxembourg, Malta, Poland, Portugal, Slovakia, Slovenia, Spain, Sweden, The Netherlands, and the United Kingdom.

In 1992, the EU decided to go for economic and monetary union (EMU), involving the introduction of a single European currency managed by a European Central Bank. The single currency—the euro—became a reality on 1 January 2002, when euro notes and coins replaced national currencies in 12 of the then 15 countries of the European Union (Belgium, Germany, Greece, Spain, France, Ireland, Italy, Luxembourg, The Netherlands, Austria, Portugal, and Finland). Since then, 10 countries have become members of the EU, but have yet to adopt the euro as their national currency.

On January 1, 1993, Czechoslovakia was succeeded by two independent countries: the Czech Republic and Slovakia. Eritrea announced its independence from Ethiopia in April 1993 and was subsequently recognized as an independent nation by the United States. In May of 2002, East Timor won independence from Indonesia, making it the world's newest independent state.

Serbia and Montenegro, both former republics of Yugoslavia, became independent of one another on May 31, 2006. This separation is seen in the population

estimates tables (Tables 1308–1310), but the majority of tables still show both countries as combined.

The population estimates and projections used in Tables 1305–1310 were prepared by the Census Bureau. For each country, the data on population, by age and sex, fertility, mortality, and international migration were evaluated and, where necessary, adjusted for inconsistencies and errors in the data. In most instances, comprehensive projections were made by the component method, resulting in distributions of the population by age and sex and requiring an assessment of probable future trends of fertility, mortality, and international migration.

Economic associations—The Organization for European Economic Co-Operation (OEEC), a regional grouping of Western European countries established in 1948 for the purpose of harmonizing national economic policies and conditions, was succeeded on September 30, 1961, by the Organization for Economic Cooperation and Development (OECD). The member nations of the OECD are Australia, Austria, Belgium, Canada, Czech Republic, Denmark, Finland, France, Germany, Greece, Hungary, Iceland, Ireland, Italy, Japan, Luxembourg, Mexico, the Netherlands, New Zealand, Norway, Poland, Portugal, Slovakia, South Korea, Spain, Sweden, Switzerland, Turkey, the United Kingdom, and the United States.

Quality and comparability of the data—The quality and comparability of the data presented here are affected by a number of factors:

(1) The year for which data are presented may not be the same for all subjects for a particular country or for a given subject for different countries, though the data shown are the most recent available. All such variations have been noted. The data shown are for calendar years except as otherwise specified.

(2) The bases, methods of estimating, methods of data collection, extent of coverage, precision of definition, scope of territory, and margins of error may vary for different items within a particular country, and for like items for different

U.S. Census Bureau, Statistical Abstract of the United States: 2007

countries. Footnotes and headnotes to the tables give a few of the major time-periods and coverage qualifications attached to the figures; considerably more detail is presented in the source publications. Many of the measures shown are, at best, merely rough indicators of magnitude.

(3) Figures shown in this section for the United States may not always agree with figures shown in the preceding sections. Disagreements may be attributable to the use of differing original sources, a difference in the definition of geographic limits (the 50 states, conterminous United States only, or the United States including certain outlying areas and possessions), or to possible adjustments made in the United States' figures by other sources in order to make them more comparable with figures from other countries.

International comparisons of national accounts data—In order to compare national accounts data for different countries, it is necessary to convert each country's data into a common unit of currency, usually the U.S. dollar. The market exchange rates, which are often used in converting national currencies, do not necessarily reflect the relative purchasing power in the various countries. It is necessary that the goods and services produced in different countries be valued consistently if the differences observed are meant to reflect real differences in the volumes of goods and services produced. The use of purchasing power parities (see Table 1325) instead of exchange rates is intended to achieve this objective.

The method used to present the data shown in Table 1325 is to construct volume measures directly by revaluing the goods and services sold in different countries at a common set of international prices. By dividing the ratio of the gross domestic products of two countries expressed in their own national currencies by the corresponding ratio calculated at constant international prices, it is possible to derive the implied purchasing power parity (PPP) between the two currencies concerned. PPPs show how many

units of currency are needed in one country to buy the same amount of goods and services that one unit of currency will buy in the other country. For further information, see *National Accounts, Main Aggregates, Volume I,* issued annually by the Organisation for Economic Cooperation and Development, Paris, France.

International Standard Industrial Classification—The original version of the International Standard Industrial Classification of All Economic Activities (ISIC) was adopted in 1948. Wide use has been made both nationally and internationally in classifying data according to kind of economic activity in the fields of production, employment, national income, and other economic statistics. A number of countries have utilized the ISIC as the basis for devising their industrial classification scheme.

Substantial comparability has been attained between the industrial classifications of many other countries, including the United States and the ISIC by ensuring, as far as practicable, that the categories at detailed levels of classification in national schemes fitted into only one category of the ISIC. The United Nations, the International Labour Organization, the Food and Agriculture Organization, and other international bodies have utilized the ISIC in publishing and analyzing statistical data. Revisions of the ISIC were issued in 1958, 1968, and 1989.

International maps—A series of regional world maps is provided on pages 824–830. References are included in Table 1308 for easy location of individual countries on the maps. The Robinson map projection is used for this series of maps. A map projection is used to portray all or part of the round Earth on a flat surface, but this cannot be done without some distortion. For the Robinson projection, distortion is very low along the Equator and within 45 degrees of the center but is greatest near the poles. For additional information on map projections and maps, please contact the Earth Science Information Center, U.S. Geological Survey, 507 National Center, Reston, VA 22092.

World

U.S. Census Bureau, Statistical Abstract of the United States: 2007

S1 (North and Central America)

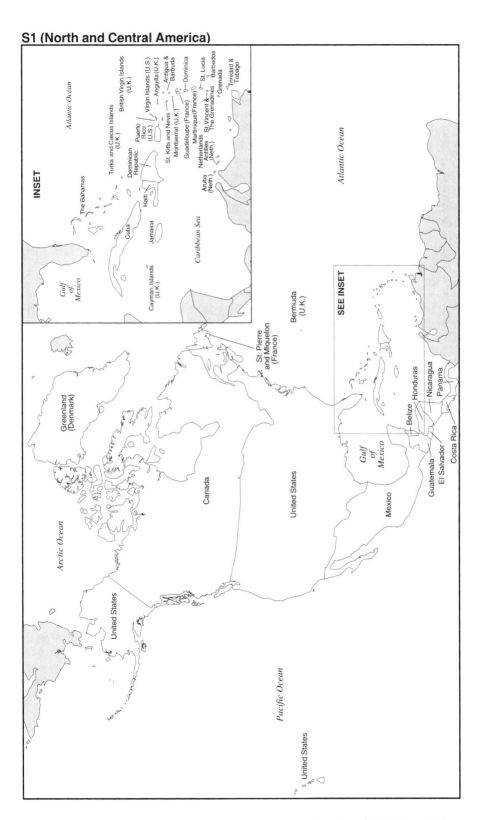

U.S. Census Bureau, Statistical Abstract of the United States: 2007

Svalbard
(Norway)

Jan Mayen
(Norway)

Arctic Ocean

Iceland

Faroe Islands
(Denmark)

Finland

Norway

Sweden

Estonia

Denmark

Latvia

Russia   Lithuania

Ireland

Belarus

Netherlands

Isle of Man   United
(U.K.)   Kingdom

Guernsey
(U.K.)

Germany   Poland

Luxembourg

Jersey
(U.K.)

Czech
Republic   Ukraine

Belgium

Moldova

Switzerland   Slovakia

*Atlantic
Ocean*

France   Austria   Romania

Slovenia   Hungary

Liechtenstein   Bosnia &
Herzegovina

Croatia

San Marino   *Black Sea*

Serbia

Andorra   Monaco   Italy   Montenegro

Spain   Albania   Bulgaria

Corsica
(France)   Holy
See

Balearic Islands
(Spain)   Sardinia
(Italy)   Greece

Portugal   Sicily
(Italy)   Macedonia

Malta

Mediterranean Sea

Comparative International Statistics   827

Atlantic Ocean

Azores
(Portugal)

Madeira Islands
(Portugal)

Canary Islands
(Spain)

Western
Sahara

Cape
Verde

The Gambia

Guinea-Bissau

Sierra Leone

Liberia

Morocco

Tunisia

Algeria

Mauritania

Senegal

Guinea

Cote
d'Ivoire

Mali

Burkina
Faso

Ghana

Togo

Sao Tome &
Principe

Equatorial
Guinea

Niger

Benin

Nigeria

Cameroon

Gabon

Mediterranean Sea

Libya

Chad

Central African
Republic

Congo
(Brazzaville)

Egypt

Red Sea

Eritrea

Sudan

Djibouti

Ethiopia

Somalia

Uganda

Rwanda

Congo
(Kinshasa)

Burundi

Kenya

Indian Ocean

Tanzania

Seychelles

Ascension
(United Kingdom)

Angola

Angola

St. Helena
(United Kingdom)

Zambia

Malawi

Comoros

Mayotte
(France)

Mauritius

Reunion
(France)

Zimbabwe

Mozambique

Namibia

Botswana

Bassas
de India
(France)

Europa
Island
(France)

Madagascar

Atlantic Ocean

Swaziland

Lesotho

South Africa

Tristan da Cunha Islands
(United Kingdom)

Prince Edward Islands
(South Africa)

French Southern and
Antarctic Lands
(France)

Heard Island and
McDonald Islands
(Australia)

U.S. Census Bureau, Statistical Abstract of the United States: 2007

Pacific Ocean

North Korea
South Korea
Japan
Taiwan
Macau
Hong Kong
China

Arctic Ocean

Mongolia

Russia

China

Bhutan
Bangladesh

Sri Lanka

India

Indian Ocean

Kyrgyzstan
Kazakhstan
Uzbekistan
Tajikistan
Turkmenistan

Nepal

Pakistan
Afghanistan

Maldives

Iran

Oman
Socotra (Yemen)

Caspian Sea

Azerbaijan
Georgia
Armenia
Iraq
Kuwait
Bahrain
Qatar
United Arab Emirates
Yemen
Saudi Arabia

Turkey
Syria
Jordan

Black Sea

Cyprus
Lebanon
West Bank
Gaza Strip
Israel

Red Sea

Pacific Ocean

Pitcairn Islands (U.K.)

French Polynesia (France)

Kingman Reef (U.S.)
Palmyra Atoll (U.S.)
Jarvis Island (U.S.)
Kiribati
Cook Islands (New Zealand)

Johnston Atoll (U.S.)

Midway Islands (U.S.)

Howland Island (U.S.)
Baker Island (U.S.)
Kiribati
Tokelau (New Zealand)
Samoa
American Samoa (U.S.)
Niue (New Zealand)
Tonga

Tuvalu

Wallis and Futuna (France)
Fiji

Wake Island (U.S.)
Kiribati
Nauru
Vanuatu
New Caledonia (France)

New Zealand

Marshall Islands

Solomon Islands

Northern Mariana Islands (U.S.)

Guam (U.S.)

Federated States of Micronesia

Papua New Guinea

Australia

Palau

Philippines

Australia

Vietnam
Brunei
Malaysia
Singapore
Cambodia
Indonesia
East Timor

Laos
Thailand

Burma

Indian Ocean

Figure 30.1
Net Additions to the World: 2006
In 2006, the world gained 2.4 people per second

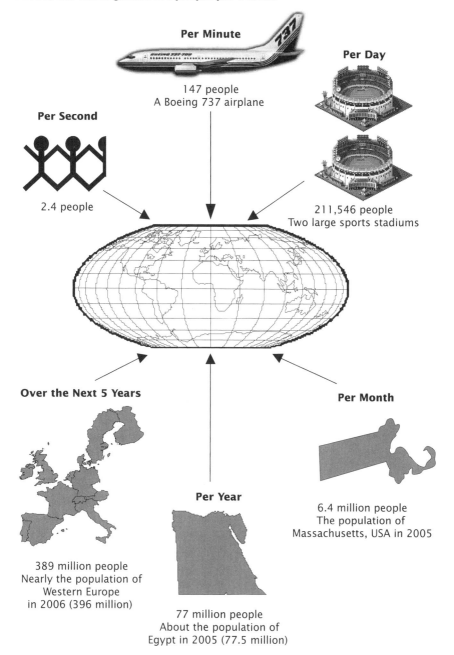

Per Minute

147 people
A Boeing 737 airplane

Per Day

Per Second

2.4 people

211,546 people
Two large sports stadiums

Over the Next 5 Years

Per Month

Per Year

6.4 million people
The population of
Massachusetts, USA in 2005

389 million people
Nearly the population of
Western Europe
in 2006 (396 million)

77 million people
About the population of
Egypt in 2005 (77.5 million)

Source: U.S. Census Bureau, International Programs Center, International Database and
unpublished tables.

Table 1305. **Total World Population: 1980 to 2050**

[As of midyear (**4,447 represents 4,447,000,000**)]

Year	Population (mil.)	Average annual [1] Growth rate (percent)	Average annual [1] Population change (mil.)	Year	Population (mil.)	Average annual [1] Growth rate (percent)	Average annual [1] Population change (mil.)
1980......	4,447	1.7	75.6	2015......	7,230	1.1	77.1
1985......	4,844	1.7	83.2	2020......	7,608	1.0	73.0
1990......	5,274	1.6	83.8	2025......	7,964	0.9	68.2
1995......	5,683	1.4	79.9	2030......	8,296	0.8	63.8
2005......	6,451	1.2	76.7	2035......	8,607	0.7	59.7
2006......	6,528	1.2	77.0	2040......	8,897	0.6	55.3
2007......	6,605	1.2	77.4	2045......	9,164	0.5	50.3
2010......	6,838	1.1	78.5	2050......	9,404	(NA)	(NA)

NA Not available. [1] Represents change from year shown to immediate succeeding year.

Source: U.S. Census Bureau, International Data Base, "Total Midyear Population for the World: 1950-2050," updated 24 August 2006; <http://www.census.gov/ipc/www/worldpop.html>.

Table 1306. **Population by Continent: 1980 to 2050**

[In millions, except percent (**4,447 represents 4,447,000,000**). As of midyear]

Year	World	Africa	North America	South America	Asia	Europe	Oceania
1980	4,447	472	371	242	2,645	694	23
1990	5,274	626	424	296	3,181	721	27
2000	6,073	801	486	348	3,678	730	31
2010	6,838	998	540	393	4,148	726	35
2020	7,608	1,220	594	431	4,610	715	38
2030	8,296	1,461	645	461	4,991	696	41
2040	8,897	1,719	692	481	5,291	671	43
2050	9,404	1,990	734	490	5,505	640	45
PERCENT DISTRIBUTION							
1980	100.0	10.6	8.4	5.4	59.5	15.6	0.5
2000	100.0	13.2	8.0	5.7	60.6	12.0	0.5
2050	100.0	21.2	7.8	5.2	58.5	6.8	0.5

Source: U.S. Census Bureau, "International Data Base" (as of 24 August 2006); <http://www.census.gov/ipc/www/idbnew.html>.

Table 1307. **Population and Population Change, by Development Status: 1950 to 2050**

[In millions, except percent (**2,557 represents 2,557,000,000**). As of midyear. Minus sign (–) indicates decrease. The "less developed" countries include all of Africa, all of Asia except Japan, the Transcaucasian and Central Asian republics of the New Independent States, all of Latin America and the Caribbean, and all of Oceania except Australia and New Zealand. This category matches the "less developed country" classification employed by the United Nations]

Year	Numbers World	Numbers Less developed countries	Numbers More developed countries	Percent of world Less developed countries	Percent of world More developed countries
POPULATION					
1950	2,557	1,750	807	68.4	31.6
1960	3,041	2,130	910	70.1	29.9
1970	3,708	2,705	1,003	72.9	27.1
1980	4,447	3,366	1,081	75.7	24.3
1990	5,274	4,131	1,143	78.3	21.7
2000	6,073	4,880	1,193	80.4	19.6
2010	6,838	5,617	1,222	82.1	17.9
2020	7,608	6,369	1,239	83.7	16.3
2030	8,296	7,052	1,244	85.0	15.0
2040	8,897	7,656	1,241	86.1	13.9
2050	9,404	8,174	1,231	86.9	13.1
POPULATION CHANGE					
1950–1960	484	380	104	78.6	21.4
1960–1970	667	574	93	86.1	13.9
1970–1980	739	662	78	89.5	10.5
1980–1990	827	765	62	92.5	7.5
1990–2000	799	749	50	93.7	6.3
2000–2010	765	736	28	96.3	3.7
2010–2020	770	753	17	97.8	2.2
2020–2030	688	683	5	99.2	0.8
2030–2040	601	604	–3	100.5	–0.5
2040–2050	507	518	–10	102.1	–2.1

Source: U.S. Census Bureau, "International Data Base" (as of 24 August 2006); <http://www.census.gov/ipc/www/idbnew.html>.

Table 1308. **Population by Country: 1990 to 2010**

[**5,274,320 represents 5,274,320,000.** Population data generally are de facto figures for the present territory. Population estimates were derived from information available as of fall 2005. See text of this section for general comments concerning the data. For details of methodology, coverage, and reliability, see source. Minus sign (–) indicates decrease]

Country or area	Map refer- ence	Mid-year population (1,000)				Popu- lation rank, 2005	Annual rate of growth, [1] 2000– 2010 (percent)	Popula- tion per sq. mile, 2005	Area (sq. mile)
		1990	2000	2005	2010, proj.				
World	S0	5,274,320	6,073,265	6,451,430	6,838,220	(X)	1.2	128	50,391,392
Afghanistan	S5	14,669	23,898	29,929	34,505	38	3.7	120	250,000
Albania	S3	3,251	3,474	3,563	3,660	129	0.5	337	10,579
Algeria	S4	25,093	30,409	32,532	34,555	37	1.3	35	919,591
Andorra	S3	53	67	71	74	203	1.0	405	174
Angola	S4	8,297	10,377	11,707	13,068	70	2.3	24	481,351
Antigua and Barbuda	S1	63	66	69	71	205	0.6	402	171
Argentina	S2	33,022	37,498	39,538	41,405	31	1.0	37	1,056,637
Armenia	S5	3,377	3,043	2,983	2,967	134	–0.3	272	10,965
Australia	S6	17,022	19,165	20,090	20,925	54	0.9	7	2,941,285
Austria	S3	7,723	8,113	8,185	8,214	90	0.1	257	31,832
Azerbaijan	S5	7,200	7,809	8,016	8,304	91	0.6	241	33,243
Bahamas, The	S1	257	290	302	311	178	0.7	78	3,888
Bahrain	S4	500	634	688	737	163	1.5	2,681	257
Bangladesh	S5	109,897	130,407	144,320	159,765	7	2.0	2,791	51,703
Barbados	S1	263	273	279	284	181	0.4	1,680	166
Belarus	S3	10,201	10,034	9,809	9,613	81	–0.4	122	80,154
Belgium	S3	9,969	10,264	10,364	10,423	76	0.2	887	11,690
Belize	S1	191	248	281	314	180	2.4	32	8,803
Benin	S4	4,676	6,628	7,649	8,731	93	2.8	179	42,710
Bhutan	S5	1,598	2,005	2,232	2,476	142	2.1	123	18,147
Bolivia	S2	6,574	8,153	8,858	9,499	87	1.5	21	418,683
Bosnia and Herzegovina	S3	4,424	4,035	4,430	4,622	118	1.4	224	19,741
Botswana	S4	1,264	1,607	1,640	1,637	147	0.2	7	226,012
Brazil	S2	151,084	175,553	186,113	195,580	5	1.1	57	3,265,061
Brunei	S6	258	336	372	408	175	1.9	183	2,035
Bulgaria	S3	8,894	7,818	7,450	7,149	95	–0.9	175	42,683
Burkina Faso	S4	8,336	11,309	13,492	15,667	63	3.3	128	105,714
Burma	S5	39,243	44,301	46,596	48,511	26	0.9	183	253,954
Burundi	S4	5,505	6,621	7,795	9,281	92	3.4	787	9,903
Cambodia	S5	9,355	12,466	13,636	14,912	62	1.8	200	68,154
Cameroon	S4	11,884	15,343	17,261	19,294	58	2.3	95	181,251
Canada	S1	27,791	31,278	32,805	34,253	35	0.9	9	3,511,006
Cape Verde	S1	349	401	418	431	173	0.7	269	1,556
Central African Republic	S4	3,084	3,935	4,238	4,567	121	1.5	18	240,533
Chad	S4	6,023	8,316	9,657	11,170	82	3.0	20	486,178
Chile	S2	13,128	15,153	15,981	16,720	60	1.0	55	289,112
China [2]	S5	1,148,364	1,268,853	1,306,314	1,347,563	1	0.6	363	3,600,930
Colombia	S2	32,859	39,686	42,954	46,109	28	1.5	107	401,042
Comoros	S4	429	578	671	773	164	2.9	801	838
Congo (Brazzaville) [3]	S4	2,265	3,102	3,602	4,124	127	2.8	27	131,853
Congo (Kinshasa) [3]	S4	39,064	52,022	60,764	70,757	20	3.1	69	875,521
Costa Rica	S2	3,027	3,711	4,016	4,306	123	1.5	205	19,560
Cote d'Ivoire	S4	11,981	15,563	17,298	19,093	57	2.0	141	122,780
Croatia	S3	4,508	4,411	4,496	4,487	117	0.2	206	21,781
Cuba	S1	10,545	11,134	11,347	11,507	72	0.3	265	42,803
Cyprus	S5	681	758	780	801	159	0.5	219	3,568
Czech Republic	S3	10,310	10,270	10,241	10,202	77	–0.1	343	29,836
Denmark	S3	5,141	5,337	5,432	5,516	108	0.3	332	16,368
Djibouti	S4	366	431	477	526	167	2.0	56	8,486
Dominica	S1	73	72	69	70	204	–0.2	238	290
Dominican Republic	S1	7,083	8,410	9,088	9,794	85	1.5	487	18,680
East Timor	S6	746	847	1,041	1,153	156	3.1	185	5,641
Ecuador	S2	10,318	12,505	13,364	14,245	64	1.3	125	106,888
Egypt	S4	56,694	70,492	77,506	84,348	15	1.8	202	384,344
El Salvador	S1	5,100	6,123	6,705	7,293	99	1.7	838	8,000
Equatorial Guinea	S4	368	473	529	585	166	2.1	49	10,830
Eritrea	S4	2,996	4,357	4,670	5,278	115	1.9	100	46,842
Estonia	S3	1,569	1,380	1,333	1,291	152	–0.7	80	16,684
Ethiopia	S4	48,197	64,690	73,053	81,754	16	2.3	169	432,310
Fiji	S6	738	832	893	958	157	1.4	127	7,054
Finland	S3	4,986	5,169	5,223	5,255	111	0.2	44	117,557
France	S3	56,735	59,382	60,656	61,638	21	0.4	288	210,668
Gabon	S4	937	1,235	1,394	1,543	150	2.2	14	99,486
Gambia, The	S4	949	1,368	1,595	1,831	148	2.9	413	3,861
Georgia	S5	5,426	4,777	4,677	4,601	114	–0.4	174	26,911
Germany [4]	S3	79,380	82,188	82,431	82,283	14	(Z)	611	134,835
Ghana	S4	15,414	19,736	22,026	24,279	50	2.1	247	89,166
Greece	S3	10,130	10,559	10,668	10,750	74	0.2	211	50,502
Grenada	S2	92	89	90	91	198	0.2	674	133
Guatemala	S1	8,966	11,085	12,183	13,550	66	2.0	291	41,865
Guinea	S4	6,279	8,639	9,453	10,758	83	2.2	100	94,927
Guinea-Bissau	S4	996	1,278	1,413	1,564	149	2.0	131	10,811
Guyana	S2	751	755	765	774	161	0.2	10	76,004
Haiti	S1	6,131	7,444	8,298	9,386	89	2.3	780	10,641
Honduras	S1	4,792	6,348	7,168	7,944	96	2.2	166	43,201
Hungary	S3	10,372	10,137	10,007	9,880	80	–0.3	281	35,653
Iceland	S1	255	281	297	309	179	0.9	8	38,707
India	S5	838,159	1,004,124	1,093,563	1,184,090	2	1.6	953	1,147,950
Indonesia	S6	181,770	213,829	228,896	242,968	4	1.3	325	705,189

See footnotes at end of table.

U.S. Census Bureau, Statistical Abstract of the United States: 2007

Table 1308. **Population by Country: 1990 to 2010**—Con.

[See headnote, page 833]

Country or area	Map reference	Mid-year population (1,000)				Population rank, 2005	Annual rate of growth,[1] 2000–2010 (percent)	Population per sq. mile, 2005	Area (sq. mile)
		1990	2000	2005	2010, proj.				
Iran	S5	56,669	63,273	64,737	67,038	18	0.6	102	631,660
Iraq	S5	18,135	22,676	26,075	29,672	44	2.7	156	166,858
Ireland	S3	3,508	3,792	4,016	4,250	124	1.1	151	26,598
Israel	S4	4,512	5,842	6,277	6,645	101	1.3	800	7,849
Italy	S3	56,743	57,719	58,103	58,091	23	0.1	512	113,521
Jamaica	S1	2,348	2,615	2,736	2,843	137	0.8	654	4,181
Japan	S5	123,537	126,700	127,417	127,195	10	(Z)	881	144,689
Jordan	S4	3,262	4,999	5,760	6,486	105	2.6	162	35,510
Kazakhstan	S5	16,398	15,032	15,186	15,460	61	0.3	15	1,030,811
Kenya	S4	23,354	30,508	34,912	40,047	34	2.7	159	219,788
Kiribati	S6	71	92	103	115	196	2.3	329	313
Korea, North	S5	20,019	21,648	22,912	23,802	47	0.9	493	46,490
Korea, South	S5	42,869	47,351	48,641	49,568	24	0.5	1,283	37,911
Kuwait	S5	2,142	1,974	2,336	2,788	140	3.5	339	6,880
Kyrgyzstan	S5	4,382	4,851	5,146	5,509	112	1.3	70	73,861
Laos	S5	4,210	5,498	6,217	6,994	102	2.4	70	89,112
Latvia	S3	2,664	2,376	2,290	2,218	141	-0.7	93	24,552
Lebanon	S4	3,147	3,578	3,826	4,056	126	1.3	969	3,950
Lesotho	S4	1,722	2,038	2,031	1,983	144	-0.3	173	11,718
Liberia	S4	2,117	2,694	2,900	3,531	135	2.7	78	37,189
Libya	S4	4,140	5,115	5,766	6,447	104	2.3	8	679,359
Liechtenstein	S3	29	32	34	35	214	0.8	542	62
Lithuania	S5	3,695	3,654	3,597	3,545	128	-0.3	143	25,174
Luxembourg	S3	383	439	469	498	168	1.3	469	998
Macedonia	S3	1,861	2,015	2,045	2,072	143	0.3	213	9,597
Madagascar	S4	11,633	15,742	18,312	21,282	56	3.0	82	224,533
Malawi	S4	9,536	11,560	12,975	14,613	65	2.3	357	36,324
Malaysia	S6	17,504	21,793	23,953	26,144	46	1.8	189	126,853
Maldives	S5	216	301	349	400	177	2.8	3,014	116
Mali	S4	8,085	10,049	11,379	13,025	71	2.6	24	471,042
Malta	S4	359	390	399	407	174	0.4	3,266	122
Marshall Islands	S6	46	53	59	66	208	2.2	845	70
Mauritania	S4	1,984	2,668	3,087	3,561	132	2.9	8	397,838
Mauritius	S4	1,074	1,179	1,231	1,280	153	0.8	1,570	784
Mexico	S1	84,914	99,927	106,203	112,469	11	1.2	143	742,486
Micronesia, Federated States of	S6	109	108	108	107	195	-0.1	399	271
Moldova	S5	4,394	4,382	4,332	4,309	120	-0.2	333	13,012
Monaco	S3	30	32	32	33	215	0.4	41,970	1
Mongolia	S5	2,216	2,601	2,791	3,004	136	1.4	5	603,906
Montenegro	S3	583	732	699	667	162	-0.9	131	5,333
Morocco	S4	24,686	30,122	32,726	35,301	36	1.6	190	172,317
Mozambique	S4	12,667	18,125	20,154	22,061	53	2.0	67	302,737
Namibia	S4	1,471	1,906	2,031	2,077	145	0.9	6	318,694
Nauru	S6	9	12	13	14	224	1.9	1,609	8
Nepal	S5	19,325	24,702	27,677	30,758	41	2.2	501	55,282
Netherlands	S3	14,952	15,908	16,407	16,783	59	0.5	1,254	13,082
New Zealand	S6	3,360	3,820	4,035	4,228	122	1.0	39	103,483
Nicaragua	S2	3,684	4,932	5,465	5,990	107	1.9	118	46,430
Niger	S4	7,945	10,516	12,163	14,054	67	2.9	25	489,073
Nigeria	S4	88,510	114,307	128,766	145,032	9	2.4	366	351,649
Norway	S3	4,242	4,492	4,593	4,676	116	0.4	39	118,865
Oman	S5	1,773	2,533	3,002	3,523	133	3.3	37	82,031
Pakistan	S5	114,578	146,343	162,420	179,592	6	2.0	540	300,664
Palau	S6	15	19	20	22	221	1.4	115	177
Panama	S2	2,390	2,889	3,140	3,393	131	1.6	107	29,340
Papua New Guinea	S6	3,825	4,927	5,545	6,171	106	2.3	32	174,849
Paraguay	S2	4,236	5,586	6,348	7,162	100	2.5	41	153,398
Peru	S2	21,511	25,980	27,926	29,758	40	1.4	57	494,208
Philippines	S6	64,318	79,740	87,857	95,868	12	1.8	763	115,124
Poland	S3	38,119	38,654	38,558	38,464	32	(Z)	328	117,554
Portugal	S3	9,923	10,336	10,566	10,736	75	0.4	298	35,502
Qatar	S5	481	744	863	970	158	2.6	195	4,416
Romania	S5	22,866	22,452	22,330	22,181	49	-0.1	251	88,934
Russia	S5	147,973	146,710	142,776	139,390	8	-0.5	22	6,562,083
Rwanda	S4	6,982	8,278	9,378	10,769	84	2.6	974	9,633
Saint Kitts and Nevis	S1	41	39	39	40	213	0.4	387	101
Saint Lucia	S1	140	156	166	177	191	1.3	711	234
Saint Vincent and the Grenadines	S1	107	115	118	119	192	0.3	783	150
Samoa	S0	170	179	177	176	189	-0.2	157	1,133
San Marino	S3	23	27	29	31	216	1.3	1,247	23
Sao Tome and Principe	S4	119	160	187	219	188	3.1	485	386
Saudi Arabia	S4	16,061	23,153	26,418	29,222	43	2.3	35	756,981
Senegal	S4	7,846	10,332	11,860	13,516	69	2.7	160	74,131
Serbia	S3	9,348	10,118	10,130	10,173	78	0.1	297	34,116
Seychelles	S4	73	79	81	83	199	0.4	461	176
Sierra Leone	S4	4,221	4,809	5,867	6,580	103	3.1	212	27,653
Singapore	S6	3,047	4,037	4,426	4,701	119	1.5	16,807	263
Slovakia	S3	5,263	5,400	5,431	5,470	109	0.1	288	18,842
Slovenia	S3	1,991	2,011	2,011	2,003	146	(Z)	258	7,780
Solomon Islands	S6	335	466	538	610	165	2.7	51	10,633
Somalia	S4	6,675	7,253	8,592	9,922	88	3.1	35	242,216

See footnotes at end of table.

U.S. Census Bureau, Statistical Abstract of the United States: 2007

Table 1308. **Population by Country: 1990 to 2010**—Con.

[See headnote, page 833]

Country or area	Map refer- ence	Mid-year population (1,000)				Popu- lation rank, 2005	Annual rate of growth,[1] 2000– 2010 (percent)	Popula- tion per sq. mile, 2005	Area (sq. mile)
		1990	2000	2005	2010, proj.				
South Africa	S4	38,391	44,066	44,344	43,333	27	-0.2	94	471,008
Spain	S3	39,351	40,016	40,341	40,549	29	0.1	209	192,873
Sri Lanka	S5	17,365	19,436	20,504	21,514	52	1.0	820	24,996
Sudan	S4	26,627	35,080	40,187	45,485	30	2.6	44	917,375
Suriname	S2	395	432	460	487	169	1.2	7	62,344
Swaziland	S4	885	1,110	1,138	1,119	154	0.1	171	6,641
Sweden	S3	8,601	8,924	9,002	9,074	86	0.2	57	158,662
Switzerland	S3	6,837	7,267	7,489	7,623	94	0.5	488	15,355
Syria	S4	12,436	16,306	18,449	20,606	55	2.3	260	71,062
Tajikistan	S5	5,272	6,230	6,815	7,487	98	1.8	124	55,097
Tanzania	S4	25,138	33,065	36,766	40,382	33	2.0	107	342,100
Thailand	S5	55,197	61,863	64,186	66,303	19	0.7	325	197,595
Togo	S4	3,505	4,712	5,400	6,185	110	2.7	257	20,998
Tonga	S0	92	102	112	123	193	1.8	406	277
Trinidad and Tobago	S2	1,198	1,118	1,075	1,029	155	-0.8	543	1,980
Tunisia	S4	8,207	9,564	10,075	10,583	79	1.0	168	59,985
Turkey	S5	56,085	65,667	69,661	73,322	17	1.1	234	297,591
Turkmenistan	S5	3,668	4,518	4,952	5,431	113	1.8	26	188,456
Tuvalu	S6	9	11	12	13	225	1.5	1,159	10
Uganda	S4	17,456	23,956	28,199	33,399	39	3.3	366	77,108
Ukraine	S5	51,622	49,005	46,959	45,416	25	-0.8	201	233,089
United Arab Emirates	S5	1,951	2,369	2,563	2,763	138	1.5	80	32,000
United Kingdom	S3	57,493	59,522	60,441	61,285	22	0.3	648	93,278
United States	S1	250,132	282,339	295,734	309,163	3	0.9	84	3,537,421
Uruguay	S2	3,106	3,324	3,416	3,491	130	0.5	51	67,035
Uzbekistan	S5	20,624	24,756	26,851	29,280	42	1.7	163	164,247
Vanuatu	S6	154	190	206	221	185	1.5	44	4,710
Venezuela	S2	19,325	23,543	25,375	27,134	45	1.4	75	340,560
Vietnam	S5	67,283	79,060	83,536	87,814	13	1.1	665	125,622
Yemen	S5	12,416	17,479	20,727	24,637	51	3.4	102	203,849
Zambia	S4	7,978	10,205	11,115	12,057	73	1.7	39	285,994
Zimbabwe	S4	10,153	11,751	12,161	12,516	68	0.6	81	149,293
OTHER									
Taiwan [2]	S5	20,279	22,151	22,894	23,562	48	0.6	1,838	12,456
AREAS OF SPECIAL SOVEREIGNTY AND DEPENDENCIES									
American Samoa	S0	47	57	58	57	209	(Z)	753	77
Anguilla	S1	8	12	13	14	223	1.8	337	39
Aruba	S1	67	70	72	73	202	0.5	960	75
Bermuda	S1	58	63	65	67	206	0.7	3,194	20
Cayman Islands	S1	26	38	44	50	212	2.7	441	100
Cook Islands	S0	18	20	21	22	219	0.9	230	93
Faroe Islands	S3	47	45	47	48	211	0.6	87	541
French Guiana	S2	116	173	196	214	186	2.1	6	34,421
French Polynesia	S0	202	249	270	291	182	1.5	191	1,413
Gaza Strip [5]	S4	643	1,132	1,376	1,651	151	3.8	9,902	139
Gibraltar	S3	29	28	28	28	217	0.2	12,037	2
Greenland	S1	56	56	56	56	210	(Z)	(Z)	131,931
Guadeloupe	S1	378	426	449	468	171	0.9	681	659
Guam	S6	134	155	169	181	190	1.5	807	209
Guernsey	S3	63	64	65	66	207	0.3	2,166	30
Hong Kong	S5	5,688	6,659	6,899	7,090	97	0.6	17,147	402
Jersey	S3	84	89	91	92	197	0.3	2,010	45
Macau	S6	352	431	449	468	170	0.8	41,551	11
Man, Isle of	S3	69	73	75	77	201	0.5	340	221
Martinique	S1	374	415	433	448	172	0.8	1,059	409
Mayotte	S4	90	156	194	231	187	3.9	1,334	145
Montserrat	S1	11	6	9	10	226	4.3	242	39
Netherlands Antilles	S2	189	210	220	228	183	0.8	593	371
New Caledonia	S6	168	202	216	230	184	1.3	30	7,172
Northern Mariana Islands	S6	44	70	80	91	200	2.6	436	184
Puerto Rico	S1	3,537	3,816	3,912	3,988	125	0.4	1,142	3,425
Reunion	S4	597	721	777	829	160	1.4	803	968
Saint Helena	S4	7	7	7	8	227	0.6	47	159
Saint Pierre and Miquelon	S1	6	7	7	7	228	0.2	75	93
Turks and Caicos Islands	S1	12	18	21	24	220	3.0	124	166
Virgin Islands	S1	104	109	109	108	194	-0.1	814	134
Virgin Islands, British	S1	16	20	23	25	218	2.0	391	58
Wallis and Futuna	S6	14	15	16	17	222	0.9	151	106
West Bank [5]	S4	1,255	2,020	2,386	2,765	139	3.1	1,095	2,178
Western Sahara	S4	221	309	361	417	176	3.0	4	102,703

X Not applicable.   Z Less than 0.05 percent or less than one person per square mile.   [1] Computed by the exponential method. For explanation of average annual percent change, see Guide to Tabular Presentation.   [2] With the establishment of diplomatic relations with China on January 1, 1979, the U.S. government recognized the People's Republic of China as the sole legal government of China and acknowledged the Chinese position that there is only one China and that Taiwan is part of China. [3] "Congo" is the official short-form name for both the Republic of Congo and the Democratic Republic of the Congo. To distinguish one from the other the U.S. Dept. of State adds the capital in parentheses. This practice is unofficial and provisional.   [4] Data for 1990 are for former West Germany and East Germany combined.   [5] The Gaza Strip and West Bank are Israeli-occupied with interim status subject to Israeli/Palestinian negotiations. The final status is yet to be determined.

Source: U.S. Census Bureau, "International Data Base" (as of 24 August 2006); <http://www.census.gov/ipc/www/idbnew .html>.

Comparative International Statistics   835

Table 1309. Age Distribution by Country: 2005 and 2010

[In percent. Covers countries with 5 million or more population in 2005]

Country or area	2005 Under 15 years old	2005 65 years old and over	2010, proj. Under 15 years old	2010, proj. 65 years old and over	Country or area	2005 Under 15 years old	2005 65 years old and over	2010, proj. Under 15 years old	2010, proj. 65 years old and over
World	**28.0**	**7.3**	**26.8**	**7.7**	Korea, North	24.2	7.9	22.2	9.5
Afghanistan	44.7	2.4	44.4	2.4	Korea, South	19.3	8.8	16.6	10.4
Algeria	29.0	4.7	24.8	5.0	Kyrgyzstan	31.6	6.2	29.4	5.5
Angola	43.8	2.8	43.4	2.7	Laos	41.6	3.2	40.5	3.1
Argentina	25.6	10.6	24.1	11.0	Libya	33.9	4.2	32.9	4.4
Australia	19.8	12.9	18.7	13.9	Madagascar	44.3	3.1	43.3	3.0
Austria	15.6	16.6	14.3	18.1	Malawi	46.4	2.7	45.6	2.7
Azerbaijan	27.3	7.0	23.4	6.6	Malaysia	33.0	4.6	31.0	5.1
Bangladesh	33.1	3.4	33.8	3.7	Mali	48.0	3.1	48.3	3.0
Belarus	15.4	14.9	14.2	14.2	Mexico	31.1	5.6	28.7	6.4
Belgium	16.9	17.4	16.0	17.8	Morocco	32.1	4.9	29.6	5.2
Benin	44.5	2.3	43.0	2.5	Mozambique	45.0	2.7	44.1	2.9
Bolivia	35.7	4.5	32.1	4.9	Nepal	39.0	3.7	37.3	3.9
Brazil	26.1	6.0	24.0	6.8	Netherlands	18.1	14.1	17.2	15.2
Bulgaria	14.1	17.2	13.8	17.9	Nicaragua	37.2	3.1	33.1	3.4
Burkina Faso	46.9	2.5	46.3	2.4	Niger	46.9	2.4	46.9	2.4
Burma	26.8	5.1	24.9	5.5	Nigeria	42.3	3.1	42.1	3.2
Burundi	46.4	2.6	46.1	2.5	Pakistan	39.6	4.1	36.7	4.2
Cambodia	36.6	3.4	32.9	3.5	Papua, New Guinea	38.1	3.8	36.6	4.1
Cameroon	41.8	3.1	40.7	3.3	Paraguay	37.9	4.8	36.5	5.1
Canada	17.9	13.2	16.7	14.2	Peru	31.5	5.2	28.5	5.8
Chad	48.0	2.8	47.5	2.7	Philippines	35.4	4.0	33.2	4.4
Chile	25.2	8.0	22.7	9.2	Poland	16.3	13.2	14.8	13.5
China [1]	21.4	7.6	19.6	8.3	Portugal	16.6	17.1	16.3	17.8
Colombia	30.7	5.1	28.5	5.7	Romania	15.9	14.6	15.5	14.7
Congo (Kinshasa) [2]	47.5	2.5	46.7	2.5	Russia	14.8	14.0	15.0	13.3
Cote d'Ivoire	41.0	2.7	40.1	3.0	Rwanda	42.1	2.6	42.4	2.4
Cuba	19.6	10.4	18.2	11.7	Saudi Arabia	38.2	2.4	38.0	2.5
Czech Republic	14.7	14.2	13.5	15.9	Senegal	42.3	3.0	41.6	3.1
Denmark	18.8	15.1	17.9	16.6	Serbia	18.1	15.1	17.6	15.1
Dominican					Sierra Leone	44.9	3.2	44.5	3.2
Republic	32.9	5.5	31.1	6.0	Slovakia	17.1	11.9	15.7	12.6
Ecuador	33.5	4.9	31.0	5.4	Somalia	44.5	2.6	45.0	2.5
Egypt	33.0	4.4	31.0	4.9	South Africa	30.3	5.2	27.6	5.8
El Salvador	36.5	5.1	35.0	5.4	Spain	14.4	17.6	14.5	18.4
Ethiopia	43.9	2.7	42.5	2.8	Sri Lanka	24.8	7.5	23.6	8.3
Finland	17.3	15.9	16.2	17.2	Sudan	43.2	2.4	40.7	2.7
France	18.4	16.4	18.0	16.7	Sweden	17.1	17.4	15.5	19.3
Germany	14.4	18.9	13.5	20.4	Switzerland	16.6	15.4	15.4	16.6
Ghana	39.2	3.5	36.9	3.6	Syria	37.4	3.3	35.5	3.4
Greece	14.4	18.8	14.2	19.4	Taiwan [1]	19.7	9.6	18.4	10.4
Guatemala	42.1	3.5	38.7	3.8	Tajikistan	36.5	3.9	34.1	3.5
Guinea	44.4	3.2	44.2	3.2	Tanzania	44.0	2.6	42.6	2.6
Haiti	42.7	3.5	41.4	3.4	Thailand	22.5	7.8	20.4	8.9
Honduras	40.4	3.4	37.4	3.7	Togo	42.6	2.6	41.3	2.8
Hong Kong	13.8	12.7	11.9	13.3	Tunisia	25.3	6.6	22.3	7.2
Hungary	15.8	15.1	14.8	16.0	Turkey	26.0	6.7	23.5	7.3
India	32.4	4.9	30.7	5.4	Uganda	50.5	2.2	50.0	2.1
Indonesia	29.4	5.4	27.7	6.1	Ukraine	14.6	16.1	13.7	15.5
Iran	25.7	5.3	21.3	5.4	United Kingdom	17.7	15.8	16.5	16.4
Iraq	40.0	3.0	38.5	3.0	**United States**	**20.6**	**12.4**	**20.0**	**13.0**
Israel	26.5	9.8	25.4	10.0	Uzbekistan	33.5	4.8	31.7	4.3
Italy	13.9	19.4	13.4	20.3	Venezuela	29.9	5.1	26.6	5.7
Japan	14.3	19.5	14.1	22.1	Vietnam	27.9	5.8	24.3	5.7
Jordan	34.5	3.8	30.5	4.3	Yemen	46.5	2.7	46.1	2.5
Kazakhstan	23.7	7.9	21.6	7.6	Zambia	46.2	2.4	44.8	2.3
Kenya	42.0	2.6	42.3	2.7	Zimbabwe	37.7	3.5	36.8	3.6

[1] See footnote 2, Table 1308.   [2] See footnote 3, Table 1308.

Source: U.S. Census Bureau, "International Data Base" (as of 24 August 2006); <http://www.census.gov/ipc/www/idbnew.html>.

U.S. Census Bureau, Statistical Abstract of the United States: 2007

Table 1310. **Vital Statistics, by Country: 2005 and 2010**

[Covers countries with 12 million or more population in 2005]

Country or area	Crude birth rate [1] 2005	2010, proj.	Crude death rate [2] 2005	2010, proj.	Expectation of life at birth (years) 2005	2010, proj.	Infant mortality rate [3] 2005	2010, proj.	Total fertility rate per woman [4] 2005	2010, proj.
United States......	14.1	14.2	8.3	8.3	77.7	78.4	6.5	6.17	2.08	2.11
Afghanistan	47.0	45.1	20.8	18.8	42.9	45.1	163.1	149.28	6.75	6.47
Algeria..........	17.1	16.7	4.6	4.7	73.0	74.3	31.0	25.74	1.92	1.76
Argentina........	16.9	15.8	7.6	7.5	75.9	76.9	15.2	13.05	2.19	2.03
Australia.........	12.3	11.7	7.4	7.7	80.4	81.0	4.7	4.39	1.76	1.75
Bangladesh	30.0	27.8	8.4	7.7	62.1	63.9	62.6	54.25	3.13	3.04
Brazil...........	16.8	15.5	6.2	6.3	71.7	73.0	29.6	24.88	1.93	1.81
Burkina Faso	46.0	44.2	15.9	14.5	48.5	50.2	92.9	85.23	6.54	6.21
Burma...........	17.9	16.7	9.5	9.1	61.6	63.8	54.0	46.15	2.01	1.86
Cambodia........	26.9	26.5	9.2	8.6	58.9	60.9	70.9	60.97	3.44	3.10
Cameroon	36.1	33.6	13.3	12.0	51.7	54.0	68.5	62.15	4.66	4.25
Canada..........	10.8	10.7	7.7	8.0	80.1	80.7	4.8	4.46	1.61	1.62
Chile............	15.4	14.5	5.8	6.1	76.6	77.5	8.8	7.74	2.02	1.90
China [5].........	13.1	14.3	6.9	7.1	72.3	73.8	24.2	19.38	1.72	1.80
Colombia	20.8	19.3	5.6	5.6	71.7	73.1	21.0	17.83	2.56	2.44
Congo (Kinshasa) [6] ..	44.1	42.3	13.5	12.3	51.1	52.9	90.7	80.90	6.54	6.11
Cote d'Ivoire......	35.5	33.3	14.9	14.5	48.6	49.5	90.8	82.38	4.58	4.20
Ecuador..........	22.7	20.8	4.2	4.2	76.2	77.2	23.7	19.94	2.72	2.50
Egypt	23.3	21.3	5.3	5.2	71.0	72.4	32.6	26.74	2.88	2.61
Ethiopia..........	38.6	35.6	15.1	14.1	48.8	49.8	95.3	86.90	5.33	4.76
France...........	12.2	11.5	9.1	9.4	79.6	80.3	4.3	4.03	1.85	1.83
Germany	8.3	8.2	10.6	11.0	78.7	79.4	4.2	3.95	1.39	1.42
Ghana	31.1	27.9	9.9	9.1	58.4	60.2	56.2	49.91	4.10	3.57
Guatemala	30.2	27.4	5.5	5.0	69.1	70.6	31.8	26.91	3.93	3.36
India...........	23.6	21.3	7.0	6.1	67.2	70.5	39.7	28.14	2.90	2.67
Indonesia	20.5	18.5	6.3	6.3	69.6	71.1	34.5	28.94	2.44	2.28
Iran.............	16.0	17.3	5.6	5.8	70.0	71.4	40.6	34.66	1.73	1.70
Iraq.............	32.5	29.4	5.5	4.9	68.7	70.3	50.3	42.21	4.28	3.76
Italy............	8.9	8.0	10.3	10.8	79.7	80.3	5.9	5.41	1.28	1.32
Japan	9.5	8.7	9.0	10.0	81.2	81.6	3.3	3.17	1.39	1.42
Kazakhstan	15.8	16.7	9.5	9.4	66.6	68.2	29.2	24.93	1.89	1.87
Kenya	40.2	35.1	12.0	9.3	53.2	58.8	60.7	53.49	4.96	4.38
Korea, North......	16.1	13.8	7.1	7.5	71.4	72.7	24.0	20.51	2.15	1.90
Korea, South	10.0	9.5	5.7	6.4	76.9	77.8	6.3	5.73	1.26	1.31
Madagascar	39.0	37.9	8.9	8.0	61.4	63.3	60.0	52.84	5.33	5.09
Malawi..........	42.7	41.2	19.4	17.4	41.6	44.1	95.4	87.58	5.90	5.51
Malaysia	23.1	22.1	5.1	5.1	72.2	73.6	17.7	15.00	3.07	2.92
Mexico..........	21.0	19.4	4.7	4.8	75.2	76.3	20.9	17.84	2.45	2.31
Morocco.........	22.3	20.6	5.6	5.4	70.7	72.1	41.6	34.68	2.73	2.46
Mozambique......	39.5	37.8	20.7	19.8	41.0	41.4	114.3	103.82	5.40	5.13
Nepal	31.5	28.8	9.5	8.7	59.8	61.7	67.0	58.66	4.19	3.73
Netherlands	11.1	10.3	8.7	8.8	78.8	79.6	5.0	4.66	1.66	1.66
Niger............	51.3	48.6	21.2	19.6	43.5	44.8	119.7	112.62	7.55	7.11
Nigeria..........	40.7	39.5	17.2	15.9	46.7	48.6	98.8	90.88	5.53	5.33
Pakistan.........	30.4	26.9	8.5	7.5	63.0	64.9	72.4	63.10	4.14	3.46
Peru	20.9	18.9	6.3	6.2	69.5	71.0	31.9	27.22	2.56	2.32
Philippines	25.3	23.2	5.5	5.2	69.9	71.4	23.5	20.18	3.16	2.89
Poland	9.7	10.0	9.8	10.1	74.7	75.9	7.4	6.66	1.24	1.29
Romania	10.7	10.4	11.7	11.9	71.4	72.7	26.4	22.09	1.36	1.40
Russia...........	10.6	11.1	15.9	16.0	65.8	66.2	11.5	10.32	1.38	1.41
Saudi Arabia.......	29.6	28.2	2.6	2.5	75.5	76.5	13.2	11.26	4.05	3.77
South Africa	18.5	17.3	21.3	22.7	43.3	42.7	61.8	56.19	2.24	2.02
Spain	10.1	9.5	9.6	10.1	79.5	80.2	4.4	4.14	1.28	1.32
Sri Lanka	17.7	15.9	5.9	6.2	74.5	75.3	20.4	18.14	2.11	1.96
Sudan	35.2	31.8	9.2	8.3	58.5	60.5	62.5	55.22	4.85	4.21
Syria	28.3	25.2	4.9	4.6	70.0	71.5	29.5	24.95	3.50	3.02
Taiwan [5]........	12.6	12.0	6.4	6.9	77.3	78.1	6.4	5.87	1.57	1.59
Tanzania	38.2	35.9	16.7	15.3	45.2	47.2	98.5	88.85	5.06	4.62
Thailand.........	14.0	13.2	7.0	7.3	72.0	73.4	20.2	17.05	1.63	1.65
Turkey..........	16.8	15.6	6.0	6.1	72.4	73.7	41.0	34.25	1.94	1.82
Uganda	48.0	47.6	13.5	11.9	50.1	53.0	69.8	63.70	6.92	6.73
Ukraine	9.2	9.6	16.5	15.7	67.5	68.5	10.0	8.73	1.23	1.27
United Kingdom.....	10.8	10.7	10.2	10.0	78.4	79.2	5.2	4.78	1.66	1.66
Uzbekistan	26.2	26.1	8.0	7.4	64.2	66.2	71.1	65.56	2.94	2.80
Venezuela	18.9	17.8	4.9	5.0	74.3	75.5	22.2	18.89	2.26	2.13
Vietnam	17.1	16.1	6.2	6.2	70.6	71.9	26.0	22.17	1.94	1.80
Yemen	43.1	41.8	8.5	7.4	61.8	63.6	61.5	53.40	6.67	6.23
Zimbabwe	28.2	26.6	21.9	21.6	39.1	40.2	52.3	49.55	3.18	2.93

[1] Number of births during 1 year per 1,000 persons (based on midyear population). [2] Number of deaths during 1 year per 1,000 persons (based on midyear population). [3] Number of deaths of children under 1 year of age per 1,000 live births in a calendar year. [4] Average number of children that would be born if all women lived to the end of their childbearing years and, at each year of age, they experienced the birth rates occurring in the specified year. [5] See footnote 2, Table 1308. [6] See footnote 3, Table 1308.

Source: U.S. Census Bureau, "International Data Base" (as of 24 August 2006); <http://www.census.gov/ipc/www/idbnew.html>.

Table 1311. **Births to Unmarried Women by Country: 1980 to 2004**

[**Percent of all live births.** For U.S. figures, marital status is inferred from a comparison of the child's and parents' surnames on the birth certificate for those states that do not report on marital status. No estimates are included for misstatements on birth records or failures to register births]

Country	1980	1990	2000	2004
United States	18.4	28.0	33.2	35.7
Canada [1]	12.8	24.4	28.3	26.0
Japan	0.8	1.1	1.6	2.0
Denmark [1]	33.2	46.4	44.6	44.9
France	11.4	30.1	42.6	46.4
Germany [2]	(NA)	15.1	23.4	27.9
Ireland [2]	5.0	14.6	31.5	32.3
Italy [1]	4.3	6.5	9.7	13.0
Netherlands	4.1	11.4	24.9	32.5
Spain [1]	3.9	9.6	17.7	23.4
Sweden	39.7	47.0	55.3	55.4
United Kingdom	11.5	27.9	39.5	42.3

NA Not available.   [1] Data are for 2003 instead of 2004.   [2] Data are for 1991 instead of 1990.
Source: U.S. Bureau of Labor Statistics, updated and revised from "Families and Work Transition in 12 Countries 1980–2001,"*Monthly Labor Review*, September 2003, with unpublished data.

Table 1312. **Marriage and Divorce Rates by Country: 1980 to 2003**

[**Per 1,000 population aged 15–64 years**]

Country	Marriage rate				Divorce rate			
	1980	1990	2000 [1]	2003 [2]	1980	1990	2000 [1]	2003 [2]
United States [3]	15.9	14.9	12.5	11.6	7.9	7.2	6.2	5.7
Canada	11.5	10.0	7.5	6.6	3.7	4.2	3.4	3.2
Japan	9.8	8.4	9.3	8.7	1.8	1.8	3.1	3.3
Denmark	8.0	9.1	10.8	9.8	4.1	4.0	4.0	4.4
France [4, 5]	9.7	7.7	7.7	7.1	2.4	2.8	3.1	3.2
Germany [6]	(NA)	8.2	7.6	7.0	(NA)	2.5	3.5	3.9
Ireland [4, 5]	10.9	8.3	7.6	7.5	([7])	([7])	1.0	1.0
Italy	8.7	8.2	7.3	6.7	0.3	0.7	1.0	1.1
Netherlands	9.6	9.3	8.2	7.2	2.7	2.8	3.2	2.9
Spain [4, 5]	9.4	8.5	7.9	7.3	(NA)	0.9	1.4	3.0
Sweden	7.1	7.4	7.0	6.7	3.7	3.5	3.8	3.6
United Kingdom [5]	11.6	10.0	8.0	7.8	4.4	4.4	4.0	4.3

NA Not available.   [1] Provisional marriage rates for France; provisional divorce rates for Spain.   [2] Provisional marriage rates for the United States and Italy. U.S. marriage rate may be understated because of incomplete reporting in Oklahoma.   [3] Divorce rates for 2000 and 2003 are estimated by the Bureau of Labor Statistics; includes unlicensed marriages in California.   [4] Marriages for 2003 are estimated by Eurostat.   [5] Divorces for 2003 are estimated by Eurostat.   [6] Data are for 1991 instead of 1990.   [7] Divorce not allowed by law prior to 1997.

Source: U.S. Bureau of Labor Statistics, updated and revised from "Families and Work in Transition in 12 Countries, 1980–2001," *Monthly Labor Review*, September 2003, with unpublished data.

Table 1313. **Single-Parent Households: 1980 to 2005**

[In thousands (6,061 represents 6,061,000). For the United Kingdom in 1981, children are defined as those under 15 and those who are 15, 16, or 17 and attended school full-time; for later years, children are defined as those under 16 and those who are 16 or 17 and attend school full-time. For Ireland, children are defined as those under 15. For all other countries, children are defined as children living at home, or away at school, under the age of 18. Data are generally for the entire year, but in some instances they are only for a particular month within the year]

Country and year	Number	Percent of all households with children	Country and year	Number	Percent of all households with children
United States:			Germany:		
1980	6,061	19.5	1991	1,429	15.2
1990	7,752	24.0	1995	2,496	18.8
1995	9,055	26.4	2000 [2]	2,274	17.6
2004	10,152	28.2	2005	2,525	20.1
Canada:			Ireland: [1]		
1981	437	12.7	1981	30	7.2
1991	572	16.2	1991	44	10.7
1996	690	18.7	1996	56	13.8
2001	707	19.3	2002	69	16.7
Japan:			Netherlands:		
1980	796	4.9	1988	179	9.6
1990	934	6.5	1995 [2]	208	11.7
1995	884	6.9	2000	240	13.0
2000	996	8.3	2005	290	14.9
Denmark: [1]			Sweden:		
1980	99	13.4	1985	117	11.2
1990	117	17.8	1990	151	14.8
1995	120	18.6	1995 [2]	189	17.4
2005	135	20.2	2003 [3]	231	21.3
France:			United Kingdom: [4]		
1988	761	11.9	1981	1,010	13.9
1990	755	11.9	1991	1,344	19.4
1995	874	14.0	1994-95	1,617	21.9
2004 [2]	638	13.8	2005	1,694	24.1

[1] Data are from family-based, rather than household-based, statistics.   [2] Break in series.   [3] Bureau of Labor Statistics estimates.   [4] Great Britain only (excludes Northern Ireland).
Source: U.S. Bureau of Labor Statistics, updated and revised from "Families and Work in Transition in 12 Countries, 1980–2001," *Monthly Labor Review*, September 2003, with unpublished data.

Table 1314. **Percent Distribution of Households by Type and Country: 1980 to 2005**

[Data are generally for the entire year, but in some instances they are only for a particular month within the year]

Year	Total	Married-couple households [1]			Single parent [2]	One-person	Other [3]
		Total	With children [2]	Without children [2]			
United States:							
1980	100.0	60.8	30.9	29.9	7.5	22.7	9.0
1990	100.0	56.0	26.3	29.8	8.3	24.6	11.1
1995	100.0	54.4	25.5	28.9	9.1	25.0	11.5
2002	100.0	51.9	23.6	28.3	9.1	26.3	12.7
2004	100.0	51.5	23.0	28.5	9.1	26.4	13.0
Canada:							
1981	100.0	66.8	36.3	30.5	5.3	20.3	7.6
1991	100.0	62.8	29.6	33.2	5.7	22.9	8.6
1996	100.0	60.5	27.8	32.7	6.4	24.2	8.9
2001	100.0	59.4	25.6	33.8	6.1	25.7	8.8
Japan:							
1980	100.0	68.4	42.9	25.6	2.2	19.8	9.5
1990	100.0	65.2	33.1	32.1	2.3	23.1	9.4
1995	100.0	62.8	27.4	35.4	2.0	25.6	9.6
2000	100.0	60.3	23.6	36.7	2.1	27.6	10.0
Denmark: [4]							
1980	100.0	50.3	25.0	25.3	3.9	44.9	1.0
1990	100.0	45.6	19.5	26.1	4.2	49.6	0.6
1995	100.0	44.9	18.2	26.6	4.2	50.4	0.5
2003	100.0	45.7	18.5	27.2	4.4	49.3	0.6
2005	100.0	45.3	18.4	26.9	4.7	49.4	0.6
France:							
1982	100.0	67.0	39.7	27.3	4.3	24.6	4.1
1990	100.0	64.9	38.6	26.2	6.6	26.1	2.5
1995	100.0	62.2	35.9	26.3	6.7	28.9	2.3
2000 [5]	100.0	60.0	32.8	27.1	7.2	30.8	2.0
2004 [5]	100.0	56.8	31.1	25.7	6.4	33.8	3.0
Germany:							
1991	100.0	55.3	31.6	23.7	7.1	33.6	4.0
1995	100.0	53.3	29.2	24.0	6.8	34.9	5.1
2000 [5]	100.0	56.8	28.0	28.8	6.0	36.1	1.2
2004	100.0	55.3	26.1	29.2	6.3	37.2	1.2
2005	100.0	54.7	25.5	29.1	6.4	37.5	1.4
Ireland:							
1981	100.0	(NA)	(NA)	(NA)	(NA)	16.9	(NA)
1991	100.0	61.6	47.9	13.7	10.6	20.2	7.6
1996	100.0	59.6	44.5	15.1	11.2	21.5	7.7
2002	100.0	59.2	41.4	17.7	11.7	21.6	7.6
Netherlands:							
1988	100.0	64.7	37.3	27.4	5.4	28.7	1.2
1993	100.0	63.1	33.3	29.9	5.0	30.9	1.0
1995 [5]	100.0	61.2	32.6	28.5	5.6	32.6	0.7
2004	100.0	58.8	29.7	29.1	6.2	34.4	0.7
2005	100.0	58.5	29.4	29.1	6.3	34.5	0.7
Sweden:							
1985	100.0	54.8	23.8	31.0	3.2	36.1	5.9
1990	100.0	52.1	21.9	30.2	3.9	39.6	4.4
1995 [5]	100.0	50.7	21.2	29.4	4.6	42.3	2.4
2000 [6]	100.0	45.8	19.1	26.7	5.3	46.5	1.9
2003 [6]	100.0	46.0	18.9	27.1	5.3	46.2	2.2
United Kingdom: [7]							
1981	100.0	65.0	31.0	34.0	5.0	22.0	8.0
1991	100.0	61.0	25.0	36.0	6.0	27.0	6.0
1994–95	100.0	58.0	25.0	33.0	7.0	27.0	8.0
2001	100.0	58.0	23.0	35.0	7.0	29.0	6.0
2005	100.0	57.0	22.0	35.0	7.0	29.0	7.0

NA Not available. [1] May include unmarried cohabiting couples. Such couples are explicitly included under married couples in Canada, Denmark, Ireland, France, the Netherlands, and Sweden. In Germany cohabitants are grouped with married couples beginning in 2000. In other countries, some unmarried cohabitants are included as marries couples, while some are classified under "other households." [2] Children are defined as unmarried children living at home according to the following age limits: under 18 years old in the United States, Canada, Japan, Denmark, Sweden, and the United Kingdom, except that the United Kingdom includes 15-, 16-, and 17-year-olds in 1981 and 16- and 17-year-olds thereafter only if they are attending school full-time; under 25 years old in France; and children of all ages in Germany, Ireland, and the Netherlands. [3] Includes both family and nonfamily households not elsewhere classified. These households comprise, for example, siblings residing together, other households composed of relatives, and households made up of roommates. Some unmarried cohabiting couples may also be included in the "other" group. See footnote 1. [4] From family-based statistics. However, one person living alone constitutes a family in Denmark. In this respect, the Danish data are closer to household statistics. [5] Break in series. [6] Bureau of Labor Statistics estimates for single-parent households. [7] Great Britain only (excludes Northern Ireland).

Source: U.S. Bureau of Labor Statistics, updated and revised from "Families and Work in Transition in 12 Countries, 1980–2001," *Monthly Labor Review*, September 2003 with unpublished data.

Table 1315. **Foreign or Foreign-Born Population and Labor Force in Selected OECD Countries: 1990 and 2002**

[33,383 represents 33,383,000. In Australia and the United States the data refer to people present in the country who are foreign born. In the European countries and Japan they generally refer to foreigners and represent the nationalities of residents]

Country	Foreign population [1]				Foreign labor force [2]			
	Number (1,000)		Percent of total population		Number (1,000)		Percent of total labor force	
	1990	2002	1990	2002	1990	2002	1990	2002
United States	(NA)	33,383	(NA)	11.8	11,565	20,964	9.4	14.6
Australia	(NA)	4,566	(NA)	23.2	(NA)	2,438	25.7	24.6
Austria	456	708	5.9	8.8	230	(NA)	7.4	(NA)
Belgium	905	850	9.1	8.2	289	(NA)	7.1	(NA)
Denmark.	161	265	3.1	4.9	69	(NA)	2.4	(NA)
France	3,597	(NA)	6.3	(NA)	1,550	(NA)	6.2	(NA)
Germany [3]	5,343	7,336	8.4	8.9	(NA)	(NA)	(NA)	(NA)
Italy	781	1,512	1.4	2.6	(NA)	(NA)	(NA)	(NA)
Japan	1,075	1,852	0.9	1.5	(NA)	(NA)	(NA)	(NA)
Luxembourg	113	171	29.4	38.1	85	(NA)	45.2	(NA)
Netherlands	692	700	4.6	4.3	197	(NA)	3.1	(NA)
Spain.	279	1,324	0.7	3.1	85	(NA)	0.6	(NA)
Sweden	484	474	5.6	5.3	246	(NA)	5.4	(NA)
Switzerland.	1,100	1,447	16.3	19.9	670	(NA)	18.9	(NA)
United Kingdom	1,723	2,681	3.2	4.5	882	(NA)	3.3	(NA)

NA Not available. [1] Data are from population registers of foreigners except for France (census), the United Kingdom (Labour Force Survey), Australia (inter-and post-censal estimates), and the United States (Current Population Survey). [2] Includes unemployed except for Italy, Luxembourg, Netherlands, and United Kingdom. Data for Austria, Germany, and Luxembourg are from social security registers, and for Denmark, from the register of population. Data for Italy, Spain, and Switzerland are from residence or work permits. Figures for Japan and Netherlands are estimates. Data for other countries are from labor force surveys. [3] Data prior to 1991 are for former West Germany.

Source: Organization for Economic Cooperation and Development, Paris, France, *Trends in International Migration* (2004 Editions) (copyright).

Table 1316. **Average Temperatures and Precipitation—Selected International Cities**

[In degrees Fahrenheit, except as noted. Data are generally based on a standard 30-year period; for details, see source. For data on U.S. cities, see Tables 378–381]

City	January					July				
	Average high	Average low	Warm-est	Coldest	Average precipi-tation (inches)	Average high	Average low	Warm-est	Coldest	Average precipi-tation (inches)
Amsterdam, Netherlands. . .	41	34	57	3	3.1	69	55	90	39	2.9
Athens, Greece	55	44	70	28	1.9	89	73	108	61	0.2
Baghdad, Iraq	58	38	75	25	1.1	110	78	122	61	–
Bangkok, Thailand	89	71	95	54	0.4	90	78	99	72	6.2
Beijing, China	34	17	54	1	0.2	86	72	104	63	8.8
Berlin, Germany	35	26	58	–11	(NA)	73	56	95	41	(NA)
Bogota, Colombia	66	43	84	27	1.9	64	47	82	32	1.8
Brasilia, Brazil.	81	64	95	54	(NA)	79	52	97	37	(NA)
Buenos Aires, Argentina . . .	85	64	104	44	4.2	58	41	88	23	2.3
Cairo, Egypt	65	49	86	32	0.2	93	72	108	63	–
Frankfurt, Germany	38	30	56	–4	1.8	75	57	97	38	2.4
Geneva, Switzerland	39	29	57	–2	2.2	77	56	96	41	2.8
Hong Kong, China	67	58	79	43	1.1	89	81	97	70	14.3
Istanbul, Turkey.	46	37	64	16	3.7	82	66	100	50	0.7
Jakarta, Indonesia	83	75	92	72	(NA)	88	74	92	67	(NA)
Karachi, Pakistan.	76	55	93	39	0.3	89	83	109	68	3.5
Lagos, Nigeria.	82	79	93	64	(NA)	79	76	88	70	(NA)
London, England	45	36	61	15	2.4	72	56	93	45	1.8
Madrid, Spain	51	32	68	14	1.8	90	61	104	46	0.4
Manila, Philippines	86	71	95	61	0.8	88	76	99	70	15.9
Mexico City, Mexico	70	45	86	26	0.3	74	56	86	37	5.1
Montreal, Canada	21	7	52	–31	2.8	79	61	93	43	3.4
Moscow, Russia	21	11	46	–33	1.4	71	55	95	41	3.2
Nairobi, Kenya	77	58	88	45	1.8	71	54	85	43	0.5
New Delhi, India	68	48	85	32	0.9	93	81	111	70	7.9
Paris, France	43	34	59	1	(NA)	75	58	95	41	(NA)
Rio De Janeiro, Brazil.	91	74	109	64	5.3	81	64	102	52	1.8
Rome, Italy.	55	39	64	19	3.2	83	66	100	55	0.5
Seoul, Korea.	33	21	55	–1	(NA)	82	71	97	55	(NA)
Singapore, Singapore	85	73	100	66	9.4	86	76	99	70	5.9
Sydney, Australia	79	65	109	49	4.0	62	44	80	32	2.5
Tel Aviv, Israel	62	46	84	32	(NA)	87	69	100	50	(NA)
Tokyo, Japan	48	35	66	25	2.0	82	71	95	55	5.3
Toronto, Canada	28	15	59	–24	1.9	79	60	99	45	2.8

– Represents zero. NA Not available.

Source: U.S. National Oceanic and Atmospheric Administration, *Climates of the World*.

Table 1317. Carbon Dioxide Emissions From Consumption of Fossil Fuels by Country: 1990 to 2004

[In million metric tons of carbon equivalent (5,843 represents 5,843,000,000). Includes carbon dioxide emissions from the consumption of petroleum, natural gas, and coal, and the flaring of natural gas]

Country	1990	1995	1998	1999	2000	2001	2002	2003	2004
World, total	5,843	6,009	6,232	6,325	6,505	6,578	6,668	6,999	7,376
Australia	72	78	91	96	96	100	102	101	105
Brazil	61	79	88	91	94	96	96	87	92
Canada	131	138	148	152	155	151	154	162	160
China [1]	611	784	801	791	827	869	902	1,063	1,284
France	101	102	111	109	109	110	109	111	111
Germany	(NA)	239	235	227	231	237	230	235	235
India	160	236	246	255	273	278	279	284	304
Indonesia	41	58	65	72	75	81	85	86	84
Iran	55	71	80	86	87	91	99	105	110
Italy	113	117	119	119	121	120	122	128	132
Japan	277	293	301	313	325	319	323	339	344
Korea, South	65	107	103	116	121	120	127	130	135
Mexico	82	87	100	98	104	103	105	107	105
Netherlands	56	60	65	64	68	75	70	70	73
Poland	90	83	85	88	79	75	74	78	78
Russia	(NA)	434	399	419	424	422	422	437	460
Saudi Arabia	57	64	70	71	79	82	84	94	100
South Africa	81	94	99	101	103	106	102	112	117
Spain	61	66	75	81	86	87	92	94	99
Taiwan [1]	32	49	60	60	68	67	73	78	84
Thailand	23	43	44	46	44	47	51	56	60
Turkey	35	41	50	49	55	50	53	56	58
Ukraine	(NA)	122	90	88	88	86	88	96	99
United Kingdom	163	151	152	150	150	154	151	154	158
United States	1,367	1,443	1,523	1,543	1,586	1,566	1,570	1,584	1,612

NA Not available.   [1] See footnote 2, Table 1308.

Source: U.S. Energy Information Administration, *International Energy Annual, 2004.* See also <http://www.eia.doe.gov/pub/international/iealf/tableh1.xls> (accessed July 2006).

Table 1318. Health Expenditures as Percent of GDP by Country: 1980 to 2003

[In percent. G.D.P. = gross domestic product; for explanation, see text, Section 13]

Country	Total health expenditures					Public health expenditures				
	1980	1990	2000	2002	2003	1980	1990	2000	2002	2003
United States	8.7	11.9	13.1	14.6	15.0	3.6	4.7	5.8	6.6	6.6
Australia	7.0	7.8	9.0	9.3	(NA)	4.4	5.2	6.2	6.3	(NA)
Austria	7.4	7.0	7.6	7.6	(NA)	5.1	5.1	5.3	5.3	(NA)
Belgium	6.4	7.4	8.7	9.1	9.6	(NA)	(NA)	(NA)	(NA)	(NA)
Canada	7.1	9.0	8.9	9.6	9.9	5.4	6.7	6.3	6.7	6.9
Czech Republic	(NA)	4.7	6.6	7.2	7.5	(NA)	4.6	6.0	6.5	6.8
Denmark	9.1	8.5	8.4	8.8	9.0	8.0	7.0	6.9	7.3	7.5
Finland	6.4	7.8	6.7	7.2	7.4	5.0	6.3	5.0	5.5	5.7
France	7.1	8.6	9.3	9.7	10.1	5.7	6.6	7.1	7.4	7.7
Germany [1]	8.7	8.5	10.6	10.9	11.1	6.8	6.5	8.3	8.6	8.6
Greece	6.6	7.4	9.9	9.8	9.9	3.7	4.0	5.2	5.0	5.1
Hungary	(NA)	(NA)	7.1	7.8	(NA)	(NA)	(NA)	5.0	5.5	(NA)
Iceland	6.2	8.0	9.3	10.0	10.5	5.5	6.9	7.7	8.3	8.8
Ireland	8.4	6.1	6.3	7.3	(NA)	6.8	4.4	4.7	5.5	(NA)
Italy	(NA)	7.9	8.1	8.4	8.4	(NA)	6.3	5.9	6.3	6.3
Japan	6.5	5.9	7.6	7.9	(NA)	4.6	4.6	6.1	6.4	(NA)
Korea, South	(NA)	4.5	4.7	5.3	5.6	(NA)	1.7	2.2	2.7	2.8
Luxembourg	5.9	6.1	5.5	6.1	(NA)	5.5	5.7	4.9	5.2	(NA)
Mexico	(NA)	4.8	5.6	6.0	6.2	(NA)	2.0	2.6	2.7	2.9
Netherlands	7.5	8.0	8.3	9.3	9.8	5.2	5.4	5.2	5.8	6.1
New Zealand	5.9	6.9	7.8	8.2	8.1	5.2	5.7	6.1	6.4	6.3
Norway	7.0	7.7	7.7	9.9	10.3	5.9	6.4	6.5	8.2	8.6
Poland	(NA)	4.9	5.7	6.0	(NA)	(NA)	4.5	4.0	4.4	(NA)
Portugal	5.6	6.2	9.2	9.3	9.6	3.6	4.1	6.4	6.6	6.7
Slovakia	(NA)	(NA)	5.5	5.7	5.9	(NA)	(NA)	4.9	5.1	5.2
Spain	5.4	6.7	7.4	7.6	7.7	4.3	5.3	5.3	5.4	5.5
Sweden	9.1	8.4	8.4	9.2	(NA)	8.4	7.5	7.2	7.9	(NA)
Switzerland	7.4	8.3	10.4	11.1	11.5	(NA)	4.3	5.8	6.4	6.7
Turkey	3.3	3.6	6.6	(NA)	(NA)	1.0	2.2	4.2	(NA)	(NA)
United Kingdom	5.6	6.0	7.3	7.7	(NA)	5.0	5.0	5.9	6.4	(NA)

NA Not available.   [1] See footnote 3, Table 1315.

Source: Organization for Economic Cooperation and Development, Paris, France, *OECD Health Data 2004, 2nd ed.* (copyright).

Table 1319. **Medical Doctors and Inpatient Care—Selected Countries: 1990 to 2003**

Country	Medical doctors per 1,000 population			Inpatient care					
				Beds per 1,000 population			Average length of stay (days)		
	1990	2000	2003	1990	2000	2003	1990	2000	2003
United States	1.8	2.2	(NA)	4.9	3.5	3.3	9.1	6.8	6.5
Australia	2.2	2.5	(NA)	(NA)	7.8	(NA)	(NA)	16.0	(NA)
Austria	2.2	3.2	3.4	10.2	8.7	8.3	12.8	8.6	7.8
Belgium	3.3	3.9	(NA)	(NA)	7.1	(NA)	13.8	(NA)	(NA)
Canada.	2.1	2.1	2.1	6.0	3.8	(NA)	13.0	(NA)	(NA)
Czech Republic	2.7	3.4	3.5	(NA)	8.8	8.8	15.4	11.4	10.9
Denmark.	2.5	2.8	(NA)	5.6	4.3	4.0	8.2	6.0	5.4
Finland	2.0	2.6	2.6	(NA)	(NA)	(NA)	18.2	10.3	10.2
France	3.1	3.3	3.4	9.7	8.1	7.7	15.1	13.2	13.4
Germany.	(NA)	3.3	3.4	(NA)	9.1	(NA)	(NA)	11.4	(NA)
Greece	3.4	4.3	(NA)	5.1	4.7	(NA)	9.9	8.4	(NA)
Hungary	2.8	(NA)	3.2	(NA)	8.1	7.8	12.6	8.9	8.4
Iceland	2.8	3.4	3.6	(NA)	(NA)	(NA)	18.3	(NA)	(NA)
Ireland	(NA)	2.2	2.6	6.1	4.6	4.3	7.9	7.4	7.6
Italy	(NA)	4.2	4.1	7.2	4.7	(NA)	11.7	7.7	(NA)
Japan.	1.7	1.9	(NA)	(NA)	14.7	14.3	50.5	39.1	36.4
Korea, South	0.8	1.3	1.6	3.1	6.1	7.1	13.0	14.0	13.5
Luxembourg.	2.0	2.5	2.7	7.6	6.2	6.0	17.6	(NA)	(NA)
Mexico	1.0	1.6	1.5	1.0	1.1	1.0	(NA)	4.2	4.1
Netherlands.	2.5	3.2	3.1	5.8	4.8	(NA)	34.1	33.4	(NA)
New Zealand	1.9	2.2	2.2	(NA)	(NA)	(NA)	9.4	8.0	6.9
Norway.	(NA)	2.9	3.1	4.6	3.8	(NA)	(NA)	8.9	8.0
Poland	2.1	2.2	2.5	(NA)	(NA)	(NA)	12.5	8.9	(NA)
Portugal	2.8	3.2	3.3	4.1	3.8	(NA)	10.8	9.2	8.7
Slovakia	(NA)	3.2	3.1	(NA)	7.9	7.2	(NA)	10.4	8.7
Spain	(NA)	3.2	3.2	4.6	4.1	3.8	12.2	9.0	(NA)
Sweden	2.9	3.1	(NA)	(NA)	(NA)	(NA)	18.0	6.4	(NA)
Switzerland	3.0	3.5	(NA)	(NA)	(NA)	(NA)	(NA)	12.8	12.4
Turkey	0.9	1.3	1.4	2.4	2.6	2.6	6.9	5.9	5.8
United Kingdom	1.6	1.9	2.2	(NA)	4.2	4.2	17.7	8.4	7.6

NA Not available.

Source: Organization for Economic Cooperation and Development, Paris, France, *OECD Health Data 2005* (copyright).

Table 1320. **People Infected With HIV and AIDS-Related Deaths, by Region: 2003 and 2005**

[In thousands (37,500 represents 37,500,000). Estimates are based on ranges which define the boundaries within which the actual numbers lie, based on the best available information]

Region	Adults and children living with HIV		Adults and children newly infected with HIV		Adult prevalence (percent)		Adult and child deaths due to AIDS	
	2003	2005	2003	2005	2003	2005	2003	2005
Total.	37,500	40,300	4,600	4,900	1.1	1.1	2,800	3,100
Sub-Saharan Africa	24,900	25,800	3,000	3,200	7.3	7.2	2,100	2,400
North Africa and Middle East	500	510	62	67	0.2	0.2	55	58
South and South-East Asia	6,500	7,400	840	990	0.6	0.7	390	480
East Asia	690	870	100	140	0.1	0.1	22	41
Oceania	63	74	8.9	8.2	0.4	0.5	2.0	3.6
Latin America	1,600	1,800	170	200	0.6	0.6	59	66
Caribbean.	300	300	29	30	1.6	1.6	24	24
Eastern Europe and Central Asia .	1,200	1,600	270	270	0.7	0.9	36	62
Western and Central Europe	700	720	20	22	0.3	0.3	12	12
North America	1,100	1,200	43	43	0.7	0.7	18	18

Source: Joint United Nations Programme on HIV/AIDS (UNAIDS) and World Health Organization (WHO), *AIDS Epidemic Update: December 2005*. See also <http://www.unaids.org/epi/2005/doc/EPIupdate2005_pdf_en/epi-update2005_en.pdf>.

Table 1321. **Percentage of the Adult Population Considered to be Obese**

[Obesity rates are defined as the percentage of the population with a Body Mass Index (BMI) over 30 kg/m². The BMI is a single number that evaluates an individual's weight status in relation to height (weight/height², with weight in kilograms and height in meters). For Australia, the United Kingdom, and the United States, figures are based on health examinations, rather than self-reported information. Obesity estimates derived from health examinations are generally higher and more reliable than those coming from self-reports because they preclude any misreporting of people's height and weight. However, health examinations are only conducted regularly in a few countries. For more information on methods by country, see <www.irdes.fr/ecosante/OCDE/814010.html>]

Country	2003	Country	2003	Country	2003
United States	[1]30.6	France	[1]9.4	Luxembourg	18.4
Australia	[2]21.7	Germany	12.9	Mexico	[4]24.2
Austria	[2]9.1	Greece	21.9	New Zealand	20.9
Belgium	[3]11.7	Hungary	18.8	Norway	[1]8.3
Canada	14.3	Ireland	[1]13.0	Spain	13.1
Czech Republic	[1]14.8	Italy	[1]8.5	Sweden	9.7
Denmark	[4]9.5	Japan	3.2	Switzerland	[1]7.7
Finland	12.8	Korea	[3]3.2	United Kingdom	23.0

[1] 2002 data.   [2] 1999 data.   [3] 2001 data.   [4] 2000 data.

Source: Organization for Economic Cooperation and Development, Paris, France, *OECD in Figures*, 2005 (copyright). See also <http://oecd.p4.siteinternet.com/publications/doifiles/012005061T003.xls>.

Table 1322. **Educational Performance: 2002 and 2003**

[Tertiary-type A includes education leading to a BA, Master's, or equivalent degree, and advanced research programs. Performance figures were gathered from the Program for International Student Assessment (PISA), which is an internationally standardized assessment that was jointly developed by participating countries and takes place in three-year cycles. To implement PISA, each of the participating countries selects a nationally representative sample of 15-year-olds, regardless of grade level. In the United States, 5,456 students from public and private schools took the PISA assessment in 2003. Tests are typically administered to between 4,500 and 10,000 students in each country]

Country	Student performance on the combined reading, scientific, and mathematical literacy scales (2003)			Educational attainment of adult population and current graduation rates (2002) (percent)	
	Mean score on the combined reading literacy scale [1]	Mean score on the mathematical literacy scale [2]	Mean score on the scientific literacy scale [3]	Upper secondary or higher attainment (25–64 year-olds) [4]	Tertiary-type A attainment (25–64 year-olds)
Australia	525.4	524.3	525.1	60.9	20.0
Austria	490.7	505.6	491.0	77.9	7.0
Canada	527.9	532.5	518.7	82.6	21.0
Czech Republic	488.5	516.5	523.3	87.9	[6]11.9
Finland	543.5	544.3	548.2	74.8	15.6
France	496.2	510.8	511.2	64.8	12.4
Germany	491.4	503.0	502.3	83.0	13.4
Greece	472.3	444.9	481.0	50.5	12.7
Italy	475.7	465.7	486.5	44.4	[6]10.4
Japan	498.1	534.1	547.6	83.7	20.1
Korea	534.1	542.2	538.4	70.8	18.5
Luxembourg	479.4	493.2	482.8	56.6	11.6
Mexico	399.7	385.2	404.9	12.6	2.5
Poland	496.6	490.2	497.8	47.0	[6]12.1
Spain	480.5	485.1	487.1	41.3	17.3
Sweden	514.3	509.0	506.1	81.6	17.7
Switzerland	499.1	526.6	513.0	82.4	16.2
United Kingdom	(NA)	(NA)	(NA)	64.3	18.6
United States	**495.2**	**482.9**	**491.3**	**87.3**	**29.0**
Country mean	494.2	500.0	499.6	64.9	15.5

NA Not available.   [1] Reading literacy is understanding, using, and reflecting on written texts, in order to achieve one's goals, to develop one's knowledge and poteential, and to participate in society.   [2] Mathematical literacy is an individual's capacity to identify and understand the role that mathematics plays in the world, to make well-founded judgements and to use and engage with mathematics in ways that meet the needs of that individual's life as a constructive, concerned, and reflective citizen.   [3] Scientific literacy is the capacity to use scientific knowledge, to identify questions and to draw evidence-based conclusions in order to understand and help make decisions about the natural world and the changes made to it through human activity.   [4] Excluding ISCED 3C short programs.   [5] All tertiary level: type A and type B (focus on practical, technical, or occupational skills).

Source: Organization for Economic Cooperation and Development, Paris, France, *OECD in Figures*, 2005 (copyright). See also <http://ocde.p4.siteinternet.com/publications/doifiles/012005061T032.xls>.

Table 1323. **Patents by Country: 2005**

[Includes only U.S. patents granted to residents of areas outside of the United States and its territories]

Country	Total [1]	Inventions	Designs	Country	Total [1]	Inventions	Designs
Total	**75,155**	**69,169**	**5,397**	Netherlands	1,200	993	63
				Sweden	1,189	1,123	65
Japan	31,834	30,341	1,384	Switzerland	1,106	995	111
Germany	9,575	9,011	474	Australia	1,033	911	90
Taiwan [2]	5,993	5,118	870	Israel	976	924	44
Korea, South	4,591	4,352	233	Finland	751	720	31
United Kingdom	3,560	3,148	370	Belgium	577	519	55
Canada	3,177	2,894	277	Austria	491	462	28
France	3,106	2,866	222	Denmark	473	358	40
Italy	1,591	1,296	294	Other countries	3,932	3,138	746

[1] Includes patents for botanical plants and reissues, not shown separately.   [2] See footnote 2, Table 1308.

Source: U.S. Patent and Trademark Office, Technology Assessment and Forecast Database.

Table 1324. Gross National Income by Country: 1990 and 2004

[61 represents $61,000,000,000. GNI (gross national product, or GNP, in the terminology of the 1968 United Nations System of National Accounts) measures the total domestic and foreign value added claimed by residents. GNI comprises GDP plus net receipts of primary income (compensation of employees and property income) from nonresident sources]

Country	Gross national income [1]				GNI on purchasing power parity basis [2]			
	Total (bil. dol.)		Per capita (dol.)		Total (bil. dol.)		Per capita (dol.)	
	1990	2004	1990	2004	1990	2004	1990	2004
Algeria	61	73	2,440	2,270	107	[3]204	4,280	[3]6,320
Argentina	104	137	3,220	3,580	227	481	6,990	12,530
Australia	302	544	17,720	27,070	278	590	16,320	29,340
Bangladesh	31	61	280	440	107	274	970	1,970
Belarus	(NA)	21	(NA)	2,140	44	68	4,310	6,970
Belgium	185	326	18,520	31,280	181	329	18,140	31,530
Brazil	415	552	2,800	3,000	757	1,460	5,120	7,940
Bulgaria	20	21	2,260	2,750	48	62	5,480	[3]7,940
Burkina Faso	3	4	330	350	6	[3]15	700	[3]1,170
Cambodia	(NA)	5	(NA)	350	(NA)	[3]32	(NA)	[3]2,310
Cameroon	11	13	950	810	19	34	1,600	2,120
Canada	551	905	19,840	28,310	511	984	18,400	30,760
Chile	29	84	2,190	5,220	58	171	4,450	[3]10,610
China [4]	368	1,938	320	1,500	1,488	[5]7,634	1,310	[5]5,890
Colombia	42	91	1,190	2,020	159	[3]312	4,550	[3]6,940
Congo (Kinshasa) [6]	2	6	880	110	2	[3]38	650	[3]680
Cote d'Ivoire	9	14	780	760	15	26	1,270	1,470
Czech Republic	(NA)	93	(NA)	9,130	112	188	10,790	18,420
Ecuador	9	29	900	2,210	26	49	2,510	3,770
Egypt	42	(NA)	810	(NA)	121	(NA)	2,310	(NA)
Ethiopia	9	8	170	110	27	[3]52	520	[3]750
France	1,142	1,888	19,620	30,370	1,011	1,779	17,820	29,460
Germany	1,601	2,532	20,160	30,690	1,427	2,324	17,960	28,170
Ghana	6	8	380	380	20	[3]48	1,300	[3]2,220
Greece	79	185	7,770	16,730	114	246	11,260	22,230
Guatemala	8	27	970	2,190	24	[3]52	2,760	[3]4,260
Hong Kong	71	184	12,520	26,660	91	217	15,980	31,560
Hungary	30	85	2,880	8,370	90	160	8,640	15,800
India	331	673	390	620	1,156	[3]3,369	1,360	[3]3,120
Indonesia	111	248	620	1,140	313	757	1,760	3,480
Iran	141	155	2,590	2,320	204	505	3,740	7,530
Iraq	39	(NA)	2,170	[7]	(NA)	(NA)	(NA)	(NA)
Italy	988	1,513	17,420	26,280	984	1,613	17,360	28,020
Japan	3,349	4,734	27,110	37,050	2,339	3,809	18,930	29,810
Kazakhstan	(NA)	34	(NA)	2,250	76	104	4,620	6,930
Kenya	9	16	380	480	20	38	880	1,130
Korea, South	246	673	5,740	14,000	317	987	7,390	20,530
Madagascar	3	5	240	290	9	15	740	840
Malawi	2	2	200	160	3	8	410	630
Malaysia	43	113	2,380	4,520	78	242	4,290	9,720
Mexico	236	705	2,830	6,790	491	1,001	5,890	9,640
Morocco	25	47	1,030	1,570	63	[3]127	2,630	[3]4,250
Mozambique	2	5	170	270	7	[3]23	480	[3]1,170
Nepal	4	7	220	250	15	39	840	1,480
Netherlands	280	523	18,710	32,130	264	[3]511	17,670	31,360
Niger	2	3	310	210	5	[3]11	710	[3]780
Nigeria	26	55	270	430	62	125	650	970
Pakistan	43	91	390	600	143	330	1,320	2,170
Peru	17	65	780	2,360	66	149	3,050	5,400
Philippines	45	95	740	1,170	191	404	3,140	4,950
Poland	(NA)	233	(NA)	6,100	215	486	5,640	12,730
Portugal	64	149	6,450	14,220	105	202	10,630	19,240
Romania	40	64	1,730	2,960	124	181	5,340	8,330
Russia	(NA)	489	(NA)	3,400	1,234	1,392	8,320	9,680
Saudi Arabia	118	243	7,490	10,140	162	[3]331	10,240	[3]13,810
Senegal	5	7	720	630	8	[3]19	1,100	[3]1,660
Singapore	36	105	11,840	24,760	37	116	12,170	27,370
South Africa	102	165	2,890	3,630	276	[3]499	7,840	[3]10,960
Spain	454	919	11,680	21,530	498	1,057	12,810	24,750
Sri Lanka	8	20	490	1,010	31	[3]82	1,880	[3]4,210
Sudan	14	19	570	530	23	[3]64	2,090	[3]1,810
Sweden	226	322	26,390	35,840	144	269	16,820	29,880
Switzerland	225	367	33,510	49,600	165	264	24,550	35,660
Syria	11	23	940	1,230	25	65	2,090	3,500
Tanzania	5	[8]12	190	[8]320	10	25	410	670
Thailand	84	158	1,520	2,490	199	505	3,580	7,930
Turkey	127	269	2,270	3,750	242	[3]554	4,300	[3]7,720
Uganda	6	7	320	250	12	[3]40	700	[3]1,450
Ukraine	(NA)	60	(NA)	1,270	368	300	7,080	6,330
United Kingdom	932	2,013	16,190	33,630	940	1,882	16,330	31,430
United States	**5,846**	**12,169**	**23,440**	**41,440**	**5,768**	**11,693**	**23,120**	**39,820**
Uzbekistan	(NA)	12	(NA)	450	30	49	1,480	1,860
Venezuela	52	105	2,650	4,030	89	152	4,580	5,830
Vietnam	9	45	130	540	61	222	920	2,700
Yemen	(NA)	11	(NA)	550	6	16	520	810
Zimbabwe	9	8	880	620	22	26	2,140	2,040

NA Not available. [1] Gross national income calculated using the World Bank Atlas method; for details, see source. [2] See footnote 1, Table 1325. [3] The estimate is based on regression; others are extrapolated from the latest International Comparison Program benchmark estimates. [4] See footnote 2, Table 1308. [5] Estimate based on bilateral comparison between China and the United States. [6] See footnote 3, Table 1308. [7] Estimated to be lower middle income ($766–$3,035). [8] Data refer to mainland Tanzania only.

Source: The World Bank, Washington, DC, *World Development Indicators CD-ROM*, annual (copyright).

Table 1325. Gross Domestic Product (GDP) by Country: 1995 to 2004

[20,673 represents $20,673,000,000,000. PPP stands for purchasing power parity. Except as noted, based on the System of National Accounts, 1993; for details, see source]

Country	Current price levels and PPPs [1] (bil. dol.)					Constant (2000) price levels [2] and PPPs [1] (bil. dol.)					GDP per capita, 2004 based on—	
	1995	2000	2002	2003	2004	1995	2000	2002	2003	2004	Current prices and PPPs [1]	Constant (2000) prices and PPPs [1]
OECD, total [3]	20,673	26,492	28,536	29,598	31,353	22,509	26,493	27,202	27,735	28,665	28,502	26,058
OECD Europe [3,4]	8,180	10,295	11,223	11,509	12,079	8,922	10,296	10,598	10,732	11,013	25,696	23,428
Australia	393	525	586	621	655	434	525	562	585	598	32,409	29,600
Austria	185	230	242	250	266	199	230	234	237	243	32,520	29,752
Belgium	226	273	303	312	327	240	273	280	283	290	31,323	27,850
Canada	657	860	925	963	1,017	702	860	902	920	947	31,828	29,640
Czech Republic	133	150	169	176	190	139	154	156	157	168	18,643	16,493
Denmark	119	154	162	165	174	134	154	156	157	160	32,141	29,578
Finland	98	134	146	150	160	106	134	138	141	147	30,594	28,028
France [5]	1,247	1,575	1,720	1,749	1,838	1,366	1,575	1,627	1,640	1,678	29,554	26,993
Germany	1,803	2,102	2,238	2,281	2,360	1,903	2,102	2,129	2,125	2,160	28,605	26,182
Greece	138	178	210	226	239	150	178	193	202	211	21,596	19,111
Hungary	96	124	147	153	161	102	124	134	138	145	15,948	14,325
Iceland	6	8	8	9	10	6	8	8	8	9	32,528	30,809
Ireland	65	109	130	136	148	69	109	123	129	134	36,341	33,133
Italy	1,190	1,443	1,528	1,542	1,588	1,312	1,443	1,474	1,478	1,496	27,312	25,731
Japan	2,832	3,302	3,466	3,582	3,775	3,100	3,302	3,299	3,342	3,432	29,567	26,875
Korea, South	578	768	879	924	993	620	768	853	880	921	20,644	19,148
Luxembourg	13	22	23	25	27	15	22	22	23	24	60,188	53,301
Mexico	627	897	951	984	1,054	688	897	904	917	957	10,139	9,200
Netherlands	349	453	505	516	537	377	453	460	460	467	32,996	28,726
New Zealand [6]	64	80	89	95	100	71	80	87	90	94	24,608	22,987
Norway	104	163	166	170	186	136	163	169	171	176	40,568	38,317
Poland	291	397	428	442	474	310	397	407	423	445	12,409	11,661
Portugal	132	178	195	184	190	147	178	181	179	181	18,098	17,194
Slovakia	44	58	68	71	74	48	58	63	66	70	13,752	12,915
Spain	631	849	981	1,042	1,105	694	849	902	929	958	25,875	22,439
Sweden	190	241	253	264	280	206	241	248	253	262	31,139	29,148
Switzerland [6]	186	219	239	246	260	198	219	222	221	226	34,710	30,169
Turkey	343	459	454	478	543	379	459	459	485	529	7,562	7,364
United Kingdom	1,152	1,506	1,719	1,763	1,843	1,285	1,506	1,571	1,610	1,661	30,806	27,765
United States	7,342	9,765	10,418	10,919	11,679	7,973	9,765	9,998	10,269	10,704	39,732	36,414

[1] The goods and services produced in different countries should be valued consistently if the differences observed are meant to reflect real differences in the volumes of goods and services produced. The use of purchasing power parities (PPP) instead of exchange rates is intended to achieve this objective. PPPs show how many units of currency are needed in one country to buy the same amount of goods and services which one unit of currency will buy in the other country. See text of this section.   [2] Based on constant (2000) price data converted to U.S. dollars using 2000 PPPs.   [3] Excluding Czech Republic, Hungary, Poland, and Slovakia.   [4] OECD Europe: Austria, Belgium, Denmark, Finland, France, Germany, Greece, Iceland, Ireland, Italy, Luxembourg, Netherlands, Norway, Portugal, Spain, Sweden, Switzerland, Turkey, United Kingdom.   [5] Includes overseas departments.   [6] Based on System of National Accounts, 1968.

Source: Organization for Economic Cooperation and Development, Paris, France, "National Accounts of OECD Countries annual, Vol. 1", published July 2006.

Table 1326. **Average Annual Percent Changes in International Economic Composite Indexes by Country: 1990 to 2005**

[Change from previous year; derived from indexes with base 1990 = 100. The coincident index changes are for calendar years and the leading index changes are for years ending June 30 because they lead the coincident indexes by about 6 months, on average. The G-7 countries are United States, Canada, France, Germany, Italy, United Kingdom, and Japan. Minus sign (–) indicates decrease]

Country	Leading index						Coincident index					
	1990	2000	2002	2003	2004	2005	1990	2000	2002	2003	2004	2005
Total, 13 countries	2.1	6.3	–4.5	2.9	7.5	4.4	4.5	5.0	–2.0	0.4	3.7	2.7
12 countries, excluding U.S.	3.8	7.7	–4.1	1.7	7.4	5.9	6.8	5.4	–1.5	0.8	3.6	2.5
G-7 countries	2.0	6.0	–5.0	2.8	7.5	4.3	4.5	4.8	–2.5	0.1	3.5	2.5
North America	–0.9	4.1	–4.8	4.9	7.4	1.9	–0.2	4.8	–2.4	0.0	3.9	3.0
United States	–1.0	3.9	–5.1	5.1	7.8	1.8	–0.1	4.4	–2.4	–0.7	3.8	2.9
Canada	–1.1	7.1	–1.3	2.0	3.1	3.9	–1.7	9.7	4.3	2.8	4.8	4.1
Four European countries	1.8	4.4	–4.7	–1.3	4.7	4.9	5.9	9.8	0.4	0.2	2.5	1.8
France.	1.5	1.5	–7.5	–2.3	5.0	6.8	5.7	14.4	–0.4	–1.1	1.4	0.6
Germany	4.5	6.2	–4.5	–1.5	6.8	6.7	7.2	7.9	–2.2	–3.0	1.2	1.0
Italy.	0.2	7.2	–3.5	0.1	1.6	3.0	9.3	16.2	5.9	4.8	5.0	4.1
United Kingdom.	–0.3	2.5	–0.4	–0.6	3.3	1.2	0.9	4.0	2.2	4.1	4.8	3.0
Seven Pacific region countries.	6.1	11.2	–4.2	4.7	10.5	7.0	8.1	1.2	–3.8	1.2	4.5	3.0
Australia [1]	–1.4	8.2	1.1	3.0	4.5	3.2	–0.4	5.1	6.8	6.0	7.9	4.5
Taiwan [1].	4.9	8.5	2.0	6.8	11.5	6.7	5.1	4.9	1.8	3.2	8.3	4.1
Thailand.	12.1	9.5	7.4	6.7	13.8	5.8	11.6	9.4	9.4	8.9	8.2	6.8
Japan	6.6	11.3	–6.2	4.5	11.1	7.4	8.6	–0.5	–6.2	0.5	4.0	2.7
Korea, South	6.5	15.9	6.1	6.6	8.9	7.5	9.9	13.7	8.8	1.9	4.6	4.0
Malaysia	–0.8	12.7	–1.9	6.2	4.6	2.7	1.5	3.5	–7.2	–2.3	–1.2	–4.0
New Zealand	0.8	4.6	2.8	–0.4	5.5	2.6	–1.2	2.7	6.7	6.2	9.3	5.2

[1] See footnote 2, Table 1308.

Source: Foundation for International Business and Economic Research, New York, NY, *International Economic Indicators*, monthly.

Table 1327. **Sectoral Contributions to Gross Value Added: 1993 and 2003**

[In percent. According to the 1993 System of National Accounts (SNA) and the International Standard Industrial Classification (ISIC), Revision 3. Value added is estimated at basic prices and excludes financial intermediation services indirectly measured (FISIM). It represents an industry's contribution to national GDP and is calculated as the difference between production and intermediate inputs. Value added comprises labor costs, consumption of fixed capital, indirect taxes less subsidies, and net operating surplus and mixed income]

Country	Agriculture		Industry					
			Total		Manufacturing		Services	
	1993	2003	1993	2003	1993	2003	1993	2003
United States [1,2] . .	1.9	1.2	[3]26.0	[3]22.3	[4]17.2	[4]13.9	[3,5]72.2	[3,5]76.5
Australia [1]	3.8	3.4	28.1	25.7	14.0	11.9	68.1	71.0
Austria [1]	2.9	2.0	30.1	30.5	19.0	19.9	67.0	67.6
Belgium	2.0	1.4	29.0	25.6	[6]21.0	18.1	69.0	73.0
Canada	2.9	[7]2.2	29.4	[7]32.4	16.2	[7]18.1	67.8	[7]65.4
Czech Republic	5.5	2.9	41.0	38.6	[6]24.0	26.5	53.8	58.5
Denmark.	3.6	2.3	25.2	25.9	17.3	15.9	71.3	71.8
Finland	5.4	3.4	30.9	31.1	23.2	23.1	63.7	65.5
France [1]	3.1	2.6	24.9	21.5	(NA)	14.0	72.8	75.9
Germany [1]	1.2	1.1	33.2	28.8	23.9	22.5	65.6	70.1
Greece.	9.8	7.0	25.1	23.5	[6]13.4	11.9	65.1	69.5
Hungary	6.5	3.4	32.2	31.3	[6]23.6	22.9	61.3	65.4
Iceland.	12.1	[8]10.0	29.2	[8]25.4	[9]16.6	[8]13.2	58.7	[8]64.6
Ireland [1]	8.5	2.7	35.1	41.2	27.1	31.2	56.5	56.2
Italy	3.4	2.7	31.4	27.8	22.5	19.7	65.2	69.6
Japan [10].	2.0	1.3	36.4	30.7	24.2	21.0	61.6	68.0
Korea [1]	7.5	4.1	41.1	38.7	26.8	26.4	51.4	57.2
Luxembourg	1.3	0.6	26.3	20.6	16.6	11.8	72.5	78.8
Mexico	6.3	3.8	26.8	25.8	19.0	18.0	66.9	70.4
Netherlands [1]	3.6	[2]2.5	28.7	[2]25.7	17.9	[2]15.0	67.7	[2]71.8
New Zealand [11] . . .	8.5	[7]9.5	27.1	[7]25.0	18.7	[7]16.7	64.5	[7]65.5
Norway.	3.1	1.5	33.8	37.7	13.1	10.0	63.1	60.8
Poland [1]	6.8	3.0	40.3	30.5	[6]22.2	18.3	52.6	66.5
Portugal	6.2	3.8	29.6	27.1	19.4	16.9	64.2	69.1
Slovakia	6.3	4.0	36.4	32.4	20.4	21.3	57.3	63.5
Spain [1]	5.8	3.7	29.8	29.1	(NA)	16.9	64.8	67.2
Sweden	2.7	1.9	29.0	28.1	19.7	[8]20.7	68.3	[8]70.1
Switzerland [13]	2.3	[8]1.4	31.3	[8]29.0	21.2	[8]20.4	66.4	[8]69.6
Turkey [11,12,13]	16.1	12.2	33.2	29.3	(NA)	(NA)	50.7	58.5
United Kingdom	1.8	1.0	31.3	26.2	21.1	[7]17.4	66.9	72.0

NA Not available. [1] FISIM (financial intermediation services indirectly measured) are included within industries. [2] Value added is estimated at factor cost. [3] Sanitary and similar services are included under industry. [4] Contribution to GDP instead of value added. [5] Includes government enterprises. [6] 1995. [7] 2001. [8] 2002. [9] 1997. [10] Value added is estimated approximately at market prices. [11] Value added is estimated at producer's prices. [12] According to 1968 SNA (System of National Accounts). [13] According to ISIC (International Standard Industrial Classification), Revision 2.

Source: Organization for Economic Cooperation and Development, Paris, France, *OECD in Figures*, 2005 (copyright). See also <http://ocde.p4.siteinternet.com/publications/doifiles/012005061T009.xls>.

Table 1328. Index of Industrial Production by Country: 1980 to 2004

[Annual averages of monthly data. Industrial production index measures output in the manufacturing, mining, and electric, gas and water utilities industries. Minus sign (–) indicates decrease]

Country	Index (2000 = 100)								Annual percent change				
	1980	1985	1990	1995	2001	2002	2003	2004	1999– 2000	2000– 2001	2001– 2002	2002– 2003	2003– 2004
OECD, total.	62.1	67.2	78.4	83.6	97.6	98.0	99.2	103.2	5.4	–2.4	0.4	1.2	4.0
Australia.	61.3	67.9	79.9	87.0	100.2	103.3	103.5	103.7	5.5	0.2	3.1	0.2	0.2
Austria	52.6	57.1	69.0	74.5	102.8	103.6	105.6	112.3	8.9	2.8	0.8	1.9	6.3
Belgium [1]	70.6	73.5	85.9	86.5	99.0	100.3	101.0	104.3	5.4	–1.0	1.3	0.7	3.3
Canada	55.8	64.6	69.1	78.6	96.0	97.6	98.6	102.5	8.6	–4.0	1.7	1.0	4.0
Czech Republic [1] . . .	(X)	(X)	119.8	90.5	106.5	116.6	123.4	135.6	5.4	6.5	9.5	5.8	9.9
Denmark.	57.5	70.3	75.8	86.5	101.6	103.0	103.2	103.2	5.4	1.6	1.4	0.2	–
Finland.	45.6	53.1	60.4	69.3	99.8	102.0	103.2	107.6	12.4	–0.2	2.2	1.2	4.3
France	76.8	77.2	87.6	87.3	101.3	99.8	99.4	101.6	3.8	1.3	–1.5	–0.4	2.2
Germany [2]	75.2	77.6	90.7	87.4	100.2	99.2	99.6	102.6	5.6	0.2	–1.0	0.4	3.0
Greece.	75.6	81.0	83.2	81.7	98.2	99.0	99.3	100.2	7.2	(NA)	0.8	0.3	0.9
Hungary [1]	69.3	76.1	67.6	59.4	103.6	106.4	113.2	121.5	18.2	3.6	2.7	6.4	7.3
Ireland	16.8	21.5	30.9	49.6	110.0	117.9	123.5	123.8	15.5	10.0	7.2	4.7	0.2
Italy	76.8	73.5	86.7	93.1	99.0	97.4	96.9	96.2	4.3	–1.0	–1.6	–0.5	–0.7
Japan [1]	66.8	79.2	98.5	95.5	93.7	92.6	95.4	100.5	5.5	–6.3	–1.2	3.0	5.3
Korea, South [1]	14.3	23.5	43.1	64.9	100.7	108.8	114.2	126.1	16.8	0.7	8.0	5.0	10.4
Luxembourg	55.4	67.3	79.5	81.3	103.1	105.2	110.7	117.8	4.3	3.1	2.0	5.2	6.4
Mexico [3]	56.9	60.1	67.7	70.8	96.5	96.4	96.3	100.0	6.0	–3.5	–0.1	–0.1	3.8
Netherlands	76.2	76.9	83.9	90.9	100.4	100.1	97.7	100.2	3.5	0.4	–0.3	–2.4	2.6
New Zealand.	(X)	(X)	83.0	95.0	100.3	105.4	106.5	110.5	3.8	–	5.1	1.0	3.8
Norway.	46.3	56.2	71.5	90.3	98.7	99.6	95.5	97.4	3.0	–1.3	0.9	–4.1	2.0
Poland	(X)	74.7	61.0	69.7	100.4	101.8	110.7	124.8	7.5	0.4	1.4	8.7	12.7
Portugal.	54.7	64.5	87.2	84.7	103.1	102.7	102.6	94.6	0.5	3.1	–0.4	–0.1	–7.8
Spain. . [4, 5].	66.9	69.1	80.6	83.7	98.6	98.7	100.1	101.7	4.4	–1.4	0.1	1.4	1.6
Sweden [4, 5].	58.4	64.7	74.8	84.0	98.9	98.8	100.2	105.4	5.7	–1.1	–0.1	1.4	5.2
Switzerland.	65.0	67.0	79.0	82.0	99.3	94.2	94.5	98.4	8.5	–0.7	–5.1	–	4.1
Turkey.	30.9	46.0	65.5	80.7	91.3	100.0	108.7	119.4	6.0	–8.7	9.5	8.7	9.8
United Kingdom	71.6	77.4	87.9	93.4	98.4	96.0	95.5	96.2	1.8	–1.6	–2.4	–0.5	0.7
United States	54.2	59.1	67.1	77.5	96.5	96.6	97.2	101.1	4.4	–3.5	0.1	0.6	4.0

– Represents or rounds to zero.   NA Not available.   X Not applicable.   [1] Not adjusted for unequal number of working days in the month.   [2] See footnote 3, Table 1315.   [3] Including construction.   [4] Mining and manufacturing.   [5] Annual figures correspond to official annual figures and differ from the average of the monthly figures.

Source: Organization for Economic Cooperation and Development, Paris, France, *Main Economic Indicators,* monthly (copyright).

Table 1329. Annual Percent Change in Labor Productivity and Hours Worked by Country: 1995 to 2005

[Change for period shown. For OECD countries and Eastern Europe, labor productivity growth refers to the growth in gross domestic product per hour worked. Data are derived from an annual database maintained by the Groningen Growth and Development Centre at the University of Groningen, Netherlands, in association with The Conference Board. Growth for regional aggregates is calculated based on the sum of gross domestic product divided by the sum of total hours worked. Gross domestic product for each country was converted based on the 2003 OECD benchmark for purchasing power parities and updated to 2005 using the aggregate inflation rate for each country relative to U.S. inflation. Minus sign (–) indicates decrease]

Country	Labor productivity		Total hours worked		Country	Labor productivity		Total hours worked	
	1995– 2000	2000– 2005	1995– 2000	2000– 2005		1995– 2000	2000– 2005	1995– 2000	2000– 2005
All OECD	2.0	1.8	1.3	0.4	European Union (EU-10, new) [3]	4.2	4.7	–0.1	–0.4
All OECD, excl. United States	1.8	1.4	1.0	0.5	Cyprus	0.7	1.0	3.0	2.2
United States	2.1	2.6	1.9	(Z)	Czech Republic	2.2	4.2	–0.7	–0.8
European Union (EU-25, enlarged) [1] . .	2.1	1.4	0.9	0.4	Estonia.	7.5	7.4	–1.8	(Z)
					Hungary	2.3	4.1	1.6	0.3
European Union (EU-15, old) [2]	1.8	1.0	1.1	0.6	Latvia	5.7	7.3	–0.3	0.4
Austria	3.3	1.9	–0.4	–0.4	Lithuania	7.3	7.9	–2.9	–0.2
Belgium	1.6	1.3	1.0	0.2	Malta	3.8	–0.3	0.7	0.3
Denmark.	1.6	1.6	1.2	–0.2	Poland	5.2	5.0	(Z)	–0.8
Finland	2.6	1.5	2.0	0.6	Slovakia	4.0	4.8	–0.3	0.4
France	2.1	1.9	0.8	–0.2	Slovenia	2.4	2.7	2.0	0.6
Germany.	2.5	1.2	–0.5	–0.5	Other OECD members. .	1.7	1.6	1.1	0.6
Greece.	2.0	2.9	1.4	1.4	Japan.	2.2	1.9	–0.9	–0.6
Ireland	5.5	3.0	3.9	2.2	Australia.	2.3	1.5	1.5	1.8
Italy	0.9	–0.3	1.0	1.0	Canada.	1.7	1.2	2.5	1.4
Luxembourg	2.9	1.0	4.0	1.9	Iceland	2.6	3.3	2.5	(Z)
Netherlands	0.4	0.8	3.3	(Z)	Mexico	1.4	0.4	4.0	1.5
Portugal.	3.4	0.2	0.7	0.4	New Zealand	1.6	0.8	1.0	2.9
Spain	–0.2	–0.6	4.4	3.8	Norway	2.3	2.2	1.2	–0.2
Sweden	2.4	2.3	0.9	–0.1	South Korea	3.7	3.7	0.6	0.8
U.K.	2.1	1.8	1.1	0.5	Switzerland	1.5	1.1	0.5	–0.2
					Turkey	2.6	3.4	1.3	0.6

Z Less than .05 percent.   [1] Referring to all members of the European Union as of 1 May 2004.   [2] Referring to membership of the European Union until April 2004.   [3] Referring to new membership of the European Union as of 1 May 2004.

Source: The Conference Board, New York, NY, *Performance 2006: Productivity, Employment, and Income in the World's Economies,* by Bart van Ark, Catherine Guillemineau and Robert H. McGuckin, 2006 (copyright). See also <http://www.conference-board.org/>.

Table 1330. **Annual Percent Changes in Consumer Prices, by Country: 2000 to 2005**

[**Change from previous year**. See text of this section for general comments concerning the data. For additional qualifications of the data for individual countries, see source. Minus sign (–) indicates decrease]

Country	2000	2002	2003	2004	2005	Country	2000	2002	2003	2004	2005
United States	3.4	1.6	2.3	2.7	3.4	Kenya	10.0	2.0	9.8	11.6	10.3
Argentina	-0.9	25.9	13.4	4.4	9.6	Korea, South	2.2	2.7	3.6	3.6	2.7
Australia	4.5	3.0	2.8	2.3	2.7	Malaysia	1.5	1.8	1.1	1.5	3.1
Austria	2.4	1.8	1.4	2.1	2.3	Mexico	9.5	5.0	4.6	4.7	4.0
Bangladesh	2.4	3.3	5.7	3.2	(NA)	Netherlands	2.5	3.3	2.1	1.3	1.7
Belgium	2.5	1.6	1.6	2.1	2.8	Nigeria	14.5	13.0	14.1	19.4	13.5
Bolivia	4.6	0.9	3.3	4.4	5.4	Norway	3.1	1.3	2.5	0.5	1.5
Brazil	7.0	8.5	14.7	6.6	6.9	Pakistan	4.4	3.3	2.9	7.4	9.1
Canada	2.7	2.3	2.8	1.8	2.2	Peru	3.8	0.2	2.3	3.7	1.6
Chile	3.8	2.5	2.8	1.1	3.1	Philippines	4.4	3.0	3.5	6.0	7.6
Colombia	9.2	6.4	7.1	5.9	5.1	Portugal	2.8	3.6	3.3	2.4	2.3
Egypt	2.7	2.7	4.5	11.3	4.9	Romania	45.7	22.5	15.3	11.9	9.0
France	1.7	1.9	2.1	2.1	1.8	Russia	20.8	15.8	13.7	10.9	12.7
Germany	1.5	1.4	1.1	1.7	2.0	South Africa	5.4	9.2	5.9	1.4	3.4
Ghana	25.2	14.8	26.7	12.6	15.1	Spain	3.4	3.1	3.0	3.0	3.4
Greece	3.1	3.6	3.5	2.9	3.6	Sri Lanka	6.2	9.6	6.3	7.6	(NA)
Guatemala	6.0	8.0	5.5	7.4	8.4	Sweden	0.9	2.2	1.9	0.4	0.5
India	4.0	4.4	3.8	3.8	4.3	Switzerland	1.5	0.6	0.6	0.8	1.2
Indonesia	4.5	11.9	6.6	6.2	10.5	Thailand	1.6	0.6	1.8	2.8	4.5
Iran	14.5	14.3	16.5	14.8	(NA)	Turkey	54.9	45.0	25.3	8.6	8.2
Israel	1.1	5.6	0.7	-0.4	1.3	United Kingdom	2.9	1.6	2.9	3.0	2.8
Italy	2.5	2.5	2.7	2.2	2.0	Venezuela	16.2	22.4	31.1	21.8	16.0
Japan	-0.7	-0.9	-0.3	0.0	-0.3						

NA Not available.

Source: International Monetary Fund, Washington, DC, *International Financial Statistics*, monthly (copyright).

Table 1331. **Comparative Price Levels—Selected OECD Countries: 2006**

[Example of data: An item that costs $1.00 in the United States would cost $1.29 (U.S. dollars) in Japan]

Country	United States (U.S. dollar)	Canada (Canadian dollar)	Mexico (Mexican peso)	Japan (yen)	France (euro)	Germany (euro)	Italy (euro)	United Kingdom (pound)
United States	100	89	148	77	86	86	92	86
Australia [1]	107	95	158	83	92	92	99	92
Austria	114	102	169	89	99	99	106	99
Belgium	112	100	166	87	97	97	104	97
Canada	113	100	166	87	97	97	104	97
Czech Republic	65	58	96	50	56	56	60	56
Denmark	147	130	217	113	126	127	136	127
Finland	130	116	192	101	112	112	120	112
France	116	103	172	90	100	100	107	100
Germany	116	103	171	90	100	100	107	100
Greece	95	85	141	74	82	82	88	82
Hungary	64	57	94	49	55	55	59	55
Iceland	148	132	219	114	127	128	137	128
Ireland	139	123	205	107	120	120	128	120
Italy	108	96	160	84	93	93	100	94
Japan	129	115	191	100	111	112	119	112
Korea, South	92	82	137	72	80	80	85	80
Luxembourg	114	101	169	88	98	99	106	99
Mexico	68	60	100	52	58	58	63	59
Netherlands	114	101	168	88	98	98	105	98
New Zealand [1]	96	85	141	74	82	83	88	83
Norway	156	138	230	121	134	134	144	135
Poland	64	57	95	50	55	56	60	56
Portugal	86	76	127	66	74	74	79	74
Slovakia	64	57	95	50	55	55	59	56
Spain	98	87	145	76	85	85	91	85
Sweden	125	111	185	97	108	108	116	108
Switzerland	147	130	217	113	126	127	136	127
Turkey	70	62	103	54	60	60	64	60
United Kingdom	116	103	171	89	100	100	107	100

[1] Estimates based on quarterly consumer prices.

Source: Organization for Economic Cooperation and Development, Paris, France, *Main Economic Indicators*, May 2006 (copyright). See also <http://www.oecd.org/dataoecd/48/18/18598721.pdf>.

848   Comparative International Statistics

Table 1332. **Gross Public Debt, Expenditures, and Receipts by Country: 1990 to 2005**

[Percent of nominal gross domestic product. 2005 data estimated. Expenditures and receipts refer to the general government sector, which is a consolidation of accounts for the central, state, and local governments plus social security. Expenditures, or total outlays, are defined as current outlays plus capital outlays. Receipts cover current receipts, but exclude capital receipts. Nontax receipts consist of property income (including dividends and other transfers from public enterprises), fees, charges, sales, fines, capital transfers received by the general government, etc.)]

Country	Gross debt			Expenditures			Receipts		
	1990	2000	2005	1990	2000	2005	1990	2000	2005
United States [1]	-4.2	1.6	-3.8	37.1	34.2	36.6	32.8	35.8	32.8
Australia	-1.7	[2]0.9	1.5	36.2	[2]34.8	34.9	34.5	35.7	36.4
Austria	-2.5	[2]-1.6	-1.6	52.1	[2]51.4	49.6	49.7	49.7	47.9
Belgium	-6.7	0.0	-0.1	53.4	49.1	50.1	46.6	49.2	50.0
Canada	-5.8	2.9	1.7	48.8	41.1	39.3	43.0	44.1	41.0
Czech Republic	(X)	-3.7	-2.6	(X)	42.0	43.9	(X)	38.3	41.3
Denmark	-1.3	2.3	4.0	57.2	53.9	53.0	56.0	56.2	56.9
Finland	5.4	7.1	2.4	48.7	48.8	50.8	54.2	55.9	53.2
France	-1.8	[2]-1.5	-2.9	50.7	51.6	54.4	48.6	50.1	51.4
Germany	-2.0	[2]1.3	-3.3	44.5	[2]45.1	46.8	42.5	46.4	43.5
Greece	-15.7	-4.2	-4.4	50.2	52.2	46.7	34.5	48.0	42.2
Hungary	(NA)	-3.0	-6.1	(NA)	47.4	50.5	(NA)	44.4	44.4
Iceland	-3.3	2.4	3.2	42.7	42.1	44.5	39.3	44.6	47.7
Ireland	-2.8	4.4	1.0	43.2	31.6	34.6	40.4	36.0	35.6
Italy	-11.5	[2]-0.9	-4.3	54.4	[2]46.1	48.2	42.6	45.3	44.0
Japan [3]	2.1	-7.7	-5.2	31.8	39.2	36.9	33.9	31.5	31.7
Korea, South	3.1	5.4	2.7	19.7	23.9	28.1	23.0	29.3	30.9
Netherlands	-5.2	[2]2.3	-0.3	54.8	[2]43.7	45.7	49.4	46.0	45.4
New Zealand	-3.5	2.5	5.8	53.3	40.4	40.6	48.9	42.8	46.5
Norway	2.2	15.6	15.8	54.0	42.7	42.9	56.2	58.2	58.6
Portugal	-6.3	[2]-3.0	-6.0	42.1	[2]43.1	47.8	35.5	40.2	41.8
Spain	-3.9	[2]-0.9	1.1	43.4	[2]39.0	38.2	39.5	38.1	39.3
Sweden	3.4	5.0	2.7	61.7	56.8	56.4	65.1	61.8	59.1
United Kingdom	-1.6	[2]3.8	-3.2	42.2	[2]37.5	45.1	40.7	41.3	41.9

NA Not available. X Not applicable. [1] Receipts exclude the operating surpluses of public enterprises and expenditures include them. [2] Financial balances include substantial one-off revenues from the sale of the mobil telephone licenses. [3] The 2000 expenditures include capital transfers to the Deposit Insurance Company. Receipts include deferred tax payments on postal savings accounts in 2000.

Source: Organization for Economic Cooperation and Development, Paris, France, OECD Economic Outlook, December 2005 (copyright).

Table 1333. **Percent Distribution of Tax Receipts by Country: 1990 to 2003**

Country	Income and profits taxes [2]				Social security contributions			Taxes on goods and services [5]		
	Total [1]	Total [3]	Indi-vidual	Corpo-rate	Total [4]	Employ-ees	Employ-ers	Total [3]	General consump-tion taxes [6]	Taxes on specific goods, and ser-vices [7]
United States:										
1990	100.0	45.4	37.7	7.7	25.9	11.0	13.4	17.3	8.0	7.1
2000	100.0	50.7	41.9	8.7	23.2	10.4	11.6	16.1	7.6	6.3
2003	100.0	43.3	35.3	8.1	26.4	11.7	13.3	18.2	8.4	7.1
Canada:										
1990	100.0	48.6	40.8	7.0	12.2	4.4	7.6	25.8	14.1	10.3
2000	100.0	50.1	36.8	12.2	13.6	5.5	7.8	24.2	14.3	8.5
2003	100.0	46.0	34.6	10.4	15.4	6.3	8.6	26.1	15.1	9.6
France:										
1990	100.0	17.2	11.8	5.3	44.1	13.2	27.2	28.4	18.8	8.7
2000	100.0	24.9	18.0	6.9	36.0	8.9	24.8	25.7	16.9	8.2
2003	100.0	23.2	17.5	5.7	37.7	9.5	25.7	25.5	16.8	8.1
Germany:										
1990	100.0	32.4	27.6	4.8	37.5	16.2	19.1	26.7	16.6	9.2
2000	100.0	30.1	25.3	4.8	39.0	17.2	19.2	28.1	18.4	8.8
2003	100.0	27.4	23.9	3.5	40.5	17.7	19.9	29.4	17.9	10.5
Italy:										
1990	100.0	36.5	26.3	10.0	32.9	6.3	23.6	28.0	14.7	10.6
2000	100.0	33.2	24.9	6.8	28.6	5.4	19.9	27.8	15.4	9.7
2003	100.0	30.9	25.1	6.6	29.5	5.4	20.6	25.7	14.2	8.9
Japan:										
1990	100.0	48.5	26.9	21.6	29.0	11.0	15.0	13.2	4.3	7.3
2000	100.0	34.8	21.1	13.8	35.1	14.7	16.4	19.3	9.1	8.0
2003	100.0	30.6	17.5	13.0	38.5	16.5	17.6	20.3	9.5	8.4
United Kingdom:										
1990	100.0	38.3	27.1	11.2	16.7	6.5	9.7	30.5	16.4	12.4
2000	100.0	39.1	29.3	9.7	16.9	6.8	9.5	32.0	18.3	12.3
2003	100.0	36.5	28.7	7.8	18.5	7.5	10.3	32.7	19.8	11.6

[1] Includes property taxes, employer payroll taxes other than social security contributions, and miscellaneous taxes, not shown separately. [2] Includes taxes on capital gains. [3] Includes other taxes not shown separately. [4] Includes contributions of self-employed not shown separately. [5] Taxes on the production, sales, transfer, leasing, and delivery of goods and services and rendering of services. [6] Primary value-added and sales taxes. [7] For example, excise taxes on alcohol, tobacco, and gasoline.

Source: Organization for Economic Cooperation and Development, Paris, France, Revenue Statistics of OECD Member Countries, annual (copyright).

Comparative International Statistics 849

Table 1334. Household Tax Burden by Country: 2005

[**Percent of gross earnings equivalent to the average production worker**. The tax burden reflects income tax plus employee contributions less cash benefits]

Country	Single person without children	One earner family with two children	Country	Single person without children	One earner family with two children
Australia	24.0	10.9	Korea, South	9.9	8.6
Austria	32.1	16.7	Luxembourg	26.5	0.3
Belgium	41.9	22.2	Mexico	7.9	7.9
Canada	23.5	12.3	Netherlands	32.2	21.7
Czech Republic	24.1	1.5	New Zealand	20.5	14.5
Denmark	41.0	29.2	Norway	29.0	20.4
Finland	31.3	23.6	Poland	32.0	30.3
France	29.0	17.1	Portugal	21.1	9.1
Germany	41.7	22.3	Slovakia	22.1	3.0
Greece	21.6	22.1	Spain	20.3	13.0
Hungary	32.9	18.4	Sweden	31.0	23.7
Iceland	24.9	5.9	Switzerland	21.7	9.6
Ireland	17.7	-1.8	Turkey	30.4	30.4
Italy	27.3	13.7	United Kingdom	26.5	19.4
Japan	18.5	15.3	**United States**	**23.6**	**5.0**

Source: Organization for Economic Cooperation and Development, Paris, France, *Taxing Wages, 2004–2005*, (copyright).

Table 1335. Income Tax and Social Security Contributions as Percent of Labor Costs: 2004

[Data are for single individual at the income level of the average production worker]

Country	Labor costs [1] (dol.)	Percent of labor costs		Social security contributions	
		Total [2]	Income tax	Employee	Employer [3]
Belgium	46,261	54	27	14	14
Germany	42,543	51	20	21	10
Australia	40,630	29	24	–	4
Netherlands	39,614	44	9	26	9
Switzerland	38,213	29	10	11	8
Norway	37,550	37	21	8	8
Denmark	37,788	41	31	11	–
Luxembourg	35,767	32	9	14	9
Canada	37,856	32	18	7	8
Korea, South	36,125	17	2	7	7
Finland	37,174	44	24	6	13
United States	**37,606**	**30**	**17**	**8**	**5**
Italy	35,005	46	19	9	18
France	35,443	47	13	14	21
Austria	34,356	45	11	18	16
United Kingdom	36,159	31	16	9	7
Japan	35,103	27	6	12	9
Sweden	34,606	48	24	7	17
Iceland	32,194	30	25	–	4
New Zealand	28,228	21	21	–	–
Ireland	30,236	24	11	5	8
Spain	29,382	38	13	6	19
Czech Republic	19,395	44	11	13	20
Greece	22,138	35	1	16	18
Turkey	20,003	43	15	15	12
Poland	17,319	43	6	25	12
Portugal	16,128	33	6	11	16
Hungary	13,229	46	12	14	20
Mexico	10,278	15	3	2	11

– Represents or rounds to zero.   [1] Adjusted for purchasing power parities, see text of this section. Labor costs include gross wages plus employers compulsory social security contributions.   [2] Due to rounding total may differ one percentage point from aggregate columns for income tax and social security contributions.   [3] Includes reported payroll taxes.

Source: Organization for Economic Cooperation and Development, Paris, France, *Taxing Wages, 2003–2004* (copyright).

850 Comparative International Statistics

Table 1336. **Civilian Labor Force, Employment, and Unemployment by Country: 1990 to 2005**

[125,840 represents 125,840,000. Data based on U.S. labor force definitions (see source) except that minimum age for population base varies as follows: United States, Canada, France, Sweden, and United Kingdom, 16 years; Australia, Japan, Netherlands, Germany, and Italy (beginning 1993), 15 years; and Italy (prior to 1993) 14 years]

Year	United States	Canada	Aus-tralia	Japan	France	Ger-many [1]	Italy	Nether-lands	Swe-den	United King-dom
Civilian labor force (1,000):										
1990	[2]125,840	14,047	8,440	63,050	[2]24,159	29,410	22,670	6,657	4,594	28,766
2000	[2]142,583	15,637	9,590	66,990	26,083	39,302	23,357	8,137	4,489	28,952
2003	[2]146,510	16,729	10,092	66,010	26,865	39,276	24,021	8,391	4,567	29,557
2004	[2]147,401	16,955	10,244	65,770	26900	39,796	24,065	8,505	4,576	29,776
2005	149,320	17,108	10,524	65,850	(NA)	(NA)	(NA)	8,441	(NA)	30,094
Labor force participation rate: [3]										
1990	[2]66.5	67.3	64.7	62.6	[2]55.7	55.3	47.2	56.2	67.3	64.3
2000	67.1	65.8	64.4	62.0	56.5	56.7	48.1	64.4	63.8	62.9
2003	66.2	67.3	64.6	60.3	57.0	56.0	49.1	65.2	64.0	63.0
2004	66.0	67.3	64.7	60.0	56.9	56.5	49.1	65.7	63.7	63.0
2005	66.0	67.0	65.4	60.0	(NA)	(NA)	(NA)	65.2	(NA)	63.1
Civilian employment (1,000):										
1990	[2]118,793	12,964	7,877	61,700	[2]22,075	27,950	21,080	6,267	4,513	26,713
2000	[2]136,891	14,681	8,989	63,790	23,698	36,236	20,969	7,907	4,229	27,368
2003	[2]137,736	15,579	9,481	62,510	24,288	35,615	21,973	8,080	4,303	28,073
2004	[2]139,252	15,861	9,677	62,640	24259	35,876	22,105	8,118	4,276	28,358
2005	141,730	16,080	9,987	62,910	(NA)	(NA)	(NA)	8,036	(NA)	28,637
Employment-population ratio: [4]										
1990	[2]62.8	62.2	60.4	61.3	[2]50.9	52.6	43.9	52.9	66.1	59.8
2000	64.4	62.0	60.3	59.0	51.4	52.2	43.2	62.6	60.1	59.4
2003	62.3	63.0	60.7	57.1	51.5	50.8	44.9	62.8	60.3	59.8
2004	62.3	63.3	61.2	57.1	51.3	50.9	45.1	62.7	59.5	60.0
2005	62.7	63.4	62.1	57.3	(NA)	(NA)	(NA)	62.0	(NA)	60.0
Unemployment rate:										
1990	[2]5.6	7.7	6.7	2.1	[2]8.6	5.0	7.0	5.9	1.8	7.1
2000	4.0	6.1	6.3	4.8	9.1	7.8	10.2	2.8	5.8	5.5
2003	6.0	6.9	6.1	5.3	9.6	9.3	8.5	3.7	5.8	5.0
2004	5.5	6.4	5.5	4.8	9.8	9.9	8.1	4.6	6.6	4.8
2005	5.1	6.0	5.1	4.5	9.7	9.7	(NA)	4.8	(NA)	4.8
Under 25 years old [5]	11.3	11.3	10.8	8.8	21.2	(NA)	(NA)	9.3	(NA)	13.0
Teenagers [6]	16.6	15.4	15.2	10.4	25.8	(NA)	(NA)	12.3	(NA)	(NA)
20 to 24 years old......	8.8	9.0	7.7	8.4	20.0	(NA)	(NA)	7.1	(NA)	(NA)
25 years old and over	4.0	5.0	3.7	4.0	8.0	(NA)	(NA)	4.5	(NA)	3.3

NA Not available. [1] Unified Germany for 1991 onward. Prior to 1991, data relate to the former West Germany. [2] Break in series. Data not comparable with prior years. [3] Civilian labor force as a percent of the civilian working-age population. Germany and Japan include the institutionalized population as part of the working-age population. [4] Civilian employment as a percent of the civilian working-age population. Germany and Japan include the institutionalized population as part of the working-age population. [5] Data for Spring only for France and Netherlands. [6] 16-to 19-year-olds in the United States, Canada, and France; 15-to 19-year-olds in Australia, Japan, and the Netherlands.

Source: U.S. Bureau of Labor Statistics, *Comparative Civilian Labor Force Statistics, Ten Countries, 1990–2005*, April 5, 2006. See also <http://www.bls.gov/fls/lfcompendium.pdf>.

Table 1337. **Percent of Persons Not in Education or at Work by Age Group and Sex: 2003**

[Represents those persons not in education and either unemployed or not in the labor force]

Country	15 to 19 years old			20 to 24 years old		
	Total	Male	Female	Total	Male	Female
Australia	6.8	6.4	7.1	13.3	10.7	15.9
Belgium	7.1	6.9	7.4	17.1	16.1	18.2
Canada..........	6.7	7.3	6.0	13.2	13.6	12.9
Czech Republic	5.7	5.4	6.2	18.0	13.3	22.9
Denmark..........	2.9	2.8	3.1	8.2	7.4	9.0
Finland	9.7	13.0	4.0	16.4	18.9	13.9
France	14.0	14.8	13.2	15.5	14.0	17.1
Germany..........	4.7	4.6	4.8	15.6	14.7	16.6
Greece	9.3	8.6	10.1	21.5	14.9	27.9
Hungary	6.8	6.6	5.7	19.9	17.7	22.1
Italy	10.5	10.7	10.3	24.3	21.8	26.8
Luxembourg	(S)	(S)	2.0	(S)	(S)	9.6
Mexico	17.8	8.1	27.8	27.6	6.8	46.8
Netherlands.......	4.6	4.7	4.5	7.9	6.4	9.5
Poland	3.3	3.8	2.7	25.5	25.8	25.2
Portugal	8.8	(S)	5.5	12.3	10.0	14.5
Spain	7.3	7.3	7.3	14.8	12.2	17.3
Sweden	4.3	5.0	3.4	11.8	12.1	11.4
Switzerland	8.0	7.1	6.7	12.7	11.3	14.2
United States	**7.0**	**6.4**	**7.6**	**16.6**	**12.6**	**20.4**

S Figure does not meet publication standards.

Source: Organization for Economic Cooperation and Development, Paris, France, *Education at a Glance 2005* (copyright).

Table 1338. Unemployment Rates by Country: 2000 to 2005

[**Annual averages.** The standardized unemployment rates shown here are calculated as the number of unemployed persons as a percentage of the civilian labor force. The unemployed are persons of working age who, in the reference period, are without work, available for work, and have taken specific steps to find work]

Country	2000	2003	2004	2005	Country	2000	2003	2004	2005
OECD, total	6.3	7.1	6.9	6.6	Ireland	4.3	4.8	4.6	4.3
OECD Europe[1]....	8.5	8.9	8.9	(NA)	Italy	10.4	8.4	8.0	(NA)
					Japan	4.7	5.3	4.7	4.4
United States	4.0	6.0	5.5	5.1	Korea, South	4.4	3.6	3.7	(NA)
Australia	6.3	6.1	5.5	5.1	Luxembourg	2.3	3.7	4.8	5.3
Austria	3.7	4.3	4.9	5.2	Netherlands......	2.9	3.7	4.6	4.8
Belgium	6.9	8.2	8.4	8.4	New Zealand	6.0	4.6	3.9	(NA)
Canada.........	6.8	7.6	7.2	6.8	Norway	3.4	4.5	4.4	(NA)
Czech Republic ...	8.7	7.8	8.3	7.9	Poland	16.4	19.6	19.0	17.9
Denmark........	4.4	5.4	5.5	4.9	Portugal	4.1	6.2	6.7	7.4
Finland	9.7	9.0	9.0	8.4	Spain	11.3	11.5	10.9	9.2
France	9.1	9.5	9.6	9.5	Sweden	5.6	5.6	6.4	(NA)
Germany........	7.8	9.1	9.5	9.5	Switzerland	2.7	4.2	4.4	(NA)
Hungary	6.3	5.9	6.1	7.1	United Kingdom ...	5.4	4.9	4.7	(NA)

NA Not available. [1] See footnote 4, Table 1325.

Source: Organization for Economic Cooperation and Development, Paris, France, *Main Economic Indicators*, April 2006 and earlier releases.

Table 1339. Female Labor Force Participation Rates by Country: 1980 to 2004

[**In percent.** Female labor force of all ages divided by female population 15–64 years old]

Country	1980	1990	2000	2004	Country	1980	1990	2000	2004
Australia	52.7	62.1	66.4	67.5	Korea, South	(NA)	51.2	54.3	57.2
Austria	48.7	55.4	62.2	64.0	Luxembourg	39.9	50.7	68.8	84.0
Belgium	47.0	52.4	59.2	57.3	Mexico	33.7	(NA)	42.4	44.2
Canada............	57.8	67.6	70.4	73.0	Netherlands........	35.5	[1]53.1	65.2	67.6
Czech Republic	(X)	69.1	64.3	62.9	New Zealand	44.6	[1]63.0	67.6	70.9
Denmark...........	(NA)	78.5	75.9	76.4	Norway	62.3	71.2	76.3	75.6
Finland	70.1	73.8	72.2	72.3	Poland	(NA)	(NA)	59.7	57.9
France	54.4	57.8	62.0	64.8	Portugal	54.3	62.9	67.2	70.6
Germany [2].........	52.8	56.7	64.0	66.6	Slovakia	(NA)	(NA)	63.0	62.7
Greece	33.0	43.6	50.2	52.8	Spain	32.2	41.2	50.7	57.0
Hungary	(NA)	(NA)	52.5	53.7	Sweden	74.1	[1]80.4	75.0	75.0
Iceland	(NA)	65.6	82.8	79.9	Switzerland	54.1	65.7	70.6	77.5
Ireland	36.3	43.8	56.2	58.5	Turkey	(NA)	36.7	26.9	27.7
Italy	39.6	45.9	46.8	51.0	United Kingdom	58.3	66.5	67.8	68.5
Japan	54.8	60.3	64.2	64.6	**United States ....**	**59.7**	[1]**68.5**	**71.7**	**69.8**

NA Not available.   X Not applicable.   [1] Break in series. Data not comparable with prior years.   [2] Prior to 1991, data are for former West Germany.

Source: Organization for Economic Cooperation and Development, Paris, France, *OECD in Figures*, annual (copyright). See also <http://ocde.p4.siteinternet.com/publications/doifiles/012005061T006.xls>.

Table 1340. Civilian Employment-Population Ratio: 1990 to 2005

[Civilian employment as a percent of the civilian working-age population. See headnote, Table 1336]

Country	Women					Men				
	1990	1995	2000	2004	2005	1990	1995	2000	2004	2005
United States [1]...	**54.3**	**55.6**	**57.5**	**56.0**	**56.2**	**72.0**	**70.8**	**71.9**	**69.2**	**69.6**
Canada	54.1	52.7	56.0	58.3	58.3	70.6	66.1	68.2	68.5	68.6
Australia........	49.5	50.5	52.5	53.8	55.0	71.4	68.2	68.4	68.8	69.4
Japan	48.0	47.7	46.4	45.5	45.7	75.4	75.0	72.5	69.6	69.7
France..	41.5	41.9	44.6	45.6	(NA)	61.4	57.4	58.8	57.6	(NA)
Germany [2]	40.9	42.7	44.4	44.9	(NA)	65.6	63.1	60.6	57.3	(NA)
Italy [1]	29.2	29.1	31.6	34.2	(NA)	60.0	56.2	55.8	57.1	(NA)
Netherlands	39.4	44.2	53.0	55.0	54.9	67.0	65.9	72.5	70.6	69.4
Sweden	61.8	54.7	56.1	56.1	(NA)	70.6	62.1	64.3	63.1	(NA)
United Kingdom. ..	50.3	49.8	52.5	53.5	53.7	70.0	64.7	66.9	66.9	66.8

NA Not available.   [1] Break in series between 1990 and 1995.   [2] Unified Germany for 1991 onward. Prior to 1991, data relate to the former West Germany. Break in series between 1995 and 2000.

Source: U.S. Bureau of Labor Statistics, *Comparative Civilian Labor Force Statistics, Ten Countries, 1960–2005*, April 5, 2006. See also <http://www.bls.gov/fls/lfcompendium.pdf>.

Table 1341. Civilian Employment by Industry and Country: 2000 and 2005

[136,891 represents 136,891,000. Civilian employment as a percent of the civilian working-age population. See headnote, Table 1336]

Industry	United States [1,2]	Canada [1]	Aus-tralia	Japan	France	Ger-many	Italy	Sweden	United Kingdom
TOTAL EMPLOYMENT (1,000)									
2000, total	136,891	14,764	8,989	63,790	23,698	36,238	20,969	4,217	27,058
Agriculture, forestry, fishing [3]	2,464	487	446	3,070	922	952	1,007	122	419
Industry [4]	30,050	3,220	1,901	19,710	5,508	11,898	6,353	999	6,637
Manufacturing [5]	19,644	2,249	1,129	13,180	4,081	8,647	4,796	761	4,612
Services [6]	104,377	11,057	6,642	41,010	17,268	23,388	13,609	3,096	20,002
2005, total	141,730	16,170	9,987	62,905	(NA)	(NA)	(NA)	(NA)	(NA)
Agriculture, forestry, fishing [3]	2,197	439	366	2,667	(NA)	(NA)	(NA)	(NA)	(NA)
Industry [4]	28,074	3,438	2,054	17,059	(NA)	(NA)	(NA)	(NA)	(NA)
Manufacturing [5]	16,253	2,207	1,073	11,393	(NA)	(NA)	(NA)	(NA)	(NA)
Services [6]	111,459	12,293	7,567	43,179	(NA)	(NA)	(NA)	(NA)	(NA)
PERCENT DISTRIBUTION									
2000, total	100.0	100.0	100.0	100.0	100.0	100.0	100.0	100.0	100.0
Agriculture, forestry, fishing [3]	1.8	3.3	5.0	4.8	3.9	2.6	4.8	2.9	1.5
Industry [4]	22.0	21.8	21.1	30.9	23.2	32.8	30.3	23.7	24.5
Manufacturing [5]	14.4	15.2	12.6	20.7	17.2	23.9	22.9	18.0	17.0
Services [6]	76.2	74.9	73.9	64.3	72.9	64.5	64.9	73.4	73.9
2005, total	100.0	100.0	100.0	100.0	100.0	100.0	100.0	100.0	100.0
Agriculture, forestry, fishing [3]	1.6	2.7	3.7	4.2	(NA)	(NA)	(NA)	(NA)	(NA)
Industry [4]	19.8	21.3	20.6	27.1	(NA)	(NA)	(NA)	(NA)	(NA)
Manufacturing [5]	11.5	13.6	10.7	18.1	(NA)	(NA)	(NA)	(NA)	(NA)
Services [6]	78.6	76.0	75.8	68.6	(NA)	(NA)	(NA)	(NA)	(NA)

NA Not available. [1] Data for the United States and Canada are based on the 2002 North American Industry Classification System (NAICS). [2] Break in series between 2000 and 2005. [3] Includes hunting. [4] Includes manufacturing, mining, and construction. [5] For Italy, some mining is included in manufacturing. [6] Transportation, communication, public utilities, trade, finance, public administration, private household services, and miscellaneous services.

Source: U.S. Bureau of Labor Statistics, *Comparative Civilian Labor Force Statistics, Ten Countries, 1960–2005*, April 5, 2006. See also <http://www.bls.gov/lf/lfcompendium.pdf>.

Table 1342. Unmanufactured Tobacco and Cigarettes—Selected Countries: 2000 to 2004

[6,400 represents 6,400,000. Tobacco is on dry weight basis]

Country	Unmanufactured tobacco (1,000 metric tons)			Country	Cigarettes (bil. pieces)		
	2000	2003	2004		2000	2003	2004
PRODUCTION				**PRODUCTION**			
World, total	6,400	5,371	5,734	World, total	5,609	5,662	5,530
China [1]	2,295	1,918	2,014	China [1]	1,699	1,793	1,793
Brazil	493	516	757	United States	595	500	498
India	599	595	598	Russia	341	385	380
United States	408	339	358	Japan	258	219	216
Indonesia	157	144	144	Indonesia	233	186	186
				Germany	207	205	185
EXPORTS				Turkey	128	126	130
World, total	2,132	2,049	2,126				
Brazil	342	466	564	**EXPORTS**			
United States	180	156	164	World, total	843	859	759
China [1]	113	146	157	United States	148	122	119
Malawi	101	121	138	Netherlands	102	105	100
India	123	125	128	Germany	91	106	90
				United Kingdom	111	68	65
IMPORTS				Korea, South	7	31	35
World, total	2,539	2,029	1,873	Hong Kong	28	28	29
Russia	285	293	275	Switzerland	23	23	23
United States	197	261	258	Japan	14	20	20
Germany	263	195	175				
United Kingdom	108	88	100	**IMPORTS**			
Netherlands	112	110	98	World, total	722	650	637
				Japan	83	83	83
CONSUMPTION				Italy	56	58	70
World, total	5,816	5,935	5,729	France	68	63	63
China [1]	1,235	2,232	2,220	Spain	25	41	43
India	474	488	491	Germany	34	34	32
United States	499	444	436	United Kingdom	69	34	32
Russia	301	294	281	United States	15	23	23
Indonesia	171	151	157				

[1] See footnote 2, Table 1308.

Source: U.S. Dept. of Agriculture, Foreign Agricultural Service, Production, Supply & Distribution Online <http://www.fas.usda.gov/psd/psdselection.asp> (accessed July 2006).

Comparative International Statistics   853

Table 1343. World Supply and Utilization of Major Crops, Livestock, and Products: 1995 to 2005

[In millions of units (214.3 represents 214,300,000). For major crops, data ending in year shown. For meat and dairy, calendar year data, selected countries]

Commodity	1995	1998	1999	2000	2001	2002	2003	2004	2005 [1]
Wheat									
Area (hectares)	214.3	228.4	225.1	215.4	217.6	214.6	214.6	209.9	218.6
Production (metric tons)	523.1	610.0	590.0	585.8	581.5	581.1	567.7	554.6	626.7
Exports (metric tons) [2]	101.5	104.5	102.0	112.6	104.0	110.7	109.9	104.5	113.0
Consumption (metric tons) [3]	545.0	577.3	579.0	585.0	583.9	585.2	604.0	588.6	609.2
Ending stocks (metric tons) [4]	160.2	197.1	208.1	208.9	206.5	202.5	166.1	132.1	149.6
Coarse grains									
Area (hectares)	323.6	311.2	308.5	300.0	296.9	301.2	293.0	306.7	302.6
Production (metric tons)	869.7	881.2	890.5	876.9	861.3	891.8	873.6	912.9	1,008.3
Exports (metric tons) [2]	98.6	85.8	96.7	104.8	104.4	102.7	104.3	102.6	101.6
Consumption (metric tons) [3]	858.8	867.1	869.1	881.9	883.8	905.5	900.4	942.2	970.0
Ending stocks (metric tons) [4]	190.8	215.8	237.2	231.8	209.3	195.6	168.8	139.4	177.7
Rice, milled									
Area (hectares)	147.4	151.2	152.7	155.3	151.5	150.5	145.8	148.1	149.5
Production (metric tons)	363.6	386.9	394.6	408.8	398.7	399.1	377.5	391.4	402.2
Exports (metric tons) [2]	20.7	27.6	24.8	22.8	24.4	27.8	27.6	27.1	28.4
Consumption (metric tons) [3]	365.2	379.4	387.6	397.6	394.6	410.1	406.5	415.7	415.3
Ending stocks (metric tons) [4]	118.3	128.0	135.1	146.2	150.4	139.4	110.3	86.0	72.9
Total grains									
Area (hectares)	685.3	690.8	686.3	670.7	666.0	666.3	653.4	664.7	670.7
Production (metric tons)	1,756.4	1,878.1	1,875.1	1,871.5	1,841.5	1,872.0	1,818.8	1,858.9	2,037.2
Exports (metric tons) [2]	220.8	217.9	223.5	240.2	232.8	241.2	241.8	234.2	243.0
Consumption (metric tons) [3]	1,769.0	1,823.8	1,835.7	1,864.5	1,862.3	1,900.8	1,910.9	1,946.5	1,994.5
Ending stocks (metric tons) [4]	469.3	540.9	580.4	586.9	566.2	537.5	445.2	357.5	400.2
Oilseeds									
Crush (metric tons)	238.3	264.3	278.4	247.3	254.4	265.0	268.9	278.4	301.6
Production (metric tons)	299.5	338.6	346.0	303.9	314.2	325.1	330.3	334.9	380.1
Exports (metric tons)	47.5	62.1	63.5	59.9	66.9	62.8	69.9	67.4	74.9
Ending stocks (metric tons)	28.1	30.2	32.9	35.1	37.1	38.6	44.8	40.6	52.2
Meals									
Production (metric tons)	166.2	183.8	194.6	168.5	174.9	182.6	185.1	189.4	205.0
Exports (metric tons)	61.5	69.6	71.6	47.2	48.8	52.8	53.7	58.5	59.9
Oils									
Production (metric tons)	73.4	82.1	87.7	86.4	90.1	92.9	96.0	101.7	110.2
Exports (metric tons)	27.3	30.5	32.4	29.0	30.9	33.2	36.3	38.6	41.7
Cotton									
Area (hectares)	32.2	33.8	32.9	32.3	32.0	33.7	30.4	32.2	35.8
Production (bales)	85.9	92.2	85.5	87.7	88.9	98.8	88.3	95.3	120.4
Exports (bales)	28.4	26.7	23.5	27.2	26.4	29.0	30.3	33.2	34.7
Consumption (bales)	84.4	87.3	84.8	91.1	92.2	94.3	94.8	98.1	108.6
Ending stocks (bales)	29.9	49.4	52.2	50.2	48.1	53.7	44.2	42.9	54.1
Beef and Pork									
Production (metric tons)	124.2	128.2	131.4	132.1	133.2	137.7	139.0	141.2	144.5
Consumption (metric tons)	123.2	126.8	131.1	131.2	132.2	136.7	137.8	140.0	141.7
Exports (metric tons) [2]	7.6	8.2	9.2	8.9	8.9	10.0	10.4	11.0	11.9
Broilers and Turkeys									
Production (metric tons)	43.6	49.5	52.3	55.3	57.1	59.0	59.0	60.7	63.2
Consumption (metric tons)	43.1	48.8	51.6	54.1	55.5	57.2	57.3	58.7	60.6
Exports (metric tons) [2]	5.0	4.7	4.9	5.4	6.1	6.3	6.5	6.6	7.6
Dairy									
Milk production (metric tons)	(NA)	373.7	376.7	381.6	384.8	392.5	396.6	403.9	413.7

NA Not available. [1] Forecast for crops, preliminary for meat & dairy. [2] Excludes intra-EU (European Union) trade but includes intra-FSU (Former Soviet Union) trade. [3] Where stocks data are not available, consumption includes stock changes. [4] Stocks data are based on differing marketing years and do not represent levels at a given date. Data not available for all countries.

Source: U.S. Dept. of Agriculture, Economic Research Service, "Agricultural Outlook: Statistical Indicators" (published February 2006); <http://www.ers.usda.gov/publications/agoutlook/aotables/>.

Table 1344. Fisheries—Commercial Catch by Country: 1990 to 2003

[In thousands of metric tons, live weight (97,852 represents 97,852,000). Catch of fish, crustaceans, mollusks (including weight of shells). Does not include marine mammals and aquatic plants]

Country	1990	2000	2002	2003	Country	1990	2000	2002	2003
World [1]	97,852	130,957	132,993	132,524	Norway	1,754	3,191	3,292	3,132
China [2]	31,136	41,568	44,320	45,648	Philippines	2,209	2,291	2,474	2,629
Peru	6,874	10,665	8,775	6,103	Vietnam	939	1,949	2,210	2,604
India	3,800	5,609	5,924	5,905	Korea, South	2,843	2,118	1,968	2,035
Indonesia	3,022	4,909	5,258	5,672	Bangladesh	846	1,661	1,890	1,998
United States	5,871	5,174	5,435	5,483	Iceland	1,508	1,986	2,133	1,984
Japan	10,361	5,751	5,191	5,456	Burma	743	1,169	1,434	1,606
Chile	5,195	4,692	4,817	4,185	Mexico	1,383	1,369	1,524	1,524
Thailand	2,790	3,736	3,464	3,590	Taiwan [2,3]	1,444	1,338	1,373	1,486
Russia	7,604	4,048	3,334	3,390	Malaysia	1,005	1,441	1,441	1,454
					Canada	1,685	1,125	1,234	1,230

[1] Includes other countries, not shown separately. [2] See footnote 2, Table 1308. [3] Taipei.

Source: U.S. National Oceanic and Atmospheric Administration, National Marine Fisheries Service, *Fisheries of the United States*, annual. Data from Food and Agriculture Organization of the United Nations, Rome, Italy.

Table 1345. Meat Production by Type and Country: 2003 to 2004

[In thousands of metric tons (49,992 represents 49,992,000). Carcass weight basis for beef, veal, and pork. Excludes offals and rabbit]

Country	Beef and veal		Country	Pork [1]		Country	Poultry meat	
	2003	2004, prel.		2003	2004, prel.		2003	2004, prel.
World [2]	49,992	51,248	World [2]	88,959	90,678	World [2]	54,067	55,846
United States	12,039	11,261	China [3]	45,186	47,016	United States	14,696	15,286
Brazil	7,385	7,975	European Union	21,150	20,851	China [3]	9,888	9,998
European Union	8,061	7,941	United States	9,056	9,312	Brazil	7,645	8,408
China [3]	6,305	6,759	Brazil	2,560	2,600	European Union	7,439	7,656
Argentina	2,800	3,130	Canada	1,882	1,936	Mexico	2,290	2,389
India	1,960	2,130	Russia	1,710	1,725	India	1,500	1,650
Australia	2,073	2,114	Japan	1,260	1,271	Japan	1,127	1,124
Mexico	1,950	2,099	Mexico	1,100	1,150	Canada	929	946
Russia	1,670	1,590	Philippines	1,145	1,145	Argentina	750	910
Canada	1,190	1,496	Korea, South	1,149	1,100	Thailand	1,340	900

[1] Includes edible pork fat, but excludes lard and inedible greases (except United States). [2] Includes other countries, not shown separately. [3] See footnote 2, Table 1308.

Source: U.S. Department of Agriculture, National Agricultural Statistics Service, *Agricultural Statistics*, annual.

Table 1346. Meat Consumption by Type and Country: 2004 to 2005

[In thousand metric tons (12,667 represents 12,667,000). Carcass weight basis for beef, veal, and pork. Broiler (chicken, 16-week-old) weight based on ready-to-cook equivalent]

Country	Beef and veal		Country	Pork		Country	Poultry meat	
	2004	2005 [1]		2004	2005 [1]		2004	2005 [1]
United States	12,667	12,666	China [2]	46,725	49,395	United States	13,080	13,455
European Union [3]	8,292	8,145	European Union [3]	19,773	19,839	China [2]	9,931	10,150
Brazil	6,400	6,774	United States	8,817	8,671	European Union [3]	7,280	7,370
China [2]	6,703	7,051	Russian	2,337	2,429	Brazil	5,992	6,622
Russia	2,308	2,200	Japan	2,562	2,512	Mexico	2,713	2,883
Mexico	2,368	2,419	Brazil	1,979	2,039	Japan	1,713	1,877
Argentina	2,512	2,446	Mexico	1,556	1,556	Russia	1,675	1,949
India [4]	1,631	1,610	South Korea	1,331	1,282	Canada	972	984
Japan	1,181	1,195	Philippines	1,170	1,130	Saudi Arabia	890	(NA)
Canada	1,054	1,052	Canada	1,072	978	Malaysia	881	(NA)
Australia	747	749	Taiwan	959	959	India	1,650	(NA)
Other Countries	3,954	3,966	Other Countries	2,548	2,464	Other Countries	7,367	7,746

NA Not available. [1] Preliminary data. [2] See footnote 2, Table 1308. [3] European Union-25: Austria, Belgium, Cyprus, Czech Republic, Denmark, Estonia, Finland, France, Germany, Greece, Hungary, Ireland, Italy, Latvia, Lithuania, Luxembourg, Malta, Netherlands, Poland, Portugal, Slovakia, Slovenia, Spain, Sweden, and United Kingdom. [4] Includes buffalo.

Source: U.S. Department of Agriculture, Foreign Agricultural Service, *Livestock and Poultry: World Markets and Trade*, annual. See also <http://www.fas.usda.gov/dlp/circular/2006/06-03LP/dlp06_03LP.pdf>.

Table 1347. World Crop Production Summary: 2004 to 2006

[In millions of metric tons, (628.77 represents 628,770,000), except as indicated]

Commodity	Unit	World [1]	North America			EU-25	Other Europe		Asia				South America		Selected Other		
			United States	Canada	Mexico		Russia	Ukraine	China	India	Indonesia	Pakistan	Argentina	Brazil	Australia	South Africa	Turkey
Wheat:																	
2004–2005 . . .	Mil. metric tons	628.77	58.74	25.86	2.42	136.77	45.40	17.50	91.95	72.06	(2)	19.50	16.00	5.85	22.60	1.68	18.50
2005–2006 prel. . .	Mil. metric tons	621.86	57.28	26.80	3.02	122.59	47.70	18.70	97.45	72.00	(2)	21.50	12.50	4.87	24.50	1.89	18.00
Coarse grains:																	
2004–2005 . . .	Mil. metric tons	1,014.62	319.42	26.45	28.95	150.75	29.60	23.00	138.25	34.15	7.20	1.98	24.90	37.87	11.57	12.21	11.05
2005–2006 prel. . .	Mil. metric tons	973.48	298.74	25.98	25.53	131.79	27.60	18.14	147.47	33.67	6.90	1.98	17.40	43.77	13.96	7.88	11.95
Rice (milled):																	
2004–2005 . . .	Mil. metric tons	400.49	7.46	(2)	0.20	1.86	0.31	0.05	125.36	83.13	34.83	4.92	0.68	9.00	0.23	(2)	0.30
2005–2006 prel. . .	Mil. metric tons	413.11	7.09	(2)	0.18	1.71	0.38	0.06	126.40	89.88	34.96	5.50	0.75	7.80	0.72	(2)	0.36
Total grains [3]:																	
2004–2005 . . .	Mil. metric tons	2,043.87	385.62	52.31	31.56	289.39	75.31	40.55	355.57	189.34	42.03	26.40	41.59	52.72	34.40	13.89	29.85
2005–2006 prel. . .	Mil. metric tons	2,008.45	363.10	52.78	28.73	256.09	75.68	36.90	371.32	195.55	41.86	28.98	30.65	56.45	39.17	9.77	30.31
Oilseeds [4]:																	
2004–2005 . . .	Mil. metric tons	381.17	95.94	10.83	0.44	21.06	5.63	3.56	57.97	28.64	1.99	5.53	43.43	55.65	2.57	1.02	2.11
2005–2006 prel. . .	Mil. metric tons	390.13	96.14	12.91	0.43	20.79	7.44	5.60	56.56	29.82	2.02	5.01	44.89	57.74	2.44	1.09	1.98
Cotton:																	
2004–2005 . . .	Mil. 480 lb. bales. . .	120.29	23.25	(2)	0.63	2.31	(2)	(2)	23.25	19.00	0.03	11.14	0.68	5.90	3.00	0.10	4.15
2005–2006 prel. . .	Mil. 480 lb. bales. . .	114.09	23.89	(2)	0.64	2.49	(2)	(2)	23.89	19.00	0.03	9.85	0.55	4.70	2.70	0.10	3.55

[1] Includes other countries not shown separately. [2] Indicates no reported or insignificant production. [3] Includes wheat, coarse grains, and rice (milled) shown above. [4] Includes soybean, cottonseed, peanut (in shell), sunflower seed, rapeseed and palm kernel. Copra and palm kernel are added to world totals.

Source: U.S. Department of Agriculture, Foreign Agricultural Service, *World Agricultural Production*, June 2006. See also <http://www.fas.usda.gov/wap/circular/2006/06-06/WldSum.pdf>.

Table 1348. **EU and U.S. Organic Land, Farm Sector, and Sales: 2001 and 2003**

[EU numbers for land and farms include those certified organic and in-conversion; U.S. numbers include only certified organic farms and land. U.S. retail sales dollars were converted to euros on an exchange rate of $1.29 = 1.00, May 2005. 1 hectare = 2.47 acres]

Country	Total organic land (hectares)	Organic farms (number)	2003 Farms under organic production (percent)	2003 Farmland under organic production (percent)	Retail sales (mil. Euros)	Per capita spending on organic food (Euros) [1]	Share of total food sales, 2001 (percent)
Austria	328,803	19,056	9.5	9.7	400	48.9	2.0
Belgium	24,000	688	1.1	1.7	300	(NA)	(NA)
Denmark.	165,146	3,510	6.1	6.1	339	113.6	([2])
Finland	159,987	5,074	6.3	7.2	212	(NA)	(NA)
France	550,000	11,377	1.7	1.9	1,578	21.2	1.0
Germany.	734,027	16,476	6.5	4.3	3,100	30.4	([3])
Greece	244,455	6,028	0.7	6.2	21	(NA)	(NA)
Ireland	28,514	899	0.6	0.7	([4])	(NA)	([5])
Italy	1,052,002	44,039	2.0	6.9	1,400	19.2	1.0
Luxembourg	3,002	59	2.0	2.4	(NA)	(NA)	(NA)
The Netherlands.	41,865	1,522	1.5	2.2	395	38.1	([6])
Portugal	120,729	1,507	0.4	3.2	(NA)	(NA)	(NA)
Spain	725,254	17,028	1.3	2.8	144	(NA)	(NA)
Sweden	225,776	3,562	4.4	7.4	420	45.0	1.0
United Kington	695,619	4,017	1.7	4.4	1,607	15.3	1.0
European Union [7]	5,099,179	134,434	2.0	3.9	9,966	(NA)	(NA)
United States [8].	889,734	8,035	0.2	0.2	8,019	35.7	1.4

NA Not available. [1] Per capita spending figures based on an exchange rate of $1.00 = 1.00. [2] 2.5–3.1 [3] 1.25–1.6 [4] 40–51 [5] less than 0.6. [6] 0.75–1.1 [7] For land data, all EU hectares are for certified organic and in-conversion land. Numbers for Sweden do not reflect the substantial hectares that are managed organically but not legally certified to market products as "organic.". In Sweden, these lands accounted for another 180,001 hectares and an estimated 12,500 farms in 2003. [8] For land data, the U.S. reports certified organic acreage, which has been converted to hectares (1 acre = 0.405 hectares).

Source: U.S. Department of Agriculture, Economic Research Service, Market-Led Versus Government-Facilitated Growth: Development of the U.S. and EU Organic Agricultural Sectors, August 2005.

Table 1349. **Wheat, Rice, and Corn—Exports and Imports of Leading Countries: 2000 to 2005**

[In thousands of metric tons (28,027 represents 28,027,000). Wheat data are for trade year beginning in July of year shown; rice data are for calendar year; corn data are for trade year beginning in October of year shown. Countries listed are the ten leading exporters or importers in 2005]

Leading exporters	Exports 2000	Exports 2004	Exports 2005	Leading importers	Imports 2000	Imports 2004	Imports 2005
WHEAT				**WHEAT**			
United States	28,027	28,464	27,500	EU-25 [1].	4,694	7,393	7,500
Canada.	17,351	15,142	16,500	Egypt	6,050	8,150	7,500
Australia	16,682	15,826	16,000	Brazil	7,453	5,309	6,000
EU-25 [1]	16,792	14,367	14,500	Japan	5,885	5,744	5,700
Russia	696	7,951	10,000	Algeria	5,600	5,398	5,500
Argentina	11,396	13,502	7,000	Indonesia.	4,069	4,661	4,600
Ukraine.	78	4,351	5,500	Korea	3,127	3,591	3,900
Kazakhstan	3,972	2,700	3,200	Nigeria	1,913	3,014	3,900
Turkey	1,601	2,217	2,000	Iraq	3,200	3,010	3,800
China	623	1,171	1,000	Mexico	3,066	3,717	3,600
RICE				**RICE**			
Thailand	7,521	7,274	7,000	Philippines	1,175	1,900	1,800
Vietnam	3,528	5,174	5,000	Nigeria	1,906	1,800	1,500
United States	2,541	3,950	3,700	Iraq	959	800	1,200
India.	1,936	4,500	3,500	Indonesia.	1,500	500	1,000
Pakistan	2,417	2,650	2,800	Saudi Arabia	1,053	1,250	1,000
Egypt	705	1,100	1,000	EU-25 [1].	1,189	1,050	975
Uruguay	806	762	700	Iran	765	950	950
China [2].	1,847	656	700	Senegal.	874	1,200	750
Australia	617	100	500	South Africa	572	850	750
Argentina	368	350	400	Bangladesh	401	800	500
CORN				**CORN**			
United States	48,329	45,223	47,500	Japan	16,340	16,485	16,500
Argentina	12,229	13,752	11,000	Korea	8,743	8,638	8,400
China [2].	7,276	7,589	6,000	Mexico	5,928	5,921	6,700
Ukraine.	397	2,334	2,300	Egypt	5,268	5,398	4,800
Brazil	3,741	1,431	1,500	Taiwan	4,924	4,500	4,600
South Africa.	1,415	1,517	1,500	EU-25 [1]	3,800	2,951	3,000
Serbia and Montenegro . . .	50	500	1,000	Malaysia	2,588	2,400	2,500
Romania	50	587	800	Colombia	1,857	2,256	2,400
EU-25 [1]	1,016	164	600	Iran	1,265	2,558	2,300
Paraguay	386	386	400	Algeria	1,265	2,046	1,900

[1] See footnote 2, Table 1346. [2] See footnote 2, Table 1308.

Source: U.S. Department of Agriculture, Economic Research Service, unpublished data from the PS&D (Production, supply, and distribution) database.

Comparative International Statistics   857

Table 1350. **Wood Products—Production, Exports, and Consumption for Selected Countries: 2000 to 2005**
[In thousand cubic meters (163,000 represents 163,000,000)]

Country	Production 2000	2004	2005	Exports 2000	2004	2005	Consumption 2000	2004	2005
SOFTWOOD LOGS									
Canada.................	163,000	187,000	183,000	2,595	3,514	3,300	164,926	187,286	183,600
United States	175,411	177,043	178,000	7,406	6,744	7,000	169,741	172,020	173,575
Russia	64,000	72,500	74,875	20,000	30,710	32,245	44,000	41,790	42,630
Sweden	30,200	34,500	35,000	1,397	1,300	1,500	31,800	35,200	35,700
Finland	29,000	25,700	26,000	700	370	370	15,186	20,350	20,350
Poland	15,300	21,000	21,000	524	850	850	36,288	35,642	37,425
China [1]	29,891	19,681	20,665	1	–	–	11,874	17,180	
Chile	12,033	16,200	17,500	159	295	320	11,488	14,417	15,102
Australia	12,475	15,750	16,500	988	1,335	1,400	8,607	9,985	9,700
New Zealand	15,500	17,080	15,395	6,897	7,100	5,700	15,905		
SOFTWOOD LUMBER									
Canada.................	68,557	81,383	79,000	48,607	55,340	53,000	20,719	26,613	26,550
United States	61,114	65,212	66,000	2,795	1,552	1,700	103,615	118,517	121,991
Sweden	14,839	17,200	17,600	11,188	11,200	11,600	3,832	6,150	6,150
Russia	14,000	15,800	17,160	4,500	12,075	13,285	9,500	3,725	3,875
Finland	11,750	13,900	14,200	8,000	8,300	8,600	3,750	5,850	5,850
Japan..................	16,403	13,800	14,000	2	6	6	25,208	21,794	22,194
Austria.................	9,960	10,625	10,625	6,070	7,000	7,000	5,000	5,125	5,125
TEMPERATE HARDWOOD LOGS									
United States	60,300	57,630	58,000	1,981	2,180	2,580	58,559	55,637	55,640
Canada.................	32,500	35,400	34,200	308	341	330	34,179	36,759	35,670
Russia	22,300	25,500	26,625	8,580	10,160	10,975	13,720	15,340	15,650
TEMPERATE HARDWOOD LUMBER									
United States	29,932	22,224	23,000	2,943	3,028	3,101	28,670	21,012	21,855
China [1]	2,217	7,850	9,420	332	274	300	4,400	8,971	10,655
Russia	4,700	4,890	5,040	320	343	360	4,380	4,547	4,680
TROPICAL HARDWOOD LOGS									
Brazil..................	27,850	31,790	33,380	236	60	40	27,986	32,110	33,790
Indonesia	25,500	25,000	25,000	–	–	–	25,500	25,000	25,000
Malaysia	23,074	21,793	22,700	6,804	5,118	5,220	16,852	16,743	17,550
TROPICAL HARDWOOD LUMBER									
Brazil..................	14,400	16,705	17,540	901	1,515	1,740	13,656	15,230	15,860
Indonesia	6,600	6,100	6,100	–	–	–	6,600	6,100	6,100
Malaysia	5,589	4,857	5,080	2,901	2,761	2,520	3,973	2,644	3,160

– Represents or rounds to zero. [1] See footnote 2, Table 1308.
Source: U.S. Dept. of Agriculture, Foreign Agricultural Service, Production, Supply & Distribution Online; <http://www.fas.usda.gov/psd/psdselection.asp> (accessed July 2006).

Table 1351. **World Production of Major Mineral Commodities: 1990 to 2004**
[5,348 represents 5,348,000,000]

Commodity	Unit	1990	2000	2003	2004	Leading producers, 2003
MINERAL FUELS						
Coal.................	Mil. short tons. .	5,348	4,935	5,648	6,079	China, United States, India
Dry natural gas	Tril. cu. ft.	73.6	88.3	95.4	98.6	Russia, United States, Canada
Natural gas plant liquids [1] . . .	Mil. barrels [2] . . .	4,640	6,608	7,325	7,631	United States, Saudi Arabia, Canada
Petroleum, crude	Mil. barrels [2] . . .	22,079	24,955	25,271	26,362	Saudi Arabia, Russian, United States
NONMETALLIC MINERALS						
Cement, hydraulic	Mil. metric tons .	1,160	1,600	2,020	2,000	China, India, United States
Diamond, gem and industrial .	Mil. carats	111	(NA)	145	152	Australia, Botswana, Russia
Nitrogen in ammonia.......	Mil. metric tons .	97.5	109.0	109.0	109.0	China, India, Russia
Phosphate rock	Mil. metric tons .	162	133	137	138	United States, China, Morocco and Western Sahara
Potash, marketable........	Mil. metric tons .	28.0	25.3	28.4	30.0	Canada, Russia, Belarus
Salt	Mil. metric tons .	183	214	210	215	United States, China, Germany
Sulfur, elemental basis	Mil. metric tons .	58.0	57.2	62.0	63.0	United States, Canada, Russia
METALS						
Aluminum [3]	Mil. metric tons .	19.3	24.0	27.7	29.8	China, Russia, Canada
Bauxite, gross weight	Mil. metric tons .	113	135	155	159	Australia, Brazil, Guinea
Chromite, gross weight [1]	1,000 metric tons.	13,200	14,400	15,500	17,500	South Africa, Kazakhstan, India
Copper, metal content [4]	1,000 metric tons.	8,950	13,200	13,600	15,000	Chile, United States, Indonesia
Gold, metal content [5]	Metric tons	2,180	2,550	2,550	2,430	South Africa, Australia, United States
Iron ore, gross weight [5]	Mil. metric tons .	983	1,060	1,190	1,340	China, Brazil, Australia
Lead, metal content [4]	1,000 metric tons.	3,370	3,100	2,950	3,150	Australia, China, United States
Nickel, metal content [4]	1,000 metric tons.	974	1,250	1,390	1,390	Russia, Australia, Canada
Tin, metal content [4]	1,000 metric tons.	223	238	207	264	Indonesia, China, Peru

NA Not available. [1] Excludes China. [2] 42-gallon barrels. [3] Unalloyed ingot metal. [4] Mine output. [5] Includes iron ore concentrates and iron ore agglomerates.
Source: Mineral fuels, U.S. Energy Information Administration, *International Energy Annual, 2004*; nonmetallic minerals and metals, 1990, U.S. Bureau of Mines, thereafter, U.S. Geological Survey, *Minerals Yearbook; Annual Reports;* and *Mineral Commodity Summaries, 2005.*

Table 1352. **World Primary Energy Production by Region and Type: 1980 to 2004**

[In quadrillion Btu (287.6 represents 287,600,000,000,000,000). Btu = British thermal unit. For Btu conversion factors, see source]

Region and type	1980	1985	1990	1995	1999	2000	2001	2002	2003	2004 [1]
World total [2]	**287.6**	**307.2**	**349.7**	**364.2**	**385.3**	**397.1**	**404.3**	**406.1**	**421.7**	**443.1**
North America	83.3	87.7	91.9	96.0	98.4	98.8	99.5	100.0	98.5	99.3
United States	67.3	67.8	70.8	71.1	71.7	71.3	71.9	70.9	70.1	70.4
Central and South America	12.1	13.7	16.7	21.1	24.5	26.0	26.0	25.3	25.7	27.2
Europe	40.2	47.6	46.9	49.1	51.0	50.8	51.4	51.2	50.7	50.6
Eurasia	56.5	65.3	72.1	52.2	53.2	55.7	57.7	59.5	63.2	66.7
Middle East	42.3	25.8	41.0	48.3	53.8	57.5	56.2	54.3	57.6	62.1
Africa	17.4	18.4	21.6	24.2	26.7	27.8	28.1	28.0	30.1	32.0
Asia and Oceania	35.9	48.7	59.4	73.3	77.7	80.5	85.5	87.9	95.9	105.2
Petroleum	133.1	121.2	136.2	141.9	150.3	156.4	155.6	153.6	159.0	166.3
Dry natural gas	54.7	64.2	75.9	80.2	87.9	91.3	93.7	96.7	98.9	102.2
Coal	71.2	82.2	90.9	88.9	90.4	91.4	96.9	97.1	104.6	113.3
Hydroelectric power	17.9	20.4	22.4	25.3	26.6	27.0	26.4	26.4	26.8	27.5
Nuclear electric power. . .	7.6	15.3	20.4	23.3	25.1	25.7	26.4	26.7	26.4	27.5
Geothermal, solar, wind, wood, and waste	0.5	0.8	1.7	2.2	2.8	3.0	3.1	3.4	3.7	3.9

[1] Preliminary.   [2] Includes geothermal, solar, and wood and waste energy produced in the United States and not used for generating electricity, not shown separately by type.

Source: U.S. Energy Information Administration, *International Energy Annual, 2004.* See also <http://www.eia.doe.gov/emeu/iea/contents.html>.

Table 1353. **World Primary Energy Consumption by Region and Type: 1980 to 2004**

[In quadrillion Btu (283.6 represents 283,600,000,000,000,000). Btu = British thermal unit. For Btu conversion factors, see source]

Region and type	1980	1985	1990	1995	1999	2000	2001	2002	2003	2004 [1]
World total [2]	**283.6**	**308.6**	**347.3**	**365.6**	**389.1**	**399.6**	**403.5**	**409.7**	**425.7**	**446.4**
North America	91.8	91.3	100.9	108.9	115.8	118.4	115.6	117.4	118.3	120.6
United States	78.3	76.6	84.7	91.2	96.8	99.0	96.5	98.0	98.3	100.4
Central and South America	11.5	12.4	14.5	17.6	20.3	20.9	21.2	21.2	21.7	22.5
Europe	71.7	73.1	76.2	76.6	80.2	81.3	82.5	82.2	84.0	85.6
Eurasia	46.7	55.7	60.9	42.4	39.8	40.6	41.0	41.7	43.4	45.2
Middle East	5.9	8.6	11.3	13.9	16.8	17.3	18.1	19.1	19.9	21.1
Africa	6.8	8.5	9.5	10.6	11.5	12.0	12.6	12.7	13.3	13.7
Asia and Oceania	49.2	59.1	74.1	95.6	104.7	109.1	112.6	115.5	125.0	137.6
Petroleum	131.0	123.1	136.2	142.4	153.4	155.4	156.8	158.1	161.5	167.5
Dry natural gas	54.0	63.6	75.2	81.0	88.2	91.4	92.8	96.1	99.6	103.4
Coal	70.2	82.4	89.4	89.1	90.9	94.9	96.1	97.0	105.6	114.5
Hydroelectric power	17.9	20.4	22.4	25.3	26.6	27.0	26.4	26.4	26.8	27.5
Nuclear electric power. . .	7.6	15.3	20.4	23.3	25.1	25.7	26.4	26.7	26.4	27.5
Geothermal, solar, wind, wood, and waste	0.5	0.8	1.7	2.2	2.8	3.0	3.1	3.4	3.7	3.9

[1] Preliminary.   [2] See footnote 2, Table 1352.

Source: U.S. Energy Information Administration, *International Energy Annual, 2004.* See also <http://www.eia.doe.gov/emeu/iea/contents.html>.

Table 1354. **World Energy Consumption by Region and Energy Source, 1990 to 2002, and Projections, 2010 to 2025**

[In quadrillion Btu (348.2 represents 348,200,000,000,000,000). Btu = British thermal units. For Btu conversion factors, see source. Energy totals include net imports of coal coke and electricity generated from biomass in the United States. Totals may not equal sum of components due to independent rounding. The electricity portion of the national consumption values consists of generation for domestic use plus an adjustment for electricity trade based on a fuel's share of total generation in the exporting country]

Region and energy source	1990	2000	2002	Projections			
				2010	2015	2020	2025
World, total	**348.2**	**398.9**	**411.5**	**503.5**	**553.5**	**598.1**	**644.6**
North America	100.9	118.7	117.7	134.2	143.6	152.9	162.1
United States	84.6	99.3	98.0	110.6	117.6	125.1	132.4
Western Europe	59.9	66.8	67.4	70.2	72.2	73.4	76.1
Industrialized Asia	22.7	27.5	28.4	30.4	31.5	32.5	33.6
Eastern Europe and former Soviet Union . . .	76.2	52.2	53.6	63.0	68.4	72.8	77.7
Developing Asia	51.5	80.5	88.4	133.6	155.8	176.3	196.7
Middle East	13.1	20.3	22.0	28.7	32.4	35.6	38.9
Africa	9.3	11.9	12.7	16.7	19.3	21.4	23.4
Central and South America	14.5	21.0	21.2	26.8	30.4	33.2	36.1
Oil	136.0	155.9	159.4	193.1	210.6	226.6	243.4
Natural gas	75.0	91.4	95.2	115.2	132.4	146.6	162.1
Coal	90.5	93.6	98.1	125.2	136.4	146.8	156.1
Nuclear	20.3	25.5	26.9	30.2	31.7	32.9	34.1
Other	26.4	32.8	32.1	39.8	42.4	45.2	48.9

Source: U.S. Energy Information Administration (EIA), *International Energy Outlook 2005.*. See also <http://www.eia.doe.gov/oiaf/ieo/pdf/ieoreftab_1.pdf>.

Comparative International Statistics   859

Table 1355. **Energy Consumption by Country: 2000 and 2004**

[**399.6 represents 399,600,000,000,000,000.** See text of this section for general comments about the data. For data qualifications for countries and Btu conversion factors, see source]

Country	Total (quad. Btu) 2000	Total 2004, prel.	Per capita (mil. Btu) 2000	Per capita 2004, prel.	Country	Total (quad. Btu) 2000	Total 2004, prel.	Per capita (mil. Btu) 2000	Per capita 2004, prel.
World total	399.6	446.4	65.7	70.1	Japan	22.4	22.6	177.2	177.7
United States	99.0	100.4	350.6	342.7	Korea, North	0.9	0.9	39.7	39.2
Algeria	1.2	1.2	40.7	38.6	Korea, South	7.9	9.0	167.3	185.5
Argentina	2.7	2.8	71.1	71.2	Kuwait	0.9	1.1	460.1	470.0
Australia	4.8	5.3	252.2	264.5	Libya	0.6	0.7	122.9	133.0
Austria	1.4	1.5	170.3	178.1	Malaysia	1.9	2.5	85.9	107.1
Bahrain	0.4	0.4	575.0	611.5	Mexico	6.3	6.6	63.3	63.0
Bangladesh	0.5	0.7	3.9	4.7	Morocco	0.4	0.4	14.8	13.8
Belarus	1.1	1.0	101.4	93.7	Netherlands	3.8	4.1	238.5	251.4
Belgium	2.7	2.8	262.4	269.0	New Zealand	0.9	0.9	226.4	221.4
Brazil	8.6	9.1	48.9	49.3	Nigeria	0.8	1.0	7.1	8.1
Bulgaria	0.9	0.8	111.1	112.6	Norway	2.0	1.9	435.2	424.2
Burma	0.2	0.2	3.7	4.4	Pakistan	1.9	2.0	12.7	12.5
Canada	13.0	13.6	417.2	418.4	Peru	0.5	0.6	20.3	20.9
Chile	1.0	1.2	66.9	74.6	Philippines	1.3	1.3	15.7	15.2
China [1]	38.8	59.6	30.6	45.9	Poland	3.6	3.7	93.9	95.1
Colombia	1.2	1.2	29.9	28.2	Portugal	1.1	1.1	103.6	105.5
Congo (Kinshasa) [2]	0.1	0.1	1.8	1.5	Romania	1.6	1.6	70.6	73.5
Cuba	0.5	0.5	41.0	41.5	Russia	27.5	30.1	187.1	208.8
Czech Republic	1.7	1.8	162.4	172.7	Saudi Arabia	4.8	6.1	209.2	236.5
Denmark	0.9	0.9	164.1	159.6	Serbia and Montenegro [3]	0.6	0.8	57.8	71.3
Ecuador	0.3	0.4	27.5	29.0	South Africa	4.6	5.1	103.3	115.2
Egypt	2.0	2.5	28.5	33.1	Spain	5.5	6.4	138.2	158.9
Finland	1.2	1.3	235.9	258.1	Sweden	2.2	2.3	246.5	257.9
France	10.9	11.2	183.0	186.1	Switzerland	1.3	1.3	177.2	172.0
Germany	14.3	14.7	173.5	178.3	Syria	0.8	0.8	48.5	45.7
Greece	1.3	1.4	126.7	135.8	Taiwan [1]	3.8	4.4	170.1	193.3
Hong Kong	0.8	1.1	120.8	159.1	Thailand	2.6	3.4	41.7	53.7
Hungary	1.0	1.1	101.3	106.1	Trinidad and Tobago	0.4	0.6	376.0	546.8
India	13.6	15.4	13.5	14.5	Tunisia	0.3	0.3	31.4	33.4
Indonesia	4.1	4.7	18.2	19.7	Turkey	3.2	3.5	48.1	51.3
Iran	5.0	6.4	76.2	95.5	Ukraine	5.8	6.5	117.4	137.1
Iraq	1.1	1.2	47.7	47.5	United Arab Emirates	1.8	2.3	757.9	925.4
Ireland	0.6	0.6	157.4	160.6	United Kingdom	9.7	10.0	162.6	166.5
Israel	0.8	0.9	144.5	140.8	Venezuela	2.8	2.9	117.5	115.3
Italy	7.6	8.3	132.2	142.3	Vietnam	0.7	0.9	9.5	11.5

[1] See footnote 2, Table 1308. [2] See footnote 3, Table 1308. [3] As of June 2006, Serbia and Montenegro are separate countries (formerly Yugoslavia).

Source: U.S. Energy Information Administration, *International Energy Annual*. See also <http://www.eia.doe.gov/emeu/iea/contents.html>.

Table 1356. **World Daily Crude Oil Production by Major Producing Country: 1980 to 2004**

[**In thousands of barrels per day (59,558 barrels represents 59,558,000 barrels)**. In prior editions, this table was located in Section 18]

Country	1980	1990	1995	1999	2000	2001	2002	2003	2004
World, total [1]	59,558	60,492	62,333	65,848	68,369	67,984	66,967	69,235	72,224
Saudi Arabia	9,900	6,410	8,231	7,833	8,404	8,031	7,634	8,775	9,101
Russia	(X)	(X)	5,995	6,079	6,479	6,917	7,408	8,132	8,805
United States	8,597	7,355	6,560	5,881	5,822	5,801	5,746	5,681	5,419
Iran [2]	1,662	3,088	3,643	3,557	3,696	3,724	3,444	3,743	4,001
China [2]	2,114	2,774	2,990	3,195	3,249	3,300	3,390	3,409	3,485
Mexico	1,936	2,553	2,618	2,906	3,012	3,127	3,177	3,371	3,383
Norway	486	1,630	2,766	3,019	3,222	3,226	3,131	3,042	2,954
Venezuela	2,168	2,137	2,750	2,826	3,155	3,010	2,604	2,335	2,557
United Arab Emirates	1,709	2,117	2,233	2,169	2,368	2,205	2,082	2,348	2,478
Canada	1,435	1,553	1,805	1,907	1,977	2,029	2,171	2,306	2,398
Kuwait	1,656	1,175	2,057	1,898	2,079	1,998	1,894	2,136	2,376
Nigeria	2,055	1,810	1,993	2,130	2,165	2,256	2,118	2,275	2,329
Iraq	2,514	2,040	560	2,508	2,571	2,390	2,023	1,308	2,011
United Kingdom	1,622	1,820	2,489	2,684	2,275	2,282	2,292	2,093	1,845
Algeria	1,106	1,175	1,202	1,202	1,254	1,310	1,306	1,611	1,677
Libya	1,787	1,375	1,390	1,319	1,410	1,367	1,319	1,421	1,515
Brazil	182	631	695	1,132	1,269	1,295	1,455	1,496	1,477
Indonesia	1,577	1,462	1,503	1,472	1,428	1,340	1,249	1,155	1,096
Angola	150	475	646	745	746	742	896	903	1,052
Kazakhstan	(X)	(X)	362	530	610	721	818	893	1,014
Qatar	472	406	442	665	737	714	679	715	783
Malaysia	283	619	682	693	690	659	698	738	755
Oman	282	685	851	910	970	913	897	819	751
Argentina	491	483	715	802	761	802	799	783	733
India	182	660	703	653	646	642	665	660	683
Egypt	595	873	920	852	748	698	631	618	594
Colombia	126	440	585	816	691	625	577	541	529
Ecuador	204	285	392	373	395	412	393	411	528
Australia	380	575	562	539	722	657	626	512	436
Yemen	–	193	345	409	440	438	443	448	424

X Not applicable. – Represents zero. [1] Includes countries not shown separately. [2] See footnote 2, Table 1308.

Source: U.S. Energy Information Administration, *International Energy Annual, 2004*. See also <http://www.eia.doe.gov/pub/international/iealf/table22.xls> (issued June 2006).

Table 1357. **World Dry Natural Gas Production by Major Producing Country: 1980 to 2004**

[In trillion cubic feet (53.35 represents 53,350,000,000,000). In prior editions, this table was located in Section 18]

Country	1980	1990	1995	1999	2000	2001	2002	2003	2004
World Total [1]	53.35	73.57	77.96	84.96	88.30	90.45	92.21	95.39	98.62
Russia	(X)	(X)	21.01	20.83	20.63	20.51	21.03	21.77	22.39
United States	19.40	17.81	18.60	18.83	19.18	19.62	18.93	19.10	18.76
Canada	2.76	3.85	5.60	6.27	6.47	6.60	6.63	6.45	6.48
United Kingdom	1.32	1.75	2.67	3.49	3.83	3.69	3.66	3.63	3.39
Netherlands	3.40	2.69	2.98	2.65	2.56	2.75	2.68	2.57	3.04
Iran	0.25	0.84	1.25	2.04	2.13	2.33	2.65	2.86	2.96
Norway	0.92	0.98	1.08	1.76	1.87	1.95	2.41	2.70	2.95
Algeria	0.41	1.79	2.05	2.88	2.94	2.79	2.80	2.85	2.83
Indonesia	0.63	1.53	2.24	2.51	2.36	2.34	2.48	2.61	2.66
Saudi Arabia	0.33	1.08	1.34	1.63	1.76	1.90	2.00	2.12	2.32
Malaysia	0.06	0.65	1.02	1.42	1.50	1.66	1.71	2.01	2.20
Uzbekistan	(X)	(X)	1.70	1.96	1.99	2.23	2.04	2.03	2.11
Turkmenistan	(X)	(X)	1.14	0.79	1.64	1.70	1.89	2.09	2.07
United Arab Emirates	0.20	0.78	1.11	1.34	1.36	1.39	1.53	1.58	1.63
Argentina	0.28	0.63	0.88	1.22	1.32	1.31	1.28	1.45	1.58
Mexico	0.90	0.90	0.96	1.29	1.31	1.30	1.33	1.40	1.46
China [2]	0.51	0.51	0.60	0.89	0.96	1.07	1.15	1.21	1.44
Qatar	0.18	0.28	0.48	0.78	1.03	0.95	1.04	1.11	1.38
Australia	0.31	0.72	1.03	1.12	1.16	1.19	1.23	1.27	1.31
Egypt	0.03	0.29	0.44	0.52	0.65	0.87	0.88	1.06	1.15
India	0.05	0.40	0.63	0.75	0.79	0.85	0.93	0.96	1.00
Trinidad and Tobago	0.08	0.18	0.27	0.41	0.49	0.54	0.61	0.87	0.99
Pakistan	0.29	0.48	0.65	0.78	0.86	0.77	0.81	0.89	0.97
Venezuela	0.52	0.76	0.89	0.95	0.96	1.12	1.00	0.86	0.96
Thailand	–	0.21	0.37	0.63	0.66	0.66	0.71	0.77	0.79
Nigeria	0.04	0.13	0.18	0.25	0.44	0.53	0.50	0.72	0.77
Germany	(X)	(X)	0.74	0.82	0.78	0.79	0.79	0.78	0.73
Kazakhstan	(X)	(X)	0.17	0.16	0.31	0.36	0.46	0.49	0.72
Ukraine	(X)	(X)	0.62	0.63	0.64	0.64	0.65	0.69	0.68
Oman	0.03	0.10	0.15	0.20	0.32	0.49	0.53	0.56	0.61

– Represents or rounds to zero.   X Not applicable.   [1] Includes countries not shown separately.   [2] See footnote 2, Table 1308.

Source: U. S. Energy Information Administration, *International Energy Annual.* See also <http://www.eia.doe.gov/pub/international /iealf/table24.xls>.

Table 1358. **World Coal Production by Major Producing Country: 1980 to 2004**

[In millions of short tons (4,181.8 represents 4,181,800,000). In prior editions, this table was located in Section 18]

Country	1980	1990	1995	1999	2000	2001	2002	2003	2004
World, total	4,181.8	5,347.5	5,095.8	4,941.2	4,935.0	5,232.9	5,265.3	5,648.3	6,078.6
China [1]	683.6	1,190.4	1,537.0	1,364.9	1,314.4	1,458.7	1,521.2	1,837.6	2,156.4
United States	829.7	1,029.1	1,033.0	1,100.4	1,073.6	1,127.7	1,094.3	1,071.8	1,112.1
India	125.8	247.6	320.6	356.3	370.0	388.7	404.9	428.9	443.7
Australia	116.1	225.8	266.5	320.8	338.2	362.9	376.8	377.3	391.0
Russia	(X)	(X)	270.9	259.2	264.9	273.4	261.9	283.3	308.9
South Africa	131.9	193.2	227.3	243.0	248.9	250.8	245.8	263.8	267.7
Germany	(X)	(X)	274.2	226.1	226.0	227.1	232.6	229.1	232.7
Poland	253.5	237.1	221.2	188.6	179.5	180.3	178.5	180.6	177.7
Indonesia	0.6	11.6	45.4	81.3	84.4	102.0	113.9	127.1	142.3
Kazakhstan	(X)	(X)	93.1	65.9	81.5	93.0	89.2	98.1	95.7
Greece	25.6	57.2	63.6	68.4	70.4	73.1	77.7	75.3	79.5
Canada	40.4	75.3	82.7	79.9	76.2	77.6	73.3	68.5	72.7
Ukraine	(X)	(X)	94.6	69.6	69.1	68.0	68.3	70.8	69.3
Czech Republic	(X)	(X)	82.6	65.2	71.8	72.9	69.8	70.4	68.1
Colombia	4.5	22.6	28.4	36.1	42.0	47.9	43.6	55.1	59.2
Turkey	20.2	52.3	60.6	73.9	69.6	68.3	59.4	53.1	51.1
Serbia and Montenegro [2].	(X)	(X)	44.7	36.5	40.8	40.0	42.3	44.4	44.9
Romania	38.8	42.1	45.3	25.2	32.3	36.7	33.5	36.4	34.8
Korea, North	48.6	51.0	34.5	30.6	32.8	33.7	31.9	32.5	33.8
Bulgaria	33.3	34.9	30.6	27.9	29.1	29.4	28.7	30.1	29.1
United Kingdom	143.8	104.1	52.5	39.9	33.7	34.7	32.6	30.6	27.0
Spain	31.2	39.6	31.4	26.8	25.9	25.0	24.3	22.7	22.6
Thailand	1.6	13.7	20.3	20.1	19.6	21.6	21.6	20.8	22.1
Vietnam	5.8	5.1	9.2	10.6	12.8	14.3	17.5	18.4	18.1
Estonia	(X)	(X)	13.7	11.8	12.9	13.0	13.7	16.4	15.4
Mexico	4.0	8.6	10.3	11.4	12.5	12.5	12.1	10.6	12.5
Hungary	28.3	19.7	16.1	16.0	15.5	15.3	14.4	14.7	12.4
Venezuela	0.0	2.4	4.5	7.7	8.7	8.4	8.1	7.3	9.0
Mongolia	5.3	7.9	5.5	6.6	6.4	6.6	7.1	7.2	7.2
Macedonia	(X)	(X)	8.0	8.1	8.3	8.9	8.4	8.1	6.8

X Not applicable.   [1] See footnote 2, Table 1308.   [2] As of June 2006, Serbia and Montenegro are separate countries (formerly Yugoslavia).

Source: U.S. Energy Information Administration, *International Energy Annual, 2004.* See also <http://www.eia.doe.gov/pub/international /iealf/table25.xls> (issued July 2006).

Table 1359. Net Electricity Generation by Type and Country: 2003

[15,883.5 represents 15,883,500,000,000. kWh = kilowatt hours]

Country	Total [1] (bil. kWh)	Thermal [2]	Hydro	Nuclear	Country	Total [1] (bil. kWh)	Thermal [2]	Hydro	Nuclear
World, total [3]	15,883.5	65.7	16.5	15.9	Norway	105.6	0.4	98.9	–
United States	3,891.7	70.9	7.1	19.6	Netherlands	91.1	90.0	0.1	4.2
China [4]	1,806.8	82.1	15.4	2.3	Venezuela	89.4	32.8	67.2	–
Japan	982.8	65.1	9.5	23.2	Argentina	88.2	52.8	38.0	8.0
Russia	869.1	65.6	18.0	16.2	Egypt	87.1	85.0	14.7	–
India	598.8	83.9	12.5	2.7	Finland	80.0	48.9	11.9	27.0
Canada	569.4	27.1	58.7	12.5	Belgium	79.1	40.7	0.3	56.9
Germany	561.6	63.2	3.4	27.9	Czech Republic	78.2	66.2	1.8	31.4
France	535.5	9.8	10.9	78.3	Pakistan	77.5	63.2	34.4	2.3
United Kingdom	373.3	74.5	0.9	22.6	Malaysia	74.0	92.3	7.7	–
Brazil	358.6	7.4	84.4	3.7	Switzerland	63.1	1.5	54.6	41.4
Korea, South	325.7	60.1	1.5	37.8	Kazakhstan	60.4	85.9	14.1	–
Italy	268.2	83.2	12.5	–	Austria	59.3	35.5	60.7	–
Spain	245.2	53.4	16.6	24.0	Greece	54.7	89.2	8.6	–
South Africa	215.9	93.7	0.4	5.9	Romania	52.4	66.3	25.0	8.7
Australia	215.0	91.7	7.4	–	Paraguay	51.3	(Z)	100.0	–
Mexico	206.7	81.6	9.5	4.8	Chile	47.0	49.0	47.6	–
Ukraine	170.0	49.5	5.4	45.1	Uzbekistan	46.8	86.6	13.4	–
Taiwan	166.0	73.4	4.1	22.5	United Arab Emirates	46.6	100.0	–	–
Saudi Arabia	143.8	100.0	–	–	Colombia	46.1	21.1	77.7	–
Iran	142.9	92.3	7.7	–	Portugal	44.5	60.0	34.9	–
Poland	141.1	98.2	1.2	–	Israel	44.2	99.9	0.1	–
Turkey	133.9	73.7	26.1	–	Denmark	43.6	80.8	(Z)	–
Sweden	130.8	6.2	40.3	49.0	Bulgaria	39.9	51.8	8.0	40.2
Thailand	110.4	91.2	6.5	–					
Indonesia	106.6	86.0	8.4	–					

– Represents zero. Z Less than 0.05 percent. [1] Geothermal, solar, wind, and wood and waste generation. [2] Electricity generated from coal, oil, and gas. [3] Includes countries not shown separately. [4] See footnote 2, Table 1308.

Source: U.S. Energy Information Administration, *International Energy Annual 2004*. See also <http://www.eia.doe.gov /pub/international/iea2004/table63.xls>.

Table 1360. Commercial Nuclear Power Generation by Country: 1990 to 2005

[Generation for calendar years; other data as of December (1,743.9 represents 1,743,900,000,000). kWh = kilowatt hours. kW = kilowatts]

Country	Reactors				Gross electricity generated (bil. kWh)				Gross capacity (1,000 kW)			
	1990	2003	2004	2005	1990	2003	2004	2005	1990	2003	2004	2005
Total	368	436	436	446	1,743.9	2,599.3	2,707.1	2690.3	301,745	381,185	382,875	391,366
United States	112	104	104	104	606.4	797.0	828.2	815.7	105,998	104,425	104,015	104,235
Argentina	2	2	2	2	7.0	1.9	7.9	6.9	1,005	1,005	1,005	1,005
Armenia	(NA)	1	1	1	(NA)	1.9	2.4	2.7	(NA)	408	408	408
Belgium	7	7	7	7	42.7	47.4	47.3	47.6	5,740	6,050	6,101	6,101
Brazil	1	2	2	2	2.0	13.3	11.5	9.8	657	2,007	2,007	2,007
Bulgaria	(NA)	4	4	4	(NA)	17	16.8	18.7	(NA)	2,880	2,880	2,880
Canada	19	21	21	21	74.0	75.7	90.9	92.5	13,855	15,396	15,426	15,341
China [1]	(NA)	2	2	9	(NA)	15.0	13.9	53.1	(NA)	1,968	1,968	7,014
Czech Republic	(NA)	6	6	6	(NA)	24.4	26.2	24.7	(NA)	3,722	3,760	3,760
Finland	4	4	4	4	18.9	22.7	22.7	23.3	2,400	2,760	2,760	2,760
France	58	59	59	59	314.1	441.1	448.2	451.5	58,862	66,042	66,042	66,042
Germany	22	19	18	18	147.2	165.1	167.1	163	23,973	22,365	21,693	21,723
Great Britain	42	25	24	23	68.8	90.6	77.2	(NA)	15,274	14,240	14,000	13,760
Hungary	4	4	4	4	13.6	11.0	11.9	13.8	1,760	1,866	1,866	1,866
India	6	14	14	15	6.0	18.3	16.9	17.6	1,330	2,720	2,770	3,310
Italy	2	(NA)	(NA)	(NA)	–	(NA)	(NA)	(NA)	1,132	(NA)	(NA)	(NA)
Japan	40	53	52	54	191.9	227.1	281.9	287.9	31,645	45,907	45,742	48,222
Korea, South	9	18	19	20	52.8	129.6	129.6	145.6	7,616	15,768	16,768	17,768
Lithuania	(NA)	2	2	1	(NA)	15.5	14.1	10.9	(NA)	3,000	3,000	1,500
Mexico	1	2	2	2	2.1	10.5	9.2	10.8	675	1,350	1,350	1,350
Netherlands	2	1	1	1	3.4	4.0	3.8	3.9	540	480	480	480
Pakistan	1	2	2	2	0.4	1.9	2.1	2.6	137	462	462	462
Romania	(NA)	1	1	1	(NA)	4.9	5.5	5.5	(NA)	706	706	706
Russia	(NA)	30	30	31	(NA)	148.6	142.9	146.8	(NA)	22,266	22,266	23,266
Slovakia	(NA)	6	6	6	(NA)	17.9	17.0	17.7	(NA)	2,640	2,640	2,640
Slovenia	1	1	1	1	4.6	5.2	4.0	5.9	664	707	707	707
South Africa	2	2	2	2	8.9	13.2	14.9	12.8	1,930	1,930	1,930	1,930
Spain	10	9	9	9	54.3	61.9	63.7	57.5	7,984	7,895	7,895	7,895
Sweden	12	11	11	11	68.2	68.4	77.3	72.5	10,344	9,844	9,852	9,852
Switzerland	5	5	5	5	23.6	27.3	26.8	23.2	3,079	3,352	3,352	3,352
Taiwan [1]	6	6	6	6	32.9	38.9	39.5	39.9	5,146	5,144	5,144	5,144
Ukraine	(NA)	13	15	15	(NA)	81.4	85.4	88.8	(NA)	11,880	13,880	13,880

– Represents zero. NA Not available. [1] See footnote 2, Table 1308.

Source: McGraw-Hill, Inc., New York, NY, *Nucleonics Week*, March issues (copyright).

U.S. Census Bureau, Statistical Abstract of the United States: 2007

Table 1361. **Selected Indexes of Manufacturing Activity by Country: 1990 to 2004**

[1992 = 100. Data relate to employees (wage and salary earners) in Belgium, and to all employed persons (employees, self-employed workers, and unpaid family workers) in the other countries. Minus sign (–) indicates decrease. For explanation of average annual percent change, see Guide to Tabular Presentation]

Index	United States	Can- ada	Japan	Bel- gium	France	Ger- many	Italy	Nether- lands	Nor- way	Swe- den	United King- dom
Output per hour:											
1990.	93.5	93.4	94.4	96.8	92.7	(NA)	96.6	98.7	98.1	94.6	90.1
1995.	112.1	112.4	111.0	113.2	116.0	110.2	107.9	117.3	100.7	125.1	106.2
2000.	147.7	131.4	135.9	129.3	148.7	132.0	113.5	132.7	106.6	176.8	120.8
2002.	165.1	134.1	139.2	136.9	158.4	137.0	112.2	136.5	112.8	190.7	127.6
2003.	176.8	137.2	154.5	141.0	158.8	142.4	111.2	138.0	122.6	204.5	132.8
2004.	186.0	141.2	165.1	145.5	164.4	149.0	110.6	145.4	125.4	224.6	140.3
Average annual percent change:											
1995–2000.	5.7	3.2	4.1	2.7	5.1	3.7	1.0	2.5	1.1	7.2	2.6
2002–2003.	7.1	2.3	11.0	2.9	0.3	3.9	–0.9	1.1	8.6	7.2	4.1
2003–2004.	5.2	2.9	6.9	3.2	3.5	4.7	–0.6	5.3	2.3	9.8	5.6
Compensation per hour, national currency basis: [1]											
1990.	90.5	88.5	90.6	90.1	91.0	(NA)	87.6	89.8	92.3	87.8	83.7
1995.	107.3	106.5	108.3	109.2	110.6	117.0	111.3	112.1	109.2	106.8	108.8
2000.	134.7	120.5	113.7	120.9	123.3	136.3	127.8	132.0	140.5	136.8	137.0
2002.	147.9	128.8	114.7	132.8	134.0	144.1	135.8	146.2	156.7	151.7	151.1
2003.	160.1	133.2	115.5	136.7	139.3	147.2	140.1	151.1	163.3	159.2	157.4
2004.	163.6	133.1	116.1	138.9	142.7	148.0	143.8	156.9	167.6	162.6	163.7
Average annual percent change:											
1995–2000.	4.7	2.5	1.0	2.1	2.2	3.1	2.8	3.3	5.2	5.1	4.7
2002–2003.	8.3	3.4	0.7	2.9	4.0	2.2	3.2	3.4	4.3	5.0	4.2
2003–2004.	2.2	–0.1	0.5	1.6	2.5	0.5	2.6	3.8	2.6	2.1	4.0
Real hourly compensation: [2]											
1990.	96.1	94.9	95.1	95.2	96.4	(NA)	98.0	95.6	97.7	97.6	91.9
1995.	100.1	102.1	106.3	102.2	104.8	107.3	97.4	104.2	102.7	97.9	101.1
2000.	112.0	105.8	109.9	104.3	109.9	117.4	99.1	110.2	118.0	120.1	111.4
2002.	117.7	107.9	112.7	110.0	115.3	120.0	100.0	113.4	126.1	127.0	118.8
2003.	124.6	108.5	113.8	111.4	117.4	121.3	100.4	114.8	128.3	130.5	120.2
2004.	124.0	106.4	114.4	110.9	117.8	120.0	100.9	117.8	131.1	133.0	121.4
Average annual percent change:											
1995–2000.	2.3	0.7	0.7	0.4	1.0	1.8	0.4	1.1	2.8	4.2	2.0
2002–2003.	5.9	0.5	1.0	1.3	1.9	1.1	0.5	1.3	1.7	2.8	1.2
2003–2004.	–0.5	–2.0	0.5	–0.5	0.4	–1.1	0.4	2.6	2.2	1.9	1.0
Unit labor costs, national currency: [1]											
1990.	96.8	94.8	95.9	93.0	98.2	(NA)	90.7	91.1	94.1	92.9	92.9
1995.	95.7	94.7	97.5	96.4	95.3	106.2	103.2	95.6	108.4	85.3	102.5
2000.	91.2	91.7	83.6	93.5	83.0	103.3	112.6	99.5	131.9	77.4	113.4
2002.	89.6	96.1	82.4	97.0	84.6	105.1	121.1	107.1	138.8	79.5	118.4
2003.	90.5	97.1	74.8	97.0	87.7	103.4	126.0	109.5	133.3	77.9	118.5
2004.	87.9	94.2	70.3	95.4	86.8	99.3	130.1	108.0	133.7	72.4	116.7
Average annual percent change:											
1995–2000.	–0.9	–0.6	–3.0	–0.6	–2.7	–0.5	1.8	0.8	4.0	–1.9	2.0
2002–2003.	1.1	1.0	–9.3	–0.1	3.7	–1.7	4.2	2.3	–4.0	–2.1	0.1
2003–2004.	–2.9	–3.0	–6.0	–1.6	–1.0	–4.0	3.2	–1.4	0.3	–7.0	–1.6
Unit labor costs, U.S. dollar basis: [1, 3]											
1990.	96.8	98.1	83.9	89.5	95.4	(NA)	93.3	87.9	93.5	91.3	93.9
1995.	95.7	83.4	131.6	105.2	101.2	115.8	78.0	104.8	106.4	69.6	91.6
2000.	91.2	74.6	98.4	68.8	61.8	76.2	66.2	73.3	93.0	49.1	97.3
2002.	89.6	74.0	83.5	73.1	64.5	79.4	72.8	80.8	108.1	47.6	100.7
2003.	90.5	83.8	81.7	87.5	80.1	93.5	90.8	98.9	117.0	56.2	109.7
2004.	87.9	87.5	82.4	94.6	87.1	98.6	103.0	107.2	123.3	57.4	121.1
Average annual percent change:											
1995–2000.	–0.9	–2.2	–5.7	–8.1	–9.4	–8.0	–3.2	–6.9	–2.7	–6.7	1.2
2002–2003.	1.1	13.3	–2.1	19.7	24.2	17.8	24.6	22.4	8.2	17.9	8.9
2003–2004.	–2.9	4.4	0.8	8.1	8.8	5.5	13.4	8.3	5.4	2.2	10.4
Employment:											
1990.	105.4	113.2	97.5	102.5	105.2	(NA)	103.7	100.0	105.2	117.2	115.0
1995.	102.8	104.8	90.1	91.9	92.6	86.1	95.8	92.1	107.0	98.0	100.9
2000.	102.5	118.2	81.7	89.1	91.0	82.7	96.1	93.1	107.5	98.1	94.3
2002.	90.6	114.9	75.8	86.6	89.6	81.2	96.9	90.4	102.7	96.4	85.8
2003.	86.3	113.3	74.2	84.1	89.1	79.1	97.1	87.5	98.0	93.9	81.6
2004.	85.3	112.2	72.4	82.1	86.9	77.9	96.8	84.0	95.2	92.2	78.6
Average annual percent change:											
1995–2000.	–0.1	2.4	–1.9	–0.6	–0.3	–0.8	0.1	0.2	0.1	–	–1.3
2002–2003.	–4.8	–1.4	–2.2	–2.9	–0.6	–2.6	0.2	–3.2	–4.6	–2.6	–4.8
2003–2004.	–1.2	–1.0	–2.4	–2.4	–2.4	–1.5	–0.3	–4.0	–2.9	–1.9	–3.7
Aggregate hours:											
1990.	105.0	113.5	102.9	104.3	105.5	(NA)	102.9	100.3	103.4	116.4	117.0
1995.	104.6	106.4	89.1	92.0	91.6	85.3	99.4	92.3	106.6	105.9	101.5
2000.	103.4	121.3	80.3	91.4	86.6	79.4	100.1	92.5	105.9	107.3	95.1
2002.	89.8	116.2	73.9	87.0	82.0	76.4	99.6	89.4	99.4	103.0	86.1
2003.	85.4	114.1	72.9	83.8	81.3	74.3	99.1	86.9	94.3	99.6	82.8
2004.	85.0	115.0	72.0	83.0	79.4	74.2	99.6	83.5	94.0	99.6	79.9
Average annual percent change:											
1995–2000.	–0.2	2.6	–2.0	–0.1	–1.1	–1.4	0.1	–	–0.1	0.3	–1.3
2002–2003.	–4.9	–1.9	–1.3	–3.7	–0.8	–2.8	–0.5	–2.7	–5.1	–3.3	–3.8
2003–2004.	–0.4	0.8	–1.3	–0.9	–2.4	–0.1	0.5	–3.9	–0.3	–	–3.5

– Represents or rounds to zero.   NA Not available.   [1] In Canada, France, Sweden, and the United Kingdom, compensation adjusted for employment taxes and government subsidies to estimate the actual labor cost to employers.   [2] Index of hourly compensation divided by the index of consumer prices to adjust for changes in purchasing power.   [3] Indexes in national currency adjusted for changes in prevailing exchange rates.

Source: U.S. Bureau of Labor Statistics, *International Comparisons of Manufacturing Productivity and Unit Labor Cost Trends*, revised data for 2004, February 15, 2006. See also <http://www.bls.gov/news.release/pdf/prod4.pdf>.

Comparative International Statistics   863

Table 1362. Indexes of Hourly Compensation Costs for Production Workers in Manufacturing by Country: 1990 to 2004

[United States = 100. Compensation costs include pay for time worked, other direct pay (including holiday and vacation pay, bonuses, other direct payments, and the cost of pay in kind), employer expenditures for legally required insurance programs and contractual and private benefit plans, and for some countries, other labor taxes. Data adjusted for exchange rates. Area averages are trade-weighted to account for difference in countries' relative importance to U.S. trade in manufactured goods. The trade weights used to compute the average compensation cost measures for selected economic groups are based on the relative dollar value of U.S. trade in manufactured commodities (exports plus imports) with each country or area in 2004; see source for detail]

Area or country	1990	1995	2000	2002	2003	2004	Area or country	1990	1995	2000	2002	2003	2004
United States	100	100	100	100	100	100	Austria	121	147	97	97	114	122
Total [1,2]	80	87	70	65	73	78	Belgium.	120	149	102	102	119	129
OECD [2,3,4]	86	93	75	70	79	84	Czech Republic	(X)	15	14	18	21	23
Europe [4]	115	125	92	93	108	117	Denmark	124	147	111	113	135	146
Asian newly industrial-							Finland	143	141	99	102	122	132
izing economies [5] . . .	25	38	36	33	34	36	France [8]	104	112	78	80	95	103
Brazil	(NA)	(NA)	18	12	12	13	Germany [8]	(X)	175	115	113	133	140
Canada	110	96	84	78	87	92	Greece	46	53	(NA)	(NA)	(NA)	(NA)
Mexico	11	9	11	12	11	11	Hungary	(NA)	16	14	18	22	25
Australia	88	89	73	72	89	100	Ireland	79	80	65	71	86	95
Hong Kong [6]	22	28	28	26	25	24	Italy	116	91	70	69	81	88
Israel	52	55	58	52	52	53	Luxembourg	108	136	89	87	104	115
Japan	84	137	112	87	91	95	Netherlands	121	140	98	103	123	133
Korea, South	25	42	42	41	45	50	Norway	147	144	115	128	142	150
New Zealand	54	57	40	40	50	56	Portugal	24	30	23	24	28	30
Singapore	25	44	37	31	32	32	Spain	76	74	54	56	67	74
Sri Lanka.	2	3	2	2	2	(NA)	Sweden	140	126	102	95	113	123
Taiwan [7]	26	34	31	26	26	26	Switzerland	139	168	107	111	125	131
							United Kingdom	85	80	85	85	95	107

NA Not available.   X Not applicable.   [1] For 1990, the trade-weighted measure includes all 31 foreign economies except for Brazil, the Czech Republic, and Hungary. For 1995, it includes all but Brazil. For 2000 onward, the measure includes all 31 foreign economies.   [2] Data pertain to the former West Germany only in the trade-weighted measures.   [3] Organization for Economic Cooperation and Development; see text of this section.   [4] Data for the Czech Republic and Hungary for 1990 are not included.   [5] Hong Kong, South Korea, Singapore, and Taiwan.   [6] Hong Kong Special Administrative Region of China.   [7] See footnote 2, Table 1308.   [8] Unified.

Source: U.S. Bureau of Labor Statistics, *International Comparisons of Hourly Compensation Costs for Production Workers in Manufacturing, 2004*, November 18, 2005. See also <http://www.bls.gov/news.release/pdf/ichcc.pdf>.

Table 1363. Key Global Telecom Indicators for the World Telecommunication Service Sector: 1995 to 2004

[All data were converted by annual average exchange rates. Country fiscal year data was aggregated to obtain calendar year estimates]

Indicators	1995	1999	2000	2001	2002	2003	2004
Telecom market total revenue (bil. dol.)	779	1,123	1,210	1,232	1,314	1,426	(NA)
Telecom telephone services revenue (bil. dol.) [1]	428	476	477	472	478	475	552
Other statistics:							
Main telephone lines (mil.)	689	905	983	1,053	1,086	1,140	1,207
Mobile cellular subscribers (mil.)	91	490	740	955	1,166	1,414	1,758
International telephone traffic minutes (bil.) [2]	63	100	118	127	131	142	145
Personal computers (mil.).	235	435	500	555	615	650	775
Internet users (mil.).	40	277	399	502	619	724	863

[1] Revenue from installation, subscription and local, trunk and international call charges for fixed telephone service.
[2] Including traffic between countries of former Soviet Union.
Source: International Telecommunication Union, Geneva Switzerland, 2005; <http://www.itu.int/ITU-D/ict/statistics/at_glance /KeyTelecom99.html>. Reproduced with the kind permission of ITU.

Table 1364. Telephones and Computers by Country: 2004

[Rates per 100 persons. See text of this section for general comments about the data. For data qualifications for countries, see source]

Country	Telephone main lines	Cellular phone sub-scribers	Personal computers [1]	Country	Telephone main lines	Cellular phone sub-scribers	Personal computers [1]
Australia	58.55	82.76	68.90	Italy	44.75	108.19	31.29
Austria	46.20	97.36	57.63	Japan.	46.00	71.58	54.15
Belgium	46.44	88.32	35.08	Korea, South	55.31	76.09	54.49
Brazil	23.46	36.32	10.71	Lebanon	17.75	25.01	11.27
Canada	64.27	46.72	69.82	Mexico	17.22	36.64	10.68
China [2]	23.98	25.76	4.08	Netherlands	48.44	91.21	68.47
Colombia.	17.14	22.95	5.53	Poland	(NA)	59.91	19.10
Cuba	6.78	0.67	2.65	Russia	27.47	51.61	13.18
Czech Republic . . .	33.58	105.64	21.55	Saudi Arabia	14.83	36.82	34.01
Egypt	13.52	10.92	3.29	Singapore	43.20	89.47	(NA)
Finland	45.40	95.63	48.22	South Africa	(NA)	43.13	8.27
France	56.04	73.72	48.66	Spain	41.52	89.46	25.36
Germany.	66.15	86.42	(NA)	Sweden	71.54	108.47	76.14
Greece	57.84	84.77	8.98	Switzerland	70.97	84.63	82.33
Hungary	35.43	86.43	14.62	Taiwan [2]	59.63	100.31	52.78
India.	4.07	4.37	1.21	Thailand	10.97	44.18	6.00
Indonesia	4.49	13.48	1.36	United Kingdom . . .	56.35	102.16	60.02
Ireland	49.94	93.49	49.74	**United States**	**60.60**	**62.11**	**76.22**
Israel	43.72	105.25	73.40				

NA Not available.   [1] In many countries mainframe computers are used extensively, and thousands of users can be connected to a single mainframe computer; thus the number of PCs understates the total use of computers.   [2] See footnote 2, Table 1308.
Source: International Telecommunications Union, Geneva, Switzerland, *World Telecommunication Indicators*, (copyright). See also <http://www.itu.int/ITU-D/ict/statistics/at_glance/main04.pdf>. Reproduced with the kind permission of ITU.

864   Comparative International Statistics

Table 1365. Dow-Jones World Stock Index by Country and Industry: 2000 to 2005

[Index figures shown are as of December 31. Based on share prices denominated in U.S. dollars. Stocks in countries that impose significant restrictions on foreign ownership are included in the world index in the same proportion that shares are available to foreign investors]

Country and industry	2000	2003	2004	2005	Country and industry	2000	2003	2004	2005
World, total.	210.9	187.0	214.0	234.1	Asia/Pacific	93.0	92.2	108.6	132.0
Americas.	299.1	259.8	289.0	307.3	Australia	156.0	218.1	280.7	312.5
United States	306.9	262.7	289.4	302.4	Hong Kong	245.6	216.8	255.8	273.6
Canada	225.3	238.7	291.2	369.4	Indonesia.	31.2	55.0	72.5	79.0
Mexico	132.2	175.6	257.3	360.1	Japan	88.3	77.7	90.6	113.5
Europe	241.2	207.9	246.7	267.4	Malaysia	88.5	108.6	120.7	119.5
Austria	86.2	165.2	277.5	335.5	New Zealand	96.7	180.8	235.1	227.3
Belgium	196.9	217.3	310.9	321.2	Singapore	135.2	133.2	158.6	176.3
Denmark	220.1	239.0	307.8	375.1	Thailand	27.2	80.0	73.0	76.7
Finland	1,537.8	788.0	834.0	948.5					
France	252.9	213.9	250.5	273.3	Basic materials.	117.6	154.1	179.4	213.8
Germany	219.1	180.9	206.8	224.3	Consumer Goods	183.8	199.2	226.4	241.9
Ireland.	312.3	341.4	470.8	470.4	Consumer Services. . . .	192.8	184.6	209.8	214.4
Italy	192.2	171.0	218.1	213.8	Energy	230.7	234.7	298.2	383.3
Netherlands	335.7	249.8	279.4	309.6	Financial.	207.1	201.6	236.3	259.8
Norway	151.8	155.8	228.2	276.1	Healthcare.	329.9	270.3	287.0	310.6
Spain	193.5	221.9	279.7	288.6	Industrial.	167.1	146.2	171.2	192.4
Sweden	339.0	261.4	348.9	378.3	Technology	552.7	347.8	355.3	375.1
Switzerland	388.8	344.9	393.8	452.5	Telecommunications . . .	273.3	185.6	217.8	201.6
United Kingdom	199.8	177.3	207.3	217.6	Utilities.	156.0	128.5	159.3	176.9

Source: Dow Jones & Company, Inc., New York, NY, *Dow Jones Indexes*, (copyright).

Table 1366. Foreign Stock Market Activity—Morgan Stanley Capital International Indexes: 2000 to 2005

[Index figures shown are as of December 31. January 1, 1970 = 100, except as noted. Minus sign (–) indicates decrease. Based on share prices denominated in U.S. dollars. EM = Emerging Markets]

Index and country	Index			Percent change [1]		Index and country	Index			Percent change [1]	
	2000	2004	2005	2004	2005		2000	2004	2005	2004	2005
ALL COUNTRY (AC) INDEXES						Sweden.	4,240	4,503	4,868	34.0	8.1
						Switzerland	2,695	2,822	3,241	13.8	14.9
AC World index [2]	289.8	284.5	309.6	13.3	8.8	United Kingdom	1,146	1,162	1,206	15.5	3.7
AC World index except						Hong Kong	5,475	5,479	5,742	20.8	4.8
USA [2]	195.4	207.5	236.4	18.3	13.9	Japan	2,552	2,460	3,053	14.7	24.1
AC Asia Pacific [2].	92.7	101.4	122.7	16.3	21.0	Singapore	2,081	2,163	2,396	18.8	10.8
AC Europe [2]	376.5	380.1	407.8	18.1	7.3						
European Union [2]	361.5	358.0	378.2	18.3	5.6	EMERGING MARKETS					
						EM Far East index [4]. . .	123.8	210.0	256.4	11.8	22.1
DEVELOPED						India [6].	114.5	193.7	262.3	16.5	35.4
MARKETS						Indonesia.	78.2	235.3	264.9	44.5	12.6
World index [3]	1,221	1,169	1,258	12.8	7.6	Korea, South	78.7	196.2	302.8	20.0	54.3
EAFE index [3]	1,492	1,515	1,680	17.6	10.9	Malaysia [6]	160.9	220.2	216.9	11.8	–1.5
Europe index	1,378	1,378	1,468	17.8	6.5	Pakistan [6]	44.3	91.8	143.6	8.6	56.5
Pacific index.	1,832	1,935	2,333	17.2	20.6	Philippines [6]	142.2	141.2	169.4	24.1	19.9
Far East index	2,583	2,501	3,061	15.2	22.4	Sri Lanka [6].	36.3	98.1	128.3	7.8	30.7
United States	1,250	1,137	1,181	8.8	3.8	Taiwan [7]	191.7	232.1	239.8	6.5	3.3
Canada	832.5	1,028.2	1,302.0	20.5	26.6	Thailand	56.9	169.5	177.7	–4.0	4.9
Australia	317.7	558.6	629.0	26.6	12.6						
New Zealand [4]	56.4	139.3	134.0	29.8	–3.8	EM Latin America.	1,002	1,484	2,150	34.8	44.9
						Argentina.	1,233	1,163.0	1,857.1	24.6	59.7
Austria	708.3	1,960	2,411	69.2	23.0	Brazil	869.9	1,046.6	1,569.4	30.5	50.0
Belgium.	1,222	1,606	1,696	39.6	5.6	Chile.	604.7	997.3	1,180.7	24.6	18.4
Denmark	2,201	2,900	3,551	28.8	22.5	Colombia [6].	42.1	245.0	495.7	125.7	102.3
Finland [4]	921.8	468.5	534.0	3.9	14.0	Mexico	1,197	2,716	3,944	45.0	45.2
France	1,509	1,446	1,558	16.3	7.8	Peru [6].	125.0	343.4	441.3	–0.2	28.5
Germany	1,436	1,328	1,430	14.4	7.7	Venezuela [6]	106.1	151.0	107.4	45.4	–28.9
Greece [4]	475.8	540.7	609.0	41.2	12.6						
Ireland [4]	308.4	412.6	393.0	39.2	–4.8	Czech Republic [8]	79.9	293.8	421.5	76.6	43.5
Italy [5]	447.2	503.0	497.0	28.6	–1.2	Hungary [8].	233.6	661.8	765.0	87.5	15.6
Luxembourg [5].	491.9	(NA)	(NA)	(NA)	(NA)	Jordan	55.1	180.4	309.8	59.1	71.7
Netherlands	2,177	1,753	1,939	9.1	10.6	Poland [6]	499.0	747.1	903.9	58.6	21.0
Norway	1,181	1,993	2,392	49.6	20.0	Russia [8]	155.2	479.9	813.4	4.1	69.5
Portugal [4]	127.8	141.1	135.0	21.9	–4.3	South Africa [6].	157.6	304.7	377.9	40.7	24.0
Spain	347.1	486.8	494.4	25.4	1.6	Turkey.	247.7	321.0	486.6	38.5	51.6

NA Not available. [1] Percent change during calendar year (e.g. December 31, 2004 through December 31, 2005). Adjusted for foreign exchange fluctuations relative to U.S. dollar. [2] January 1, 1988 = 100. [3] Europe, Australasia, Far East Index. Comprises all European and Far East countries listed under developed markets plus Australia and New Zealand. [4] January 1, 1988 = 100. [5] MSCI Luxembourg Index discontinued as of March 29, 2002. [6] January 1, 1993 = 100. [7] See footnote 2, Table 1308. [8] January 1, 1995 = 100.

Source: Morgan Stanley Capital International, New York, NY, <http://www.mscibarra.com/about/indexdata_tou.jsp?/products /indices/stdindex/performance.jsp> (copyright). This information may not be reproduced or redisseminated in any form without prior written permission from Morgan Stanley Capital International. This information is provided on an "as is" basis. Neither Morgan Stanley nor any other party makes any representation or warranty of any kind either express or implied, with respect to this information (or the results to be obtained by the use thereof) and Morgan Stanley expressly disclaims any and all warranties of originality, accuracy, completeness, merchantability, and fitness for any particular purpose. The user of this information assumes the entire risk of any use made of the information. In no event shall Morgan Stanley or any other part be liable to the user for any direct or indirect damages, including without limitation, any lost profits, lost savings, or other incidental or consequential damages arising out of use of this information.

Comparative International Statistics 865

Table 1367. **Foreign Stock Market Indices: 1980 to 2005**

[**As of year end.** The DAX-30 index is a total return index which includes dividends, whereas the other foreign indices are price indices which exclude dividends]

Year	London FTSE 100	Tokyo Nikkei 225	Hong Kong Hang Seng	Germany DAX-30	Paris CAC-40	Dow Jones Europe STOXX 50
1980	647	7,116	1,477	481	(X)	(X)
1985	1,413	13,113	1,752	1,366	(X)	(X)
1990	2,144	23,849	3,025	1,398	1,518	835
1991	2,493	22,984	4,297	1,578	1,766	1,000
1992	2,847	16,925	5,512	1,545	1,858	1,058
1993	3,418	17,417	11,888	2,267	2,268	1,429
1994	3,066	19,723	8,191	2,107	1,881	1,299
1995	3,689	19,868	10,073	2,254	1,872	1,538
1996	4,119	19,361	13,452	2,889	2,316	1,850
1997	5,136	15,259	10,723	4,250	2,999	2,634
1998	5,883	13,842	9,507	5,002	3,943	3,320
1999	6,930	18,934	16,962	6,958	5,958	4,742
2000	6,223	13,786	15,096	6,434	5,926	4,557
2001	5,217	10,543	11,397	5,160	4,625	3,707
2002	3,940	8,579	9,321	2,893	3,064	2,408
2003	4,477	10,677	12,576	3,965	3,558	2,660
2004	4,814	11,489	14,230	4,256	3,821	2,775
2005	5,619	16,111	14,876	5,408	4,715	3,349

X Not applicable.

Source: Global Financial Data, Los Angeles, CA, <http://www.globalfinancialdata.com>, unpublished data (copyright).

Table 1368. **United States and Foreign Stock Markets—Market Capitalization and Value of Shares Traded: 2000 to 2005**

[In billions of U.S. dollars (15,104.0 represents $15,104,000,000,000). Market capitalization is the market value of all domestic listed companies at the end of the year. The market value of a company is the share price times the number of shares outstanding. Value of shares traded is the annual total turnover of listed company shares]

Country	Market capitalization				Value of shares traded			
	2000	2003	2004	2005	2000	2003	2004	2005
United States	15,104.0	14,266.3	16,323.7	16,998.0	31,862.5	15,547.4	19,354.9	21,510.0
Argentina	166.1	38.9	46.4	61.5	6.0	4.9	7.6	16.4
Australia	372.8	585.5	776.4	804.1	226.3	369.8	514.2	616.1
Austria	29.9	54.5	85.8	126.3	9.4	10.8	23.8	45.9
Belgium	182.5	173.6	768.4	327.1	38.0	37.5	70.3	113.7
Brazil	226.2	234.6	330.3	474.6	101.3	60.4	93.6	154.2
Canada	841.4	894.0	1,177.5	1,480.9	634.7	467.8	653.9	845.0
Chile	60.4	86.3	117.1	136.4	6.1	6.5	11.6	18.9
China [1]	581.0	681.2	639.8	780.8	721.5	476.8	748.3	586.3
Denmark	107.7	128.0	151.3	178.0	91.6	67.0	97.5	152.0
Egypt	28.7	27.1	38.5	79.7	11.1	3.3	5.6	25.4
Finland	293.6	170.3	183.8	209.5	206.6	163.5	220.0	273.5
France	1,446.6	1,355.6	1,857.2	1,710.0	1,083.3	995.4	1,311.7	1,475.5
Germany	1,270.2	1,079.0	1,194.5	1,221.3	1,069.1	1,147.2	1,406.1	1,763.2
Greece	110.8	106.8	125.2	145.0	95.1	38.6	43.5	65.3
Hong Kong	623.4	714.6	861.5	1,006.2	377.9	331.6	439.0	460.1
India	148.1	279.1	387.9	553.1	509.8	284.8	379.1	443.2
Indonesia	26.8	54.7	73.3	81.4	14.3	14.8	27.6	41.9
Iran	34.0	34.4	47.0	38.7	5.0	5.3	13.3	8.2
Ireland	81.9	85.1	114.1	114.1	14.4	44.0	44.3	64.7
Israel	64.1	75.7	95.5	120.1	23.4	41.6	46.2	59.9
Italy	768.4	614.8	789.6	798.2	778.4	663.2	804.3	1,115.2
Japan	3,157.2	3,040.7	3,678.3	4,736.5	2,693.9	2,273.0	3,430.4	4,997.4
Korea, South	171.6	329.6	428.6	718.2	1,067.7	682.7	638.9	1,203.0
Luxembourg	34.0	37.3	50.1	51.3	1.2	0.3	0.4	0.2
Malaysia	116.9	168.4	190.0	181.2	58.5	50.1	59.9	49.9
Mexico	125.2	122.5	171.9	239.1	45.3	23.5	42.8	52.7
Morocco	10.9	13.2	25.1	27.2	1.1	0.7	1.7	4.1
Netherlands	640.5	488.6	622.3	727.5	677.2	463.5	604.2	757.4
New Zealand	18.6	33.1	43.7	40.6	10.8	10.5	15.4	17.4
Norway	65.0	94.7	141.4	191.0	60.1	70.0	135.5	194.8
Philippines	51.6	23.6	28.9	40.2	8.2	2.6	3.7	7.0
Poland	31.3	37.2	71.1	93.9	14.6	8.5	16.6	30.0
Portugal	60.7	58.3	73.4	67.0	54.4	21.4	34.6	38.9
Russia	38.9	230.8	268.0	548.6	20.3	81.0	130.8	159.3
Saudi Arabia	67.2	157.3	306.2	646.1	17.3	159.1	473.0	1,103.5
Singapore	152.8	145.1	171.6	208.3	91.5	87.9	81.3	119.8
Sweden	328.3	287.5	376.8	403.9	390.0	263.8	412.4	464.0
Switzerland	792.3	725.7	825.8	938.6	609.1	575.6	727.1	883.3
Taiwan [1]	247.6	379.0	441.4	485.6	983.5	592.0	718.6	618.2
Thailand	29.5	118.7	115.4	123.5	23.3	96.6	109.9	89.3
Turkey	69.7	68.4	98.3	161.5	179.2	99.6	147.4	201.3
United Kingdom	2,580.0	2,412.4	2,815.9	3,058.2	1,835.3	2,150.8	3,707.2	4,167.0

[1] See footnote 2, Table 1308.

Source: Standard and Poor's, New York, NY, *Standard & Poor's Emerging Stock Markets Factbook 2006* (copyright).

Table 1369. **Foreign Exchange Rates: 2004**

[**Foreign currency units per U.S. dollar.** Rates shown include market, official, principal, and secondary rates, as published by the International Monetary Fund in *International Financial Statistics*]

Country	Currency	2004	Country	Currency	2004
Afghanistan [1]	Afghanis	3,000.00	Laos	Kip	10,820.0
Albania	Leks	102.65	Latvia	Lats	0.54
Algeria	Algerian Dinars	72.06	Lebanon	Lebanese Pounds	1,507.50
Antigua and Barbuda	E.Caribbean Dollars	2.70	Lesotho	Maloti	6.46
Argentina	Argentine Pesos	2.92	Liberia	Liberian Dollars	54.91
Armenia	Drams	533.45	Libya [1]	Libyan Dinars	1.30
Aruba	Aruban Florins	1.79	Lithuania	Litai	2.78
Australia	Australian Dollars	1.36	Luxembourg [2]	Euro	0.81
Austria [2]	Euro	0.81	Macedonia	Denars	49.41
Bahamas, The	Bahamian Dollars	1.00	Madagascar	Malagasy Ariary	1,868.86
Bahrain	Bahrain Dinars	0.38	Malaysia	Ringgit	3.80
Bangladesh	Taka	59.51	Mali	CFA Francs	528.29
Barbados	Barbados Dollars	2.00	Malta	Maltese Liri	0.34
Belarus	Belarusian Rubel	2,160.26	Mauritania	Ouguiyas	267.00
Belgium [2]	Euro	0.81	Mauritius	Mauritian Rupees	27.50
Belize	Belize Dollars	2.00	Mexico	Mexican Pesos	11.29
Benin	CFA Francs	528.29	Moldova	Lei	12.33
Bolivia	Bolivianos	7.94	Mongolia	Togrogs	1,185.28
Botswana	Pula	4.69	Morocco	Dirhams	8.87
Brazil	Reais	2.93	Mozambique	Meticais	22,581.3
Bulgaria	Leva	1.58	Namibia	Namibia Dollars	6.46
Burkina Faso	CFA Francs	528.29	Nepal	Nepalese Rupees	73.67
Burma [1]	Kyats	5.75	Netherlands [2]	Euro	0.81
Cambodia	Riel	4,016.25	Netherlands Antilles	Guilders	1.79
Cameroon	CFA Francs	528.29	New Zealand	New Zealand Dollars	1.51
Canada	Canadian Dollars	1.30	Nicaragua	Cordobas	15.94
Central African Republic	CFA Francs	528.29	Niger	CFA Francs	528.29
Chad	CFA Francs	528.29	Nigeria	Naira	132.89
Chile	Chilean Pesos	609.37	Norway	Norwegian Kroner	6.74
China [3]	Yuan	8.28	Oman	Rials Omani	0.38
Colombia	Colombian Pesos	2,628.61	Pakistan	Pakistan Rupees	58.26
Comoros	Comorian Francs	396.21	Panama	Balboas	1.00
Congo (Brazzaville) [4]	CFA Francs	528.29	Papua New Guinea	Kina	3.22
Costa Rica	Colones	437.91	Paraguay	Guaranies	5,974.58
Cote d'Ivoire	CFA Francs	528.29	Peru	Nuevos Soles	3.41
Croatia	Kunas	6.04	Philippines	Philippine Pesos	56.04
Cyprus	Cyprus Pounds	0.47	Poland	Zlotys	3.66
Czech Republic	Koruny	25.70	Portugal [2]	Euro	0.81
Denmark	Kroner	5.99	Qatar	Qatar Riyals	3.64
Djibouti	Djibouti Francs	177.72	Romania	Lei	32,636.6
Dominica	E.Caribbean Dollars	2.70	Russia	Russian Rubles	28.81
Dominican Republic	Dominican Pesos	42.12	Rwanda	Rwanda Francs	574.62
Ecuador	U.S. Dollars	25,000.0	Saint Kitts and Nevis	E.Caribbean Dollars	2.70
Egypt	Egyptian Pounds	6.20	Saint Lucia	E.Caribbean Dollars	2.70
El Salvador	Colones	8.75	Saint Vincent and the		
Equatorial Guinea	CFA Francs	528.29	Grenadines	E.Caribbean Dollars	2.70
Estonia	Krooni	12.60	Saudi Arabia	Saudi A. Riyals	3.75
Ethiopia [1]	Birr	8.64	Senegal	CFA Francs	528.29
Euro area (EMU-11) [2]	Euro	0.81	Sierra Leone	Leones	2,701.30
Fiji	Fiji Dollars	1.73	Singapore	Singapore Dollar	1.69
Finland [2]	Euro	0.81	Slovakia	Koruny	32.26
France [2]	Euro	0.81	Slovenia	Tolars	192.38
Gabon	CFA Francs	528.29	South Africa	Rand	6.46
Georgia	Lari	1.92	Spain [2]	Euro	0.81
Germany [2]	Euro	0.81	Sri Lanka	Sri Lanka Rupees	101.19
Greece [2]	Euro	0.81	Sudan	Sudanese Dinars	257.91
Guatemala	Quetzales	7.95	Suriname [1]	Suriname Dollar	2.73
Guyana	Guyana Dollars	198.31	Swaziland	Emalangeni	6.46
Haiti	Gourdes	38.35	Sweden	Swedish Kronor	7.35
Honduras	Lempiras	18.21	Switzerland	Swiss Francs	1.24
Hong Kong	Hong Kong Dollars	7.79	Syria	Syrian Pounds	11.23
Hungary	Forint	202.75	Tanzania	Tanzania Shillings	1,089.33
Iceland	Kronur	70.19	Thailand	Baht	40.22
India	Indian Rupees	45.32	Togo	CFA Francs	528.29
Indonesia	Rupiah	8,938.85	Trinidad and Tobago	Tt Dollars	6.30
Iran	Rials	8,613.99	Tunisia	Tunisian Dinars	1.25
Iraq	Dinars	(NA)	Turkey	Liras	1,425,540
Ireland [2]	Euro	0.81	Uganda	Uganda Shillings	1,810.30
Israel	New Sheqalim	4.48	Ukraine	Hryvnias	5.32
Italy [2]	Euro	0.81	United Arab Emirates	Dirhams	3.67
Jamaica	Jamaica Dollars	61.20	United Kingdom	Pounds Sterling	0.55
Japan	Yen	108.19	Uruguay	Uruguayan Pesos	28.70
Jordan	Jordinian Dinars	0.71	Vanuatu	Vatu	111.79
Kazakhstan	Tenge	136.04	Venezuela	Bolivares	1,891.33
Kenya	Kenya Shillings	79.17	Yemen	Yemeni Rials	184.78
Korea, South	Won	1,145.32	Zambia	Zambian Kwacha	4,778.88
Kuwait	Kuwaiti Dinars	0.29	Zimbabwe	Zimbabwe Dollar	4,303.28
Kyrgyzstan	Soms	42.65			

NA Not available.   [1] End-of year values were used if annual averages were unavailable. Some values were estimated using partial year data.   [2] The euro became the official currency of the 11 Euro Area (EMU) nations on January 1, 1999, and Greece in 2001.   [3] See footnote 2, Table 1308.   [4] See footnote 3, Table 1308.

Source: U.S. Dept. of Commerce, International Trade Administration, "Foreign Exchange Rates, 1997-04"; accessed July 2006. Also see <http://www.ita.doc.gov/td/industry/otea/usfth/aggregate/H04T34.html>.

Comparative International Statistics   867

Table 1370. Reserve Assets and International Transaction Balances by Country: 2000 to 2005

[In millions of U.S. dollars (56,600 represents $56,600,000,000). Assets include holdings of convertible foreign currencies, special drawing rights, and reserve position in International Monetary Fund and exclude gold holdings. Minus sign (–) indicates debits]

Country	Total reserve assets				Current account balance			Merchandise trade balance		
				2005						
	2000	2004	Total	Cur-rency hold-ings[1]	2000	2004	2005	2000	2004	2005
United States	56,600	75,890	54,080	37,840	–416,000	–668,070	(NA)	–449,780	–668,070	(NA)
Algeria	12,024	43,246	56,303	56,178	(NA)	(NA)	(NA)	(NA)	(NA)	(NA)
Argentina	25,147	18,884	27,179	22,742	–8,981	3,281	(NA)	2,452	13,239	(NA)
Australia	18,118	35,803	41,941	40,972	–15,306	–40,021	(NA)	–4,841	–18,142	(NA)
Austria	14,319	7,858	6,839	6,298	–4,864	765	(NA)	–2,737	3,048	(NA)
Bangladesh.	1,486	3,172	2,767	2,766	–306	–279	(NA)	–1,654	–3,007	(NA)
Belgium[2]	9,994	10,361	8,241	6,815	11,381	(NA)	(NA)	2,591	(NA)	(NA)
Brazil	32,488	52,740	53,574	53,545	–24,225	11,711	14,199	–698	33,641	44,757
Burma	223	672	771	771	–212	112	(NA)	–504	928	(NA)
Cameroon.	212	829	949	946	(NA)	(NA)	(NA)	(NA)	(NA)	(NA)
Canada	32,102	34,429	32,962	30,664	19,622	22,000	25,268	45,047	50,682	55,303
Chile	15,035	15,994	16,929	16,689	–898	1,390	(NA)	2,119	9,019	(NA)
China[3].	168,278	614,500	821,514	818,872	20,518	68,659	(NA)	34,474	58,982	(NA)
Colombia	8,916	13,394	14,787	14,206	761	–950	(NA)	2,633	1,368	(NA)
Congo (Brazzaville)[4]	222	120	732	729	648	(NA)	(NA)	2,037	(NA)	(NA)
Cote d'Ivoire	668	1,694	(NA)	(NA)	–241	303	(NA)	1,486	2,734	(NA)
Denmark	15,108	39,084	32,930	32,510	2,262	5,941	(NA)	6,641	9,527	(NA)
Ecuador	947	1,070	1,714	1,667	921	–157	(NA)	1,395	321	(NA)
Egypt.	13,118	14,273	20,609	20,508	–971	3,922	(NA)	–8,321	–6,576	(NA)
Finland.	7,977	12,318	10,588	10,143	8,975	9,698	(NA)	13,684	12,840	(NA)
France	37,039	35,314	27,753	23,996	18,580	–8,380	(NA)	–3,620	–7,940	(NA)
Germany	56,890	48,823	45,140	39,765	–29,600	103,770	(NA)	57,220	189,970	(NA)
Ghana	232	1,627	1,753	1,752	–387	–236	(NA)	–830	–1,513	(NA)
Greece.	13,424	1,191	506	309	–9,820	–13,148	(NA)	–20,239	–31,621	(NA)
Hungary	11,190	15,908	18,539	18,283	–4,004	–8,842	(NA)	–2,913	–2,998	(NA)
India	37,902	126,593	131,924	131,018	–4,601	(NA)	(NA)	–10,640	(NA)	(NA)
Indonesia	28,502	34,952	32,989	32,774	7,992	3,108	(NA)	25,042	21,552	(NA)
Ireland	5,360	2,831	779	514	–516	–1,423	(NA)	25,010	39,506	(NA)
Israel	23,281	27,094	28,006	27,786	–1,230	1,474	(NA)	–3,540	–2,902	(NA)
Italy	25,567	27,859	25,515	23,528	–5,781	–15,137	(NA)	9,549	10,911	(NA)
Japan	354,902	833,891	834,275	828,813	119,660	172,060	(NA)	116,720	132,130	(NA)
Kenya	898	1,519	1,799	1,781	–199	–379	(NA)	–1,262	–1,598	(NA)
Korea, South	96,131	198,997	210,317	209,968	12,251	27,613	(NA)	16,954	38,161	(NA)
Kuwait	7,082	8,242	8,863	8,380	14,672	18,884	(NA)	13,027	19,301	(NA)
Malaysia.	29,523	66,384	70,172	69,691	8,488	(NA)	(NA)	20,827	(NA)	(NA)
Mexico	35,509	64,141	74,054	73,015	–18,652	–7,195	–5,723	–8,337	–8,811	–7,559
Morocco.	4,823	16,337	16,187	16,008	–501	922	(NA)	–3,235	–6,487	(NA)
Nepal.	945	1,462	1,499	1,490	–299	52	(NA)	–814	–1,049	(NA)
Netherlands	9,643	10,102	9,074	7,167	7,264	54,414	(NA)	17,800	42,946	(NA)
Nigeria	9,911	16,956	28,280	28,279	7,429	12,264	(NA)	10,415	12,561	(NA)
Norway.	27,597	44,308	46,986	46,377	25,851	34,445	(NA)	25,975	33,576	(NA)
Pakistan	1,513	9,799	10,033	9,817	–85	–817	(NA)	–1,157	–3,396	(NA)
Peru	8,374	12,176	13,599	13,599	–1,526	–11	1,030	–411	2,792	5,163
Philippines	13,090	13,116	15,928	15,802	6,258	2,080	(NA)	3,814	–6,381	(NA)
Poland.	26,562	35,324	40,864	40,487	–9,981	–10,357	(NA)	–12,307	–5,622	(NA)
Portugal	8,909	5,174	3,479	3,173	–11,748	–13,158	(NA)	–14,532	–18,666	(NA)
Romania.	2,470	14,616	19,872	19,872	–1,355	–6,382	(NA)	–1,684	–6,665	(NA)
Saudi Arabia	19,585	27,291	26,530	24,074	14,317	51,926	87,131	49,777	84,947	123,308
Singapore	80,132	112,232	115,794	115,334	11,936	27,897	(NA)	12,723	31,239	(NA)
South Africa	6,083	13,141	18,579	18,260	–191	–7,442	(NA)	4,698	–281	(NA)
Spain.	30,989	12,389	9,678	8,594	–23,076	–55,380	(NA)	–37,087	–65,830	(NA)
Sri Lanka	1,039	2,132	2,651	2,581	–1,044	–677	(NA)	–1,044	–1,443	(NA)
Sudan	247	1,626	2,450	2,450	–557	–871	3,013	440	192	1,122
Sweden	14,863	22,129	22,063	21,355	6,617	27,485	(NA)	15,215	23,415	(NA)
Switzerland	32,272	55,497	36,297	35,421	33,562	58,294	(NA)	2,071	15,737	(NA)
Syria	(NA)	(NA)	(NA)	(NA)	1,061	205	(NA)	1,423	–374	(NA)
Thailand	32,016	48,664	50,691	50,502	9,313	6,632	(NA)	11,701	10,583	(NA)
Trinidad and Tobago	1,386	3,168	4,856	4,781	544	(NA)	(NA)	969	(NA)	(NA)
Turkey	22,488	35,669	50,579	50,402	–9,819	–15,543	(NA)	–21,959	–23,924	(NA)
United Kingdom	43,890	45,340	43,530	40,920	–36,680	–42,300	(NA)	–49,850	–110,600	(NA)
Venezuela.	13,088	18,375	23,919	23,454	11,853	13,830	25,359	16,664	21,430	31,532

NA Not available. [1] Holdings of convertible foreign currencies. [2] Balance of payments current account and trade balance data for 2000 are for Belgium-Luxembourg. Thereafter, data is for Belgium only. [3] See footnote 2, Table 1308. [4] See footnote 3, Table 1308.

Source: International Monetary Fund, Washington, DC, *International Financial Statistics*, monthly, (copyright).

868 Comparative International Statistics

Table 1371. Foreign Trade—Destination of Exports and Source of Imports for Selected Countries: 2004

[In billions of dollars (4.1 represents $4,100,000,000)]

Country	United States		Canada		Australia		Japan		France		Germany		Italy		United Kingdom	
	Imports	Exports	Imports	Exports	Imports	Exports	Imports	Exports	Imports	Exports	Imports	Exports	Imports	Exports	Imports	Exports
Argentina	4.1	3.4	0.2	0.1	0.1	0.1	0.5	0.4	0.5	0.7	1.2	1.1	1.2	0.7	0.5	0.3
Australia	7.9	14.3	1.4	1.2	0.4	—	19.5	11.8	1.2	2.9	1.5	5.7	1.4	3.1	3.3	4.4
Austria	5.9	2.0	1.0	0.2	0.6	(Z)	1.3	1.3	4.0	4.4	28.7	47.9	8.9	8.3	4.3	2.0
Belgium	12.8	16.9	1.0	1.7	0.9	0.5	2.1	7.2	31.6	31.7	34.9	50.4	15.4	8.5	23.2	18.6
Brazil	22.7	13.9	1.8	0.7	0.4	0.4	3.7	2.3	3.1	2.3	5.7	5.7	3.3	2.2	2.8	1.5
Canada [1]	259.7	189.1	2.7	(NA)	1.4	1.4	8.4	7.6	2.2	3.0	2.9	5.9	1.7	3.0	6.7	6.1
China	210.5	34.7	18.5	5.1	13.2	8.1	94.3	73.9	20.5	6.6	40.2	25.8	14.7	5.4	26.4	4.4
Colombia	7.8	4.5	0.3	0.3	(Z)	(Z)	0.3	0.7	0.3	0.3	0.5	0.7	0.6	0.3	0.5	0.2
Czech Republic	1.8	0.8	0.2	0.1	0.1	0.1	0.3	1.2	2.5	2.8	21.0	21.6	2.1	3.2	2.3	1.8
Denmark	4.0	2.1	0.8	0.2	0.7	0.1	2.8	0.8	3.5	3.2	10.9	13.5	2.5	2.6	5.6	3.7
Egypt	1.4	2.1	0.8	0.2	(Z)	0.5	0.1	0.8	0.4	1.3	0.6	1.7	1.6	1.8	0.9	1.2
Finland	4.1	2.1	0.7	0.2	0.5	0.4	1.4	1.7	2.7	2.2	7.5	9.1	1.9	1.8	4.3	2.5
France	32.6	21.2	4.1	1.8	3.1	0.7	8.3	8.4	5.2	(NA)	64.6	92.2	38.0	42.7	36.9	33.7
Germany	79.1	31.4	7.2	2.1	6.0	1.0	17.1	19.0	75.4	62.2	(NA)	(NA)	62.2	47.2	63.8	39.4
Hungary	2.6	1.1	0.2	(Z)	0.1	(Z)	0.5	1.5	2.7	2.5	16.6	15.4	2.9	3.3	2.8	1.7
India	16.4	6.1	0.7	0.7	0.8	4.0	2.6	3.0	2.1	1.6	3.6	3.9	2.5	1.5	4.3	4.1
Indonesia	11.7	2.7	1.2	0.5	2.7	2.4	18.7	9.1	1.4	0.5	2.8	2.0	1.5	0.6	1.9	0.7
Ireland	27.6	8.2	1.3	0.4	1.3	0.1	3.8	2.0	8.0	3.2	18.7	5.3	5.3	1.7	18.6	25.5
Israel	14.8	9.2	0.5	0.3	0.4	0.1	0.8	1.2	1.0	1.2	1.5	2.9	1.1	1.7	1.6	2.6
Italy	29.4	10.7	3.5	1.3	3.3	1.0	6.9	6.5	39.0	38.6	43.2	63.3	(NA)	(NA)	22.2	15.3
Japan	133.3	54.4	10.3	6.6	12.3	16.3	(NA)	(NA)	13.3	6.6	26.0	15.4	6.9	5.4	15.1	6.9
Luxembourg	0.3	0.7	0.1	0.1	(Z)	(Z)	0.1	0.2	2.0	2.3	2.7	6.0	0.4	0.7	1.5	0.5
Mexico	157.8	110.8	10.3	2.3	0.5	0.3	2.2	5.2	0.8	1.9	2.0	6.0	0.4	2.2	1.2	1.1
Netherlands	13.2	24.3	1.2	1.6	0.9	1.1	2.0	13.4	19.1	16.4	55.7	53.5	19.9	8.1	33.0	21.9
Norway	6.9	1.6	3.8	1.2	0.2	0.1	1.2	1.1	8.6	1.6	9.3	6.3	4.4	1.4	15.4	3.7
Poland	2.8	0.9	0.3	0.2	0.2	(Z)	0.2	3.1	3.9	5.3	19.7	22.9	4.1	6.1	3.2	2.6
Russia	12.6	3.0	1.1	0.3	(Z)	0.2	5.7	2.9	9.1	3.9	14.5	18.3	8.1	6.2	7.0	2.7
Saudi Arabia	(NA)	(NA)	(NA)	(NA)	(NA)	(NA)	(NA)	(NA)	(NA)	(NA)	(NA)	(NA)	(NA)	(NA)	(NA)	(NA)
South Africa	6.2	3.2	0.5	0.9	0.9	1.2	4.6	2.9	1.3	2.1	3.8	7.2	2.5	1.4	5.6	3.4
Spain	7.9	6.6	1.0	0.9	0.9	0.5	1.7	5.0	32.0	41.4	21.4	45.1	16.0	24.9	16.1	16.6
Sweden	13.1	3.3	1.7	0.3	1.3	0.2	2.1	1.9	5.6	5.6	12.5	19.4	4.7	3.5	9.4	7.9
Switzerland	11.8	9.3	1.3	0.5	1.0	0.2	4.8	2.2	9.9	12.7	25.6	33.4	11.6	14.6	4.8	5.4
Thailand	18.6	6.4	1.6	0.4	2.8	2.3	14.1	20.3	1.8	1.6	3.0	2.4	1.5	0.9	3.2	1.2
United Kingdom	47.7	36.0	7.4	6.0	4.2	3.7	6.7	15.0	28.1	38.7	42.1	74.3	14.9	24.0	5.4	(NA)
United States	**(NA)**	**(NA)**	**160.8**	**267.8**	**15.1**	**7.0**	**62.6**	**127.0**	**27.9**	**28.7**	**48.3**	**79.2**	**12.3**	**27.7**	**41.8**	**52.1**

– Represents zero.   NA Not available.   Z Less than 50,000,000.   [1] See footnote 2, Table 1308.

Source: Organization for Economic Cooperation and Development, Paris, France, OECD International Trade by Commodities Statistics, 2005.

Table 1372. International Tourism Arrivals, Expenditures, and Receipts—Leading Countries: 1990 to 2004

[Expenditures and receipts in millions of dollars; arrivals in thousands of nonresident tourists at national borders, excluding same-day visitors (52,497 represents 52,497,000). Receipts are dollars spent by foreign tourists on travel inside the country shown. Expenditures are dollars visitors (same-day visitors and tourists) from a given country of origin spend on travel outside their country of residence. Excludes international transport receipts]

Country	Arrivals					Expenditures				Receipts				
	1990	2000	2002	2003	2004	2000	2002	2003	2004	1990	2000	2002	2003	2004
France	52,497	77,190	77,012	75,048	75,121	17,906	19,518	23,396	28,520	20,184	30,981	32,437	36,617	40,686
Spain	34,085	47,898	52,327	50,854	52,430	5,476	6,662	8,285	11,078	18,593	30,979	33,783	41,770	46,202
United States	39,362	51,237	43,582	41,218	46,085	67,043	61,738	60,970	69,516	43,007	97,943	84,752	83,254	93,922
China[1]	10,484	31,229	36,803	32,970	41,761	13,114	15,398	15,187	19,149	2,218	16,231	20,385	17,406	25,739
Italy	26,679	41,181	39,799	39,604	37,071	15,685	16,924	20,589	20,460	16,458	27,493	26,873	31,247	35,378
United Kingdom[2]	18,013	25,209	24,180	24,715	27,755	38,262	41,744	47,853	56,428	15,375	21,769	20,549	22,668	28,188
Mexico[2]	17,172	20,641	19,667	18,665	20,618	5,499	6,060	6,253	6,959	5,467	8,294	8,858	9,362	10,753
Germany	17,045	18,983	17,969	18,399	20,137	52,824	52,660	64,629	70,614	14,245	18,611	19,278	23,125	27,601
Russia[3]	(NA)	(NA)	21,279	20,443	19,892	8,848	11,284	12,880	15,730	(NA)	3,430	4,168	4,502	5,226
Austria	19,011	17,982	18,611	19,078	19,373	8,463	9,460	11,757	11,252	13,417	9,998	11,137	13,842	15,306
Canada	15,209	19,627	20,057	17,534	19,095	12,438	11,679	13,393	15,985	6,339	10,778	10,691	10,602	12,817
Turkey	4,799	9,586	12,790	13,341	16,826	1,713	1,881	2,113	2,524	3,225	7,636	11,901	13,203	15,888
Malaysia	7,446	10,222	13,292	10,577	15,703	2,075	2,618	2,846	3,093	1,667	5,011	7,118	5,901	8,198
Poland	(NA)	17,400	13,980	13,720	14,290	3,313	3,202	2,801	3,841	358	5,677	4,314	4,069	5,833
Greece	8,873	13,096	14,180	13,969	(NA)	4,558	2,436	2,431	2,872	2,587	9,219	9,909	10,766	12,715
Hong Kong	6,581	8,814	10,689	9,676	13,655	(NA)	(NA)	(NA)	(NA)	5,032	5,868	7,412	7,106	8,948
Ukraine	(NA)	6,341	10,517	12,514	(NA)	470	657	789	996	(NA)	394	788	935	1,141
Hungary	20,510	(NA)	(NA)	(NA)	12,212	1,651	2,133	2,594	2,848	824	3,733	3,728	4,061	4,034
Thailand	5,299	9,579	10,873	10,082	11,737	2,772	3,303	2,921	4,514	4,326	7,483	7,901	7,856	10,043
Portugal	8,020	12,097	11,644	11,707	11,617	2,228	2,125	2,409	2,762	3,555	5,243	5,762	6,580	7,758
Netherlands	5,795	10,003	9,595	9,181	9,646	12,191	12,976	14,583	17,216	4,155	7,197	7,710	9,249	10,417
Saudi Arabia[4]	2,209	6,585	7,511	7,332	8,599	(NA)	3,418	(NA)	6,540	(NA)	3,205	3,418	(NA)	6,540
Macao[5]	2,513	5,197	6,565	6,309	8,324	(NA)	(NA)	(NA)	(NA)	1,473	3,205	4,440	5,303	7,344
Croatia[3]	(NA)	5,831	6,944	7,409	7,912	568	781	672	839	1,704	2,758	3,812	6,377	6,973
Sweden	(NA)	(NA)	7,458	7,627	(NA)	8,048	7,301	8,296	9,946	2,906	4,064	4,710	5,304	6,056
Egypt[3]	2,411	5,116	4,906	5,746	7,795	1,072	1,266	1,321	1,257	1,100	4,345	3,098	4,584	6,125
Ireland[3]	3,666	6,646	6,476	6,764	6,982	2,525	3,755	4,736	5,173	1,459	2,615	3,862	4,064	4,262
Belgium[3]	(NA)	6,457	6,720	6,690	6,710	9,429	10,176	12,159	13,884	3,721	6,592	6,931	8,163	9,171
South Africa[6]	1,029	5,872	6,430	6,505	6,678	2,085	1,811	2,889	2,680	992	2,677	2,923	5,185	5,672
Switzerland[6]	13,200	7,821	6,868	6,530	(NA)	6,335	6,674	7,463	8,779	7,411	7,788	7,885	9,169	11,265
Japan	3,236	4,757	5,239	5,212	6,138	31,884	26,656	28,959	38,252	419	3,373	3,497	8,849	11,265
Czech Republic[3]	3,204	4,666	4,579	5,076	6,061	1,276	1,597	1,934	2,279	948	2,973	2,964	3,556	4,183
Tunisia	973	5,058	5,064	5,114	5,998	263	260	300	340	315	1,683	1,332	1,439	1,970
United Arab Emirates[5,6]	(NA)	3,907	5,445	5,871	(NA)	3,019	3,654	3,959	4,475	(NA)	1,063	1,524	1,583	1,594
Korea, South[2]	2,959	5,322	5,347	4,753	5,818	7,132	10,465	10,103	11,986	3,559	6,834	5,936	5,358	5,713
Singapore	4,842	6,917	6,997	5,705	(NA)	4,535	6,343	5,470	7,750	4,937	5,142	4,437	3,790	5,093
Morocco	4,024	4,240	4,303	4,761	5,516	426	444	548	575	1,259	2,039	2,646	3,221	3,923
Indonesia	2,178	5,064	5,033	4,467	5,321	3,197	3,289	3,082	3,507	2,105	4,975	5,285	4,037	4,798
Brazil	1,091	5,313	3,785	4,133	4,794	3,894	2,396	2,261	2,871	1,492	1,810	1,998	2,479	3,222
Australia	2,215	4,530	4,420	4,354	4,774	6,103	6,104	7,347	9,410	4,088	8,469	8,577	10,312	12,703

NA Not available. [1] See footnote 2, Table 1308. [2] Arrivals of nonresident visitors at national borders, including tourists and same-day visitors. [3] Arrivals are of nonresident tourists in all types of accommodation establishments. [4] Receipts include both travel and passenger transport. [5] Expenditures and receipts include both travel and passenger transport. [6] Arrivals of nonresident tourists in hotels and similar establishments.

Source: World Tourism Organization, Madrid, Spain, Yearbook of Tourism Statistics, 2005 (copyright).

Table 1373. **Net Flow of Financial Resources to Developing Countries and Multilateral Organizations: 1995 to 2004**

[165,182 represents $165,182,000,000. Net flow covers loans, grants, and grant-like flows minus amortization on loans. Military flows are excluded. Developing countries are designated by Development Assistance Committee as developing. GNI = gross national income]

Type of aid and country	Amount (mil. dol.)					Percent of GNI		
	1995	2000	2002	2003	2004	1995	2000	2004
Total net flows	165,182	134,485	73,267	126,009	148,646	0.75	0.56	0.48
United States	46,984	25,252	24,410	37,860	32,283	0.65	0.25	0.28
Australia.	2,536	1,961	834	3,010	2,466	0.76	0.53	0.41
Austria	906	1,135	1,910	1,445	1,352	0.39	0.61	0.46
Belgium	−234	2,281	1,337	1,221	816	−0.09	1.00	0.23
Canada	5,724	6,483	2,044	4,949	5,986	1.04	0.95	0.62
Denmark.	1,799	2,176	1,577	1,896	2,634	1.07	1.39	1.10
Finland	604	1,087	−180	−44	(NA)	0.50	0.91	(NA)
France	12,477	5,557	4,729	6,936	12,599	0.81	0.41	0.61
Germany	21,197	12,331	7,207	5,224	11,830	0.87	0.66	0.43
Greece	−	229	322	403	472	−	0.20	0.23
Ireland	247	740	1,469	2,334	3,851	0.46	0.93	2.47
Italy	2,800	10,846	1,399	4,218	3,239	0.26	1.01	0.19
Japan	42,295	11,423	4,659	6,335	11,351	0.82	0.24	0.24
Luxembourg	72	129	148	201	242	0.40	0.75	0.86
Netherlands	6,795	6,947	−1,487	15,196	14,106	1.71	1.85	2.46
New Zealand.	166	142	164	208	271	0.31	0.32	0.30
Norway	1,670	1,437	2,279	3,306	2,785	1.16	0.87	1.11
Portugal	395	4,622	175	1,145	676	0.38	4.45	0.41
Spain	2,025	23,471	8,171	6,667	12,762	0.37	4.25	1.25
Sweden	2,224	3,952	2,232	1,255	2,954	1.00	1.76	0.84
Switzerland	1,118	2,054	2,234	3,684	−949	0.35	0.80	−0.25
United Kingdom	13,382	10,230	7,634	18,561	26,922	1.19	0.72	1.24

NA Not Available.   – Represents zero.

Source: Organization for Economic Cooperation and Development, Paris, France, *Annual Reports of the Development Assistance Committee* (copyright).

Table 1374. **External Debt by Country: 1990 to 2004**

[In millions of dollars (28,149 represents $28,149,000,000). Total external debt is debt owed to nonresidents repayable in foreign currency, goods, or services. Total external debt is the sum of public, publicly guaranteed, and private nonguaranteed long-term debt, use of IMF credit, and short-term debt. Short-term debt includes all debt having an original maturity of one year or less and interest in arrears on long-term debt]

Country	1990	2000	2003	2004	Country	1990	2000	2003	2004
Algeria	28,149	25,272	23,386	21,987	Mexico	104,442	150,314	140,004	138,689
Angola	8,592	9,410	9,698	9,521	Morocco	25,004	20,721	18,795	17,672
Argentina	62,233	145,879	166,207	169,247	Nigeria	33,439	31,355	34,963	35,890
Bangladesh.	12,439	15,682	18,778	20,344	Pakistan	20,663	32,779	36,345	35,687
Brazil.	119,964	238,793	235,431	222,026	Panama	6,493	7,046	8,770	9,469
Bulgaria	(NA)	10,188	13,289	15,661	Peru	20,044	28,710	29,857	31,296
Cameroon.	6,657	9,277	9,496	9,496	Philippines	30,580	57,429	62,663	60,550
Chile [1]	19,226	37,048	43,231	44,058	Poland	49,364	63,259	95,219	99,190
China [1]	55,301	145,706	193,567	248,934	Romania.	1,140	10,498	21,280	30,034
Colombia . . . . . . [2] .	17,222	33,934	32,979	37,732	Russia [3]	(NA)	160,027	175,257	197,335
Congo (Kinshasa) [2] .	10,259	4,887	5,516	11,841	Serbia and				
Cote d'Ivoire	17,251	12,138	12,187	11,739	Montenegro [4, 5] . . .	(NA)	11,851	14,885	15,882
Croatia	(NA)	11,344	23,452	31,548	Slovakia	(NA)	12,140	18,379	22,068
Czech Republic	(NA)	21,526	34,630	45,561	South Africa	(NA)	24,861	27,807	28,500
Ecuador	12,107	13,717	16,864	16,868	Sri Lanka	5,863	9,155	10,238	10,887
Egypt	33,017	29,187	31,383	30,291	Sudan	14,762	15,741	17,496	19,332
Ghana	3,734	6,625	7,957	7,035	Syria	17,259	21,657	21,566	21,521
Hungary	21,202	29,520	45,785	63,159	Tanzania.	6,454	7,394	7,516	7,799
India	83,628	99,098	113,467	122,723	Thailand.	28,095	79,716	51,793	51,307
Indonesia	69,872	144,407	134,389	140,649	Tunisia	7,688	10,629	15,502	18,700
Iran	9,020	7,982	11,601	13,622	Turkey	49,424	117,431	145,662	161,595
Jordan	8,333	7,354	8,337	8,175	Ukraine	(NA)	12,190	16,309	21,652
Kazakhstan.	(NA)	11,805	22,835	32,310	Uruguay	4,415	8,196	11,764	12,376
Lebanon.	1,779	9,856	18,598	22,177	Venezuela.	33,171	38,152	34,851	35,570
Malaysia.	15,328	41,941	49,074	52,145	Vietnam	23,270	12,822	15,817	17,825

NA Not available.   [1] See footnote 2, Table 1308.   [2] See footnote 3, Table 1308.   [3] External debt data presented for the Russian Federation prior to 2000 are for the former Soviet Union. The debt of the former Soviet Union is included in the Russian Federation data after 1990 on the assumption that 100 percent of all outstanding external debt as of December 1991 has become a liability of the Russian Federation. Beginning in 2000, the data for the Russian Federation has also been revised to include obligations to members of the former Council for Mutual Economic Assistance and other countries in the form of trade-related credits amounting to $15.4 billion as of the end of 1996.   [4] External debt obligations, excluding IBRD, IMF, and short-term, of Bosnia and Herzegovina before 2000 are included under Serbia and Montenegro. Data prior to 2000 refer to the former Socialist Federal Republic of Yugoslavia. Data from 2000 onwards are estimates and reflect borrowing by the former Yugoslavia that are not yet allocated to the successor republics.   [5] As of June 2006, Serbia and Montenegro are separate countries (formerly Yugoslavia).

Source: The World Bank, Washington, DC, *2006 World Development Indicators CD-ROM* (copyright).

Table 1375. **Foreign Direct Investment Flows in OECD Countries: 2000 to 2003**

[In billions of dollars (1,288.0 represents $1,288,000,000,000). Data are converted to U.S. dollars using the yearly average exchange rate]

Country	Inflows				Outflows			
	2000	2002	2003 [1]	Cumulative, 1994–2003	2000	2002	2003 [1]	Cumulative, 1994–2003
OECD, total.	1,288.0	535.0	384.4	5,194.2	1,235.8	566.7	576.3	6,081.0
Australia.	13.2	16.5	7.8	82.3	0.7	7.6	14.3	57.4
Austria	8.8	1.0	6.9	41.2	5.7	5.3	7.1	33.6
Belgium	(NA)	13.1	31.3	44.4	(NA)	11.0	39.0	49.9
Canada	66.8	21.0	6.6	208.3	44.7	26.4	21.6	237.5
Czech Republic	5.0	8.5	2.6	37.9	(Z)	0.2	0.2	1.2
Denmark.	33.8	6.6	2.6	91.8	26.5	5.7	1.2	82.1
Finland.	8.8	7.9	2.8	45.9	24.0	7.6	-7.4	72.7
France	43.3	48.9	47.0	351.9	177.5	49.5	57.3	653.3
Germany	198.3	36.0	12.9	387.4	56.6	8.6	2.6	453.1
Greece.	1.1	0.1	0.7	8.7	2.1	0.7	(Z)	3.7
Hungary	2.8	2.8	2.5	32.4	0.6	0.3	1.6	3.9
Iceland.	0.2	0.1	0.1	1.0	0.4	0.2	0.2	1.5
Ireland	25.8	24.4	25.5	120.1	4.6	3.1	1.9	26.7
Italy	13.4	14.6	17.0	86.6	12.3	17.1	9.1	112.5
Japan	8.3	9.2	6.3	50.5	31.5	32.3	28.8	268.3
Korea, South.	9.3	2.4	3.2	41.0	5.0	2.6	3.4	37.6
Luxembourg	(NA)	117.1	73.2	190.4	(NA)	126.2	81.8	[2]5.4
Mexico	16.4	14.4	10.7	138.4	(NA)	1.0	(NA)	[2]5.4
Netherlands	63.9	25.6	19.7	286.7	75.6	34.6	36.1	383.1
New Zealand.	1.3	-0.6	0.8	19.9	0.6	-1.0	-0.1	2.9
Norway.	6.9	0.7	2.2	35.5	7.6	4.2	2.6	37.7
Poland	9.3	4.1	4.2	52.0	(Z)	0.2	0.4	1.1
Portugal	6.8	1.8	1.0	25.8	7.5	3.3	0.1	29.2
Spain	37.5	35.9	25.6	183.6	54.7	31.5	23.4	230.1
Sweden	23.2	11.6	3.4	168.4	40.7	10.7	10.6	150.3
Switzerland.	19.3	5.7	12.2	82.0	44.7	7.6	10.9	190.6
Turkey	1.0	1.0	0.6	10.6	0.9	0.2	0.5	3.6
United Kingdom.	118.8	27.8	14.6	463.5	233.5	35.2	55.3	879.5
United States.	321.3	72.4	39.9	1,366.4	159.2	134.8	173.8	1,354.6

NA Not available.   Z Less than 50,000,000.   [1] Preliminary.   [2] Based on outflow data for 2001 and 2002 only.
Source: Organization for Economic Cooperation and Development, Paris, France, *Financial Market Trends*, June 2005.

Table 1376. **Military Manpower Fit for Military Service, by Country: 2005**

[In thousands (5,172 represents 5,172,000). Covers males ages 15–49]

Country	Total	Male	Female	Country	Total	Male	Female
Afghanistan	5,172	2,663	2,509	Israel	2,468	1,256	1,212
Albania	1,317	669	648	Italy	21,416	10,964	10,452
Algeria	13,301	6,590	6,711	Jamaica.	983	479	505
Argentina.	14,759	7,316	7,443	Japan	43,730	22,235	21,495
Australia.	8,076	4,093	3,983	Kazakhstan	5,642	2,474	3,168
Austria	3,066	1,550	1,515	Korea, North.	9,664	4,811	4,853
Bahrain	287	161	125	Korea, South.	19,838	10,116	9,722
Belarus	3,761	1,658	2,103	Kuwait.	1,142	737	405
Belgium.	3,939	1,998	1,941	Laos.	1,961	955	1,006
Bolivia.	2,814	1,311	1,502	Lebanon	1,688	822	866
Bosnia and Herzegovina. .	1,792	911	881	Libya	2,522	1,292	1,231
Brazil	71,199	33,119	38,080	Malaysia	9,188	4,575	4,613
Bulgaria.	2,667	1,302	1,365	Mexico	41,025	19,058	21,967
Burma.	16,490	7,947	8,544	Morocco	13,161	6,485	6,676
Cambodia	4,004	1,955	2,049	Mozambique	(NA)	1,751	(NA)
Canada.	13,321	6,740	6,581	Netherlands	5,643	2,857	2,786
Chile.	6,252	3,123	3,128	New Zealand	1,612	810	802
China [1]	550,266	281,240	269,026	Nicaragua	2,181	1,051	1,130
Colombia.	15,781	6,986	8,794	Nigeria	28,914	15,053	13,861
Congo (Brazzaville) [2]	801	406	395	Norway.	1,628	827	801
Cote d'Ivoire.	3,885	1,973	1,912	Oman	1,017	581	435
Croatia	1,550	726	824	Pakistan	57,821	29,429	28,392
Cuba	4,839	2,442	2,397	Peru	10,217	4,938	5,279
Czech Republic.	3,920	1,997	1,924	Philippines	32,101	15,170	16,931
Denmark.	1,891	955	936	Poland	15,599	7,739	7,859
Dominican Republic.	3,208	1,671	1,536	Russia.	50,106	21,050	29,056
Ecuador	4,719	2,338	2,380	Saudi Arabia	11,252	6,593	4,659
Egypt	30,480	15,540	14,939	Singapore	(NA)	982	(NA)
El Salvador	2,271	960	1,310	South Africa	9,537	4,928	4,609
Ethiopia.	15,975	8,073	7,903	Spain	15,058	7,623	7,434
Finland	1,789	914	876	Sudan	11,077	5,427	5,650
France	22,342	11,263	11,079	Sweden.	2,935	1,494	1,441
Germany	29,702	15,259	14,443	Switzerland	2,719	1,376	1,343
Greece	4,019	2,019	2,001	Syria	6,875	3,454	3,422
Guatemala.	3,982	1,911	2,071	Thailand	21,884	10,396	11,488
Honduras.	2,223	1,101	1,122	Turkey.	27,242	13,906	13,336
Hungary	3,645	1,781	1,865	Ukraine	16,689	7,376	9,313
India	429,390	219,472	209,918	United Arab Emirates. . . .	947	527	420
Indonesia.	98,940	48,687	50,253	United Kingdom	23,602	12,046	11,556
Iran	30,671	15,666	15,006	United States	109,306	54,609	54,697
Iraq	9,701	4,930	4,771	Venezuela	10,060	4,908	5,152
Ireland	1,629	815	814	Vietnam	33,954	16,032	17,921

NA Not available.   [1] See footnote 2, Table 1308.   [2] See footnote 3, Table 1308.
Source: Central Intelligence Agency, *The World Factbook, 2006*. See also <https://www.cia.gov/cia/publications/factbook/index.html> (accessed July 2006).

Appendix I
Guide to Sources of Statistics, State Statistical Abstracts, and Foreign Statistical Abstracts

Alphabetically arranged, this guide contains references to important primary sources of statistical information for the United States. Secondary sources have been included if the information contained in them is presented in a particularly convenient form or if primary sources are not readily available. Nonrecurrent publications presenting compilations or estimates for years later than 1990, or types of data not available in regular series, are also included. Data are also available in press releases.

Valuable information may also be found in state reports, foreign statistical abstracts, which are included at the end of this appendix, and in reports for particular commodities, industries, or similar segments of our economic and social structures, many of which are not included here.

Publications listed under each subject are divided into two main groups: "U.S. Government" and "Nongovernment." The location of the publisher of each report is given except for federal agencies located in Washington, DC. Most federal publications may be purchased from the Superintendent of Documents, U.S. Goverment Printing Office, Washington, DC, tel. 202-512-1800, (Web site <http://www.access.gpo.gov>) or from Government Printing Office bookstores in certain major cities. In some cases, federal publications may be obtained from the issuing agency.

Title	Frequency	Paper	Internet	
			PDF	Other Formats
U.S. GOVERNMENT				
Administrative Office of the United States Courts <http://www.uscourts.gov>				
Calendar Year Reports on Authorized Wiretaps (state and federal)	Annual	X	X	X
Federal Court Management Statistics.	Annual	X		X
Federal Judicial Caseload Statistics.	Annual	X		
Judicial Business of the United States Courts	Annual	X	X	
Statistical Tables for the Federal Judiciary.	Semiannual	X		
Agency for International Development <http://www.usaid.gov>				
U.S. Overseas Loans and Grants and Assistance From International Organizations .	Annual	X	X	
Army, Corps of Engineers <http://www.usace.army.mil>				
Waterborne Commerce of the United States (in five parts).	Annual	X		X
Board of Governors of the Federal Reserve System <http://www.federalreserve.gov>				
Assets and Liabilities of Commercial Banks in the United States H8	Weekly	X	X	X
Consumer Credit. G.19	Weekly	X	X	X
Federal Reserve Bulletin	Annual	X	X	X
Foreign Exchange Rates. H.10.	Weekly	X	X	X
Flow of Funds Accounts of the United States. Z.1.	Quarterly	X	X	X
Industrial Production and Capacity Utilization. G.17.	Monthly	X	X	X
Money Stock and Debt Measures. H.6.	Weekly	X	X	X
Statistical Supplement to the Federal Reserve Bulletin	Monthly	X	X	X
Bureau of Economic Analysis <http://www.bea.gov>				
Survey of Current Business	Monthly	X	X	X
U.S. Direct Investment Abroad: 1999 Benchmark Survey, 2004.	Periodic	X	X	X
Bureau of Justice Statistics <http://www.ojp.usdoj.gov/bjs>				
American Indians and Crime: A BJS Statistical Profile, December 2004	Periodic	X	X	X
Background Checks for Firearm Transfers	Annual	X	X	X
Capital Punishment.	Annual	X	X	X
Carjacking, 1993–2002, July 2004.	Periodic		X	X
Census of Publicly Funded Forensic Crime Laboratories, February 2005	Periodic	X	X	X
Census of State and Federal Correctional Facilities, 2000, August 2003.	Periodic		X	X
Civil Rights Complaints in U.S. District Courts, July 2002.	Periodic	X	X	X
Civil Trial Cases and Verdicts in Large Counties, 2001, April 2004.	Periodic	X	X	X

Title	Frequency	Paper	Internet PDF	Internet Other Formats
Bureau of Justice Statistics—Con.				
Compendium of Federal Justice Statistics, 2003	Annual	X	X	X
Contacts Between Police and Public: Findings from the 2002 National Survey	Periodic	X	X	X
Contract Trials and Verdicts in Large Counties, 2001, February 2005	Periodic	X	X	X
Crime and the Nation's Households, 2004. April 2006	Annual	X	X	X
Crimes Against Persons Age 65 or Older, 1993–2002, January 2005	Periodic	X	X	X
Criminal Victimization in the United States	Annual	X	X	X
Cross-National Studies in Crime and Justice, September 2004	Periodic	X	X	X
Defense Counsel in Criminal Cases, November 2000	Periodic	X	X	X
Education and Correctional Populations, January 2003	Periodic	X	X	X
Family Violence Statistics	Annual		X	X
Federal Criminal Case Processing	Biennial		X	X
Federal Law Enforcement Officers, 2002, July 2003	Biennial	X	X	X
Felony Defendants in Large Urban Counties, 2002, February 2006	Biennial	X	X	X
Felony Sentences in State Courts, 2002, December 2004	Periodic	X	X	X
Firearm Use by Offenders, November 2001	Periodic	X	X	X
Hepatitis Testing and Treatment in State Prisons, April 2004	Periodic	X	X	X
Hispanic Victims of Violent Crime, 1993–2000, April 2002	Annual	X	X	X
HIV in Prisons and Jails	Annual	X	X	X
Homicide Trends in the United States	Periodic	X	X	X
Identity Theft, 2004. April 2006	Periodic	X	X	X
Immigration Offenders in the Federal Criminal Justice System, August 2002	Periodic	X	X	X
Incarcerated Parents and Their Children, August 2000	Annual	X	X	X
Indicators of School Crime and Safety	Periodic	X	X	X
Intimate Partner Violence, 1993–2001, February 2003	Annual	X	X	X
Jails in Indian Country, 2002, November 2003	Periodic	X	X	X
Justice Expenditure and Employment in the United States, 2003, April 2004	Periodic	X	X	X
Juvenile Offenders and Victims	Periodic	X	X	X
Juvenile Victimization and Offending, 1993–2003	Periodic		X	X
Law Enforcement Management and Administrative Statistics 2000: Data for Individual State and Local Agencies with 100 or More Officers	Periodic	X	X	X
Local Police Departments, 2003, May 2006	Periodic	X	X	X
Medical Malpractice Trials and Verdicts in Large Counties, April 2004	Periodic	X	X	X
Money Laundering Offenders, 1994–2001, July 2003	Periodic	X	X	X
Prevalence of Imprisonment in the U.S. Population, 1974–2001, August 2003	Periodic	X	X	X
Prison and Jail Inmates at Midyear	Annual	X	X	X
Prisoners in 2004	Annual	X	X	X
Probation and Parole in the United States	Annual	X	X	X
Profile of Jail Inmates, 2002, July 2004	Periodic		X	X
Prosecutors in State Courts, 2001, May 2002	Biennial		X	X
Rape and Sexual Assault: Reporting to Police and Medical Attention, August 2002	Periodic	X	X	X
Reentry Trends in the United States Current Data Electronic	Periodic		X	X
Sheriffs' Offices, 2000, January 2003	Periodic	X	X	X
Sourcebook of Criminal Justice Statistics	Annual		X	X
State Court Prosecutors in Large Districts, December 2001	Periodic	X	X	X
State Court Prosecutors in Small Districts, 2001, January 2003	Periodic		X	X
State Court Sentencing of Convicted Felons, 2000, June 2003	Biennial	X	X	X
State Prison Expenditures, 2001, June 2004	Periodic	X	X	X
Summary of State Sex Offender Registries, 2001, March 2002	Periodic		X	X
Survey of DNA Crime Laboratories, 2001, January 2002	Periodic	X	X	X
Survey of State Criminal History Information Systems, September 2003	Biennial		X	X
Survey of State Procedures Related to Firearm Sales	Annual		X	X
Tort Trials and Verdicts in Large Counties, November 2004	Periodic	X	X	X
Traffic Stop Data Collection Policies for State Police, 2004, June 2005	Periodic		X	X
Violent Victimization of College Students, 1995–2002, January 2005	Periodic		X	X
Weapon Use and Violent Crime, 1993–2001, September 2003	Periodic	X	X	X
Bureau of Labor Statistics				
<http://www.bls.gov>				
100 Years of U.S. Consumer Spending: Data for the Nation, New York City and Boston, Report 991	Periodic	X	X	
College Enrollment and Work Activity of High School Graduates	Annual	X		
Comparative Labor Force Statistics, Ten Countries	Annual	X	X	X
Compensation and Working Conditions	Quarterly	X	X	X
Consumer Expenditure Survey, Integrated Diary and Interview Survey data	Annual	X	X	X
Consumer Prices: Energy and Food	Monthly	X	X	X
CPI Detailed Report	Monthly	X	X	X
Employee Benefits in Private Industry	Annual	X	X	X
Employer Costs for Employee Compensation	Annual	X	X	X
Employment and Earnings	Monthly	X	X	X
Employment and Wages	Annual	X	X	X
Employment Characteristics of Families	Annual	X	X	X
Employment Cost Index	Quarterly	X	X	X
Employment Cost Indexes and Levels	Annual	X	X	X
The Employment Situation	Monthly	X	X	X
Geographic Profile of Employment and Unemployment	Annual	X	X	
International Comparisons of Hourly Compensation Costs for Production Workers in Manufacturing	Annual	X	X	X
International Comparisons of Manufacturing Productivity and Unit Labor Cost Trends	Annual	X	X	X
Metropolitan Area Employment and Unemployment	Monthly	X	X	X
Monthly Labor Review	Monthly	X	X	X
Occupational Injuries and Illnesses in the United States by Industry	Annual	X	X	X
Occupational Projections and Training Data	Biennial	X	X	X
Producer Price Indexes Detailed Report	Monthly	X	X	X
Productivity Measures for Selected Industries and Government Services	Annual	X	X	X
Real Earnings	Monthly	X	X	

874   Appendix I

Title	Frequency	Paper	Internet PDF	Internet Other Formats
Bureau of Labor Statistics—Con.				
Regional and State Employment and Unemployment	Monthly	X	X	X
Relative Importance of Components in the Consumer Price Indexes	Annual	X	X	X
Union Members	Annual	X	X	X
U.S. Import and Export Price Indexes	Monthly	X	X	X
Usual Weekly Earnings of Wage and Salary Workers	Quarterly	X	X	X
Work Experience of the Population	Annual	X	X	X
Bureau of Land Management				
<http://www.blm.gov>				
Public Land Statistics	Annual	X	X	
Census Bureau				
<http://www.census.gov>				
2002 Economic Census				
Comparative Statistics	Quinquennial	X	X	X
Bridge Between NAICS and SIC	Quinquennial	X	X	X
Business Expenses	Quinquennial	X	X	X
Industry/Geography	Quinquennial		X	X
2002 Economic Census, Company Statistics Series, Survey of Business Owners	Quinquennial	X	X	X
American Indian- and Alaska Native-Owned Firms	Quinquennial	X	X	X
Asian-Owned Firms	Quinquennial	X	X	X
Black-Owned Firms	Quinquennial	X	X	X
Hispanic-Owned Firms	Quinquennial	X	X	X
Native Hawaiian- and other Pacific Islander-Owned Firms	Quinquennial	X	X	X
Annual Revision of Monthly Retail and Food Services: Sales and Inventories	Annual	X	X	
Annual Revision of Monthly Wholesale Distributors: Sales and Inventories	Annual	X	X	X
Annual Survey of Manufactures	Annual	X	X	
Census of Governments	Quinquennial	X	X	
Volume 3, No. 2 Compendium of Public Employment	Quinquennial	X	X	
Volume 4, No. 6 Employee-Retirement Systems of State and Local Governments	Quinquennial	X	X	
Volume 3, No. 1 Employment of Major Local Governments	Quinquennial	X	X	
Volume 4, No. 3 Finances of County Governments	Quinquennial	X	X	
Volume 1, No. 1 Government Organization	Quinquennial	X	X	
Volume 4, No. 1 Public Education Finances	Quinquennial	X	X	
Census of Housing Decennial (2000, most recent)	Decennial	X	X	X
Census of Population Decennial (2000, most recent)	Decennial	X	X	X
CFFR Consolidated Federal Funds Report	Annual	X	X	X
State and County Areas	Annual	X	X	X
County Business Patterns	Annual		X	X
Current Construction Reports:				
New Residential Construction and New Residential Sales:	Annual	X	X	
Value of Construction Put in Place, C30	Monthly	X	X	
Residential Improvements and Repairs, C50	Monthly	X	X	
Current Housing Reports:				
Housing Vacancies, H111	Quarterly	X	X	
Who Can Afford to Buy a House, H121	Biennial	X	X	
Market Absorption of Apartments, H130	Quarterly	X	X	
Characteristics of Apartments Completed, H131	Annual	X	X	
American Housing Survey for the United States, H150	Biennial	X	X	
American Housing Survey for Selected Metropolitan Areas, H170	Biennial	X	X	
Current Industrial Reports			X	
Current Population Reports (Series P20)		X	X	X
Consumer Income and Poverty, P60, and Household Economic Studies, P70		X	X	
Alternative Poverty Estimates in the United States: 2003	Periodic	X	X	
Alternative Income Estimates in the United States: 2003	Periodic	X	X	
Income, Poverty, and Health Insurance Coverage in the United States	Annual	X	X	X
Economic Census of Outlying Areas	Quinquennial	X	X	
Federal Aid to States for Fiscal Year	Annual	X	X	X
Global Population Profile: 2002 (Series WP)		X	X	X
International Briefs (Series IB)		X	X	
International Population Reports (Series IPC)		X	X	
Manufacturers' Shipments, Inventories, and Orders	Monthly	X	X	
Manufacturers' Shipments, Inventories, and Orders: 1992–2005	Annual	X	X	
Minority- and Women-Owned Business Enterprises	Quinquennial	X	X	X
Nonemployer Statistics	Annual		X	X
Quarterly Financial Report for Manufacturing, Mining, and Trade Corporations	Quarterly	X	X	
Service Annual Survey Report	Annual	X	X	
Survey of Plant Capacity Utilization (Current Industrial Reports MQ-C1)	Annual	X	X	
U.S. International Trade in Goods and Services: includes cumulative data		X	X	X
U.S. Trade with Puerto Rico and U.S. Possessions (FT 895)	Monthly	X	X	
Vehicle Inventory and Use Survey	Quinquennial	X	X	X
Centers for Disease Control and Prevention, Atlanta, GA				
<http://www.cdc.gov>				
Injury Fact Book, 2001–2002		X	X	X
Morbidity and Mortality Weekly Report	Annual	X	X	X
Centers for Medicare and Medicaid Services (CMS)				
<http://www.cms.hhs.gov>				
CMS Statistics	Annual	X	X	
Data Compendium	Annual	X	X	
Health Care Financing Review Medicare and Medicaid Statistical Supplement	Quarterly	X	X	
Health Care Financing Review	Quarterly	X	X	
Trustees' Report	Annual	X	X	
Central Intelligence Agency				
<http://www.cia.gov>				
World Factbook	Annual	X	X	X
Coast Guard (See Department of Homeland Security)				

U.S. Census Bureau, Statistical Abstract of the United States: 2007

Title	Frequency	Paper	PDF	Other Formats
Comptroller of the Currency <http://www.occ.treas.gov>				
Quarterly Journal	Quarterly		X	X
Office of the Clerk U.S. House of Representatives <http://clerk.house.gov>				
Statistics of the Presidential and Congressional Election	Biennial		X	X
Council of Economic Advisers <http://www.whitehouse.gov>				
Economic Indicators	Monthly	X	X	X
Economic Report of the President	Annual	X	X	
Department of Agriculture <http://www.usda.gov>				
Agricultural Chemical Usage	Periodic	X	X	X
Agricultural Income and Finance (Situation and Outlook Report)	Quarterly	X	X	X
Agricultural Land Values and Cash Rents	Annual	X	X	X
Agricultural Price Reports	Annual	X	X	X
Agricultural Statistics	Annual	X	X	
Amber Waves	Periodic	X	X	X
America's Diverse Family Farms: Structure and Finances	Periodic	X	X	
Catfish Production	Annual	X	X	X
Cattle	Biennial	X	X	X
Census of Agriculture	Quinquennial	X	X	
Cherry Production	Annual	X	X	X
Chickens and Eggs	Annual	X	X	X
Citrus Fruits	Annual	X	X	X
Cotton and Wool Yearbook	Annual	X	X	
Cotton Ginnings	Periodic	X	X	X
Cranberries	Annual	X	X	X
Crop Production Reports	Monthly	X	X	X
Crop Values Report	Annual	X	X	X
Dairy Products	Annual	X	X	X
Farm Labor	Quarterly	X	X	X
Farms, Land in Farms, and Livestock Operations	Annual	X	X	X
Floriculture Crops	Annual	X	X	X
Food Marketing Review, (Agricultural Economic Report No. 743)	Annual	X	X	X
Food Spending in American Households (Statistical Bulletin No. 824)	Annual	X	X	X
Income, Wealth, and the Economic Well-Being of Farm Households (ERS)	Periodic	X	X	X
Livestock and Poultry World Markets and Trade	Annual			
Livestock Slaughter	Annual	X	X	X
Meat Animals: Production, Disposition, and Income	Annual	X	X	X
Milk Production	Annual	X	X	X
Noncitrus Fruits and Nuts	Biennial	X	X	X
Poultry: Production and Value Summary	Annual	X	X	X
Rural Development Perspectives		X	X	
Situation and Outlook Reports Issued for agricultural exports, cotton and wool, dairy, feed, fruit and tree nuts, agricultural resources, livestock and poultry, oil crops, rice, aquaculture, sugar and sweeteners, tobacco, vegetables, wheat, and world agriculture	Periodic	X	X	
Stock Reports, stocks of grain, peanuts, potatoes, and rice	Periodic	X	X	X
Structure and Finances of U.S. Farms: 2005 Family Farm Report	Periodic	X	X	
Tobacco: World Markets and Trade	Annual			
Trout Production	Annual	X	X	X
Turkeys: Hatchery and Raised	Annual	X	X	X
Usual planting and harvesting dates	Periodic	X	X	X
Vegetable Reports	Periodic	X	X	X
Weekly Weather and Crop Bulletin Report	Weekly	X	X	
Winter Wheat Seedlings	Monthly	X	X	X
World Agricultural Supply and Demand	Monthly	X	X	X
Department of Agriculture, Food and Nutrition Service <http://www.fns.usda.gov>				
Annual Historical Review	Annual	X		
Characteristics of Food Stamp Households	Annual			
Food and Consumer Service Programs		X	X	X
Department of Agriculture, Natural Resources and Conservation Service <http://www.nrcs.usda.gov>				
National Resources Inventory	Periodic	X		X
Department of Defense <http://www.defenselink.mil/pubs>				
Foreign Military Sales and Military Assistance Facts	Annual			X
Personnel Statistics	Annual		X	
Department of Education <http://www.ed.gov>				
Department of Education, Rehabilitation Services Administration				
Caseload Statistics of State Vocational Rehabilitation Agencies in Fiscal Year	Annual	X	X	X
Department of Health and Human Services <http://www.os.hhs.gov>				
Annual Report	Annual	X		
Department of Homeland Security (DHS) <http://www.dhs.gov>				
Budget in Brief	Annual	X	X	
Department of Homeland Security, Coast Guard <http://www.uscg.mil/USCG.shtm>				
Fact File		X	X	X
Department of Homeland Security, Office of Immigration Statistics <http://uscis.gov/graphics/shared/statistics/index.htm>				

Title	Frequency	Paper	Internet PDF	Internet Other Formats
Department of Homeland Security, Office of Immigration Statistics—Con.				
Yearbook of Immigration Statistics	Annual	X	X	
Department of Housing and Urban Development <http://www.hud.gov>				
Survey of Mortgage Lending Activity	Monthly	X		X
Department of Labor <http://www.dol.gov>				
Annual Report of the Secretary	Annual	X	X	X
Department of State <http://www.state.gov>				
United States Contribution to International Organizations	Annual			X
Department of Transportation <http://www.dot.gov>				
Air Travel Consumer Report	Monthly	X	X	X
Airport Activity Statistics of Certified Route Air Carriers	Annual	X		X
Transportation Safety Information Report	Quarterly	X		X
U.S. International Air Travel Statistics	Quarterly	X	X	X
Wage Statistics of Class I Railroads in the United States	Annual	X	X	
Department of the Treasury <http://www.treasury.gov>				
Department of the Treasury, Alcohol and Tobacco Tax and Trade Bureau <http://www.atf.treas.gov>				
Alcohol and Tobacco Summary Statistics	Annual	X		
Tobacco Products Monthly Statistical Releases		X		
Department of the Treasury, Bureau of Public Debt <http://www.publicdebt.treas.gov>				
Monthly Statement of the Public Debt of the United States	Monthly	X	X	X
Department of the Treasury, Financial Management Services <http://www.fms.treas.gov>				
Active Foreign Credits of the United States Government	Quarterly	X		
Combined Statement of Receipts, Outlays, and Balances	Annual	X	X	X
Monthly Treasury Statement of Receipts and Outlays of the United States Government	Monthly	X	X	X
Treasury Bulletin	Quarterly	X	X	X
Financial Report of the United States Government	Annual	X	X	
Department of Veterans Affairs <http://www.va.gov>				
Disability Compensation, Pension, and Death Pension Data	Annual	X		X
Government Life Insurance Programs for Veterans and Members of the Service	Annual	X		X
Selected Compensation and Pension Data by State of Residence	Annual	X		X
Veterans Affairs Annual Accountability Report	Annual	X	X	X
Drug Enforcement Administration <http://www.whitehousedrugpolicy.gov>				
Drug Abuse and Law Enforcement Statistics	Irregular	X	X	X
Employment and Training Administration <http://www.doleta.gov>				
Unemployment Insurance Claims	Weekly			X
Energy Information Administration <http://www.eia.doe.gov>				
Annual Energy Outlook	Annual	X	X	X
Annual Energy Review	Annual	X	X	X
Annual Coal Report	Annual		X	X
Electric Power Annual	Annual		X	X
Electric Power Monthly	Monthly	X	X	X
Electric Sales, Revenue and Retail Price	Annual		X	X
Emissions of Greenhouse Gases in the U.S.	Annual		X	X
International Energy Annual	Annual			X
International Energy Outlook	Annual		X	X
Monthly Energy Review, 2005	Monthly	X	X	X
Performance Profiles of Major Energy Producers	Annual		X	X
Petroleum Marketing Annual	Monthly		X	X
Petroleum Supply Annual Volume 1	Annual		X	X
Petroleum Supply Annual Volume 2 (Web only)	Annual		X	X
Petroleum Supply Monthly 2005	Monthly		X	X
Quarterly Coal Report, 2004	Quarterly		X	X
Renewable Energy Annual	Annual		X	
Residential Energy Consumption Survey	Quadrennial		X	X
State Electricity Profiles, 2002	Annual		X	X
State Energy Data Report	Annual		X	X
State Energy Price and Expenditure Report	Annual		X	X
U.S. Crude Oil, Natural Gas, and Natural Gas Liquids Reserves	Annual		X	X
Weekly Coal Production, 2005 (Web only)	Weekly		X	X
Environmental Protection Agency <http://www.epa.gov>				
Air Quality Data	Annual			X
Drinking Water Infrastructure Needs Survey	Periodic	X	X	
Needs Survey, Conveyance and Treatment of Municipal Wastewater Summaries of Technical Data	Biennial		X	
Toxics Release Inventory	Annual		X	X
National Water Quality Inventory: 2000 Report (EPA-841-T-01-001)	Biennial	X	X	
Export-Import Bank of the United States <http://www.exim.gov>				
Annual Report	Annual	X	X	
Report to the U.S. Congress on Export Credit Competition and the Export-Import Bank of the United States	Annual	X	X	

U.S. Census Bureau, Statistical Abstract of the United States: 2007

Title	Frequency	Paper	Internet PDF	Internet Other Formats
Farm Credit Administration <http://www.fca.gov>				
Annual Report on the Work of the Cooperative Farm Credit System	Annual	X	X	
Loans and Discounts of Farm Credit Banks and Associations.	Annual	X		
Production Credit Association: Summary of Operations	Annual	X		
Report to the Federal Land Bank Associations.	Annual	X		
Federal Bureau of Investigation <http://www.fbi.gov/ucr/ucr.htm>				
Bomb Summary.	Annual			
Crime in the United States.	Annual	X	X	X
Hate Crime Statistics	Annual	X	X	X
Law Enforcement Officers Killed and Assaulted	Annual	X	X	X
Federal Communications Commission <http://www.fcc.gov>				
Annual Report	Annual	X	X	
Statistics of Communications Common Carriers.	Annual	X	X	
Federal Deposit Insurance Corporation <http://www.fdic.gov>				
Annual Report	Annual	X	X	
Bank and Thrift Branch Office Data Book	Annual	X	X	X
Banking Review.	Quarterly	X	X	
Historical Statistics on Banking.	Quarterly			
Quarterly Banking Profile.	Quarterly	X	X	
Statistics on Banking.	Annual	X	X	X
Summary of Deposits	Annual	X	X	X
Trust Assets of Financial Institutions	Annual	X		X
Federal Highway Administration <http://www.fhwa.dot.gov>				
Highway Statistics	Annual	X	X	
Federal Railroad Administration <http://www.fra.dot.gov> <http://safetydata.fra.dot.gov/officeofsafety>				
Accident/Incident Bulletin Summary, statistics, and analysis of accidents on railroads in the United States	Annual	X	X	
Rail-Highway Crossing Accident/Incident and Inventory Bulletin	Annual	X	X	
Railroad Safety Statistics.	Annual	X	X	X
Fish and Wildlife Service <http://www.fws.gov>				
Federal Aid in Fish and Wildlife Restoration	Annual	X	X	
National Survey of Fishing, Hunting, and Wildlife Associated Recreation.	Quinquennial	X	X	
Forest Service <http://www.fs.fed.us>				
An Analysis of the Timber Situation in the United States 1996–2050	Periodic			X
Land Areas of the National Forest System	Annual	X		X
The 1993 RPA Timber Assessment Update.	Periodic			
U.S. Timber Production, Trade, Consumption, and Price Statistics 2001	Biennial	X	X	
General Services Administration <http://www.gsa.gov>				
Inventory Report on Real Property Leased to the United States Throughout the World	Annual	X	X	
Inventory Report on Real Property Owned by the United States Throughout the World	Annual	X	X	
Geological Survey <http://ask.usgs.gov>				
A Statistical Summary of Data from the U.S. Geological Surveys National Water Quality Networks (Open-File Report 83-533).		X		
Estimated Use of Water in the United States in 2000	Quinquennial	X	X	X
Mineral Commodity Summaries.	Annual	X		X
Mineral Industry Surveys.	Monthly	X	X	X
Minerals Yearbook	Monthly	X	X	X
Internal Revenue Service <http://www.irs.gov>				
Corporation Income Tax Returns.	Annual	X	X	X
Individual Income Tax Returns	Annual	X	X	X
IRS Data Book.	Annual	X	X	X
Statistics of Income Bulletin	Quarterly	X	X	X
International Trade Administration <http://www.ita.doc.gov>				
U.S. Foreign Trade Highlights.	Annual			X
International Trade Administration, Office of Travel and Tourism Industries <http://www.tinet.ita.doc.gov>				
Travel Data reports.		X		
International Trade Commission <http://www.usitc.gov>				
Recent Trends in U.S. Services	Periodic	X	X	
Synthetic Organic Chemicals, U.S. Production and Sales	Annual	X	X	
Library of Congress <http://www.loc.gov>				
Annual Report.	Annual	X	X	
Maritime Administration <http://www.marad.dot.gov>				
Annual Report.	Annual	X	X	
Cargo-Carrying U.S. Flag Fleet by Area of Operation	Semiannual	X	X	X

U.S. Census Bureau, Statistical Abstract of the United States: 2007

Title	Frequency	Paper	Internet PDF	Internet Other Formats
Maritime Administration—Con.				
Merchant Fleet Ocean-Going Vessels 1,000 Gross Tons and Over	Quarterly			X
Seafaring Wage Rates	Biennial	X	X	
Mine Safety and Health Administration				
<http://www.msha.gov>				
Informational Reports by Mining Industry: Coal; Metallic Minerals; Nonmetallic Minerals (except stone and coal); Stone, Sand, and Gravel	Annual			X
Mine Injuries and Worktime (Some preliminary data)......................	Quarterly	X		X
National Aeronautics and Space Administration				
<http://ifmp.nasa.gov>				
Annual Procurement Report......................................	Annual	X	X	
The Civil Service Work Force		X	X	
National Center for Education Statistics				
<http://nces.ed.gov>				
Characteristics of the 100 Largest Public Elementary and Secondary School Districts in the United States..	Annual	X	X	X
College and University Library Survey				X
Computer and Internet Use by Children and Adolescents	Biennial	X	X	
The Condition of Education	Annual	X	X	
Digest of Education Statistics..	Annual	X	X	
Earned Degrees Conferred	Annual		X	X
Elementary and Secondary Education	Annual	X	X	X
Faculty Salaries, Tenure, and Benefits	Annual	X	X	
Fall Enrollment in Degree-Granting Institutions..........................	Annual	X	X	X
Fall Staff in Postsecondary Institutions	Biennial	X	X	
Federal Support for Education	Annual		X	
Financial Statistics of Higher Education	Annual	X	X	
Indicators of School Crime and Safety	Annual	X	X	
National Assessment of Educational Progress	Annual	X	X	
National Education Statistics Quarterly (last edition 4th quarter 2005)	Quarterly			X
National Household Education Survey:..................................	Annual	X	X	
Early Childhood Program Participation Survey	Periodic	X	X	
The Nation's Report Card: Mathematics Highlights 2003	Periodic	X	X	
The Nation's Report Card: Reading Highlights 2003	Periodic	X	X	
The Nation's Report Card: Geography 2004	Periodic	X	X	
The Nation's Report Card: Science 2000	Periodic	X	X	
The Nation's Report Card: History 2001	Periodic	X	X	
The Nation's Report Card: Writing 2002	Periodic	X	X	
Private School Survey..	Biennial	X		X
Projections of Education Statistics....................................	Annual	X	X	X
Revenues and Expenditures for Public Elementary and Secondary Education	Annual	X	X	X
School and Staffing Survey:..	Quadrennial			X
Characteristics of Schools, Districts, Teachers, Principals, and School Libraries in the United States	Annual	X	X	
Statistics of Public Elementary and Secondary School Systems Fall	Annual	X	X	X
Status and Trends in the Education of Blacks		X	X	
National Center for Health Statistics				
<http://www.cdc.gov/nchs/>				
Ambulatory Care Visits to Physician Offices, Hospital Outpatient Departments and Emergency Departments...........................	Annual	X	X	
Health: United States	Annual	X	X	
Health Characteristics of Adults 55 Years of Age and Over	Periodic	X	X	
Fertility, Family Planning, and Reproductive Health of U.S. Women:				
Data from the 2002 National Survey of Family Growth..................	Periodic		X	X
National Hospital Discharge Survey: Annual Summary	Annual		X	
National Vital Statistics Reports (NVRS)................................	Monthly		X	
Vital and Health Statistics			X	
Series 10: Health Interview Survey Statistics..........................	Annual	X	X	
Series 11: Health and Nutrition Examination Survey Statistics..............	Irregular	X	X	
Series 13: Data from National Health Care Survey	Irregular	X	X	
Series 14: Data on Health Resources: Manpower and Facilities	Irregular	X	X	
Series 20: Mortality Data	Irregular	X	X	
Series 21: Natality, Marriage, and Divorce Data	Irregular	X	X	
Series 23: Data from the National Survey of Family Growth	Irregular	X	X	
National Credit Union Administration				
<http://www.ncua.gov>				
Annual Report..	Annual	X	X	
Midyear Statistics..	Semiannual	X	X	
Yearend Statistics..	Annual		X	
National Endowment for the Arts				
<http://www.nea.gov>				
National Endowment for the Arts, Annual Report	Annual			X
The Performing Arts in the GDP, 2002	Periodic	X	X	
Artist Labor Force by State, 2000	Periodic	X	X	
Artist Employment, 2000–2002......................................	Periodic	X	X	
The Arts in the GDP...	Periodic	X	X	
Demographic Characteristics of Art Attendance, 2002	Periodic	X	X	
2002 Survey of Public Participation in the Arts..........................	Periodic	X	X	
National Endowment for the Humanities				
<ttp://www.neh.gov>				
Budget Request..	Annual	X		X
National Guard Bureau				
<http://www.ngb.army.mil/>				
Annual Review of the Chief	Annual	X	X	
National Highway Traffic Safety Administration				
<http://www.nhtsa.dot.gov>				

Title	Frequency	Paper	PDF	Other Formats
National Highway Traffic Safety Administration—Con.				
Traffic Safety Facts.	Annual	X	X	
The National Library of Medicine (for clinical medical reports)				
<http://www.nlm.nih.gov>				
Annual Report	Annual		X	
National Oceanic and Atmospheric Administration				
<http://www.lib.noaa.gov>				
Climates of the World, HCS 6-4	Monthly	X		
Climatological Data Issued in sections for states and outlying areas	Monthly	X		X
Comparative Climatic Data.	Annual	X		X
Daily Normals of Temp, Precip, HDD, & CDD/Clim 84.	Periodic			X
Fisheries of the United States.	Annual	X	X	
General Summary of Tornadoes	Annual			X
Hourly Precipitation Data Monthly with annual summary; for each state	Monthly			X
Local Climatological Data Monthly with annual summary; for major cities	Monthly			X
Monthly Climatic Data for the World.	Monthly			X
Monthly Normals of Temp, Precip, HDD, & CDD/Clim 84.	Periodic		X	X
Our Living Oceans	Periodic	X	X	
Storm Data	Monthly			X
U.S. Climate Normals	Daily	X	X	X
Weekly Weather and Crop Bulletin National Summary	Weekly	X	X	
National Park Service				
<http://www.nps.gov>				
Federal Recreation Fee Report.	Annual	X		
National Park Statistical Abstract.	Annual	X	X	
National Science Foundation				
<http://www.nsf.gov>				
Academic Research and Development Expenditures	Annual	X	X	X
Academic Science and Engineering: Graduate Enrollment and Support	Annual	X	X	X
Characteristics of Doctoral Scientists and Engineers in the United States	Biennial	X	X	X
Characteristics of Recent Science/Engineering Graduates	Biennial	X	X	
Federal Funds for Research and Development	Annual	X	X	X
Federal R&D Funding by Budget Function Report	Annual	X	X	X
Federal Science and Engineering Support to Universities, Colleges, and				
Nonprofit Institutions: Detailed statistical tables	Annual	X	X	X
Federal Support to Universities, Colleges, and Nonprofit Institutions	Annual		X	
Graduate Science and Engineering Students and Postdoctorates	Annual		X	X
Graduate Students and Postdoctorates in Science and Engineering	Annual	X	X	X
Immigrant Scientists, Engineers, and Technicians.	Annual	X	X	X
International Science and Technology Data Update Report	Annual	X		
National Patterns of Research & Development Resources Report	Annual	X	X	X
Planned R&D Expenditures of Major U.S. Firms Special Report (NSF 91-306)		X		
Research and Development in Industry	Annual	X	X	X
Science and Engineering Degrees.	Annual	X	X	
Science and Engineering Degrees, by Race/Ethnicity of Recipients: Detailed				
Statistical Tables.	Annual	X	X	
Science and Engineering Doctorate Awards	Annual	X	X	X
Science and Engineering Indicators Report.	Biennial	X	X	X
Science and Engineering Personnel: A National Overview Report	Biennial		X	X
Science and Engineering Profiles	Annual	X	X	X
Science and Technology Pocket Data Book Report.	Annual	X	X	X
Science Resources Studies Data Brief.	Frequent			X
Scientific and Engineering Research Facilities at Universities and Colleges.	Biennial		X	X
Scientists, Engineers, and Technicians in the United States: Detailed				
Statistical Tables.	Triennial	X	X	X
U.S. Scientists and Engineers.	Biennial	X	X	X
Women, Minorities in Science and Engineering Report	Biennial	X	X	
National Transportation Safety Board				
<http://www.ntsb.gov>				
Accidents; Air Carriers.	Annual	X	X	
Accidents; General Aviation	Annual	X	X	
Office of Juvenile Justice and Delinquency Prevention				
<http://ojjdp.ncjrs.org>				
Highlights of the 2002 National Youth Gang Survey (FS-200401)	Annual		X	X
Juvenile Arrests 2002 (Bulletin, NCJ 204608)	Annual		X	X
Victims of Violent Juvenile Crime (Bulletin, NCJ 201628).	Periodic	X	X	X
Office of Management and Budget				
<http://www.whitehouse.gov/omb>				
The Budget of the United States Government	Annual	X	X	
Office of Personnel Management				
<http://www.opm.gov>				
Civil Service Retirement and Disability Fund Report	Annual	X		
Demographic Profile of the Federal Workforce.	Biennial	X	X	X
Employment and Trends	Bimonthly	X	X	X
Employment by Geographic Area	Biennial	X	X	X
The Fact Book.	Annual	X	X	X
Federal Employment Statistics	Annual			X
Occupations of Federal White-Collar and Blue-Collar Workers	Biennial		X	X
Pay Structure of the Federal Civil Service.	Annual		X	X
Statistical Abstract for the Federal Employee Benefit Programs.	Annual			X
Work Years and Personnel Costs	Annual	X	X	
Patent and Trademark Office				
<http://www.uspto.gov>				
Technology Assessment and Forecast Reports		X	X	X
All Technologies (Utility Patents)	Annual	X	X	X
Patent Counts by Country/State and Year, Utility Patents Report.	Annual	X	X	X

880 Appendix I

Title	Frequency	Paper	Internet PDF	Internet Other Formats
Patent and Trademark Office—Con.				
Patenting Trends in the United States	Annual	X		
Railroad Retirement Board, Chicago, IL				
<http://www.rrb.gov/default.asp>				
Annual Report.	Annual	X	X	
Monthly Benefit Statistics.	Monthly	X	X	
Statistical Supplement to the Annual Report	Annual	X	X	
Securities and Exchange Commission				
<http://www.sec.gov>				
Annual Report	Annual		X	
Small Business Administration				
<http://www.sba.gov>				
Annual Report.	Annual	X		X
Handbook of Small Business Data.		X	X	
The State of Small Business	Annual	X	X	
Social Security Administration				
<http://www.ssa.gov>				
Annual Statistical Report on the Social Security Disability Insurance Program	Annual	X	X	X
Annual Statistical Supplement to the Social Security Bulletin	Annual	X	X	X
Children Receiving SSI	Annual	X	X	X
Congressional Statistics, 2005	Annual	X	X	X
Income of the Population 55 and over	Biennially	X	X	X
SSI Annual Statistical Report	Annual	X	X	X
SSI Disabled Recipients Who Work	Annual	X	X	X
SSI Recipients by State and County	Annual	X	X	X
Social Security Beneficiaries State and County Data.	Annual	X	X	X
Social Security Bulletin	Quarterly	X	X	X
State Assistance Programs for SSI Recipients	Annual	X	X	X
Supplemental Security Income, State and County Data.	Annual	X	X	X
OASDI Beneficiaries by State and County.	Annual	X	X	X
Substance Abuse and Mental Health Services Administration				
<http://www.samhsa.gov>				
National Survey on Drug Use and Health	Annual	X	X	X
National Survey on Substance Abuse Treatment Services (N-SSATS)	Annual	X	X	X

NONGOVERNMENT

Title	Frequency	Paper	Internet PDF	Internet Other Formats
Aerospace Industries Association, Washington, DC				
<http://www.aia-aerospace.org>				
Aerospace Facts and Figures.	Annual	X	X	
Aerospace Industry Year-End Review and Forecast	Annual	X	X	X
Commercial Helicopter Shipments	Triennial	X	X	
Employment in the Aerospace Industry.	Monthly		X	
Exports of Aerospace Products	Quarterly	X	X	
Imports of Aerospace Products	Quarterly	X	X	
Manufacturing Production, Capacity, and Utilization in Aerospace and Aircraft and Parts	Monthly	X	X	
Orders, Shipments, Backlog, and Inventories for Aircraft, Missiles, and Parts	Monthly	X	X	
Air Transport Association of America, Inc., Washington, DC				
<http://www.airlines.org>				
Air Transport Association, Annual Report	Annual	X	X	
The Alan Guttmacher Institute, New York, NY				
<http://www.guttmacher.org>				
Perspectives on Sexual and Reproductive Health.	Bimonthly	X	X	X
American Bureau of Metal Statistics, Inc., Secaucus, NJ				
<http://www.abms.com>				
Nonferrous Metal Yearbook	Annual	X		X
American Council on Education, Washington, DC				
<http://www.acenet.edu>				
A Fact Book on Higher Education	Quarterly	X		
National Norms for Entering College Freshmen	Annual	X		
American Council of Life Insurers, Washington, DC				
<http://www.acli.com>				
Life Insurers Fact Book	Annual	X		
American Dental Association, Chicago, IL				
<http://www.ada.org>				
Dental Students Register.	Annual	X		
Distribution of Dentists in the United States by Region and State	Triennial	X		
Survey of Dental Practice	Annual	X		
American Forest & Paper Association, Washington, DC				
<http://www.afandpa.org>				
Annual Statistical Summary of Recovered Paper Utilization	Annual	X	X	
Statistical Roundup.	Monthly	X	X	
Statistics of Paper, Paperboard, and Wood Pulp	Annual	X		
U.S. Wood Pulp Data Report	Annual	X		
U.S. Forest Facts and Figures	Annual	X		
American Frozen Food Institute, Burlingame, CA				
<http://www.affi.com>				
Frozen Food Pack Statistics.	Annual	X		
American Gas Association, Washington, DC				
<http://www.aga.org>				
Gas Facts.	Annual	X		X

U.S. Census Bureau, Statistical Abstract of the United States: 2007

			Internet	
Title				
	Frequency	Paper	PDF	Other Formats
America's Health Insurance Plans, Washington, DC <http://www.ahip.org>				
Source Book of Health Insurance Data...........................	Annual	X		
American Iron and Steel Institute, Washington, DC <http://www.steel.org>				
Annual Statistical Report.....................................	Annual	X		
American Jewish Committee, New York, NY <http://www.ajc.org>				
American Jewish Year Book....................................	Annual	X		
American Medical Association, Chicago, IL <http://www.ama-assn.org>				
Physician Characteristics and Distribution in the U.S..................	Annual	X		
Physician Marketplace Statistics..............................	Annual	X		
U.S. Medical Licensure Statistics, and License Requirements..........	Annual	X		
American Metal Market, New York, NY <http://www.amm.com>				
Metal Statistics..	Annual	X		
American Osteopathic Association, Chicago, IL <http://www.osteopathic.org/index.cfm>				
American Osteopathic Association Fact Sheet.....................	Biennial	X	X	
American Petroleum Institute, Washington, DC <http://www.api.org>				
The Basic Petroleum Data Book (online subscription)...............	Annual	X		
Joint Association Survey on Drilling Costs (JA5)...................	Annual	X		
Petroleum Industry Environmental Report.......................	Annual	X		X
Quarterly Well Completion Report (online subscription)..............	Quarterly	X		
American Public Transportation Association, Washington, DC <http://www.apta.com>				
Public Transportation Fact Book...............................	Annual	X	X	
Association for Manufacturing Technology, McLean, VA <http://www.amtonline.org>				
Economic Handbook of the Machine Tool Industry 2003–2004 (online version by subscription only)...........................	Annual			X
Association of American Railroads, Washington, DC <http://www.aar.org>				
Analysis of Class I Railroads.................................	Annual	X	X	X
Cars of Revenue Freight Loaded...............................	Weekly		X	X
Freight Commodity Statistics, Class I Railroads in the United States.....	Annual	X	X	X
Yearbook of Railroad Facts...................................	Annual	X	X	
Association of Racing Commissioners International, Inc., Lexington, KY <http://www.arci.com>				
Statistical Reports on Greyhound Racing in the United States........	Annual	X		
Statistical Reports on Horse Racing in the United States............	Annual	X		
Statistical Reports on Jai Alai in the United States................	Annual	X		
Book Industry Study Group, Inc., New York, NY <http://www.bisg.org>				
Book Industry Trends..	Annual	X		
Used-Book Sales..	Periodic	X		
Boy Scouts of America, Irving, TX <http://www.scouting.org>				
Annual Report..	Annual	X		
The Bureau of National Affairs, Inc., Washington, DC <http://www.bna.com>				
Basic Patterns in Union Contracts.............................	Annual	X		
BNA's Employment Outlook...................................	Quarterly	X		
BNA's Job Absence and Turnover..............................	Quarterly	X		
Directory of U.S. Labor Organizations..........................	Annual	X		
National Labor Relations Board Election Statistics.................	Annual	X		
Union Membership & Earnings Data Book........................	Annual	X		
Source Book on Collective Bargaining..........................	Annual	X		
Carl H. Pforzheimer & Co, New York, NY				
Comparative Oil Company Statistics Annual......................	Annual	X		
Chronicle of Higher Education, Inc., Washington, DC <http://chronicle.com>				
Almanac...	Annual	X		
College Board, New York, NY <http://www.collegeboard.com>				
National Report on College-Bound Seniors.......................	Annual	X	X	
Commodity Research Bureau, Logical Systems, Inc., Chicago, IL <http://www.crbtrader.com>				
Commodity Year Book Update CD..............................	Quarterly			
CRB Commodity Index Report.................................	Weekly	X		
CRB Commodity Year Book...................................	Annual	X		
CRB Futures Perspective.....................................	Weekly	X	X	
CRB Infotech CD..	Monthly			
Electronic Futures Trend Analyzer..............................	Daily			X
Final Markets-End-of-Day Data................................	Daily			X
Futures Market Service.......................................	Weekly		X	
Futures Market Service Fundamental & Technical Commentary (online subscription)..	Daily			X
The Conference Board, New York, NY <http://www.conference-board.org> <http://www.conference-board.org/economics/bci>				

882   Appendix I

Title	Frequency	Paper	Internet PDF	Internet Other Formats
The Conference Board, New York, NY—Con.				
Business Cycle Indicators	Monthly	X	X	
Corporate Contributions	Annual	X	X	
Productivity, Employment, and Income, in the World's Economies	Annual	X	X	
CQ Press, Washington, DC				
<http://www.cqpress.com>				
America Votes	Biennial	X		
Consumer Electronics Association (Electronic Industries Alliance), Arlington, VA				
<http://www.ce.org>				
Consumer Electronics Association (CEA) Sales and Forecasts	Semiannual	X	X	
The Council of State Governments, Lexington, KY				
<http://www.csg.org>				
The Book of the States	Annual	X	X	
State Administrative Officials Classified by Function	Annual	X		
State Elective Officials and the Legislatures	Annual	X		
State Legislative Leadership, Committees, and Staff	Annual	X		
Credit Union National Association, Inc., Madison, WI				
<http://www.cuna.org>				
The Credit Union Ranking Report	Annual	X		
Credit Union Services Profile	Annual	X		
Operating Ratios and Spreads	Semiannual	X		
Dow Jones & Co., New York, NY.				
<http://www.dj.com>				
Wall Street Journal	Daily	X		
Edison Electric Institute, Washington, DC				
<http://www.eei.org>				
Statistical Yearbook of the Electric Power Industry	Annual	X	X	X
Editor & Publisher Co., New York, NY				
<http://www.editorandpublisher.com>				
Editor & Publisher	Monthly	X		
International Year Book	Annual	X		X
Market Guide	Annual	X		
Euromonitor International, London, England				
<http://www.euromonitor.com>				
Consumer Asia	Annual	X		
Consumer China	Annual	X		
Consumer Eastern Europe	Annual	X		
Consumer Europe	Annual	X		
Consumer International	Annual	X		
Consumer Latin America	Annual	X		
European Marketing Data and Statistics	Annual	X		
International Marketing Data and Statistics	Annual	X		
Latin America Marketing Data and Statistics	Annual	X		
World Consumer Expenditure Patterns	Annual	X		
World Consumer Income Patterns	Annual	X		
World Economic Factbook	Annual	X		
World Retail Data and Statistics	Annual	X		
Federal National Mortgage Association, Washington, DC				
<http://www.fanniemae.com>				
Annual Report	Annual	X		
Food and Agriculture Organization of the United Nations, Rome, Italy				
<http://www.fao.org>				
Fertilizer Yearbook	Annual	X		
Production Yearbook	Annual	X		
Trade Yearbook	Annual	X		
Yearbook of Fishery Statistics	Annual	X		
Yearbook of Forest Products	Annual	X		
The Foundation Center, New York, NY				
<http://www.foundationcenter.org>				
Foundation Yearbook	Annual	X		
General Aviation Manufacturers Association, Washington, DC				
<http://www.gama.aero/home.php>				
Shipment Report	Quarterly	X		X
Statistical Databook	Annual	X	X	
Girl Scouts of the USA, New York, NY				
<http://www.girlscouts.org>				
Annual Report	Annual	X	X	
Giving Institute (previously AAFRC), Indianapolis, IN				
<http://www.aafrc.org>				
Giving USA	Annual	X		
Health Forum, an American Hospital Association Company, Chicago, IL				
<http://www.healthforum.com>				
Annual Report	Annual	X		
Hospital Statistics	Annual	X		X
Independent Petroleum Association of America, Washington, DC				
<http://www.ipaa.org>				
Domestic Oil and Gas Trends	Monthly	X		
Oil & Natural Gas Production in Your State	Annual	X		X
U.S. Petroleum Statistics	Annual	X		X
Information Today, Inc., Medford, NJ				
<http://www.infotoday.com>				
American Library Directory	Annual	X		

Appendix I 883

Title	Frequency	Paper	Internet PDF	Internet Other Formats
Information Today, Inc., Medford, NJ—Con.				
Bowker Annual Library and Book Trade Almanac	Annual	X		
Institute for Criminal Justice Ethics, New York, NY				
<http://www.lib.jjay.cuny.edu/cje>				
Criminal Justice Ethics	Semiannual	X		
Insurance Information Institute, New York, NY				
<http://www.iii.org>				
The I.I.I. Insurance Fact Book	Annual	X	X	
Inter-American Development Bank, Washington, DC				
<http://www.iadb.org>				
Annual Report	Annual	X	X	
Economic and Social Progress in Latin America	Annual	X		
International Air Transport Association				
<http://www.iata.org>				
World Air Transport Statistics	Annual	X	X	X
International City Management Association, Washington, DC				
<http://www.icma.org>				
Compensation: An Annual Report on Local Government Executive Salaries and Fringe Benefits	Annual			X
Municipal Year Book	Annual	X		
International Labour Organization, Geneva, Switzerland				
<http://www.ilo.org>				
Yearbook of Labour Statistics	Annual	X		
International Monetary Fund, Washington, DC				
<http://www.imf.org>				
Annual Report	Annual	X	X	X
Balance of Payments Statistics	Monthly	X		
Direction of Trade Statistics	Monthly	X		
Government Finance Statistics Yearbook	Annual	X		
International Financial Statistics	Monthly	X		
International Telecommunication Union, Geneva, Switzerland				
<http://www.itu.int/home/index.html>				
ITU Yearbook of Statistics	Annual	X		
World Telecommunication Indicators	Annual	X		
Investment Company Institute, Washington, DC				
<http://www.ici.org>				
Mutual Fund Fact Book	Annual	X	X	
Jane's Information Group, Coulsdon, UK, and Alexandria, VA				
<http://www.janes.com>				
Jane's Air-Launched Weapons	Monthly			X
Jane's All the World's Aircraft	Annual			X
Jane's Armour and Artillery	Annual			X
Jane's Avionics	Annual			X
Jane's Fighting Ships	Annual			X
Jane's Infantry Weapons	Annual			X
Jane's Merchant Ships	Annual			X
Jane's Military Communications	Annual			X
Jane's Military Logistics	Annual			X
Jane's Military Training Systems	Annual			X
Jane's NATO Handbook	Annual			X
Jane's Spaceflight Directory	Annual			X
Joint Center for Political and Economic Studies, Washington, DC				
<http://www.jointcenter.org>				
Black Elected Officials: A Statistical Summary	Annual	X	X	
McGraw-Hill Construction Dodge, a Division of the McGraw-Hill Companies, New York, NY				
<http://www.construction.com>				
<http://www.dodge.construction.com/Analytics/>				
Dodge Construction Potential (online subscription)	Monthly	X	X	
National Academy of Sciences, Washington, DC				
<http://www.pnas.org>				
Summary Report Doctorate Recipients from United States Universities	Annual	X		
National Academy of Social Insurance, Washington, DC				
<http://www.nasi.org>				
Workers' Compensation, Benefits, Coverage, and Costs	Annual	X	X	
National Association of Home Builders, Washington, DC				
<http://www.nahb.org>				
Home Builders Forecast (online subscription)	Monthly			X
Housing Economics (online subscription)	Monthly			X
Housing Market Statistics (online subscription)	Monthly			X
National Association of Latino Elected and Appointed Officials, Washington, DC				
<http://www.naleo.org>				
National Roster of Hispanic Elected Officials	Annual	X		
National Association of Realtors. Washington, DC				
<http://www.realtor.org>				
<http://realtor.org/reinsights>				
Real Estate Outlook: Market Trends & Insights (discontinued)	Monthly	X		X
Real Estate Insights	Monthly		X	X
National Association of State Budget Officers, Washington, DC				
<http://www.nasbo.org>				
State Expenditure Report	Annual	X	X	
Fiscal Survey of the States	Semi-annual	X	X	

884   Appendix I

Title	Frequency	Paper	PDF	Other Formats
			Internet	
National Association of State Park Directors, Raleigh, NC <http://www.naspd.org>				
Annual Information Exchange.			X	X
National Catholic Educational Association, Washington, DC <http://www.ncea.org>				
Catholic Schools in America.	Annual		X	X
U.S. Catholic Elementary and Secondary Schools Staffing and Enrollment	Annual	X		X
U.S. Catholic Elementary Schools and Their Finances	Biennial	X		
U.S. Catholic Secondary Schools and Their Finances.	Biennial	X		
National Center for State Courts, Williamsburg, VA <http://www.ncsconline.org>				
State Court Caseload Statistics.	Annual	X	X	
National Council of Churches USA, New York, NY <http://www.ncccusa.org>				
Yearbook of American and Canadian Churches	Annual	X		X
National Education Association, Washington, DC <http://www.nea.org>				
Rankings of the States and Estimates of School Statistics	Annual	X	X	
Status of the American Public School Teacher, 2000–2001	Quinquennial	X	X	
National Fire Protection Association, Quincy, MA <http://www.nfpa.org>				
NFPA Journal	Bimonthly			X
National Golf Foundation, Jupiter, FL <http://www.ngf.org>				
Golf Consumer Profile.	Annual		X	
Golf Facilities in the U.S.	Annual	X	X	
National Marine Manufacturers Association, Chicago, IL <http://www.nmma.org>				
Boating (A Statistical Report on America's Top Family Sport)	Annual	X	X	X
U.S. Recreational Boat Registration Statistics	Annual	X	X	
National Restaurant Association, Washington, DC <http://www.restaurant.org>				
Compensation for Salaried Personnel in Restaurants 2001				
Holiday Dining 2004				
Quick-Service Restaurant Trends	Annual	X		
Restaurant Economic Trends (online subscriptions)	Monthly			X
Restaurant Industry Forecast	Annual	X		
Restaurant Industry in Review	Annual	X	X	X
Restaurant Industry Operations Report.	Annual	X		
Restaurant Industry Pocket Factbook.	Annual			
Restaurant Industry 2015, 2005	Annual	X		
Restaurant Performance Index	Monthly	X		X
Restaurant Spending	Annual	X		
State of the Restaurant Industry Work Force	Annual	X		
Tableservice Restaurant Trends	Annual	X		
The Economic Impact of the Nation's Eating and Drinking Places	Annual	X		
Hourly Wages for Food Service Occupations.	Annual	X		
Research News and Numbers	Monthy	X		
National Safety Council, Itasca, IL <http://www.nsc.org>				
Injury Facts	Annual	X		
National Sporting Goods Association, Mt. Prospect, IL <http://www.nsga.org>				
The Sporting Goods Market in 2004	Annual	X	X	
Sports Participation in 2003	Annual	X	X	
New York Stock Exchange, Inc., New York, NY <http://www.nyse.com>				
Fact Book (online subscription).	Annual	X	X	
The New York Times Almanac, 2004.	Annual	X		
Organisation for Economic Cooperation and Development, Paris, France <http://www.sourceoecd.org>				
Agricultural Outlook	Annual	X		X
Bank Profitability: Financial Statements of Banks	Annual	X		X
Central Government Debt: Statistical Yearbook	Annual	X		X
Coal Information.	Annual	X		X
CO_2 Emissions From Fuel Combustion, 1971–2001 2003 Edition		X		X
Communications Outlook	Annual	X		X
Economic Outlook	Biennial	X		X
Economic Studies.	Annual	X		X
Economic Surveys	Annual	X		X
Education at a Glance: OECD Indicators	Annual	X		X
Electricity Information	Annual	X		X
Employment Outlook.	Annual	X		X
Energy Balances of Non-OECD Countries	Annual	X		X
Energy Balances of OECD Countries.	Annual	X		X
Energy Prices and Taxes	Quarterly	X	X	
Energy Statistics of Non-OECD Countries.	Annual	X	X	X
Energy Statistics of OECD Countries.	Annual	X	X	X
Environmental Data Compendium	Annual	X		X
Environmental Outlook		X	X	
External Debt Statistics	Annual			
Financial Market Trends	Triennial	X	X	
Geographical Distribution of Financial Flows to Aid Recipients, 1998–02	Annual	X		
Health Data.	Annual	X	X	X

U.S. Census Bureau, Statistical Abstract of the United States: 2007

Title	Frequency	Paper	PDF	Other Formats
Organisation for Economic Cooperation and Development, Paris, France—Con.				
Historical Statistics, 1970–2000 2001 Edition (discontinued as of 2001)		X	X	X
Information Technology Outlook, 2002 Edition	Biennial	X	X	X
Insurance Statistics Yearbook	Annual	X	X	X
International Development Statistics	Annual			X
International Trade by Commodities	Annual	X	X	
Iron and Steel Industry in 2002, 2004 Edition				
Labor Force Statistics	Annual	X	X	
Main Economic Indicators	Monthly	X	X	
Main Science and Technology Indicators, Vol. 2003	Biennial	X	X	
Measuring Globalization: The Role of Multinationals in OECD Countries 2001 Edition	Biennial			
Monthly Statistics of International Trade Series A	Monthly	X	X	
National Accounts of OECD Countries	Annual			
Vol I: Main Aggregates		X	X	X
Vol II: Detailed Tables		X	X	X
Natural Gas Information	Annual	X	X	X
Nuclear Energy Data	Annual	X	X	
OECD in Figures	Bimonthly	X		X
Oil Information 2003 Edition	Annual	X	X	
Oil, Gas, Coal, and Electricity Quarterly Statistics	Quarterly	X	X	
Quarterly Labor Force Statistics (discontinued as of 4th quarter 2004)	Quarterly	X	X	
Quarterly National Accounts	Quarterly	X	X	
Research and Development Statistics		X	X	X
Revenue Statistics of OECD Member Countries	Annual	X	X	
Review of Fisheries in OECD Member Countries	Annual	X	X	
Science, Technology, and Industry: Scoreboard, 2003	Biennial	X	X	X
Small and Medium Enterprise Outlook 2002 Edition	Biennial	X	X	
Structural Statistics for Industry and Services	Annual	X	X	
Taxing Wages	Annual	X	X	
The DAC Journal	Quarterly	X	X	
Trends in International Migration 2004 Edition	Annual	X	X	
Trends in the Transport Sector, 1970–2002, 2004 Edition		X	X	
Uranium Resources Production and Demand, 2001	Biennial	X	X	
Pan American Health Organization, Washington, DC				
<http://www.paho.org>				
Health Conditions in the Americas	Quadrennial	X	X	X
PennWell Corporation, Tulsa, OK				
<http://www.pennwell.com>				
Offshore (online subscription)	Monthly	X	X	
Oil and Gas Journal (online subscription)	Weekly	X		
Population Association of America, Washington, DC				
<http://www.popassoc.org>				
Demography	Quarterly	X	X	X
Puerto Rico Planning Board, San Juan, PR				
<http://www.jp.gobierno.pr>				
Balance of Payments Puerto Rico	Annual	X		
Selected Statistics on External Trade	Annual	X		
Selected Statistics on Construction Industry	Annual	X		
Activity Index	Monthly	X		X
Projections	Annual	X		
Economic Report to the Governor	Annual	X		
Statistical Appendix—Economic Report to the Governor	Annual	X		X
Income and Product	Annual	X		
Radio Advertising Bureau, New York, NY				
<http://www.rab.com>				
Media Facts	Biennial	X	X	
Radio Marketing Guide and Fact Book	Annual	X	X	
Reed Business Information, New York, NY				
<http://www.reedbusiness.com>				
Library Journal	Semimonthly	X		X
Publishers Weekly		X		X
School Library Journal	Monthly	X		X
Regional Airline Association, Washington, DC				
<http://www.raa.org>				
Statistical Report	Annual	X		X
Magazine	Bimonthly	X	X	
Securities Industry Association, New York, NY				
<http://www.sia.com>				
Foreign Activity Report	Quarterly	X		
Securities Industry Trends	Periodic	X		
Securities Industry Yearbook	Annual	X		X
Standard and Poor's Corporation, New York, NY				
<http://www.standardandpoors.com>				
Analysts Handbook	Monthly	X		
Corporation Records	Daily	X		
Daily Stock Price Records	Quarterly	X		
Standard and Poor's Global Stock Market Factbook	Annual	X		
United Nations Statistics Division, New York, NY				
<http://unstats.un.org/unsd/>				
Compendium of Human Settlements Statistics (Series N)	Annual	X		
Demographic Yearbook (Series R)	Annual	X	X	X
Energy Balances and Electricity Profiles (Series W)	Annual	X	X	
Energy Statistics Yearbook (Series J)	Annual	X	X	

Title	Frequency	Paper	Internet PDF	Internet Other Formats
United Nations Statistics Division, New York, NY—Con.				
Industrial Statistics Yearbook: (Series P)				
Commodity Production Statistics	Annual	X		
International Trade Statistics Yearbook (Series G)	Annual	X		
Monthly Bulletin of Statistics (Series Q)	Monthly	X		
National Accounts Statistics: (Series X)				
Main Aggregates and Detailed Tables.	Annual	X		
Analysis of Main Aggregates.	Annual	X		
Population and Vital Statistics Report (Series A)	Quarterly	X		
Social Statistics and Indicators: (Series K)	Occasional	X		X
The World's Women: Progress in Statistics, 2005.		X	X	X
Statistical Yearbook (Series; also available in CD-ROM, Series S/CD)	Annual	X		X
World Statistics Pocketbook (Series V).	Annual	X		
United Nations Conference on Trade and Development,				
Geneva Switzerland				
<http://www.unctad.org>				
Development and Globalization: Facts and Figures.	Annual	X	X	X
Handbook of Statistics	Annual	X	X	X
United States Telecom Association, Washington, DC				
<http://www.usta.org>				
Statistics of the Local Exchange Carriers	Annual	X		
University of Michigan, Center for Political Studies, Institute for				
Social Research, Ann Arbor, MI				
<http://www.umich.edu>				
National Election Studies Cumulative Datafile	Biennial	X		X
Warren Communications News, Washington, DC				
<http://www.warren-news.com>				
Cable and Station Coverage Atlas.	Annual			X
Television and Cable Action Update.	Weekly			X
Television and Cable Factbook	Annual	X		X
World Almanac, New York, NY				
<http://www.worldalmanac.com>				
The World Almanac and Book of Facts.	Annual	X		
The World Bank Group, Washington, DC				
<http://www.worldbank.org>				
Global Development Finance, 2006.	Annual	X		
The Little Data Book.	Annual	X		
World Bank Atlas, 2004.	Annual	X		
World Development Indicators	Annual	X		
World Health Organization, Geneva, Switzerland				
<http://www.who.int/en/>				
Epidemiological and Vital Statistics Report	Monthly	X		
World Health Statistics	Quarterly	X		
World Trade Organization				
<http://www.wto.org>				
International Trade Statistics	Annual	X	X	X

Appendix I   887

Guide to State Statistical Abstracts

This bibliography includes the most recent statistical abstracts for states published since 1999, plus those that will be issued in late 2006. For some states, a near equivalent has been listed in substitution for, or in addition to, a statistical abstract. All sources contain statistical tables on a variety of subjects for the state as a whole, its component parts, or both. Internet sites also contain statistical data.

Alabama

University of Alabama, Center for Business and Economic Research, Box 870221, Tuscaloosa, AL 35487-0221. 205-348-6191. Fax: 205-348-2951. Internet site <http://cber.cba.ua.edu/>.

Economic Abstract of Alabama, 2000.

Alabama Economic Outlook, 2006. Revised annually.

Alaska

Department of Commerce, Community, and Economic Development, Division of Community Advocacy, 550 W. 7th Avenue, Suite 1770, Anchorage, AK 99501-2341. 907-269-4580. Fax: 907-269-4539. Internet site <http://www.dced.state.ak.us/dca/home.htm>.

The Alaska Economic Performance Report, 2005. Online.

Arizona

Economic and Business Research Center, University of Arizona, 1130 East Helen Street, McClelland Hall, Rm. 103, P. O. Box 210108, Tucson, AZ 85721-0108. 520-621-2155. Fax: 520-621-2150. Internet site <http://www.ebr.eller.arizona.edu/>.

Arizona Statistical Abstract, 2003.

Arizona's Economy. Quarterly newsletter.

Arizona Economic Indicators. Semiannual. Online.

Arkansas

University of Arkansas at Little Rock, Institute for Economic Advancement, Economic Research, 2801 South University Avenue, Little Rock, AR 72204-1099. 501-569-8519. Fax: 501-5698538. Internet site <http://www.aiea.ualr.edu/default.html>.

Arkansas State and County Economic Data, 2003.

Arkansas Personal Income Handbook, 2005.

Arkansas Statistical Abstract, 2004. Revised biennially.

California

Department of Finance, 915 L Street, Sacramento, CA 95814. 916-445-3878. Internet site <http://www. dof.ca.gov/HTML/FSDATA/Fshome.asp>.

California Statistical Abstract, 2005. Annual. Online only.

Colorado

University of Colorado, University Libraries, 184 UCB, 1720 Pleasant St., Boulder, CO 80309-0184. 303-492-8705. Internet site <http://www.colorado.edu/libraries/govpub/online.htm>.

Colorado by the Numbers. Online only.

Colorado Office of Economic Development and International Trade, 1625 Broadway, Suite 1700, Denver, CO 80202. 303-892-3840. Fax: 303-892-3848. Internet site <http://www.state.co.us/oed/business-development/colorado-databook.cfm>.

Colorado Data Book. Online only.

Connecticut

Connecticut Department of Economic & Community Development, 505 Hudson St., Hartford, CT 06106-7107. 1-860-270-8000. Internet site <http://www.ct.gov/ecd/site/default.asp>.

Connecticut Town Profiles, 2005.

Delaware

Delaware Economic Development Office, 99 Kings Highway, Dover, DE 19901. 302-739-4271. Fax: 302-739-5749. Internet site <http://www.state.de.us/dedo/default.shtml>.

Delaware Statistical Overview. Online only.

District of Columbia

Business Resource Center, John A. Wilson Building, 1350 Pennsylvania Avenue, NW, Washington, DC 20004. 202-727-1000. Internet site <http://brc.dc.gov/resources/facts.asp>.

Market Facts and Statistics. Online only.

Florida

University of Florida, Bureau of Economic and Business Research, P. O. Box 117145, 221 Matherly Hall, Gainesville, FL 32611-7145. 352-392-0171, ext. 219. Internet site <http://www.bebr.ufl.edu/>.

Florida Statistical Abstract, 2005. Annual. Also available on CD-ROM.

Florida County Perspective, 2005. One profile for each county. Annual. Also available on CD-ROM.

Florida County Rankings, 2005. Annual. Also available on CD-ROM.

Georgia

University of Georgia, Selig Center for Economic Growth, Terry College of Business, Athens, GA 30602. 706-542-4085. Internet site <http://www.selig.uga.edu/>.
Georgia Statistical Abstract, 2004–05.

University of Georgia, Center for Agribusiness and Economic Development, 301 Lumpkin House, Athens, GA 30602-7509. 706-542-2434. Fax: 706-542-0770. Internet site <http://www.georgiastats.uga.edu/>.
The Georgia County Guide, 2005–2006. Annual.

Hawaii

Hawaii State Department of Business, and Economic Development & Tourism, Research and Economic Analysis Division, Statistics and Data Support Branch, P. O. Box 2359, Honolulu, HI 96804. 808-586-2423. Internet site <http://www2.hawaii.gov/dbedt/>.
The State of Hawaii Data Book 2004. Annual. Periodically updated.

Idaho

Idaho Commerce & Labor, 700 West State St., P. O. Box 83720, Boise, ID 83720-0093. 208-334-2650. Internet site <http://cl.idaho.gov/DNN/Default .aspx?alias=cl.idaho.gov/dnn/idcl >.
County Profiles Idaho. Online.
Idaho Community Profiles. Online.
Profile of Rural Idaho, 1999.

Illinois

Institute of Government and Public Affairs, 1007 W. Nevada Street, Urbana, IL 61801. 217-333-3340. Internet site <http://www .igpa.uiuc.edu/default.htm>.
Illinois Statistical Abstract, 2004. Online only.

Indiana

Indiana University, Indiana Business Research Center, Kelley School of Business, Ste 3110, 1275 E. 10th Street, Bloomington, IN 47405. 812-855-5507. Internet site <http://www.stats .indiana.edu/>.
STATS Indiana. Online only.

Iowa

Office of Social and Economic Trend Analysis, 303 East Hall, Ames, IA 50010-1070. 515-294-9903. Fax: 515-294-0592. Internet site <http://www.seta.iastate.edu/>.
Iowa by the Numbers, 2005. CD-ROM.

State Library of Iowa, State Data Center, Ola Babcock Miller Building, East 12th and Grand, Des Moines, IA 50319. 800248-4483. Fax: 515-242-6543. Internet site <http://www.iowadatacenter.org>.

Kansas

University of Kansas, Policy Research Institute, 1541 Lilac Lane, 607 Blake Hall, Lawrence, KS 66044-3177. 785-864-3701. Fax: 785-864-3683. Internet site <http://www.ipsr.ku.edu/>.
Kansas Statistical Abstract, 2004. 39th ed. Online only.

Kentucky

Kentucky Cabinet for Economic Development, Division of Research, 300 West Broadway, Frankfort, KY 40601. 800-626-2930. Internet site <http://www .thinkkentucky.com/kyedc/resandstat.asp/>.
Kentucky Deskbook of Economic Statistics. Online only.

Louisiana

Louisiana State Census Data Center, Office of Electronic Services, P. O. Box 94095, Baton Rouge, LA 70804-9095. 225-219-4025. Fax: 225-219-4027. Internet site <http://www.louisiana.gov/wps/portal/>.

Maine

Maine State Planning Office, 38 State House Station, 184 State Street, Augusta, ME 04333. 800-662-4545. Fax: 207-287-6489. Internet site <http://www.state .me.us/spo/economics/economics/>.

Maryland

RESI, Towson University, 8000 York Road, Towson, MD 21252-7097. 410-704-7374. Fax 410-704-4115. Internet site <http://wwwnew.towson.edu/outreach/resi /default.asp/>.
Maryland Statistical Abstract, 2006.

Massachusetts

MassCHIP, Massachusetts Department of Public Health, 250 Washington Street, Boston, MA 02108-4619. 617-624-5629. Internet site <http://masschip.state .ma.us/>.
Instant Topics. Online only.

Michigan

Michigan Economic Development Corporation, 300 North Washington Square, Lansing, MI 48913. 1-888-522-0103. Internet site <http://www.michigan.org/medc /miinfo>.
Economic Profiler. Online only.

Minnesota

Minnesota Department of Employment and Economic Development, 1st National Bank Building, 332 Minnesota Street Suite E200, Saint Paul, MN 55101-1351. 800-657-3858. Internet site <http://www .deed.state.mn.us/facts/index.htm>.
Compare Minnesota: Profiles of Minnesota's Economy & Population, 2002–2003. Online only.

State Demographic Center, 658 Cedar Street, Saint Paul, MN 55155. 651-296-2557. Internet Site <http://www.demography.state.mn.us/>.

Mississippi
Mississippi State University, College of Business and Industry, Division of Research, P. O. Box 5288, Mississippi State, MS 39762. 662-325-3817. Internet site <http://www.cbi.msstate.edu/dept/bizserv/abstract/>.
Mississippi Statistical Abstract, 2005. 38th ed. Also available on CD-ROM.

Missouri
University of Missouri, Economic and Policy Analysis Research Center, 10 Professional Building, Columbia, MO 65211. 573-882-4805. Fax: 573-882-5563. Internet site <http://econ.missouri.edu/eparc/>.
Statistical Abstract for Missouri, 2003. 13th ed. Biennial. Online only.

Montana
Census and Economic Information Center, Montana Department of Commerce, 301 S. Park Ave., P. O. Box 200505, Helena, MT 59620-0505. 406-841-2740. Fax: 406-841-2741. Internet site <http://ceic.commerce.state.mt.us/>.

Nebraska
Nebraska Department of Economic Development, P. O. Box 94666, 301 Centennial Mall South, Lincoln, NE 68509-4666. 800-426-6505. Fax 402-471-3778. Internet site <http://info.neded.org/>.
Nebraska Data Book. Online only.

Nevada
Department of Administration, Budget and Planning Division, 209 East Musser Street, Room 200, Carson City, NV 89701. 775-684-0222. Fax: 775-684-0260. Internet site <http://www.budget.state.nv.us/>.
Nevada Statistical Abstract. Online only.

New Hampshire
New Hampshire Office of Energy and Planning, 57 Regional Drive, Suite 3, Concord, NH 03301-8519. 603-271-2155. Fax 603271-2615. Internet site <http://www.nh.gov/oep/index.htm>.

New Jersey
New Jersey State Data Center, NJ Department of Labor and Workforce Development, P. O. Box 388, Trenton, NJ 08625-0388. 609-984-2595. Fax: 609-984-6833. Internet site <http://www.state.nj.us/labor/lra/>.
Labor Market Information. Online only.

New Mexico
University of New Mexico, Bureau of Business and Economic Research, MSC02 1720, 1 University of New Mexico, Albuquerque, NM 87131-0001. 505-277-2216. Fax 505-277-7066. Internet site <http://www.unm.edu/~bber/>.
New Mexico Business, Current Economic Report Monthly.
FOR-UNM Bulletin. Quarterly.

New York
Nelson A. Rockefeller Institute of Government, 411 State Street, Albany, NY 12203-1003. 518-443-5522. Fax: 518-443-5788. Internet site <http://www.rockinst.org/>.
New York State Statistical Yearbook, 2005. 30th ed.

North Carolina
Office of Governor, Office of State Budget and Management, 116 West Jones Street, Raleigh, NC 27603-8005. 919-807-4700. Fax 919-733-0640. Internet site <http://www.osbm.state.nc.us/osbm/>.
How North Carolina Ranks, 2004. Online only.

North Dakota
University of North Dakota, Bureau of Business and Economic Research, P. O. Box 8369, Grand Forks, ND 58202. 800-225-5863. Fax 701-777-3365. Internet site <http://business.und.edu/bber/>.
North Dakota Statistical Abstract. Online only.

Ohio
Office of Strategic Research, Ohio Department of Development, P. O. Box 1001, Columbus, OH 43216-1001. 1-800-848-1300. Internet site <http://www.odod.state.oh.us/research>.
Research products and services. Updated continuously.
Ohio County Profiles. Updated periodically.
Ohio County Indicators. Updated periodically.

Oklahoma
University of Oklahoma, Center for Economic and Management Research, Michael F. Price College of Business, 307 West Brooks, Norman, OK 73019. 405-325-2933. Fax: 405-325-7688. Internet site <http://cemr.ou.edu/cemr/index.asp>.
Statistical Abstract of Oklahoma, 1999.

Oregon
Secretary of State, Archives Division, Archives Bldg., 800 Summer Street, NE, Salem, OR 97310. 503-373-0701. Fax: 503373-0953. Internet site <http://www.sos.state.or.us/bbook>.
Oregon Blue Book. 2005–2006. Biennial.

Pennsylvania
Pennsylvania State Data Center, Institute of State and Regional Affairs, Penn State Harrisburg, 777 West Harrisburg Pike, Middletown, PA 17057-4898. 717-948-6336. Fax: 717-948-6754 Internet site <http://pasdc.hbg.psu.edu>.
Pennsylvania Statistical Abstract, 2005.

Rhode Island

Rhode Island Economic Development Corporation, One West Exchange Street, Providence, RI 02903. 401-222-2601. Internet site <http://www.riedc.com/r/index.html>.

RI Databank. Online only.

South Carolina

Budget and Control Board, Office of Research and Statistics, 1919 Blanding Street, Columbia 29201. 803-898-9940. Internet site <http://www.ors2.state.sc.us/abstract/index.asp>.

South Carolina Statistical Abstract, 2006.

South Dakota

South Dakota State Data Center, Business Research Bureau, The University of South Dakota, 414 E. Clark Street, Vermillion, SD 57069. 605-677-5287. Fax: 605-677-5427. Internet site <http://www.usd.edu/brbinfo/>.

2005 South Dakota Community Abstracts.

Tennessee

College of Business Administration, The University of Tennessee, Temple Court, Suite 100, 804 Volunteer Blvd., Knoxville, Tennessee 37996-4334. 865-974-5441. Fax: 865-974-3100. Internet site <http://cber.bus.utk.edu/Default.htm>.

Tennessee Statistical Abstract, 2003. Biennial.

Texas

Dallas Morning News, Communications Center, P. O. Box 655237, Dallas, TX 75265-5237. 214-977-8262. Internet site <http://www.texasalmanac.com/>.

Texas Almanac, 2006-2007. 63rd ed.

Texas State Data Center and Office of the State Demographer, Institute for Demographic and Socioeconomic Research, University of Texas at San Antonio, One UTSA Circle, San Antonio, TX 78249-0704. 210-458-6543. Fax: 210-458-6541. Internet site <http://txsdc.utsa.edu/>.

Utah

Governor's Office of Planning and Budget, Demographic & Economic Analysis, State Capitol Complex, Suite 210, East Office Building, Salt Lake City, UT 84114. 801-538-1027. Fax: 801-5381547. Internet site <http://www.governor.utah.gov/dea/>.

2006 Economic Report to the Governor. Annual.

Utah Data Guide Newsletter. Quarterly.

Vermont

Department of Labor, Labor Market Information, P. O. Box 488, Montpelier, VT 05601-0488. 802-828-4202. Fax: 802-828-4050. Internet site <http://www.vtlmi.info/>.

Vermont Economic-Demographic Profile, 2005. Annual.

Virginia

Weldon Cooper Center for Public Service, P. O. Box 400206, Charlottesville, VA 22904-4206. 434-982-5582. Fax: 434-982-5536. Internet site <http://www.coopercenter.org/demographics/>.

Virginia Statistical Abstract. Online only.

Washington

Washington State Office of Financial Management, Forecasting Division, P. O. Box 43113, Olympia, WA 98504-3113. 360-902-0555. Internet site <http://www.ofm.wa.gov/>.

Washington State Data Book. Online only.

West Virginia

West Virginia University, College of Business and Economics, Bureau of Business and Economic Research, P. O. Box 6025, Morgantown, WV 26506-6025. 304-293-4092. Fax: 304-293-5652. Internet site <http://www.bber.wvu.edu/bbr/>.

2005 West Virginia County Data Profiles.

West Virginia Economic Outlook, 2006. Annual.

Wisconsin

Wisconsin Legislative Reference Bureau, One East Main Street, Suite 200, Madison, WI 53701-2037. 608-266-3561. Internet site <http://www.legis.state.wi.us/lrb/bb/>.

2005–2006 Wisconsin Blue Book. Biennial.

Wyoming

Department of Administration and Information, Economic Analysis Division, 1807 Capitol Avenue, Suite 206, Cheyenne, WY 82002-0060. 307-777-7504. Fax: 307-632-1819. Internet site <http://eadiv.state.wy.us/>.

The Equality State Almanac, 2002.

Guide to Foreign Statistical Abstracts

This bibliography presents recent statistical abstracts for member nations of the Organization for Economic Cooperation and Development and Russia. All sources contain statistical tables on a variety of subjects for the individual countries. Many of the following publications provide text in English as well as in the national language(s). For further information on these publications, contact the named statistical agency which is responsible for editing the publication.

Australia
Australian Bureau of Statistics, Canberra. <http://www.abs.gov.au>.
Year Book Australia. Annual. 2006. With CD-ROM. (In English.)

Austria
Statistik Austria, A-1033 Wien. <http://www.statistik.at/index.shtml>.
Statistisches Jahrbuch Osterreichs. Annual. 2006. With CD-ROM. (In German.) With English translations of table headings.

Belgium
Institut National de Statistique, Rue de Louvain; 44-1000 Bruxelles. <http://statbel.fgov.be/info/linksen.asp>.
Annuaire statistique de la Belgique. Annual. 1995. (In French.)

Canada
Statistics Canada, Ottawa, Ontario, KIA OT6. <http://www.statcan.ca/start.html>.
Canada Yearbook: A review of economic, social and political developments in Canada. 2001. Irregular. (In English.)

Czech Republic
Czech Statistical Office, Sokolovska 142, 186 04 Praha 8; <http://www.czso.cz/>.
Statisticka Rocenka Ceske Republiky 2005. With CD-ROM. (In English and Czech.)

Denmark
Danmarks Statistik, Sejrogade 11, 2100 Kobenhavn O. <http://www.dst.dk/665>.
Statistisk ARBOG. 2006. Annual. English version available only on internet and is free of charge at: <www.dst.dk/yearbook>. (Printed version—in Danish only.)

Finland
Statistics Finland, Helsinki. <http://www.stat.fi/tk/tilastotietoaen.html>.
Statistical Yearbook of Finland, Annual. 2005. With CD-ROM. (In English, Finnish, and Swedish.)

France
Institut National de la Statistique et des Etudes Economiques, Paris 18, Bld. Adolphe Pinard, 75675 Paris (Cedex 14). <http://www.insee.fr/fr/home/homepage.asp>.
Annuaire Statistique de la France. Annual. 2003. (In French.) 2005 CD-ROM only.

Germany
Statistische Bundesamt, D-65180 Wiesbaden. <http://www.destatis.de>.
Statistisches Jahrbuch fur die Bundesrepublic Deutschland. Annual. 2005. (In German.)
Statistisches Jahrbuch fur das Ausland. 2005. *Statistisches Jahrbuch 2005 Fur die Bundesreublik Deutschland und fur das ausland*—CD-ROM.

Greece
National Statistical Service of Greece, Athens. <http:// www.statistics.gr/>.
Concise Statistical Yearbook 2004. (In English and Greek.)
Statistical Yearbook of Greece. Annual. 2004. (In English and Greek.)

Hungary
Hungarian Central Statistical Office, 1024 Budapest. <http://www.ksh.hu>.
Statistical Yearbook of Hungary, 2004. With CD-ROM. (In English and Hungarian.)

Iceland
Hagstofa Islands/Statistics Iceland; <http://www.hagstofa.is/template41.asp?PageID=251>.
Statistical Yearbook of Iceland. 2005 with CD-ROM. Irregular. (In English and Icelandic.)

Ireland
Central Statistics Office, Skehard Road, Cork. <http://www.cso.ie>.
Statistical Yearbook of Ireland. Annual. 2005. (In English.)

Italy
ISTAT (Istituto Centrale di Statistica); <http://www.istat.it>. Via Cesare Balbo 16 Roma.
Annuario Statistico Italiano. Annual. 2004. With CD-ROM. (In Italian.)

Japan

Statistics Bureau, Ministry of Internal Affairs and Communications, Statistical Research and Training Institute, Ministry of Internal Affairs and Communications, Japan. <http://www.stat.go.jp/english/data/index.htm>.

Japan Statistical Yearbook. Annual. 2006. (In English and Japanese.)

Korea, South

National Statistical Office, Government Complex, #920 Dunsan-dong Seo-gu Daejeon 302-701. <http://www.nso.go.kr/>. *Korea Statistical Yearbook.* Annual. 2005. (In Korean and English.)

Luxembourg

STATEC (Service Central de la Statistique et des Etudes economiques), 13 rue Erasme, B.P. 304, L-2013, Luxembourg. <www.statec.public.iu/>.

Annuaire Statistique du Luxembourg. 2004. (In French.) (Alphabetical numbering system).

Mexico

Instituto Nacional de Estadistica Geografia e Informatica, Av. Heroe Nacozari Num. 2301 Sur Fracc. Jardines del Parque, CP 20270 Aguascalientes, Ags. <http://www.inegi.gob.mx/difusion/ingles/fiest.html>.

Anuario estadistico de los Estados Unidos Mexicanos. Annual. 1998. Also on disc. (In Spanish.) *Agenda Estadistica 1999.*

Netherlands

Statistics Netherlands, R L Vellekoop. Prinses Beatrixiaan 428, 2273 X Z Voorburg; <http://www.cbs.nl/en/>. *Statistical Yearbook 2005 of the Netherlands.* (In English.)

Statistisch Jaarboek 2006. With CD-ROM.

New Zealand

Department of Statistics, Wellington. <http://www.stats.govt.nz/>.

New Zealand Official Yearbook. Annual. 2004. (In English.)

Norway

Statistics Norway, Oslo/Kongsvinger. <http://www.ssb.no/english/subjects/>.

Statistical Yearbook. Annual. 2005. (In English.)

Poland

Central Statistical Office al. Niepodleglosci 208, 00-925 Warsaw. <http://www.stat.gov.pl/english/index.htm>.

Concise Statistical Yearbook 2005. CD-ROM only. (In Polish and English.) *Statistical Yearbook of the Republic of Poland* 2004. CD-ROM only. (In Polish and English.)

Portugal

INE (Instituto Nacional de Estatistica.) <http://www.ine.pt/indexeng.htm>. Avenida Antonio Jose de Almeida P-1000-043 Lisboa.

Anuario Estatistico de Portugal. 2001. (In Portuguese and English.)

Russia

State Committee of Statistics of Russia, Moscow. <http://www.gks.ru/eng/>.

Statistical Yearbook. 2005. (In Russian.)

Slovakia

Statistical Office of the Slovak Republic, Bradacova 7, 852 86 Bratislava. <http://www.statistics.sk/webdata/english/index2a.htm>.

Statisticka Rocenka Slovenskej Republiky. 2005. (In English and Slovak.) With CD-ROM.

Spain

INE (Instituto Nacional de Estadistica); Paseo de la Castellana, 183, Madrid 16. <http://www.ine.es/welcoing.htm>

Anuario Estadistico de Espana. 2006. CD-ROM only. (In Spanish.)

Sweden

Statistics Sweden, S-11581 Stockholm. <http://www.scb.se/indexeng.asp>.

Statistisk Arsbok for Sverige. Annual. 2006. With CD-ROM. (In English and Swedish.)

Switzerland

Bundesamt fur Statistik, Hallwylstrasse 15, CH-3003, Bern.

Statistisches Jahrbuch der Schweiz. Annual. 2006. With CD-ROM. (In French and German.)

Turkey

State Institute of Statistics, Prime Ministry, Necatibey Cad/Ankara. No. 114 06100.

Statistical Yearbook of Turkey. 2004. With CD-ROM. (In English and Turkish.) *Turkey in Statistics.* 1999. (In English only.)

United Kingdom

The Stationary Office; P. O. Box 29, Norwich, NR3 1GN. <http://www.statistics.gov.uk/>.

Annual Abstract of Statistics. Annual. 2002. (In English.)

Metropolitan and Micropolitan Statistical Areas: Concepts, Components, and Population

The United States Office of Management and Budget (OMB) defines metropolitan and micropolitan statistical areas according to published standards that are applied to Census Bureau data. The general concept of a metropolitan or micropolitan statistical area is that of a core area containing a substantial population nucleus, together with adjacent communities having a high degree of economic and social integration with that core. Currently defined metropolitan and micropolitan statistical areas are based on application of 2000 standards (which appeared in the Federal Register on December 27, 2000) to 2000 decennial census data. Current metropolitan and micropolitan statistical area definitions were announced by OMB effective June 6, 2003, and subsequently updated as of December 2003, November 2004, and December 2005.

Standard definitions of metropolitan areas were first issued in 1949 by the then Bureau of the Budget (predecessor of OMB), under the designation "standard metropolitan area" (SMA). The term was changed to "standard metropolitan statistical area" (SMSA) in 1959 and to "metropolitan statistical area" (MSA) in 1983. The term "metropolitan area" (MA) was adopted in 1990 and referred collectively to metropolitan statistical areas (MSAs), consolidated metropolitan statistical areas (CMSAs), and primary metropolitan statistical areas (PMSAs). The term "core-based statistical area" (CBSA) became effective in 2000 and refers collectively to metropolitan and micropolitan statistical areas.

OMB has been responsible for the official metropolitan areas since they were first defined, except for the period 1977 to 1981, when they were the responsibility of the Office of Federal Statistical Policy and Standards, Department of Commerce. The standards for defining metropolitan areas were modified in 1958, 1971, 1975, 1980, 1990, and 2000.

Defining Metropolitan and Micropolitan Statistical Areas—The 2000 standards provide that each CBSA must contain at least one urban area of 10,000 or more population. Each metropolitan statistical area must have at least one urbanized area of 50,000 or more inhabitants. Each micropolitan statistical area must have at least one urban cluster of at least 10,000 but less than 50,000 population.

Under the standards, the county (or counties) in which at least 50 percent of the population resides within urban areas of 10,000 or more population, or that contain at least 5,000 people residing within a single urban area of 10,000 or more population, is identified as a "central county" (counties). Additional "outlying counties" are included in the CBSA if they meet specified requirements of commuting to or from the central counties. Counties or equivalent entities form the geographic "building blocks" for metropolitan and micropolitan statistical areas throughout the United States and Puerto Rico.

If specified criteria are met, a metropolitan statistical area containing a single core with a population of 2.5 million or more may be subdivided to form smaller groupings of counties referred to as "metropolitan divisions."

As of December 2005, there are 361 metropolitan statistical areas and 577 micropolitan statistical areas in the United States. In addition, there are eight metropolitan statistical areas and five micropolitan statistical areas in Puerto Rico.

Principal Cities and Metropolitan and Micropolitan Statistical Area Titles—

The largest city in each metropolitan or micropolitan statistical area is designated a "principal city." Additional cities qualify if specified requirements are met concerning population size and employment. The title of each metropolitan or micropolitan statistical area consists of the names of up to three of its principal cities and the name of each state into which the metropolitan or micropolitan statistical area extends. Titles of metropolitan divisions also typically are based on principal city names, but in certain cases consist of county names.

U.S. Census Bureau, Statistical Abstract of the United States: 2007

Defining New England City and Town Areas—In view of the importance of cities and towns in New England, the 2000 standards also provide for a set of geographic areas that are defined using cities and towns in the six New England states. The New England city and town areas (NECTAs) are defined using the same criteria as metropolitan and micropolitan statistical areas and are identified as either metropolitan or micropolitan, based, respectively, on the presence of either an urbanized area of 50,000 or more population or an urban cluster of at least 10,000 but less than 50,000 population. If the specified criteria are met, a NECTA containing a single core with a population of at least 2.5 million may be subdivided to form smaller groupings of cities and towns referred to as New England city and town area divisions.

Changes in Definitions Over Time— Changes in the definitions of these statistical areas since the 1950 census have consisted chiefly of (1) the recognition of new areas as they reached the minimum required city or urbanized area population and (2) the addition of counties (or cities and towns in New England) to existing areas as new decennial census data showed them to qualify.

In some instances, formerly separate areas have been merged, components of an area have been transferred from one area to another, or components have been dropped from an area. The large majority of changes have taken place on the basis of decennial census data. However, Census Bureau data serve as the basis for intercensal updates in specified circumstances.

Because of these historical changes in geographic definitions, users must be cautious in comparing data for these statistical areas from different dates. For some purposes, comparisons of data for areas as defined at given dates may be appropriate; for other purposes, it may be preferable to maintain consistent area definitions. Historical metropolitan area definitions are available for 1999, 1993, 1990, 1983, 1981, 1973, 1970, 1963, 1960, and 1950.

Excluding Tables 25 through 28 in the Population section; Table 580 in the Labor Force section; Table 662 in the Income section, and the tables that follow in this appendix, the tables presenting data for metropolitan areas in this edition of the *Statistical Abstract* are based on the 1999 or earlier metropolitan area definitions. For a list of component counties according to the 1999 definition, see Appendix II in the 2002 edition of the *Statistical Abstract* or <http://www.census.gov /population /www/estimates/pastmetro .html>.

Figure A1
Metropolitan and Micropolitan Statistical Areas of the United States
As defined by the U.S. Office of Management and Budget, December 2005

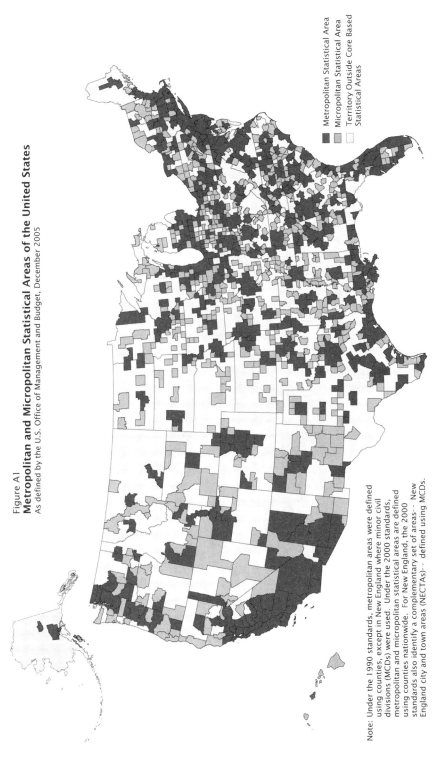

Metropolitan Statistical Area
Micropolitan Statistical Area
Territory Outside Core Based
Statistical Areas

Note: Under the 1990 standards, metropolitan areas were defined using counties, except in New England where minor civil divisions (MCDs) were used. Under the 2000 standards, metropolitan and micropolitan statistical areas are defined using counties nationwide. For New England, the 2000 standards also identify a complementary set of areas—New England city and town areas (NECTAs)—defined using MCDs.

U.S. Census Bureau, Statistical Abstract of the United States: 2007

Metropolitan and Micropolitan New England City and Town Areas (NECTAs)
As defined by the U.S. Office of Management and Budget, December 2005

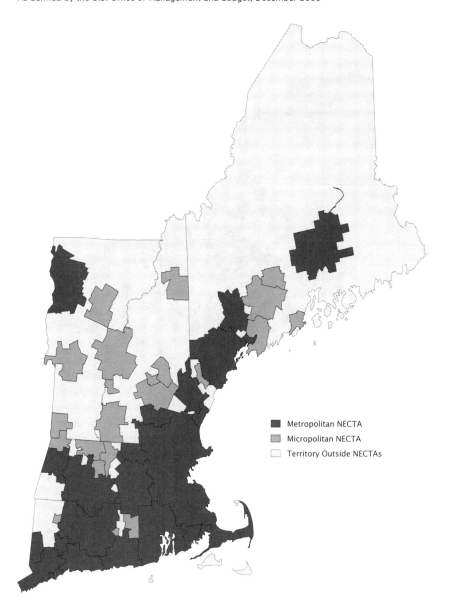

Legend:
- ■ Metropolitan NECTA
- ▨ Micropolitan NECTA
- ☐ Territory Outside NECTAs

Note: Under the 2000 standards, metropolitan and micropolitan statistical areas are defined using
counties nationwide. For New England, the 2000 standards also identify a complementary
set of areas- - New England city and town areas (NECTAs) - - defined using MCDs.

Table A. **Metropolitan Statistical Areas and Components as of December 2005**

[Population as of **July 2005. 158 represents 158,000**. All metropolitan areas are arranged alphabetically]

Metropolitan statistical area / Metropolitan division / Component county	Population, 2005 (1,000)	Metropolitan statistical area / Metropolitan division / Component county	Population, 2005 (1,000)	Metropolitan statistical area / Metropolitan division / Component county	Population, 2005 (1,000)
Abilene, TX	**158**	**Athens-Clarke County, GA**	**175**	**Baton Rouge, LA**	**734**
Callahan County, TX	14	Clarke County, GA	104	Ascension Parish, LA	91
Jones County, TX	20	Madison County, GA	27	East Baton Rouge	
Taylor County, TX	125	Oconee County, GA	30	Parish, LA	411
		Oglethorpe County, GA	14	East Feliciana Parish,	
Akron, OH	**702**			LA	21
Portage County, OH	156	**Atlanta-Sandy Springs-**		Iberville Parish, LA	32
Summit County, OH	547	**Marietta, GA**	**4,918**	Livingston Parish, LA	109
		Barrow County, GA	60	Pointe Coupee Parish,	
Albany, GA	**163**	Bartow County, GA	89	LA	22
Baker County, GA	4	Butts County, GA	21	St. Helena Parish, LA	10
Dougherty County, GA	95	Carroll County, GA	105	West Baton Rouge	
Lee County, GA	31	Cherokee County, GA	184	Parish, LA	22
Terrell County, GA	11	Clayton County, GA	268	West Feliciana Parish,	
Worth County, GA	22	Cobb County, GA	664	LA	15
		Coweta County, GA	110		
Albany-Schenectady-Troy,		Dawson County, GA	20	**Battle Creek, MI**	**139**
NY	**849**	DeKalb County, GA	678	Calhoun County, MI	139
Albany County, NY	297	Douglas County, GA	113		
Rensselaer County, NY	155	Fayette County, GA	104	**Bay City, MI**	**109**
Saratoga County, NY	215	Forsyth County, GA	140	Bay County, MI	109
Schenectady County,		Fulton County, GA	916		
NY	149	Gwinnett County, GA	726	**Beaumont-Port Arthur, TX**	**384**
Schoharie County, NY	32	Haralson County, GA	28	Hardin County, TX	51
		Heard County, GA	11	Jefferson County, TX	248
Albuquerque, NM	**798**	Henry County, GA	168	Orange County, TX	85
Bernalillo County, NM	604	Jasper County, GA	13		
Sandoval County, NM	107	Lamar County, GA	16	**Bellingham, WA**	**183**
Torrance County, NM	18	Meriwether County, GA	23	Whatcom County, WA	183
Valencia County, NM	69	Newton County, GA	87		
		Paulding County, GA	112	**Bend, OR**	**141**
Alexandria, LA	**148**	Pickens County, GA	28	Deschutes County, OR	141
Grant Parish, LA	20	Pike County, GA	16		
Rapides Parish, LA	128	Rockdale County, GA	79	**Billings, MT**	**147**
		Spalding County, GA	61	Carbon County, MT	10
Allentown-Bethlehem-		Walton County, GA	76	Yellowstone County, MT	137
Easton, PA-NJ	**791**				
Warren County, NJ	110	**Atlantic City, NJ**	**271**	**Binghamton, NY**	**248**
Carbon County, PA	62	Atlantic County, NJ	271	Broome County, NY	197
Lehigh County, PA	330			Tioga County, NY	51
Northampton County,		**Auburn-Opelika, AL**	**123**		
PA	288	Lee County, AL	123	**Birmingham-Hoover, AL**	**1,090**
				Bibb County, AL	22
Altoona, PA	**127**	**Augusta-Richmond County,**		Blount County, AL	56
Blair County, PA	127	**GA-SC**	**520**	Chilton County, AL	42
		Burke County, GA	23	Jefferson County, AL	657
Amarillo, TX	**239**	Columbia County, GA	104	St. Clair County, AL	72
Armstrong County, TX	2	McDuffie County, GA	22	Shelby County, AL	171
Carson County, TX	7	Richmond County, GA	196	Walker County, AL	70
Potter County, TX	120	Aiken County, SC	150		
Randall County, TX	110	Edgefield County, SC	26	**Bismarck, ND**	**99**
				Burleigh County, ND	74
Ames, IA	**80**	**Austin-Round Rock, TX**	**1,453**	Morton County, ND	26
Story County, IA	80	Bastrop County, TX	70		
		Caldwell County, TX	37	**Blacksburg-Christiansburg-**	
Anchorage, AK	**351**	Hays County, TX	124	**Radford, VA**	**151**
Anchorage Borough, AK	275	Travis County, TX	888	Giles County, VA	17
Matanuska-Susitna		Williamson County, TX	333	Montgomery County, VA	84
Borough, AK	76			Pulaski County, VA	35
		Bakersfield, CA	**757**	Radford city, VA	15
Anderson, IN	**130**	Kern County, CA	757		
Madison County, IN	130			**Bloomington, IN**	**178**
		Baltimore-Towson, MD	**2,656**	Greene County, IN	33
Anderson, SC	**176**	Anne Arundel County,		Monroe County, IN	121
Anderson County, SC	176	MD	511	Owen County, IN	23
		Baltimore County, MD	786		
Ann Arbor, MI	**342**	Carroll County, MD	169	**Bloomington-Normal, IL**	**159**
Washtenaw County, MI	342	Harford County, MD	239	McLean County, IL	159
		Howard County, MD	269		
Anniston-Oxford, AL	**112**	Queen Anne's County,		**Boise City-Nampa, ID**	**544**
Calhoun County, AL	112	MD	46	Ada County, ID	345
		Baltimore city, MD	636	Boise County, ID	8
Appleton, WI	**215**			Canyon County, ID	165
Calumet County, WI	44	**Bangor, ME**	**147**	Gem County, ID	16
Outagamie County, WI	171	Penobscot County, ME	147	Owyhee County, ID	11
Asheville, NC	**393**	**Barnstable Town, MA**	**227**	**Boston-Cambridge-Quincy,**	
Buncombe County, NC	219	Barnstable County, MA	227	**MA-NH**	**4,412**
Haywood County, NC	56			**Boston-Quincy, MA**	**1,800**
Henderson County, NC	97			Norfolk County, MA	654
Madison County, NC	20				

U.S. Census Bureau, Statistical Abstract of the United States: 2007

Metropolitan statistical area / Metropolitan division / Component county	Population, 2005 (1,000)
Boston-Cambridge-Quincy, MA-NH—Con.	
Boston-Quincy, MA—Con. . .	
Plymouth County, MA. . .	492
Suffolk County, MA	654
Cambridge-Newton-Framingham, MA	1,459
Middlesex County, MA . .	1,459
Essex County, MA	738
Essex County, MA.	738
Rockingham County-Strafford County, NH . . .	414
Rockingham County, NH.	295
Strafford County, NH . . .	119
Boulder, CO	280
Boulder County, CO. . . .	280
Bowling Green, KY	111
Edmonson County, KY . .	12
Warren County, KY	99
Bremerton-Silverdale, WA . .	241
Kitsap County, WA.	241
Bridgeport-Stamford-Norwalk, CT	903
Fairfield County, CT. . . .	903
Brownsville-Harlingen, TX. .	378
Cameron County, TX . . .	378
Brunswick, GA	98
Brantley County, GA . . .	15
Glynn County, GA	72
McIntosh County, GA . .	11
Buffalo-Niagara Falls, NY . .	1,148
Erie County, NY	931
Niagara County, NY. . . .	217
Burlington, NC	141
Alamance County, NC . .	141
Burlington-South Burlington, VT	205
Chittenden County, VT . .	150
Franklin County, VT	48
Grand Isle County, VT . .	8
Canton-Massillon, OH	410
Carroll County, OH	29
Stark County, OH	381
Cape Coral-Fort Myers, FL .	545
Lee County, FL	545
Carson City, NV	56
Carson City, NV	56
Casper, WY.	70
Natrona County, WY . . .	70
Cedar Rapids, IA.	246
Benton County, IA	27
Jones County, IA	21
Linn County, IA	199
Champaign-Urbana, IL	216
Champaign County, IL . .	185
Ford County, IL	14
Piatt County, IL	17
Charleston, WV.	306
Boone County, WV	26
Clay County, WV.	10
Kanawha County, WV . .	194
Lincoln County, WV	22
Putnam County, WV . . .	54
Charleston-North Charleston, SC	595
Berkeley County, SC . . .	152
Charleston-North Charleston, SC—Con.	
Charleston County, SC. .	330
Dorchester County, SC. .	113
Charlotte-Gastonia-Concord, NC-SC	1,521
Anson County, NC	25
Cabarrus County, NC . .	150
Gaston County, NC	196
Mecklenburg County, NC.	796
Union County, NC	163
York County, SC	190
Charlottesville, VA	188
Albemarle County, VA . .	91
Fluvanna County, VA . . .	25
Greene County, VA	17
Nelson County, VA.	15
Charlottesville city, VA . .	40
Chattanooga, TN-GA.	492
Catoosa County, GA . . .	61
Dade County, GA	16
Walker County, GA	64
Hamilton County, TN . . .	311
Marion County, TN.	28
Sequatchie County, TN. .	13
Cheyenne, WY	85
Laramie County, WY . . .	85
Chicago-Naperville-Joliet, IL	9,443
Chicago-Naperville-Joliet, IL	7,883
Cook County, IL	5,304
DeKalb County, IL	98
DuPage County, IL	929
Grundy County, IL	44
Kane County, IL	482
Kendall County, IL	80
McHenry County, IL. . . .	304
Will County, IL.	643
Gary, IN.	697
Jasper County, IN	32
Lake County, IN	493
Newton County, IN.	14
Porter County, IN.	158
Lake County-Kenosha County, IL-WI.	863
Lake County, IL.	703
Kenosha County, WI . . .	161
Chico, CA.	214
Butte County, CA.	214
Cincinnati-Middletown, OH-KY-IN	2,070
Dearborn County, IN . . .	49
Franklin County, IN	23
Ohio County, IN.	6
Boone County, KY	106
Bracken County, KY . . .	9
Campbell County, KY. . .	87
Gallatin County, KY	8
Grant County, KY	25
Kenton County, KY	154
Pendleton County, KY . .	15
Brown County, OH.	44
Butler County, OH.	350
Clermont County, OH. . .	191
Hamilton County, OH. . .	807
Warren County, OH	197
Clarksville, TN-KY.	244
Christian County, KY . . .	70
Trigg County, KY	13
Montgomery County, TN.	147
Stewart County, TN	13
Cleveland, TN.	108
Bradley County, TN	92
Polk County, TN	16
Cleveland-Elyria-Mentor, OH	2,126
Cuyahoga County, OH . .	1,335
Geauga County, OH . . .	95
Lake County, OH.	232
Lorain County, OH	296
Medina County, OH	167
Coeur d'Alene, ID	128
Kootenai County, ID. . . .	128
College Station-Bryan, TX. .	190
Brazos County, TX.	156
Burleson County, TX . . .	17
Robertson County, TX . .	16
Colorado Springs, CO.	588
El Paso County, CO. . . .	566
Teller County, CO	22
Columbia, MO.	153
Boone County, MO	143
Howard County, MO . . .	10
Columbia, SC	690
Calhoun County, SC . . .	15
Fairfield County, SC. . . .	24
Kershaw County, SC . . .	56
Lexington County, SC . .	235
Richland County, SC . . .	340
Saluda County, SC	19
Columbus, GA-AL.	284
Russell County, AL	49
Chattahoochee County, GA.	15
Harris County, GA	28
Marion County, GA	7
Muscogee County, GA . .	185
Columbus, IN	74
Bartholomew County, IN.	74
Columbus, OH	1,709
Delaware County, OH . .	150
Fairfield County, OH . . .	138
Franklin County, OH . . .	1,091
Licking County, OH	155
Madison County, OH . . .	41
Morrow County, OH	34
Pickaway County, OH . .	53
Union County, OH	46
Corpus Christi, TX	414
Aransas County, TX. . . .	25
Nueces County, TX	320
San Patricio County, TX.	69
Corvallis, OR	79
Benton County, OR	79
Cumberland, MD-WV.	101
Allegany County, MD . . .	74
Mineral County, WV	27
Dallas-Fort Worth-Arlington, TX	5,819
Dallas-Plano-Irving, TX . .	3,893
Collin County, TX.	659
Dallas County, TX	2,305
Delta County, TX	5
Denton County, TX	555
Ellis County, TX.	133
Hunt County, TX	83
Kaufman County, TX . . .	89
Rockwall County, TX . . .	63
Fort Worth-Arlington, TX .	1,926
Johnson County, TX. . . .	146
Parker County, TX.	103
Tarrant County, TX.	1,620
Wise County, TX	57
Dalton, GA	132
Murray County, GA	41
Whitfield County, GA . . .	91
Danville, IL	82

900   Appendix II

Metropolitan statistical area / Metropolitan division / Component county	Popu- lation, 2005 (1,000)	Metropolitan statistical area / Metropolitan division / Component county	Popu- lation, 2005 (1,000)	Metropolitan statistical area / Metropolitan division / Component county	Popu- lation, 2005 (1,000)
Vermilion County, IL. . . .	82	**Eau Claire, WI.**	154	**Fort Walton Beach-**	
Danville, VA	108	Chippewa County, WI. . .	60	**Crestview-Destin, FL.**	182
Pittsylvania County, VA. .	62	Eau Claire County, WI . .	94	Okaloosa County, FL . . .	182
Danville city, VA	46	**El Centro, CA**	156	**Fort Wayne, IN**	404
Davenport-Moline-Rock		Imperial County, CA. . . .	156	Allen County, IN	344
Island, IA-IL	376	**Elizabethtown, KY.**	111	Wells County, IN	28
Henry County, IL.	51	Hardin County, KY.	97	Whitley County, IN.	32
Mercer County, IL	17	Larue County, KY	14	**Fresno, CA**	878
Rock Island County, IL. .	148	**Elkhart-Goshen, IN**	195	Fresno County, CA	878
Scott County, IA	161	Elkhart County, IN	195	**Gadsden, AL.**	103
Dayton, OH.	844	**Elmira, NY**	90	Etowah County, AL	103
Greene County, OH	152	Chemung County, NY . .	90	**Gainesville, FL**	240
Miami County, OH	102	**El Paso, TX.**	722	Alachua County, FL. . . .	224
Montgomery County,		El Paso County, TX	722	Gilchrist County, FL	16
OH.	547	**Erie, PA**	280	**Gainesville, GA.**	166
Preble County, OH.	43	Erie County, PA.	280	Hall County, GA	166
Decatur, AL.	148	**Eugene-Springfield, OR.** . . .	335	**Glens Falls, NY.**	129
Lawrence County, AL. . .	35	Lane County, OR.	335	Warren County, NY	66
Morgan County, AL	114	**Evansville, IN-KY**	350	Washington County, NY .	63
Decatur, IL	110	Gibson County, IN	33	**Goldsboro, NC**	114
Macon County, IL	110	Posey County, IN	27	Wayne County, NC	114
Deltona-Daytona Beach-		Vanderburgh County, IN .	173	**Grand Forks, ND-MN.**	97
Ormond Beach, FL	490	Warrick County, IN.	56	Polk County, MN	31
Volusia County, FL.	490	Henderson County, KY. .	46	Grand Forks County,	
		Webster County, KY. . . .	14	ND.	66
Denver-Aurora, CO	2,360	**Fairbanks, AK.**	88	**Grand Junction, CO**	130
Adams County, CO	399	Fairbanks North Star		Mesa County, CO	130
Arapahoe County, CO . .	529	Borough, AK	88	**Grand Rapids-Wyoming, MI.**	771
Broomfield County, CO. .	43	**Fargo, ND-MN.**	185	Barry County, MI	60
Clear Creek County, CO.	9	Clay County, MN	54	Ionia County, MI	65
Denver County, CO	558	Cass County, ND.	131	Kent County, MI	597
Douglas County, CO . . .	249	**Farmington, NM**	126	Newaygo County, MI . . .	50
Elbert County, CO	23	San Juan County, NM . .	126	**Great Falls, MT.**	80
Gilpin County, CO	5	**Fayetteville, NC**	346	Cascade County, MT . . .	80
Jefferson County, CO. . .	527	Cumberland County, NC.	305	**Greeley, CO**	229
Park County, CO	17	Hoke County, NC.	41	Weld County, CO.	229
Des Moines-West Des		**Fayetteville-Springdale-**		**Green Bay, WI.**	297
Moines, IA.	522	**Rogers, AR-MO.**	405	Brown County, WI	239
Dallas County, IA.	52	Benton County, AR	187	Kewaunee County, WI . .	21
Guthrie County, IA	12	Madison County, AR . . .	15	Oconto County, WI	38
Madison County, IA	15	Washington County, AR .	180	**Greensboro-High Point, NC.**	675
Polk County, IA	401	McDonald County, MO . .	23	Guilford County, NC. . . .	444
Warren County, IA	43	**Flagstaff, AZ.**	124	Randolph County, NC . .	138
Detroit-Warren-Livonia, MI. .	4,488	Coconino County, AZ . . .	124	Rockingham County,	
Detroit-Livonia-Dearborn,		**Flint, MI**	444	NC.	93
MI.	1,998	Genesee County, MI . . .	444	**Greenville, NC**	163
Wayne County, MI	1,998	**Florence, SC.**	198	Greene County, NC	20
Warren-Troy-Farmington		Darlington County, SC . .	67	Pitt County, NC	143
Hills, MI.	2,490	Florence County, SC . . .	131	**Greenville, SC.**	591
Lapeer County, MI	93	**Florence-Muscle Shoals,**		Greenville County, SC . .	407
Livingston County, MI. . .	182	**AL**	142	Laurens County, SC . . .	70
Macomb County, MI . . .	829	Colbert County, AL.	55	Pickens County, SC	114
Oakland County, MI	1,214	Lauderdale County, AL. .	88	**Gulfport-Biloxi, MS**	255
St. Clair County, MI	171	**Fond du Lac, WI**	99	Hancock County, MS . . .	47
Dothan, AL.	137	Fond du Lac County, WI.	99	Harrison County, MS . . .	194
Geneva County, AL	26	**Fort Collins-Loveland, CO.** . .	272	Stone County, MS	15
Henry County, AL	17	Larimer County, CO. . . .	272	**Hagerstown-Martinsburg,**	
Houston County, AL. . . .	94	**Fort Smith, AR-OK**	285	**MD-WV**	251
Dover, DE.	144	Crawford County, AR . . .	58	Washington County, MD.	142
Kent County, DE	144	Franklin County, AR. . . .	18	Berkeley County, WV . . .	93
Dubuque, IA	92	Sebastian County, AR . .	119	Morgan County, WV. . . .	16
Dubuque County, IA. . . .	92	Le Flore County, OK . . .	50	**Hanford-Corcoran, CA.**	143
Duluth, MN-WI	275	Sequoyah County, OK . .	41	Kings County, CA	143
Carlton County, MN	34			**Harrisburg-Carlisle, PA**	522
St. Louis County, MN. . .	197			Cumberland County, PA .	223
Douglas County, WI . . .	44			Dauphin County, PA. . . .	254
Durham, NC	456				
Chatham County, NC. . .	58				
Durham County, NC. . . .	243				
Orange County, NC	118				
Person County, NC	37				

Metropolitan statistical area Metropolitan division Component county	Population, 2005 (1,000)	Metropolitan statistical area Metropolitan division Component county	Population, 2005 (1,000)	Metropolitan statistical area Metropolitan division Component county	Population, 2005 (1,000)
Harrisburg-Carlisle, PA—Con.		**Iowa City, IA**	139	**Killeen-Temple-Fort Hood, TX**	352
Perry County, PA	45	Johnson County, IA	117	Bell County, TX	256
		Washington County, IA	21	Coryell County, TX	76
Harrisonburg, VA	112			Lampasas County, TX	20
Rockingham County, VA	71	**Ithaca, NY**	100		
Harrisonburg city, VA	40	Tompkins County, NY	100	**Kingsport-Bristol-Bristol, TN-VA**	301
				Hawkins County, TN	56
Hartford-West Hartford-East Hartford, CT	1,188	**Jackson, MI**	164	Sullivan County, TN	153
Hartford County, CT	877	Jackson County, MI	164	Scott County, VA	23
Middlesex County, CT	163			Washington County, VA	52
Tolland County, CT	148	**Jackson, MS**	523	Bristol city, VA	17
		Copiah County, MS	29		
Hattiesburg, MS	132	Hinds County, MS	249	**Kingston, NY**	183
Forrest County, MS	75	Madison County, MS	84	Ulster County, NY	183
Lamar County, MS	45	Rankin County, MS	132		
Perry County, MS	12	Simpson County, MS	28	**Knoxville, TN**	655
				Anderson County, TN	72
Hickory-Lenoir-Morganton, NC	356	**Jackson, TN**	111	Blount County, TN	116
Alexander County, NC	35	Chester County, TN	16	Knox County, TN	405
Burke County, NC	89	Madison County, TN	95	Loudon County, TN	43
Caldwell County, NC	79			Union County, TN	19
Catawba County, NC	152	**Jacksonville, FL**	1,248		
		Baker County, FL	25	**Kokomo, IN**	101
Hinesville-Fort Stewart, GA	69	Clay County, FL	171	Howard County, IN	85
Liberty County, GA	58	Duval County, FL	826	Tipton County, IN	16
Long County, GA	11	Nassau County, FL	65		
		St. Johns County, FL	162	**La Crosse, WI-MN**	129
Holland-Grand Haven, MI	255			Houston County, MN	20
Ottawa County, MI	255	**Jacksonville, NC**	152	La Crosse County, WI	109
		Onslow County, NC	152		
Honolulu, HI	905			**Lafayette, IN**	183
Honolulu County, HI	905	**Janesville, WI**	158	Benton County, IN	9
		Rock County, WI	158	Carroll County, IN	20
Hot Springs, AR	94			Tippecanoe County, IN	154
Garland County, AR	94	**Jefferson City, MO**	144		
		Callaway County, MO	43	**Lafayette, LA**	248
Houma-Bayou Cane-Thibodaux, LA	200	Cole County, MO	73	Lafayette Parish, LA	197
Lafourche Parish, LA	92	Moniteau County, MO	15	St. Martin Parish, LA	50
Terrebonne Parish, LA	107	Osage County, MO	13		
				Lake Charles, LA	195
Houston-Sugar Land-Baytown, TX	5,280	**Johnson City, TN**	189	Calcasieu Parish, LA	185
Austin County, TX	26	Carter County, TN	59	Cameron Parish, LA	10
Brazoria County, TX	278	Unicoi County, TN	18		
Chambers County, TX	28	Washington County, TN	113	**Lakeland, FL**	543
Fort Bend County, TX	464			Polk County, FL	543
Galveston County, TX	278	**Johnstown, PA**	148		
Harris County, TX	3,693	Cambria County, PA	148	**Lancaster, PA**	491
Liberty County, TX	75			Lancaster County, PA	491
Montgomery County, TX	378	**Jonesboro, AR**	112		
San Jacinto County, TX	25	Craighead County, AR	87	**Lansing-East Lansing, MI**	455
Waller County, TX	35	Poinsett County, AR	25	Clinton County, MI	69
				Eaton County, MI	107
Huntington-Ashland, WV-KY-OH	286	**Joplin, MO**	166	Ingham County, MI	279
Boyd County, KY	50	Jasper County, MO	111		
Greenup County, KY	37	Newton County, MO	56	**Laredo, TX**	225
Lawrence County, OH	63			Webb County, TX	225
Cabell County, WV	94	**Kalamazoo-Portage, MI**	319		
Wayne County, WV	42	Kalamazoo County, MI	241	**Las Cruces, NM**	189
		Van Buren County, MI	79	Dona Ana County, NM	189
Huntsville, AL	369				
Limestone County, AL	70	**Kankakee-Bradley, IL**	108	**Las Vegas-Paradise, NV**	1,711
Madison County, AL	298	Kankakee County, IL	108	Clark County, NV	1,711
Idaho Falls, ID	113	**Kansas City, MO-KS**	1,948	**Lawrence, KS**	103
Bonneville County, ID	92	Franklin County, KS	26	Douglas County, KS	103
Jefferson County, ID	22	Johnson County, KS	507		
		Leavenworth County, KS	73	**Lawton, OK**	112
Indianapolis-Carmel, IN	1,641	Linn County, KS	10	Comanche County, OK	112
Boone County, IN	52	Miami County, KS	30		
Brown County, IN	15	Wyandotte County, KS	156	**Lebanon, PA**	126
Hamilton County, IN	241	Bates County, MO	17	Lebanon County, PA	126
Hancock County, IN	63	Caldwell County, MO	9		
Hendricks County, IN	127	Cass County, MO	94	**Lewiston, ID-WA**	59
Johnson County, IN	128	Clay County, MO	202	Nez Perce County, ID	38
Marion County, IN	863	Clinton County, MO	21	Asotin County, WA	21
Morgan County, IN	70	Jackson County, MO	663		
Putnam County, IN	37	Lafayette County, MO	33	**Lewiston-Auburn, ME**	108
Shelby County, IN	44	Platte County, MO	82	Androscoggin County, ME	108
		Ray County, MO	24		
				Lexington-Fayette, KY	430
		Kennewick-Richland-Pasco, WA	221	Bourbon County, KY	20
		Benton County, WA	158	Clark County, KY	35
		Franklin County, WA	63	Fayette County, KY	268

U.S. Census Bureau, Statistical Abstract of the United States: 2007

Metropolitan statistical area Metropolitan division Component county	Population, 2005 (1,000)	Metropolitan statistical area Metropolitan division Component county	Population, 2005 (1,000)	Metropolitan statistical area Metropolitan division Component county	Population, 2005 (1,000)
Lexington-Fayette, KY—Con.		**Manchester-Nashua, NH ...**	401	**Montgomery, AL ....**	357
Jessamine County, KY . .	43	Hillsborough County, NH . . .	401	Autauga County, AL. . . .	49
Scott County, KY	39			Elmore County, AL. . . .	74
Woodford County, KY. . .	24	**Mansfield, OH. . . . .**	128	Lowndes County, AL . . .	13
		Richland County, OH . . .	128	Montgomery County, AL .	222
Lima, OH	106				
Allen County, OH.	106	**McAllen-Edinburg-Mission, TX . . . .**	678	**Morgantown, WV . . . .**	115
		Hidalgo County, TX	678	Monongalia County, WV . .	84
Lincoln, NE.	282			Preston County, WV . . .	30
Lancaster County, NE . .	265	**Medford, OR. . . . .**	195		
Seward County, NE	17	Jackson County, OR . . .	195	**Morristown, TN. . . . .**	131
				Grainger County, TN . . .	22
Little Rock-North Little Rock, AR	643	**Memphis, TN-MS-AR. . . . . .**	1,261	Hamblen County, TN . . .	60
Faulkner County, AR . . .	97	Crittenden County, AR . .	52	Jefferson County, TN . . .	48
Grant County, AR	17	DeSoto County, MS. . . .	137		
Lonoke County, AR	61	Marshall County, MS . . .	36	**Mount Vernon-Anacortes, WA . . . .**	113
Perry County, AR	10	Tate County, MS	27	Skagit County, WA.	113
Pulaski County, AR	366	Tunica County, MS	10		
Saline County, AR	91	Fayette County, TN	34	**Muncie, IN . . . .**	116
		Shelby County, TN.	909	Delaware County, IN . . .	116
Logan, UT-ID.	110	Tipton County, TN	56		
Franklin County, ID	12			**Muskegon-Norton Shores, MI . . . .**	176
Cache County, UT	98	**Merced, CA. . . . .**	242	Muskegon County, MI . .	176
		Merced County, CA	242		
Longview, TX	202			**Myrtle Beach-Conway-North Myrtle Beach, SC . . . .**	227
Gregg County, TX	116	**Miami-Fort Lauderdale-Miami Beach, FL. . . . .**	5,422	Horry County, SC	227
Rusk County, TX	48	**Fort Lauderdale-Pompano Beach-Deerfield Beach, FL. . . .**	1,778		
Upshur County, TX	38	Broward County, FL. . . .	1,778	**Napa, CA . . . .**	133
		Miami-Miami Beach-Kendall, FL	2,376	Napa County, CA	133
Longview, WA.	97	Miami-Dade County, FL . .	2,376		
Cowlitz County, WA	97	**West Palm Beach-Boca Raton-Boynton Beach, FL. . . . .**	1,269	**Naples-Marco Island, FL . . .**	307
		Palm Beach County, FL . .	1,269	Collier County, FL	307
Los Angeles-Long Beach-Santa Ana, CA	12,924				
Los Angeles-Long Beach-Glendale, CA. . .	9,935	**Michigan City-La Porte, IN. .**	111	**Nashville-Davidson—Murfreesboro, TN . . . .**	1,423
Los Angeles County, CA.	9,935	La Porte County, IN	111	Cannon County, TN	13
Santa Ana-Anaheim-Irvine, CA	2,988			Cheatham County, TN . .	39
Orange County, CA	2,988	**Midland, TX . . . .**	121	Davidson County, TN . . .	575
		Midland County, TX	121	Dickson County, TN	46
Louisville-Jefferson County, KY-IN	1,208			Hickman County, TN . . .	24
Clark County, IN	102	**Milwaukee-Waukesha-West Allis, WI . . . .**	1,513	Macon County, TN.	22
Floyd County, IN	72	Milwaukee County, WI . .	922	Robertson County, TN . .	60
Harrison County, IN	37	Ozaukee County, WI . . .	86	Rutherford County, TN . .	218
Washington County, IN. .	28	Washington County, WI . .	126	Smith County, TN	19
Bullitt County, KY.	68	Waukesha County, WI . .	379	Sumner County, TN	145
Henry County, KY	16			Trousdale County, TN . .	8
Jefferson County, KY . . .	700	**Minneapolis-St. Paul-Bloomington, MN-WI . . . . . .**	3,143	Williamson County, TN . .	154
Meade County, KY.	28	Anoka County, MN.	324	Wilson County, TN.	101
Nelson County, KY	41	Carver County, MN	85		
Oldham County, KY. . . .	54	Chisago County, MN . . .	49	**New Haven-Milford, CT . . . .**	847
Shelby County, KY.	38	Dakota County, MN	384	New Haven County, CT .	847
Spencer County, KY . . .	16	Hennepin County, MN . . .	1,119		
Trimble County, KY	9	Isanti County, MN	38	**New Orleans-Metairie-Kenner, LA . . . .**	1,319
		Ramsey County, MN . . .	495	Jefferson Parish, LA . . .	453
Lubbock, TX.	259	Scott County, MN	120	Orleans Parish, LA	455
Crosby County, TX	7	Sherburne County, MN. . .	82	Plaquemines Parish, LA .	29
Lubbock County, TX. . . .	252	Washington County, MN. .	220	St. Bernard Parish, LA . .	65
		Wright County, MN	111	St. Charles Parish, LA . .	51
Lynchburg, VA	237	Pierce County, WI	39	St. John the Baptist Parish, LA.	46
Amherst County, VA. . . .	32	St. Croix County, WI . . .	77	St. Tammany Parish, LA.	220
Appomattox County, VA .	14				
Bedford County, VA	65	**Missoula, MT . . . .**	100	**New York-Northern New Jersey-Long Island, NY-NJ-PA . . . .**	18,747
Campbell County, VA . . .	52	Missoula County, MT . . .	100	**Edison, NJ . . . .**	2,304
Bedford city, VA.	6			Middlesex County, NJ . .	790
Lynchburg city, VA.	67	**Mobile, AL . . . .**	401	Monmouth County, NJ . .	636
		Mobile County, AL	401	Ocean County, NJ	558
Macon, GA	229			Somerset County, NJ . . .	320
Bibb County, GA	155	**Modesto, CA. . . . .**	506	**Nassau-Suffolk, NY . . . . . .**	2,808
Crawford County, GA. . .	13	Stanislaus County, CA . .	506	Nassau County, NY	1,333
Jones County, GA	27			Suffolk County, NY	1,475
Monroe County, GA	24	**Monroe, LA. . . . .**	171	**Newark-Union, NJ-PA . . . .**	2,153
Twiggs County, GA	10	Ouachita Parish, LA. . . .	148	Essex County, NJ	791
		Union Parish, LA	23	Hunterdon County, NJ . .	130
Madera, CA.	143			Morris County, NJ	491
Madera County, CA	143	**Monroe, MI . . . .**	154	Sussex County, NJ	153
		Monroe County, MI	154	Union County, NJ	531
Madison, WI	537			Pike County, PA	56
Columbia County, WI . . .	55			**New York-White Plains-Wayne, NY-NJ . . . .**	11,483
Dane County, WI	458				
Iowa County, WI	24				

U.S. Census Bureau, Statistical Abstract of the United States: 2007

Metropolitan statistical area Metropolitan division Component county	Population, 2005 (1,000)	Metropolitan statistical area Metropolitan division Component county	Population, 2005 (1,000)	Metropolitan statistical area Metropolitan division Component county	Population, 2005 (1,000)
Bergen County, NJ	903	**Parkersburg-Marietta-**		**Port St. Lucie-Fort Pierce,**	
Hudson County, NJ	604	**Vienna, WV-OH**	163	**FL.**	381
Passaic County, NJ	499	Washington County, OH . .	62	Martin County, FL	140
Bronx County, NY	1,358	Pleasants County, WV . .	7	St. Lucie County, FL . . .	241
Kings County, NY	2,486	Wirt County, WV	6		
New York County, NY. . .	1,593	Wood County, WV	87	**Poughkeepsie-Newburgh-**	
Putnam County, NY. . . .	101			**Middletown, NY.**	668
Queens County, NY	2,242	**Pascagoula, MS**	157	Dutchess County, NY. . .	295
Richmond County, NY . .	465	George County, MS. . . .	21	Orange County, NY	373
Rockland County, NY. . .	293	Jackson County, MS . . .	136		
Westchester County, NY.	941			**Prescott, AZ**	199
		Pensacola-Ferry Pass-		Yavapai County, AZ	199
Niles-Benton Harbor, MI . . .	163	**Brent, FL**	440		
Berrien County, MI.	163	Escambia County, FL.. .	297	**Providence-New Bedford-**	
		Santa Rosa County, FL .	143	**Fall River, RI-MA**	1,623
Norwich-New London, CT . .	267			Bristol County, MA.	546
New London County,		**Peoria, IL**	369	Bristol County, RI.	53
CT	267	Marshall County, IL	13	Kent County, RI.	172
		Peoria County, IL.	182	Newport County, RI	84
Ocala, FL	303	Stark County, IL	6	Providence County, RI . .	640
Marion County, FL.	303	Tazewell County, IL	130	Washington County, RI. .	128
		Woodford County, IL . . .	37		
Ocean City, NJ	99			**Provo-Orem, UT**	453
Cape May County, NJ . .	99	**Philadelphia-Camden-**		Juab County, UT	9
		Wilmington, PA-NJ-DE-MD.	5,823	Utah County, UT	444
Odessa, TX.	125	**Camden, NJ**	1,246		
Ector County, TX.	125	Burlington County, NJ . .	451	**Pueblo, CO.**	151
		Camden County, NJ. . . .	518	Pueblo County, CO	151
Ogden-Clearfield, UT.	487	Gloucester County, NJ . .	277		
Davis County, UT	268	**Philadelphia, PA**	3,890	**Punta Gorda, FL**	158
Morgan County, UT	8	Bucks County, PA	621	Charlotte County, FL . . .	158
Weber County, UT.	211	Chester County, PA	474		
		Delaware County, PA. . .	556	**Racine, WI**	196
Oklahoma City, OK	1,157	Montgomery County, PA.	776	Racine County, WI.	196
Canadian County, OK . .	99	Philadelphia County, PA .	1,463		
Cleveland County, OK . .	225	**Wilmington, DE-MD-NJ** . .	687	**Raleigh-Cary, NC**	950
Grady County, OK	49	New Castle County, DE .	523	Franklin County, NC. . . .	54
Lincoln County, OK	32	Cecil County, MD.	98	Johnston County, NC. . .	146
Logan County, OK.	37	Salem County, NJ	66	Wake County, NC.	749
McClain County, OK . . .	30				
Oklahoma County, OK . .	685	**Phoenix-Mesa-Scottsdale,**		**Rapid City, SD**	118
		AZ	3,865	Meade County, SD	25
Olympia, WA.	229	Maricopa County, AZ . . .	3,636	Pennington County, SD .	94
Thurston County, WA. . .	229	Pinal County, AZ	230		
				Reading, PA	396
Omaha-Council Bluffs,		**Pine Bluff, AR.**	105	Berks County, PA	396
NE-IA	813	Cleveland County, AR . .	9		
Harrison County, IA	16	Jefferson County, AR. . .	82	**Redding, CA.**	180
Mills County, IA.	15	Lincoln County, AR	14	Shasta County, CA	180
Pottawattamie County,					
IA	90	**Pittsburgh, PA**	2,386	**Reno-Sparks, NV**	394
Cass County, NE.	26	Allegheny County, PA. . .	1,236	Storey County, NV.	4
Douglas County, NE . . .	487	Armstrong County, PA . .	71	Washoe County, NV. . . .	390
Sarpy County, NE	139	Beaver County, PA	177		
Saunders County, NE. . .	20	Butler County, PA	182	**Richmond, VA.**	1,176
Washington County, NE .	20	Fayette County, PA	146	Amelia County, VA.	12
		Washington County, PA .	206	Caroline County, VA. . . .	26
Orlando-Kissimmee, FL. . . .	1,933	Westmoreland County,		Charles City County, VA .	7
Lake County, FL	277	PA	368	Chesterfield County, VA .	289
Orange County, FL	1,023			Cumberland County, VA .	9
Osceola County, FL. . . .	232	**Pittsfield, MA**	132	Dinwiddie County, VA. . .	25
Seminole County, FL . . .	402	Berkshire County, MA . .	132	Goochland County, VA. .	19
				Hanover County, VA. . . .	97
Oshkosh-Neenah, WI	159	**Pocatello, ID.**	86	Henrico County, VA	281
Winnebago County, WI. .	159	Bannock County, ID. . . .	78	King and Queen County,	
		Power County, ID	8	VA	7
Owensboro, KY.	112			King William County, VA.	15
Daviess County, KY	93	**Portland-South Portland-**		Louisa County, VA	30
Hancock County, KY . . .	9	**Biddeford, ME.**	514	New Kent County, VA . . .	16
McLean County, KY. . . .	10	Cumberland County, ME.	275	Powhatan County, VA . .	27
		Sagadahoc County, ME .	37	Prince George County,	
Oxnard-Thousand Oaks-		York County, ME	202	VA	37
Ventura, CA	796			Sussex County, VA	12
Ventura County, CA. . . .	796	**Portland-Vancouver-**		Colonial Heights city, VA.	18
		Beaverton, OR-WA	2,096	Hopewell city, VA.	23
Palm Bay-Melbourne-		Clackamas County, OR .	368	Petersburg city, VA. . . .	33
Titusville, FL.	531	Columbia County, OR . .	48	Richmond city, VA	194
Brevard County, FL	531	Multnomah County, OR .	673		
		Washington County, OR .	500	**Riverside-San Bernardino-**	
Panama City-Lynn Haven,		Yamhill County, OR	92	**Ontario, CA.**	3,910
FL.	162	Clark County, WA	404	Riverside County, CA. . .	1,946
Bay County, FL	162	Skamania County, WA . .	11	San Bernardino County,	
				CA.	1,964

U.S. Census Bureau, Statistical Abstract of the United States: 2007

Metropolitan statistical area / Metropolitan division / Component county	Population, 2005 (1,000)
Roanoke, VA	293
Botetourt County, VA	32
Craig County, VA	5
Franklin County, VA	50
Roanoke County, VA	88
Roanoke city, VA	93
Salem city, VA	25
Rochester, MN	177
Dodge County, MN	20
Olmsted County, MN	135
Wabasha County, MN	22
Rochester, NY	1,039
Livingston County, NY	64
Monroe County, NY	733
Ontario County, NY	104
Orleans County, NY	43
Wayne County, NY	94
Rockford, IL	339
Boone County, IL	50
Winnebago County, IL	289
Rocky Mount, NC	146
Edgecombe County, NC	54
Nash County, NC	91
Rome, GA	94
Floyd County, GA	94
Sacramento—Arden-Arcade—Roseville, CA	2,042
El Dorado County, CA	177
Placer County, CA	317
Sacramento County, CA	1,363
Yolo County, CA	185
Saginaw-Saginaw Township North, MI	208
Saginaw County, MI	208
St. Cloud, MN	181
Benton County, MN	39
Stearns County, MN	143
St. George, UT	119
Washington County, UT	119
St. Joseph, MO-KS	122
Doniphan County, KS	8
Andrew County, MO	17
Buchanan County, MO	85
DeKalb County, MO	12
St. Louis, MO-IL [1]	2,779
Bond County, IL	18
Calhoun County, IL	5
Clinton County, IL	36
Jersey County, IL	22
Macoupin County, IL	49
Madison County, IL	264
Monroe County, IL	31
St. Clair County, IL	260
Franklin County, MO	99
Jefferson County, MO	214
Lincoln County, MO	48
St. Charles County, MO	330
St. Louis County, MO	1,005
Warren County, MO	29
Washington County, MO	24
St. Louis city, MO	344
Salem, OR	376
Marion County, OR	305
Polk County, OR	70
Salinas, CA	412
Monterey County, CA	412
Salisbury, MD	116
Somerset County, MD	26
Wicomico County, MD	90
Salt Lake City, UT	1,034
Salt Lake County, UT	948
Summit County, UT	35
Tooele County, UT	51
San Angelo, TX	105
Irion County, TX	2
Tom Green County, TX	104
San Antonio, TX	1,890
Atascosa County, TX	43
Bandera County, TX	20
Bexar County, TX	1,518
Comal County, TX	96
Guadalupe County, TX	103
Kendall County, TX	29
Medina County, TX	43
Wilson County, TX	38
San Diego-Carlsbad-San Marcos, CA	2,933
San Diego County, CA	2,933
Sandusky, OH	79
Erie County, OH	79
San Francisco-Oakland-Fremont, CA	4,153
Oakland-Fremont-Hayward, CA	2,467
Alameda County, CA	1,449
Contra Costa County, CA	1,018
San Francisco-San Mateo-Redwood City, CA	1,686
Marin County, CA	247
San Francisco County, CA	739
San Mateo County, CA	700
San Jose-Sunnyvale-Santa Clara, CA	1,755
San Benito County, CA	56
Santa Clara County, CA	1,699
San Luis Obispo-Paso Robles, CA	255
San Luis Obispo County, CA	255
Santa Barbara-Santa Maria, CA	401
Santa Barbara County, CA	401
Santa Cruz-Watsonville, CA	250
Santa Cruz County, CA	250
Santa Fe, NM	141
Santa Fe County, NM	141
Santa Rosa-Petaluma, CA	466
Sonoma County, CA	466
Sarasota-Bradenton-Venice, FL	673
Manatee County, FL	307
Sarasota County, FL	366
Savannah, GA	314
Bryan County, GA	29
Chatham County, GA	238
Effingham County, GA	47
Scranton—Wilkes-Barre, PA	551
Lackawanna County, PA	210
Luzerne County, PA	313
Wyoming County, PA	28
Seattle-Tacoma-Bellevue, WA	3,203
Seattle-Bellevue-Everett, WA	2,450
King County, WA	1,794
Snohomish County, WA	656
Tacoma, WA	754
Pierce County, WA	754
Sebastian-Vero Beach, FL	129
Indian River County, FL	129
Sheboygan, WI	115
Sheboygan County, WI	115
Sherman-Denison, TX	117
Grayson County, TX	117
Shreveport-Bossier City, LA	383
Bossier Parish, LA	106
Caddo Parish, LA	251
De Soto Parish, LA	26
Sioux City, IA-NE-SD	143
Woodbury County, IA	103
Dakota County, NE	20
Dixon County, NE	6
Union County, SD	13
Sioux Falls, SD	208
Lincoln County, SD	33
McCook County, SD	6
Minnehaha County, SD	160
Turner County, SD	9
South Bend-Mishawaka, IN-MI	318
St. Joseph County, IN	266
Cass County, MI	52
Spartanburg, SC	267
Spartanburg County, SC	267
Spokane, WA	441
Spokane County, WA	441
Springfield, IL	206
Menard County, IL	13
Sangamon County, IL	193
Springfield, MA	687
Franklin County, MA	72
Hampden County, MA	462
Hampshire County, MA	153
Springfield, MO	398
Christian County, MO	67
Dallas County, MO	16
Greene County, MO	251
Polk County, MO	29
Webster County, MO	35
Springfield, OH	142
Clark County, OH	142
State College, PA	141
Centre County, PA	141
Stockton, CA	664
San Joaquin County, CA	664
Sumter, SC	106
Sumter County, SC	106
Syracuse, NY	652
Madison County, NY	70
Onondaga County, NY	458
Oswego County, NY	123
Tallahassee, FL	335
Gadsden County, FL	46
Jefferson County, FL	14
Leon County, FL	246
Tallahassee, FL—Con.	

Metropolitan statistical area / Metropolitan division / Component county	Popu-lation, 2005 (1,000)	Metropolitan statistical area / Metropolitan division / Component county	Popu-lation, 2005 (1,000)	Metropolitan statistical area / Metropolitan division / Component county	Popu-lation, 2005 (1,000)
Wakulla County, FL	28	Victoria, TX—Con.		**Wausau, WI**	**129**
		Goliad County, TX	7	Marathon County, WI . . .	129
Tampa-St. Petersburg-		Victoria County, TX	86		
Clearwater, FL.	**2,648**			**Weirton-Steubenville,**	
Hernando County, FL. . .	158	**Vineland-Millville-Bridgeton,**		**WV-OH**	**126**
Hillsborough County, FL.	1,132	**NJ**	**153**	Jefferson County, OH. . .	71
Pasco County, FL	429	Cumberland County, NJ .	153	Brooke County, WV . . .	25
Pinellas County, FL	928			Hancock County, WV . . .	31
		Virginia Beach-Norfolk-			
Terre Haute, IN	**168**	**Newport News, VA-NC.** . . .	**1,647**	**Wenatchee, WA.**	**105**
Clay County, IN.	27	Currituck County, NC . . .	23	Chelan County, WA . . .	70
Sullivan County, IN	22	Gloucester County, VA . .	38	Douglas County, WA . . .	35
Vermillion County, IN . . .	17	Isle of Wight County, VA.	33		
Vigo County, IN.	103	James City County, VA. .	58	**Wheeling, WV-OH**	**149**
		Mathews County, VA . . .	9	Belmont County, OH . . .	69
Texarkana, TX-Texarkana,		Surry County, VA.	7	Marshall County, WV . . .	34
AR	**134**	York County, VA	62	Ohio County, WV.	45
Miller County, AR.	43	Chesapeake city, VA . . .	219		
Bowie County, TX	91	Hampton city, VA.	146	**Wichita, KS.**	**587**
		Newport News city, VA . .	180	Butler County, KS	62
		Norfolk city, VA	232	Harvey County, KS	34
Toledo, OH	**657**	Poquoson city, VA	12	Sedgwick County, KS. . .	466
Fulton County, OH	43	Portsmouth city, VA	100	Sumner County, KS	25
Lucas County, OH	448	Suffolk city, VA	79		
Ottawa County, OH	42	Virginia Beach city, VA . .	438	**Wichita Falls, TX.**	**146**
Wood County, OH	124	Williamsburg city, VA . . .	12	Archer County, TX	9
				Clay County, TX	11
Topeka, KS.	**229**	**Visalia-Porterville, CA**	**411**	Wichita County, TX	126
Jackson County, KS. . . .	14	Tulare County, CA	411		
Jefferson County, KS . . .	19			**Williamsport, PA**	**118**
Osage County, KS.	17	**Waco, TX**	**225**	Lycoming County, PA. . .	118
Shawnee County, KS. . .	172	McLennan County, TX . .	225		
Wabaunsee County, KS .	7			**Wilmington, NC.**	**315**
		Warner Robins, GA	**126**	Brunswick County, NC . .	89
Trenton-Ewing, NJ	**366**	Houston County, GA . . .	126	New Hanover County,	
Mercer County, NJ.	366			NC.	180
		Washington-Arlington-		Pender County, NC	46
Tucson, AZ.	**925**	**Alexandria, DC-VA-MD-WV.**	**5,215**		
Pima County, AZ	925	**Bethesda-Gaithersburg-**		**Winchester, VA-WV**	**116**
		Frederick, MD	**1,148**	Frederick County, VA . . .	69
Tulsa, OK	**888**	Frederick County, MD . .	221	Winchester city, VA . . .	25
Creek County, OK	69	Montgomery County,		Hampshire County, WV .	22
Okmulgee County, OK . .	40	MD	928		
Osage County, OK.	45	**Washington-Arlington-**		**Winston-Salem, NC.**	**449**
Pawnee County, OK . . .	17	**Alexandria, DC-VA-MD-**		Davie County, NC	39
Rogers County, OK	81	**WV**	**4,066**	Forsyth County, NC	326
Tulsa County, OK	572	District of Columbia, DC.	551	Stokes County, NC	46
Wagoner County, OK . . .	64	Calvert County, MD	88	Yadkin County, NC	38
		Charles County, MD. . . .	139		
Tuscaloosa, AL.	**197**	Prince George's County,		**Worcester, MA**	**783**
Greene County, AL . . .	10	MD	846	Worcester County, MA . .	783
Hale County, AL	18	Arlington County, VA . . .	196		
Tuscaloosa County, AL. .	169	Clarke County, VA	14	**Yakima, WA**	**232**
		Fairfax County, VA	1,007	Yakima County, WA	232
Tyler, TX.	**191**	Fauquier County, VA . . .	65		
Smith County, TX	191	Loudoun County, VA . . .	256	**York-Hanover, PA**	**409**
		Prince William County,		York County, PA	409
Utica-Rome, NY	**298**	VA	349		
Herkimer County, NY . . .	64	Spotsylvania County, VA.	117	**Youngstown-Warren-**	
Oneida County, NY	234	Stafford County, VA	118	**Boardman, OH-PA.**	**593**
		Warren County, VA	36	Mahoning County, OH . .	254
Valdosta, GA.	**125**	Alexandria city, VA	135	Trumbull County, OH . . .	219
Brooks County, GA	16	Fairfax city, VA	22	Mercer County, PA.	120
Echols County, GA	4	Falls Church city, VA . . .	11		
Lanier County, GA	8	Fredericksburg city, VA. .	21	**Yuba City, CA**	**156**
Lowndes County, GA. . .	97	Manassas city, VA	38	Sutter County, CA	89
		Manassas Park city, VA .	12	Yuba County, CA.	67
Vallejo-Fairfield, CA	**412**	Jefferson County, WV . . .	49		
Solano County, CA	412			**Yuma, AZ**	**181**
		Waterloo-Cedar Falls, IA . . .	**162**	Yuma County, AZ	181
Victoria, TX.	**113**	Black Hawk County, IA. .	126		
Calhoun County, TX. . . .	21	Bremer County, IA.	24		
		Grundy County, IA	12		

[1] The portion of Sullivan city in Crawford County, Missouri, is legally part of the St. Louis, MO-IL MSA. The estimate shown here for the St. Louis, MO-IL Metropolitan Statistical Area does not include this area.

Source: U.S. Census Bureau, "July 1, 2005 Population Estimates for Metropolitan, Micropolitan, and Combined Statistical Areas (Areas Defined by the Office of Management and Budget as of December 2005)"; published 21 August 2006; <http://www.census.gov/population/www/estimates/Estimates%20pagesfinal.html>.

Table B. **Micropolitan Statistical Areas and Components as of December 2005**

[Population as of **July 2005**. **55 represents 55,000**. All micropolitan areas are arranged alphabetically]

Micropolitan statistical area Component county	Population, 2005 (1,000)	Micropolitan statistical area Component county	Population, 2005 (1,000)	Micropolitan statistical area Component county	Population, 2005 (1,000)
Abbeville, LA	55	**Astoria, OR.**	37	**Big Rapids, MI**	42
Vermilion Parish, LA	55	Clatsop County, OR.	37	Mecosta County, MI.	42
Aberdeen, SD	39	**Atchison, KS**	17	**Big Spring, TX**	33
Brown County, SD.	35	Atchison County, KS	17	Howard County, TX.	33
Edmunds County, SD	4	**Athens, OH**	62	**Bishop, CA**	18
Aberdeen, WA.	71	Athens County, OH	62	Inyo County, CA	18
Grays Harbor County, WA .	71	**Athens, TN**	51	**Blackfoot, ID.**	44
Ada, OK	35	McMinn County, TN.	51	Bingham County, ID	44
Pontotoc County, OK.	35	**Athens, TX**	80	**Bloomsburg-Berwick, PA** . .	83
Adrian, MI.	102	Henderson County, TX. . . .	80	Columbia County, PA.	65
Lenawee County, MI	102	**Auburn, IN**	42	Montour County, PA	18
Alamogordo, NM.	64	De Kalb County, IN	42	**Bluefield, WV-VA.**	106
Otero County, NM.	64	**Auburn, NY.**	81	Tazewell County, VA	45
Albany-Lebanon, OR.	109	Cayuga County, NY.	81	Mercer County, WV.	62
Linn County, OR	109	**Augusta-Waterville, ME.** . . .	121	**Blytheville, AR**	48
Albemarle, NC	59	Kennebec County, ME. . . .	121	Mississippi County, AR . . .	48
Stanly County, NC.	59	**Austin, MN**	39	**Bogalusa, LA**	45
Albert Lea, MN	32	Mower County, MN	39	Washington Parish, LA . . .	45
Freeborn County, MN	32	**Bainbridge, GA.**	29	**Bonham, TX**	33
Albertville, AL.	86	Decatur County, GA	29	Fannin County, TX	33
Marshall County, AL	86	**Baraboo, WI**	58	**Boone, IA.**	27
Alexander City, AL	52	Sauk County, WI.	58	Boone County, IA	27
Coosa County, AL.	11	**Barre, VT**	59	**Boone, NC**	42
Tallapoosa County, AL. . . .	41	Washington County, VT . . .	59	Watauga County, NC.	42
Alexandria, MN	35	**Bartlesville, OK.**	49	**Borger, TX.**	22
Douglas County, MN	35	Washington County, OK. . .	49	Hutchinson County, TX . . .	22
Alice, TX.	41	**Bastrop, LA**	30	**Bozeman, MT**	78
Jim Wells County, TX	41	Morehouse Parish, LA. . . .	30	Gallatin County, MT.	78
Allegan, MI.	113	**Batavia, NY**	59	**Bradford, PA.**	44
Allegan County, MI	113	Genesee County, NY.	59	McKean County, PA	44
Alma, MI.	42	**Batesville, AR.**	35	**Brainerd, MN**	89
Gratiot County, MI.	42	Independence County, AR .	35	Cass County, MN	29
Alpena, MI	30	**Bay City, TX**	38	Crow Wing County, MN . . .	60
Alpena County, MI.	30	Matagorda County, TX. . . .	38	**Branson, MO**	74
Altus, OK	27	**Beatrice, NE**	23	Stone County, MO.	31
Jackson County, OK	27	Gage County, NE	23	Taney County, MO	43
Americus, GA.	37	**Beaver Dam, WI**	88	**Brenham, TX.**	32
Schley County, GA	4	Dodge County, WI.	88	Washington County, TX . . .	32
Sumter County, GA	33	**Beckley, WV**	79	**Brevard, NC**	30
Amsterdam, NY.	49	Raleigh County, WV	79	Transylvania County, NC . .	30
Montgomery County, NY . .	49	**Bedford, IN.**	46	**Brigham City, UT**	46
Andrews, TX.	13	Lawrence County, IN.	46	Box Elder County, UT	46
Andrews County, TX	13	**Beeville, TX**	33	**Brookhaven, MS**	34
Angola, IN	34	Bee County, TX	33	Lincoln County, MS.	34
Steuben County, IN.	34	**Bellefontaine, OH**	47	**Brookings, OR**	22
Arcadia, FL.	35	Logan County, OH	47	Curry County, OR	22
DeSoto County, FL	35	**Bemidji, MN**	43	**Brookings, SD**	28
Ardmore, OK	56	Beltrami County, MN	43	Brookings County, SD	28
Carter County, OK.	47	**Bennettsville, SC**	28	**Brownsville, TN**	20
Love County, OK.	9	Marlboro County, SC.	28	Haywood County, TN.	20
Arkadelphia, AR	23	**Bennington, VT.**	37	**Brownwood, TX**	39
Clark County, AR	23	Bennington County, VT . . .	37	Brown County, TX.	39
Ashland, OH.	54	**Berlin, NH-VT**	40	**Bucyrus, OH.**	46
Ashland County, OH	54	Coos County, NH	34	Crawford County, OH	46
Ashtabula, OH	103	Essex County, VT	7		
Ashtabula County, OH. . . .	103				

U.S. Census Bureau, Statistical Abstract of the United States: 2007

Micropolitan statistical area Component county	Popu- lation, 2005 (1,000)	Micropolitan statistical area Component county	Popu- lation, 2005 (1,000)	Micropolitan statistical area Component county	Popu- lation, 2005 (1,000)
Burley, ID	40	**Clarksburg, WV.**	92	**Cullman, AL**	80
Cassia County, ID	21	Doddridge County, WV . . .	7	Cullman County, AL.	80
Minidoka County, ID	19	Harrison County, WV	68	**Culpeper, VA.**	43
Burlington, IA-IL	49	Taylor County, WV	16	Culpeper County, VA	43
Henderson County, IL	8	**Clarksdale, MS**	29	**Danville, KY**	53
Des Moines County, IA . . .	41	Coahoma County, MS	29	Boyle County, KY	28
Butte-Silver Bow, MT	33	**Clearlake, CA**	65	Lincoln County, KY	25
Silver Bow County, MT . . .	33	Lake County, CA.	65	**Daphne-Fairhope, AL**	163
Cadillac, MI.	47	**Cleveland, MS.**	39	Baldwin County, AL.	163
Missaukee County, MI	15	Bolivar County, MS	39	**Decatur, IN**	34
Wexford County, MI.	32	**Clewiston, FL**	40	Adams County, IN.	34
Calhoun, GA.	50	Hendry County, FL	40	**Defiance, OH**	39
Gordon County, GA.	50	**Clinton, IA**	50	Defiance County, OH.	39
Cambridge, MD.	31	Clinton County, IA.	50	**Del Rio, TX.**	48
Dorchester County, MD . . .	31	**Clovis, NM**	46	Val Verde County, TX	48
Cambridge, OH.	41	Curry County, NM	46	**Deming, NM**	26
Guernsey County, OH	41	**Coffeyville, KS**	35	Luna County, NM	26
Camden, AR	33	Montgomery County, KS . .	35	**De Ridder, LA.**	35
Calhoun County, AR	6	**Coldwater, MI**	46	Beauregard Parish, LA . . .	35
Ouachita County, AR	27	Branch County, MI	46	**Dickinson, ND.**	23
Campbellsville, KY	24	**Columbia, TN**	76	Billings County, ND	1
Taylor County, KY	24	Maury County, TN.	76	Stark County, ND	22
Canon City, CO.	48	**Columbus, MS**	60	**Dillon, SC.**	31
Fremont County, CO	48	Lowndes County, MS.	60	Dillon County, SC	31
Canton, IL.	38	**Columbus, NE**	31	**Dixon, IL.**	36
Fulton County, IL.	38	Platte County, NE	31	Lee County, IL	36
Cape Girardeau-Jackson,		**Concord, NH.**	147	**Dodge City, KS.**	34
MO-IL	92	Merrimack County, NH. . . .	147	Ford County, KS	34
Alexander County, IL.	9	**Connersville, IN**	25	**Douglas, GA.**	48
Bollinger County, MO.	12	Fayette County, IN	25	Atkinson County, GA	8
Cape Girardeau County,		**Cookeville, TN**	98	Coffee County, GA	40
MO	71	Jackson County, TN	11	**Dublin, GA**	56
Carbondale, IL	58	Overton County, TN.	21	Johnson County, GA	10
Jackson County, IL	58	Putnam County, TN.	67	Laurens County, GA	47
Carlsbad-Artesia, NM	51	**Coos Bay, OR.**	65	**DuBois, PA.**	83
Eddy County, NM	51	Coos County, OR	65	Clearfield County, PA.	83
Cedar City, UT	38	**Corbin, KY**	38	**Dumas, TX**	20
Iron County, UT	38	Whitley County, KY	38	Moore County, TX.	20
Cedartown, GA.	40	**Cordele, GA**	22	**Duncan, OK**	43
Polk County, GA.	40	Crisp County, GA	22	Stephens County, OK	43
Celina, OH	41	**Corinth, MS**	35	**Dunn, NC**	104
Mercer County, OH	41	Alcorn County, MS	35	Harnett County, NC	104
Central City, KY	32	**Cornelia, GA.**	40	**Durango, CO.**	47
Muhlenberg County, KY. . .	32	Habersham County, GA. . .	40	La Plata County, CO	47
Centralia, IL	40	**Corning, NY**	99	**Durant, OK**	38
Marion County, IL	40	Steuben County, NY	99	Bryan County, OK.	38
Centralia, WA	72	**Corsicana, TX.**	49	**Dyersburg, TN**	38
Lewis County, WA.	72	Navarro County, TX.	49	Dyer County, TN.	38
Chambersburg, PA	137	**Cortland, NY.**	49	**Eagle Pass, TX.**	51
Franklin County, PA.	137	Cortland County, NY	49	Maverick County, TX	51
Charleston-Mattoon, IL	62	**Coshocton, OH.**	37	**East Liverpool-Salem, OH .**	111
Coles County, IL	51	Coshocton County, OH . . .	37	Columbiana County, OH . .	111
Cumberland County, IL . . .	11	**Crawfordsville, IN**	38	**Easton, MD.**	36
Chester, SC	33	Montgomery County, IN . . .	38	Talbot County, MD.	36
Chester County, SC.	33	**Crescent City, CA**	29	**East Stroudsburg, PA**	163
Chillicothe, OH	75	Del Norte County, CA	29	Monroe County, PA	163
Ross County, OH	75	**Crossville, TN.**	51	**Edwards, CO**	55
City of The Dalles, OR.	24	Cumberland County, TN. . .	51	Eagle County, CO.	48
Wasco County, OR	24	**Crowley, LA**	60	Lake County, CO	8
Claremont, NH	43	Acadia Parish, LA	60		
Sullivan County, NH	43				

908   Appendix II

Micropolitan statistical area Component county	Popu- lation, 2005 (1,000)	Micropolitan statistical area Component county	Popu- lation, 2005 (1,000)	Micropolitan statistical area Component county	Popu- lation, 2005 (1,000)
Effingham, IL	35	**Fort Leonard Wood, MO** . . .	44	**Great Bend, KS.**	28
Effingham County, IL	35	Pulaski County, MO.	44	Barton County, KS	28
El Campo, TX	42	**Fort Madison-Keokuk,**		**Greeneville, TN.**	65
Wharton County, TX	42	**IA-MO.**	44	Greene County, TN.	65
El Dorado, AR.	44	Lee County, IA	37	**Greensburg, IN**	25
Union County, AR	44	Clark County, MO	7	Decatur County, IN	25
Elizabeth City, NC	59	**Fort Morgan, CO.**	28	**Greenville, MS**	59
Camden County, NC	9	Morgan County, CO.	28	Washington County, MS. . .	59
Pasquotank County, NC. . .	38	**Fort Payne, AL**	67	**Greenville, OH**	53
Perquimans County, NC. . .	12	DeKalb County, AL	67	Darke County, OH.	53
Elk City, OK	19	**Fort Polk South, LA**	49	**Greenwood, MS**	47
Beckham County, OK	19	Vernon Parish, LA.	49	Carroll County, MS	10
Elko, NV	47	**Fort Valley, GA**	25	Leflore County, MS	36
Elko County, NV	46	Peach County, GA	25	**Greenwood, SC.**	68
Eureka County, NV	1	**Frankfort, IN**	34	Greenwood County, SC . . .	68
Ellensburg, WA.	37	Clinton County, IN.	34	**Grenada, MS.**	23
Kittitas County, WA	37	**Frankfort, KY**	69	Grenada County, MS.	23
Emporia, KS	39	Anderson County, KY	20	**Guymon, OK.**	20
Chase County, KS.	3	Franklin County, KY.	48	Texas County, OK.	20
Lyon County, KS.	36	**Freeport, IL.**	48	**Hammond, LA.**	107
Enid, OK.	57	Stephenson County, IL . . .	48	Tangipahoa Parish, LA. . . .	107
Garfield County, OK	57	**Fremont, NE**	36	**Hannibal, MO**	38
Enterprise-Ozark, AL.	94	Dodge County, NE	36	Marion County, MO.	28
Coffee County, AL.	46	**Fremont, OH.**	62	Ralls County, MO	10
Dale County, AL	49	Sandusky County, OH	62	**Harriman, TN**	53
Escanaba, MI	38	**Gaffney, SC**	54	Roane County, TN	53
Delta County, MI	38	Cherokee County, SC	54	**Harrisburg, IL.**	26
Espanola, NM	41	**Gainesville, TX**	39	Saline County, IL.	26
Rio Arriba County, NM. . . .	41	Cooke County, TX.	39	**Harrison, AR.**	44
Eufaula, AL-GA	31	**Galesburg, IL**	71	Boone County, AR.	36
Barbour County, AL.	28	Knox County, IL	53	Newton County, AR.	8
Quitman County, GA	2	Warren County, IL	18	**Hastings, NE.**	40
Eureka-Arcata-Fortuna, CA .	128	**Gallup, NM**	72	Adams County, NE	33
Humboldt County, CA	128	McKinley County, NM	72	Clay County, NE	7
Evanston, WY.	20	**Garden City, KS**	39	**Havre, MT.**	16
Uinta County, WY	20	Finney County, KS	39	Hill County, MT.	16
Fairmont, MN	21	**Gardnerville Ranchos, NV.** .	47	**Hays, KS**	27
Martin County, MN	21	Douglas County, NV	47	Ellis County, KS	27
Fairmont, WV	57	**Georgetown, SC**	61	**Heber, UT**	19
Marion County, WV	57	Georgetown County, SC . .	61	Wasatch County, UT	19
Fallon, NV.	25	**Gettysburg, PA**	100	**Helena, MT**	70
Churchill County, NV	25	Adams County, PA	100	Jefferson County, MT	11
Faribault-Northfield, MN . . .	61	**Gillette, WY**	37	Lewis and Clark County,	
Rice County, MN.	61	Campbell County, WY	37	MT	58
Farmington, MO	62	**Glasgow, KY.**	50	**Henderson, NC**	44
St. Francois County, MO . .	62	Barren County, KY	40	Vance County, NC.	44
Fergus Falls, MN.	58	Metcalfe County, KY	10	**Hereford, TX.**	19
Otter Tail County, MN	58	**Gloversville, NY**	56	Deaf Smith County, TX . . .	19
Fernley, NV.	48	Fulton County, NY.	56	**Hilo, HI.**	167
Lyon County, NV.	48	**Granbury, TX**	56	Hawaii County, HI	167
Findlay, OH.	74	Hood County, TX	48	**Hilton Head Island-**	
Hancock County, OH.	74	Somervell County, TX	8	**Beaufort, SC.**	159
Fitzgerald, GA.	27	**Grand Island, NE**	70	Beaufort County, SC	138
Ben Hill County, GA	17	Hall County, NE	55	Jasper County, SC	21
Irwin County, GA.	10	Howard County, NE.	7	**Hobbs, NM**	57
Forest City, NC	64	Merrick County, NE	8	Lea County, NM	57
Rutherford County, NC . . .	64	**Grants, NM.**	28	**Homosassa Springs, FL** . . .	134
Forrest City, AR	28	Cibola County, NM	28	Citrus County, FL	134
St. Francis County, AR . . .	28	**Grants Pass, OR.**	81	**Hood River, OR.**	21
Fort Dodge, IA	39	Josephine County, OR. . . .	81	Hood River County, OR . . .	21
Webster County, IA	39				

Appendix II 909

Micropolitan statistical area Component county	Popu- lation, 2005 (1,000)	Micropolitan statistical area Component county	Popu- lation, 2005 (1,000)	Micropolitan statistical area Component county	Popu- lation, 2005 (1,000)
Hope, AR	33	**Keene, NH**	77	**Levelland, TX**	23
Hempstead County, AR . . .	23	Cheshire County, NH.	77	Hockley County, TX.	23
Nevada County, AR.	10				
		Kendallville, IN	47	**Lewisburg, PA**	43
Houghton, MI	38	Noble County, IN.	47	Union County, PA	43
Houghton County, MI.	36				
Keweenaw County, MI. . . .	2	**Kennett, MO**	33	**Lewisburg, TN**	28
		Dunklin County, MO	33	Marshall County, TN	28
Hudson, NY	64				
Columbia County, NY	64	**Kerrville, TX**	46	**Lewistown, PA**	46
		Kerr County, TX	46	Mifflin County, PA	46
Humboldt, TN	48				
Gibson County, TN	48	**Ketchikan, AK.**	13	**Lexington, NE.**	27
		Ketchikan Gateway		Dawson County, NE	25
Huntingdon, PA	46	Borough, AK.	13	Gosper County, NE	2
Huntingdon County, PA . . .	46				
		Key West-Marathon, FL. . . .	76	**Lexington Park, MD**	97
Huntington, IN	38	Monroe County, FL	76	St. Mary's County, MD. . . .	97
Huntington County, IN	38				
		Kill Devil Hills, NC	34	**Liberal, KS**	23
Huntsville, TX.	63	Dare County, NC.	34	Seward County, KS.	23
Walker County, TX	63				
		Kingsville, TX	31	**Lincoln, IL**	31
Huron, SD.	16	Kenedy County, TX	(Z)	Logan County, IL.	31
Beadle County, SD	16	Kleberg County, TX.	31		
				Lincolnton, NC	70
Hutchinson, KS.	64	**Kinston, NC**	58	Lincoln County, NC	70
Reno County, KS	64	Lenoir County, NC.	58		
				Lock Haven, PA	37
Hutchinson, MN	37	**Kirksville, MO**	29	Clinton County, PA	37
McLeod County, MN	37	Adair County, MO	25		
		Schuyler County, MO.	4	**Logansport, IN**	40
Indiana, PA.	89			Cass County, IN	40
Indiana County, PA	89	**Klamath Falls, OR.**	66		
		Klamath County, OR	66	**London, KY**	56
Indianola, MS	32			Laurel County, KY.	56
Sunflower County, MS. . . .	32	**Kodiak, AK.**	13		
		Kodiak Island Borough, AK.	13	**Los Alamos, NM**	19
Iron Mountain, MI-WI.	33			Los Alamos County, NM. . .	19
Dickinson County, MI.	28	**Laconia, NH**	62		
Florence County, WI	5	Belknap County, NH	62	**Lufkin, TX.**	82
				Angelina County, TX	82
Jackson, WY-ID	26	**La Follette, TN**	41		
Teton County, ID	7	Campbell County, TN	41	**Lumberton, NC**	128
Teton County, WY	19			Robeson County, NC.	128
		La Grande, OR	25		
		Union County, OR.	25	**Macomb, IL.**	32
Jacksonville, IL.	41			McDonough County, IL . . .	32
Morgan County, IL.	36	**LaGrange, GA.**	62		
Scott County, IL	5	Troup County, GA	62	**Madison, IN**	32
				Jefferson County, IN	32
Jacksonville, TX	48	**Lake City, FL**	64		
Cherokee County, TX	48	Columbia County, FL.	64	**Madisonville, KY.**	47
				Hopkins County, KY	47
Jamestown, ND.	21	**Lake Havasu City-Kingman,**			
Stutsman County, ND	21	**AZ**	187	**Magnolia, AR**	25
		Mohave County, AZ.	187	Columbia County, AR	25
Jamestown-Dunkirk-					
Fredonia, NY.	136	**Lamesa, TX**	14	**Malone, NY.**	51
Chautauqua County, NY . .	136	Dawson County, TX.	14	Franklin County, NY	51
Jasper, IN.	54	**Lancaster, SC**	63	**Manhattan, KS**	107
Dubois County, IN.	41	Lancaster County, SC	63	Geary County, KS.	25
Pike County, IN.	13			Pottawatomie County, KS. .	19
		Laramie, WY.	31	Riley County, KS.	63
Jennings, LA	31	Albany County, WY	31		
Jefferson Davis Parish, LA.	31			**Manitowoc, WI**	82
		Las Vegas, NM	30	Manitowoc County, WI. . . .	82
Jesup, GA	28	San Miguel County, NM. . .	30		
Wayne County, GA	28			**Mankato-North Mankato,**	
		Laurel, MS	84	**MN**	89
Juneau, AK.	31	Jasper County, MS	18	Blue Earth County, MN . . .	58
Juneau City and Borough,		Jones County, MS.	66	Nicollet County, MN.	31
AK.	31				
		Laurinburg, NC	37	**Marinette, WI-MI.**	68
Kahului-Wailuku, HI	140	Scotland County, NC.	37	Menominee County, MI . . .	25
Maui County, HI	140			Marinette County, WI.	43
		Lawrenceburg, TN	41		
Kalispell, MT.	83	Lawrence County, TN	41	**Marion, IN.**	71
Flathead County, MT.	83			Grant County, IN.	71
		Lebanon, MO	34		
Kapaa, HI	63	Laclede County, MO	34	**Marion, OH.**	66
Kauai County, HI.	63			Marion County, OH	66
		Lebanon, NH-VT	172		
Kearney, NE.	50	Grafton County, NH.	85	**Marion-Herrin, IL.**	64
Buffalo County, NE	44	Orange County, VT.	29	Williamson County, IL	64
Kearney County, NE	7	Windsor County, VT	58		

910 Appendix II

Micropolitan statistical area Component county	Popu- lation, 2005 (1,000)	Micropolitan statistical area Component county	Popu- lation, 2005 (1,000)	Micropolitan statistical area Component county	Popu- lation, 2005 (1,000)
Marquette, MI	65	**Mineral Wells, TX**	27	**Newberry, SC**	37
Marquette County, MI	65	Palo Pinto County, TX	27	Newberry County, SC	37
Marshall, MN.	24	**Minot, ND**	64	**New Castle, IN**	47
Lyon County, MN	24	McHenry County, ND.	6	Henry County, IN	47
Marshall, MO	23	Renville County, ND	2	**New Castle, PA.**	93
Saline County, MO	23	Ward County, ND	56	Lawrence County, PA	93
Marshall, TX.	63	**Mitchell, SD**	23	**New Iberia, LA**	74
Harrison County, TX	63	Davison County, SD	19	Iberia Parish, LA	74
Marshalltown, IA.	39	Hanson County, SD.	4	**New Philadelphia-Dover,**	
Marshall County, IA	39	**Moberly, MO**	25	**OH**	92
Marshfield-Wisconsin		Randolph County, MO	25	Tuscarawas County, OH . .	92
Rapids, WI	75	**Monroe, WI.**	35	**Newport, TN**	35
Wood County, WI	75	Green County, WI	35	Cocke County, TN.	35
Martin, TN.	34	**Montrose, CO.**	37	**Newton, IA**	38
Weakley County, TN	34	Montrose County, CO	37	Jasper County, IA	38
Martinsville, VA.	71	**Morehead City, NC**	63	**New Ulm, MN**	27
Henry County, VA	57	Carteret County, NC	63	Brown County, MN	27
Martinsville city, VA	15	**Morgan City, LA**	51	**Nogales, AZ**	42
Maryville, MO	22	St. Mary Parish, LA.	51	Santa Cruz County, AZ . . .	42
Nodaway County, MO	22	**Moscow, ID.**	35	**Norfolk, NE.**	50
Mason City, IA	52	Latah County, ID.	35	Madison County, NE	35
Cerro Gordo County, IA . .	45	**Moses Lake, WA**	81	Pierce County, NE.	8
Worth County, IA.	8	Grant County, WA	81	Stanton County, NE.	7
Mayfield, KY	38	**Moultrie, GA**	44	**North Platte, NE**	37
Graves County, KY	38	Colquitt County, GA.	44	Lincoln County, NE	36
Maysville, KY	31	**Mountain Home, AR**	40	Logan County, NE.	1
Lewis County, KY	14	Baxter County, AR.	40	McPherson County, NE . . .	1
Mason County, KY	17	**Mountain Home, ID.**	29	**North Vernon, IN.**	28
McAlester, OK.	45	Elmore County, ID.	29	Jennings County, IN	28
Pittsburg County, OK.	45	**Mount Airy, NC**	73	**North Wilkesboro, NC**	67
McComb, MS	53	Surry County, NC	73	Wilkes County, NC	67
Amite County, MS.	13	**Mount Pleasant, MI**	66	**Norwalk, OH.**	60
Pike County, MS.	39	Isabella County, MI	66	Huron County, OH.	60
McMinnville, TN	40	**Mount Pleasant, TX.**	29	**Oak Harbor, WA**	79
Warren County, TN	40	Titus County, TX	29	Island County, WA.	79
McPherson, KS.	30	**Mount Sterling, KY**	43	**Oak Hill, WV**	47
McPherson County, KS . . .	30	Bath County, KY	12	Fayette County, WV	47
Meadville, PA	89	Menifee County, KY.	7	**Ocean Pines, MD**	49
Crawford County, PA.	89	Montgomery County, KY . .	24	Worcester County, MD. . . .	49
Menomonie, WI.	42	**Mount Vernon, IL**	49	**Ogdensburg-Massena, NY. .**	111
Dunn County, WI.	42	Hamilton County, IL.	8	St. Lawrence County, NY. .	111
Meridian, MS.	105	Jefferson County, IL	40	**Oil City, PA.**	56
Clarke County, MS	18	**Mount Vernon, OH**	58	Venango County, PA	56
Kemper County, MS	10	Knox County, OH	58	**Okeechobee, FL**	40
Lauderdale County, MS . . .	77	**Murray, KY**	35	Okeechobee County, FL . .	40
Merrill, WI.	30	Calloway County, KY.	35	**Olean, NY.**	83
Lincoln County, WI	30	**Muscatine, IA**	55	Cattaraugus County, NY . .	83
Mexico, MO	26	Louisa County, IA	12	**Oneonta, NY.**	63
Audrain County, MO	26	Muscatine County, IA.	43	Otsego County, NY	63
Miami, OK.	33	**Muskogee, OK**	71	**Ontario, OR-ID**	54
Ottawa County, OK	33	Muskogee County, OK. . . .	71	Payette County, ID	22
Middlesborough, KY	30	**Nacogdoches, TX**	60	Malheur County, OR	31
Bell County, KY	30	Nacogdoches County, TX. .	60	**Opelousas-Eunice, LA.**	90
Midland, MI.	84	**Natchez, MS-LA**	51	St. Landry Parish, LA	90
Midland County, MI	84	Concordia Parish, LA.	19	**Orangeburg, SC**	92
Milledgeville, GA.	55	Adams County, MS	32	Orangeburg County, SC. . .	92
Baldwin County, GA	45	**Natchitoches, LA**	39	**Oskaloosa, IA**	22
Hancock County, GA	10	Natchitoches Parish, LA. . .	39	Mahaska County, IA	22
Minden, LA.	41	**New Bern, NC**	114	**Ottawa-Streator, IL**	154
Webster Parish, LA	41	Craven County, NC	91	Bureau County, IL.	35
		Jones County, NC.	10	La Salle County, IL	113
		Pamlico County, NC	13		

Appendix II 911

Micropolitan statistical area / Component county	Popu-lation, 2005 (1,000)	Micropolitan statistical area / Component county	Popu-lation, 2005 (1,000)	Micropolitan statistical area / Component county	Popu-lation, 2005 (1,000)
Ottawa-Streator, IL—Con.		**Plattsburgh, NY**	82	**Rolla, MO**	42
Putnam County, IL	6	Clinton County, NY	82	Phelps County, MO.......	42
Ottumwa, IA	36	**Plymouth, IN**.	47	**Roseburg, OR**.	104
Wapello County, IA	36	Marshall County, IN......	47	Douglas County, OR	104
Owatonna, MN	36	**Point Pleasant, WV-OH**	57	**Roswell, NM**	62
Steele County, MN	36	Gallia County, OH	31	Chaves County, NM	62
Owosso, MI	73	Mason County, WV	26	**Ruidoso, NM**.	21
Shiawassee County, MI ...	73	**Ponca City, OK**	46	Lincoln County, NM......	21
Oxford, MS..............	41	Kay County, OK	46	**Russellville, AR**	78
Lafayette County, MS	41	**Pontiac, IL**	39	Pope County, AR........	57
Paducah, KY-IL...........	98	Livingston County, IL.....	39	Yell County, AR.	21
Massac County, IL	15	**Poplar Bluff, MO**	41	**Ruston, LA**.	57
Ballard County, KY	8	Butler County, MO.	41	Jackson Parish, LA	15
Livingston County, KY	10	**Portales, NM**.	18	Lincoln Parish, LA.	42
McCracken County, KY ...	65	Roosevelt County, NM....	18	**Rutland, VT**	64
Pahrump, NV	40	**Port Angeles, WA**	70	Rutland County, VT......	64
Nye County, NV	40	Clallam County, WA	70	**Safford, AZ**..............	41
Palatka, FL..............	74	**Portsmouth, OH**	77	Graham County, AZ......	33
Putnam County, FL......	74	Scioto County, OH	77	Greenlee County, AZ.....	8
Palestine, TX	56	**Pottsville, PA**	147	**St. Marys, GA**...........	46
Anderson County, TX	56	Schuylkill County, PA.....	147	Camden County, GA	46
Palm Coast, FL.	76	**Price, UT**	19	**St. Marys, PA**	34
Flagler County, FL.	76	Carbon County, UT	19	Elk County, PA	34
Pampa, TX	22	**Prineville, OR**	22	**Salina, KS**.	60
Gray County, TX........	21	Crook County, OR.......	22	Ottawa County, KS	6
Roberts County, TX......	1	**Pullman, WA**.	40	Saline County, KS.......	54
Paragould, AR	39	Whitman County, WA.....	40	**Salisbury, NC**	135
Greene County, AR......	39	**Quincy, IL-MO**.	77	Rowan County, NC	135
Paris, TN	32	Adams County, IL	67	**Sanford, NC**	56
Henry County, TN	32	Lewis County, MO.......	10	Lee County, NC	56
Paris, TX	50	**Raymondville, TX**	20	**Sault Ste. Marie, MI**.......	39
Lamar County, TX.......	50	Willacy County, TX	20	Chippewa County, MI	39
Parsons, KS	22	**Red Bluff, CA**	61	**Sayre, PA**	63
Labette County, KS......	22	Tehama County, CA	61	Bradford County, PA	63
Payson, AZ..............	52	**Red Wing, MN**.	46	**Scottsbluff, NE**	37
Gila County, AZ	52	Goodhue County, MN	46	Banner County, NE	1
Pecos, TX.	12	**Rexburg, ID**	43	Scotts Bluff County, NE ...	37
Reeves County, TX	12	Fremont County, ID......	12	**Scottsboro, AL**	54
Pella, IA	33	Madison County, ID......	31	Jackson County, AL.......	54
Marion County, IA	33	**Richmond, IN**	69	**Scottsburg, IN**	24
Pendleton-Hermiston, OR ..	86	Wayne County, IN	69	Scott County, IN	24
Morrow County, OR.	12	**Richmond-Berea, KY**.	94	**Seaford, DE**	177
Umatilla County, OR	74	Madison County, KY	78	Sussex County, DE	177
Peru, IN	36	Rockcastle County, KY ...	17	**Searcy, AR**	71
Miami County, IN	36	**Rio Grande City-Roma, TX** .	61	White County, AR	71
Phoenix Lake-Cedar Ridge, CA	59	Starr County, TX........	61	**Sebring, FL**.	95
Tuolumne County, CA	59	**Riverton, WY**	36	Highlands County, FL	95
Picayune, MS	53	Fremont County, WY.....	36	**Sedalia, MO**	40
Pearl River County, MS ...	53	**Roanoke Rapids, NC**......	78	Pettis County, MO.	40
Pierre, SD..............	20	Halifax County, NC	56	**Selinsgrove, PA**	38
Hughes County, SD......	17	Northampton County, NC..	21	Snyder County, PA	38
Stanley County, SD......	3	**Rochelle, IL**	54	**Selma, AL**...............	44
Pierre Part, LA	23	Ogle County, IL.	54	Dallas County, AL	44
Assumption Parish, LA ...	23	**Rockingham, NC**.	47	**Seneca, SC**	70
Pittsburg, KS	38	Richmond County, NC	47	Oconee County, SC	70
Crawford County, KS.....	38	**Rockland, ME**	41	**Seneca Falls, NY**.	35
Plainview, TX	36	Knox County, ME	41	Seneca County, NY......	35
Hale County, TX........	36	**Rock Springs, WY**........	38	**Sevierville, TN**	79
Platteville, WI	50	Sweetwater County, WY ..	38	Sevier County, TN.	79
Grant County, WI	50				

912   Appendix II

Micropolitan statistical area Component county	Popu- lation, 2005 (1,000)	Micropolitan statistical area Component county	Popu- lation, 2005 (1,000)	Micropolitan statistical area Component county	Popu- lation, 2005 (1,000)
Seymour, IN	42	**Sturgis, MI**	63	**Ukiah, CA**	88
Jackson County, IN	42	St. Joseph County, MI	63	Mendocino County, CA . . .	88
Shawnee, OK	68	**Sulphur Springs, TX**	33	**Union, SC**	29
Pottawatomie County, OK .	68	Hopkins County, TX.	33	Union County, SC	29
Shelby, NC	98	**Summerville, GA**	27	**Union City, TN-KY**	39
Cleveland County, NC	98	Chattooga County, GA. . . .	27	Fulton County, KY.	7
Shelbyville, TN	42	**Sunbury, PA**	93	Obion County, TN	32
Bedford County, TN.	42	Northumberland County,		**Urbana, OH**.	40
Shelton, WA	54	PA.	93	Champaign County, OH. . .	40
Mason County, WA	54	**Susanville, CA**	35	**Uvalde, TX**	27
Sheridan, WY	27	Lassen County, CA	35	Uvalde County, TX	27
Sheridan County, WY	27	**Sweetwater, TX**.	15	**Valley, AL**	35
Sidney, OH	49	Nolan County, TX	15	Chambers County, AL	35
Shelby County, OH	49	**Tahlequah, OK**	45	**Van Wert, OH**	29
Sierra Vista-Douglas, AZ . . .	126	Cherokee County, OK	45	Van Wert County, OH	29
Cochise County, AZ.	126	**Talladega-Sylacauga, AL** . . .	80	**Vermillion, SD**	13
Sikeston, MO	41	Talladega County, AL.	80	Clay County, SD	13
Scott County, MO	41	**Tallulah, LA**	12	**Vernal, UT**.	27
Silver City, NM	30	Madison Parish, LA.	12	Uintah County, UT.	27
Grant County, NM	30	**Taos, NM**	32	**Vernon, TX**	14
Silverthorne, CO.	25	Taos County, NM	32	Wilbarger County, TX	14
Summit County, CO.	25	**Taylorville, IL**	35	**Vicksburg, MS**	49
Snyder, TX	16	Christian County, IL.	35	Warren County, MS.	49
Scurry County, TX.	16	**The Villages, FL**	64	**Vidalia, GA**	36
Somerset, KY	59	Sumter County, FL	64	Montgomery County, GA . .	9
Pulaski County, KY	59	**Thomaston, GA.**	28	Toombs County, GA	27
Somerset, PA	79	Upson County, GA	28	**Vincennes, IN**	38
Somerset County, PA	79	**Thomasville, GA.**	45	Knox County, IN	38
Southern Pines-Pinehurst,		Thomas County, GA	45	**Wabash, IN**.	34
NC	82	**Thomasville-Lexington, NC** .	155	Wabash County, IN	34
Moore County, NC	82	Davidson County, NC	155	**Wahpeton, ND-MN.**	24
Spearfish, SD	22	**Tiffin, OH**	57	Wilkin County, MN.	7
Lawrence County, SD	22	Seneca County, OH	57	Richland County, ND.	17
Spencer, IA	17	**Tifton, GA.**	41	**Walla Walla, WA**	58
Clay County, IA.	17	Tift County, GA.	41	Walla Walla County, WA . .	58
Spirit Lake, IA.	17	**Toccoa, GA.**	25	**Walterboro, SC**	40
Dickinson County, IA	17	Stephens County, GA	25	Colleton County, SC	40
Starkville, MS	41	**Torrington, CT**	190	**Wapakoneta, OH**.	47
Oktibbeha County, MS. . . .	41	Litchfield County, CT	190	Auglaize County, OH.	47
Statesboro, GA.	61	**Traverse City, MI.**	141	**Warren, PA**	42
Bulloch County, GA.	61	Benzie County, MI.	18	Warren County, PA	42
Statesville-Mooresville, NC .	141	Grand Traverse County,		**Warrensburg, MO**	51
Iredell County, NC.	141	MI	84	Johnson County, MO.	51
Staunton-Waynesboro, VA. . .	114	Kalkaska County, MI	17	**Warsaw, IN**	76
Augusta County, VA	70	Leelanau County, MI	22	Kosciusko County, IN	76
Staunton city, VA	23	**Troy, AL**	30	**Washington, IN**	30
Waynesboro city, VA	21	Pike County, AL	30	Daviess County, IN	30
Stephenville, TX	34	**Truckee-Grass Valley, CA** . .	98	**Washington, NC**	46
Erath County, TX	34	Nevada County, CA.	98	Beaufort County, NC	46
Sterling, CO	21	**Tullahoma, TN**	98	**Washington, OH**	28
Logan County, CO	21	Coffee County, TN.	51	Fayette County, OH.	28
Sterling, IL	60	Franklin County, TN.	41	**Watertown, SD**	32
Whiteside County, IL	60	Moore County, TN.	6	Codington County, SD	26
Stevens Point, WI	68	**Tupelo, MS**	130	Hamlin County, SD	6
Portage County, WI.	68	Itawamba County, MS	23	**Watertown-Fort Atkinson,**	
Stillwater, OK	69	Lee County, MS	79	**WI.**	79
Payne County, OK	69	Pontotoc County, MS.	28	Jefferson County, WI	79
Storm Lake, IA	20	**Tuskegee, AL**	23	**Watertown-Fort Drum, NY** . .	116
Buena Vista County, IA . . .	20	Macon County, AL.	23	Jefferson County, NY.	116
		Twin Falls, ID	89		
		Jerome County, ID	20		
		Twin Falls County, ID.	69		

Appendix II　913

Micropolitan statistical area Component county	Popu- lation, **2005** (1,000)	Micropolitan statistical area Component county	Popu- lation, **2005** (1,000)	Micropolitan statistical area Component county	Popu- lation, **2005** (1,000)
Wauchula, FL	**28**	**Willimantic, CT**	**116**	**Winona, MN**	**49**
Hardee County, FL	28	Windham County, CT	116	Winona County, MN	49
Waycross, GA.	**52**	**Williston, ND.**	**19**	**Woodward, OK**	**19**
Pierce County, GA	17	Williams County, ND	19	Woodward County, OK . . .	19
Ware County, GA	34				
		Willmar, MN	**41**	**Wooster, OH**.	**114**
West Helena, AR.	**24**	Kandiyohi County, MN. . . .	41	Wayne County, OH	114
Phillips County, AR	24				
		Wilmington, OH	**43**	**Worthington, MN.**	**21**
West Plains, MO	**38**	Clinton County, OH	43	Nobles County, MN.	21
Howell County, MO	38				
		Wilson, NC	**76**	**Yankton, SD**	**22**
West Point, MS.	**21**	Wilson County, NC	76	Yankton County, SD	22
Clay County, MS.	21				
		Winfield, KS	**35**	**Yazoo City, MS**	**28**
Whitewater, WI	**100**	Cowley County, KS	35	Yazoo County, MS	28
Walworth County, WI.	100				
				Zanesville, OH	**86**
				Muskingum County, OH. . .	86

Z Less than 500.

Source: U.S. Census Bureau, "July 1, 2005 Population Estimates for Metropolitan, Micropolitan, and Combined Statistical Areas (Areas Defined by the Office of Management and Budget as of December 2005)"; published 21 August 2006; <http://www.census.gov/population/www/estimates/Estimates%20pagesfinal.html>.

Appendix III
Limitations of the Data

Introduction The data presented in this *Statistical Abstract* came from many sources. The sources include not only federal statistical bureaus and other organizations that collect and issue statistics as their principal activity, but also governmental administrative and regulatory agencies, private research bodies, trade associations, insurance companies, health associations, and private organizations such as the National Education Association and philanthropic foundations. Consequently, the data vary considerably as to reference periods, definitions of terms and, for ongoing series, the number and frequency of time periods for which data are available.

The statistics presented were obtained and tabulated by various means. Some statistics are based on complete enumerations or censuses while others are based on samples. Some information is extracted from records kept for administrative or regulatory purposes (school enrollment, hospital records, securities registration, financial accounts, social security records, income tax returns, etc.), while other information is obtained explicitly for statistical purposes through interviews or by mail. The estimation procedures used vary from highly sophisticated scientific techniques, to crude "informed guesses."

Each set of data relates to a group of individuals or units of interest referred to as the *target universe* or *target population*, or simply as the *universe* or *population*. Prior to data collection the target universe should be clearly defined. For example, if data are to be collected for the universe of households in the United States, it is necessary to define a "household." The target universe may not be completely tractable. Cost and other considerations may restrict data collection to a *survey universe* based on some available list, such list may be inaccurate or out of date. This list is called a *survey frame* or *sampling frame*.

The data in many tables are based on data obtained for all population units, *a census,* or on data obtained for only a portion, or *sample,* of the population units. When the data presented are based on a sample, the sample is usually a scientifically selected *probability sample*. This is a sample selected from a list or sampling frame in such a way that every possible sample has a known chance of selection and usually each unit selected can be assigned a number, greater than zero and less than or equal to one, representing its likelihood or probability of selection.

For large-scale sample surveys, the probability sample of units is often selected as a multistage sample. The first stage of a multistage sample is the selection of a probability sample of large groups of population members, referred to as primary sampling units (PSUs). For example, in a national multistage household sample, PSUs are often counties or groups of counties. The second stage of a multistage sample is the selection, within each PSU selected at the first stage, of smaller groups of population units, referred to as secondary sampling units. In subsequent stages of selection, smaller and smaller nested groups are chosen until the ultimate sample of population units is obtained. To qualify a multistage sample as a probability sample, all stages of sampling must be carried out using probability sampling methods.

Prior to selection at each stage of a multistage (or a single stage) sample, a list of the sampling units or sampling frame for that stage must be obtained. For example, for the first stage of selection of a national household sample, a list of the counties and county groups that form the PSUs must be obtained. For the final stage of selection, lists of households, and sometimes persons within the households, have to be compiled in the field. For surveys of economic entities and for the economic censuses the Bureau generally uses a frame constructed from the Bureau's Business Register. The Business Register contains all establishments with payroll in the United States including small single establishment firms as well as large multi-establishment firms.

Wherever the quantities in a table refer to an entire universe, but are constructed from data collected in a sample survey, the table quantities are referred to as *sample estimates*. In constructing a sample estimate, an attempt is made to come as close as is feasible to the corresponding universe quantity that would be obtained from a complete census of the universe. Estimates based on a sample will, however, generally differ from the hypothetical census figures. Two classifications of errors are associated with estimates based on sample surveys: (1) *sampling error*—the error arising from the use of a sample, rather than a census, to estimate population quantities and (2) *nonsampling error*—those errors arising from nonsampling sources. As discussed below, the magnitude of the sampling error for an estimate can usually be estimated from the sample data. However, the magnitude of the nonsampling error for an estimate can rarely be estimated. Consequently, actual error in an estimate exceeds the error that can be estimated.

The particular sample used in a survey is only one of a large number of possible samples of the same size which could have been selected using the same sampling procedure. Estimates derived from the different samples would, in general, differ from each other. The *standard error* (SE) is a measure of the variation among the estimates derived from all possible samples. The standard error is the most commonly used measure of the sampling error of an estimate. Valid estimates of the standard errors of survey estimates can usually be calculated from the data collected in a probability sample. For convenience, the standard error is sometimes expressed as a percent of the estimate and is called the relative standard error or *coefficient of variation* (CV). For example, an estimate of 200 units with an estimated standard error of 10 units has an estimated CV of 5 percent.

A sample estimate and an estimate of its standard error or CV can be used to construct interval estimates that have a prescribed confidence that the interval includes the average of the estimates derived from all possible samples with a known probability. To illustrate, if all possible samples were selected under essentially the same general conditions, and using the same sample design, and if an estimate and its estimated standard error were calculated from each sample, then: 1) approximately 68 percent of the intervals from one standard error below the estimate to one standard error above the estimate would include the average estimate derived from all possible samples; 2) approximately 90 percent of the intervals from 1.6 standard errors below the estimate to 1.6 standard errors above the estimate would include the average estimate derived from all possible samples; and 3) approximately 95 percent of the intervals from two standard errors below the estimate to two standard errors above the estimate would include the average estimate derived from all possible samples.

Thus, for a particular sample, one can say with the appropriate level of confidence (e.g., 90 percent or 95 percent) that the average of all possible samples is included in the constructed interval. Example of a confidence interval: An estimate is 200 units with a standard error of 10 units. An approximately 90 percent confidence interval (plus or minus 1.6 standard errors) is from 184 to 216.

All surveys and censuses are subject to nonsampling errors. Nonsampling errors are of two kinds—*random* and *nonrandom*. Random nonsampling errors arise because of the varying interpretation of questions (by respondents or interviewers) and varying actions of coders, keyers, and other processors. Some randomness is also introduced when respondents must estimate. Nonrandom nonsampling errors result from total nonresponse (no usable data obtained for a sampled unit), partial or item nonresponse (only a portion of a response may be usable), inability or unwillingness on the part of respondents to provide correct information, difficulty interpreting questions, mistakes

U.S. Census Bureau, *Statistical Abstract of the United States: 2007*

in recording or keying data, errors of collection or processing, and coverage problems (overcoverage and undercoverage of the target universe). Random nonresponse errors usually, but not always, result in an understatement of sampling errors and thus an overstatement of the precision of survey estimates. Estimating the magnitude of nonsampling errors would require special experiments or access to independent data and, consequently, the magnitudes are seldom available.

Nearly all types of nonsampling errors that affect surveys also occur in complete censuses. Since surveys can be conducted on a smaller scale than censuses, nonsampling errors can presumably be controlled more tightly. Relatively more funds and effort can perhaps be expended toward eliciting responses, detecting and correcting response error, and reducing processing errors. As a result, survey results can sometimes be more accurate than census results.

To compensate for suspected nonrandom errors, adjustments of the sample estimates are often made. For example, adjustments are frequently made for nonresponse, both total and partial. Adjustments made for either type of nonresponse are often referred to as *imputations*. Imputation for total nonresponse is usually made by substituting for the questionnaire responses of the nonrespondents the "average" questionnaire responses of the respondents. These imputations usually are made separately within various groups of sample members, formed by attempting to place respondents and nonrespondents together that have "similar" design or ancillary characteristics. Imputation for item nonresponse is usually made by substituting for a missing item the response to that item of a respondent having characteristics that are "similar" to those of the nonrespondent.

For an estimate calculated from a sample survey, the *total error* in the estimate is composed of the sampling error, which can usually be estimated from the sample, and the nonsampling error, which usually cannot be estimated from the

sample. The total error present in a population quantity obtained from a complete census is composed of only nonsampling errors. Ideally, estimates of the total error associated with data given in the *Statistical Abstract* tables should be given. However, due to the unavailability of estimates of nonsampling errors, only estimates of the levels of sampling errors, in terms of estimated standard errors or coefficients of variation, are available. To obtain estimates of the estimated standard errors from the sample of interest, obtain a copy of the referenced report which appears at the end of each table.

Source of Additional Material: The Federal Committee on Statistical Methodology (FCSM) is an interagency committee dedicated to improving the quality of federal statistics <http://www.fcsm.gov>.

Principal data bases—Beginning below are brief descriptions of 35 of the sample surveys and censuses that provide a substantial portion of the data contained in this *Abstract*.

U.S. DEPARTMENT OF AGRICULTURE, National Agriculture Statistics Service

Basic Area Frame Sample

Universe, Frequency, and Types of Data: June agricultural survey collects data on planted acreage and livestock inventories. The survey also serves to measure list incompleteness and is subsampled for multiple frame surveys.

Type of Data Collection Operation: Stratified probability sample of about 11,000 land area units of about 1 sq. mile (range from 0.1 sq. mile in cities to several sq. miles in open grazing areas). Sample includes 42,000 parcels of agricultural land. About 20 percent of the sample replaced annually.

Data Collection and Imputation Procedures: Data collection is by personal enumeration. Imputation is based on enumerator observation or data reported by respondents having similar agricultural characteristics.

Estimates of Sampling Error: Estimated CVs range from 1 percent to 2 percent for regional estimates to 3 percent to 6 percent for state estimates of major crop acres and livestock inventories.

Other (nonsampling) Errors: Minimized through rigid quality controls on the collection process and careful review of all reported data.

Sources of Additional Material: U.S. Department of Agriculture, National Agricultural Statistics Service, USDA's National Agricultural Statistics Service: The Fact Finders of Agriculture, January 2004.

Census of Agriculture

Universe, Frequency, and Types of Data: Complete count of U.S. farms and ranches conducted once every 5 years with data at the national, state, and county level. Data published on farm numbers and related items/characteristics.

Type of Data Collection Operation: Complete census for number of farms; land in farms; agriculture products sold; total cropland; irrigated land; farm operator characteristics; livestock and poultry inventory and sales; and selected crops harvested. Market value of land and buildings, total farm production expenses, machinery and equipment, fertilizer and chemicals, and farm labor are estimated from a sample of farms.

Data Collection and Imputation Procedures: Data collection is by mailing questionnaires to all farmers and ranchers. Nonrespondents are contacted by telephone and correspondence follow-ups. Imputations were made for all non-response item/characteristics. Coverage adjustments were made to account for missed farms and ranches.

Estimates of Sampling Error: Variability in the estimates is due to the sample selection and estimation for items collected by sample and census nonresponse and coverage estimation procedures. The CVs for national and state estimates are generally very small. Approximately 81 percent response rate.

Other (nonsampling) Errors: Nonsampling errors are due to incompleteness of the census mailing list, duplications on the list, respondent reporting errors, errors in editing reported data, and in imputation for missing data. Evaluation studies are conducted to measure certain non-sampling errors such as list coverage and classification error. Results from the

evaluation program for the 2002 census indicate the net under coverage amounted to about 18 percent of the nation's total farms.

Sources of Additional Material: U.S. Department of Agriculture (NASS), *2002 Census of Agriculture,* Volume 1, *Subject Series C* Part 1, *Agriculture Atlas of the U.S.;* Part 2, *Coverage Evaluation;* Part 3, *Rankings of States and Counties;* Part 4, *History;* Part 5, *ZIP Code Tabulation of Selected Items;* and Volume 3 *Special Studies,* Part 1, *Farm and Ranch Irrigation Survey;* Part 2, *Census of Horticultural Specialties;* Part 3, *Census of Aquaculture.*

Multiple Frame Surveys

Universe, Frequency, and Types of Data: Surveys of U.S. farm operators to obtain data on major livestock inventories, selected crop acreage and production, grain stocks, and farm labor characteristics; farm economic data and chemical use data.

Type of Data Collection Operation: Primary frame is obtained from general or special purpose lists, supplemented by a probability sample of land areas used to estimate for list incompleteness.

Data Collection and Imputation Procedures: Mail, telephone, or personal interviews used for initial data collection. Mail nonrespondent follow-up by phone and personal interviews. Imputation based on average of respondents.

Estimates of Sampling Error: Estimated CV for number of hired farm workers is about 3 percent. Estimated CVs range from 1 percent to 2 percent for regional estimates to 3 percent to 6 percent for state estimates of livestock inventories and crop acreage.

Other (nonsampling) Errors: In addition to above, replicated sampling procedures used to monitor effects of changes in survey procedures.

Sources of Additional Material: U.S. Department of Agriculture, National Agricultural Statistics Service), USDA's National Agricultural Statistics Service: The Fact Finders of Agriculture, January 2004.

Objective Yield Surveys

Universe, Frequency, and Types of Data: Surveys for data on corn, cotton, potatoes, soybeans, and wheat, to forecast and estimate yields.

Type of Data Collection Operation: Random location of plots in probability sample. Corn, cotton, soybeans, spring wheat, and durum wheat selected in June from Basic Area Frame Sample (see above). Winter wheat and potatoes selected from March and June multiple frame surveys, respectively.

Data Collection and Imputation Procedures: Enumerators count and measure plant characteristics in sample fields. Production measured from plots at harvest. Harvest loss measured from post harvest gleanings.

Estimates of Sampling Error: CVs for national estimates of production are about 2–3 percent.

Other (nonsampling) Errors: In addition to above, replicated sampling procedures used to monitor effects of changes in survey procedures.

Sources of Additional Material: U.S. Department of Agriculture, National Agricultural Statistics Service), USDA's National Agricultural Statistics Service: The Fact Finders of Agriculture, January 2004.

U.S. BUREAU OF JUSTICE STATISTICS (BJS)

National Crime Victimization Survey

Universe, Frequency, and Types of Data: Monthly survey of individuals and households in the United States to obtain data on criminal victimization of those units for compilation of annual estimates.

Type of Data Collection Operation: National probability sample survey of about 42,000 interviewed households in 203 PSUs selected from a list of addresses from the 1990 census, supplemented by new construction permits and an area sample where permits are not required.

Data Collection and Imputation Procedures: Interviews are conducted every 6 months for 3 years for each household

in the sample; 7,000 households are interviewed monthly. Personal interviews are used in the first interview; the intervening interviews are conducted by telephone whenever possible.

Estimates of Sampling Error: CVs for 2005 estimates are: 4.1 percent for personal crimes (includes all crimes of violence plus purse snatching crimes), 4.2 percent for crimes of violence; 16.2 percent for estimate of rape/sexual assault counts; 9.7 percent for robbery counts; 4.4 percent for assault counts; 15.1 percent for purse snatching/pocket picking; 2.2 percent for property crimes; 4.2 percent for burglary counts; 2.5 percent for theft (of property); and 6.6 percent for motor vehicle theft counts.

Other (nonsampling) Errors: Respondent recall errors which may include reporting incidents for other than the reference period; interviewer coding and processing errors; and possible mistaken reporting or classifying of events. Adjustment is made for a household noninterview rate of about 9 percent and for a within-household noninterview rate of 16 percent.

Sources of Additional Material: U.S. Bureau of Justice Statistics, *Criminal Victimization in the United States,* annual.

U.S. Bureau of Labor Statistics

Consumer Expenditure Survey (CE)

Universe, Frequency and Types of Data: Consists of two continuous components: a quarterly Interview survey and a weekly diary or recordkeeping survey. They are nationwide surveys that collect data on consumer expenditures, income, characteristics, and assets and liabilities. Samples are national probability samples of households that are representative of the civilian noninstitutional population. The surveys have been ongoing since 1980.

Type of Data Collection Operation: The Interview Survey is a panel rotation survey. Each panel is interviewed for five quarters and then dropped from the survey. About 7,500 consumer units are interviewed each quarter. The Diary Survey sample is new each year and consists of about 7,500 consumer units. Data are collected on an ongoing basis in 105 PSUs since 1996.

Data Collection and Imputation Procedures: For the Interview Survey, data are collected by personal interview with each consumer unit interviewed once per quarter for five consecutive quarters. Designed to collect information that respondents can recall for 3 months or longer, such as large or recurring expenditures. For the Diary Survey, respondents record all their expenditures in a self-reporting diary for two consecutive one-week periods. Designed to pick up items difficult to recall over a long period, such as detailed food expenditures. Missing or invalid attributes, expenditures, or incomes are imputed. Assets and liabilities are not imputed. The U.S. Census Bureau collects the data for the Bureau of Labor Statistics.

Estimates of Sampling Error: Standard error tables are available since 2000.

Other (nonsampling) Errors: Includes incorrect information given by respondents, data processing errors, interviewer errors, and so on. They occur regardless of whether data are collected from a sample or from the entire population.

Sources of Additional Material: Bureau of Labor Statistics, Internet site <http://www.bls.gov/cex>.

Consumer Price Index (CPI)

Universe, Frequency, and Types of Data: Monthly survey of price changes of all types of consumer goods and services purchased by urban wage earners and clerical workers prior to 1978, and urban consumers thereafter. Both indexes continue to be published.

Type of Data Collection Operation: Prior to 1978, and since 1998, sample of various consumer items in 87 urban areas; from 1978–1997, in 85 PSUs, except from January 1987 through March 1988, when 91 areas were sampled.

Data Collection and Imputation Procedures: Prices of consumer items are obtained from about 50,000 housing units, and 23,000 other reporters in 87

areas. Prices of food, fuel, and a few other items are obtained monthly; prices of most other commodities and services are collected every month in the three largest geographic areas and every other month in others.

Estimates of Sampling Error: Estimates of standard errors are available.

Other (nonsampling) Errors: Errors result from inaccurate reporting, difficulties in defining concepts and their operational implementation, and introduction of product quality changes and new products.

Sources of Additional Material: U.S. Bureau of Labor Statistics, Internet site <http://www.bls.gov/cpi/home.htm> and *BLS Handbook of Methods,* Chapter 17, Internet site <http://www.bls.gov /opub/hom/homch17_a.htm>.

Current Employment Statistics (CES) Program

Universe, Frequency, and Types of Data: Monthly survey drawn from a sampling frame of over 8 million unemployment insurance tax accounts in order to obtain data by industry on employment, hours, and earnings.

Type of Data Collection Operation: In 2006, the CES sample included about 160,000 businesses and government agencies, which represent approximately 400,000 individual worksites.

Data Collection and Imputation Procedures: Each month, the state agencies cooperating with BLS, as well as BLS Data Collection Centers, collect data through various automated collection modes and mail. BLS Washington staff prepares national estimates of employment, hours, and earnings while states use the data to develop state and area estimates.

Estimates of Sampling Errors: The relative standard error for total nonfarm employment is 0.2 percent.

Other (nonsampling) Errors: Estimates of employment adjusted annually to reflect complete universe. Average adjustment is 0.2 percent over the last decade, with an absolute range from less than 0.05 percent to less than 0.5 percent.

Sources of Additional Material: U.S. Bureau of Labor Statistics, Employment and Earnings, monthly, Explanatory Notes and Estimates of Errors, Tables 2-A through 2-F.

National Compensation Survey (NCS)

Universe, Frequency, and Types of Data: NCS collects data from establishments of all employment size classes in private industries as well as state and local governments. The survey stratifies its data by geographic area and industry. NCS collects data on work schedules, wages, salaries, and employer costs for employee benefits. For approximately 80 metropolitan areas and the nation, NCS produces information on workers' earnings and benefits in a variety of occupations at different work levels. NCS is also responsible for two quarterly releases: the Employment Cost Index (ECI), which measures percent changes in the cost of employment, and the Employer Costs for Employee Compensation (ECEC), which measures costs per hour worked for individual benefits. The survey provides data by industry sector, industry division, occupational group, bargaining status, metropolitan area status, census region, and census division. ECEC also provides data by establishment size class.

Type of Data Collection Operation: Establishments are selected for the survey based on a probability-proportionate-to-employment technique. NCS replaces its sample on a continual basis. Private industry establishments are in the survey for approximately 5 years.

Data Collection and Imputation Procedures: A personal visit to the establishment is the initial source for collecting data. Communication via mail, fax, and telephone provide quarterly updates. Imputation is done for individual benefits.

Estimates of Sampling Error: NCS uses standard errors to evaluate published series. These standard errors are available at <http://www.bls.gov/ncs/ect /home.htm>.

Other (nonsampling) Errors: Nonsampling errors have a number of potential sources. The primary sources are:

(1) survey nonresponse and (2) data collection and processing errors. Nonsampling errors are not measured. The use of quality assurance programs reduces the potential for nonsampling errors. These programs include the use of reinterviews, interview observations, and the systematic professional review of reports. The programs also serve as a training device that provides feedback on errors for field economists (or data collectors). Quality assurance programs also provide information on sources of error. This information is used to improve procedures that result in fewer errors. NCS also conducts extensive training of field economists to maintain high standards in data collection.

Sources of Additional Material: Bureau of Labor Statistics, *BLS Handbook of Methods,* Chapter 8 <http://www.bls/gov /opub/hom/pdf/homch8.pdf> or <http://www.bls.gov/opub/hom /homch8_a.htm>.

Producer Price Index (PPI)

Universe, Frequency, and Types of Data: Monthly survey of producing companies to determine price changes of all commodities and services produced in the United States for sale in commercial transactions. Data on agriculture, forestry, fishing, manufacturing, mining, gas, electricity, construction, public utilities, wholesale trade, retail trade, transportation, healthcare, and other services.

Type of Data Collection Operation: Probability sample of approximately 30,000 establishments that result in about 100,000 price quotations per month.

Data Collection and Imputation Procedures: Data are collected by mail and facsimile. If transaction prices are not supplied, list prices are used. Some prices are obtained from trade publications, organized exchanges, and government agencies. To calculate index, price changes are multiplied by their relative weights taken from the Census Bureau's 1997 shipment values from their Census of Industries.

Estimates of Sampling Error: Not applicable.

Other (nonsampling) Errors: Not available at present.

Sources of Additional Material: U.S. Bureau of Labor Statistics, *BLS Handbook of Methods*, Chapter 14, Bulletin 2490. U.S. Bureau of Labor Statistics Internet site <http://www.bls.gov/opub/hom/homch14_a.htm>.

BOARD OF GOVERNORS OF THE FEDERAL RESERVE SYSTEM

Survey of Consumer Finances

Universe, Frequency, and Types of Data: Periodic sample survey of families. In this survey a given household is divided into a primary economic unit and other economic units. The primary economic unity, which may be a single individual, is generally chosen as the person or couple who either holds the title to the home or is listed on the lease, along with all other people in the household who are financially dependent on that person or couple. The primary unit is used as the reference family. The survey collects detailed data on the composition of family balance sheets, the terms of loans, and relationships with financial institutions. It also gathers information on the employment history and pension rights of the survey respondent and the spouse or partner of the respondent.

Type of Data Collection Operation: The survey employs a two-part strategy for sampling families. Some families are selected by standard multistage area probability sampling methods applied to all 50 states. The remaining families in the survey are selected using statistical records derived from tax returns, under the strict rules governing confidentiality and the rights of potential respondents to refuse participation.

Data Collection and Imputation Procedures: National Opinion Research Center (NORC) at the University of Chicago has collected data for the survey since 1992. Since 1995, the survey has used computer-assisted personal interviewing. Adjustments for nonresponse are made through multiple imputation of unanswered questions and through weighting adjustments based on data used in the sample design for families that refused participation.

Estimates of Sampling Error: Because of the complex design of the survey, the estimation of potential sampling errors is not straightforward. A replicate-based procedure is available.

Other (nonsampling) Errors: The survey aims to complete 4,500 interviews, with about two thirds of that number deriving from the area-probability sample. The response rate is typically about 70 percent for the area-probability sample and about 35 percent over all strata in the tax-data sample. Proper training and monitoring of interviewers, careful design of questionnaires, and systematic editing of the resulting data were used to control inaccurate survey responses.

Sources of Additional Material: Board of Governors of the Federal Reserve System, "Recent Changes in U.S. Family Finances: Evidence from the 2001 and 2004 Survey of Consumer Finances," *Federal Reserve Bulletin*, 2006, pp. A-1–A-38.

U.S. CENSUS BUREAU

2002 Economic Census (Industry Series, Geographic Area Series and Subject Series Reports) (for NAICS sectors 22, 42, 44–45, 48–49, and 51–81)

Universe, Frequency, and Types of Data: Conducted every 5 years to obtain data on number of establishments, number of employees, total payroll size, total sales/receipts/revenue, and other industry-specific statistics. In 2002, the universe was all employer and nonemployer establishments primarily engaged in wholesale, retail, utilities, finance & insurance, real estate, transportation & warehousing, information, education, health care, and other service industries.

Type of Data Collection Operation: All large employer firms were surveyed (i.e., all employer firms above payroll-size cutoffs established to separate large from small employers) plus a 5 percent to 25 percent sample of the small employer firms. Firms with no employees were not required to file a census return.

Data Collection and Imputation Procedures: Mail questionnaires were used with both mail and telephone follow-ups for nonrespondents. Data for nonrespondents and for small employer firms not mailed a questionnaire were obtained from administrative records of other federal agencies or imputed. Nonemployer data were obtained exclusively from IRS 2002 income tax returns.

Estimates of Sampling Error: Not applicable for basic data such as sales, revenue, receipts, payroll, etc. Other (nonsampling) errors: establishment response rates by NAICS sector in 2002 ranged from 80 percent to 89 percent. Item response rates generally ranged from 50 percent to 90 percent with lower rates for the more detailed questions. Nonsampling errors may occur during the collection, reporting, and keying of data, and due to industry misclassification.

Sources of Additional Material: U.S. Census Bureau, *2002 Economic Census: Industry Series, Geographic Area Series and Subject Series Reports* (by NAICS sector), Appendix C and <http://www .census.gov/econ/census02/guide /index.html>.

American Community Survey (ACS)

Universe, Frequency, and Types of Data: Nationwide survey to obtain data about demographic, social, economic, and housing characteristics of people, households, and housing units. Covers household population and excludes the population living in institutions, college dormitories, and other group quarters.

Type of Data Collection Operation: Two-stage stratified annual sample of approximately 838,000 housing units. The ACS samples housing units from the Master Address File (MAF). The first stage of sampling involves dividing the United States into primary sampling units (PSUs) most of which comprise a metropolitan area, a large county, or a group of smaller counties. Every PSU falls within the boundary of a state. The PSUs are then grouped into strata on the basis of independent information, that is, information obtained from the decennial census or other sources. The strata are constructed so that they are as homogeneous as possible with respect to social and economic characteristics

that are considered important by ACS data users. A pair of PSUs were selected from each stratum. The probability of selection for each PSU in the stratum is proportional to its estimated 1996 population. In the second stage of sampling, a sample of housing units within the sample PSUs is drawn. Ultimate sampling units (USUs) are housing units. The USUs sampled in the second stage consist of housing units which are systematically drawn from sorted lists of addresses of housing units from the MAF.

Data Collection and Imputation Procedures: The American Community Survey is conducted every month on independent samples. Each housing unit in the independent monthly samples is mailed a prenotice letter announcing the selection of the address to participate, a survey questionnaire package, and a reminder postcard. These sample units receive a second (replacement) questionnaire package if the initial questionnaire has not been returned by a scheduled date. In the mail-out/mail-back sites, sample units for which a questionnaire is not returned in the mail and for which a telephone number is available are defined as the telephone nonresponse follow-up universe. Interviewers attempt to contact and interview these mail nonresponse cases. Sample units from all sites that are still unresponsive two months after the mailing of the survey questionnaires and directly after the completion of the telephone follow-up operation are subsampled at a rate of 1 in 3. The selected nonresponse units are assigned to Field Representatives (FRs), who visit the units, verify their existence or declare them nonexistent, determine their occupancy status, and conduct interviews. After data collection is completed, any remaining incomplete or inconsistent information was imputed during the final automated edit of the collected data.

Estimates of Sampling Error: The data in the ACS products are estimates of the actual figures that would have been obtained by interviewing the entire population using the same methodology. The estimates from the chosen sample also differ from other samples of housing units and persons within those housing units.

Other (nonsampling) Errors: Nonsampling Error—In addition to sampling error, data users should realize that other types of errors may be introduced during any of the various complex operations used to collect and process survey data. An important goal of the ACS is to minimize the amount of nonsampling error introduced through nonresponse for sample housing units. One way of accomplishing this is by following up on mail nonrespondents.

Sources of Additional Material: U.S. Census Bureau, American Community Survey Web site available on Internet, <http://census.gov/acs/www/index.html> U.S. Census Bureau, American Community Survey Accuracy of the Data documents available on the Internet, <http://www.census.gov/acs/www /UseData/Accuracy/Accuracy1.htm>.

American Housing Survey (AHS)

Universe, Frequency, and Types of Data: Conducted nationally in the fall in odd numbered years to obtain data on the approximately 121 million occupied or vacant housing units in the United States (group quarters are excluded). Data include characteristics of occupied housing units, vacant units, new housing and mobile home units, financial characteristics, recent mover households, housing and neighborhood quality indicators, and energy characteristics.

Type of Data Collection Operation: The national sample was a multistage probability sample with about 57,000 units eligible for interview in 2005. Sample units, selected within 394 PSUs, were surveyed over a 4-month period.

Data Collection and Imputation Procedures: For 2005, the survey was conducted by personal interviews. The interviewers obtained the information from the occupants or, if the unit was vacant, from informed persons such as landlords, rental agents, or knowledgeable neighbors.

Estimates of Sampling Error: For the national sample, illustrations of the Standard Errors (SE) of the estimates are provided in the Appendix D of the 2003 report. As an example, the estimated CV is about 0.2 percent for the estimated percentage of owner-occupied units with two persons.

Other (nonsampling) Errors: Response rate was about 92 percent. Nonsampling errors may result from incorrect or incomplete responses, errors in coding and recording, and processing errors. For the 2005 national sample, approximately 2.2 percent of the total housing inventory was not adequately represented by the AHS sample.

Sources of Additional Material: U.S. Census Bureau, *Current Housing Reports,* Series H-150 and H-170, American Housing Survey <http://www.census.gov /hhes/www/ahs.html>.

Annual Survey of Manufactures (ASM)

Universe, Frequency, and Types of Data: The Annual Survey of Manufactures is conducted annually, except for years ending in 2 and 7 for all manufacturing establishments having one or more paid employees. The purpose of the ASM is to provide key intercensal measures of manufacturing activity, products, and location for the public and private sectors. The ASM provides statistics on employment, payroll, worker hours, payroll supplements, cost of materials, value added by manufacturing, capital expenditures, inventories, and energy consumption. It also provides estimates of value of shipments for 1,800 classes of manufactured products.

Type of Data Collection Operation: The ASM includes approximately 50,000 establishments selected from the census universe of 346,000 manufacturing establishments. Some 24,000 large establishments are selected with certainty, and some 26,000 other establishments are selected with probability proportional to a composite measure of establishment size. The survey is updated from two sources: Internal Revenue Service administrative records are used to include new single-unit manufacturers and the Company Organization Survey identifies new establishments of multiunit forms.

924   Appendix III

Data Collection and Imputation Procedures: Survey is conducted by mail with phone and mail follow-ups of nonrespondents. Imputation (for all nonresponse items) is based on previous year reports, or for new establishments in survey, on industry averages.

Estimates of Sampling Error: Estimated standard errors for number of employees, new expenditures, and for value added totals are given in annual publications. For U.S. level industry statistics, most estimated standard errors are 2 percent or less, but vary considerably for detailed characteristics.

Other (nonsampling) Errors: Response rate is about 85 percent. Nonsampling errors include those due to collection, reporting, and transcription errors, many of which are corrected through computer and clerical checks.

Sources of Additional Material: U.S. Census Bureau, *Annual Survey of Manufactures,* and Technical Paper 24.

Annual Surveys of State and Local Government

Universe, Frequency, and Types of Data: Sample survey conducted annually to obtain data on revenue, expenditure, debt, and employment of state and local governments. Universe is all governmental units in the United States (about 87,500).

Type of Data Collection Operation: Sample survey includes all state governments, county governments with 100,000+ population, municipalities with 75,000+ population, townships with 50,000+ population, all independent school districts with 10,000+ enrollment in March 2002, all school districts providing college level (postsecondary) education, and other governments meeting certain criteria; probability sample for remaining units.

Data Collection and Imputation Procedures: Field and office compilation of data from official records and reports for states and large local governments; central collection of local governmental financial data through cooperative agreements with a number of state governments; mail canvass of other units with mail and telephone follow-ups of nonrespondents. Data for nonresponses are imputed from previous year data or obtained from secondary sources, if available.

Estimates of Sampling Error: State and local government totals are generally subject to sampling variability of less than 3 percent.

Other (nonsampling) Errors: Nonresponse rate is less than 10 percent for local governments. Other possible errors may result from undetected inaccuracies in classification, response, and processing.

Sources of Additional Material: U.S. Census Bureau, *Public Employment in 1992,* GE 92, No. 1, *Governmental Finances in 1991–1992,* GF 92, No. 5, and *Census of Governments, 1997 and 2002,* various reports. Web site references: Census of Governments <http://www.census.gov /govs/www/cog2002.html>; <http://www.census.gov/govs/www /cog.html>;Employment—state and local site: <http://www.census.gov/govs /www/apes.html>; Finance—state and local site: <http://www.census.gov /govs/www/estimate.html>.

Census of Population

Universe, Frequency, and Types of Data: Complete count of U.S. population conducted every 10 years since 1790. Data obtained on number and characteristics of people in the U.S.

Type of Data Collection Operation: In 1980, 1990, and 2000, complete census for some items: age, date of birth, sex, race, and relationship to householder. In 1980, approximately 19 percent of the housing units were included in the sample; in 1990 and 2000, approximately 17 percent.

Data Collection and Imputation Procedures: In 1980, 1990, and 2000, mail questionnaires were used extensively with personal interviews in the remainder. Extensive telephone and personal follow-up for nonrespondents was done in the censuses. Imputations were made for missing characteristics.

Estimates of Sampling Error: Sampling errors for data are estimated for all items collected by sample and vary by characteristic and geographic area. The coefficients of variation (CVs) for national and state estimates are generally very small.

Other (nonsampling) Errors: Since 1950, evaluation programs have been conducted to provide information on the magnitude of some sources of nonsampling errors such as response bias and undercoverage in each census. Results from the evaluation program for the 1990 census indicated that the estimated net undercoverage amounted to about 1.5 percent of the total resident population. For Census 2000, the evaluation program indicated a net overcount of 0.5 percent of the resident population.

Sources of Additional Material: U.S. Census Bureau, The Coverage of Population in the 1980 Census, PHC80-E4; *Content Reinterview Study: Accuracy of Data for Selected Population and Housing Characteristics as Measured by Reinterview,* PHC80-E2; *1980 Census of Population, Vol. 1,* (PC80-1), Appendixes B, C, and D. Content *Reinterview Survey: Accuracy of Data for Selected Population and Housing Characteristics as Measured by Reinterview,* 1990, CPH-E-1; *Effectiveness of Quality Assurance,* CPH-E-2; *Programs to Improve Coverage in the 1990 Census,* 1990, CPH-E-3. For Census 2000 evaluations, see <http://www.census.gov/pred/www>.

County Business Patterns

Universe, Frequency, and Types of Data: County Business Patterns is an annual tabulation of basic data items extracted from the Business Register, a file of all known single- and multilocation companies maintained and updated by the Census Bureau. Data include number of establishments, number of employees, first quarter and annual payrolls, and number of establishments by employment size class. Data are excluded for self-employed persons, domestic service workers, railroad employees, agricultural production workers, and most government employees.

Type of Data Collection Operation: The annual Company Organization Survey provides individual establishment data for multilocation companies. Data for single establishment companies are obtained from various Census Bureau programs, such as the Annual Survey of Manufactures and Current Business Surveys, as well as from administrative records of the Internal Revenue Service and the Social Security Administration.

Estimates of Sampling Error: Not applicable.

Other (nonsampling) Error: The data are subject to nonsampling errors, such as industry classification errors, as well as errors of response, keying, and nonreporting.

Sources of Additional Materials: U.S. Census Bureau, *General Explanation of County Business Patterns.*

Current Population Survey (CPS)

Universe, Frequency, and Types of Data: Nationwide monthly sample survey of civilian noninstitutional population, 15 years old or over, to obtain data on employment, unemployment, and a number of other characteristics.

Type of Data Collection Operation: Multistage probability sample that currently includes 60,000 households in 824 sample areas. Over-sampling in some states and the largest MSAs to improve data reliability for those areas on an annual average basis. A continual sample rotation system is used. Households are in sample 4 months, out for 8 months, and in for 4 more. Month-to-month overlap is 75 percent; year-to-year overlap is 50 percent.

Data Collection and Imputation Procedures: For first and fifth months that a household is in sample, personal interviews; other months, approximately 87 percent of the data collected by phone. Imputation is done for both item and total nonresponse. Adjustment for total nonresponse is done by a predefined cluster of units, by MSA size and residence; for item nonresponse imputation varies by subject matter.

Estimates of Sampling Error: Estimated CVs on national annual averages for labor force, total employment, and nonagricultural employment, 0.2 percent; for total unemployment and agricultural employment, 1.0 percent to 2.5 percent. The estimated CVs for family income and poverty rate for all persons in 1986 are 0.5 percent and 1.5 percent, respectively. CVs for subnational areas, such as states, would be larger and would vary by area.

Other (nonsampling) Errors: Estimates of response bias on unemployment are not available, but estimates of unemployment are usually 5 percent to 9 percent lower than estimates from reinterviews. Six to 7.0 percent of sample households unavailable for interviews.

Sources of Additional Material: U.S. Census Bureau and Bureau of Labor Statistics, *Current Population Survey: Design and Methodology,* (Tech. Paper 63), available on the Internet <http://www .census.gov/prod/2002pubs/tp63rv.pdf> and Bureau of Labor Statistics, *Employment and Earnings,* monthly, and *BLS Handbook of Methods,* Chapter 1, available on the Internet at <http://www .bls.gov/opub/hom/homch1_a.htm>.

Foreign Trade—Import Statistics

Universe, Frequency, and Types of Data: The import entry documents collected by U.S. Bureau of Customs and Border Protection are processed each month to obtain data on the movement of merchandise imported into the United States. Data obtained include value, quantity, and shipping weight by commodity, country of origin, district of entry, and mode of transportation.

Type of Data Collection Operation: Import entry documents, either paper or electronic, are required to be filed for the importation of goods into the United States valued over $2,000 or for articles which must be reported on formal entries. U.S. Bureau of Customs and Border Protection officials collect and transmit statistical copies of the documents to the Census Bureau on a flow basis for data compilation. Estimates for shipments valued under $2,001 and not reported on formal entries are based on estimated established percentages for individual country totals.

Data Collection and Imputation Procedures: Statistical copies of import entry documents, received on a daily basis from ports of entry throughout the country, are subjected to a monthly processing cycle. They are fully processed

to the extent they reflect items valued at $2,001 and over or items which must be reported on formal entries.

Estimates of Sampling Error: Not applicable.

Other (nonsampling) Errors: The goods data are a complete enumeration of documents collected by the U.S. Bureau of Customs and Border Protection and are not subject to sampling errors; but they are subject to several types of non-sampling errors. Quality assurance procedures are performed at every stage of collection, processing and tabulation; however the data are still subject to several types of nonsampling errors. The most significant of these include reporting errors, undocumented shipments, timeliness, data capture errors, and errors in the estimation of low-valued transactions. Additional information on errors affecting import data can be found at <http://www.census.gov /foreign-trade/PressRelease /current_press_release/explain.pdf>.

Sources of Additional Material: U.S. Census Bureau, FT 900 U.S. International Trade in Goods and Services, FT 895 U.S. Trade with Puerto Rico and U.S. Possessions, FT920 U.S. Merchandise Trade: selected highlights, and Information Section on Goods and Services at <http: //www.census.gov/ft900>.

Foreign Trade—Export Statistics

Universe, Frequency, and Types of Data: The export declarations collected by U.S. Bureau of Customs and Border Protection are processed each month to obtain data on the movement of U.S. merchandise exports to foreign countries. Data obtained include value, quantity, and shipping weight of exports by commodity, country of destination, district of exportation, and mode of transportation.

Type of Data Collection Operation: Shipper's Export Declarations (paper and electronic) are generally required to be filed for the exportation of merchandise valued over $2,500. U.S. Bureau of Customs and Border Protection officials collect and transmit the documents to the Census Bureau on a flow basis for data compilation. Data for shipments valued under $2,501 are estimated, based on established percentages of individual country totals.

Data Collection and Imputation Procedures: Statistical copies of Shipper's Export Declarations are received on a daily basis from ports throughout the country and subjected to a monthly processing cycle. They are fully processed to the extent they reflect items valued over $2,500. Estimates for shipments valued at $2,500 or less are made, based on established percentages of individual country totals.

Estimates of Sampling Error: Not applicable.

Other (nonsampling) Errors: The goods data are a complete enumeration of documents collected by the U.S. Bureau of Customs and Border Protection and are not subject to sampling errors; but they are subject to several types of nonsampling errors. Quality assurance procedures are performed at every stage of collection, processing and tabulation; however the data are still subject to several types of nonsampling errors. The most significant of these include reporting errors, undocumented shipments, timeliness, data capture errors, and errors in the estimation of low-valued transactions. Additional information on errors affecting export data can be found at <http://www.census.gov/foreign-trade/PressRelease/current_press_release/explain.pdf>.

Sources of Additional Material: U.S. Census Bureau, FT 900 U.S. International Trade in Goods and Services, FT 895 U.S. Trade with Puerto Rico and U.S. Possessions, FT 920 U.S. Merchandise trade: selected highlights, and Information Section on Goods and Services at <http://census.gov/ft900>.

Monthly Retail Trade and Food Service Survey

Universe, Frequency, and Types of Data: Provides monthly estimates of retail and food service sales by kind of business and end of month inventories of retail stores.

Type of Data Collection Operation: Probability sample of all firms from a list frame. The list frame is the Bureau's

Business Register updated quarterly for recent birth Employer Identification (EI) Numbers issued by the Internal Revenue Service and assigned a kind of business code by the Social Security Administration. The largest firms are included monthly; a sample of others is included every month also.

Data Collection and Imputation Procedures: Data are collected by mail questionnaire with telephone follow-ups and fax reminders for nonrespondents. Imputation is made for each nonresponse item and each item failing edit checks.

Estimates of Sampling Error: For the 2005 monthly surveys, CVs are about 0.6 percent for estimated total retail sales and 1.2 percent for estimated total retail inventories. Sampling errors are shown in monthly publications.

Other (nonsampling) Errors: Imputation rates are about 22 percent for monthly retail and food service sales, and 30 percent for monthly retail inventories.

Sources of Additional Material: U.S. Census Bureau, Current Business Reports, Annual Revision of Monthly Retail and Food Services: Sales and Inventories.

Monthly Survey of Construction

Universe, Frequency, and Types of Data: Survey conducted monthly of newly constructed housing units (excluding mobile homes). Data are collected on the start, completion, and sale of housing. (Annual figures are aggregates of monthly estimates.)

Type of Data Collection Operation: A multistage probability sample of approximately 900 of the 20,000 permit-issuing jurisdictions in the U.S. was selected. Each month in each of these permit offices, field representatives list and select a sample of permits for which to collect data. To obtain data in areas where building permits are not required, a multistage probability sample of 80 land areas (Census tracts or subsections of Census tracts) was selected. All roads in these areas are canvassed and data are collected on all new residential construction found. Sampled buildings are followed up until they are completed (and sold, if for sale).

928   Appendix III

Data Collection and Imputation Procedures: Data are obtained by telephone inquiry and/or field visit. Nonresponse/undercoverage adjustment factors are used to account for late reported data.

Estimates of Sampling Error: Estimated CV of 3 percent to 4 percent for estimates of national totals of units started, but may be higher than 20 percent for estimated totals of more detailed characteristics, such as housing units in multiunit structures.

Other (nonsampling) Errors: Response rate is over 90 percent for most items. Nonsampling errors are attributed to definitional problems, differences in interpretation of questions, incorrect reporting, inability to obtain information about all cases in the sample, and processing errors.

Sources of Additional Material: All data are available on the Internet at <http://www.census.gov/const/www/newressalesindex.html>, or <http://www.census.gov/const/www/newresconstindex.html>. Further documentation of the survey is also available at those sites.

Nonemployer Statistics

Universe, Frequency, and Types of Data: Nonemployer statistics are an annual tabulation of economic data by industry for active businesses without paid employees that are subject to federal income tax. Data showing the number of establishments and receipts by industry are available for the U.S., states, counties, and metropolitan areas. Most types of businesses covered by the Census Bureau's economic statistics programs are included in the nonemployer statistics. Tax-exempt and agricultural-production businesses are excluded from nonemployer statistics.

Type of Data Collection Operation: The universe of nonemployer establishments is created annually as a byproduct of the Census Bureau's Business Register processing for employer establishments. If a business is active but without paid employees, then it becomes part of the potential nonemployer universe. Industry classification and receipts are available for each potential nonemployer

business. These data are obtained primarily from the annual business income tax returns of the Internal Revenue Service (IRS). The potential nonemployer universe undergoes a series of complex processing, editing, and analytical review procedures at the Census Bureau to distinguish nonemployers from employers, and to correct and complete data items used in creating the data tables.

Estimates of Sampling Error: Not applicable.

Other (nonsampling) Errors: The data are subject to nonsampling errors, such as errors of self-classification by industry on tax forms, as well as errors of response, keying, nonreporting, and coverage.

Sources of Additional Material: U. S. Census Bureau, Nonemployer Statistics: see <http://www.census.gov/epcd/nonemployer/view/cov&meth.htm>.

Service Annual Survey

Universe, Frequency, and Types of Data: The U.S. Census Bureau conducts the Service Annual Survey to provide nationwide estimates of revenues and expenses for selected service industries. Estimates are summarized by industry classification based on the 1997 North American Industry Classification System (NAICS). Selected service industries covered by the Service Annual Survey include all or part of the following NAICS sectors: Transportation and Warehousing (NAICS 48–49); Information (NAICS 51); Finance and Insurance (NAICS 52); Real Estate and Rental and Leasing (NAICS 53); Professional, Scientific, and Technical Services (NAICS 54); Administrative and Support and Waste Management and Remediation Services (NAICS 56); Health Care and Social Assistance (NAICS 62); Arts, Entertainment, and Recreation (NAICS 71); and Other Services, except Public Administration (NAICS 81). Data collected include total revenue, revenue from e-commerce transactions; and for selected industries, revenue from detailed service products, total expenses, and expenses by major type, revenue from exported services, and inventories. For industries with a significant nonprofit component, separate estimates are developed for taxable firms and firms and organizations exempt from federal income taxes. Questionnaires are mailed in January and request annual data for the prior year. Estimates are published approximately 12 months after the initial survey mailing.

Type of Data Collection Operation: The Service Annual Survey estimates are developed from a probability sample of employer firms and administrative records for nonemployers. Service Annual Survey questionnaires are mailed to a probability sample that is periodically reselected from a universe of firms located in the United States and having paid employees. The sample includes firms of all sizes and covers both taxable firms and firms exempt from federal income taxes. Updates to the sample are made on a quarterly basis to account for new businesses. Firms without paid employees, or nonemployers, are included in the estimates through imputation and/or administrative records data provided by other federal agencies. Links to additional information about confidentiality protection, sampling error, nonsampling error, sample design, definitions, and copies of the questionnaires may be found on the Internet at <http://www.census.gov /econ/www/servmenu.html.

Estimates of Sampling Error: Coefficients of variation for the 2004 Service Annual Survey estimates range from 0.03% to 1.5% for total revenue estimates computed at the NAICS sector (2-digit NAICS code) level. Sampling errors for more detailed industries are shown in the corresponding publications. The full 2004 Service Annual Survey results, including coefficients of variations, can be found at <http://www.census.gov/econ/www /servmenu.html>. Links to additional information regarding sampling error may be found at: <http://www.census .gov/svsd/www/cv.html>.

Other (nonsampling) Errors: Data are imputed for unit nonresponse, item nonresponse, and for reported data that fails edits. The percent of imputed data for total revenue for the 2004 Service Annual Survey is approximately 13%.

Sources of Additional Material: U.S. Census Bureau, Current Business Reports,

Service Annual Survey, Census Bureau Web site: <http://www.census.gov /econ/www/servmenu.html>.

Survey of Business Owners (SBO)

Universe, Frequency, and Types of Data: This survey, formerly known as the Surveys of Minority- and Women-Owned Business Enterprises (SMOBE/SWOBE), provides statistics that describe the composition of U.S. businesses by gender, Hispanic or Latino origin, and race. Data are presented for businesses owned by American Indians and Alaska Natives, Asians, Blacks, Hispanics, Native Hawaiians and Other Pacific Islanders, and Women. All U.S. firms operating during 2002 with receipts of $1,000 or more, which are classified by the North American Industry Classification System (NAICS) codes 11 through 99, are represented, except for the following: NAICS 111, 112, 4811 (part), 482, 491, 525 (part), 813, 814, and 92. The lists of all firms (or sample frames) are compiled from a combination of business tax returns and data collected on other economic census reports. The published data include the number of firms, gross receipts, number of paid employees, and annual payroll. Data are presented by industry classifications and/or geographic area (states, metropolitan and micropolitan statistical areas, counties, and corporate municipalities (places) including cities, towns, townships, villages, and boroughs), and size of firm (employment and receipts).

Type of Data Collection Operation: The survey is based on a stratified probability sample of approximately 2.3 million firms from a universe of approximately 23 million firms. There were 5.5 million firms with paid employees and 17.4 million firms with no paid employees. The data are based on the entire firm rather than on individual locations of a firm.

Data Collection and Imputation Procedures: Data were collected through a mailout/mailback operation. Compensation for missing data is addressed through reweighting, edit correction, and standard statistical imputation methods.

Estimates of Sampling Error: Variability in the estimates is due to the sample selection and estimation for items collected

930   Appendix III

by the SBO. *Standard errors* (SE) are measures of the variation among the estimates derived from all possible samples. For convenience, the data collected in the SBO probability samples are expressed as a percent of the estimate and are called the relative standard errors or *coefficient of variations* (CVs). CVs are applied only to published cells in which sample cases are tabulated. The CVs for number of firms and receipts at the national level range from 1 to 4 percent.

Other (nonsampling) Error: Nonsampling errors are attributed to many sources: inability to obtain information for all cases in the universe, adjustments to the weights of respondent to compensate for nonrespondents, imputation for missing data, data errors and biases, mistakes in recording or keying data, errors in collection or processing, and coverage problems.

Sources of Additional Materials: U.S. Census Bureau, Guide to the 2002 Economic Census and Related Statistics; <http://www.census.gov/econ/census02/guide/index.html>.

U.S. DEPARTMENT OF EDUCATION, National Center for Education Statistics

Higher Education General Information Survey (HEGIS), Degrees and Other Formal Awards Conferred. Beginning 1986, Integrated Postsecondary Education Data Survey (IPEDS), Completions

Universe, Frequency, and Types of Data: Annual survey of all institutions and branches listed in the *Education Directory, Colleges and Universities* to obtain data on earned degrees and other formal awards, conferred by field of study, level of degree, sex, and by racial/ethnic characteristics (every other year prior to 1989, then annually).

Type of Data Collection Operation: Complete census.

Data Collection and Imputation Procedures: Data are collected through a Web-based survey in the fall of every year. Missing data are imputed by using data of similar institutions.

Estimates of Sampling Error: Not applicable.

Other (nonsampling) Errors: For 2003–04, approximately 99.6 percent response rate for degree granting institutions.

Sources of Additional Material: U.S. Department of Education, National Center for Education Statistics, *Postsecondary Institutions in the United States: Fall 2004 and Degrees and Other Awards Conferred: 200304*; <http://www.nces.ed.gov/ipeds/>.

National Household Education Surveys (NHES) Program

Universe, Frequency, and Types of Data: The National Household Education Surveys Program is a system of telephone surveys of the noninstitutionalized civilian population of the United States. Surveys in NHES have varying universes of interest depending on the particular survey. Specific topics covered by each survey are at the NHES Web site <http://nces.ed.gov/nhes>. A list of the surveys fielded as part of NHES, each universe, and the years they were fielded is provided below. 1) Adult Education Interviews were conducted with a representative sample of civilian, noninstitutionalized persons age 16 and older who were not enrolled in grade 12 or below (1991, 1995, 1999, 2001, 2003, 2005, and planned for 2007). 2) Before-and After-School Programs and Activities Interviews were conducted with parents of a representative sample of students in grades K through 8 (1999, 2001, 2005). 3) Civic Involvement Interviews were conducted with representative samples of parents, youth, and adults (1996, 1999). 4) Early Childhood Program Participation Interviews were conducted with parents of a representative sample of children from birth through grade 3, with the specific age groups varying by survey year (1991, 1995, 1999, 2001, 2005). 5) Household and Library Use Interviews were conducted with a representative sample of U.S. households (1996). 6) Parent and Family Involvement in Education Interviews were conducted with parents of a representative sample of children age 3 through grade 12 or in grades K through 12 depending on the survey year (1996, 1999, 2003, and planned for 2007).

7) School Readiness Interviews were conducted with parents of a representative sample of 3- to 7-year-old children (1993, 1999, and planned for 2007).
8) School Safety and Discipline Interviews were conducted with a representative sample of students in grades 6–12, their parents, and the parents of a representative sample of students in grades 3–12 (1993).

Type of Data Collection Operation: NHES uses telephone interviews to collect data.

Data Collection and Imputation Procedures: Telephone numbers are selected using random digit dialing (RDD) techniques. Approximately 45,000 to 64,000 households are contacted in order to identify persons eligible for the surveys. Data are collected using computer-assisted telephone interviewing (CATI) procedures. Missing data are imputed using hot-deck imputation procedures.

Estimates of Sampling Error: Unweighted sample sizes range between 2,250 and 55,708. The average root design effects of the surveys in NHES range from 1.1 to 4.5.

Other (nonsampling) Errors: Because of unit nonresponse and because the samples are drawn from households with telephone instead of all households, nonresponse and/or coverage bias may exist for some estimates. However, both sources of potential bias are adjusted for in the weighting process. Analyses of both potential sources of bias in the NHES collections have been studied and no significant bias has been detected.

Sources of Additional Material: Please see the NHES Web site at <http://nces.ed .gov/nhes>.

U.S. FEDERAL BUREAU OF INVESTIGATION

Uniform Crime Reporting (UCR) Program

Universe, Frequency, and Types of Data: Monthly reports on the number of criminal offenses that become known to law enforcement agencies. Data are collected on crimes cleared by arrest or exceptional means; by age, sex, and race of arrestees and for victims and offenders for homicides, on fatal and nonfatal assaults against law enforcement officers, and on hate crimes reported.

Type of Data Collection Operation: Crime statistics are based on reports of crime data submitted either directly to the FBI by contributing law enforcement agencies or through cooperating state UCR programs.

Data Collection and Imputation Procedures: States with UCR programs collect data directly from individual law enforcement agencies and forward reports, prepared in accordance with UCR standards, to FBI. Accuracy and consistency edits are performed by FBI.

Estimates of Sampling Error: Not applicable.

Other (nonsampling) Errors: Coverage of 94 percent of the population (95 percent in MSAs, 87 percent in "cities outside of metropolitan areas," and 89 percent in nonmetropolitan counties) by UCR Program, through varying number of agencies reporting.

Sources of Additional Material: U.S. Federal Bureau of Investigation, *Crime in the United States,* annual, *Hate Crime Statistics,* annual, *Law Enforcement Officers Killed & Assaulted,* annual, <http://www.fbi.gov/ucr/05cius/index .html>.

U.S. INTERNAL REVENUE SERVICE

Corporation Income Tax Returns

Universe, Frequency, and Types of Data: Annual study of unaudited corporation income tax returns, Forms 1120, 1120-A, 1120-F, 1120-L, 1120-PC, 1120-REIT, 1120-RIC, and 1120S, filed by corporations or businesses legally defined as corporations. Data provided on various financial characteristics by industry and size of total assets, and business receipts.

Type of Data Collection Operation: Stratified probability sample of approximately 142,000 returns for Tax Year 2003, allocated to sample classes which are based on type of return, size of total assets size of net income or deficit, and selected business activity. Sampling rates for sample classes varied from .25 percent to 100 percent.

Data Collection and Imputation Procedures: Computer selection of sample of tax return records. Data adjusted during editing for incorrect, missing, or inconsistent entries to ensure consistency with other entries on return and to comply with statistical definitions.

Estimates of Sampling Error: Estimated CVs for Tax Year 2003: Returns with assets over $10 million are self-representing. Coefficients of variation are published in the 2003 Statistics of Income Corporation Income Tax Returns, Table 1, by industry group.

Other (nonsampling) Errors: Nonsampling errors include coverage errors, processing errors, and response errors.

Sources of Additional Material: U.S. Internal Revenue Service, *Statistics of Income, Corporation Income Tax Returns,* annual.

Partnership Income Tax Returns

Universe, Frequency, and Types of Data: Annual study of unaudited income tax returns of partnerships, Form 1065. Data provided on various financial characteristics by industry.

Type of Data Collection Operation: Stratified probability sample of approximately 39,000 partnership returns from a population of 2.7 million filed during calendar year 2004. The sample is classified based on combinations of gross receipts, net income or loss, and total assets, and on industry. Sampling rates vary from 0.09 percent to 100 percent.

Data Collection and Imputation Procedures: Computer selection of sample of tax return records. Data are adjusted during editing for incorrect, missing, or inconsistent entries to ensure consistency with other entries on return. Data not available due to regulations are not imputed.

Estimates of Sampling Error: Estimated CVs for tax year 2004 (latest available): For number of partnerships, 0.30 percent; business receipts, 0.30 percent; net income, 0.73 percent; net loss, 1.87 percent.

Other (nonsampling) Errors: Processing errors and errors arising from the use of tolerance checks for the data.

Sources of Additional Material: U.S. Internal Revenue Service, *Statistics of Income, Partnership Returns and Statistics of Income Bulletin,* Vol. 25, No. 2 (fall 2005).

Sole Proprietorship Income Tax Returns

Universe, Frequency, and Types of Data: Annual study of unaudited income tax returns of nonfarm sole proprietorships, Form 1040 with business schedules. Data provided on various financial characteristics by industry.

Type of Data Collection Operation: Stratified probability sample of approximately 56,000 sole proprietorships for tax year 2003. The sample is classified based on presence or absence of certain business schedules; the larger of total income or loss; and size of business plus farm receipts. Sampling rates vary from 0.05 percent to 100 percent.

Data Collection and Imputation Procedures: Computer selection of sample of tax return records. Data adjusted during editing for incorrect, missing, or inconsistent entries to ensure consistency with other entries on return.

Estimates of Sampling Error: Estimated CVs for tax year 2003 are available. For sole proprietorships, business receipts, 0.66 percent; depreciation 1.37 percent.

Other (nonsampling) Errors: Processing errors and errors arising from the use of tolerance checks for the data.

Sources of Additional Material: U.S. Internal Revenue Service, *Statistics of Income, Sole Proprietorship Returns* (for years 1980 through 1983) and *Statistics of Income Bulletin,* Vol. 25, No. 1 (summer 2005, as well as bulletins for earlier years).

Individual Income Tax Returns

Universe, Frequency, and Types of Data: Annual study of unaudited individual income tax returns, Forms 1040, 1040A, and 1040EZ, filed by U.S. citizens and residents. Data provided on various financial characteristics by size of adjusted gross income, marital status, and by taxable and nontaxable returns. Data by state, based on 100 percent file, also include returns from 1040NR, filed by nonresident aliens plus certain self-employment tax returns.

Type of Data Collection Operation: Annual 2003 stratified probability sample of approximately 183,000 returns broken into sample strata based on the larger of total income or total loss amounts as well as the size of business plus farm receipts. Sampling rates for sample strata varied from 0.05 percent to 100 percent.

Data Collection and Imputation Procedures: Computer selection of sample of tax return records. Data adjusted during editing for incorrect, missing, or inconsistent entries to ensure consistency with other entries on return.

Estimates of Sampling Error: Estimated CVs for tax year 2003: Adjusted gross income less deficit 0.12 percent; salaries and wages 0.21 percent; and tax exempt interest received 1.77 percent. (State data not subject to sampling error.)

Other (nonsampling) Errors: Processing errors and errors arising from the use of tolerance checks for the data.

Sources of Additional Material: U.S. Internal Revenue Service, *Statistics of Income, Individual Income Tax Returns,* annual.

U.S. NATIONAL CENTER FOR HEALTH STATISTICS (NCHS)

National Health Interview Survey (NHIS)

Universe, Frequency, and Types of Data: Continuous data collection covering the civilian noninstitutional population to obtain information on demographic characteristics, conditions, injuries, impairments, use of health services, health behaviors, and other health topics.

Type of Data Collection Operation: Multi-stage probability sample of 49,000 households (in 198 PSUs) from 1985 to 1994; 36–40,000 households (358 design PSUs) from 1995 to 2005.

Data Collection and Imputation Procedures: Some missing data items (e.g., race, ethnicity) are imputed using a hot deck imputation value. Sequential regression models are used to create multiple imputation files for family income. Unit nonresponse is compensated for by an adjustment to the survey weights.

Estimates of Sampling Error: Estimates of Standard Error (SE): For 2004 medically attended injury episodes rates in the past 12 months by falling for: females 46.38 (3.50), and males 36.87 (3.24) per 1,000 population; for 2004 injury episodes rates during the past 12 months inside the home—29.72 (2.11) per 1,000 population.

Other (nonsampling) Errors: The response rate was 93.8 percent in 1996; in 2004, the total household response rate was 86.9 percent, with the final family response rate of 86.5 percent, and the final sample adult response rate of 83.8 percent. (Note: The NHIS sample redesign was conducted in 1995, and the NHIS questionnaire was redesigned in 1997.)

Sources of Additional Material: National Center for Health Statistics, Summary Health Statistics for the U.S. Population: National Health Interview Survey, 2004, Vital and Health Statistics, Series 10 #229; National Center for Health Statistics, Summary Health Statistics for U.S. Children: National Health Interview Survey, 2004, Vital and Health Statistics, Series 10 #227; National Center for Health Statistics, Summary Health Statistics for U.S. Adults: National Health Interview Survey, 2004, Vital and Health Statistics, Series 10 #228; U.S. National Center for Health Statistics, Design and Estimation for the National Health Interview Survey, 1995–2004, Vital and Health Statistics, Series 2 #130.

National Survey of Family Growth (NSFG)

Universe, Frequency, and Types of Data: Periodic survey of men and women 15–44 years of age in the household population of the United States. Interviews were conducted in 2002 in person by trained female interviewers. Interview topics covered include births and pregnancies, marriage, divorce, and cohabitation, sexual activity, contraceptive use, and medical care. For men, data on father involvement with children were collected. The most sensitive data on sexual behavior related to HIV and Sexually Transmitted Disease risk were collected in a self-administered form in which the data are entered into a computer.

Type of Data Collection Operation: In the 2002 (Cycle 6) NSFG, the sample was a multistage area probability sample of men and women 15–44 years of age in the household population of the United States. Only one person 15–44 was selected from households with one or more persons 15–44. Data were collected and entered into laptop (notebook) computers. In the self-administered portion, the respondent entered his or her own answers into the computer. Sample included 12,571 interviews. The response rate was 79 percent. Hispanic and Black persons, as well as those 15–19 years of age, were sampled at higher rates than White adults. All percentages and other statistics shown for the NSFG are weighted to make national estimates. The weights adjust for the different rates of sampling for each group, and for nonresponse.

Data Collection and Imputation Procedures: When interviews are received, they are reviewed for consistency and quality, and analysis variables (recodes) are created. Missing data on these recodes were imputed using multiple regression techniques and checked again for consistency. Variables indicating whether a value has been imputed ("imputation flags") are included on the data file.

Estimates of Sampling Error: Sampling error codes are included on the data file so that users can estimate sampling errors for their own analyses. Sampling error estimates for nine illustrative analyses are shown on the NSFG Web site. <http://www.cdc.gov/nchs.nsfg.htm>. Sampling error estimates are also shown in most NCHS reports.

Other (nonsampling) Errors: In any survey, errors can occur because the respondent (the person being interviewed) does not recall the specific fact or event being asked about. The NSFG questionnaire in 2002 was programmed to check the consistency of many variables during the interview, so that the interviewer and respondent had a chance to correct any inconsistent information. Further checking occurred after the interview and during recoding and imputation. Typically, less than 1 percent of cases need imputation because of missing data.

Sources of Additional Material: The following references can be found at <http://www.cdc.gov/nchs/hsfg.htm>. "National Survey of Family Growth, Cycle 6: Sample Design, Weighting, and Variance Estimation." *Vital and Health Statistics*, Series 2, Number 142, July 2006. "Plan and Operation of Cycle 6 of the National Survey of Family Growth." *Vital and Health Statistics*, Series 1, No. 42. August 2005. "Sexual Behavior and Selected Health Measures: Men and Women 15–44 Years of Age, United States, 2002." *Advance Data from Vital and Health Statistics*, No. 362, Sept 15, 2005.

National Vital Statistics System

Universe, Frequency, and Types of Data: Annual data on births and deaths in the United States.

Type of Data Collection Operation: Mortality data based on complete file of death records, except 1972, based on 50 percent sample. Natality statistics 1951–71, based on 50 percent sample of birth certificates, except a 20 percent to 50 percent sample in 1967, received by NCHS. Beginning 1972, data from some states received through Vital Statistics Cooperative Program (VSCP) and complete file used; data from other states based on 50 percent sample. Beginning 1986, all reporting areas participated in the VSCP.

Data Collection and Imputation Procedures: Reports based on records from registration offices of all states, District of Columbia, New York City, Puerto Rico, Virgin Islands, Guam, American Samoa, and Northern Marianas.

Estimates of Sampling Error: For recent years, there is no sampling for these files; the files are based on 100 percent of events registered.

Other (nonsampling) Errors: Data on births and deaths believed to be at least 99 percent complete.

Sources of Additional Material: U.S. National Center for Health Statistics, *Vital Statistics of the United States,* Vol. I and Vol. II, annual, and *National Vital Statistics Reports.* NCHS Web site at <http://www.cdc.gov/nchs/nvss.htm>.

National Highway Traffic Safety Administration (NHTSA)

Fatality Analysis Reporting System (FARS)

Universe, Frequency, and Types of Data: FARS is a census of all fatal motor vehicle traffic crashes that occur throughout the United States including the District of Columbia and Puerto Rico on roadways customarily open to the public. The crash must be reported to the state/jurisdiction and at least one directly related fatality must occur within thirty days of the crash.

Type of Data Collection Operation: One or more analysts, in each state, extract data from the official documents and enter the data into a standardized electronic database.

Data Collection and Imputation Procedures: Detailed data describing the characteristics of the fatal crash, the vehicles and persons involved are obtained from police crash reports, driver and vehicle registration records, autopsy reports, highway department, etc. Computerized edit checks monitor the accuracy and completeness of the data. The FARS incorporates a sophisticated mathematical multiple imputation procedure to develop a probability distribution of missing blood alcohol concentration (BAC) levels in the database for drivers, pedestrians and cyclists.

Estimates of Sampling Error: Since this is census data, there are no sampling errors.

Other (nonsampling) Errors: FARS represents a census of all police reported crashes and captures all data reported at the state level. FARS data undergo a rigorous quality control process to prevent inaccurate reporting. However, these data are highly dependent on the accuracy of the police accident reports. Errors or omissions within police accident reports may not be detected.

Sources of Additional Material: The FARS Coding and Validation Manual, ANSI D16.1 Manual on Classification of Motor Vehicle Traffic Accidents (Sixth Edition).

936   Appendix III

Weights and Measures

[For assistance on metric usage, call or write:

Kenneth S. Butcher
NIST
Weights and Measures Division
100 Bureau Drive – Mail Stop 2600
Gaithersburg, MD 20899-2600

Telephone: 301-975-4859 or 4004   FAX: 301-926-0647

E-mail: kbutcher@nist.gov

Internet site <http://www.nist.gov/metric>

Symbol	When you know conventional	Multiply by	To find metric	Symbol
in	inches	2.54	centimeters	cm
ft	feet	30.48	centimeters	cm
yd	yards	0.91	meters	m
mi	miles	1.61	kilometers	km
in^2	square inches	6.45	square centimeters	cm^2
ft^2	square feet	0.09	square meters	m^2
yd^2	square yards	0.84	square meters	m^2
mi^2	square miles	2.59	square kilometers	km^2
	acre	0.41	hectare	ha
oz	ounces [1]	28.35	grams	g
lb	pounds [1]	.45	kilograms	kg
oz (troy)	ounces [2]	31.10	grams	g
	short tons (2,000 lb)	0.91	metric tons	t
	long tons (2,240 lb)	1.02	metric tons	t
fl oz	fluid ounces	29.57	milliliters	mL
c	cups	0.24	liters	L
pt	pints	0.47	liters	L
qt	quarts	0.95	liters	L
gal	gallons	3.78	liters	L
ft^3	cubic feet	0.03	cubic meters	m^3
yd^3	cubic yards	0.76	cubic meters	m^3
F	degrees Fahrenheit (subtract 32)	0.55	degrees Celsius	C

Symbol	When you know metric	Multiply by	To find conventional	Symbol
cm	centimeters	0.39	inches	in
cm	centimeters	0.03	feet	ft
m	meters	1.09	yards	yd
km	kilometers	0.62	miles	mi
cm^2	square centimeters	0.15	square inches	in^2
m^2	square meters	10.76	square feet	ft^2
m^2	square meters	1.20	square yards	yd^2
km^2	square kilometers	0.39	square miles	mi^2
ha	hectares	2.47	acre	
g	grams	.035	ounces [1]	oz
kg	kilograms	2.21	pounds [1]	lb
g	grams	.032	ounces [2]	oz (troy)
t	metric tons	1.10	short tons (2,000 lb)	
t	metric tons	0.98	long tons (2,240 lb)	
mL	milliliters	0.03	fluid ounces	fl oz
L	liter	4.24	cups	c
L	liters	2.13	pints (liquid)	pt
L	liters	1.05	quarts (liquid)	qt
L	liters	0.26	gallons	gal
m^3	cubic meters	35.32	cubic feet	ft^3
m^3	cubic meters	1.32	cubic yards	yd^3
C	degrees Celsius (after multiplying, add 32)	1.80	degrees Fahrenheit	F

[1] For weighing ordinary commodities.   [2] For weighing precious metals, jewels, etc.

Appendix V
Tables Deleted From the
2006 Edition of the Statistical Abstract

U.S. Census Bureau, Statistical Abstract of the United States: 2007

Index

NOTE: Index citations refer to **table** numbers, not page numbers.

U.S. Census Bureau, Statistical Abstract of the United States: 2007

NOTE: Index citations refer to **table** numbers, not page numbers.

NOTE: Index citations refer to **table** numbers, not page numbers.

NOTE: Index citations refer to **table** numbers, not page numbers.

U.S. Census Bureau, Statistical Abstract of the United States: 2007

NOTE: Index citations refer to **table** numbers, not page numbers.

NOTE: Index citations refer to **table** numbers, not page numbers.

U.S. Census Bureau, Statistical Abstract of the United States: 2007

NOTE: Index citations refer to **table** numbers, not page numbers.

NOTE: Index citations refer to **table** numbers, not page numbers.

NOTE: Index citations refer to **table** numbers, not page numbers.

U.S. Census Bureau, Statistical Abstract of the United States: 2007

NOTE: Index citations refer to **table** numbers, not page numbers.

NOTE: Index citations refer to **table** numbers, not page numbers.

U.S. Census Bureau, Statistical Abstract of the United States: 2007

NOTE: Index citations refer to **table** numbers, not page numbers.

NOTE: Index citations refer to **table** numbers, not page numbers.

U.S. Census Bureau, Statistical Abstract of the United States: 2007

NOTE: Index citations refer to **table** numbers, not page numbers.

NOTE: Index citations refer to **table** numbers, not page numbers.

Index   957

NOTE: Index citations refer to **table** numbers, not page numbers.

U.S. Census Bureau, Statistical Abstract of the United States: 2007

NOTE: Index citations refer to **table** numbers, not page numbers.

U.S. Census Bureau, Statistical Abstract of the United States: 2007

NOTE: Index citations refer to **table** numbers, not page numbers.

NOTE: Index citations refer to **table** numbers, not page numbers.

NOTE: Index citations refer to **table** numbers, not page numbers.

NOTE: Index citations refer to **table** numbers, not page numbers.

Index 963

NOTE: Index citations refer to **table** numbers, not page numbers.

U.S. Census Bureau, Statistical Abstract of the United States: 2007

NOTE: Index citations refer to **table** numbers, not page numbers.

NOTE: Index citations refer to **table** numbers, not page numbers.

NOTE: Index citations refer to **table** numbers, not page numbers.

U.S. Census Bureau, Statistical Abstract of the United States: 2007

NOTE: Index citations refer to **table** numbers, not page numbers.

NOTE: Index citations refer to **table** numbers, not page numbers.

NOTE: Index citations refer to **table** numbers, not page numbers.

NOTE: Index citations refer to **table** numbers, not page numbers.

U.S. Census Bureau, Statistical Abstract of the United States: 2007

NOTE: Index citations refer to **table** numbers, not page numbers.

NOTE: Index citations refer to **table** numbers, not page numbers.

U.S. Census Bureau, Statistical Abstract of the United States: 2007

NOTE: Index citations refer to **table** numbers, not page numbers.

NOTE: Index citations refer to **table** numbers, not page numbers.

U.S. Census Bureau, Statistical Abstract of the United States: 2007

NOTE: Index citations refer to **table** numbers, not page numbers.

NOTE: Index citations refer to **table** numbers, not page numbers.

U.S. Census Bureau, Statistical Abstract of the United States: 2007

NOTE: Index citations refer to **table** numbers, not page numbers.

NOTE: Index citations refer to **table** numbers, not page numbers.

U.S. Census Bureau, Statistical Abstract of the United States: 2007

NOTE: Index citations refer to **table** numbers, not page numbers.

U.S. Census Bureau, *Statistical Abstract of the United States: 2007*

NOTE: Index citations refer to **table** numbers, not page numbers.

U.S. Census Bureau, Statistical Abstract of the United States: 2007

NOTE: Index citations refer to **table** numbers, not page numbers.

U.S. Census Bureau, Statistical Abstract of the United States: 2007

NOTE: Index citations refer to **table** numbers, not page numbers.

U.S. Census Bureau, Statistical Abstract of the United States: 2007

NOTE: Index citations refer to **table** numbers, not page numbers.

U.S. Census Bureau, Statistical Abstract of the United States: 2007

NOTE: Index citations refer to **table** numbers, not page numbers.

U.S. Census Bureau, Statistical Abstract of the United States: 2007

NOTE: Index citations refer to **table** numbers, not page numbers.

NOTE: Index citations refer to **table** numbers, not page numbers.

U.S. Census Bureau, Statistical Abstract of the United States: 2007

NOTE: Index citations refer to **table** numbers, not page numbers.

NOTE: Index citations refer to **table** numbers, not page numbers.

NOTE: Index citations refer to **table** numbers, not page numbers.

NOTE: Index citations refer to **table** numbers, not page numbers.

U.S. Census Bureau, Statistical Abstract of the United States: 2007

NOTE: Index citations refer to **table** numbers, not page numbers.

992   Index

NOTE: Index citations refer to **table** numbers, not page numbers.

U.S. Census Bureau, Statistical Abstract of the United States: 2007

NOTE: Index citations refer to **table** numbers, not page numbers.

994   Index

NOTE: Index citations refer to **table** numbers, not page numbers.

NOTE: Index citations refer to **table** numbers, not page numbers.

U.S. Census Bureau, Statistical Abstract of the United States: 2007

NOTE: Index citations refer to **table** numbers, not page numbers.

U.S. Census Bureau, *Statistical Abstract of the United States: 2007*

NOTE: Index citations refer to **table** numbers, not page numbers.

U.S. Census Bureau, Statistical Abstract of the United States: 2007